25-L

REED'S
NAUTICAL ALMANAC

CARIBBEAN
1995

W9-BXZ-438

REED'S
NAUTICAL ALMANAC

CARIBBEAN
1995

Editor: Catherine Degnon

Second Edition 1995

THOMAS REED
PUBLICATIONS INC

BOSTON

© 1994 Thomas Reed Publications, Inc.
120 Lewis Wharf
Boston MA 02110
U.S.A.
Tel: 617-248-0700 Fax: 617-248-5855

ISBN 1-884666-04-3

Composition and Layout by:

DeNee Reiton Skipper
24 Essex Road
Belmont, MA 02178

Printed in the U.S.A. by:

The Banta Company
114 First Avenue
Needham, MA 02194

Contents

PREFACE 1995

That we are able to bring you this second edition of *Reed's Nautical Almanac, Caribbean edition,* is testament to the loyalty and enthusiastic support of you, our readers, and our dealers.

We announced the first edition of *Reed's Caribbean* in the fall of 1994 with high expectations and little warning of a financial dilemma that would last for several months. Thankfully, we passed that test and owe a large measure of our success to you who rely on *Reed's.* Your overwhelming support and patience while waiting for delivery of the 1994 edition says as much about you, our readers, as it does about the quality of the publication you've chosen.

And so, with great pride, we present to you our 1995 edition of *Reed's Nautical Almanac* for the Caribbean. Researched with the same care and attention you have come to expect from *Reed's,* this edition includes modest improvements, many suggested by readers' letters and by comments on the *Supplement* reply card bound into each edition. Among the improvments in this year's edition are a completely rewritten introduction to the Nautical Ephemeris (Chapter 6), with notes comparing *Reed's* presentation of data to that found in the U.S. government's nautical almanac; source numbers and edition dates for harbor chartlets; and latitudes and longitudes on most chartlets. We also, of course, incorporated updates and corrections to the coast pilot, electronic aids, and communication services chapters. Best of all, we have published this year's edition on time!

So enjoy this 1995 edition, and please continue to send us your comments, suggestions, and updates. We try to incorporate as many as we can because while we believe that *Reed's* is the most comprehensive nautical almanac available anywhere, there is always room for improvement.

Thank you again, and smooth sailing in 1995.

Jerald D. Knopf, President
Thomas Reed Publications, Inc.

LEGAL NOTES

Although the greatest care has been taken in compilation and preparation of this almanac, the publisher and editors respectively accept no responsibility or liability for any errors, omissions, or alterations or for any consequences ensuing upon the use of, or reliance upon, any information given in this almanac.

This almanac is copyrighted, and the rights respecting the tidal and other information in the almanac are strictly reserved. This information may not be reproduced in almanacs, calendars, tide cards, or any publication without the permission of the publisher.

ACKNOWLEDGEMENTS

The publisher and editor would like to thank the many people, government agencies, and businesses that have helped in the preparation of this second edition of the almanac. Without their assistance, this project would not have been possible.

Micronautics Inc., Rockport, ME: Jim Mays and Ben Ellison; Ben Ellison; Cynthia Flanagan; Chris Doyle; David Moynihan; Dr. Bernard Yallop; U.S. Customs Service; U.S. Coast Guard; L.J. Harri Nautical Booksellers, Boston, MA; Maryland Nautical, Baltimore, MD; AT&T High Seas Radio Telephone Service Coast Stations WOO, W0M, and KMI; WLO Radio, Alabama; Virgin Islands Radio; Bermuda Harbour Radio; Voice of America; The British Broadcasting Corporation; and the dozens of tremendously helpful and courteous people at foreign consulates in the U.S., at U.S. goverment offices around the country, and at government and customs offices, tourist bureaus, and marinas throughout the Caribbean basin.

Mexican hydrographic and cartographic information is courtesy of the Secretaría de Marina, Dirección de Oceanografía Naval, of Mexico.

GOVERNMENT PUBLICATIONS

Government publications for the waters covered in this almanac include:

U.S. Government Printing Office: Light List Volume III: Atlantic and Gulf Coasts; The Nautical Almanac

Defense Mapping Agency: Pub. 110, List of Lights, Radio Aids and Fog Signals; Pub. 117, Radio Navigational Aids; Pub. 140, Sailing Directions North Atlantic Ocean; Pub. 147, Sailing Directions for the Caribbean Sea, Volume I; Pub. 148, Sailing Directions for the Caribbean Sea, Volume II; Pub. 150, World Port Index; Pub. 151, Distances Between Ports; Notices to Mariners

U.S. Coast Guard: Local Notices to Mariners, District 7

National Oceanic and Atmospheric Administration: United States Coast Pilot, Volumes 4 and 5; Selected Worldwide Marine Weather Broadcasts; Tide Tables, East Coast of North and South America; Tidal Current Tables, Atlantic Coast of North America

Data given in the Ephemeris has been supplied by H.M. Nautical Almanac Office, the Particle Physics and Astronomy Research Council, Royal Greenwich Observatory, England, and is reproduced with permission.

The best way to learn seamanship

Navigation

Weather

Seamanship

Marine Electronics

Here it is, the most serious magazine in the boating field. No travelogs, no bikini-clad models, nothing about what to feed the crew or what to wear when it rains. A hardcore magazine about running a vessel at sea.

You'll learn coastal and celestial navigation, radar navigation, radio communications, electronics, weather forecasting, star finding and hear countless stories about open-ocean voyaging. You'll get detailed serious information on liferafts, EPIRBs, storm equipment and other safety equipment. Build your own illustrated encyclopedia of navigation and seamanship. You can't help but become a better mariner.

Special offer:
Send payment of $24 today for your six regular issues of *Ocean Navigator* and receive a free copy of our annual bluewater handbook *Ocean Voyager* PLUS a bonus issue of *Ocean Navigator*.

Ocean Navigator

Marine navigation & ocean voyaging

P.O. Box 4733, Portland, ME 04112
207-772-2466   Fax 207-772-2879

CRUISING COMPANIONS

Whether your next cruise is to the Virgin Islands, the Leewards Islands, Windward Islands, or destinations further south, Cruising Guide publications are the ideal companions.

Providing colorful photography, award winning design and the most up-to-date information on marinas, haul out facilities, anchorages, resorts, restaurants, shops and watersports activities, Cruising Guide's publications are a must for Caribbean cruising.

The guides are illustrated with sketch charts for safe, comfortable passages and anchorages, as well as being packed with information, tips and pointers that will help you make the most out of your voyages.

Ideally suited for the chartering yachtsman or the yacht owner travelling the Caribbean, the guides are updated regularly to ensure the most accurate information available.

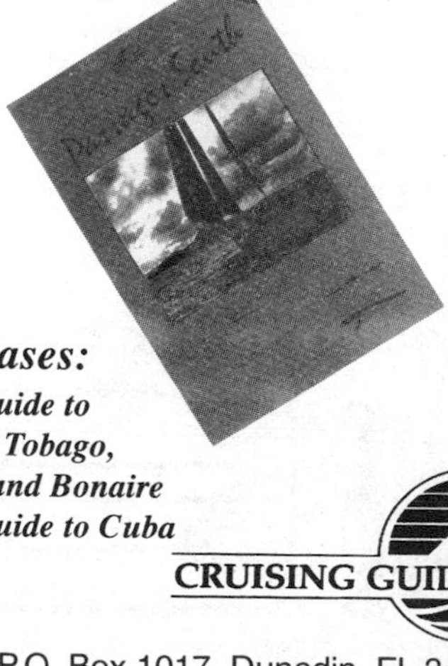

New Releases:
- *Cruising Guide to Trinidad & Tobago, Venezuela and Bonaire*
- *Cruising Guide to Cuba*

CRUISING GUIDE PUBLICATIONS

P.O. Box 1017, Dunedin, FL 34697-1017 • Phone: (813) 733-5322
PHONE 1-800-330-9542 (Orders Only)

WE STOCK WHAT SAILORS WANT !

Achilles - ACR - Apelco - Aquata - Artigiana Battelli
ASA - Autohelm - Baldwin - Blue Wave - Boat Armor
Boatlife - Bruce - Bruynzeel - Caframo - Camp
Chillington Marine - Cole Hersee - Dahl - Danforth
Dan Hill - Davis - Drivesaver - Dutch Hydrographic
Charts - Edson - ENO - Epifanes - Force 10 - Forespar
Fram - G & B Garelick - Goit - Harken - Hella
Henderson - HYE - Imray - Indian Head - International
Paint - Itt/Jabeco - Johnson Marine - Kent Marine
Laser - Leatherman - Lewmar - Lofrans - 3M - Magma
March Pumps - Marinco - Marine Muffler - Marlow
Mercury - Nautix - Newmar - Nicro Marine - Orion
Ormiston - Pelican Products - Plastimo - Prindle
Pro-Line Paint - R & D Marine - Raritan - Raske &
Van Der Meyde - Raytheon - Rule - S & J Products
SP Systems - Sailing Angles - Scanmarine - Shearwater
Siemens Solar - Simpson Lawrence - Slam - Sowester
Sta-Lok Terminals - Starbrite - Statpower - Sunfish
Synchro Start - T-Jett - Taco - Teleflex - Thomas
Reed - Titan - Ultraflex - United Solar Systems
Vetus - Wellington Puritan - West System - Whale
Wichard - Wilcox Crittenden - Windbugger - Yanmar

TECHNICALLY THE BEST CHANDLERY IN THE CARIBBEAN

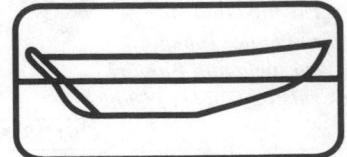

ST. MAARTEN: OPPOSITE BOBBYS MARINA TEL.: 22068 FAX 23804
ANTIGUA: JOLLY HARBOUR TEL: 462-7727

Need Charts?
Call Bluewater

- Over 35,000 nautical books and charts in stock
- Worldwide chart coverage in stock for immediate delivery
- All major chart publishers, both government and private
- America's largest selection of cruising guides
- Courtesy flags for over 100 countries
- Worldwide shipping - over 95% of orders shipped same day

Call our friendly cruising experts for help!

 **Bluewater**
BOOKS & CHARTS

1481 SE 17th Street Causeway, Fort Lauderdale, FL 33316,
Tel. (305) 763-6533 ☎ Fax. (305) 522-2278

Toll Free Orders 1-800-942-2583

JSI ▶ THE SAILING SOURCE

**P.O. BOX 20926
ST PETERSBURG, FL 33742**

SAILS
SPARS
CANVAS
RIGGING
CUSHIONS
INTERIORS
HARDWARE

**STORES: 3000 Gandy Blvd. ST. Petersburg, FL
417 10th Ave. W. Palmetto, FL**

- •KNOWLEDGEABLE STAFF OF SAILORS
- •COMPLETE OUTFITTING PACKAGE DISCOUNTS
- •ONE STOP SHOPPING •SAME DAY SHIPPING

1-800-234-3220

**LOCAL (813) 577-3220   FAX (813) 576-1306
HOURS: M-F 8AM–6PM SAT 10AM–2PM EST**

Whether racing around the world alone...

Sponsored by The BOC Group. Presented by IBM.

...or chartering with friends,

The Moorings®

with MEDICAL SEA PAK®

THE LAST WORD
MEDICAL SEA PAK
IN FIRST AID

you have
what you need
and you know
what to do.

MEDICAL SEA PAK
1945 Ridge Road East
Suite 105
Rochester, NY 14622
(800)832-6054•(716) 266-3136

Medical Sea Pak is an official supplier to the BOC Challenge and The Moorings.

REED'S
NAUTICAL COMPANION

THE HANDBOOK
TO COMPLEMENT
REED'S ALMANACS

A comprehensive nautical handbook designed as the essential complement to the Caribbean and North American East Coast Almanacs. Full of practical information for the experienced or novice mariner, with topics such as:

The Complete New Rules of the Road
Seamanship • Navigation • Buoyage Systems
Distance Tables • Distress and Rescue
First Aid • Safety at Sea

The Companion combines all the essential elements of a complete marine library in one handy volume for only $19.95. This is the reference book every boat can carry — and should!

CALL OR WRITE

THOMAS REED
PUBLICATIONS INC

120 Lewis Wharf, Boston, MA 02110
Tel: (800) 995-4995; (617) 248-0700
Fax: (617) 248-5855

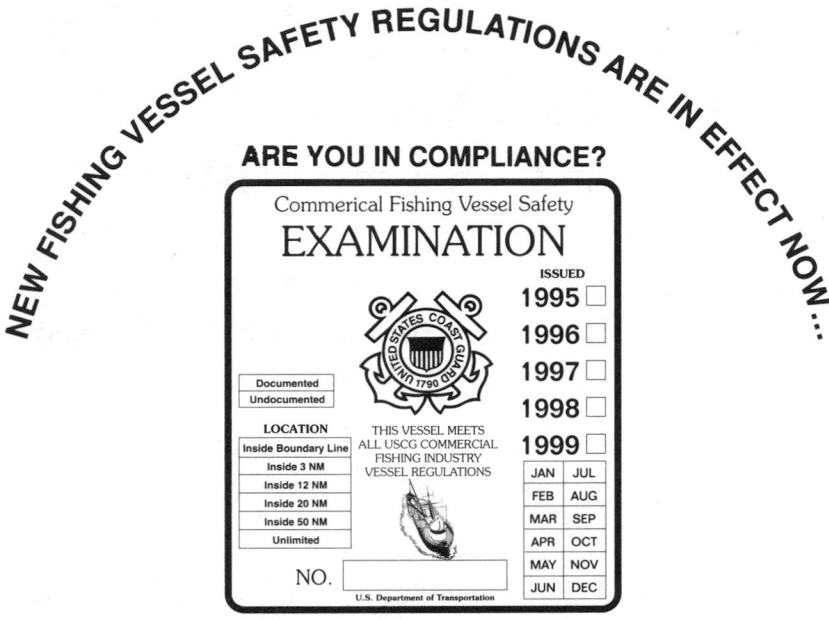

NEW FISHING VESSEL SAFETY REGULATIONS ARE IN EFFECT NOW...

ARE YOU IN COMPLIANCE?

Commerical Fishing Vessel Safety

EXAMINATION

ISSUED

1995 ☐
1996 ☐
1997 ☐
1998 ☐
1999 ☐

Documented
Undocumented

LOCATION
Inside Boundary Line
Inside 3 NM
Inside 12 NM
Inside 20 NM
Inside 50 NM
Unlimited

THIS VESSEL MEETS
ALL USCG COMMERCIAL
FISHING INDUSTRY
VESSEL REGULATIONS

JAN	JUL
FEB	AUG
MAR	SEP
APR	OCT
MAY	NOV
JUN	DEC

NO.

U.S. Department of Transportation

THESE NEW SAFETY
REQUIREMENTS CAN HELP
SAVE YOUR LIFE!

The Coast Guard is conducting examinations to help YOU make sure your boat complies and to help explain the regulations. This can help reduce the chance of boarding violations or maybe even termination of your fishing voyage.

Exams are done dockside. They are FREE. NO VIOLATIONS will be issued. Boats in compliance will be issued a SAFETY DECAL.

Exams are voluntary.
Exams are done by request only.
FOR MORE INFORMATION CALL YOUR LOCAL MARINE
SAFETY OFFICE

SAFETY DECAL: DON'T LEAVE PORT WITHOUT IT

REED'S
NAUTICAL ALMANAC

NORTH AMERICAN
EAST COAST 1995

The most complete, compact, easy-to-use onboard reference for the Atlantic and Gulf Coast of North America.

- More than $300 worth of vital information from government & private resources in one handy volume. Meets many USCG rules for navigation information required on board.
- Coast pilot information — organized geographically for 24 regions along the Atlantic and Gulf Coasts of North America

Nova Scotia • New Brunswick • Maine • Isles of Shoals
New Hampshire • Massachusetts • Rhode Island • Connecticut
New York • Hudson River • New Jersey • Delaware Bay
Delmarva Coast • Chesapeake Bay • North Carolina • South Carolina
Georgia • Florida • Alabama • Mississippi • Louisiana
Texas • Bermuda • Bahamas

- Comprehensive tide tables and current information *adjusted for daylight saving time!*
- Aids to navigation — all major aids to navigation with latitude/longitude positions
- Selected harbor chartlets — more than 200, with descriptions for the most popular ports and anchorages
- Communication and weather service information — VHF, SSB, high-seas radiotelephone, NOAA weather radio, and weatherfax broadcast services
- Celestial navigation tables — a complete nautical ephemeris for 1995

Call (800) 995-4995 to find out where you can order your Reed's

L.J. HARRI
SINCE 1730

L. J. HARRI
NAUTICAL BOOKSELLERS

PURVEYORS
OF
CHARTS
&
NAUTICAL
BOOKS
SINCE 1730

CHARTS ◆ Authorized agent for NOAA, DMA, and Canadian charts. Worldwide coverage for charts, pilot charts, sailing directions, almanacs, sight reduction tables, and other government publications

CRUISING GUIDES ◆ Comprehensive selection covering New England, East Coast, Caribbean, European, South Pacific, and other popular destinations around the world

BOOKS ◆ Maintenance how-tos, fishing, navigation, nautical fiction, kayaking, license study guides, marine reference, design, boatbuilding, seamanship, children's books, magazines, videos, and more

HISTORIC PHOTOGRAPHS ◆ Exclusive distributor of Beken of Cowes marine photographs and unusual nautical gifts

We specialize in service. MC/Visa/Amex accepted. Open seven days a week. Free catalogue. Call us today!

Phone orders: **1-800-242-3352**
Fax orders (24 hrs): **1-617-248-5855**

LOCATED ON BOSTON'S
HISTORIC WATERFRONT
**120 LEWIS WHARF
BOSTON, MA 02110**

L. J. HARRI, a worldwide nautical resource
120 LEWIS WHARF, BOSTON, MA 02110
and
PRINS HENDRIKKADE 94-95,
1012 AE AMSTERDAM, NETHERLANDS

The Lewis Wharf building is on the harbor side of Atlantic Avenue, halfway between the Aquarium and North Station. Take advantage of free 15-minute parking for quick pickup service.

NOTICES TO MARINERS

SPECIAL WARNING ON HAITI EMBARGO

In accordance with UN Security Council Resolution 917, on May 21, 1994, allied naval forces, including U.S. forces, participating in the Haiti Multinational Interception Force (MIF) will begin enforcing the comprehensive trade sanctions on Haiti contained in the resolution.

The resolution prohibits all imports from Haiti, except for trade in informational materials, and also prohibits all imports to Haiti, except for supplies intended strictly for medical purposes, foodstuffs, and informational materials. Other products may be exported to Haiti if they have the express approval of the UN Security Council Haiti Sanctions Committee.

Vessels are prohibited from entering or leaving the territory or the territorial sea of Haiti carrying commodities or products that violate the embargo. While the sanctions regime remains in effect, vessels found to be in violation of sanctions may be denied entry to U.S. ports.

MIF operations are being conducted in a rectangular area that is bounded by the following coordinates: 20 45N, 75 20W; 17 20N, 75 20W; 17 20N, 70 50W: and 20 45N, 70 50W. *(NOTE: This rectangle encompasses the Windward Passage.)*

All merchant ships perceived to be proceeding to or originating from Haitian ports will be intercepted and may be searched. The intercepting ship may use all available communication, primarily VHF channel 16, but including international code signals, flag hoists, other radio equipment, signal lamps, loudspeakers, and other appropriate means to communicate directions to a ship. Failure of a ship to proceed as directed will result in the use of such force as is necessary to assure compliance.

All vessels operating in the vicinity should remain clear of and avoid interference with ships engaged in enforcing U.N. sanctions.

SPECIAL WARNING FOR CUBA

Cuba claims a 12-mile territorial sea extending from straight baselines drawn from Cuban coastal points. The effect is that Cuba's claimed territorial sea extends in many areas well beyond 12 miles from Cuba's physical coastline. These claims are not in conformance with international law and are not recognized by the United States. Nonetheless, within distances extending in some cases upwards of 20 miles from the Cuban coast, United States vessels have been stopped and boarded by Cuban authorities. Within the limits of prudence and good judgment, mariners are advised to protest (but not physically resist) any improper attempt to stop, board, or seize U.S. vessels in international waters. Notify the U.S. Coast Guard of your status so that it can relay information about your situation to the U.S. Department of State for diplomatic attention.

On September 1, 1990, seven Traffic Separation Schemes, approved by the International Maritime Organization, were implemented off the eastern, western, and northern coasts of Cuba. The government of Cuba has unilaterally established a mandatory ship-reporting system within the Old Bahama Channel to govern vessel movement within the area. While it is the U.S. position that the mandatory provisions of the ship-reporting system are inconsistent with international law, vessels should exercise caution while transiting the Old Bahama Channel.

The Traffic Separation Schemes are located:
Off Cabo San Antonio
Off La Tabla
Off Costa de Matanzas
In the Old Bahama Channel
Off Punta Maternillos
Off Punta Lucrecia
Off Cabo Maisi

FCC STATION LICENSE CHECK

In an effort to improve maritime safety, the Federal Communications Commission (FCC) and the U.S. Coast Guard are jointly enforcing existing radio regulations to help reduce the growing problem of hoaxes and other violations interfering with distress operations.

Because of evidence that many boaters and operators of uninspected vessels disregard FCC maritime radio licensing and usage rules, or are unaware of such rules, the Coast Guard will check a FCC Ship Station License on radio-equipped vessels during boarding inspections.

Recreational boaters with a VHF-FM radio, EPIRB, tunable radar, HF single-sideband radio, or portable radio installed aboard their vessels are required to have a Ship Station License to operate any of this equipment. To operate any equipment other than a VHF-FM radio or if you plan to visit a foreign port, you must also have a Restricted Radiotelephone Operator's Permit. You are required to post the original or a clearly legible copy of the Ship Station License at the principal control point of each station. A copy must indicate the location of the original. If you cannot post the license, it must be kept where it will be readily available for inspection.

To obtain a Ship Station License you should request FCC Form 506, fee-type code PASR. New and renewal licenses are now valid for 10 years; the filing fee is now $115. If you install additional radio equipment that is not covered by the original ship's license, you must request a modification, also on Form 506, fee type code PASM; the filing fee for a modification is $45. To obtain a Restricted Radiotelephone Operators Permit, request FCC Form 753. This license is valid for your lifetime and the cost is currently $45. Applications may be obtained by visiting your FCC Field Operations Bureau or by phoning the FCC Forms Distribution Center in Hyattsville, MD (202 418-3676). For information about fees, call the Fees Hotline (202-418-0220); for more information concerning ship's licenses or the status of applications, call the FCC office in Gettysburg, PA (717-337-1212).

Those who fail to obtain an FCC authorization to operate maritime equipment are liable for a criminal misdemeanor penalty of up to $1,000, one year in prison, or both. CB radios, cellular telephones, and receive-only equipment are exempted.

PROPER USE OF CHANNEL 16 VHF-FM

Channel 16 VHF-FM (156.8 MHz) is designated by the Federal Communications Commission (FCC) as the National Distress, Safety, and Calling frequency. It must be monitored at all times by vessels underway. Calls to other vessels are normally initiated on channel 16 (except by recreational vessels, see below), and except in an emergency, vessels should shift to another channel to communicate. If a vessel cannot be raised on channel 16 for communications concerning navigational safety, an attempt can be made on channel 13.

The Coast Guard has received complaints concerning the failure of vessels to answer calls from other vessels on channel 16 VHF-FM. Incidents of failure to respond on channel 16 involving safety communications should be reported to the nearest Coast Guard Marine Safety Office.

FCC Regulations prohibit radio checks with the Coast Guard on channel 16 VHF-FM except when conducted by FCC representatives, qualified radio technicians installing or repairing equipment, or when requested by the Coast Guard.

CHANNEL 9 VHF-FM CALLING CHANNEL

In an effort to eliminate traffic congestion on channel 16 VHF-FM, the Federal Communications Commission (FCC) has recently designated channel 9 VHF-FM as the nationwide *Recreational Calling Channel* for use by noncommercial boaters within the United States. Use of this channel by recreational boaters is strictly voluntary but is strongly encouraged by the Coast Guard and the FCC.

It is important to note, however, the Coast Guard does **not** monitor channel 9 VHF-FM for distress calls. Vessels in distress should make their calls on channel 16 VHF-FM. Additional information can be obtained from your nearest Coast Guard facility.

WARNING ON USE OF FLOATING AIDS TO NAVIGATION

The aids to navigation depicted on charts comprise a system consisting of fixed and floating aids with varying degrees of reliability. Therefore, prudent mariners will not rely solely on any single aid to navigation, particularly a floating aid.

The buoy symbol is used to indicate the approximate position of the buoy body and the sinker that secures the buoy to the seabed. The approximate position is used because of practical limitations in positioning and maintaining buoys and their sinkers in precise geographical locations. These limitations include, but are not limited to: inherent imprecisions in position-fixing methods, prevailing atmospheric and sea conditions, the slope of and the material of the seabed, the fact that buoys are moored to sinkers by varying lengths of chain, and the fact that buoy and/or sinker positions are not under continuous surveillance but are normally checked only during periodic maintenance visits, which often occur more than a year apart. The position of the buoy body can be expected to shift inside and outside the charting symbol due to the forces of nature. The mariner is also cautioned that buoys are liable to be carried away, shifted, capsized, sunk, etc. Lighted buoys may be extinguished or sound signals may not function as the result of ice or other natural causes, collisions, or other accidents.

For the foregoing reasons, a prudent mariner must not rely completely upon the position or operation of floating aids to navigation, but will utilize bearings from fixed objects and aids to navigation on shore. Further, a vessel attempting to pass close aboard always risks collision with a yawing buoy or with the obstruction that the buoy marks.

CHART NOTES REGARDING DIFFERENT DATUMS

Particular attention should be exercised during a passage when transferring the navigational plot to an adjacent chart upon a different geodetic datum or when transferring positions from one chart to another chart of the same area that is based upon a different datum. The transfer of positions should be done by bearings and distances from common features.

Notes on charts should be read with care, as they give important information not graphically presented. Notes in connection with chart title include the horizontal geodetic datum that serves as a reference for the values of the latitude and longitude of any point or object on the chart. The latitude and longitudes of the same points or objects on a second chart of the same area that is based upon a different datum will differ from those of the first chart. The difference may be navigationally significant.

IALA MARITIME BUOYAGE SYSTEM

The IALA Maritime (combined Cardinal/Lateral) Buoyage System has been, is being, or will be imlemented by nearly every maritime buoyage jurisdiction worldwide as either REGION A buoyage (red to port) or REGION B buoyage (red to starboard). The actual conversion in REGION A began in 1977 and is continuing. Conversion in REGION B has begun, and it can be anticipated that several years will be required to complete the transformation.

The terms "REGION A" and "REGION B" are used to determine which type of buoyage region is in effect or undergoing conversion in a particular area. The major difference between the two buoyage regions concerns the lateral marks. When viewed from sea, the lateral marks in REGION A will be red to port; in REGION B they will be red to starboard. Shapes of lateral marks will be the same in both regions: can to port; cone (nun) to starboard. Cardinal and other marks will continue to follow current guidelines and may be found in both regions. A modified lateral mark, indicating the preferred channel where a channel divides has been introduced for use in both regions. It is intended that after a reasonable period, each chart will make reflection to REGION A or REGION B to indicate which type of lateral buoyage is in use in that particular area. The precise limits between the two regions cannot be defined at this time. *(NOTE: All North American, Central American, South American, and Caribbean coasts fall well inside IALA REGION B; and Bermuda has now completed its changeover to IALA REGION B.)*

Mariners are advised that the U.S. maritime aids to navigation system has been modified to incorporate the IALA system for REGION B.

WARNING ON POSSIBLE DANGER FROM UNLABELED DRUMS

With the many exotic chemicals being transported in drums as deck cargo, increasingly more reports are received of loss overboard of these potentially dangerous containers. Even empty drums may contain residues that are extremely hazardous to touch or smell, and a few vapors may be explosive.

When coming upon derelict drums, whether afloat or from the sea bottom, this danger should be considered. Identifying labels will give adequate warning, but containers are more likely to be found with caution labels washed off. Avoid direct contact, and notify the U.S. Coast Guard's National Response Center of any sightings in U.S. coastal waters (24-hour toll-free reporting number, 800-424-8802; oil and chemical spills in U.S. waters should also be called into this center) or government authorities of the nearest port state if the sighting is near any foreign shores.

CLARIFICATION OF RULES CONCERNING DIVE FLAGS

There has been some confusion over the status of the traditional sport diver's flag because of a change to the U.S. Inland Navigation rules concerning the use of a 1-meter rigid replica of the International Code Flag ALFA (a blue and white swallow-tailed flag).

The ALFA flag is to be flown on small vessels engaged in diving operations whenever the vessels are restricted in their ability to maneuver. However, in sport diving, where divers are usually free swimming, the ALFA flag does not have to be shown, and the Coast Guard encourages the continued use of the traditional sports diver flag. Divers in U.S. waters should also review state laws as these may have different requirements for dive flags and operations.

The distinction the Coast Guard wants to make clear is: The ALFA is a navigational signal intended to protect the vessel from collision. The sport diver flag is an unofficial signal that, through custom, has come to be used to protect the diver in the water. It is the responsibility of the operator of a diving vessel to determine if his or her craft's movements are restricted. To be most effective, the sport diver flag should be exhibited on a float in the water to mark the approximate location of the diver.

COAST GUARD DROP/FLOAT PUMPS

The U.S. Coast Guard often provides vessels in distress with emergency pumps by parachute drop, helicopter hoist, or vessel. The most commonly used type of pump comes complete in a sealed aluminum drum about half the size of a 55-gallon drum.

A single lever on the top opens the drum. *Do not allow smoking or open flames in the vicinity while opening the drum, as there may be gas fumes inside the can.* The pump draws about 90 gallons of water per minute. There should be a waterproof flashlight on top of the pump for night use. Operating instructions are provided inside the pump container.

U.S. COAST GUARD WARNING ON POTENTIAL MASS MIGRATION: CUBA

In late August 1994 the U.S. Coast Guard issued a warning notice of potential mass migration from Cuba to the U.S. The warning cautioned persons contemplating voyages to Cuba to bring back persons who have not been authorized to enter the U.S. by immigration officials that such actions violate numerous U.S. civil and criminal laws. In addition, such actions subject individuals involved to arrest, seizure of any vessels used, heavy fines (up to $250,000) or penalties, and imprisonment (from one to ten years). Specific prohibitions include:

1. Assisting or attempting to assist a foreign national to enter the U.S. without prior permission (visa) from U.S. immigration officials.

2. Failure to comply with the terms of a security zone that may be established by the U.S. Coast Guard or failure to obey orders controlling the movement or anchoring of vessels within such zone. When a security zone is necessary for south Florida, information about it and any operating permits that may be required will be announced in the Coast Guard Broadcast Notice to Mariners.

3. Carrying goods or passengers to or from Cuba (penalties include vessel forfeiture and up to $100,000 fine and ten years in prison).

4. Resisting or impeding U.S. law enforcement officers engaged in the performance of their duties.

5. Tampering with seized property.

6. Overloading vessels or failure to have adequate safety equipment for the number of persons aboard.

Coast Pilot

COAST PILOT

INTRODUCTION TO THE COAST PILOT

The Coast Pilot chapter is organized geographically, beginning with Bermuda and then proceeding clockwise around the Caribbean from southeast Florida, the Bahamas, and the Turks and Caicos through the Greater Antilles and Lesser Antilles to the north coast of South America and the Caribbean coasts of Central America and Mexico. Refer to the chapter table of contents on the preceding page or the Index in the back of the almanac to find a particular country or island section. Each section contains information on entry procedures and selected major lights, buoys, daymarks, and harbors, plus harbor descriptions for selected ports and harbor chartlets for reference purposes.

WAYPOINTS

Whenever available, Reed's has listed the latitude and longitude of major aids to navigation. The listings are in degrees, minutes, and tenths of a minute. These positions have been obtained from the government light lists and are for reference only. Many navigators will be tempted to use these as waypoints in their LORAN or GPS units. If doing so, the listed position should be plotted on a large-scale chart of the area to ascertain its relationship to navigational hazards in the vicinity. It must be kept in mind that floating aids to navigation, such as buoys, move about on their anchor rodes. The positions of buoys should be regarded as approximate. Reed's does not guarantee the accuracy of any latitude or longitude position. Prudent navigators will use these waypoints with caution and will not rely upon them as their sole means of position-fixing.

HARBOR DESCRIPTIONS

Information included in the many brief harbor descriptions has been gathered from a variety of sources, including actual visits by editors. Individual harbors may be found by referring to the Index in the back of the almanac or by referring to the geographic section appropriate for that harbor. Whenever possible, the harbors have been placed near the buoys and lights leading to the harbors.

CHARTLETS

As a further aid to mariners Reed's has included in this almanac more than 200 chartlets of major harbors. Each chartlet coincides with a harbor description and a listing of the major aids to navigation in the area. Although in many cases these chartlets are actual reproductions of government charts, prudent mariners will not rely upon them for navigation. While those reproduced from government sources are from the most current editions as of press time, they incorporate no corrections to navigational aids, depths, or hazards since the edition publication date. While these chartlets can be very useful in planning your trip and familiarizing yourself with the area, your vessel should be equipped with up-to-date charts of your intended route. You should also keep abreast of chart changes as posted in the various regional Notices to Mariners.

LIGHTS, BUOYS, AND DAYMARKS

The information in Reed's regarding aids to navigation is derived from official government sources and is current through Notice to Mariners No. 32/94 (August 6, 1994).

Lights may vary from simple poles to major stone towers over 100 feet high. In general, a "light" is a fixed structure that is lighted at night. Some major lights remain lit 24 hours a day; this information is generally noted in the listings. Where available, Reed's has included a brief description of all aids, which in the case of lights can often help with identification during the day.

Buoys are floating aids to navigation. Within the United States and Canada, all even-numbered buoys (i.e., 2, 4, 6, etc.) are colored red and all odd-numbered buoys (i.e., 1, 3, 5, etc.) are colored green. In some areas, especially in the Caribbean, you may encounter a few black buoys that have not yet been given a coat of green paint. The color of the light shown by the buoy will usually match the color of its hull. Center of channel buoys are often red and white. Buoys marking hazards are often yellow.

Large navigational buoys are designated as LNBs in the listings. These are 40 feet in diameter and were designed to replace lightships. They are red in color to aid their visibility. They are equipped with lights, radiobeacons, sound signals, and racons.

An unlit red buoy is usually a nun, while an unlit green buoy is a can. Other variations are generally indicated.

Daymarks are colored signs that can be seen during the day—and sometimes at night if illuminated by a spotlight—that are fixed to posts, lighthouses, buildings, and other structures. There are many types of daymarks, which can be very confusing to even the most informed navigators. The list of abbreviations that follows this introduction should help alleviate some of the confusion.

Information is presented for all aids to navigation in a set order. The first item is the *name of the light* and *its designation,* followed by its *latitude* and *longitude,* usually given to the nearest tenth of a minute. Sometimes there is a brief description of the aid's location relative to fixed identifiable objects (i.e., piers, shoals, etc.).

For those aids to navigation that are lighted, the descriptive information that follows the location includes *light characteristics,* the *height of the light* (as measured above high water and generally given in feet [ft] but sometimes in meters [m]), and its *visible range* in nautical miles (abbreviated M). A brief description of the aid's *physical characteristics,* or structure, generally follows the light characteristics information. Any *additional notes,* such as limits of visibility or the presence of radar reflectors, racons, or other potentially confusing lights, follow the structure description. When bearings are given (usually for ranges), they are true bearings, not adjusted for magnetic variation. Limits of light sectors and arcs of visibility *as observed from a vessel* are given in clockwise order. Note that not all information is known for all aids to navigation.

Here is an example of a typical listing:
SMITH SHOAL LIGHT, on NE end of shoal, 24 43.2N, 81 55.0W. Fl W 6s, 47ft, 9M. Small black house on white hexagonal pyramidal skeleton tower on piles.

The name of the aid to navigation is SMITH SHOAL LIGHT. Its position is 24 degrees, 43.2 minutes north latitude, 81 degrees, 55.0 minutes west longitude, at the northeast end of Smith Shoal. The light is white and flashes every 6 seconds and is located 47 feet above sea level. It has a range of 9 nautical miles. The light is located on a small black house on a white hexagonal pyramidal skeleton tower set on piles.

A list of abbreviations for various types of daybeacons and lights used in the descriptions of aids to navigation begins on this page. A light

characteristics table follows. Both are useful references to both this almanac and information frequently found on government charts.

ABBREVIATIONS

The following is a list of standard abbreviations used to describe aids to navigation. These abbreviations are used in the Coast Pilot chapter of this almanac.

N=north S=south W=west E=east

R=red   G=green W=white B=black
Y=yellow Or=orange

Al=alternating
Dir=directional
F=fixed
Fl=flashing
Fl (2)=group flashing (two lights)
IQ=interrupted quick flashing
Iso=isophase (equal interval)
IVQ=interrupted very quick flashing
Km=kilometer
L Fl=long flashing
Lt=light
M=nautical mile
Mo=Morse code
min=minute (or minimum in Tidal Current Tables)
m=meters
obsc=obscured
Oc=occulting
ODAS=anchored oceangraphic data buoy
Q=quick flashing
s=seconds
UQ=ultra quick flashing
vert=vertical
vis=visible
VQ=very quick flashing

DAYMARKS
The first letter of the daymark listing indicates its basic purpose, following the U.S. System:

S=Square. Used to mark the port (left) side of channels when entering from seaward.

T=Triangle. Used to mark the starboard (right) side of channels when entering from seaward.

J=Junction. May be a square or a triangle. Used to mark channel junctions or bifurcations in the channel. May be used to mark wrecks or other obstructions, which may be passed on either side. The color of the top band has lateral significance for the preferred channel.

M=Safe water. Octagonal. Used to mark the fairway, or middle of the channel.

K=Range. Rectangular. When the front and rear daymarks are aligned on the same bearing, you are on the azimuth of the range, which usually marks safe water.

N=No lateral significance. Diamond or rectangular shaped. Used for special purposes as a warning, distance, or location marker.

The second letter in a daymark abbreviation indicates its color. The following abbreviations cover many of the major designations used particularly for aids in U.S. waters:

SG=Square green daymark with a green reflective border.

SG-I=Square green daymark with a green reflective border and a yellow reflective horizontal strip.

SG-SY=Square green daymark with a green reflective border and a yellow reflective square.

SG-TY=Square green daymark with a green reflective border and a yellow reflective triangle.

SR=Square red daymark with a red reflective border.

TG=Triangular green daymark with a green reflective border.

TR=Triangular red daymark with a red reflective border.

TR-I=Triangular red daymark with a red reflective border and a yellow reflective horizontal strip.

TR-SY=Triangular red daymark with a red reflective border and a yellow reflective square.

TR-TY=Triangular red daymark with a red reflective border and a yellow reflective triangle.

JG=Daymark with horizontal bands of green and red, green band topmost, with a green reflective border.

JG-I=Daymark with horizontal bands of green and red, green band topmost, with a green reflective border and a yellow reflective horizontal strip.

JG-SY=Daymark with horizontal bands of green and red, green band topmost, with a green reflective border and a yellow reflective square.

JG-TY=Daymark with horizontal bands of green and red, green band topmost, with a green reflective border and a yellow reflective triangle.

JR=Daymark with horizontal bands of green and red, red band topmost, with a red reflective border.

JR-I=Daymark with horizontal bands of green and red, red band topmost, with a red reflective border with a yellow horizontal strip.

JR-SY=Triangular daymark with horizontal bands of green and red, red band topmost, with a red reflective border and a yellow reflective square.

JR-TY=Triangular daymark with horizontal bands of green and red, red band topmost, with a red reflective border and a yellow reflective triangle.

MR=Octagonal daymark with stripes of white and red with a white reflective border.

MR-I=Octagonal daymark with stripes of white and red, with a white reflective border and a yellow reflective horizontal strip.

CG=Diamond-shaped green daymark bearing small green diamond-shaped reflectors at each corner.

CR=Diamond-shaped red daymark bearing small red diamond-shaped reflectors at each corner.

KBG=Rectangular black daymark bearing a central green stripe.

KBG-I=Rectangular black daymark bearing a central green stripe and a yellow reflective horizontal strip.

KBR=Rectangular black daymark bearing a central red stripe.

KBR-I=Rectangular black daymark bearing a central red stripe and a yellow reflective horizontal strip.

KBW=Rectangular black daymark bearing a central white stripe.

KBW-I=Rectangular black daymark bearing a central white stripe and a yellow reflective horizontal strip.

KGB=Rectangular green daymark bearing a central black stripe.

KGB-I=Rectangular green daymark bearing a central black stripe and a yellow reflective horizontal strip.

KGR=Rectangular green daymark bearing a central red stripe.

KGR-I=Rectangular green daymark bearing a central red stripe and a yellow reflective horizontal strip.

KGW=Rectangular green daymark bearing a central white stripe.

KGW-I=Rectangular green daymark bearing a central white stripe and a yellow reflective horizontal strip.

KRB=Rectangular red daymark bearing a central black stripe.

KRB-I=Rectangular red daymark bearing a central black stripe and a yellow reflective horizontal strip.

KRG=Rectangular red daymark bearing a central green stripe.

KRG-I=Rectangular red daymark bearing a central green stripe and a yellow reflective horizontal strip.

KRW=Rectangular red daymark bearing a central white stripe.

KRW-I=Rectangular red daymark bearing a central white stripe and a yellow reflective horizontal strip.

KWB=Rectangular white daymark bearing a central black stripe.

KWB-I=Rectangular white daymark bearing a central black stripe and a yellow reflective horizontal strip.

KWG=Rectangular white daymark bearing a central green stripe.

KWG-I=Rectangular white daymark bearing a central green stripe and a yellow reflective horizontal strip.

KWR=Rectangular white daymark bearing a central red stripe.

KWR-I=Rectangular white daymark bearing a central red stripe and a yellow reflective horizontal strip.

NB=Diamond-shaped daymark divided into four diamond-shaped colored sectors with the sectors at the side corners white and the sectors at the top and bottom corners black, with a white reflective border.

NG=Diamond-shaped daymark divided into four diamond-shaped colored sectors with the sectors at the side corners white and the sectors at the top and bottom corners green, with a white reflective border.

NR=Diamond-shaped daymark divided into four diamond-shaped colored sectors with the sectors at the side corners white and the sectors at the top and bottom corners red, with a white reflective border.

NW=Diamond-shaped white daymark with an orange reflective border and black letters describing the information, or regulatory nature, of the mark.

ND=Rectangular white mileage marker with black numerals indicating the mile number.

NL=Rectangular white location marker with an orange reflective border and black letters indicating the location.

NY=Diamond-shaped yellow daymark with a yellow reflective border.

LIGHT CHARACTERISTICS

Abbrev	Old Abbrev		Period shown ————
F		FIXED a continuous steady light	
		OCCULTING total duration of light more than dark and total eclipse at regular intervals.	
Oc	Occ	SINGLE OCCULTING steady light with eclipse regularly repeated	
Oc (2)	Gp Occ (2)	GROUP OCCULTING two or more eclipses in a group, regularly repeated	
Oc (2+3)	Gp Occ (2+3)	COMPOSITE GROUP OCCULTING in which successive groups in a period have different number of eclipses	
Iso		ISOPHASE a light where duration of light and darkness are equal	
		FLASHING single flash at regular intervals. Duration of light less than dark.	
Fl		SINGLE FLASHING light in which flash is regularly repeated at less than 50 flashes per minute	
L Fl		LONG FLASHING a flash of 2 or more seconds, regularly repeated	
Fl (3)	Gp Fl (3)	GROUP FLASHING successive groups, specified in number, regularly repeated	
Fl (2+1)	Gp Fl (2+1)	COMPOSITE GROUP FLASHING in which successive groups in a period have different number of flashes	
		QUICK usually 50 or 60 flashes per minute.	
Q	Qk Fl	CONTINUOUS QUICK in which a flash is regularly repeated	
Q (3)	Qk Fl (3)	GROUP QUICK in which a specified group of flashes is regularly repeated.	
IQ	Int Qk Fl	INTERUPTED QUICK sequence of flashes interrupted by regularly repeated eclipses of constant and long duration	
		VERY QUICK usually either 100 or 120 flashes per minute.	
VQ	Q Qk Fl	CONTINUOUS VERY QUICK flash is regularly repeated	
VQ (3)	V Qk (3)	GROUP VERY QUICK specified group of flashes regularly repeated	
IVQ	Int V Qk Fl	INTERRUPTED VERY QUICK FLASH in groups with total eclipse at regular intervals of constant and long duration	
		ULTRA QUICK usually not less than 160 flashes per minute.	
UQ		CONTINUOUS ULTRA QUICK in which flash is regularly repeated	
IUQ		INTERRUPTED ULTRA QUICK in groups with total eclipse at intervals of long duration	
Mo (K)		MORSE CODE in which appearances of light of two clearly different durations are grouped to represent a character(s) in the Morse code	
F Fl		FIXING AND FLASHING steady light with one brilliant flash at regular intervals	
Al WR	Alt WR	ALTERNATING a light that alters in color in successive flashing (in this case white and red)	R W R W R W

U.S. CUSTOMS PROCEDURES

The harbor descriptions indicate when a port is a designated Customs Port of Entry. When a pleasure boat arrives in the United States for the first time, the first landfall must be at a designated Customs Port of Entry. If you must make an emergency stop at some other port first, customs should be notified immediately via telephone. U.S. vessels may proceed to any port, but must report to customs by phone at the first landfall and await instructions. (Note: contacting customs by mobile phone while approaching but before actually arriving at the landfall does not fulfill customs requirements.) For both foreign and U.S. vessels, nothing should be allowed ashore from the vessel and no person should be allowed ashore other than the master until customs has been have been notified.

U.S.-documented or -registered vessels do not need to report their departure from the United States for foreign destinations.

Pleasure boats of certain countries may obtain a cruising license for the United States. This license exempts them from formal reporting and clearance procedures at every port of call. The license can be obtained from the District Director of Customs at the first port of arrival in the United States. The licenses are issued for no more than a one-year period. They do not exempt a vessel from applicable duties. Vessels from the following countries are eligible to obtain a cruising license:

Argentina
Australia
Austria
Bahamas
Belgium
Bermuda
Canada
Denmark
Germany
France
Greece
Honduras
Ireland
Jamaica
Liberia
Netherlands
New Zealand
Norway
Sweden

Great Britain is also eligible (including Turks and Caicos, St. Vincent, Northern Grenadine Islands, Cayman Islands, British Virgin Islands, and St. Christopher-Nevis-Anguilla islands).

In the absence of a cruising license, foreign vessels must report at each U.S. port and must obtain clearance to proceed to the next port. When these vessels depart the U.S., they must clear customs.

There is no charge for customs inspection during normal working hours (0800 to 1700, Monday through Saturday, except holidays). After hours, Sunday, and holidays, inspection service costs a maximum of $25 per boat.

Failure to report to customs as required may result in a fine of up to $5,000 for the first violation and $10,000 for subsequent violations.

Effective July 6, 1986, pleasure craft 30 feet long or longer must purchase from the U.S. Customs Service an annual $25 Customs User Fee Decal in order to clear customs. If the decal is not obtained before returning to U.S. waters, the vessel operator will be directed to the nearest customs office to purchase one within 48 hours of arriving.

The special regulations governing reporting requirements for the southern Florida region in effect since 1986 were suspended in May 1994. Private vessels arriving in Florida from foreign destinations now follow the same procedures as those arriving elsewhere in the rest of the country (see Florida listing below for appropriate telephone numbers). For more information on U.S. customs procedures contact the nearest customs regional or district office.

The following is a *partial* list of U.S. customs offices where you may report your arrival. In most instances, the 800 number ties into a district office that can provide up-to-date reporting information and phone numbers for all locations throughout the district. Note that some numbers are manned 24 hours a day, and some have answering machines for off-duty hours. Others are answered only during office hours, which vary according to location.

Maine: Portland, 207-780-3328 (800-743-7416)
Massachusetts: Boston, 617-937-2380 (800-743-7416)
Rhode Island: Newport, 401-847-2744 (800-743-7416)

Connecticut: Bridgeport, 203-579-5606
(800-743-7416)
New York: New York City, 212-466-5472
(800-522-5270, New York locations only, or
800-221-4265, out-of-state).
New Jersey: Newark, 201-645-3770
(800-221-4265). Arrivals in New Jersey south of
Manasquan Inlet should contact Philadelphia.
Pennsylvania: Philadelphia, 215-597-4648
Maryland area (includes all of Chesapeake
Bay, Maryland, and the Atlantic coast of
Delmarva peninsula): Baltimore district,
410-962-2806
Virginia: Alexandria, 703-557-1950
Newport News, 804-245-6470
Norfolk, 804-441-6741
North Carolina: Morehead City, 919-726-5845;
after hours, -726-3651
Wilmington, 910-343-4616
South Carolina: Charleston 803-723-1272
Georgia: Savannah, 912-652-4400, -4430;
after hours, -232-7507
Florida: Jacksonville, 904-291-2775
Port Canaveral, 407-783-2066
Miami, Ft. Lauderdale, and Key West,
800-432-1216, -458-4239, or -451-0393
Ft. Myers, 813-768-4318
St. Petersburg, 813-536-7311
Panama City, 904-785-4688, -291-2775
Pensacola, 904-432-6811
Alabama: Mobile, 205-441-5102; after hours,
504-589-3771
Mississippi: Gulfport, 601-864-6794
Pascagoula, 601-762-7311, 504-589-3771
Louisiana: New Orleans, 504-589-6804; after
hours, 504-589-3771
Texas: Port Arthur, 409-727-0285
Galveston, 409-766-3624
Freeport, 409-233-3004
Corpus Christi, 512-888-3352
Brownsville, 210-831-4121; after hours,
512-542-4232
Puerto Rico: Aguadilla, 809-882-3556
Mayaguez, 809-831-3342
San Juan, 809-253-4533, -4534, 4537, -4538
Ponce, 809-841-3130
Fajardo, 809-863-0950
Vieques, 809-741-8366
Culebra, 809-742-3531
*Note: In Puerto Rico all vessels arriving after
1700 hours, or on Sunday and holidays, must
report to the San Juan station via telephone.
All vessels arriving from the U.S. Virgin Islands
must report to customs. U.S. vessels traveling
from Puerto Rico to the U.S. Virgin Islands
need not clear out on departure.*

U.S. Virgin Islands: St. Croix, 809-773-1011,
Sunday, -778-0216
St. Thomas, 809-774-6755; after hours, Sunday,
holidays, -774-4554
St. John, 809-776-6741

TIDE AND TIDAL CURRENT TABLES

Sir Charles Darwin wrote in the *Admiralty
Manual of Tides* in 1891:
"When we consider that the incessant variability
of the tidal forces, the complex outlines of our
coasts, the depth of the sea and the earth's
rotation are all involved, we should regard
good tidal prediction as one of the greatest
triumphs of the theory of universal gravitation."

Reed's tide and current tables are now
computed independently by Micronautics, Inc.
Micronautics' predictions apply a slightly more
accurate algorithm to the same harmonic
constituent information used by the U.S.
National Ocean Service. Hence, there are small
differences between the times, heights, and
current velocities cited in these tables and those
published by NOS. Mariners will not find these
differences to be of navigational significance
and should, in fact, find these tables to be a
slightly more accurate representation of the
real-world phenomenon. Above all, prudent
mariners understand that all tide and current
predictions are approximations and are also
subject to weather influences that cannot be
predicted in the long term.

Complete tide and tidal current tables covering
the full year of 1995 for more than a dozen
primary reference stations throughout the
Caribbean are located in this Coast Pilot chapter
at the end of the geographical section where
that station is located (i.e., the tide tables and
tidal current tables for Florida stations follow
the coast pilot information for Florida).

The 1995 tide tables provide the time and
height of each low and high tide for every
day of the year. Times given are standard, on
a 24-hour clock, for each particular location as
noted; be sure to adjust for Daylight Saving
Time where and when appropriate. Tide heights
are given in feet and are referenced to the
chart datum of soundings for the particular
location.

The 1995 tidal current tables indicate the times of all slacks (i.e., minimum current flow), times of maximum flood for both ebbs and floods, and the maximum current speeds, in knots, for both ebb and flood currents. The direction in degrees true of the ebb and flood currents are also indicated at the top of each tidal current table. As with the tide tables, be sure to adjust for Daylight Saving Time when appropriate.

An additional feature found in both the tide and current tables are symbols indicating the days of new moon, quarter moons, and full moon. And because the tide tables are calculated for each day of the year, they also coincidentally serve as a yearly calendar!

Tide predictions for many additional secondary reference stations are provided in Chapter 3, Tide and Tidal Current Difference Tables. The differences noted in the Chapter 3 tables are applied to primary reference tables in this Coast Pilot chapter to obtain estimates of the tidal situation in a desired location. For instructions on how to use the Tide and Current Differences tables, see Chapter 3.

CAUTION: The time and height differences in the Chapter 3 tables are average differences derived from comparisons of simultaneous tide observations at the subordinate location and its reference station. Because these figures are constant, they may not always provide for the daily variations of the actual tide, especially if the subordinate station is some distance from the primary reference station. Therefore, although the application of the time and height differences will generally provide fairly accurate approximations, they cannot result in predictions as accurate as those at the reference station. The reference stations are based upon much larger periods of analyses.

For more information on tides and tidal currents, see Chapter 10 in *Reed's Nautical Companion.*

GULF STREAM INFORMATION

The region where the Gulf of Mexico narrows to form the channel between the Florida Keys and Cuba may be regarded as the head of the Gulf Stream. From this region the stream sets eastward and northward through the Straits

of Florida and after passing Little Bahama Bank continues northward and then northeastward, following the general direction of the 100-fathom curve as far as Cape Hatteras, North Carolina. The flow in the Straits is frequently referred to as the Florida Current. Shortly after emerging from the Straits of Florida, the stream is joined by the Antilles Current, which flows northwesterly along the open ocean side of the West Indies before uniting with the water that has passed through the Straits. Beyond Cape Hatteras the combined current turns more and more eastward under the combined effects of the deflecting force of the Earth's rotation and the eastward-trending coastline, until it reaches the region of the Grand Banks of Newfoundland.

Eastward of the Grand Banks the whole surface is slowly driven eastward and northeastward by the prevailing westerly winds to the coastal waters of northwestern Europe. For distinction, this broad and variable wind-driven surface movement is sometimes referred to as the North Atlantic Drift or Gulf Stream Drift.

In general, the Gulf Stream as it issues into the sea through the Straits of Florida may be characterized as a swift, highly saline current of blue water whose upper stratum is composed of warm water.

On its western or inner side, the Gulf Stream is separated from the coastal waters by a zone of rapidly falling temperature, to which the term "cold wall" has been applied. It is most clearly marked north of Cape Hatteras, but extends more or less well defined from the Straits of Florida to the Grand Banks.

Throughout the whole stretch of 400 miles in the Straits of Florida, the stream flows with considerable speed. Abreast of Havana, the average surface speed in the axis of the stream is about 2.5 knots. As the cross-sectional area of the stream decreases, the speed increases gradually, until abreast of Cape Florida it becomes about 3.5 knots. From this point within the narrows of the Straits, the speed along the axis gradually decreases to about 2.5 knots off Cape Hatteras. These values are for the axis of the stream where the current is a maximum; the speed of the stream decreases gradually from the axis as the edges of the stream are approached. The speed of the stream, furthermore, is subject to fluctuations brought about by variations in winds and barometric pressure.

The Gulf Stream Mean Surface Speed table below gives the mean surface speed of the Gulf Stream in two cross-sections in the Straits of Florida. Vessels crossing the Gulf Stream at Jupiter or Fowey Rocks should make an average allowance of 2.5 knots in a northerly direction for the current. Vessels crossing the stream from Havana should make a fair allowance for the average current between 100-fathom curves of 1.1 knots in an east-northeasterly direction. From within the Straits, the axis of the Gulf Stream runs approximately parallel with the 100-fathom curve as far as Cape Hatteras. Since this stretch of coastline sweeps northward in a sharper curve than does the 100-fathom line, the stream lies at varying distances from the shore. The lateral boundaries of the current within the Straits are fairly well fixed, but when the stream flows into the sea the eastern boundary becomes somewhat vague. On the western side, the limits can be defined approximately since the waters of the stream differ in color, temperature, salinity, and flow from the inshore coastal waters. On the east, however, the Antilles Current combines with the Gulf Stream, so that its waters here merge gradually with the waters of the open Atlantic. Observations of the National Ocean Service indicate that, in general, the average position of the inner edge of the Gulf Stream as far as Cape Hatteras lies inside the 50-fathom curve. The Gulf Stream, however, shifts somewhat with the seasons and is considerably influenced by the winds, which cause fluctuations in its position, direction, and speed; consequently any limits that are assigned refer to mean or average positions. For the approximate mean positions of the inner edge and axis (point where greatest speed may be found) see the Approximate Mean Position of the Gulf Stream table on the next page.

At the western edge of the Straits of Florida the limits of the Gulf Stream are not well defined, and for this reason the location of the inner edge has been omitted for Havana, Cuba, and Key West, Florida, in this table. Between Fowey Rocks and Jupiter Inlet the inner edge is deflected westward and lies very close to the shoreline.

Along the Florida Reefs, between Alligator Reef and Dry Tortugas, the distance of the northerly edge of the Gulf Stream from the edge of the reefs gradually increases towards the west. Off Alligator Reef it is quite close inshore, while off Rebecca Shoal and Dry Tortugas it is possibly 15 to 20 miles south of the 100-fathom curve. Between the reefs and the northern edge of the Gulf Stream, the currents are ordinarily tidal and are subject at all times to considerable modification by local winds and barometric conditions. This neutral zone varies in both length and breadth; it may extend along the reefs a greater or lesser distance than stated, and its width varies as the northern edge of the Gulf Stream approaches or recedes from the reefs.

The approximate position of the axis of the Gulf Stream for various regions is shown on the following National Ocean Service charts: No. 11013, Straits of Florida; No. 411, South Carolina to Cuba; No. 11460, Cape Canaveral to Key West; No. 11420, Alligator Reef to Havana. Chart No. 11009 shows the axis and the position of the inner edge of the Gulf Stream from Cape Hatteras to the Straits of Florida.

GULF STREAM
MEAN SURFACE SPEED

Between Rebecca Shoal and Cuba		Between Fowey Rocks and Gun Cay	
Distance south of Rebecca Shoal	Mean surface speed observed	Distance east of Fowey Rocks	Mean surface speed observed
Nautical miles	Knots	Nautical Miles	Knots
20	0.3	8	2.7
35	0.7	11.5	3.5
50	2.2	15	3.2
68	2.2	22	2.7
86	0.8	29	2.1
		36	1.7

AREA DESCRIPTIONS

FLORIDA, EAST COAST

Florida's east coast varies in character from north to south. North of St. Lucie there are open sounds and rivers interspersed with short stretches of canal. Sailors can often raise sail and enjoy a good run. Anchorages are not frequent, but they are well spaced. South of St. Lucie the character of the waterway changes. High-rise buildings begin to intrude upon the natural landscape. Anchorages are infrequent and often restricted by local laws. Most boats will have to proceed under power. The many opening bridges have restricted schedules. However, here the many marine facilities are top notch—among the finest in the country.

For boaters crossing the Gulf Stream to the Bahamas, Palm Beach is a favorite spot to depart for West End and the Abacos. Fort Lauderdale and Miami are good departure points for Bimini, Cat Cay, or Nassau.

FLORIDA, THE KEYS

The Keys are Florida's answer to the Bahamas. They are an archipelago of tropical islets surrounded by beautiful, but shallow, water. For those boats drawing less than 4 or 5 feet, the inside route is possible. For deeper-draft boats, the often-boisterous Hawk Channel route is preferred. Passes between the two are restricted to a few good openings. Channel Five near Long Key and the Moser Channel near Marathon are the only choices for sailors.

The John Pennekamp Park, near Key Largo, is an undersea coral reef park. Everywhere, the coral is protected and should not be anchored upon or even touched. Those who go aground in coral are liable for fines.

Key West is the end of the line for most boaters in the Keys. The adventurous make the 60-mile passage to the Dry Tortugas to find a true "out island." Fort Jefferson guards a beautiful sandy lagoon sheltered by coral reefs. The nesting ground of the frigate bird is on aptly named Bird Key. There are no facilities for boaters—you must even remove your own trash.

BERMUDA

This archipelago is a favorite offshore destination for U.S. boaters. Whether as a stopover

APPROXIMATE MEAN POSITION OF THE GULF STREAM

Locality	Inner Edge Nautical miles	Axis Nautical miles
North of Havana, Cuba		25
Southeast of Key West, FL		45
East of Fowey Rocks, FL		10
East of Miami Beach, FL		15
East of Palm Beach, FL		15
East of Jupiter Inlet, FL		20
East of Cape Canaveral, FL	10	45
East of Daytona Beach, FL	25	75
East of Ormond Beach, FL	25	75
East of St. Augustine, FL (coast line)	40	85
East of Jacksonville, FL (coast line)	55	90
Southeast of Savannah, GA (coast line)	65	95
Southeast of Charleston, SC (coast line)	55	90
Southeast of Myrtle Beach, SC	60	100
Southeast of Cape Fear, NC (light)	35	75
Southeast of Cape Lookout, NC (light)	20	50
Southeast of Cape Hatteras, NC	10	35
Southeast of Virginia Beach, VA	85	115
Southeast of Atlantic City, NJ	120	
Southeast of Sandy Hook, NJ	150	

on the way to the Caribbean or as a cruising ground of its own, Bermuda is a favorite port of call. It lies just under 700 miles from both Newport, Rhode Island, and Norfolk, Virginia, and is approximately 900 miles north of St. Thomas in the Virgin Islands.

The major consideration voyaging to Bermuda is always the weather. Routes to the islands cross the major hurricane tracks. In addition, boats sailing from the U.S. must cross the Gulf Stream.

The approaches to Bermuda are generally well marked. You will be beyond the range of reliable LORAN coverage, but the island does have several powerful radiobeacons and long-range lights. Bermuda Harbour Radio is always standing by to aid those in trouble.

It is wise to stand well off Bermuda in heavy weather. Many vessels have encountered severe seas when deep ocean waves began tumbling on the Bermuda shelf waters. It is often hard to spot the edge of the reefs surrounding Bermuda. Keep in mind that the major beacons are situated on the reef itself; they should be given a wide berth in bad weather.

Bermuda offers a warm welcome to the visiting cruiser. The island is beautiful and safe. Most boating supplies are readily available. This is a great place to break up an offshore trip and recoup for the next leg.

THE BAHAMAS
Cruising in the Bahamas is very different from cruising U.S. waters. The waters are shallow and filled with shifting sands and coral reefs. Aids to navigation are few and far between, and none should be trusted. LORAN is also unreliable.

The tools of Bahama navigation are simple—a good depthsounder and your eyes. Most boaters will quickly learn to read the water depth ahead, utilizing the beautiful colors visible through the crystal clear water. Experienced Bahamas cruisers learn to travel when the sun is high to prevent glare on the water from impeding visibility.

The VHF radio can be a handy tool. If you leave it on channel 16 while entering an unfamiliar harbor, advice will often be radioed out to you from a boater inside. During storms boaters

relay information on location, wind speeds, and wind direction. Evenings an informal chat-hour invariably commences around 1700. Working your way from island to island you will encounter wild places with few people. The island chain is around 500 miles long, and most of the islands are uninhabited. Despite a few, often-repeated horror stories, most cruisers here are much safer than in their home towns. Bahamians are friendly and helpful people.

THE CARIBBEAN
The islands of the Caribbean are many and varied. From the gorgeous reef diving of the Caymans to the old-world charm of San Juan to the crowded harbors of the Virgins and the boisterous sailing of the Grenadines, this is an area of contrasts. You will encounter many new cultures. Some people speak Spanish and others French, but most know at least a smattering of English. You must be more self-sufficient to travel here. You may have to travel 200 miles to get fuel (Bahamas to Dominican Republic), and you may have to jug your water from an inland spigot. You learn to stock up when the food is plentiful and low in price (Puerto Rico, the Dominican Republic, and Venezuela). You will want to carry lots of heavy ground tackle, with plenty of anchor chain, to resist the chafe on coral bottoms.

Many of the harbors are not geared strictly to transient boaters, although charter areas do have marinas with stateside-type facilities. But many of the islands cater to boaters only as a courtesy; the harbors are designed for the handling of commercial ships and cruise liners. You may have to tie to a crumbling concrete wharf while clearing customs, or you may have to anchor out for weeks at a time. Of course, this is part of the great charm. Despite decades of tourism, Caribbean people have often maintained their own cultures in the face of mounting pressures to change.

Navigation in the Caribbean often involves simply sailing to the next island. Visibility is usually excellent. There is often plenty of wind—in the winter, 20 to 30 knots almost every day. The trades blow from the east day after day, week after week, month after month. When the wind switches, many harbors become uncomfortable for a few days. There are many harbors that are simply coves on the leeward side of an island.

The currents of the Caribbean tend to be the result of the constant northeast trade winds. However, they do vary with the strength of the wind, its direction, and the season. See the two current charts on the following pages for an indication of the general pattern to be expected. (Note: speeds are given in knots.)

Hurricanes are the scourge of the Caribbean. Experienced boaters plan to be south in the Grenadines or Venezuela from August through October. If you must stay in the islands during the hurricane season, plan your strategy well ahead of time. Find your hurricane hole and retreat to it early if hurricane winds threaten.

PREVAILING SURFACE CURRENTS, SUMMER (JULY, AUGUST, SEPTEMBER)

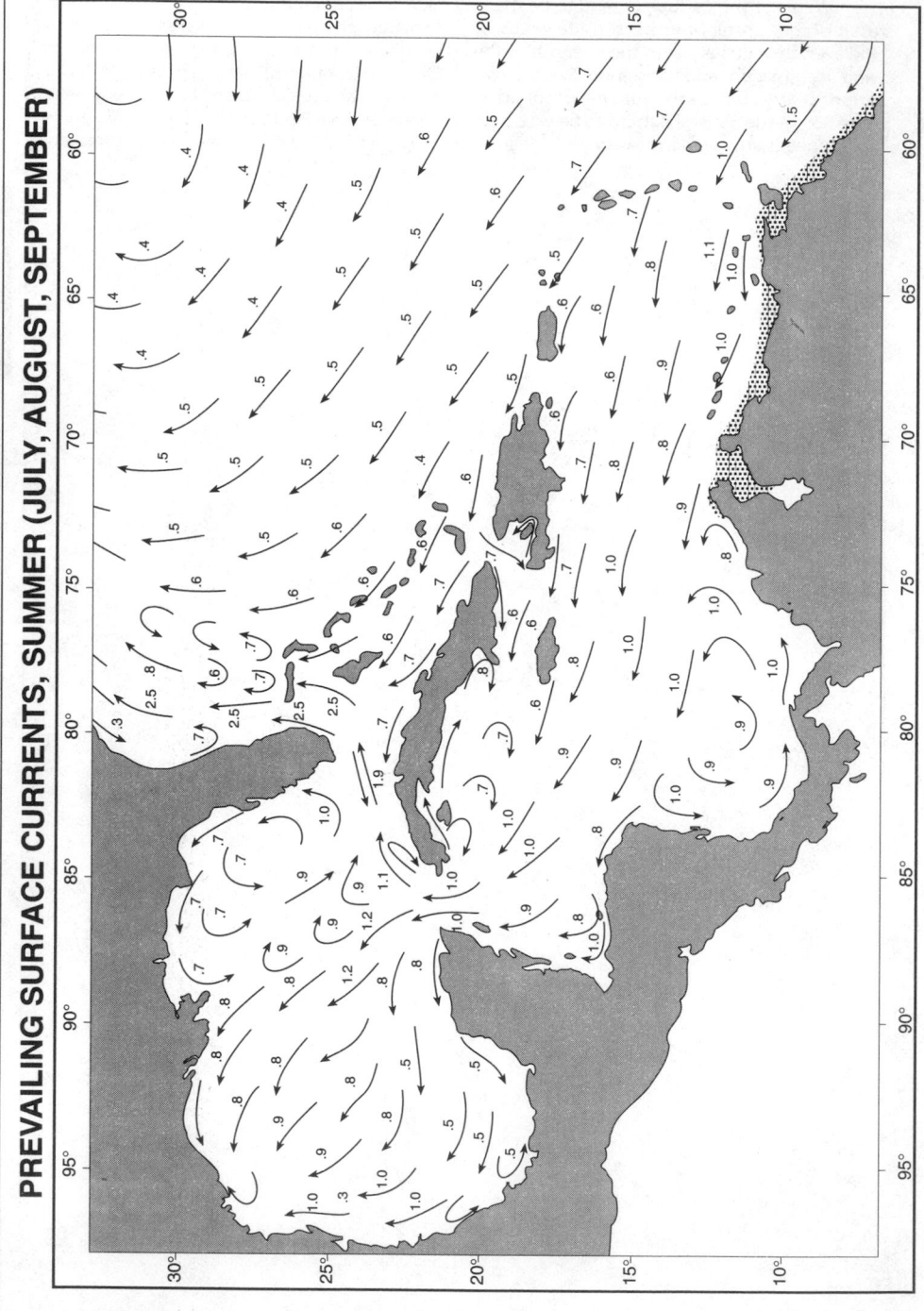

COAST PILOT

PREVAILING SURFACE CURRENTS, WINTER (JANUARY, FEBRUARY, MARCH)

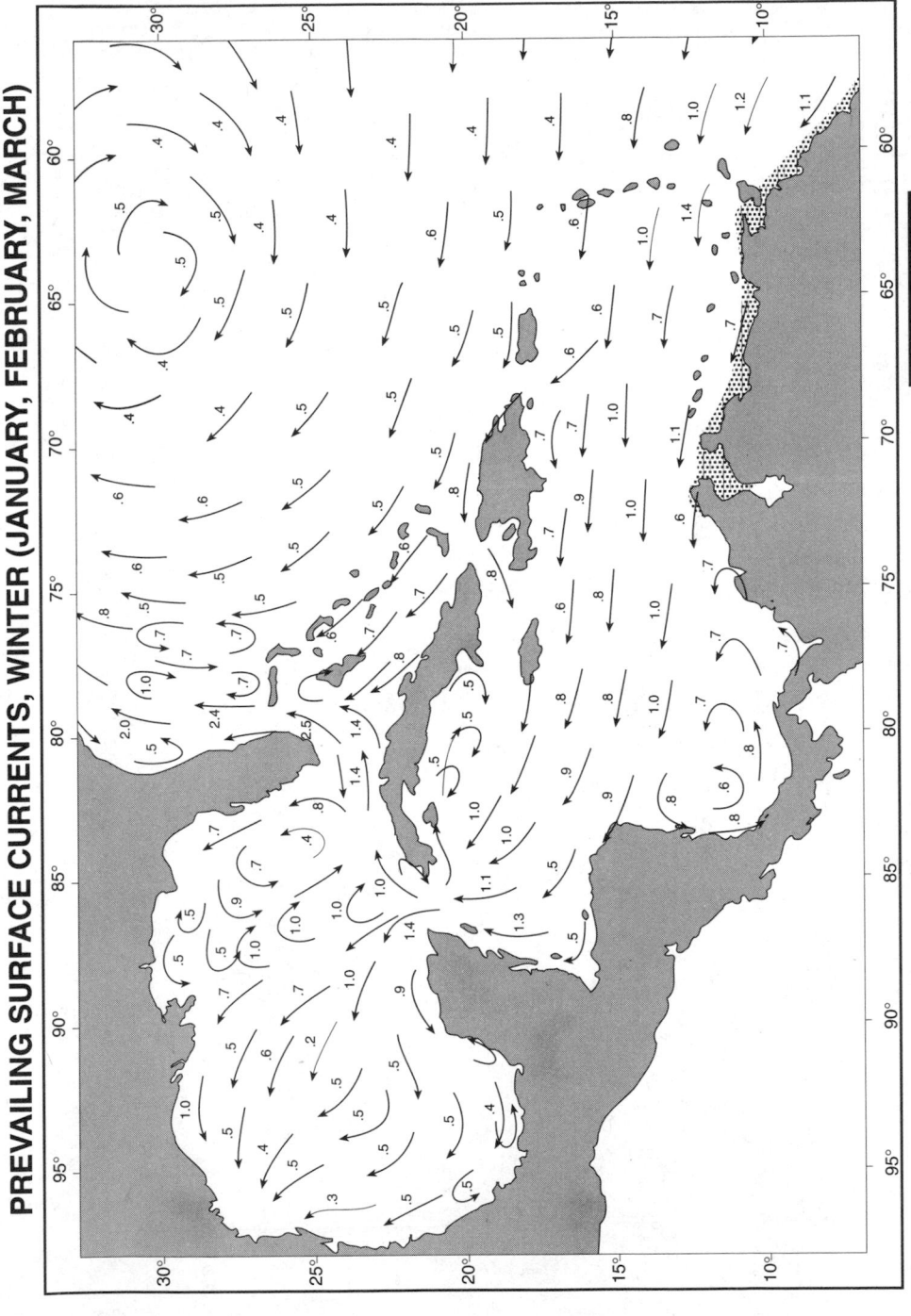

BERMUDA

APPROACHES

NOTE: In Bermuda, offshore light towers are referred to as beacons.

NORTH ROCK BEACON, 32 28.5N, 64 46.0W. Fl (4) W 20s, 70 ft, 12M. Black over yellow tower. Radar reflector; words NORTH ROCK in white letters on black background near the top of the tower.

NORTH EAST BREAKER BEACON, 32 28.7N, 64 40.9W. Fl W 2.5s, 45 ft,12M. Red tower on red tripod base. Radar reflector; words NORTH EAST in red letters on a white background near the base of the tower. RACON: **N(‒·).**

KITCHEN SHOAL BEACON, 32 26.0N, 64 37.6W. Fl (3) W 15s, 45 ft, 12M. East cardinal mark; red-and-white horizontal striped tower on a tripod. Radar reflector; word KITCHEN in red letters on a white background at the base of the tower.

Mills Breaker Buoy, 32 23.9N, 64 36.8W. V Q Fl (3) 5s. Black with a single horizontal yellow band; topmark: 2 black cones base to base; word MILLS in black on a yellow background.

Spit Buoy, 32 22.6N, 64 38.4W. Q Fl (3) W 10s. Black with a single horizontal yellow band; topmark: 2 black cones base to base; word SPIT in black on a yellow background.

ST. DAVIDS ISLAND LIGHTHOUSE, 32 21.8N, 64 39.0W. Fl (2) W 20s on top, F R+G sectored light below, 212 ft, 15M white, 20M red and green. White tower with red band. R 135°–221°, G 221°– 276°, R 276°– 044°, R 044°–135°; W+R partially obscured 044°–135°. F R lights 0.95 mile SSW, 0.63 mile SW, 0.75 mile and 1.12 mile WNW.

ST. DAVIDS RADIOBEACON, 32 22.0N, 64 38.9W. BSD (‒··· ··· ‒··), 323kHz A2A, 150M.

KINDLEY FIELD AVIATION LIGHT, on control tower at airport, 32 21.9N, 64 40.5W. Al Fl W W G 10s, 140ft, 15M. F R on tank 0.5 mile WNW; 2 F R at Swing Bridge Ferry Reach 0.8 mile WNW.

GIBBS HILL LIGHTHOUSE, summit, 32 15.1N, 64 50.0W. Fl W 10s, 354 ft, 26M. White round iron tower. Obscured 223°–228° and 229°–237°; F R obstruction light shown on top of lantern.

CHUBB HEADS BEACON, 32 17.2N, 64 58.7W. V Q Fl (9) W 15s, 60 ft, 12M. West cardinal; yellow and black horizontal striped tower on tripod; words CHUB HEADS in white letters on black central band, RACON: C(‒·‒·).

EASTERN BLUE CUT BEACON, 32 24.0N, 64 52.6W. Fl W Morse U(··‒) 10s, 60 ft, 12M. Black and white horizontal striped tower on black tripod; words EASTERN BLUE CUT in black letters on white central band; radar reflector.

TOWN CUT CHANNEL

GATES FORT LIGHT, N side, outer, 32 22.7N, 64 39.7W. F R, 46 ft, 8M. White metal framework tower with black and white checkered daymark. Visible 250°–080°.

HIGGS ISLAND LIGHT, NE corner, 32 22.6N, 64 39.7W. F G, 48 ft, 8M. Red and white checkered square on red metal framework tower, white bands. FR lights shown from Fort George flagstaff 1 mile W.

CHALK WHARF LIGHT, on NW side of channel, 32 22.7N, 64 39.9W. F R, 52ft, 8M. White metal framework tower with black and white checkered daymark. Visible 250°–095°.

HORSESHOE ISLAND LIGHT, on W corner of island, 32 22.6N, 64 39.8W. F G, 8M.

ST. GEORGE'S HARBOUR

THREE SISTERS SHOAL BEACON, 32 22.6N, 64 40.0W. V Q G (80 per minute), 4M. White beacon with green band.

HEN ISLAND BEACON, 32 22.5N, 64 40.5W. Fl G 1.5s, 16 ft, 4M. White metal framework tower with green band; Red and white checkered daymark.

ST. GEORGE'S

Bermuda Harbour Radio: Contact BHR on VHF channel 16 (working 27) or 2182kHz (working 2582kHz) when approaching the islands and when moving vessels within Bermuda. BHR is also the Airsea Rescue Coordination Center for the Bermuda area and is in contact with the U.S. Coast Guard 24 hours a day.

Weather Reports: Available from the Bermuda Yacht Reporting Service on Ordnance Island in St. George's. A dedicated phone line connects directly to the U.S. Naval Oceanography Command Facility for recorded weather and special warnings. Departure weather packages are also available from the Yacht Reporting Service. BHR transmits local and high-seas weather on VHF channel 27 at 1235 and 2035 GMT.

Bermuda Radio VRT: VHF channel 26 or 28 for marine phone calls.

H.M. Customs: Contact on VHF channel 16 (working channel 68). Pleasure vessels clear at the customs wharf on the northeast end of Ordnance Island; the facility operates 24 hours a day. All firearms must be declared and will be held or sealed by officials until the vessel departs Bermuda. This regulation includes flare guns. A fee of $15 is levied for each person aboard a visiting yacht. Fruit and vegetables from other countries are prohibited.

Dockage: The concrete wharves on the north side of Ordnance Island provide side-to dockage. Rafting boats several deep is common. More dockage is available at bulkheads west of the island. St. George's Dinghy Club may have some space at its docks near Town Cut.

Anchorage: There are designated yacht anchorages east of Ordnance Island and west of Hen Island. H.M. Customs can supply a map of the harbor area.

Fuel: Fuel is available at the bulkhead west of Ordnance Island and at the west end of the harbor. Vessels must register in advance to obtain duty-free fuel upon departure.

Repairs: Good services are available. There are some haulout facilities near the west end of the harbor and elsewhere in Bermuda in the Dockyard, in Hamilton, and in other locations. (Also in Bermuda are several sail repair agents, a rigger, and an electronics specialist. Most marine supplies are available. BHR may be able to help in locating repair services.)

Supplies: A small, but well stocked, grocery is located in St. George's. Larger supermarkets are a short drive away.

Currency: The Bermuda dollar is on a par with the U.S. dollar. U.S. currency is accepted everywhere, and credit cards are widely accepted. The Bank of Bermuda has 18 ATM machines linked to the MasterCard/Cirrus and Visa/Plus systems, 13 of which are available 24 hours a day.

Entering St. George's after dark is not recommended. If in any doubt, it is wise to stand off until daylight. All vessels must contact Bermuda Harbour Radio on VHF channel 16 before approaching the island for entry and berthing instructions. BHR can provide valuable navigational and traffic safety advice. Keep in mind the possibility of encountering a large cruise ship or commercial vessel when approaching or transiting Town Cut Channel. The anchorages in St. George's are secure in most conditions, but there are other sheltered harbors nearby if severe weather threatens. Most hurricanes pass to the west of Bermuda, with the peak season being August 15 to October 15. For the latest information sheet for yachts sailing to Bermuda contact: Bermuda Department of Tourism, P.O. Box HM 465, Hamilton, Bermuda, HM BX.

THE NARROWS

Buoy 1, Fl R 2.5s. Red.
Buoy 2, Fl G 2.5s. Green.
BEACON 10, 32 23.4N, 64 39.9W. Fl G 4s. Green port-hand beacon with topmark.
Buoy 15, Fl R 4s. Red.
Buoy 16, Fl (2) G 7.5s. Green.

SOUTH CHANNEL

BEACON 20, 32 20.9N, 64 44.4W. Fl G 2.5s. Green column.
Buoy 21, Fl R 2.5s. Red, to be replaced with a beacon.
BEACON 22, Fl G 4s. Green.
SHELLY BAY SHOAL BEACON, Fl (2) W 7.5s. Black beacon with one broad horizontal red band; topmark: 2 black spheres. Middle ground mark.
GIBBET ISLAND LIGHT, 32 19.3N, 64 44.6W. Fl R 4., 24 ft, 2M. Wood column, white base, 11ft.
DEVONSHIRE DOCK LIGHT, W side of entrance, 32 18.4N, 64 46.3W. F G, 27 ft, 2M. White post. F R on radio mast 0.7 mile and 1.2 mile ENE and 0.55 mile and 0.7 mile SE; 2 F R mark chimney 460 meters ENE.
BEACON 26, 32 18.7N, 64 47.5W. Fl G 2.5s. Green column.
Elbow Buoy, Q Fl W (6) plus one long every 10s. Yellow and black pillar; 2 cones point down; word ELBOW.
BEACON 30, 32 19.1N, 64 48.7W. Fl G 4s, 16ft. Green.
HOGFISH BEACON, 32 18.6N, 64 49.3. Fl (2) Y 10s, 16 ft, 5M. White masonry structure with black band around top. F R on radio mast 1.07 mile 290°.

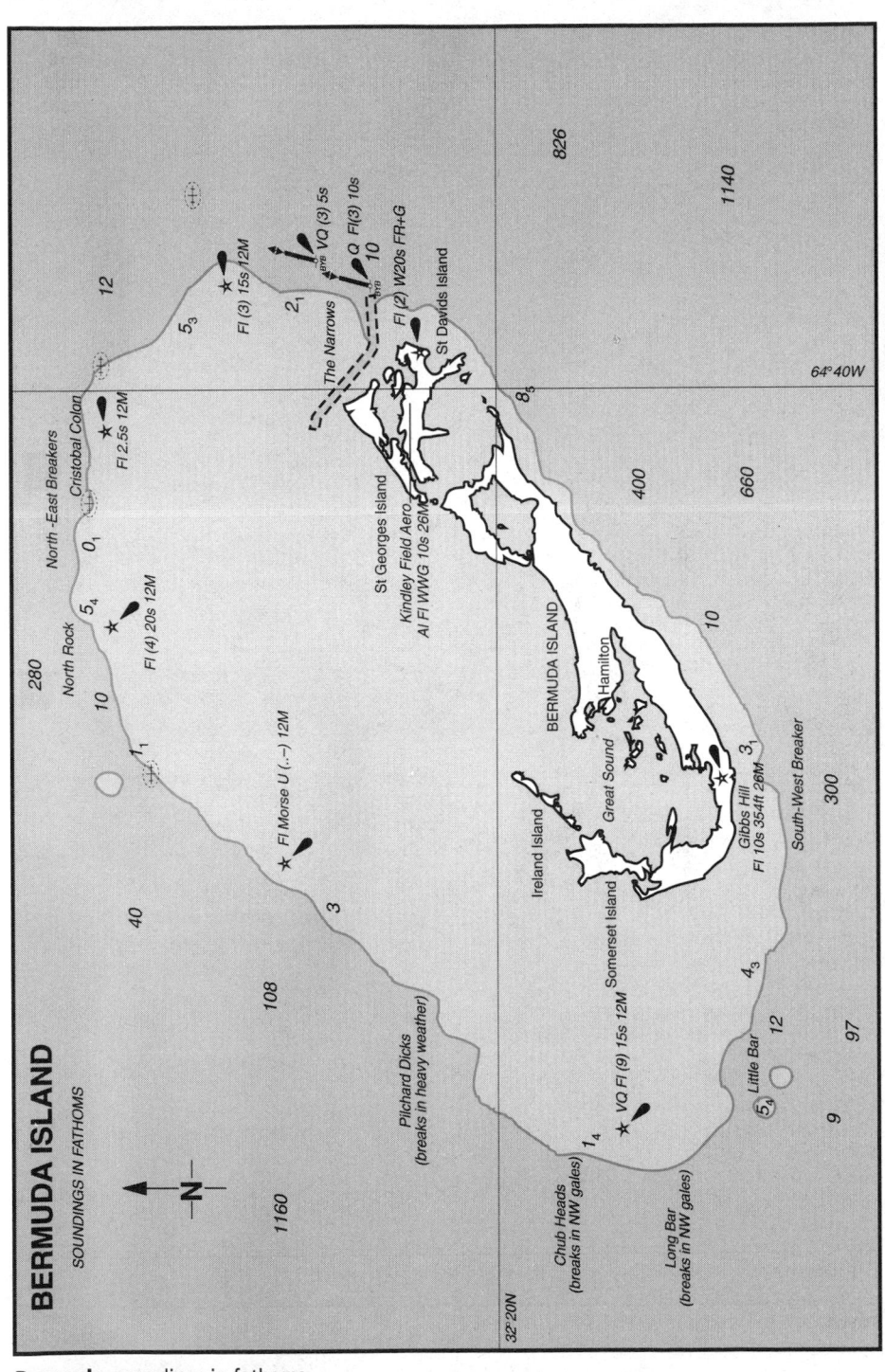

BERMUDA ISLAND
SOUNDINGS IN FATHOMS

N

1160

280

40

108

1160

10

3

1

Pilchard Dicks
(breaks in heavy weather)

Fl Morse U (..–) 12M

Fl (4) 20s 12M

5

North Rock

0

North-East Breakers

Cristobal Colan

Fl 2.5s 12M

5

12

Fl (3) 15s 12M

VQ (3) 5s

Q Fl(3) 10s

10

Fl (2) W20s FR+G

The Narrows

2

St Davids Island

8

826

1140

400

660

10

St Georges Island

Kindley Field Aero
Al Fl WWG 10s 26M

BERMUDA ISLAND

Hamilton

Great Sound

Ireland Island

Somerset Island

VQ Fl (9) 15s 12M

1

Chub Heads
(breaks in NW gales)

Long Bar
(breaks in NW gales)

Little Bar

5

12

9

97

300

South-West Breaker

4

3

Gibbs Hill
Fl 10s 354ft 26M

32°20N

64°40W

Bermuda, soundings in fathoms

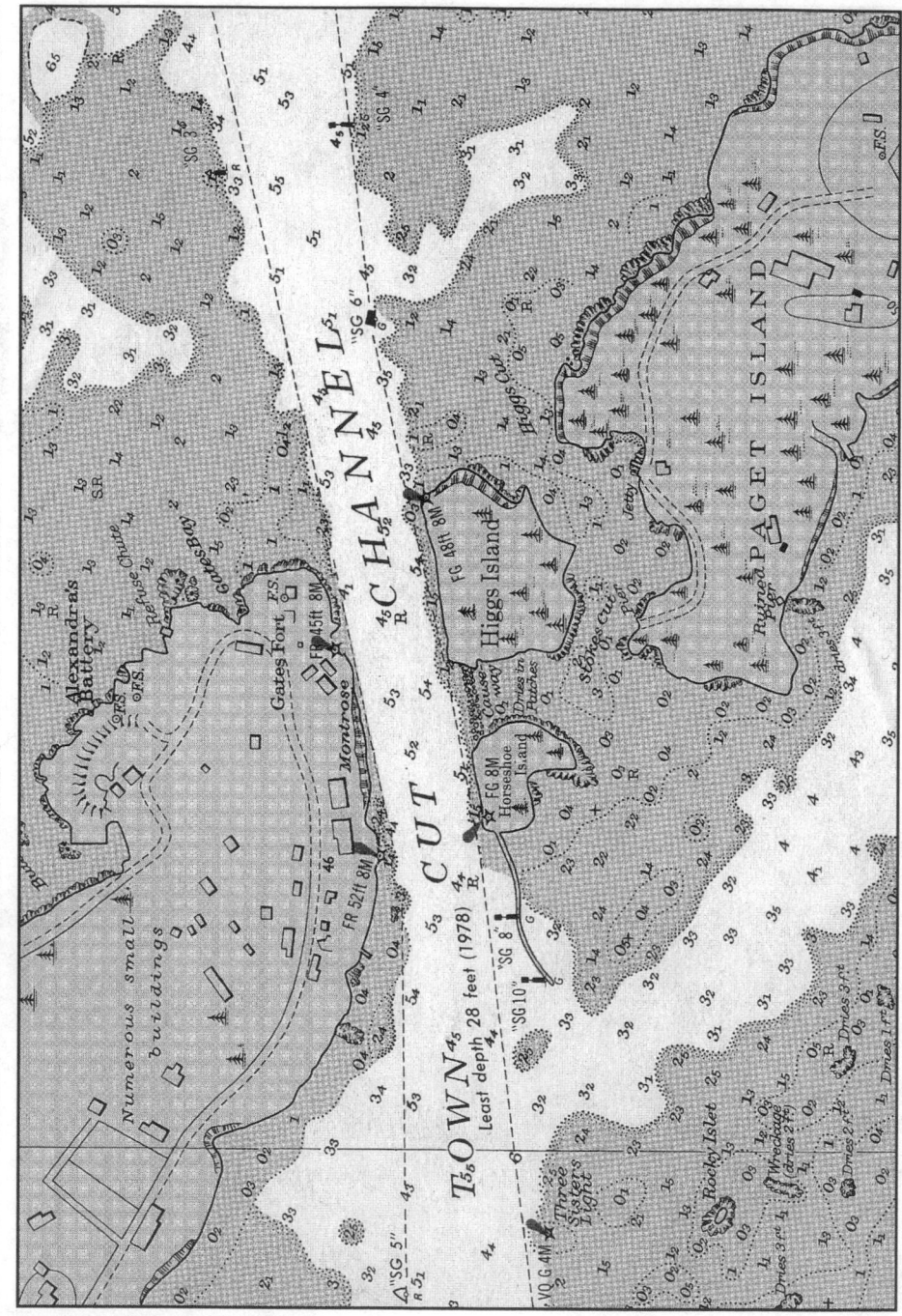

Town Cut, soundings in fathoms

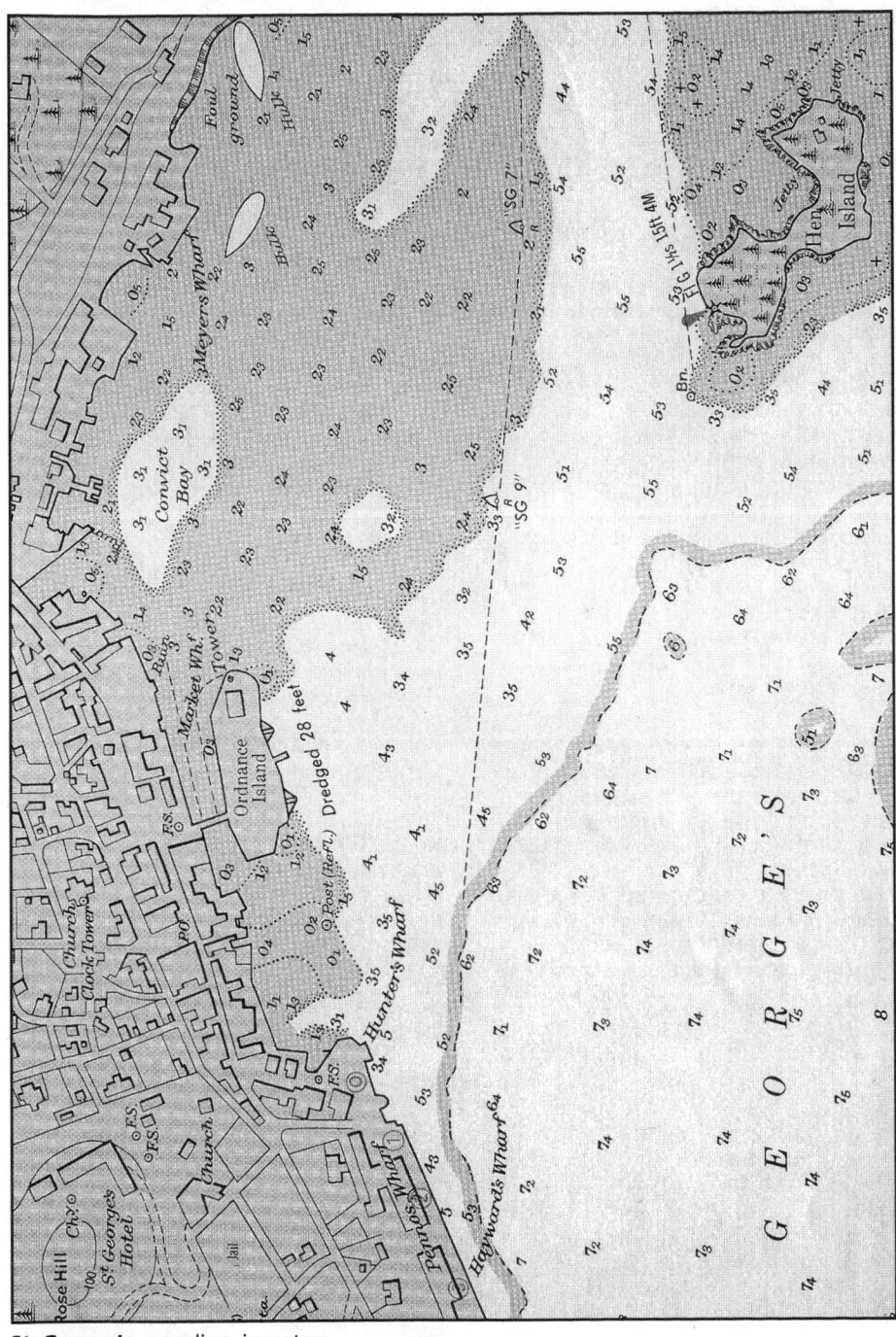

St. George's, soundings in meters

THE DOCKYARD

NORTH BREAKWATER LIGHT, 32 19.3N, 64 50.0W. Fl R 4s, 12 ft, 2M. Black structure on white bollard.
SOUTH BREAKWATER LIGHT, 32 19.2N, 64 49.9W. Fl G 4s, 12 ft, 3M. Black structure on white bollard.
WEST CORNER OF SOUTH BASIN LIGHT, Dockyard gate, 32 19.2N, 64 50.3W. F G, 27ft, 2M. Visible 322°–350°.
IRELAND ISLAND WHARF LIGHT, on pier in front of captain-in-charge residence, 32 19.1N, 64 50.4W. F R, 11ft, 2M.

DUNDONALD CHANNEL

Buoy 33, Fl R 2.5s. Red.
BEACON 35, 32 18.8N, 64 49.7W. Fl R 4s. White column with a red band.
Buoy 38, Fl G 2.5s. Green.
Buoy 40, V Q Fl (9) W 15s. West cardinal mark; yellow with a broad black band; topmark: 2 black cones point to point.
Buoy 99, Fl R 1.5s. Red.
Buoy 102, Fl G 4s. Green.
PEARL ISLAND LIGHT, 32 17.5N, 64 50.2W. Fl Y 4s, 20 ft, 5M. White concrete beacon.
Buoy 103, Fl R 4s, Red.

GREAT SOUND

PLAICES POINT LIGHT, Somerset Island, 32 17.8N, 64 51.5W. F R, 20 ft, 2M. Iron column. A F R light is shown from the center of Watford Bridge.
TWO ROCKS PASSAGE LIGHT, on N side of channel on islet off SW point of Agars Island, 32 17.5N, 64 48.6W. V Q G (80 per minute), 21ft, 5M. White structure with a green band.

TWO ROCKS PASSAGE SOUTH SIDE LIGHT, 32 17.4N, 64 48.6W. V Q R (80 per minute), 21ft, 5M. White structure with a red band.
HEAD OF THE LANE CHANNEL NORTH SIDE, 32 17.3N, 64 48.8W. Fl W 4s, 15ft, 1M. Black circular stone beacon with a white base.
TEE ROCK LIGHT, SW of Royal Bermuda Yacht Club dock, 32 17.3N, 64 47.2W. Fl G 4s, 8ft, 3M. White circular concrete tower.
HINSON ISLAND LIGHT, NW point, Timlins Narrows, 32 17.0N, 64 48.3W. F R, 12ft, 5M. White structure with a red band.
DAGGER ROCK LIGHT, 32 16.5N, 64 48.8W. Fl R 4s, 13ft, 4M. White column with red band.
RICKETTS ISLAND LIGHT, 32 16.5N, 64 49.7W. Fl R 2.5s, 18ft, 4M. White column with red top.
RIDDELLS BAY LIGHT, N side of entrance, 32 15.7N, 64 49.8W. Fl R 4s, 12ft, 1M. White circular stone tower with red top.
PEROTS ISLAND LIGHT, SW end, 32 15.5N, 64 49.9W. F W. Occasional.

HOGFISH CUT CHANNEL

NOTE: This channel is not recommended. Boaters should not attempt it without local knowledge. All arriving yachts must report to customs in St. George's.

POMPANO BEACON, 32 15.0N, 64 52.6W. V Q G (80 per minute). Green square on beacon. Turning mark for entrance into Hogfish Channel.
HOGFISH TRIPOD, 32 15.3N, 64 52.7W. Fl G 4s.
HOGFISH CUT BEACON, 32 15.5N, 64 52.9W. Fl R 4s, 13ft, 5M. Post.
WRECK HILL BEACON, 32 16.8N, 64 53.3W. V Q R. Red triangular daymark on beacon.

ST GEORGE'S, BERMUDA

HIGH & LOW WATER 1995 32°23'N 64°42'W

ATLANTIC STANDARD TIME (GMT -4H). ADD 1H DAYLIGHT SAVING APR 2 - OCT 28

BERMUDA

JANUARY

Day	Time ft	Time ft	Time ft	Time ft
1 Su ●	0135 0.4	0803 4.3	1434 0.5	2025 3.4
16 M ○	0137 0.9	0805 3.7	1428 1.0	2026 3.1
2 M	0228 0.4	0852 4.3	1523 0.5	2115 3.5
17 Tu	0214 0.9	0845 3.8	1504 0.9	2106 3.2
3 Tu	0319 0.5	0939 4.2	1610 0.5	2203 3.5
18 W	0252 0.8	0924 3.8	1539 0.8	2146 3.3
4 W	0410 0.6	1026 4.0	1656 0.6	2251 3.5
19 Th	0331 0.8	1002 3.7	1613 0.8	2226 3.3
5 Th	0501 0.8	1112 3.7	1741 0.7	2340 3.4
20 F	0413 0.9	1040 3.6	1650 0.8	2306 3.3
6 F	0553 1.0	1159 3.4	1826 0.9	
21 Sa	0459 0.9	1118 3.4	1725 0.8	2350 3.3
7 Sa	0031 3.3	0648 1.2	1245 3.2	1912 1.0
22 Su	0551 1.0	1201 3.2	1815 0.8	
8 Su ☾	0125 3.2	0746 1.3	1335 2.9	2001 1.1
23 M	0041 3.3	0654 1.1	1251 3.0	1909 0.8
9 M	0223 3.1	0846 1.4	1428 2.7	2052 1.1
24 Tu ☽	0141 3.3	0809 1.1	1351 2.9	2012 0.9
10 Tu	0325 3.1	0948 1.5	1527 2.6	2144 1.2
25 W	0247 3.4	0924 1.1	1500 2.8	2122 0.8
11 W	0425 3.1	1048 1.4	1628 2.6	2236 1.2
26 Th	0356 3.5	1033 1.0	1614 2.8	2230 0.7
12 Th	0516 3.2	1142 1.4	1725 2.7	2326 1.1
27 F	0503 3.6	1136 0.8	1725 2.9	2334 0.8
13 F	0601 3.4	1229 1.3	1815 2.8	
28 Sa	0604 3.8	1234 0.7	1826 3.1	
14 Sa	0013 1.1	0643 3.5	1311 1.2	1900 2.9
29 Su	0033 0.5	0658 3.9	1327 0.6	1920 3.3
15 Su	0057 1.0	0724 3.6	1351 1.1	1944 3.0
30 M ●	0127 0.4	0748 4.0	1416 0.5	2009 3.4
31 Tu	0218 0.4	0834 4.0	1500 0.5	2055 3.5

FEBRUARY

Day	Time ft	Time ft	Time ft	Time ft
1 W	0305 0.5	0918 3.9	1542 0.5	2140 3.6
16 Th	0235 0.7	0900 3.7	1508 0.7	2122 3.6
2 Th	0350 0.6	1000 3.8	1621 0.6	2224 3.5
17 F	0316 0.7	0939 3.7	1544 0.6	2202 3.6
3 F	0435 0.7	1041 3.5	1659 0.7	2307 3.4
18 Sa	0400 0.7	1017 3.6	1622 0.6	2244 3.6
4 Sa	0519 0.9	1121 3.3	1737 0.8	2352 3.3
19 Su	0447 0.7	1057 3.4	1704 0.6	2330 3.6
5 Su	0606 1.1	1203 3.0	1819 0.9	
20 M	0541 0.8	1142 3.2	1750 0.7	
6 M	0039 3.2	0659 1.3	1247 2.8	1905 1.0
21 Tu	0022 3.5	0644 1.0	1234 3.0	1844 0.7
7 Tu ☾	0130 3.0	0757 1.4	1337 2.6	1957 1.1
22 W ☽	0120 3.4	0757 1.0	1336 2.8	1952 0.8
8 W	0227 3.0	0900 1.5	1436 2.5	2056 1.2
23 Th	0226 3.4	0909 1.1	1447 2.7	2109 0.9
9 Th	0329 3.0	1002 1.5	1542 2.5	2156 1.2
24 F	0338 3.4	1017 1.0	1604 2.8	2221 0.8
10 F	0430 3.1	1100 1.4	1647 2.5	2253 1.2
25 Sa	0449 3.5	1121 0.9	1715 2.9	2327 0.7
11 Sa	0525 3.2	1152 1.3	1744 2.7	2345 1.1
26 Su	0552 3.6	1218 0.8	1815 3.1	
12 Su	0613 3.4	1237 1.2	1833 2.9	
27 M	0026 0.6	0645 3.7	1308 0.6	1905 3.3
13 M	0032 1.0	0657 3.5	1318 1.0	1918 3.1
28 Tu	0119 0.6	0732 3.7	1353 0.6	1951 3.5
14 Tu	0115 0.9	0739 3.7	1356 0.9	2001 3.3
15 W ○	0155 0.8	0820 3.7	1432 0.8	2042 3.4

MARCH

Day	Time ft	Time ft	Time ft	Time ft
1 W ●	0206 0.5	0815 3.7	1433 0.5	2034 3.6
16 Th ○	0134 0.8	0753 3.7	1358 0.7	2016 3.7
2 Th	0250 0.5	0855 3.7	1510 0.5	2115 3.7
17 F	0218 0.6	0834 3.7	1437 0.6	2058 3.9
3 F	0330 0.6	0933 3.7	1544 0.6	2155 3.6
18 Sa	0303 0.6	0915 3.7	1516 0.5	2141 3.9
4 Sa	0410 0.7	1010 3.4	1618 0.7	2235 3.5
19 Su	0350 0.6	0957 3.5	1558 0.5	2225 3.9
5 Su	0449 0.9	1047 3.2	1654 0.8	2316 3.4
20 M	0441 0.6	1041 3.4	1642 0.5	2314 3.9
6 M	0531 1.0	1126 3.0	1732 0.9	2359 3.2
21 Tu	0537 0.7	1130 3.2	1732 0.6	
7 Tu	0617 1.2	1209 2.8	1812 1.0	
22 W	0006 3.7	0639 0.8	1226 3.0	1832 0.8
8 W	0045 3.1	0711 1.3	1258 2.6	1900 1.2
23 Th ☽	0105 3.6	0746 0.9	1329 2.9	1946 0.9
9 Th ☾	0138 3.0	0813 1.4	1357 2.5	2001 1.3
24 F	0210 3.4	0853 1.0	1440 2.8	2103 1.0
10 F	0238 2.9	0916 1.5	1503 2.5	2113 1.3
25 Sa	0322 3.3	0959 1.0	1555 2.9	2213 0.9
11 Sa	0342 3.0	1015 1.4	1610 2.6	2218 1.3
26 Su	0435 3.3	1101 0.9	1704 3.1	2317 0.9
12 Su	0444 3.1	1109 1.3	1710 2.8	2314 1.2
27 M	0536 3.4	1156 0.8	1800 3.3	
13 M	0538 3.3	1156 1.2	1802 3.0	
28 Tu	0015 0.8	0627 3.4	1244 0.7	1848 3.4
14 Tu	0004 1.1	0626 3.4	1239 1.0	1849 3.3
29 W	0107 0.7	0712 3.5	1325 0.7	1931 3.6
15 W	0050 0.9	0710 3.6	1319 0.9	1933 3.5
30 Th ●	0152 0.7	0752 3.5	1402 0.6	2011 3.7
31 F	0233 0.7	0829 3.4	1435 0.6	2049 3.7

APRIL

Day	Time ft	Time ft	Time ft	Time ft
1 Sa	0311 0.7	0905 3.3	1509 0.7	2127 3.7
16 Su	0251 0.5	0853 3.5	1451 0.4	2121 4.2
2 Su	0348 0.8	0942 3.2	1543 0.7	2205 3.6
17 M	0342 0.5	0940 3.5	1537 0.4	2209 4.1
3 M	0425 0.9	1019 3.0	1618 0.8	2245 3.5
18 Tu	0435 0.5	1029 3.3	1627 0.5	2259 4.0
4 Tu	0504 1.0	1059 2.9	1654 0.9	2326 3.3
19 W	0531 0.6	1122 3.2	1723 0.6	2353 3.8
5 W	0546 1.1	1142 2.7	1732 1.1	
20 Th	0631 0.7	1219 3.1	1828 0.8	
6 Th	0010 3.2	0634 1.2	1231 2.6	1815 1.2
21 F ☽	0051 3.6	0732 0.8	1321 3.0	1940 0.9
7 F	0059 3.0	0730 1.3	1326 2.6	1912 1.3
22 Sa	0154 3.4	0834 0.9	1430 3.0	2051 1.0
8 Sa ☾	0155 3.0	0830 1.4	1428 2.6	2027 1.4
23 Su	0304 3.3	0935 0.9	1541 3.0	2158 1.0
9 Su	0257 3.0	0929 1.3	1532 2.7	2139 1.3
24 M	0412 3.2	1034 0.9	1646 3.2	2301 0.9
10 M	0400 3.0	1023 1.2	1632 2.9	2239 1.2
25 Tu	0512 3.2	1126 0.8	1740 3.3	2359 0.9
11 Tu	0458 3.2	1112 1.1	1727 3.2	2333 1.0
26 W	0603 3.2	1212 0.8	1826 3.5	
12 W	0550 3.3	1157 0.9	1817 3.5	
27 Th	0050 0.8	0647 3.2	1252 0.7	1908 3.6
13 Th	0024 0.9	0638 3.4	1241 0.7	1904 3.7
28 F	0134 0.8	0726 3.1	1328 0.7	1947 3.7
14 F	0113 0.7	0723 3.6	1324 0.6	1949 4.0
29 Sa ●	0214 0.8	0803 3.1	1403 0.7	2024 3.7
15 Sa ○	0202 0.6	0808 3.6	1407 0.5	2035 4.1
30 Su	0251 0.8	0839 3.1	1438 0.7	2102 3.6

TIME MERIDIAN 60°W   0000h is midnight, 1200h is noon.
Heights in feet are referenced to the chart datum of soundings.

ST GEORGE'S, BERMUDA

HIGH & LOW WATER 1995 32°23'N 64°42'W

ATLANTIC STANDARD TIME (GMT -4H).   ADD 1H DAYLIGHT SAVING APR 2 - OCT 28

MAY

Day	Time	ft	Day	Time	ft
1 M	0328 / 0917 / 1514 / 2140	0.8 / 3.0 / 0.8 / 3.6	16 Tu	0331 / 0925 / 1521 / 2153	0.4 / 3.4 / 0.3 / 4.2
2 Tu	0405 / 0957 / 1549 / 2219	0.8 / 2.9 / 0.8 / 3.5	17 W	0425 / 1017 / 1616 / 2245	0.4 / 3.3 / 0.4 / 4.1
3 W	0444 / 1038 / 1625 / 2300	0.9 / 2.8 / 0.9 / 3.4	18 Th	0519 / 1111 / 1716 / 2338	0.5 / 3.3 / 0.5 / 3.9
4 Th	0524 / 1122 / 1703 / 2343	1.0 / 2.7 / 1.0 / 3.2	19 F	0615 / 1207 / 1820	0.6 / 3.2 / 0.7
5 F	0607 / 1209 / 1747	1.1 / 2.7 / 1.1	20 Sa	0035 / 0712 / 1307 / 1926	3.6 / 0.7 / 3.1 / 0.9
6 Sa	0029 / 0654 / 1259 / 1841	3.1 / 1.2 / 2.6 / 1.2	21 Su	0134 / 0809 / 1411 /) 2030	3.4 / 0.7 / 3.1 / 1.0
7 Su	0119 / 0746 / 1354 / (1947	3.0 / 1.2 / 2.7 / 1.3	22 M	0237 / 0905 / 1517 / 2134	3.2 / 0.8 / 3.1 / 1.0
8 M	0215 / 0841 / 1453 / 2058	3.0 / 1.2 / 2.8 / 1.2	23 Tu	0340 / 0959 / 1619 / 2237	3.0 / 0.8 / 3.2 / 1.0
9 Tu	0314 / 0935 / 1552 / 2202	3.0 / 1.1 / 3.0 / 1.1	24 W	0438 / 1049 / 1713 / 2335	3.0 / 0.8 / 3.3 / 1.0
10 W	0413 / 1027 / 1649 / 2302	3.0 / 0.9 / 3.3 / 1.0	25 Th	0530 / 1134 / 1800	2.9 / 0.8 / 3.4
11 Th	0509 / 1116 / 1743 / 2358	3.1 / 0.8 / 3.5 / 0.8	26 F	0027 / 0616 / 1215 / 1842	0.9 / 2.9 / 0.8 / 3.5
12 F	0602 / 1204 / 1834	3.2 / 0.6 / 3.8	27 Sa	0111 / 0657 / 1254 / 1921	0.9 / 2.9 / 0.8 / 3.5
13 Sa	0052 / 0653 / 1252 / 1924	0.6 / 3.3 / 0.4 / 4.1	28 Su	0151 / 0736 / 1333 / 1959	0.9 / 2.9 / 0.8 / 3.6
14 Su	0145 / 0743 / 1340 / O 2013	0.5 / 3.4 / 0.3 / 4.2	29 M	0229 / 0815 / 1411 / ● 2038	0.8 / 2.9 / 0.8 / 3.6
15 M	0238 / 0834 / 1430 / 2103	0.4 / 3.4 / 0.3 / 4.3	30 Tu	0307 / 0855 / 1449 / 2117	0.8 / 2.9 / 0.8 / 3.6
			31 W	0345 / 0937 / 1526 / 2157	0.8 / 2.9 / 0.8 / 3.5

JUNE

Day	Time	ft	Day	Time	ft
1 Th	0424 / 1019 / 1603 / 2238	0.9 / 2.8 / 0.9 / 3.4	16 F	0501 / 1054 / 1704 / 2320	0.4 / 3.4 / 0.5 / 3.9
2 F	0502 / 1102 / 1642 / 2320	0.9 / 2.8 / 1.0 / 3.3	17 Sa	0553 / 1148 / 1803	0.5 / 3.3 / 0.7
3 Sa	0540 / 1146 / 1725	1.0 / 2.8 / 1.0	18 Su	0012 / 0645 / 1244 / 1903	3.6 / 0.6 / 3.3 / 0.8
4 Su	0002 / 0621 / 1232 / 1816	3.2 / 1.0 / 2.8 / 1.1	19 M	0106 / 0736 / 1342 /) 2003	3.4 / 0.7 / 3.2 / 1.0
5 M	0047 / 0706 / 1321 / 1915	3.1 / 1.0 / 2.8 / 1.1	20 Tu	0202 / 0827 / 1443 / 2103	3.1 / 0.8 / 3.2 / 1.1
6 Tu	0135 / 0756 / 1414 / (2021	3.0 / 1.0 / 2.9 / 1.1	21 W	0259 / 0918 / 1544 / 2204	2.9 / 0.9 / 3.2 / 1.1
7 W	0229 / 0849 / 1513 / 2129	3.0 / 0.9 / 3.1 / 1.1	22 Th	0356 / 1006 / 1640 / 2302	2.8 / 0.9 / 3.2 / 1.1
8 Th	0327 / 0944 / 1612 / 2233	2.9 / 0.8 / 3.3 / 0.9	23 F	0451 / 1054 / 1730 / 2355	2.7 / 0.9 / 3.3 / 1.1
9 F	0427 / 1039 / 1711 / 2334	3.0 / 0.6 / 3.6 / 0.8	24 Sa	0541 / 1139 / 1814	2.7 / 0.9 / 3.4
10 Sa	0528 / 1132 / 1807	3.0 / 0.5 / 3.8	25 Su	0041 / 0626 / 1224 / 1855	1.1 / 2.8 / 0.9 / 3.5
11 Su	0032 / 0626 / 1226 / 1901	0.6 / 3.1 / 0.4 / 4.1	26 M	0123 / 0709 / 1307 / 1934	1.0 / 2.8 / 0.9 / 3.5
12 M	0128 / 0722 / 1320 / 1953	0.5 / 3.2 / 0.3 / 4.2	27 Tu	0203 / 0751 / 1348 / ● 2014	1.0 / 2.9 / 0.9 / 3.6
13 Tu	0222 / 0816 / 1414 / O 2045	0.4 / 3.3 / 0.2 / 4.3	28 W	0242 / 0833 / 1428 / 2054	0.9 / 2.9 / 0.9 / 3.6
14 W	0316 / 0909 / 1509 / 2136	0.3 / 3.4 / 0.3 / 4.2	29 Th	0321 / 0915 / 1506 / 2135	0.9 / 3.0 / 0.9 / 3.6
15 Th	0408 / 1001 / 1606 / 2228	0.3 / 3.4 / 0.4 / 4.1	30 F	0358 / 0957 / 1543 / 2216	0.9 / 3.0 / 0.9 / 3.5

JULY

Day	Time	ft	Day	Time	ft
1 Sa	0434 / 1039 / 1622 / 2256	0.9 / 3.0 / 0.9 / 3.4	16 Su	0523 / 1122 / 1739 / 2344	0.6 / 3.6 / 0.7 / 3.6
2 Su	0510 / 1120 / 1705 / 2336	0.9 / 3.0 / 1.0 / 3.3	17 M	0610 / 1213 / 1833	0.7 / 3.5 / 0.9
3 M	0547 / 1202 / 1753	0.9 / 3.0 / 1.0	18 Tu	0032 / 0656 / 1307 / 1929	3.3 / 0.8 / 3.4 / 1.1
4 Tu	0016 / 0629 / 1248 / 1848	3.2 / 0.9 / 3.1 / 1.1	19 W	0121 / 0744 / 1402 /) 2026	3.1 / 0.9 / 3.3 / 1.2
5 W	0100 / 0716 / 1340 / (1952	3.1 / 0.9 / 3.2 / 1.1	20 Th	0213 / 0833 / 1500 / 2124	2.9 / 1.0 / 3.2 / 1.3
6 Th	0151 / 0810 / 1438 / 2102	3.0 / 0.8 / 3.3 / 1.0	21 F	0309 / 0924 / 1559 / 2221	2.8 / 1.1 / 3.2 / 1.4
7 F	0249 / 0908 / 1541 / 2209	2.9 / 0.7 / 3.4 / 1.0	22 Sa	0407 / 1016 / 1654 / 2316	2.7 / 1.1 / 3.3 / 1.4
8 Sa	0354 / 1009 / 1643 / 2313	2.9 / 0.6 / 3.6 / 0.9	23 Su	0503 / 1107 / 1742	2.7 / 1.1 / 3.4
9 Su	0501 / 1109 / 1744	3.0 / 0.5 / 3.8	24 M	0005 / 0555 / 1156 / 1826	1.3 / 2.8 / 1.1 / 3.5
10 M	0013 / 0604 / 1208 / 1841	0.7 / 3.1 / 0.4 / 4.0	25 Tu	0050 / 0641 / 1242 / 1908	1.2 / 2.9 / 1.1 / 3.6
11 Tu	0110 / 0703 / 1306 / 1936	0.6 / 3.3 / 0.4 / 4.2	26 W	0132 / 0726 / 1326 / 1949	1.2 / 3.1 / 1.0 / 3.7
12 W	0205 / 0758 / 1403 / O 2028	0.5 / 3.4 / 0.3 / 4.2	27 Th	0212 / 0809 / 1406 / ● 2030	1.1 / 3.2 / 1.0 / 3.7
13 Th	0257 / 0851 / 1458 / 2118	0.4 / 3.5 / 0.4 / 4.2	28 F	0250 / 0851 / 1444 / 2111	1.0 / 3.3 / 1.0 / 3.7
14 F	0347 / 0941 / 1552 / 2208	0.4 / 3.6 / 0.4 / 4.1	29 Sa	0326 / 0932 / 1522 / 2151	1.0 / 3.3 / 1.0 / 3.7
15 Sa	0435 / 1032 / 1646 / 2256	0.5 / 3.6 / 0.6 / 3.9	30 Su	0401 / 1013 / 1601 / 2230	1.0 / 3.4 / 1.0 / 3.6
			31 M	0436 / 1053 / 1644 / 2308	0.9 / 3.4 / 1.0 / 3.5

AUGUST

Day	Time	ft	Day	Time	ft
1 Tu	0514 / 1134 / 1733 / 2348	0.9 / 3.4 / 1.0 / 3.3	16 W	0611 / 1227 / 1852	1.0 / 3.5 / 1.3
2 W	0555 / 1220 / 1828	0.9 / 3.4 / 1.1	17 Th	0040 / 0658 / 1318 /) 1946	3.1 / 1.2 / 3.4 / 1.4
3 Th	0032 / 0643 / 1313 / (1933	3.2 / 0.9 / 3.5 / 1.1	18 F	0130 / 0749 / 1413 / 2043	3.0 / 1.3 / 3.3 / 1.5
4 F	0124 / 0739 / 1412 / 2044	3.1 / 0.9 / 3.5 / 1.2	19 Sa	0224 / 0844 / 1511 / 2140	2.8 / 1.4 / 3.3 / 1.6
5 Sa	0225 / 0843 / 1517 / 2152	3.0 / 0.9 / 3.6 / 1.1	20 Su	0325 / 0941 / 1611 / 2235	2.8 / 1.4 / 3.3 / 1.6
6 Su	0334 / 0951 / 1623 / 2256	3.0 / 0.8 / 3.7 / 1.0	21 M	0426 / 1037 / 1706 / 2327	2.9 / 1.4 / 3.4 / 1.5
7 M	0444 / 1057 / 1727 / 2356	3.1 / 0.8 / 3.9 / 0.9	22 Tu	0522 / 1129 / 1755	3.0 / 1.4 / 3.5
8 Tu	0549 / 1159 / 1826	3.3 / 0.7 / 4.0	23 W	0014 / 0612 / 1217 / 1839	1.5 / 3.2 / 1.3 / 3.7
9 W	0052 / 0647 / 1257 / 1920	0.8 / 3.5 / 0.6 / 4.1	24 Th	0057 / 0657 / 1301 / 1922	1.4 / 3.4 / 1.2 / 3.8
10 Th	0145 / 0740 / 1352 / O 2010	0.7 / 3.6 / 0.6 / 4.2	25 F	0137 / 0741 / 1342 / 2003	1.3 / 3.5 / 1.2 / 3.9
11 F	0234 / 0830 / 1444 / 2058	0.6 / 3.8 / 0.6 / 4.1	26 Sa	0214 / 0823 / 1421 / ● 2044	1.2 / 3.7 / 1.1 / 3.9
12 Sa	0320 / 0918 / 1534 / 2143	0.6 / 3.9 / 0.6 / 4.0	27 Su	0251 / 0905 / 1501 / 2124	1.1 / 3.8 / 1.0 / 3.9
13 Su	0404 / 1005 / 1623 / 2228	0.7 / 3.9 / 0.8 / 3.8	28 M	0326 / 0945 / 1542 / 2203	1.1 / 3.8 / 1.0 / 3.8
14 M	0446 / 1052 / 1711 / 2311	0.8 / 3.8 / 0.9 / 3.6	29 Tu	0403 / 1026 / 1627 / 2242	1.0 / 3.9 / 1.1 / 3.7
15 Tu	0528 / 1139 / 1800 / 2355	0.9 / 3.7 / 1.1 / 3.4	30 W	0443 / 1110 / 1717 / 2324	1.0 / 3.8 / 1.1 / 3.5
			31 Th	0527 / 1158 / 1815	1.0 / 3.8 / 1.2

TIME MERIDIAN 60°W

0000h is midnight, 1200h is noon.

Heights in feet are referenced to the chart datum of soundings.

REED'S NAUTICAL ALMANAC

Get Your Free
REED'S Supplement

Dear REED'S Customer,
Please take a moment to complete this questionnaire so we can continue to make REED'S your most important nautical resource. Thank you!

[ ] Please send me my **free** annual supplement to REED'S 1995 Almanac.

Name _____

Address _____

City _____ State _____ Zip _____

Type of boat owned? _____

[ ] Power [ ] Sail Builder _____ Length _____

In what type of boating activity do you participate? [ ] Daysailing [ ] Fishing
[ ] Racing [ ] Coastal Cruising [ ] Offshore [ ] Commercial [ ] Other _____

How many days of the year do you spend on the water?
[ ] <20 [ ] 20 - 39 [ ] 40 - 59 [ ] 60 - 89 [ ] > 90 [ ] All Year

Where do you go? _____

Topics or features in REED'S that are of particular interest or use to you?
[ ] Coast Pilot [ ] Harbor Charts [ ] Tides/Currents [ ] Communications
[ ] Electronics Navigation [ ] Nautical Ephemeris [ ] Other _____

How many years have you been buying REED'S? [ ] 1 - 3 [ ] 4 - 6 [ ] 7 - 10 [ ] >10

Fold along dotted line

How many times throughout the year do you refer to REED'S?
[ ] <20 [ ] 20 - 50 [ ] 51 - 100 [ ] >100

Would you find it valuable for REED'S to issue supplements more frequently than once a year? [ ] Yes [ ] No   How often? [ ] Semi-Annually [ ] Quarterly

What other areas would you like REED'S to cover in future editions?
[ ] North California   [ ] South California   [ ] Baja   [ ] Mexico (Pacific Coast)
[ ] Hawaii [ ] South America [ ] Canada [ ] Other _____

Do you have a copy of REED'S Nautical Companion? [ ] Yes   [ ] No

Would you like more information on REED'S Companion? [ ] Yes [ ] No

What improvements can you suggest for REED'S Almanacs? _____
_____
_____

Other comments _____
_____

Please see reverse side

Are you planning a charter? [ ] Yes   [ ] No   [ ] Bareboat   [ ] Crewed

Average days spent on a charter per year? [ ] 3 - 7 [ ] 8 - 14 [ ] >14

Where do you intend to charter? [ ] Caribbean   [ ] East Coast   [ ] Europe
[ ] Pacific Northwest [ ] West Coast [ ] Mexico [ ] Other _____

In the next 12 months what do you expect to spend on all boating expenses?
[ ] <$1,000   [ ] $1,000 - $3,000   [ ] $3,001 - $5,000   [ ] over $5,000

What equipment do you have/intend to buy in the next 12 months?

	Have	Intend to Buy		Have	Intend to Buy
Navigation	[ ]	[ ]	Hardware	[ ]	[ ]
Marine Radio	[ ]	[ ]	Rigging	[ ]	[ ]
Sails	[ ]	[ ]	Weather	[ ]	[ ]
Canvas	[ ]	[ ]	Inflatable	[ ]	[ ]
Fishing Gear	[ ]	[ ]	Outboard	[ ]	[ ]

Thank you for taking the time to help us improve REED'S Nautical Almanac!

-------------------- **Fold along dotted line and seal** --------------------

NO POSTAGE
NECESSARY
IF MAILED IN THE
UNITED STATES

BUSINESS REPLY MAIL
FIRST CLASS MAIL PERMIT NO. 8237 BOSTON MA

POSTAGE WILL BE PAID BY ADDRESSEE

THOMAS REED PUBLICATIONS, INC.
120 LEWIS WHARF
BOSTON MA 02110-9838

ST GEORGE'S, BERMUDA

HIGH & LOW WATER 1995 · 32°23'N 64°42'W

ATLANTIC STANDARD TIME (GMT -4H). ADD 1H DAYLIGHT SAVING APR 2 - OCT 28

BERMUDA

SEPTEMBER

Day	Time	ft	Time	ft	Time	ft	Time	ft
1 F	0012	3.3	0619	1.0	1253	3.8	1922	1.3
2 Sa	0109	3.2	0720	1.1	1353	3.7	(2031	1.3
3 Su	0213	3.1	0832	1.1	1500	3.7	2138	1.3
4 M	0324	3.2	0945	1.1	1609	3.8	2241	1.2
5 Tu	0434	3.3	1051	1.0	1714	3.9	2340	1.1
6 W	0537	3.5	1152	0.9	1812	4.0		
7 Th	0034	1.0	0632	3.7	1249	0.9	1904	4.1
8 F	0123	0.9	0722	3.9	1341	0.8	O 1951	4.1
9 Sa	0208	0.9	0809	4.0	1429	0.8	2035	4.0
10 Su	0249	0.9	0854	4.1	1515	0.9	2117	3.9
11 M	0328	0.9	0938	4.1	1559	1.0	2157	3.8
12 Tu	0406	1.0	1021	4.0	1642	1.1	2237	3.6
13 W	0445	1.2	1104	3.8	1726	1.3	2319	3.4
14 Th	0526	1.2	1149	3.7	1814	1.4		
15 F	0003	3.2	0612	1.4	1236	3.5	1906	1.6
16 Sa	0052	3.1	0704	1.5	1328	3.4	) 2002	1.7
17 Su	0147	3.0	0804	1.6	1425	3.3	2100	1.8
18 M	0248	3.0	0906	1.7	1526	3.4	2156	1.8
19 Tu	0350	3.0	1005	1.6	1626	3.4	2248	1.7
20 W	0448	3.2	1059	1.6	1719	3.6	2336	1.6
21 Th	0540	3.4	1148	1.5	1806	3.7		
22 F	0019	1.5	0627	3.6	1233	1.4	1851	3.8
23 Sa	0059	1.4	0712	3.8	1316	1.2	1933	3.9
24 Su	0137	1.2	0755	4.0	1358	1.1	● 2015	4.0
25 M	0215	1.1	0837	4.2	1442	1.1	2056	3.9
26 Tu	0253	1.0	0920	4.2	1527	1.1	2137	3.8
27 W	0333	1.0	1003	4.2	1615	1.1	2220	3.7
28 Th	0417	1.0	1050	4.2	1709	1.2	2307	3.6
29 F	0506	1.1	1141	4.1	1808	1.2		
30 Sa	0000	3.4	0603	1.2	1237	4.0	1913	1.3

OCTOBER

Day	Time	ft	Time	ft	Time	ft	Time	ft
1 Su	0100	3.3	0712	1.3	1339	3.9	(2019	1.4
2 M	0206	3.3	0829	1.3	1447	3.8	2123	1.4
3 Tu	0316	3.4	0939	1.3	1557	3.8	2224	1.3
4 W	0425	3.5	1044	1.2	1702	3.8	2321	1.2
5 Th	0525	3.7	1143	1.1	1757	3.9		
6 F	0013	1.1	0617	3.9	1238	1.1	1845	3.9
7 Sa	0058	1.1	0704	4.0	1328	1.0	1929	3.9
8 Su	0139	1.0	0748	4.1	1413	1.0	O 2010	3.8
9 M	0217	1.0	0830	4.2	1455	1.0	2049	3.7
10 Tu	0252	1.1	0911	4.2	1535	1.1	2128	3.6
11 W	0329	1.1	0951	4.2	1615	1.2	2206	3.5
12 Th	0406	1.2	1032	3.9	1656	1.4	2247	3.3
13 F	0446	1.3	1114	3.7	1740	1.5	2331	3.2
14 Sa	0529	1.5	1159	3.6	1829	1.6		
15 Su	0020	3.1	0618	1.6	1249	3.5	1922	1.7
16 M	0114	3.0	0719	1.7	1343	3.4	) 2019	1.8
17 Tu	0212	3.0	0826	1.8	1442	3.4	2114	1.8
18 W	0313	3.1	0928	1.7	1542	3.4	2206	1.7
19 Th	0412	3.3	1024	1.7	1638	3.5	2254	1.6
20 F	0506	3.5	1116	1.5	1729	3.6	2338	1.4
21 Sa	0555	3.8	1204	1.4	1816	3.7		
22 Su	0019	1.3	0642	4.0	1251	1.2	1902	3.8
23 M	0100	1.1	0727	4.2	1338	1.1	1946	3.8
24 Tu	0141	1.0	0812	4.4	1425	1.0	● 2030	3.8
25 W	0224	0.9	0857	4.5	1514	1.0	2115	3.8
26 Th	0309	0.9	0944	4.5	1606	1.0	2202	3.7
27 F	0357	0.9	1033	4.4	1701	1.0	2254	3.6
28 Sa	0451	1.0	1125	4.2	1759	1.1	2349	3.5
29 Su	0554	1.1	1222	4.1	1900	1.2		
30 M	0050	3.4	0706	1.3	1323	3.9	(2002	1.3
31 Tu	0155	3.4	0818	1.3	1430	3.7	2104	1.3

NOVEMBER

Day	Time	ft	Time	ft	Time	ft	Time	ft
1 W	0305	3.5	0926	1.3	1538	3.6	2203	1.2
2 Th	0413	3.6	1030	1.3	1642	3.6	2257	1.2
3 F	0511	3.7	1131	1.2	1736	3.6	2347	1.1
4 Sa	0601	3.9	1225	1.2	1824	3.6		
5 Su	0030	1.1	0646	4.0	1314	1.1	1906	3.5
6 M	0109	1.1	0728	4.1	1357	1.1	1946	3.5
7 Tu	0146	1.0	0807	4.1	1436	1.1	O 2024	3.4
8 W	0221	1.1	0846	4.0	1514	1.1	2101	3.4
9 Th	0258	1.1	0924	4.0	1551	1.2	2141	3.3
10 F	0335	1.2	1004	3.9	1630	1.3	2222	3.2
11 Sa	0413	1.3	1044	3.7	1711	1.4	2305	3.1
12 Su	0453	1.4	1127	3.6	1754	1.5	2352	3.0
13 M	0536	1.5	1213	3.5	1841	1.5		
14 Tu	0042	3.0	0628	1.6	1303	3.3	1932	1.6
15 W	0136	3.0	0732	1.7	1357	3.3	) 2025	1.6
16 Th	0233	3.1	0841	1.7	1454	3.2	2117	1.5
17 F	0332	3.3	0943	1.6	1551	3.3	2207	1.4
18 Sa	0429	3.5	1041	1.5	1647	3.3	2254	1.2
19 Su	0522	3.7	1136	1.3	1739	3.4	2341	1.1
20 M	0612	4.0	1228	1.1	1830	3.5		
21 Tu	0027	0.9	0701	4.2	1320	1.0	1919	3.6
22 W	0113	0.8	0749	4.4	1411	0.8	● 2007	3.6
23 Th	0201	0.7	0837	4.5	1502	0.8	2057	3.7
24 F	0251	0.7	0926	4.5	1554	0.8	2148	3.6
25 Sa	0343	0.7	1016	4.4	1648	0.8	2240	3.6
26 Su	0441	0.8	1108	4.2	1743	0.9	2336	3.5
27 M	0544	1.0	1203	4.0	1840	0.9		
28 Tu	0034	3.5	0652	1.1	1302	3.8	1938	1.0
29 W	0137	3.4	0759	1.2	1404	3.5	(2036	1.1
30 Th	0244	3.4	0906	1.3	1508	3.3	2132	1.1

DECEMBER

Day	Time	ft	Time	ft	Time	ft	Time	ft
1 F	0352	3.5	1011	1.3	1612	3.2	2226	1.1
2 Sa	0451	3.6	1114	1.3	1709	3.2	2315	1.1
3 Su	0542	3.7	1210	1.2	1759	3.1	2359	1.0
4 M	0627	3.8	1258	1.1	1843	3.1		
5 Tu	0040	1.0	0707	3.8	1340	1.1	1923	3.1
6 W	0118	1.0	0745	3.9	1417	1.1	O 2001	3.1
7 Th	0156	1.0	0823	3.9	1453	1.1	2039	3.1
8 F	0234	1.0	0900	3.8	1529	1.1	2119	3.1
9 Sa	0311	1.1	0939	3.8	1606	1.1	2200	3.1
10 Su	0347	1.1	1018	3.7	1643	1.2	2241	3.1
11 M	0424	1.2	1059	3.5	1720	1.2	2324	3.0
12 Tu	0503	1.3	1140	3.4	1757	1.2		
13 W	0009	3.0	0549	1.4	1223	3.3	1838	1.3
14 Th	0057	3.0	0643	1.4	1308	3.1	1925	1.3
15 F	0150	3.0	0748	1.5	1400	3.0	2018	1.2
16 Sa	0248	3.2	0900	1.4	1457	3.0	2115	1.1
17 Su	0348	3.3	1008	1.3	1559	3.0	2210	1.0
18 M	0448	3.6	1110	1.2	1701	3.1	2305	0.8
19 Tu	0544	3.9	1207	1.0	1800	3.2	2359	0.7
20 W	0637	4.1	1302	0.8	1856	3.3		
21 Th	0052	0.5	0728	4.3	1355	0.6	● 1949	3.4
22 F	0145	0.5	0819	4.4	1447	0.5	2041	3.5
23 Sa	0238	0.4	0908	4.4	1538	0.5	2132	3.6
24 Su	0333	0.5	0958	4.3	1629	0.5	2224	3.6
25 M	0430	0.6	1049	4.1	1720	0.6	2316	3.6
26 Tu	0528	0.8	1140	3.9	1812	0.7		
27 W	0011	3.5	0630	1.0	1233	3.6	1905	0.8
28 Th	0110	3.4	0733	1.1	1329	3.3	(1959	0.9
29 F	0213	3.0	0838	1.2	1428	3.0	2053	1.0
30 Sa	0320	3.3	0943	1.3	1532	2.8	2147	1.0
31 Su	0423	3.3	1049	1.3	1636	2.8	2238	1.1

TIME MERIDIAN 60°W · 0000h is midnight, 1200h is noon.
Heights in feet are referenced to the chart datum of soundings.

FLORIDA

NOTE: For information on parts of the Florida coast not covered here, as well as the entire eastern coast of North America from Halifax, Nova Scotia, to Brownsville, Texas, refer to Reed's Nautical Almanac, East Coast 1995 edition. For more information on U.S. customs and immigration procedures refer to the introduction to this chapter.

CAUTION: The chartlets in this section are not intended for navigation and are included for reference and planning purposes only. While chartlets reproduced from government sources are from the most current editions as of press time, they incorporate no corrections to navigational aids, depths, or hazards since the edition publication date.

FORT PIERCE INLET

Fort Pierce Inlet Lighted Whistle Buoy 2, 27 28.5N, 80 16.2W. Fl R 4s, 4M. Red.
ENTRANCE RANGE (Front Light), 27 28.1N, 80 18.2W. Q R, 15ft. KRW on skeleton tower on piles. Visible 2° each side of rangeline. **(Rear Light),** 1,285 yards, 259.6° from front light. Iso R 6s, 50ft. KRW on skeleton tower on piles. Visible 2° each side of rangeline.
Buoy 3, Green can.
Buoy 4, Red nun.
Buoy 4A, Red nun.
Buoy 5, Green can.
Buoy 6, Red nun.
Lighted Buoy 7, Fl G 4s, 4M. Green.
INNER RANGE (Front Light), 27 28.3N, 80 17.8W. Q W, 20ft. KRW on skeleton tower on piles. Obscured 129°–355°; higher intensity on rangeline. **(Rear Light),** 266 yards, 061.6° from front light. Iso W 6s, 32ft. KRW on skeleton tower on piles. Visible all around; higher intensity on rangeline.
CENTER RANGE (Front Light), 27 27.5N, 80 19.4W. F R, 53ft. On warehouse. Visible 2° each side of rangeline. **(Rear Light),** 630 yards, 242° from front light. F R, 90ft. On telephone pole. Visible 2° each side of rangeline.
Buoy 8, Red nun.
Buoy 9, Green can.

Buoy 10, Red nun.
Buoy 11, Green can.
Buoy 12, Red nun with yellow square.
LIGHT 13, 27 27.6N, 80 19.1W. Fl G 4s, 12ft, 4M. SG-SY on pile.

FORT PIERCE

27 28N, 80 19W
U.S. Coast Guard: Station located just inside Ft. Pierce inlet.
Dockage: Extensive selection of marinas both north and south on the ICW. Care should be used when approaching the marinas because of strong currents on the beam.
Anchorage: This city is attempting to outlaw anchoring through local ordinances.
Fuel: Available at marinas.
Repairs: Extensive. Haulout facilities.
Supplies: Extensive.

Ft. Pierce Inlet is considered to be navigable by most craft under ordinary conditions. Caution should be used when an ebb current meets heavy seas outside. Contact the Coast Guard if unsure of conditions. The boatyards and marinas in this area can provide any marine service. The city is a major sportfishing center. The nearby inlet provides easy access to the Gulf Stream.

FORT PIERCE TO ST. LUCIE

Capron Shoal Buoy 10A, E side of 18-foot shoal, 27 26.6N, 80 13.3W. Red nun.
Fort Pierce Yacht Club Race Course Buoy, 27 26.4N, 80 16.1W. Orange and white bands, nun. Private aid.
St. Lucie Shoal Lighted Whistle Buoy 12, 27 23.3N, 80 08.0W. Fl R 6s, 4M. Red.
St. Lucie Power Plant Ocean Discharge Pipeline Obstruction Lighted Buoy, 27 21.3N, 80 13.8W. Q Y, Yellow, words DANGER SUBMERGED DISCHARGE STRUCTURE. Private aid.
St. Lucie Power Plant Intake Pipe North Obstruction Lighted Buoy, 27 20.9N, 80 14.0W. Q Y. Yellow, words DANGER SUBMERGED INTAKE STRUCTURE. Private aid.

COAST PILOT

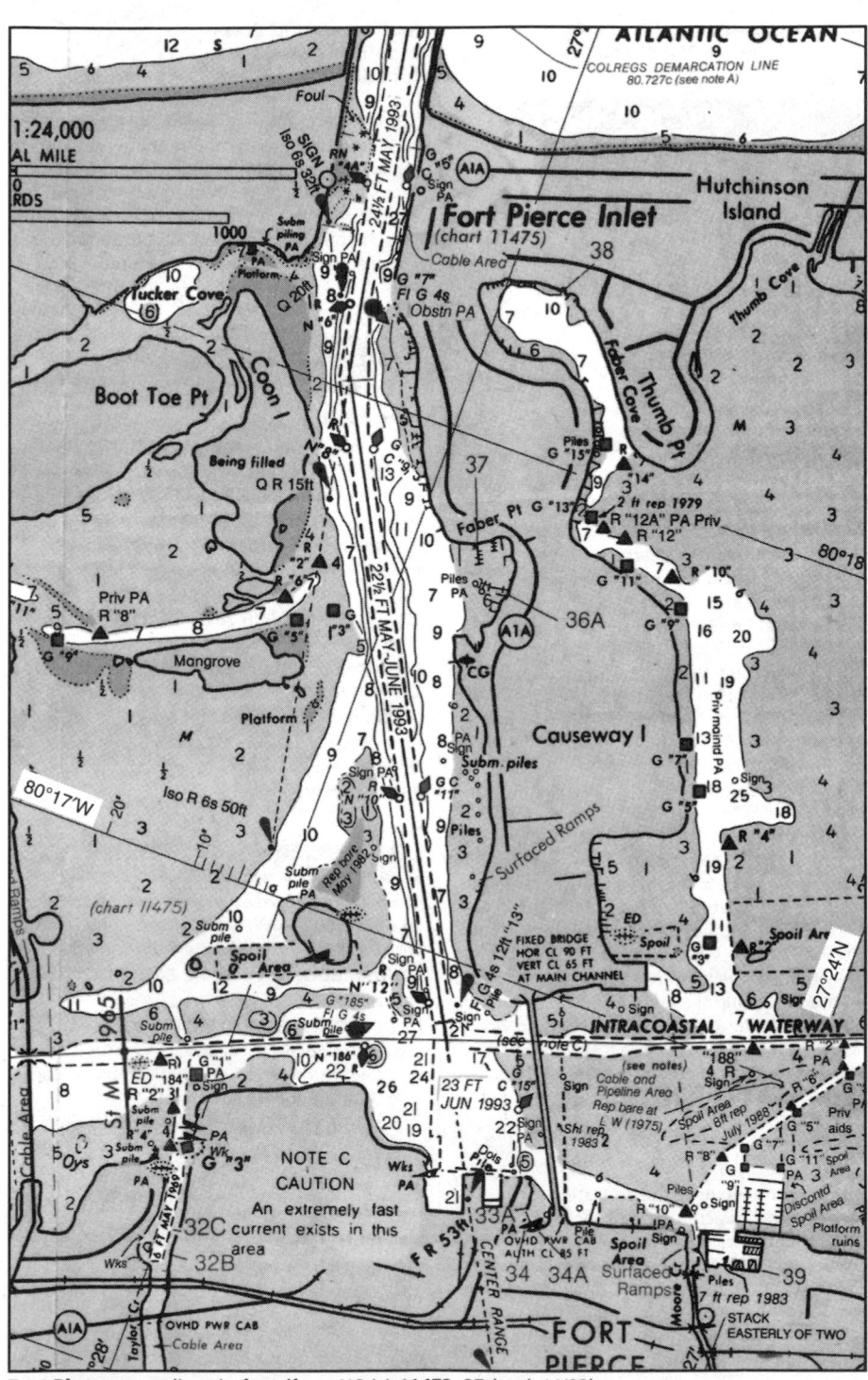

Fort Pierce, soundings in feet (*from NOAA 11472, 27th ed, 11/93*)

St. Lucie Shoal Buoy 14, near SE end of shoal, 27 18.6N, 80 08.7W. Red nun.

ST. LUCIE INLET

St. Lucie Entrance Lighted Whistle Buoy 2, 27 10.0N, 80 08.4W. Fl R 4s, 3M. Red.
Buoy 3, Green can.
Buoy 4, Red nun.
Lighted Buoy 5, Fl G 2.5s, 3M. Green.
Buoy 6, 27 10.1N, 80 09.6W. Red nun.
Buoy 8, Red nun.
Buoy 9, Green can.
Daybeacon 10, TR on pile.
Daybeacon 12, TR on pile.
Daybeacon 14, TR on pile.
Daybeacon 16, TR on pile.
Daybeacon 17, SG on pile.

ST. LUCIE

27 10N, 80 10W
U.S. Coast Guard: Ft. Pierce station.
Dockage: Large number of marinas in Manatee Pocket.
Anchorage: Excellent, well-sheltered anchorage in Manatee Pocket. The Coast Pilot considers this a hurricane hole.
Fuel: At marinas in Manatee Pocket or farther up river at Stuart.
Repairs: Extensive. Haulout facilities. More repairs at Stuart.
Supplies: Good.

St. Lucie Inlet is a "local knowledge"-only entrance. Sportfishermen use the inlet constantly; it may be possible to follow one if you are trying to locate the best channel. Buoys are shifted frequently to match the changing conditions. Use care when negotiating the ICW in the vicinity of the inlet. Strong currents hit boats on the beam, and the area is prone to shoaling. Manatee Pocket is a pleasant anchorage well away from the traffic of the ICW. The St. Lucie River is the eastern end of the cross-Florida Okeechobee Waterway.

STUART

27 12N, 80 14W
U.S. Coast Guard: Ft. Pierce station.
Town Dock: Concrete dock is located before the railroad bridge.
Dockage: Marinas on both the North and South Forks.
Anchorage: Good anchorage on both the North and South Forks. The city is trying to restrict anchoring with local ordinances.

Fuel: Several fuel docks.
Repairs: Extensive.
Supplies: Good.

The Stuart area is well serviced by a variety of marinas and repair facilities. There are good anchoring opportunities, which are rare from here south to Miami. The beginning of the Okeechobee Waterway passes down the South Fork. If you can clear the 49-foot bridge, this is an excellent way to voyage to Florida's west coast.

JUPITER INLET TO LAKE WORTH

JUPITER INLET LIGHT, 26 56.9N, 80 04.9W. Fl (2) W 30s, 146ft, 25M. Red brick tower. Obscured 231°–234° when within 5.5 miles.
JUPITER INLET RADIOBEACON, 27 04.5N, 80 07.1W. **J** (·–––), 110M, 294kHz.
Jupiter Inlet South Jetty Daybeacon 1, 26 56.6N, 80 04.3W. SG on pile on jetty. Private aid.
Jupiter Inlet North Jetty Daybeacon 2, TR on pile on jetty. Private aid.
Palm Beach Sailing Club Race Course Buoy B, 26 49.6N, 80 00.3W. Orange and white bands, nun. Private aid.
Palm Beach Sailing Club Race Course Buoy D, 26 42.0N, 80 01.7W. Orange and white bands, nun. Private aid.

LAKE WORTH INLET

Lake Worth Lighted Whistle Buoy LW, 26 46.3N, 80 00.6W. Mo (A) W, 6M. Red and white stripes with red spherical topmark.
Lighted Buoy 2, 26 46.4N, 80 01.5W. Fl R 2.5s, 4M. Red.
LAKE WORTH ENTRANCE RANGE (Front Light), 26 46.3N, 80 02.5W. Q W, 30ft. KRW on skeleton tower on dolphin. Visible 4° each side of rangeline. **(Rear Light),** 440 yards, 271.5° from front light. Iso W 6s, 55ft. KRW on skeleton tower. Visible 4° each side of rangeline.
Lighted Buoy 3, Fl G 4s, 3M. Green.
Buoy 4, Red nun.
LIGHT 5, Fl G 6s, 19ft, 4M. SG on dolphin.
Lighted Buoy 7, Fl G 2.5s, 3M. Green.
LIGHT 8, Fl R 4s, 16ft, 3M. TR on pile.
Palm Beach Channel Daybeacon 2, TR on pile.
Palm Beach Channel Daybeacon 4, TR on pile.

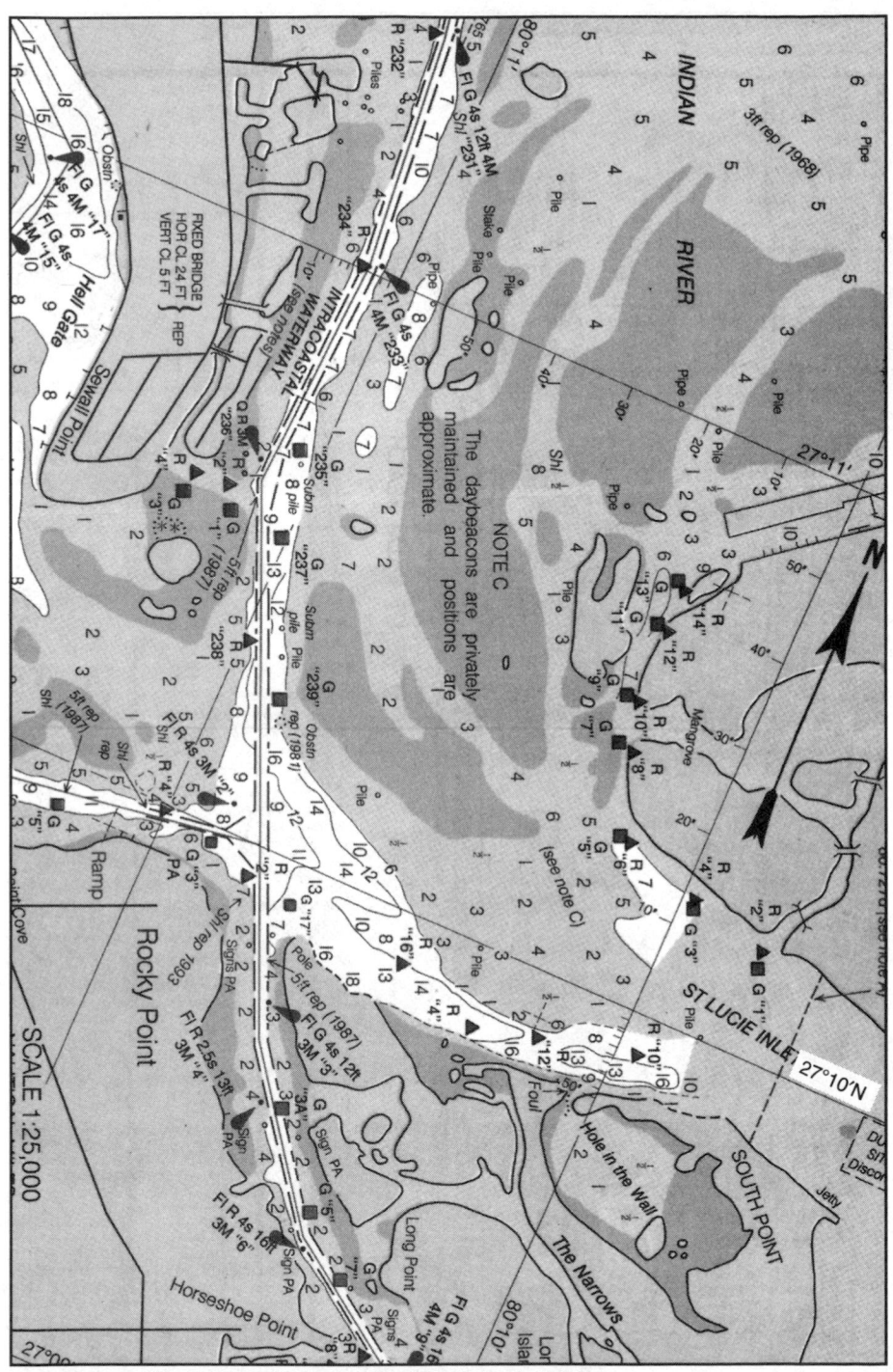

St. Lucie, soundings in feet *(from NOAA 11472, 27th ed, 11/93)*

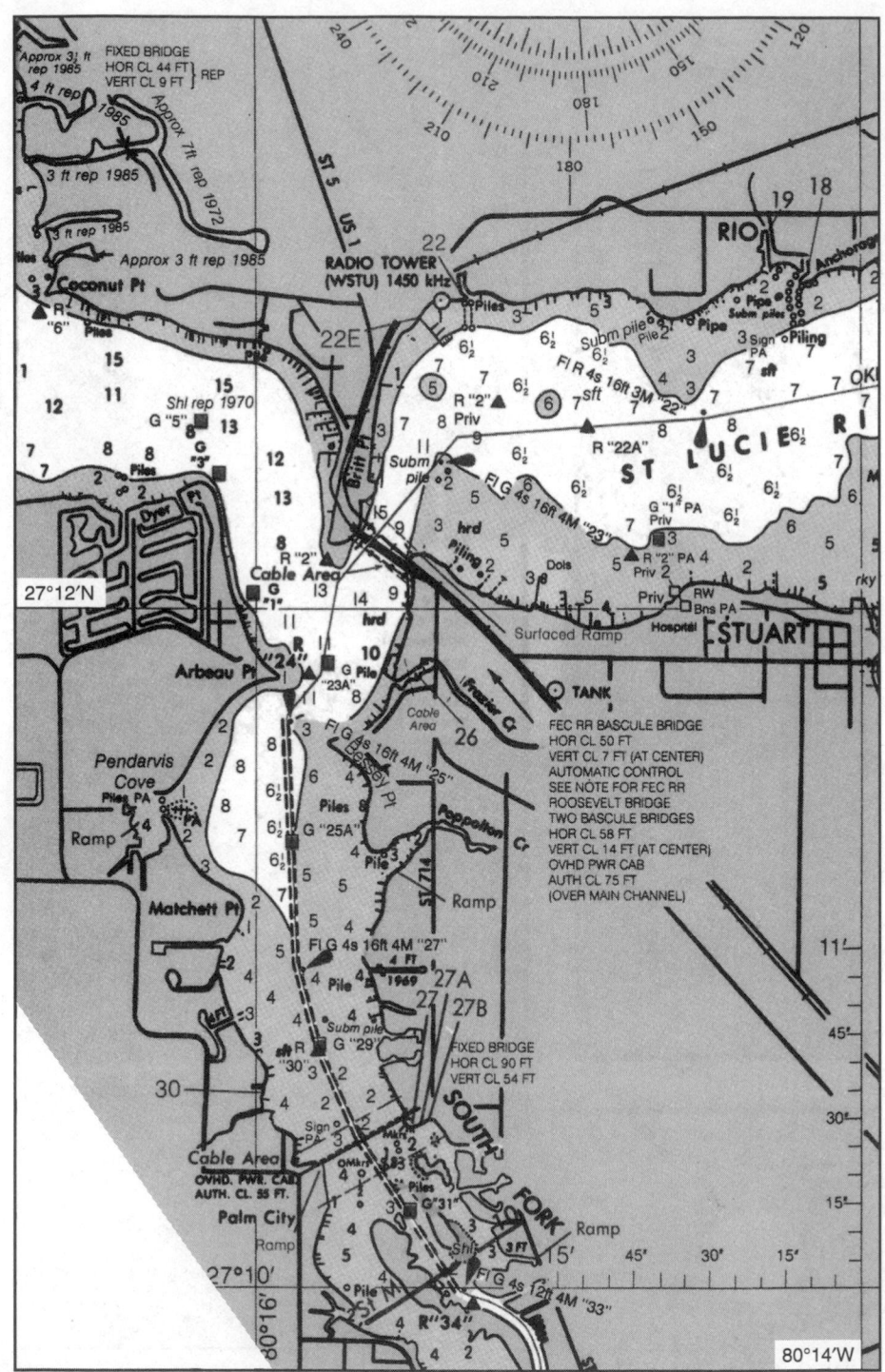

Stuart, soundings in feet *(from NOAA 11428, 28th ed, 1/94)*

Palm Beach Channel Daybeacon 6, TR on pile.
LIGHT 9, Fl G 6s, 16ft, 3M. SG on dolphin.
LIGHT 10, Fl R 6s, 16ft, 3M. TR on dolphin.
LIGHT 11, Fl G 4s, 16ft, 3M. SG on pile.
LIGHT 12, Fl R 4s, 12ft, 3M. TR on pile.
LIGHT 13, Fl G 2.5s, 16ft, 3M. SG on pile.
LAKE WORTH SOUTH LIGHT 1, 26 45.9N,
80 02.9W. Q G, 12ft, 4M. SG-SY on pile.

PALM BEACH

26 46N, 80 03W
U.S. Coast Guard: Lake Worth Inlet station
south side of Peanut Island.
Customs: Port of Entry
Dockage: Many luxurious marinas.
Anchorage: Good anchorage in the northern-
most portion of Lake Worth. Possible to anchor
just east of Peanut Island.
Fuel: Many fuel docks.
Repairs: Extensive. Haulout facilities.
Supplies: Extensive.

The Palm Beach and West Palm Beach area
form one of the wealthiest and most luxurious
communities in the United States. Every con-
ceivable marine service is available for yachts
of any size. The shopping on Palm Beach is
absolutely top-notch in both quality and price.
Lake Worth Inlet is one of the best on Florida's
coast. This is a favorite jumping-off spot for
those heading to West End in the Bahamas.

BOCA RATON INLET

NORTH JETTY LIGHT 2, 26 20.1N, 80 04.2W.
Q R, 14ft. TR on pile. Private aid.
SOUTH JETTY LIGHT 1, Q G, 14ft. SG on pile.
Private aid.
DEERFIELD FISHING PIER, NORTH LIGHT,
26 19.0N, 80 04.4W. F R, 20ft. On pier. Private
aid.
DEERFIELD FISHING PIER, SOUTH LIGHT, F R,
20ft. On pier. Private aid.

HILLSBORO INLET

HILLSBORO INLET LIGHT, 26 15.6N, 80 04.9W.
Fl W 20s, 136ft, 28M. Octagonal pyramidal
iron skeleton tower with central stair cylinder;
lower third of structure white, upper two-thirds
black. Obscured 015°–186°.
Hillsboro Inlet Entrance Lighted Buoy HI,
26 15.1N, 80 04.5W. Mo (A) W, 5M. Red and
white stripes with red spherical topmark.
ENTRANCE LIGHT 1, 26 15.3N, 80 04.8W.
Fl G 4s, 8ft, 4M. SG on dolphin.

ENTRANCE LIGHT 2, Fl R 4s, 16ft, 4M. TR on
dolphin.
Entrance Daybeacon 3, SG on pile.

PORT EVERGLADES

APPROACH LIGHT, 26 05.7N, 80 06.4W. Fl W 5s,
349ft, 17M. On building. Obscured 030°–180°.
Lighted Buoy PE, 26 05.5N, 80 04.8W.
Mo (A) W, 7M. Red and white stripes with red
spherical topmark.
Spoil Bank Daybeacon, 26 05.8N, 80 06.0W.
NW on pile worded DANGER SHOAL.
Spoil Bank West Daybeacon, 26 05.8N,
80 06.2W. NW on pile worded DANGER SHOAL.
Lighted Buoy 2, Fl R 2.5s, 3M. Red.
Lighted Buoy 3, Fl G 2.5s, 3M. Green.
ENTRANCE RANGE (Front Light), 26 05.6N,
80 07.5W. F G, 85ft. KRW on skeleton tower.
Visible 2° each side of rangeline. **(Rear Light),**
924 yards, 269.5° from front light. F G, 135ft.
KRW on skeleton tower. Visible 2° each side of
rangeline.
LIGHT 4, 26 05.7N, 80 06.1W. Fl R 4s, 16ft, 3M.
TR on pile.
LIGHT 5, Fl G 4s, 21ft, 4M. SG on dolphin.
LIGHT 6, Fl R 2.5s, 16ft, 4M. TR on dolphin.
LIGHT 7, 26 05.6N, 80 06.7W. Fl G 4s, 16ft, 4M.
SG on dolphin.
LIGHT 9, Fl G 6s, 16ft, 4M. SG on piles.
TURNING BASIN LIGHT 11, Fl G 4s, 16ft, 4M.
SG-SY on pile.
TURNING BASIN LIGHT 12, Q R, 16ft, 3M.
TR-SY on dolphin.
Stranahan River Lighted Buoy 30, Fl R 4s,
3M. Red with yellow triangle.

FT. LAUDERDALE

26 06N, 80 07W
City Dockmaster: Contact the dockmaster at
the city docks up the New River. Try VHF channel
09. Dockmaster is in charge of the mooring area
near the Las Olas Boulevard bridge.
U.S. Coast Guard: On the east side of the
ICW at mile 1066.8.
Customs: Port of Entry
Dockage: Very extensive for any size pleasure
boat.
Moorings: Near Las Olas Boulevard bridge. The
city regulates the moorings and collects the fees.
A dinghy dock and fresh water are provided.
Anchorage: Possible near moorings by Las Olas
Boulevard bridge. You'll probably be asked to
move or pick up a mooring if available.
Fuel: Large fueling docks can handle any
request.

COAST PILOT

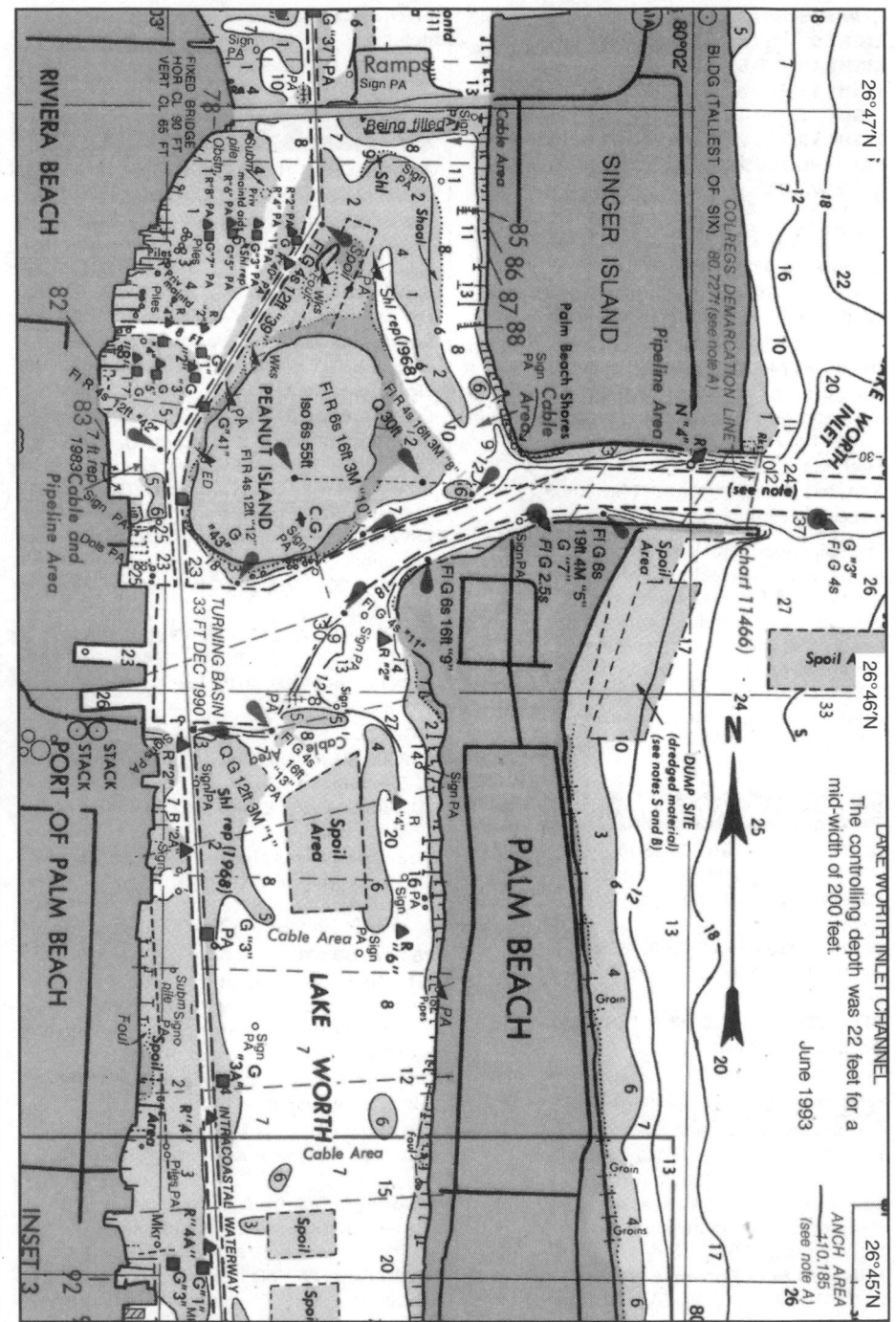

Palm Beach, soundings in feet *(from NOAA 11472, 27th ed, 11/93)*

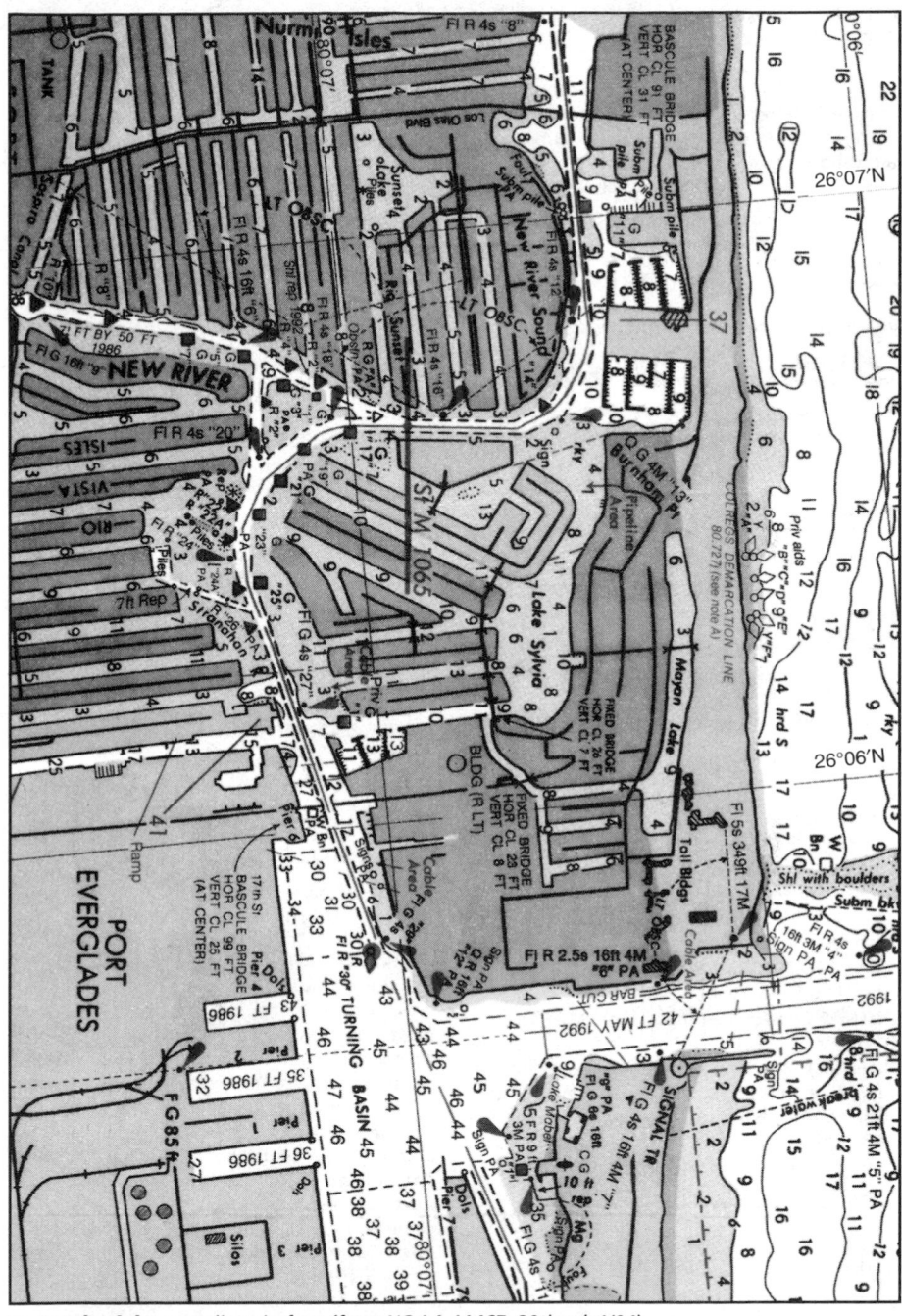

Ft. Lauderdale, soundings in feet *(from NOAA 11467, 30th ed, 1/94)*

Repairs: Very extensive. Large haulout facilities.
Supplies: Very extensive.

Fort Lauderdale provides the most complete marine facilities on the U.S. east coast. The marinas accommodate the largest luxury yachts alongside the ordinary. Despite the huge number of berths, reservations are always recommended. Ashore are many luxury hotels, restaurants, and endless shops. Port Everglades is a safe and well-marked inlet. This is an excellent departure port for trips to the Bahamas.

PORT EVERGLADES TO MIAMI

Parker Dorado Association Obstruction Daybeacon, 25 58.5N, 80 07.1W. NW on pile worded DANGER SUBMERGED OUTFALL. Private aid.
BAKERS HAULOVER INLET JETTY LIGHT, 25 53.9N, 80 07.2W. Q W, 13ft. NW on pile worded DANGER JETTY. Private aid.

MIAMI ENTRANCE

Miami Anchorage Buoy A, 25 48.3N, 80 05.7W. Yellow nun. Marks anchorage area east of Miami Beach.
Miami Anchorage Buoy B, 25 46.4N, 80 06.2W. Yellow nu., Marks anchorage area east of Miami Beach.
MIAMI APPROACH LIGHT, 25 46.0N, 80 08.0W. Fl (2) W 30s, 240ft, 17M. On building, Obscured 065°–195°.
Miami Lighted Whistle Buoy M, 25 46.1N, 80 05.0W. Mo (A) W, 7M. Red and white stripes with red spherical topmark. RACON **M** (– –).
MIAMI RADIOBEACON, 25 43.9N, 80 09.6W. RACON **U** (··–), 100M, 322kHz.
ENTRANCE RANGE (Front Light), 25 45.1N, 80 07.7W. Q G, 25ft, Fl W 4s, 27ft, 5M. KRB on skeleton tower on piles. Visible 4° each side of rangeline; passing light visible around horizon. **(Rear Light),** 670 yards, 249.5° from front light. Iso G 6s, 49ft, KRB on skeleton tower on piles. Visible 4° each side of rangeline.
Lighted Buoy 1, Fl G 6s, 4M. Green.
Lighted Buoy 2, Fl R 4s, 4M. Red.
Lighted Buoy 3, Fl G 4s, 4M. Green.
Lighted Buoy 4, Q R, 4M. Red.
Lighted Buoy 5, Fl G 2.5s, 4M. Green.
Lighted Buoy 6, Fl R 2.5s, 4M. Red.
Lighted Buoy 7, Q G, 4M. Green.
GOVERNMENT CUT RANGE (Front Light), 25 45.2N, 80 06.5W. Q W, 25ft, Fl W 4s, 28ft,

5M. KRW on tower on piles. Visible 2° each side of rangeline; passing light visible around horizon. **(Rear Light),** 785 yards, 114.8° from front light. Iso W 6s, 50ft, Fl W 4s, 25ft, 5M. KRW on tower on piles. Visible 2° each side of rangeline; passing light visible around horizon.
Lighted Buoy 6A, Fl R 2.5s, 4M. Red.
Lighted Buoy 9, Fl G 2.5s, 4M. Green.
Lighted Buoy 8, Q R, 4M. Red.
Lighted Buoy 11, Q G, 4M. Green.
Lighted Buoy 10, Fl R 4s, 4M. Red.
NORTH JETTY FISHING PIER EAST OBSTRUCTION LIGHT, 25 45.8N, 80 07.8W. F W, 17ft, On jetty. Private aid.
NORTH JETTY FISHING PIER WEST OBSTRUCTION LIGHT, F W, 17ft. On jetty. Private aid.
LIGHT 13, Fl G 4s, 16ft, 4M. SG on dolphin.
Buoy 12, Red nun.
Lighted Buoy 14, Fl R 4s, 4M. Red.
LIGHT 15, Fl G 2.5s, 16ft, 3M. SG on dolphin.

MIAMI HARBOR

INTERNATIONAL YACHT HARBOR BREAKWATER SOUTH LIGHT, 25 46.0N, 80 08.4W. Q W, 12ft. On pile. Private aid.
INTERNATIONAL YACHT HARBOR BREAKWATER BARRIER SOUTH LIGHT, Q W, 12ft. On pile. Private aid.
INTERNATIONAL YACHT HARBOR BREAKWATER BARRIER NORTH LIGHT, Q W, 12ft. On pile. Private aid.
Lighted Buoy 16, 25 46.0N, 80 08.5W. Fl R 4s, 4M. Red.

MIAMI

25 46N, 80 08W
U.S. Coast Guard: Miami Beach Coast Guard on Causeway Island.
Customs: Port of Entry
Dockage: Extensive dockage available at Miami Beach just inside Government Cut. Be careful in the strong currents running through the marina. Many marinas and repair facilities along the ICW and in the Miami River.
Anchorage: Good anchorage possibilities exist north of the MacArthur Causeway. Beware of cable and pipeline areas marked on the charts.
Fuel: Many fuel docks. Beware strong currents in the marina just inside Government Cut.
Repairs: Extensive. Haulout facilities.
Supplies: Extensive.

Miami is the largest city in Florida and has become the de-facto capital of the Caribbean in

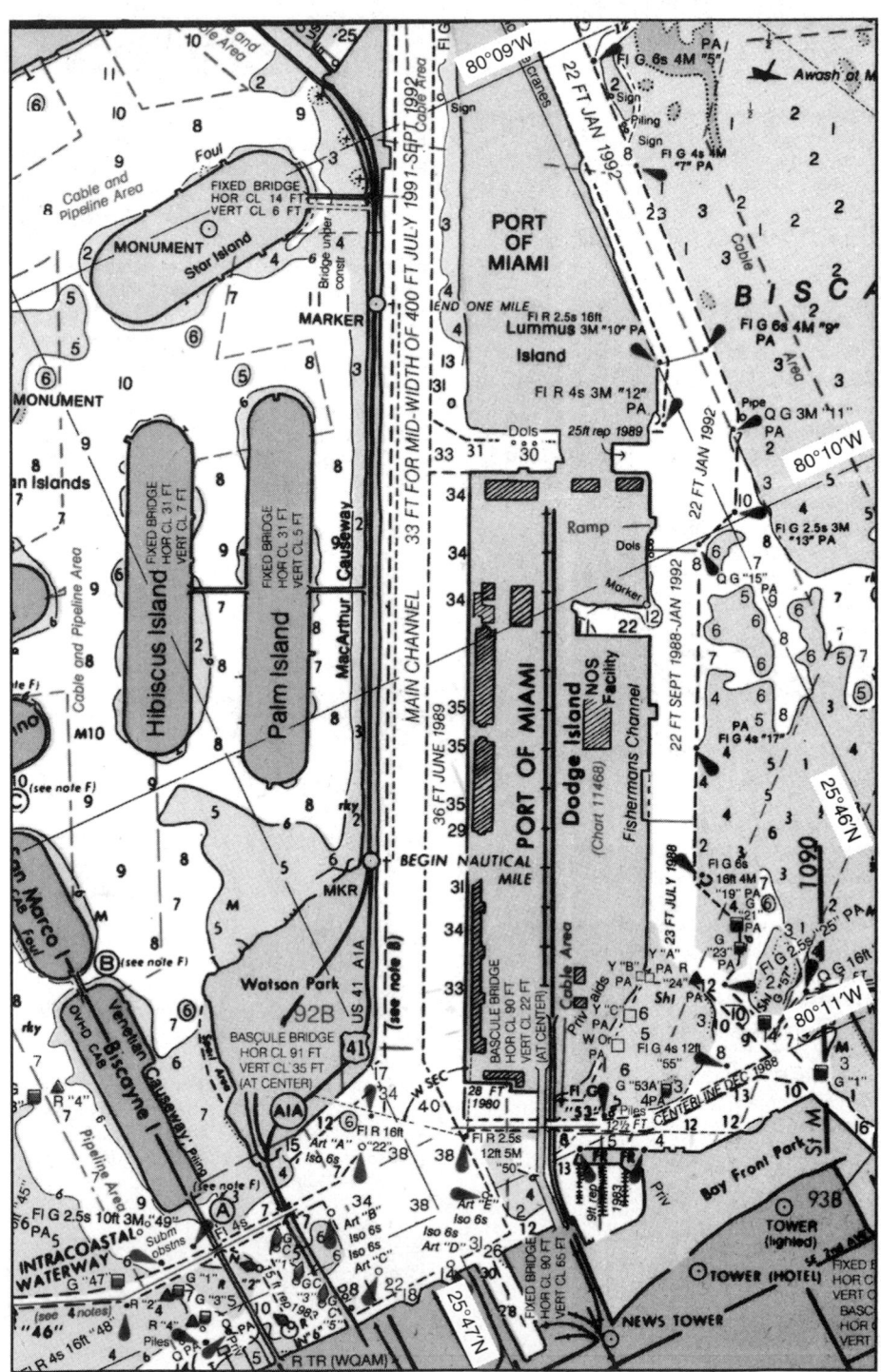

Miami, soundings in feet *(from NOAA 11467, 30th ed, 1/94)*

recent years. A large volume of commercial traffic steams through Government Cut day and night. The channel is safe and almost too well marked. The profusion of buoyage and lights can be confusing at night. From the marina at Miami Beach you can walk to museums, restaurants, and shops. The downtown marina complex is in the heart of Miami's revitalized waterfront. Shops and restaurants overlook the harbor. Visitors should be careful where they walk, especially at night.

MIAMI TO FOWEY ROCKS

Bear Cut Daybeacon 2, 25 43.5N, 80 08.0W. TR on pile.
CASA DEL MAR LIGHT, 25 41.1N, 80 09.4W. Fl W 6s, 350ft, 8M. On building. Obscured 017°–180°.
Cape Florida Daybeacon 2, TR on pile.
CAPE FLORIDA LIGHT 4, 25 41.1N, 80 11.0W. Fl R 2.5s, 16ft, 4M. TR on pile.
Biscayne National Park North Lighted Buoy N, 25 38.7N, 80 05.4W. Fl Y 2.5s, 4M. Yellow.
FOWEY ROCKS LIGHT, on outer line of reefs, 25 35.4N, 80 05.8W. Fl W 10s (2R sectors), 110ft, 16M white, 12M red. Brown octagonal pyramidal skeleton tower enclosing white stair; cylinder and octagonal dwelling; pile foundation. W 188°–359° and 022°–180°, R in intervening sectors.

BISCAYNE CHANNEL

LIGHT, 25 38.3N, 80 07.9W. Fl W 4s, 37ft, 5M. NG on skeleton tower on piles.
LIGHT 1, 25 38.7N, 80 08.0W. Fl G 2.5s, 16ft, 4M. SG on dolphin.
LIGHT 2, Fl R 2.5s, 16ft, 4M. TR on dolphin.
LIGHT 3, Fl G 4s, 12ft, 3M. SG on pile.
Daybeacon 4, TR on pile.
LIGHT 6, Fl R 4s, 12ft, 3M. TR on dolphin.
Daybeacon 7, SG on pile.
Daybeacon 8, TR on pile.
Daybeacon 10, TR on pile.
Daybeacon 12, TR on pile.
Daybeacon 14, TR on pile.
LIGHT 15, 25 39.1N, 80 10.5W. Fl G 4s, 16ft, 4M. SG on pile.
Daybeacon 16, TR on pile.
Daybeacon 18, TR on pile.
Daybeacon 19, SG on pile.
Daybeacon 20, TR on pile.
LIGHT 21, Fl G 2.5s, 12ft, 3M. SG on pile.

FOWEY ROCKS TO ALLIGATOR REEF

TRIUMPH REEF LIGHT 2TR, 25 28.6N, 80 06.7W. Fl R 2.5s, 19ft, 6M. TR on dolphin.
PACIFIC REEF LIGHT, 25 22.2N, 80 08.5W. Fl W 4s, 44ft, 9M. Black skeleton tower on piles.
Turtle Harbor Lighted Whistle Buoy 4, marks entrance between shoal patches, 25 17.5N, 80 09.9W. Fl R 6s, 5M. Red.
CARYSFORT REEF LIGHT, on outer line of reefs, 25 13.3N, 80 12.7W. Fl (3) W 60s (3R sectors), 100ft, 15M white, 13M red. Brown octagonal pyramidal skeleton tower enclosing stair cylinder and conical dwelling; pile foundation. W 211°–018°, 049°–087°, and 145°–184°, R in intervening sectors.
ELBOW REEF LIGHT 6, 25 08.7N, 80 15.5W. Fl R 2.5s, 36ft, 6M. TR on skeleton tower on piles.
Dixie Shoal Buoy 8, on seaward edge of reef, 25 04.6N, 80 18.7W. Red nun.

MOLASSES REEF BOUNDARY
Northwest Buoy, 25 00.7N, 80 22.4W. Yellow nun worded NO ANCHOR ZONE. Private aid.
Northeast Buoy, 25 00.6N, 80 22.4W. Yellow nun worded NO ANCHOR ZONE. Private aid.
Southwest Buoy, 25 00.6N, 80 22.4W. Yellow nun worded NO ANCHOR ZONE. Private aid.
Southeast Buoy, 25 00.6N, 80 22.4W. Yellow nun worded NO ANCHOR ZONE. Private aid.

MOLASSES REEF LIGHT 10, 25 00.7N, 80 22.6W. Fl R 10s, 45ft, 13M. TR on square brown pyramidal skeleton tower; pile foundation.
Conch Reef Buoy 12, near seaward edge of reef, 24 57.0N, 80 27.5W. Red nun.
DAVIS REEF LIGHT 14, 24 55.5N, 80 30.2W. Fl R 4s, 20ft, 6M. TR on dolphin.
Crocker Reef Buoy 16, 24 54.5N, 80 31.5W. Red nun.
ALLIGATOR REEF LIGHT, on outer line of reef, 24 51.1N, 80 37.1W. Fl (4) W 60s (2R sectors), 136ft, 16M white, 13M red. White octagonal pyramid skeleton tower enclosing stair cylinder and square dwelling; black pile foundation. R 223°–249° and 047°–068°.

HAWK CHANNEL: SOLDIER KEY TO CHANNEL FIVE

Soldier Key Daybeacon 2, 25 35.8N, 80 07.6W. TR on pile.

Fowey Rocks Daybeacon 3, 25 35.7N, 80 06.9W. SG on pile.
Soldier Key Daybeacon 4, 25 34.2N, 80 07.9W. TR on pile.
Ragged Key Daybeacon 7, 25 31.0N, 80 08.3W. SG on pile.
BOWLES BANK LIGHT 8, 25 30.4N, 80 08.7W. Fl R 4s, 16ft, 3M. TR on pile.
Bache Shoal Daybeacon 9, SG on pile.
BACHE SHOAL LIGHT 11BS, on southwest edge of shoal, 25 29.2N, 80 08.9W. Fl G 6s, 18ft, 5M. SG on dolphin.
Bache Shoal Daybeacon 13, SG on pile.

ELLIOT KEY
Daybeacon 14, TR on pile.
Daybeacon 15, SG on pile.
Daybeacon 16, 25 26.8N, 80 10.2W. TR on pile.
Daybeacon 17, SG on pile.
Daybeacon 18, TR on pile.
Daybeacon 19, SG on pile.
Pacific Reef Daybeacon 2, TR on pile.
Pacific Reef Daybeacon 3, 25 22.4N, 80 09.6W. SG on pile.
Pacific Reef Daybeacon 4, TR on pile.
LIGHT 20, 25 23.1N, 80 11.5W. Fl R 4s, 16ft, 3M. TR on pile.

CAESAR CREEK
Caesar Creek Daybeacon 1, 25 23.1N, 80 11.6W. SG on pile. Maintained by National Park Service.

NOTE: A series of 36 more daybeacons, maintained by the National Park Service, mark Caesar Creek to the Junction Buoy, which is a black and red can. West Buoys 1 through 4, which are black cans and red nuns, mark the remainder of the channel.

OLD RHODES KEY
Daybeacon 21, SG on pile.
LIGHT 22, Fl R 2.5s, 12ft, 4M. TR on pile.
Daybeacon 23, SG on pile.
Daybeacon 24, TR on pile.

ANGELFISH CREEK
LIGHT 2, 25 19.7N, 80 15.0W. Fl R 4s, 12ft, 3M. TR on pile.
Daybeacon 1, SG on pile.
Daybeacon 2A, TR on pile.
Daybeacon 3, SG on pile.
Daybeacon 3A, SG on pile.
Daybeacon 4, TR on pile.
Daybeacon 5, SG on pile.
LIGHT 6, Fl R 4s, 12ft, 3M. TR on pile.

Daybeacon 8, TR on pile.
Daybeacon 10, TR on pile.
Daybeacon 12, TR on pile.
LIGHT 14, 25 20.1N, 80 16.8W. Fl R 4s, 12ft, 3M. TR on pile.

VILLA CHANNEL
Daybeacon 1, 25 18.8N, 80 15.9W. SG on pile. Private aid.

NOTE: A series of 20 more red and green daybeacons mark the Villa Channel. These are private aids.

OCEAN REEF HARBOR ENTRANCE LIGHT 2, 25 18.5N, 80 16.0W. Fl R 4s, 16ft, 3M. TR on pile.

DISPATCH CREEK CHANNEL
Daybeacon 3, 25 18.3N, 80 16.2W. SG on pile. Private aid.

NOTE: A series of 17 more daybeacons, alternating red triangles and green squares on pilings, mark the Dispatch Creek Channel. These are private aids.

HARBOR COURSE CREEK
Daybeacon 1, 25 18.6N, 80 17.0W. SG on pile. Private aid.
Daybeacon 2, TR on pile. Private aid.

TURTLE HARBOR
West Shoal Daybeacon 2, 25 19.4N, 80 12.7W. TR on pile.
WEST SHOAL PREFERRED CHANNEL LIGHT, 25 18.3N, 80 12.8W. Fl (2+1) G 6s, 16ft, 3M. JG on pile.
Daybeacon 1, SG on pile.
Daybeacon 3, SG on pile.
Daybeacon 4, TR on pile.
Daybeacon 5, SG on pile.
Daybeacon 6, TR on pile.

Key Largo Daybeacon 25, SG on pile.
Key Largo Daybeacon 27, SG on pile.
Key Largo Daybeacon 29, 25 14.3N, 80 17.0W. SG on pile.

WORLDS BEYOND MARINA
Daybeacon 1, SG on pile. Private aid.
Daybeacon 2, TR on pile. Private aid.
Daybeacon 3, SG on pile. Private aid.
Daybeacon 4, TR on pile. Private aid.
Daybeacon 6, TR on pile. Private aid.
Daybeacon 7, SG on pile. Private aid.

BASIN HILLS LIGHT 31BH, Fl G 4s, 27ft, 4M. SG on skeleton structure on piles.
KEY LARGO LIGHT 32, 25 10.6N, 80 20.3W. FL R 2.5s, 16ft, 3M. TR on pile.

BASIN HILLS CHANNEL
Daybeacon 2, 12ft. TR on pile. Private aid.
Daybeacon 3, 12ft. SG on pile. Private aid.
Daybeacon 5, 12ft. SG on pile. Private aid.
Daybeacon 7, 12ft. SG on pile. Private aid.
Daybeacon 9, 12ft. SG on pile. Private aid.
Daybeacon 11, 12ft. SG on pile. Private aid.

GARDEN COVE
Daybeacon 1, SG on pile. Private aid.

NOTE: A series of 15 more daybeacons, alternating red triangles and green squares on pilings, mark the Garden Cove channel. These are private aids.

North Largo Yacht Club Marina Daybeacon 18A, 25 10.2N, 80 22.0W. TR on pile. Private aid.
North Largo Yacht Club Marina Daybeacon 18B, TR on pile. Private aid.

NORTH SOUND CREEK
Daybeacon 21, SG on pile. Private aid.
Daybeacon 22, TR on pile. Private aid.
Daybeacon 24, TR on pile. Private aid.
Daybeacon 25, SG on pile. Private aid.
Daybeacon 26, TR on pile. Private aid.
Daybeacon 27, SG on pile. Private aid.
Daybeacon 29, SG on pile. Private aid.

Key Largo Daybeacon 32A, 25 08.8N, 80 21.2W. TR on pile.
Key Largo Daybeacon 33, SG on pile.

JOHN PENNEKAMP
CORAL REEF STATE PARK
Buoy D, 25 07.4N, 80 18.0W. Orange and white bands, barrel. Private aid.
Buoy E, 25 06.7N, 80 18.5W. Orange and white bands, barrel. Private aid.
Buoy F, 25 06.6N, 80 20.7W. Orange and white bands, barrel. Private aid.
Buoy G, 25 03.2N, 80 20.2W. Orange and white bands, barrel. Private aid.
Carysfort North Reef North Obstruction Daybeacon, 25 13.5N, 80 12.5W. NW on pile worded DANGER SHOAL. Private aid.
Carysfort North Reef South Obstruction Daybeacon, 25 13.2N, 80 12.7W. NW on pile worded DANGER SHOAL. Private aid.

Carysfort South Reef North Obstruction Daybeacon, 25 12.8N, 80 13.1W. NW on pile worded DANGER SHOAL. Private aid.
Carysfort South Reef South Obstruction Daybeacon, 25 12.4N, 80 13.3W. NW on pile worded DANGER SHOAL. Private aid.
Key Largo Dry Rocks Obstruction Daybeacon, NW on pile worded DANGER SHOAL. Private aid.
Grecian Rocks Obstruction Daybeacon, NW on pile worded DANGER SHOAL. Private aid.
Cannon Patch Obstruction Daybeacon, NW on pile worded DANGER SHOAL. Private aid.
Mosquito Bank Obstruction Daybeacon, NW on pile worded DANGER SHOAL. Private aid.
White Banks Obstruction Daybeacon, 25 02.4N, 80 22.3W. NW on pile worded DANGER SHOAL. Private aid.
French Reef Obstruction Daybeacon, 25 02.1N, 80 21.1W. NW on pile worded DANGER SHOAL. Private aid.
Sand Island Obstruction Daybeacon, 25 01.1N, 80 22.0W. NW on pile worded DANGER SHOAL. Private aid.
Molasses Reef North Obstruction Daybeacon, 25 00.8N, 80 22.4W. NW on pile worded DANGER SHOAL. Private aid.
Molasses Reef South Obstruction Daybeacon, 25 00.6N, 80 22.7W. NW on pile worded DANGER SHOAL. Private aid.

LARGO SOUND CHANNEL
LIGHT 2, 25 05.6N, 80 23.8W. Fl R 4s, 16ft, 4M. TR on dolphin.
Daybeacon 3, SG on pile.
Daybeacon 4, TR on pile.
Daybeacon 5, SG on pile.
Daybeacon 6, TR on pile.
Daybeacon 6A, TR on pile.
Daybeacon 7, SG on pile.
Daybeacon 7A, SG on pile.
Daybeacon 8, TR on pile.
LIGHT 9, Fl G 4s, 16ft, 3M. SG on pile.
Daybeacon 10, TR on pile.
Daybeacon 11, SG on pile.
Daybeacon 12, TR on pile.
Daybeacon 13, SG on pile.
Daybeacon 14, TR on pile.
Daybeacon 16, TR on pile.
Daybeacon 17, SG on pile.
Daybeacon 19, SG on pile.
Daybeacon 20, TR on pile.
Daybeacon 21, SG on pile.
Daybeacon 22, TR on pile.
Daybeacon 23, SG on pile.

MARVIN D. ADAMS WATERWAY LIGHT A, 25 08.2N, 80 23.7W. Fl W 6s, 12ft, 4M. NR on pile.

MARVIN D. ADAMS WATERWAY LIGHT B, Fl W 6s, 12ft, 4M. NR on pile.

MOSQUITO BANK LIGHT 35, 25 04.3N, 80 23.6W. Fl G 4s, 37ft, 5M. SG on triangular pyramidal skeleton structure on piles.

MOSQUITO BANK LIGHT 2, Fl R 2.5s, 16ft, 4M. TR on pile.

PORT LARGO PROPERTY OWNERS LIGHT, 25 05.3N, 80 25.9W. F G, 4s, 16ft. On pile. Private aid.

Hidden Bay Daybeacon 2, 25 04.8N, 80 26.2W. TR on pile. Private aid.

Hidden Bay Daybeacon 4, TR on pile. Private aid.

KAWAMA MARINA AND YACHT CLUB LIGHT, 25 04.6N, 80 26.4W. Q R, 25ft. On roof of thatched hut. Private aid.

HARBORAGE YACHT CLUB ENTRANCE LIGHT 2, 25 04.1N, 80 27.7W. Fl R 4s, 12ft. TR on steel tower. Private aid.

Key Largo Daybeacon 37, SG on pile.

Key Largo Daybeacon 39, NW of shoal. SG on pile.

KEY LARGO

25 06N, 80 26W

U.S. Coast Guard: Islamorada Station at the southwest end of Plantation Key.

Dockage: The marinas are in a series of canals northwest of Mosquito Bank on Key Largo. Approach depths are 4 to 5 feet.

Anchorage: Good anchorage in the lee of Rodriguez Key.

Fuel: At marina up the canal.

Repairs: Good. Haulout facilities.

Supplies: Good.

The big attraction on Key Largo is the John Pennekamp Coral Reef State Park. Dive boats take visitors out to the reefs—anchoring is forbidden on the reefs. Ashore many restaurants and shops are strung out along Route 1. The marinas are small and low key, but provide most services. When approaching any docks do so at slow speed—shoaling occurs frequently.

MOLASSES REEF

Daybeacon 1, on south side of passage between shoals, 25 01.6N, 80 23.7W. SG on pile.

Daybeacon 3, SG on pile.

Daybeacon 5, SG on pile.

KEY LARGO OCEAN RESORT LIGHT 2, 25 02.5N, 80 29.3W. Fl R 4s. TR on pile. Private aid.

BLUE WATERS TRAILER VILLAGE

LIGHT 1, 25 00.8N, 80 30.3W. Fl G 6s, 12f., SG on pile. Private aid.

Daybeacon 2, TR on pile. Private aid.

Daybeacon 3, SG on pile. Private aid.

Daybeacon 4, TR on pile. Private aid.

Daybeacon 5, SG on pile. Private aid.

Daybeacon 6, TR on pile. Private aid.

TAVERNIER KEY LIGHT 2, 25 00.2N, 80 29.0W. Fl R 4s, 16ft, 3M. TR on pile.

Tavernier Key Daybeacon 3, SG on pile.

Tavernier Key Daybeacon 4, TR on pile.

Tavernier Ocean Shores Daybeacon 2, TR on pile. Private aid.

Tavernier Ocean Shores Daybeacon 4, TR on pile. Private aid.

TAVERNIER CREEK

LIGHT, 24 59.2N, 80 31.4W. Fl W 6s, 16ft, 5M. NR on pile.

Daybeacon 1, SG on pile.

Daybeacon 2, TR on pile.

NOTE: Tavernier Creek is marked by a series of 15 more red and green daymarks, numbered to 18. These are private aids.

Coral Harbor Club Daybeacon 1, SG on pile. Private aid.

Coral Harbor Club Daybeacon 2, TR on pile. Private aid.

HEN AND CHICKENS SHOAL LIGHT 40, Southeast of shoal, 24 55.9N, 80 32.9W. Fl R 2.5s, 35ft, 5M. TR on triangular pyramidal structure on piles.

SNAKE CREEK

LIGHT 2, 24 56.5N, 80 34.8W. Fl R 4s, 16ft, 4M. TR on pile.

Daybeacon 1, SG on pile.

Daybeacon 3, SG on pile.

Daybeacon 4, TR on pile.

Daybeacon 4A, TR on pile.

Daybeacon 5, SG on pile.

Daybeacon 6, TR on pile.

Daybeacon 6A, TR on pile.

Daybeacon 7, SG on pile.

Daybeacon 7A, SG on pile.

Daybeacon 8, TR on pile.

Daybeacon 9, SG on pile.

Daybeacon 10, TR on pile.

LIGHT 12, Fl R 2.5s, 16ft, 3M. TR on pile.

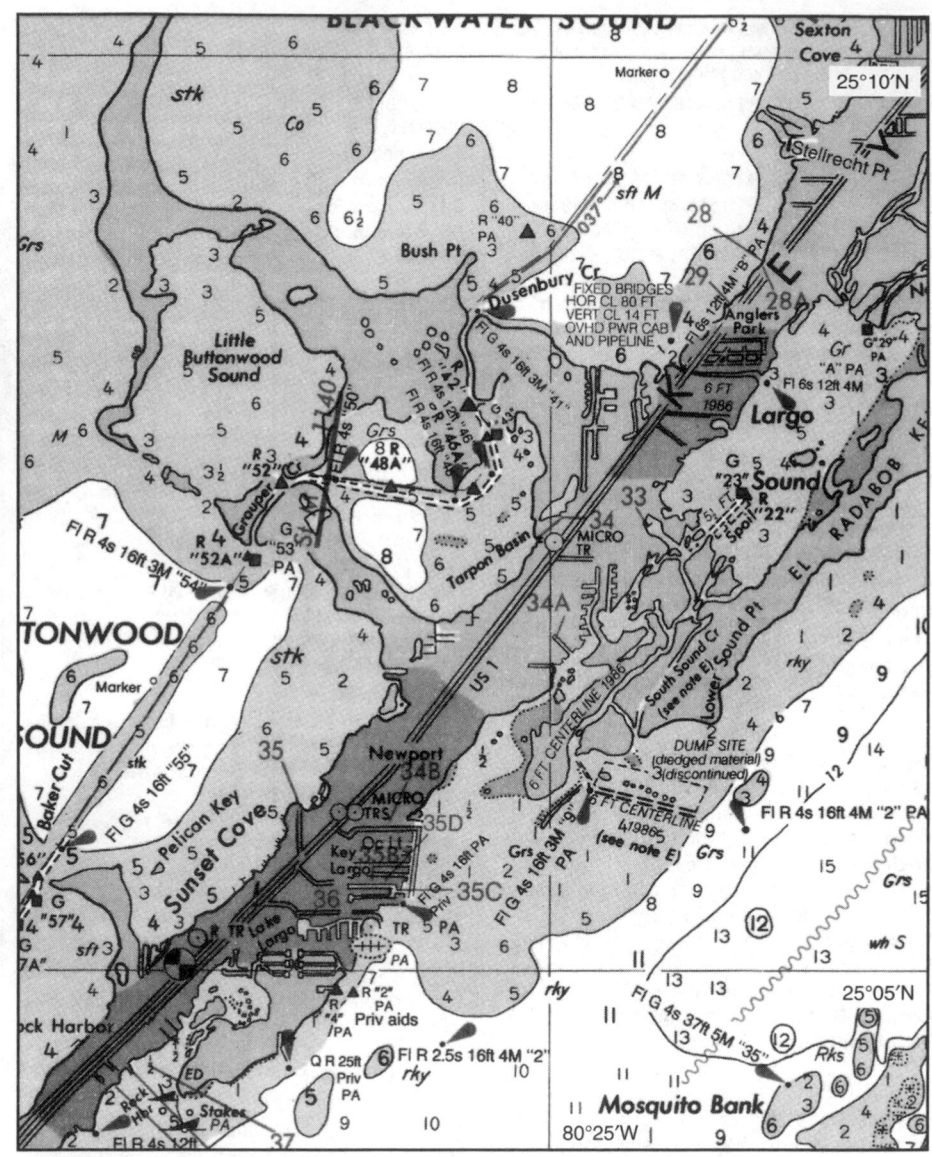

Key Largo, soundings in feet *(from NOAA 11451, 26th ed, 2/94)*

WHALE HARBOR
LIGHT 1, 24 55.8N, 80 35.7W. Fl G 2.5s, 14ft, 3M. SG on pile.
Daybeacon 2, TR on pile.
Daybeacon 3, SG on pile.
Daybeacon 4, TR on pile.
Daybeacon 4A, TR on pile.
Daybeacon 5, SG on pile.
Daybeacon 6, TR on pile.

Daybeacon 7, SG on pile.
Daybeacon 8, TR on pile.
Daybeacon 9, SG on pile.

WINDLEY PASS
Daybeacon 11, SG on pile. Private aid.
Daybeacon 12, TR on pile. Private aid.
Daybeacon 13, SG on pile. Private aid.
Daybeacon 15, SG on pile. Private aid.

Daybeacon 16, TR on pile. Private aid.

HOLIDAY ISLE MARINA
Daybeacon 1, 24 56.3N, 80 36.5W. SG on pile. Private aid.

NOTE: A series of 5 more red and green daybeacons, numbered 2 through 6, mark the Holiday Isle Marina channel. These are private aids.

BEACON REEF PIER LIGHT, 24 55.8N, 80 37.0W. Q W, 10ft. On pile. Private aid.
Upper Matecumbe Daybeacon 41, SG on pile.

LA SIESTA RESORT
Daybeacon 1, SG on pile. Private aid.
Daybeacon 2, TR on pile. Private aid.
Daybeacon 3, SG on pile. Private aid.
Daybeacon 4, TR on pile. Private aid.

BUD AND MARY'S FISHING MARINA
Daybeacon 1, 24 53.5N, 80 39.2W. SG on pile. Private aid.

NOTE: A series of 9 more red and green daybeacons, beginning with number 2 and ending with 14, mark this channel. These are private aids.

YELLOW SHARK CHANNEL
Buoy 15, 24 53.9N, 80 39.7W. Green can. Private aid.

NOTE: A series of 11 more alternating green cans and red nuns, beginning with number 15 and ending with 27, mark this channel. These are private aids.

TEA TABLE CHANNEL
Teatable Key Daybeacon 42, TR on pile.

NOTE: Several series of alternating green cans and red nuns, all private aids, mark Tea Table Channel, Flagler Channel, Plant Channel, Shell Key, and Race Channel.

Alligator Reef Daybeacon 43, SG on pile.

NOTE: Several series of alternating numbered green cans and red nuns, all private aids, mark Lignumvitae Channel and Wheel Ditch Channel. Between Buoys 8 and 9 in Lignumvitae Channel are Shoal Buoys A (24 53.2N, 80 41.3W) and B (24 53.2N, 80 41.5W), which display orange and white

bands with an orange diamond. These two are also private aids.

INDIAN KEY CHANNEL
Daybeacon 2, 24 52.6N, 80 40.2W. TR on pile.
Daybeacon 4, TR on pile.
Daybeacon 6, TR on pile.
Daybeacon 7, SG on pile.
Daybeacon 8, TR on pile.
Daybeacon 9, SG on pile.
Daybeacon 10, TR on pile.

CALOOSA COVE CHANNEL
LIGHT 2, 24 50.1N, 80 44.8W. Fl R 6s, 10ft. TR and NL on dolphin; NL worded CALOOSA COVE. Private aid.

NOTE: A series of 16 more red and green daybeacons, beginning with number 4 and ending with 21, mark the Caloosa Cove channel. These are private aids.

CHANNEL FIVE
Channel Five Daybeacon 1, SG on pile.
CHANNEL FIVE LIGHT 2, 24 49.6N, 80 46.4W. Fl R 4s, 16ft., 4M, TR on pile.

ALLIGATOR REEF TO SOMBRERO KEY

Tennessee Reef East Lighted Buoy 18, 24 47.5N, 80 41.6W. Fl R 2.5s, 5M. Red.
TENNESSEE REEF LIGHT, on west side of shoal, 24 44.7N, 80 46.9W. Fl W 4s, 49ft, 8M. Small black house on hexagonal pyramidal skeleton tower on piles.
COFFINS PATCH LIGHT 20, 24 40.5N, 80 57.4W. Fl R 6s, 20ft, 6M. TR on dolphin.
SOMBRERO KEY LIGHT, 24 37.6N, 81 06.6W. Fl (5) W 60s (3R sectors), 142ft, 15M white, 12M red. Brown octagonal pyramidal skeleton tower enclosing stair cylinder and square dwelling; pile foundation. W 222°–238°, 264°–066°, and 094°–163°, R in intervening sectors.

HAWK CHANNEL: LONG KEY TO MARATHON

LONG KEY LIGHT 44, FL R 6s, 4M. TR on pile.
Layton Canal Channel Daybeacon 1, SG on pile. Private aid.
Layton Canal Channel Daybeacon 2, TR on pile. Private aid.
Layton Canal Channel Daybeacon 3, SG on pile. Private aid.

DUCK KEY INLET CHANNEL
LIGHT 1, Fl W 4s, SG on pile. Private aid.

NOTE: A series of six more red and green daybeacons, beginning with number 2 and ending with 8, mark the Duck Key Inlet channel. These are private aids.

Duck Key Channel Daybeacon 2, TR on pile. Private aid.
Duck Key Channel Daybeacon 4, TR on pile. Private aid.

LITTLE CRAWL KEY CHANNEL
Daybeacon 1, 24 44.4N, 80 58.2W. SG on pile. Private aid.

NOTE: A series of 12 more red and green daybeacons, beginning with number 2 and ending with 15, mark the Little Crawl Key Channel. These are private aids.

EAST TURTLE SHOAL LIGHT 45, 24 43.5N, 80 56.0W. Fl G 4s, 27ft, 5M. SG on tower.
West Turtle Shoal Daybeacon 47, SG on pile.
Coco Plum Channel Daybeacon 1, SG on pile. Private aid.
Coco Plum Channel Daybeacon 3, SG on pile. Private aid.

KEY COLONY BEACH
East Channel Daybeacon 2A, TR on pile. Private aid.
East Channel Daybeacon 3A, SG on pile. Private aid.
West Channel Daybeacon 1, SG on pile. Private aid.
West Channel Daybeacon 3, SG on pile. Private aid.
West Channel Daybeacon 6, TR on pile. Private aid.

Fat Deer Key Daybeacon 48, 24 41.5N, 81 01.5W. TR on pile.
EAST WASHERWOMAN SHOAL LIGHT 49, on north side of shoal, 24 40.0N, 81 04.0W. Fl G 4s, 36ft, 5M. SG on black triangular pyramidal structure on piles.

SISTER CREEK
LIGHT 2, 24 41.2N, 81 05.2W. Fl R 4s, 16ft, 3M. TR on pile.
Daybeacon 3, SG on pile.
Daybeacon 4, TR on pile.
Daybeacon 6, TR on pile.
Daybeacon 8, TR on pile.

BOOT KEY HARBOR
LIGHT 1, 24 42.0N, 81 07.3W. Fl G 4s, 16ft, 4M. SG on pile.

NOTE: A series of 13 red and green day-beacons, beginning with number 2 and ending with 21, mark the Boot Key Harbor channel. A series of 7 private daybeacons, beginning with number 1 and ending with 9, mark the channel in the eastern part of the harbor.

MARATHON

24 42N, 81 06W
U.S. Coast Guard: Marathon station on the north side of Vaca Key, east of Knight Key Channel.
Dockage: Many marinas line the shores of Boot Key Harbor.
Anchorage: Good anchorage in Boot Key Harbor. Beware of the local authorities conducting surprise boat inspections.
Fuel: Many fuel docks.
Repairs: Extensive.
Supplies: Extensive. Haulout facilities.

This is one of the few sheltered harbors on the Hawk Channel side of the Keys. Elaborate marine facilities provide most services. Nearby Moser Channel is one of only two high-level bridges allowing access to the waters of Florida Bay. This is a possible route for those headed north to the west coast of Florida. Ashore are many stores and restaurants. Marathon is your best bet for restocking in the Keys. In recent years the authorities have made a practice of mass boat inspections in the harbor.

SOMBRERO KEY TO KEY WEST

BIG PINE SHOAL LIGHT 22, on seaward edge of reef, 24 34.1N, 81 19.6W. Fl R 2.5s, 16ft, 6M. TR on dolphin.
LOOE KEY LIGHT 24, 24 32.8N, 81 24.2W. Fl R 4s, 20ft., 6M. TR on dolphin.
AMERICAN SHOAL LIGHT, 24 31.5N, 81 31.2W. Fl (3) W 15s (2R sectors), 109ft, 13M white, 10M red. Brown octagonal pyramidal skeleton tower enclosing white stair cylinder and brown ocagonal dwelling; pile foundation. W 270°–067°, R 067°–090°, obscured 090°–125°, W 125°–242°, R 242°–270°.
PELICAN SHOAL LIGHT 26, on seaward edge of reef, 24 30.3N, 81 36.0W. Fl R 6s, 20ft, 7M. TR on dolphin.
Eastern Sambo Daybeacon 28, 24 29.5N, 81 39.8W. TR on pile.

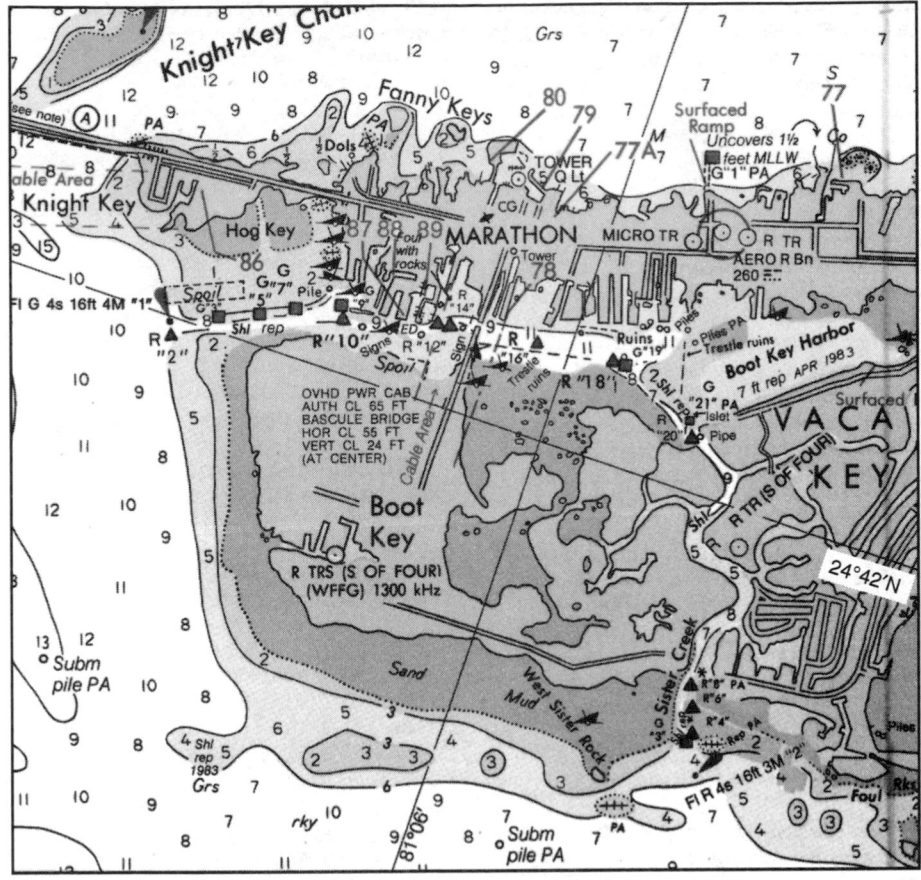

Marathon, soundings in feet *(from NOAA 11451, 26th ed, 2/94)*

Western Sambo Daybeacon 30, 24 28.9N, 81 42.3W. TR on pile.
STOCK ISLAND APPROACH CHANNEL LIGHT 32, 24 28.4N, 81 44.5W. Fl R 2.5s, 19ft, 6M. TR on dolphin.
Key West Entrance Lighted Whistle Buoy KW, 24 27.7N, 81 48.1W. Mo (A) W, 6M. Red and white stripes with red spherical topmark.

HAWK CHANNEL: MOSER CHANNEL TO KEY WEST

MOSER CHANNEL
South Daybeacon 2, 24 41.1N, 81 10.0W. TR on pile.
South Daybeacon 4, TR on pile.
South Daybeacon 5, SG on pile.
South Daybeacon 6, TR on pile.

BAHIA HONDA KEY LIGHT 49A, 24 37.5N, 81 14.2W. Fl G 6s, 20ft, 6M. SG on piles.
NEWFOUND HARBOR KEYS LIGHT 50, 24 36.8N, 81 23.6W. Fl R 2.5s, 16ft, 4M. TR on pile.

NEWFOUND HARBOR CHANNEL
ENTRANCE LIGHT 2, 24 37.1N, 81 24.4W. Fl R 4s, 16ft, 3M. TR on dolphin.
Daybeacon 3, SG on pile.
Daybeacon 4, TR on pile.
Daybeacon 5, SG on pile.
Daybeacon 6, TR on pile.
Daybeacon 8, TR on pile.

RAMROD KEY
Approach Daybeacon 2, TR on pile. Private aid.
Shoal Daybeacon, 24 31.5N, 81 23.7W. NW on pile worded SHOAL. Private aid.

Channel Daybeacon 1, SG on pile. Private aid.
Channel Daybeacon 2, TR on pile. Private aid.
Channel Daybeacon 3, SG on pile. Private aid.
Channel Daybeacon 5, SG on pile. Private aid.

NILES CHANNEL
Daybeacon 4, TR on pile.
Daybeacon 5, SG on pile.
Daybeacon 6, TR on pile.
North Shoal Daybeacon, NW on pile.
South Shoal Daybeacon, 24 39.7N, 81 25.9W.
NW on pile worded SHOAL.

TROPICAL MARINA
Daybeacon 2, TR on pile. Private aid.
Daybeacon 4, TR on pile. Private aid.
Daybeacon 6, TR on pile. Private aid.
Daybeacon 8, TR on pile. Private aid.
LOGGERHEAD KEY LIGHT 50A, 24 35.8N,
81 27.3W Fl R 6s, 16ft, 4M. TR on pile.

KEMP CHANNEL
*This channel is marked by a series of 20
red and green private daymarks, begin-
ning with number 1 and ending with 25.
Near the end of the channel is an
Obstruction Daybeacon, worded DANGER
SUBMERGED PILES.*

SUMMERLAND KEY
Daybeacon 1, 24 36.5N, 81 30.7W. SG on pile.
Private aid.
Daybeacon 2, TR on pile. Private aid.
Daybeacon 4, TR on pile. Private aid.
Daybeacon 5, SG on pile. Private aid.

PIRATES COVE
AND CUDJOE KEY

*This channel is marked by a series of 19
red and green daymarks beginning with
number 1, increasing to 24, and ending
with 1A. Numbers 11 through 24 and 1A
are private aids.*

NINEFOOT SHOAL LIGHT, 24 34.1N, 81 33.1W.
Fl W 2.5s, 18ft, 6M. NG on dolphin.
West Washerwoman Daybeacon 51,
24 33.3N, 81 33.8W. SG on pile.
West Washerwoman Daybeacon 53, SG on
pile.
Pelican Key Daybeacon 55, SG on pile.

SADDLEBUNCH
HARBOR
Daybeacon 1, 24 34.5N, 81 37.6W. SG on pile.
Private aid.

*NOTE: This channel is marked by a series of
8 more red and green daymarks beginning
with number 2 and ending with 18. These
are private aids.*

TAMARAC PARK CHANNEL
Obstruction East Daybeacon, NW on pile.
Private aid.
Obstruction West Daybeacon, NW on pile.
Private aid.
Daybeacon 1, SG on pile. Private aid.
Daybeacon 2, TR on pile. Private aid.
Daybeacon 3, SG on pile. Private aid.
Daybeacon 4, TR on pile. Private aid.
Daybeacon 6, TR on pile. Private aid.
BOCA CHICA LIGHT 56, 24 33.1N, 81 41.2W.
Fl R 4s, 14ft, 3M. TR on pile.

STOCK ISLAND APPROACH CHANNEL
LIGHT 32, 24 28.4N, 81 44.5W. Fl R 2.5s, 19ft,
6M. TR on dolphin.
Daybeacon 2, TR on pile.
HAWK CHANNEL LIGHT 57, 24 31.9N,
81 45.5W. Fl G 4s, 16ft, 4M. SG on dolphin.

BOCA CHICA CHANNEL
LIGHT 1, 24 32.8N, 81 43.6W. Fl G 4s, 16ft, 4M.
SG on pile.
Daybeacon 2, TR on pile.
Daybeacon 3, SG on pile.
Daybeacon 4, TR on pile.
Daybeacon 5, SG on pile.
Daybeacon 6, TR on pile.
Daybeacon 7, SG on pile.
LIGHT 8, Fl R 4s, 16ft, 3M. TR on pile.
Daybeacon 9, SG on pile.
Daybeacon 10, TR on pile.
Daybeacon 11, SG on pile.
Daybeacon 12, TR on pile.
Daybeacon 13, SG on pile.
Daybeacon 14, TR on pile.
Daybeacon 15, SG on pile.
LIGHT 16, Fl R 4s, 16ft, 3M. TR on pile.
Daybeacon 17, SG on pile.

STOCK ISLAND
EAST CHANNEL
A Daybeacon 1A, 24 33.3N, 81 43.4W. SG on
pile. Private aid.
A Daybeacon 3A, SG on pile. Private aid.
A Daybeacon 4A, TR on pile. Private aid.
A Daybeacon 5A, SG on pile. Private aid.
B Daybeacon 1B, 24 33.7N, 81 43.1W. SG on
pile. Private aid.
B Daybeacon 2B, TR on pile. Private aid.
B Daybeacon 3B, SG on pile. Private aid.

B Daybeacon 4B, TR on pile. Private aid.
B Daybeacon 5B, SG on pile. Private aid.
B Daybeacon 6B, TR on pile. Private aid.
B Daybeacon 7B, SG on pile. Private aid.

SAFE HARBOR CHANNEL
LIGHT 2, 24 32.5N, 81 43.9W. Fl R 4s, 16ft, 3M. TR on dolphin.
LIGHT 3, Fl G 6s, 16ft, 4M. SG on dolphin.
LIGHT 4, Fl R 2.5s, 16ft, 3M. TR on pile.
Daybeacon 5, SG on pile.

KEY WEST OCEANSIDE MARINA
This channel is marked by 8 alternating red and green daybeacons numbered from 1 through 9. These are private aids.

COW KEY CHANNEL
Daybeacon 1, 24 33.3N, 81 44.7W. SG on pile. Private aid.

This channel is marked by 11 more red and green daybeacons, beginning with number 2 and ending with 20. These are private aids.

COW KEY WEST CHANNEL
Daybeacon 1A, 24 33.9N, 81 45.0W. SG on pile. Private aid.
Daybeacon 3A, SG on pile. Private aid.

CASA MARINA
Daybeacon 1, 24 32.4N, 81 47.4W. SG on pile. Private aid.
Daybeacon 2, TR on pile. Private aid.
Daybeacon 3, SG on pile. Private aid.
Daybeacon 4, TR on pile. Private aid.

KEY WEST HARBOR
MAIN CHANNEL
Entrance Lighted Whistle Buoy KW, 24 27.7N, 81 48.1W. Mo (A) W, 6M. Red and white stripes with red spherical topmark.
Lighted Bell Buoy 2, Fl R 4s, 3M. Red.
Lighted Buoy 3, Fl G 4s, 4M. Green.
RANGE (Front Light), 24 32.2N, 81 48.4W. Q G, Fl R 4s, 32ft., 3M red. KRW on skeleton tower on piles. Visible 2° each side of rangeline; passing light obscured 326°–026°.
(Rear Light), 1310 yards, 356° from front light. Iso G 6s, 75ft. KRW on skeleton tower on piles. Visible 2° each side of rangeline.
Lighted Bell Buoy 3A, 24 29.8N, 81 48.3W. Fl G 6s, 4M. Green.
EASTERN TRIANGLE LIGHT, 24 30.5N, 81 48.2W. Fl R 2.5s, 36ft, 5M. Red skeleton tower on piles.

Western Triangle Lighted Bell Buoy 5, at edge of shoal. Fl G 4s, 4M. Green.
Lighted Buoy 7, Fl G 4s, 4M. Green.
CUT A RANGE (Front Light), 24 33.2N, 81 50.0W. Q G, 44ft. KRW on tower on piles, Visible 2° each side of rangeline. **(Rear Light),** 1000 yards, 325° from front light. Iso G 6s, 70ft, KRW on tower on piles. Visible 2° each side of rangeline.
Lighted Buoy 8, Q R 3M. Red.
North Spoil Bank Buoy A, Yellow can.
Lighted Buoy 9, Fl G 4s, 4M. Green.
CUT B RANGE (Front Light), 24 33.6N, 81 48.9W. Q R, 25ft. KRW on tower, Visible 4° each side of rangeline. **(Rear Light),** 300 yards, 003° from front light. Iso R 6s, 40ft. KRW on tower. Visible 4° each side of rangeline.
Lighted Buoy 12, 24 32.0N, 81 48.9W. Q R, 3M. Red.
Lighted Buoy 13, Fl G 4s, 4M. Green.
Lighted Buoy 14, Q R, 3M. Red.
Lighted Buoy 15, Fl G 4s, 4M. Green.
KEY WEST HARBOR RANGE (Front Light), 24 34.7N, 81 48.0W. Q W, 19ft. KRW on dolphin. Visible all around; higher intensity on range-line. **(Rear Light),** 781 yards, 024.3° from front light. Iso W 6s, 36ft. KRW on piles. Visible 4° each side of rangeline.
Buoy 17, Green can.
Buoy 19, Green can.
TRUMAN ANNEX BARRIER PIER LIGHT, 24 33.4N, 81 48.5W. F W, 5ft. On pier. Private aid.
Daybeacon 21, SG on pile.
Lighted Buoy 23, Fl G 2.5s, 3M. Green.
Lighted Buoy 24, Fl R 4s, 3M. Red.
Lighted Buoy 25, Fl G 4s, 3M. Red.
TURNING BASIN LIGHT 27, 24 34.0N, 81 48.5W. Fl G 4s, 16ft, 4M. SG on dolphin.
Turning Basin Lighted Buoy 29, Fl G 4s, 4M. Green.
Turning Basin Daybeacon 31, SG on pile.

KEY WEST

24 34N, 81 48W
U.S. Coast Guard: Key West Station located at Pier D2, north of main waterfront.
Port of Entry
Dockage: There is a marina in the old Truman Annex basin and a couple in Key West Bight. Others are located in Garrison Bight.
Anchorage: The best anchorage is just east of Wisteria Island. There may be some room near Light 2, but the holding is poor and the area crowded with moorings. A public dinghy landing is southwest of Light 2.
Fuel: Garrison Bight has fuel.

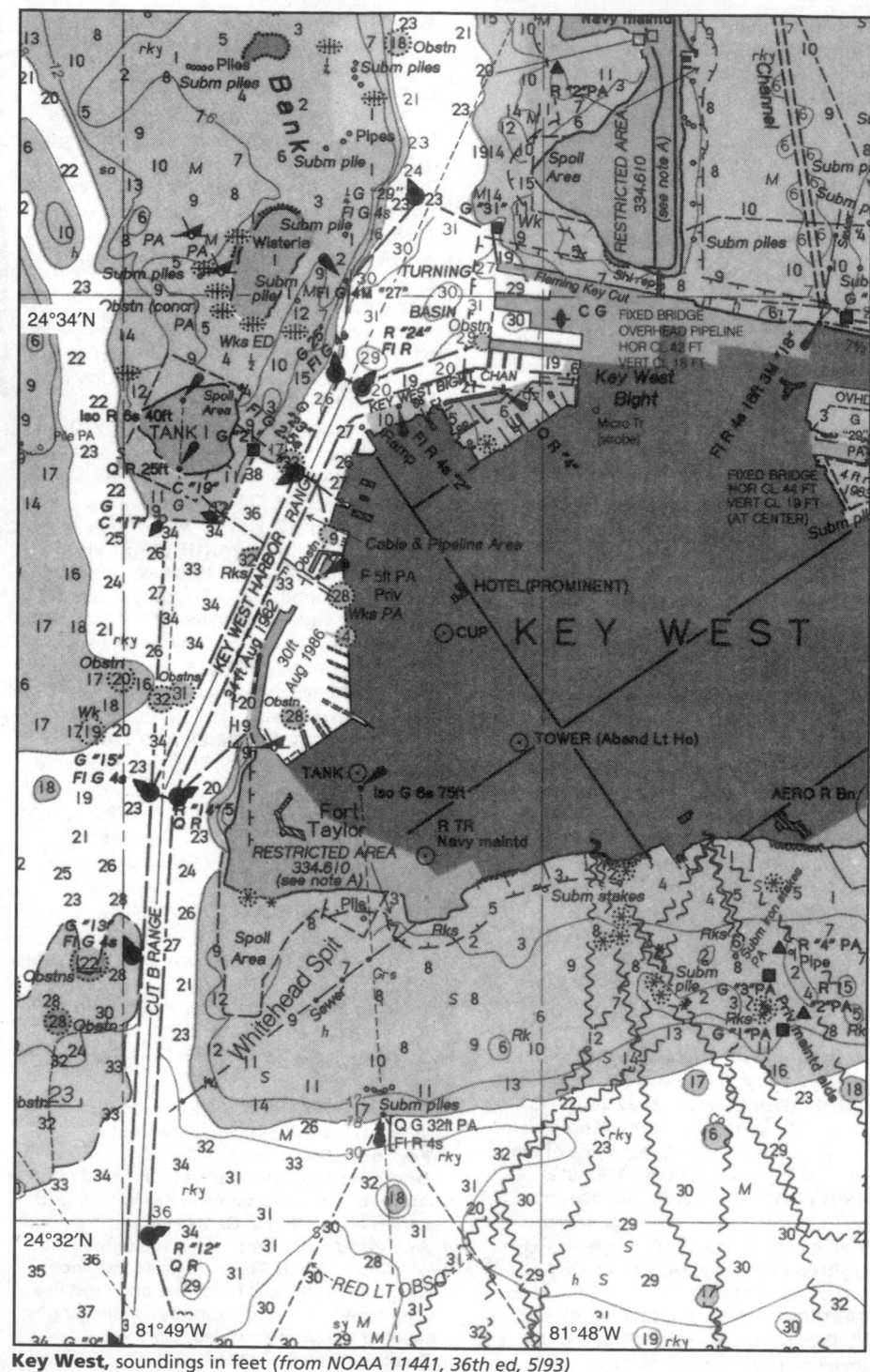

Key West, soundings in feet *(from NOAA 11441, 36th ed, 5/93)*

Repairs: Good. Haulout facilities.
Supplies: Good. Walking distance to most shops.
Key West is the final stop for boats cruising the
Keys. It has several well-marked approaches.
The southern channel is the easiest. The northwest channel is shallower and has several
hazards, including a submerged breakwater.
Study the chart well if using the northwest
channel after dark. The anchorage off Wisteria
Island offers poor shelter and holding, but is
within dinghy distance of town. If bad weather
threatens, you are better off in a marina or
some other harbor. This is no place to be in a
hurricane. Ashore is a collage of everything
touristy and entertaining. Live music, tie-die
shirts, open-air bars, and the Hemingway house
all vie for your attention. There is always something interesting happening in Key West.

FLEMING KEY
RANGE (Front Daybeacon), 24 34.5N,
81 47.8W. KRW on dolphin. Maintained by
U.S. Navy. **(Rear Daybeacon),** 45 yards, 256°
from front daybeacon. KRW on dolphin. Maintained by U.S. Navy.
Daybeacon 2, TR on pile. Maintained by U.S.
Navy.
KEY WEST BIGHT CHANNEL LIGHT 2,
24 33.7N, 81 48.3W. Fl R 4s, 16ft, 4M. TR on
dolphin.
KEY WEST BIGHT CHANNEL LIGHT 4, Q R,
16ft., 4M. TR on dolphin.

GARRISON BIGHT CHANNEL
APPROACH LIGHT 2, 24 35.0N, 81 48.3W.
Fl R 4s, 16ft, 3M. TR on pile.
LIGHT 3, Fl G 4s, 16ft, 4M. SG on pile.
Daybeacon 4, TR on pile.
Daybeacon 6, TR on pile.
LIGHT 8, Fl R 4s, 12ft, 3M. TR on pile.
Daybeacon 10, TR on pile.
Daybeacon 12, TR on pile.
LIGHT 13, Fl G 4s, 16ft, 4M. SG on dolphin.
Daybeacon 14, TR on pile.
LIGHT 16, Fl R 4s, 16ft, 3M. TR on pile.
LIGHT 17, Fl G 4s, 13ft, 4M. SG on pile.
LIGHT 18, Fl R 4s, 16ft, 3M. TR on pile.
Daybeacon 19, SG on pile.
Daybeacon 20, TR on pile.
LIGHT 21, Fl G 4s, 16ft, 4M. SG on pile.
Daybeacon 22, TR on pile.

GARRISON BIGHT CHANNEL
TURNING BASIN
Daybeacon 24, 24 33.7N, 81 47.0W. TR on
pile.
Daybeacon 25, SG on pile.

Daybeacon 26, TR on pile.
Daybeacon 27, SG on pile.
Daybeacon 29, SG on pile.

KEY WEST NORTHWEST CHANNEL
Entrance Lighted Bell Buoy 1, 24 38.8N,
81 54.0W. Fl G 2.5s, 4M. Green.
ENTRANCE RANGE (Front Light 6),
24 37.9N, 81 53.8W. Q R, 22ft, 4M. TR and
KRW on piles. Visible all around. **(Rear Light),**
787 yards, 166° from front light. Iso R 6s, 36ft.
KRW on triangular pyramidal structure on
piles. Visible all around; higher intensity on
rangeline.
JETTY LIGHT A, 24 38.4N, 81 53.6W. Q Y,
16ft, 7M. NY on dolphin worded DANGER
SUBMERGED JETTY.
Buoy 2, Red nun.
Lighted Buoy 3, Q G, 5M. Green.
Buoy 4, Red nun.
Lighted Buoy 5, Fl G, 2.5s, 4M. Green.
Daybeacon 8, TR on pile.
Buoy 9, Green can.
LIGHT 10, 24 36.9N, 81 52.6W. Fl R 4s, 12ft,
4M. TR on pile.
Daybeacon 11, SG on pile.
LIGHT 12, Fl R 2.5s, 16ft, 4M. TR on pile.
LIGHT 14, Fl R 6s, 16ft, 4M. TR on pile.
Daybeacon 15, SG on pile.
LIGHT 15A, Fl G 4s, 14ft, 4M. SG on pile.
Daybeacon 16, TR on pile.
LIGHT 17, Fl G 2.5s, 16ft, 4M. SG on pile.
LIGHT 18, on east point of shoals, 24 33.4N,
81 49.7W. Fl R 2.5s, 36ft, 4M. TR on red trian-
gular pyramidal skeleton structure on piles.
LIGHT 19, on southeast end of middle
ground. Fl G 4s, 16ft, 4M. SG on pile.

LAKE PASSAGE CHANNEL
Daybeacon 1, 24 34.2N, 81 50.5W. SG on pile.
Private aid.

*NOTE: This channel is marked by a series
of 13 more private red and green daymarks,
beginning with number 2 and ending
with 18.*

CALDA CHANNEL
LIGHT 1, 24 37.8N, 81 49.6W. Fl G 4s, 16ft, 4M.
SG on pile.
Daybeacon 3, SG on pile.
Daybeacon 5, SG on pile.
Daybeacon 6, TR on pile.
Daybeacon 6A, TR on pile.
Daybeacon 8, TR on pile.
Daybeacon 9, SG on pile.

Daybeacon 11, SG on pile.
Daybeacon 12, TR on pile.
Daybeacon 13, SG on pile.
Daybeacon 14, TR on pile.
Shoal Daybeacon, 24 36.7N, 81 48.3W. NW on pile worded SHOAL.
Daybeacon 16, TR on pile.
Daybeacon 17, SG on pile.
Daybeacon 18, TR on pile.
Daybeacon 20, TR on pile.
Daybeacon 21, SG on pile.
Daybeacon 22, TR on pile.
Daybeacon 24, TR on pile.
Daybeacon 25, SG on pile.

SAND KEY CHANNEL

Daybeacon 2, 24 27.6N, 81 52.8W. TR on pile.
Middle Ground Daybeacon 3, 24 29.0N, 81 52.9W. SG on pile.
Preferred Channel Buoy, red and green bands, nun.

KEY WEST
SOUTHWEST CHANNEL

Buoy A, 24 26.6N, 81 58.8W. Red and white stripes, spherical buoy.
Buoy B, Red and white stripes, spherical buoy.
Buoy C, Red and white stripes, spherical buoy.
Buoy D, Red and white stripes, spherical buoy.
Buoy 2, Red nun.
Buoy 3, Green can.
Buoy 4, Red nun.
Buoy E, Red and white stripes, spherical buoy.
Buoy F, Red and white stripes, spherical buoy.
Buoy G, Red and white stripes, spherical buoy.
Wreck Lighted Buoy WR5, 24 32.6N, 81 49.6W. Q G, 3M. Green.

KEY WEST TO
THE DRY TORTUGAS

SAND KEY LIGHT, 24 27.2N, 81 52.6W. Fl (2) W 15s, 40ft, 13M. NR on square skeleton tower.
Western Dry Rocks Daybeacon K, 24 26.8N, 81 55.6W. NB on pile.
Boca Grande Channel Daybeacon 1, 24 37.4N, 82 04.2W. SG on pile.
Boca Grande Channel Daybeacon 2, TR on pile.
Coalbin Rock Buoy CB, on south side of shoal, 24 27.0N, 82 05.3W. Red and green bands, nun.
COSGROVE SHOAL LIGHT, 24 27.5N, 82 11.1W. Fl W 6s, 49ft, 9M. Small black house on red hexagonal skeleton tower on piles.

Marquesas Rock Buoy MR, on south side of reef, Red and green bands, nun.
Twenty-Eight Foot Shoal Lighted Bell Buoy, on southwest side of shoal, 24 25.6N, 82 25.5W. Fl (2+1) R 6s, 4M. Red and green bands.
HALFMOON SHOAL LIGHT WR2, 24 33.5N, 82 28.5W. Fl R 6s, 19ft, 4M. TR on dolphin.
REBECCA SHOAL LIGHT, 24 34.7N, 82 35.2W. Fl W 6s, (R sector), 66ft, 9M white, 6M red. Square skeleton tower on brown pile foundation, Red 254°–302°.
DRY TORTUGAS LIGHT, 24 38.0N, 82 55.2W. Fl W 20s, 151ft, 24M. Conical tower, lower half white, upper half black. Emergency light of reduced intensity when main light is extinguished.

NORTHWEST CHANNEL TO
THE DRY TORTUGAS

SMITH SHOAL LIGHT, on northeast end of shoal, 24 43.2N, 81 55.0W. Fl W 6s, 47ft, 9M. Small black house on white hexagonal pyramidal skeleton tower on piles.
ELLIS ROCK LIGHT, 24 39.2N, 82 11.2W. Fl W 2.5s, 16ft, 3M. NB on dolphin.
NEW GROUND ROCKS LIGHT, 24 40.1N, 82 26.7W. Fl W 4s, 19ft, 7M. NB on pile.

DRY TORTUGAS

Lighted Buoy A, 24 34.0N, 82 54.0W. Fl Y 2.5s, 4M. Yellow.
Buoy B, Yellow can.
Lighted Buoy C, 24 34.0N, 82 58.0W. Fl Y 4s, 4M. Yellow.
Buoy D, Yellow can.
Lighted Buoy E, 24 39.0N, 82 58.0W. Fl Y 6s, 5M. Yellow.
Buoy F, Yellow can.
Buoy G, Yellow can.
Lighted Buoy H, 24 43.0N, 82 54.0W. Fl Y 2.5s, 4M. Yellow.
Lighted Buoy I, 24 43.5N, 82 52.0W. Fl Y 4s, 4M. Yellow.
Buoy J, Yellow can.
Lighted Buoy K, 24 43.5N, 82 48.0W. Fl Y 6s, 5M. Yellow.
Lighted Buoy L, 24 42.0N, 82 46.0W. Fl Y 2.5s, 4M. Yellow.
Lighted Buoy M, 24 40.0N, 82 46.0W. Fl Y 4s, 4M. Yellow.
Buoy N, Yellow can.
Lighted Buoy O, 24 37.0N, 82 48.0W. Fl Y 6s, 5M. Yellow.
Buoy P, Yellow can.
Buoy Q, Yellow can.

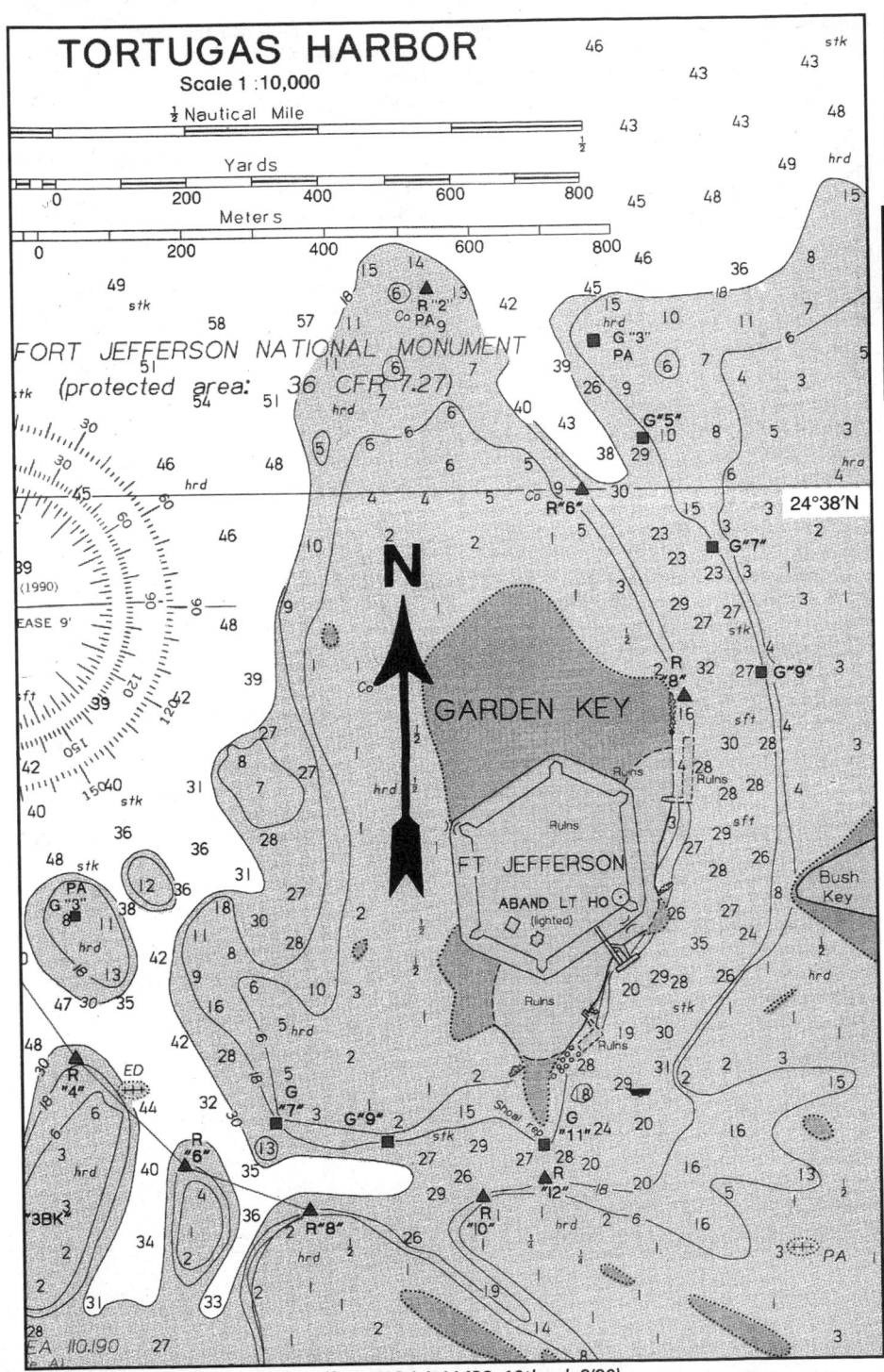

TORTUGAS HARBOR
Scale 1:10,000

½ Nautical Mile

Yards

Meters

Dry Tortugas, soundings in feet *(from NOAA 11438, 10th ed, 8/90)*

PULASKI SHOAL LIGHT, on east side of shoal, 24 41.6N, 82 46.4W. Fl W 6s, 49ft, 9M. Small black house on hexagonal pyramidal skeleton tower on piles.

SOUTHEAST CHANNEL
LIGHT 1, 24 35.6N, 82 52.4W. Fl G, 2.5s, 19ft, 3M. SG on dolphin.
Lighted Buoy 2, Fl R 4s, 3M. Red.
LIGHT 3, 24 38.3N, 82 51.7W. Fl G 4s, 16ft, 4M. SG on dolphin.
Daybeacon 4, TR on pile.
Middle Ground Daybeacon, on east side of shoal. JR on pile.

EAST CHANNEL
Daybeacon 2, 24 38.1N, 82 52.5W. TR on pile.
Daybeacon 3, SG on pile.
Daybeacon 5, SG on pile.
Daybeacon 6, TR on pile.
Daybeacon 7, SG on pile.
Daybeacon 8, TR on pile.
Daybeacon 9, SG on pile.

SOUTHWEST CHANNEL
Buoy 1, Green can.
Daybeacon 3, 24 37.6N, 82 54.5W. SG on pile.
Daybeacon 4, TR on pile.
Daybeacon 6, TR on pile.
White Shoal North Daybeacon 7, SG on pile.

WEST CHANNEL
Daybeacon 2, 24 37.7N, 82 52.9W. TR on pile.
Daybeacon 3, SG on pile.
Daybeacon 4, TR on pile.
Daybeacon 6, TR on pile.
Daybeacon 7, SG on pile.
Daybeacon 8, TR on pile.
Daybeacon 9, SG on pile.
Daybeacon 10, TR on pile.
Daybeacon 11, SG on pile.
Daybeacon 12, TR on pile.

BIRD KEY HARBOR
Daybeacon 2BK, TR on pile.
Daybeacon 3BK, SG on pile.
Daybeacon 5BK, SG on pile.

DRY TORTUGAS
24 38N, 82 52W
U.S. Coast Guard: Key West station. Lighthouse keepers on Loggerhead Key monitor VHF channel 16.
National Park Service: Station located in Fort Jefferson. Call on VHF channel 16. The NPS is in charge of the Fort Jefferson National Monument and surrounding waters.
Dockage: Temporary landings may be made at the National Park Service dock. There is no overnight dockage.
Anchorage: Directly east of Fort Jefferson and south of Bird Key. The surrounding shallows are not marked, but may be easily seen when the sun is high. The holding is good. Although there is no protection from high ground the shoals break up most seas. Dinghy ashore near the Park Service dock.
Fuel, Repairs, Supplies: None. No water is available. All trash must be taken away.

The Dry Tortugas are a small slice of the Bahamas brought to the U.S. Beautiful sandy beaches and crystal-clear water are the reward for the often-rough 65-mile trip from Key West. The approaches are best made in daylight because of the many surrounding shoals that may be easily seen. Large areas of coral reef should be carefully avoided. A Coast Guard mooring may be available for those wishing to visit the 151-foot-high lighthouse on Loggerhead Key. Check ahead with the Coast Guard personnel stationed at the lighthouse.

MIAMI, FLORIDA (Harbor Entrance)

HIGH & LOW WATER 1995 25°46'N 80°08'W

EASTERN STANDARD TIME (GMT -5H).   ADD 1H DAYLIGHT SAVING APR 2 - OCT 28

FLORIDA

JANUARY

Day	Time	ft	Day	Time	ft
1 Su ●	0127 / 0750 / 1400 / 2002	-0.7 / 3.2 / -0.3 / 3.0	**16** O	0128 / 0751 / 1357 / 1954	-0.2 / 2.6 / 0.1 / 2.4
2 M	0218 / 0840 / 1450 / 2054	-0.7 / 3.2 / -0.3 / 3.0	**17** Tu	0207 / 0827 / 1435 / 2034	-0.3 / 2.6 / 0.0 / 2.5
3 Tu	0309 / 0929 / 1540 / 2146	-0.6 / 3.1 / -0.3 / 2.9	**18** W	0246 / 0904 / 1512 / 2115	-0.3 / 2.6 / -0.1 / 2.5
4 W	0358 / 1017 / 1630 / 2237	-0.4 / 3.0 / -0.2 / 2.8	**19** Th	0326 / 0941 / 1552 / 2158	-0.3 / 2.6 / -0.1 / 2.5
5 Th	0448 / 1104 / 1720 / 2330	-0.3 / 2.8 / -0.2 / 2.6	**20** F	0407 / 1021 / 1633 / 2243	-0.2 / 2.6 / -0.2 / 2.5
6 F	0539 / 1153 / 1811	-0.0 / 2.7 / -0.0	**21** Sa	0452 / 1103 / 1719 / 2333	-0.1 / 2.5 / -0.2 / 2.4
7 Sa	0024 / 0631 / 1242 / 1903	2.5 / 0.2 / 2.5 / 0.1	**22** Su	0541 / 1150 / 1810	-0.0 / 2.5 / -0.2
8 Su ☾	0120 / 0725 / 1333 / 1957	2.3 / 0.4 / 2.3 / 0.1	**23** M	0029 / 0806 / 1243 / 1907	2.4 / 0.1 / 2.4 / -0.2
9 M	0219 / 0823 / 1427 / 2052	2.2 / 0.5 / 2.2 / 0.2	**24** Tu	0132 / 0738 / 1344 / 2011	2.4 / 0.2 / 2.3 / -0.3
10 Tu	0318 / 0922 / 1521 / 2146	2.2 / 0.5 / 2.1 / 0.2	**25** W	0239 / 0846 / 1450 / 2117	2.4 / 0.2 / 2.3 / -0.3
11 W	0414 / 1018 / 1614 / 2236	2.2 / 0.5 / 2.1 / 0.1	**26** Th	0347 / 0955 / 1558 / 2223	2.4 / 0.1 / 2.4 / -0.4
12 Th	0505 / 1110 / 1703 / 2323	2.3 / 0.5 / 2.1 / 0.0	**27** F	0452 / 1100 / 1702 / 2325	2.5 / 0.0 / 2.5 / -0.5
13 F	0551 / 1156 / 1749	2.3 / 0.4 / 2.2	**28** Sa	0551 / 1200 / 1802	2.7 / -0.2 / 2.6
14 Sa	0007 / 0633 / 1239 / 1833	-0.1 / 2.4 / 0.3 / 2.3	**29** Su	0022 / 0645 / 1254 / 1858	-0.6 / 2.8 / -0.3 / 2.7
15 Su	0048 / 0713 / 1319 / 1914	-0.2 / 2.5 / 0.2 / 2.3	**30** M ●	0115 / 0735 / 1345 / 1950	-0.7 / 2.9 / -0.4 / 2.8
			31 Tu	0204 / 0822 / 1433 / 2039	-0.7 / 2.9 / -0.5 / 2.8

FEBRUARY

Day	Time	ft	Day	Time	ft
1 W	0252 / 0907 / 1519 / 2127	-0.7 / 2.9 / -0.3 / 2.7	**16** Th	0225 / 0837 / 1447 / 2056	-0.4 / 2.6 / -0.4 / 2.6
2 Th	0337 / 0951 / 1603 / 2213	-0.5 / 2.8 / -0.3 / 2.6	**17** F	0306 / 0916 / 1527 / 2139	-0.4 / 2.6 / -0.5 / 2.7
3 F	0422 / 1033 / 1647 / 2259	-0.4 / 2.6 / -0.4 / 2.5	**18** Sa	0349 / 0957 / 1610 / 2225	-0.4 / 2.6 / -0.5 / 2.6
4 Sa	0506 / 1115 / 1732 / 2346	-0.2 / 2.5 / -0.3 / 2.3	**19** Su	0434 / 1041 / 1657 / 2315	-0.3 / 2.6 / -0.5 / 2.6
5 Su	0552 / 1159 / 1818	0.0 / 2.3 / -0.1	**20** M	0523 / 1129 / 1749	-0.2 / 2.5 / -0.4
6 M	0036 / 0640 / 1245 / 1907	2.2 / 0.2 / 2.1 / 0.0	**21** Tu	0011 / 0618 / 1223 / 1847	2.5 / -0.0 / 2.4 / -0.3
7 Tu ☾	0130 / 0733 / 1335 / 2000	2.0 / 0.4 / 2.0 / 0.1	**22** W	0113 / 0720 / 1326 / 1952	2.4 / 0.1 / 2.3 / -0.3
8 W	0228 / 0832 / 1430 / 2056	2.0 / 0.5 / 1.9 / 0.2	**23** Th	0221 / 0830 / 1435 / 2102	2.3 / 0.2 / 2.3 / -0.3
9 Th	0328 / 0933 / 1529 / 2153	2.0 / 0.5 / 1.9 / 0.1	**24** F	0331 / 0941 / 1546 / 2211	2.4 / 0.1 / 2.3 / -0.3
10 F	0425 / 1031 / 1626 / 2247	2.0 / 0.4 / 1.9 / 0.0	**25** Sa	0438 / 1048 / 1654 / 2314	2.4 / 0.0 / 2.4 / -0.4
11 Sa	0516 / 1122 / 1718 / 2336	2.1 / 0.3 / 2.0 / -0.1	**26** Su	0537 / 1147 / 1754	2.6 / -0.2 / 2.5
12 Su	0601 / 1208 / 1806	2.2 / 0.2 / 2.2	**27** M	0011 / 0630 / 1240 / 1847	-0.5 / 2.7 / -0.3 / 2.7
13 M	0021 / 0642 / 1249 / 1850	-0.2 / 2.4 / 0.0 / 2.3	**28** Tu	0102 / 0717 / 1327 / 1936	-0.5 / 2.7 / -0.4 / 2.7
14 Tu	0104 / 0722 / 1329 / 1932	-0.3 / 2.5 / -0.1 / 2.4			
15 W O	0145 / 0759 / 1408 / 2014	-0.4 / 2.6 / -0.3 / 2.6			

MARCH

Day	Time	ft	Day	Time	ft
1 W ●	0149 / 0801 / 1411 / 2022	-0.5 / 2.8 / -0.5 / 2.8	**16** Th	0119 / 0728 / 1338 / 1951	-0.3 / 2.7 / -0.4 / 2.8
2 Th	0232 / 0842 / 1453 / 2105	-0.5 / 2.8 / -0.5 / 2.7	**17** F	0202 / 0809 / 1420 / 2035	-0.4 / 2.8 / -0.5 / 2.9
3 F	0314 / 0921 / 1533 / 2147	-0.4 / 2.7 / -0.5 / 2.7	**18** Sa	0245 / 0851 / 1504 / 2121	-0.4 / 2.8 / -0.6 / 3.0
4 Sa	0354 / 1000 / 1613 / 2228	-0.2 / 2.6 / -0.4 / 2.5	**19** Su	0330 / 0935 / 1549 / 2209	-0.3 / 2.8 / -0.6 / 2.9
5 Su	0434 / 1038 / 1653 / 2310	-0.1 / 2.4 / -0.2 / 2.4	**20** M	0417 / 1021 / 1638 / 2300	-0.3 / 2.8 / -0.5 / 2.8
6 M	0515 / 1117 / 1734 / 2354	0.1 / 2.3 / -0.1 / 2.3	**21** Tu	0508 / 1112 / 1731 / 2356	-0.1 / 2.7 / -0.4 / 2.7
7 Tu	0559 / 1200 / 1819	0.3 / 2.1 / 0.1	**22** W	0605 / 1209 / 1831	0.0 / 2.5 / -0.3
8 W	0043 / 0648 / 1247 / 1909	2.1 / 0.4 / 2.0 / 0.2	**23** Th	0058 / 0708 / 1314 / 1937	2.6 / 0.2 / 2.4 / -0.1
9 Th ☾	0137 / 0744 / 1343 / 2006	2.0 / 0.5 / 1.9 / 0.2	**24** F	0206 / 0818 / 1426 / 2048	2.5 / 0.2 / 2.4 / -0.1
10 F	0237 / 0846 / 1445 / 2107	2.0 / 0.6 / 1.9 / 0.2	**25** Sa	0315 / 0929 / 1538 / 2158	2.5 / 0.2 / 2.4 / -0.1
11 Sa	0337 / 0947 / 1548 / 2207	2.0 / 0.5 / 2.0 / 0.2	**26** Su	0421 / 1034 / 1645 / 2301	2.5 / 0.1 / 2.5 / -0.1
12 Su	0433 / 1042 / 1645 / 2301	2.0 / 0.4 / 2.1 / 0.1	**27** M	0519 / 1131 / 1743 / 2356	2.6 / -0.1 / 2.6 / -0.1
13 M	0522 / 1131 / 1736 / 2350	2.3 / 0.2 / 2.3 / -0.1	**28** Tu	0609 / 1221 / 1834	2.7 / -0.2 / 2.7
14 Tu	0606 / 1215 / 1823	2.4 / 0.0 / 2.5	**29** W	0045 / 0654 / 1306 / 1919	-0.2 / 2.7 / -0.3 / 2.8
15 W	0035 / 0648 / 1257 / 1907	-0.2 / 2.6 / -0.2 / 2.7	**30** Th ●	0129 / 0735 / 1347 / 2002	-0.3 / 2.7 / -0.3 / 2.8
			31 F	0210 / 0814 / 1425 / 2041	-0.2 / 2.7 / -0.3 / 2.8

APRIL

Day	Time	ft	Day	Time	ft
1 Sa	0248 / 0851 / 1503 / 2120	-0.1 / 2.7 / -0.3 / 2.8	**16** Su	0224 / 0827 / 1441 / 2103	-0.3 / 3.0 / -0.6 / 3.2
2 Su	0326 / 0927 / 1539 / 2158	0.0 / 2.6 / -0.2 / 2.7	**17** M	0312 / 0914 / 1530 / 2153	-0.3 / 3.0 / -0.6 / 3.2
3 M	0404 / 1003 / 1616 / 2237	0.1 / 2.5 / -0.1 / 2.6	**18** Tu	0402 / 1005 / 1622 / 2245	-0.2 / 2.9 / -0.5 / 3.1
4 Tu	0443 / 1041 / 1655 / 2318	0.3 / 2.4 / 0.0 / 2.4	**19** W	0456 / 1059 / 1717 / 2342	-0.1 / 2.8 / -0.4 / 2.9
5 W	0524 / 1122 / 1738	0.4 / 2.2 / 0.2	**20** Th	0554 / 1159 / 1817	0.1 / 2.7 / -0.2
6 Th	0002 / 0610 / 1208 / 1825	2.3 / 0.5 / 2.1 / 0.3	**21** F ☽	0043 / 0657 / 1305 / 1923	2.8 / 0.2 / 2.5 / 0.0
7 F	0053 / 0703 / 1302 / 1921	2.2 / 0.6 / 2.1 / 0.4	**22** Sa	0148 / 0805 / 1416 / 2033	2.6 / 0.2 / 2.5 / 0.2
8 Sa	0149 / 0801 / 1404 / 2022	2.2 / 0.6 / 2.0 / 0.4	**23** Su	0255 / 0912 / 1526 / 2141	2.6 / 0.2 / 2.5 / 0.2
9 Su	0248 / 0902 / 1509 / 2124	2.2 / 0.6 / 2.1 / 0.4	**24** M	0358 / 1014 / 1630 / 2242	2.6 / 0.1 / 2.6 / 0.2
10 M	0345 / 0959 / 1609 / 2222	2.3 / 0.4 / 2.3 / 0.3	**25** Tu	0454 / 1109 / 1726 / 2336	2.6 / 0.0 / 2.7 / 0.2
11 Tu	0437 / 1050 / 1703 / 2315	2.4 / 0.2 / 2.5 / 0.2	**26** W	0543 / 1157 / 1815	2.6 / -0.1 / 2.7
12 W	0525 / 1138 / 1753	2.5 / -0.0 / 2.7	**27** Th	0023 / 0626 / 1240 / 1859	0.1 / 2.7 / -0.1 / 2.8
13 Th	0004 / 0611 / 1224 / 1841	0.0 / 2.7 / -0.2 / 2.9	**28** F	0106 / 0706 / 1319 / 1939	0.1 / 2.7 / -0.2 / 2.8
14 F	0051 / 0656 / 1309 / 1928	-0.1 / 2.9 / -0.4 / 3.1	**29** Sa ●	0145 / 0744 / 1356 / 2017	0.1 / 2.6 / -0.2 / 2.8
15 Sa O	0137 / 0741 / 1355 / 2015	-0.2 / 3.0 / -0.6 / 3.2	**30** Su	0223 / 0820 / 1432 / 2053	0.2 / 2.6 / -0.2 / 2.8

TIME MERIDIAN 75°W

0000h is midnight, 1200h is noon.

Heights in feet are referenced to the chart datum of soundings.

MIAMI, FLORIDA (Harbor Entrance)

HIGH & LOW WATER 1995　　　　　　　　　　25°46'N　80°08'W

EASTERN STANDARD TIME (GMT -5H).　ADD 1H DAYLIGHT SAVING APR 2 - OCT 28

MAY

Day	Time ft	Time ft	Time ft	Time ft
1 M	0300 0.2	0856 2.6	1508 -0.1	2130 2.7
2 Tu	0337 0.3	0932 2.5	1545 -0.0	2208 2.6
3 W	0415 0.4	1010 2.4	1623 0.1	2247 2.6
4 Th	0455 0.5	1051 2.3	1704 0.2	2329 2.5
5 F	0539 0.5	1137 2.2	1750 0.3	
6 Sa	0015 2.4	0628 0.6	1229 2.2	1842 0.4
7 Su	0105 2.3	0721 0.5	1328 2.2	(1940 0.5
8 M	0200 2.3	0818 0.5	1430 2.2	2041 0.5
9 Tu	0256 2.4	0915 0.3	1532 2.4	2142 0.4
10 W	0351 2.5	1010 0.1	1629 2.6	2239 0.3
11 Th	0444 2.6	1102 -0.1	1723 2.8	2332 0.1
12 F	0535 2.8	1152 -0.3	1815 3.0	
13 Sa	0024 -0.0	0625 2.9	1242 -0.5	1905 3.2
14 Su	0114 -0.2	0715 3.0	1332 -0.7	O 1955 3.3
15 M	0204 -0.3	0805 3.1	1422 -0.7	2046 3.3
16 Tu	0255 -0.2	0857 3.1	1514 -0.7	2137 3.3
17 W	0348 -0.1	0950 3.0	1607 -0.6	2231 3.1
18 Th	0443 -0.1	1047 2.9	1703 -0.4	2326 3.0
19 F	0540 -0.0	1147 2.7	1802 -0.2	
20 Sa	0025 2.8	0642 0.1	1251 2.6	1905 0.0
21 Su	0126 2.7	0745 0.1	1358 2.5	) 2011 0.2
22 M	0227 2.6	0836 0.1	1505 2.4	2115 0.3
23 Tu	0327 2.5	0947 0.1	1607 2.5	2215 0.3
24 W	0421 2.5	1041 0.0	1702 2.6	2309 0.3
25 Th	0510 2.5	1128 -0.0	1751 2.6	2357 0.3
26 F	0555 2.5	1211 -0.1	1834 2.7	
27 Sa	0040 0.3	0635 2.5	1250 -0.1	1914 2.7
28 Su	0119 0.3	0714 2.5	1328 -0.1	1952 2.7
29 M	0158 0.3	0751 2.5	1405 -0.1	● 2029 2.7
30 Tu	0235 0.3	0828 2.4	1441 -0.1	2105 2.7
31 W	0312 0.3	0906 2.4	1504 -0.0	2142 2.6

JUNE

Day	Time ft	Time ft	Time ft	Time ft
1 Th	0350 0.3	0945 2.3	1557 0.0	2220 2.6
2 F	0429 0.4	1026 2.3	1637 0.1	2259 2.5
3 Sa	0511 0.4	1110 2.2	1721 0.2	2341 2.4
4 Su	0556 0.4	1200 2.2	1809 0.3	
5 M	0027 2.4	0645 0.3	1255 2.2	1903 0.4
6 Tu	0118 2.3	0739 0.2	1355 2.2	(2003 0.4
7 W	0213 2.4	0836 0.2	1457 2.4	2104 0.3
8 Th	0310 2.4	0933 -0.1	1558 2.5	2205 0.2
9 F	0408 2.6	1030 -0.3	1656 2.7	2303 0.1
10 Sa	0504 2.7	1125 -0.5	1752 2.9	2359 -0.0
11 Su	0600 2.8	1219 -0.6	1845 3.1	
12 M	0053 -0.2	0654 2.9	1313 -0.7	O 1938 3.2
13 Tu	0147 -0.3	0748 3.0	1406 -0.8	2030 3.3
14 W	0239 -0.3	0842 3.0	1459 -0.7	2122 3.2
15 Th	0325 -0.2	0937 2.9	1552 -0.6	2214 3.1
16 F	0427 -0.3	1033 2.8	1647 -0.5	2307 3.0
17 Sa	0522 -0.2	1130 2.7	1743 -0.2	
18 Su	0001 2.8	0619 -0.1	1231 2.6	1841 -0.0
19 M	0057 2.6	0717 -0.1	1333 2.5	) 1941 0.2
20 Tu	0153 2.5	0815 0.0	1435 2.4	2042 0.3
21 W	0249 2.4	0912 0.0	1536 2.4	2141 0.4
22 Th	0344 2.3	1006 0.0	1632 2.4	2236 0.4
23 F	0434 2.3	1055 -0.0	1722 2.4	2326 0.4
24 Sa	0521 2.3	1140 -0.1	1807 2.5	
25 Su	0011 0.4	0604 2.3	1221 -0.1	1848 2.5
26 M	0053 0.3	0646 2.3	1301 -0.1	1927 2.6
27 Tu	0132 0.3	0725 2.3	1339 -0.2	● 2004 2.6
28 W	0211 0.2	0804 2.4	1417 -0.2	2041 2.6
29 Th	0248 0.2	0843 2.4	1455 -0.1	2117 2.6
30 F	0325 0.2	0923 2.4	1533 -0.1	2153 2.5

JULY

Day	Time ft	Time ft	Time ft	Time ft
1 Sa	0403 0.2	1003 2.3	1613 0.0	2231 2.5
2 Su	0442 0.2	1046 2.3	1655 0.1	2310 2.5
3 M	0525 0.1	1134 2.3	1741 0.2	2354 2.4
4 Tu	0612 0.1	1226 2.3	1832 0.3	
5 W	0042 2.4	0704 0.0	1324 2.3	(1930 0.3
6 Th	0137 2.4	0802 -0.1	1427 2.4	2032 0.3
7 F	0237 2.4	0903 -0.2	1531 2.5	2136 0.2
8 Sa	0339 2.5	1004 -0.3	1633 2.7	2239 0.1
9 Su	0441 2.6	1104 -0.5	1732 2.8	2339 -0.0
10 M	0541 2.8	1202 -0.6	1828 3.0	
11 Tu	0036 -0.2	0638 2.9	1258 -0.7	1922 3.1
12 W	0131 -0.3	0734 3.0	1351 -0.7	O 2013 3.1
13 Th	0223 -0.4	0828 3.0	1444 -0.7	2104 3.1
14 F	0315 -0.4	0922 3.0	1535 -0.6	2153 3.1
15 Sa	0406 -0.4	1015 2.9	1626 -0.4	2242 2.9
16 Su	0457 -0.3	1108 2.8	1718 -0.2	2332 2.8
17 M	0549 -0.2	1203 2.6	1811 0.0	
18 Tu	0022 2.6	0642 -0.1	1259 2.5	1905 0.2
19 W	0114 2.4	0736 0.0	1358 2.3	) 2003 0.4
20 Th	0207 2.3	0831 0.1	1457 2.3	2101 0.5
21 F	0302 2.2	0926 0.2	1555 2.3	2159 0.6
22 Sa	0356 2.2	1018 0.1	1648 2.3	2252 0.5
23 Su	0447 2.2	1107 0.1	1736 2.4	2341 0.5
24 M	0535 2.2	1152 0.1	1819 2.5	
25 Tu	0025 0.4	0619 2.3	1235 -0.0	1859 2.5
26 W	0105 0.3	0701 2.4	1315 -0.1	1937 2.6
27 Th	0144 0.2	0742 2.5	1354 -0.1	● 2013 2.7
28 F	0221 0.2	0821 2.5	1432 -0.1	2049 2.7
29 Sa	0258 0.1	0900 2.6	1511 -0.1	2125 2.7
30 Su	0335 0.1	0941 2.6	1550 0.0	2202 2.7
31 M	0414 0.2	1024 2.6	1631 0.1	2241 2.6

AUGUST

Day	Time ft	Time ft	Time ft	Time ft
1 Tu	0456 0.0	1110 2.6	1716 0.2	2324 2.6
2 W	0543 0.0	1201 2.5	1807 0.3	
3 Th	0013 2.6	0636 0.0	1259 2.5	(1904 0.4
4 F	0110 2.5	0735 -0.0	1402 2.5	2008 0.4
5 Sa	0213 2.5	0840 -0.1	1509 2.6	2116 0.4
6 Su	0320 2.6	0946 -0.1	1615 2.7	2223 0.3
7 M	0426 2.7	1050 -0.2	1717 2.9	2325 0.1
8 Tu	0529 2.8	1150 -0.4	1813 3.0	
9 W	0022 -0.0	0627 3.0	1245 -0.4	1906 3.1
10 Th	0115 -0.2	0722 3.1	1338 -0.5	O 1955 3.2
11 F	0206 -0.3	0814 3.1	1427 -0.4	2043 3.2
12 Sa	0254 -0.3	0904 3.1	1515 -0.3	2128 3.1
13 Su	0341 -0.3	0953 3.1	1602 -0.2	2213 3.0
14 M	0427 -0.2	1041 2.9	1649 0.0	2258 3.0
15 Tu	0514 -0.1	1130 2.8	1737 0.3	2343 2.7
16 W	0602 0.1	1221 2.6	1826 0.5	
17 Th	0031 2.5	0652 0.3	1315 2.5	) 1920 0.7
18 F	0122 2.4	0745 0.4	1413 2.4	2018 0.8
19 Sa	0218 2.3	0842 0.5	1512 2.4	2118 0.8
20 Su	0316 2.3	0939 0.5	1609 2.4	2216 0.8
21 M	0413 2.3	1033 0.5	1700 2.5	2307 0.7
22 Tu	0505 2.5	1122 0.4	1746 2.6	2353 0.6
23 W	0552 2.5	1207 0.3	1827 2.7	
24 Th	0034 0.5	0636 2.7	1248 0.2	1905 2.8
25 F	0113 0.3	0717 2.8	1328 0.1	● 1942 2.9
26 Sa	0150 0.2	0757 2.9	1407 0.1	2019 3.0
27 Su	0228 0.2	0837 3.0	1447 0.1	2056 3.0
28 M	0306 0.1	0918 3.0	1527 0.2	2134 3.0
29 Tu	0347 0.0	1002 3.0	1609 0.2	2215 3.0
30 W	0430 0.0	1049 3.0	1655 0.4	2300 2.9
31 Th	0518 0.1	1140 2.9	1747 0.5	2351 2.8

TIME MERIDIAN 75°W

Heights in feet are referenced to the chart datum of soundings.

0000h is midnight, 1200h is noon.

MIAMI, FLORIDA (Harbor Entrance)

HIGH & LOW WATER 1995 25°46'N 80°08'W

EASTERN STANDARD TIME (GMT -5H).   ADD 1H DAYLIGHT SAVING APR 2 - OCT 28

FLORIDA

SEPTEMBER

Day	Time	ft	Time	ft	Time	ft	Time	ft
1	0613	0.2	1239	2.9	F 1846	0.6		
16	0038	2.6	0658	0.7	Sa 1326	2.6	) 1934	1.1
2	0051	2.8	0715	0.2	Sa 1344	2.8	(1952	0.6
17	0134	2.5	0755	0.8	Su 1425	2.6	2035	1.1
3	0158	2.7	0824	0.3	Su 1453	2.8	2103	0.6
18	0236	2.5	0855	0.8	M 1524	2.6	2135	1.1
4	0309	2.6	0933	0.2	M 1601	2.9	2211	0.5
19	0337	2.5	0954	0.8	Tu 1618	2.7	2229	1.1
5	0418	2.9	1039	0.2	Tu 1702	3.0	2313	0.4
20	0433	2.7	1047	0.7	W 1706	2.8	2316	0.8
6	0521	3.1	1139	0.1	W 1758	3.2		
21	0523	2.8	1135	0.6	Th 1749	3.0	2359	0.6
7	0008	0.2	0618	3.1	Th 1233	-0.0	1848	3.3
22	0608	3.0	1219	0.5	F 1829	3.1		
8	0059	0.1	0710	3.1	F 1322	-0.0	O 1934	3.3
23	0039	0.5	0650	3.2	Sa 1300	0.4	1908	3.2
9	0145	-0.0	0758	3.4	Sa 1409	0.0	2018	3.4
24	0118	0.3	0732	3.3	Su 1341	0.4	● 1947	3.3
10	0230	-0.1	0844	3.4	Su 1453	0.1	2100	3.3
25	0158	0.2	0813	3.4	M 1422	0.3	2026	3.3
11	0313	-0.0	0928	3.3	M 1536	0.2	2142	3.2
26	0239	0.1	0857	3.5	Tu 1505	0.4	2108	3.4
12	0355	0.1	1011	3.2	Tu 1618	0.4	2222	3.0
27	0322	0.1	0942	3.5	W 1550	0.4	2152	3.3
13	0437	0.2	1055	3.0	W 1702	0.6	2304	2.9
28	0408	0.1	1030	3.4	Th 1638	0.5	2241	3.2
14	0520	0.4	1141	2.9	Th 1747	0.8	2348	2.7
29	0459	0.2	1123	3.3	F 1732	0.7	2336	3.1
15	0606	0.6	1231	2.8	F 1838	1.0		
30	0556	0.4	1223	3.2	Sa 1833	0.8		

OCTOBER

Day	Time	ft	Time	ft	Time	ft	Time	ft
1	0039	3.0	0701	0.5	Su 1329	3.1	(1941	0.8
16	0052	2.6	0708	1.0	M 1336	2.8	) 1951	1.2
2	0149	3.0	0811	0.6	M 1438	3.1	2052	0.8
17	0154	2.6	0809	1.1	Tu 1434	2.8	2050	1.2
3	0302	3.0	0922	0.6	Tu 1545	3.1	2200	0.7
18	0257	2.7	0910	1.0	W 1530	2.8	2145	1.0
4	0411	3.1	1028	0.5	W 1646	3.2	2259	0.5
19	0356	2.8	1007	1.0	Th 1621	2.9	2235	0.9
5	0513	3.3	1126	0.5	Th 1739	3.3	2352	0.4
20	0449	3.0	1058	0.8	F 1707	3.1	2320	0.7
6	0607	3.4	1218	0.4	F 1827	3.4		
21	0536	3.2	1145	0.7	Sa 1751	3.2		
7	0039	0.3	0655	3.5	Sa 1305	0.4	1911	3.4
22	0004	0.4	0622	3.4	Su 1230	0.6	1833	3.3
8	0123	0.2	0740	3.5	Su 1348	0.4	O 1952	3.4
23	0047	0.3	0706	3.6	M 1314	0.5	● 1916	3.5
9	0204	0.2	0822	3.6	M 1430	0.5	2031	3.4
24	0130	0.1	0751	3.7	Tu 1359	0.4	2000	3.5
10	0244	0.2	0902	3.6	Tu 1509	0.6	2110	3.3
25	0215	0.0	0837	3.7	W 1445	0.4	2046	3.5
11	0323	0.3	0942	3.4	W 1549	0.7	2148	3.1
26	0301	0.0	0924	3.7	Th 1533	0.5	2134	3.5
12	0401	0.5	1023	3.2	Th 1629	0.9	2227	3.0
27	0351	0.1	1015	3.6	F 1625	0.5	2227	3.4
13	0442	0.6	1105	3.1	F 1712	1.0	2310	2.9
28	0444	0.2	1109	3.5	Sa 1721	0.6	2325	3.3
14	0525	0.8	1150	3.0	Sa 1759	1.1	2357	2.7
29	0543	0.4	1208	3.4	Su 1822	0.7		
15	0613	0.9	1240	2.9	Su 1852	1.2		
30	0029	3.1	0648	0.5	M 1312	3.2	(1929	0.8
31	0140	3.1	0757	0.7	Tu 1419	3.2	2038	0.7

NOVEMBER

Day	Time	ft	Time	ft	Time	ft	Time	ft
1	0252	3.1	0907	0.7	W 1524	3.1	2142	0.6
16	0214	2.6	0823	1.0	Th 1437	2.7	2058	0.8
2	0359	3.1	1012	0.7	Th 1623	3.2	2241	0.5
17	0314	2.7	0922	0.9	F 1531	2.8	2151	0.7
3	0459	3.2	1109	0.7	F 1716	3.2	2332	0.4
18	0411	2.9	1018	0.8	Sa 1623	2.9	2241	0.4
4	0551	3.3	1200	0.6	Sa 1803	3.2		
19	0503	3.1	1111	0.7	Su 1712	3.1	2330	0.2
5	0018	0.3	0638	3.4	Su 1245	0.6	1846	3.2
20	0553	3.3	1201	0.5	M 1801	3.2		
6	0100	0.3	0720	3.4	M 1327	0.6	1925	3.2
21	0018	0.0	0642	3.5	Tu 1249	0.4	1849	3.3
7	0139	0.3	0800	3.4	Tu 1406	0.6	O 2003	3.2
22	0106	-0.2	0730	3.6	W 1338	0.3	● 1938	3.4
8	0216	0.3	0838	3.4	W 1444	0.7	2040	3.1
23	0155	-0.3	0819	3.7	Th 1427	0.2	2028	3.4
9	0253	0.4	0916	3.3	Th 1522	0.8	2118	3.0
24	0245	-0.3	0909	3.6	F 1518	0.2	2120	3.4
10	0331	0.4	0954	3.2	F 1601	0.8	2156	2.9
25	0337	-0.2	1000	3.6	Sa 1611	0.2	2215	3.3
11	0409	0.6	1033	3.1	Sa 1642	0.9	2238	2.8
26	0431	-0.1	1054	3.4	Su 1708	0.3	2313	3.2
12	0450	0.7	1114	3.0	Su 1726	1.0	2323	2.7
27	0529	0.1	1151	3.3	M 1807	0.4		
13	0535	0.8	1159	2.9	M 1814	1.0		
28	0017	3.0	0631	0.3	Tu 1251	3.1	1910	0.4
14	0014	2.6	0626	0.9	Tu 1249	2.8	1906	1.0
29	0124	2.9	0737	0.5	W 1354	3.0	(2015	0.4
15	0112	2.6	0722	1.0	W 1342	2.7	) 2002	1.0
30	0233	2.9	0844	0.6	Th 1456	2.9	2118	0.4

DECEMBER

Day	Time	ft	Time	ft	Time	ft	Time	ft
1	0339	2.9	0948	0.6	F 1555	2.9	2215	0.3
16	0232	2.5	0837	0.7	Sa 1443	2.5	2108	0.3
2	0439	2.9	1046	0.6	Sa 1648	2.8	2307	0.3
17	0333	2.6	0939	0.6	Su 1541	2.6	2205	0.1
3	0531	3.0	1138	0.6	Su 1736	2.8	2353	0.2
18	0431	2.8	1037	0.6	M 1638	2.8	2300	-0.1
4	0618	3.0	1223	0.6	M 1819	2.8		
19	0527	3.0	1134	0.5	Tu 1733	2.9	2354	-0.3
5	0035	0.1	0700	3.0	Tu 1305	0.6	1900	2.8
20	0620	3.1	1227	0.1	W 1827	3.0		
6	0114	0.1	0738	3.0	O 1344	0.5	1938	2.8
21	0047	-0.5	0712	3.3	● 1320	-0.1	1921	3.1
7	0152	0.1	0815	3.0	Th 1422	0.5	2016	2.8
22	0139	-0.6	0803	3.4	F 1412	-0.2	2014	3.2
8	0229	0.1	0852	3.0	F 1459	0.5	2053	2.7
23	0231	-0.6	0853	3.4	Sa 1504	-0.2	2108	3.2
9	0305	0.2	0928	2.9	Sa 1537	0.6	2132	2.6
24	0323	-0.6	0944	3.3	Su 1557	-0.2	2202	3.1
10	0343	0.3	1005	2.9	Su 1615	0.6	2212	2.6
25	0417	-0.4	1036	3.2	M 1650	-0.2	2259	3.0
11	0422	0.4	1043	2.8	M 1655	0.6	2254	2.5
26	0512	-0.2	1130	3.0	Tu 1746	-0.1	2358	2.8
12	0503	0.5	1123	2.7	Tu 1738	0.6	2341	2.4
27	0609	-0.0	1225	2.8	W 1845	-0.0		
13	0549	0.6	1207	2.6	W 1824	0.6		
28	0100	2.7	0710	0.2	Th 1322	2.7	(1945	0.0
14	0033	2.4	0640	0.6	Th 1254	2.5	1915	0.5
29	0205	2.5	0813	0.3	F 1421	2.5	2045	0.1
15	0131	2.4	0737	0.7	F 1347	2.5	) 2011	0.4
30	0310	2.5	0916	0.2	Sa 1520	2.4	2144	0.1
31	0411	2.5	1017	0.5	Su 1616	2.4	2238	0.1

TIME MERIDIAN 75°W

0000h is midnight, 1200h is noon.

Heights in feet are referenced to the chart datum of soundings.

MIAMI, FLORIDA (Harbor Entrance)

CURRENT TABLES 1995   **FLOOD 292° EBB 112°**

EASTERN STANDARD TIME (GMT -5H).   ADD 1H DAYLIGHT SAVING APR 2 - OCT 28

JANUARY

Day	Slack time	Max time	Fld knots	Ebb knots
1 Su ●	0306 / 0918 / 1538 / 2125	0030 / 0632 / 1308 / 1849	2.5 / 2.2	2.2 / 2.1
2 M	0357 / 1008 / 1628 / 2219	0117 / 0716 / 1354 / 1936	2.5 / 2.2	2.3 / 2.2
3 Tu	0446 / 1056 / 1716 / 2310	0205 / 0804 / 1442 / 2031	2.4 / 2.1	2.2 / 2.1
4 W	0534 / 1140 / 1803 / 2359	0256 / 0859 / 1530 / 2129	2.3 / 2.0	2.1 / 2.0
5 Th	0621 / 1224 / 1852	0346 / 0950 / 1615 / 2218	2.1 / 1.9	1.9 / 1.9
6 F	0048 / 0711 / 1308 / 1943	0435 / 1033 / 1700 / 2303	1.9 / 1.8	1.7 / 1.7
7 Sa	0139 / 0803 / 1354 / 2035	0531 / 1107 / 1800 / 2352	1.6 / 1.6	1.4 / 1.5
8 Su ☾	0232 / 0856 / 1442 / 2125	0648 / 1120 / 1913	1.4	1.3 / 1.4
9 M	0326 / 0949 / 1533 / 2216	0056 / 0752 / 1315 / 2010	1.2 / 1.2	1.5 / 1.4
10 Tu	0423 / 1043 / 1625 / 2309	0159 / 0845 / 1419 / 2059	1.2 / 1.1	1.4 / 1.3
11 W	0522 / 1139 / 1721	0254 / 0935 / 1514 / 2148	1.2 / 1.1	1.5 / 1.3
12 Th	0002 / 0619 / 1234 / 1816	0347 / 1030 / 1608 / 2243	1.5 / 1.2	1.2 / 1.4
13 F	0054 / 0708 / 1326 / 1905	0439 / 1123 / 1700 / 2334	1.6 / 1.3	1.3 / 1.4
14 Sa	0143 / 0752 / 1413 / 1951	0526 / 1209 / 1744	1.7 / 1.4	1.4
15 Su	0228 / 0833 / 1457 / 2035	0017 / 0605 / 1248 / 1818	1.8 / 1.5	1.5 / 1.5
16 M ○	0311 / 0915 / 1540 / 2120	0049 / 0633 / 1319 / 1819	1.8 / 1.6	1.5 / 1.5
17 Tu	0354 / 0955 / 1621 / 2205	0102 / 0629 / 1330 / 1837	1.9 / 1.7	1.6 / 1.5
18 W	0435 / 1036 / 1701 / 2249	0100 / 0656 / 1324 / 1914	2.0 / 1.8	1.6 / 1.6
19 Th	0516 / 1116 / 1741 / 2334	0125 / 0735 / 1348 / 1958	2.0 / 1.9	1.7 / 1.7
20 F	0558 / 1156 / 1824	0201 / 0821 / 1425 / 2048	2.0 / 2.0	1.7 / 1.8
21 Sa	0020 / 0644 / 1239 / 1912	0246 / 0910 / 1509 / 2139	2.0 / 2.0	1.7 / 1.8
22 Su	0110 / 0735 / 1325 / 2005	0334 / 1000 / 1556 / 2229	1.9 / 2.0	1.7 / 1.8
23 M ☽	0205 / 0832 / 1418 / 2102	0424 / 1048 / 1646 / 2320	1.8 / 1.9	1.5 / 1.8
24 Tu	0304 / 0930 / 1514 / 2200	0520 / 1140 / 1746	1.7 / 1.6	1.4
25 W	0407 / 1030 / 1615 / 2300	0020 / 0746 / 1242 / 1945	1.6 / 1.6	1.8 / 1.3
26 Th	0513 / 1133 / 1720	0200 / 0904 / 1407 / 2109	1.5 / 1.7	1.8 / 1.4
27 F	0002 / 0618 / 1236 / 1824	0335 / 1012 / 1558 / 2225	1.9 / 1.6	1.6 / 1.8
28 Sa	0102 / 0717 / 1334 / 1923	0439 / 1117 / 1702 / 2332	2.1 / 1.8	1.8 / 2.0
29 Su	0158 / 0809 / 1428 / 2018	0533 / 1210 / 1754	2.3 / 2.0	2.0
30 M ●	0250 / 0859 / 1519 / 2111	0025 / 0620 / 1256 / 1840	2.4 / 2.2	2.2 / 2.1
31 Tu	0340 / 0947 / 1607 / 2202	0111 / 0704 / 1339 / 1924	2.4 / 2.2	2.2 / 2.2

FEBRUARY

Day	Slack time	Max time	Fld knots	Ebb knots
1 W	0427 / 1032 / 1653 / 2251	0155 / 0746 / 1422 / 2011	2.3 / 2.1	2.2 / 2.1
2 Th	0511 / 1114 / 1737 / 2336	0240 / 0832 / 1504 / 2100	2.2 / 2.0	2.0 / 2.0
3 F	0555 / 1154 / 1821	0323 / 0918 / 1542 / 2146	2.0 / 1.9	1.9 / 1.9
4 Sa	0020 / 0640 / 1234 / 1907	0402 / 0953 / 1610 / 2222	1.7 / 1.8	1.7 / 1.8
5 Su	0105 / 0728 / 1316 / 1955	0433 / 1002 / 1620 / 2232	1.6 / 1.5	1.4 / 1.7
6 M	0152 / 0819 / 1401 / 2045	0443 / 1032 / 1636 / 2301	1.5 / 1.3	1.2 / 1.5
7 Tu ☾	0243 / 0910 / 1450 / 2131	0504 / 1111 / 1711 / 2344	1.3 / 1.1	1.0 / 1.4
8 W	0337 / 1004 / 1543 / 2229	0811 / 1158 / 2024	1.1	1.0 / 1.1
9 Th	0435 / 1059 / 1640 / 2325	0212 / 0903 / 1432 / 2114	1.0 / 1.0	1.3 / 1.2
10 F	0535 / 1157 / 1739	0310 / 0955 / 1532 / 2208	1.1 / 1.1	1.3 / 1.2
11 Sa	0021 / 0631 / 1253 / 1836	0406 / 1051 / 1628 / 2305	1.4 / 1.2	1.2 / 1.3
12 Su	0114 / 0720 / 1343 / 1926	0457 / 1140 / 1717 / 2352	1.5 / 1.4	1.3 / 1.4
13 M	0202 / 0803 / 1428 / 2012	0540 / 1221 / 1755	1.7 / 1.5	1.4
14 Tu	0247 / 0845 / 1512 / 2058	0029 / 0613 / 1251 / 1816	1.8 / 1.7	1.5 / 1.5
15 W ○	0331 / 0927 / 1554 / 2144	0052 / 0619 / 1306 / 1823	1.9 / 1.9	1.6 / 1.6
16 Th	0413 / 1009 / 1635 / 2230	0059 / 0639 / 1309 / 1857	2.0 / 2.1	1.7 / 1.8
17 F	0455 / 1050 / 1716 / 2316	0119 / 0715 / 1333 / 1938	2.1 / 2.2	1.8 / 1.9
18 Sa	0538 / 1132 / 1800	0152 / 0759 / 1408 / 2027	2.1 / 2.2	1.9 / 2.0
19 Su	0002 / 0623 / 1216 / 1848	0234 / 0848 / 1452 / 2119	2.1 / 2.2	1.9 / 2.0
20 M	0051 / 0714 / 1303 / 1941	0321 / 0939 / 1539 / 2211	2.0 / 2.1	1.8 / 2.0
21 Tu	0145 / 0810 / 1356 / 2039	0410 / 1029 / 1629 / 2302	1.9 / 2.0	1.6 / 1.8
22 W ☽	0243 / 0910 / 1454 / 2139	0506 / 1120 / 1729 / 2400	1.7 / 1.8	1.4 / 1.6
23 Th	0345 / 1010 / 1557 / 2240	0751 / 1222 / 2006	1.5	1.3 / 1.6
24 F	0452 / 1113 / 1704 / 2344	0212 / 0857 / 1439 / 2114	1.5 / 1.5	1.7 / 1.7
25 Sa	0559 / 1217 / 1811	0321 / 0958 / 1548 / 2220	1.6 / 1.6	1.8 / 1.8
26 Su	0045 / 0659 / 1316 / 1912	0422 / 1059 / 1648 / 2321	2.0 / 1.8	1.8 / 1.9
27 M	0141 / 0750 / 1410 / 2006	0517 / 1153 / 1740	2.1 / 2.0	2.0
28 Tu	0232 / 0837 / 1458 / 2056	0013 / 0604 / 1238 / 1825	2.2 / 2.2	2.1 / 2.1

TIME MERIDIAN 75°W

0000h is midnight, 1200h is noon.

REED'S NAUTICAL ALMANAC

MIAMI, FLORIDA (Harbor Entrance)

CURRENT TABLES 1995 **FLOOD 292° EBB 112°**

EASTERN STANDARD TIME (GMT -5H). ADD 1H DAYLIGHT SAVING APR 2 - OCT 28

FLORIDA

MARCH

Day	Slack time	Max time	Fld	Ebb
1 W ●		0058		2.1
	0320	0646	2.2	
	0921	1319		2.1
	1544	1906	2.2	
	2144			
2 Th		0139		2.1
	0405	0725	2.2	
	1004	1358		2.1
	1627	1946	2.1	
	2228			
3 F		0219		2.0
	0448	0802	2.0	
	1044	1434		2.0
	1708	2026	2.0	
	2310			
4 Sa		0257		1.8
	0529	0831	1.9	
	1122	1502		1.8
	1749	2100	1.9	
	2351			
5 Su		0327		1.6
	0611	0838	1.7	
	1200	1507		1.7
	1831	2108	1.8	
6 M ☾	0032	0331		1.4
	0655	0915	1.6	
	1240	1519		1.5
	1916	2143	1.7	
7 Tu	0115	0344		1.3
	0742	0956	1.5	
	1323	1549		1.4
	2005	2223	1.6	
8 W	0203	0415		1.1
	0834	1038	1.4	
	1411	1627		1.3
	2057	2305	1.5	
9 Th ☾	0255	0456		1.0
	0927	1123	1.2	
	1504	1713		1.1
	2151	2354	1.3	
10 F	0351	0829		0.9
	1022	1216	1.1	
	1602	2040		1.0
	2247			
11 Sa		0055	1.2	
	0450	0918		1.0
	1119	1321	1.1	
	1704	2130		1.1
12 Su		0325	1.3	
	0549	1009		1.1
	1216	1549	1.2	
	1805	2226		1.2
13 M	0041	0420	1.4	
	0642	1101		1.2
	1309	1642	1.4	
	1859	2320		1.4
14 Tu	0133	0507	1.6	
	0729	1144		1.4
	1356	1725	1.6	
	1948			
15 W		0000		1.5
	0220	0543	1.8	
	0812	1215		1.6
	1441	1753	1.9	
	2035			
16 Th ○		0029		1.7
	0305	0558	1.9	
	0855	1232		1.8
	1524	1808	2.1	
	2122			
17 F		0049		1.8
	0350	0620	2.1	
	0939	1248		1.9
	1608	1840	2.3	
	2209			
18 Sa		0112		1.9
	0434	0656	2.2	
	1024	1316		2.1
	1652	1920	2.4	
	2257			
19 Su		0145		2.0
	0518	0738	2.2	
	1109	1353		2.1
	1737	2007	2.4	
	2344			
20 M		0226		1.9
	0605	0827	2.1	
	1155	1438		2.1
	1826	2101	2.3	
21 Tu	0033	0315		1.8
	0656	0921	2.0	
	1244	1528		2.0
	1920	2156	2.2	
22 W	0126	0407		1.7
	0752	1014	1.9	
	1338	1621		1.8
	2020	2249	2.0	
23 Th ☽	0224	0509		1.5
	0852	1108	1.7	
	1438	1729		1.6
	2120	2350	1.8	
24 F	0325	0741		1.4
	0953	1227	1.5	
	1542	2005		1.6
	2222			
25 Sa		0159	1.7	
	0430	0843		1.5
	1055	1430	1.6	
	1651	2106		1.7
	2324			
26 Su		0303	1.8	
	0536	0939		1.7
	1158	1531	1.7	
	1759	2205		1.8
27 M		0026		
	0636	0401	1.9	
	1256	1036		1.8
	1900	1629	1.9	
		2304		1.9
28 Tu		0122	2.0	
	0726	0455		
		1130		1.9
	1347	1720	2.0	
	1952	2355		2.0
29 W	0212	0543	2.0	
	0810	1216		2.0
	1434	1805	2.1	
	2038			
30 Th ●		0040		2.0
	0258	0625	2.0	
	0852	1257		2.0
	1518	1845	2.2	
	2122			
31 F		0121		2.0
	0342	0702	2.0	
	0932	1333		2.0
	1559	1921	2.1	
	2203			

APRIL

Day	Slack time	Max time	Fld	Ebb
1 Sa		0158		1.9
	0423	0732	1.8	
	1012	1403		1.8
	1639	1949	2.0	
	2243			
2 Su		0232		1.7
	0503	0731	1.7	
	1050	1415		1.7
	1718	1948	1.9	
	2322			
3 M		0251		1.6
	0543	0756	1.6	
	1129	1411		1.6
	1758	2021	1.8	
4 Tu	0002	0241		1.4
	0625	0837	1.6	
	1208	1436		1.5
	1840	2104	1.8	
5 W	0043	0305		1.3
	0710	0923	1.5	
	1250	1512		1.5
	1927	2149	1.7	
6 Th	0128	0342		1.2
	0801	1008	1.4	
	1338	1554		1.3
	2020	2234	1.6	
7 F	0217	0423		1.1
	0854	1054	1.3	
	1431	1640		1.2
	2115	2321	1.4	
8 Sa ☾	0311	0511		1.0
	0947	1144	1.2	
	1529	1734		1.1
	2210			
9 Su		0014	1.3	
	0407	0835		1.0
	1042	1243	1.2	
	1630	2046		1.0
	2308			
10 M		0118	1.3	
	0504	0912		1.1
	1138	1352	1.3	
	1732	2129		1.2
11 Tu	0006	0226	1.4	
	0600	0944		1.2
	1232	1504	1.5	
	1830	2227		1.3
12 W	0100	0347	1.5	
	0651	1031		1.4
	1322	1641	1.7	
	1922	2322		1.5
13 Th	0150	0455	1.7	
	0738	1119		1.6
	1409	1720	2.0	
	2010			
14 F		0000		1.7
	0238	0525	1.9	
	0823	1153		1.9
	1455	1750	2.3	
	2059			
15 Sa ○		0031		1.9
	0325	0559	2.1	
	0910	1226		2.1
	1542	1824	2.5	
	2148			
16 Su		0103		2.0
	0412	0637	2.2	
	0958	1301		2.2
	1629	1904	2.5	
	2238			
17 M		0140		2.0
	0459	0720	2.2	
	1047	1342		2.2
	1717	1951	2.5	
	2327			
18 Tu		0225		2.0
	0547	0810	2.1	
	1136	1430		2.1
	1807	2048	2.4	
19 W	0017	0320		1.9
	0639	0909	2.0	
	1228	1526		2.0
	1902	2151	2.2	
20 Th	0109	0419		1.7
	0736	1011	1.9	
	1324	1627		1.8
	2001	2249	2.0	
21 F ☽	0205	0544		1.6
	0836	1112	1.7	
	1424	1823		1.6
	2101			
22 Sa		0014	1.8	
	0304	0722		1.6
	0936	1301	1.6	
	1529	1951		1.6
	2201			
23 Su		0137	1.7	
	0405	0823		1.7
	1035	1411	1.7	
	1636	2049		1.6
	2301			
24 M		0239	1.7	
	0507	0916		1.7
	1134	1510	1.8	
	1744	2144		1.7
25 Tu	0001	0335	1.7	
	0605	1009		1.8
	1230	1605	1.9	
	1844	2240		1.7
26 W	0058	0429	1.8	
	0656	1103		1.9
	1321	1656	2.0	
	1933	2333		1.8
27 Th	0148	0518	1.8	
	0739	1151		1.9
	1407	1742	2.1	
	2017			
28 F		0020		1.8
	0233	0601	1.8	
	0820	1233		1.9
	1449	1822	2.1	
	2057			
29 Sa ●		0100		1.8
	0316	0638	1.7	
	0859	1309		1.8
	1530	1857	2.0	
	2137			
30 Su		0138		1.7
	0358	0707	1.7	
	0939	1337		1.7
	1610	1920	2.0	
	2217			

TIME MERIDIAN 75°W

0000h is midnight, 1200h is noon.

MIAMI, FLORIDA (Harbor Entrance)

CURRENT TABLES 1995   **FLOOD 292° EBB 112°**

EASTERN STANDARD TIME (GMT -5H).   ADD 1H DAYLIGHT SAVING APR 2 - OCT 28

MAY

Day	Slack time	Max time	Fld knots	Ebb knots
1 M		0210		1.6
	0438	0659	1.6	
	1019	1338		1.6
	1649	1916	1.9	
	2256			
2 Tu		0227		1.5
	0518	0725	1.6	
	1100	1337		1.6
	1729	1948	1.8	
	2335			
3 W		0209		1.4
	0559	0805	1.5	
	1140	1404		1.5
	1810	2031	1.8	
4 Th	0015	0236		1.4
	0642	0852	1.5	
	1223	1442		1.5
	1855	2119	1.7	
5 F	0058	0314		1.3
	0730	0941	1.4	
	1309	1526		1.4
	1946	2206	1.6	
6 Sa	0144	0356		1.3
	0822	1029	1.4	
	1401	1613		1.3
	2040	2252	1.6	
7 Su ☾	0234	0442		1.2
	0914	1117	1.4	
	1458	1704		1.2
	2135	2342	1.5	
8 M	0327	0537		1.2
	1006	1211	1.4	
	1558	1810		1.1
	2231			
9 Tu		0039	1.4	
	0422	0655		1.2
	1100	1314	1.5	
	1659	2002		1.2
	2329			
10 W		0142	1.4	
	0518	0813		1.4
	1154	1420	1.6	
	1759	2102		1.3
11 Th	0026	0242	1.5	
	0612	0902		1.6
	1248	1524	1.9	
	1855	2211		1.5
12 F	0119	0343	1.7	
	0704	0959		1.8
	1339	1640	2.1	
	1946	2329		1.7
13 Sa	0210	0448	1.9	
	0753	1113		1.9
	1428	1733	2.4	
	2037			
14 Su ○		0015	1.9	
	0300	0540		2.0
	0843	1208	2.1	
	1518	1814		2.5
	2128			
15 M		0056	2.0	
	0350	0623		2.1
	0934	1252	2.2	
	1608	1854		2.6
	2219			
16 Tu		0139		2.1
	0440	0707	2.2	
	1027	1338		2.2
	1658	1942	2.5	
	2310			
17 W		0230		2.0
	0530	0759	2.1	
	1120	1432		2.1
	1750	2047	2.4	
18 Th	0000	0329		2.0
	0622	0917	2.0	
	1213	1536		2.0
	1843	2200	2.2	
19 F	0051	0428		1.9
	0718	1028	1.9	
	1309	1642		1.8
	1940	2256	2.1	
20 Sa	0144	0536		1.7
	0816	1130	1.8	
	1408	1809		1.6
	2039	2358	1.9	
21 Su ☽	0239	0655		1.7
	0914	1240	1.7	
	1510	1928		1.6
	2137			
22 M		0109	1.7	
	0335	0757		1.7
	1010	1346	1.7	
	1614	2027		1.6
	2234			
23 Tu		0210	1.6	
	0432	0849		1.8
	1105	1443	1.7	
	1719	2120		1.6
	2332			
24 W		0306	1.6	
	0528	0939		1.7
	1159	1536	1.8	
	1819	2213		1.6
25 Th	0028	0359	1.5	
	0620	1032		1.7
	1250	1628	1.9	
	1909	2307		1.6
26 F	0119	0450	1.6	
	0706	1123		1.7
	1337	1716	1.9	
	1951	2356		1.6
27 Sa	0206	0536	1.6	
	0748	1208		1.7
	1420	1759	2.0	
	2031			
28 Su		0039	1.6	
	0250	0615		1.6
	0828	1246	1.7	
	1502	1835		1.9
	2111			
29 M ●		0118	1.6	
	0332	0647		1.5
	0909	1317	1.6	
	1544	1902		1.9
	2151			
30 Tu		0152	1.5	
	0414	0640		1.5
	0951	1325	1.5	
	1624	1854		1.8
	2231			
31 W		0216	1.4	
	0454	0701		1.5
	1034	1315	1.5	
	1704	1922		1.8
	2310			

JUNE

Day	Slack time	Max time	Fld knots	Ebb knots
1 Th		0151	1.4	
	0535	0739		1.5
	1116	1340	1.5	
	1745	2003		1.8
	2350			
2 F		0212	1.4	
	0616	0825		1.5
	1159	1418	1.5	
	1827	2051		1.8
3 Sa	0030	0249	1.4	
	0701	0915		1.5
	1244	1503	1.4	
	1915	2139		1.7
4 Su	0113	0332	1.4	
	0750	1004		1.6
	1334	1550	1.4	
	2007	2226		1.7
5 M	0200	0417	1.4	
	0841	1052		1.6
	1429	1639	1.3	
	2102	2313		1.6
6 Tu ☾	0250	0506	1.4	
	0932	1143		1.6
	1527	1736	1.2	
	2157			
7 W		0006		1.5
	0343	0607	1.4	
	1025	1241		1.7
	1627	1859	1.2	
	2254			
8 Th		0105		1.5
	0439	0726	1.5	
	1120	1347		1.8
	1729	2027	1.4	
	2352			
9 F		0208		1.6
	0537	0830	1.7	
	1217	1453		1.9
	1828	2130	1.5	
10 Sa	0050	0309		1.7
	0634	0927	1.8	
	1312	1612		2.1
	1923	2302	1.6	
11 Su	0145	0420		1.8
	0727	1047	2.0	
	1405	1724		2.3
	2016			
12 M ○		0003		1.8
	0238	0532	2.0	
	0820	1200		2.1
	1458	1811	2.5	
	2108			
13 Tu		0050		2.0
	0330	0621	2.1	
	0914	1251		2.2
	1549	1855	2.6	
	2201			
14 W		0137		2.1
	0421	0706	2.2	
	1010	1340		2.2
	1641	1943	2.5	
	2252			
15 Th		0228		2.1
	0512	0805	2.1	
	1104	1437		2.2
	1731	2048	2.4	
	2341			
16 F		0323		2.1
	0603	0921	2.1	
	1157	1537		2.0
	1823	2149	2.2	
17 Sa	0030	0416		2.0
	0656	1019	2.0	
	1251	1635		1.8
	1917	2241	2.1	
18 Su	0119	0511		1.9
	0752	1112	1.9	
	1347	1742		1.6
	2013	2331	1.9	
19 M ☽	0210	0619		1.7
	0847	1210	1.8	
	1445	1858		1.5
	2108			
20 Tu		0032	1.6	
	0301	0726		1.7
	0940	1314	1.7	
	1544	2000		1.5
	2203			
21 W		0136	1.5	
	0353	0820		1.7
	1032	1412	1.7	
	1644	2052		1.4
	2258			
22 Th		0233	1.4	
	0447	0909		1.6
	1125	1506	1.7	
	1744	2144		1.4
	2354			
23 F		0326	1.4	
	0541	0959		1.6
	1217	1558	1.7	
	1837	2238		1.4
24 Sa	0047	0419	1.4	
	0631	1053		1.5
	1306	1649	1.7	
	1923	2331		1.5
25 Su	0137	0509	1.4	
	0717	1143		1.5
	1352	1734	1.8	
	2004			
26 M		0017		1.5
	0223	0552	1.4	
	0800	1225		1.5
	1436	1814	1.8	
	2044			
27 Tu ●		0057		1.5
	0307	0628	1.4	
	0843	1300		1.5
	1519	1846	1.8	
	2125			
28 W		0133		1.5
	0349	0644	1.5	
	0927	1322		1.5
	1601	1842	1.8	
	2206			
29 Th		0200		1.4
	0430	0642	1.5	
	1010	1307		1.5
	1641	1901	1.8	
	2245			
30 F		0141		1.4
	0510	0717	1.6	
	1054	1324		1.5
	1722	1939	1.8	
	2324			

TIME MERIDIAN 75°W

0000h is midnight, 1200h is noon.

MIAMI, FLORIDA (Harbor Entrance)

CURRENT TABLES 1995 FLOOD 292° EBB 112°

EASTERN STANDARD TIME (GMT -5H). ADD 1H DAYLIGHT SAVING APR 2 - OCT 28

JULY

Day	Slack time	Max time	Fld	Ebb
1 Sa		0153		1.5
	0551	0800	1.6	
	1137	1359		1.5
	1803	2024	1.8	
2 Su		0226		1.6
	0633	0849	1.7	
	1222	1442		1.5
	1848	2112	1.8	
3 M		0308		1.6
	0718	0939	1.7	
	1309	1528		1.5
	1937	2200	1.8	
4 Tu		0353		1.6
	0808	1028	1.8	
	1402	1617		1.5
	2031	2247	1.7	
5 W (		0440		1.6
	0901	1117	1.8	
	1459	1709		1.4
	2126	2337	1.7	
6 Th		0535		1.6
	0955	1212	1.8	
	1559	1819		1.3
	2223			
7 F		0034	1.6	
	0407	0648		1.6
	1051	1317	1.8	
	1701	2007		1.3
	2323			
8 Sa		0138	1.6	
	0508	0810		1.7
	1151	1431	1.9	
	1804	2121		1.5
9 Su	0024	0246	1.6	
	0609	0916		1.8
	1250	1608	2.1	
	1903	2249		1.6
10 M	0122	0421	1.8	
	0707	1048		1.9
	1346	1715	2.3	
	1957	2352		1.8
11 Tu	0217	0533	2.0	
	0803	1200		2.1
	1440	1806	2.4	
	2050			
12 W O		0042	2.0	
	0311	0623		2.1
	0858	1251	2.2	
	1532	1851		2.5
	2141			
13 Th		0128	2.2	
	0402	0710		2.2
	0954	1339	2.2	
	1623	1937		2.5
	2231			
14 F		0216	2.2	
	0452	0802		2.2
	1047	1431	2.2	
	1712	2031		2.3
	2319			
15 Sa		0305	2.2	
	0541	0903		2.1
	1139	1524	2.0	
	1801	2127		2.2
16 Su	0004	0354		2.1
	0630	0958	2.1	
	1229	1615		1.8
	1850	2216	2.0	
17 M	0049	0440		1.9
	0721	1046	2.0	
	1320	1708		1.6
	1943	2259	1.8	
18 Tu	0136	0533		1.7
	0813	1134	1.8	
	1413	1818		1.4
	2036	2342	1.6	
19 W)	0224	0644		1.5
	0905	1232	1.6	
	1507	1927		1.3
	2129			
20 Th		0050	1.4	
	0314	0747		1.5
	0956	1336	1.5	
	1603	2024		1.3
	2222			
21 F		0157	1.2	
	0406	0839		1.4
	1048	1432	1.5	
	1701	2114		1.3
	2317			
22 Sa		0253	1.2	
	0501	0928		1.4
	1142	1526	1.5	
	1759	2207		1.3
23 Su	0013	0347	1.2	
	0556	1021		1.4
	1235	1619	1.6	
	1851	2302		1.3
24 M	0106	0440	1.3	
	0648	1116		1.4
	1325	1708	1.7	
	1935	2351		1.4
25 Tu	0155	0528	1.4	
	0735	1203		1.5
	1411	1751	1.7	
	2017			
26 W		0033	1.5	
	0240	0608		1.5
	0819	1241	1.5	
	1455	1826		1.8
	2057			
27 Th ●		0109	1.5	
	0323	0636		1.5
	0904	1309	1.5	
	1537	1841		1.8
	2138			
28 F		0134	1.5	
	0404	0628		1.6
	0948	1309	1.5	
	1619	1843		1.9
	2218			
29 Sa		0126	1.5	
	0444	0657		1.7
	1032	1314	1.6	
	1659	1916		1.9
	2257			
30 Su		0133	1.6	
	0523	0737		1.8
	1115	1343	1.6	
	1740	1958		1.9
	2336			
31 M		0204	1.7	
	0604	0823		1.9
	1200	1423	1.7	
	1823	2046		1.9

AUGUST

Day	Slack time	Max time	Fld	Ebb
1 Tu	0017	0244		1.8
	0648	0914	1.9	
	1246	1508		1.6
	1910	2135	1.9	
2 W	0100	0330		1.8
	0738	1004	2.0	
	1338	1556		1.6
	2004	2223	1.8	
3 Th (	0149	0417		1.8
	0832	1053	1.9	
	1434	1647		1.4
	2100	2313	1.7	
4 F	0244	0510		1.7
	0929	1147	1.9	
	1534	1751		1.3
	2159			
5 Sa		0008	1.6	
	0343	0621		1.6
	1028	1252	1.8	
	1637	2017		1.3
	2300			
6 Su		0115	1.5	
	0446	0814		1.6
	1130	1441	1.8	
	1743	2127		1.5
7 M	0003	0247	1.6	
	0551	0932		1.8
	1231	1602	2.0	
	1844	2238		1.6
8 Tu	0103	0426	1.8	
	0653	1054		1.9
	1329	1703	2.2	
	1939	2339		1.9
9 W	0159	0526	2.0	
	0750	1155		2.1
	1423	1754	2.4	
	2030			
10 Th O		0029	2.1	
	0252	0615		2.2
	0844	1245	2.2	
	1514	1839		2.4
	2120			
11 F		0113	2.2	
	0342	0700		2.3
	0937	1330	2.2	
	1604	1922		2.4
	2207			
12 Sa		0156	2.2	
	0430	0745		2.3
	1029	1416	2.1	
	1651	2007		2.3
	2252			
13 Su		0240	2.1	
	0516	0836		2.2
	1117	1503	2.0	
	1736	2057		2.1
	2335			
14 M		0324	2.1	
	0601	0928		2.1
	1203	1549	1.9	
	1822	2143		1.9
15 Tu	0017	0403		1.8
	0647	1013	1.9	
	1248	1631		1.6
	1910	2218	1.7	
16 W	0100	0435		1.6
	0736	1050	1.8	
	1336	1720		1.3
	2001	2229	1.5	
17 Th)	0145	0454		1.4
	0827	1105	1.6	
	1427	1845		1.1
	2053	2301	1.3	
18 F	0234	0706		1.2
	0919	1137	1.4	
	1520	1952		1.1
	2146			
19 Sa	0327	0809		1.2
	1011	1355	1.3	
	1617	2045		1.1
	2241			
20 Su		0218	1.1	
	0423	0900		1.2
	1106	1452	1.3	
	1716	2135		1.1
	2338			
21 M		0315	1.1	
	0522	0951		1.3
	1202	1546	1.4	
	1813	2229		1.2
22 Tu	0034	0409	1.2	
	0619	1046		1.3
	1255	1638	1.5	
	1903	2321		1.3
23 W	0124	0500	1.4	
	0710	1136		1.4
	1344	1724	1.6	
	1946			
24 Th		0004	1.4	
	0210	0542		1.5
	0756	1217	1.5	
	1429	1802		1.7
	2027			
25 F ●		0039	1.5	
	0253	0614		1.7
	0841	1248	1.6	
	1513	1823		1.8
	2107			
26 Sa		0102	1.6	
	0334	0615		1.8
	0925	1300	1.6	
	1555	1823		1.9
	2147			
27 Su		0059	1.7	
	0415	0638		2.0
	1009	1304	1.7	
	1636	1854		2.0
	2228			
28 M		0111	1.8	
	0455	0715		2.1
	1054	1329	1.8	
	1717	1934		2.0
	2309			
29 Tu		0142	1.9	
	0536	0759		2.1
	1138	1406	1.8	
	1800	2020		2.0
	2351			
30 W		0222	1.9	
	0621	0850		2.1
	1225	1451	1.7	
	1847	2111		1.9
31 Th	0036	0308	1.9	
	0711	0942		2.1
	1316	1539	1.6	
	1941	2202		1.8

TIME MERIDIAN 75°W

0000h is midnight, 1200h is noon.

FLORIDA

MIAMI, FLORIDA (Harbor Entrance)

CURRENT TABLES 1995 **FLOOD 292° EBB 112°**

EASTERN STANDARD TIME (GMT -5H). ADD 1H DAYLIGHT SAVING APR 2 - OCT 28

SEPTEMBER

Day	Slack time	Max time	Fld knots	Ebb knots
1 F	0126	0358		1.8
	0808	1033	2.0	
	1412	1631		1.5
	2039	2253	1.7	
2 Sa (	0223	0451		1.7
	0908	1127	1.9	
	1513	1736		1.3
	2140	2348	1.6	
3 Su	0325	0607		1.5
	1009	1234	1.7	
	1617	2023		1.4
	2241			
4 M		0103	1.5	
	0430	0838		1.6
	1111	1445	1.8	
	1723	2123		1.5
	2345			
5 Tu		0312	1.6	
	0538	0942		1.7
	1214	1549	1.9	
	1825	2224		1.7
6 W	0046	0416	1.8	
	0642	1047		1.9
	1313	1647	2.1	
	1920	2322		1.9
7 Th	0141	0512	2.1	
	0739	1144		2.1
	1406	1738	2.2	
	2009			
8 F O		0011		2.1
	0232	0600	2.2	
	0831	1232		2.2
	1456	1822	2.3	
	2055			
9 Sa		0054		2.2
	0319	0643	2.3	
	0920	1316		2.2
	1543	1902	2.2	
	2140			
10 Su		0134		2.2
	0405	0724	2.3	
	1007	1357		2.1
	1628	1941	2.1	
	2223			
11 M		0212		2.1
	0448	0805	2.2	
	1052	1439		1.9
	1711	2017	1.9	
	2304			
12 Tu		0248		1.9
	0530	0848	2.0	
	1134	1519		1.7
	1753	2035	1.8	
	2344			
13 W		0314		1.7
	0613	0925	1.9	
	1216	1550		1.5
	1838	2104	1.6	
14 Th	0024	0322		1.6
	0658	0937	1.7	
	1300	1558		1.3
	1926	2144	1.5	
15 F	0108	0343		1.4
	0748	1012	1.6	
	1347	1613		1.1
	2018	2225	1.3	
16 Sa)	0156	0417		1.2
	0841	1052	1.5	
	1439	1648		1.0
	2112	2309	1.2	
17 Su	0250	0500		1.1
	0935	1139	1.3	
	1534	2014		1.0
	2206			
18 M	0347	0831	1.1	
	1030	1413		1.2
	1632	2103	1.1	
	2302			
19 Tu		0240		1.1
	0448	0920	1.1	
	1127	1510		1.3
	1730	2151	1.2	
	2358			
20 W		0335		1.2
	0549	1011	1.2	
	1223	1602		1.4
	1824	2242	1.3	
21 Th	0050	0426		1.4
	0643	1103	1.4	
	1314	1651		1.5
	1910	2327	1.4	
22 F	0137	0511		1.6
	0731	1147	1.6	
	1401	1730		1.7
	1952			
23 Sa		0002	1.5	
	0221	0545		1.8
	0816	1220	1.6	
	1446	1752		1.8
	2034			
24 Su ●		0022	1.7	
	0303	0555		2.0
	0901	1239	1.7	
	1529	1800		1.9
	2115			
25 M		0028	1.8	
	0345	0619		2.2
	0946	1252	1.8	
	1612	1833		2.0
	2158			
26 Tu		0050	2.0	
	0428	0655		2.3
	1032	1317	1.9	
	1655	1912		2.1
	2243			
27 W		0123	2.1	
	0512	0738		2.3
	1118	1354	1.9	
	1739	1957		2.0
	2328			
28 Th		0204	2.1	
	0558	0828		2.3
	1206	1438	1.8	
	1828	2049		1.8
29 F	0016	0252	2.0	
	0650	0923		2.2
	1257	1530	1.7	
	1922	2144		1.9
30 Sa	0108	0345	1.8	
	0748	1017		2.0
	1353	1625	1.5	
	2022	2238		1.7

OCTOBER

Day	Slack time	Max time	Fld knots	Ebb knots
1 Su (	0207	0443	1.6	
	0850	1112		1.9
	1453	1848	1.6	
	2123	2336		
2 M	0311	0725	1.5	
	0951	1311		1.7
	1556	2013	1.5	
	2225			
3 Tu		0154		1.5
	0418	0836	1.6	
	1053	1431		1.8
	1701	2109	1.7	
	2327			
4 W		0301		1.7
	0528	0934	1.7	
	1156	1530		1.9
	1803	2204	1.8	
5 Th	0026	0359		1.9
	0632	1033	1.9	
	1254	1626		2.0
	1858	2300	2.0	
6 F	0120	0454		2.1
	0727	1128	2.0	
	1347	1717		2.1
	1945	2350	2.1	
7 Sa	0209	0542		2.2
	0815	1216	2.1	
	1435	1802		2.1
	2028			
8 Su O		0033	2.1	
	0255	0624		2.3
	0901	1259	2.0	
	1520	1842		2.0
	2110			
9 M		0111	2.1	
	0338	0702		2.3
	0944	1338	2.0	
	1604	1916		1.9
	2151			
10 Tu		0145	1.9	
	0419	0736		2.1
	1026	1416	1.8	
	1645	1935		1.8
	2232			
11 W		0211	1.8	
	0500	0747		2.0
	1106	1449	1.6	
	1726	1943		1.7
	2312			
12 Th		0212	1.6	
	0541	0807		1.9
	1146	1501	1.5	
	1808	2020		1.6
	2352			
13 F		0226	1.5	
	0623	0848		1.8
	1227	1501	1.3	
	1854	2105		1.4
14 Sa	0035	0259	1.4	
	0710	0933		1.6
	1312	1531	1.2	
	1944	2152		1.4
15 Su	0122	0340	1.3	
	0803	1018		1.5
	1400	1610	1.1	
	2038	2238		1.3
16 M)	0215	0424	1.1	
	0858	1104		1.4
	1453	1656	1.0	
	2132	2327		1.2
17 Tu	0313	0516	1.0	
	0953	1155		1.3
	1548	2027	1.0	
	2225			
18 W		0024		1.2
	0413	0846	1.0	
	1050	1434		1.2
	1644	2109	1.1	
	2320			
19 Th		0250		1.2
	0515	0931	1.1	
	1146	1511		1.3
	1740	2147	1.2	
20 F	0013	0342		1.4
	0612	1019	1.3	
	1241	1601		1.4
	1831	2226	1.4	
21 Sa	0102	0429		1.7
	0703	1108	1.4	
	1330	1644		1.6
	1917	2302	1.5	
22 Su	0148	0508		1.9
	0750	1147	1.6	
	1417	1705		1.7
	2000	2329	1.7	
23 M ●	0233	0530		2.1
	0836	1215	1.8	
	1502	1735		1.9
	2045	2359	1.9	
24 Tu	0318	0601		2.3
	0923	1240	1.9	
	1548	1812		2.1
	2131			
25 W		0032	2.1	
	0403	0638		2.5
	1012	1310	1.9	
	1634	1853		2.1
	2219			
26 Th		0110	2.2	
	0450	0721		2.5
	1100	1348	1.9	
	1721	1939		2.1
	2308			
27 F		0153	2.1	
	0539	0810		2.4
	1149	1437	1.9	
	1810	2032		2.0
	2359			
28 Sa		0245	2.0	
	0631	0909		2.2
	1240	1534	1.8	
	1905	2133		1.9
29 Su	0053	0344	1.8	
	0729	1009		2.1
	1334	1638	1.6	
	2005	2233		1.8
30 M (	0153	0452	1.6	
	0831	1109		1.9
	1433	1838	1.6	
	2106	2357		1.6
31 Tu	0258	0715	1.5	
	0932	1258		1.7
	1533	1954	1.6	
	2206			

TIME MERIDIAN 75°W

0000h is midnight, 1200h is noon.

MIAMI, FLORIDA (Harbor Entrance)

CURRENT TABLES 1995   FLOOD 292° EBB 112°

EASTERN STANDARD TIME (GMT -5H).   ADD 1H DAYLIGHT SAVING APR 2 - OCT 28

NOVEMBER

Day	Slack time	Max time	Fld knots	Ebb knots
1 W	0405	0140	1.7	
	1032	0822		1.6
	1635	1409	1.7	
	2305	2049		1.8
2 Th	0513	0242	1.8	
	1133	0917		1.7
	1735	1507	1.7	
		2141		1.9
3 F	0003	0338	1.9	
	0618	1012		1.8
	1232	1602	1.8	
	1830	2234		1.9
4 Sa	0057	0431	2.0	
	0712	1107		1.8
	1324	1654	1.8	
	1917	2326		2.0
5 Su	0145	0520	2.1	
	0758	1157		1.9
	1412	1740	1.9	
	2000			
6 M	0229	0011		2.0
	0840	0603	2.2	
	1457	1241		1.9
	2041	1821	1.8	
7 Tu ◯	0311	0050		1.9
	0920	0641	2.2	
	1540	1320		1.8
	2121	1855	1.7	
8 W	0352	0124		1.8
	1000	0713	2.1	
	1621	1356		1.7
	2202	1911	1.6	
9 Th	0432	0145		1.7
	1040	0716	1.9	
	1701	1428		1.6
	2243	1913	1.6	
10 F	0512	0137		1.6
	1119	0734	1.9	
	1742	1424		1.4
	2324	1948	1.5	
11 Sa	0553	0153		1.5
	1159	0813	1.8	
	1825	1427		1.4
		2033	1.5	
12 Su	0007	0227		1.4
	0637	0900	1.7	
	1240	1500		1.3
	1912	2123	1.4	
13 M	0052	0309		1.3
	0727	0947	1.6	
	1325	1540		1.3
	2004	2211	1.4	
14 Tu	0143	0355		1.2
	0821	1034	1.5	
	1414	1624		1.2
	2056	2258	1.4	
15 W ☽	0239	0444		1.1
	0916	1121	1.4	
	1506	1714		1.1
	2148	2350	1.3	

Day	Slack time	Max time	Fld knots	Ebb knots
16 Th	0338	0543		1.0
	1011	1214	1.3	
	1600	1822		1.1
	2240			
17 F	0438	0050	1.4	
	1107	0840		1.1
	1655	1316	1.3	
	2333	2002		1.3
18 Sa	0538	0157	1.5	
	1204	0910		1.2
	1749	1418	1.4	
		2045		1.5
19 Su	0026	0300	1.7	
	0633	0954		1.4
	1258	1515	1.5	
	1841	2130		1.6
20 M	0116	0407	2.0	
	0724	1107		1.5
	1348	1615	1.7	
	1929	2231		1.8
21 Tu	0205	0507	2.2	
	0813	1154		1.7
	1437	1711	1.9	
	2017	2335		2.0
22 W ●	0253	0548	2.4	
	0902	1231		1.9
	1525	1756	2.1	
	2107			
23 Th	0342	0022		2.2
	0952	0627	2.5	
	1614	1309		2.0
	2159	1839	2.1	
24 F	0432	0105		2.2
	1043	0710	2.5	
	1703	1352		2.0
	2252	1926	2.1	
25 Sa	0522	0153		2.2
	1132	0800	2.4	
	1754	1446		2.0
	2345	2023	2.0	
26 Su	0614	0251		2.0
	1223	0907	2.3	
	1848	1546		1.9
		2141	2.0	
27 M	0040	0357		1.9
	0710	1016	2.1	
	1315	1648		1.8
	1946	2251	1.9	
28 Tu	0138	0512		1.7
	0809	1116	1.9	
	1409	1810		1.7
	2045			
29 W ☾	0240	0001	1.8	
	0909	0652		1.6
	1506	1231	1.7	
	2142	1927		1.7
30 Th	0345	0115	1.7	
	1007	0800		1.6
	1603	1341	1.6	
	2239	2024		1.8

DECEMBER

Day	Slack time	Max time	Fld knots	Ebb knots
1 F	0451	0217	1.8	
	1105	0855		1.6
	1701	1440	1.6	
	2335	2115		1.8
2 Sa	0555	0312	1.9	
	1204	0948		1.6
	1757	1534	1.6	
		2207		1.8
3 Su	0029	0406	1.9	
	0650	1043		1.7
	1258	1628	1.6	
	1847	2300		1.8
4 M	0118	0456	2.0	
	0736	1136		1.7
	1347	1717	1.7	
	1931	2349		1.8
5 Tu	0203	0542	2.0	
	0817	1221		1.7
	1433	1800	1.6	
	2013			
6 W ○	0246	0031		1.8
	0857	0621	2.0	
	1516	1302		1.7
	2054	1837	1.6	
7 Th	0328	0107		1.7
	0936	0655	2.0	
	1558	1339		1.6
	2136	1903	1.5	
8 F	0408	0134		1.6
	1015	0710	1.9	
	1638	1412		1.5
	2218	1853	1.5	
9 Sa	0448	0127		1.5
	1054	0711	1.8	
	1718	1421		1.4
	2300	1924	1.5	
10 Su	0528	0133		1.5
	1133	0746	1.8	
	1759	1405		1.4
	2343	2006	1.5	
11 M	0610	0204		1.5
	1212	0830	1.8	
	1842	1434		1.4
		2054	1.5	
12 Tu	0026	0244		1.4
	0655	0918	1.7	
	1254	1513		1.4
	1929	2144	1.5	
13 W	0114	0329		1.4
	0745	1005	1.6	
	1338	1556		1.4
	2019	2231	1.6	
14 Th	0206	0416		1.3
	0839	1051	1.6	
	1426	1642		1.4
	2110	2319	1.6	
15 F ☽	0303	0508		1.2
	0933	1140	1.5	
	1518	1735		1.4
	2202			

Day	Slack time	Max time	Fld knots	Ebb knots
16 Sa	0402	0013	1.6	
	1029	0614		1.1
	1612	1236	1.4	
	2255	1844		1.4
17 Su	0502	0115	1.6	
	1127	0754		1.2
	1710	1337	1.4	
	2351	1959		1.5
18 M	0603	0221	1.8	
	1225	0900		1.3
	1807	1439	1.5	
		2056		1.7
19 Tu	0047	0328	2.0	
	0659	1020		1.5
	1320	1542	1.7	
	1902	2200		1.8
20 W	0141	0454	2.2	
	0751	1138		1.7
	1413	1656	1.9	
	1955	2326		2.0
21 Th ●	0233	0547	2.4	
	0843	1226		1.9
	1504	1753	2.0	
	2048			
22 F	0324	0023		2.2
	0934	0629	2.5	
	1556	1309		2.1
	2142	1838	2.2	
23 Sa	0415	0110		2.3
	1025	0711	2.5	
	1646	1355		2.1
	2237	1925	2.2	
24 Su	0506	0201		2.2
	1115	0802	2.5	
	1736	1447		2.1
	2331	2032	2.1	
25 M	0556	0259		2.1
	1203	0911	2.3	
	1828	1541		2.1
		2146	2.1	
26 Tu	0024	0359		2.0
	0649	1009	2.2	
	1252	1634		2.0
	1922	2242	2.0	
27 W	0119	0500		1.7
	0744	1059	2.0	
	1342	1735		1.8
	2019	2337	1.9	
28 Th ☾	0217	0619		1.6
	0841	1155	1.7	
	1434	1852		1.7
	2114			
29 F	0317	0042	1.8	
	0937	0732		1.5
	1528	1306	1.5	
	2208	1955		1.7
30 Sa	0418	0146	1.7	
	1034	0830		1.5
	1623	1409	1.4	
	2302	2048		1.7
31 Su	0521	0243	1.7	
	1131	0922		1.5
	1719	1505	1.4	
	2357	2139		1.6

TIME MERIDIAN 75°W   0000h is midnight, 1200h is noon.

FLORIDA

KEY WEST, FLORIDA

HIGH & LOW WATER 1995 24°33'N 81°49'W

EASTERN STANDARD TIME (GMT -5H). ADD 1H DAYLIGHT SAVING APR 2 - OCT 28

JANUARY

Day	Time	ft	Time	ft	Day	Time	ft	Time	ft
1 Su ●	0324	-0.5	1009	1.2	16	0333	-0.3	1003	1.1
	1446	0.2	2133	2.2		O 2131	1.8		
2 M	0410	-0.5	1050	1.3	17 Tu	0404	-0.3	1036	1.1
	1538	0.1	2223	2.1		1529	0.2	2209	1.8
3 Tu	0454	-0.4	1131	1.3	18 W	0435	-0.3	1109	1.2
	1631	0.1	2311	2.0		1610	0.1	2248	1.7
4 W	0536	-0.3	1211	1.3	19 Th	0507	-0.3	1142	1.2
	1725	0.1	2358	1.8		1654	0.1	2329	1.6
5 Th	0618	-0.2	1252	1.4	20 F	0540	-0.2	1216	1.3
	1823	0.2				1743	0.1		
6 F	0047	1.5	0700	-0.0	21 Sa	0014	1.5	0615	-0.1
	1333	1.4	1926	0.2		1252	1.4	1839	0.0
7 Sa	0139	1.3	0744	0.1	22 Su	0104	1.3	0653	0.0
	1417	1.4	2036	0.2		1331	1.4	1943	0.0
8 Su ☾	0239	1.1	0829	0.3	23 M	0205	1.1	0736	0.1
	1505	1.4	2150	0.2		1418	1.5	2057	-0.0
9 M	0354	0.9	0920	0.4	24 Tu	0322	0.9	0827	0.2
	1558	1.4	2302	0.2		1514	1.6	2216	-0.1
10 Tu	0525	0.8	1014	0.5	25 W	0458	0.8	0928	0.3
	1655	1.5				1621	1.6	2332	-0.2
11 W	0006	0.1	0644	0.8	26 Th	0628	0.8	1036	0.3
	1109	0.5	1752	1.5		1734	1.7		
12 Th	0059	0.0	0740	0.9	27 F	0038	-0.3	0735	0.8
	1201	0.5	1844	1.6		1144	0.3	1843	1.8
13 F	0145	-0.1	0821	0.9	28 Sa	0135	-0.4	0826	0.9
	1248	0.4	1930	1.7		1247	0.2	1945	1.9
14 Sa	0225	-0.2	0857	1.0	29 Su	0224	-0.5	0909	1.0
	1331	0.4	2012	1.7		1345	0.1	2039	1.9
15 Su	0300	-0.2	0930	1.0	30 M ●	0308	-0.5	0949	1.1
	1411	0.3	2052	1.8		1440	-0.0	2129	1.9
					31 Tu	0349	-0.5	1025	1.2
						1532	-0.1	2216	1.8

FEBRUARY

Day	Time	ft	Time	ft	Day	Time	ft	Time	ft
1 W	0428	-0.4	1101	1.3	16 Th	0403	-0.3	1034	1.3
	1622	-0.2	2300	1.7		1600	-0.2	2239	1.6
2 Th	0505	-0.3	1135	1.4	17 F	0434	-0.3	1106	1.4
	1712	-0.2	2342	1.5		1645	-0.2	2323	1.5
3 F	0541	-0.2	1208	1.4	18 Sa	0507	-0.2	1139	1.5
	1803	-0.1				1734	-0.3		
4 Sa	0024	1.3	0617	-0.1	19 Su	0009	1.3	0542	-0.1
	1243	1.4	1856	-0.1		1214	1.5	1828	-0.3
5 Su	0108	1.1	0653	0.1	20 M	0100	1.1	0620	0.0
	1319	1.4	1955	0.0		1255	1.6	1929	-0.3
6 M	0157	0.9	0731	0.2	21 Tu	0200	0.9	0703	0.2
	1401	1.4	2101	0.1		1343	1.6	2040	-0.2
7 Tu	0257	0.8	0815	0.3	22 W	0316	0.8	0755	0.3
	1451	1.3	☾ 2215	0.1		1444	1.6	☽ 2158	-0.2
8 W	0420	0.7	0911	0.4	23 Th	0451	0.7	0903	0.3
	1553	1.3	2326	0.1		1600	1.6	2316	-0.2
9 Th	0559	0.7	1018	0.4	24 F	0617	0.8	1022	0.3
	1702	1.3				1724	1.6		
10 F	0028	-0.0	0707	0.7	25 Sa	0023	-0.3	0719	0.9
	1123	0.4	1809	1.4		1138	0.3	1840	1.7
11 Sa	0117	-0.1	0752	0.8	26 Su	0118	-0.3	0806	1.0
	1220	0.4	1904	1.5		1246	0.1	1943	1.7
12 Su	0158	-0.2	0827	0.8	27 M	0204	-0.3	0846	1.1
	1309	0.3	1952	1.6		1344	0.0	2037	1.7
13 M	0232	-0.2	0900	1.0	28 Tu	0244	-0.3	0922	1.3
	1353	0.2	2035	1.6		1437	-0.1	2124	1.7
14 Tu	0303	-0.3	0932	1.1					
	1424	0.1	2117	1.7					
15 W	0333	-0.3	1003	1.2					
	1517	-0.1	O 2158	1.7					

MARCH

Day	Time	ft	Time	ft	Day	Time	ft	Time	ft
1 W ●	0321	-0.3	0954	1.4	16 Th O	0253	-0.1	0923	1.4
	1525	-0.2	2207	1.6		1504	-0.2	2146	1.6
2 Th	0356	-0.2	1025	1.4	17 F	0325	-0.1	0955	1.6
	1611	-0.3	2247	1.5		1549	-0.4	2231	1.5
3 F	0430	-0.1	1055	1.5	18 Sa	0359	-0.1	1028	1.7
	1656	-0.3	2326	1.4		1635	-0.5	2317	1.4
4 Sa	0503	-0.0	1125	1.5	19 Su	0434	-0.0	1104	1.8
	1740	-0.3				1724	-0.5		
5 Su	0003	1.2	0535	0.1	20 M	0005	1.3	0511	0.1
	1156	1.5	1826	-0.2		1143	1.9	1818	-0.4
6 M	0043	1.1	0607	0.2	21 Tu	0058	1.1	0552	0.2
	1230	1.5	1916	-0.1		1228	1.8	1917	-0.4
7 Tu	0125	0.9	0640	0.3	22 W	0159	1.0	0639	0.3
	1310	1.4	2013	0.0		1321	1.8	2025	-0.3
8 W	0217	0.8	0718	0.4	23 Th	0312	0.9	0738	0.4
	1357	1.4	2121	0.1		1426	1.7	☽ 2140	-0.2
9 Th	0326	0.7	0809	0.5	24 F	0438	0.9	0855	0.4
	1457	1.3	☾ 2236	0.1		1548	1.6	2253	-0.1
10 F	0500	0.7	0925	0.5	25 Sa	0555	0.9	1022	0.4
	1610	1.3	2343	0.1		1718	1.5	2357	-0.1
11 Sa	0619	0.8	1047	0.5	26 Su	0652	1.1	1141	0.3
	1727	1.3				1836	1.5		
12 Su	0035	0.0	0709	0.9	27 M	0050	-0.1	0737	1.2
	1154	0.4	1833	1.4		1247	0.2	1939	1.5
13 M	0116	-0.0	0747	1.0	28 Tu	0133	-0.1	0815	1.4
	1248	0.3	1928	1.5		1343	-0.0	2031	1.5
14 Tu	0151	-0.1	0820	1.1	29 W	0211	-0.1	0849	1.5
	1335	0.1	2016	1.5		1432	-0.2	2116	1.5
15 W	0222	-0.1	0852	1.3	30 Th	0247	0.0	0919	1.6
	1420	-0.1	2102	1.6		1516	-0.3	● 2156	1.5
					31 F	0320	0.1	0948	1.6
						1558	-0.3	2234	1.4

APRIL

Day	Time	ft	Time	ft	Day	Time	ft	Time	ft
1 Sa	0353	0.1	1016	1.7	16 Su	0324	0.1	0956	2.0
	1638	-0.3	2309	1.3		1625	-0.6	2311	1.4
2 Su	0424	0.2	1045	1.7	17 M	0403	0.2	1037	2.1
	1717	-0.3	2345	1.2		1715	-0.6		
3 M	0455	0.3	1116	1.7	18 Tu	0001	1.3	0446	0.2
	1758	-0.2				1121	2.1	1808	-0.5
4 Tu	0022	1.1	0526	0.3	19 W	0054	1.2	0532	0.3
	1151	1.6	1843	-0.1		1211	2.0	1906	-0.4
5 W	0103	1.0	0558	0.4	20 Th	0153	1.1	0626	0.4
	1230	1.6	1932	0.0		1307	1.9	2009	-0.2
6 Th	0152	0.9	0636	0.5	21 F	0300	1.0	0733	0.5
	1316	1.5	2031	0.1		1414	1.7	☽ 2115	-0.1
7 F	0253	0.9	0726	0.6	22 Sa	0413	1.1	0856	0.5
	1412	1.4	2138	0.2		1536	1.5	2221	0.0
8 Sa	0409	0.9	0843	0.6	23 Su	0520	1.2	1024	0.4
	1521	1.4	☾ 2243	0.2		1706	1.4	2320	0.1
9 Su	0521	0.9	1012	0.6	24 M	0616	1.3	1142	0.3
	1636	1.3	2336	0.2		1825	1.4		
10 M	0615	1.1	1127	0.5	25 Tu	0010	0.2	0701	1.5
	1756	1.4				1245	0.1	1929	1.4
11 Tu	0020	0.1	0656	1.2	26 W	0054	0.2	0739	1.6
	1900	1.4				1337	-0.0	2021	1.4
12 W	0058	0.1	0732	1.4	27 Th	0132	0.2	0813	1.7
	1317	0.1	1955	1.5		1423	-0.1	2105	1.3
13 Th	0134	0.1	0807	1.6	28 F	0208	0.3	0843	1.8
	1404	-0.2	2046	1.5		1504	-0.2	2144	1.3
14 F	0210	0.1	0842	1.7	29 Sa ●	0243	0.3	0912	1.8
	1505	-0.3	2135	1.5		1543	-0.3	2220	1.3
15 Sa	0246	0.1	0917	1.9	30 Su	0316	0.3	0942	1.9
	1537	-0.5	O 2223	1.4		1620	-0.3	2254	1.2

TIME MERIDIAN 75°W

0000h is midnight, 1200h is noon.

Heights in feet are referenced to the chart datum of soundings.

KEY WEST, FLORIDA

HIGH & LOW WATER 1995   24°33'N   81°49'W

EASTERN STANDARD TIME (GMT -5H).   **ADD 1H DAYLIGHT SAVING APR 2 - OCT 28**

FLORIDA

MAY

Day	Time ft	Time ft	Time ft	Time ft		Day	Time ft	Time ft	Time ft	Time ft
1	0348 0.4	1013 1.9	M 1658 -0.2	2329 1.2		16	0338 0.3	1018 2.3	Tu 1705 -0.6	2352 1.2
2	0420 0.4	1046 1.8	Tu 1736 -0.2			17	0426 0.3	1107 2.2	W 1756 -0.5	
3	0006 1.1	0452 0.5	W 1122 1.8	1816 -0.1		18	0043 1.2	0519 0.3	Th 1200 2.1	1850 -0.3
4	0047 1.1	0527 0.5	Th 1201 1.7	1900 0.0		19	0137 1.2	0619 0.4	F 1257 1.9	1946 -0.2
5	0133 1.0	0607 0.6	F 1245 1.6	1949 0.1		20	0235 1.2	0730 0.5	Sa 1402 1.7	2044 -0.0
6	0227 1.0	0700 0.6	Sa 1336 1.5	2042 0.2		21	0336 1.3	0853 0.5	Su 1518 1.4	) 2141 0.1
7	0325 1.1	0814 0.7	Su 1439 1.4	(2137 0.2		22	0436 1.4	1017 0.4	M 1643 1.3	2235 0.2
8	0424 1.1	0940 0.6	M 1555 1.3	2230 0.2		23	0531 1.5	1132 0.3	Tu 1805 1.2	2324 0.3
9	0516 1.3	1058 0.5	Tu 1717 1.3	2318 0.3		24	0618 1.6	1234 0.1	W 1913 1.2	
10	0601 1.4	1201 0.2	W 1831 1.3			25	0010 0.4	0659 1.7	Th 1325 0.0	2007 1.2
11	0002 0.3	0642 1.6	Th 1256 0.0	1935 1.3		26	0051 0.4	0736 1.8	F 1410 -0.1	2051 1.2
12	0045 0.3	0723 1.8	F 1347 -0.2	2032 1.3		27	0130 0.4	0809 1.8	Sa 1450 -0.2	2130 1.2
13	0127 0.3	0804 2.0	Sa 1436 -0.4	2124 1.3		28	0207 0.4	0842 1.9	Su 1527 -0.2	2204 1.2
14	0209 0.3	0846 2.2	Su 1525 -0.6	O 2214 1.3		29	0242 0.4	0915 1.9	● 2238 1.2	
15	0253 0.3	0931 2.2	M 1614 -0.6	2303 1.3		30	0317 0.4	0949 1.9	Tu 1640 -0.2	2313 1.2
						31	0351 0.5	1025 1.9	W 1716 -0.2	2349 1.1

JUNE

Day	Time ft	Time ft	Time ft	Time ft		Day	Time ft	Time ft	Time ft	Time ft
1	0426 0.5	1101 1.8	Th 1753 -0.1			16	0022 1.3	0510 0.3	F 1151 2.0	1828 0.3
2	0029 1.1	0505 0.5	F 1140 1.8	1831 -0.1		17	0110 1.3	0612 0.3	Sa 1245 1.8	1916 -0.1
3	0111 1.1	0549 0.6	Sa 1222 1.7	1911 0.0		18	0200 1.4	0721 0.4	Su 1344 1.6	2005 0.1
4	0155 1.2	0643 0.6	Su 1309 1.5	1953 0.1		19	0251 1.5	0838 0.4	M 1451 1.3	) 2055 0.2
5	0242 1.2	0752 0.6	M 1407 1.4	2039 0.2		20	0345 1.5	0957 0.3	Tu 1610 1.1	2145 0.3
6	0329 1.3	0911 0.5	Tu 1518 1.3	(2128 0.3		21	0439 1.6	1111 0.3	W 1736 1.0	2236 0.4
7	0418 1.4	1029 0.4	W 1642 1.2	2219 0.3		22	0531 1.7	1214 0.2	Th 1850 1.0	2326 0.5
8	0507 1.6	1137 0.2	Th 1806 1.1	2310 0.4		23	0618 1.7	1307 0.1	F 1948 1.0	
9	0556 1.8	1237 -0.1	F 1919 1.1			24	0012 0.5	0701 1.8	Sa 1353 -0.0	2033 1.0
10	0000 0.4	0646 2.0	Sa 1332 -0.3	2019 1.2		25	0056 0.5	0741 1.9	Su 1434 -0.1	2111 1.1
11	0050 0.4	0735 2.1	Su 1424 -0.5	2113 1.2		26	0136 0.5	0819 1.9	M 1512 -0.1	2145 1.1
12	0139 0.3	0826 2.3	M 1514 -0.6	O 2202 1.2		27	0215 0.5	0856 1.9	Tu 1547 -0.2	● 2218 1.1
13	0229 0.3	0916 2.3	Tu 1603 -0.6	2249 1.2		28	0253 0.5	0932 1.9	W 1621 -0.2	2252 1.2
14	0320 0.3	1007 2.2	W 1651 -0.5	2336 1.3		29	0330 0.5	1009 1.9	Th 1654 -0.1	2326 1.2
15	0413 0.3	1058 2.2	Th 1740 -0.4			30	0408 0.5	1046 1.9	F 1726 -0.1	

JULY

Day	Time ft	Time ft	Time ft	Time ft		Day	Time ft	Time ft	Time ft	Time ft
1	0002 1.2	0449 0.5	Sa 1124 1.8	1759 -0.1		16	0034 1.5	0600 0.2	Su 1229 1.7	1839 0.0
2	0039 1.3	0535 0.5	Su 1205 1.7	1833 0.0		17	0116 1.6	0703 0.3	M 1321 1.5	1922 0.2
3	0116 1.3	0628 0.5	M 1251 1.5	1910 0.1		18	0200 1.6	0811 0.3	Tu 1419 1.3	2006 0.3
4	0156 1.4	0731 0.4	Tu 1346 1.4	1950 0.2		19	0248 1.6	0925 0.3	W 1528 1.1	) 2054 0.5
5	0239 1.5	0844 0.4	W 1453 1.2	(2036 0.3		20	0341 1.7	1038 0.3	Th 1654 1.0	2147 0.6
6	0327 1.6	1002 0.3	Th 1617 1.1	2129 0.4		21	0438 1.7	1146 0.3	F 1819 1.0	2243 0.6
7	0421 1.8	1115 0.1	F 1749 1.0	2226 0.5		22	0536 1.7	1244 0.2	Sa 1923 1.0	2337 0.6
8	0520 1.9	1221 -0.1	Sa 1907 1.0	2325 0.5		23	0630 1.8	1333 0.1	Su 2008 1.0	
9	0620 2.1	1319 -0.2	Su 2008 1.1			24	0027 0.6	0717 1.9	M 1414 0.1	2045 1.1
10	0024 0.4	0719 2.2	M 1412 -0.4	2059 1.1		25	0113 0.6	0800 1.9	Tu 1451 0.0	2118 1.2
11	0120 0.4	0815 2.3	Tu 1501 -0.4	2145 1.2		26	0155 0.5	0840 2.0	W 1524 -0.0	2150 1.3
12	0216 0.3	0909 2.3	W 1554 -0.4	O 2229 1.3		27	0235 0.5	0918 2.0	Th 1554 -0.0	● 2222 1.3
13	0310 0.2	1000 2.3	Th 1632 -0.4	2310 1.4		28	0314 0.4	0955 2.0	F 1624 -0.0	2254 1.4
14	0405 0.2	1050 2.2	F 1715 -0.3	2352 1.5		29	0354 0.4	1033 1.9	Sa 1653 0.0	2326 1.5
15	0501 0.2	1139 2.0	Sa 1757 -0.1			30	0437 0.4	1112 1.9	Su 1723 0.1	2359 1.5
						31	0523 0.3	1154 1.7	M 1755 0.2	

AUGUST

Day	Time ft	Time ft	Time ft	Time ft		Day	Time ft	Time ft	Time ft	Time ft
1	0033 1.6	0614 0.3	Tu 1240 1.6	1830 0.3		16	0107 1.8	0736 0.4	W 1345 1.4	1916 0.6
2	0110 1.7	0713 0.3	W 1333 1.4	1909 0.4		17	0150 1.8	0843 0.4	Th 1443 1.2	) 2001 0.7
3	0153 1.8	0822 0.3	Th 1439 1.2	(1954 0.5		18	0241 1.8	0956 0.5	F 1601 1.1	2056 0.8
4	0244 1.9	0939 0.3	F 1605 1.1	2050 0.6		19	0342 1.8	1109 0.5	Sa 1736 1.1	2201 0.8
5	0346 1.9	1057 0.2	Sa 1740 1.0	2156 0.6		20	0452 1.8	1213 0.4	Su 1847 1.1	2307 0.8
6	0457 2.0	1206 0.1	Su 1856 1.1	2305 0.6		21	0557 1.8	1304 0.4	M 1934 1.2	
7	0608 2.1	1306 -0.0	M 1954 1.0			22	0005 0.8	0653 1.9	Tu 1345 0.3	2010 1.3
8	0012 0.5	0713 2.2	Tu 1358 -0.1	2041 1.3		23	0055 0.7	0739 2.0	W 1420 0.3	2042 1.4
9	0113 0.4	0811 2.3	W 1443 -0.1	2122 1.4		24	0139 0.6	0822 2.1	Th 1450 0.2	2113 1.5
10	0210 0.3	0908 2.3	Th 1526 -0.1	O 2201 1.6		25	0220 0.5	0901 2.1	F 1519 0.2	● 2144 1.6
11	0305 0.2	0954 2.2	F 1605 -0.1	2238 1.7		26	0300 0.4	0941 2.1	Sa 1547 0.2	2214 1.7
12	0358 0.2	1040 2.1	Sa 1644 0.0	2315 1.8		27	0341 0.3	1020 2.0	Su 1616 0.3	2245 1.8
13	0450 0.2	1126 1.9	Su 1721 0.2	2351 1.8		28	0424 0.3	1102 1.9	M 1646 0.3	2317 1.9
14	0542 0.2	1210 1.7	M 1758 0.3			29	0510 0.2	1145 1.8	Tu 1719 0.4	2352 2.0
15	0028 1.8	0637 0.3	Tu 1256 1.5	1836 0.4		30	0600 0.2	1233 1.6	W 1754 0.5	
						31	0030 2.0	0657 0.3	Th 1328 1.5	1835 0.6

TIME MERIDIAN 75°W   0000h is midnight, 1200h is noon.
Heights in feet are referenced to the chart datum of soundings.

KEY WEST, FLORIDA

HIGH & LOW WATER 1995　　　　　　　　　　　　　　　　　　　24°33'N　81°49'W

EASTERN STANDARD TIME (GMT -5H).　ADD 1H DAYLIGHT SAVING APR 2 - OCT 28

SEPTEMBER

	Time	ft		Time	ft
1 F	0116	2.1	**16** Sa	0148	1.9
	0804	0.3		0908	0.6
	1435	1.3		1512	1.3
	1923	0.7	☽	2004	1.0
2 Sa	0213	2.1	**17** Su	0249	1.9
	0921	0.3		1023	0.7
	1601	1.2		1640	1.3
☾	2025	0.8		2120	1.0
3 Su	0324	2.1	**18** M	0403	1.9
	1040	0.3		1130	0.7
	1731	1.2		1758	1.3
	2142	0.8		2239	1.0
4 M	0446	2.1	**19** Tu	0518	1.9
	1150	0.3		1223	0.6
	1841	1.3		1849	1.4
	2301	0.8		2344	0.9
5 Tu	0605	2.2	**20** W	0622	1.9
	1248	0.2		1303	0.6
	1933	1.5		1926	1.5
6 W	0012	0.6	**21** Th	0037	0.8
	0712	2.2		0714	2.0
	1336	0.2		1337	0.5
	2015	1.6		1959	1.7
7 Th	0114	0.5	**22** F	0122	0.7
	0809	2.3		0801	2.1
	1418	0.2		1407	0.5
	2053	1.8		2031	1.8
8 F	0209	0.4	**23** Sa	0204	0.5
	0900	2.2		0844	2.1
	1456	0.3		1436	0.5
○	2129	1.9		2101	2.0
9 Sa	0300	0.3	**24** Su	0245	0.4
	0946	2.2		0926	2.1
	1533	0.3	●	1506	0.5
	2202	2.0		2133	2.1
10 Su	0348	0.2	**25** M	0327	0.3
	1029	2.1		1009	2.1
	1608	0.4		1537	0.5
	2235	2.1		2205	2.2
11 M	0435	0.2	**26** Tu	0411	0.2
	1110	1.9		1053	2.0
	1643	0.5		1610	0.6
	2307	2.1		2240	2.3
12 Tu	0521	0.2	**27** W	0457	0.1
	1150	1.8		1139	1.8
	1717	0.6		1646	0.6
	2341	2.1		2317	2.3
13 W	0609	0.3	**28** Th	0548	0.1
	1231	1.6		1229	1.7
	1752	0.7		1725	0.7
14 Th	0017	2.1	**29** F	0000	2.4
	0700	0.4		0645	0.2
	1314	1.5		1325	1.6
	1828	0.8		1810	0.8
15 F	0059	2.0	**30** Sa	0052	2.3
	0759	0.6		0749	0.3
	1405	1.4		1433	1.4
	1910	0.9		1905	0.9

OCTOBER

	Time	ft		Time	ft
1 Su	0154	2.2	**16** M	0202	1.9
	0903	0.4		0926	0.7
	1553	1.4		1546	1.4
☾	2016	1.0	☽	2038	1.1
2 M	0312	2.2	**17** Tu	0312	1.8
	1018	0.5		1031	0.7
	1712	1.5		1658	1.5
	2143	0.9		2206	1.1
3 Tu	0441	2.1	**18** W	0430	1.8
	1125	0.5		1125	0.7
	1815	1.4		1753	1.6
	2306	0.8		2318	1.0
4 W	0602	2.1	**19** Th	0543	1.8
	1220	0.5		1207	0.7
	1904	1.7		1835	1.7
5 Th	0016	0.7	**20** F	0014	0.8
	0709	2.1		0645	1.9
	1305	0.5		1244	0.7
	1945	1.9		1911	1.9
6 F	0115	0.5	**21** Sa	0102	0.6
	0805	2.1		0738	1.9
	1345	0.5		1317	0.7
	2022	2.0		1945	2.0
7 Sa	0206	0.4	**22** Su	0146	0.4
	0854	2.1		0826	2.0
	1423	0.6		1350	0.7
	2055	2.2		2019	2.2
8 Su	0253	0.3	**23** M	0230	0.2
	0937	2.0		0913	2.0
	1500	0.6		1425	0.7
○	2127	2.2	●	2054	2.3
9 M	0336	0.2	**24** Tu	0313	0.1
	1017	1.9		0958	1.9
	1532	0.7		1500	0.7
	2157	2.3		2131	2.5
10 Tu	0418	0.2	**25** W	0359	-0.0
	1055	1.9		1044	1.8
	1606	0.7		1538	0.7
	2228	2.3		2211	2.5
11 W	0500	0.3	**26** Th	0447	-0.0
	1131	1.8		1132	1.8
	1639	0.8		1619	0.7
	2301	2.3		2254	2.5
12 Th	0542	0.3	**27** F	0538	0.0
	1208	1.7		1223	1.6
	1712	0.9		1704	0.8
	2337	2.2		2343	2.5
13 F	0628	0.4	**28** Sa	0633	0.1
	1249	1.6		1318	1.6
	1747	0.9		1755	0.8
14 Sa	0018	2.1	**29** Su	0038	2.4
	0718	0.4		0733	0.3
	1336	1.5		1421	1.5
	1827	1.0		1858	0.9
15 Su	0105	2.0	**30** M	0143	2.2
	0818	0.7		0839	0.4
	1434	1.4		1530	1.5
	1920	1.1	☾	2017	0.9
			31 Tu	0302	2.0
				0946	0.5
				1640	1.6
				2146	0.9

NOVEMBER

	Time	ft		Time	ft
1 W	0431	1.9	**16** Th	0339	1.6
	1048	0.6		1012	0.7
	1740	1.7		1650	1.6
	2308	0.7		2244	0.8
2 Th	0554	1.9	**17** F	0459	1.6
	1142	0.6		1100	0.7
	1829	1.9		1737	1.7
				2346	0.6
3 F	0016	0.6	**18** Sa	0613	1.6
	0703	1.8		1144	0.7
	1228	0.7		1820	1.9
	1912	2.0			
4 Sa	0112	0.4	**19** Su	0039	0.4
	0759	1.8		0716	1.6
	1309	0.7		1225	0.7
	1949	2.1		1900	2.1
5 Su	0200	0.3	**20** M	0127	0.2
	0846	1.8		0811	1.6
	1348	0.7		1306	0.6
	2023	2.2		1941	2.2
6 M	0243	0.2	**21** Tu	0214	-0.1
	0928	1.8		0901	1.6
	1424	0.7		1347	0.6
	2055	2.3		2023	2.4
7 Tu	0324	0.1	**22** W	0301	-0.2
	1005	1.7		0948	1.6
	1459	0.7	●	1430	0.6
○	2126	2.3		2107	2.5
8 W	0402	0.1	**23** Th	0348	-0.3
	1040	1.7		1035	1.6
	1533	0.7		1514	0.6
	2158	2.3		2153	2.5
9 Th	0441	0.2	**24** F	0436	-0.3
	1114	1.6		1122	1.5
	1607	0.8		1600	0.5
	2232	2.2		2242	2.5
10 F	0520	0.2	**25** Sa	0526	-0.2
	1149	1.5		1211	1.5
	1641	0.8		1651	0.6
	2308	2.2		2333	2.4
11 Sa	0601	0.3	**26** Su	0618	-0.1
	1228	1.5		1302	1.5
	1717	0.9		1748	0.6
	2348	2.1			
12 Su	0644	0.4	**27** M	0029	2.2
	1311	1.4		0712	0.1
	1758	0.9		1357	1.5
				1855	0.6
13 M	0032	2.0	**28** Tu	0133	2.0
	0732	0.5		0808	0.2
	1401	1.4		1455	1.5
	1849	1.0		2014	0.6
14 Tu	0123	1.8	**29** W	0246	1.7
	0824	0.6		0906	0.4
	1457	1.4		1556	1.6
	2000	1.0	☽	2140	0.6
15 W	0225	1.7	**30** Th	0411	1.6
	0919	0.6		1003	0.5
	1556	1.5		1655	1.7
☾	2126	0.9		2300	0.5

DECEMBER

	Time	ft		Time	ft
1 F	0538	1.5	**16** Sa	0416	1.2
	1057	0.6		0952	0.5
	1749	1.8		1637	1.6
				2314	0.3
2 Sa	0008	0.3	**17** Su	0542	1.2
	0651	1.4		1044	0.5
	1147	0.6		1728	1.8
	1836	1.9			
3 Su	0103	0.3	**18** M	0015	0.1
	0750	1.4		0656	1.2
	1232	0.6		1137	0.5
	1917	2.0		1820	1.9
4 M	0150	0.1	**19** Tu	0109	-0.1
	0837	1.4		0757	1.2
	1314	0.6		1227	0.5
	1955	2.0		1911	2.1
5 Tu	0232	0.0	**20** W	0200	-0.3
	0917	1.4		0849	1.3
	1354	0.6		1317	0.4
	2030	2.1		2002	2.2
6 W	0311	-0.0	**21** Th	0249	-0.4
	0952	1.4		0937	1.3
	1431	0.6	●	1407	0.3
○	2104	2.1		2053	2.3
7 Th	0348	-0.1	**22** F	0337	-0.5
	1024	1.4		1022	1.3
	1507	0.6		1458	0.3
	2138	2.1		2144	2.3
8 F	0425	-0.0	**23** Sa	0424	-0.5
	1056	1.3		1106	1.3
	1543	0.6		1550	0.2
	2213	2.0		2235	2.3
9 Sa	0500	0.0	**24** Su	0510	-0.4
	1130	1.3		1150	1.3
	1619	0.6		1645	0.2
	2250	2.0		2327	2.1
10 Su	0536	0.1	**25** M	0557	-0.3
	1206	1.3		1235	1.4
	1656	0.6		1744	0.2
	2328	1.9			
11 M	0613	0.1	**26** Tu	0021	1.9
	1244	1.3		0643	-0.1
	1738	0.6		1322	1.4
				1849	0.2
12 Tu	0009	1.8	**27** W	0119	1.6
	0650	0.2		0731	0.0
	1326	1.3		1412	1.5
	1828	0.7		2001	0.3
13 W	0054	1.6	**28** Th	0224	1.4
	0729	0.3		0821	0.2
	1410	1.3		1506	1.5
	1930	0.7	☾	2121	0.2
14 Th	0148	1.5	**29** F	0343	1.2
	0812	0.4		0914	0.3
	1456	1.4		1603	1.6
	2044	0.6		2239	0.2
15 F	0255	1.3	**30** Sa	0513	1.0
	0900	0.4		1009	0.4
	1546	1.5		1701	1.6
☽	2203	0.5		2349	0.1
			31 Su	0634	1.0
				1104	0.5
				1757	1.7

TIME MERIDIAN 75°W

Heights in feet are referenced to the chart datum of soundings.

0000h is midnight, 1200h is noon.

KEY WEST, FLORIDA (0.3 nm West of Fort Taylor)

CURRENT TABLES 1995 **FLOOD 022° EBB 194°**

EASTERN STANDARD TIME (GMT -5H).   ADD 1H DAYLIGHT SAVING APR 2 - OCT 28

FLORIDA

JANUARY

Day	Slack time	Max time	Fld (kn)	Ebb (kn)
1 Su ●		0035		2.6
	0415	0720	1.8	
	1015	1319		2.1
	1647	1924	1.2	
	2155			
2 M		0122		2.5
	0502	0803	1.8	
	1058	1402		2.1
	1733	2008	1.2	
	2244			
3 Tu		0208		2.4
	0548	0844	1.6	
	1139	1444		2.0
	1819	2053	1.2	
	2332			
4 W		0252		2.2
	0634	0924	1.4	
	1218	1526		2.0
	1906	2138	1.1	
5 Th	0020	0338		2.0
	0722	1004	1.2	
	1257	1608		1.8
	1957	2226	0.9	
6 F	0110	0425		1.7
	0813	1046	0.9	
	1337	1654		1.7
	2052	2320	0.8	
7 Sa	0204	0516		1.5
	0909	1133	0.7	
	1418	1743		1.6
	2152			
8 Su ☾		0028	0.6	
	0305	0613		1.3
	1014	1230	0.5	
	1504	1839		1.5
	2257			
9 M		0152	0.6	
	0412	0721		1.1
	1126	1348	0.4	
	1557	1941		1.5
10 Tu	0001	0307	0.7	
	0521	0839		1.1
	1239	1508	0.3	
	1655	2046		1.5
11 W	0057	0407	0.8	
	0624	0949		1.1
	1339	1609	0.4	
	1754	2144		1.6
12 Th	0145	0456	0.9	
	0720	1043		1.2
	1426	1656	0.5	
	1847	2233		1.7
13 F	0227	0538	1.1	
	0808	1126		1.4
	1504	1734	0.6	
	1935	2315		1.9
14 Sa	0305	0613	1.2	
	0851	1201		1.5
	1538	1806	0.7	
	2019	2353		2.0
15 Su	0341	0643	1.3	
	0929	1234		1.6
	1610	1834	0.8	
	2100			
16 M ○		0030		2.1
	0416	0710	1.4	
	1005	1306		1.7
	1642	1903	0.9	
	2139			
17 Tu		0107		2.2
	0451	0736	1.4	
	1038	1339		1.8
	1715	1936	1.0	
	2218			
18 W		0146		2.2
	0527	0806	1.4	
	1111	1415		1.9
	1750	2013	1.1	
	2259			
19 Th		0226		2.2
	0605	0840	1.4	
	1143	1453		2.0
	1828	2053	1.2	
	2343			
20 F		0309		2.1
	0646	0917	1.3	
	1216	1535		2.0
	1912	2138	1.1	
21 Sa	0032	0355		1.9
	0759	0959	1.1	
	1252	1620		2.0
	2003	2229	1.1	
22 Su ☽	0129	0447		1.7
	0826	1046	0.9	
	1332	1712		1.9
	2102	2329	1.0	
23 M ☽	0236	0546		1.5
	0930	1142	0.7	
	1422	1810		1.9
	2210			
24 Tu		0042	0.9	
	0354	0655		1.4
	1045	1249	0.6	
	1525	1917		1.9
	2322			
25 W		0214	1.0	
	0514	0814		1.3
	1204	1413	0.5	
	1640	2029		1.9
26 Th	0032	0342	1.1	
	0628	0935		1.4
	1315	1542	0.6	
	1755	2141		2.0
27 F	0134	0448	1.4	
	0731	1043		1.6
	1414	1651	0.8	
	1903	2244		2.2
28 Sa	0229	0541	1.5	
	0825	1137		1.8
	1504	1746	1.0	
	2003	2339		2.4
29 Su	0319	0628	1.7	
	0912	1224		1.9
	1549	1834	1.2	
	2057			
30 M ●		0028		2.4
	0406	0710	1.7	
	0954	1305		2.1
	1631	1917	1.3	
	2146			
31 Tu		0112		2.4
	0449	0748	1.6	
	1033	1343		2.1
	1712	1957	1.3	
	2233			

FEBRUARY

Day	Slack time	Max time	Fld (kn)	Ebb (kn)
1 W		0153		2.4
	0531	0823	1.5	
	1110	1419		2.1
	1752	2034	1.3	
	2316			
2 Th		0232		2.2
	0612	0856	1.4	
	1145	1455		2.1
	1834	2111	1.2	
	2359			
3 F		0311		2.0
	0653	0927	1.2	
	1218	1532		2.0
	1917	2149	1.1	
4 Sa	0042	0352		1.8
	0736	1000	0.9	
	1251	1611		1.8
	2004	2230	0.9	
5 Su	0127	0435		1.5
	0824	1037	0.7	
	1324	1655		1.7
	2058	2319	0.7	
6 M	0219	0524		1.3
	0921	1121	0.5	
	1401	1745		1.5
	2200			
7 Tu ☾		0022	0.6	
	0320	0622		1.1
	1031	1217	0.3	
	1447	1843		1.4
	2310			
8 W		0203	0.5	
	0431	0734		1.0
	1153	1340	0.2	
	1552	1950		1.4
9 Th	0017	0328	0.6	
	0542	0859		1.0
	1308	1526	0.3	
	1707	2101		1.5
10 F	0115	0427	0.8	
	0645	1009		1.1
	1359	1628	0.4	
	1814	2202		1.6
11 Sa	0202	0512	1.0	
	0738	1057		1.3
	1438	1711	0.6	
	1911	2251		1.8
12 Su	0242	0549	1.1	
	0822	1135		1.5
	1511	1745	0.8	
	2000	2333		2.0
13 M	0320	0620	1.2	
	0901	1208		1.7
	1542	1816	0.9	
	2045			
14 Tu		0012		2.1
	0355	0647	1.3	
	0936	1241		1.9
	1614	1847	1.1	
	2128			
15 W ○		0050		2.3
	0431	0714	1.4	
	1009	1315		2.0
	1647	1920	1.3	
	2209			
16 Th		0128		2.3
	0507	0744	1.4	
	1042	1350		2.2
	1722	1957	1.4	
	2252			
17 F		0209		2.3
	0545	0818	1.4	
	1114	1428		2.2
	1802	2037	1.5	
	2337			
18 Sa		0251		2.2
	0626	0855	1.3	
	1147	1510		2.3
	1846	2121	1.4	
19 Su	0025	0337		2.0
	0711	0936	1.2	
	1223	1555		2.2
	1936	2211	1.3	
20 M	0119	0427		1.8
	0804	1022	0.9	
	1303	1646		2.1
	2035	2308	1.1	
21 Tu	0222	0525		1.5
	0908	1117	0.7	
	1352	1744		1.9
	2145			
22 W ☽		0021	1.0	
	0336	0633		1.3
	1027	1226	0.5	
	1458	1853		1.8
	2302			
23 Th		0202	0.9	
	0455	0757		1.2
	1152	1404	0.5	
	1622	2012		1.8
24 F	0019	0333	1.0	
	0608	0926		1.3
	1307	1544	0.6	
	1745	2133		1.9
25 Sa	0126	0438	1.2	
	0711	1033		1.5
	1404	1650	0.8	
	1856	2240		2.0
26 Su	0222	0530	1.4	
	0803	1125		1.7
	1451	1741	1.1	
	1956	2333		2.2
27 M	0311	0614	1.5	
	0848	1207		1.9
	1532	1825	1.3	
	2049			
28 Tu		0019		2.3
	0354	0654	1.5	
	0927	1244		2.1
	1611	1905	1.4	
	2135			

TIME MERIDIAN 75°W

0000h is midnight, 1200h is noon.

KEY WEST, FLORIDA (0.3 nm West of Fort Taylor)

CURRENT TABLES 1995
FLOOD 022° EBB 194°

EASTERN STANDARD TIME (GMT -5H). ADD 1H DAYLIGHT SAVING APR 2 - OCT 28

MARCH

Day	Slack time	Max time	Fld knots	Ebb knots
1 W ●	0434	0058		2.3
		0728	1.5	
	1647	1318		2.1
	2218	1940	1.4	
2 Th	0511	0135		2.2
	1037	0758	1.4	
	1724	1350		2.2
	2258	2012	1.4	
3 F	0547	0209		2.1
	1108	0825	1.2	
	1801	1422		2.1
	2336	2043	1.3	
4 Sa	0624	0244		2.0
		0851	1.1	
	1138	1456		2.0
	1840	2114	1.2	
5 Su	0014	0320		1.8
	0702	0921	0.9	
	1207	1533		1.9
	1922	2150	1.0	
6 M	0054	0400		1.6
	0746	0955	0.7	
	1235	1614		1.8
	2010	2232	0.8	
7 Tu	0138	0445		1.3
	0838	1036	0.5	
	1306	1701		1.6
	2107	2323	0.7	
8 W	0944	0538		1.1
	1344	1126	0.3	
	2216	1756		1.4
9 Th ☾	0340	0032	0.5	
	1105	0643		1.0
	1446	1234	0.2	
	2330	1902		1.3
10 F	0454	0226	0.5	
	1225	0802		1.0
	1620	1417	0.2	
		2015		1.4
11 Sa	0036	0345	0.6	
	0601	0919		1.1
	1321	1548	0.4	
	1741	2125		1.5
12 Su	0129	0435	0.8	
	0657	1015		1.3
	1400	1638	0.6	
	1846	2221		1.7
13 M	0213	0514	1.0	
	0744	1058		1.6
	1435	1717	0.9	
	1940	2308		1.9
14 Tu	0253	0547	1.2	
	0824	1135		1.8
	1508	1751	1.1	
	2028	2349		2.1
15 W	0331	0616	1.3	
	0900	1210		2.0
	1542	1825	1.4	
	2114			
16 Th ○	0408	0030		2.3
		0647	1.4	
	1618	1247		2.2
	2158	1902	1.6	
17 F	0446	0110		2.3
	1009	0719	1.4	
	1656	1324		2.4
	2243	1940	1.7	
18 Sa	0526	0151		2.3
	1044	0755	1.4	
	1738	1404		2.5
	2328	2021	1.7	
19 Su	0608	0234		2.2
	1120	0834	1.3	
	1824	1447		2.4
		2106	1.6	
20 M	0017	0321		2.0
	0656	0916	1.1	
	1159	1533		2.3
	1916	2156	1.4	
21 Tu	0110	0411		1.8
	0750	1004	0.9	
	1243	1625		2.1
	2015	2254	1.2	
22 W	0211	0509		1.5
	0856	1102	0.7	
	1336	1725		1.9
	2126			
23 Th ☽)	0319	0008	1.0	
	1016	0619		1.3
	1448	1218	0.5	
	2245	1836		1.7
24 F	0433	0150	0.9	
	1141	0744		1.3
	1616	1411	0.5	
		2001		1.6
25 Sa	0005	0317	1.0	
	0542	0910		1.4
	1253	1538	0.7	
	1738	2125		1.7
26 Su	0114	0419	1.1	
	0643	1014		1.6
	1347	1639	0.9	
	1848	2231		1.9
27 M	0210	0510	1.2	
	0733	1103		1.8
	1432	1728	1.1	
	1946	2322		2.0
28 Tu	0257	0554	1.3	
	0816	1143		1.9
	1511	1810	1.3	
	2036			
29 W	0338	0004		2.1
	0854	0631	1.3	
	1547	1217		2.0
	2120	1847	1.4	
30 Th ●	0415	0041		2.1
	0929	0703	1.2	
	1622	1249		2.1
	2200	1920	1.4	
31 F	0450	0114		2.0
	1001	0729	1.1	
	1656	1319		2.1
	2238	1948	1.4	

APRIL

Day	Slack time	Max time	Fld knots	Ebb knots
1 Sa	0523	0145		2.0
	1031	0753	1.1	
	1731	1350		2.1
	2314	2015	1.3	
2 Su	0558	0218		1.9
	1059	0818	1.0	
	1807	1423		2.1
	2349	2045	1.2	
3 M	0635	0252		1.7
	1127	0847	0.8	
	1846	1500		2.0
		2118	1.1	
4 Tu	0027	0331		1.6
	0716	0922	0.7	
	1155	1540		1.8
	1931	2157	0.9	
5 W	0108	0415		1.4
	0806	1002	0.5	
	1225	1626		1.6
	2023	2244	0.8	
6 Th	0156	0505		1.2
	0906	1052	0.4	
	1304	1719		1.5
	2127	2342	0.6	
7 F	0255	0604		1.1
	1019	1154	0.3	
	1405	1821		1.4
	2238			
8 Sa ☾ (	0404	0058	0.5	
	1132	0712		1.1
	1540	1315	0.3	
	2348	1932		1.4
9 Su	0510	0233	0.6	
	1230	0823		1.2
	1708	1450	0.4	
		2043		1.5
10 M	0047	0339	0.7	
	0607	0924		1.4
	1315	1554	0.7	
	1818	2145		1.7
11 Tu	0137	0425	0.9	
	0656	1013		1.7
	1355	1641	1.0	
	1917	2237		1.9
12 W	0221	0504	1.0	
	0740	1056		1.9
	1433	1722	1.3	
	2009	2323		2.1
13 Th	0303	0540	1.2	
	0820	1137		2.2
	1512	1802	1.5	
	2058			
14 F	0344	0007		2.2
	0859	0617	1.3	
	1552	1218		2.4
	2145	1843	1.7	
15 Sa ○	0425	0051		2.3
	0938	0654	1.3	
	1634	1300		2.6
	2232	1925	1.8	
16 Su	0508	0135		2.3
	1017	0734	1.3	
	1718	1343		2.6
	2319	2008	1.8	
17 M	0554	0220		2.2
	1058	0816	1.2	
	1807	1428		2.5
		2055	1.7	
18 Tu	0008	0308		2.0
	0644	0902	1.1	
	1142	1516		2.4
	1900	2146	1.5	
19 W	0101	0400		1.8
	0741	0954	0.9	
	1232	1609		2.1
	2000	2245	1.3	
20 Th	0158	0457		1.6
	0847	1055	0.7	
	1332	1710		1.9
	2109	2358	1.0	
21 F)	0259	0605		1.4
	1003	1219	0.5	
	1446	1821		1.7
	2225			
22 Sa	0405	0129	0.9	
	1121	0724		1.4
	1608	1404	0.6	
	2344	1946		1.6
23 Su	0508	0249	0.9	
	1228	0841		1.5
	1726	1520	0.8	
		2108		1.6
24 M	0054	0352	0.9	
	0605	0943		1.6
	1322	1619	1.0	
	1833	2212		1.7
25 Tu	0151	0443	1.0	
	0655	1032		1.8
	1407	1708	1.2	
	1930	2303		1.8
26 W	0238	0526	1.0	
	0738	1112		1.9
	1446	1750	1.3	
	2019	2344		1.8
27 Th	0318	0604	1.0	
	0817	1147		2.0
	1522	1827	1.4	
	2102			
28 F	0354	0020		1.8
	0852	0635	1.0	
	1556	1218		2.0
	2141	1859	1.4	
29 Sa ●	0428	0052		1.8
	0924	0701	0.9	
	1630	1249		2.1
	2217	1927	1.4	
30 Su	0502	0122		1.8
	0955	0724	0.9	
	1704	1321		2.1
	2253	1953	1.3	

TIME MERIDIAN 75°W

0000h is midnight, 1200h is noon.

REED'S NAUTICAL ALMANAC

KEY WEST, FLORIDA (0.3 nm West of Fort Taylor)

CURRENT TABLES 1995   **FLOOD 022° EBB 194°**

EASTERN STANDARD TIME (GMT -5H).   ADD 1H DAYLIGHT SAVING APR 2 - OCT 28

MAY

Day	Slack time	Max time	Fld knots	Ebb knots
1 M	0536	0154		1.7
		0750	0.8	
	1025	1355		2.0
	1740	2021	1.2	
	2329			
2 Tu	0613	0229		1.7
		0820	0.8	
	1054	1432		2.0
	1818	2054	1.1	
3 W	0005	0307		1.6
	0653	0856	0.7	
	1124	1513		1.9
	1900	2132	1.0	
4 Th	0044	0350		1.5
	0740	0937	0.6	
	1159	1558		1.7
	1949	2215	0.9	
5 F	0127	0437		1.4
	0834	1025	0.5	
	1242	1649		1.6
	2045	2307	0.8	
6 Sa	0217	0531		1.3
	0935	1123	0.4	
	1344	1747		1.5
	2149			
7 Su (		0007	0.7	
	0314	0630		1.3
	1039	1233	0.4	
	1509	1852		1.4
	2256			
8 M		0116	0.6	
	0414	0733		1.4
	1137	1352	0.6	
	1635	2000		1.5
9 Tu	0000	0226	0.7	
	0511	0833		1.6
	1229	1505	0.8	
	1749	2105		1.6
10 W	0057	0327	0.8	
	0604	0928		1.8
	1316	1604	1.1	
	1852	2204		1.8
11 Th	0147	0418	0.9	
	0653	1018		2.1
	1400	1654	1.4	
	1949	2257		1.9
12 F	0235	0504	1.1	
	0740	1106		2.3
	1445	1741	1.6	
	2041	2346		2.1
13 Sa	0320	0548	1.2	
	0825	1152		2.5
	1529	1827	1.8	
	2131			
14 Su ○		0033		2.1
	0406	0632	1.2	
	0910	1238		2.6
	1615	1912	1.9	
	2220			
15 M		0120		2.2
	0452	0717	1.2	
	0955	1324		2.6
	1703	1959	1.9	
	2308			
16 Tu		0207		2.1
	0540	0804	1.2	
	1042	1412		2.6
	1753	2047	1.8	
	2357			
17 W		0256		2.0
	0632	0853	1.1	
	1132	1503		2.4
	1847	2138	1.6	
18 Th	0047	0348		1.9
	0729	0948	0.9	
	1226	1556		2.1
	1945	2235	1.3	
19 F	0139	0443		1.7
	0831	1051	0.8	
	1327	1655		1.9
	2049	2340	1.1	
20 Sa	0233	0544		1.6
	0939	1210	0.7	
	1436	1802		1.6
	2159			
21 Su)		0056	0.9	
	0329	0652		1.5
	1050	1338	0.7	
	1551	1919		1.5
	2313			
22 M		0211	0.8	
	0426	0801		1.5
	1155	1452	0.8	
	1704	2037		1.4
23 Tu	0023	0315	0.7	
	0520	0902		1.6
	1250	1552	0.9	
	1810	2143		1.5
24 W	0123	0409	0.7	
	0610	0954		1.7
	1338	1643	1.1	
	1907	2236		1.5
25 Th	0213	0455	0.8	
	0656	1038		1.8
		1727	1.2	
	1956	2320		1.6
26 F	0256	0535	0.8	
	0738	1115		1.9
	1458	1806	1.3	
	2040	2358		1.6
27 Sa	0333	0608	0.8	
	0816	1149		2.0
	1533	1840	1.3	
	2120			
28 Su		0031		1.6
	0408	0636	0.8	
	0851	1222		2.0
	1608	1909	1.3	
	2158			
29 M ●		0102		1.6
	0442	0701	0.7	
	0925	1256		2.0
	1643	1936	1.3	
	2234			
30 Tu		0135		1.6
	0517	0728	0.7	
	0958	1332		2.0
	1718	2003	1.2	
	2310			
31 W		0209		1.6
	0553	0759	0.7	
	1031	1409		2.0
	1756	2034	1.2	
	2346			

JUNE

Day	Slack time	Max time	Fld knots	Ebb knots
1 Th		0246		1.6
	0631	0835	0.7	
	1105	1450		1.9
	1836	2110	1.1	
2 F	0022	0327		1.6
	0713	0916	0.7	
	1144	1534		1.8
	1920	2150	1.0	
3 Sa	0100	0411		1.5
	0800	1002	0.6	
	1231	1622		1.7
	2010	2236	0.9	
4 Su	0141	0459		1.5
	0853	1055	0.6	
	1330	1716		1.6
	2106	2327	0.8	
5 M	0227	0552		1.5
	0950	1157	0.6	
	1444	1816		1.5
	2209			
6 Tu (		0025	0.7	
	0319	0649		1.6
	1049	1307	0.7	
	1604	1921		1.5
	2314			
7 W		0128	0.7	
	0415	0749		1.7
	1147	1422	0.9	
	1720	2028		1.5
8 Th	0017	0234	0.7	
	0514	0848		1.9
	1241	1531	1.1	
	1829	2133		1.6
9 F	0116	0336	0.8	
	0610	0945		2.1
	1333	1631	1.4	
	1930	2233		1.8
10 Sa	0209	0433	0.9	
	0705	1039		2.3
	1423	1725	1.6	
	2025	2327		1.9
11 Su	0300	0526	1.0	
	0758	1131		2.5
	1512	1815	1.8	
	2117			
12 M ○		0018		2.0
	0349	0617	1.1	
	0850	1221		2.6
	1601	1903	1.9	
	2207			
13 Tu		0107		2.1
	0438	0706	1.2	
	0941	1310		2.6
	1651	1951	1.9	
	2254			
14 W		0155		2.1
	0527	0755	1.2	
	1032	1400		2.5
	1741	2038	1.8	
	2341			
15 Th		0243		2.0
	0617	0846	1.1	
	1124	1450		2.4
	1832	2126	1.6	
16 F	0027	0331		2.0
	0710	0939	1.0	
	1218	1541		2.2
	1926	2216	1.3	
17 Sa	0113	0421		1.9
	0806	1037	0.9	
	1315	1635		1.9
	2023	2310	1.1	
18 Su	0200	0514		1.7
	0907	1143	0.8	
	1417	1734		1.6
	2126			
19 M)		0010	0.8	
	0248	0610		1.6
	1010	1300	0.8	
	1523	1840		1.4
	2233			
20 Tu		0118	0.7	
	0338	0710		1.6
	1114	1414	0.8	
	1632	1952		1.3
	2343			
21 W		0227	0.6	
	0430	0812		1.6
	1215	1519	0.8	
	1737	2104		1.2
22 Th	0049	0329	0.5	
	0522	0910		1.6
	1308	1615	0.9	
	1837	2204		1.3
23 F	0146	0421	0.5	
	0613	1001		1.7
	1354	1703	1.1	
	1930	2254		1.3
24 Sa	0233	0506	0.6	
	0700	1045		1.8
	1435	1745	1.1	
	2017	2335		1.4
25 Su	0312	0544	0.6	
	0744	1124		1.9
	1513	1822	1.2	
	2059			
26 M		0011		1.5
	0348	0616	0.7	
	0825	1200		1.9
	1549	1854	1.2	
	2138			
27 Tu ●		0044		1.6
	0423	0643	0.7	
	0903	1236		2.0
	1624	1921	1.3	
	2214			
28 W		0116		1.6
	0456	0711	0.7	
	0940	1312		2.0
	1659	1947	1.3	
	2249			
29 Th		0149		1.7
	0530	0742	0.8	
	1016	1350		2.0
	1735	2016	1.2	
	2323			
30 F		0224		1.7
	0605	0817	0.8	
	1054	1429		2.0
	1813	2048	1.2	
	2356			

FLORIDA

TIME MERIDIAN 75°W   0000h is midnight, 1200h is noon.

KEY WEST, FLORIDA (0.3 nm West of Fort Taylor)

CURRENT TABLES 1995 **FLOOD 022° EBB 194°**

EASTERN STANDARD TIME (GMT -5H).   ADD 1H DAYLIGHT SAVING APR 2 - OCT 28

JULY

Day	Slack time	Max time	Fld knots	Ebb knots
1 Sa		0302		1.7
	0643	0856	0.9	
	1135	1511		1.9
	1854	2125	1.1	
2 Su	0029	0343		1.7
	0725	0939	0.9	
	1221	1557		1.8
	1939	2206	1.0	
3 M	0104	0427		1.7
	0813	1029	0.9	
	1316	1648		1.7
	2030	2252	0.9	
4 Tu	0144	0517		1.7
	0907	1126	0.8	
	1422	1744		1.5
	2128	2344	0.8	
5 W ☾	0230	0612		1.8
	1008	1232	0.9	
	1537	1847		1.4
	2235			
6 Th		0045	0.7	
	0325	0712		1.8
	1111	1347	0.9	
	1655	1956		1.4
	2344			
7 F		0153	0.6	
	0429	0815		1.9
	1214	1507	1.1	
	1808	2108		1.5
8 Sa	0051	0306	0.7	
	0536	0919		2.1
	1313	1617	1.3	
	1912	2215		1.6
9 Su	0151	0414	0.8	
	0641	1020		2.3
	1408	1715	1.6	
	2010	2314		1.8
10 M	0245	0515	1.0	
	0741	1117		2.4
	1500	1807	1.7	
	2102			
11 Tu		0006		1.9
	0335	0609	1.1	
	0838	1209		2.5
	1550	1855	1.8	
	2150			
12 W ○		0055		2.0
	0423	0659	1.2	
	0931	1259		2.6
	1639	1940	1.8	
	2235			
13 Th		0140		2.1
	0509	0747	1.3	
	1023	1347		2.5
	1727	2024	1.7	
	2318			
14 F		0224		2.1
	0556	0834	1.3	
	1114	1434		2.4
	1814	2106	1.5	
	2359			
15 Sa		0307		2.1
	0644	0921	1.2	
	1204	1521		2.1
	1903	2148	1.3	
16 Su	0040	0351		2.0
	0734	1010	1.1	
	1255	1609		1.9
	1953	2231	1.1	
17 M	0120	0436		1.8
	0828	1104	0.9	
	1349	1659		1.6
	2048	2317	0.8	
18 Tu	0201	0524		1.7
	0926	1207	0.8	
	1447	1755		1.4
	2149			
19 W ☽		0011	0.6	
	0246	0618		1.6
	1029	1324	0.7	
	1551	1859		1.2
	2259			
20 Th		0120	0.4	
	0336	0718		1.5
	1134	1440	0.7	
	1658	2013		1.1
21 F	0012	0241	0.4	
	0432	0822		1.5
	1235	1544	0.8	
	1802	2127		1.1
22 Sa	0118	0348	0.4	
	0531	0924		1.6
	1328	1638	0.9	
	1900	2226		1.2
23 Su	0209	0440	0.5	
	0628	1017		1.7
	1413	1723	1.0	
	1950	2311		1.3
24 M	0250	0523	0.6	
	0719	1101		1.8
	1453	1802	1.1	
	2034	2349		1.4
25 Tu	0325	0558	0.7	
	0804	1141		1.9
	1529	1834	1.2	
	2113			
26 W		0022		1.6
	0358	0627	0.8	
	0847	1218		2.0
	1605	1902	1.3	
	2149			
27 Th ●		0053		1.7
	0430	0654	0.9	
	0926	1254		2.1
	1639	1926	1.3	
	2223			
28 F		0125		1.8
	0502	0724	1.0	
	1005	1331		2.1
	1714	1953	1.3	
	2254			
29 Sa		0158		1.9
	0535	0758	1.1	
	1044	1409		2.1
	1750	2023	1.3	
	2325			
30 Su		0234		1.9
	0611	0835	1.1	
	1125	1450		2.1
	1829	2058	1.2	
	2355			
31 M		0314		2.0
	0651	0917	1.1	
	1211	1534		1.9
	1911	2137	1.1	

AUGUST

Day	Slack time	Max time	Fld knots	Ebb knots
1 Tu	0028	0357		2.0
	0737	1004	1.1	
	1302	1622		1.8
	2000	2220	1.0	
2 W	0105	0445		1.9
	0832	1059	1.0	
	1404	1717		1.6
	2057	2311	0.8	
3 Th ☾	0149	0539		1.9
	0934	1203	1.0	
	1516	1820		1.4
	2206			
4 F		0012	0.6	
	0246	0641		1.9
	1044	1322	1.0	
	1634	1932		1.3
	2322			
5 Sa		0125	0.6	
	0357	0750		1.9
	1154	1453	1.1	
	1749	2050		1.3
6 Su	0036	0251	0.6	
	0516	0902		2.0
	1300	1609	1.2	
	1856	2203		1.5
7 M	0139	0411	0.8	
	0629	1009		2.2
	1358	1708	1.5	
	1953	2303		1.7
8 Tu	0232	0513	1.0	
	0733	1109		2.3
	1451	1759	1.6	
	2043	2354		1.9
9 W	0320	0605	1.2	
	0831	1201		2.4
	1540	1844	1.7	
	2128			
10 Th ○		0038		2.1
	0405	0652	1.3	
	0923	1249		2.5
	1626	1925	1.7	
	2210			
11 F		0120		2.2
	0448	0735	1.4	
	1012	1333		2.4
	1710	2003	1.6	
	2249			
12 Sa		0159		2.2
	0530	0816	1.4	
	1059	1415		2.3
	1753	2039	1.4	
	2325			
13 Su		0237		2.2
	0613	0856	1.3	
	1144	1456		2.1
	1836	2113	1.2	
14 M	0001	0315		2.1
	0658	0937	1.2	
	1229	1538		1.9
	1921	2148	1.0	
15 Tu	0036	0356		1.9
	0746	1020	1.0	
	1316	1622		1.6
	2009	2226	0.8	
16 W	0111	0439		1.8
	0840	1109	0.8	
	1407	1710		1.3
	2106	2310	0.5	
17 Th ☽	0150	0528		1.6
	0941	1213	0.6	
	1506	1808		1.1
	2214			
18 F		0006	0.4	
	0237	0626		1.5
	1049	1347	0.6	
	1613	1918		1.0
	2334			
19 Sa		0132	0.2	
	0340	0733		1.4
	1158	1509	0.6	
	1722	2042		1.0
20 Su	0048	0313	0.3	
	0452	0845		1.4
	1258	1608	0.8	
	1824	2152		1.1
21 M	0143	0414	0.4	
	0559	0948		1.6
	1347	1656	0.9	
	1917	2241		1.3
22 Tu	0222	0459	0.6	
	0656	1038		1.7
	1429	1735	1.1	
	2002	2320		1.5
23 W	0256	0535	0.7	
	0746	1119		1.9
	1506	1807	1.2	
	2042	2353		1.6
24 Th	0327	0605	0.9	
	0830	1157		2.0
	1541	1834	1.2	
	2117			
25 F ●		0024		1.8
	0358	0633	1.1	
	0912	1233		2.1
	1616	1859	1.3	
	2149			
26 Sa		0056		2.0
	0429	0703	1.2	
	0952	1310		2.2
	1651	1926	1.3	
	2220			
27 Su		0130		2.1
	0503	0737	1.3	
	1032	1348		2.2
	1727	1956	1.3	
	2250			
28 M		0206		2.2
	0540	0814	1.4	
	1114	1429		2.1
	1805	2031	1.2	
	2321			
29 Tu		0245		2.2
	0621	0856	1.4	
	1200	1512		2.0
	1848	2110	1.1	
	2355			
30 W		0329		2.2
	0708	0943	1.3	
	1251	1600		1.8
	1936	2154	1.0	
31 Th	0032	0417		2.1
	0803	1037	1.2	
	1349	1655		1.6
	2036	2246	0.8	

TIME MERIDIAN 75°W

0000h is midnight, 1200h is noon.

REED'S NAUTICAL ALMANAC

KEY WEST, FLORIDA (0.3 nm West of Fort Taylor)

CURRENT TABLES 1995

FLOOD 022° EBB 194°

EASTERN STANDARD TIME (GMT -5H).   ADD 1H DAYLIGHT SAVING APR 2 - OCT 28

SEPTEMBER

Day	Slack time	Max time	Fld knots	Ebb knots
1 F	0118	0513		1.9
	0909	1142	1.0	
	1459	1759		1.4
	2149	2349	0.6	
2 Sa (	0220	0618		1.8
	1023	1307	0.9	
	1616	1915		1.3
	2311			
3 Su		0113	0.5	
	0342	0733		1.8
	1140	1447	1.0	
	1731	2040		1.3
4 M	0027	0256	0.6	
	0508	0853		1.9
	1250	1601	1.2	
	1836	2154		1.5
5 Tu	0129	0413	0.8	
	0624	1004		2.0
	1350	1657	1.3	
	1931	2251		1.7
6 W	0219	0510	1.1	
	0728	1103		2.2
	1442	1745	1.5	
	2019	2337		2.0
7 Th	0303	0558	1.3	
	0824	1152		2.3
	1528	1827	1.5	
	2101			
8 F O		0018		2.1
	0344	0640	1.5	
	0913	1236		2.3
	1610	1904	1.5	
	2139			
9 Sa		0055		2.2
	0424	0719	1.5	
	0959	1315		2.3
	1651	1938	1.4	
	2215			
10 Su		0130		2.2
	0503	0754	1.5	
	1041	1353		2.2
	1729	2008	1.3	
	2248			
11 M		0204		2.2
	0542	0829	1.4	
	1122	1429		2.0
	1808	2037	1.1	
	2320			
12 Tu		0239		2.1
	0622	0903	1.3	
	1202	1506		1.8
	1849	2108	0.9	
	2352			
13 W		0317		2.0
	0706	0939	1.1	
	1243	1546		1.6
	1933	2142	0.7	
14 Th	0023	0358		1.8
	0755	1021	0.9	
	1328	1632		1.4
	2026	2223	0.5	
15 F	0056	0445		1.6
	0852	1113	0.7	
	1421	1724		1.2
	2133	2315	0.3	

Day	Slack time	Max time	Fld knots	Ebb knots
16 Sa)	0138	0540		1.4
	1000	1226	0.5	
	1526	1829		1.0
	2253			
17 Su		0026	0.2	
	0244	0646		1.3
	1114	1417	0.5	
	1636	1949		1.0
18 M	0012	0226	0.2	
	0412	0802		1.3
	1221	1529	0.6	
	1741	2106		1.1
19 Tu	0107	0341	0.4	
	0529	0912		1.5
	1315	1620	0.8	
	1837	2200		1.3
20 W	0146	0428	0.6	
	0632	1008		1.7
	1359	1659	0.9	
	1923	2241		1.5
21 Th	0220	0505	0.8	
	0725	1052		1.8
	1438	1731	1.1	
	2003	2316		1.8
22 F	0252	0537	1.1	
	0811	1132		2.0
	1514	1759	1.2	
	2039	2350		2.0
23 Sa	0324	0608	1.3	
	0855	1210		2.2
	1550	1827	1.3	
	2112			
24 Su ●		0025		2.2
	0358	0641	1.5	
	0937	1248		2.2
	1626	1857	1.3	
	2145			
25 M		0101		2.3
	0434	0717	1.6	
	1020	1328		2.2
	1704	1930	1.3	
	2217			
26 Tu		0139		2.4
	0513	0756	1.6	
	1104	1410		2.2
	1744	2007	1.2	
	2251			
27 W		0220		2.4
	0556	0839	1.6	
	1150	1454		2.0
	1829	2048	1.1	
	2328			
28 Th		0305		2.3
	0645	0926	1.5	
	1241	1543		1.8
	1920	2134	0.9	
29 F	0010	0355		2.2
	0742	1021	1.3	
	1338	1638		1.6
	2023	2229	0.7	
30 Sa	0101	0453		2.0
	0849	1127	1.1	
	1444	1743		1.4
	2138	2338	0.5	

OCTOBER

Day	Slack time	Max time	Fld knots	Ebb knots
1 Su (	0210	0600		1.8
	1006	1257	0.9	
	1556	1902		1.3
	2301			
2 M		0117	0.5	
	0338	0721		1.7
	1126	1435	0.9	
	1707	2028		1.4
3 Tu	0016	0300	0.6	
	0505	0846		1.7
	1238	1545	1.1	
	1809	2138		1.6
4 W	0114	0407	0.9	
	0619	0958		1.9
	1338	1639	1.2	
	1903	2231		1.8
5 Th	0202	0500	1.2	
	0721	1054		2.0
	1429	1725	1.3	
	1949	2315		2.0
6 F	0244	0545	1.4	
	0814	1140		2.1
	1513	1805	1.3	
	2029	2353		2.1
7 Sa	0323	0625	1.5	
	0900	1220		2.1
	1553	1840	1.2	
	2106			
8 Su O		0028		2.2
	0400	0701	1.5	
	0943	1256		2.1
	1630	1911	1.2	
	2140			
9 M		0100		2.2
	0436	0733	1.5	
	1022	1330		2.0
	1706	1937	1.1	
	2212			
10 Tu		0133		2.2
	0513	0803	1.4	
	1100	1403		1.9
	1742	2003	1.0	
	2242			
11 W		0207		2.1
	0551	0833	1.3	
	1137	1438		1.7
	1820	2033	0.8	
	2311			
12 Th		0243		2.0
	0631	0906	1.1	
	1215	1516		1.6
	1903	2107	0.7	
	2341			
13 F		0323		1.8
	0716	0944	1.0	
	1255	1559		1.4
	1953	2148	0.5	
14 Sa	0013	0409		1.6
	0808	1030	0.8	
	1343	1649		1.2
	2054	2237	0.4	
15 Su	0053	0502		1.5
	0911	1128	0.6	
	1440	1748		1.1
	2208	2341	0.3	

Day	Slack time	Max time	Fld knots	Ebb knots
16 M)	0156	0604		1.3
	1022	1246	0.5	
	1545	1857		1.1
	2321			
17 Tu		0109	0.2	
	0329	0715		1.3
	1132	1424	0.5	
	1650	2008		1.2
18 W	0019	0249	0.4	
	0454	0827		1.4
	1232	1527	0.7	
	1747	2108		1.4
19 Th	0102	0346	0.6	
	0602	0929		1.6
	1322	1611	0.8	
	1835	2155		1.6
20 F	0140	0429	0.9	
	0700	1020		1.8
	1405	1647	1.0	
	1918	2237		1.9
21 Sa	0216	0507	1.2	
	0750	1104		1.9
	1445	1721	1.1	
	1957	2316		2.1
22 Su	0252	0543	1.5	
	0837	1146		2.1
	1524	1754	1.2	
	2034	2355		2.3
23 M ●	0330	0621	1.7	
	0923	1228		2.2
	1603	1829	1.3	
	2111			
24 Tu		0035		2.5
	0410	0700	1.8	
	1008	1310		2.2
	1644	1907	1.3	
	2149			
25 W		0116		2.6
	0452	0742	1.8	
	1053	1354		2.1
	1727	1948	1.2	
	2228			
26 Th		0200		2.5
	0538	0826	1.7	
	1141	1440		2.0
	1815	2032	1.1	
	2311			
27 F		0248		2.4
	0629	0915	1.6	
	1231	1530		1.8
	1909	2122	0.9	
	2359			
28 Sa		0339		2.2
	0726	1010	1.4	
	1326	1625		1.7
	2012	2220	0.7	
29 Su	0057	0437		2.0
	0832	1116	1.1	
	1426	1729		1.5
	2125	2334	0.6	
30 M (	0209	0545		1.7
	0947	1241	0.9	
	1530	1844		1.4
	2243			
31 Tu		0117	0.6	
	0333	0706		1.6
	1106	1410	0.9	
	1635	2003		1.5
	2354			

FLORIDA

TIME MERIDIAN 75°W

0000h is midnight, 1200h is noon.

1995 CARIBBEAN

KEY WEST, FLORIDA (0.3 nm West of Fort Taylor)

CURRENT TABLES 1995

FLOOD 022° EBB 194°

EASTERN STANDARD TIME (GMT -5H). ADD 1H DAYLIGHT SAVING APR 2 - OCT 28

NOVEMBER

Day	Slack time	Max time	Fld knots	Ebb knots
1 W	0455, 1220, 1735	0246, 0832, 1519, 2111	0.7, 0.9	1.6, 1.6
2 Th	0052, 0607, 1322, 1827	0351, 0943, 1615, 2205	1.0, 1.0	1.7, 1.8
3 F	0141, 0708, 1413, 1914	0443, 1039, 1702, 2249	1.2, 1.0	1.8, 1.9
4 Sa	0223, 0800, 1457, 1955	0529, 1124, 1742, 2327	1.4, 1.0	1.8, 2.1
5 Su	0302, 0845, 1535, 2032	0609, 1203, 1817	1.5, 1.0	1.9
6 M	0338, 0926, 1611, 2107	0001, 0644, 1237, 1846	1.5, 1.0	2.1, 1.8
7 Tu O	0414, 1004, 1646, 2139	0033, 0715, 1309, 1911	1.4, 0.9	2.2, 1.8
8 W	0449, 1040, 1721, 2210	0106, 0743, 1341, 1937	1.4, 0.8	2.1, 1.7
9 Th	0525, 1115, 1758, 2241	0140, 0810, 1415, 2007	1.3, 0.8	2.1, 1.7
10 F	0603, 1151, 1838, 2312	0216, 0841, 1452, 2041	1.2, 0.7	2.0, 1.6
11 Sa	0645, 1229, 1924, 2346	0256, 0917, 1533, 2121	1.0, 0.6	1.9, 1.5
12 Su	0731, 1310, 2017	0340, 0958, 1619, 2208	0.9, 0.5	1.7, 1.4
13 M	0028, 0826, 1357, 2118	0429, 1047, 1711, 2304	0.7, 0.4	1.6, 1.3
14 Tu	0126, 0929, 1451, 2222	0525, 1145, 1809	0.6	1.4, 1.3
15 W ☽	0247, 1036, 1549, 2322	0012, 0629, 1253, 1911	0.4, 0.6	1.3, 1.3
16 Th	0413, 1141, 1647	0133, 0738, 1405, 2012	0.5, 0.6	1.4, 1.5
17 F	0013, 0528, 1239, 1741	0250, 0844, 1507, 2107	0.7, 0.7	1.5, 1.7
18 Sa	0059, 0632, 1329, 1830	0348, 0944, 1557, 2157	1.0, 0.8	1.6, 2.0
19 Su	0142, 0728, 1415, 1915	0436, 1036, 1642, 2243	1.3, 0.9	1.8, 2.2
20 M	0224, 0819, 1459, 2000	0521, 1124, 1725, 2328	1.5, 1.1	1.9, 2.4
21 Tu	0307, 0908, 1542, 2044	0604, 1210, 1807	1.7, 1.2	2.1
22 W ●	0351, 0956, 1627, 2128	0013, 0647, 1255, 1850	1.9, 1.2	2.6, 2.1
23 Th	0437, 1043, 1713, 2214	0059, 0732, 1341, 1936	1.9, 1.2	2.7, 2.1
24 F	0525, 1130, 1802, 2303	0146, 0818, 1428, 2023	1.8, 1.1	2.6, 2.1
25 Sa	0616, 1218, 1856, 2356	0235, 0907, 1518, 2115	1.7, 1.0	2.5, 1.9
26 Su	0712, 1308, 1956	0326, 1000, 1611, 2214	1.4, 0.9	2.3, 1.8
27 M	0055, 0813, 1401, 2102	0423, 1059, 1709, 2325	1.2, 0.7	2.0, 1.7
28 Tu	0203, 0922, 1457, 2212	0527, 1210, 1814	0.9	1.7, 1.6
29 W ☾	0318, 1036, 1554, 2322	0055, 0641, 1331, 1925	0.7, 0.8	1.5, 1.6
30 Th	0435, 1151, 1652	0220, 0803, 1444, 2033	0.8, 0.7	1.4, 1.6

DECEMBER

Day	Slack time	Max time	Fld knots	Ebb knots
1 F	0024, 0546, 1258, 1746	0327, 0918, 1544, 2131	0.9, 0.7	1.4, 1.7
2 Sa	0117, 0648, 1354, 1835	0423, 1018, 1635, 2220	1.1, 0.8	1.5, 1.8
3 Su	0202, 0741, 1440, 1920	0510, 1106, 1719, 2301	1.2, 0.8	1.6, 1.9
4 M	0243, 0827, 1519, 2001	0553, 1147, 1756, 2338	1.3, 0.8	1.6, 2.0
5 Tu	0320, 0908, 1555, 2039	0629, 1221, 1828	1.4, 0.8	1.6
6 W O	0356, 0946, 1629, 2114	0011, 0701, 1253, 1854	1.4, 0.8	2.0, 1.7
7 Th	0431, 1022, 1703, 2148	0045, 0729, 1323, 1920	1.3, 0.8	2.1, 1.7
8 F	0506, 1056, 1738, 2221	0119, 0755, 1356, 1948	1.3, 0.8	2.1, 1.7
9 Sa	0542, 1131, 1815, 2255	0155, 0823, 1431, 2022	1.2, 0.7	2.1, 1.6
10 Su	0620, 1205, 1855, 2332	0234, 0855, 1509, 2059	1.1, 0.7	1.9, 1.6
11 M	0701, 1240, 1939	0315, 0931, 1550, 2142	1.0, 0.7	1.8, 1.5
12 Tu	0013, 0748, 1317, 2029	0400, 1013, 1636, 2231	0.9, 0.6	1.7, 1.5
13 W	0105, 0841, 1359, 2125	0451, 1100, 1726, 2329	0.8, 0.6	1.6, 1.5
14 Th	0212, 0941, 1446, 2225	0548, 1154, 1821	0.7	1.4, 1.5
15 F ☽	0332, 1048, 1541, 2324	0036, 0652, 1256, 1921	0.6, 0.6	1.4, 1.6
16 Sa	0451, 1153, 1641	0152, 0800, 1403, 2021	0.7, 0.6	1.4, 1.8
17 Su	0020, 0603, 1254, 1741	0306, 0907, 1509, 2120	1.0, 0.7	1.5, 2.0
18 M	0112, 0706, 1348, 1838	0409, 1009, 1608, 2215	1.2, 0.8	1.6, 2.2
19 Tu	0202, 0802, 1438, 1933	0503, 1104, 1702, 2307	1.5, 1.0	1.8, 2.4
20 W	0250, 0854, 1526, 2025	0553, 1155, 1752, 2357	1.7, 1.1	1.9, 2.6
21 Th ●	0338, 0943, 1612, 2116	0639, 1243, 1841	1.9, 1.2	2.1
22 F	0426, 1029, 1659, 2207	0046, 0725, 1330, 1929	1.9, 1.3	2.7, 2.1
23 Sa	0514, 1115, 1748, 2258	0135, 0811, 1416, 2018	1.9, 1.3	2.7, 2.1
24 Su	0604, 1200, 1838, 2351	0224, 0857, 1503, 2108	1.7, 1.2	2.5, 2.1
25 M	0656, 1244, 1932	0314, 0944, 1551, 2202	1.5, 1.1	2.3, 2.0
26 Tu	0047, 0751, 1330, 2031	0406, 1034, 1642, 2303	1.2, 0.9	2.0, 1.9
27 W	0147, 0851, 1417, 2134	0502, 1130, 1736	0.9	1.8, 1.7
28 Th ☾	0253, 0959, 1508, 2242	0017, 0606, 1237, 1837	0.8, 0.7	1.5, 1.6
29 F	0404, 1114, 1602, 2349	0141, 0720, 1355, 1943	0.8, 0.5	1.3, 1.6
30 Sa	0514, 1228, 1658	0256, 0841, 1507, 2050	0.8, 0.5	1.2, 1.6
31 Su	0050, 0620, 1333, 1754	0358, 0950, 1607, 2148	0.9, 0.5	1.2, 1.7

TIME MERIDIAN 75°W

0000h is midnight, 1200h is noon.

BAHAMAS

COAST PILOT

CAUTION: Our information on aids to navigation comes from official government sources. The latitudes and longitudes of these marks may not correspond to the readings from GPS or LORAN receivers. Some aids have been reported as unreliable, missing, off position, or showing incorrect characteristics. No single aid to navigation, or waypoint, should be relied upon as a sole means of fixing your position.

NOTE: The chartlets in this section are <u>not</u> <u>intended for navigation</u> and are incuded for reference and planning purposes only. While chartlets reproduced from government sources are from the most current editions as of press time, they incorporate <u>no corrections</u> to navigational aids, depths, or hazards since the edition publication date.

ENTRY PROCEDURES

Vessels may clear in with customs at the following Ports of Entry: on New Providence Island, Nassau; in the Abacos, Walkers Cay, Green Turtle Cay, Treasure Cay, Marsh Harbour, and Sandy Point; on Grand Bahama, Freeport Harbour, Bell Channel, and West End; on Great Bahama Bank, Alice Town (North Bimini) and Cat Cay; in the Berry Islands, Great Harbour Cay and Chub Cay; on Andros, Andros Harbour, Fresh Creek, and Congo Town; on Eleuthera, Governor's Harbour, Rock Sound, Hatchet Bay, Spanish Wells, and Harbour Island; in the Exumas, Georgetown; on Cat Island, Smith's Bay; on San Salvador, Cockburn Town; on Long Island, Stella Maris; and on Great Inagua Island, Matthew Town.

You should have proof of ownership of your boat. Vessels may remain in the Bahamas for up to one year duty free; duty exemptions may be granted for additional years upon application; application fees are $500 a year. Vessels between 30 and 100 feet long and less than 150 gross tons that remain in the Bahamas longer than three years are subject to a 7.5% duty and 1% stamp tax; duty rates and stamp taxes vary

for vessels of other sizes. Vessels that have temporary cruising permits may bring in equipment and repair materials duty free. All firearms must be declared. For more information, contact customs headquarters in Nassau (809-325-6551 or -326-4401).

Immigration requires a passport or original birth certificate and photo identification for each person. The immigration officer may use discretion in determining the period of stay, but in any event, no stays may exceed eight months. For more information, call immigration headquarters in Nassau (809-322-7530).

Fishing licenses for the boat are obtained when you clear customs. Licenses are $20 per vessel for the duration of your stay or $150 per calendar year. There are stiff fines for fishing without a license. For more information on fishing rules and regulations, as well as a fishing guide, contact the Bahamas Sports and Aviation Office in Florida (800-327-7678).

The official currency is the Bahamian dollar, which is on par with the U.S. dollar. The language spoken is English.

WEST END AND LITTLE BAHAMA BANK

MEMORY ROCK LIGHT, 26 56.8N, 79 06.8W. Fl W 3s, 37ft, 11M. Metal tower.
INDIAN CAY LIGHT, 26 43.0N, 79 00.1W. Fl W 6s, 40ft, 8M. Aluminum tower.
SETTLEMENT POINT LIGHT, 26 41.5N, 78 59.9W. Fl W 4s, 44ft, 6M. White steel tower.
LITTLE SALE CAY LIGHT, 27 02.5N, 78 10.5W. Fl W 3s, 47ft, 9M. Metal tower. Unreliable.

WEST END

26 42N, 78 59W
Emergencies: Call the Bahamas Air Sea Rescue Association (BASRA) on VHF channels 16 or 22 or on 2182kHz. The Nassau headquarters can be reached at 809-325-8864 (809-322-3877 after hours).
Port of Entry: Customs is located in the yacht basin, near the marina docks. You may tie up in the marina and walk to the office.

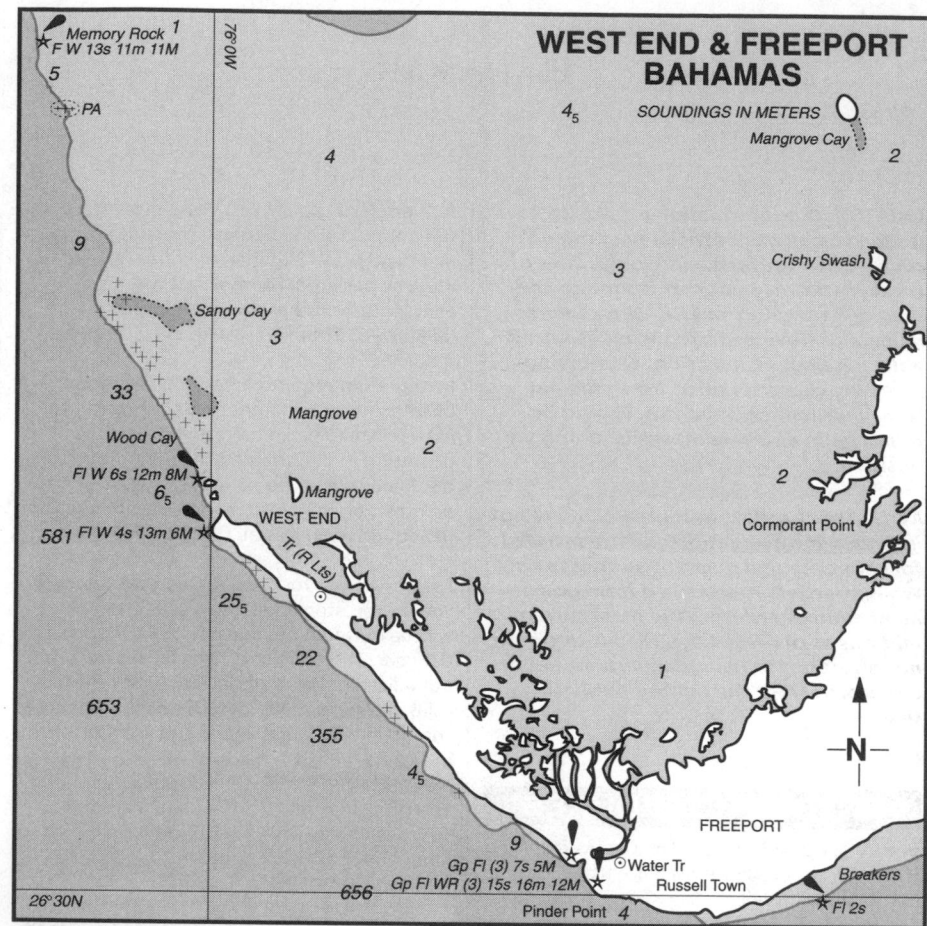

West End and Freeport Approaches, soundings in meters

Dockage: Available at the Jack Tar Marina in the Yacht Basin. The marina monitors VHF channel 16. Entering the marina after dark may be difficult.

Anchorage: Possible between North Point and Settlement Point. This is a good anchorage if arriving after dark. Most vessels anchor outside the channel into the marina.

Services: Fuel and water are available. Some groceries available in town. More extensive supplies are available in Freeport.

This is a convenient port of entry for many vessels traveling to the northern Bahamas. At night the tall television tower makes a good leading light. Approaching the marina, the first channel to the south is for the commercial harbor. The second channel leads into the marina. The passages onto the Little Bahama Bank are very shoal here. Depths of less than 5 feet have been reported in the channel north of Indian Cay. Deeper draft boats should enter the bank near Memory Rock.

WALKERS CAY

27 16N, 78 24W

Emergencies: Call the Bahamas Air Sea Rescue Association (BASRA) on VHF channels 16 or 22 or on 2182kHz. The Nassau headquarters can be reached at 809-325-8864 (809-322-3877 after hours).

Port of Entry: The marina can contact customs, who may be at the airstrip.

Dockage: Walkers Cay Marina (from the U.S., 800-432-2092, or locally, VHF channels 16 and 68) encompasses the protected basin on the

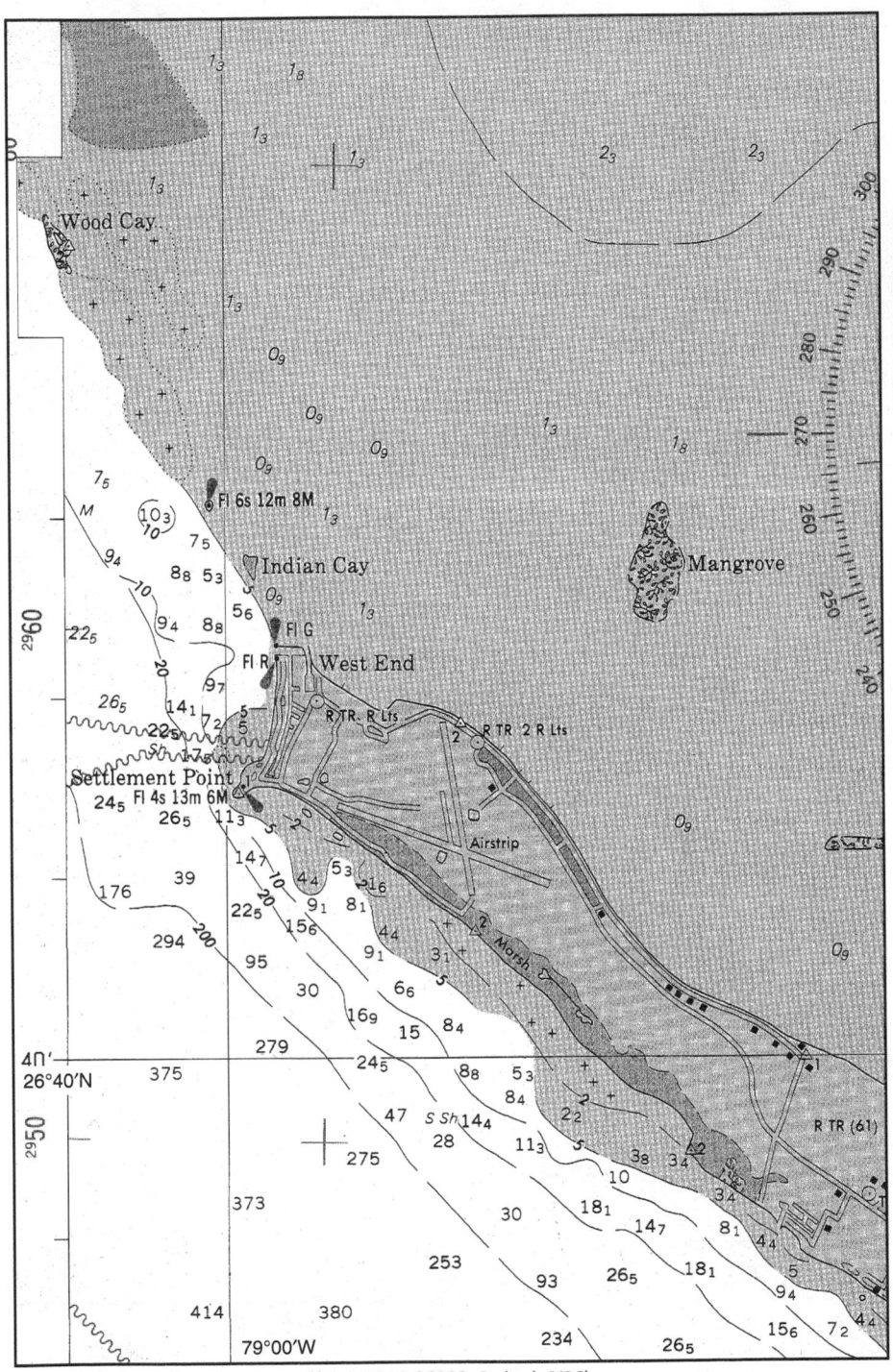

West End, soundings in meters *(from DMA 26323, 3rd ed, 8/86)*

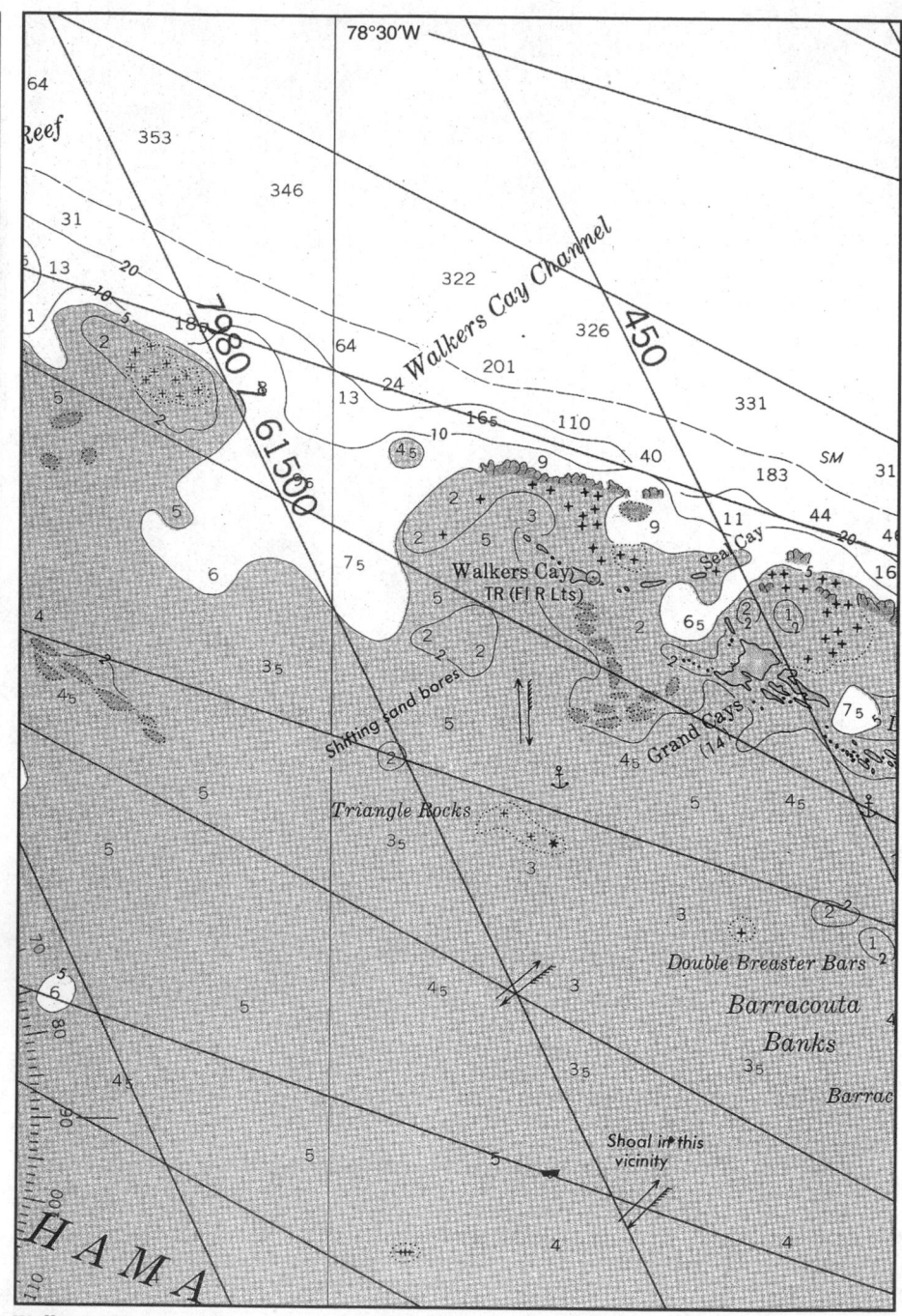

Walkers Cay, soundings in meters *(from DMA 26300, 6th ed, 7/81)*

GAMEFISH OF THE BAHAMAS

The following table will give you a general idea of the fishing prospects in the Bahamas. Check with Bahamian officials for the latest bag limits and other restrictions.

E = Excellent   G = Good   F = Fair   O = Occasional   N = None

	Jan	Feb	Mar	Apr	May	June	July	Aug	Sept	Oct	Nov	Dec
Blue Marlin	O	O	G	G	E	E	E	G	F	O	O	O
White Marlin	O	F	G	E	E	G	F	F	F	F	F	O
Sailfish	F	F	G	E	G	F	F	O	O	F	F	F
Swordfish	F	F	F	F	G	E	E	E	E	F	F	F
Dolphin	F	F	G	E	G	F	F	G	G	G	F	F
Wahoo	E	E	E	F	O	O	O	O	O	F	E	E
Kingfish	F	F	F	F	F	G	G	F	F	F	F	F
Mackeral	G	G	E	E	F	F	F	F	F	F	F	F
Allison Tuna	O	O	E	E	E	E	F	O	O	O	O	O
Blackfin Tuna	F	F	F	F	G	F	F	F	O	F	F	F
Bluefin Tuna	N	N	O	G	E	N	N	N	N	N	N	N
Bonito	F	F	F	E	G	E	E	F	N	F	F	F
Bonefish	G/E	G/E	E	E	G/E	G/E	G/E	G/E	G/E	G/E	G/E	G/E
Permit	F	F	G	E	E	E	E	G	F	F	G	G
Tarpon	O	O	O	F	E	G	F	F	O	O	O	O
Amberjack	F	F	E	E	E	E	F	E	F	F	F	F
Grouper	E	E	G	G	G	G	G	G	G	G	G	G
Snapper	G	G	G	E	E	E	E	E	E	G	G	G
Barracuda	G	G	G	G	G	E	E	G	G	G	G	G
Shark	G	G	G	E	E	E	G	G	G	G	G	G

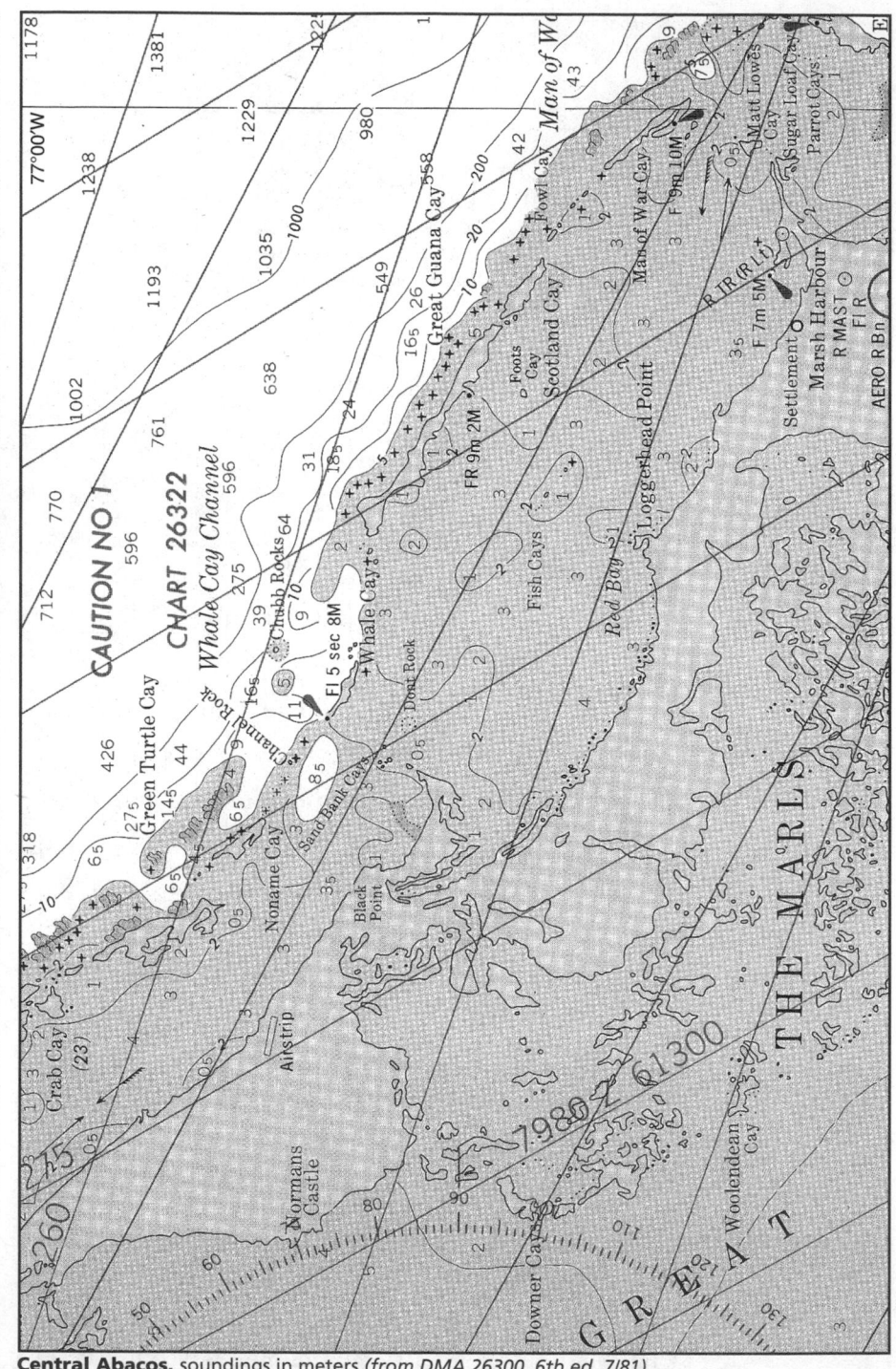

Central Abacos, soundings in meters *(from DMA 26300, 6th ed, 7/81)*

south side of the island. Dock space fills quickly during fishing tournaments, and reservations are advised.

Anchorage: There may be some room to anchor west of the western breakwater forming the marina. This area is shallow.

Services: Fuel, water, fishing supplies, and some limited groceries are available. The resort has accommodations and a restaurant.

This island and resort are dedicated to sport fishing. The entry channel is very shoal and shifting. Stakes are moved to mark the deep water, but an approach in good light is recommended. Approach depths have been reported as less than 5 feet from the banks side.

GREAT ABACO

CRAB CAY LIGHT, Angel Fish Point, 26 55.6N, 77 36.3W. Fl W 5s, 33ft, 8M. Metal tower.

GREEN TURTLE CAY

26 46N, 77 20W

Emergencies: Call the Bahamas Air Sea Rescue Association (BASRA) on VHF channels 16 or 22 or on 2182kHz. The Nassau headquarters can be reached at 809-325-8864 (809-322-3877 after hours).

Port of Entry

Dockage: In White Sound there is the Bluff House Marina (809-365-4247) and the Green Turtle Club (809-365-4271 or -4272). The Other Shore Club (809-365-4195) and Abaco Yacht Services (809-365-4033) are located in Black Sound. All marinas monitor VHF channel 16.

Anchorage: Good anchorage is available in both Black Sound and White Sound. Some boats anchor west of New Plymouth or in shallow Settlement Creek to the east of town.

Services: Fuel, water, electricity, showers, and repairs are available. There are haulout facilities in Black Sound. Plymouth has a good selection of shops and restaurants.

WHALE CAY LIGHT, Western point, 26 42.9N, 77 14.8W. Fl W 5s, 40ft, 8M. Black and aluminum structure.

WHALE CAY PASS

26 42N, 77 14W

Emergencies: Call the Bahamas Air Sea Rescue Association (BASRA) on VHF channels 16 or 22 or on 2182kHz. The Nassau headquarters can be reached at 809-325-8864 (809-322-3877 after hours).

CAUTION: This is a dangerous passage during periods of heavy onshore seas and winds. These conditions are known locally as a "rage." Large vessels have been capsized during these conditions.

A marked ship channel used by cruise ships leads in the direction of Guana Cay. Several large spoil banks have been created south of the channel from dredged material. The shallow "Don't Rock Passage" leads across the banks inside of Whale Cay, but is very poorly defined. Depths are reported to be less than 3 feet.

TREASURE CAY

26 40N, 77 17W

Emergencies: Call the Bahamas Air Sea Rescue Association (BASRA) on VHF channels 16 or 22 or on 2182kHz. The Nassau headquarters can be reached at 809-325-8864 (809-322-3877 after hours).

Port of Entry

Dockage: Treasure Cay Marina (809-367-2570 or VHF channel 16; in the U.S., 800-327-1584) offers luxurious dockage with all amenities.

Anchorage: Anchor outside of the channel before reaching the marina. There may be some moorings available for rent.

Services: Fuel, water, and basic supplies are available. The resort attached to the marina has a restaurant and a few shops.

GREAT GUANA CAY LIGHT, 26 39.8N, 77 06.8W. F W, 30ft, 2M. White pole.
MARSH HARBOR, N side, 26 33.1N, 77 03.4W. Fl W 4s, 23ft, 5M. White mast.
MAN OF WAR CAY LIGHT, 26 35.2N, 77 00.0W. Q W, 30ft, 5M. White pole.

MARSH HARBOUR

26 33N, 77 03W

Port of Entry: Use the government wharf at the western end of the harbor. A separate channel leads to the wharf.

Dockage: Several marinas offer dockage: Boat Harbour Marina (809-367-2736), Conch Inn Marina (809-367-4000), Harbour View Marina and D & E Boat Rentals (809-367-2182 or -2117), Marsh Harbour Marina (809-367-2700), Triple J Marina (809-367-2163), and Admiral Yacht Haven (809-367-2765). All marinas monitor VHF channel 16.

Anchorage: Anchor anywhere depths permit without blocking the marked channels.

Services: All services available. Nearby Man of War Cay has haulout facilities. This is the

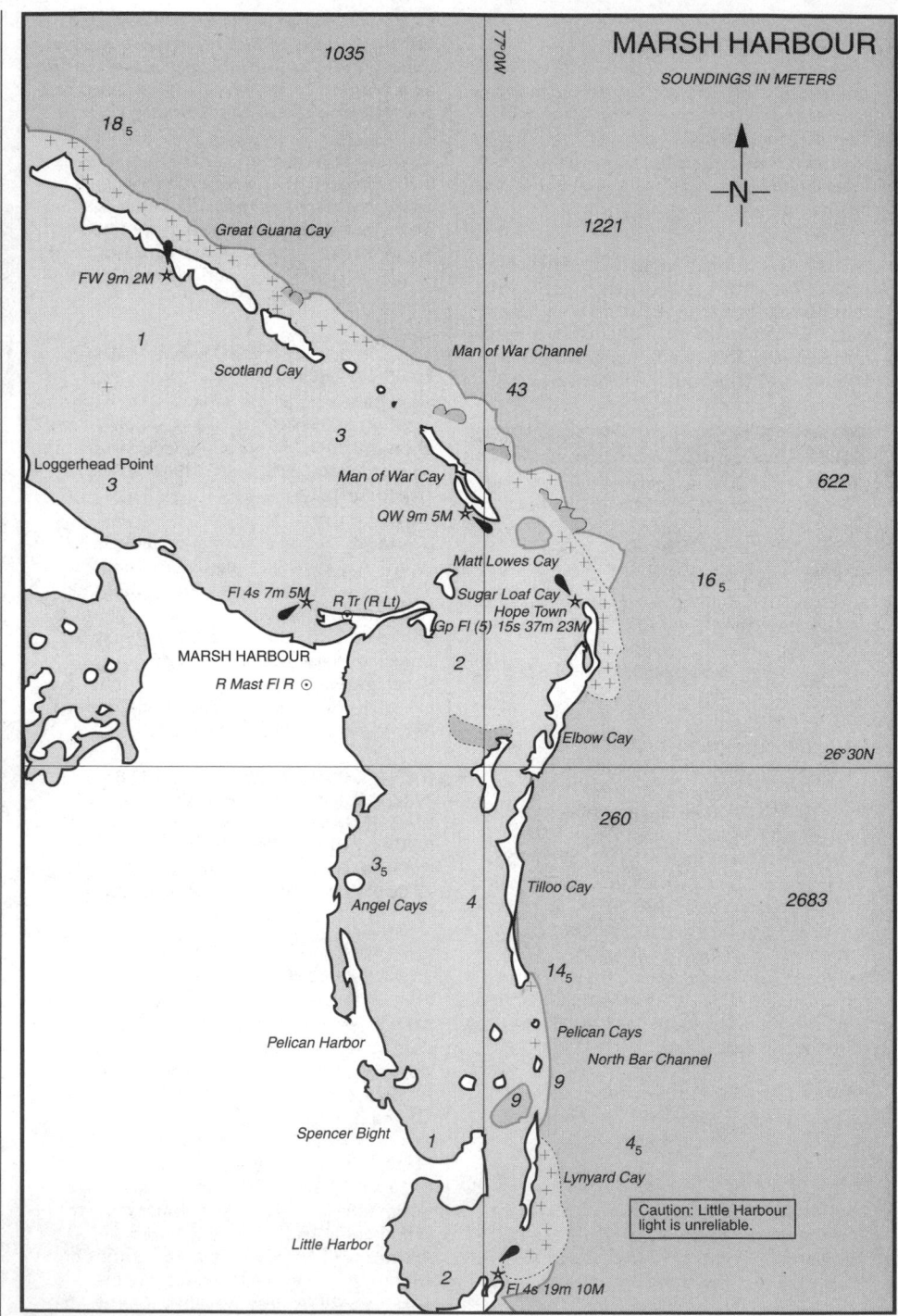

MARSH HARBOUR

SOUNDINGS IN METERS

—N—

1035

77°W

18₅

Great Guana Cay

FW 9m 2M ★

1221

Scotland Cay

Man of War Channel

43

1

3

Man of War Cay

622

Loggerhead Point

3

QW 9m 5M ★

Matt Lowes Cay

16₅

Fl 4s 7m 5M ★ R Tr (R Lt)

Sugar Loaf Cay
Hope Town
Gp Fl (5) 15s 37m 23M

MARSH HARBOUR

R Mast Fl R ⊙

2

Elbow Cay

26°30N

260

3₅

Angel Cays

4

Tilloo Cay

2683

14₅

Pelican Harbor

Pelican Cays
North Bar Channel

9

9

Spencer Bight

1

4₅

Lynyard Cay

Caution: Little Harbour
light is unreliable.

Little Harbor

2

Fl 4s 19m 10M

Marsh Harbour Area, soundings in meters

commercial center of the Abacos and is your best port for major stocking of groceries, doing laundry, obtaining parts, receiving mail, and making travel arrangements. Fresh water is available in large quantities.

Marsh Harbour is one of the largest towns in the Bahamas. There is also a good selection of shops, restaurants, and nightlife ashore.

MAN OF WAR CAY

26 35N, 77 00W
Emergencies: Call the Bahamas Air Sea Rescue Association (BASRA) on VHF channels 16 or 22 or on 2182kHz. The Nassau headquarters can be reached at 809-325-8864 (809-322-3877 after hours).
Dockage: Contact Man-O-War Marina (809-365-6008 or VHF channel 16). They are located in the western arm of the harbor. Approach depths are reported to be about 5 feet.
Anchorage: A popular anchorage is in Eastern Harbour. There may be some moorings available here. It may be possible to anchor among the moored boats in the main harbor to the west. Beware of shoal spots.
Services: All boat services are available. This is one of the best places for major repairs in the Bahamas. There are haulout facilities and services for major repairs of all sorts. The boatyards are expert in wood repairs, and there is a sail loft and a well-stocked hardware store. Most groceries are available, although the selection is not as great as in Marsh Harbour.

ELBOW CAY LIGHT (Hope Town), 26 32.4N, 76 58.0W. Fl (5) W 15s, 120ft, 23M. White tower, red bands, white lantern.

HOPE TOWN

26 33N, 76 58W
Emergencies: Call the Bahamas Air Sea Rescue Association (BASRA) on VHF channels 16 or 22 or on 2182kHz. The Nassau headquarters can be reached at 809-325-8864 (809-322-3877 after hours).
Dockage: Contact Hope Town Marina (809-366-0003; fax, -366-0254) or Lighthouse Marina (809-366-0154). The marinas monitor VHF channel 16. Approach depths have been reported as about 5 feet at low tide.
Moorings: A profusion of moorings now cover most of Hope Town harbor. Contact Hope Town Marina.
Anchorage: It may be possible to find room among the moored boats, but be prepared for poor holding and limited swinging room.

Services: Fuel, water, and a good selection of groceries are available. There is a bakery and several restaurants.

SANDY CAY BEACON, 26 24.0N, 76 59.1W. Fl G 3s. Beacon.
LITTLE HARBOR LIGHT, S side of entrance, 26 19.7N, 76 59.6W. Fl W 4s, 61ft, 10M. White building.

LITTLE HARBOUR

26 20N, 77 00W
Emergencies: Call the Bahamas Air Sea Rescue Association (BASRA) on VHF channels 16 or 22 or on 2182kHz. The Nassau headquarters can be reached at 809-325-8864 (809-322-3877 after hours).
Moorings: Contact Pete's Pub at the dock on the western side of the harbor. The channel depths have been reported to be 3 to 4 feet.
Anchorage: Anchor off the docks or wherever depths allow.
Services: Meals and drinks are available at Pete's Pub. No other services are available.

This is the location of the famous Johnston Studios, where the late Randolph Johnston created his famous lost-wax-process bronzes. Bronzes and jewelry are sold at the studios. This harbor is well sheltered in most weather, but the entrance channel is quite shoal. The pass from the ocean is tricky and should be attempted only in good light. If conditions are not ideal, North Bar Channel is a better pass.

CHEROKEE SOUND LIGHT, on Duck Cay, 26 16.0N, 77 04.0W. F R, 29ft, 6M. White stone building. Visible 229°–094° except where obscured to the east by the high land of Cherokee Point.
ABACO LIGHT, HOLE IN THE WALL, 25 51.5N, 77 11.2W. Fl W 10s, 168ft, 23M. White tower, red top, white lantern.
ROCKY POINT LIGHT, 25 59.9N, 77 24.3W. Fl W 6s, 33ft, 10M. Black metal framework.
SANDY POINT LIGHT, 26 01.6N, 77 24.0W. F W, 25ft, 5M. Pole.
CHANNEL CAY LIGHT, 26 15.0N, 77 37.8W. Fl W 2.5s, 38ft, 7M. Black steel lattice structure.

GRAND BAHAMA ISLAND

SWEETINGS CAY LIGHT, 26 36.7N, 77 54.0W. Fl W 6s, 23ft, 8M. Black tower.
RIDING POINT AVIATION LIGHT, 26 42.7N, 78 09.5W. Oc R 3s, 269ft. Red and white tower.

SOUTH RIDING POINT HARBOR RANGE (Front Light), 26 37.5N, 78 13.1W. Oc G 3s, 39ft. Orange triangle on framework tower. **(Rear Light),** 60 meters, 340° from front. Oc G 3s, 52ft. Orange diamond on framework tower.
COMMUNICATIONS TOWER LIGHTS, 26 37.7N, 78 14.3W. 2 F R, 239ft. Red and white tower; lights in vertical line on tower.
PLATFORM LIGHT, 26 36.8N, 78 13.7W. Fl R 3s. Control building. Two Q R lights on east and west dolphins.
HIGH ROCK LIGHT, S side of Grand Bahama, 26 37.3N, 78 16.1W. F W, 25ft, 6M. White pole.
IONOSPHERIC TOWER AVIATION LIGHT, 26 37.1N, 78 18.8W. F R, Oc R 8s, 210ft.
BASSETT COVE TOWER AVIATION LIGHT, 26 36.8N, 78 19.4W. Q R, 2 F R, 407ft. Red and white tower; lights in vertical line.
BORE SITE TOWER AVIATION LIGHT, 26 36.7N, 78 20.9W. F W, 2 F R, Oc R 4s, 174ft. Red and white tower; lights in vertical line.
GRAND LUCAYAN WATERWAY LIGHT, W breakwater head, 26 32.4N, 78 33.4W. Fl (3) G 10s, 13ft, 3M. Concrete column.
GRAND LUCAYAN WATERWAY LIGHT, E breakwater head, 26 32.4N, 78 33.3W. Fl (3) R 10s, 13ft, 3M. Concrete column.
BAHAMIA MARINA LIGHT, Xanadu Marina, E breakwater head, 26 29.3N, 78 42.1W. Q R, 3M. Concrete pedestal.
BAHAMIA MARINA LIGHT, Xanadu Marina, W breakwater head, 26 29.3N, 78 42.2W. Q G, 3M. Concrete pedestal.

XANADU, RUNNING MON, OCEAN REEF, LUCAYA

26 29N 78 42W
Emergencies: Call the Bahamas Air Sea Rescue Association (BASRA) on VHF channels 16 or 22 or on 2182kHz. The Nassau headquarters can be reached at 809-325-8864 (809-322-3877 after hours).
Ports of Entry: Pleasure boats may clear at Xanadu in the first marked channel east of Freeport. You may also clear at the two marinas in the Bell Channel area.
Harbormasters: Contact Xanadu (809-352-6782), Running Mon Hotel and Marina (809-352-6834), Ocean Reef Resort (809-373-4662), Port Lucaya (809-373-9090), and Lucayan Marina (809-373-8888) on VHF channel 16.
Dockage: Available at all of the marinas mentioned above; Lucayan Marina's docks are undergoing major renovation, which is expected to be completed by December 1994.

Services: All services available in this area. A short bus or taxi ride will take you to Freeport proper. Many tourist shops and restaurants are located near the marinas.

The first marked channel east of Freeport leads to Xanadu marina. This area is listed as Bahamia Marina on the charts. A little farther east is the entrance to Running Mon Marina; the entrance to the Ocean Reef Club is about 2.2 miles farther east at about 78 39.6W. The waterway labeled Bell Channel is the home of the Port Lucaya and Lucayan marinas. The entrance to the Lucayan Waterway is located about 5 miles east of the Bell Channel. The waterway provides a protected inside route to the Little Bahama Bank for those who can clear a 27-foot fixed bridge. Controlling depth is reported to be about 4 or 5 feet.

FREEPORT INTERNATIONAL AIRPORT AVIATION LIGHT, 26 32.9N, 78 42.3W. Alt W G 10s, 98ft, 40M.
FREEPORT LIGHT, Pinder Point, 26 30.4N, 78 45.9W. Fl (3) W R 15s, 54ft, 12M. White structure; black bands. W 301°–113°, R 113°–301°. Occasional. Reported obscured to seaward by jetties and ships.
BORCO OIL TERMINAL LIGHT, NO 1, jetty SE end, 26 30.0N, 78 46.2W. Q W.
BORCO OIL TERMINAL LIGHT, NO 1, jetty NW end, 26 30.3N, 78 46.7W. Fl (3) W 7s, 5M. Dolphin.
BORCO OIL TERMINAL LIGHT, NO 2, jetty NW end, 26 30.5N, 78 46.7W. Q W. Dolphin.
FREEPORT WEST BREAKWATER LIGHT, 26 31.1N, 78 46.7W. Fl W 4s, 23ft, 2M. Metal structure.
FREEPORT CHANNEL ENTRANCE, W side, 26 31.2N, 78 46.6W. Fl G 4s, 12ft, 2M. Metal structure.
FREEPORT CHANNEL ENTRANCE, E side, 26 31.2N, 78 46.5W. Fl R 4s, 12ft, 2M. Metal structure.

FREEPORT

26 31N 78 47W
Emergencies: Call the Bahamas Air Sea Rescue Association (BASRA) on VHF channels 16 or 22 or on 2182kHz. The Nassau headquarters can be reached at 809-325-8864 (809-322-3877 after hours).
Port of Entry: Vessels may clear customs here, although the harbor is oriented to large commercial vessels. Pleasure boats usually clear at one of the marinas east of Freeport.

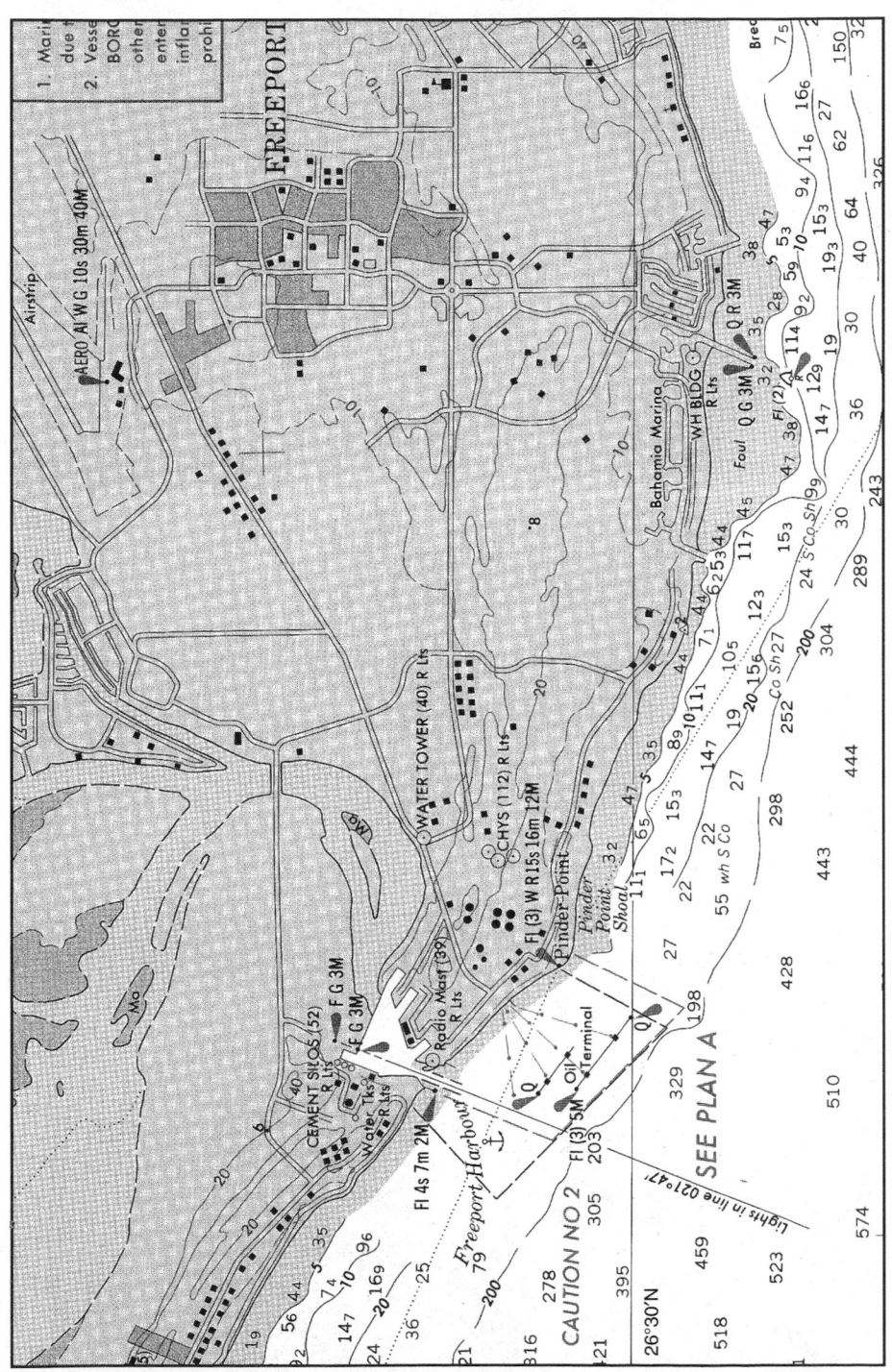

Freeport and Xanadu, soundings in meters *(from DMA 26323, 3rd ed, 8/86)*

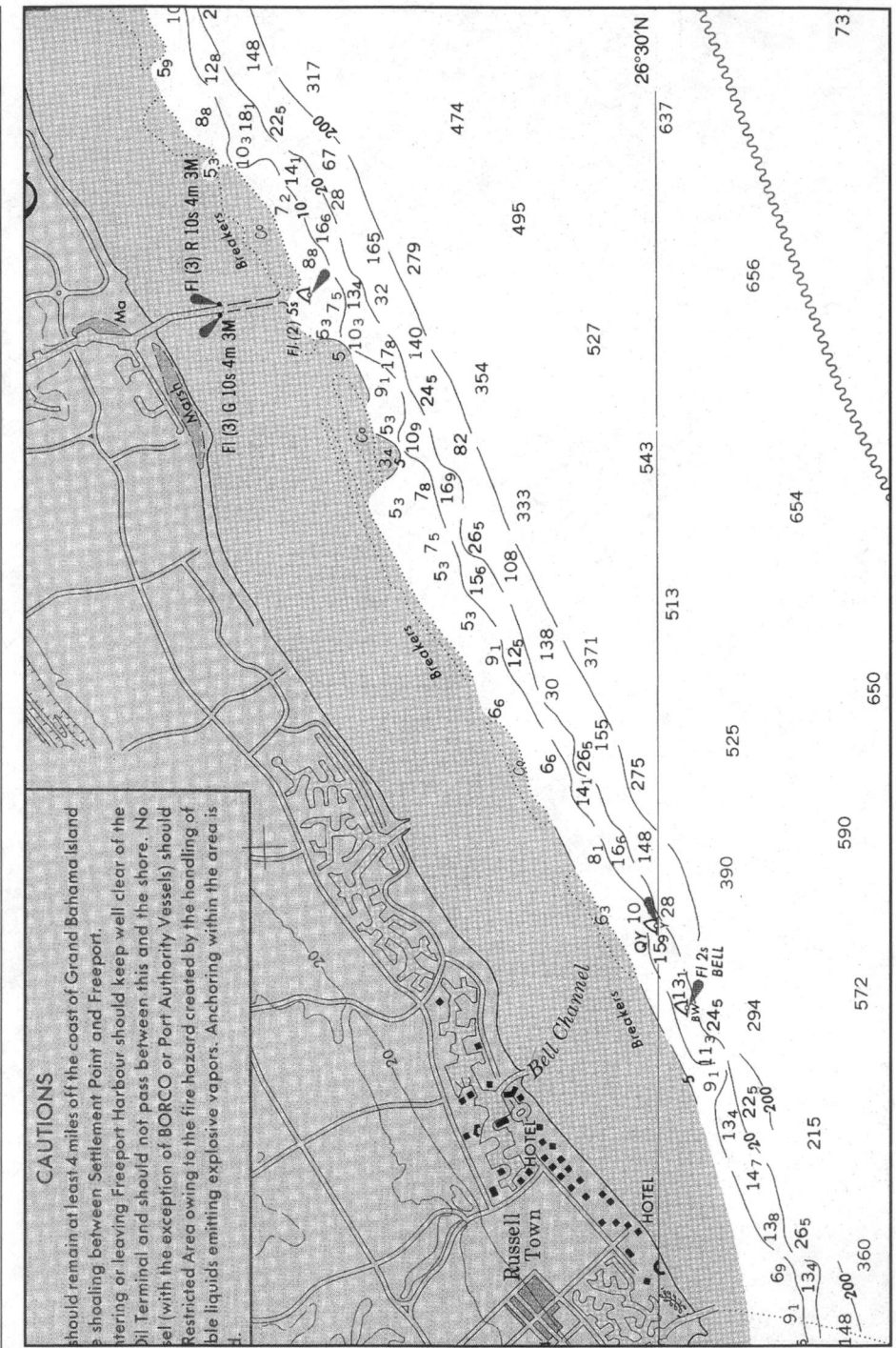

Bell Channel, soundings in meters *(from DMA 26323, 3rd ed, 8/86)*

Freeport Harbour Control: Call on VHF channel 16 when approaching the harbor.
Dockage: Contact Freeport Harbour Control for details. Most pleasure boats dock at one of the marinas to the east of Freeport.
Anchorage: None in the harbor.
Services: Fuel and water are available at the marinas to the east. Freeport has a good selection of supplies, including a variety of tourist oriented shops. The town is located well to the northeast of the harbor and will be a cab ride away for most boaters.

Freeport is one of the leading commercial harbors in the Bahamas. Large cruise ships, cargo vessels, and oil tankers call here.

PINDER POINT RANGE (Front Light),
26 31.5N, 78 46.4W. F G, 26ft, 3M. Orange and white diamond-shaped daymark on beacon. **(Rear Light),** 255 meters, 021°47′ from front. 26 31.6N, 78 46.4W. F G, 45ft, 3M. Orange and white diamond-shaped daymark on beacon.
SETTLEMENT POINT LIGHT, 26 41.5N, 78 59.9W. Fl W 4s, 44ft, 6M. White steel tower.

BIMINI AND CAT CAY APPROACHES

GREAT ISAAC LIGHT, 26 01.8N, 79 05.4W. Fl W 15s, 152ft, 23M. White tower.
NORTH ROCK LIGHT, 1.9 km N of North Bimini, 25 48.2N, 79 16.7W. Fl W 3s, 40ft, 8M. White skeleton steel tower. Visible 022°–343°.
NORTH BIMINI ISLAND LIGHT, head of wharf, 25 43.7N, 79 19.1W. F W, 20ft, 5M. Gray steel framework tower. Two F R range lights indicate channel through reef on South Bimini. These lights are considered unreliable.
BIMINI AVIATION LIGHT, 25 42.5N, 79 16.3W. Mo (B) R 20s, 284ft, 23M. Steel framework tower.

BIMINI

25 43N, 79 18W
Emergencies: Call the Bahamas Air Sea Rescue Association (BASRA) on VHF channels 16 or 22 or on 2182kHz. The Nassau headquarters can be reached at 809-325-8864 (809-322-3877 after hours).
Port of Entry: You may clear customs after securing your boat in a marina. Check with the dockmaster for the location of customs.
Dockage: Contact Bimini Blue Water (809-347-3166 or VHF channel 68), Bimini Big Game

Fishing Club and Hotel (809-347-3391 or VHF channels 16 and 9), or Weech's Bimini Dock (809-347-3028). Care should be taken when approaching any slip because of the strong currents running through the harbor.
Anchorage: Good anchorage is available off of the marina docks. Be careful not to block access to the marinas or the seaplane ramp. There are strong currents, and the bottom shoals rapidly to the east and north.
Services: Fuel, water, groceries, liquor, hardware, and some marine supplies are available.

Bimini is only 45 miles from Miami and makes a convenient first port of call for boaters. The entrance channel is frequently shifted to follow the deepest water. A range on the South Bimini beach directs boaters over the bar. The channel then parallels the beach running north into the harbor. If in any doubt, call one of the marinas on the VHF radio for directions. It is best to arrive with good light, when the shoals will be most visible.

GUN CAY LIGHT, 25 34.5N, 79 18.8W. Fl W 10s, 80ft, 23 M. Tower, upper red, lower white. Obscured by Bimini between 176° and 198° when 8 miles distant.

GUN CAY CAT CAY

25 34N, 79 18W
Emergencies: Call the Bahamas Air Sea Rescue Association (BASRA) on VHF channels 16 and 22 or on 2182kHz. The Nassau headquarters can be reached at 809-325-8864 or -322-3877.
Port of Entry: Clear customs at the docks on the east side of North Cat Cay. The Cay Cay Yacht Club dockmaster (VHF channel 16) will contact customs for you.
Dockage: The docks of the Cat Cay Yacht Club (305-359-8272 or VHF channel 16), which were heavily damaged by Hurricane Andrew, are now totally restored.
Anchorage: The best anchorages are on either side of Gun Cay, depending upon the weather. Honeymoon Harbor, on the north end of Gun Cay, is another favorite spot, but be careful not to get caught in a north wind.
Services: Fuel, water, electricity, a commissary, liquor, and a restaurant are available at the Cat Cay Yacht Club.

Transients may use the yacht club marina and restaurant for a 24-hour period, but otherwise are not allowed on the island. This is a good

COAST PILOT

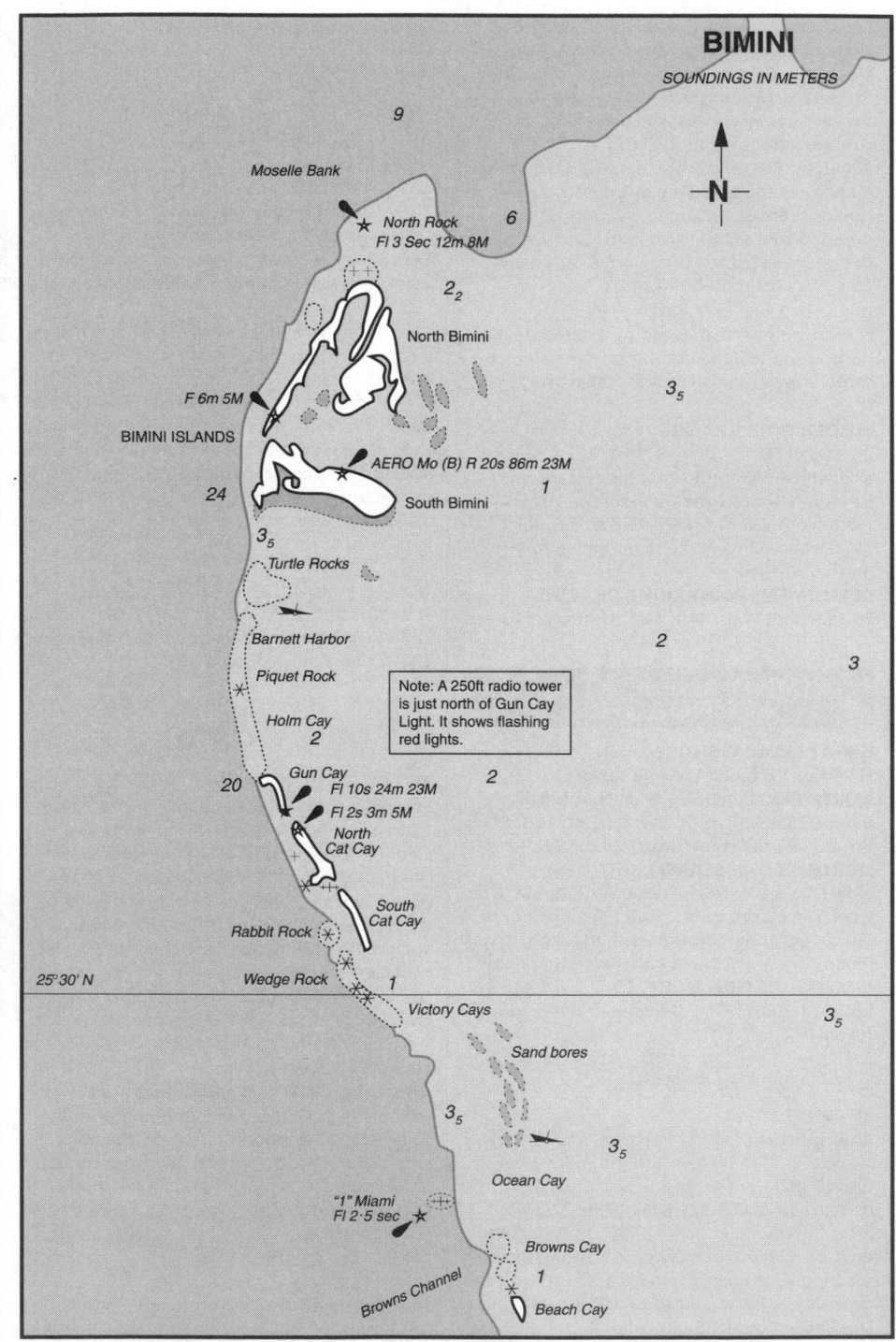

BIMINI

SOUNDINGS IN METERS

—N—

9

Moselle Bank

6

★ *North Rock*
Fl 3 Sec 12m 8M

2₂

North Bimini

3₅

F 6m 5M

BIMINI ISLANDS

AERO Mo (B) R 20s 86m 23M

1

South Bimini

24

3₅

Turtle Rocks

Barnett Harbor

2

3

Piquet Rock

Holm Cay 2

Note: A 250ft radio tower
is just north of Gun Cay
Light. It shows flashing
red lights.

Gun Cay
Fl 10s 24m 23M

20

2

Fl 2s 3m 5M

*North
Cat Cay*

*South
Cat Cay*

Rabbit Rock

25°30' N

Wedge Rock

1

Victory Cays

3₅

Sand bores

3₅

3₅

Ocean Cay

"1" Miami
Fl 2·5 sec

Browns Cay

1

Browns Channel

Beach Cay

Bimini and Cat Cay Approaches, soundings in meters

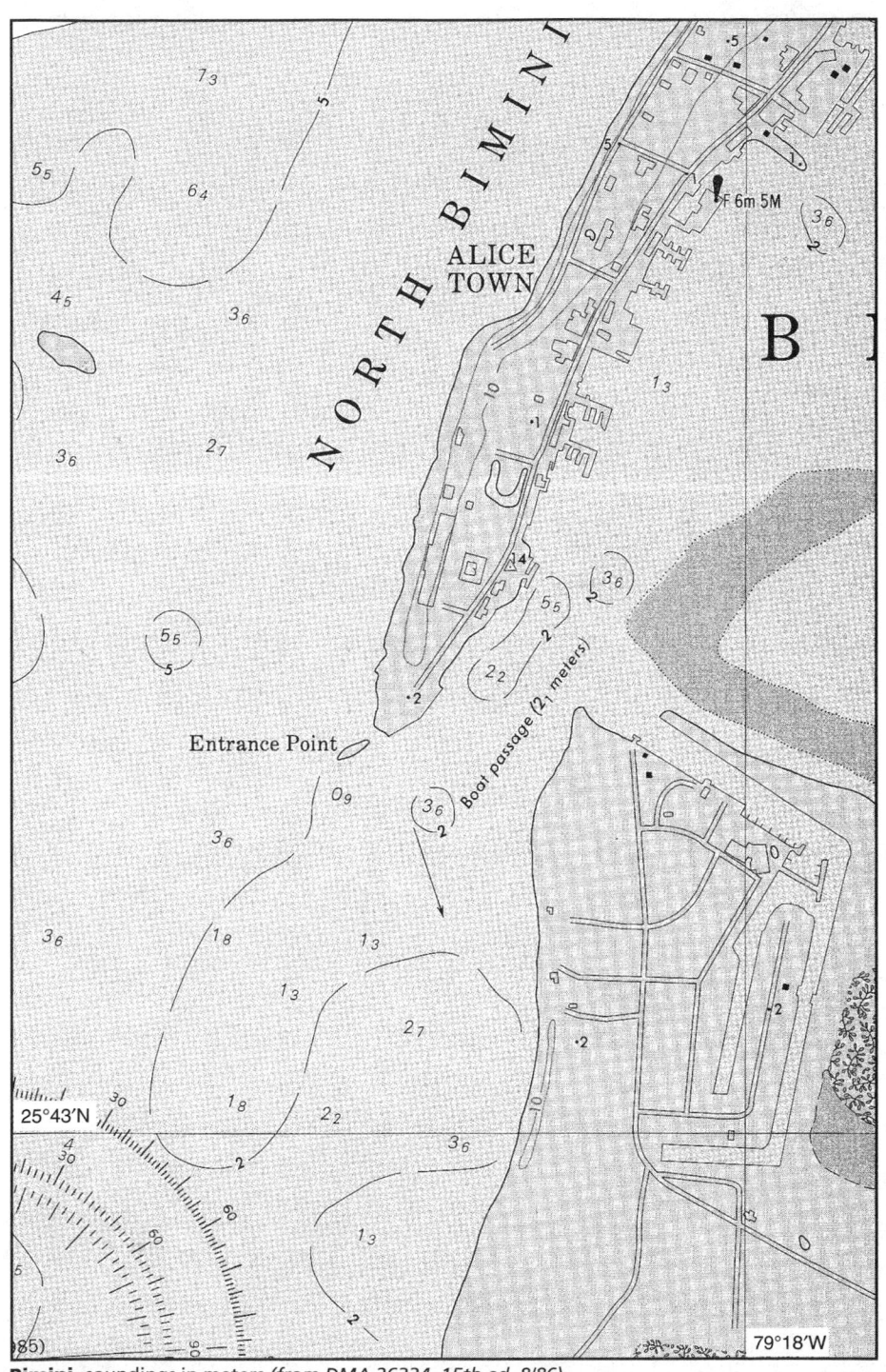

Bimini, soundings in meters *(from DMA 26324, 15th ed, 8/86)*

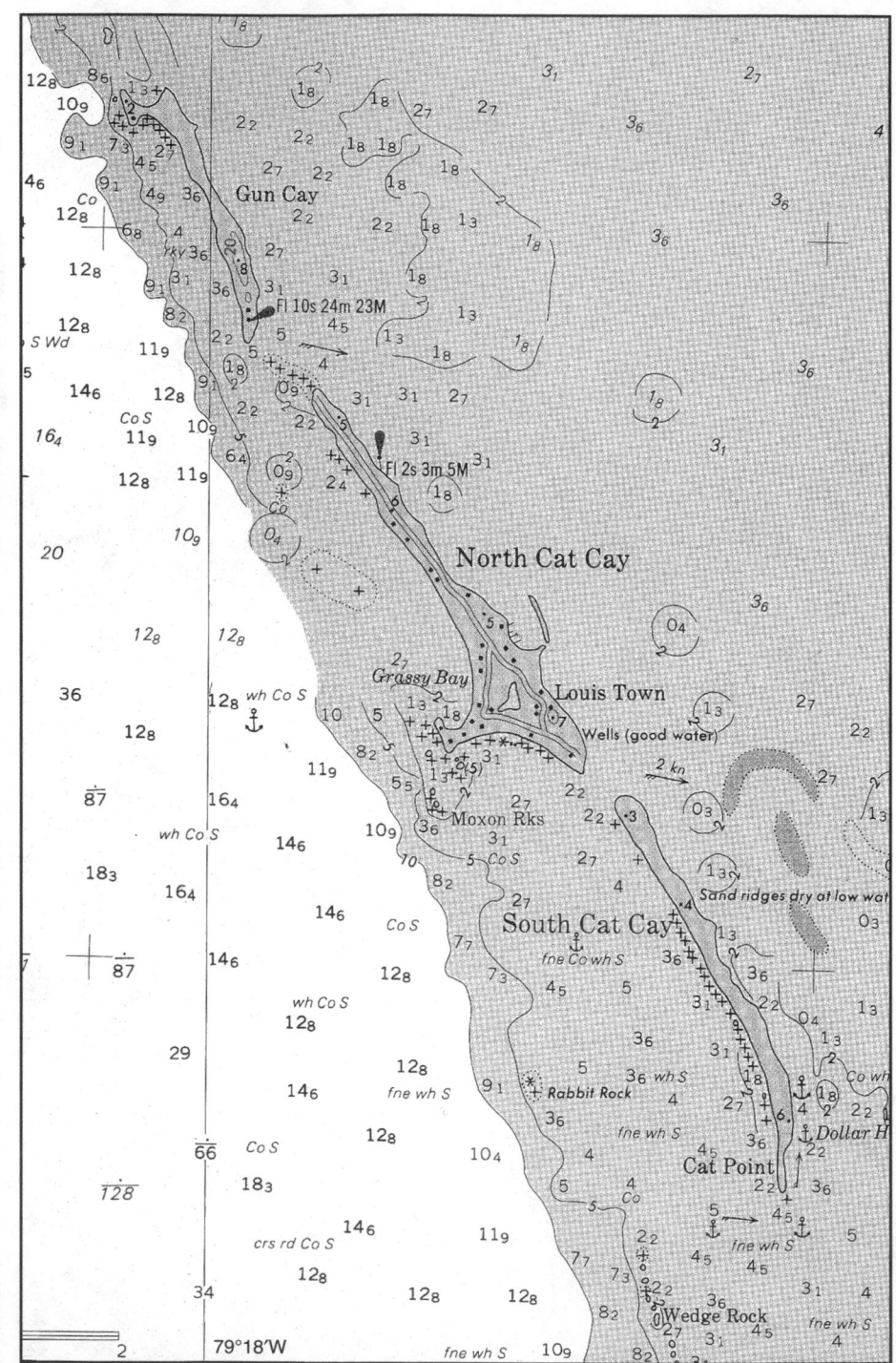

Gun Cay and Cat Cay, soundings in meters *(from DMA 26324, 15th ed, 8/86)*

place to anchor before crossing the Great Bahama Bank. The channel between Gun Cay and North Cat Cay is easy when the sun is high. Hug the shore of Gun Cay closely until past the bar extending north from North Cat Cay. You can receive NOAA weather radio from Florida; it is advisable to cross the banks with a favorable forecast.

GREAT BAHAMA BANK

NORTH CAT CAY, head of breakwater, 25 34.0N, 79 18.3W. Fl W 2s, 10ft, 5M. Beacon. Not visible W or SW of Cat Cay.
SOUTH RIDING ROCK LIGHT, 25 13.8N, 79 10.0W. Fl W 5s, 35ft, 11M. White framework structure.
SYLVIA BEACON, 25 28.0N, 79 01.0W. FL W 5s, 33ft, 8M. Beacon on piles.
MACKIE SHOAL LIGHT, 25 41.2N, 78 39.2W. Fl W 2s, 15ft, 10M. White tripod, yellow top.
RUSSELL BEACON, 25 28.6N, 78 25.5W. Beacon has been destroyed; use caution as the remains are dangerous.
Russell Lighted Buoy, 25 28.6N, 78 25.5W. Replaces Russell Beacon. Vessels anchor here at night. Use caution when approaching after dark. Reported missing 1993.
NORTHWEST CHANNEL LIGHT, 25 27.2N, 78 09.8W. Fl W 5s, 33ft, 8M. White skeleton tower. Reported destroyed 1993.

GREAT BAHAMA BANK

Emergencies: Call the Bahamas Air Sea Rescue Association (BASRA) on VHF channels 16 or 22 or on 2182kHz. The Nassau headquarters can be reached at 809-325-8864 (809-322-3877 after hours).
Pilotage: Many boaters cross the banks from Gun Cay Light (25 34.5N, 79 18.8W) to the remains of Northwest Channel Light (25 27.2N, 78 09.8W), a distance of about 62 miles. Mariners are cautioned that the aids to navigation on the banks cannot be considered reliable. They may be missing, off station, or showing incorrect characteristics due to hurricane damage.

Leaving Gun Cay, you encounter a series of sand ridges within the first 10 miles. The controlling depth of this route has been reported as 6 feet. The water depths improve approximately 10 miles east of Gun Cay. Deeper-draft vessels may want to travel from North Rock Light (25 48.2N, 79 16.7W) to Northwest Channel, taking care to avoid Mackie Shoal in approximate position

25 41.2N, 78 39.2W. On the southern route, Russell Beacon and buoy are reported as missing. Vessels anchoring on the banks are advised to show an anchor light.

Good depths have been reported on the route from South Riding Rock Light (25 13.8N, 79 10.0W) to the vicinity of the Russell Beacon, then on to Northwest Channel. Vessels may get some protection anchoring between South Riding Rock and Castle Rock.

THE BERRY ISLANDS

CHUB POINT LIGHT, 25 23.8N, 77 54.2W. Fl W R 10s, 44ft, 7M. Aluminum-colored lattice structure. W 320°–054°, R 054°–320°. Fl W and Fl G on water tower 0.8M to the NE.
FRAZERS HOG CAY AVIATION LIGHT, 25 25.0N, 77 53.7W. Fl W G. Radiobeacon.

CHUB CAY

25 24N, 77 54W
Emergencies: Call the Bahamas Air Sea Rescue Association (BASRA) on VHF channels 16 or 22 or on 2182kHz. The Nassau headquarters can be reached at 809-325-8864 (809-322-3877 after hours).
Port of Entry: Tie up in Chub Cay Club Marina to clear customs. The officials may have to travel from the airstrip.
Dockage: Chub Cay Club Marina (809-325-1490 or VHF channel 68), which was damaged by Hurricane Andrew, has restored all its docks. The boat basin is protected, and 6 feet of water are reported in the entrance channel.
Anchorage: Boats crossing the banks and headed to Nassau often anchor in the bight just south of the marina entrance channel. This area is subject to a surge, and depths run less than 6 feet in some spots. Shallow-draft boats can get good protection between Mama Rhoda Cay and Chub Cay. Controlling depth in this channel is reported to be about 3 feet. Good anchorage is found in the channel along the eastern shore of Frazer's Hog Cay.
Services: Fuel, water, electricity, ice, and minor repairs are available in the marina. Some groceries are sold in the marina store, and there is a restaurant and bar.

This is a good spot to break up the long journey from Nassau across the banks. From here it is about 50 miles to Nassau and 76 miles to Gun Cay. The main anchorage may become untenable in strong westerlies.

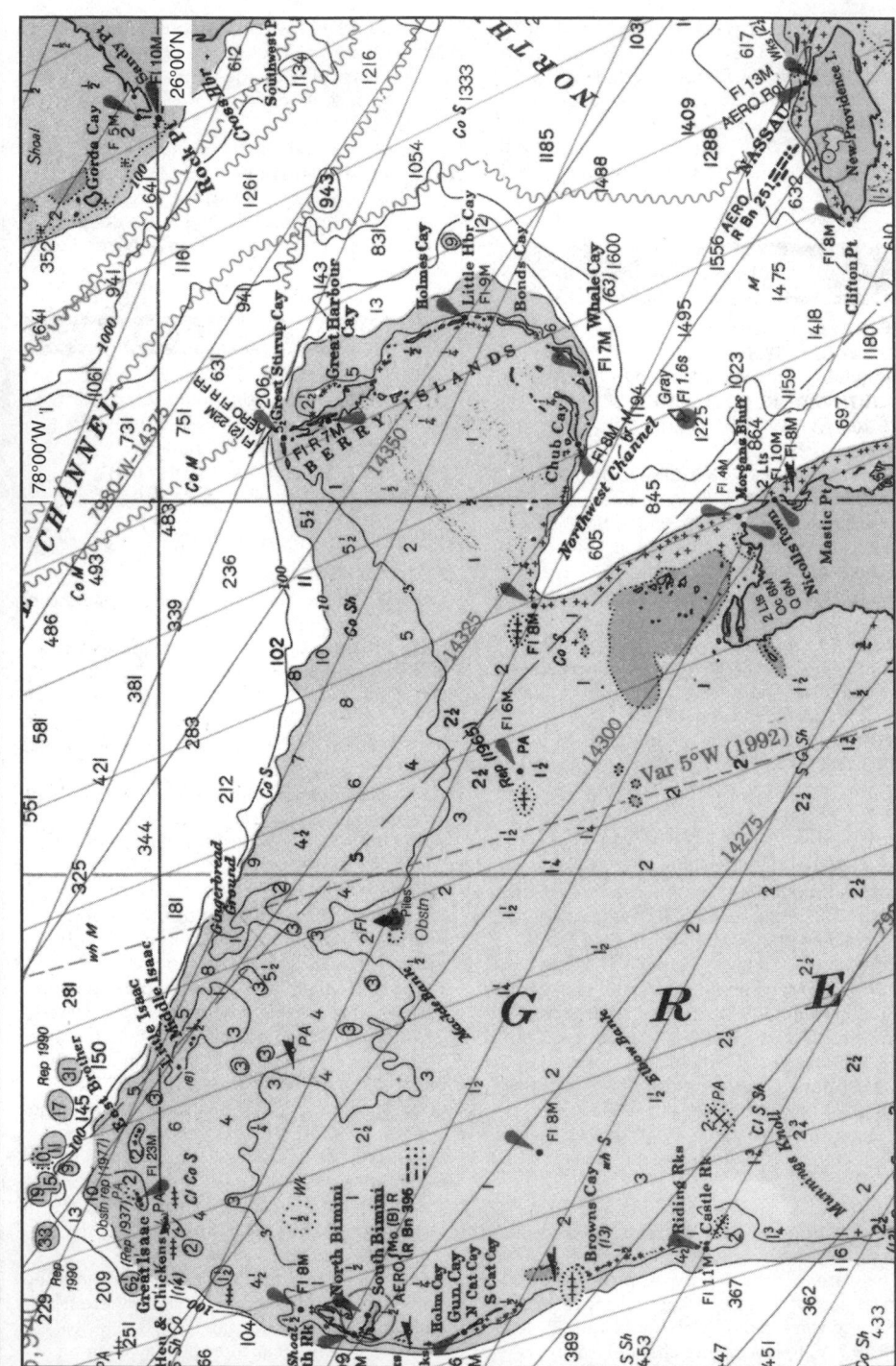

Great Bahama Bank, soundings in fathoms *(from NOAA 11013, 40th ed, 10/93)*

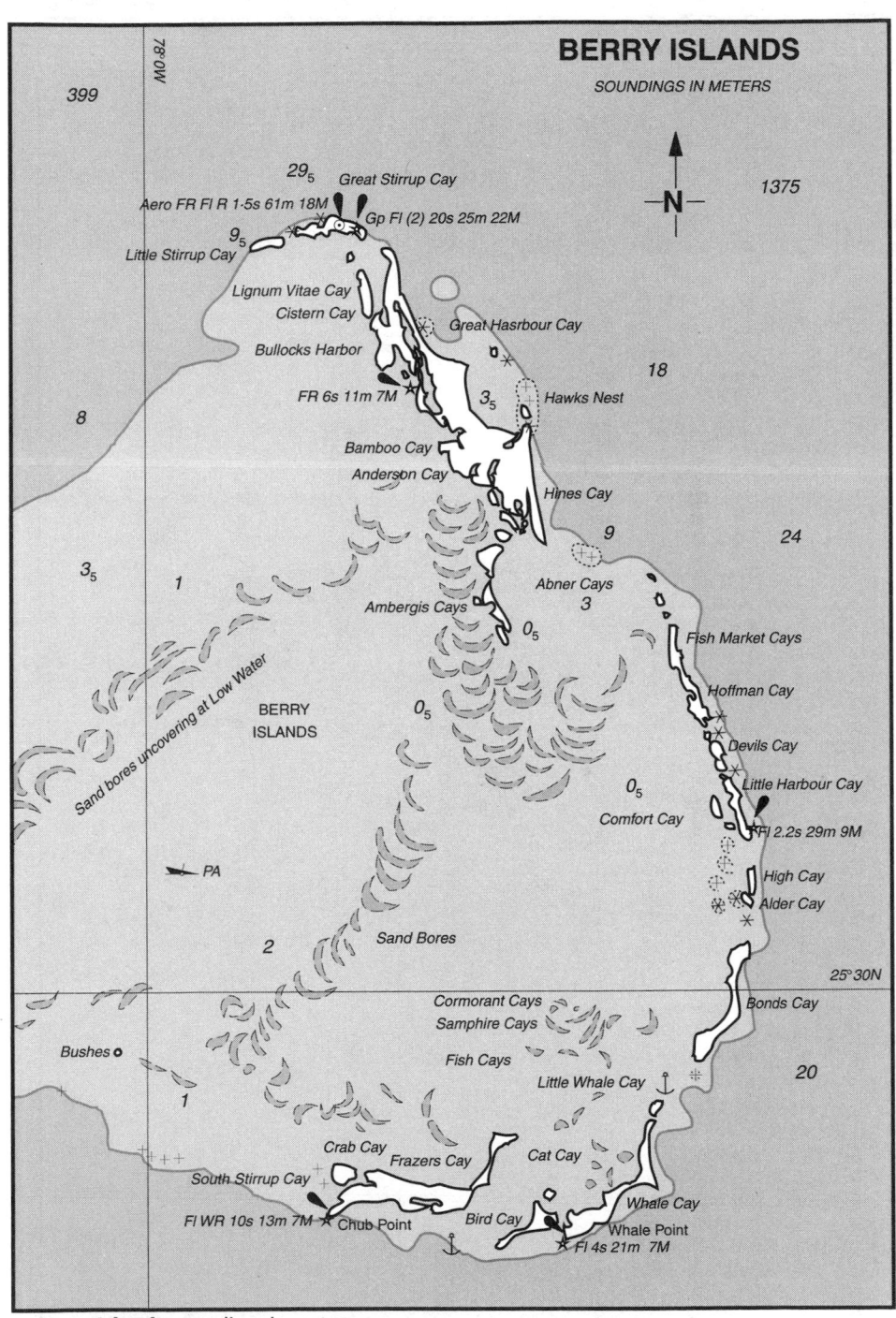

BERRY ISLANDS

SOUNDINGS IN METERS

—N—

399

78°00'W

29₅ Great Stirrup Cay

Aero FR Fl R 1·5s 61m 18M   Gp Fl (2) 20s 25m 22M

9₅

Little Stirrup Cay

Lignum Vitae Cay

Cistern Cay

Bullocks Harbor

Great Hasrbour Cay

FR 6s 11m 7M

3₅   Hawks Nest

Bamboo Cay

Anderson Cay

Hines Cay

Ambergis Cays

Abner Cays

0₅

Fish Market Cays

Hoffman Cay

Devils Cay

Little Harbour Cay

Fl 2.2s 29m 9M

0₅

Comfort Cay

High Cay

Alder Cay

Sand bores uncovering at Low Water

BERRY
ISLANDS

0₅

PA

2

1

3₅

8

1375

18

24

9

3

Sand Bores

25°30N

Cormorant Cays

Samphire Cays

Fish Cays

Little Whale Cay

Bonds Cay

20

Bushes ○

Crab Cay

Frazers Cay

Cat Cay

South Stirrup Cay

Fl WR 10s 13m 7M Chub Point

Bird Cay

Whale Cay

Whale Point
Fl 4s 21m 7M

Berry Islands, soundings in meters

COAST PILOT

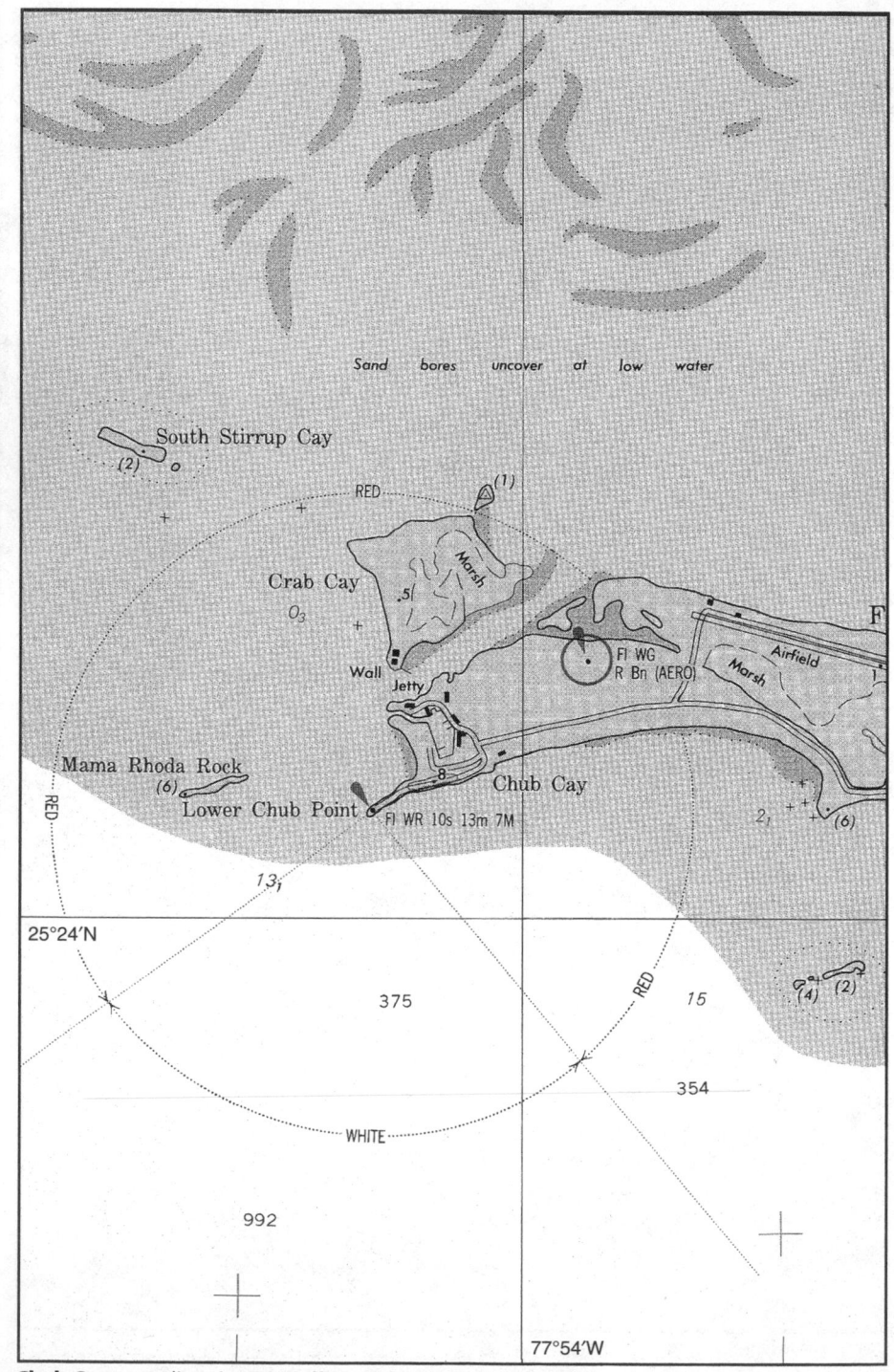

Sand   bores   uncover   at   low   water

South Stirrup Cay
(2)   o

RED

(1)

Crab Cay
            Marsh
        .5(
    O₃

Wall
    Jetty

Fl WG
R Bn (AERO)

Airfield
Marsh

F

Mama Rhoda Rock
    (6)

RED

Lower Chub Point

8

Chub Cay

Fl WR 10s 13m 7M

2₁

(6)

1.3₁

25°24'N

375

15

RED

(4) (2)

354

WHITE

992

77°54'W

Chub Cay, soundings in meters *(from DMA 26328, 1st ed, 10/86)*

WHALE POINT LIGHT, SW point of Whale Cay, 25 23.0N, 77 47.8W. Fl W 4s, 70ft, 7M. Stone tower, white steel superstructure.
LITTLE HARBOR CAY LIGHT, 25 33.6N, 77 42.4W. Fl W 2.2s, 94ft, 9M. Black and white banded pipe.

LITTLE HARBOUR CAY

25 34N, 77 43W
Anchorage: Anchor between Little Harbour Cay and Cabbage Cay. A shallow channel with a reported depth of less than 3 feet leads north to a private dock on Little Harbour.

BULLOCK HARBOR LIGHT, 25 45.8N, 77 52.1W. Fl R 6s, 36ft, 7M. Iron pyramidal structure, upper half white, lower half black.

GREAT HARBOUR CAY

25 45N, 77 52W
Emergencies: Call the Bahamas Air Sea Rescue Association (BASRA) on VHF channels 16 or 22 or on 2182kHz. The Nassau headquarters can be reached at 809-325-8864 (809-322-3877 after hours).
Pilotage: On a course of 180° run for 2 3/4 miles from the western tip of Little Stirrup Cay to an unlit piled mark with a radar reflector. From here a course of 110° leads through a well-marked channel to the marina.
Port of Entry: Tie up in Great Harbour Cay Marina, and call customs via telephone (809-367-8566). Officials must come in from the airstrip.
Dockage: Contact Great Harbour Cay Marina (809-367-8123 or VHF channel 68; in the U.S., 800-343-7256). Call the U.S. number for reservations.
Anchorage: Anchor west of Bullock's Harbour or south of the marina channel or off the beach club on the east side of the island.
Services: Fuel, water, groceries, and several restaurants are available.

GREAT STIRRUP CAY LIGHT, 640 meters from E end, 25 49.7N, 77 54.0W. Fl (2) W 20s, 82ft, 22M. White circular tower. Reported extinguished 1993.
GREAT STIRRUP CAY AVIATION LIGHT, 1,189 meters from E end, 25 49.8N, 77 54.4W. Fl R 1.5s, 200ft, 18M. Radio mast. Obstruction light.

GREAT STIRRUP CAY

25 50N, 77 54W
Anchorage only: Enter the anchorage at the eastern end of the cay. Cruise ships discharge passengers in the coves on the north side of the island. Caution: The light has been reported as unreliable.

NASSAU AND APPROACHES

CLIFTON TERMINAL LIGHT, commercial harbor on SW end of New Providence Island, 25 00.4N, 77 32.5W. 2 Q R (horiz.), 121ft, 13M. 2 F R (horiz.), 59ft, 10M. Orange mast with white bands.
GOULDING CAY LIGHT, off W end of New Providence Island, 25 01.6N, 77 35.8W. Fl W 2s, 36ft, 8M. Gray structure.
FORT FINCASTLE AVIATION LIGHT, 25 04.4N, 77 20.3W. Fl W 5s, 219ft, 28M. Gray concrete tower.
PARADISE ISLAND LIGHT, W point, 25 05.2N, 77 21.1W. Fl W or R 5s, 68ft, 13M white. White conical stone tower. Changed to Fl R 5s when bar is dangerous; obscured 334°–025°.
NASSAU EAST BREAKWATER HEAD LIGHT, 25 05.3N, 77 21.2W. Fl G 5s, 29ft. Reported destroyed February 1991.
NASSAU WEST BREAKWATER HEAD LIGHT, 25 05.1N, 77 21.3W. Fl R 5s, 29ft. Tower.
NASSAU HARBOR RANGE (Front Light), 25 04.7N, 77 21.0W. F G, 37ft, 7M. Red framework tower. **(Rear Light),** 260 meters, 151°36' from front.F G, 61ft, 7M. Red framework tower.
GOVERNMENT HOUSE LIGHT, 25 04.5N, 77 20.7W. Fl R 3s, 122ft, 10M. Green cupola on building.
THE NARROWS LIGHT, between Paradise Island and Athol Island, 25 05.0N, 77 18.5W. Fl R 5s, 12ft, 2M. Red post.
PORGEE ROCKS LIGHT, 25 04.3N, 77 15.8W. Fl W 3s, 25ft, 5M. Gray structure.
CHUB ROCKS LIGHT, 25 06.9N, 77 15.6W. Fl W 5s, 32ft, 4M. White framework tower.
EAST END POINT LIGHT, on point S of East End Point on New Providence Island, 25 02.3N, 77 16.8W. Fl W 6s, 57ft, 8M. White square stone building. Visible 180°–056°.

NASSAU

25 05N, 77 21W
Emergencies: Call the Bahamas Air Sea Rescue Association (BASRA) on VHF channels 16 or 22 or on 2182kHz. The Nassau headquarters can be reached at 809-325-8864 (809-322-3877 after hours). BASRA headquarters is located just west of the Paradise Island Bridge and Potter's Cay. Its dock is a favorite dinghy landing site. For more information contact: BASRA, P.O. Box SS-6247, Nassau, Bahamas.

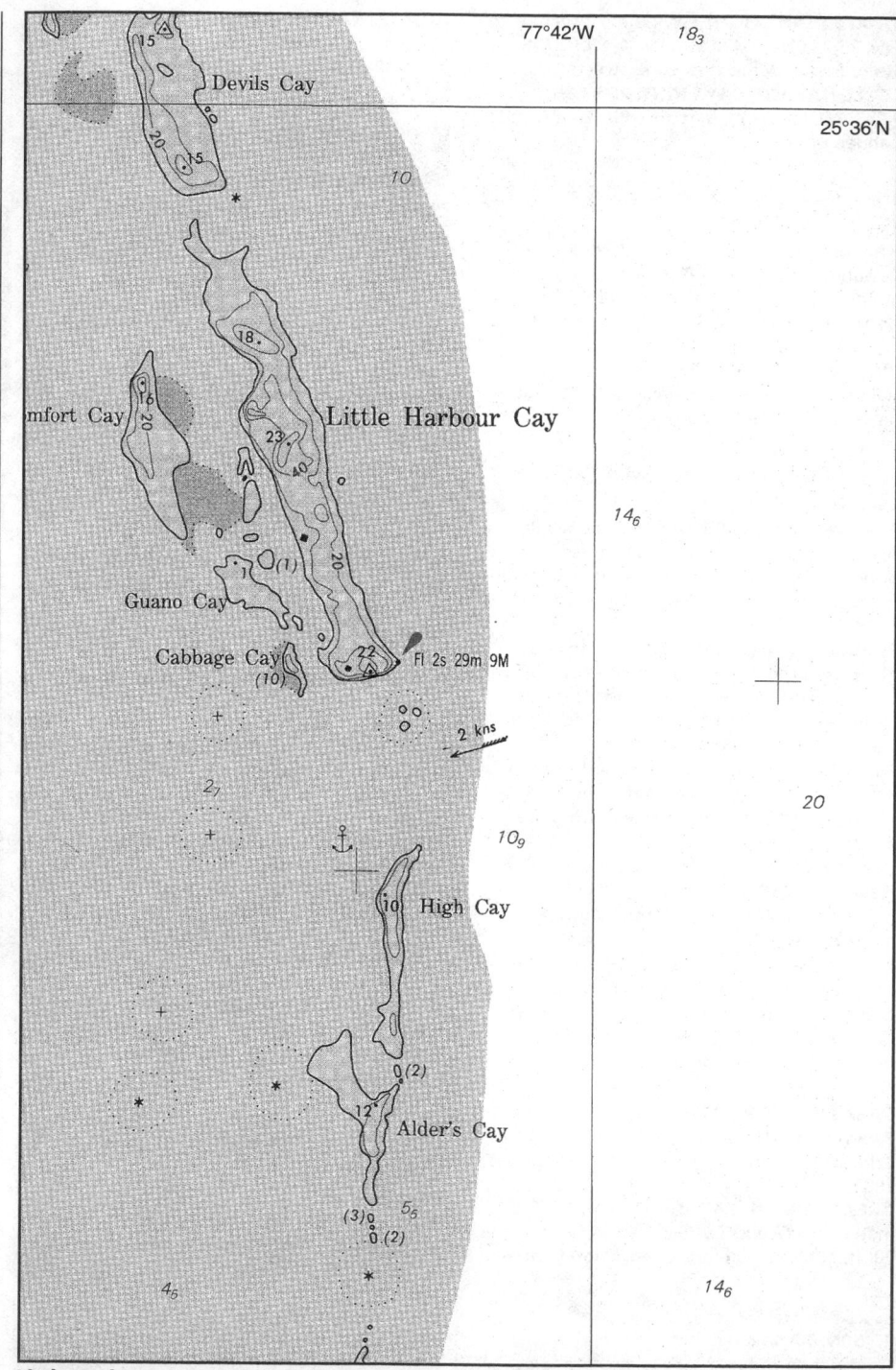

77°42'W 18₃

25°36'N

Devils Cay

15

20
15

10

18

mfort Cay   16
20

Little Harbour Cay

23
40

14₆

(1)

20

Guano Cay

Cabbage Cay
(10)

22

Fl 2s 29m 9M

2 kns

+

2₇

+

10₉

10 High Cay

20

+

+

*

*

0 (2)

12°

Alder's Cay

(3)0   5₅
0 (2)

4₅

14₆

Little Harbour Cay, soundings in meters *(from DMA 26328, 1st ed, 10/86)*

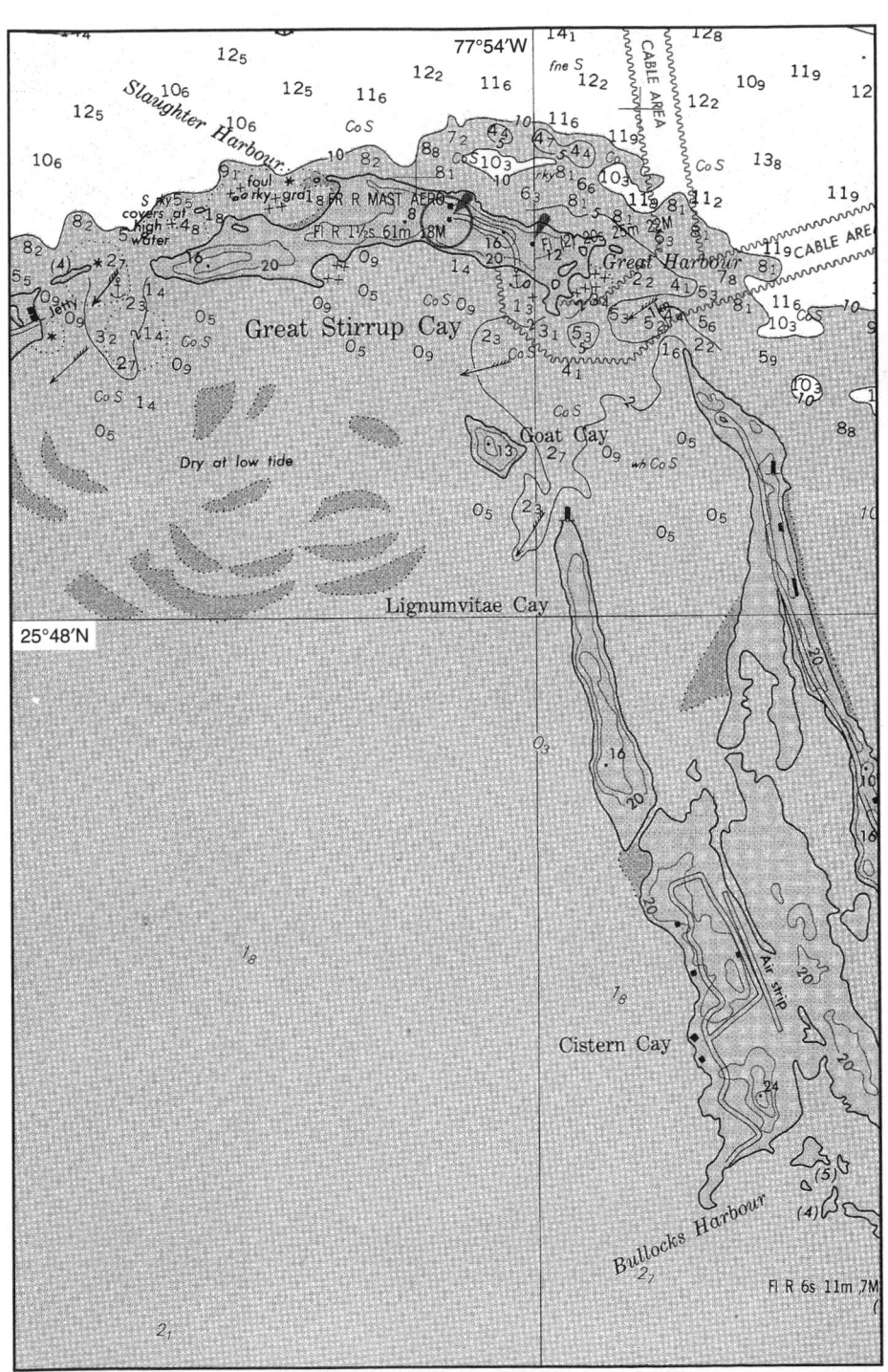

Great Stirrup Cay and Great Harbour Cay, soundings in meters *(from DMA 26328, 1st ed, 10/86)*

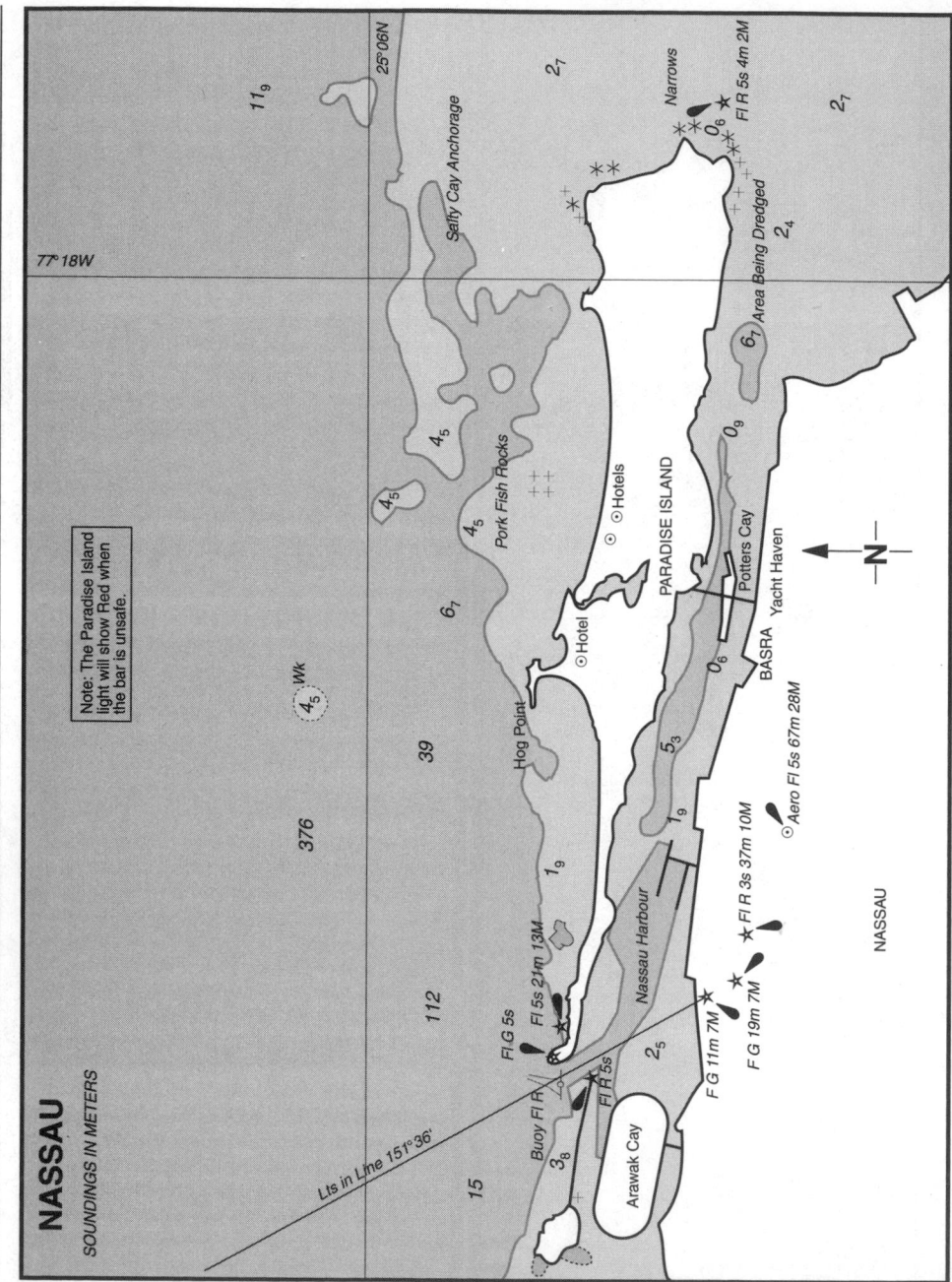

Nassau Approaches, soundings in meters *(after DMA 26309, 25th ed, 8/86)*

Note: The Paradise Island light will show Red when the bar is unsafe.

NASSAU
SOUNDINGS IN METERS

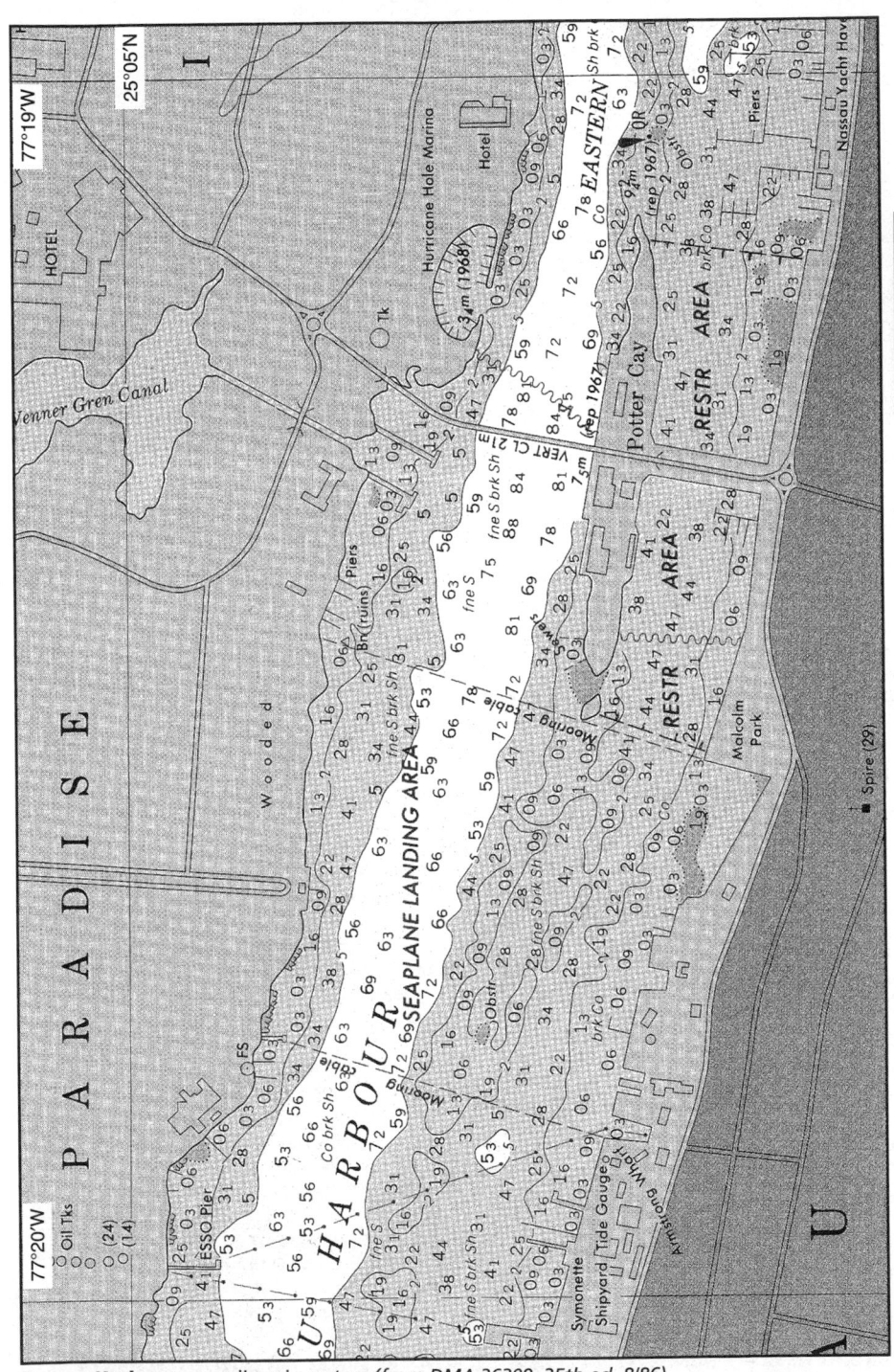

Nassau Harbour, soundings in meters *(from DMA 26309, 25th ed, 8/86)*

Nassau Harbour Control: All vessels must report on VHF channel 16 when entering the harbor or when moving within the harbor.

Port of Entry: The office is located on the cruise ship docks. You may tie up here (use lots of fenders) or call customs from a marina.

Dockage: Contact East Bay Marina (809-322-3754), Hurricane Hole (809-363-3600), Nassau Yacht Haven (809-393-8173), or Nassau Harbour Club (809-393-0771). All monitor VHF channel 16. All the marinas are east of the Paradise Island Bridge except East Bay Marina, which is in the basin just west of the bridge.

Anchorage: The holding ground in most of Nassau Harbour has been reported to be very poor. Boats must stay clear of the cruise ship docks, the marinas, and the seaplane landing area. Some boats anchor south of Paradise Island near the Club Med docks or at the eastern end of the harbor. There are also charted shoal areas and cable areas to be avoided.

Services: All services are available. Major repairs and haulouts may be done here. There are several large grocery stores, hardware stores, marine supply stores, and many restaurants, bars, casinos, shops, and modern services of all types.

Nassau Harbor has a bar across the entrance channel. If the Paradise Island bar light shows red, the channel is considered dangerous. In general, approaching the harbor after dark is not considered safe because of the difficulty of spotting the navigation aids against the background of city lights. Boaters should be prepared to encounter large cruise ships, freighters, and barges in the harbor. Nassau Harbour Control will advise you of any traffic problems.

This is the capital of the Bahamas and is an exciting port of call. There are many historic sights and interesting attractions ashore. This is also a good place to conduct banking, place phone calls, and make travel arrangements.

PORT NEW PROVIDENCE MARINA LIGHT, 25 00.2N, 77 15.7W. Fl W 4s, 7ft, 4M. Wooden pile.

MARINA CHANNEL NO 1, 25 00.3N, 77 15.7W. Fl W 4s, 7ft, 4M. Wooden pile.

MARINA CHANNEL NO 2, 25 00.4N, 77 15.8W. Fl W 4s, 7ft, 4M. Wooden pile.

ANDROS

MORGANS BLUFF RANGE (Front Light), 25 10.5N, 78 02.1W. Q W, 29ft, 6M. Intensified on rangeline. **(Rear Light),** 223°44' from front. Oc W 4s, 60ft, 6M. Intensified on rangeline.

MORGANS BLUFF DOCK LIGHT, 25 10.8N, 78 01.6W. Fl W 4s, 20ft, 4M.

NICOLLS TOWN RANGE (Front Light), 25 07.8N, 78 00.5W. Fl W 5s, 60ft, 8M. Red and aluminum colored structure. **(Rear Light),** 24 meters, 247° from front Fl W 5s, 65ft, 10M. Red and aluminum colored structure.

STANIARD ROCK LIGHT, 24 51.1N, 77 52.5W. Fl W 4s, 18ft, 6M. Gray structure.

STANIARD CREEK LIGHT, 24 50.8N, 77 54.0W. F R, 26ft, 6M. Wooden framework structure.

FRESH CREEK ISLET LIGHT, S side, 24 44.3N, 77 46.9W. Fl W 6s, 10ft, 5M. Metal mast.

ANDROS TOWN LIGHT, S side of entrance, 24 43.7N, 77 47.8W. F W, 27ft, 6M. White quadrangular stone building.

SITE 1 N ITT TOWER, 24 43.9N, 77 46.3W. Fl Y 4s, 5M. Steel skeleton tower.

SITE 1 S ITT TOWER, 24 42.4N, 77 45.3W. Fl Y 4s, 5M. Steel skeleton tower.

AVIATION LIGHT, 24 42.3N, 77 46.4W. Al Fl W G Y 2s, 136ft. Tower.

AUTEC SITE 1 RANGE (Front Light), 24 42.3N, 77 45.9W. Q W, 25ft, 10M. White tower, red daymark with white stripe. **(Rear Light),** 335 meters, 223°48' from front. Iso W 6s, 33ft, 10M. White tower, red daymark with white stripe.

HIGH CAY LIGHT, 24 39.3N, 77 42.6W. Fl W 4s, 70ft, 6M. Metal mast.

AUTEC SITE 1 LIGHT 5, 24 42.8N, 77 45.3W. Fl G 4s, 18ft, 4M. Dolphin, green square daymark with green reflective border. Fl G and Fl R lights mark channel.

AUTEC SITE 2 RANGE (Front Light), 24 29.9N, 77 43.1W. Q W, 22ft, 10M. White skeletal tower, red daymark with white stripes. **(Rear Light),** 745 meters, 269°54' from front. Iso W 6s, 42ft, 10M. White skeletal tower, red daymark with white stripes.

AUTEC SITE 2 LIGHT 3, 24 29.9N, 77 42.1W. Fl G 4s, 19ft, 4M. Dolphin, green square daymark with green reflective border. Fl G and Fl R lights mark channel.

SITE 3 ITT TOWER, 24 20.9N, 77 40.4W. Fl Y 4s, 33ft, 5M.

AUTEC SITE 3 LIGHT 3, 24 20.1N, 77 40.4W. Fl G 4s, 19ft, 4M. Dolphin, green square daymark with green reflective border. Fl G and Fl R lights mark channel.

NOTE: AUTEC (ATLANTIC UNDERSEA TEST AND EVALUATION CENTER) SITES

ARE OFF LIMITS TO BOATERS, EXCEPT IN AN EMERGENCY.

MIDDLE BIGHT LIGHT, on rock S side of channel, 24 18.8N, 77 40.3W. Fl W 5s, 17ft, 7M. White steel framework tower.

MANGROVE CAY PEATS WHARF LIGHT, 24 14.8N, 77 39.2W. F R, 20ft, 7M.

SIRIOUS ROCK LIGHT, 24 13.5N, 77 37.0W. Fl W 3s, 29ft, 7M. Black and white mast on white cylindrical structure.

SITE 4 ITT TOWER, 24 13.3N, 77 36.0W. Fl Y 4s, 33ft, 5M.

AUTEC SITE 4 LIGHT 1, 24 13.3N, 77 36.3W. Fl G 4s, 23ft, 4M.

AUTEC SITE 4 LIGHT 2, 24 13.3N, 77 36.2W. Fl R 4s, 22ft, 3M.

GREEN CAY LIGHT, W end, 24 02.2N, 77 11.2W. Fl W 3s, 33ft, 7M. Black structure, white house.

AUTEC SITE 6 RANGE (Front Light), 24 00.4N, 77 31.7W. Q W, 34ft, 10M. Skeleton tower. **(Rear Light),** 760 meters, 257° from front. Iso W 6s, 68ft. Skeleton tower.

AUTEC SITE 6 LIGHT 4, 24 00.5N, 77 30.1W. Fl R 4s, 16ft, 3M. Fl G and Fl R lights mark channel.

TINKER ROCKS LIGHT, 23 59.0N, 77 29.6W. Fl W (14 flashes per minute), 32ft, 8M. Black mast on white cylindrical housing.

HIGH POINT CAY LIGHT, 23 55.6N, 77 29.0W. Fl W 5s. White building on piles.

BILLY ISLAND LIGHT, N end of Williams Island, 24 39.3N, 78 28.7W. F W, 22ft, 5M. Mast. Fishing light.

SITE 7 ITT TOWER, 23 54.5N, 77 28.5W. Fl Y 4s, 33ft, 5M.

AUTEC SITE 7 LIGHT 4, 23 53.9N, 77 28.7W. Fl R 4s, 20ft, 3M.

AUTEC SITE 7 LIGHT 5, 23 53.9N, 77 28.7W. Fl G 4s, 20ft, 4M.

NASSAU TO ELEUTHERA

SIX SHILLING CHANNEL LIGHT, 4.3 km. 235°30′ from Six Shilling Cays Light, 25 15.1N, 76 56.4W. Fl R 4s, 16ft, 8M. Red and yellow structure.

SIX SHILLING CAYS LIGHT, 25 16.7N, 76 55.1W. Fl W 8s, 32ft, 10M. Gray steel framework tower.

CURRENT ROCK LIGHT, 25 25.0N, 76 52.0W. Fl W 8s, 41ft, 7M. Framework structure.

EGG ISLAND LIGHT, on summit of island, Northeast Providence Channel, 25 30.0N, 76 53.0W. Fl W 3s, 112ft, 12M. White metal tower.

ELEUTHERA

MAN ISLAND LIGHT, 25 32.8N, 76 38.5W. Fl (3) W 15s, 93ft, 12M. Aluminum framework tower.

HARBOUR ISLAND

25 30N, 76 38W

Emergencies: Call the Bahamas Air Sea Rescue Association (BASRA) on VHF channels 16 or 22 or on 2182kHz. The Nassau headquarters can be reached at 809-325-8864 (809-322-3877 after hours).

Port of Entry: The marinas will alert customs to your arrival.

Dockage: You may tie up temporarily to the government dock at Dunmore Town. South of the dock is Valentine's Yacht Club and Marina (809-333-2142 or VHF channel 16). Farther south is Harbour Island Club and Marina (809-333-2427 or VHF channel 16).

Services: There is fuel, water, and ice at the marinas. There are several good grocery stores and, in general, a very good selection of supplies. The town's resorts have a variety of bars, restaurants, and nightclubs.

The approaches to Harbour Island from Spanish Wells through Devil's Backbone are notoriously difficult. See the section on Spanish Wells for information on obtaining a local pilot to guide you. This route should not be attempted in strong north winds.

SPANISH WELLS LIGHT, 25 53.0N, 76 46.0W. F W, 6ft, 1M. Concrete column.

SPANISH WELLS

25 33N, 76 45W

Emergencies: Call the Bahamas Air Sea Rescue Association (BASRA) on VHF channels 16 or 22 or on 2182kHz. The Nassau headquarters can be reached at 809-325-8864 (809-322-3877 after hours).

Port of Entry

Dockage: Contact Spanish Wells Yacht Haven (809-333-4255 or VHF channel 16).

Anchorage: A few boats squeeze into the small pocket of deep water near the east end of town. Do not block the channel. Good anchorage is found in nearby Royal Harbour.

Services: Fuel, water, groceries, hardware, and restaurants are ashore. Dockage is available at the Yacht Haven for those leaving their boats for extended periods. Pilots may be hired to assist vessels headed to Harbour Island; contact

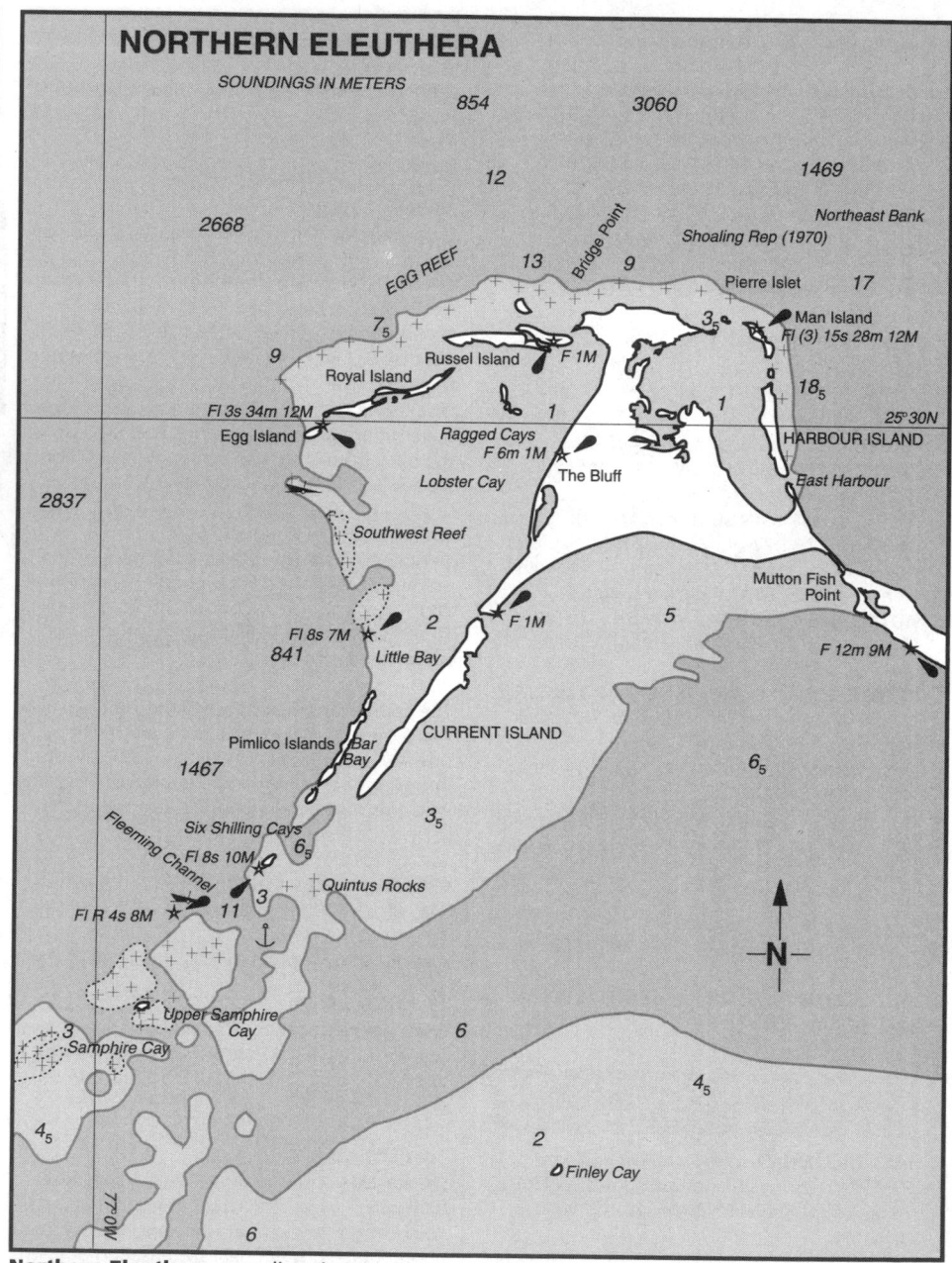

NORTHERN ELEUTHERA

SOUNDINGS IN METERS

854   3060

12   1469

2668   Northeast Bank
                                    Shoaling Rep (1970)

EGG REEF   13   Bridge Point   9   Pierre Islet   17

7₅   3₅   Man Island
9   Russel Island   F 1M   Fl (3) 15s 28m 12M
     Royal Island   18₅

Fl 3s 34m 12M   25° 30N
Egg Island   Ragged Cays   1   HARBOUR ISLAND
                    F 6m 1M
     Lobster Cay   The Bluff   1   East Harbour

2837
              Southwest Reef

                                                Mutton Fish
                                                    Point
          Fl 8s 7M   2   F 1M   5
     841   Little Bay   F 12m 9M

     Pimlico Islands   Bar   CURRENT ISLAND
                       Bay   6₅
     1467
                              3₅
     Six Shilling Cays
Fleeming Channel Fl 8s 10M
                   6₅
Fl R 4s 8M   11   3   Quintus Rocks

                                            N

          Upper Samphire
              Cay   6
     3
  Samphire Cay

4₅   2

77° 0W   D Finley Cay
          6

Northern Eleuthera, soundings in meters

A-1 Broadshad, Cinnabar, Dolphin, Reef Reader, or Blue Marlin on VHF channel 16.

THE BLUFF LIGHT, 25 31.0N, 76 45.0W. F W, 20ft, 1M. Mast.
CURRENT ISLAND LIGHT, W side of island, 25 23.0N, 76 49.0W. F W, 20ft, 1M. Mast.
CURRENT LIGHT, at town of Current, 25 25.0N, 76 48.0W. F W, 12ft, 1M. Mast.
STAFFORD LIGHT, GREGORY TOWN, 25 23.5N, 76 34.5W. F W, 41ft, 9M. Mast.
HATCHET BAY LIGHT, W side of entrance, 25 20.5N, 76 29.8W. Fl W 15s, 57ft, 8M. Tapered cast iron pipe mast; 2 F R range lights in line on 022° are shown from the E side of the bay.

HATCHET BAY

25 21N, 76 30W
Emergencies: Call the Bahamas Air Sea Rescue Association (BASRA) on VHF channels 16 or 22 or on 2182kHz. The Nassau headquarters can be reached at 809-325-8864 (809-322-3877 after hours).
Port of Entry
Dockage: Eleuthera Bahamas Charters (VHF channel 16; in the U.S., 508-255-8930) has a concrete bulkhead that may be available for transient dockage.
Moorings: Contact Eleuthera Bahamas Charters.
Anchorage: This harbor offers notoriously poor holding, although there is good shelter from the wind and seas. Stay clear of the commercial docks in the northwest portion of the bay.
Services: Fuel, water, and some supplies are available. There are several small groceries.

AVIATION LIGHT, 25 16.1N, 76 19.1W. Iso R 3s. Radio mast.
CUPID CAY LIGHT, Governor's Harbour, 25 12.0N, 76 16.0W. Fl W 4s, 40ft, 8M. Aluminum colored steel tower.

GOVERNOR'S HARBOUR

25 12N, 76 15W
Emergencies: Call the Bahamas Air Sea Rescue Association (BASRA) on VHF channels 16 or 22 or on 2182kHz. The Nassau headquarters can be reached at 809-325-8864 (809-322-3877 after hours).
Port of Entry
Anchorage only: The holding ground is reported to be poor here. There may be some moorings available, but their holding power is also uncertain.
Services: Groceries, stores, and restaurants are ashore.

NORTH PALMETTO POINT LIGHT, 25 10.8N, 76 11.4W. Iso W 4s, 73ft, 12M. White tower with black top and dwelling.
TARPUM BAY LIGHT, S end, 25 00.0N, 76 13.1W. F W, 35ft, 7M. Mast.
POISON POINT LIGHT, 24 52.4N, 76 13.7W. Fl W 15s, 29ft, 7M. White mast.
ROCK SOUND SETTLEMENT LIGHT, 24 54.4N, 76 12.3W. F R, 25ft. Mast.

ROCK SOUND

24 52N, 76 10W
Emergencies: Call the Bahamas Air Sea Rescue Association (BASRA) on VHF channels 16 or 22 or on 2182kHz. The Nassau headquarters can be reached at 809-325-8864 (809-322-3877 after hours).
Port of Entry
Dockage: You may be able to tie up temporarily to the government wharf. Check your depths carefully as you approach.
Anchorage: Anchor wherever depths permit. There are many shallow spots sprinkled throughout the harbor. Some of these shoal areas are hard coral.
Services: There is a good selection of groceries and shops ashore. You may be able to obtain water via jugs or hose at the wharf. Fuel may be jugged from a service station.

POWELL POINT LIGHT, 24 52.4N, 76 21.9W. Fl W 3s, 38ft, 8M. Aluminum-colored steel framework tower.
FREE TOWN LIGHT, 24 48.1N, 76 18.2W. F W, 19ft, 7M. White pole.
WEMYSS BIGHT LIGHT, 24 45.0N, 76 14.1W. F W, 27ft, 2M. White pole.

DAVIS HARBOUR

24 44N, 76 14W
Emergencies: Call the Bahamas Air Sea Rescue Association (BASRA) on VHF channels 16 or 22 or on 2182kHz. The Nassau headquarters can be reached at 809-325-8864 (809-322-3877 after hours).
Dockage: A privately marked channel leads to a marina in a small dredged basin. It is reported to have fuel, water, a restaurant, and limited supplies. The Cotton Bay Club has a golf course and accommodations. The marina monitors VHF channel 16.

ELEUTHERA POINT, SE extremity of island, 24 36.8N, 76 08.8W. Fl W 4.6s, 61ft, 6M. Light colored framework structure on white house.

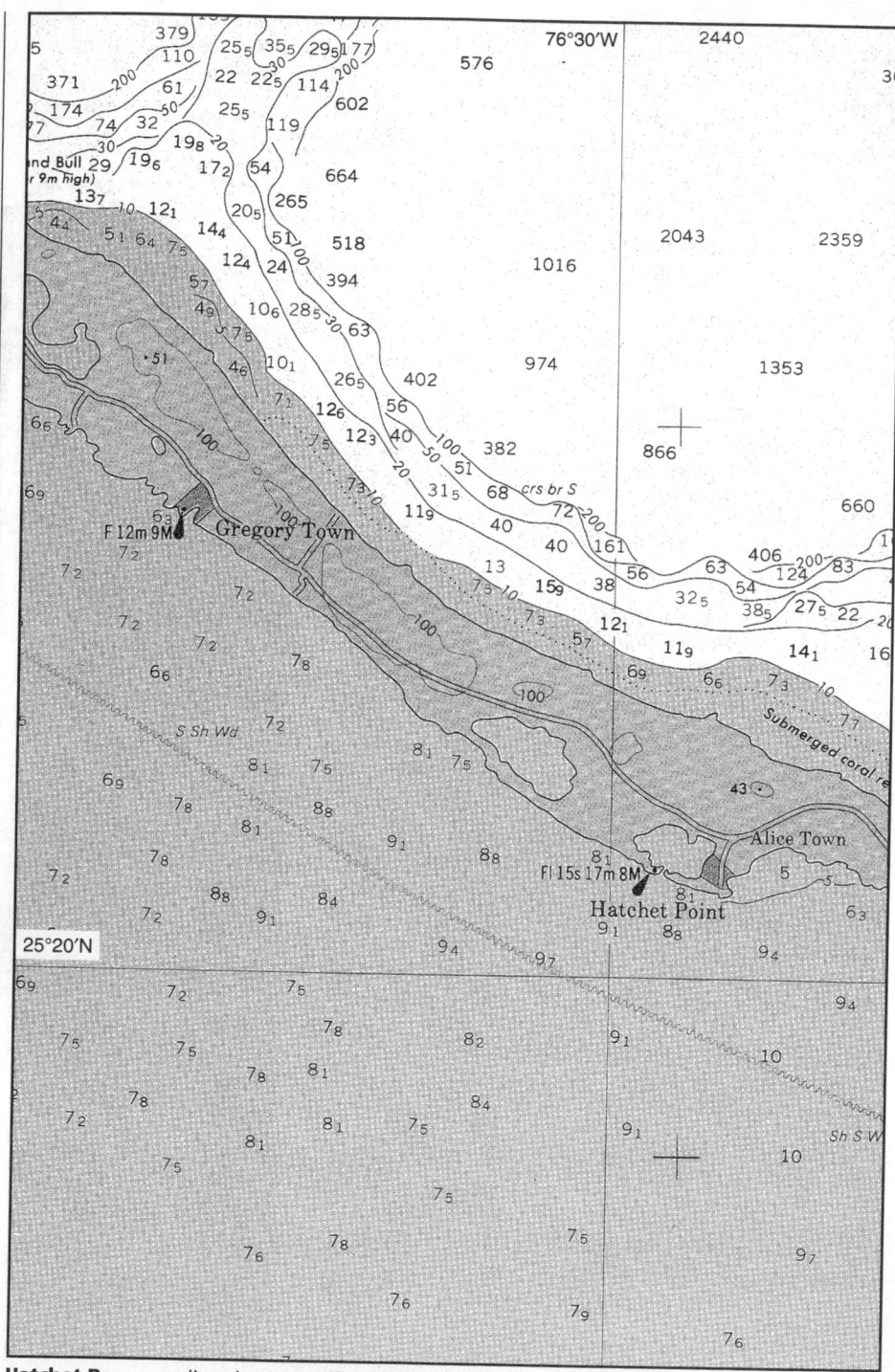

Hatchet Bay, soundings in meters *(from DMA 26307, 15th ed, 8/86)*

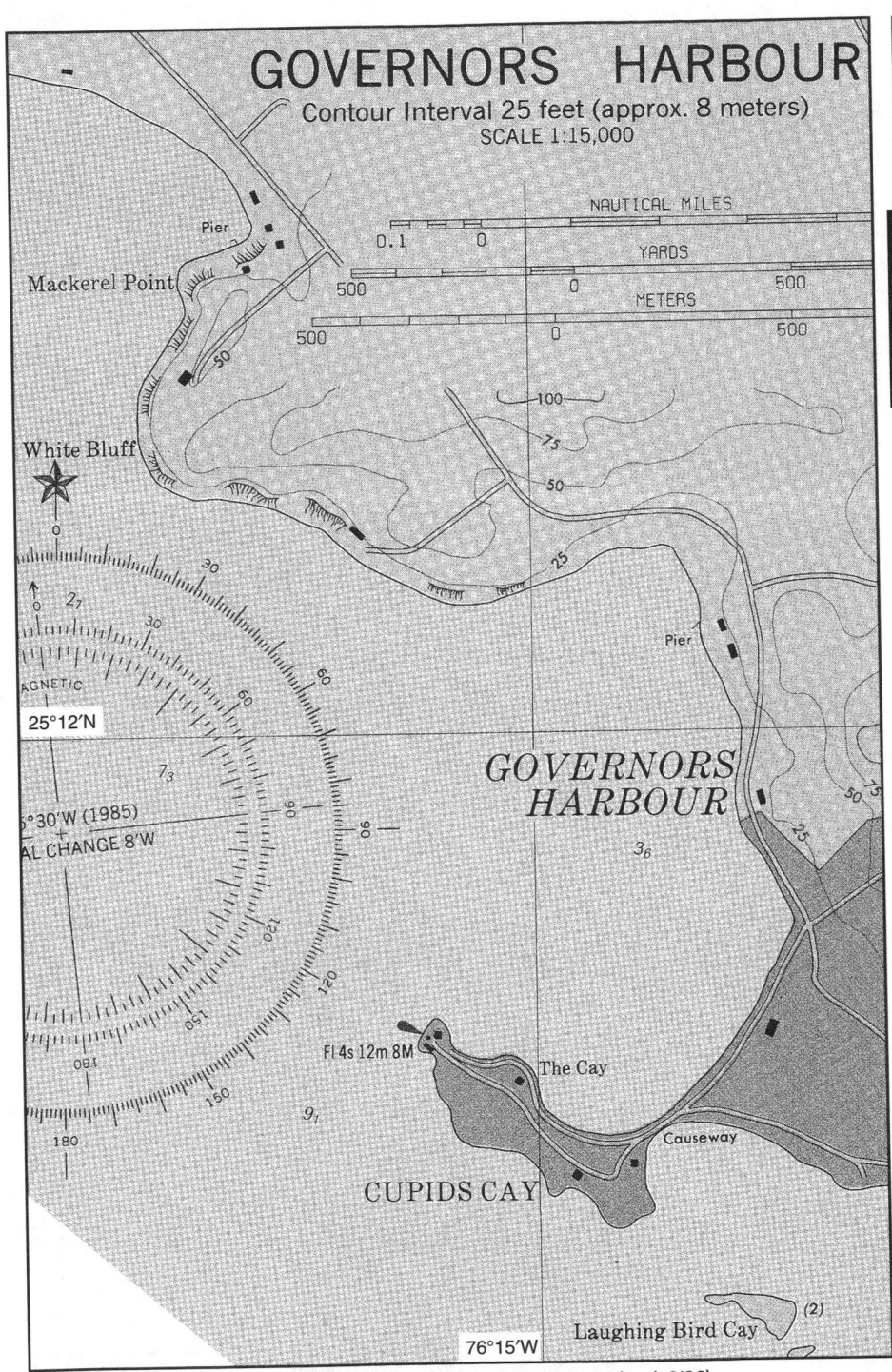

GOVERNORS HARBOUR
Contour Interval 25 feet (approx. 8 meters)
SCALE 1:15,000

NAUTICAL MILES

0.1   0

YARDS

500   0   500

METERS

500   0   500

Pier

Mackerel Point

White Bluff

MAGNETIC

25°12′N

°30′W (1985)

AL CHANGE 8′W

Pier

GOVERNORS HARBOUR

3₆

Fl 4s 12m 8M

The Cay

Causeway

CUPIDS CAY

9₁

Laughing Bird Cay   (2)

76°15′W

Governor's Harbour, soundings in meters *(from DMA 26307, 15th ed, 8/86)*

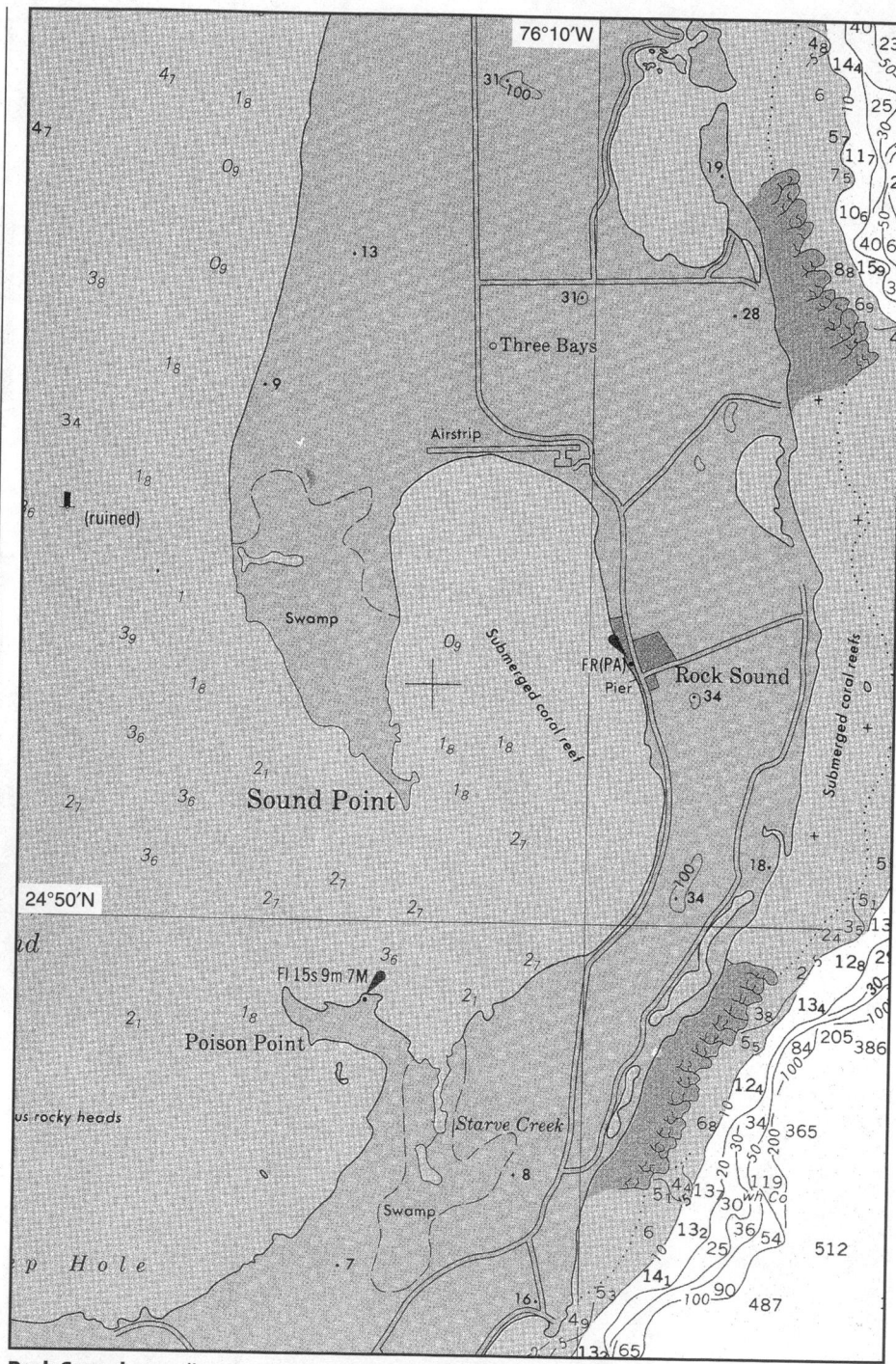

Rock Sound, soundings in meters *(from DMA 26307, 15th ed, 8/86)*

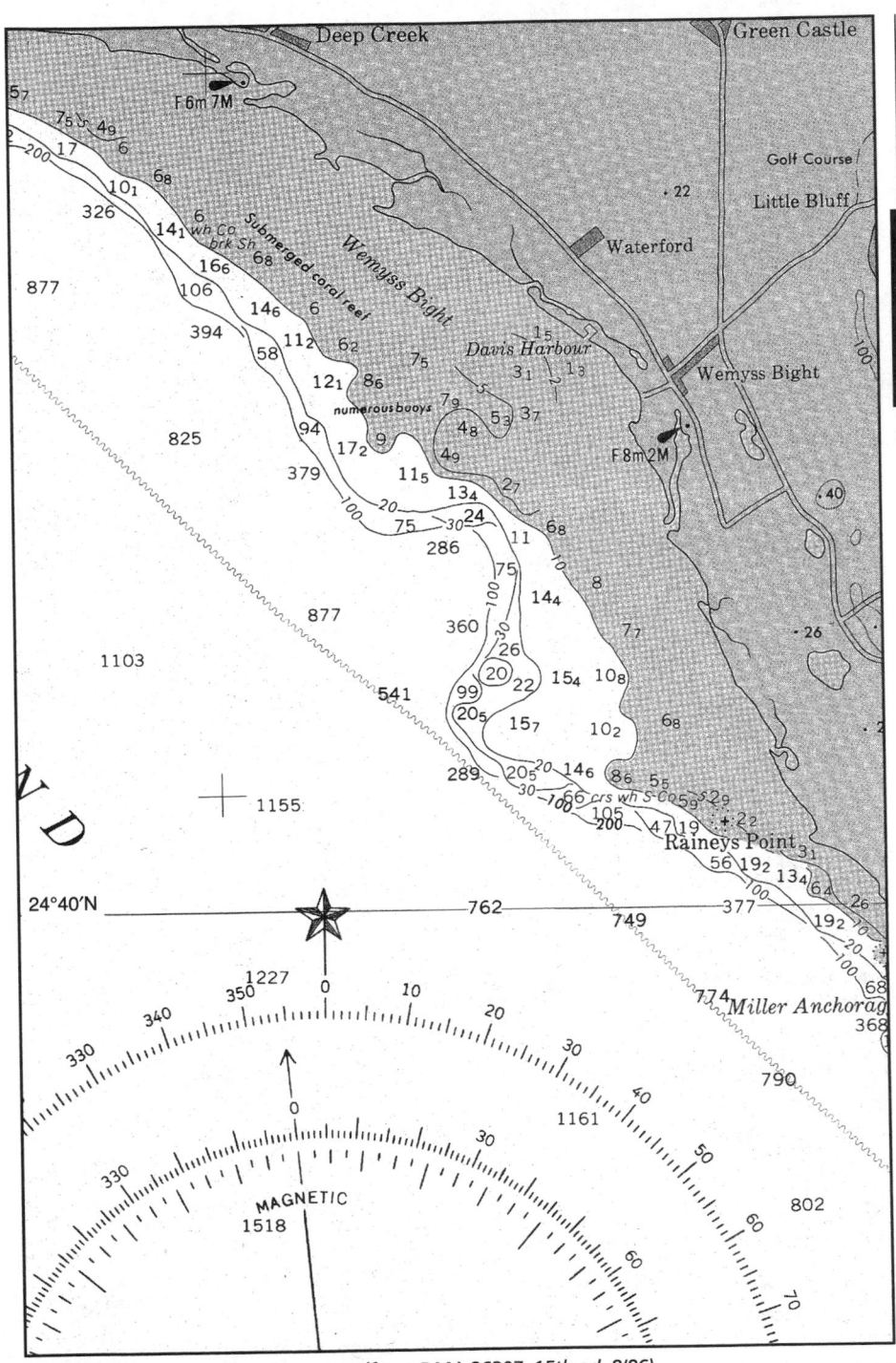

Davis Harbour, soundings in meters *(from DMA 26307, 15th ed, 8/86)*

LITTLE SAN SALVADOR

LITTLE SAN SALVADOR LIGHT, 24 35.0N, 75 56.0W. Fl W 2.4s, 69ft, 13M. Aluminum-colored steel skeleton structure. Visible 240°–110°, obscured 110°–130°, visible 130°–140°, obscured 140°–170°, visible 170°–190°, obscured 190°–200°, visible 200°–220°, obscured 220°–240°.

LITTLE SAN SALVADOR

24 34N, 75 56W

Emergencies: Call the Bahamas Air Sea Rescue Association (BASRA) on VHF channels 16 or 22 or on 2182kHz. The Nassau headquarters can be reached at 809-325-8864 (809-322-3877 after hours).

Anchorage only: The anchorage in West Bay, by a spectacular crescent-shaped beach, is popular.

EXUMAS

BEACON CAY LIGHT, North Rock, Ship Channel, 24 52.4N, 76 49.8W. Fl W R 3s, 58ft, 8M. Gray structure. R 292°–303°, W 303°–292°; partially obscured by neighboring islands 319°–006°.

HIGHBORNE CAY AVIATION LIGHT, 24 42.9N, 76 49.3W. Oc R 2s, 216ft, F R, 161ft, Radio mast.

ALLAN'S CAY

24 45N, 76 50W

Emergencies: Call the Bahamas Air Sea Rescue Association (BASRA) on VHF channels 16 or 22 or on 2182kHz. The Nassau headquarters can be reached at 809-325-8864 (809-322-3877 after hours).

Anchorage only: This is a popular stop at the northern end of the Exumas chain of islands. The easiest approach is from the west. As there are no aids to navigation, the approach should be made in good light. Some coral will be spotted in the entrance channel at the south end of Allan's Cay. Once inside, most boats anchor on either side of the shallow sandbar in the middle of the harbor. It is possible to anchor in the bight on the north end of Southwest Allan's Cay. The small cay to the east of Allan's is famous for the large iguanas that wander its beaches.

HIGHBORNE CAY

24 42N, 76 49W

Emergencies: Call the Bahamas Air Sea Rescue Association (BASRA) on VHF channels 16 or 22 or on 2182kHz. The Nassau headquarters can

be reached at 809-325-8864 (809-322-3877 after hours).

Dockage: Some dockage is available in the basin at the south end of the cay. Contact Wee Watin on VHF channel 16. A range on the hill may lead you clear of the coral shoals to the west of the marina. An approach in good light is recommended.

Anchorage: There is some room to anchor in the small basin off the docks. Be careful to limit your swinging room if a wind shift is expected.

Services: Fuel, water, and some groceries are available.

ELBOW CAY LIGHT, W end, 24 31.0N, 76 49.0W. Fl W 2s, 46ft, 11M. Gray structure.

WARDERICK WELLS

24 24N, 76 38W

Emergencies: Call the Bahamas Air Sea Rescue Association (BASRA) on VHF channels 16 or 22 or on 2182kHz. The Nassau headquarters can be reached at 809-325-8864 (809-322-3877 after hours).

Exuma Cays Land and Sea Park: The Bahamas National Trust administers the park that has its headquarters here in Warderick Wells. Park rangers monitor VHF channel 16, and you may see the park warden's boat *Moby* nearby. Several park moorings available to visitors. All fishing and collection of wildlife is prohibited within the park. For more information contact: The Bahamas National Trust, P.O. Box 4105, Nassau, Bahamas.

Anchorage: Approach only in good light to find the narrow deepwater channel. Boats can anchor all along the channel, but should use two anchors to limit swinging room. This is where the classic Bahamian Moor is desirable.

Services: The park headquarters provides maps of the trails ashore and descriptive information on the flora and fauna.

SAMPSON CAY

24 13N, 77 29W

Emergencies: Call the Bahamas Air Sea Rescue Association (BASRA) on VHF channels 16 or 22 or on 2182kHz. The Nassau headquarters can be reached at 809-325-8864 (809-322-3877 after hours).

Dockage: Contact Sampson Cay Club (809-355-2034 or VHF channel 16), where very protected dockage is available in the lagoon for those leaving boats for extended periods.

Anchorage: Anchor west of the docks in good holding, but be wary of several shoal spots, and do not block access to the docks.

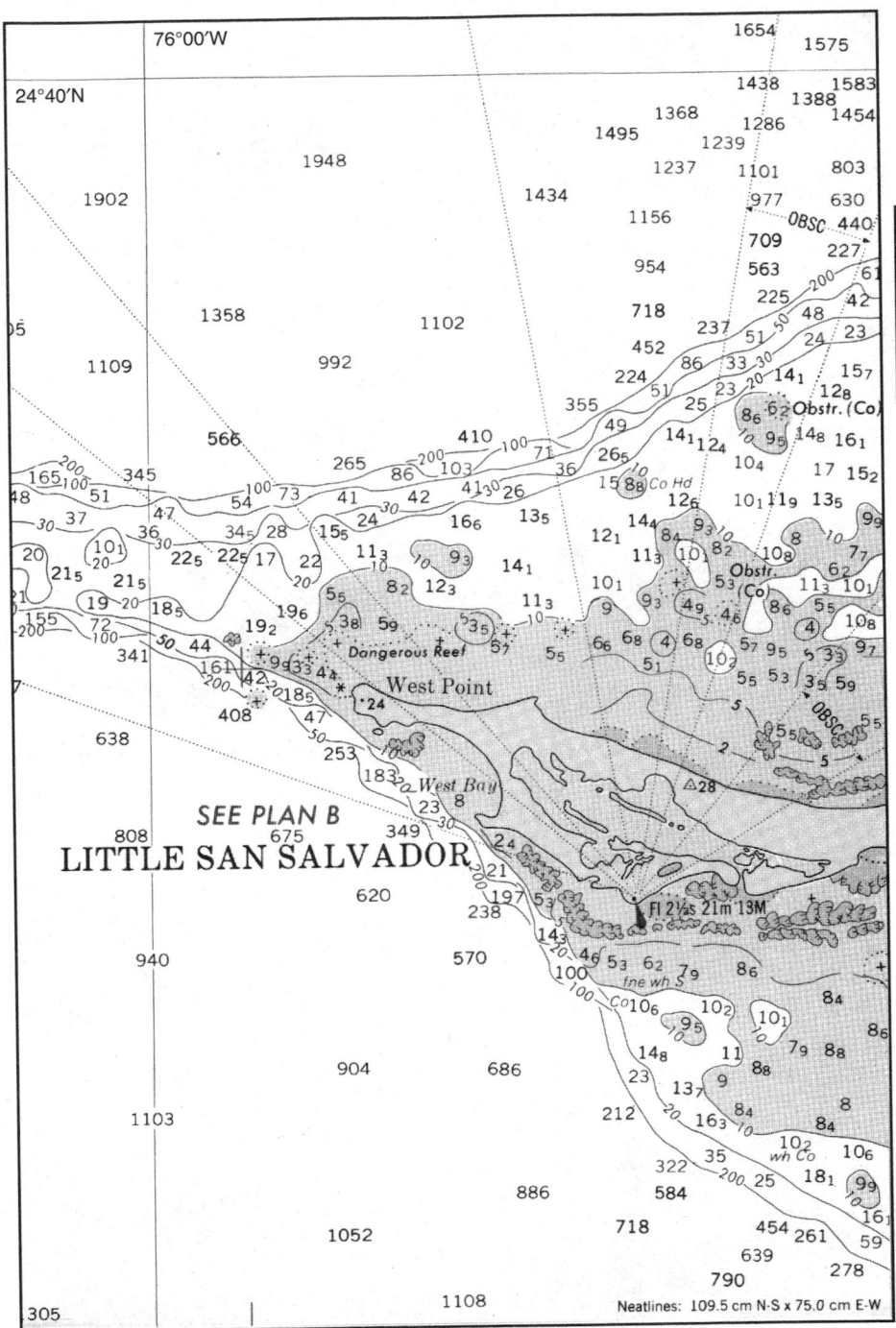

Little San Salvador, soundings in meters *(from DMA 26307, 15th ed, 8/86)*

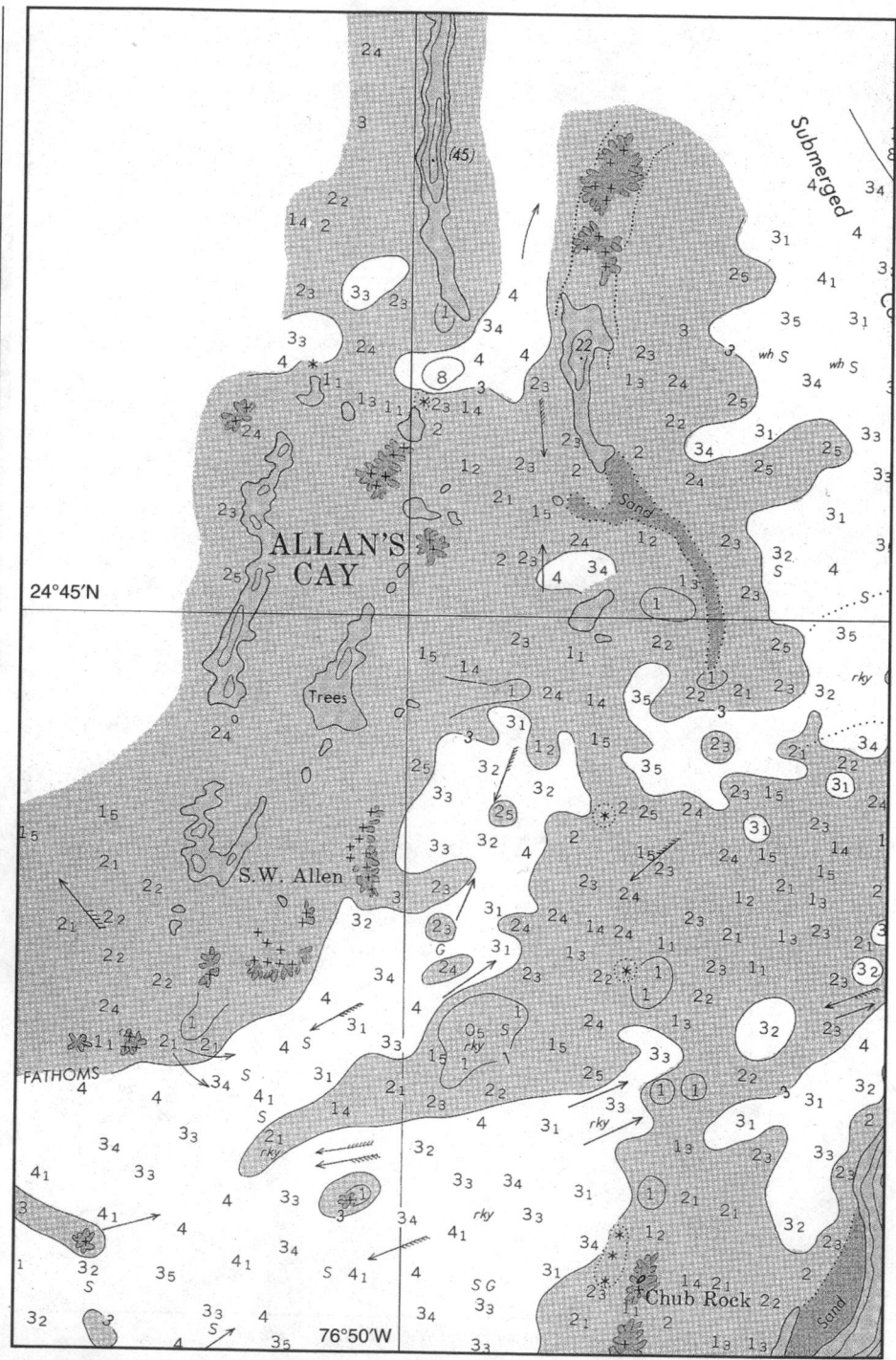

Allan's Cay, soundings in fathoms and feet *(from DMA 26257, 14th ed, 12/69)*

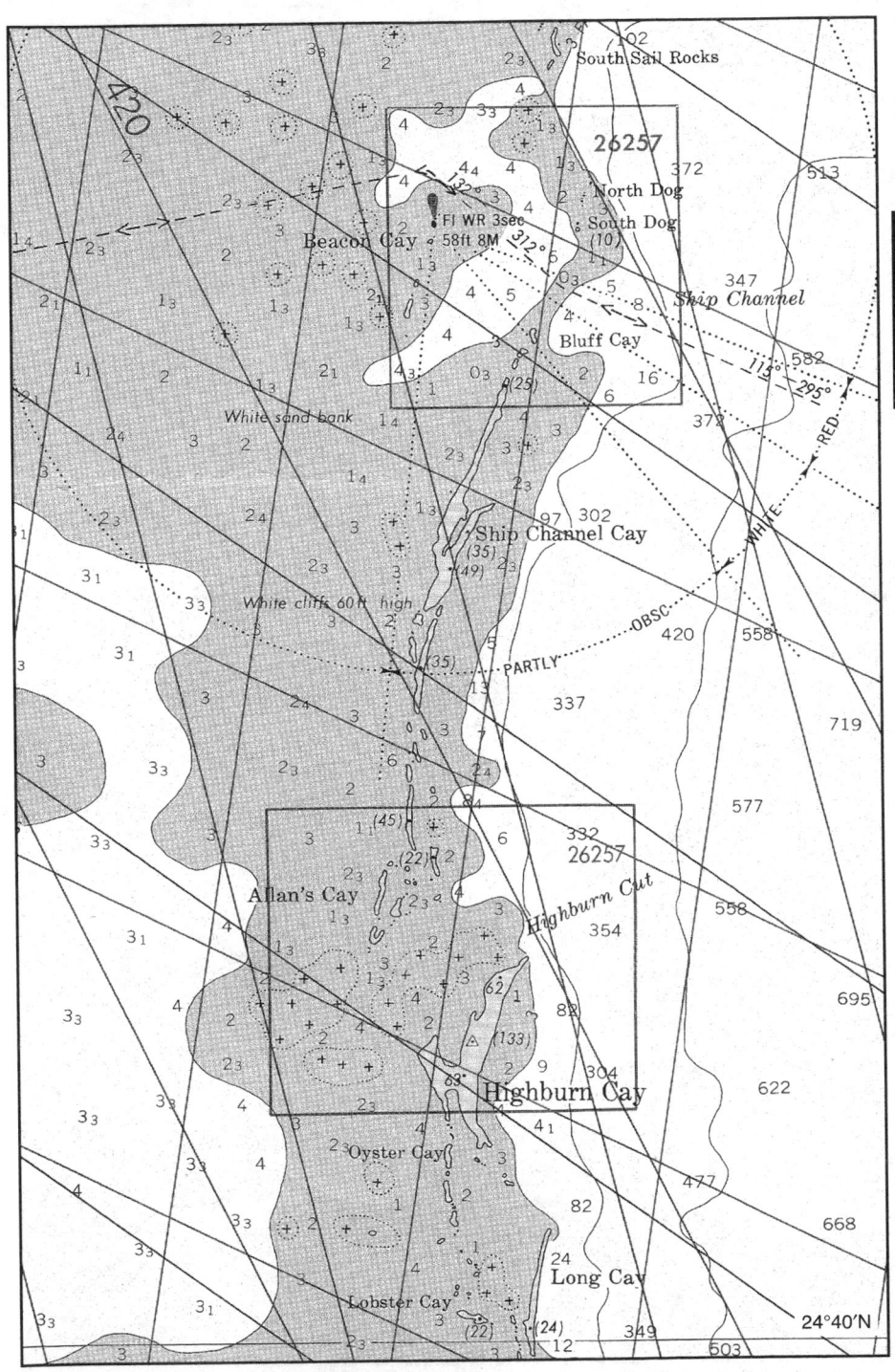

Highborne Cay, soundings in fathoms *(from DMA 26305, 4th ed, 3/80)*

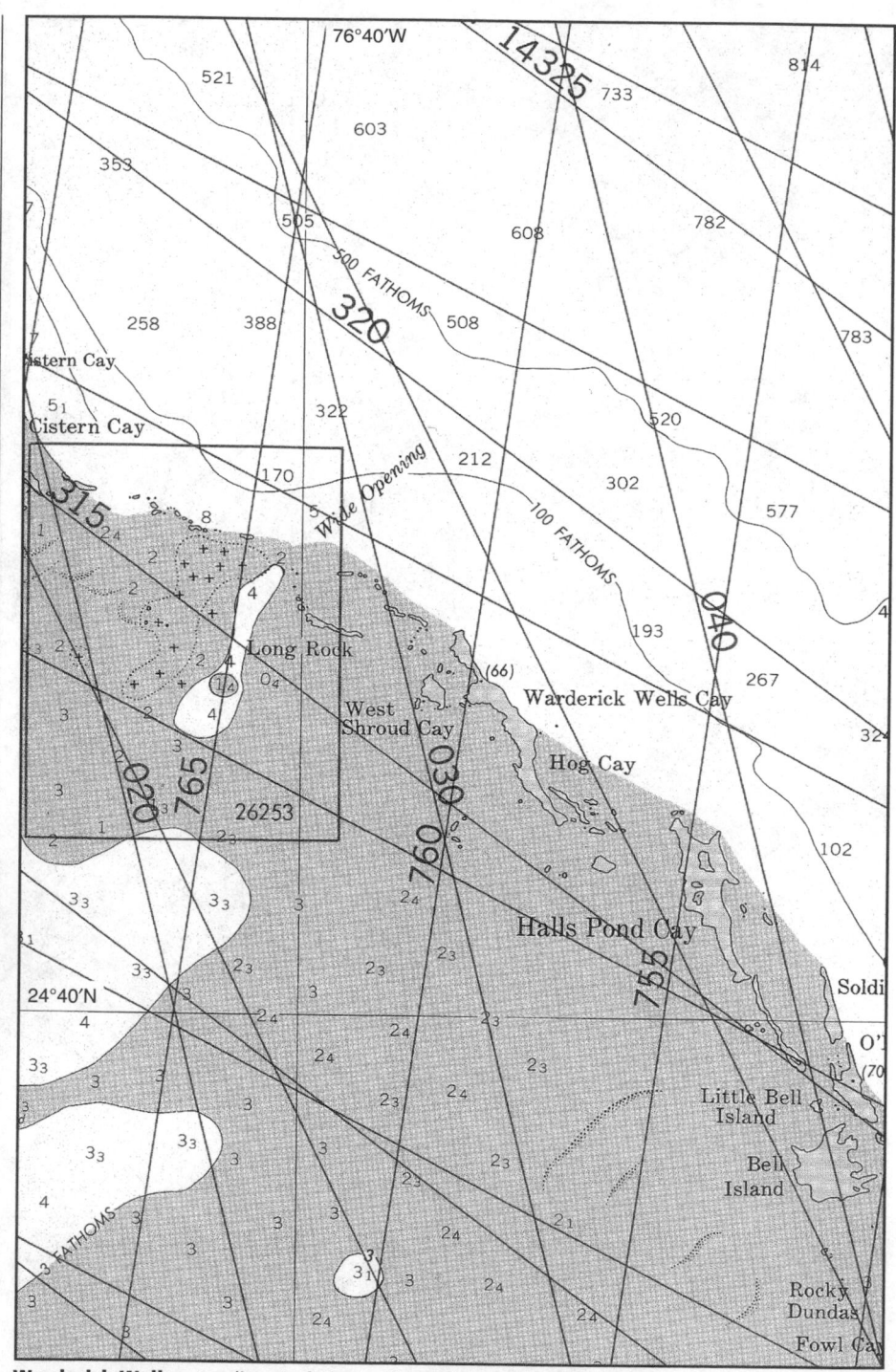

Warderick Wells, soundings in fathoms *(from DMA 26305, 4th ed, 3/80)*

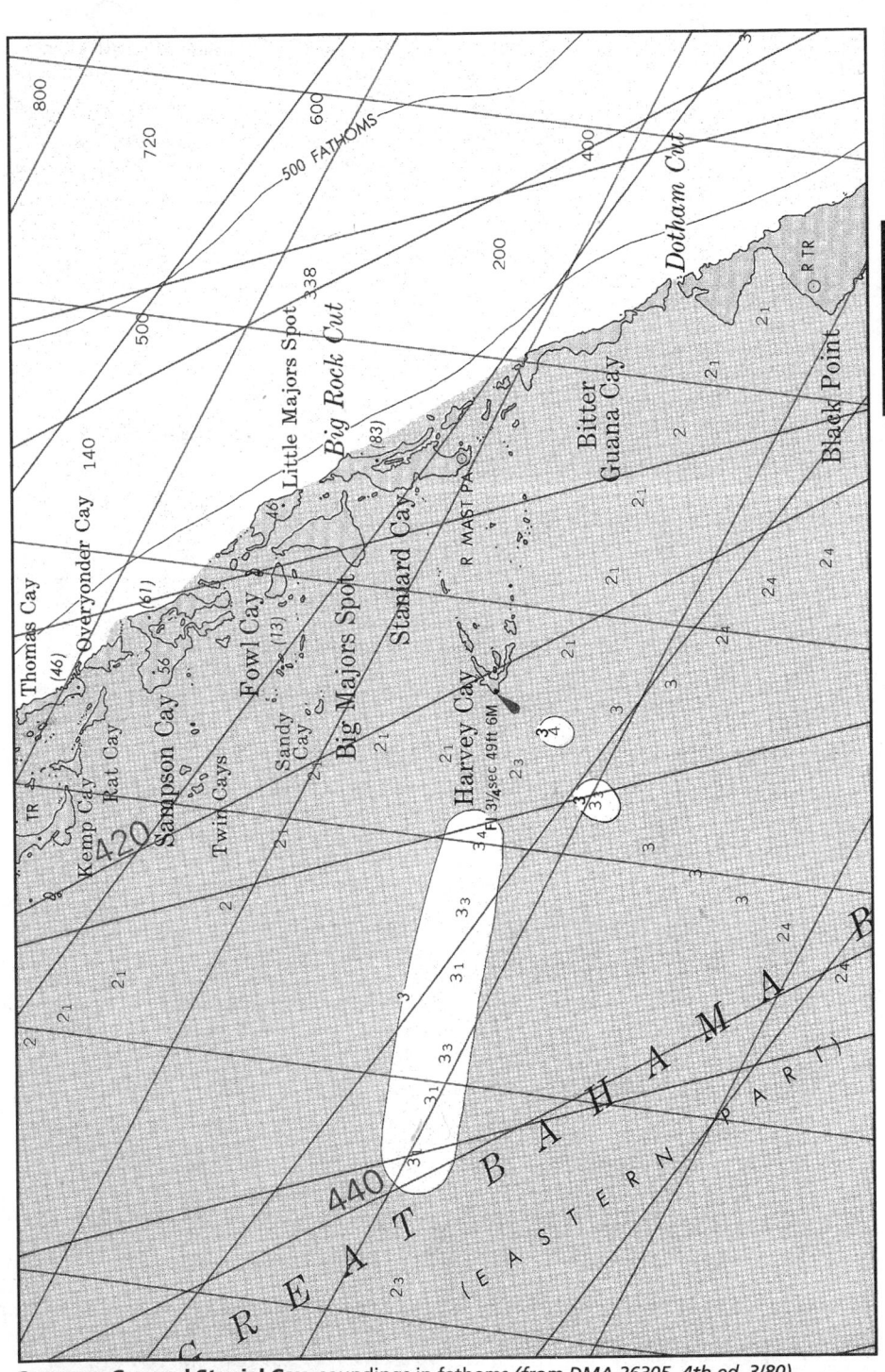

Sampson Cay and Staniel Cay, soundings in fathoms *(from DMA 26305, 4th ed, 3/80)*

Services: The club has fuel, water, ice, some groceries, liquor, diving supplies, air refills, and a restaurant and bar. Reservations are recommended for the restaurant. A seaplane is available for chartered flights and emergencies. This is also the headquarters of a salvage operation complete with a mobile crane.

STANIEL CAY

24 10N, 76 27W (Charted as Staniard Cay)
Emergencies: Call the Bahamas Air Sea Rescue Association (BASRA) on VHF channels 16 or 22 or on 2182kHz. The Nassau headquarters can be reached at 809-325-8864 (809-322-3877 after hours).
Dockage: Contact the Staniel Cay Yacht Club (809-355-2024) or the Happy People Marina (809-355-2008). Both monitor VHF channel 16. Strong currents run parallel to the yacht club docks.
Anchorage: Boats anchor in several places here. A favorite bad-weather spot is in the narrow channel east of Big Majors Spot. Some boats anchor east of the yacht club docks or in the shallow basin south of the docks. Be wary of old moorings and coral south of the docks. The approach depths to all areas are reported to be around 6 feet.
Services: Fuel, water, limited groceries, marine supplies, and a telephone are available. General repair services are available.

HARVEY CAY LIGHT, 24 09.0N, 76 28.0W. Fl W 3.3s, 49ft, 6M. Gray beacon.
BITTER GUANA CAY LIGHT, N side of Dotham Cut, 24 07.0N, 76 23.0W. Fl W 5s, 33ft.

LITTLE FARMER'S CAY

23 57N, 76 19W
Emergencies: Call the Bahamas Air Sea Rescue Association (BASRA) on VHF channels 16 or 22 or on 2182kHz. The Nassau headquarters can be reached at 809-325-8864 (809-322-3877 after hours).
Dockage: Contact Farmer's Cay Yacht Club.
Anchorage: Make your approach in good light as this area is loaded with shoals and coral areas. There is a narrow strip of deep water along the shore of Great Guana Cay and one along the east side of Little Farmer's. The mouth of the cove on the end of Big Farmer's is a good anchorage. Farmer's Cay Cut is a good passage to the deeper waters of Exuma Sound. The passage on the banks side gets quite shallow south of Little Farmers.
Services: There are a couple of small restaurants and bars. The well-known Ocean Cabin may

be reached at 809-355-4006 or via VHF channel 16. There's a telephone, an air strip, and a diver available.

GALLIOT CUT, N end of Cave Cay, 23 54.0N, 76 14.0W. Fl W 4s, 49ft, 7M. Aluminum colored steel framework tower.
CONCH CAY LIGHT, approach to Georgetown, 23 34.0N, 75 49.0W. Fl W 5s, 40ft, 8M. Aluminum and steel framework structure; housing at base.
SIMON POINT LIGHT, approach to Georgetown, 23 32.0N, 75 48.0W. F W, 40ft, 5M. Mast.

GEORGETOWN

23 31N, 75 47W
Emergencies: Call the Bahamas Air Sea Rescue Association (BASRA) on VHF channels 16 or 22 or on 2182kHz. The Nassau headquarters can be reached at 809-325-8864 (809-322-3877 after hours).
Port of Entry: Customs is located in the government building near the head of the government wharf. You may tie to the wharf temporarily.
Dockage: Available at Exuma Docking Services in Kidd Cove (809-336-2578 or VHF channel 16, call sign Sugar One). The approaches to the dock have been reported to have depths under 6 1/2 feet.
Anchorage: Hundreds of cruising boats may be found here during the winter. A popular spot is off the "holes" at Stocking Island or in one of the "holes" themselves. Boats with drafts of around 6 feet may enter the holes with local knowledge. It is wise to scout the channels with your dinghy. Many boats anchor off the Peace and Plenty Hotel, where there is a convenient dinghy dock.
Services: Fuel, water, ice, propane, groceries, some marine supplies, a telephone, restaurants, and bars are available. Good air connections can be made via Nassau. During the regattas open-air snack bars line the streets.

Georgetown is the southern terminus of many Bahamas cruisers. A large gathering of boats is bound to be here, but there always seems to be room for more. The popularity of this port has promoted the development of a good selection of shops oriented towards boaters. This is the best restocking port in the southern Bahamas.

HAWKSBILL ROCKS, on banks side, 23 26.0N, 76 07.0W. Fl W 3.3s, 32ft, 6M. White conical metal structure, black bands.

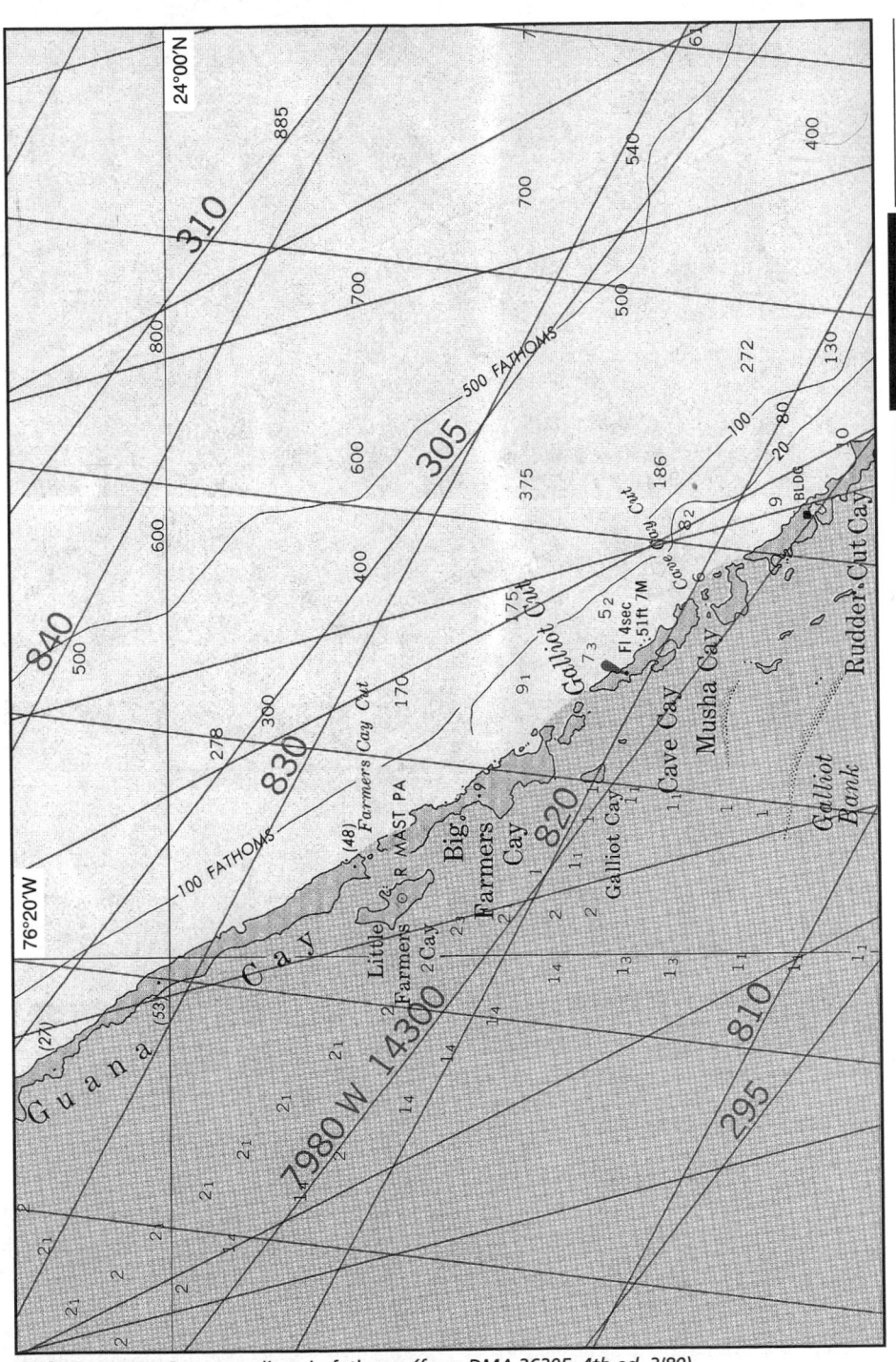

Little Farmer's Cay, soundings in fathoms *(from DMA 26305, 4th ed, 3/80)*

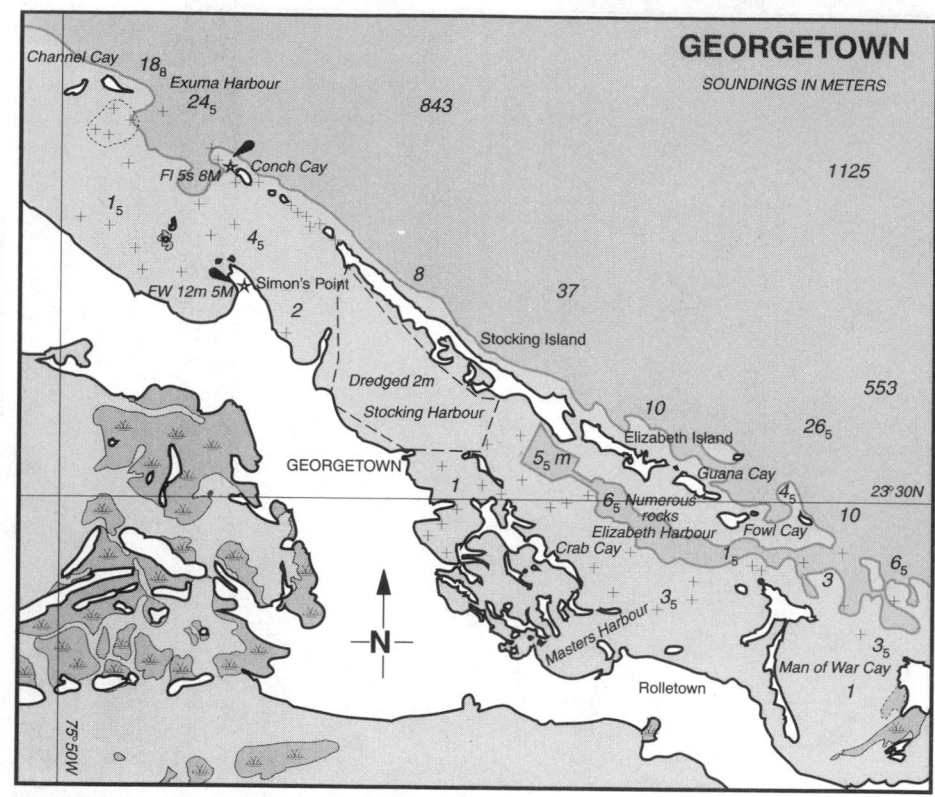

Georgetown Approaches, soundings in meters

JEWFISH CUT, on banks side, 23 27.0N, 75 58.0W. Fl W 2.5s, 38ft, 8M. White metal conical structure, black bands.

CAT ISLAND

BENNETTS HARBOR, entrance to Harbor Creek, 24 33.5N, 75 38.3W. Fl W 4s, 53ft, 12M. Light gray structure. Visible 350°–130°.

BENNETT'S HARBOR

24 33N, 75 38W

Emergencies: Call the Bahamas Air Sea Rescue Association (BASRA) on VHF channels 16 or 22 or on 2182kHz. The Nassau headquarters can be reached at 809-325-8864 (809-322-3877 after hours).

Dockage: You may be able to tie up temporarily to the government wharf.

Anchorage: There is not a lot of shelter off the west coast of Cat Island. Some of the creeks may offer shelter to shallow-draft boats.

Services: Services are very limited.

SMITH TOWN, 24 19.8N, 75 28.5W. Fl W 3.3s, 38ft, 7M. Light gray steel structure.

DEVILS POINT LIGHT, on summit, 823 meters NW of point, 24 08.0N, 75 29.0W. Fl W 5s, 143ft, 12M. Aluminum colored steel skeleton structure.

HAWKSNEST CREEK

24 09N, 75 32W

Emergencies: Call the Bahamas Air Sea Rescue Association (BASRA) on VHF channels 16 or 22 or on 2182kHz. The Nassau headquarters can be reached at 809-325-8864 (809-322-3877 after hours).

Dockage: Contact the Hawks Nest Club Marina on VHF channel 16. Depths are reported to be about 6 feet.

COAST PILOT

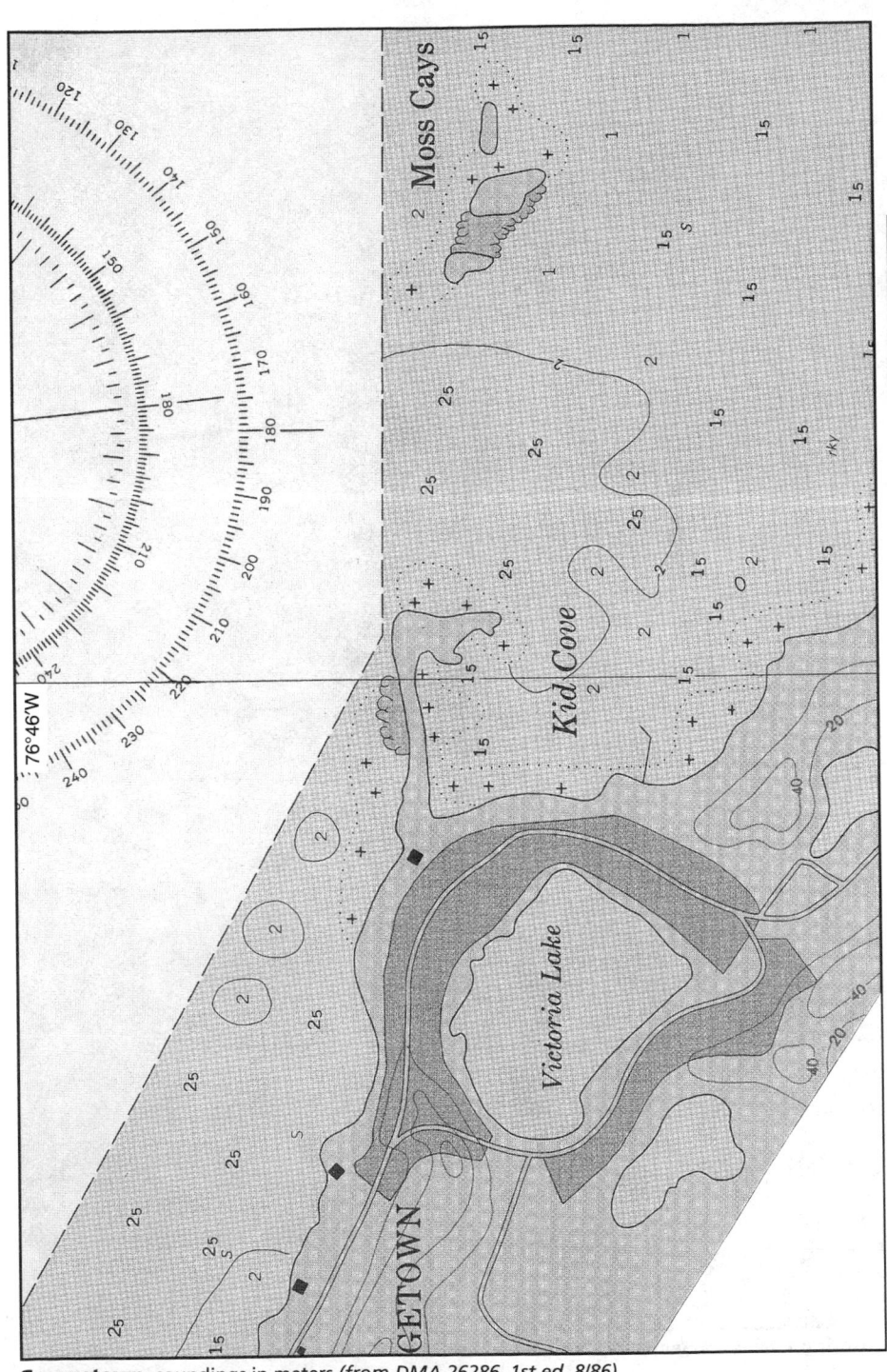

Georgetown, soundings in meters *(from DMA 26286, 1st ed, 8/86)*

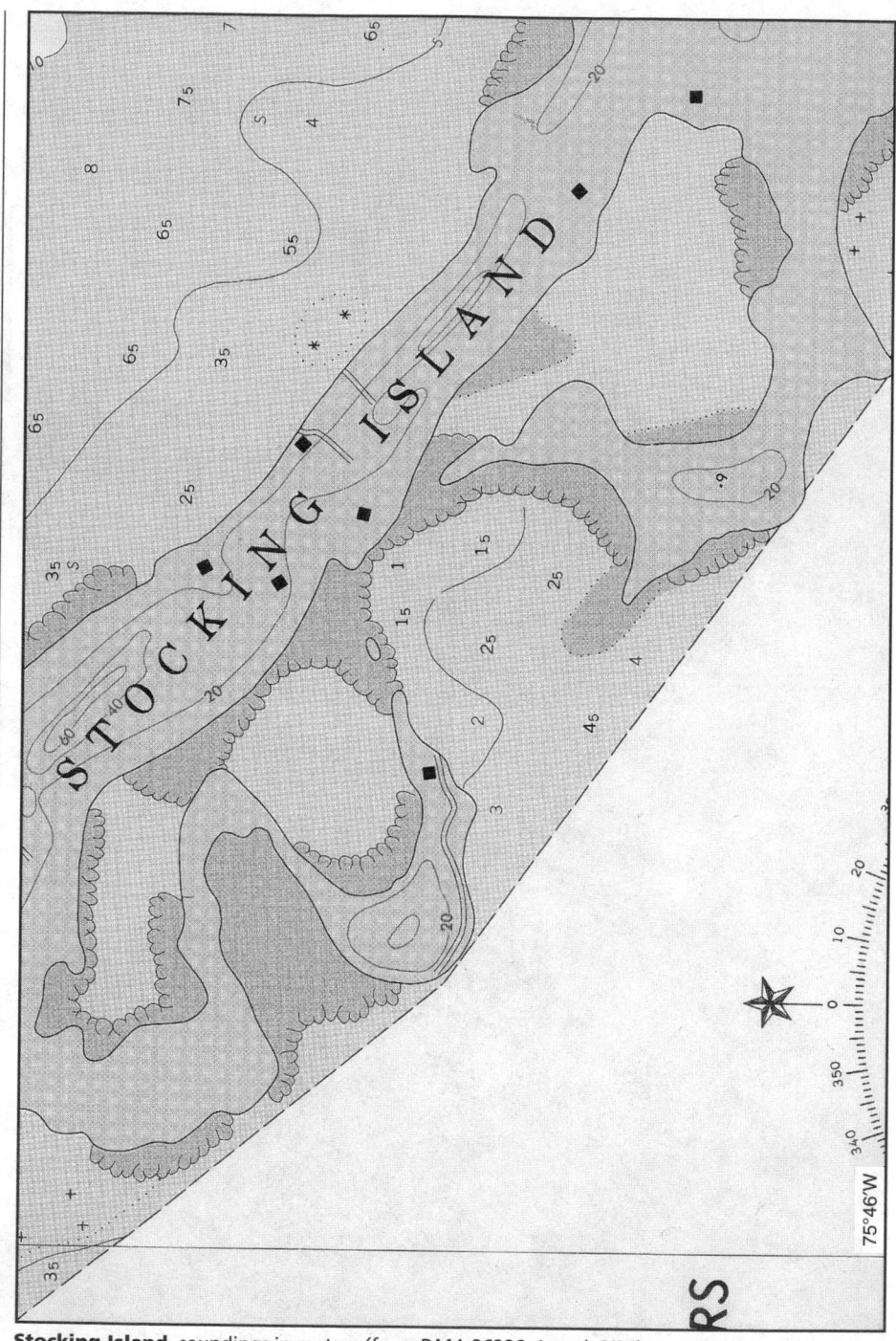

Stocking Island, soundings in meters *(from DMA 26286, 1st ed, 8/86)*

COAST PILOT

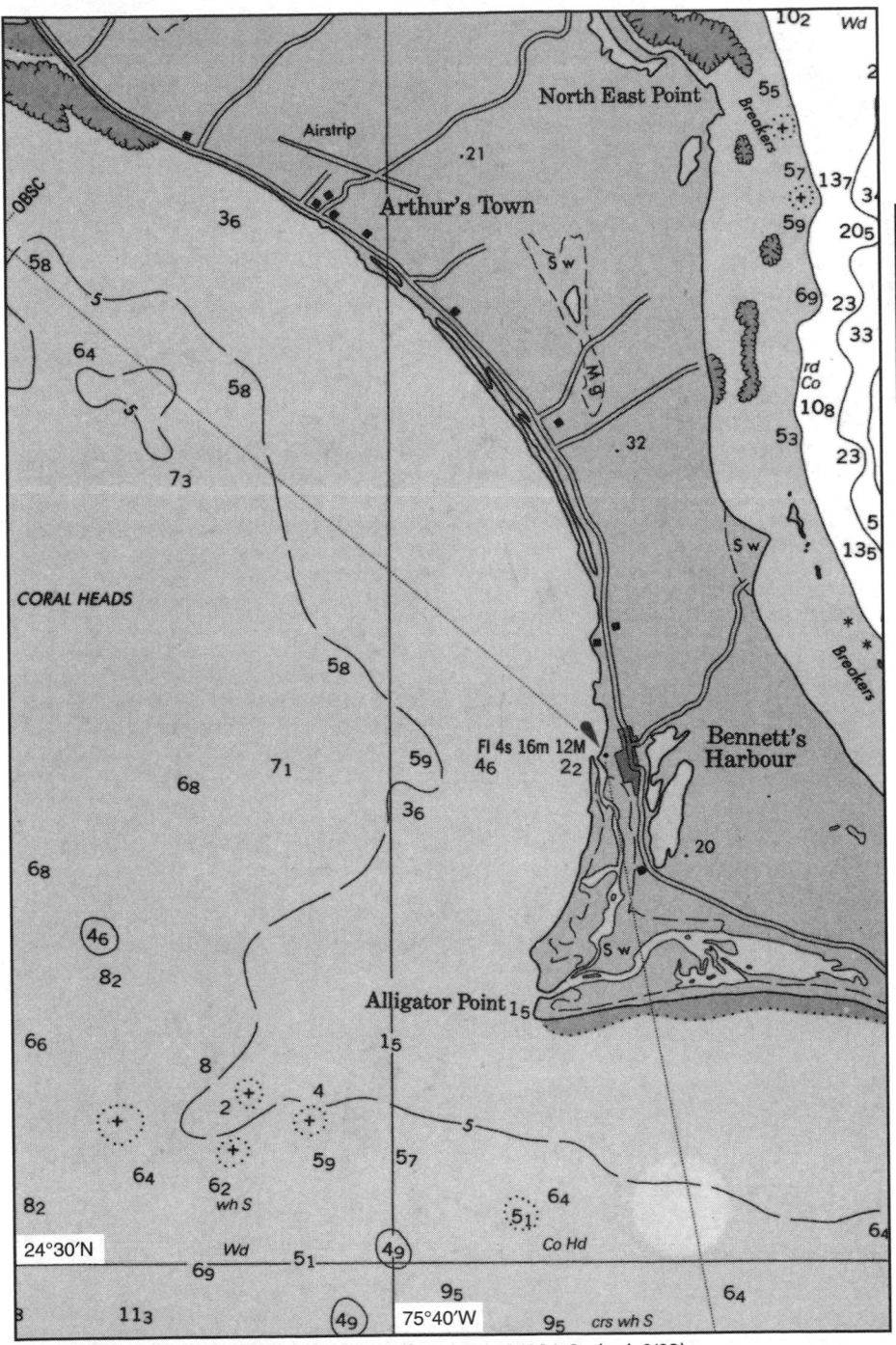

Bennett's Harbour, soundings in meters *(from DMA 26284, 2nd ed, 9/93)*

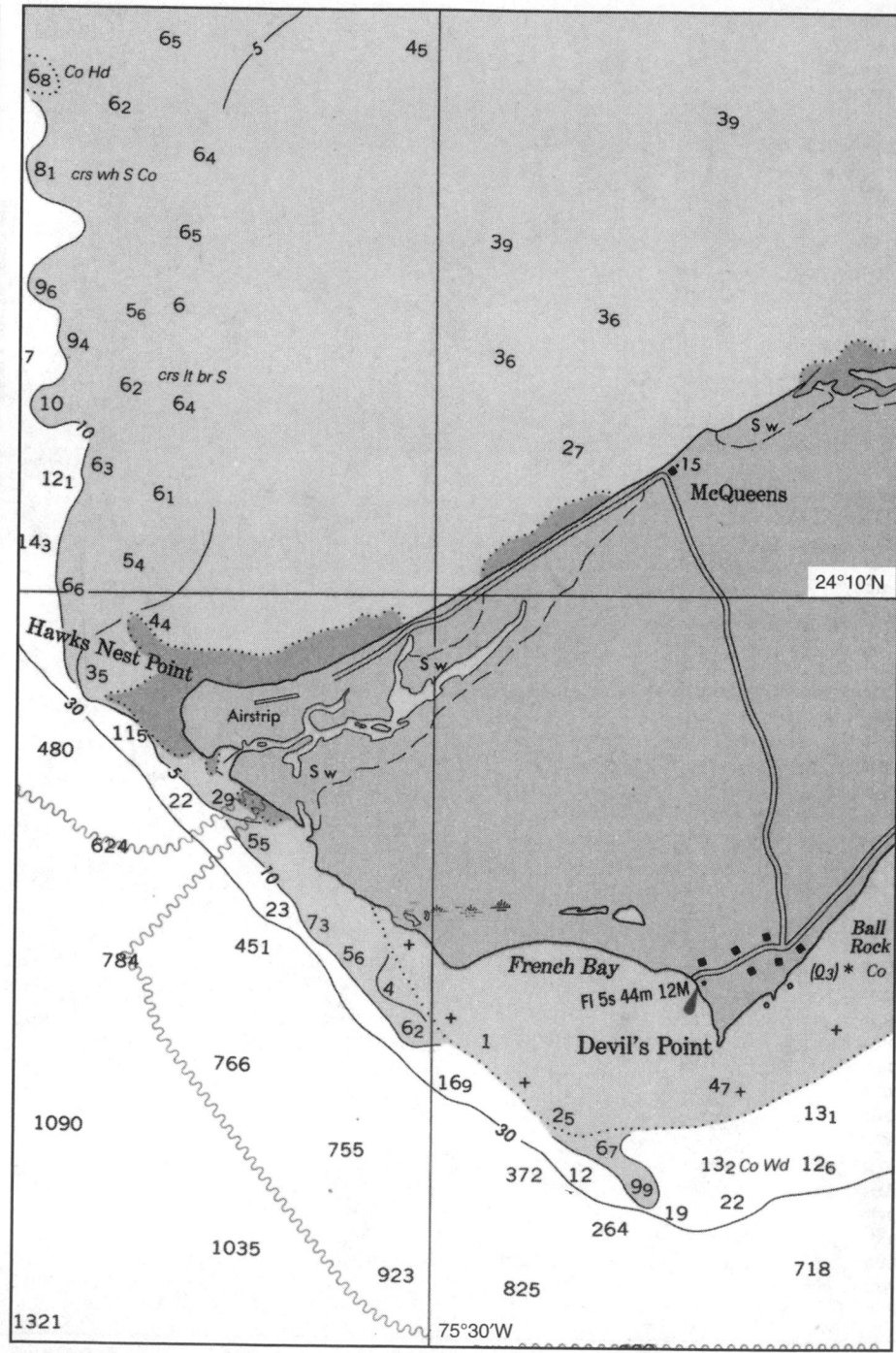

Hawksnest Creek, soundings in meters *(from DMA 26284, 2nd ed, 9/93)*

Anchorage: You can anchor in the narrow channel between the shoals. Don't block the channel to the marina.

Services: Fuel, water, and ice are available.

CONCEPTION ISLAND

CONCEPTION ISLAND LIGHT, 23 50.0N, 75 08.0W. Fl W 2s, 84ft, 6M. Gray structure.

CONCEPTION

23 50N, 75 07

Emergencies: Call the Bahamas Air Sea Rescue Association (BASRA) on VHF channels 16 or 22 or on 2182kHz. The Nassau headquarters can be reached at 809-325-8864 (809-322-3877 after hours).

Bahamas National Trust: This uninhabited island is a land and sea park, with similar regulations to the Exumas park. For more information contact: The Bahamas National Trust, P.O. Box 4105, Nassau, Bahamas.

Anchorage only: Anchor in the bay at the northwest end of the island. Proceed in slowly as coral heads have been reported. The coral becomes thicker within 1/4 mile of the beach.

RUM CAY

COTTON FIELD POINT LIGHT, 23 39.2N, 74 51.6W. L Fl W Y R 10s, 75ft, 10M. R 083°30'–006°30', W 006°30'–014°30', Y 014°30'–075°30', W 075°30'–083°30'.

PORT NELSON LIGHT, near wharf, 23 38.4N, 74 49.8W. F W, 18ft, 5M. Pole.

PORT NELSON

23 40N, 74 50W

Emergencies: Call the Bahamas Air Sea Rescue Association (BASRA) on VHF channels 16 or 22 or on 2182kHz. The Nassau headquarters can be reached at 809-325-8864 (809-322-3877 after hours).

Dockage: You may be able to tie up temporarily to the government dock. Depths are reported to be less than 6 feet.

Anchorage: Anchor west of town, as depths permit. The charted approach takes you through a deep passage between several coral reefs. A bearing of 013°T on Cotton Field Point brings you safely across the reef. When the dock at Port Nelson bears 081°T, steer for the dock.

Services: There are limited supplies and a bar and restaurant. The town has fewer than 100 residents.

SAN SALVADOR

DIXON HILL LIGHT, near NE point, 24 05.4N, 74 27.0W. Fl (2) W 10s, 163ft, 23M. White stone tower, dwelling each side. Partially obscured 001°–008°, 010°–068°, and 076°–095°.

COCKBURN TOWN LIGHT, near landing, 24 03.0N, 74 32.0W. F W, 23ft, 1M. White mast.

COCKBURN TOWN

24 03N, 74 32W

Emergencies: Call the Bahamas Air Sea Rescue Association (BASRA) on VHF channels 16 or 22 or on 2182kHz. The Nassau headquarters can be reached at 809-325-8864 (809-322-3877 after hours).

Port of Entry

Dockage: There may be some space at the tiny Riding Rock Marina (809-331-2631 or -2632 or VHF channel 06) in a basin located about half-way between town and Riding Rock Point. A range (about 075°) leads boats safely in.

Anchorage: In good weather boats can anchor in the bay off of town. Be prepared to leave if bad weather threatens.

Services: Fuel, water, a telephone, and some supplies available.

This island is considered the first landing place of Columbus in the New World. A monument has been erected on the eastern side of the island. Its charted location makes a good landmark.

LONG ISLAND

CAPE ST. MARIA, near N extremity of island, 23 41.0N, 75 21.0W. Fl W 3.3s, 99ft, 14M. Light gray iron framework structure. Obscured 240°–340°.

STELLA MARIS

23 33N, 75 16W

Emergencies: Call the Bahamas Air Sea Rescue Association (BASRA) on VHF channels 16 or 22 or on 2182kHz. The Nassau headquarters can be reached at 809-325-8864 (809-322-3877 after hours).

Port of Entry

Dockage: Between them, the Stella Maris Inn and Marina (809-336-2106 or VHF channel 16; or from the United States only, 800-426-0466) have all facilities. The approach depths to the marina are reported to be about 3 1/2 feet at low tide and 6 feet at high tide. Tides run approximately 2 hours after Nassau. Boaters

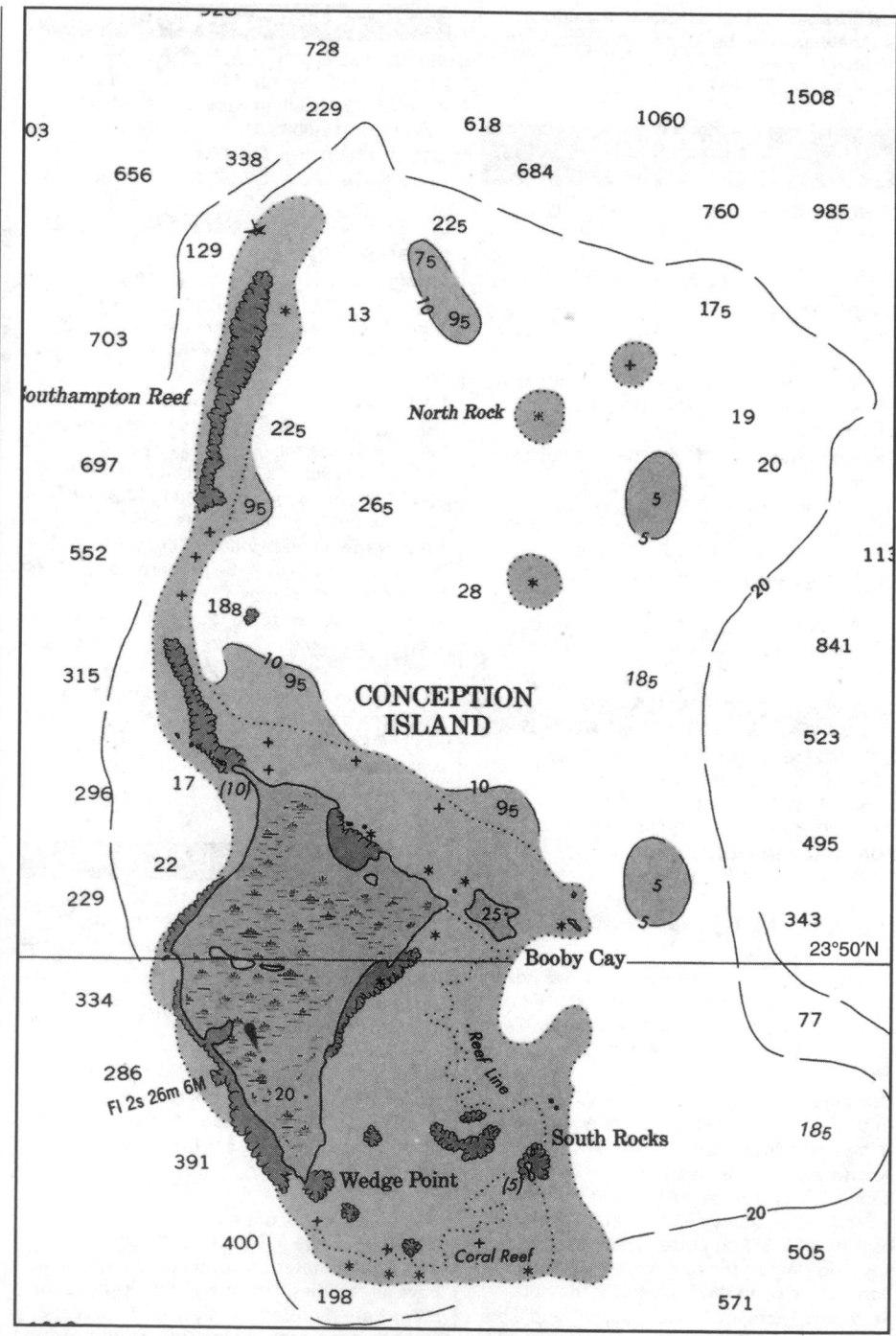

928
728
229
618
1060
1508
03
656
338
229
760
985
684
129
225
7₅
175
703
13
10
95
19
Southampton Reef
North Rock
*
20
225
697
95
265
5
5
552
188
28
*
113
10
95
841
315
185
CONCEPTION
ISLAND
523
296
17 (10)
10
495
22
95
229
25
343
Booby Cay
23°50′N
334
77
286
Reef Line
Fl 2s 26m 6M
20
391
South Rocks
185
Wedge Point
(5)
400
Coral Reef
20
505
198
571

Conception, soundings in meters *(from DMA 26284, 2nd ed, 9/93)*

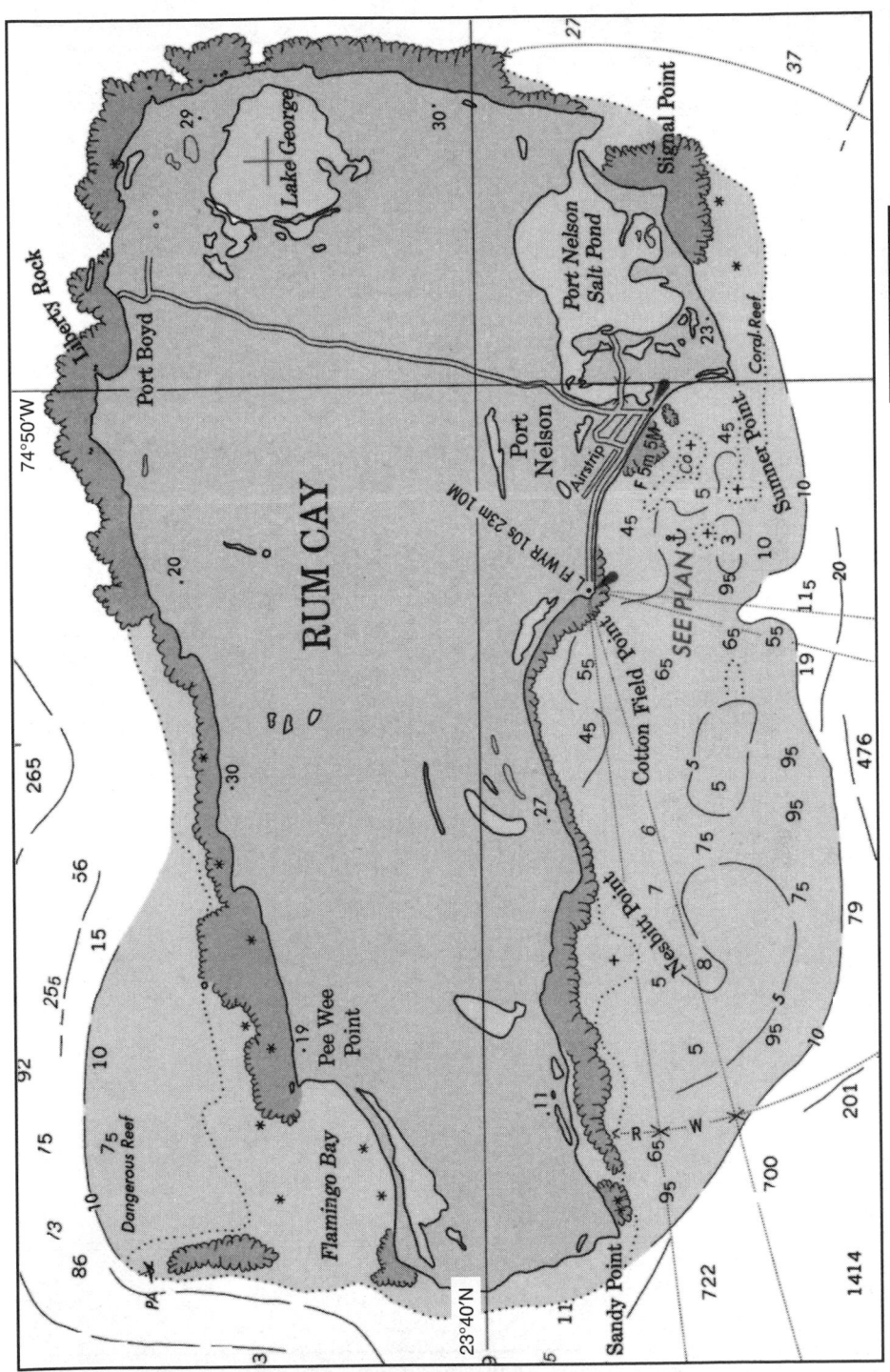

Rum Cay, soundings in meters *(from DMA 26284, 2nd ed, 9/93)*

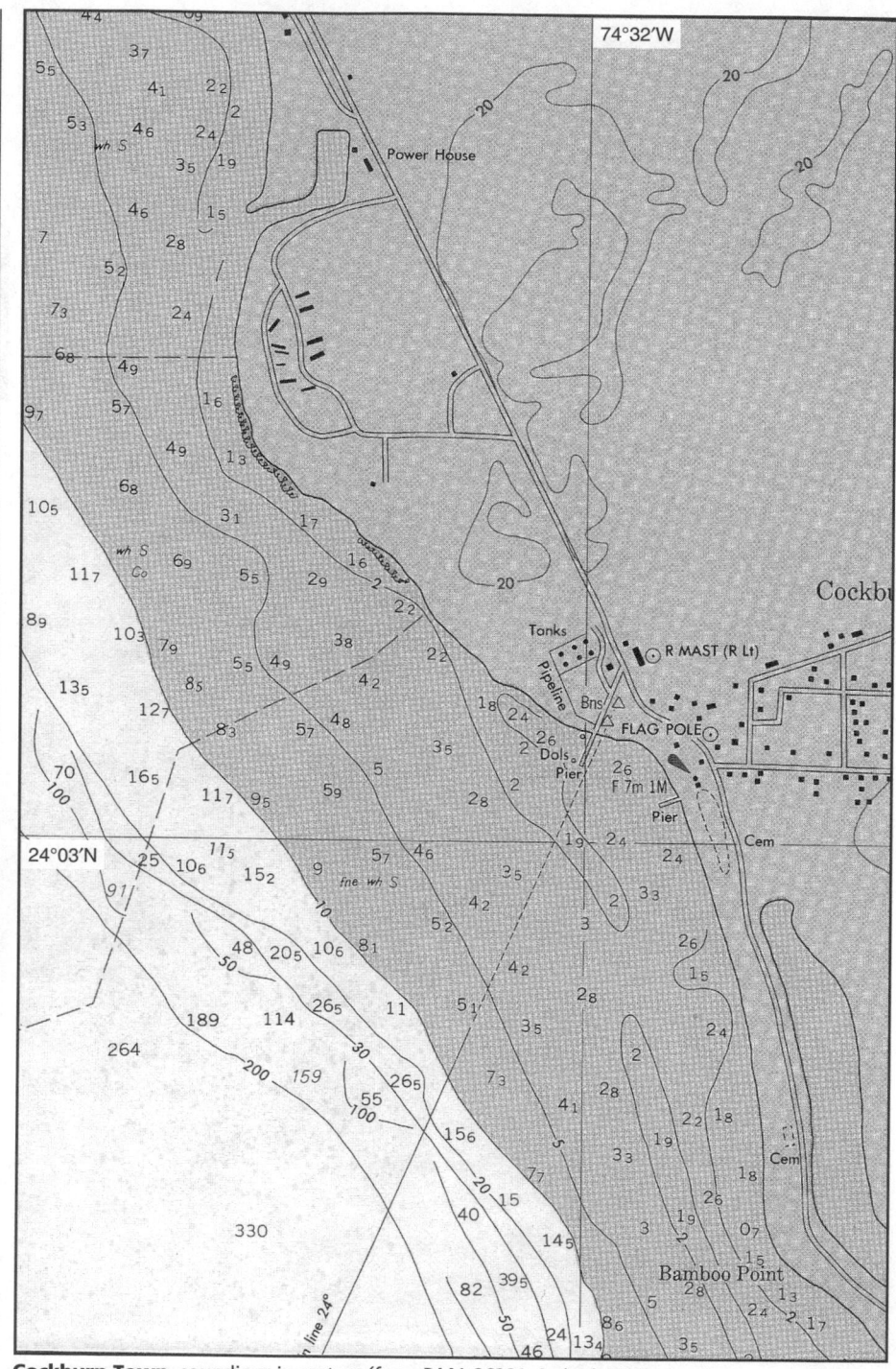

Cockburn Town, soundings in meters *(from DMA 26281, 3rd ed, 7/86)*

should head south about 1 1/2 miles past Dove Cay, until the sandbar to the east ends. Then turn to the east and head toward the bright yellow sign at the marina entrance.

Services: A marine railway makes Stella Maris the only full-repair facility south of Nassau in the Bahamas. It also has fuel, water, ice, and supplies and offers engine and fiberglass repair services. Elsewhere on the island are banking services, a post office, and restaurants. Stella Maris Inn can arrange car and bicycle rentals for exploring the island.

SIMMS LIGHT, 23 29.0N, 75 14.0W. F W, 23ft, 4M. Mast.

BOOBY ROCK LIGHT, approach to Clarence Town, 23 07.0N, 74 58.3W. Fl W 2s, 39ft, 8M. Red and white structure.

HARBOR POINT LIGHT, approach to Clarence Town, 23 06.2N, 74 57.5W. F W, 25ft, 3M. White mast and hut.

CLARENCE TOWN

23 06N, 74 58W

Emergencies: Call the Bahamas Air Sea Rescue Association (BASRA) on VHF channels 16 or 22 or on 2182kHz. The Nassau headquarters can be reached at 809-325-8864 (809-322-3877 after hours).

Dockage: You may be able to tie up temporarily to the government wharf.

Anchorage: Anchor off town, avoiding the charted cables. This area is wide open to north and west winds and may be untenable in bad weather.

Services: Fuel, water, groceries, ice, a telephone, and a restaurant are available.

The best approach is from the north, passing west of Booby Rocks. Approach in good light to avoid the many reefs and shoals in the area. As the administrative center of Long Island, it has a good variety of services.

SOUTH POINT LIGHT, Turbot Hill, 22 51.3N, 74 51.2W. Fl W 2.5s, 61ft, 12M. Gray metal structure. Partially obscured 140°–245°.

GALLOWAY LANDING LIGHT, 23 04.0N, 75 00.0W. F W, 14ft, 2M. White post and lantern. Marks landing place for small boats.

JUMENTOS CAYS

NUEVITAS ROCKS LIGHT, on eastern Jumentos Cays, 23 09.0N, 75 23.0W. Fl W 4s, 38ft, 10M. Gray structure.

FLAMINGO CAY LIGHT, on hill, 22 53.0N, 75 52.0W. Fl W 6s, 138ft, 8M. Aluminum colored steel tower.

RAGGED ISLAND LIGHT, Duncan Town, Man-O-War Hill, 22 11.0N, 75 44.0W. Fl W 3s, 118ft, 12M. Black pipe, platform. F W light shown from settlement wharf. Unreliable.

RAGGED ISLAND HARBOR

22 14N, 75 44W

Emergencies: Call the Bahamas Air Sea Rescue Association (BASRA) on VHF channels 16 or 22 or on 2182kHz. The Nassau headquarters can be reached at 809-325-8864 (809-322-3877 after hours).

Dockage: The narrow, shallow channel to Duncan Town should be attempted with local knowledge only.

Anchorage: Anchor in a sandy spot away from the coral. The sailing directions recommend an anchoring spot in a position where the south extremity of Little Ragged Island bears 097°T and Point Wilson, on Ragged Island, bears 004°T. The latter anchorage is not shown on the chartlet in this almanac.

Services: There are some limited supplies, a bar, and a restaurant.

Ragged Island is at the southern end of the Jumentos Cays, in one of the most remote areas of the Bahamas.

CAY SANTO DOMINGO LIGHT, 21 42.0N, 75 44.0W. Fl W 5s, 29ft, 7M. Aluminum and red steel structure. Reported extinguished 1990.

OLD BAHAMA CHANNEL

CAY LOBOS, near W end, 22 22.9N, 77 35.9W. Fl (2) W 20s, 145ft, 22M. White round metal tower. Reported extinguished 1991.

CROOKED AND ACKLINS ISLAND

WINDSOR POINT LIGHT, 22 34.0N, 74 22.5W. Fl W 3s, 36ft, 8M. Black structure.

BIRD ROCK LIGHT, on summit, 22 50.9N, 74 21.5W. Fl W 15s, 112ft, 23M. White conical stone tower.

MAJORS CAY LIGHT, 22 45.0N, 74 09.0W. F W, 30ft, 4M. Mast. Unreliable.

ATTWOOD HARBOR LIGHT, W of NE point of Acklins Island, 22 44.2N, 73 52.6W. Fl W 4.5s, 20ft, 5M. Metal tower.

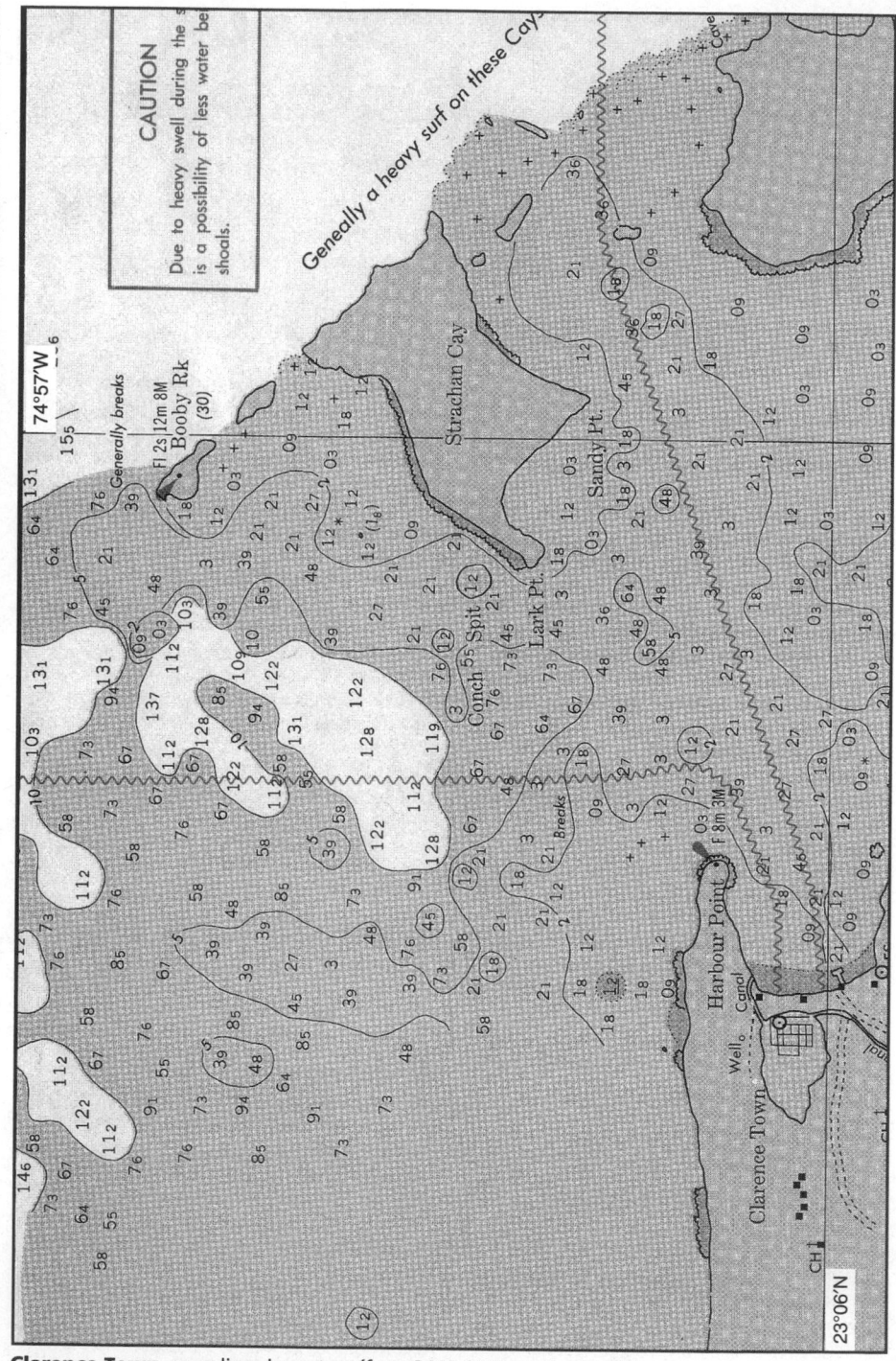

Clarence Town, soundings in meters *(from DMA 26280, 6th ed, 2/91)*

COAST PILOT

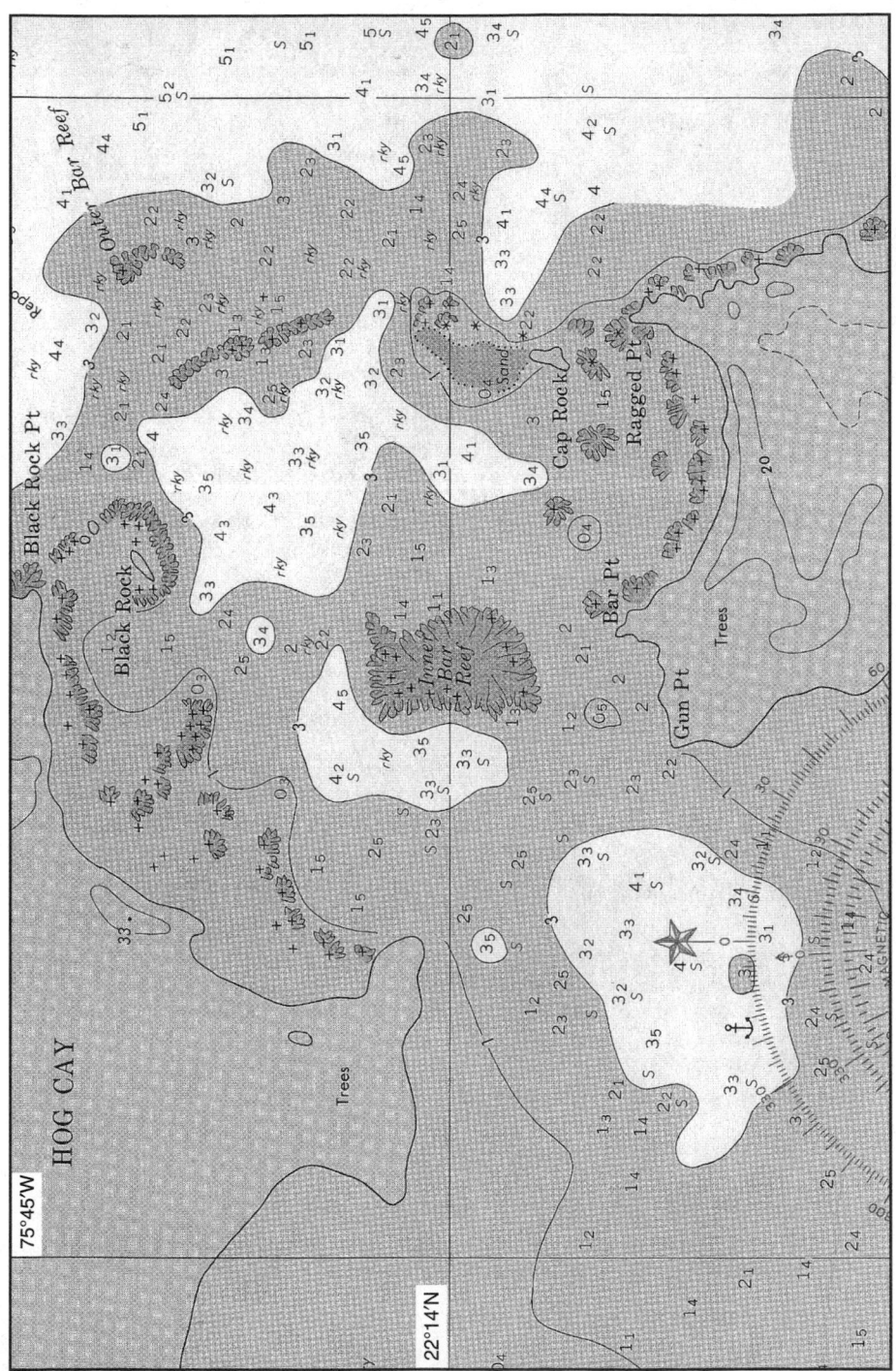

Ragged Island Harbour, soundings in fathoms and feet *(from DMA 26257, 14th ed, 12/69)*

ACKLINS ISLAND NORTHEAST POINT LIGHT, Hell Gate, 22 43.8N, 73 50.8W. Fl W 6s, 56ft, 10M. Gray steel tower.
CASTLE ISLAND LIGHT, near SW point, 22 07.3N, 74 19.6W. Fl (2) W, 20s, 131ft, 22M. White cylindrical tower.
SPRING POINT LIGHT, 22 28.5N, 73 57.7W. F W, 19ft, 7M. White pole.
LONG CAY LIGHT, E side of cay, 22 37.0N, 74 19.3W. F W, 60ft, 4M. White post.

MAYAGUANA

NORTHWEST POINT LIGHT, 22 27.8N, 73 07.6W. Fl W 5s, 70ft, 12M. White framework tower; red lantern.
GUANO POINT LIGHT, Abraham Bay, 22 21.1N, 72 57.9W. Fl W 3s, 14ft, 8M. Gray structure.

ABRAHAM'S BAY

22 21N, 73 00W
Emergencies: Call the Bahamas Air Sea Rescue Association (BASRA) on VHF channels 16 or 22 or on 2182kHz. The Nassau headquarters can be reached at 809-325-8864 (809-322-3877 after hours).
Anchorage: The best area to anchor is in Abraham's Bay, southwest of the settlement. There are two channels through the reef, one near Guano Point and the other southeast of Low Point. An approach in good light is recommended. Keep a good lookout for coral throughout Abraham's Bay.
Services: There is a telephone and limited supplies. You can jug fuel or water to your boat.

HOGSTY REEF

HOGSTY REEF LIGHT, on Northwest Cay, 21 41.4N, 73 50.8W. Fl W 4s, 29ft, 8M. Red mast, white bands.

GREAT INAGUA ISLAND

MAN OF WAR BAY RANGE (Front Light), 21 03.3N, 73 39.2W. F Y, B and W square daymark. **(Rear Light),** 320 meters 087° from front. F Y. Black and white square daymark.
MAN OF WAR BAY RANGE (Front Light), 21 03.3N, 73 39.3W. F Y. Black and white square daymark. **(Rear Light),** 120 meters 130° from front. F Y. Black and white square daymark.
MATTHEW TOWN LIGHT, 20 56.5N, 73 40.2W. Fl (2) W 10s, 120ft, 22M. White cylindrical stone tower. Partially obscured 165°–183°.

MATTHEW TOWN

21 00N, 73 30W
Emergencies: Call the Bahamas Air Sea Rescue Association (BASRA) on VHF channels 16 or 22 or on 2182kHz. The Nassau headquarters can be reached at 809-325-8864 (809-322-3877 after hours).
Port of Entry: Located in Matthew Town at the southwest corner of the island.
Bahamas National Trust: The Inagua Park is the home of a huge colony of flamingoes. For more information contact: The Bahamas National Trust, P.O. Box 4105, Nassau, Bahamas.
Anchorage: There is anchorage in Man of War Bay on the western side of the island. The wharf, extending 400 yards seaward, is owned by the Morton Salt Co. and is private. Vessels up to 35,000 tons call here. The terminal may be contacted on 2182kHz or VHF channel 16 (call sign, Morton Salt). Matthew Town is the administrative center of the island An open roadstead anchorage is available off the town.
Services: Some supplies and a telephone are available. There is an airstrip with flights available to Nassau.

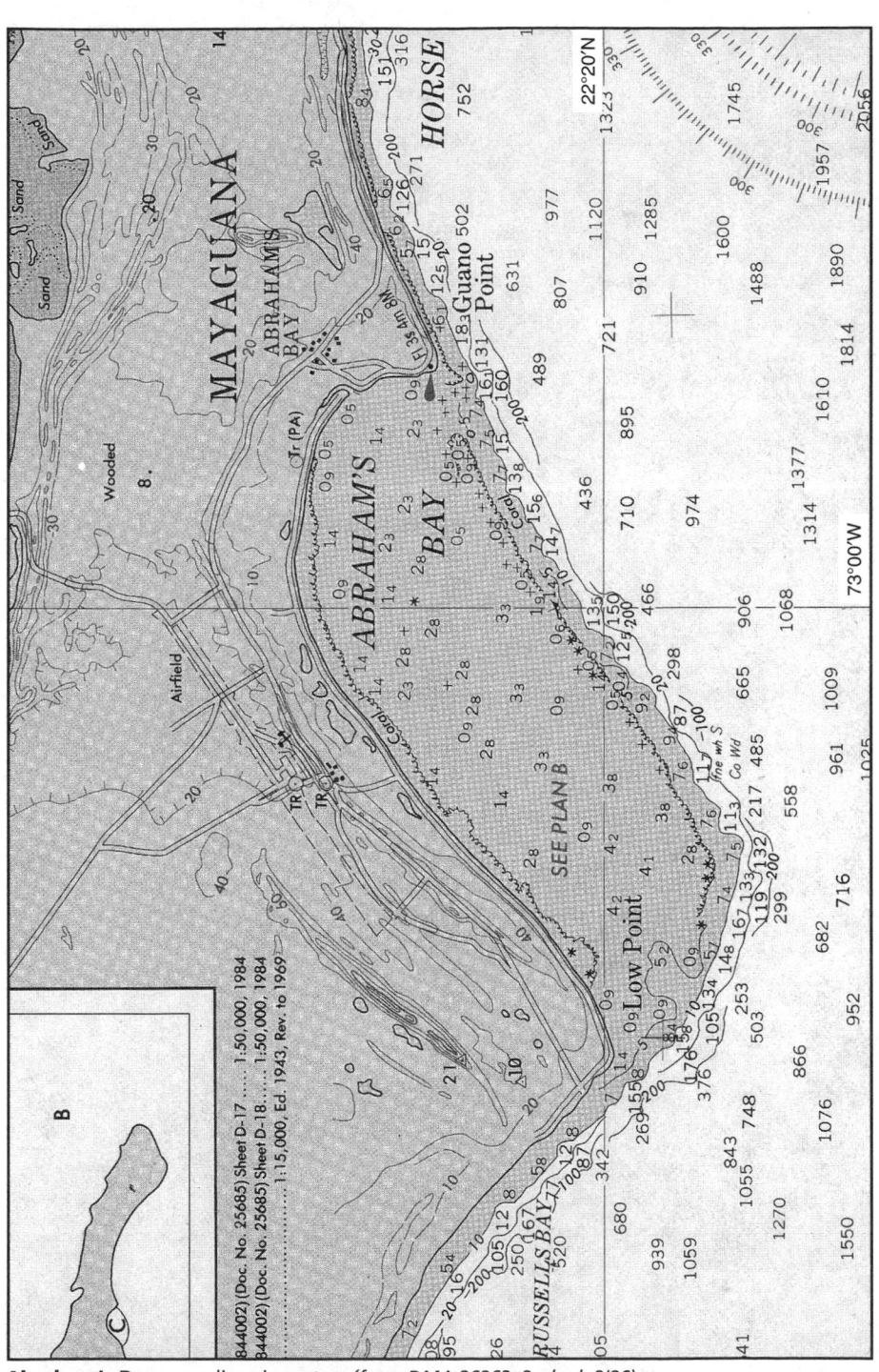

Abraham's Bay, soundings in meters *(from DMA 26263, 2nd ed, 8/86)*

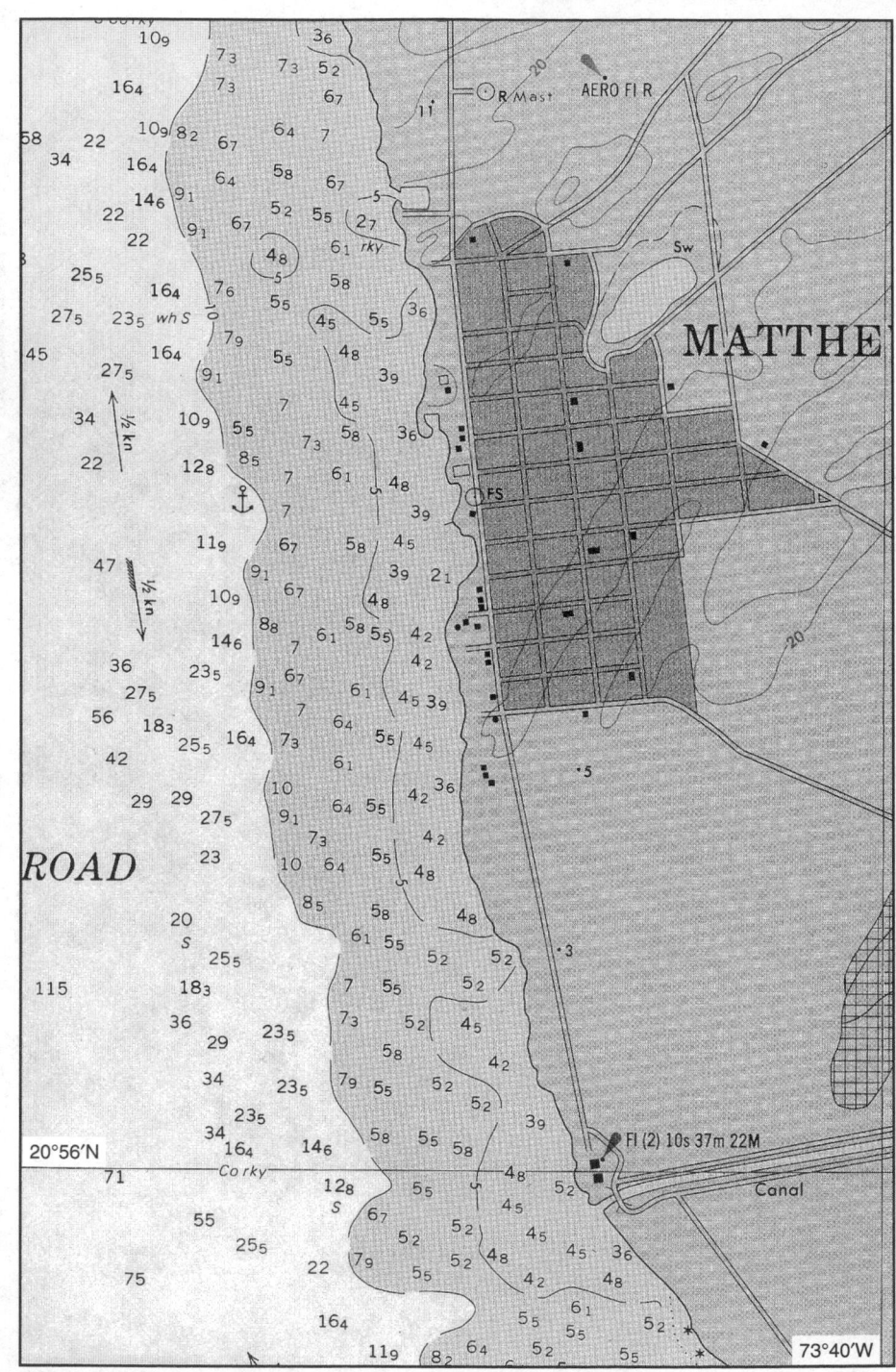

Matthew Town, soundings in meters *(from DMA 26267, 1st ed, 8/86)*

NASSAU, BAHAMAS

HIGH & LOW WATER 1995 25°05'N 77°21'W

EASTERN STANDARD TIME (GMT -5H). ADD 1H DAYLIGHT SAVING APR 2 - OCT 28

JANUARY

Day	Time ft	Time ft	Time ft	Time ft
1 Su ●	0045 0.6	0720 4.7	1347 0.9	1939 3.7
2 M	0139 0.6	0812 4.7	1438 0.8	2034 3.8
3 Tu	0233 0.7	0902 4.6	1528 0.8	2128 3.7
4 W	0327 0.9	0951 4.4	1617 0.9	2222 3.7
5 Th	0421 1.1	1039 4.1	1705 0.9	2316 3.7
6 F	0515 1.3	1127 3.9	1752 1.0	
7 Sa	0010 3.6	0611 1.5	1215 3.6	1839 1.1
8 Su (	0105 3.6	0710 1.6	1304 3.4	1925 1.2
9 M	0200 3.6	0809 1.7	1354 3.2	2012 1.2
10 Tu	0253 3.7	0908 1.7	1446 3.1	2059 1.3
11 W	0344 3.7	1005 1.7	1538 3.1	2145 1.2
12 Th	0431 3.8	1056 1.6	1629 3.0	2231 1.2
13 F	0515 3.9	1143 1.5	1718 3.1	2316 1.2
14 Sa	0558 4.0	1226 1.4	1804 3.1	
15 Su	0000 1.1	0638 4.1	1306 1.3	1848 3.2
16 M O	0043 1.1	0718 4.1	1345 1.2	1932 3.3
17 Tu	0127 1.0	0757 4.2	1423 1.1	2014 3.4
18 W	0210 1.0	0837 4.1	1500 1.1	2057 3.5
19 Th	0255 1.1	0916 4.1	1539 1.0	2141 3.6
20 F	0341 1.1	0958 4.0	1619 1.0	2228 3.7
21 Sa	0430 1.2	1041 3.9	1701 1.0	2318 3.8
22 Su	0524 1.2	1129 3.7	1748 0.9	
23 M)	0013 3.9	0623 1.3	1221 3.6	1839 0.9
24 Tu	0112 3.9	0727 1.4	1319 3.5	1935 0.9
25 W	0215 4.0	0834 1.4	1422 3.4	2036 0.9
26 Th	0318 4.1	0942 1.3	1637 3.4	2138 0.8
27 F	0420 4.3	1046 1.2	1632 3.4	2239 0.7
28 Sa	0519 4.4	1145 1.1	1733 3.5	2338 0.7
29 Su	0614 4.5	1239 1.0	1831 3.6	
30 M ●	0035 0.7	0706 4.5	1329 0.9	1925 3.7
31 Tu	0128 0.7	0755 4.4	1417 0.8	2017 3.8

FEBRUARY

Day	Time ft	Time ft	Time ft	Time ft
1 W	0220 0.8	0842 4.3	1502 0.8	2106 3.8
2 Th	0309 1.0	0926 4.1	1545 0.9	2154 3.8
3 F	0358 1.1	1009 3.9	1627 1.0	2242 3.8
4 Sa	0447 1.3	1051 3.7	1709 1.1	2330 3.7
5 Su	0536 1.5	1134 3.5	1750 1.2	
6 M	0019 3.6	0628 1.6	1218 3.3	1834 1.3
7 Tu	0110 3.6	0723 1.7	1306 3.2	(1920 1.3
8 W	0202 3.6	0821 1.8	1359 3.1	2010 1.4
9 Th	0256 3.6	0920 1.8	1456 3.0	2102 1.4
10 F	0348 3.7	1014 1.7	1552 3.1	2155 1.3
11 Sa	0437 3.8	1104 1.6	1646 3.2	2246 1.2
12 Su	0523 3.9	1148 1.4	1735 3.3	2335 1.2
13 M	0607 4.0	1230 1.3	1822 3.4	
14 Tu	0022 1.1	0649 4.1	1310 1.1	1906 3.6
15 W	0108 1.0	0731 4.2	1349 1.0	O 1949 3.8
16 Th	0154 0.9	0811 4.2	1427 0.9	2033 3.9
17 F	0239 0.9	0853 4.1	1507 0.9	2118 4.0
18 Sa	0327 1.0	0936 4.0	1549 0.9	2206 4.1
19 Su	0417 1.1	1021 3.9	1634 0.9	2256 4.1
20 M	0510 1.2	1110 3.7	1722 0.9	2352 4.1
21 Tu	0609 1.3	1204 3.6	1816 1.0	
22 W	0052 4.1	0713 1.4	1305 3.5	) 1916 1.0
23 Th	0157 4.1	0821 1.4	1411 3.4	2021 1.1
24 F	0303 4.1	0929 1.3	1520 3.4	2128 1.0
25 Sa	0407 4.2	1033 1.3	1626 3.5	2232 1.0
26 Su	0506 4.2	1129 1.2	1726 3.7	2332 1.0
27 M	0600 4.3	1220 1.1	1820 3.8	
28 Tu	0027 0.9	0649 4.3	1307 1.0	1910 3.9

MARCH

Day	Time ft	Time ft	Time ft	Time ft
1 W ●	0118 0.9	0735 4.2	1350 1.0	1957 4.0
2 Th	0205 1.0	0818 4.1	1430 1.0	2041 4.0
3 F	0251 1.1	0858 4.0	1509 1.1	2124 4.0
4 Sa	0334 1.2	0937 3.8	1546 1.1	2206 4.0
5 Su	0418 1.4	1015 3.6	1623 1.2	2248 3.9
6 M	0502 1.6	1054 3.5	1702 1.3	2332 3.8
7 Tu	0549 1.7	1136 3.3	1743 1.4	
8 W	0019 3.8	0640 1.8	1224 3.2	1830 1.5
9 Th	0110 3.7	0735 1.8	1318 3.1	(1923 1.6
10 F	0205 3.7	0833 1.8	1418 3.2	2021 1.6
11 Sa	0301 3.8	0928 1.7	1518 3.2	2120 1.5
12 Su	0354 3.9	1019 1.6	1614 3.4	2217 1.4
13 M	0444 4.0	1106 1.5	1705 3.6	2310 1.3
14 Tu	0532 4.1	1149 1.3	1753 3.8	
15 W	0617 4.2	1231 1.1	1838 4.1	
16 Th	0048 1.0	0701 4.2	1312 1.0	O 1923 4.3
17 F	0135 1.0	0744 4.2	1353 0.9	2009 4.4
18 Sa	0223 0.9	0829 4.2	1436 0.9	2056 4.5
19 Su	0312 1.0	0914 4.1	1521 0.9	2145 4.5
20 M	0404 1.1	1003 4.0	1609 0.9	2237 4.5
21 Tu	0458 1.2	1055 3.8	1701 1.0	2333 4.4
22 W	0558 1.3	1153 3.7	1759 1.1	
23 Th	0034 4.3	0702 1.4	1257 3.6	) 1903 1.3
24 F	0140 4.2	0809 1.5	1406 3.6	2012 1.3
25 Sa	0247 4.2	0915 1.5	1515 3.6	2122 1.3
26 Su	0351 4.2	1015 1.4	1619 3.8	2226 1.3
27 M	0449 4.1	1108 1.3	1716 3.9	2325 1.3
28 Tu	0541 4.1	1156 1.3	1807 4.1	
29 W	0017 1.2	0628 4.1	1239 1.2	1852 4.2
30 Th ●	0105 1.2	0711 4.0	1318 1.2	1935 4.2
31 F	0149 1.3	0750 3.9	1355 1.2	2015 4.3

APRIL

Day	Time ft	Time ft	Time ft	Time ft
1 Sa	0231 1.4	0828 3.8	1430 1.3	2053 4.2
2 Su	0311 1.5	0904 3.7	1505 1.3	2131 4.2
3 M	0351 1.6	0941 3.6	1540 1.4	2210 4.1
4 Tu	0432 1.7	1019 3.5	1617 1.5	2250 4.0
5 W	0515 1.8	1101 3.4	1658 1.6	2334 4.0
6 Th	0602 1.8	1149 3.3	1746 1.7	
7 F	0022 3.9	0654 1.9	1244 3.3	1841 1.8
8 Sa	0116 3.9	0748 1.8	1344 3.4	(1942 1.8
9 Su	0212 3.9	0841 1.7	1444 3.5	2045 1.7
10 M	0308 3.9	0932 1.6	1541 3.7	2146 1.6
11 Tu	0402 4.0	1020 1.4	1633 4.0	2242 1.5
12 W	0453 4.1	1106 1.3	1723 4.2	2335 1.3
13 Th	0542 4.2	1151 1.1	1810 4.5	
14 F	0026 1.1	0629 4.2	1236 1.0	1858 4.7
15 Sa	0116 1.0	0717 4.2	1321 0.9	O 1946 4.9
16 Su	0206 1.0	0805 4.2	1408 0.8	2035 4.9
17 M	0258 1.0	0854 4.1	1457 0.9	2126 4.9
18 Tu	0351 1.1	0947 4.0	1548 1.0	2219 4.8
19 W	0447 1.2	1043 3.9	1644 1.1	2316 4.7
20 Th	0546 1.3	1144 3.8	1745 1.3	
21 F	0017 4.5	0648 1.4	1250 3.8	) 1851 1.5
22 Sa	0121 4.3	0752 1.5	1359 3.8	2002 1.6
23 Su	0226 4.2	0854 1.5	1506 3.9	2112 1.6
24 M	0328 4.1	0950 1.4	1607 4.0	2216 1.6
25 Tu	0425 4.0	1041 1.4	1700 4.1	2313 1.6
26 W	0516 4.0	1126 1.4	1748 4.3	
27 Th	0004 1.5	0601 3.9	1206 1.4	1831 4.4
28 F	0049 1.5	0642 3.8	1244 1.4	1911 4.4
29 Sa ●	0131 1.6	0721 3.7	1319 1.4	1948 4.4
30 Su	0211 1.6	0758 3.7	1353 1.4	2024 4.4

BAHAMAS

TIME MERIDIAN 75°W

0000h is midnight, 1200h is noon.

Heights in feet are referenced to the chart datum of soundings.

HIGH & LOW WATER 1995   25°05'N   77°21'W

EASTERN STANDARD TIME (GMT -5H).   ADD 1H DAYLIGHT SAVING APR 2 - OCT 28

MAY

Day	Time ft	Day	Time ft
1 M	0249 1.6 / 0834 3.6 / 1428 1.5 / 2100 4.4	**16** Tu	0243 1.1 / 0836 4.1 / 1436 0.9 / 2109 5.1
2 Tu	0327 1.7 / 0911 3.5 / 1503 1.6 / 2137 4.3	**17** W	0337 1.1 / 0932 4.1 / 1531 1.0 / 2203 5.0
3 W	0406 1.7 / 0950 3.5 / 1541 1.7 / 2215 4.2	**18** Th	0433 1.2 / 1030 4.0 / 1629 1.2 / 2259 4.8
4 Th	0447 1.8 / 1033 3.4 / 1623 1.8 / 2257 4.1	**19** F	0530 1.3 / 1132 3.9 / 1731 1.4 / 2357 4.6
5 F	0530 1.8 / 1121 3.4 / 1711 1.8 / 2342 4.1	**20** Sa	0629 1.3 / 1237 3.9 / 1837 1.6
6 Sa	0617 1.8 / 1215 3.5 / 1806 1.9	**21** Su	0058 4.3 / 0727 1.4 / 1343 4.0 /) 1945 1.7
7 Su	0033 4.0 / 0706 1.8 / 1312 3.6 / (1907 1.9	**22** M	0158 4.1 / 0824 1.5 / 1446 4.0 / 2053 1.8
8 M	0127 4.0 / 0756 1.7 / 1410 3.7 / 2012 1.9	**23** Tu	0258 4.0 / 0918 1.5 / 1545 4.1 / 2157 1.8
9 Tu	0223 4.0 / 0847 1.5 / 1507 4.0 / 2114 1.7	**24** W	0353 3.9 / 1006 1.5 / 1637 4.2 / 2254 1.8
10 W	0319 4.0 / 0937 1.4 / 1601 4.2 / 2214 1.6	**25** Th	0443 3.8 / 1050 1.5 / 1724 4.3 / 2344 1.8
11 Th	0414 4.0 / 1026 1.2 / 1653 4.5 / 2310 1.4	**26** F	0529 3.7 / 1131 1.5 / 1806 4.4
12 F	0507 4.1 / 1115 1.1 / 1744 4.8	**27** Sa	0030 1.8 / 0611 3.6 / 1209 1.5 / 1845 4.5
13 Sa	0004 1.3 / 0559 4.2 / 1204 0.9 / 1835 5.0	**28** Su	0111 1.8 / 0651 3.6 / 1245 1.5 / 1922 4.5
14 Su	0057 1.1 / 0651 4.2 / 1254 0.8 / O 1925 5.1	**29** M	0150 1.7 / 0729 3.6 / 1321 1.5 / ● 1958 4.6
15 M	0150 1.1 / 0743 4.2 / 1344 0.8 / 2016 5.2	**30** Tu	0228 1.7 / 0808 3.5 / 1357 1.6 / 2034 4.5
		31 W	0305 1.7 / 0847 3.5 / 1435 1.6 / 2110 4.4

JUNE

Day	Time ft	Day	Time ft
1 Th	0342 1.7 / 0927 3.5 / 1514 1.7 / 2148 4.4	**16** F	0414 1.2 / 1015 4.1 / 1614 1.3 / 2239 4.8
2 F	0420 1.7 / 1010 3.5 / 1557 1.8 / 2227 4.3	**17** Sa	0508 1.2 / 1114 4.1 / 1713 1.5 / 2333 4.6
3 Sa	0500 1.7 / 1056 3.6 / 1645 1.9 / 2310 4.2	**18** Su	0601 1.3 / 1215 4.1 / 1816 1.7
4 Su	0542 1.7 / 1146 3.7 / 1738 1.9 / 2356 4.1	**19** M	0029 4.3 / 0655 1.4 / 1316 4.1 /) 1920 1.8
5 M	0627 1.6 / 1240 3.8 / 1837 1.9	**20** Tu	0124 4.1 / 0747 1.5 / 1417 4.1 / 2025 2.0
6 Tu	0047 4.0 / 0715 1.6 / 1337 4.0 / (1940 1.9	**21** W	0220 3.9 / 0838 1.5 / 1514 4.2 / 2128 2.0
7 W	0142 4.0 / 0805 1.5 / 1434 4.2 / 2044 1.8	**22** Th	0314 3.7 / 0927 1.6 / 1607 4.3 / 2226 2.0
8 Th	0240 4.0 / 0857 1.3 / 1531 4.4 / 2147 1.7	**23** F	0405 3.6 / 1012 1.6 / 1654 4.3 / 2318 2.0
9 F	0338 4.0 / 0951 1.2 / 1627 4.4 / 2247 1.6	**24** Sa	0454 3.6 / 1055 1.6 / 1738 4.4
10 Sa	0436 4.0 / 1044 1.0 / 1721 4.9 / 2344 1.4	**25** Su	0004 2.0 / 0539 3.5 / 1136 1.6 / 1818 4.5
11 Su	0533 4.1 / 1138 0.9 / 1815 5.1	**26** M	0046 1.9 / 0622 3.5 / 1215 1.6 / 1856 4.5
12 M	0040 1.3 / 0629 4.2 / 1232 0.9 / O 1908 5.2	**27** Tu	0125 1.8 / 0703 3.6 / 1255 1.6 / ● 1933 4.6
13 Tu	0134 1.2 / 0725 4.2 / 1326 0.9 / 2000 5.2	**28** W	0203 1.8 / 0744 3.6 / 1334 1.6 / 2009 4.6
14 W	0228 1.1 / 0821 4.2 / 1421 1.0 / 2053 5.2	**29** Th	0239 1.7 / 0824 3.7 / 1414 1.7 / 2046 4.5
15 Th	0321 1.1 / 0917 4.2 / 1516 1.1 / 2146 5.0	**30** F	0315 1.7 / 0905 3.7 / 1455 1.7 / 2123 4.5

JULY

Day	Time ft	Day	Time ft
1 Sa	0352 1.7 / 0947 3.8 / 1538 1.8 / 2201 4.4	**16** Su	0439 1.3 / 1050 4.3 / 1652 1.6 / 2305 4.5
2 Su	0429 1.6 / 1031 3.8 / 1625 1.8 / 2242 4.3	**17** M	0527 1.4 / 1145 4.2 / 1749 1.8 / 2355 4.3
3 M	0508 1.6 / 1118 3.9 / 1715 1.9 / 2326 4.2	**18** Tu	0616 1.5 / 1241 4.2 / 1848 2.0
4 Tu	0551 1.6 / 1210 4.1 / 1811 1.9	**19** W	0045 4.0 / 0704 1.6 / 1338 4.2 /) 1949 2.1
5 W	0015 4.1 / 0638 1.5 / 1305 4.2 / (1913 1.9	**20** Th	0137 3.8 / 0753 1.7 / 1434 4.2 / 2051 2.2
6 Th	0109 4.0 / 0729 1.4 / 1404 4.4 / 2017 1.9	**21** F	0231 3.7 / 0842 1.8 / 1528 4.2 / 2150 2.2
7 F	0207 4.0 / 0824 1.3 / 1504 4.6 / 2123 1.8	**22** Sa	0325 3.6 / 0931 1.8 / 1618 4.3 / 2244 2.2
8 Sa	0309 3.9 / 0922 1.3 / 1604 4.8 / 2226 1.7	**23** Su	0417 3.6 / 1019 1.8 / 1704 4.4 / 2332 2.1
9 Su	0412 4.0 / 1021 1.2 / 1702 4.9 / 2327 1.6	**24** M	0507 3.6 / 1105 1.8 / 1747 4.5
10 M	0513 4.1 / 1119 1.1 / 1758 5.1	**25** Tu	0015 2.0 / 0554 3.7 / 1149 1.7 / 1827 4.5
11 Tu	0024 1.4 / 0612 4.1 / 1216 1.0 / 1852 5.2	**26** W	0054 1.9 / 0637 3.7 / 1232 1.7 / 1906 4.6
12 W	0118 1.3 / 0710 4.2 / 1313 1.0 / O 1945 5.2	**27** Th	0132 1.8 / 0719 3.9 / 1314 1.7 / ● 1944 4.6
13 Th	0210 1.2 / 0806 4.3 / 1408 1.1 / 2036 5.1	**28** F	0208 1.7 / 0800 4.0 / 1356 1.7 / 2021 4.6
14 F	0301 1.2 / 0901 4.4 / 1502 1.2 / 2126 5.0	**29** Sa	0244 1.7 / 0841 4.1 / 1438 1.7 / 2059 4.6
15 Sa	0350 1.2 / 0955 4.4 / 1557 1.4 / 2216 4.8	**30** Su	0319 1.6 / 0922 4.2 / 1522 1.7 / 2137 4.5
		31 M	0356 1.6 / 1005 4.2 / 1608 1.8 / 2217 4.4

AUGUST

Day	Time ft	Day	Time ft
1 Tu	0436 1.6 / 1052 4.3 / 1657 1.8 / 2301 4.3	**16** W	0532 1.7 / 1200 4.4 / 1812 2.1
2 W	0518 1.5 / 1142 4.4 / 1752 1.9 / 2350 4.2	**17** Th	0005 4.0 / 0617 1.8 / 1252 4.3 /) 1908 2.3
3 Th	0607 1.5 / 1238 4.5 / 1852 2.0 / (	**18** F	0054 3.8 / 0705 1.9 / 1346 4.3 / 2007 2.4
4 F	0044 4.1 / 0700 1.5 / 1339 4.6 / 1957 2.0	**19** Sa	0147 3.7 / 0756 2.0 / 1441 4.3 / 2106 2.4
5 Sa	0145 4.0 / 0800 1.5 / 1442 4.7 / 2104 2.0	**20** Su	0245 3.6 / 0849 2.0 / 1534 4.3 / 2202 2.3
6 Su	0251 4.0 / 0903 1.5 / 1545 4.8 / 2210 1.9	**21** M	0342 3.7 / 0943 2.0 / 1624 4.4 / 2251 2.2
7 M	0357 4.0 / 1006 1.4 / 1646 4.9 / 2311 1.7	**22** Tu	0435 3.7 / 1035 2.0 / 1710 4.5 / 2335 2.1
8 Tu	0501 4.1 / 1108 1.4 / 1744 5.0	**23** W	0524 3.9 / 1124 2.0 / 1753 4.5
9 W	0007 1.6 / 0601 4.3 / 1207 1.2 / 1838 5.1	**24** Th	0016 2.0 / 0609 4.0 / 1210 1.8 / 1835 4.6
10 Th	0100 1.5 / 0657 4.4 / O 1929 5.1	**25** F	0054 2.0 / 0652 4.2 / 1254 1.7 / ● 1914 1.7
11 F	0149 1.4 / 0750 4.5 / 1356 1.3 / 2017 5.0	**26** Sa	0131 1.7 / 0733 4.4 / 1338 1.6 / 1953 4.7
12 Sa	0236 1.4 / 0841 4.6 / 1448 1.4 / 2104 4.8	**27** Su	0208 1.6 / 0814 4.5 / 1421 1.6 / 2033 4.6
13 Su	0321 1.4 / 0931 4.6 / 1538 1.5 / 2149 4.6	**28** M	0245 1.6 / 0857 4.6 / 1506 1.6 / 2113 4.6
14 M	0405 1.5 / 1020 4.5 / 1628 1.7 / 2234 4.4	**29** Tu	0324 1.5 / 0941 4.6 / 1552 1.7 / 2155 4.4
15 Tu	0449 1.6 / 1110 4.5 / 1719 1.9 / 2319 4.2	**30** W	0405 1.5 / 1028 4.5 / 1642 1.8 / 2241 4.3
		31 Th	0451 1.6 / 1119 4.7 / 1737 1.9 / 2332 4.2

TIME MERIDIAN 75°W   0000h is midnight, 1200h is noon.

Heights in feet are referenced to the chart datum of soundings.

NASSAU, BAHAMAS

HIGH & LOW WATER 1995 **25°05'N 77°21'W**

EASTERN STANDARD TIME (GMT -5H). ADD 1H DAYLIGHT SAVING APR 2 - OCT 28

BAHAMAS

SEPTEMBER

Day	Time	ft	Time	ft	Time	ft	Time	ft
1 F	0542	1.6	1216	4.7	1837	2.0		
2 Sa	0029	4.1	0640	1.7	1318	4.7	(1943	2.0
3 Su	0134	4.0	0744	1.7	1424	4.7	2050	2.0
4 M	0243	4.0	0851	1.7	1530	4.7	2156	1.9
5 Tu	0350	4.1	0959	1.6	1632	4.8	2255	1.8
6 W	0454	4.3	1102	1.5	1729	4.8	2348	1.7
7 Th	0551	4.5	1200	1.5	1821	4.9		
8 F	0038	1.6	0644	4.6	1253	1.4	O 1910	4.8
9 Sa	0123	1.5	0733	4.7	1344	1.5	1955	4.7
10 Su	0206	1.5	0819	4.8	1432	1.6	2039	4.6
11 M	0247	1.5	0904	4.8	1518	1.7	2120	4.4
12 Tu	0328	1.6	0948	4.7	1604	1.8	2201	4.2
13 W	0407	1.7	1032	4.6	1650	2.0	2242	4.1
14 Th	0447	1.9	1117	4.5	1737	2.2	2326	3.9
15 F	0530	2.0	1205	4.4	1828	2.3		
16 Sa	0014	3.8	0617	2.1	1255	4.3	) 1923	2.3
17 Su	0108	3.7	0709	2.2	1349	4.2	2019	2.3
18 M	0207	3.7	0807	2.2	1445	4.2	2114	2.3
19 Tu	0307	3.8	0907	2.2			2204	2.2
20 W	0402	3.9	1003	2.1	1648	4.4	2250	2.0
21 Th	0452	4.1	1056	1.9	1715	4.5	2332	1.9
22 F	0538	4.3	1145	1.8	1759	4.5		
23 Sa	0012	1.7	0622	4.5	1231	1.7	1841	4.6
24 Su	0051	1.6	0705	4.7	1317	1.6	● 1923	4.6
25 M	0131	1.5	0748	4.9	1403	1.5	2006	4.6
26 Tu	0212	1.4	0832	5.0	1449	1.5	2049	4.5
27 W	0254	1.4	0918	5.0	1538	1.6	2135	4.4
28 Th	0339	1.4	1007	5.0	1630	1.7	2225	4.3
29 F	0429	1.5	1100	4.9	1725	1.8	2320	4.1
30 Sa	0524	1.6	1158	4.8	1826	1.8		

OCTOBER

Day	Time	ft	Time	ft	Time	ft	Time	ft
1 Su	0021	4.1	0626	1.6	1301	4.7	(1931	1.9
2 M	0129	4.0	0734	1.8	1408	4.6	2036	1.9
3 Tu	0239	4.1	0845	1.8	1513	4.6	2138	1.8
4 W	0345	4.2	0953	1.8	1615	4.6	2235	1.7
5 Th	0445	4.4	1055	1.7	1710	4.5	2325	1.6
6 F	0539	4.6	1152	1.6	1801	4.5		
7 Sa	0012	1.6	0628	4.7	1243	1.6	1847	4.4
8 Su	0054	1.5	0714	4.8	1330	1.6	O 1930	4.3
9 M	0134	1.5	0756	4.8	1415	1.7	2011	4.2
10 Tu	0212	1.5	0837	4.8	1458	1.8	2050	4.1
11 W	0250	1.7	0917	4.7	1540	1.9	2129	3.9
12 Th	0327	1.8	0957	4.6	1622	2.0	2209	3.8
13 F	0405	1.9	1038	4.5	1705	2.1	2252	3.7
14 Sa	0446	2.0	1121	4.3	1752	2.1	2340	3.6
15 Su	0533	2.1	1208	4.2	1841	2.2		
16 M	0033	3.6	0626	2.2	1259	4.2	) 1933	2.1
17 Tu	0132	3.6	0726	2.2	1353	4.1	2024	2.1
18 W	0230	3.8	0829	2.1	1448	4.1	2114	1.9
19 Th	0326	3.9	0929	2.0	1541	4.2	2201	1.8
20 F	0417	4.2	1025	1.9	1631	4.2	2246	1.6
21 Sa	0505	4.4	1117	1.7	1720	4.3	2329	1.5
22 Su	0551	4.7	1207	1.6	1806	4.3		
23 M	0013	1.3	0637	4.9	1255	1.4	● 1853	4.3
24 Tu	0057	1.2	0723	5.0	1344	1.3	1939	4.3
25 W	0142	1.1	0810	5.1	1433	1.3	2028	4.3
26 Th	0229	1.1	0859	5.1	1524	1.3	2118	4.2
27 F	0318	1.2	0950	5.1	1618	1.4	2212	4.1
28 Sa	0412	1.3	1044	4.9	1714	1.5	2311	4.0
29 Su	0511	1.5	1143	4.8	1814	1.5		
30 M	0015	4.0	0615	1.6	1244	4.6	(1916	1.6
31 Tu	0122	4.0	0725	1.7	1349	4.4	2017	1.6

NOVEMBER

Day	Time	ft	Time	ft	Time	ft	Time	ft
1 W	0230	4.1	0836	1.7	1452	4.3	2116	1.6
2 Th	0334	4.2	0944	1.7	1552	4.2	2209	1.5
3 F	0431	4.3	1045	1.7	1647	4.1	2258	1.5
4 Sa	0523	4.5	1140	1.6	1736	4.0	2342	1.4
5 Su	0610	4.6	1230	1.6	1822	3.9		
6 M	0023	1.4	0653	4.6	1315	1.6	1904	3.9
7 Tu	0102	1.4	0733	4.6	1358	1.6	O 1943	3.8
8 W	0139	1.5	0811	4.6	1438	1.7	2022	3.7
9 Th	0215	1.5	0849	4.5	1517	1.7	2101	3.6
10 F	0252	1.6	0926	4.4	1557	1.8	2141	3.5
11 Sa	0330	1.7	1004	4.3	1637	1.8	2223	3.5
12 Su	0411	1.8	1044	4.2	1718	1.8	2310	3.5
13 M	0457	1.9	1127	4.1	1802	1.8		
14 Tu	0001	3.5	0550	2.0	1214	4.0	1849	1.8
15 W	0056	3.6	0648	2.0	1305	3.9	) 1936	1.7
16 Th	0152	3.7	0750	2.0	1359	3.9	2025	1.6
17 F	0247	3.9	0852	1.9	1454	3.9	2113	1.4
18 Sa	0340	4.1	0951	1.7	1548	3.9	2202	1.3
19 Su	0431	4.4	1047	1.6	1641	3.9	2250	1.1
20 M	0521	4.6	1141	1.4	1732	4.0	2338	1.0
21 Tu	0611	4.8	1234	1.2	1824	4.0		
22 W	0027	0.9	0700	5.0	1325	1.1	● 1916	4.0
23 Th	0117	0.8	0750	5.1	1417	1.1	2008	4.0
24 F	0208	0.8	0842	5.0	1510	1.0	2103	4.0
25 Sa	0302	0.9	0934	4.9	1604	1.1	2200	4.0
26 Su	0359	1.0	1029	4.8	1659	1.1	2300	3.9
27 M	0459	1.2	1125	4.6	1756	1.2		
28 Tu	0003	3.9	0603	1.4	1224	4.3	1854	1.2
29 W	0108	3.8	0711	1.5	1325	4.1	(1951	1.2
30 Th	0213	4.0	0820	1.6	1425	3.9	2047	1.3

DECEMBER

Day	Time	ft	Time	ft	Time	ft	Time	ft
1 F	0314	4.0	0927	1.6	1524	3.7	2139	1.3
2 Sa	0411	4.1	1028	1.6	1618	3.6	2227	1.3
3 Su	0502	4.2	1124	1.6	1708	3.5	2311	1.3
4 M	0548	4.3	1213	1.6	1754	3.4	2353	1.3
5 Tu	0631	4.3	1258	1.6	1837	3.4		
6 W	0031	1.3	0710	4.3	1339	1.5	O 1917	3.4
7 Th	0109	1.3	0747	4.3	1417	1.5	1957	3.3
8 F	0146	1.4	0823	4.3	1455	1.5	2036	3.3
9 Sa	0224	1.4	0859	4.2	1531	1.5	2116	3.3
10 Su	0303	1.5	0935	4.1	1608	1.5	2158	3.3
11 M	0345	1.6	1013	4.0	1646	1.5	2242	3.3
12 Tu	0430	1.6	1053	3.9	1725	1.4	2329	3.4
13 W	0519	1.7	1136	3.8	1807	1.4		
14 Th	0020	3.5	0614	1.7	1224	3.7	1852	1.3
15 F	0114	3.6	0714	1.7	1315	3.7	) 1939	1.2
16 Sa	0209	3.8	0817	1.7	1410	3.6	2030	1.1
17 Su	0305	4.0	0919	1.5	1508	3.6	2122	1.0
18 M	0400	4.3	1019	1.4	1606	3.6	2216	0.8
19 Tu	0455	4.5	1117	1.2	1703	3.7	2310	0.7
20 W	0548	4.5	1213	1.1	1800	3.7		
21 Th	0004	0.6	0641	4.8	1307	0.9	● 1856	3.8
22 F	0058	0.6	0733	4.9	1400	0.8	1952	3.8
23 Sa	0153	0.6	0826	4.8	1453	0.8	2048	3.9
24 Su	0249	0.7	0918	4.7	1545	0.8	2145	3.9
25 M	0346	0.8	1011	4.6	1638	0.8	2243	3.9
26 Tu	0445	1.0	1105	4.3	1731	0.9	2343	3.9
27 W	0546	1.2	1200	4.1	1825	0.9		
28 Th	0045	3.8	0650	1.3	1256	3.8	(1918	1.0
29 F	0146	3.8	0756	1.5	1353	3.6	2012	1.1
30 Sa	0247	3.9	0902	1.6	1450	3.4	2103	1.1
31 Su	0343	3.9	1004	1.6	1545	3.2	2153	1.2

TIME MERIDIAN 75°W   0000h is midnight, 1200h is noon.
Heights in feet are referenced to the chart datum of soundings.

TURKS AND CAICOS

CAUTION: Our information on aids to navigation comes from official government sources. The latitudes and longitudes of these marks may not correspond to the readings from GPS or LORAN receivers. Lights in the Turks and Caicos islands hare reported to be unreliable. No single aid to navigation, or waypoint, should be relied upon as a sole means of fixing your position.

NOTE: The chartlets in this section are <u>not</u> <u>intended for navigation</u> and are included for reference and planning purposes only. While chartlets reproduced from government sources are from the most current editions as of press time, they incorporate <u>no corrections</u> to navigational aids, depths, or hazards since the edition publication date.

ENTRY PROCEDURES

On the Caicos island of Providenciales, temporary permission to stay for 7 days may be obtained directly from the harbormaster, who moniters VHF channel 16 or who may be paged through any of the marinas, who also monitor VHF channel 16. For longer stays, you must go to the immigration office in town.

Other ports of entry are Cockburn Harbour on South Caicos and Cockburn Town on Grand Turk, the capital of the islands. Boaters will need passports, but no visas. Firearms should be declared, and those wishing to fish should check on the latest sportfishing regulations. There are restrictions regarding the use of all types of fishing spears. Overtime charges apply to vessels clearing in after hours, Saturday, Sunday, and holidays.

The Turks and Caicos are a British Crown Colony. For the latest information on clearing-in and departure procedures and entrance and boarding fees, on Providenciales contact customs at 809-946-4776 and immigration at 809-946-4233; on South Caicos, immigration at 809-946-3355; and on Grand Turk, immigration

at 809-946-2972. The Turks and Caicos Tourist Board on Providenciales may be reached at 809-946-4970; on Grand Turk, at 809-946-2321.

The U.S. dollar is legal tender in the Turks and Caicos Islands. Language spoken: English.

CAICOS

NORTHWEST POINT LIGHT, on NW point of Providenciales Island, 21 51.9N, 72 20.0W. Fl (3) W 15s, 14M. Reported Q (3) W 15s (Aug 1988).
WEST CAICOS LIGHT, S end, 21 37.9N, 72 27.9W. Q R, 52ft. Pillar.
PROVIDENCIALES ISLAND LIGHT, E end, 21 48.6N, 72 07.8W. Fl W 10s, 12M.
FRENCH CAY LIGHT, 21 30.3N, 72 12.1W. Fl R, 10ft. Pillar.
CAPE COMETE LIGHT, East Caicos Island, 21 43.4N, 71 28.3W. Fl (2) W 20s, 12M.
SOUTH CAICOS ISLAND LIGHT, Cockburn Harbor on Government Hill, 21 29.9N, 71 30.7W. F W, 50ft, 9M. White building; flat roof. Visible 180°–090°.
LONG CAY LIGHT, E end, 21 29.0N, 71 32.1W. Fl R 2.5s, 5M.
DOVE CAY LIGHT, W end, 21 29.0N, 71 32.1W. Fl G 2.5s, 5M. White tower.
BUSH CAY LIGHT, 21 11.0N, 71 38.0W. Fl (2) W 10s, 14M.

PROVIDENCIALES

21 47N, 72 17W
Port of Entry: Contact the harbormaster via Turtle Cove Marina, Provo Aquatic Centre, or Leeward Yacht Club and Marina. The harbormaster and marinas stand by on VHF channel 16.
Dockage: Located on the north side of Providenciales are Turtle Cove Marina (809-946-4232), with new docks in 1994, and the Leeward Yacht Club and Marina (809-946-5553). Located on the south side are the Provo Aquatic Centre (VHF channel 68), with limited dock space, and Caicos Marina and Shipyard (809-946-5600).

The approach to Turtle Cove through the reef is made via Sellers Cut. The marina advises new visitors to call ahead for a paid guide for

COAST PILOT

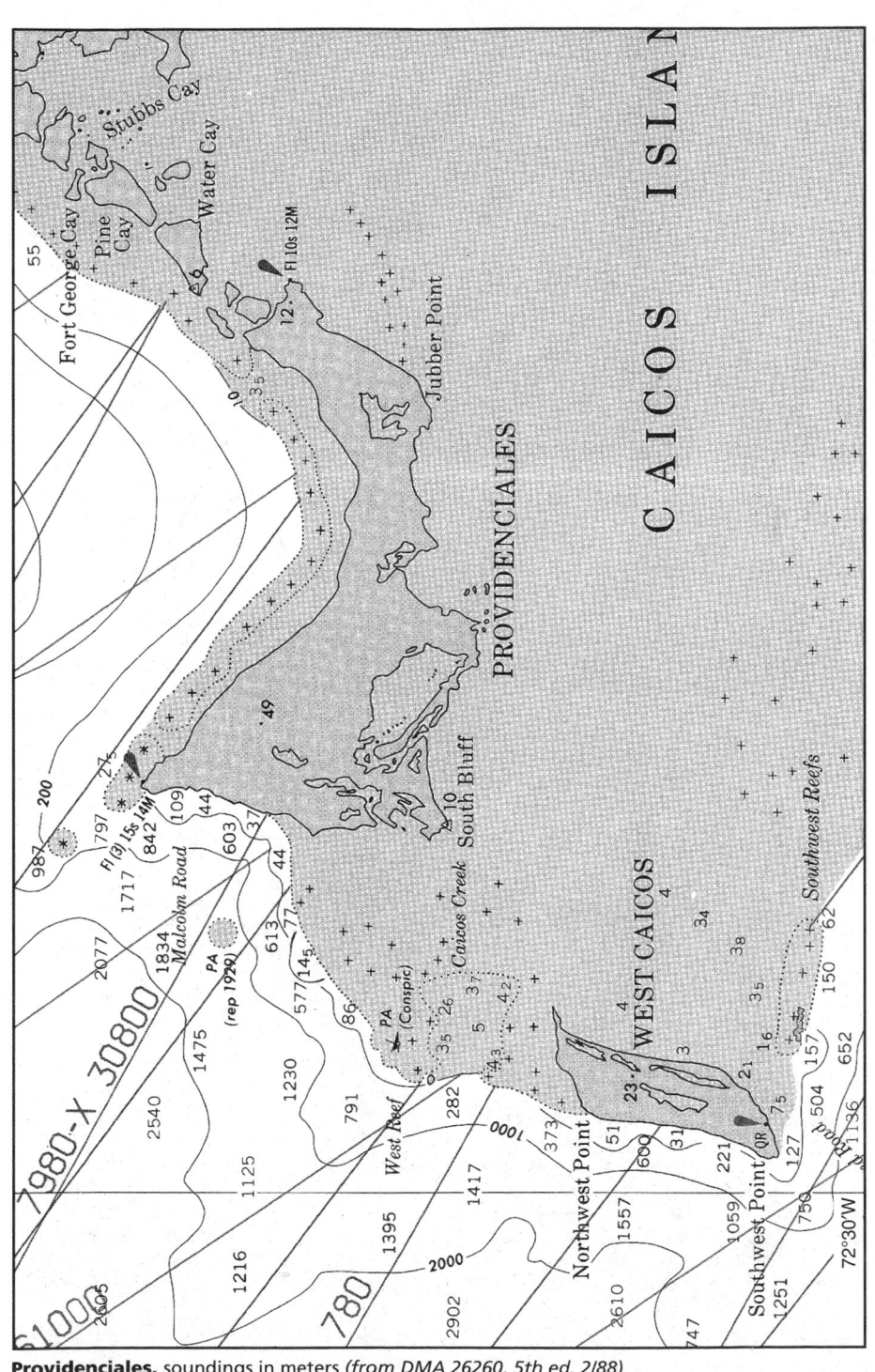

Providenciales, soundings in meters *(from DMA 26260, 5th ed, 2/88)*

this passage. The approach to Leeward Marina is also through a cut in the reef marked with a red and white striped buoy. The channel from the cut to the marina is marked by red and green buoys. Both marinas report approach depths of over 6 feet. The approaches to the marinas on the south side are mentioned in the Anchorage section.

Anchorage: A popular anchorage is off the Sand Bore Channel, which leads into the harbors on the south side of Providenciales. Enter the Sand Bore Channel through West Reef via a break south of a visible wreck. The channel then runs about 103°T towards the southern point of Providenciales. If in doubt, contact one of the marinas on the VHF. You can also make the approach to the south side of Providenciales via Clear Sand Road. This channel is reported to run about 068° from the southern end of West Caicos. You can anchor in Clear Sand Road on the edge of the banks. Sapodilla Bay is located west of the Caicos Marina. It has up to 8 feet of water for anchoring. The Government Dock is nearby.

Services: All services are available, including haulouts and major repairs. There is a good selection of parts and supplies. Regular air service to the U.S. can bring in special items. There is good telephone service.

Providenciales has become a tourist, dive, and boating destination in recent years. The expansion of all facilities has made the Turks and Caicos Islands a good stop for those traveling between eastern North America and the Caribbean.

COCKBURN HARBOR, SOUTH CAICOS

21 29N, 71 32W
Port of Entry: Vessels may call Sea View Marina (809-946-3219 or VHF channel 16), who will then contact officials. The immigration office on South Caicos can be reached at 809-946-3355.
Dockage: Sea View Marina (809-946-3219 or VHF channel 16) has 6–7 feet of water off its dock. Vessels with greater draft may be able to tie up at the government wharf.
Anchorage: Anchor off the town dock or north of Long Cay. Be wary of shallow spots and the charted reef north of Long Cay. The protection is good in most conditions.

Services: Sea View Marina can provide fuel at its docks or the government wharf. It can also make arrangements for fresh water delivery, laundry, and small repairs; its market sells some groceries. Customers may use the marina's telelphone, and restaurants are near by.

TURKS

GRAND TURK LIGHT, 21 30.9N, 71 07.9W. Fl W 7.5s, 108ft, 18M. White cylindrical iron tower. Signal station.
SALT CAY LIGHT, NW point, 21 20.2N, 71 12.7W. Fl (4) W 20s, 8M.
SAND CAY LIGHT, 21 11.9N, 71 14.8W. Fl W 2s, 85ft, 10M. Red steel framework structure. Reported extinguished (1985).

COCKBURN TOWN, GRAND TURK

21 28N, 71 09W
Port of Entry: Contact the harbormaster on VHF channel 16 for instructions on clearing in. If officials are not available, the harbormaster may perform customs and immigration duties in either the south dock or town areas.
Pilotage: There are reported to be two lighted ranges on the west coast of the island. The northern range leads through the reef on a course of 084°T to Cockburn Town, while the southern range leads on a course of 056°T to a large government wharf. Mariners are urged to make their approach in good light.
Anchorage: The best anchorage is reported to be north of the wharf at the southern end of the island. A cut has been made through the reef at the island's north end, which allows access to sheltered North Creek. The entrance is marked by a pile of black stones on the east. Local knowledge is recommended for those attempting this pass. The Hawks Nest anchorage at the south end of the island requires local knowledge.
Services: Most supplies are available, and there is good telephone service. There are small shops, restaurants, and hotels. Call sign Flagstaff Grand Turk runs a radio net on 21.4MHz, providing weather and other information.

Grand Turk is the administrative center of the Turks and Caicos, although the anchorages are not as sheltered as some in the Caicos area.

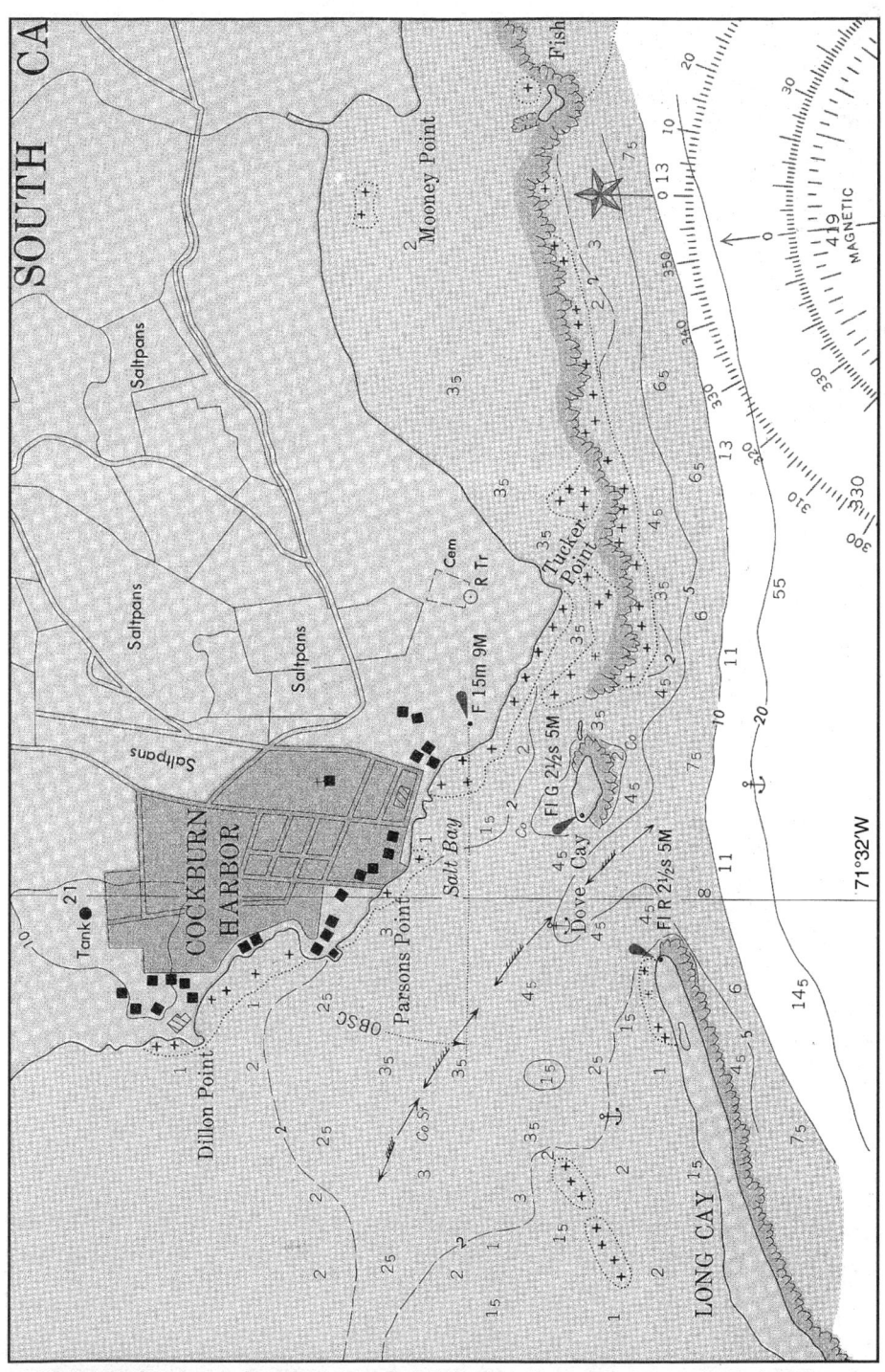

Cockburn Harbour, South Caicos, soundings in meters *(from DMA 26261, 26th ed, 8/84)*

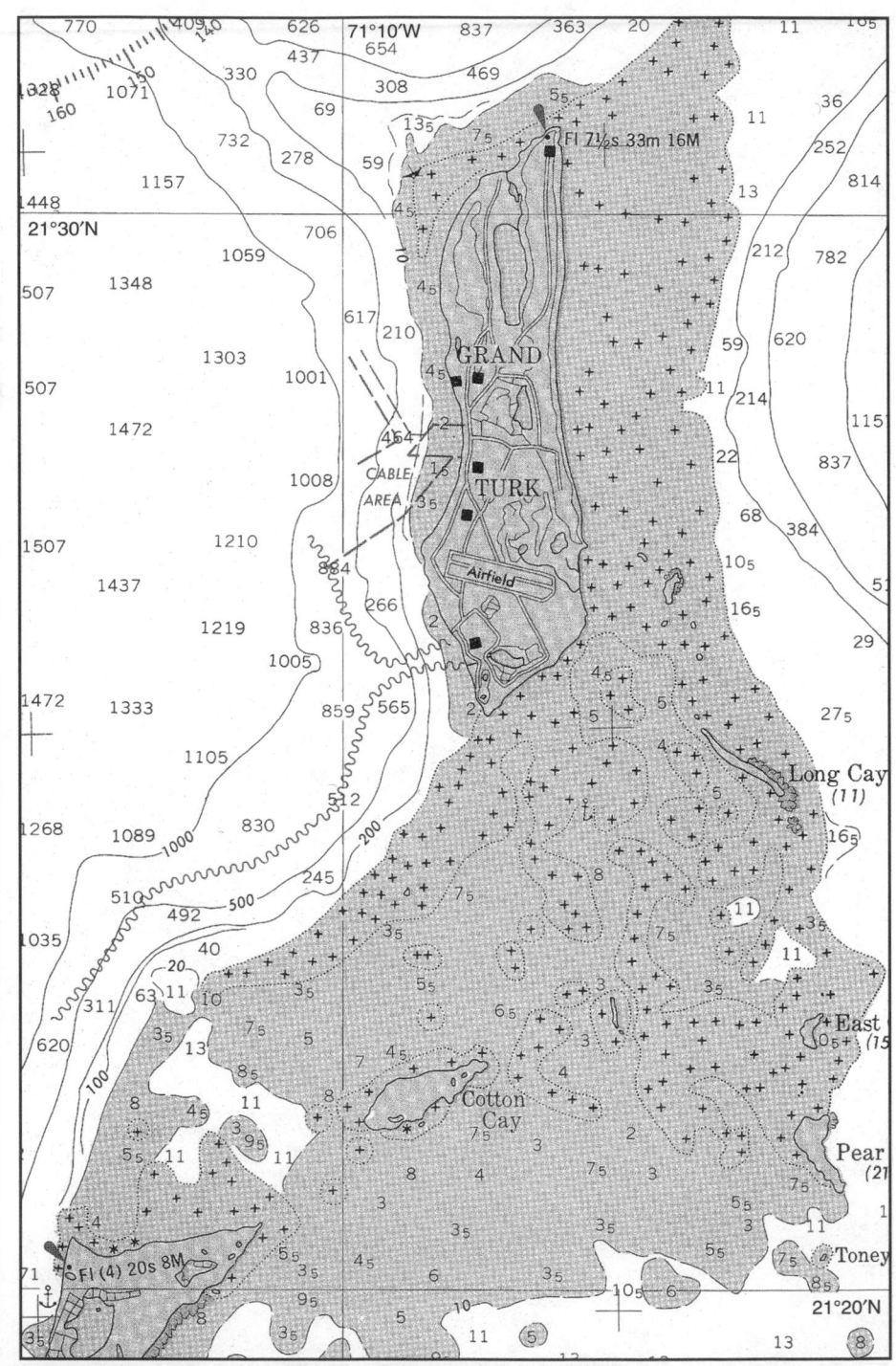

Grand Turk, soundings in meters *(from DMA 26261, 26th ed, 8/84)*

CUBA

WARNING: Cuba claims a 12-mile territorial sea extending from straight baselines drawn from Cuban coastal points. The effect is that Cuba's claimed territorial sea extends in many areas well beyond the 12 miles from Cuba's physical coastline. These claims are not in conformance with international law and are not recognized by the United States. Nonetheless, United States vessels have been stopped and boarded by Cuban authorities more than 20 miles from the Cuban coast in some cases. Within the limits of prudence and good judgment, mariners are advised to protest (but not physically resist) any improper attempt to stop, board, or seize U.S. vessels in international waters. Notify the U.S. Coast Guard of your status so that it can relay information about your situation to the Department of State for diplomatic attention.

TRAFFIC SEPARATION SCHEMES: On September 1, 1990, seven Traffic Separation Schemes, approved by the International Maritime Organization, were implemented off the eastern, western, and northern coasts of Cuba. The government of Cuba has unilaterally established a mandatory ship-reporting system within the Old Bahama Channel to govern vessel movement within the area. While it is the U.S. position that the mandatory provisions of the ship-reporting system are inconsistent with international law, vessels should exercise caution while transiting the Old Bahama Channel.

The Traffic Separation Schemes are in the following areas:

Off Cabo San Antonio
Off La Tabla
Off Costa de Matanzas
In the Old Bahama Channel
Off Punta Maternillos
Off Punta Lucrecia
Off Cabo Maisi

CAUTION: Our information on aids to navigation comes from official government sources. The latitudes and longitudes of

these marks may not correspond to the readings from GPS or LORAN receivers. Some aids have been reported as unreliable, missing, off position, or showing incorrect characteristics. No single aid to navigation, or waypoint, should be relied upon as a sole means of fixing your position.

NOTE: The chartlets in this section are <u>not intended for navigation</u> and are included for reference and planning purposes only. While chartlets reproduced from government sources are from the most current editions as of press time, they incorporate <u>no corrections</u> to navigational aids, depths, or hazards since the edition publication date.

CUBAN ASSETS CONTROL REGULATIONS

The Cuban Assets Control Regulations were issued by the U.S. government on July 8, 1963, under the Trading With the Enemy Act in response to certain hostile actions by the Cuban government. They are still in force today and affect all U.S. citizens and permanent residents wherever they are located, all people and organizations physically in the United States, and all branches and subsidiaries of U.S. organizations throughout the world. The regulations are administered by the U.S. Treasury Department's Office of Foreign Assets Control. The basic goal of the sanctions is to isolate Cuba economically and deprive it of U.S. dollars. Penalties for violating the sanctions range up to 10 years in prison and up to $500,000 in corporate and $250,000 in individual fines. The regulations require those dealing with Cuba to maintain records and, upon request from the U.S. Treasury Department, to furnish information regarding such dealings.

Spending money in connection with tourist, business, or recreational trips is prohibited, whether travelers go directly to Cuba or via a third country. In April 1992 the Treasury Department further tightened these sanctions with a new regulation. Vessels are prohibited entry into any U.S. port if they are carrying passengers or goods to or from Cuba. There are certain exceptions to these rules for family visitors, official government travelers, news gatherers, professional researchers, and sponsored travelers. Certain types of humanitarian assistance may be carried to Cuba. For the latest information on these regulations contact: Office of Foreign Assets Control, U.S. Department of the Treasury, 1500 Pennsylvania Avenue NW, Washington, DC 20220 (202-622-2520).

When in Cuba U.S. citizens should contact and register with the United States Interests Section, Embassy of Switzerland, Calzada between L&M, Vedado Section, Havana, telephone: 320551, 320543.

ENTRY PROCEDURES

Mariners are advised to enter the country at a marina where officials are familiar with the procedures for pleasure boats. Ports of Entry (circling the island in a clockwise direction) include Santa Lucía, the Marina Hemingway in Barlovento, the marinas in Veradero, Bahía Naranjo Marina, Punta Gorda in Bahía de Santiago de Cuba, Trinidad, Cienfuegos, Cayo Largo, and Isla de Pinos. You must clear in and out whenever moving the boat from one point to another, and you should always check with the authorities ashore, whether or not in a Port of Entry. Havana is a commercial port only and has no facilities for clearing yachts.

You should have passports, a clearance from your last port, crew lists, and ship's papers. Make sure the crew list includes each crew's birthdate and nationality. When you are inside the 12-mile limit of Cuban waters, you must notify the authorities on VHF channel 16. A patrol boat may come out to meet you. You will be met by many officials, usually including an armed member of the national guard.

Most visitors are granted a temporary tourist card for a three-day visit, which can be renewed for periods of up to several months. For more information on traveling to Cuba contact the Cuba Interests Section in the Swiss Embassy (16th Street NW, Washington, DC 20009; tel, 202-797-8518).

Mariners are issued a coastwise clearance stating where they can go—be careful to avoid unplanned intermediate stops.

When telephoning Cuba from the U.S. you must use an international operator. Recent restrictions have been placed on companies routing calls through Canada to avoid the congestion on the limited number of circuits available. In general, the phone system is reported to be slow and cumbersome.

The official currency is the Cuban peso, but U.S. dollars are accepted in many places—in fact, U.S. currency is preferred by many. There are special stores for visitors that take only dollars. The official exchange rate is 1 peso to US$1. U.S. citizens should check the restrictions on spending money discussed previously. You cannot use U.S. credit cards, and you should change all Cuban currency before leaving the country. Non-U.S. citizens may be able to use their credit cards and traveler's checks.

Spanish is the main language, but visitors report many people can speak some English or French. English is taught to all students in school. Marina personnel and tourist office staff can be helpful with language problems.

Visitors to Cuba can obtain official Cuban charts, pilots, and other information at the Marina Hemingway.

THE YUCATAN CHANNEL

21 30N, 86 00W
Pilotage: This channel between Cabo San Antonio on Cuba and Isla Contoy off the Mexican coast is about 108 miles wide. It serves as the main route for shipping between the Gulf of Mexico and the Panama Canal. The east side of the channel is deep, shoaling gradually toward the Mexican coast.

There is a tremendous flow of water from the Caribbean Sea through the Yucatán Channel toward the Gulf of Mexico. Currents reach velocities of up to 4 knots on the stream's axis. The eastern border of the flow is about 20 miles off Cabo San Antonio, which is just beyond Cuba's 12-mile territorial limit. Twenty to 35 miles from Cabo San Antonio the rate is 1 knot; at 50 miles, 2 knots; at 65 miles, 3 knots; at 78 miles, 4 knots, and at 90 miles, or about 25 miles from Yucatán, 1 knot. The current axis is located about 35 miles off the Yucatán coast, or about 6 miles beyond the 100-fathom curve. The mean rate during April, May and June along the axis is about 4 knots. The current increases in the summer and decreases in the winter. When the current is stronger, the width of the flow is wider, and when the flow is weaker, the width shrinks. There is also a noticeable daily variation in flow, particularly on the west side. The flow has been known to increase or decrease by as much as 3 knots in 5 hours time.

Within 20 miles of Cabo San Antonio the flow is either northeast toward the Straits of Florida or southeast along the south coast of Cuba. At times the east-setting current can reach velocities of 4 knots, especially during southerly winds.

CAUTION: During periods of southerly winds it is advisable to avoid the coast of Cuba from Cabo San Antonio to Cabo Corrientes, due to dangerous currents.

NORTH COAST: CABO SAN ANTONIO TO BAHIA HONDA

CABO SAN ANTONIO LIGHT, W extremity of Cuba, 21 52.0N, 84 57.2W. Fl (2) W 10s, 103ft, 40M. Yellow tower, marked RONCALI; masonry house. Radar reflector. Aeromarine light.

CABO SAN ANTONIO
21 52N, 84 57W
Pilotage: This is the western extremity of Cuba. It is low and covered by trees from 69 to 79 feet in height. The trees will be visible before the land, frequently having the appearance of vessels under sail. The curve of the coast is so gradual that the position of the cape can only be determined by the lighthouse. The area is reported to be radar conspicuous at a distance of 15 miles. Currents near the outer edge of the bank are confused, while near shore they flow north on a rising tide and south on a falling tide. Tide rips are also present.
Anchorage: Temporary anchorage is available south of the lighthouse, with the southeast extremity of the land bearing 135° and the west extremity, 023°.

BANCO SANCHO PARDO, 22 09.6N, 84 45.0W. Fl W 8s, 36ft, 11M. Yellow aluminum skeleton tower.
LA TABLA, 22 18.3N, 84 40.1W. Fl W 5s, 33ft, 11M. Metal framework tower on white concrete base. RACON: **M** (– –), 30s, 12M.
ZORRITA, 22 23.2N, 84 34.8W. FL W 7S, 33ft, 11M. Metal framework tower on white concrete base.

EL PINTO, 22 25.0N, 84 31.2W. Fl W 15s, 33ft, 11M. Metal framework tower, yellow and red bands on white concrete base.
CAYO BUENAVISTA, 22 24.1N, 84 26.7W. Fl W 5s, 108ft, 8M. White metal framework tower.
QUEBRADO DE BUENAVISTA, 22 28.1N, 84 28.0W. Fl W 7s, 33ft, 11M. Metal framework tower on white concrete base.
CABEZO SECA, 22 32.0N, 84 20.0W. Fl W 12s, 33ft, 11M. Metal framework tower, red and white bands on concrete platform on piles.
PUERTO DE LOS ARROYOS, BAJA LA PAILA, 22 21.4N, 84 22.8W. Fl G 5s, 16ft, 4M. Green port-hand beacon with topmark.

GOLFO DE GUANAHACABIBES
22 08N, 84 35W
Pilotage: This area is located just to the northeast of Cabo San Antonio. The area is much encumbered with shoals and cays, and the intricate channels indicate local knowledge may be necessary.

LA FE
22 03N, 84 16W
Pilotage: This is a small port situated on the east bank 2 miles from the Río Guadiana in the southeast part of Golfo de Guanahacabibes. Vessels drawing up to 9 feet can anchor here. The area is marked with navigational aids, but they are considered unreliable. There is a wharf with fresh water available.

FONDEADERO LOS ARROYOS
22 22N, 84 26W
Pilotage: This anchorage is located in the extreme northeast part of Golfo de Guanahacabibes. The holding ground is reported to be good, and there is shelter from the prevailing winds. It is a loading place for the inland community of Mantua.

PUNTA TABACO, 22 34.7N, 84 15.3W. Fl W 8s, 33ft, 11M. Yellow metal framework tower on concrete platform on piles.
RONCADORA, 22 38.3N, 84 11.6W. Fl W 10s, 33ft, 15M. Yellow metal framework on concrete platform on piles.

ARCHIPIELAGO LOS COLORADOS
Pilotage: This group of sunken dangers fronts about 100 miles of the northeastern coast of Cuba from Golfo de Guanahacabibes to Bahia

Honda. It consists of an almost uninterrupted series of reefs rising steeply from seaward. The shallow area between the reefs and the coast is also full of hazards and low-lying islets. The shore beyond the dangers is low and the dangers rarely marked by breakers, except during heavy weather. Boats should approach this coast with extreme caution. Those with local knowledge can use some shallow channels to proceed to towns along the coast. The coast becomes generally steep-to when east of the archipelago.

CAYO JUTIAS LIGHT, NE point, 22 42.9N, 84 01.4W. L Fl W 15s, 138ft, 36M. Octagonal skeleton steel tower. Yellow and black bands, lower part enclosed. Masonry structure to S. *Bahía de Santa Lucia, Buoy 1,* 22 45.7N, 83 59.1W. L Fl W 10s. SAFE WATER, RW, pillar with topmark.

BAHÍA SANTA LUCIA

22 42N, 83 58W
Pilotage: This shallow water bay is located about 73 miles northeast of Cabo San Antonio. It is fronted by fields of mangroves and a low-lying terrain that rises gradually to hills in the interior. Seaward of the bay are the many dangers of the Archipiélago Los Colorados. The island of Cayos Jutias is marked by a light, and the intricate entrance channel, Pasa Honda, begins 2 1/2 miles to its northeast. Many sunken dangers are scattered in this area, and a radar-conspicuous wreck lies on the reef about 2 1/2 miles northeast of Pasa Honda.

This port is under the jurisdiction of Bahía de Mariel, located about 72 miles to the east-northeast. Ore is lightered out to larger vessels from the town of Santa Lucia.

PUNTA BANO, offshore on W side of entrance to channel, 22 41.2N, 83 58.2W. Fl R 4s, 16ft, 4M. Red starboard-hand beacon with topmark.
CAYO ARENAS LIGHT, 22 50.2N, 83 39.3W. Fl W 10s, 46ft, 12M. Aluminum framework tower.
PUNTA GOBERNADORA LIGHT, 3 miles W of Bahía Honda entrance, 22 59.6N, 83 12.9W. Fl W 5s, 108ft, 16M. Red and white banded conical tower. Radar reflector. Aeromarine light.

BAHÍA HONDA

BAHIA HONDA, N of old fort on Punta del Morillo, 22 58.9N, 83 09.2W. Fl (2) W 10s, 89ft, 12M. White iron skeleton.

BAHIA HONDA RANGE (Front Light), W end of Cayo del Muerto, 22 57.4N, 83 09.8W. Q W, 16ft, 9M. Yellow diamond with black border on white skeleton structure on piles. **(Rear Light),** W end of Cayo del Muerto, head of bay, 3.9 km, 183° from front, 22 55.3N, 83 10.0W. Fl W 6s, 46ft, 16M. White diamond with black border on white skeleton structure on piles. Visible 6° each side of range line.

BAHÍA HONDA

22 58N, 83 10W
Pilotage: This "pocket bay" is located about 120 miles northeast of Cabo San Antonio and 45 miles west of Havana. The saddle-shaped 2,270-foot summit of El Pan de Guajiaibon (22° 47′N, 83° 10′W) is a conspicuous landmark when approaching the bay from offshore.

The deep entrance channel leads through a coral reef into the bay. The port is part of the jurisdiction of Bahía de Mariel, located 23 miles to the east. There are several deepwater (up to 27-foot-draft) docks and anchorages within the bay.

BAHIA CABANAS LIGHT, Cerro Frias W side of entrance, 22 59.7N, 82 58.9W. Fl W 6s, 174ft, 19M. Aluminum skeleton tower, gray hut.

CABANAS

23 00N, 82 58W
Pilotage: This is another sub-port of Mariel, which is located about 12 miles to the east. Puerto Cabanas is divided into east and west parts by the Península Juan Tomas. The Canal Orozco leads into the western part and the Canal Cabanas into the eastern part. Fuerte Reina Amalia stands in ruins on the north extremity of the peninsula and serves as a conspicuous landmark when approaching these channels from the sea.

Tidal currents in the entrance have a flow of about 1 1/2 knots during the ebb, with a some-what stronger flow during the rainy season. There is a bulk sugar pier within the bay.

PUNTA ARENAS, edge of shoal S of Punta Arena (No.2A), 22 59.2N, 82 59.0W. Fl R 6s, 16ft, 4M. Red starboard-hand beacon with topmark.
PUNTA AFRICANA, NE point of Cayo Juan Tomas (No. 6), 22 59.2N, 82 58.4W. Fl R 4s, 16ft, 4M. Red starboard-hand beacon with topmark.

PIEDRA GLORIA, Lighted Beacon No. 8, 22 59.5N, 82 56.7W. Fl R 6s, 16ft, 4M. Red starboard-hand beacon with topmark.

BAHÍA DEL MARIEL

Puerto Mariel, Buoy 1, E side of entrance. 23 01.7N, 82 45.4W. Fl G 5s. Green buoy.
PUERTO DEL MARIEL LIGHT, W side of entrance, 23 01.3N, 82 45.6W. Fl W 12s, 134ft, 15M. Metal framework tower.
PUNTA REGULA ENTRANCE RANGE (Front Light), 23 00.9N 82.45.5W. Q W, 16ft, 9M. Black diamond with white border on triangular structure. **(Rear Light),** 620 meters 182°54′ from front. Q Y, 29ft, 8M. Black diamond wtih white border on triangular structure. Visible 6° each side of range line.

MARIEL

22 59N, 82 45W

Pilotage: This is one of the major "pocket bays" found along the north coast of Cuba. The terrain on either side of the narrow entrance channel is low-lying, except for the east side of the bay where hills slope steeply upward directly from the water's edge. The west face of these hills has been quarried into a conspicuous white cliff.

Mesa del Mariel is a conspicuous plateau located about 8 miles east-northeast of the entrance to Bahía del Mariel. There is a distinctive terrace at the high elongated plateau's eastern end and a remarkable steep slope at its west extremity. It has been reported as radar conspicuous.

There are several tall chimneys in a cement works on the east side of the bay; they may be seen up to 12 miles offshore. The light-colored smoke forms a dense distinctive cloud, which can be sighted from up to 25 miles. This is the best landmark on the north coast of Cuba.

The Cuban Naval Academy, a large group of white buildings, is located on the southeast side of the bay on the slopes behind the community of Mariel. This serves as a good landmark for the approach to the bay's entrance channel. Line up the center of the academy with a large white tower on the bay's entrance point. Range lights also mark the channel.

Mariel is an important port, particularly for cement and sugar cargoes. The harbor pilots may be contacted by VHF radio (call sign, Mariel Practice).

BOCA DEL RÍO BANES

23 02N, 82 38W

Pilotage: This small inlet is about 6 1/2 miles east of Bahía del Mariel. The channel is short and unencumbered. On its eastern shore there is a small sugar-loading facility.

RÍO SANTA ANA, 23 03.3N, 82 32.4W. Fl W 12s, 30ft, 11M. White framework tower.
RÍO SANTA ANA, BEACON NO. 5, 23 03.5N, 82 31.9W. Fl G 3s, 9ft, 3M. Green port-hand beacon with topmark.
RÍO SANTA ANA, BEACON NO. 6, 23 03.5N, 82 32.0W. Fl R 4s, 9ft, 4M. Red starboard-hand beacon with topmark.
RÍO SANTA ANA, BEACON NO. 8, 23 03.5N, 82 32.0W. Fl R 6s, 9ft, 3M. Red starboard-hand beacon with topmark.
DARSENA DE BARLOVENTO, 23 05.5N, 82 29.6W. Fl W 7s, 118ft, 25M. W skeleton tower on building. Reserve light range 10M.
BOCA DE JAIMANITAS BEACON, 23 05.6N, 82 29.4W. Fl G 3s, 16ft, 4M. Round concrete structure, green square topmark.

MARINA HEMINGWAY

23 04N, 82 30W

Pilotage: The entrance to the marina is located about 8 miles west of the entrance to Havana and about 90 miles south-southwest of Key West, Florida. The light at Barlovento is a good position indicator. An entrance range of 140.1° will help guide you in. You should contact the harbor authorities on VHF channels 12 or 16 when within the 12-mile territorial limit. They may send out a patrol boat to escort you in.
Port of Entry: The officials are located right in the marina. This is reported to be one of the best places for pleasure vessels to enter the country.
Dockage: Contact Marina Hemingway (VHF channel 12 or 16 or telephone 22 5590-3). The dockage rate at Cuban marinas is reported to be US$0.35 per foot, per day.
Facilities: There is a special market for visitors with U.S. dollars, and there are supermarkets nearby and in Havana. Repair facilities for yachts may be available, but services tend to be geared toward fishing and commercial vessels. Cuban charts, publications, and guides are available at the marina.

This is the first stop for many boaters in Cuba and is a good place to clear with the officials and collect information. The city of Havana is a short bus or taxi ride away.

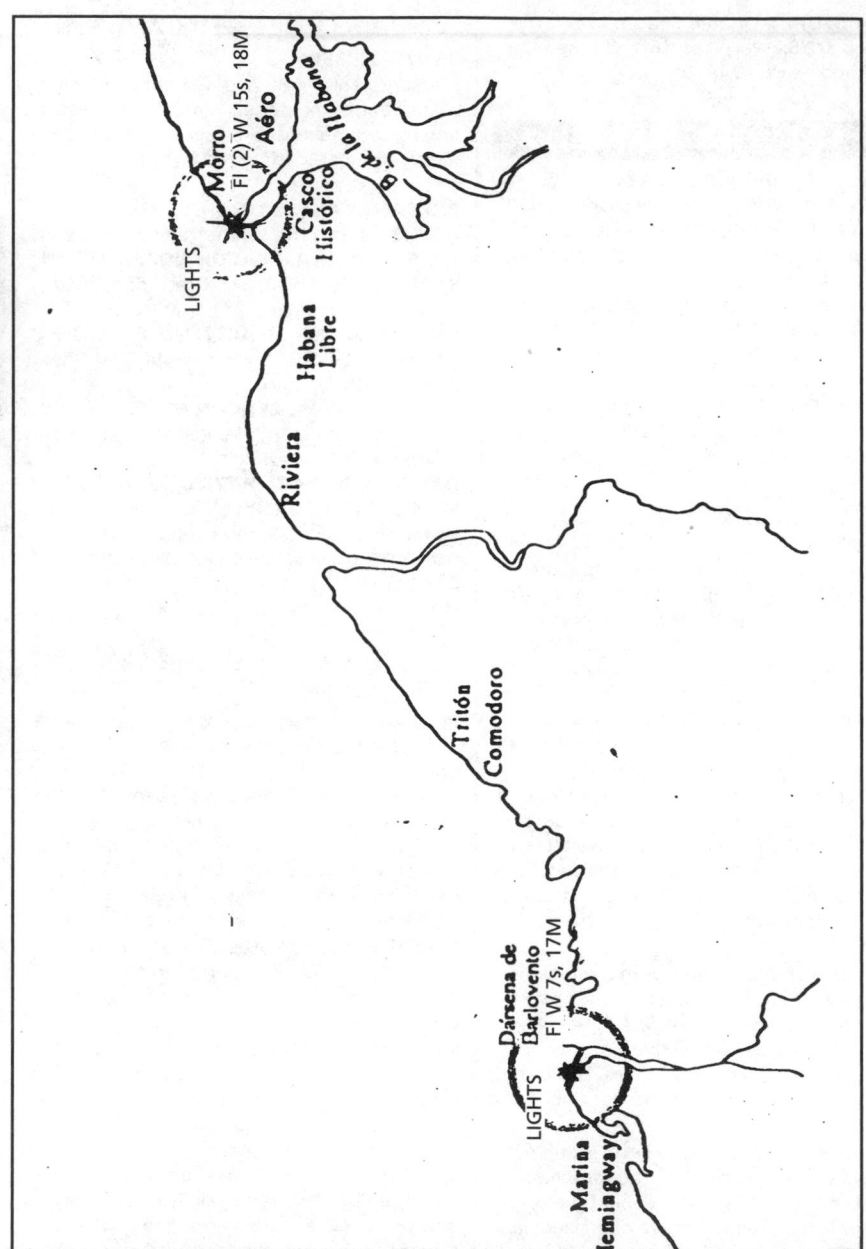

Approaches to Marina Hemingway *(after T-114, Instituto Cubano de Hidrografía, 1991)*

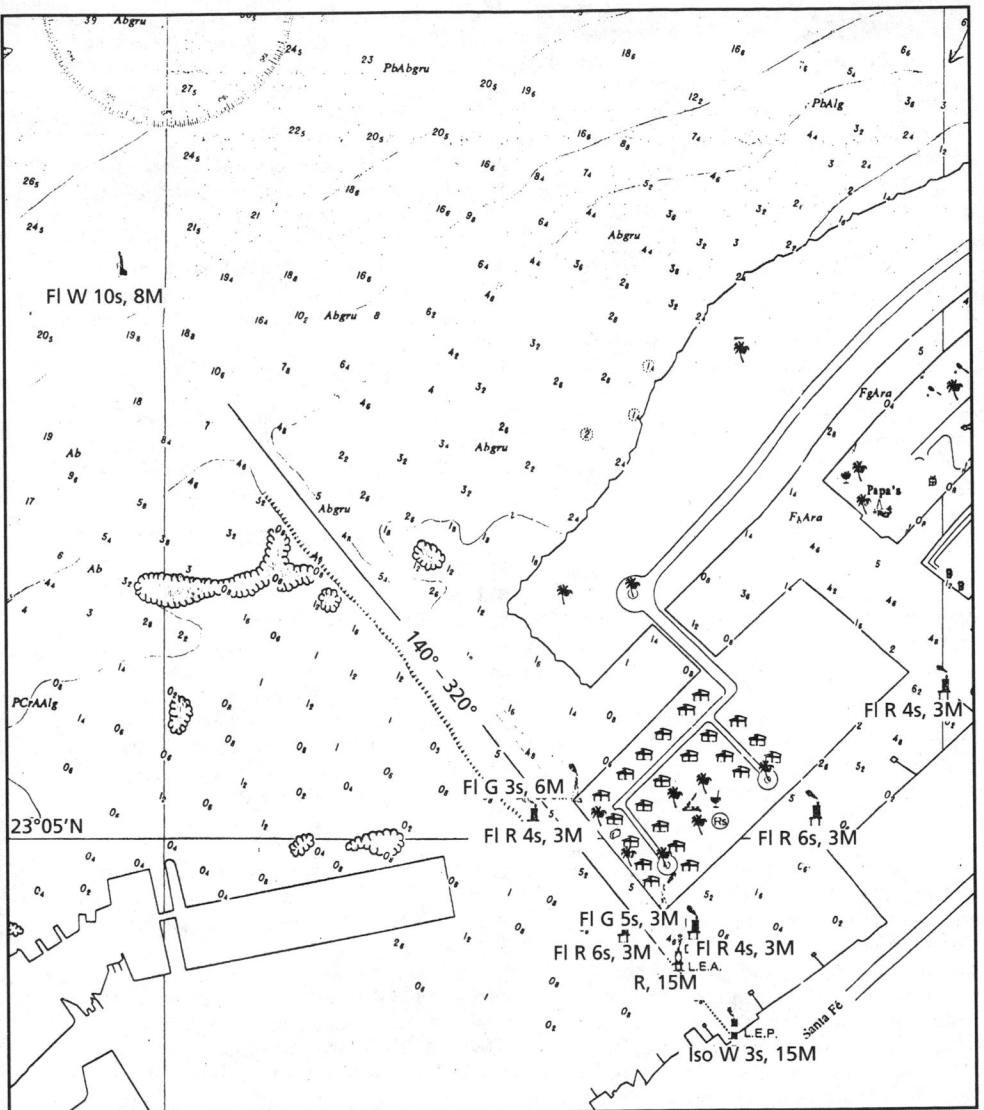

Marina Hemingway, soundings in meters *(after T-114, Instituto Cubano de Hidrografia, 1991)*

LA HABANA (HAVANA)

BAHÍA CHORRERA, W side of entrance (No. 2). 23 08.0N, 82 24.6W. Fl R 6s, 33ft, 4M. Red starboard-hand beacon with topmark. Reported destroyed (1994).

BAHÍA CHORRERA, NO. 3 BEACON, on mole., 23 07.9N, 82 24.7W. Fl G 3s, 10ft, 4M. Green port-hand beacon with topmark.

BAHÍA DE LA CHORRERA

23 08N, 82 25W

Pilotage: This inlet is about 3 miles west of the entrance to Bahía de La Habana. The Río Almenderes flows into the harbor. The coast in the vicinity is low and ragged, with blackened coral honeycombed by the sea. Depths in the bay average 20 to 30 feet over coral sand, in a position just within the entrance. With winds from the northeast through northwest, through north, the anchorage is subject to surge.

CASTILLO DEL MORRO, E side of entrance, 23 09.0N, 82 21.4W. Fl (2) W 15s, 144ft, 43M. White truncated conical tower. Storm signals; signal station. Aeromarine light. Reserve light range 21M.

RANGE (Front Light), 23 07.9N, 82 19.8W. Q Y, 42ft, 14M. White pyramidal framework tower; yellow diamond daymark. **(Rear Light),** 300 meters 124°48′ from front, 23 07.8N, 82 19.7W. Iso Y 6s, 62ft, 14M. White pyramidal framework tower; yellow diamond daymark.

LA HABANA

23 08N, 82 20W

Pilotage: This is one of the largest sugar shipping ports in the world and is the commercial and shipping center for all of Cuba. Castillo Del Morro is east of the entrance and La Punta Castle is located to the west. A powerful light is shown from Castillo Del Morro. The land east of Castillo Del Morro is about 197 feet high and flat, with a prominent ridge, Sierras de Jaruco, located about 19 miles farther east. About the same distance west of the entrance is a distinctive notch in the east end of Mesa de Mariel. At night, the loom of the metropolis is reported visible up to 25 miles offshore.

CAUTION: Occasionally, powerful lights are displayed from the dome of the capitol in La Habana; these lights may be confused with the navigation light on Castillo Del Morro.

The pilot station may be contacted on VHF channels 3 and 16 (call sign, Habana Practicos).

The port signal station is located in Castillo Del Morro (VHF channels 13, 16, and 68; call sign Morro Habana). The port authorities may be reached on VHF channels 16 and 68 (call sign, Habana Capitonia).

NOTE: Pleasure vessels should enter at Marina Hemingway, where facilities are geared to their needs.

BOCA DE COJIMAR BEACON, E side of entrance, 23 10.0N, 82 17.6W. Fl G 5s, 36ft, 4M. Square concrete structure, green square topmark.

BOCA DE GUANABO BEACON, E side of entrance, 23 10.4N, 82 07.4W. Fl G 3s, 26ft, 4M. Green port-hand beacon with topmark.

RÍO JARUCO BEACON, W side of entrance, 23 10.8N, 82 00.6W. Fl R 4s, 23ft, 4M. Red starboard-hand beacon with topmark.

SANTA CRUZ DE NORTE

23 09N, 81 55W

Pilotage: This is a small community located about 24 miles east of Bahía de La Habana. A distillery has a tall chimney and two storage tanks, which can be clearly seen from sea. Central Hershey sugar mill is located 2 miles southwest of Santa Cruz del Norte and has three tall chimneys standing on an elevation of 387 feet, which make an excellent landmark. Between January and June the sugar mill is brightly lit for nighttime operations.

CANASI LIGHT, 23 08.8N, 81 48.0W. Fl W 7s, 374ft, 19M. Red framework tower on platform.

PUNTA SEBORUCO LIGHT, 23 09.1N, 81 36.4W. Fl W 15s, 115ft, 15M. Round concrete tower, red and white bands.

PUNTA MAYA LIGHT, E side of entrance to Bahía de Matanzas, 23 05.6N, 81 28.5W. Fl W 8s, 112ft, 17M. White cylindrical tower. A F W light is shown from a wharf on the N side of port.

MATANZAS

23 03N, 81 35W

Pilotage: This is an important port and city located about 45 miles east of La Habana. It is situated near the head of one of the north coast's largest bays. Two aeronautical lights shown from the high ground on the west side of the bay are visible for up to 35 miles.

Bajo Nuevo, a shoal with a least depth of 10 feet, and Bajo La Laja, with a least depth of 6 feet, lie offshore near the head of Bahía de Matanzas. Several deepwater passages lead in

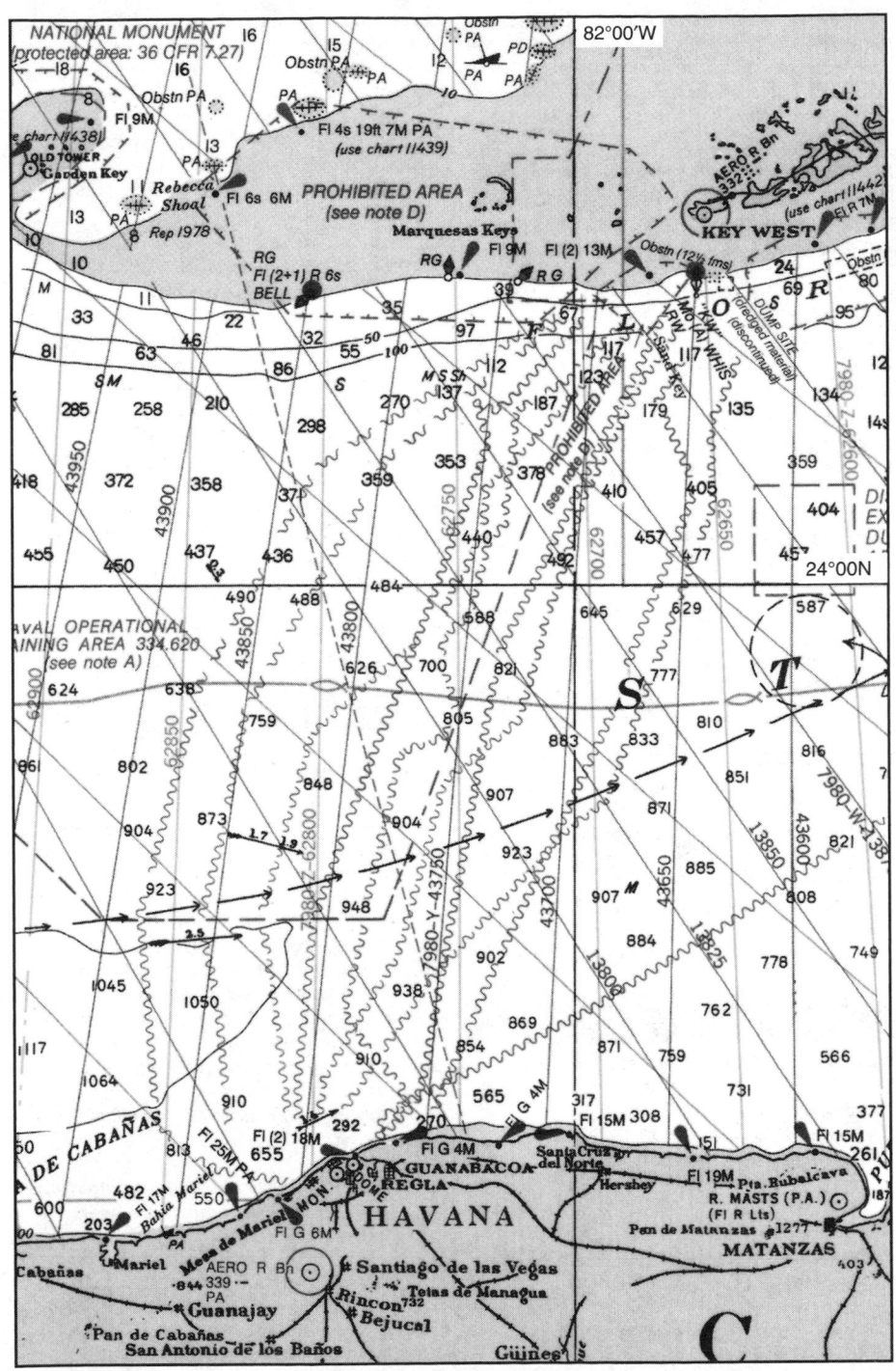

Approaches to Havana, soundings in fathoms *(from NOAA 11013, 40th ed, 10/93)*

from the sea around and between these rocky dangers.

The pilots may be contacted on VHF channels 13, 16, and 68 (call sign, Matanzas Practicos).

CANALIZO PASO MALO

KAWAMA WEST JETTY, 23 08.8N, 81 18.8W. Fl R 4s, 23ft, 4M. Red starboard-hand beacon with topmark.
EAST JETTY, 23 08.0N, 81 18.7W. Fl G 3s, 23ft, 4M. Green port-hand beacon with topmark.
RANGE (Front Light), 23 07.8N, 81 18.6W, Q W, 9ft, 7M. White concrete tower, square base. **(Rear Light),** 108 meters 152°36' from front. Iso W 6s, 23ft, 7M. White concrete tower, square base.
LAGUNA DE PASO MALO, NO. 3, 23 07.8N, 81 18.3W. Fl G 3s, 20ft, 4M. Green port-hand beacon with topmark.
LAGUNADE PASO MALO, NO. 6, 23 07.8N, 81 18.1W. Fl R 6s, 20ft, 4M. Red starboard-hand beacon with topmark.
LAGUNA DE PASO MALO, NO. 9, 23 07.8N, 81 17.7W. Fl G 5s, 20ft, 4M. Green port-hand beacon with topmark.
CAYO MONITO, 23 13.8N, 81 08.6W. Fl (2) W 10s, 20ft, 7M. ISOLATED DANGER BRB, beacon w/topmark.
LAGUNA DE PASO MALO, NO. 11, 23 07.8N, 81 17.6W. Fl G 3s, 20ft, 4M. Green port-hand beacon with topmark.
LAGUNA DE PASO MALO, NO. 21, 23 07.8N, 81 16.7W. Fl G 3s, 20ft, 4M. Green port-hand beacon with topmark.
LAGUNA DE PASO MALO, NO. 22, 23 07.8N, 81 16.7W. Fl R 4s, 7ft, 4M. Red starboard-hand beacon with topmark.

BAHIA DE CARDENAS

CAYO PIEDRAS LIGHT, entrance to bay, 23 14.5N, 81 07.2W. Fl W 10s, 79ft, 15M. White cylindrical masonry tower.
Cabezo del Coral Buoy, 23 15.1N, 81 06.3W. Fl G 3s. Green port-hand pillar with topmark. Radar reflector.
Buoy 1, 23 13.6N, 81 05.3W. Fl G 5s. Green port-hand pillar with topmark.
CAYO DIANA, S side, 23 09.9N, 81 06.2W. Fl W 8s, 49ft, 12M. White framework tower.

PUNTA HICACOS
23 12N, 81 09W
Pilotage: This is the northern extremity of Península de Hicacos, which guards the northern border of Bahía De Cardenas. It is low and sandy but can be identified by the buildings of a salt works near it. Punta de Molas is the low-lying eastern extremity of the peninsula. The seaward side of the peninsula is a long fine beach, broken only in a few places by low cliffs. The highest cliff is situated 4 1/2 miles southwest of Punta Hicacos and is named Bernardino.

VARADERO
23 08N, 81 15W (approx.)
Pilotage: This resort community is located on a low part of the Península de Hicacos, near where it connects with the mainland. It is about 7 1/2 miles southwest of Punta Hicacos. This is one of the premier boating areas on the north coast of Cuba. From seaward this community is identified by its tall trees, houses, windmills, a club house, and a large white building with a red roof. At night, the lights of the settlement are conspicuous.
Port of Entry: This is a recommended place for pleasure boats to clear in.
Dockage: Cayo Largo Marina is located just outside Veradero. Marina Veradero has more complete repair facilities, including a crane for hauling. Marina Chapelin is in a mangrove-protected basin.
Facilities: This being a tourist area, there are nightclubs, restaurants, and shops.

CARDENAS
23 02N, 81 12W
Pilotage: This is the second biggest sugar exporting port in Cuba and also the location of a significant fishing industry. It is the northern-most port in Cuba. The port is located on the western side of Bahía de Cardenas, which lies under the shelter of Península de Hicacos to the northwest. The bay is scattered with low-lying mangrove-fringed islands, but there are several deepwater passages among them. The tall buildings in the resort of Varadero are prominent when approaching the bay from the north. The lighthouse on the low reef-fringed islet Cayo Piedras de Norte marks the entrance to the bay.

CAUTION: The lights and other navigational aids in Bahía de Cardenas have been reported as unreliable.

CAYO DIANA, BEACON NO. 2, 23 10.8N, 81 07.7W. Fl R 6s, 13ft, 3M. Red starboard-hand beacon with topmark.
CAYO DIANA, BEACON NO. 3, 23 11.5N, 81 07.8W. Fl G 3s, 13ft, 3M. Green port-hand beacon with topmark.

CAYO DIANA, BEACON NO. 4, 23 11.2N, 81 07.7W. Fl R 4s, 13ft, 3M. Red starboard-hand beacon with topmark.

CHANNEL BEACON 4A, PUNTA GORDA, 23 10.0N, 81 10.3W. Fl R 4s, 13ft, 4M. Red starboard-hand beacon with topmark.

BEACON NO. 6A, 23 09.9N, 81 11.2W. Fl R 6s, 13ft, 4M. Red starboard-hand beacon with topmark.

CANAL DE LA MANUY, NO. 1, 23 08.6N, 81 01.2W. Fl G 3s, 16ft. Green port-hand beacon with topmark.

CANAL DE LA MANUY, NO. 2, 23 08.3N, 81 01.1W. Fl R 4s, 16ft. Red starboard-hand beacon with topmark.

CANAL DE LA MANUY, NO. 3, 23 08.2N, 81 00.8W. Fl G 5s, 16ft. Green port-hand beacon with topmark.

CANAL DE LA MANUY, NO. 4, 23 07.8N, 81 00.6W. Fl R 6s, 16ft. Red starboard-hand beacon with topmark.

CANAL DE LA MANUY, NO. 7, 23 07.1N, 80 59.8W. Fl G 3s, 16ft. Green port-hand beacon with topmark.

CANAL DE LA MANUY, NO. 9, 23 05.2N, 80 57.8W. Fl G 5s, 16ft. Green port-hand beacon with topmark.

CANAL DE LOS BARCOS, NO. 2, 23 11.8N, 80 42.2W. Fl R 4s, 16ft. Red starboard-hand beacon with topmark.

CANAL DE LOS BARCOS, NO. 3, 23 10.1N, 80 42.1W. Fl G 5s, 16ft. Green port-hand beacon with topmark.

CAYO CRUZ DEL PADRE LIGHT, 23 16.9N, 80 53.9W. Fl W 7s, 82ft. 14M. White concrete tower on square base. RACON **C** (– · – ·), 16M.

CAYO CRUZ DEL PADRE

23 16N, 80 55W

Pilotage: This small mangrove-fringed piece of land is located about 13 miles east-northeast of Punta Hicacos, making it the northernmost islet along the north coast of Cuba. To seaward of it is a dangerous partially drying reef, which can be distinguished in calm weather by discoloration in the surrounding water. In heavy weather, waves break over it.

CAYO BAHÍA DE CADIZ LIGHT, N side of cay, 23 12.3N, 80 28.9W. Fl (3) W 15s, 177ft. 19M. Pyramidal tower with white and black stripes.

CAYO BAHÍA DE CADIZ

23 12N, 80 29W

Pilotage: This flat islet is located about 24 miles east-southeast of Cayo Cruz del Padre. It is rocky on its north side and somewhat higher than other islets in the vicinity.

Anchorage: Bahía de Cadiz is a shoal bay located close southwest of the islet. Vessels with local knowledge can anchor here with some protection from the prevailing northeast winds. The anchorage is open to winds from the north.

Megano de Nicolas Buoy, 23 13.2N, 80 19.3W. Fl (2) W 6s. ISOLATED DANGER BRB, pillar w/topmark.

SAGUA LA GRAND

CAYO HICACAL, ON PUNTA DE LA RANCHERIA, 23 04.3N, 80 05.2W. Fl W 8s, 36ft, 8M. White framework tower.

NO. 4, 23 03.5N, 80 07.4W. Fl R 6s, 13ft, 4M. Red starboard-hand beacon with topmark.

CAYO DEL CRISTO, ON PUNTA DE LOS PRACTICOS, 23 02.0N, 79 59.4W. Fl W 10s, 50ft, 12M. White framework tower.

RÍO SAGUA ENTRANCE BEACON, E side, 22 56.8N, 80 00.0W. Fl G 3s, 13ft. Green port-hand mark with topmark.

RÍO SAGUA, NO. 21, 22 56.9N. 80 00.6W. Fl G 5s, 13ft. Green port-hand beacon with topmark.

RÍO SAGUA, NO. 22, 22 56.9N. 80 00.6W. Fl R 6s, 13ft. Red starboard-hand beacon with topmark.

RÍO SAGUA, NO. 26, 22 56.8N. 80 01.0W. Fl R 6s, 13ft. Red starboard-hand beacon with topmark.

PUERTO SAGUA LA GRANDE

22 58N, 80 03W

Pilotage: The main entrance to this port, which fronts the Río Sagua la Grande, is through Canal Boca de Maravillas. The dredged channel passes between Cayo dela Cruz and Cayo Maravillas. Cayo del Cristo light, located about 6 miles north of Río Sagua la Grande, is the major identifying mark along this coast. The area off the coast consists of small mangrove-covered islands.

Being open to the northeast, there is frequently a very heavy sea in the entrance channel.

CAUTION: Dredged material has been deposited on each side of the channel where it lies uncharted and built up in the form of partially drying banks.

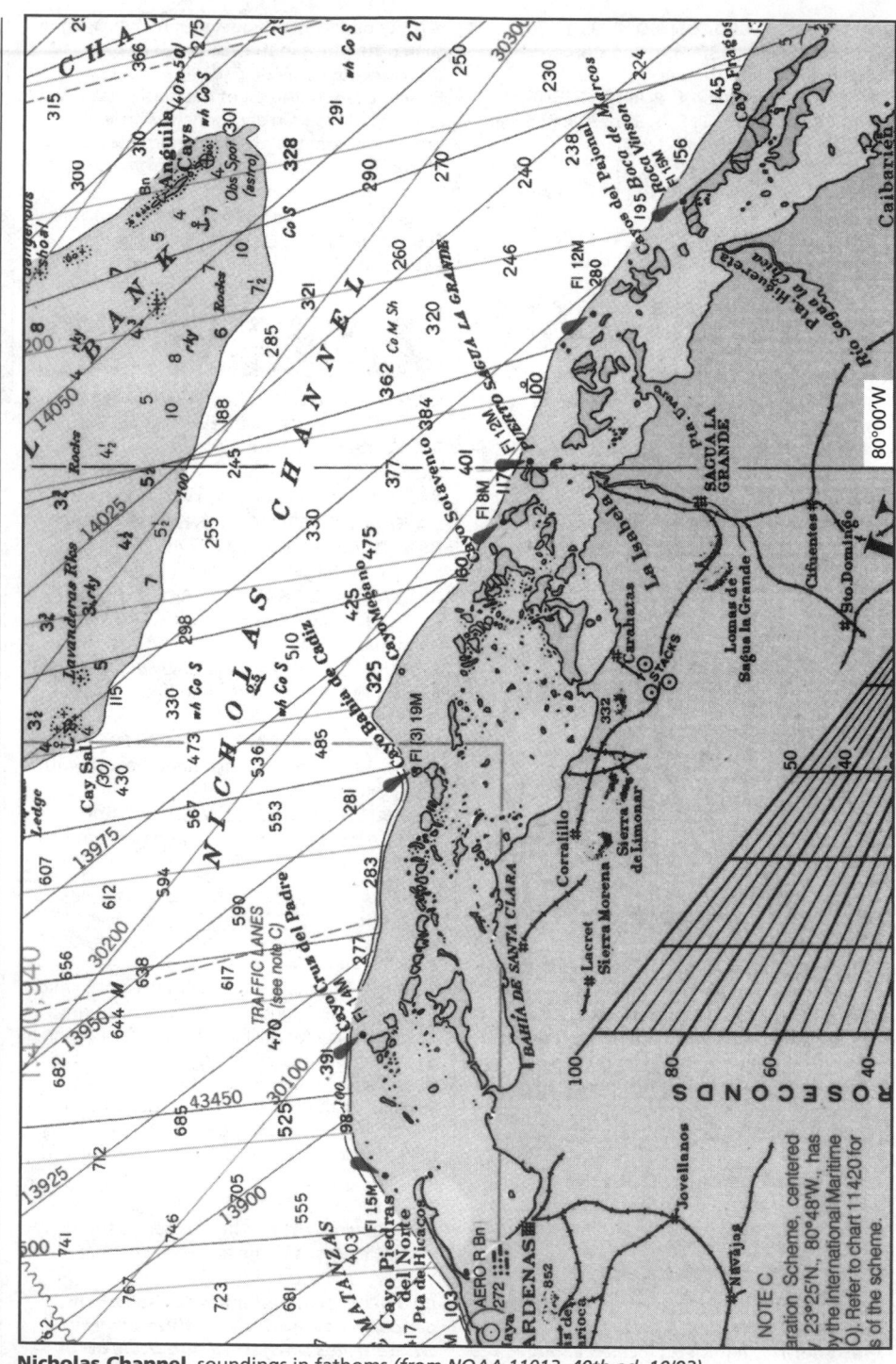

Nicholas Channel, soundings in fathoms *(from NOAA 11013, 40th ed, 10/93)*

LA ISABELLA

22 57N, 80 00W

Pilotage: This small community is located at the entrance to Río Sagua la Grande. It is a sugar-shipping center for Sagua la Grande, a well populated community located about 12 miles upstream. The pilot may be contacted on VHF channel 16.

CANAL DEL SERON BEACON, E side, 22 58.0N, 79 55.6W. Fl G 5s, 10ft, 3M. Green port-hand mark with topmark.
BOCA DE JUTIAS BEACON, 22 58.0N, 79 51.9W. Fl G 5s, 16ft, 3M. Green port-hand mark with topmark.
CANAL DE CILINDRIN BEACON, 22 56.3N 79 49.0W. Fl G 5s, 16ft, 4M. Green port-hand mark with topmark.
CANAL DE LAS BARZAS BEACON, 22 54.0N, 79 45.6W. Fl G 3s, 16ft, 4M. Green port-hand mark with topmark.
CAYO ALTO BEACON, 22 51.9N, 79 46.5W. Fl G 5s, 16ft, 5M. Green port-hand mark with topmark.
CAYO LA VELA, 22 56.6N, 79 45.4W. Fl W 12s, 39ft, 14M. White round metal column.
CAYO FRAGOSO, NW end, 22 48.4N, 79 34.6W. Fl W 15s, 68ft, 15M. White framework tower.
CAYO FRAGOSO, BEACON NO. 2, 22 44.6N, 79 36.9W. Fl R 6s, 19ft, 4M. Red starboard-hand mark with topmark.
CAYO FRAGOSO, BEACON NO. 3, 22 42.6N, 79 36.2W. Fl G 5s, 16ft, 4M. Green port-hand mark with topmark.
CAYO FRAGOSO, BEACON NO. 5, 22 41.0N, 79 35.0W. Fl G 3s, 16ft, 4M. Green port-hand mark with topmark.
CAYO FRAGOSO, BEACON NO. 8, 22 40.1N, 79 34.2W. Fl R 4s, 16ft, 4M. Red starboard-hand mark with topmark.
CAYO FRANCES, W end at entrance to Caibarien, 22 38.5N, 79 13.8W. Fl W 10s, 32ft, 9M. White square concrete tower.
Buoy 1, West of Cayo Frances Light, 22 38.3N, 79 15.1W. Fl G 5s, 13ft. Green port-hand pillar with topmark.
Cayo Frances Anchorage, 22 37.8N 79 13.2W. Fl G 5s, 13ft, 4M. Green port-hand mark with topmark.
CAYO FRANCES, BEACON NO. 4, 22 35.6N, 79 17.4W. Fl R 4s, 16ft, 4M. Red starboard-hand mark with topmark.
CAYO FRANCES, BEACON NO. 6, 22 34.4N, 79 18.5W. Fl R 6s, 16ft, 4M. Red starboard-hand mark with topmark.
CAYO FRANCES, BEACON NO. 8, 22 33.4N, 79 22.8W. Fl R 4s, 16ft, 4M. Red starboard-hand mark with topmark.

PUERTO DE CAIBARIEN

22 37N, 79 15W

Pilotage: This is the sugar port for the city of Caibarien, located 16 miles to the west-southwest. It is located about 46 miles east-southeast of Puerto Sagua La Grande, with its seaward entrance near Cayo Frances (22° 38′N, 79° 13′W).

PUNTA BRAVA BEACON, NO 9, 22 31.9N, 79 26.7W. Fl G 5s, 39ft, 4M. Green port-hand mark with topmark.
PUNTA BRAVA BEACON, NO 11, 22 31.9N, 79 28.5W. Fl G 5s, 16ft, 4M. Green port-hand mark with topmark.
CAYO FIFA BEACON, SE, 22 35.5N, 79 28.5W. Fl R 6s, 16ft, 4M. Red starboard-hand mark with topmark.
CAYO FIFA BEACON, NE, 22 36.1N, 79 27.9W. Fl G 3s, 13ft, 3M. Green square daymark on concrete tower.
CANAL DEL REFUGIO, E BEACON, NO 1, 22 31.8N, 79 27.5W. Fl G 5s, 16ft, 4M. Green port-hand beacon with topmark.
CANAL DEL REFUGIO, W BEACON, NO 2, 22 31.5N, 79 27.3W. Fl R 6s, 16ft, 4M. Red starboard-hand beacon with topmark.
CANAL DE LAS PIRAGUAS BEACON, 22 37.0N, 79 13.2W. Fl R 4s, 13ft, 4M. Red starboard-hand beacon with topmark.
CANALIZO DE LOS BARCOS BEACON, NO 2, 22 31.7N, 79 18.8W. Fl R 4s, 13ft, 4M. Red starboard-hand beacon with topmark.
CANALIZO DE LOS BARCOS BEACON, NO 3, 22 31.0N, 79 18.9W. Fl G 3s, 19ft, 4M. Red starboard-hand beacon with topmark.
BAJO DEL MEDIO BEACON, NO 5, off SW end, 22 29.8N, 79 17.4W. Fl G 5s, 16ft, 4M. Green port-hand beacon with topmark.
BAHIA DE BUENAVISTA BEACON, NO 6, 22 27.4N, 78 56.7W. Fl R 4s, 13ft, 4M. Red starboard-hand beacon with topmark.
CAYO BORACHO BEACON, W END, 22 39.0N, 79 09.4W. Fl G 5s, 28ft, 4M. Green port-hand beacon with topmark.
CAYO CAIMAN GRANDE DE SANTA MARIA LIGHT, 22 41.1N, 78 53.0W. Fl W 5s, 158ft, 19M. Conical tower, black and white bands. Radiobeacon. Aeromarine light.

OLD BAHAMA CHANNEL

Pilotage: This channel separates the Great Bahama Bank from the north coast of Cuba and allows passage from the Atlantic via Crooked Island Passage to the Straits of Florida or the Gulf of Mexico. An IMO Traffic Separation

Scheme has been established in the channel, which can best be seen on the appropriate chart.

The government of Cuba has unilaterally established a mandatory ship reporting system to govern vessel movement in the area. See the introduction to this chapter for more information.

Two hours before entering the Scheme vessels should contact the appropriate shore station in Cuba. The message should be prefixed "OLDBACHA" and should include information on the type of vessel, nationality, position, course, speed, and so on. For the western approach call "CLG-50 CAIMAN." For the eastern approach call "CLG-60 CONFITES." Communication with the stations is conducted on VHF channel 13, which should be monitored continuously while within the Traffic Separation Scheme. Vessels may contact the station in English or Spanish.

The southwest side of the channel is composed of low-lying islands and other dangers. There are a number of small lagoons suitable for exploration by small craft only. The southwest side of the channel from Cayo Paredon Grande Light (22° 30'N, 78° 10'W) to Cayo Confites (22° 11'N, 77° 40'W) is considered quite dangerous. For this 34-mile stretch vessels are recommended to stay in the middle of the channel and proceed with caution.

PASO MANUY WEST BEACON, 22 24.9N, 78 41.4W. Fl R 6s, 13ft, 4M. Red starboard-hand beacon with topmark.
CAYO JAULA, 22 34.2N, 78 30.9W. Fl W 10s, 68ft, 14M. Aluminum skeleton tower, white concrete base. Reported extinguished (1983).
BOCO DE MANATI, E SIDE MANATI CHANNEL ENTRANCE, 22 15.7N, 78 29.8W. Fl G 5s, 13ft, 4M. Green port-hand mark with topmark.
CAYO PAREDON GRANDE LIGHT, N side, 22 29.0N, 78 09.9W. Fl (3) W 15s, 157ft, 19M. Black and yellow checkered iron column.
CAYO CONFITES, 22 11.4N, 77 39.7W. Fl W 7.5s, 75ft, 14M. Gray metal framework tower.
CAYO CONFITES, NO 2, 22 10.3N, 77 39.2W. Fl R 6s, 13ft, 3M. Red starboard-hand mark with topmark.
CAYO CONFITES, NO 3, 22 10.2N, 77 38.6W. Fl G 5s, 13ft, 3M. Green port-hand mark with topmark.
CAYO CONFITES BEACON, 22 08.7N, 77 41.6W. Fl Y 7s, 13ft, 5M. Special yellow with topmark.

CAYO CONFITES

22 10N, 77 40W

Pilotage: This low islet lies close within the outer edge of the bank along the south side of the Old Bahama Channel. A drying reef extends 1 mile south-southeast from the cay, and a channel 300 yards wide separates the cay from a reef that dries, which extends from it. A light is shown from a 66-foot-high tower standing on the north side of the cay.
Anchorage: Proceed to a position on the coastal edge of the bank where the light of Cayo Verde bears 191° and Cayo Confites's extremity bears 314°. From this point a vessel steers 270° until the south extremity of Cayo Confites bears 344°. The vessel then hauls to starboard and takes a heading of about 323° until Cayo Confites's extremity bears 050°, distant 1/2 mile. Anchor in a charted depth of 22 feet.

BAHÍA DE NUEVITAS

PUNTA MATERNILLOS LIGHT, 21 39.8N, 77 08.5W. Fl W 15s, 174ft, 40M. White conical tower. Aeromarine light.
PUNTA PRACTICOS, E side of entrance, 21 36.3N, 77 05.9W. Fl W 10s, 32ft, 8M. White concrete tower.

NUEVITAS

21 33N, 77 16W

Pilotage: The coast from Cayo Confites to Cayo Sabinal consists of sandy beaches, punctuated by numerous lagoons and swamps, with broken reefs adding to the dangers. Punta Maternillos light is about 4 miles northwest of the entrance to Puerto de Nuevitas and is the principal landmark in the area.

Bahía de Nuevitas is entered through a narrow deepwater channel 7 miles long. The bay is divided by a somewhat hilly and heavily scrub-covered peninsula extending 3 miles east from the southwest side of the bay. Bahía Nuevitas lies southeast of the peninsula and Bahía de Mayanabo lies northwest of it. The towns of Pastelillo and Puerto Tarafa, sub-ports of Nuevitas, lie respectively on the southeast and northwest sides of the peninsula. The terminal of Bufadero lies on the northeast side.

The surrounding coastal terrain is low-lying, flat, and without distinguishing features, except for the hills on the dividing peninsula and the nearby conical islets Cayo Ballenatos, which, rising above the lowland, are visible from the sea.

COAST PILOT

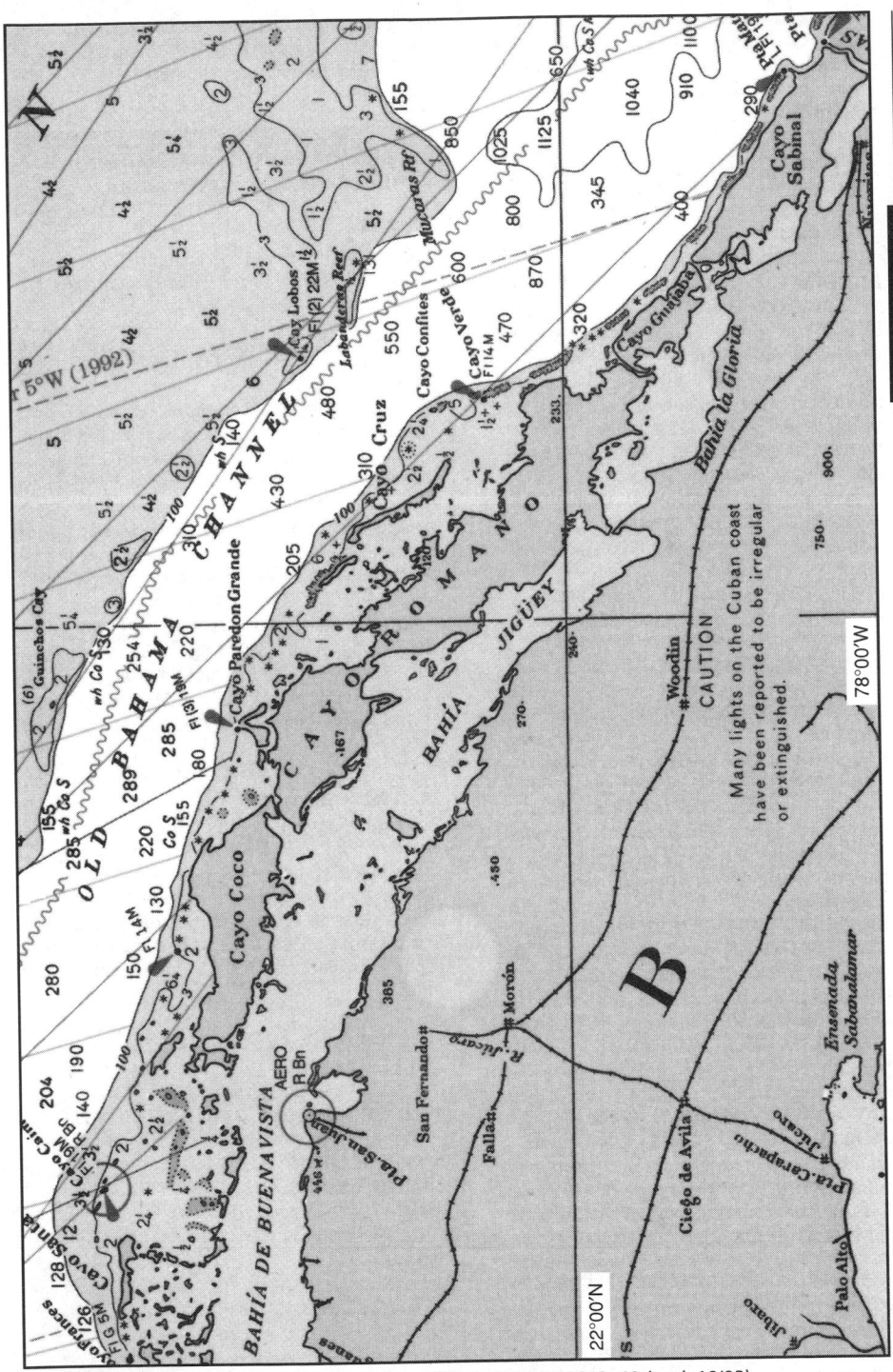

Old Bahama Channel, soundings in fathoms *(from NOAA 11013, 40th ed, 10/93)*

The entrance channel to Nuevitas has four right-angle turns in it and has a tidal current reaching 3 to 4 1/2 knots about 2 to 3 hours after high or low water. There is about a 20-minute slack.

The ports in Bahía de Nuevitas are the major sugar-shipping centers of Cuba. There is an IMO Traffic Separation Scheme in the waters off Bahía de Nuevitas.

ENTRANCE RANGE (Front Light), 21 35.5N, 77 06.4W. Q W, 6ft, 7M. White diamond with black border on triangular concrete structure. **(Rear Light),** 175 meters 185°36′ from front. Iso W 3s, 22ft, 10M. White diamond with black border on triangular concrete structure. Visible 6° each side of range line.
PUNTA SALTEADORES LIGHTED BEACON, NO. 3, 21 35.8N, 77 06.2W. Fl G 3s, 13ft, 4M. Green port-hand beacon with topmark.
PENA REDONDA BEACON NO 4, 21 35.7N, 77 06.4W. Fl R 4s, 16ft, 4M. Red starboard-hand beacon with topmark.
PLAYA CHUCHU RANGE (Front Light), 21 35.6N, 77 06.9W. Q W, 20ft, 9M. White diamond with black border on triangular concrete structure. **(Rear Light),** 195 meters 000°54′ from front. Iso W 3s, 33ft, 9M. White diamond with black border on square concrete structure. Visible 6° each side of range line.
LAS CALABAZAS RANGE (Front Light), 21 33.9N, 77 06.9W. Q W, 23ft, 9M. White diamond with black border on triangular concrete structure. **(Rear Light),** 190 meters 180°54′ from front. Iso W 3s, 33ft, 12M. White diamond with black border on triangular concrete structure.
BAJO DEL MEDIO RANGE (Front Light), 21 34.2N, 77 08.3W. Q W, 20ft, 10M. White diamond with black border on triangular concrete structure on pilings. **(Rear Light),** 265 meters 269°30′ from front. Iso W 3s, 33ft, 11M. White diamond with black border on triangular concrete structure. Visible 6° each side of range line.
CAYO CAYITA, COMMON (Front Light), 21 32.8N, 77 08.1W. Q W, 16ft, 5M. White diamond with black border on triangular concrete structure. **(Rear Light),** 290 meters 179°30′ from common front. Iso W 3s, 22ft, 10M. White diamond with black border on square concrete column on pilings. Visible 6° each side of range **(Rear Light),** 225 meters 057°48′ from common front. Iso W 3s, 33ft, 11M. White diamond with black border on square concrete column. Visible 6° on each side of range line.

BAJO DEL RÍO LIGHT BEACON, NO 7A, 21 31.2N, 77 14.8W. Fl G 5s, 16ft, 4M. Green port-hand column with topmark.

BAHÍA DE MANATI

BAHIA DE MANATI, PUNTA ROMA, 21 23.4N, 76 48.8W. Fl W 12s, 43ft, 12M. Iron conical tower, aluminum and red bands.
Buoy 1, E side of entrance channel, 21 23.5N, 76 48.5W. Fl G 3s. Green pillar can with topmark.

PUERTO MANATI
21 22N, 76 50W
Pilotage: This small community is located on the west side of the "pocket bay" called Bahía de Manati. The bay is located about 21 miles southeast of Puerto de Nuevitas and 165 miles west-northwest of Cabo Maisi. The light structure is reported to be visible by day up to 8 miles, and there is a gray brick chimney in the port. The port is a major sugar-shipping center.

PUERTO PADRE, PUNTA MASTERLERO, W side of entrance, 21 16.5N, 76 32.2W. Fl W 8s, 50ft, 12M. White round metal tower.
Puerto Padre Buoy 1, 21 16.5N, 76 31.9W. Fl G 5s. Green pillar can with topmark.

PUERTO PADRE
21 12N, 76 36W
Pilotage: This community is at the head of Bahía de Puerto Padre and is another major sugar-shipping point. Punta Mastelero light structure stands at the seaward entrance to the bay and is reported visible during the day at a distance of 6 miles. The entrance itself is reported radar conspicuous at a distance of 5 miles.

PUNTA PIEDRA DEL MANGLE, 21 15.0N, 76 18.7W. Fl W 10s, 76ft, 15M. White metal framework tower.
PUNTA RASA LIGHT, 21 09.0N, 76 07.8W. Fl W 15s, 112ft, 16M. White cylindrical concrete tower, red bands.
PUERTO GIBARA, ON PUNTA PEREGRINA, E side of entrance, 21 06.7N, 76 06.7W. Fl G 5s, 26ft, 5M. Green square on round green tower.

GIBARA
21 07N, 76 08W
Pilotage: This is the port for Holguin, the third largest city in Cuba. Silla de Gibara (21° 02′N, 76° 05′W) lies about 6 miles south-

southeast of the entrance to Puerto Gibara. This saddle-shaped hill has a gray rocky summit rising to over 1,000 feet. Cerro Colorado (834 feet) and Cerro Yabazon (808 feet) are two conspicuous hills lying within miles west-southwest of Silla de Gibara. Lomas de Cupeicillo are a series of forested hills and conspicuous ridges rising to heights of 492 to 805 feet. They extend up to 10 miles west of Puerto Gibara.

Tidal currents are negligible in the entrance, but the flow from rivers in the rainy season can sometimes create a 1/4-knot current setting north.

BAHÍA DE BARIAY AND BAHÍA DE JURURU

21 05N, 76 01W

Pilotage: Bahía de Bariay is entered between Punta La Mula (Desiree) and a point 3/4 mile southwest. It is a shoal-water bay providing temporary anchorage for vessels with local knowledge in about 30 feet of water over white sand and coral.

Anchorage: Anchor close inshore off the second sandy beach south of Punta La Mulla. This anchorage is fully open to the north and is considered dangerous in the winter. Bahía de Jururu is located west of Bahía de Bariay and is completely sheltered. It is entered through a narrow channel blocked by a bar and is only suitable for small craft.

PUERTO DE VITA, PUNTA BARLOVENTO, E side of entrance, 21 05.8N, 75 57.7W. Fl W 10s, 115ft, 14M. White cylindrical tower.

PUERTO VITA

21 05N, 75 57W

Pilotage: The "pocket bay" of Bahía Vita is located about 9 miles east of Puerto Gibara and 115 miles west-northwest of the eastern extremity of Cuba. A narrow and intricate channel leads to a deepwater berthing facility at Puerto Vita. Because of the flat terrain in the area, vessels at Puerto Vita are discernible from sea.

The port is a sub-port of Gibara and another in the string of sugar-shipping centers. An excellent landmark on the approach is the tall white chimney of Central Rafael Friere sugar mill located about 4 miles south-southwest of the entrance. An isolated 397-foot-high hill, with a conspicuous outcropping of white rock on its top, is another good mark. The white rock looks like a vertical white stripe. The

summit is reported to be visible 10 to 12 miles at sea. At night the Punta Barlovento light, on the east side of the port entrance, can be seen up to 10 miles.

BAHIA NARANJO, E side of entrance, 21 06.8N, 75 52.6W. Fl W 6s, 59ft, 8M. White metal framework tower.

BAHÍA DE NARANJO

21 06N, 75 53W

Pilotage: This is another "pocket bay" with no facilities except for a well-sheltered anchorage. On the west side of the bay is a flattened wooded hill rising to 344 feet. On the east side is an isolated sugarloaf hill. About 3 miles southeast of the entrance is a high flat-topped ridge having a white, precipitous west slope. A conspicuous red scarp at Punta Barlovento marks the entrance. The drying coastal reef northnortheast of Punta Barlovento extends almost 3/4 mile offshore.

BAHIA SAMA, ON PUNTA BOTA FUERTE, E side of entrace, 21 07.5N, 75 46.1W. Fl W 8s, 98ft, 10M. White metal framework tower.

SAMA

21 07N, 75 46W

Pilotage: This small community is located on the west side of Bahía Sama, which is about 11 miles east of Bahía Vita. The inlet is shoal, allowing vessels drawing less than 14 1/2-feet to enter. The mean tidal range here is about 2 feet. Pan de Sama, a rounded hill about 4 miles south-southwest of Bahía Sama, stands out well against a terrain of wooded flats and small undulations. This anchorage is open to winds from the north.

CABO LUCRECIA LIGHT, near extremity, 21 04.3N, 75 37.2W. Fl W 5s, 132ft, 18M. White stone tower on octagonal base. Aeromarine light. RACON G (– – ·) 14M.

CABO (PUNTA) LUCRECIA

21 04N, 75 37W

Pilotage: This is one of the principal landfalls for vessels proceeding along the north coast of Cuba. For a mile or two either side of the point the coast has a low profile and consists of a low white scarp partially interrupted by sandy beaches. Trees and mangroves are inland. A light is shown from a prominent stone tower standing 121 feet in height. A stone dwelling stands behind the light tower. In 1990 a RACON was reported at the tower. There is an IMO Traffic Separation Scheme off Cabo Lucrecia.

BAHIA DE BANES, ON CARACOLILLO BEACH, S side of entrance, 20 52.6N, 75 39.7W. Fl W 8s, 43ft, 8M. White cylindrical tower.
BAHIA DE BANES, BEACON NO 2, 20 52.9N, 75 39.8W. Fl R 4s, 13ft, 3M. Red starboard-hand column with topmark.
BAHIA DE BANES, BEACON NO 3, 20 52.8N, 75 39.8W. Fl G 5s, 13ft. Green port-hand column with topmark.
BAHIA DE BANES, BEACON NO 5, 20 52.8N, 75 39.9W. Fl G 3s, 13ft, 4M. Green port-hand column with topmark.
BAHIA DE BANES, BEACON NO 7, 20 52.7N, 75 40.1W. Fl G 5s, 13ft, 3M. Green port-hand column with topmark.
BAHIA DE BANES, BEACON NO 9, 20 52.4N, 75 40.3W. Fl G 3s, 10ft, 3M. Green port-hand column with topmark.
BAHIA DE BANES, BEACON NO 10, 20 52.5N, 75 40.3W. Fl R 6s, 13ft, 3M. Red starboard-hand column with topmark.
BAHIA DE BANES, BEACON NO 11, 20 52.9N, 75 40.6W. Fl G 3s, 13ft, 3M. Green port-hand column with topmark.
BAHIA DE BANES, BEACON NO 12, 20 52.8N, 75 40.8W. Fl R 4s, 15ft, 4M. Red starboard-hand column with topmark.
BAHIA DE BANES, BEACON NO 15, 20 53.0N, 75 41.1W. Fl G 5s, 15ft, 3M. Red starboard-hand column with topmark.
BAHIA DE BANES, BEACON NO 16, 20 53.4N, 75 41.4W. Fl R 4s, 20ft, 3M. Red starboard-hand column with topmark.
BAHIA DE BANES, BEACON NO 23, 20 54.6N, 75 42.5W. Fl G 3s, 15ft, 4M. Green port-hand column with topmark.

PUERTO BANES

20 55N, 75 42W
Pilotage: The deepwater "pocket bay" called Bahía de Banes is well sheltered and almost totally landlocked. The entrance channel is one of the most intricate on the Cuban coast. The bay is difficult to recognize from the sea, but from a position about 12 miles to the west three grouped hills, equal in elevation, can be seen. They are serrated in appearance and steep-to on the northeast side, but sloping on the southwest. Close northeast of the hills is a conspicuous rounded, or somewhat saddle-shaped, hill.

The entrance channel is marked by a light, but it should not be confused with the nearby light marking Bahía de Nipe. The sharp hairpin turns

of the channel are crucial, and the seaward end is open to the northeast. Tidal currents run up to 6 knots, so vessels are advised to enter only at slack water during the day. The currents continue to run along the sides of the channel 40 to 45 minutes after high and low water.

Traffic signals are flown from Boca de la Bahía de Banes seaward entrance on the south side. A white flag means the channel is clear; a red flag means anchor and wait; a gray flag means wait, a vessel is outbound.

BAHÍA DE NIPE

PUNTA MAYARI LIGHT, E side of entrance, 20 47.5N, 75 31.5W. Fl W 6s, 115ft, 16M. White metal framework tower.
PUNTA MAYARI RANGE (Front Light), 20 46.3N, 75 32.8W. Q W, 25ft, 8M. Aluminum skeleton tower, red daymark yellow border. **(Rear Light),** 230 meters 201°36′ from front. Fl W 4s, 90ft, 9M. White skeleton tower enclosing gray box on concrete base. Visible 6° on each side of range line.

BAHÍA DE NIPE

20 47N, 75 42W
Pilotage: This is one of the largest "pocket bays" on the entire Cuban coast. The bay is extensive, well sheltered, and almost landlocked. The entrance channel is deep and easy, although strong tidal currents continue to run up to 45 minutes after high or low water. From the east the entrance appears as a steep-sided notch, while from the north it cannot be distinguished at any great distance. The Río Mayari empties into the bay and has cut a notch into Sierra de Cristal. This notch is visible well out at sea.

PUNTA PIEDRA, NO 4, 20 47.7N, 75 35.2W. Fl R 6s, 15ft, 4M. Red starboard-hand mark with topmark.
PUNTA BERRACO, NO 6, 20 48.5N, 75 36.0W. Fl R 8s, 16ft, 4M. Red starboard-hand mark with topmark.
BAJO LA ESTRELLA, NO 9, 20 47.5N, 75 36.7W. Fl G 5s, 15ft, 4M. Green port-hand mark with topmark.
BAJO SALINA GRANDE, NO 10, S end, 20 48.5N, 75 41.8W. Fl R 4s, 13ft, 4M. Red starboard-hand mark with topmark.

ANTILLA CHANNEL

LENGUA TIERRA BEACON, NO 11, 20 48.7N, 75 42.6W. Fl G 5s, 13ft, 4M. Green port-hand beacon with topmark.

BAJO MANATI, NO 12, S end, 20 49.0N, 75 43.2W. Fl R 8s, 13ft, 4M. Red starboard-hand mark with topmark.

BAJO LENGUA DE TIERRA, NO 13, N end, 20 48.9N, 75 43.8W. Fl G 5s, 13ft, 4M. Green port-hand mark with topmark.

BAJO MARABELLA, NO 14, S end, 20 49.1N, 75 43.8W. Fl R 6s, 13ft, 4M. Red starboard-hand mark with topmark.

BAJO MARABELLA, NO 15, 20 48.9N, 75 44.8W. Fl G 5s, 13ft, 4M. Green port-hand mark with topmark.

BAJO MARABELLA, NO 17, 20 49.1N, 75 45.2W. Fl G 7s, 13ft, 4M. Green port-hand mark with topmark.

CANAL A, BEACON NO 1A, 20 46.0N, 75 34.7W. Fl G 7s, 13ft, 4M. Green port-hand beacon with topmark.

BAJO PLANACA BEACON, NO 3A, 20 44.7N, 75 34.6W. Fl G 5s, 13ft, 4M. Green port-hand beacon with topmark.

PUNTA LIBERAL, 20 44.8N, 75 28.8W. Fl W 10s, 56ft, 9M. White framework tower.

ANTILLA

20 50N, 75 44W

Pilotage: This is the principal shipping center for Bahía de Nipe and is located on the north side of the bay.

PRESTON

20 46N, 75 39W

Pilotage: This is another important sugar port located about 7 1/2 miles west-southwest of Punta Mayari. It is a sub-port of Antilla. The Río Miyari discharges near the berthing facilities causing a great deal of silting.

FELTON

20 45N, 75 36W

Pilotage: This small community is on the west side of Bahía de Cajinaya and about 1 mile east of the mouth of the Río Mayari. Another sub-port of Antilla, it specializes in iron ore.

SAETIA

20 47N, 75 34W

Pilotage: This is the site of a small banana plantation and shipping facility.

BAHÍA DE LEVISA

BAHIA DE LEVISA BEACON, NO 17, 20 43.2N, 75 29.3W. Fl G 3s, 13ft, 3M. Green port-hand beacon with topmark.

BAHÍA DE LEVISA BEACON, NO 19, 20 43.4N, 75 29.8W. Fl G 5s, 13ft, 3M. Green port-hand beacon with topmark.

BAHÍA DE LEVISA BEACON, NO 22, 20 43.6N, 75 30.4W. Fl R 4s, 13ft, 3M. Red starboard-hand beacon with topmark.

BAHÍA DE LEVISA BEACON, NO 23, 20 43.4N, 75 30.7W. Fl G 3s, 13ft, 3M. Green port-hand beacon with topmark.

BAHÍA DE LEVISA BEACON, NO 27, 20 43.2N, 75 31.8W. Fl G 5s, 13ft, 3M. Green port-hand beacon with topmark.

BAHÍA DE LEVISA BEACON, NO 28, 20 43.4N, 75 31.8W. Fl R 4s, 13ft, 3M. Red starboard-hand beacon with topmark.

BAHÍA DE LEVISA BEACON, NO 29, 20 43.1N, 75 32.2W. Fl G 3s, 13ft, 3M. Green port-hand beacon with topmark.

BAHÍA DE LEVISA BEACON, NO 32, 20 43.2N, 75 32.9W. Fl R 4s, 13ft, 3M. Red starboard-hand beacon with topmark.

CAYO GRANDE, 20 43.1N, 75 29.4W. Fl G 5s, 13ft, 3M. Framework tower.

BAHÍA DE LEVISA

20 43N, 75 31W

Pilotage: This "pocket bay" is entered about 5 miles southwest of Bahía de Nipe. It is well sheltered and almost totally landlocked. It is entered by a very narrow and intricate channel. Nicaro (20° 43'N, 75 33'W) is the main shipping port in the bay. It is another sub-port of Antilla in Bahía de Nipe. Sugar and nickel ore are handled here.

BAHÍA DE SAGUA DE TANAMO

PUNTA BARLOVENTO, E point of entrance, 20 43.2N, 75 19.2W. Fl W 8s, 42ft, 12M. White conical skeleton tower.

BAHÍA DE SAGUA DE TANAMO RANGE (Front Light), 20 43.6N, 75 19.5W. Q W, 22ft, 6M. Aluminum skeleton structure on concrete base. **(Rear Light),** 210 meters 180° from front. Iso W 6s, 39ft, 6M. White shield with black border on silver three-faced lattice tower on concrete base.

BAHÍA DE SAGUA DE TANAMO, NO 3, W point, 20 42.6N, 75 19.8W. Fl G 3s, 15ft. Green port-hand beacon with topmark.

BAHÍA DE SAGUA DE TANAMO, NO 5, Cayo Juanillo, W side, 20 42.3N, 75 20.2W. Fl G 5s, 15ft. Green port-hand beacon with topmark.

BAHÍA DE SAGUA DE TANAMO, NO 8, Cayo Alto, E side, 20 41.7N, 75 20.2W. Fl R 6s, 15ft. Red starboard-hand beacon with topmark.

BAHÍA DE SAGUA DE TANAMO, NO 11,
Cayo Medio, W side, 20 41.1N, 75 19.4W.
Fl G 3s, 15ft. Green port-hand beacon with
topmark.

DE SAGUA DE TANAMO
20 42N, 75 19W
Pilotage: Bahía de Sagua de Tanamo is located
about 9 1/2 miles east-southeast of Bahía de
Levisa. It is entered via a deep, but intricate
channel. The surrounding terrain is hilly and
rises inland in a succession of uneven hills to
Sierra del Cristal, a conspicuous mountain range
some 13 miles to the south. The entrance is
concealed and difficult to identify from offshore.
The light at the east entrance point is difficult
to see by day at a distance greater than 3 miles.
The tidal current runs over 3 knots in the
channel.

The port is a shipping center for sugar and
molasses.

PUERTO CAYO MOA

CAYO MOA GRANDE, 20 41.6N, 74 54.4W.
Fl W 10s, 76ft, 13M. Aluminum framework
tower.
Buoy 1, E side of entrance channel, 20 41.0N,
74 52.0W. Fl G 5s, 13ft. Green port-hand mark
with topmark.
BAJO GRANDE RANGE (Front Light),
entrance, 20 40.1N, 74 52.9W. Q W, 13ft, 7M.
Red and yellow checkered rectangular daymark
on aluminum framework tower on concrete
piles. **(Rear Light),** 615 meters 211° from front.
Iso W 6s, 26ft, 7M. Red and yellow checkered
redctangular daymark on aluminum framework tower on concrete piles.

PUERTO CAYO MOA
20 41N, 74 52W
Pilotage: Between Bahía de Sagua de Tanamo
and Puerto Cayo Moa are several shallow inlets
suitable for small craft with local knowledge.
An unbroken barrier of drying reefs and sand
flats extends about 2 miles offshore and is
marked by breakers. There is a shoal-water
lagoon between the reefs and the coastline.
Behind the coastline the terrain rises rapidly to
lofty interior mountains known as Cuchillas de
Toa.

This port lies inshore of the outer barrier and
is somewhat sheltered by it. An extremely deep

gut passes east of the low-lying mangrove-
covered islet Cayo Moa Grande and leads to
the deepwater port facilities at Darsena de
Yaguasey and Punta Gorda. Tidal currents seaward of the entrance set southwest on a rising
tide at a velocity of about 1 knot and north on
a falling tide. In the anchorage area south of
Cayo Moa the currents set basically east and
west.

PUNTA GORDA
20 38N, 74 51W
Pilotage: This small mining community is
located about 2 3/4 miles southeast of Puerto
Cayo Moa. Ships load chromium ore from
lighters while on moorings. Punta Gorda is a
sub-port of Bahía de Barocoa.

BAHÍA DE YAMANIQUEY
20 34N, 74 43W
Pilotage: This bay is located about 3 miles
south of Punta Guarico. It is approached via a
break in the offshore reefs and is suitable for
small craft only. The entrance is dangerous,
except in very calm weather. This is a sub-port
of Baracoa.

BAHÍA DE TACO
20 31N, 74 40W
Pilotage: This another miniature "pocket bay,"
providing anchorage for small vessels with
local knowledge. A short dog-legged channel
has depths of about 30 feet. The sea breaks
with considerable force on the rocky coast to
the west of the entrance and tends to obscure
the channel. Approaching vessels steer for the
conspicuous south extremity of Punta Sotavento
(20° 32'N, 74° 40'W) on a heading of 240°,
then proceed in mid-channel to the anchorage.

PUNTA GUARICO, 20 37.1N, 74 43.9W. Fl W 6s,
37ft, 11M. Aluminum tower.

BAHÍA (PUERTO) NAVAS
Pilotage: This "pocket bay" is located about
10 1/2 miles southeast of Punta Guarico. It has
an easy deepwater entrance and provides
anchorage protected from the prevailing
winds. The bay is open to the north.

BAHÍA DE (PUERTO) MARAVI
Pilotage: This deepwater estuary is located
about 15 miles southeast of Punta Guarico.
Anchorage is available in calm conditions, but
the bay is open to the prevailing winds.

BAHIA DE BARACOA, S entrance point, 20 21.1N, 74 29.9W. Fl W 6s, 63ft, 14M. Concrete pedestal on mansonry structure.

BARACOA

20 21N, 74 30W

Pilotage: Bahía de Baracoa is located about 21 miles west-northwest of Cabo Maisi. It is a very small but deep "pocket bay," open to the east and directly accessible from the open sea. The surrounding terrain is hilly and heavily scrub covered. Baracoa, on the east side of the bay, is one of the oldest communities in Cuba. Bahía Miel is a deepwater cove east of Baracoa, backed inland by a broad flat river valley leading to high interior hills.

Loma El Yunque, located 4 miles to the west, is the best approach landmark to the bay. It is a conspicuous steep-sided, flat-topped hill, rising to 1,932 feet. It is remarkable in its profile and can be seen for distances of 40 miles in clear weather. It is particularly visible from the northeast. Testas de Santa Teresa, two hills about 3 3/4 miles south-southeast of the bay, and Loma Majayara, close southeast of Bahía Miel, are three conspicuous hills, remarkable at a distance of 24 miles, with clear visibility.

CAUTION: This anchorage is subject to a heavy swell sent in by the prevailing winds, particularly during strong north and northeast winds in the winter.

Bahía Miel has anchorage somewhat sheltered from east winds, where vessels can anchor if they do not want to enter Baracoa.

BAHÍA DE MATA

20 18N, 74 23N

Pilotage: This bay will accommodate vessels up to about 300 feet, with drafts less than 15 feet. It has a deepwater entrance and is the first anchorage west of Cabo Maisi. Small vessels commonly drop anchor when abeam Punta Cuartel, tying their sterns to moorings farther in the bay. This is not a well-sheltered anchorage, particularly during the winter when a heavy sea can set in.

ROCA BUREN, 20 21.3N, 74 30.1W. Fl G 5s, 39ft, 4M. Green port-hand mark with topmark.
QUEBRADO DEL MANGLE, 20 15.2N, 74 08.6W. Fl G 5s, 13ft, 4M. Green beacon, square daymark.
PUNTA MAISI LIGHT, on Punta de la Hembra, 20 14.6N, 74 08.6W. Fl W 5s, 122ft, 17M.

White conical masonry tower and dwelling. RACON **K** (– · –) 16M.

CABO MAISI

20 13N, 74 08W

Pilotage: This is the eastern extremity of Cuba. It has a low-lying shore of white sand and is rounded. The land within the cape begins to rise 3/4 mile from the coast and when viewed from the north appears to form three steps, making useful landmarks. The terrain southwest of Punta Pintado becomes progressively steeper and more abrupt.

CAUTION: Cabo Maisi is a lee shore open to the effects of the sea and the prevailing east wind. Vessels navigating in the vicinity are cautioned to stand well offshore and are reminded that, if proceeding at night from the south, Cabo Maisi light is obscured to the west of a line bearing 359°.

An IMO Traffic Separation Scheme is in effect off Cabo Maisi.

WINDWARD PASSAGE

Pilotage: This passage lies between the eastern end of Cuba and the western part of Hispaniola, 45 miles to the east-southeast. An IMO Traffic Separation Scheme lies off Cabo Maisi, and the appropriate chart should be consulted when in the area. Vessels not using the traffic separation scheme should avoid it by as wide a margin as possible.

The current set through the middle of the channel is to the southwest at a rate usually less than 3/4 knot but may attain speeds of up to 2 knots. Near the coasts on either side of the passage tidal currents are strong and irregular.

On the east side of the passage (near Haiti) the current sets north at about 3/4 knot around Pearl Point (19° 40′N, 73° 25′W), but 6 miles offshore the current will be found to set west or west-southwest. North of Cap du Mole, on Haiti, there are ripples where the northerly flow meets the current running west along the north shore of the island.

On the west side of the passage (near Cuba) a north current sets around Cabo Maisi. This flow is affected by the tides and the wind. During the summer months and with southerly winds an east set is experienced. With northerly winds a southerly set is found. Frequently, especially during the winter, a westerly current of considerable strength will be experienced.

SOUTH COAST

PUNTA CALETA LIGHT, 20 04.0N, 74 17.8W. Fl W 10s, 149ft, 15M. White skeleton tower.
BAHIA DE BAITIQUIRI, N, 20 01.5N, 74 51.2W. Fl W 6s, 29ft, 11M. Red metal framework tower.

PUERTO BAITIQUERI

20 01N, 74 51W
Pilotage: This very well sheltered "pocket bay" is located about 42 miles west of Cabo Maisi. It is clearly indicated by the opening between the hills on either side of the entrance. The entrance channel has a least depth of about 10 feet and is only 49 feet wide between the reefs on either side. The sea breaks heavily over these reefs and can be seen from 1/4 mile away.

PUERTO ESCONDIDO

19 55N, 75 03W
Pilotage: This port is located about 6 miles east of Bahía de Guantanamo. The entrance is quite deep but narrow, and the bay is landlocked. The coast on either side of the entrance appears as a continuous jagged bluff, and the entrance itself cannot be distinguished until very close in. A tower is situated on the summit of Mogate Peak, a hill that rises to 520 feet about 1 3/4 miles northwest of the entrance. A hill to the east of the entrance has a well-defined saddle-shaped summit. Vessels entering the port steer 336° and head for the extremity of a rocky scarp that lines up with the middle of the entrance channel.

Inside, the bay branches into numerous mangrove-fringed deepwater inlets that lead off into surrounding fields of drying tidal flats.

GUANTANAMO BAY

PUNTA BARLOVENTO (WINDWARD POINT LIGHT), on 110 meters peak, E side of entrance to bay, 19 53.6N, 75 09.6W. Fl W 5s, 378ft, 15M. Gray building.
WINDWARD POINT OLD LIGHT HOUSE LIGHT, 19 53.6N, 75 09.8W. Fl W 2.5s, 90ft, 5M. White conical steel tower. Obscured 270°–110°.

HICACAL BEACH RANGE (Front Light), N side of entrance to bay, 19 56.5N, 75 09.9W. Q W, 57ft, 13M. Red rectangular daymark, white stripe on skeleton tower. Higher intensity on range line. **(Rear Light),** 405 meters 021°30' from front. Iso W 6s, 80ft, 15M. Red rectangular daymark, white stripe on skeleton tower. Higher intensity on range line.
LEEWARD POINT, AVIATION LIGHT, 19 54.2N, 75 12.3W. Alt Fl W G, 118ft. On NE corner of hangar.
FISHERMAN POINT LIGHT, E side of entrance to bay, 19 55.2N, 75 09.7W. Fl W 4s, 28ft, 5M. Red skeleton tower on pyramidal base, red and white diamond-shaped daymark. Visible all around. Marks point for leaving Hicacal Range. Various lights mark the channel in the cove south of Deer Light. A F R light is shown at each end of fuel berth N of Deer Point.
CORINASO POINT LIGHT, 19 55.1N, 75 09.3W. Fl G 6s, 42ft, 3M. Black steel framework tower. Visible all around.
McCALLA HILL, 19 54.9N, 75 09.6W. F R, 175ft, 4M. Black steel framework tower, yellow bands. Maintained by the US Navy.
RADIO POINT LIGHT, NO 1, 19 55.3N, 75 09.0W. Fl G 4s, 15ft, 3M. Green square on black piling. Obscured 240°–310°.
RADIO POINT LIGHT, NO 2, Q R, 14ft, 3M. Red triangular daymark on piles. Obscured 310°–050°.
RADIO POINT LIGHT 4, FL R 4s, 11ft, 3M. Red triangular daymark on dolphin. Obscured 334°–139°.
DEER POINT LIGHT, NO 1, 19 55.4N, 75 08.8W. Fl G 4s, 10ft, 3M. Green square daymark on dolphin.
DEER POINT LIGHT, NO 2, Q R, 14ft, 3M. Red triangle on dolphin. Obscured 310°–050°.
DEER POINT LIGHT, NO 3, Q G, 12ft, 2M. Green square daymark on dolphin.
DEER POINT LIGHT, NO 4, Fl R 4s, 11ft, 3M. Red trangle on dolphin. Obscured 334°–139°.
DEER POINT LIGHT, NO 5, Fl G 4s, 14ft, 3M. Green square daymark on dolphin.
JUNCTION LIGHT DP, 19 55.9N, 75 08.7W. Fl (2+1) R 6s, 13ft, 4M. Preferred channel, red-green-red daymark on dolphin with topmark.
EVANS POINT LIGHT, NO 8, Fl R 4s, 10ft, 3M. Red triangular daymark on piles.
MUD ISLAND LIGHT 1, 19 55.9N, 75 08.1W. Fl G 6s, 7ft, 3M. Green square on pile.
MARINE SITE TWO CHANNEL LIGHT, NO 1, 1.9 kilometers SE of Hospital Cay South Light, 19 55.9N, 75 08.1W. Fl G 4s, 10ft, 3M. Green square daymark on dolphin.

COAST PILOT

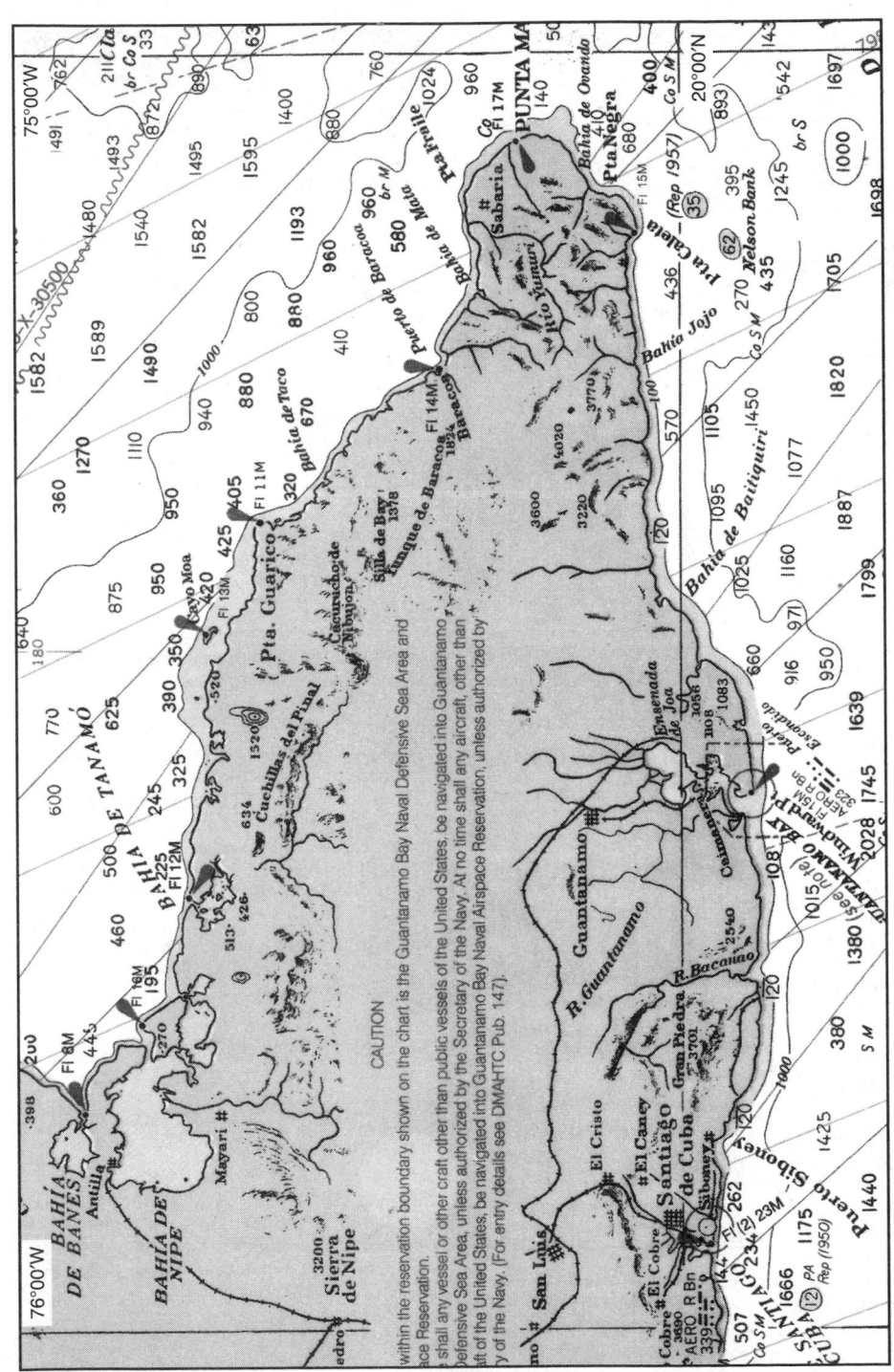

Southeast End, soundings in fathoms *(from NOAA 11013, 40th ed, 10/93)*

BAHÍA DE GUANTANAMO

19 56N, 75 10W

Pilotage: This bay is located about 62 miles west-southwest of Cabo Maisi. It is spacious, well-sheltered, easily entered, and largely landlocked. The bay is about 11 miles long and divides into Outer and Inner harbors. It is deep enough for any vessel.

REGULATIONS: Most of the bay is leased by the United States Government and is part of the Guantanamo Bay Naval Defensive Sea Area. This area is closed to the public. Full details concerning entry control and application requirements will be found in Title 32, Code of Federal Regulations, Part 761.

Harbor Control Post: The U.S. Navy maintains a Harbor Entrance Control Post that challenges and identifies all vessels approaching Guantanamo Bay. Permission to enter the U.S. Naval Reservation boundaries should be secured in advance of your arrival. Vessels sailing to Boqueron should forward their ETA and request permission to transit the waters of the Naval Reservation. Such passage is only permitted in daylight.

The Harbor Entrance Control Post operates from the signal station atop a building on McCalla Hill (19ª 55'N, 75° 09' 5W); the post monitors VHF channel 12 (call sign, Port Control). The pilots stand by on VHF channel 74.

MARINE BOAT CHANNEL LIGHT, NO. 2, 457 meters S of Caravela Point, 19 56.0N, 75 08.0W, Fl R 4s, 13ft, 3M. Triangular-shaped red daymark on dolphin.

GRANADILLO BAY LIGHT 2, 19 56.8N, 75 07.5W. Fl R 4s, 13ft, 3M. Red triangle on dolphin.

GRANADILLO BAY, EAGLE CHANNEL (CAYO TOMATE JUNCTION LIGHT CT), 19 56.9N, 75 07.9W, Fl R (2+1) 6s, 14ft, 3M. Preferred channel, red-green-red on dolphin with topmark.

HOSPITAL CAY (WATERGATE CHANNEL NO 2), 19 56.5N, 75 08.7W. Q R, 13ft, 3M. Red starboard-hand mark with topmark.

WATERGATE CHANNEL NO 4, 19 57.1N, 75 08.7W. Fl R 4s, 11ft, 5M. Red starboard mark with topmark.

PALMA POINT SHOAL, NO 13, 19 57.8N, 75 08.9W. Fl G 4s, 14ft, 4M. Three-pile cluster, black battery box.

BAHÍA DE SANTIAGO DE CUBA

MORRO DE CUBA LIGHT, on El Morro E side of entrance to Santiago de Cuba, 19 58.0N, 75 52.1W. Fl (2) W 10s, 269ft, 23M. White cylindrical concrete tower. Aeromarine light.

SANTIAGO DE CUBA

20 01N, 75 50W

Pilotage: This is one of the oldest and most important port cities in Cuba. The bay is well sheltered and land-locked. A number of coves and inlets indent this natural harbor, which is entered by way of a 263-foot-wide channel. The entrance is marked by the fortifications of El Morro on the east side. Lower-lying fortifications at Punta Estrella are below the fort. When entering, head for Punta Estrella on a course of 043° and proceed in mid-channel through most of the entrance fairway. The pilots monitor VHF channels 13 and 16 (call sign, Santiago Practicos).

A signal mast at the fortifications of El Morro indicates traffic conditions in the channel. International Code Flag P (see *Reed's Nautical Companion)* indicates a power-driven vessel is outbound; Flag P under a red pennant indicates a sailing vessel is outbound; and Flag P over a red pennant indicates the outbound vessel has anchored. *CAUTION: When a signal is displayed indicating a vessel is outbound, inbound vessels must not attempt to enter.* Contact the harbor authorities on VHF channel 16 before entering the harbor.

Port of Entry

Dockage: The yacht club Bases Nautico is in nearby Punta Gorda.

PUNTA ROMPE CANILLAS, 19 59.2N, 75 53.1W. Fl Y 7s, 13ft, 3M. Special yellow beacon with topmark.

PUERTO NIMA NIMA

19 57N, 75 59W

Pilotage: This port is located about 1 1/4 miles west-northwest of Punta Cabrera. There are numerous mooring buoys and a pier, which connects to the mines inland. A good mark on this part of the coast is a red hill excavated in terraces located about 1 1/2 miles west of Puerto Nima Nima.

Bahía Aserradero indents the coast 9 miles west-northwest of Puerto Nima Nima. Río Aserradero

COAST PILOT

flows into this bay. The wreck of the Spanish cruiser *Vizcaya* is located on the west side of the bay.

ASERRADERO, 19 59.0N, 76 10.3W. Fl W 19s, 197ft, 14M. White framework tower.
PUERTO DE CHIRIVICO RANGE (Front Light), 19 58.2N, 76 23.8W. Q W, 13ft, 4M. Aluminum-painted triangular skeleton structure on ruins of pier. **(Rear Light),** 255 meters 337° from front. Fl W 4s, 33ft, 5M. Aluminum-painted skeleton structure. Visible 6° each side of range line.

PUERTO DE CHIVIRICO

19 58N, 76 24W
Pilotage: This port is located about 30 miles west of Bahía de Santiago de Cuba. It is west of Punta Tabacal, a 425-foot-high wooded conical hill with a grassy summit, which is easily identified from the east. The coast in this area is dominated by the rugged mountainous Sierra Maestra, which rise steeply. Pico Turquino (20° 00'N, 76° 50'W) is the culminating summit of the mountain range and is the highest summit in Cuba at 6,560 feet. In clear weather the summit can be seen in Jamaica, 93 miles away.

The entrance to Puerto de Chivirico is between Cayo de Damas to the east and a peninsula that extends 600 yards from the coast to the west. The entrance channel is narrow. An abandoned ore-loading facility is in the harbor.

PUERTO PILON RANGE (Front Light), 19 54.0N, 77 17.2W. Q W, 16ft, 6M. White quadrangular daymark with yellow border on black metal framework tower. **(Rear Light),** on shore 1.5 kilometers 355°30' from front. L Fl W 10s, 26ft, 8M. White quadrangular daymark with yellow border on metal framework tower.
PUERTO PILON BEACON, NO 11, 19 54.0N, 77 19.0W. Fl G 5s, 13ft, 4M. Green port-hand mark with topmark.

PILON

19 54N, 77 19W
Pilotage: This is the small town on the west side of Ensenada de Mora where the sugar mill is located. The maximum draft for this sub-port of Manzanillo is 20 feet.

ENSENADA MAREA DEL PORTILLO, NO 4, 19 54.7N, 77 11.2W. Fl R 6s, 10ft, 3M. Red starboard-hand beacon with topmark.

PUERTO PORTILLO

19 55N, 77 11W
Pilotage: The harbor is 45 miles west of Puerto de Chivirico. It is entered between Punta de Piedras and Punta de Los Farallones, 1/2 mile to the west-southwest. Puerto Portillo can be identified by low, swampy mangrove-covered land on its east side and by the three perpendicular white cliffs on its west point. The bay is small and much encumbered.

BAJO PUNTA DEL MEDIO, 19 54.6N, 77 11.4W. Fl (2) W 6s, 10ft, 4M. ISOLATED DANGER BRB, beacon with topmark.
PUNTA RASA, 19 54.8N, 77 11.1W. Fl Y 7s, 10ft, 3M. Special yellow beacon with topmark.

ENSENADA DE MORA

19 54N, 77 18W
Pilotage: This break in the coast is located about 5 miles west of Puerto Portillo. Its entrance is between Cayo Blanco on the east, and Punta Icacos, 2 miles to the west-southwest. The bight consists of deep water indenting the low-lying coastal plain, with the westernmost part of the Sierra Maestra backing it. Close to the northeast is 1,248-foot-high Loma Aguada, which provides an excellent landmark. There are prominent cane fields west of the peak and a sugar mill on the northwest shore of the bay. The white spire of a church and a water tower with a red tank are north and northwest of the sugar mill.

The entrance is rather intricate, with a fairway partially blocked by rocky heads. The bay is encumbered with dangers. Head for Loma Aguada on a heading of 005°, then when abeam of Punta Icacos, the low mangrove-covered west entrance of the bight, ease to port and steer for the light charted northeast of Cayo Pajaro. Pass north and east of Cayo Pajaro, then proceed to your destination.

Río Toro cuts a remarkable gorge through the coastal terraces 7 miles west of Ensenada de Mora. Just west of the river Ojo del Toro rises to a height of 1,750 feet. This is the westernmost peak of the Sierra Maestra and is very prominent. When viewed from the southwest, the summit of this mountain appears as two or three hummocks.

CABO CRUZ LIGHT, 914 meters E of SW extremity of cape, 19 50.4N, 77 43.6W. Fl W 5s, 111ft, 37M. Yellow stone tower and dwelling. Aeromarine light.

CABO CRUZ
19 51N, 77 44W
Pilotage: The point is low and sandy, backed by a relatively level, somewhat forested, plain. The plain continues inland as flat tableland, eventually rising into the foothills of the Sierra Maestra to the east. There is a pilot station at the village located on the sandy spit of Cabo Cruz, which consists of a few huts and a flagstaff. The light is about 1/2 mile east of the cape's extremity, on the rear of a large rectangular building. East of Punta Del Ingles the light is obscured by high land when bearing less than 285°. It is reported the light is also beamed for use by aircraft. The sea breaks heavily on an awash reef located 1 1/2 miles west of the lighthouse. A light marks the outer end of the reef.
Anchorage: Anchorage is available in a depth of 24 feet over sand, northwest of Cabo Cruz.
Pilots: Contact the pilot station on VHF channels 13 and 16.

RESTINGA CABO CRUZ BEACON, 19 50.1N, 77 44.9W. Fl R 4s, 20ft, 5M. Red starboard-hand beacon with topmark.
RESTINGA CABO CRUZ BEACON, NO 2, 19 50.3N, 77 44.7W. Fl R 6s, 10ft, 2M. Red starboard-hand beacon with topmark.
RESTINGA CABO CRUZ BEACON, NO 3, 19 50.4N, 77 44.5W. Fl G 3s, 10ft., 3M. Green port-hand beacon with topmark.

GOLFO DE GUACANAYABO
20 28N, 77 30W
Pilotage: This large gulf on the south coast of Cuba lies between Cabo Cruz and Punta de las Angosturas, about 66 miles to the north-northwest. The gulf is interrupted by many shoals, reefs, and cays, including Bajo de Buena Esperanza in the center. Numerous channels lead through the groupings of above and below-water dangers. These channels may be affected by silting caused by the rivers flowing into the gulf.

NIQUERO
20 03N, 77 35W
Pilotage: Bahía de Niquero is entered about 15 miles northeast of Cabo Cruz. Niquero is a sugar port, and the tall chimney of the sugar mill is an outstanding landmark. The pier is reported to be 525 feet long, taking a maximum draft of 23 feet alongside.

MEDIA LUNA
20 09N, 77 26W
Pilotage: This port lies about 25 miles northeast of Cabo Cruz. It is composed of a community and a sugar mill with several prominent chimneys. The sugar-loading pier is connected by rail to the town 1 1/4 miles inland. There is an anchorage northwest of the pier, with poor holding in soft mud reported. This bay is wide open to the northwest.

SAN RAMON
20 13N, 77 22W
Pilotage: This port is located 31 miles northeast of Cabo Cruz. The sugar mill is marked by a prominent chimney. There is a 660-foot wooden pier with a minimum depth of 21 feet alongside.

CANAL DE PALOMINO
CANAL DE PALOMINO BEACON, NO 9, 20 10.0N, 77 44.9W. Fl G 5s, 13ft, 5M. Green port-hand mark with topmark.
CANAL DE PALOMINO BEACON, NO 10, 20 09.2N, 77 45.1W. Fl R 6s, 13ft, 5M. Red starboard-hand mark with topmark.
CANAL DE PALOMINO BEACON, NO 12, 20 09.5N, 77 40.9W. Fl R 4s, 13ft, 5M. Red starboard-hand mark with topmark.
CANAL DE PALOMINO BEACON, NO 13, 20 09.8N, 77 39.8W. Fl G 5s, 13ft, 5M. Green port-hand mark with topmark.
BANCO FUSTETE BEACON, 20 11.3N, 77 35.6W. Fl G 3s, 13ft, 6M. Green port-hand mark with topmark.
CANAL DE CEIBA HUECA, NO 5, 20 14.0N, 77 19.6W. Fl G 3s, 13ft, 4M. Green port-hand beacon with topmark.

CIEBA HUECA
20 13N, 77 19W
Pilotage: This sugar-loading port is located 33 miles northeast of Cabo Cruz. A conspicuous chimney marks the location of a large sugar mill. Small tankers also use a pier here. Vessels anchor northwest of the pier.

CAMPECHUELA
20 14N, 77 17W
Pilotage: This is another sugar-loading town, located about 35 miles northeast of Cabo Cruz. There are berthing facilities for small craft only.

PUNTA GUA, 20 17.3N, 77 15.5W. Fl R 6s, 13ft, 5M. Red starboard-hand beacon with topmark.

ENSENADA GUA, 20 18.4N, 77 10.2W. Fl Y 7s, 13ft, 7M. Yellow framework tower on piles.

CAYOS MANZANILLO
CAYO PERLA, on S point, approach to Manzanillo, 20 21.4N, 77 14.6W. Fl W 5s, 36ft, 11M. Aluminum skeleton structure enclosing gray hut; gray wooden house.
PUNTA SOCORRO, 20 20.8N, 77 12.9W. Fl G 5s, 12ft, 3M. Square concrete pile.
PUNTA CAIMANERA, 20 19.8N, 77 09.4W. Fl R 4s, 12ft, 5M. Red concrete tower.
CAYITA, 20 22.2N, 77 08.7W. Fl G 3s, 12ft, 5M. Square concrete pile.
BAJO CUCHARILLAS, SW of Medano de Cauto, 20 31.6N, 77 17.3W. Fl R 4s, 13ft, 6M. Red starboard-hand beacon with topmark.
CHINCHORRO BANK, 20 32.7N, 77 22.5W. Fl R 6s, 13ft, 6M. Red starboard-hand beacon with topmark.

MANZANILLO
20 21N, 77 07W
Pilotage: This small metropolis and sugar-shipping center is located in Bahía de Caimanera, about 40 miles northeast of Cabo Cruz. It is the port for Bayamo, one of the oldest cities in Cuba. The bay is fronted offshore by several low-lying, reef-fringed, mangrove-covered islets known as Cayos Manzanillo. The light colored buildings of Manzanillo, at the head of the bight, may be seen over the cays at distances up to 20 miles under favorable conditions.

PASO DE CHINCHORRO
BAJO DE SANTA CLARA, NE side of shoal, 20 31.6N, 77 24.0W. Fl G 3s, 13ft, 4M. Green port-hand beacon with topmark.
BANCO VIBORA BEACON, 20 33.8N, 77 41.5W. Fl R 6s, 13ft, 4M. Red starboard-hand beacon with topmark.
BANCO VIBORA BEACON, NO 2, 20 41.7N, 77 58.1W. Fl R 4s, 16ft, 4M. Red starboard-hand beacon with topmark.
PUNTA BONITA, NO 3, 20 41.8N, 77 58.6W. Fl G 5s, 16ft, 4M. Green port-hand beacon with topmark.
PUNTA BONITA, NO 4, 20 41.9N, 77 58.5W. Fl R 6s, 16ft, 4M. Red starboard-hand beacon with topmark.

MEDIA LUNA CHANNEL
CAYO GUIZASO BEACON, 20 35.8N, 77 49.6W. Fl G 5s, 13ft, 3M. Green port-hand beacon with topmark.
CAYO CULEBRA BEACON, 20 33.6N, 77 50.0W. Fl R 4s, 16ft, 4M. Red starboard-hand beacon with topmark.

CAYO MEDIO LUNA BEACON, 20 33.0N, 77 53.5W. Fl G 5s, 13ft, 4M. Green port-hand beacon with topmark.
CAYO ALACRAN BEACON, 20 39.4N, 77 44.8W. Q W, 10ft, 5M. North cardinal, black and yellow beacon with topmark.
CAYO BAJO BAYAMESES BEACON, 20 40.6N, 77 49.5W. Fl G 3s, 10ft, 3M, Green port-hand beacon with topmark.
CAYO LOS TRES LACIOS, 20 40.6N, 77 57.2W. Fl G 5s, 10ft, 3M. Green port-hand beacon with topmark.
CAYO JUAN SUAREZ BEACON, NO 2, 20 32.5N, 78 01.8W. Fl R 6s, 13ft, 3M. Red starboard-hand beacon with topmark.
CAYO JUAN SUAREZ BEACON, NO 3, 20 33.5N, 78 04.1W. Fl G 5s, 13ft, 3M, Port Green, beacon w/topmark.
CAYO JUAN SUAREZ BEACON, NO 4, 20 36.3N, 78 06.2W. Fl R 4s, 16ft, 4M. Red starboard-hand beacon with topmark.
CAYO JUAN SUAREZ BEACON, NO 5, 20 35.9N, 78 06.8W. Fl G 5s, 13ft, 3M. Green port-hand beacon with topmark.

CANAL DE CUATRO REALES
CAYO CARAPACHO, 20 26.9N, 78 02.5W. Fl W 10s, 47ft, 9M. Red iron skeleton structure enclosing gray hut with red band.

SANTA CRUZ DEL SUR
20 42N, 77 59W
Pilotage: This community is located on the northwest shore of Golfo de Guacanayabo. The entrance channel is between La Ceiba bank and Carapacho Cay Lighthouse.

MUELLE MANOPLA
20 43N, 77 52W
Pilotage: This sub-port of Santa Cruz is located about 6 1/2 miles to the east. It is approached via Canal Media Luna and Bayameses Passage.

Cayo Carapacho, Buoy 2, 20 25.0N, 78 01.0W. Fl R 4s. Red buoy.
CAYO CARAPACHO BEACON, NO 5, 20 28.5N, 77 59.7W. Fl G 5s, 13ft, 6M. Green port-hand beacon with topmark.
CAYO CARAPACHO BEACON, NO 8, 20 28.6N, 77 58.9W. Fl R 4s, 13ft, 6M. Red starboard-hand beacon with topmark.
CAYO CARAPACHO BEACON, NO 9, 20 29.2N, 77 58.8W. Fl G 5s, 13ft, 4M. Green port-hand beacon with topmark.
CANAL DE CABEZA DEL ESTE, W side of entrance on Cabeza del Este Cay, 20 31.0N, 78 19.8W. Fl W 12s, 47ft, 13M. Aluminum skeleton structure.

MEDANO DE MANUEL GOMEZ, 21 01.5N, 78 51.8W. Fl R 6s, 13ft, 4M. Red starboard-hand beacon with topmark.

CAYO MANUEL GOMEZ, NW extremity of reef, 21 04.5N, 78 50.8W. Fl R 4s, 13ft, 7M. Red starboard-hand beacon with topmark.

CAYO SANTA MARIA, SW part of the bank, 21 11.0N, 78 39.2W. Fl W 5s, 43ft, 10M. Aluminum skeleton tower. Reported Fl W 10s (1993).

PUERTO VERTIENTES LIGHTED BEACON, 21 24.5N, 78 34.5W. Fl G 3s, 13ft, 4M. Green port-hand beacon with topmark.

CANAL BALANDRAS
CANAL BALANDRAS LIGHT BEACON NO 1, 21 25.6N, 78 45.0W. Fl G 5s, 13ft, 4M. Green port-hand beacon with topmark.

CANAL BALANDRAS LIGHT BEACON NO 3, 21 26.4N, 78 46.1W. Fl G 3s, 13ft, 5M. Green port-hand beacon with topmark.

MEDANO DE BALANDRAS, 21 26.0N, 78 49.0W. Fl G 5s, 13ft, 4M. Green port-hand beacon with topmark.

CANAL BALANDRAS LIGHT BEACON NO 6, 21 27.8N, 78 47.0W. Fl R 6s, 16ft, 4M. Red starboard-hand beacon with topmark.

CAYUELO SABICU, NO 9, 21 30.1N, 78 50.1W. Fl G 5s, 13ft, 4M. Green port-hand beacon with topmark.

CABEZO DEL FLAMENCO, 21 24.8N, 78 53.2W. Fl R 6s, 10ft, 4M. Red starboard-hand beacon with topmark.

GOLFO DE ANA MARIA

21 25N, 78 40W

Pilotage: This is part of a broad coastal indentation lying between Punta de Las Angostura and Punta Maria Aguilar about 112 miles to the west-northwest. The coast is similar to the Golfo de Guacanayabo in that it is low-lying and consists of a muddy shore, overgrown by mangroves. Behind the shore is a coastal plain largely cultivated for sugar cane. In the far west-northwest the coast gradually rises into the foothills of the mountainous Sierra de Saneti Spiritus and Sierra de Trinidad. Conspicuous on this coast is Loma de Banao, one of the highest peaks in the chain of the Sierra de Sancti Spiritus. Also conspicuous is Pico Porterillo, the summit peak of Sierra de Trinidad.

The 70-mile islet chains, Jardines de la Reina and Laberinto de Las Doce Leguas, form the south side of the area. These islets are steep-to, reef fringed, and mangrove covered. A line of sunken dangers continues to Punta Maria Aguilar, and more islets string along to Punta de las Angosturas. Inside these barriers the area is somewhat obstructed by a considerable scattering of above- and below-water dangers, particularly in the east-southeast and west-northwest portions. The muddy bottom often discolors the water, making it difficult to see the dangers.

PASA ANA MARIA, S side, 21 30.7N, 78 46.4W. Fl G 5s, 13ft, 5M. Green port-hand beacon with topmark.

FUERA CHANNEL
Fuera Channel Buoy 3, 21 32.0N, 78 53.0W. Fl W 4s. Black buoy.

BOCA GRANDE INLET, E side of entrance, 21 33.0N, 78 40.6W. Fl G 5s, 13ft, 5M. Green port-hand beacon with topmark.

BOCA GRANDE INLET, BEACON NO 13, 21 34.8N, 78 58.3W. Fl G 3s, 10ft, 3M. Green port-hand mark with topmark.

BOCA GRANDE INLET, BEACON NO 14, 21 34.8N, 78 58.3W. Fl R 4s, 10ft, 3M. Red starboard-hand mark with topmark.

BOCA GRANDE INLET, BEACON NO 15, 21 34.9N, 78 58.3W. Fl G 5s, 10ft, 3M. Green port-hand mark with topmark.

BOCA GRANDE INLET, BEACON NO 16, 21 35.0N, 78 58.1W. Fl R, 6s, 10ft, 3M. Red starboard-hand mark with topmark.

CAYO ENCANTADO, 21 33.6N, 78 49.7W. Fl G 3s, 12ft, 5M. Green port-hand beacon with topmark.

CAYO ENCANTADO, NO 6, 21 36.9N, 78 51.4W. Fl R 6s, 7ft, 3M. Red starboard-hand beacon with topmark.

JUCARO, W side of channel, 21 36.6N, 78 51.2W. Fl G 5s, 13ft, 4M. Green port-hand beacon with topmark.

JUCARO

21 37N, 78 51W

Pilotage: This port is located about 123 miles northwest of Cabo Cruz. It is a sugar-shipping port and the harbor for the larger community of Ciego de Avila. The shipping anchorage (21° 31'N, 78° 53'W) lies west of the low-lying, mangrove-covered Cayo Guinea. This anchorage is about 40 miles northeast of the entrance to Canal de Breton.

ENSENADA DE SANTA MARIA

21 16N, 78 31W

Pilotage: This is a shoal coastal indentation located about 28 miles southeast of Jucaro.

Vessels have sugar lightered out to them from the harbor.

PALO ALTO

21 36N, 78 58W

Pilotage: This is a sub-port of Jucaro. It is marked by a conspicuous chimney that stands near the commercial pier. There are also four prominent gray molasses tanks.

Arrecife Palo Alto lies about 2 1/4 miles south of Palo Alto. It is awash near its south end, and a light marks its southeast side.

MUELLE DE MAMBISAS, 21 36.9N, 78 51.2W. Fl R 4s, 13ft, 3M. Red starboard-hand mark with topmark.
TOMEGUIN, N end of shoal, 21 19.1N, 79 13.0W. Fl R 6s, 13ft, 4M. Red starboard-hand mark with topmark.
CAYO CACHIBOCA LIGHT, 20 40.7N, 78 45.0W. Fl W 15s, 111ft, 15M. Aluminum framework tower on piles.

CANAL DE BRETON

21 10N, 79 30W

Pilotage: This is the primary deepwater access to the Golfo De Ana Maria area. It is entered about 127 miles northwest of Cabo Cruz. The east side of the entrance is marked by Cayo Breton, which is low and mangrove covered. There is a barely awash reef to seaward that breaks in heavy seas but is hard to see in calm weather. The conspicuous remains of a white concrete tower stand on the west of the reef.

Vessels bound for Jucaro steer for the summit of Sierra de Sancti Spiritus on a heading of 354° and proceed so as to avoid the dangerous reef fronting Cayo Breton. When the light bears 098°, distant 4 miles, haul to starboard and proceed through Canal de Breton. It was reported in 1990 that a RACON was on the light at Cayo Breton.

CAYO BRETON, on W side, 21 07.3N, 79 26.9W. Fl W 10s, 108ft, 13M. White metal skeleton tower, concrete base. RACON **K** (–·–) 12M.
Canal de Breton, Buoy 2, 21 08.3N, 79 30.5W. Fl R 6s. Red starboard-hand pillar with topmark.
Canal de Breton, Buoy 3, 21 11.4N, 79 29.0W. Fl G 5s. Green port-hand pillar with topmark.

MEDANOS DE LA VELA, 21 13.3N, 79 33.3W. Fl R 4s, 16ft, 4M. Red starboard-hand beacon with topmark.
MEDANOS DE LA VELA BEACON, NO 6, 21 13.8N, 79 26.3W. Fl R 4s, 13ft. Red starboard-hand mark with topmark. Reported destroyed (1994).
MEDANOS DE LA VELA BEACON, NO 8, 21 24.1N, 79 22.1W. Fl R 4s, 10ft, 4M. Red starboard-hand beacon with topmark.

CANAL TUNAS

21 31N, 79 40W

Pilotage: This access to Golfo de Ana Maria is located about 148 miles northwest of Cabo Cruz. This is the most direct route to the port of Tunas de Zaza. Cayo Zaza de Fuera is the first above-water landmass southeast of Canal Tunas. It is low-lying, heavily wooded, and sandy. Cayos Machos de Fuera lie northwest of the passage and are equally low and wooded. A sunken danger with visible boulders is reported to lie about 6 3/4 miles west-southwest of Cayo Zaza de Fuera.

Vessels proceed to a position about 9 1/2 miles west-northwest of Cayo Zaza de Fuera, then steer east-northeast until Cayo Blanco de Zaza light bears 351°, distant about 3 miles. If heading for Tunas de Zaza, steer for Central Siete de Noviembre chimney and proceed until Cayo Blanco de Zaza light bears 305°, before heading toward town.

BOCA ESTERO DE TUNAS, NO 8, 21 37.9N, 79 33.6W. Fl R 6s, 13ft, 4M. Red starboard-hand column with topmark.
CAYO BLANCO DE ZAZA, 21 35.9N, 79 35.9W. Fl W 12s, 48ft, 11M. Skeleton tower on concrete base.

CANAL MULATAS

ESTERO TUNAS DE ZAZA, NO 6, 21 36.4N, 79 33.0W. Fl R 4s, 13ft, 3M. Red starboard-hand beacon with topmark.
Landfall Buoy, 21 30.9N, 79 41.4W. Fl R 4s. Red starboard-hand pillar with topmark.
Buoy 4, 21 31.8N, 79 37.5W. Fl R 6. Red starboard-hand pillar with topmark.

TUNAS DE ZAZA

21 38N, 79 33W

Pilotage: This sugar-shipping port is located about 149 miles northwest of Cabo Cruz.

CANAL DE JOBABO

21 38N, 79 52W

Pilotage: This is the principal passage to Casilda. The entry is easy and the passage deep, but intricate. Cayo Blanco de Casilda is on the west side of the entrance. It is a reef-fringed wooded islet of white rock and sand, which has the appearance of a wedge when seen from the southwest. A largely uninterrupted line of awash and sunken dangers extends from the islet north-west to Punta Maria Aguilar. Banco Cascajal, a shoal-water sandbank, continues the islet northeast to the mainland.

CASILDA

21 45N, 79 59W

Pilotage: This port is located just east of Punta Maria Aguilar and is entered by the previously mentioned Canal de Jobabo. This is the port for the inland city of Trinidad. Sugar is the main product being shipped here. The quay is about 650 feet long with depths of 24 feet alongside.

CAYO BLANCO DE CASILDA, E end, 21 38.3N, 79 53.0W. Fl W 7s, 46ft, 12M. White metal framework tower.

Les Guairos Channel Buoy 1, 21 38.8N, 79 52.4W. Fl G 3s, 21ft, 5M. Green port-hand pillar with topmark.

BAJO LOS GUAIROS BEACON, 21 40.3N, 79 53.4W. Fl G 5s, 14ft, 4M. Green port-hand column with topmark.

BAJO JOBABOS BEACON NO.4, 21 40.5N, 79 53.2W. Fl R 4s, 14ft, 4M. Red starboard-hand beacon with topmark.

CANAL DE LOS GUAIROS BEACON, NO 5, 21 40.7N, 79 53.8W. Fl G 3s, 20ft, 4M. Green port-hand column with topmark.

CANAL DE LOS GUAIROS BEACON, NO 9, 21 40.7N, 79 54.0W. Fl G 3s, 21ft, 4M. Green port-hand column with topmark.

CANAL DE LOS GUAIROS BEACON, NO 11, 21 40.6N, 79 54.1W. Fl G 5s, 20ft, 4M. Green port-hand beacon with topmark.

CANAL DE LOS GUAIROS BEACON, NO 12, 21 40.7N, 79 54.2W. Fl R 6s, 13ft. Red starboard-hand beacon with topmark.

Canal Las Mulatas, Buoy 2, 21 41.7N, 79 58.6W. Fl R 4s. Red starboard-hand pillar with topmark.

BANCO DERRIBADA, 21 42.0N, 79 57.9W. Fl G 5s, 13ft, 4M. Green port-hand beacon with topmark.

BANO DEL GUEYO BEACON, NO 14, 21 42.3N, 79 56.6W. Fl R 6s, 20ft. Red starboard-hand beacon with topmark.

BANO DEL MEDIO BEACON, NO 17, 21 43.6N, 79 57.7W. Fl G 3s, 20ft, 4M. Green port-hand column with topmark.

PUNTA CASILDA BEACON, NO 21, 21 43.8N, 79 58.2W. Fl G 3s, 14ft, 4M. Green port-hand column with topmark.

Punta Lastre Beacon, No 25, 21 44.4N, 79 59.2W. 14ft. Green port-hand beacon with topmark.

BASE NAUTICA ANCON, NO 2, 21 44.4N, 79 59.7W. Fl R 4s, 13ft, 3M. Starboard-hand pile with topmark.

BASE NAUTICA ANCON, NO 3, 21 44.3N, 79 59.6W. Fl G 3s, 13ft, 3M. Port-hand pile with topmark.

BASE NAUTICA ANCON, NO 5, 21 44.3N, 79 59.6W. Fl G 5s, 13ft, 3M. Port-hand pile with topmark.

CAYO RATON BEACON, NO 26, 21 44.4N, 79 59.1W. 14ft. Red starboard-hand column with topmark.

CAYO RATON BEACON, NO 28, 21 44.5N, 79 59.2W. 14ft, 4M. Red starboard-hand column with topmark.

CAYO RATON BEACON, NO 31, 21 45.5N, 79 59.5W. Fl G 3s, 14ft, 4M. Green port-hand beacon with topmark.

CAYO RATON BEACON, NO 32, 21 44.9N, 79 59.4W. Fl R 4s, 14ft, 4M. Red starboard-hand column with topmark.

Cayo Raton Beacon, No 37, 21 45.1N, 79 59.6W. 14ft, 4M. Green port-hand mark with topmark.

ANCON, PUNTA MARIA ANGUILAR, 21 44.6N, 80 01.3W. Fl W 5s, 56ft, 25M. Pedestal on white water tank.

RÍO YAGUANABO LIGHT, E entrance point, 21 51.4N, 80 12.4W. Fl W 10s, 190ft, 15M. White round concrete tower with hut at base.

CIENFUEGOS, PUNTA DE LOS COLORADOS LIGHT, E side of entrance, 22 02.0N, 80 26.6W. Fl W 5s, 83ft, 15M. White conical masonry tower. Radiobeacon.

CIENFUEGOS, PUNTA DE LOS COLORADOS RANGE (Front Light), 22 03.5N, 80 27.5W. F R, 14M. White concrete structure. **(Rear Light),** 220 meters, 350°12' from front. F R, 14M. White concrete structure.

CIENFUEGOS, PUNTA DE LOS COLORADOS RANGE, NO 2 (Front Light), 22 03.8N, 80 27.9W. Fl W 1.5s, 11M. White concrete structure. **(Rear Light),** 60 meters 322°48' from front. Fl W 1.5s, 11M. White concrete structure.

JURAGUA LIGHT, NO 5, 22 03.6N, 80 27.9W. Fl G 3s, 22ft, 4M. White triangular pyramidal tower, square house.

PASA CABALLOS, 22 03.7N, 80 27.7W. Fl R 2s, 33ft, 4M. Red starboard-hand beacon with top-mark.
CIENFUEGOS, PUNTA DE LOS COLORADOS RANGE, NO 3 (Front Light), 22 03.6N, 80 27.8W. F W, 11M. White concrete structure. **(Rear Light),** 50 meters 204°54' from front. F W, 11M. White concrete structure.
CAYO ALCATRAZ, SSW side, 22 04.3N, 80 26.6W. Fl G 5s, 16ft, 8M. Black square concrete tower on platform on piles.
CIENFUEGOS, PUNTA DE LOS COLORADOS RANGE, NO 4, ON CAYO CARENAS (Front Light), 22 05.1 N, 80 27.5W. Fl W 1.5s, 11M. White concrete structure. **(Rear Light),** 60 meters 358°30' from front. Fl W 1.5s, 11M. White concrete structure.

CIENFUEGOS

22 09N, 80 27W
Pilotage: This harbor is located about midway along the eastern side of Bahía de Cienfuegos. The bay is surrounded by level or undulating land, which is heavily cultivated with sugar cane, especially to the east. This is considered one of the most important cities on Cuba. Punta Colorados light marks the east side of the entrance to the bay. Pico Cuevita, 15 1/2 miles east-southeast, is an excellent landmark, with its sharp conspicuous crest, which seen from the west appears as the highest peak of Sierra de San Juan. Loma Guamo, about 6 miles north-northwest, is an irregular peak and useful mark for determining position offshore when plotted together with Pico La Cuevita and the light at Punta Colorados.

Tidal currents average 1 to 2 knots during the dry season, but can increase to 4 knots during the wet season. The ebb can be particularly strong when runoff adds to the flow. Entry on an ebb tide is recommended. Range lights mark the channel.
Port of Entry

PASA BAJO DE LA CUEVA, NO 1, 22 05.8N, 80 27.3W. Fl G 3s, 13ft, 4M. Green port-hand pile with topmark.
PASA BAJO DE LA CUEVA, NO 2, 22 05.7N, 80 27.3W. Fl R 4s, 13ft, 3M. Red starboard-hand pile with topmark.
PASA BAJO DE LA CUEVA, NO 3, 22 05.7N, 80 27.2W. Fl G 5s, 13ft, 3M. Green port-hand pile with topmark.
PASA BAJO DE LA CUEVA, NO 4, 22 05.6N, 80 27.2W. Fl R 6s, 13ft, 3M. Red starboard-hand pile with topmark.

JUNCO SUR, 22 06.6N, 80 26.3W. Fl G 5s, 13ft, 3M. Green port-hand beacon with topmark.

ENSENADA DE COTICA, NO 5B, 22 09.3N, 80 27.9W. Fl G 5s, 30ft. Green port-hand column with topmark.
ENSENADA DE COTICA, NO 6B, 22 09.4N, 80 27.8W. Fl R 4s, 14ft, 4M. Red starboard-hand column with topmark.
ENSENADA DE COTICA, NO 7B, 22 09.3N, 80 27.5W. Fl G 3s, 14ft, 4M. Green port-hand column with topmark.
ENSENADA DE COTICA, NO 8B, 22 09.1N, 80 27.4W. Fl R 4s, 14ft, 4M. Red starboard-hand column with topmark.

BANCO DE JAGUA

21 35N, 80 40W
Pilotage: This bank lies well offshore and to the east of Banco de los Jardines. It is an isolated shoal-water patch of coral that rises steep-to. During the day, it can be seen at a distance of about 1 mile, but at night it is hard to spot.

CAYO PIEDRAS, W side of entrance to Bahía de Cochinos, 21 58.2N, 81 07.4W. Fl W 10s, 55ft, 13M. Aluminum framework tower.

BAHÍA DE COCHINOS

22 07N, 81 10W
Pilotage: This is the deepest and most extensive of all the sleeve-like inlets indenting the Cuban coastline. Depths of over 100 fathoms are found over most of its area. Its west entrance point is Punta Palmillas, which is extended seaward to Cayo Piedras by a shoal-water spit that forms the only known danger in the immediate approaches. Playa Buenaventura lies at the head of the bay and is the only community of significance here. Anchorage near the inlet is not considered safe.

MUELLE, 21 58.0N, 81 07.5W. Fl G 3s, 13ft, 3M. Green port-hand beacon with topmark.
CAYO PIEDRAS, 21 58.1N, 81 07.6W, Fl G 5s, 4M. Green port-hand beacon with topmark.
REEF, SW side, 21 57.7N, 81 09.4W. Fl R 4s, 4M. Red starboard-hand beacon with topmark.
CAYO GUANO DEL ESTE LIGHT, near E extremity of Banco los Jardines, 21 39.7N, 81 02.5W. Fl (2) W 15s, 177ft, 43M. White cylindrical concrete tower with red bands on building. Aeromarine light.
CALETA DE TORO, 22 02.4N, 80 53.6W. Fl W 15s, 72ft, 14M. White metal framework tower.

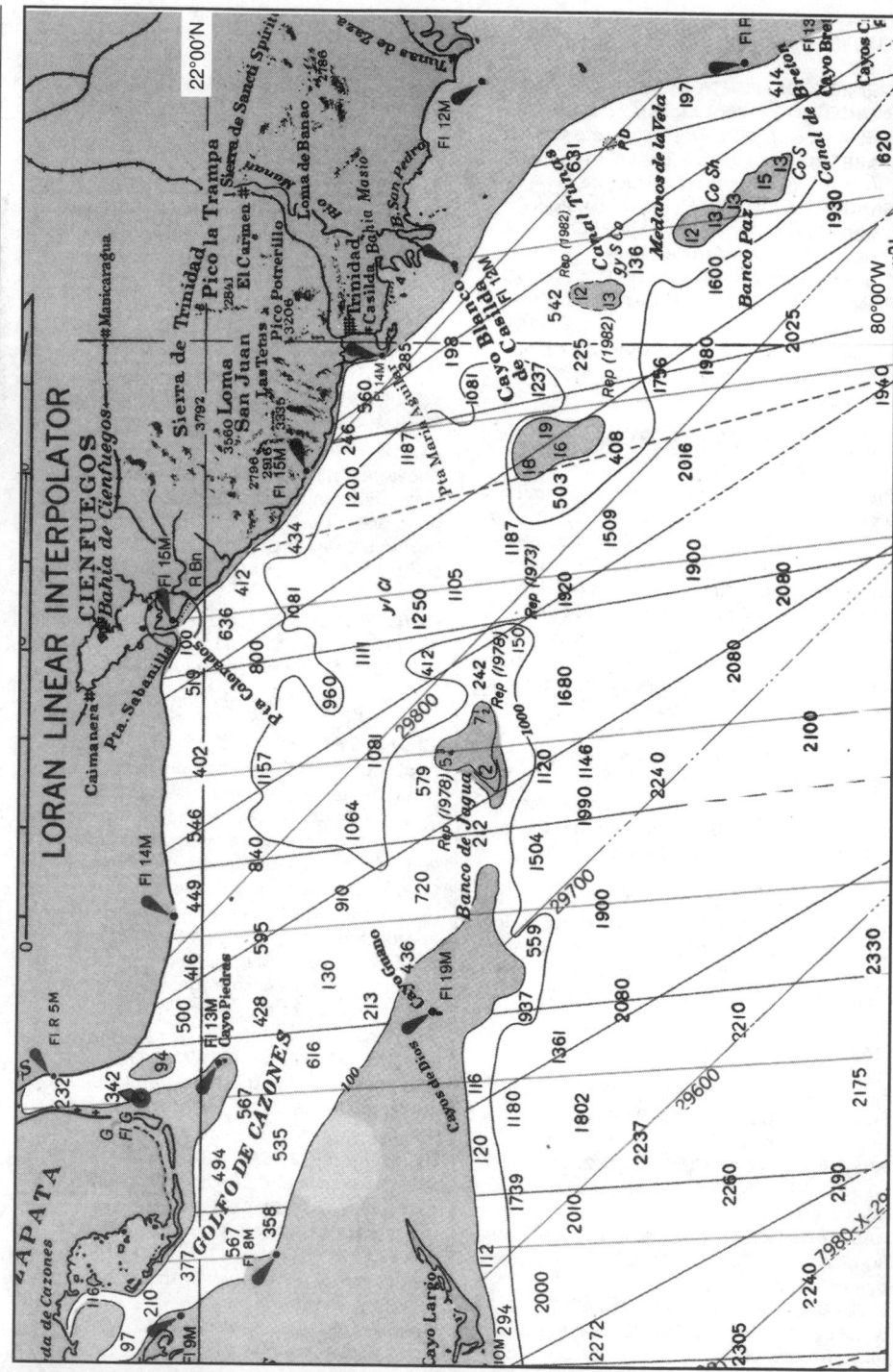

Approaches to Cienfuegos, soundings in fathoms *(from NOAA 11013, 40th ed, 10/93)*

BEACON NO 1, 22 13.5N, 81 08.8W. Fl G 3s, 23ft, 4M. Green port-hand mark with topmark.
NO 2, 22 13.6N, 81 08.7W. Fl R 6s, 13ft, 3M. Red starboard-hand beacon with topmark.
BEACON NO 2, 22 12.6N, 81 08.4W. Fl R 4s, 26ft, 4M. Red framework tower, concrete base.
CABETA DE BUENAVENTURA, NO 1, 22 12.6N, 81 08.4W. Fl G 3s, 13ft, 4M. Green port-hand beacon with topmark.
CABETA DE BUENAVENTURA, NO 2, 22 16.7N, 81 12.5W. Fl R 4s, 13ft, 3M. Red starboard-hand beacon with topmark.
CABETA DE BUENAVENTURA, NO 5, 22 16.9N, 81 12.6W. Fl G 5s, 13ft, 3M. Green port-hand beacon with topmark.
CABETA DE BUENAVENTURA, NO 6, 22 16.9N, 81 12.6W. Fl R 4s, 13ft, 3M. Red starboard-hand beacon with topmark.
CAYO SIGUA, 21 53.4N, 81 25.1W. Fl W 7s, 28ft, 8M. Aluminum-colored skeleton structure.
PASA DE DIEGO PEREZ, on reef at entrance, 22 01.4N. 81 30.9W. Fl W 5s, 38ft, 9M. Red iron skeleton structure enclosing gray hut with red stripe.
CABEZO DEL VAPOR, 22 01.5N, 81 36.5W. Fl G 5s, 13ft, 4M. Green port-hand beacon with topmark.
CABEZO DEL CARBONERO, 22 05.9N, 81 46.0W. Fl G 3s, 13ft, 4M. Green port-hand beacon with topmark.
MEDANO DON CRISTOBAL, 22 07.3N, 81 49.2W. Fl R 6s, 13ft, 3M. Red starboard-hand beacon with topmark.
CAYOS BALLENATOS (LOS BALLENATOS), 21 34.7N, 81 38.3W. Fl W 10s, 31ft, 9M. Red iron skeleton structure enclosing gray hut with red stripe.
CAYOS BALLENATOS BEACON 25, 22 03.8N, 81 59.6W. Fl G 5s. Green port-hand beacon with topmark.
CAYOS BALLENATOS BEACON 28, 22 08.5N, 82 05.4W. Fl R 6s. Red starboard-hand beacon with topmark.
BAJO LAS GORDAS, off SW side, 22 13.0N, 82 08.7W. Fl R 6s, 13ft, 3M, Red on column on platform on piles with topmark.
CAYO AMBER, off SE side, 22 19.1N, 82 09.6W. Fl G 5s. Green port-hand beacon with topmark.
PUNTA GORDA, 22 23.6N, 82 09.5W. Fl R 4s. Red starboard-hand beacon with topmark.
CAYO LARGO, 21 38.4N, 81 33.9W. Fl W 6s, 42ft, 11M. White concrete tower.
CAYO LARGO, NO 6, 21 36.2N, 81 34.4W. Fl R 4s, 13ft, 4M. Red starboard-hand beacon with topmark.
CAYO LARGO, NO 11, 21 37.5N, 81 34.2W. Fl G 3s, 13ft, 3M. Green port-hand beacon with topmark.

PLAYA SIRENA, 21 36.2N, 81 34.1W. FL (2) W 10S, 6M. Black, red, black, beacon with topmark. Marks isolated danger.
CAYO AVALOS, S end, 21 32.3N, 82 09.9W. Fl W 8s, 31ft, 12M. Aluminum-colored iron skeleton structure enclosing gray hut with red stripe.

CAYO AVALOS

21 33N, 82 10W
Pilotage: This small sandy islet is located about 22 miles east of Isla de Pinos. It has good anchorage in 27 feet over sand and rock, when Cayo Avalos light bears northeast, distant about 1 3/4 miles. Vessels make their approach with the light bearing between 045° and 070° so as to pass northwest of the drying rock Sambo Head.

CALETA DE CARAPACHIBEY LIGHT, S side of Isla de la Juventud, 21 26.9N, 82 55.5W. Fl W 7.5s, 184ft, 29M. White cylindrical concrete tower, yellow band. Aeromarine light.

GOLFO DE BATABANO

PETATILLOS DEL NORTE, 22 28.0N, 82 39.8W. Q W, 20ft, 4M. North cardinal, black and yellow beacon with topmark.
BAJO LA PIPA, 22 09.5N, 82 58.0W. Fl R 5s, 13ft, 4M. Red starboard-hand beacon with topmark.
CAYO HAMBRE, 22 10.2N, 82 51.6W. Fl G 5s, 13ft, 4M. Green port-hand beacon with topmark.
PUNTA DO LOS BARCOS, 21 56.3N, 82 59.7W. Fl R 5s, 13ft, 3M. Red starboard-hand beacon with topmark.
PUNTA BUENAVISTA, 21 46.9N, 83 05.7W. Fl R 6s, 13ft, 4M. Red starboard-hand beacon with topmark.
DARSENA DE SIGUANEA, N entrance, 21 37.0N, 82 59.1W. Fl G 5s. Red structure.
DARSENA DE SIGUANEA, S entrance. Fl R 6s. Red structure.
CAYOS LOS INDIOS, 21 43.1N, 83 10.0W. Fl G 12s, 13ft, 5M. Green port-hand beacon with topmark.
Ensenade de la Siguanea Buoy, 21 41.0N, 83 12.0W. Fl W 7.5s. Black and white striped buoy.
LOS COYUELOS, 21 38.4N, 83 11.2W. Q W, 16ft, 4M. North Cardinal Black and yellow beacon w/topmark.
GOLFO DE BATABANO LIGHT, NO 1, 21 59.5N, 82 43.4W. Fl G 3s, 13ft. Green port-hand beacon.

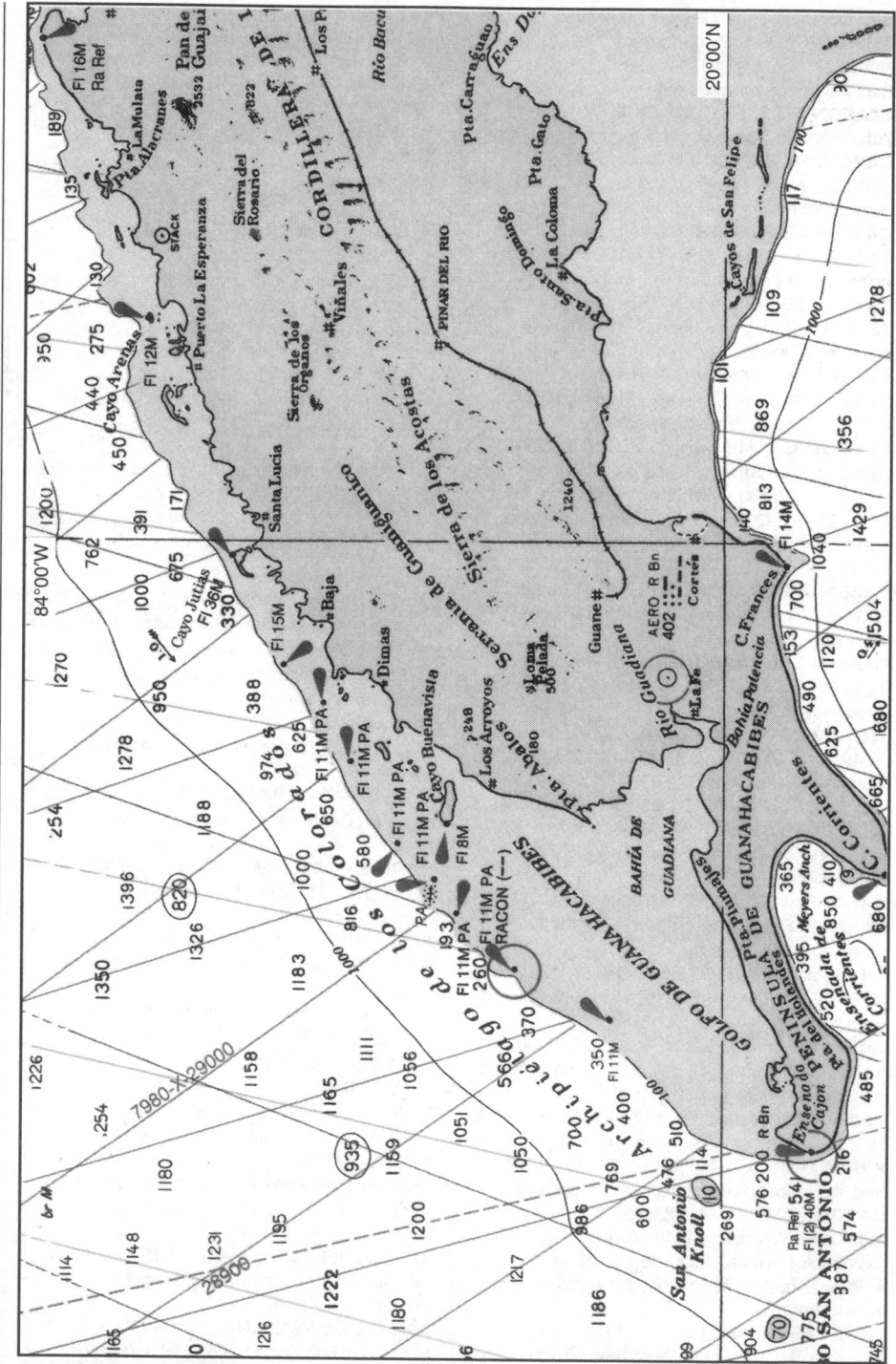

Western End, soundings in fathoms *(from NOAA 11013, 40th ed, 10/93)*

COAST PILOT

GOLFO DE BATABANO BEACON, NO 2,
21 59.7N, 82 43.2W. Fl R 4s, 13ft, 4M. Red starboard-hand beacon with topmark.
GOLFO DE BATABANO LIGHT, NO 13,
22 00.3N, 82 42.8W. Fl G 5s, 3M. Black skeleton tower.
GOLFO DE BATABANO LIGHT, NO 14,
22 00.2N, 82 42.7W. Fl R 4s, 7ft, 4M. Red skeleton tower.
GOLFO DE BATABANO LIGHT, NO 21,
22 01.2N, 82 42.4W. Fl G 3s, 13ft. Green port-hand beacon.
GOLFO DE BATABANO LIGHT, NO 22,
22 01.3N, 82 42.3W. Fl R 4s, 13ft, 3M. Green port-hand beacon with topmark. Temporarily replaced by buoy (1994).
GOLFO DE BATABANO BEACON, NO 2,
21 55.7N, 82 39.4W, Fl R 4s, 13ft., 3M. Red starboard-hand beacon with topmark.
GOLFO DE BATABANO BEACON, NO 30,
21 56.0N, 82 37.3W. Fl R 4s, 13ft, 3M. Red starboard-hand beacon with topmark. Pasa Quitasol marked by lights and beacons between "2" and "30."
CANAL DEL INGLES, NE of Pasa de Quitasol, 21 57.2N, 82 36.5W. Fl G 5s, 19ft, 4M. Green port-hand mark with topmark.
SURGIDERO DE BATABANO LIGHT,
22 41.1N, 82 17.8W. Fl W 3s, 101ft, 10M. White water tank.
COMETA, 22 40.3N, 82 17.5W. Fl R 4s, 13ft, 3M. Red starboard-hand beacon with topmark.

SURGIDERO DE BATABANO

22 41N, 82 18W
Pilotage: This city on the north side of the Golfo de Batabano has a partially sheltered roadstead anchorage. The area is exposed to southeast winds, which are common between July and October. The Golfo de Batabano lies between the mangrove-fringed island Cabo Diego Perez and Cabo Frances, 142 miles to the west. The numerous islets east and west of Isla de Pinos form the southern boundary of the relatively shallow gulf. Tidal action here is slight, but currents and water levels are strongly influenced by the wind direction. A northeast wind lowers water levels, while a southeast wind raises them. Extreme lows occur with a northwest wind, while extreme highs occur with a southwest breeze. Currents outside the gulf can be of concern as they tend to set vessels to the northwest, which is toward the dangers between Banco de Jardinillos and Isla de Pinos. This is particularly the case with southeast winds.

ISLA DE PINOS

21 40W, 82 50W
Pilotage: This is the largest of the islands lying off the Cuban coast. It is quite flat, with the south part being very low, swampy, and densely wooded. The north two-thirds of the island has a wide, very flat, coastal plain that merges with a scattering of high, often heavily forested, interior hills and mountains. Loma la Canada (1,017 feet) is the highest, and the first sighted when coming from the south. From the west it appears as a domed summit flanked by two sharp peaks. Loma Daguilla is the highest peak (612 feet) on the east side of the island; from the southeast it appears as a steep-sided isolated hill.

The Cayos Jardines are the numerous islets lying scattered east of Isla de Pinos for a distance of about 67 miles to the heavily wooded islet Cayo Largo. They continue on to Cayo Guamo del Este, a group of high, closely spaced barren rocks, which form the easternmost above-water dangers fronting this section of the coast.

Ensenada de la Siguanea (21° 38′N, 83° 05′W) is a spacious deepwater inlet on the west side of Isla de Pinos. It is entered between Punta Frances, the low-lying, mangrove-covered west extremity of the island, and Cayos los Indios, a group of low-lying heavily wooded islets that give a measure of shelter from the west. If approaching from the west, steer for Loma la Canada on a heading of 084°. When approaching from the south or southwest, pass no less than 2 1/4 miles northwest of Punta Frances before turning into the entrance.

Nueva Gerona (21° 53′N, 82° 48′W) is a small riverine community lying somewhat inland on the north coast of Isla de Pinos. This is the principal community on the island. Vessels can approach this area by passaging around the west side of Isla de Pinos, via Ensenada de la Siguanea.

REFUGE CANAL, E breakwater, 22 40.6N, 82 17.9W. Fl R 6s, 19ft, 4M. Red concrete pyramid.
REFUGE CANAL, W side, 22 40.8N, 82 17.9W. Fl G 3s, 13ft, 4M. Green port-hand column with topmark.
SUR BAJO BOQUERON, 22 21.1N, 82 25.7W. Fl G 5s, 14ft, 3M. Green port-hand beacon with topmark.
MONTERREY, 22 20.2N, 82 20.5W. Fl R 6s, 14ft, 7M. Red starboard-hand beacon with topmark.

CUBA

CAYO CRUZ, 22 28.1N, 82 16.8W. Fl G 3s, 13ft, 6M. Green port-hand beacon with topmark.
BUENAVISTA, 22 30.0N, 82 21.2W. Fl R 6s, 13ft, 3M. Red starboard-hand beacon with topmark.
CAYO CULEBRA, 22 24.1N, 82 33.8W. L Fl R 6s, 13ft, 4M. Red starboard-hand beacon with topmark.
CAYO CARABELA, 22 29.2N, 82 28.7W, Fl G 3s, 13ft, 4M. Green port-hand beacon with topmark.
BOQUERON DEL HACHA, 22 29.3N, 82 27.8W. Fl R 4s, 13ft, 4M. Red starboard-hand beacon with topmark.

ENSENADA DE COLOMA

LA COLOMA, 22 14.3N, 83 34.3W. Fl W 5s, 25M. Tower on green metal tank; 13ft.
SANTO DOMINGO, APPROACH BEACON, 22 09.5N, 83 36.5W. L Fl W 10s, 19ft, 5M. Red metal tower, white stripes, on platform on piles, ball topmark.
ENSENADA DE COLOMA, NO 1, W side, 22 11.9N, 83 35.6W. Fl G 3s, 13ft, 4M. Green port-hand beacon with topmark.
ENSENADA DE COLOMA, NO 4, E side, 22 12.4N, 83 35.3W. Fl R 4s, 13ft, 4M. Red starboard-hand beacon with topmark.

ENSENADA DE COLOMA, NO 5, W side, 22 13.0N, 83 34.9W. Fl G 5s, 13ft, 4M. Green port-hand beacon with topmark.
ENSENADA DE COLOMA, NO 8, E side, 22 13.5N, 83 34.6W. Fl R 4s, 13ft, 4M. Red starboard-hand beacon with topmark.
ENSENADA DE COLOMA, NO 10, E side, 22 14.1N, 83 34.2W. Fl R 6s, 13ft, 4M. Red starboard-hand beacon with topmark.

ENSENADA DE CORTES

Pilotage: This coastal bight is located in the far western part of Golfo de Batabano. The approaches are obstructed by a string of dangers extending west from Isla de Pinos to the mainland. It is entered by means of a narrow passage west of a partially emerged sunken wreck charted about 12 1/2 miles north-northeast of Cabo Frances.

CABO FRANCES, 21 54.4N, 84 02.1W. Fl W 10s, 28ft, 15M. Aluminum framework tower.
CABO CORRIENTES, 21 45.7N, 84 31.0W. Fl W 5s, 88ft, 13M. Aluminum-colored iron skeleton structure enclosing gray hut with red band.

CAYMAN ISLANDS

COAST PILOT

CAUTION: Our information on aids to navigation comes from official government sources. The latitudes and longitudes of these marks may not correspond to the readings from GPS receivers. Some aids have been reported as extinguished. No single aid to naavigation, or waypoint, should be relied upon as a sole means of fixing your position.

NOTE: The chartlet on the following page is not intended for navigation and is included for reference and planning purposes only. While it is reproduced from the most current edition as of press time, it incorporates no corrections to navigational aids, depths, or hazards since the edition publication date.

ENTRY PROCEDURES

All vessels should clear customs and immigration at George Town on Grand Cayman. Call the Port Authority on VHF channel 16, who will alert customs to your arrival. Anchor off the town or tie up to the government wharf. If bad weather makes anchoring off George Town untenable, call the Port Authority for information on an alternative port. The harbor is wide open to northwest winds.

To clear, vessels and crew are required to have clearance from the last port of call, the ship's documents, proof of ownership, and passports. There is a US$40 fee for vessels arriving after 1600 weekdays, after 12 noon Saturday, and on Sunday and holidays. All guns, spear guns, pole spears, and Hawaiian slings will be held for the duration of your stay. There are strict environmental rules and regulations that must be complied with while in the islands. For more information, customs may reached at 809-949-2473.

The Cayman dollar is the official currency, but U.S. dollars are accepted everywhere. Credit cards are widely accepted, and more than 500 banks conduct business in the Caymans. The language spoken is English.

GRAND CAYMAN

GRAND CAYMAN LIGHT, Georgetown near church, 19 17.8N, 81 23.0W. Q R, 41ft, 7M. Black steel tower, white base.

BOATSWAIN POINT LIGHT, NW end of island, 19 23.1N, 81 24.6W. Fl W 15s, 90ft, 15M. White steel tower, black base. Partially obscured 241°–257°; obscured 257°–shore.

GORLING BLUFF LIGHT, at SE end of island, 19 18.0N, 81 06.3W. Fl (2) W 20s, 72ft, 12M. White steel tower, black base.

GEORGETOWN AVIATION LIGHT, 19 17.5N, 81 21.5W. Al W G, 40ft, 20M.

GEORGE TOWN

19 18N, 81 23W

Port of Entry: Contact the Port Authority on VHF channel 16 upon arrival. See Entry Procedures for more information.

Dockage: You may be able to tie up temporarily to the government wharf while clearing customs. The Cayman Islands Yacht Club on North Sound (809-947-4322 or fax, -4432) has more than 130 slips, many for transients. For small or shallow-draft vessels, Ralphie's for the Love of Diving (809-949-3099) at Morgan's Harbour Marina in West Bay has one small dock. Harbour House Marine (809-947-1307 or VHF channel 16) at the south end of North Sound can offer emergency dockage for vessels drawing less than 6 feet and less than 24 feet in width.

Anchorage: There are sheltered anchorages in North Sound. In good weather you can anchor west of West Bay. When a norther threatens, boats anchored off George Town move around to the south end of the island.

Services: The Cayman Islands Yacht Club offers water, electricity, and fuel; plans are underway for a dockhouse and related facilities. Harbour House Marina offers fuel, water, a fully stocked chandlery, repair and some rigging services, and haulouts for vessels to 70 tons. Fuel and water are available at Morgan's Harbour, where Ralphie's provides dive services and Bay Side Water Sports (809-949-3200) charters boats to

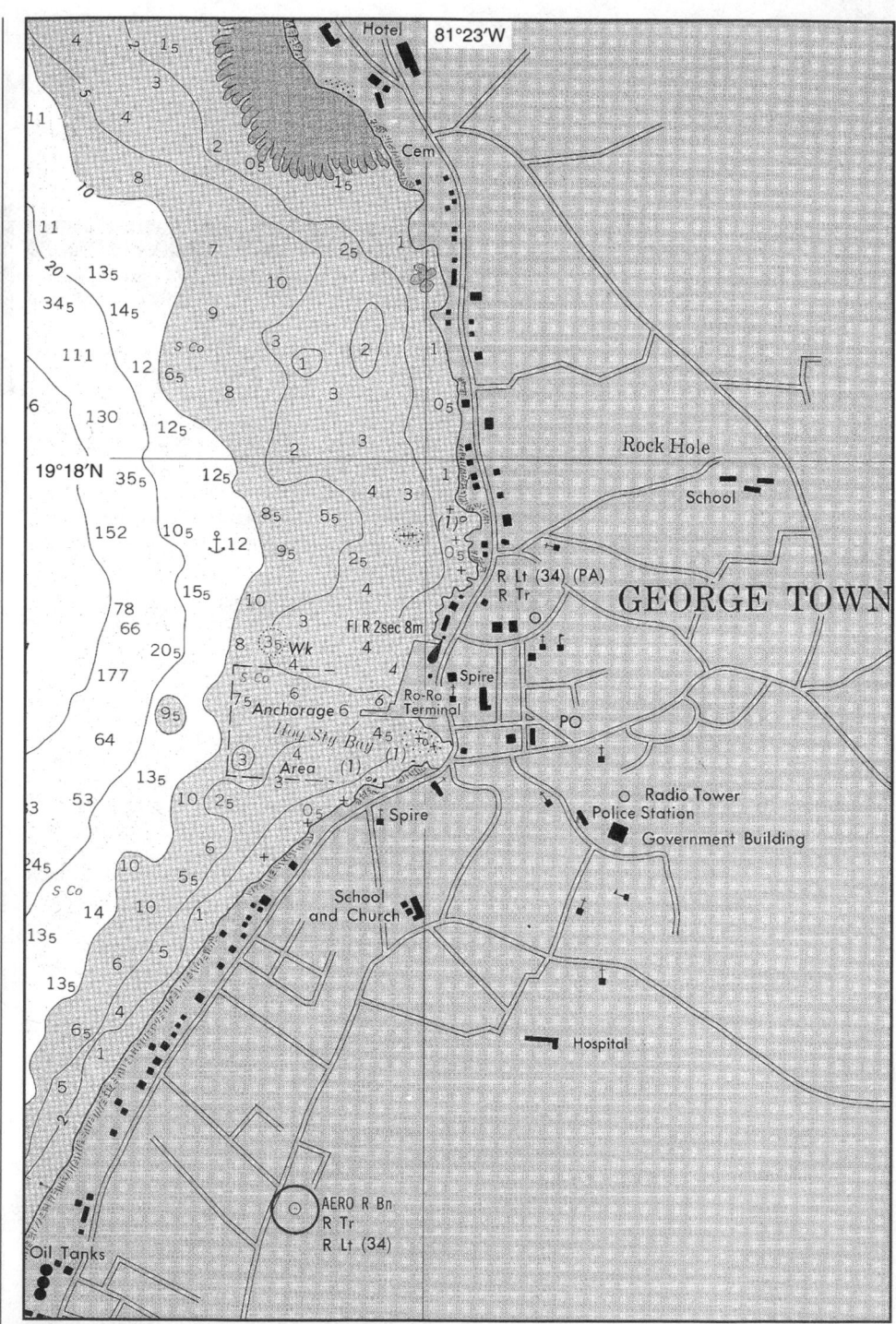

George Town, soundings in meters *(from DMA 27243, 1st ed, 3/81)*

54 feet for snorkeling, fishing, and sailing. There are good chandleries and grocery stores on the island. The offshore banking industry has promoted the development of modern facilities of all sorts.

Being situated well off the normal trade wind routes of the Caribbean, the Cayman Islands are less visited by transient yachts than other islands. The islands have world-famous diving opportunities and good shoreside facilities. The Lesser Caymans (Little Cayman and Cayman Brac) are located more than 60 miles northeast of Grand Cayman. They hold little attraction for private yachts, as there are few possibilities for shelter without local knowledge. Commercial transfer operations are carried out off both islands.

LITTLE CAYMAN

SOUTH WEST POINT LIGHT, 19 15.7N, 81 23.2W. Fl (2) W 10s, 30ft, 15M. White metal tower and base. Visible 253°–150°.
LITTLE CAYMAN LIGHT, South West Point, 19 39.5N, 80 06.8W. Fl W 5s, 30ft, 10M. White steel tower, black base.
EAST POINT LIGHT, 19 42.4N, 79 58.2W, Fl W 10s, 36ft, 10M. White tower and base.

CAYMAN BRAC

CAYMAN BRAC LIGHT, SW point, 19 41.0N, 79 53.5W, Fl (2) W 15s, 41ft, 15M. Mast. Reported extinguished (1993).
CAYMAN BRAC LIGHT, North East Point, 19 45.0N, 79 44.0W, L Fl W 20s, 150ft, 12M. White steel tower, black base.

COAST PILOT

JAMAICA

CAUTION: Our information on aids to navigation comes from official government sources. The latitudes and longitudes of these marks may not correspond to the readings from GPS receivers. Some aids have been reported as unreliable, missing, off position, or showing incorrect characteristics. No single aid to navigation, or waypoint, should be relied upon as a sole means of fixing your position.

NOTE: The chartlets in this section are <u>not</u> intended for navigation and are included for reference and planning purposes only. While chartlets from government sources are reproduced from the most current editions as of press time, they incorporate <u>no corrections</u> to navigational aids, depths, or hazards since the edition publication date.

ENTRY PROCEDURES

Arriving yachts should proceed to a Port of Entry for customs and immigration clearance. Ports of Entry include Port Royal, Kingston Harbour; Port Morant; Port Antonio; Montego Bay; Ocho Rios; and Port Esquival.

You should have a clearance from your last port of call, passports or identification for the crew, three copies of the crew's list, a stores list (and a cargo manifest for boats carrying cargo) and documentation and proof of ownership for the boat. Vessels with pets aboard will also be required to carry documents for their animals and visit a veternarian ashore. You may apply for a three-month stay in the country, with another three-month extension possible. Additional extensions may be requested. Normal working hours are 0800 to 1600, Monday through Friday. Overtime charges apply for after-hours clearances, with double time charged on Saturday, Sunday, and public holidays. Charges are based upon the number of officials involved and the amount of time needed.

To move about the island you will need a coastwise clearance stating your itinerary and schedule. You must report to customs upon arriving in each port of call and then get another coastwise clearance for the next port.

When leaving the country you can wait for up to 24 hours after receiving your clearance if you do not have any firearms being held. Customs holds all firearms and ammunition for the duration of your stay.

In Port Royal you should anchor out with the Q flag flying or go to the ferry dock. Customs officials will come out to see you. After customs, you will be visited by immigration and quarantine officials. For more information contact customs at Port Royal (809-924-8633).

The official currency in Jamaica is the Jamaican dollar. Credit cards are widely used in tourist areas. The language is English.

NORTH COAST: LUCEA HARBOR TO OCHO RIOS BAY

LUCEA HARBOR LIGHT, on Flagstaff Reef, 18 27.1N, 78 09.8W. Fl R 4s, 12ft, 5M. Triangular steel skeleton structure.
MONTEGO BAY LOWER RANGE (Front Light), 18 28.1N, 77 55.4W. F R, 22ft, 5M. Cylindrical iron structure, triangular shaped. Visible 108°–128°. **(Rear Light)** 323 meters 118.5° from front. F R, 57ft, 5M. Black structure. Visible 108°–128°.
MONTEGO BAY UPPER RANGE (Front Light), 18 28.7N, 77 55.6W. F R, 44ft, 5M. Cylindrical iron structure, ball topmark. Visible 026°–046°. Stopping lights. Reported destroyed 1991. **(Rear Light),** 104 meters 035.2° from front. F R, 113ft, 5M. Cylindrical iron structure, ball topmark. Visible 026°–046°. Stopping lights.
MONTEGO BAY ENTRANCE CHANNEL RANGE (Front Light), 18 27.5N, 77 56.3W. Oc W 2s, 26ft. Red triangle daymark on post. **(Rear Light),** 300 meters 200.8° from front. Oc W 3s, 43ft. Red triangular daymark on post.
AVIATION LIGHT, 18 29.9N, 77 55.1W. Fl W 4s, 59ft, 10M. Control tower.
MONTEGO PORT LIGHT 2, W side, 18 27.8N, 77 56.2W. Fl R 5s, 16ft. Red pile.

MONTEGO PORT LIGHT 3, W side, 18 27.8N, 77 56.3W. Fl R 3s, 16ft. Red pile.
MONTEGO PORT LIGHT 4, 18 27.7N, 77 56.5W. Fl R 5s, 16ft. Red steel column on pile.
MONTEGO PORT LIGHT 5, 18 27.6N, 77 56.5W. Fl R 3s, 16ft. Red steel column on pile.
MONTEGO PORT LIGHT 6, 18 27.7N, 77 56.2W. F G, 20ft. Green steel column.

MONTEGO BAY

18 28N, 7756W

Port of Entry: If you anchor off or dock at the Montego Bay Yacht Club, club staff will call the officials for you. Otherwise customs officials can be reached at 809-952-2469 and immigration officials at 809-952-5456.
Dockage: The Montego Bay Yacht Club (809-979-8038 or VHF channel 16) is located in the bay west of town that forms the commercial port. The club wharf has up to 30 feet of water at the outer end, but depths vary as you progress toward shore. There is a fee for anchoring off the club and using its facilities.
Services: At this writing diesel fuel only is available at the Montego Bay Yacht Club. With 24 hours' notice, the club can arrange for delivery of ice in large quantities. Club facilities include a bar, restaurant, showers, tennis, and swimming. Minor repairs may be carried out at the docks; for emergencies, the club may be able to arrange for a mobile crane for haulouts. There are no other haulout facilities here. All sorts of tourist diversions are available at the club, in town, and nearby.

Though the yacht club is situated several miles from downtown, its good facilities make it a popular stop for boaters. Montego Bay is a well-sheltered harbor.

ROSE HALL LIGHT, 18 32.1N, 77 49.2W. Fl (5) W 30s, 106ft, 22M. Metal framework tower.
FALMOUTH HARBOR LIGHT, 18 29.3N, 77 39.1W. F R, 37ft. White round structure.
DISCOVERY BAY RANGE (Front Light) (DRY HARBOR), 18 27.7N, 77 24.6W. F R, 25ft. White triangular daymark, point up, on post. **(Rear Light),** 220 meters 193.9° from front. F R, 40ft. Framework tower, white triangular daymark, point down.
ST. ANNS BAY RANGE (Front Light), on Custom House, 18 26.1N, 77 12.1W. F R, 59ft, 11M. Roof of Custom House. Visible 186°–206°. Destroyed 1966. **(Rear Light),** 580 meters 193.5° from front. F R, 275ft, 11M. White iron column. Visible 186°–206°.

OCHO RIOS BAY

Buoy, 18 25.0N, 77 07.0W. Fl G, 3s. Red buoy with triangular topmark. Radar reflector.
RANGE (Front Light), 18 24.5N, 77 06.9W. Oc R 5s, 42ft, 10M. Red and white triangular daymark. Shown when vessels are expected. **(Rear Light),** 384 meters 169° from front. Oc R 5s, 150ft, 10M. Steel column, red and white triangular daymark. Synchronized with front. Shown when vessels are expected.
BEACON, 18 24.7N, 77 06.7W. Fl G 5s, 16ft. Square topmark on three-pile beacon.
BEACON, 18 24.6N, 77 06.6W. Fl G 1.5s, 16ft. Square topmark on three-pile beacon.

ORACABESSA BAY

RANGE (Front Light), E side of bay, 18 24.3N, 76 56.8W. Fl W 2.5s, 25ft, 7M. White circular iron column, white circular daymark. **(Rear Light),** 46 meters 093.2° from front. Q W, 41ft, 7M. White circular iron column, white circular daymark.
RANGE (Front Light), S part of bay, 18 24.0N, 76 57.1W. Fl W 5s, 12ft, 7M. White circular iron column, white diamond daymark. **(Rear Light),** 55 meters 175.7° from front. Q W, 18ft, 7M. White circular iron column, white diamond daymark.
GALINA POINT LIGHT, 18 25.2N, 76 55.1W. Fl W 12s, 62ft, 22M. White round concrete tower and hut. F R on radio masts close W.

PORT ANTONIO

FOLLY POINT LIGHT, 18 11.3N, 76 26.6W. L Fl W 10s, 54ft, 23M. Concrete tower, red and white bands. Obscured by Wood Island.
FOLLY POINT RANGE (Front Light), 18 11.2N, 76 26.6W. F R. Beacon. When required. **(Rear Light),** 146 meters 068.8° from front. F R. Beacon. When required.
WEST HARBOR RANGE (Front Light), on the shore, 18 10.9N, 76 27.6W. F R, 25ft. White structure. **(Rear Light),** 1271 meters 249° from front. F R, 277ft. White structure.
TITCHFIELD LIGHT, 18 11.0N, 76 27.1W. Q G. Beacon.

PORT ANTONIO

18 11N, 76 27W

Port of Entry: Port Antonio Marina (809-993-3209 or VHF channel 68) and Huntress Marina (809-993-3053 or VHF channel 16) will contact officials for yachts arriving at their docks. Other vessels should clear with officials in town;

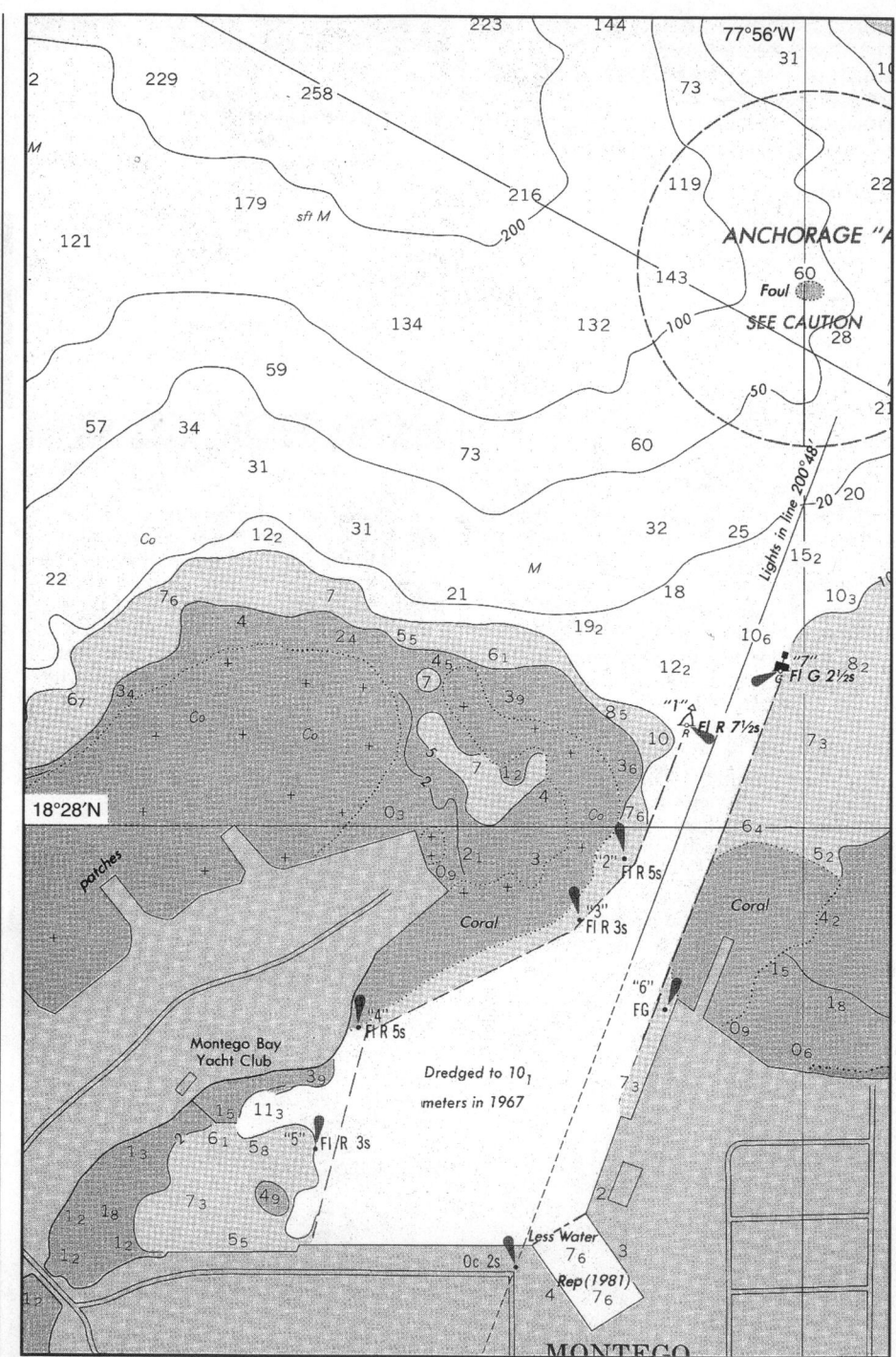

Montego Bay, soundings in meters *(from DMA 26122, 28th, 5/84)*

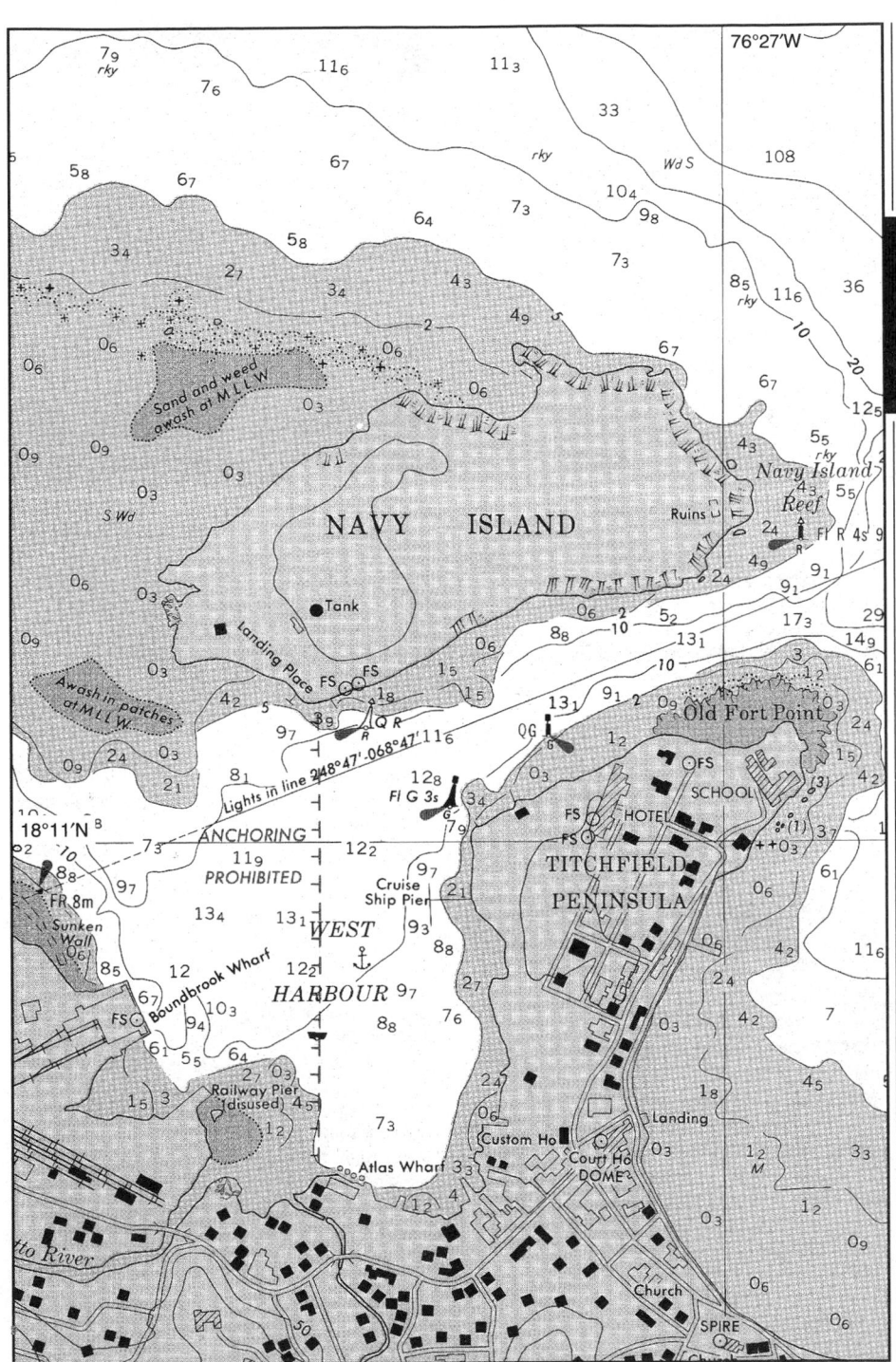

Port Antonio, soundings in meters *(from DMA 26129, 10th ed, 9/87)*

customs can be reached at 809-993-2305; immigration at 809-993-2527; and the quarantine office at 809-993-2557.

Dockage: Navy Island Marina and Resort (809-993-2667 or VHF channel 72) on Navy Island and Port Antonio Marina (809-993-3209 or VHF channel 68) and Huntress Marina (809-993-3053 or VHF channel 16) near the Boundbrook Wharf area all have dock space for transients. A ferry offers transporation between Navy Island and the market area of town.

Services: All three marinas have water and electricity. Diesel is available at Navy Island, and Huntress and Port Antonio can arrange fuel delivery by truck. Both Port Antonio Marine and Huntress Marina have a bar and restaurant. Huntress also has showers and can help you make arrangements for repair services. Port Antonio also can arrange for minor repair services on site. Grocery stores and general supplies are available in town.

Port Antonio is one of the most beautiful towns on the island, and the marinas are a popular stop for cruisers. The mountain scenery is spectacular and makes a visit inland worthwhile. It is also a good place for yachts from the north to clear customs after a voyage down the Windward Passage.

MORANT POINT LIGHT, SE extremity of Jamaica, 17 54.9N, 76 11.1W. Fl (3) W 20s, 115ft, 22M. White metal tower, red bands. Obscured when bearing more than 067°. Reported Fl (2) W, 20s (April 1993).

SOUTH COAST: MORANT POINT TO KINGSTON

MORANT CAYS LIGHT, Northeast Cay, 17 25.0N, 75 59.2W. L Fl W 10s, 75ft, 12M. Aluminum framework tower. Radar reflector.
PORT MORANT RANGE (Front Light), 17 53.3N, 76 19.4W. F R, 34ft, 5M. White beacon. **(Rear Light),** 418 meters 005.8° from front. F R, 95ft, 5M. White beacon.
HARBOR SHOAL SOUTH LIGHT, 17 52.4N, 76 19.6W. Fl G 5s. Beacon.
MORANT BAY LIGHT, 17 53.0N, 76 24.0W. Fl W 5s, 244ft, 14M. Red framework tower. Visible 283°–078°; only top of tower is visible above trees.
HARBOR SHOAL NORTH, Fl G 1.5s. Beacon.
COTTON TREE SPIT, Fl R 1.5s. Beacon.
LEITH HALL SPIT, Fl G 3s. Beacon.
WATSON SPIT, Fl G 5s. Beacon.

KINGSTON AND APPROACHES

PLUMB POINT LIGHT, 17 55.6N, 76 46.7W. Fl W R 9s, 70ft, 19M. White tower. W 297°–010°, R 010°–36°, W 136°–81°; obscured elsewhere.
NORMAN MANLEY AVIATION LIGHT, 17 56.1N, 76 46.8W. Al Fl W G 8s, 55ft. Tower. Occasional.
Lime Cay Buoy, 17 55.0N, 76 49.0W. Q R. Red buoy.
East Middle Ground Buoy, 17 55.0N, 76 47.0W. Fl R. Red buoy. Radar reflector.

PORT ROYAL

GUN CAY LIGHT, S end of shoal, 17 55.6N, 76 50.2W. Fl R 4s, 20ft, 5M. White triangular topmark on pile structure.
RACKHAMS CAY RANGE (Front Light), N extremity of shoal, 17 55.5N, 76 50.3W. Fl G 5s, 28ft, 8M. Green beacon. **LAZARETTO (Rear),** 3.9 km 284° from front, 17 56.0N, 76 52.5W. Fl W 3s, 92ft. White cairn. Lights mark the boat channel off Gallows Point when required.
BEACON SHOAL LIGHT, S extremity, 17 55.7N, 76 50.8W. Q R, 18ft. White tripod structure, black base.
HARBOR SHOAL BEACON, SW edge of shoal, 17 55.9N, 76 51.0W. Fl R 3s, 16ft, 5M. Red starboard-hand beacon.
CHEVANNES BEACON, 17 56.2N, 76 50.8W. Q R. Red starboard-hand beacon. F R lights on four masts 600 meters south.

PORT ROYAL

17 56N, 76 50W
Emergencies: Call the Jamaican Coast Guard on VHF channel 16.
Port of Entry: Tie up to the customs wharf at the Coast Guard station or anchor out with the Q flag flying. Morgan's Harbour (809-924-8464) can also make arrangements for customs, immigration, and quarantine officials to clear in vessels. See Entry Procedures for more information.
Dockage: Morgan's Harbour Hotel and Yacht Marina (809-924-8464) offers safe dockage and moorings in Port Royal at the entrance to Kingston harbor near the Coast Guard station. Or after clearing in, proceed to the Royal Jamaica Yacht Club (809-924-8685) located east of the airport on the north side of the Palisadoes Peninsula.

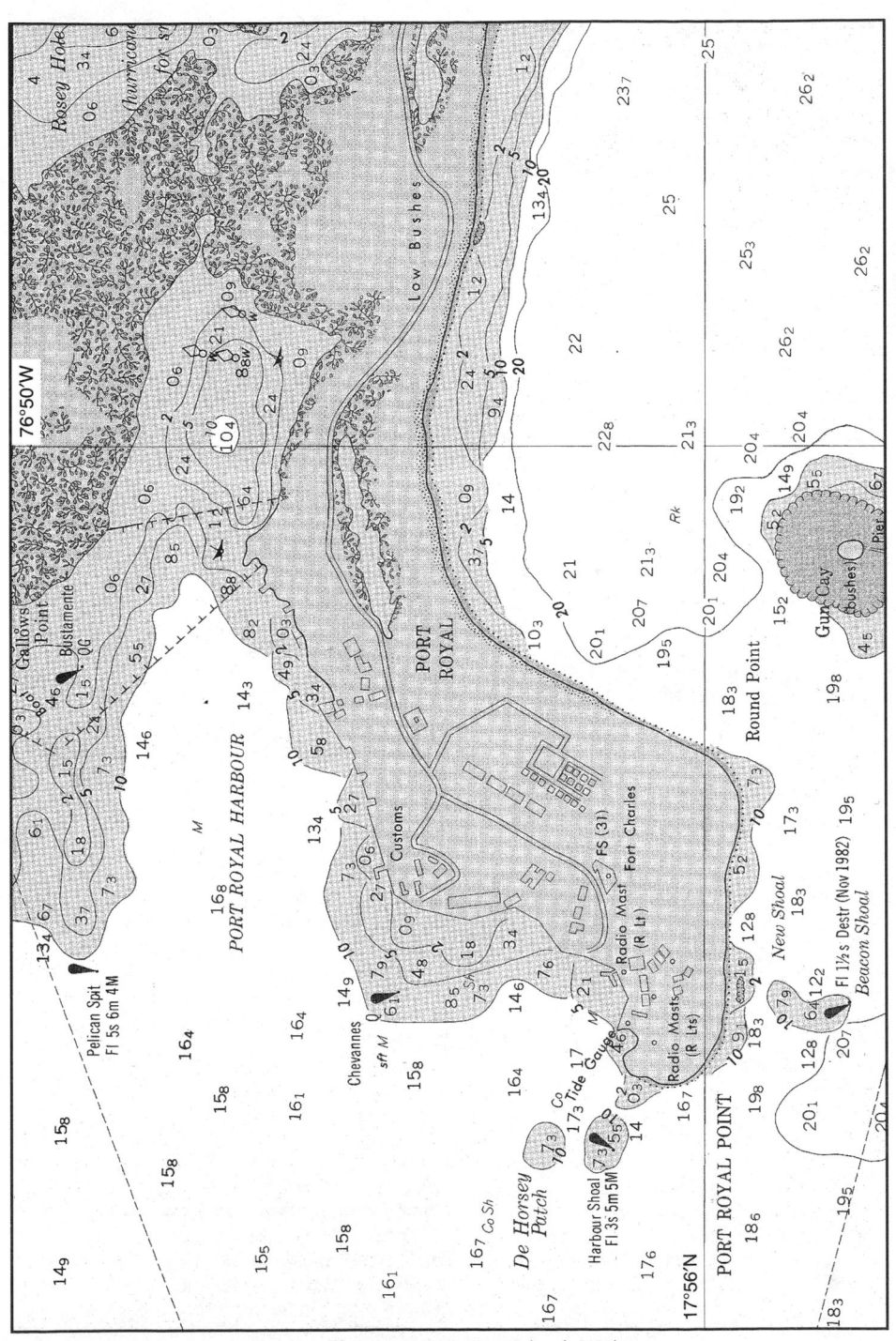

Port Royal, soundings in meters *(from DMA 26128, 48th ed, 3/85)*

Services: Morgan's Harbour and the yacht club both offer diesel, water, electricity, ice, and a restaurant and bar. Morgan's Harbour can arrange for repairs at the small marina next door. All other services are available in Port Royal or Kingston; from Port Royal a ferry offers service to Pier 2 in Kingston. It is about 12 miles to town by taxi.

Kingston is a busy commercial port and boaters should be aware of encountering large ships in the channels. It is a good idea to monitor VHF channel 16 when under way here. Port Royal is the former hangout of Captain Morgan, the pirate, and other nefarious characters. The area was subsequently converted to a naval base and features a maritime museum and a castle. The vibrant streets of Kingston are but a ferry ride away.

PELICAN SPIT, N side of Port Royal Harbor, 17 56.6N, 76 50.7W. Fl R 5s, 21ft, 4M. Red starboard-hand beacon.

BUSTAMENTE LIGHT, SW of Gallows Point, 17 56.6N, 76 50.3W. Fl R 3s. Red starboard-hand beacon.

KINGSTON HARBOUR

CURREYS GATE LIGHT, 17 57.0N, 76 50.9W. Fl W 1.5s. Red starboard-hand beacon.

DELBERT SICARD, 17 56.7N, 76 51.5W. Fl G 5s. Green port-hand beacon.

MORTON, Fl G 1.5s, 22ft, 6M. Green port-hand beacon.

BLOOMFIELD, 17 56.8N, 76 50.0W. Q R. Red starboard-hand beacon. In line 249.5° with Lazaretto, rear.

ANGEL BEACON, 17 57.0N, 76 49.6W. Q R. Red starboard-hand beacon. In line 249.5° with Lazaretto, rear.

TWO SISTERS LIGHT, Near W extremity of Middle Ground, E side of ship channel, 17 57.5N, 76 50.7W. Q R, 18ft. Red starboard-hand beacon.

BURIAL GROUND LIGHT, W side of channel, 17 57.5N, 76 50.9W. Fl G 3s, 22ft. Green port-hand beacon.

SPHINX LIGHT, 17 57.6N, 76 50.6W. Fl R 3s, 18ft. Red starboard-hand beacon.

AUGUSTA, Fl G 5s. Green port-hand beacon. Reported destroyed (1988).

MAMMEE, E side of Ship Channel, Fl R 1.5s, 18 ft. Red starboard-hand beacon.

ST. ALBANS, W side of Ship Channel. Fl G 1.5s, 22ft. Green port-hand beacon; 20ft. Reported

destroyed, marked by green buoy 38 meters NNE (1988).

EAST HORSESHOE, N extremity of Middle Ground. Fl R 3s, 26 ft. Red starboard-hand beacon; 20ft.

HUNTS BAY BEACON, 17 57.9N, 76 49.9W. Fl G 1.5s. Green port-hand beacon.

GREENWICH, 17 58.3N, 76 49.6W. Fl R 3s, 17ft. Red starboard-hand beacon.

NEWPORT B, Q R. Red starboard-hand beacon.

MIDDLE GROUND, 17 57.6N, 76 49.5W. Fl R 5s, 17ft. Red starboard-hand beacon.

POND MOUTH, Fl G 1.5s, 22ft. Green port-hand beacon, 20ft.

PICKERING, 17 57.0N, 76 48.4W. Fl R 1.5s. Red starboard-hand beacon.

TUPPER, 17 56.9N, 76 47.9W. Fl R 3s. Red starboard-hand beacon.

ROYAL JAMAICAN YACHT CLUB MARINA LIGHT, E side of entrance, 17 56.6N, 76 46.5W. Fl G 3s. Pile.

SHELL PIER LIGHTS, on each end of pier, 17 57.8N, 76 44.7W. 2 QR, QR shown from eastern dolphin.

WRECK REEF, 17 49.7N, 76 55.3W. Fl R 5s, 25ft, 6M. Red and white banded iron column. Radar reflector.

PORTLAND BIGHT

Approach Buoy, 17 46.0N, 77 01.0W. Q W. Conical-shaped black and white checkered buoy.

BARE BUSH CAY LIGHT, 17 45.2N, 77 02.0W. Fl R 10s, 28ft, 6M. White metal column, red bands. Radar reflector.

PIGEON ISLAND RANGE (Front Light), common front, 17 47.5N, 77 04.4W. Fl W 3s, 25ft, 9M. White iron column, circular daymark for East Channel; white triangle point up for South Channel. **(Rear Light),** on pumping station 11.3 km 294.7° from common front, 17 50.1N, 77 10.2W. Oc W 5s, 131ft, 16M. White steel structure. Marks East Channel. **(Rear Light),** 878 meters 343.3° from common front. L Fl W 6s, 80ft, 10M. White lattice tower, daymark white triangle, point down, Visible 004.25° either side of range line. Marks South Channel.

ROCKY POINT PIER LIGHT, 17 49.1N, 77 08.4W. 2 F R. 1 light shows from each end.

RANGE (Front Light), 17 53.4N, 77 08.4W. Fl R 3s, 26ft. White conical beacon. Q W and Q R are shown in harbor. **(Rear Light),** 677 meters 300° from front, 17 53.5N, 77 08.8W. Q R, 41ft, W conical beacon.

SALT ISLAND LIGHT, N end, 17 50.0N, 77 08.2W. Fl W 5s, 21ft, 7M. White iron column, white disk topmark.
SALT RIVER LIGHT, near mouth, 17 50.0N, 77 09.7W. Q W, 31ft, 7M. White iron column.
PORTLAND RIDGE LIGHT, summit, 17 44.4N, 77 09.5W. Fl (2) W 15s, 650ft, 20M. Steel framework tower. Reported Fl (2) W 27s.

SOUTH COAST: PORTLAND BIGHT TO SOUTH NEGRIL POINT

KAISER PIER RANGE (Front Light), outer end of pier, 17 51.5N, 77 36.2W. F R, 34ft. **(Rear Light)** 690 meters 347.5° from front. F R, 138ft. Framework tower.
LOVERS LEAP LIGHT, 17 52.0N, 77 39.7W Fl W 10s, 530 meters, 40M. White round tower, red bands. Reported Fl W 18.5s 1985.

SAVANNA LA MAR LIGHT, N extremity at Boat Stag Reef, 18 11.6N, 78 07.8W. Fl R 5s, 23ft, 9M. Iron column on concrete base.
Southeast Channel Buoy, 18 12.0N, 78 08.0W. F W. Black buoy, white bands.
SAVANNA LA MAR RANGE (Front Light), On S side of ruined fort, 18 12.4N, 78 08.1W. F R, 13ft, Occasional. **(Rear Light),** 1006 meters 032.2° from front. F R, 40ft. Occasional.
SOUTH NEGRIL POINT LIGHT, W end of Jamaica, 18 14.7N, 78 21.7W. Fl W R 2s, 100ft, 15M, White tower. R 297°–305°, W305°–161°, red thence to the coast to the north; Partially obscured by trees in the latter sector.
PEDRO BANK LIGHT, Northeast Cay, NW extremity of Cay, 17 03.1N, 77 45.8W. Fl W 5s, 35ft, 11M. Beacon; square topmark, red and white bands.

NAVASSA ISLAND, U.S.A

NAVASSA ISLAND LIGHT, summit, 18 23.8N, 75 00.8W. Fl W 10s, 395ft, 9M. Light gray tower.

NAVASSA ISLAND, U.S.A.

18 24N, 75 01W
Navassa Island lies about 30 miles west of the western extremity of Haiti and is reported to be radar conspicuous at a distance of 20 miles. It is about 1.9 miles long and 1.1 miles wide. The island's shores are white cliffs that rise as much as 50 feet directly from the sea. The lighthouse is on the southeast side of the island.

The U.S. claimed possession of Navassa Island in 1857, and it was formally annexed in January 1916 by presidential proclamation. It is uninhabited, except for a few goats, and there is no water.

Lulu Bay, a small indentation on the southwest side of the island, is the safest place to make a landing. It was the site of a phosphate mining operation. Small craft can anchor here, but should be careful because of the frequent surge. Vessels can also anchor about 0.4 mile west-southwest of Lulu Bay with the light bearing about 080°T. The bottom is sand and coral in depths of around 85 feet.

A current with a rate of 1 to 2 knots sets along the southwest side of the island, in a northwesterly direction, changing to west at the last of the east-going tidal current.

The island is a reservation administered by the U.S. Coast Guard. Entry and landing are prohibited, except by permit. Contact the Commander, Seventh Coast Guard District, 909 Southeast First Avenue, Miami, FL, 33131-3050.

HAITI

WARNING: The U.S. Department of State warns U.S. citizens against all travel to Haiti. As of late June 1994, the U.S. embassy in Port-au-Prince is operating on a very limited basis, and all U.S. citizens not affiliated with international humanitarian programs are urged to depart. The political situation in Haiti remains unstable with the potential throughout the country for random violence. Police and the judiciary are unable to provide adequate levels of security and due process. In August 1994, the United Nations Security Council authorized a multinational invasion force to restore political power to the exiled government of Haiti. In response, Haiti's military leaders declared a state of siege.

SPECIAL MARITIME WARNING: In accordance with UN Security Council Resolution 917, on May 21, 1994, allied naval forces, including U.S. forces, participating in the Haiti Multinational Interception Force (MIF) began enforcing the comprehensive trade sanctions on Haiti contained in Resolution 917. This resolution prohibits all but humanitarian and informational imports and exports to and from Haiti. While the sanctions remain in place, vessels found to be in violation may be denied entry to U.S. ports. The MIF operations are being conducted in a rectangular area bounded by the following coordinates: 20 45N, 75 20W; 17 20N, 75 20W; 17 20N, 70 50W; and 20 45N, 70 50W. All merchant ships perceived to be proceeding to or originating from Haitian ports will be intercepted and may be searched. The intercepting ship may use all available communication to give directions to a ship. All vessels operating in the vicinity should remain clear of and avoid interference with ships engaged in enforcing UN sanctions.

U.S. citizens seeking information about the current status of the trade embargo should contact the U.S. Department of Treasury Office of Foreign Assets Control (202-622-2520).

Haiti is the poorest nation in the Western Hemisphere, and visitors may be targeted by criminals, especially in urban areas. Fuel, propane, and electricity are subject to sporadic availability even under normal circumstances. As sanitation may not be up to standards, visitors are advised to drink only bottled water and bottled drinks. Medical facilities are generally substandard. Those seeking medical treatment should be prepared to pay in cash, as medical insurance may not be honored. Tropical diseases are prevalent, including malaria, typhoid, and dengue fever. There is a special alert concerning AIDS.

CAUTION: Our information on aids to navigation comes from official government sources. The latitudes and longitudes of these marks may not correspond to the readings from GPS or LORAN receivers. Some aids have been reported as unreliable, missing, off position, or showing incorrect characteristics. No single aid to navigation, or waypoint, should be relied upon as a sole means of fixing your position.

NOTE: The chartlets in this section are <u>not intended for navigation</u> and are included for reference and planning purposes only. While chartlets reproduced from government sources are from the most current editions as of press time, they incorporate <u>no corrections</u> to navigational aids, depths, or hazards since the edition publication date.

ENTRY PROCEDURES

NOTE: Specific information concerning current clearing-in procedures could not be confirmed at press time (August 1994). Cruisers planning visits to Haiti are advised to keep themselves informed of the current state of governmental affairs and military activities in Haiti.

The principal ports of entry are Port-au-Prince and Cap-Haitién. Cruising permits issued at other ports may or may not be honored by Haitian officials. A cruising permit is necessary to visit other ports in the country and may or may not be granted. You must have a clearance from your last port of call, ship's papers, crew lists, and passports. All firearms should be declared and may be held for the duration of your stay.

Clearing in at other places has been reported as difficult and dangerous. Ports on Haiti's south coast are reported to be particularly poor, and boaters are advised not to cruise the area. Jacmel and Les Cayes are ports of entry but are not recommended because of difficulties encountered by private yachts. Other possibilities are Fort Liberté, Port-de-Paix, Gonaives, St. Marc, Petit Goave, Miragoane, and Jérémie. Penalties for failing to comply with regulations are reported to be severe.

U.S. citizens over the age of 18 need proof of identification to enter Haiti. Those under 18 must have a passport, which is the preferred means of identification for everyone. A departure tax of $25, payble in cash only, is levied on everyone leaving the country.

Boats should not be left unattended if at all possible. During periods when large numbers of "boat people" are leaving, private yachts become possible targets of theft.

For assistance in Haiti, U.S. citizens may contact the consular section of the U.S. Embassy on Harry Truman Boulevard, Port-au-Prince (P.O. Box 1761; tel., 509-22-0200, -22-0354, -22-0368, or 22-0612; fax, 509-23-1641) or the Consular Section Annex (509-22-0200, -23-8971, fax, -23-9665). The international telephone country code for Haiti is 509; within the country you need dial only the last six digits.

For information from the government of Haiti contact the Embassy of Haiti, 2311 Massachusetts Avenue, Washington, DC 20008 (202-332-4090). Haiti also maintains consulates in Miami, Los Angeles, Chicago, New York, Boston, and San Juan, Puerto Rico.

The Haitian government permits a free-market exchange of U.S. dollars for the official currency, the gourde, which is equal to US$5. A "Haitian dollar" is actually 5 gourdes. Carrying large amounts of cash and valuables is not recommended.

French is the official language, but Haitian Creole is widely spoken.

CAP-HAITIÉN

19 46N, 72 12W

Emergencies: U.S. citizens may contact the consular section of the U.S. embassy in Port-au-Prince (see Entry Procedures, above).

Pilotage: The marked channel runs along the shore southward from Point Picolet. South of the main pier is an area where small craft and yachts can tie up. There are shoals east of the marked channel. The pilot boats monitor VHF channel 16.

Port of Entry: Customs is located on the main wharf.

Dockage: Dockage may be available at the south side of the main docking basin.

Anchorage: Although the anchorage off town is unsheltered, Baie de L'Acul, 10 miles to the west of Pointe Picolet, is reported to be a good hurricane hole. Also, see Fort Liberté.

Services: You may have to jug water from ashore. There are groceries and general stores, but no marine supplies. Because of the embargo, it is doubtful that fuel is available to pleasure yachts.

Somewhere between Cap-Haitién and Passe Caracol, to the east, Columbus put the *Santa Maria* on the reefs. This area has many unmarked shoals and reefs and should be transited in good light if possible. San Souci and the Citadelle, King Christophe's palace and fort, are historically interesting. The Citadelle is an enormous fort built at the cost of many lives to protect Christophe from an imagined attack by Napoléon's legions.

FORT LIBERTÉ

19 40N, 71 50W

Emergencies: U.S. citizens may contact the consular section of the U.S. embassy in Port-au-Prince (see Entry Procedures, above).

Pilotage: The coast between Baie de Fort Liberté entrance and Pointe Jacquezy, about 8 miles west, is low with a sandy beach, fringed with reefs, and backed by mangroves. A long reef then extends another 8 miles in a west-northwest direction. The entrance to the bay is in position 19 43N, 71 50.8W.

Port of Entry: You can clear customs in the town, but there are reports your cruising permit may not be honored in Cap-Haitién or other ports. Boaters are advised to obtain a cruising permit in Cap-Haitién before visiting other ports on the north coast.

Dockage: Depths are reported as shallow off the town docks.

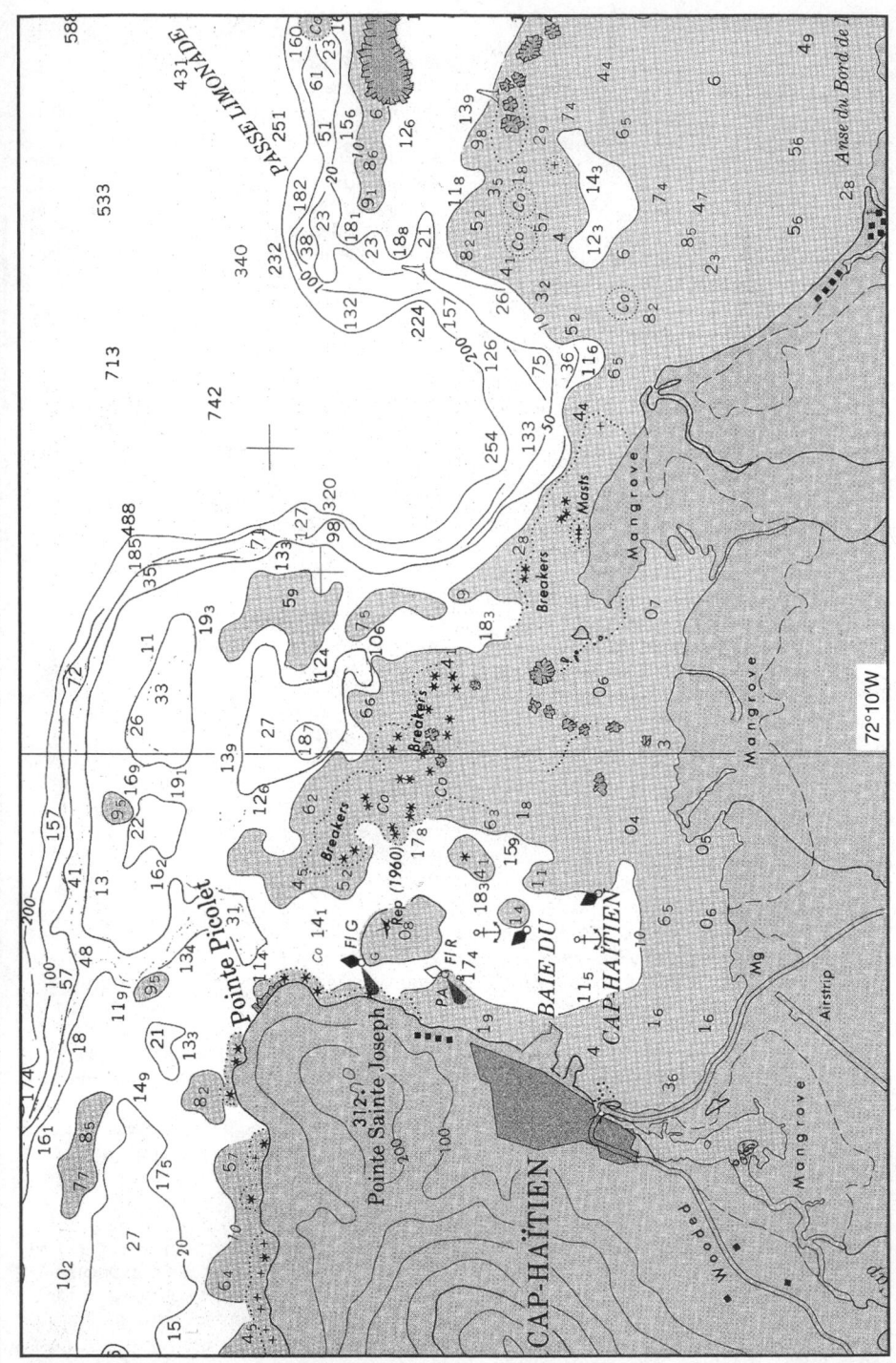

Cap-Haitién, soundings in meters *(from DMA 26142, 9th ed, 7/90)*

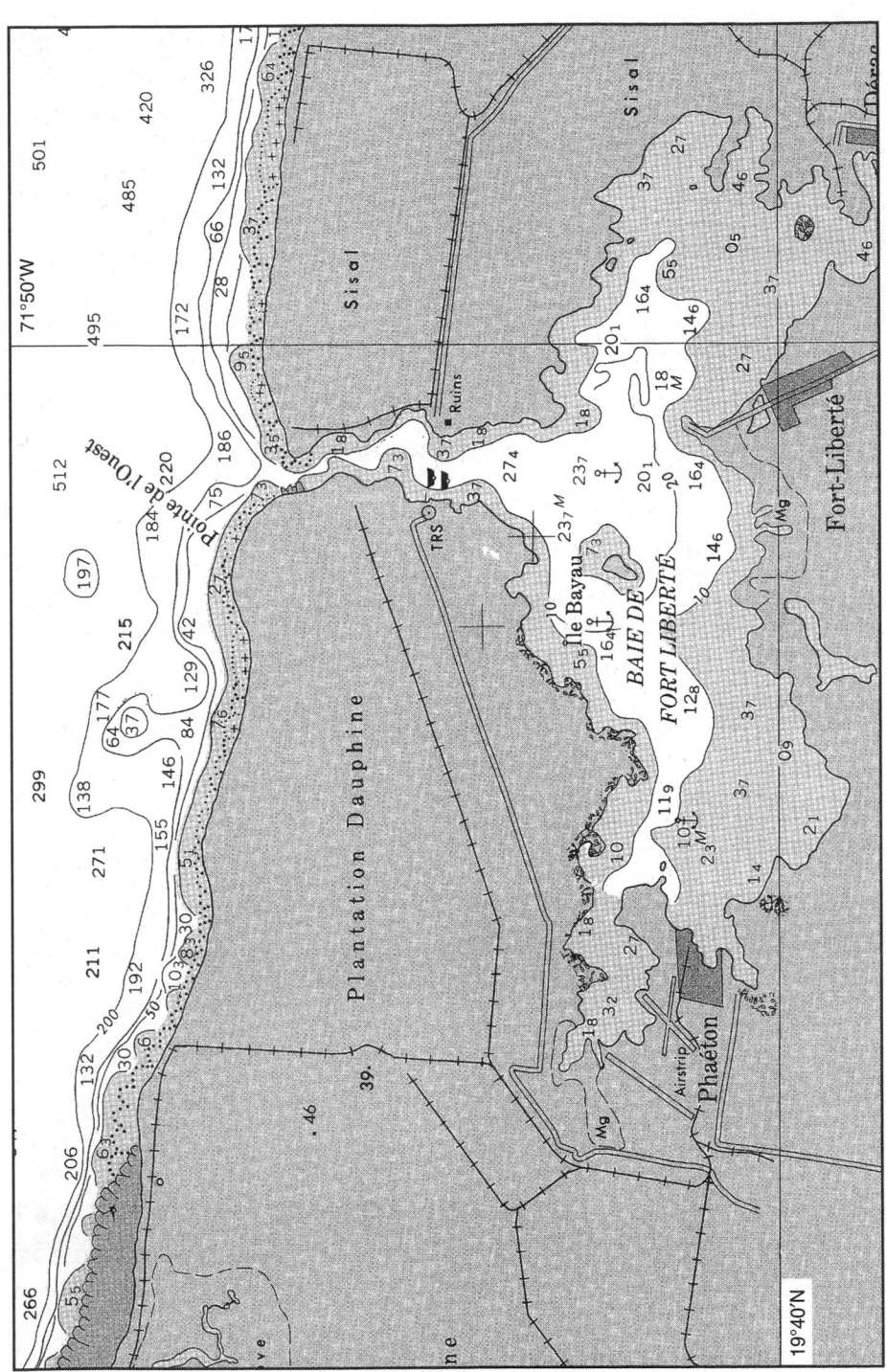

Fort Liberté, soundings in meters *(from DMA 26142, 9th ed, 7/90)*

COAST PILOT

Anchorage: This area is a good hurricane hole, with excellent holding ground reported.
Services: The trade embargo may have curtailed the availability of fuel and general supplies; water may be available. You will probably have to carry everything in the dinghy out to your anchored boat.

NORTH COAST

ILE DE LA TORTUGA LIGHT, E point, 20 01.0N, 72 38.0W. Fl (2) W 6s, 77ft, 14M. White metal framework tower, triangular base.
ILE DE LA TORTUGA LIGHT, W point, 20 04.4N, 72 58.2W. V Q W.
PORT-DE-PAIX, W side of pier, 19 57.1N, 72 50.1W. F R, 7M. On second story of building. A F R light is shown from a post on NW corner of pier.
CAP DU MOLE ST. NICOLAS LIGHT, 19 49.4N, 73 25.0W. Oc W, 3s, 15M. White tower. Reported extinguished (October 1993).

WEST COAST

POINT LAPIERRE LIGHT, N side of entrance to Gonaives Bay, 19 27.0N, 72 46.0W. Fl W 6s, 318ft, 11M. White square stone tower.
POINTE DE ST. MARC LIGHT, 19 02.7N, 72 49.0W. Q (9) W 15s, 96ft, 9M. White framework tower.
LES ARCADINS LIGHT, NW point, 18 48.4N, 72 38.9W. Fl (2) W 5s, 41ft, 9M. Circular white iron tower. Obscured 358°–012°.

PORT-AU-PRINCE AND APPROACHES

LAFITEAU RANGE (Front Light), on head of pier, 18 41.7N, 72 21.2W. F R. Black and white beacon on structure. **(Rear Light),** 304 meters 044.5° from front. F R. Black and white beacon on building.
RANGE (Front Light), head of navy yard dock, 18 32.3N, 72 22.7W. F R. **(Rear Light),** inner end of dock, 120 meters 183° from front, F G.
RANGE (Front Light), N tower of cathedral, 18 32.9N, 72 20.3W. Oc W 3s, 12M. F R on Port Captains office 0.5 mile WNW. **(Rear Light),** near SW corner of Fort Alexander, 823 meters 104 degrees from front. Oc W 3s, 12M.
POINTE DU LAMENTIN LIGHT, 18 33.4N, 72 24.5W. Fl W 3s, 106ft, 16M. White circular iron tower. Obscured by trees 109°–126°.

PORT-AU-PRINCE

18 33N, 72 21W
Emergencies: U.S. citizens may contact the consular section of the U.S. embassy in Port-au-Prince (see Entry Procedures, above).
Pilotage: Mariners are warned that numerous fishing vessels may be encountered between Ile de Gonave and the southeast head of Baie de Port-au-Prince. The forenoon haze may obscure the inner entrance range at distances greater than 4 miles. The most favorable time to enter port is in the afternoon or at dawn. Aids to navigation have been reported extinguished, missing, or showing incorrect characteristics.
Port of Entry: Tie up at the commercial wharf or anchor out as directed by port control.
Port Control: Contact port control on 2182kHz or VHF channel 16. The pilot boats can also be reached on these channels. They are reported to respond to three whistle blasts.
Dockage: A small marina near the main wharf in Port-au-Prince may be able to furnish dockage. About 10 miles north of Port-au-Prince, a marina is located at Ibo Beach on the north side of Ile á Cabrit, also known as Carenage Island. The island is surrounded by reefs and must be approached with care.
Anchorage: Anchoring is possible but not recommended off Port-au-Prince. There are good spots to anchor on the north side of Ibo Beach.
Supplies: The trade embargo may have curtailed fuel availability, as well as availability of some groceries. Water should be available. There are no marine supplies or repair facilities.

Port-au-Prince is the capital and principal city of Haiti. Although it has many political and economic problems, it has traditionally been a fascinating city to visit. Especially popular are the art galleries displaying the distinctive "primitivist" Haitian art. Visitors should be prepared for much haggling and many requests for handouts—you may be carrying more cash than an average Haitian's yearly wages.

PORT-AU-PRINCE TO CAP DAME MARIE

POINTE FANTASQUE LIGHT, SE end of Ile de la Gonave, 18 41.8N, 72 49.2W. Q (6) + L Fl W 15s, 50ft, 9M. Skeleton tower, black and white bands.

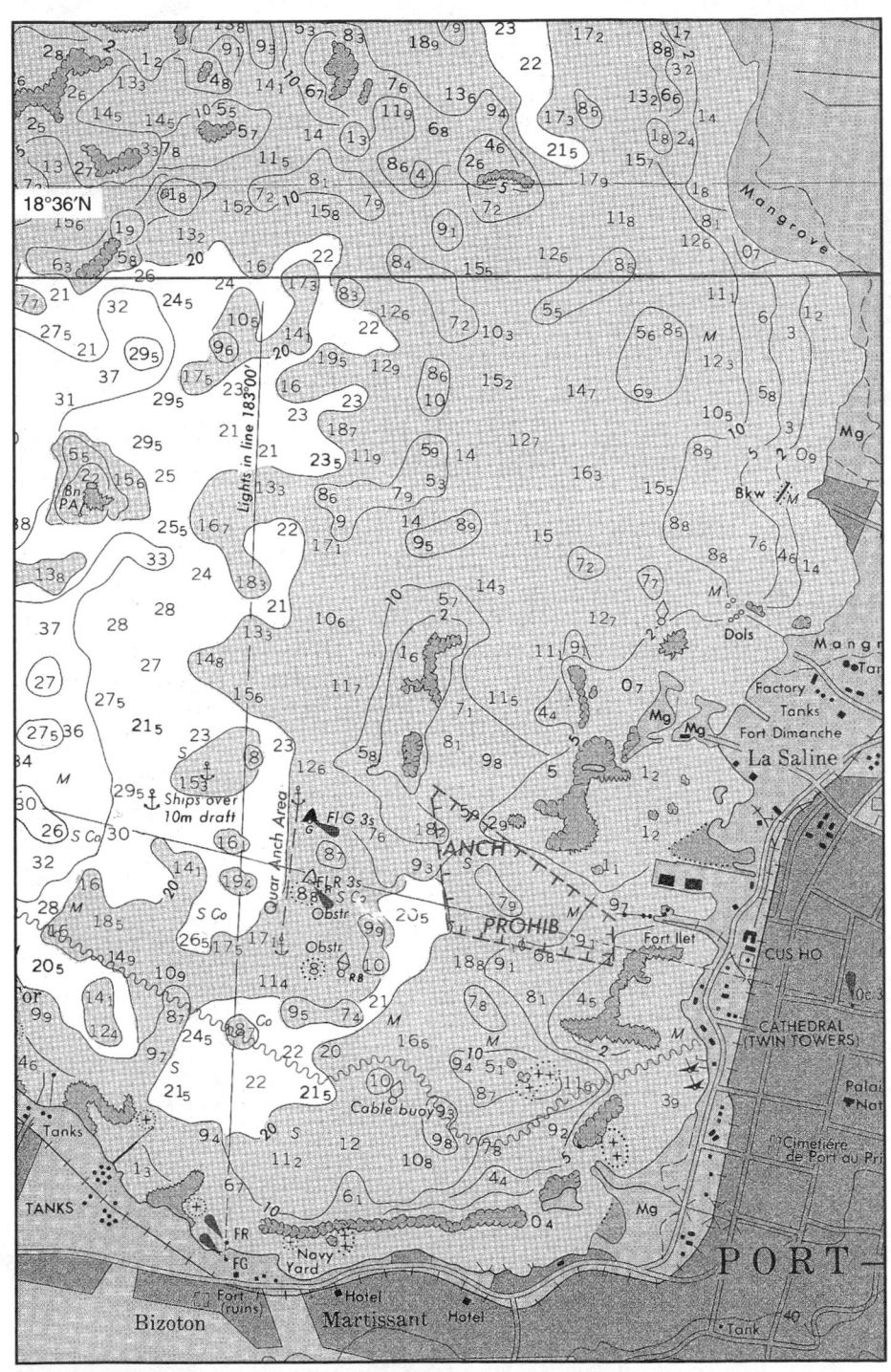

Port-au-Prince, soundings in meters *(from DMA 26184, 3rd ed, 7/89)*

Baie de Miragoane Lighted Buoy, 18 29.0N, 73 05.0W. Fl W 3s. Red buoy.

Miragoane Approach Buoy, 18 29.0N, 73 04.0W. Fl W 5s. Red buoy with topmark.

MIRAGOANE LIGHT, 18 27.2N, 73 06.4W. F R, 20ft. Corner of loading chute.

BANC DE ROCHELOIS LIGHT, in Canal de Sud, on Les Pirogues, 18 38.9N, 73 12.0W. Mo (A) W 10s, 30ft, 9M. White framework tower, black band, red lantern, hut on S side.

POINTE OUEST (WEST POINT) LIGHT, W end of Ile de la Gonave, 18 55.6N, 73 18.0W. Fl (4) W 15s, 279ft, 20M. White iron framework tower.

GRANDE CAYEMITE LIGHT, N. point, 18 38.6N, 73 45.5W. V Q W 3s, 54ft, 12M. White iron tower, triangular base.

CAP DAME MARIE LIGHT, 18 36.3N, 74 25.7W. Iso W 5s, 123ft, 9M. White square concrete structure surmounted by skeleton framework.

SOUTH COAST

ILE VACHE LIGHT, 18 03.5N, 73 34.0W. Q (6) + L Fl W 15s, White square tower.

CAP JACMEL LIGHT, 18 10.0N, 72 32.0W. F W 6s, 127ft, 9M. White skeleton tower, red lantern.

Dominican Republic

CAUTION: Our information on aids to navigation comes from official government sources. The latitudes and longitudes of these marks may not correspond to the readings from GPS or LORAN receivers. Some aids have been reported as unreliable, missing, off position, or showing incorrect characteristics. No single aid to navigation, or waypoint, should be relied upon as a sole means of fixing your position.

NOTE: The chartlets in this section are not *intended for navigation and are included for reference and planning purposes only. While chartlets reproduced from government sources are from the most current editions as of press time, they incorporate* no corrections *to navigational aids, depths, or hazards since the edition publication date.*

ENTRY PROCEDURES

Arriving yachts must enter the Dominican Republic at an official Port of Entry. Ports of Entry on the north coast are Pepillo Salcedo, in Manzanillo Bay; Luperon in Puerto Blanco; Puerto Plata; and Samaná. On the south coast they are La Romana, San Pedro de Macoris, Santo Domingo, and Haina. Boats should fly the Q flag and await the arrival of officials. It is illegal to go ashore before you have cleared into the country.

You should have a clearance from your last port of call and the usual identification for all crew-members and the boat. Firearms should be declared and will most likely be held until your departure. Each person will have to purchase a tourist card if they do not have a visa. Tourist cards are good for 60 days and are renewable. You should obtain clearance to your next port of call, whether or not it is within the country.

The U.S. State Department is warning tourists of the danger of petty street crime. There is also some danger from malaria, particularly near the Haitian border. AIDS is also a growing health problem.

U.S. citizens in need of assistance may contact the U.S. Embassy in Santo Domingo (809-221-2171) or the consular agent in Puerto Plata (809-586-4204). The U.S. consulate in Santo Domingo has an American Citizens Service Department (809-474-3789). Information on the Dominican Republic may be obtained from the Consulate of the Dominican Republic, 1715 22nd St. NW, Washington, DC 20008 (tel., 202-332-6280).

The official currency is the peso, and the language spoken is Spanish. Travelers are advised to have at least a rudimentary knowledge of the language.

NORTH COAST: CAYO ARENAS TO PUERTO PLATA

CAYO ARENAS LIGHT, on Bahía de Monte Cristi, 19 52.9N, 71 52.0W. L Fl W 6s, 65ft, 13M. Red tower, black lantern.
PUERTO LIBERATADOR LIGHT, on head of steel pier, 19 43.2N, 71 44.7W. Iso R 20s, 50ft, 10M. White tower, red lantern. Reported removed 1992.

PEPILLO SALCEDO

19 43N, 71 45W
Port of Entry
Pilotage: A light is shown from the end of the pier. A water tank 3/4 mile southwest of the pier and two oil tanks 600 yards southeast of the pier are good landmarks.
Dockage: If the surge is not too bad, you may be able to obtain permission to tie to the pier. It is about 740 feet long, with depths of 34 feet reported alongside. The pier is reported to be a good radar target for up to 15 miles.
Anchorage: With local knowledge you can bring boats into Estero Balsa, which is reported to be a good hurricane hole.
Services: Fuel should be available by truck. Water and groceries are available in limited quantities.

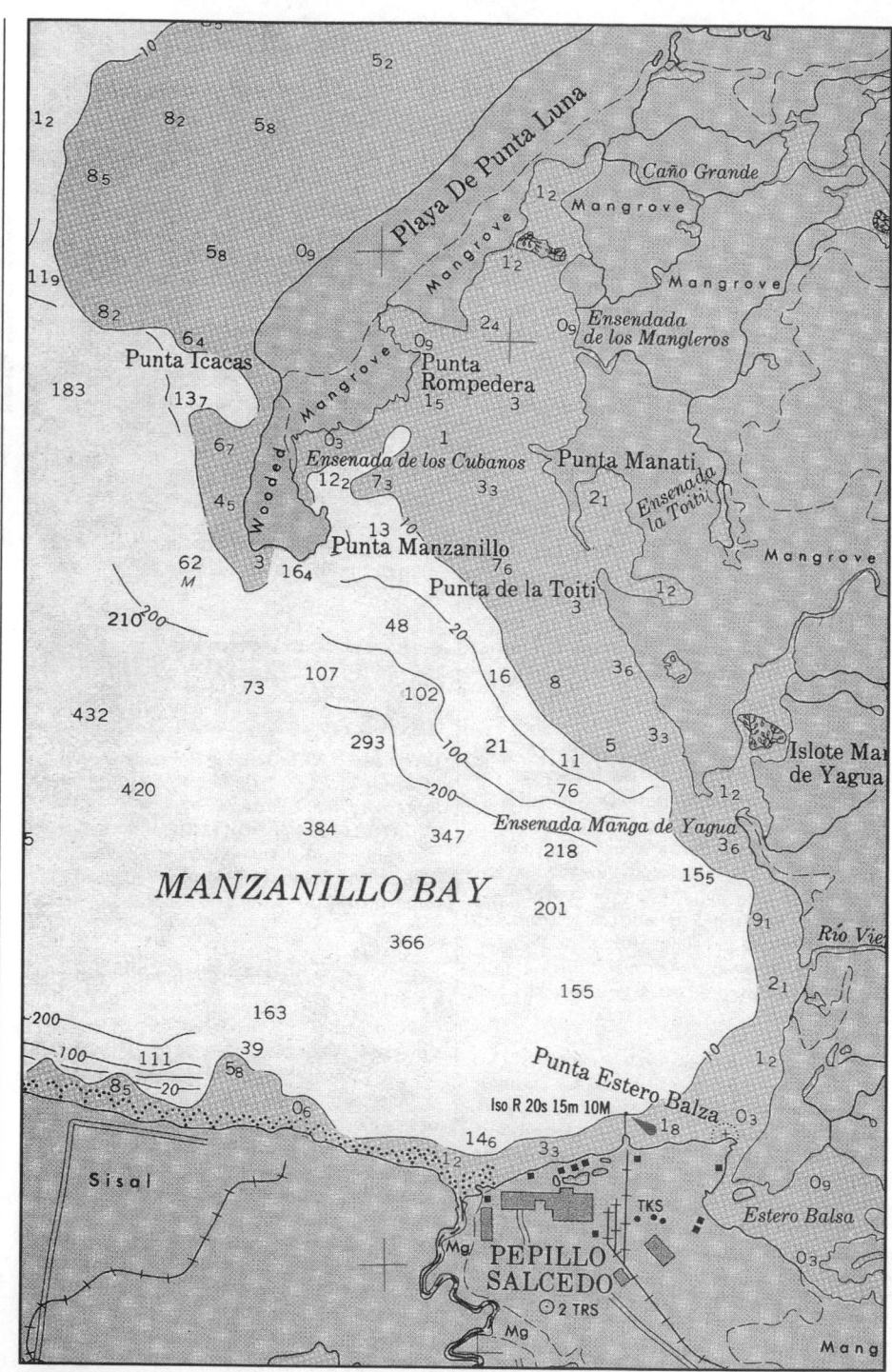

Pepillo Salcedo, soundings in meters *(from DMA 26142, 9th ed, 7/90)*

CABRA ISLAND LIGHT, NW side of Bahía de Monte Cristi, 19 54.1N, 71 40.3W. L Fl W 12s, 110ft, 13M. White pyramidal steel tower.
EL MORRO DE MONTE CRISTI LIGHT, 19 54.2N, 71 39.1W. L Fl W 8s, 860ft, 25M. White metal tower, square base. Reported destroyed 1992.
PUNTA RUCIA AVIATION LIGHT, 19 52.3N, 71 12.7W. Al Fl W G 10s.

LUPERON

19 54N, 70 57W
Port of Entry
Pilotage: The small town of Luperon is situated in the southwestern arm of Puerto Blanco. The entrance to Puerto Blanco is about 4 miles east-southeast of Cabo Isabela, the northern-most point of Hispaniola. A coastal reef extends 1,200 yards seaward from the northwest side of the cape. Punta Patilla, about 5 miles east of Puerto Blanco, has a light and a reef extending 1 mile west of the point.
Anchorage: This anchorage offers excellent protection, and the holding ground is reported to be excellent.
Services: Fuel and water will have to be jugged to the boat. Other supplies are limited.

PUNTA PATILLA LIGHT, 19 54.8N, 70 49.9W. Mo (A) W 10s, 80ft, 12M. Yellow and black concrete tower. Reported extinguished 1992.
PUERTO PLATA LIGHT, on hill near signal station, 19 48.8N, 70 41.5W. L Fl W 6s, 137ft, 18M. Yellow steel skeleton tower, black lantern. Signal station occasional.
PUERTO PLATA RANGE (Front Light), 19 48.6N, 70 42.0W. Fl R. White concrete tower, red lantern. **(Rear Light),** 230 meters 218° from front. Fl R. White concrete tower, red lantern.
PUERTO PLATA AVIATION LIGHT, 19 46.2N, 70 33.5W. Al Fl W G 10s, 10M.

PUERTO PLATA

19 48N, 70 42W
Port of Entry
Pilotage: A set of range lights stand at the head of the bay and when in line bearing 218°T lead through the entrance channel. The pilot boat may be contacted on VHF channel 16 (call sign HIW8). The pilot boat is black and flies a blue flag with a white P.
Dockage: The yacht dock is on the western side of the wharf to the east. Boats usually use a Mediterranean moor here to avoid damage from the surge.

Anchorage: There is some room to anchor near the yacht dock.
Services: Puerto Plata is the best place to restock along the north coast of the Dominican Republic. Fuel, water, and all groceries should be available. You may have to jug fuel. General repairs may be possible, but marine supplies are not available. There is a U.S. consular agent here (809-586-4204).

Puerto Plata is a popular stop for those trying to beat into the headwinds down the "Thorny Path" to the islands. The coastline is high (with elevations to 3,000 feet), and the water is deep close to shore. There are few official ports of entry on this coast, so you should plan your passage carefully. A good selection of charts is necessary to avoid the many reefs—it is wise to keep a good offing until sure of your position. The docking situation is rather rough and requires careful placement of anchors and heavy gear. Once you get the boat settled, you'll find an interesting city ashore, with further exploring possibilities inland.

NORTH COAST: PUERTO PLATA TO CABO ENGANO

CABO VIEJO FRANCES LIGHT, near edge of cliff, 19 40.5N, 69 54.6W. L Fl W 10s, 163ft, 18M. White pyramidal steel tower. Visible 132°–304°.
PORT SANCHEZ LIGHT, at end of pier, 19 13.6N, 69 36.6W. Fl R 6s, 30ft, 6M. White pyramidal tower. Reported removed 1992.
CABO SAMANA LIGHT, 19 18.5N, 69 08.6W. Fl W 5s, 463ft, 10M. White pyramidal skeleton tower, red lantern.
PUNTA BALANDRA LIGHT, on the bluff, 19 11.2N, 69 13.4W. Fl W 4s, 155ft, 10M. White tower, black lantern. Reported extinguished 1992.
CAYO VIGIA LIGHT, 19 11.7N, 69 19.6W. Fl R, 23ft, 8M. White pyramidal metal tower. Reported extinguished 1992.

SAMANA

19 12N, 69 20W
Charted Name: Santa Bárbara de Samaná.
Port of Entry: Tie up to the wharf and await the arrival of the officials. Approach carefully, as there are unconfirmed reports of depths less than 6 feet in the area.
Dockage: You may be able to tie up to the wharf for refueling, water, and loading supplies.

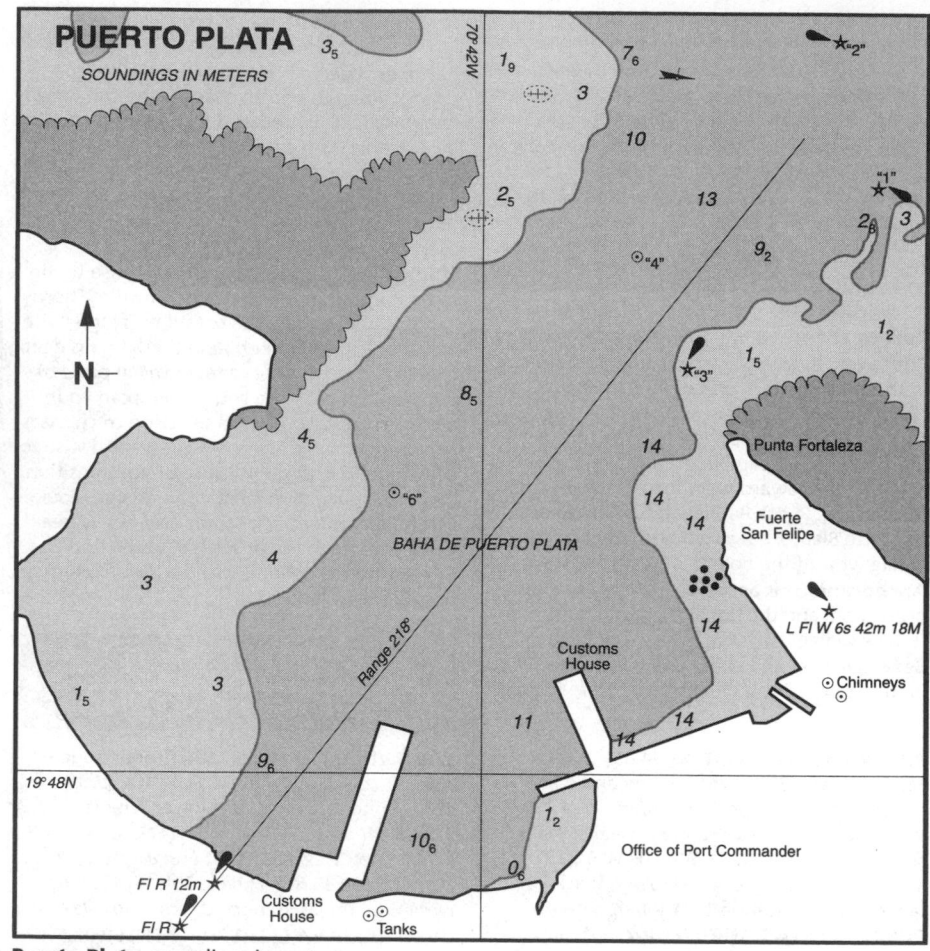

Puerto Plata, soundings in meters

Anchorage: There is reported to be good holding in depths of 12 to 25 feet. Stay clear of the channel to the main wharf.

Services: Fuel, water, ice, water, and groceries are available. A farmer's market offers fresh fruits and vegetables. There is a telephone station for placing calls. There is a ferry from Samaná to Sabana de la Mar.

This is a good spot to plan your passage across the notorious Mona Passage or to clear in to the Dominican Republic from Puerto Rico. The scenery is reported to be spectacular, and a trip outside of town is recommended. Los Haitises National Park, on the other side of the bay, is reported to be quite interesting.

PUNTA NISIBON LIGHT, 18 58.5N, 68 46.2W. Fl (2) W 10s, 50ft, 12M. White pyramidal tower, red lantern. Reported extinguished 1992.

CABO ENGANO LIGHT, E point of island, 18 36.8N, 68 19.5W. Fl W 5s, 141ft, 11M. Red and white steel tower.

SOUTH COAST: CABO ENGANO TO PUERTO DE ANDRES

PUNTA BARRACHANA LIGHT, 18 32.7N, 68 21.3W. Iso R 2s. Tower.

BOCA DE YUMA LIGHT, 18 23.1N, 68 35.5W. Fl R 11s, 30ft, 10M. Red pyramidal steel tower. Reported extinguished 1992.

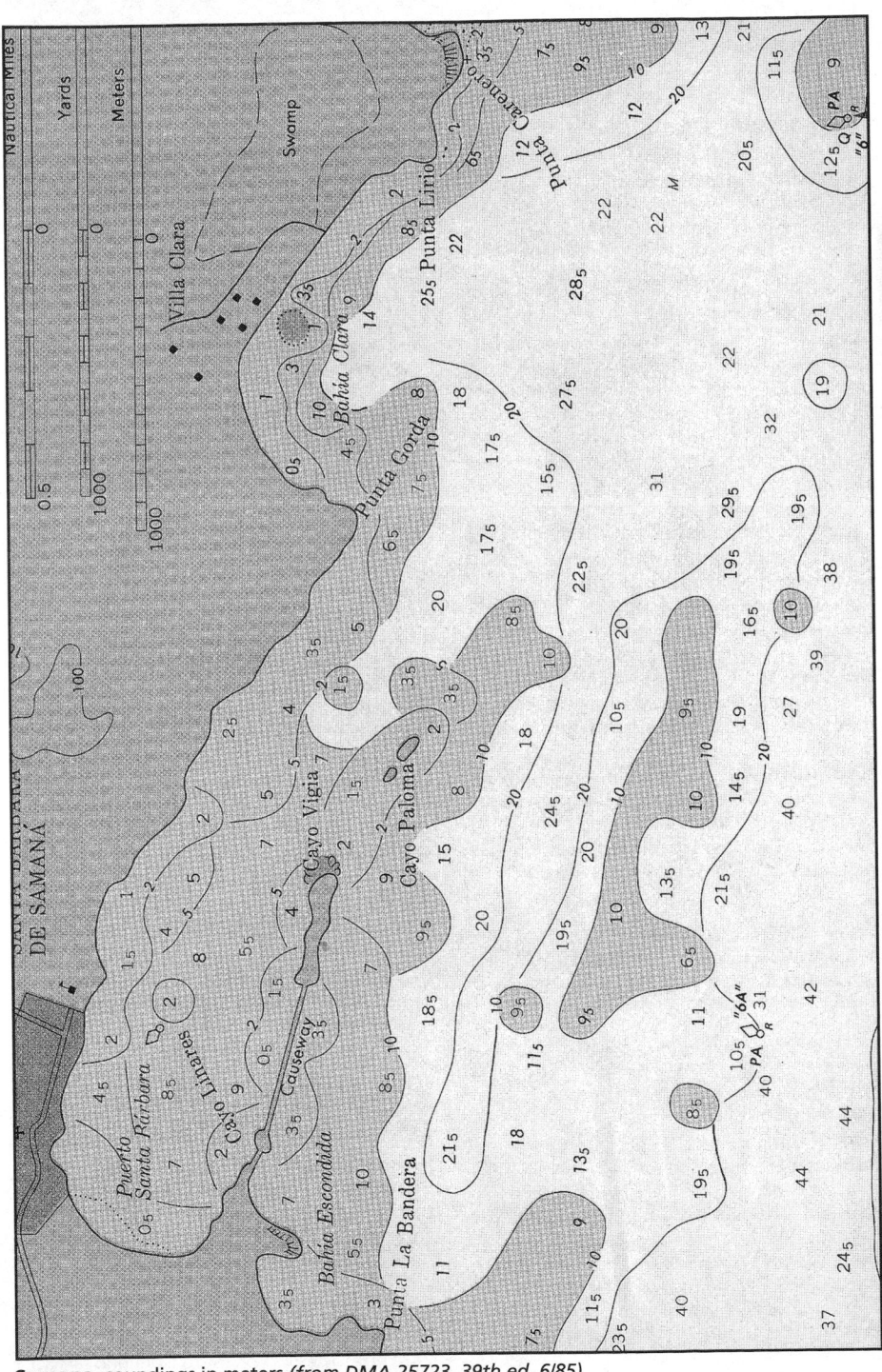

Samana, soundings in meters *(from DMA 25723, 39th ed, 6/85)*

ISLA SAONA LIGHT, E end on Punta Cana, 18 06.6N, 68 34.5W. Fl W 10s, 105ft, 16M. White concrete tower. Reported destroyed 1992.

PUNTA LAGUNA LIGHT, 18 08.3N, 68 44.8W. Fl W 4s, 45ft, 10M. White concrete tower.

LA ROMANA LIGHT, E point at entrance to river, 18 24.8N, 68 57.1W. Fl W 6s, 90ft, 15M. Yellow metal tower, red lantern.

LA ROMANA

18 25N, 68 57W

Pilotage: The sugar mill on the west side of the mouth of the Río Dulce is conspicuous day or night. Its lights have been reported to be visible at up to 20 miles, and the smokestacks will be visible during the day. A navigation light is shown on the east side of the entrance to the river. The first large wharf to the west is for the sugar plant. The next wharf north is the government dock. Pilot boats monitor VHF channel 16, call sign HIW 9.

Bridge Height: Reported as 28 feet.

Port of Entry: The government wharf is on the west side of the river before the bridge. Depths are reported as 5 to 6 feet alongside.

Dockage: There is a shipyard and a marina near the bridge on the eastern side of the river. There is a yacht club north of the bridge, on the eastern shore.

Anchorage: There is a possible anchorage in the small cove on the eastern side of the river about 200 yards inside the mouth.

Services: The shipyard can haul your boat and has a fuel dock. Most supplies are available.

SAN PEDRO DE MACORIS LIGHT, E point, 18 26.1N, 69 17.7W. L Fl W 10s, 49ft, 12M. White and red tower. Reported extinguished 1992.

SAN PEDRO DE MACORIS

18 27N, 69 19W
Port of Entry

Pilotage: Entry is recommended before 1100, as there is decreased swell in the channel entrance. The pilot boat monitors VHF radio, call sign HIW 19.

Dockage and Anchorage: This is primarily a commercial harbor, serving the needs of the sugar industry. Anchoring is possible, but no dockage is reported. Visiting yachtsmen may be better off visiting Club Nautico, in Boca Chica, about 17 miles to the west.

ISLA CATALINA LIGHT, Punta Berroa, 18 20.5N, 68 59.3W. L Fl W 8s, 40ft, 10M. Yellow and black concrete tower. Reported destroyed 1992.

PUERTO DE ANDRES

LA CALETA AVIATION LIGHT, 18 25.9N, 69 40.2W. Al Fl W G 5s, 14M. On aero radiobeacon tower. On request.

RANGE (Front Light), 18 26.1N, 69 38.0W. Fl R, 6M. Yellow metal tower. Reported extinguished 1992. **(Rear Light),** 118 meters 300° from front. Fl R, 6M. Yellow metal tower. Reported extinguished 1992.

BOCA CHICA

18 26N, 69 38W

Pilotage: Boca Chica is also called Andrés on charts. The harbor is about 18 miles east of Santo Domingo at the head of a small bay. The port consists of a basin 500 yards long and 200 yards wide with wharves on its northwest and northeast sides and protected on its south-west side by a reef that has been reinforced to form a breakwater. The village of Andrés has a sugar factory with a conspicuous chimney, marked by a red obstruction light, with the name BOCA CHICA painted prominently on it. Range lights located on the south side of the port lead to the entrance channel when in line bearing 300°T. Vessels may enter only during the day. The port is under the jurisdiction of the Commander of the Port, Santo Domingo.

Dockage: Club Nautico yacht club has dockage, repair facilities, and luxurious facilities.

Services: Haulouts, fuel, water, repairs, and most supplies available. Boca Chica is not a Port of Entry.

PUNTA TORRECILLA LIGHT, 18 27.8N, 69 52.6W. L Fl (2) W 10s, 135ft, 13M. White tower, black diagonal bands.

PUERTO DE SANTO DOMINGO

Approach Buoy, 18 27.0N, 69 53.0W. Fl R.
ENTRANCE RANGE (Front Light), E side of harbor, 18 28.3N, 69 52.6W. F R. White concrete tower. **(Rear Light),** 155 meters 047° from front. F R. White concrete tower.

SANTO DOMINGO

18 28N, 69 53W

Pilotage: The port of Santo Domingo lies at the mouth of the Río Ozama. West of the river

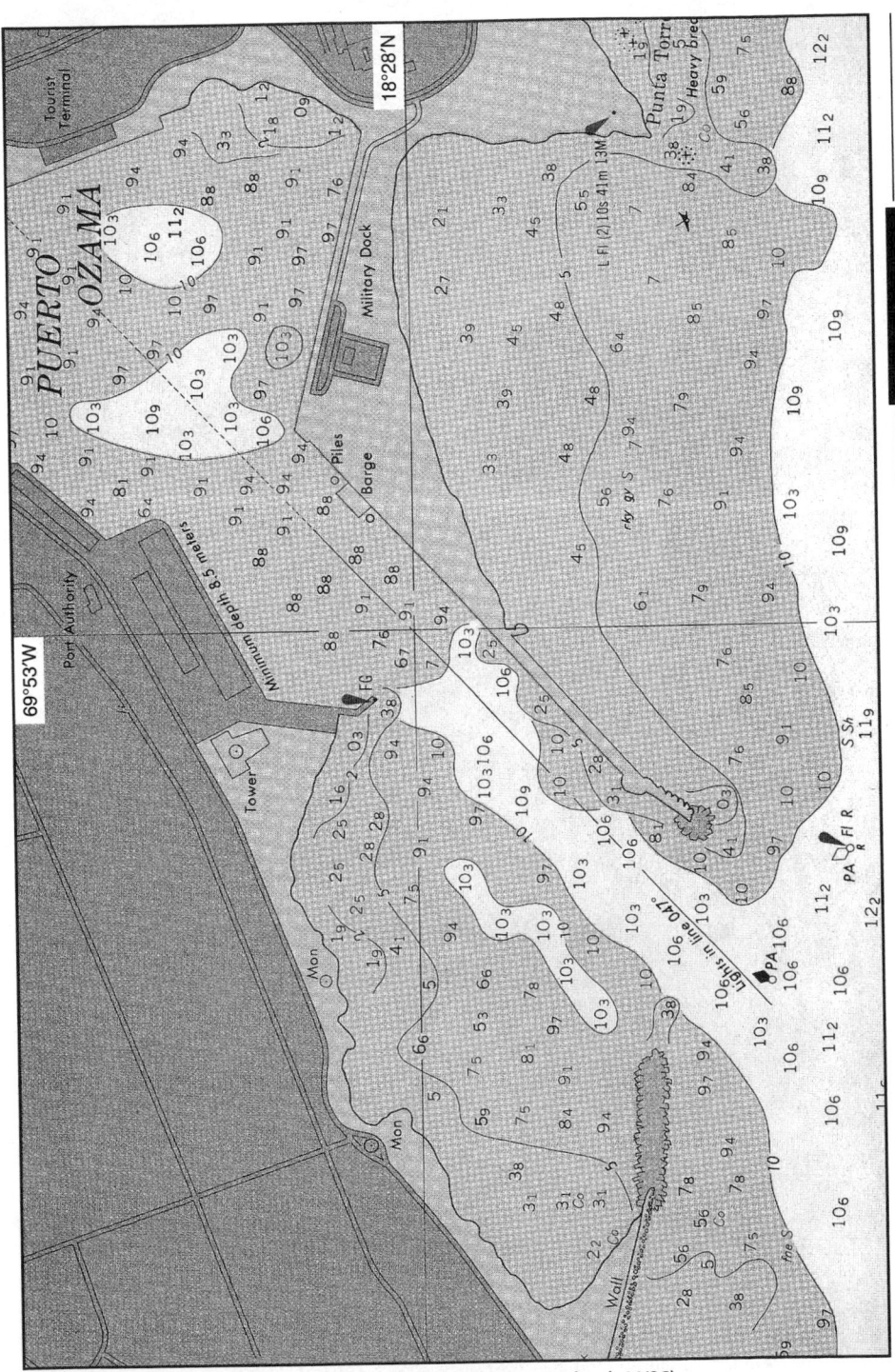

Santo Domingo, soundings in meters *(from DMA 25848, 24th ed, 11/86)*

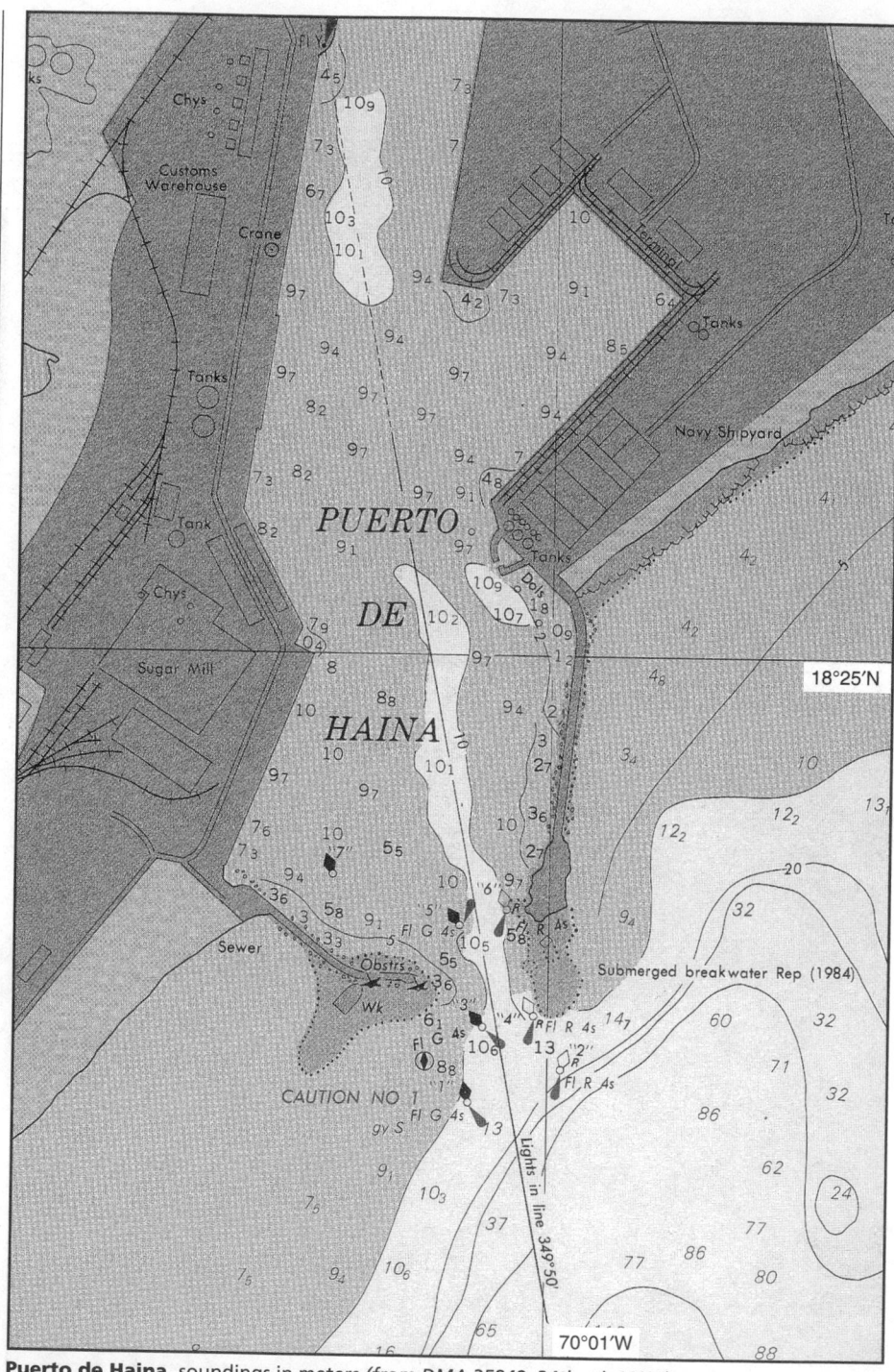

Puerto de Haina, soundings in meters *(from DMA 25848, 24th ed, 11/86)*

the coast is low and rocky, with foothills rising 4 or 5 miles inland. East of the river, a coastal plain extends for 15 or 20 miles. Strong onshore winds can cause a rise in sea level considerably above normal in the bay. Currents in the river average 1 1/2 knots; however, during the rainy season (May to September) the current is reported to reach rates of 4 1/2 knots. The port may be entered from 0600 to 2100. Harbor authorities may be reached on the VHF radio.

Port of Entry
Dockage and Anchorage: This is primarily a commercial harbor. Boaters may be better off at Boca Chica, which is 18 miles by highway to the east.

Santo Domingo is one of the oldest cities in the Caribbean and one of the largest, with a population of around 2 million. The son of Christopher Columbus, Don Diego, began building a palace and fort here in 1510, as well as the first church in the New World, which is the supposed final resting place of the Navigator himself.

PUERTO DE HAINA TO CABO ROJO

PUERTO DE HAINA ENTRANCE RANGE (Front Light), 18 25.4N, 70 01.2W. Fl Y. Yellow framework tower. Bearing is not reliable. Reported extinguished 1989. **(Rear Light),** 150 meters 349.8° from front. Fl Y. Yellow framework tower. Reported extinguished 1989.

PUERTO DE HAINA

18 25N, 70 01W
Pilotage: Two conspicuous chimneys, which show red lights, stand 450 yards north-northwest of the root of the west breakwater. The lights on the chimneys are visible for about 20 miles. There is an obstruction about 3/4 mile

southeast of the harbor entrance. The river currents increase to 2 1/2 knots during the rainy season (May to September). The pilot boat may be contacted on VHF channel 16 or on 2182kHz (call sign HIW20).

Port of Entry
Dockage and Anchorage: Haina is primarily a commercial harbor.

PUNTA PALENQUE LIGHT, 18 13.5N, 70 09.0W. Fl W 7s, 45ft, 12M. White pyramidal concrete tower, red lantern.
BOCA CANASTA LIGHT, 18 14.4N, 70 19.6W. F R, Fl R vertical, 22M.
PUNTA SALINAS LIGHT, Bahía de las Calderas, 18 12.3N, 70 31.8W. Fl W 3s, 98ft, 10M. Red pyramidal steel tower. Reported extinguished 1992.
PUERTO VIEJO DE AZUA LIGHT, 18 19.5N, 70 49.1W. L Fl (2) W 10s, 75ft, 15M. Black steel tower on concrete base. Reported destroyed 1992.
BARAHONA HARBOR RANGE (Front Light), 18 12.1N, 71 04.5W. F R, 6M. White pyramidal tower. Occasional. **(Rear Light),** 85 meters 243° from front. F R. White pyramidal tower. Occasional.
ISLA ALTO VELO, summit, 17 28.3N, 71 38.5W. Fl (2) W 10s, 535ft, 13M. Yellow truncated concrete tower, black triangular projections on each side. Reported extinguished.
PUNTA BEATA LIGHT, 17 36.1N, 71 25.2W. Fl W 9s, 80ft, 14M. Concrete tower. Extinguished.
LOS FRAILES LIGHT, 17 38.0N, 71 40.9W. Q R, 32ft, 5M. Reported removed 1992.
ANSE JOSEPH LIGHT, head of jetty, 17 55.2N, 71 39.0W. F R, 8M.
PEDERNALES LIGHT, 18 02.2N, 71 44.9W. L Fl W 12s, 40ft, 11M, White pyramidal steel tower, red lantern.
Cabo Rojo Entrance Buoy, 17 56.0N, 71 40.0W. Fl W 4s. Red buoy. Radar reflector.

PUERTO RICO

CAUTION: Our information on aids to navigation comes from official government sources. The latitudes and longitudes of these marks may not correspond to readings from GPS or LORAN receivers. Some aids have been reported as unreliable, missing, off position or showing incorrect characteristics. No single aid to navigation, or waypoint, should be relied upon as a sole means of fixing a position.

NOTE: The chartlets in this section are <u>not intended for navigation</u> and are included for reference and planning purposes only. While chartlets reproduced from government sources are from the most current editions as of press time, they incorporate <u>no corrections</u> to navigational aids, depths, or hazards since the edition publication date.

ENTRY PROCEDURES

The Commonwealth of Puerto Rico is voluntarily associated with the United States. Many of the laws, rules, and regulations, including clearing in, are similar to those in effect in the mainland U.S. U.S. vessels returning from foreign waters, including the U.S. Virgins, should purchase the annual $25 customs user's decal in advance of arrival in Puerto Rico, if possible (see the introduction to the Coast Pilot).

Ports of entry are Aguadilla (809-882-3556), Mayagüez (809-831-3342), Guánica (call Ponce office), Ponce (809-841-3130), Puerto de Jobos (call Ponce office), Humacao (call Fajardo office), Fajardo (809-863-0950), and San Juan (809-253-4533, -4534, -4537, or 4538). There are also customs inspectors on Vieques (809-741-8366) and on Culebra (809-742-3531).

Vessels arriving after 1700 hours, on Sunday, or on holidays must report to the San Juan station via telephone. All vessels arriving from the U.S. Virgin Islands must report to customs. Vessels traveling from Puerto Rico to the U.S. Virgin Islands need not clear customs.

The U.S. dollar is the official currency. The language spoken is Spanish. English is widely spoken as a second language.

WEST COAST

PUNTA BORINQUEN LIGHT, 18 29.8N, 67 08.9W. Fl (2) W 15s, 292ft, 24M. Gray cylindrical tower.

AGUADILLA

18 26N, 67 09W

Emergencies: Contact the U.S. Coast Guard (VHF channel 16 or 2182kHz). A Coast Guard air station is at Borinquen Airport, north of Aguadilla.

Pilotage: A 1,208-foot-high naval communication tower south of town is quite prominent. Large vessels load raw sugar and molasses at the pier 1.1 miles north of town, and an Air Force pier is 1.8 miles north of town. The bay is exposed to north and west winds and experiences a frequent surge.

Port of Entry: Call customs at 809-882-3556.

Dockage: None for pleasure craft.

Anchorage: Anchor off town, but be prepared for rough conditions in north winds.

Services: There are no yacht facilities. General supplies are available ashore.

PUNTA HIGUERO LIGHT, 18 21.7N, 67 16.2W. Oc W 4s, 90ft, 9M. Gray cylindrical tower.

RINCON SEWER EXTENSION LIGHT, on seaward side of sewer outfall, 18 20.1N, 67 15.4W. Q R, 12ft. On pile. Private aid.

BAHÍA DE MAYAGÜEZ

Manchas Exteriores Buoy 1, 18 14.6N, 67 12.7W. Green can.

Entrance Lighted Buoy 3, Fl G 4s, 4M. Green.

Entrance Lighted Buoy 4, Fl R 4s, 4M. Red.

RANGE (Front Light), 18 13.3N, 67 09.8W. Q G, 54 ft. KRW on tower on roof of warehouse. Visible 4° each side of rangeline. **(Rear Light),** 310 yards, 092° from front light. Oc G 4s, 87ft.

COAST PILOT

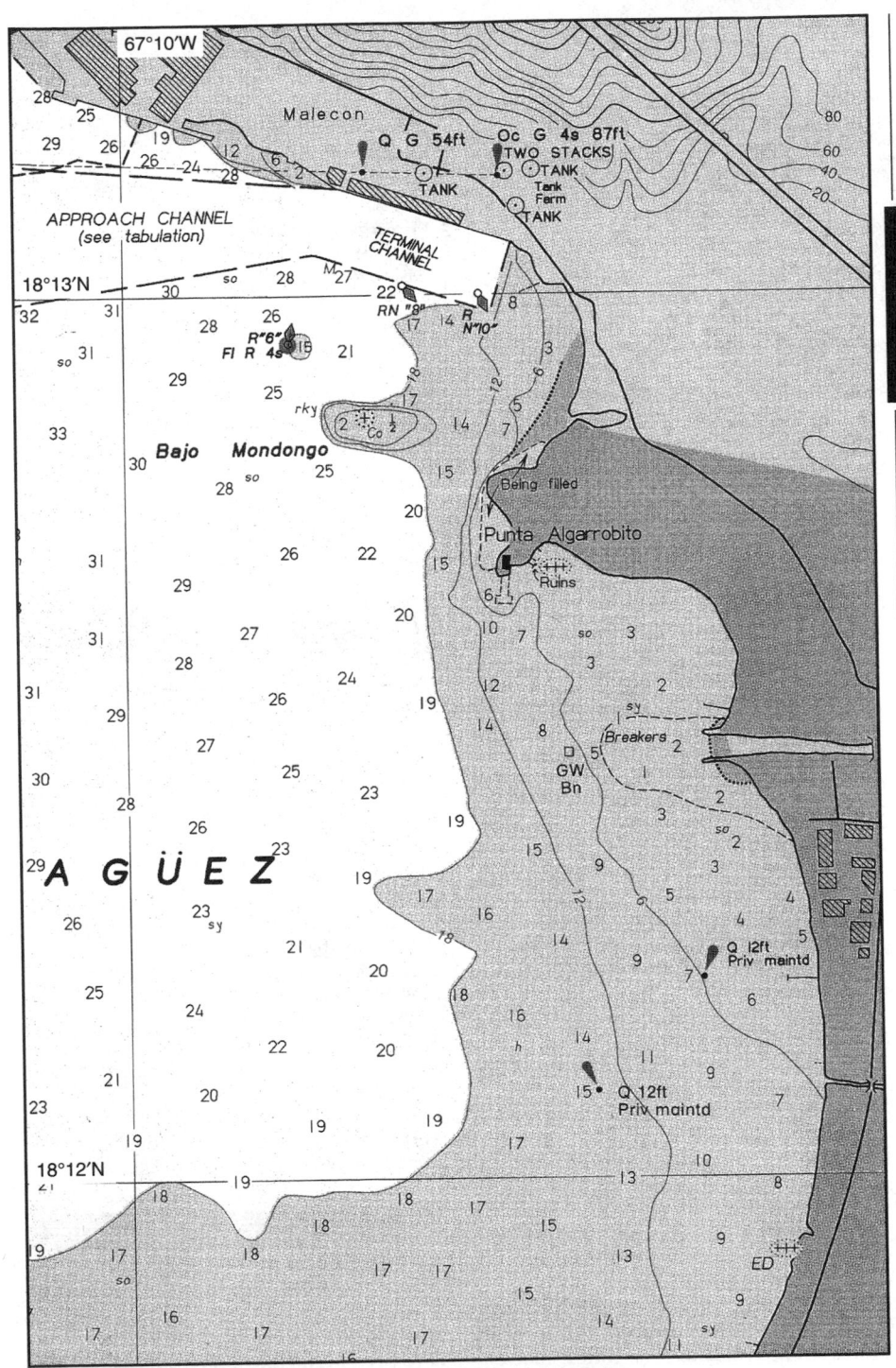

Mayagüez, soundings in feet *(from NOAA 25673, 14th ed, 10/90)*

KRW on tower on building. Visible 4° each side of rangeline.

Lighted Buoy 5, Fl G 4s, 4M. Green.

NORTH BREASTING DOLPHIN ONE OBSTRUCTION LIGHT, FL W 2.5s, 13M. On dolphin. Private aid.

SOUTH BREASTING DOLPHIN SIX OBSTRUCTION LIGHT, Fl W 2.5s, 13M. On dolphin. Private aid.

Lighted Buoy 6, Fl R 4s, 3M. Red.

Buoy 8, Red nun.

Buoy 10, marks southeast end of 18-foot spot. Red nun.

Mayagüez Harbor Daybeacon, 18 12.6N, 67 09.5W. NG on tower on house.

NORTH SEWER EXTENSION LIGHT, marks edge of sewer outfall. QW, 12 ft. On pile. Private aid.

SOUTH SEWER EXTENSION LIGHT, marks end of sewer outfall, 18 12.2N, 67 09.4W. Q W, 12M. On pile. Private aid.

MAYAGÜEZ

18 12N, 67 09W

Emergencies: Contact the U.S. Coast Guard (VHF channel 16 or 2182kHz).

Pilotage: At Punta Guanajibo, 2 miles south of Mayagüez, is a 165-foot-high, flat-topped ridge with a prominent reform school on top. Cerro Anterior is a 433-foot-high saddle-shaped hill 1.5 miles inshore of the city. The city hall clock tower and a church are conspicuous above the other buildings. Several red and white radio towers are visible along the south shore of the bay.

Port of Entry: Call 809-831-3342. Boats should tie to the commercial wharf north of town to clear customs and immigration.

Dockage: None for pleasure craft in town. Club Deportivo marina (809-851-8880), about 6.5 miles south of the city, is for members only.

Anchorage: Pleasure boats anchor south of the charted private lights off of town.

Services: There are no pleasure-boat facilities in Mayagüez. The large city has all general supplies, good transportation, banking, and communications.

Mayagüez is primarily a commercial port, but makes a convenient first port of call for boats arriving from the west. The city is one of Puerto Rico's major ports and commercial centers.

CANAL DE GUANAJIBO

Punta Arenas Buoy 6, at northwest edge of shoal point. Red nun.

Punta Ostiones Buoy 4, at southwest edge of shoal spot off point. Red nun.

Punta Melones Shoal Buoy 1, Green can.

PUERTO REAL

18 04N, 67 12W

Emergencies: Contact the U.S. Coast Guard (VHF channel 16 or 2182kHz).

Pilotage: The harbor is located about 2 miles north of the Bahía de Boquerón. It is a circular basin 0.7 miles in diameter used by local fishing vessels and small pleasure craft. Depths in the basin are 6 to 15 feet with shoal water toward the eastern end. The town of Puerto Real is on the north shore of the basin.

Dockage: There are a couple of small marinas with dockage and most services.

Anchorage: This is a well-protected spot.

Services: Water, fuel, some marine supplies, and groceries are available. There are haulout facilities for fishing boats that pleasure boats may be able to use. Take a *publico* (small bus) to Cabo Rojo for more extensive shopping.

BAHÍA DE BOQUERÓN

Bajo Enmedio South Lighted Buoy 1, at south end of shoal, 18 00.8N, 67 12.5W. Fl G 4s, 3M. Green.

BOQUERÓN

18 01N, 67 11W

Emergencies: Contact the U.S. Coast Guard (VHF channel 16 or 2182kHz).

Pilotage: For boats coming from the west the primary obstruction is Bajo Enmedio, stretching for about a mile across the entrance to the bay. It is marked by a buoy at its south end.

Dockage: The Club Nautico de Boquerón (809-851-1336) may have some space at the docks near the north end of the waterfront.

Anchorage: Anchor south of the club docks. Hurricane protection among the mangroves is available in the Cano Boquerón a mile south. Depths of 10 feet are reported in the channel.

Services: Fuel, water, general supplies, and some marine supplies are available.

MONA PASSAGE

ISLA DE MONA LIGHT, 18 16.6N, 67 54.5W. Fl W 5s, 323ft, 14M. On steel tower. Light may be obscured by land masses when viewed from approximate bearings 140° and 270°.

Arrecife Tourmaline Lighted Buoy 8, 18 09.7N, 67 20.7W. Fl R 6s, 4M. Red.

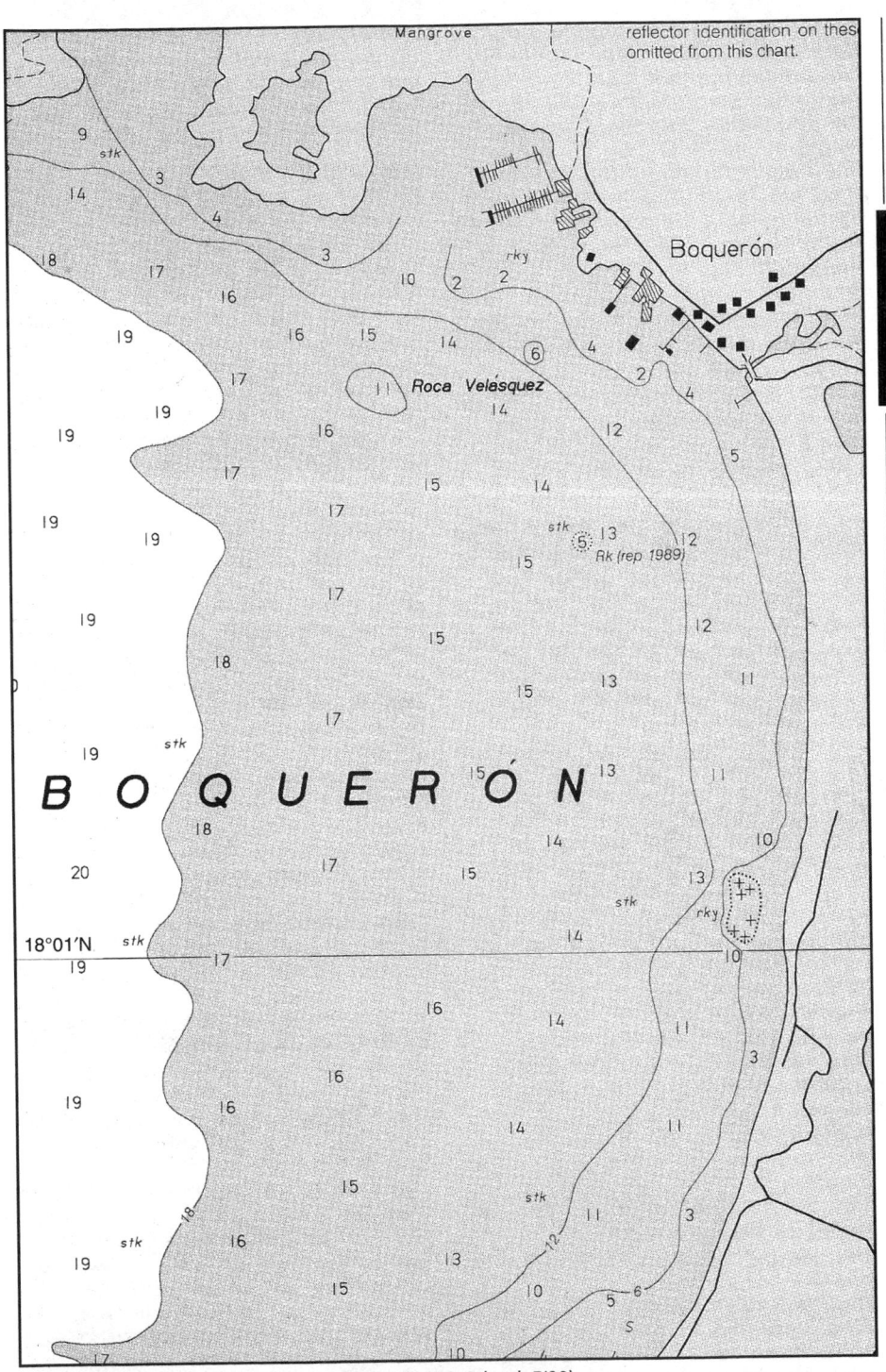

Boquerón, soundings in feet *(from NOAA 25675, 8th ed, 5/90)*

Canal de la Mona East Shoal Lighted Buoy 6, 18 05.3N, 67 25.4W. Fl R 6s, 4M. Red.
Canal de la Mona East Shoal Lighted Buoy 4, 18 00.4N, 67 23.0W. Fl R 6s, 4M. Red.
Canal de la Mona East Shoal Lighted Buoy 2, Fl R 6s, 4M. Red.
CABO ROJO LIGHT, 17 56.0N, 67 11.6W. Fl W 20s, 121ft, 20M. Gray hexagonal tower attached to flat-roofed dwelling. Emergency light when main light is extinguished shows Fl W 6s, 9M.

ISLA MAGUEYES

Buoy 1, Black can. Private aid.
Buoy 2, Red nun. Private aid.
Buoy 4, Red nun. Private aid.
Buoy 6, Red nun. Private aid.
Buoy 7, Black can. Private aid.

BAHÍA DE GUÁNICA

Entrance Lighted Buoy 2, 17 55.2N, 66 54.6W. Fl R 4s, 4M. Red.
Buoy 3, Green can.
GUÁNICA LIGHT, 17 57.1N, 66 54.3W. Fl W 6s, 132ft, 7M. White skeleton tower. Obscured by Punta Brea to seacoast traffic westward to 044°.
Lighted Buoy 4, on west end of shoal, 17 56.2N, 66 54.4W. Fl R 4s, 3M. Red.
Buoy 5, marks 27-foot shoal. Green can.
RANGE (Front Light), 17 57.9N, 66 54.6W. Q R, 27ft, 4M. KRW on skeleton tower. Visible 4° each side of rangeline. **(Rear Light),** 560 yards, 354.5° from front light. Iso R 6s, 48ft, 5M. KRW on skeleton tower. Visible 4° each side of rangeline.
Lighted Buoy 6, Fl R 6s, 3M. Red.
Buoy 7, Green can.
Buoy 8, Red nun.
Buoy 9, 17 57.6N, 66 54.6W. Green can.
Buoy 10, At south end of shoal. Red nun.
Buoy 11, Green can.
Buoy 12, Red nun.
SUGAR PIER LIGHTS (2), 17 57.9N, 66 55.5W. F R, 16ft. On pier. Private aids.

GUÁNICA

17 58N, 66 56W
Emergencies: Contact the U.S. Coast Guard (VHF channel 16 or 2182kHz).
Pilotage: A range of 354° 30″ leads up the main dredged channel to the town.
Port of Entry: Call customs in Ponce (809-841-3130). The port captain is near Playa de Guánica.

Anchorage: Anchor outside the dredged ship channels in well-protected waters. Depths become quite shallow in the north end of the bay off Playa de Guánica.
Services: General supplies available ashore.

BAHÍA DE GUAYANILLA

CAYO MARIA LANGA LIGHT, 17 58.0N, 66 45.2W. Fl W 2.5s, 42ft, 8M. NR on skeleton tower.
ENTRANCE RANGE (Front Light), 17 58.6N, 66 45.8W. Q Y, 16ft. KRW on dolphin. Visible all around. Higher intensity on rangeline. **(Rear Light),** 1,000 yards, 358° from front light. Iso Y 6s, 36ft. KRW on tower on piles. Visible 15° each side of rangeline.
Lighted Buoy 1, Fl G 2.5s, 3M. Green.
Lighted Buoy 2, 17 58.0N, 66 45.8W. Fl R 4s, 3M. Green.
Lighted Buoy 3, Fl G 4s, 4M. Green.
PUNTA GOTAY SOUTH MOORING DOLPHIN LIGHT, 17 58.8N, 66 45.8W. F R, 15ft. On square concrete deck. Private aid.
PUNTA GOTAY NORTH MOORING DOLPHIN LIGHT, 17 58.9N, 66 45.8W. F R, 15ft. On square concrete deck. Private aid.
Lighted Buoy 5, Fl G 6s, 4M. Green.
Lighted Buoy 6, marks end of shoal, Fl R 4s, 4M. Red.
Buoy 7, Green can.
Buoy 8, marks end of shoal. Red nun.
Buoy 9, Green can.
COMMONWEALTH OIL REFINING COMPANY SOUTH LOADING DOCK LIGHT, 17 59.6N, 66 46.0W. F R, 12ft. Private aid.
COMMONWEALTH OIL REFINING COMPANY NORTH LOADING DOCK LIGHTS (3), 17 59.8N, 66 45.9W. F R, 19ft. On pile. Private aids.

PPG INDUSTRIES

RANGE (Front Light), 18 00.3N, 66 46.0W. Q W, 20ft. Visible 4° each side of rangeline. Private aid. **(Rear Light),** 158 yards, 014° from front light. Oc W 4s, 40ft. Visible 2° each side of rangeline. Private aid.
Lighted Buoy 1, 17 57.8N, 66 46.2W. Fl G 2.5s, Black. Private aid.
Lighted Buoy 2, Fl R 2.5s. Red. Private aid.
Lighted Buoy 3, Fl G 2.5s. Black. Private aid.
Lighted Buoy 4, Fl R 2.5s. Red. Private aid.
PIER LIGHT, F R, 13ft. On dolphin. Private aid.
TEXACO WEST MOORING DOLPHIN ONE LIGHT, 18 00.0N, 66 45.9W. Fl R 6s, 15ft. On dolphin. Private aid.

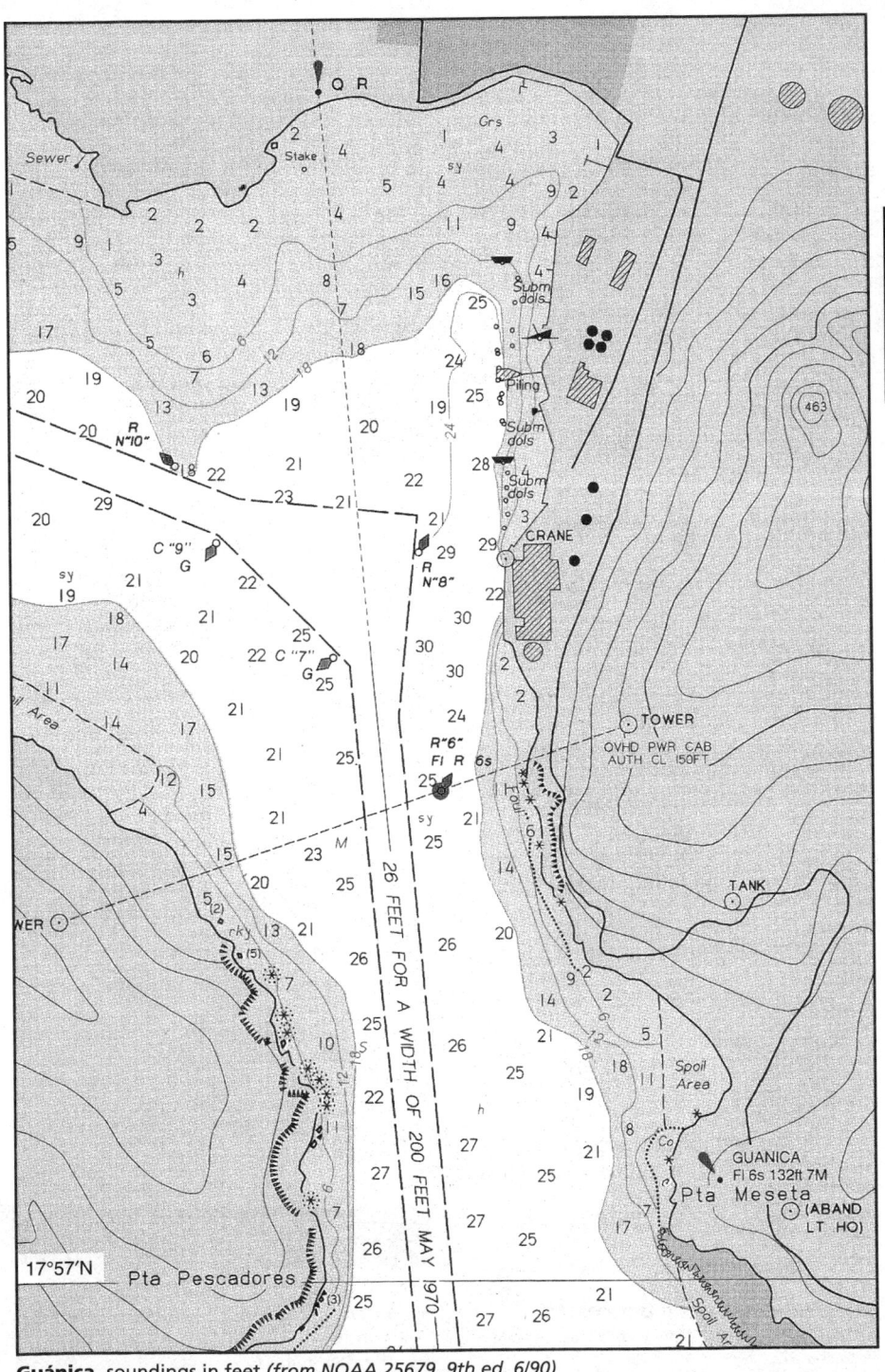

Guánica, soundings in feet *(from NOAA 25679, 9th ed, 6/90)*

TEXACO LOADING DOCK LIGHT, F R, 30ft. On pile. Private aid.
TEXACO EAST MOORING DOLPHIN FOUR LIGHT, 18 00.0N, 66 45.8W. Fl R 6s, 15ft. On dolphin. Private aid.

BAHÍA DE TALLABOA

Lighted Buoy 1, 17 57.7N, 66 44.3W. Fl G 4s, 4M. Green.
Buoy 2, Red nun.
Lighted Buoy 4, Fl R 4s, 3M. Red.
Lighted Buoy 5, 17 58.2N, 66 44.3W. Fl G 2.5s, 4M. Green.
Lighted Buoy 6, Q R, 2M. Red.
LIGHT 7A, 17 58.8N, 66 44.2W. Fl G 2.5s, 15ft. SG on pile. Private aid.
Buoy 7, Green can.
LOADING PLATFORM LIGHTS (4), 17 59.0N, 66 44.5W. F W. Platform. Private aids.
Buoy 8, 17 58.7N, 66 43.7W. Red nun. Private aid.
Lighted Buoy 10, 17 59.0N, 66 43.8W. Fl R 2.5s. Red. Private aid.
PIER LIGHT, 17 59.2N, 66 43.9W. F R, 20ft. On pier. Private aid.
Buoy 12, 17 59.3N, 66 43.8W. Red nun. Private aid.

BAHÍA DE PONCE AND APPROACHES

ISLA DE CARDONA LIGHT, 17 57.4N, 66 38.1W. Fl W 4s, 46ft, 8M. White cylindrical tower on center of front of flat-roofed dwelling.
Lighted Buoy 1, Fl G 4s, 4M. Green.
RANGE (Front Light), 17 58.8N, 66 37.2W. Q G, 49ft. KRW on pyramidal skeleton tower. Visible 15° each side of rangeline. **(Rear Light),** 305 yards, 015° from front light. Iso G 6s, 75ft. KRW on roof of building. Visible 4° each side of rangeline.
Lighted Buoy 3, Fl G 4s, 3M. Green.
Lighted Buoy 4, on SW side of shoal. Fl R 2.5s, 3M. Red.
MUELLE MUNICIPAL PIER LIGHTS (2), 17 58.0N, 66 37.3W. F W, 10ft. On pier. Private aids.
PONCE HARBOR PIER 4 OBSTRUCTION LIGHT, 17 58.1N, 66 37.3W. F W, 5ft. Square white case. Light not visible 360°; may be obscured by vessels moored at pier. Private aid.
TRAILER WHARF OBSTRUCTION LIGHT, 17 58.4N, 66 37.1W. F W, 10 ft. On steel pile. Private aid.

Lighted Buoy 5, Fl G 4s, 4M. Green.
SEWER EXTENSION LIGHT, marks end of sewer outfall, 17 58.9N, 66 37.8W. F W, 12ft. White rectangular framework on piles. Private aid.
ISLA CAJA DE MUERTOS LIGHT, 17 53.6N, 66 31.3W. Fl W 30s, 297ft, 12M. Gray cylindrical tower on center of flat-roofed dwelling.
RÍO BUCANA EAST JETTY LIGHT, 17 58.0N, 66 36.0W. Fl W 5s, 19ft. On tripod. Private aid.
RÍO BUCANA JETTY LIGHT, 17 58.1N, 66 36.0W. Fl W 5s, 19ft. On tripod. Private aid.

PONCE

17 59N, 66 37W
Emergencies: Contact the U.S. Coast Guard (VHF channel 16 or 2182kHz).
Pilotage: Prominent from offshore are the cement facotry stacks west of Ponce, the large microwave tower in Ponce, and the hotel on the hill back of Ponce. The charted radio towers can be seen from well offshore. The eastern entrance channel marked by a lighted range running 015°T leads to the waterfront.
Port of Entry: Call customs at 809-841-3120; tie up at the yacht club on Isla de Gata.
Dockage: The Ponce Yacht and Fishing Club located on Isla de Gata (VHF channel 16 or 809-842-9003) has all facilities. Anchored boats can use the club for a small fee.
Anchorage: A designated anchorage is shown on the chart. Many cruisers anchor off the club, so they can use its facilities (fee).
Services: All facilities are available. Haulouts up to 50 tons can be handled, and repairs are readily available. Fuel, water, and ice are available at the yacht club, and good grocery stores are in town. There is good transportation to any point on the island.

Ponce is the second largest city in Puerto Rico and one of its most important ports. There are art museums, historic buildings, shops and restaurants, and excellent transportation facilities. You may want to leave your boat here while visiting San Juan or use this as a crew transfer point. Here is your best bet for marine supplies and repairs on the south coast.

BAHÍA DE JOBOS AND APPROACHES

CAYOS DE RATONES LIGHT, 17 56.0N, 66 17.0W. Fl W 2.5s, 48 ft, 5M. NR on triangular skeleton tower.
Buoy 2, Red nun.

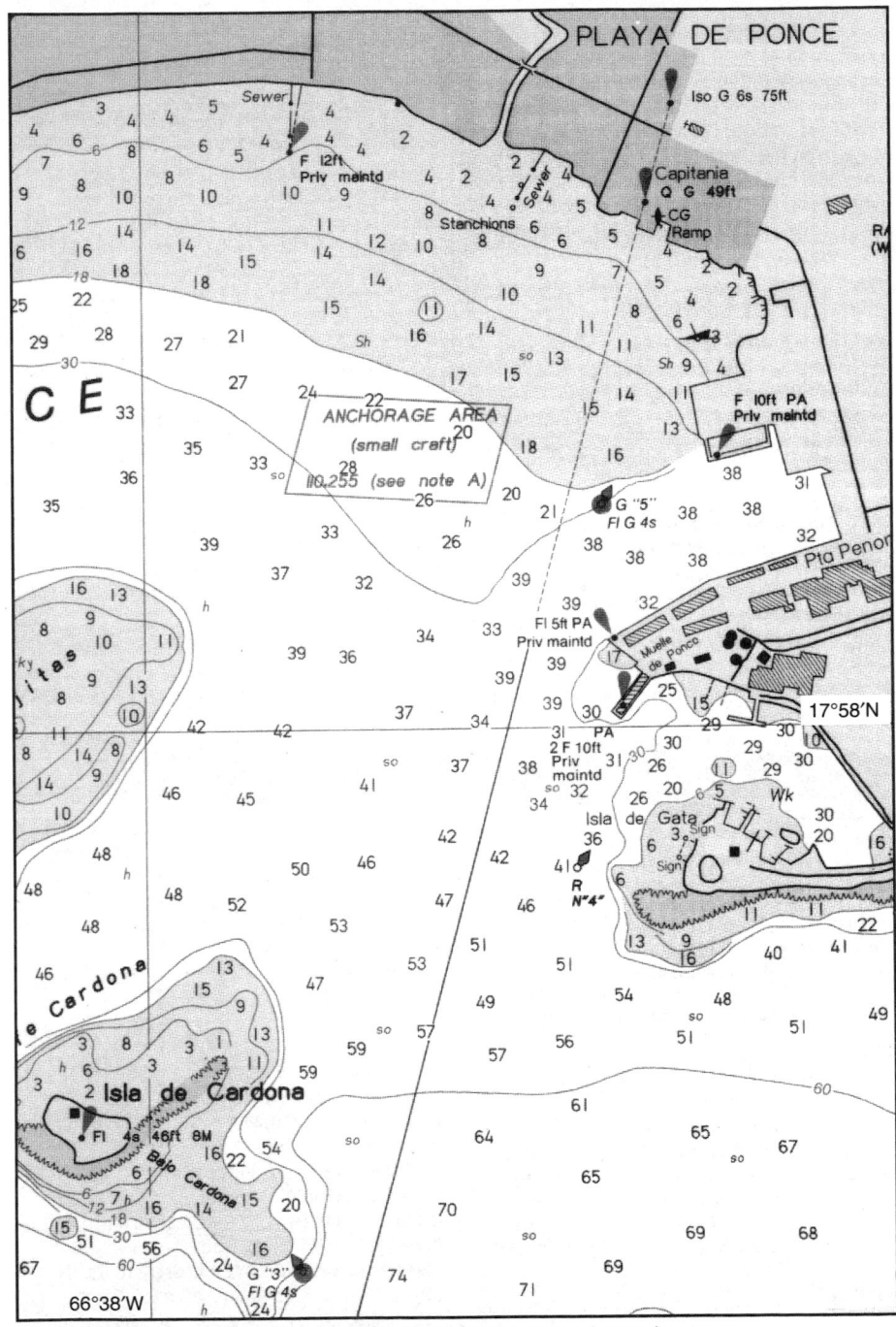

Playa de Ponce, soundings in feet *(from NOAA 25683, 14th ed, 12/91)*

SALINAS

17 58N, 66 18W

Emergencies: Contact the U.S. Coast Guard (VHF channel 16 or 2182kHz).

Pilotage: Enter the small bay east of Cayo Mata from the south.

Dockage: The Marina de Salinas (809-824-3185) may be able to offer some space.

Anchorage: Good protection and good holding are reported. Anchor anywhere off Playa de Salinas and dinghy in to the marina.

Services: Fuel, water, ice, canvas work, and general supplies are available. Take the *publico* (local bus) to the town of Salinas a mile away or to Ponce for major shopping.

This is a favorite anchorage on the south coast. Cruisers stop here for rest, repairs, and protection from the weather.

Cayo Puerca Buoy 3, Green can.
Punta Colchones Cut Buoy 5, Green can.
Punta Colchones Cut Buoy 6, Red nun.
DISCHARGE PIPE EAST OBSTRUCTION LIGHT, on rock mound, 17 56.0N, 66 13.7W. Q R, 12ft. On piles. Private aid.
DISCHARGE PIPE WEST OBSTRUCTION LIGHT, on rock mound. Q R, 12ft. On piles. Private aid.

AGUIRRE POWER PLANT

Lighted Buoy 1, 17 56.6N, 66 13.5W. Q G, Black. Private aid.
Lighted Buoy 2, Q R. Red. Private aid.
Lighted Buoy 3, Fl G 4s. Black. Private aid.
Lighted Buoy 4, Fl R 4s. Red. Private aid.
Lighted Buoy 5, Fl G 4s. Black. Private aid.
Lighted Buoy 6, Fl R 4s. Red. Private aid.

PUERTO DE JOBOS

17 57N, 66 12W

Emergencies: Contact the U.S. Coast Guard (VHF channel 16 or 2182kHz).

Pilotage: The main buoyed entrance leads to the commercial wharves at Central Aguirre. The stacks of the sugar plant show up well from offshore. The southern channel through the reefs is known as Boca del Inferno. There is 11 feet of water over the bar, which breaks in heavy weather.

Port of Entry: Call customs in Ponce (809-841-3130).

Dockage: There may be some dockage at a small yacht club in the indentation about 0.7 miles east of Punta Rodeo.

Anchorage: Good throughout the bay. Avoid the commercial area of Central Aguirre.

LAS MAREAS TO PUNTA TUNA

Lighted Buoy LM, 17 54.1N, 66 10.6W. Mo (A) W. Red and white stripes with red spherical topmark. Private aid.
RANGE (Front Light), 17 56.4N, 66 09.4W. Q W, 86ft. KRW on tower. Visible on rangeline only. Private aid. **(Rear Light),** 635 yards, 017.7° from front light. Iso W 6s, 124ft. KRW on tower. Visible on rangeline only. Private aid.
Lighted Buoy 1, 17 55.6N, 66 09.9W. Fl G 4s, Black. Private aid.
Lighted Buoy 2, Fl R 2.5s, Red, Private aid.
LIGHT 3, Fl G 4s, 25ft. SG on pile. Private aid.
LIGHT 4, Fl R 2.5s, 50ft. TR on tower. Private aid.
ARTICULATED LIGHT 5, Q G. On mast. Private aid.
LIGHT 6, Q R, 25ft. TR on pile. Private aid.
PIER LIGHTS (3), F R, 10ft. On dolphin. Private aids.
PUNTA TUNA LIGHT, 17 59.4N, 65 53.1W. Fl (2) W 30s, 111ft, 16M. White octagonal tower on square flat-roofed dwelling.

PUERTO YABUCOA

CHANNEL RANGE (Front Light), 18 03.4N, 65 50.2W. Q W, 75ft. KRW on tower. Visible 1° each side of rangeline. Private aid. **(Rear Light),** 910 yards, 296.8° from front light. Iso W 6s, 140ft. KRW on tower. Visible 1° each side of rangeline. Private aid.
Channel Lighted Buoy 2, 18 02.7N, 65 48.6W. Fl R 4s. Red. Private aid.
Channel Lighted Buoy 3, Q G. Black. Private aid.
CHANNEL LIGHT 5, Fl G 4s, 15ft. SG on dolphin. Radar reflector. Private aid.
CHANNEL LIGHT 6, Fl R 4s, 15ft. TR on dolphin. Radar reflector. Private aid.
CHANNEL LIGHT 7, Fl G 4s, 15ft. SG on pile. Radar reflector. Private aid.
CHANNEL LIGHT 8, Fl R 4s, 15ft. TR on pile. Radar reflector. Private aid.
CHANNEL BREAKWATER LIGHT, 18 03.3N, 65 49.7W. F R, 51ft. Radar reflector. Private aid.
CHANNEL LIGHT 9, Fl G 4s, 15ft. SG on pile. Radar reflector. Private aid.
CHANNEL LIGHT 10, Fl R 4s, 15ft. TR on pile. Radar reflector. Private aid.

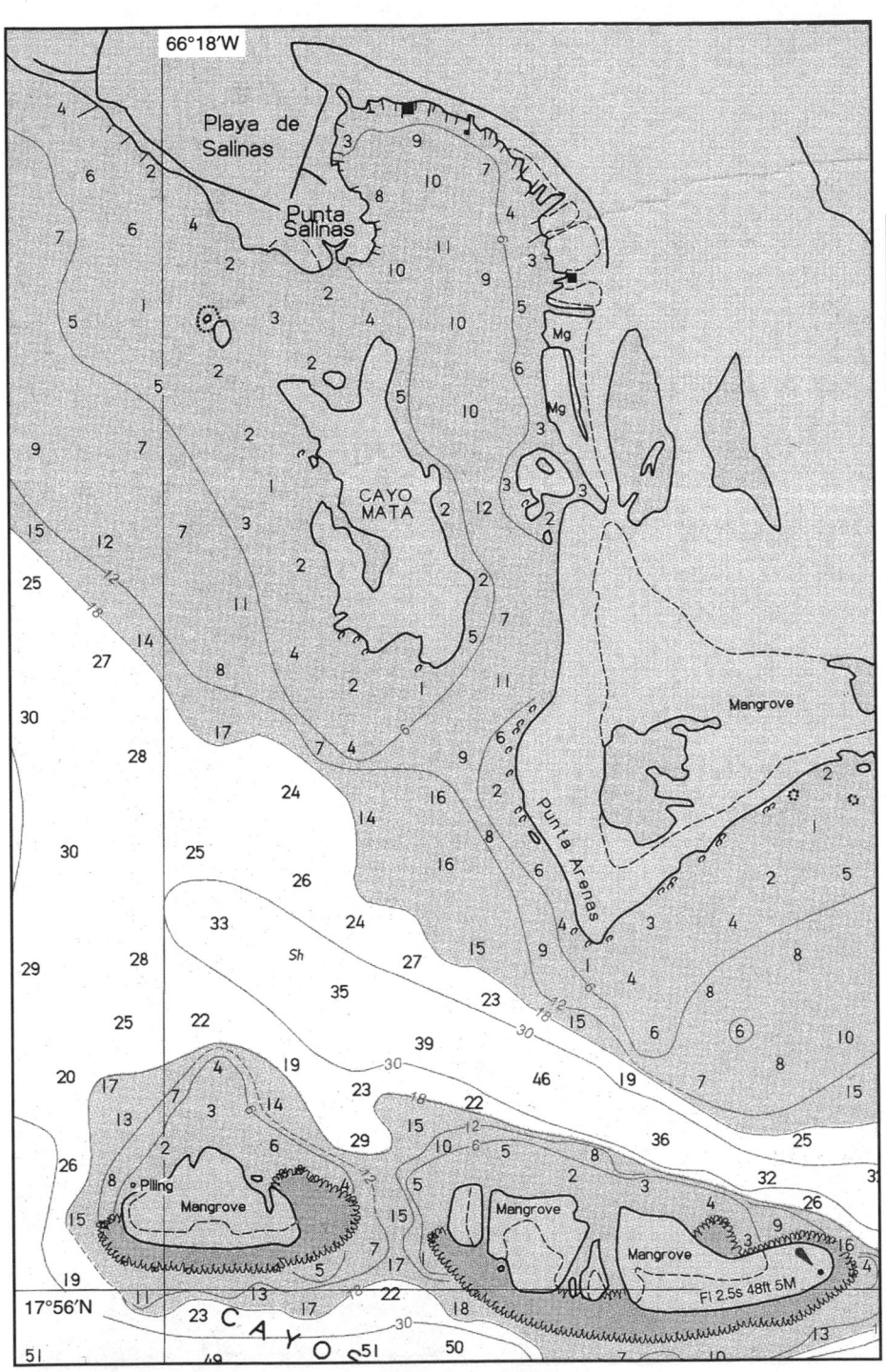

Salinas, soundings in feet *(from NOAA 25687, 11th ed, 1/91)*

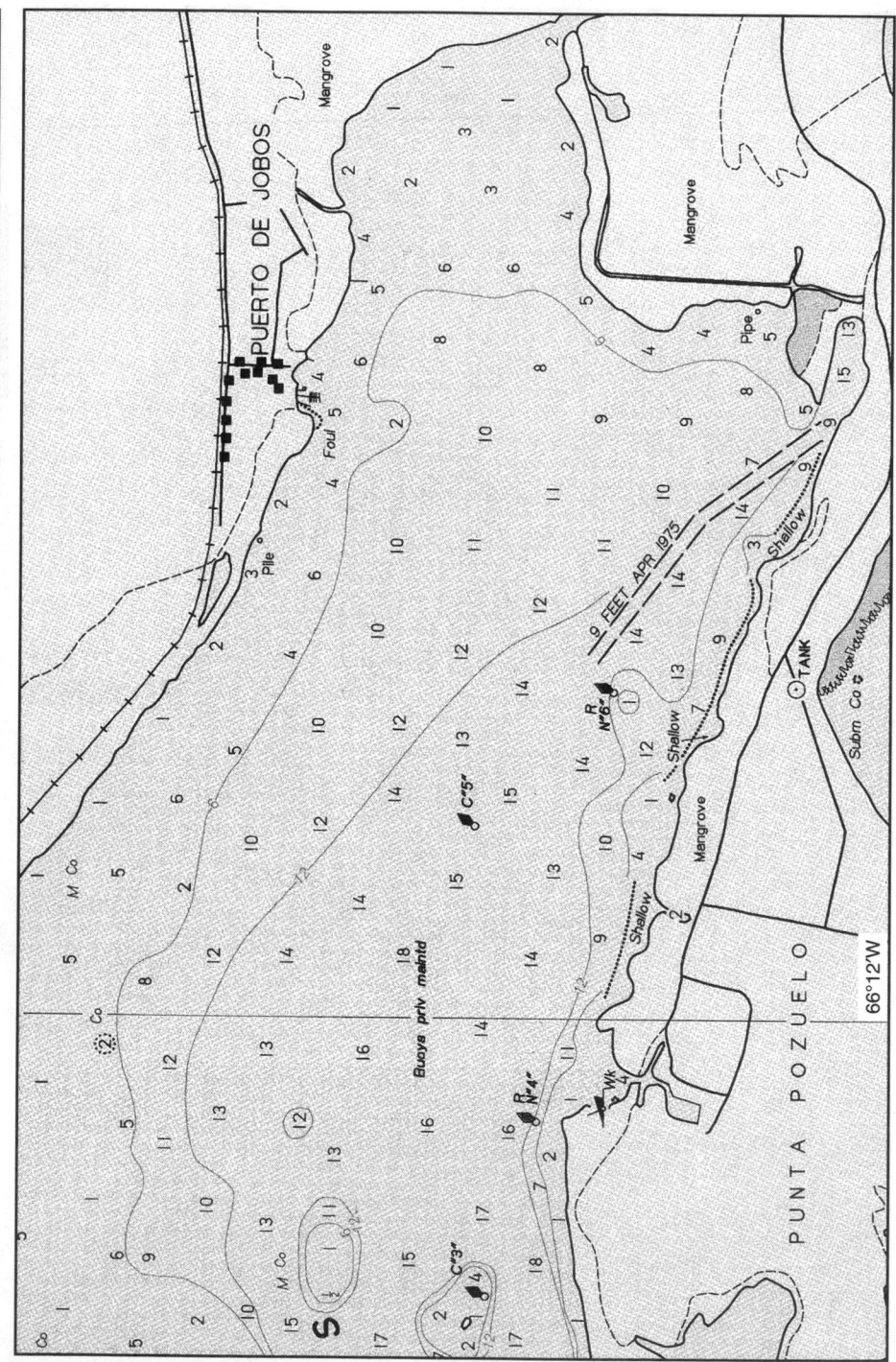

Puerto de Jobos, soundings in feet *(from NOAA 25687, 11th ed, 1/91)*

PALMAS DEL MAR

LIGHT 1, Fl G 6s, 12ft. SG on pile. Private aid.
LIGHT 2, Q W, 16ft. TR on pile. R 203.5°–295. Private aid.
LIGHT 3, Q G, 6ft. SG on pile. Private aid.
LIGHT 4, Q W, 6ft. TR on pile. Private aid.

PALMAS DEL MAR

18 05N, 65 48W
Emergencies: Contact the U.S. Coast Guard (VHF channel 16 or 2182kHz).
Pilotage: The harbor entrance is marked by private lights. The marina is on the south side of the harbor. It is reported that strong easterly winds cause breaking seas in the harbor entrance and surge inside the harbor.
Dockage: Available at the marina (VHF channel 16) with all facilities.
Anchorage: Anchor in the small basin north of the marina.
Services: All services are available, including haulouts.

This artificial harbor is formed by a group of luxurious resorts clustered around a small dredged basin.

RADAS ROOSEVELT PASSAGE

Lighted Buoy 9, Fl G 4s, 4M. Green.
Lighted Buoy 8, Fl R 4s, 3M. Red.
Lighted Buoy 7, Fl G 4s, 3M. Green.
Lighted Buoy 6, Fl R 2.5s, 2M. Red.
Lighted Buoy 5, Fl G 6s, 4M. Green.
Lighted Buoy 4, Q R, 3M. Red.
Lighted Buoy 3, Q G, 3M. Green.
Lighted Buoy 2, Fl R 4s, 3M. Red.
Lighted Buoy 1, on west end of shoal, 18 13.6N, 65 28.2W. Fl G 6s, 4M. Green.
Sonde de Vieques Obstruction Lighted Buoy LAE, marks end of sewer outfall. IQ W. Black and red bands. Private aid.

ISLA DE VIEQUES

VIEQUES NAVAL PIER LIGHTS (2), 18 08.9N, 65 30.9W. F R, 15ft. On pier. Maintained by U.S. Navy.
VIEQUES NAVAL BREAKWATER LIGHT, 18 09.1N, 65 30.9W. Q R, 10ft. On pile. Maintained by U.S. Navy.
PUNTA MULAS LIGHT, 18 09.3N, 65 26.6W. Oc R 4s, 68ft, 7M. White octagonal tower on top of flat-roofed dwelling.

PUNTA ESTE LIGHT, 18 08.2N, 65 16.1W. Fl W 6s, 43ft, 7M. NR on tower.
PUNTA CONEJO LIGHT, 18 06.6N, 65 22.6W. Fl W 6s, 58ft, 7M. NR on tower.
PUERTO FERRO LIGHT, 18 05.9N, 65 25.4W. Fl W 4s, 56 ft, 7M. NR on skeleton tower.
Puerto Real Shoal Buoy 1, on east end of shoal, 18 04.9N, 65 29.0W. Green can.

PASAJE DE VIEQUES

RANGE (Front Light), 18 12.7N, 65 36.0W. Q W, 70 ft. KWR on skeleton tower. Visible all around. Higher intensity on rangeline. **(Rear Light),** 1,715 yards, 025.4° from front light. Iso W 6s, 142ft. KWR on tower. Visible 4° each side of rangeline.
NAVY PIER LIGHTS (2), W of Punta Puerca, 18 13.6N, 65 36.1W. F R. Maintained by U.S. Navy.
Lighted Buoy 2, Fl R 2.5s, 4M. Red.
Lighted Buoy 3, Fl G 2.5s, 4M. Green.
Buoy 4, Red nun.
Lighted Buoy 6, Fl R 2.5s, 3M. Red.

ROOSEVELT ROADS HARBOR

Channel Lighted Buoy 1, 18 11.8N, 65 36.6W. Fl G 6s, 4M. Green.
Channel Lighted Buoy 2, Fl R 6s, 3M. Red.
ENTRANCE CHANNEL RANGE (Front Light), 18 13.7N, 65 38.1W. Q W, 37ft. KWR on skeleton tower on piles. Visible 2° each side of rangeline. **(Rear Light),** 800 yards, 315° from front light. Iso W, 6s, 66ft. KWR on tower. Visible 2° each side of rangeline.
Channel Lighted Buoy 3, Fl G 4s, 3M. Green.
Channel Buoy 4, Red nun.
Channel Buoy 5, Green can.
Channel Lighted Buoy 6, Fl R 2.5s, 2M. Red.
CHANNEL LIGHT 7, Fl G 4s, 16 ft, 4M. SG on dolphin.
ROOSEVELT ROADS PIER 3 LIGHTS (2), F R, 10ft. On pier. Maintained by U.S. Navy.
Turning Basin Buoy 8, Red nun.
Anchorage Buoy A, Yellow nun.
Anchorage Buoy B, Yellow can.
Turning Basin Lighted Buoy 9, Fl G 4s, 3M. Green.
Turning Basin Buoy 11, Green can.
Turning Basin Lighted Buoy 13, Fl G 4s, 4M. Green.
Anchorage Buoy C, Yellow nun.
Anchorage Buoy D, Yellow nun.

COAST PILOT

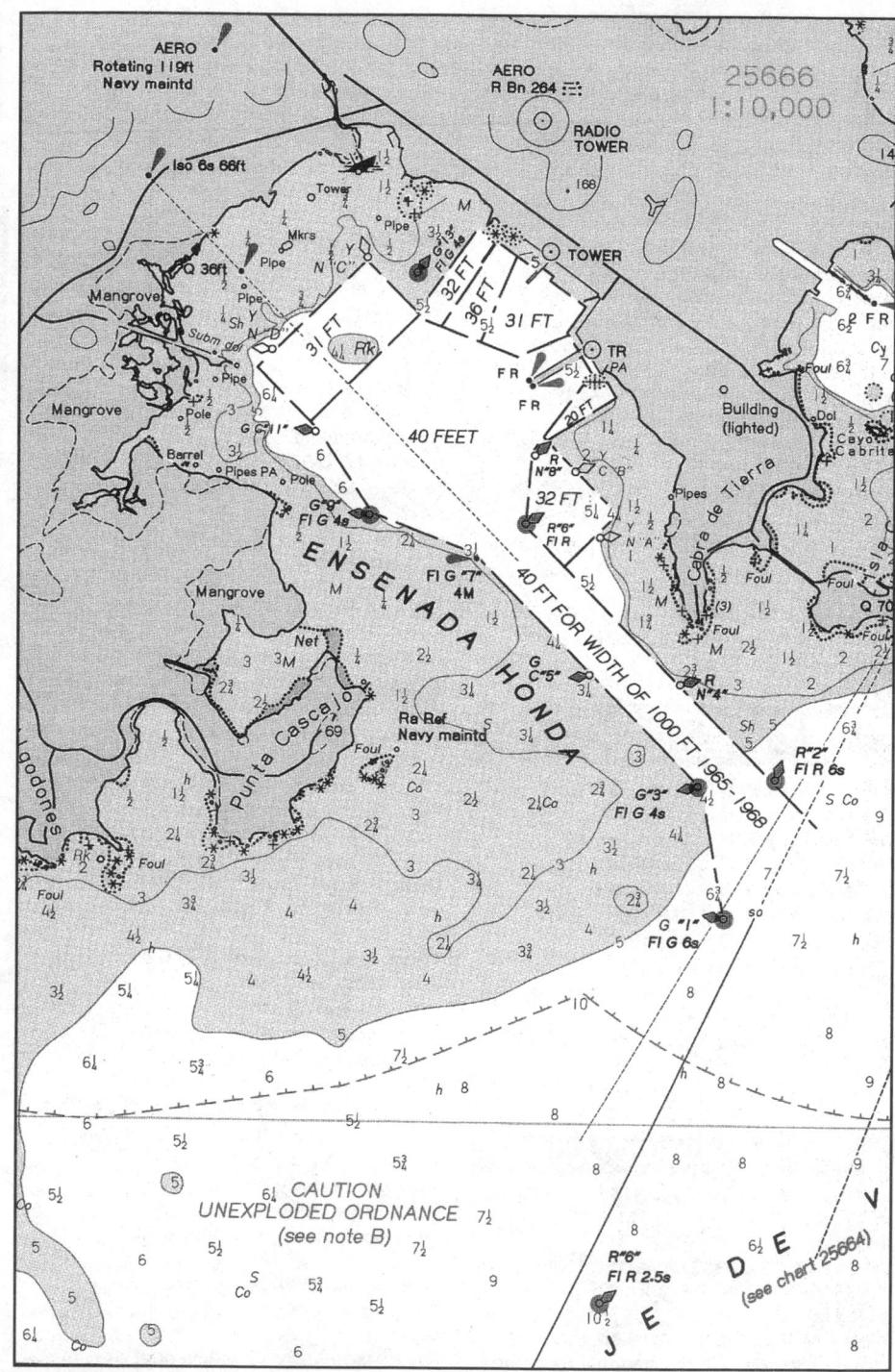

Roosevelt Roads, soundings in feet *(from NOAA 25663, 26th ed, 1/92)*

ROOSEVELT ROADS

18 13N, 65 37W

Emergencies: Contact the U.S. Coast Guard (VHF channel 16 or 2182kHz).

Pilotage: No vessel shall enter or remain within the charted restricted areas extending about 1 mile to 1 1/2 miles offshore from the naval base unless on official business. Fishing is not permitted in the restricted areas. Naval personnel may obtain permission to use the small-craft facilities of the base by calling the Roosevelt Roads Marina (809-865-3297). Make reservations before approaching the area.

Port Control: Contact port control on VHF channel 12 before entering the naval base.

Dockage: The marina monitors VHF channel 16. There is also a Roosevelt Roads Yacht Club.

Services: Fuel, water, and general supplies are available.

The Roosevelt Roads U.S. Naval Station (809-865-2000) is a convenient, safe port for active and retired military personnel, reservists, Department of Defense personnel, and those able to obtain a sponsor on the base.

ROOSEVELT ROADS TO FAJARDO

Cabeza de Perro Lighted Buoy 7, 18 13.6N, 65 33.7W. Fl G 6s, 4M. Green.

BAJOS CHINCHORRO DEL SUR LIGHT, 18 14.1N, 65 31.2W. Fl W 4s, 25ft, 8M. NR on tower on piles.

CABEZA DE PERRO LIGHT, 18 15.0N, 65 34.6W. Fl W 6s, 80ft, 8M white, 6M red. R 021°–031° and 066°–161°, obscured 031°–066°.

Roca Lavandera del Oeste Buoy 5, Green can.

Punta Figueras Buoy 4, on shoal. Red nun. Buoy edge of red sector of Cabeza de Perro Light.

Bajos Largo Buoy 3, Green can.

Isla de Ramos Buoy 2, Red nun.

Cayo Largo Lighted Buoy 1A, midway of westerly shoal, 18 18.9N, 65 35.3W. Fl G 4s, 4M. Green.

Cayo Largo Buoy 1, N side of shoals. Green can.

Isla Palominos Lighted Buoy 2, 18 21.1N, 65 33.6W. Fl R 4s, 3M. Red.

FAJARDO

Fifteen-foot Spot Lighted Buoy 1, Fl G 2.5s, 4M. Green.

Bajo Onaway Buoy 3, Green can.

PUERTO CHICO MARINA BREAKWATER LIGHT, 18 20.8N, 65 38.0W. F R, 13ft. On pile. Private aid.

SEA LOVERS PIER A EAST LIGHT, 18 20.8N, 65 38.1W. F R, 10ft. On pier pile. Private aid.

SEA LOVERS PIER A WEST LIGHT, F R, 10ft. On pier pile. Private aid.

SEA LOVERS PIER B EAST LIGHT, F R, 10ft. On pier pile. Private aid.

SEA LOVERS PIER B WEST LIGHT, F R, 10ft. On pier pile. Private aid.

FAJARDO HARBOR PIER OBSTRUCTION LIGHTS (2), 18 20.1N, 65 37.8W. F R, 10ft. On pile. Private aids.

ISLETA MARINA, FAJARDO

PIER A LIGHT, 18 20.4N, 65 37.3W. Q W, 12ft. On pile. Private aid.

PIER B LIGHT, F G, 12ft. On pile. Private aid.

PIER C LIGHT, F G, 12ft. On pile. Private aid.

PIER D LIGHT, F G, 12ft. On pile. Private aid.

Daybeacon 2, TR on pile. Private aid.

FAJARDO

18 20N, 65 38W

Emergencies: Contact the U.S. Coast Guard (VHF channel 16 or 2182kHz).

Pilotage: The easiest entrance is from the north, via the unmarked ferry channel. There are fixed red lights, privately maintained, on the ferry dock. The controlling depth is 11 feet to the public wharf. Depths at the dock are 12 feet at the outer end and 8 feet alongside. The southern approach has more hazards and fewer marks, but should have about 9 to 11 feet.

Port of Entry: Customs is on the waterfront near the ferry dock (809-863-0950). Boats arriving from the Virgin Islands should clear here if they haven't done so in Culebra. If you tie up to the public wharf be prepared to move quickly upon the arrival of a ferry.

Dockage: This area has a profusion of repair yards, marinas, and boating services. At Las Croabas, about 1 1/2 miles south of Cabo San Juan, is Marina Lanais, entered via a marked channel through the reef. At the north end of Playa Sardinera is the Puerto Chico marina for smaller, local boats. Villa Marina (809-863-5131 or VHF channels 16 and 68) is located in a small dredged basin behind a breakwater just north of the public wharf. Isleta Marina is on the island across from town. Puerto del Rey marina (809-860-1000 or VHF channel 71) is behind a breakwater in Bahía Demajagua, about 3 miles south of the main waterfront.

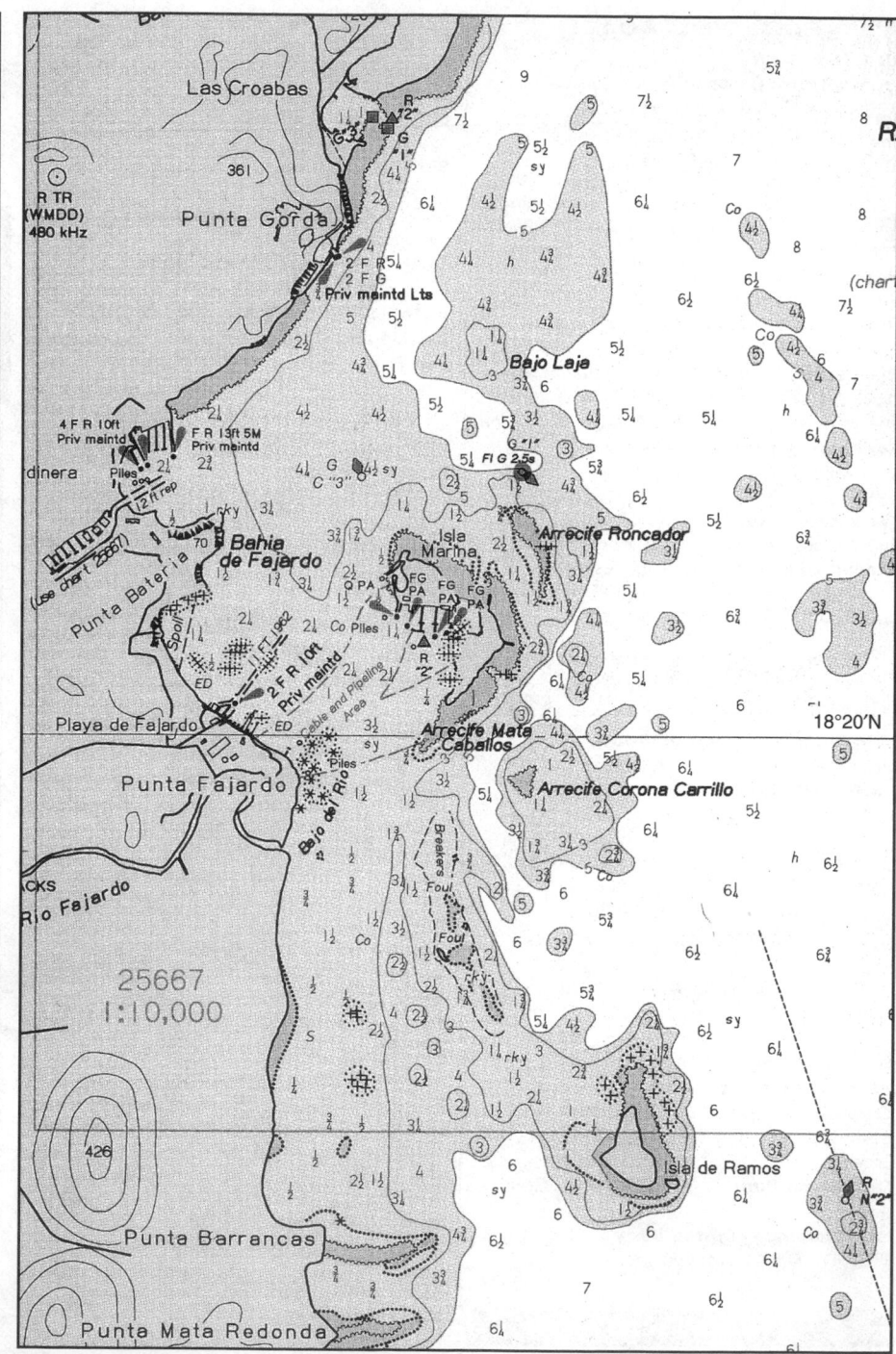

Fajardo, soundings in fathoms *(from NOAA 25663, 26th ed, 1/92)*

Anchorage: There is good anchorage south of the island with the marina. Note the charted cable and pipeline areas between the island and Fajardo.

Services: All services are available. This is one of the best places in Puerto Rico to obtain supplies and accomplish repairs on your boat.

LAS CROABAS

Daybeacon 1, 18 21.8N, 65 37.3W. SG on pile.
Daybeacon 2, TR on pile.
Daybeacon 3, SG on pile.

FAJARDO TO CULEBRA

Isla Palominos Lighted Buoy 2, 18 21.2N, 65 33.5W. Fl R, 4s, 3M. Red.
Bajo Blake South Buoy 3, 18 20.5N, 65 31.9W. Green can.
CAYO LOBITO LIGHT, 18 20.1N, 65 23.5W. Fl W 6s, 110ft, 8M. NR on skeleton tower.

CULEBRA

PUNTA MELONES LIGHT, 18 18.1N, 65 18.7W. Fl W 6s, 45ft, 6M. NR on tower.
PUNTA DEL SOLDADO LIGHT, 18 16.7N, 65 17.2W. Fl W 2.5s, 65ft, 5M. NR on tower.
Bajo Amarillo Lighted Buoy 2, 18 16.7N, 65 16.5W. Fl R 4s, 3M. Red.
Canal del Este Buoy 2, 18 16.6N, 65 15.1W. Red nun.
Cabezas Crespas Lighted Buoy 3, 18 16.8N, 65 15.4W. Fl G 4s, 4M. Green.
Cabezas Puercas Buoy 4, Red nun.
ISLA DE CULEBRA OUTER RANGE (Front Daybeacon), 18 17.7N, 65 17.0W. KRW on skeleton tower. **(Rear Daybeacon),** 750 yards, 296° from front daybeacon. KRW on skeleton tower.
Bajo Grouper Buoy 5, Green can.
Bajo Camaron Buoy 6, Red nun.
Bajo Snapper Lighted Buoy 8, 18 17.4N, 65 16.3W. Q R, 3M. Red.
ISLA DE CULEBRA INNER RANGE (Front Daybeacon), on Punta Cemeterio, 18 18.6N, 65 17.3W. KRW on skeleton tower. **(Rear Daybeacon),** 1,200 yards, 323° from front daybeacon. KRW on skeleton tower.
Punta Colorada Lighted Buoy 9, Fl G 4s, 4M. Green.
Punta Caranero Buoy 10, Red nun.
Punta Caranero Buoy 12, Red nun.
Punta Caranero Buoy 14, Red nun.

CULEBRA

18 18N, 65 18W
Emergencies: Contact the U.S. Coast Guard (VHF channel 16 or 2182kHz).

Pilotage: The area charted as Bahía de Sardinas is the location of the town's waterfront and ferry dock. You can anchor in the bay and dinghy in to the ferry wharf or the small creek just south of the wharf. This area is prone to a surge, or roll, under certain conditions. Most boaters prefer to enter Ensenada Honda and anchor west or southwest of Cayo Pirata. A large bay on the eastern side of Ensenada Honda has good hurricane anchorage among the mangroves at its head.

Customs Station: Mariners should call the airport office (809-742-3531). Hours are 0900 to 12 noon and 1300 to 1600, Monday through Saturday. All boats coming from the U.S. Virgin Islands must clear customs when entering Puerto Rico.

Dockage: You may be able to tie temporarily to the ferry wharf for fuel and supplies. There is no dockage for large boats in Ensenada Honda.

Anchorage: Excellent anchorages abound in Culebra. The most popular spot is east of town in Ensenada Honda. Dinghy ashore near the head of the small creek that passes through town. Anchorage can also be found in any of the bays along the shores of Ensenada Honda. A cool spot is west of the reef blocking the entrance to Ensenada Honda.

Services: There is fuel and water (via jugs), a hardware store, a canvas shop, a dive shop, several small restaurants, groceries, a post office, a bank, and telephones. Supplies can be limited. A ferry runs daily to Fajardo.

Culebra is only 20 miles west of St. Thomas, yet it is in another cruising world. The island is only quietly interested in tourists, but offers marvelous gunkholing and peaceful anchorages.

CULEBRA TO ST. THOMAS

ISLA CULEBRITA LIGHT, 18 18.8N, 65 13.7W. Fl W 10s, 305ft, 13M. Stone-colored cylindrical tower with red trim on flat-roofed dwelling. Obscured by Cayo Norte 125°–142°.

CULEBRITA

18 19N, 65 14W
Emergencies: Contact the U.S. Coast Guard (VHF channel 16 or 2182kHz).

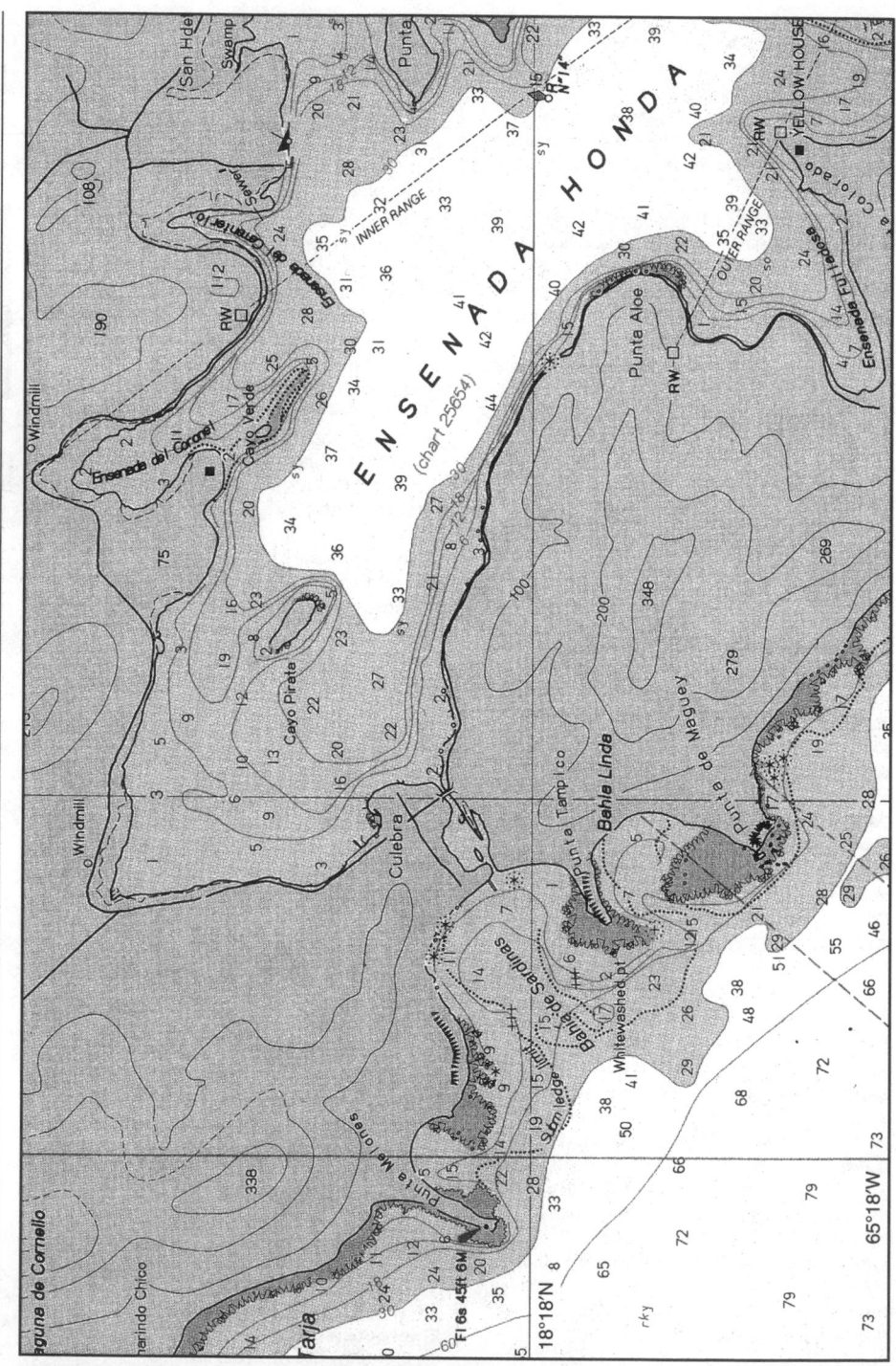

Culebra, soundings in feet *(from NOAA 25653, 11th ed, 12/92)*

Pilotage: A powerful light marks the summit of Isla Culebrita. Approaching from the northeast, large seas may become steep breakers on the bar. Be prepared to leave if a norther threatens.
Anchorage: This is a lovely anchorage, off a crescent-shaped sandy beach. The island is all park land preserved in its natural state. There are no facilities here.

Bajos Grampus South Lighted Buoy 2, S side of shoals, 18 14.3N, 65 12.5W. Fl R 4s, 3M. Red.
Sail Rock Lighted Buoy 1, 18 17.1N, 65 06.5W. Fl G 6s, 4M, Green.
SAVANA ISLAND LIGHT, 18 20.4N, 65 05.0W. Fl W 4s, 300ft, 7M. White tower.

CABO SAN JUAN TO SAN JUAN HARBOR

CABO SAN JUAN LIGHT, 18 22.9N, 65 37.1W. Fl W 15s, 260ft, 26M. Cylindrical tower on front of white rectangular dwelling. Black band around base.
LAS CUCARACHAS LIGHT, 18 24.0N, 65 36.7W. Fl W 6s, 38ft, 7M. NG on skeleton tower.
Punta Picua Lighted Buoy WR2, NE of 2 1/2-fathom shoal. 18 26.6N, 65 45.6W. Fl R 4s, 4M. Red.
Lighted Buoy BC, 18 28.1N, 66 00.6W. Mo (A) W, 5M. Red and white stripes with red spherical topmark. Use only with local knowledge.
CABALLO CHANNEL RANGE (Front Lights), 2 lights, 18 26.9N, 65 59.9W. F R, 20ft. Red and orange diamond daymark. Private aids. **(Rear Lights),** 2 lights, 29 yards, 146.5° from front light, F R, 25ft. Red and orange round daymark. Private aids.
PLATFORM LIGHT, 18 27.1N, 65 59.2W. F W, 12ft. On pile. Maintained by the FAA.

SAN JUAN HARBOR

PUERTO SAN JUAN LIGHT, 18 28.4N, 66 07.4W. Fl (3) W 40s, 181ft. 24M. Buff-colored square tower, octagonal base, on Morro Castle. Obscured 281°–061°.
CABRAS LIGHT, 18 28.5N, 66 08.4W. Iso W 6s, 44 ft, 9M. NR on tower.
RANGE (Front Light), 18 27.3N, 66 07.8W. Q G, 23ft. KRW on skeleton tower on piles. Visible 2° each side of rangeline. **(Rear Light),** 1,335 yards, 187.7° from front light. Oc G 4s, 56ft. KRW on skeleton tower. Visible 2° each side of rangeline.
Lighted Buoy 1, 18 28.3N, 66 07.6W. Fl G 4s, 4M. Green.

Lighted Buoy 2, Fl R 6s, 3M. Red.
Lighted Buoy 3, 18 28.2N, 66 07.6W. Q G, 3M. Green.
Lighted Buoy 4, Fl R 4s, 3M. Red.
Lighted Buoy 5, 18 28.1N, 66 07.6W. Fl G 2.5s, 3M. Green.
Lighted Buoy 6, Fl R 2.5s, 2M. Red.
Buoy 6A, Red nun.
Lighted Buoy 7, Fl G 4s, 4M. Green.
Lighted Buoy 8, Fl R 2.5s, 4M. Red.
Lighted Buoy 10, Fl R 2.5s, 4M. Red.
Lighted Buoy 11, Q G, 2M. Green.
Lighted Buoy 13, Fl G 4s, 3M. Green.
San Juan Harbor Anchorage F Buoy A, 18 27.0N, 66 07.0W. Yellow can.
Lighted Buoy 14, Q R, 2M. Red.
TMT OUTER DOLPHIN OBSTRUCTION LIGHT, 18 27.1N, 66 06.2W. Q W, 12ft. On mooring dolphin. Private aid.
TMT MIDDLE DOLPHIN OBSTRUCTION LIGHT, Q W, 12ft. On mooring dolphin. Private aid.
San Juan Harbor Anchorage E Buoy A, Yellow can.
San Juan Harbor Anchorage E Buoy B, 18 27.0N, 66 06.1W. Yellow nun.

SAN ANTONIO CHANNEL
LA PUNTILLA FINGER PIER B LIGHT, 18 27.6N, 66 06.9W. F G, 10ft. On pier.
LA PUNTILLA FINGER PIER A LIGHT, F G, 10ft. On pier.
PIER 1 LIGHTS (3), 18 27.6N, 66 06.8W. F G, 10 ft. On dolphins. Private aids.
PIER 3 LIGHTS (3), F G, 13ft. On dolphins. Private aids.

SAN JUAN

18 28N, 66 07W
Emergencies: Contact the U.S. Coast Guard (VHF channel 16 or 2182kHz).
Pilotage: The harbor entrance is deep and well marked. Approaching from offshore, be careful to stay well off the land until you are sure of your position, as there are many hazardous reefs along the coast. It can be hard to spot the charted landmarks from offshore, but you may be lucky enough to see a cruise ship entering or leaving. Steep seas can pile up on the bar at the entrance to the harbor.
Puerto Rico Ports Authority: The signal station at Fort San Cristobal is manned 24 hours a day, and boaters should contact the authorities on VHF channel 16 (switching to channel 14) for permission to enter or leave the harbor.
Port of Entry: Call 809-253-4533, -4534, -4537, or -4538 to reach customs and immigration.

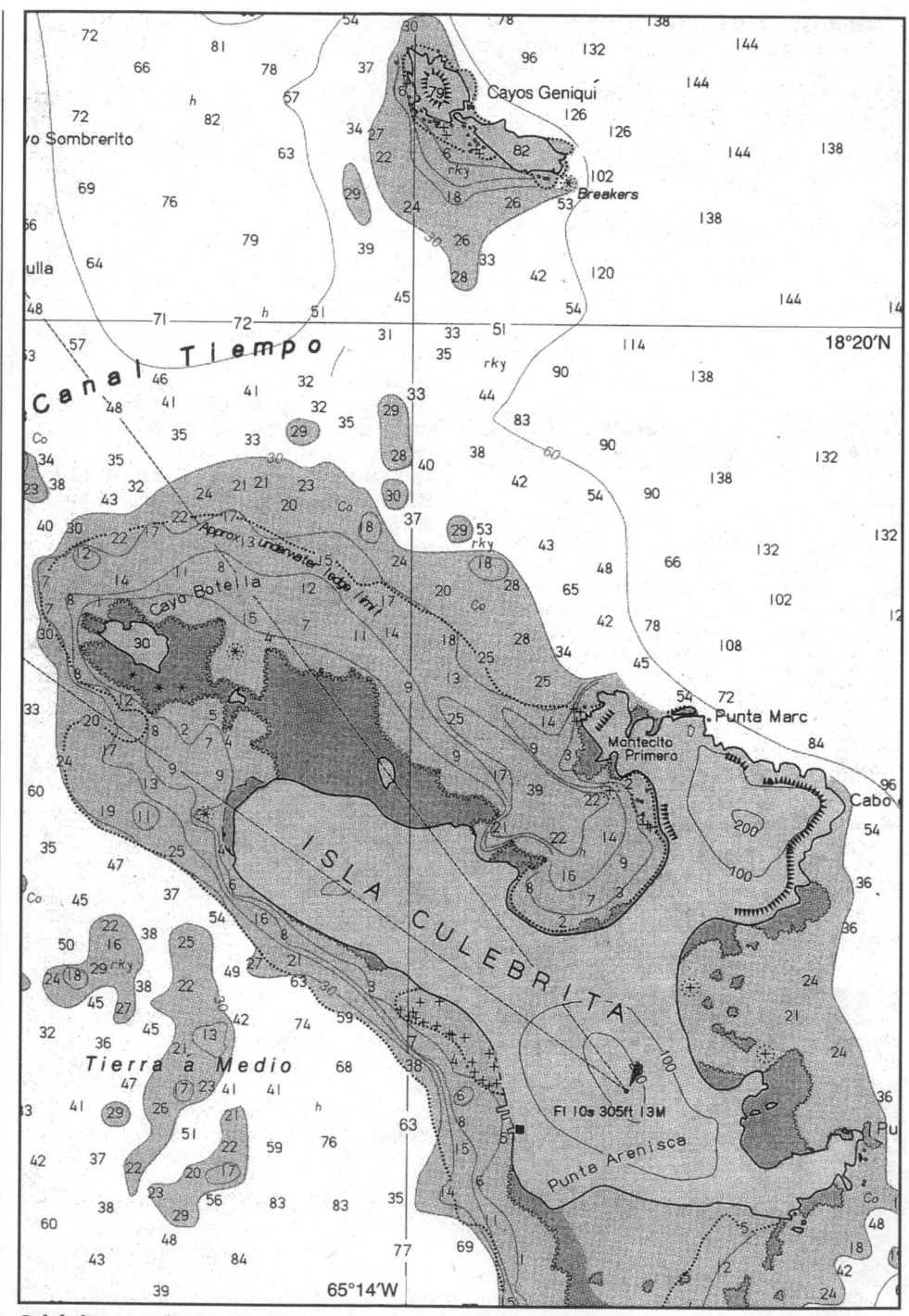

Culebrita, soundings in feet *(from NOAA 25653, 11th ed, 12/92)*

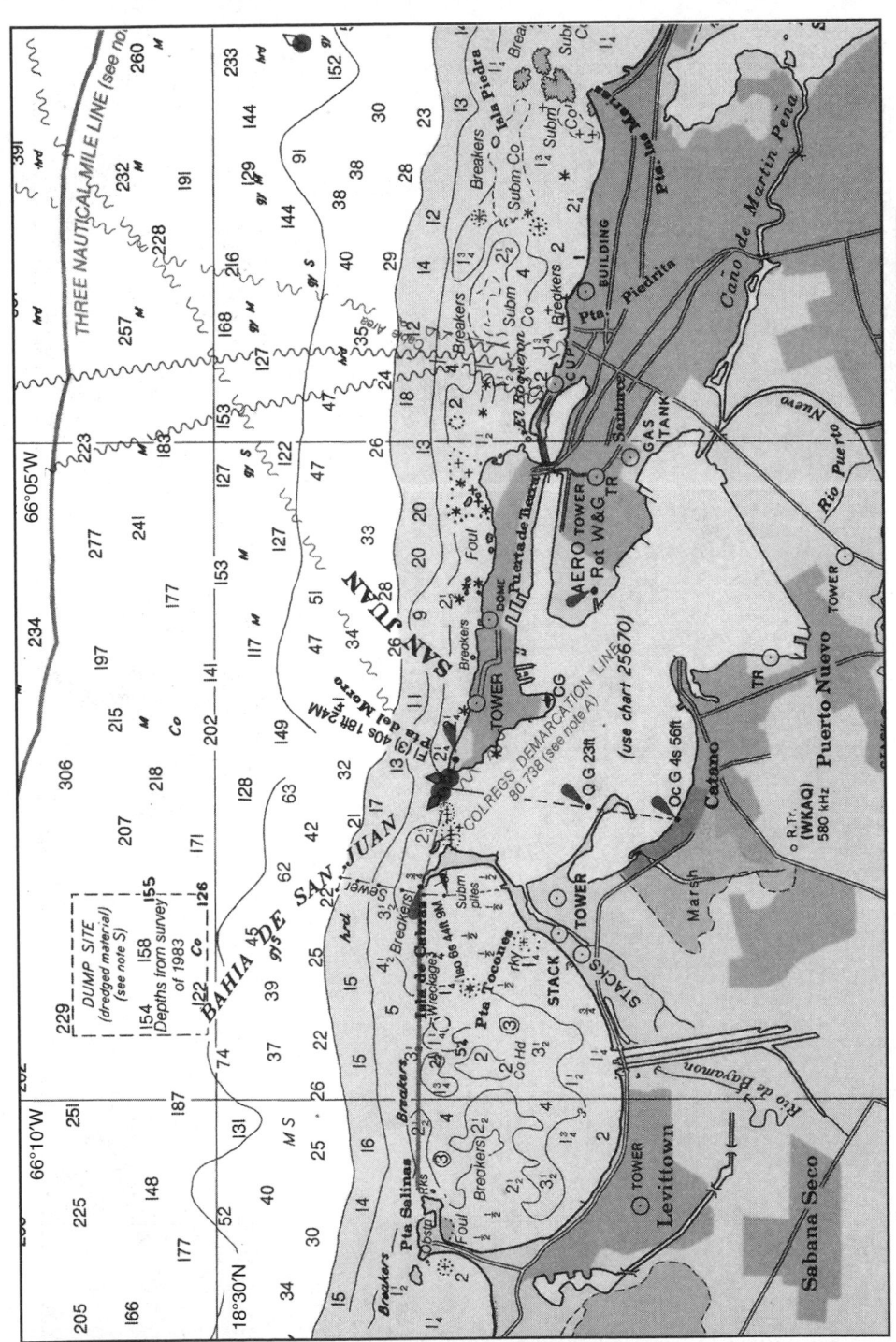

San Juan Approaches, soundings in fathoms *(from NOAA 25668, 14th ed, 6/93)*

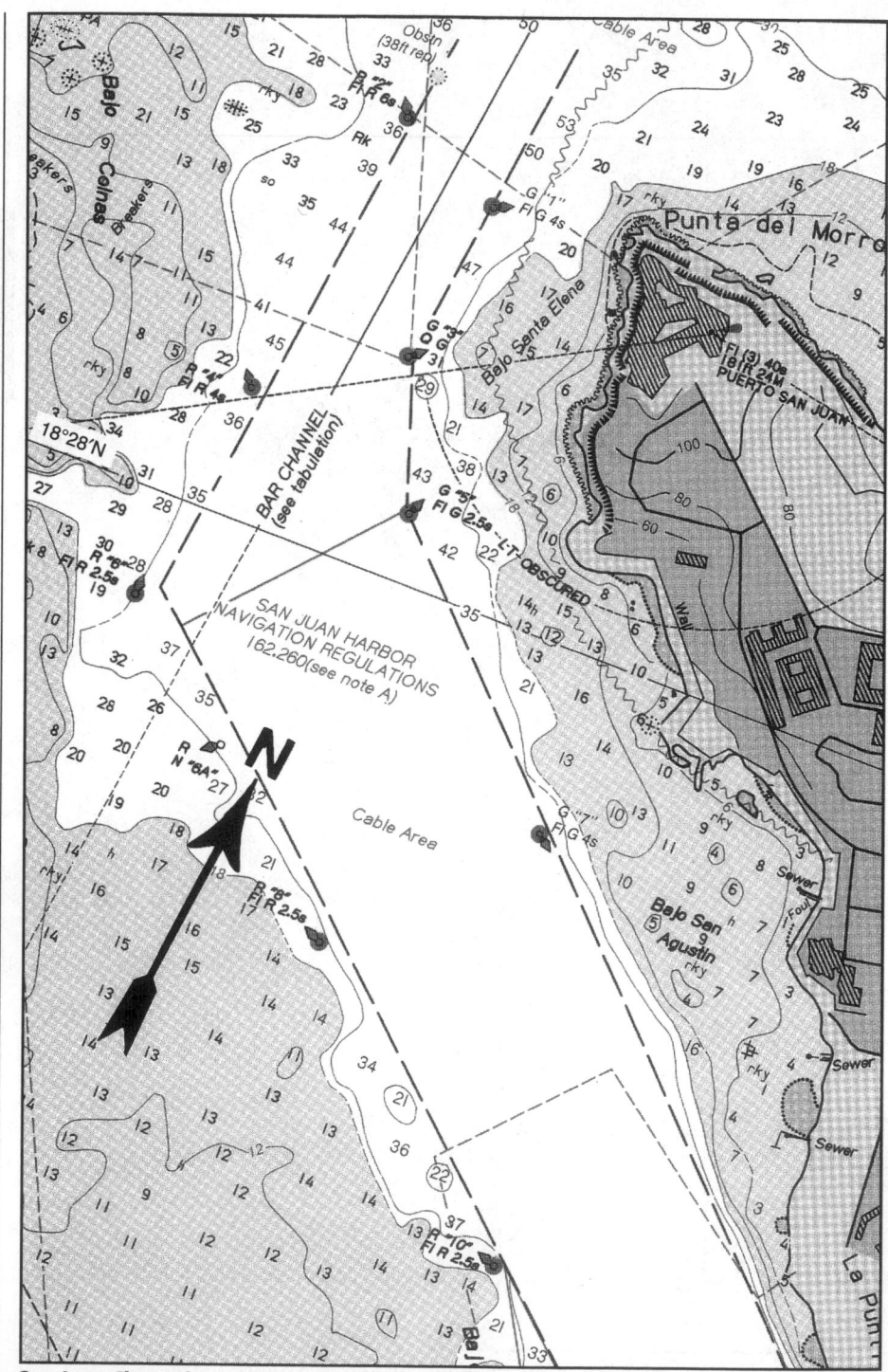

San Juan Channel, soundings in feet *(from NOAA 25670, 37th ed, 1/94)*

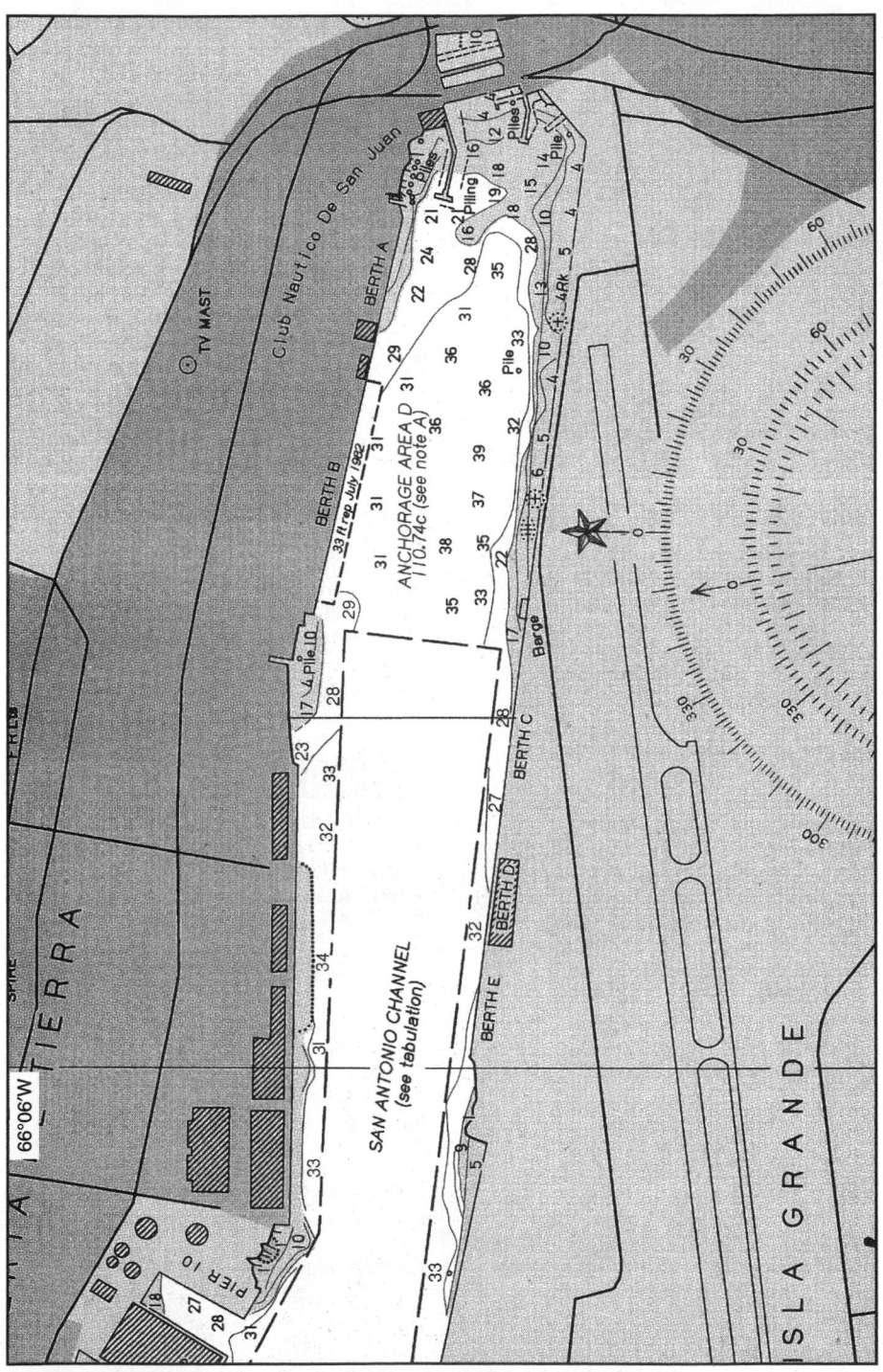

San Juan Harbor, soundings in feet *(from NOAA 25670, 37th ed, 1/94)*

You can dock at one of the marinas at the eastern end of the San Antonio Channel.

Dockage: There are two marinas at the eastern end of the San Antonio Channel. The Club Nautico de San Juan (809-722-0177 or VHF channel 16) is on the north side. Across the channel is the San Juan Bay Marina (VHF channel 16) offering both slips and some moorings. Room for transients tends to be limited.

Anchorage: There is some room to anchor west of the marinas, among the moorings. Small white buoys with orange markings limit the anchoring area. The bottom is poor holding, and the area is swept by strong currents. You can dinghy in to the marina to the south.

Services: All services are available. Haulouts can be done, and there are facilities for major repairs of engines, electronics, and hulls. There are several good chandleries and nearby grocery stores. This is a good place for major restocking of the ship's larder.

San Juan was founded in 1421 and is a delight for historically minded boaters. The approach to the harbor takes you dramatically below the ramparts of El Morro castle and past the walls of Old San Juan. Although limited in its cruising amenities, it is a fascinating port.

ARMY TERMINAL CHANNEL
Lighted Buoy A, Fl (2+1) G 6s, 3M. Green and red bands.
Lighted Buoy 2, Fl R 4s, 3M. Red.
Lighted Buoy 3, Fl R 4s, 3M. Red.
Buoy 4, Red nun.
RANGE (Front Light), 18 25.7N, 66 06.5W. Q R, 28 ft., KRW on tower. Visible 2° each side of rangeline. **(Rear Light),** 380 yards, 175.6° from front light. Oc R 4s, 43ft. KRW on tower. Visible 2° each side of rangeline.
Lighted Buoy 5, Fl G 4s, 3M. Green.
Lighted Buoy 6, Fl R 4s, 3M. Red.
Lighted Buoy 7, Fl G 4s, 3M. Green.
Turning Basin Lighted Buoy 9, Fl G 2.5s, 3M. Green.

PUERTO NUEVO CHANNEL
Lighted Buoy 1, Fl G 4s, 4M. Green.
RANGE (Front Light), 18 26.5N, 66 05.2W. Q G, 45ft. KRW on tower on piles. Visible 2° each side of rangeline. **(Rear Light),** 610 yards, 058.4° from front light. Oc G 4s, 79ft. KRW on tower. Visible 2° each side of rangeline.

LIGHT 3, Fl G 4s, 16ft, 4M. SG on dolphin.
LIGHT 5, Q G, 16ft, 2M. SG on dolphin.
Turning Basin Buoy 7, Green can.
Turning Basin Lighted Buoy 9, Q G, 3M. Green.
TURNING BASIN LIGHT 10, Fl R 4s, 19ft, 2M. TR on dolphin.

MARTIN PENA CHANNEL
LIGHT 2, 18 26.5N, 66 05.1W. Fl R 4s, 10ft. TR on pile. Private aid.

NOTE: A series of 24 more flashing green and red lights on piles mark Martin Pena Channel. These lights are all private aids.

GRAVING DOCK CHANNEL
RANGE (Front Light), 18 26.5N, 66 05.2W. Q R, 41ft. KRW on skeleton tower. Visible all around; higher intensity on rangeline. **(Rear Light),** 535 yards, 111.1° from front light. Oc R, 4s, 83ft. KRW on tower. Visible 2° each side of rangeline.
Buoy 1, Green can.
Lighted Buoy 2, Fl R 4s, 3M. Red.
Lighted Buoy 3, Fl G 4s, 4M. Green.
Buoy 5, Green can.
Turning Basin Buoy 6, Red nun.

SAN JUAN TO PUNTA BORINQUEN

ARECIBO LIGHT, 18 29.0N, 66 41.9W. Fl W 5s, 120ft. 14M. White hexagonal tower attached to square flat-roofed dwelling.
Puerto Arecibo Buoy 1, Green can.
Puerto Arecibo Buoy 2, Red nun.

ARECIBO
18 29N, 66 42W
Emergencies: Contact the U.S. Coast Guard (VHF channel 16 or 2182kHz).
Pilotage: Arecibo, located about 33 miles west of San Juan and marked by a powerful light, is one of the few places to take shelter on Puerto Rico's north coast. A 600-foot-wharf, where depths range from 5 to 20 feet, projects from Punta Morrillos, providing some protection.
Anchorage: Anchor south of the breakwater.

PUNTA BORINQUEN LIGHT, 18 29.8N, 67 08.9W, Fl (2) W 15s, 292ft, 24M. Gray cylindrical tower.

COAST PILOT

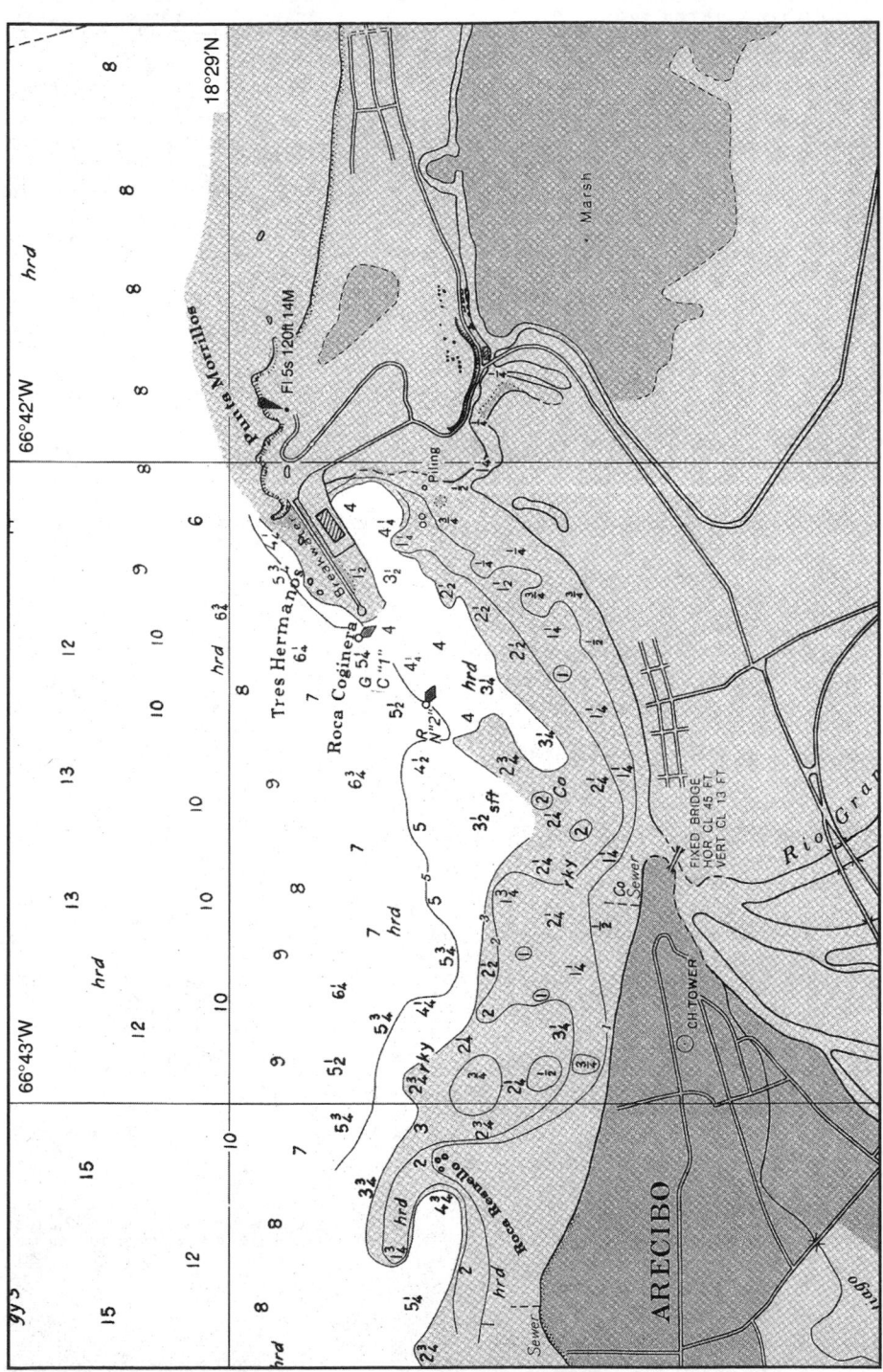

Arecibo, soundings in fathoms *(from NOAA 25668, 14th ed, 6/93)*

SAN JUAN, PUERTO RICO

HIGH & LOW WATER 1995   18°28'N   66°01'W

ATLANTIC STANDARD TIME (GMT -4H)

JANUARY

Day	Time	ft	Time	ft	Time	ft	Time	ft
1 Su ●	0149	-0.5	0905	1.9	1536	0.3	2029	1.0
2 M	0244	-0.5	0953	1.9	1624	0.2	2129	1.0
3 Tu	0338	-0.4	1039	1.8	1711	0.1	2229	1.0
4 W	0432	-0.3	1124	1.7	1756	0.1	2330	1.0
5 Th	0526	-0.1	1207	1.6	1841	0.0		
6 F	0033	1.1	0623	0.1	1249	1.4	1925	-0.0
7 Sa	0138	1.1	0724	0.2	1331	1.2	2010	-0.1
8 Su ☾	0244	1.1	0830	0.4	1413	1.1	2055	-0.1
9 M	0349	1.2	0942	0.5	1457	1.0	2140	-0.1
10 Tu	0450	1.2	1055	0.5	1544	0.9	2225	-0.1
11 W	0546	1.3	1205	0.5	1633	0.8	2309	-0.2
12 Th	0636	1.4	1305	0.5	1722	0.7	2352	-0.2
13 F	0720	1.4	1356	0.4	1809	0.7		
14 Sa	0034	-0.2	0801	1.5	1439	0.4	1854	0.7
15 Su	0114	-0.3	0838	1.5	1516	0.4	1937	0.7
16 M ○	0152	-0.3	0913	1.5	1549	0.3	2019	0.7
17 Tu	0232	-0.3	0946	1.5	1618	0.3	2103	0.8
18 W	0312	-0.3	1018	1.5	1646	0.2	2150	0.8
19 Th	0355	-0.2	1049	1.4	1714	0.1	2241	0.9
20 F	0441	-0.1	1121	1.3	1746	0.0	2337	1.0
21 Sa	0533	0.0	1154	1.2	1822	-0.1		
22 Su	0038	1.1	0631	0.1	1231	1.1	1904	-0.2
23 M	0143	1.2	0737	0.2	1313	1.0	1952	-0.3
24 Tu ☾)	0252	1.3	0852	0.3	1402	0.9	2046	-0.4
25 W	0402	1.4	1011	0.4	1459	0.9	2144	-0.5
26 Th	0509	1.5	1128	0.4	1603	0.8	2245	-0.6
27 F	0611	1.6	1236	0.3	1712	0.8	2346	-0.6
28 Sa	0708	1.6	1334	0.2	1819	0.8		
29 Su ●	0046	-0.6	0800	1.7	1425	0.2	1924	0.9
30 M	0143	-0.6	0848	1.6	1512	0.1	2024	0.9
31 Tu	0238	-0.5	0933	1.6	1555	0.0	2122	1.0

FEBRUARY

Day	Time	ft	Time	ft	Time	ft	Time	ft
1 W	0331	-0.4	1015	1.5	1637	-0.1	2218	1.0
2 Th	0422	-0.3	1055	1.4	1717	-0.1	2313	1.1
3 F	0514	-0.1	1133	1.2	1756	-0.2	2326	1.2
4 Sa	0008	1.1	0605	0.0	1209	1.1	1836	-0.2
5 Su	0104	1.1	0700	0.2	1246	1.0	1917	-0.2
6 M	0202	1.1	0759	0.3	1325	0.9	2000	-0.2
7 Tu ☾	0302	1.1	0904	0.4	1407	0.8	2047	-0.2
8 W	0403	1.1	1014	0.4	1455	0.7	2136	-0.4
9 Th	0501	1.1	1120	0.5	1549	0.7	2227	-0.2
10 F	0555	1.2	1224	0.4	1645	0.6	2316	-0.2
11 Sa	0643	1.3	1313	0.3	1739	0.6		
12 Su	0004	-0.3	0725	1.3	1353	0.3	1830	0.7
13 M	0050	-0.3	0803	1.3	1427	0.2	1918	0.7
14 Tu	0134	-0.3	0838	1.3	1457	0.2	2005	0.8
15 W	0218	-0.3	0911	1.3	1526	0.1	2052	0.9
16 Th	0303	-0.3	0942	1.3	1555	0.0	2141	1.0
17 F	0350	-0.2	1014	1.2	1627	-0.1	2232	1.1
18 Sa	0439	-0.1	1047	1.1	1703	-0.2	2326	1.2
19 Su	0532	-0.0	1123	1.0	1743	-0.3		
20 M	0024	1.3	0631	0.1	1204	1.0	1830	-0.4
21 Tu	0126	1.3	0736	0.2	1250	0.9	1922	-0.4
22 W ☾)	0233	1.4	0849	0.3	1344	0.8	2022	-0.5
23 Th	0343	1.4	1004	0.3	1440	0.7	2127	-0.5
24 F	0450	1.4	1116	0.3	1602	0.8	2234	-0.5
25 Sa	0553	1.5	1218	0.2	1715	0.8	2340	-0.5
26 Su	0650	1.5	1312	0.1	1824	0.9		
27 M	0043	-0.4	0740	1.4	1358	0.1	1926	1.0
28 Tu	0141	-0.4	0826	1.4	1440	-0.0	2023	1.1

MARCH

Day	Time	ft	Time	ft	Time	ft	Time	ft
1 W ●	0236	-0.3	0907	1.3	1519	-0.1	2116	1.1
2 Th	0327	-0.2	0946	1.2	1556	-0.1	2205	1.2
3 F	0416	-0.1	1021	1.1	1632	-0.2	2253	1.2
4 Sa	0503	0.0	1055	1.0	1707	-0.2	2340	1.2
5 Su	0550	0.1	1128	0.9	1743	-0.2		
6 M	0027	1.2	0638	0.2	1203	0.8	1822	-0.2
7 Tu	0117	1.2	0731	0.3	1240	0.8	1904	-0.1
8 W	0211	1.1	0829	0.4	1323	0.7	1951	-0.1
9 Th	0308	1.1	0933	0.4	1414	0.7	2044	-0.1
10 F	0407	1.1	1037	0.4	1513	0.7	2141	-0.1
11 Sa	0503	1.2	1133	0.4	1616	0.7	2238	-0.1
12 Su	0553	1.2	1219	0.3	1716	0.7	2334	-0.1
13 M	0637	1.3	1257	0.3	1812	0.8		
14 Tu	0026	-0.2	0716	1.2	1330	0.2	1903	0.9
15 W	0117	-0.2	0753	1.2	1401	0.1	1952	1.1
16 Th ○	0207	-0.2	0827	1.2	1433	-0.0	2041	1.2
17 F	0256	-0.1	0902	1.1	1507	-0.2	2130	1.3
18 Sa	0346	-0.1	0937	1.1	1544	-0.3	2220	1.5
19 Su	0438	-0.0	1015	1.0	1625	-0.4	2313	1.5
20 M	0533	0.1	1056	1.0	1711	-0.4		
21 Tu	0009	1.6	0632	0.2	1143	0.9	1802	-0.4
22 W	0110	1.6	0736	0.2	1237	0.9	1859	-0.4
23 Th ☾)	0214	1.5	0844	0.3	1341	0.8	2004	-0.3
24 F	0321	1.5	0953	0.3	1454	0.8	2114	-0.3
25 Sa	0426	1.5	1057	0.2	1612	0.9	2227	-0.2
26 Su	0527	1.4	1153	0.2	1725	1.0	2338	-0.2
27 M	0622	1.4	1242	0.1	1831	1.1		
28 Tu	0043	-0.1	0712	1.3	1325	0.0	1928	1.2
29 W	0142	-0.1	0755	1.2	1404	-0.1	2020	1.3
30 Th	0235	-0.0	0835	1.1	1440	-0.1	2107	1.4
31 F	0325	0.0	0910	1.0	1513	-0.1	2150	1.4

APRIL

Day	Time	ft	Time	ft	Time	ft	Time	ft
1 Sa	0411	0.1	0944	1.0	1546	-0.1	2231	1.4
2 Su	0454	0.2	1016	0.9	1619	-0.1	2312	1.4
3 M	0537	0.3	1048	0.8	1653	-0.1	2353	1.4
4 Tu	0621	0.3	1122	0.8	1729	-0.1		
5 W	0037	1.3	0708	0.4	1200	0.8	1810	-0.0
6 Th	0124	1.3	0800	0.4	1245	0.7	1857	0.0
7 F	0216	1.3	0855	0.4	1340	0.7	1951	0.1
8 Sa	0309	1.2	0949	0.4	1444	0.7	2052	0.1
9 Su	0402	1.2	1038	0.4	1552	0.8	2157	0.1
10 M	0452	1.2	1120	0.3	1657	0.9	2302	0.1
11 Tu	0538	1.2	1157	0.2	1755	1.1		
12 W	0003	0.1	0620	1.2	1233	0.1	1848	1.2
13 Th	0101	0.1	0700	1.1	1309	-0.1	1938	1.4
14 F	0156	0.1	0740	1.1	1346	-0.2	2028	1.6
15 Sa	0249	0.1	0820	1.1	1426	-0.3	2117	1.7
16 Su	0342	0.1	0901	1.0	1509	-0.4	2208	1.8
17 M	0436	0.1	0946	1.0	1556	-0.4	2300	1.8
18 Tu	0531	0.2	1035	1.0	1646	-0.4	2355	1.8
19 W	0629	0.2	1129	0.9	1741	-0.4		
20 Th	0053	1.8	0730	0.2	1232	0.9	1842	-0.3
21 F ☾)	0153	1.7	0832	0.2	1343	0.9	1949	-0.2
22 Sa	0254	1.6	0933	0.2	1501	0.9	2103	-0.0
23 Su	0355	1.5	1030	0.1	1619	1.0	2220	0.1
24 M	0453	1.4	1121	0.1	1729	1.2	2333	0.1
25 Tu	0546	1.3	1207	0.0	1831	1.3		
26 W	0041	0.2	0634	1.2	1248	-0.1	1924	1.4
27 Th	0141	0.2	0717	1.1	1325	-0.1	2012	1.5
28 F	0234	0.2	0756	1.0	1400	-0.1	2054	1.6
29 Sa ●	0322	0.3	0831	0.9	2134	1.6		
30 Su ○	0406	0.3	0904	0.9	1505	-0.1	2211	1.6

TIME MERIDIAN 60°W

0000h is midnight, 1200h is noon.

Heights in feet are referenced to the chart datum of soundings.

SAN JUAN, PUERTO RICO

HIGH & LOW WATER 1995 **18°28'N 66°01'W**

ATLANTIC STANDARD TIME (GMT -4H)

MAY

Day	Time	ft	Day	Time	ft
1 M	0447 / 0936 / 1536 / 2248	0.3 / 0.8 / -0.1 / 1.6	**16** Tu	0429 / 0923 / 1535 / 2247	0.2 / 1.0 / -0.5 / 2.0
2 Tu	0526 / 1009 / 1610 / 2325	0.4 / 0.8 / -0.1 / 1.5	**17** W	0523 / 1019 / 1628 / 2340	0.2 / 1.0 / -0.4 / 1.9
3 W	0607 / 1044 / 1646	0.4 / 0.8 / -0.0	**18** Th	0618 / 1121 / 1725	0.2 / 1.0 / -0.3
4 Th	0004 / 0649 / 1124 / 1726	1.5 / 0.4 / 0.8 / 0.8	**19** F	0033 / 0713 / 1228 / 1827	1.8 / 0.2 / 1.0 / -0.2
5 F	0045 / 0732 / 1213 / 1811	1.4 / 0.4 / 0.8 / 0.1	**20** Sa	0128 / 0809 / 1342 / 1935	1.7 / 0.1 / 1.0 / 0.0
6 Sa	0129 / 0817 / 1312 / 1905	1.4 / 0.4 / 0.8 / 0.2	**21** Su	0223 / 0904 / 1459 /) 2049	1.6 / 0.1 / 1.1 / 0.2
7 Su	0214 / 0900 / 1419 / (2008	1.3 / 0.4 / 0.8 / 0.2	**22** M	0318 / 0956 / 1614 / 2207	1.4 / 0.0 / 1.2 / 0.3
8 M	0301 / 0942 / 1529 / 2118	1.3 / 0.3 / 0.9 / 0.3	**23** Tu	0411 / 1044 / 1722 / 2323	1.3 / -0.0 / 1.3 / 0.4
9 Tu	0348 / 1022 / 1636 / 2231	1.2 / 0.2 / 1.1 / 0.3	**24** W	0502 / 1129 / 1821	1.1 / -0.1 / 1.4
10 W	0435 / 1102 / 1736 / 2340	1.2 / 0.1 / 1.3 / 0.3	**25** Th	0033 / 0550 / 1210 / 1912	0.4 / 1.0 / -0.1 / 1.5
11 Th	0521 / 1142 / 1831	1.1 / -0.1 / 1.5	**26** F	0135 / 0634 / 1248 / 1957	0.4 / 0.9 / -0.1 / 1.6
12 F	0044 / 0607 / 1225 / 1923	0.3 / 1.1 / -0.2 / 1.7	**27** Sa	0228 / 0714 / 1324 / 2038	0.4 / 0.9 / -0.1 / 1.6
13 Sa	0144 / 0653 / 1309 / 2014	0.3 / 1.0 / -0.4 / 1.8	**28** Su	0315 / 0751 / 1358 / 2116	0.4 / 0.8 / -0.1 / 1.6
14 Su	0240 / 0741 / 1355 / O 2105	0.3 / 1.0 / -0.4 / 1.9	**29** M	0357 / 0826 / 1431 / ● 2151	0.4 / 0.8 / -0.1 / 1.6
15 M	0335 / 0831 / 1444 / 2155	0.2 / 1.0 / -0.5 / 2.0	**30** Tu	0436 / 0900 / 1504 / 2226	0.4 / 0.8 / -0.1 / 1.6
			31 W	0513 / 0935 / 1538 / 2301	0.4 / 0.8 / -0.1 / 1.6

JUNE

Day	Time	ft	Day	Time	ft
1 Th	0548 / 1013 / 1614 / 2335	0.4 / 0.8 / -0.0 / 1.6	**16** F	0557 / 1113 / 1713	0.2 / 1.0 / -0.2
2 F	0623 / 1057 / 1654	0.4 / 0.8 / 0.0	**17** Sa	0010 / 0647 / 1221 / 1814	1.8 / 0.1 / 1.1 / -0.0
3 Sa	0011 / 0658 / 1148 / 1739	1.5 / 0.4 / 0.8 / 0.1	**18** Su	0059 / 0737 / 1332 / 1920	1.7 / 0.1 / 1.1 / 0.1
4 Su	0047 / 0733 / 1249 / 1832	1.5 / 0.3 / 0.8 / 0.2	**19** M	0147 / 0827 / 1444 /) 2031	1.5 / 0.0 / 1.2 / 0.3
5 M	0125 / 0810 / 1356 / 1935	1.4 / 0.3 / 0.9 / 0.3	**20** Tu	0236 / 0915 / 1555 / 2148	1.3 / -0.0 / 1.3 / 0.4
6 Tu	0206 / 0848 / 1505 / (2047	1.3 / 0.2 / 1.1 / 0.4	**21** W	0325 / 1003 / 1701 / 2305	1.2 / -0.1 / 1.4 / 0.5
7 W	0249 / 0930 / 1612 / 2204	1.2 / 0.2 / 1.2 / 0.5	**22** Th	0415 / 1049 / 1800	1.1 / -0.1 / 1.5
8 Th	0336 / 1014 / 1715 / 2319	1.1 / -0.1 / 1.4 / 0.5	**23** F	0016 / 0503 / 1132 / 1851	0.5 / 1.0 / -0.1 / 1.5
9 F	0427 / 1102 / 1813	1.1 / -0.3 / 1.6	**24** Sa	0119 / 0550 / 1214 / 1937	0.5 / 0.9 / -0.1 / 1.6
10 Sa	0029 / 0520 / 1151 / 1908	0.5 / 1.0 / -0.4 / 1.8	**25** Su	0212 / 0634 / 1253 / 2018	0.5 / 0.8 / -0.1 / 1.6
11 Su	0132 / 0615 / 1242 / 2001	0.4 / 1.0 / -0.5 / 1.9	**26** M	0258 / 0715 / 1330 / 2055	0.5 / 0.8 / -0.1 / 1.7
12 M	0229 / 0712 / 1334 / 2052	0.4 / 1.0 / -0.5 / 2.0	**27** Tu	0338 / 0754 / 1405 / ● 2130	0.5 / 0.8 / -0.1 / 1.7
13 Tu	0323 / 0809 / 1427 / O 2142	0.3 / 1.0 / -0.5 / 2.0	**28** W	0414 / 0832 / 1441 / 2203	0.5 / 0.8 / -0.1 / 1.7
14 W	0415 / 0908 / 1521 / 2232	0.3 / 1.0 / -0.5 / 2.0	**29** Th	0446 / 0911 / 1516 / 2235	0.5 / 0.8 / -0.1 / 1.6
15 Th	0506 / 1009 / 1616 / 2321	0.2 / 1.0 / -0.4 / 1.9	**30** F	0516 / 0953 / 1554 / 2306	0.4 / 0.8 / -0.0 / 1.6

JULY

Day	Time	ft	Day	Time	ft
1 Sa	0545 / 1039 / 1635 / 2337	0.4 / 0.9 / 0.1 / 1.5	**16** Su	0611 / 1206 / 1802	0.1 / 1.3 / 0.1
2 Su	0614 / 1131 / 1721	0.4 / 0.9 / 0.2	**17** M	0026 / 0657 / 1311 / 1903	1.6 / 0.1 / 1.3 / 0.3
3 M	0009 / 0645 / 1229 / 1814	1.5 / 0.3 / 1.0 / 0.3	**18** Tu	0109 / 0743 / 1417 / 2009	1.4 / 0.0 / 1.3 / 0.5
4 Tu	0042 / 0720 / 1333 / 1915	1.4 / 0.2 / 1.1 / 0.4	**19** W	0153 / 0830 / 1510 /) 2121	1.3 / 0.0 / 1.4 / 0.6
5 W	0119 / 0800 / 1440 / (2026	1.3 / 0.0 / 1.3 / 0.5	**20** Th	0239 / 0918 / 1628 / 2236	1.1 / 0.0 / 1.4 / 0.6
6 Th	0201 / 0846 / 1548 / 2144	1.2 / -0.1 / 1.4 / 0.6	**21** F	0327 / 1006 / 1727 / 2347	1.0 / 0.0 / 1.5 / 0.7
7 F	0250 / 0936 / 1654 / 2302	1.1 / -0.2 / 1.6 / 0.6	**22** Sa	0418 / 1054 / 1821	1.0 / 0.0 / 1.6
8 Sa	0346 / 1031 / 1755	1.1 / -0.3 / 1.7	**23** Su	0050 / 0510 / 1140 / 1908	0.7 / 0.9 / 0.0 / 1.6
9 Su	0014 / 0447 / 1127 / 1853	0.6 / 1.0 / -0.4 / 1.9	**24** M	0142 / 0601 / 1224 / 1950	0.6 / 0.9 / 0.0 / 1.6
10 M	0117 / 0551 / 1224 / 1946	0.5 / 1.0 / -0.5 / 2.0	**25** Tu	0226 / 0647 / 1306 / 2028	0.6 / 0.9 / 0.0 / 1.7
11 Tu	0213 / 0655 / 1321 / 2037	0.5 / 1.1 / -0.5 / 2.0	**26** W	0303 / 0731 / 1345 / 2102	0.6 / 0.9 / 0.0 / 1.7
12 W	0305 / 0758 / 1417 / O 2126	0.4 / 1.1 / -0.4 / 2.0	**27** Th	0335 / 0814 / 1424 / ● 2134	0.6 / 1.0 / 0.0 / 1.7
13 Th	0353 / 0900 / 1512 / 2213	0.3 / 1.1 / -0.4 / 1.9	**28** F	0403 / 0856 / 1503 / 2205	0.5 / 1.0 / 0.1 / 1.6
14 F	0440 / 1002 / 1608 / 2258	0.2 / 0.2 / -0.2 / 1.8	**29** Sa	0429 / 0939 / 1543 / 2233	0.5 / 1.1 / 0.1 / 1.6
15 Sa	0526 / 1103 / 1704 / 2342	0.1 / 1.2 / -0.1 / 1.7	**30** Su	0456 / 1026 / 1626 / 2302	0.4 / 1.2 / 0.2 / 1.5
			31 M	0524 / 1116 / 1713 / 2332	0.3 / 1.2 / 0.3 / 1.5

AUGUST

Day	Time	ft	Day	Time	ft
1 Tu	0556 / 1211 / 1806	0.2 / 1.3 / 0.4	**16** W	0030 / 0654 / 1341 / 1945	1.4 / 0.2 / 1.6 / 0.6
2 W	0005 / 0634 / 1312 / 1906	1.4 / 0.1 / 1.4 / 0.5	**17** Th	0110 / 0739 / 1441 /) 2049	1.3 / 0.2 / 1.5 / 0.7
3 Th	0043 / 0719 / 1417 / (2015	1.3 / 0.0 / 1.5 / 0.6	**18** F	0155 / 0828 / 1542 / 2158	1.2 / 0.2 / 1.6 / 0.8
4 F	0127 / 0810 / 1525 / 2131	1.2 / -0.1 / 1.6 / 0.7	**19** Sa	0244 / 0920 / 1643 / 2307	1.1 / 0.2 / 1.6 / 0.8
5 Sa	0221 / 0908 / 1633 / 2248	1.2 / -0.1 / 1.7 / 0.7	**20** Su	0340 / 1013 / 1738	1.1 / 0.3 / 1.6
6 Su	0324 / 1009 / 1737 / 2358	1.1 / -0.2 / 1.8 / 0.7	**21** M	0007 / 0439 / 1105 / 1828	0.8 / 1.1 / 0.2 / 1.7
7 M	0434 / 1113 / 1836	1.1 / -0.2 / 1.9	**22** Tu	0057 / 0535 / 1155 / 1911	0.8 / 1.1 / 0.2 / 1.7
8 Tu	0059 / 0545 / 1215 / 1929	0.6 / 1.2 / -0.2 / 2.0	**23** W	0138 / 0626 / 1242 / 1950	0.7 / 1.1 / 0.2 / 1.7
9 W	0151 / 0653 / 1315 / 2019	0.5 / 1.2 / -0.2 / 2.0	**24** Th	0212 / 0714 / 1326 / 2024	0.7 / 1.2 / 0.2 / 1.7
10 Th	0239 / 0756 / 1412 / O 2105	0.4 / 1.3 / -0.2 / 1.9	**25** F	0242 / 0758 / 1409 / 2056	0.6 / 1.3 / 0.2 / 1.7
11 F	0324 / 0856 / 1508 / 2149	0.3 / 1.4 / -0.1 / 1.9	**26** Sa	0309 / 0842 / 1452 / ● 2126	0.6 / 1.4 / 0.3 / 1.7
12 Sa	0407 / 0954 / 1602 / 2231	0.3 / 1.5 / 0.1 / 1.7	**27** Su	0336 / 0926 / 1536 / 2156	0.5 / 1.5 / 0.3 / 1.6
13 Su	0448 / 1050 / 1656 / 2311	0.2 / 1.5 / 0.2 / 1.6	**28** M	0404 / 1013 / 1622 / 2226	0.4 / 1.6 / 0.4 / 1.5
14 M	0530 / 1146 / 1750 / 2350	0.2 / 1.6 / 0.4 / 1.5	**29** Tu	0437 / 1102 / 1711 / 2258	0.4 / 1.7 / 0.5 / 1.5
15 Tu	0611 / 1242 / 1846	0.2 / 1.6 / 0.5	**30** W	0513 / 1155 / 1805 / 2335	0.2 / 1.8 / 0.6 / 1.4
			31 Th	0556 / 1253 / 1905	0.1 / 1.8 / 0.7

TIME MERIDIAN 60°W   0000h is midnight, 1200h is noon.

Heights in feet are referenced to the chart datum of soundings.

PUERTO RICO

SAN JUAN, PUERTO RICO

HIGH & LOW WATER 1995   18°28'N   66°01'W

ATLANTIC STANDARD TIME (GMT -4H)

SEPTEMBER

Day	Time / ft	Day	Time / ft
1 F	0017 1.4 / 0646 0.1 / 1356 1.8 / 2011 0.8	16 Sa	0114 1.3 / 0735 0.4 / 1450 1.7 /) 2119 0.9
2 Sa	0108 1.3 / 0743 0.1 / 1503 1.9 / (2123 0.8	17 Su	0207 1.2 / 0828 0.5 / 1548 1.7 / 2221 0.9
3 Su	0210 1.3 / 0847 0.1 / 1610 1.9 / 2235 0.8	18 M	0308 1.2 / 0927 0.5 / 1644 1.7 / 2316 0.9
4 M	0323 1.3 / 0956 0.1 / 1715 1.9 / 2339 0.7	19 Tu	0412 1.2 / 1026 0.5 / 1734 1.7
5 Tu	0439 1.3 / 1105 0.1 / 1814 1.9	20 W	0003 0.8 / 0512 1.1 / 1123 0.5 / 1820 1.7
6 W	0035 0.7 / 0552 1.4 / 1212 0.1 / 1906 1.9	21 Th	0041 0.8 / 0607 1.4 / 1216 0.5 / 1859 1.7
7 Th	0123 0.6 / 0658 1.5 / 1314 0.1 / 1955 1.9	22 F	0114 0.7 / 0656 1.5 / 1307 0.5 / 1935 1.7
8 F	0208 0.5 / 0758 1.6 / 1412 0.2 / O 2039 1.8	23 Sa	0144 0.6 / 0742 1.6 / 1355 0.5 / 2009 1.7
9 Sa	0249 0.4 / 0853 1.7 / 1507 0.3 / 2120 1.7	24 Su	0214 0.5 / 0827 1.8 / 1443 0.5 / ● 2041 1.6
10 Su	0329 0.3 / 0945 1.8 / 1559 0.4 / 2159 1.6	25 M	0245 0.4 / 0912 1.9 / 1531 0.5 / 2114 1.6
11 M	0407 0.3 / 1034 1.8 / 1649 0.5 / 2236 1.5	26 Tu	0319 0.3 / 0959 2.0 / 1620 0.6 / 2149 1.5
12 Tu	0445 0.3 / 1123 1.8 / 1739 0.6 / 2313 1.5	27 W	0357 0.2 / 1048 2.1 / 1711 0.7 / 2228 1.5
13 W	0523 0.3 / 1211 1.8 / 1829 0.7 / 2350 1.4	28 Th	0439 0.2 / 1140 2.1 / 1805 0.7 / 2311 1.4
14 Th	0603 0.4 / 1301 1.8 / 1921 0.8	29 F	0528 0.2 / 1237 2.1 / 1904 0.8
15 F	0029 1.3 / 0647 0.4 / 1354 1.7 / 2018 0.9	30 Sa	0002 1.4 / 0622 0.2 / 1337 2.1 / 2008 0.8

OCTOBER

Day	Time / ft	Day	Time / ft
1 Su	0103 1.4 / 0724 0.2 / 1441 2.1 / (2114 0.8	16 M	0134 1.2 / 0736 0.6 / 1450 1.8 /) 2134 0.9
2 M	0214 1.4 / 0833 0.3 / 1545 2.0 / 2217 0.8	17 Tu	0239 1.3 / 0836 0.6 / 1541 1.7 / 2222 0.8
3 Tu	0333 1.4 / 0948 0.3 / 1647 2.0 / 2315 0.7	18 W	0346 1.3 / 0942 0.7 / 1631 1.7 / 2303 0.8
4 W	0451 1.5 / 1102 0.4 / 1745 1.9	19 Th	0449 1.4 / 1047 0.7 / 1716 1.7 / 2340 0.7
5 Th	0006 0.6 / 0600 1.6 / 1212 0.4 / 1837 1.8	20 F	0545 1.5 / 1149 0.7 / 1759 1.6
6 F	0052 0.5 / 0702 1.8 / 1316 0.5 / 1924 1.8	21 Sa	0015 0.6 / 0636 1.7 / 1247 0.7 / 1838 1.6
7 Sa	0133 0.4 / 0757 1.9 / 1414 0.5 / 2007 1.7	22 Su	0049 0.5 / 0724 1.9 / 1341 0.7 / 1916 1.5
8 Su	0213 0.4 / 0847 2.0 / 1507 0.6 / O 2046 1.6	23 M	0124 0.3 / 0811 2.0 / 1433 0.7 / 1954 1.5
9 M	0250 0.3 / 0933 2.0 / 1557 0.6 / 2124 1.5	24 Tu	0202 0.2 / 0857 2.2 / 1524 0.7 / 2034 1.5
10 Tu	0326 0.3 / 1017 2.0 / 1644 0.7 / 2159 1.4	25 W	0242 0.1 / 0945 2.3 / 1615 0.7 / 2117 1.4
11 W	0401 0.4 / 1059 2.0 / 1729 0.8 / 2234 1.4	26 Th	0327 0.1 / 1035 2.3 / 1707 0.7 / 2204 1.4
12 Th	0437 0.4 / 1141 2.0 / 1814 0.8 / 2311 1.3	27 F	0415 0.1 / 1126 2.3 / 1801 0.7 / 2256 1.4
13 F	0515 0.4 / 1224 1.9 / 1900 0.9 / 2351 1.3	28 Sa	0507 0.1 / 1221 2.3 / 1858 0.7 / 2356 1.4
14 Sa	0556 0.5 / 1310 1.9 / 1950 0.9	29 Su	0606 0.2 / 1317 2.2 / 1957 0.7
15 Su	0038 1.2 / 0643 0.5 / 1359 1.8 / 2042 0.9	30 M	0105 1.4 / 0711 0.3 / 1416 2.1 / (2056 0.6
		31 Tu	0222 1.4 / 0823 0.4 / 1515 1.9 / 2153 0.6

NOVEMBER

Day	Time / ft	Day	Time / ft
1 W	0342 1.5 / 0940 0.5 / 1614 1.8 / 2245 0.5	16 Th	0317 1.3 / 0858 0.7 / 1524 1.6 / 2204 0.5
2 Th	0456 1.6 / 1058 0.6 / 1709 1.7 / 2334 0.4	17 F	0421 1.4 / 1010 0.7 / 1609 1.5 / 2242 0.4
3 F	0602 1.8 / 1211 0.6 / 1800 1.6	18 Sa	0520 1.6 / 1120 0.7 / 1654 1.4 / 2321 0.3
4 Sa	0018 0.3 / 0700 1.9 / 1317 0.6 / 1847 1.5	19 Su	0614 1.7 / 1225 0.7 / 1739 1.4
5 Su	0059 0.3 / 0751 2.0 / 1415 0.7 / 1931 1.4	20 M	0001 0.1 / 0704 1.9 / 1325 0.7 / 1824 1.3
6 M	0138 0.2 / 0837 2.0 / 1507 0.7 / 2010 1.3	21 Tu	0044 0.0 / 0754 2.1 / 1420 0.6 / 1911 1.3
7 Tu	0214 0.2 / 0920 2.1 / 1554 0.7 / O 2047 1.3	22 W	0129 -0.1 / 0842 2.2 / 1513 0.6 / ● 2000 1.3
8 W	0249 0.2 / 0959 2.0 / 1638 0.7 / 2122 1.2	23 Th	0216 -0.2 / 0931 2.3 / 1605 0.6 / 2052 1.2
9 Th	0324 0.3 / 1037 2.0 / 1719 0.8 / 2157 1.2	24 F	0306 -0.2 / 1021 2.3 / 1656 0.5 / 2147 1.2
10 F	0358 0.3 / 1114 2.0 / 1759 0.8 / 2235 1.1	25 Sa	0358 -0.2 / 1111 2.2 / 1749 0.5 / 2247 1.2
11 Sa	0435 0.3 / 1152 1.9 / 1839 0.8 / 2317 1.1	26 Su	0454 -0.1 / 1203 2.1 / 1842 0.4 / 2353 1.2
12 Su	0514 0.4 / 1232 1.8 / 1921 0.8	27 M	0554 0.0 / 1255 2.0 / 1935 0.4
13 M	0006 1.1 / 0558 0.5 / 1313 1.8 / 2003 0.7	28 Tu	0105 1.3 / 0700 0.2 / 1348 1.9 / 2029 0.3
14 Tu	0103 1.1 / 0650 0.5 / 1355 1.7 / 2045 0.7	29 W	0222 1.3 / 0813 0.4 / 1442 1.7 / (2121 0.2
15 W	0209 1.2 / 0750 0.6 / 1439 1.6 / 2125 0.6	30 Th	0339 1.4 / 0931 0.5 / 1536 1.5 / 2211 0.2

DECEMBER

Day	Time / ft	Day	Time / ft
1 F	0450 1.5 / 1051 0.6 / 1629 1.4 / 2259 0.1	16 Sa	0350 1.3 / 0937 0.6 / 1507 1.2 / 2150 0.0
2 Sa	0554 1.7 / 1206 0.6 / 1720 1.3 / 2344 0.1	17 Su	0453 1.4 / 1052 0.6 / 1555 1.1 / 2236 -0.1
3 Su	0650 1.8 / 1313 0.6 / 1808 1.2	18 M	0550 1.6 / 1203 0.6 / 1647 1.1 / 2324 -0.3
4 M	0027 0.0 / 0739 1.8 / 1411 0.6 / 1853 1.1	19 Tu	0645 1.8 / 1307 0.6 / 1742 1.0
5 Tu	0107 0.0 / 0824 1.9 / 1502 0.6 / 1934 1.0	20 W	0014 -0.4 / 0737 1.9 / 1404 0.5 / 1839 1.0
6 W	0144 0.0 / 0904 1.9 / 1546 0.6 / O 2013 1.0	21 Th	0106 -0.5 / 0827 2.0 / 1457 0.4 / ● 1937 1.0
7 Th	0220 0.0 / 0941 1.8 / 1626 0.6 / 2050 0.9	22 F	0159 -0.5 / 0916 2.1 / 1548 0.3 / 2037 1.1
8 F	0255 0.1 / 1016 1.8 / 1703 0.6 / 2127 0.9	23 Sa	0253 -0.5 / 1005 2.0 / 1637 0.3 / 2138 1.1
9 Sa	0329 0.1 / 1050 1.7 / 1737 0.6 / 2206 0.9	24 Su	0348 -0.4 / 1053 2.0 / 1726 0.2 / 2241 1.1
10 Su	0405 0.1 / 1124 1.7 / 1811 0.5 / 2250 0.9	25 M	0445 -0.3 / 1141 1.9 / 1815 0.1 / 2348 1.1
11 M	0444 0.2 / 1157 1.7 / 1904 0.5 / 2339 0.9	26 Tu	0545 -0.1 / 1229 1.7 / 1904 0.0
12 Tu	0527 0.3 / 1231 1.6 / 1918 0.5	27 W	0058 1.2 / 0650 0.1 / 1317 1.5 / 1954 -0.0
13 W	0036 1.0 / 0616 0.3 / 1306 1.5 / 1952 0.4	28 Th	0210 1.2 / 0800 0.2 / 1406 1.4 / (2044 -0.1
14 Th	0138 1.0 / 0714 0.4 / 1344 1.4 / 2028 0.3	29 F	0322 1.3 / 0916 0.2 / 1456 1.2 / 2134 -0.1
15 F	0245 1.1 / 0822 0.5 / 1423 1.3 / 2108 0.2	30 Sa	0431 1.4 / 1036 0.5 / 1547 1.0 / 2223 -0.2
		31 Su	0535 1.5 / 1152 0.5 / 1639 0.9 / 2311 -0.2

TIME MERIDIAN 60°W   0000h is midnight, 1200h is noon.

Heights in feet are referenced to the chart datum of soundings.

VIEQUES PASSAGE, PUERTO RICO

CURRENT TABLES 1995 **FLOOD 250° EBB 056°**

ATLANTIC STANDARD TIME (GMT -4H)

JANUARY

Day	Slack time	Max time	Fld knots	Ebb knots
1 Su ●	0129 0655 1343 2055	0417 1028 1713 2336	0.9 1.1	0.6 0.6
2 M	0229 0756 1433 2140	0517 1123 1802	0.9 1.1	0.6
3 Tu	0327 0858 1521 2222	0027 0614 1216 1850	0.7 0.8	0.6 1.0
4 W	0422 1000 1608 2303	0116 0711 1309 1936	0.7 0.7	0.6 1.0
5 Th	0516 1103 1654 2343	0204 0807 1402 2021	0.8 0.6	0.6 0.9
6 F	0608 1207 1739	0251 0903 1456 2106	0.8 0.5	0.6 0.8
7 Sa	0022 0659 1313 1825	0337 0959 1550 2151	0.8 0.4	0.6 0.7
8 Su ☾	0101 0748 1421 1914	0423 1054 1647 2236	0.8 0.4	0.6 0.6
9 M	0140 0837 1529 2006	0509 1149 1745 2324	0.8 0.3	0.7 0.5
10 Tu	0220 0923 1633 2103	0555 1243 1845	0.7 0.3	0.7
11 W	0301 1009 1732 2205	0013 0642 1335 1944	0.7 0.3	0.4 0.7
12 Th	0343 1053 1824 2307	0105 0728 1424 2039	0.7 0.3	0.4 0.8
13 F	0428 1135 1910	0157 0814 1510 2131	0.7 0.3	0.4 0.8
14 Sa	0007 0515 1217 1950	0249 0859 1553 2217	0.7 0.4	0.3 0.8
15 Su	0101 0604 1258 2027	0339 0944 1634 2300	0.7 0.4	0.3 0.8
16 M ○	0150 0654 1338 2101	0427 1028 1713 2339	0.7 0.9	0.4 0.5
17 Tu	0234 0745 1418 2132	0513 1112 1751	0.7 0.9	0.4
18 W	0316 0838 1458 2202	0016 0559 1156 1828	0.6	0.5 0.4 0.8
19 Th	0357 0933 1538 2232	0053 0645 1242 1906	0.6	0.6 0.5 0.8
20 F	0439 1030 1620 2304	0131 0733 1329 1945	0.6	0.6 0.6 0.8
21 Sa	0523 1130 1704 2338	0211 0823 1419 2026	0.6	0.7 0.5 0.7
22 Su	0611 1234 1751	0253 0916 1513 2111	0.7	0.8 0.5 0.7
23 M	0017 0702 1341 1843	0340 1012 1611 2200	0.7 0.4	0.8 0.6
24 Tu ☽	0100 0755 1450 1940	0430 1111 1713 2254	0.8 0.3	0.9 0.6
25 W	0148 0851 1558 2044	0524 1212 1818 2353	0.8 0.4	0.9 0.6
26 Th	0242 0949 1703 2153	0622 1313 1924	0.9 0.4	0.9
27 F	0341 1046 1801 2303	0057 0721 1413 2027	0.9 0.9	0.5 0.4
28 Sa	0443 1142 1855	0201 0821 1509 2127	0.9 0.9	0.5 0.5
29 Su	0010 0547 1236 1943	0305 0920 1603 2222	0.9 1.0	0.5 0.6
30 M ●	0113 0651 1327 2027	0406 1016 1653 2314	0.8 1.0	0.6 0.6
31 Tu	0210 0754 1416 2109	0505 1111 1741	0.8	0.6 0.9

FEBRUARY

Day	Slack time	Max time	Fld knots	Ebb knots
1 W	0304 0854 1503 2149	0002 0600 1203 1826	0.7 0.7	0.6 0.9
2 Th	0355 0953 1547 2227	0048 0653 1253 1909	0.7 0.7	0.7 0.8
3 F	0444 1051 1630 2304	0132 0744 1342 1951	0.8 0.7	0.6 0.8
4 Sa	0531 1149 1713 2341	0216 0834 1431 2032	0.8 0.5	0.7 0.7
5 Su	0618 1247 1757	0258 0924 1521 2115	0.8 0.4	0.7 0.6
6 M	0018 0704 1347 1843	0342 1015 1613 2158	0.7 0.4	0.7 0.5
7 Tu ☾	0057 0750 1448 1934	0426 1106 1708 2245	0.7 0.3	0.7 0.5
8 W	0138 0836 1547 2030	0512 1158 1805 2336	0.7 0.3	0.7 0.4
9 Th	0222 0923 1644 2131	0600 1251 1903	0.7 0.3	0.7
10 F	0310 1011 1736 2233	0030 0649 1342 1958	0.7 0.3	0.4 0.7
11 Sa	0401 1058 1822 2331	0125 0740 1430 2050	0.7 0.3	0.4 0.7
12 Su	0455 1144 1903	0220 0830 1516 2137	0.7 0.4	0.4 0.8
13 M	0024 0551 1229 1939	0312 0919 1559 2219	0.7 0.5	0.4 0.8
14 Tu	0111 0646 1313 2013	0402 1007 1640 2259	0.7 0.5	0.5
15 W ○	0154 0740 1356 2045	0450 1054 1720 2338	0.7	0.5 0.8 0.6
16 Th	0237 0835 1439 2116	0537 1140 1758	0.6	0.6 0.8
17 F	0319 0929 1522 2150	0016 0624 1227 1838	0.7 0.6	0.7 0.8
18 Sa	0404 1025 1606 2225	0056 0712 1316 1919	0.7 0.6	0.7 0.7
19 Su	0451 1123 1652 2304	0138 0802 1406 2003	0.8 0.6	0.8 0.7
20 M	0540 1222 1741 2347	0224 0854 1459 2050	0.8 0.5	0.8 0.7
21 Tu	0633 1325 1834	0313 0950 1556 2142	0.9 0.5	0.8 0.6
22 W ☽	0036 0728 1429 1933	0406 1049 1657 2240	0.9 0.4	0.8 0.6
23 Th	0131 0827 1533 2038	0504 1150 1801 2342	0.8 0.4	0.8 0.5
24 F	0231 0927 1634 2146	0605 1251 1906	0.8 0.4	0.8
25 Sa	0337 1026 1730 2254	0048 0708 1351 2008	0.8 0.8	0.5 0.5
26 Su	0445 1124 1822 2357	0155 0811 1448 2106	0.8 0.8	0.6 0.5
27 M	0552 1220 1908	0258 0911 1541 2159	0.8 0.8	0.6 0.6
28 Tu	0055 0656 1311 1951	0358 1007 1630 2247	0.7 0.8	0.6 0.7

TIME MERIDIAN 60°W   0000h is midnight, 1200h is noon.

PUERTO RICO

VIEQUES PASSAGE, PUERTO RICO

CURRENT TABLES 1995 **FLOOD 250° EBB 056°**

ATLANTIC STANDARD TIME (GMT -4H)

MARCH

Day	Slack time	Max time	Fld knots	Ebb knots
1 W ●	0148	0453		0.7
	0756	1100	0.7	
	1359	1716		0.8
	2031	2333	0.7	
2 Th	0237	0544		0.7
	0852	1149	0.6	
	1445	1759		0.8
	2109			
3 F		0015	0.7	
	0323	0632		0.7
	0946	1237	0.6	
	1528	1839		0.7
	2145			
4 Sa		0056	0.7	
	0407	0718		0.7
	1038	1322	0.5	
	1610	1919		0.7
	2221			
5 Su		0137	0.7	
	0449	0803		0.7
	1128	1408	0.5	
	1651	1959		0.6
	2257			
6 M		0217	0.7	
	0532	0848		0.7
	1219	1454	0.4	
	1735	2040		0.5
	2335			
7 Tu		0258	0.7	
	0614	0934		0.7
	1310	1542		
	1821	2124		0.5
8 W	0015	0342	0.7	
	0658	1021		0.7
	1403	1633	0.4	
	1912	2212		0.4
9 Th ☾	0059	0428	0.6	
	0745	1111		0.7
	1456	1726	0.3	
	2007	2304		0.4
10 F	0148	0518	0.6	
	0833	1202		0.7
	1548	1821	0.3	
	2105	2400		0.4
11 Sa	0243	0611	0.6	
	0924	1254		0.7
	1637	1914	0.4	
	2202			
12 Su		0057		0.4
	0342	0707	0.6	
	1016	1345		0.7
	1722	2005	0.4	
	2256			
13 M		0153		0.4
	0443	0801	0.6	
	1107	1433		0.7
	1803	2051	0.5	
	2346			
14 Tu		0247		0.5
	0543	0855	0.6	
	1158	1518		0.7
	1840	2134	0.5	
15 W	0032	0338		0.6
	0641	0946	0.6	
	1246	1602		0.7
	1916	2216	0.6	
16 Th ○	0116	0427		0.7
	0737	1036	0.6	
	1334	1644		0.7
	1952	2257	0.7	
17 F	0200	0514		0.8
	0831	1125	0.6	
	1420	1727		0.7
	2028	2339	0.8	
18 Sa	0245	0602		0.8
	0925	1213	0.6	
	1506	1810		0.7
	2107			
19 Su		0023	0.8	
	0332	0651		0.9
	1018	1303	0.6	
	1554	1855		0.7
	2148			
20 M		0109	0.9	
	0421	0741		0.9
	1113	1354	0.6	
	1643	1943		0.6
	2234			
21 Tu		0158	0.9	
	0512	0834		0.9
	1209	1448	0.6	
	1735	2034		0.6
	2324			
22 W		0250	0.9	
	0605	0928		0.9
	1306	1544	0.5	
	1832	2131		
23 Th ☽	0020	0346		0.8
	0702	1026		
	1404	1644		0.9
	1933	2232	0.5	
24 F	0122	0447		0.8
	0801	1126	0.8	
	1502	1745		0.5
	2037	2337	0.5	
25 Sa	0230	0551		0.7
	0902	1227	0.8	
	1559	1847		0.5
	2143			
26 Su		0045	0.6	
	0342	0657		0.7
	1004	1326	0.8	
	1652	1946		0.6
	2245			
27 M		0150	0.6	
	0453	0801		0.6
	1104	1422	0.7	
	1741	2040		0.6
	2343			
28 Tu		0251	0.7	
	0601	0901		0.6
	1200	1514	0.7	
	1826	2131		0.7
29 W	0035	0347	0.7	
	0702	0957		0.6
	1253	1602	0.7	
	1907	2217		0.7
30 Th ●	0123	0438	0.8	
	0759	1048		0.6
	1341	1647	0.6	
	1946	2259		0.7
31 F	0207	0525	0.8	
		1135		0.5
	1426	1728	0.6	
	2023	2340		0.7

APRIL

Day	Slack time	Max time	Fld knots	Ebb knots
1 Sa	0249	0608	0.8	
	0938	1220		0.5
	1510	1808	0.6	
	2059			
2 Su		0018		0.7
	0328	0650	0.8	
	1024	1303		0.5
	1552	1848	0.5	
	2135			
3 M		0056		0.7
	0407	0731	0.8	
	1108	1346		0.5
	1635	1927	0.5	
	2212			
4 Tu		0135		0.7
	0445	0812	0.8	
	1152	1429		0.4
	1719	2009	0.4	
	2252			
5 W		0216		0.7
	0525	0854	0.8	
	1236	1514		0.4
	1806	2054	0.4	
	2335			
6 Th		0259		0.6
	0607	0938	0.7	
	1321	1601		0.4
	1856	2143	0.4	
7 F	0024	0346		0.6
	0653	1025	0.7	
	1407	1650		0.4
	1948	2236	0.4	
8 Sa ☾	0120	0438		0.5
	0742	1114	0.7	
	1452	1740		0.4
	2041	2333	0.4	
9 Su	0222	0534		0.5
	0834	1204	0.7	
	1536	1830		0.5
	2133			
10 M		0031	0.4	
	0328	0633		0.5
	0930	1255	0.6	
	1618	1918		0.5
	2222			
11 Tu		0127	0.5	
	0434	0732		0.5
	1026	1345	0.6	
	1658	2004		0.6
	2310			
12 W		0222	0.6	
	0537	0829		0.5
	1122	1434	0.6	
	1738	2050		0.7
	2357			
13 Th		0313	0.7	
	0636	0924		0.5
	1216	1521	0.6	
	1818	2135		0.7
14 F	0043	0403	0.8	
	0731	1017		0.6
	1308	1608	0.6	
	1859	2220		0.8
15 Sa ○	0129	0453	0.9	
	0825	1108		0.6
	1359	1655	0.6	
	1942	2306		0.9
16 Su	0216	0542	1.0	
	0917	1159		0.6
	1450	1743	0.6	
	2028	2353		0.9
17 M	0305	0631	1.0	
	1008	1250		0.6
	1542	1833	0.6	
	2117			
18 Tu		0043		0.9
	0355	0722	1.0	
	1100	1342		0.6
	1635	1926	0.6	
	2209			
19 W		0135		0.9
	0446	0814	1.0	
	1152	1436		0.6
	1731	2022	0.6	
	2307			
20 Th		0230		0.8
	0540	0908	1.0	
	1245	1531		0.6
	1830	2122	0.6	
21 F ☽	0010	0328		0.8
	0636	1003	0.9	
	1337	1629		0.6
	1931	2226	0.6	
22 Sa	0119	0431		0.7
	0734	1100	0.9	
	1429	1727		0.6
	2033	2332	0.6	
23 Su	0232	0537		0.6
	0834	1158	0.8	
	1520	1824		0.6
	2134			
24 M		0038	0.6	
	0348	0643		0.5
	0936	1255	0.7	
	1609	1920		0.7
	2231			
25 Tu		0142	0.5	
	0500	0748		0.6
	1036	1350	0.7	
	1655	2011		0.7
	2324			
26 W		0240	0.7	
	0606	0848		0.5
	1134	1442	0.6	
	1738	2059		0.7
27 Th	0012	0332	0.8	
	0705	0943		0.5
	1229	1529	0.6	
	1819	2143		0.7
28 F	0056	0420	0.8	
	0758	1034		0.5
	1319	1614	0.6	
	1858	2224		0.7
29 Sa ●	0137	0503	0.8	
	0845	1120		0.5
	1407	1656	0.5	
	1935	2303		0.7
30 Su	0215	0544	0.9	
	0928	1203		0.5
	1452	1737	0.4	
	2012	2341		0.7

TIME MERIDIAN 60°W

0000h is midnight, 1200h is noon.

VIEQUES PASSAGE, PUERTO RICO

CURRENT TABLES 1995 **FLOOD 250° EBB 056°**

ATLANTIC STANDARD TIME (GMT -4H)

MAY

Day	Slack time	Max time	Fld knots	Ebb knots
1 M	0251	0623		0.9
	1008	1245	0.5	
	1537	1817		0.4
	2049			
2 Tu		0019	0.7	
	0327	0701		0.9
	1047	1325	0.5	
	1621	1858		0.4
	2129			
3 W		0057	0.7	
	0404	0739		0.8
	1126	1406	0.5	
	1706	1942		0.4
	2212			
4 Th		0138	0.6	
	0442	0819		0.8
	1204	1448	0.5	
	1751	2028		0.4
	2300			
5 F		0221	0.6	
	0523	0900		0.8
	1242	1531	0.5	
	1838	2117		0.4
	2355			
6 Sa		0309	0.5	
	0607	0943		0.7
	1321	1615	0.5	
	1926	2210		0.4
7 Su ☾	0056	0402	0.5	
	0654	1029		0.7
	1359	1701	0.5	
	2014	2306		0.4
8 M	0204	0459	0.4	
	0746	1117		0.6
	1438	1747	0.6	
	2102			
9 Tu		0004		0.5
	0314	0600	0.4	
	0843	1206		0.6
	1518	1834	0.6	
	2150			
10 W		0100		0.6
	0423	0702	0.4	
	0942	1257		0.6
	1559	1921	0.7	
	2238			
11 Th		0156		0.7
	0527	0802	0.4	
	1042	1349		0.6
	1642	2010	0.8	
	2326			
12 F		0249		0.8
	0627	0900	0.5	
	1142	1441		0.6
	1727	2058	0.9	
13 Sa	0014	0341	0.5	
	0722	0956		0.9
	1240	1534	0.6	
	1814	2147		0.9
14 Su ○	0103	0432		1.0
	0815	1050	0.6	
	1337	1626		0.6
	1904	2238	1.0	
15 M	0153	0522		1.1
	0905	1143	0.6	
	1433	1720		0.6
	1957	2329	1.0	
16 Tu	0242	0612		1.1
	0955	1235	0.6	
	1529	1815		0.6
	2053			
17 W		0021		0.9
	0333	0703		1.1
	1044	1328	0.7	
	1626	1912		0.6
	2152			
18 Th		0116		0.9
	0424	0754		1.1
	1132	1421	0.7	
	1724	2011		0.6
	2255			
19 F		0212		0.8
	0516	0846		1.0
	1220	1515	0.7	
	1823	2112		0.6
20 Sa	0002	0311		0.7
	0610	0939		0.9
	1307	1609	0.7	
	1922	2216		0.6
21 Su ☽	0115	0413		0.6
	0705	1033		0.8
	1354	1703	0.7	
	2021	2321		0.6
22 M	0230	0518	0.5	
	0803	1127		0.7
	1440	1757	0.7	
	2117			
23 Tu		0024		0.7
	0346	0623	0.4	
	0902	1220		0.6
	1525	1849	0.8	
	2210			
24 W		0125		0.7
	0458	0728	0.4	
	1002	1313		0.6
	1609	1938	0.8	
	2259			
25 Th		0220		0.7
	0602	0828	0.4	
	1101	1404		0.5
	1651	2025	0.8	
	2345			
26 F		0311		0.8
	0659	0924	0.4	
	1159	1453		0.4
	1731	2108	0.8	
27 Sa	0027	0357		0.8
	0749	1014	0.4	
	1253	1539		0.4
	1811	2149	0.7	
28 Su	0106	0439		0.9
	0833	1100	0.4	
	1345	1623		0.4
	1850	2229	0.7	
29 M ●	0143	0519		0.9
	0912	1143	0.4	
	1433	1706		0.3
	1930	2307	0.7	
30 Tu	0219	0556		0.9
	0949	1224	0.4	
	1520	1749		0.3
	2011	2346	0.7	
31 W	0254	0633		0.9
	1024	1304	0.5	
	1604	1832		0.3
	2055			

JUNE

Day	Slack time	Max time	Fld knots	Ebb knots
1 Th		0026	0.6	
	0331	0710		0.9
	1058	1342	0.5	
	1647	1917		0.3
	2143			
2 F		0107	0.6	
	0408	0748		0.8
	1132	1421	0.5	
	1730	2003		0.4
	2235			
3 Sa		0151	0.6	
	0448	0826		0.8
	1205	1500	0.5	
	1813	2052		0.4
	2334			
4 Su		0239	0.5	
	0530	0906		0.8
	1238	1540	0.6	
	1857	2144		0.4
5 M		0331	0.4	
	0038	0949		0.7
	0615	1623	0.6	
	1312	2239		0.5
	1942			
6 Tu ☾	0147	0428	0.4	
	0705	1034		0.6
	1348	1707	0.7	
	2029	2335		0.6
7 W	0258	0529	0.4	
	0800	1123		0.6
	1427	1755	0.8	
	2118			
8 Th		0033		0.7
	0407	0632	0.4	
	0900	1215		0.6
	1510	1844	0.8	
	2208			
9 F		0129		0.8
	0513	0735	0.4	
	1004	1310		0.5
	1557	1936	0.9	
	2259			
10 Sa		0225		0.9
	0613	0836	0.4	
	1109	1407		0.5
	1648	2028	0.9	
	2350			
11 Su		0319		1.0
	0709	0935	0.5	
	1213	1505		0.5
	1742	2122	1.0	
12 M		0042		1.1
	0800	0412		1.1
	1315	1031	0.6	
	1838	1603		0.6
		2216	1.0	
13 Tu ○	0133	0503		1.1
	0849	1125	0.6	
	1415	1701		0.6
	1937	2310	1.0	
14 W	0223	0554		1.1
	0936	1218	0.7	
	1514	1800		0.6
	2038			
15 Th		0005	0.9	
	0314	0644		1.1
	1022	1310	0.7	
	1612	1858		0.6
	2141			
16 F		0100		0.8
	0404	0734		1.1
	1107	1401	0.7	
	1709	1958		0.6
	2246			
17 Sa		0156		0.8
	0454	0823		1.0
	1151	1453	0.8	
	1806	2058		0.6
	2354			
18 Su		0253		0.6
	0545	0913		0.9
	1235	1544	0.8	
	1902	2159		0.6
19 M ☽	0105	0353		0.5
	0636	1002		0.8
	1318	1635	0.8	
	1957	2300		0.7
20 Tu	0219	0454		0.4
	0729	1052		0.7
	1400	1725	0.8	
	2050			
21 W		0000		0.7
	0332	0557	0.4	
	0824	1143		0.6
	1442	1814	0.8	
	2141			
22 Th		0058		0.7
	0442	0659	0.3	
	0923	1234		0.5
	1524	1902	0.8	
	2228			
23 F		0152		0.7
	0545	0800	0.3	
	1023	1325		0.4
	1606	1949	0.8	
	2313			
24 Sa		0243		0.8
	0640	0856	0.3	
	1125	1416		0.4
	1649	2033	0.7	
	2355			
25 Su		0329		0.8
	0728	0948	0.3	
	1224	1505		0.3
	1732	2116	0.7	
26 M		0411		0.8
	0035	1035	0.4	
	0810	1553		0.3
	1318	2158	0.7	
	1815			
27 Tu ●	0113	0451		0.9
	0848	1118	0.4	
	1409	1639		0.3
	1900	2239	0.7	
28 W	0150	0529		0.9
	0922	1158	0.4	
	1455	1724		0.3
	1947	2320	0.7	
29 Th	0227	0606		0.9
	0955	1236	0.5	
	1537	1809		0.4
	2035			
30 F		0002	0.6	
	0304	0642		0.9
	1026	1313	0.5	
	1618	1854		0.4
	2126			

PUERTO RICO

TIME MERIDIAN 60°W

0000h is midnight, 1200h is noon.

VIEQUES PASSAGE, PUERTO RICO

CURRENT TABLES 1995 **FLOOD 250° EBB 056°**

ATLANTIC STANDARD TIME (GMT -4H)

JULY

Day	Slack time	Max time	Fld (kn)	Ebb (kn)
1 Sa		0044	0.6	
	0342	0718		0.8
	1056	1349	0.6	
	1658	1939		0.4
	2221			
2 Su		0129	0.5	
	0421	0755		0.8
	1125	1426	0.6	
	1739	2027		0.5
	2320			
3 M		0216	0.5	
	0502	0833		0.7
	1156	1504	0.7	
	1822	2117		0.5
4 Tu	0023	0307	0.4	
	0546	0914		0.7
	1229	1546	0.7	
	1908	2211		0.6
5 W (☾)	0129	0403	0.4	
	0634	0959		0.6
	1306	1632	0.8	
	1956	2307		0.7
6 Th	0238	0502	0.4	
	0728	1048		0.6
	1347	1721	0.8	
	2048			
7 F		0005		0.7
	0347	0605	0.3	
	0828	1142		0.6
	1434	1813	0.9	
	2141			
8 Sa		0104		0.8
	0453	0710	0.4	
	0934	1241		0.5
	1526	1909	0.9	
	2235			
9 Su		0202		0.9
	0553	0813	0.4	
	1042	1342		0.5
	1623	2006	0.9	
	2330			
10 M		0258		1.0
	0648	0914	0.5	
	1150	1445		0.5
	1723	2103	1.0	
11 Tu	0023	0352		1.0
	0739	1011	0.5	
	1255	1547		0.6
	1825	2200	0.9	
12 W (○)	0116	0445		1.1
	0827	1106	0.6	
	1357	1647		0.6
	1929	2256	0.9	
13 Th	0207	0535		1.1
	0912	1158	0.7	
	1456	1746		0.6
	2032	2351	0.9	
14 F	0257	0624		1.0
	0955	1248	0.7	
	1552	1844		0.7
	2135			
15 Sa		0046	0.8	
	0346	0711		1.0
	1037	1337	0.8	
	1646	1941		0.7
	2239			
16 Su		0140	0.7	
	0434	0758		0.9
	1119	1425	0.8	
	1740	2038		0.7
	2343			
17 M		0234	0.6	
	0521	0844		0.8
	1159	1513	0.8	
	1832	2134		0.7
18 Tu	0049	0329	0.5	
	0608	0930		0.7
	1240	1600	0.8	
	1923	2230		0.7
19 W (☽)	0156	0426	0.4	
	0657	1017		0.6
	1320	1648	0.8	
	2014	2327		0.7
20 Th	0304	0525	0.3	
	0749	1105		0.5
	1401	1736	0.8	
	2103			
21 F		0022		0.7
	0410	0625	0.3	
	0846	1156		0.5
	1444	1824	0.7	
	2150			
22 Sa		0116		0.7
	0511	0724	0.3	
	0947	1248		0.4
	1529	1912	0.7	
	2236			
23 Su		0206		0.7
	0605	0821	0.3	
	1050	1342		0.4
	1615	1959	0.7	
	2320			
24 M		0254		0.8
	0652	0914	0.3	
	1151	1435		0.3
	1704	2046	0.7	
25 Tu	0003	0338		0.8
	0733	1002	0.4	
	1246	1526		0.3
	1754	2131	0.7	
26 W	0044	0420		0.8
	0810	1045	0.4	
	1336	1614		0.4
	1844	2216	0.7	
27 Th (●)	0124	0459		0.8
	0844	1124	0.5	
	1420	1701		0.4
	1935	2259	0.6	
28 F	0204	0537		0.8
	0915	1201	0.5	
	1501	1746		0.4
	2027	2343	0.6	
29 Sa	0243	0613		0.8
	0945	1237	0.6	
	1540	1830		0.5
	2119			
30 Su		0026	0.6	
	0322	0649		0.8
	1014	1312	0.6	
	1620	1915		0.6
	2213			
31 M		0111	0.6	
	0402	0726		0.7
	1044	1350	0.7	
	1701	2002		0.6
	2310			

AUGUST

Day	Slack time	Max time	Fld (kn)	Ebb (kn)
1 Tu		0158	0.5	
	0443	0804		0.7
	1116	1429	0.7	
	1745	2051		0.7
2 W	0009	0249	0.5	
	0527	0846		0.7
	1151	1513	0.8	
	1833	2144		0.7
3 Th (☾)	0112	0343	0.4	
	0616	0932		0.6
	1232	1600	0.8	
	1924	2240		0.8
4 F	0217	0441	0.4	
	0709	1023		0.6
	1318	1653	0.8	
	2019	2339		0.8
5 Sa	0323	0543	0.4	
	0810	1120		0.6
	1410	1749	0.9	
	2115			
6 Su		0039		0.8
	0427	0648	0.4	
	0917	1223		0.5
	1509	1849	0.9	
	2213			
7 M		0139		0.9
	0526	0752	0.4	
	1026	1328		0.5
	1612	1950	0.9	
	2311			
8 Tu		0237		0.9
	0620	0853	0.5	
	1135	1433		0.6
	1718	2050	0.9	
9 W	0007	0332		0.9
	0710	0950	0.6	
	1239	1536		0.6
	1824	2149	0.9	
10 Th (○)	0101	0425		1.0
	0756	1043	0.6	
	1338	1637		0.7
	1929	2245	0.8	
11 F	0152	0514		0.9
	0840	1133	0.7	
	1434	1734		0.7
	2031	2340	0.8	
12 Sa	0241	0601		0.9
	0922	1221	0.7	
	1527	1828		0.7
	2131			
13 Su		0032	0.7	
	0328	0647		0.9
	1002	1307	0.8	
	1617	1921		0.8
	2230			
14 M		0123	0.6	
	0414	0731		0.8
	1041	1352	0.8	
	1706	2012		0.7
	2329			
15 Tu		0213	0.6	
	0459	0814		0.7
	1120	1437	0.8	
	1754	2103		0.7
16 W	0027	0304	0.5	
	0544	0858		0.6
	1200	1522	0.8	
	1842	2155		0.7
17 Th (☽)	0126	0356	0.4	
	0631	0943		0.6
	1240	1607	0.7	
	1929	2246		0.7
18 F	0226	0451	0.3	
	0722	1030		0.5
	1323	1654	0.7	
	2017	2339		0.7
19 Sa	0325	0547	0.3	
	0818	1121		0.4
	1408	1743	0.7	
	2105			
20 Su		0031		0.7
	0422	0645	0.3	
	0918	1216		0.4
	1458	1834	0.6	
	2153			
21 M		0123		0.7
	0514	0741	0.3	
	1019	1312		0.4
	1551	1925	0.6	
	2241			
22 Tu		0212		0.7
	0601	0833	0.4	
	1118	1408		0.4
	1647	2017	0.6	
	2328			
23 W		0259		0.7
	0642	0920	0.4	
	1210	1501		0.4
	1743	2106	0.6	
24 Th	0014	0343		0.7
	0720	1003	0.5	
	1257	1550		0.5
	1837	2154	0.6	
25 F	0058	0424		0.7
	0754	1042	0.5	
	1339	1637		0.5
	1931	2241	0.6	
26 Sa (●)	0141	0503		0.7
	0825	1120	0.6	
	1420	1722		0.6
	2023	2326	0.6	
27 Su	0223	0541		0.7
	0856	1157	0.6	
	1500	1806		0.7
	2115			
28 M		0011	0.6	
	0305	0618		0.7
	0927	1234	0.7	
	1541	1851		0.7
	2207			
29 Tu		0056	0.6	
	0347	0657		0.7
	1001	1314	0.8	
	1625	1938		0.8
	2301			
30 W		0144	0.5	
	0430	0739		0.7
	1037	1357	0.8	
	1711	2027		0.8
	2356			
31 Th		0234	0.5	
	0516	0823		0.8
	1118	1443	0.8	
	1801	2119		0.8

TIME MERIDIAN 60°W

0000h is midnight, 1200h is noon.

VIEQUES PASSAGE, PUERTO RICO

CURRENT TABLES 1995 **FLOOD 250° EBB 056°**

ATLANTIC STANDARD TIME (GMT -4H)

SEPTEMBER

Day	Slack time	Max time	Fld	Ebb knots
1 F	0054	0327	0.5	
	0607	0913		0.6
	1205	1534	0.8	
	1854	2215		0.8
2 Sa ☾	0154	0425	0.4	
	0703	1008		0.6
	1258	1630	0.8	
	1951	2314		0.8
3 Su	0255	0526	0.4	
	0805	1109		0.5
	1359	1730	0.8	
	2051			
4 M		0014		0.8
	0355	0629	0.4	
	0911	1214		0.5
	1505	1834	0.8	
	2151			
5 Tu		0115		0.8
	0452	0732	0.5	
	1019	1322		0.6
	1615	1938	0.8	
	2252			
6 W		0214		0.8
	0545	0831	0.6	
	1123	1427		0.6
	1724	2041	0.7	
	2350			
7 Th		0309		0.8
	0634	0926	0.6	
	1223	1529		0.7
	1831	2140	0.7	
8 F ○	0045	0401		0.8
	0719	1017	0.7	
	1318	1626		0.7
	1934	2236	0.7	
9 Sa	0136	0450		0.8
	0802	1105	0.7	
	1410	1720		0.8
	2033	2329	0.7	
10 Su	0225	0536		0.8
	0842	1151	0.8	
	1458	1810		0.8
	2128			
11 M		0018	0.6	
	0311	0619		0.7
	0921	1234	0.8	
	1544	1858		0.8
	2221			
12 Tu		0106	0.6	
	0356	0701		0.7
	1000	1316	0.8	
	1628	1944		0.8
	2312			
13 W		0153	0.5	
	0440	0743		0.6
	1038	1358	0.8	
	1711	2030		0.8
14 Th	0003	0240	0.5	
	0525	0826		0.5
	1118	1440	0.7	
	1755	2116		0.8
15 F	0053	0328	0.4	
	0612	0911		0.5
	1200	1525	0.7	
	1839	2203		0.7
16 Sa ☽	0144	0418	0.4	
	0703	0959		0.4
	1245	1611	0.6	
	1925	2252		0.7
17 Su	0235	0510	0.4	
	0757	1051		0.4
	1336	1702	0.6	
	2013	2343		0.7
18 M	0326	0604	0.4	
	0854	1147		0.4
	1433	1755	0.6	
	2104			
19 Tu		0034		0.7
	0414	0657	0.4	
	0951	1245		0.5
	1533	1851	0.5	
	2156			
20 W		0125		0.7
	0459	0747	0.4	
	1044	1342		0.5
	1635	1947	0.5	
	2248			
21 Th		0214		0.7
	0540	0833	0.5	
	1132	1435		0.5
	1735	2040	0.5	
	2339			
22 F		0300		0.6
	0618	0916	0.5	
	1217	1525		0.6
	1832	2132	0.5	
23 Sa	0029	0343		0.6
	0654	0957	0.6	
	1259	1612		0.7
	1926	2221	0.6	
24 Su ●	0116	0425		0.6
	0729	1037	0.7	
	1341	1657		0.7
	2018	2308	0.6	
25 M	0202	0506		0.6
	0803	1117	0.7	
	1423	1743		0.8
	2108	2355	0.6	
26 Tu	0247	0547		0.6
	0840	1158	0.8	
	1507	1828		0.9
	2159			
27 W		0042		0.6
	0332	0630	0.6	
	0920	1242	0.8	
	1553	1916		0.9
	2250			
28 Th		0130		0.6
	0420	0716	0.6	
	1004	1328	0.9	
	1641	2005		0.9
	2342			
29 F		0221		0.6
	0510	0806	0.6	
	1052	1418	0.8	
	1732	2057		0.9
30 Sa	0036	0315		0.5
	0604	0900	0.6	
	1147	1513	0.8	
	1827	2152		0.9

OCTOBER

Day	Slack time	Max time	Fld	Ebb knots
1 Su ☾	0130	0411	0.5	
	0702	0959		0.6
	1248	1612	0.8	
	1925	2250		0.8
2 M	0226	0511	0.5	
	0805	1104		0.6
	1357	1716	0.7	
	2025	2350		0.8
3 Tu	0321	0611	0.6	
	0909	1211		0.6
	1510	1822	0.7	
	2128			
4 W		0050	0.8	
	0414	0711	0.6	
	1012	1318		0.6
	1624	1929	0.6	
	2230			
5 Th		0148	0.7	
	0504	0807	0.7	
	1112	1422		0.6
	1734	2032	0.6	
	2330			
6 F		0243	0.7	
	0552	0900	0.7	
	1206	1521		0.7
	1839	2132	0.6	
7 Sa	0026	0334	0.7	
	0636	0949	0.7	
	1257	1614		0.8
	1939	2226	0.6	
8 Su ○	0119	0422	0.6	
	0718	1034	0.8	
	1344	1704		0.8
	2033	2317	0.6	
9 M	0208	0507	0.6	
	0758	1118	0.8	
	1427	1750		0.9
	2123			
10 Tu		0004	0.5	
	0254	0550		0.6
	0837	1159	0.8	
	1509	1833		0.9
	2210			
11 W		0049	0.5	
	0339	0631		0.5
	0915	1239	0.7	
	1549	1915		0.9
	2254			
12 Th		0133	0.5	
	0424	0713		0.5
	0955	1319	0.7	
	1628	1956		0.8
	2338			
13 F		0217	0.5	
	0510	0756		0.4
	1036	1400	0.7	
	1708	2038		0.8
14 Sa	0021	0301	0.5	
	0557	0842		0.4
	1121	1443	0.6	
	1749	2122		0.8
15 Su	0104	0348	0.5	
	0647	0931		0.4
	1211	1530	0.6	
	1833	2207		0.7
16 M ☽	0147	0435	0.5	
	0738	1024		0.4
	1308	1621	0.5	
	1921	2255		0.7
17 Tu	0231	0524	0.5	
	0830	1120		0.4
	1410	1717	0.5	
	2012	2344		0.6
18 W	0314	0613	0.5	
	0921	1218		0.4
	1517	1816	0.4	
	2107			
19 Th		0034		0.6
	0355	0700	0.5	
	1009	1314		0.5
	1623	1915	0.4	
	2203			
20 F		0123		0.6
	0435	0746	0.6	
	1055	1407		0.6
	1725	2012	0.5	
	2259			
21 Sa		0212		0.6
	0514	0830	0.7	
	1140	1457		0.7
	1823	2106	0.5	
	2354			
22 Su		0258		0.6
	0553	0913	0.7	
	1223	1546		0.7
	1918	2158	0.5	
23 M	0046	0345		0.6
	0632	0957	0.8	
	1308	1633		0.9
	2009	2248	0.5	
24 Tu ●	0137	0431		0.6
	0714	1041	0.9	
	1352	1720		1.0
	2059	2337	0.6	
25 W	0227	0518		0.6
	0758	1127	0.9	
	1439	1807		1.0
	2148			
26 Th		0027		0.6
	0318	0606	0.6	
	0846	1215	0.9	
	1527	1856		1.0
	2236			
27 F		0117		0.6
	0410	0658	0.6	
	0938	1305	0.9	
	1616	1945		1.0
	2325			
28 Sa		0208		0.6
	0504	0752	0.6	
	1034	1358	0.8	
	1708	2037		1.0
29 Su	0015	0302		0.6
	0601	0851	0.6	
	1136	1456	0.8	
	1802	2131		0.9
30 M ☾	0105	0357		0.6
	0647	0953	0.6	
	1245	1557	0.7	
	1859	2226		0.9
31 Tu	0155	0454	0.7	
	0802	1059		0.6
	1359	1702	0.6	
	1959	2324		0.8

PUERTO RICO

TIME MERIDIAN 60°W 0000h is midnight, 1200h is noon.

VIEQUES PASSAGE, PUERTO RICO

CURRENT TABLES 1995 **FLOOD 250° EBB 056°**

ATLANTIC STANDARD TIME (GMT -4H)

NOVEMBER

Day	Slack time	Max time	Fld (knots)	Ebb (knots)
1 W	0245 0903 1516 2101	0551 1206 1810	0.7 0.5	 0.6
2 Th	0334 1001 1631 2203	0021 0647 1311 1917	 0.7 0.5	0.7 0.7
3 F	0422 1056 1741 2305	0118 0741 1412 2020	 0.7 0.5	0.6 0.7
4 Sa	0508 1147 1844	0212 0831 1508 2119	 0.8 0.5	0.6 0.8
5 Su	0003 0551 1233 1939	0303 0919 1559 2213	 0.8 0.5	0.5 0.8
6 M	0058 0633 1317 2029	0351 1003 1645 2303	 0.8 0.5	0.5 0.9
7 Tu ○	0149 0713 1357 2114	0436 1044 1728 2348	 0.8 0.5	0.5 0.9
8 W	0237 0753 1435 2155	0520 1124 1808	 0.8	0.4 0.9
9 Th	0324 0833 1512 2234	0031 0602 1203 1847	0.5 0.7	 0.4 0.9
10 F	0410 0914 1549 2312	0113 0645 1243 1925	0.5 0.7	 0.4 0.9
11 Sa	0455 0959 1627 2349	0154 0729 1323 2004	0.5 0.6	 0.4 0.8
12 Su	0541 1047 1706	0235 0815 1407 2044	0.5 0.6	 0.4 0.8
13 M	0026 0628 1142 1748	0317 0905 1454 2126	0.5 0.5	 0.4 0.8
14 Tu	0103 0715 1243 1833	0401 0957 1545 2210	0.5 0.5	 0.5 0.7
15 W ☽	0140 0801 1349 1923	0444 1052 1641 2256	0.6 0.4	 0.4 0.6
16 Th	0218 0848 1459 2017	0529 1148 1740 2344	0.6 0.4	 0.5 0.6
17 F	0256 0934 1607 2115	0614 1243 1841	0.6 0.4	 0.6
18 Sa	0335 1020 1711 2215	0033 0700 1337 1941	 0.7 0.4	0.6 0.7
19 Su	0416 1106 1810 2314	0124 0747 1429 2039	 0.8 0.4	0.5 0.8
20 M	0459 1152 1905	0215 0834 1519 2134	 0.8 0.4	0.5 0.9
21 Tu	0013 0545 1239 1956	0307 0922 1609 2227	 0.9 0.5	0.5 1.0
22 W ●	0110 0634 1327 2044	0359 1011 1658 2319	 0.9 0.5	0.5 1.1
23 Th	0206 0726 1416 2132	0452 1101 1747	 1.0	0.5 1.1
24 F	0302 0822 1505 2219	0010 0546 1153 1836	0.6 0.9	 0.6 1.1
25 Sa	0358 0921 1556 2305	0101 0642 1247 1926	0.6 0.9	 0.6 1.1
26 Su	0455 1023 1647 2351	0153 0741 1342 2017	0.7 0.8	 0.6 1.0
27 M	0552 1130 1740	0245 0841 1441 2109	0.7 0.7	 0.6 0.9
28 Tu	0038 0651 1242 1835	0339 0944 1542 2202	0.7 0.6	 0.7 0.9
29 W ☾	0124 0750 1358 1932	0433 1049 1646 2256	0.8 0.5	 0.6 0.8
30 Th	0210 0847 1515 2031	0527 1154 1752 2350	0.8 0.5	 0.7 0.7

DECEMBER

Day	Slack time	Max time	Fld (knots)	Ebb (knots)
1 F	0256 0942 1629 2132	0620 1256 1858	0.8 0.4	 0.7
2 Sa	0341 1034 1738 2234	0045 0712 1355 2002	 0.8 0.4	0.6 0.8
3 Su	0425 1123 1838 2335	0138 0801 1449 2101	 0.8 0.4	0.5 0.8
4 M	0508 1208 1931	0230 0847 1538 2155	 0.8 0.4	0.4 0.9
5 Tu	0033 0551 1249 2018	0319 0931 1623 2244	 0.8 0.4	0.4 0.9
6 W ○	0127 0632 1328 2059	0406 1013 1704 2329	 0.8 0.4	0.4 0.9
7 Th	0218 0715 1405 2136	0451 1053 1743	 0.7	0.4 0.9
8 F	0306 0758 1441 2211	0011 0536 1133 1820	0.4 0.7	 0.3 0.9
9 Sa	0351 0843 1517 2244	0050 0620 1213 1856	0.5 0.6	 0.3 0.9
10 Su	0435 0931 1554 2317	0129 0705 1254 1933	0.5 0.6	 0.3 0.8
11 M	0517 1023 1632 2349	0207 0750 1337 2011	0.5 0.5	 0.4 0.8
12 Tu	0600 1120 1712	0245 0838 1423 2049	0.6 0.5	 0.4 0.8
13 W	0021 0642 1222 1755	0324 0928 1513 2130	0.6 0.4	 0.4 0.7
14 Th	0054 0726 1328 1842	0405 1021 1608 2213	0.6 0.4	 0.4 0.6
15 F ☽	0128 0812 1437 1934	0447 1115 1706 2259	0.7 0.3	 0.6 0.6
16 Sa	0204 0857 1546 2031	0532 1210 1807 2349	0.7 0.3	 0.6 0.5
17 Su	0244 0946 1651 2132	0620 1306 1909	0.8 0.3	 0.7
18 M	0329 1035 1751 2237	0042 0710 1400 2010	 0.9 0.4	0.5 0.8
19 Tu	0418 1125 1846 2341	0138 0801 1454 2108	 0.9 0.4	0.5 0.9
20 W	0511 1216 1937	0235 0854 1546 2204	 0.9 0.5	0.5 1.0
21 Th ●	0044 0608 1306 2025	0333 0948 1637 2258	 1.0 0.6	0.5 1.1
22 F	0145 0707 1357 2111	0432 1042 1727 2350	 1.0 0.6	0.6 1.1
23 Sa	0244 0809 1448 2156	0530 1137 1817	 0.9	0.6 1.1
24 Su	0341 0912 1538 2240	0042 0629 1232 1907	0.7 0.9	 0.6 1.1
25 M	0438 1017 1629 2324	0133 0728 1328 1956	0.7 0.8	 0.6 1.0
26 Tu	0535 1125 1719	0224 0828 1426 2046	0.8 0.7	 0.7 0.9
27 W	0007 0632 1235 1811	0315 0929 1525 2136	0.8 0.6	 0.7 0.7
28 Th ☾	0051 0727 1348 1904	0406 1030 1626 2226	0.8 0.5	 0.5 0.7
29 F	0134 0822 1502 2000	0458 1132 1729 2318	0.8 0.4	 0.4 0.6
30 Sa	0218 0915 1614 2059	0549 1232 1833	0.8 0.3	 0.3
31 Su	0302 1006 1721 2200	0010 0639 1329 1936	 0.8 0.7	0.5 0.8

TIME MERIDIAN 60°W 0000h is midnight, 1200h is noon.

U.S. VIRGIN ISLANDS

COAST PILOT

CAUTION: Our information on aids to navigation comes from official government sources. The latitudes and longitudes of these marks may not correspond to the readings from GPS or LORAN receivers. Some aids have been reported as unreliable, missing, off position, or showing incorrect characteristics. No single aid to navigation, or waypoint, should be relied upon as a sole means of fixing your position.

Note: The chartlets in this section are <u>not</u> <u>intended for navigation</u> and are included for reference and planning purposes only. While chartlets reproduced from government sources are from the most current editions as of press time, they incorporate <u>no corrections</u> to navigational aids, depths, or hazards since the edition publication date.

ENTRY PROCEDURES

The U.S. Virgin Islands are a territory of the United States, but constitute a separate customs district. The three principal islands are St. Thomas, St. John, and St. Croix. U.S. vessels arriving from a foreign port (including the British Virgin Islands) and all foreign vessels must clear customs with authorities at Charlotte Amalie, St. Thomas (809-774-6755; on Sundays, holidays, and after hours, 809-774-4554); Christiansted, St. Croix (809-773-1011; on Sundays, 809-778-0216); or Cruz Bay, St. John (809-776-6741). U.S. vessels arriving directly from mainland U.S. and Puerto Rico do not need to clear in. Most foreign yachts have to obtain a cruising permit. See the Coast Pilot introduction for more information on U.S. Customs and Immigration procedures.

Normal working hours are 8:00AM to 5:00PM, Monday through Saturday. Overtime is charged for Sunday, holiday, and after-hours arrivals. U.S.-registered vessels do not need to obtain a clearance when leaving the U.S. Virgin Islands, but may need one when checking in with authorities in another country.

The local currency is the U.S. dollar, and credit cards or traveler's checks are widely accepted.

The language spoken is English.

APPROACHES TO ST. THOMAS

Sail Rock Lighted Buoy 1, 18 17.1N, 65 06.5W. Fl G 6s, 4M. Green.

SAVANA ISLAND LIGHT, 18 20.4N, 65 05.0W. Fl W 4s, 300ft, 7M. White tower.

WEST GREGERIE CHANNEL

Lighted Buoy 2, 18 18.4N, 65 33.5W. Fl R, 4s, 3M. Red.

Buoy 3, Green can.

Lighted Buoy 4, Fl R 2.5s, 3M. Red.

Lighted Buoy 5, Fl G 4s, 4M. Green.

LIGHT 6, 18 19.9N, 64 56.9W. Fl R 4s, 16ft, 4M. TR on dolphin.

CROWN BAY MOORING CELL LIGHT, 18 19.9N, 64 57.1W. F R. On dolphin. Private aid.

KRUM BAY

SOUTH DOLPHIN OBSTRUCTION LIGHT, 18 19.6N, 64 57.7W. Q W. On dolphin. Sychronized with Krum Bay Pier Obstruction Light; private aid.

PIER OBSTRUCTION LIGHT, 18 19.6N, 64 57.7W. Q W. On end of pier. Synchronized with Krum Bay North Mooring Dolphin Obstruction Light; private aid.

NORTH MOORING DOLPHIN OBSTRUCTION LIGHT, 18 19.6N, 64 57.7W. Q W. On dolphin. Synchronized with Krum Bay Pipeway Obstruction Light; private aid.

PIPEWAY OBSTRUCTION LIGHT, 18 19.6N, 64 57.7W. Q W. On end of pipeway. Synchronized with Krum Bay Pier Obstruction Light; private aid.

EAST GREGERIE CHANNEL

Lighted Buoy WR1, 18 18.6N, 64 56.1W. Q G, 3M. Green.

Lighted Buoy 2, westerly side of shoal. Fl R 2.5s, 3M. Red.

Lighted Buoy 3, Fl G 4s, 4M. Green.

ST. THOMAS HARBOR

Entrance Lighted Buoy 2, S of rocks. Fl R 6s, 4M. Red.

BERG HILL RANGE (Front Light), 18 20.6N, 64 56.0W. Q G, 197ft. KRW on skeleton tower. Visible 2° each side of rangeline. **(Rear Light),** 125 yards, 344° from front light. Oc G 4s, 302ft. KRW on skeleton tower. Visible 2° each side of rangeline.

Lighted Buoy 3, on shoal about center of entrance to harbor. Fl G 4s, 4M. Green.

Buoy 4, W of bank. Red nun.

Rupert Rock Daybeacon, NW on pile worded DANGER.

Lighted Buoy 6, off E side of entrance to harbor. Fl R 4s, 3M. Red.

HARBOR AREA BOUNDARY

Buoy B, 18 20.3N, 64 55.9W. Yellow sphere. Private aid.

Buoy C, Yellow sphere. Private aid.

Buoy D, Yellow sphere. Private aid.

Buoy E, Yellow sphere. Private aid.

Buoy F, Yellow sphere. Private aid.

Buoy G, Yellow sphere. Private aid.

CHARLOTTE AMALIE

18 20N, 64 56W

Emergencies: Contact the U.S. Coast Guard on VHF channel 16 or 2182kHz. There is a vessel documentation office in town, and a patrol vessel is often based at Kings Wharf. Virgin Islands Radio can assist in emergencies.

Pilotage: Approaching from the north, St. Thomas's prominent, 1500-plus-foot-high mountains make the island highly visible. At night, its loom is visible for many miles. The western approach to the main harbor of Charlotte Amalie, on the island's south side, passes through Savana Passage, marked by a light on Savana Island. At night, it is safer to pass west of the light to avoid unlit rocks in the passage. Several other unlit rocks clutter the approach from the west, but a safe bearing can be taken on the lights of the airport. Boats often anchor in West Gregerie Channel, while the channel east of Hassel Island is kept clear for the many cruise ships calling at the West Indian Docks. The entrance range of 344° will bring you safely into the main harbor.

Port of Entry: See Entry Procedures and the introduction to the Coast Pilot. You may tie up in a marina and call customs at 809-774-6755.

The Customs Office is along the downtown waterfront in the Marine Terminal Building.

Virgin Islands Radio: This private station provides an important communication link in the islands. It broadcasts weather reports, makes telephone calls, and provide emergency assistance. Contact the station on VHF channel 16. For more information refer to the Communications and Weather Services chapter.

Dockage: There are several marinas in and around Charlotte Amalie, and all services are available. On the west side of Crown Bay contact Crown Bay Marina (809-774-2255). Avery's Marine (809-776-0113) is on the west side of Haulover Cut. Yacht Haven Marina (809-774-9700 or 774-6050) is located in the head of Long Bay, east of the cruise ship docks. The Haulover Marine Yachting Center (809-776-2078) is located in West Gregerie Channel. Contact any of the marinas on VHF channel 16 or through Virgin Islands Radio.

Moorings: The numerous moorings scattered around the harbor are privately owned.

Anchorages: There is usually room to anchor among the moored boats in Long Bay, taking care to stay clear of the cruise ship docks and approaches to the marina and turning basin. The holding is good, but the harbor can be rough from wakes and surge from the south. Boats anchor all along West Gregerie Channel, so many at times they practically block passage. Other anchoring spots include Hassel Island and the cove on the west side of Water Island known locally as Honeymoon Harbor. A crowded dinghy dock is available at Yacht Haven. Locking your tender is recommended.

Services: All services are available. Large supermarkets, banks, a post office, hardware stores, marine stores, drug stores, and liquor stores are all within easy walking distance of the harbor front. A major airport has good connections to all points. If the part you need is not here, U.S. mail can get it to you quickly.

Charlotte Amalie is the capital of commerce and biggest city in the Virgins. It is the place to take care of major repairs, stock up, and conduct business. The harbors are crowded with cruisers and charterboats from around the world, bringing fascinating variety to the waterfront. Ashore are all the pleasures of a major tourist destination, including historical sights and good restaurants. This is the center of action, but visitors should also exercise common sense during evening hours. Crime problems led the government to launch an anti-crime campaign in 1994, including additional

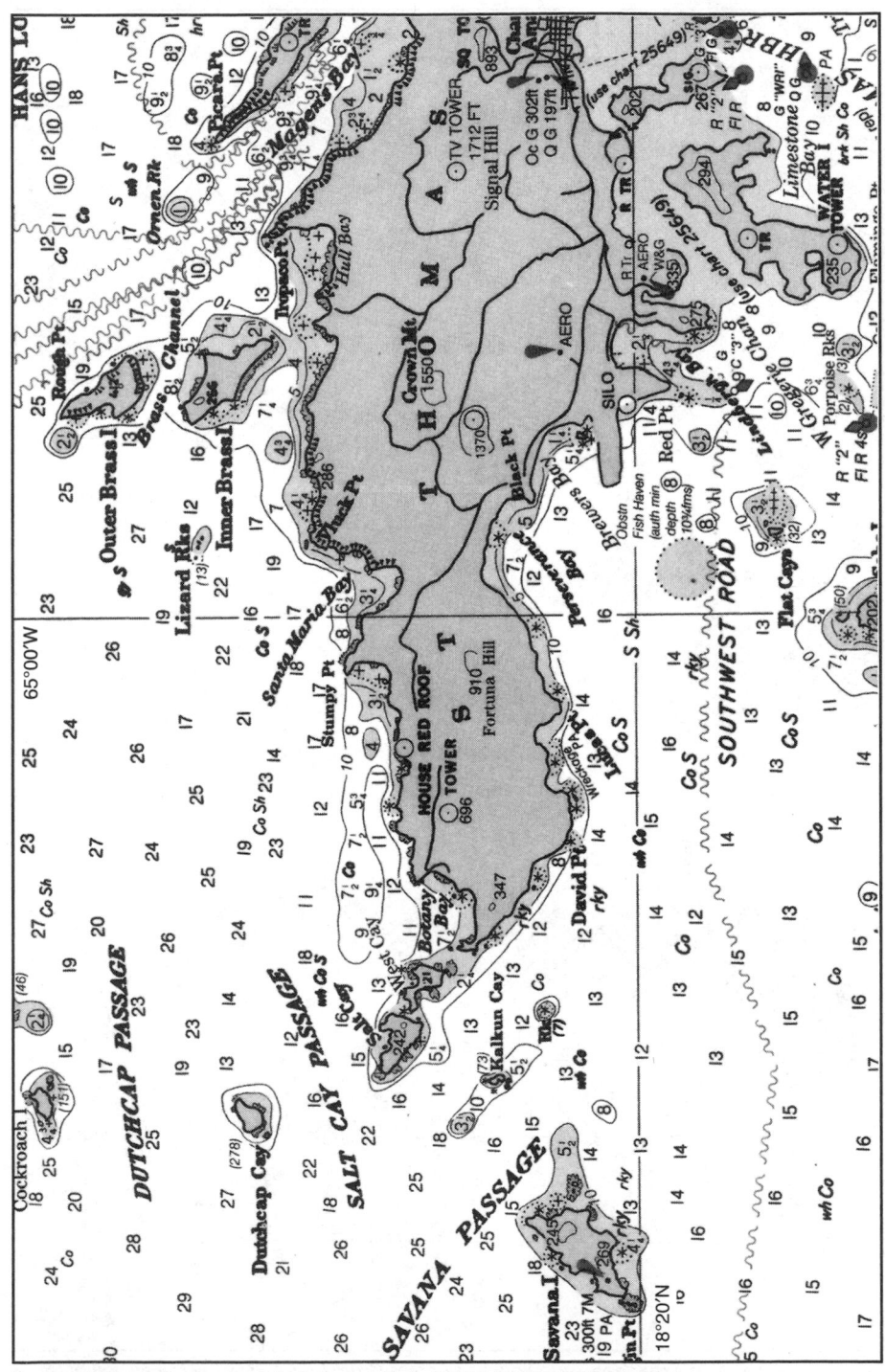

Savana Passage, soundings in fathoms *(from NOAA 25650, 30th ed, 7/93)*

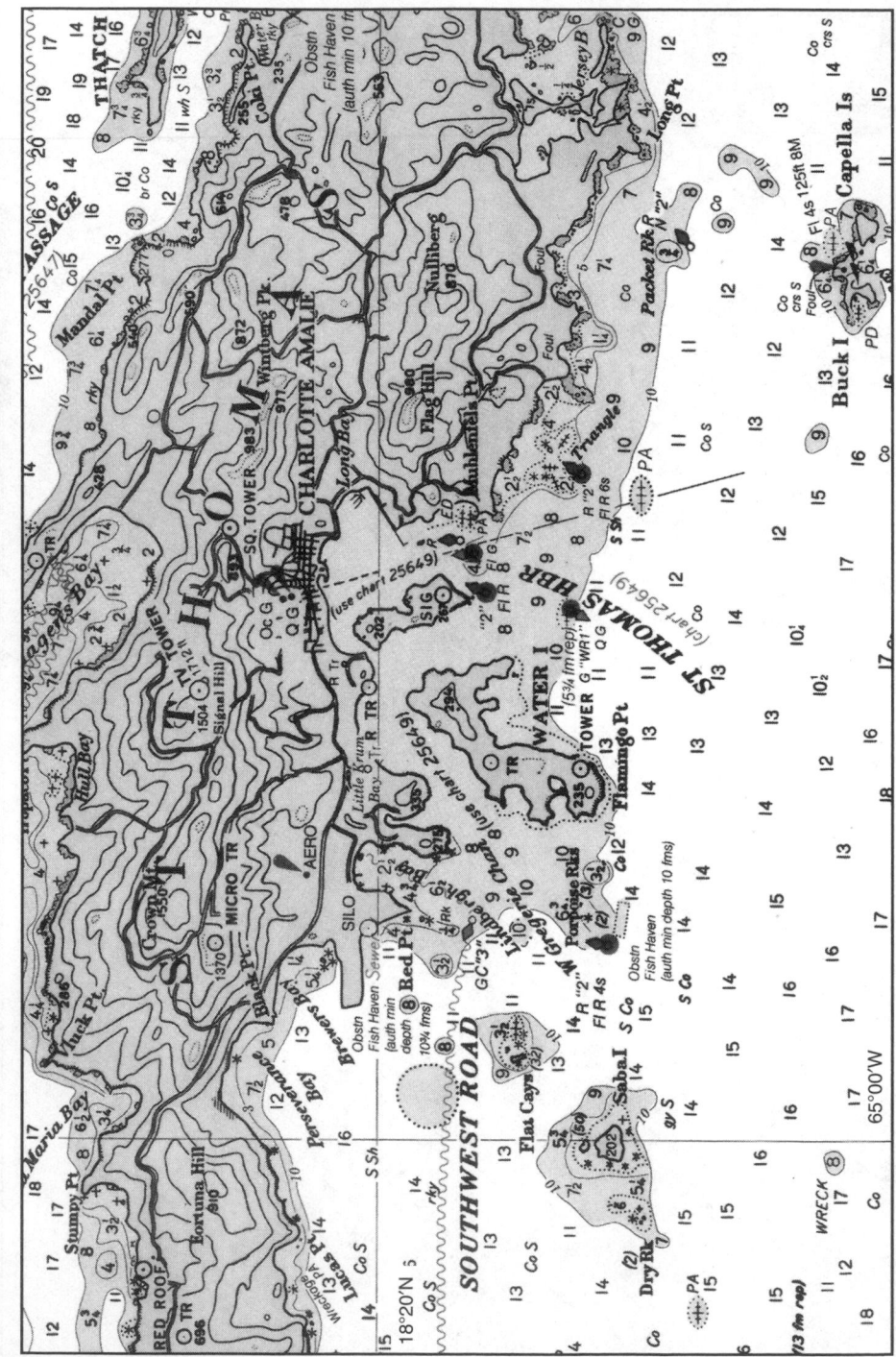

Charlotte Amalie Approaches, soundings in fathoms *(from NOAA 25641, 22nd ed, 8/93)*

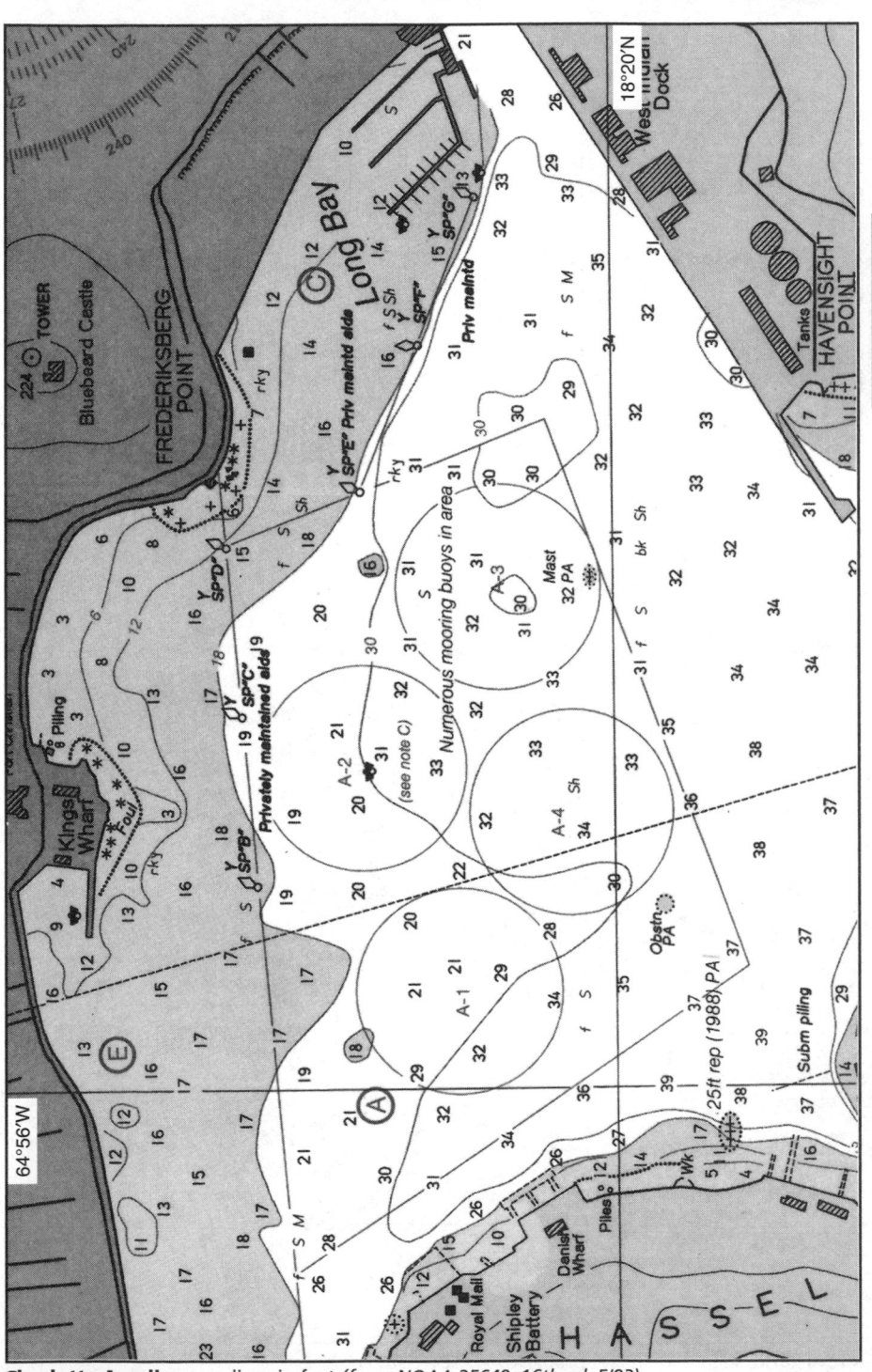

Charlotte Amalie, soundings in feet *(from NOAA 25649, 16th ed, 5/93)*

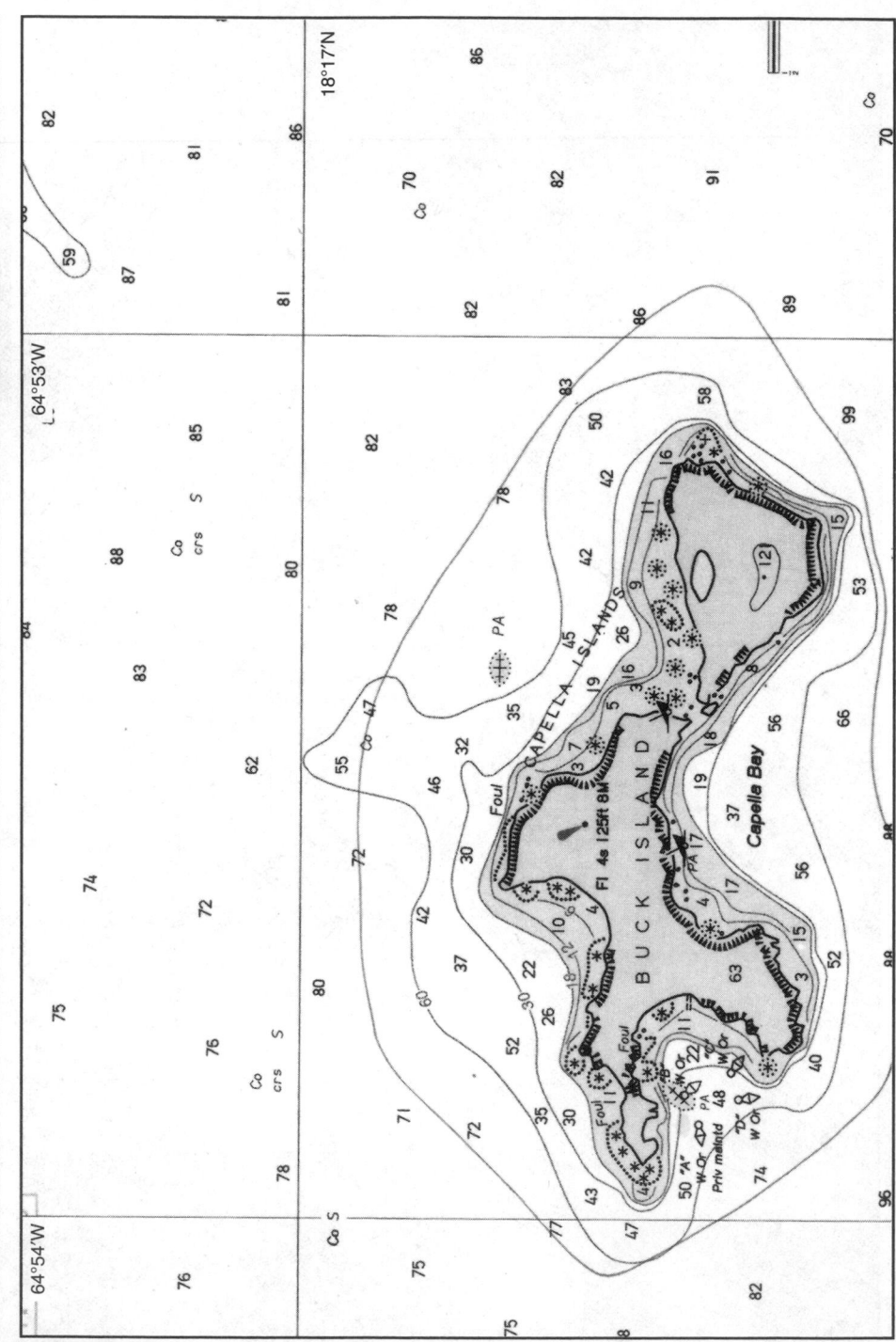

Buck Island, soundings in feet *(from NOAA 25647, 9th ed, 7/92)*

police, improved lighting, and other precautions. A visitor safety pamphlet has been published by the St. Thomas Hotel Association.

SOUTHEAST COAST OF ST. THOMAS

BUCK ISLAND LIGHT, 18 16.7N, 64 53.6W. Fl W 4s, 125ft, 8M. White square tower.
Packet Rock Buoy 2, on south side of rock, 18 17.8N, 64 53.4W. Red nun.
Red Point Buoy 1, 18 18.4N, 64 51.6W. Green can.

BENNER BAY CHANNEL

Lighted Buoy 1, 18 19.0N, 64 52.1W. Fl G 2s. Green. Private aid.
Lighted Buoy 2, Fl R 2s. Red. Private aid.
Buoy 3, Green can. Private aid.
Buoy 4, Red nun. Private aid.
Buoy 5, Green can. Private aid.
Buoy 6, Red nun. Private aid.
Buoy 7, Green can. Private aid.
Buoy 8, Red nun. Private aid.
Buoy 9, Green can. Private aid.
Buoy 10, Red nun. Private aid.
Buoy 12, Red nun. Private aid.
Buoy 13, Green can. Private aid.
Buoy 14, Red nun. Private aid.
Buoy 15, Green can. Private aid.
Buoy 16, Red nun. Private aid.
Buoy 18, Red nun. Private aid.

BENNER BAY

18 19N, 64 52W
Emergencies: Contact the U.S. Coast Guard on VHF channel 16 or 2182kHz. Virgin Islands Radio, VHF channel 16 (see information under Charlotte Amalie), can assist in emergencies.
Pilotage: Do not pass between Cas Cay and Patricia Cay. The green can off the east end of Cas Cay is the main entrance mark. The channel into Benner Bay (known locally as the Lagoon) is privately marked by red and green buoys. The channel is reported to be shoal in places, with possible broken-off pilings outside the deeper water. You may want to call ahead for the latest depth information if you draw more than 6 feet.
Dockage: This area features several marinas and repair yards. Contact Limnos Marina (809-775-6901), Tropical Marine (809-775-6595), and Ruan's Marine (809-775-6346). For repairs contact Independent Boat Yard (809-776-0466).

Anchorage: There may be some room to anchor along the channel leading into Benner Bay. The water shoals rapidly outside the dredged area, and broken-off pilings have been reported.
Services: All services are available here or nearby on the island. More sheltered than Charlotte Amalie or Red Hook, Benner Bay is a good place for major repairs or boat storage, being more sheltered than Charlotte Amalie or Red Hook.

CURRENT CUT TO RED HOOK

CURRENT ROCK LIGHT, 18 18.9N, 64 50.1W. Fl W 6s, 20ft, 6M, NR on skeleton tower. Higher intensity beams towards Buck Island and Two Brothers.
Cabrita Point Buoy 1, Green can.
Vessup Bay Buoy 1, 18 19.7N, 64 50.6W. Black can. Private aid.
Buoy 2, Red nun. Private aid.
Buoy 3, Black can. Private aid.
Buoy 4, Red nun. Private aid.
Buoy 5, Black can. Private aid.
Buoy 6, Red nun. Private aid.

RED HOOK

18 20N, 64 51W
Emergencies: Contact the U.S. Coast Guard on VHF channel 16 or 2182kHz. Virgin Islands Radio, VHF channel 16 (see information under Charlotte Amalie), can assist in emergencies.
Dockage: Contact American Yacht Harbor (809-775-6454) or Sapphire Beach Resort and Marina in a small bay just north of Redhook Point (809-775-6100) or on VHF channel 16.
Anchorage: Many private moorings limit the available anchoring area, but some boats find room in Muller Bay. Boat traffic is heavy, and the ferries running to St. John kick up wakes.
Services: Most services are available here, except for haulouts. Supplies can be found near the docks or elsewhere on the island.

PILLSBURY SOUND

TWO BROTHERS LIGHT, 18 20.6N, 64 49.0W. Fl W 6s, 23ft, 6M. NR on skeleton tower.
STEVENS CAY LIGHT, 18 19.9N, 64 48.5W. Fl W 4s, 14ft, 5M. NR on skeleton tower.
Mingo Rock Lighted Buoy 2, 18 19.4N, 64 48.2W. Fl R 4s, 4M. Red.

COAST PILOT

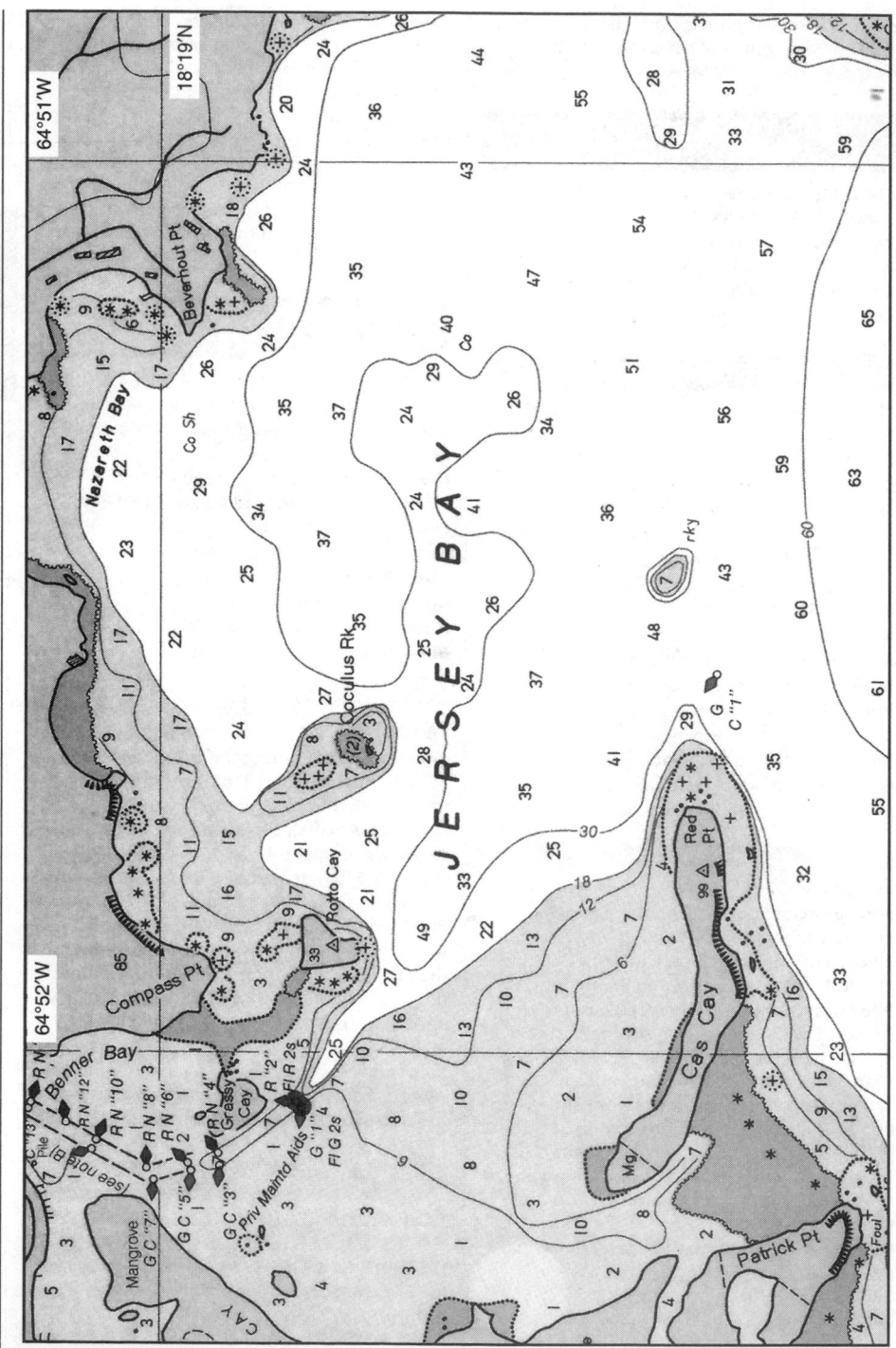

Benner Bay, soundings in feet *(from NOAA 25647, 9th ed, 7/92)*

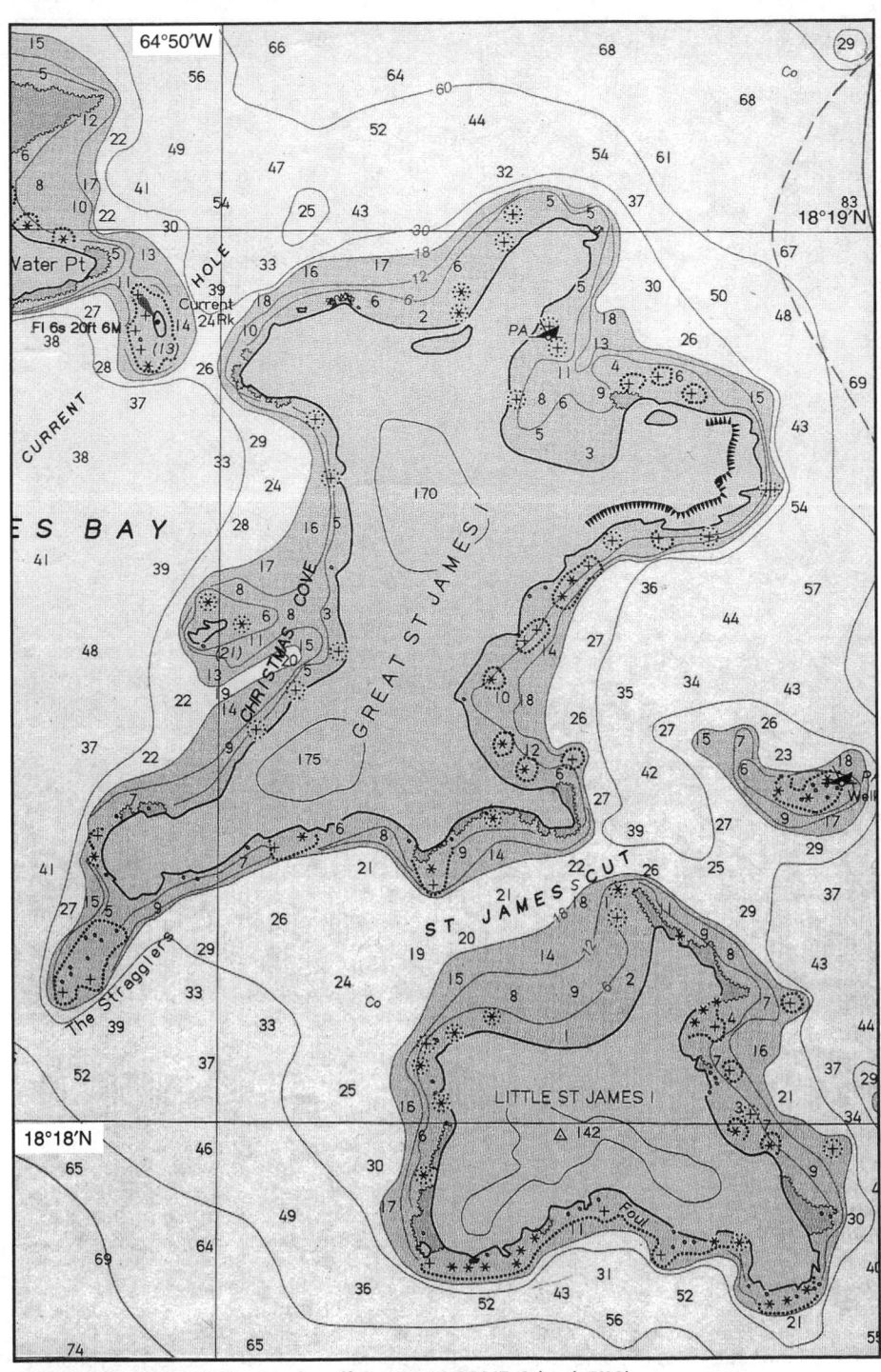

Christmas Cove, soundings in feet *(from NOAA 25647, 9th ed, 7/92)*

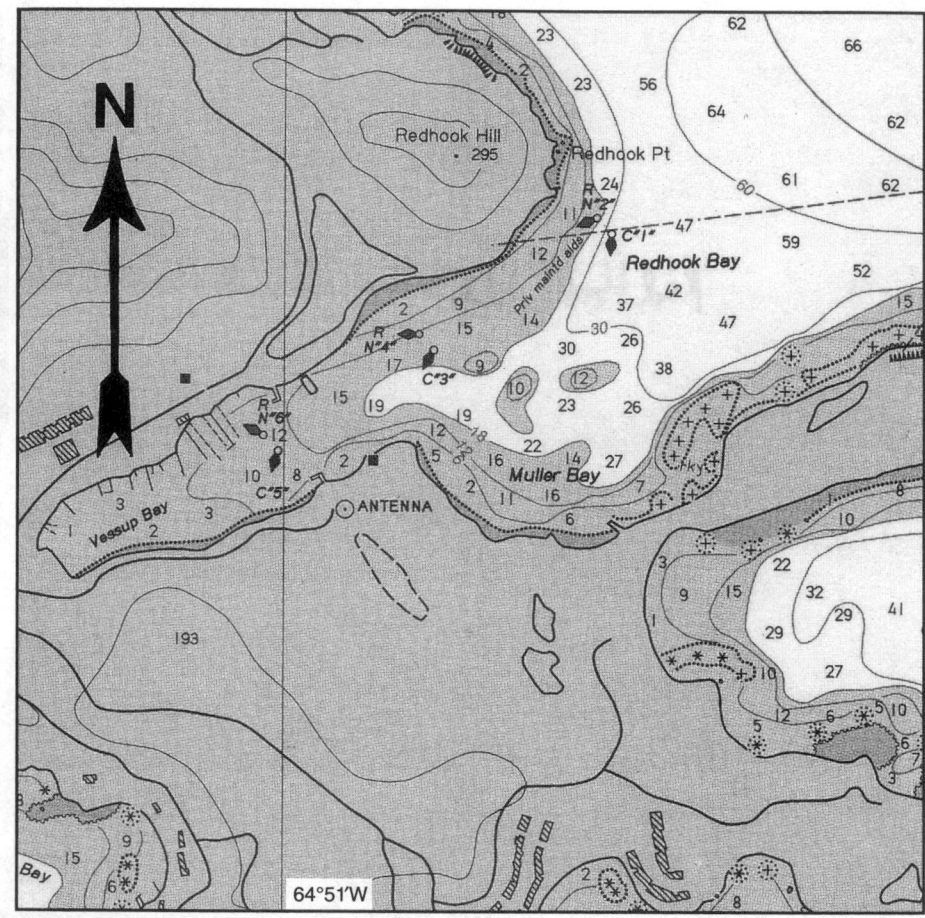

Red Hook, soundings in feet *(from NOAA 25647, 9th ed, 7/92)*

CRUZ BAY

CRUZ BAY LIGHT, 18 20.0N, 64 47.9W. Fl W, 4s, 12ft, 5M. NR on pile.
Buoy 1, 18 20.0N, 64 47.9W. Black can. Private aid.
Buoy 2, Red nun. Private aid.
Buoy 4, Red nun. Private aid.
Junction Buoy, black and red bands. Private aid.
Buoy 5, Black can. Private aid.
Buoy 6, Red nun. Private aid.
Viss Channel Buoy 1S, 18 20.1N, 64 47.8W. Black can. Private aid.
Viss Channel Buoy 2S, Red nun. Private aid.
Battery Point Buoy 1, N of point, 18 20.0N, 64 47.7W. Black can. Private aid.

Battery Point Buoy 2, N of point. Red nun. Private aid.

CRUZ BAY

18 20N, 64 48W
Emergencies: Contact the U.S. Coast Guard on VHF channel 16 or 2182kHz. Virgin Islands Radio, VHF channel 16 (see information under Charlotte Amalie), can assist in emergencies.
Port of Entry: Dinghy in to the customs dock in the northern arm of the harbor. Customs may be contacted at 809-776-6741. Vessels arriving from the British Virgin Islands must check in with customs.
National Park Service: A dock and visitors center are located in the northern arm of the

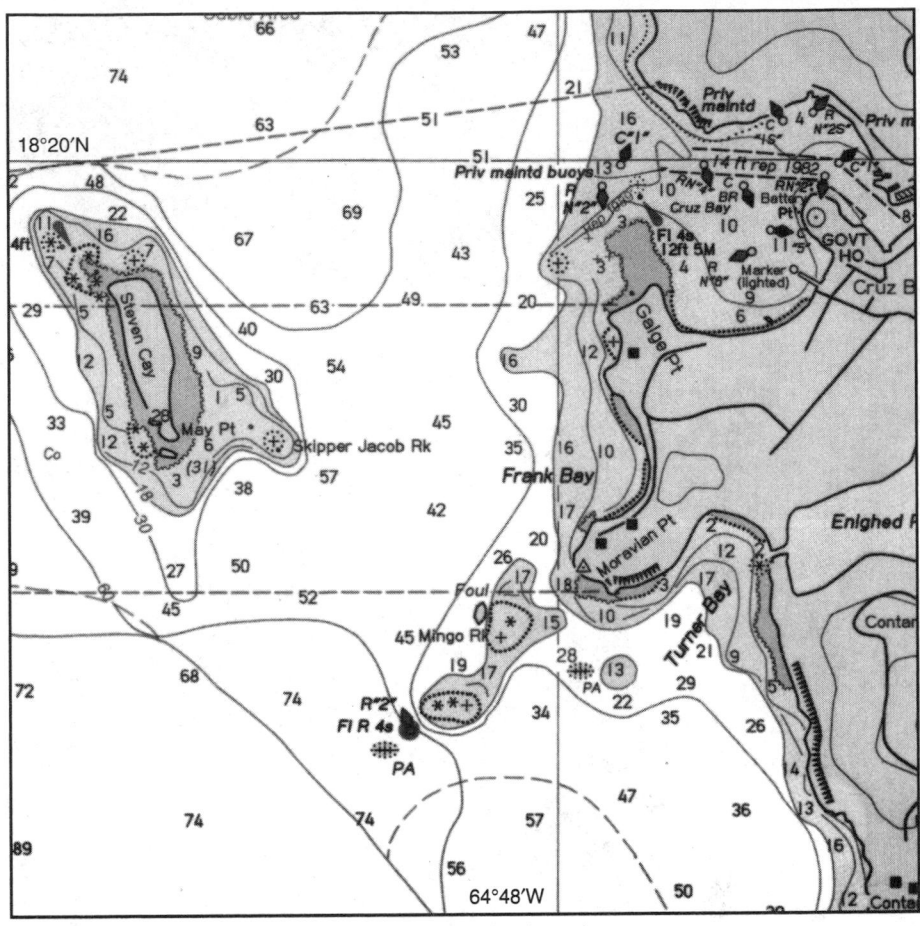

Cruz Bay, soundings in feet *(from NOAA 25647, 9th ed, 7/92)*

harbor. Contact the office (809-776-6201) for the latest park boating regulations. The current limit on anchoring in the park is two weeks a year. For boats to 55 feet overall, there are now 4 park moorings in Little Lameshur Bay, 5 in Great Lameshur Bay, 4 in Leinster Bay, 3 in I Bay, 1 in Reef Bay, 7 in Salt Pond Bay, 1 in Ram's Head Cove, 2 in Maho Bay, 1 in north Francis Bay, 1 off the southwest corner of Whistling Cay, and 1 in Jumbie Bay, all available on a first-come, first-served basis. To protect critical habitat areas, anchoring is now prohibited in Reef, Litte Lameshur, Great Lameshur, and Salt Pond bays.

Dockage: You can tie up for 10 minutes to the National Park Service dock in the cove off the northern channel in the harbor.

Anchorage: The anchorage areas are very small, crowded, and swept by wakes from the frequent ferries. Boats anchor both north and south of the main ferry channel in the southern arm of the harbor. Stay clear of the marked channels and the reef extending north from Galge Point. Temporary anchorage is available south of Lind Point. There may not be enough room to anchor safely in any of these spots. Dinghies may be landed north of the ferry wharf in the harbor's southern arm.

Services: Caneel Bay Shipyard (809-693-8771) provides haulouts, fuel, water, supplies, and repairs. Limited groceries and general stores are available from several small shops in town. Connections (809-776-6922) specializes in providing communication services for boaters.

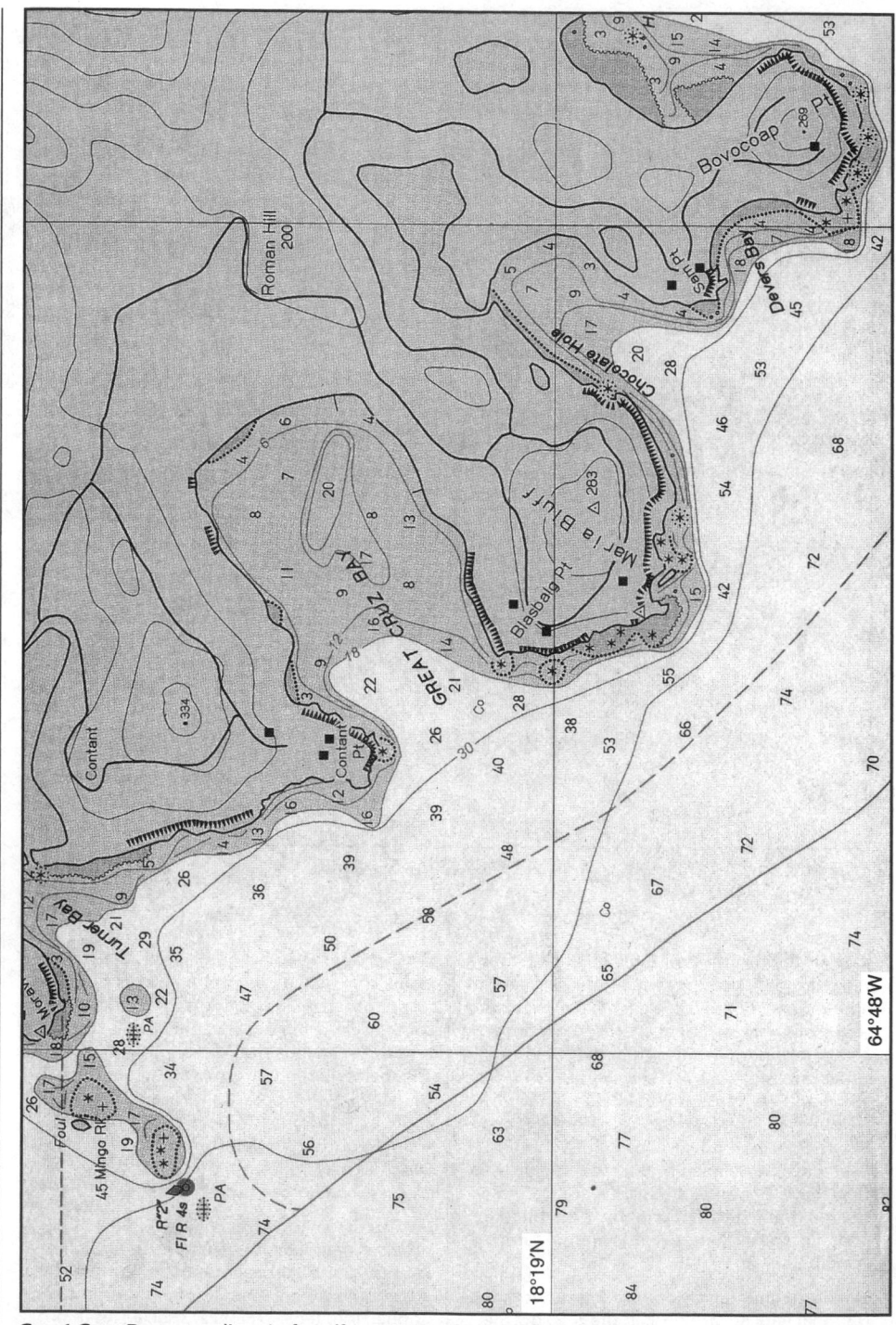

Great Cruz Bay, soundings in feet *(from NOAA 25647, 9th ed, 7/92)*

There are many small specialty shops, boutiques, and informal eateries.

Many people prefer the calmer pace of St. John to the big-city rush of Charlotte Amalie. Unfortunately, Cruz Bay is tiny, crowded, and much stirred up by ferries. With much of St. John being national park, the island's natural beauty is spectacular. It is well worth climbing one of the 1000-foot-high peaks for a glimpse of the Virgin Islands spread before you.

CANEEL BAY

Buoy 1, 18 20.6N, 64 47.3W. Black can. Private aid.
Buoy 2, Red nun. Private aid.
Buoy 3, Black can. Private aid.
Buoy 4, Red nun. Private aid.
Buoy 5, Black can. Private aid.
Buoy 6, Red nun. Private aid.

HAWKSNEST BAY

Buoy 1, 18 20.8N, 64 46.7W. Black can. Private aid.
Buoy 2, Red nun. Private aid.

TRUNK BAY

Buoy 1, 18 21.1N, 64 46.2W. Black can. Private aid.
Buoy 2, Red nun. Private aid.

WINDWARD PASSAGE

Johnson Reef Lighted Buoy 1JR, 18 21.9N, 64 46.4W. Fl G 4s, 4M. Green.
Johnson Reef South Buoy 2, 18 21.5N, 64 46.4W. Orange and white can worded DANGER SHOAL.

FRANCIS BAY

Buoy 1, 18 21.9N, 64 44.7W. Black can. Private aid.
Buoy 2, Red nun. Private aid.

FRANCIS BAY

18 22N, 64 45W
Emergencies: Contact the U.S. Coast Guard on VHF channel 16 or 2182kHz. Virgin Islands Radio, VHF channel 16 (see information under Charlotte Amalie), can assist in emergencies.
National Park Service: Refer to the section on Cruz Bay for information on park headquarters.

Anchoring is limited to two weeks a year in the park. NPS boats patrol this area regularly.
Anchorage: This is an excellent anchorage area, with wonderful swimming, snorkeling, and beaching. Several private buoys mark an area where dinghies may proceed in to the beach. From here you can hike the road to the Annaberg Sugar Mill ruins near Leinster Bay.
Services: You may be able to purchase a few basic supplies or make a phone call at the resort in nearby Maho Bay.

CORAL HARBOR CHANNEL

Buoy 1, 18 20.6N, 64 42.7W. Green can. Private aid.
Buoy 2, Red nun. Private aid.
Buoy 3, Green can. Private aid.
Buoy 4, Red nun. Private aid.
Buoy 5, Green can. Private aid.
Buoy 6, Red nun. Private aid.
Buoy 7, Green can. Private aid.
Buoy 8, Red nun. Private aid.

CORAL BAY AND HURRICANE HOLE

18 20N, 64 42W
Emergencies: Contact the U.S. Coast Guard on VHF channel 16 or 2182kHz. Virgin Islands Radio, VHF channel 16 (see information under Charlotte Amalie), can assist in emergencies.
Anchorage: There are many excellent possibilities for anchoring in any of the arms of the harbor. The area to the north is known as Hurricane Hole, because of the excellent protection afforded by the mangroves. The small boat wharf at the head of the bay is reported to have 3 feet of depth alongside.
Services: Coral Bay Marine (809-776-6859) and Coral Bay Sails (809-776-6665) can offer some repairs, although there is no haulout facility. There are a few small shops, a grocery, and casual eateries, plus buses and taxis that run to Cruz Bay if you need something.

ST. CROIX

HAMS BLUFF LIGHT, W end of island, 17 46.3N, 64 52.3W. Fl (2) W 30s, 394ft, 16M. White cylindrical tower. Visible 053°–265°; partially obscured 053°–062°.
National Undersea Research Habitat Lighted Buoy, off entrance to Salt River Bay, 17 47.5N, 64 45.3W. Q W. Large white hull lettered NOAA. Maintained by NOAA.

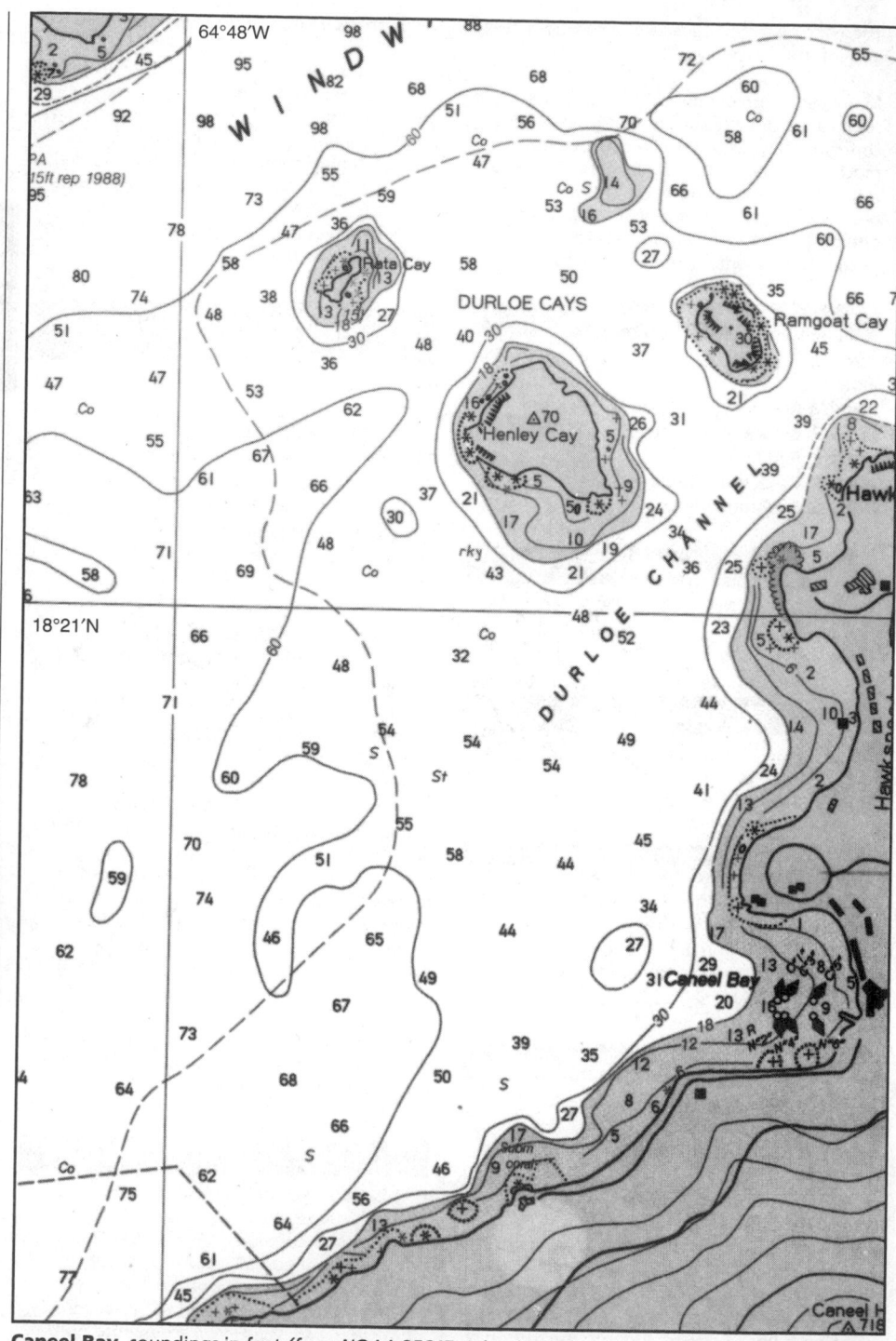

Caneel Bay, soundings in feet *(from NOAA 25647, 9th ed, 7/92)*

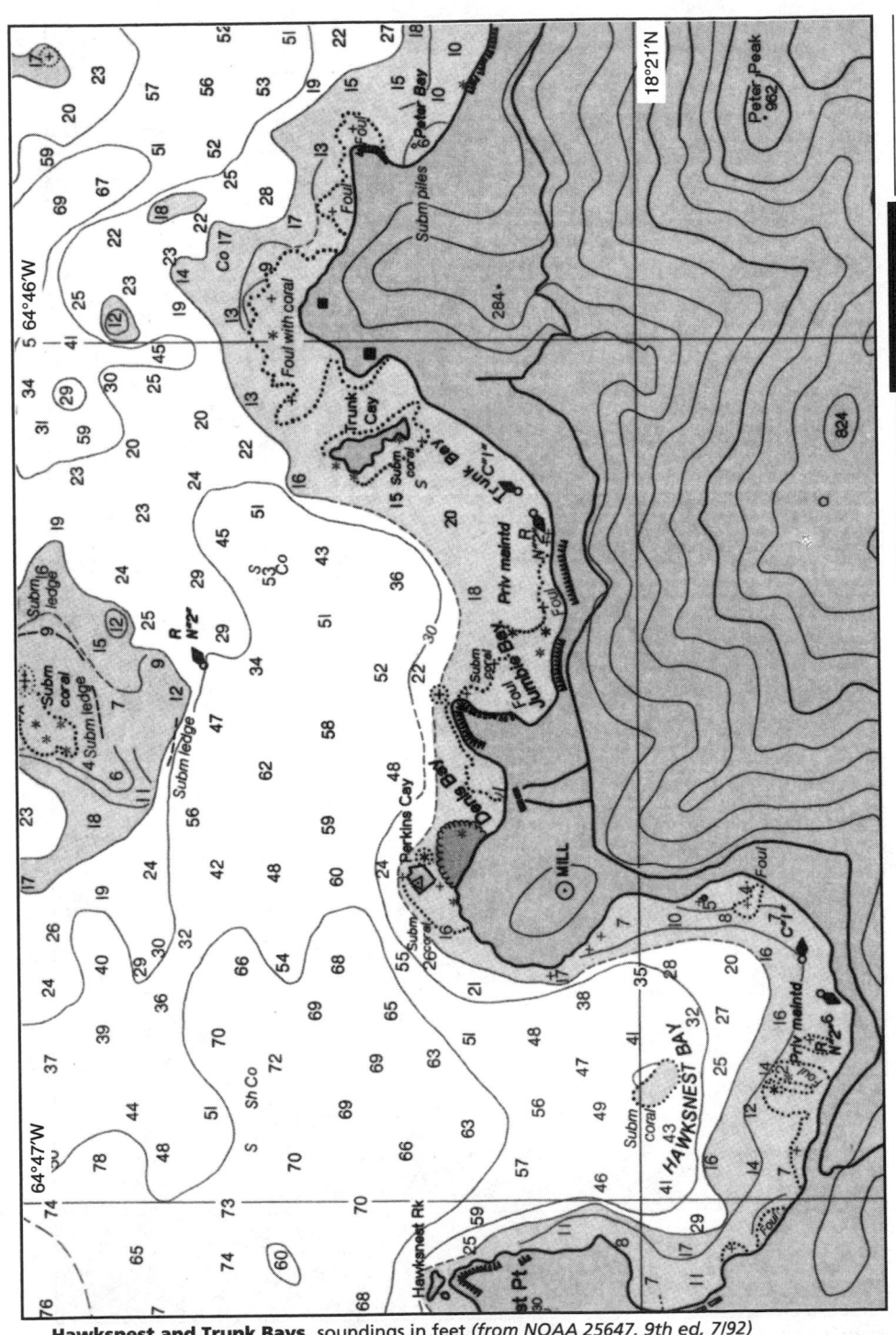

Hawksnest and Trunk Bays, soundings in feet *(from NOAA 25647, 9th ed, 7/92)*

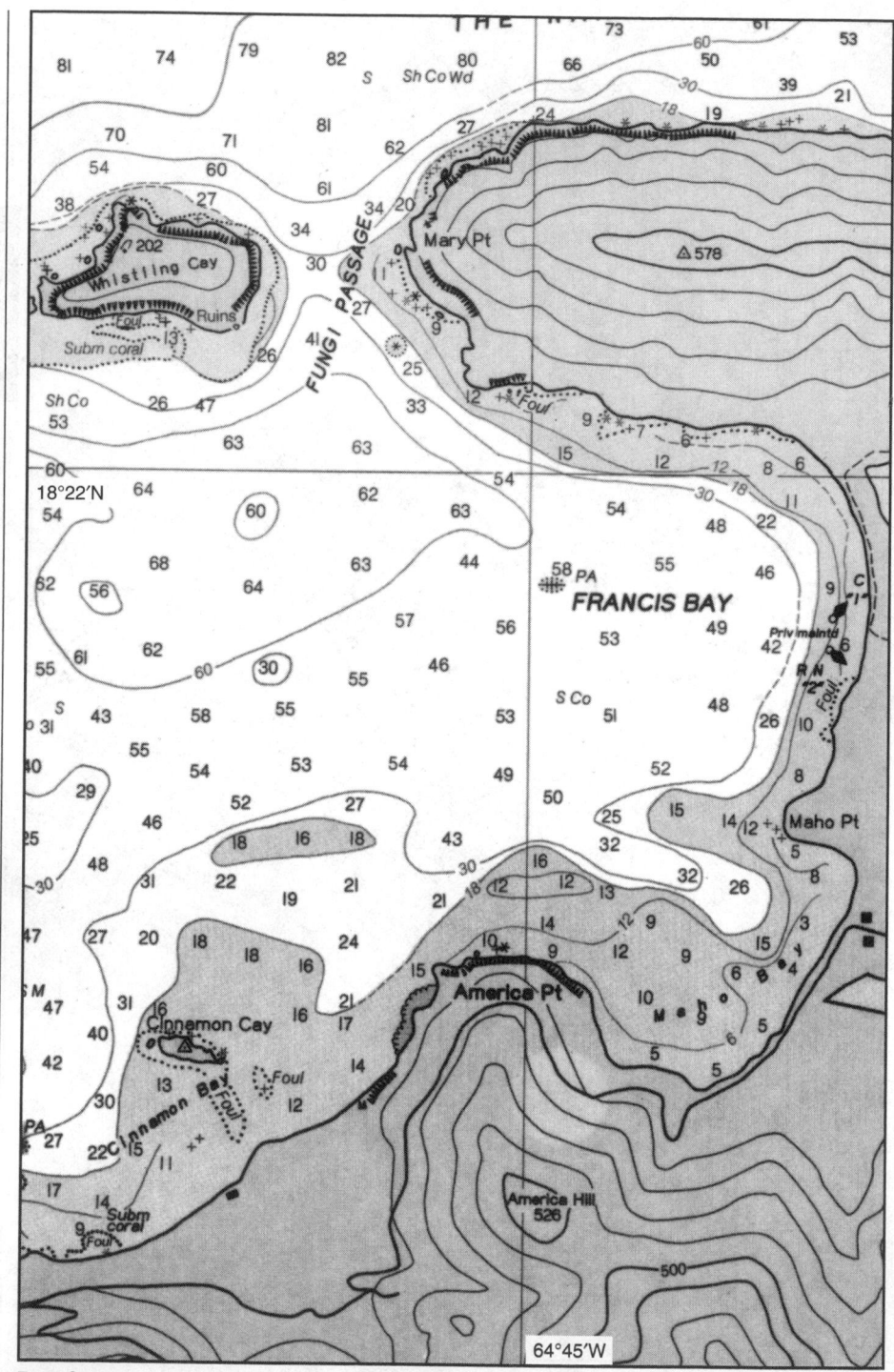

Francis Bay, soundings in feet *(from NOAA 25647, 9th ed, 7/92)*

COAST PILOT

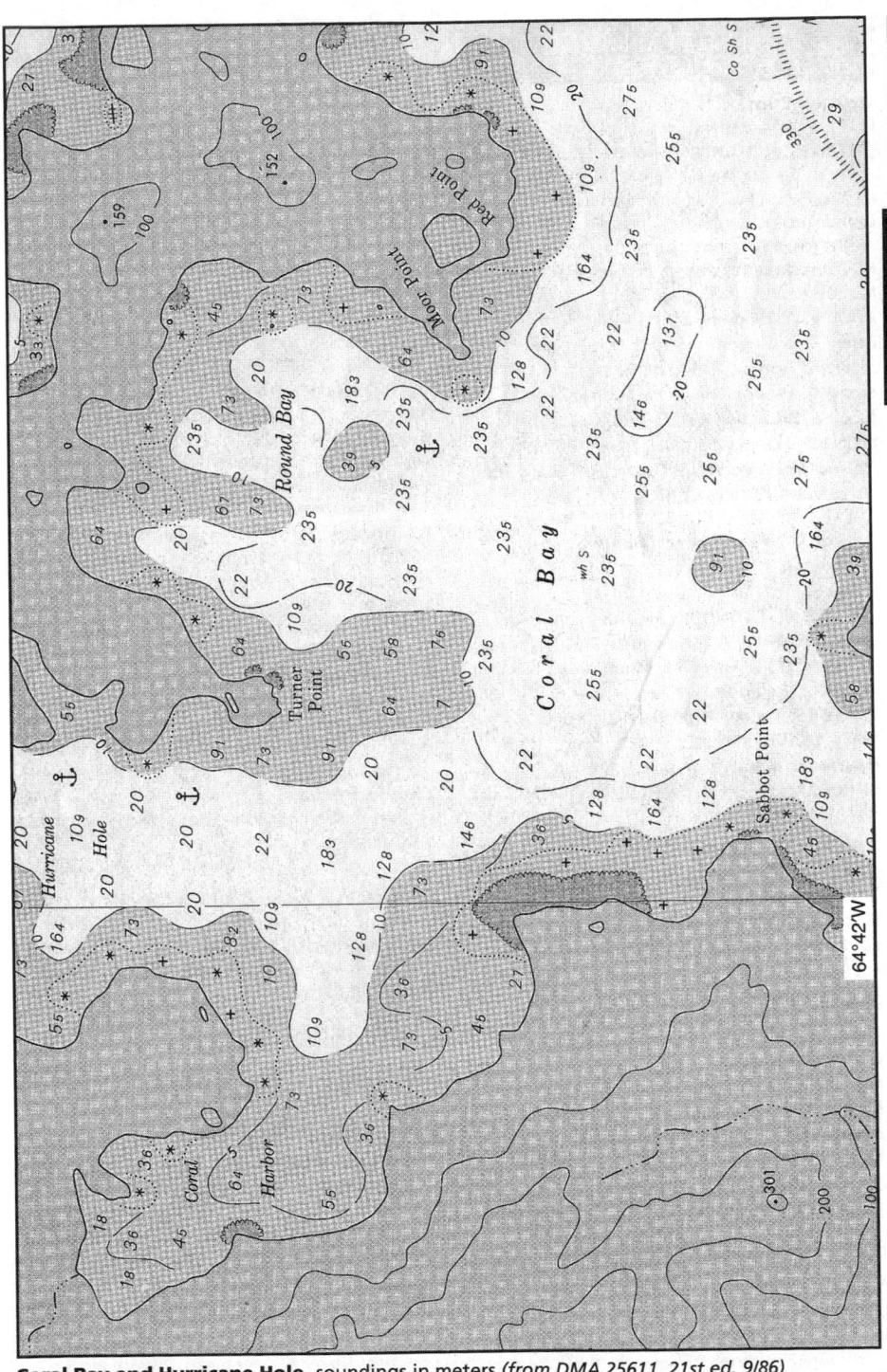

Coral Bay and Hurricane Hole, soundings in meters *(from DMA 25611, 21st ed, 9/86)*

CHRISTIANSTED APPROACHES

Lighted Buoy 1, 17 45.8N, 64 41.8W. Fl G 2.5s, 4M. Green.

ENTRANCE CHANNEL RANGE (Front Light), Fort Louisa Agusta, 17 45.4N, 64 41.7W. Q W, 45ft. KRW on skeleton tower. Visible all around; higher intensity on rangeline. **(Rear Light),** 735 yards, 164° from front light. Iso W, 6s, 93ft. KRW on skeleton tower. Visible all around; higher intensity on rangeline.

Buoy 2, at NE point of shoal. Red nun.

Buoy 3, at W point of bank. Green can.

Lighted Buoy 4, Q R, 3M. Red.

Buoy 5, at SW point of bank. Green can.

Buoy 6, Red nun.

LIGHT 7, Fl G, 4s, 16ft, 4M. SG on dolphin.

Round Reef Northeast Junction Buoy RR, at NE point of reef, 17 45.4N, 64 41.7W. Green and red banded can.

Round Reef Southwest Daybeacon 2, TR on dolphin.

Buoy 8, Red nun.

LIGHT 9, Fl G 2.5s, 16ft, 5M. SG on dolphin.

Daybeacon 10, TR on pile.

LIGHT 11, Q G, 10ft, 2M. SG on dolphin.

Buoy 12, Red nun.

LIGHT 13, Fl G 4s, 16ft, 4M. SG on pile.

Buoy 15, Green can.

Daybeacon 16, TR on pile.

CHRISTIANSTED HARBOR WHARF LIGHTS (2), F W, 12ft. Private aids.

SCHOONER CHANNEL

This privately marked channel runs from east of Round Reef to the main harbor area.

Lighted Buoy 5, 17 45.3N, 64 41.8W. Q G, Green. Private aid.

Lighted Buoy 6, Q R. Red. Private aid.

Lighted Buoy 7, Q G. Green. Private aid.

Lighted Buoy 8, Q R. Red. Private aid.

Lighted Buoy 9, Fl G 4s. Green. Private aid.

Lighted Buoy 10, Fl R 4s. Red. Private aid.

Lighted Buoy 11, Fl G 4s. Green. Private aid.

Lighted Buoy 14, Fl R 4s. Red. Private aid.

CHRISTIANSTED

17 45N, 64 42W

Emergencies: Contact the U.S. Coast Guard on VHF channel 16 or 2182kHz. Virgin Islands Radio, VHF channel 16 (see information under Charlotte Amalie), can assist in emergencies.

Pilotage: St. Croix is located about 37 miles south of St. Thomas. Because of extensive off-lying reefs, vessels should stay a mile or two offshore until sure of their position. When crossing from St. Thomas, allow for a westerly set to the current of about 1/2 knot—it is often prudent to lay a course for the east end of the island to avoid a final slog to windward. The initial entrance range is 164° and gets you through the reef. The channel then zigzags to the west and south to the waterfront.

Port of Entry: Contact customs at (809-773-1011).

Dockage: Northeast of the main wharf, St. Croix Marine (809-773-0289 or VHF channel 16) is a full-service yard with a 300-ton railway and 60-ton Travelift. East of Christiansted is Green Cay Marina (809-773-1452 or VHF channel 16). Enter via the channel west of Green Cay. Salt River Marina (809-778-9650) is in Salt River Bay, 4 miles west of Christiansted.

Anchorage: In Christiansted anchor southwest of Protestant Cay, avoiding the charted cable area. Salt River is a hurricane hole, with about 6 feet of water in the tricky reef entrance. Call ahead to Salt River Marina (VHF channel 16) for the latest directions before entering. Private marks help define the channel.

Services: All services are available, including haulouts and repairs. A chandlery is located at St. Croix Marina. Within walking distance from the marina is Chandler's Wharf, with eateries, a hardware store, a travel agent, a post office, and other services. Public bus service is available on the island.

Because it is 37 miles south of the beaten track, Christiansted is less visited by cruisers. There are many historic buildings worth seeing, and the countryside is more open outside the towns. The combination of Danish, British, and West Indian heritage is more visible here than elsewhere in the U.S. Virgins.

DEVCON INTERNATIONAL CHANNEL

This channel begins north of Protestant Cay and runs west to the industrial plant.

Channel Buoy 1, 17 45.3N, 64 42.2W. Green can. Private aid.

Channel Buoy 2, Red nun. Private aid.

Channel Buoy 3, Green can. Private aid.

Channel Buoy 4, Red nun. Private aid.

Channel Buoy 5, Green can. Private aid.

Channel Buoy 6, Red nun. Private aid.

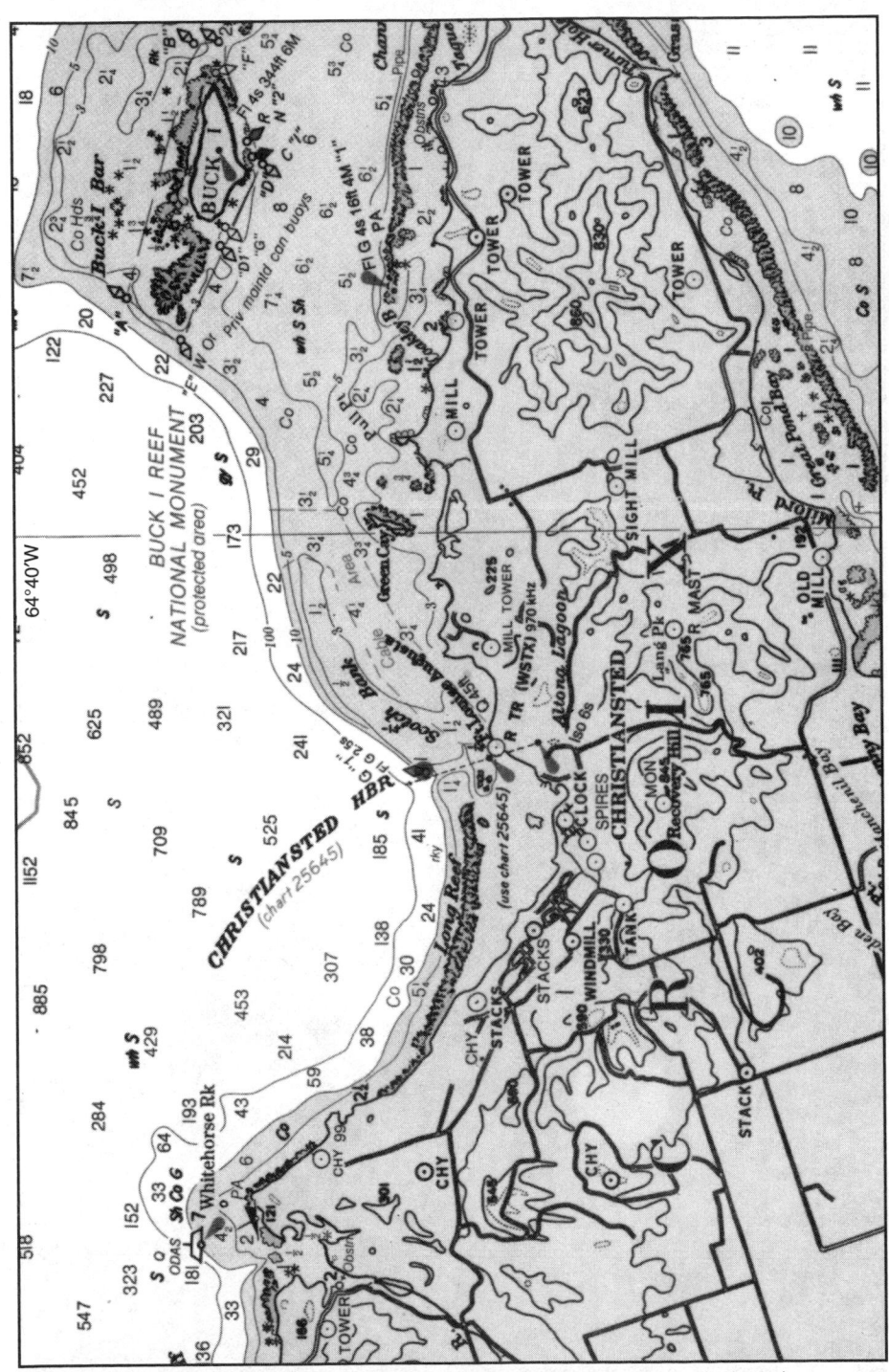

Christiansted Approaches, soundings in fathoms *(from NOAA 25641, 22nd ed, 8/93)*

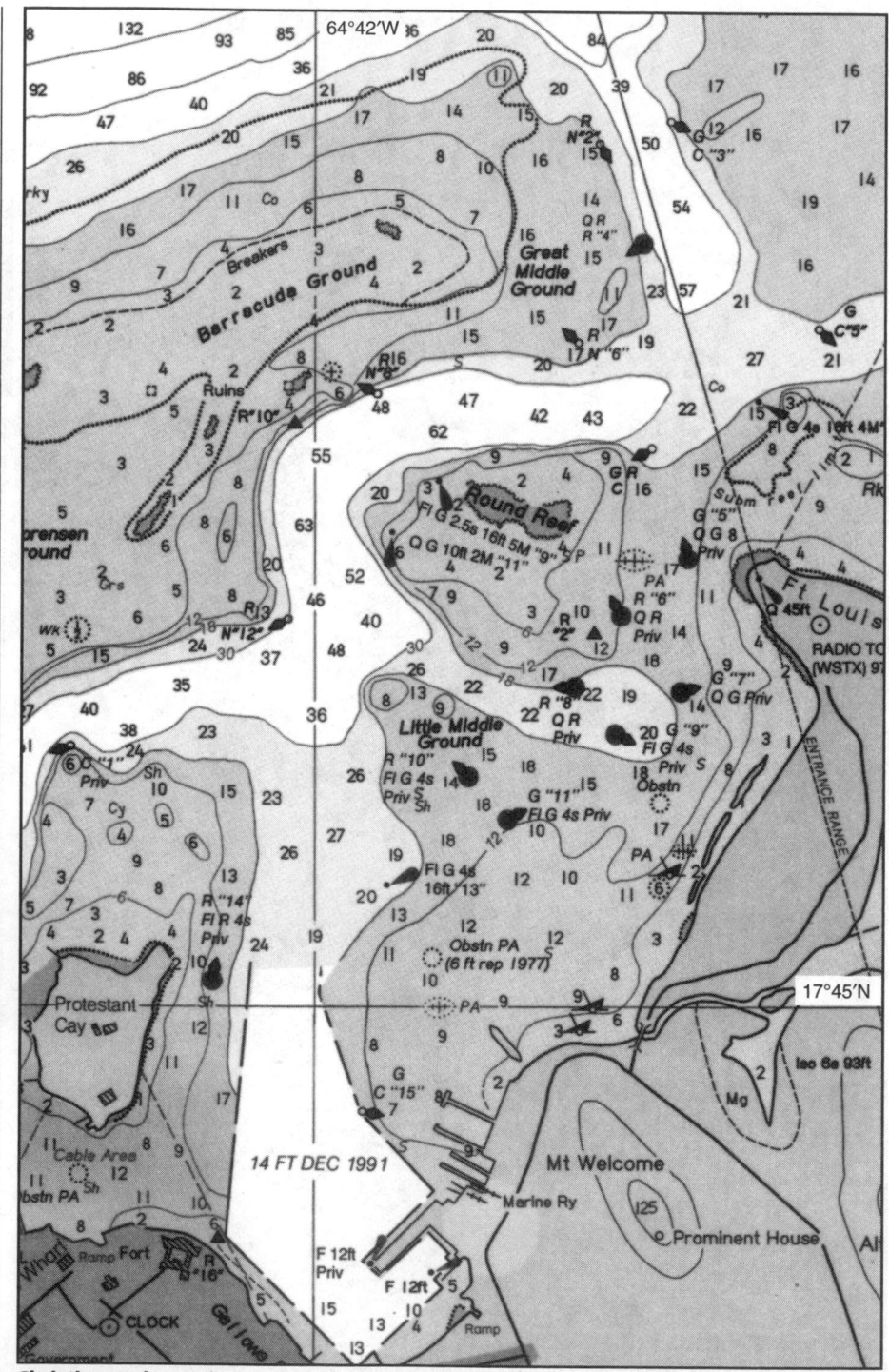

Christiansted, soundings in feet *(from NOAA 25645, 13th ed, 8/93)*

Channel Buoy 7, Green can. Private aid.
Channel Buoy 8, Red nun. Private aid.
Channel Buoy 9, Green can. Private aid.
Channel Buoy 10, Red nun. Private aid.
CHRISTIANSTED WATER INTAKE LIGHTS (4), 17 45.2N, 64 42.8W. F W, 12ft. On pile. Private aids.
CHRISTIANSTED WATER INTAKE SOUTH LIGHTS (4), 17 45.1N, 64 42.8W. F W. On piles. Private aids.

ST. CROIX: NORTHEAST COAST

COAKLEY BAY LIGHT 1, 17 46.1N, 64 38.2W. Fl G 4s, 16ft., 3M. SG on pile.
BUCK ISLAND LIGHT, 17 47.3N, 64 37.1W. Fl W 4s, 344ft, 6M. Red pyramidal skeleton tower.
Buck Island Channel Buoy 1, Black can. Private aid.
Buck Island Channel Buoy 2, Red nun. Private aid.

BUCK ISLAND REEF NATIONAL MONUMENT

Buoy A, 17 48.0N, 64 38.3W. Orange and white banded can. Private aid.
Buoy B, Orange and white banded can. Private aid.
Buoy C, Orange and white banded can. Private aid.
Buoy D, Orange and white banded can. Private aid.
Buoy D1, Orange and white banded can. Private aid.
Buoy E, Orange and white banded can. Private aid.
Buoy F, Orange and white banded can. Private aid.
Buoy G, 17 47.3N, 64 37.7W. Orange and white banded can. Private aid.

LIME TREE BAY

CHANNEL RANGE (Front Light), 17 42.2N, 64 45.0W. F G, 165ft. KRW on skeleton tower. Visible 4° each side of rangeline. Private aid. **(Rear Light),** 500 yards, 334° from front light. F G, 195ft. KRW on skeleton tower. Visible 4° each side of rangeline. Private aid.
CHANNEL EAST AUXILIARY RANGE (Front Light), 17 42.2N, 64 45.0W. F R, 55ft. Black and yellow bands, pole. Visible 4° each side of rangeline. Private aid. **(Rear Light),** 303 yards, 334° from front light. F R, 70ft. Black and yellow

bands, pole. Visible 4° each side of rangeline. Private aid.
Channel Lighted Buoy 1, 17 40.7N, 64 44.3W. Q G. Green, spar station buoy. Private aid.
Channel Lighted Buoy 2, Q R. Red, spar station buoy. Private aid.
Channel Lighted Buoy 3, Fl G 5s. Green. Private aid.
Channel Lighted Buoy 4, Fl R 5s. Red. Private aid.

Note: The following lights are located 35 feet outside the channel limits.

CHANNEL LIGHT 5, Fl G 4s, 14ft. SG on pile. Private aid.
Channel Lighted Buoy 6, Fl R 4s, Red. Private aid.
CHANNEL LIGHT 7, Fl G 2.5s, 14ft. SG on pile. Private aid.
CHANNEL LIGHT 8, Fl R 2.5s, 14ft. TR on pile. Private aid.
CHANNEL LIGHT 9, Fl G 2.5s, 14ft. SG on pile. Private aid.
CHANNEL LIGHT 11, Fl G 2.5s, 14ft. SG on pile. Private aid.
CHANNEL JUNCTION LIGHT LK, Fl (2+1) G 6s, 14ft. JG on pile. Obscured 296°–026°. Private aid.
CONTAINER PORT BASIN LIGHT 13, Fl G 5s, 14ft. SG on pile. Private aid.
CONTAINER PORT BASIN LIGHT 15, Fl G 4s, 14 ft. SG on pile. Private aid.
CONTAINER PORT BASIN LIGHT 17, Fl G 2.5s, 14 ft. SG on pile. Private aid.

KRAUSE LAGOON CHANNEL

Entrance Lighted Buoy 1, 17 40.7N, 64 45.2W. Fl G 4s. Black. Private aid.
Entrance Lighted Buoy 2, Fl R 6s. Red. Private aid.
LIGHT 3, Fl W 4s, 18ft. SG on pile. Private aid.
LIGHT 4, Fl R 4s, 18ft. TR on pile. Private aid.
LIGHT 4A, Q R, 14 ft. TR on pile. Obscured 227°–317°. Private aid.
LIGHT 5, Q G, 14ft. SG on pile; on same structure as Krause Lagoon Cross Channel Range Front Light. Private aid.
LIGHT 6, Q W, 14ft. TR on pile. Private aid.
LIGHT 7, Fl G 4s, 15ft. SG on pile. Private aid.
LIGHT 8, Fl R 2.5s, 15ft. TR on pile. Private aid.
LIGHT 9, Fl G 4s, 16 ft. SG on pile. Private aid.
LIGHT 10, Fl R 2.5s, 16ft. TR on pile. Private aid.

LIGHT 11, Fl G 4s, 16ft. SG on pile. Private aid.
LIGHT 12, Fl R 2.5s, 16ft. TR on pile. Private aid.
LIGHT 13, Fl W 4s, 16ft. SG on pile. Private aid.
LIGHT 14, Fl R 2.5s, 16ft. TR on pile. Private aid.
LIGHT 16, Fl R 2.5s, 16ft. TR on pile. Private aid.
LIGHT 17, Fl G 4s, 16ft. SG on pile. Private aid.
EAST MOORING DOLPHIN SIX LIGHT, Fl R 5s, 12ft. On dolphin. Private aid.
WEST TURNING DOLPHIN LIGHT, Fl W 5s, 12ft. On dolphin. Private aid.

KRAUSE LAGOON CROSS CHANNEL

RANGE (Front Light), 17 41.4N, 64 45.6W. Q G, 14ft. KWB on pile; on same structure as Krause Lagoon Channel Light 5. Private aid.
(Rear Light), 153 yards, 244° from front light, Oc G 4s, 28ft. KWB on pile. Private aid.

Note: The following lights are located 35 outside the channel limits.

LIGHT 1, Fl G 4s, 14ft. SG on pile. Private aid.
LIGHT 2, 17 41.4N, 64 45.5W. Fl W 4s, 14ft. TR on pile. Obscured 260°–350°. Private aid.
LIGHT 3, Fl G 2.5s, 14ft. SG on pile. Private aid.
LIGHT 4, Fl R 2.5s, 14ft. TR on pile. Obscured 288°–018°. Private aid.
LIGHT 5, Q G, 14ft. SG on pile. Private aid.

TEXACO CARIBBEAN

Buoy 1, 17 39.6N, 64 52.1W. Black can. Private aid.
Buoy 2, Red nun. Private aid.
Buoy 3, Black can. Private aid.
Buoy 4, Red nun. Private aid.
Buoy 5, Black can. Private aid.
Buoy 6, Red nun. Private aid.
Buoy 7, Black can. Private aid.
Buoy 8, Red nun. Private aid.

FREDERIKSTED ROAD

SOUTHWEST CAPE LIGHT, 17 40.8N, 64 54.0W. Fl W 6s, 45ft, 7M. Gray skeleton tower.
Southwest Cape Shoal Buoy 2, marks shoal off cape. Red nun.
U.S. Navy Radar Reflector Buoy, 17 41.3N, 64 54.2W. Platform of 3 yellow spherical buoys. Orange radar reflector; maintained by U.S. Navy.
FREDERIKSTED HARBOR LIGHT, 17 43.0N, 64 53.1W. Fl W 4s (2 red sectors), 42ft, 8M white, 6M red. NR on skeleton tower. Red 000°–044.5° and 137°–180°.
FREDERIKSTED PIER LIGHTS, F R, 12ft. Private aids.

CHARLOTTE AMALIE, U.S.V.I.

HIGH & LOW WATER 1995　　　　　　　　18°20'N　64°56'W

ATLANTIC STANDARD TIME (GMT -4H)

JANUARY

Day	Time ft	Time ft	Time ft	Time ft
1 Su ●	0110 -0.4	0945 0.8		
16 M ○	0046 -0.4	0929 0.6		
2 M	0154 -0.4	1028 0.7		
17 Tu	0126 -0.4	0959 0.6		
3 Tu	0238 -0.3	1108 0.7		
18 W	0209 -0.3	1029 0.5	1839 0.0	2019 0.0
4 W	0323 -0.2	1145 0.6	2004 0.0	2223 0.0
19 Th	0257 -0.3	1101 0.5	1834 0.0	2210 0.0
5 Th	0410 -0.1	1218 0.5	2012 -0.0	
20 F	0353 -0.2	1132 0.4	1849 -0.1	2357 0.1
6 F	0041 0.1	0503 0.0	1243 0.4	2028 -0.1
21 Sa	0502 -0.1	1202 0.2	1913 -0.1	
7 Sa	0308 0.1	0621 0.1	1258 0.3	2048 -0.1
22 Su	0143 0.1	0638 0.1	1229 0.2	1944 -0.2
8 Su ☾	0455 0.2	0909 0.2	1244 0.2	2112 -0.2
23 M	0316 0.3	0857 0.1	1248 0.2	2021 -0.3
9 M	0553 0.3	2137 -0.2		
24 Tu ☽	0431 0.4	2103 -0.4		
10 Tu	0634 0.4	2204 -0.3		
25 W	0531 0.5	2148 -0.4		
11 W	0708 0.5	2232 -0.3		
26 Th	0625 0.6	2236 -0.5		
12 Th	0739 0.5	2303 -0.4		
27 F	0714 0.6	2325 -0.5		
13 F	0807 0.6	2335 -0.4		
28 Sa	0759 0.6			
14 Sa	0834 0.6			
29 Su	0014 -0.5	0843 0.6		
15 Su ●	0009 -0.4	0901 0.6		
30 M ●	0103 -0.5	0924 0.6	1745 -0.0	
31 Tu	0152 -0.4	1001 0.5	1739 -0.0	2012 -0.0

FEBRUARY

Day	Time ft	Time ft	Time ft	Time ft
1 W	0241 -0.3	1035 0.4	1752 -0.1	2137 0.0
16 Th	0222 -0.3	0951 0.4	1636 -0.1	2124 0.1
2 Th	0331 -0.2	1103 0.3	1809 -0.1	2307 0.0
17 F	0320 -0.2	1020 0.3	1656 -0.1	2241 0.1
3 F	0425 -0.1	1124 0.3	1830 -0.1	
18 Sa	0428 -0.1	1048 0.2	1723 -0.2	
4 Sa	0048 0.1	0532 0.0	1133 0.2	1854 -0.2
19 Su	0002 0.2	0551 -0.0	1111 0.1	1757 -0.2
5 Su	0236 0.2	0723 0.1	1115 0.1	1922 -0.2
20 M	0125 0.3	0743 0.0	1127 0.1	1837 -0.3
6 M	0406 0.2	1952 -0.3		
21 Tu	0245 0.4	1924 -0.3		
7 Tu ☾	0507 0.3	2025 -0.3		
22 W ☽	0358 0.4	2016 -0.4		
8 W	0551 0.4	2102 -0.3		
23 Th	0501 0.5	2114 -0.4		
9 Th	0626 0.4	2141 -0.4		
24 F	0557 0.6	2213 -0.4		
10 F	0657 0.5	2222 -0.4		
25 Sa	0647 0.6	2312 -0.4		
11 Sa	0725 0.5	2305 -0.4		
26 Su	0733 0.6	1530 -0.0	1712 -0.0	
12 Su	0753 0.5	2350 -0.4		
27 M	0010 -0.4	0814 0.5	1531 -0.0	1838 0.0
13 M	0822 0.5			
28 Tu	0107 -0.3	0851 0.4	1543 -0.0	1950 0.1
14 Tu	0038 -0.4	0851 0.5	1627 -0.0	1846 0.0
15 W ●	0128 -0.3	0921 0.4	1624 -0.0	2009 0.0

MARCH

Day	Time ft	Time ft	Time ft	Time ft
1 W	0203 -0.3	0924 0.4	1558 -0.1	2058 0.1
16 Th ○	0147 -0.2	0835 0.3	1454 -0.1	2044 0.1
2 Th	0300 -0.2	0950 0.3	1616 -0.1	2206 0.2
17 F	0251 -0.1	0904 0.3	1516 -0.1	2145 0.3
3 F	0359 -0.1	1008 0.2	1635 -0.1	2317 0.2
18 Sa	0400 -0.1	0931 0.2	1543 -0.0	2248 0.4
4 Sa	0507 0.0	1013 0.1	1657 -0.2	
19 Su	0519 0.0	0953 0.1	1615 -0.2	2355 0.4
5 Su	0030 0.3	0643 0.1	0954 0.1	1722 -0.2
20 M	0657 0.1	1006 0.1	1654 -0.3	
6 M	0145 0.3	1750 -0.3		
21 Tu	0103 0.5	1738 -0.3		
7 Tu	0255 0.3	1824 -0.3		
22 W	0213 0.5	1831 -0.3		
8 W	0355 0.4	1903 -0.3		
23 Th ☽	0321 0.6	1933 -0.3		
9 Th ☾	0443 0.4	1950 -0.3		
24 F	0423 0.6	2042 -0.3		
10 F	0522 0.4	2044 -0.3		
25 Sa	0520 0.6	1402 0.0	2156 -0.2	
11 Sa	0557 0.5	2143 -0.3		
26 Su	0610 0.5	1343 0.0	1658 0.1	2309 -0.2
12 Su	0630 0.5	2243 -0.2		
27 M	0654 0.5	1351 0.0	1817 0.1	
13 M	0702 0.5	1442 0.0	1718 0.0	2344 -0.2
28 Tu	0019 -0.2	0732 0.4	1404 -0.0	1923 0.2
14 Tu	0734 0.4	1432 0.0	1837 0.1	
29 W	0126 -0.1	0804 0.3	1420 -0.0	2023 0.3
15 W ●	0045 -0.2	0805 0.4	1439 -0.0	1943 0.2
30 Th ●	0232 -0.0	0828 0.3	1437 -0.1	2120 0.3
31 F	0339 0.0	0843 0.2	1456 -0.1	2214 0.4

APRIL

Day	Time ft	Time ft	Time ft	Time ft
1 Sa	0454 0.1	0844 0.1	1516 -0.2	2308 0.4
16 Su	0455 0.1	0824 0.1	1448 -0.2	2245 0.6
2 Su	0642 0.1	0809 0.1	1538 -0.2	
17 M	0631 0.1	0832 0.1	1524 -0.3	2342 0.7
3 M	0001 0.5	1602 -0.2		
18 Tu	1605 -0.3			
4 Tu	0054 0.5	1629 -0.2		
19 W	0041 0.7	1652 -0.3		
5 W	0145 0.5	1702 -0.2		
20 Th	0141 0.7	1746 -0.2		
6 Th	0235 0.5	1741 -0.2		
21 F ☽	0241 0.6	1853 -0.2		
7 F	0321 0.5	1833 -0.2		
22 Sa	0339 0.6	1223 0.0	2014 -0.1	
8 Sa ☾	0404 0.5	1943 -0.1		
23 Su	0432 0.5	1214 0.0	1628 0.1	2147 -0.0
9 Su	0445 0.5	1348 0.0	1503 0.0	2108 -0.1
24 M	0519 0.5	1223 0.0	1750 0.2	2319 0.0
10 M	0524 0.5	1258 0.0	1707 0.1	2234 -0.0
25 Tu	0558 0.4	1237 -0.0	1854 0.3	
11 Tu	0601 0.4	1256 0.0	1815 0.2	2354 0.0
26 W	0045 0.1	0629 0.3	1253 -0.1	1949 0.4
12 W	0636 0.4	1307 -0.0	1912 0.3	
27 Th	0206 0.1	0651 0.2	1312 -0.0	2038 0.5
13 Th	0109 0.0	0708 0.3	1315 -0.1	2005 0.4
28 F	0327 0.1	0701 0.2	1331 -0.1	2124 0.5
14 F	0222 0.0	0738 0.3	1348 -0.1	2057 0.5
29 Sa ●	0504 0.1	0644 0.1	1352 -0.2	2208 0.6
15 Sa ○	0336 0.1	0804 0.2	1416 -0.2	2150 0.6
30 Su	1413 -0.2	2249 0.6		

TIME MERIDIAN 60°W　　　　　　　　0000h is midnight, 1200h is noon.
Heights in feet are referenced to the chart datum of soundings.

U.S.V.I.

CHARLOTTE AMALIE, U.S.V.I.

HIGH & LOW WATER 1995　　　　　　　　　　　　　　　　18°20'N　64°56'W

ATLANTIC STANDARD TIME (GMT -4H)

MAY

Day	Time	ft	Day	Time	ft
1 M	1436 / 2329	-0.2 / 0.6	**16** Tu	1449 / 2327	-0.3 / 0.8
2 Tu	1501	-0.2	**17** W	1532	-0.3
3 W	0008 / 1528	0.6 / -0.2	**18** Th	0018 / 1619	0.8 / -0.2
4 Th	0047 / 1600	0.6 / -0.2	**19** F	0109 / 1712	0.7 / -0.2
5 F	0126 / 1638	0.6 / -0.1	**20** Sa	0200 / 1100 / 1254 / 1820	0.6 / 0.1 / 0.1 / -0.0
6 Sa	0207 / 1728	0.6 / -0.1	**21** Su	0248 / 1049 / 1535 /)1954	0.6 / 0.6 / 0.1 / 0.1
7 Su	0249 / 1209 / 1420 / (1849	0.5 / 0.1 / 0.1 / 0.0	**22** M	0332 / 1100 / 1714 / 2155	0.5 / 0.0 / 0.2 / 0.1
8 M	0331 / 1129 / 1637 / 2048	0.5 / 0.0 / 0.1 / 0.1	**23** Tu	0409 / 1116 / 1820 / 2355	0.4 / -0.0 / 0.4 / 0.2
9 Tu	0412 / 1130 / 1744 / 2244	0.4 / 0.0 / 0.3 / 0.1	**24** W	0437 / 1134 / 1912	0.3 / -0.1 / 0.5
10 W	0451 / 1144 / 1836	0.4 / -0.0 / 0.4	**25** Th	0147 / 0450 / 1155 / 1957	0.2 / 0.2 / -0.1 / 0.6
11 Th	0024 / 0526 / 1205 / 1924	0.1 / 0.3 / -0.1 / 0.5	**26** F	1217 / 2038	-0.2 / 0.6
12 F	0151 / 0557 / 1230 / 2011	0.1 / 0.2 / -0.2 / 0.6	**27** Sa	1239 / 2116	-0.2 / 0.7
13 Sa	0315 / 0623 / 1300 / 2059	0.1 / 0.2 / -0.2 / 0.7	**28** Su	1302 / 2151	-0.2 / 0.7
14 Su	0442 / 0638 / 1333 / O2147	0.1 / 0.1 / -0.3 / 0.8	**29** M ●	1327 / 2224	-0.3 / 0.7
15 M	1410 / 2236	-0.3 / 0.8	**30** Tu	1353 / 2255	-0.3 / 0.7
			31 W	1420 / 2327	-0.2 / 0.7

JUNE

Day	Time	ft	Day	Time	ft
1 Th	1451 / 2359	-0.2 / 0.7	**16** F	1601	-0.2
2 F	1524	-0.2	**17** Sa	0035 / 0917 / 1115 / 1655	0.7 / 0.1 / 0.1 / -0.0
3 Sa	0032 / 1604	0.6 / -0.1	**18** Su	0115 / 0917 / 1356 / 1804	0.6 / 0.1 / 0.2 / 0.1
4 Su	0107 / 1035 / 1216 / 1657	0.6 / 0.1 / 0.1 / 0.0	**19** M	0150 / 0932 /)1609 / 1957	0.5 / 0.2 / 0.3 / 0.2
5 M	0144 / 0958 / 1526 / 1832	0.5 / 0.0 / 0.1 / 0.1	**20** Tu	0218 / 0951 / 1731 / 2239	0.4 / -0.0 / 0.4 / 0.3
6 Tu	0221 / 1004 / 1654 / (2100	0.5 / 0.0 / 0.3 / 0.2	**21** W	0230 / 1014 / 1826	0.3 / -0.1 / 0.5
7 W	0257 / 1022 / 1748 / 2321	0.4 / -0.1 / 0.4 / 0.2	**22** Th	1038 / 1910	-0.1 / 0.6
8 Th	0331 / 1046 / 1836	0.3 / -0.1 / 0.5	**23** F	1104 / 1949	-0.2 / 0.7
9 F	0119 / 0359 / 1116 / 1921	0.2 / 0.2 / -0.2 / 0.7	**24** Sa	1130 / 2024	-0.2 / 0.7
10 Sa	0314 / 1149 / 2007	0.2 / -0.3 / 0.8	**25** Su	1157 / 2055	-0.2 / 0.8
11 Su	1226 / 2052	-0.3 / 0.8	**26** M	1225 / 2125	-0.2 / 0.8
12 M	1305 / 2137	-0.3 / 0.9	**27** Tu ●	1254 / 2153	-0.2 / 0.8
13 Tu O	1346 / 2223	-0.3 / 0.9	**28** W	1325 / 2221	-0.2 / 0.8
14 W	1429 / 2308	-0.3 / 0.8	**29** Th	1358 / 2249	-0.2 / 0.7
15 Th	1514 / 2352	-0.2 / 0.8	**30** F	1435 / 2317	-0.1 / 0.7

JULY

Day	Time	ft	Day	Time	ft
1 Sa	1516 / 2347	-0.1 / 0.7	**16** Su	0725 / 1204 / 1701	0.2 / 0.3 / 0.2
2 Su	0815 / 1046 / 1605	0.1 / 0.2 / 0.0	**17** M	0024 / 0747 / 1409 / 1823	0.6 / 0.1 / 0.4 / 0.3
3 M	0018 / 0811 / 1314 / 1715	0.6 / 0.1 / 0.2 / 0.2	**18** Tu	0041 / 0812 / 1600 / 2048	0.5 / 0.1 / 0.5 / 0.4
4 Tu	0049 / 0827 / 1514 / 1909	0.5 / 0.1 / 0.3 / 0.3	**19** W)	0036 / 0841 / 1715	0.4 / 0.0 / 0.6
5 W	0117 / 0851 / 1633 / (2150	0.4 / 0.2 / 0.4 / 0.3	**20** Th	0911 / 1807	-0.0 / 0.7
6 Th	0140 / 0922 / 1731	0.4 / -0.1 / 0.6	**21** F	0943 / 1848	-0.1 / 0.7
7 F	0054 / 0958 / 1821	0.3 / -0.1 / 0.7	**22** Sa	1015 / 1924	-0.1 / 0.8
8 Sa	1038 / 1908	-0.2 / 0.8	**23** Su	1048 / 1955	-0.1 / 0.8
9 Su	1120 / 1954	-0.2 / 0.9	**24** M	1122 / 2024	-0.1 / 0.8
10 M	1204 / 2038	-0.3 / 0.9	**25** Tu	1156 / 2050	-0.1 / 0.8
11 Tu	1249 / 2122	-0.3 / 0.9	**26** W	1233 / 2116	-0.1 / 0.8
12 W O	1335 / 2204	-0.2 / 0.9	**27** Th ●	1311 / 2143	-0.1 / 0.8
13 Th	1422 / 2244	-0.2 / 0.8	**28** F	1353 / 2210	0.0 / 0.8
14 F	0706 / 0818 / 1511 / 2322	0.2 / 0.2 / -0.1 / 0.7	**29** Sa	0601 / 0816 / 1440 / 2237	0.3 / 0.3 / 0.1 / 0.7
15 Sa	0709 / 1010 / 1602 / 2356	0.2 / 0.2 / 0.0 / 0.7	**30** Su	0559 / 0954 / 1533 / 2305	0.3 / 0.3 / 0.2 / 0.7
			31 M	0613 / 1130 / 1638 / 2331	0.2 / 0.4 / 0.3 / 0.6

AUGUST

Day	Time	ft	Day	Time	ft
1 Tu	0637 / 1308 / 1806 / 2355	0.2 / 0.5 / 0.4 / 0.5	**16** W	0648 / 1518	0.2 / 0.7
2 W	0708 / 1441 / 2016	0.1 / 0.6 / 0.4	**17** Th)	0722 / 1630	0.2 / 0.8
3 Th (	0011 / 0745 / 1558	0.5 / 0.1 / 0.7	**18** F	0759 / 1724	0.1 / 0.8
4 F	0828 / 1701	0.0 / 0.8	**19** Sa	0839 / 1806	0.1 / 0.9
5 Sa	0916 / 1756	-0.0 / 0.9	**20** Su	0921 / 1841	0.1 / 0.9
6 Su	1006 / 1846	-0.1 / 1.0	**21** M	1005 / 1911	0.1 / 0.9
7 M	1058 / 1933	-0.1 / 1.0	**22** Tu	1050 / 1939	0.1 / 0.9
8 Tu	1151 / 2017	-0.1 / 1.0	**23** W	1136 / 2006	0.1 / 0.9
9 W	1244 / 2059	-0.1 / 1.0	**24** Th	1224 / 2032	0.2 / 0.9
10 Th O	0442 / 0644 / 1336 / 2137	0.4 / 0.4 / 0.0 / 0.9	**25** F	0356 / 0649 / 1314 / 2059	0.5 / 0.5 / 0.2 / 0.9
11 F	0452 / 0805 / 1429 / 2212	0.4 / 0.4 / 0.1 / 0.8	**26** Sa ●	0354 / 0803 / 1407 / 2126	0.4 / 0.5 / 0.4 / 0.8
12 Sa	0508 / 0924 / 1525 / 2243	0.4 / 0.5 / 0.2 / 0.7	**27** Su	0404 / 0912 / 1505 / 2152	0.4 / 0.6 / 0.3 / 0.8
13 Su	0528 / 1045 / 1624 / 2306	0.3 / 0.5 / 0.3 / 0.7	**28** M	0423 / 1021 / 1611 / 2217	0.4 / 0.7 / 0.4 / 0.7
14 M	0551 / 1214 / 1737 / 2319	0.3 / 0.6 / 0.4 / 0.6	**29** Tu	0448 / 1134 / 1731 / 2239	0.3 / 0.7 / 0.5 / 0.6
15 Tu	0618 / 1348 / 1926 / 2308	0.2 / 0.6 / 0.5 / 0.5	**30** W	0520 / 1250 / 1915 / 2253	0.3 / 0.8 / 0.5 / 0.6
			31 Th	0559 / 1407	0.2 / 0.9

TIME MERIDIAN 60°W　　　　　　　　　　　　0000h is midnight, 1200h is noon.

Heights in feet are referenced to the chart datum of soundings.

CHARLOTTE AMALIE, U.S.V.I.

HIGH & LOW WATER 1995 18°20'N 64°56'W

ATLANTIC STANDARD TIME (GMT -4H)

SEPTEMBER

Day	Time	ft	Time	ft	Time	ft	Time	ft
1 F	0645	0.2	1520	0.9				
2 Sa (	0738	0.2	1625	1.0				
3 Su	0838	0.1	1723	1.1				
4 M	0941	0.1	1816	1.1				
5 Tu	1045	0.1	1903	1.1				
6 W	0245	0.5	0505	0.5	1149	0.2	1946	1.0
7 Th	0251	0.5	0628	0.6	1250	0.2	2025	1.0
8 F O	0305	0.5	0738	0.6	1351	0.3	2059	0.9
9 Sa	0322	0.5	0845	0.7	1453	0.4	2128	0.8
10 Su	0341	0.4	0950	0.8	1557	0.5	2148	0.7
11 M	0403	0.4	1055	0.8	1711	0.5	2158	0.7
12 Tu	0427	0.4	1203	0.8	1850	0.6	2142	0.6
13 W	0453	0.3	1313	0.9				
14 Th	0523	0.3	1422	0.9				
15 F	0556	0.3	1524	0.9				
16 Sa)	0635	0.3	1616	1.0				
17 Su	0721	0.3	1700	1.0				
18 M	0816	0.3	1737	1.0				
19 Tu	0918	0.3	1810	1.0				
20 W	1023	0.4	1840	1.0				
21 Th	0217	0.5	0527	0.5	1127	0.4	1910	0.9
22 F	0206	0.5	0638	0.6	1231	0.4	1938	0.9
23 Sa	0211	0.5	0738	0.7	1334	0.4	2006	0.8
24 Su ●	0225	0.5	0833	0.8	1439	0.5	2033	0.8
25 M	0246	0.4	0929	0.8	1547	0.5	2057	0.7
26 Tu	0312	0.4	1027	1.0	1705	0.6	2118	0.7
27 W	0343	0.3	1127	1.0	1839	0.6	2130	0.6
28 Th	0419	0.3	1230	1.1				
29 F	0502	0.2	1336	1.1				
30 Sa	0553	0.2	1442	1.1				

OCTOBER

Day	Time	ft	Time	ft	Time	ft	Time	ft
1 Su (	0653	0.3	1545	1.1				
2 M	0804	0.3	1643	1.1				
3 Tu	0119	0.5	0241	0.6	0922	0.3	1735	1.1
4 W	0107	0.5	0441	0.6	1042	0.4	1822	1.0
5 Th	0117	0.5	0602	0.7	1159	0.4	1902	0.9
6 F	0131	0.5	0708	0.8	1312	0.4	1936	0.8
7 Sa	0149	0.5	0808	0.8	1423	0.5	2003	0.8
8 Su O	0209	0.4	0904	0.9	1536	0.5	2021	0.7
9 M	0230	0.4	0958	1.0	1656	0.6	2025	0.6
10 Tu	0252	0.3	1050	1.0				
11 W	0316	0.3	1142	1.0				
12 Th	0341	0.3	1234	1.0				
13 F	0408	0.3	1324	1.0				
14 Sa	0437	0.3	1411	1.0				
15 Su	0512	0.3	1456	1.0				
16 M (	0556	0.4	1538	1.0				
17 Tu	0659	0.4	1617	0.9				
18 W	0124	0.5	0329	0.5	0829	0.5	1654	0.9
19 Th	0039	0.5	0517	0.6	1007	0.5	1728	0.9
20 F	0034	0.5	0617	0.7	1136	0.5	1802	0.8
21 Sa	0043	0.4	0707	0.8	1256	0.5	1832	0.8
22 Su	0059	0.4	0755	0.9	1411	0.5	1901	0.7
23 M	0121	0.3	0843	1.0	1526	0.5	1925	0.6
24 Tu ●	0148	0.3	0932	1.0	1646	0.5	1944	0.6
25 W	0220	0.2	1023	1.1	1825	0.5	1947	0.5
26 Th	0255	0.2	1115	1.1				
27 F	0335	0.1	1210	1.1				
28 Sa	0420	0.2	1307	1.1				
29 Su	0512	0.2	1404	1.1				
30 M (	0616	0.2	1501	1.0	2349	0.5		
31 Tu	0143	0.5	0736	0.3	1554	1.0	2340	0.4

NOVEMBER

Day	Time	ft	Time	ft	Time	ft	Time	ft
1 W	0401	0.5	0912	0.4	1643	0.9	2351	0.4
2 Th	0529	0.6	1053	0.4	1724	0.8		
3 F	0007	0.4	0635	0.7	1228	0.5	1759	0.7
4 Sa	0026	0.3	0731	0.8	1356	0.5	1823	0.6
5 Su	0047	0.3	0821	0.9	1523	0.5	1835	0.5
6 M	0110	0.2	0909	1.0	1717	0.5		
7 Tu O	0133	0.2	0953	1.0				
8 W	0157	0.1	1035	1.0				
9 Th	0221	0.1	1115	1.0				
10 F	0246	0.1	1154	1.0				
11 Sa	0311	0.1	1230	1.0				
12 Su	0339	0.2	1306	0.9				
13 M	0409	0.2	1342	0.9				
14 Tu	0445	0.3	1418	0.8				
15 W))	0000	0.4	0227	0.4	0544	0.3	1455	0.8
16 Th	0453	0.4	0753	0.4	1532	0.7	2309	0.3
17 F	0548	0.5	1015	0.5	1608	0.6	2321	0.2
18 Sa	0631	0.7	1208	0.5	1641	0.6	2340	0.2
19 Su	0714	0.8	1344	0.5	1711	0.5		
20 M	0005	0.1	0757	0.9	1512	0.4	1734	0.4
21 Tu	0035	0.0	0841	1.0				
22 W ●	0108	-0.0	0926	1.0				
23 Th	0145	-0.1	1013	1.0				
24 F	0224	-0.1	1101	1.0				
25 Sa	0307	-0.1	1149	1.0				
26 Su	0354	-0.0	1238	1.0				
27 M	0446	0.0	1327	0.9	2222	0.3		
28 Tu	0008	0.3	0551	0.1	1414	0.8	2215	0.2
29 W (	0251	0.3	0720	0.3	1458	0.7	2228	0.2
30 Th	0441	0.4	0921	0.3	1536	0.6	2246	0.1

DECEMBER

Day	Time	ft	Time	ft	Time	ft	Time	ft
1 F	0554	0.5	1130	0.4	1605	0.5	2308	0.1
2 Sa	0649	0.7	1333	0.4	1619	0.4	2332	0.0
3 Su	0737	0.7	2357	-0.0				
4 M	0821	0.8						
5 Tu	0023	-0.1	0901	0.9				
6 W O	0049	-0.1	0938	0.9				
7 Th	0115	-0.1	1013	0.9				
8 F	0142	-0.1	1044	0.8				
9 Sa	0208	-0.1	1114	0.8				
10 Su	0236	-0.1	1143	0.8				
11 M	0305	-0.0	1212	0.7				
12 Tu	0338	0.0	1241	0.7	2227	0.1	2342	0.1
13 W	0417	0.1	1312	0.6	2137	0.1		
14 Th	0325	0.2	0526	0.2	1342	0.5	2140	0.1
15 F))	0453	0.3	0809	0.3	1412	0.4	2157	0.0
16 Sa	0540	0.4	1057	0.3	1439	0.4	2221	-0.1
17 Su	0622	0.6	1321	0.3	1453	0.3	2251	-0.2
18 M	0705	0.7	2325	-0.2				
19 Tu	0748	0.8						
20 W	0002	-0.3	0831	0.8				
21 Th ●	0042	-0.3	0915	0.9				
22 F	0124	-0.3	0959	0.9				
23 Sa	0208	-0.3	1042	0.8				
24 Su	0254	-0.3	1126	0.8				
25 M	0344	-0.2	1207	0.7	2027	0.1	2245	0.1
26 Tu	0439	-0.1	1247	0.6	2036	0.0		
27 W	0105	0.1	0548	0.0	1322	0.5	2055	-0.0
28 Th	0315	0.2	0731	0.2	1351	0.4	2119	-0.1
29 F	0450	0.2	1005	0.2	1405	0.3	2145	-0.1
30 Sa	0555	0.4	2214	-0.2				
31 Su	0645	0.5	2244	-0.3				

U.S.V.I.

TIME MERIDIAN 60°W
Heights in feet are referenced to the chart datum of soundings.

0000h is midnight, 1200h is noon.

BRITISH VIRGIN ISLANDS

CAUTION: Our information on aids to navigation comes from official government sources. The latitudes and longitudes of these marks may not correspond to the readings from GPS receivers. Some aids have been reported as unreliable, missing, off position, or showing incorrect characteristics. No single aid to navigation, or waypoint, should be relied upon as a sole means of fixing your position.

Note: The chartlets in this section are not intended for navigation and are included for reference and planning purposes only. While chartlets reproduced from government sources are from the most current editions as of press time, they incorporate no corrections to navigational aids, depths, or hazards since the edition publication date.

ENTRY PROCEDURES

The British Virgin Islands (B.V.I.) include the islands of Jost Van Dyke, Tortola, Norman, Peter, Salt, Cooper, Ginger, Virgin Gorda, Guana, Great Camanoe, and Anegada and numerous small cays. The country is a British dependency.

Ports of Entry are located on Jost Van Dyke (Great Harbour), Tortola (Road Town and West End/Soper's Hole), and Virgin Gorda (Virgin Gorda Yacht Harbour). Normal working hours are 0830 to 1530, Monday through Friday and 0830 to 1230 on Saturday. An overtime charge applies after hours and on Sunday and holidays. Office hours at the individual customs offices can vary during these overtime hours. Check with Road Town Customs at 809-494-3475 for information. Boats must clear customs and immigration when traveling between the U.S. Virgin Islands and the B.V.I.

You should have a clearance from your last port of call, although this is not strictly necessary when arriving from the U.S. Virgin Islands. You should also obtain a clearance before departing the B.V.I.s.

Immigration clearance will be given for 30 days, with extensions possible for $10 per person.

You can generally get permission for visits of up to six months, provided you can prove adequate finances. Visitors from some countries may need a visa. For the latest information contact Road Town Customs at 809-494-3475 and Road Town Immigration at 809-494-3471.

There is a small fee for private cruising boats and a per diem charge for charterboats. From December 1 through April 30 B.V.I.-registered charterboats pay $2 per person, per day. Boats registered elsewhere pay $4 per person, per day. From May 1 through November 30 the rates are, respectively, $0.75 and $4 per person, per day.

Dive boats, sportfishing boats, and day charterboats should contact the B.V.I. customs department regarding cruising permits. All non-B.V.I. residents planning to fish must have a recreational fishing permit. Contact the Conservation and Fisheries Department in Road Town at 809-494-3429.

A system of approximately 180 National Parks Trust moorings for day stops only has been placed in reef-sensitive areas and near many dive sites. To use these moorings, it is necessary to have a permit, which is available from customs, charter and dive companies, and the National Parks Trust office in Road Town. Fees vary depending on the type of yacht. Contact the Trust at 809-494-3904 or -2069 for more information.

The currency of the B.V.I. is the U.S. dollar, and major credit cards are widely accepted, especially in tourist areas. The language spoken is English.

GREAT HARBOUR
18 27N, 64 45W
Emergencies: Contact Virgin Islands Search and Rescue (VISAR) on VHF channel 16 or 809-494-4357 or dial 999 on the telephone. Call Tortola Radio on VHF channel 16.
Pilotage: This bay is easy to enter with depths of 15 to 20 feet. A reef extends across most of the head of the bay, so don't venture too far in. A gap in the middle of the reef creates a safe route for dinghies traveling to the wharf. When anchoring, check your set well, as the

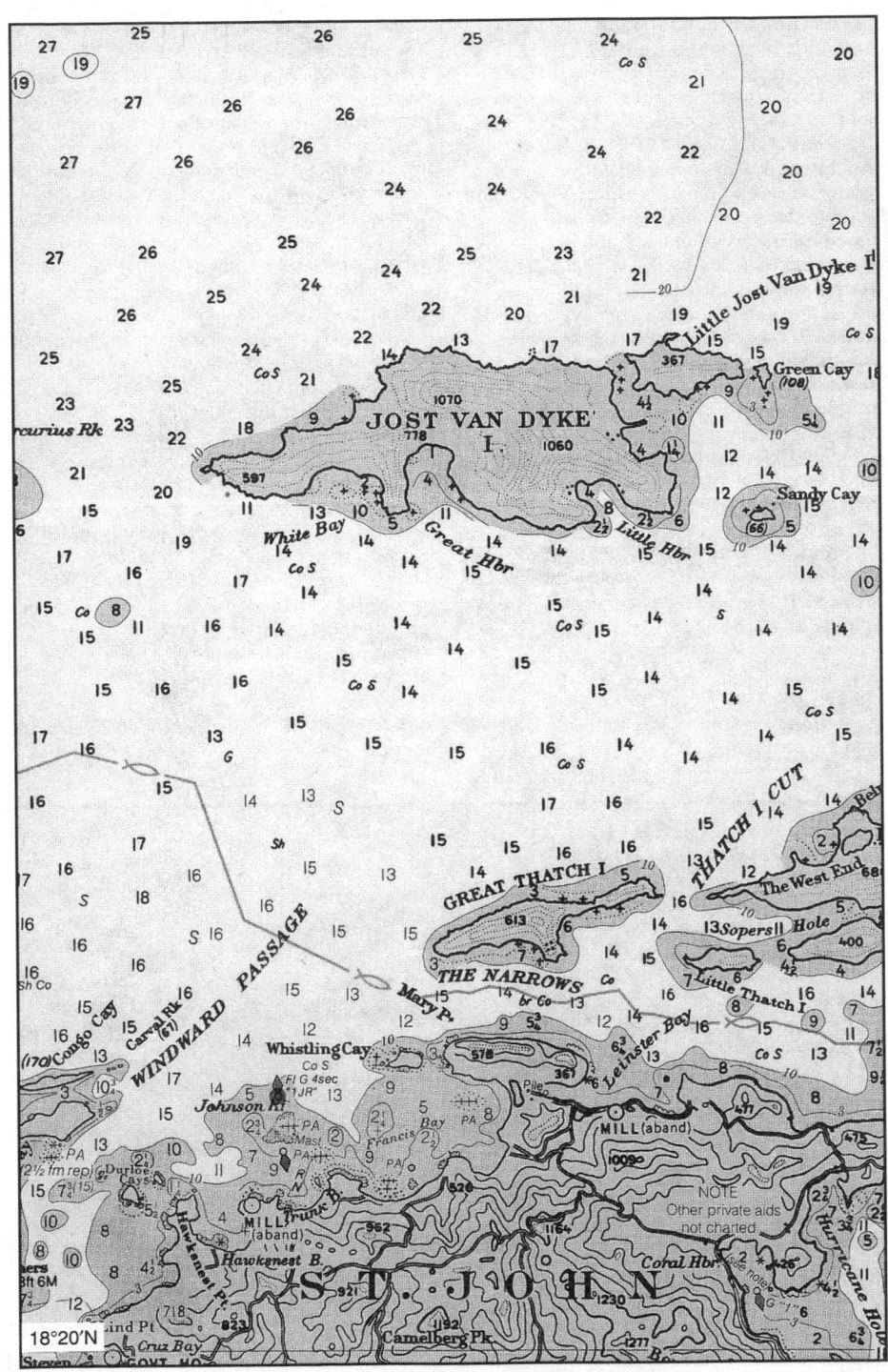

Jost Van Dyke, soundings in fathoms *(from NOAA 25611, 22nd ed, 8/93)*

holding is not all good and the wind tends to swing the boats in strange ways.

Port of Entry: Dinghy in to the main dock. The Customs and Immigration offices are located near the wharf.

Dockage: None on Jost Van Dyke.

Anchorage: There are good anchorages in White Bay, Great Harbour, Little Harbour, and south of Little Jost Van Dyke. Green Cay and Sandy Cay are favorite day stops.

Services: There are several well-known restaurant/bars here, famous for their pig roasts and entertainment. Probably the best known "yachty" hangout is Foxy's, where you may be serenaded by Foxy himself. There are a few small stores, some groceries, and a couple of telephones.

Jost Van Dyke is famous for its watering holes and relaxed atmosphere. It is probably the easiest place to clear customs in the B.V.I.

TORTOLA

SOPERS HOLE LIGHT, passenger terminal, SW end, 18 23.4N, 64 42.2W. F R, 16ft.

WEST END

18 23N, 64 43W

Emergencies: Contact Virgin Islands Search and Rescue (VISAR) on VHF channel 16 or 809-494-4357 or dial 999 on the telephone. Call Tortola Radio on VHF channel 16.

Pilotage: This popular harbor is charted as Soper's Hole, and both names are used interchangeably. The entrance is deep and free of obstructions, except close to shore. Be prepared for currents up to 3 or 4 knots in the mouth of Soper's Hole, in Thatch Island Cut, and in the pass between Little Thatch and Frenchman's Cay. Stay clear of the docking ferries at the wharf on the north side of the harbor.

Port of Entry: The officials are located in the building on the ferry wharf. Due to the constant flow of traffic at the wharf, it is best to dinghy over from your moored boat.

Dockage: Contact Sunsail (809-495-4740 or VHF channels 12 and 16).

Moorings: There are so many moorings here, you may have trouble finding room to anchor. Generally, you can pick up a mooring and a boat will come to collect the fee. Short-term rates are available for those waiting to clear customs only. Sunsail and Frenchman's Cay Shipyard on VHF channel 16 rent moorings.

Anchorage: With depths of 25 to 65 feet, lots of moorings, and frequent crowds of boats, anchoring is problematic at best. Renting a mooring is a viable alternative.

Services: Frenchman's Cay Shipyard (809-495-4353 or VHF channel 16), has a 200-ton marine railway and complete repair facilities

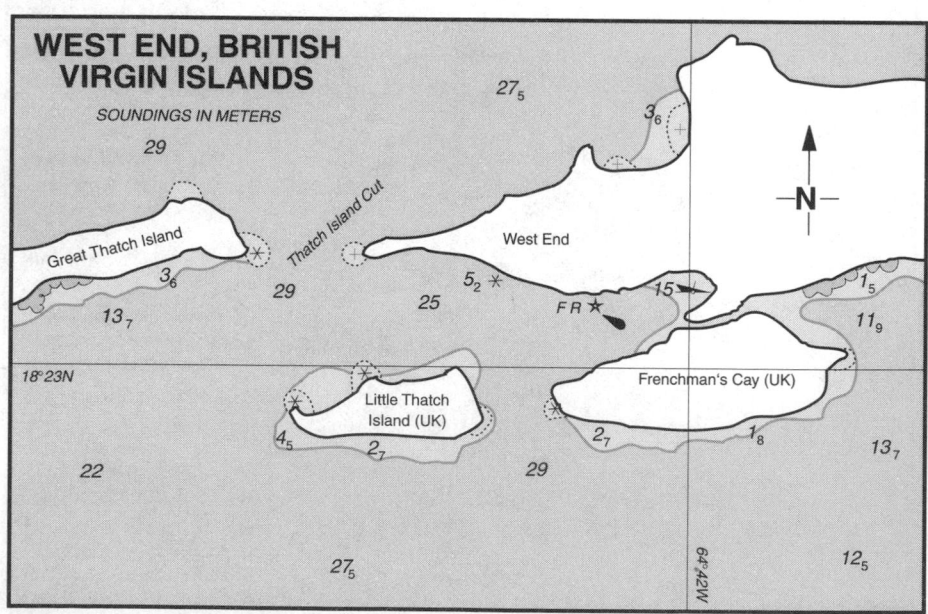

West End, soundings in meters (*after DMA 25611, 21st ed, 9/86*)

for boats of all types. The yard's speciality is woodworking and wooden vessels There are chandlers on-site, and parts can be messengered from Road Town. Pusser's Rum and the Jolly Roger are popular bars and restaurants, and the Ample Hamper can supply most food and liquor needs. Call the Ample Hamper (809-495-4684) for provisioning information if you are on a bareboat charter. Baskin in the Sun (809-495-4582 or VHF channel 16), is a full-service dive shop. There are taxis to Road Town, telephones, and in the complex near the Sunsail docks, several shops.

West End is a popular and busy spot. The yacht facilities are good, and the entertainment ashore is geared to the many charterboats visiting here. The presence of first-class wooden boat specialists and repair facilities of all sorts makes this a unique harbor. The Sweethearts of the Caribbean race features classic yachts racing in these beautiful waters.

ROAD TOWN RANGE (Front Light), 18 25.3N, 64 37.1W. F R, 37ft, 3M. Administration building. F R lights on radio mast 1.5M WNW; aero F R, F W (occasional) 3M E. **(Rear Light),** about 40 meters 290° from front. F R 52ft, 3M. Administration building.

ROAD TOWN

18 26N, 64 37W

Emergencies: Contact Virgin Islands Search and Rescue (VISAR) on VHF channel 16 or 809-494-4357 or dial 999 on the telephone. Call Tortola Radio on VHF channel 16.
Pilotage: The range of 290°T will take you in to the government wharf safely. There are several shoal areas within the harbor, some of which may not be marked. There is shallow water both north and south of the main wharf, off Baugher's Bay, and all along the shore north of the Fort Burt Marina area. Note that anchoring is prohibited in the central harbor area.
Port of Entry: You may tie up temporarily to the main passenger wharf while clearing customs and immigration, but there may be a surge. The office is located just across the street from the wharf. Contact Road Town Customs at 809-494-3475 and Road Town Immigration at 809-494-3471.
Dockage: The Nanny Cay Resort and Marina (809-494-2512) is located about 2 miles southwest of Road Harbor on the south coast of Tortola. Prospect Reef Resort and Marina is entered through a reef just a bit southwest of Fort Burt Point. Depths are reported to be less

than 6 feet in the entrance channel. Fort Burt Marina can be contacted at 809-494-4200. Road Reef Marina (809-494-2751) is located in the small cove south of Fort Burt Marina. In the Wickhams Cay basin are Village Cay Marina (809-494-2771) and Inner Harbour Marina (809-494-4502). The Moorings is located on Wickham's Cay 2 (809-494-2331 or VHF channel 12.)

Anchorage: Most boaters find room north of the Fort Burt Marina, where there is a dinghy dock. Check depths carefully, as the bottom shoals rapidly towards shore. There may be some room among the many moored boats in the Wickham's Cay basin. There is a dinghy dock near the Village Cay Marina. It is also possible to anchor south of the charterboat marina in Baugher's Bay. Most of the harbor is subject to surge and swells, especially when the wind comes in south of east.

Services: Tortola Yacht Services (809-494-2124), on Wickham's Cay 2, is a full-service boatyard. Nanny Cay also has hauling and repair services. There are several chandlers. Fuel, water, and ice are available at Nanny Cay, Road Reef Marina, The Moorings, and Inner Harbour Marina. There is a propane fill-up within walking distance of Wickham's Cay 2. Road Town is the capital and commercial center of the British Virgin Islands. There are good telephone connections, banks, a post office, several grocery stores, many eateries, and good shopping. Everything is available in a compact area, easily accessible to those on foot.

Road Town is a delightful Caribbean city of small winding streets, with colorful wooden buildings leaning over the narrow sidewalks. Without the hectic pace of Charlotte Amalie, it is a pleasant place to stock up on supplies. The small bars and restaurants are often full of cruisers from around the world. Try a visit to the botanical garden or a trip into the hills via taxi or rental car.

FAT HOGS BAY LIGHT, 18 26.1N, 64 33.6W. Fl (2) W, 5s, 25ft, 5M.
BELLAMY CAY LIGHT, off Beef Island, 18 27.0N, 64 31.9W. F W. White mast.

TRELLIS BAY

18 27N, 64 32W

Emergencies: Contact Virgin Islands Search and Rescue (VISAR) on VHF channel 16 or 809-494-4357 or dial 999 on the telephone. Call Tortola Radio on VHF channel 16.

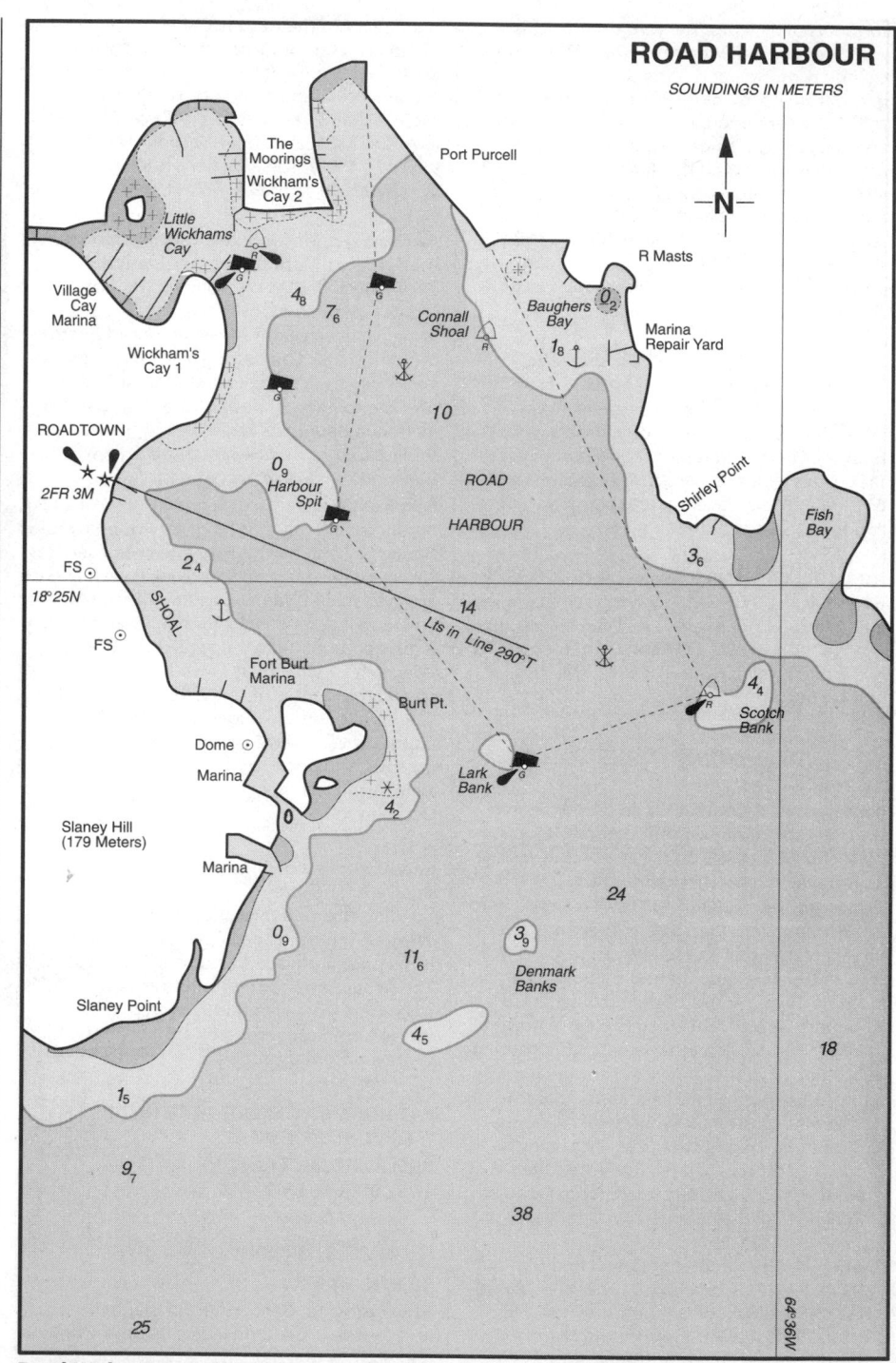

ROAD HARBOUR

SOUNDINGS IN METERS

-N-

The
Moorings
Wickham's
Cay 2

Port Purcell

Little
Wickhams
Cay

R Masts

Village
Cay
Marina

Wickham's
Cay 1

Connall
Shoal

Baughers
Bay

0₂

Marina
Repair Yard

4₈ 7₆

1₈

ROADTOWN

2FR 3M

0₉
Harbour
Spit

10

ROAD

HARBOUR

Shirley Point

Fish
Bay

FS

18°25N

2₄

SHOAL

FS

14   Lts in Line 290° T

3₆

Fort Burt
Marina

Burt Pt.

4₄
Scotch
Bank

Dome

Marina

Lark
Bank

Slaney Hill
(179 Meters)

Marina

0

4₂

24

0₉

3₉

Denmark
Banks

Slaney Point

11₆

1₅

4₅

18

9₇

38

25

64°36W

Road Harbour, soundings in meters *(after DMA 25611, 21st ed, 9/86)*

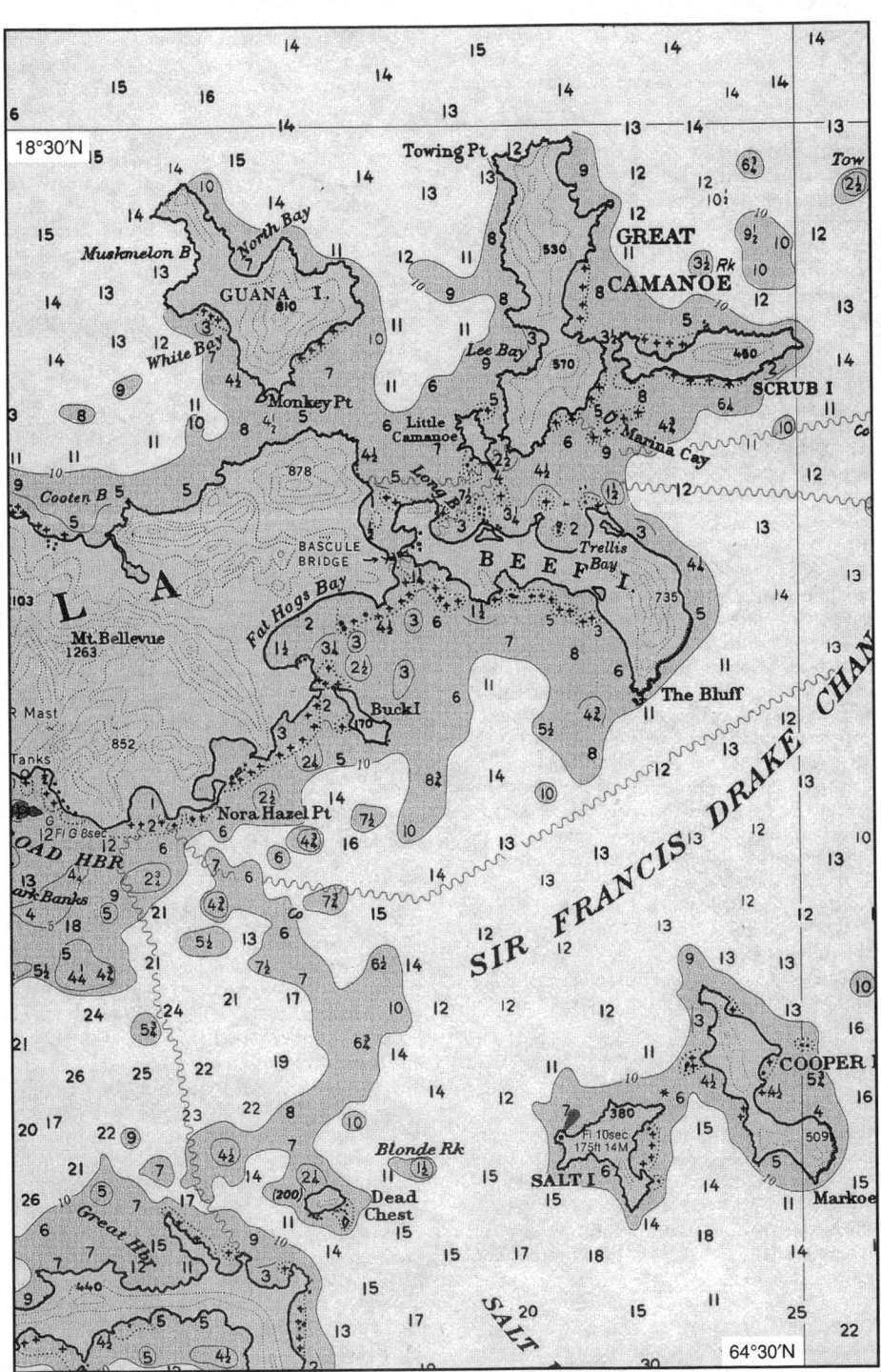

Trellis Bay, soundings in fathoms *(from NOAA 25641, 22nd ed, 8/93)*

Pilotage: Entering from the north there are some rocks off Sprat Point, on the east side of Trellis Bay and a 3-foot-deep reef extending north from Conch Shell Point on the west side of the bay. A cable extends from Bellamy Cay west to shore, and there is a small shallow patch south of the cay.

Anchorage: Good anchorage is available throughout the bay. The airport is within walking distance off the docks on the west side of the bay.

Services: The well-known Last Resort Island Restaurant offers a huge buffet and an evening of laughs when the owner parodies the foibles of visitors to the islands.

NORMAN ISLAND

18 19N, 64 37W

Emergencies: Contact Virgin Islands Search and Rescue (VISAR) on VHF channel 16 or 809-494-4357 or dial 999 on the telephone. Call Tortola Radio on VHF channel 16.

Pilotage: The tall rocks west of Pelican Island are known as the Indians. This is a favorite dive site, where the National Parks Trust has placed moorings to prevent further damage to the coral. You must have a permit to use the moorings. South of Treasure Point is another reef and a series of caves, which are also a dive site. Use the moorings if possible.

Anchorage: Anchor as far in the Bight as you can to avoid the more-than-30-foot depths farther out. You can dinghy in to the small beach at the head of the cove. This anchorage is often crowded with charterboats in the winter. In settled weather, Benures Bay, on the north coast of the island, is a pleasant anchorage. Pass west of the reefs before looping up inside the hook of land.

Services: An anchored boat serves as a bar and restaurant. Contact the *William Thornton* on VHF channel 16.

PETER ISLAND

18 21N, 64 35W

Emergencies: Contact Virgin Islands Search and Rescue (VISAR) on VHF channel 16 or 809-494-4357 or dial 999 on the telephone. Call Tortola Radio on VHF channel 16.

Pilotage: The only yacht facility on the island is located east of the spit of land forming the eastern boundary of Great Harbour. This body of water is called Sprat Bay.

Dockage: Peter Island Resort and Yacht Harbour (809-494-2561) or VHF channel 16, offers dockage for yachts up to 170 feet, with 12-foot draft.

Moorings: Peter Island Resort has some rental moorings in Sprat Bay.

Anchorage: Anchorages include Sprat Bay, Great Harbour, and Little Harbour. In settled weather you can anchor in White Bay on the south shore or west of Key Cay.

Services: Diesel, water, ice, and electricity are available at the Peter Island Resort docks. The resort's restaurant serves lunch, dinner, and cocktails (jackets and ties at dinner are now optional).

SALT ISLAND

SALT ISLAND LIGHT, NW corner of island, 18 22.5N, 64 32.1W. Fl W 10s, 175ft, 14M.

SALT ISLAND

18 22N, 64 32W

Emergencies: Contact Virgin Islands Search and Rescue (VISAR) on VHF channel 16 or 809-494-4357 or dial 999 on the telephone. Call Tortola Radio on VHF channel 16.

Pilotage: Salt Island rises to a height of 380 feet. There is a rock awash off the northeast point of the island. There is a small settlement in Salt Island Bay on the north shore where workers once mined the island's salt ponds. The wreck of the *Rhone* is a favorite dive site located southwest of the island. Boaters can anchor in Lee Bay to dinghy to the site, where the *Rhone* is located in more than 30 feet of water. No anchoring is allowed, and visitors must use the National Parks Trust moorings.

Anchorage: Anchor in Salt Island Bay or Lee Bay.

COOPER ISLAND

18 23N, 64 31W

Emergencies: Contact Virgin Islands Search and Rescue (VISAR) on VHF channel 16 or 809-494-4357 or dial 999 on the telephone. Call Tortola Radio on VHF channel 16.

Pilotage: Cooper Island is 1.7 miles long and rises to 530 feet at its south end. The passage between Salt and Cooper is constricted by a rock awash off the northeast point of Salt. A small islet off the west coast of Cooper forms the southern boundary of Manchioneel Bay.

Moorings: Available in Manchioneel Bay from Cooper Island Beach Club on VHF channel 16.

Anchorage: The swirling winds, deep waters, and crowded moorings make this anchorage uncomfortable at times. You can dinghy in to the beach club dock.

Services: The Cooper Island Beach Club, with bar and restaurant, is often the site of lively charterboat parties.

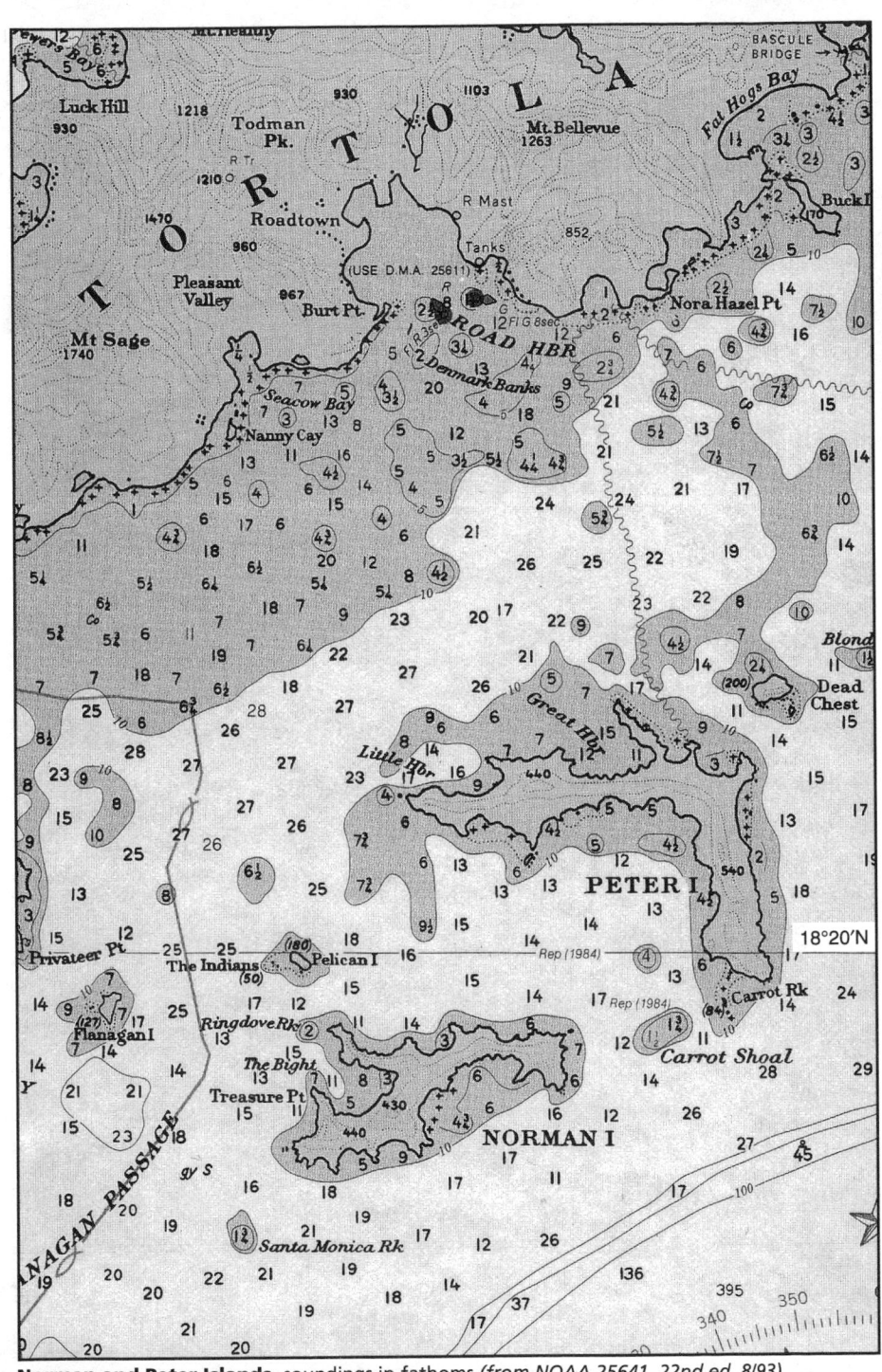

Norman and Peter Islands, soundings in fathoms *(from NOAA 25641, 22nd ed, 8/93)*

COAST PILOT

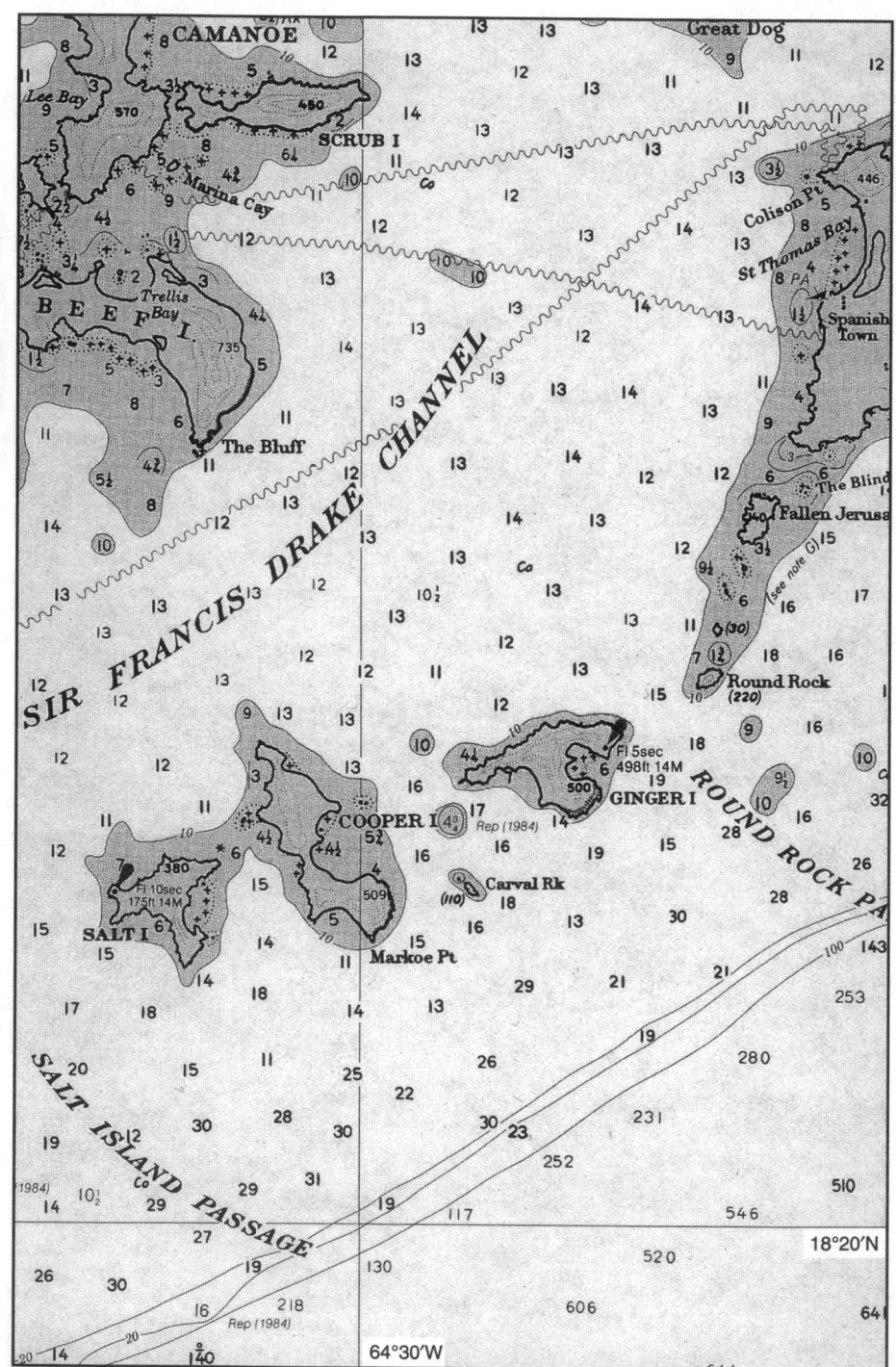

Salt, Cooper, and Ginger Islands, soundings in fathoms *(from NOAA 25641, 22nd ed, 8/93)*

GINGER ISLAND

GINGER ISLAND LIGHT, NE end of island, 18 23.6N, 64 28.3W. Fl W 5s, 498ft, 14M. Yellow tower.

VIRGIN GORDA

PAJAROS POINT LIGHT, 18 30.2N, 64 19.5W. Fl (3) W 15s, 200ft, 16M.

THE BATHS AND VIRGIN GORDA YACHT HARBOUR

18 26N, 64 27W

Emergencies: Contact Virgin Islands Search and Rescue (VISAR) on VHF channel 16 or 809-494-4357 or dial 999 on the telephone. Call Tortola Radio on VHF channel 16.

Pilotage: The Baths are located about 1/2 mile north of the southern tip of Virgin Gorda. Virgin Gorda Yacht Harbour is located about 1 1/2 miles farther north. The marina is reached through a privately marked channel that takes you safely through the reef.

Port of Entry: Contact customs officials at the marina.

Dockage: Contact Virgin Gorda Yacht Harbour (809-495-5500 or on VHF channel 16).

Anchorage: Anchor off the huge boulders that form the Baths. Be very careful to avoid the many snorkelers if you motor in to the beach in your dinghy. There is a marked dinghy channel. This anchorage can be very rolly and is only a day stop.

Services: Virgin Gorda Yacht Harbour is a full-service marina with fuel, water, ice, haulouts, repairs, and a chandlery. A shopping center, a grocery store, and several restaurants are nearby. You can buy stamps and post letters in the Yacht Harbour complex. For additional postal services, the post office is a short taxi ride away. Taxi service to the Baths and the rest of the island is also available.

GORDA SOUND

18 30N, 64 22W

Emergencies: Contact Virgin Islands Search and Rescue (VISAR) on VHF channel 16 or 809-494-4357 or dial 999 on the telephone. Call Tortola Radio on VHF channel 16.

Pilotage: The west entrance to the sound passes through a narrow channel south of Mosquito Island. Just east of the narrowest part (175 yards wide) is a shallow bar to the north. Controlling depth is about 5 or 6 feet. Attempt this passage only in good light. The northern entrance passes east of Colquhoun Reef and is marked by a red and green buoy at its narrowest point. Least depth is about 17 feet on this route.

Dockage: Pusser's Leverick Bay has dockage and moorings in Leverick Bay along the south shore of Gorda Sound. A free bottle of Pusser's Rum comes with every 25-gallon fuel purchase. The Bitter End Yacht Club (809-494-2746 or VHF channel 16), located on the eastern side of the sound, offers moorings and dockage. Biras Creek Marina (809-494-3555 or VHF channel 16) is south of the Bitter End.

Moorings: Rental moorings are available at Pusser's, the Bitter End, Biras Creek, and Drake's Anchorage (809-494-2254 or VHF channel 16) on Mosquito Island.

Anchorage: There are many excellent places to anchor in Gorda Sound. In addition to anchorages off the establishments mentioned above, favorite spots include west of Prickly Pear Island, in Gun Creek, and near Saba Rock. Choose your spot according to the wind direction, and watch for coral heads in the shallows.

Services: All of the marinas and resorts have excellent bars and restaurants. Fuel, water, and ice are available at Pusser's, the Bitter End, and Biras Creek. Some provisions are available at the Bitter End. There are interesting shops at Pusser's and the Bitter End. Kilbride's Underwater Tours (809-495-9638 or VHF channel 16), leads snorkeling and diving expeditions from the Bitter End. Pirates Pub, a favorite "yachty" hangout on Saba Rock, can be contacted via VHF channel 16.

Gorda Sound is a miniature cruising ground all by itself. There are interesting anchorages, good restaurants, and beautiful views in all directions. Despite its popularity, a good anchoring spot always seems to be available.

ANEGADA

ANEGADA LIGHT, W end, 18 44.8N, 64 24.7W. Fl W 10s, 62ft, 10M. Caution: This light may be inoperative.

ANEGADA

18 44N, 64 23W

Emergencies: Contact Virgin Islands Search and Rescue (VISAR) on VHF channel 16 or 809-494-4357 or dial 999 on the telephone. Call Tortola Radio on VHF channel 16.

Pilotage: Anegada is only 30 feet high and very difficult to spot from a distance. It is surrounded by coral reefs and shoals. Never approach the island after dark or in poor visibility. The

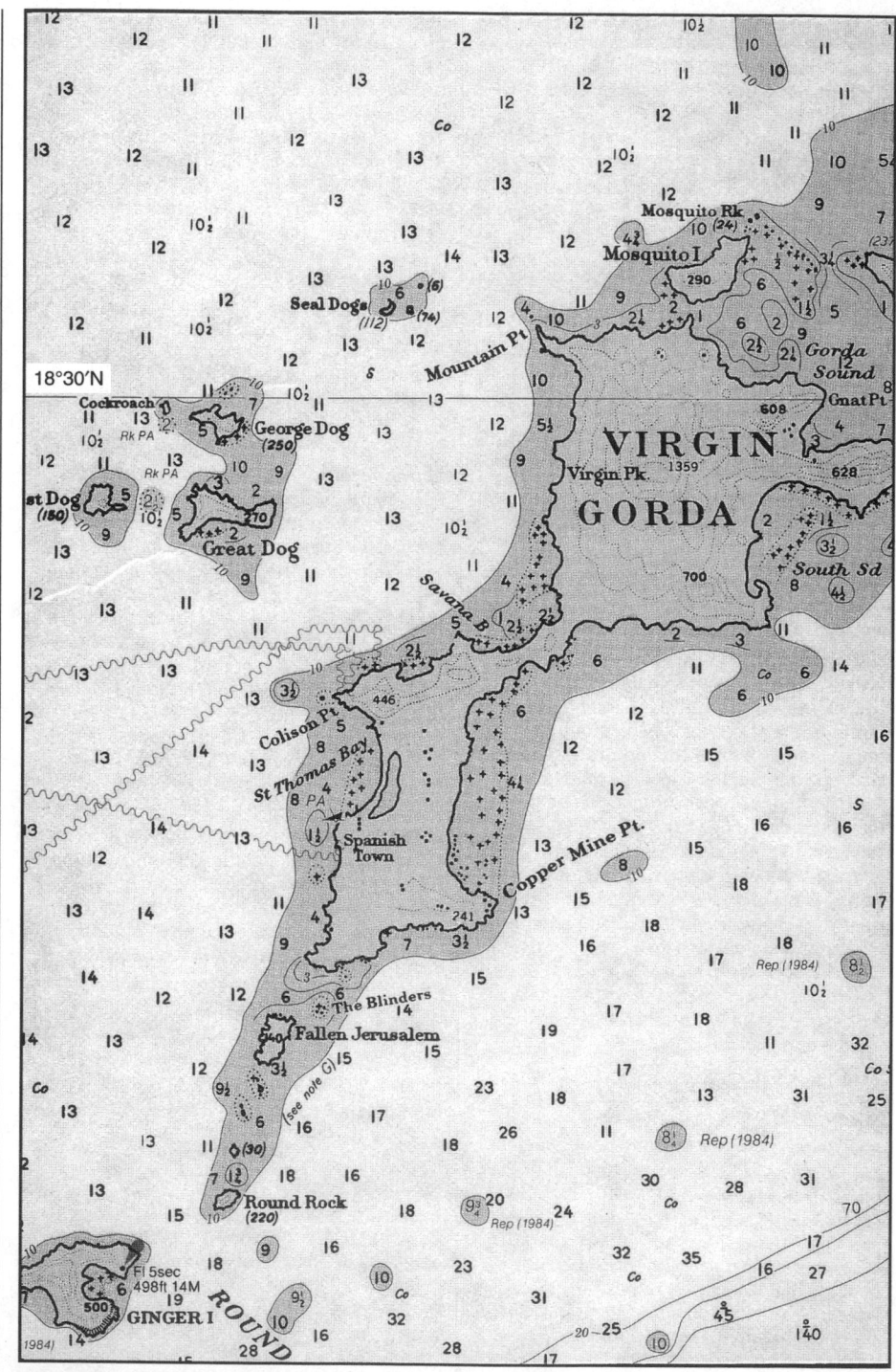

The Baths, soundings in fathoms *(from NOAA 25641, 22nd ed, 8/93)*

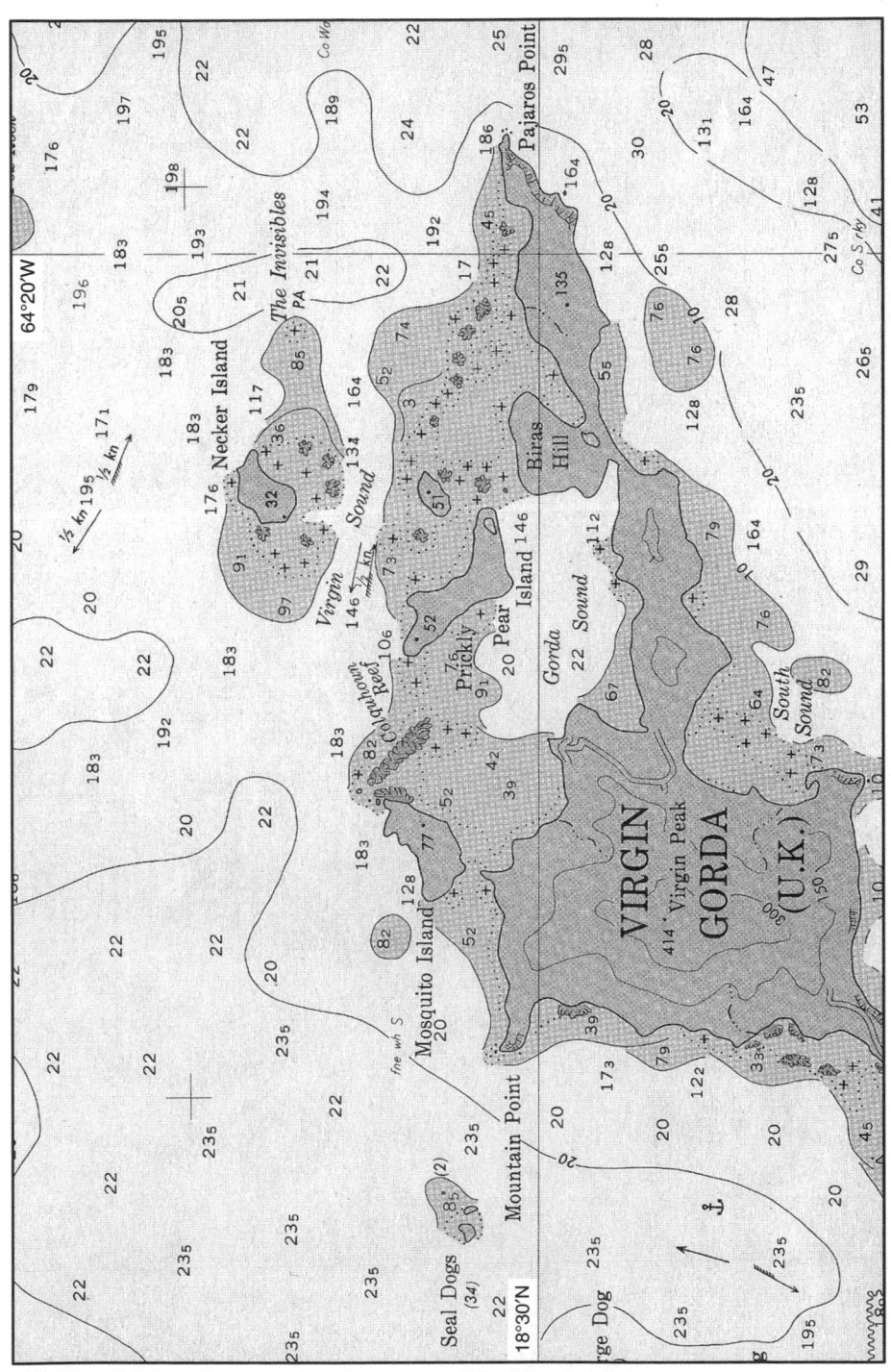

Gorda Sound, soundings in meters *(from DMA 25609, 4th ed, 10/86)*

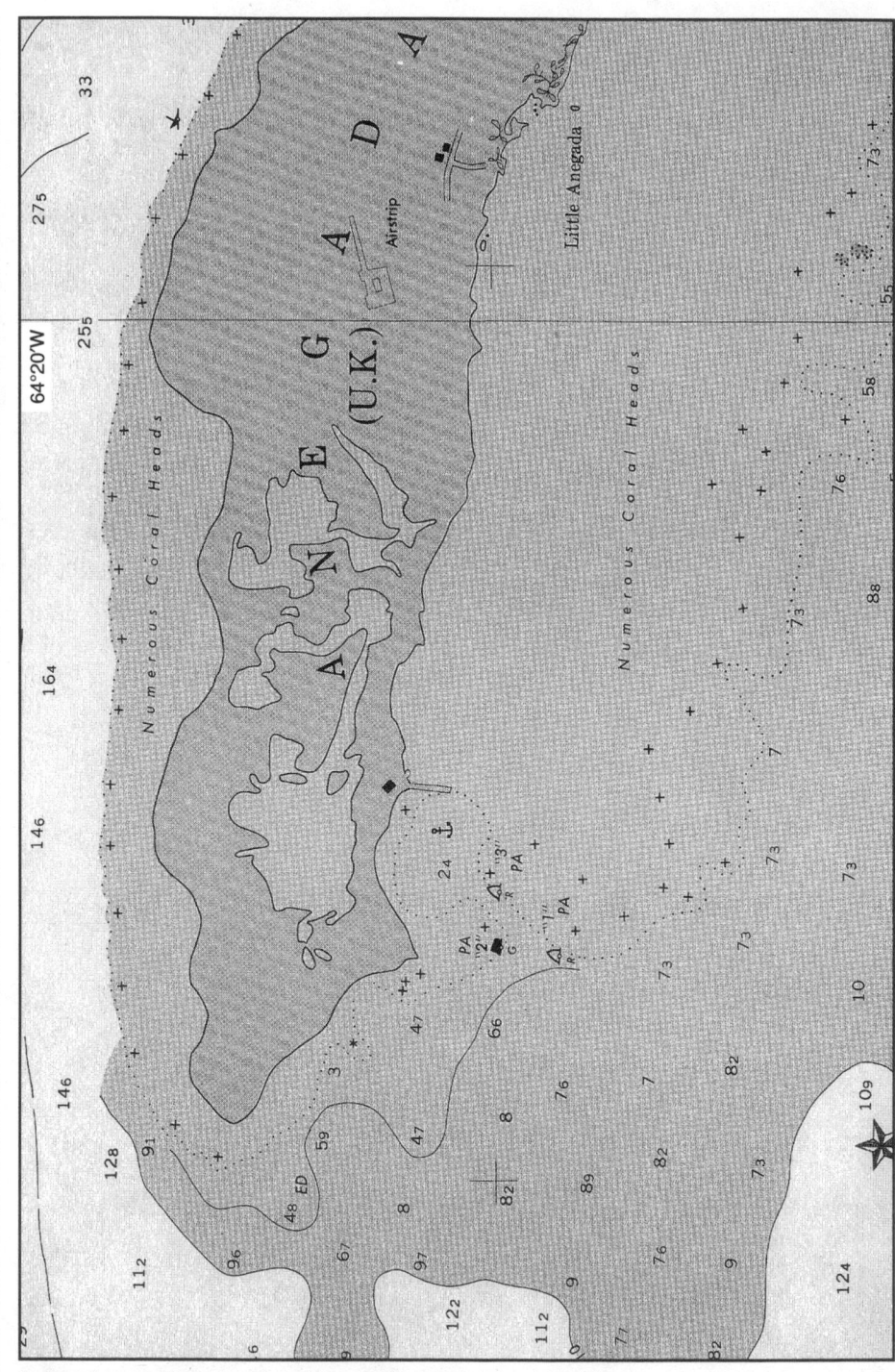

Anegada, soundings in meters *(from DMA 25609, 4th ed, 10/86)*

direct course from Gorda Sound to the west end of Anegada is about 352°T. With the west end of Anegada lined up on your bow and Gorda Sound on your stern, you should clear all the coral heads. The currents are notoriously irregular, and you should judge leeway by watching Virgin Gorda behind you. Chances are you will be set well to the west. Once you can see the island, you may be able to spot the buoys marking the channel into the anchorage on the south side of the island. Stay in deep water until you are sure of your course. Several buoys should lead you on a course of about 60° or 70°T towards the wharf and hotels on shore. Jost Van Dyke should be on your stern when you are headed towards the hotel. If in doubt, call the Anegada Reef Hotel on VHF channel 16 or one of the boats in the anchorage. The controlling depth is about 7 feet to the hotel and then 6 feet in the anchorage area west of the hotel.

Anchorage: Anchor in the cove west of the hotel, watching for coral heads. This area is surprisingly sheltered, even in high winds.

Boats sometimes anchor west of the restaurant on Pomato Point. Enter when the restaurant bears approximately 90°. Call Pomato Point on VHF channel 16 for directions.

Services: Neptune's Treasure (809-495-9439 or VHF channel 16), rents tents and rooms and has a restaurant and small bakery. The Anegada Reef Hotel (809-495-8002 or VHF channel 16), offers rooms and meals. Pomato Point Restaurant (809-495-9466 or VHF channel 16), has an interesting museum of local artifacts. The Anegada Beach Club, which also monitors VHF channel 16, has dining. Call ahead for reservations at these establishments.

Anegada's fringing reefs have always been a treacherous trap for passing ships, creating a diving and treasure hunter's paradise. Most bareboat charters aren't permitted to visit here, so the anchorage tends to be less crowded. Note that anchoring and fishing on Horseshoe Reef have been prohibited while fish stocks are restored.

SOMBRERO, UNITED KINGDOM

18 36N, 63 25W
SOMBRERO LIGHT, SE side, 18 35.8N, 63 25.6W. Fl W 10s, 157ft, 23M. Red iron framework tower.

This small island lies about 30 miles northwest of Anguilla. Its lighthouse is the only mark in the Anegada Passage. It lies on a small circular bank with depths of 10 to 30 fathoms. The island has precipitous sides and rises in sharp jagged points. Vegetation is sparse, but there is abundant bird life on the island.

A light is exhibited from a square metal framework tower on a white concrete base situated near the center of the island. The keeper's dwellings and a flag staff stand north of the light tower. A 20-foot-high circular concrete base of a former light tower stands east of the light. A ruined chimney about 33 feet high is about 175 yards southwest of the light.

There is an anchorage off the west side of the island in depths of about 12 fathoms.

ANGUILLA

CAUTION: Our information on aids to navigation comes from official government sources. The latitudes and longitudes of these marks may not correspond to the readings from GPS receivers. Some aids have been reported as unreliable, missing, off position, or showing incorrect characteristics. No single aid to navigation, or waypoint, should be relied upon as a sole means of fixing your position.

NOTE: The chartlet in this section is <u>not intended for navigation</u> and is included for reference and planning purposes only. Reproduced from government sources, it is from the most current edition as of press time, but incorporates <u>no corrections</u> to navigational aids, depths, or hazards since the edition publication date.

ENTRY PROCEDURES

Anguilla is a British dependency, although it is basically self governing.

Ports of Entry are Road Bay, on the north coast, and Blowing Point, on the south coast. Road Bay is the preferred place of entry for pleasure vessels. Customs and immigration

offices are open from 0830 to 1200 and from 1330 to 1600, Monday through Friday. Saturday hours are 1330 to 1600, and the offices are closed on Sundays and holidays.

Vessels over 20 tons must pay port and lighthouse dues. The charge is $20 for vessels from 20 to 50 tons, $60 for vessels from 50 to 100 tons, and $150 for vessels from 100 to 250 tons. Charterboats must purchase a cruising permit for the duration of their stay. For vessels up to 5 tons the charge is $25 per day or $150 per week. For vessels from 5 to 20 tons the charge is $100 per day or $600 per week. For vessels over 20 tons the charge is $150 per day or $900 per week. All charges are based on registered tonnage and are quoted in Eastern Caribbean, or EC, dollars. The exchange rate of EC dollars to U.S. dollars is about .40.

Privately owned boats are not currently subject to charges in Anguilla. Spearfishing and commercial fishing are prohibited aboard foreign boats. Check with customs for the areas where anchoring is prohibited.

For further information contact customs in Road Bay (809-497-5461). The language spoken is English, and the official currency is the Eastern Caribbean dollar.

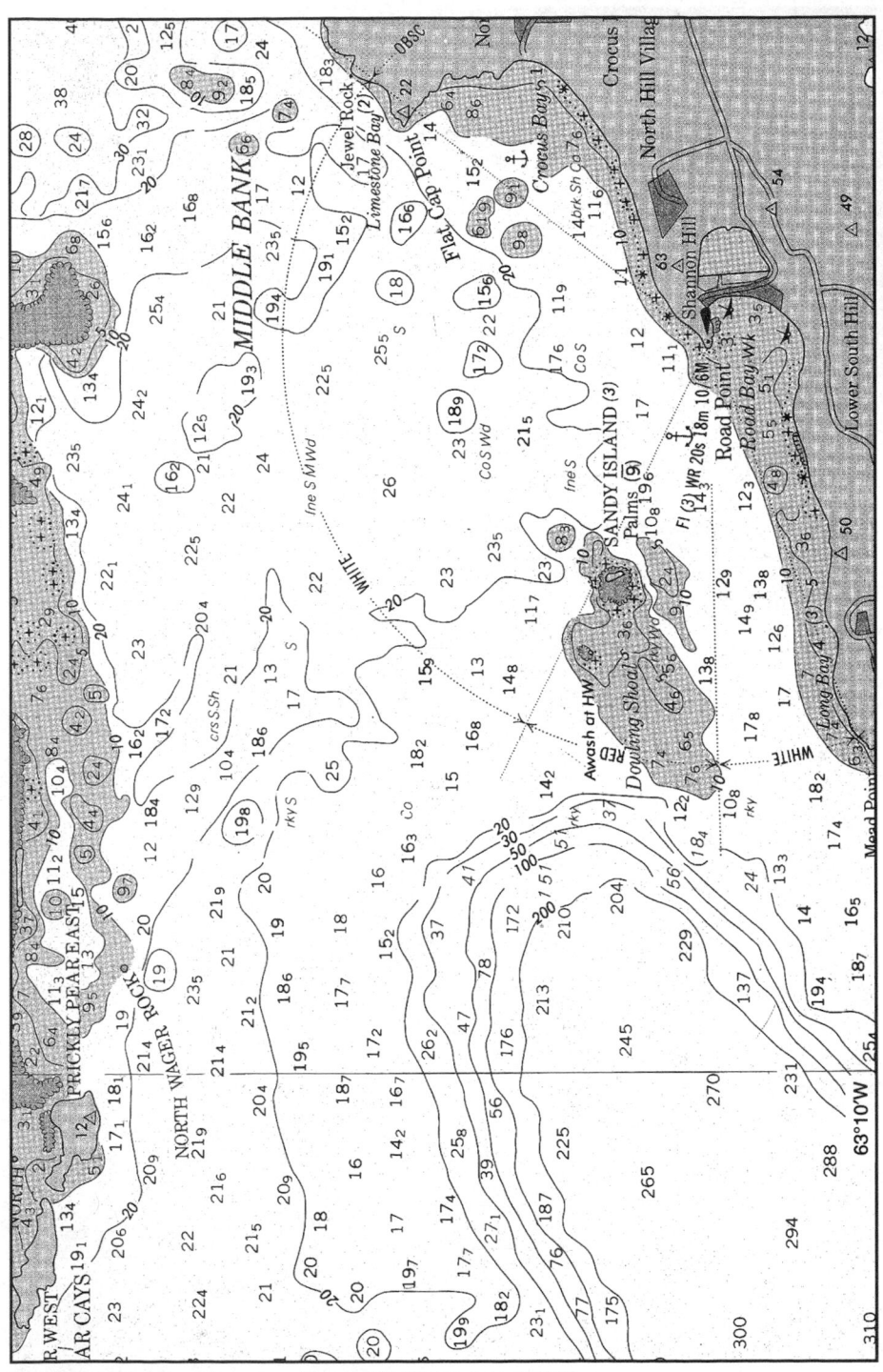

Road Bay, soundings in meters *(from DMA 25613, 1st ed, 9/84)*

ANGUILLA APPROACHES

ANGUILLITA ISLAND LIGHT, 18 09.4N, 63 10.6W. Fl (2) W 15s, 48ft, 5M. Aluminum skeleton tower, red top.

ANGUILLA ISLAND LIGHT, Road Point, 18 12.2N, 63 05.7W. Fl (3) W R 20s, 59ft, 10M white, 6M red. White concrete triangular structure, W 070°–089°, R 089°–116°, W 116°–218°.

WINDWARD POINT LIGHT, 18 16.8N, 62 58.1W. Fl (3) W, 14.5s, 82ft.

ROAD BAY

18 12N, 63 06W

Emergencies: Call Saba Radio on VHF channel 16.

Pilotage: Anguilla is quite low, with no conspicuous hills. The approach should be made in good light. Hazards include Dog Island, located about 10 miles northwest of Road Bay, and Prickly Pear Cays, located 5 miles north of the harbor. Seal Island Reefs extend about 5 miles in an easterly direction from Prickly Pear Cays. The water is quite deep right up to the edge of the reefs. Dowling Shoals and Sandy Island lie about 2 miles northwest of the harbor. The white-and-red sectored light shown from Road Point helps direct you around the hazards.

Boats are warned to watch for anchored vessels not showing anchor lights in the bay.

Port of Entry: The customs offices (809-497-5461) are located near the main commercial wharf.

Anchorage: There is good anchorage in depths of 7 to 20 feet. Keep the channel to the commercial wharf clear. In the area immediately inside the hook of Road Point are a coral reef and shallows extending towards town. You can dinghy in to the dock in the north part of the bay. There is a wide variety of uncrowded anchorages on other parts of the island and on nearby cays.

Services: There are few services oriented directly to yachts, but there are sources for fuel, water, ice, and groceries ashore. You'll have to ferry supplies to your boat via dinghy. There is a good variety of restaurants, bars, and shops. Tamarian Watersports (809-497-2020 or VHF channel 16) is a full-service scuba center.

Because Anguilla is somewhat off the beaten track and has a charterboat fee, it is visited by fewer boats than most islands in this area. There are few yacht-oriented services, but there are interesting anchorages, abundant dive sites, and pleasant eateries.

ST. MARTIN

CAUTION: Our information on aids to navigation comes from official government sources. The latitudes and longitudes of these marks may not correspond to the readings from GPS receivers. Some aids have been reported as unreliable, missing, off position, or showing incorrect characteristics. No single aid to navigation, or waypoint, should be relied upon as a sole means of fixing your position.

NOTE: The chartlet on the following page is not intended for navigation and is included for reference and planning purposes only.

ENTRY PROCEDURES

St. Martin, the French half of the island by the same name, is part of the French overseas department of Guadeloupe. You should fly the French courtesy flag here. The Dutch portion of the island, Sint Maarten, is discussed in the next section of this chapter. The procedures for arriving yachts are handled informally, but you should check in with officials when arriving and leaving—this means clearing in and out when passing between French St. Martin and Dutch Sint Maarten as well.

Yachts can clear in Marigot or Anse Marcel. Officials in the harbors are located in the port authority offices. In Marigot the office is near the ferry wharf. St. Martin has no duty on imports, so is a good place to do shopping or have parts shipped to your boat.

The telephone country code for St. Martin is 590. When calling within French St. Martin or to St. Barts (also part of the department of Guadeloupe), you dial only the six-digit local number. To call St. Martin from Dutch Sint Maarten, use the code 06 before the six-digit number. To call Sint Maarten from St. Martin, you must dial the international access code, 19; then the country code, 599, then the island code, 5; and finally the five-digit Dutch number. Calls are routed through Guadeloupe.

The official currency is the French franc, which trades at about 5.24 to the dollar (summer 1994). U.S. dollars are widely accepted. The language spoken is French.

ST. MARTIN APPROACHES

BREAKWATER LIGHT, N end, head of breakwater, 18 06.9N, 63 03.0W. Fl R 2.5s, 10ft, 5M. White framework tower, red top.
SPUR LIGHT, 18 06.9N, 63 03.0W. Fl G 2.5s, 10ft, 5M. White framework tower, green top.
BAIE DU MARIGOT LIGHT, 18 04.1N, 63 05.7W. Fl W R G 4s, 66ft, 8M. White tower, red top. R 104°–120°, W 120°–132°, G 132°–185°, obscured 185°–104°.

MARIGOT

18 04N, 63 05W
Emergencies: Contact Saba Radio on VHF channel 16.
Pilotage: A flashing white, red, and green light is shown from the 200-foot-high hill topped by the ruins of Fort de Marigot. You can approach the commercial pier, below the light, on a bearing of 143°T. Anchor away from the approaches to the pier.
Port of Entry: The port authority office is near the ferry and commercial wharf.
Bridge to Simpson Bay Lagoon: The bridge that allows access into Simpson Bay Lagoon from the French side formerly opened twice a day. In summer 1994, the bridge and channel into the Lagoon were still closed for repairs, with an anticipated official opening date sometime before year's end. The harbormaster's office (590-87-20-43) may have updated information. The bridge at the Dutch Simpson Bay end opens at 0600, 1100, 1600, and 1800 (there is no 1600 opening on weekends). The Simpson Bay bridge operator monitors VHF channel 12.
Dockage: Most of the marinas are on the Dutch side of the lagoon. In the east end of the lagoon, off Marigot, try the Marina Port La Royal (590-87-20-43) or Caraibes Sport Boats (590-87-89-38). There is a dinghy dock here.

COAST PILOT

1995 CARIBBEAN

277

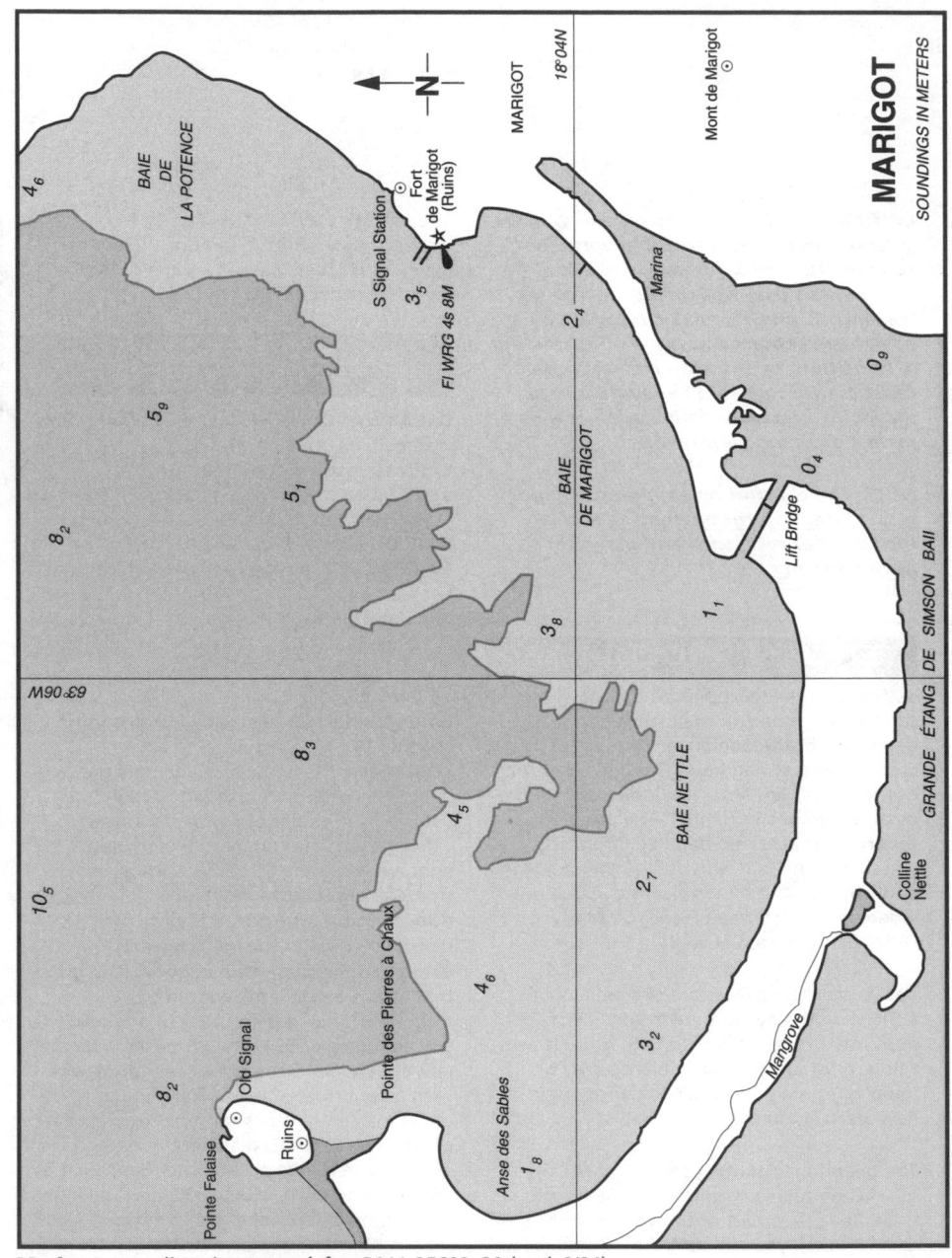

Marigot, soundings in meters *(after DMA 25608, 20th ed, 9/84)*

Anchorage: Marigot Bay is a good anchorage, though it can be subject to swells from the north. Simpson Bay Lagoon is very sheltered, but watch depths carefully. This is a possible hurricane hole, being very sheltered from wave action, yet open to the breeze.

Services: There is an extensive variety of yacht services here, and there are more in nearby Sint Maarten. Egreteau Marine Services (590-87-23-92 or VHF channel 77) is an inflatable and liferaft specialist. Boat rentals as well as dockage are available from Caraibes Sport Boats. The St. Martin Marine Center (590-87-86-32 or VHF channel 72), near the Marigot bridge, is a Mercury engine dealer and service center. There are excellent grocery, liquor, and gourmet shops, as befits a French island. UPS and Federal Express (590-87-03-71) also maintain offices here if you need something in a hurry from the United States.

Being only 74 miles from Virgin Gorda, St. Martin is often a first port of call in the Leeward Islands. Marigot is the capital of the French half of the island and has a good harbor where you may clear in quite easily. Ashore are many fine restaurants and shops, which stock a wide variety of items at duty-free prices. With the sheltered waters of Simpson Bay Lagoon nearby and a continental atmosphere, Marigot is a favorite long-term stop for many cruisers.

GRANDE CASE

18 06N, 63 03W

Emergencies: Contact Saba Radio on VHF channel 16. You may not be able to call very far on the VHF because of the surrounding high hills.

Pilotage: A shoal area north of the point forming the south end of Baie Grande Case is reported to be as shallow as 5 feet.

Anchorage: Anchor well in towards shore in the southeast part of the bay to avoid any swells rolling around Roche Crole off Bell Point. Depths are 15 to 20 feet, shoaling to 6 to 8 feet close to the beach. There is a dinghy dock on the beach.

Services: Marine services are limited, but dozens of fine restaurants line the main street. Provisions can be purchased, and there are general shops for browsing.

ANSE MARCEL

18 07N, 63 02W

Emergencies: Contact Saba Radio on VHF channel 16. You may not be able to call very far on the VHF because of the surrounding high hills.

Pilotage: This small bay is located west of the northernmost part of the island. It is the only major indentation on the northern coast. Do not pass between Marcel Rock located in the mouth of the bay and the mainland to the southwest, as the waters are quite shoal.

Port of Entry: Check in at the port authority office.

Dockage: Port Lonvilliers is entered by way of a narrow channel that begins in the southeast corner of the bay. Contact Port Lonvilliers Marina (590-87-31-94 or VHF channel and 16). This is a very protected spot.

Anchorage: There is sheltered anchorage in the bay, north of town. Depths run from 8 to 15 feet.

Services: Port Lonvilliers Marina has fuel, water and ice. For repairs and marine supplies contact Yachting Maintenance (590-87-43-48). There is a small grocery store and several shops. Several restaurants are nearby.

OYSTER POND

18 03N, 63 01W

Emergencies: Contact Saba Radio on VHF channel 16. You may not be able to call very far on the VHF because of the surrounding high hills.

Pilotage: This small pond is located near the middle of the east coast of the island. With an east-facing entrance surrounded by reefs, it is no place to enter after dark or in rough conditions. The entrance channel is privately marked by Captain Oliver's Marina. Controlling depth is reported to be about 10 feet as far as the fuel dock. If you are in doubt as to your navigation or the conditions, call the marina on VHF channels 16 and 67.

Dockage: Contact Captain Oliver's Marina (590-87-30-00 or VHF channels 16 and 67). The Moorings (590-87-32-55) charter fleet is also located here.

Anchorage: The harbor is quite shoal, except for the area near the docks. There is a shoal in the middle of the harbor, with depths of 5 to 6 feet around most of the perimeter. Captain Oliver's Dinghy Dock is north of the marina.

Services: The Moorings has its own ship's store and grocery, which visitors are welcome to use. Captain Oliver's has a gourmet restaurant (590-87-30-00) and hotel (590-87-40-26), and there are other shops and restaurants nearby. Fuel, water, and ice are available at the marina, and Captain Oliver's runs a scuba center as well.

WE STOCK WHAT SAILORS WANT!

Achilles - ACR - Apelco - Aquata - Artigiana Battelli
ASA - Autohelm - Baldwin - Blue Wave - Boat Armor
Boatlife - Bruce - Bruynzeel - Caframo - Camp
Chillington Marine - Cole Hersee - Dahl - Danforth
Dan Hill - Davis - Drivesaver - Dutch Hydrographic
Charts - Edson - ENO - Epifanes - Force 10 - Forespar
Fram - G & B Garelick - Goit - Harken - Hella
Henderson - HYE - Imray - Indian Head - International
Paint - Itt/Jabeco - Johnson Marine - Kent Marine
Laser - Leatherman - Lewmar - Lofrans - 3M - Magma
March Pumps - Marinco - Marine Muffler - Marlow
Mercury - Nautix - Newmar - Nicro Marine - Orion
Ormiston - Pelican Products - Plastimo - Prindle
Pro-Line Paint - R & D Marine - Raritan - Raske &
Van Der Meyde - Raytheon - Rule - S & J Products
SP Systems - Sailing Angles - Scanmarine - Shearwater
Siemens Solar - Simpson Lawrence - Slam - Sowester
Sta-Lok Terminals - Starbrite - Statpower - Sunfish
Synchro Start - T-Jett - Taco - Teleflex - Thomas
Reed - Titan - Ultraflex - United Solar Systems
Vetus - Wellington Puritan - West System - Whale
Wichard - Wilcox Crittenden - Windbugger - Yanmar

TECHNICALLY THE BEST CHANDLERY IN THE CARIBBEAN

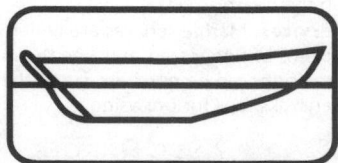

BUDGET MARINE

ST. MAARTEN: OPPOSITE BOBBYS MARINA TEL.: 22068 FAX 23804
ANTIGUA: JOLLY HARBOUR TEL: 462-7727

SINT MAARTEN

CAUTION: Our information on aids to navigation comes from official government sources. The latitudes and longitudes of these marks may not correspond to the readings from GPS receivers. Some aids have been reported as unreliable, missing, off position, or showing incorrect characteristics. No single aid to navigation, or waypoint, should be relied upon as a sole means of fixing your position.

The chartlets in this section are <u>not</u> <u>intended for navigation</u> and are included for reference and planning purposes only. While chartlets reproduced from government sources are from the most current editions as of press time, they incorporate <u>no corrections</u> to navigational aids, depths, or hazards since the edition publication date.

ENTRY PROCEDURES

Dutch Sint Maarten, which lies on the southern side of the same island as French St. Martin, is part of the Netherlands Antilles. You should fly the Dutch courtesy flag while in these waters. Sint Maarten is a duty-free port and has no customs as such, but you should clear with immigration officials (599-5-22740) in the police station near the ferry dock in Philipsburg. You can reach the Philipsburg police at 599-5-22222. You should check in when traveling back and forth to the French side of the island. Formalities are swift and simple.

The telephone country code for the northern Netherlands Antilles is 599, and the island code for Sint Maarten, 5. When calling from the French side of the island, begin with the international access code of 19. The calls are routed through Guadeloupe. When calling the French side from the Dutch side, use the code 06 before the six-digit French number.

The official language is Dutch, but English is widely spoken. Dutch guilders currently trade at 1.73 to the U.S. dollar (summer 1994), but U.S. currency is widely accepted.

SINT MAARTEN APPROACHES

SIMSON BAAI AVIATION LIGHT, 18 02.4N, 63 06.7W. Al Fl W G 6s, 52ft, 13M. On station building.
GROOT BAAI, on side of old Fort Amsterdam, 18 00.8N, 63 03.6W. Fl (2) W 10s, 120ft, 15M. Wooden post. Visible 300°–096°.

PHILIPSBURG

18 01N, 63 03W
Emergencies: Contact Saba Radio on VHF channel 16.
Pilotage: Groot Baai (Grand Bay) is the main port and the location of Sint Maarten's capital, Philipsburg. A light is shown from old Fort Amsterdam on the western point of land at the mouth of the bay. There is a stranded wreck about 200 yards south of Fort Amsterdam. There is a 300-yard-long, L-shaped cruise ship pier at the south end of the eastern part of the bay. Groot Baai is generally free of obstructions, except for some shoaling in the northwest portion.
Port of Entry: Contact immigration officials (599-5-22740) in the police station near the ferry dock.
Dockage: Bobby's Marina (599-5-22366) and Great Bay Marina (599-5-22167 or VHF channels 71 and 16) are on the eastern side of Groot Baai.
Anchorage: There is good anchorage in the bay, with depths from about 6 to 20 feet.
Services: Almost anything is available here and at very good prices for the Caribbean. Fuel, water, and ice are available at the marinas, and Bobby's can haul boats to 90 tons. Among the many marine-oriented businesses, Dockside Management (599-5-24096, or fax, -22858) is a telephone, fax, information, message, and shipping center. The staff are very helpful and speak English. Dockside will also hold mail for you (P.O. Box 999, Philipsburg, Sint Maarten, Netherlands Antilles), is an agent for Outfitters International, from whom you can order parts, and handles liferaft reconditioning. Necol (599-5-23571) is an electronics specialist, and the Trade Winds Dive Center (599-5-54387) can handle your tanks. Budget Marine (599-5-22068

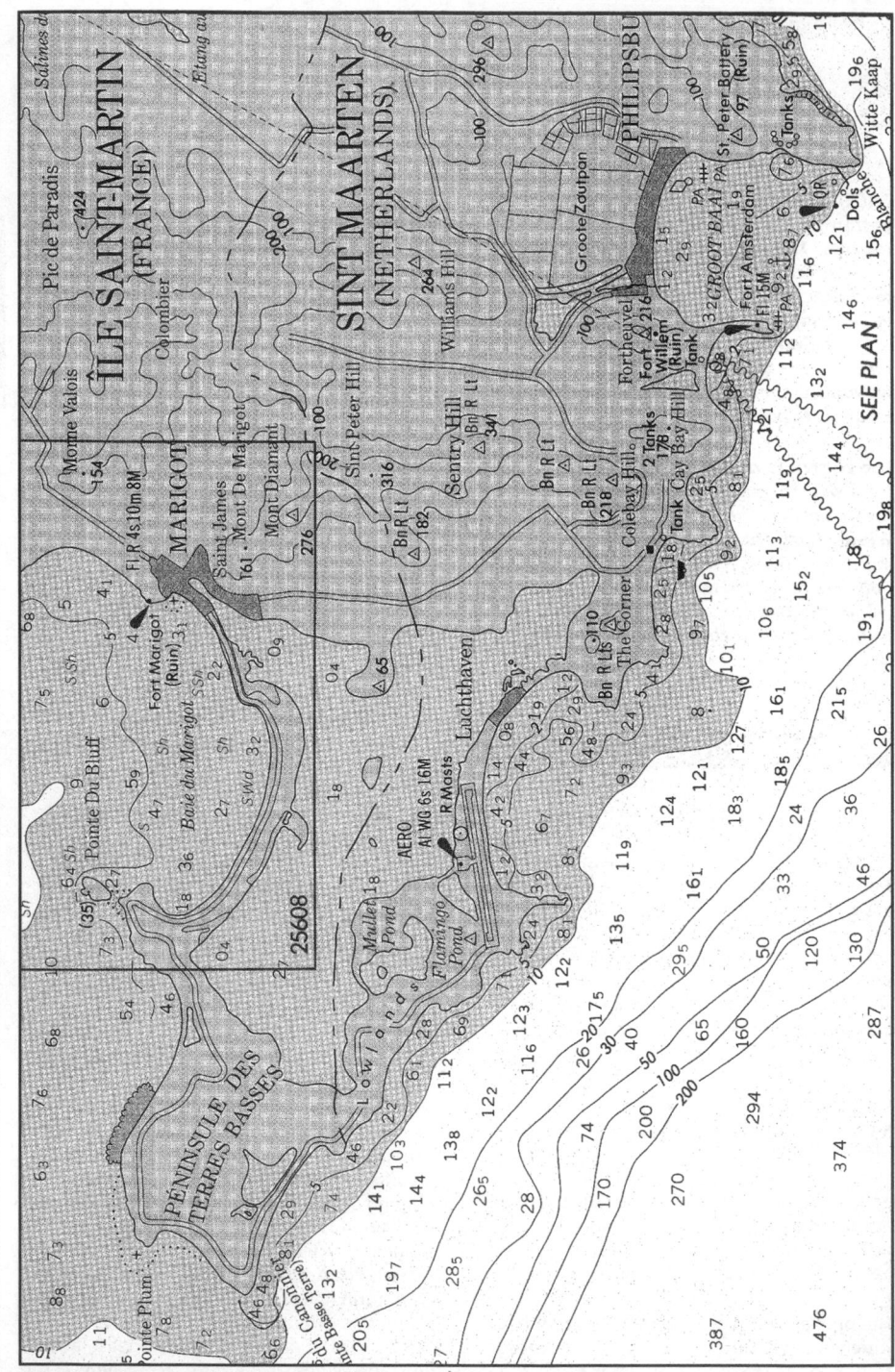

Sint Maarten, soundings in meters *(from DMA 25613, 1st ed, 9/84)*

and VHF channel 68) has most equipment and can get anything you need. Tropical Sails (599-5-22842) specializes in navigation equipment, books, charts, and general marine gear. There are Federal Express (599-5-42810) and UPS offices on the island, so it is easy to get gear quickly from the United States. There are several good grocery stores.

Philipsburg is a favorite stop for cruising yachtsmen and one of the best places in the Caribbean for repairs or stocking up. The harbor is sometimes rolly, but is generally a good anchorage. Nearby Simpson Bay Lagoon provides better shelter and more marine services.

SIMSON BAAI

18 02N, 63 06W
Emergencies: Contact Saba Radio on VHF channel 16.
Pilotage: Simson Baai, or Simpson Bay, is about 3 miles to the northwest of Groot Baai and Philipsburg. Prinses Juliana Airport lies

along the north side of the bay, and there is an aviation light shown from just north of the runway. The entrance to Simpson Bay Lagoon is on the eastern side of the bay.

Bridge to Simpson Bay Lagoon: The bridge to the lagoon at the Simpson Bay end opens at 0600, 1100, 1600, and 1800 (there is no 1600 opening on weekends). The Simpson Bay bridge operator monitors VHF channel 12 (for information on the Marigot bridge entrance, see the St. Marten section of this chapter).

Dockage: There are several marinas in the Lagoon. Contact the Simpson Bay Yacht Club Marina (599-5-43378 or VHF channel 16), the Port Plaisance Marina (599-5-45222), which has luxurious services, and Island Water World (599-5-45310 or VHF channel 74). Lagoon Marina (599-5-45210) is for shoal-draft boats.

Anchorage: The various anchorages in the lagoon are some of the most protected around. It is considered a hurricane hole.

Services: Extensive marine services are available here, in Philipsburg, and in Marigot on the

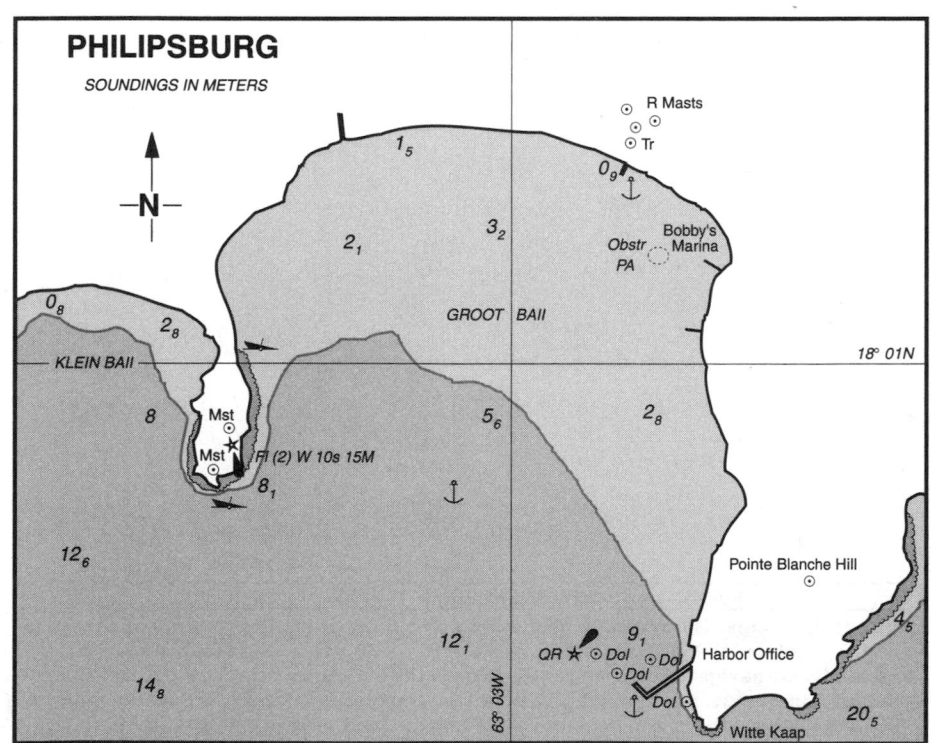

Philipsburg, soundings in meters *(after DMA 25613, inset, 1st ed, 9/84)*

French side. Fuel, water, and ice are available at the marinas. Among the many marine services here are: Tropicold (599-5-53411), specializing in refrigeration and air conditioning; Island Water World (599-5-45310 or VHF channel 74), an Evinrude dealer and chandlery; and FKG Yacht Rigging and Marine Fabricating (599-5-42171 or VHF channel 70, call sign Squarerigger). There are good grocery stores and restaurants nearby.

Simson Bay Lagoon is one of the best places in the Caribbean for restocking and repairs. It is also a sheltered place to stay while enjoying the continental atmosphere ashore. If you tire of being in Dutch waters, simply cross the lagoon to the French side.

USE NOTICES TO MARINERS!

Your 1995 almanac is up-to-date at the time of publication, but prudent mariners use Notices to Mariners and Local Notices to Mariners to keep abreast of the latest navigational changes. To obtain these notices contact the Coast Guard District Commanders for the areas where you travel. See *Reed's Nautical Companion* for more information, and be sure to send in the post-paid reply card bound in this book to receive your *FREE 1995 Supplement* for updates to this almanac.

SABA

CAUTION: Our information on aids to navigation comes from official government sources. The latitudes and longitudes of these marks may not correspond to the readings from GPS receivers. Some aids have been reported as unreliable, missing, off position, or showing incorrect characteristics. No single aid to navigation, or waypoint, should be relied upon as a sole means of fixing your position.

NOTE: The chartlet on the following page is not intended for navigation and is included for reference and planning purposes only. Reproduced from government sources, it is from the most current edition as of press time, but incorporates no corrections to navigational aids, depths, or hazards since the edition publication date.

ENTRY PROCEDURES

Saba lies about 26 miles southwest of St. Barthélemy and is part of the Netherlands Antilles. You should fly the Dutch courtesy flag while in its waters. Saba is a duty-free port and has no customs as such, but you should clear with the harbormaster (599-46-3294 or VHF channels 11 and 16) in Fort Baai. You must check in with the Saba Marine Park (599-46-3295 or VHF channel 16) before proceeding to the mooring area in the Ladder Baai/Wells Baai area. Formalities are swift and simple.

The telephone country code for the northern Netherlands Antilles is 599 and the Saba code, 46. Local numbers have four digits. (To call Dutch Sint Maarten from Saba you dial the prefix 05, and then the five-digit local number.)

English is widely spoken, but you may encounter Dutch as well. The official currency is the Dutch guilder, which currently trades at 1.73 to the U.S. dollar (summer 1994), but U.S. currency is widely accepted.

SABA

17 38N, 63 14W
AVIATION LIGHT, 17 38.1N, 63 14.3W. Fl W, 1.5s, 940ft. Radio mast. Height of light 3084ft.
ST. JOHN'S LIGHT, 17 37.1N, 63 14.6W. Fl (2) W 10s, 15M.

Emergencies: Contact Saba Radio on VHF channel 16.

Pilotage: The coast of the island rises nearly perpendicular from the sea, with the 2,853-foot summit of the island usually enveloped in clouds. The island is a mass of rugged mountains, with deep precipitous ravines. Two conspicuous radio masts stand on the island. St. Johns Light is exhibited about 1/2 mile east-northeast of Fort Baai. The Saba Bank, located south and west of the island, is deep enough to sail over, but should be avoided in heavy weather.

Port of Entry: Check with the harbor officials in Fort Baai, who monitor VHF channels 11 and 16.

Saba Radio, Call Sign PJS: Saba Radio is the main communications service in this part of the Caribbean, with a 200-mile range on VHF (its antenna is 3,083 feet above sea level). It covers an area extending from the British Virgin Islands to Antigua. For emergencies Saba Radio is in contact with the U.S. Coast Guard and other rescue agencies. During hurricane season it broadcasts reports as received. The station can be contacted on VHF channels 16, 26, and 84 seven days a week from 0600 to 2400. It will accept international phone credit cards (AT&T international charge numbers beginning with 891) or place collect calls for you. To make calls from a land line to a boat, call the station at 599-46-3402. For more information on Saba Radio's services call 599-46-3211.

Dockage: You may be able to tie up inside the 100-yard-long jetty at Fort Baai. Check first with the harbormaster; because the pier is small, it is for loading and unloading goods only, unless the harbormaster gives you permission.

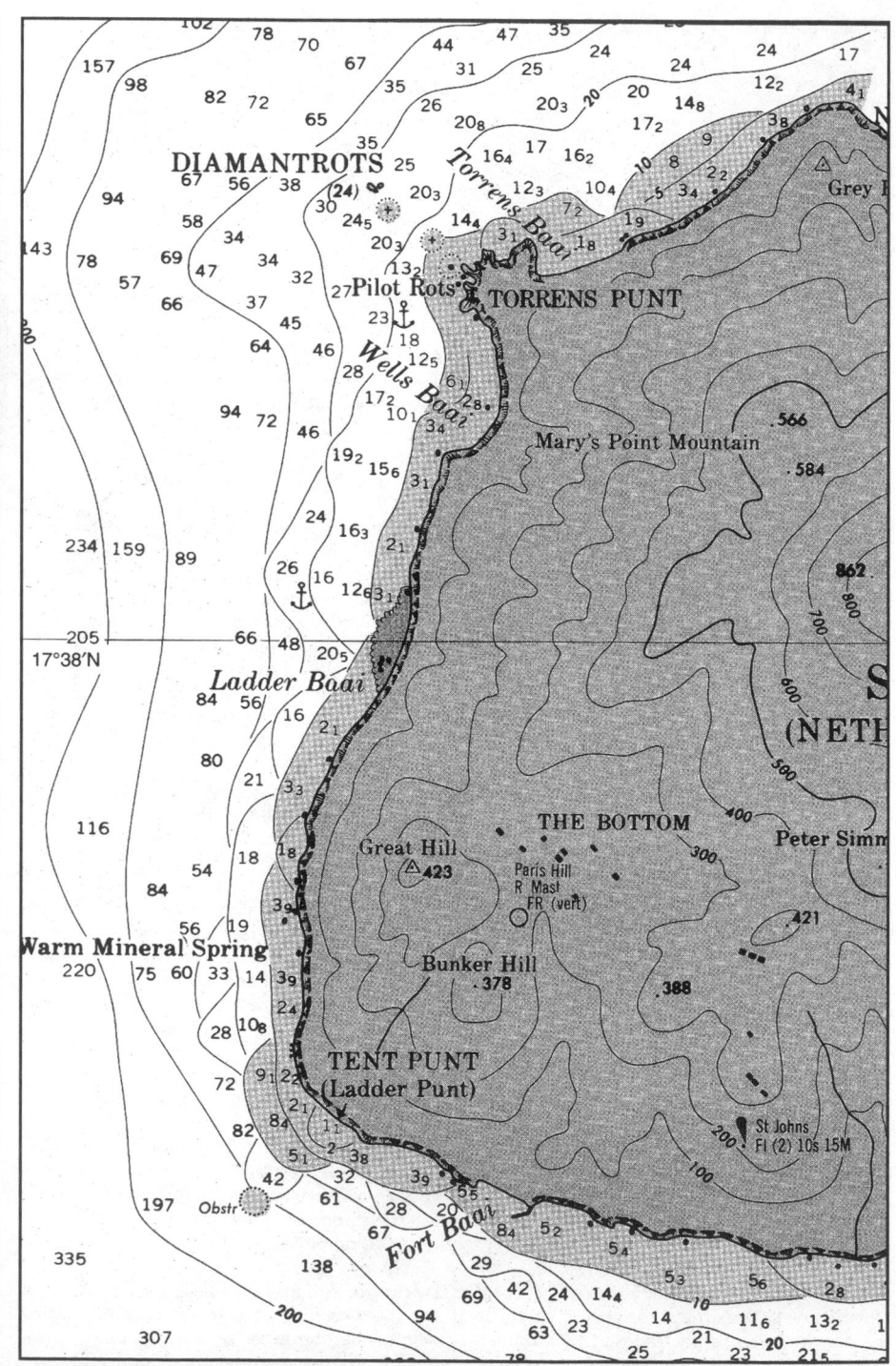

Saba, West Coast, soundings in meters *(from DMA 25607, 3rd ed, 7/84)*

COAST PILOT

Anchorage and Moorings: Much of the coastline is part of the Saba Marine Park, and anchoring is restricted. You must check in with the Saba Marine Park office in Fort Baai before proceeding to the mooring area. At this time you can anchor outside of Fort Baai and from Ladder Baai to the southern part of Wells Baai. The center of Wells Baai offers excellent holding in clear sand with plenty of swinging room. Ladder Baai offers good holding in depths of about 20 feet. There are rocks close in to shore, and the swirling winds require a stern anchor if you are leaving the boat unattended.

There are two orange moorings outside Fort Baai and five yellow moorings with blue stripes in the Wells Baai/Ladder Baai area. The latter are for boats under 60 feet long or under 50 tons and consist of two 1-ton blocks chained together. Orange and white buoys with blue stripes are for commercial and private dive boats. White buoys are for boats actively diving that less than 50 feet long; orange buoys are for diving vessels up to 110 feet. There is a yacht visitor fee of $2 per person, per week, for boats under 30 meters and a fee

of $0.10 per registered ton, per week, for boats over 30 meters in length. When diving or snorkeling you should display the dive flag, and you should stay 150 yards seaward of any dive operations when underway. There is a fee of $2 per dive (snorkeling is included in the boat fee). No fishing or collecting of any marine life, dead or alive, is allowed in the park. Legislation restricting boats without holding-tank capabilities to certain areas was under discussion in summer 1994. For the latest regulations check with the park office in Fort Baai (599-46-3295).

Services: You may be able to get some fuel via jug. Provisions are available at The Bottom, the first village you come to as you travel up the island road. There are several interesting restaurants and shops. Take a taxi tour of the island via the famous road that winds among the mountains. There are two dive shops in Fort Baai: Saba Deep (599-46-3347) and Wilson's Dive Shop (599-46-3410). Sea Saba (599-46-2246) is in Windwardside. Information on some of the island's great diving opportunities is available from the Saba Tourist Bureau, P.O. Box 527, Windwardside, Saba, Netherlands Antilles (tel: 599-46-2231).

REED'S NAUTICAL COMPANION

The perfect complement to this almanac is *Reed's Nautical Companion* — a one-volume, onboard reference library. Included are chapters on Rules of the Road, seamanship, first-aid, celestial navigation, weather, and much more! Visit your chandlery or nautical bookstore or call Thomas Reed Publications at 800-995-4995.

St. Barthelemy

CAUTION: Our information on aids to navigation comes from official government sources. The latitudes and longitudes of these marks may not correspond to the readings from GPS receivers. Some aids have been reported as unreliable, missing, off position, or showing incorrect characteristics. No single aid to navigation, or waypoint, should be relied upon as a sole means of fixing your position.

NOTE: The chartlets on the following pages are not intended for navigation and are included for reference and planning purposes only. While chartlets reproduced from government sources are from the most current editions as of press time, they incorporate no corrections to navigational aids, depths, or hazards since the edition publication date.

ENTRY PROCEDURES

The island of St. Barthélemy (St. Barts) is part of the French overseas department of Guadeloupe. You should fly the French courtesy flag here. The procedures for arriving yachts are handled informally, but you should check in with the officials when arriving from another country and when leaving.

Clear in at the port captain's office (590-27-66-97 or VHF channel 16) on the east side of Gustavia harbor.

The telephone country code for St. Barts is 590. Local phone numbers have six digits, which is all you dial when on the island or calling from St. Martin. The official currency is the French franc, which is currently trading at about 5.37 to the dollar (summer 1994). U.S. dollars are widely accepted. The language spoken is French.

GUSTAVIA

17 54N, 62 51W
FORT GUSTAVIA LIGHT, 17 54.3N, 62 51.2W. Fl (3) W R G, 12s, 210ft, 10M white, 7M red, 6M green. White truncated tower, red top. W 054°–071°, R 071°–095°, W 095°–111°, G 111°–160°, obscured 160°–340°, G 340°–054°.

Emergencies: Call Saba Radio on VHF channel 16.

Pilotage: The port lies on the west coast of the island. The light is shown from Fort Gustave, which is north of the inner harbor. The safest approaches are made by coming in on the white sectors of the light. The port captain monitors VHF channel 16.

Port of Entry: Check in with the port captain, on the east side of the inner harbor.

Dockage: It may be possible to tie up stern-to one of the quays (Mediterranean style) in the inner harbor. Check with the port captain for availability and the daily charge.

Anchorage: You can anchor in the inner harbor if there is room or outside the marked channel into the inner harbor. Daily charges will be collected by a patrol boat or at the port captain's office.

Services: Fuel is available at the commercial wharf north of Fort Gustave by contacting St. Barth Marine (590-27-60-38). Le Shipchandler (590-27-86-29 or VHF channel 16) is a chandlery that represents Wichard, International Paint, Raytheon, and other manufacturers; parts not in stock can be ordered. Other services include sending faxes and renting cars. The AMC supermarket (590-27-60-09) is a source for groceries; call in advance and your provisions will be gathered for your arrival. There's a good selection of French restaurants. Being a duty-free port, Gustavia offers a wide variety of stores of all types. Prices are very good for the Caribbean.

Gustavia is a popular harbor, but can get very crowded in season. You may have some difficulty finding a secure spot for your boat. Once ashore, you'll find a good variety of services and supplies, although not as extensive as in St. Martin and Sint Maarten. Because St. Barts is a French island, the dining can be particularly enjoyable.

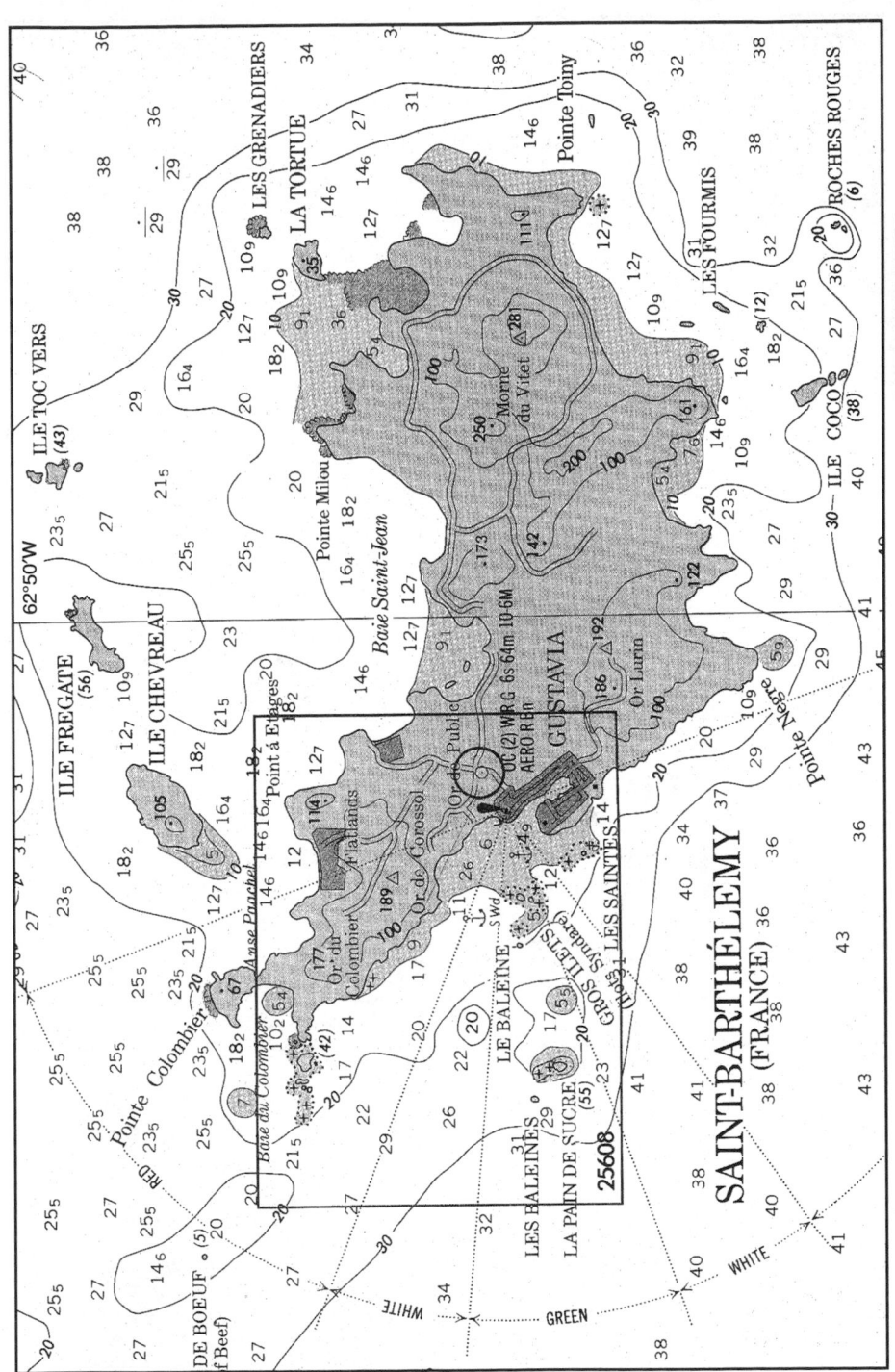

St. Barthélemy, soundings in meters *(from DMA 25613, 1st ed, 9/84)*

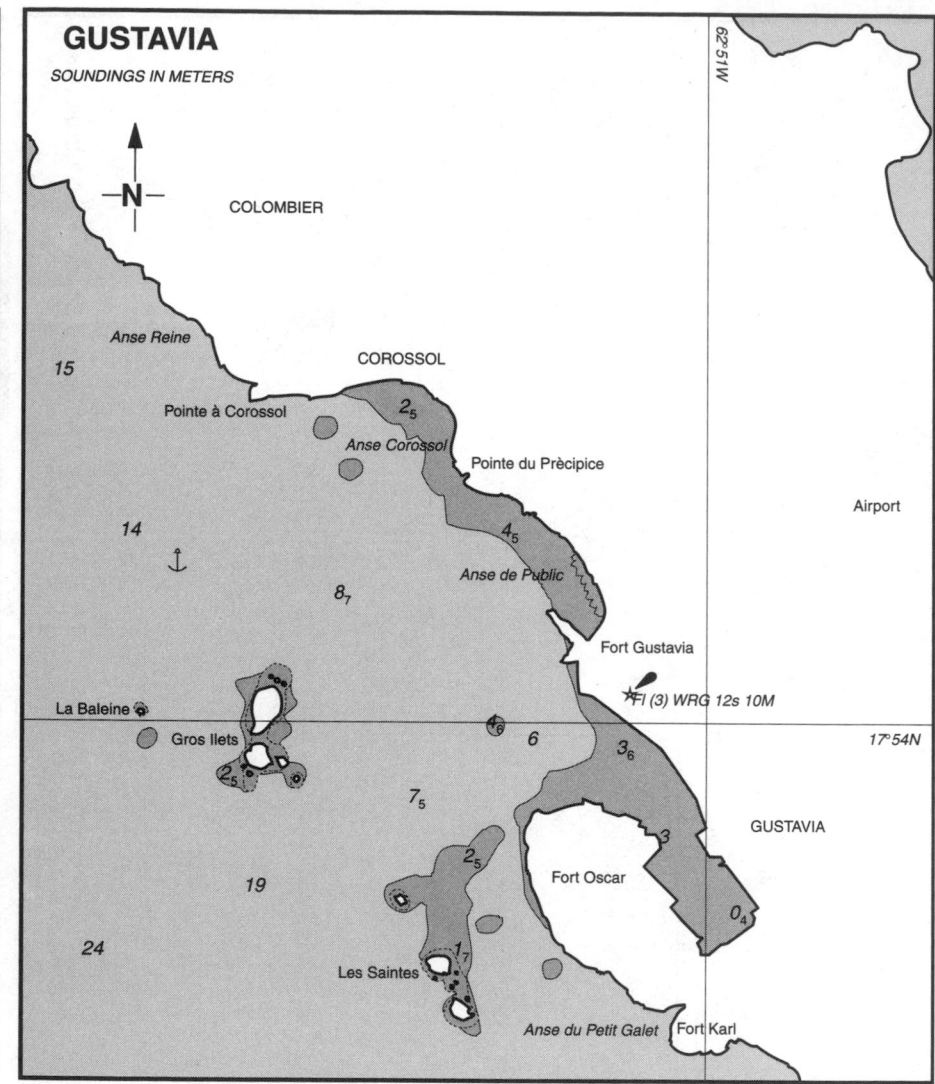

Gustavia, soundings in meters *(after DMA 25608, 20th ed, 9/84)*

SINT EUSTATIUS

CAUTION: Our information on aids to navigation comes from official government sources. The latitudes and longitudes of these marks may not correspond to the readings from GPS receivers. Some aids have been reported as unreliable, missing, off position, or showing incorrect characteristics. No single aid to navigation, or waypoint, should be relied upon as a sole means of fixing your position.

NOTE: The chartlet on the following page is not intended for navigation. Reproduced from government sources, it is from the most current edition as of press time, but incorporates no corrections to navigational aids, hazards, or depths since the edition publication date.

ENTRY PROCEDURES

Sint Eustatius, known as Statia, is located about 30 miles south of Sint Maarten and is part of the Netherlands Antilles. You should fly the Dutch courtesy flag while in its waters. Statia is a duty-free port and has no customs as such, but you should clear immigration with the harbor office in Oranjestad (599-3-82205 or VHF channel 16). Formalities are swift and simple. The harbormaster can be reached at 599-3-82888 or on VHF channel 16.

The telephone country code is 599, and the island code, 3. Local numbers have five digits. When calling Dutch Sint Maarten from Statia, dial the prefix 05 and then the five-digit local number.

English is widely spoken, but you may encounter Dutch as well. The Dutch guilder is the official currency, which currently (summer 1994) trades at 1.73 to the U.S. dollar. U.S. currency is also widely accepted.

ORANJESTAD

17 29N, 62 59W
TUMBLEDOWN DICK BAY LIGHT, head of oil pier, 17 29.4N, 63 00.1W. Fl W 5s, 10M.
ORANJESTAD LIGHT, 17 28.8N, 62 59.2W. Fl (3) W 15s, 131ft, 17M.

Emergencies: Contact Saba Radio on VHF channel 16.

Pilotage: The island is dominated by an extinct 1,900-foot-high volcano near its southeast extremity. Except for the slopes of the volcano, the island is devoid of trees. A group of rugged hills is located on the northwest portion of the island. Fish pots may be encountered up to 3 miles off the west coast. Tumbledown Dick Bay Light is located at the end of a 1/2-mile-long jetty located about 1 mile northwest of Oranjestad. The oil terminal at the jetty stands by on the VHF radio.

Port of Entry: Contact the harbor office (599-3-82205 or VHF channel 16) near the foot of the large dock.

Anchorage: The anchorage off town, Oranje Baai, can be rolly. You may want to try a stern anchor to hold your boat into the swells.

Services: You can jug water and fuel to your boat, and there are good markets ashore. For a trip to Statia's delightful reefs, contact Dive Statia (599-3-82435 or VHF channel 16). There are many historic buildings to see and several good restaurants, although the tourist industry is quite small. Statia is a great place to "get away from it all."

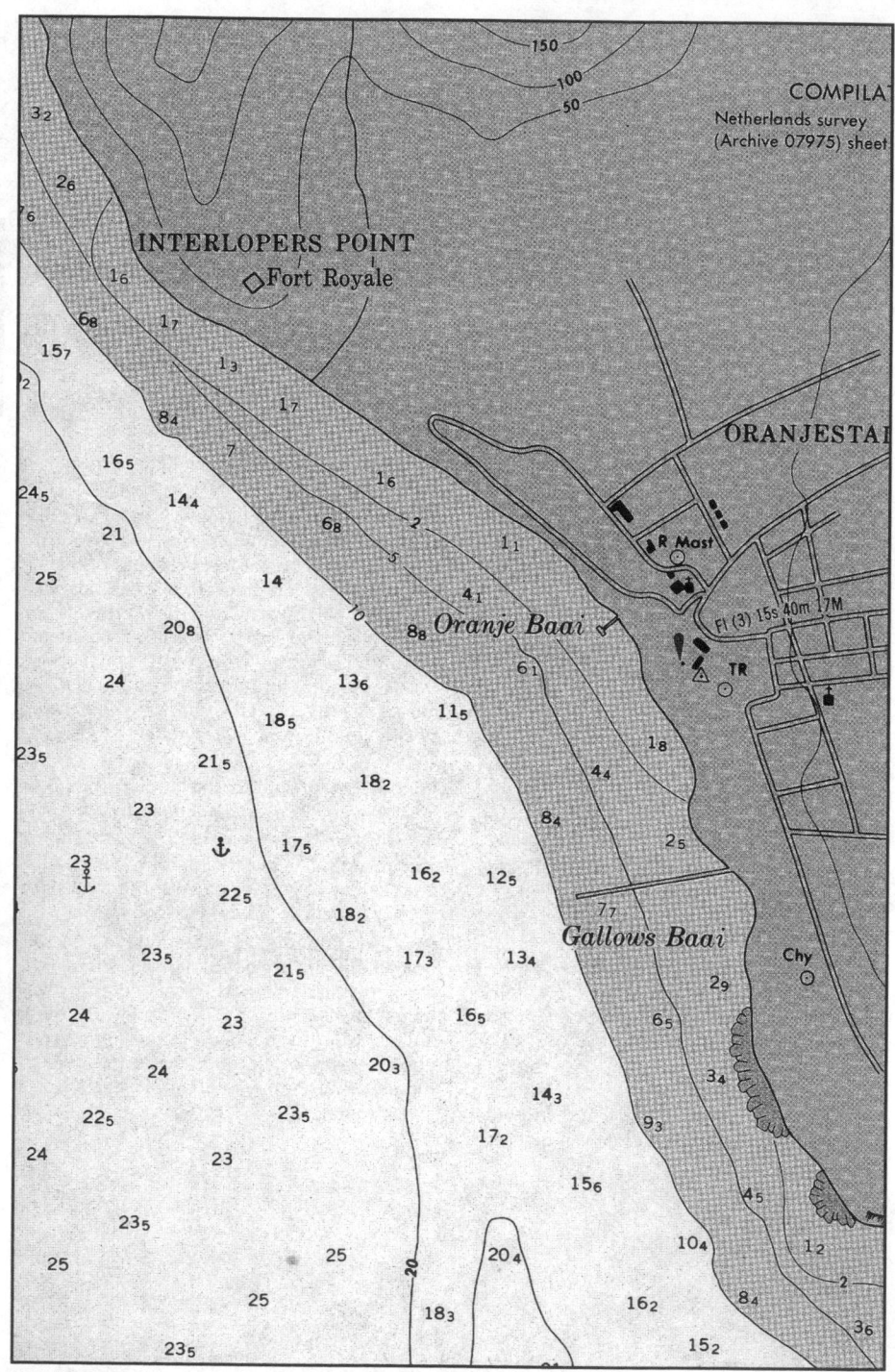

COMPILA
Netherlands survey
(Archive 07975) sheet

INTERLOPERS POINT
◇Fort Royale

ORANJESTAI

Oranje Baai

R Mast

Fl (3) 15s 40m 17M

TR

Gallows Baai

Chy

Oranjestad, soundings in meters *(from DMA 25607, 3rd ed, 7/84)*

St. Christopher and Nevis

CAUTION: Our information on aids to navigation comes from official government sources. The latitudes and longitudes of these marks may not correspond to the readings from GPS receivers. Some aids have been reported as unreliable, missing, off position, or showing incorrect characteristics. No single aid to navigation, or waypoint, should be relied upon as a sole means of fixing your position.

NOTE: The chartlet in this section is <u>not</u> <u>intended for navigation</u> and is included for reference and planning purposes only. Reproduced from government sources, it is from the current edition as of press time, but incorporates <u>no corrections</u> to navigational aids, depths, or hazards since the edition publication date.

ENTRY PROCEDURES

St. Christopher, known as St. Kitts, and Nevis are located about 40 miles west of Antigua. They are separate islands, but one country, sharing a British heritage.

The Port of Entry on St. Kitts is Basseterre; on Nevis it is Charlestown. A cruising permit must be obtained to visit anchorages other than the Ports of Entry. The cost is US$10 for boats under 20 tons and is valid for both islands. Port authority charges apply to vessels over 20 tons. Charterboats must pay $3 per passenger. When traveling between the islands you must obtain a boat pass and check in with the authorities when you arrive.

In Basseterre the customs (809-465-2521, extensions 1076 and 1077) and immigration offices are in the Port Authority building. The Charlestown office can be reached at 809-469-9343. Normal hours in both ports are 0800 to 1630 on Monday and Tuesday and 0800 to 1600 on Wednesday, Thursday, and Friday. In Basseterre, if you arrive on a weekend or after hours, contact one of the guards at the Port Authority, who will summon officials.

You should have your passports, clearance from last port of call, ship's papers, and two crew lists. Firearms must be secured under lock and key while in port.

The telephone area code for the islands is 809. St. Kitts phones use a prefix of 465; Nevis, 469. The official currency is the Eastern Caribbean, or EC, dollar, although U.S. dollars are widely accepted. EC dollars exchange with U.S. dollars at a rate of about .40 to 1. Registered tonnage is the basis for all clearance charges.

HALF MOON POINT LIGHT, 17 19.1N, 62 42.2W. Oc R 2s, F R. Tower.

BASSETERRE

17 18N, 62 43W
FORT THOMAS LIGHT, W side of harbor, 17 17.3N, 62 44.2W. F R, 67ft. Metal mast. Aero Al Fl W G (occasional) 1.6M NE.
TREASURY BUILDINGS LIGHT, F R, 46ft, 10M.
FORT SMITH LIGHT, E side of harbor, 17 17.3N, 62 42.6W. F G, 35ft, 2M. Concrete block. Fl W 2s 2M on dolphin 300 meters NW.

Emergencies: Contact Saba Radio on VHF channel 16.
Pilotage: The north end of the island rises to the 3,798-foot-high Mount Misery. The summit is usually covered with clouds. The southeast end of the island is connected by only a narrow neck of sand. Caution is advised as the hydrography is incomplete around St. Kitts and Nevis. The port is situated on the southwest side of the island. A 283-foot-high white chimney is located about 1/2 mile north-northeast of the east end of town. Contact the port authority on VHF channels 6 and 16.
Port of Entry: Check in with customs (809-465-2521, extensions 1076 and 1077) and immigration in the Port Authority building.
Anchorage: The anchorage area is subject to swells when the wind shifts to the south. You might want to try the area off the Salt Ponds about a mile southeast of Basseterre.
Services: You can jug water and fuel to your boat. Caribe Yachts Ltd. (809-465-8411 or VHF channel 16) is located on the waterfront and does repairs. This yard can haul catamarans up to 14 tons and sells marine supplies. There is a good variety of restaurants, grocery stores, and general shops. The tourist office can be

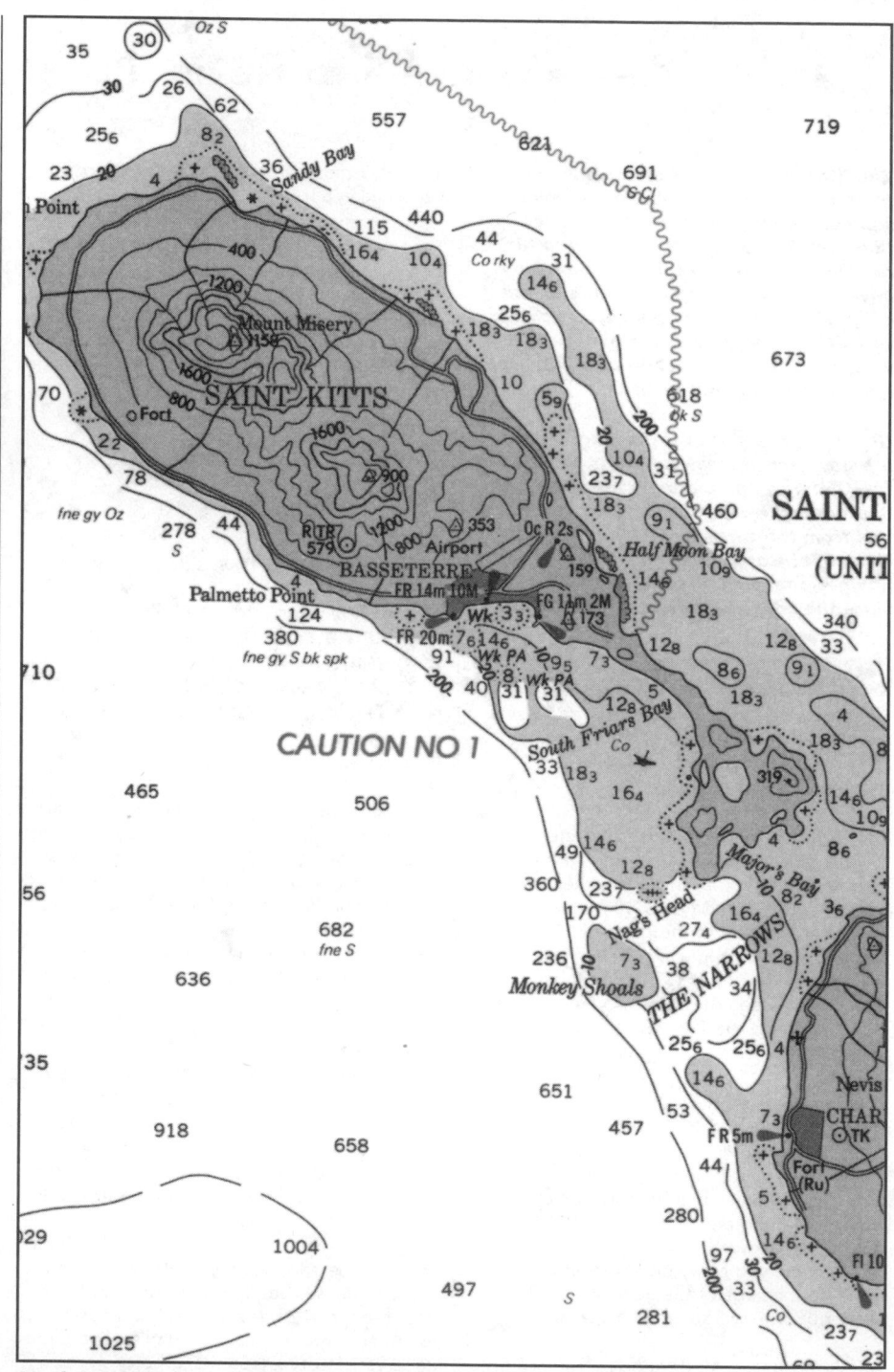

St. Christopher, soundings in meters *(from DMA 25550, 2nd ed, 11/93)*

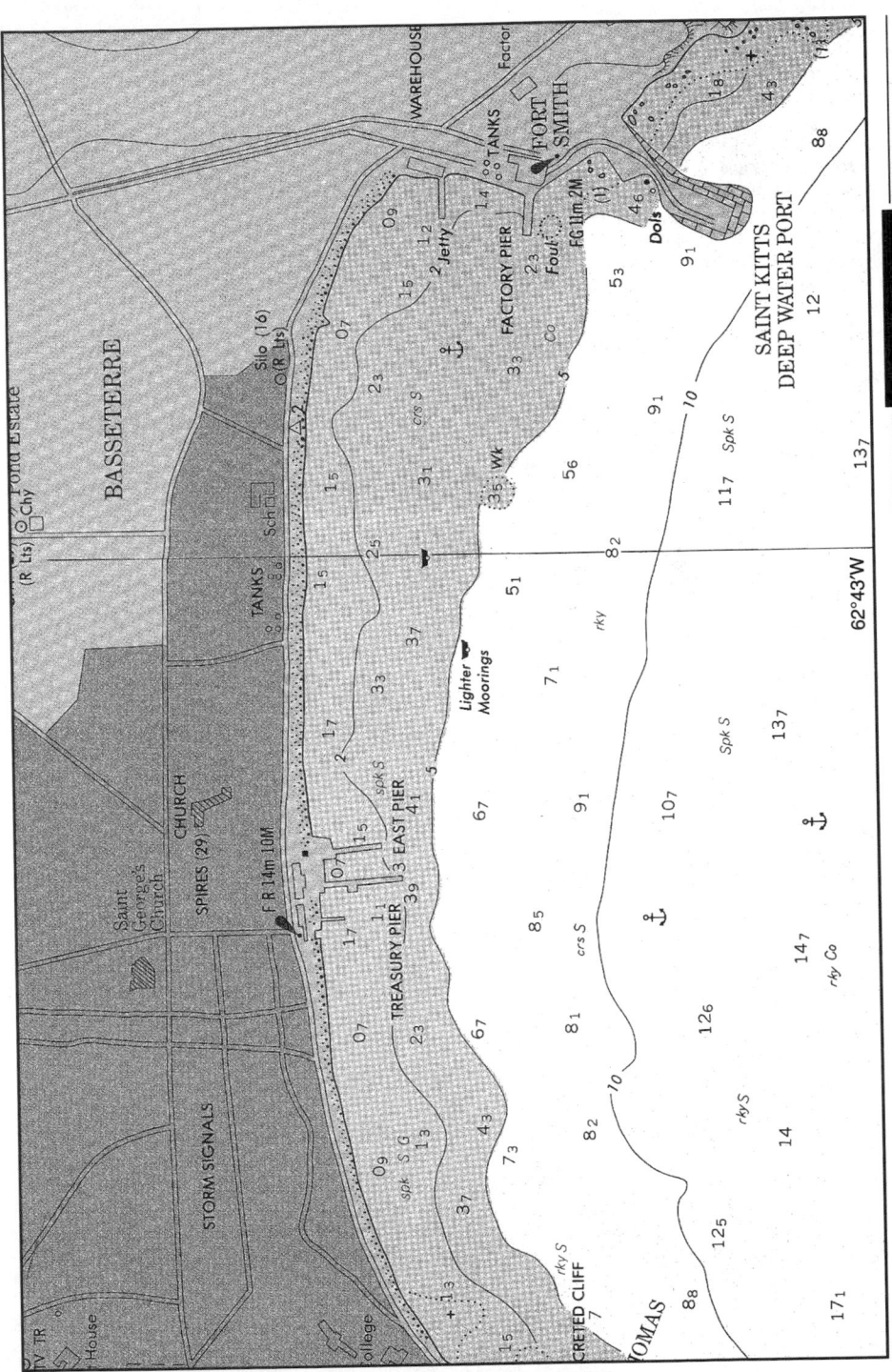

Basseterre, soundings in meters *(from DMA 25608, 20th ed, 9/84)*

reached at 809-465-4040; it is located in the center of Basseterre, about five minutes by taxi from the Port Authority.

CHARLESTOWN

17 08N, 62 28W
CHARLESTOWN LIGHT, root of pier, 17 08.2N, 62 36.9W. F R, 15ft. Post. Iso R light on radio mast 0.7M SSE.
DOGWOOD POINT LIGHT, south end of island, 17 05.7N, 62 36.4W. Fl W 10s, 29ft.

Emergencies: Contact Saba Radio on VHF channel 16.

Pilotage: Caution is advised as the hydrography is incomplete around St. Kitts and Nevis. Charlestown is located on the west coast of Nevis and is the capital of the island. Nevis peak rises to 3,230 feet in the center of the island and is usually hidden in the clouds. A concrete pier with depths from 11 to 15 feet alongside projects from the town waterfront. A prominent radio mast stands near the root of the pier.

Port of Entry: Contact customs at 809-469-9343.

Anchorage: Anchor right off the town waterfront. There is a ladder on the pier, where you can land your dinghy.

Services: Fuel and water are available by jug or at the wharf via truck if you are getting a large quantity. There is a good variety of shops, restaurants, and grocery stores on the island. Contact the tourist office at 809-469-1042; the office is within walking distance of the pier.

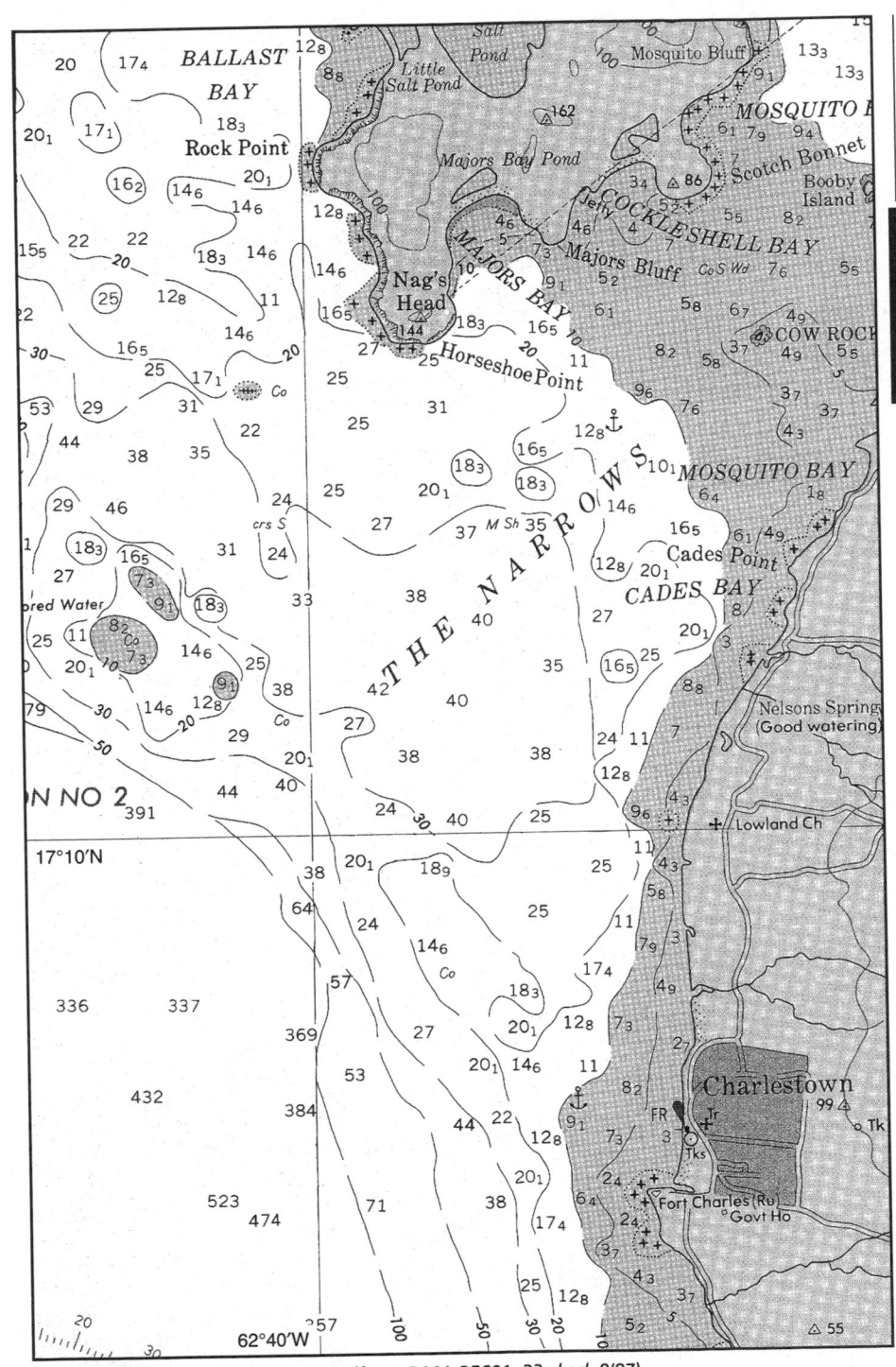

Charlestown, soundings in meters *(from DMA 25601, 33rd ed, 8/87)*

MONTSERRAT

CAUTION: Our information on aids to navigation comes from official government sources. The latitudes and longitudes of these marks may not correspond to the readings from GPS receivers. Some aids have been reported as unreliable, missing, off position, or showing incorrect characteristics. No single aid to navigation, or waypoint, should be relied upon as a sole means of fixing your position.

The chartlet on the following page is <u>not intended for navigation</u> and is included for reference and planning purposes only. Reproduced from government sources, it is from the most current edition as of press time, but incorporates <u>no corrections</u> to navigational aids, depths, or hazards since the edition publication date.

ENTRY PROCEDURES

Montserrat lies about 25 miles southwest of Antigua and is a British crown colony.

The Port of Entry is Plymouth, on the southwest side of the island. You should check in with customs and immigration (809-491-2456 or -2452) in the port authority office near the main wharf. Hours are 0800 to 1600 Monday to Friday. Overtime charges apply for clearances outside of normal working hours.

You should apply for a coastwise clearance if you are planning a visit to harbors on Monserrat other than Plymouth. Firearms must be locked on board, or for stays longer than a couple of days, are held at the police station. A departure fee is charged; as of summer 1994, the fee was to be raised from EC$5, but the amount had not been set. Contact customs and immigration or the comptroller at (809-491-3211) for the latest information.

Montserrat's area code is 809, and the island code is 491. Local numbers have four digits and are all you need for calls within the island.

The official currency is the Eastern Caribbean, or EC, dollar, though U.S. dollars are widely accepted. The exchange rate, when converting EC dollars to U.S. dollars, is about .40.

MONTSERRAT APPROACHES

AVIATION LIGHT, 16 45.9N, 62 09.9W. Oc R 1.5s, 197ft. Occasional.
BLACKBURNE AIRPORT LIGHT, 16 45.5N, 62 09.5W. Aero Al Fl W G 6s, 33ft. Occasional.
CASTLE PEAK LIGHT, 16 42.5N, 62 10.9W. Aero Fl R 1.5s, 3179 ft, 6M. Mast. Obstruction light.
AVIATION LIGHT, 16 40.7N, 62 11.7W. Oc R 2s, 341ft, 22M. Radio tower.

PLYMOUTH

16 43N, 62 13W
PLYMOUTH LIGHT, jetty root, 16 42.3N, 62 13.3W. F R. Terminal building.

Emergencies: Call Saba Radio on VHF channel 16.
Pilotage: The island presents a rugged and uneven appearance from seaward. The Soufriere Hills at the south end rise to almost 3,000 feet. The hills are wooded and may rise into the clouds. The coasts tend to be bold and steep-to. An L-shaped jetty projects 100 yards seaward at Plymouth. The ruins of an old dolphin near the end of the wharf have been reported to be a hazard. Another obstruction is marked by a buoy located about 115 feet northwest of the jetty head. The yacht club is situated south of the jetty. Anchoring is prohibited in much of the area off the town.
Port of Entry: You can raise the port authority on VHF channel 16 for entry instructions. Customs and immigration (809-491-2456 or -2452) are located in the Port Authority building near the main wharf.
Radio Antilles: Called the "Big RA" by many boaters, this station broadcasts on 930kHz at 20kw. Marine weather is forecast at 1335 and 2225 UTC. Radio Antilles is a good source of weather information for the eastern Caribbean.
Dockage: You may be able to get permission from the port authority to tie alongside the wharf while taking on fuel or supplies. Be careful if a swell is running.

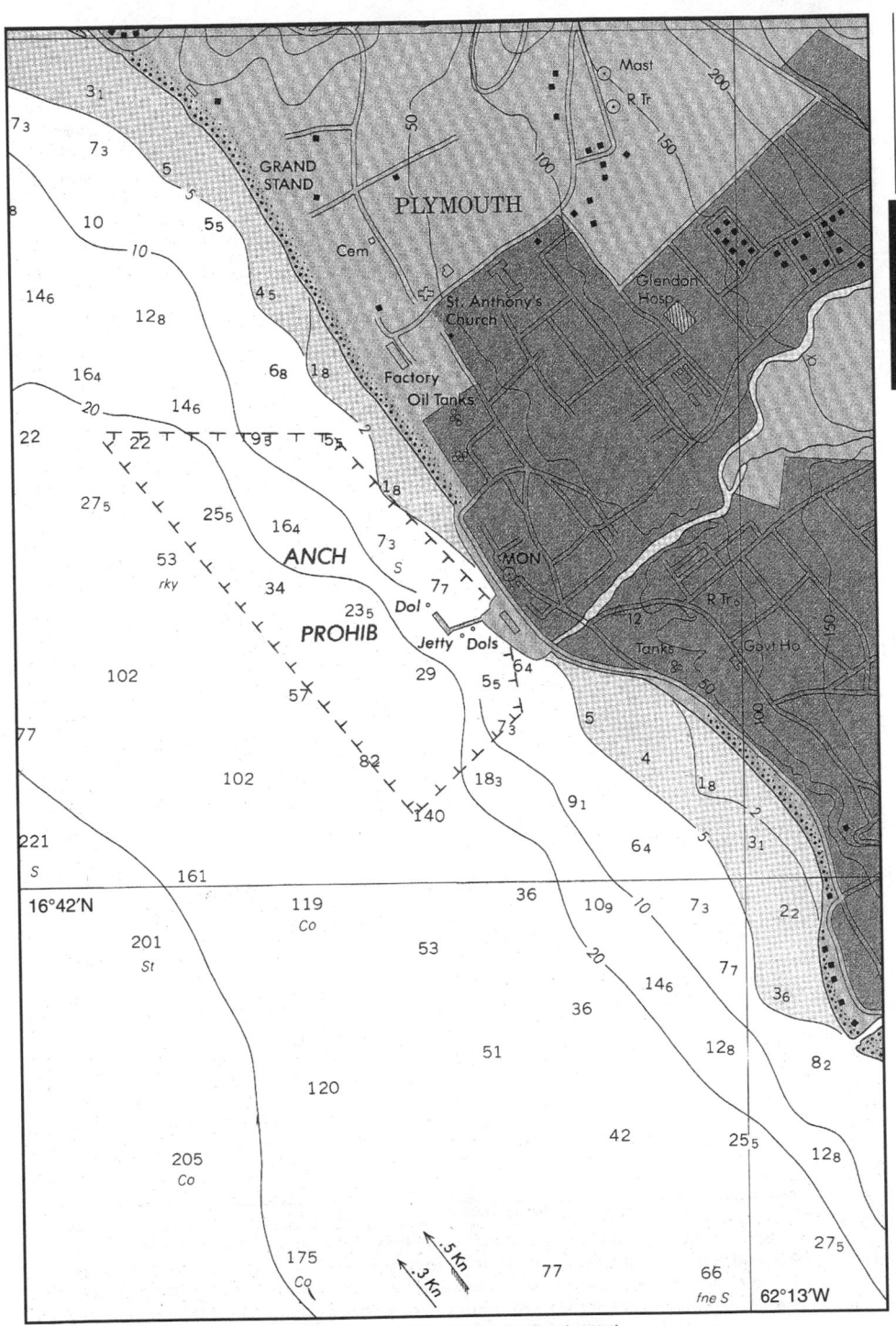

Plymouth, soundings in meters *(from DMA 25608, 20th ed, 9/84)*

Anchorage: Anchorage is prohibited in much of the area directly off Plymouth. You might want to try directly off the yacht club, south of the main wharf. This area is reported to be very rolly. Old Road Bay, north of town, is reported to be a better anchorage, but you still may need a stern anchor to hold your boat into the swells. You can dinghy in to the Vue Pointe Hotel dock in Old Road Bay.

Services: Large quantities of fuel and water can be obtained at the wharf by truck, but you'll have to jug smaller amounts. The Sea Wolf Diving School (809-491-7807) offers dive services. The tourist office (809-491-2230), which is within walking distance of the Port Authority building, can be very helpful. There is a good variety of supermarkets, restaurants, and general shops. The Vue Pointe Hotel (809-491-5210 or -5211), located near the north end of Old Road Bay, is reported to be very friendly to yachtsmen. It has a landing, water, a telephone, garbage facilities, ice, and a bus into town. The hotel may be able to hold mail for you (c/o the Vue Pointe Hotel, P.O. Box 65, Montserrat).

KEEP YOUR ALMANAC UP-TO-DATE

Return the post-paid reply card bound in this almanac to receive your free *1995 Supplement* updating information since this edition went to press. Always use Notices To Mariners and Local Notices to Mariners. To obtain these notices contact the Coast Guard District Commanders for the areas where you travel.
See *Reed's Nautical Companion* for more information.

ANTIGUA AND BARBUDA

CAUTION: Our information on aids to navigation comes from official government sources. The latitudes and longitudes of these marks may not correspond to the readings from GPS receivers. Some aids have been reported as unreliable, missing, off position or showing incorrect characteristics. No single aid to navigation, or waypoint, should be relied upon as a sole means of fixing your position.

The chartlets in this section are not intended for navigation and are included for reference and planning purposes only. While chartlets reproduced from government sources are from the most current editions as of press time, they incorporate no corrections to navigational aids, depths, or hazards since the edition publication date.

ENTRY PROCEDURES

Antigua and Barbuda form an independent country, having formerly been British colonies. The small island of Redonda is also part of the country.

Ports of Entry are English Harbour, Crabb's Marina in the Parham area, St. John's, and Jolly Harbour at Mosquito Cove. There is a customs station near the boat harbor south of Codrington on Barbuda, but you can only clear out here; to obtain a cruising permit you must go to one of the Ports of Entry on Antigua.

When clearing in English Harbour you may anchor in Freeman Bay flying the Q flag. If customs and immigration officials do not arrive in a reasonable amount of time, you may proceed to their office in Nelson's Dockyard, on the western side of the channel leading in to the harbor. The official hours of operation are 0600 to 1700 daily, but actual opening times may vary. Port entry fees range from EC$10 to $20. There is a fee of EC$5 per person to enter the Dockyard here. You must obtain a cruising permit to visit other places in the country. For boats in the 30- to 40-foot range the fee is EC$20 a month. There are fees based on vessel length both for tying up stern-to and anchoring.

Contact the officials (809-460-1397) for the latest information.

Jolly Harbour, a recently developed, sizable marina/condominium complex at Mosquito Cove on the western side of the island between Johnson Point and St. Johns, is a new port of entry. Customs (809-462-6042 or VHF channel 16) here is open between 0800 and 1600 daily.

St. John's is primarily a commercial port, but vessels can clear with officials at the wharf on the north side of the harbor. Hours of operation are 0800 to 1600 most days. The local phone number for the boarding officer is 462-0814.

Crabb's Marina is located on the northeast part of the island. Officials' hours of operation are 0830 to 1630, Monday through Friday. The local phone number for officials is 463-2372.

If you are visiting Barbuda, contact the customs and immigration authorities in the small boat harbor on the west side of this island. They are reported to monitor VHF channel 16. You must have obtained a cruising permit in Antigua before visiting Barbuda. You can get an outward clearance here, however.

The area code for the island is 809, and island numbers are seven digits. On the island you only need dial the last seven digits. Many phone numbers are restricted to local calls only, which means you may not be able to reach every number from overseas (local numbers are so designated in this section).

The official currency is the Eastern Caribbean, or EC, dollar, although U.S. dollars are widely accepted. The exchange rate of EC dollars to U.S. dollars is about .40 to 1.

BARBUDA

17 36N, 61 50W
Emergencies: Call the Antigua Coast Guard on VHF channels 16 and 68 or contact Saba Radio on VHF channel 16.
Pilotage: The small-boat landing on Barbuda lies about 28 miles north of St. John's, Antigua. A hotel, partly obscured by tall shrubs, is prominent on Cocoa Point, the southern

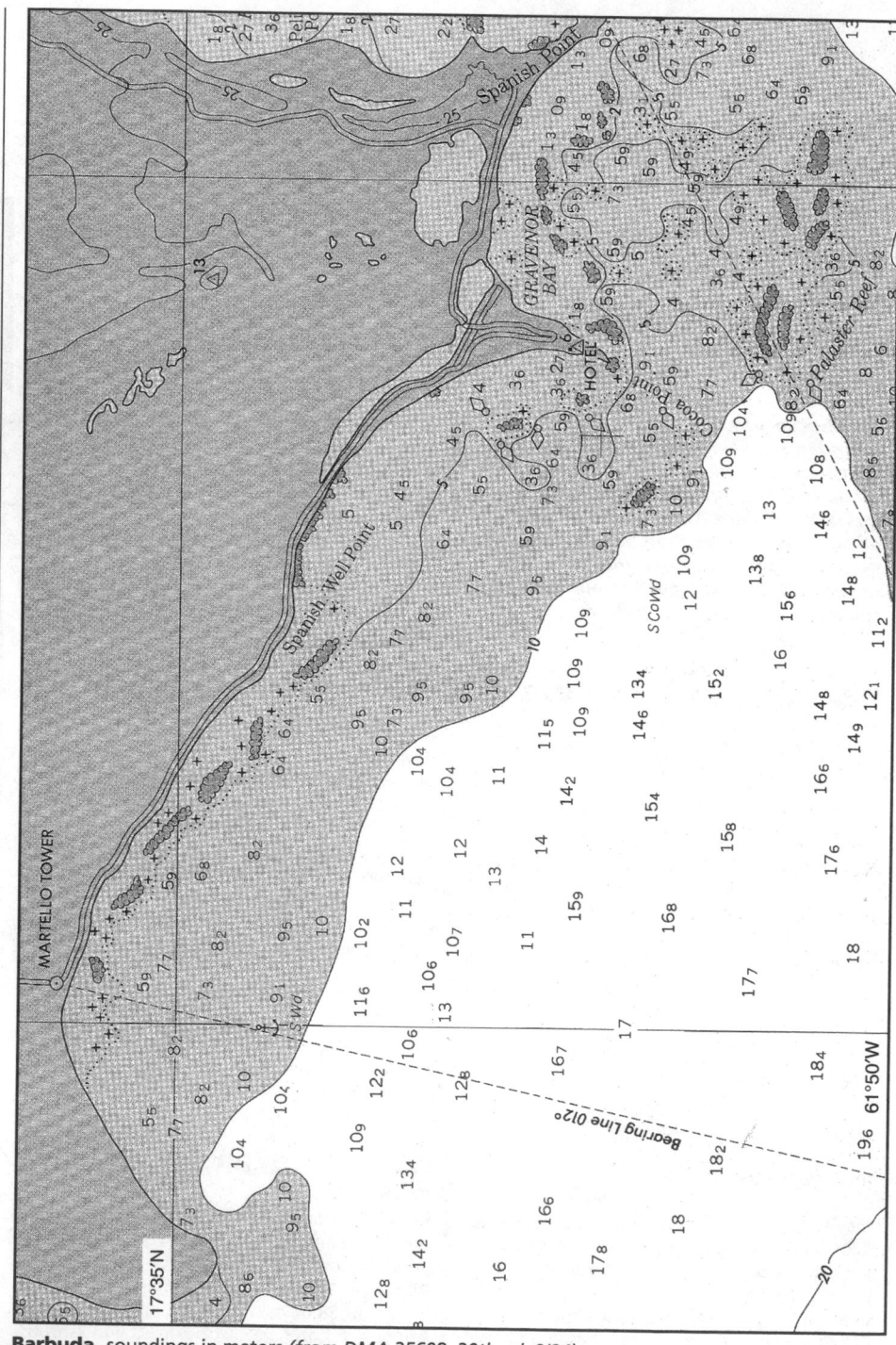

Barbuda, soundings in meters *(from DMA 25608, 20th ed, 9/84)*

point of the island. A Martello tower, partly ruined, is visible about 2 miles east of Palmetto Point. The boat harbor is located about 3/4 mile east of the Martello tower. Sand piles, from a sand mining operation, indicate the location of the harbor. There are numerous reefs around the island, including ones along the shore near the boat harbor. The channel into the dock is locally marked. Many coral heads are found up to 2 1/2 miles off the northwestern part of the island.

Customs Station: You can clear out of the country from here, but you should have a cruising permit from Antigua before visiting. The station is located near the boat harbor.

Anchorages: You can anchor in the small basin at the boat harbor, in depths reported to be 5 to 9 feet. The town of Codrington is almost 3 miles north of the harbor by road. Most boats will want to anchor north of Palmetto Point or among the reefs along the south coast. This is an area where "eyeball navigation" is critical. You should never be underway around Barbuda at night or in poor visibility.

Services: A couple of hotels and restaurants are all that might interest boaters. There are some small stores and a telephone in Codrington. Barbuda is a place for "getting away from it all."

Palaster Reef, off the south coast of Barbuda, is a national park, where no fishing is permitted. This a wonderful place for snorkeling and diving on the coral reefs and coral heads. These add both to the beauty and to the difficulties. Be sure of your navigation, your charts, and your guides before heading to Barbuda.

NORTH ANTIGUA

PRICKLY PEAR ISLAND LIGHT, 17 10.5N, 68 48.9W. Q W, 26ft. Black round metal structure.
SANDY ISLAND LIGHT, near center of island, 17 08.1N, 61 55.4W. Fl W 15s, 53ft. 13M. White iron framework structure. Reported irregular (April 1985).

PARHAM

17 08N, 61 45W
Emergencies: Call the Antigua Coast Guard on VHF channels 16 and 68 or contact Saba Radio on VHF channel 16.
Pilotage: Approach the harbors on the north coast of Antigua via Boon Channel starting north of St. John's. The major hazards are the reefs surrounding Prickly Pear Island, which is marked by a light. After passing Prickly Pear you can head to the southeast. You'll see some

buoys that lead toward the vicinity of Crabb's Marina on North Sound Point. Parham harbor is south of the west side of the point. Because of the many shoals and reefs, the north shore should be approached only in good light.

Port of Entry: Clear in at Crabb's Marina. The officials may be reached at their local number, 463-2372.

Dockage: Crabb's Marina (809-463-2113) offers some dockage, fuel, and water, but there is no electricity at the docks.

Anchorage: You can anchor off Crabb's or further south near town. This area is well protected in most conditions.

Services: Crabb's can do repairs and haul boats on its Travelift, which handles vessels to 50 tons with a maximum beam of 16 feet and draft of 10 feet. Parham Marine (809-463-2148) is located near the commercial wharf. It handles repairs of all kinds and has a chandlery. There is a supermarket ashore.

ST. JOHN'S

17 08N, 61 52W
PILLAR ROCK LIGHT, S side of entrance to harbor, 17 07.8N, 61 52.6W. Fl G 4s, 106ft, 5M. White house, words PILLAR ROCK in black. Visible 067°–093°, obscured 093°–108°, visible thence to shore southeast of light.
RANGE (Front Light), 17 07.1N, 61 50.5W. Iso R 6s, 62ft, 6M. Metal framework tower. **(Rear Light),** 440 meters, 113° from front light. Iso R 6s, 92ft, 6M. Metal framework tower.
FORT JAMES LIGHT, N side of entrance to harbor, 17 07.9N, 61 51.7W. Fl R 4s, 48ft, 5M. White pillar. Visible between Ledwell Point and center of Week Bay.
RANGE (Front Light), 17 01.4N, 61 46.3W. Q G, 35ft. Wooden pile. **(Rear Light),** 290 meters, 029° from front light. Iso G 2s, 75ft. Wooden pile.

Emergencies: Call the Antigua Coast Guard on VHF channels 16 and 68 or contact Saba Radio on VHF channel 16.
Pilotage: If approaching from the north, be careful to stay west of the reefs and Diamond Bank. Sandy Island, marked by a light, lies in the western approaches. When coming from the northwest, Fort James Light in alignment with the cathedral spires bearing 110° should keep you clear of dangers. When you get closer there is a charted range on a bearing of 113°. Warrington Bank, north of the channel, is less than 3 feet deep. The harbor pilot and harbor authorities monitor VHF channel 16 and the

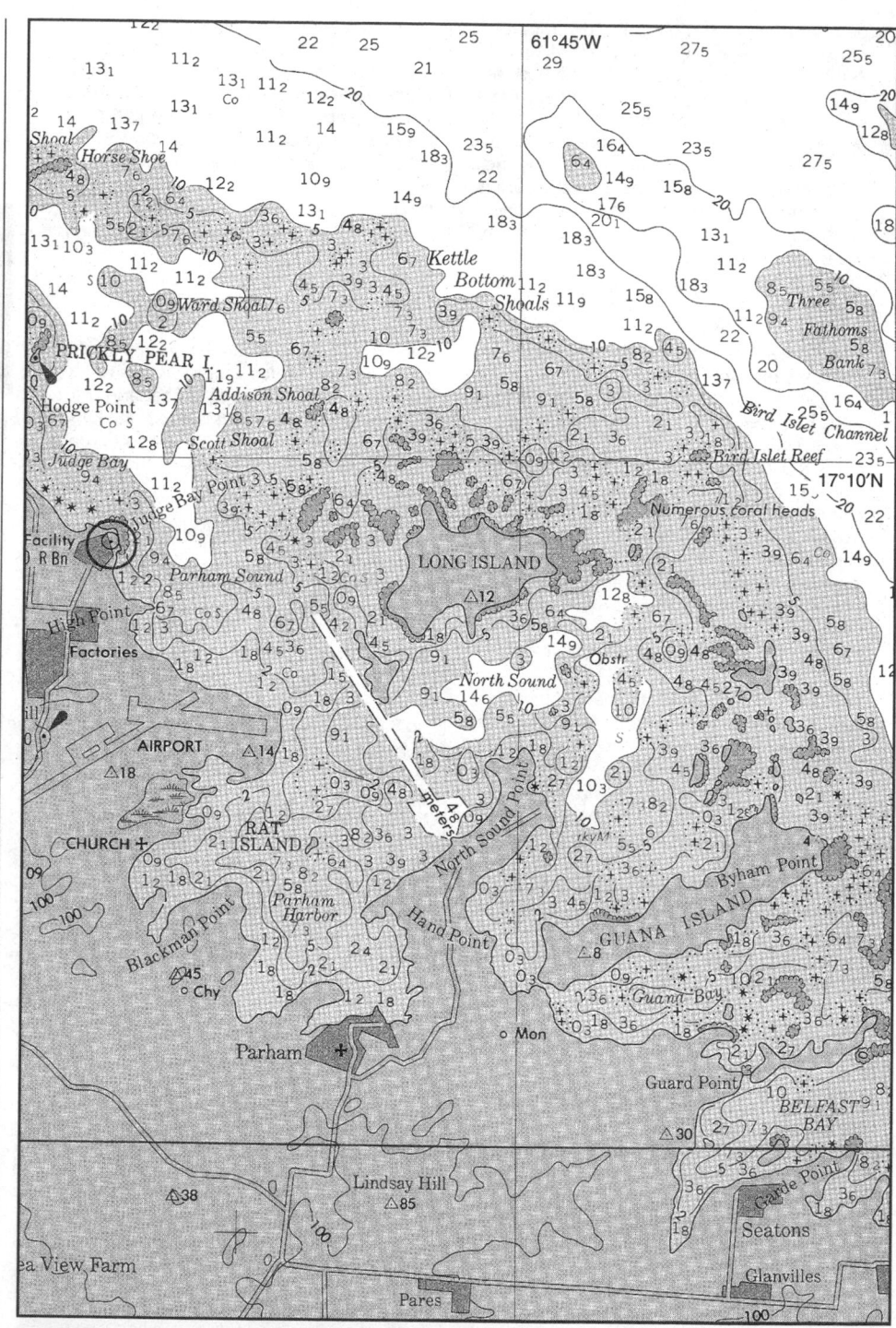

Parham, soundings in meters *(from DMA 25570, 2nd ed, 8.84)*

COAST PILOT

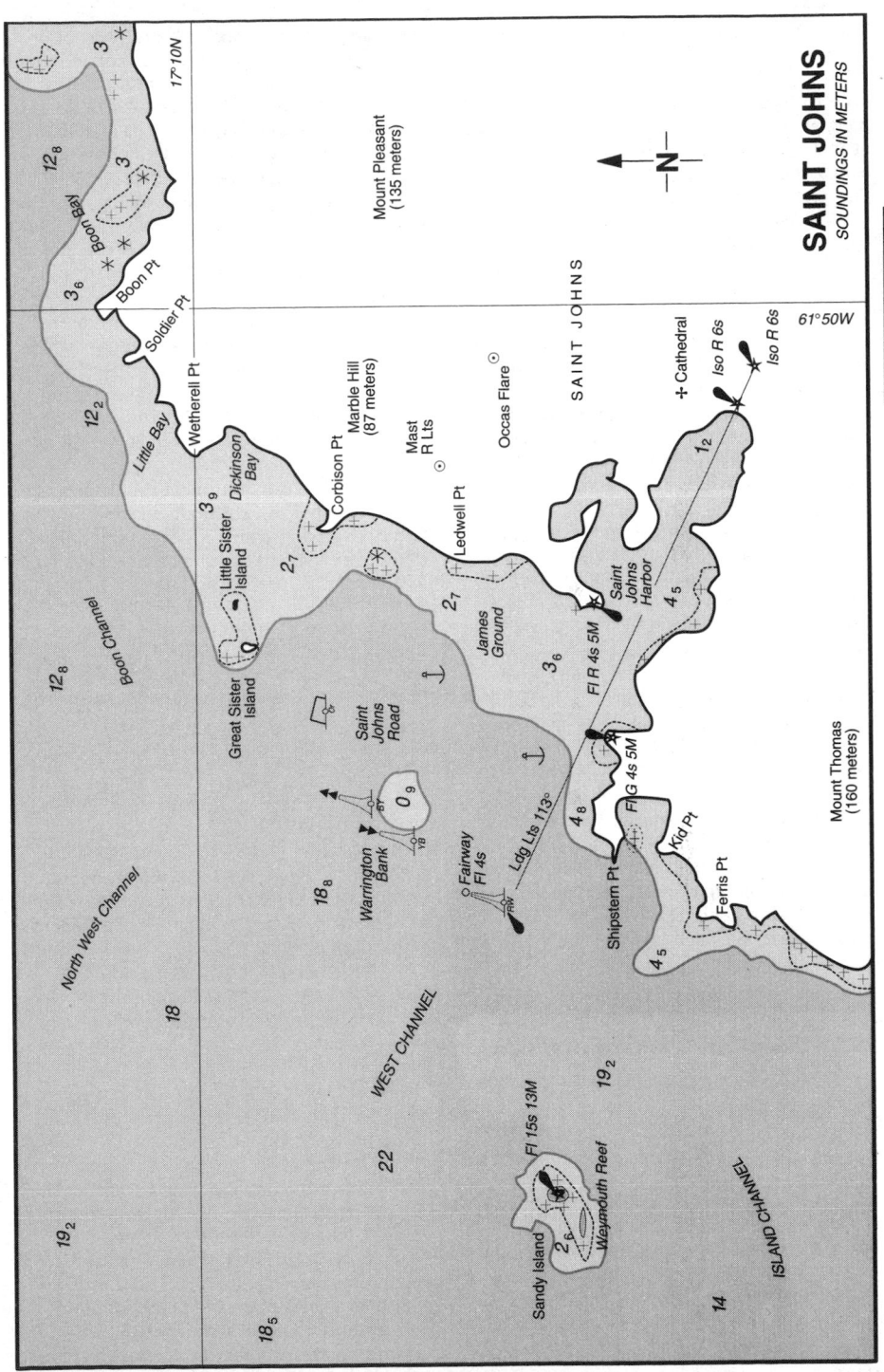

SAINT JOHNS
SOUNDINGS IN METERS

17°10N

3

12₈

Boon Bay

3

3₆

Boon Pt

Soldier Pt

Mount Pleasant
(135 meters)

—N—

SAINT JOHNS

61°50W

+ Cathedral

Iso R 6s

Iso R 6s

1₂

12₂

Little Bay

Wetherell Pt

Marble Hill
(87 meters)

Corbison Pt

Occas Flare ⊙

Mast
R Lts ⊙

Ledwell Pt

3₉

Dickinson Bay

Little Sister
Island

2₁

2₁

James
Ground

Saint
Johns
Harbor

4₅

12₈

Boon Channel

Great Sister
Island

3₆

Fl R 4s 5M

Mount Thomas
(160 meters)

Saint
Johns
Road

8

Fl G 4s 5M

4₈

Kid Pt

Ferris Pt

North West Channel

Warrington
Bank

0₉

8V

6V

Fairway
Fl 4s

FW

Ldg Lts 113°

Shipstern Pt

4₅

18

18₈

WEST CHANNEL

22

Fl 15s 13M

19₂

19₂

Sandy Island

2₆

Weymouth Reef

ISLAND CHANNEL

14

18₅

St. John's, soundings in meters *(after DMA 25570, 2nd ed, 8/84)*

latter 2182kHz. The oil terminal monitors 2182kHz and VHF channel 16 (call sign Marine Center).

Port of Entry: St. John's is primarily a commercial port, but vessels can clear with officials at the wharf on the north side of the harbor. Hours of operation are 0800 to 1600 most days. The local phone number for the boarding officer is 462-0814.

Dockage: A marina is under development in the Redcliffe Quay area, south of the cruise ship dock. The dinghy dock has been completed, and docks for transient yachts are scheduled for completion in late 1994/early 1995. Call Redcliffe Quay (809-462-1847) for updates if you are visiting here.

Anchorage: Anchor either north or south of the main ship channel. At times, you may encounter a swell from the north.

Services: Pleasure boats can get fuel at the commercial dock in the harbor basin. There is good general shopping in St. John's. The Redcliffe Quay area is oriented toward cruise ship passengers. Island Motors Limited (809-462-2138 or VHF channel 82) is a Yamaha dealer. The Epicurean (809-462-2565 or -1546) does gourmet provisioning. Other provisions can be obtained at the Joseph Dew Supermarket and Liquor stores (809-462-1210). Govee's Marine Supplies (809-462-2975) is the local chandlery. There is a Radio Shack (809-462-2685). There are many bars, restaurants, and hotels here or nearby.

St. John's is the capital and major port of Antigua. The harbor is not yet fully geared for pleasure boaters, but a marina is under development near the cruise ship dock. There is an excellent variety of shops and restaurants, so you may want to visit here even if you are based in English Harbour.

SOUTH ANTIGUA

FALMOUTH HARBOUR

17 01N, 61 47W

Emergencies: Call the Antigua Coast Guard on VHF channels 16 and 68 or contact Saba Radio on VHF channel 16.

Pilotage: Falmouth is located 1 mile west of English Harbour, on the south coast of Antigua. There may be a lighted range of 029° leading into the harbor. Several private buoys indicate shoal areas in the harbor, but some of the shallow patches are not marked. There is a prominent shoal extending west from Blacks Point, at the mouth of the harbor.

English Harbour Radio V2MA2: Nicholson Yacht Charters provides the local communications link for many boaters. Contact the company on VHF channel 68 or on 8294.0kHz Monday through Friday from 9AM to 4:30PM and on Saturdays from 9AM until noon.

Dockage: The Catamaran Club (809-460-1503 or VHF channels 16 and 68) at the head of the bay offers stern-to dockage. The Antigua Yacht Club Marina (809-460-1444 or VHF channel 68) is in the eastern portion of the bay.

Anchorage: There is good anchorage in the southeast portion of the bay. Be careful to observe the many shoal areas when searching for an anchoring spot. There is a fee of $0.03 per foot, per night, in the low season (June 1 to mid-November) and $.05 per foot, per night, in the high season to anchor in Falmouth or English Harbour.

Services: You can get fuel at the Catamaran Club. For other services see the listings under English Harbour, which is located right next door. Every type of boating service is available in this area.

Falmouth and English harbors share many of the same shops and facilities. Falmouth may offer more room for those who want to anchor out. This harbor is the center of many activities during the famous Antigua Race Week.

ENGLISH HARBOUR

17 00N, 61 45W

RANGE (Front Light), 17 00.4N, 61 45.4W. Q R, 35ft. Wooden pile. Reported extinguished (1985). **(Rear Light),** 100 meters, 055° from front light. Iso R 2s, 85ft. Wooden pile. Reported extinguished (1985).

CAPE SHIRLEY LIGHT, 17 00.1N, 61 44.7W. Fl (4) W 20s, 494ft, 20M. Metal mast. Visible 264°–084°. Reported extinguished (February 1987).

Emergencies: Call the Antigua Coast Guard on VHF channels 16 and 68 or contact Saba Radio on VHF channel 16.

Pilotage: The approaches to the south coast of Antigua are generally clear, except for the reefs extending east and south from Johnson Point. The harbor is entered between Charlotte Point and Barclay Point, where a range leads you in on a bearing of 055°T. The front light is near a large anchor on the beach. Contact the port authorities on VHF channel 16.

Communications: Many businesses and services stand by on VHF channel 68 in this area.

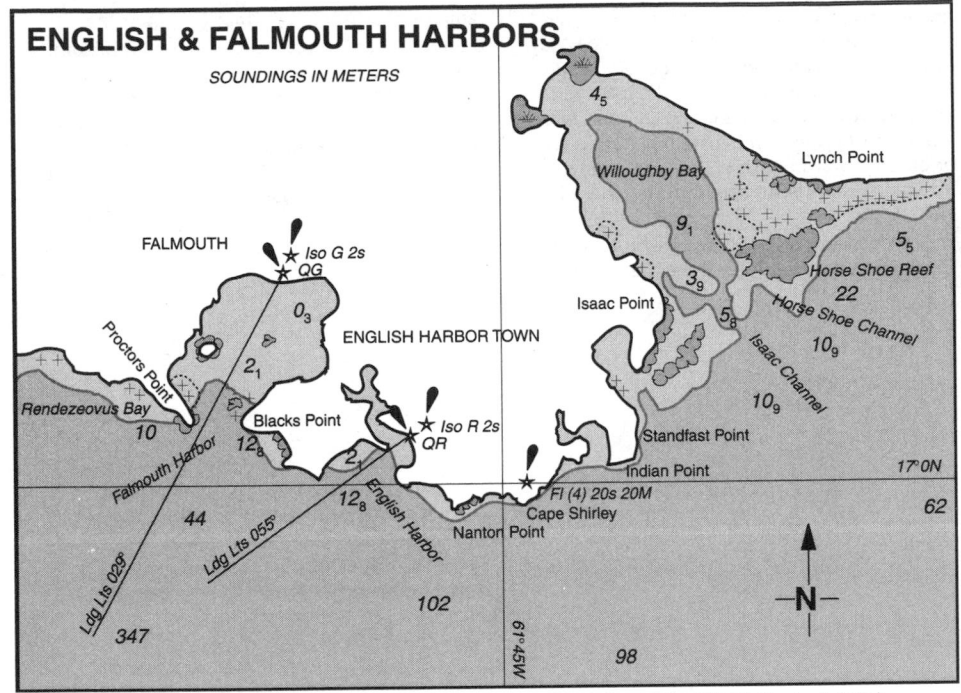

ENGLISH & FALMOUTH HARBORS
SOUNDINGS IN METERS

Falmouth and English Harbours, soundings in meters *(after DMA 25570, 2nd ed, 8/84)*

English Harbour Radio V2MA2: Nicholson Yacht Charters provides the local communications link for many boaters. Contact the company on VHF channel 68 or on 8294.0kHz Monday through Friday from 9AM to 4:30PM and on Saturdays from 9AM until noon.

Port of Entry: When clearing with the officials in English Harbour you may anchor in Freeman Bay flying the Q flag. If customs and immigration officials do not arrive in a reasonable amount of time, you can proceed to their office (809-460-1397) in Nelson's Dockyard, on the western side of the channel leading in to the inner harbor.

Dockage: Contact Antigua Slipway (809-460-1056 or VHF channels 12 and 68), located on the eastern side of the inner harbor mouth, for stern-to dockage at $0.50 per day or side-to dockage at $0.75 per day. You can tie up stern-to in the Dockyard area for $0.25 per foot, per day in the low season (June 1–mid-November) and $0.50 per foot, per day in the high season. Longer term rates are available. The Dockyard has public toilets and showers.

Anchoring: There is some room to anchor in Freeman Bay, outside the channel, or in the inner harbor. This can be a good hurricane hole, if you can get in before the crowd. There is a fee of $0.03 per foot, per night in the low season and $0.05 in the high season to anchor in Falmouth or English Harbour.

Services: All services are available here or in Falmouth. Antigua Slipway (809-460-1056 or VHF channels 12 and 68) can haul boats up to 120 feet long, 125 tons in displacement, and 13 foot draft and has full repair facilities, a chandlery, and a fuel dock. Pumps and Power (809-460-1242 or VHF channel 68) can fill propane bottles. Bailey's Supermarket is opposite the Catamaran Club in Falmouth. For sail repairs, contact A&F Sails (809-460-1522 or VHF channel 68) and Antigua Sails (809-460-1527 or VHF channel 68). Nicholson Yacht Services (809-460-1055 or VHF channel 68) provides message and mail services of all types. Mail can be addressed c/o Nicholson Yacht Services, English Harbour, Antigua, West Indies. Carib Marine (809-460-1521 or -1532) is a combination grocery and hardware store that can handle major provisioning. Seagull Services (809-460-3050) is a complete engine and general repair facility that also does dinghy and rigging repairs and liferaft servicing. This listing contains just a sample of some of the many fine services oriented toward boaters. There are many interesting bars and restaurants here as well.

English Harbour is the location of the famous shipyard that once serviced the great British sailing fleets and now services some of the premier luxury charter yachts in the Caribbean. Consequently, there is limited anchoring and docking room. Many formal and informal regattas originate here, including the famous Antigua Sailing Week, which begins the last Sunday in April. This area is a favorite watering hole for Caribbean "yachties."

REED'S NEEDS YOU!

It is difficult to obtain accurate and up-to-date information on many areas in the Caribbean. To provide the mariner with the best possible product we use many sources. Reed's welcomes your contributions, suggestions, and updates. Please be as specific as possible, and include your address and phone number.
Send your comments to:
Editor, Thomas Reed Publications,
120 Lewis Wharf, Boston, MA 02110, U.S.A.
Thank you!

GUADELOUPE

CAUTION: Our information on aids to navigation comes from official government sources. The latitudes and longitudes of these marks may not correspond to the readings from GPS receivers. Some aids have been reported as unreliable, missing, off position, or showing incorrect characteristics. No single aid to navigation, or waypoint, should be relied upon as a sole means of fixing your position.

NOTE: The chartlets in this section are <u>not</u> <u>intended for navigation</u> and are included for reference and planning purposes only. While chartlets reproduced from government sources are from the most current editions as of press time, they incorporate <u>no corrections</u> to navigational aids, depths, or hazards since the edition publication date.

ENTRY PROCEDURES

Guadeloupe is located about 40 miles south of English Harbour, Antigua. An overseas department of France, it consists of two large islands, Basse-Terre and Grande-Terre, and the off-lying islands of Iles des Saintes, Marie-Galante, and La Désirade. The islands of St. Barts and St. Martin are also part of this department. You should fly the French courtesy flag here.

On the two big islands, the Ports of Entry are Deshaies, Basse-Terre, and Pointe-à-Pitre; Grand-Bourg on Marie-Galante is also a port of entry.

There is no charge for entering the country. The officials may not allow the entry of boats from the U.S. that have only a state registration, so U.S. vessels should have federal documentation. No chartering is allowed by foreign yachts, although charterboats may pass through with non-French passengers.

You should check in with the local police *(les gendarmes)* if you are visiting Iles des Saintes before clearing in officially in Guadeloupe.

The telephone country code for Guadeloupe is 590. Local numbers have six digits. On the island you dial only the six digits. You can call St. Barts, St. Martin, La Désirade, Marie Galante, and Iles des Saintes directly using only their six-digit local numbers. To make phone calls you need to purchase a phone card, sold at the post office and in many shops.

The official currency is the French franc, which currently (summer 1994) trades at about 5.37 to the dollar. The language spoken is French, and some proficiency in French is recommended.

BASSE-TERRE

ANSE A LA BARQUE, head of cove, 16 05.4N, 61 46.1W. Fl (2) W R G 6s, 36ft, 8M white, 5M red, 5M green. White tower, green top. R 050°–064°, W 064°–081°, G 081°–115°.
NORTH SIDE OF ENTRANCE LIGHT, 16 05.4N, 61 46.4W. Q (9) W 15s, 91ft, 9M. West cardinal, YB.
BASSE TERRE LIGHT, on quay near customs house, 15 59.8N, 61 43.8W. Fl W G 4s, 46ft, 10M white, 7M green. White metal pylon, red lantern, W 325°–110°, G 110°–135°.

BASSE-TERRE

15 59N, 61 44W
Pilotage: Between Guadeloupe and Antigua the current is basically west-going and off the southwest point of the island of Basse-Terre reaches speeds of 2 knots. The southwest part of the island is dark rock and quite steep-to. The three peaks of Soufrière may be visible if they are not obscured by clouds. A tower on a church and the steeple of the cathedral are prominent. A statue and a cross are on the church tower. The port authority monitors VHF channel 16.
Port of Entry: Officials are in the Marina de Rivière Sens or in town.
Dockage: Marina de Rivière Sens (590-81-88-71) is located in a protected basin about 1 1/4 miles southeast of the commercial wharf. All services are available.

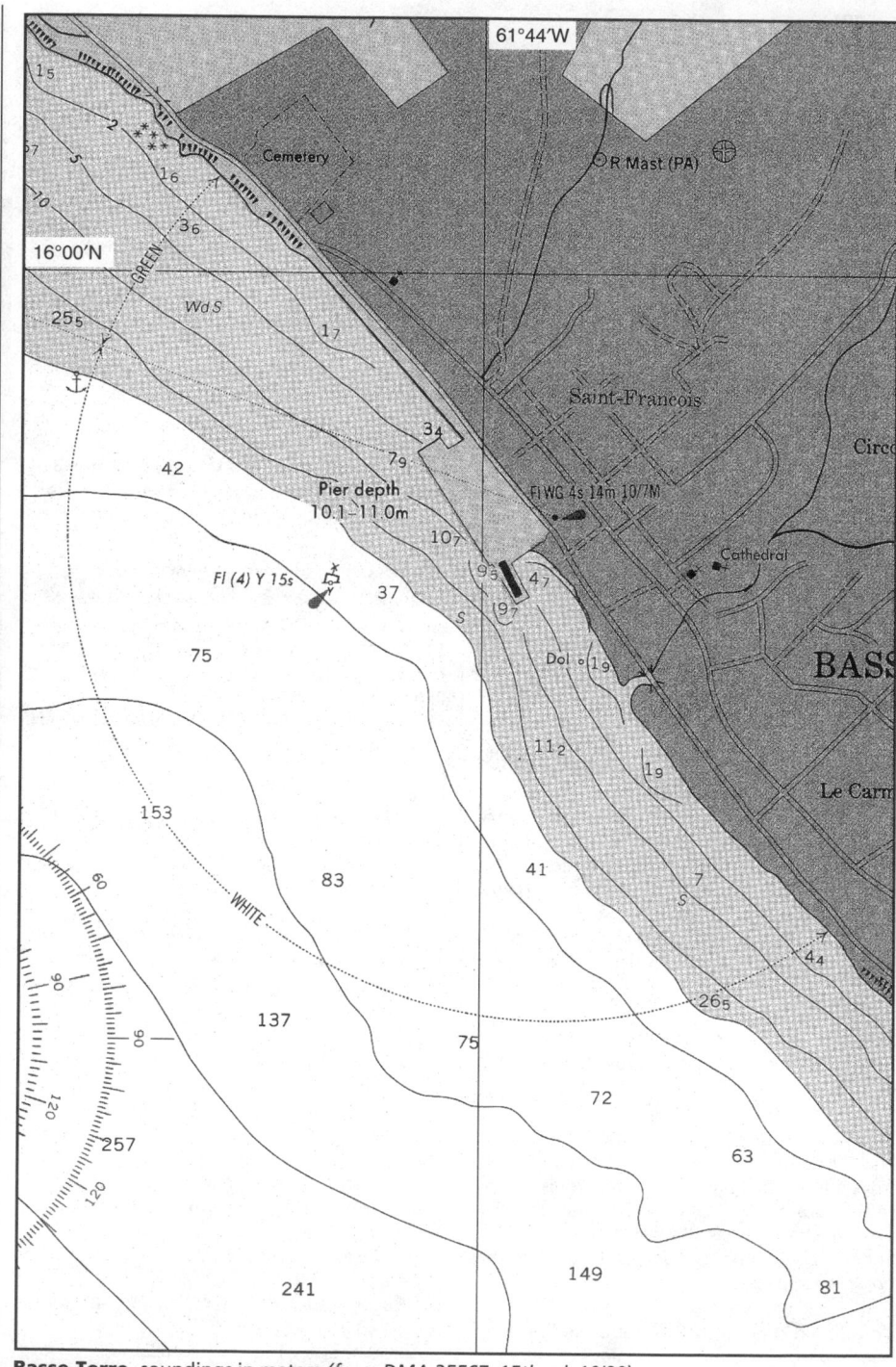

Basse-Terre, soundings in meters *(from DMA 25567, 15th ed, 10/90)*

Anchorage: Anchor north or south of the town wharf or off the entrance to the marina. There is no shelter in south or west winds.
Services: There are good yacht services in the area around the marina. The town has good general shopping and groceries.

Basse-Terre, the capital of Guadeloupe, was founded in 1643. The historic city rests in a dramatic setting below towering volcanic peaks. There are good markets and supplies for those who can find room in the marina.

POINTE DU VIEUX FORT, 15 56.9N, 61 42.6W. Fl (2+1) W 15s, 85ft, 22M. White tower, gray top. Obscured 297°–331° by Les Saintes. Reserve light F W.
TROIS RIVIERES LIGHT, on the point, 15 58.1N, 61 38.8W. Iso W R G 4s, 82ft, 10M white, 7M red, 7M green. White tower, red top. R 275°–349°, W 349°–054°,G 054°–068°.
Passe de la Baleine, West Pass Buoy BA, 15 52.8N, 61 35.5W. Fl (2) G 6s. Green pillar, can topmark. Radar reflector.
SAINTE MARIE LIGHT, root of E pier, 16 06.1N, 61 33.9W. Fl G 4s, 36ft, 6M. White square tower, green top.
PETIT BOURG LIGHT, on jetty, 16 11.5N, 61 35.1W. Fl (2) G 6s, 4M. White tripod, green top.

POINTE-A-PITRE APPROACHES

ENTRANCE RANGE (Front Light), S end Monroux peninsula, 16 13.3N, 61 31.6W. Dir. Q W, 49ft, 13M. White pylon, white rectangular topmark. Intensified 4° either side of range.
(Rear Light), Pointe Fouillole 640 meters 348° from front. Q W, 69ft, 13M. White mast, topmark white slats.
AVIATION LIGHT, 16 15.8N, 61 31.7W. Mo (P) W 30s. Aero radiobeacon. Occasional.

POINTE-A-PITRE

16 14N, 61 32W
Pilotage: The approaches to the commercial port of Pointe-à-Pitre are well marked by buoys, lights, and ranges. The buoyage is laid out on the red-right-returning scheme. Beware of the coral reefs extending from the shore of Basse-Terre in the approaches. The west side of the inner harbor is commercial in nature, while the pleasure boat facilities are concentrated to the east. The captain of the port monitors VHF channel 16.
Port of Entry: Customs offices (*bureaux de douane*) are in the marina and in town.

Dockage: Marina Bas du Fort (590-90-84-85 or VHF channel 9) is located in the first bay to the east as you enter the harbor. This area is known as Port du Plaisance.
Anchorage: There are various places to anchor tucked just outside of the marked channels near shore. Most boats try to be near the shipyard and marina complexes on the east side of the harbor. The marina rents moorings.
Services: Extensive services are available here, including several places for haulouts. There are many marine businesses in the Port du Plaisance area, rivaling the facilities available in Antigua. Karukera Marine (590-90-90-96) and Electro Nautique (590-82-18-35) are chandleries. The North Sails loft can be reached at 590-90-80-44. Sorema (590-90-88-77) offers diesel engine, electrics, and general engineering service. LGEM Electronic Marine (590-90-89-19) repairs electronics. There are supermarkets, restaurants, and shops in the area around the marina and in town.

This is a well-sheltered harbor, offering some of the best facilities and services for boaters available in the Caribbean. It is also a busy commercial port and center of commerce for Guadeloupe.

GRANDE-TERRE

PORT LOUIS LIGHT, on the beach, 16 25.1N, 61 32.2W. Q (9) W 15s, 33ft, 9M. West cardinal YBY, beacon. Visible 252°–162°.
ANSE BERTRAND LIGHT, 16 28.4N, 61 30.7W. Fl (2) W R G 6s, 46ft, 9M white, 6M red, 6M green. White concrete tower. R 120°–163°, W 163°–170°, G 170°–200°.
PORT DU MOULE LIGHT, W side of entrance, 16 20.0N, 61 20.8W. Fl W R 4s, 39ft, 9M white, 6M red. White concrete pylon, green lantern. R 110°–202°, W 202°–312°, R 312°–340°.
EAST SIDE OF ENTRANCE LIGHT, Fl (2) W R G 6s, 23ft, 7M white, 5M red, 5M green. White pillar, R top. R 353°–133°, W 133°–138°, G 138°–165° (W on Hastings Pass).
PORT DE SAINT FRANCOIS LIGHT, Directional light, 16 15.1N, 61 16.7W. Dir Q W R G, 33ft, 9M white, 7M red, 7M green. White tower. R 345°–358°, W 358°–002°, G 002°–015°.
PORT DE SAINT FRANCOIS, on wharf, 16 15.1N, 61 16.6W. Fl G 4s, 30ft, 6M. White metal post, green top.
ILET A GOZIER, 16 12.0N, 61 29.2W. Fl (2) R 10s, 79ft, 26M. White cylindrical masonry tower. Visible 259°–115°, obscured on certain bearings toward Pointe Caraibe.

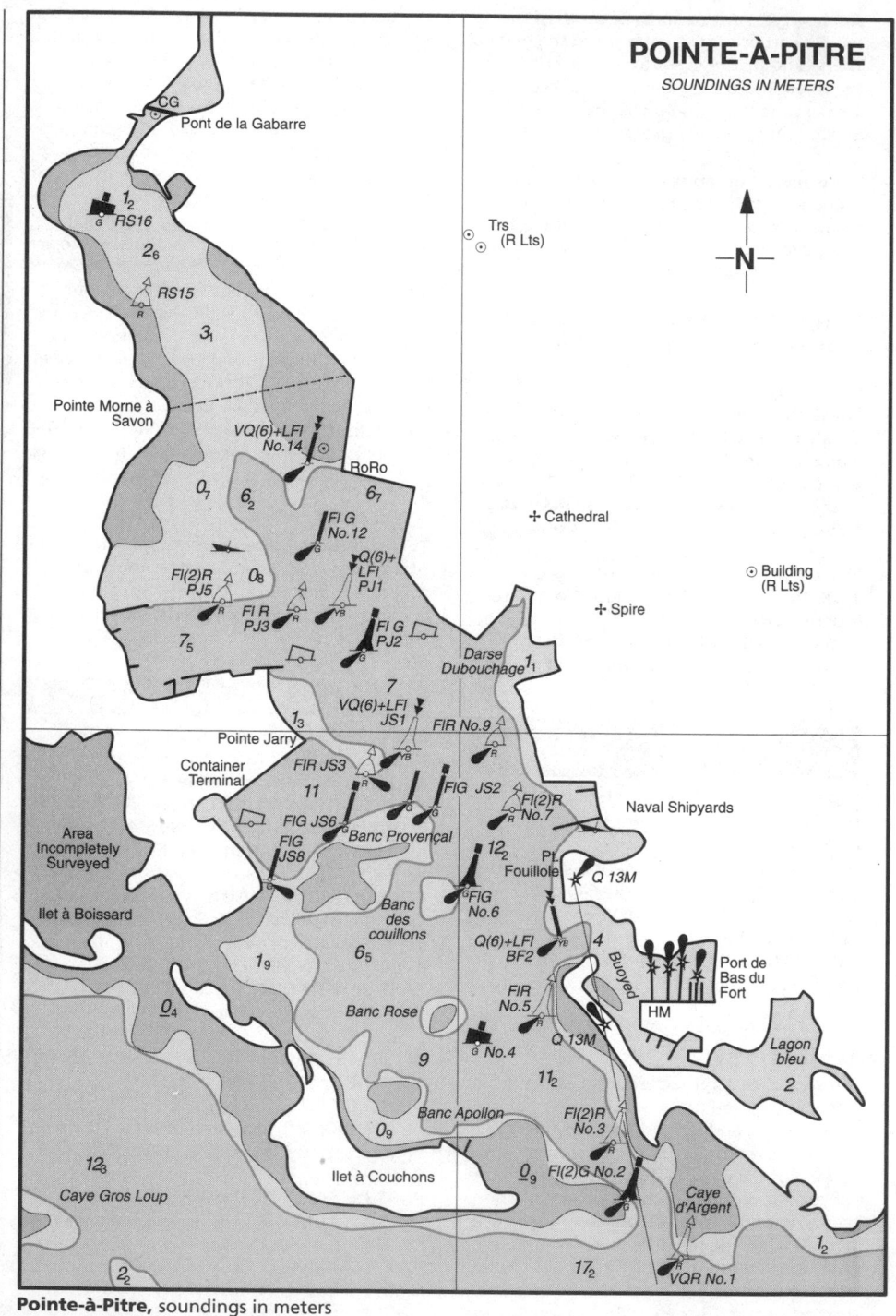

POINTE-À-PITRE

SOUNDINGS IN METERS

CG
Pont de la Gabarre

1_2
G RS16
2_6

RS15
R

3_1

Pointe Morne à Savon

VQ(6)+LFl No.14
RoRo

0_7 6_2 6_7

Trs (R Lts)

✝ Cathedral

⊙ Building (R Lts)

Fl G No.12

Fl(2)R PJ5 0_8 Q(6)+ LFl PJ1

Fl R PJ3   R   ⊙

✝ Spire

Fl G PJ2

7_5

Darse Dubouchage 1_1

7

VQ(6)+LFl JS1   FlR No.9

Pointe Jarry 1_3

Container Terminal   FlR JS3

11

Fl G JS2   Fl(2)R No.7

Naval Shipyards

FlG JS6   Banc Provençal

FIG JS8

Area Incompletely Surveyed

12_2

Pt. Fouillole   ✦ Q 13M

Ilet à Boissard

Banc des couillons   G FIG No.6

Q(6)+LFl BF2   4   Buoyed

1_9 6_5

0_4

Banc Rose   FIR No.5

9   G No.4   Q 13M

Port de Bas du Fort

HM

Lagon bleu   2

11_2

Banc Apollon

Fl(2)R No.3

0_9 Fl(2)G No.2

12_3
Caye Gros Loup

Ilet à Couchons

0_9 Caye d'Argent

1_2

2_2 17_2 VQR No.1

Pointe-à-Pitre, soundings in meters

ISLANDS OF GUADELOUPE

LA DESIRADE LIGHT, near SE point of island, 16 19.6N, 61 00.7W. Fl (2) W 10s, 165ft, 20M. White framework tower, red top, upper part enclosed, dwelling.

BAIE MAHAULT RANGE (Front Light), 16 19.7N, 61 01.1W. Fl R 2s, 16ft, 4M. White pylon, red top. **(Rear Light),** 35 meters 327° from front. Fl R 2s, 23ft, 4M. White pylon, red top, synchronized with front.

GRANDE ANSE LIGHT, head of pier, 16 18.2N, 61 04.8W. Fl G 2.5s, 23ft, 1M. White mast.

LEADING LIGHT, dir. Oc (2) W R G 6s, 23ft, 8M white, 6M red, 6M green. White stone structure, red top. R 250°–335°, W 335°–339°, G 339°–056°.

ILES DE PETITE TERRE, E extremity of Ilot Terre d'en Bas, 16 10.3N, 61 06.8W. Fl (3) W 12s, 108ft, 15M. Gray cylindrical tower. Square stone base. Obscured by Ile La Desinade 185°–213°.

LES SAINTES

BOURG DES SAINTES LIGHT, Terre d'en Haut, root of wharf, 15 52.1N, 61 35.2W. Fl W R G 4s, 30ft, 10M white, 7M red, 7M green. White metal framework tower. R 075°–142°, W 142°–154°, G 154°–160°. Obstruction light on aerial.

BOURG DES SAINTES

15 52N, 61 35W

Pilotage: The town is located on the western side of Terre d'en Haut, near the middle of the island. A large conspicuous cross is illuminated at night and stands south of the church. Note the shoal patch, halfway to Ilet à Cabrit, marked by a buoy. There is a 100-foot-long pier projecting from the waterfront, where a light is shown from near the root of the pier.

Vessel Clearance: Check with the gendarmes if arriving here from another country before clearing with the authorities on Guadeloupe.

Anchorage: Anchor away from the ferry dock and ferry channels.

Services: There is little in the way of marine services, but there is a good selection of boutiques, restaurants, and general stores.

MARIE-GALANTE

GRAND-BOURG LIGHT, on wharf, 15 52.9N, 61 19.2W. Fl (2) G 6s, 30ft, 6M. White metal post, green top.

GRAND BOURG

15 53N, 61 19W

Pilotage: This town lies on the southwest side of Marie-Galante. The fort and the hospital on the northwest side of the town and the church with a belfry on its northeast side are all prominent landmarks. A conspicuous lighted TV tower stands about 1 mile north of the town. Lighted buoys mark the edge of the reefs in the approach to the pier from the west.

Port of Entry: You can clear in here, but you must get your outward clearance on Guadeloupe.

Anchorage: Anchor in or near the small basin near the ferry dock.

Services: General supplies are available.

ST. LOUIS LIGHT, W of church, 15 57.4N, 61 19.3W. Fl G 4s, 36ft, 6M. White square tower, green top.

CAPESTERRE RANGE (Front Light), 15 53.9N, 61 13.2W. Q R, 39ft, 6M. Square tower, red and white bands. Visible 246.5°–051.5°. **(Rear Light),** 100 meters 313° from front. Q R, 52ft, 6M. Square tower, red and white bands. Visible 246.5°–051.5°.

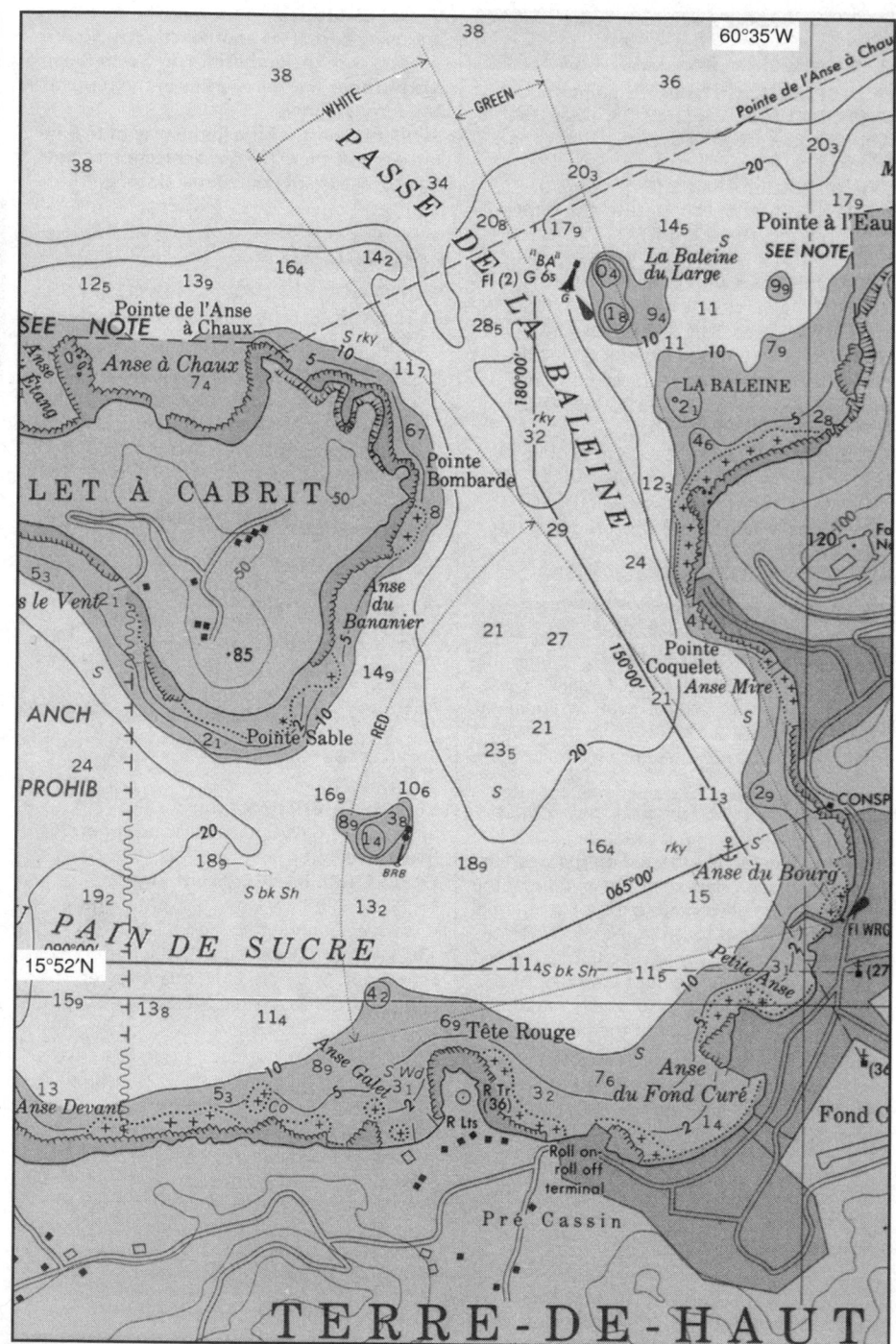

Bourg des Saintes, soundings in meters *(from DMA 25564, 6th ed, 3/90)*

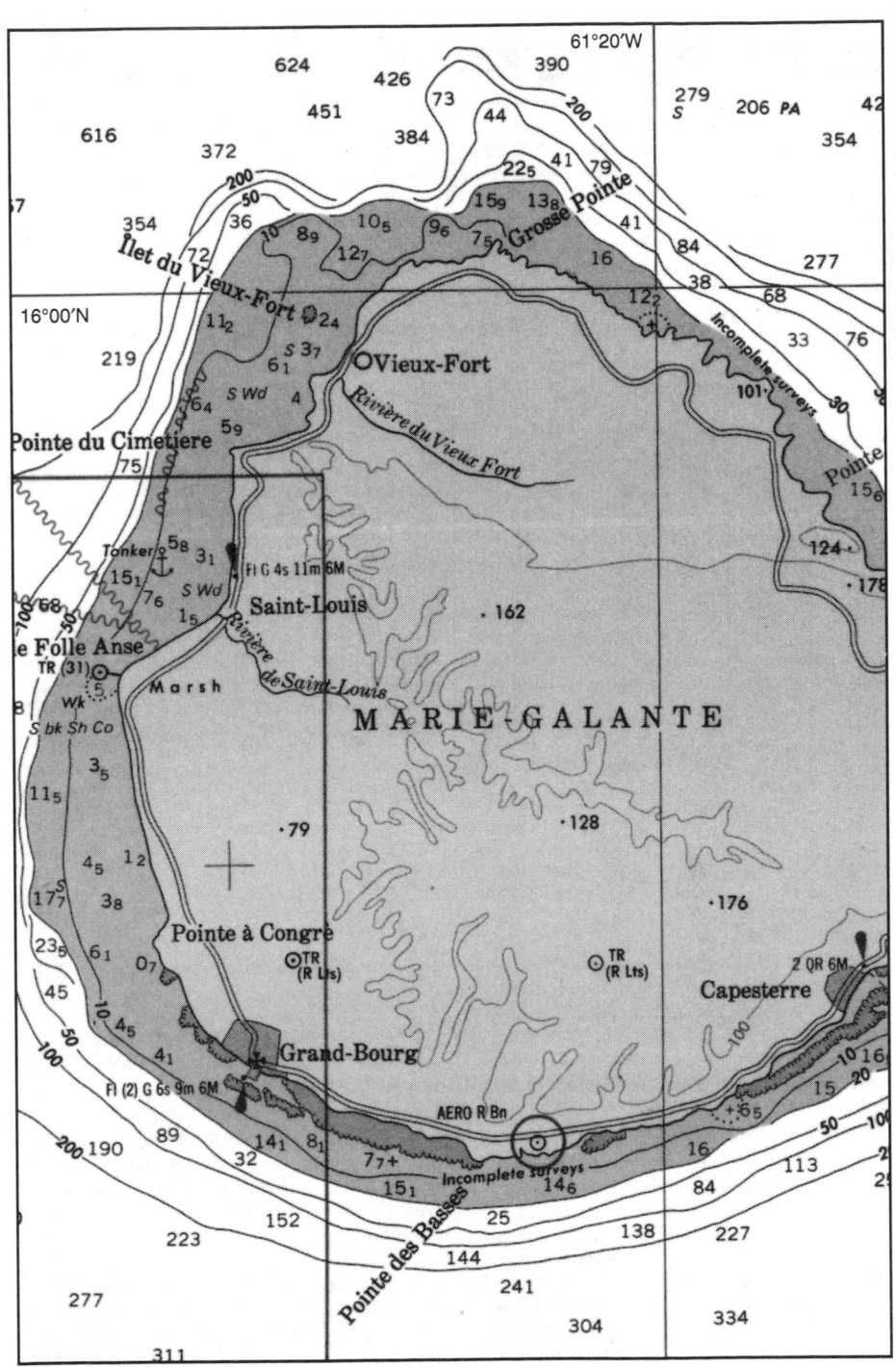

Marie-Galante, soundings in meters *(from DMA 25563, 49th ed, 8/93)*

ISLA AVES, VENEZUELA

CAUTION: It has been reported that much of this island was washed away in a 1979 hurricane, leaving two sand cays bordered by coral reefs, with a pool between. The latitude and longitude of this island has been reported to be inaccurate by some yachtsmen. All of the following information should, therefore, be used with great caution.

15 40N, 63 37W
ISLA AVES LIGHT, 15 40.1N, 63 37.0W. FL W 5s, 49f., 13M. RACON: A (–).

Venezuelan Coast Guard: Call sign Simon Bolivar Coast Guard Station.

Isla Aves is a Venezuelan possession with a latitude slightly north of the northern tip of Dominica, but 128 miles to the west. It is nearly 600 yards long in a north–south direction and 100 yards wide. The maximum elevation of about 10 feet is near its northern end, and the sea breaks across the center in anything more than a moderate swell. The island is formed of coral, overlaid with sand, which supports some vegetation. Birds abound, and the island is a protected nature sanctuary.

An oil-rig style-Texas tower with a radar reflector stands on the island. The structure on top of the tower is the size of an average house. The platform is approximately 60 feet high. This is a manned Venezuelan Coast Guard Station, call sign Simon Bolivar Coast Guard Station. The island has been reported as a good radar target up to 30 miles distant. There is also a transmitting radar beacon (RACON).

About 100 yards from the south end of the island, a jetty with a depth of about 9 feet alongside its head projects from land about 88 yards. Depths less than 5 feet are found on several shoal patches in the western approaches to the jetty. In moderate weather you may be able to land near the center of the western side of the island. Here, a narrow sandy beach extends down to the low water line here.

Vessels without local knowledge are advised to give the islands a berth of at least 1 1/2 miles. If you wish to anchor, the best approach is from the south–southwest. Keep a good lookout for coral heads. The recommended anchorage is with the mast bearing 077°, distant 600 yards. Depths should be about 17 feet in this area, though there is a 9-foot patch reported about 100 yards east-northeast of this position.

DOMINICA

CAUTION: Our information on aids to navigation comes from official government sources. The latitudes and longitudes of these marks may not correspond to the readings from GPS receivers. Some aids have been reported as unreliable, missing, off position, or showing incorrect characteristics. No single aid to navigation, or waypoint, should be relied upon as a sole means of fixing your position.

NOTE: The chartlets in this section are not intended for navigation and are included for reference and planning purposes only. While chartlets reproduced from government sources are from the most current editions as of press time, they incorporate no corrections to navigational aids, depths,
or hazards since the edition publication date.

ENTRY PROCEDURES

The northern tip of Dominica is located about 38 miles south of Pointe-à-Pitre, Guadeloupe. Although the island has most recently been a British possession, a strong French influence seeps in from neighboring islands. The Commonwealth of Dominica is now an independent country.

Ports of Entry are Portsmouth in Prince Rupert Bay and Roseau, the capital. Both are on the west coast of the island. Contact customs in Portsmouth at 809-44-55340 and in Roseau at 809-44-84462. Immigration in Portsmouth can be reached at 809-44-55222.

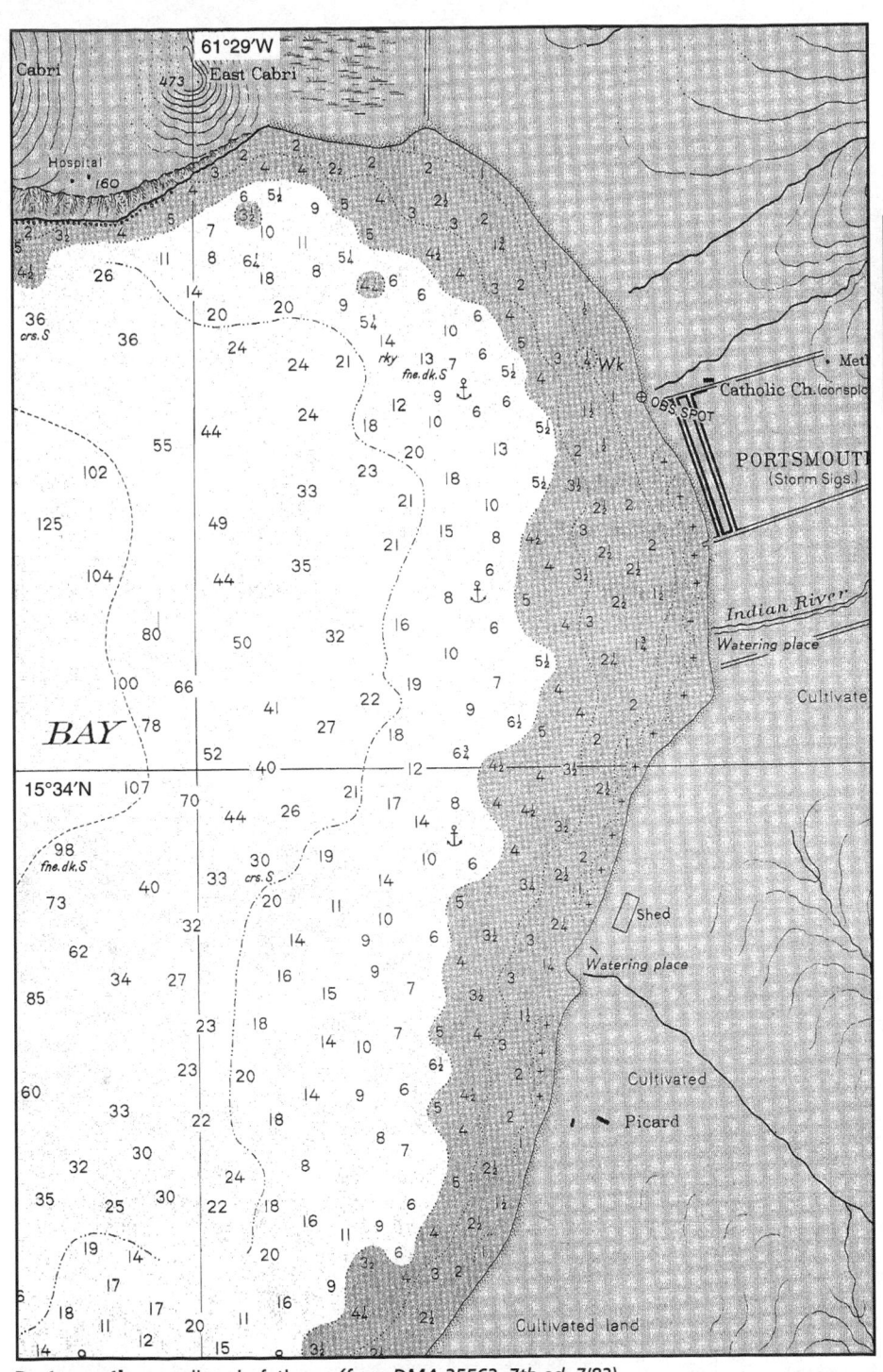

Portsmouth, soundings in fathoms *(from DMA 25562, 7th ed, 7/82)*

In Roseau you might want to call the Anchorage Hotel (809-44-82638 or VHF channel 16) to see if you can contact the officials from the facility's anchorage. In Portsmouth try calling the Portsmouth Beach Hotel (809-44-55142 or VHF channel 16) for the same reason. These facilities are owned by the same family and specialize in making yachtsmen feel welcome. They can assist with most of your needs while on the island.

In Roseau call the port manager on VHF channel 16 to obtain permission to anchor off the commercial wharves, which are north of town. You can then dinghy in to clear with officials. The area north of the mouth of the Roseau River, including the commercial wharves, is a Restricted Anchorage. In Portsmouth you should visit the officials near the commercial wharf south of town. Normal working hours for the officials are about 0800 to 1200 and 1300 to 1600, Monday through Friday. Overtime charges apply outside of these hours.

A cruising permit should be obtained for your itinerary on the island. There is a departure charge of EC$5 per boat.

If you are calling from outside the island, the telephone area code for Dominica is 809, followed by the island code of 44. On the island you dial only the five-digit local number. The Eastern Caribbean, or EC, dollar is the official currency. The exchange rate with the U.S. dollar is about .40. U.S. dollars may be accepted in tourist areas. The official language is English, but you will also encounter French Creole because of the proximity of French territories.

PORTSMOUTH

15 34N, 61 29W
Pilotage: Prince Rupert Bay is a well-sheltered bay near the north end of the west coast of the island. There are no dangers in the approach to this steep-to coast. The gray spire and red roof of the Catholic Church in town are conspicuous. The white Methodist Chapel, east of the Catholic Church, is prominent from offshore. There are two jetties and a prominent warehouse 1 mile south of Portsmouth (not shown on the Portsmouth chartlet) and a cruise ship dock to the north.
Port of Entry: See Entry Procedures above.
Dockage: The Portsmouth Beach Hotel (809-44-55142 or VHF channel 16) may have some dockage, either bow- or stern-to, at its facility about 1 mile south of town. Rental moorings are also available.
Anchorage: Anchor near the Portsmouth Beach Hotel and dinghy in to the hotel dock. Other boats anchor north of town near the Purple Turtle or Mamie's on the Beach. You can probably dinghy in to one of these restaurants.
Services: Contact the Portsmouth Beach Hotel to obtain fuel or water at its wharf. The hotel also offers a mail drop, showers, a restaurant, telephones, and assistance with most projects on the island. Ask for recommendations on guides or taxis. Basic supplies and groceries are available in town. Mamie's (809-44-55997) and The Purple Turtle (809-44-55296) will assist yachtsmen. "Boat boys" will offer you their services here.

BARROUI LIGHT, 15 26.0N, 61 26.8W. 2 F R (vertical).

ROSEAU

15 18N, 61 24W
ROSEAU LIGHT, on Fort Young, 15 17.4N, 61 23.7W. Oc R 3s, 80ft, 8M. White concrete structure. Partially obscured 117°–125°; obscured 125°–shore. Temporarily extinguished (1983).

Pilotage: The port of Roseau comprises Woodbridge Bay and Roseau Roads. A deepwater wharf is situated 1600 yards north of the mouth of the Roseau River. This area is a Restricted Anchorage, and boaters should contact the Port Manager on VHF channel 16 for permission to drop the hook. Morne Bruce, a tableland, rises to a height of 475 feet east of town. There are several old military buildings on its summit. There is a prominent flagstaff on the west corner of Fort Young at the south end of town. The Catholic Church and Wesleyan Church spires are also prominent. The red bridge crossing the mouth of the Roseau River is a good landmark.
Port of Entry: Contact Customs at 809-44-84462.
Anchorage: Anchor near the Anchorage Hotel (809-44-82638 or VHF channel 16) located about 1 mile south of town. The hotel has moorings, a dinghy dock, showers, water, telephones and a mail drop. The staff can also assist you in obtaining fuel or other services.
Services: There are few yachting services here, but you can obtain most general supplies

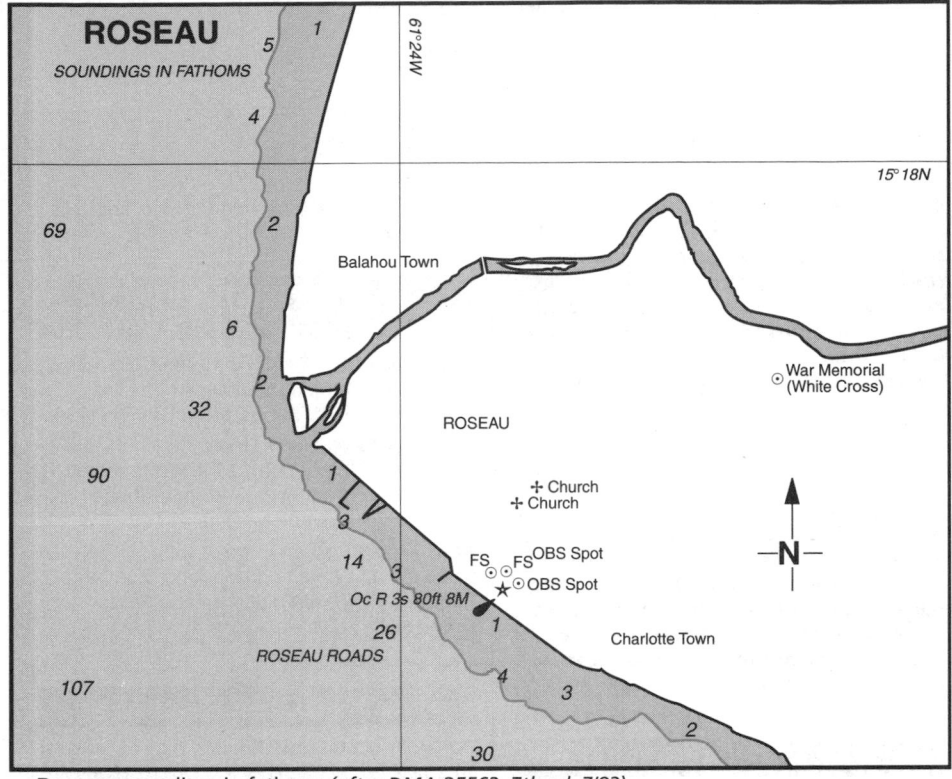

Roseau, soundings in fathoms *(after DMA 25562, 7th ed, 7/82)*

and groceries. Contact the government's National Development Corporation, Division of Tourism (809-44-82045, -82351, or -82186) for information on visiting the "Nature Island of the Caribbean." The Castaways Beach Hotel (809-44-96244 or VHF channel 16, call sign Castaways), located about 7 miles north of town, is a dive and watersports center. There are also dive facilities at the Anchorage Hotel. The "boat boys" will offer you their services here.

MARTINIQUE

CAUTION: Our information on aids to navigation comes from official government sources. The latitudes and longitudes of these marks may not correspond to the readings from GPS receivers. Some aids have been reported as unreliable, missing, off position, or showing incorrect characteristics. No single aid to navigation, or waypoint, should be relied upon as a sole means of fixing your position.

NOTE: The chartlets in this section are <u>not</u> <u>intended for navigation</u> and are included for reference and planning purposes only. While chartlets reproduced from government sources are from the most current editions as of press time, they incorporate <u>no corrections</u> to navigational aids, depths, or hazards since the edition publication date.

ENTRY PROCEDURES

This island country is a department of France. With a population of more than 350,000, it is one of the commercial centers of the Antilles. You should fly the French courtesy flag here.

The main port of entry is Fort-de-France, but you can also check in at St. Pierre or Marin. Hours are about 0800 to 1100 and 1500 to 1730. The main customs office can be reached at 596 63 04 82 (fax, 596 63 61 80) and the main immigration office at 596 51 48 85.

You will need a clearance from your last port of call, several crew lists, your boat documents, and your passports. Check on the latest regulations if you plan on staying in the country or leaving your boat for more than six months. You may be liable for duty after this period.

The country code for Martinique is 596. Local numbers use six digits. To make phone calls you will need to purchase a phone card, which is sold at the post office and in many shops. The official currency is the French franc, which is currently (summer 1994) trading at about 5.37 to the U.S. dollar. The language spoken is French, and some proficiency in the language is recommended.

MARTINIQUE, WEST COAST

PRECHEUR POINT LIGHT, 14 48.0N, 61 13.8W. Fl R 1s, 72ft, 14M. Iron tower, stone base, Visible 338°–162°. Temporarily Fl R 6.5s (1994).

POINTE DES NEGRES LIGHT, 14 35.9N, 61 05.6W. Fl W 5s, 118ft, 25M. White metal framework tower, gray lantern. Visible 276°–126°. Aero radiobeacon.

Banc Mitan Buoy, W side of shoal, 14 35.0N, 61 05.0W. Q W. Red and black horizontally banded buoy, black ball topmark. Radar reflector.

FORT-DE-FRANCE

FORT ST. LOUIS LIGHT, in SW part of fortress, 14 35.9N, 61 04.4W. Fl W R G, 102ft, 17M white, 13M red, 13 green. White iron framework structure. R 320°–057°, W 057°–087°, G 087°–140°; obscured 140°–320°.

BAIE DU CARENAGE RANGE (Front Light), 14 36.3N, 61 03.7W. Iso G 4s, 138ft, 14M. Yellow rectangle, white metal framework tower, black bands. Intensified 001°–007°. **(Rear Light)** 145 meters 004° from front. Iso G 4s, 164ft, 14M. Yellow rectangle, white metal framework tower, black bands. Synchronized with front. Intensified 001°–007°.

OIL PIER LIGHT, SW corner, 14 35.9N, 61 04.1W. F R, 3ft, 6M. Red pedestal.

BEACON, 14 36.0N, 61 03.0W. 2 F R, 3 F R vertical 20 feet below and 20 feet apart. Red and white banded radio mast. Obstruction light.

BEACON, 2 F R, 3 F R vertical 20 feet below and 20 feet apart, red and white banded radio mast. Obstruction light.

BEACON, 2 F R, 3 F R vertical 20 feet below and 20 feet apart. Red and white banded radio mast. Obstruction light.

LE LAMENTIN AVIATION LIGHT, 14 35.7N, 61 00.0W. Fl (3+1) W 12s, 105ft, 20M. Occasional.

COAST PILOT

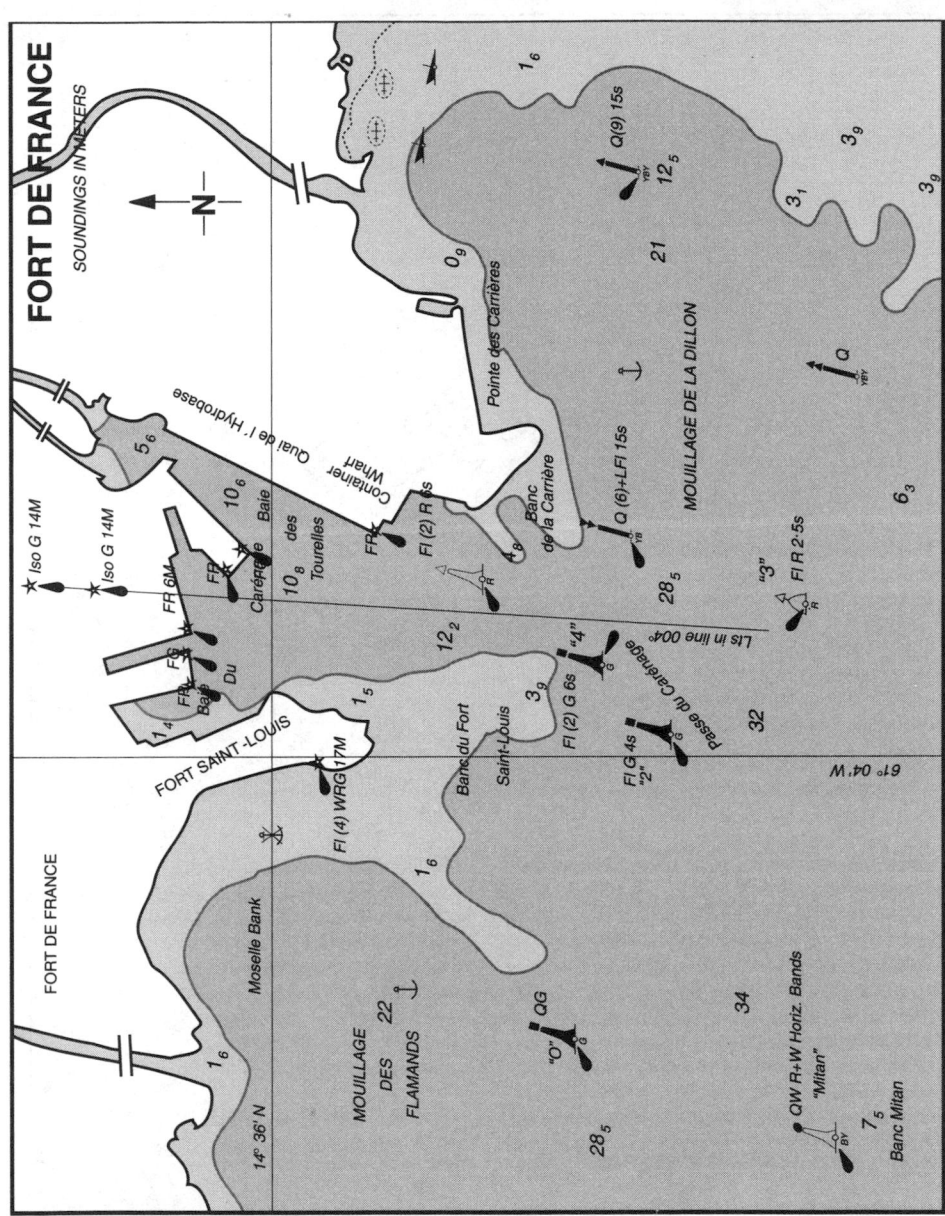

Fort-de-France, soundings in meters *(after DMA 25527, 30th ed, 10/88)*

FORT-DE-FRANCE

14 36N, 61 04W

Pilotage: The island is very mountainous and is easily identified by three outstanding peaks towering above the main mountain chain that traverses it in a northwest to southeast direction. Shoals, banks, and other dangers are marked by buoys in the approaches to the city. Note the 004° range leading into the main harbor. Local port authorities and pilots may be contacted on VHF channels 13 and 16. This city of 100,000 inhabitants is a very busy port.

Port of Entry: The officials are located behind the new cruise ship dock in the western portion of the waterfront.

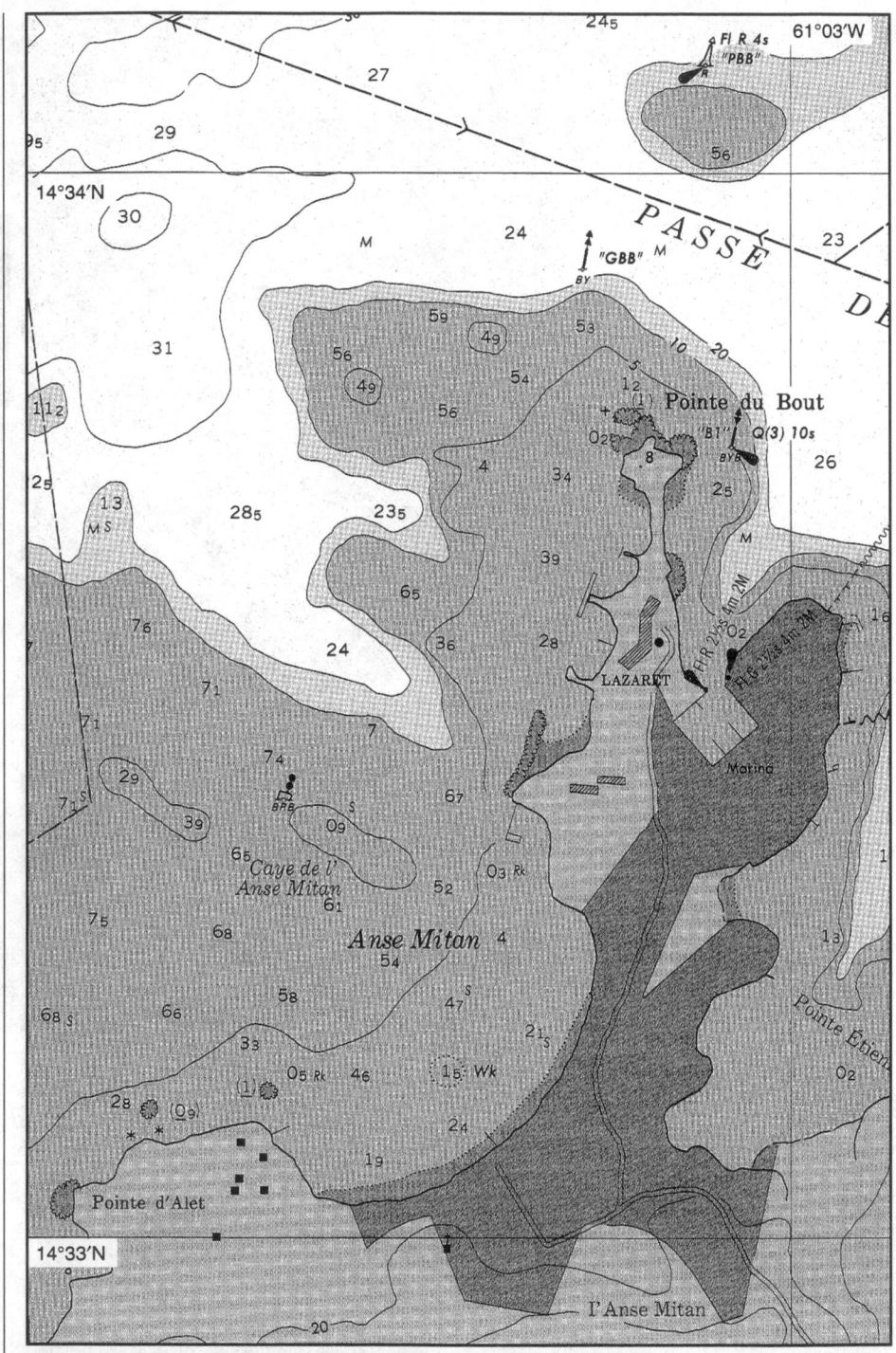

Anse Mitan, soundings in meters *(from DMA 25527, 30th ed, 10/88)*

Dockage: There may be some stern-to dockage on the wharf east of Fort Saint-Louis, but most boats anchor out. There should be some dockage available across the way on the Pointe du Bout at Anse Mitan.

Anchorage: Most boats anchor in the western part of Baie des Flamands. For a more peaceful anchorage try one of the nearby bays or the area around Anse Mitan.

Ferry: Several ferries run across the bay to Anse Mitan. Service is frequent.

Services: Every type of marine service is here or nearby. Fuel and water are available at Anse Mitan. Sea Services (596 70 26 69), Littoral (596 70 28 70), Martinique Ship Chandler (596 60 49 01), and the Ship Shop (596 71 43 40) are all chandleries. Puces Nautiques (596 60 58 48) describes itself as a "nautical fleamarket." Sailmakers include North Sails (596 68 03 34) and R. Helenon (596 60 22 05). The repair yards are Martinique Drydock (596 72 69 40) and the Ship Shop, which has a Travelift. Engine repairs are done by Madia Boat (596 63 10 61), metalwork by Chalemessin Enterprise (596 60 03 75), and woodwork or fiberglass (and supplies) by Polymar (596 70 62 88). There are large first-class supermarkets and general stores of all types.

Fort-de-France is the busy and very European capital of Martinique. It is also the largest city in the Antilles and a great place to find the items and services a modern city can provide. Nearby are peaceful anchorages when you tire of all the hustle-bustle.

POINT DU BOUT

POINTE DU BOUT LIGHT, marina E jetty head, 14 33.4N, 61 03.5W. Fl G 2.5s, 13ft, 2M. Green post.
POINTE DU BOUT LIGHT, marina W jetty head. Fl R 2.5s, 13ft, 2M. Red post.

ANSE MITAN

14 34N, 61 03W

Pilotage: There is a buoyed reef, Caye de l'Anse Mitan, west of Pointe du Bout, where Anse Mitan is located. There are also some reefs close to shore around Pointe du Bout. A ferry runs from the marina basin to Fort-de-France and another from a dock in the big bay on the southern end of the western side of the peninsula.

Dockage: The Ponton du Bakoua (596 66 05 45 or VHF channel 16) has some dockage about halfway down the peninsula on the western

side. The Somatras Marina (596 66 07 74) is in the square dredged basin.

Anchorage: Anchor along the western shore of the peninsula, taking care to avoid the small reef marked by a buoy. The reef is located west of the Ponton du Bakoua dock.

Ferry: Frequent ferries run to Fort-de-France from the marina basin and from the dock at the southwestern end of Pointe du Bout.

Services: Fuel and water are available at the Ponton du Bakoua. Mecanique Plaisance (596 66 05 40) is located in the marina and does inboard engine repairs. The Captain's Shop (596 66 06 77) is a chandlery and repair shop. The local sail shop is Voilerie Caraibe Martinique (596 66 07 24 or VHF channel 16). Nearby are supermarkets and general shops. For anything you can't find, take the ferry across to Fort-de-France.

Anse Mitan is a convenient anchorage and is less commercial than Fort-de-France. The facilities are good and the atmosphere less hectic than in the big city across the way.

MARTINIQUE, SOUTH COAST

POINT DU MARIN, On W side of point, 14 26.9N, 60 53.2W. Dir Q W R G, 23ft, 9M white, 6M red, 6M green. White structure, green top. R 015°–071°, W 071°–075°, G 075°–080°.
NORTH HEAD LIGHT, 14 27.1N, 60 53.1W. Fl R 2.5s, 16ft, 2M. Red starboard-hand beacon with topmark.
BANC MAJOR LIGHT, 14 27.7N, 60 52.6W. Fl G 2.5s, 7ft, 2M. Green port-hand beacon with topmark.
BANC DU MILIEU LIGHT, 14 27.7N, 60 52.5W. Fl R 2.5s, 7ft, 2M. Red starboard-hand beacon with topmark.
BANC DE LA DOUANE LIGHT, S side, 14 28.0N, 60 52.2W. V Q (3) G 5s, 7ft, 2M. Green port-hand beacon with topmark.
E SIDE LIGHT, 14 28.1N, 60 52.2W. Q (3) G 10s, 7ft, 2M. Green port-hand beacon with top-mark.

LE MARIN

14 28N, 60 52W

Pilotage: There are quite a few reefs in Cul-de-Sac Marin, but the clear water and good aids to navigation should make the approach easy. There are three conspicuous chimneys west of town, and a light is shown from Pointe du Marin. Because of the shoals, an approach

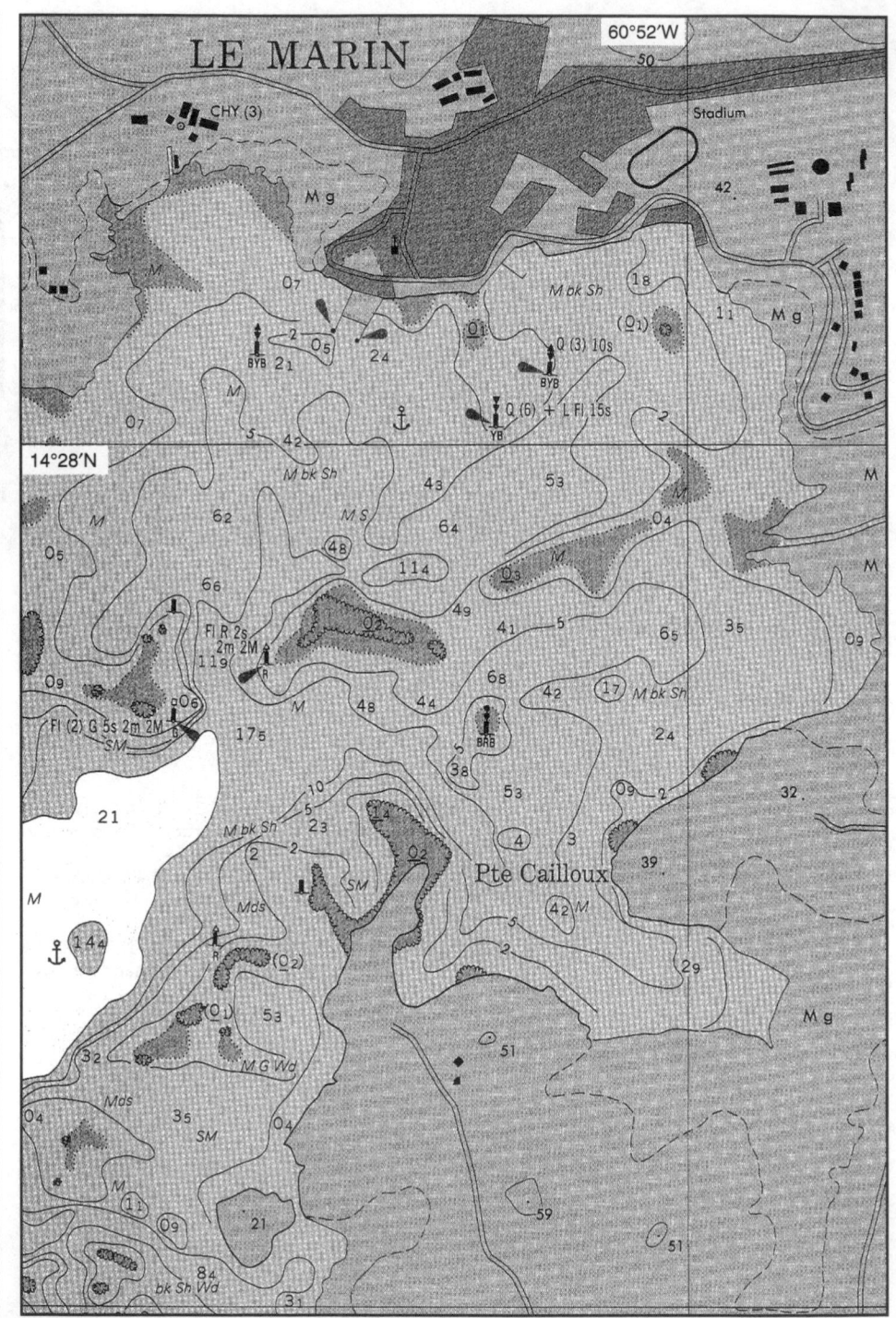

Le Marin, soundings in meters *(from DMA 25524, 42nd ed, 2/89)*

in good light is recommended. There are channels to Carene Antilles and the SAEPP marina.

Port of Entry: Officials maintain office hours from 0700 to 1200.

Dockage: The SAEPP marina (596 74 85 33) is located in the lagoon at the eastern end of the waterfront. Space is apt to be tight due to the many charter operations in this area.

Anchorage: Anchor directly south of the waterfront, keeping the designated channels clear.

Services: Marin is the main base of the Martinque charter fleet, and all manner of repair facilities can be found here. Fuel and water are available at the SAEPP marina. Carene Antilles (596 74 77 70) is a large repair yard located west of the main docks. There is also a large chandlery here and for sail repair, Nautic Tech Care (596 74 74 64). Nearby is the Marine Paint Factory (596 74 84 14). Another sailmaker is La Voilerie du Marin (596 74 73 10), which also does laundry. Captain's Ship Chandlery (596-74-87-55) is another source of marine hardware. There is a good selection of supermarkets and general shops ashore.

The harbor of this small city offers good shelter and is a good alternative to busy Fort-de-France.

MARTINIQUE, EAST COAST

BAIE TRINITE RANGE (Front Light), 14 45.2N, 60 58.2W. Iso W 4s, 20ft, 8M. White structure. **(Rear Light)** 284.2° from front. Iso W 4s, 23ft, 8M. White structure.

LA CARAVELLE LIGHT, 14 46.2N, 60 53.1W. Fl (3) W 15s, 423ft, 10M. Yellow square tower, white lantern. Visible 113°–345°.

BAIE DU FRANCOIS DIRECTIONAL LIGHT, 14 38.0N, 60 53.7W. Dir Q W R G, 108ft, 8M white, 6M red, 6M green. White tower, green top. R 200°–245°, W 245°–248°, G 248°–280°; white sector indicates preferred channel.

PORT VAUCLIN LIGHT, N point, 14 33.0N, 60 50.4W. Q W R G, 46ft, 11M white, 9M red, 9M green. R 220°–230°, W 230°–232°, G 232°–250°.

DIQUE EST LIGHT, head, 14 32.7N, 60 50.1W. Fl G 2.5s, 13ft, 2M. White tower, green top.

EPI OUEST LIGHT, Head, 14 32.8N, 60 50.1W. Fl R 2.5s, 10ft, 2M. White tower, red top.

PORT VAUCLIN DIRECTIONAL LIGHT, 305°, 14 26.0N, 60 49.8W. Dir Q W R G, 10M white, 7M red, 7M green. White pole. R 291°–304°, W 304°–306°, G 306°–319°.

ILET CABRIT LIGHT, N part, 14 23.4N, 60 52.3W. Fl R 5s, 138ft, 16M. Red pylon, hexagonal base. Visible 235°–106° and 107°–108°.

FORT-DE-FRANCE, MARTINIQUE

HIGH & LOW WATER 1995   14°35'N   61°03'W

ATLANTIC STANDARD TIME (GMT -4H)

JANUARY

Day	Time	ft	Day	Time	ft
1 Su ●	1402 / 2222	2.2 / 0.9	16 M ○	1352 / 2221	2.0 / 1.1
2 M	1450 / 2303	2.2 / 1.0	17 Tu	1432 / 2250	2.0 / 1.1
3 Tu	0652 / 0835 / 1538 / 2343	1.6 / 1.6 / 2.1 / 1.0	18 W	0657 / 0810 / 1514 / 2319	1.6 / 1.6 / 2.0 / 1.1
4 W	0711 / 0957 / 1627	1.7 / 1.6 / 2.0	19 Th	0646 / 0944 / 1601 / 2348	1.7 / 1.6 / 1.9 / 1.2
5 Th	0019 / 0735 / 1121 / 1718	1.1 / 1.7 / 1.6 / 1.9	20 F	0656 / 1105 / 1653	1.7 / 1.6 / 1.9
6 F	0053 / 0802 / 1251 / 1813	1.2 / 1.7 / 1.6 / 1.8	21 Sa	0016 / 0715 / 1228 / 1754	1.2 / 1.7 / 1.5 / 1.8
7 Sa	0123 / 0832 / 1431 / 1918	1.3 / 1.8 / 1.6 / 1.7	22 Su	0044 / 0741 / 1354 / 1908	1.3 / 1.8 / 1.5 / 1.7
8 Su (	0147 / 0905 / 1613 / 2049	1.3 / 1.8 / 1.5 / 1.5	23 M	0111 / 0813 / 1521 / 2045	1.4 / 1.9 / 1.4 / 1.6
9 M	0203 / 0939 / 1740 / 2308	1.4 / 1.9 / 1.4 / 1.5	24 Tu)	0134 / 0851 / 1642 / 2252	1.4 / 1.9 / 1.3 / 1.5
10 Tu	0200 / 1015 / 1845	1.5 / 1.9 / 1.3	25 W	0151 / 0935 / 1751	1.5 / 2.0 / 1.2
11 W	1051 / 1935	2.0 / 1.2	26 Th	1023 / 1851	2.1 / 1.1
12 Th	1126 / 2015	2.0 / 1.1	27 F	1114 / 1944	2.1 / 1.0
13 F	1202 / 2050	2.0 / 1.1	28 Sa	1207 / 2032	2.1 / 1.0
14 Sa	1237 / 2122	2.1 / 1.1	29 Su	1300 / 2117	2.2 / 1.0
15 Su	1314 / 2152	2.1 / 1.0	30 M ●	0503 / 0628 / 1353 / 2158	1.6 / 1.6 / 2.1 / 1.0
			31 Tu	0514 / 0756 / 1445 / 2236	1.6 / 1.6 / 2.1 / 1.1

FEBRUARY

Day	Time	ft	Day	Time	ft
1 W	0534 / 0912 / 1537 / 2311	1.7 / 1.6 / 2.0 / 1.2	16 Th	0459 / 0908 / 1519 / 2238	1.7 / 1.6 / 1.9 / 1.3
2 Th	0557 / 1026 / 1630 / 2342	1.7 / 1.6 / 1.9 / 1.2	17 F	0514 / 1015 / 1615 / 2306	1.8 / 1.6 / 1.9 / 1.3
3 F	0624 / 1141 / 1725	1.8 / 1.5 / 1.8	18 Sa	0535 / 1122 / 1715 / 2332	1.8 / 1.5 / 1.8 / 1.4
4 Sa	0009 / 0653 / 1259 / 1825	1.3 / 1.8 / 1.5 / 1.7	19 Su	0602 / 1231 / 1824 / 2357	1.9 / 1.4 / 1.7 / 1.5
5 Su	0030 / 0725 / 1422 / 1938	1.4 / 1.9 / 1.4 / 1.6	20 M	0635 / 1343 / 1945	1.9 / 1.4 / 1.7
6 M	0044 / 0759 / 1546 / 2123	1.5 / 1.9 / 1.4 / 1.5	21 Tu	0020 / 0714 / 1458 / 2127	1.5 / 2.0 / 1.3 / 1.6
7 Tu (	0041 / 0836 / 1702	1.5 / 2.0 / 1.3	22 W	0037 / 0800 / 1610 / 2356	1.6 / 2.1 / 1.2 / 1.6
8 W	0915 / 1804	2.0 / 1.3	23 Th	0851 / 1718	2.1 / 1.2
9 Th	0955 / 1853	2.0 / 1.3	24 F	0948 / 1819	2.1 / 1.2
10 F	1037 / 1933	2.0 / 1.2	25 Sa	1049 / 1913	2.1 / 1.1
11 Sa	1120 / 2008	2.0 / 1.2	26 Su	1151 / 2002	2.1 / 1.2
12 Su	1204 / 2040	2.0 / 1.2	27 M	0319 / 0555 / 1252 / 2045	1.7 / 1.7 / 2.1 / 1.2
13 M	1250 / 2111	2.0 / 1.2	28 Tu	0336 / 0719 / 1352 / 2124	1.7 / 1.6 / 2.1 / 1.3
14 Tu	0516 / 0620 / 1338 / 2140	1.7 / 1.7 / 2.0 / 1.2			
15 W ○	0454 / 0756 / 1427 / 2209	1.7 / 1.6 / 2.0 / 1.2			

MARCH

Day	Time	ft	Day	Time	ft
1 W ●	0358 / 0832 / 1451 / 2159	1.8 / 1.6 / 2.0 / 1.3	16 Th ○	0320 / 0832 / 1437 / 2120	1.8 / 1.6 / 1.9 / 1.4
2 Th	0422 / 0940 / 1548 / 2229	1.8 / 1.5 / 1.9 / 1.4	17 F	0338 / 0931 / 1539 / 2149	1.9 / 1.5 / 1.9 / 1.5
3 F	0448 / 1044 / 1647 / 2255	1.9 / 1.5 / 1.9 / 1.5	18 Sa	0401 / 1028 / 1642 / 2216	1.9 / 1.5 / 1.9 / 1.6
4 Sa	0516 / 1148 / 1747 / 2315	1.9 / 1.5 / 1.8 / 1.5	19 Su	0429 / 1126 / 1749 / 2241	2.0 / 1.4 / 1.8 / 1.6
5 Su	0546 / 1252 / 1855 / 2328	2.0 / 1.4 / 1.7 / 1.6	20 M	0502 / 1226 / 1903 / 2304	2.1 / 1.3 / 1.8 / 1.7
6 M	0618 / 1357 / 2021 / 2329	2.0 / 1.4 / 1.7 / 1.6	21 Tu	0541 / 1328 / 2028 / 2324	2.1 / 1.3 / 1.7 / 1.7
7 Tu	0651 / 1502	2.0 / 1.4	22 W	0625 / 1432 / 2215 / 2336	2.2 / 1.3 / 1.7 / 1.7
8 W	0727 / 1605	2.0 / 1.3	23 Th)	0715 / 1536	2.2 / 1.2
9 Th (	0807 / 1701	2.1 / 1.3	24 F	0812 / 1639	2.2 / 1.2
10 F	0851 / 1750	2.0 / 1.3	25 Sa	0917 / 1738	2.1 / 1.3
11 Sa	0941 / 1833	2.0 / 1.3	26 Su	0125 / 0325 / 1028 / 1831	1.8 / 1.8 / 2.1 / 1.3
12 Su	1036 / 1911	2.0 / 1.3	27 M	0141 / 0514 / 1141 / 1918	1.8 / 1.7 / 2.1 / 1.4
13 M	1135 / 1946	2.0 / 1.3	28 Tu	0202 / 0641 / 1253 / 2000	1.8 / 1.7 / 2.0 / 1.4
14 Tu	0311 / 0612 / 1236 / 2019	1.8 / 1.7 / 2.0 / 1.4	29 W	0225 / 0754 / 1402 / 2036	1.9 / 1.6 / 2.0 / 1.5
15 W	0310 / 0729 / 1337 / 2050	1.8 / 1.7 / 2.0 / 1.4	30 Th ●	0251 / 0858 / 1508 / 2107	1.9 / 1.5 / 1.9 / 1.6
			31 F	0318 / 0956 / 1613 / 2132	2.0 / 1.5 / 1.9 / 1.6

APRIL

Day	Time	ft	Day	Time	ft
1 Sa	0346 / 1051 / 1718 / 2152	2.0 / 1.4 / 1.8 / 1.7	16 Su	0304 / 1031 / 1719 / 2114	2.1 / 1.3 / 1.8 / 1.7
2 Su	0415 / 1144 / 1827 / 2205	2.1 / 1.4 / 1.8 / 1.7	17 M	0339 / 1123 / 1830 / 2139	2.2 / 1.3 / 1.8 / 1.8
3 M	0444 / 1235 / 1949 / 2205	2.1 / 1.3 / 1.8 / 1.7	18 Tu	0417 / 1216 / 1947 / 2202	2.2 / 1.2 / 1.8 / 1.8
4 Tu	0514 / 1325	2.1 / 1.3	19 W	0459 / 1310 / 2114 / 2221	2.2 / 1.2 / 1.8 / 1.8
5 W	0546 / 1415	2.1 / 1.3	20 Th	0546 / 1405	2.2 / 1.2
6 Th	0620 / 1503	2.1 / 1.3	21 F)	0639 / 1500 / 2326	2.2 / 1.2 / 1.8
7 F	0658 / 1550	2.1 / 1.4	22 Sa	0739 / 1555 / 2344	2.2 / 1.3 / 1.8
8 Sa (	0743 / 1636	2.1 / 1.4	23 Su	0226 / 0849 / 1648	1.8 / 2.1 / 1.4
9 Su	0841 / 1719	2.0 / 1.4	24 M	0007 / 0421 / 1011 / 1737	1.9 / 1.8 / 2.0 / 1.4
10 M	0148 / 0342 / 0953 / 1800	1.8 / 1.8 / 2.0 / 1.4	25 Tu	0032 / 0556 / 1139 / 1820	1.9 / 1.7 / 1.9 / 1.5
11 Tu	0128 / 0540 / 1114 / 1839	1.8 / 1.8 / 1.9 / 1.5	26 W	0058 / 0713 / 1305 / 1858	2.0 / 1.6 / 1.9 / 1.6
12 W	0134 / 0655 / 1234 / 1915	1.9 / 1.7 / 1.9 / 1.5	27 Th	0126 / 0816 / 1426 / 1929	2.0 / 1.5 / 1.9 / 1.7
13 Th	0148 / 0755 / 1350 / 1948	1.9 / 1.6 / 1.9 / 1.6	28 F	0154 / 0912 / 1542 / 1955	2.1 / 1.4 / 1.8 / 1.7
14 F	0209 / 0849 / 1501 / 2019	2.0 / 1.5 / 1.9 / 1.6	29 Sa ●	0224 / 1001 / 1656 / 2013	2.1 / 1.4 / 1.8 / 1.8
15 Sa ○	0234 / 0940 / 1610 / 2048	2.0 / 1.4 / 1.9 / 1.7	30 Su	0253 / 1047 / 1814 / 2022	2.2 / 1.3 / 1.9 / 1.8

TIME MERIDIAN 60°W   0000h is midnight, 1200h is noon.

Heights in feet are referenced to the chart datum of soundings.

FORT-DE-FRANCE, MARTINIQUE

HIGH & LOW WATER 1995 14°35'N 61°03'W

ATLANTIC STANDARD TIME (GMT -4H)

MAY

Day	Time	ft	Day	Time	ft
1 M	0322 / 1131	2.2 / 1.3	16 Tu	0303 / 1114 / 1922 / 2021	2.3 / 1.2 / 1.8 / 1.8
2 Tu	0351 / 1212	2.2 / 1.3	17 W	0345 / 1201	2.3 / 1.1
3 W	0420 / 1251	2.2 / 1.3	18 Th	0430 / 1249	2.3 / 1.2
4 Th	0450 / 1329	2.2 / 1.3	19 F	0519 / 1336 / 2145 / 2325	2.3 / 1.2 / 1.9 / 1.9
5 F	0523 / 1407	2.1 / 1.3	20 Sa	0612 / 1423 / 2209	2.2 / 1.3 / 1.9
6 Sa	0600 / 1446	2.1 / 1.4	21 Su ☽	0113 / 0714 / 1508 / 2236	1.9 / 2.1 / 1.4 / 1.9
7 Su ☾	0647 / 1525 / 2358	2.0 / 1.4 / 1.9	22 M	0308 / 0828 / 1551 / 2304	1.8 / 2.0 / 1.5 / 2.0
8 M	0236 / 0751 / 1604 / 2352	1.9 / 2.0 / 1.5 / 1.9	23 Tu	0456 / 1002 / 1631 / 2333	1.7 / 1.9 / 1.6 / 2.0
9 Tu	0446 / 0921 / 1644	1.8 / 1.9 / 1.5	24 W	0623 / 1149 / 1705	1.6 / 1.8 / 1.6
10 W	0002 / 0610 / 1107 / 1722	2.0 / 1.7 / 1.8 / 1.6	25 Th	0004 / 0730 / 1336 / 1733	2.1 / 1.5 / 1.8 / 1.7
11 Th	0021 / 0711 / 1249 / 1759	2.0 / 1.6 / 1.8 / 1.6	26 F	0036 / 0825 / 1517 / 1753	2.2 / 1.4 / 1.8 / 1.8
12 F	0045 / 0803 / 1419 / 1833	2.1 / 1.5 / 1.8 / 1.7	27 Sa	0107 / 0912 / 1710	2.2 / 1.4 / 1.8
13 Sa	0114 / 0852 / 1539 / 1904	2.1 / 1.4 / 1.8 / 1.8	28 Su	0138 / 0955	2.3 / 1.4
14 Su ○	0147 / 0939 / 1654 / 1932	2.2 / 1.3 / 1.8 / 1.8	29 M ●	0209 / 1034	2.3 / 1.3
15 M	0224 / 1027 / 1807 / 1958	2.3 / 1.2 / 1.8 / 1.8	30 Tu	0239 / 1110	2.3 / 1.3
			31 W	0309 / 1144	2.3 / 1.3

JUNE

Day	Time	ft	Day	Time	ft
1 Th	0339 / 1216	2.3 / 1.3	16 F	0414 / 1225 / 2011 / 2227	2.4 / 1.3 / 1.9 / 1.9
2 F	0411 / 1248	2.2 / 1.3	17 Sa	0504 / 1305 / 2035	2.3 / 1.3 / 2.0
3 Sa	0446 / 1319	2.2 / 1.4	18 Su	0000 / 0559 / 1343 / 2103	1.9 / 2.2 / 1.4 / 2.0
4 Su	0526 / 1351 / 2210	2.1 / 1.4 / 2.0	19 M ☽	0142 / 0701 / 1419 / 2133	1.9 / 2.1 / 1.5 / 2.1
5 M	0106 / 0617 / 1424 / 2214	1.9 / 2.0 / 1.5 / 2.0	20 Tu	0331 / 0820 / 1450 / 2206	1.8 / 2.0 / 1.6 / 2.1
6 Tu ☾	0315 / 0728 / 1457 / 2231	1.9 / 1.9 / 1.5 / 2.0	21 W	0511 / 1008 / 1515 / 2240	1.7 / 1.9 / 1.7 / 2.2
7 W	0458 / 0914 / 1530 / 2254	1.8 / 1.9 / 1.6 / 2.1	22 Th	0630 / 1224 / 1528 / 2316	1.6 / 1.8 / 1.8 / 2.3
8 Th	0612 / 1122 / 1602 / 2323	1.7 / 1.8 / 1.7 / 2.2	23 F	0730 / 2351	1.5 / 2.3
9 F	0708 / 1324 / 1631 / 2356	1.5 / 1.8 / 1.8 / 2.3	24 Sa	0818	1.5
10 Sa	0758 / 1512 / 1655	1.4 / 1.8 / 1.8	25 Su	0026 / 0900	2.4 / 1.4
11 Su	0033 / 0845	2.3 / 1.3	26 M	0100 / 0937	2.4 / 1.4
12 M	0113 / 0931	2.4 / 1.2	27 Tu ●	0133 / 1011	2.4 / 1.4
13 Tu ○	0156 / 1016	2.4 / 1.2	28 W	0206 / 1042	2.4 / 1.4
14 W	0240 / 1100	2.4 / 1.2	29 Th	0239 / 1111	2.4 / 1.4
15 Th	0326 / 1143 / 1954 / 2058	2.4 / 1.2 / 1.9 / 1.9	30 F	0313 / 1140	2.4 / 1.4

JULY

Day	Time	ft	Day	Time	ft
1 Sa	0350 / 1208 / 2020 / 2209	2.3 / 1.5 / 2.0 / 2.0	16 Su	0502 / 1230 / 1926	2.3 / 1.6 / 2.2
2 Su	0431 / 1236 / 2019 / 2350	2.3 / 1.5 / 2.1 / 2.0	17 M	0023 / 0600 / 1300 / 1957	2.0 / 2.2 / 1.7 / 2.2
3 M	0519 / 1304 / 2032	2.2 / 1.6 / 2.1	18 Tu	0154 / 0706 / 1325 / 2031	1.9 / 2.1 / 1.8 / 2.3
4 Tu	0130 / 0619 / 1332 / 2053	2.0 / 2.1 / 1.6 / 2.2	19 W ☽	0330 / 0833 / 1344 / 2108	1.9 / 2.0 / 1.9 / 2.3
5 W ☾	0311 / 0741 / 1358 / 2121	1.9 / 2.0 / 1.7 / 2.2	20 Th	0459 / 1039 / 1346 / 2147	1.8 / 1.9 / 1.9 / 2.4
6 Th	0440 / 0936 / 1422 / 2155	1.8 / 1.9 / 1.8 / 2.3	21 F	0612 / 2227	1.7 / 2.5
7 F	0552 / 1159 / 1438 / 2234	1.7 / 1.9 / 1.9 / 2.4	22 Sa	0709 / 2307	1.6 / 2.5
8 Sa	0650 / 2317	1.6 / 2.5	23 Su	0754 / 2346	1.6 / 2.5
9 Su	0742	1.5	24 M	0833	1.6
10 M	0002 / 0830	2.5 / 1.4	25 Tu	0025 / 0907	2.5 / 1.5
11 Tu	0050 / 0915	2.6 / 1.4	26 W	0103 / 0938	2.5 / 1.5
12 W ○	0139 / 0958	2.6 / 1.3	27 Th	0141 / 1007	2.5 / 1.6
13 Th	0228 / 1039 / 1817 / 2017	2.6 / 1.4 / 2.0 / 2.0	28 F	0221 / 1034 / 1825 / 2017	2.5 / 1.6 / 2.1 / 2.1
14 F	0318 / 1119 / 1835 / 2138	2.5 / 1.4 / 2.1 / 2.0	29 Sa	0303 / 1101 / 1821 / 2138	2.4 / 1.6 / 2.2 / 2.1
15 Sa	0409 / 1156 / 1859 / 2258	2.4 / 1.5 / 2.1 / 2.0	30 Su	0348 / 1127 / 1830 / 2253	2.4 / 1.7 / 2.2 / 2.1
			31 M	0438 / 1153 / 1848	2.3 / 1.8 / 2.2

AUGUST

Day	Time	ft	Day	Time	ft
1 Tu	0009 / 0536 / 1218 / 1912	2.0 / 2.3 / 1.8 / 2.3	16 W	0149 / 0730 / 1227 / 1928	1.9 / 2.2 / 2.0 / 2.5
2 W	0128 / 0646 / 1242 / 1942	2.0 / 2.2 / 1.9 / 2.4	17 Th ☽	0308 / 0909 / 1230 / 2007	1.9 / 2.1 / 2.1 / 2.5
3 Th	0250 / 0816 / 1303 / 2019	1.9 / 2.1 / 2.0 / 2.4	18 F	0424 / 2048	1.8 / 2.5
4 F	0409 / 1017 / 1317 / 2103	1.8 / 2.0 / 2.0 / 2.5	19 Sa	0531 / 2132	1.8 / 2.6
5 Sa	0520 / 2151	1.7 / 2.6	20 Su	0626 / 2217	1.8 / 2.6
6 Su	0621 / 2244	1.7 / 2.6	21 M	0711 / 2304	1.7 / 2.6
7 M	0716 / 2339	1.6 / 2.7	22 Tu	0750 / 2351	1.7 / 2.6
8 Tu	0805	1.6	23 W	0823	1.7
9 W	0035 / 0851 / 1627 / 1811	2.7 / 1.6 / 2.1 / 2.1	24 Th	0038 / 0853 / 1637 / 1839	2.5 / 1.8 / 2.2 / 2.2
10 Th ○	0130 / 0933 / 1638 / 1939	2.7 / 1.6 / 2.2 / 2.1	25 F	0126 / 0922 / 1629 / 1959	2.5 / 1.8 / 2.2 / 2.2
11 F	0226 / 1011 / 1658 / 2055	2.6 / 1.6 / 2.2 / 2.1	26 Sa ●	0216 / 0949 / 1634 / 2104	2.5 / 1.8 / 2.3 / 2.1
12 Sa	0321 / 1047 / 1722 / 2207	2.5 / 1.7 / 2.2 / 2.1	27 Su	0308 / 1016 / 1648 / 2206	2.5 / 1.9 / 2.3 / 2.1
13 Su	0417 / 1119 / 1749 / 2318	2.5 / 1.8 / 2.3 / 2.0	28 M	0402 / 1041 / 1707 / 2307	2.4 / 1.9 / 2.4 / 2.0
14 M	0514 / 1147 / 1819	2.4 / 1.9 / 2.4	29 Tu	0502 / 1106 / 1733	2.3 / 2.0 / 2.4
15 Tu	0032 / 0617 / 1210 / 1852	2.0 / 2.3 / 2.0 / 2.4	30 W	0010 / 0608 / 1129 / 1804	2.0 / 2.3 / 2.0 / 2.5
			31 Th	0116 / 0725 / 1151 / 1841	1.9 / 2.2 / 2.1 / 2.5

TIME MERIDIAN 60°W

0000h is midnight, 1200h is noon.

Heights in feet are referenced to the chart datum of soundings.

MARTINIQUE

FORT-DE-FRANCE, MARTINIQUE

HIGH & LOW WATER 1995　　　　　　　　　　　　　　**14°35'N　61°03'W**

ATLANTIC STANDARD TIME (GMT -4H)

SEPTEMBER

Day	Time ft	Time ft	Time ft	Time ft		Day	Time ft	Time ft	Time ft	Time ft
1 F	0225 1.8	0901 2.2	1207 2.1	1925 2.6 ☽		16 Sa	0335 1.8	1943 2.5		
2 Sa ☾	0335 1.8	1116 2.2	2016 2.6			17 Su	0432 1.8	2028 2.5		
3 Su	0442 1.7	2113 2.7				18 M	0523 1.8	2118 2.5		
4 M	0544 1.7	2216 2.7				19 Tu	0608 1.8	2215 2.5		
5 Tu	0640 1.7	2321 2.6				20 W	0648 1.8	1511 2.2	1633 2.2	2317 2.4
6 W	0731 1.7	1444 2.2	1735 2.2			21 Th	0723 1.8	1445 2.2	1822 2.2	
7 Th	0027 2.6	0816 1.7	1501 2.2	1901 2.1		22 F	0021 2.4	0755 1.9	1446 2.3	1932 2.1
8 F ○	0131 2.6	0856 1.8	1523 2.3	2015 2.1		23 Sa	0124 2.4	0825 1.9	1456 2.3	2030 2.1
9 Sa	0234 2.5	0932 1.9	1548 2.3	2122 2.0		24 Su ●	0226 2.4	0854 1.9	1513 2.3	2123 2.0
10 Su	0335 2.5	1004 1.9	1615 2.4	2225 2.0		25 M	0328 2.3	0921 1.9	1534 2.4	2216 1.9
11 M	0436 2.4	1032 2.0	1645 2.4	2327 1.9		26 Tu	0431 2.3	0946 2.0	1601 2.5	2309 1.8
12 Tu	0540 2.3	1054 2.1	1716 2.5			27 W	0537 2.2	1010 2.1	1633 2.5	
13 W	0029 1.9	0650 2.2	1110 2.1	1750 2.5		28 Th	0004 1.7	0648 2.2	1033 2.1	1710 2.6
14 Th	0131 1.8	0814 2.2	1116 2.1	1825 2.5		29 F	0101 1.7	0810 2.2	1053 2.1	1752 2.6
15 F	0234 1.8	1902 2.6				30 Sa	0200 1.7	0950 2.2	1106 2.2	1840 2.6

OCTOBER

Day	Time ft	Time ft	Time ft	Time ft		Day	Time ft	Time ft	Time ft	Time ft
1 Su ☾	0301 1.6	1936 2.6				16 M	0326 1.6	1918 2.3		
2 M	0402 1.6	2040 2.5				17 Tu	0410 1.7	2011 2.3		
3 Tu	0500 1.7	1248 2.2	1459 2.2	2152 2.5		18 W	0452 1.7	1316 2.1	1600 2.1	2123 2.2
4 W	0555 1.7	1305 2.2	1651 2.1	2309 2.4		19 Th	0531 1.7	1306 2.1	1749 2.1	2248 2.2
5 Th	0644 1.8	1328 2.2	1821 2.0			20 F	0608 1.8	1312 2.2	1859 2.0	
6 F	0027 2.4	0728 1.8	1353 2.3	1935 1.9		21 Sa	0016 2.1	0643 1.8	1325 2.2	1953 1.9
7 Sa	0142 2.3	0820 1.9	1420 2.3	2040 1.9		22 Su	0137 2.1	0715 1.9	1345 2.3	2042 1.7
8 Su ○	0253 2.3	0906 2.0	1448 2.4	2139 1.8		23 M	0251 2.1	0745 1.9	1409 2.3	2129 1.6
9 M	0402 2.2	0929 2.0	1518 2.4	2233 1.7		24 Tu ●	0401 2.1	0813 1.9	1438 2.4	2216 1.5
10 Tu	0510 2.2	0944 2.1	1549 2.5	2326 1.7		25 W	0510 2.1	0839 2.0	1512 2.4	2304 1.5
11 W	0621 2.1	1621 2.5				26 Th	0620 2.0	0903 2.0	1549 2.5	2353 1.4
12 Th	0017 1.6	0744 2.1	0948 2.1	1653 2.5		27 F	0735 2.0	0926 2.0	1630 2.5	
13 F	0106 1.6	1726 2.5				28 Sa	0044 1.4	0900 2.0	1716 2.5	
14 Sa	0154 1.6	1759 2.4				29 Su	0135 1.4	1806 2.4		
15 Su	0241 1.6	1836 2.4				30 M ☾	0228 1.4	1048 2.0	1157 2.0	1904 2.4
						31 Tu	0320 1.5	1108 2.0	1356 2.0	2012 2.3

NOVEMBER

Day	Time ft	Time ft	Time ft	Time ft		Day	Time ft	Time ft	Time ft	Time ft
1 W	0412 1.5	1132 2.1	1551 1.9	2134 2.2		16 Th	0335 1.5	1131 2.0	1651 1.9	2039 1.9
2 Th	0500 1.6	1158 2.1	1731 1.9	2306 2.1		17 F	0410 1.6	1141 2.0	1813 1.8	2235 1.8
3 F	0545 1.7	1226 2.1	1851 1.7			18 Sa	0444 1.6	1159 2.1	1909 1.6	
4 Sa	0039 2.0	0624 1.7	1256 2.2	1956 1.6		19 Su	0029 1.8	0518 1.7	1222 2.1	1956 1.5
5 Su	0208 2.0	0658 1.8	1327 2.2	2053 1.5		20 M	0208 1.7	0549 1.7	1250 2.2	2040 1.4
6 M	0329 2.0	0725 1.9	1358 2.3	2144 1.4		21 Tu	0334 1.8	0619 1.8	1322 2.2	2124 1.3
7 Tu ○	0448 1.9	0746 1.9	1430 2.3	2231 1.4		22 W ●	0453 1.8	0645 1.8	1358 2.3	2209 1.2
8 W	0610 1.9	0756 1.9	1502 2.3	2315 1.3		23 Th	1438 2.3	2253 1.1		
9 Th	1534 2.3	2357 1.3				24 F	1519 2.3	2338 1.1		
10 F	1605 2.3					25 Sa	1604 2.3			
11 Sa	0036 1.3	1635 2.3				26 Su	0024 1.1	1652 2.3		
12 Su	0114 1.4	1707 2.2				27 M	0109 1.2	0911 1.8	1100 1.8	1745 2.2
13 M	0150 1.4	1740 2.2				28 Tu	0154 1.2	0934 1.8	1242 1.8	1844 2.1
14 Tu	0225 1.4	1820 2.1				29 W	0238 1.3	1001 1.9	1433 1.8	☾ 1956 1.9
15 W ☽	0300 1.5	1134 2.0	1440 1.9	1914 2.0		30 Th	0319 1.4	1030 1.9	1622 1.7	2126 1.8

DECEMBER

Day	Time ft	Time ft	Time ft	Time ft		Day	Time ft	Time ft	Time ft	Time ft
1 F	0358 1.5	1101 2.0	1754 1.5	2316 1.7		16 Sa	0254 1.4	1030 1.9	1803 1.5	2248 1.6
2 Sa	0432 1.6	1134 2.0	1905 1.4			17 Su	0320 1.5	1058 2.0	1857 1.4	
3 Su	0110 1.9	0501 1.6	1209 2.1	2004 1.3		18 M	0108 1.5	0340 1.5	1131 2.0	1944 1.2
4 M	0300 1.7	0520 1.7	1243 2.1	2053 1.2		19 Tu	1208 2.1	2028 1.1		
5 Tu	1318 2.2	2138 1.2				20 W	1248 2.2	2112 1.0		
6 W ○	1352 2.2	2219 1.1				21 Th ●	1331 2.2	2155 1.0		
7 Th	1425 2.2	2256 1.1				22 F	1416 2.2	2238 1.0		
8 F	1457 2.2	2331 1.1				23 Sa	1503 2.2	2319 1.0		
9 Sa	1528 2.1					24 Su	0722 1.7	0837 1.7	1551 2.1	
10 Su	0003 1.1	1559 2.1				25 M	0000 1.0	0737 1.7	1005 1.7	1642 2.1
11 M	0033 1.2	1632 2.0				26 Tu	0040 1.1	0800 1.7	1134 1.6	1737 2.0
12 Tu	0103 1.2	1708 1.9				27 W	0118 1.2	0827 1.7	1309 1.6	1839 1.8
13 W	0131 1.2	0946 1.8	1300 1.8	1751 1.8		28 Th	0152 1.3	0858 1.8	1451 1.7	☾ 1955 1.7
14 Th	0159 1.3	0952 1.8	1504 1.7	1853 1.7		29 F	0223 1.3	0932 1.9	1631 1.4	2135 1.6
15 F ☽	0227 1.4	1008 1.8	1650 1.6	2032 1.6		30 Sa	0249 1.4	1009 1.9	1756 1.3	2347 1.5
						31 Su	0304 1.5	1047 2.0	1902 1.2	

TIME MERIDIAN 60°W　　　　　　　　　　　　　　0000h is midnight, 1200h is noon.
Heights in feet are referenced to the chart datum of soundings.

　　　　　　　REED'S NAUTICAL ALMANAC

St. Lucia

COAST PILOT

CAUTION: Our information on aids to navigation comes from official government sources. The latitudes and longitudes of these marks may not correspond to the readings from GPS receivers. Some aids have been reported as unreliable, missing, off position, or showing incorrect characteristics. No single aid to navigation, or waypoint, should be relied upon as a sole means of fixing your position.

NOTE: The chartlets in this section are not intended for navigation and are included for reference and planning purposes only. While chartlets reproduced from government sources are from the most current editions as of press time, they incorporate no corrections to navigational aids, depths, or hazards since the edition publication date.

ENTRY PROCEDURES

With France, England, and the Caribs battling for control of St. Lucia for three hundred years, the island has a dramatic history. St. Lucia was an English colony until it gained independence in 1979. It remains a member nation of the British Commonwealth. See *Reed's Nautical Companion* for an illustration of the country flag.

Ports of Entry are Rodney Bay, Castries, Marigot, and Vieux Fort. Fees are now charged at all ports of entry: navigational aids, EC$15 to 750 tons; practique, EC$10 to 100 tons; clearance, EC$5 to 40 feet, EC$15 greater than 40 feet; port fee, EC$30 per boat. Yachts on charter pay an additional EC$20 to 40 feet, EC$30 between 41 and 70 feet, and EC$40 greater than 70 feet.

In Rodney Bay customs officials (809-452-0235) are located at Rodney Bay Marina. The office is open from 0800 to 1800 every day; overtime fees are charged for after-hours, weekend, and holiday clearances.

In Castries customs officials (809-452-3487) are located on the north wharf. In Marigot contact customs at 809-451-4257. In Vieux Fort call

809-454-6074; on weekends, you will have to clear in with customs at the airport (809-454-5882). Hours of operation are usually 0800 to 1800.

You should have a clearance from your last port of call, ship's papers, and passports. A permit to moor is needed if you are planning to visit any harbors on St. Lucia other than your port of entry.

St. Lucia's currency is the Eastern Caribbean, or EC, dollar. The EC-to-US exchange rate is about .40. In other words, EC$100 = US$40. U.S. dollars are often accepted, especially in tourist areas. The telephone area code for St. Lucia is 809. The official language is English, but you will also encounter a French patois because of the proximity of French territories and the island's tumultuous history.

ST. LUCIA, WEST COAST

MARINA LIGHT, N entrance, 14 04.6N, 60 57.3W. Q G, 3ft, 2M.
MARINA LIGHT, S entrance, 14 04.6N, 60 57.2W. Q R, 3ft, 2M.
MARINA RANGE (Front Light), 14 04.6N, 60 57.0W. Fl W 15ft, 2M. **(Rear Light),** 251 meters 098.6° from front. Fl W 31ft, 2M.

RODNEY BAY

14 05N, 60 57W
Pilotage: Rodney Bay is a dredged basin off Gros Islet Bay on the northwest coast of the island. A light is shown from Foureur Islet in the approaches. There are lights at the entrance, and a range of 098.6° leads into Rodney Bay Marina. Approach depths are reported to be about 10 feet, with 6 to 12 feet in the lagoon. The tidal range averages about 0.8 foot to 1.2 feet. Call Rodney Bay Marina if you need assistance getting in.
Port of Entry: The customs office (809-452-0235) is located in Rodney Bay Marina.
Dockage: Rodney Bay Marina (809-452-0324 or VHF channel 16) has more than 230 berths and all facilities.
Anchorage: You can anchor in Rodney Bay or outside along the beach south of the channel.

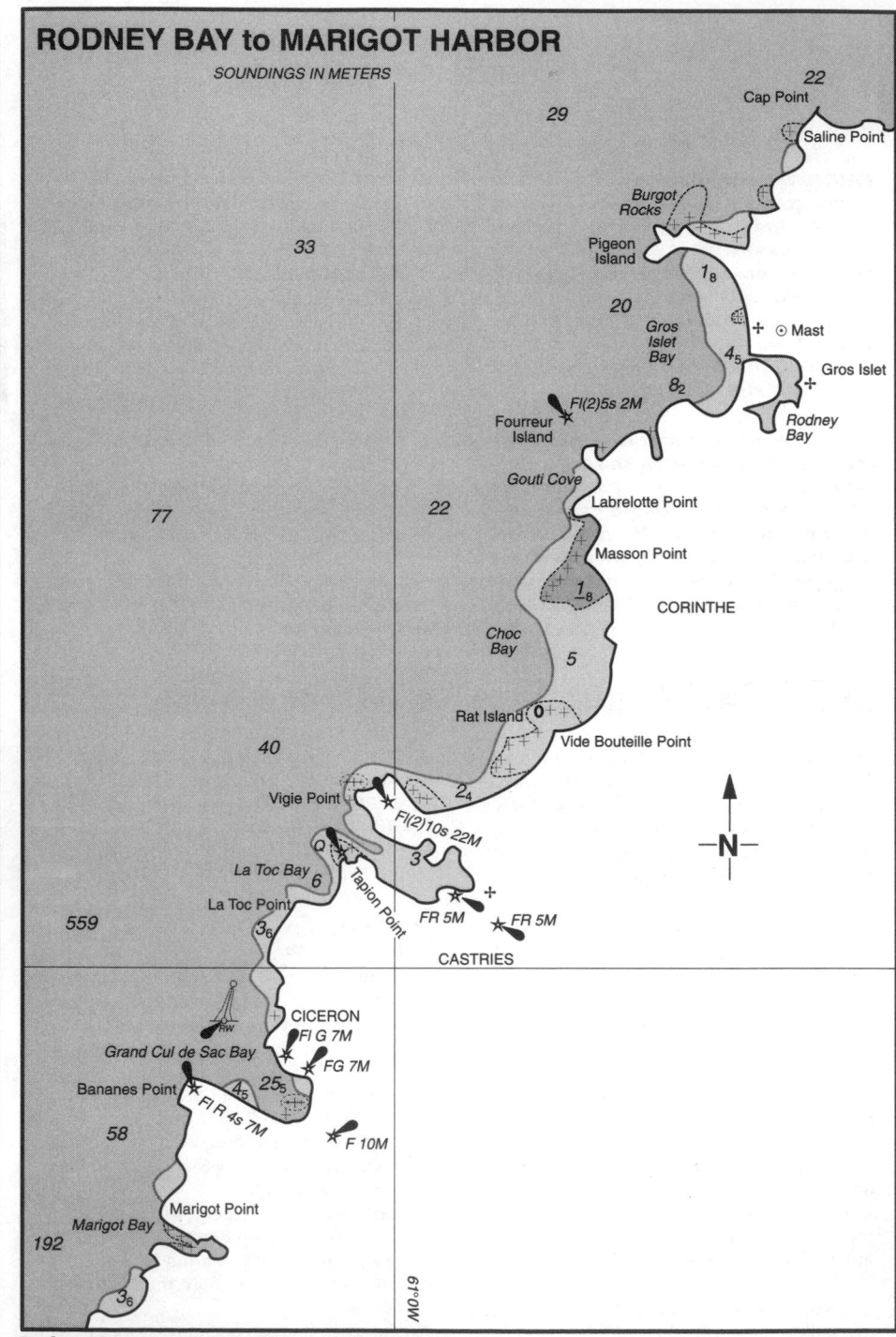

RODNEY BAY to MARIGOT HARBOR

SOUNDINGS IN METERS

22

Cap Point

Saline Point

29

Burgot
Rocks

Pigeon
Island

33

20

1₈

Gros
Islet
Bay

4₅

+ ⊙ Mast

Gros Islet

8₂

+

Rodney
Bay

Fl(2)5s 2M

Fourreur
Island

Gouti Cove

Labrelotte Point

77

22

Masson Point

1₈

CORINTHE

Choc
Bay

5

Rat Island O

Vide Bouteille Point

40

Vigie Point

2₄

Fl(2)10s 22M

N

3

La Toc Bay

O

6

Tapion Point

La Toc Point

FR 5M

+

FR 5M

559

3₆

CASTRIES

CICERON

Rw

Fl G 7M

Grand Cul de Sac Bay

FG 7M

Bananes Point

4₅ 25₅

Fl R 4s 7M

58

F 10M

Marigot Point

Marigot Bay

192

3₆

61°0'W

Rodney Bay to Marigot Bay, soundings in meters

Services: All marine services are available here. Rodney Bay Marina offers fuel, water, dry storage, haulouts, repairs, banking, car rental, and provisioning—all on site. Rodney Bay Ship Services Ltd. (809-452-9973 or VHF channels 16, call sign RBSS) is a major chandlery. Cay Electronics (809-452-9922) services and sells all sorts of electric and electronic devices. Sunsail (809-452-8648) specializes in servicing charter yachts, but can do repairs for anyone. There are many other marine-related services on the island that travel to Rodney Bay. Good supermarkets and general shops are nearby.

Rodney Bay is a favorite place to leave a boat while making an extended trip back home. There are good in-the-water and dry storage facilities, and the island is south of the most frequented hurricane tracks. A large charter industry has spawned an excellent variety of marine services.

FOUREUR ROCK LIGHT, 14 04.2N, 60 58.7W. Fl (2) W 5s, 23ft, 2M.

PORT OF CASTRIES

VIGIE LIGHT, summit N side of entrance to Castries, 14 01.2N, 61 00.0W. Fl (2) W 10s, 320ft, 22M. White circular masonry tower, red roof. Visible 039°–212°; partially obscured by Pigeon Island 206°–209°.
TAPION ROCK LIGHT, S side of entrance to Castries, 14 00.9N, 61 00.4W. Q W, 50ft, 8M. Old battery. Visible outside harbor 046°–192°, inside harbor 192°–287°.
AIRFIELD EXTENSION LIGHT, 14 00.9N, 61 00.1W. Q G, 14ft, 2M. On sunken barge.
WEST WHARF (Front Light), 14 00.5N, 60 59.5W. F R, 43ft, 5M. White triangle, orange stripe, on metal skeleton tower. **(Rear Light),** 740 meters 121° from front. F R, 110ft, 5M. White triangle, orange stripe, on metal skeleton tower.
NORTH WHARF LIGHT, corner of Berth No. 4 and 5, 14 00.6N, 60 59.6W. F Y, 1M.

CASTRIES

14 01N, 61 00W
Pilotage: Castries is the capital and principal commercial port on St. Lucia. On the north side of the harbor entrance Vigie Point, with Vigie Light on its summit, rises to a height of about 295 feet. To the south, Morne Fortune rises to 852 feet, with Fort Charlotte on its summit. The range of 121° should guide you in safely to the main wharf area. The pilots and port authorities (call sign, Castries Lighthouse) stand by on VHF channel 16 and 2182kHz.
Port of Entry: Proceed to the custom's wharf on North Wharf or anchor off and dinghy in. Customs may be contacted at 809-452-3487.
Dockage: There is no dockage for transients.
Anchorage: The yacht anchorage is in Vigie Yacht Harbour or to its west. Many of Castries' boating services are concentrated in the Vigie area. (Note that the shoal area off Point Serafin by the yacht harbor entrance shown on the Vigie Harbor chartlet, next page, is now reclaimed land.)
Services: St. Lucia Yacht Services (809-452-5057) in Vigie Yacht Harbour usually has fuel and water and rental cars. Several yacht services are nearby, including: International Diesel and Marine Services Ltd. (809-453-1311), A.F. Valmont Yamaha Outboards (809-452-3817), Johnsons Hardware (809-452-2392), Andrew Tyson Cabinet Maker and Joiner (809-452-5794; but usually found around Rodney Bay) Richard Cox Fiberglass Repair Specialist (809-453-2361, also usually found around Rodney Bay), and Castries Yacht Center (809-452-6234 or VHF channel 16), which has a small chandlery and a 35-ton Travelift for haulouts and repairs just west of the yacht harbor. In Castries, there are good supermarkets and general shops, and the Castries airport is right next to the yacht harbor.

GRAND CUL DE SAC BAY

CICERON POINT LIGHT, 14 00.0N, 61 01.0W. Fl G 6s, 39ft, 7M. Green square on tower.
BANANES POINT LIGHT, 13 59.0N, 61 02.0W. Fl R 4s, 85ft, 7M. Red triangle on tower.
DIRECTIONAL LIGHT, 13 59.0N, 61 01.0W. F W, 115ft, 10M.

MARIGOT

13 58N, 61 02W
Pilotage: The entrance to this bay is located about a mile south of the Hess oil terminal in Grande Cul de Sac Bay.
Port of Entry: Customs (809-451-4257) is located on the south shore of the harbor, west of the docks.
Dockage: The Moorings Marina (809-451-4357 or VHF channels 16 and 85) is in the inner harbor.
Anchorage: Anchor anywhere, avoiding the Cable Crossing at the narrow point in the harbor. The shelter is excellent, and some consider Marigot a hurricane hole.
Services: The Moorings complex features all the amenities of a modern resort including

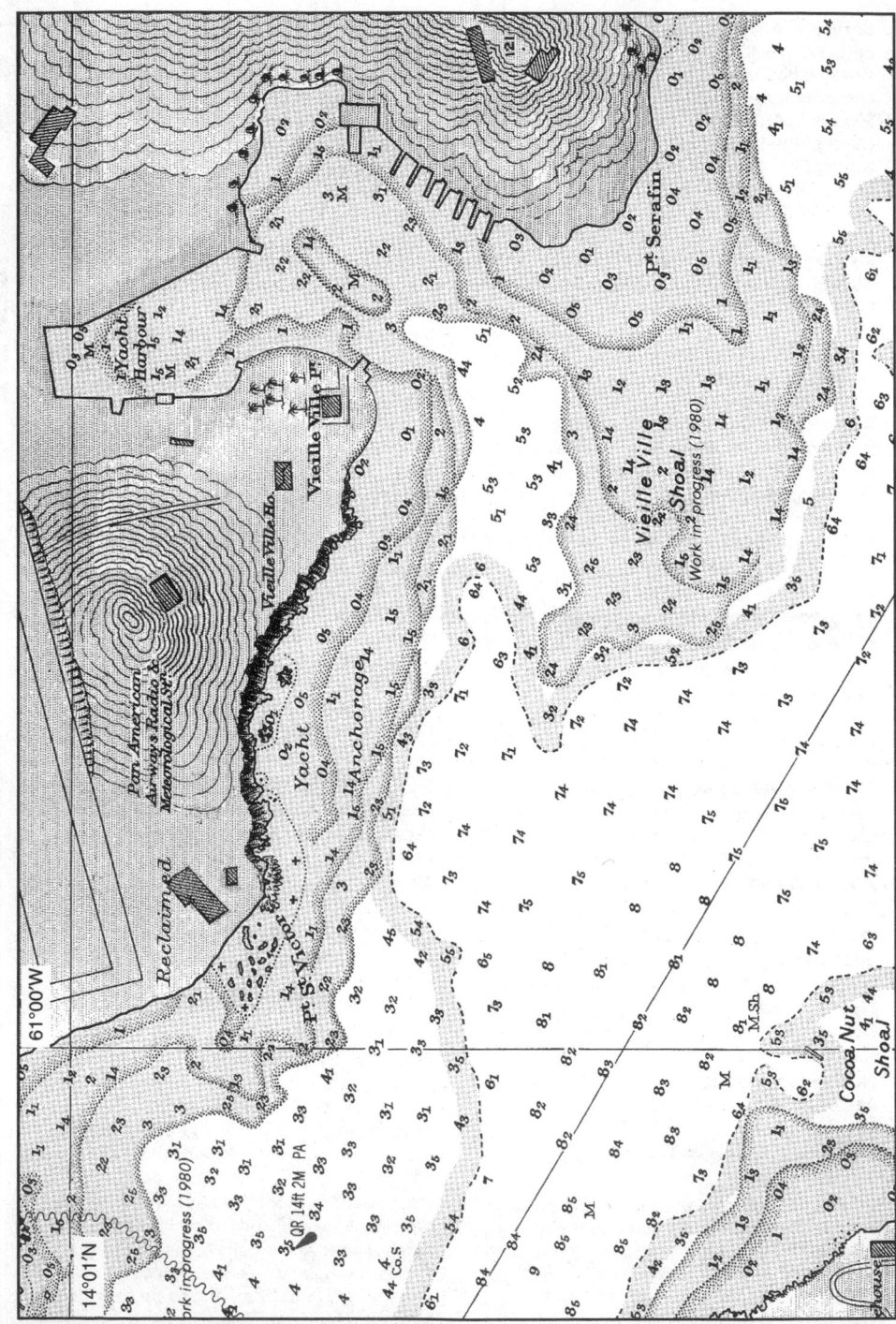

Castries, Vigie Yacht Harbour, soundings in fathoms *(from DMA 25528, 4th ed, 7/84)*

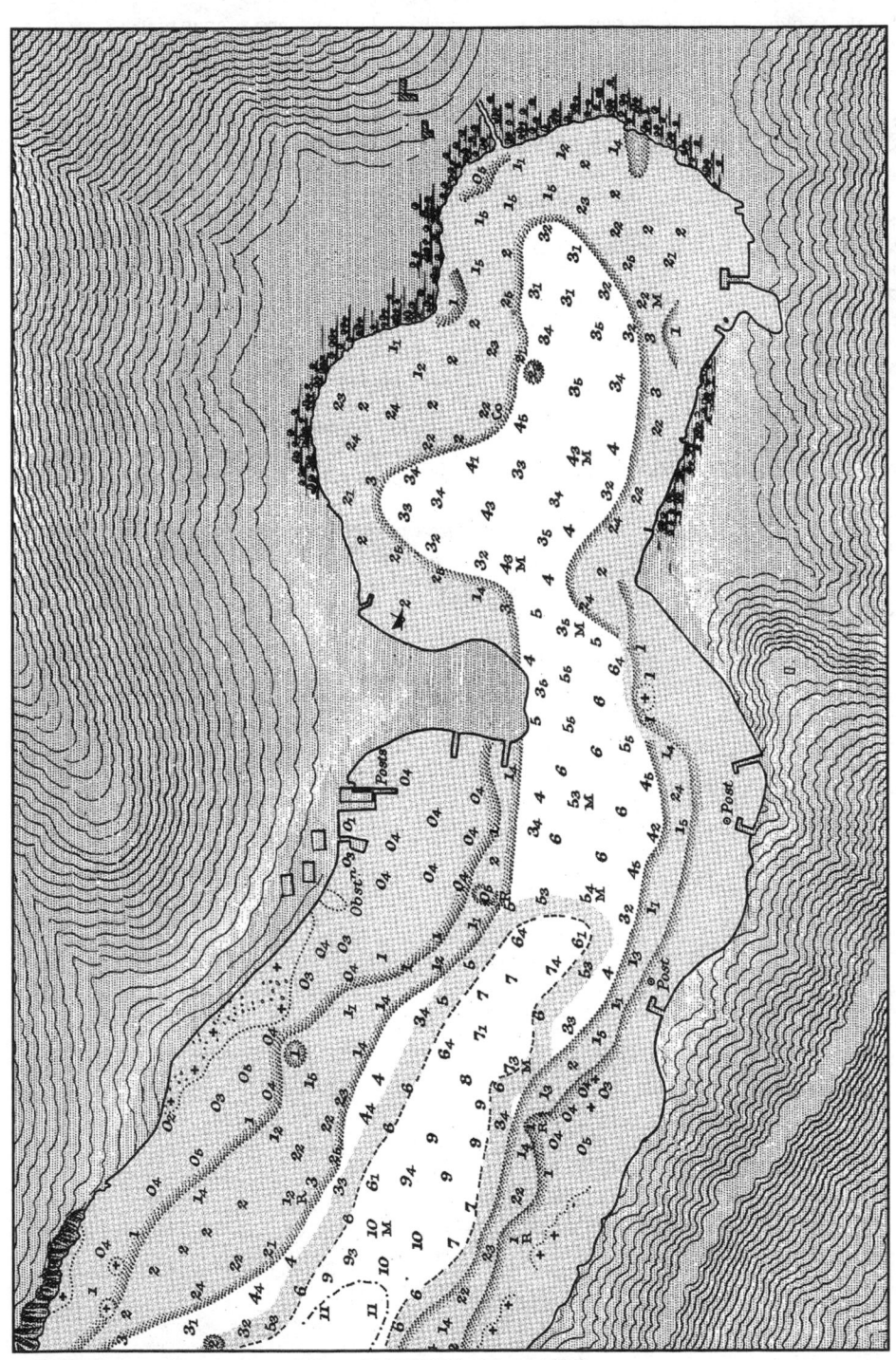

Marigot, soundings in meters *(from DMA 25528, 4th ed, 7/84)*

hotels, swimming pools, restaurants, and a dive center. There is fuel, gasoline, propane, and a commissary and laundry at the docks.

VIEUX FORT BAY

MATHURIN POINT LIGHT, 13 42.6N, 60 57.5W. Fl (2) W 5s, 16ft, 2M. Red skeleton tower, concrete base.

VIEUX FORT BAY RANGE (Front Light), head of wharf, 13 43.1N, 60 57.2W. F R, 16ft, 2M. Orange rectangle on building. **(Rear Light),** 500 meters 059.9° from front. F R, 65ft. Red metal framework tower, white bands.

NO. 1, 13 43.3N, 60 57.5W. Q G, 15ft, 5M. Green port-hand beacon.

NO. 2, 13 43.1N, 60 57.2W. Q R, 15ft, 5M. Red starboard-hand beacon.

NO. 3, 13 43.3N, 60 57.3W. Fl Y, 15ft, 5M. Yellow beacon.

NO. 4, 13 43.1N, 60 57.2W. Fl Y, 15ft, 5M. Yellow beacon.

CAPE MOULE A CHIQUE LIGHT, Brandon Point, 13 42.6N, 60 56.5W. Fl W 5s, 745ft, 19M. Masonry tower. Visible 197°–123°.

VIEUX FORT

13 43N, 60 57W

Pilotage: The town is located on the south tip of St. Lucia. Several obstructions in the bay are marked by buoys, and a range of 059.9° leads you in safely. The charted dome of the Custom House is prominent. The pilots and port officials (call sign, Vieux Fort Lighthouse) monitor VHF channel 16 and 2182kHz.

Port of Entry: Contact customs (809-454-6074) near the commercial wharf. On weekends you must clear with officials at the Vieux Fort airport (809-454-5882).

Anchorage: The recommended area is in the southeast portion of the bay, under the lee of Moule à Chique. This is south of the commercial wharf. Anchoring is prohibited in an area north of the wharf, as there are pipelines and commercial moorings in the area.

Services: There are few yacht services in Vieux Fort, but there are several restaurants and most general supplies are available. The Il Pirata Restaurant (809-454-6610) has a dock northwest of town and showers for yachtsmen.

ST. LUCIA, EAST COAST

CAPE MARQUIS LIGHT, 14 03.3N, 60 53.6W. Fl (2) W 20s, 197ft. White square support.

MOUNT TOURNEY AVIATION LIGHT, 13 44.4N, 60 57.9W. Iso R 485ft. Red skeleton tower, white bands.

MOUNT BELLEVUE AVIATION LIGHT, 13 44.4N, 60 56.7W. Al Fl W G 5s, 351ft. Beacon.

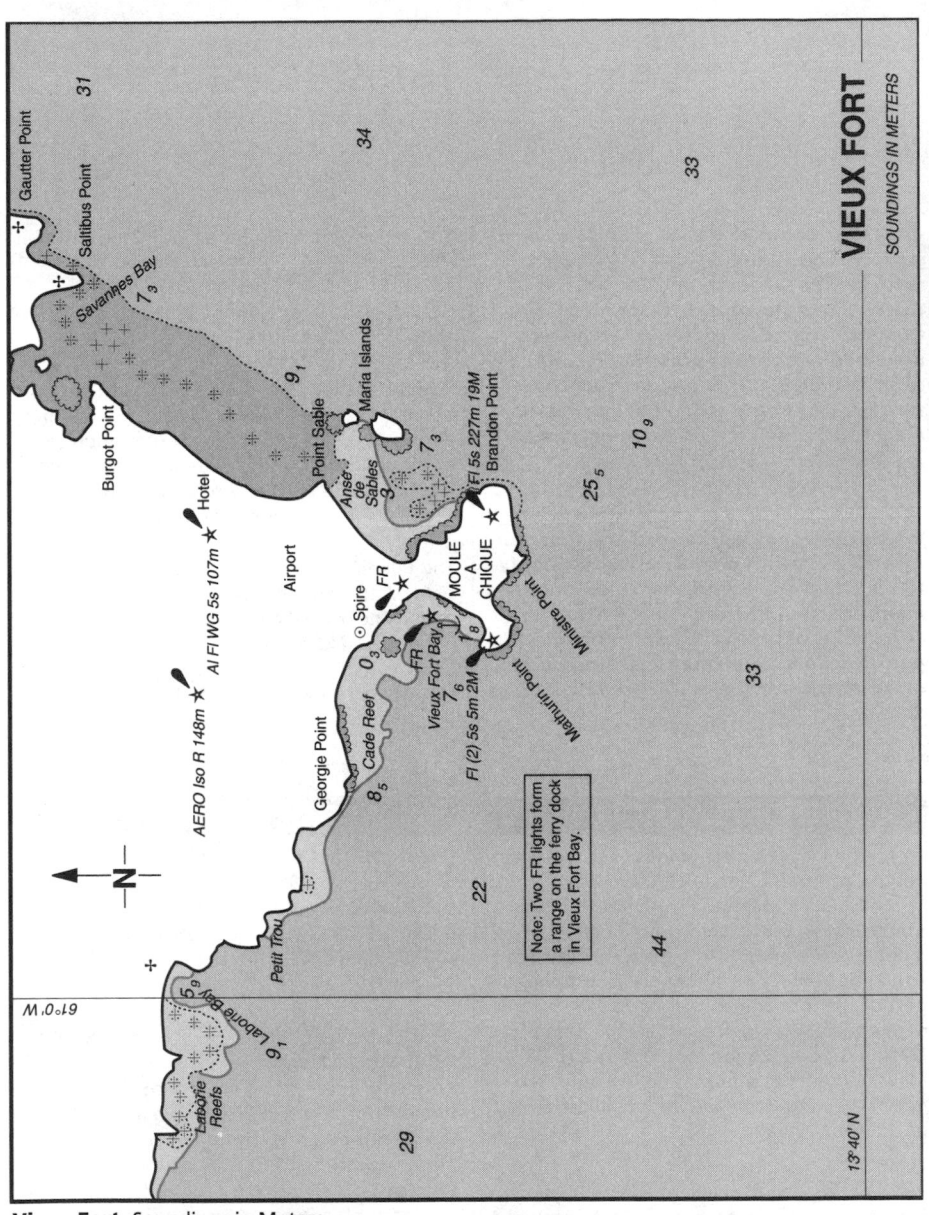

Vieux Fort, Soundings in Meters

VIEUX FORT

SOUNDINGS IN METERS

COAST PILOT

Gautter Point

Saltibus Point

Savannes Bay

7 ₃

Burgot Point

Hotel

Point Sable

Maria Islands

Anse de Sables

9 ₁

7 ₃

3

Fl 5s 227m 19M
Brandon Point

25 ₅

10 ₉

33

34

31

Al Fl WG 5s 107m

Airport

FR

MOULE
A
CHIQUE

Ministre Point

AERO Iso R 148m

⊙ Spire

FR

Vieux Fort Bay

7 ₆ *8*

Marburin Point

Georgie Point

0 ₃ Cade Reef

FR

Fl (2) 5s 5m 2M
5 2M

33

8 ₅

N

Petit Trou

Laborie Bay

5 ₉

6 ₁

Laborie
Reefs

22

Note: Two FR lights form
a range on the ferry dock
in Vieux Fort Bay.

44

29

61°0′W

13°40′N

ST. VINCENT AND THE GRENADINES

CAUTION: Our information on aids to navigation comes from official government sources. The latitudes and longitudes of these marks may not correspond to the readings from GPS receivers. Some aids have been reported as unreliable, missing, off position, or showing incorrect characteristics. No single aid to navigation, or waypoint, should be relied upon as a sole means of fixing your position.

NOTE: The chartlets in this section are <u>not</u> <u>intended for navigation</u> and are included for reference and planning purposes only. While chartlets reproduced from government sources are from the most current editions as of press time, they incorporate <u>no corrections</u> to navigational aids, depths, or hazards since the edition publication date.

You can contact customs officials in Kingstown at 809-456-1083, in Port Elizabeth at 809-457-3044, and in Clifton at 809-458-8360. Generally, hours are about 0800 to 1600 or 1800, with a break for lunch.

You should have a clearance from your last port of call, ship's papers, and passports. A cruising permit is required for further exploration within the country. There is a fee for charterboats, but no charge for pleasure vessels. There is a charge of EC$10 per person on board.

The telephone area code for all of the islands of St. Vincent is 809. Local numbers use seven digits. The official currency is the Eastern Caribbean (EC) dollar; the EC dollar is equivalent to about US$.40. Especially in tourist areas, many people also accept U.S. dollars. The official language is English.

ENTRY PROCEDURES

This nation includes the islands of St. Vincent, Bequia, Mustique, Canouan, the Tobago Cays, Union Island, and Petit St. Vincent (PSV). St. Vincent was a British colony until gaining independence in 1979. The islands of Carriacou and Petit Martinique, although geographically part of the Grenadines, belong to the nation of Grenada. All told, more than 100 islands, islets, and rocks extend for a distance of 52 miles between St. Vincent and Grenada. See *Reed's Nautical Companion* for an illustration of the country flag.

Ports of Entry on St. Vincent are Wallilabou Bay and Kingstown; on Bequia, Port Elizabeth; and on Union, Clifton. Customs also plans to extend Port of Entry status to the new Ottley Hall Marina just west of Kingstown once it officially opens in late fall 1994. It may be possible to clear on Mustique and Canouan by finding the officials at the airports. Cruisers recommend Wallilabou Bay, Port Elizabeth, and Clifton as the most convenient places to handle the clearing-in process.

ST. VINCENT

OWIA LIGHT (Cow and Calves), 13 22.3N, 61 09.0W. Fl W 10s, 118ft, 8M. White metal framework tower. Visible 101°–307°.
DARK HEAD LIGHT, 13 16.8N, 61 16.0W. Fl W 5s, 338ft, 12M. Metal framework tower. Visible 020°–211°.

WALLILABOU BAY, ST. VINCENT
13 15N, 61 17W
Pilotage: Located on the west coast of St. Vincent north of Kingstown, Wallilabou Bay can be distinguished by a radio tower near the point of land that forms its southern entrance.
Port of Entry: Customs officials here are geared to clearing in pleasure boats; Wallilabou Anchorage Restaurant will contact them on your behalf.
Moorings: Contact Wallilabou Anchorage Restaurant (809-458-7270 or VHF channel 68).
Anchorage: Because the bottom drops to depths of 35 to 50 feet right off the beach, you might hire a boat boy to take a stern line ashore. Contact the restaurant if you are in doubt about a good location.

Services: The Wallilabou Anchorage Restaurant has ice and a bar and can assist with phone calls and tours of the island in addition to customs and moorings.

KINGSTOWN, ST. VINCENT

13 09N, 61 14W
FORT CHARLOTTE LIGHT, 13 09.4N, 61 15.0W. Fl (3) W 20s, 640ft, 16M. Octagonal structure. Visible from shore to 143°. Aero Oc R (occasional) 1.5M SE of light.
KINGSTOWN WHARF LIGHT, NW end of wharf, 13 09.1N, 61 14.1W. F R. Column.
KINGSTOWN WHARF LIGHT, SE end of wharf, 13 08.9N, 61 14.0W. F R. Column.

Pilotage: Kingstown is the capital of St. Vincent and its major port. The cathedral's square white tower in the northwestern part of town is conspicuous. The clock on the tower is lighted at night. The red cupola on the police station located north of the main wharf is also conspicuous. The pilots and port authorities use call sign ZQS and monitor VHF channel 16 and 2182kHz. Entry to Blue Lagoon, about 2 miles south of Kingstown, is by a narrow dredged channel whose depth varies between 5.6 and 7.6 feet.
Port of Entry: Contact the officials (809-456-1083) in their office near the main wharf. When the new Ottley Hall Marina is officially opened (scheduled for fall 1994), the government plans to declare it a port of entry as well.
Dockage: Proceed either south to the Lagoon Marina (809-458-4308 or VHF channel 68), in the Blue Lagoon about 2 miles southeast of Kingstown, or west to the new Ottley Hall Marina (809-457-2178 or VHF 68), a major facility under construction (summer 1994) in a small bay in the shadow of Fort Charlotte.
Anchorage: Anchor north or south of the main commercial wharf. During the day strong gusts of wind may blow down St. Vincent's mountain valleys with great violence. At night the breeze will usually be light.
Services: In Kingstown you can get fuel at the fish boat dock, but it is easier at the Lagoon Marina in Blue Lagoon. Lagoon Marina also has laundry, showers, ice, and water and a scuba shop and hotel on site. The new Ottley Hall Marina expects to offer fuel, in addition to major haul-out, boat construction, and repair services. In Kingstown, St. Vincent Sales and Service (809-457-1820) is a Yamaha dealer and general chandlery. Nichols Marine (809-456-4118 or VHF channel 68) repairs starters and alternators and also handles welding. A

branch of Ross Lulley & Son (809-456-2735) offers fishing and diving gear. There is a good selection of supermarkets and general provisioning stores in Kingstown.

Although the harbor of Kingstown offers few amenities for yachtsmen, the nearby areas feature a good variety. Many boaters visit Kingstown by road or ferry, as it is more pleasant to clear customs elsewhere. The wild interior of the island is well worth a sightseeing tour or hiking trip. For general information about any of the islands, contact the main government tourist office in Kingstown (809-457-1502).

CALLIAQUA

YOUNG ISLAND CARENAGE LIGHT, 13 07.7N, 61 12.6W. Fl G 4s. Green port-hand pillar with topmark.
ROOKES POINT SHOAL LIGHT, 13 07.7N, 61 12.5W. V Q (6) and L Fl W 10s. South cardinal; yellow and black, pillar with topmark.
DUVERNETTE ISLAND LIGHT, 13 07.5N, 61 12.8W. V Q (2) W 2s, 229ft, 6M. White metal framework tower.
CALLIAQUA BAY LIGHT, 13 07.5N, 61 12.3W. Fl R 4s. Red starboard-hand mark, pillar with topmark.
BRIGHTON LIGHT, 13 07.3N, 61 10.6W. Fl W 4s, 118ft, 8M. White metal framework tower. Visible 217°–077°.

ADMIRALTY BAY, BEQUIA

DEVIL'S TABLE LIGHT, 13 00.7N, 61 15.6W. V Q (9) W 10s. West cardinal; yellow black yellow, pillar with topmark.
ADMIRALTY BAY LIGHT, root of jetty, 13 00.5N, 61 14.7W. Fl W R G 4s, 19ft, 5M. White metal framework tower. R shore–048°, W 048°–058°, G 058°–shore.
WEST CAY LIGHT, 12 59.3N, 61 18.0W. Fl W 10s, 42ft, 8M. White metal framework tower.

PORT ELIZABETH, BEQUIA

13 00N, 61 15W
Pilotage: The town of Port Elizabeth is situated near the head of Admiralty Bay, on the west coast of Bequia. A conspicuous radio mast stands south-southeast of the town. A reef, charted as Belmont Shoal, extends from the eastern shore of the bay south of the main wharf. A light is shown from the commercial wharf.

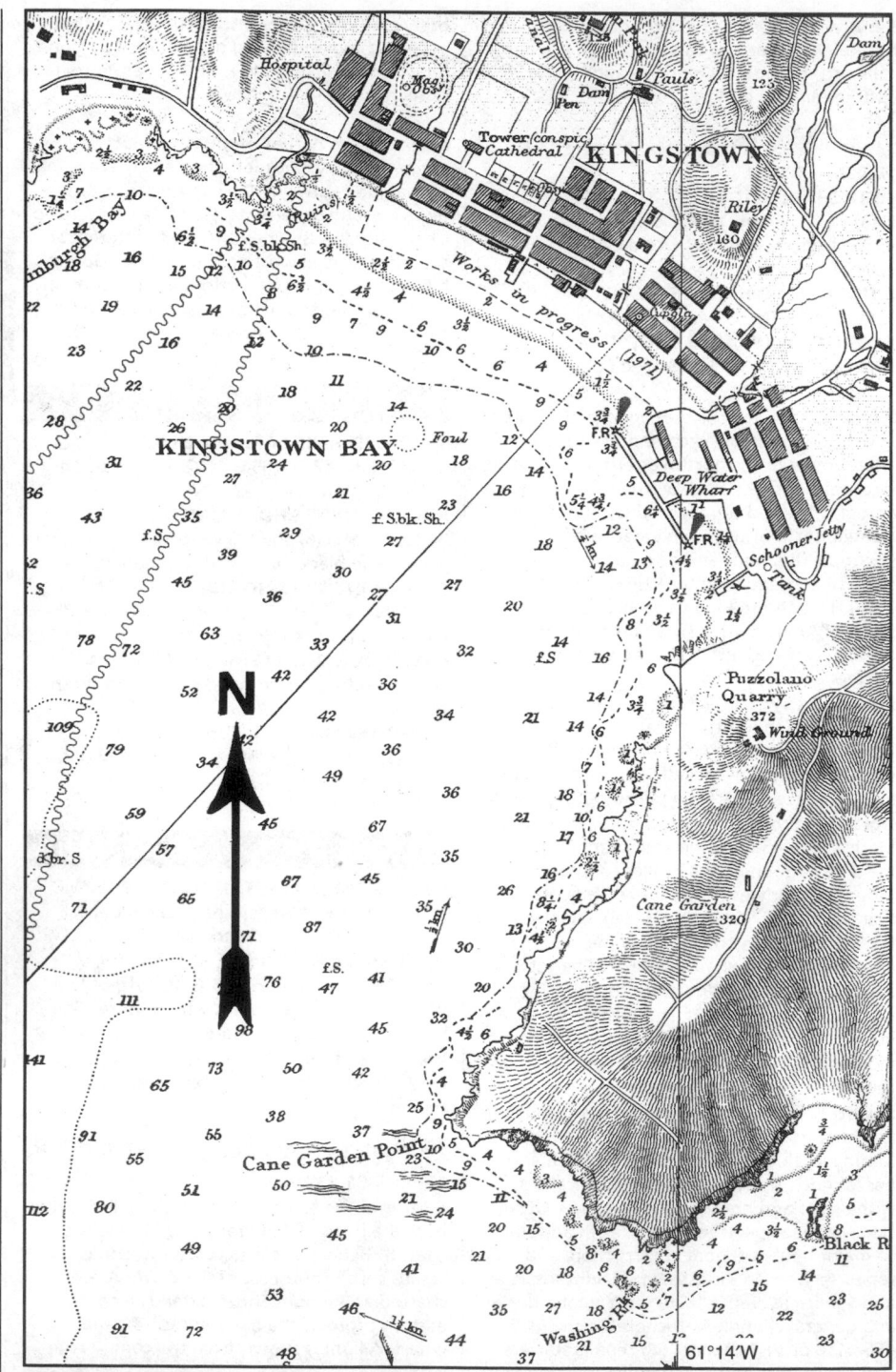

Kingstown, St. Vincent, soundings in fathoms *(from DMA 25483, 19th ed, 8/77)*

COAST PILOT

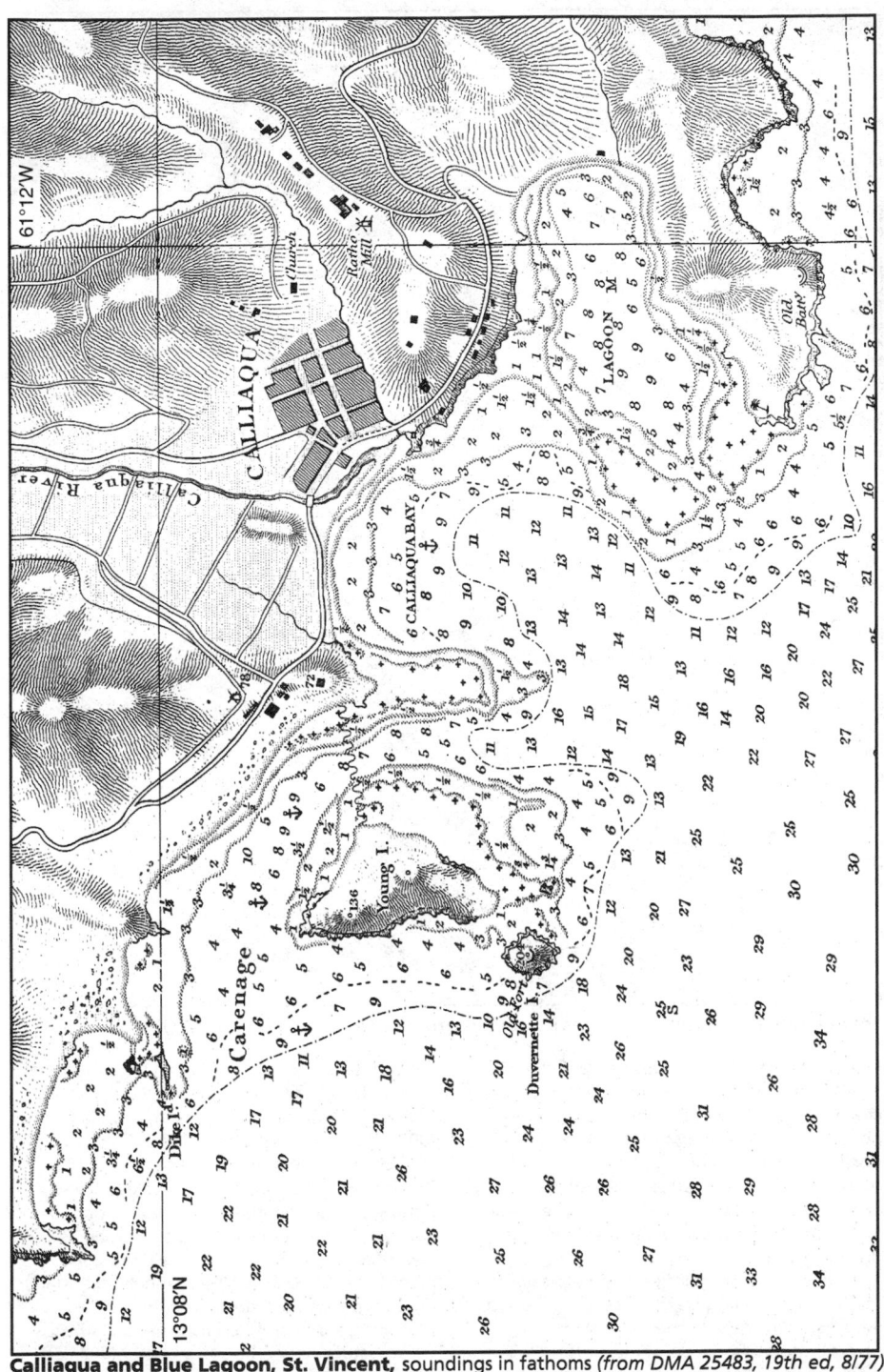

Calliaqua and Blue Lagoon, St. Vincent, soundings in fathoms *(from DMA 25483, 19th ed, 8/77)*

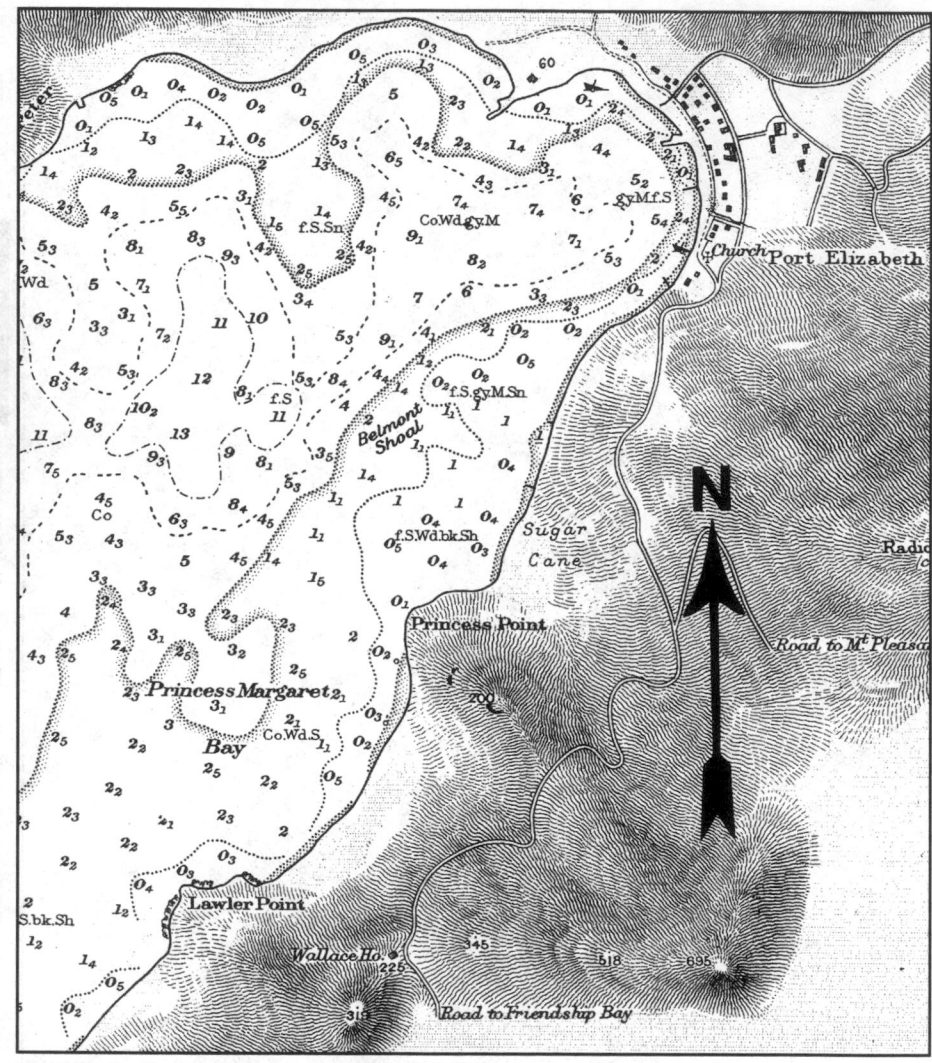

Port Elizabeth, Bequia, soundings in fathoms *(from DMA 25483, 19th ed, 8/77)*

Port of Entry: The customs office (809-457-3044) is located near the commercial wharf.

Dockage: You may be able to tie up temporarily at the Bequia Marina (809-458-3272), north of the main wharf.

Anchorage: You can anchor west of the marina or south of the commercial wharf. Check your charts carefully for the shoal areas extending out from shore.

Services: You can get diesel and water at the marina or by calling Daffodil's Marine Service (809-458-3942 or VHF channel 68), which offers a mobile service station. Daffodil's also offers mechanical and dinghy repairs and

laundry services. Sail repairs can be undertaken by North Sails (809-457-3213) and Allick Sails (809-458-3992); canvas repairs, by Bequia Canvas (809-458-3369). Sunsports (809-458-3577 or VHF channel 68) and Dive Bequia (809-458-3504 or VHF channel 68) are dive agencies. Fishing and diving gear is available from Ross Lulley & Son at two locations on Bequia (809-458-3420 or -3088). Grenadines Yacht Equipment (809-458-3347 or VHF channels 16 and 68) do all types of mechanical repairs and sell plumbing supplies and hardware, including West system epoxy. Bo'sun's Locker (809-458-3246 or -3634) is a complete chandlery. Handy

Andy's (809-458-3722 or 3370) has bike rentals, showers, and laundry, and performs boat repairs. The Bequia Bookshop (809-458-3905) stocks charts, courtesy flags, and cruising guides. There is a good variety of boutiques, restaurants, and supermarkets.

Bequia is a favorite port of call with sailors. The waters are often windy and boisterous, with gusts over 30 knots a matter of course. The gaps between some of the islands tend to funnel the wind into pockets of higher intensity. On Bequia you may be able find traditional West Indian boats being built under the trees on the beach.

BATTOWIA TO PETIT CANOUAN

BATTOWIA ISLAND LIGHT, 12 57.7N, 61 08.3W. Fl (2) W 20s, 708ft, 8M. White metal framework tower.

MUSTIQUE LIGHT, Montezuma Shoal, 12 52.7N, 61 12.5W. Fl (2) W. Isolated danger, Black red black, pillar with topmark.

PETIT CANOUAN ISLAND LIGHT, 12 47.5N, 61 17.0W. Fl (4) W 40s, 252ft, 8M. White metal framework tower.

CANOUAN

CHARLESTOWN BAY RANGE (Front Light), Canouan Island, 12 42.1N, 61 19.9W. F W, 18ft. Beacon. **(Rear Light),** 500 meters, 158° 32' from front light. F W, 165ft. Beacon.

RANGE (Front Light), marks the approach to the pier in Charlestown Bay, 12 42.7N, 61 19.5W. Iso W 4s, 46ft, 5M. Black and white square on white framework tower. Visible on rangeline only. **(Rear Light),** 60 meters, 060° from front light. Fl W 5s, 91ft, 5M. Black and white square on white framework tower. Visible on rangeline only.

CHARLESTOWN BAY PIER HEAD LIGHT, 12 42.2N, 61 19.8W, F W.

CATHOLIC ISLAND TO UNION ISLAND

CATHOLIC ISLAND, 12 39.6N, 61 24.1W. Fl (2) W 20s, 144ft., 8M, White metal framework tower.

MAYREAU, Grand Col Point, 12 38.3N, 61 24.1W. V Q (9) W, 10s. West cardinal, YBY beacon with topmark.

JONDELL, 12 39.5N, 61 23.7W. V Q (3) 5s, East cardinal. BYB beacon, topmark.

CLIFTON HARBOR RANGE (Front Light), 12 35.8N, 61 25.0W. F W, 13ft. White concrete tower. Lighted beacons mark reef and shoal. **(Rear Light),** 555 meters, 327.5° from front light. F W, 125ft. White concrete tower.

THOMPSON REEF, SE edge, 12 35.6N, 61 24.7W. Fl R. Red starboard-hand beacon with topmark.

THOMSPON REEF, SW edge, 12 34.5N, 61 24.7W. FL R. Red starboard-hand beacon with topmark.

ROUNDABOUT REEF, SW edge, 12 35.6N, 61 24.8W. Fl R. Red starboard-hand beacon with topmark.

WESTWARD, 12 35.6N, 61 25.0W. Fl G. Green port-hand beacon with topmark.

GRAND DE COI LIGHT, 12 35.1N, 61 24.9W. V Q (9) W, 10s. West cardinal, yellow black yellow; pillar with topmark.

MISS IRENE POINT LIGHT, 12 35.5N, 61 27.8W. Fl (2) W, 20s, 410ft, 8M. Metal framework tower.

CLIFTON, UNION

12 36N, 61 25W

Pilotage: Clifton lies in a bay on the southeast end of Union Island. It is protected to the east by Thompson Reef. The new buoyage leading in to the harbor is the IALA B system, indicating you should follow the "red-right-returning" rule. This may vary with what charts show. (Note: The list of navigational aids above is more accurate than shown on the Union Island chartlet; also an airport now extends from the island towards Red Island.) Copper Reef, with a ruined concrete structure on its southwest end, lies in the middle of the harbor. There may be a range of 327.5° leading safely into the harbor.

Port of Entry: Union Island is the southern check-in point for boats headed north through the Grenadines towards St. Vincent. Report to the customs (809-458-8360) and immigration officials located at the airport.

Dockage: Contact Anchorage Yacht Club (809-458-8221 or VHF channels 16 and 68).

Anchorage: There is good anchorage in most of the harbor, but take care to avoid the various reefs. Depths are from 16 to 40 feet, with a sand bottom.

Services: You can jug fuel, but water and ice is available at Anchorage Yacht Club. The marina also has a mechanic, a sailmaker, and a marine railway. There is a good selection of small shops, restaurants, and supermarkets.

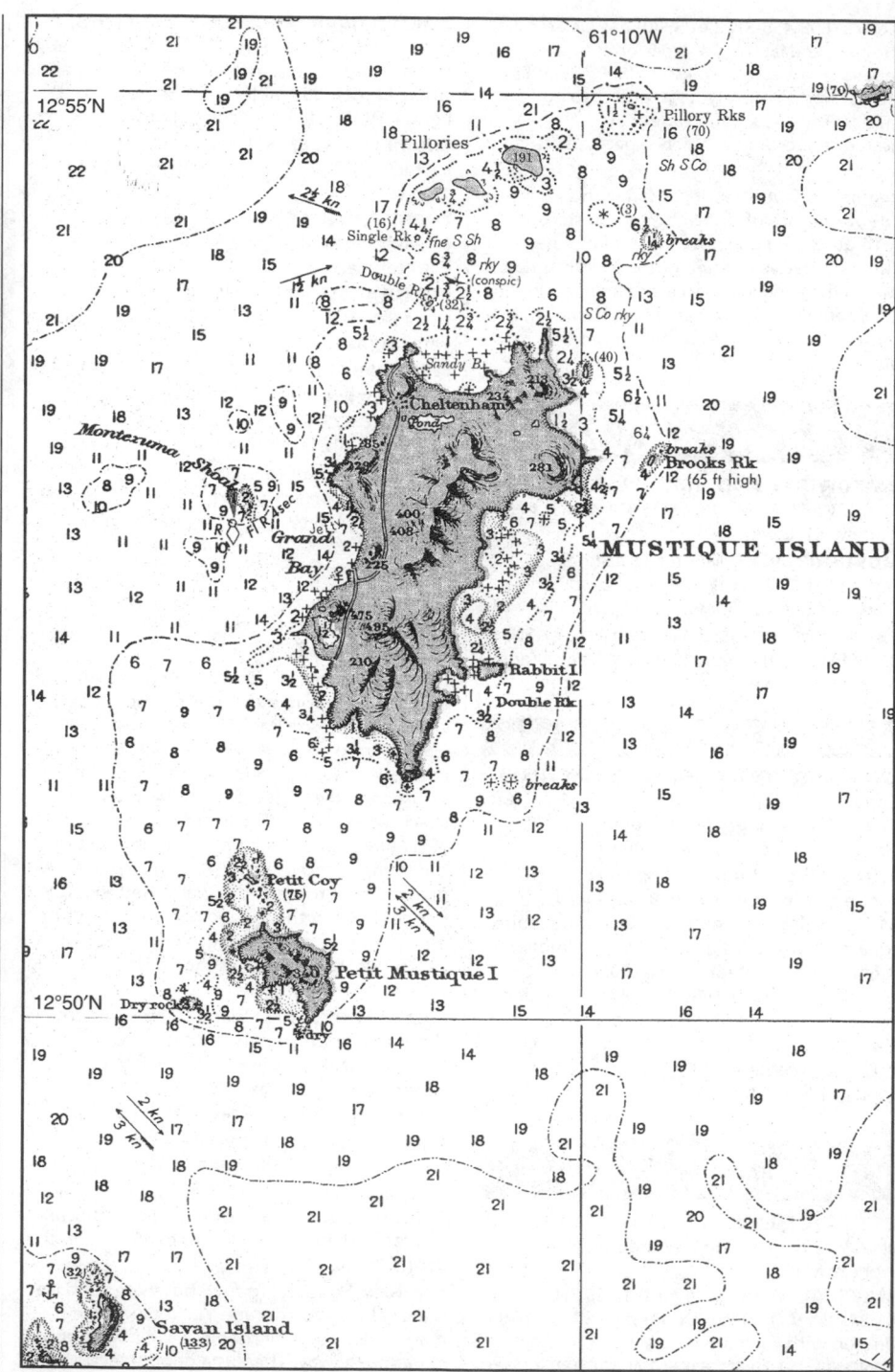

Mustique, soundings in fathoms *(from DMA 25482, 15th ed, 5/79)*

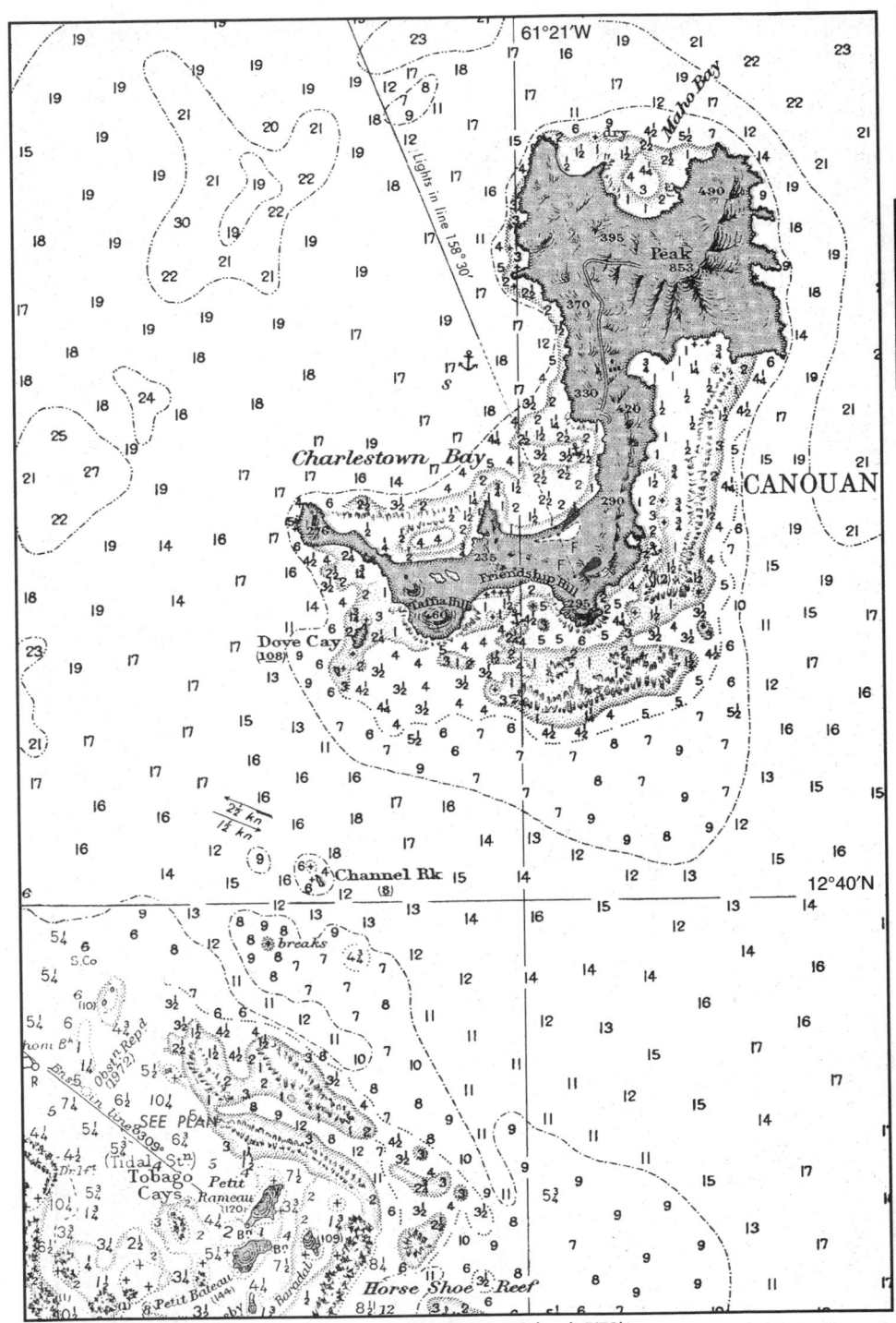

Canouan, soundings in fathoms *(from DMA 25482, 15th ed, 5/79)*

PETIT ST. VINCENT (PSV)

12 32N, 61 23W

Pilotage: Extensive reefs lie east, north, and northwest of the island. The anchorage is near the east end of the south coast of the island. Although PSV is a private resort island, yachtsmen are invited to visit. You can contact the Petit St. Vincent Resort at 809-458-8801 or on VHF channel 16.

Services: You may be able to purchase fuel from the resort in an emergency. Ice, bread, and phones are available during office hours. You can visit the bar, restaurant, and boutique, or ask about joining a hotel barbecue on the beach. Cottage rentals are available.

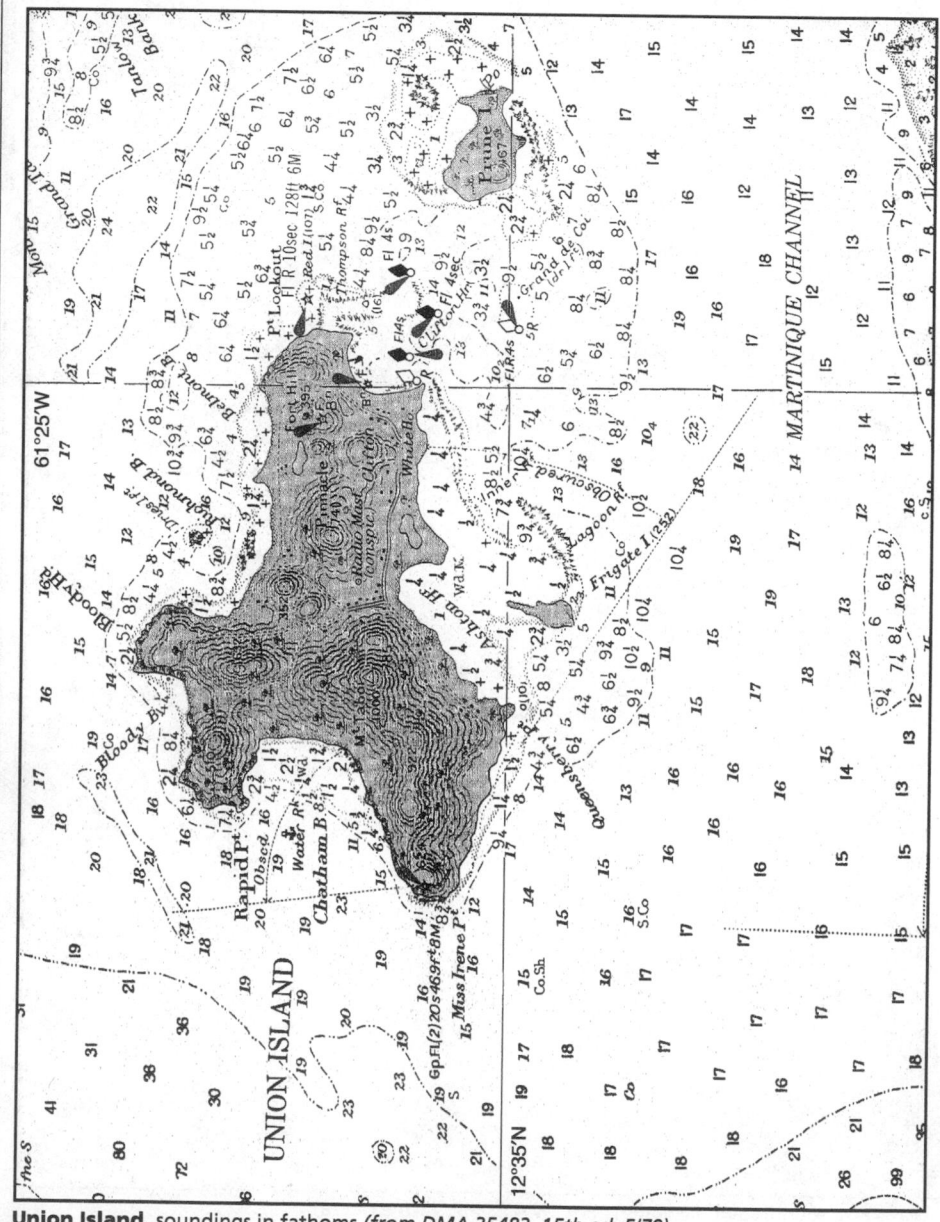

Union Island, soundings in fathoms *(from DMA 25482, 15th ed, 5/79)*

GRENADA

COAST PILOT

CAUTION: Our information on aids to navigation comes from official government sources. The latitudes and longitudes of these marks may not correspond to the readings from GPS receivers. Some aids have been reported as unreliable, missing, off position, or showing incorrect characteristics. No single aid to navigation, or waypoint, should be relied upon as a sole means of fixing your position.

NOTE: The chartlets in this section are <u>not</u> <u>intended for navigation</u> and are included for reference and planning purposes only. While chartlets reproduced from government sources are from the most current editions at press time, they incorporate <u>no corrections</u> to navigational aids, depths, or hazards since the edition publication date.

ENTRY PROCEDURES

This country includes the islands of Grenada, the two Grenadine islands of Petit Martinique and Carriacou, and Ronde Island, Isle de Caille, The Sisters, and a handful of smaller islets. Grenada was a British colony until gaining independence in 1974. After a difficult period in the early 1980s, the government today is stable, and the island is an independent nation member of the British Commonwealth. See *Reed's Nautical Companion* for an illustration of the country flag.

The Port of Entry on Carriacou is Hillsborough. Unfortunately, you cannot clear customs on nearby Petit Martinique. On Grenada, the Ports of Entry are St. George's, Prickly Bay, and Grenville. Customs office hours are about 0800 to 1600, with a break for lunch from 1200 to 1300. Contact customs in St. George's at 809-440-3270, -2239 or -2240; in Prickly Bay, at 809-444-4509.

You should have a clearance from your last port of call, ship's papers, crew lists, and passports. A coastwise clearance allows you to visit other ports in the country. Port fees range

from EC$10 for boats to 50 feet and EC$15 for boats over 50 feet. Fee amounts charged to charterboats depend on whether the boats are based in Grenada. Charterboats should contact the Port Authority in St. George's at 809-440-3013 or -3015 for the latest information. All departing boats pay an EC$15 fee. Charter fees are charged in all Ports of Entry, but on the island of Grenada other fees may not be collected, owing to a shortage of port officers.

For general information call the tourism office at 809-440-2872. This office specializes in cruise ship and yacht information.

The telephone area code for all the Grenadan islands is 809. The official currency is the Eastern Caribbean, or EC, dollar, which has an exchange rate to the U.S. dollar of about .40. Many people accept U.S. dollars, however, especially in tourist areas. The official language is English.

CARRIACOU

JACK A DAN LIGHT, 12 29.7N, 61 28.3W. Q G, 14ft, 3M. Visible 243°–182°.
SANDY ISLAND LIGHT, 12 29.2N, 61 28.7W. Q R. Red starboard-hand beacon with topmark.

HILLSBOROUGH, CARRIACOU

12 29N, 61 28W
Pilotage: Hillsborough Bay is entered between Jack a Dan and Sandy Island, both of which have lights on them. The town has a 210-foot-long jetty with a depth of about 8 feet alongside its head. A church and tower stands at the southwest end of the village.
Port of Entry: Clear here if you are headed south to Grenada or if you want to visit Petit Martinique. Obtain your coastwise clearance for proceeding south.
Moorings: The Silver Beach Resort (809-443-7337 or VHF channel 16) has free moorings and a dinghy dock.
Anchorage: The anchorage along the waterfront beach in depths of 10 to 20 feet is good.

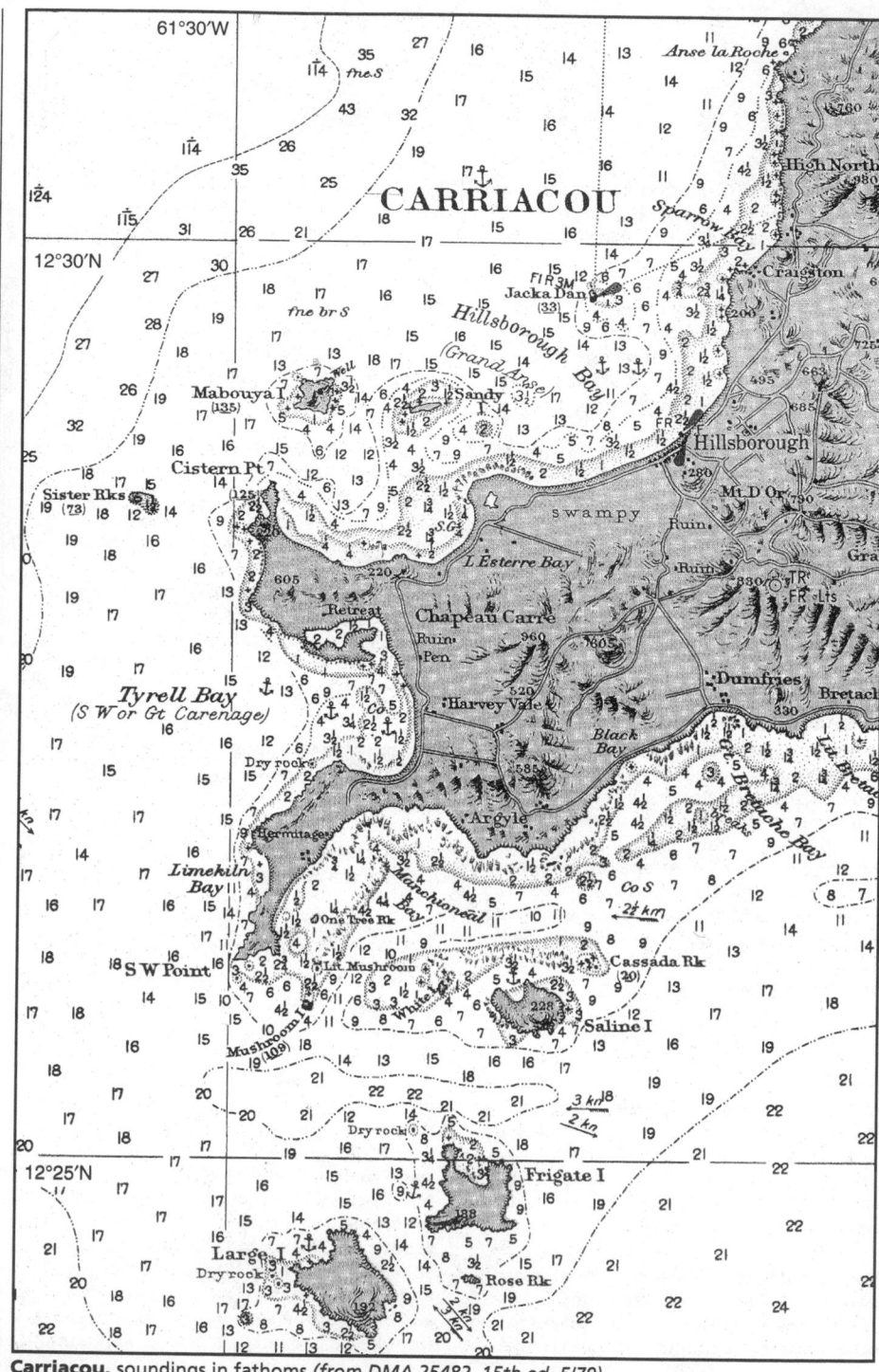

Carriacou, soundings in fathoms *(from DMA 25482, 15th ed, 5/79)*

Services: The Silver Beach Resort provides showers, laundry, a boutique, a small market, a bar and restaurant, and a liquor store. Silver Beach Diving (VHF channel 16) can take you on a dive tour. There is a good selection of small markets and restaurants.

PETITE MARTINIQUE

12 33N, 61 23W

Petit Martinique, a small island 2 1/4 miles east of the north end of Carriacou and adjacent to Petit St. Vincent, is a good place to take on fuel and water. B & C Fuels (809-443-9110 or VHF channel 16, call sign Golf Sierra) on the northwest corner of the island has a convenient dock with about 14 feet of water alongside that is easily approached into the wind.

CARRIACOU TO GRENADA

RONDE ISLAND

12 18N, 61 35W

This small islet lies about 5 miles northeast of the north coast of Grenada. Reefs fringe the shores in places and extend across the bays on its north and east sides. Yachts may be able to anchor off the northwest side of the island, north of a shoal that extends along the western coast.

ISLE DE CAILLE

12 17N, 61 35W

This small islet lies south of Ronde Island. The narrow channel between the two islands has depths of 12 to 30 feet. During strong winds the sea breaks in this channel. You may be able to anchor under the lee of the island in an emergency.

THE SISTERS

12 18N, 61 36W

The Sisters are two groups of small islets just west of Ronde Island. *CAUTION: Volcanic activity has been reported in an area about 1 3/4 miles west of The Sisters. Eruptions have been reported as recently as 1986, 1988, and 1989.*

ST. GEORGE'S APPROACHES

West Buoy, 750 meters, 251.5° from St. George's Harbour Light, 12 03N, 61 46W. Q R. Red starboard-hand mark.

East Buoy, 530 meters, 238° from St. George's Harbor Light, 12 03N, 61 46W. Q G. Green port-hand mark.

ST. GEORGE'S HARBOUR LIGHT, extremity of north bastion of Fort George Point, 12 03.0N, 61 45.3W. F R, 188ft, 15M. Brick building. Visible 056.5°–151°. Red light on tower 1 mile E.

ST. GEORGE'S RANGE (Front Light), 12 02.5N, 61 45.2W, F R, 46ft. Red square daymark, white stripe on framework tower. Red lights on radio masts 1.7 miles SW. **(Rear Light),** 28 meters, 132° from front. F R 92ft. Red triangular daymark, white stripe on framework tower.

RANGE (Front Light), 12 03.0N, 61 44.7W. F R, 102ft. Red triangular daymark, white stripe on framework tower. **(Rear Light),** 91 meters, 68°30' from front. F R, 299ft. Red square daymark, white stripe on framework tower.

ST. GEORGE'S, GRENADA

12 03N, 61 45W

Pilotage: St. George's is the capital of Grenada and the country's most important harbor. The inner part of the harbor has two basins; the small-craft facilities are located in the southern one known as the Lagoon. Two pairs of range lights are shown. The first pair, bearing 132°, lead from the north into Martins Bay. The second pair, bearing 068°, lead from Martins Bay into the inner harbor. Be careful not to cut the corner too close when turning into the channel leading to the Lagoon or you may discover Harbour Reef firsthand. You can contact Port Control (call sign J3YA) on VHF channel 16.

Port of Entry: Yachts should proceed to the Grenada Yacht Services docks in the Lagoon, where a customs office is located (809-440-3270). The main customs office can be reached at 809-440-2239 or -2240.

Dockage: Grenada Yacht Services (809-440-2508), located in the Lagoon, may have dock space.

Anchorage: The best shelter is in the Lagoon, but you can also try in the Carenage, which is very busy with commercial traffic.

Services: Grenada Yacht Services has haulout facilities, water, fuel, and some repair shops. Lagoon Marine (809-440-3381) specializes in refrigeration. There are other marine services here and in nearby Prickly Bay. Ashore you'll find a good variety of general shops, supermarkets, and restaurants.

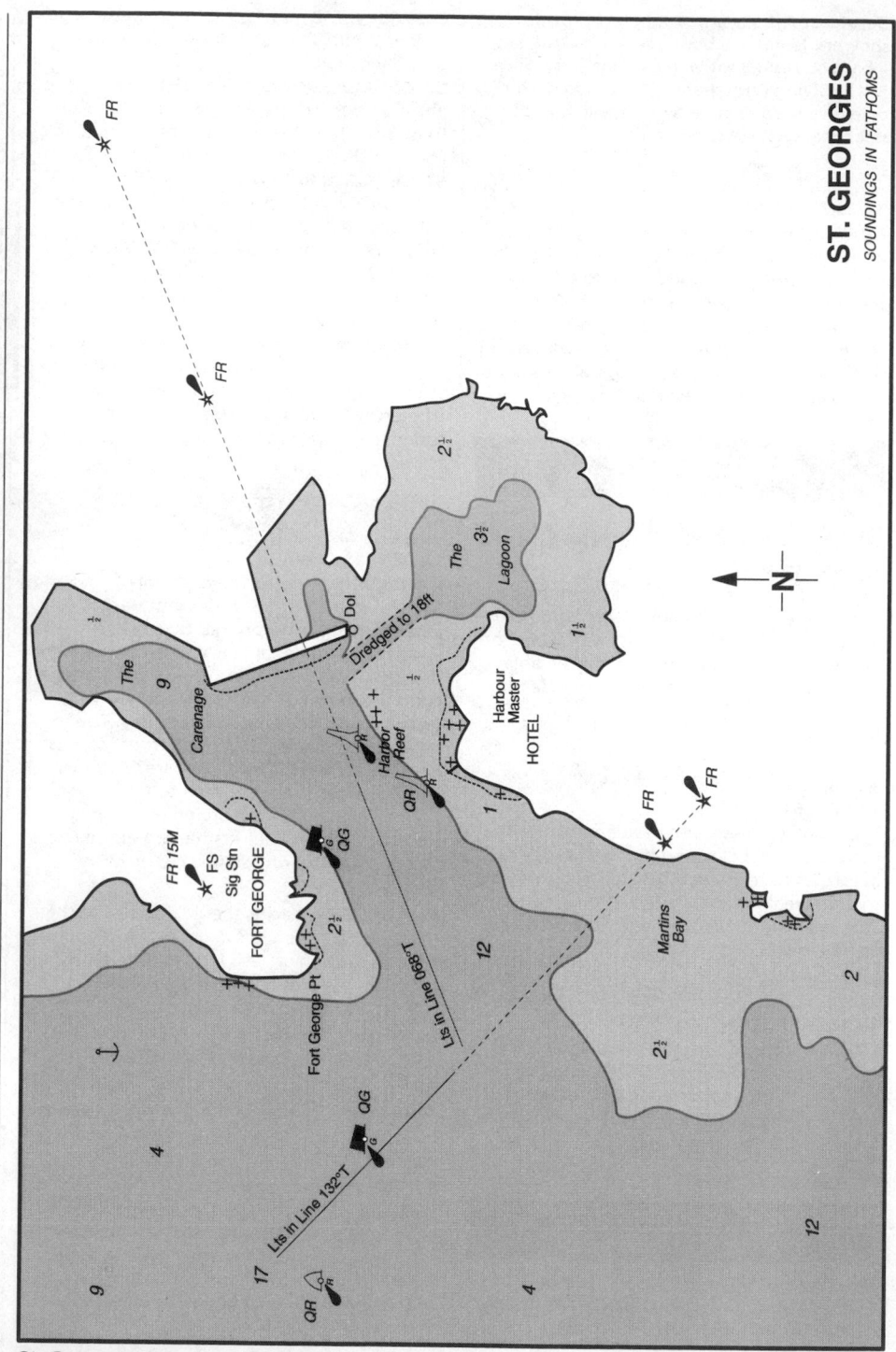

ST. GEORGES
SOUNDINGS IN FATHOMS

St. George's, soundings in fathoms

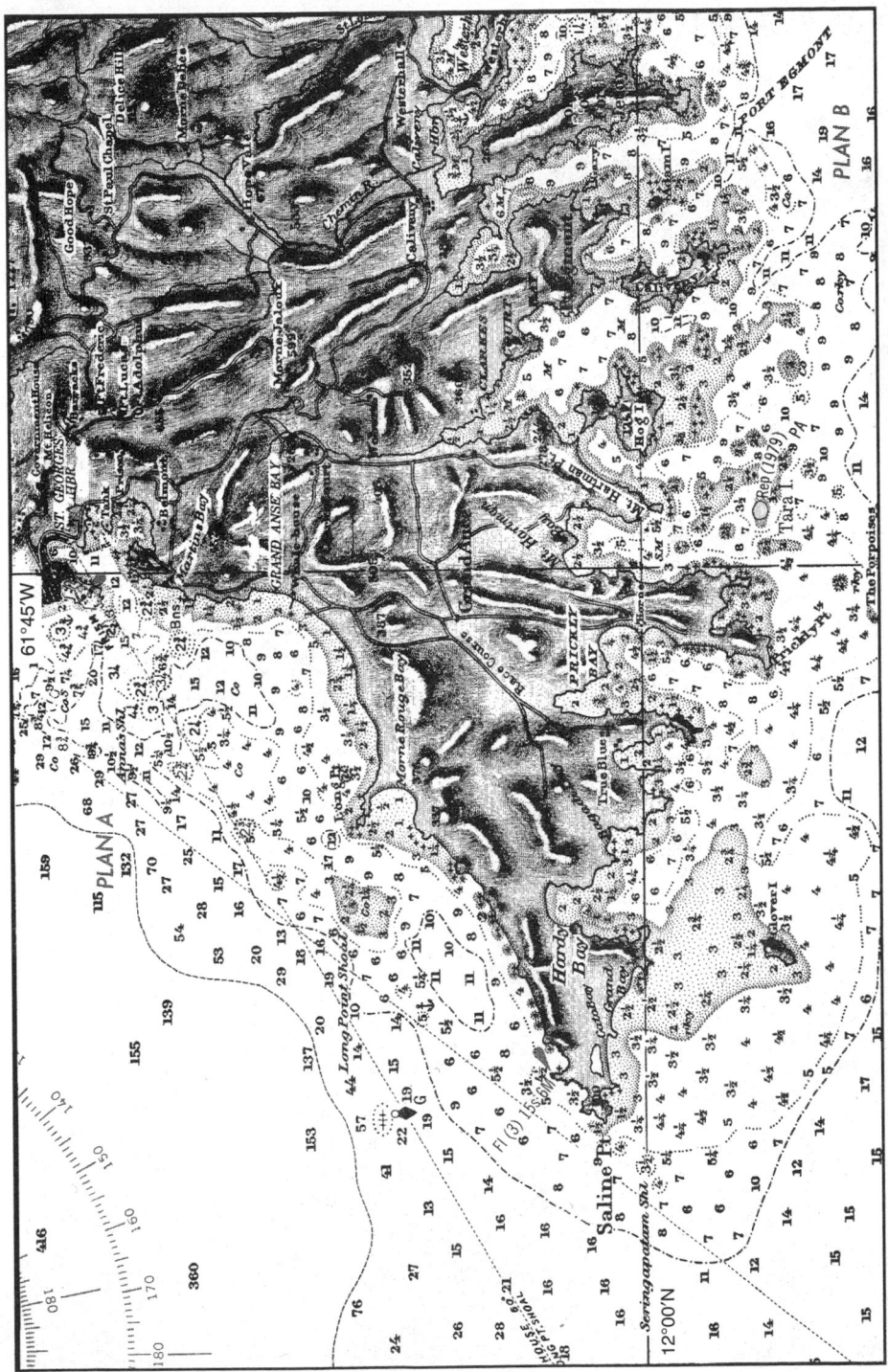

Grenada, South Coast, soundings in fathoms *(from DMA 25481, 24th ed, 11/84)*

St. George's is well sheltered and south of most hurricane tracks. The island may once again become a favorite of yachtsmen now that the political situation seems to have stabilized.

ST. GEORGE'S TO PRICKLY BAY

PETIT CABRITS LIGHT, 12 01.0N, 61 46.4W. Fl (2+1) W 20s, 354ft, 18M. Red framework tower.

POINT SALINE LIGHT, 12 00.2N, 61 47.8W. Q (9) W 15s, 7M. West cardinal.

GLOVER ISLAND LIGHT, 11 59.2N, 61 47.2W. Q (6) and L Fl W 15s, 7M. South cardinal.

PRICKLY BAY, GRENADA

12 00N, 61 46W

Pilotage: Prickly Bay is located on the south coast of Grenada, about 2 1/2 miles east of Saline Point. When traveling from St. George's to Prickly Bay be sure to stay well outside Long Point Shoal. A course of 240°T, with Ft. George Point in line with Government House (in St. George's), is reported to keep you clear of the shoal. There is a shoal spot in Prickly Bay, due west of Spice Island Marine Services.

Port of Entry: Customs officials (809-444-4509) are located at Spice Island Marine Services.

Dockage: Contact Spice Island Marine Services (809-444-4257 or -4342 or VHF channels 16 or 68 or SSB 4125kHz), on the eastern side of the bay. There is also some dockage at the True Blue Inn (809-444-2000 or VHF channel 68), in the small bay west of Prickly Bay. The Moorings Secret Harbour Marina (809-444-4549 or VHF channels 16 and 71) is located in the next cove to the east, known as Mount Hartmann Bay.

Anchorage: There is good anchorage in both True Blue and Prickly bays.

Services: Fuel, water, ice, showers, haulouts, repairs, a chandlery, sail repairs, a canvas shop, and a telephone are all available at Spice Island Marine Services. The Moorings operation also

has fuel, laundry, showers, and a commissary. There are markets and restaurants nearby. Other services include: Johnny Sails (809-444-1108 or VHF channels 16 and 66), Power Tripper (809-444-1351 or VHF channel 16) for mechanical repairs, and Cottle Boat Builders (809-444-1108 or from 0800 to 0900 VHF channel 72), for woodworking.

The south coast of Grenada has several good anchorages, with convenient yachting services nearby. You are a short taxi or bus ride from St. George's, but in a much more natural setting. These harbors are also convenient to the airport near Saline Point.

GRENVILLE BAY

12 07N, 61 37W

Pilotage: This harbor, about midway up the east coast of the island, is protected by coral reefs to the east. The entrance channel is difficult to negotiate and should be attempted only in good weather, good light, and with local knowledge. During strong winds the sea breaks right across the entrance. There are reported to be two white beacons, on a bearing of 291°, that lead through the outer reef. The channel through the inner reef, called Luffing Channel, leads in a northerly direction. There may be some buoys marking these channels. The town pier is reported to have depths of 10 feet alongside its head.

Port of Entry: This is the only Port of Entry on the east coast of the island. The officials are located near the pier.

Anchorage: Anchor in the area clear of reefs off the town pier.

Services: This is not a yachting area, but there are good markets and general shops.

This harbor is not visited by many yachtsmen, because of its location on the east coast and its tricky reef entrance. It is a Port of Entry, and might be worth visiting for those who want to get off the beaten track.

BARBADOS

CAUTION: Our information on aids to navigation comes from official government sources. The latitudes and longitudes of these marks may not correspond to the readings from GPS receivers. Some aids have been reported as unreliable, missing, off position, or showing incorrect characteristics. No single aid to navigation, or waypoint, should be relied upon as a sole means of fixing your position.

NOTE: The chartlets in this section are <u>not</u> intended for navigation and are included for reference and planning purposes only. While chartlets reproduced from government sources are from the most current editions as of press time, they incorporate <u>no corrections</u> to navigation aids, depths, or hazards since the edition publication date.

ENTRY PROCEDURES

Barbados is the easternmost of the Windward Islands, lying about 89 miles to windward of St. Vincent. A former British colony, it gained independence in 1966. See *Reed's Nautical Companion* for an illustration of the country flag.

The Port of Entry is Bridgetown, located on the southwest side of the island. Vessels should contact the Port Authority's Signal Station (call sign 8PA on VHF channels 12, 16, and 2182kHz) for permission to enter Deepwater Harbour, east of the breakwater where the station is located. Yachts should fly the Q flag. Customs officials (809-426-2604) are on duty from 0600 to 2200, seven days a week; the customs area is well sign-posted. The main customs office in Bridgetown (809-427-5940) is open weekdays only from 0815 to 1630.

You should have clearance from your last port of call, ship's papers, crew lists, and passports. Request a coastwise clearance if you wish to anchor elsewhere on the island. Current fees are Barbados$50 (US$25) per boat, plus a Barbados$7 light charge when departing. No overtime fees are charged for weekend or holiday clearances.

For general information call the Barbados Tourist Office at (809-427-2623). The telephone area code for Barbados is 809. The official currency is the Barbados dollar, which is roughly equivalent to US$.49. The official language is English.

BARBADOS, WEST COAST

HARRISON POINT LIGHT, NW side of island, 13 18.3N, 59 39.0W. Fl (2) W 15s, 193ft, 22M. White stone tower.
MAYCOCKS BAY LIGHT, jetty N end, 13 16.8N, 59 39.3W. Q R, 3M.
MAYCOCKS BAY LIGHT, jetty S end, 13 16.9N, 59 39.3W. Q G, 3M.

APPROACHES TO BRIDGETOWN

BULK FACILITY LIGHT, 13 06.5N, 59 37.8W. Fl G 5s, 29ft. Red metal mast.
SHALLOW DRAFT JETTY, N, 13 06.4N, 59 37.5W. F R, 18M. Red mast.
SHALLOW DRAFT JETTY, S. 13 06.4N, 59 37.5W. F R, 18M. Red mast.
CONTAINER BERTH LIGHT, 13 06.2N, 59 37.9W. Q G, 26ft, 6M.
BRIDGETOWN BREAKWATER LIGHT, 13 06.3N, 59 38.0W. Q (3) R 10s, 49ft, 12M. F W shown when required, on flagstaff at shore end of pipeline at Spring Garden anchorage, 1.15M north.
OIL PIER LIGHT, SE end, 13 05.9N, 59 37.8W. Q R, 16ft, 5M. Silver metal mast.
OIL PIER LIGHT, center. F R, 39ft, 5M. Silver metal mast.
OIL PIER LIGHT, NW end. Q R, 16ft, 5M. Silver metal mast.
FISHING HARBOR ENTRANCE LIGHT, S side, 13 05.7N, 59 37.2W. F G.
FISHING HARBOR ENTRANCE LIGHT, N side, 13 05.7N, 59 37.2W. F R.
BRIDGETOWN CAREENAGE LIGHT, S side of entrance, 13 05.6N, 59 37.1W. Fl (2) G 10s, 26ft, 2M. Silver metal framework structure.

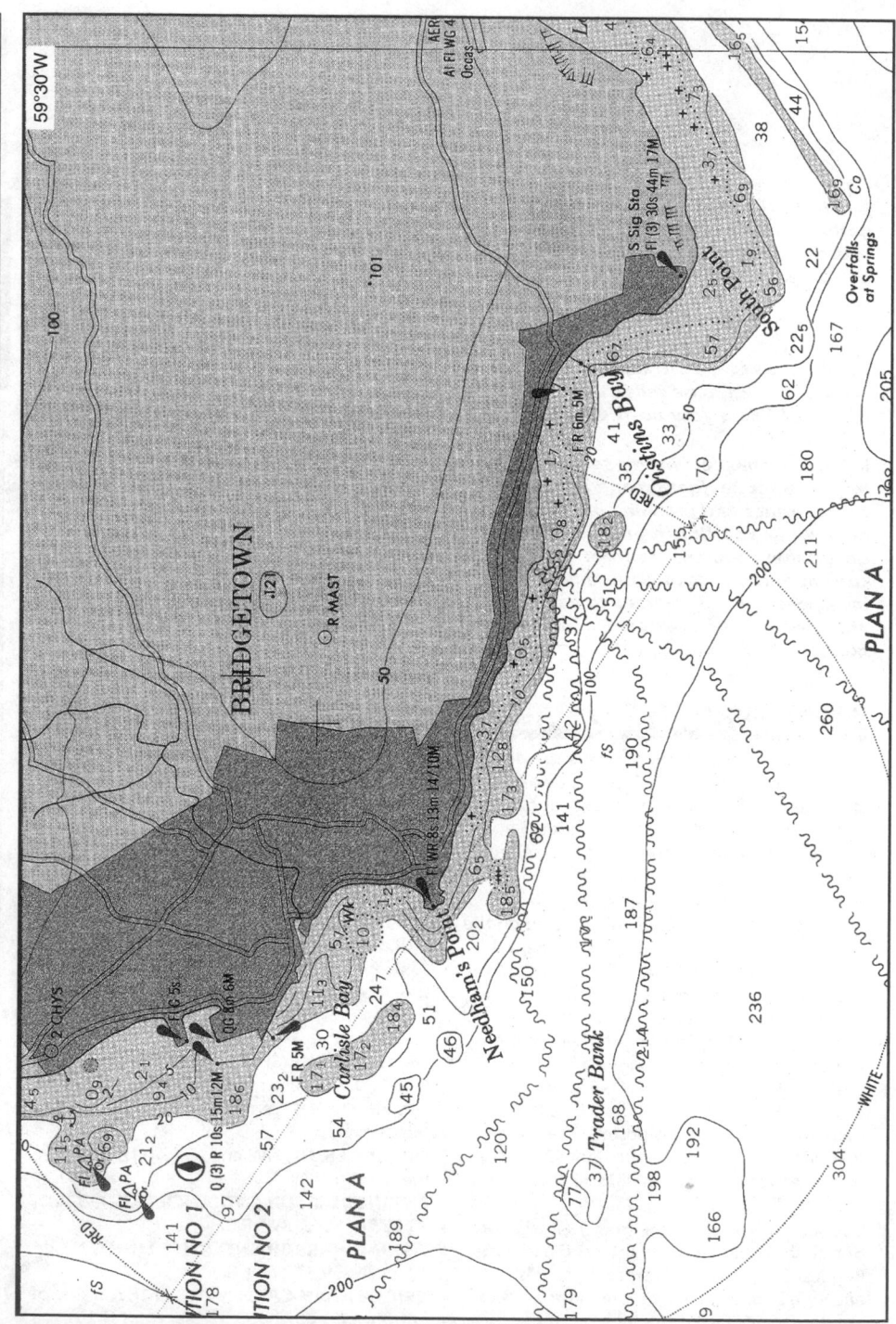

Approaches to Bridgetown, soundings in meters *(from DMA 25485, 44th ed, 12/91)*

COAST PILOT

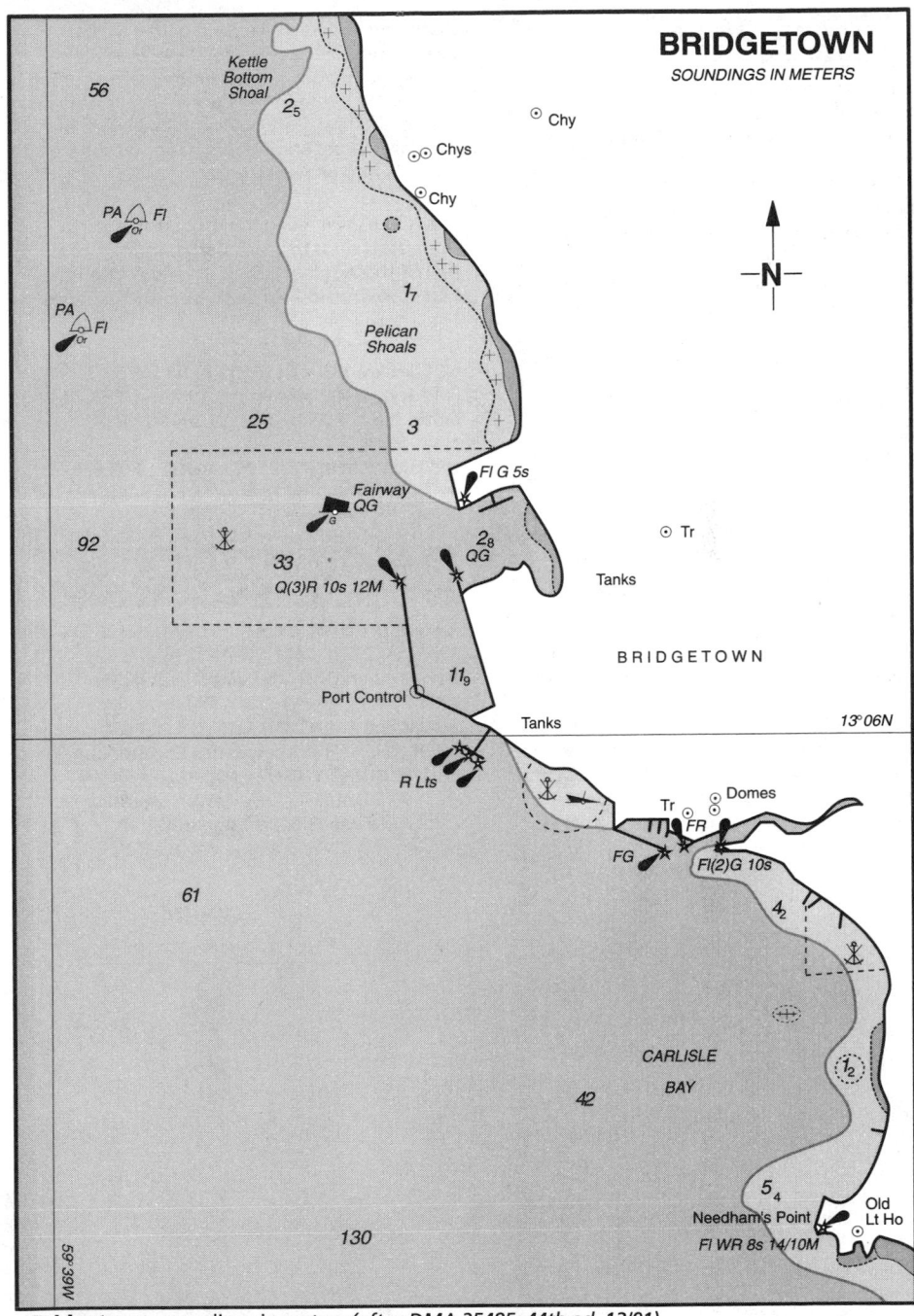

BRIDGETOWN

SOUNDINGS IN METERS

—N—

56

Kettle Bottom Shoal

2₅

⊙ Chy

⊙⊙ Chys

⊙ Chy

PA △ Fl
Or

1₇

Pelican Shoals

PA △ Fl
Or

25

3

⊙ Tr

92

Fl G 5s

Fairway QG

G

2₈ QG

Tanks

33

Q(3)R 10s 12M

B R I D G E T O W N

11₉

Port Control

Tanks

13°06N

R Lts

Tr ⊙ ⊙ Domes
⊙
FR

61

FG   Fl(2)G 10s

4₂

CARLISLE
BAY

42

1½

5₄

59°39W

130

Needham's Point
Fl WR 8s 14/10M

Old
Lt Ho
⊙

Bridgetown, soundings in meters *(after DMA 25485, 44th ed, 12/91)*

BRIDGETOWN

13 06N, 59 38W

Pilotage: The approaches to Bridgetown are generally free of hazards. The area known as The Shallows and the reef along the east coast of the island can generate very heavy seas when rounding South Point. Overfalls have been reported near the point.

Port of Entry: See Entry Procedures at the start of the Barbados section.

Public Correspondence: Call Barbados Radio, call sign 8PO, on 2182kHz or VHF channel 16.

Dockage: It may be possible to tie up in the Careenage, which has a flashing green light at the entrance. Call the Port Signal Station (809-436-6883) for information on tying up.

Anchorage: After clearing in, most yachts pro-cede to the anchorage in Carlisle Bay, north of Needham Point. You can land your dinghy at the Boatyard, the Yacht Club, Bay Boat Supplies, the Cruising Club, or in the Careenage.

Services: The Boatyard (809-436-2622 or 426-4241) in the northern part of Carlisle Bay can assist yachtsmen with many services, including water, ice, laundry, communications, and making arrangements for repair. In summer 1994, the whole property, including a restau-rant and bar and the dinghy dock, was being rebuilt, with expected completion by Novem-ber. You might want to contact the Barbados Yacht Club (809-427-1125) or the small Barba-dos Cruising Club for assistance. They are located on either side of a hotel pier at the south end of Carlisle Bay, and both have bars overlooking the anchorage. Diesel is available in the Careenage and also in the fishing harbor on the north side of the Careenage, as is fresh water. Shallow-draft boats can be hauled in the Careenage. Bridgetown has good super-markets and general stores.

Few sailors will make the rough trip against the trade winds to reach Barbados from the rest of the Antilles, but this island is often the first stop for those crossing from the Canaries. The approaches are easy.

NEEDHAM POINT LIGHT, 13 04.5N, 59 36.9W. Fl W R 8s, 43ft, 14M white, 10M red. Red metal mast. R 274°–304°, W 304°–124°, R 124°–154°.

OISTINS FISHING JETTY LIGHT, 13 03.6N, 59 32.8W. F R, 20ft, 5M.

BARBADOS, EAST COAST

RAGGED POINT LIGHT, 13 09.6N, 59 26.1W. Fl W 15s, 213ft, 21M. White circular coral stone tower. Obscured when bearing less than 135°.

SEAWALL AVIATION LIGHT, 13 04.5N, 59 29.7W. Al Fl W G 4s, 210ft. Occasional.

SOUTH POINT LIGHT, 13 02.8N, 59 31.8W. Fl (3) W 30s, 145ft, 17M. Tower, alternate red and white bands. Storm signal station.

TRINIDAD AND TOBAGO

COAST PILOT

CAUTION: Our information on aids to navigation comes from official government sources. The latitudes and longitudes of these marks may not correspond to the readings from GPS receivers. Some aids have been reported as unreliable, missing, off position, or showing incorrect characteristics. No single aid to navigation, or waypoint, should be relied upon as a sole means of fixing your position.

NOTE: The chartlets in this section are <u>not</u> <u>intended for navigation</u> and are included for reference and planning purposes only. While chartlets reproduced from government sources are from the most current editions as of press time, they incorporate <u>no corrections</u> to navigational aids, depths, or hazards since the edition publication date.

ENTRY PROCEDURES

The islands of Trinidad and Tobago lie east of the Venezuelan coast. They form an independent country, with ties to the British Commonwealth. See *Reed's Nautical Companion* for an illustration of the country flag.

The Port of Entry for Tobago is Scarborough, located on the southwest end of the island. Customs can be reached at 809-639-2415; immigration at 809-639-2681 (airport office, 809-639-0006).

In Trinidad most yachtsmen will clear in with officials in Port of Spain or the new customs station in Chaguaramas. For details see the Port of Entry headings for those areas on the following pages.

For all ports, you should have a clearance from your last port of call, ship's papers, crew and stores lists, and passports. Any guns and ammunition (including flare guns) must be declared and turned over to officials for the duration of your stay. If you move your boat from one harbor to another on the islands, be sure to call the nearest customs. When arriving on either island, having already cleared on the other, be sure to notify immigration of your presence. Check with officials for the latest regulations governing boats passing between the two islands.

For general information about either island, call the tourist offices in Trinidad (809-623-1932, -1933, or -1934) or Tobago (809-639-2125). The telephone area code for both islands is 809.

The official currency is the Trinidad and Tobago (TT) dollar. One US$ is equivalent roughly to 5.6 TT$. The use of U.S. dollars is not legal, although you may be approached by money-changers on the streets. You may be required to produce exchange receipts from official exchange offices upon your departure.

The official language is English, although you may hear many other languages, reflecting the varied origins of the islands' inhabitants.

TOBAGO, NORTH COAST

ST. GILES ISLAND LIGHT, E end, 11 21.2N, 60 31.1W. Fl W 7.5s, 16M.
LITTLE TOBAGO LIGHT, 11 17.5N, 60 29.5W. Fl (3) W 10s, 59ft, 5M.
MAN OF WAR BAY LIGHT, 11 19.1N, 60 32.8W. Q W R G, 82ft, 5M white, 4M red, 4M green. R 098°–108°, W 108°–131°, G 131°–141°.
THE SISTERS LIGHT, 11 19.7N, 60 38.7W. Fl (2) W 10s, 8M.
COURTLAND POINT LIGHT, 11 13.2N, 60 46.8W. L Fl W 10s, 8M.
BOOBY POINT LIGHT, 11 10.9N, 60 48.8W. Fl Y 3s, 4M.
MILFORD BAY LIGHT, 11 09.4N, 60 50.4W. Q W R G, 23ft, 5M white, 4M red, 4M green. R 073°–083°, W 083°–128°, G 128°–138°.
CROWN POINT LIGHT, SW extremity of island, 11 08.7N, 60 50.7W. Fl (4) W 20s, 115ft, 11M. Steel lattice tower painted aluminum.

TOBAGO, SOUTH COAST

SMITHS ISLAND LIGHT, 11 11.0N, 60 39.1W. Fl W R 5s, 59ft, 7M white, 5M red. R 068°–276°, W 276°–068°.

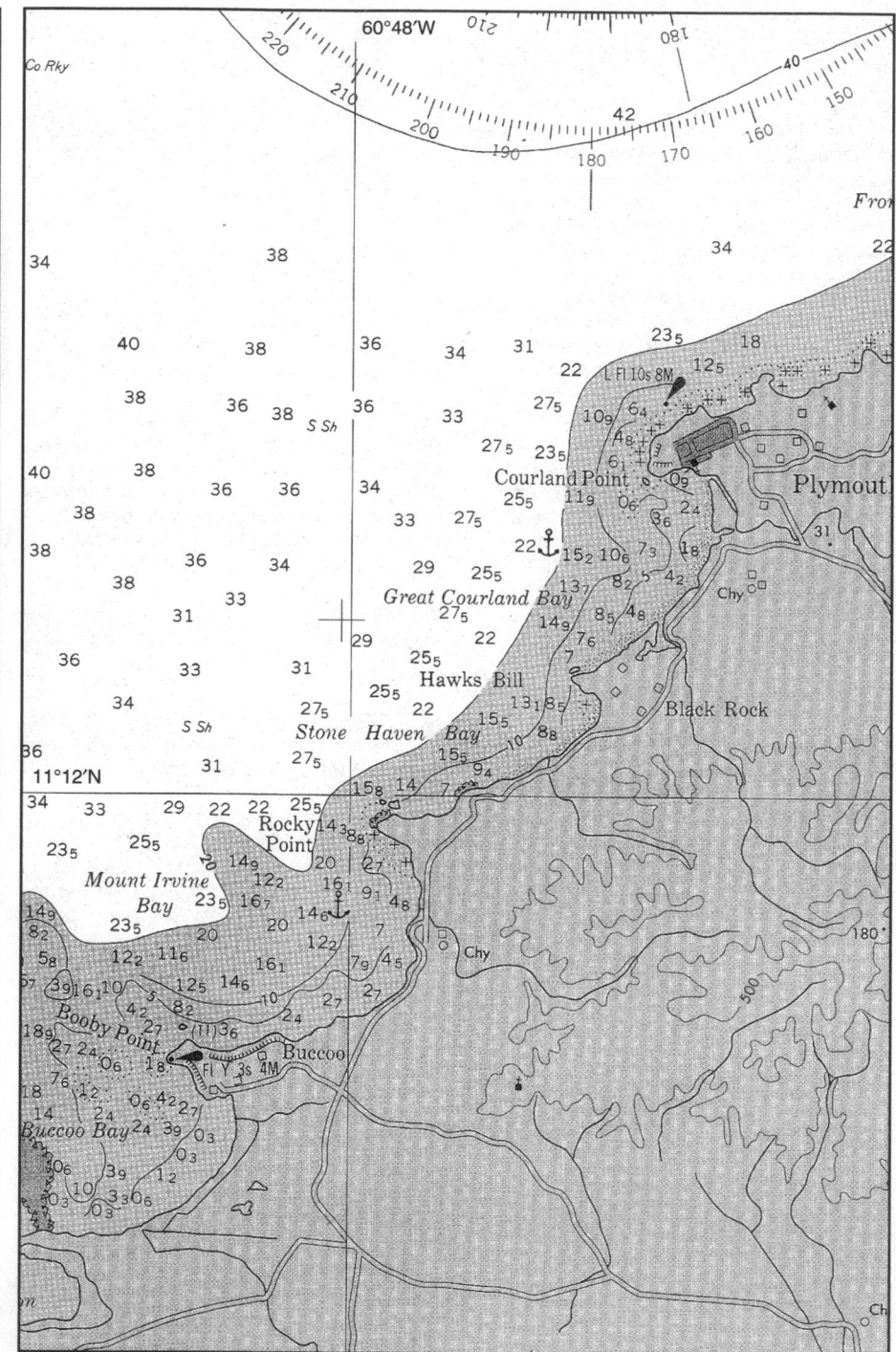

Plymouth, Tobago, soundings in meters *(from DMA 24402, 16th ed, 9/87)*

SCARBOROUGH LIGHT, on Fort George Point, 11 10.4N, 60 43.7W. Fl (2) W 20s, 462ft, 30M. White rectangular building with tower. Visible 258°–090°.

SCARBOROUGH HARBOR LIGHT, East Beacon, 11 10.6N, 60 44.2W. Q R, 18ft, 2M. White steel structure on piles.

RANGE (Front Light), 11 11.0N, 60 44.5W. V Q G, 13ft, 5M. Pile. **(Rear Light),** 115 meters 329.5° from front. Iso W R G 2s, 49ft, 7M white, 5M red, 5M green. R 313.5°–323.5°, W 323.5°–335.5°, G 335.5°–345.5°.

LOWER TOWN LIGHT, 11 11.1N, 60 44.5W. Oc W 5s, 66ft, 11M. White triangular daymark, point down, on beacon.

ROCKLY BAY LIGHT, 11 10.9N, 60 44.4W. Oc W 5s, 33ft, 11M.

SCARBOROUGH, TOBAGO

11 11N, 60 44W

Pilotage: Tobago lies about 19 miles north-northeast of Trinidad and 78 miles southeast of Grenada. The equatorial current runs in a northwesterly direction between Tobago and Grenada and is very variable and unpredictable, running strong at some places and barely existent at others. Take careful note of the charted and buoyed shoals to the east and west of the entrance to Rockly Bay. Fort George and several nearby radio towers are conspicuous. A lighted range of 329.5° should lead you in safely. Watch for strong easterly currents entering Scarborough. When sailing to Trinidad avoid Wasp Shoal and Drew Bank located about 3 miles off the southwestern tip of the island.

Port of Entry: Scarborough is the only Port of Entry on Tobago. Customs (809-639-2415) is located near the docks. Immigration can be reached at 809-639-2681 or at the airport at 809-639-0006. If you are coming from Trinidad, you should call immigration upon your arrival.

Coast Station: The coast station monitors VHF channel 16 and 2182kHz (call sign 9YL, North Post). For the daily weather schedule see Communications and Weather Services.

Dockage: You may be able to tie up Mediterranean style (stern-to) behind the breakwater (not shown on the Scarborough chartlet on the following page).

Anchorage: Anchor outside the jetty in depths of around 10–12 feet. This area is reported to suffer from surge.

Services: You can get water and jug your fuel. There are few yacht-oriented services of any kind, but there are good general stores, markets, and restaurants. There are several dive shops on the island.

TRINIDAD SOUTH COAST

SOLDADO ROCK, 10 04.2N, 62 00.9W. Fl W 10s, 8M.

WOLF ROCK, 10 03.0N, 61 56.1W. Q (6) + L Fl W 15s, 13ft, 5M. Temporarily extinguished (1988).

PUNTA DEL ARENAL, 10 02.8N, 61 55.7W. Fl W 7.5s, 72ft, 16M. White steel structure. Obscured when bearing less than 301°.

CHATHAM JETTY HEAD, 10 04.8N, 61 44.1W. F R, 3M.

TAPARO POINT, 10 03.4N, 61 37.7W. Fl (3) W 15s, 226ft, 14M.

LA LUNE POINT, 10 04.5N, 61 18.9W. Fl (4) W 20s, 148ft, 14M.

GALEOTA POINT, 10 08.5N, 60 59.7W. Fl W 5s, 285ft, 16M. White steel framework tower.

TRINIDAD EAST COAST

BRIGAND HILL, 10 29.4N, 61 04.2W. Fl (2+1) W 30s, 712ft, 20M. White steel framework tower.

GALERA POINT, 10 50.0N, 60 54.3W. Oc W 10s, 141ft, 16M. White concrete tower.

TRINIDAD, NORTH COAST

PETITE MATELOT POINT, 10 49.2N, 61 07.7W. Fl (3) W 15s, 7M.

CHUPARA POINT, 10 48.2N, 61 22.0W. Fl (2) W 10s, 325ft, 12M. White metal framework tower and hut.

SAUT D'EAU ISLAND, 10 46.2N, 61 30.7W. Q W, 7M.

NORTH POST, POINT A DIABLE, 10 44.7N, 61 33.8W. Fl W 5s, 747ft, 14M. Beacon. Visible 087°–252°.

NOTE: The current between Trinidad and Tobago sets to the northwest, usually with sufficient strength to prevent a sailing vessel from working through against it. The strength of the current is somewhat lessened by the ebb tidal stream. Current runs to the westward along the north shore of Trinidad.

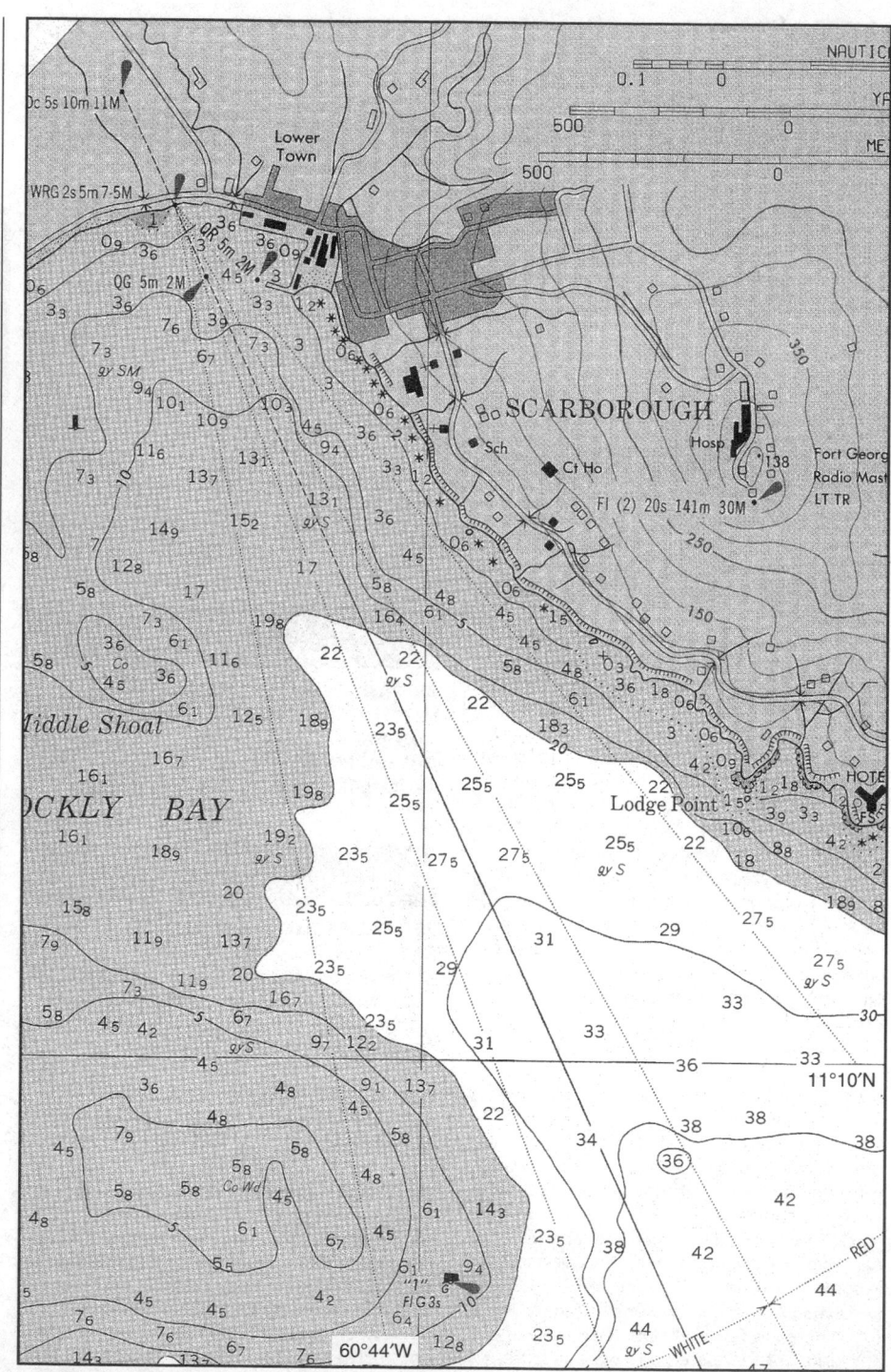

Scarborough, Tobago, soundings in meters *(from DMA 24402, 16th ed, 9/87)*

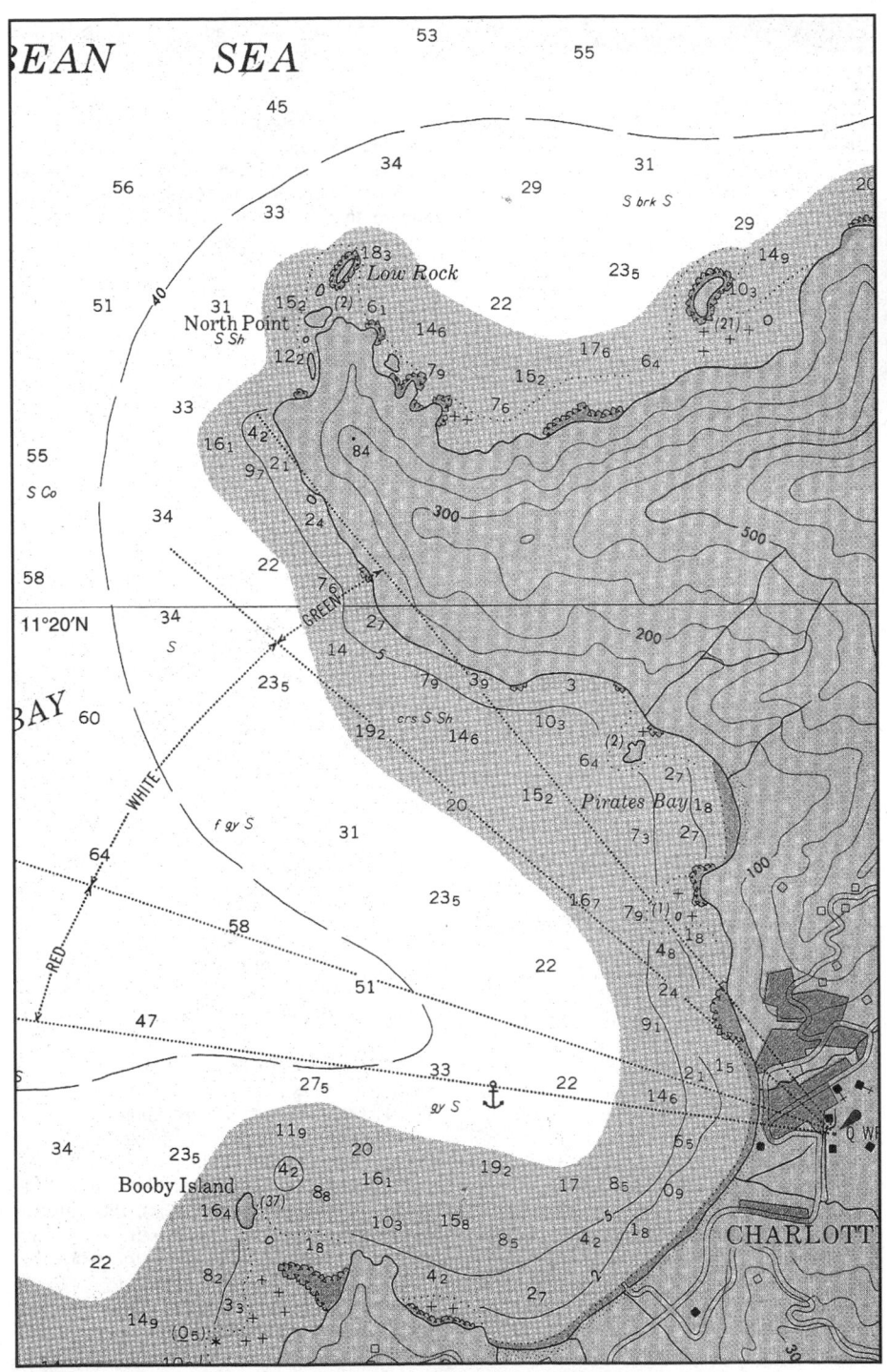

Charlotteville, Tobago, soundings in meters *(from DMA 24402, 16th ed, 9/87)*

COAST PILOT

GULF OF PARIA

CHACACHACARE, 10 41.7N, 61 45.2W.
Fl W 10s, 825ft, 26M. White concrete tower.
CHACACHACARE BEACON, about 640 meters
216° from main light, 10 41.4N, 61 45.4W.
Fl W 2s, 503ft, 11M. White square on white
metal framework tower. In line 036° with
Chacachacare.
POINT DE CABRAS, S end of Huevos, 10 40.9N,
61 43.2W. V Q (6) + L Fl W 10s, 40ft, 5M.
LE CHAPEAU ROCK, 10 42.3N, 61 40.6W.
Fl (3) W 10s.
TETERON ROCK, 10 40.8N, 61 40.1W. Fl G 4s,
24ft, 4M. White metal structure on concrete
base. Reported extinguished.
LA RETRAITE COAST GUARD STATION,
10 40.7N, 61 39.5W. 2 F R.
GASPARILLO ISLAND, W end, 10 40.4N,
61 39.4W. Q W, 36ft. White mast.
ESPOLON POINT, SW point of Gaspar Grande
Island, 10 39.8N, 61 40.1W. Fl W 4s, 42ft, 12M.
White framework tower. Reported extin-
guished (December 1981).
CRONSTADT ISLAND, W end, 10 39.4N,
61 37.9W. Q R, 4M.
REYNA POINT, 10 40.0N, 61 38.8W. Q G, 33ft,
4M.
ESCONDIDA COVE, off N point, 10 40.3N,
61 38.3W. Q R, 17ft. White tripodal beacon.
Unreliable.
FURNESS SMITH FLOATING DOCK, 10 40.7N,
61 38.9W. 2 F R.
ON S END OF ALUMINUM COMPANY PIER,
W side of Point Gourde, Chaguaramas Bay,
10 40.5N, 61 38.1W. F G, 13ft. Unreliable.

CHAGUARAMAS, TRINIDAD

10 41N, 61 39W
Pilotage: Off the north coast of Trinidad the
north- and northwest-going tidal streams attain
velocities of 2 to 3 knots. Between July and
October the influence may be felt 15 to 20
miles offshore. The Dragons Mouth has several
channels leading south into the Gulf of Paria.
In Boca de Monos (the easternmost channel)
there is no south current during the flood, but
the north-running ebb attains speeds of 2 to 3
knots. The tidal currents create eddies around
piers 4 and 5 in Chaguaramas. A tidal surge,
known locally as the Re-Mou, is strongest in
July and August. It may appear as a clear line
moving through the channel north of Gaspar
Grande, achieving speeds of 1 to 5 knots. The
customs office and the yacht facilities are
located in the northeast portion of the bay.

Port of Entry: Call Chaguaramas customs on
VHF channel 16 to announce your arrival
(phone, 809-634-4223 or -4279). The customs
dock is near the aluminum plant. Immigration
officers must be summoned from Port of Spain,
for which there is a traveling fee. There is also
an overtime fee for customs for arrivals outside
business hours (0800 to 1600, with an hour for
lunch). If you are arriving from Tobago, you
should call immigration in Port of Spain (809-
623-8147).
Coast Station: The station monitors VHF
channel 16 and 2182kHz (call sign 9YL, North
Post). For the daily weather schedule see Communications and Weather Services.
Dockage: Contact Trinity Yacht Service (809-
634-4303, or fax, -4327, or VHF channel 72),
which is primarily a repair yard, or Peake
Marine (809-634-4388 or fax, -4387), whose
new docks can service large private yachts.
Anchorage: Anchor near the Trinity Yacht
Service.
Services: Trinity Yacht Service (also called
Power Boats, but not limited to power vessels)
is a significant boat-hauling operation in
Trinidad. The company also has fuel, ice, water,
showers, grocery, and launderette; repair
services are available. Peake Marine, which
specializes in fiberglass repair, has a new 150-
ton Travelift and new 120-foot paint shed, a
major chandlery (with a second store in Port
of Spain), and small on-site hotel (scheduled
for completion fall 1994). Fuel, water, and
electricity are also available here. Other
marine-related services in the area include
marine paint supplies, hardware, propeller
repair, sailmakers, and upholsterers.

Chaguaramas has become a popular place
to clear customs and immigration for those
arriving from abroad. It is also the best place
to accomplish major repairs or maintenance.

NELSON, E end, 10 39.4N, 61 36.0W. Fl W 2.5s,
61ft, 5M. White pole beacon.
POINT SINET RANGE (Front Light),
10 40.9N, 61 36.0W. Oc W 2.5s, 98ft, 14M.
White square daymark, black stripe. Visible
038°–046°. Reduced visibility (5M) due to dust
(occas). Unreliable. **(Rear Light),** 180 meters
042°14′ from front. Oc W 5s, 102ft, 14M. White
square daymark, black stripe. Visible 038°–
046°. Unreliable.
PIER 2 RANGE (Front Light), 10 41.0N,
61 36.5W, F R, 23ft. **(Rear Light),** about 290
meters 346°30′ from front. F R, 39ft.

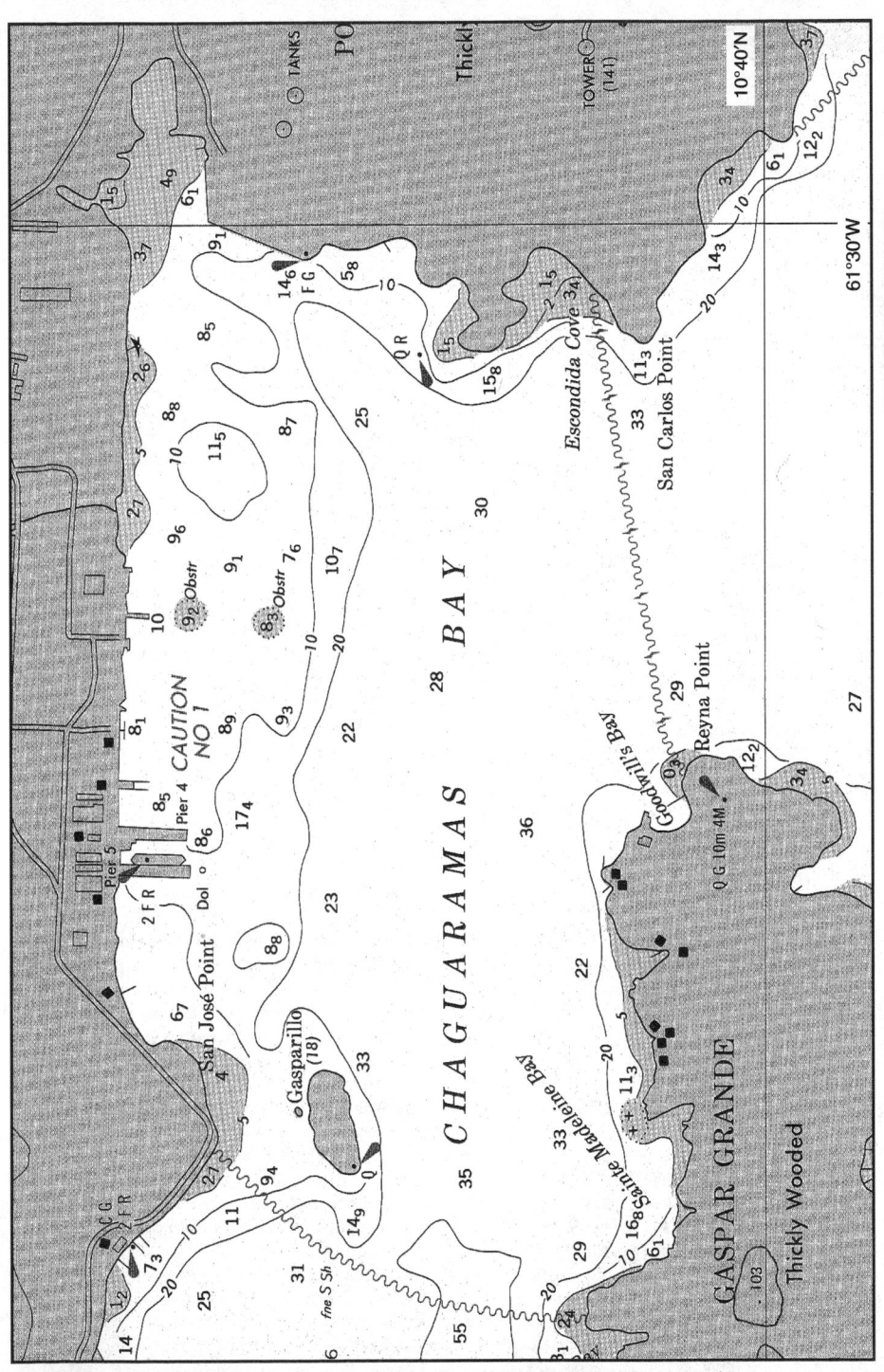

Chaguaramas, Trinidad, soundings in meters *(from DMA 24406, 29th ed, 7/91)*

PORT OF SPAIN

GRIER CHANNEL RANGE (Front Light),
10 39.2N, 61 31.4W. Oc W 4s, 135ft, 10M,
F G 6M. White and orange checkered rectangular daymark on white framework tower.
(Rear Light), 181 meters 061°32' from front.
Iso W 2s, 157ft, 11M. F R 6M. Orange rectangular daymark on white framework tower.
Visible 058°24'–064°24'.
DREDGED CHANNEL ENTRANCE, 10 37.8N,
61 33.9W. Iso Y 10s, 20ft, 8M. Concrete platform on pilings.
GRIER CHANNEL NO 1, entrance, N side, 10
38.2N, 61 33.2W. Fl G 3s. Concrete platform on pilings.
NO 2, entrance S side, 10 38.1N, 61 33.2W.
Fl R 3s. Concrete platform on pilings.
NO 3, 10 38.4N, 61 32.9W. Q G. Concrete platform on pilings.
NO 4, 10 38.3N, 61 32.8W. Q R. Concrete platform on pilings.
NO 5, 10 38.7N, 61 32.3W. Q G. Concrete platform on pilings.
NO 6, 10 38.6N, 61 32.3W. Q R. Concrete platform on pilings.
NO 7, 10 38.9N, 61 31.9W. Fl G 5s. Concrete platform on pilings.
NO 8, 10 38.8N, 61 31.9W. Fl R 5s. Concrete platform on pilings.
NO 9, 10 39.1N, 61 31.9W. Q G. Concrete platform on pilings.
NO 10, 10 38.9N, 61 31.5W. Q R. Concrete platform on pilings.
NO 12, 10 38.8N, 61 31.3W. Q R. Concrete platform on pilings.
NO 14, 10 38.7N, 61 31.1W. Q R. Concrete platform on pilings.
HEAD OF ST VINCENT JETTY, 10 38.6N,
61 30.9W. F R, 23ft, 4M. Wooden post.
SEA LOTS CHANNEL NO 1, entrance,
N side, 10 37.6N, 61 32.0W. Fl (2) G 7.5s. Pile.
NO 2, entrance S side, 10 37.6N, 61 31.9W.
V Q (9) W 10s. Pile.
NO 3, 10 37.7N, 61 31.6W. Q G. Pile.
NO 4, 10 37.7N, 61 31.6W. Q R. Pile.
NO 5, 10 37.9N, 61 31.1W. V Q G. Pile.
NO 6, 10 37.9N, 61 31.1W. V Q R. Pile.
NO 7, 10 38.1N, 61 30.6W. Q G. Pile.
NO 8, 10 38.1N, 61 30.6W. Q R. Pile.
NO 9, 10 38.3N, 61 30.3W. L Fl G 5s. Pile.
NO 10, 10 38.2N, 61 30.3W. L Fl R 5s. Pile.
NO 12, 10 38.2N, 61 30.1W. Q R. Pile.
NO 13, 10 38.0N, 61 29.9W. Q G. Pile.
NO 14, 10 38.1N, 61 30.0W. Q R. Pile.
SEA LOTS CHANNEL RANGE (Front Light),
10 38.4N, 61 29.8W. Oc W 10s, 85ft, 6M. F R.
Orange rectangular daymark on white frame-

work tower. **(Rear Light),** 640 meters 069°10'
from front. Fl W 2s, 128ft, 6M. F R. Orange
rectangular daymark on white framework
tower.

PORT OF SPAIN, TRINIDAD

10 39N, 61 31W
Pilotage: Port of Spain is the principal port in
Trinidad and also one of the most important
ports in the West Indies. The Grier Channel
range lights are often obscured by smoke, and
there are several submerged obstructions outside the marked channels. Tidal currents set
southeast at about 1/2 knot on the flood and
1 1/2 knots on the ebb. The harbormaster,
Maritime Services Division of the Ministry of
Works and Transport, monitors VHF channels
10 and 16 (call sign, Maritime Services).
Coast Station: The station monitors VHF
channel 16 and 2182kHz (call sign 9YL, North
Post). For the daily weather schedule see
Communications and Weather Services.
Port of Entry: The customs dock is located
inshore of the dredged area at the southeast
end of the Grier Channel. The main customs
office in Port of Spain can be reached at 809-
625-3311, -3312, -3314, or -3315. Customs at
the harbor is through the tide surveyor's office
(809-625-2501). Immigration can reached at
809-623-8147; vessels arriving from Tobago
must check in with immigration. Note that
clearances to leave Trinidad involve visits to
immigration, the harbormaster's office on
Sackville Street, and customs, although some
visits make take place in Chaguaramas.
Dockage: You may be able to tie up right in
Port of Spain. For information contact the
Maritime Services Division (809-625-3858 or
VHF channels 10 and 16). Many boaters prefer
to dock at the Trinidad and Tobago Yacht
Club (809-637-4260) in Cumana Bay, 4 miles
northwest of town. During Carnival, the docks
are likely to be very crowded, if not full. If you
are headed for the yacht club, be sure to clear
in with officials first.
Anchorage: Anchor off the Trinidad and
Tobago Yachting Association (809-634-4376,
634-4217, or VHF channel 68) docks in the
northwest part of Carenage Bay or off the
yacht club docks. Both clubs offer the use of
their facilities to visitors who purchase temporary memberships.
Services: Most services are available. Fuel,
water, and showers are available at the Yacht
Club, while the Yachting Association offers
haulouts, water, and showers but no fuel.
Either place would be a good place to start if
searching for a particular marine service.

COAST PILOT

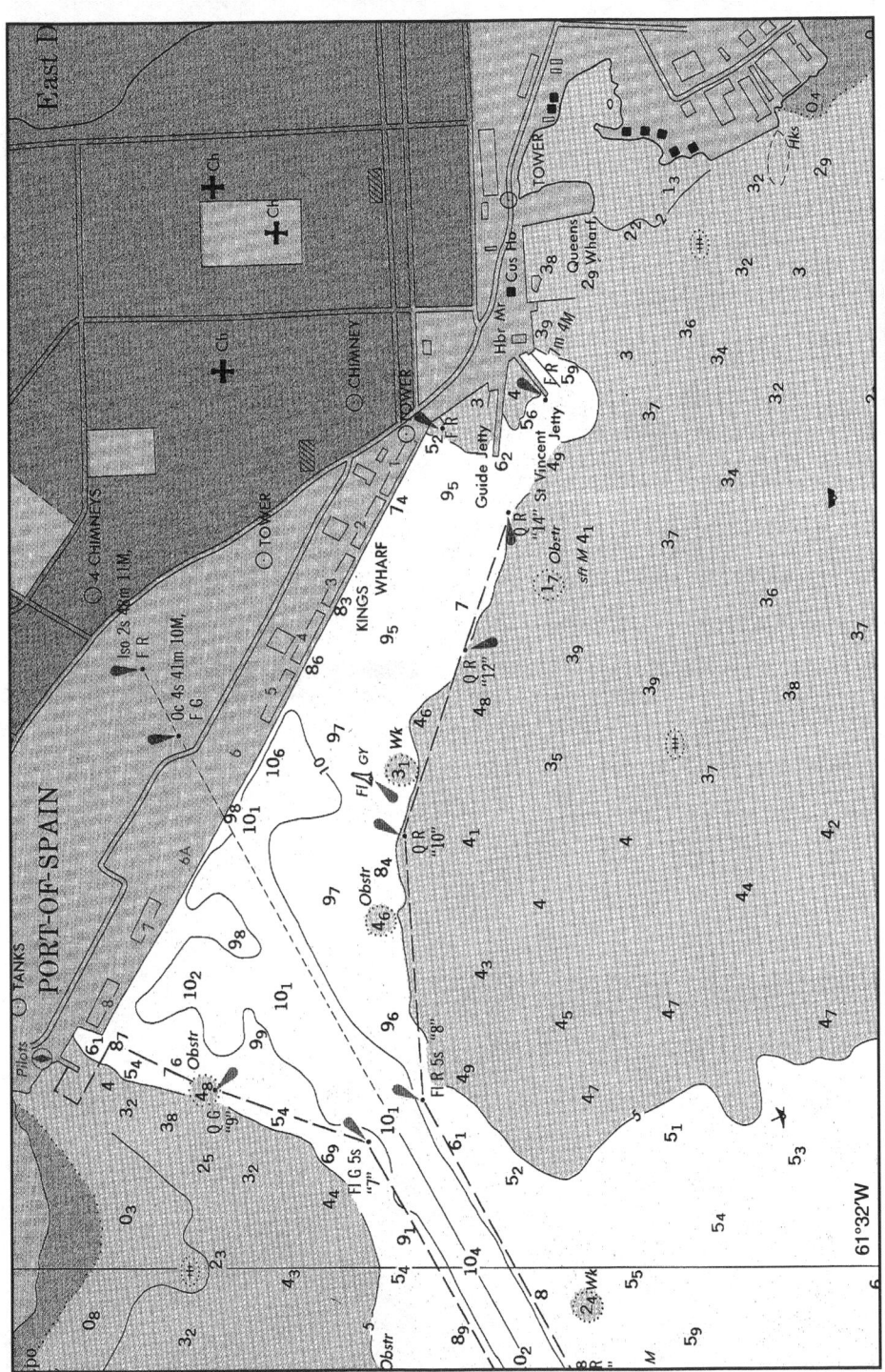

Port of Spain, Trinidad, soundings in meters *(from DMA 24406, 29th ed, 7/91)*

Venezuelan Embassy: If you are planning to visit Venezuela, you must have a visa before entering; contact the Venezuelan Embassy at 809-627-9821 or -9823.

Port of Spain, with a population of over 300,000, is a bustling commercial city. In the weeks following Christmas it is the location for a world-famous Carnival, or *Mas*. For this reason alone yachtsmen have begun to flock to the area in increasing numbers, but they also enjoy the advantage of being south of the hurricane belt. For those heading to Venezuela, this is a good place to obtain visas.

POINT LISAS

RANGE (Front Light), No 13, 10 22.7N, 61 29.0W. Q W, 30ft, 8M, F R, 30ft, 4M. Visible 083°48'–098°48'. **(Rear Light),** No 14, 530 meters 091°20' from front. Oc W 5s, 52ft, 8M. F R, 56ft, 4M. Visible 087°18'–095°18'.
MARINE TERMINAL RANGE (Front Light), 10 20.9N, 61 27.9W. Q Y, 69ft, 10M. Building. **(Rear Light),** 260 meters 081°25' from front. Oc Y 3s, 82ft, 10M. Silo.
CHANNEL ENTRANCE, N side, No 1, 10 22.7N, 61 31.0W. Fl (2) G 5s, 26ft, 8M. White beacon.
CHANNEL ENTRANCE, S side, No 2, 10 22.6N, 61 31.0W. Fl W 3s, 26ft, 8M. White beacon.
SAVONNETA RANGE (Front Light), 10 24.2N, 61 29.5W. Fl W 2s, 98ft, 8M. Orange rectangle stripe. Visible 049°18'–055°18'. Identification light Fl R 4s. **(Rear Light),** 700

meters 052°16' from front. Fl W 2s, 135ft, 8M. Orange rectangle, white stripe. Synchronized with front. Identification light Fl R 4s.

POINTE-A-PIERRE

LA CARRIERE, 10 19.3N, 61 27.6W. Fl W 2.5s, 233ft, 23M. White water tower. Emergency light range 18M.
HEAD OF PIPELINE VIADUCT, 10 18.8N, 61 28.8W. Fl (4) W 10s, 98ft, 14M. White metal tower.
TURNING BASIN, 10 18.8N, 61 28.7W. Fl R. Wood pile.
OROPUCHE BANK BEACON, 10 16.8N, 61 33.9W. V Q W, 4M. Steel caisson.
BRIGHTON (Front Light), head of pier, 10 14.9N, 61 38.1W. Fl (3) W 10s, 52ft, 15M. White metal tower. Visible 134°12'–144°12'. Berthing signals. **(Rear Light),** 852 meters 139°15' from front. Fl W 5s, 100ft, 8M. Visible 134°12'–144°12'.
LA BREA, head of Pitch Point pier, 10 15.2N, 61 37.1W. Iso W 2s, 26ft, 10M. White framework tower.

POINT FORTIN

HEAD OF PIPELINE PIER, 10 12.6N, 61 42.2W. Fl (2) W 10s, 98ft, 14M. Aluminum framework tower.
N BREAKWATER, 10 11.3N, 61 41.6W. Fl G 3s.
S BREAKWATER, head, 10 11.2N, 61 41.6W. Fl R 3s.

PORT OF SPAIN, TRINIDAD

HIGH & LOW WATER 1995 **10°39'N   61°31'W**

ATLANTIC STANDARD TIME (GMT -4H)

JANUARY

Day	Time	ft	Day	Time	ft
1 Su ●	0400 / 0930 / 1545 / 2221	3.4 / 1.3 / 4.2 / 0.3	**16** M ○	0414 / 0939 / 1551 / 2229	3.1 / 1.4 / 3.7 / 0.6
2 M	0447 / 1020 / 1634 / 2307	3.5 / 1.2 / 4.2 / 0.3	**17** Tu	0449 / 1018 / 1630 / 2304	3.2 / 1.3 / 3.7 / 0.6
3 Tu	0530 / 1108 / 1721 / 2351	3.5 / 1.2 / 4.1 / 0.4	**18** W	0524 / 1057 / 1708 / 2339	3.3 / 1.2 / 3.8 / 0.6
4 W	0613 / 1156 / 1806	3.5 / 1.2 / 3.9	**19** Th	0559 / 1137 / 1747	3.4 / 1.2 / 3.7
5 Th	0034 / 0654 / 1245 / 1851	0.6 / 3.5 / 1.3 / 3.6	**20** F	0013 / 0636 / 1220 / 1829	0.7 / 3.5 / 1.1 / 3.6
6 F	0116 / 0736 / 1335 / 1937	0.8 / 3.4 / 1.4 / 3.4	**21** Sa	0050 / 0714 / 1307 / 1914	0.8 / 3.5 / 1.1 / 3.4
7 Sa	0159 / 0820 / 1429 / 2026	1.1 / 3.3 / 1.5 / 3.1	**22** Su	0128 / 0756 / 1400 / 2006	0.9 / 3.5 / 1.1 / 3.2
8 Su (	0242 / 0906 / 1531 / 2124	1.4 / 3.3 / 1.5 / 2.8	**23** M	0212 / 0844 / 1500 / 2106	1.1 / 3.5 / 1.1 / 3.0
9 M	0329 / 0956 / 1640 / 2234	1.6 / 3.2 / 1.5 / 2.6	**24** Tu)	0302 / 0937 / 1608 / 2217	1.3 / 3.5 / 1.1 / 2.8
10 Tu	0424 / 1052 / 1752	1.7 / 3.2 / 1.5	**25** W	0402 / 1037 / 1720 / 2337	1.4 / 3.5 / 1.0 / 2.8
11 W	0002 / 0525 / 1152 / 1857	2.5 / 1.8 / 3.2 / 1.4	**26** Th	0512 / 1142 / 1830	1.5 / 3.6 / 0.8
12 Th	0119 / 0629 / 1251 / 1952	2.6 / 1.8 / 3.3 / 1.2	**27** F	0058 / 0622 / 1248 / 1935	2.8 / 1.5 / 3.6 / 0.7
13 F	0215 / 0726 / 1343 / 2036	2.7 / 1.8 / 3.4 / 1.0	**28** Sa	0205 / 0728 / 1350 / 2031	3.0 / 1.4 / 3.8 / 0.5
14 Sa	0259 / 0816 / 1430 / 2116	2.8 / 1.7 / 3.5 / 0.9	**29** Su	0259 / 0826 / 1445 / 2119	3.1 / 1.3 / 3.9 / 0.4
15 Su	0338 / 0859 / 1512 / 2153	3.0 / 1.6 / 3.6 / 0.7	**30** M ●	0345 / 0918 / 1535 / 2204	3.3 / 1.2 / 3.9 / 0.3
			31 Tu	0426 / 1005 / 1621 / 2245	3.4 / 1.0 / 3.9 / 0.3

FEBRUARY

Day	Time	ft	Day	Time	ft
1 W	0504 / 1050 / 1703 / 2324	3.5 / 0.9 / 3.8 / 0.4	**16** Th	0454 / 1039 / 1653 / 2311	3.5 / 0.9 / 3.7 / 0.5
2 Th	0541 / 1134 / 1743	3.6 / 0.9 / 3.7	**17** F	0528 / 1120 / 1733 / 2346	3.6 / 0.7 / 3.7 / 0.6
3 F	0002 / 0616 / 1217 / 1822	0.6 / 3.5 / 0.9 / 3.4	**18** Sa	0604 / 1204 / 1816	3.7 / 0.7 / 3.6
4 Sa	0038 / 0652 / 1302 / 1902	0.8 / 3.4 / 1.0 / 3.2	**19** Su	0023 / 0643 / 1252 / 1902	0.7 / 3.7 / 0.7 / 3.4
5 Su	0114 / 0728 / 1349 / 1945	1.0 / 3.3 / 1.1 / 2.9	**20** M	0103 / 0725 / 1344 / 1955	0.9 / 3.6 / 0.7 / 3.1
6 M	0150 / 0808 / 1442 / 2036	1.2 / 3.2 / 1.2 / 2.6	**21** Tu	0147 / 0813 / 1443 / 2056	1.1 / 3.5 / 0.8 / 2.9
7 Tu (	0227 / 0853 / 1545 / 2140	1.4 / 3.1 / 1.3 / 2.4	**22** W)	0240 / 0909 / 1549 / 2208	1.3 / 3.4 / 0.9 / 2.7
8 W	0315 / 0947 / 1658 / 2305	1.6 / 3.0 / 1.3 / 2.3	**23** Th	0345 / 1014 / 1701 / 2330	1.5 / 3.3 / 0.9 / 2.7
9 Th	0425 / 1053 / 1813	1.8 / 2.8 / 1.3	**24** F	0501 / 1127 / 1814	1.6 / 3.3 / 0.8
10 F	0045 / 0548 / 1206 / 1918	2.4 / 1.8 / 3.0 / 1.1	**25** Sa	0051 / 0616 / 1240 / 1921	2.8 / 1.5 / 3.4 / 0.8
11 Sa	0152 / 0658 / 1312 / 2008	2.5 / 1.7 / 3.1 / 1.0	**26** Su	0154 / 0724 / 1345 / 2017	3.0 / 1.4 / 3.5 / 0.7
12 Su	0237 / 0753 / 1406 / 2049	2.7 / 1.6 / 3.3 / 1.0	**27** M	0243 / 0821 / 1439 / 2102	3.1 / 1.2 / 3.6 / 0.6
13 M	0313 / 0838 / 1452 / 2127	2.9 / 1.4 / 3.4 / 1.0	**28** Tu	0324 / 0909 / 1527 / 2142	3.3 / 1.0 / 3.7 / 0.6
14 Tu	0347 / 0919 / 1533 / 2202	3.1 / 1.2 / 3.6 / 0.6			
15 W ○	0420 / 0959 / 1613 / 2236	3.3 / 1.0 / 3.7 / 0.5			

MARCH

Day	Time	ft	Day	Time	ft
1 W ●	0401 / 0953 / 1609 / 2219	3.4 / 0.9 / 3.7 / 0.6	**16** Th ○	0345 / 0939 / 1556 / 2205	3.5 / 0.8 / 3.6 / 0.7
2 Th	0434 / 1034 / 1647 / 2255	3.5 / 0.7 / 3.6 / 0.6	**17** F	0419 / 1020 / 1638 / 2241	3.7 / 0.5 / 3.7 / 0.7
3 F	0506 / 1113 / 1723 / 2329	3.5 / 0.7 / 3.5 / 0.8	**18** Sa	0455 / 1104 / 1721 / 2319	3.8 / 0.4 / 3.6 / 0.7
4 Sa	0537 / 1152 / 1759	3.5 / 0.7 / 3.3	**19** Su	0533 / 1149 / 1806 / 2359	3.9 / 0.3 / 3.5 / 0.8
5 Su	0002 / 0609 / 1231 / 1836	0.9 / 3.4 / 0.8 / 3.1	**20** M	0613 / 1237 / 1855	3.8 / 0.3 / 3.3
6 M	0035 / 0642 / 1313 / 1917	1.1 / 3.3 / 0.9 / 2.8	**21** Tu	0043 / 0658 / 1329 / 1949	1.0 / 3.7 / 0.4 / 3.1
7 Tu	0106 / 0717 / 1359 / 2005	1.3 / 3.2 / 1.0 / 2.6	**22** W	0131 / 0749 / 1426 / 2051	1.2 / 3.6 / 0.6 / 2.9
8 W (	0140 / 0759 / 1454 / 2105	1.5 / 3.0 / 1.2 / 2.4	**23** Th)	0230 / 0849 / 1531 / 2202	1.4 / 3.4 / 0.8 / 2.8
9 Th	0224 / 0851 / 1602 / 2221	1.7 / 2.9 / 1.3 / 2.3	**24** F	0339 / 1000 / 1642 / 2322	1.6 / 3.2 / 0.9 / 2.8
10 F	0335 / 0959 / 1721	1.8 / 2.8 / 1.3	**25** Sa	0458 / 1120 / 1757	1.6 / 3.2 / 1.0
11 Sa	0000 / 0510 / 1121 / 1834	2.4 / 1.9 / 2.8 / 1.2	**26** Su	0039 / 0617 / 1236 / 1904	2.9 / 1.6 / 3.2 / 1.0
12 Su	0117 / 0630 / 1239 / 1930	2.6 / 1.8 / 2.9 / 1.1	**27** M	0136 / 0726 / 1341 / 1957	3.1 / 1.4 / 3.3 / 1.0
13 M	0202 / 0729 / 1340 / 2014	2.8 / 1.6 / 3.1 / 1.0	**28** Tu	0221 / 0819 / 1433 / 2040	3.3 / 1.2 / 3.4 / 1.0
14 Tu	0238 / 0816 / 1430 / 2053	3.0 / 1.3 / 3.3 / 0.9	**29** W	0258 / 0902 / 1518 / 2117	3.4 / 1.0 / 3.5 / 0.9
15 W	0311 / 0858 / 1514 / 2129	3.3 / 1.0 / 3.5 / 0.7	**30** Th ●	0332 / 0931 / 1558 / 2152	3.5 / 0.8 / 3.5 / 1.0
			31 F	0403 / 1017 / 1634 / 2226	3.6 / 0.7 / 3.4 / 1.0

APRIL

Day	Time	ft	Day	Time	ft
1 Sa	0433 / 1053 / 1707 / 2259	3.6 / 0.6 / 3.3 / 1.0	**16** Su	0423 / 1047 / 1711 / 2255	4.0 / 0.2 / 3.6 / 1.0
2 Su	0502 / 1129 / 1741 / 2332	3.5 / 0.6 / 3.2 / 1.1	**17** M	0505 / 1134 / 1758 / 2339	4.0 / 0.1 / 3.5 / 1.0
3 M	0532 / 1205 / 1817	3.5 / 0.7 / 3.0	**18** Tu	0549 / 1222 / 1848	4.0 / 0.2 / 3.4
4 Tu	0003 / 0603 / 1243 / 1858	1.3 / 3.3 / 0.8 / 2.8	**19** W	0027 / 0637 / 1314 / 1942	1.2 / 3.8 / 0.3 / 3.2
5 W	0035 / 0637 / 1325 / 1944	1.4 / 3.2 / 0.9 / 2.7	**20** Th	0121 / 0731 / 1410 / 2042	1.4 / 3.6 / 0.6 / 3.1
6 Th	0111 / 0716 / 1412 / 2039	1.6 / 3.0 / 1.1 / 2.5	**21** F	0222 / 0834 / 1512 / 2149	1.5 / 3.3 / 0.8 / 3.0
7 F	0157 / 0805 / 1511 / 2146	1.8 / 2.9 / 1.3 / 2.5	**22** Sa	0333 / 0948 / 1620 / 2304	1.7 / 3.1 / 1.1 / 3.0
8 Sa	0305 / 0915 / 1624 / 2304	1.9 / 2.7 / 1.4 / 2.5	**23** Su	0453 / 1110 / 1731	1.7 / 3.1 / 1.2
9 Su	0432 / 1038 / 1739	1.9 / 2.7 / 1.4	**24** M	0013 / 0615 / 1228 / 1836	3.1 / 1.6 / 3.1 / 1.3
10 M	0020 / 0555 / 1201 / 1841	2.7 / 1.8 / 2.8 / 1.3	**25** Tu	0108 / 0723 / 1333 / 1930	3.2 / 1.4 / 3.1 / 1.3
11 Tu	0111 / 0659 / 1309 / 1930	2.9 / 1.6 / 3.0 / 1.2	**26** W	0151 / 0813 / 1425 / 2013	3.3 / 1.2 / 3.2 / 1.4
12 W	0151 / 0749 / 1405 / 2013	3.2 / 1.3 / 3.2 / 1.1	**27** Th	0228 / 0853 / 1509 / 2050	3.4 / 1.0 / 3.3 / 1.3
13 Th	0229 / 0834 / 1453 / 2053	3.5 / 0.9 / 3.4 / 1.0	**28** F	0302 / 0928 / 1547 / 2126	3.5 / 0.8 / 3.3 / 1.3
14 F	0306 / 0918 / 1539 / 2132	3.7 / 0.6 / 3.5 / 1.0	**29** Sa ●	0333 / 1001 / 1622 / 2200	3.6 / 0.7 / 3.2 / 1.3
15 Sa	0344 / 1002 / 1625 / 2213	3.9 / 0.3 / 3.6 / 0.9	**30** Su ○	0403 / 1035 / 1655 / 2234	3.6 / 0.6 / 3.2 / 1.3

TIME MERIDIAN 60°W
0000h is midnight, 1200h is noon.

Heights in feet are referenced to the chart datum of soundings.

TRINIDAD

PORT OF SPAIN, TRINIDAD

HIGH & LOW WATER 1995 10°39'N 61°31'W

ATLANTIC STANDARD TIME (GMT -4H)

MAY

Day				
1 M	0433 3.5	1109 0.6	1729 3.1	2308 1.4
16 Tu	0442 4.1	1118 0.1	1748 3.5	2322 1.2
2 Tu	0504 3.5	1145 0.7	1805 3.0	2340 1.5
17 W	0530 4.0	1207 0.2	1837 3.4	
3 W	0535 3.3	1221 0.8	1844 2.9	
18 Th	0014 1.3	0621 3.8	1258 0.4	1929 3.3
4 Th	0014 1.6	0609 3.2	1259 0.9	1927 2.8
19 F	0108 1.4	0717 3.6	1351 0.7	2025 3.2
5 F	0052 1.7	0648 3.1	1341 1.1	2016 2.7
20 Sa	0209 1.6	0819 3.4	1448 1.0	2125 3.2
6 Sa	0139 1.8	0736 2.9	1430 1.3	2111 2.7
21 Su	0318 1.7	0929 3.1	1549 1.2	) 2230 3.1
7 Su	0239 1.8	0840 2.8	1529 1.4	(2213 2.8
22 M	0436 1.7	1048 3.0	1653 1.5	2333 3.2
8 M	0352 1.9	0957 2.8	1636 1.5	2315 2.9
23 Tu	0558 1.6	1208 2.9	1756 1.6	
9 Tu	0510 1.8	1117 2.8	1741 1.5	
24 W	0029 3.3	0707 1.4	1317 3.0	1852 1.7
10 W	0011 3.1	0621 1.5	1233 2.9	1838 1.5
25 Th	0116 3.3	0759 1.2	1412 3.0	1939 1.7
11 Th	0100 3.3	0719 1.2	1338 3.1	1928 1.4
26 F	0156 3.4	0839 1.1	1456 3.0	2021 1.7
12 F	0145 3.6	0810 0.8	1433 3.3	2015 1.3
27 Sa	0233 3.5	0914 0.9	1535 3.1	2100 1.6
13 Sa	0228 3.8	0857 0.5	1523 3.4	2101 1.2
28 Su	0307 3.5	0946 0.8	1610 3.1	2137 1.6
14 Su	0312 4.0	0944 0.3	1644 ...	○ 2147 1.2
29 M	0340 3.5	1019 0.8	1644 3.1	● 2213 1.6
15 M	0356 4.1	1031 0.1	1659 3.5	2234 1.2
30 Tu	0412 3.5	1053 0.7	1718 3.1	2248 1.6
31 W	0445 3.5	1128 0.6	1753 3.1	2322 1.6

JUNE

Day				
1 Th	0519 3.4	1204 0.8	1830 3.0	2357 1.7
16 F	0606 3.9	1238 0.5	1907 3.5	
2 F	0554 3.3	1240 1.0	1909 3.0	
17 Sa	0051 1.4	0659 3.7	1327 0.8	1956 3.4
3 Sa	0036 1.7	0633 3.2	1317 1.1	1951 3.0
18 Su	0147 1.5	0755 3.4	1417 1.1	2048 3.3
4 Su	0120 1.8	0718 3.1	1357 1.3	2037 3.0
19 M	0251 1.6	0857 3.1	1509 1.4	) 2142 3.3
5 M	0213 1.8	0813 3.0	1443 1.4	2127 3.1
20 Tu	0403 1.7	1009 2.9	1606 1.7	2240 3.3
6 Tu	0316 1.8	0920 2.9	1537 1.6	(2221 3.1
21 W	0522 1.6	1133 2.8	1705 1.8	2339 3.3
7 W	0429 1.7	1035 2.8	1640 1.7	2317 3.3
22 Th	0636 1.5	1252 2.8	1805 1.9	
8 Th	0544 1.5	1155 2.9	1743 1.7	
23 F	0033 3.3	0735 1.4	1353 2.8	1901 1.9
9 F	0012 3.5	0649 1.2	1311 3.0	1844 1.6
24 Sa	0122 3.4	0821 1.2	1441 2.9	1951 1.9
10 Sa	0105 3.7	0747 0.9	1414 3.1	1941 1.6
25 Su	0205 3.4	0858 1.1	1521 3.0	2035 1.8
11 Su	0157 3.9	0838 0.6	1508 3.3	2034 1.5
26 M	0244 3.5	0931 1.0	1556 3.0	2116 1.8
12 M	0247 4.1	0928 0.3	1558 3.4	2125 1.4
27 Tu	0321 3.6	1004 0.9	1630 3.1	● 2154 1.7
13 Tu	0336 4.2	1015 0.2	1646 3.5	○ 2216 1.3
28 W	0357 3.6	1038 0.8	1703 3.2	2229 1.7
14 W	0426 4.2	1103 0.2	1733 3.5	2306 1.3
29 Th	0432 3.6	1112 0.9	1736 3.2	2304 1.7
15 Th	0516 4.1	1150 0.3	1820 3.5	2357 1.4
30 F	0507 3.6	1145 0.9	1810 3.3	2340 1.7

JULY

Day				
1 Sa	0543 3.5	1219 1.0	1845 3.3	
16 Su	0028 1.4	0636 3.8	1256 1.0	1918 3.6
2 Su	0018 1.7	0621 3.4	1253 1.1	1922 3.3
17 M	0120 1.5	0725 3.5	1339 1.3	2002 3.5
3 M	0101 1.7	0703 3.3	1328 1.3	2002 3.3
18 Tu	0216 1.6	0817 3.2	1424 1.6	2047 3.4
4 Tu	0150 1.7	0752 3.2	1407 1.5	2047 3.3
19 W	0320 1.7	0919 2.9	1512 1.8	) 2138 3.4
5 W	0249 1.7	0852 3.0	1455 1.6	(2138 3.4
20 Th	0432 1.7	1039 2.7	1609 2.0	2236 3.3
6 Th	0359 1.6	1004 2.9	1553 1.7	2235 3.5
21 F	0549 1.7	1214 2.7	1715 2.1	2340 3.3
7 F	0513 1.4	1126 2.9	1700 1.8	2335 3.6
22 Sa	0700 1.5	1328 2.7	1822 2.2	
8 Sa	0624 1.2	1249 2.9	1810 1.8	
23 Su	0043 3.3	0755 1.4	1420 2.9	1922 2.1
9 Su	0036 3.8	0726 0.9	1358 3.1	1915 1.8
24 M	0137 3.4	0836 1.3	1501 3.0	2012 2.0
10 M	0135 4.0	0822 0.7	1454 3.3	2015 1.6
25 Tu	0223 3.6	0911 1.2	1536 3.2	2055 1.9
11 Tu	0230 4.1	0912 0.5	1543 3.5	2109 1.5
26 W	0303 3.7	0944 1.1	1609 3.3	2133 1.8
12 W	0323 4.2	1000 0.2	1629 3.6	○ 2200 1.4
27 Th	0341 3.8	1017 1.0	1640 3.4	● 2209 1.7
13 Th	0413 4.2	1045 0.4	1713 3.7	2250 1.3
28 F	0417 3.8	1049 1.0	1711 3.5	2244 1.6
14 F	0502 4.2	1129 0.5	1755 3.7	2339 1.3
29 Sa	0454 3.8	1122 1.0	1743 3.6	2321 1.6
15 Sa	0549 4.0	1213 0.7	1836 3.7	
30 Su	0530 3.8	1154 1.1	1816 3.6	
31 M	0000 1.5	0608 3.7	1227 1.2	1851 3.7

AUGUST

Day				
1 Tu	0044 1.5	0649 3.6	1301 1.4	1929 3.7
16 W	0139 1.5	0739 3.3	1338 1.7	1953 3.6
2 W	0133 1.5	0738 3.4	1340 1.5	2013 3.7
17 Th	0234 1.6	0833 3.0	1420 2.0	) 2039 3.5
3 Th	0230 1.5	0836 3.2	1426 1.7	(2104 3.7
18 F	0338 1.7	0942 2.8	1512 2.2	2135 3.4
4 F	0337 1.5	0947 3.0	1525 1.9	2204 3.7
19 Sa	0452 1.8	1119 2.7	1626 2.3	2243 3.3
5 Sa	0450 1.4	1110 3.0	1637 2.0	2310 3.8
20 Su	0609 1.7	1253 2.8	1746 2.3	2359 3.4
6 Su	0602 1.3	1234 3.1	1753 2.0	
21 M	0715 1.6	1351 3.0	1854 2.3	
7 M	0017 3.9	0709 1.1	1343 3.2	1902 1.9
22 Tu	0105 3.5	0802 1.5	1432 3.2	1948 2.1
8 Tu	0122 4.0	0806 0.9	1438 3.5	2002 1.8
23 W	0157 3.6	0840 1.4	1506 3.4	2032 2.0
9 W	0221 4.2	0856 0.8	1525 3.7	2056 1.6
24 Th	0241 3.8	0914 1.3	1537 3.6	2110 1.8
10 Th	0313 4.3	0941 0.7	1607 3.8	○ 2146 1.4
25 F	0321 3.9	0947 1.2	1607 3.7	2146 1.6
11 F	0401 4.3	1023 0.8	1646 3.9	2233 1.3
26 Sa	0359 4.0	1020 1.2	1637 3.9	● 2223 1.5
12 Sa	0447 4.2	1103 0.9	1723 4.0	2318 1.3
27 Su	0437 4.0	1052 1.2	1709 4.0	2302 1.4
13 Su	0530 4.1	1143 1.0	1759 3.9	2343 1.3
28 M	0515 4.0	1125 1.3	1743 4.0	2343 1.3
14 M	0003 1.3	0612 3.8	1221 1.2	1836 3.9
29 Tu	0556 3.9	1200 1.4	1819 4.1	
15 Tu	0050 1.4	0654 3.6	1259 1.5	1913 3.8
30 W	0029 1.3	0640 3.7	1237 1.5	1859 4.0
31 Th	0119 1.3	0731 3.5	1320 1.7	1945 4.0

TIME MERIDIAN 60°W 0000h is midnight, 1200h is noon.

Heights in feet are referenced to the chart datum of soundings.

PORT OF SPAIN, TRINIDAD

HIGH & LOW WATER 1995

10°39'N 61°31'W

ATLANTIC STANDARD TIME (GMT -4H)

SEPTEMBER				OCTOBER				NOVEMBER				DECEMBER			
1 F	0215 1.4 0831 3.4 1410 1.9 2040 3.9	**16** Sa	0249 1.7 0901 3.0 1426 2.3) 2044 3.5	**1** Su	0303 1.4 0933 3.4 1510 2.2 (2130 3.9	**16** M	0306 1.8 0935 3.1 1503 2.4 2110 3.4	**1** W	0453 1.6 1131 3.7 1727 2.0 2343 3.7	**16** Th	0415 1.8 1049 3.3 1642 2.2 2246 3.3	**1** F	0514 1.7 1148 3.6 1815 1.7	**16** Sa	0408 1.7 1044 3.4 1704 1.7 2309 3.0
2 Sa (	0319 1.4 0941 3.2 1514 2.1 2144 3.8	**17** Su	0356 1.8 1021 2.9 1542 2.4 2152 3.4	**2** M	0411 1.5 1048 3.4 1624 2.2 2245 3.9	**17** Tu	0413 1.9 1050 3.1 1622 2.5 2224 3.4	**2** Th	0556 1.7 1229 3.8 1837 1.8	**17** F	0513 1.9 1142 3.5 1751 2.0 2356 3.3	**2** Sa	0026 3.3 0610 1.8 1239 3.7 1916 1.5	**17** Su	0506 1.7 1138 3.6 1812 1.4
3 Su	0430 1.5 1101 3.2 1629 2.2 2255 3.8	**18** M	0512 1.9 1159 3.0 1709 2.5 2311 3.4	**3** Tu	0522 1.5 1201 3.5 1740 2.1 2359 3.9	**18** W	0521 1.9 1200 3.3 1738 2.4 2338 3.4	**3** F	0050 3.7 0651 1.7 1318 3.9 1935 1.7	**18** Sa	0607 1.9 1231 3.7 1850 1.7	**3** Su	0129 3.3 0701 1.8 1325 3.8 2006 1.4	**18** M	0024 3.1 0606 1.7 1232 3.8 1914 1.1
4 M	0543 1.4 1221 3.3 1746 2.1	**19** Tu	0622 1.8 1306 3.2 1822 2.4	**4** W	0628 1.6 1302 3.7 1849 2.0	**19** Th	0619 1.9 1250 3.5 1840 2.2	**4** Sa	0148 3.8 0738 1.8 1359 4.0 2022 1.5	**19** Su	0101 3.4 0657 1.8 1317 3.9 1943 1.4	**4** M	0221 3.3 0748 1.8 1407 3.8 2048 1.2	**19** Tu	0133 3.2 0705 1.6 1326 4.0 2009 0.8
5 Tu	0008 3.9 0651 1.3 1326 3.5 1855 2.0	**20** W	0026 3.5 0716 1.7 1349 3.4 1919 2.2	**5** Th	0106 4.0 0723 1.5 1350 3.9 1947 1.8	**20** F	0044 3.5 0707 1.8 1330 3.7 1930 1.9	**5** Su	0237 3.8 0820 1.8 1437 4.1 2104 1.3	**20** M	0200 3.5 0745 1.7 1401 4.1 2032 1.1	**5** Tu	0306 3.3 0831 1.8 1445 3.9 2126 1.1	**20** W	0234 3.3 0801 1.5 1418 4.2 2101 0.5
6 W	0115 4.0 0748 1.2 1417 3.7 1955 1.8	**21** Th	0125 3.6 0758 1.7 1423 3.6 2004 2.0	**6** F	0202 4.0 0810 1.5 1431 4.0 2036 1.6	**21** Sa	0140 3.7 0749 1.6 1407 3.9 2014 1.6	**6** M	0321 3.7 0859 1.8 1511 4.1 2142 1.2	**21** Tu	0253 3.7 0832 1.6 1446 4.3 2120 0.8	**6** W	0346 3.3 0912 1.7 1521 3.9 ○ 2202 1.0	**21** Th	0327 3.4 0855 1.4 1510 4.3 ● 2150 0.3
7 Th	0213 4.2 0836 1.2 1500 3.9 2046 1.6	**22** F	0213 3.8 0835 1.6 1455 3.8 2044 1.8	**7** Sa	0251 4.1 0850 1.5 1508 4.2 2118 1.4	**22** Su	0229 3.9 0829 1.7 1443 4.2 2057 1.3	**7** Tu	0400 3.7 0936 1.8 1544 4.1 ○ 2218 1.1	**22** W	0344 3.8 0919 1.5 1531 4.5 ● 2207 0.6	**7** Th	0423 3.3 0952 1.7 1557 3.9 2238 0.9	**22** F	0417 3.5 0948 1.3 1602 4.4 2239 0.2
8 F ○	0303 4.2 0918 1.1 1539 4.0 2132 1.4	**23** Sa	0256 4.0 0910 1.5 1526 4.0 2122 1.5	**8** Su ○	0335 4.1 0928 1.6 1542 4.2 2158 1.3	**23** M	0315 4.0 0908 1.6 1520 4.3 2140 1.1	**8** W	0437 3.6 1014 1.8 1617 4.1 2255 1.1	**23** Th	0433 3.8 1006 1.5 1618 4.5 2255 0.5	**8** F	0459 3.3 1030 1.7 1633 3.8 2315 0.9	**23** Sa	0505 3.7 1039 1.3 1653 4.4 2327 0.2
9 Sa	0349 4.3 0957 1.2 1614 4.1 2215 1.3	**24** Su ●	0337 4.1 0945 1.4 1559 4.2 2202 1.3	**9** M	0415 4.0 1005 1.6 1614 4.2 2237 1.2	**24** Tu ●	0401 4.0 0948 1.6 1559 4.5 2225 0.9	**9** Th	0513 3.5 1051 1.8 1651 4.0 2332 1.1	**24** F	0521 3.8 1056 1.5 1707 4.5 2344 0.5	**9** Sa	0535 3.3 1108 1.7 1710 3.8 2352 1.0	**24** Su	0552 3.7 1131 1.2 1744 4.3
10 Su	0431 4.2 1034 1.3 1648 4.2 2257 1.2	**25** M	0419 4.1 1020 1.4 1633 4.3 2243 1.1	**10** Tu	0453 3.9 1041 1.6 1646 4.2 2315 1.2	**25** W	0447 4.0 1029 1.6 1641 4.5 2311 0.8	**10** F	0551 3.5 1127 1.9 1727 3.9	**25** Sa	0611 3.8 1147 1.5 1759 4.4	**10** Su	0613 3.3 1145 1.7 1748 3.7	**25** M	0014 0.4 0640 3.7 1223 1.3 1835 4.1
11 M	0510 4.0 1111 1.4 1721 4.1 2338 1.2	**26** Tu	0501 4.1 1056 1.5 1710 4.4 2327 1.0	**11** W	0529 3.7 1116 1.7 1718 4.1 2354 1.2	**26** Th	0534 4.0 1114 1.6 1725 4.5 2359 0.8	**11** Sa	0011 1.2 0631 3.4 1205 2.0 1805 3.8	**26** Su	0034 0.6 0702 3.7 1241 1.6 1853 4.2	**11** M	0029 1.1 0652 3.3 1224 1.8 1828 3.6	**26** Tu	0102 0.6 0727 3.7 1318 1.3 1929 3.8
12 Tu	0549 3.8 1147 1.5 1754 4.0	**27** W	0545 4.0 1135 1.5 1749 4.4	**12** Th	0607 3.6 1152 1.9 1752 4.0	**27** F	0624 3.9 1202 1.7 1814 4.4	**12** Su	0052 1.3 0714 3.3 1245 2.1 1847 3.6	**27** M	0126 0.8 0755 3.7 1339 1.7 1952 4.0	**12** Tu	0107 1.2 0733 3.2 1305 1.8 1911 3.5	**27** W	0150 0.9 0816 3.6 1416 1.4 2025 3.5
13 W	0020 1.3 0628 3.6 1223 1.7 1828 3.9	**28** Th	0014 1.0 0633 3.9 1218 1.7 1833 4.3	**13** F	0035 1.3 0649 3.4 1228 2.0 1829 3.8	**28** Sa	0050 0.9 0717 3.8 1255 1.8 1908 4.2	**13** M	0136 1.5 0802 3.2 1331 2.2 1935 3.5	**28** Tu	0221 1.0 0852 3.6 1442 1.8 2054 3.7	**13** W	0147 1.3 0816 3.2 1353 1.9 1959 3.3	**28** Th	0240 1.1 0907 3.5 1510 1.5 (2126 3.2
14 Th	0104 1.4 0710 3.4 1258 1.9 1906 3.8	**29** F	0105 1.1 0726 3.7 1306 1.8 1924 4.2	**14** Sa	0118 1.5 0736 3.3 1308 2.2 1912 3.6	**29** Su	0145 1.0 0815 3.6 1354 2.0 2009 4.0	**14** Tu	0224 1.6 0855 3.2 1426 2.2 2033 3.4	**29** W	0317 1.3 0950 3.6 1550 1.8 (2203 3.5	**14** Th	0228 1.5 0903 3.3 1448 1.9 2055 3.2	**29** F	0332 1.4 1000 3.4 1629 1.5 2236 3.0
15 F	0152 1.6 0800 3.2 1337 2.1 1949 3.6	**30** Sa	0201 1.2 0826 3.5 1403 2.0 2023 4.0	**15** Su	0208 1.6 0831 3.1 1357 2.3 2005 3.5	**30** M	0244 1.2 0918 3.6 1500 2.1 (2116 3.9	**15** W)	0317 1.7 0951 3.2 1530 2.3 2138 3.3	**30** Th	0416 1.5 1050 3.6 1703 1.8 2315 3.4	**15** F)	0315 1.6 0952 3.3 1553 1.8 2159 3.1	**30** Sa	0426 1.6 1056 3.4 1741 1.5 2353 2.8
						31 Tu	0348 1.4 1025 3.6 1612 2.1 2229 3.8							**31** Su	0524 1.8 1154 3.4 1849 1.4

TIME MERIDIAN 60°W

0000h is midnight, 1200h is noon.

Heights in feet are referenced to the chart datum of soundings.

TRINIDAD

VENEZUELA

CAUTION: Our information on aids to navigation comes from official government sources. The latitudes and longitudes of these marks may not correspond to the readings from GPS receivers. Some aids have been reported as unreliable, missing, off position, or showing incorrect characteristics. No single aid to navigation, or waypoint, should be relied upon as a sole means of fixing your position.

NOTE: The chartlets in this section are <u>not intended for navigation</u> and are included for reference and planning purposes only. While chartlets reproduced from government sources are from the most current editions as of press time, they incorporate <u>no corrections</u> to navigational aids, depths, or hazards since the edition publication date.

ENTRY PROCEDURES

As the crow flies, it is almost 600 nautical miles from the Gulf of Paria to the Colombian border. The entire Caribbean coast of Venezuela measures about 1,700 miles. This area has become a popular cruising ground, especially during the hurricane season. See *Reed's Nautical Companion* for an illustration of the country flag.

Before sailing to Venezuela you must obtain a visa. Application should be made at a Venezuelan embassy or consulate, such as the ones in Port of Spain, Trinidad (809-627-9821 or -9823); on Bonaire; or on Grenada. You will need passport photos and financial references to submit with the application; passports should have at least six months remaining before expiration. There are processing fees. Generally, a visa is good for a two-month stay initially, with two-month extensions available for Bs1000. Check current policy when you arrive in the country. It is wise to request clearance for a stay longer than you intend, as the best laid plans tend to change. Your stay is timed from the day you enter the country.

For more information on visas contact the Embassy of Venezuela, Consular Section, 1099

30th Street NW, Washington, DC, 20007 (202-342-2214). In the U.S. there are additional Venezuelan consulates in Boston, New York, Miami, New Orleans, Houston, Chicago, San Francisco, and San Juan, Puerto Rico.

Ports of Entry include Güiria (10° 34'N, 62° 18'W), Carúpano (10° 40'N, 63° 15'W), Pampatar (10° 59'N, 63° 48'W), Cumaná (10° 28'N, 64° 11'W), Puerto La Cruz (10° 14'N, 64° 38'W), La Guaira (10° 37'N, 66° 56'W), Puerto Cabello (10° 29'N, 68° 00'W), La Vela (11° 28'N, 69° 35'W), Las Piedras (11° 43'N, 70° 13'W), and Maracaibo (10° 38'N, 71° 36'W). A pilot must be used when entering Maracaibo. The Islas Los Testigos are not an official Port of Entry, but you can try reporting to local officials. You should present your clearances in every harbor that has a port captain or customs office. Business hours are general 0830 to 1600, with a break for lunch.

Upon arrival in port you should proceed to customs *(aduana)*, the national guard, immigration, and then the port captain. Any weapons must be declared to the national guard and will be sealed on board. You should repeat this process in each new port, showing your clearance, or *zarpe,* from the last port. When requesting clearance to your next port, ask for permission to stop at any intermediate harbor along the way. To speed and simplify this process you might want to hire one of the commercial agents found in many ports.

Some areas of the Orinoco basin suffer from malaria, and some cholera is reported in Venezuela.

For U.S. citizens, the U.S. embassy is in Caracas (58-2-285-3111, -2222, or consulate general's office, -2475).

The monetary unit is the bolivar (Bs). There are 100 centimos in 1 bolivar. The current exchange rate (summer 1994) is about 180 bolivars to 1 U.S. dollar.

Venezuela's telephone country code 58. A one- or two-digit city code follows, then a local number. The language spoken is Spanish.

RÍO ORINOCO

Orinoco Entrance Buoy EO, 9 00.0N, 60 18.0W. Fl W 6s. Black buoy marked EO. Radar reflector.
Río Orinoco Approach Lighted Buoy "O.1.", 8 56.1N, 60 11.0W. Fl W 10s, 4M. SAFE WATER RW, pillar. Radar reflector 14M. RACON O (– – –).

GULF OF PARIA

PUNTA GORDA, 10 09.8N, 62 37.8W. Fl R 5s, 19ft, 3M. Aluminum and white column.

RÍO SAN JUAN

Buoy "E-1.", 10 19.0N, 62 28.0W. Fl W 5s, 11ft. Black buoy.
LIGHT 1, 10 18.5N, 62 29.2W. Q W, 13ft, 6M.
LIGHT 1-B, 10 18.4N, 62 31.0W. Q W, 14ft, 6M.
Güiria Approach Lighted Buoy, 10 34.0N, 62 15.0W. Fl W 3s. White buoy.
GÜIRIA EAST BREAKWATER, S extremity, 10 33.7N, 62 17.3W. Fl R 4.3s, 30ft, 8M. Gray round concrete tower. F R lights on radio tower 0.9 mile N.
SOUTH BREAKWATER, E extremity, 10 33.8N, 62 17.5W. Fl G 9s, 16ft, 4M. Gray round concrete tower.

GÜIRIA

10 34N, 62 18W
Pilotage: This small harbor located in the northwestern portion of the Gulf of Paria is about 30 miles west of the tip of the Península de Paria. The port may be identified by the red-roofed towers of a church, the radio towers north of the harbor, and the white tank on the high cliffs north of town. Several lights mark the harbor entrance. The pilot station for the Río San Juan and Orinoco area is here.
Port of Entry: This is the closest port to Trinidad for those headed west. The customs house is inshore of the western docks.
Dockage: You may be able to tie up along the breakwater in the western part of the harbor.
Anchorage: The best shelter is inside the breakwaters, if there is room. Depths are reported to be better than 15 feet.
Services: Supplies, including fuel, are limited.

PUERTO DE HIERRO, 10 38.2N, 62 05.6W. Fl W 6s, 262ft, 12M. White metal framework tower, red bands. Fl R on dolphin 789 meters ESE. Reported extinguished (1989).
ISLA DE PATOS, 10 38.1N, 61 52.1W. Fl W 6s, 374ft, 16M. White metal framework tower, black bands. Q R marks platform 15 miles S.

ENSENADA MACURO, E head of pier, 10 39.0N, 61 56.6W. Fl W 2s, 52ft, 9M. Metal tower.

NORTH COAST

ISLA TESTIGO GRANDE, 11 22.8N, 63 07.1W. Fl W 4.5s, 814ft, 10M. Tower, black and white bands.

LOS TESTIGOS

11 23N, 63 07W
Pilotage: This group of several islets and above-water rocks is located about 48 miles northeast of Isla de Margarita, on the direct route from Grenada. Isla Testigo Grande, the largest island, rises to a height of more than 800 feet on its northwest part. A light stands near the summit, but it has been reported as not visible from a distance of 5 miles. The island has been reported to be a good radar target at distances up to 22 miles.

The channels between some of the islands are deep and clear. The north islands are mostly unlighted and surrounded by deep water. They should be given a wide berth at night, keeping in mind the constant northwestward-going current. This current varies in intensity and set. In August the rate may be as much as 1 1/2 knots. In February the set is more north-northwest, at a rate of 2 knots. In July, it may attain speeds up to 3 knots.

There are several potential anchorages on the lee side of Isla Testigo Grande during periods of settled weather. Vessels should report to authorities ashore, but it is not a Port of Entry.

CARÚPANO, Cerro Miranda SW extremity of Hernan Vasquez Bay, 10 40.5N, 63 14.6W. Fl W 9s, 190ft, 24M. Black metal framework tower.
HERNAN VASQUEZ, head of breakwater, 10 40.7N, 63 14.8W. Fl G 3.5s, 10ft, 3M. White metal tower black bands.

CARÚPANO

10 40N, 63 15W
Pilotage: This harbor lies near the western end of the Península de Paria about 40 miles southeast of Isla de Margarita. Depths of 4 to 36 feet can be found up to a mile offshore in this area. To avoid the shoals and foul areas on either side of the harbor boats should stay in depths of more than 36 feet until directly off the port. Vessels should stay at least 1 1/2 miles off the

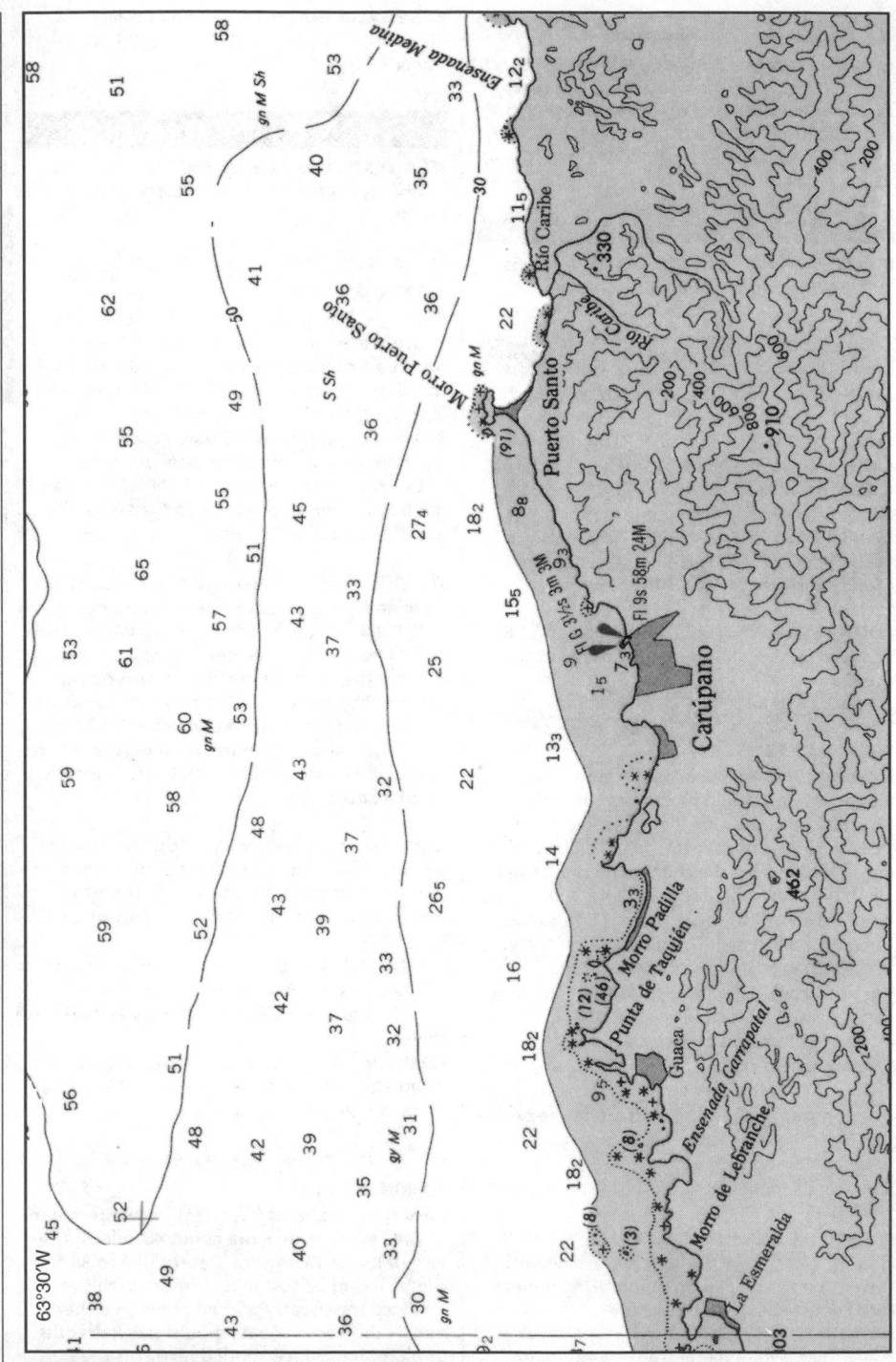

Carúpano, soundings in meters *(from DMA 24430, 5th ed, 8/93)*

coast from here to Morro de Chacopata, 33 miles to the west. A strong westward-setting current will be found all along this coast. Some radio masts 3/4 mile south of the breakwater, a cathedral, and a white church with twin spires are prominent landmarks. The port has a pier protected by a breakwater on its northeast side.

Port of Entry: This is the first Port of Entry west of Trinidad and north of the Península de Paria.

Dockage: You may be able to tie up stern-to on one of the wharves.

Anchorage: Anchor off the docks. Reports of swells and rough conditions are frequent.

Services: Most basic supplies are available.

MORRO DE CHACOPATA, 10 42.5N, 63 48.8W. Fl W 15s, 164ft, 16M. White metal framework tower, black bands. Reported extinguished (1990).
Isla Coche Buoy, 10 50.0N, 64 01.0W. Fl W 4s. Black buoy.

ISLA CUBAGUA

PUNTA CHARAGATO, NE extremity, 10 50.5N, 64 09.4W. Fl W 3s, 20ft, 10M. White concrete hexagonal tower with black bands.
PUNTA PALANQUETE, NW side of island, 10 49.8N, 64 12.6W. Fl W 8s, 42ft, 10M. Fiberglass tower.

LOS FRAILES

11 12N, 63 44W

Pilotage: This group of rocky islets is located about 7 to 9 miles east-northeast of Cabo de La Isla on Isla de Margarita. The islets have sparse vegetation and are steep-to. The south islet is the largest, rising to a height of 300 feet. The group has been reported to be a good radar target at distances up to 24 miles. Roca del Norte (11° 16′N, 63° 45′W) is a small rock about 10 feet high located about 3 miles north of Los Frailes. La Sola is a small rock about 25 feet high located about 10 3/4 miles east-northeast of Roca del Norte.

ISLA DE MARGARITA

CABO DE LA ISLA (Cabo Negro), on summit of hill at point, 11 10.5N, 63 53.1W. Fl W 10s, 236ft, 12M. White fiberglass tower, orange boards.
AVIATION LIGHT, 10 55.0N, 63 58.2W. Al Fl W G 10s. On roof of control tower.

PUNTA MOSQUITO, 10 54.0N, 63 53.7W. Fl W 5.5s, 95ft, 12M. White fiberglass tower, orange bands. R lights mark mast 7 miles NNW.

PAMPATAR

10 59N, 63 48W

Pilotage: The harbor is located on the eastern end of Isla de Margarita and is convenient for those voyaging from the Lesser Antilles via the Islas Los Testigos. The bay is generally clear of dangers. A fort with two towers stands on the shore and is a good landmark. The bay is very exposed to the prevailing easterly winds, but a new breakwater provides some protection. You can land at the public pier.

Port of Entry: You may clear in here or proceed directly to Porlamar to clear in if you use the local agent in Porlamar (Centro Nautico Margarita, VHF channel 72, call sign Ricardo).

Dockage: There are a couple of small marinas in Porlamar, about 4 miles beyond Pampatar.

Anchorage: The anchorage area has some protection from the east but is wide open to the southeast.

Services: Limited supplies are available in Pampatar. You can take a bus to the larger Porlamar for the supermarkets and open-air market. In Porlamar, for repairs and marine supplies, contact Venezuelan Marine Supply (58-95-631-072 or VHF channel 72).

MORRO DEL ROBLEDAR, 11 02.8N, 64 22.4W. Fl W 5s, 262ft, 16M. White fiberglass tower, orange bands.
Araya Bank Lighted Buoy, outer end of bank, 10 39.0N, 64 19.0W. Fl W 3s. Red buoy.
CUMANA, Puerto Sucre, SE corner of pier, 10 27.6N, 64 11.7W. Fl W 4.4s, 33ft, 6M. Concrete hexagonal pyramid black and white bands.

CUMANÁ

10 28N, 64 11W

Pilotage: The harbor is located on Punta Caranero at the entrance to the Golfo de Cariaco. There is a light at the airport reported on the chart to be Al Fl W G. This is located south and inland of the commercial port known as Puerto Sucre. The main pier projects southwest from the coast for 400 yards. The customs office is near the root of the pier. The yacht marina is located on the north side of the point, a bit northeast of the fishing harbor. There are reported to be red and green private marks indicating the dredged channel into the marina.

Port of Entry

Anchorage: You can anchor off town, near the commercial pier.

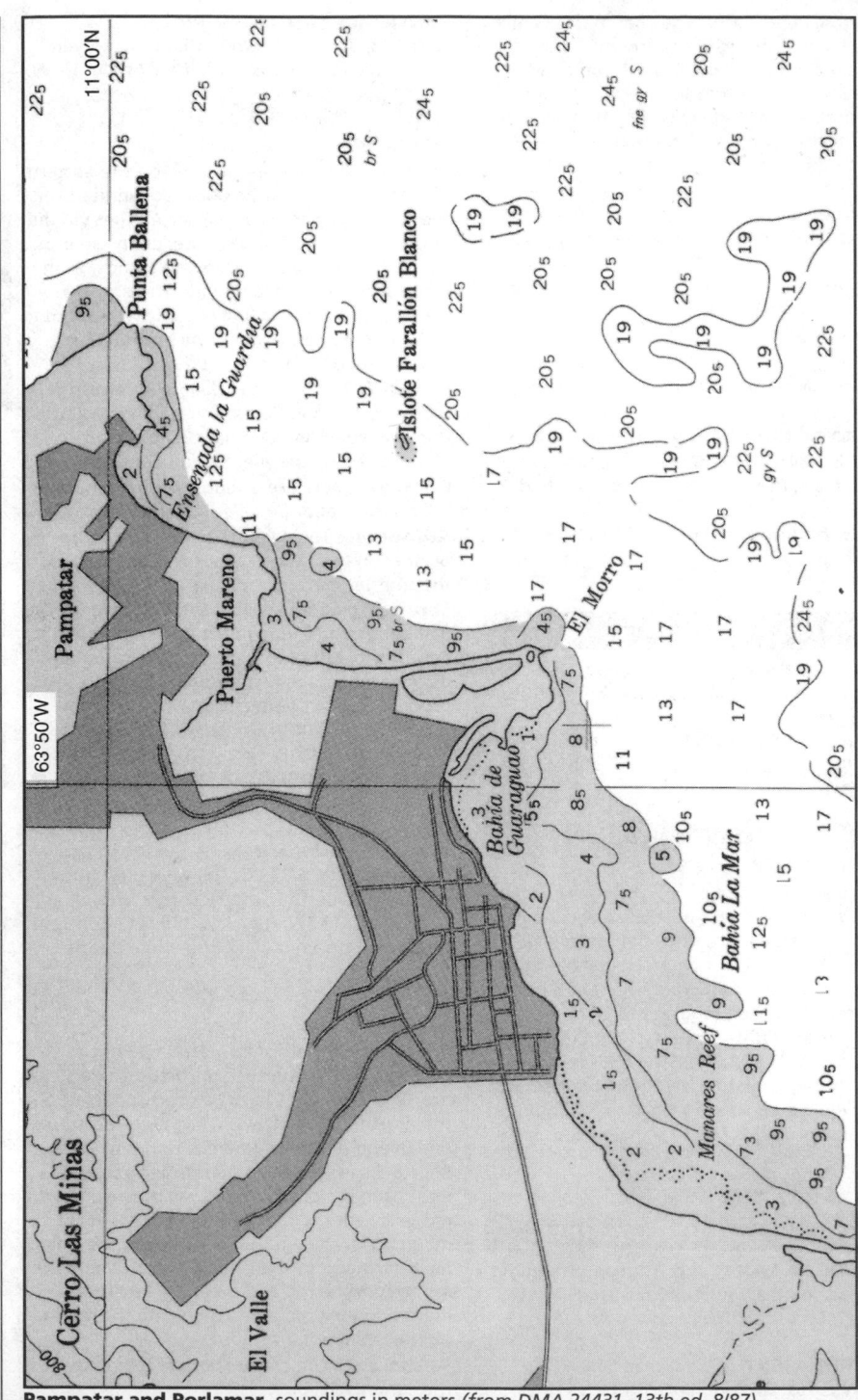

Pampatar and Porlamar, soundings in meters *(from DMA 24431, 13th ed, 8/87)*

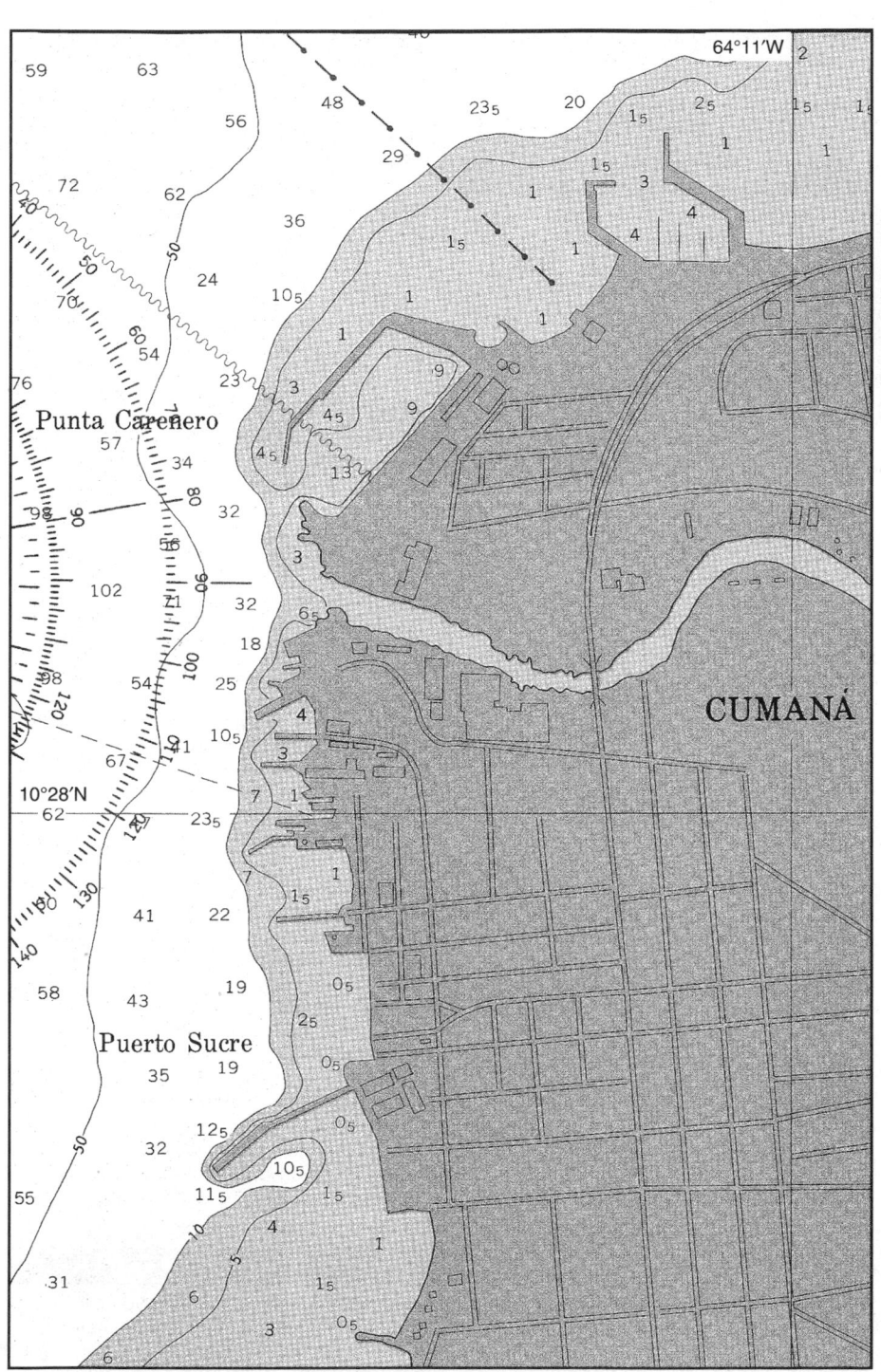

Cumaná, soundings in meters *(from DMA 24431, 13th ed, 8/87)*

Services: Fuel and water are available in the marina. There are haulout facilities and workboat-oriented repair shops. There are several good chandleries.

BAHÍA GUANTA

ISLA REDONDA, 10 15.4N, 64 35.6W. Fl G 6s, 27ft, 5M. Concrete hexagonal pyramid tower, red and white bands.
MORRO DE PITAHAYA, 10 15.4N, 64 35.7W. Fl R 3.5s, 65ft, 6M. Concrete hexagonal pyramid tower, red and white bands.

PUERTO LA CRUZ

10 14N, 64 38W
Pilotage: This is a major commercial and oil port, as well as a growing recreational boating center. The adjacent islands are relatively high and rocky with sparse vegetation. The radio towers 4 miles southwest and 3 miles south of the town are prominent. There is a major light on the summit of Morro Pelotas 2 miles east of town.
Port of Entry: For an agent's assistance with formalities, call Marisol on VHF channel 77 (or telephone 58-81-691-334).
Dockage: There are several marinas in this area including Paseo Colón, El Morro, and Americo Vespucio.
Anchorage: Many boats anchor off the beach. Dinghy theft has been reported in this area. This is a favorite area for those waiting out the hurricane season.
Services: Fuel is available in the marinas. Most marine services are available, including haulouts. There are good supermarkets and general stores of all types.

ISLA CHIMANA SEGUNDA, W end, 10 17.8N, 64 36.4W. Fl W 10s, 157ft, 10M. White fiberglass tower, orange bands.
ISLA LA BLANQUILLA, S end, 11 49.7N 64 36.1W. Fl W 11s, 66ft, 12M. Round fiberglass tower, white and orange bands. Visible 090°–260°.

LA BLANQUILLA

11 52N, 64 36W
Pilotage: This roundish island is about 5 miles in diameter, rising to a height of about 60 feet. It is located about 50 miles north-northwest of the western end of Isla de Margarita. The island is reported to be a good radar target at distances of up to 13 miles. The radar image is better when approaching from the west. There is a light on the south side.

There are several possible anchorages on the southeastern side of the island.

LOS HERMANOS

11 47N, 64 25W
Pilotage: This chain of seven barren, rocky islets lie about 45 miles north of the west end of Isla de Margarita. All of the islets are steep-to and have clear deep passages between them. Isla Grueso, the largest, rises to a height of 650 feet and is reported to be a good radar target at distances up to 25 miles. Isla Chiquito at the southern end of the group is the smallest islet.

BAHÍA BERGANTIN

Entrance Buoy, 10 15.0N, 64 39.0W. Fl W 3s.
ISLA BURRO LIGHT "3", 10 14.7N, 64 38.2W. Fl R 3s, 13ft, 2M. Yellow hut on concrete platform.
LIGHT "4", 10 14.6N, 64 38.1W. Fl R 3s, 13ft, 2M. Yellow hut on concrete platform.
LIGHT "5", 10 14.7N, 64 37.9W. Fl R 3s, 13ft, 2M. Yellow hut on concrete platform. F R on radio mast 1 mile ESE.
LIGHT "6", 10 14.8N, 64 37.8W. Fl W 3s, 13ft, 2M. Yellow hut on concrete platform.
LIGHT "7", 10 14.8N, 64 37.9W. Fl R 3s, 13ft, 2M. Yellow hut on concrete platform.
CARGO DOCK, W end, 10 14.4N, 64 38.1W. Q R, 3M.
BARCELONA AVIATION LIGHT, 10 07.2N, 64 41.0W. Al Fl W G 20s. Fl R on radio tower 4 miles N, 5 F R on radio tower 1 mile NW, F R on radio towers 5 miles NE, F W and F R on radio towers 9 miles NE.
Punta Puinare Buoy, about 274 meters S of point on Chimana del Oeste, 10 17.0N, 64 41.0W. Fl W 3s. Black buoy.
MORRO PELOTA, summit, 10 18.3N, 64 41.1W. Fl (2) W 12s, 250ft, 15M. White framework tower. Visible 320°–056°, 101°–180°. Irregular (1979).
CAYO BARRACHO, 10 18.2N, 64 44.1W. 30M. RACON B(– · · ·).
ISLAS PIRITU, W end of W island, 10 10.1N, 64 58.7W. Fl W 10s, 36ft, 11M. Cylindrical fiberglass tower, white and orange bands.

ISLA LA TORTUGA

PUNTA ORIENTAL, 10 53.9N, 65 12.1W. Fl W 7s, 56ft, 14M. White metal framework tower, black bands. F R on radio towers 3.7 miles W, 8 miles WNW, and 4.1 miles NW.

COAST PILOT

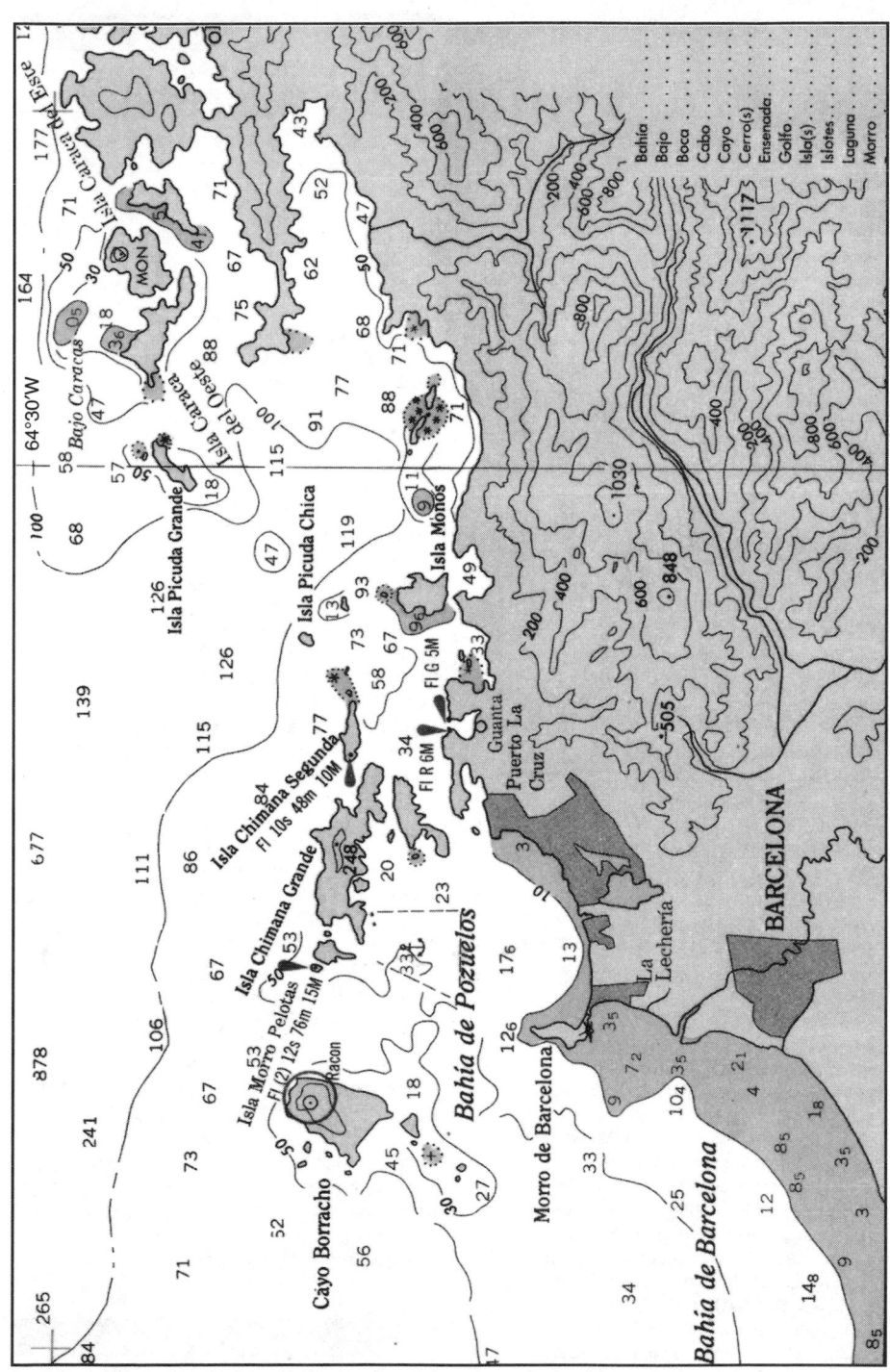

Puerto La Cruz Area, soundings in meters *(from DMA 24430, 5th ed, 8/93)*

CAYO HERRADURA, 10 59.5N, 65 23.7W. Fl W 12s, 59ft, 9M. Black metal framework tower. Reported Fl W, 10s (1993).

ISLA LA TORTUGA

10 56N, 65 18W

Pilotage: This barren island is about 12 miles long (east to west) and 6 miles wide. It rises to a height of over 130 feet. The island is located about 46 miles west of Isla de Margarita.

The south coast of the island is bold and steep-to, but the west and northwest sides are fringed by a sand and coral shoal that extends up to 2 miles offshore. Las Tortuguillas (two small islets) and Cayo Herradura lie near the outer edge of this shoal area. Several lighted radio towers stand in various locations on the island, and there are lights on Punta Oriental and Cayo Herradura. The island has been reported to be a good radar target at distances up to 24 miles.

There are several possible anchorages along the west and north coasts.

ISLA FARALLIN, "El Centinela," 10 48.9N, 66 05.5W. Fl (2) W 15s, 125ft, 15M. White fiberglass tower, orange bands.

FARALLON CENTINELA

10 49N, 66 05W

Pilotage: This prominent, light-colored rock, from which a light is shown, rises to an elevation of about 90 feet. It lies about 14 miles north of Cabo Codera on the Venezuelan coast. The northeast side is steep, but the southwest side slopes gradually to the sea. A rock, which breaks, lies 1/4 mile to the northwest. Farallon Centinella has been reported to be a poor radar target at a distance of 7 miles.

HIGUEROTE, E breakwater, head, 10 29.7N, 66 05.7W. Fl R.
PUERTO CARENERO, 10 32.3N, 66 06.8W. Fl W 9s, 138ft, 10M. Skeleton tower building.
CABO CODERA, 10 34.7N, 66 02.9W. Fl W 6s, 876ft, 25M. Black skeleton tower.
PUNTA CAMURI-GRANDE, 10 37.7N, 66 43.0W. Fl W R 3s, 43ft, 7M. Yellow masonry tower, black bands. W 029–063°, R 029°.
NAIGUATA, 10 36.9N, 66 45.0W. Iso W R G 2s, 52ft, 8M. White concrete tower, black bands.
PUERTO DEL GUAICAMACUTO HOTEL, W head, main breakwater, 10 37.6N, 66 50.7W. Fl W 5s, 22ft, 8M. White concrete tower, red bands. F R on hotel 5.55 miles 204°, Extinguished (1984).

LA GUAIRA

AVIATION LIGHT, 10 36.4N, 67 00.3W. Al Fl W G, 10s, 465ft, 15M. Metal framework tower.
LA GUAIRA, 10 34.9N, 66 56.8W. L Fl W, 15.5s, 1,394ft, 25M. Orange barrel,black "I" in center. Visible 291°–028°.
N BREAKWATER, 10 36.6N, 66 56.9W. Fl G 3.7s, 33ft, 6M. Green metal tower. Extinguished (1984).
S BREAKWATER, 10 36.1N, 66 57.3W. Fl R 3s, 29ft, 5M. Pyramid tower, red and white bands.
BREAKWATER, head, 10 36.3N, 66 56.6W. Fl R 2.5s, 23ft, 5M. Concrete pyramid tower, red and white bands.

LA GUAIRA

10 37N, 66 56W

Pilotage: This is an artificial harbor created by breakwaters to serve the city of Caracas. The north breakwater is 1500 meters long. From October to March especially, the harbor experiences heavy ground swell with considerable scend. This harbor is very commercial and is generally avoided by pleasure boats except those wishing to clear in to the country. The nearby marinas offer better shelter to yachts.

Port of Entry

Dockage: There are marinas at Caraballeda, 6 miles to the east, and in Catia La Mar, 4 miles to the west. There is another marina at Punta Naiguata, 6 miles east of Caraballeda. Most yachts will want to berth at one of these locations if visiting Caracas or La Guaira. You may be able to tie up at the main docks in La Guaira while clearing with the officials.

Anchorage: This would be an emergency anchorage only. You can anchor near one of the marinas mentioned above.

Services: There are no yacht-oriented facilities in La Guaira, but you can find most services at the marinas.

PLAYA GRANDE YACHT BASIN WESTERN LIGHT, 10 37.2N, 67 00.9W. Fl G 6s, 30ft, 11M. Truncated tower, red bands.
EASTERN LIGHT, Q R, 16ft, 4M. Metal tower.
CATIA LA MAR, outer end of pier, 10 36.4N, 67 02.4W. Fl R 2s, 20ft, 9M. Triangular daymark point upward.
TACOA, 10 35.5N, 67 04.9W. Fl R.

LA ORCHILLA

CERRO WALKER, 11 49.1N, 66 11.0W. Fl W 11.5s, 449ft, 15M. Black metal structure.

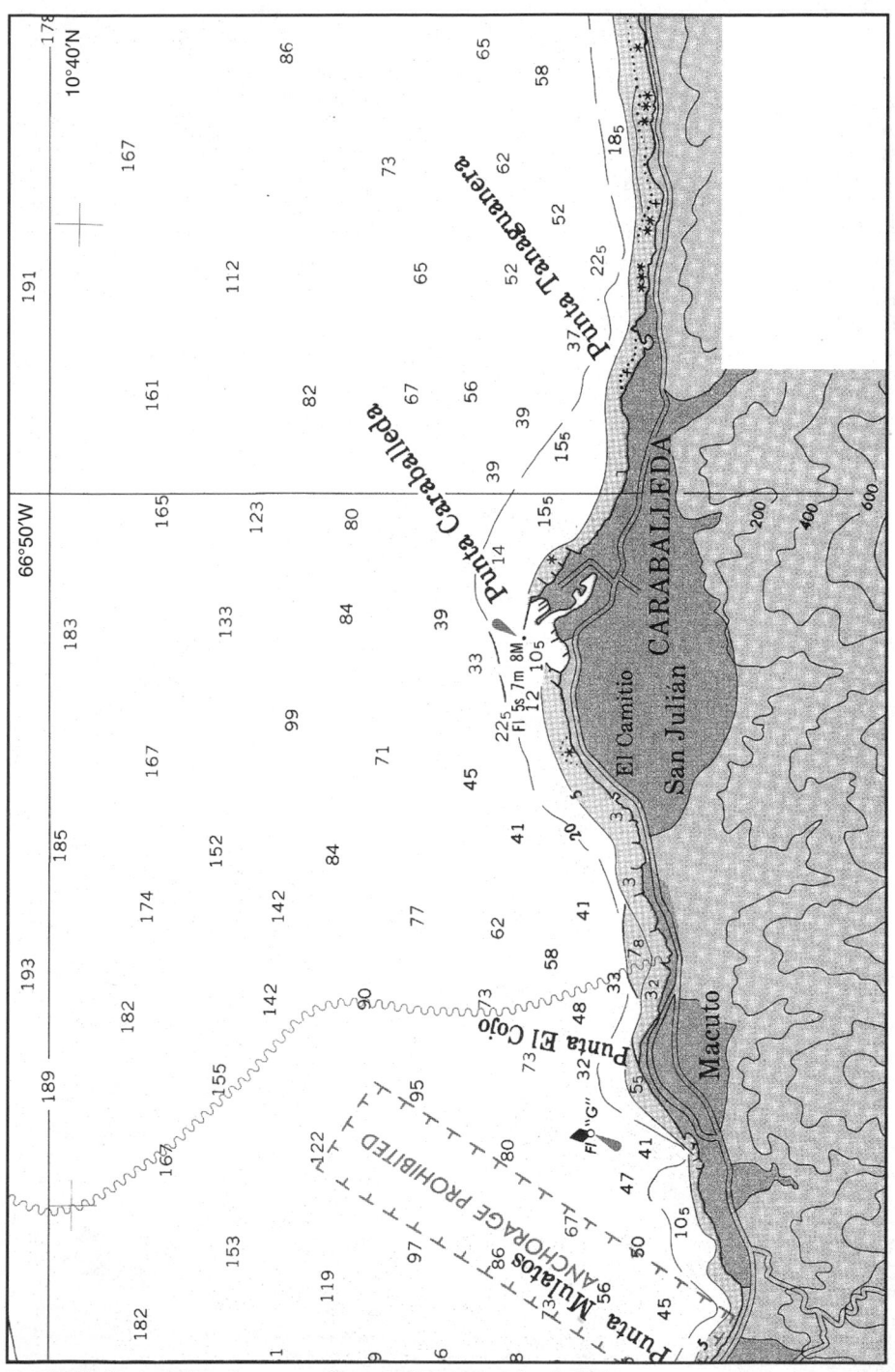

Caraballeda, soundings in meters *(from DMA 24452, 6th ed, 8/86)*

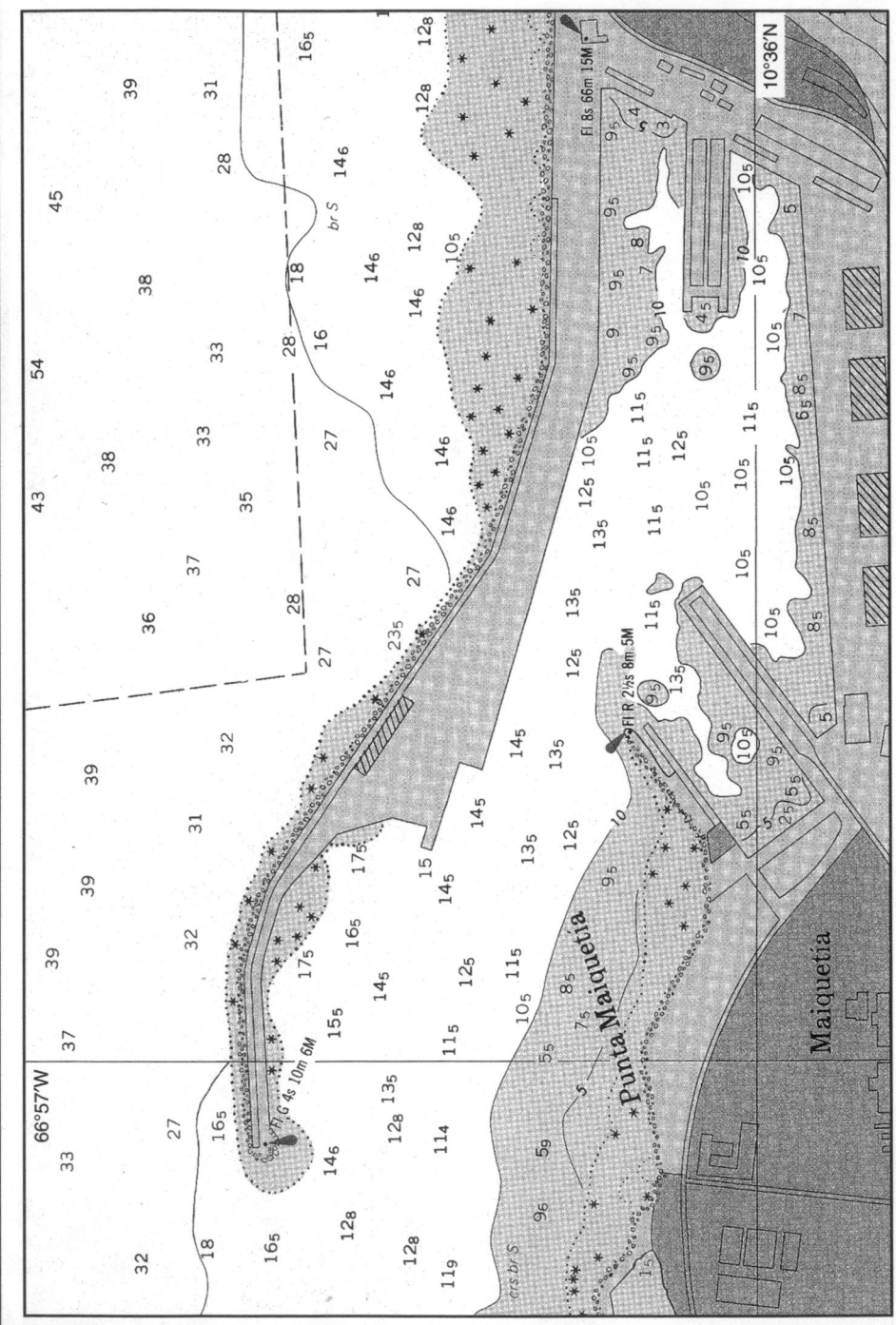

La Guaira, soundings in meters *(from DMA 24452, 6th ed, 8/86)*

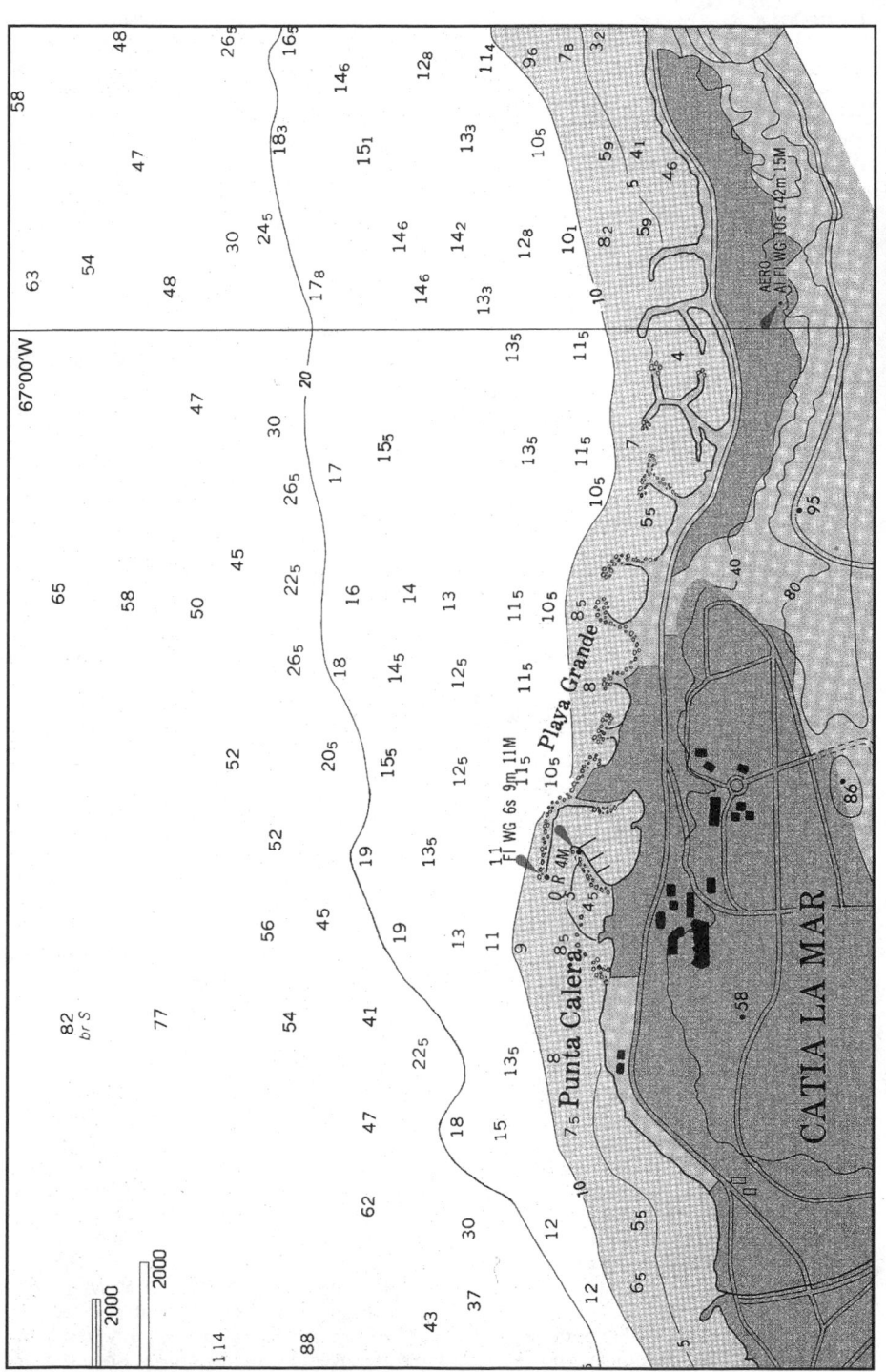

Catia La Mar, soundings in meters *(from DMA 24452, 6th ed, 8/86)*

LA ORCHILLA, head of pier, 11 48.6N, 66 11.9W. Fl W 4s, 19ft, 5M. Concrete pyramid tower, orange and white bands.

LA ORCHILLA

11 48N, 66 08W

Pilotage: This small (6 miles long) island is generally low and flat, but has seven distinct hills on its north side. These hills are visible from 15 miles and when first sighted from the north or south appear as separate islands. A 262-foot-high hill stands on the west end of the island, and Cerro Walker, the summit of the island, rises to 457 feet about 1 mile to its east. The island is reported to be a good radar target at distances up to 16 miles.

Cayo Nordeste (11° 52'N, 66° 06'W) is the largest of a series of small cays lying on a bank extending north-northeast from the northeast end of La Orchilla. Some ruined buildings can be seen on the north end of Cayo Nordeste.

CAUTION: Due to a naval base, the area around La Orchilla is restricted and closed to general navigation.

ISLAS LOS ROQUES

CAYO GRANDE, Sebastopol, 11 46.8N, 66 34.9W. Fl W, 6s, 42ft, 8M. Round fiberglass tower. white and black bands.
CAYO DE AGUA, 11 50.3N, 66 57.2W. Fl W 9s, 49ft, 10M. Cylindrical, fiberglass tower white and orange bands.
EL GRAN ROQUE, 11 57.5N, 66 41.1W. Fl W 10s, 220ft, 15M. White fiberglass tower with orange bands.

ISLAS LOS ROQUES

11 50N, 66 43W

Pilotage: This group of many cays and an extensive and dangerous coral reef lie 22 miles west of La Orchilla and about 70 miles north of La Guaira. The cays are all lower than 25 feet except for El Roque, which rises to 380 feet. El Roque lies on the northern extremity of the reef. The north extremity of the cay is in position 11° 58'N, 66° 41'W. A light is shown from this cay, and a prominent disused lighthouse is nearby. It has been reported as a good radar target at distances up to 23 miles.

A light is also shown from the southeast point of Cayo Grande, at the southeast end of the island group. There is a light at the western end of the group in at 11° 50'N, 66° 57'W. The south side of the group is steep-to. Be careful approaching the eastern side as the strong west-northwest-going current and easterly winds can make it a dangerous lee shore.

Puerto El Roque (11° 57'N, 66° 39'W) is an anchorage area near the north part of Los Roques. Vessels should obtain local knowledge before entering. Los Roques makes an excellent cruising area in good conditions once you are behind the outer reefs.

ISLAS DE AVES

AVES DE BARLOVENTO, on S island of group, 11 56.6N, 67 26.6W. Fl W 8.5s, 72ft, 12M. Black metal framework tower.
AVE DE SOTAVENTO, on N island of group, 12 03.6N, 67 41.0W. Fl W 15s, 75ft, 14M. Black metal framework tower.
MORRO CHORONI, 10 30.6N, 67 36.1W. Fl W 5s, 246ft, 10M. White metal framework tower.
ISLA TURIAMO, 10 29.0N, 67 50.4W. Fl W 9s, 66ft, 10M. White framework tower.
BAHÍA DE TURIAMO, pier head, 10 27.5N, 67 50.7W. Fl W 3.3s, 17ft, 6M. Black metal structure.
ISLA ALCATRAZ, 10 30.5N, 67 58.6W. Fl W 6s, 69ft, 10M. Black metal framework tower, black stripes.

ISLA DE AVES

12 00N, 67 24W

Pilotage: Another island with this name, also a Venezuelan possession, lies in position 15° 40'N, 63° 37'W (128 miles west of Dominica). This group of cays lies about 28 1/2 miles west of Islas Los Roques. There are two groups of low cays, about 8 1/2 miles apart lying on dangerous coral reefs.

The eastern group (11° 58'N, 67° 26'W), called Ave de Barlovento, is an area of small cays and shoals forming a circle about 5 miles in diameter. The east and north sides of the group form an almost continuous drying reef along which heavy breakers occur. The group is reported to be a good radar target up to 15 miles. There are good local-knowledge-only anchorages on the north sides of the cays.

Ave de Sotavento (12° 00'N, 67° 40'W) is the western group and is only about 33 miles east of Bonaire. A large cay on its southern side is mostly covered with mangroves. An unbroken drying reef extends from this cay along the east and north sides of the group. Heavy surf breaks along the entire reef, and there is foul ground up to 1/2 mile from it. The cay is reported to be a good radar target at distances up to 14 miles. There are possible anchorages within the reefs for those with local knowledge.

PUERTO CABELLO

PUNTA BRAVA, 10 29.4N, 68 00.6W. Fl W 8s, 95ft, 18M. White metal framework tower on white square tower, red bands. Visible 105°–255°. F R lights on radio mast 0.6 mile S. Reported Fl W 6s (1987).
ISLA GUAIGUAZA, 10 29.6N, 68 02.6W. Fl W 7.5s, 34ft, 8M. Black metal framework tower.
FORT LIBERTADOR, on pier, 10 29.0N, 68 00.7W. Fl G 7s, 6ft, 1M. Black concrete tower, white bands.
NAVAL QUAY SW END, 10 29.1N, 68 00.2W. Fl G, 20ft, 4M. Black framework tower.
PIER P.I.,10 29.0N, 68 00.5W. Oc R. Red mast.
Buoy, S side of channel entrance, 10 29.0N, 68 01.0W. Fl R 7s, 7ft, 1M. Red buoy.
PIER HEAD, 10 29.3N, 68 00.0W. F G, 20ft. White concrete pyramid tower, green bands.
FORTIN SOLANO, 10 27.8N, 68 01.2W. Fl (3) W 15.5s, 525ft, 18M. Metal framework tower.

PUERTO CABELLO

10 29N, 68 00W
Pilotage: Puerto Cabello is the third ranking port in Venezuela. Bajo Larne, a 19- to 20-foot-deep shoal located about 1/4 mile northeast of Isla Goaigoaza, breaks when any sea is raised. There is a prominent power plant about 2 miles west of town. The marina is located in the outer harbor, south of the main ship channel. The northern part of the inner harbor is a prohibited naval area. The port authority and customs house is located on the wharves to the south, near the entrance.
Port of Entry
Dockage: Tie up in the Marina Puerto Cabello, located west of the charted steeple.
Anchorage: Anchor near the marina.
Services: Most services are available, and there are some marine supplies In town are good supermarkets and general shops.

PIERHEAD, 10 29.4N, 68 02.1W. Fl R. Reported Fl Y (December 1985).

PUERTO CABELLO AVIATION LIGHT, 10 28.6N, 68 04.5W. Al Fl W G 4s, 73ft, 14M. On airport control tower.
PUNTA CHAVEZ, NW head of pier, 10 29.6N, 68 07.4W. Oc R 3s, 80ft, 10M. Aluminum tower. Reported extinguished (1980).
PUNTA CHAVEZ, SE head of pier. Fl G 3s, 80ft, 10M. Aluminum tower. Reported extinguished (1980).
MORON OIL TERMINAL, 10 31.1N, 68 11.3W. Fl W 3s, 10M. Red post, white bands.
CAYO BORRACHO, 10 59.0N, 68 14.9W. Fl W 8s, 46ft, 12M. Black metal tower.
CAYO NOROESTE, N side, 11 13.2N, 68 26.9W. Fl W, 6s, 49ft, 11M. Black pyramidal framework tower.
PUNTA AGUIDE, 11 21.0N, 68 41.1W. L Fl W R 15s, 190ft, 18M white, 7M red. White metal framework tower, black bands. W shore–198°, R 198°–218°, W 218°–shore.
PUNTA ZAMURO, 11 26.6N, 68 50.0W. Fl W 10s, 36ft, 12M. White metal and concrete framework tower, black top.
PUNTA MANZANILLO, 11 32.0N, 69 16.2W. Fl W 6s, 150ft, 15M. White metal framework tower, black bands.
PUEBLO CUMAREBO, 11 29.0N, 69 21.2W. F R, 57ft, 9M. White masonry tower.
PUNTA TAIMA TAIMA, 11 30.2N, 69 30.0W. Fl W 7s, 191ft, 12M. White metal framework tower, black bands.
LA VELA, 11 27.7N, 69 34.1W. Fl W, 65ft, 6M.

LA VELA

11 28N, 69 35W
Pilotage: The harbor, located in the southeast portion of Bahía Vela de Coro, is the last harbor before rounding the Península de Paraguaná. There is a pier located about 1 3/4 miles northeast of the town. The customhouse is a conspicuous white building with a red roof and the word "Aduana" painted on top.

CAUTION: An abnormal magnetic disturbance has been observed between Puerto Cumarebo and La Vela.

Port of Entry
Anchorage: Punta Taimataima is reported to provide little shelter to the east. This harbor can be rough to untenable in strong winds. This is the last shelter for many miles if headed west along the Venezuela coast.
Services: General supplies are available.

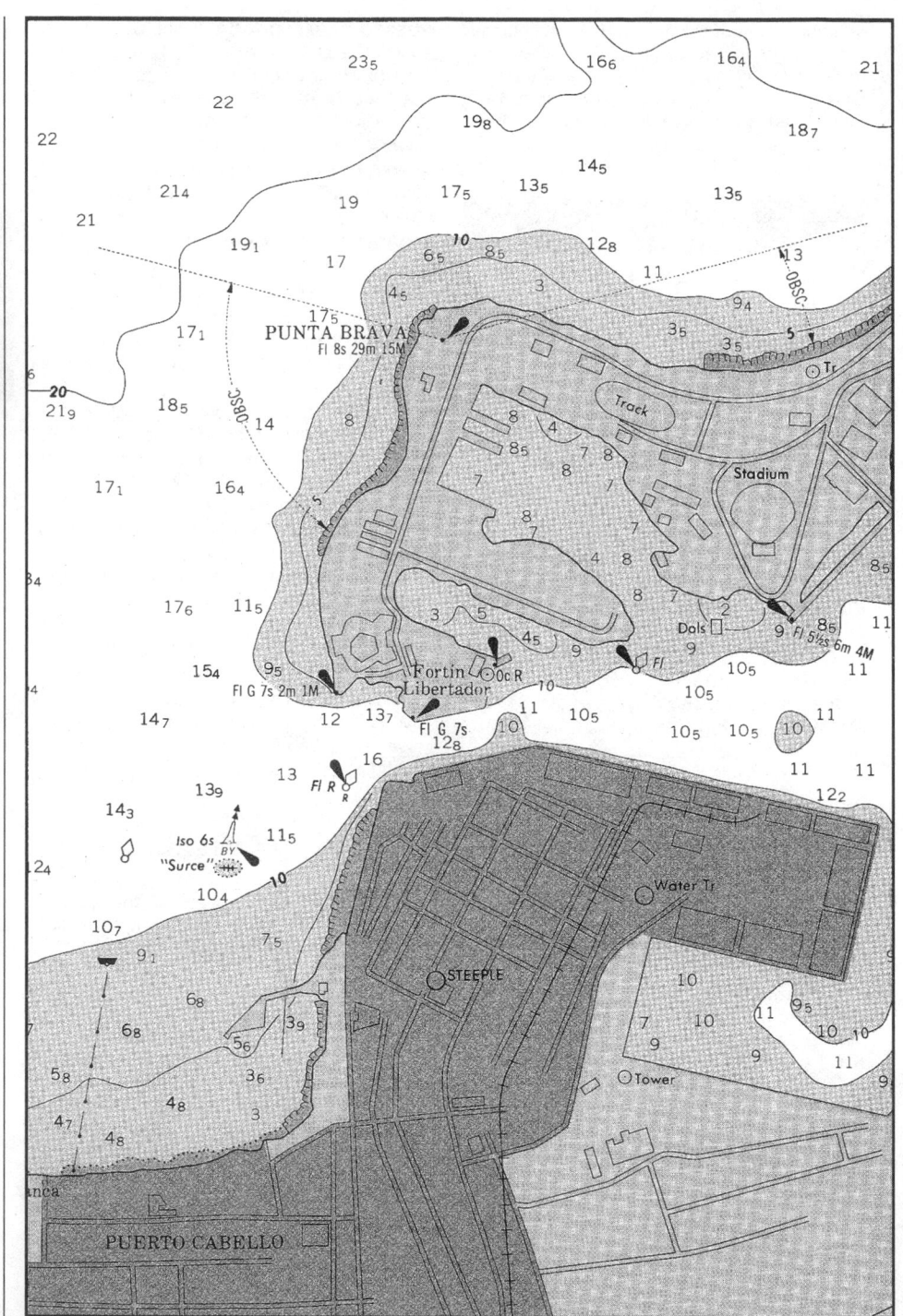

Puerto Cabello, soundings in meters *(from DMA 24454, 4th ed, 9/86)*

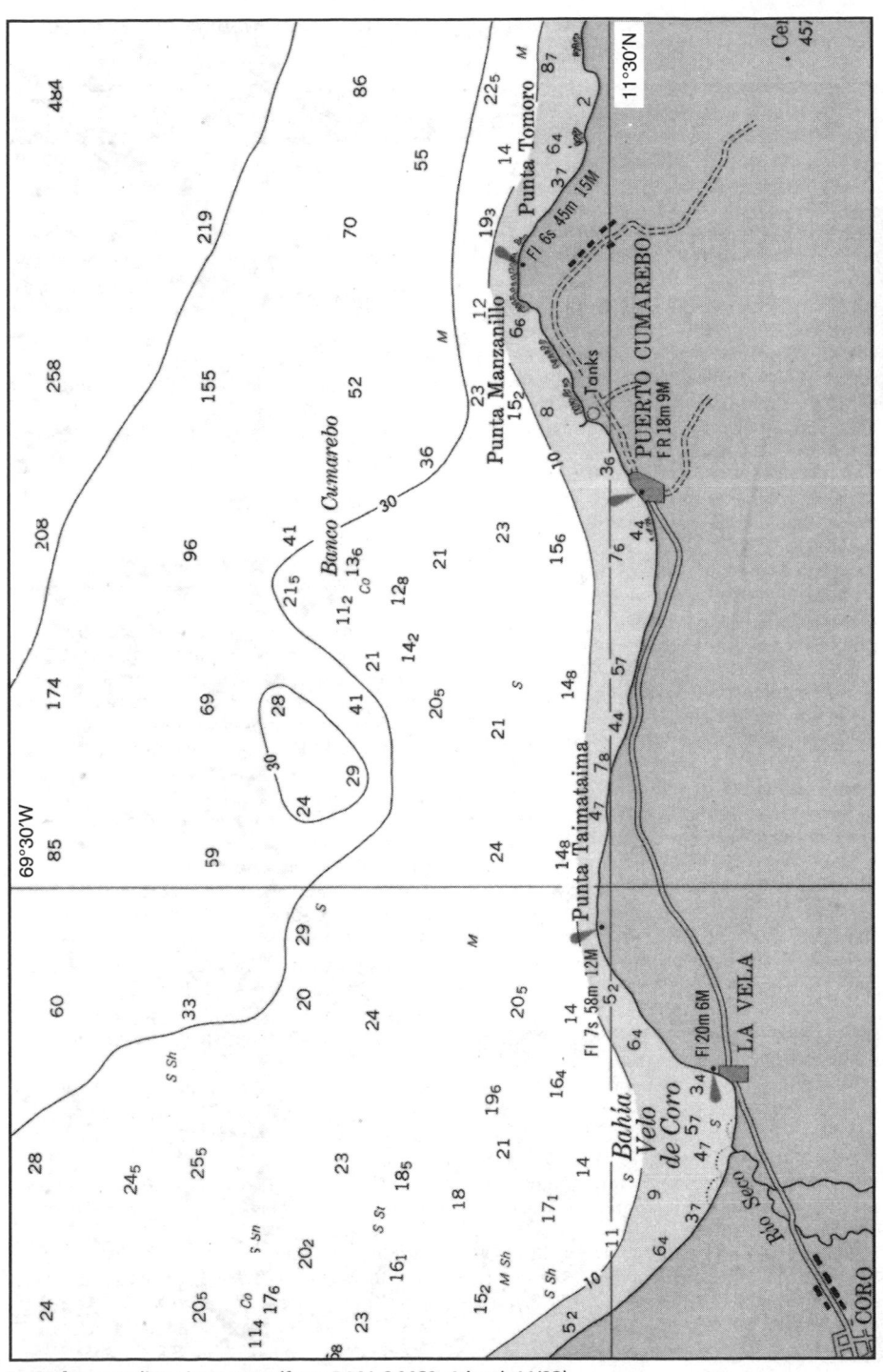

La Vela, soundings in meters *(from DMA 24460, 4th ed, 11/93)*

PUNTA ADICORA, 11 56.7N, 69 48.2W. Fl W 16s, 66ft, 16M. Black metal framework tower.

PENÍNSULA DE PARAGUANA

CABO SAN ROMAN, N side of peninsula, 12 11.3N, 70 00.1W. Fl W 6s, 79ft, 16M. Black metal framework tower.
MACOLLA, NW side of peninsula, 12 05.7N, 70 12.5W. Fl (2) W 15s, 131ft, 25M. Black metal tower, concrete base.
BAHÍA DE AMUAY (Front Light), 11 45.1N, 70 12.4W. F G, 122ft, 5M. Orange diamond daymark on aluminum tank. Oc R 2s and 2 F R on each of 2 towers, 0.93 and 1.2 miles ESE.
(Rear Light), 365 meters 074°45′ from front. F G, 156ft, 5M. Orange diamond daymark on aluminum tank.
LAS PIEDRAS, head of Naval Pier, 11 42.2N, 70 13.2W. Fl G 3s, 24ft, 8M. Concrete pyramid tower, white and green bands.

LAS PIEDRAS

11 43N, 70 13W
Pilotage: This village is located on the west side of the Península de Paraguaná. There is a dangerous wreck located about 1 mile west-southwest of Punta Piedras. Conspicuous water tanks stand on the eastern shore of Bahía Boca de Las Piedras. There are several commercial piers projecting from the town.
Port of Entry: Customs is about 2 miles south of Boca de Las Piedras in Caleta Guaranao.
Anchorage: Strong northeast trade winds have been reported here, but you should have good shelter with the land to the east.

PUNTA GORDA, 11 38.1N, 70 13.9W. Fl W R 10s, 204ft, 21M. Radio tower. R 340°–009°, W 009–202°. Reported extinguished (1992).

PUNTA BOTIJA

PIER NO 3, 11 37.1N, 70 14.0W. F W, 7ft, 5M. Concrete structure. Chimneys marked by red lights 0.6 mile and 1.5 miles NE.
PIER NO 1 (Front Light), 11 37.3N, 70 14.0W. F G, 13ft, 5M. Concrete structure. **(Rear Light),** 160 meters 061° from front. F G, 43ft, 5M. Metal structure.
PIER NO 2 (Front Light), 11 37.5N, 70 14.2W. F R, 13ft, 5M. Concrete structure. **(Rear Light),** 160 meters 061° from front. F R, 43ft, 5M. Metal structure.

PIER NO 4, 11 37.7N, 70 14.3W. F Blue, 13ft, 5M. Concrete structure.

PUERTO DE GUARANAO

GUARANAO PIER, S side, 11 40.3N, 70 13.0W. F R, 16ft, 3M.
N SIDE, 11 40.3N, 70 13.0W. F G, 16ft, 3M.

LAGO DE MARACAIBO ENTRANCE

MALECON DEL ESTE, E breakwater head, 11 01.4N, 71 34.9W. Fl Y 4s, 51ft, 10M. Fiberglass tower, white and orange bands.
Approach Whistle Buoy EM, 11 13.6N, 71 33.5W. Fl (2) W 10s. SAFE WATER RW, pillar, topmark. Radar reflector, whistle.

MARACAIBO

10 38N, 71 36W
Pilotage: This very commercial city is one of the busiest ports in Venezuela and a major oil industry center. Be wary of large commercial ships in the marked channels. When within 10 miles of "EM" buoy you should establish contact with the pilot station on VHF channel 16 (call San Carlos Pilot). You may be required to carry a pilot to Maracaibo. In any case, it is wise to monitor the VHF while in this area. Squalls, known locally as *chubascos,* occur frequently from May to August, usually between 1400 and 1900 hours. Winds are generally south to southeast with speeds up to 50 knots. They may last for 1/2 to 1 hour. A heavy rain usually follows. The Golfo de Venezuela is reported to be very rough with frequent high winds.
Port of Entry
Dockage: Contact the Club Nautico de Maracaibo or the Los Andes Yacht Club.
Anchorage: You may be able to anchor near the clubs, but the depths are reported to be less than 6 feet.
Services: There is fuel, water, and a haulout facility at Club Nautico. The city has good supermarkets, general stores, and restaurants.

PUNTA PERRET, 11 47.7N, 71 20.3W. Fl W, 15s, 22ft, 14M. Fiberglass tower, white and orange stripes.
MONJES DEL SUR, 12 21.3N, 70 54.1W. Fl W 10.6s, 253ft, 10M. Conical stone tower, white and orange bands, 29ft.

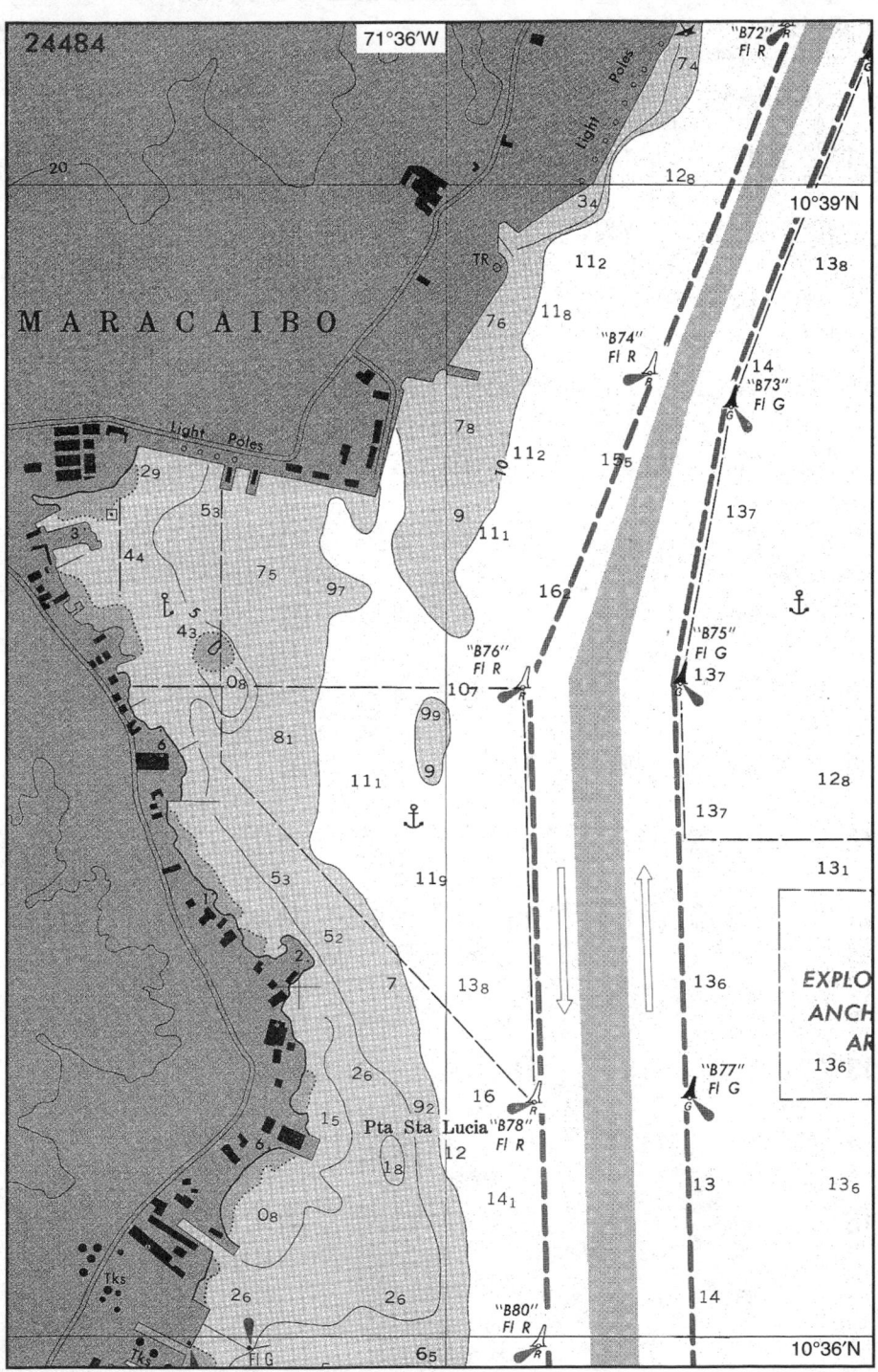

Maracaibo, soundings in meters *(from DMA 24482, 1st ed, 7/88)*

PUNTA GORDA, VENEZUELA

HIGH & LOW WATER 1995　　　　　　　　　　　　　　　　　**10°10'N　62°38'W**

ATLANTIC STANDARD TIME (GMT -4H)

JANUARY

Day	Time ft	Day	Time ft
1 Su ●	0505 6.5 / 1122 -0.3 / 1712 7.3 / 2353 -1.7	**16** O	0505 5.6 / 1124 0.2 / 1700 6.3 / 2351 -0.8
2 M	0552 6.7 / 1210 -0.4 / 1758 7.4	**17** Tu	0538 5.8 / 1202 0.1 / 1735 6.5
3 Tu	0039 -1.7 / 0635 6.7 / 1256 -0.4 / 1842 7.2	**18** W	0026 -0.8 / 0610 6.0 / 1238 -0.0 / 1810 6.6
4 W	0124 -1.5 / 0717 6.6 / 1343 -0.3 / 1926 6.9	**19** Th	0100 -0.8 / 0643 6.2 / 1314 -0.1 / 1847 6.6
5 Th	0208 -1.1 / 0758 6.4 / 1430 -0.1 / 2010 6.5	**20** F	0135 -0.6 / 0718 6.3 / 1352 -0.1 / 1927 6.5
6 F	0254 -0.6 / 0840 6.1 / 1519 0.2 / 2055 6.0	**21** Sa	0211 -0.4 / 0756 6.1 / 1435 -0.1 / 2011 6.2
7 Sa	0341 -0.1 / 0923 5.9 / 1611 0.5 / 2145 5.5	**22** Su	0251 -0.1 / 0840 6.2 / 1527 0.1 / 2101 5.8
8 Su ☾	0433 0.4 / 1010 5.6 / 1708 0.7 / 2241 5.0	**23** M	0342 0.3 / 0930 6.0 / 1629 0.2 / 2159 5.4
9 M	0528 0.8 / 1104 5.4 / 1809 0.7 / 2346 4.7	**24** Tu ☽	0447 0.6 / 1029 5.8 / 1741 0.2 / 2310 5.0
10 Tu	0628 1.0 / 1204 5.2 / 1910 0.6	**25** W	0603 0.9 / 1140 5.6 / 1854 0.0
11 W	0057 4.6 / 0727 1.1 / 1308 5.3 / 2009 0.4	**26** Th	0033 4.9 / 0718 0.8 / 1258 5.7 / 2003 -0.4
12 Th	0205 4.7 / 0824 1.0 / 1407 5.4 / 2102 0.1	**27** F	0156 5.0 / 0826 0.6 / 1413 5.9 / 2105 -0.9
13 F	0302 4.9 / 0915 0.8 / 1459 5.6 / 2150 -0.2	**28** Sa	0307 5.4 / 0926 0.1 / 1518 6.3 / 2200 -1.3
14 Sa	0349 5.1 / 1002 0.6 / 1544 5.9 / 2233 -0.5	**29** Su	0405 5.8 / 1020 -0.3 / 1614 6.6 / 2250 -1.6
15 Su	0429 5.4 / 1045 0.3 / 1624 6.1 / 2313 -0.7	**30** M ●	0454 6.1 / 1109 -0.6 / 1703 6.8 / 2336 -1.8
		31 Tu	0537 6.4 / 1155 -0.9 / 1747 6.9

FEBRUARY

Day	Time ft	Day	Time ft
1 W	0020 -1.8 / 0616 6.5 / 1238 -0.9 / 1828 6.8	**16** Th	0002 -1.0 / 0546 6.1 / 1217 -0.7 / 1755 6.5
2 Th	0101 -1.6 / 0653 6.4 / 1320 -0.9 / 1907 6.6	**17** F	0037 -1.0 / 0619 6.4 / 1255 -0.9 / 1833 6.6
3 F	0142 -1.2 / 0728 6.3 / 1402 -0.7 / 1945 6.2	**18** Sa	0112 -0.8 / 0655 6.5 / 1334 -0.9 / 1913 6.5
4 Sa	0222 -0.8 / 0803 6.1 / 1445 -0.4 / 2024 5.8	**19** Su	0150 -0.6 / 0733 6.5 / 1417 -0.8 / 1957 6.2
5 Su	0304 -0.3 / 0839 5.9 / 1531 -0.1 / 2105 5.4	**20** M	0232 -0.3 / 0816 6.4 / 1507 -0.6 / 2046 5.8
6 M	0349 0.3 / 0920 5.5 / 1622 0.3 / 2152 4.9	**21** Tu	0322 0.2 / 0905 6.1 / 1607 -0.3 / 2143 5.3
7 Tu	0441 0.7 / 1006 5.2 / 1720 0.5 / ☾ 2248 4.5	**22** W	0427 0.6 / 1004 5.7 / 1718 -0.1 / 2253 4.9
8 W	0541 1.0 / 1102 5.0 / 1824 0.6 / 2358 4.3	**23** Th	0544 0.9 / 1117 5.4 / 1832 -0.1
9 Th	0645 1.2 / 1209 4.8 / 1929 0.5	**24** F	0017 4.7 / 0701 0.8 / 1241 5.3 / 1943 -0.4
10 F	0114 4.2 / 0748 1.1 / 1320 4.9 / 2028 0.3	**25** Sa	0143 4.9 / 0811 0.5 / 1402 5.5 / 2046 -0.7
11 Sa	0223 4.4 / 0845 0.8 / 1424 5.1 / 2120 -0.1	**26** Su	0255 5.3 / 0912 0.0 / 1510 5.9 / 2142 -1.1
12 Su	0318 4.8 / 0935 0.5 / 1516 5.5 / 2206 -0.4	**27** M	0351 5.7 / 1005 -0.5 / 1605 6.2 / 2231 -1.4
13 M	0401 5.1 / 1020 0.1 / 1601 5.8 / 2248 -0.7	**28** Tu	0437 6.6 / 1053 -0.9 / 1651 6.5 / 2316 -1.5
14 Tu	0439 5.5 / 1101 / 1641 6.1 / 2326 -0.9		
15 W O	0513 5.8 / 1140 -0.5 / 1718 6.4		

MARCH

Day	Time ft	Day	Time ft
1 W ●	0516 6.3 / 1136 -1.1 / 1733 6.6 / 2357 -1.5	**16** Th O	0442 6.1 / 1115 -0.9 / 1658 6.4 / 2335 -0.8
2 Th	0551 6.4 / 1217 -1.2 / 1810 6.6	**17** F	0518 6.5 / 1155 -1.2 / 1738 6.6
3 F	0036 -1.3 / 0624 6.4 / 1256 -1.2 / 1845 6.4	**18** Sa	0013 -0.8 / 0554 6.8 / 1234 -1.3 / 1818 6.7
4 Sa	0114 -0.9 / 0655 6.1 / 1334 -1.0 / 1919 6.1	**19** Su	0051 -0.7 / 0632 6.9 / 1316 -1.4 / 1900 6.6
5 Su	0151 -0.5 / 0726 6.2 / 1412 -0.7 / 1953 5.8	**20** M	0132 -0.4 / 0713 6.8 / 1401 -1.2 / 1945 6.3
6 M	0229 -0.1 / 0759 6.0 / 1453 -0.3 / 2030 5.5	**21** Tu	0217 -0.1 / 0757 6.6 / 1452 -0.9 / 2035 5.9
7 Tu	0310 0.4 / 0836 5.7 / 1538 0.1 / 2112 5.1	**22** W	0311 0.3 / 0848 6.2 / 1551 -0.6 / 2133 5.5
8 W	0357 0.8 / 0918 5.4 / 1632 0.4 / 2201 4.7	**23** Th	0416 0.7 / 0947 5.8 / 1659 -0.2 / ☽ 2242 5.1
9 Th	0455 1.2 / 1010 5.0 / 1736 0.7 / ☾ 2304 4.4	**24** F	0531 0.9 / 1102 5.4 / 1811 -0.1
10 F	0603 1.3 / 1114 4.8 / 1844 0.7	**25** Sa	0004 4.9 / 0646 0.9 / 1228 5.2 / 1921 -0.2
11 Sa	0020 4.3 / 0711 1.2 / 1229 4.7 / 1948 0.5	**26** Su	0127 5.1 / 0755 0.5 / 1350 5.4 / 2024 -0.4
12 Su	0135 4.4 / 0812 0.9 / 1342 4.9 / 2044 0.2	**27** M	0235 5.5 / 0854 0.0 / 1457 5.7 / 2119 -0.7
13 M	0236 4.8 / 0905 0.5 / 1443 5.3 / 2133 -0.1	**28** Tu	0329 5.8 / 0946 -0.5 / 1551 6.0 / 2207 -0.8
14 Tu	0324 5.3 / 0952 0.0 / 1533 5.7 / 2216 -0.4	**29** W	0412 6.2 / 1032 -0.9 / 1636 6.3 / 2251 -0.9
15 W	0405 5.7 / 1035 -0.5 / 1617 6.1 / 2257 -0.7	**30** Th ●	0449 6.4 / 1114 -1.1 / 1715 6.4 / 2331 -0.8
		31 F	0522 6.5 / 1153 -1.2 / 1750 6.4

APRIL

Day	Time ft	Day	Time ft
1 Sa	0009 -0.7 / 0553 6.5 / 1200 -1.1 / 1822 6.3	**16** Su	0530 7.1 / 1216 -1.6 / 1804 6.8
2 Su	0046 -0.4 / 0622 6.5 / 1307 -1.0 / 1854 6.1	**17** M	0032 -0.3 / 0612 7.2 / 1300 -1.6 / 1849 6.7
3 M	0122 -0.1 / 0653 6.4 / 1343 -0.7 / 1927 5.9	**18** Tu	0117 -0.2 / 0655 7.1 / 1348 -1.4 / 1936 6.5
4 Tu	0158 0.3 / 0724 6.2 / 1420 -0.4 / 2001 5.7	**19** W	0206 0.2 / 0743 6.8 / 1439 -1.1 / 2028 6.1
5 W	0236 0.7 / 0800 6.0 / 1501 0.0 / 2040 5.4	**20** Th	0302 0.5 / 0835 6.4 / 1537 -0.7 / 2125 5.8
6 Th	0320 1.0 / 0841 5.7 / 1550 0.4 / 2126 5.1	**21** F	0406 0.8 / 0936 5.9 / 1641 -0.3 / ☽ 2231 5.5
7 F	0415 1.3 / 0929 5.3 / 1649 0.7 / 2222 4.8	**22** Sa	0516 0.9 / 1048 5.5 / 1748 -0.0 / 2345 5.4
8 Sa	0522 1.5 / 1029 5.0 / 1757 0.8 / ☾ 2330 4.7	**23** Su	0626 0.8 / 1210 5.3 / 1854 0.1
9 Su	0631 1.4 / 1140 4.9 / 1903 0.9	**24** M	0100 5.5 / 0732 0.5 / 1329 5.3 / 1955 0.0
10 M	0042 4.8 / 0734 1.1 / 1256 5.0 / 2002 0.6	**25** Tu	0204 5.7 / 0831 0.1 / 1436 5.6 / 2050 -0.1
11 Tu	0146 5.1 / 0831 0.6 / 1404 5.3 / 2054 0.3	**26** W	0256 6.0 / 0922 -0.3 / 1530 5.8 / 2139 -0.2
12 W	0240 5.6 / 0920 0.0 / 1501 5.7 / 2141 0.0	**27** Th	0340 6.2 / 1008 -0.9 / 1615 6.0 / 2223 -0.2
13 Th	0326 6.1 / 1006 -0.5 / 1551 6.1 / 2225 -0.2	**28** F	0417 6.4 / 1050 -0.9 / 1653 6.1 / 2304 -0.1
14 F	0408 6.5 / 1050 -1.0 / 1637 6.4 / 2307 -0.2	**29** Sa	0451 6.5 / 1129 -1.0 / 1728 6.1 / ● 2343 -0.0
15 Sa	0449 6.9 / 1132 -1.4 / 1720 6.7 / 2349 -0.4	**30** Su O	0522 6.5 / 1206 -0.9 / 1800 6.1

TIME MERIDIAN 60°W　　　　　　　　　　　　　0000h is midnight, 1200h is noon.

Heights in feet are referenced to the chart datum of soundings.

PUNTA GORDA, VENEZUELA

HIGH & LOW WATER 1995 10°10'N 62°38'W

ATLANTIC STANDARD TIME (GMT -4H)

MAY

Day	Time	ft	Time	ft	Time	ft	Time	ft
1 M	0020	0.2	0552	6.5	1242	-0.8	1832	6.1
16 Tu	0015	-0.1	0555	7.4	1246	-1.7	1839	6.7
2 Tu	0056	0.4	0623	6.5	1318	-0.6	1904	6.0
17 W	0104	0.0	0642	7.3	1334	-1.5	1928	6.6
3 W	0132	0.6	0656	6.4	1354	-0.3	1938	5.8
18 Th	0155	0.2	0731	7.0	1426	-1.2	2019	6.4
4 Th	0210	0.9	0731	6.2	1432	-0.0	2015	5.7
19 F	0251	0.5	0824	6.5	1520	-0.8	2113	6.1
5 F	0252	1.2	0811	5.9	1515	0.3	2058	5.5
20 Sa	0351	0.7	0923	6.0	1618	-0.3	2213	5.9
6 Sa	0342	1.4	0858	5.7	1607	0.6	2148	5.3
21 Su	0455	0.8	1029	5.6	1719	0.0	2317	5.8
7 Su	0443	1.5	0953	5.4	1708	0.8	2247	5.3
22 M	0600	0.7	1143	5.3	1821	0.3		
8 M	0550	1.4	1058	5.2	1813	0.9	2351	5.3
23 Tu	0022	5.7	0703	0.5	1258	5.2	1921	0.4
9 Tu	0654	1.1	1211	5.1	1915	0.9		
24 W	0123	5.8	0801	0.2	1406	5.3	2016	0.5
10 W	0055	5.6	0754	0.6	1323	5.3	2012	0.7
25 Th	0217	6.0	0854	-0.1	1503	5.5	2107	0.5
11 Th	0154	6.0	0848	0.0	1427	5.6	2105	0.5
26 F	0303	6.2	0941	-0.4	1550	5.7	2153	0.4
12 F	0247	6.4	0938	-0.6	1524	6.0	2154	0.2
27 Sa	0343	6.3	1025	-0.6	1630	5.8	2236	0.4
13 Sa	0336	6.8	1025	-1.1	1616	6.4	2241	0.0
28 Su	0420	6.4	1105	-0.7	1706	5.9	2317	0.5
14 Su	0423	7.2	1112	-1.5	1704	6.6	2328	-0.1
29 M	0454	6.5	1143	-0.7	1739	5.9	2355	0.6
15 M	0509	7.4	1158	-1.7	1752	6.8		
30 Tu	0526	6.5	1220	-0.7	1812	6.0		
31 W	0033	0.7	0559	6.5	1256	-0.5	1844	6.0

JUNE

Day	Time	ft	Time	ft	Time	ft	Time	ft
1 Th	0110	0.8	0632	6.4	1332	-0.3	1917	5.9
16 F	0141	0.1	0720	7.0	1408	-1.3	2004	6.7
2 F	0147	1.0	0708	6.3	1408	-0.1	1953	5.9
17 Sa	0234	0.2	0811	6.6	1459	-0.8	2053	6.5
3 Sa	0227	1.1	0747	6.2	1446	0.2	2032	5.9
18 Su	0329	0.4	0904	6.2	1551	-0.3	2144	6.2
4 Su	0313	1.2	0832	5.9	1529	0.4	2117	5.8
19 M	0427	0.5	1003	5.7	1646	0.2	2238	6.0
5 M	0407	1.2	0923	5.7	1621	0.7	2208	5.8
20 Tu	0527	0.6	1107	5.3	1744	0.6	2336	5.9
6 Tu	0509	1.2	1023	5.4	1722	0.9	2306	5.8
21 W	0628	0.6	1216	5.1	1843	0.8		
7 W	0614	0.9	1131	5.3	1828	1.0		
22 Th	0034	5.8	0727	0.4	1326	5.0	1940	1.0
8 Th	0009	6.0	0718	0.5	1245	5.4	1932	1.0
23 F	0131	5.9	0822	0.2	1428	5.1	2034	1.0
9 F	0112	6.2	0817	-0.0	1356	5.5	2032	0.8
24 Sa	0224	6.0	0912	-0.1	1521	5.3	2124	0.9
10 Sa	0212	6.5	0912	-0.6	1500	5.8	2127	0.6
25 Su	0310	6.1	0959	-0.3	1605	5.5	2210	0.8
11 Su	0309	6.9	1004	-1.1	1558	6.2	2220	0.3
26 M	0352	6.3	1041	-0.5	1644	5.7	2253	0.8
12 M	0402	7.2	1054	-1.5	1651	6.5	2311	0.2
27 Tu	0429	6.4	1121	-0.6	1719	5.8	2333	0.7
13 Tu	0453	7.4	1143	-1.7	1741	6.7		
28 W	0505	6.5	1159	-0.6	1751	6.0		
14 W	0001	0.0	0542	7.4	1231	-1.1	1829	6.8
29 Th	0011	0.7	0538	6.5	1235	-0.5	1823	6.1
15 Th	0051	0.0	0631	7.3	1319	-1.6	1916	6.8
30 F	0048	0.8	0613	6.6	1309	-0.4	1855	6.2

JULY

Day	Time	ft	Time	ft	Time	ft	Time	ft
1 Sa	0125	0.8	0648	6.5	1343	-0.2	1929	6.2
16 Su	0212	-0.0	0752	6.8	1432	-0.7	2024	6.8
2 Su	0203	0.8	0727	6.4	1418	0.0	2006	6.3
17 M	0301	0.2	0839	6.3	1520	-0.2	2108	6.5
3 M	0245	0.9	0809	6.2	1455	0.3	2047	6.3
18 Tu	0354	0.4	0929	5.8	1610	0.4	2154	6.3
4 Tu	0333	0.9	0857	6.0	1540	0.6	2134	6.3
19 W	0450	0.6	1025	5.4	1704	0.9	2245	6.0
5 W	0432	0.9	0953	5.7	1637	0.9	2228	6.2
20 Th	0549	0.7	1128	5.0	1802	1.2	2341	5.8
6 Th	0537	0.8	1058	5.4	1746	1.2	2330	6.2
21 F	0649	0.7	1238	4.9	1902	1.4		
7 F	0645	0.5	1213	5.3	1858	1.2		
22 Sa	0043	5.7	0748	0.6	1348	4.9	2000	1.4
8 Sa	0038	6.3	0750	0.1	1331	5.4	2006	1.1
23 Su	0143	5.8	0842	0.4	1449	5.1	2054	1.3
9 Su	0146	6.5	0850	-0.5	1442	5.7	2107	0.8
24 M	0238	6.0	0931	0.1	1538	5.4	2144	1.1
10 M	0250	6.8	0946	-0.9	1545	6.1	2204	0.5
25 Tu	0325	6.2	1016	-0.1	1619	5.7	2228	0.9
11 Tu	0348	7.1	1038	-1.3	1639	6.5	2257	0.2
26 W	0407	6.4	1057	-0.3	1655	5.9	2310	0.8
12 W	0442	7.3	1127	-1.6	1729	6.8	2347	-0.0
27 Th	0444	6.6	1135	-0.4	1728	6.2	2348	0.6
13 Th	0532	7.4	1215	-1.6	1815	7.0		
28 F	0519	6.7	1211	-0.4	1759	6.4		
14 F	0035	-0.1	0620	7.4	1301	-1.5	1859	7.0
29 Sa	0025	0.6	0554	6.8	1245	-0.3	1830	6.6
15 Sa	0123	-0.1	0706	7.1	1346	-1.2	1941	6.9
30 Su	0102	0.5	0629	6.8	1317	-0.1	1902	6.7
31 M	0138	0.5	0707	6.7	1350	0.1	1938	6.8

AUGUST

Day	Time	ft	Time	ft	Time	ft	Time	ft
1 Tu	0218	0.5	0748	6.5	1426	0.4	2017	6.8
16 W	0317	0.4	0853	6.0	1531	0.8	2107	6.5
2 W	0304	0.6	0835	6.3	1508	0.7	2102	6.7
17 Th	0409	0.8	0941	5.6	1622	1.3	) 2153	6.2
3 Th	0401	0.7	0929	5.9	1604	1.1	(2155	6.6
18 F	0506	1.0	1038	5.2	1720	1.7	2247	5.9
4 F	0507	0.7	1033	5.5	1717	1.5	2259	6.4
19 Sa	0608	1.1	1146	4.9	1824	1.9	2351	5.8
5 Sa	0619	0.6	1150	5.3	1835	1.6		
20 Su	0711	1.1	1302	4.9	1927	1.9		
6 Su	0012	6.3	0729	0.3	1314	5.4	1948	1.4
21 M	0100	5.8	0809	0.9	1411	5.2	2025	1.7
7 M	0129	6.5	0832	-0.2	1430	5.8	2053	1.1
22 Tu	0203	5.9	0901	0.6	1505	5.5	2116	1.4
8 Tu	0239	6.8	0930	-0.7	1534	6.2	2150	0.6
23 W	0257	6.2	0948	0.3	1549	5.9	2202	1.1
9 W	0339	7.1	1022	-1.0	1627	6.7	2243	0.2
24 Th	0342	6.5	1029	0.1	1625	6.2	2244	0.8
10 Th	0433	7.4	1110	-1.3	1713	7.0	O 2331	-0.1
25 F	0422	6.8	1108	-0.1	1659	6.6	2323	0.5
11 F	0521	7.5	1155	-1.3	1755	7.3 ●		
26 Sa	0459	7.0	1143	-0.1	1730	6.9		
12 Sa	0017	-0.3	0605	7.5	1239	-1.1	1835	7.3
27 Su	0001	0.3	0535	7.1	1217	-0.1	1802	7.1
13 Su	0101	-0.3	0648	7.3	1321	-0.8	1912	7.2
28 M	0037	0.2	0611	7.2	1251	0.1	1835	7.3
14 M	0146	-0.1	0729	6.9	1403	-0.3	1949	7.1
29 Tu	0114	0.2	0649	7.1	1325	0.3	1910	7.4
15 Tu	0230	0.1	0810	6.5	1446	0.3	2027	6.8
30 W	0155	0.2	0730	6.9	1402	0.6	1950	7.3
31 Th	0241	0.4	0811	6.6	1446	1.0	2036	7.1

TIME MERIDIAN 60°W
0000h is midnight, 1200h is noon.
Heights in feet are referenced to the chart datum of soundings.

VENEZUELA

PUNTA GORDA, VENEZUELA

HIGH & LOW WATER 1995 10°10'N 62°38'W

ATLANTIC STANDARD TIME (GMT -4H)

SEPTEMBER

Day	Time	ft	Time	ft	Time	ft	Time	ft
1 F	0337	0.6	0910	6.2	1544	1.5	2130	6.8
2 Sa	0445	0.7	1016	5.8	1700	1.8	(2236	6.5
3 Su	0558	0.8	1136	5.5	1821	1.9	2356	6.4
4 M	0710	0.6	1303	5.6	1935	1.6		
5 Tu	0119	6.5	0815	0.2	1419	6.1	2040	1.2
6 W	0231	6.8	0912	-0.2	1520	6.6	2136	0.7
7 Th	0331	7.1	1003	-0.5	1610	7.0	2227	0.2
8 F	0422	7.4	1050	-0.7	1652	7.4	O 2313	-0.1
9 Sa	0507	7.5	1133	-0.7	1731	7.6	2356	-0.3
10 Su	0548	7.5	1214	-0.5	1806	7.6		
11 M	0037	-0.3	0626	7.3	1253	-0.2	1840	7.5
12 Tu	0118	-0.1	0703	7.1	1332	0.3	1913	7.4
13 W	0159	0.2	0740	6.7	1412	0.7	1947	7.1
14 Th	0241	0.5	0818	6.3	1454	1.3	2024	6.8
15 F	0328	0.9	0900	5.9	1541	1.7	2106	6.5
16 Sa	0423	1.3	0951	5.5	1638	2.1	) 2157	6.2
17 Su	0525	1.5	1055	5.3	1744	2.3	2300	5.9
18 M	0630	1.5	1210	5.2	1851	2.3		
19 Tu	0013	5.8	0731	1.4	1324	5.4	1952	2.0
20 W	0124	6.0	0826	1.1	1423	5.8	2046	1.6
21 Th	0224	6.2	0914	0.8	1510	6.2	2134	1.2
22 F	0313	6.6	0958	0.5	1550	6.6	2217	0.8
23 Sa	0357	6.9	1037	0.3	1625	7.0	2257	0.4
24 Su	0436	7.2	1114	0.3	● 2335	0.1		
25 M	0514	7.4	1150	0.3	1733	7.7		
26 Tu	0014	-0.1	0553	7.4	1226	0.4	1809	7.8
27 W	0053	-0.1	0633	7.4	1303	0.6	1847	7.9
28 Th	0136	-0.1	0716	7.2	1344	0.9	1929	7.7
29 F	0224	0.2	0804	6.8	1433	1.3	2017	7.4
30 Sa	0321	0.5	0859	6.4	1535	1.7	2113	7.0

OCTOBER

Day	Time	ft	Time	ft	Time	ft	Time	ft
1 Su	0427	0.7	1005	6.1	1650	2.0	(2221	6.6
2 M	0539	0.9	1125	5.9	1809	2.0	2344	6.4
3 Tu	0649	0.8	1249	6.0	1921	1.7		
4 W	0108	6.4	0754	0.5	1403	6.4	2024	1.2
5 Th	0221	6.7	0850	0.2	1500	6.8	2119	0.7
6 F	0319	7.0	0941	0.0	1547	7.2	2208	0.2
7 Sa	0409	7.3	1027	-0.1	1628	7.5	2252	-0.1
8 Su	0451	7.4	1109	-0.1	1704	7.7	O 2334	-0.2
9 M	0529	7.4	1149	0.1	1737	7.7		
10 Tu	0013	-0.2	0605	7.2	1226	0.4	1809	7.6
11 W	0052	-0.0	0639	7.0	1304	0.7	1840	7.5
12 Th	0130	0.2	0712	6.8	1341	1.1	1912	7.3
13 F	0209	0.6	0747	6.5	1420	1.5	1947	7.0
14 Sa	0252	0.9	0827	6.2	1504	1.9	2028	6.7
15 Su	0341	1.3	0913	5.8	1558	2.2	2115	6.4
16 M	0439	1.6	1009	5.6	1703	2.4	) 2213	6.1
17 Tu	0544	1.7	1117	5.5	1811	2.4	2322	5.9
18 W	0647	1.6	1229	5.6	1915	2.1		
19 Th	0036	5.9	0745	1.4	1332	5.9	2011	1.7
20 F	0143	6.1	0836	1.2	1425	6.4	2101	1.2
21 Sa	0239	6.5	0922	0.9	1509	6.8	2147	0.6
22 Su	0328	6.8	1005	0.7	1550	7.3	2230	0.2
23 M	0412	7.1	1045	0.6	1629	7.7	2311	-0.2
24 Tu	0455	7.3	1125	0.5	1707	8.0	● 2353	-0.4
25 W	0537	7.4	1205	0.6	1747	8.1		
26 Th	0036	-0.5	0620	7.4	1247	0.7	1829	8.1
27 F	0121	-0.4	0706	7.2	1333	1.0	1914	7.9
28 Sa	0211	-0.2	0755	6.9	1426	1.3	2004	7.5
29 Su	0307	0.2	0850	6.6	1528	1.6	2101	7.0
30 M	0409	0.5	0954	6.3	1638	1.8	(2209	6.6
31 Tu	0517	0.7	1108	6.1	1751	1.8	2329	6.2

NOVEMBER

Day	Time	ft	Time	ft	Time	ft	Time	ft
1 W	0624	0.8	1225	6.2	1901	1.5		
2 Th	0051	6.2	0727	0.7	1335	6.5	2003	1.0
3 F	0203	6.4	0824	0.6	1433	6.8	2058	0.6
4 Sa	0303	6.6	0915	0.5	1520	7.1	2147	0.2
5 Su	0352	6.8	1002	0.4	1601	7.3	2231	-0.1
6 M	0433	6.9	1044	0.4	1637	7.4	2312	-0.3
7 Tu	0511	6.9	1124	0.5	1710	7.5	O 2351	-0.2
8 W	0545	6.9	1202	0.7	1741	7.4		
9 Th	0028	-0.1	0617	6.7	1239	0.9	1812	7.3
10 F	0105	0.1	0649	6.6	1315	1.2	1844	7.2
11 Sa	0142	0.4	0723	6.4	1353	1.4	1919	7.0
12 Su	0222	0.7	0759	6.2	1434	1.7	1957	6.8
13 M	0305	1.0	0841	6.0	1521	2.0	2042	6.5
14 Tu	0354	1.3	0929	5.8	1624	2.1	2133	6.1
15 W	0453	1.5	1026	5.7	1725	2.1	) 2235	5.9
16 Th	0555	1.6	1130	5.7	1831	1.9	2345	5.7
17 F	0656	1.5	1235	5.9	1932	1.5		
18 Sa	0057	5.8	0753	1.4	1334	6.3	2027	1.0
19 Su	0202	6.1	0845	1.1	1427	6.7	2117	0.4
20 M	0259	6.4	0933	0.9	1516	7.2	2204	-0.2
21 Tu	0350	6.7	1019	0.6	1602	7.5	2250	-0.6
22 W	0438	7.0	1104	0.5	1646	7.8	● 2335	-0.9
23 Th	0524	7.1	1149	0.4	1731	8.0		
24 F	0021	-1.0	0610	7.2	1235	0.4	1817	7.9
25 Sa	0108	-1.0	0657	7.1	1324	0.6	1904	7.7
26 Su	0158	-0.7	0747	6.9	1417	0.9	1955	7.3
27 M	0251	-0.2	0839	6.6	1515	1.0	2050	6.9
28 Tu	0348	0.0	0937	6.4	1619	1.2	2153	6.4
29 W	0450	0.4	1041	6.2	1726	1.4	2305	5.9
30 Th	0553	0.6	1149	6.1	1833	1.1		

DECEMBER

Day	Time	ft	Time	ft	Time	ft	Time	ft
1 F	0023	5.7	0655	0.8	1257	6.2	1935	0.8
2 Sa	0136	5.8	0754	0.8	1357	6.3	2032	0.4
3 Su	0239	5.9	0847	0.7	1449	6.5	2122	0.1
4 M	0331	6.1	0936	0.6	1533	6.7	2208	-0.2
5 Tu	0415	6.2	1020	0.6	1611	6.8	2250	-0.4
6 W	0452	6.3	1101	0.6	1646	6.9	O 2330	-0.4
7 Th	0526	6.3	1140	0.6	1719	6.9		
8 F	0008	-0.4	0558	6.3	1218	0.7	1751	6.9
9 Sa	0044	-0.3	0630	6.2	1254	0.8	1823	6.9
10 Su	0120	-0.1	0702	6.2	1330	1.0	1857	6.8
11 M	0156	0.1	0736	6.1	1408	1.1	1934	6.6
12 Tu	0233	0.4	0812	6.0	1449	1.3	2014	6.4
13 W	0313	0.6	0854	5.9	1538	1.4	2101	6.1
14 Th	0400	0.4	0942	5.8	1637	1.5	2155	5.7
15 F	0458	1.2	1036	5.8	1743	1.4	) 2258	5.5
16 Sa	0603	1.3	1138	5.8	1849	1.1		
17 Su	0010	5.4	0708	1.3	1244	6.0	1951	0.6
18 M	0123	5.5	0809	1.1	1348	6.3	2048	0.1
19 Tu	0231	5.7	0905	0.8	1446	6.7	2142	-0.5
20 W	0330	6.1	0957	0.5	1540	7.1	2232	-1.0
21 Th	0424	6.4	1047	0.2	1631	7.4	● 2320	-1.4
22 F	0513	6.7	1135	-0.0	1720	7.6		
23 Sa	0007	-1.6	0601	6.9	1224	-0.2	1808	7.6
24 Su	0055	-1.5	0647	6.9	1312	-0.2	1856	7.4
25 M	0142	-1.3	0734	6.8	1403	-0.1	1945	7.1
26 Tu	0232	-1.0	0822	6.6	1456	0.1	2036	6.6
27 W	0323	-0.5	0912	6.3	1553	0.4	2131	6.1
28 Th	0418	-0.0	1006	6.0	1654	0.5	(2234	5.6
29 F	0517	0.4	1105	5.8	1758	0.6	2344	5.2
30 Sa	0619	0.7	1209	5.6	1901	0.5		
31 Su	0058	5.0	0719	0.8	1313	5.6	2001	0.3

TIME MERIDIAN 60°W

0000h is midnight, 1200h is noon.

Heights in feet are referenced to the chart datum of soundings.

AMUAY, VENEZUELA

HIGH & LOW WATER 1995 | **11°45'N   70°13'W**

ATLANTIC STANDARD TIME (GMT -4H)

JANUARY

Day	Time ft	Time ft	Time ft	Time ft
1 Su ●	0539 0.7	0907 0.5	1519 1.4	2255 -0.7
2 M	0634 0.8	1010 0.5	1613 1.3	2344 -0.6
3 Tu	0726 0.8	1117 0.5	1712 1.1	
4 W	0033 -0.5	0817 0.9	1231 0.5	1824 1.0
5 Th	0120 -0.4	0904 0.9	1350 0.4	1950 0.8
6 F	0206 -0.2	0949 1.0	1515 0.3	2121 0.6
7 Sa	0250 -0.1	1031 1.0	1637 0.2	2246 0.6
8 Su ◐	0333 0.0	1110 1.1	1747 0.0	
9 M	0002 0.5	0413 0.2	1147 1.1	1840 -0.1 ◑
10 Tu	0111 0.5	0453 0.2	1221 1.1	1923 -0.2
11 W	0214 0.5	0531 0.3	1251 1.1	2000 -0.3
12 Th	0311 0.5	0608 0.4	1316 1.1	2034 -0.3
13 F	0406 0.4	0645 0.4	1334 1.1	2107 -0.4
14 Sa	0459 0.5	0722 0.5	1344 1.1	2140 -0.4
15 Su	0550 0.5	0800 0.5	1357 1.1	2214 -0.4
16 M ○	0638 0.5	0842 0.5	1420 1.0	2248 -0.4
17 Tu	0720 0.5	0931 0.5	1452 1.0	2323 -0.4
18 W	0753 0.6	1030 0.5	1531 0.9	2358 -0.3
19 Th	0818 0.6	1137 0.4	1619 0.8	
20 F	0035 -0.3	0837 0.6	1250 0.3	1720 0.7
21 Sa	0114 -0.2	0854 0.7	1405 0.2	1849 0.5
22 Su	0156 -0.1	0914 0.8	1517 0.0	2135 0.4
23 M	0242 -0.0	0943 0.9	1624 -0.2	2319 0.4
24 Tu	0331 0.1	1022 1.0	1725 -0.4	
25 W	0033 0.4	0423 0.1	1107 1.2	1822 -0.5
26 Th	0136 0.5	0517 0.2	1155 1.2	1915 -0.7
27 F	0232 0.5	0612 0.2	1246 1.3	2006 -0.7
28 Sa	0324 0.5	0707 0.2	1337 1.3	2055 -0.8
29 Su	0414 0.6	0803 0.2	1429 1.2	2143 -0.7
30 M ●	0503 0.6	0901 0.2	1522 1.1	2230 -0.7
31 Tu	0552 0.6	1001 0.2	1619 1.0	2315 -0.5

FEBRUARY

Day	Time ft	Time ft	Time ft	Time ft
1 W	0640 0.7	1104 0.2	1723 0.8	2359 -0.4
2 Th	0727 0.7	1211 0.2	1837 0.7	
3 F	0043 -0.3	0814 0.7	1323 0.1	2002 0.5
4 Sa	0125 -0.1	0859 0.8	1439 0.0	2127 0.5
5 Su	0208 0.0	0943 0.8	1553 -0.1	2245 0.4
6 M	0252 0.1	1025 0.8	1659 -0.1	2354 0.4
7 Tu	0337 0.2	1104 0.8	1751 -0.2 ◐	
8 W	0054 0.4	0421 0.2	1140 0.9	1833 -0.3
9 Th	0147 0.4	0506 0.3	1213 0.9	1911 -0.4
10 F	0235 0.5	0549 0.3	1242 0.9	1947 -0.4
11 Sa	0319 0.5	0631 0.3	1307 0.9	2022 -0.4
12 Su	0400 0.5	0713 0.3	1331 0.9	2056 -0.4
13 M	0438 0.4	0756 0.3	1356 0.9	2130 -0.4
14 Tu	0512 0.4	0842 0.3	1428 0.9	2205 -0.4
15 W	0540 0.5	0933 0.2	1508 0.8	2240 -0.3
16 Th ○	0602 0.5	1029 0.1	1558 0.7	2317 -0.2
17 F	0619 0.5	1130 0.1	1704 0.6	2357 -0.1
18 Sa	0638 0.6	1236 -0.0	1845 0.5	
19 Su	0040 -0.0	0710 0.7	1345 -0.2	2046 0.4
20 M	0129 0.1	0756 0.8	1454 -0.3	2216 0.5
21 Tu	0222 0.1	0852 0.9	1600 -0.4	2327 0.5
22 W	0320 0.2	0952 1.0	1702 -0.5 ◑	
23 Th	0027 0.5	0419 0.2	1051 1.1	1759 -0.6
24 F	0119 0.6	0518 0.2	1150 1.1	1852 -0.7
25 Sa	0207 0.6	0615 0.2	1247 1.1	1943 -0.6
26 Su	0253 0.6	0711 0.1	1343 1.1	2030 -0.6
27 M	0337 0.7	0806 0.1	1440 1.0	2115 -0.5
28 Tu	0419 0.7	0901 0.0	1538 0.9	2158 -0.4

MARCH

Day	Time ft	Time ft	Time ft	Time ft
1 W	0501 0.7	0957 0.0	1640 0.8	2239 -0.2
2 Th	0542 0.7	1053 -0.0	1748 0.7	2319 -0.1
3 F	0624 0.7	1152 -0.0	1903 0.6	2359 0.1
4 Sa	0705 0.7	1253 -0.1	2021 0.5	
5 Su	0041 0.2	0749 0.7	1355 -0.1	2137 0.5
6 M	0126 0.3	0834 0.7	1457 -0.1	2244 0.5
7 Tu	0215 0.3	0920 0.7	1555 -0.2	2342 0.5
8 W	0306 0.4	1006 0.7	1646 -0.2	
9 Th	0030 0.6	0358 0.4	1048 0.8	1731 -0.2 ◐
10 F	0113 0.6	0448 0.4	1127 0.8	1812 -0.3
11 Sa	0150 0.6	0535 0.3	1204 0.8	1851 -0.3
12 Su	0224 0.6	0620 0.3	1239 0.8	1928 -0.3
13 M	0254 0.6	0705 0.2	1317 0.9	2004 -0.3
14 Tu	0318 0.6	0751 0.2	1359 0.8	2040 -0.2
15 W	0337 0.6	0839 0.1	1448 0.8	2116 -0.1
16 Th ○	0349 0.7	0929 -0.0	1546 0.8	2155 -0.0
17 F	0403 0.7	1023 -0.1	1658 0.7	2235 0.1
18 Sa	0428 0.8	1121 -0.2	1824 0.6	2320 0.2
19 Su	0505 0.9	1222 -0.3	1953 0.6	
20 M	0011 0.3	0554 0.9	1326 -0.4	2112 0.7
21 Tu	0109 0.4	0657 1.0	1431 -0.4	2219 0.7
22 W	0213 0.4	0811 1.0	1534 -0.5	2317 0.8
23 Th	0319 0.4	0929 1.0	1635 -0.5 ◑	
24 F	0008 0.8	0424 0.4	1042 1.1	1731 -0.5
25 Sa	0054 0.9	0526 0.3	1149 1.1	1823 -0.4
26 Su	0136 0.9	0625 0.2	1253 1.0	1912 -0.4
27 M	0217 0.9	0720 0.1	1355 1.0	1956 -0.2
28 Tu	0255 0.9	0813 0.0	1457 0.9	2038 -0.1
29 W	0331 0.9	0905 -0.0	1600 0.9	2117 0.1
30 Th	0405 0.9	0955 -0.1	1707 0.8	2155 0.2
31 F	0434 0.9	1044 -0.1	1817 0.7	2231 0.4

APRIL

Day	Time ft	Time ft	Time ft	Time ft
1 Sa	0457 0.8	1133 -0.1	1929 0.7	2309 0.5
2 Su	0457 0.8	1223 -0.1	2041 0.7	2350 0.6
3 M	0438 0.8	1314 -0.1	2146 0.7	
4 Tu	0040 0.6	0457 0.8	1405 -0.1	2240 0.8
5 W	0137 0.6	0540 0.8	1456 -0.1	2325 0.8
6 Th	0239 0.6	0643 0.8	1544 -0.1	
7 F	0003 0.8	0338 0.6	0819 0.8	1629 -0.1
8 Sa	0035 0.8	0433 0.5	1005 0.8	1711 -0.1 ◐
9 Su	0103 0.8	0523 0.5	1113 0.8	1751 -0.1
10 M	0126 0.9	0611 0.4	1211 0.8	1830 -0.0
11 Tu	0144 0.9	0657 0.2	1309 0.8	1908 0.0
12 W	0157 0.9	0744 0.1	1409 0.8	1947 0.1
13 Th	0209 1.0	0832 -0.0	1514 0.8	2026 0.2
14 F	0227 1.1	0922 -0.2	1624 0.8	2108 0.3
15 Sa	0255 1.2	1015 -0.3	1738 0.9	2154 0.4
16 Su ○	0332 1.2	1110 -0.4	1854 0.8	2246 0.5
17 M	0417 1.2	1207 -0.4	2005 0.9	2346 0.6
18 Tu	0511 1.2	1307 -0.5	2109 0.9	
19 W	0054 0.7	0618 1.2	1407 -0.5	2205 1.0
20 Th	0207 0.6	0741 1.1	1507 -0.4	2255 1.1
21 F	0321 0.6	0912 1.1	1604 -0.4	2341 1.1 ◑
22 Sa	0431 0.5	1035 1.0	1658 -0.3	
23 Su	0023 1.2	0537 0.4	1150 1.0	1748 -0.2
24 M	0103 1.2	0636 0.2	1300 1.0	1834 0.0
25 Tu	0140 1.2	0730 0.1	1408 0.9	1916 0.2
26 W	0214 1.2	0821 0.0	1514 0.9	1954 0.3
27 Th	0244 1.2	0907 -0.1	1621 0.9	2030 0.5
28 F	0308 1.1	0952 -0.1	1730 0.9	2103 0.6
29 Sa	0319 1.1	1034 -0.1	1839 0.9	2136 0.7 ●
30 Su	0300 1.1	1115 -0.1	1949 0.9	2212 0.8

VENEZUELA

TIME MERIDIAN 60°W | 0000h is midnight, 1200h is noon.

Heights in feet are referenced to the chart datum of soundings.

AMUAY, VENEZUELA

HIGH & LOW WATER 1995 11°45'N 70°13'W

ATLANTIC STANDARD TIME (GMT -4H)

MAY

Day	Time ft	Time ft	Time ft	Time ft
1 M	0253 1.1	1157 -0.1	2054 0.9	2254 0.9
16 Tu	0351 1.5	1151 -0.6	1954 1.1	2325 0.8
2 Tu	0312 1.1	1239 -0.1	2148 0.9	2349 0.9
17 W	0448 1.4	1247 -0.5	2049 1.1	
3 W	0344 1.1	1322 -0.1	2230 1.0	
18 Th	0039 0.8	0556 1.3	1342 -0.5	2140 1.2
4 Th	0056 0.9	0425 1.0	1406 -0.1	2303 1.0
19 F	0158 0.7	0722 1.2	1437 -0.4	2226 1.3
5 F	0208 0.9	0518 1.0	1449 -0.1	2331 1.0
20 Sa	0319 0.6	0900 1.0	1531 -0.2	2309 1.3
6 Sa	0316 0.8	0626 0.9	1532 -0.0	2354 1.0
21 Su	0436 0.5	1030 1.0	1621 -0.1	) 2350 1.4
7 Su (	0417 0.7	0757 0.8	1613 0.0	
22 M	0544 0.3	1151 0.9	1708 0.1	
8 M	0012 1.1	0510 0.5	1006 0.8	1654 0.1
23 Tu	0028 1.4	0644 0.2	1306 0.9	1751 0.3
9 Tu	0026 1.1	0559 0.4	1154 0.8	1734 0.2
24 W	0103 1.4	0736 0.0	1417 0.9	1831 0.4
10 W	0036 1.2	0647 0.2	1313 0.8	1814 0.3
25 Th	0135 1.4	0822 -0.1	1526 0.9	1907 0.6
11 Th	0049 1.3	0735 -0.0	1424 0.8	1856 0.4
26 F	0202 1.3	0904 -0.1	1633 0.9	1940 0.7
12 F	0110 1.4	0823 -0.2	1533 0.8	1939 0.5
27 Sa	0219 1.3	0943 -0.2	1740 0.9	2012 0.8
13 Sa	0141 1.4	0912 -0.3	1642 0.9	2027 0.6
28 Su	0216 1.3	1019 -0.2	1847 0.9	2043 0.9
14 Su	0218 1.5	1004 -0.5	1749 0.9	O 2119 0.7
29 M	0202 1.3	1055 -0.2	1953 1.0	● 2117 0.9
15 M	0302 1.5	1057 -0.5	1854 0.9	2218 0.7
30 Tu	0212 1.3	1130 -0.2	2052 1.0	2201 1.0
31 W	0237 1.2	1207 -0.1	2134 1.0	2302 1.0

JUNE

Day	Time ft	Time ft	Time ft	Time ft
1 Th	0310 1.2	1245 -0.1	2205 1.0	
16 F	0024 0.8	0546 1.3	1315 -0.4	2106 1.3
2 F	0016 1.0	0350 1.1	1323 -0.1	2230 1.1
17 Sa	0145 0.7	0715 1.1	1406 -0.2	2151 1.3
3 Sa	0134 0.9	0438 1.0	1402 -0.0	2250 1.1
18 Su	0310 0.6	0856 0.9	1455 -0.1	2234 1.4
4 Su	0249 0.8	0539 0.9	1441 0.0	2305 1.1
19 M	0431 0.4	1029 0.9	1542 0.1	) 2314 1.4
5 M	0355 0.7	0704 0.8	1521 0.1	2316 1.2
20 Tu	0542 0.2	1152 0.8	1627 0.3	2353 1.4
6 Tu	0453 0.5	0931 0.7	1601 0.2	(2324 1.2
21 W	0641 0.1	1308 0.8	1709 0.4	
7 W	0544 0.3	1204 0.3	1643 0.3	2337 1.4
22 Th	0028 1.4	0729 -0.1	1419 0.8	1748 0.6
8 Th	0633 0.1	1326 0.7	1727 0.4	
23 F	0100 1.4	0812 -0.1	1524 0.8	1825 0.7
9 F	0001 1.5	0722 -0.2	1436 0.8	1814 0.5
24 Sa	0126 1.4	0849 -0.2	1626 0.9	1900 0.8
10 Sa	0034 1.6	0810 -0.3	1540 0.8	1903 0.6
25 Su	0144 1.4	0924 -0.2	1726 0.9	1934 0.8
11 Su	0113 1.6	0859 -0.5	1640 0.9	1957 0.7
26 M	0145 1.3	0956 -0.2	1824 0.9	2010 0.9
12 M	0158 1.7	0949 -0.6	1738 1.0	2055 0.7
27 Tu	0142 1.3	1028 -0.2	1919 0.9	● 2049 0.9
13 Tu	0246 1.6	1040 -0.6	1834 1.0	O 2158 0.8
28 W	0157 1.3	1101 -0.2	2007 1.0	2137 1.0
14 W	0338 1.6	1132 -0.6	1927 1.1	2308 0.8
29 Th	0223 1.3	1134 -0.1	2045 1.1	2238 1.0
15 Th	0437 1.4	1223 -0.5	2018 1.2	
30 F	0256 1.2	1208 -0.1	2113 1.0	2348 0.9

JULY

Day	Time ft	Time ft	Time ft	Time ft
1 Sa	0336 1.1	1243 -0.0	2135 1.0	
16 Su	0128 0.6	0723 1.0	1331 0.0	2109 1.3
2 Su	0103 0.9	0425 1.0	1318 0.1	2151 1.1
17 M	0251 0.5	0901 0.9	1417 0.2	2153 1.4
3 M	0218 0.7	0527 0.9	1356 0.1	2201 1.1
18 Tu	0412 0.3	1031 0.8	1503 0.3	2235 1.4
4 Tu	0328 0.6	0658 0.7	1435 0.2	2208 1.2
19 W	0523 0.2	1152 0.8	1548 0.5	) 2315 1.4
5 W (	0429 0.4	1047 0.6	1518 0.3	2223 1.3
20 Th	0619 0.1	1303 0.8	1632 0.6	2352 1.4
6 Th	0524 0.1	1223 0.7	1604 0.4	2251 1.5
21 F	0705 -0.0	1407 0.9	1714 0.7	
7 F	0616 -0.1	1333 0.7	1654 0.5	2329 1.6
22 Sa	0026 1.4	0744 -0.1	1503 0.9	1756 0.8
8 Sa	0705 -0.3	1433 0.8	1747 0.6	
23 Su	0056 1.4	0818 -0.1	1556 0.9	1836 0.8
9 Su	0012 1.7	0754 -0.4	1528 0.9	1843 0.6
24 M	0118 1.4	0850 -0.1	1645 0.9	1917 0.8
10 M	0059 1.7	0843 -0.5	1620 0.9	1941 0.7
25 Tu	0130 1.3	0922 -0.1	1731 0.9	1959 0.9
11 Tu	0149 1.7	0931 -0.6	1710 1.0	2042 0.7
26 W	0138 1.3	0953 -0.1	1814 1.0	2043 0.9
12 W	0241 1.6	1020 -0.5	1800 1.1	O 2147 0.7
27 Th	0156 1.3	1024 -0.1	1853 1.0	● 2132 0.9
13 Th	0336 1.5	1108 -0.5	1849 1.1	2255 0.7
28 F	0223 1.2	1056 -0.0	1926 1.0	2229 0.9
14 F	0438 1.4	1156 -0.3	1937 1.2	
29 Sa	0259 1.2	1129 0.1	1952 1.0	2331 0.8
15 Sa	0009 0.7	0552 1.2	1244 -0.2	2024 1.3
30 Su	0343 1.1	1202 0.2	2010 1.0	
31 M	0039 0.7	0438 0.9	1238 0.3	2020 1.1

AUGUST

Day	Time ft	Time ft	Time ft	Time ft
1 Tu	0150 0.6	0558 0.8	1316 0.4	2030 1.2
16 W	0336 0.3	1035 0.9	1424 0.6	2149 1.4
2 W	0258 0.4	0938 0.7	1400 0.5	2053 1.3
17 Th	0442 0.2	1147 0.9	1513 0.7	) 2232 1.4
3 Th	0401 0.2	1119 0.7	1449 0.6	(2131 1.4
18 F	0536 0.2	1248 1.0	1602 0.8	2313 1.4
4 F	0459 0.0	1229 0.8	1543 0.6	2218 1.5
19 Sa	0620 0.1	1341 1.0	1651 0.8	2350 1.4
5 Sa	0553 -0.1	1325 0.9	1640 0.7	2309 1.6
20 Su	0657 0.1	1427 1.0	1738 0.9	
6 Su	0644 -0.3	1415 0.9	1739 0.7	
21 M	0024 1.4	0731 0.1	1509 1.1	1824 0.9
7 M	0002 1.7	0734 -0.4	1502 1.0	1839 0.7
22 Tu	0052 1.4	0804 0.1	1548 1.1	1908 0.9
8 Tu	0055 1.7	0822 -0.4	1547 1.1	1938 0.7
23 W	0116 1.4	0836 0.1	1625 1.1	1953 0.9
9 W	0150 1.7	0908 -0.4	1632 1.1	2039 0.7
24 Th	0138 1.3	0908 0.1	1657 1.1	2039 0.8
10 Th	0246 1.6	0954 -0.3	1716 1.2	O 2141 0.6
25 F	0206 1.3	0940 0.2	1725 1.1	2128 0.8
11 F	0347 1.4	1039 -0.1	1801 1.2	2246 0.6
26 Sa	0241 1.2	1012 0.3	1745 1.1	● 2222 0.7
12 Sa	0454 1.3	1124 0.0	1846 1.3	2355 0.5
27 Su	0327 1.1	1046 0.4	1755 1.1	2319 0.8
13 Su	0613 1.1	1208 0.2	1932 1.3	
28 M	0428 1.0	1121 0.5	1759 1.2	
14 M	0107 0.5	0742 1.0	1252 0.4	2018 1.3
29 Tu	0021 0.5	0620 0.9	1159 0.6	1818 1.3
15 Tu	0222 0.4	0912 0.9	1337 0.5	2104 1.3
30 W	0125 0.4	0843 0.9	1444 0.7	1856 1.4
31 Th	0230 0.3	1014 0.9	1336 0.8	1949 1.5

TIME MERIDIAN 60°W

0000h is midnight, 1200h is noon.

Heights in feet are referenced to the chart datum of soundings.

AMUAY, VENEZUELA

HIGH & LOW WATER 1995

11°45'N 70°13'W

ATLANTIC STANDARD TIME (GMT -4H)

SEPTEMBER

Time	ft		Time	ft
1 0333	0.1	**16** 0437	0.3
1122	1.0	1226	1.2
F 1435	0.8	Sa 1538	1.0
2050	1.6	☽ 2219	1.4
2 0432	0.0	**17** 0520	0.3
1216	1.1	1307	1.2
Sa 1538	0.9	Su 1633	1.0
☾ 2155	1.6	2302	1.4
3 0527	-0.1	**18** 0559	0.2
1304	1.1	1344	1.2
Su 1642	0.8	M 1725	1.0
2259	1.7	2343	1.4
4 0619	-0.1	**19** 0635	0.3
1347	1.2	1418	1.3
M 1744	0.8	Tu 1814	0.9
5 0001	1.7	**20** 0021	1.4
0708	-0.1	0709	0.3
Tu 1428	1.3	W 1448	1.3
1844	0.8	1900	0.9
6 0101	1.6	**21** 0059	1.4
0755	-0.1	0743	0.3
W 1509	1.3	Th 1513	1.3
1943	0.7	1946	0.8
7 0201	1.6	**22** 0141	1.3
0839	0.0	0816	0.4
Th 1549	1.3	F 1533	1.3
2042	0.6	2033	0.7
8 0304	1.5	**23** 0228	1.3
0922	0.2	0850	0.5
F 1628	1.4	Sa 1544	1.3
○ 2141	0.6	2122	0.6
9 0410	1.4	**24** 0326	1.2
1004	0.3	0924	0.6
Sa 1708	1.4	Su 1550	1.4
2240	0.5	● 2213	0.5
10 0522	1.2	**25** 0441	1.1
1045	0.5	1000	0.7
Su 1747	1.4	M 1602	1.4
2341	0.5	2307	0.4
11 0642	1.1	**26** 0613	1.1
1126	0.6	1040	0.8
M 1828	1.4	Tu 1629	1.5
12 0044	0.4	**27** 0004	0.3
0805	1.1	0745	1.1
Tu 1208	0.8	W 1125	0.9
1910	1.4	1710	1.6
13 0148	0.4	**28** 0104	0.2
0925	1.1	0905	1.1
W 1254	0.9	Th 1219	1.0
1955	1.4	1801	1.6
14 0250	0.3	**29** 0206	0.1
1037	1.1	1011	1.2
Th 1344	1.0	F 1322	1.0
2043	1.4	1906	1.6
15 0347	0.3	**30** 0306	0.1
1136	1.1	1105	1.3
F 1440	1.0	Sa 1432	1.0
2132	1.4	2022	1.6

OCTOBER

Time	ft		Time	ft
1 0404	0.0	**16** 0418	0.3
1152	1.3	1231	1.3
Su 1542	1.0	M 1616	1.1
☾ 2142	1.6	☽ 2113	1.3
2 0458	0.0	**17** 0458	0.3
1234	1.4	1300	1.4
M 1650	0.9	Tu 1712	1.0
2257	1.6	2239	1.3
3 0549	0.0	**18** 0535	0.4
1314	1.5	1325	1.4
Tu 1754	0.8	W 1803	0.9
		2344	1.2
4 0007	1.6	**19** 0611	0.4
0637	0.1	1345	1.4
W 1353	1.5	Th 1850	0.8
1855	0.7		
5 0114	1.5	**20** 0046	1.2
0722	0.2	0647	0.5
Th 1430	1.5	F 1400	1.4
1952	0.6	1937	0.7
6 0221	1.4	**21** 0149	1.2
0804	0.4	0722	0.6
F 1506	1.6	Sa 1409	1.5
2048	0.5	2023	0.5
7 0328	1.4	**22** 0255	1.1
0845	0.5	0758	0.7
Sa 1540	1.6	Su 1419	1.6
2142	0.4	2111	0.4
8 0438	1.3	**23** 0407	1.1
0923	0.7	0836	0.8
Su 1612	1.5	M 1439	1.6
○ 2235	0.4	2201	0.2
9 0552	1.2	**24** 0523	1.1
1000	0.9	0916	0.9
M 1640	1.5	Tu 1509	1.7
2328	0.3	● 2253	0.1
10 0709	1.2	**25** 0639	1.1
1037	1.0	1002	1.0
Tu 1702	1.5	W 1548	1.7
		2348	0.0
11 0020	0.3	**26** 0752	1.2
0825	1.2	1057	1.0
W 1117	1.1	Th 1635	1.7
1709	1.5		
12 0112	0.3	**27** 0045	-0.1
0936	1.2	0856	1.3
Th 1203	1.2	F 1201	1.1
1712	1.4	1732	1.7
13 0203	0.3	**28** 0142	-0.1
1035	1.3	0950	1.3
F 1301	1.2	Sa 1314	1.1
1737	1.4	1841	1.6
14 0251	0.3	**29** 0239	-0.1
1121	1.3	1038	1.4
Sa 1407	1.2	Su 1431	1.1
1823	1.4	2005	1.6
15 0336	0.3	**30** 0334	-0.1
1159	1.3	1121	1.5
Su 1514	1.2	M 1548	1.0
1932	1.4	☾ 2136	1.5
		31 0427	0.0
		1202	1.5
		Tu 1700	0.8
		2300	1.4

NOVEMBER

Time	ft		Time	ft
1 0516	0.1	**16** 0438	0.3
1241	1.6	1229	1.3
W 1806	0.7	Th 1748	0.7
		2313	1.0
2 0017	1.3	**17** 0515	0.4
0603	0.3	1241	1.4
Th 1318	1.6	F 1836	0.5
1906	0.5		
3 0129	1.3	**18** 0045	0.9
0646	0.4	0553	0.5
F 1353	1.6	Sa 1250	1.5
2002	0.4	1923	0.3
4 0240	1.2	**19** 0200	0.9
0726	0.6	0631	0.5
Sa 1426	1.6	Su 1304	1.6
2053	0.3	2010	0.1
5 0350	1.2	**20** 0311	0.9
0803	0.7	0711	0.6
Su 1456	1.6	M 1328	1.6
2142	0.2	2057	-0.0
6 0501	1.1	**21** 0420	0.9
0837	0.9	0753	0.7
M 1520	1.6	Tu 1401	1.7
2229	0.2	2147	-0.2
7 0614	1.1	**22** 0527	1.0
0910	1.0	0841	0.8
Tu 1532	1.5	W 1441	1.7
○ 2314	0.1	● 2238	-0.3
8 0727	1.1	**23** 0632	1.0
0943	1.1	0934	0.9
W 1526	1.5	Th 1527	1.7
2357	0.1	2330	-0.3
9 0839	1.2	**24** 0733	1.1
1019	1.1	1037	0.9
Th 1528	1.5	F 1618	1.7
10 0039	0.1	**25** 0024	-0.4
0941	1.2	0827	1.2
F 1107	1.2	Sa 1147	0.9
1549	1.4	1718	1.6
11 0121	0.2	**26** 0118	-0.3
1026	1.2	0917	1.2
Sa 1212	1.2	Su 1305	0.9
1622	1.4	1830	1.4
12 0202	0.2	**27** 0212	-0.3
1059	1.2	1003	1.3
Su 1329	1.2	M 1427	0.8
1704	1.3	2000	1.3
13 0242	0.2	**28** 0304	-0.2
1127	1.3	1047	1.4
M 1445	1.1	Tu 1548	0.7
1758	1.2	2137	1.2
14 0322	0.2	**29** 0354	-0.1
1152	1.3	1128	1.5
Tu 1554	1.0	W 1704	0.5
1909	1.1	☾ 2305	1.1
15 0400	0.3	**30** 0442	0.1
1212	1.3	1207	1.5
W 1655	0.9	Th 1812	0.3
☽ 2051	1.0		

DECEMBER

Time	ft		Time	ft
1 0026	1.0	**16** 0425	0.2
0527	0.3	1137	1.2
F 1244	1.5	Sa 1816	0.2
1912	0.2		
2 0140	0.9	**17** 0055	0.6
0609	0.4	0506	0.3
Sa 1320	1.5	Su 1154	1.3
2005	0.0	1904	-0.1
3 0251	0.9	**18** 0206	0.6
0647	0.6	0549	0.4
Su 1353	1.5	M 1222	1.5
2053	-0.1	1952	-0.3
4 0400	0.9	**19** 0310	0.7
0722	0.7	0635	0.4
M 1421	1.5	Tu 1258	1.5
2137	-0.1	2040	-0.4
5 0508	0.9	**20** 0410	0.5
0755	0.8	0725	0.5
Tu 1441	1.4	W 1341	1.6
2217	-0.1	2129	-0.6
6 0617	0.9	**21** 0507	0.6
0825	0.9	0819	0.6
W 1445	1.4	Th 1427	1.6
○ 2255	-0.1	● 2219	-0.6
7 0726	0.9	**22** 0603	0.8
0855	0.9	0918	0.6
Th 1439	1.3	F 1518	1.5
2331	-0.1	2309	-0.6
8 0833	0.9	**23** 0656	0.9
1451	1.3	1024	0.6
F		Sa 1614	1.4
9 0006	-0.1	**24** 0000	-0.6
0926	1.0	0747	0.9
Sa 1515	1.3	Su 1136	0.6
		1717	1.3
10 0042	-0.1	**25** 0051	-0.5
0958	1.0	0836	1.0
Su 1131	1.0	M 1254	0.6
1549	1.2	1834	1.1
11 0118	-0.1	**26** 0142	-0.4
1024	1.0	0923	1.1
M 1251	0.9	Tu 1416	0.5
1629	1.1	2008	0.9
12 0154	-0.0	**27** 0233	-0.3
1046	1.0	1008	1.2
Tu 1410	0.9	W 1539	0.3
1719	1.0	2143	0.8
13 0231	0.0	**28** 0322	-0.1
1104	1.0	1051	1.2
W 1525	0.7	Th 1657	0.1
1825	0.8	☾ 2311	0.7
14 0308	0.1	**29** 0409	0.1
1119	1.1	1133	1.3
Th 1630	0.6	F 1806	-0.0
2004	0.7		
15 0346	0.2	**30** 0030	0.7
1726	0.4	0454	0.2
F 1726	0.4	Sa 1213	1.3
☽ 2322	0.6	1905	-0.2
		31 0141	0.7
		0536	0.3
		Su 1250	1.3
		1955	-0.3

TIME MERIDIAN 60°W
Heights in feet are referenced to the chart datum of soundings.

0000h is midnight, 1200h is noon.

VENEZUELA

1995 CARIBBEAN

391

MALECON-ZAPARA, VENEZUELA

HIGH & LOW WATER 1995 **11°00'N 71°35'W**

ATLANTIC STANDARD TIME (GMT -4H)

JANUARY

Day	Time ft	Time ft	Time ft	Time ft
1 Su ●	0447 4.3	1038 1.5	1643 5.0	2324 0.2
16 M ○	0458 3.8	1031 2.0	1648 4.3	2309 1.0
2 M	0550 4.3	1144 1.6	1745 4.9	2347 1.1
17 Tu	0541 3.8	1112 2.0	1729 4.2	
3 Tu	0024 0.3	0654 4.3	1252 1.6	1849 4.7
18 W	0624 3.8	1158 2.0	1814 4.2	
4 W	0125 0.5	0759 4.3	1401 1.6	1954 4.6
19 Th	0028 1.1	0708 3.8	1249 1.9	1902 4.1
5 Th	0227 0.7	0902 4.4	1509 1.5	2101 4.4
20 F	0113 1.2	0753 3.8	1344 1.8	1954 4.0
6 F	0329 1.0	1000 4.4	1613 1.4	2205 4.3
21 Sa	0200 1.3	0839 3.9	1441 1.6	2050 3.9
7 Sa	0428 1.2	1054 4.4	1712 1.3	2307 4.1
22 Su	0251 1.3	0926 4.0	1539 1.4	2149 3.9
8 Su ☾	0524 1.3	1143 4.4	1806 1.1	
23 M	0345 1.4	1016 4.1	1637 1.1	2249 3.9
9 M	0003 4.0	0616 1.5	1226 4.4	1855 1.1
24 Tu	0441 1.4	1106 4.3	1734 0.8	☽ 2348 0.8
10 Tu	0053 3.9	0702 1.6	1305 4.3	1939 1.0
25 W	0538 1.4	1159 4.5	1830 0.5	
11 W	0137 3.8	0743 1.7	1341 4.3	2018 1.0
26 Th	0046 4.1	0636 1.3	1252 4.6	1925 0.3
12 Th	0218 3.8	0819 1.8	1417 4.3	2054 1.0
27 F	0143 4.1	0734 1.3	1346 4.8	2020 0.2
13 F	0257 3.8	0851 1.9	1453 4.3	2127 1.0
28 Sa	0240 4.2	0832 1.3	1441 4.8	2115 0.1
14 Sa	0336 3.8	0922 1.9	1530 4.3	2200 1.0
29 Su	0336 4.2	0931 1.3	1537 4.8	2211 0.2
15 Su	0417 3.8	0954 2.0	1608 4.3	2233 1.0
30 M ●	0433 4.2	1032 1.3	1634 4.7	2308 0.4
31 Tu	0531 4.2	1134 1.3	1733 4.6	

FEBRUARY

Day	Time ft	Time ft	Time ft	Time ft
1 W	0006 0.6	0630 4.1	1237 1.3	1835 4.4
16 Th	0533 3.8	1128 1.4	1747 4.1	2351 1.1
2 Th	0106 0.8	0730 4.1	1342 1.3	1938 4.2
17 F	0617 3.8	1221 1.3	1839 4.0	
3 F	0207 1.1	0829 4.0	1445 1.3	2042 4.1
18 Sa	0041 1.2	0705 3.8	1318 1.1	1936 4.0
4 Sa	0308 1.3	0925 4.0	1546 1.2	2144 3.9
19 Su	0135 1.3	0758 3.9	1418 1.0	2038 3.9
5 Su	0408 1.4	1017 4.0	1642 1.1	2242 3.8
20 M	0233 1.3	0854 3.9	1519 0.8	2141 3.9
6 M	0503 1.5	1104 3.9	1733 1.1	2334 3.7
21 Tu	0335 1.4	0953 4.0	1620 0.6	2244 3.9
7 Tu	0552 1.6	1147 4.0	1818 1.0	
22 W ☾	0437 1.3	1052 4.2	1719 0.4	2344 4.0
8 W	0020 3.7	0634 1.6	1226 4.0	1858 1.0
23 Th	0539 1.3	1150 4.3	1817 0.2	
9 Th	0101 3.7	0710 1.7	1304 4.0	1934 0.9
24 F	0042 4.1	0638 1.2	1247 4.4	1913 0.2
10 F	0139 3.7	0742 1.7	1340 4.1	2006 0.9
25 Sa	0137 4.1	0736 1.1	1342 4.5	2008 0.2
11 Sa	0217 3.7	0811 1.7	1417 4.2	2038 0.9
26 Su	0231 4.2	0833 1.0	1437 4.5	2102 0.3
12 Su	0254 3.8	0842 1.6	1455 4.2	2111 0.9
27 M	0323 4.2	0929 1.0	1532 4.5	2156 0.5
13 M	0333 3.8	0917 1.6	1534 4.2	2146 0.9
28 Tu	0415 4.1	1026 1.0	1628 4.4	2251 0.7
14 Tu	0411 3.8	0956 1.5	1615 4.2	2224 0.9
15 W ○	0451 3.8	1040 1.5	1659 4.2	2306 1.0

MARCH

Day	Time ft	Time ft	Time ft	Time ft
1 W ●	0507 4.0	1123 1.0	1725 4.2	2348 1.0
16 Th ○	0403 4.0	1013 0.9	1634 4.1	2228 1.0
2 Th	0600 3.9	1221 1.0	1824 4.1	
17 F	0445 4.0	1103 0.7	1725 4.1	2318 1.1
3 F	0046 1.2	0654 3.8	1319 1.0	1924 3.9
18 Sa	0532 4.0	1157 0.6	1822 4.0	
4 Sa	0147 1.4	0748 3.7	1417 1.0	2024 3.8
19 Su	0014 1.2	0624 3.9	1256 0.5	1924 4.0
5 Su	0249 1.6	0842 3.6	1512 1.0	2122 3.7
20 M	0115 1.3	0723 3.9	1357 0.4	2029 4.0
6 M	0347 1.7	0933 3.5	1604 1.0	2216 3.6
21 Tu	0221 1.4	0827 3.9	1500 0.3	2134 4.0
7 Tu	0440 1.7	1020 3.5	1650 1.0	2303 3.6
22 W	0329 1.4	0934 4.0	1602 0.2	2238 4.1
8 W	0526 1.7	1104 3.6	1731 1.0	2344 3.6
23 Th	0437 1.3	1039 4.1	1703 0.1	☽ 2339 4.2
9 Th ☾	0604 1.7	1145 3.6	1808 0.9	
24 F	0540 1.2	1141 4.2	1802 0.1	
10 F	0023 3.7	0635 1.6	1224 3.7	1841 0.9
25 Sa	0035 4.2	0640 1.0	1241 4.3	1858 0.2
11 Sa	0059 3.7	0704 1.6	1302 3.9	1913 0.9
26 Su	0128 4.3	0737 0.9	1338 4.3	1953 0.4
12 Su	0135 3.8	0734 1.5	1341 4.0	1946 0.9
27 M	0218 4.3	0832 0.8	1434 4.3	2047 0.6
13 M	0211 3.9	0807 1.3	1421 4.1	2022 0.8
28 Tu	0306 4.2	0926 0.7	1529 4.2	2140 0.8
14 Tu	0247 3.9	0844 1.2	1502 4.1	2101 0.9
29 W	0353 4.1	1018 0.7	1624 4.1	2234 1.1
15 W	0324 4.0	0926 1.0	1546 4.1	2143 0.9
30 Th ●	0440 4.0	1111 0.7	1719 3.9	2329 1.4
31 F	0526 3.8	1203 0.7	1815 3.8	

APRIL

Day	Time ft	Time ft	Time ft	Time ft
1 Sa	0027 1.6	0614 3.6	1254 0.8	1911 3.7
16 Su	0456 4.3	1137 0.0	1808 4.1	2351 1.4
2 Su	0126 1.8	0702 3.5	1344 0.8	2006 3.6
17 M	0553 4.2	1236 -0.0	1912 4.1	
3 M	0227 1.9	0752 3.4	1433 0.9	2058 3.6
18 Tu	0059 1.5	0657 4.1	1338 -0.1	2019 4.1
4 Tu	0324 1.9	0842 3.3	1518 0.9	2146 3.6
19 W	0211 1.5	0805 4.1	1441 -0.1	2125 4.2
5 W	0414 1.9	0930 3.3	1559 1.0	2229 3.6
20 Th	0323 1.4	0916 4.1	1544 0.0	2228 4.3
6 Th	0455 1.9	1016 3.4	1636 1.0	2308 3.7
21 F ☽	0433 1.3	1025 4.1	1645 0.1	2328 4.5
7 F	0529 1.8	1100 3.4	1710 1.0	2345 3.8
22 Sa	0537 1.1	1131 4.1	1745 0.3	
8 Sa ☾	0558 1.7	1142 3.6	1744 1.0	
23 Su	0022 4.5	0637 0.9	1233 4.2	1842 0.5
9 Su	0020 3.9	0627 1.6	1223 3.7	1818 0.9
24 M	0113 4.5	0733 0.7	1332 4.3	1937 0.7
10 M	0054 4.0	0659 1.4	1304 3.8	1856 0.9
25 Tu	0201 4.5	0826 0.6	1429 4.1	2030 1.0
11 Tu	0128 4.1	0736 1.1	1347 3.9	1935 0.9
26 W	0245 4.4	0917 0.5	1525 4.0	2123 1.3
12 W	0202 4.2	0816 0.9	1432 4.0	2018 1.0
27 Th	0328 4.2	1006 0.5	1618 3.9	2215 1.6
13 Th	0239 4.2	0901 0.6	1520 4.1	2105 1.0
28 F	0409 4.1	1054 0.5	1711 3.8	2308 1.8
14 F	0320 4.3	0949 0.4	1612 4.1	2155 1.1
29 Sa ●	0451 3.9	1140 0.6	1803 3.7	
15 Sa ○	0405 4.3	1042 0.2	1708 4.1	2250 1.3
30 Su	0002 2.0	0533 3.7	1224 0.7	1853 3.6

TIME MERIDIAN 60°W

Heights in feet are referenced to the chart datum of soundings.

0000h is midnight, 1200h is noon.

MALECON-ZAPARA, VENEZUELA

HIGH & LOW WATER 1995   11°00'N 71°35'W

ATLANTIC STANDARD TIME (GMT -4H)

VENEZUELA

MAY

Day	Time	ft	Day	Time	ft
1 M	0058	2.1	16 Tu	0530	4.5
	0616	3.5		1218	-0.3
	1307	0.8		1859	4.3
	1943	3.6			
2 Tu	0155	2.2	17 W	0044	1.6
	0703	3.4		0636	4.4
	1348	0.9		1319	-0.2
	2029	3.6		2005	4.4
3 W	0248	2.2	18 Th	0159	1.6
	0750	3.3		0746	4.3
	1426	0.9		1422	-0.1
	2113	3.7		2111	4.5
4 Th	0335	2.2	19 F	0313	1.5
	0839	3.3		0857	4.2
	1503	1.0		1524	0.1
	2154	3.7		2213	4.6
5 F	0415	2.1	20 Sa	0423	1.3
	0927	3.3		1008	4.2
	1538	1.0		1626	0.3
	2232	3.8		2311	4.7
6 Sa	0448	2.0	21 Su	0527	1.1
	1013	3.4		1117	4.1
	1613	1.1		1726	0.6
	2307	3.9		)	
7 Su	0519	1.9	22 M	0004	4.8
	1058	3.5		0627	0.8
	1650	1.1		1222	4.1
	(2341	4.1		1823	0.8
8 M	0551	1.6	23 Tu	0054	4.8
	1144	3.6		0722	0.6
	1729	1.1		1323	4.0
				1918	1.1
9 Tu	0013	4.2	24 W	0139	4.7
	0628	1.3		0814	0.5
	1229	3.7		1421	4.0
	1810	1.1		2011	1.4
10 W	0047	4.3	25 Th	0221	4.6
	0708	1.0		0903	0.4
	1316	3.8		1515	3.9
	1854	1.1		2102	1.7
11 Th	0122	4.5	26 F	0300	4.4
	0752	0.6		0948	0.4
	1406	3.9		1606	3.8
	1942	1.2		2152	1.9
12 F	0202	4.6	27 Sa	0338	4.2
	0839	0.3		1031	0.5
	1458	4.0		1655	3.7
	2033	1.2		2240	2.1
13 Sa	0246	4.7	28 Su	0416	4.0
	0930	0.0		1112	0.6
	1553	4.1		1741	3.7
	2127	1.4		2328	2.3
14 Su	0335	4.7	29 M	0454	3.9
	1023	-0.2		1150	0.7
	1652	4.2		1825	3.7
	O 2227	1.5		●	
15 M	0429	4.6	30 Tu	0017	2.4
	1119	-0.3		0535	3.8
	1754	4.2		1226	0.8
	2333	1.6		1910	3.7
			31 W	0106	2.5
				0618	3.6
				1301	0.9
				1953	3.7

JUNE

Day	Time	ft	Day	Time	ft
1 Th	0154	2.5	16 F	0145	1.7
	0703	3.6		0727	4.5
	1335	1.0		1402	0.1
	2036	3.8		2051	4.7
2 F	0239	2.5	17 Sa	0258	1.5
	0750	3.5		0839	4.3
	1409	1.0		1504	0.4
	2116	3.9		2152	4.8
3 Sa	0321	2.4	18 Su	0408	1.3
	0838	3.5		0951	4.2
	1445	1.1		1606	0.7
	2154	4.0		2249	4.9
4 Su	0400	2.2	19 M	0512	1.1
	0928	3.5		1101	4.1
	1523	1.2		1706	0.9
	2229	4.1		) 2342	4.9
5 M	0438	2.0	20 Tu	0611	0.8
	1018	3.5		1208	4.0
	1604	1.2		1804	1.2
	2302	4.3			
6 Tu	0518	1.7	21 W	0029	4.8
	1108	3.6		0705	0.7
	1647	1.3		1309	3.9
	(2335	4.4		1859	1.5
7 W	0600	1.3	22 Th	0113	4.7
	1159	3.7		0755	0.5
	1733	1.3		1405	3.9
				1950	1.7
8 Th	0010	4.6	23 F	0153	4.6
	0644	0.9		0841	0.5
	1251	3.8		1456	3.8
	1822	1.3		2038	1.9
9 F	0050	4.7	24 Sa	0230	4.5
	0731	0.5		0923	0.5
	1344	3.9		1542	3.8
	1914	1.4		2122	2.1
10 Sa	0134	4.9	25 Su	0307	4.4
	0820	0.1		1002	0.6
	1440	4.0		1625	3.7
	2009	1.5		2204	2.3
11 Su	0222	5.0	26 M	0342	4.3
	0912	-0.1		1037	0.6
	1537	4.1		1706	3.7
	2107	1.6		2244	2.4
12 M	0314	5.0	27 Tu	0420	4.1
	1006	-0.3		1110	0.7
	1637	4.3		1747	3.8
	2211	1.6		● 2324	2.5
13 Tu	0411	4.9	28 W	0458	4.0
	1102	-0.3		1142	0.8
	1739	4.4		1828	3.8
	O 2318	1.7			
14 W	0512	4.8	29 Th	0005	2.5
	1200	-0.3		0539	3.9
	1843	4.5		1214	0.9
				1911	3.9
15 Th	0030	1.7	30 F	0050	2.5
	0618	4.6		0622	3.8
	1300	-0.1		1248	1.0
	1948	4.6		1953	3.9

JULY

Day	Time	ft	Day	Time	ft
1 Sa	0137	2.5	16 Su	0240	1.5
	0708	3.7		0822	4.2
	1323	1.1		1444	0.8
	2033	4.0		2127	4.7
2 Su	0225	2.4	17 M	0348	1.3
	0757	3.6		0934	4.1
	1402	1.2		1546	1.1
	2112	4.1		2223	4.8
3 M	0312	2.2	18 Tu	0452	1.1
	0850	3.6		1044	4.0
	1443	1.3		1647	1.3
	2148	4.2		2315	4.8
4 Tu	0400	1.9	19 W	0549	0.9
	0944	3.6		1150	3.9
	1528	1.4		1744	1.5
	2224	4.4		)	
5 W	0447	1.5	20 Th	0001	4.7
	1040	3.6		0642	0.7
	1616	1.4		1249	3.8
	(2301	4.5		1837	1.7
6 Th	0535	1.2	21 F	0043	4.7
	1137	3.7		0729	0.7
	1707	1.5		1340	3.8
	2342	4.7		1925	1.9
7 F	0623	0.8	22 Sa	0122	4.6
	1233	3.8		0811	0.6
	1800	1.5		1425	3.8
				2008	2.0
8 Sa	0027	4.9	23 Su	0158	4.5
	0713	0.4		0849	0.7
	1329	3.9		1506	3.8
	1856	1.6		2046	2.2
9 Su	0115	5.0	24 M	0234	4.5
	0804	0.1		0924	0.7
	1426	4.1		1544	3.8
	1955	1.6		2122	2.2
10 M	0207	5.1	25 Tu	0309	4.4
	0857	-0.1		0955	0.8
	1523	4.2		1622	3.8
	2056	1.7		2156	2.3
11 Tu	0301	5.1	26 W	0346	4.3
	0950	-0.2		1026	0.8
	1621	4.3		1701	3.9
	2200	1.7		2232	2.4
12 W	0359	5.1	27 Th	0425	4.3
	1046	-0.2		1057	0.9
	1722	4.4		1741	3.9
	O 2307	1.7		2312	2.4
13 Th	0459	4.9	28 F	0505	4.1
	1143	-0.0		1129	1.0
	1823	4.5		1822	4.0
				2357	2.3
14 F	0017	1.7	29 Sa	0548	4.0
	0604	4.7		1205	1.1
	1242	0.2		1903	4.0
	1926	4.6			
15 Sa	0129	1.6	30 Su	0046	2.3
	0711	4.5		0635	3.9
	1342	0.5		1244	1.2
	2028	4.7		1945	4.1
			31 M	0138	2.1
				0727	3.8
				1326	1.3
				2025	4.2

AUGUST

Day	Time	ft	Day	Time	ft
1 Tu	0232	1.9	16 W	0426	1.1
	0823	3.7		1026	3.8
	1412	1.4		1628	1.7
	2107	4.3		2242	4.5
2 W	0326	1.6	17 Th	0521	1.0
	0922	3.6		1127	3.8
	1503	1.5		1724	1.8
	2150	4.4		) 2328	4.5
3 Th	0420	1.3	18 F	0611	0.9
	1023	3.6		1220	3.7
	1557	1.6		1813	1.9
	(2235	4.5			
4 F	0513	0.9	19 Sa	0009	4.5
	1123	3.7		0655	0.8
	1653	1.6		1306	3.7
	2323	4.7		1856	2.0
5 Sa	0605	0.6	20 Su	0047	4.5
	1222	3.8		0733	0.8
	1751	1.7		1346	3.8
				1934	2.1
6 Su	0013	4.9	21 M	0123	4.5
	0657	0.3		0807	0.8
	1318	4.0		1422	3.8
	1850	1.6		2007	2.1
7 M	0105	5.0	22 Tu	0159	4.5
	0750	0.1		0838	0.9
	1414	4.2		1458	3.9
	1950	1.6		2039	2.1
8 Tu	0158	5.1	23 W	0236	4.5
	0842	0.0		0908	0.9
	1510	4.3		1535	4.0
	2051	1.6		2112	2.1
9 W	0253	5.1	24 Th	0314	4.4
	0935	0.0		0938	0.9
	1606	4.4		1612	4.0
	2153	1.6		2149	2.1
10 Th	0350	5.0	25 F	0353	4.4
	1030	0.1		1011	1.0
	1703	4.5		1651	4.1
	O 2258	1.6		2231	2.0
11 F	0450	4.4	26 Sa	0435	4.3
	1126	0.4		1047	1.1
	1801	4.5		1730	4.1
				● 2317	1.9
12 Sa	0004	1.5	27 Su	0520	4.1
	0552	4.6		1126	1.2
	1223	0.6		1811	4.1
	1900	4.5			
13 Su	0112	1.5	28 M	0008	1.8
	0658	4.3		0610	4.0
	1324	0.9		1209	1.3
	1959	4.5		1854	4.2
14 M	0220	1.4	29 Tu	0102	1.6
	0808	4.1		0705	3.9
	1425	1.2		1257	1.4
	2057	4.5		1940	4.2
15 Tu	0325	1.2	30 W	0200	1.4
	0918	3.8		0806	3.8
	1528	1.5		1350	1.6
	2152	4.5		2029	4.3
			31 Th	0258	1.2
				0909	3.8
				1447	1.7
				2121	4.4

TIME MERIDIAN 60°W
Heights in feet are referenced to the chart datum of soundings.

0000h is midnight, 1200h is noon.

MALECON-ZAPARA, VENEZUELA

HIGH & LOW WATER 1995 11°00'N 71°35'W

ATLANTIC STANDARD TIME (GMT -4H)

SEPTEMBER

Day	Time ft	Day	Time ft
1 F	0356 0.9 / 1013 3.8 / 1548 1.7 / 2215 4.6	**16** Sa	0532 1.1 / 1145 3.7 / 1745 2.1 /) 2329 4.2
2 Sa	0453 0.7 / 1115 3.9 / 1650 1.7 / (2310 4.7	**17** Su	0612 1.1 / 1226 3.8 / 1823 2.1
3 Su	0548 0.5 / 1214 4.0 / 1752 1.7	**18** M	0008 4.3 / 0646 1.0 / 1302 3.9 / 1856 2.1
4 M	0005 4.8 / 0642 0.3 / 1310 4.2 / 1852 1.6	**19** Tu	0046 4.4 / 0717 1.0 / 1337 4.0 / 1927 2.0
5 Tu	0059 4.9 / 0735 0.2 / 1404 4.3 / 1951 1.5	**20** W	0123 4.4 / 0747 1.0 / 1412 4.0 / 1959 1.9
6 W	0154 5.0 / 0828 0.3 / 1457 4.4 / 2050 1.5	**21** Th	0202 4.4 / 0817 1.0 / 1448 4.1 / 2034 1.8
7 Th	0249 4.9 / 0921 0.4 / 1549 4.5 / 2150 1.4	**22** F	0241 4.4 / 0850 1.1 / 1524 4.2 / 2114 1.7
8 F	0345 4.8 / 1015 0.6 / 1642 4.5 / O 2250 1.4	**23** Sa	0323 4.4 / 0927 1.1 / 1601 4.3 / 2158 1.6
9 Sa	0444 4.6 / 1109 0.9 / 1736 4.5 / 2352 1.3	**24** Su	0408 4.3 / 1007 1.2 / 1640 4.3 / ● 2246 1.4
10 Su	0545 4.3 / 1207 1.2 / 1831 4.4	**25** M	0457 4.2 / 1051 1.3 / 1722 4.3 / 2338 1.3
11 M	0055 1.3 / 0648 4.1 / 1306 1.4 / 1927 4.3	**26** Tu	0550 4.1 / 1140 1.4 / 1809 4.4
12 Tu	0157 1.2 / 0755 3.9 / 1408 1.7 / 2022 4.3	**27** W	0034 1.1 / 0649 4.0 / 1234 1.6 / 1901 4.4
13 W	0258 1.2 / 0901 3.8 / 1509 1.8 / 2115 4.2	**28** Th	0133 1.0 / 0752 4.0 / 1334 1.7 / 1958 4.5
14 Th	0354 1.1 / 1003 3.7 / 1608 1.9 / 2204 4.2	**29** F	0234 0.8 / 0858 4.0 / 1439 1.8 / 2058 4.5
15 F	0446 1.1 / 1058 3.7 / 1700 2.0 / 2248 4.2	**30** Sa	0335 0.6 / 1004 4.0 / 1545 1.8 / 2159 4.6

OCTOBER

Day	Time ft	Day	Time ft
1 Su	0434 0.5 / 1106 4.2 / 1651 1.7 / (2259 4.7	**16** M	0520 1.3 / 1144 3.9 / 1744 2.2 /) 2327 4.2
2 M	0532 0.4 / 1205 4.3 / 1754 1.6 / 2358 4.8	**17** Tu	0552 1.3 / 1219 4.0 / 1816 2.1
3 Tu	0627 0.4 / 1300 4.4 / 1854 1.5	**18** W	0007 4.2 / 0622 1.3 / 1253 4.1 / 1847 2.0
4 W	0055 4.8 / 0721 0.5 / 1352 4.5 / 1953 1.4	**19** Th	0046 4.3 / 0654 1.2 / 1327 4.2 / 1922 1.8
5 Th	0151 4.8 / 0815 0.6 / 1442 4.6 / 2049 1.3	**20** F	0127 4.3 / 0728 1.2 / 1401 4.3 / 2001 1.8
6 F	0247 4.7 / 0907 0.8 / 1532 4.6 / 2146 1.2	**21** Sa	0210 4.4 / 0805 1.2 / 1437 4.4 / 2044 1.4
7 Sa	0343 4.5 / 0957 1.1 / 1621 4.5 / 2242 1.2	**22** Su	0255 4.4 / 0847 1.3 / 1514 4.5 / 2130 1.1
8 Su	0441 4.3 / 1055 1.4 / 1710 4.4 / O 2359 1.1	**23** M	0343 4.3 / 0931 1.3 / 1556 4.6 / 2220 0.9
9 M	0539 4.1 / 1151 1.6 / 1800 4.3	**24** Tu	0435 4.3 / 1021 1.5 / 1642 4.6 / ● 2314 0.8
10 Tu	0035 1.2 / 0639 4.0 / 1249 1.9 / 1851 4.2	**25** W	0532 4.2 / 1115 1.6 / 1733 4.7
11 W	0131 1.2 / 0740 3.8 / 1349 2.0 / 1942 4.1	**26** Th	0011 0.6 / 0633 4.2 / 1215 1.7 / 1831 4.7
12 Th	0226 1.2 / 0840 3.7 / 1447 2.2 / 2031 4.0	**27** F	0111 0.6 / 0738 4.2 / 1321 1.8 / 1933 4.7
13 F	0317 1.2 / 0935 3.7 / 1541 2.2 / 2119 4.0	**28** Sa	0212 0.5 / 0845 4.2 / 1430 1.8 / 2038 4.7
14 Sa	0403 1.2 / 1023 3.7 / 1629 2.3 / 2203 4.0	**29** Su	0314 0.5 / 0951 4.3 / 1541 1.8 / 2144 4.7
15 Su	0444 1.3 / 1106 3.8 / 1710 2.2 / 2246 4.1	**30** M	0415 0.5 / 1054 4.5 / 1648 1.6 / (2248 4.7
		31 Tu	0515 0.5 / 1152 4.6 / 1752 1.5 / 2351 4.7

NOVEMBER

Day	Time ft	Day	Time ft
1 W	0612 0.6 / 1246 4.7 / 1852 1.3	**16** Th	0529 1.4 / 1211 4.2 / 1810 1.9
2 Th	0051 4.7 / 0708 0.8 / 1337 4.8 / 1950 1.2	**17** F	0010 4.2 / 0605 1.4 / 1244 4.4 / 1848 1.6
3 F	0149 4.6 / 0802 1.0 / 1426 4.7 / 2045 1.0	**18** Sa	0055 4.2 / 0644 1.4 / 1318 4.5 / 1931 1.3
4 Sa	0245 4.5 / 0855 1.3 / 1513 4.7 / 2138 1.0	**19** Su	0140 4.3 / 0727 1.4 / 1355 4.6 / 2016 1.0
5 Su	0341 4.3 / 0947 1.5 / 1558 4.6 / 2230 1.0	**20** M	0229 4.3 / 0812 1.4 / 1436 4.8 / 2105 0.8
6 M	0436 4.1 / 1040 1.8 / 1643 4.4 / 2322 1.0	**21** Tu	0320 4.3 / 0902 1.4 / 1521 4.9 / 2157 0.5
7 Tu	0531 4.0 / 1133 2.0 / 1728 4.3 / O	**22** W	0415 4.3 / 0956 1.5 / 1612 4.9 / ● 2252 0.4
8 W	0012 1.1 / 0626 3.9 / 1227 2.2 / 1813 4.2	**23** Th	0513 4.3 / 1054 1.6 / 1708 4.9 / 2349 0.3
9 Th	0101 1.2 / 0719 3.8 / 1321 2.3 / 1859 4.1	**24** F	0615 4.3 / 1158 1.7 / 1808 4.9
10 F	0148 1.2 / 0811 3.7 / 1414 2.4 / 1946 4.0	**25** Sa	0049 0.3 / 0721 4.4 / 1307 1.8 / 1913 4.9
11 Sa	0232 1.3 / 0859 3.8 / 1504 2.4 / 2031 4.0	**26** Su	0151 0.4 / 0828 4.4 / 1419 1.7 / 2021 4.8
12 Su	0313 1.4 / 0944 3.8 / 1548 2.5 / 2117 4.0	**27** M	0254 0.4 / 0934 4.6 / 1531 1.6 / 2129 4.8
13 M	0350 1.4 / 1024 3.9 / 1626 2.4 / 2201 4.0	**28** Tu	0356 0.6 / 1036 4.7 / 1639 1.5 / 2237 4.7
14 Tu	0423 1.4 / 1102 4.0 / 1700 2.3 / 2244 4.0	**29** W	0458 0.7 / 1135 4.8 / 1744 1.3 / (2342 4.5
15 W	0455 1.4 / 1137 4.1 / 1734 2.1 /) 2327 4.1	**30** Th	0557 0.9 / 1229 4.8 / 1844 1.1

DECEMBER

Day	Time ft	Day	Time ft
1 F	0044 4.5 / 0654 1.1 / 1319 4.2 / 1940 0.9	**16** Sa	0525 1.5 / 1203 4.4 / 1818 1.4
2 Sa	0144 4.4 / 0749 1.3 / 1407 4.8 / 2034 0.9	**17** Su	0026 4.1 / 0609 1.5 / 1241 4.5 / 1904
3 Su	0240 4.3 / 0842 1.5 / 1452 4.7 / 2124 0.8	**18** M	0115 4.1 / 0656 1.4 / 1322 4.7 / 1952 0.7
4 M	0333 4.1 / 0932 1.8 / 1534 4.6 / 2212 0.9	**19** Tu	0206 4.2 / 0746 1.4 / 1407 4.7 / 2043 0.4
5 Tu	0424 4.0 / 1022 2.0 / 1615 4.4 / 2259 0.9	**20** W	0259 4.3 / 0840 1.4 / 1457 5.0 / 2136 0.3
6 W	0513 3.9 / 1109 2.1 / 1656 4.3 / O 2343 1.0	**21** Th	0354 4.4 / 0937 1.5 / 1551 5.1 / ● 2231 0.2
7 Th	0600 3.8 / 1156 2.3 / 1737 4.2	**22** F	0453 4.4 / 1038 1.5 / 1649 5.1 / 2329 0.2
8 F	0025 1.2 / 0646 3.7 / 1242 2.4 / 1819 4.1	**23** Sa	0555 4.4 / 1144 1.6 / 1751 5.0
9 Sa	0105 1.3 / 0731 3.7 / 1327 2.5 / 1902 4.0	**24** Su	0029 0.2 / 0659 4.4 / 1253 1.6 / 1856 4.9
10 Su	0143 1.4 / 0816 3.8 / 1411 2.5 / 1946 4.0	**25** M	0131 0.4 / 0805 4.5 / 1405 1.5 / 2005 4.8
11 M	0219 1.4 / 0859 3.8 / 1453 2.5 / 2032 3.9	**26** Tu	0235 0.5 / 0911 4.6 / 1517 1.4 / 2115 4.6
12 Tu	0253 1.5 / 0940 3.9 / 1533 2.4 / 2118 3.9	**27** W	0339 0.7 / 1014 4.6 / 1625 1.2 / 2224 4.5
13 W	0328 1.5 / 1018 4.0 / 1613 2.2 / 2205 3.9	**28** Th	0442 0.9 / 1113 4.7 / 1729 1.0 / (2331 4.4
14 Th	0404 1.5 / 1054 4.1 / 1652 2.0 / 2251 4.0	**29** F	0543 1.1 / 1208 4.7 / 1829 0.9
15 F	0443 1.5 / 1128 4.2 / 1734 1.7 /) 2338 4.0	**30** Sa	0034 4.3 / 0641 1.3 / 1258 4.7 / 1924 0.8
		31 Su	0133 4.2 / 0735 1.4 / 1344 4.6 / 2015 0.7

TIME MERIDIAN 60°W
Heights in feet are referenced to the chart datum of soundings.

0000h is midnight, 1200h is noon.

REED'S NAUTICAL ALMANAC

BONAIRE

CAUTION: Our information on aids to navigation comes from official government sources. The latitudes and longitudes of these marks may not correspond to the readings from GPS receivers. Some aids have been reported as unreliable, missing, off position, or showing incorrect characteristics. No single aid to navigation, or waypoint, should be relied upon as a sole means of fixing your position.

NOTE: The chartlets on the following page are not intended for navigation and are included for reference and planning purposes only. While chartlets reproduced from government sources are from the most current editions as of press time, they incorporate no corrections to navigational aids, depths, or hazards since the edition publication date.

ENTRY PROCEDURES

Bonaire, off the coast of Venezuela, is part of the Netherlands Antilles, an autonomous part of the Netherlands. It is also the easternmost of what are familiarly known as the ABC islands, making it a good first stop for vessels headed from Venezuela to Panama.

The Port of Entry is Kralendijk, located midway up the western side of the island. Yachts can enter the marina north of town to clear in. Customs and immigration are open 24 hours a day, seven days a week. You may contact the officials from Harbour Village Marina (VHF channel 17 or 599-7-7419 or -8384) 1 mile north of the commercial pier and await their arrival from town or tie up to the customs wharf at the commercial pier, an area that can be quite rough. Mariners have reported no problem in traveling to town to visit the offices in person. Formalities are reported to be simple and swift once you reach the officials.

Firearms and spearguns will be held during your stay. There are strict rules preventing the taking of marine life, as most of the islands reefs are part of Bonaire Marine Park.

The country code for the Netherlands Antilles is 599 and the island code for Bonaire , 7. The local numbers consist of four digits. The official currency is the Netherlands Antilles florin, but U.S. currency is widely accepted. The exchange rate is 1.79 florins to 1 U.S. dollar. Dutch is the official language, but many people speak English. The local dialect, known as Papiamento, is also heard.

Venezuela maintains a consulate in Bonaire where the required visa applications to visit that country may be submitted.

BONAIRE

BOCA SPELONK, NE side of island, 12 13.0N, 68 11.7W. Fl W 5s, 100ft, 15M. White circular stone structure. Visible 127°–002°; visibility variable on account of salt deposits which constantly form on the lenses.
LACRE PUNT, S point of island, 12 01.9N, 68 14.1W. Fl W, 9s, 75ft, 13M. White round stone tower, red stripes. Visible 203°–147°; visibility variable on account of salt deposits which constantly form on the lenses.
PUNT VIERKANT, 12 07.0N, 68 17.6W. Fl (3) W 22s, 30ft, 5M. Gray square tower, red lantern.
KRALENDIJK, W side of island opposite Klein Bonaire, 12 09.1N, 68 16.5W. Fl W 2s, 44ft, 5M. White square stone structure. Visible 027°–150°.
KLEIN BONAIRE, SW point, 12 09.4N, 68 19.8W. Fl (2) W 20s, 19ft, 9M. White round tower. Visible 278°–143°; obscured elsewhere.

KRALENDIJK

12 09N, 68 17W
Pilotage: The island is high at the north end, but low and sandy to the south. The highest peak is Brandaris, about 787 feet above sea level, and located on the northwest part of the island. The coast is all steep-to with no off-lying hazards. However, the east coast of the island was where longtime voyager Peter Tangvald put his boat on the reefs and lost his life. There have been many reports of confusion in identifying the lights of the island when approaching from offshore. The lights have been reported to be

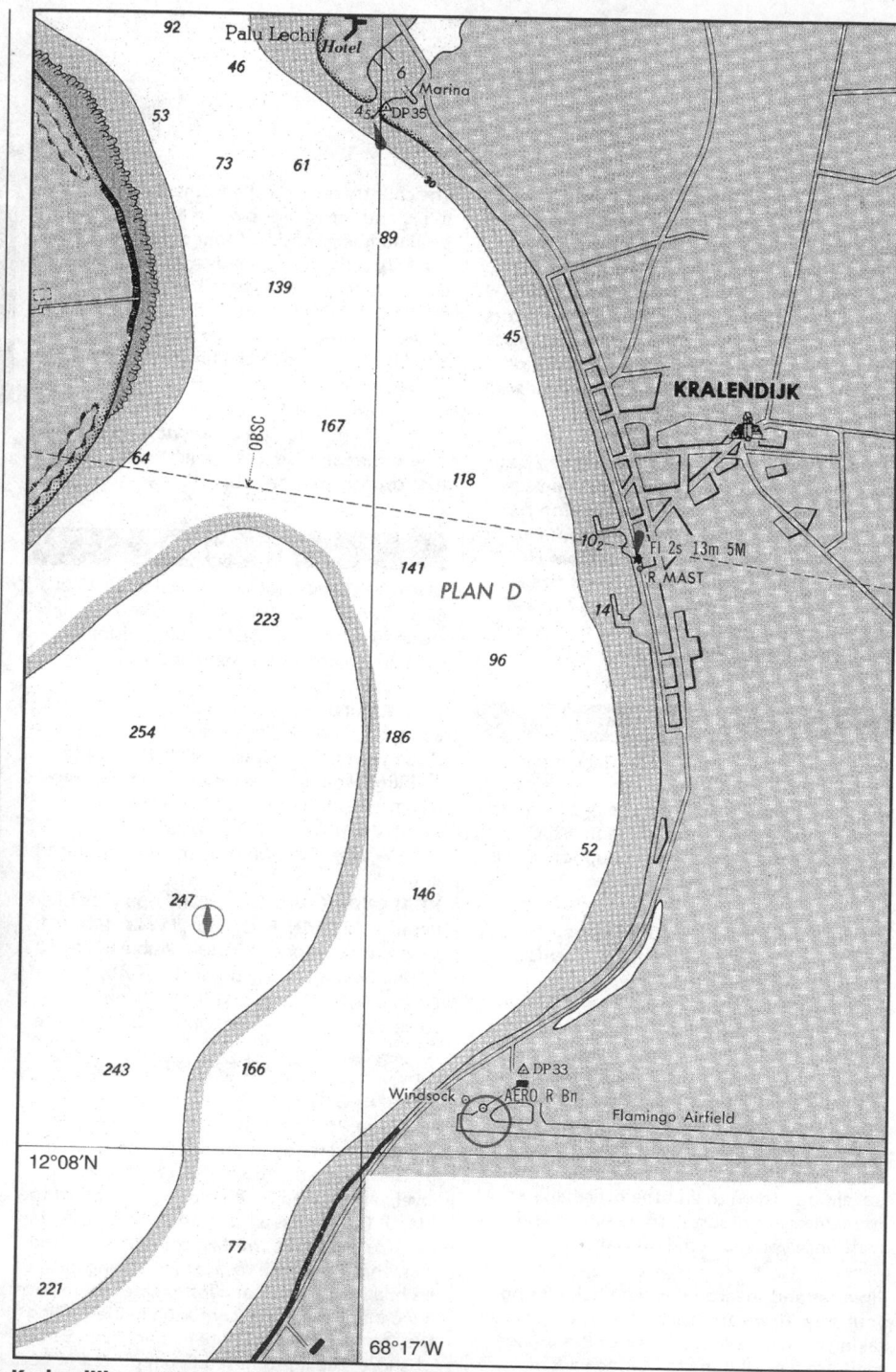

Kralendijk, soundings in meters *(from DMA 24461, 3rd ed, 7/80)*

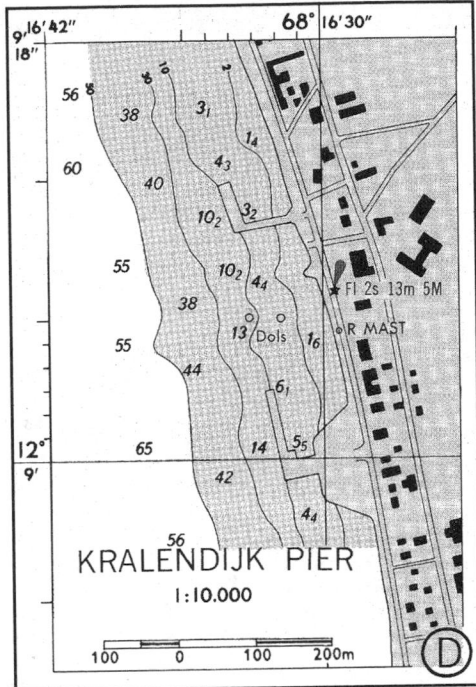

Kralendijk Pier Area, soundings in meters *(from DMA 24461, 3rd ed, 7/80)*

unreliable. Contact the harbor master on VHF channel 16.

Port of Entry: See Entry Procedures, preceding page.

Communications: See Communications and Weather Services for information on Trans World Radio. Yachts use VHF channel 77 for calling, switching to channel 71 to talk.

Dockage: Contact Harbour Village Marina (599-7-7419 or -8384 or fax, -7506 or -5028, or VHF channel 17). The marina is located in a small basin about 1 mile north of the commercial docks. Boaters report it is a safe place to leave your boat for extended periods.

Anchorage: Most boats anchor on the narrow shelf of shallow water between the marina and the commercial docks. Check your anchor set carefully and set two anchors if in doubt. The holding has been reported to be poor, and there isn't much dragging room before you're off the shelf. Strong southwest winds can make the anchorage unsafe. These are usually experienced from September through early November. If you anchor out, dinghy in to the main wharf area or the dinghy dock at the Zee Zicht restaurant, located just north of the commercial wharves.

Services: Fuel and water (desalinized and expensive) is available in the marina. There is a bank, some restaurants, markets, and most general supplies. The island is a world-famous diving center, so those services are excellent. Contact the Tourist Board (599-7-8322) for information on the island's parks and recreation opportunities. The large flocks of pink flamingoes are well worth seeing.

GOTO, 12 13.5N, 68 23.8W. Q W 6ft, 5M.

RANGE No 1 (Front), 12 13.3N, 68 23.0W. F G, 46ft, 9M. **(Rear),** 197 meters, 067°47′ from front. F R, 82ft, 9M.

GOTO RANGE No 2 (Front), 12 13.4N, 68 21.4W. Q R, 26ft, 8M. **(Rear),** 126 meters 081°04′ from front. Q G, 33ft, 6M.

PUNT WEKOEWA, 12 14.0N, 68 25.0W. Fl (3) W 20s, 49ft, 12M. Visible 285°–155°; obscured elsewhere.

CERU BENTANA, 12 18.2N, 68 22.8w. Fl (4) W 22s, 144ft, 17M. Square building, yellow tower. Visible 069°30′–073° and 074°–303°; obscured elsewhere.

CURAÇAO

CAUTION: *Our information on aids to navigation comes from official government sources. The latitudes and longitudes of these marks may not correspond to the readings from GPS receivers. Some aids have been reported as unreliable, missing, off position, or showing incorrect characteristics. No single aid to navigation, or waypoint, should be relied upon as a sole means of fixing your position.*

NOTE: *The chartlets in this section are <u>not</u> <u>intended for navigation</u> and are included for reference and planning purposes only. While chartlets reproduced from government sources are from the most current editions as of press time, they incorporate <u>no corrections</u> to navigational aids, depths, or hazards since the edition publication date.*

ENTRY PROCEDURES

Located about 35 miles north of the coast of Venezuela and 30 miles west of Bonaire, Curaçao is the administrative center of the Netherlands Antilles. It is the middle island geographically of the so-called ABC group.

Ports of Entry are Spaansche (Spanish) Water and Willemstad. Private yachts generally prefer to clear customs in Spaansche Water, because of the commercial nature of Willemstad harbor. You still must travel overland to Willemstad to clear with immigration.

The entrance channel at Willemstad is called Sint Anna Baai and is crossed by two bridges. The port officials (call sign Fort Nassau on VHF channels 12 and 16) are near the fuel dock, after the high-level bridge on the starboard side of the channel; call them for information and berthing instructions. In Spaansche Water, Sarifundy's Marina will call officials on behalf of visiting yachts.

Immigration will generally grant you three months in the country. All firearms will be held during your stay. Formalities are reported to be simple and swift, once you get in touch with the officials.

The country code for Curacao is 599; the island code is 9; local numbers have five or six digits. The official currency is the Netherlands Antilles florin, but U.S. currency is widely accepted.

Dutch is the official language, but you will find many people who speak English. The local dialect, known as Papiamento, is also spoken.

CURAÇAO

KLEIN CURAÇAO, near center of island. 11 59.5N, 68 39.0W. Fl (2) W 15s, 82ft, 15M. White circular stone tower, lower part red.
PUNT KANON, SE point of island, 12 02.5N, 68 44.5W. Fl W 4s, 39ft, 8M. Red and white banded round stone tower.
FUIK BAAI, Range (Front), 12 03.2N, 68 49.7W. F G, 32ft, 2M. Red and white beacon with cross topmark. **(Rear),** 50 meters, 027°30' from front. F R, 42ft, 4M. Red and white beacon with triangular topmark.

SPAANSCHE WATER
12 04N, 68 51W
Pilotage: Spaanse Haven, the narrow channel leading into Spaansche (Spanish) Water, is reported to be hard to spot from offshore. The obscure entrance is identified by a cluster of oil storage tanks atop and fringing the side of the hill on the left bank of the entrance. The channel is 1 1/2 miles northwest of the marked entrance to Fuikbaai and 1 1/4 miles southeast of Lijhoek Light in Caracasbaai. The channel is reported to be privately marked and flanked by several shallow spots and reefs. An approach in good light is recommended.
Port of Entry: Contact customs officials upon your arrival at Sarifundy's Marina. You will have to travel to Willemstad to visit the immigration office.
Dockage: Sarifundy's Marina (599-9-677643 or fax, -674672) is located in the northwest arm of Spaansche Water. The Curaçao Yacht Club is located nearby, as are several small clubs. They may be able to provide dockage.
Anchorage: Anchor near Sarifundy's, where customers can dinghy in.
Services: Sarifundy's has water, ice, laundry, showers, a dinghy dock, telephones, message

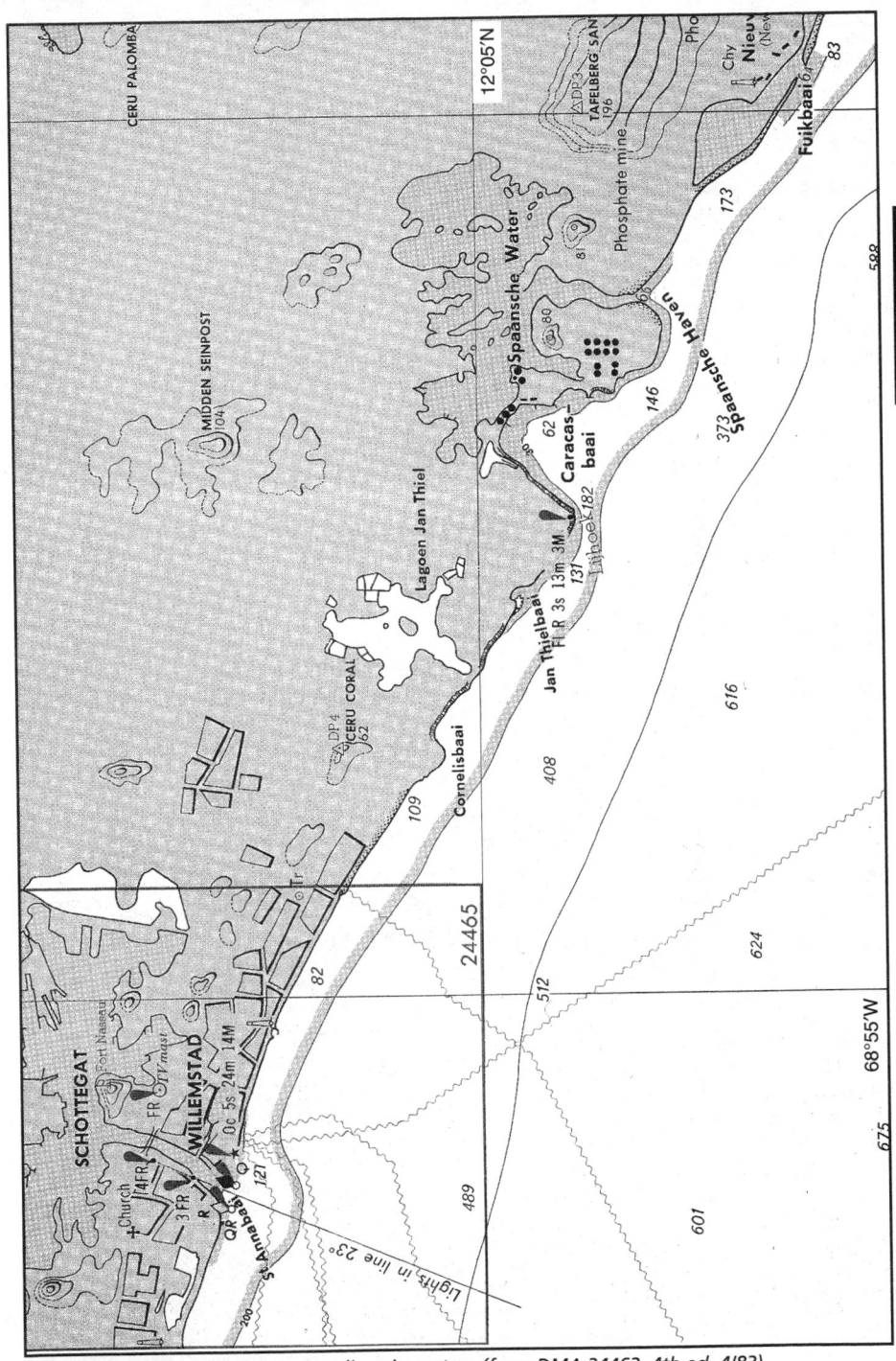

Spaansche Water, Curaçao, soundings in meters *(from DMA 24462, 4th ed, 4/82)*

services, rental cars, and a small selection of groceries and can help you find what you need on the island. There are several chandleries in nearby Willemstad, and buses run four times a week into town. All general supplies are available.

CARACAS BAAI ON LIJ HOEK, W point of bay, Fl R 3s, 42ft, 4M. Red and white metal framework tower, red lantern,
Range (Front), 12 04.8N, 68 51.8W. F R. Beacon with cross topmark. **(Rear),** 90 meters, 043°30′ from front. F G. Beacon with triangular topmark, point down.
DR. ALBERT PLESMAN FIELD, aviation light, 12 11.0N, 68 57.1W. Al Fl W G, 10s, 148ft, 26M white, 21M green. Iron skeleton tower. Occasional.
Buoy, E side entrance to St. Anna Baai, 12 06.0N, 68 56.0W. Q W, 5M. Black buoy.
Buoy, W side entrance to harbor, 12 06.0N, 68 56.0W. Q R, 5M. Red buoy.
WILLEMSTAD, about 247 meters, 263° from Riffort Light, 12 06.2N, 68 56.3W. Fl G 4s, 6ft, 1M. Black pole.
RIFFORT, SINT ANNA (WILLEMSTAD), E side of entrance, 12 06.4N, 68 55.9W. Oc W 5s, 83ft, 14M. Gray structure on battery wall.
RANGE (Front), 12 06.8N, 68 55.7W. F R. Orange diamond daymark. **(Rear),** 580 meters, 042° from front. F R. Orange diamond daymark.
W SIDE OF ENTRANCE, F R, 23ft. Red iron structure.
E SIDE OF ENTRANCE, F G, 26ft. Orange column, black bands.
RANGE (Front), 12 06.6N, 68 56.0W. 3 F R, 54ft. Black metal mast, yellow bands, orange square, rectangular shape. **(Rear),** 480 meters, 023°30′ from front. 4 F R, 108ft. Steel mast, yellow circular shape. Lights arranged in diamond shape.
W SIDE, NEAR W WHARF, SINT ANNA BAY, F R, 23ft. Iron post.
E SIDE OF ENTRANCE TO SCHOTTEGAT, F G, 67ft. Aluminum painted structure. Visible only when entering or leaving Schottegat.
N SIDE, 12 07.5N, 68 55.1W. F G.
BAAI MACOLA, 12 07.1N, 68 55.1W. Q W.

WILLEMSTAD

12 07N, 68 56W
Pilotage: The well-marked entrance to the harbor is called Sint Anna Baai. Approaching vessels should contact the harbor control

office on VHF channels 12 or 16 (call sign Fort Nassau). The first bridge is a floating pontoon structure and can be opened only by calling Fort Nassau. A single siren blasts alerts local land-based traffic 1 minute prior to the bridge's opening; no siren signals are used for boat traffic. The second bridge has a vertical clearance of 180 feet. At night Fort Nassau shows a green and white signal when vessel traffic can enter the port; a red and white signal means outgoing traffic is en route and incoming traffic must wait. By island decree, no small boats or yachts are allowed to enter or leave the port of Willemstad between 1800 and 0600 hours; the bridge will not open for smaller vessels during this period.
Port of Entry: Tie up to the fueling wharf along the starboard side of Sint Anna Baai north of the high-level bridge. The harbor official's office (call sign Fort Nassau on VHF channels 12 or 16) is nearby.
Dockage: Contact the harbor officials about the possibility of mooring to the bulkhead between the bridges, on the starboard side of the channel. The wharves are named Kleine Wharf, Groote Wharf, and Salazar Wharf, proceeding from seaward. The wharves on the west side of the channel are for larger ships.
Anchorage: Anchor in nearby Spaansche Water (see previous description).
Services: Willemstad is the commercial center of Curaçao and a major port. Most services are available, including haulouts and repairs. There are several chandleries.

BULLENBAAI

BULLENBAAI, 12 10.9N, 69 00.9W. Q W.
FIRST RANGE (Front), 12 12.1N, 69 02.1W. F R. Red daymark. **(Rear),** 251 meters, 043° from front, 12 12.2N, 69 01.9W. F G. Red daymark.
SECOND RANGE (Front), 12 11.7N, 69 01.2W. Q R. On tank. **(Rear),** 640 meters 095° from front. Q R. On tank.
THIRD RANGE (Front), 12 11.2N, 69 00.9W. F G. **(Rear),** 200 meters, 123° from front. F R.
KAAP ST. MARIE, 12 11.4N, 69 03.4W. Fl (2) W 9s, 41ft, 9M. Red rectangular iron tower.
NOORDPUNT, 12 23.2N, 69 09.5W.
Fl (3) W 15s, 138ft, 12M. White masonry structure. Visible 006°–271°, also on certain bearings N of 271°.

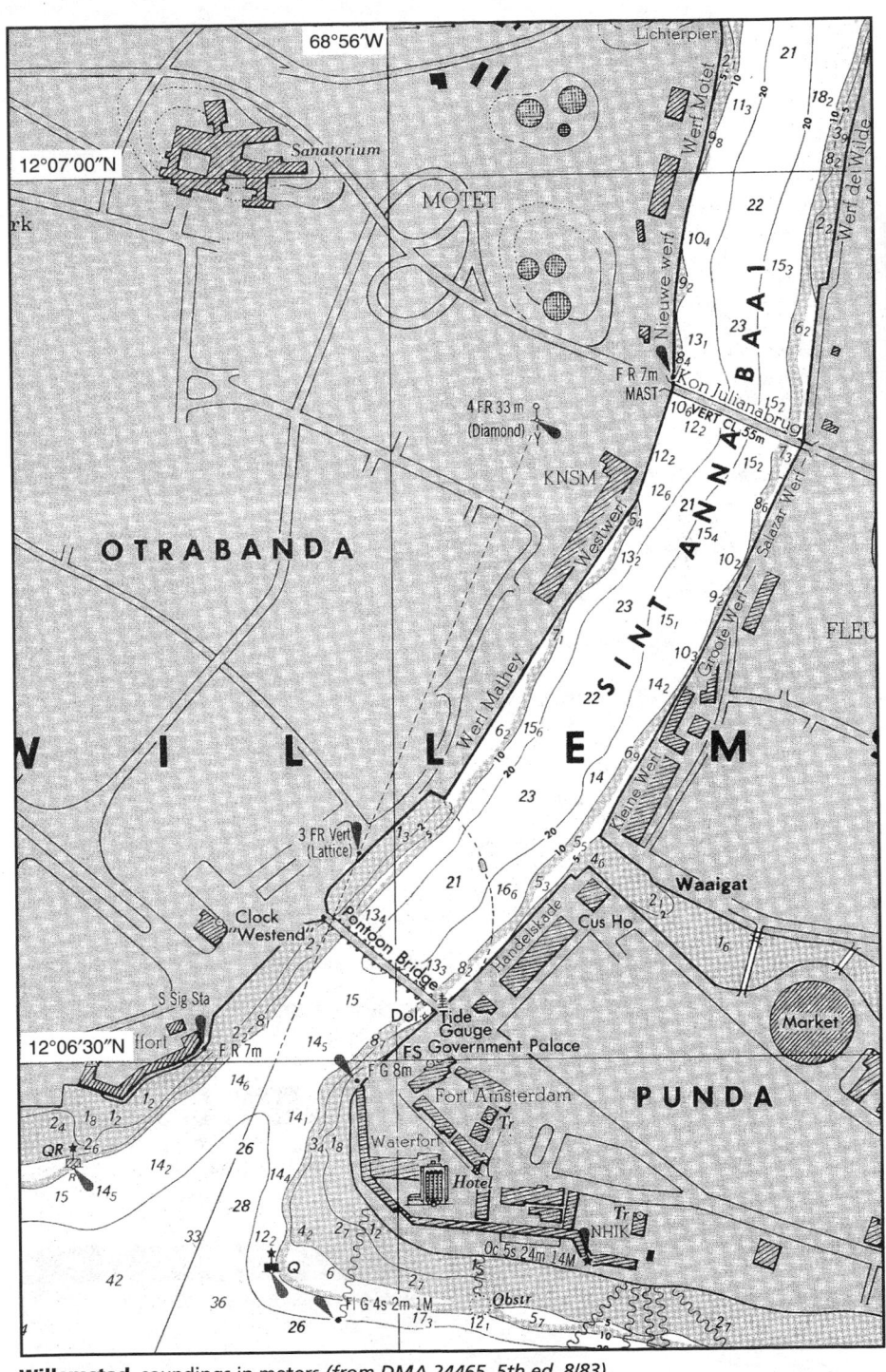

Willemstad, soundings in meters *(from DMA 24465, 5th ed, 8/83)*

ARUBA

CAUTION: Our information on aids to navigation comes from official government
sources. The latitudes and longitudes of
these marks may not correspond to the
readings from GPS receivers. Some aids
have been reported as unreliable, missing,
off position, or showing incorrect characteristics. No single aid to navigation, or
waypoint, should be relied upon as a sole
means of fixing your position.

NOTE: The chartlet in this section is <u>not</u>
<u>intended for navigation</u> and is included
for reference and planning purposes only.
Reproduced from government sources, it
is from the most current edition as of
press time, but incorporates <u>no corrections</u>
to navigational aids, depths, or hazards
since the edition publication date.

ENTRY PROCEDURES

Aruba, the westernmost island of the ABC
group, is located about 15 miles north of the
Peninsula de Paraguaná on the Venezuelan
coast and about 60 miles west-northwest of
the Willemstad area on Curaçao. The island is
frequently the last stop for cruisers headed to
Panama. Aruba has separated from the Netherlands Antilles and is scheduled to become an
independent nation in 1996.

The Port of Entry is Oranjestad, about 12 miles
northwest of the southern tip of the island.
Tie up to the southern end of the main commercial wharves. The officials with whom you
clear in are located nearby. Call Oranjestad
port radio on VHF channel 16 for instructions.
Firearms will be held until your departure.

The country code for Aruba is 297 and the
island code 8. Local numbers use five digits.
The official currency is the Aruban florin, but
U.S. currency is widely accepted. Dutch is the
official language, but many residents speak
English. The local dialect, known as Papiamento,
is also spoken.

ARUBA

PUNT BASORA (COLORADO POINT), SE
extremity of island, 12 25.3N, 69 52.1W.
Fl W 6s, 167ft, 21M. Gray square stone tower.
Visible 160°–109°. Reported extinguished
(1992).
INDIAANSKOP, No 10, 12 25.1N, 69 53.6W.
Q G, 10 ft. Steel trellis mast.

ST NICHOLAS BAAI

East Channel Entrance Buoy, 12 25.0N,
69 54.0W. Fl W 3s, 10ft. Red buoy.
Buoy Janet, E side of entrance, 12 25.0N,
69 54.0W. Fl R 4s, 10 ft. Red buoy.
BEACON NO. 6, W side of entrance, E channel,
12 25.7N, 69 54.1W. Fl R 2s, 11ft. Beacon.
BEACON NO. 5, W side of Entrance E channel,
12 25.6N, 69 54.2W. Q G, 11ft. Dolphin. F R
and F G lights are shwon from heads of laker
piers.
West Channel Entrance Buoy, 12 26.0N,
69 55.0W. Fl W 3s. Black buoy.
W ENTRANCE RANGE, near marine railway,
(Front), 12 26.0N, 69 54.3W. 4 F R, 102ft.
Occasional. Lights arranged in diamond shape.
(Rear), 240 meters, 083°14′ from front. 4 F R,
134ft. Occasional. Lights arranged in diamond
shape. N side of channel marked by Fl R light on
dolphin and two F R lights on dock. F G and F R
lights are shown from outer corners of finger
piers.
ENTRANCE, N SIDE, NO. 2, 12 26.1N, 69 54.9W.
Fl R 2s, 23ft, 7M.

COMMANDEURS BAAI

RANGE (Front), 12 27.1N, 69 56.8W. 2 F G (vert),
19ft. 1M. Pole. **(Rear),** 34 meters, 059° from
front. 2 F R (vert), 23ft, 1M. Pole.

BACADERA

North Entrance Buoy, 12 29.0N, 70 00.0W.
Fl R 5s. Red buoy.

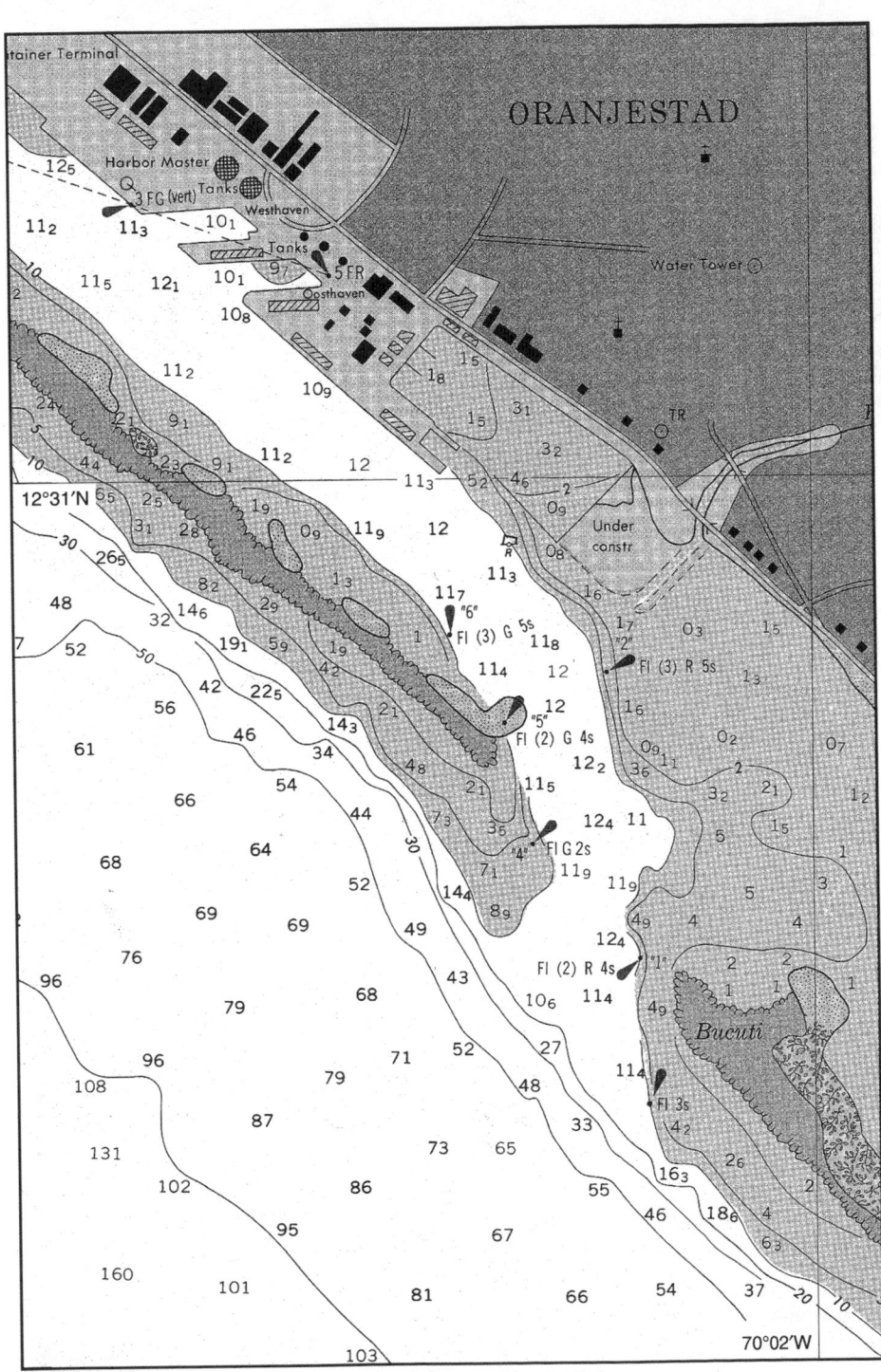

Oranjestad, soundings in meters *(from DMA 24463, 5th ed, 1/87)*

PAARDEN BAAI

South Entrance Buoy, 12 29.0N, 70 00.0W. Fl W 5s. Red buoy.

ORANJESTAD, PRINSES BEATRIX AVIATION LIGHT, 12 31.0N, 70 00.0W. F R, 669ft. Tower.

SOUTH ENTRANCE, 12 30.5N, 70 02.1W. Q W. Concrete column.

SOUTH ENTRANCE LIGHT "1", 12 30.7N, 70 02.1W. Fl (2) R 4s. Concrete column.

SOUTH ENTRANCE LIGHT "4", 12 30.8N, 70 02.2W. Q G. Concrete column.

SOUTH ENTRANCE LIGHT "5", 12 30.9N, 70 02.2W. Fl (2) G 4s, 10ft. Concrete column.

SOUTH ENTRANCE LIGHT "2", 12 31.0N, 70 02.1W. Fl (3) R 5s, 10ft. Concrete column.

SOUTH ENTRANCE LIGHT "6", 12 31.0N, 70 02.3W. Fl (3) G 5s. Concrete column.

WEST ENTRANCE, N side of channel, 12 31.8N, 70 03.3W. Fl R 2s. Concrete column.

WEST ENTRANCE, 12 31.7N, 70 03.1W. Fl (2) R 4s.

West Entrance Buoy, S side of channel, 12 32.0N, 70 03.0W. Fl W 3s. Yellow buoy.

WEST ENTRANCE LIGHT "3", N side of channel, 12 31.6N, 70 03.4W. Fl R, 2s. Concrete column.

WEST ENTRANCE LIGHT "7", S side of entrance, 12 31.5N, 70 02.9W. Fl (2) G 4s. Concrete column.

WESTERN ENTRANCE RANGE (Front), 12 31.5N, 70 02.6W. 3 F G (vert). Triangle on black mast with orange bands on N side of building. **(Rear),** 430 meters, 110° from front, 5 F G. Orange diamond on black mast, orange bands, F R lights are shown from NW and SW corners of Oosthaven.

ORANJESTAD

12 31N, 70 02W

Pilotage: The harbor is located in Paarden Baai and is protected by a barrier reef on its west side. Oranjestad is the capital of Aruba. There is a westward-flowing current in this area of 2 to 3 knots. Prominent landmarks are the white circular water tower and close by and to the northwest, the Roman Catholic church. Contact Oranjestad port radio on VHF channel 16 for information on entering the harbor.

Port of Entry: Tie up at the southern end of the main piers. The main customs office can be reached at 297-8-31414.

Dockage: Harbour Town Marina is opposite the commercial wharves. Two yacht clubs (Aruba Nautical Club, 297-8-23022; and Bucuti Yacht Club, 297-8-23793) located to the south-east inside the reefs. Inquire locally for directions to these areas.

Anchorage: You can anchor southeast of the harbor area in the patch of deeper water extending east from marker 1. There are reports that boats anchor close in to the beach, avoiding the shallow spots on the way in. The depths in this area may be poorly charted.

Services: There are good supermarkets and general supplies. Air connections are excellent. Marine supplies are rather limited. Fuel and water are available at Harbor Town Marina.

COLOMBIA

CAUTION: Our information on aids to navigation comes from official government sources. The latitudes and longitudes of these marks may not correspond to the readings from GPS receivers. Some aids have been reported as unreliable, missing, off position, or showing incorrect characteristics. No single aid to navigation, or waypoint, should be relied upon as a sole means of fixing your position.

NOTE: The chartlets in this section are not intended for navigation and are included for reference and planning purposes only. While chartlets reproduced from government sources are from the most current editions as of press time, they incorporate no corrections to navigational aids, depths, or hazards since the edition publication date. Colombian authorities advise vessels to exercise caution sailing in coastal waters with depths of less than 30 meters, as the hydrographic information shown on the charts is derived from old survey data.

ENTRY PROCEDURES

From Punta Gallinas to the Panama Canal is about 530 miles. From Aruba to the Canal is about 630 miles. Increasing numbers of cruisers are breaking up this long run with a voyage along the Colombian coast at least a stop in Cartagena, Turbo, Zapzurro, and the island of San Andrés, which is discussed later in this chapter in the section *Western Caribbean: Offshore Islands*.

Citizens of the U.S., Germany, the Netherlands, the United Kingdom, and many other countries are granted 90-day visas when they clear in; citizens of other countries are required to have a visa on arrival. Those traveling on business should check the latest visa requirements. For more information contact the Colombian Consulate at 1825 Connecticut Avenue, Suite 218, Washington, DC, 20008 (202-332-7476). In the United States, Colombia also maintains consulates in San Juan, Puerto Rico; Miami; New Orleans; Houston; Chicago; Los Angeles; and New York.

The importation of firearms into the country is strictly forbidden, and all weapons must be declared.

Yachts are generally required to use the services of an agent to handle clearing-in paperwork. A cruising permit, or *zarpe*, will be issued and should be presented in every port visited.

WARNING: The U.S. State Department is warning U.S. citizens against travel to Colombia until further notice. With the exception of several popular tourist areas, violence continues to affect significant portions of the country. Recent attacks have targeted U.S. citizens and institutions. Colombia's north coast is among the areas considered particularly dangerous and unstable, except the tourist centers of Santa Marta, Barranquilla, Cartegena, and San Andres. For the current status of this travel warning, call the U.S. Department of State Citizens Emergency Center (202-647-5225).

Some boaters advise staying well offshore when underway, and all boats should avoid anchoring in remote areas.

U.S. citizens can seek advice and assistance at the U.S. Embassy in Bogotá (57-1-320-1300) or the U.S. Consulate in Barranquilla (57-58-457-088).

Cholera has been reported in Colombia, generally outside the big cities and tourist areas. For the latest information contact the Centers for Disease Control International Travelers Hotline (404-332-4559) in Atlanta, Georgia.

Ports of Entry on Colombia's Caribbean coast include Riohacha, Santa Marta, Barranquilla, 324 miles from Cartagena to the Canal. The country's long Spanish heritage and beautiful scenery provide an interesting contrast to some of the Caribbean countries to the east. See *Reed's Nautical Companion* for an illustration of the country flag.

The telephone area code for the country is 57; a one-, two-, or three-digit city code follows, then the local number. The city code for Cartagena is 536; Bogotá, 1; Cali, 2; Medellín, 4; and Palmira, 22.

The currency is the peso, which is divided into 100 centavos. The exchange rate in summer 1994 was about 820 pesos per U.S. dollar. The language spoken is Spanish.

PENINSULA DE LA GUAJIRA

CASTILLETES, 11 51.4N, 71 19.5W. Fl W 9s, 72ft, 15M. Metal structure, black and white bands.

PUNTA ESPADA, 12 05.5N, 71 06.8W. Fl W 8s, 105ft, 18M. White metal tower.

CHICHIBACOA, 12 17.7N, 71 13.1W. Fl W 10s, 89ft, 20M. Black and white tower.

PUERTO ESTRELLA, 12 21.4N, 71 18.6W. FL W 15s, 85ft, 18M. White tower, 72ft.

CHIMARE, 12 23.2N, 71 26.5W. Fl W 12s, 82ft, 20M. Orange tower.

PUNTA GALLINAS, 12 28.0N, 71 40.0W. Fl W 10s, 110ft, 16M. Aluminum square tower.

Puerto Bolivar, Buoy No 1, 12 17.5N, 71 58.4W. Fl G 2s. Green buoy. RACON **M** (– –).

PUERTO BOLIVAR, on pier, 12 15.5N, 71 57.7W. Iso W, 2s, 148ft, 16M. Coal loading gantry.

PUNTA LATATA, Fl W 3s, 5M.

CABO DE LA VELA, 12 13.1N, 72 10.5W. Fl W, 10s, 302ft, 16M. White round masonry tower, red band. Visible 358° to 268°.

CABO DE LA VELA

12 13N, 72 11W

Pilotage: The cape is reported to give a good radar return up to a distance of 21 miles. There is a light on the point. There is possible anchorage partially sheltered from the wind and seas south of the outer extremity of the cape.

PUNTA MANAURE TO POZOS COLORADO

PUNTA MANAURE, 11 45.2N, 72 33.2W. Fl (2) W 15s, 74ft, 14M. Aluminum framework tower, black bands.

PIPELINE BEACON 1, 11 44.4N, 72 44.1W. Fl (2) Y 10s, 16ft, 3M.

BEACON 2, L Fl Y 10s, 16ft, 3M.

RIOHACHA, 11 32.7N, 72 50.0W. Fl W 10s, 115ft, 20M. White metal tower, 98ft. Aero radiobeacon about 2 miles ENE.

RIOHACHA

11 34N, 72 55W

Pilotage: The town lies about 60 miles southwest of Cabo de la Vela. The river is reported to have a navigable depth of about 12 feet, but cargo is lightered out to the anchorage to be loaded. Only small coasters frequent this port. There is a small pier off town.

Port of Entry: This is reported to be the first Port of Entry west of the Venezuelan border.

Anchorage: Basically an open roadstead, the harbor can be rolly.

Services: Some supplies are available.

MORRO GRANDE, summit N side of bay, 11 15.1N, 74 13.8W. Fl (3) W 15s, 269ft, 20M. Tower on white square building. Obscured E of 203° by the high land of Aguja Island; visible over a small arc between the island and the mainland at 212°.

SANTA MARTA

11 15N, 74 13W

Pilotage: The harbor is located about 40 miles east-northeast of the entrance to Barranquilla. It is a small but commercially important port. Isla El Morro is a steep-sided islet about 1/2 mile west of the harbor. A light marks the island, and there are the ruins of a fort on it. A small rock, Morro Chico, lies just west of Punta Morrito at the harbor entrance. The northeast trades are reported to be gusty here. Between the months of March and December a local wind blows from the southwest between the hours of 1000 and 1300. A cathedral with two domes and a radio tower are conspicuous. A white stone monument stands on the summit of a hill about 3/4 mile north-northwest of the cathedral. There are also several tanks in the vicinity of the monument.

Port of Entry: The customs house is near the wharves on the eastern side of the harbor.

Anchorage: Drop the hook south of the wharf area.

Services: Basic supplies are available.

POZOS COLORADOS (Front Light), 11 09.3N, 74 12.8W. Q R, 5M. White, orange, and red rectangular daymark on metal tower. **(Rear Light),** 395 meters 085°30' from front. Iso R 6s, 5M. White, orange, and red rectangular daymark on metal tower.

SIMON BOLIVAR AVIATION LIGHT, 11 07.0N, 74 14.0W. Al Fl W G 10s. Airport control tower.

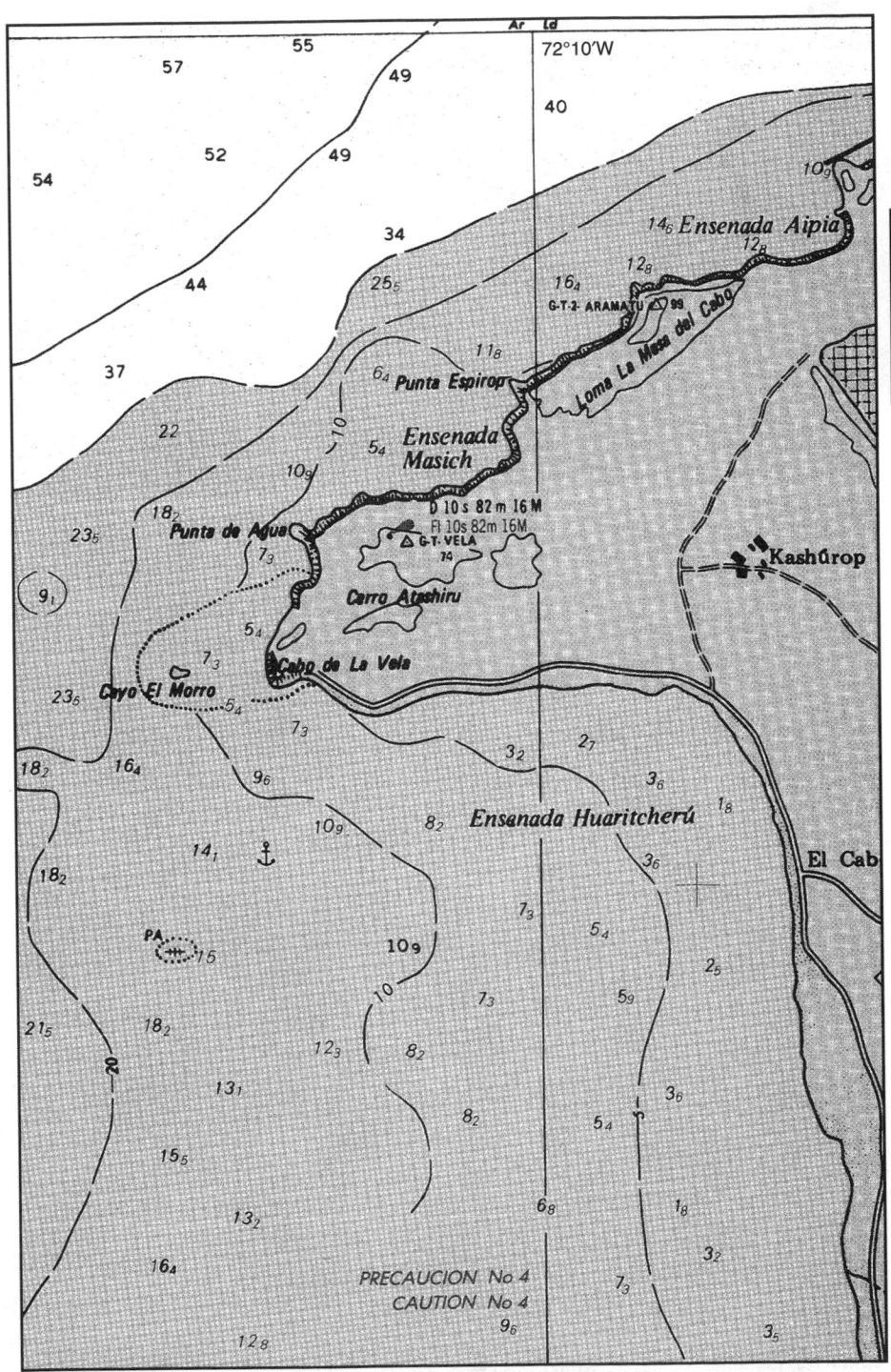

Cabo de la Vela, soundings in meters *(from DMA 24469, 1st ed, 8/87)*

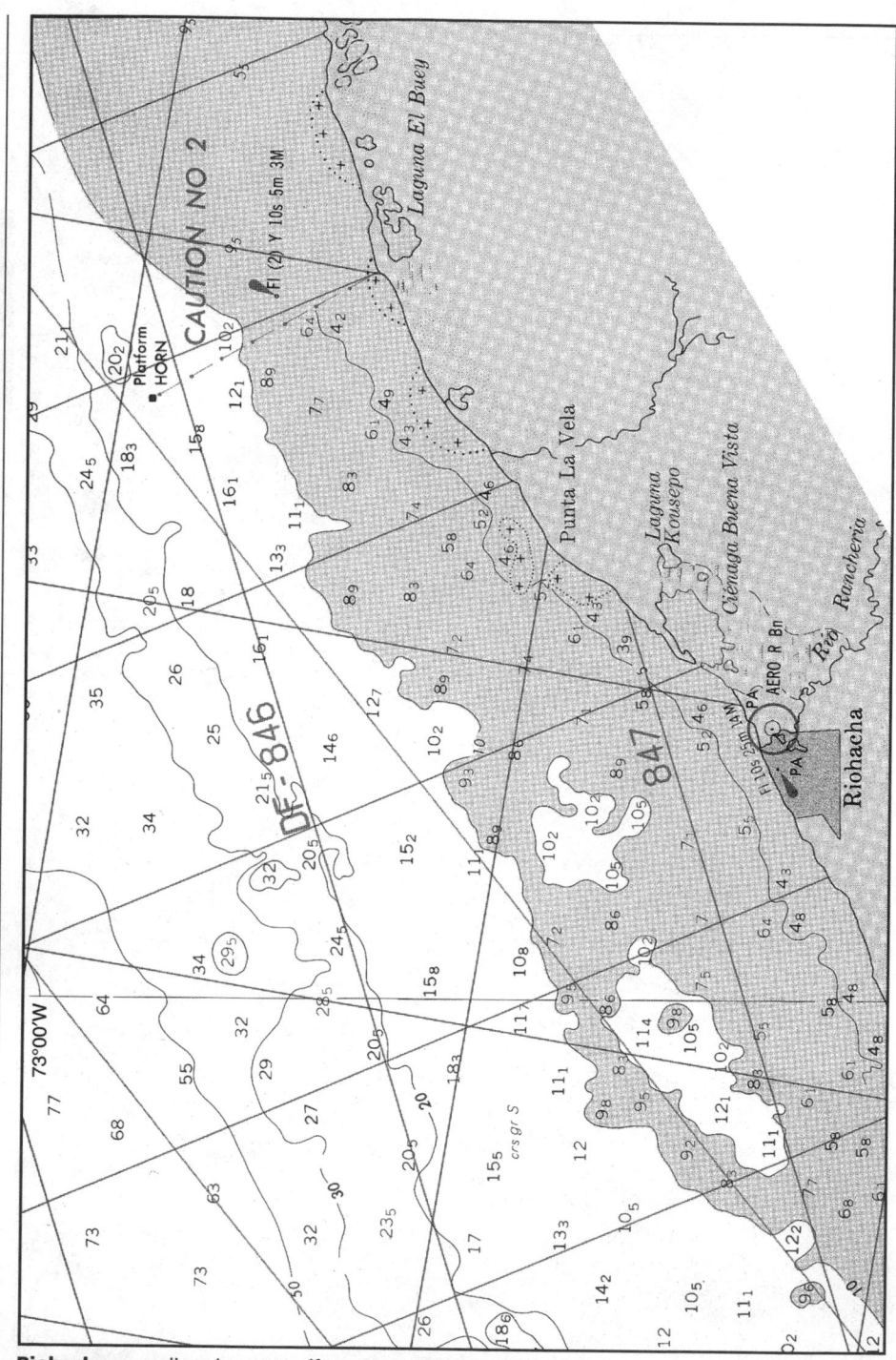

Riohacha, soundings in meters *(from DMA 24490, 2nd ed, 9/86)*

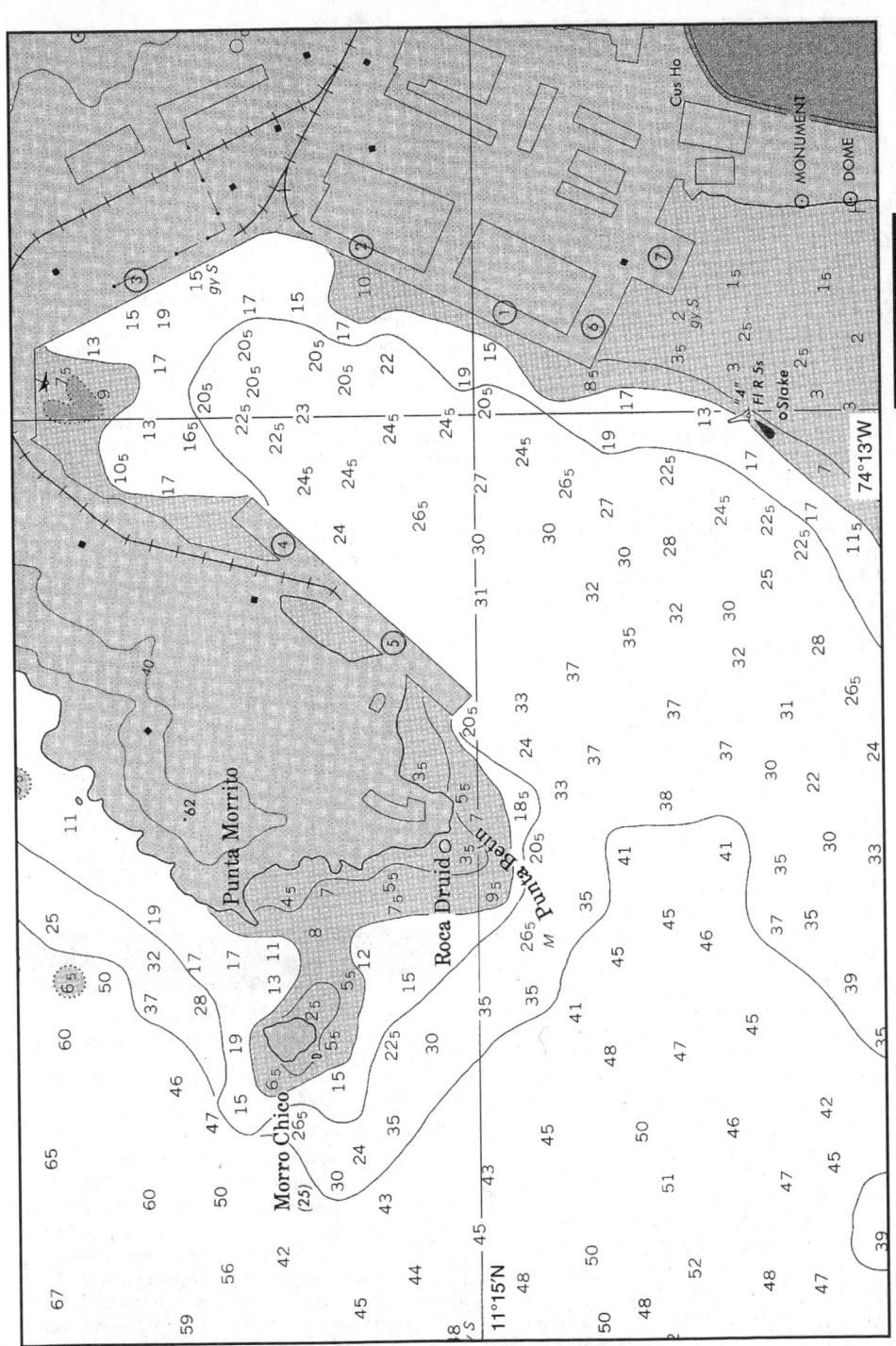

Santa Marta, soundings in meters *(from DMA 24492, 19th ed, 5/92)*

RÍO MAGDALENA

F-2, head of W breakwater, 11 06.5N, 74 51.3W. Fl R 5s, 72ft, 12M. White metal tower.

F-1, head of E breakwater, 11 06.6N, 74 51.3W. Fl G W 5s, 72ft, 12M. White metal tower.

Z-3 RANGE (Front Light), on E breakwater, 11 06.4N, 74 50.9W. Fl G 5s, 27ft, 6M. White metal tower, red bands. **(Rear Light),** Z-5, 310 meters 135° from front. Fl G 5s, 59ft, 7M. White metal tower.

X-2, W side of river, 11 05.6N, 74 51.1W. Fl R 5s, 20ft, 6M. Red and white bands on white metal tower.

X-4, W side of river, 11 04.9N, 74 51.0W. Fl R 5s, 23ft, 6M. Red and white bands on metal tower.

LAS FLORES RANGE (Front Light) (down river), on W breakwater, 11 04.2N, 74 50.8W. Fl W, 5s, 23ft, 3M. White mast, red bands. **(Rear Light),** 393 meters 322°54' from front. Iso G 6s, 33ft, 7M. Red and white square on square metal tower.

X-6, W side of river, 11 04.1N, 74 50.6W. Fl R 5s, 23ft, 6M. White metal tower, red bands.

ENTRANGE RANGE (Front Light), spur of W jetty, 11 03.9N, 74 50.7W. Fl W 5s, 40ft, 6M. White metal tower. **(Rear Light),** 697 meters 168° from front. Fl W 5s, 66ft, 6M. White metal tower.

X-8, W side of river, 11 03.5N, 74 50.4W. Fl R 5s, 23ft, 6M. Red and white bands on metal tower.

X-10, W side of river below Las Flores, 11 03.1N, 74 49.9W. Fl R 5s, 23ft, 6M. White metal tower, red bands.

LAS FLORES RANGE (Front Light) (up river), W side of river, 11 02.6N, 74 49.6W. Fl G, 18ft, 7M. White square on metal mast, white square concrete base. **(Rear Light),** 500 meters 142°54' from front. Iso G 6s, 36ft, 7M. Red and white square on square metal tower.

X-1, 11 01.9N, 74 47.9W. Fl G 5s, 23ft, 6M. White metal tower, red bands.

LAS FLORES, on pier, 11 02.5N, 74 49.2W. 2 F R (vert), 30ft, 3M. Tower.

A-1 RANGE (Front Light), 11 01.0N, 71 46.5W. Fl W 5s, 23ft, 5M. White metal tower, red bands. **(Rear Light),** A-2, 118° from front. Fl W 5s, 36ft, 5M. White metal tower, red bands.

X-3, 11 00.6N, 74 45.0W. Fl G 5s, 23ft, 6M. White metal tower, red bands.

X-5, E side of river below new canal to Cienaga, 10 59.9N, 74 45.8W. Fl G 5s, 23ft, 6M. White metal tower, red bands.

X-7, E side of river below Isla de Trupillo, 10 58.6N, 74 45.3W. Fl G 5s, 23ft, 6M. White metal tower, red bands. Marks the eastern limit turning basin off Isla de Trupillo.

BARRANQUILLA

11 00N, 74 48W

Pilotage: The port is in the outer 10 miles of the Río Magdalena, the main artery of commercial traffic in Colombia. The river is navigable for 800 miles inland. Being in an area of strong northeast trades, it is sometimes not possible to enter the river safely. The waves at the entrance can be very short and steep. Generally, the winds and seas moderate at night.

When the water level is low in the river from February to April and August to October, the current does not exceed 2 knots. When the water level is high in July and November the current can reach 6 knots, and floating debris can be a problem.

The coast east of the river entrance is backed by low flat sand dunes. West of the entrance the coast consists of flat partly wooded islands. The breakwater heads are reported to give good radar returns up to 10 miles off.

Port of Entry: Proceed 10 miles upstream to the city of Barranquilla.

Dockage: There may be some room at the yacht clubs.

U.S. Consulate: Call 57-58-457-088.

Services: This is a large city and has good stocks of general supplies. Repairs and parts should be more available here than in the ports farther east.

PUNTA HERMOSA TO CARTAGENA

PUNTA HERMOSA, 10 57.8N, 75 01.0W. Fl (3) W 20s, 440ft, 22M. White square concrete tower, black stripe.

ISLA VERDE

11 02N, 75 00W

Pilotage: Isla Verde is actually a sandspit covered at all stages of the tide. This coast has many shoal areas within a distance of 3 miles from shore. Vessels should plot courses carefully until past the shoals along the coast for the 13 miles between the Río Magdalena and Punta Hermosa. Generally, sailing beyond the 10-fathom line is safe. There is a light on Punta Hermosa and one on Punta de La Garita, as well as one on Punta Canoas.

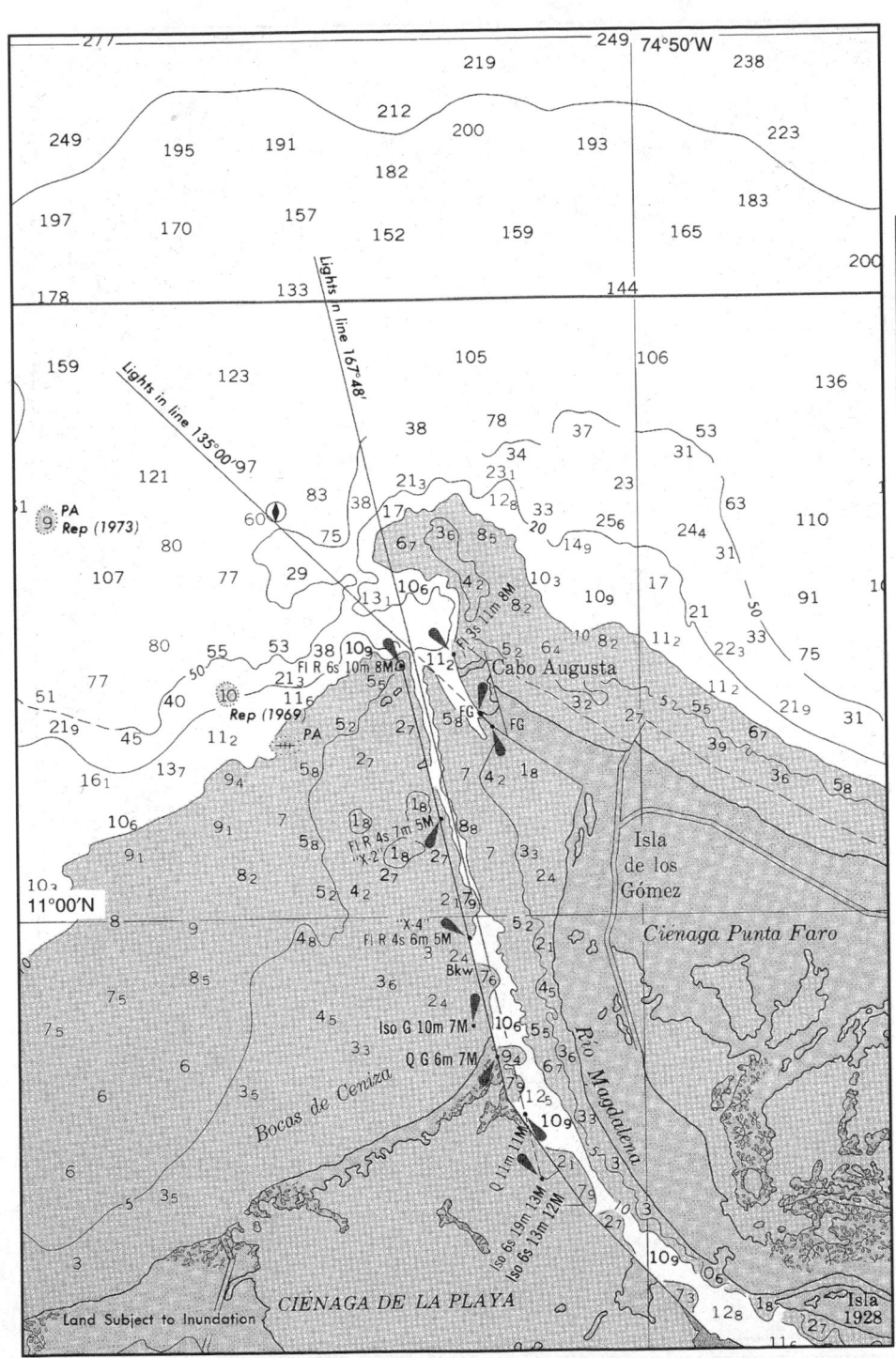

Approaches to Barranquilla, soundings in meters *(from DMA 24490, 2nd ed, 9/86)*

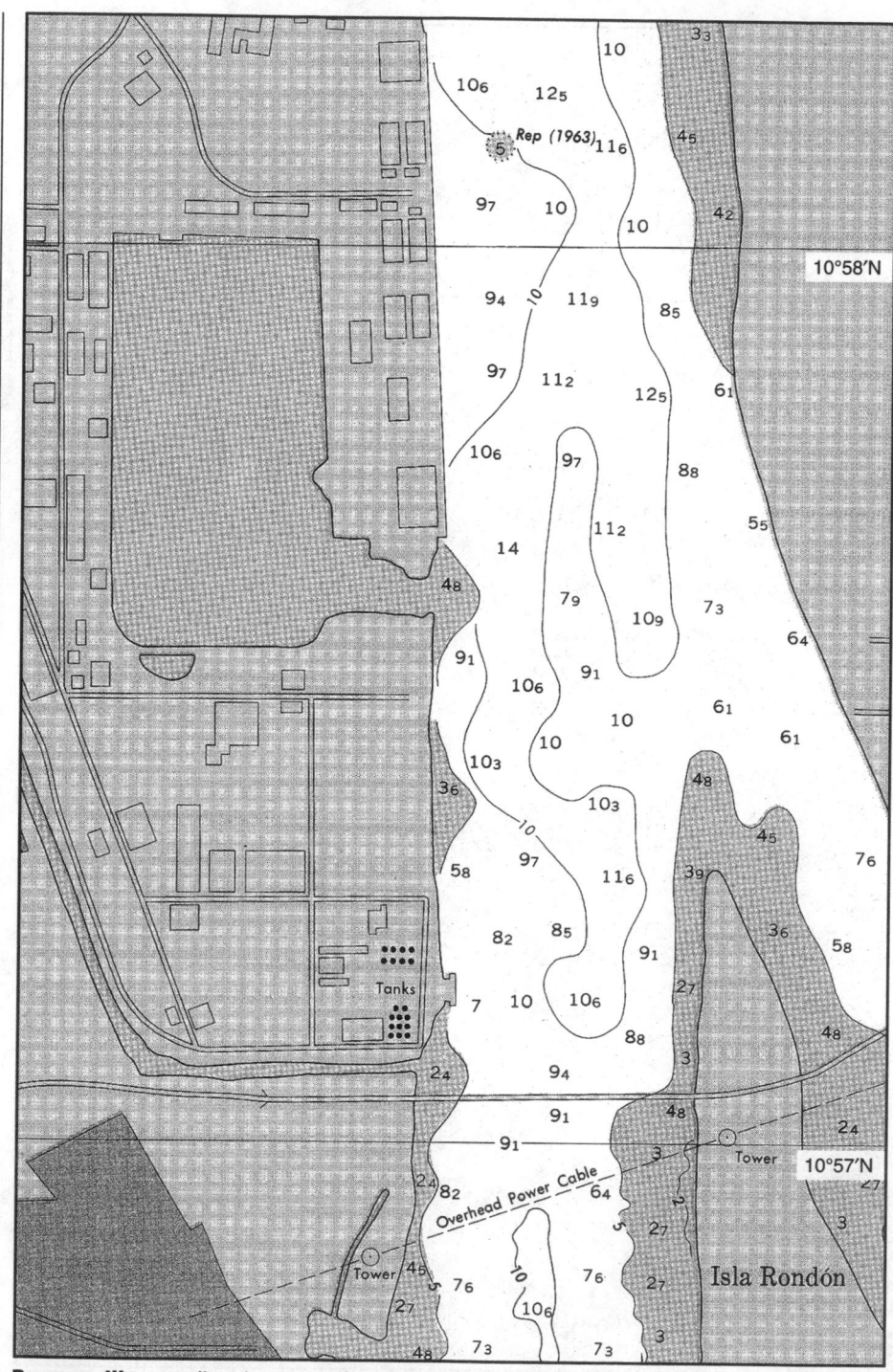

Barranquilla, soundings in meters *(from DMA 24502, 4th ed, 7/87)*

PUNTA GALERA, 10 48.4N, 75 19.8W. Fl W 7s, 60ft, 13M. White metal framework tower.
PUNTA CANOAS, N side of point, 10 34.5N, 75 30.0W. Fl W 10s, 289ft, 24M. White cylindrical tower, black bands.
CRESPO AVIATION LIGHT, 10 27.2N, 75 31.0W. Al FL W G 10s, 20M.

BANCOS DE SALMEDINA

10 23N, 75 40W

Pilotage: Two detached shoal areas of sand and coral lie about 5 miles northwest of the Boca Chica entrance buoy to Cartagena. Breakers have been reported on the western shoals, which have a least depth of about 15 feet. There is a light on the eastern bank.

CARTAGENA

ISLA TIERRA BOMBA, 10 20.6N, 75 35.1W. Fl (2) W 20s, 259ft, 23M. White metal framework tower, red bands. Radiobeacon.
BOYA DE MAR, 10 19.1N, 75 36.2W. Fl W 8s. Red and white stripes. Radar reflector. Reported extinguished (1991).
Buoy 1, W end of Boca Chica entrance, 10 19.2N, 75 35.5W. Fl G 3s. Green buoy.
Buoy 2, S side of W entrance to dredged channel. Fl R 3s. Red buoy.
ISLA BRUJAS, NO 2, 10 20.0N, 75 31.1W. Fl W 3s, 65ft, 10M. White metal tower, F W on water tower 0.48 mile ENE.
CANAL DEL DIQUE, E side of canal, 10 17.8N, 75 31.6W. Fl W 10s, 59ft, 10M. White tower.
CASTILLO GRANDE, 10 23.6N, 75 32.9W. Fl W 4s, 79ft, 14M. Stone tower.

CARTAGENA

10 25N, 75 32W

Pilotage: This is the largest and most secure port on the north coast of Colombia. It is located about 324 miles east-northeast of the Panama Canal. The main entrance to the bay is Boca Chica, lying between two islands about 6 3/4 miles south-southwest of the city. The northern entrance, known as Boca Grande, has a submerged rock barrier across its entire width. The small boat passages through the barrier should be attempted only with local knowledge.

In the season of strong winds, January to June, the sea breeze sets in from the west and then veers northwest. At about noon it blows parallel to the coast. During the wet season, April to October, the climate is hot and early morning land breezes are usually preceded by rainsqualls of short duration. During the dry season from November to March the winds are stronger.

The maximum tide range is about 2.6 feet and the mean range about 1 foot. The tidal current off the entrance to the inner harbor sets east-southeast on the flood at a velocity of 1/2 knot and west at the same speed during the maximum ebb.

There are several Restricted Areas in the harbor, and vessels should not travel or anchor in these areas. One of them fills most of the western harbor off Boca Grande and Castillo Grande, extending almost all the way east to Manga island.

Port of Entry: Many cruisers dock or anchor at the Club Nautico, where you can contact an agent.
Dockage: Cruisers recommend Club Nautico located on the west coast of Manga island. Depths are reported to be less than 7 feet at the docks. The Club de Pesca is nearby on the north end of the island. Be prepared if strong winds come in from the south.
Anchorage: Yachts anchor off Club Nautico, or north of the northeast corner of Manga island. Be prepared if strong winds come in from the south.
Services: Fuel is available at the Club de Pesca, and you can get water, ice, and showers at Club Nautico. Repair facilities or assistance in finding services are all found at Club Nautico. Haulouts can be arranged at several shipyards. There are good supermarkets and general supplies of all types.

This city has a five-hundred-year history and has done a good job of preserving memories of it. The old walled city is a short walk from the marinas and is reported to be fascinating. The strategic location that so attracted the Spanish galleons still brings in the cruisers.

ISLAS DEL ROSARIO

ISLA DEL TESORO, 10 14.2N, 75 44.4W. Fl (3) W 12s, 75ft, 15M. White metal framework tower. RACON C (– · – ·).
ROSARIO LIGHTHOUSE, 10 09.7N, 75 48.6W. Fl W 6s, 39ft, 10M. White tower.
ISLA DEL ROSARIO, 10 10.1N, 75 48.2W. Fl R 5s, 16ft, 5M. Tower.
ISLA ARENAS, 10 08.8N, 75 43.7W. Fl W 8s, 72ft, 10M. White metal framework tower.

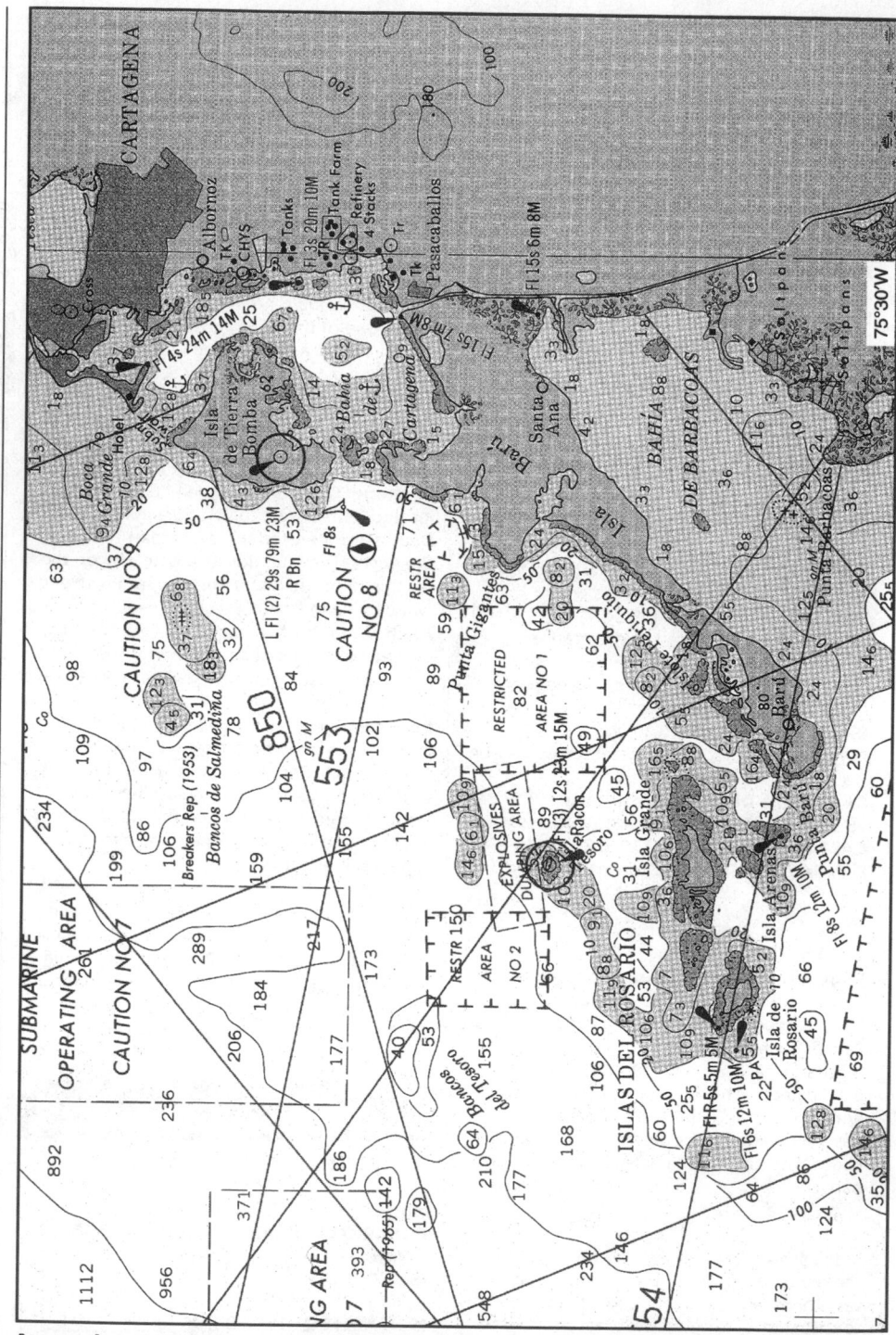

Approaches to Cartagena and Islas del Rosario, soundings in meters *(fr. DMA 24480, 1st ed, 6/90)*

COAST PILOT

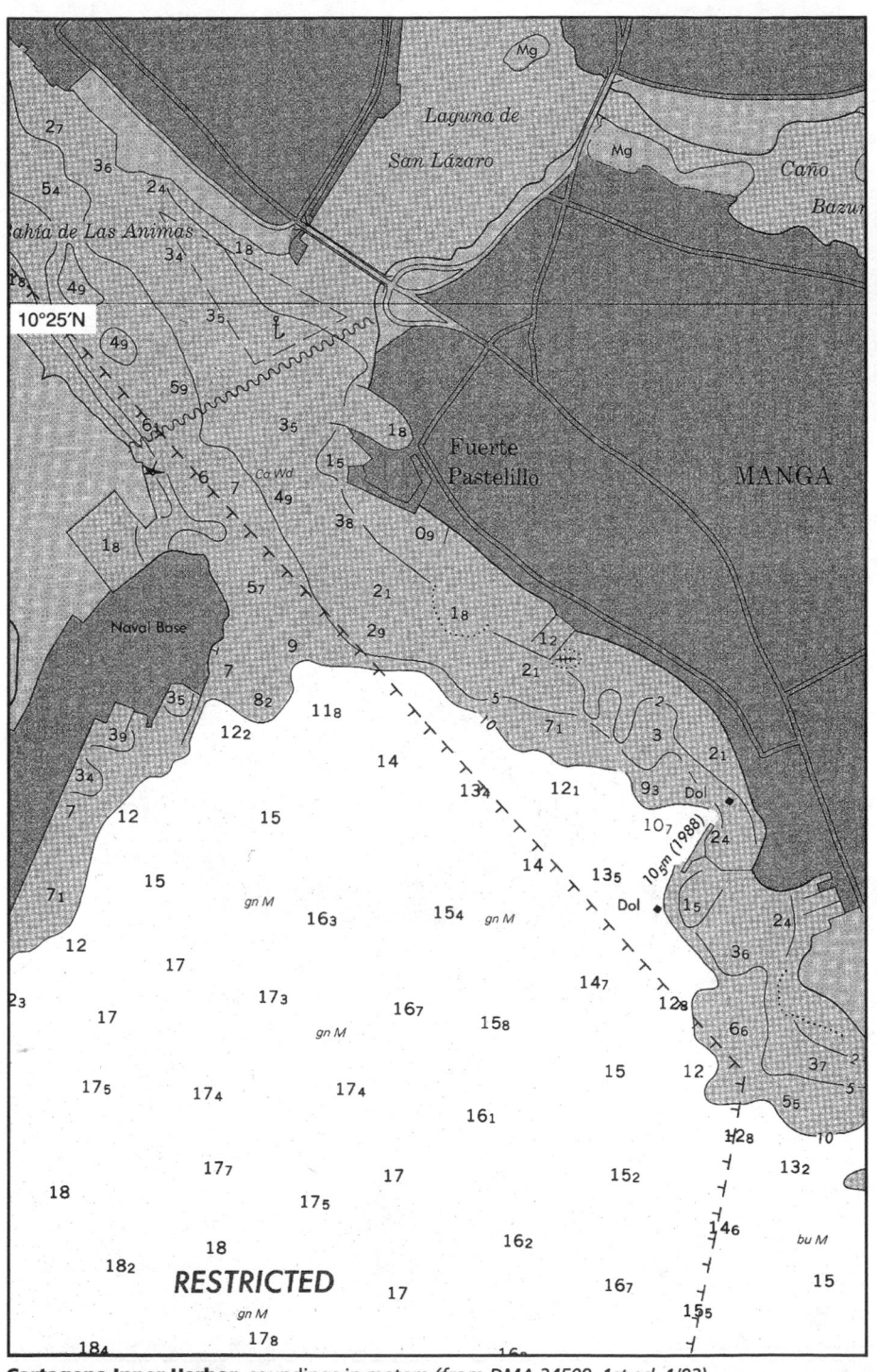

Cartagena Inner Harbor, soundings in meters *(from DMA 24509, 1st ed, 1/92)*

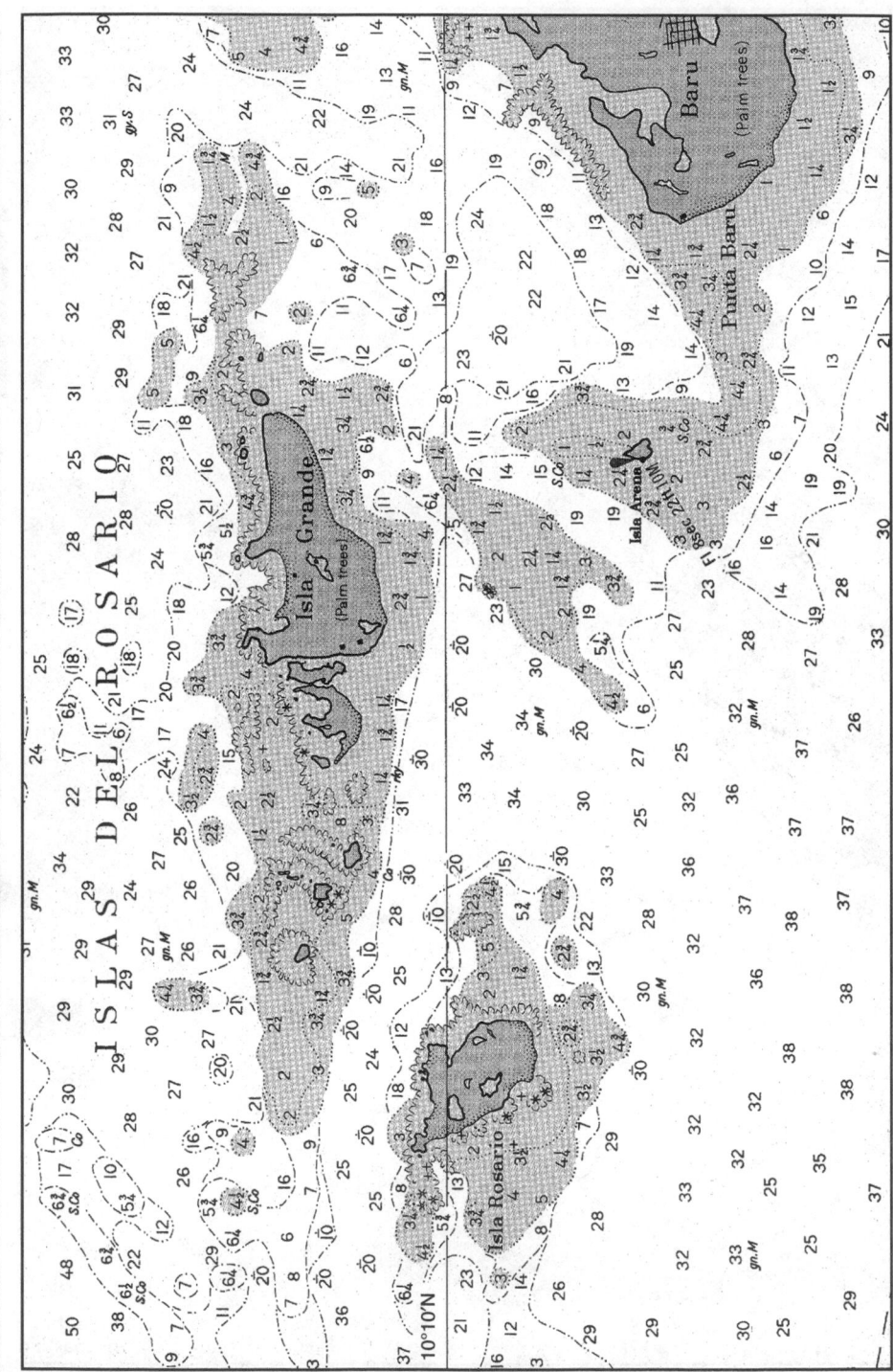

Islas del Rosario, soundings in fathoms *(from DMA 24511, 2nd ed, 4/76)*

ISLAS DEL ROSARIO

10 11N, 75 45W

Pilotage: This group of small islands is located about 12 miles southwest of the Boca Chica entrance to Cartagena. They are surrounded by banks and shoals, making the area a danger to those approaching Cartagena from the southwest. This area is a popular cruising ground for local boaters.

The north island of the group, Isla Tesoro, is marked by a light. There are two lights on the west end of the group and one on Isla Arenas. Note the charted Restricted Areas north and south of the islands.

Isla del Rosario, the south island of the group, lies about 5 miles west of Punta Baru and is covered by palm trees. Isla Grande, the largest of the group, lies about 2 1/4 miles east-northeast of Isla del Rosario. There are several good anchorages within the group, but bear in mind the depths between the islands are very irregular, and there are many rocks and reefs.

BAHÍA DE BARBACOAS, head of the bay, 10 14.5N, 75 31.4W. Fl W 15s, 19ft, 8M. Beacon.
ISLA MUCURA, 9 47.1N, 75 52.3W, Fl (2) W 8s, 79ft, 10M. White square metal tower.
ISLA CEYCEN, 9 41.8N, 75 51.3W. Fl W 10s, 78ft, 15M. White metal tower.

ISLAS SAN BERNARDO

9 45N, 75 50W

Pilotage: This group of low rocks, wooded cays, and shoals lies about 20 miles south of Islas del Rosario. They extend for about 13 1/2 miles west of Punta San Bernardo. Note the Target and Restricted Areas in the vicinity of the group. There are lights on Isla Mucura and Isla Ceycen.

There is a small village, Islote, on a tiny island south of Isla Tintipan. There are several possible anchorages in this vicinity, but the many shoals and reefs must be avoided. An approach in good light is recommended.

There are several deepwater channels between the group and the mainland.

COVENAS, 9 24.5N, 75 41.3W. Fl W 5s, 100ft, 14M. Top of cooling plant. F R on water tank 0.1 mile SW.
PIER HEAD, 9 25.0N, 75 41.2W. 2 F R (vert), 50ft, 2M.

Covenas Buoy, 9 26.0N, 75 42.0W. Fl W 3s. Red buoy.

ROCA MORROSQUILLO

9 36N, 76 00W

Pilotage: This is a coral shoal consisting of two major heads. One has a depth of about 30 feet over it and the other about 69 feet. The group is marked by a lighted buoy. This would make a good position indicator if approaching the Islas San Bernardo from the south.

ISLA FUERTE, 9 23.6N, 76 10.6W. Fl W 10s, 135ft, 18M. Metal framework tower.

ISLA FUERTE

9 23N, 76 11W

Pilotage: This low, wooded islet lies about 6 1/2 miles west-northwest of Punta Piedras and is surrounded by foul ground that extends up to 2 1/2 miles from the south side and nearly 1 1/2 miles from its west side. The islet is difficult to distinguish when approaching from the west, but there is a light on its eastern side.

There is a small village on the south side of the islet and an area suitable for anchoring on the east side.

ISLA TORTUGUILLA, 9 01.9N, 76 20.6W. Fl W 10s, 59ft, 15M. White metal tower.

ISLA TORTUGUILLA

9 02N, 76 20W

Pilotage: This tiny wooded islet lies about 5 miles west of Colina Tortugon. There is a navigation light shown from its northwest extremity. Depths of less than 30 feet lie within 3/4 miles of its shores. It may be possible to anchor here.

GOLFO DE URABÁ

PUNTA CARIBANA, 8 37.5N, 76 53.1W. Fl W 12s, 275ft, 20M. White square concrete tower.

PUNTA CARIBANA

8 37N, 76 53W

Pilotage: This is the eastern point of the entrance to the Golfo de Urabá. It is low, wooded, and marked by a light. Cerro Aguilla, at over 1,100 feet high, makes an excellent landmark. Foul ground, with some rocks awash, extends about 3 3/4 miles north-northwest from the point. This reef can be dangerous for coasting vessels, and a good offing is recommended.

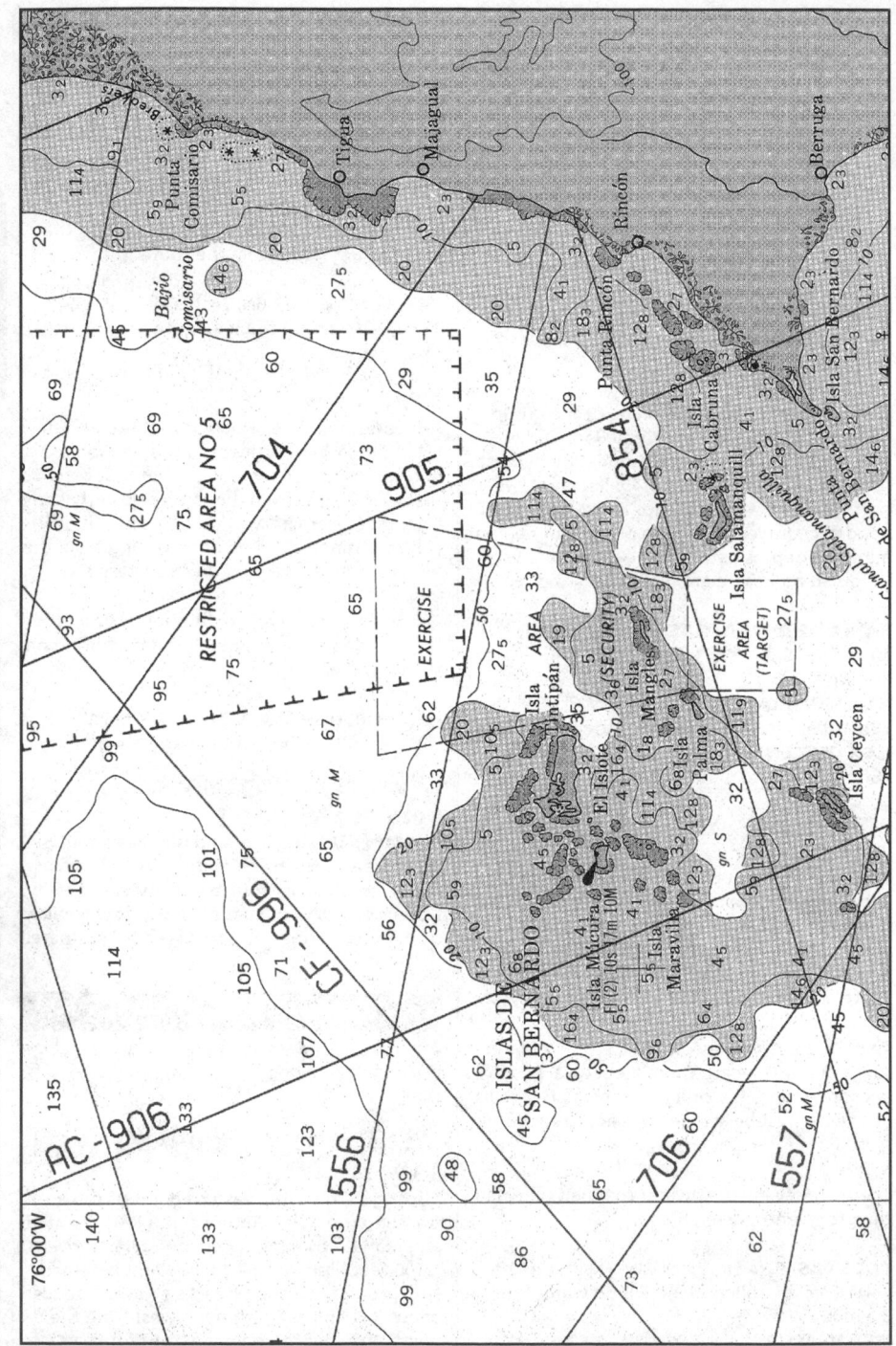

Approaches to Islas San Bernardo, soundings in meters *(from DMA 24480, 1st ed, 6/90)*

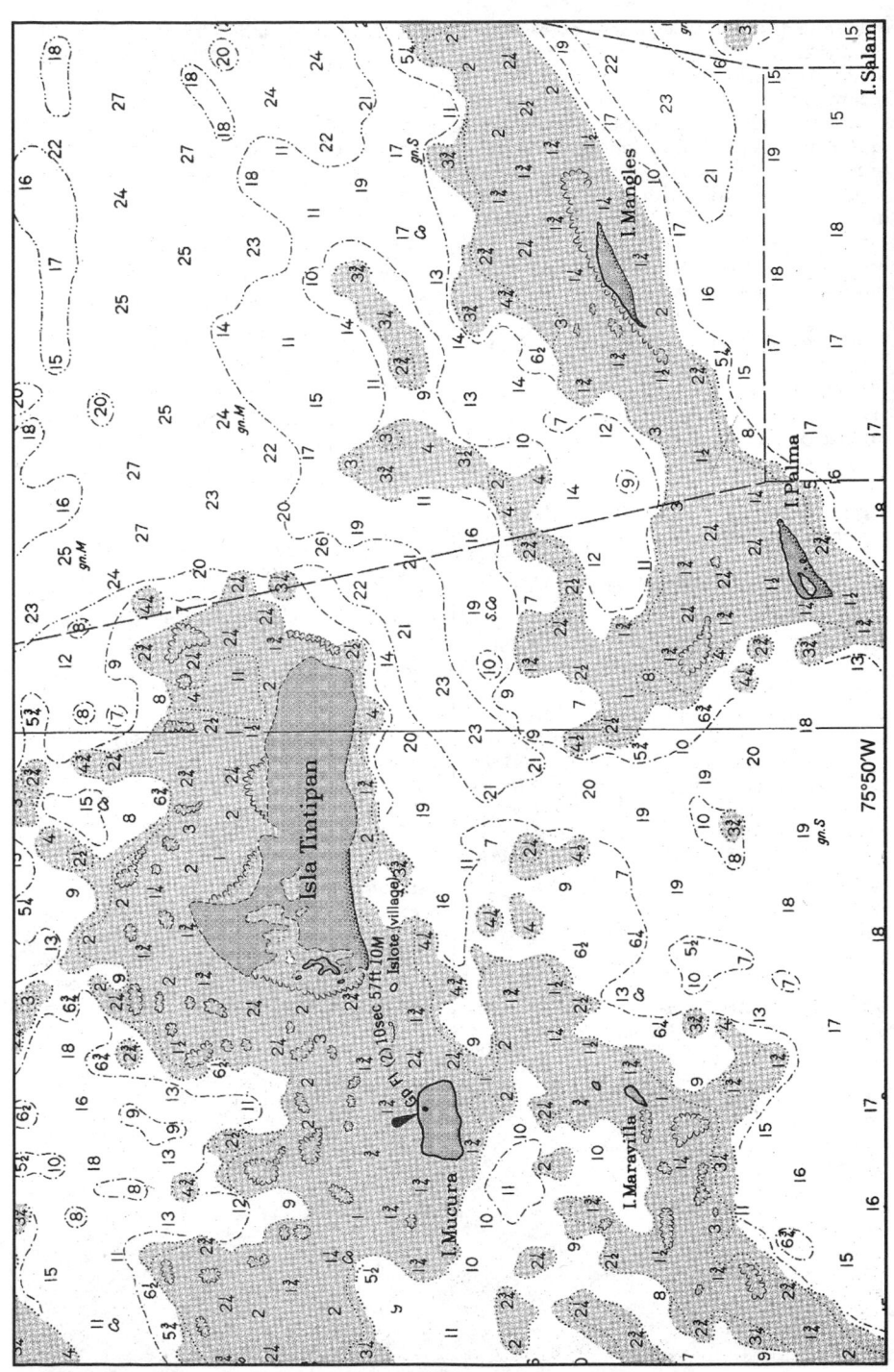

Islas San Bernardo, soundings in fathoms *(from DMA 24511, 2nd ed, 4/76)*

The Golfo de Urubá experiences a northward-flowing current of up to 2 knots at times. This area experiences a severe local storm in the months from June to October. It is called Choco-sanas and occurs most frequently between 2200 and 2400. It is preceded by light north winds and general lightning around the horizon. The wind gradually shifts from the north to the south and increases to near hurricane force in some instances. The storm lasts about 1/2 hour and is accompanied by heavy rain and lightning. As much as 4 inches of rain may fall in one storm.

PUNTA ARENAS, 8 32.5N, 76 56.1W. Fl W 9s, 44ft, 11M. White metal tower.
PUNTA CAIMAN, 8 16.5N, 76 46.4W. Fl W 7.5s, 59ft, 12M. White tower, black bands.
PUNTA DE LAS VACAS, 8 04.2N, 76 44.6W. Fl W 6s, 59ft, 12M. White metal framework tower.
TURBO AIRFIELD TOWER, 8 04.5N, 76 44.1W. F R, 40M. Tower. Obstruction light. Radiobeacon.

TURBO

8 06N, 76 43W
Pilotage: The harbor is located about 30 miles south of Punta Arenas del Norte. This coast is reported to be gradually creeping to the west. Vessels should keep a good offing to avoid shoal areas. There is a light shown from Punta Las Vacas at the entrance to Bahía Turbo. The bay is quite shallow. Check with the port officials for the latest depths in the channel. Officials board commercial vessels west of Punta Las Vacas, so you could anchor in this area to wait for clearance.
Port of Entry
Services: Basic supplies and fuel are reported to be available.

BOCAS RÍO LEON, 7 55.9N, 76 45.0W. Fl W 8s, 59ft, 12M. White metal framework tower.

PUNTA YARUMAL, 8 07.0N, 76 45.1W. Fl W 5s, 65ft, 15M. White metal tower, black bands.
MATUTUNGO, 8 07.6N, 76 50.6W. Fl W 10s, 52ft, 12M. White tower.
ISLA DE LOS MUERTOS, E end, 8 07.9N, 76 49.3W. Fl R 6s, 72ft, 6M. White metal framework tower.

ISLA NAPU

8 25N, 77 07W
Pilotage: This is a steep rocky island lying about 2 3/4 miles east-southeast of Punta de La Goleta. It is covered with brush and small trees.

ACANDI

8 31N, 77 16W
Pilotage: This town lies at the mouth of the Río Acandi about 11 miles southeast of Cabo Tiburón. An excellent landmark between Cabo Tiburón and Acandi is Terron de Azucar, a precipitous dark rock lying about 1 1/4 miles offshore midway between the two positions. A rocky ridge, upon which the sea breaks, connects the rock with the coast. South of Acandi is a sandy beach broken by hills 2 miles southeast of town.

CABO TIBURON, 8 40.5N, 77 21.6W. Fl (2) W 15s, 275ft, 15M. White square concrete tower.

CABO TIBURÓN

8 41N, 77 22W
Pilotage: This bold promontory marks the west entrance point of Golfo de Uraba and the border between Colombia and Panama. It rises to a height of about 405 feet, and there are two concrete beacons on its northwest extremity marking the border. The seaward beacon stands on a pinnacle rock.

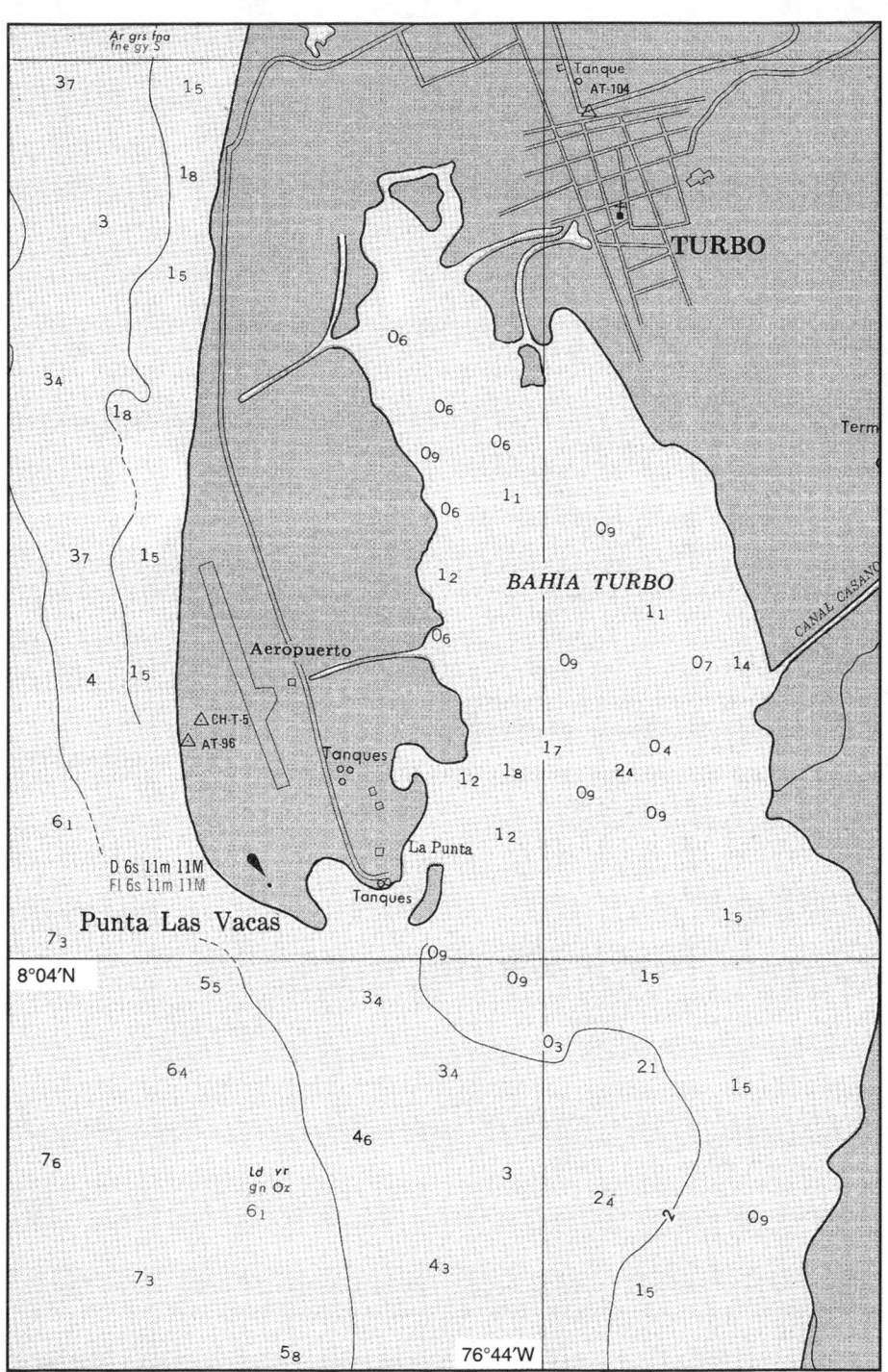

Turbo, soundings in meters *(from DMA 24517, 1st ed, 6/84)*

PANAMA

CAUTION: Our information on aids to navigation comes from official government sources. The latitudes and longitudes of these marks may not correspond to the readings from GPS receivers. Some aids have been reported as unreliable, missing, off position, or showing incorrect characteristics. No single aid to navigation, or waypoint, should be relied upon as a sole means of fixing your position.

NOTE: The chartlets in this section are not intended for navigation and are included for reference and planning purposes only. While chartlets reproduced from government sources are from the most current editions as of press time, they incorporate no corrections to navigational aids, depths, or hazards since the edition publication date.

ENTRY PROCEDURES

The Panama Canal in Panama is a natural crossroads for many Caribbean cruisers. Some are headed across the Pacific or around the world. Others will attempt the hard slog north up the west coast of North America. Some are headed to Hawaii, and others are just arriving in the Caribbean from the Pacific side. The Canal is about 1,072 miles from Charlotte Amalie, 1,202 from Martinique, 1,202 from Trinidad, 661 from Aruba, 324 from Cartagena, and 594 from Jamaica. See *Reed's Nautical Companion* for distance tables and an illustration of the country flag.

The Port of Entry in the San Blas Islands is Porvenir. On the Panamanian mainland clear at either end of the Canal: Colón on the Caribbean side and Balboa on the Pacific. The town of Colón is located in Puerto Cristóbal on a peninsula of land jutting northward into the eastern part of Bahía Limón.

Most nationals will need visas, which should be applied for in advance of arrival. U.S. citizens need at least proof of birth in the U.S. and a tourist card. There are reports visas can be purchased in Colón if you do not have one on

arrival. A fee may be charged, depending on your nationality and where you obtain the visa. Visas are granted for varying lengths of time, from 30 days to one year, depending on the expiration date of your passport and the consulate where you obtain the visa. Extensions are possible. For more information and visa applications contact the Panama Consulate at 2862 McDill Terrace NW, Washington, DC 20008 (202-483-1407). Panama also maintains consulates in New York, Miami, Tampa, Atlanta, Houston, San Francisco, and in Puerto Rico.

In Colón the immigration office is next to the Panama Canal Yacht Club and should be your first stop in the clearance procedure. You will also pay a fee for quarantine inspection. You will be given a map showing you where to proceed for customs and the Port Authority. You must purchase a cruising permit from the Port Authority. You need this permit to visit the San Blas Islands. Firearms will be held until your departure.

The international country code for Panama is 507. Local numbers use six digits. The currency used is the U.S. dollar.

Cholera is present in the country. To obtain the latest health information contact the U.S. Centers for Disease Control (404-332-4559) in Atlanta, Georgia.

The U.S. Southern Command Network broadcasts current travel advisories for Panama on both television and radio. The U.S. embassy is in Panama City; for assistance, contact the consular section (507-27-1777) or the U.S. consulate in Cristóbal (507-41-2440 or -2478). Office hours are 0900 to 1200 and 1300 to 1500.

Spanish is the main language of Panama, but English is widely spoken. Canal operations are conducted in English.

WARNING: The U.S. State Department warns of high rates of crime in Panama. The streets of Colón and Panama City are not considered safe after dark, and many visitors prefer to take taxis even during

---

the day. Cruisers report many crimes in these areas. Police presence in the Darien peninsula area, which is reported to be frequented by Colombian criminals, is scarce and is not considered safe. For the latest advisory contact the U.S. Department of State Citizens Emergency Center (202-647-5225).

THE PANAMA CANAL

After you have cleared into the country you can proceed to the Panama Canal Commission Admeasurers Office (507-43-7293). You make an appointment to have your boat measured, which is usually a quick process. These measurements determine the fee you will pay to transit the canal.

Next, you proceed to Canal Operations Captain's Office (507-52-4211 or -4215). You will be informed of the equipment requirements for passage, given a schedule of passage, and notified of other safety information. Yachts are currently being allowed to transit every day, but there is a limit of four pleasure boats per day. You will usually be able to make your transit within two days of making your application.

You should have four lines (the Operations Office recommends 7/8" nylon) over 100 feet long and four line handlers. The captain of the boat is not counted as a line handler. Line handlers are often crews from other boats who wish to get a preview of the trip. Paid line handlers are available for about $50 per day. They must also be housed, fed, and returned (via public transport) to Colón.

On the day before (preferably 24 hours prior to) your transit you must contact the Marine Traffic Control Office (507-52-4202 or the Cristóbal Signal Station on VHF channels 12 and 16). This office will confirm your transit and schedule the arrival of your pilot. You should be ready to go on time, as there are stiff fines for delays or cancellation.

There are basically three ways to negotiate the locks: sidewall tie-up, center tie-up, or rafted to a tug. Yachts report a preference for one of the first two options, as there seems to be less chance of damage. However, some people report being alongside a tug as the easiest method, as you don't constantly need to be handling your lines. Don't let the tug pull away from the lock wall with your boat tied alongside! Sometimes a group of yachts will be rafted together in the center of the lock. You will be given a choice of these methods at the Operations Office, but be prepared to change to one of the other methods along the way.

You are required to maintain a speed of at least 5 knots. Slower boats will probably have to anchor overnight in Gatún Lake at Gamboa. If you are planning on stopping at the Pedro Miguel Yacht Club (507-32-4509 or fax, 507-52-8105), you must make arrangements in advance and be able to show written confirmation of your reservations to your pilot. The club is located in Miraflores Lake near the Pedro Miguel Locks. Call the Canal Operations office when you are ready to resume your passage through the Canal.

There are three up-locks on the Caribbean side, and three down-locks on the Pacific side. They lift you 85 feet from sea level to Gatún Lake, then lower you into the Pacific Ocean on the other side. The lock chambers measure 1,000 feet long by 110 feet wide. The entire trip is about 50 miles in length.

The system of lighting and buoyage in the Canal utilizes range lights, generally green, in the longest reaches and light buoys and beacons along the sides. In general, there are red lights on one side and white lights on the other. The IALA (Region B) Maritime Buoyage System is used. The direction of buoyage changes at Puedro Miguel Locks (9° 01', 79° 37'W).

The Panama Canal Commission rigidly controls all radio communications in this area. All radio communications between vessels in the Panama Canal operating area or calls to stations outside the area must be forwarded through the Canal Radio Station (call sign HPN) located in Balboa. Except for emergency traffic and routine bridge-to-bridge VHF communications, no vessel in transit through the canal shall communicate with any other station.

The Canal is currently controlled jointly by the United States and Panama, but will become the sole responsibility of Panama on January 1, 2000.

NORTHEAST COAST

PUERTO OBALDIA, 8 40.0N, 77 25.0W. L Fl W 10s, 39ft, 8M. White framework tower.

PUERTO OBALDIA

8 40N, 77 26W

Pilotage: This is a small cove located about 4 miles west of Cabo Tiburon and the Colombian border. There is a small village in the cove. The coast between here and the cape is steep-to and rocky, with heavily wooded hills rising inland. A prominent rock lies about 1 mile north of the east entrance point to the cove.

PUERTO PERME

8 45N, 77 32W

Pilotage: This is a narrow cove about 8 miles northwest of Puerto Obaldia. A village is located about 1 mile south-southwest of Puerto Perme. The port is abandoned but anchorage can be taken.

PUERTO CARRETO

Pilotage: This small cove is just west of Punta Carreto. Two steep-to rocky patches lie about 2 1/2 miles north of Punta Carreto, and seas break here in fresh breezes. The cove has depths of 18 to 54 feet. There is a small village near the mouth of a river on the west side of the cove.

Between Punta Carreto and Punta Brava located 39 1/2 miles to the northwest the coast is fronted by many dangers extending up to 5 miles offshore. A prominent headland in this area is Punta Escoces, rising to a height of 580 feet, about 5 1/2 miles northwest of Puerto Carreto.

There are several roadstead anchorages along this coast. Isla de Pinos is prominent at 400 feet high. It stands about 1/4 mile offshore, about 2 1/2 miles northwest of Punta Sasardi. Isla Pajaros, a low islet surrounded by reefs, lies about 2 1/2 miles farther northwest. This island has been reported as a good landmark, as it is covered with tall palm trees.

PUNTA BRAVA

9 15N, 78 03W

Pilotage: Between here and Punta Mandinga, 56 1/2 miles to the west-northwest, the coast is fronted by the Archipiélago De Las Mulatas. This is a group of small cays, reefs, and banks lying within 10 miles of the coast. There are a number of navigable channels in the group. Many vessels with local knowledge navigate this area.

RÍO DIABLO

9 26N, 78 29W

Pilotage: This village stands on two small islands near shore. They are located about 34 miles west-northwest of Punta Brava. Depths in this area are reported to be less than charted.

GOLFO DE SAN BLAS

9 30N, 79 00W

Pilotage: This area lies between Punta San Blas and Punta Mandinga. It can be entered from the north via Canal De San Blas, located about 2 1/2 miles east of Punta San Blas. There are numerous detached dangers in the south and west parts of the gulf. Numerous creeks and rivers discharge into the gulf, but their entrances are obstructed by bars. The north shore of the gulf is swampy and fringed with mangroves. The south shore is low, but east of Punta Mandinga the high land approaches the coast. This area has been reported to be poorly charted.

PUNTA SAN BLAS

9 34N, 78 58W

Pilotage: This point has a low extremity, but a 150-foot-high hill stands about 1/2 mile to the northwest. A 200-foot-high hill, the highest of a group of four, stands about 1 1/2 miles west-southwest of the end of the point. A conspicuous tower stands about 3/4 mile southwest of the end.

Between Punta San Blas and Punta Macolla, 28 miles to the west, the coast is low and wooded.

PORVENIR

9 33.5N, 78 57W

Pilotage: Isla Porvenir lies about 1 mile east of Punta San Blas and 1/4 mile north-northwest of Sail Rock. A government compound with two conspicuous buff-colored buildings and several lesser structures stands on the west side of the islet. All vessels in the Golfo De San Blas must clear in and out of this station.

CAUTION: The charts in this area are reported to be inaccurate. Passages should be made in good light.

Port of Entry: You should check in at this station, whether or not you have obtained a cruising permit in Colón. This is the administrative center for the San Blas area.

COAST PILOT

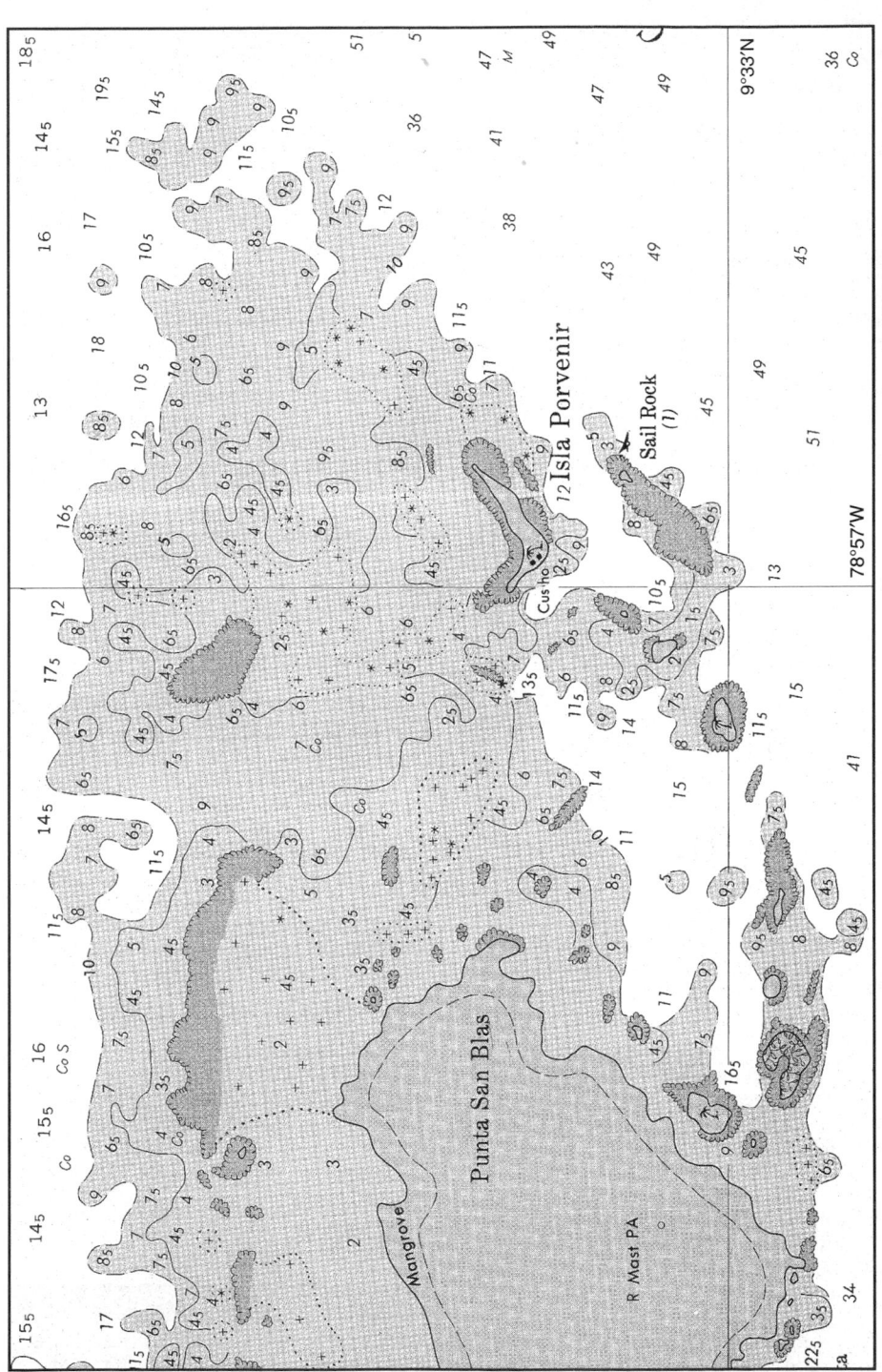

Porvenir, soundings in meters *(from DMA26065, 3rd ed, 6/84)*

PUNTA MACOLLA

9 36N, 79 26W
Pilotage: This point is bold, high, and easily identified. Near the point the mountains, two of which have conspicuous high peaks, begin to approach the coast. From the west it appears as a dark bluff.

PUNTA PESCADOR

9 36N, 79 28W
Pilotage: This point is located a bit west of Punta Macolla. It is fringed by reefs.

PUNTA MANZANILLA

9 38N, 79 33W
Pilotage: This is the northernmost point in Panama. It is a high, precipitous projection, with two conical hillocks resembling a saddle. This is the termination of a mountain ridge that extends along the coast to the mouth of the Río Piedras.

Several offlying rocks and islets are northeast and northwest of the point, including Islas Los Magotes and Isla Tambor, which is connected to Isla Grande by reefs.

ISLA GRANDE

9 38N, 79 34W
Pilotage: This high, palm-tree-covered island lies about 1 mile west of Punta Manzanilla and is reported to give a good radar return up to a distance of 20 miles. There is a light on the northeast part of the island. A confused sea and tide rips are found in the vicinity.

Isla Tambor is connected to the island by reefs. The coast of the island is foul ground except for the northeast part, but a deep channel runs between the island and Punta Manzanilla.

PUERTO GAROTE

9 36N, 79 35W
Pilotage: This small harbor is entered about 1/2 mile west of Isla Grande. It is formed by the coast and several offlying islands. The narrow entrance has depths of 36 to 72 feet, while the inlet leading into the harbor has a depth of 34 feet. The center of the harbor is about 20 feet deep. There is a small pier and room for vessels to anchor.

ISLA GRANDE, off Punta Manzanillo, 9 38.0N, 79 34.0W. Fl W 5s, 305ft, 12M. White metal tower, stone base.

FARALLON SUCIO ROCK, summit, 9 39.0N, 79 38.0W. Fl R, 5s, 107ft, 12M. White concrete pyramidal tower. Reported at reduced intensity (1984).

LOS FARALLONES

9 39N, 79 38W
Pilotage: This group of rocks lies about 2 miles offshore to the north-northwest of Punta Cacique. They are about 4 miles west of Isla Tambor. There is a light on the westernmost rock.

PORTOBELO

9 33N, 79 40W
Pilotage: This good harbor of refuge lies about 18 miles northeast of the entrance to Puerto Cristóbal and 11 miles southwest of Isla Grande. Bajo Salmedina, a coral reef upon which the sea breaks, is located about 3/4 mile west of Punta Mantilla. Depths in the harbor may be less than charted due to silting. A church with a large red roof and small white tower is conspicuous. This is reported to be a good anchorage, with some supplies available in town. Without local knowledge, vessels should stay at least 3 miles offshore from here to the entrance to Puerto Cristóbal.

BAHÍA LAS MINAS

RANGE (Front), 9 23.9N, 79 49.5W. F G. Orange diamond daymark on beacon. **(Rear),** 80 meters 170° from front. F G. Orange diamond daymark on beacon.
RANGE (Front), 9 23.4N, 79 48.8W. F G. Orange diamond daymark on beacon. **(Rear),** 160 meters, 148°45′ from front. F G. Orange diamond daymark on beacon.
NW PIER, N end, 9 23.8N, 79 49.1W. F R.
TANKER JETTY, N end. 9 23.6N, 79 49.1W. F R.

PUERTO DE BAHÍA DE LAS MINAS

9 24N, 79 49W
Pilotage: This commercial port is entered via a well-marked channel located about 6 miles northeast of the entrance to Puerto Cristóbal. There is a large refinery located in the bay. Without local knowledge, vessels should stay at least 3 miles offshore from here to the entrance to Puerto Cristóbal.

COLÓN — CRISTÓBAL

TORO POINT, W. side of entrance to Limón Bay, 9 22.4N, 79 57.1W. L Fl W, 30s, 108ft, 16M. White metal tower, stone base.

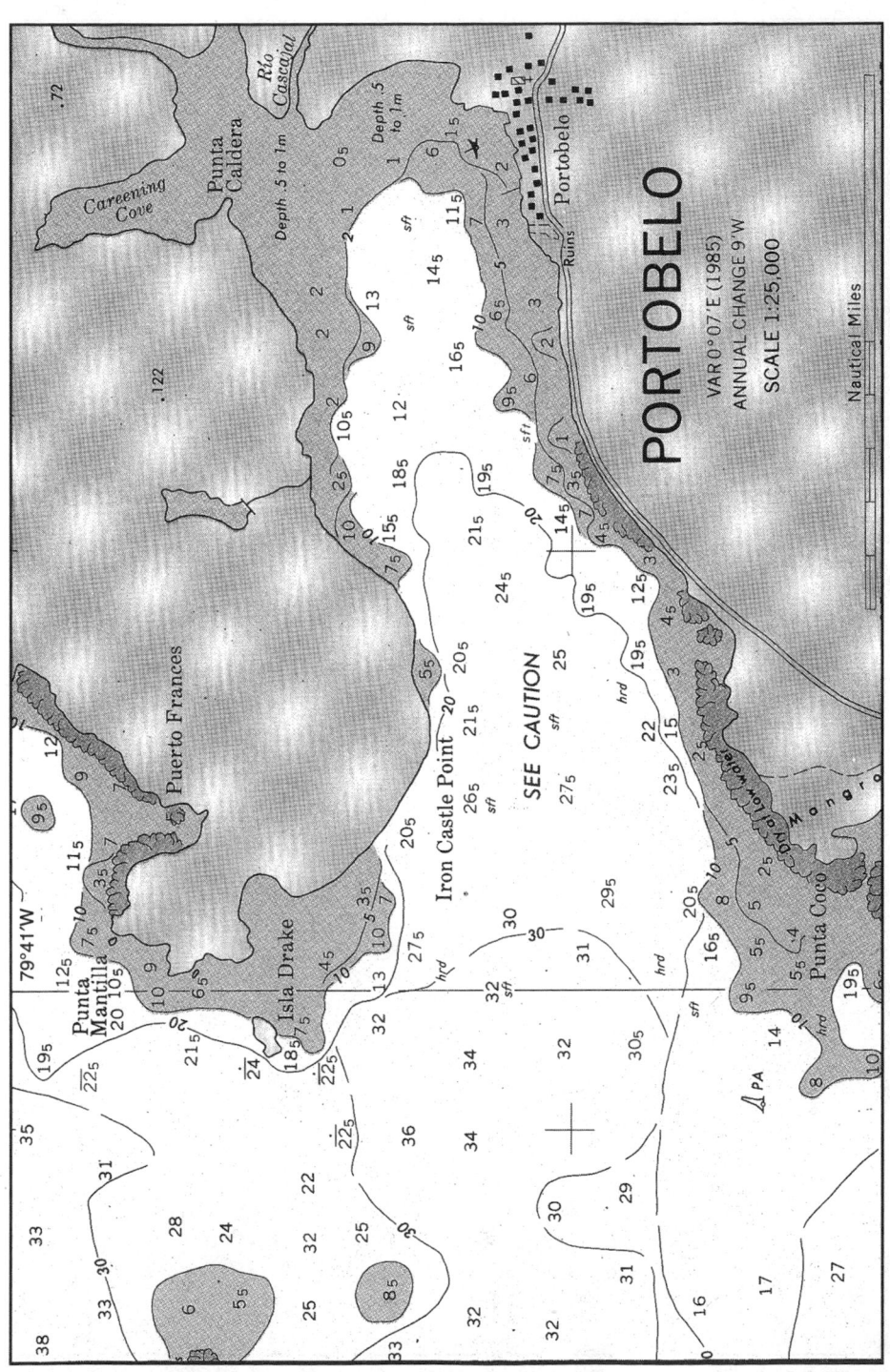

Portobelo, soundings in meters *(from DMA 26066, 11th ed, 7/90)*

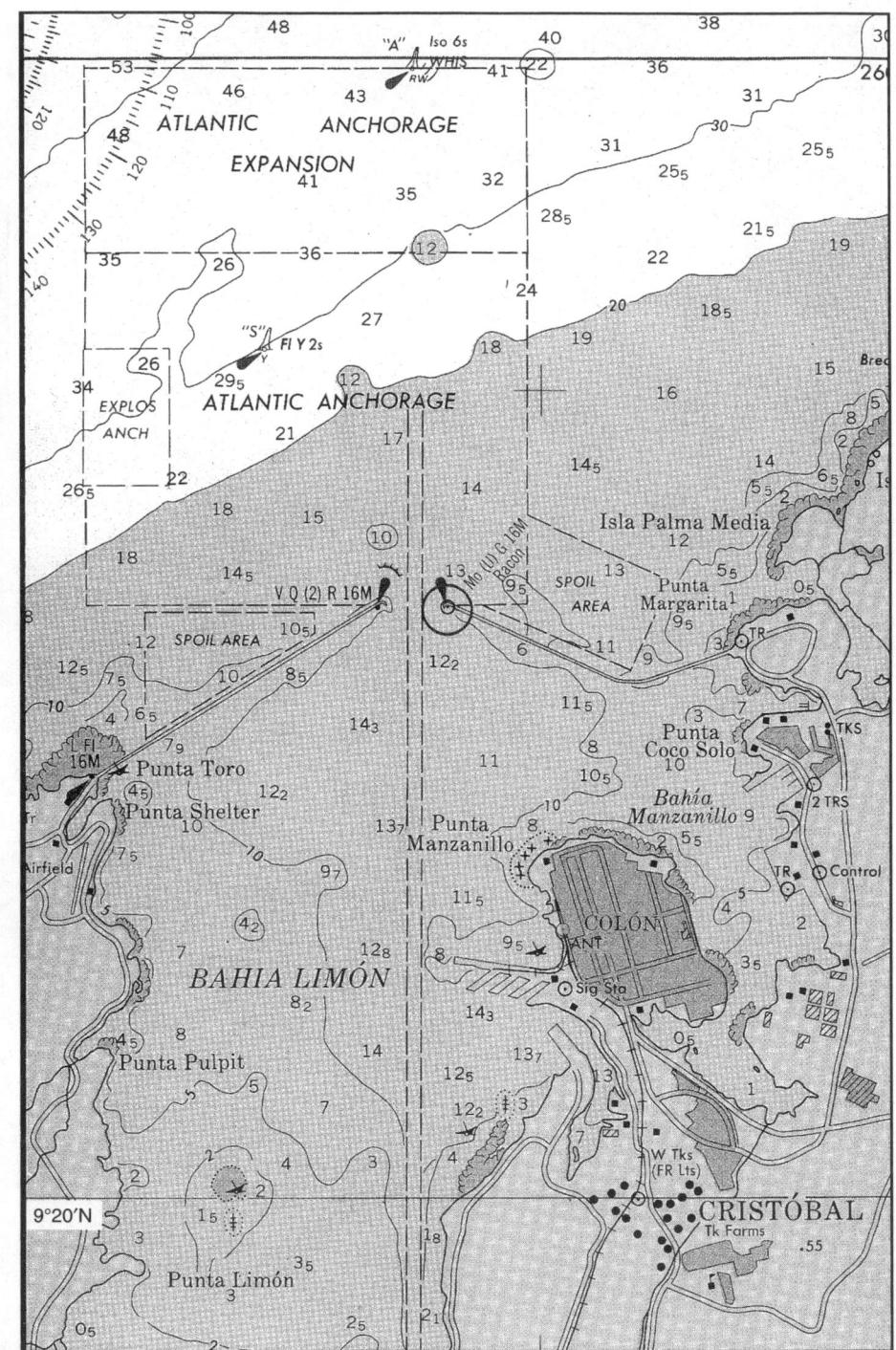

Approaches to Cristóbal, soundings in meters *(from DMA 26066, 11th ed, 7/90)*

COAST PILOT

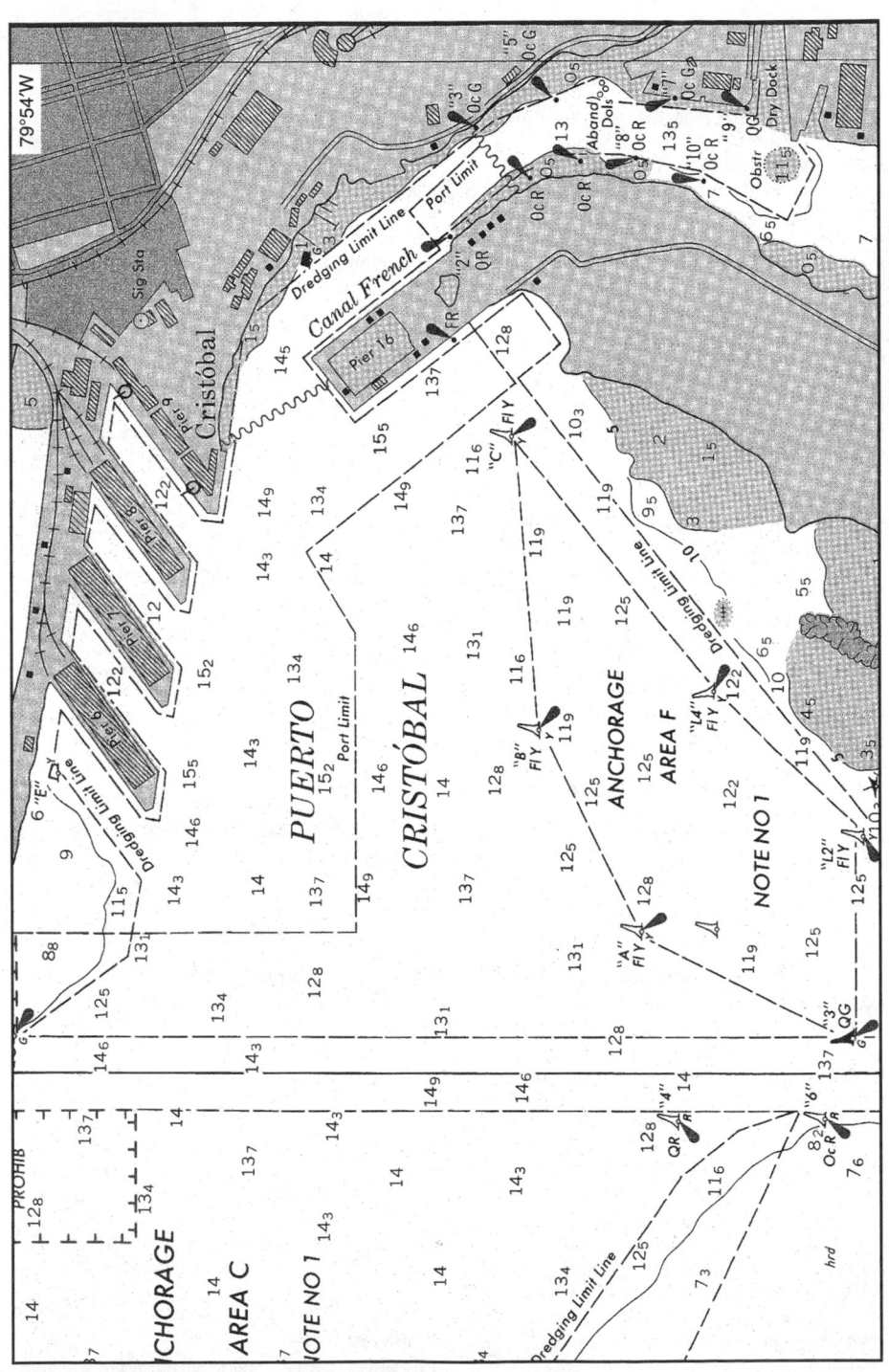

Cristóbal, soundings in meters *(from DMA 26068, 8th ed, 2/90)*

Cristóbal Approach, Lighted Whistle Buoy A, 9 26.3N, 79 55.1W. Iso W 6s. Red and white stripes. Reported missing (1989).
W BREAKWATER, head, 9 23.4N, 79 55.5W. V Q (2) R 2s, 100ft, 16M. Red square on metal tower. Radar reflector.
E BREAKWATER, head, 9 23.3N, 79 54.9W. Mo (U) G 20s, 100ft, 16M. Green triangle on green metal tower. F R on chimney 5.9M E; F R on signal station 1.7M E; Q R and 3 F R (vert) on mast 1.9M SSE; 4 F R on each of 2 water tanks, 3.5M SSE; F R 2.1M SSE. Racon **C** (− · − ·)
EXPLOSIVE ANCHORAGE, near W limit, 9 22.4N, 79 56.7W. Fl Y 2s, 15ft. Special Yellow.
CRISTÓBAL HARBOR, BEACON NO 2, 9 20.9,N, 79 54.4W. Q R. Red starboard-hand mark.
BEACON NO 3, 9 20.8N, 79 54.4W. Oc G 5s. Green port-hand mark.
BEACON NO 4, 9 20.8N, 79 54.3W. Oc R 5s. Red starboard-hand mark.
BEACON NO 5, 9 20.8N, 79 54.2W. Oc G 5s. Green port-hand mark.
BEACON NO 6, 9 20.8N, 79 54.3W. Oc R 5s. Red starboard-hand mark.
BEACON NO 8, 9 20.7N, 79 54.3W. Oc R 5s. Red starboard-hand mark.
BEACON NO 7, 9 20.6N, 79 54.2W. Oc G 5s. Green port-hand mark.
BEACON NO 9, Q G. Green port-hand mark.
BEACON NO 10, 9 20.6N, 79 54.3W. Oc R 5s. Red starboard-hand mark.
BEACON E OF TORO POINT LIGHT, 9 22.3N, 79 56.3W. Fl Y 2s, 15ft. Yellow beacon.
PANAMA CANAL, ATLANTIC ENTRANCE RANGE (Front), 9 17.7N, 79 55.4W. F G. Red lights shown on W side and green lights shown on E side of dredged channel and in Limón Bay. The canal is marked by lights, and leading lights mark the center of the channel.
PANAMA CANAL, ENTRANCE RANGE (Middle), 1037 meters, 180° 15' from front. F G, 98ft, 15M. Concrete conical tower. Visible on range line only. **(Rear),** 2278 meters, 180° 15' from front. Oc G, 158ft, 15M. Concrete conical tower. Visible on range line only. F R lights shown on each of 2 radio towers 1.1 miles NE.

PUERTO CRISTÓBAL

9 21N, 79 55W
Pilotage: This is the entrance to the Panama Canal. Entrance to the harbor is made between two breakwaters about 1/4 mile apart. There are lights at the end of both breakwaters and an offshore approach buoy. All vessels must contact the Cristóbal Signal Station (VHF channels 12 or 16) before entering the harbor. The station is located on the western end of the Muelle Cristóbal, which extends westward into the harbor from Colón. Vessels should maintain a continuous watch on channel 12 while in the harbor.
Dockage: The Panama Canal Yacht Club is located on the east side of Canal French, northeast of Anchorage Area F. This is where you can begin your trek to the various port offices. Check with the club for their advice on street crime before heading out. If planning a stop at the Pedro Miguel Boat Club (507-32-4509 or fax, 507-52-8105), you must obtain written permission in advance, or your Canal pilot will not let you stop. They reserve a certain number of slips for transients. Club Nautico is located on the eastern shore of Colón.
Anchorage: Yachts should anchor in Anchorage Area F, located south of the Muelle Cristóbal. This area is marked by flashing yellow buoys and is known as "The Flats."
Services: Fuel, water, showers, laundry, haul-out facilities, and a bar and restaurant can all be found at the yacht club. This is also the place to get advice on transiting the canal or locating something you might need. The Pedro Miguel Boat Club is set up for those who want "do-it-yourself" type repairs, including haulouts. This is reported to be a good place to store your boat while traveling ashore.
The Panama Canal: See the information at the beginning of the Panama section.

LAGUNA DE CHIRIQUÍ

ESCUDO DE VERAGUAS, 9 05.3N, 81 32.2W. Fl W 7s, 120ft, 6M. White square framework tower.
CHIRIQUÍ RANGE (Front), 8 56.5N, 82 06.8W. Q W. White cylindrical tower with black stripe. F R obstruction lights on tower 1.4M W; F Y on oil tanks 1.5 miles W. Visible 202°–222°.
(Rear), 60m, 212° from front. Fl W 4s. White cylindrical tower with black stripe. Visible 202°–222°.

LAGUNA DE BLUEFIELD

9 09N, 81 54W
Pilotage: Located south of Punta Valiente, in the entrance to Laguna Chiriquí, this is a possible anchorage. The ground is foul west of Punta Valiente, and along the shores in the Laguna. The bottom is reported to be mud.

LAGUNA DE CHIRIQUÍ

8 56N, 82 07W
Pilotage: There are many anchoring possibilities in the Laguna De Chiriquí. The entrance, through

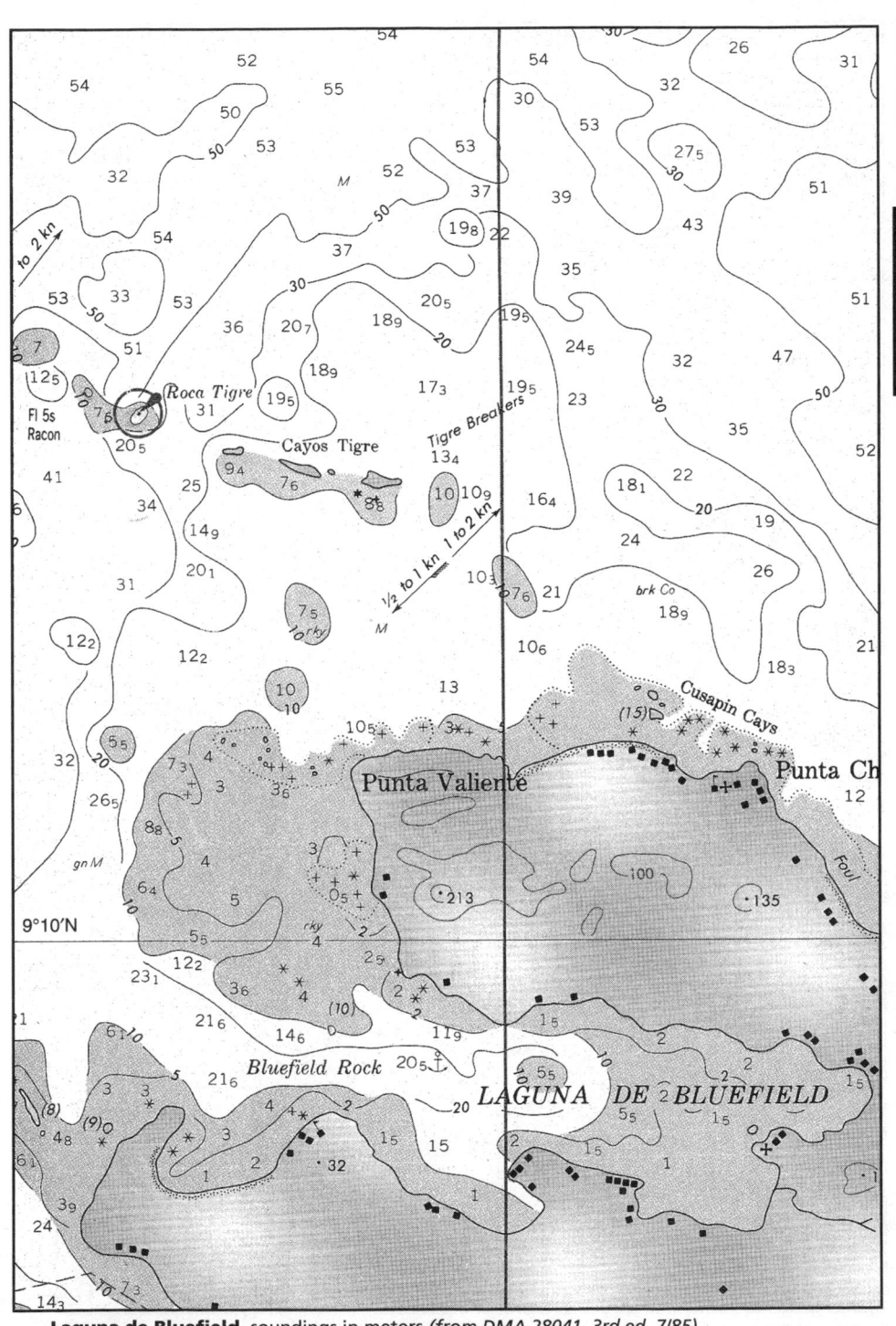

Laguna de Bluefield, soundings in meters *(from DMA 28041, 3rd ed, 7/85)*

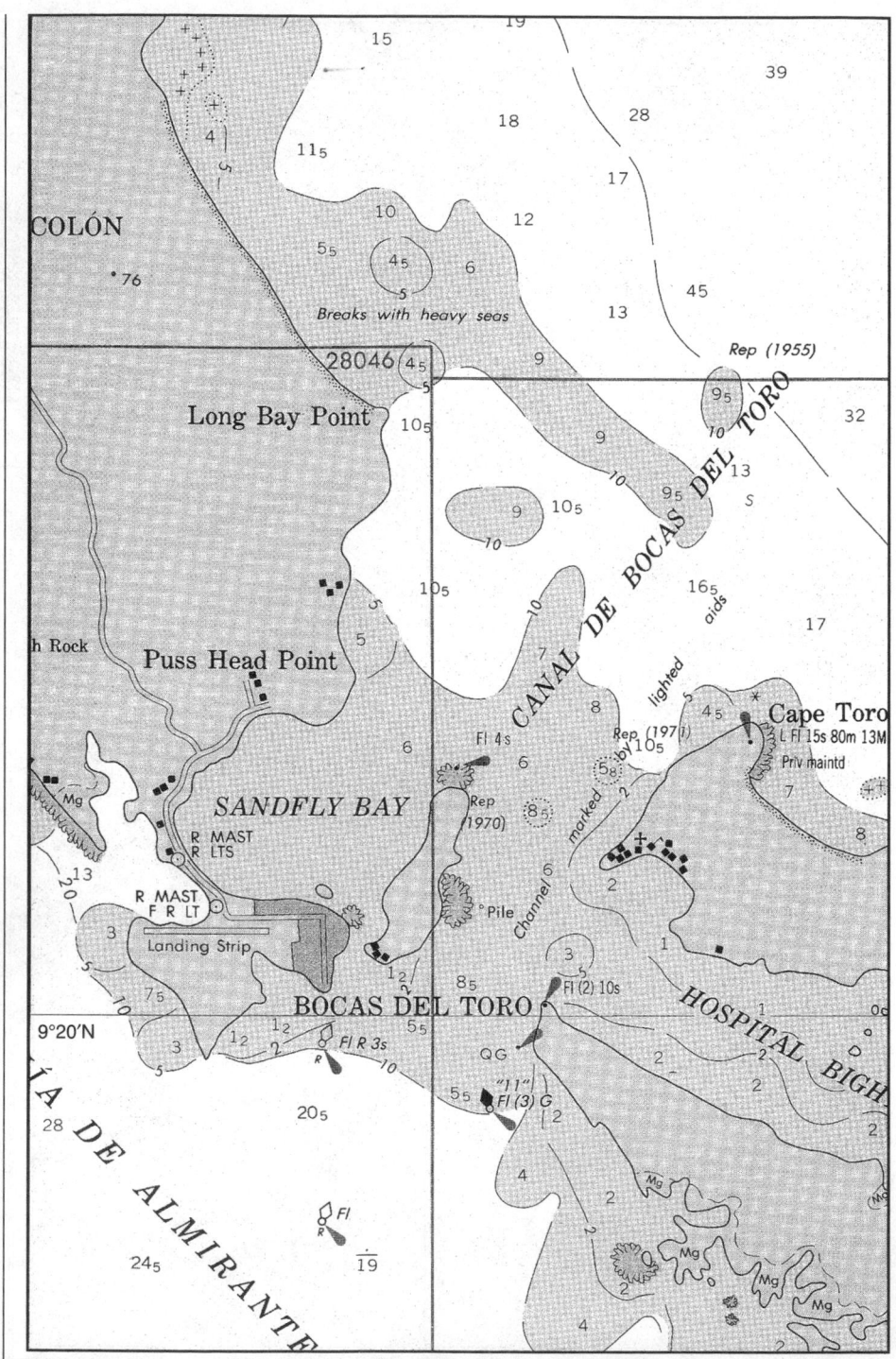

Bocas Del Toro, soundings in meters *(from DMA 28041, 3rd ed, 7/85)*

Canal Del Tigre, is well marked because of the oil terminal at Chiriquí Grande. Currents in the inlet are generally weaker than 1 knot. The Chiriquí Grande pilots stand by on VHF channel 14, and the terminal can be contacted by calling "Rambala Control" on VHF channel 16. The terminal is located on the south side of the bay. There are several lit moorings and a range of 212° for the terminal.

PUNTA VALIENTE

9 11N, 81 55W

Pilotage: This is the eastern point at the entrance to Laguna De Chiriquí. It is about 120 miles west of the entrance to the Canal. There is foul ground west of the point, extending south to the entrance to Laguna De Bluefield. Valiente Peak, a conspicuous 758-foot-high peak, stands about 1 mile south of Punta Valiente.

ROCA TIGRE, 9 13.0N, 81 56.5W. Fl W 5s, 50ft. Metal tower. Racon **P** (· — — ·).

BAHÍA DE ALMIRANTE

HOSPITAL POINT, 9 19.9N, 82 13.2W. Fl (2) W 10s, 36ft, 13M. Metal pedestal, F R lights on radio masts 1.2M, 1.9M, and 2.2M WNW.
BEACON 8, 9 20.4N, 82 13.6W. Q R. 15ft.

BEACON 9, 9 19.9N, 82 13.5W. Q G.
BOCAS DEL TORO, pier NE corner, 9 20.0N, 82 14.4W. Fl G, 27ft. White pedestal.
PIER, SW corner. Fl R.

BOCAS DEL TORO

9 21N, 82 14W

Pilotage: The harbor is entered via Canal De Bocas Del Toro, which begins west of Cabo Toro (9° 22'N, 82° 12'W). There is a breaking reef around the shores of Cabo Toro, and Toro lies awash about 350 yards northeast of the cape. Heavy seas break on the shoals extending up to a mile off Long Bay Point to the north. The channel to town is marked with lighted aids to navigation. The pilot boat can be called on VHF channel 12.

Anchorage: Anchor off town as depths permit. Some general supplies may be available. This is the last good anchorage before reaching the border of Costa Rica.

JUAN POINT, 9 18.2N, 82 17.8W. Fl G 4s, 15ft, 5M. Green tower.
PONDSOCK REEF, 9 17.3N, 82 19.8W. Fl W 6s, 15ft, 5M. Black tower, red bands.
ALMIRANTE, pier, 9 17.3N, 82 23.5W. Fl R. Post. Occasional.
ISLA PASTORES, NW end, 9 14.7N, 82 21.2W Fl W 10s, 60ft, 9M. Metal windmill tower.

CRISTÓBAL-COLÓN, PANAMA

HIGH & LOW WATER 1995

9°21'N 79°55'W

EASTERN STANDARD TIME (GMT -5H)

JANUARY

Day	Time ft	Time ft	Time ft	Time ft	Day	Time ft	Time ft	Time ft	Time ft
1 Su ●	0041 0.2	0405 0.1	1159 1.4	2001 -0.3	16 M ○	1150 1.1	2046 -0.1		
2 M	0205 0.3	0517 0.2	1254 1.3	2050 -0.3	17 Tu	1230 1.0	2113 -0.1		
3 Tu	0317 0.4	0645 0.3	1351 1.2	2134 -0.3	18 W	1314 0.9	2134 -0.1		
4 W	0415 0.5	0821 0.3	1448 1.1	2215 -0.3	19 Th	0505 0.4	0637 0.4	1401 0.8	2152 -0.1
5 Th	0504 0.7	0953 0.3	1545 0.9	2253 -0.3	20 F	0452 0.5	0857 0.4	1452 0.7	2211 -0.1
6 F	0548 0.8	1118 0.3	1641 0.8	2328 -0.2	21 Sa	0509 0.7	1033 0.5	1546 0.6	2232 -0.1
7 Sa	0628 0.9	1234 0.2	1735 0.6	2359 -0.2	22 Su	0536 0.8	1150 0.2	1643 0.5	2258 -0.2
8 Su (	0706 1.0	1342 0.2	1828 0.5		23 M	0610 1.0	1256 0.1	1740 0.4	2329 -0.2)
9 M	0026 -0.1	0743 1.1	1445 0.1	1920 0.4	24 Tu	0649 1.1	1356 -0.0	1837 0.3	
10 Tu	0051 -0.1	0818 1.1	1545 0.1	2012 0.3	25 W	0004 -0.2	0731 1.3	1453 -0.1	1936 0.3
11 W	0111 -0.0	0852 1.1	1643 0.0	2107 0.2	26 Th	0044 -0.2	0816 1.3	1549 -0.2	2037 0.2
12 Th	0127 0.0	0926 1.1	1740 -0.0	2210 0.1	27 F	0127 -0.2	0904 1.4	1645 -0.2	2142 0.2
13 F	0136 0.1	1000 1.1	1836 -0.1	2336 0.1	28 Sa	0215 -0.1	0954 1.4	1740 -0.2	2253 0.2
14 Sa	0130 0.1	1035 1.1	1927 -0.1		29 Su	0309 -0.1	1046 1.3	1834 -0.3	
15 Su	1112 1.1	2011 -0.1			30 M ●	0009 0.2	0412 0.0	1141 1.2	1925 -0.2
					31 Tu	0125 0.3	0529 0.1	1238 1.1	2014 -0.2

FEBRUARY

Day	Time ft	Time ft	Time ft	Time ft	Day	Time ft	Time ft	Time ft	Time ft
1 W	0234 0.4	0701 0.2	1338 0.9	2058 -0.2	16 Th	0206 0.3	0608 0.2	1258 0.7	2019 -0.0
2 Th	0333 0.5	0836 0.2	1439 0.8	2139 -0.2	17 F	0247 0.5	0758 0.2	1359 0.6	2045 -0.0
3 F	0423 0.7	1004 0.2	1540 0.6	2216 -0.2	18 Sa	0326 0.6	0930 0.1	1502 0.5	2115 -0.1
4 Sa	0507 0.8	1119 0.1	1639 0.5	2250 -0.1	19 Su	0406 0.8	1045 0.0	1604 0.4	2148 -0.1
5 Su	0547 0.9	1224 0.1	1733 0.4	2321 -0.1	20 M	0448 0.9	1147 -0.1	1703 0.4	2225 -0.1
6 M	0624 0.9	1320 0.0	1823 0.4	2349 -0.1	21 Tu	0532 1.1	1243 -0.2	1758 0.3	2307 -0.1
7 Tu	0659 1.0	1410 -0.0	1909 0.3		22 W	0618 1.2	1335 -0.2	1852 0.3	2351 -0.2)
8 W	0015 -0.0	0734 1.0	1458 -0.0	1953 0.2	23 Th	0705 1.2	1425 -0.3	1945 0.3	
9 Th	0039 -0.0	0808 1.0	1546 -0.1	2035 0.2	24 F	0039 -0.2	0753 1.2	1516 -0.3	2038 0.3
10 F	0103 -0.0	0842 1.0	1633 -0.1	2120 0.1	25 Sa	0130 -0.1	0843 1.2	1606 -0.3	2135 0.3
11 Sa	0126 0.0	0918 1.0	1720 -0.1	2210 0.1	26 Su	0225 -0.1	0935 1.1	1656 -0.2	2235 0.3
12 Su	0151 0.0	0955 1.0	1806 -0.1	2309 0.1	27 M	0327 -0.0	1029 1.0	1746 -0.2	2339 0.4
13 M	0221 0.1	1034 1.0	1848 -0.1		28 Tu	0439 0.0	1127 0.8	1835 -0.1	
14 Tu	0016 0.2	0307 0.1	1117 0.9	1923 -0.1					
15 W ○	0118 0.2	0422 0.2	1204 0.8	1952 -0.1					

MARCH

Day	Time ft	Time ft	Time ft	Time ft	Day	Time ft	Time ft	Time ft	Time ft
1 W ●	0044 0.4	0603 0.1	1231 0.7	1923 -0.1	16 Th ○	0531 0.1	1144 0.5	1810 0.0	
2 Th	0146 0.5	0734 0.2	1339 0.6	2008 -0.0	17 F	0039 0.6	0703 0.1	1254 0.4	1847 0.0
3 F	0241 0.6	0900 0.1	1449 0.5	2050 0.0	18 Sa	0131 0.7	0828 -0.0	1410 0.4	1928 0.0
4 Sa	0330 0.7	1013 0.0	1556 0.4	2129 0.0	19 Su	0223 0.8	0938 -0.1	1522 0.3	2014 0.0
5 Su	0414 0.8	1113 -0.1	1654 0.4	2204 0.0	20 M	0315 1.0	1038 -0.2	1625 0.3	2104 0.0
6 M	0454 0.8	1203 -0.1	1743 0.3	2237 0.1	21 Tu	0406 1.1	1131 -0.3	1721 0.3	2157 -0.0
7 Tu	0531 0.9	1247 -0.1	1826 0.3	2308 0.1	22 W	0457 1.1	1220 -0.4	1812 0.3	2251 -0.0
8 W	0607 0.9	1327 -0.1	1903 0.3	2338 0.0	23 Th	0547 1.2	1307 -0.4	1901 0.4	2346 -0.1
9 Th (	0642 0.9	1405 -0.1	1938 0.3		24 F	0638 1.1	1353 -0.4	1949 0.4	
10 F	0009 0.0	0717 0.9	1443 -0.0	2013 0.3	25 Sa	0044 -0.1	0729 1.1	1438 -0.3	2038 0.4
11 Sa	0042 0.0	0753 0.9	1520 -0.1	2049 0.3	26 Su	0144 -0.0	0821 1.0	1522 -0.3	2128 0.5
12 Su	0119 0.0	0830 0.9	1556 -0.1	2127 0.3	27 M	0249 0.0	0915 0.8	1605 -0.2	2220 0.6
13 M	0202 0.1	0910 0.8	1631 -0.1	2209 0.3	28 Tu	0401 0.0	1013 0.7	1648 -0.1	2313 0.6
14 Tu	0256 0.1	0954 0.7	1704 -0.0	2256 0.4	29 W	0521 0.0	1120 0.5	1729 -0.0	
15 W	0406 0.1	1044 0.7	1737 0.0	2346 0.5	30 Th ●	0005 0.7	0646 0.0	1237 0.4	1811 0.1
					31 F	0057 0.7	0808 -0.1	1403 0.3	1852 0.1

APRIL

Day	Time ft	Time ft	Time ft	Time ft	Day	Time ft	Time ft	Time ft	Time ft
1 Sa	0146 0.8	0917 -0.1	1527 0.3	1933 0.2	16 Su	0045 1.0	0832 -0.2	1421 0.2	1812 0.1
2 Su	0232 0.8	1013 -0.2	1636 0.3	2014 0.2	17 M	0140 1.1	0930 -0.3	1535 0.2	1916 0.1
3 M	0314 0.8	1059 -0.2	1728 0.3	2055 0.2	18 Tu	0235 1.2	1022 -0.4	1635 0.3	2025 0.1
4 Tu	0354 0.8	1137 -0.2	1806 0.3	2136 0.2	19 W	0330 1.2	1109 -0.5	1727 0.3	2134 0.1
5 W	0431 0.9	1212 -0.2	1837 0.3	2216 0.2	20 Th	0424 1.2	1154 -0.5	1814 0.4	2241 0.1
6 Th	0508 0.9	1244 -0.2	1904 0.3	2256 0.2	21 F)	0518 1.1	1238 -0.5	1901 0.5	2348 0.1
7 F	0544 0.9	1315 -0.2	1930 0.3	2339 0.2	22 Sa	0611 1.0	1319 -0.4	1946 0.6	
8 Sa	0621 0.8	1344 -0.2	1957 0.4		23 Su	0056 0.1	0703 0.9	1359 -0.4	2032 0.7
9 Su (	0025 0.1	0659 0.8	1412 -0.2	2026 0.4	24 M	0206 0.1	0758 0.7	1436 -0.3	2117 0.7
10 M	0117 0.1	0739 0.7	1439 -0.1	2058 0.5	25 Tu	0320 0.1	0855 0.6	1512 -0.2	2202 0.8
11 Tu	0217 0.1	0822 0.6	1505 -0.1	2134 0.6	26 W	0438 0.0	1000 0.4	1543 -0.1	2247 0.9
12 W	0312 0.2	0912 0.5	1532 -0.1	2215 0.7	27 Th	0600 -0.0	1119 0.3	1611 0.0	2331 0.9
13 Th	0444 0.1	1012 0.4	1602 -0.0	2301 0.8	28 F	0717 -0.1	1301 0.2	1631 0.1	
14 F	0606 -0.0	1127 0.3	1636 0.0	2351 0.9	29 Sa ●	0014 0.9	0825 -0.2	1516 0.2	1630 0.2
15 Sa ○	0724 -0.1	1254 0.2	1719 0.0		30 Su	0056 0.9	0919 -0.2		

TIME MERIDIAN 75°W

0000h is midnight, 1200h is noon.

Heights in feet are referenced to the chart datum of soundings.

CRISTÓBAL-COLÓN, PANAMA

HIGH & LOW WATER 1995 9°21'N 79°55'W

EASTERN STANDARD TIME (GMT -5H)

MAY

Day	Time	ft	Day	Time	ft
1 M	0136 / 1004	0.9 / -0.3	16 Tu	0108 / 0912 / 1531 / 1831	1.3 / -0.5 / 0.2 / 0.1
2 Tu	0216 / 1041	0.9 / -0.3	17 W	0204 / 1000 / 1630 / 1955	1.3 / -0.5 / 0.3 / 0.2
3 W	0254 / 1112	0.9 / -0.3	18 Th	0301 / 1045 / 1720 / 2118	1.2 / -0.5 / 0.4 / 0.2
4 Th	0332 / 1141 / 1906 / 2100	0.9 / -0.3 / 0.3 / 0.3	19 F	0356 / 1127 / 1806 / 2238	1.2 / -0.5 / 0.5 / 0.2
5 F	0410 / 1206 / 1909 / 2210	0.9 / -0.3 / 0.4 / 0.3	20 Sa	0451 / 1207 / 1851 / 2355	1.0 / -0.5 / 0.7 / 0.2
6 Sa	0448 / 1229 / 1921 / 2314	0.8 / -0.3 / 0.4 / 0.3	21 Su ☽	0546 / 1245 / 1934	0.9 / -0.4 / 0.8
7 Su ☾	0526 / 1251 / 1939	0.8 / -0.2 / 0.5	22 M	0111 / 0641 / 1321 / 2017	0.2 / 0.7 / -0.3 / 0.9
8 M	0018 / 0606 / 1313 / 2002	0.3 / 0.7 / -0.2 / 0.6	23 Tu	0227 / 0737 / 1353 / 2059	0.1 / 0.5 / -0.2 / 1.0
9 Tu	0125 / 0649 / 1334 / 2031	0.2 / 0.6 / -0.2 / 0.7	24 W	0344 / 0837 / 1421 / 2140	0.0 / 0.4 / -0.1 / 1.0
10 W	0236 / 0738 / 1357 / 2106	0.2 / 0.5 / -0.2 / 0.9	25 Th	0500 / 0947 / 1443 / 2219	-0.0 / 0.2 / -0.0 / 1.0
11 Th	0350 / 0835 / 1423 / 2146	0.1 / 0.4 / -0.1 / 1.0	26 F	0615 / 1115 / 1454 / 2258	-0.1 / 0.1 / 0.1 / 1.0
12 F	0505 / 0944 / 1453 / 2231	-0.0 / 0.2 / -0.1 / 1.1	27 Sa	0722 / 2336	-0.2 / 1.0
13 Sa	0617 / 1109 / 1529 / 2320	-0.1 / 0.1 / -0.1 / 1.2	28 Su	0820	-0.2
14 Su ○	0723 / 1245 / 1615	-0.3 / 0.1 / -0.0	29 M	0013 / 0908	1.0 / -0.3
15 M	0013 / 0820 / 1417 / 1715	1.3 / -0.4 / 0.1 / 0.1	30 Tu	0050 / 0947	1.0 / -0.3
			31 W	0127 / 1019	1.0 / -0.3

JUNE

Day	Time	ft	Day	Time	ft
1 Th	0204 / 1047	1.0 / -0.3	16 F	0237 / 1017 / 1659 / 2114	1.2 / -0.5 / 0.5 / 0.2
2 F	0242 / 1109	0.9 / -0.3	17 Sa	0334 / 1058 / 1746 / 2242	1.1 / -0.5 / 0.7 / 0.2
3 Sa	0320 / 1129 / 1901 / 2138	0.9 / -0.3 / 0.4 / 0.4	18 Su	0431 / 1136 / 1830	0.9 / -0.4 / 0.8
4 Su	0400 / 1146 / 1858 / 2308	0.8 / -0.3 / 0.5 / 0.4	19 M ☽	0004 / 0528 / 1212 / 1913	0.2 / 0.8 / -0.4 / 0.9
5 M	0441 / 1203 / 1911	0.7 / -0.2 / 0.6	20 Tu	0121 / 0624 / 1245 / 1953	0.1 / 0.6 / -0.3 / 1.0
6 Tu ☾	0026 / 0525 / 1222 / 1933	0.3 / 0.6 / -0.2 / 0.8	21 W	0234 / 0722 / 1314 / 2033	0.1 / 0.4 / -0.2 / 1.1
7 W	0139 / 0614 / 1243 / 2003	0.2 / 0.5 / -0.2 / 0.9	22 Th	0345 / 0821 / 1339 / 2111	0.0 / 0.3 / -0.1 / 1.1
8 Th	0250 / 0708 / 1308 / 2039	0.1 / 0.4 / -0.2 / 1.1	23 F	0453 / 0927 / 1357 / 2148	-0.1 / 0.2 / -0.0 / 1.1
9 F	0358 / 0810 / 1337 / 2120	0.0 / 0.2 / -0.2 / 1.2	24 Sa	0558 / 1047 / 1403 / 2224	-0.1 / 0.1 / 0.0 / 1.1
10 Sa	0504 / 0923 / 1412 / 2206	-0.1 / 0.2 / -0.2 / 1.3	25 Su	0659 / 2300	-0.2 / 1.1
11 Su	0607 / 1047 / 1453 / 2256	-0.2 / 0.1 / -0.1 / 1.4	26 M	0754 / 2336	-0.2 / 1.1
12 M ○	0705 / 1220 / 1543 / 2348	-0.3 / 0.1 / -0.1 / 1.4	27 Tu	0841	-0.2
13 Tu	0758 / 1350 / 1647	-0.4 / 0.2 / 0.0	28 W	0012 / 0919	1.1 / -0.2
14 W	0043 / 0848 / 1507 / 1808	1.4 / -0.5 / 0.2 / 0.1	29 Th	0048 / 0950	1.0 / -0.2
15 Th	0140 / 0934 / 1608 / 1941	1.3 / -0.5 / 0.4 / 0.2	30 F	0126 / 1013	1.0 / -0.2

JULY

Day	Time	ft	Day	Time	ft
1 Sa	0206 / 1032	0.9 / -0.2	16 Su	0321 / 1026 / 1714 / 2249	0.9 / -0.3 / 0.8 / 0.2
2 Su	0247 / 1047 / 1809 / 2151	0.8 / -0.2 / 0.5 / 0.4	17 M	0421 / 1103 / 1759	0.7 / -0.3 / 0.9
3 M	0331 / 1102 / 1813 / 2322	0.7 / -0.2 / 0.6 / 0.4	18 Tu	0007 / 0520 / 1138 / 1841	0.1 / 0.6 / -0.2 / 1.0
4 Tu	0418 / 1118 / 1832	0.6 / -0.2 / 0.8	19 W ☽	0116 / 0617 / 1211 / 1921	0.1 / 0.5 / -0.2 / 1.1
5 W	0037 / 0509 / 1139 / 1859	0.3 / 0.5 / -0.2 / 1.0	20 Th	0220 / 0712 / 1239 / 1959	0.0 / 0.4 / -0.1 / 1.1
6 Th ☾	0144 / 0603 / 1204 / 1933	0.2 / 0.4 / -0.2 / 1.1	21 F	0319 / 0806 / 1305 / 2036	-0.0 / 0.3 / -0.1 / 1.1
7 F	0246 / 0700 / 1235 / 2013	0.1 / 0.3 / -0.2 / 1.3	22 Sa	0416 / 0900 / 1326 / 2112	-0.0 / 0.2 / 0.1 / 1.1
8 Sa	0345 / 0802 / 1311 / 2057	0.0 / 0.2 / -0.2 / 1.4	23 Su	0512 / 0958 / 1341 / 2148	-0.1 / 0.1 / 0.0 / 1.1
9 Su	0443 / 0910 / 1353 / 2144	-0.0 / 0.1 / -0.2 / 1.4	24 M	0608 / 1109 / 1347 / 2223	-0.1 / 0.1 / 0.1 / 1.1
10 M	0539 / 1025 / 1440 / 2234	-0.2 / 0.1 / -0.1 / 1.4	25 Tu	0701 / 2300	-0.1 / 1.1
11 Tu	0634 / 1147 / 1536 / 2328	-0.3 / 0.1 / -0.1 / 1.4	26 W	0749 / 2337	-0.1 / 1.0
12 W ○	0726 / 1311 / 1645	-0.3 / 0.2 / 0.1	27 Th	0828	-0.1
13 Th	0024 / 0816 / 1427 / 1810	1.3 / -0.3 / 0.3 / 0.2	28 F	0017 / 0858	1.0 / -0.1
14 F	0122 / 0902 / 1532 / 1946	1.2 / -0.4 / 0.5 / 0.2	29 Sa	0100 / 0920 / 1657 / 1817	0.9 / -0.1 / 0.4 / 0.4
15 Sa	0221 / 0945 / 1626 / 2122	1.0 / -0.3 / 0.6 / 0.2	30 Su	0146 / 0938 / 1638 / 2042	0.8 / -0.1 / 0.5 / 0.4
			31 M	0237 / 0954 / 1651 / 2219	0.7 / -0.0 / 0.6 / 0.3

AUGUST

Day	Time	ft	Day	Time	ft
1 Tu	0330 / 1012 / 1715 / 2333	0.6 / -0.1 / 0.8 / 0.2	16 W	0524 / 1103 / 1759	0.5 / -0.0 / 1.0
2 W	0425 / 1035 / 1746	0.5 / -0.1 / 0.9	17 Th	0056 / 0617 / 1136 / 1838	0.0 / 0.5 / 0.0 / 1.1
3 Th ☾	0035 / 0519 / 1103 / 1823	0.1 / 0.4 / -0.1 / 1.1	18 F	0148 / 0706 / 1207 / 1916	-0.0 / 0.4 / 0.1 / 1.1
4 F	0131 / 0613 / 1138 / 1903	0.0 / 0.3 / -0.1 / 1.2	19 Sa	0236 / 0750 / 1236 / 1953	-0.0 / 0.4 / 0.1 / 1.1
5 Sa	0224 / 0708 / 1217 / 1947	-0.1 / 0.3 / -0.1 / 1.3	20 Su	0322 / 0833 / 1303 / 2029	-0.0 / 0.3 / 0.1 / 1.1
6 Su	0316 / 0804 / 1300 / 2033	-0.1 / 0.3 / -0.1 / 1.4	21 M	0408 / 0916 / 1329 / 2105	0.0 / 0.3 / 0.1 / 1.1
7 M	0408 / 0904 / 1349 / 2123	-0.2 / 0.2 / -0.1 / 1.4	22 Tu	0453 / 1002 / 1357 / 2142	0.0 / 0.3 / 0.2 / 1.0
8 Tu	0500 / 1009 / 1444 / 2215	-0.2 / 0.3 / -0.1 / 1.3	23 W	0538 / 1054 / 1430 / 2220	0.0 / 0.3 / 0.2 / 1.0
9 W	0552 / 1119 / 1548 / 2310	-0.2 / 0.3 / 0.0 / 1.2	24 Th	0620 / 1153 / 1515 / 2303	0.1 / 0.3 / 0.2 / 0.9
10 Th ○	0644 / 1232 / 1704	-0.2 / 0.4 / 0.1	25 F ●	0657 / 1251 / 1625 / 2350	0.1 / 0.4 / 0.1 / 0.8
11 F	0008 / 0733 / 1343 / 1833	1.1 / -0.2 / 0.5 / 0.2	26 Sa	0728 / 1341 / 1804	0.1 / 0.4 / 0.3
12 Sa	0111 / 0821 / 1447 / 2008	1.0 / -0.1 / 0.6 / 0.2	27 Su	0044 / 0754 / 1421 / 1949	0.7 / 0.1 / 0.6 / 0.3
13 Su	0216 / 0906 / 1543 / 2137	0.8 / -0.1 / 0.7 / 0.2	28 M	0146 / 0819 / 1500 / 2118	0.6 / 0.1 / 0.7 / 0.2
14 M	0322 / 0947 / 1632 / 2254	0.7 / -0.1 / 0.9 / 0.1	29 Tu	0250 / 0846 / 1538 / 2229	0.5 / 0.1 / 0.8 / 0.1
15 Tu	0426 / 1026 / 1717 / 2359	0.6 / -0.0 / 1.0 / 0.1	30 W	0351 / 0918 / 1619 / 2327	0.5 / 0.1 / 1.0 / 0.1
			31 Th	0448 / 0954 / 1702	0.4 / 0.1 / 1.1

TIME MERIDIAN 75°W

Heights in feet are referenced to the chart datum of soundings.

0000h is midnight, 1200h is noon.

CRISTÓBAL-COLÓN, PANAMA

HIGH & LOW WATER 1995 9°21'N 79°55'W

EASTERN STANDARD TIME (GMT -5H)

SEPTEMBER

Time	ft	Time	ft
1 0018	-0.0	**16** 0108	-0.0
0540	0.4	0702	0.5
F 1035	0.1	Sa 1132	0.2
1746	1.2	) 1825	1.1
2 0107	-0.1	**17** 0146	-0.0
0629	0.4	0737	0.5
Sa 1121	0.0	Su 1206	0.2
(1833	1.3	1901	1.1
3 0154	-0.1	**18** 0223	-0.0
0718	0.4	0812	0.5
Su 1210	0.0	M 1242	0.2
1920	1.3	1937	1.0
4 0240	-0.1	**19** 0258	0.0
0808	0.4	0846	0.5
M 1302	0.0	Tu 1320	0.3
2010	1.3	2015	1.0
5 0327	-0.1	**20** 0332	0.1
0901	0.5	0923	0.5
Tu 1400	0.0	W 1405	0.3
2101	1.2	2054	0.9
6 0414	-0.1	**21** 0405	0.1
0957	0.5	1001	0.5
W 1503	0.1	Th 1459	0.3
2156	1.1	2136	0.8
7 0502	-0.1	**22** 0436	0.2
1057	0.6	1042	0.6
Th 1616	0.1	F 1607	0.3
2255	1.0	2226	0.7
8 0550	0.0	**23** 0505	0.2
1159	0.7	1126	0.7
F 1739	0.2	Sa 1729	0.3
O		2325	0.6
9 0001	0.8	**24** 0534	0.2
0638	0.1	1213	0.8
Sa 1301	0.7	Su 1858	0.2
1909	0.2	●	
10 0113	0.7	**25** 0038	0.5
0726	0.1	0606	0.2
Su 1359	0.8	M 1302	0.9
2034	0.1	2018	0.2
11 0229	0.6	**26** 0158	0.5
0813	0.2	0644	0.3
M 1453	0.9	Tu 1352	1.0
2148	0.1	2125	0.1
12 0341	0.6	**27** 0312	0.4
0858	0.2	0729	0.3
Tu 1542	1.0	W 1442	1.1
2250	0.0	2220	-0.1
13 0444	0.5	**28** 0414	0.4
0940	0.2	0821	0.3
W 1627	1.0	Th 1532	1.2
2342	-0.0	2309	-0.1
14 0538	0.5	**29** 0506	0.4
1020	0.2	0917	0.2
Th 1708	1.1	F 1622	1.3
		2355	-0.2
15 0027	-0.0	**30** 0553	0.5
0623	0.5	1014	0.2
F 1057	0.2	Sa 1713	1.3
1747	1.1		

OCTOBER

Time	ft	Time	ft
1 0039	-0.2	**16** 0059	-0.1
0638	0.5	0729	0.6
Su 1113	0.2	M 1136	0.4
(1803	1.3	) 1804	1.0
2 0121	-0.2	**17** 0127	-0.0
0723	0.6	0756	0.6
M 1213	0.2	Tu 1224	0.4
1854	1.3	1841	1.0
3 0203	-0.2	**18** 0154	0.0
0810	0.7	0823	0.7
Tu 1316	0.2	W 1317	0.4
1946	1.2	1920	0.9
4 0245	-0.1	**19** 0219	0.1
0858	0.7	0853	0.7
W 1423	0.2	Th 1417	0.4
2041	1.0	2002	0.8
5 0326	-0.0	**20** 0242	0.1
0947	0.8	0925	0.8
Th 1536	0.2	F 1525	0.3
2139	0.9	2050	0.7
6 0406	0.1	**21** 0305	0.1
1039	0.9	1001	0.9
F 1657	0.2	Sa 1641	0.3
2246	0.7	2147	0.6
7 0447	0.1	**22** 0329	0.2
1131	0.9	1041	1.0
Sa 1821	0.2	Su 1801	0.2
		2301	0.4
8 0005	0.6	**23** 0355	0.2
0528	0.2	1126	1.1
Su 1223	1.0	M 1915	0.1
O 1942	0.1		
9 0135	0.5	**24** 0032	0.4
0609	0.3	0429	0.2
M 1313	1.0	Tu 1215	1.2
2053	0.0	2019	-0.0
10 0306	0.5	**25** 0206	0.3
0654	0.4	0515	0.3
Tu 1402	1.1	W 1308	1.3
2151	-0.0	2113	-0.1
11 0423	0.5	**26** 0324	0.4
0741	0.4	0617	0.3
W 1448	1.1	Th 1401	1.3
2239	-0.1	2201	-0.2
12 0520	0.5	**27** 0422	0.4
0830	0.4	0732	0.3
Th 1531	1.1	F 1456	1.4
2320	-0.1	2246	-0.3
13 0602	0.5	**28** 0510	0.5
0918	0.4	0848	0.3
F 1612	1.1	Sa 1550	1.4
2356	-0.1	2329	-0.3
14 0635	0.6	**29** 0554	0.6
1005	0.4	1002	0.3
Sa 1650	1.1	Su 1643	1.3
15 0029	-0.1	**30** 0010	-0.3
0703	0.5	0637	0.7
Su 1050	0.4	M 1114	0.3
1727	1.1	(1736	1.2
		31 0049	-0.3
		0721	0.8
		Tu 1225	0.3
		1830	1.1

NOVEMBER

Time	ft	Time	ft
1 0127	-0.2	**16** 0057	-0.0
0805	0.9	0757	0.8
W 1338	0.3	Th 1323	0.4
1924	1.0	1829	0.8
2 0204	-0.1	**17** 0116	-0.0
0849	1.0	0823	0.9
Th 1454	0.2	F 1432	0.4
2022	0.8	1915	0.6
3 0239	-0.0	**18** 0136	0.0
0934	1.1	0853	1.0
F 1612	0.2	Sa 1544	0.3
2127	0.6	2008	0.5
4 0312	0.1	**19** 0158	0.0
1019	1.1	0929	1.2
Sa 1733	0.1	Su 1656	0.2
2244	0.5	2113	0.4
5 0341	0.2	**20** 0223	0.1
1104	1.2	1009	1.3
Su 1850	0.1	M 1805	0.1
		2234	0.3
6 0021	0.4	**21** 0252	0.1
0405	0.3	1054	1.4
M 1149	1.2	Tu 1907	-0.0
1959	-0.0		
7 0227	0.4	**22** 0010	0.2
0414	0.3	0329	0.1
Tu 1233	1.2	W 1144	1.4
O 2057	-0.1	● 2001	-0.2
8 1316	1.2	**23** 0148	0.2
2144	-0.1	0420	0.2
W		Th 1237	1.5
		2051	-0.2
9 1357	1.2	**24** 0308	0.3
2224	-0.1	0533	0.3
Th		F 1331	1.5
		2136	-0.3
10 1437	1.1	**25** 0407	0.4
2258	-0.1	0701	0.3
F		Sa 1427	1.4
		2219	-0.4
11 1516	1.1	**26** 0456	0.5
2327	-0.1	0833	0.4
Sa		Su 1523	1.3
		2301	-0.4
12 0708	0.5	**27** 0540	0.7
0845	0.5	1000	0.4
Su 1553	1.1	M 1619	1.2
2353	-0.1	2340	-0.3
13 0709	0.6	**28** 0624	0.8
1002	0.5	1122	0.4
M 1631	1.0	Tu 1714	1.1
14 0016	-0.1	**29** 0018	-0.3
0720	0.6	0708	0.9
Tu 1110	0.5	W 1242	0.3
1708	0.9	(1811	0.9
15 0037	-0.1	**30** 0053	-0.2
0737	0.7	0750	1.1
W 1216	0.5	Th 1359	0.3
) 1747	0.9	1908	0.7

DECEMBER

Time	ft	Time	ft
1 0127	-0.1	**16** 0025	-0.1
0833	1.2	0750	1.0
F 1516	0.2	Sa 1439	0.3
2010	0.6	1844	0.5
2 0158	-0.0	**17** 0047	-0.1
0915	1.2	0822	1.2
Sa 1631	0.1	Su 1543	0.2
2118	0.4	1941	0.3
3 0224	0.0	**18** 0113	-0.1
0956	1.3	0859	1.3
Su 1745	0.0	M 1646	0.1
2240	0.3	2048	0.2
4 0243	-0.0	**19** 0145	-0.1
1037	1.3	0942	1.4
M 1853	-0.0	Tu 1745	-0.1
		2205	0.2
5 0030	0.2	**20** 0222	-0.0
0243	0.2	1029	1.5
Tu 1118	1.3	W 1840	-0.1
1954	-0.1	2333	0.1
6 1157	1.2	**21** 0308	0.0
2046	-0.1	1119	1.5
O		Th 1932	-0.2
		●	
7 1235	1.2	**22** 0104	0.2
2129	-0.2	0406	0.2
Th		F 1212	1.5
		2020	-0.3
8 1313	1.2	**23** 0226	0.3
2204	-0.2	0523	0.2
F		Sa 1308	1.4
		2106	-0.3
9 1350	1.1	**24** 0331	0.4
2233	-0.2	0656	0.3
Sa		Su 1406	1.3
		2149	-0.4
10 1428	1.1	**25** 0426	0.6
2257	-0.2	0834	0.3
Su		M 1504	1.2
		2230	-0.4
11 1505	1.0	**26** 0515	0.7
2317	-0.1	1007	0.3
M		Tu 1603	1.0
		2309	-0.3
12 0700	0.6	**27** 0600	0.9
0930	0.8	1133	0.3
Tu 1544	0.9	W 1702	0.9
2334	-0.1	2346	-0.3
13 0655	0.7	**28** 0644	1.0
1102	0.9	1252	0.2
W 1624	0.8	Th 1801	0.7
2350	-0.1	(	
14 0705	0.8	**29** 0021	-0.2
1220	0.8	0727	1.1
Th 1707	0.7	F 1405	0.1
		1900	0.5
15 0007	-0.1	**30** 0054	-0.2
0724	0.9	0809	1.2
F 1331	0.4	Sa 1515	0.1
1753	0.6	2002	0.4
		31 0123	-0.1
		0849	1.2
		Su 1622	-0.0
		2106	0.3

TIME MERIDIAN 75°W

0000h is midnight, 1200h is noon.

Heights in feet are referenced to the chart datum of soundings.

COSTA RICA

CAUTION: Our information on aids to navigation comes from official government sources. The latitudes and longitudes of these marks may not correspond to the readings from GPS receivers. Some aids have been reported as unreliable, missing, off position, or showing incorrect characteristics. No single aid to navigation, or waypoint, should be relied upon as a sole means of fixing your position.

NOTE: The chartlet on the following page is <u>not intended for navigation</u> and is included for reference and planning purposes only. Reproduced from government sources, it is from the most current edition as of press time, but incorporates <u>no corrections</u> to navigational aids, depths, or hazards since the edition publication date.

ENTRY PROCEDURES

The only harbor of interest on the Caribbean coast of Costa Rica is Puerto Limón. It is a Port of Entry and a major shipping center for the country. Bananas and cocoa are the principal exports, but a considerable amount of general cargo is handled. See *Reed's Nautical Companion* for an illustration of the country flag.

Visitors should have the usual papers—passports, ship's documents, clearance from your last port, and crew lists. U.S. citizens can get a visa upon arrival; citizens of other countries should check with Costa Rican officials before heading for this port. For more information on entry requirements contact the Consulate General of Costa Rica, 2112 S Street NW, Washington, DC 20008 (tel, 202-328-6628).

For assistance within Costa Rica, U.S. citizens might want to call the U.S. Embassy in Pava, San José (506-220-3939).

Cases of malaria have been reported from the Puerto Limón area. Travelers should contact the U.S. Center for Disease Control's International Traveler's Hotline (404-332-4559).

Costa Rica's telephone country code is 506.

City codes are not required; local numbers now have seven digits.

The currency is the colon, which is divided into 100 centimos. Currently (summer 1994) the exchange rate is about 155–160 colons to 1 U.S. dollar. The language spoken is Spanish, but English is frequently heard, especially in tourist areas and cities.

COSTA RICA

SIXAOLA, 9 34.1N, 82 33.6W. Fl W 10s, 46 ft, 11M. White skeleton steel tower. Visible 114°–315°. RACON K (– · –), 20M.
LIMÓN, ISLA UVITA, summit, 9 59.6N, 83 00.7W. Fl W 10s, 134ft, 5M. White metal framework tower. Fl R 2s and F R on radio tower 0.9M WNW; Aero Al Fl W G 10s, 2M SW; R lights on radio tower 1.5M SW.
CONTAINER PIER, S end. 9 59.0N, 83 01.0W. F R, 49ft, 10M.
BAHÍA MOÍN, ISLA PAJAROS, 10 01.0N, 83 04.6W. Fl W 2.5s. Tower.
PUERTO MOÍN RANGE (Front), 10 00.2N, 83 04.6W. F W. Tower. **(Rear),** 130 meters, 151° from front. F W. Tower.

PUERTO LIMÓN

10 00N, 83 01W
Pilotage: This open coastal harbor is about 234 miles west-northwest of the entrance to the Panama Canal. The approaches are safe and easy of access. At night the loom of the bright pier lights is seen well out to sea. Two radio masts on Punta Blanca are reported to be prominent. A south-setting current is generally experienced between Isla Uvita and Puerto Limón. During the dry season it attains a velocity of less than 1 knot, but during the rainy season may run at 3/4 to 1 1/4 knots. In general, the current sets southeast along this stretch of coast. There is a strong discharge from the rivers during the rainy season. A continual swell from the northeast breaks along the beaches of this entire coast.

Volcan Turrialba (10° 01'N, 83° 45'W) is an 11,349-foot-high inactive volcano located about 43 miles west of Puerto Limón. When seen from the east, the peak and crater appear clearly

COAST PILOT

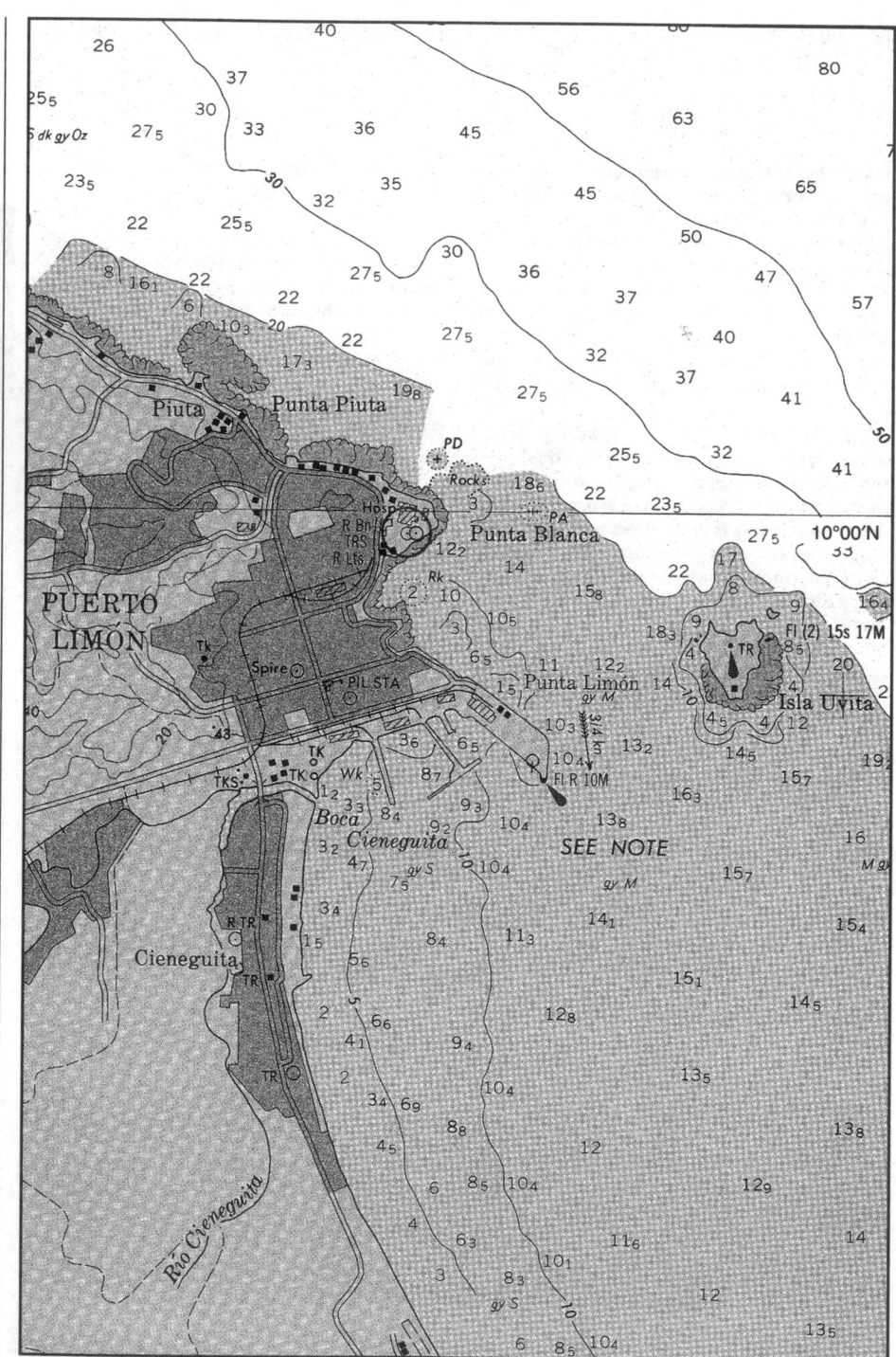

Puerto Limón, soundings in meters *(from DMA 28049, 12th ed, 10/89)*

defined, with the hollow of the crater being on the north side. The peak is generally hidden by clouds.

Monte Irazu, an 11,897-foot-high mountain, stands close south of the volcano. On a clear day, these conspicuous peaks can be seen for a considerable distance.

Port of Entry: The customs office is across the street from the gates of the port area.
Radio Communications: You can contact Puerto Limón on VHF channel 16 or 2182kHz. (call sign TIM).
Anchorage: The anchorage is rather exposed and open to swells. There is some shelter from Isla Uvita. There is reported to be a strong surge along the docks here. Be prepared to leave quickly if bad weather threatens.

Services: There are good markets and general stores. You can make rail connections to San José and other parts of the country. Many people here speak English.

BAHÍA MOÍN

10 00N, 83 05W
Pilotage: This bay is the location of the commercial port facility, Puerto Moín, which is located on the western side of the same peninsula as Puerto Limón. It is primarily a banana exporting and oil importing terminal. There is a light on Isla Pájaros and a rock close to the northwest. The tanker moorings in the bay are subject to frequent changes of positions, colors, and characteristics. There is a continual surge in this harbor, and this entire coast has a continual swell breaking on the beach.

REED'S NEEDS YOU!

It is difficult to obtain accurate and up-to-date information on many areas in the Caribbean. To provide mariners with the best possible almanac, *Reed's* uses many sources. *Reed's* welcomes your contributions, suggestions, and updates. Please be as specific as possible and include your address and phone number. Send this information to: Editor, Thomas Reed Publications, 120 Lewis Wharf, Boston, MA 02110, U.S.A. *Thank you!*

NICARAGUA

CAUTION: Mariners are advised to avoid both the Caribbean and Pacific ports and waters of Nicaragua until further notice. There have been several cases of foreign flag vessels seized off the Nicaraguan coast by Nicaraguan authorities. While in all cases the ships, passengers, and crews have been released within a short period of time, prompt U.S. embassy consular access to detained U.S. citizens may not be possible because of non-notification of the embassy by the Nicaraguan government. It should also be noted that there have been recent incidents of piracy in the Caribbean waters off the coast of Nicaragua.

Inland travelers should be aware of occasional flare-ups of armed violence, especially in the northern part of the country. The roads connecting Nicaragua and Honduras may be dangerous. All roads are considered dangerous at night.

ENTRY PROCEDURES

The Port of Entry on the Caribbean coast is Bluefields. This harbor is located about 275 miles northwest of the Panama Canal and 120 miles north of Puerto Limón, Costa Rica. For an illustration of the country flag see *Reed's Nautical Companion*.

Passports should be valid at least six months beyond your intended departure date, and all persons should be prepared to demonstrate financial resources of at least about US$200. You should also have the usual papers: clearance from your last port, ship's documents, and crew lists. Visas may or may not be required, depending on your nationality. Many nationals can get a tourist card upon entering the country. For visa information contact the Nicaraguan Consulate at 1627 New Hampshire

Avenue NW, Washington, DC, 20009 (202-939-6531 or 6532). The Nicaraguan Embassy at the same address can be reached by calling 202-939-6570.

For information or assistance while in the country, U.S. citizens might want to contact the United States Embassy in Managua (505-2-666-010).

Credit cards and traveler's checks are not widely accepted, even in the larger cities. In Managua the large tourist hotels may accept credit cards or change traveler's checks. Traveler's checks may be changed at banks and other official exchange stations. The currency is the cordoba, which is divided into 100 centavos. Currently (summer 1994) the exchange rate is 6.5 cordobas to 1 U.S. dollar.

Cases of malaria have been reported. For more information travelers should contact the U.S. Centers for Disease Control's International Travelers Hotline (404-332-4559).

The telephone calling code for Nicaragua is 505; a one-, two-, three-, or four-digit city code follows, and then the local number. The city code for Leone is 311; Managua, 2; San Juan Del Sur, 4682; and San Marcos, 43.

The main language spoken is Spanish, but English is heard in some Caribbean coastal areas.

CAUTION: Our information on aids to navigation comes from official government sources. The latitudes and longitudes of these marks may not correspond to the readings from GPS receivers. Some aids have been reported as unreliable, missing, off position, or showing incorrect characteristics. No single aid to navigation, or waypoint, should be relied upon as a sole means of fixing your position.

CURRENTS

Between Punta Mico and Punta Gorda the currents on the edge of the 200-meter depth curve are affected by the equatorial current. Generally, part of the current recurves to the southwest in the vicinity of Isla de Providencia, while the main flow continues northwest across Miskito Bank.

The currents along the coast are variable and subject to great and sudden change. They are influenced to a large extent by the wind, but they do tend to run south at a velocity varying from 1/2 to 3 knots. This southerly set sometimes reverses its direction for several days before resuming its normal flow.

The current is stronger in the vicinity of Punta Mico, where it sometimes sets east, than between Cayos de Perlas and Puerto Cabezas. Between Puerto Cabezas and Punta Gorda the current is variable, but tends to set north. However, this current may be completely reversed by a norther. A countercurrent setting south may be experienced close inshore.

PUNTA CASTILLO
10 56N, 83 40W
Pilotage: This low point marked by breakers is about 10 miles north-northwest of the Río Colorado. The entrance to San Juan del Norte is located about 2 3/4 miles west of the point. Morris shoal, about 4 miles long and 1 mile wide, lies about 10 miles east of the point. Depths over the shoal range from 60 feet to about 72 feet.

SAN JUAN DEL NORTE
10 56N, 83 42W
Pilotage: This harbor was once the proposed terminus of the Nicaraguan ship canal. The project was abandoned in 1893, and the harbor is now closed to ocean-shipping because of silting, but it is still possible for small craft to enter. The village and equipment are reported to be obscured by trees.

North of the harbor the coast is low and sandy for about 29 miles to a bold rocky point. A small wooded island lies near the point. The surf breaks constantly along these sandy beaches. The twin peaks of Round Hill rise to about 617 feet about 20 miles northwest of

Punta Castillo. The coast then becomes higher and extends irregularly northeast to Punta Gorda.

PUNTA GORDA
11 26N, 83 48W
Pilotage: This is a prominent rocky point with several steep-to islets lying close offshore. Río de Punta Gorda discharges into the sea about 4 1/2 miles northeast of the point. There are several settlements at the river mouth. From the point the coast extends irregularly for 12 1/2 miles northeast to Punta Mico.

ISLA DEL PAJARO BOBO
11 30N, 83 43W
Pilotage: This 154-foot-high wooded islet lies about 5 3/4 miles southwest of Punta Mico and 3 miles offshore. When seen from the east it appears as a small green conical hill, but from the south it appears wedge-shaped, with the higher end to the west.

PUNTA MICO
11 36N, 83 40W
Pilotage: This is the south extremity of a bold rocky peninsula, which extends about 1 1/2 miles southeast and is about 2 miles wide. In the middle of the promontory stands Red Hill, about 100 feet high and red in color. Red cliffs extend about 1 mile northwest from Black Bluff on the northeast end of the promontory. Shoal water and several cays lie within 1 mile of Punta Mico.

From the point the low coast extends about 45 miles north to Punta Mosquito at the entrance to Laguna de Perlas. El Bluff, a bold promontory, stands about midway along this stretch of coast.

FRENCH CAY
11 44N, 83 37W
Pilotage: This small, flat, wooded islet rises to a height of 90 feet. It stands about 7 1/2 miles north-northeast of Black Bluff, on the north part of a narrow reef about 1 1/4 miles long. Sister cays, three small islets, stand 8 1/2 miles north of Black Bluff. Two breaking reefs lie about 3 miles southeast and 2 1/2 miles east of Green Point. Cayo de la Paloma is a 108-foot high cay with a saddle-shaped summit lying about 1 1/2 miles east-northeast of Green Point.

It is the largest cay in this area. Other hazards in the area include White Rock and Guano Cay—caution should be used in this area because of the many reefs and dangers.

EL BLUFF

12 00N, 83 41W

EL BLUEFIELDS BLUFF SUMMIT LIGHT, 12 00N, 83 41W. Fl W 3.8s, 163ft, 14M. Red metal framework tower.

Pilotage: This bold promontory is over 137 feet high and wooded. It stands on the east side of the entrance to Laguna De Blue-fields, but looks like an island from seaward. Red cliffs stand on the east side of the promontory.

BLUEFIELDS

12 01N, 83 45W

Pilotage: Cayo Casaba, a low wooded islet with a smaller islet to its west, lies in the middle of the entrance to Laguna De Blue-fields. The navigable channel between this islet and El Bluff is about 200 to 400 yards wide. The town of Bluefields is located on the west side of the lagoon about 3 1/2 miles inside the entrance. The port for the town is on the west and northwest sides of El Bluff. This is where all cargo is handled. The entrance bar has a minimum depth of about 9 feet, and the harbor has depths of less than 18 feet. Currents off the entrance generally set south at about 1 1/2 to 2 knots, but can reverse for a day for no apparent reason. A conspicuous white house on the northwest side of El Bluff and the radio towers in town are conspicuous. The pilots monitor VHF channel 16.

Port of Entry: Check in at the office on the El Bluff docks.

THE MISKITO BANK

Pilotage: From a position about 25 miles south of Punta Mico the 200-meter-depth curve extends north-northeast to a position 28 miles east of the point and then extends north-northeast to a position about 72 miles east of Punta Gorda. The Miskito Bank lies within this 200-meter-depth curve.

The depths within the curve are irregular and numerous cays, islands, and other dangers exist in the area. There are numerous detached shallow patches—some with depths of less than 6 feet. Most of the bank has depths of around 78 to 108 feet. Coral reefs grow about two tenths of a foot annually, and depths may be less than charted in some areas.

The turtle fishermen in this area are reported to know where most of the rocks are and are adept at estimating depths. This is an area for eyeball navigation during the day. You should travel when the sun is high and preferably behind you.

CAUTION: Great care is required in navigating this area because of reef growth and the unreliability and/or age of the chart surveys. New shoals have been reported.

BLOWING ROCK

12 02N, 83 02W

Pilotage: This rock is about 4 feet high and has a hole through the center from which water is occasionally forced, which looks like the spouting of a whale. It lies about 38 miles east of El Bluff.

ISLA DEL MAIZ GRANDE

12 10N, 83 03W

Pilotage: This island is about 2 1/2 miles long by 2 miles wide and lies about 38 miles east-northeast of El Bluff. Mount Pleasant rises to a 371-foot wooded peak in the middle of the north part of the island. A 98-foot-high rocky bluff stands at the south end of the island. The island is fringed by foul ground extending about 1/4 to 1 1/2 miles offshore. A stranded wreck is located about 1 1/4 miles north-northeast of Mount Pleasant, which is reported to give a good radar return.

Anchorage: There is an anchorage in South-west Bay on the southwest side of the island. Depths run about 27 to 30 feet. There are also anchorages in Brig Bay on the island's west side and in Long Bay on the southeast side. Care must be taken to avoid the reefs and shoal patches in or near these anchorages.

A 321-foot-long pier extends from the shore near a shrimp processing plant in the head of Southwest Bay. Depths range from 6 to 13 feet alongside. There is a conspicuous building that is lighted at night. A similar building stands at the head of Brig Bay.

ISLA DEL MAIZ PEQUENA

12 18N, 82 59W

Pilotage: This 125-foot-high island is about 1/2 mile long and 1/2 mile wide. It lies about 7 1/2 miles north-northeast of Isla del Maiz Grande. The north and northeast sides of the island are fringed by reefs extending about 1/2 to 1 mile offshore. The west side of the island is fairly steep-to seaward of the 10-meter curve, which lies between 1/4 and 1/2 mile offshore.

Anchorage: There is an anchorage in Pelican Bay on the southwest side of the island. Depths are reported to be about 36 feet with the west tangent of the island bearing 342° and the south tangent of the island bearing 106°.

SEAL CAY

12 25N, 83 17W

Pilotage: This is the most southeastern of the Cayos de Perlas. It is a small coral ridge about 3 feet high, lying about 12 1/2 miles east of Punta de Perlas. Foul ground extends about 1/2 mile northwest and about 1 mile south-southwest from the cay, but the southeast side is steep-to.

The south limits of Cayos de Perlas are marked by Columbilla Cay, a steep-to reef-fringed islet, 110 feet high to the tops of the trees, located about 6 1/2 miles southwest of Seal Cay. Maroon Cay, a similar islet on the edge of a reef extending about 2 miles east from Punta de Perlas, marks the southwest extremity of the area.

CAYOS DE PERLAS

12 29N, 83 19W

Pilotage: These cays and reefs lie between Punta de Perlas and a position about 13 1/2 miles east. They extend about 12 miles to the north within the 20-meter-depth curve, which runs about 8 to 17 miles offshore.

Although there are depths of 36 to 60 feet in this area, navigation is very hazardous because of the numerous charted and uncharted reefs and shoals. Some of these may not be visible because of the turbid waters. A mud bottom may be only a thin covering over coral, and you should anchor with care.

BODEN REEF

12 30N, 83 19W

Pilotage: This area is about 3/4 mile long, with a least depth of 14 feet. It lies along the eastern edge of the Cayos de Perlas about midway between Seal Cay and the Northeast Cays located 8 miles northwest of Seal Cay. The Northeast Cays are a small group of reef-fringed islets with several rocks awash about 1 mile to the northwest. They mark the north-eastern extremity of the Cayos de Perlas. Numerous rocks awash and 9- to 18-foot patches lie up to about 5 miles west-southwest of these cays. Within this area lie the Crawl Cays and the Tungawarra Cays, as well as numerous small cays and shoals.

Anchorage: Good anchorage can be taken about 1/4 mile southwest of a mooring buoy lying 1/4 mile west of Little Tungawarra Cay. This anchorage should be approached from the south. Other anchorages may be found in the lee of the larger cays.

GREAT KING CAY

12 45N, 83 21W

Pilotage: This 70-foot-high cay is the largest of a group of islets lying about 12 miles north of the Cayos de Perlas and about 9 to 13 miles off the mainland. Little King Cay is about 32 feet high and stands about 3/4 of a mile east of Great King. The two Rocky Cays lie about 1 mile to the northwest, and 8-foot-high Little Tyra Cay lies about 2 to 3 miles west-southwest of Great King.

GREAT TYRA CAY

12 52N, 83 23W

Pilotage: This cay is about 60 feet high to the tops of the trees. There is foul ground extend-ing about 1/2 mile north from it. It is the largest of a group of islets and shoals lying about 8 miles north of Great King Cay. Seal Cay, two barren rocks about 10 feet high, lies about 3/4 of a mile south of Great Tyra, and a dangerous shoal patch lies about 1 mile east of Seal Cay. Several detached reefs lie between 1 and 3 miles southwest of Great Tyra Cay. There are two shoals located about 1 mile and 5 miles northwest of Great Tyra.

Tyra Rock is about 8 feet high and located about 4 1/2 miles northeast of Great Tyra Cay. Numerous detached reefs and shoals, over which the sea breaks, lie up to 3 1/2 miles west and 1 mile north of Tyra Rock.

RÍO GRANDE

12 54N, 83 32W

Pilotage: This river is navigable by barges for 106 miles upstream. The bar entrance has a depth of about 5 feet. Río Grande village stands on the north bank of the river near the entrance. A fruit station and a wharf are on the south bank, and two radio towers to the south are conspicuous. Sandy bay village is 3 1/2 miles north of the river.

CAYOS MAN O WAR

13 01N, 83 23W

Pilotage: This cluster of islets stands about 11 miles offshore and 6 3/4 miles northwest of Tyra Rock. The largest rises to a height of about 50 feet. An old oil barge, formerly used as a storage tank, stands on the west cay. A sheltered bight on the west side of this cay has pilings where vessels formerly moored to load lightered cargo. Depths alongside range from 13 feet to 22 feet.

Numerous detached reefs and shoals lie up to about 3 miles south-southwest and west-northwest of Cayos Man O War.

CAUTION: Many vessels have reported striking coral heads inside the 20-meter curve in the vicinity of Cayos Man O War and between the cay and Puerto Cabezas.

EGG ROCK

13 02N, 83 22W

Pilotage: This 6-foot-high steep-to rock is located about 1 1/3 miles northeast of Cayos Man O War. A dangerous shoal lies about 13 miles north-northwest of Cayos Man O War.

PUERTO ISABEL

13 22N, 83 34W

PUERTO ISABEL RANGE (Front Light), 13 21N, 83 33W. F R. Roof of shed. **(Rear Light),** 90 meters, 276° from front light, F W.

Pilotage: This open roadstead is a privately owned port. There is a 1/2-mile-long pier extending east from shore. From March to April currents run north; from May to February, south at a velocity of 1 to 2 knots.

RÍO PRINZAPOLCA

13 25N, 83 34W

Pilotage: There is a small village on the south bank of the river. Shoal water, with depths of less than 6 feet, extends 1 mile east from the river.

RÍO WALPASIXA

13 29N, 83 33W

Pilotage: The sea breaks heavily on the bar at the entrance to this river, which is located about 4 miles north of the Río Prinzapolca. There is a village at the river mouth and another called Wounta on the south side of a small lagoon about 4 miles north of the river. Foul ground extends about 3 miles east from just north of the lagoon entrance.

Several prominent mounds, each about 80 feet high, stand near the coast about 14 miles north of Wounta. From east of the mounds, south to 11 miles north of the Río Grande, the area within the 20 meter curve is restricted by numerous dangers. From the mounds, north to Puerto Cabezas, there are few dangers within the 10 meter curve, which lies within 2 to 4 miles from the coast.

RÍO HUAHUA

13 53N, 83 27W

Pilotage: This river is about 21 miles north of Wounta. After heavy rains, muddy river water discolors the sea for some distance offshore. From the river the coast extends about 10 miles north to Bragman Bluff, a bold headland about 98 feet high with red cliffs extending about 1/2 mile along its east edge.

PUERTO CABEZAS

14 01N, 83 23W

BRAGMAN BLUFF LIGHT, 14 02N, 83 25W. Mo (B) W 10.6s, 168ft, 14M. Southern square water tower. Visible 201° 30′–021° 30′. Private light.

Pilotage: This harbor is an open roadstead with a government wharf extending about 1/2 mile southeast from Bragman Bluff. It is a banana and lumber exporting port. Some water towers, the radio towers on the east side of town, and several chimneys in its southeast part are prominent landmarks. At night, the loom of the town's lights may be seen long before the navigational light can be spotted. The beach shows poorly on radar, although the railroad cars on the siding are reported to make an excellent return. The pier is reported to have a good radar return up to 14 miles. The current in the vicinity of the pier sets south or south-southwest at a velocity of about 1 1/4 knots. This is a possible Port of Entry, although the harbor is not sheltered and makes a poor anchorage.

NED THOMAS CAY
14 10N, 82 48W

Pilotage: This cay and The Witties lie about in the center of a group of reefs. The group is about 8 miles in diameter and lies about 11 1/2 miles south of Cayos Miskitos. Sea Devil Reef and Franklin Reef lie on the south limits of the Cayos Miskitos group. They have depths of at least 15 feet over them.

SOUTHEAST ROCK
14 10N, 82 29W

Pilotage: This rock lying within 9 feet of the surface is on the southeast extremity of the Cayos Miskitos.

TSIANKUALAIA ROCK
14 20N, 83 04W

Pilotage: This rock, with a depth of about 9 feet over it, lies on the southwest side of the Cayos Miskito group about 7 3/4 miles east of Punta Gorda. Several rocks within 6 feet of the surface lie within 1/2 mile south and southeast of this rock. Waham Cay, 3 feet high, stands about 3 1/2 miles north-northeast of the rock. Toro Cay and Kisura Cay, two similar islets, stand about 2 miles north-northwest and 2 miles north, respectively, of Waham Cay.

Alice Agnes Rocks consist of several awash rocks that lie on the southwest limits of the Cayos Miskitos group. They are about 13 miles west-southwest of Cayos Miskitos and about the same distance southeast of Punta Gorda.

PUNTA GORDA
14 21N, 83 12W

Pilotage: This mainland point is low and wooded and has almost no identifying features. The Cayos Miskitos group lies about 7 1/2 miles to the east.

CAYOS MISKITOS
14 23N, 82 46W

Pilotage: This is the center of a group of cays and reefs with a diameter of about 19 miles. Approaches to this area are dangerous because of the many detached reefs and shoals and the lack of any navigational aids. Cayos Miskitos is the largest of the group, being about 2 1/2 miles in diameter. Several smaller islands and islets lie adjacent to it. This area is part of a reef that extends 19 miles north-northeast from a position about 21 miles east of Punta Gorda. Currents in this vicinity generally run north to northwest at speeds of 1/4 to 1 knot. Inside the 20-meter curve close to the coast there may be a southerly countercurrent. These currents are variable and may even reverse, especially with a norther.

Porgee Channel (14° 26'N, 82° 41'W) is a narrow and intricate route bisecting the reef from east to west about 1/2 mile northeast of the northeasternmost island.

BLUE CHANNEL
14 25N, 82 50W

Pilotage: This channel is about 1 1/2 to 3 miles wide and runs parallel to the west side of Miskito Reef. Depths range from 30 to 84 feet. The Morrison Dennis Cays and the Valpatara Reefs (14° 27'N, 82° 58'W) extend about 12 miles north.

HANNIBAL SHOALS
14 26N, 82 31W

Pilotage: This 25-foot-deep shoal marks the eastern side of the Cayos Miskitos.

AUIAPUNI REEF
14 31N, 83 05W

Pilotage: This group of shoal patches about 1 1/2 miles in extent lies about 7 1/2 miles southwest of Outer Mohegan. They are at the west extremity of the Cayos Miskitos group.

HAMKERA
14 34N, 82 58W

Pilotage: This small group of islets and reefs lies about 15 miles north-northwest of Cayos Miskitos. From Outer Mohegan, the largest of the Hamkera group, numerous detached reefs extend about 3 1/2 miles north to several rocks awash. This group is the most northwestern portion of the Cayos Miskitos.

EDINBURGH REEF
14 50N, 82 39W

Pilotage: This 4-mile-long reef lies awash about 8 1/4 miles north of the northern limits of the Cayos Miskitos group. Edinburgh Cay is about 1 1/2 miles west-northwest of the south-west end of the reef. Edinburgh Channel is a clear passage between this reef and the ones to the south.

Cock Rocks are a series of drying rocks about 1/2 mile in extent that lie about 4 1/2 miles north of Edinburgh Reef.

CABO GRACIAS A DIOS
15 00N, 83 10W

Pilotage: This is a small town on the south side of the cape, at the mouth of the Río Coco. The river is obstructed by several cays at its mouth. The depth over the bar is about 6 feet, but is subject to change because of silting. This town, which is the seat of the governor, is a timber- and banana-exporting port. Except for some radio masts, the town cannot be seen from the south because of heavy foliage.

WESTERN CARIBBEAN:
OFFSHORE ISLANDS AND BANKS

CAUTION: Our information on aids to navigation comes from official government sources. The latitudes and longitudes of these marks may not correspond to the readings from GPS receivers. Some aids have been reported as unreliable, missing, off position, or showing incorrect characteristics. No single aid to navigation, or waypoint, should be relied upon as a sole means of fixing your position.

NOTE: The chartlets in this section are not intended for navigation and are included for reference and planning purposes only. While chartlets reproduced from government sources are from the most current editions as of press time, they incorporate no corrections to navigational aids, depths, or hazards since the edition publication date.

ENTRY PROCEDURES

For information on entry procedures to the various countries that govern these islands refer to the separate section on that country. The Cayos de Albuquerque, Cayos del Este Sudeste, Isla de San Andrés, and Isla de Providencia are all under the jurisdiction of Colombia. Only San Andrés Island and Isla de Providencia have settlements with customs stations where formalities may be complicated, but you should be prepared to check in with any officials found on the smaller cays. The Swan Islands are under the jurisdiction of Honduras.

CAYOS DE ALBUQUERQUE (COLOMBIA)

12 10N, 81 51W
CAYOS DE ALBUQUERQUE LIGHT, on Cayo del Norte, 12 10.2N, 81 50.0W. Fl (2) W 20s, 72ft, 14M. Black and white banded tower.

Pilotage: These small cays are about 111 miles east-northeast of Punta Mico on the Nicaraguan coast and about 204 miles northwest of the Panama Canal. They lie on a bank about 5 miles in extent, with steep-to sides. Numerous rocky heads and drying reefs exist, particularly near the east and south sides of the bank.

Cayo del Norte and Cayo del Sur, near the east side of the bank, stand about 6 feet high and 4 feet high respectively and are reported to give a good radar return at distances of up to 12 miles. Both cays are reported to be heavily wooded with palm trees about 60 feet high. A light is shown from Cayo del Norte.

CAYOS DEL ESTE SUDESTE (COLOMBIA)

12 24N, 81 28W
CAYOS DEL ESTE SUDESTE LIGHT, Courtown Cays, Cayo Bolivar, 12 24.0N, 81 27.9W. Fl W 15s, 107ft, 17M. Metal tower. Radar reflector.

Pilotage: These cays lie on a 7-mile-long (north-south), 2-mile-wide coral bank about 24 miles northeast of Cayos de Albuquerque. A reef extends across the northern portion of the bank, and a broken reef extends along the bank's eastern side. The middle and western parts have numerous shoal patches. There is a stranded wreck about 3 1/4 miles northwest of the light on Cayo Bolivar.

Cayo del Este is on the southeast portion of the bank and is thickly wooded with palm trees. Cayo Bolivar, about 1 1/4 miles west of Cayo del Este, is about 6 feet high with several palms on it. West Cay is a small low cay about 800 yards west-northwest of Cayo del Este. Cayo Arena, a small dry sandbank about 1 1/4 miles northwest of Cayo del Este, is reported to give a good radar return at 14 miles. Fishermen's huts may be found on these cays. You can anchor, with care, on the western part of the banks.

ISLA DE SAN ANDRÉS (COLOMBIA)

12 33N, 81 43W
PUNTA SUR LIGHT, 12 28.9N, 81 43.8W. Fl W 10s, 82ft, 14M. White tower.

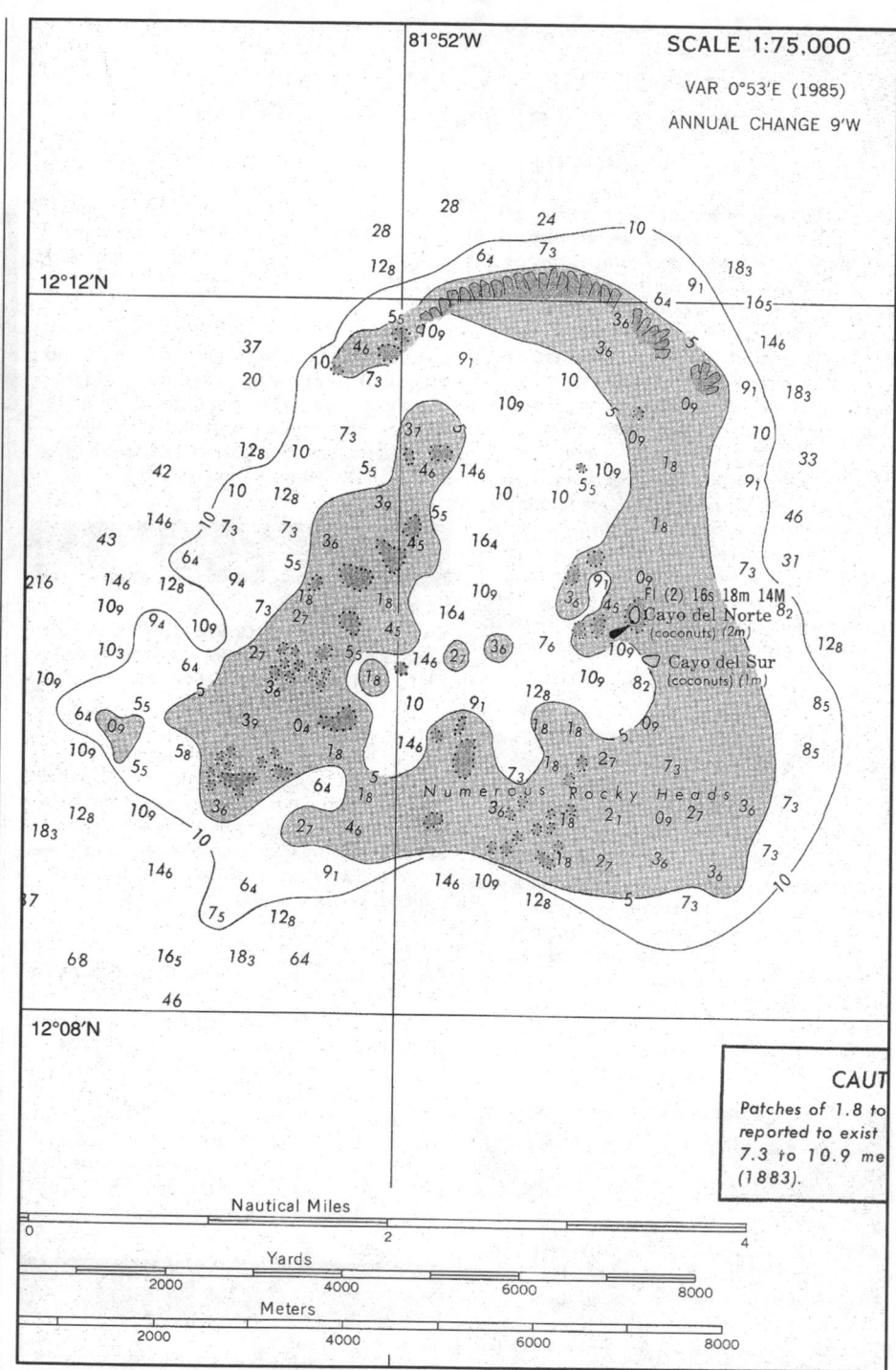

Cayos de Albuquerque, soundings in meters *(from DMA 26081, 8th ed, 5/85)*

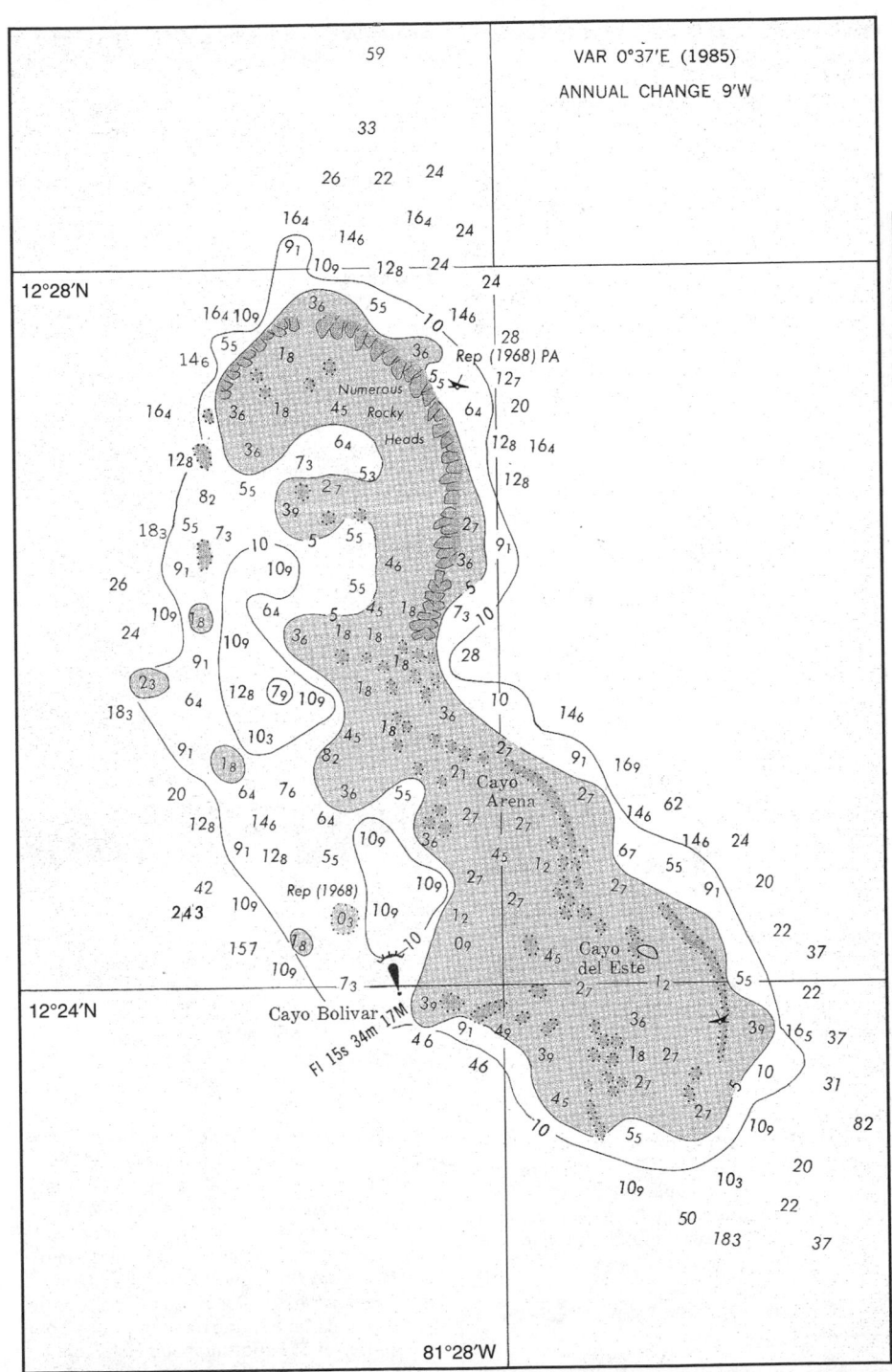

Cayos del Este Sudeste, soundings in meters *(from DMA 26081, 8th ed, 5/85)*

COVE LIGHT, 12 31.0N, 81 43.8W. Fl R 3s, 65ft, 8M. Red tower.

PUNTA EVANS LIGHT, 12 31.9N, 81 44.1W. Fl G 5s, 65ft, 8M. Green tower, white bands.

AVIATION LIGHT, 12 35.1N, 81 41.7W. Al Fl W G 10s, 16M. Radio mast.

RADIOBEACON, 12 35.1N, 81 42.3W. SPP (··· ·——· ·——·), 387kHz NON, A2A, 192M.

CAYO CORDOBA LIGHT, SE end, 12 33.1N, 81 41.3W. Fl W 5s, 72ft, 10M. White tower.

Pilotage: The island lies about 16 miles west-northwest of Cayos del Este Sudeste, or about 218 miles northwest of the Panama Canal. It is about 7 miles long (north-south) and 1 1/2 miles wide. A ridge of hills extends most of the length of the island. Three flat-topped summits rise above the ridge, but they appear as only two hills when viewed from north or south. A cliff at the north end of the ridge is distinctive. The island is reported to give a good radar return at distances to 23 miles away.

PUNTA NORTE
12 36N, 81 42W
Pilotage: Punta Norte, the northern extremity of the island, is fringed by foul ground up to 1 mile north of the point. Blowing Rocks, where the sea breaks heavily during north winds, are located about 3/4 mile north of the point.

Cayo Johnny (Cayo Sucre) is low and covered by palm trees. It stands on the the northwest end of a detached reef about 1 mile east-northeast of Punta Norte. The coastal reef extends about 1/2 mile north and east of Cayo Johnny, then about 4 miles south to a position about 1 3/4 miles east-northeast of Punta Sterthemberg. The south side of this reef is indented by a narrow, irregular channel that leads north to Bahía de San Andrés. South of Punta Sterthemberg the reef lies within 1/4 mile of the eastern coastline of the island. The west side of the island is steep-to and free of dangers.

PUNTA SUR
12 29N, 81 44W
Pilotage: This south extremity of the island is wooded. The western side of the island is mainly rocky cliffs. It is indented about 2 1/2 miles north of Punta Sur by Rada El Cove. Temporary anchorage may be found off the mouth of the cove or for small craft, inside.

BAHÍA DE SAN ANDRÉS
12 35N, 81 42W
Pilotage: This bay is formed by the reef to the east of the island and the east side of Isla de San

Andrés. A 300-meter-long wharf lies parallel to the shore in the southwest part of the bay. Proceed with caution when entering the channel and when maneuvering within the harbor—the charted depths and shoals may be inaccurate.

Port of Entry: Fees were reported to be about US$12, plus a US$35 agent fee. An agent is required.

Dockage: Several marinas are located here.

Anchorage: Yachts can anchor on either side of Cayo Santander, but should pass around the south side of the cay, as a shallow bar connects to the mainland on the north side. Yachts report anchoring off Club Nautico in the deep water east of the cay. Dinghies can be landed at the marina east of Club Nautico. Proceed cautiously in this area, as depths and shoals may not be charted accurately. The anchorage is reported to be cool and comfortable, with clean water.

Services: This is a duty-free port and a tourist center for Colombians. There are good supermarkets, fine restaurants, and very good shops.

With its good anchorage and fine shopping, Isla de San Andrés makes a good stopping point for boats making the run between Honduras and Panama.

ISLA DE PROVIDENCIA (COLOMBIA)

13 21N, 81 22W
PROVIDENCE ISLAND LIGHT, 13 19.3N, 81 23.5W. Fl (2) W 14s, 180ft, 15M. White metal tower. Visible 318°–157°. Reported at reduced intensity (August 1986).

PALMA CAY LIGHT, 13 24.0N, 81 22.1W. Fl W 10s, 82ft, 15M. White tower, 59ft.

LOW CAY LIGHT, 13 31.6N, 81 20.6W. Fl W 10s, 66ft, 14M. White tower, 59ft.

Pilotage: The island lies about 50 miles northeast of Isla de San Andrés. Isla de Providencia and Isla Santa Catalina, nearby to the north, together extend about 4 1/2 miles in a north-south direction. The mountainous center rises to three peaks of about the same elevation, with the highest being over 1,190 feet. The north extremity of Isla de Providencia is Jones Point. On a spur extending south from this point rises 551-foot-high Spit Hill. From the northwest or southeast a rocky chasm is prominent on Spit Hill.

The island is reported to give a good radar return up to 37 miles. A reef lies within about 2 miles of the east and south sides of the island and up to 8 miles north from its north end. The west side of the island is foul except for an area about 1 1/2 miles wide west of Catalina Harbor. Strong and irregular currents exist in the vicinity of Isla de Providencia.

CATALINA HARBOR

13 23N, 81 23W

Pilotage: This harbor is located on the west side of the northern part of Isla de Providencia. Morgan Head, the west extremity of the island, is a prominent 40-foot-high rock. Isla Santa Catalina forms the northern side of the harbor area. Basalt Cay and Palm Cay are located about 1/4 mile north of Isla Santa Catalina. The suggested approach from the northwest is with Morgan Head in line with Fairway Hill bearing 143°. The approach from the southwest may be marked by some buoys and runs very close to shore. Any approach should be made in good light, with the sun behind you, as there are many shoal patches and reefs.

Port of Entry: Check with the government officials in Isabel Village, located in the northeastern part of Catalina Harbor.

Anchorage: The harbor is reported to be well sheltered, with good holding in sand. Depths off of Isabel Village range from 6 to 9 feet across most of the anchorage area.

Services: This is a quiet little island settlement. There are telephones, general stores, a post office, and a government office.

LOW CAY

13 32N, 81 21W

Pilotage: This cay is located on the northwest extremity of the reef, about 8 1/2 miles north of Jones Point on Isla de Providencia. A reef that dries in places extends about 1/2 mile south. There is a light on the cay.

Anchorage: The area 1 mile south of the cay is reported to be a good anchorage. There are shoal patches in this area.

RONCADOR BANK

13 34N, 80 04W

RONCADOR BANK LIGHT, on Roncador Cay, N end of bank, 13 34.9N, 80 05.3W. Fl W 11s, 79ft, 15M. Red metal tower.

Pilotage: The bank lies about 75 miles east-northeast of Isla de Providencia. It is very steep-to and is about 7 miles long (north-

south) with a maximum width of about 3 1/2 miles. Roncador Cay, composed of sand and blocks of coral, lies on the north part of the bank and is 13 feet high. A light is shown from the cay. The bank is mostly covered by reefs, drying sandbanks, and coral heads. A conspicuous stranded wreck lies on the south end of the bank. A strong northwest current usually sets over the bank. *CAUTION: The wreck and the south end of the bank were reported (1981) to be 1 1/2 miles southeast of their charted positions.*

Anchorage: Good anchorage can be taken on the bank's west edge, but take care to avoid the coral heads, which can be easily seen.

SERRANA BANK

14 24N, 80 16W

SERRANA BANK LIGHT, Southwest Cay, 14 16.3N, 80 23.5W. Fl W 10s, 82ft, 15M. White metal tower, black band.

Pilotage: This extensive dangerous shoal area lies with its southwest end about 44 miles north-northwest of Roncador Cay. The bank is steep-to and about 20 miles long (northeast to southwest) and about 6 miles wide. All sides, except the west and southwest edges, are fringed by a nearly unbroken reef. The sea breaking over the reef on the east side of the bank is visible for several miles farther than the cays that stand on it. Mariners are advised to use extreme caution in the vicinity of Serrana Bank because of strong currents. On the west and southwest side of the bank are numerous live coral heads with less than a meter of water over them. *CAUTION: It has been reported (1989) that Serrana Bank might lie about 5 miles east of its charted position.*

SOUTHWEST CAY

14 16N, 80 24W

Pilotage: This small cay, composed of sand covered with grass and stunted brushwood, is about 32 feet high and the largest of the few cays on Serrana Bank. It is reported to be a good radar target at distances up to 10 miles. A steep-to reef extends about 9 miles northeast from the cay, but is not always visible. A ledge on the edge of the reef 6 miles northeast of Southwest Cay is about 2 feet high. A drying sandbank stands about 1 1/2 miles farther northeast.

SOUTH CAY CHANNEL

14 21N, 80 15W

Pilotage: This 1/4-mile-wide channel is located about midway along the southeast side of

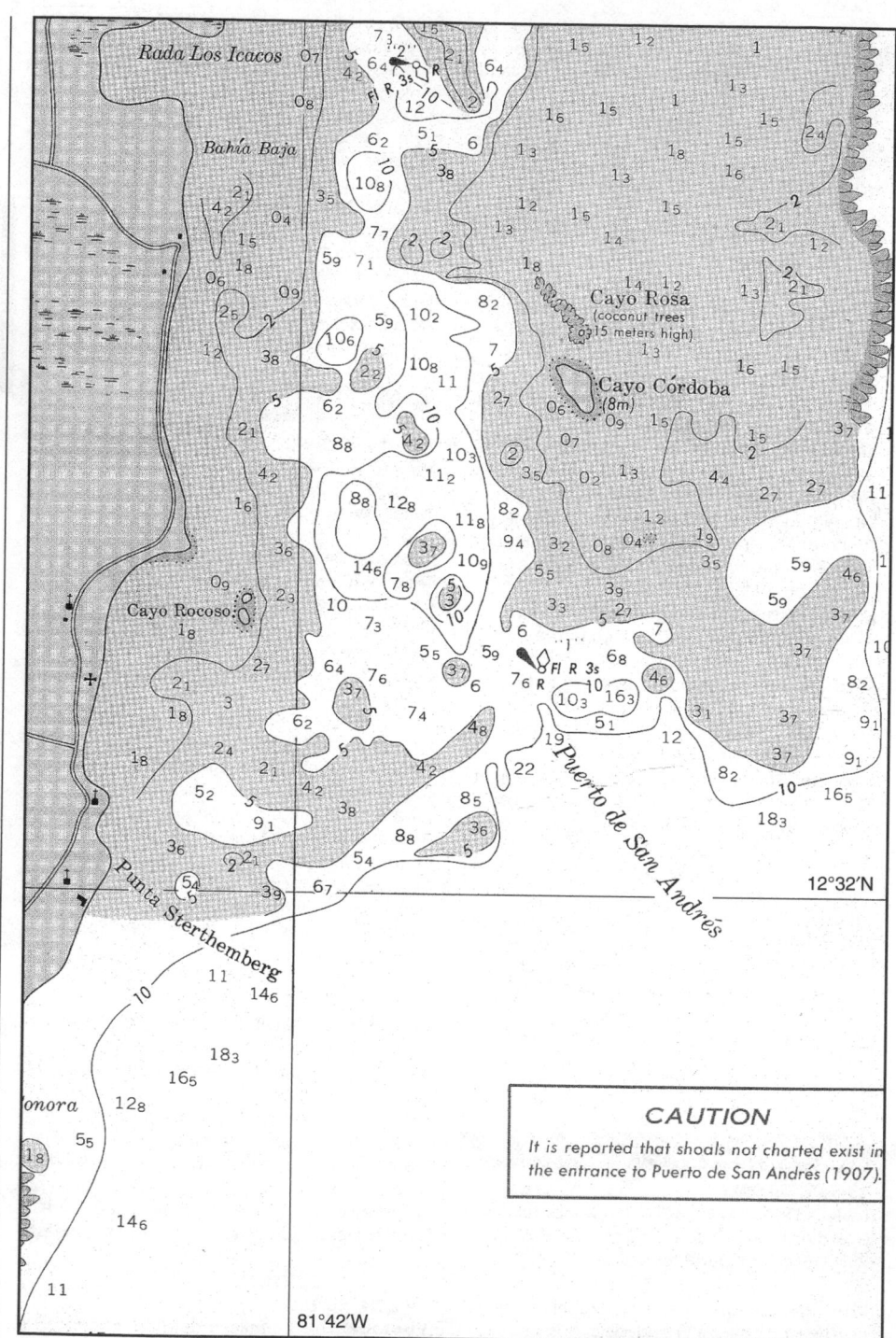

Approaches to San Andrés, soundings in meters *(from DMA 26081, 8th ed, 5/85)*

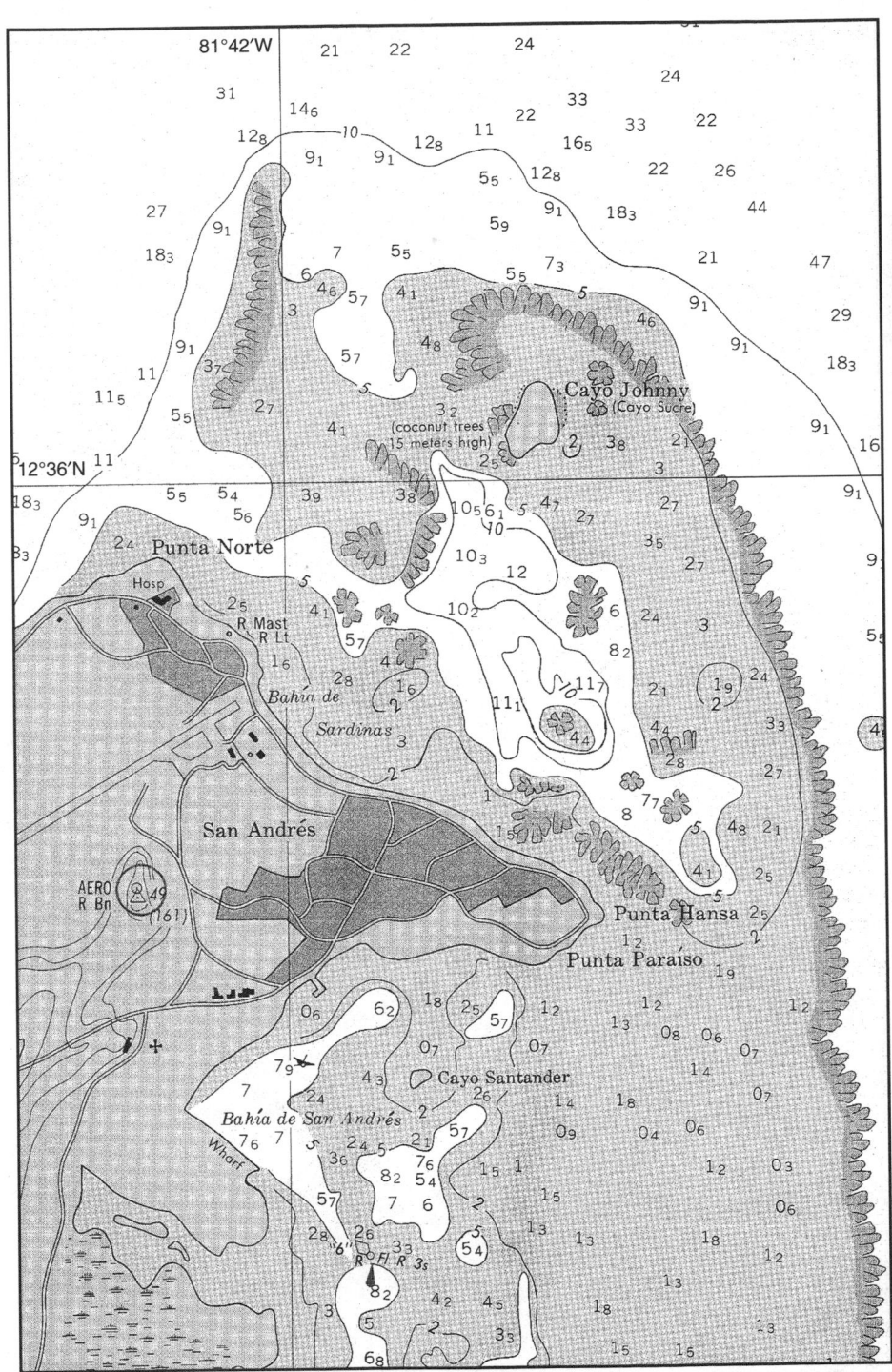

San Andrés, soundings in meters *(from DMA 26081, 8th ed, 5/85)*

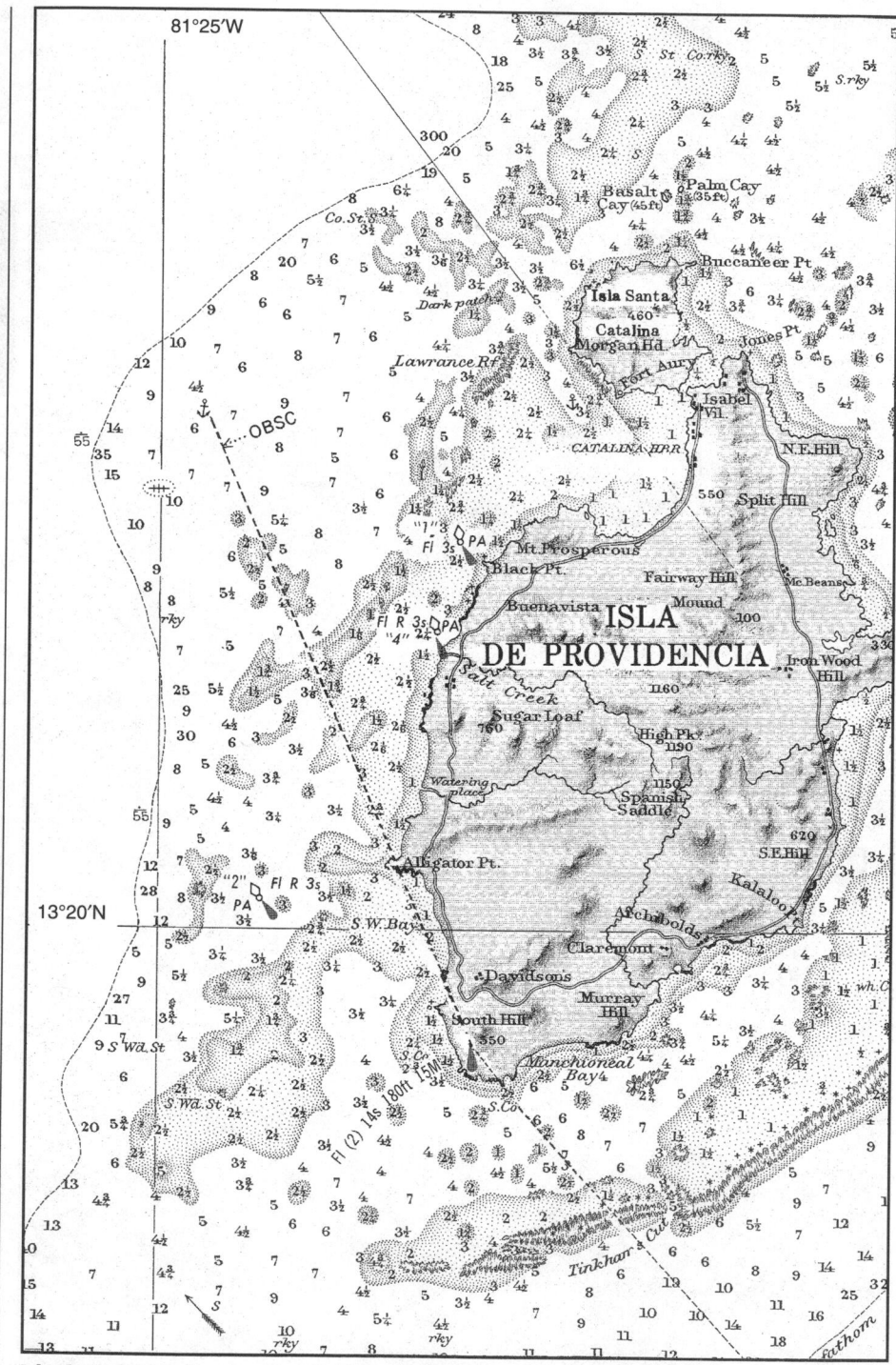

Isla de Providencia, soundings in fathoms *(from DMA 26083, 14th ed, 11/83)*

Serrana Bank. Depths in the fairway range from 24 feet to 42 feet. The currents in the channel run from 1 1/2 to 2 knots.

Anchorage: Temporary anchorage can be found with a depth of about 27 feet in a position 1 mile northeast of the channel entrance. You can anchor in depths of about 42 feet midway between the cays at the channel entrance.

EAST CAY CHANNEL
14 21N, 80 11W

Pilotage: This channel is located about 4 miles east of South Cay Channel. It is about 1/2 mile wide, with depths of 60 to 84 feet in the fairway. East Cay lies on the west side of the entrance and a spur of the reef extends about 2 miles north from it.

NORTH CAY
14 28N, 80 17W

Pilotage: This cay is about 13 1/2 miles northeast of Southwest Cay on the north end of the reef. It is small and low, with a reef extending about 3 miles from the cay to the southwest. A stranded wreck was reported (1971) to lie about 1 mile southwest of North Cay. Northwest Rocks and the border of the bank are visible by radar from distances of less than 10 miles. Turtle fishermen visit this area from March to August. On occasion, the masts of their vessels and their temporary huts may be sighted before the reefs themselves. Currents run at 1 1/2 to 2 knots.

QUITA SUENO BANK

14 15N, 81 15W
QUITA SUENO BANK LIGHT, N end, 14 29.2N, 81 08.2W. Fl W 9s, 75ft, 15M. White metal tower.

Pilotage: The bank's south end is about 39 miles north-northeast of Isla de Providencia. It is very steep-to and dangerous. A 22-mile-long reef lies along its east side. *CAUTION: Take great care when passing east of the bank as the current here sets strongly to the west.* Two wrecks stranded on the reef are reported to give a good radar return. There are reported to be other wrecks on the reef. A detached shoal with depths of 17 to 22 feet lies about 14 miles west-northwest of the north edge of the reef. A vessel struck a coral head about 14 miles southwest, and a dangerous sunken rock is charted about 19 miles south-southwest of the north edge of the reef. It seems probable that another unsurveyed reef exists west of

Quita Sueno Bank. A depth of 60 feet was reported (1964) to lie 38 miles west-northwest of Quita Sueno Light.

Anchorage: Good anchorage can be taken in about 60 feet, clear sand, and coral west of the rocky ground that lies near the middle of the reef.

SERRANILLA BANK

15 55N, 79 54W
SERRANILLA BANK LIGHT, 15 47.7N, 79 50.7W. Fl (2) W 20s, 65ft, 15M. White metal tower.

Pilotage: This bank lies about 78 miles north-northeast of Serrana Bank. It is very steep-to, with depths generally ranging between 30 feet and 120 feet. There are shoal areas in the vicinity of the cays on the east and south parts of the bank. There is no perceptible current on the bank, but the current runs west-northwest at 1/4 to 1 knot in the vicinity.

BEACON CAY
15 47N, 79 50W

Pilotage: This is the largest of the three cays on Serranilla Bank. It lies about 7 1/2 miles southwest of East Cay. It is about 8 feet high, covered by grass, and marked with a coral stone beacon on its west end. A light is shown from this cay. A 7-foot-deep shoal is located about 5 miles south of the light. There are numerous obstructions north of Beacon and East cays for a distance of about 4 1/2 miles.

Anchorage: Good anchorage is reported in depths of 36 feet about 1 mile northwest of Beacon Cay. Take care to avoid the coral heads on the bank.

WEST BREAKER
15 48N, 79 59W

Pilotage: This dangerous breaking ledge about 2 feet high lies almost 8 miles west of Beacon Cay and is the westernmost danger on the bank.

EAST CAY
15 52N, 79 44W

Pilotage: This is the easternmost above-water feature on Serranilla Bank. It is small, covered by bushes, and about 7 feet high. It lies about 3 miles west of the east edge of the bank. Foul ground extends about 2 1/2 miles north and northeast from the cay. Three miles northeast of East Cay lies Northeast Breaker, a coral ledge with a rock awash on its south side.

BAJO NUEVO (HONDURAS)

15 53N, 78 33W (East End)
BAJO NUEVO LIGHT, located on Low Cay, 15 51.2N, 78 38.0W. Fl (2) W 15s, 69ft, 15M. White tower, black stripes.

Pilotage: This bank has not been well surveyed. It has been reported (1967) to extend west to about 15° 48'N, 78° 55'W. Its southwest end is not well defined, but the northwest side of the bank is reported to be clear of known dangers. Depths of 12 feet are reported to extend up to 10 miles west of Bajo Nuevo. Seals gather on the reefs here and are hunted in March and April.

East Reef and West Reef, separated by a 1/2-mile-wide opening, extend along the southeast side of the bank. They are over 2 1/2 miles wide and steep-to on the southeast and north sides. Sand accumulates on the reefs, forming low ridges, sometimes barely awash. A stranded wreck at the northeast end of East Reef is reported to be visible on radar. Another stranded wreck lies on the west end of West Reef. Currents in the vicinity of the bank set west and southwest at speeds of up to 2 knots.

LOW CAY
15 52N, 78 39W
Pilotage: This cay, which lies at the north end of West Reef, is about 5 feet high and barren. It is composed of broken coral, driftwood, and sand.
Anchorage: In moderate weather exposed anchorage can be taken in depths of 42 to 48 feet. This sand and coral bottom can be found about 1 1/2 miles west of Low Cay. Approach the anchorage from the west, taking care to avoid coral heads.

ROSALIND BANK

16 26N, 80 31W
Pilotage: The south extremity of the bank is located about 167 miles east-northeast of Cabo Gracias a Dios. As defined by the 200-meter-depth curve, the bank is about 63 miles long and 35 miles wide. General depths range from 60 feet to 121 feet over coarse sand and coral. The shallowest spots are about 35 feet deep.

The current generally sets northwest at a velocity of 1 1/2 knots over the bank. On striking the ledge near the southeast edge, the current causes a race that has the appearance of breakers.

An extensive bank, about 41 miles long and 10 miles wide, lies about 11 miles west of Rosalind Bank. Depths range from 24 feet to 216 feet. The shallowest detached patches are found along the east edge of the bank. A detached 36-foot-patch lies on the north part of the bank.

THUNDER KNOLL

16 27N, 81 20W
Pilotage: This bank is about 11 miles in extent and composed of coral sand. It lies about 4 miles west of the extensive bank mentioned in the section on Rosalind Bank. Depths range from 79 feet to 230 feet. Two detached shoals with depths of 42 feet to 51 feet and 115 feet to 121 feet lie between 4 1/2 and 8 1/2 miles west of Thunder Knoll. A detached 36-foot patch was reported to lie about 4 miles southwest of the southwest part of Thunder Knoll.

SWAN ISLANDS (HONDURAS)

17 25N, 83 56W
ISLAS DE EL CISNE, aviation light, near the W end of the largest island, 17 24.5N, 83 56.5W. Fl W 5s, 70ft, 28M. 3 Fl R 1.5s (vertical) on tower 1 mile E. Occasional.

Pilotage: The Swan Islands (Islas Santanilla) are located about 150 miles north-northwest of Cabo Gracias a Dios. There are two small islands lying close together near the west part of a narrow bank about 18 miles long. The east island is 1 1/2 miles long and 60 feet high and has a bold rocky shore. The island is densely covered by trees and bushes. The west island is flat, about 1 3/4 miles long, and covered by trees about 60 feet high. A Honduran navy post and a cattle farm exist on the southwest end of the west island. The passage separating the islands is foul. The islands have been reported to be good radar targets at distances up to 25 miles. The light with an aero light stands on the northwest side of the west island.
Anchorage: When the wind is in the northeast or east, anchor off the sandy bay at the west end of the west island. During north winds anchor south of the west end of the island. During south and southwest gales

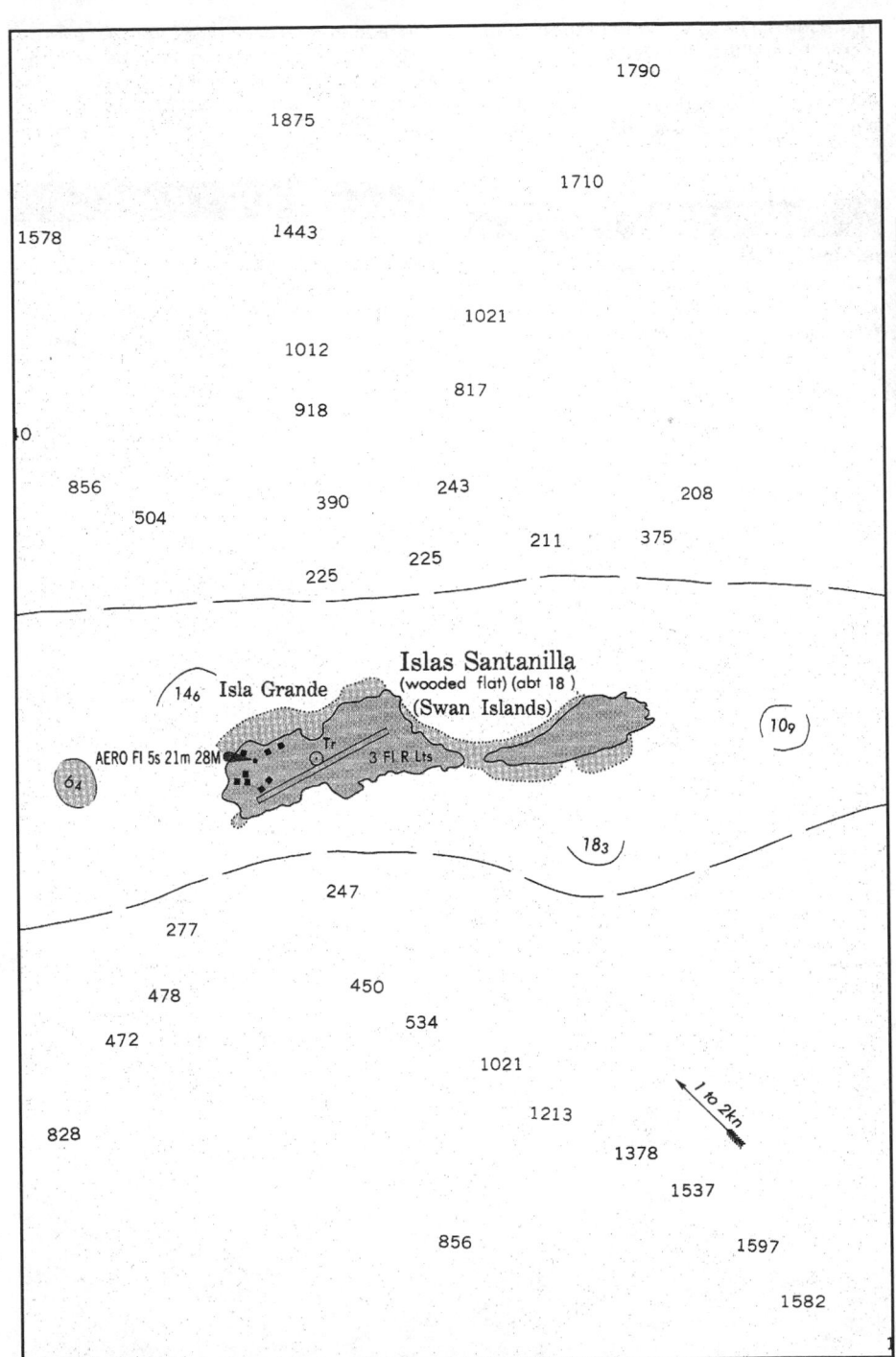

Swan Islands, soundings in meters *(from DMA 28150, 2nd ed, 4/89)*

COAST PILOT

anchorage can be taken north of the islands, nearer the east than the west end.

This island was formerly a U.S. weather station and has been handed over to Honduras to oversee.

MISTERIOSA BANK

18 51N, 83 50W

Pilotage: This bank is about 24 miles long and from 2 to 7 miles wide. It is centered about 87 miles north of the Swan Islands. Depths over

the reddish coral bank range from 42 feet to 161 feet. There are other shallow banks in the vicinity. A detached 24-foot patch was reported to lie about 6 miles east of the east side of Rosario Bank.

ROSARIO BANK

18 30N, 84 04W

Pilotage: This bank is about 10 miles in extent and lies about 62 miles north of the Swan Islands. Depths range from 60 feet to 210 feet. There are other shallow banks in the vicinity.

HONDURAS

CAUTION: Our information on aids to navigation comes from official government sources. The latitudes and longitudes of these marks may not correspond to the readings from GPS receivers. Some aids have been reported as unreliable, missing, off position, or showing incorrect characteristics. No single aid to navigation, or waypoint, should be relied upon as a sole means of fixing your position.

NOTE: The chartlets in this section are <u>not</u> <u>intended for navigation</u> and are included for reference and planning purposes only. While chartlets reproduced from government sources are from the most current editions as of press time, they incorporate <u>no corrections</u> to navigational aids, depths, or hazards since the edition publication date.

ENTRY PROCEDURES

Ports of Entry in the Bay Islands include Guanaja and Coxen's Hole on Roatán. On the mainland, you may clear at Puerto Castilla, La Ceiba, and Puerto Cortés. See *Reed's Nautical Companion* for an illustration of the country flag.

You should have passports, your clearance from the last port of call, ship's papers, and the proper courtesy flag. Fly the yellow Q flag upon arrival. Obtain a *zarpe*, or cruising permit, from officials, and be sure to list any place you are planning to visit. You will have to clear in and out of each port as you cruise through Honduras.

Visas are usually issued for stays of 90 days, with renewals possible. For the latest information on entry requirements contact the Honduran Consulate, 1612 K Street NW, Suite 310, Washington, DC, 20006 (202-223-0185).

The border areas between Nicaragua or El Salvador and Honduras are considered quite dangerous and should be avoided. There are mine fields in some of these areas. U.S. citizens should check with the U.S. Embassy in Tegucigalpa (504-36-93-20, 38-51-14, or fax,

36-90-37) if you are planning an overland trip across these borders.

The international telephone country code for Honduras is 504; local numbers have six digits. The currency is the lempira, which in mid-summer 1994 was trading at about 8.6 lempiras to 1 US dollar. The main language is Spanish, but English is widely spoken in the Bay Islands area.

CABO GRACIÁS A DIOS

15 00N, 83 09W
Pilotage: This point marks the border between Nicaragua and Honduras. It is low, swampy, and covered with trees that attain a height of about 79 feet. The 151-foot-high radio masts standing close west of the disused lighthouse are the best landmarks during the day.

CAUTION: The cape was reported in 1969 and 1973 to lie about 2 miles east of its charted position. Less depths than charted have been reported to lie 4 miles southeast and from 4 to 10 miles east of the cape. Vessels should give the cape a berth of at least 10 miles and in thick weather should keep in depths of over 60 feet.

ARRECIFE DE LA MEDIA LUNA (HALF MOON REEF)
15 13N, 82 38W
Pilotage: The north extremity of this group of reefs and cays is about 34 miles east-northeast of Cabo Graciás a Dios. This area extends about 20 miles on the north-south axis and about 11 miles on the east-west, as defined by the 20-meter curve. The southern extremity is marked by Cock Rocks. Logwood Cay (Cayo Modera) stands on the west side of the bank.

Cayo Media Luna (Half Moon Cay) lies about 2 1/2 miles south of Logwood Cay, and a crescent shaped reef extends about 1/2 mile east, then 3/4 mile north from it.

Bobel Cay stands about 4 miles southsoutheast of Cayo Media Luna. Two cays stand close together between 6 1/4 and 7 miles east-southeast of Cayo Media Luna. Several rocky heads lie in the vicinity of these cays.

Savanna Cut is a narrow passage with depths of 36 to 60 feet. It lies between Arrecife de Media Luna and Savanna Reefs (15° 10′N, 82° 25′W), which are located about 5 miles to the east.

Arrecife Alagardo (Alargate Reefs) are the easternmost visible danger on the Miskito bank. They lie about 5 miles east of the Savanna Reefs, where they are marked by heavy breakers. During periods of fresh northeast winds there is often a strong set toward the east side of the reef.

NOTE: It has been reported that Arrecife Alagardo lies 2 miles east of its charted position.

BANCO DEL CABO
(MAIN CAPE SHOAL)
15 16N, 82 57W
Pilotage: This nearly awash shoal lies about 17 miles northeast of Cabo Gracías a Dios. It is about 4 miles long. The sea seldom breaks over it, but it may be spotted by the discoloration of the water in the area.

Main Cape Channel is the passage between Banco del Cabo and Arrecife de La Media Luna. It is clear of known dangers and has depths ranging from 60 feet to 95 feet.

GORDA BANK
15 36N, 82 13W
Pilotage: This bank, with depths of less than 66 feet, extends for about 52 miles northwest of a position about 18 miles east-northeast of the northeast extremity of Arrecife Alagardo. Shallower depths than those charted may exist on the bank. The bottom is clearly visible, and on the north side there are a number of patches of flat coral covered with dark weed.

CAYO GORDA
15 52N, 82 24W
Pilotage: This barren cay stands on the north edge of Gorda Bank. It is about 12 feet high and is composed of sand, broken coral, and large stones. A reef extends about 1 3/4 miles northwest from it, but its east and south sides are steep-to.

CAUTION: An obstruction was reported to lie about 4 1/2 miles southwest of Cayo Gorda.

Farral Rock, located 5 miles east of Cayo Gorda, breaks in heavy weather and can be identified by its dark appearance, in contrast to the white sandy bank on which it lies. The two parts of the stranded wreck near the rock were reported to be good radar targets up to 10 miles distant.

BANCOS DEL CABO FALSO
(FALSE CAPE BANK)
15 32N, 83 03W
Pilotage: This is a dangerous, steep-to, breaking bank, lying about 32 miles north-northeast of Cabo Gracías a Dios.

CAYOS COCOROCUMA
15 43N, 83 00W
Pilotage: This reef lies about 44 miles north-northeast of Cabo Gracías a Dios. It is about 5 miles long, but a detached coral patch, on which the sea breaks, lies about 3/4 mile west of its north end. A group of seven small cays, not over 2 feet high and 1 mile in extent, lie on the south end of the reef. The southernmost, and largest, cay, is covered with bushes and some coconut trees on its east end. Another cay, about 1 mile to the north, has a square clump of brushwood about 15 feet high on it. This clump resembles an isolated rock when seen from a distance.

CAYOS PICHONES
(PIGEON CAYS)
15 45N, 82 56W
Pilotage: These two cays lie 3 miles east of Cayos Cocorocuma. The westernmost is a small islet at the south end of a dangerous, steep-to, half-moon-shaped reef. The reef is about 3/4 mile in extent, and the sea breaks heavily here in stormy weather. A steep-to reef lies about 2 3/4 miles southeast of this islet.

BANCO VIVORILLO (VIVARIO BANK)
15 54N, 83 22W
Pilotage: This 10-mile-long coral bank lies with its northwest extremity about 59 miles north of Cabo Gracías a Dios. Depths over the bank range from about 9 feet to 33 feet.

CAYOS VIVORILLO
(VIVARIO CAYS)
15 50N, 83 18W
CAYOS VIVORILLO LIGHT, 15 50.0N, 83 17.7W. Fl W 10s, 13M.

Pilotage: These bush- and tree-covered cays lie on a coral reef at the southeast end of Banco

Vivorillo. A continuous line of breakers front the steep-to east side of the reef. Practically all of this reef is usually dry or awash.

CAYOS BECERRO

15 55N, 83 16W
Pilotage: This group of eight small cays lie about 5 1/2 miles northeast of Cayos Vivorillo. They lie on a coral ledge about 3 1/2 miles long by 1 mile wide. The sea always breaks along the east and north sides of the reef.

Grand Becerro, the largest cay, consists of two parts. It stands near the south part of the ledge and is marked by mangroves and a conspicuous palm tree on its west side.

El Becerro, a rock over which the sea usually breaks, stands 1 1/4 miles southeast of Grand Becerro. It is surrounded by a coral reef with depths of 12 to 30 feet. Rocky pinnacles, with depths of about 30 feet, lie about 5 1/2 miles north-northeast of El Becerro.

Hannibal Banks consists of two small shoals about 3/4 mile apart, lying in the southeast part of the passage between Cayos Vivorillo and Cayos Becerro. The north shoal has a least depth of 34 feet and the south shoal a least depth of 42 feet.

CAYOS CARATASCA

16 02N, 83 20W
Pilotage: This group of seven small cays lies about in the middle of a shoal bank located about 9 miles northwest of Cayos Becerro. The southernmost cay has some vegetation, but the others are barren.

CAYOS CAJONES (HOBBIES)

16 06N, 83 13W
Pilotage: This steep-to reef, about 13 miles long in an east-west direction, lies centered about 11 miles north of El Becerro. The narrow west part nearly always dries, but it does not always break. A small cay with bushes and coconut trees stands about 3 miles west of the east end of the reef. A 23-foot patch is reported (1970) to lie about 5 1/2 miles northwest of the middle part of Cayos Cajones. Another 30-foot patch lies about 6 miles south of the middle of the reef.

CAUTION: Exercise great caution when approaching this reef. A vessel approaching from the north at night or in hazy weather should not come within depths of less than 180 feet, which lie up to 11 miles north of the reef. Depths of 121 feet will be found about 4 miles off. Within that depth the bottom is coral and sand, and outside it is mud.

During periods of strong northeast winds there is often a strong current set toward the north side of Cayos Cajones, which adds considerably to their danger.

CABO FALSO

15 12N, 83 20W
CABO FALSO LIGHT, 15 15.2N, 83 23.7W. Fl W 5s, 75ft, 19M.

Pilotage: This low point is about 21 1/2 miles northwest of Cabo Graciás a Dios. It is backed by several isolated trees and brushwood. It should be approached with caution, as a hard sandbank, with depths of less than 18 feet, lies about 3 miles to its northeast. The sea usually breaks over this bank, and the inner part dries in places. The 36-foot-line lies about 6 1/2 miles northeast of the cape.

CAUTION: Cabo Falso has been reported to lie about 3 miles west of its charted position. The area in the vicinity of the cape has not been thoroughly examined, and passing vessels should give it a wide berth.

The Río Cruta lies about 3 1/2 miles northwest of Cabo Falso. Its shallow mouth is marked by high trees, which have the appearance of a bluff. When viewed from the west, they may be mistaken for Cabo Falso. In 1973 the mouth of the river was easily identified by radar. A light is shown from the mouth of the river.

PUNTA PATUCA

15 49N, 84 17W
PUNTA PATUCA LIGHT, 15 49.0N, 84 18.2W. Fl W 10s, 73ft, 19M.

Pilotage: This low, but prominent, point lies about 64 miles northwest of Río Cruta. The coast presents the same generally low aspect as the coast southeast of Río Cruta.

The southern entrance to the Laguna Caratasca lies about 27 miles west-northwest of the Río

Cruta and can be identified by a large group of 89-foot-high trees on either side. This large freshwater lagoon parallels the coast for about 35 miles and is separated from the sea by a low, narrow, thinly wooded ridge of sand. In 1973, the prominent point on the east side of the entrance was reported to be a good radar target.

Estero Tabacunta, the west outlet for the Laguna Caratasca, lies about 28 miles northwest of the more southerly entrance. Both entrances are fronted by shallow bars, but the latter entrance has a channel with a depth of about 6 feet. Low white sand cliffs serve to identify the coast in the vicinity of Estero Tabacunta.

Río Patuca lies about 9 miles north-northwest of Estero Tabacunta. Punta Patuca marks the west entrance to the 150-mile-long river, one of the longest in Honduras. The mouth is about 225 yards wide, but is difficult to make out unless a vessel is close-in. A light stands at the mouth. The controlling depth over the bar is about 6 feet during the dry season and from 8 to 10 feet in the wet season. The outgoing current, even in the dry season, attains a rate of 1 1/2 knots. The only landmarks are a series of light-colored bluffs, which stand southeast of the river mouth, and a low rounded hill in the which the land to the east seems to end. The east entrance point of the river is low and sandy.

LAGUNA DE BRUS

Pilotage: The entrance to this lagoon is at its western end, which is about 22 miles west of Punta Patuca. The entrance is marked on its west side by a clump of trees, higher than those elsewhere in the vicinity. This entrance is hard to spot from seaward. The bar across the entrance has depths of 6 to 7 feet in the dry season and is usually fronted by heavy breakers. There are depths of 10 to 11 feet within the lagoon, but there are many shoals and shallow areas.

RÍO SICO

Pilotage: The river entrance is about 16 miles west-northwest of the entrance to the Laguna de Brus, or about 38 miles from Punta Patuca. This is about where 3,700-foot-high Cerro Payas (15° 45'N, 84° 56'W) rises abruptly from the low land along the coast. This mountain forms the eastern end of the Sierras La Cruz, an irregular

mountain chain. The peak is frequently obscured by clouds, but 2,050-foot-high Pico Panoche, about 5 miles to the north, is usually visible. A vessel proceeding west will sight these peaks soon after passing Punta Patuca.

The bar at the river entrance has a least depth of about 5 feet in the dry season and as much as 9 feet in the rainy season. It is passable by boats only in moderate weather.

The land rises abruptly on both sides of the river, and the mountains approach fairly close to the coast. The flat, swampy part of Honduras ends here, and the land to the west is traversed by numerous ridges that reach the coast in places.

CABO CAMARÓN

16 00N, 85 00W
CABO CAMARÓN LIGHT, 15 59.2N, 85 01.9W. Fl W 5s, 73ft, 19M.

Pilotage: This point is located about 5 miles west-northwest of the Río Sico. It is low, rounded, and topped by trees 79 feet high. The land is flat for some distance inland. A light is shown from the cape.

The coast between Cabo Camarón and the Río Aquan, 42 miles to the west, is indented by a bight extending about 6 miles to the south. The east part of the bight is low and sandy, and the west part is a low, thinly wooded beach topped by some sand hills 40 to 60 feet high.

From Cabo Camarón the coast trends about 15 miles west-southwest to Piedracito, a small distinctive rocky bluff. Cabeza Piedra Grande (15° 54'N, 85° 29'W), a rocky bluff about 400 feet high, is located a further 11 miles to the west. Cerro Sangrelaya (15° 52'N, 85° 09'W) rises to 6,150 feet in a position about 5 miles southeast of Piedracito. Seven miles south of the same point, a conical peak rises to 3,149 feet. A saddle-shaped summit stands about 5 miles southwest of the latter peak.

Iriona is a small settlement located 8 miles southwest of Cabo Camarón. This is the seat of government for the territory east to the Nicaraguan border.

A lower ridge of mountains rises south of Iriona and extends west to a position close south of Cabeza Piedra Grande. From a position about midway between Cabo Camarón and Piedracito, as far west as Cabeza Piedra Grande, the lower slopes of the mountains nearly reach the coast.

RÍO AQUAN

Pilotage: This river enters the sea via two mouths located about 2 1/2 miles apart. The river extends 120 miles inland. The east mouth is located 16 miles west-northwest of Cabeza Piedra Grande and is shallow. The east side of this entrance forms a distinctive point; about 3 miles to its southeast is a 79-foot-high hill close to the coast. The hill appears round when seen from the east or west, but from the north its west end appears as a flattened summit and its east end as a sugarloaf hill. The two ends are separated by a chasm.

The settlement of Santa Rosa de Aquan stands on the east bank of the river, about 1 mile within the east entrance.

Vessels bound for the Río Aquan should call at Trujillo for clearance in entering and departing.

PUNTA CAXINAS

16 02N, 86 01W
PUNTA CAXINAS LIGHT, 16 01.5N, 86 00.6W. Fl W 7s, 75ft, 19M.

Pilotage: This point (referred to in some sources as Punta Castilla) is located at the west extremity of Cabo de Honduras, a narrow, 5-mile-long neck of low land some 24 miles south of Isla de Guanaja in the Bay Islands. The cape is bordered by a scantily wooded beach with some scattered 40- to 60-foot sand hills. A light is shown from here.

Depths are about 60 feet, 3 miles offshore and less than 240 feet up to 17 miles out. Within 17 miles of Cabo de Honduras the depths become irregular, with shoals of between 30 and 60 feet to the northeast, 57 feet to the north, and 30 to 56 feet to the northwest.

The mountain range south of Cabeza Piedra Grande extends west for about 14 miles and then appears to terminate rather abruptly in a saddle-shaped summit 2,499 feet high. This summit is about 8 miles south of the mouth of the Río Aquan. A much smaller sugarloaf peak

stands west of the summit. A wide valley lies between this peak and Montanas de Trujillo.

ISLA DE LA BAHÍA (THE BAY ISLANDS)

Pilotage: This group of islands fronts the coast for a distance of about 75 miles in a west-southwest direction from a position about 30 miles north-northeast of Punta Caxinas. The group consists of Isla Guanaja, Isla Roatán, Isla Utila, and three small islands.
Currents: The currents in and around the islands are extremely uncertain, particularly during the summer. The equatorial current north of the islands sets west, but when the northers have ceased, its surface influence is felt on the islands. The countercurrent generally sets in the opposite direction south of the islands.

Currents in the area may be greatly altered, or even reversed, by winds and tides. The range of the tropic tide at Isla Roatán is greater than anywhere else in the area. The current sets west and north with a rising tide and south and east with a falling tide. A counterclockwise eddy is observed north of Isla Utila.
Winds: The prevailing winds on the sheltered south sides of the islands are from the southeast and at times attain a maximum velocity of 45 knots. During the winter months the winds may come from any direction.

ISLA DE GUANAJA (BONACCA ISLAND)

16 28N, 85 54W
BLACK ROCK POINT LIGHT, 16 29.9N, 85 49.0W. Fl W 10s, 200ft, 25M.
POND CAY LIGHT, Isla de Guanaja, 16 26.3N, 85 52.8W. Q G, 2M. Gray concrete column.

Pilotage: This easternmost island of the Bay Islands group is about 8 1/4 miles long and 2 1/2 miles wide at its widest part. The island is composed of densely wooded hills that rise to a height of 1,200 feet near its center. The northeast extremity is a bold peninsula terminating in 102-foot-high East Cliff, which is ochre in color. Ochre Bluff at the southwest end of the island is of the same height and color. Several anchorages are available within the coastal reefs, especially on the southeast side of the island. Numerous reefs, shoals, and small cays fringe the island, especially on its southeast side.

GUANAJA SETTLEMENT

16 26N, 85 54W

Pilotage: This small town is located on Sheen Cays, about 1/4 mile off the southeast side of the island. Some of the buildings stand on piles around the cays. The approach depths are reported to be around 30 feet, with depths of 9 to 18 feet alongside the piers. You should be able to contact the port captain by VHF radio.

Port of Entry

Anchorage: Anchor west of the main cay, in depths of 8 to 30 feet.

Services: Fuel, water, groceries, and basic supplies should be available. There are restaurants, a post office, and communication facilities.

ISLA DE ROATÁN

16 25N, 86 23W

Pilotage: The largest island of the Bay Islands group, Roatán lies about 15 miles west of Isla Guanaja and is about 28 miles long and 2 miles wide. Isla Santa Elena, Isla Morat, and Isla Barbareta stand close off its east end.

The island is densely wooded and hilly, with general elevations rising 298 to 499 feet. A 735-foot-high peak rises about 7 miles from the east end, and an 800-foot-high peak rises about 6 miles from the west end.

Punta Oueste is the southwest extremity of the island. A light is shown from the point. A conspicuous white church with a red roof and a square bell tower stands about 2 miles east-northeast of Punta Oueste.

The south shore of the island is indented with bays and coves suitable for small craft. The west and southwest parts of the island are steep-to, but elsewhere the island is fringed by a steep-to reef that extends up to about 1 mile offshore. Isla Barbareta, off the east end, is fronted by a reef that lies up to about 2 miles off its east and south sides.

By keeping the west extremity of Isla de Roatán bearing 272°, a vessel will pass south of all off-lying dangers when approaching from the east.

PUERTO REAL

16 25N, 86 19W

Pilotage: This harbor is located on the south side of the island, near the eastern end. Shelter is provided from the south by George Reef, George Cay, and Long Reef. George Reef extends about 1 mile west from the east side of the harbor entrance. George Cay, low and wooded with the ruins of a fort at its west end, stands about 250 yards from the west end of the reef. Long reef is separated from George Reef by a channel 200 yards wide. Long Reef is a nearly dry ledge, 3/4 mile long, that protects the west side of the harbor. Enter the harbor via the channel between the reefs, which has reported depths of 18 to 27 feet. The reefs are steep-to and easily seen. A good landmark is the 735-foot-peak that stands about 3/4 mile west of the harbor.

Anchorage: Anchor in the eastern part of the protected water north of the reefs.

OAK RIDGE HARBOR

Pilotage: This anchorage is located about 4 miles west of Puerto Real. It is entered through a narrow channel with a least depth of 20 feet, which leads north to the town. Depths off town are about 20 feet. A conspicuous stranded wreck lies close west of the entrance to the channel and is a good mark in the approach. A pier extends from the shore of the harbor.

Services: Fuel and water should be available at the fish docks.

FRENCH HARBOUR

FRENCH HARBOUR LIGHT, 16 23.5N, 86 23.0W. Q W, 15M. Mast.

Pilotage: This harbor is about 10 miles west of Puerto Real. The town is almost surrounded by water, as extensive lagoons back it.

Dockage: Contact the French Harbour Yacht Club.

Anchorage: Anchor off the French Harbour Yacht Club in the lagoon east of town.

Services: Fuel, water, ice, groceries and general supplies are available.

COXEN HOLE

16 18N, 86 35W

COXEN HOLE REEF LIGHT, SW extremity of reef at entrance, 16 18.6N, 86 32.3W. F W, 25ft. Reported extinguished 1989.

Pilotage: This is the principal town on the island and the seat of government for the Bay Islands. It occupies the east part of a bight on the south shore of the island, about 3 3/4 miles east-northeast of Punta Oueste. Its west side is bordered by dark 20-foot-high cliffs and its east and south sides by the reef upon which Coxen Cay stands. Carib Point, about in the middle of the bight, has high coconut trees on it. Hendricks Hill rises to 298 feet about 1/2 mile north of the

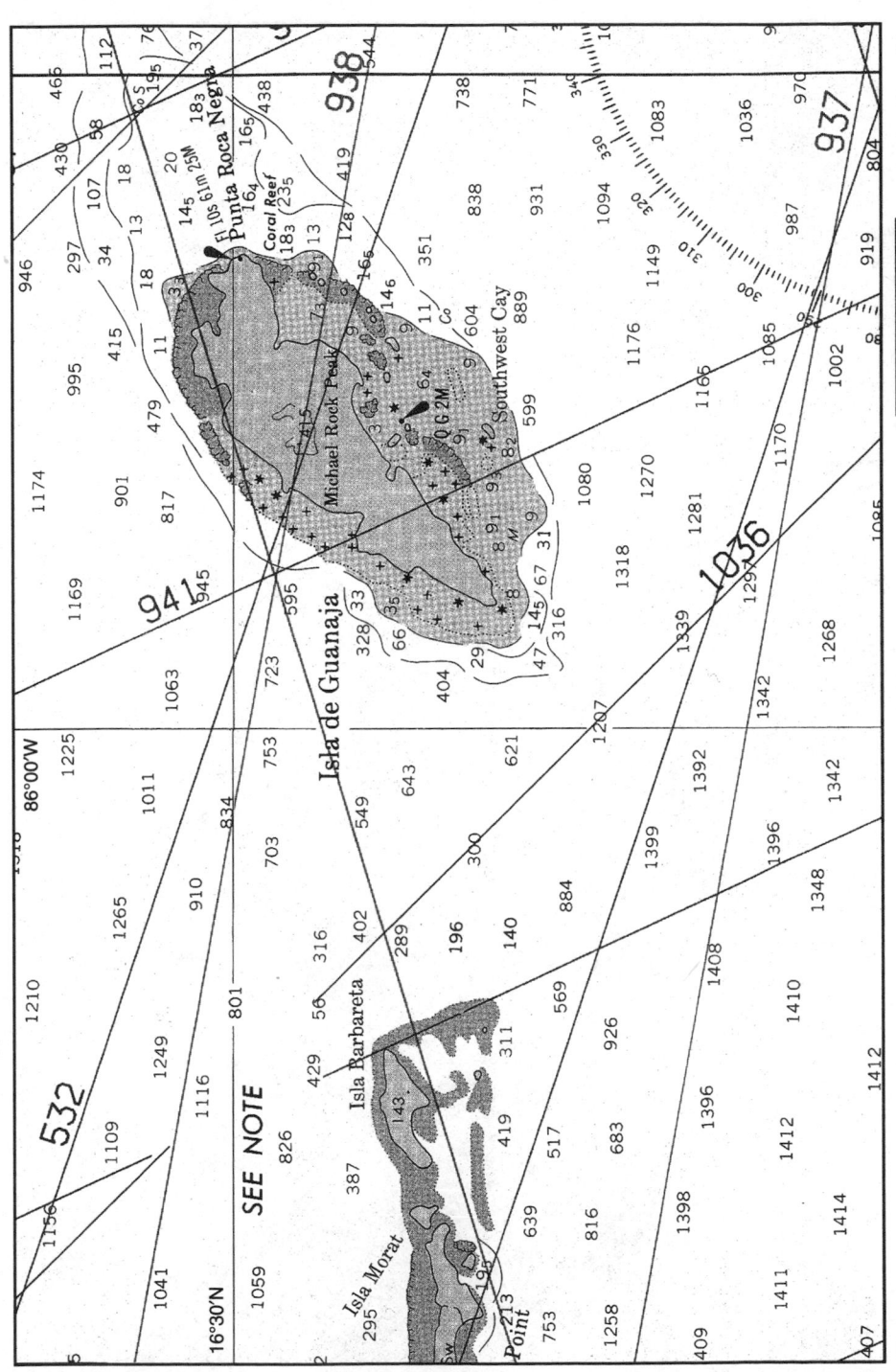

Isla de Guanaja, soundings in meters *(from DMA 28150, 2nd ed, 4/89)*

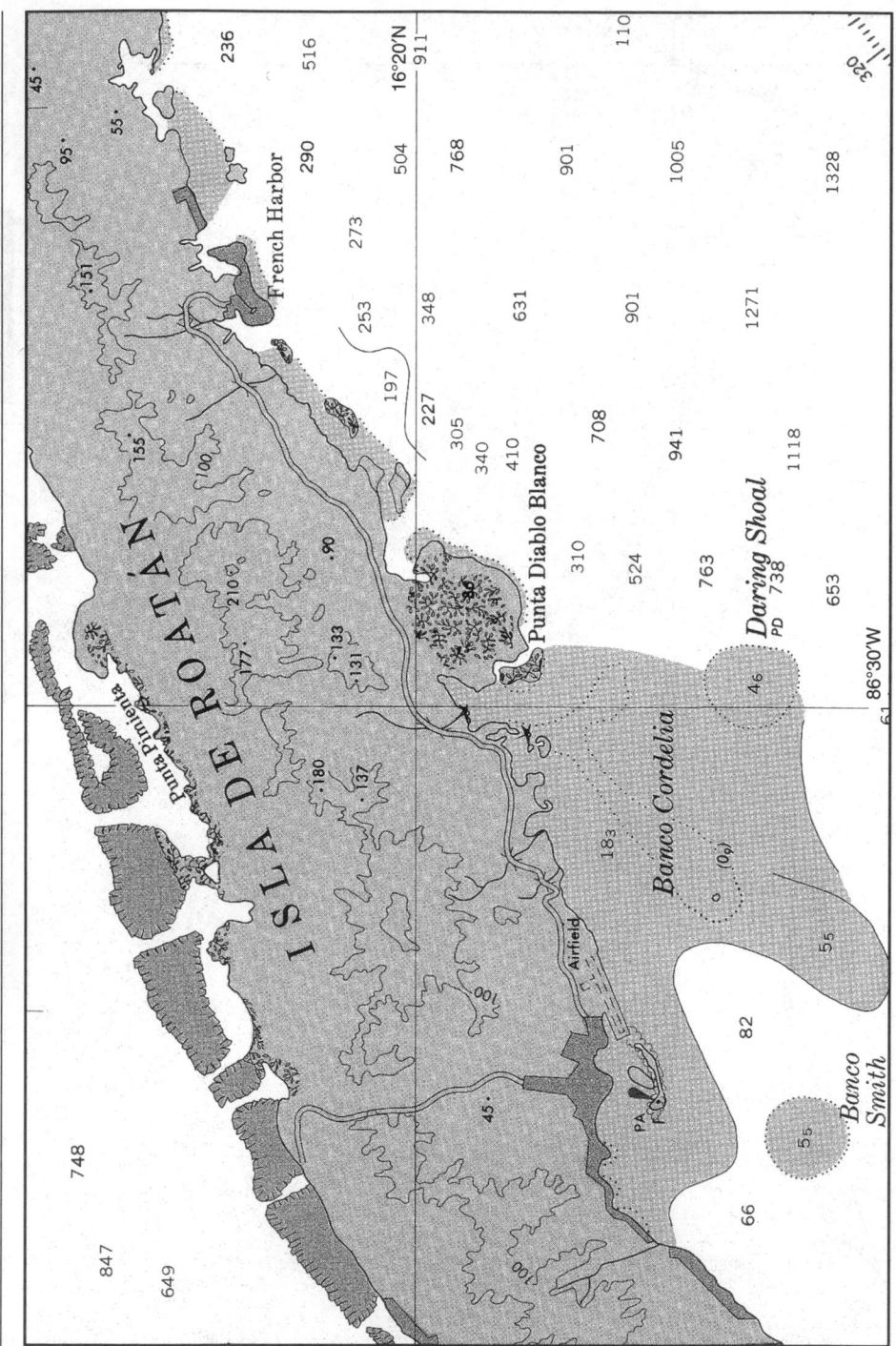

French Harbour and Coxen Hole, soundings in meters *(from DMA 28154, 1st ed, 3/88)*

COAST PILOT

point. An 899-foot-peak rises about 3/4 mile northeast of Hendricks Hill. When Hendricks Hill bears 020° a vessel will be in the fairway of the west channel and may steer in on this bearing until abeam of Coxen Cay. Care should be taken to clear the reef off the west side of the cay. The settlement is on the north shore of the bight, north of the cay.

Banco Becerro (Seal Bank) lies nearly awash about 1/3 mile southwest of Coxen Cay. The channel between this reef and the reef southwest of Coxen Cay is about 300 yards wide.

Banco Smith (16° 17′N, 86° 35′W) lies about 1 mile south-southwest of Coxen Cay. It has a least depth of about 21 feet.

Banco Cordelia, which dries, lies about 1 mile east-southeast of Banco Smith. A bank about 1 mile in extent with depths of 18 to 72 feet lies 1 1/2 miles southeast of Coxen Cay.

Daring Shoal is a detached 15-foot patch about 2 1/2 miles east of Coxen Cay. It is reported joined to Banco Cordelia by a narrow ridge, with depths of less than 60 feet.

Port of Entry: Coxen Hole is the administrative center for the Bay Islands.
Dockage: The town wharf is reported to have depths of 6 to 10 feet alongside.
Anchorage: Anchor either northwest or northeast of Coxen Cay. The airport runway partially extends along the reef toward Coxen Cay in the eastern part of the harbor. The bottom is reported to be sand and coral heads.
Services: Fuel, water, ice, groceries, and general supplies should be available. There are banks, a post office, and communication facilities.

PUNTA OUESTE LIGHT, 16 16.1N, 86 36.1W. Fl W 5s, 74ft, 19M. Reported extinguished 1989.
ISLA DE ROATÁN WEST END LIGHT, 16 18.0N, 86 35.3W. Fl W 20s, 10M. Red framework tower. Visible 320°–190°. Reported extinguished 1989.

ISLA DE UTILA

16 06N, 86 56W
UTILA PEAK LIGHT, NE end of island on summit, 16 07N, 86 53W. Fl W 10s, 325ft, 20M. Red metal framework tower.

Pilotage: This is the westernmost of the Bay Islands. It lies about 18 miles southwest of Isla de Roatán. The island is about 7 1/2 miles long and from 1 1/4 to 2 3/4 miles wide. It is generally low, swampy, and thickly wooded. A range of 60- to 70-foot-high hills is located near its east end. Pumpkin Hill, 289 feet high and conical, stands near the northeast extremity of the island. A disused, black framework light structure, 102 feet high, stands near the west extremity of the island.

NOTE: In 1962, Isla de Utila and Isla de Roatán were reported to lie 2 to 4 miles farther apart than charted.

The island is steep-to, except for its southwest side. The north side of the island is indented by several shallow bays. An area of foul ground extends about 4 3/4 miles southwest from the southwest side of the island and is about 3 to 4 miles wide. Several good anchorages lie within this area, for those with local knowledge.

PUERTO ESTE

16 06N, 86 54W
PUERTO ESTE LIGHT, East Reef, 16 05N, 86 55W. F W, 4M. Wooden building.

Pilotage: This harbor lies about 1 mile west of the 20-foot black and red cliffs that form the southeast extremity of Isla de Utila. The harbor is about 3/4 mile in extent and provides anchorage in depths of 12 to 40 feet, with a clay bottom over coral.

Reefs narrow the entrance to about 300 yards, but depths run 30 to 36 feet. Two small coral heads lie about 1/4 mile from the east shore of the harbor. A church steeple in range 020° with a prominent tree is the leading mark used by local pilots.

It has been reported that entering vessels should steer 040°, passing about 200 yards off a stake on the coral reef to the east.

BAHÍA DE TRUJILLO

15 58N, 86 00W
Pilotage: This bay is about 7 miles wide between Punta Caxinas at the end of Cabo de Honduras and the coast to the south. From the south entrance point of the bay the coast extends west for about 115 miles to Punta Caballos. The shore is generally low, wooded, and bordered by sandy beaches. Mountain ranges reach the shore in places, but are 10 miles inland in others. The mountains extend west to Tela, about 85

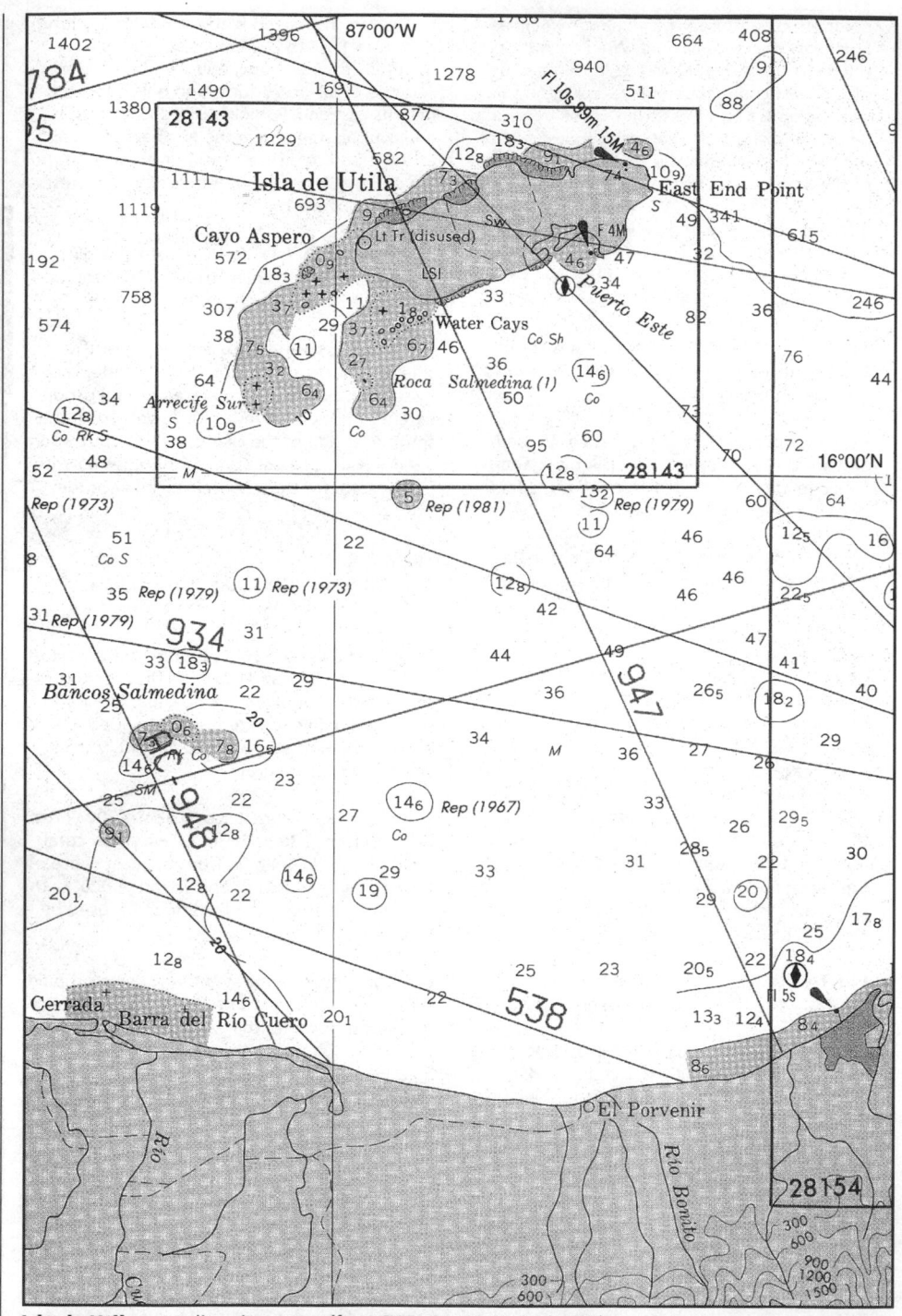

Isla de Utila, soundings in meters *(from DMA 28150, 2nd ed, 4/89)*

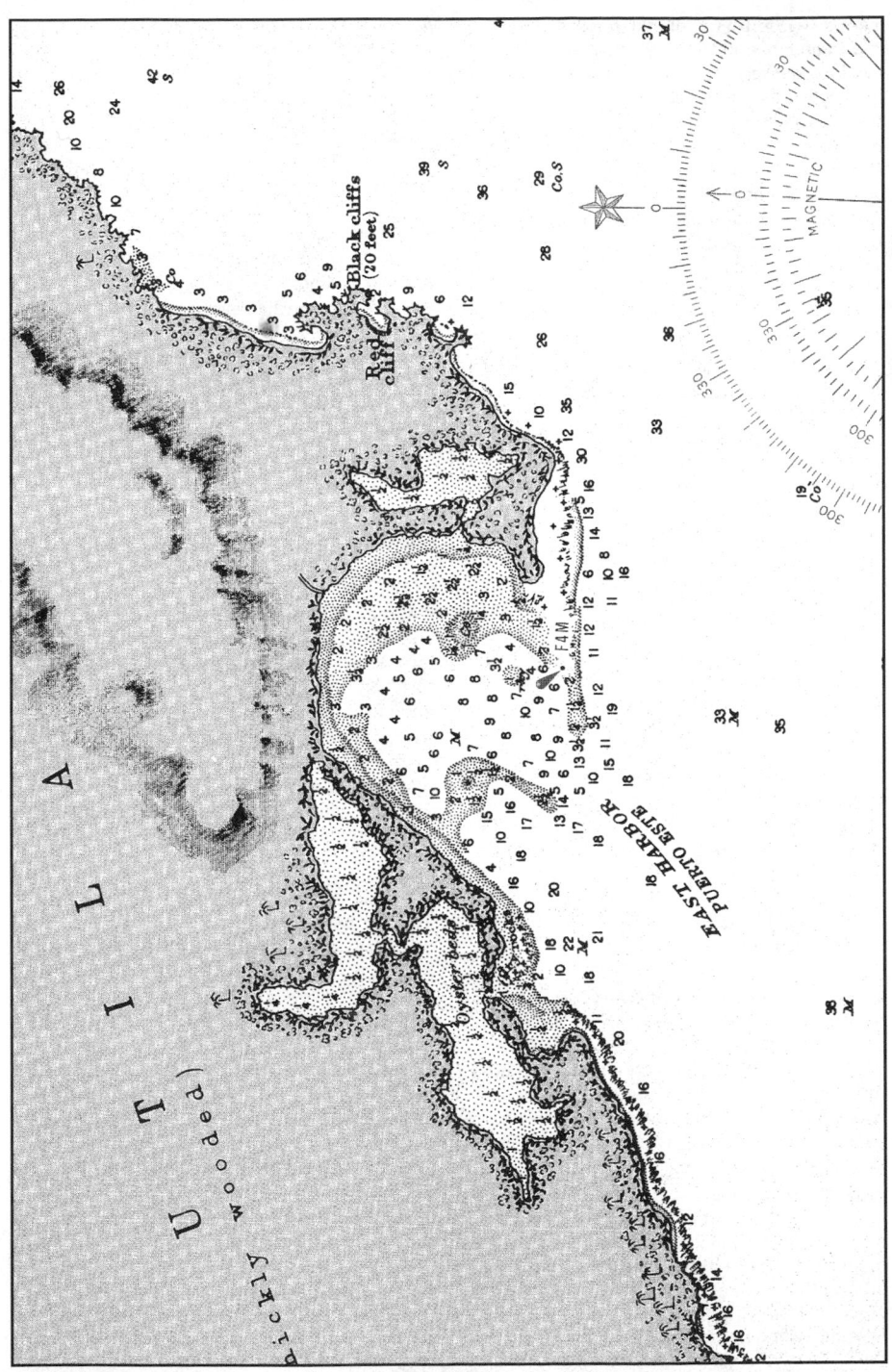

Puerto Este, soundings in fathoms *(from DMA 28143, 6th ed, 3/85)*

miles away. South of Tela the ranges curve inland and extend to the southwest. An extensive low, densely wooded plain lies between the base of the ranges and Montanas de Omoa, about 30 miles to the west.

The mountain ranges rise to high prominent peaks south and southwest of Bahía de Trujillo and south and southeast of Punta Congrejal. These peaks are good landmarks from offshore, particularly Cerro Congrejal, an 8,049-foot-high mountain that is located about 10 miles southwest of Punta Congrejal.

There are few navigational aids along this coast. Puerto Castilla is on the north side of the bay, and Trujillo on the southeast side. A shallow channel at the eastern end of the bay leads into a spacious lagoon. Depths in the central part of the bay average 39 to 184 feet. When approaching from the north give Punta Caxinas a berth of 1 to 1 1/2 miles. The tank in Puerto Castilla is higher than the surrounding vegetation and can be seen from about 12 miles to the north.

The north and east shores of the bay are low, swampy, and wooded, with no prominent landmarks. The south shore is backed by a high mountain chain that extends almost to the shore at Trujillo. Pico Colentura, a 3,198-foot peak, rises 3 miles south of the town. A *vigia*, or lookout hill, 2,499 feet high, stands at the northeast end of the mountain chain. These mountains are sometimes referred to as Montanas de Trujillo.

Callo Blanco is a dangerous reef located about 5 miles south of Punta Caxinas.

Currents: The usual set of the current off this coast is east within the 100-fathom curve. This current is uncertain due to the influence of the tides and winds. Within Bahía de Trujillo there is very little current during calms or east winds. With west winds the current sets east and counter-clockwise around the bay at rates up to 2 knots.

Winds: The winds along the coast of Honduras are easterly for most of the year, with a pronounced diurnal variation. Calms and light offshore winds are frequent during the late night and early morning. Strong winds seldom blow in the early morning, except during November and December. During these months there are several days with northerly winds that attain gale force. During periods of strong

northwest to northeast winds a heavy swell enters Bahía de Trujillo.

PUERTO CASTILLA
16 00N, 85 58W
Pilotage: This port is located on the south side of Cabo de Honduras, about 2 miles southeast of Punta Caxinas, on the north side of Bahía de Trujillo. There are several piers on the waterfront and others under construction.
Port of Entry
Anchorage: Anchor east of the commercial port area. Check locally for the latest depths over the bar at the entrance to the lagoon in the eastern part of the bay.
Services: Fuel, water, and general supplies should be available.

TRUJILLO
15 55N, 85 57W
Pilotage: The port is located on the southeast shore of Bahía de Trujillo. The twin spires of the church in town are conspicuous when making your approach. A small fort looks out over the bay. The town pier is about 200 feet long and has a least depth of 16 feet along its south side.
Port of Entry
Anchorage: In calm weather you can anchor here, but you should move north in the bay when swells invade.
Services: Fuel, water, and general supplies should be available.

CAYOS COCHINOS
15 58N, 86 34W
COCHINO GRANDE LIGHT, 15 58.6N, 86 28.5W. Fl W 7s, 516ft, 40M.

Pilotage: This group of cays lies about 27 miles west of Punta Caxinas and 9 miles north of Punta Catchabutan. The island farthest to the east is densely wooded and rises to a height of 430 feet. The north side of the island is steep-to, but a coral spit with depths of 24 to 36 feet extends 1 1/4 miles from the east side. A group of cays and rocks lie a short distance off the south side. A light stands on the east side of the island.

A wooded island about 1 mile farther southwest rises to a height of 499 feet. A steep-to coral ledge with numerous cays and sandbanks extends about 3 miles southwest from the islands. The channel between the islands has

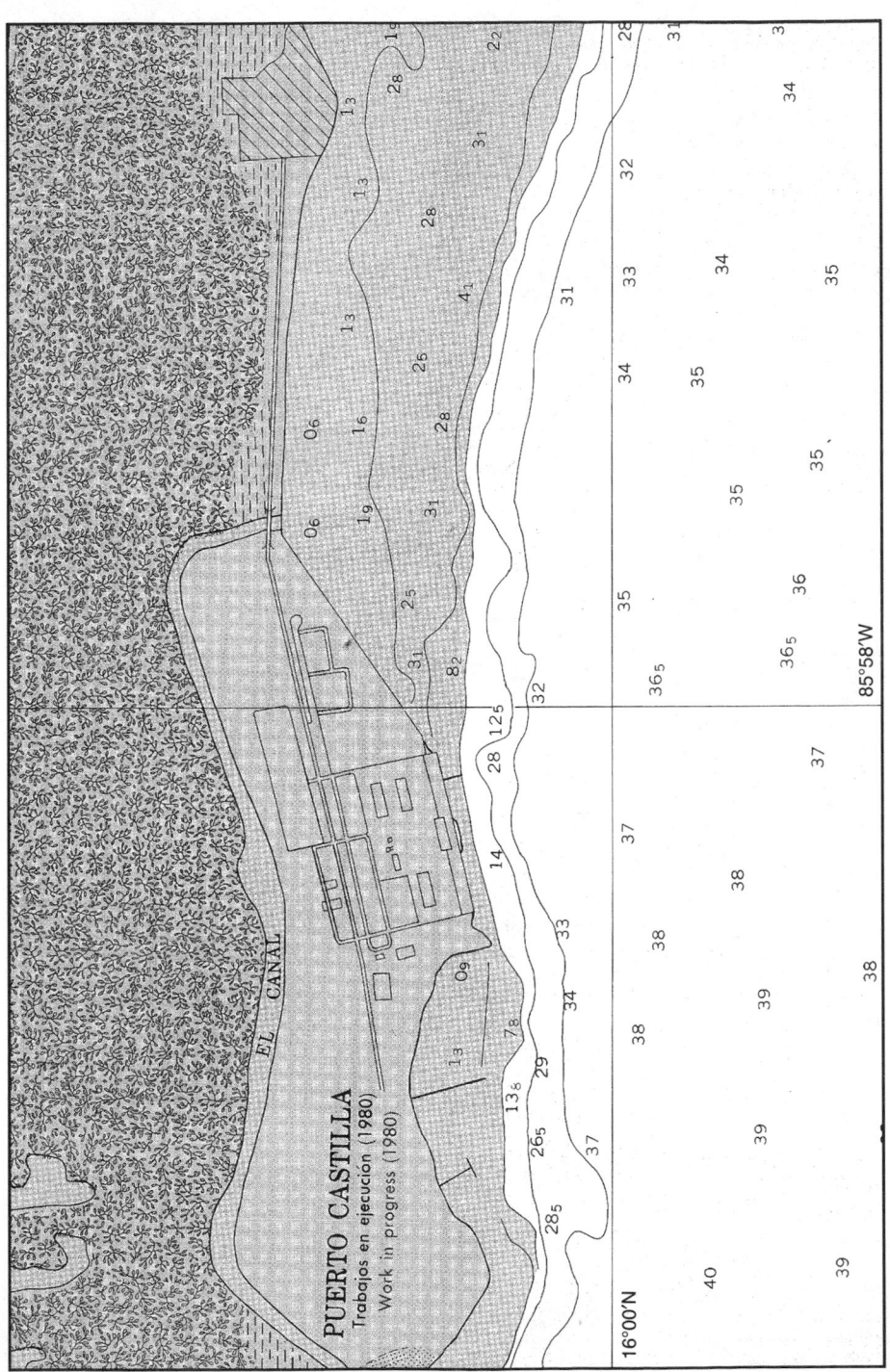

Puerto Castilla, soundings in meters *(from DMA 28142, 4th ed, 9/80)*

depths of 85 to 95 feet. Depths of 25 to 37 feet lie off the northwest side of these two islands.

BANCO PROVIDENCIA
15 55N, 86 38W

Pilotage: This dangerous bank lies 9 miles northwest of Punta Catchabutan.

CAUTION: Dangerous uncharted shoals are likely to be encountered anywhere within the 200-meter contour in this area.

BANCO SALMEDINA
15 55N, 87 05W

Pilotage: This bank lies 25 miles west of Banco Providencia and about 10 miles offshore. It is a dangerous steep-to patch of coral, with a least depth of 2 feet near its east end. This reef breaks when there is any swell. A detached 24-foot patch lies 1 mile south-southeast of the bank and a 15-foot patch lies 6 miles northeast of it. Banco Salmedina should be given a berth of at least 2 miles.

PUNTA CONGREJAL
15 47N, 86 51W

Pilotage: This low sandy point is marked by the trunks of trees and the discolored water from the Río Congrejal, which extends some distance out to sea. Depths of less than 36 feet extend up to 1 1/2 miles off the point. A tall tree, prominent from the east, stands about 3/4 mile west of the point.

The mountain chain that backs this part of the coast rises to Cerro Nana Cruz, a 6,098-foot peak located 9 miles southeast of the point. Cerro Congrejal (Bonito Peak) is 8,049 feet high and lies about 10 miles southwest of the point. This peak appears as a well-defined, sharp cone when seen from the northeast, but when seen from the northwest has a small, flat shoulder projecting east from just below the summit.

PUERTO LA CEIBA
15 46N, 86 48W

LA CEIBA LIGHT, head of pier, 15 47.5N, 86 47.8W. Fl W 5s, 16ft. Wooden tower.

Pilotage: This open roadstead harbor is located about 1 mile southwest of Punta Congrejal. It is one of the principal ports of Honduras. A 1,423-foot-long wooden pier projects from the town.

Currents: The current in the area has been reported to be westward, attaining a velocity of 2 knots at times. During northers the current sets south.

Winds: The prevailing winds during the day are northeast and at night southwest. Normally the weather is calm with gentle breezes, except during the season of the northers (November and December) when winds of gale force occur.

Port of Entry

Anchorage: Anchorage is prohibited east of the pier. On the approach of a norther vessels are advised to proceed to sea. Swells are likely to be felt in this anchorage.

PUNTA OBISPO
15 51N, 87 23W

PUNTA OBISPO LIGHT, 15 50.9N, 87 22.5W. Fl W 5s, 132ft, 20M. White framework tower.

Pilotage: Punta Obispo is about 34 miles west of Punta Congrejal. The flat coastal plain along this coast gradually widens as the mountains become more sloping and recede inland. There are swamps and marshes a short distance inland, and numerous streams discharge into the sea. The shore is covered with trees and thick vegetation that almost reach the water's edge.

The point is a bluff, rocky, tree-covered headland that is the termination of a conspicuous, conical, grassy hill. The Clerks, a group of 20-foot-high rocks, lie close off the point. Depths of 121 feet lie within 1/2 mile of the rocks.

The entire area northeast to northwest of the point has depths of as little as 21 feet in places.

Cabo Triunfo, a bold rocky projection, stands about 4 miles southwest of Punta Obispo.

BAHÍA DE TELA
15 47N, 87 27W

Pilotage: This bay is entered between Cabo Triunfo and Punta Sal, about 12 1/2 miles to the northwest. It is bordered by a low sandy coast, but is backed by a high mountain ridge about 8 miles south of Punta Obispo. A range of mountains 2,000 to 3,000 feet high backs the coast in the vicinity of Tela, but just west of the town it veers inland and extends south.

COAST PILOT

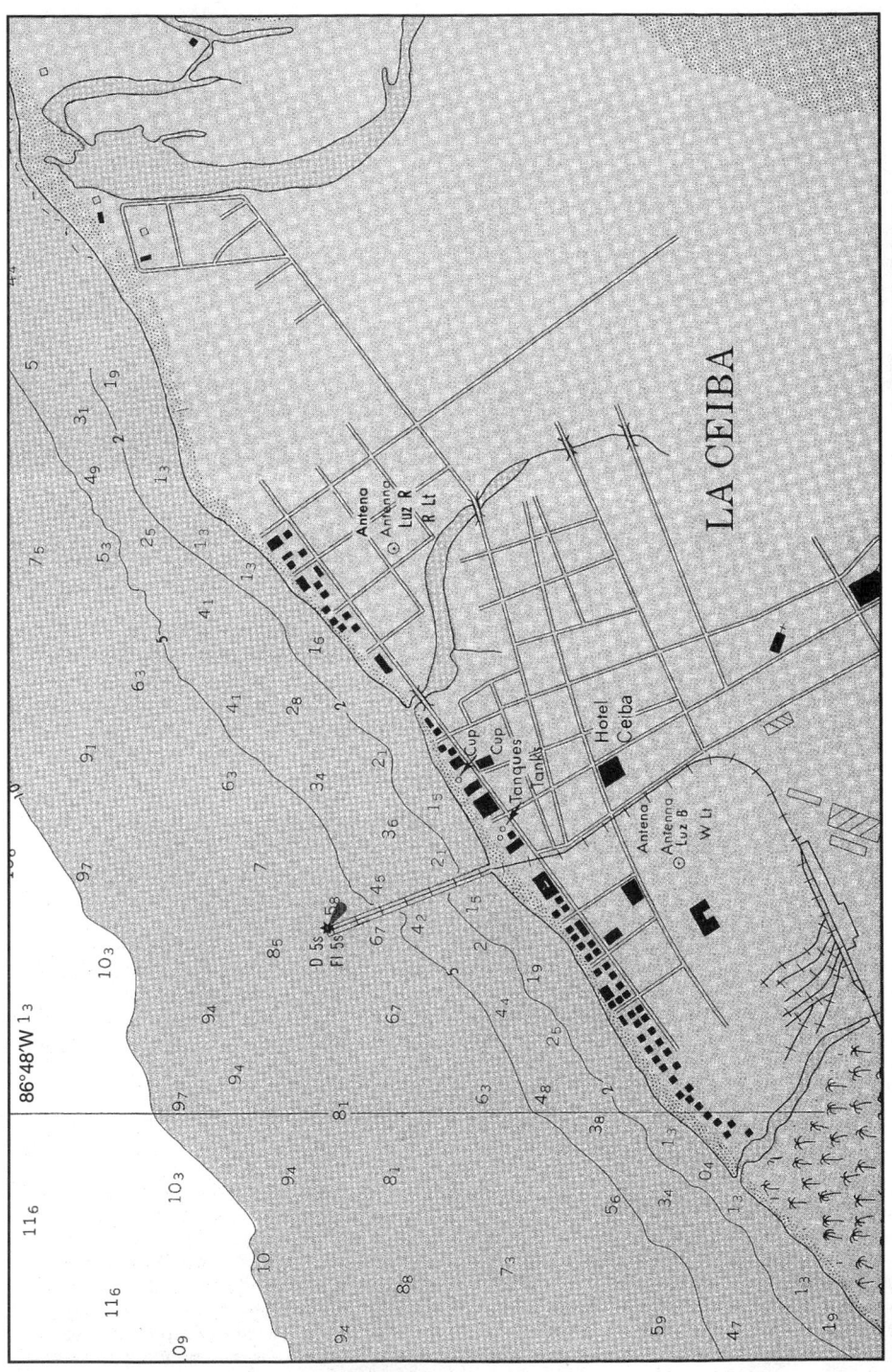

La Ceiba, soundings in meters *(from DMA 28144, 3rd ed, 10/85)*

Laguna de los Micos, a large, shallow, body of water, backs the bay and is entered about 6 miles northwest of Tela.

TELA

15 47N, 87 27W
TELA LIGHT, head of pier, 15 47.2N, 87 27.6W. Fl W 10s, 45ft, 6M. Red metal tower.

Pilotage: This open roadstead harbor is located in the southeast part of Bahía de Tela, near the eastern entrance point. It is the second ranking port in Honduras. The prevailing winds are east and northeast, but strong northers may be experienced in the winter months. The average tidal range is about 1 foot, but the water level is also raised or lowered by the wind. The current off the pier has been reported to set west in the morning and east in the afternoon. A pier about 2,000 feet long extends north from shore in front of the town. During north winds it is impossible to remain at the dock.
Anchorage: You are probably best off anchored west of the pier, but a swell is likely here. Be prepared to put to sea if a norther threatens.

PUNTA SAL

15 55N, 87 36W
PUNTA SAL LIGHT, 15 55.5N, 87 36.1W. Fl (4) W 30s, 275ft, 15M. White framework tower.

Pilotage: This bold, rocky promontory is the western boundary of Bahía de Tela. It projects 2 miles northeast from the coast, rising to wooded, irregular hills. It appears as an island when viewed against the low land to the south. A light is shown from the north end of the point. Three or four rocks, similar to The Clerks but much higher, lie about 1/2 mile off the east extremity of the point.

The coast between Punta Sal and Punta Caballos, about 22 miles to the west-southwest, is low, sandy, and densely wooded. Montanas de Omoa back the western part of this coast.

Puerto Escondido lies 2 miles southwest of Punta Sal. This small cove is a good anchorage for small craft.

Laguna Tinto lies 1 mile southwest of Puerto Escondido. This small bay should be approached with local knowledge. There is reported to be good anchorage for small craft.

Río Ulua is entered about 4 miles west of the entrance to Laguna Tinto. Punta Ulua, at the river entrance, is low and well defined. This large river is navigable by small river steamers for about 139 miles. The muddy discharge from the river discolors the sea for some distance offshore. A dangerous rock lies about 8 miles south-southwest of Punta Ulua. It lies within the 10-meter curve, about 1 mile offshore.

Río Chamelecon is located about 6 miles west-southwest of the Río Ulua. An isolated 636-foot conical hill is nearby. This is about 9 miles east-northeast of Punta Caballos.

PUNTA CABALLOS

15 50N, 87 58W
PUNTA CABALLOS LIGHT, 15 51.0N, 87 57.7W. Fl W 5s, 190ft, 20M. Tower. F R lights 0.22, 0.25, and 3 miles ESE; Fl R on tank 2.34 miles SE. Reported to lie 0.25 mile NNE (1993).
NO. 1 LIGHT, 15 51.2N, 87 57.8W. Q (3) G. Green articulated light. Reported missing (March 1986).
NO. 2 LIGHT, 15 51.0N, 87 58.2W. Q (3) R. Red articulated light. Reported Q R (1993).
NO. 3 LIGHT, 15 51.2N, 87 57.7W. Q (3) G. Articulated light. Reported destroyed (1993).
NO. 4 LIGHT, 15 50.5N, 87 58.3W. Q (3) R. Articulated light. Reported Q R (1993).
PIER LIGHT, on shoal off head, 15 50.3N, 87 57.3W. Fl R 2s. Red cylindrical daymark on pile. Destroyed.

Pilotage: This is the west extremity of a low, wooded peninsula that forms the north side of the harbor of Puerto Cortés. The radio masts on the point are good landmarks, as are the towers of a refinery located about 1/4 mile east of the light. Caution is necessary when navigating in this area as it has not been completely examined. A dangerous below-water rock lies 1 1/2 miles northwest of Cerro Cardona (15° 53'N, 87° 51'W), an isolated conical 518-foot-high hill situated 7 1/2 miles east-north-east of Punta Caballos.

The coast from Punta Caballos to Cabo Tres Puntas, about 39 miles west-northwest, forms a bight that indents the coast about 11 miles to the south. Puerto Cortés occupies the east part of this bight and Ensenada de Omoa occupies the south part. The Río Montagua enters the sea near the west part of Ensenada de Omoa and forms the boundary between Honduras and Guatemala. The east side of the

COAST PILOT

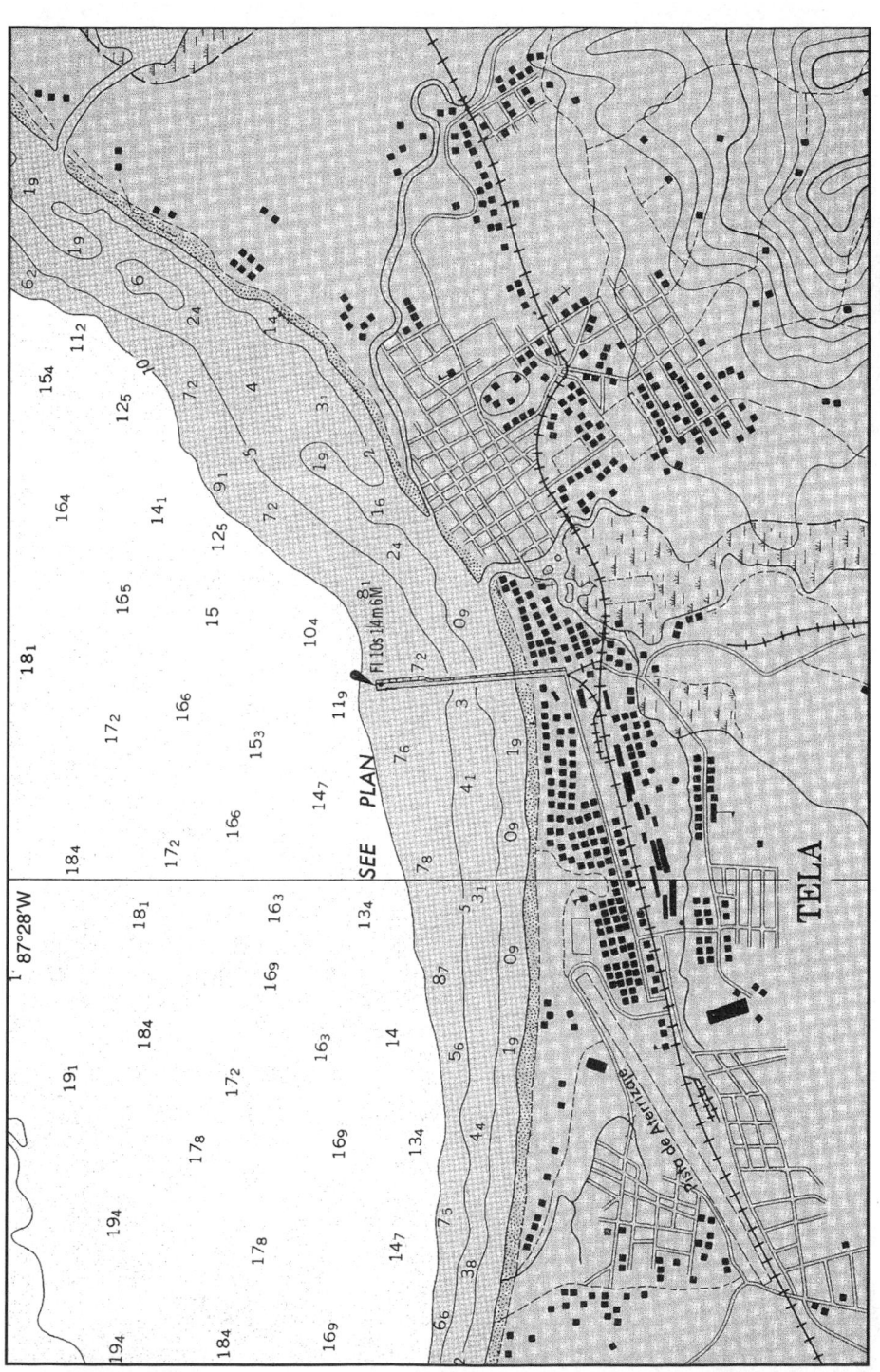

Puerto de Tela, soundings in meters *(from DMA 28161, 3rd ed, 12/82, corr. to 1/86)*

bight is bounded by the base of the Montanas de Omoa, which rise to several prominent peaks. This range extends inland to the southwest from the head of the bight, and the land to the west becomes low and swampy.

PUERTO CORTÉS

15 50N, 87 57W

Pilotage: This is the major port of Honduras. It is situated on the north side of Bahía de Cortés. The red roof of a hotel and a water tank 2 1/4 miles southeast of Punta Caballos are good landmarks. The pilots monitor VHF channels 6 and 16.

Port of Entry

Anchorage: The best anchorage is reported to be off the naval base southeast of town. This area is near the charted "Coast Guard Pier."

Services: There is reported to be fuel, water, provisions, and some repairs available. There are banks, a post office, restaurants, and communication facilities. The naval base may be able to haul your vessel and assist with repairs. Contact the base on VHF channel 21.

PUNTA DE OMOA

15 47N, 88 03W

Pilotage: This low but prominent point is about 6 1/4 miles southwest of Punta Caballos.

Red cliffs stand on the coast about 3 miles east of the point. The coast is low and sandy and backed by high, wooded ground and mountains. A disused lighthouse stands on Punta de Omoa.

Omoa is a small sheltered port that stands close south of Punta de Omoa. A small wharf extends from the town.

Ensenada de Omoa is a bight that lies between Punta de Omoa and the mouth of the Río Montagua, about 10 1/2 miles to the westsouthwest. A heavy swell rolls in during northers.

Montanas de Omoa backs this section of coast. Pico de Montagua, a 7,308-foot peak, lies about 9 miles southwest of the head of Ensenada de Omoa. This is the termination of the mountain chain. The other prominent peaks in this range are usually obscured.

RÍO MONTAGUA

15 44N, 88 13W

Pilotage: This river marks the boundary between Honduras and Guatemala. It is a fairly large, shallow river, navigable by river boats up to about 35 miles above its mouth.

COAST PILOT

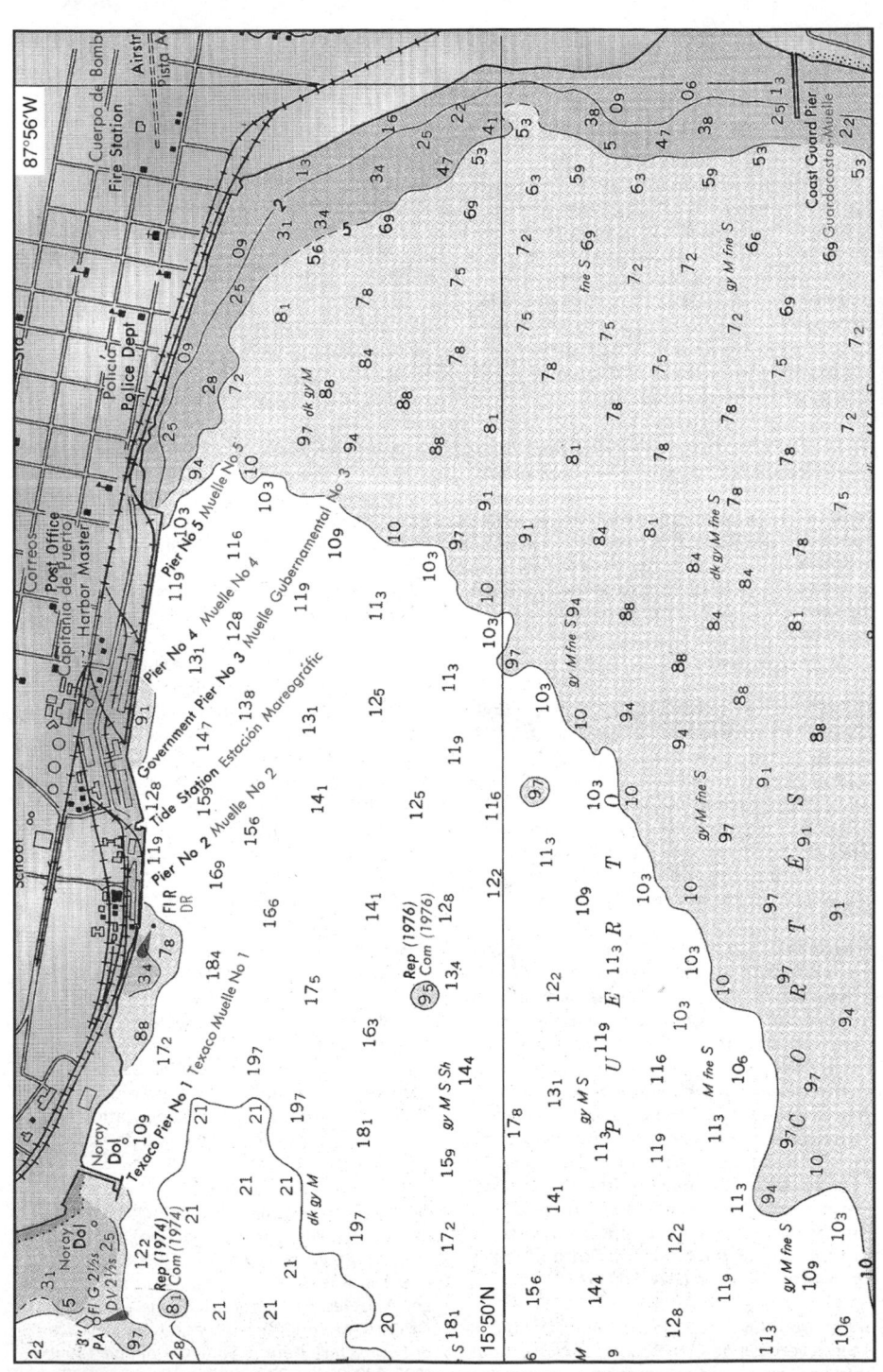

Puerto Cortés, soundings in meters *(from DMA 28163, 22nd ed, 3/84)*

GUATEMALA

CAUTION: Our information on aids to navigation comes from official government sources. The latitudes and longitudes of these marks may not correspond to the readings from GPS receivers. Some aids have been reported as unreliable, missing, off position, or showing incorrect characteristics. No single aid to navigation, or waypoint, should be relied upon as a sole means of fixing your position.

NOTE: The chartlets in this section are <u>not intended for navigation</u> and are included for reference and planning purposes only. While chartlets reproduced from government sources are from the most current editions as of press time, they incorporate <u>no corrections</u> to navigational aids, depths, or hazards since the edition publication date.

ENTRY PROCEDURES

Guatemala has a democratic government, which was temporarily suspended in May 1993, but was quickly restored. Clashes between guerilla and government forces occur periodically, and much of the countryside is currently considered unsafe for travel. In addition, theft, robbery, and violent attacks by criminals are frequent.

WARNING: In June 1994, the U.S. Department of State was warning of possible dangers of travel to Guatemala. Unfounded rumors that foreigners are involved in the theft of children for the purposes of using their organs for transplant has led to threats and incidents of mob violence in several areas of the country. However, these have not occurred in the traditional tourist areas, including Santo Thomas de Castillo. U.S. citizens should in particular avoid contact with Guatemalan children. For the current status of this warning, call the U.S. Department of State Citizens Emergency Center (202-647-5225).

In general, travel outside of major cities is considered very dangerous. Reports of car-jackings, hold-ups, rapes, and murders are frequent. For assistance or information while in the country, U.S. citizens may contact the Consular Section of the U.S. Embassy in Guatemala City (505-2-31-15-41); office hours are 0800 to noon and 1300 to 1500.

Cholera is present in Guatemala. For updated health information contact the U.S. Centers for Disease Control International Travelers Hotline (404-332-4559).

Cruising visitors seem to be able to avoid some of the problems on land; many report pleasant visits to Guatemala and the Río Dulce. Ports of Entry include Puerto Barrios, Santo Tomas de Castilla, and Livingston. For an illustration of the country flag see *Reed's Nautical Companion*. Port officials are reported to be strict about showing the proper flags.

You should have passports, a clearance from your last port, and ship's papers. You must declare any firearms, which will be held by the port captain. Citizens of the U.S. and some other countries are not required to have visas in advance of their arrival. Tourist cards can be purchased upon arrival and are usually good for 30 days; you may be granted a longer stay and you can apply for extensions in Guatemala City. You should request a cruisng permit, or *zarpe,* stating where you intend to visit. Permits are usually good for 90 days. You should carry some form of identification with you, other than your passport, in case of robbery or theft.

U.S. citizens must have a passport to <u>depart</u> Guatemala. If your passport is stolen, you must immediately contact the U.S. Embassy in Guatemala City and the local police. You will need to show your passport application and the police report before you will be allowed to depart the country.

For the latest regulations contact the Guatemalan Embassy, Consular Section, at 2220 R Street NW, Washington, DC, 20008 (202-745-4952) or any of the Guatemalan consulates in Los Angeles, San Francisco, Houston, New Orleans, Miami, Chicago, and New York, or the consular agent in Duaynabo, Puerto Rico (809-782-0558, -273-0303, or fax 273-0333).

The unit of currency is the quetzal, which in summer 1994 traded at between 5.8 and 6 quetzals to US$1. Currency values are subject to change.

The telephone code for the country is 502. The city code for Guatemala City is 2; all other locations in the country use 9. Local numbers have six digits.

RÍO MONTAGUA

15 44N, 88 13W

Pilotage: This river marks the boundary between Honduras and Guatemala. It is a fairly large, shallow river, navigable by river boats up to about 35 miles above its mouth.

Between the Río Montagua and Cabo Tres Puntas, about 27 miles to the northwest, the low, swampy coast is bordered by a dark sandy beach, backed by trees.

Río San Francisco del Mar discharges about 14 miles northwest of the Río Montagua, and a branch of the river leads to Bahía La Graciosa. A conspicuous 600 foot high tableland stands about 8 miles southwest of the mouth of this river.

CABO TRES PUNTAS (CAPE THREE POINTS)

15 58N, 88 37W

CABO TRES PUNTAS LIGHT, 15 57.4N, 88 36.2W. Fl W 10s, 132ft, 17M. White framework tower.

Pilotage: This is a prominent, well-wooded point, which is the northwest extremity of a low, wooded peninsula about 11 miles long that borders the northeast side of Bahía de Amatique. A conspicuous tower stands on the cape. Steep-to foul ground, which usually breaks, extends about 1/2 mile west from the cape.

BAHÍA DE AMATIQUE (HONDURAS BAY)

15 56N, 88 44W

Pilotage: The bay is entered between Cabo Tres Puntas and Punta Gorda, about 13 1/2 miles to the northwest in Belize. It has general depths of 30 feet to 102 feet over its central portion, with gradual shoaling toward the eastern shore. The east side of the bay recedes about 13 miles south to the narrow entrance of Bahía de Santo Tomas de Castilla, which recedes an additional

2 1/2 miles south to its head. The land on the east side of the bay is generally flat, swampy, and densely wooded. From the entrance to Bahía de Santo Tomas de Castilla the west side of the bay extends about 23 miles northwest and then about 10 miles northeast to Punta Gorda. The land on the west side of the bay is higher, densely wooded, and backed by mountain ranges.

From Cabo Tres Puntas the east side of the bay extends about 1 1/2 miles south-southeast to Punta Manabique, and then about 5 3/4 miles southeast to Firewood Point.

Bahía La Graciosa (Hospital Bight) is a shallow bight that recedes about 4 miles to the southeast and is entered between Firewood Point and Punta Manglar. A sandbar with a depth of 14 feet extends across the entrance. From Punta Manglar, the coast, which is low and swampy, extends about 7 1/2 miles south-southwest to the east entrance point of Bahía de Santo Tomas de Castilla.

OX TONGUE SHOAL

15 53N, 88 38W

OX TONGUE SHOAL LIGHT, 15 53.9N, 88 41.1W. Fl W 3s, 13ft, 12M. White and orange framework structure. Radar reflector.

Pilotage: This narrow shoal has depths of 18 feet and less. It extends about 7 1/2 miles west-northwest from Punta Manglar. A light stands on the west extremity of the shoal. It has been reported (1984) that because of reef buildup, this light should be kept at least 1 1/4 miles to the east when entering or leaving port.

HEREDIA SHOAL LIGHT, 15 50.8N, 88 40.4W. Fl R 6s, 20ft. White and orange framework structure. Reported extinguished 1989.

Heredia Shoal, with a least depth of 18 feet, lies about 3 miles south-southeast of the light on Ox Tongue Shoal. A buoy marks the north side of the shoal.

A shoal with depths of 28 feet lies about 3 1/4 miles southeast of Heredia Shoal, and another with depths of 42 feet lies a further 1 1/2 miles southeast.

BAJO VILLEDO

15 45N, 88 37W

BAJO VILLEDO LIGHT, 15 44.7N, 88 36.9W. Fl W 2s, 17ft. Aluminum framework tower. Radar reflector.

Pilotage: This reef has a least charted depth of about 15 feet. It is marked by a light and lies west of the range lights leading to Puerto Barrios.

BAHÍA SANTO TOMAS DE CASTILLA

Pilotage: The bay is entered between Punta Manglar and Punta Palma about 1 1/2 miles west-northwest. Its densely wooded shores are bordered by a mud flat, leaving a navigable basin about 2 miles in extent within the 5-meter-depth curve.

PUERTO BARRIOS

15 44N, 88 36W
PUERTO BARRIOS LIGHT, 15 43.8N, 88 35.8W. Fl W 8s, 25M.
HEAD OF PIER LIGHT, 15 44.5N, 88 36.6W. Oc W 4s, 5M. Three F R mark jetty ruins (1982).

Pilotage: This port, formerly the busiest in Guatemala, is located on the east side of Bahía de Santo Tomas de Castilla. A dredged channel leads south from a position 2 miles north-northeast of Bajo Villedo. Lights at Santo Tomas de Castilla lead through this channel, bearing 189° 30'. A 1,000-foot-long pier extends west from the shore. Ruins, marked by lights, extend 1,100 feet farther to the west-northwest. There is a minimum depth of about 24 feet at the pier.

Winds: Land and sea breezes are the predominating winds at Puerto Barrios. The sea breeze blows from the north during the day, gradually diminishing toward evening. The land breeze blows from the south from about midnight to sunrise. This regular cycle is altered by northers during the winter months.

Currents: The current off the pier is reported to be diurnal in nature. During the morning the current sets northwest at a rate of 0.4 knots and occasionally at 2.3 knots. The velocity increases after a strong norther has abated and during periods of heavy rain. In the afternoon the current reverses and sets southeast at a rate of 0.2 to 0.6 knots. The mean rise and fall of the tide is less than 1 foot.

Port of Entry
Anchorage: Anchorage is prohibited north of the pier, due to incoming traffic. Anchor south of the pier.
Services: Fuel, water, groceries, and general supplies should be available.

PUERTO SANTO TOMAS DE CASTILLA

15 42N, 88 37W
MATIAS DE GALVEZ RANGE (Front),
15 41.6N, 88 37.2W. Q Y, 35ft. Metal framework tower, red triangular-shaped daymark, Point up. Visible on rangeline only. **(Rear),** S, about 347 meters 189° 30' from front, 15° 41.4'N, 88° 37.3'W. Oc Y 4s, 80ft. Metal framework tower, red triangular-shaped daymark, point up. Visible on rangeline only.

Pilotage: This is the main commercial port facility for Guatemala. It is located on the south shore of Bahía de Santo Tomas de Castilla. There is a single 3000-foot-long wharf with a depth of about 33 feet alongside. Commercial vessels often moor stern-to this wharf. The wharf may be extended beyond this length.
Winds: Sea breezes predominate between 1100 and sunset, reaching force 4, or occasionally force 6, at about 1500. At other times it is calm, or there are light southerly breezes. This pattern is disturbed by the passage of a depression to the north, when squalls and southwest winds may be expected.
Currents: A weak current, seldom exceeding 1/2 knot, sets southwest across the turning basin.
Port of Entry: This is the primary commercial port of entry for Guatemala, but cruisers report that pleasure boats are discouraged from entering here. You can enter at nearby Puerto Barrios.

PUNTA HERRERIA
15 49N, 88 44W
Pilotage: This point is located about 7 miles northwest of Punta Palma, which is the western point at the entrance to Bahía de Santo Tomas de Castilla. The south shore of Bahía de Amatique is backed by high ground that reaches an elevation of 1,118 feet about 3 miles south of Livingston Bay.

LIVINGSTON BAY

Pilotage: The bay is entered between Punta Herreria and a point 1 1/4 miles northwest. The Río Dulce enters the head of the bay. The 6-foot-depth contour extends across the entrance to the bay and about 1/2 mile farther seaward. Depths reach about 18 feet a further 1/2 mile offshore.

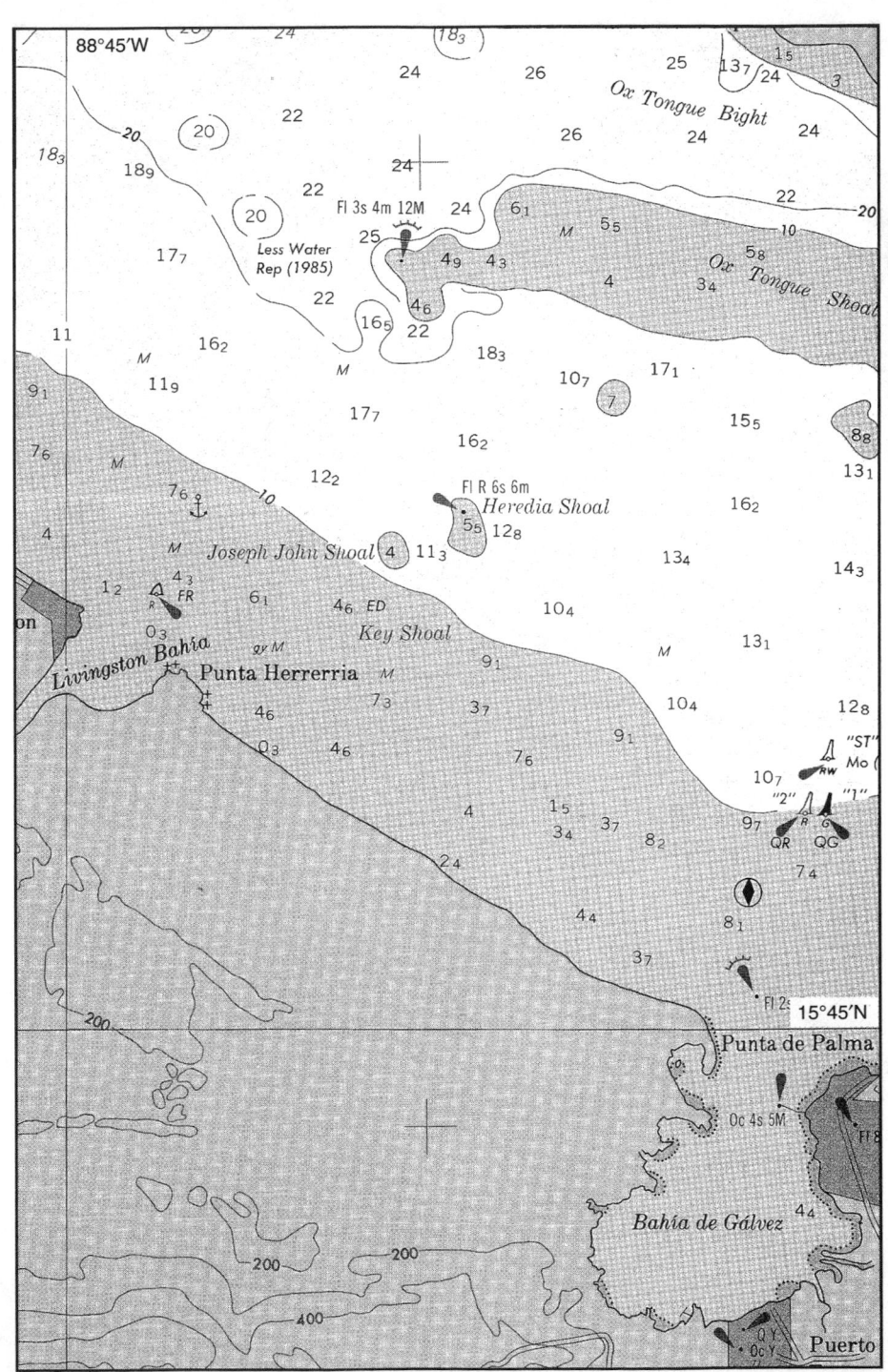

Approaches to Livingston and Puerto Barrios, *soundings in meters (fr. DMA 28162, 29th ed, 2/85)*

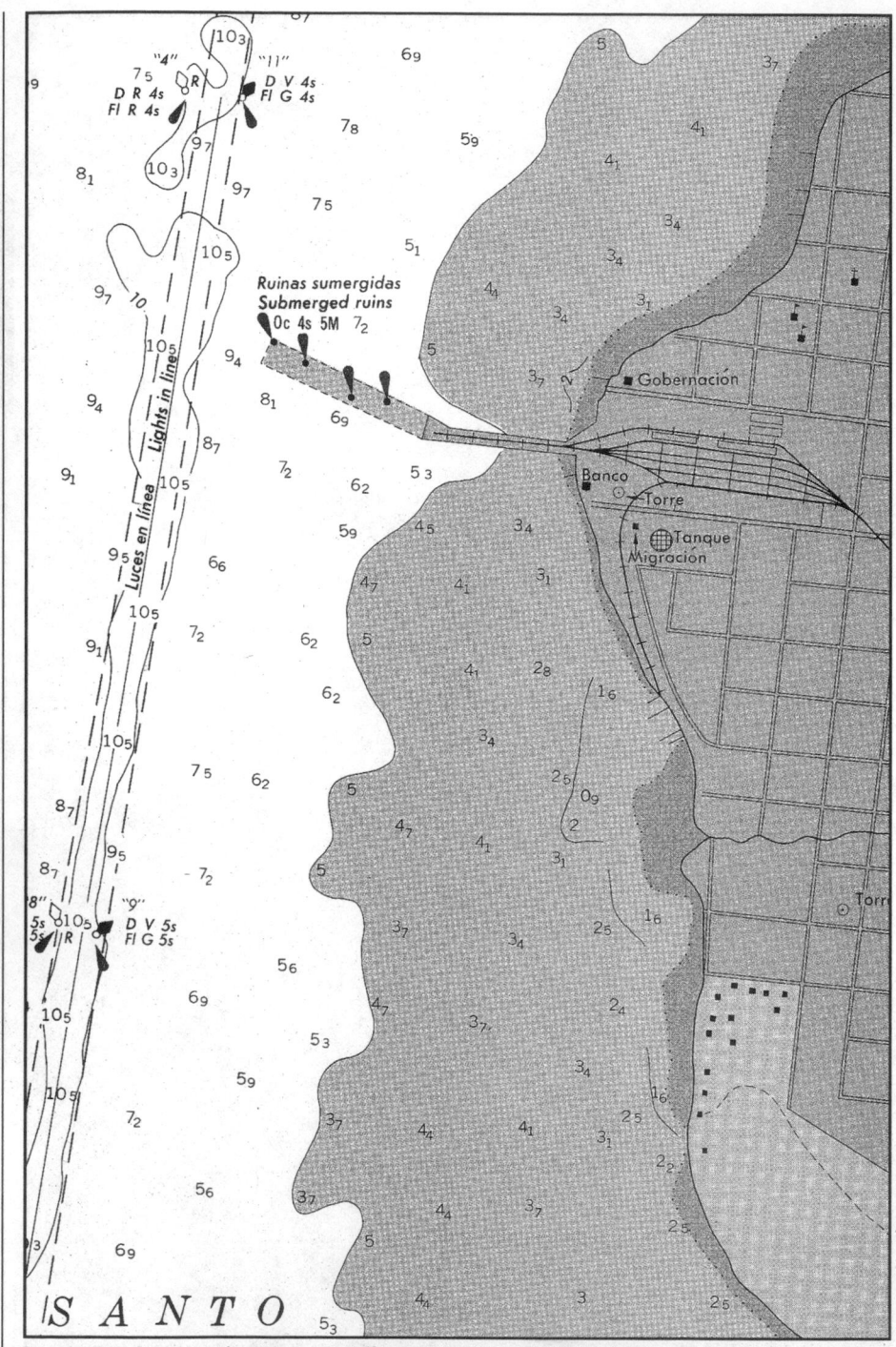

Puerto Barrios, soundings in meters *(from DMA 28165, 18th ed, 1/84)*

COAST PILOT

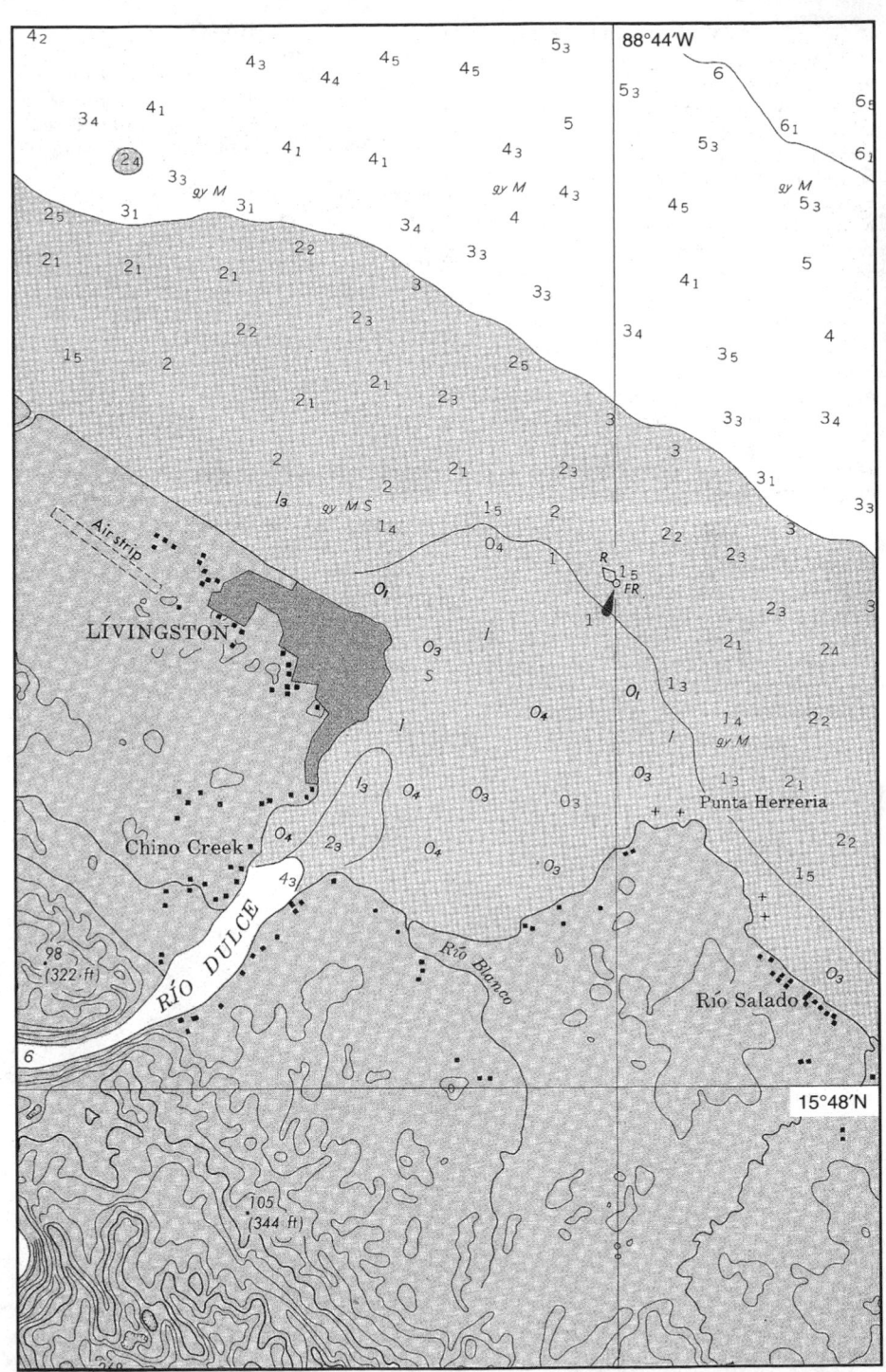

Livingston and Río Dulce, soundings in fathoms and feet *(from DMA 28164, 16th ed, 2/85)*

LIVINGSTON

15 50N, 88 45W

Pilotage: This is an important city for the transit of goods on the Río Dulce and a port of entry. A marked 6-foot-deep channel leads across the entrance bar and to the custom house wharf in Livingston. A refinery with four conspicuous chimneys is situated 1 mile northwest of Livingston.

Winds: The winds in this area are mostly northeast, with the strongest breezes being from May to September, with frequent heavy thunder squalls at night. The air is moist in all seasons, but May to October is the wettest.

Port of Entry

Anchorage: Cruisers generally anchor near the Texaco fuel dock, which is located a bit southwest of the town dock.

Services: Fuel, water, groceries, and general supplies are available.

RÍO QUEHUECHE

15 51N, 88 46W

Pilotage: This river discharges into the sea about 1 1/4 miles northwest of Livingston. It may be identified by a waterfall located 1 mile to its northwest and by the refinery with four conspicuous chimneys located about 1/4 mile to the southeast.

PUNTA COCOLI

15 53N, 88 49W

Pilotage: This prominent round bluff is located about 3 3/4 miles northwest of the entrance to Río Quehueche. Río Cocoli flows into the sea about 3/4 of a mile southwest of the bluff.

From Punta Cocoli the coast trends 2 1/2 miles west-southwest to Punta San Martin and then about 3 miles north-northwest to the mouth of the Sarstoon River. The coast is low, but about 2 miles inland it is backed by heavily wooded mountains, which rise to a height of 1,394 feet. These mountains are about 2 3/4 miles southsouthwest of the mouth of the Sarstoon River. They extend about 6 miles to the west at the same height.

SARSTOON RIVER

Pilotage: This river forms the boundary between Guatemala and Belize. The river's banks are low, swampy, and covered with mangroves. The entrance is about 1/2 mile wide, with a bar across the mouth. The bar has a depth of about 6 feet and generally breaks heavily. Depths of less than 18 feet lie about 1 mile east-northeast of the river's mouth.

BELIZE

CAUTION: Our information on aids to navigation comes from official government sources. The latitudes and longitudes of these marks may not correspond to the readings from GPS receivers. Some aids have been reported as unreliable, missing, off position, or showing incorrect characteristics. No single aid to navigation, or waypoint, should be relied upon as a sole means of fixing your position.

NOTE: The chartlets in this section are not intended for navigation and are included for reference and planning purposes only. While chartlets reproduced from government sources are from the most current editions as of press time, they incoroporate no corrections to navigational aids, depths, or hazards since the edition publication date.

ENTRY PROCEDURES

Belize was formerly a British Crown Colony, but gained independence in 1981. For an illustration of the country flag see *Reed's Nautical Companion.*

Ports of entry include Punta Gorda, Dangriga (formerly Stann Creek), and Belize City. In addition, there are reports you can have the officials flown out to San Pedro on Ambergris Cay. This would be an advantage if you are coming from the north into Belize, as it would save a trip to Belize City before you can begin exploring. The charges for this process are reported to be about US$50 to $60. When coming from the south, vessels check in at Punta Gorda or Dangriga, where the formalities are easier than in Belize City, which is geared to big commercial traffic.

You should have passports, clearance from the last port of call, crew lists, stores lists, and the ship's papers. Citizens of most countries, including the U.S., are granted a 30-day stay, but a permit is needed for longer visits. U.S. citizens do not need a visa for stays of less than 3 months. You may be requested to prove you have sufficient funds for your visit.

For the latest information on entry procedures contact the Belize Embassy, 2535 Massachusetts Avenue, Washington, DC 20008 (202-332-9636). The Belize Government Tourism Office (800-624-0686) in the U.S. can provide tourist information and general fact sheets.

Tropical diseases may be encountered in Belize. Contact the U.S. Centers for Disease Control International Travelers Hotline (404-332-4559) for the latest travel advisory.

For assistance in Belize, U.S. citizens may contact the Consular Section of the United States Embassy in Belize City (501-2-77-16-1).

The telephone code for the country is 501; a district code follows and then the local number. The district code for Punta Gorda is 7; Dangriga, 5; Placentia, 6; Belize City, 2; San Pedro, 026; Corozal, 04; and San Ignacio, 92.

The currency is the Belize dollar. The exchange rate (mid-1994) is about .50; Belize$2 is equivalent to about US$1. Exchange rates are subject to change.

SARSTOON RIVER

Pilotage: This river forms the boundary between Guatemala and Belize. The river's banks are low, swampy, and covered with mangroves. The entrance is about 1/2 mile wide, with a bar across the mouth. The bar has a depth of about 6 feet and generally breaks heavily. Depths of less than 18 feet lie about 1 mile east-northeast of the river's mouth.

From the mouth of the river the coast trends about 5 miles north-northwest to the mouth of the Temash River. The sea breaks heavily on the bar at the mouth of this river. Its banks are swampy and fringed with impenetrable mangroves for about 40 or 50 miles inland; then the banks become firm and covered with mahogany trees. The current in the river runs about 1 knot.

The coast then trends about 5 miles northeast to Mother Point, a prominent high bluff. About 9 miles north-northwest of the Sarstoon River, a small isolated hill rises to a height of 400 feet. There are red cliffs between the Temash River and Mother Point.

River Moho enters the sea about 1 1/2 miles north-northeast of Mother Point and about 2 3/4 miles southwest of Orange Point. Like the Temash River, the bar breaks heavily here and the banks of the river have similar vegetation. The current in the river runs about 1 knot.

ORANGE POINT

16 05N, 88 49W
Pilotage: This point is located about 12 miles north-northeast of the Sarstoon River and the Guatemala border. This is about 2 3/4 miles northeast of the River Moho and just south of Punta Gorda. The point is readily identified, as the land is about 30 feet high, dropping abruptly to the coast. The coast and the land are flat and densely wooded for a considerable distance inland. Some of the trees reach a height of around 200 feet.

PUNTA GORDA

16 06N, 88 48W
PUNTA GORDA LIGHT, at Carib Settlement, 16 06.3N, 88 47.9W. F W, 56ft, 9M. White mast; red lights on radio tower 0.6 mile SW.

Pilotage: The town is located just north of Orange Point. Gorda Hill is a conspicuous saddle-shaped hill located about 2 3/4 miles north-northwest of Punta Gorda. A mountain range rises to an elevation of 1,000 feet about 6 miles west of Gorda Hill. This range forms part of a chain of mountains that parallels the coast, from 10 to 20 miles inland, to within 13 miles southwest of Belize City. A light is shown from Punta Gorda.
Port of Entry: Formalities are reported to be easier here than in Belize City. This is a good place to clear in if you are arriving from Guatemala or Honduras.
Anchorage: Anchor off the town dock, where you can dinghy in. The dock is reported to have less than 6 feet of water alongside. This is an open roadstead and is subject to swells. Be prepared to get under way if conditions get too rough.
Services: Groceries, communications, and general supplies are available.

PORK AND DOUGHBOY POINT
16 11N, 88 44W
Pilotage: This point lies about 6 miles northeast of Punta Gorda on the mainland. The Río Grande flows into the sea about 2 1/4 miles south-southwest of the point.

Between Pork and Doughboy Point and Punta Ycacos (Icacos Point), 9 1/2 miles northeast, is Port Honduras. This extensive bay is fouled with many dangers.

Deep River, or Río Hondo, flows into the north part of Port Honduras, about 4 1/2 miles northwest of Punta Ycacos. Depths over the bar are about 2 feet, and inside depths run about 12 to 18 feet.

PUNTA YCACOS

16 15N, 88 35W
Pilotage: This is the southern extremity of a small cay situated close south of a tongue of land that extends 1 mile south. The cay is covered with pine trees.

Wilson Cay is located about 3/4 mile south of Punta Ycacos, and about 1 1/2 miles west of the point are the Bedford Cays. There are numerous other cays in Port Honduras.

SNAKE CAYS
16 12N, 88 32W
EAST SNAKE CAY LIGHT, 16 12.5N, 88 30.4W. Fl W 3s, 65ft, 13M. Concrete framework tower.

Pilotage: These cays lie just outside the 20-meter-depth curve, about 30 miles northeast of Punta Gorda and 4 miles southeast of Punta Ycacos. They cover an area about 8 miles long from southwest to northeast and about 4 miles from southeast to northwest. There are four densely wooded cays and numerous shoal patches with depths of 6 to 30 feet. East Snake Cay, the farthest northeast, is marked by a light.

PUNTA NEGRA
16 16N, 88 33W
Pilotage: This is a conspicuous bluff, which stands about 2 3/4 miles northeast of Punta Ycacos. Between Punta Negra and Monkey River, 6 1/2 miles to the north-northeast, the coast is more elevated and bordered by a sandy beach.

COAST PILOT

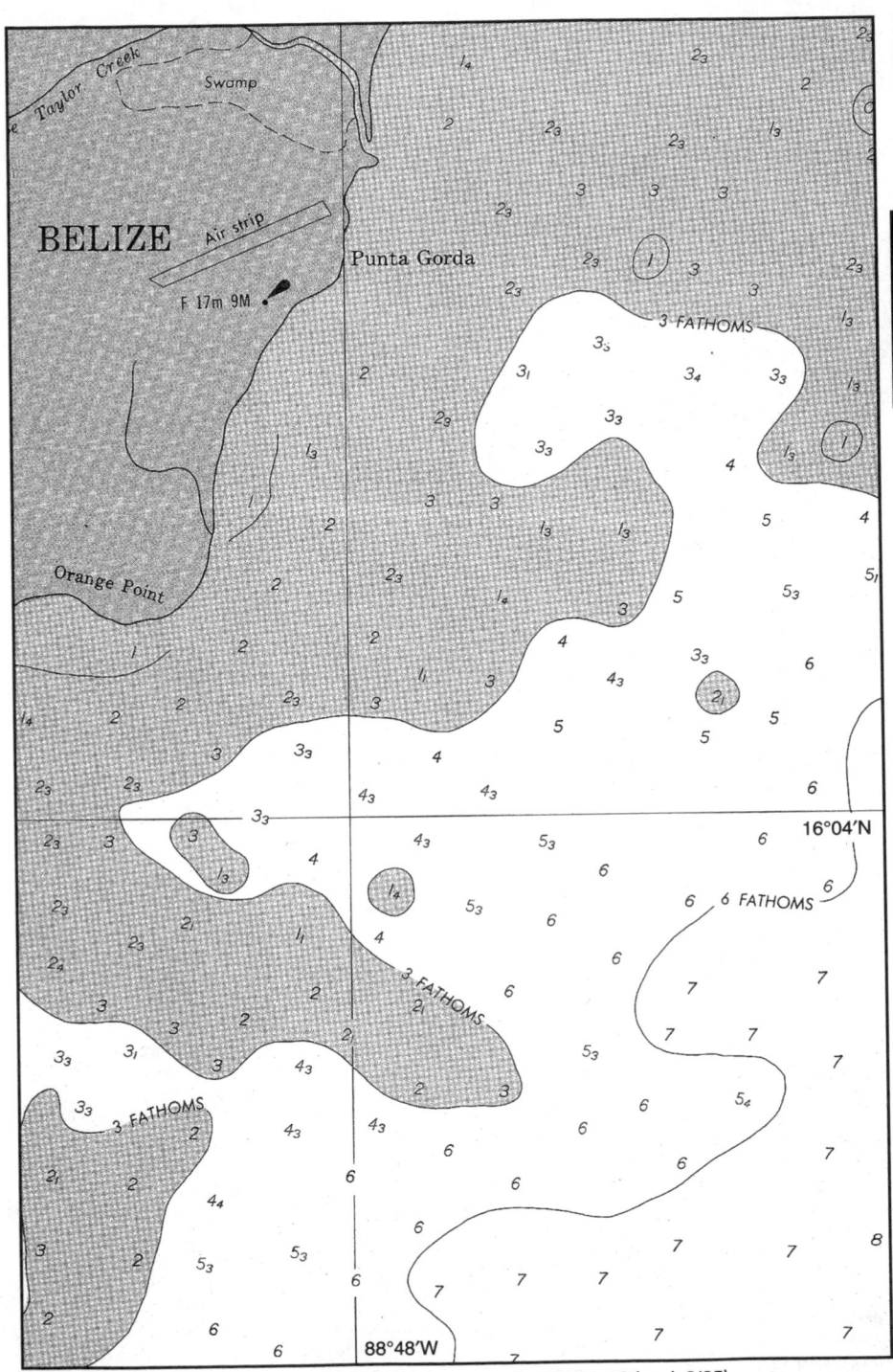

Punta Gorda, soundings in fathoms and feet *(from DMA 28164, 16th ed, 2/85)*

MONKEY RIVER

MONKEY RIVER LIGHT, N side of entrance,
16 22.0N, 88 29.1W. F W, 52ft, 8M. White mast.
Reported extinguished 1985.

Pilotage: This area may be identified by some
of the prominent houses in the town, centered
principally on the south bank of the river. A
light is also on the south bank of the river, at
its entrance.

The 10-meter-depth curve is well defined and
lies 1 mile east of the mouth of the river.
Numerous dangers lie within the 10-meter curve
along this coast.

From Monkey River the coast extends in a north-
northeast direction about 11 miles to Placentia
Point and then continues north-northeast
another 19 miles to Sittee Point. This coast is
low, swampy, and wooded. The shore is fringed
by low, wooded cays and intersected by numerous
small creeks and streams.

MONKEY SHOAL
16 23N, 88 25W
Pilotage: A light buoy is moored 1 mile east
of Monkey Shoal, which has general depths
over 13 feet.

Penguin Shoals has a least depth of about 10
feet and lies about 3 miles north-northeast of
Monkey Shoal.

Middle Shoal is about 1/2 mile north-northeast
of Penguin Shoal, with a least depth of about
13 feet. A light buoy is moored 1 mile northeast of Middle Shoal.

Potts Shoal, with a least depth of 12 feet, lies
about 1 1/2 miles north of Middle Shoal.

BUGLE CAYS
16 29N, 88 19W
BUGLE CAYS LIGHT, SW cay, E side of the
Narrows, main channel leading to Belize City
from the S, 16 29.4N, 88 19.2W. Fl (2) W 10s,
61ft, 10M. White framework tower.

Pilotage: These two cays lie about 3 miles
southeast of Placentia Point, on the east side
of the channel. Without local knowledge, these
cays will not be distinguished from a distance
of more than 4 miles.

Shoals with depths of 6 feet to 18 feet extend
about 4 3/4 miles south of Bugle Cays. The

Narrows lie between these dangers, Potts
Shoal, and the other dangers on the west side
of the passage. The Narrows are about 1 1/2
miles wide, with general depths of 33 to 85 feet.

HARVEST CAY
Pilotage: This cay is about 2 miles south of
the entrance to Placentia Lagoon and has a
conspicuous 79-foot-high table hill on it. This
is just south of the buoyed channel leading
into Big Creek.

BIG CREEK
16 30N, 88 25W
Pilotage: This narrow river lies about 2 1/2
miles west of Placentia Point. It is approached
by a buoyed channel, dredged to a depth of
22 feet, entered east of Harvest Cay. A small
34-foot-long pier with depths of 18 feet alongside extends from the right bank of the creek.
Vessels up to 230-feet-long berth port-side-to,
heading downstream. Pilots from Belize City
operate here, and you may be able to contact
one on VHF channel 16. This is primarily a
commercial port.

PLACENTIA POINT
16 31N, 88 22W
PLACENTIA LAGOON AVIATION LIGHT,
16 32.0N, 88 25.2W. F R, 315ft, 35M. Mast.

Pilotage: This is the southern point on the
narrow ridge of low land that protects the
east side of Placentia Lagoon. This shallow
lagoon parallels the coast for about 10 miles
to the north.

Placentia Cay stands close east of the point,
and the bight thus formed is a good anchorage for small craft. There is a small settlement
on Placentia Point with some groceries, a post
office, a hotel, and some restaurants.

FALSE CAY
16 36N, 88 20W
Pilotage: This cay is about 3/4 mile offshore
and about 5 miles north-northeast of Placentia
Point. The cay is low, narrow, and covered
with bushes and palms. Foul ground extends
about 1/4 mile from it to the northeast
through east, to its southwest side. The west
and northwest sides are steep-to, with depths
up to 34 feet between the cay and shore.
Anchorage: There is reported to be good
anchorage between the cay and shore, in
depths of about 34 feet.

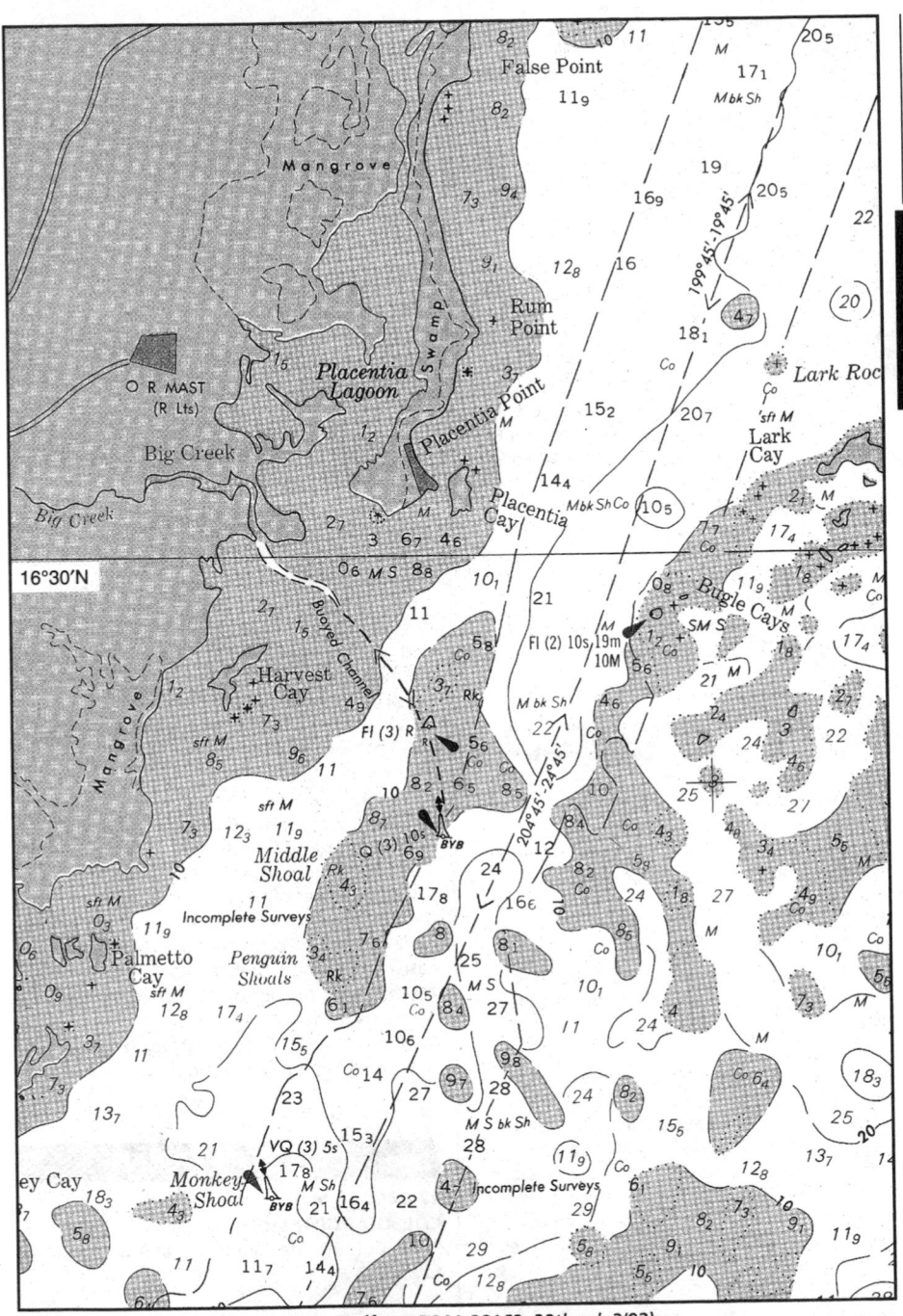

Placentia Area, soundings in meters *(from DMA 28162, 29th ed, 3/92)*

From Placentia Point the coast runs about 8 3/4 miles north-northeast to Jonathan Point. A series of small bays are formed on this coast by Rum Point, False Point, and Rocky Point. They lie 1 3/4 miles, 4 1/4 miles, and 5 1/4 miles north of Placentia Point, respectively. A pier extends about 499 feet from shore at the village of Riverdale, about 2 3/4 miles north of Jonathan Point. A fixed white light is shown from the pier head.

From Jonathan Point the coast trends about 4 miles north to the mouth of South Stann Creek, then about 3 miles north to the entrance to Sapodilla Lagoon. The coast between Placentia Point and the mouth of South Stann Creek is backed by an extensive plain of ridges from 49 to 98 feet high. About 10 miles inland is a ridge of mountains rising to a height of 3,680 feet about 18 miles west of Sapodilla Lagoon. Two peaks of 2,034 feet and 1,679 feet rise, respectively, about 11 1/4 miles northwest and 9 1/2 miles west-southwest of the entrance to Sapodilla Lagoon. A fixed white light is shown in Sapodilla Lagoon.

South Stann Creek flows into the sea across a shallow bar about 2 miles north-northeast of Riverdale.

SITTEE POINT

16 48N, 88 15W
SITTEE POINT LIGHT, 16 48.4N, 88 14.8W. Fl W 5s, 30ft, 8M. White metal framework tower. F W shown at all times in Sapodilla Lagoon 3 miles WSW and on pier head at Riverdale 7.8 miles SSW.

Pilotage: This is a well-defined, wooded point that extends about 3/4 mile from the coast. It forms the south entrance point to the Sittee River.

The river has a depth of about 3 feet over the bar at its entrance. Dead tree stumps rise from the bottom. Depths of less than 18 feet extend about 1/2 mile east from the river. Some ledges situated 3 3/4 miles southeast and 4 miles northeast have depths over them of 13 and 15 feet respectively. The ledges restrict the fairway of the Inner Channel to 3 miles in width.

False Sittee Point is a narrow projection of land located about 2 miles north-northwest of Sittee Point. Shoal ground extends about 3/4 mile east and northeast from the point.

Commerce Bight is entered north of False Sittee Point and extends about 3 miles to the west. The depths within the bight decrease gradually from 36 feet in the entrance to 18 feet about 1/4 mile to 1/2 mile offshore. *Caution: Less water than charted has been reported (1994).* A conspicuous white building is close to the coast, about 2 miles north-northwest of False Sittee Point.

A pier with depths of 5 feet alongside the west and south sides lies 1/2 mile east of the mouth of Yemeri Creek. This is about 5 1/4 miles north-northeast of False Sittee Point. A road connects the pier with Stann Creek 2 1/4 miles to the northeast. A light stands on the pier.

STANN CREEK

16 58N, 88 13W
Pilotage: The town, known as Dangriga, is located on North Stann Creek, just north of Commerce Bight. The village is on both shores of the creek and fronts the coast for about 1 mile. This is the seat of government for the district of Stann Creek. There is a 400-foot pier, with shallow depths alongside, located about 1/4 mile north-northwest of the mouth of the creek. There are many prominent buildings between the jetty and the creek. A private 600-foot jetty is located about 1/2 mile south of the creek.

In 1972 it was reported that a church with a white tower and a conspicuous square tank on a metal framework tower stood in the town. A conspicuous radio mast stands close west of the tank.

Port of Entry: Formalities are reported to be easier here than in Belize City.
Anchorage: Anchor off the town docks north of the river mouth.
Services: Groceries, fuel (by jug), a post office, telephones and general supplies are available.

COLSON POINT

17 04N, 88 15W
COLSON POINT LIGHT, 17 04.4N, 88 14.2W. Fl W 10s, 39ft, 9M. White metal framework tower.

Pilotage: The point is located about 6 1/4 miles north-northwest of North Stann Creek. The 10-meter depth curve lies about 2 1/4 miles off the point. There is a light marking the point.

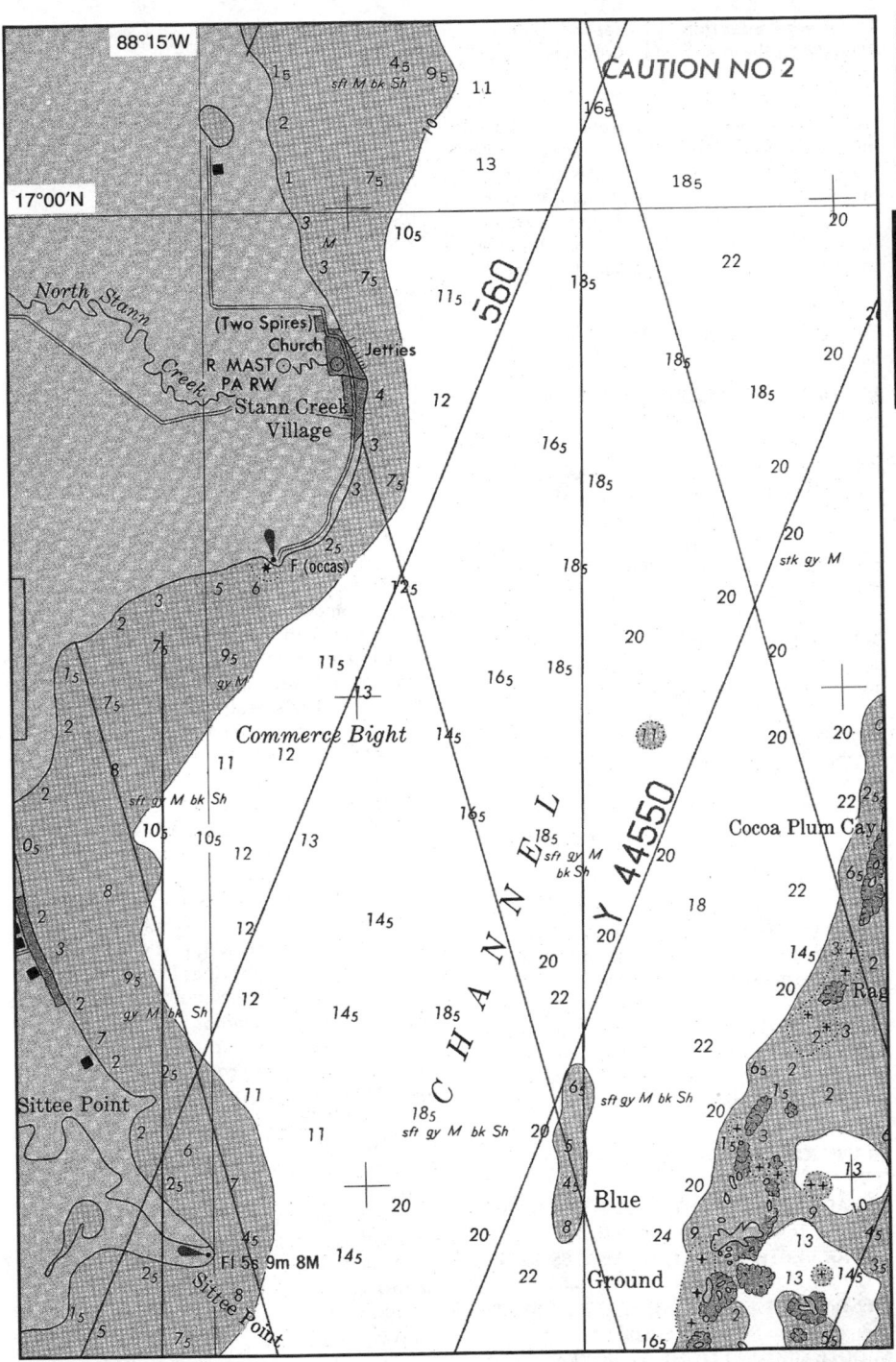

Stann Creek, soundings in meters *(from DMA 28167, 4th ed, 1/84)*

A rock with a depth of 6 1/2 feet over it lies 1/4 mile north-northwest of Colson Point light structure.

From Colson Point the coast trends about 1 1/4 miles west, then turns north-northwest. Mullins River flows into the sea 2 3/4 miles northwest of Colson Point. The town of Mullins River is located on the north shore of the river near the mouth. The bar at the mouth of this river shifts frequently and is considered dangerous.

MANATEE RIVER

17 13N, 88 18W

MANATEE RIVER LIGHT, 17 13.8N, 88 18.2W. F W, 33ft, 2M.

Pilotage: This river discharges about 7 3/4 miles north of Mullins River. It leads to a shallow lagoon, and the shifting bar at the mouth is considered dangerous. A light is occasionally exhibited from a post on the south side of the river mouth.

Dolphin Head, a 400-foot-high hill, is located about 5 miles northwest of the Manatee River light structure. The Paps, a 351-foot-high hill, and 298-foot Saddle Hill are two hummocks situated about 2 and 5 1/4 miles north-northwest of Dolphin Head. These hills are the terminus of the mountain range that backs the coast of Belize. The coast to the north and the terrain well into the interior is low and swampy in places.

There are several shoals with depths of around 20 feet located west of the Manatee River. The Río Sibun flows into the sea about 12 miles north-northeast of Manatee River.

TRIANGLES LIGHT, 17 21.5N, 88 12.3W. Fl G 5s, 16ft, 5M. Black concrete pile.

ROBINSON POINT LIGHT, W point of island, 17 22.0N, 88 11.7W. Q W, 38ft, 8M. White framework tower.

FRANK KNOLL LIGHT, 17 23.8N, 88 11.7W. Q W, 16ft, 5M. Concrete pile.

SUGAR BERTH B LIGHT, 17 23.5N, 88 10.6W. Fl R 2.5s, 16ft, 5M. Black concrete pile.

SUGAR BERTH A LIGHT, 17 25.5N, 88 08.9W. Fl G 2.5s, 16ft, 5M. Black concrete pile.

WESTWARD PATCH LIGHT, 17 25.5N, 88 11.3W. Q R, 16ft, 5M. Red concrete pile.

MIDDLE GROUND LIGHT, 17 28.0N, 88 10.5W. Fl R 2.5s, 16ft, 5M. Red concrete pile.

BELIZE CITY

17 30N, 88 11W

FORT GEORGE LIGHT, 17 29.6N, 88 10.7W. Fl R 5s, 52ft, 8M. White concrete pillar, red band on base. F R lights on radio mast 670 meters WNW; F R and FL R lights on radio mast 1.3 miles NW.

BELIZE CITY AVIATION LIGHT, 17 32.5N, 88 18.5W. Q W, 30M. Radio mast.

Pilotage: The city is located on the south branch of the Belize River, about 17 miles north-northeast of the Manatee River. The harbor is an open roadstead with limited docking facilities for large vessels. It is approached from inside the reef via Inner or Main Channel and from outside the reef via Eastern Channel (see the description later in this section).

The city is situated on both sides of Haulover Creek, which is the southern part of the Belize River.

Winds: Easterly and southeast winds prevail from the middle of February to the end of September, with the greatest period of calm occurring at the end of February. Northeast through northwest winds prevail during the rest of the year. The average wind velocity is about 10 knots. Northers are most likely to occur in November and December, but they rarely exceed force 4 or 5.

Currents: The current generally sets south through the harbor at a rate of 1 1/2 knots, but during the season of the northers this rate may increase to 3 knots. North currents, which attain a velocity of 1 1/2 to 2 knots, may be experienced during the rainy season. The mean range of the tide is negligible; however, east winds raise the water level and north winds lower it. During northers the fall may be as much as 2 to 2 1/2 feet.

Port of Entry: This harbor is geared to the needs of commercial ships, and the formalities for yachts may be less convenient than at some other ports. Customs is near the pier at Ft. George Point.

Dockage: The 1,500-foot wharf at Ft. George Point is reported to have depths of 1 to 6 feet alongside. Cruisers dinghy in here, but report there is a problem with petty theft. There is reported to be a shallow-draft marina near the Ramada Inn.

Anchorage: Cruisers usually anchor off the pier at Fort George Point. This area is open to the wind and swells.

Services: Fuel and water are available at the pier on Fort George Point. There are good

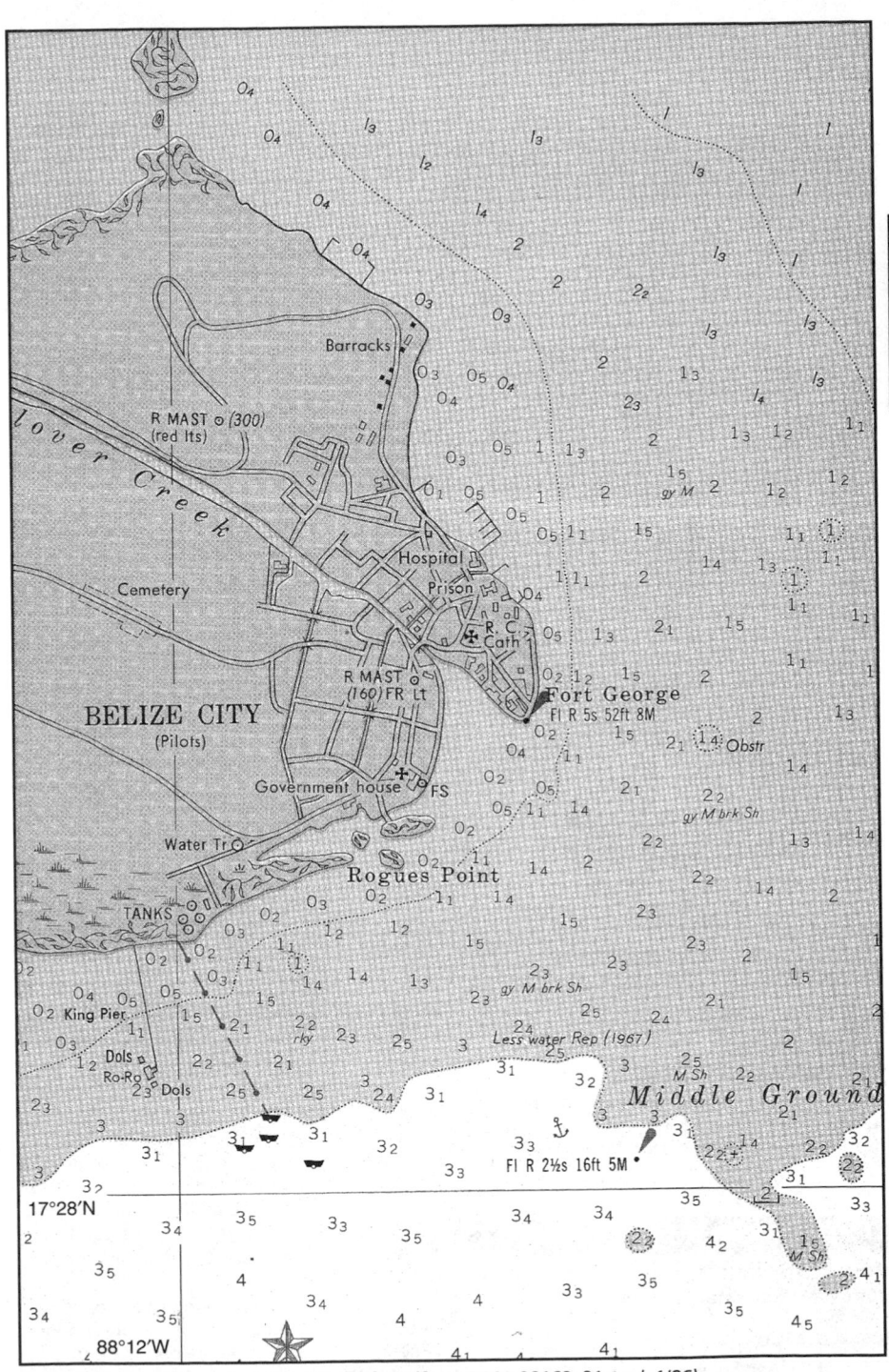

Belize City, soundings in fathoms and feet *(from DMA 28168, 21st ed, 1/86)*

grocery stores, general supplies, communication links, banks, a post office, and a U.S. Embassy. There are hardware stores, and there is a marine railway in Haulover Creek.

BELIZE CITY TO AMBERGRIS CAY

Pilotage: From Saint George's Cay the reef trends about 19 miles north to abreast the south end of Ambergris Cay. The reef's eastern edge is steep-to. The area west of the barrier reef is shoal, with general depths of 4 to 15 feet. The route between Belize City and Ambergris Cay, inside the reef, is shoal and should only be attempted by boats drawing less than 6 or 7 feet. Numerous cays are located in this shoal area.

ROCK POINT
17 40N, 88 15W
Pilotage: This point is about 12 miles north-northwest of Fort George in Belize City. Between Belize City and here lie Peter's Bluff, a low cay covered with trees about 2 1/2 miles north of Fort George, and Riders Cay, a small islet north of the former cay. There are depths of about 6 to 7 feet in the area east of the cays.

Hicks Cays lie east of Rock Point and about mid-way between the coast and the barrier reef. Depths in the area run 6 to 10 feet.

CAY CORKER (CAY CAULKER)
17 47N, 88 01W
Pilotage: This cay is about 5 miles south of the south end of Ambergris Cay. There is a small town and an anchorage in the bight on the southwest part of the island.

CANGREJO CAY
17 52N, 88 02W
Pilotage: This cay is located about 2 1/2 miles out on the reef extending southwest from the southern end of Ambergris Cay. The description of Ambergris Cay follows, under the heading "The Barrier Reef."

CHETUMAL BAY

BULKHEAD LIGHT, 17 56N, 88 08W. Fl W 1.5s, 30ft, 10M. Red metal framework tower.

Pilotage: This area is entered via an intricate channel located between Cangrejo Cay and

Northern River, 10 miles away on the mainland to the west. It is about 22 miles from Belize to the Northern River, as the crow flies. The coast is low and covered with mangroves, which extend to the shore. The water is shoal.

The channel leading north into Chetumal Bay has a least charted depth of about 6 feet. This channel takes you to the mouth of the Hondo River, which forms part of the boundary with Mexico. Parts of the channel are marked with stake beacons, but its use is recommended only to those with local knowledge.

COROZAL
18 22N, 88 24W
COROZAL LIGHT, 18 22N, 88 27W. F R, 5M.

Pilotage: This small town stands near the west head of Chetumal Bay and is fronted by a small pier with a depth of 4 feet alongside. Anchorage can be taken about 300 yards to the southeast of the pier.

HONDO RIVER (RÍO HONDO)
CONSEJO POINT LIGHT, 18 27N, 88 20W. F W, 50ft, 5M. Mast.

Pilotage: Consejo Point, about 8 miles northeast of Corozal, is the south entrance point to the Hondo River, which forms part of the border with Mexico. The Mexican settlement of Payo Obispo is located about 2 1/2 miles north of Consejo Point. The river is navigable by small craft drawing less than 4 feet for about 70 miles. A bar with a depth of about 5 feet fronts the river mouth.

THE BARRIER REEF

Pilotage: This reef fronts the coast of Belize and lies from 10 to 22 miles east of the coast. It extends from the Sapodilla Cays, which lie about 31 miles east of Punta Gorda, north for 118 miles to Ambergris Cay. Abreast of Belize City the reef lies about 8 miles offshore. There are general depths of 6 to 18 feet on the reef, but numerous small cays, rocks, and coral banks are interspersed along its entire length.

The seaward side is extremely steep-to, with depths over 656 feet close off the outer edge. A heavy sea usually breaks along the entire seaward extremity.

In the area west of the reef between Sapodilla Cays and Blue Ground Range, about 44 miles to the north-northeast, foul ground with numerous cays and shoals extends west to the fairway of the Inner or Main Channel. In the vicinity of Blue Ground Range the west side of the reef becomes regular and fairly steep-to as it extends north to the dangers on the south side of Belize City.

NOTE: Navigation through the various intricate openings in the barrier reef should not be attempted without local knowledge or the assistance of a pilot.

Many of the cays have been planted with coconut palms, and some have houses on them. Hurricanes periodically devastate the area, or some part of it, and the descriptions of the cays that follow may be out of date. Although the vegetation usually recovers quickly, the shape of individual cays may be permanently altered and some may disappear completely.

SAPODILLA CAYS
16 07N, 88 16W
HUNTING CAY LIGHT, 16 06.6N, 88 15.8W. L Fl W 10s, 57ft, 13M. White metal framework tower.

Pilotage: This group of small cays is located about 20 miles southeast of Punta Ycacos. This group is the farthest south on the great barrier reef. They extend about 3 3/4 miles northeast from Sapodilla Cay to Grassy Cay. The reef extends about 32 miles north-northeast from here to Gladden Spit. Between Sapodilla Cays and Gladden Spit the barrier reef is generally broken and there are numerous cays, rocks and openings along its entire length.

Sapodilla Cay (16° 05'N, 88° 17'W) has a conspicuous clump of coconut trees on it. Hunting and Nicolas cays, the middle cays of the group, are densely wooded with coconut trees. They are inhabited.

There are numerous dangerous heads and irregular depths in the area.

SEAL CAY
16 10N, 88 20W
Pilotage: This islet has a few trees on it. It is situated on the northeast part of a small circular reef enclosing a lagoon. The former Seal Cays, 2 1/2 miles south, are reported to have been destroyed by a hurricane in 1945, and in 1972

only a sand bore remained. Shoal patches are in the area.

LAWRENCE ROCK
16 10N, 88 20W
Pilotage: This rock lies about 3 1/4 miles west of Seal Cay and has a least depth of under four feet. This rock is dangerous because the water over it is not sufficiently discolored to indicate its position. The ground is foul between the rock and Seal Cay.

RANGUANA CAY
16 20N, 88 10W
Pilotage: This cay lies about midway along the section of reef between Sapodilla Cay and Gladden Spit and about 1 1/4 miles from the seaward side. Trees up to 50 feet high cover the cay. Ranguana Entrance, an opening through the reef about 1/4 mile wide, lies about 1 1/2 miles southeast of the cays. There are depths of 20 to 24 feet in this passage.

POMPION CAY
16 24N, 88 06W
Pilotage: This group of wooded islands that lie about 4 3/4 miles northeast of Ranguana Cay is reported to be inhabited.

Little Water Cay and Hatchet Cay are two wooded cays lying about 3 miles north and 4 1/4 miles north-northeast of Pompion Cay, respectively. The two cays have been reported to be good radar targets.

GLADDEN SPIT

16 31N, 87 59W
Pilotage: This is the easternmost projection of the barrier reef.

CAUTION: This spit has been reported to lie about 2 miles east of its charted position.

Gladden and Queen Cay entrances lie about 1 1/2 and 4 1/2 miles southwest of Gladden Spit. They have least charted depths of about 8 feet and 13 feet, respectively. These openings lead to the Inner or Main Channel through narrow intricate passages. They should not be attempted without local knowledge or the services of a pilot.

Victoria Channel is the navigable passage that lies between the dangers extending east from Bugle Cays and those extending west from

Gladden Spit. Victoria Channel may be used as an alternate route to Inner or Main Channel. Laughing Bird Cay (16° 26′N, 88° 12′W), Moho Cay (16° 30′N, 88° 10′W), Bakers Rendezvous, and Crawl Cay are all on the western side of Victoria Channel. Quamino Cay (16° 39′N, 88° 13′W) is located on the north side of the northwest end of Victoria Channel.

For about 14 miles to South Cut, the barrier reef extends north-northwest in a solid coral barrier, with no cays. Then for about 6 miles farther north-northwest to Water Cay, it is broken with numerous drying sandbanks and some above-water rocky heads. There are several cuts along this part of the barrier reef, which are usable by small vessels that have local knowledge. The west side of the reef is irregular and the area west to Inner or Main Channel is interspersed with numerous cays and shoals.

WATER CAY
16 49N, 88 05W
Pilotage: This is a fairly large, wooded cay, with trees about 59 feet high.

BLUE GROUND RANGE
16 48N, 88 09W
Pilotage: This group of cays is located on the west side of the reef opposite South Water Cay and about 5 1/2 miles east of Sittee Point. They are about 2 1/2 miles in extent in a north/south direction.

TOBACCO CAY
16 54N, 88 09W
Pilotage: This small wooded cay lies on the north side of Tobacco Cay Entrance, 5 miles north of Water Cay.

Tobacco Cay Entrance is a 13-foot-deep passage that leads west toward Tobacco Range, 1 mile west of the entrance. The passage leads to the Inner or Main Channel, where it joins about 2 1/2 miles north of Cocoa Plum Cay (16° 53′N, 88° 07′W).

Tobacco Reef, which is nearly dry in many places, lies between Water Cay and Tobacco Cay Entrance.

From Tobacco Cay to Glory Cay, about 12 1/2 miles to the north, the reef is almost continuous and practically dry. This section of the reef is known as Columbus Reef.

Cross Cay, with trees 59 feet high, and Columbus Cay, with trees 49 feet high, lie close west of the barrier reef. They lie 5 miles and 6 1/2 miles north-northeast of Tobacco Cay, respectively. Several cays lie west of Cross and Columbus Cays.

GLORY CAY
17 06N, 88 01W
Pilotage: This small, sandy cay is located 3/4 mile northwest of Columbus Reef. Southern Long Cay is a wooded cay located inside the barrier reef 1 mile southwest of Glory Cay.

From Glory Cay the barrier reef, which is broken in many places, trends north-northwest about 28 miles to Saint George's Cay, which is north of Eastern Channel. The cays west of the barrier reef and those northwest to north-northwest of Glory Cay are wooded.

SKIFF SAND
17 13N, 88 03W
Pilotage: Skiff Sand is about 1 meter high. It is located 7 1/4 miles north-northwest of Glory Cay.

Rendezvous Cay stands about 1 1/2 miles north of Skiff Sand in the middle of a break in the barrier reef. It is covered with bushes and coconut trees and a clump of palm trees.

Bluefield Range, a group of mangrove-covered cays, stand near the west side of the barrier reef west-northwest of Skiff Sand.

The barrier reef between Rendezvous Cay and English Cay, about 5 miles to the north, is broken and marked by numerous banks, cays, and coral reefs. Immediately north of English Cay is Eastern Channel. Goffs Cay is located about 1 1/4 miles north of English Cay and north of the entrance to Eastern Channel. This cay is small and sandy, and a drying coral head lies about 1/2 mile to its southeast.

EASTERN CHANNEL

17 20N, 88 02W (ENGLISH CAY)
EASTERN CHANNEL RANGE (Front),
17 19.7N, 88 02.6W. Q W, 23ft, 9M. Concrete pillar. **(Rear),** on English Cay, 300 meters 300° from front. Fl W 2.5s, 62ft, 11M. White tower.
GOFFS CAY SANDBORE LIGHT, 17 20.4N, 88 02.0W. Fl R 5s, 16ft, 3M. Red concrete pile.

WATER CAY SPIT LIGHT, 17 21.4N, 88 04.4W. Q R, 16ft, 5M. Red concrete pile.

NORTHEAST SPIT LIGHT, 17 23.0N, 88 05.3W. Q G, 16ft. Black concrete pile.

WHITE GROUNDS SPIT LIGHT, 17 22.8N, 88 06.8W. Fl W 2.5s, 16ft, 5M. Red concrete pile.

SPANISH CAY SPIT LIGHT, 17 22.7N, 88 08.2W. Q G, 16ft, 5M. Black concrete pile.

HALFWAY LIGHT, marks One Man Cay Channel, 17 22.2N, 88 09.5W. Q R, 16ft, 5M. Red concrete pile.

SOUTHWEST SIDE LIGHT, marks One Man Cay Channel, 17 22.0N, 88 09.7W. Q G, 16ft, 5M. Black concrete pile.

Pilotage: When approaching Eastern Channel from the north, steer for a position about 7 1/2 miles west of Mauger Cay (17° 36'N, 87° 46'W), which is the northernmost of the Turneffe Islands. Steer a south-southwest course to pass near mid-channel between Turneffe Islands and the barrier reef, until the lights on English Cay are in line on a bearing of 300°.

When approaching Eastern Channel from the south, steer for a position 2 3/4 miles south of Cay Bokel (17° 10'N, 87° 54'W), at the southern end of the Turneffe Islands. Then steer a mid-channel course between the Turneffe Islands Reef and Rendezvous Cay until the lights on English Cay are in line on a bearing of 300°.

To enter Eastern Channel steer for the lights on English Cay bearing 300°, until the east side of Water Cay (17° 23'N, 88° 04'W) bears 340°. Alter course to 340° and maintain it until Eastern Channel opens to the west-northwest. Then proceed through the sinuous passage, maintaining a mid-channel course until One Man Cay Channel is reached.

The east entrance to One Man Cay Channel is about 400 yards wide between the reefs, each of which is marked by a light. Steer a north-west course through the channel until Robinson Point (17° 22'N, 88° 12'W), marked by a light, bears 233°. Then steer as required to the anchorage off Belize City.

PAUNCH CAY

17 24N, 88 02W

Pilotage: This barren cay lies close to the edge of the reef about 3 miles north of Goffs Cay. From Paunch Cay the steep-to reef extends

about 9 1/2 miles north to Saint George's Cay. This low sandy cay is easily identified by the houses and coconut palms on it. From Saint George's Cay the reef trends about 19 miles north to abreast the south end of Ambergris Cay.

Drowned Cays are located about 1 to 2 miles west of the barrier reef.

AMBERGRIS CAY

18 02N, 87 55W

Pilotage: This cay's northern end is separated from Mexico, and the mainland, by Boca Bacalar Chico, a narrow boat channel with very shallow depths. The island appears to be part of the coast from offshore. The east extremity of the island, known as Reef Point, is about 1/2 to 1 1/2 miles inside the reefline. The reefs gradually approach the coast of the mainland about 9 miles north of Reef Point.

CAUTION: The current generally sets strongly west toward the barrier reef, accompanied by a heavy swell, so that every possible caution should be observed here.

San Pedro: This settlement is on the east side of Ambergris Cay, toward the south end. This is inside the barrier reef, and the only approaches from the sea are via reef channels. This is reported to be a dangerous entrance when a sea is running and should not be attempted without local knowledge. A shallow channel leads south from here, inside the reefs to Belize City. It is reported that you can fly government officials to here from Belize City to complete your entrance clearance.

OFFSHORE REEFS

Pilotage: The dangers offshore consist of Glover Reef, Lighthouse Reef, and the Turneffe Islands. They are all located east of the barrier reef described previously. There are deep passages between all three reefs and the barrier reef.

Currents: In the vicinity of the reefs, currents in November, December, and January depend on the winds. A north-setting current is experienced during west winds and a south-setting current with north winds. During February and March the current usually sets north at a rate of about 1 1/2 knots. In April and May it usually sets south at a rate of 1 1/2 knots. In June, July, and August the current usually sets

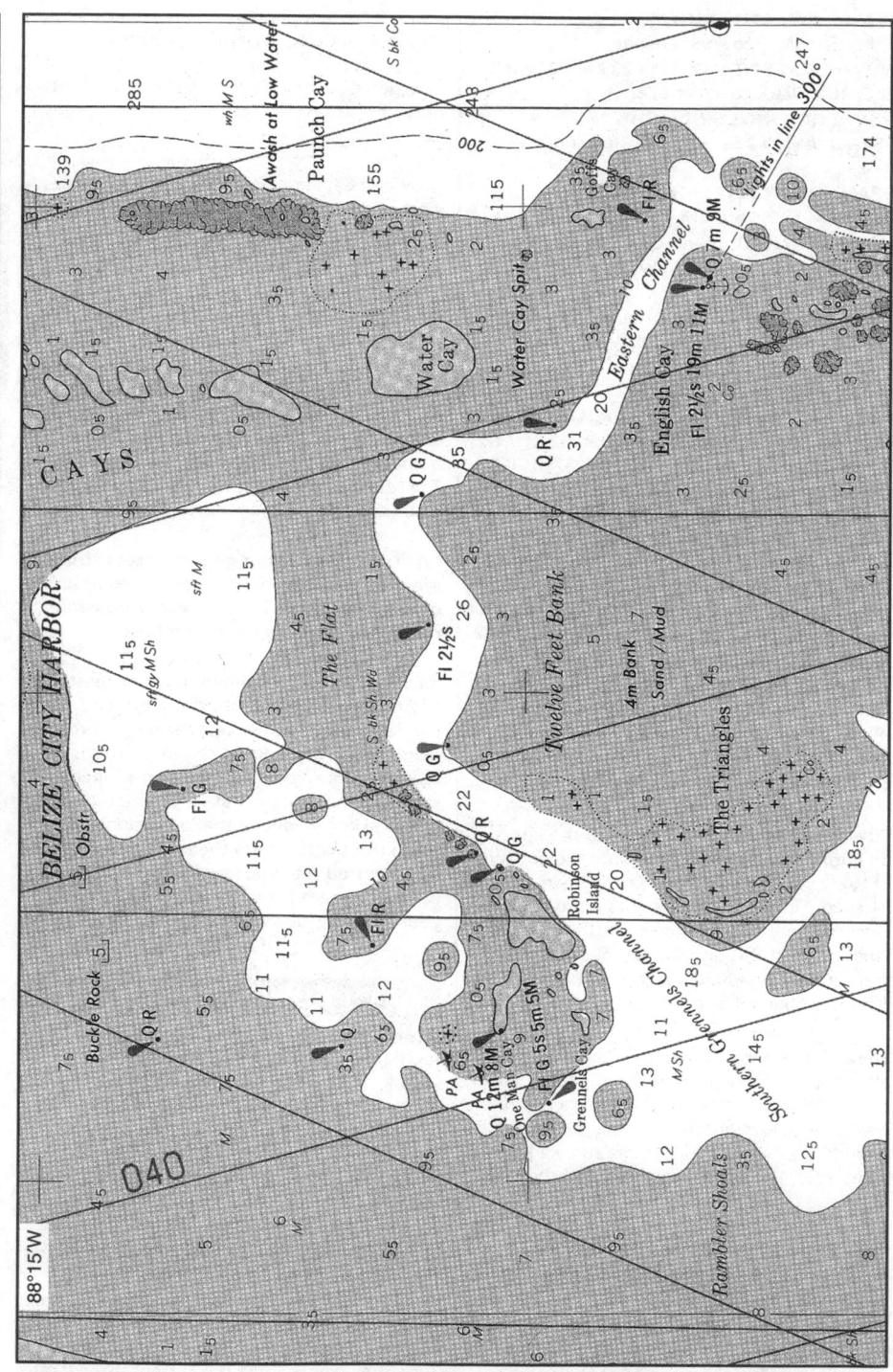

Eastern Channel, soundings in meters *(from DMA 28167, 4th ed, 1/84)*

north at a rate of 1 1/2 knots. In September and October the north-setting current increases to 2 knots.

GLOVER REEF

16 50N, 87 47W
SOUTHWEST CAYS LIGHT, 16 42.9N, 87 50.6W. Fl (2) W 5s, 9M. White metal framework tower.
NORTHEAST SIDE OF REEF LIGHT, 16 54.6N, 87 42.0W. Fl W 5s, 9M. White metal framework tower.

Pilotage: The south extremity of this reef is located about 13 miles north-northeast of Gladden Spit, on the barrier reef. It is about 14 miles long and 6 miles wide. There is a barrier reef around the perimeter, which is impassable except for a small opening at its southern extremity, west of Southwest Cays, and another north of Long Cay on the southeastern side. The latter entrance is dangerous because of its location on the windward side of the reef.

CAUTION: Glover Reef must be approached with great care, especially from the north, as the reef is low and not always visible from a distance. The reef is steep-to, and soundings give little warning. A strong west-going current has been experienced on several occasions between Glover Reef and Lighthouse Reef.

The north point of the reef is known as Amounme Point. A light is exhibited on the northeast edge of the reef, 4 miles southeast of Amounme Point.

Southwest Cays (16° 43′N, 87° 51′W) are the farthest south of the five cays situated on the south extremity of Glover Reef. The opening in the reef west of Southwest Cays accommodates vessels drawing up to 12 feet, with local knowledge.

LIGHTHOUSE REEF

17 16N, 87 32W
HALF MOON CAY LIGHT, E end, 17 12.3N, 87 31.6W. Fl (4) W 15s, 80ft, 14M. White metal framework tower.
SANDBORE CAY LIGHT, N end of reef, 17 28.1N, 87 29.2W. Fl W 10s, 83ft, 17M. Red metal framework tower.

Pilotage: This reef is the danger farthest to the east of Belize's barrier reef. It lies about 13 1/2 miles north-northeast of the northeast

extremity of Glover Reef. The reef is steep-to and unbroken except in the vicinity of Half Moon Cay, where there is a passage. There is reported to be a pass at the northwest tip of the reef.

CAUTION: Lighthouse Reef should be approached with great care as there is considerable doubt about the exact position of the edges of the reef. The western edge and the southern part of the reef are reported to lie up to 1 mile west of their charted positions.

Half Moon Cay (17° 12′N, 87° 32′W) is marked by a light. It lies within the southeast part of the reef. Numerous coral heads surround the islet, but there is a shallow opening about 1/2 mile to the west. The islet has been reported to give a good radar return at distances up to 20 miles.

Sandbore Cay (17° 28′N, 87° 30′W) lies near the north extremity of the reef. It is a small, tree-covered islet. Four small white buildings and a wooden jetty stand close to the lighthouse on the north side of the cay. Northern Cay, about 3/4 mile southwest of Sandbore Cay, is wooded.

TURNEFFE ISLANDS

17 22N, 87 51W
CAY BOKEL LIGHT, S extremity of Turneffe Islands, 17 09.8N, 87 54.4W. Fl (3) W 15s, 33ft, 8M. White metal framework tower.
MAUGER CAY LIGHT, 17 36.5N, 87 46.2W. Fl (2) W 10s, 61ft, 13M. White metal framework tower.

Pilotage: This extensive group of mangrove-covered islands and cays on a coral and sand reef lies about 12 miles west of Lighthouse Reef. The barrier reef surrounding these islands is about 30 miles long and up to 10 miles wide. These islands are so closely grouped that from a distance they appear as one large flat island. It was reported in 1964 that radar returns from Grand Point, the south end of the islands, may be easily mistaken for Cay Bokel.

CAUTION: The east side of the Turneffe Islands is charted from old surveys and should be approached with caution.

The reef that fringes this group lies at an average distance of 1/2 mile off the east side and 1 mile off the west side. The reef on the west side is awash in many places, but the seaward edge on all sides is steep-to. There are several shallow openings and numerous lagoons between the various islands, which are used by small craft with local knowledge.

Cay Bokel (17° 10′N, 87° 54′W) is a small patch of sand that lies at the south extremity of the reef extending south from Grand Point. There are several detached cays near the south extremity of the reef, but from a distance, they appear as part of the main group of islands. On one of these, Big Cay Bokel, there are several fishing lodges.

Several detached cays stand on the reef north of the main group of islands. Mauger Cay (17° 36′N, 87° 46′W) is the northernmost cay in the Turneffe group. The lighthouse on the cay is prominent and is a good landmark if heading toward Eastern Channel from the north.

MEXICO

Hydrographic and cartographic information in this section has been supplied, in part, courtesy of the Secretaría de Marina, Dirección de Oceanografía Naval of Mexico.

CAUTION: Our information on aids to navigation comes from official government sources. The latitudes and longitudes of these marks may not correspond to the readings from GPS receivers. Some aids have been reported as unreliable, missing, off position or showing incorrect characteristics. No single aid to navigation, or waypoint, should be relied upon as a sole means of fixing your position.

NOTE: The lights of Mexico are characterized by the number of flashes, the periods being subject to fluctuation.

NOTE: The chartlets in this section are <u>not</u> <u>intended for navigation</u> and are included for reference and planning purposes only. While chartlets reproduced from government sources are from the most current editions as of press time, they incorporate <u>no corrections</u> to navigational aids, depths, or hazards since the edition publication date.

ENTRY PROCEDURES

The Yucatán coast of Mexico is becoming a more popular cruising destination, as it is located only about 340 miles southwest of Key West, Florida. Some cruisers slog out against the current from Florida, while others visit the Yucatán as part of a clockwise circuit of the Caribbean basin. The area west of the Yucatán Peninsula is still seldom visited by pleasure boaters. See *Reed's Nautical Companion* for an illustration of the country flag.

Ports of Entry on the Yucatán coast include Xcalak, San Miguel on Cozumel, Puerto Morelos, and Puerto Mujeres on Isla Mujeres. On the north side of the Yucatán and in the Gulf of Mexico, you can clear at Progreso, Campeche, Frontera, Coatzacoalcos, Veracruz, and Tampico. When you check in you will be issued a coastwise clearance, or *zarpe*, on which you should list all the ports you are planning to visit while in Mexico. You should have the officials grant permission to visit intermediate ports, if possible.

You will have to check in with the port officials in any port you stop at along the way.

Mexican paperwork is reported to be time consuming and exacting. You should have multiple copies of your crew list typed in *Spanish*, which you will probably have to give to officials in each port. For each crewmember, you should have either a tourist card or visa (which depends on each crew's nationality). If you are arriving from Belize, these items are available from the Mexican Consulate in Belize City. Generally a tourist card is good for 30 to 90 days. Citizens of the U.S., the United Kingdom, Canada, and most West European countries do not need a visa for entry. Citizens of many countries can obtain tourist cards when they enter the country. You must turn in your tourist card when leaving the country.

You should have passports, ship's papers, and a clearance from your last port of call outside the country. U.S. citizens can get by with just a driver's license or other positive identification, but having a passport is always best. All firearms must be declared and have proper permits in advance from a Mexican consulate. Your guns will be held for the duration of your stay, unless you have a Mexican hunting license for them, which you should apply for in advance of your arrival. For more information on hunting licenses write to Direccion General de Caza, Serdan 27, Mexico, D.F.

Fishing licenses must be purchased for each crewmember and the boat if you have any fishing gear on board. Again, this license is best applied for before arriving in the country. For more information on fishing write to General de Pesca, Av. Alvaro Obregón 269, Mexico 7, D.F.

To obtain information on the latest entry requirements contact the Mexican Consulate at 2827 16th Street NW, Washington, DC 20009 (202-736-1000). When in Mexico, U.S. citizens might want to contact the United States Embassy in Mexico City (52-5-211-0042). The U.S. also maintains a number of consulates

and consular agents in Mexico, including in
Cancún and Tampico.

Tropical diseases may be encountered in Mexico;
visitors should contact the U.S. Centers for
Disease Control International Travelers Hotline
(404-332-4559) for up-to-date health notices.
Care should be taken to drink only sterile water,
well-cooked vegetables, and well-cooked
shellfish.

The international telephone country code for
Mexico is 52; a city code follows, and then the
local number. The city code for Cancún is 98;
Veracruz, 29; and Mexico City, 5.

Mexican currency is the peso, currently worth
about 0.29 U.S. dollars (summer 1994). Exchange
rates are subject to change. The main language
is Spanish, but many people speak some English
in tourist areas.

BAHÍA DE CHETUMAL

CIUDAD CHETUMAL (Payo Obispo),
18 30.0N, 88 20.0W. Fl W 6s, 59ft, 17M. White
cylindrical concrete tower. Visible 115°–064°.
HEAD OF FISCAL MOLE, Q W, 23ft. Wooden
post.
AVIATION LIGHT, 18 30.0N, 88 22.0W.
Al Fl W G 10s, 57ft. Tower. Radiobeacon.

PAYO OBISPO (CIUDAD CHETUMAL)

18 30N, 88 17W
Pilotage: This settlement is in Chetumal on
the north side of the Río Hondo, which forms
the border with Belize. It is the site of a Mexican
naval base, which maintains the radio station
in the town. A T-Head pier, about 130 feet long
and 80 feet across the face, with a depth of
6 feet alongside the face and 3 feet alongside
its west side, extends from the shore in front
of town. Lighters and tugs are used to unload
cargo from freighters anchored off the west
side of Cay Corker, in Belize.

Chetumal Bay extends about 26 miles north-
northeast from the Río Hondo. It narrows in its
northern part where the Río Kik flows into it.

LA AGUADA, 18 14.0N, 87.55.0W. Fl (2) W 10s,
40ft, 11M. Concrete cylindrical tower.
XCALAK, 18 16.0N, 87 50.0W. Fl (3) W 12s,
43ft, 17M. Cylindrical concrete tower. Visible
214°–360°. A Fl W light shows close by.

BOCA BACALAR CHICO

18 11N, 87 52W
Pilotage: This narrow boat passage separates
the north end of Ambergris Cay, in Belize, from
the Mexican mainland to the north. Xcalak is a
small coastal port of entry located about 6 miles
north of Boca Bacalar Chico. Vessels drawing
less than 15 feet can enter and anchor inside
the reef; local knowledge is recommended.
The bottom is reported to be mud and rock,
with patches of white sand, providing good
holding.

From Xcalak the coast trends about 65 miles
north-northeast to Punta Herrero. It is low,
flat, and wooded. Nearly all of this stretch of
coast is fronted by a reef that lies from 1 to 1 1/2
miles offshore. There are several channels through
the reef, but they should not be attempted
without local knowledge.

CAYO LOBOS, center of cay, 18 23.0N,
87 23.0W. Fl (3) W 12s, 50ft, 11M. Square
galvanized tower.
PUNTA GAVILAN, 18 25.0N, 87 45.0W.
Fl W 6s, 36ft, 11M. White cylindrical concrete
tower.
CAYO CENTRO, 18 36.0N, 87 20.0W.
Fl (2) W 10s, 50ft, 11M. Square galvanized
tower.
EL MAJAHUAL, 18 43.0N, 87 41.0W.
Fl (4) W 16s, 33ft, 11M. Square galvanized
tower.
BANCO CHINCHORRO, N of the two islets
which form Cayo Norte, 18 46.0N, 87 19.0W.
Fl W 6s, 52ft, 11M. Cylindrical concrete tower.

BANCO CHINCHORRO

18 35N, 87 27W
Pilotage: This dangerous steep-to shoal lies
about 28 miles northeast of Ambergris Cay in
Belize. It is about 14 to 16 miles offshore. The
greater part of the shoal has depths ranging
from 6 to 24 feet, but there are numerous rocky
heads and sandbanks. The stranded wrecks
that lie along the east side of the shoal have
been reported to be conspicuous visually and
on radar. It has been reported that Banco
Chinchorro is a good radar target for south-
bound vessels.

Cayo Lobos is a small cay near the south
extremity of the bank. There are several openings
through the reef to the west and northwest of
the cay; local knowledge is recommended.

Cayo Centro (18° 36'N, 87° 20'W) lies in the middle of the bank, about 1 1/2 miles from its east side. This low cay is about 2 1/2 miles long. It is composed of sand with a covering of bushes and coconut trees. A 1-mile-long salt water lagoon lies in the middle of the cay. A dangerous strong current sets into Firefly Bight, about 2 miles southeast of Cayo Centro.

Cayo Norte (18° 45'N, 87° 19'W) lies about 1 1/2 miles south of the northern extremity of the bank. It actually consists of two cays, covered with dense vegetation and trees about 40 to 50 feet high. A disused lighthouse and building stand close south of the current lighthouse.

CAUTION: In the vicinity of Banco Chinchorro there is usually a very strong current setting toward its east side.

The passage between the bank and the coast of the mainland to the west is clear of dangers and deep.

EL UVERO, 19 04.0N, 87 33.0W. Fl (3) W 12s, 33ft, 11M. Square aluminum tower.
PUNTA HERRERO, S side of entrance to Bahía del Espiritu Santo, 19 18.0N, 87 27.0W. Fl W 6s, 75ft, 15M. White metal framework tower. Visible 090°–022°.

PUNTA HERRERO

19 18N, 87 26W

Pilotage: This is the southern entrance point to Bahía del Espiritu Santo. It is fronted by foul ground extending about 1 mile offshore. The entrance to the bay to the north is also generally foul.

The coast extends about 53 miles north from here to Salta Iman. The southern part of this coast is indented by Bahía del Espiritu Santo, about 10 miles wide, and by Bahía de La Ascension, about 10 miles farther north.

The coast between Bahía de La Ascension and Salta Iman is quite regular, low, and densely wooded. Punta Yaan is a group of conspicuous cliffs, which stand on an otherwise flat section of the coast.

The coast from Punta Yaan extends northeast for about 50 miles to Puerto Morelos. Moderately elevated land extends about 6 miles north from Punta Yaan, then becomes low and flat. Isla Cozumel lies about 17 miles south of Puerto

Morelos and 9 miles offshore. The coast about 5 miles southwest of Puerto Morelos is fringed by a steep-to reef which extends up to 1 1/4 miles offshore.

The coast from Puerto Morelos extends north-northeast about 14 miles and then gradually curves north-northwest for about 36 miles to Cabo Catoche. Numerous islands, cays, and other dangers lie within 1 to 15 miles offshore in this area.

BAHÍA DEL ESPIRITU SANTO

19 22N, 87 28W

Pilotage: The bay is entered between Punta Herrero and Punta Fupar, about 11 miles to the north. It recedes about 16 miles to the southwest and is about 7 to 10 miles wide. The depths in the entrance and for a short distance within the bay range from 20 to 30 feet, but in 1943, it was reported the actual depths in this area were 45 to 48 feet. The general depths within the bay range from 8 to 15 feet, about 2 3/4 miles northwest of Punta Herrero.

From Punta Fupar the coast, which is bordered by a rocky ledge, trends about 7 3/4 miles northnortheast to Punta Pájaros (19° 34'N, 87° 25'W). A drying reef extends about 1/2 mile east from Punta Pájaros.

PUNTA OWEN, 19 20.0N, 87 27.0W. Fl (3) W 12s, 39ft, 11M. White cylindrical concrete tower.
PUNTA PÁJAROS, 19 34.0N, 87 25.0W. Fl W 6s, 36ft, 10M. Aluminum tower.
PUNTA NOHKU, 19 38.0N, 87 27.0W. Fl (2) W 10s, 39ft, 11M. White cylindrical concrete tower.
CAYO CULEBRAS, 19 42.0N, 87 28.0W. Fl (3) W 12s, 46ft, 11M. White cylindrical concrete tower.
PUNTA VIGIA CHICO, 19 48.0N, 87 30.0W. Fl (4) W 16s, 39ft, 11M. White cylindrical concrete tower.
PUNTA ALLEN, Bahía de la Ascension, 19 47.0N, 87 28.0W. Fl (4) W 16s, 72ft, 16M. White concrete tower. Visible 200°–070°.

BAHÍA DE LA ASCENSION

19 41N, 87 30W

Pilotage: This bay is entered between Punta Nohku (19° 37'N, 87° 28'W), about 3 1/4 miles northwest of Punta Pájaros, and Punta Allen, about 8 miles north. The bay recedes about 16 miles southwest and is from 5 to 11 miles wide.

The opening through the reef stretching across the entrance is about 2 miles wide. Depths are reported to be 18 to 22 feet through this opening, and as far west as the seaward side of the bar blocking the entrance to the bay itself. The opening north of Cayos Culebra is about 3 3/4 miles wide, but the entrance to the bay is obstructed by a bar with a depth of under 8 feet. Cayos Culebra are a group of mangrove cays that stand in the middle of the entrance just within the bar. Two yellow range beacons stand on these cays. There are depths of 10 to 18 feet within the bar, but the inner reaches of the bay have not been examined.

The opening south of Cayos Culebra, between them and Punta Nohku, is shallow and should not be attempted.

The coast between Punta Allen and Punta Yaan, about 23 miles to the north, is low, flat, and densely wooded.

TULUM, Salta Iman, 20 13.0N, 87 25.0W. Fl W 6s, 79ft, 15M. White square concrete tower.

PUNTA YAAN

20 11N, 87 27W
Pilotage: Punta Yaan is conspicuous, with the only cliffs along this coast. They are about 79 feet high and front the coast for about 3 miles. The ruins of a large, square watchtower stand at their north end.

Tulum is a small settlement fronted by a white beach located about 4 miles north-northeast of Punta Yaan. A small pier extends from the shore abreast of the settlement. A conspicuous, small stone temple on a truncated pyramid stands about 1/2 mile inland. It is overgrown with vegetation. There is a lighthouse at Tulum, and some cruisers report anchoring inside the reef here.

The coast between Tulum and Puerto Morelos extends about 45 miles northeast and again becomes low and flat.

The only known off-lying dangers are Isla de Cozumel and Cozumel Bank, which together front the coast for almost 30 miles and lie from 9 to 13 miles offshore. The passage between the island and the mainland is deep and clear of any known dangers.

Puerto Aventura is a marina located on the mainland about 11 1/2 miles southwest of Playa del Carmen (20° 37'N, 87° 04'W). Cruisers report anchoring off the latter town, inside the barrier reef. Ferries run from here to San Miguel, on Isla de Cozumel, so there are good navigational aids in the approach to the pier.

ISLA DE COZUMEL

20 26N, 86 53W
Pilotage: The south extremity of the island lies about 25 miles east-northeast of Punta Yaan on the mainland. The island is generally low and densely wooded and extends for 24 miles along the coast. The average width is about 9 miles. The passage between the island and the mainland to the west is deep and clear of dangers.

Punta Celerain (South Point) is low but well defined. It is fringed by a steep-to reef, which extends about 1/2 mile offshore.

The east side of the island is composed of sandy beaches separated by rocky points. The coast extends about 24 miles northeast to Punta Molas.

The west side of the island extends about 8 miles north-northwest, and then about 13 miles north-northeast to its northwest extremity. The shore is bordered by a narrow coral beach, with vegetation extending down almost to the water's edge.

Caleta Bay is a small body of water, lying about 8 miles south-southwest of the northwest extremity of the island. The entrance channel is narrow and shoal. A wharf, some buildings, and some fuel tanks stand on the shores of the bay, and a conspicuous hotel lies close southwest of it. It may be possible to anchor inside the small bay, but check locally for the latest information on the rocks and depths inside. The controlling depth is reported to be less than 6 feet.

The town of San Miguel lies about 3 miles north-northeast of Caleta Bay.

Punta Norte, the northwest extremity of Isla de Cozumel, lies about 3 1/4 miles northeast of the entrance to Banco Playa yacht harbor. The shore between is lined with numerous hotels,

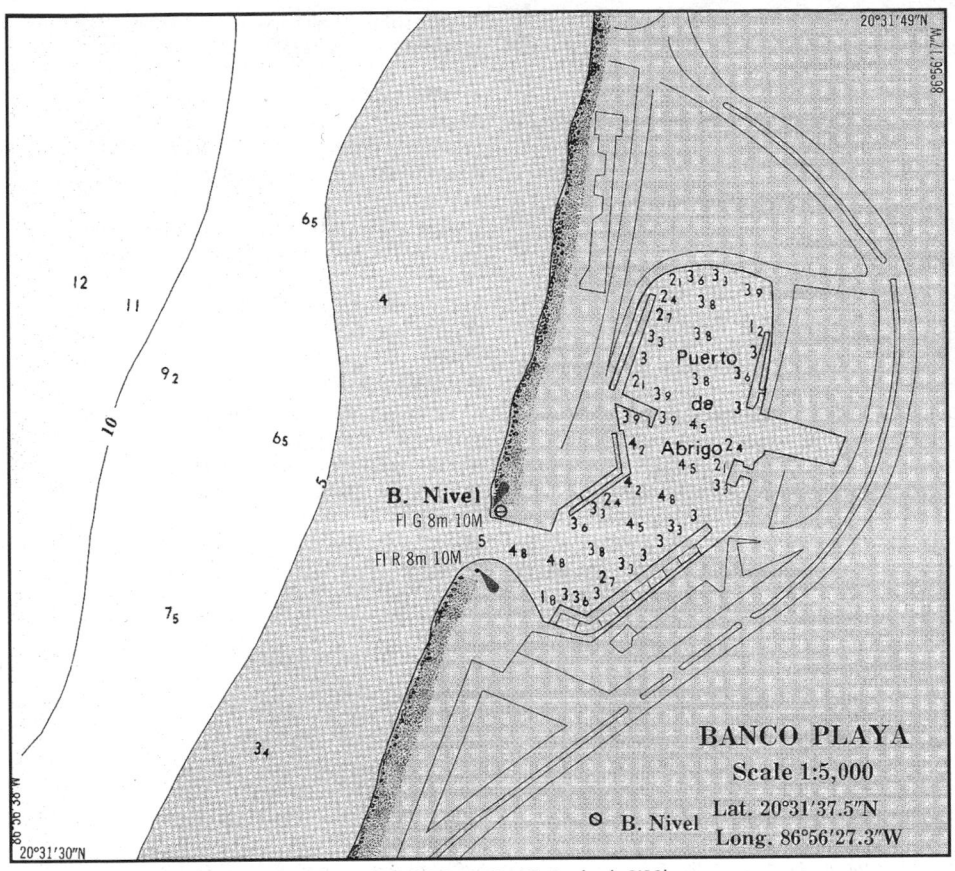

Banco Playa, soundings in meters *(after DMA 28197, 2nd ed, 6/88)*

one of which, a white building, is conspicuous and can be seen from a considerable distance seaward. A conspicuous clump of trees stands about 2 1/2 miles east of the northwest extremity of the island. A reef extends up to 1 3/4 miles offshore. Some coral heads lie within the 10-meter-depth curve, which lies up to 2 3/4 miles offshore.

La Laguna is an almost landlocked body of water lying across the northern part of the island.

The north side of the island extends about 10 miles east-northeast from its northwest extremity to Punta Molas (20° 35'N, 86° 44'W), the northeastern extremity of the island. It may be identified by a tall isolated tree and some huts. The point is marked by a light.

Cozumel Bank extends north from the north side of the island and lies up to 6 miles north of Punta Molas. The bank has been reported to extend up to 14 miles north-northeast and 4 miles east from Punta Molas. General depths on the bank range from 30 to 132 feet. Ripples, which at times have the appearance of breakers, mark the east edge of this bank.

PUNTA CELARAIN, S point of island, 20 16.3N, 86 59.3W. Fl W 5s, 87ft, 20M. White masonry tower, white house. Visible 240°–155°.
BANCO PLAYA, entrance N side, 20 32.0N, 86 58.0W. Fl G 5s, 30ft, 6M. Metal tower.
BANCO PLAYA, S side. Fl R 5s, 28ft, 6M. Metal tower.
GOVERNMENT WHARF, 20 30.7N, 86 57.1W. Iso R 2s, 20ft, 6M.

SAN MIGUEL DE COZUMEL, 20 30.2N, 86 57.0W. Fl (2) W 5s, 56ft, 15M. White concrete tower. Visible 031°–182°.
AVIATION LIGHT, 20 30.6N, 86 56.6W. Al Fl W G 10s, 82ft, 14M. Skeleton tower. Aero Radiobeacon.

SAN MIGUEL DE COZUMEL

20 30N, 86 58W
Pilotage: The town lies about 3 miles north-northeast of Caleta Bay. It is the principal settlement on the island and a popular tourist destination. The International Pier, known as Mulle del Transbordador, is located about 1 mile northeast of Caleta Bay. This is the primary cruise ship dock. A radiobeacon is located close southeast of the International Pier. A light is shown from the 43-foot-high lighthouse located 2 miles northeast of the International Pier. There is a dolphin berth for small tankers near the lighthouse. An aeronautical lightbeacon is shown from a 72-foot-high tower standing about 1 1/2 miles east of the lighthouse. An aeronautical radiobeacon is near the aeronautical lightbeacon. A pier extends northwest from the shore adjacent to town about 1 mile northeast of the lighthouse. It is 180 feet long, with a depth of about 11 feet at its head. Ferries run from here to Playa del Carmen and Puerto Morelos.
Landmarks: A conspicuous hotel stands close east of the International Pier. A conspicuous clock tower, painted white and dimly illuminated at night, stands near the root of the town pier at San Miguel. A blue-domed water tower and a framework radio tower, both conspicuous, stand close northeast and 1/2 mile southwest respectively, of the clock tower. A prominent airport control tower stands about 1 1/2 miles northeast of the town.
Port of Entry: Cruisers report that formalities can be difficult here. Some people report good success using the services of an agent available to those docked in the marina. Other agents are available to those anchored out.
Dockage: The Club Nautico marina is entered about 1 mile northeast of the town dock in San Miguel. This basin is charted as the Banco Playa Yacht Harbor. The marina is reported to respond to "Puerto Abbrigo" on the VHF radio. The docks are likely to be crowded with sportfishing boats.
Anchorage: Cruisers usually anchor north of the town dock. Be prepared to leave quickly if the wind is shifting to the north or northwest.
Services: Fuel and water are available in the marina. There are boutiques, restaurants, and tourist shops of all sorts ashore. Most types of groceries and general supplies are available.

PUNTA MOLAS, N point of island, 20 35.2N, 86 44.6W. Fl (3) W 12s, 72ft, 20M. White concrete tower, red bands, 66ft. Visible 070°–337°.
CALETA DE XEL-HA, 20 28.0N, 87 16.0W. Fl W 6s, 39ft, 11M. Aluminum tower.
CALETA DE CHACHALET, 20 34.0N, 87 09.0W. Fl (2) W 10s, 36ft, 11M. Square aluminum tower.
PLAYA DEL CARMEN, 20 37.2N, 87 04.5W. Fl (3) W 12s, 40ft, 11M. Silver metal framework tower.
PUNTA MAROMA, 20 43.7N, 86 52.8W. Fl (2) W 10s, 36ft, 11M. Silver metal framework tower.
PUNTA BRAVA, 20 48.4N, 86 56.3W. Fl (4) W 16s, 35ft, 11M. Silver metal framework tower.
PUERTO MORELOS, near wharf, 20 50.0N, 86 53.0W. Fl W 6s, 56ft, 18M. White concrete tower. Visible 205°–035°.

PUERTO MORELOS

20 51N, 86 54W
Pilotage: This is a small fishing and ferry port, with depths of 22 to 33 feet. Ferries run from here out to San Miguel de Cozumel. The village is on the mainland about 1 1/2 miles north of the reef entrance. The reefs lie about 1/4 mile offshore from the village and up to 1 mile offshore abreast the south part of the harbor. Some of these reefs are 2 to 3 feet high in places. A small pier with depths of 16 feet at its head extends from the shore north of the village.

The coast should be approached from the east to a position about 1 3/4 miles south of the light, which stands north of the village. When this light bears 024° a vessel should steer for it on that bearing.

The coast between Puerto Morelos and Cabo Catoche extends about 14 miles northeast and then curves north-northwest for 36 miles. The terrain is generally low and wooded. Sand hills stand along some parts of the coast. The terrain in the north part of this area becomes more elevated.
Port of Entry
Anchorage: Anchor north of the town pier, where the ferries come in from Isla de Cozumel. The offlying reef provides adequate shelter.
Services: Water, fuel, and some basic supplies of groceries and general stores are available.

COAST PILOT

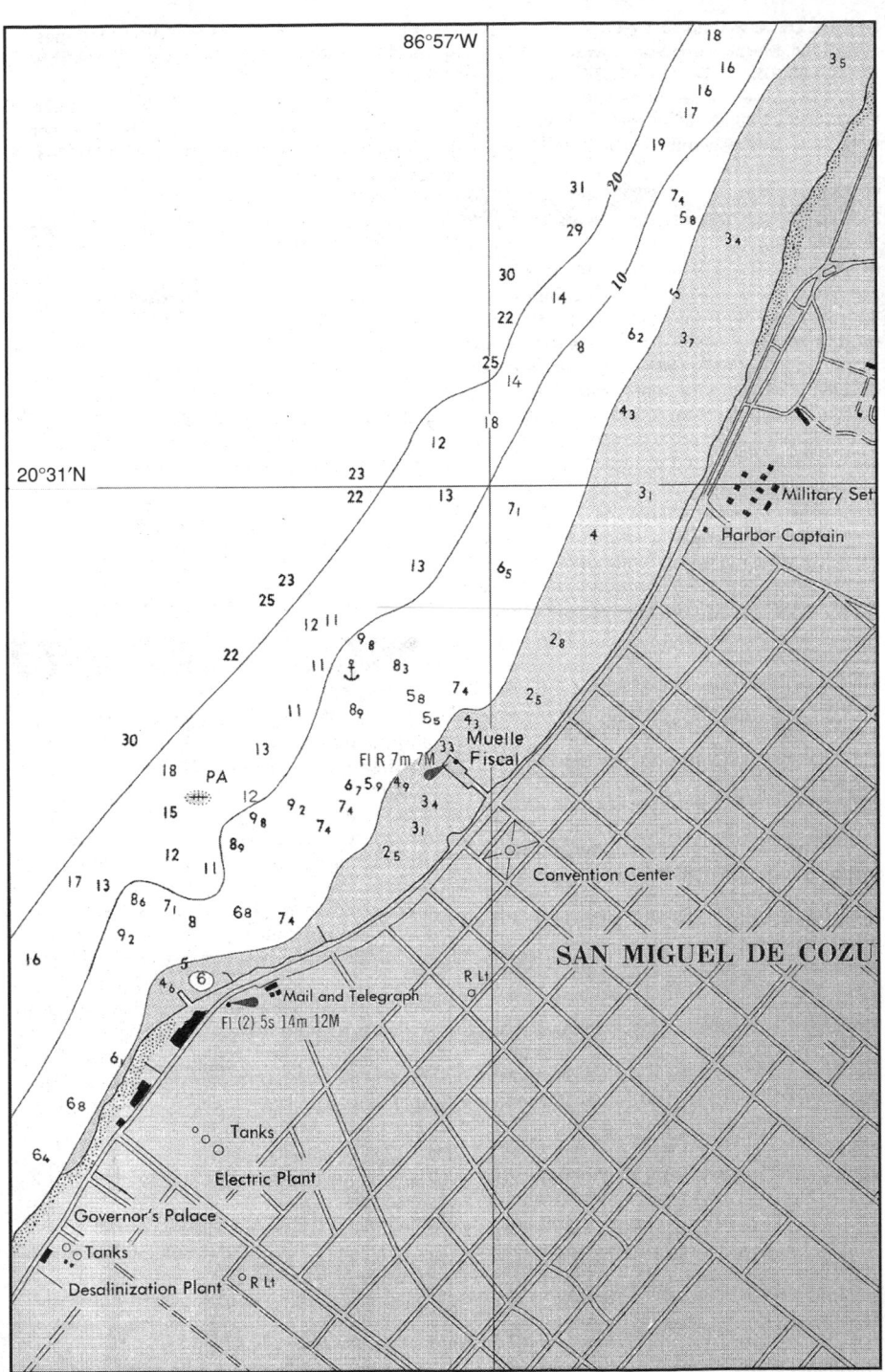

San Miguel de Cozumel, soundings in meters *(from DMA 28197, 2nd ed, 6/88)*

DUQUE DE ALBA, 20 50.4N, 86 52.7W. Iso R 2s, 17ft, 11M. Metal framework tower.
PUNTA NIZUK, 21 02.1N, 86 46.7W. Fl (4) W 16s, 36ft, 11M. Silver metal framework tower.
CANCÚN, 21 08.3N, 86 44.5W. Fl (3) W 12s, 49ft, 11M. White cylindrical concrete tower.

ISLA CANCÚN

21 05N, 86 47W

Pilotage: This island lies about 14 miles north-northeast of Puerto Morelos. It is composed of 40- to 60-foot-high sand hills. The north and south extremities of the island curve to the west and almost reach the mainland. There are two bridges connecting the island with the mainland. A 1970 report stated that the south end of the island appeared to be connected to the mainland when viewed by radar.

A conspicuous tower, marked by a fixed red obstruction light and a structure in the shape of a truncated pyramid, stand near Punta Cancún. Another tower, marked by a fixed red obstruction light, stands 2 3/4 miles south-southwest of the point.

Isla Cancún encloses a series of interconnected lagoons having shallow channels to the sea. A natural harbor for small craft is located south of Punta Nizuk, the south extremity of the island, and is protected by a reef. Local knowledge is required to enter this harbor. Club Med has a facility located on Punta Nizuk. The harbors on Isla Cancún are suitable only for shallow-draft craft that can clear the low bridges to the mainland. This is a major international tourist destination.

ARROWSMITH BANK
21 05N, 86 25W

Pilotage: This bank lies about 16 miles east of Isla Cancún. The bank is about 20 miles long and from 1 1/2 to 5 miles wide. There are depths of 54 to 150 feet over it, with the shoalest part lying on the center of its west part.

CAUTION: The east edge of this bank lies about 2 miles farther east than charted.

A north-northeast-setting current crosses Arrowsmith Bank, attaining a rate of from 2 to 3 knots. The south end of the bank is marked by strong rips.

In 1980 an area of heavily breaking seas was reported centered in position 20° 50'N, 86° 35'W.

This is south of the bank, and there was a moderate southeast breeze at the time of the observation.

A shoal with a depth of 27 feet over it was reported to lie near the northeast extremity of Arrowsmith Bank.

EL MECO, 7.4 kilometers N of ruins, 21 13.0N, 86 49.0W. Fl W 6s, 26ft, 11M. Square white tower.

ROCA DE LA BANDERA (Becket Rock), 21 10.0N, 86 44.5W. Fl (2) W 10s, 13ft, 11M. Tower, black and white bands. Visible 306°–077°.
ROCA YUNKE, N point of island, 21 16.0N, 86 45.0W. Fl G 5s, 16ft, 6M. Red tower.
PIEDRA LA CARBONERA RANGE (Front Light), 21 14.8N, 86 45.4W. Fl R 3s, 20ft, 6M. Masonry tower. **(Rear Light),** 980 meters 000° from front, 21 15.3N, 86 45.4W. Fl (2) W 10s, 62ft, 20M. White masonry tower, red stripes.
ISLA MUJERES, S extremity, 21 12.0N, 86 43.0W. Fl (4) W 16s, 75ft, 14M. White masonry tower, 39ft. Visible 150°–131°.

BAHÍA MUJERES

21 13N, 86 46W

Pilotage: This bay lies between Isla Mujeres and the mainland. It is entered between the northeast extremity of Isla Cancún and the south extremity of Isla Mujeres. A sandbank extends about 2 miles west from the south extremity of Isla Mujeres, then trends north about 2 miles toward the island. The 5-meter depth curve marks this sandbank. There are many coral heads on this bank, and some of them near the south end nearly dry. The southwest edge of the bank is marked by a light buoy.

A passage between this bank and the shoals to the west is about 1/4 mile wide and leads north past Puerto Mujeres where it joins Canal las Pailas. This passage rounds the north end of Isla Mujeres and turns back towards the sea about 1/2 mile north of El Yunque.

The general depths in this bay are from 6 1/2 feet to 26 feet.

Puerto Juarez is located in the southwest part of Bahía Mujeres, on the mainland about 5 1/2 miles west-southwest of the lighthouse on the south end of Isla Mujeres. The town serves as a terminal for ferries servicing Isla Mujeres. An 800-foot-long pier has depths of about 6 feet alongside.

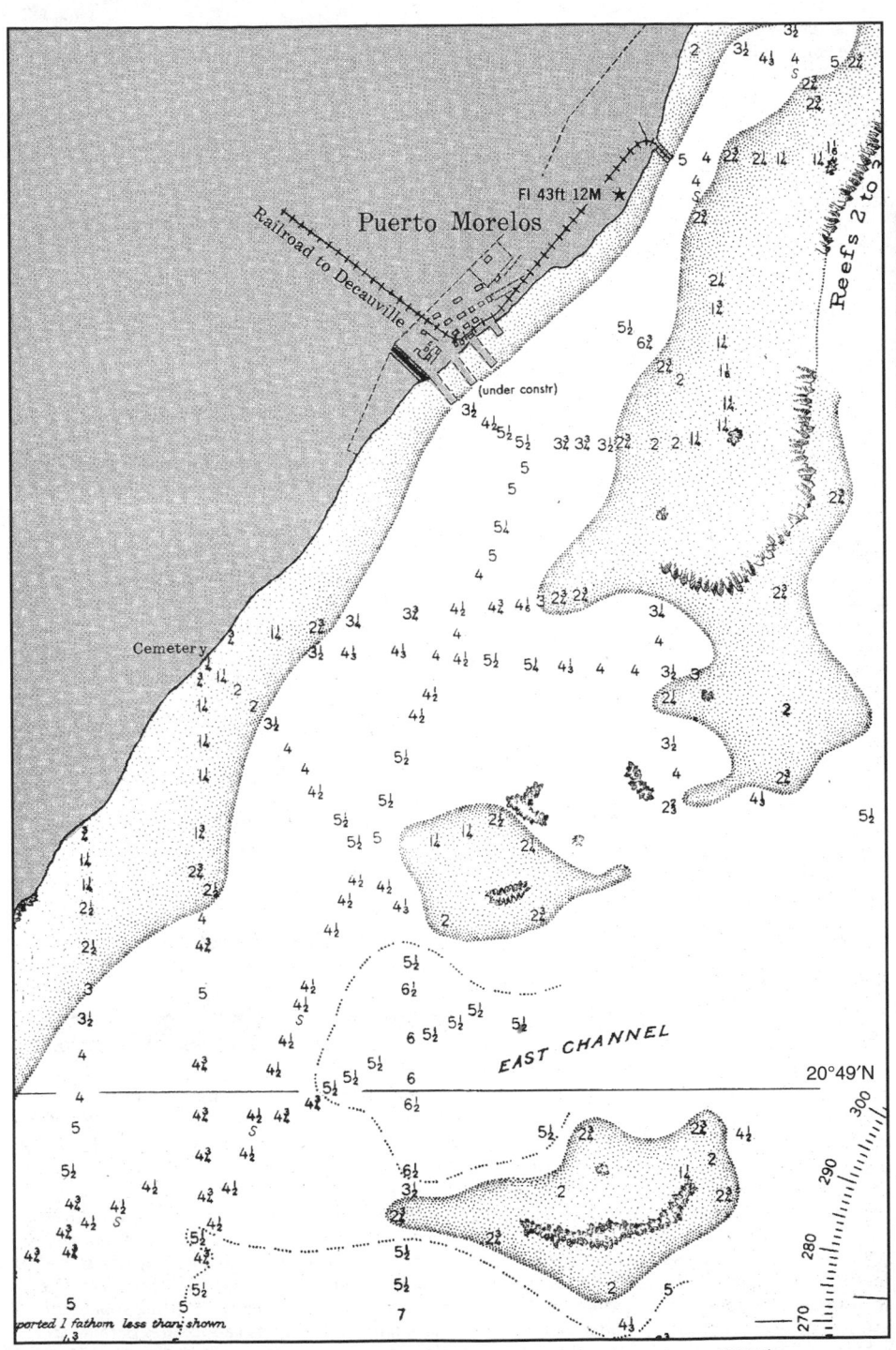

Puerto Morelos, soundings in fathoms (*from DMA 28201, 7th ed, 11/20, rev. 12/74*)

Punta Sam is located 3 miles north of Puerto Juarez and is also a ferry terminal.

ISLA MUJERES

21 14N, 86 45W

Pilotage: This island lies about 4 1/2 miles north-northeast of Isla Cancún. Its location is strategic for cruisers arriving from or departing to the United States via the Yucatán Channel. See the section on Cuba for more information on the Yucatán Channel.

The island is about 4 miles long, low, narrow, and wooded. The south part is slightly elevated and has trees about 89 feet above sea level. The ruins of a square watch tower stand near the south part of the island. The east side of the island is composed of fairly steep-to rocky shelves. They terminate at the north end in El Yunque (Anvil Rock), which is square, black, and about 6 feet high. Some white cliffs stand about midway along the east side of the island. A large, square, white hotel stands on the north extremity of the island and has been reported to be a good radar target.

The channel leads along the western shore of the island into the harbor. There is a shoal area north of the light on Roca La Carbonera.
Port of Entry: Enter at Puerto Mujeres (21° 16′N, 86° 45′W), located at the north end of the island, on its west side.
Dockage: Marina Paraiso is located in the southern part of the harbor, with reported dockside depths of about 9 feet. It has showers and a laundry.
Anchorage: Anchor south of the main commercial piers.
Services: The fuel dock is located just southeast of the light in the harbor. There are reported to be good supplies of groceries and general stores. You can take a ferry across to the tourist pleasures of Cancún.

ISLA BLANCA

21 22N, 86 49W

Pilotage: This is a narrow ridge of sand, about 7 feet high, which is a continuation of the ridge extending south into Bahía Mujeres. From the south end of the sand ridge a reef fringes the coast extending past Isla Blanca to Isla Contoy, about 4 miles farther north. This reef begins about 3 miles north-northwest of the northern extremity of Isla Mujeres. There are one or two openings for boats in this reef.

ISLA CONTOY, near N point, 21 32.2N, 86 49.4W, Fl W 7s, 105ft., 21M, White masonry tower, white house, Visible 010°– 350°, RACON T (–).

ISLA CONTOY

21 30N, 86 49W

Pilotage: This island lies about 4 miles north-northeast of Isla Blanca and 6 1/2 miles offshore. Its east side is composed of a narrow ridge of sandhills covered with bushes and trees to within 1 1/2 miles of its northwest extremity. A narrow ridge of coral with depths of 18 feet extends about 3 miles north-northwest from two rocks close off the northwest extremity of the island. The greater part of the west side of the island is intersected by numerous small lagoons. This island is a bird and wildlife sanctuary.
Anchorage: Cruisers take temporary anchorage off the west side of the island. You may be checked by the Mexican navy or other government officials if anchored here.

CABO CATOCHE, 21 36.0N, 87 04.0W. Fl (4) W 20s, 49ft, 25M. White concrete tower, masonry dwelling. Visible 080°–285°.

CAYO SUCIO

21 25N, 86 53W

Pilotage: This cay is close to the coast, about 3 miles northwest of Isla Blanca. The coast trends about 8 miles to the northwest from here and is more elevated with dense woods ashore. Some trees stand up to 131 feet above sea level. The conspicuous ruins of a church stand at the north end of this coast.

From the ruins of the church the coast extends about 6 miles west-northwest to abreast of Cabo Catoche, which is on the north side of Isla Holbox.

CABO CATOCHE

21 36N, 87 04W

Pilotage: This is a sand projection on the northern side of Isla Holbox. Depths of 18 to 30 feet extend 10 miles to the north and east.

The coast extends from here about 85 miles west to Punta Yalkubul and then about 105 miles west-southwest to Punta Boxcohuo. This north coast of the Peninsula de Yucatán is low and arid, with few conspicuous landmarks. The coast is fringed with many detached shoals and coral patches. Lagartos Lagoon lies parallel to almost all of this section of coast.

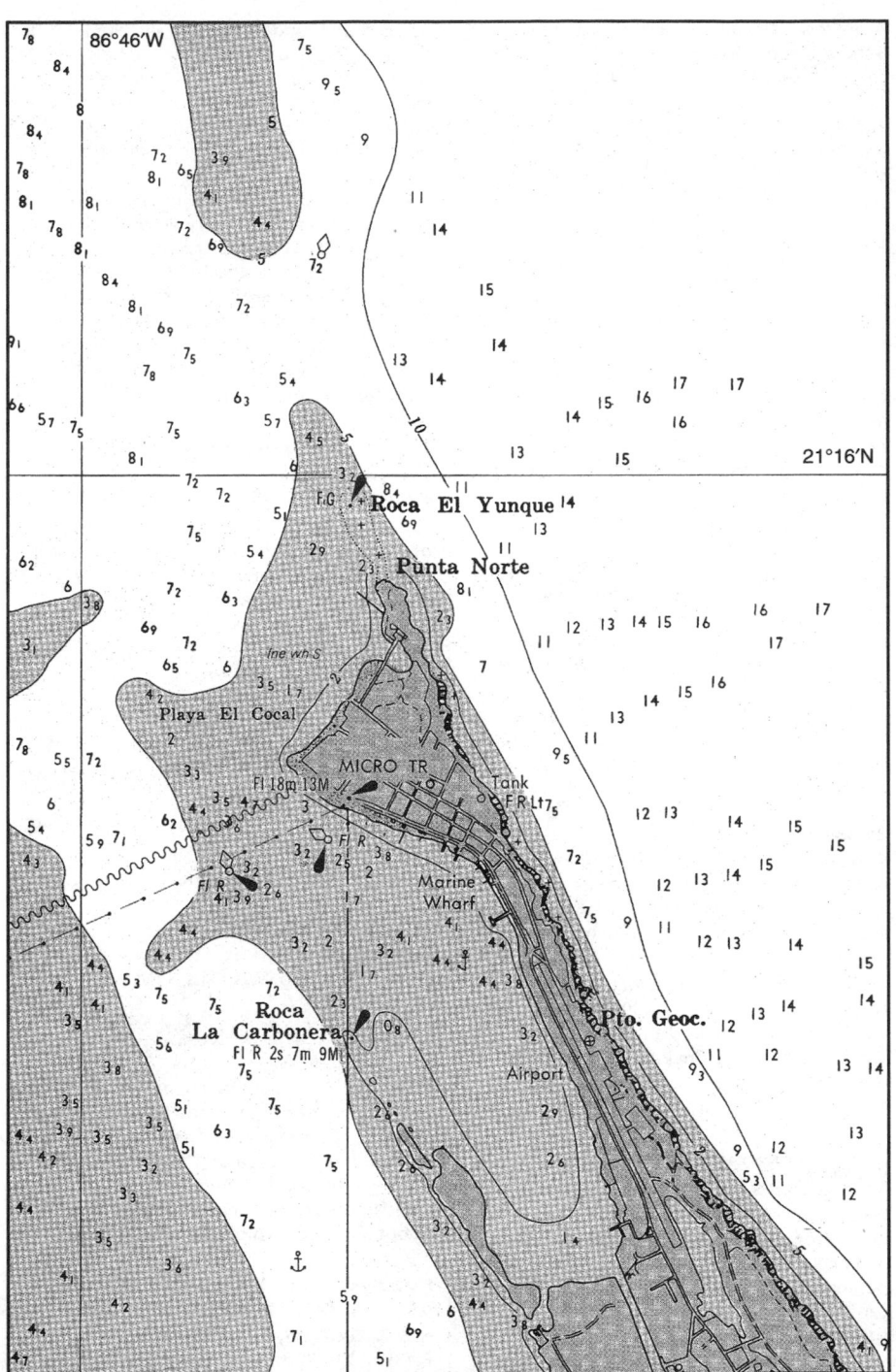

Isla Mujeres, soundings in meters *(from DMA 28202, 20th ed, 1/84)*

A shallow coastal bank, as defined by the 5-meter-depth curve, lies between 1 and 5 miles from this shore.

Tides and Currents: Between Cabo Catoche and Punta Boxcohuo the current sets west at a rate of 1/2 to 1 knot, following the trend of the coast about 30 miles offshore.

The mean rise at springs ranges from about 1.3 to 2.3 feet. The water on the off-lying banks is influenced by the winds as well as the tides. The wind may offset the normal tides for several days.

CHIQUILA, 21 26.0N, 87 15.0W. Fl W, 29ft, 9M. Red iron column, hut. Marks outer limit of anchorage.
CHIQUILA RANGE (Front Light), 21 26.0N, 87 17.0W. Fl W 3s, 15ft, 11M. Aluminum tower. **(Rear Light),** Iso W 2s, 46ft, 11M. Aluminum tower.
ISLA HOLBOX, W end 21 32.8N, 87 18.0W. Fl W 6s, 26ft, 14M. White concrete tower.
HOLBOX RANGE (Front Light), 21 33.0N, 87 18.0W. Fl W 3s, 44ft, 12M. Metal tower. **(Rear Light),** Iso W 2s, 61ft. 12M. Metal tower.
PUNTA FRANCISCA (Mosquito), 21 33.0N, 87 18.5W. Fl (2) W 10s, 39ft, 14M. Red skeleton tower.

ISLA HOLBOX
21 33N, 87 14W
Pilotage: This is one of a chain of low, narrow islands that front the coast between Cabo Catoche and Boca de Conil to the west. Punta Francisca is the northwest extremity of the island.

A chain of cays, fronted by numerous sand ridges, with depths of 8 to 30 feet, extends 8 miles northeast from Cabo Catoche and 9 miles northwest from Punta Francisca. Bajo Corsario, with a least depth of 15 feet, lies 8 miles north of Punta Francisca.

CAMPECHE BANK

Pilotage: This bank extends about 155 miles north from the north coast of the Yucatán Peninsula and about 120 miles west from the peninsula's west side. The limits of the bank can best be seen on the appropriate chart, such as NOAA 411.

This steep-to bank has very irregular depths and is marked on its east and north edges by heavy ripples and a confused sea. Some of the dangers on the banks are marked by discolored water. Many cays, shoals, and reefs are found within its limits. Small vessels have reported encountering very heavy seas on parts of the bank during periods of stormy weather.

CAUTION: Banco de Campeche has not been surveyed for many years, and as reports of new shoals are constantly received, it is reasonable to assume that many more dangers exist than are shown on the charts. Many isolated shallow patches, with depths of as little as 18 feet, have been reported north of the Yucatán Peninsula.

BOCA DE CONIL
21 29N, 87 35W
Pilotage: This is the 3-mile-wide west entrance to Laguna de Yalahua, which is a shallow body of water lying between Isla Holbox and the mainland. Foul ground extends about 7 miles northwest from Boca de Conil.

The low, sandy coast between Boca de Conil and Cuyo, about 16 miles to the west, is marked by conspicuous groves of trees near its east end.

MONTE DE CUYO, summit, 21 31.0N, 87 43.0W. Fl (3) W 12s, 86ft, 14M. Red concrete tower. Visible 100°–273°.
PIER, W side, 21 30.0N, 87 12.0W. Fl R 5s, 39ft, 7M. Metal tower.
PIER, E side, 21 30.0N, 87 12.0W. Fl G 5s, 39ft, 7M. Metal tower.
EL CUYO RANGE (Front Light), 21 30.9N, 87 41.9W. Fl W 3s, 51ft, 11M. Metal tower. **(Rear Light),** Iso W 2s, 64ft, 11M. Metal tower.

CUYO
21 32N, 87 41W
Pilotage: This town has a wharf over 350 feet long, with a depth of almost 7 feet at its outer end. The town stands on the narrow strip of land between the sea and the lagoon that parallels this coast. El Cuyo, a 40-foot-high hill, stands close to the town. A 12-foot shoal lies about 5 miles north of town.

COLORADAS, 21 36.0N, 87 59.0W. Fl (2) W 10s, 43ft, 11M. Metal tower.
RÍO LAGARTOS, 21 36.0N, 88 12.0W. Fl (3) W 12s, 59ft, 11M. Red metal tower.
BREAKWATER, W side, 21 40.0N, 88 12.0W. Fl R 3s, 33ft, 6M. Tubular tower.

BREAKWATER, E side, 21 40.0N, 88 12.0W.
Fl G 3s, 33ft, 6M. Tubular tower.
PIER, W side, 21 36.0N, 88 12.0W. Fl R 5s, 40ft,
7M. Aluminum tower.
PIER, E side, 21 36.0N, 88 12.0W. Fl W 5s, 40ft,
7M. Aluminum tower.
RIO LAGARTOS SOUTH, 21 35.1N, 88 12.1W.
Fl (2) W 10s, 69ft. Square concrete tower; 59ft.

LAS COLORADOS
21 37N, 88 01W
Pilotage: This open roadstead harbor has two
small piers. The principal export is salt, which
is barged out to the anchorage. From the north,
depths in the approach range from 24 to 30
feet, and are quite regular. The two piers form
good radar targets from a distance of about
17 miles.

The coast between Cuyo and the Río Lagartos,
30 miles to the west, is fronted by a low, sandy
beach. The Río Lagartos is the outlet of the
narrow lagoon that parallels this coast.

Bajo Antonieta is a shoal that uncovers to a
height of 2 feet. It is located about 4 miles west-
northwest of the Río Lagartos.

Between the Río Lagartos and Punta Yalkubul,
about 22 miles to the west, the coast is more
elevated. It is 170 feet higher about 6 miles
east of the point.

YALKUBUL, 21 32.0N, 88 37.0W. Fl (4) W 16s,
69ft, 14M. Concrete tower, red and white
bands, dwelling. Visible 057°–251°.
DZILAM DE BRAVO, 21 22.0N, 88 54.0W.
Fl W 6s, 59ft, 14M. White concrete tower.
BREAKWATER, W side, 21 22.2N, 88 53.6W.
Fl R 5s, 40ft, 7M. Aluminum tower.
BREAKWATER, E side, 21 22.2N, 88 53.3W.
Fl G 5s, 40ft, 7M. Aluminum tower.
DZILAM DE BRAVO RANGE (Front Light),
21 21.9N, 88 53.6W. Fl W 3s, 46ft, 11M.
Aluminum tower. **(Rear Light),** Iso W 2s, 59ft,
11M. Metal tower.

PUNTA YALKUBUL
21 32N, 88 37W
Pilotage: This point is low and marked by trees.
Bajo Carmelita, a shoal with depths of less than
15 feet, lies 11 miles northwest of the point.
Bajo Pawashick, a shoal with a least depth of
9 feet, lies 9 miles west of the point.

The coast between Punta Yalkubul and Punta
Arenas, 13 miles to the southwest, remains
low. A shallow lagoon entrance lies close east
of the latter point.

Dzilam (Silan) is a small town fronted by a pier
located 6 miles west of Punta Arenas.

Between Punta Arenas and Progreso, about 48
miles to the west, the coast consists of low
sandy beach, slightly wooded, and backed by
swampy ground. Several villages lie along this
section of coast.

Chicxulub is a small village fronted by a pier
located about 2 miles east of Progreso.

TELCHAC, 21 20.0N, 89 14.0W. Fl (3) W 8s,
72ft, 14M. White tower.
BREAKWATER, W side, 21 20.0N, 89 16.0W.
Fl R 5s, 40ft, 7M. Aluminum tower.
BREAKWATER, E side, 21 20.0N, 89 16.0W.
Fl G 5s, 40ft, 7M. Metal tower.
TELCHAC RANGE (Front Light), 21 20.0N,
89 16.0W. Fl W 3s, 46ft, 11M. Metal tower.
(Rear Light), Iso W 2s, 59ft, 11M. Metal tower.

PROGRESO
PROGRESO, near pier, 21 17.2N, 89 40.1W.
Fl W 6s, 108ft, 16M. Gray concrete tower.
Visible 066°–250°.
HEAD OF PIER, W side, 21 17.0N, 89 40.0W.
Iso R 2s, 33ft, 6M. Concrete tower.
HEAD OF PIER, E side, 21 17.0N, 89 40.0W.
Iso G 2s, 33ft, 6M. Concrete tower.
PIER LIGHT, 21 18.9N, 89 40.04W. Fl (2) R 10s,
16ft, 7M. Iron tower.
HEAD OF PIER, W side, 21 20.7N, 89 40.5W.
Fl (2) W 10s, 26ft, 9M. Metal tower.
HEAD OF PIER, E side, 21 20.7N, 89 40.8W.
Fl (2) W 10s, 26ft, 9M. Metal tower.
TERMINAL REMOTA, NW corner, 21 20.7N,
89 40.9W. Iso R 2s, 79ft, 6M. On corner of
warehouse.
NE CORNER, 21 20.7N, 89 40.6W. Iso R 2s,
79ft, 6M. On corner of warehouse. RACON
Y (– · – –), 20M.

PROGRESO
21 17N, 89 40W
Pilotage: Progreso is the most important port
on the Yucatán Peninsula. The harbor is an
open roadstead, with a long pier fronting the
town. Sisal is the principal export.

The major danger to small craft is a wreck lying 1 1/2 miles north of New Pier. When approaching the port, the lighthouse is usually the first object sighted. A square gray tower, about 60 feet high, stands close west of the lighthouse. East of the town, and somewhat detached from it, is a large square building close to the coast and partly surrounded by trees. The town itself appears as a group of low gray or white buildings. The piers, together with the warehouses on them, are prominent from a distance of 4 miles.

Terminal Remota has two berths (for commercial vessels) protected by an artificial island. It is situated at the north end of a long causeway and pier, about 1/4 mile in length, with its root near Progreso Light. Muelle Fiscal also has two berths located on the same causeway about 5,970 feet from shore. Pino Suárez Pier is located close to the west of the other two piers. It is about 200 yards long with depths of 8 to 9 feet alongside.

Winds: The prevailing winds are from the northeast to southeast. Northers occur between October and March. Storm signals are displayed from a flagstaff near the lighthouse.
Currents: The current along this coast sets to the west.
Port of Entry

Puerto de Yucalpeten Approach Buoy No 1, 21 18.0N, 89 43.0W. Fl (2) W 10s. Black and red banded buoy.
PUERTO DE YUCALPETEN RANGE (Front Light), 21 16.0N, 89 42.0W. Fl W 3s, 45ft, 5M. Red metal tower. **(Rear Light),** 169° from front. Fl (2) W 16s, 58ft, 5M. Red metal tower.
HEAD OF JETTY, E side, 21 16.1N, 89 42.1W. Fl G 5s, 38ft, 7M. Red metal tower.
HEAD OF JETTY, W side, 21 16.1N, 89 41.1W. Fl R 5s, 38ft, 7M. Red metal tower.

PUERTO DE YUKALPETÉN

21 17N, 89 43W
Pilotage: This new "free port" is located about 3 miles west of Progreso. The east breakwater extends approximately 600 feet from the shore, while the west breakwater is less prominent. The least depth between the breakwaters is just under 8 feet. Inside the harbor, alongside the two piers, there is a least depth of under 7 feet.

The coast between Puerto de Yukalpetén and Sisal, about 20 miles to the west-southwest, is marked by several villages and is more wooded than elsewhere in the vicinity.

ARRECIFE SISAL

21 21N, 90 09W
Pilotage: This is a coral reef with an obstruction on it located about 12 miles north-northwest of Sisal. It may be marked by discolored water under certain weather conditions. A 21-foot-deep coral shoal lies about 6 1/2 miles west-northwest of Sisal.

The coast between Sisal and Punta Boxcohuo, about 17 miles southwest, is low and sandy. A building in ruins, about 5 miles southwest of Sisal, is the only conspicuous landmark. The coast between Sisal and a position about 5 miles south of Celestun is radar conspicuous. Sisal is now nearly abandoned.

CHUBERNA, 21 14.0N, 89 50.0W. Fl G 5s, 23ft, 7M.
SISAL, on old white fort, 21 10.0N, 90 01.09W. Fl (3) W 12s, 72ft, 12M. Circular concrete tower, red and white bands. Visible 055°–260°.
HEAD OF PIER, W side, 21 10.0N, 90 02.0W. Iso R 2s, 33ft, 9M. Fiberglass post.
HEAD OF PIER, E side, Iso G 2s, 33ft, 9M. Fiberglass post.

ARRECIFE ALACRÁN

22 29N, 89 42W
ISLA PEREZ, on S part of Alacrán Reef, 22 23.5N, 89 41.5W. Fl (2) W 8s, 69ft, 13M. Red concrete tower. RACON Z (– – · ·).
ISLA DESTERREDA, on N part of Alacrán Reef, 22 31.7N, 89 47.4W. Fl (4) W 16s, 46ft, 10M. Tubular metal tower.

Pilotage: This steep-to, half-moon-shaped reef lies about 34 miles northwest of Granville Shoal. This is about 68 miles north-northwest of Progreso, on the Campeche Bank. The main part of the reef consists of a compact mass of coral heads about 14 miles long and 8 miles wide. The entire northeast side of the reef is awash. Isla Chica and Isla Pájaros, two small, low cays about 1/4 mile apart, stand near the south end of the reef. Isla Desterrada is a small 10-foot-high cay located on the northwest end of Arrecife Alacrán.

Isla Perez is a narrow cay about 14 feet high. It lies near the south end of the reef. The light structure on this cay has been reported to be a good radar target at distances up to 18 miles. The light is shown from a round red masonry tower with a parapet. A gray masonry tower

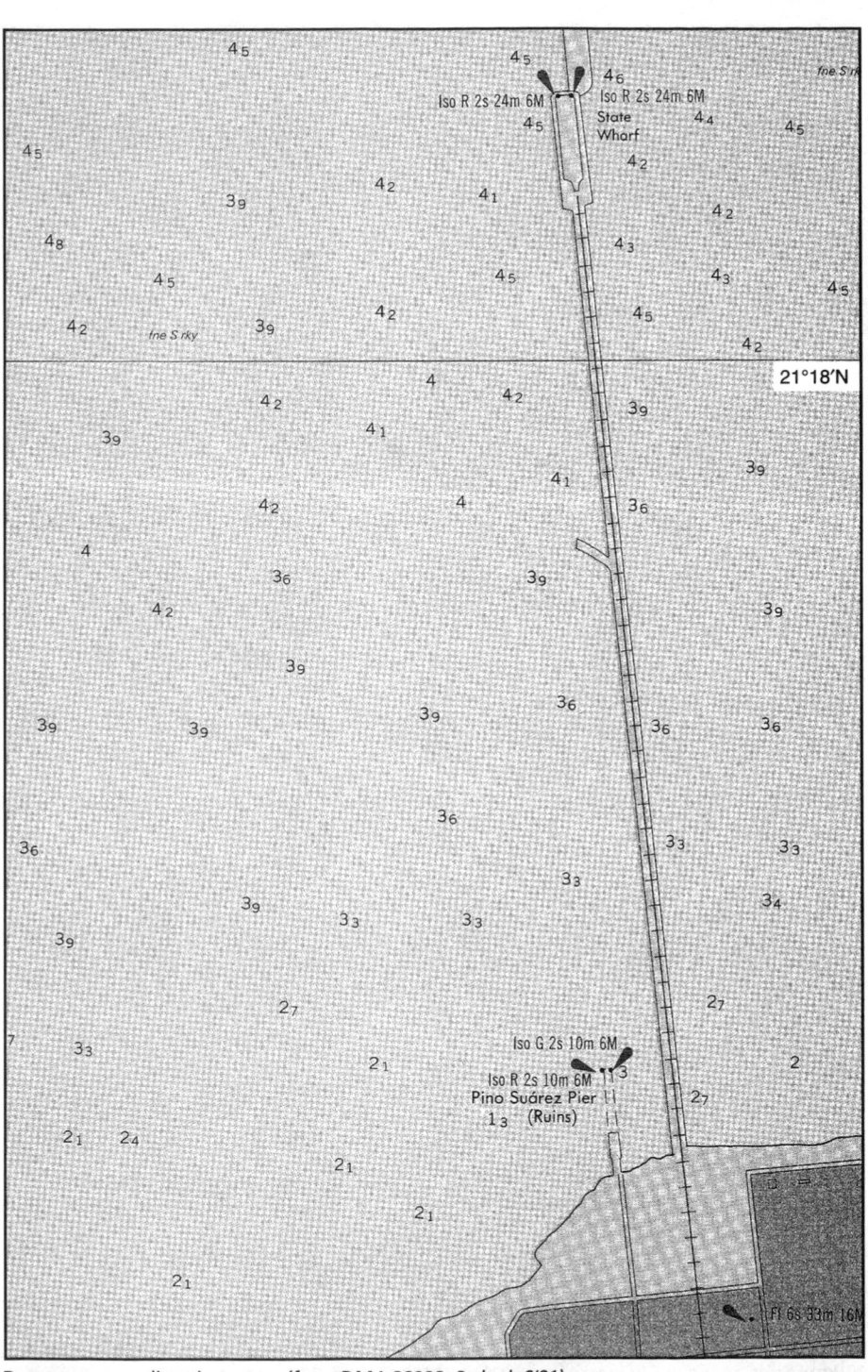

21°18'N

Progreso, soundings in meters *(from DMA 28223, 3rd ed, 6/91)*

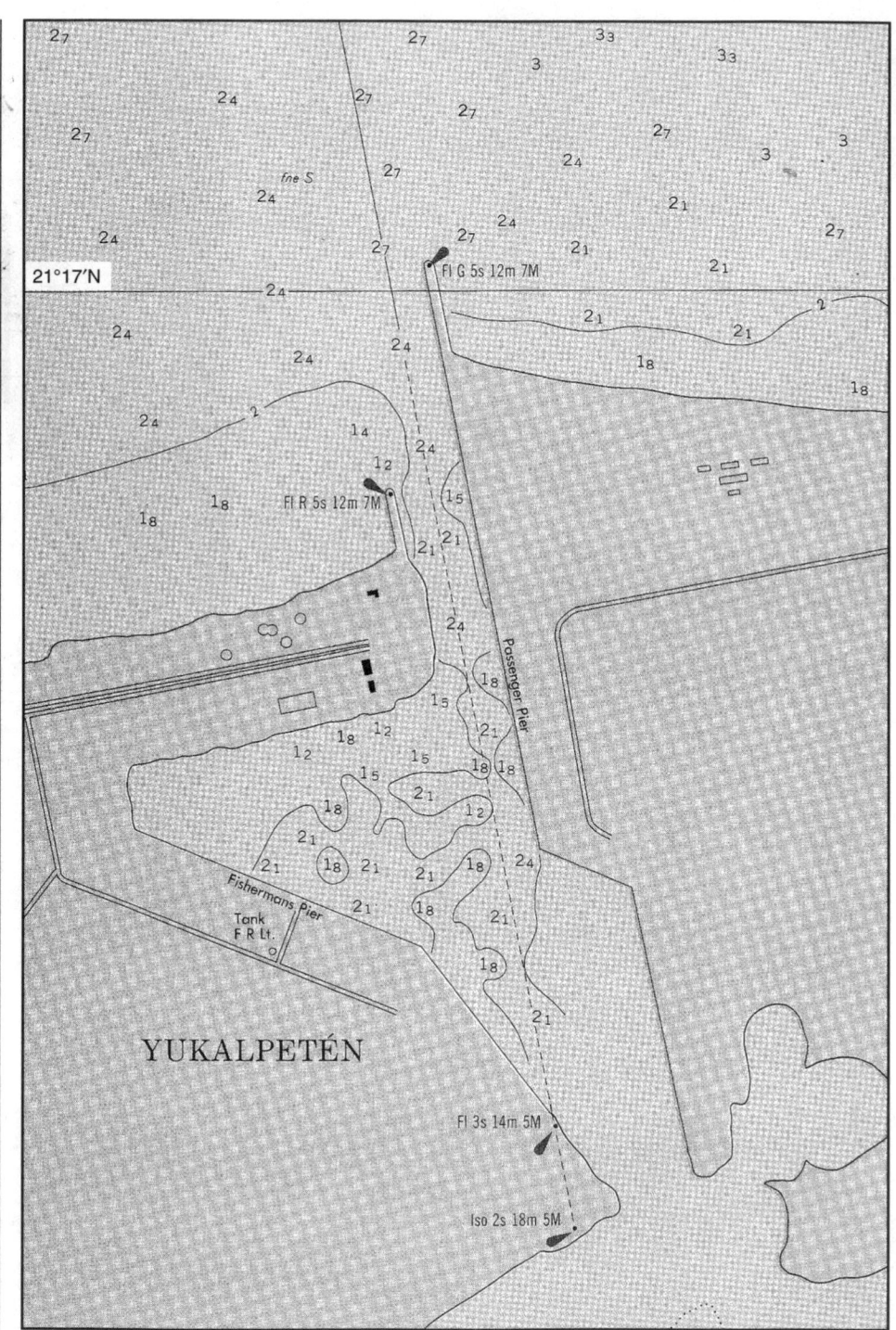

Yukalpetén, soundings in meters *(from DMA 28223, 3rd ed, 6/91)*

stands adjacent to the light. The lighthouse and tower are fully visible when approaching from the west. A stranded wreck close east of the light structure was reported to be a good radar target at distances up to 13 miles.

Anchorage: Small vessels anchor in depths of 36 to 60 feet over fine sand, mud, and coral, about 1/4 mile east of Isla Perez. The anchorage is approached from the south through an unmarked channel with a depth of about 24 feet. This channel should not be attempted without local knowledge.

Isla Desertora (not to be confused with Isla Desterrada farther to the north-northwest) is a small 12-foot-high cay located about 3 miles northwest of Isla Perez.

Currents: The current usually sets west at about 1 knot in the vicinity of these reefs, but may set north or south, depending upon the wind.

ARRECIFE MADAGASCAR
21 26N, 90 18W

Pilotage: This narrow coral ledge, with a least depth of under 9 feet, lies about 69 miles south-southwest of Arrecife Alacrán. The sea does not break on this ledge, which is covered with weed that appears the same color as the water.

Breakers were reported about 6 miles north-northeast of the ledge in 1909.

Arrecife de La Serpiente, with a least depth of 27 feet, lies about 11 1/2 miles west of Arrecife Madagascar.

PUNTA PALMAS, 21 02.0N, 90 18.0W. Fl (2) W 10s, 138ft, 12M. White concrete tower, on white house. Visible 048°–236°.
CELESTUN, center of town, near shore, 20 51.0N, 90 24.0W. Fl (3) W 12s, 69ft, 10M. White round concrete tower. Visible 002°–188°.
NORTH BREAKWATER, 20 51.0N, 90 53.0W. Fl G 5s, 33ft., 7M, White tubular tower.
SOUTH BREAKWATER, 20 51.0N, 90 53.0W, Fl R 5s, 33ft, 7M. White tubular tower.
CELESTUN RANGE (Front Light), 20 51.0N, 90 23.0W. Fl W 3s, 46ft, 9M. Aluminum tower. **(Rear Light),** Iso W 2s, 59ft, 9M. Aluminum tower.
ISLA ARENA, 20 36.0N, 90 28.0W. Fl W 6s, 46ft, 10M. White round concrete tower.
CAYO ARENAS, 22 08.0N, 91 24.0W. L Fl W 12s, 79ft, 12M. White concrete tower. RACON **X** (– · · –).

CAYO ARENAS
22 0?, 91 24W

feet high. This guano-covered cay is about 20 a detached located on the southeast edge of 93 miles we 3/4 mile long. The cay lies about The horns of the west of Arrecife Alacrán. west and 1/4 m extend 1/2 mile north- wharf stands on from the cay. A small west side of the cay.

A detached reef, 1 1, west side of the cay. patch 7 feet high on it coral patch 2 feet high ng with a rocky lies 1 mile east of Cayo And and a small channel is about 1/2 mile west end, entrance. At its south end are ntervening with depths of 14 to 19 feet. Torth are about 3/4 mile southeast of tches,

Anchorage: Vessels can anchor in in depths of 60 to 72 feet, about 1/2 of the cay. Depths of 24 to 36 feet can between the horns of the reef 1/4 mile west of the cay.

BAJO NUEVO
21 50N, 92 05W

Pilotage: This reef has depths of less than 6 feet. It lies about 40 miles west-southwest of Cayo Arenas and is marked by breakers.

BANCOS INGLESES
21 49N, 91 56W

Pilotage: These two banks lie with their least depths of 30 to 133 feet about 8 miles southeast of Bajo Nuevo.

ISLA TRIANGULOS OEST, 20 59.0N, 92 18.0W. Fl (3) W 20s, 70ft, 12M. Red rectangular concrete tower.

ARRECIFES TRIÁNGULOS
20 57N, 92 14W

Pilotage: This group of two reefs lie about 82 miles southwest of Cayos Arenas. The two groups are about 6 miles apart.

Triángulo Oest is a 3/4-mile-long reef with an 11-foot-high cay on its southwest end. A disused lighthouse stands near the lighthouse on the cay near the southwest end.

CAUTION: A dangerous wreck lies about 22 miles northeast of the lighthouse on Triángulo Oest. An awash rock was reported to lie about 18 miles north-northeast of Triángulo Oest.

COAST PILOT

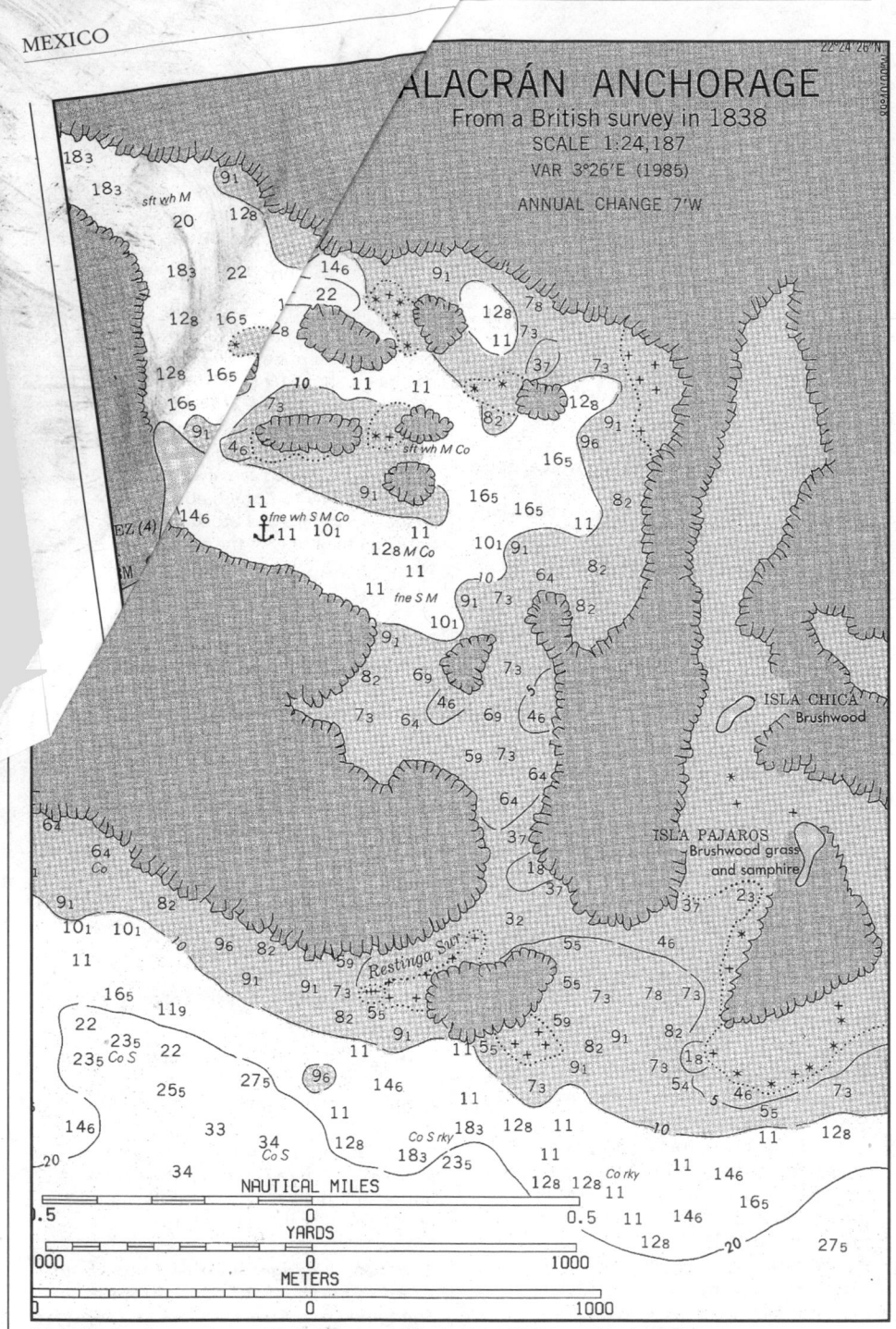

ALACRÁN ANCHORAGE

From a British survey in 1838

SCALE 1:24,187

VAR 3°26'E (1985)

ANNUAL CHANGE 7'W

22°24'26"N

ISLA CHICA
Brushwood

ISLA PAJAROS
Brushwood grass
and samphire

Restinga Sur

NAUTICAL MILES

0.5   0   0.5

YARDS

000   0   1000

METERS

0   1000

Alacrán Anchorage, soundings in meters *(from DMA 28221, 16th ed, 8/90)*

Triángulo Este (20° 55'N, 92° 13'W) and Triángulo Sur (20° 54'N, 92° 14'W), which nearly dry, are separated by a channel 1/4 mile wide with depths of 42 to 60 feet. A 24-foot-high cay stands on the south end of Triángulo Este. A reef extends about 1 mile northeast from the cay, and a coral ledge extends about 1 mile farther northeast. Triángulo Sur has a ledge extending about 1 mile southwest from the southwesternmost cay.

Anchorage: Vessels can anchor off the southwestern end of Triángulo Sur.

OBISPO NORTE
AND OBISPO SUR
20 29N, 92 12W

Pilotage: These shoals lie about 25 miles south of Triángulo Oest. They have depths of 24 to 60 feet. They are marked by discolored water. Obispo Norte has a depth of 15 feet near its north end. A dangerous wreck lies between the two shoals.

BANCO PERA
20 42N, 91 56W

Pilotage: This shoal bank has depths of 54 feet and is located about 28 miles southeast of Triángulo Oest. Banco Nuevo has a depth of 48 feet in a position about 38 miles southeast of Triángulo Oest.

CAYOS ARCAS RANGE (Front Light), W side of Cay del Centro, 20 12.7N, 91 58.2W. Fl W 3s, 42ft, 10M. Metal tower. **(Rear Light),** 80 meters 107° from front. Fl (2) W 15s, 72ft, 13M. White round concrete tower and house. Radar reflector.

CAYOS ARCAS
20 13N, 91 58W

Pilotage: This is the southernmost group of dangers on the Banco de Campeche. It consists of a group of three islets, with surrounding reefs. They lie about 44 miles south-southeast of Triángulo Este.

Cayo del Centro is the northernmost and largest. It is composed of sand and rises at its south end to a height of 21 feet. It lies on the southeast end of a reef that extends about 1 mile northwest and about 1/2 mile west from it. This reef is always visible. The islet is scantily covered with grass, some bushes, and several clumps of palm trees. A pair of lighted beacons in range 107° stand on the cay. A stranded wreck stands on the reef about 800 yards northwest of the north extremity of Cayo del Centro.

Anchorage: Vessels use the range to work into the anchorage west-northwest of the cay.

Cayo del Este is a small 10-foot-high cay on a detached reef about 1/4 mile southeast of Cayo del Centro. The intervening channel has depths of 36 to 84 feet. A stranded wreck stands on the edge of the reef about 300 yards northeast of the islet.

Cayo del Oeste is a small 6-foot-high cay lying on a small detached reef about 3/4 mile west of the south end of Cayo del Centro. The narrow intervening passage has depths of 24 to 27 feet.

PLATFORM PR-1 REBOMBEO, 18 56.7N, 92 37.2W. Q W, 56ft, 10M. Four lights, one installed on each corner of platform.
PLATFORM POOL-C, 19 13.4N, 92 15.8W. Q W, 56ft, 10M. Four lights, one installed on each corner of platform.
PLATFORM CAAN-A, 19 13.3N, 92 05.4W. Q W, 56ft, 10M. Four lights, one installed on each corner of platform.
PLATFORM ECO-1, 19 01.8N, 92 01.1W. Q W, 56ft, 10M. Four lights, one installed on each corner of platform.
PLATFORM CHUC-1, 19 10.3N, 92 17.1W. Q W, 56ft, 10M. Four lights, one installed on each corner of platform.
PLATFORM POOL-D, 19 14.5N, 92 17.3W. Q W, 56ft, 10M. Four lights, one installed on each corner of platform.
PLATFORM POOL-B, 19 14.2N, 92 16.6W. Q W, 56ft, 10M. Four lights, one installed on each corner of platform.
PLATFORM ABKATUM-D, 19 17.9N, 92 12.1W. Q W, 56ft, 10M. Four lights, one installed on each corner of platform.
PLATFORM ABKATUM-C, 19 19.7N, 92 11.3W. Q W, 56ft, 10M. Four lights, one installed on each corner of platform.
PLATFORM ABKATUM-F, 19 16.7N, 92 09.5W. Q W, 56ft, 10M. Four lights, one installed on each corner of platform.
PLATFORM ABKATUM-G, 19 18.0N, 92 08.4W. Q W, 56ft, 10M. Four lights, one installed on each corner of platform.
PLATFORM ABKATUM-J, 19 16.4N, 92 07.9W. Q W, 56ft, 10M. Four lights, one installed on each corner of platform.
PLATFORM AKAL-F, 19 23.9N, 92 03.7W. Q W, 56ft, 10M. Four lights, one installed on each corner of platform.
PLATFORM ABKATUM-H, 19 20.5N, 92 13.2W. Q W, 56ft, 10M. Four lights, one installed on each corner of platform.

PLATFORM ABKATUM-93, 19 18.0N, 92 10.9W. Q W, 56ft, 10M. Four lights, one installed on each corner of platform.

PLATFORM ABKATUM-E, 19 16.4N, 92 11.1W. Q W, 56ft, 10M. Four lights, one installed on each corner of platform.

PLATFORM ABKATUM-A, 19 17.7N, 92 10.2W. Q W, 56ft, 10M. Four lights, one installed on each corner of platform.

PLATFORM NOHOCH-A, 19 22.0N, 92 00.3W. Q W, 56ft, 10M. Four lights, one installed on each corner of platform.

PLATFORM ABKATUM-I, 19 15.3N, 92 10.0W. Q W, 56ft, 10M. Four lights, one installed on each corner of platform.

PLATFORM AKAL-J, 19 25.5N, 92 04.6W. Q W, 56ft, 10M. Four lights, one installed on each corner of platform.

PLATFORM AKAL-G, 19 22.8N, 92 03.0W. Q W, 56ft, 10M. Four lights, one installed on each corner of platform.

PLATFORM KU-1, 19 29.9N, 92 08.3W. Q W, 56ft, 10M. Four lights, one installed on each corner of platform.

PLATFORM AKAL-L, 19 23.9N, 92 00.9W. Q W, 56ft, 10M. Four lights, one installed on each corner of platform.

PLATFORM AKAL-M, 19 27.7N, 92 03.7W. Q W, 56ft, 10M. Four lights, one installed on each corner of platform.

PLATFORM IXTOC-1, 19 24.4N, 92 12.7W. Q W, 56ft, 10M. Four lights, one installed on each corner of platform.

PLATFORM AKAL-E, 19 25.1N, 92 03.0W. Q W, 56ft, 10M. Four lights, one installed on each corner of platform.

PLATFORM AKAL-N, 19 26.2N, 92 03.7W. Q W, 56ft, 10M. Four lights, one installed on each corner of platform.

PLATFORM AKAL-O, 19 24.4N, 92 04.9W. Q W, 56ft, 10M. Four lights, one installed on each corner of platform.

PLATFORM AKAL-D, 19 25.0N, 92 01.6W. Q W, 56ft, 10M. Four lights, one installed on each corner of platform.

PLATFORM POOL-A, 19 14.3N, 92 15.2W. Q W, 56ft, 10M. Four lights, one installed on each corner of platform.

PLATFORM AKAL-R, 19 20.9N, 92 02.9W. Q W, 56ft, 10M. Four lights, one installed on each corner of platform.

PLATFORM NOHO CH-B, 19 20.6N, 92 00.3W. Q W, 56ft, 10M. Four lights, one installed on each corner of platform.

PLATFORM KU-A, 19 31.2N, 92 11.3W. Q W, 56ft, 10M. Four lights, one installed on each corner of platform.

PLATFORM AKAL-C, 19 23.9N, 92 02.3W. Q W, 56ft, 10M. Four lights, one installed on each corner of platform. RACON Y (– · – –).

PLATFORM KU-H, 19 35.3N, 92 12.0W. Q W, 56ft, 10M. Four lights, one installed on each corner of platform.

PLATFORM KU-F, 19 29.7N, 92 10.4W. Q W, 56ft, 10M. Four lights, one installed on each corner of platform.

PLATFORM KU-G, 19 30.8N, 92 09.3W. Q W, 56ft, 10M. Four lights, one installed on each corner of platform.

PLATFORM KU-M, 19 33.8N, 92 11.0W. Q W, 56ft, 10M. Four lights, one installed on each corner of platform.

PLATFORM ECO-1, 19 01.8N, 92 01.1W. Q W, 56ft, 10M. Four lights, one installed on each corner of platform. RACON Q (– – · –).

PLATFORM AKAL-P, 19 22.8N, 92 04.4W. Q W, 56ft, 10M. Four lights, one installed on each corner of platform.

PLATFORM CHUC-A, 19 10.8N, 92 17.2W. Q W, 56ft, 10M. Four lights, one installed on each corner of platform.

PLATFORM CHUC-B, 19 08.7N, 92 18.3W. Q W, 56ft, 10M. Four lights, one installed on each corner of platform.

CAYO ARCAS OIL TERMINAL, 20 11.5N, 91 59.9W. Q W, 56ft, 10M. Four lights, one installed on each corner of platform.

CAYO ARCAS TERMINAL

20 10N, 91 59W

Pilotage: This oil production and export facility lies about 1 to 3 miles south of Cayos Arcas. The distribution platform is the north end of a pipeline carrying oil from a marine oil field 45 miles to the south. Pipelines are laid from this platform to two tanker moorings, known as SBMs. The terminal monitors VHF channel 9.

CAUTION: A major offshore oilfield is located between 40 and 58 miles south-southwest of Cayos Arcas. A number of production platforms interconnected by submarine pipelines are located throughout this area. Mobile drilling rigs, platforms, and associated structures, sometimes unlit, may be encountered anywhere in the area. Numerous pipelines, many uncharted, exist within the oilfields and between them and shore.

An oil platform is located at 19° 24'N, 92° 02'W.

Akbatum A Oil/Gas Platform is located in position 19° 17.9′N, 92° 10.3′W. Contact "Marine Control" on VHF channels 9 and 16.

PLATFORM ABKATUM-O, 19 16.9N, 92 13.7W. Q W, 56ft, 10M. Four lights, one installed on each corner of platform.
PLATFORM AKAL-H, 19 22.4N, 92 01.9W. Q W, 56ft, 10M. Four lights, one installed on each corner of platform.
PLATFORM AKAL-L, 19 26.9N, 92 05.0W. Q W, 56ft, 10M. Four lights, one installed on each corner of platform.
PLATFORM AKAL-S, 19 21.7N, 92 04.2W. Q W, 56ft, 10M. Four lights, one installed on each corner of platform.
PLATFORM BATAB-1A, 19 17.6N, 92 18.6W. Q W, 56ft, 10M. Four lights, one installed on each corner of platform.
PLATFORM BATAB-A, 19 17.8N, 92 19.0W. Q W, 56ft, 10M. Four lights, one installed on each corner of platform.
PLATFORM CAAN-1, 19 12.2N, 92 05.1W. Q W, 56ft, 10M. Four lights, one installed on each corner of platform.
PLATFORM VECH-A, 19 05.8N, 92 31.9W. Q W, 56ft, 10M. Four lights, one installed on each corner of platform.
PLATFORM YUM-1, 18 46.9N, 92 34.1W. Q W, 56ft, 10M. Four lights, one installed on each corner of platform.
BAY OF CAMPECHE RADAR STATION PR-1, 18 56.6N, 92 37.3W. Q W, 56ft, 10M. Four lights, one installed on each corner of platform. RACON **C** (– · – –).

PUNTA BOXCOHUO

21 02N, 90 18W
Pilotage: This is the northwest extremity of the Yucatán Peninsula. It is a low and sandy projection. Several shoals are reported to lie near the 10-meter depth curve, about 9 miles seaward of the point. A 9-foot shoal lies 3 miles north of the point. A shoal, with depth unknown, is reported to lie 20 miles west-northwest of the lighthouse on the point.

The section of coast forming the west side of the Yucatán Peninsula and the east side of the Bay of Campeche extends 13 miles south-southwest from Punta Boxcohua to Celeston, then 60 miles farther south to the town of Campeche. A wide and shallow bank fronts this portion of the coast.

Between Campeche and Punta Morro, about 13 miles to the southwest, and Champoton, 20 miles farther south, the coast is bolder and backed by prominent ridges of hills.

Between Champoton and Punta Xicalango, about 80 miles to the southwest, the coast is low, wooded, and fronted by a continuous sandy beach. Laguna de Terminos indents the south part of the coast. For a distance of 30 miles southwest of Champoton numerous sand and shell patches, with depths of 14 to 30 feet, extend as far as 12 miles offshore.

From Punta Xicalango the coast extends to the west for about 45 miles to Punta Buey and is low and free of dangers. There are no ports of importance along this section of coast.

Winds: During the rainy season, from June to September, squalls blow at times with considerable force. The prevailing winds are from northeast to southeast.
Currents: There is seldom any current off the west coast of the Yucatán Peninsula.

REAL DE LAS SALINAS
20 45N, 90 26W
Pilotage: This is the west entrance to the lagoon that parallels the north coast of the Yucatán Peninsula. It lies about 6 miles south of Celestun.

Between Real Salinas and Campeche, about 55 miles to the south, the low coast is bordered by swampy ground for about 25 miles and then becomes more elevated, rising to heights of 100 to 280 feet north of Campeche.

Isla de Piedras is about 30 feet high and located close offshore about 23 miles north of Campeche.

SAN BARTOLO HILL, Campeche, 19 48.9N, 90 35.0W. Fl (2) W 12s, 256ft, 26M. Square white concrete tower. A F W light is shown from the mole.
LERMA RANGE (Front Light), 19 48.3N, 90 36.0W. Fl W 3s, 85ft, 8M. Metal framework tower. **(Rear Light),** 178 meters 139° from front. Iso W 2s, 245ft, 9M. Metal framework tower.
WHARF, at head, 19 49.0N, 90 35.7W. Iso W 2s, 30ft, 9M. Column.
PIER, Lerma No 2, 19 48.8N, 90 35.9W. Iso R 2s, 21ft, 6M. Concrete tower.

PIER, Lerma No 1, 19 48.8N, 90 35.9W. Iso R 2s, 21ft, 6M. Concrete tower.
PIER, Breton No 3, 19 49.1N, 90 35.6W. Iso R 2s, 30ft, 6M. Green pipe.
PIER, Breton No 2, 19 49.1N, 90 35.7W. Iso R 2s, 30ft, 6M. Red pipe.

CAMPECHE

19 51N, 90 33W

Pilotage: This is the capital of the state of Campeche and a major sisal-exporting port. It stands on a plain bordered on three sides by a small amphitheater of hills. Two forts stand 1 1/4 miles northeast, and two similar forts stand 1 3/4 miles southwest of the city.

A signal station is located atop an old fort near the waterfront. A blue flag indicates bad weather and a red flag indicates that the port is closed.

A pier extending from the shore abreast of the city was reported to have a dredged channel with a depth of 18 feet leading up to it.

Port of Entry

Muelle Castillo Breton, a new 550-yard-long pier with a depth of 12 feet alongside stands at the village of Lerma, about 3 1/2 miles southwest of Campeche.

Puerto de Abrigo is situated about 1/4 mile southeast of Muelle Castillo Breton, and there is a small pier 1/4 mile northeast of the same jetty.

Between Campeche and Punta Mastun Grande, a wooded 423-foot-high headland about 9 miles southwest, and Punta Morro, about 5 miles farther south-southwest, the coast is bold and backed by ridges of hills.

CAUTION: Dangerous wrecks lie 10 miles northwest and 18 miles west of Punta Mastun.

Between Punta Morro and the Río Champoton, about 20 miles to the south, the coast is backed by a ridge of hills that are more broken than those to the north. The ridge terminates in a prominent 360-foot-high hill about 8 miles south of the river.

PUNTA MORRO, 19 41.4N, 90 42.1W. Fl (3) W 6s, 177ft, 27M. White octagonal masonry tower, white dwelling. Visible 000°–197°.

RÍO CHAMPOTON, S side of entrance, 19 20.8N, 90 43.2W. Fl W 5s, 82ft, 25M. White square concrete tower. Visible 045°–180°.

CHAMPOTON

19 22N, 90 43W

Pilotage: This is a small village on the south side of the entrance to the Río Champoton. An old fort and two churches stand in the town. Observation Cay, 5 feet high, stands close off the river entrance.

Between the Río Champoton and Barra de Puerto Real, about 55 miles to the southwest, the low, wooded coast is fronted by a continuous stretch of sandy beach. Numerous sand and shell patches, with depths of 8 to 18 feet, lie up to 5 miles off this section of coast.

BANCOS CHAMPOTON
19 23N, 90 50W

Pilotage: This is a group of detached patches with depths of 14 to 27 feet extending 10 to 15 miles west from Champoton.

BANCOS DE SABUNCUY
19 10N, 91 16W

Pilotage: This is a group of patches with depths of 14 to 30 feet lying about 32 miles southwest of Champoton. They extend up to 12 miles offshore.

SABANCUY, 19 00.0N, 91 11.0W. Fl (3) W 12s, 42ft, 11M. White concrete tower.

LAGUNA DE TERMINOS

ISLA AGUADA RANGE (Front Light), on Punta del Tigre entrance, 18 47.8N, 91 30.2W. Fl W 3s, 33ft, 11M. White concrete tower. **(Rear Light),** 400 meters 151° from front, Fl (4) W 12s, 66ft, 9M. White concrete tower. Radar reflector.
BOCA DE LOS PARGOS, 18 37.0N, 91 16.0W. Fl W 6s, 36ft, 11M. Masonry tower.
LAGUNA DE TERMINOS, Tio Campo, S end, 18 31.5N, 91 47.7W. Fl W 6s, 30ft, 11M. Round masonry tower.
PUNTA DEL ZACATAL, 18 37.3N, 91 51.9W. Fl W 5s, 49ft, 17M. Aluminum tower with concrete base.
PUNTA ATALAYA, W end of Isla del Carmen, 18 39.4N, 91 51.2W. Fl (3) W R 12s, 69ft, 21M. White masonry tower, red cupola, R 086°–113°, W 113°–086°.

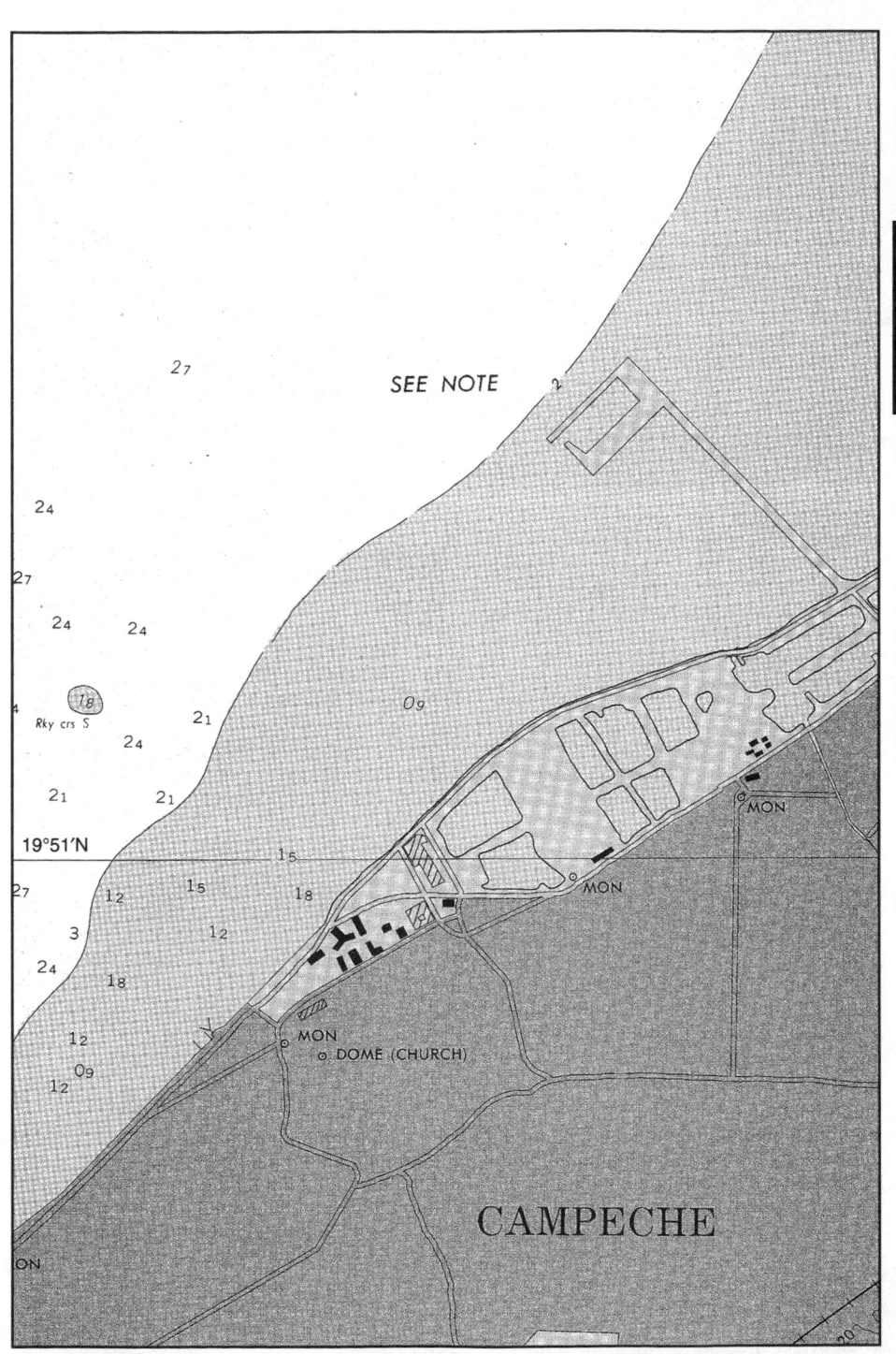

Campeche, soundings in meters *(from DMA 28265, 1st ed, 9/88)*

BARRA DE PUERTO REAL
18 47N, 91 30W

Pilotage: This is the east entrance to Laguna de Terminos. It is 2 miles wide and has depths ranging from 6 to 12 feet. A pair of lighted beacons in range 152° stand on Punta del Tigre on the north side of the entrance. A shallow, breaking spit extends 2 1/2 miles west-northwest from the point. A channel for vessels drawing less than 10 feet leads to an anchorage off Punta del Tigre, but should not be attempted without local knowledge.

Isla del Carmen, low and sparsely wooded, fronts Laguna de Terminos between Barra de Puerto Real and Barra Principal, the west entrance of the lagoon, which is located about 20 miles west-southwest.

CARMEN
18 39N, 91 50W

Pilotage: Barra Principal is about 6 miles wide between Punta Atalaya, 1/2 mile southeast of the southwest end of Isla del Carmen, and Punta Xicalango to the northwest. A breaking spit extends 4 1/2 miles northwest from Punta Atalaya, and depths of 6 to 12 feet extend 3 miles north from Punta Xicalango. A buoyed channel, with depths of 12 to 14 feet, leads through these shoals to the town of Carmen on the southeast side of Punta Atalaya. Two lighted beacons in range 180° stand on the west side of the entrance and indicate the fairway of this channel.

CAUTION: Considerable changes to depths, navigation aids, and the coastline have taken place in the approaches to Carmen. The most recent editions of appropriate charts should be consulted.

The wharves that front the town have a depth of 11 feet alongside. A pier, with a depth of 18 feet alongside, extends from the shore at the naval base near the southeast end of the town. In 1979 an artificial harbor was under construction in the area north of Punta Atalaya.

Between Barra Principal and the Río Grijalva, about 46 miles to the west, the coast is low and has no prominent features.

Entrance Buoy, 18 41.0N, 92 42.0W. Fl W 2s. Black buoy.
XICALANGO RANGE (Front Light), 18 38.5N, 91 54.5W. Fl W 3s, 42ft, 11M. Metal frame-work tower. **(Rear Light),** 330 meters 180° from front. Fl W 6s, 104ft, 20M. Red concrete tower.
GOVERNMENT PIER, at head, N side, 18 38.9N, 91 50.7W. Iso G 2s, 26ft, 4M. Cylindrical concrete tower.
GOVERNMENT PIER, S Side, 18 38.9N, 91 50.7W. Iso G 2s, 26ft, 4M. Cylindrical concrete tower.
FRONTERA, 18 36.8N, 92 41.5W. Fl W 6s, 98ft, 14M. White skeleton iron tower with eight columns. Visible 045°–245°. Two F W range lights mark entrance to Grijalva Canal. Radar reflector.
E BREAKWATER, 18 37.1N, 92 41.2W. Fl G 5s, 25ft, 6M. White concrete tower.
FRONTERA RANGE (Front Light), 18 37.0N, 92 41.0W. Fl W 3s, 38ft, 10M. White tower. **(Rear Light),** Iso W 2s, 55ft, 10M. White tower.

PUNTA BUEY
18 39N, 92 43W

Pilotage: This low point has been reported to be extending north and northwest. Depths of 18 to 24 feet extend about 1 1/2 miles north and northwest from the point.

The coast recedes about 8 miles southwest from Punta Buey, then extends in a general west-southwest direction for about 95 miles to Coatzacoalcos, then west for 10 miles, then north-northwest for an additional 25 miles to Punta Zapotitlan. This low, marshy coast is indented by several lagoons and is covered with very heavy vegetation except in the tidal marshes. Several rivers discharge into the gulf, and hills stand 3 to 8 miles inland on the west part of this coast.

Winds: The winds tend to blow from the north. Northers occur at about eight-day intervals between October and March.
Current: From October to March the current near the shore sets east at a rate of 1 to 1 1/2 knots.

FRONTERA
(ALVARO OBREGÓN)
18 35N, 92 39W

Pilotage: Puerto Frontera stands on the east bank of the Río Grijalva about 5 miles south of the entrance. The port is used mainly by small coast vessels.

Depths of less than 18 feet extend about 3/4 mile north and 1 mile northwest from the east entrance point, and similar depths extend about 1 1/2 miles north and 1/2 mile west from Punta Buey. The bar lying north of the entrance points has been reported to be dredged to a depth of 20 feet. The buoyed channel within the river has a navigable width of about 250 yards with depths ranging from 32 to 40 feet. The preferred channel passes east of Isla Buey about 3 miles south of the entrance.

Grijalva Canal, which crosses thé peninsula about 1 1/2 miles south of Punta Buey, was formerly used to enter the river. In 1974 this canal was reported no longer in use.

When the river is at its highest level the bar has the least depth over it, and when the river is at its lowest the channel is scoured out, so the depths are better. At the end of the rainy season in December, the least depths may be expected, but the first norther will increase the depth by about 3 feet. A freshet can reduce the depth by as much as 3 feet.

There is only one tidal rise every 24 hours, and the rise at springs is only about 2 feet. An over-head cable north of Frontera has a clearance of about 118 feet. Fiscal Wharf parallels the shore abreast town, with depths of 18 to 20 feet alongside. Anchorage can be taken in the river off the town, according to the direction of the port authority.

Port of Entry

Between Punta Buey and Coatzacoalcos, about 100 miles to the west-southwest, the coast is low, fairly steep-to, and bordered by mangroves and palm trees.

CHILTEPEC, at river entrance, 18 26.5N, 93 05.0W. Fl (3) W 12s, 49ft, 14M. White cylindrical tower. Radar reflector.

DOS BOCAS, 18 26.1N, 93 11.5W. RACON B (– · · ·).

RÍO GONZALEZ
18 26N, 93 04W
Pilotage: This river is located about 23 miles southwest of Punta Buey. It is shallow, but is navigated by small draft craft up to 90 miles inland. Barra de Chiltepec is the east entrance of this river and has the village of Chiltepec on its west entrance point. Small coastal vessels frequent this port.

Barra de dos Bocas is the entrance to a lagoon about 3 1/2 miles west of the Río Gonzalez. A dangerous wreck lies about 9 miles northeast of Barra de dos Bocas.

Dos Bocas Terminal, 5 miles west of the Chiltepec lighthouse, lies at the end of the pipeline from the marine oil field to the north. See the previous section on the Cayo Arcas Terminal. The terminal here has a 3,600-foot-long berth and three moorings for large tankers located 11 miles to the north. Pipelines connect the tanker moorings to shore. Anchoring is prohibited within an area shown on the chart enclosing the moorings and pipelines.

TUPILCO, 18 25.0N, 93 25.0W. Fl (4) W 16s, 79ft, 14M. Cylindrical concrete tower.

BARRA DE TUPILCO
18 26N, 93 25W
Pilotage: This is a shallow entrance to a lagoon. It is located about 16 miles west of Barra de dos Bocas. A tower stands on the west side of the entrance.

Laguna del Carmen is located about 26 miles west of Barra de Tupilco. In 1976 an awash rock was reported to lie 17 miles north-northwest of Laguna del Carmen.

TONALA, W side of entrance to Río Tonala, 18 13.0N, 94 07.3W. Fl (3) W 12s, 75ft, 16M. Concrete tower and dwelling, red and white bands. Visible 081°–246°. Two F W range lights mark entrance to Tonala River.

RÍO TONALA
18 13N, 94 08W
Pilotage: This river has a bar with depths of under 8 feet at its entrance. It lies about 16 miles west of Laguna del Carmen. Each entrance point is marked by a conspicuous sand hill. Local knowledge is needed to enter the river. Vessels anchor here to load mahogany.

COATZACOALCOS

CERRO DEL GAVILAN, 18 08.9N, 94 24.0W. Fl (2) W 18s, 177ft, 20M. White octagonal tower with dwelling. Radar reflector. Iso R 2s marks top of mast.
RANGE (Front Light), E side of river, 18 08.1N, 94 24.2W. Fl W 3s, 147ft, 9M. White skeleton iron tower, orange bands. Radar

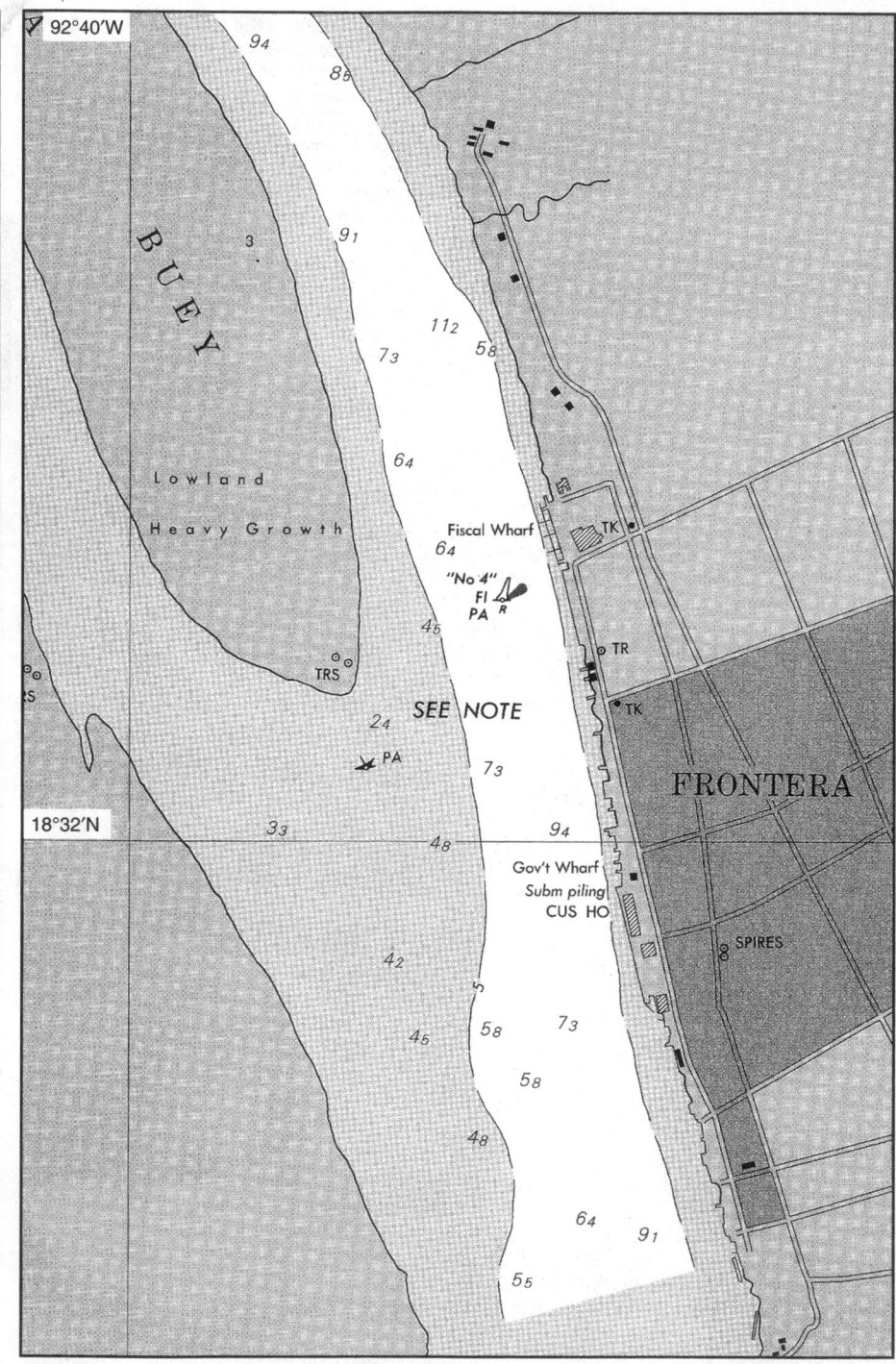

92°40'W

9₄

8₅

B U E Y

3

9₁

11₂

7₃   5₈

6₄

Lowland

Heavy Growth   Fiscal Wharf

6₄

"No 4"
Fl
PA   R

4₅

TRS   TR

SEE NOTE

TK

2₄

PA   7₃

FRONTERA

18°32'N   3₃

4₈   9₄

Gov't Wharf
Subm piling
CUS HO

SPIRES

4₂

5

4₅   5₈   7₃

5₈

4₈

6₄   9₁

5₅

Frontera, soundings in meters *(from DMA 28261, 8th ed, 7/88)*

reflector. **(Rear Light),** 310 meters 162° from front. Iso W 2s, 168ft, 9M. White skeleton iron tower, orange bands. Radar reflector.
PIEDRA NANCHITAL, 18 06.0N, 94 25.0W. Fl (2) W 10s, 33ft, 10M. White framework tower.
E BREAKWATER HEAD, 18 09.9N, 94 24.8W. Fl G 5s, 59ft, 7M. White column on concrete base.
W BREAKWATER HEAD, 18 09.9N, 94 24.7W. Fl R 5s, 46ft, 7M. White column on concrete base.
DARSENA DE PAJARITOS RANGE (Front Light), 18 07.0N, 94 24.0W. Fl W 3s, 61ft, 10M. White framework tower. **(Rear Light),** 300 meters 180° from front. Iso W 2s, 85ft, 10M. White framework tower.
BERTH 6 RANGE (Front Light), 18 07.5N, 94 24.4W. Q Y. White metal column, red bands. **(Rear Light),** 100 meters 270° from front. Fl (3) Y 10s. White metal column, red bands.
BASIN LIGHT E, 18 07.9N, 94 24.2W. Fl G 3s. Metal column.
BASIN LIGHT W, 18 07.9N, 94 24.3W. Fl R 3s. Metal column.

COATZACOALCOS

18 08N, 94 25W
Pilotage: This port was formerly known as Puerto Mexico. It lies on the west bank of the Río Coatzacoalcos, close within the entrance. There is a free port on the same side of the river, south of town. The town, with its buildings and radio towers, is prominent from seaward and can be identified during the day by smoke and at night by the loom of its lights. Approaching from seaward several high dark green hills are observed east of the entrance. On the east side of the entrance is a round hill. Westward of the entrance appear some low sandhills, the tops of which are covered with green vegetation. Low land fronts the hills on either side. The water is muddy for about 1 1/2 miles outside the heads of the breakwater. The breakwaters are con-spicuous, and the east side of the river mouth is a radar target at 40 miles. The range leads up the main channel bearing 162°.

This port is occasionally closed for up to several days during strong northers, which generally occur from November to March. These storms can raise the water level considerably in the port.

Maximum draft crossing the bar is 37 feet, but it has been reported that the depths over the bar are liable to decrease considerably because of unusually strong currents setting to the west. When the river is flooding from June to October, depths are liable to decrease even more.

The wharf along the west side of the river is over 6,200 feet long, with depths of over 28 feet alongside. There are strong currents in the vicinity of the wharves in the river. The inner harbor basin on the east side of the river is called Darsena de Pajaritos. Several oil loading facilities lie upriver.

Between Coatzacoalcos and the Río Barilla, about 12 miles to the west, the coast is low and unvaried. The Río Barilla is the entrance to a lagoon, which is connected to Coatzacoalcos by a river south of the city.
Port of Entry

Tides and Currents: Offshore the current sets northwest, but near the breakwaters it sets east. The current in the river varies with the stage of the tide, attaining its maximum rate of 5 to 5 1/2 knots about 2 hours after high water. During the first 3 hours of the flood the rate ranges from 2 1/2 to 3 knots. The rise of the tide is about 2 feet.

PUNTA SAN JUAN
18 17N, 94 37W
Pilotage: This point is located about 5 miles north of the Río Barilla and has a small islet lying close off it.

Between Punta San Juan and Punta Zapotitlan, about 20 miles north-northwest, the coast is backed by mountain ranges about 3 to 8 miles inland. Cerro San Martin, conspicuous from seaward, stands about 8 miles inland west of Punta San Juan.

PUNTA ZAPOTITLAN, 18 31.2N, 94 48.0W. Fl W 6s, 98ft, 20M. White round masonry tower. Visible 116°–324°.

PUNTA ZAPOTITLAN

18 33N, 94 48W
Pilotage: This prominent point is bordered by a reef that extends 1/2 mile offshore. Depths of greater than 60 feet lie about 1 1/2 miles off the point. An old disused lighthouse stands near the lighthouse on the point.

The coast between Punta Zapotitlan and Cabo Rojo extends in a general northwest direction

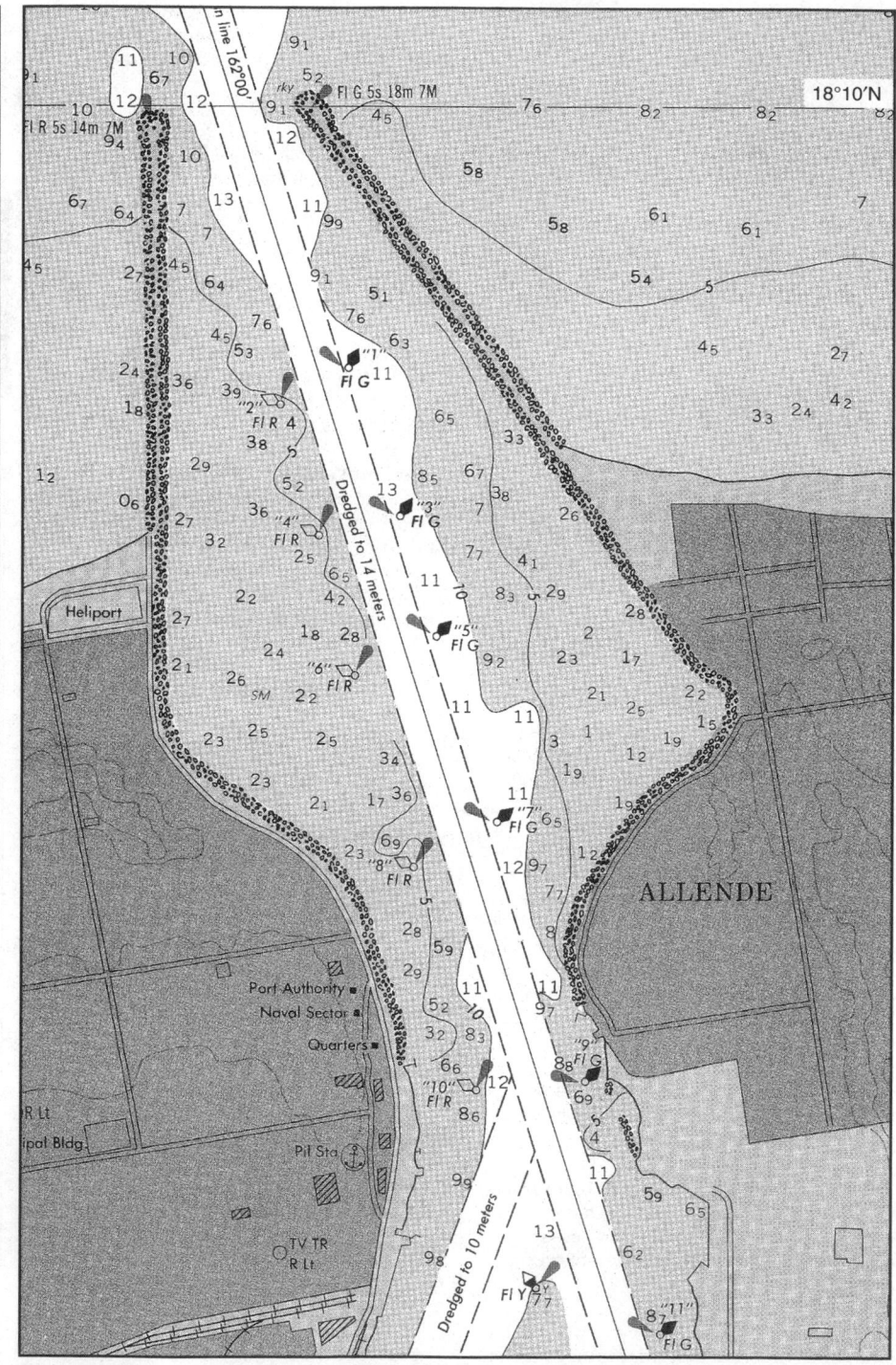

Coatzacoalcos, soundings in meters *(from DMA 28281, 31st ed, 4/92)*

for about 230 miles. Mountain ranges with some conspicuous peaks back the coastal plain. The more prominent coastal features and dangers are lighted. Numerous islets, shoals, and other dangers lie off this section of the coast.

Between Punta Zapotitlan and Alvarado, about 56 miles west-northwest, the first 33 miles of coast are backed by ranges of hills about 3 to 8 miles inland. The remaining part of the coast is lower, being composed of sand hills 50 to 200 feet high.

Barra Zontecomapan obstructs the entrance to the Laguna Coxcoapan, about 10 miles west of Punta Zapotitlan. This bar has a depth of about 6 feet over it. The entrance may be identified by a conspicuous umbrella-shaped tree that stands on a bluff a little to the west of it.

Punta Morrillo is a bold, rounded bluff standing about 15 miles west-northwest of Punta Zapotitlan.

Punta Roca Partida (18° 42'N, 95° 11'W) is a group of perpendicular cliffs that stand about 8 miles west-northwest of Punta Morrillo. A rocky islet stands close off the point.

Volcan San Martin Tuxtla (18° 33'N, 95° 12'W) is a 4,600-foot-high volcano about 10 miles south of Punta Roca Partida. This can be seen from a great distance in clear weather. When active, the column of smoke by day and the flames at night make this volcano an excellent landmark.

Currents: The currents off this coast are variable and uncertain. They are usually dependent on the force and direction of the wind. The coastal current usually sets south in the winter and north in the summer.
Winds: The trade winds blow from northeast to east-northeast. After the season of the northers, from October to March, there are light north breezes, calms, squally rains, and thick weather up to the middle of August, when the trades resume again.

ROCA PARTIDA, 18 42.0N, 94 11.0W. Fl (4) W 16s, 318ft, 22M. White masonry tower, house. Visible 112°–294°. Radar reflector.
ALVARADO, GASODUCTO DE PEMEX, 18 47.0N, 94 45.0W. Fl Y 2s, 29ft, 11M. Yellow round tower.
E FORTIN (Punta Alvarado), on point SE of town, 18 46.3N, 95 45.9W. Fl W 6s, 30ft, 13M.

White square concrete tower. Visible 005°30'–021°30'.
ALVARADO, on E entrance point of Río Papaloapan, 18 47.2N, 95 45.3W. Fl (3) W 12s, 125ft, 21M. Square concrete tower and dwelling. Visible 136°–274°. Radar reflector.
ALVARADO, E BREAKWATER, 18 47.4N, 95 44.5W. Fl G 5s, 29ft, 11M. Green aluminum tower.
W BREAKWATER, 18 47.7N, 95 45.0W. Fl R 5s, 29ft, 11M. Red aluminum tower.

ALVARADO

18 47N, 95 46W

Pilotage: This is primarily a fishing port. It lies within the entrance to a lagoon of the same name located about 32 miles west-northwest of Punta Roca Partida. A 14-foot-deep shoal lies 1 3/4 miles north of the east entrance point. Two patches with depths of 8 and 7 feet lie in mid-channel about 1/4 mile northwest and 3/4 mile south-southwest of the east entrance point. Depths of less than 36 feet extend 1 mile north of the east entrance point.

The bar is situated about 1/2 mile outside the entrance points. It is constantly shifting and the sea nearly always breaks on it. In 1985 a depth of 26 feet was reported over the bar.

A conspicuous sandy bluff and a beacon stand on the east entrance point. A beacon stands on the west entrance point.

The coast between Alvarado and Punta Coyal, about 20 miles northwest, is bordered by two large lagoons along its southern half and by low land along its northwest half.

ANEGADA DE AFUERA, on NW point of reef, 19 10.3N, 95 52.2W. Fl (4) W 16s, 36ft, 11M. Metal structure, red and black bands.
ARRECIFE SANTIAGUILLO, center of island, 19 08.6N, 95 48.4W. Fl (2) W R 10s, 118ft, 22M. Red concrete cylindrical tower. R 002°–056°, W 056°–084°, R 084°– 126°, W 126°–002°. RACON O (– – –).
ARRECIFE DE CABEZO, N end, 19 05.6N, 95 51.9W. Fl (2) W 10s, 30ft, 11M. Square concrete tower. Reported extinguished (1989).
ARRECIFE DE CABEZO, S end, 19 03.1N, 95 49.7W. Fl R 6s, 26ft, 8M. Square concrete tower.
ARRECIFE EL RIZO, S end, 19 03.2N, 95 55.4W. Fl (3) W 12s, 39ft, 11M. Rectangular concrete tower.

PUNTA COYAL
19 03N, 95 58W
Pilotage: This blunt point is composed of low sand hills. A 262-foot-high sand hill stands about 3 miles west of the point. The village of Anton Lizardo stands on the north side of this point. Arrecife El Giote extends 3/4 mile from the coast close west of Anton Lizardo.

Anton Lizardo Anchorage (19° 04'N, 95° 59'W) lies between Arrecife Chopas and Punta Coyal. This anchorage is used by commercial vessels sheltering from northers.

Between Punta Coyal and Punta Mocambo, about 9 miles to the northwest, the coast recedes about 2 miles to form a sandy bay bordered by low sand hills. A reef lies about 3/4 mile southeast of Punta Mocambo. The Río Jamapa, with depths of 3 to 6 feet over the bar, discharges into the gulf about 2 1/2 miles south of Punta Mocambo.

The coast between Punta Mocambo and Puerto Veracruz, 4 miles to the northwest, is low and sandy.

ARRECIFE SANTIAGUILLO
19 09N, 95 48W
Pilotage: This reef stands at the northeast end of a group of reefs located 11 miles east-northeast of Punta Coyal. It stands about 8 feet high.

Arrecife Anegadilla is the outermost reef of the group off Punta Coyal. It lies 1/2 mile east-southeast of Arrecife Santiaguillo.

ARRECIFE ANEGADA DE AFUERA
19 09N, 95 51W
Pilotage: This reef is about 2 1/2 miles long, and it lies about 1 1/2 miles west-northwest of Arrecife Santiaguillo. There is a cay on a small reef close off its south end.

Arrecife Cabeza is about 3 1/2 miles long and 1 1/2 miles wide. It lies about 4 miles south-southwest of Arrecife Santiaguillo.

Arrecife de Enmedio, with shoal patches close off its west side and a small reef and another patch close off its north end, lies about 3 1/2 miles northeast of Punta Coyal. A small cay stands on the south end of the reef.

Arrecife Rizo, about 1 1/2 miles long, lies 1 1/2 miles south of Arrecife de Enmedio. A spit with a depth of 10 feet over its outer end extends a little more than 1/2 mile north from the north extremity of Arrecife Rizo.

ANTON LIZARDO ANCHORAGE

BLANCA REEF, 19 05.0N, 96 00.0W. Fl (2) W 10s, 35ft, 11M. Concrete pyramidal tower.
EL GIOTE REEF, 19 04.0N, 96 00.0W. Fl R 6s, 30ft, 8M. Square concrete tower.
ISLA SALMEDINA, S part, 19 04.1N, 95 57.2W. Fl W 1.5s, 23ft, 3M. Metal mast, black and red bands.
ISLA DE ENMEDIO, 19 06.0N, 95 56.3W. Fl (3) W R G, 46ft, 13M white, 8M red, 7M green. White cylindrical concrete tower, with dwelling. W 147°–220°, R 220°–260°, W 260°–268°, G 268°–299°, W 299°–327°, R 327°–032°, W 032°–057°, R 057°–147°.

ARRECIFE CHOPAS
19 05N, 95 58W
Pilotage: This reef is about 3 1/4 miles long and lies about 2 miles north of Punta Coyal. A small reef lies close south of a grass-covered cay on the south end of the reef. Several small reefs lie close off the north and northwest ends.

Arrecife Blanca is about 1/4 mile in extent with a small cay on it. It lies about 1 mile west of Arrecife Chopas.

NOTE: Vessels without local knowledge should not attempt the passages between Arrecife Rizo, Arrecife de Enmedio, and Arrecife Chopas. Foul ground lies in the passage between Arrecife Chopas and Arrecife Blanca; this passage should not be used.

ARRECIFE ANEGADA DE LA ADENTRO
19 14N, 96 04W
Pilotage: This is the outermost reef in the approaches to Veracruz. These reefs all break and are easily identified in clear weather. This one is located 4 miles east-northeast of the harbor entrance.

Isla Verde is a low white cay standing on the south end of a reef about 1 1/2 miles south-southwest of Arrecife Anegada de La Adentro. The intervening channel is about 1 mile wide and deep.

Bajo Paducah (19° 12'N, 96° 05'W) is a shoal with a least depth of almost 15 feet. It lies about 1/4 mile west of the north end of the reef on which Isla Verde stands.

Arrecife de Pájaros is about 1 mile long and lies about 1 1/4 mile west-southwest of Isla Verde.

Isla de Sacrificios is a small cay on the south end of a reef close south of Arrecife de Pájaros. The passage between here and Arrecife de Pájaros is narrow and foul.

Bajo Mersey (19° 11'N, 96° 06'W) has a least depth of 15 feet.

Arrecife Blanquilla lies about 1 3/4 miles west of Arrecife Anegada de La Adentro. The channel between the two reefs is 1 1/2 miles wide and deep. The channel west of Arrecife Blanquilla has depths of 60 feet and is 3/4 mile wide.

Arrecife de La Gallega extends 1 1/4 miles north from the north side of the harbor entrance, and Arreciffe Galleguilla lies close northeast of its north end.

Arrecife Hornos extends about 1/4 mile east from the root of the southeast breakwater.

RÍO JAMAPA, N breakwater, 19 06.2N, 96 05.8W. Fl R 5s, 29ft, 7M. Red metal tower.
S BREAKWATER, 19 06.0N, 96 05.9W. Fl G 5s, 23ft, 7M. Green metal tower.

VERACRUZ

LA GALLEGUILLA, on E side of reef, 19 13.8N, 96 07.3W. Fl (2) 10s, 36ft, 15M. White cylindrical concrete tower.
ARRECIFE BLANQUILLA, 19 13.6N, 96 06.1W. Fl (4) R 16s, 52ft, 9M. Red concrete tower with white bands.
ARRECIFE LA BLANQUILLA, S side of reef, 19 13.4N, 96 05.8W. Fl (2) R 10s, 49ft, 9M. Red cylindrical concrete tower. Occasional. RACON B (– · · ·).
ANEGADA DE ADENTRO, NW extremity, 19 13.7N, 96 03.7W. Fl (3) G 12s, 36ft, 9M. Green cylindrical concrete tower.
ISLA VERDE, on bands S of island, 19 11.9N, 96 04.9W. Fl (4) W 16s, 26ft, 15M. Red concrete tower.
ARRECIFE PAJAROS, NW end, 19 11.6N, 96 05.7W. Fl W 6s, 23ft, 15M. White concrete tower.

ISLA DE SACRIFICIOS, 19 10.4N, 96 05.5W. Fl W 6s, 127ft, 22M. Cylindrical concrete tower, black and white bands. R 134°–157°, W 157°–163°, G 163°–187°, W 187°–195°, R 195°–238°, W 238°– 334°, obscured 334°–134°. RACON Z (– – · ·), 25M.
ARRECIFE HORNOS, 19 11.5N, 96 07.3W. Fl (2) W 10s, 10ft, 7M. Black framework tower with 2 red bands.
EL MAREGRAPO, 19 11.4N, 96 07.4W. Fl G 2s, 19ft, 6M. Green square concrete tower.
HEAD OF NE BREAKWATER, 19 12.2N, 96 07.2W. Fl R 5s, 39ft, 10M. Red pyramidal tower, concrete base.
HEAD OF SE BREAKWATER, 19 12.0N, 96 07.3W. Fl G 5s, 33ft, 10M. Green pyramidal tower, concrete base.
HEAD OF INNER BREAKWATER NO 3, 19 12.1N, 96 07.6W. Iso W 2s, 49ft, 11M. White concrete tower with small house.
PILOT PIER, N side, 19 12.0N, 96 08.0W. Iso G 2s, 16ft, 7M. White concrete tower.
PILOT PIER, S side, 19 12.0N, 96 08.0W. Iso G 2s, 16ft, 7M. White concrete tower.
MUELLE DE PEMEX, E HEAD, 19 12.2N, 96 07.4W. Iso R 2s, 13ft, 7M. Red tower.
MUELLE DE PEMEX, W side, 19 12.2N, 96 07.4W. Iso R 2s, 13ft, 7M. Red tower.
HOTEL PUERTO BELLO RANGE (Front Light), 19 11.0N, 96 08.0W. Fl W 3s, 81ft, 20M.
(Rear Light), Iso W 2s, 102ft, 25M. On hotel.

PUERTO VERACRUZ

19 12N, 96 08W
Pilotage: This is one of the principal ports of Mexico. The harbor is an artificial basin protected by breakwaters on three sides.

Volcan Citaletepet (Pico de Orizaba) is a 17,392-foot-high volcano located 63 miles west of the city. The volcano is inactive, but its 3 1/2 mile-diameter crater can easily be distinguished from a considerable distance on a clear day. Cerro Nauhcampatepetl (19° 29'N, 97° 08'W) is a 14,040-foot-high mountain with a peculiar shape. It stands about 25 miles north-northeast of the above volcano. Snow falls on isolated spots at higher elevations.

A prominent high radio tower stands about 3/4 mile south of the root of the southeast breakwater. To enter the harbor steer for the cathedral dome about 1/3 mile west-southwest of Benito Juarez tower on a heading of 261°. At night steer for the light on Muro de Pesca-dores on a heading of 270° until the light structure on the east corner of Muelle de La Terminal bears 290°, which will lead through the entrance in mid-channel between the breakwater heads.

Storm signals are displayed from a red and white banded flagstaff on Benito Juarez tower. **Port of Entry**

Winds: With the exception of land breezes at night, the winds usually blow from seaward and are heavily saturated with moisture. March and April are the least humid months. Offshore the tradewinds blow from northeast to east-southeast. During the season of the northers, from October to March, winds of up to 50 knots occur, making it impossible for vessels to enter the harbor. After April, there are light north winds, calms, squally rains, and unsettled weather, until about the middle of August when the tradewinds resume. Land and sea breezes alternate regularly, even in the intervals between northers. The former begin shortly after sunset and the latter at about 0900.

Tides and Currents: The diurnal range of the tide is about 1.6 feet, but the water level is influenced by the force and direction of the winds. The tidal currents are weak and are overcome by the coastal currents, which are also affected by the winds. During the winter, the current usually sets south, and in the summer it sets north.

VERACRUZ TO RÍO TUXPAN

Pilotage: Between Arrecife de La Gallega, which extends north from Puerto Veracruz, and Punta Gorda about 3 miles northwest, the coast recedes about 2 miles, forming Bahía de Veragua.

From Punta Gorda the coast extends about 6 3/4 miles west-northwest to Punta Antigua, on the south side of the entrance to the Río de La Antigua. It then extends about 9 1/2 miles to Punta Zempoala. Punta Antigua has been reported to be a good radar target at distances up to 29 miles and is reported to be identifiable with charted features by radar at distances up to 19 miles.

Bajo Zempoala has depths of 16 to 26 feet about 4 miles north of Punta Zempoala and 2 miles offshore.

Between Punta Zempoala and Punta del Morro, about 25 miles north-northwest, the coast has several reef-fringed points and is marked by several conspicuous peaks. Pico Zempoala (19° 33'N, 96° 27'W) is the southernmost peak. It is 2,299-feet high and stands about 10 miles northwest of Punta Zempoala. Los Dos Antriscos, a peak 2,620 feet high, stands 5 miles southwest of Punta del Morro. A bare chimney rock, 875 feet high and prominent, stands 2 miles west-northwest of Punta Penon, which lies about 9 miles north-northwest of Punta Zempoala.

Isla Bernal Chico (19° 40'N, 96° 23'W) is a 144-foot-high island lying close offshore about 12 miles north-northwest of Punta Zempoala. A prominent bare rocky hill, over 300 feet high, stands on the coast 1 3/4 miles west-southwest of this island.

The coast between Punta Gorda and the Río Nautla, about 30 miles to the northwest, and the Río Tecolutla 18 miles farther northwest, is fronted by a narrow, thickly wooded strip of land paralleled by a narrow lagoon. A range of hills stands about 5 miles inland.

Dos Hermanos (20° 06'N, 96° 52'W) is a conspicuous peak rising to an elevation of 1,169 feet about 9 miles south-southwest of the Río Nautla. Cerro Burras stands about 9 miles southwest of the Río Tecolutla. A dangerous wreck lies 4 miles east of the north side of the mouth of Río Tecolutla.

Between the Río Tecolutla and Punta de Piedras, a reef-fringed point about 25 miles northwest, several rivers discharge into the gulf from the lagoon that backs the coast.

Between Punta Piedras and the Río de Tuxpan, about 9 miles northwest, the coast is about 100 feet high.

CHACHALACAS, 19 24.8N, 96 19.3W. Fl W 6s, 30ft, 15M. White framework tower.
PUNTA DELGADA, located on Punta del Morro, 19 51.0N, 96 28.0W. Fl (3) W 12s, 151ft, 19M. White cylindrical concrete tower.
RÍO NAUTLA, S bank, 20 14.0N, 96 47.0W. Fl W 6s, 98ft, 25M. White concrete cylindrical tower. Visible 150°–300°. Radiobeacon (about 5 miles SSE).
TECOLUTLA, N side of Río Tecolutla, 20 29.0N, 97 00.0W. Fl (2) W 10s, 82ft, 25M. White round concrete tower. Visible 149°–301°. Radar reflector.

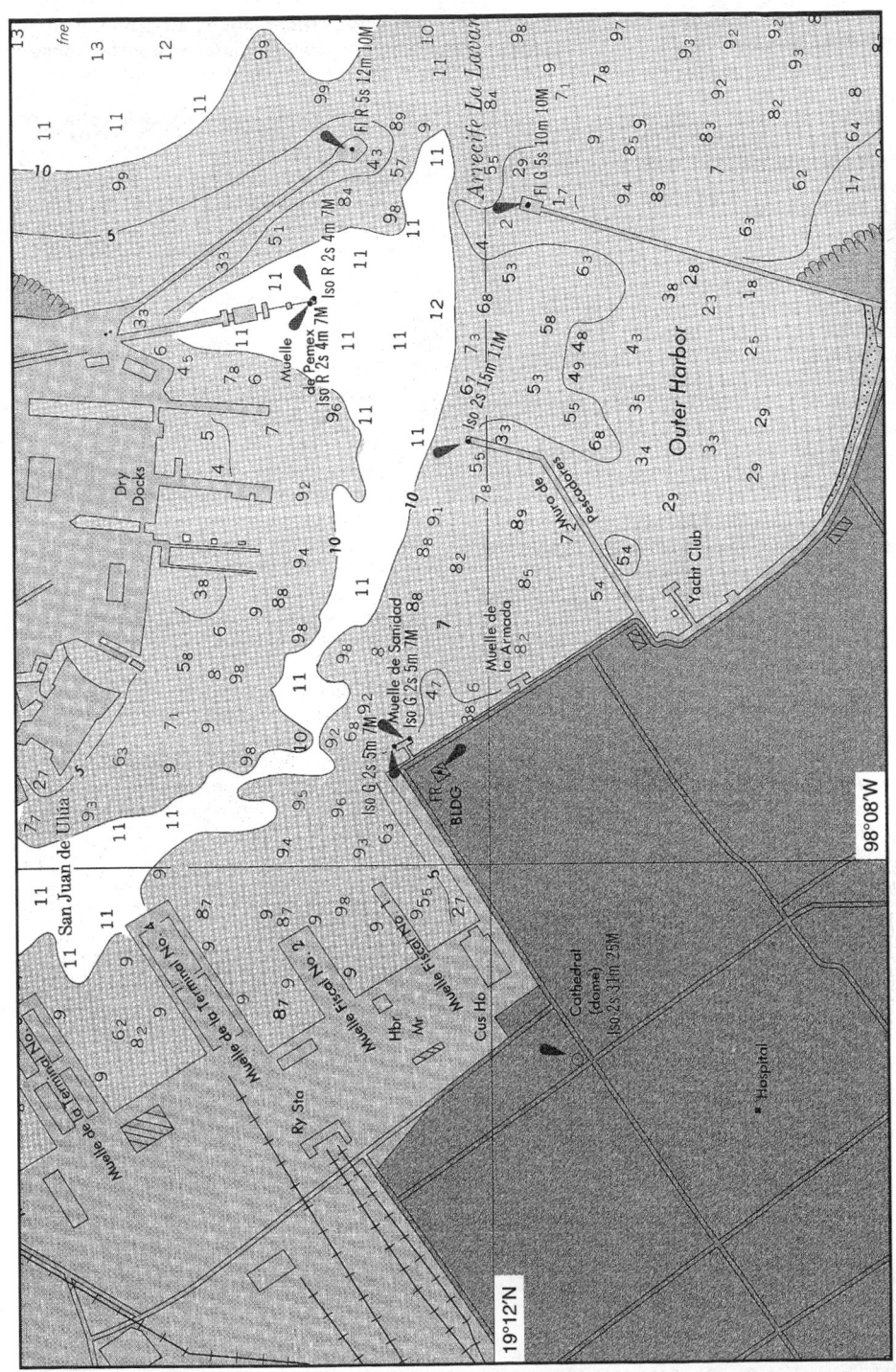

Veracruz, soundings in meters *(from DMA 28302, 14th ed, 8/91)*

BAJO BLAKE
20 45N, 96 58W
Pilotage: This shoal has a depth of 26 feet in a location about 13 miles southeast of Punta de Piedras.

S BREAKWATER, Fl G 5s, 27ft, 8M. Silver metal tower.
N BREAKWATER, Fl R 5s, 27ft, 8M. Silver metal tower.
ESCUALO, 20 41.5N, 97 56.5W. Q W, 84ft, 10M. Yellow rectangular metal tower.
MORSA, 20 46.2N, 97 58.2W. Q W, 84ft, 10M. Yellow rectangular metal platform.
ATUM "C", 20 53.6N, 97 01.0W. Q W, 84ft, 10M. Yellow rectangular metal tower.
ATUM "B", 20 52.6N, 97 00.9W. Q W, 84ft, 10M. Yellow rectangular metal tower.
ATUM "A", 20 51.6N, 97 00.1W. Q W, 84ft, 10M. Yellow rectangular metal tower.
BARGE "B", 20 57.9N, 97 02.3W. Q W, 84ft, 10M. Yellow rectangular metal tower.
BARGE "A", 20 56.6N, 97 02.3W. Q W, 84ft, 10M. Yellow rectangular metal tower.
MARSOPA, 21 03.5N, 97 02.5W. Q W, 84ft, 10M. Yellow rectangular metal tower.
TIBURON, 21 24.1N, 97 08.0W. Q W, 84ft, 10M. Yellow rectangular metal tower.
ARENQUE "B", 22 16.7N, 97 31.0W. Q W, 84ft, 10M. Yellow rectangular metal tower.
ARENQUE "A", 22 14.0N, 97 30.1W. Q W, 84ft, 10M. Yellow rectangular metal tower.
BARRA DE CAZONES, 20 45.0N, 97 12.0W. Fl W 5s, 86ft, 14M. Concrete tower.
PUNTA CAZONES, 20 46.0N, 97 12.0W. Fl (2) 10s, 49ft, 9M. Metal framework tower.

TUXPAN

N BREAKWATER, 20 58.4N, 97 18.2W. Fl R 5s, 27ft, 8M. Metal column.
S BREAKWATER, 20 58.1N, 97 18.1W. Fl G 5s, 27ft, 8M. Metal column.
N SIDE, mouth of river, 20 58.0N, 97 19.0W. Fl (4) W 7s, 79ft, 14M. White truncated conical masonry tower and hut.
RANGE (Front Light), 20 57.3N, 97 20.6W. Fl W 3s, 38ft, 16M. White metal tower. **(Rear Light),** 95 meters 248° from front. Iso W 2s, 55ft, 16M. White metal tower.
S SIDE RANGE (Front Light), 20 57.6N, 97 19.2W. Fl W 3s, 30ft, 20M. Metal framework tower. **(Rear Light),** 270 meters 238° from front. Iso W 2s, 75ft, 20M. Metal framework tower.
N SIDE RANGE 1 (Front Light), 20 57.5N, 97 20.1W. Fl W 3s, 30ft, 20M. Metal frame-work tower. **(Rear Light),** 250 meters 255° from front. Iso W 2s, 56ft, 16M. Metal framework tower.

RÍO TUXPAN
20 58N, 97 19W
Pilotage: The entrance has a maximum depth of 16 feet over the bar and is fronted by break-waters that extend 1/4 mile offshore from the entrance points. It was reported in 1991 the breakwaters were being lengthened and the harbor was to be dredged to 36 feet to accom-modate a new container terminal. Within the bar depths increase considerably. The least depth, as far as the town of Tuxpan, is under 9 feet. Vessels drawing under 7 feet can proceed up to 36 miles above the entrance.

From seaward several tall stacks and oil tanks on the banks of the river are conspicuous. The navigation lights at the river entrance are hard to identify and are often confused with the numerous fishing vessels found in the vicinity.

Tuxpan is located about 5 miles above the entrance to the river and is a Port of Entry.

Between the Río Tuxpan and Cabo Rojo the low coast extends northwest for about 19 miles, then north-northeast an additional 18 miles forming a bight called Puerto Lobos. This bight provides some protection from the northers that blow with considerable strength during the winter.

ARRECIFE TUXPAN, BAJO CENTRO,
21 01.1N, 97 12.6W. Fl (2) W 10s, 36ft, 11M. Truncated pyramidal concrete tower. Reported to lie 1.1 miles further NE (1981). RACON **X** (– · · –).
ARRECIFE TANGUIJO, 21 07.0N, 97 17.0W. Fl (3) W 12s, 36ft, 11M. Concrete truncated pyramidal tower.

BAJO DE TUXPAN
21 01N, 97 12W
Pilotage: This small steep-to reef has a low cay on it, in a position about 6 miles east-northeast of the Río de Tuxpan.

Bajo de Enmedio is a small reef lying about 3 miles northwest of Bajo de Tuxpan.

Bajo de Tanguijo lies about 7 miles northwest of Bajo de Tuxpan. It is a small, steep-to drying reef.

COAST PILOT

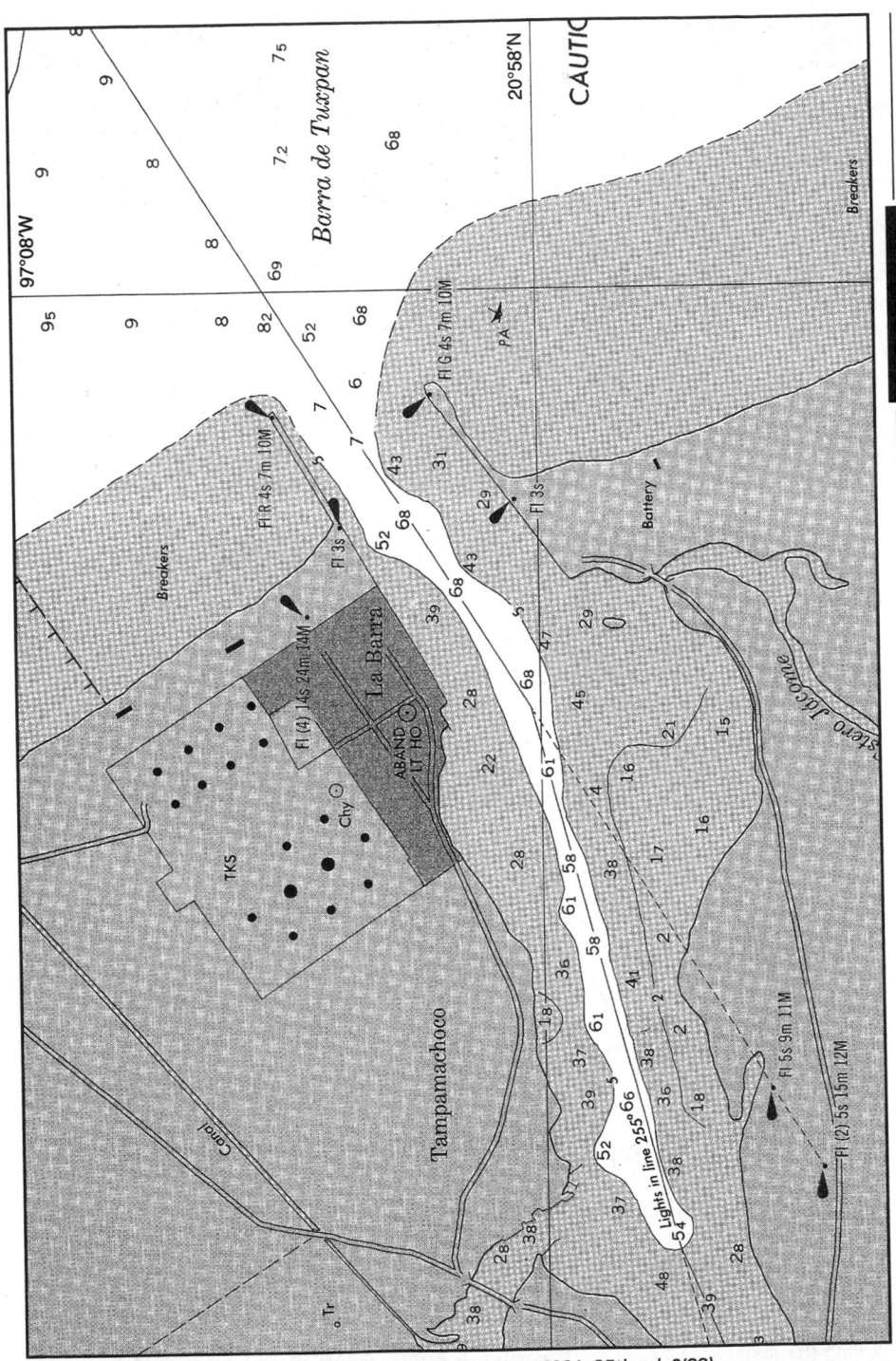

Río Tuxpan Entrance, soundings in meters *(from DMA 28321, 35th ed, 9/88)*

ARRECIFE MEDIO, 21 31.0N, 97 14.0W. Fl R 3s, 33ft, 8M. Silver metal tower.
ARRECIFE LA BLANQUILLA, 21 32.3N, 97 16.5W. Fl W 6s, 33ft, 11M. Concrete tower.
ISLA DE LOBOS, 21 27.2N, 97 13.7W. Fl W 5s, 105ft, 20M. Cylindrical concrete tower. RACON O (– – –), 25M.
LOBOS, outer light off sw shore of Isla de Lobos, 21 27.2N, 97 13.5W. Fl R 3s, 13ft, 8M. Cylindrical concrete tower. Visible 250°–090°.

ISLA LOBOS
21 28N, 97 13W
Pilotage: This small islet is about 30 feet high to the tops of the trees. It lies 9 miles southeast of Cabo Rojo. A reef extends about 1 mile north from the islet.

Arrecife Medio is a small, steep-to, breaking reef, lying about 2 1/2 miles north-northwest of Isla Lobos.

BAJO DE LA BLANQUILLA
21 32N, 97 16W
Pilotage: This is a breaking reef with a drying sandbank on it. It lies 6 miles northwest of Isla Lobos. A disused light structure stands on the reef. The passage between here and Cabo Rojo is of doubtful safety as the soundings are irregular.

CABO ROJO

21 33N, 97 20W
Pilotage: This blunt headland is composed of sand hills about 35 feet high. It is bordered by a reef that extends about 1 3/4 miles east from it.

The coast trends northwest for 49 miles to the Río Panuco, then about 160 miles north and an additional 67 miles north-northeast to the Río Grande. In general, the coast is composed of sand dunes and wooded hummocks. Mountain ranges with conspicuous peaks lie farther inland along the south part of this coast. Several extensive lagoons, separated from the coast by narrow strips of land, lie along this section. Several rivers discharge into the gulf.

Between Cabo Rojo and the Río Panuco the coast is bordered by a narrow strip of land, a few hundred feet to 5 miles wide, fronting the Laguna de Tamiahua. Canal del Chijol crosses this lagoon and is frequented by small craft going from Tuxpan to Tampico. The sand hills backing the coast about 4 miles north of Cabo Rojo are 70 feet high and rise to heights of 348 feet about 18 miles farther north. The coast then becomes very low as far north as the Río Panuco.

An 8-foot shoal lies 5 miles south-southeast of the entrance to Tampico.

Winds: The winds are east-southeast from August to April and east from April to June. During the summer the land breezes blow from midnight to 0900 and then yield to the sea breezes as far north as 26°, where the mountain ranges terminate.
Currents: During the winter the current sets north and in the opposite direction during the summer. About 15 to 20 miles offshore the current generally sets north at a rate of about 1 knot.

BAJOS DE BURROS, 21 42.5N, 97 36.2W. Fl (2) W 10s, 19ft, 5M. Fiberglass tower, white and orange bands.
LA LAJA, 21 42.1N, 97 41.4W. Fl R 6s, 19ft, 8M. White metal tower.
MOCTEZUMA, 21 44.2N, 97 45.5W. Fl R 5s, 19ft, 11M. White concrete tower.
PUNTA MORALES, 21 46.5N, 97 37.2W. Fl W 5s, 19ft, 11M. White concrete tower.
PUNTA MANGLES, 21 54.6N, 97 41.7W. Fl W 5s, 19ft, 11M. White concrete tower.

TAMPICO

TAMPICO, N point of river entrance, 21 15.8N, 97 47.7W. Fl (3) W 6s, 141ft, 24M. Aluminum colored tower. Fl R and Fl G lights mark the bridge at Tamos, above Tampico. RACON Q (– – · –).
ENTRANGE RANGE (Front Light), N bank of river, 22 15.5N, 97 48.0W. Fl W 3s, 69ft, 24M. Iron framework tower, red and white square daymark. **(Rear Light),** 420 yards 256°30′ from front. Iso W 2s, 119ft, 24M. Iron framework tower, red and white square daymark, 92ft.
HEAD OF N BREAKWATER, ESCOLLERA NORTE, 22 16.1N, 97 46.3W. Fl R 5s, 39ft, 9M. White square tower. Visible 188°–322°.
HEAD OF S BREAKWATER, ESCOLLERA SUR, 22 15.7N, 97 46.3W. Fl G 5s, 33ft, 9M. Concrete tower. Visible 188°–322°.
ROOT OF S BREAKWATER DIRECTIONAL LIGHT, 22 15.6N, 97 47.2W. Dir Fl W 3s, 33ft, 11M. White concrete tower.
CANAL DE CHIJOL, on W bank, 22 14.8N, 97 49.0W. Fl W 3s, 29ft, 10M. Concrete tower.
ARBOL GRANDE, on E bank, 22 14.0N, 97 50.0W. Fl W 3s, 23ft, 10M. Concrete tower.

COLONIA DEL GOLFO, on E bank, 22 13.8N, 97 50.2W. Fl W 3s, 33ft, 10M. Concrete tower.
COLONIA DE LA ISLETA, on E bank, 22 12.9N, 97 50.0W. Fl W 3s, 23ft, 10M. Concrete tower.
ISLA PEREZ, on E bank, 22 12.5N, 97 50.2W. Fl W 3s, 30ft, 10M. Concrete tower.
CANAL DE PUEBLO VIEJO RANGE (Front Light), 22 12.5N, 07 50.7W. Fl W 3s, 22ft, 11M. White concrete tower. **(Rear Light),** 660 meters 110°30′ from front. Fl W 4s, 69ft, 13M. Concrete tower.
RIHL FIELD AVIATION LIGHT, 22 12.0N, 97 49.0W. Al Fl W G 5s, 78ft, Beacon.

TAMPICO

22 16N, 97 50W

Pilotage: Tampico is on the lower reaches of the Río Panuco. This is an important petroleum port. A 100-yard-wide channel leads across the bar and mid-way between the breakwaters. The bar has a least depth of about 30 feet. During the rainy season, depths decrease due to heavy silting. The harbor can be identified from offshore by the numerous chimneys and tanks of the oil refineries. The hills to the south of the river are grass covered and higher than those to the north, which are composed of whitish-gray sand. On closer approach Tampico lighthouse, on the north side of the river entrance, and the light structures on the breakwater heads, will be sighted.

CAUTION: The smoke from the refineries may make Tampico light appear red when the wind is from the southwest and the humidity is high.

The entrance range is on a bearing of 257°. The current sets north across the entrance at times, and vessels usually enter at a good speed to offset its effect.

Several offshore oil platforms lie about 18 miles in a generally easterly direction from the harbor. Submarine pipelines run from these platforms to the shore. Anchorage in the vicinity of these platforms and pipelines is prohibited.

Winds: Hot southwest winds blow in the months of March and April from about 1100, sometimes lasting until 1500 or 1600, before switching back to the east-southeast. Northers are frequent during the winter season and usually last from 8 to 24 hours. At such times the port is closed.
Tides and Currents: The tides are irregular and in the vicinity of the bar are greatly affected by the prevailing winds and the rate

of discharge of the Río Panuco. The maximum rise above meanlow water is about 2 feet. When the river is in flood, currents attain a velocity of 8 1/2 knots between the seawalls and a velocity of 6 knots in the upper reaches. Normally the current in the river flows at a rate of 3 knots.

ALTAMIRA

ALTAMIRA, 22 29.5N, 97 51.7W. Fl W 6s, 138ft, 14M. Concrete octagonal tower.
ESCOLLERA SUR, 22 28.9N, 97 50.9W. Fl G 5s, 36ft, 9M. Silver truncated tower.
ESCOLLERA NORTE, 22 29.5N, 97 51.2W. Fl R 5s, 42ft, 9M. Truncated tower.
RANGE (Front Light), 22 29.2N, 97 53.3W. Fl W 3s, 39ft, 11M. White framework. **(Rear Light),** 229 meters 270° from front. Iso W 2s, 59ft, 11M. White framework tower.
ESPIGON SUR, 22 29.1N, 97 51.4W. Fl G 5s, 36ft, 9M. Silver truncated tower.
ESPIGON NORTE, 22 29.3N, 97 51.4W. Fl R 5s, 36ft, 9M. Silver truncated tower.
CANAL DE NAVIGATION, NO 3, 22 28.7N, 97 53.1W. Fl G 3s, 42ft, 7M. Aluminum tower.
NO 1, 22 29.7N, 97 52.7W. Fl G 3s, 33ft, 7M. Aluminum tower.
NO 6, 22 28.7N, 97 53.4W. Fl R 3s, 41ft, 7M. Aluminum tower.
NO 4, 22 29.4N, 97 52.8W. Fl R 3s, 28ft, 7M. Metal tower.
NO 2, 22 29.5N, 97 52.1W. Fl R 3s, 33ft, 7M. Metal tower.

ALTAMIRA

22 25N, 97 55W

Pilotage: This port was reported to be under construction in 1985. It will be a general cargo terminal when complete.

TAMPICO TO RÍO SAN FERNANDO

Pilotage: Between Tampico and Barra de Chavarria and Barra de La Trinidad, two shallow lagoon entrances about 23 and 30 miles north, the coast is backed by wooded hills about 200 feet high. Shallow water lies up to 1 1/2 miles offshore between the entrances to the lagoons.

An 18-foot patch was reported to lie about 9 miles north of Tampico entrance in 1912. An obstruction was reported in 1928 about 17 miles north of Tampico entrance.

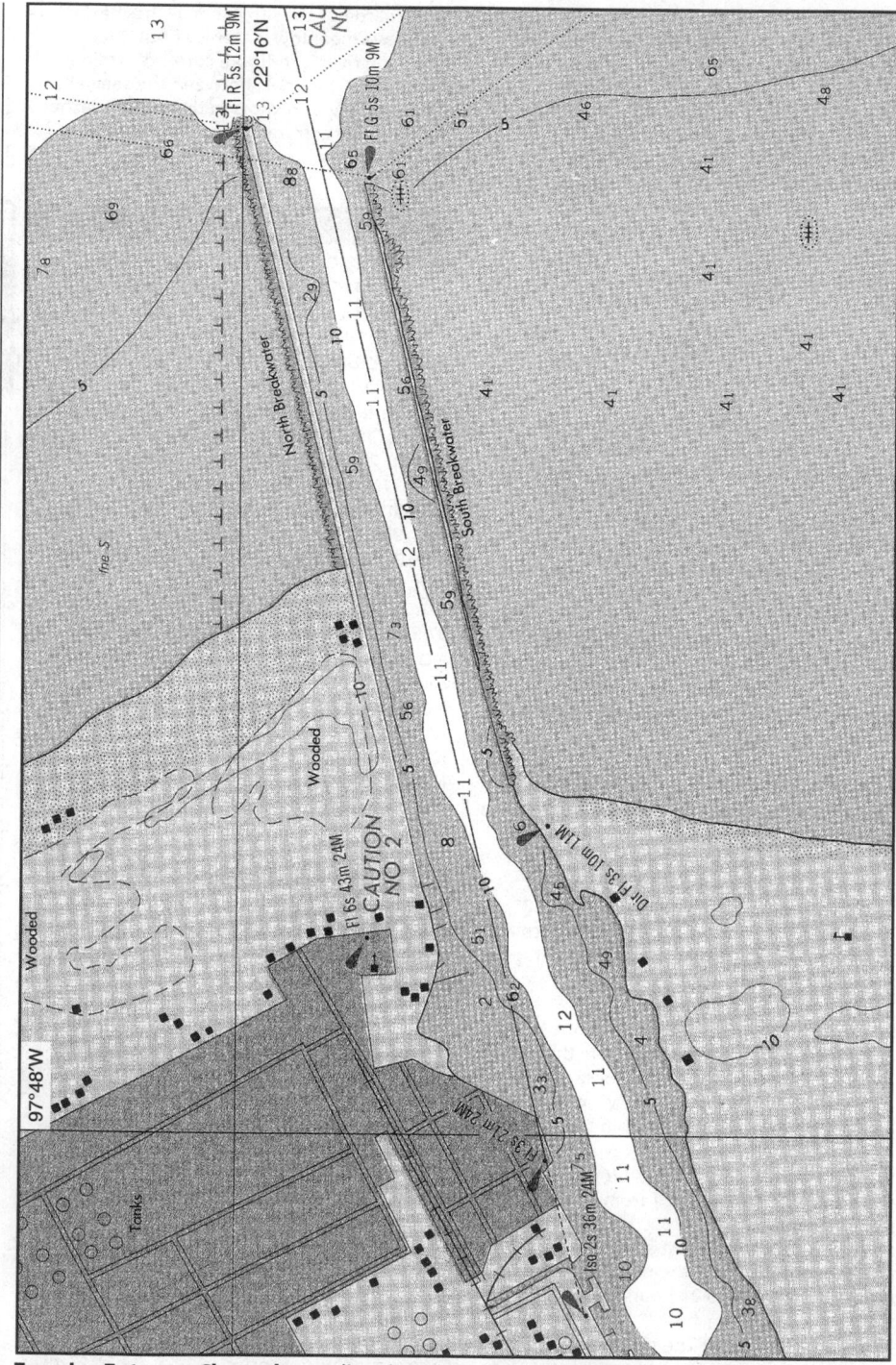

Tampico Entrance Channel, soundings in meters *(from DMA 28325, 1st ed, 3/91)*

Cerro Metate (22° 47'N, 97° 58'W) is a flat topped hill 866 feet high, located about 32 miles north-northwest of Tampico.

Between Barra de La Trinidad and Barra del Torda, a shallow lagoon entrance about 18 miles north, the coast is low and sandy. Some rocks lie up to 2 miles offshore in places.

Between Barra del Torda and Río Indios Morales (23° 24'N, 97° 46'W), about 28 miles to the north, the coast is backed by wooded hummocks 70 feet high. From abreast Punta Jerez a range of hills, Sierra de San Jose de Las Rusias, extends about 52 miles north at a distance of from 7 to 12 miles inland. A conspicuous sugarloaf peak stands about 18 miles southwest of the Río Indios Morales.

The coast between the Río Indios Morales and the Río Soto La Marina, about 21 miles to the north, is bordered by a narrow strip of land that fronts a lagoon.

Between the Río Soto La Marina and Boquillas Ceradas (25° 02'N, 97° 30'W), about 77 miles to the north, and the Río Fernando, about 25 miles farther north-northeast, the coast is bordered by a strip of land 1 to 5 miles wide fronting Laguna de La Madre. The high hills in the interior terminate about 24 miles north of the Río Soto de La Marina.

A shoal, about 3 miles in extent with a least depth of 15 feet, lies about 25 miles north of the Río Soto La Marina and 2 miles offshore.

Boquillas Ceradas are four nearly closed entrances to Laguna de La Madre.

The Río Fernando (25° 58'N, 97° 09'W), with a depth of 3 feet over the bar, drains a lagoon in the interior.

A shoal, 3 miles long with a least depth of 10 feet, lies with its south end 5 miles north of the Río San Fernando and about 3 miles offshore.

PUNTA JEREZ, on low sandy beach, 22 53.5N, 97 46.1W. Fl W 6s, 78ft, 24M. Concrete tower, white dwelling. Visible 176°–014°.

BARRA CARRIZO, 23 21.5N, 97 46.0W. Fl (2) W 10s, 30ft, 11M. Metal tower.

LA PESA RANGE (Front Light), 23 46.7N, 97 45.1W. Fl W 3s, 28ft, 11M. Aluminum colored metal tower. **(Rear Light),** Iso W 2s, 56ft, 11M. Aluminum colored metal tower.

LA CARBONERA, 23 37.6N, 97 43.0W. Fl W 6s, 38ft, 14M. concrete tower, red and white stripes.

N BREAKWATER, 23 46.2N, 97 43.9W. Fl R 5s, 22ft, 9M. Tubular metal tower.

S BREAKWATER, 23 46.0N, 97 44.1W. Fl G 5s, 25ft, 9M. Metal tower.

LA PESCA, 23 46.5N, 97 44.2W. Fl (4) W 16s, 60ft, 24M. Concrete tower.

SOTO LA MARINA, 23 46.5N, 97 47.5W. Fl W 2s, 52ft, 13M. Metal tower. Radar reflector.

CANAL DE CHAVEZ, 25 52.0N, 97 10.1W. Fl W 6s, 38ft, 14M. White round concrete tower.

EL MEZQUITAL, 25 17.0N, 97 23.0W. Fl (3) W 10s, 89ft, 24M. White concrete tower and hut.

SOUTH, breakwater, 25 14.0N, 97 25.5. Fl G 5s, 22ft, 5M. Round concrete tower.

RÍO BRAVO, 25 57.1N, 97 09.0W. Fl W 5.5s, 59ft, 24M. Concrete tower and hut.

RÍO GRANDE

25 58N, 97 09W

Pilotage: This river is located about 36 miles north of the Río San Fernando. It forms the boundary with the United States. By international agreement the river is closed to navigation.

TAMPICO, MEXICO

HIGH & LOW WATER 1995 22°13'N 97°51'W

CENTRAL STANDARD TIME (GMT -6H)

JANUARY

Day	Time ft			Day	Time ft		
1 Su ●	0807 -0.9	1700 1.3	2218 1.0 / 2326 1.0	**16** M ○	0808 -0.6	1653 1.0	2147 0.8 / 2337 0.8
2 M	0854 -0.8	1732 1.2	2233 0.9	**17** Tu	0841 -0.5	1708 1.0	2207 0.7
3 Tu	0055 0.9 / 0940 -0.7	1759 1.1	2307 0.8	**18** W	0047 0.8 / 0915 -0.5	1722 0.9	2235 0.6
4 W	0216 0.8 / 1025 -0.4	1820 1.0	2351 0.6	**19** Th	0157 0.7 / 0950 -0.3	1736 0.9	2310 0.5
5 Th	0341 0.7 / 1107 -0.2	1836 0.9		**20** F	0316 0.7 / 1028 -0.2	1747 0.8	2350 0.3
6 F	0041 0.4 / 0520 0.6	1148 0.1	1848 0.8	**21** Sa	0449 0.6	1109 0.1	1757 0.8
7 Sa	0135 0.2 / 0726 0.5	1226 0.3	1856 0.8	**22** Su	0037 0.1 / 0646 0.6	1154 0.3	1803 0.8
8 Su ☾	0230 0.1 / 1018 0.6	1302 0.5	1858 0.8	**23** M	0129 -0.1 / 0915 0.6	1248 0.6	1804 0.8
9 M	0323 -0.1	1848 0.8		**24** Tu	0226 -0.3 / 1152 0.8	1427 0.8	1755 0.8
10 Tu	0414 -0.3	1427 0.9		**25** W	0326 -0.5	1317 1.0	
11 W	0501 -0.4	1458 0.9		**26** Th	0426 -0.7	1408 1.1	
12 Th	0545 -0.4	1529 1.0		**27** F	0524 -0.8	1449 1.2	
13 F	0625 -0.5	1556 1.0		**28** Sa	0619 -0.8	1525 1.2	
14 Sa	0701 -0.5	1618 1.0		**29** Su	0712 -0.8	1554 1.1	2037 0.9 / 2317 1.0
15 Su	0735 -0.6	1637 1.0		**30** M ●	0801 -0.7	1618 1.0	2057 0.8
				31 Tu	0041 0.9 / 0847 -0.6	1637 0.9	2128 0.6

FEBRUARY

Day	Time ft			Day	Time ft		
1 W	0156 0.9 / 0930 -0.4	1652 0.9	2205 0.5	**16** Th	0155 0.9 / 0906 -0.1	1607 0.9	2133 0.4
2 Th	0309 0.8 / 1011 -0.1	1703 0.9	2246 0.3	**17** F	0303 0.9 / 0946 0.0	1616 0.8	2210 0.2
3 F	0424 0.7 / 1049 0.1	1712 0.7	2332 0.2	**18** Sa	0418 0.9 / 1028 0.2	1623 0.8	2253 0.1
4 Sa	0550 0.7 / 1123 0.4	1717 0.7		**19** Su	0545 0.8 / 1113 0.5	1627 0.8	2343 -0.1
5 Su	0022 0.0 / 0738 0.6	1152 0.5	1717 0.8	**20** M	0732 0.8	1205 0.7	1627 0.9
6 M	0118 -0.1 / 1049 0.7	1710 0.8		**21** Tu	0040 -0.3 / 0947 1.0	1322 0.9	1613 0.9
7 Tu ☾	0219 -0.1	1643 0.8		**22** W ☽	0146 -0.4	1151 1.1	
8 W	0321 -0.2	1451 0.9		**23** Th	0256 -0.4	1258 1.2	
9 Th	0420 -0.3	1449 1.0		**24** F	0406 -0.5	1341 1.2	
10 F	0512 -0.3	1502 1.0		**25** Sa	0512 -0.5 / 1412 1.2	1934 1.0	2046 1.0
11 Sa	0558 -0.4	1514 1.0		**26** Su	0611 -0.5 / 1436 1.1	1923 0.9	2255 1.0
12 Su	0638 -0.4 / 1524 1.0	2000 0.8	2223 0.9	**27** M	0705 -0.4 / 1455 1.0	1943 0.7	
13 M	0715 -0.4 / 1535 1.0	2011 0.8	2341 0.9	**28** Tu	0022 1.0 / 0754 -0.2	1509 0.9	2012 0.6
14 Tu	0751 -0.3	1545 0.9	2033 0.7				
15 W ○	0049 0.9 / 0828 -0.3	1556 0.9	2101 0.6				

MARCH

Day	Time ft			Day	Time ft		
1 W ●	0135 1.0	1520 0.9	2044 0.4	**16** Th ○	0136 1.0 / 0817 0.2	1430 0.9	2016 0.3
2 Th	0242 1.0 / 0922 0.2	1529 0.8	2119 0.2	**17** F	0241 1.1 / 0903 0.3	1438 0.9	2051 0.1
3 F	0347 1.0 / 1002 0.3	1535 0.8	2156 0.1	**18** Sa	0349 1.2 / 0951 0.5	1445 0.9	2131 -0.1
4 Sa	0453 1.0 / 1039 0.5	1537 0.8	2235 0.1	**19** Su	0501 1.2 / 1043 0.7	1448 0.9	2216 -0.2
5 Su	0606 0.9 / 1113 0.7	1536 0.8	2319 0.0	**20** M	0622 1.2 / 1143 0.9	1446 1.0	2307 -0.3
6 M	0738 0.9 / 1141 0.8	1530 0.9		**21** Tu	0757 1.2	1319 1.1	
7 Tu ☾	0009 -0.0 / 1009 0.9	1144 0.9	1514 0.9	**22** W	0006 -0.3	0942 1.3	
8 W	0107 -0.0	1417 1.0		**23** Th ☽	0114 -0.3	1108 1.3	
9 Th	0214 -0.0	1334 1.0		**24** F	0228 -0.3	1203 1.3	
10 F	0323 -0.0	1338 1.0		**25** Sa	0344 -0.2 / 1238 1.2	1845 0.9	1946 0.9
11 Sa	0425 -0.1	1344 1.0		**26** Su	0455 -0.1 / 1302 1.1	1822 0.8	2226 1.1
12 Su	0518 -0.1 / 1352 1.0	1854 0.9	2142 0.9	**27** M	0559 0.0 / 1319 1.0	1842 0.6	
13 M	0605 -0.1 / 1401 1.0	1900 0.8	2316 0.9	**28** Tu	0001 1.0 / 0656 0.1	1332 0.9	1909 0.4
14 Tu	0649 -0.0 / 1410 1.0	1920 0.6		**29** W	0116 1.1 / 0748 0.3	1342 0.9	1939 0.3
15 W ●	0029 1.0 / 0733 0.1	1420 0.9	1946 0.5	**30** Th	0221 1.1 / 0836 0.5	1349 0.9	2011 0.1
				31 F	0321 1.2 / 0922 0.6	1352 0.9	2043 0.0

APRIL

Day	Time ft			Day	Time ft		
1 Sa	0418 1.2 / 1005 0.7	1352 0.9	2117 -0.1	**16** Su	0422 1.4 / 1013 0.9	1303 1.0	2105 -0.4
2 Su	0515 1.2 / 1048 0.9	1348 0.9	2152 -0.1	**17** M	0530 1.4 / 1128 1.0	1255 1.0	2153 -0.5
3 M	0618 1.1 / 1131 0.9	1337 1.0	2230 -0.1	**18** Tu	0642 1.4	2245 -0.5	
4 Tu	0731 1.1	2313 -0.0		**19** W	0759 1.3	2343 -0.4	
5 W	0906 1.1			**20** Th	0911 1.3		
6 Th	0003 0.0	1041 1.1		**21** F ☽	0047 -0.3	1008 1.3	
7 F ☾	0102 0.0	1125 1.1		**22** Sa	0158 -0.1	1048 1.2	
8 Sa	0209 0.1	1145 1.1		**23** Su	0314 0.0 / 1114 1.1	1722 0.7	2138 0.8
9 Su	0318 0.1 / 1159 1.0	1826 0.8	1957 0.8	**24** M	0431 0.2 / 1133 1.0	1742 0.5	2333 0.9
10 M	0424 0.2 / 1212 1.0	1800 0.7	2227 0.8	**25** Tu	0542 0.4 / 1146 0.9	1811 0.2	
11 Tu	0524 0.2 / 1224 1.0	1815 0.5	2355 0.9	**26** W	0056 1.0 / 0648 0.5	1156 0.9	1842 0.1
12 W	0622 0.3 / 1236 0.9	1839 0.3		**27** Th	0203 1.1 / 0749 0.7	1201 0.8	1913 -0.1
13 Th	0107 1.1 / 0718 0.4	1246 0.9	1909 0.1	**28** F	0301 1.2 / 0847 0.8	1202 0.9	1945 -0.2
14 F	0213 1.2 / 0814 0.6	1254 0.9	1943 -0.1	**29** Sa ●	0353 1.2 / 0945 0.9	1156 0.9	2017 -0.2
15 Sa	0317 1.3 / 0912 0.7	1301 0.9	2022 -0.3	**30** Su ○	0443 1.2	2049 -0.3	

TIME MERIDIAN 90°W

0000h is midnight, 1200h is noon.

Heights in feet are referenced to the chart datum of soundings.

REED'S NAUTICAL ALMANAC

TAMPICO, MEXICO

HIGH & LOW WATER 1995 22°13'N 97°51'W

CENTRAL STANDARD TIME (GMT -6H)

MAY

Day	Time ft	Time ft	Time ft	Time ft
1 M	0533 1.2	2122 -0.3		
16 Tu	0544 1.5	2139 -0.8		
2 Tu	0625 1.2	2157 -0.2		
17 W	0643 1.4	2230 -0.7		
3 W	0720 1.1	2234 -0.2		
18 Th	0737 1.3	2324 -0.5		
4 Th	0814 1.1	2316 -0.1		
19 F	0823 1.2			
5 F	0859 1.1			
20 Sa	0021 -0.3	0858 1.1		
6 Sa	0003 -0.1	0932 1.1		
21 Su	0123 -0.0	0923 1.0	) 2010 0.6	
7 Su (	0058 0.0	0955 1.0		
22 M	0234 0.2	0942 0.9	2243 0.7	
8 M	0204 0.2	1014 1.0	1704 0.6	2057 0.6
23 Tu	0354 0.5	0955 0.9	1707 0.1	
9 Tu	0320 0.3	1030 0.9	1710 0.4	2306 0.8
24 W	0029 0.9	0521 0.6	1004 0.8	1742 -0.1
10 W	0440 0.4	1044 0.9	1733 0.1	
25 Th	0144 1.0	0648 0.8	1007 0.8	1817 -0.3
11 Th	0032 0.9	0558 0.6	1055 0.9	1804 -0.1
26 F	0243 1.1	0817 0.9	0957 0.9	1852 -0.4
12 F	0141 1.1	0713 0.7	1104 0.9	1840 -0.3
27 Sa	0333 1.2	1925 -0.4		
13 Sa	0244 1.3	0827 0.8	1109 0.9	1920 -0.5
28 Su	0419 1.2	1958 -0.4		
14 Su ○	0344 1.4	0947 1.0	1105 1.0	2003 -0.7
29 M ●	0502 1.2	2030 -0.4		
15 M	0444 1.5	2050 -0.8		
30 Tu	0542 1.2	2102 -0.4		
31 W	0620 1.2	2134 -0.4		

JUNE

Day	Time ft	Time ft	Time ft	Time ft
1 Th	0653 1.1	2208 -0.3		
16 F	0654 1.2	1234 0.9	1419 0.9	2307 -0.3
2 F	0721 1.1	2243 -0.2		
17 Sa	0720 1.1	1317 0.7	1608 0.8	2355 -0.1
3 Sa	0745 1.1	2322 -0.1		
18 Su	0740 1.0	1406 0.5	1823 0.7	
4 Su	0805 1.0			
19 M)	0046 0.2	0756 1.0	1456 0.3	2103 0.7
5 M	0007 0.0	0823 1.0	1542 0.5	1831 0.5
20 Tu	0143 0.5	0807 0.9	1544 0.1	2338 0.8
6 Tu (	0103 0.2	0839 0.9	1551 0.3	2142 0.6
21 W	0303 0.7	0813 0.9	1629 -0.1	
7 W	0219 0.5	0852 0.9	1619 0.1	2347 0.8
22 Th	0121 1.0	0504 0.9	0808 0.9	1713 -0.2
8 Th	0359 0.7	0902 0.9	1655 -0.2	
23 F	0223 1.1	1754 -0.3		
9 F	0109 1.0	0548 0.8	0908 0.9	1735 -0.4
24 Sa	0310 1.2	1833 -0.4		
10 Sa	0212 1.2	0739 1.0	0903 1.0	1818 -0.6
25 Su	0351 1.2	1910 -0.4		
11 Su	0309 1.4	1904 -0.8		
26 M	0428 1.3	1944 -0.4		
12 M ○	0402 1.5	1952 -0.9		
27 Tu ●	0501 1.2	2016 -0.4		
13 Tu	0452 1.5	2041 -0.9		
28 W	0528 1.2	2047 -0.3		
14 W	0539 1.4	2129 -0.8		
29 Th	0549 1.2	2117 -0.3		
15 Th	0620 1.3	2218 -0.6		
30 F	0606 1.2	2148 -0.2		

JULY

Day	Time ft	Time ft	Time ft	Time ft
1 Sa	0620 1.2	1218 0.9	1325 0.9	2221 -0.1
16 Su	0606 1.2	1159 0.7	1708 1.0	2332 0.4
2 Su	0634 1.1	1244 0.8	1505 0.8	2257 0.1
17 M	0617 1.1	1253 0.5	1902 0.9	
3 M	0647 1.1	1319 0.6	1706 0.7	2337 0.3
18 Tu	0013 0.7	0626 1.1	1351 0.4	2133 1.0
4 Tu	0659 1.1	1359 0.4	1938 0.7	
19 W)	0053 0.9	0629 1.2	1449 0.2	
5 W (	0025 0.6	0708 1.0	1443 0.2	2228 0.9
20 Th	0622 1.2	1547 0.1		
6 Th	0132 0.8	0714 1.1	1531 0.0	
21 F	0206 1.3	1641 0.0		
7 F	0032 1.1	0336 1.0	0714 1.1	1621 -0.2
22 Sa	0242 1.4	1730 -0.0		
8 Sa	0141 1.3	1712 -0.4		
23 Su	0315 1.4	1815 -0.0		
9 Su	0233 1.5	1803 -0.6		
24 M	0344 1.4	1854 -0.1		
10 M	0319 1.6	1855 -0.7		
25 Tu	0408 1.4	1929 -0.0		
11 Tu	0400 1.6	1945 -0.6		
26 W	0426 1.4	0915 1.3	1036 1.3	2001 0.0
12 W ○	0437 1.5	0937 1.3	1122 1.3	2034 -0.6
27 Th ●	0439 1.4	0918 1.3	1151 1.3	2032 0.1
13 Th	0507 1.5	0955 1.2	1250 1.3	2121 -0.4
28 F	0449 1.4	0937 1.2	1254 1.3	2102 0.1
14 F	0532 1.4	1028 1.1	1411 1.2	2206 -0.1
29 Sa	0458 1.4	1004 1.1	1358 1.2	2134 0.3
15 Sa	0551 1.3	1110 0.9	1534 1.1	2250 0.1
30 Su	0508 1.4	1037 1.0	1508 1.2	2209 0.4
31 M	0517 1.3	1115 0.8	1630 1.2	2246 0.6

AUGUST

Day	Time ft	Time ft	Time ft	Time ft
1 Tu	0526 1.3	1159 0.7	1811 1.1	2327 0.9
16 W	0450 1.5	1245 0.6	2138 1.4	
2 W	0532 1.3	1249 0.5	2023 1.2	
17 Th)	0025 1.4	0443 1.5	1347 0.5	
3 Th	0014 1.1	1347 0.3	(2307 1.4	
18 F	0403 1.6	1454 0.5		
4 F	0125 1.4	0529 1.4	1449 0.2	
19 Sa	0156 1.6	1600 0.5		
5 Sa	0053 1.6	1552 0.0		
20 Su	0220 1.7	1658 0.5		
6 Su	0145 1.7	1654 -0.1		
21 M	0241 1.7	1748 0.5		
7 M	0226 1.8	1752 -0.2		
22 Tu	0256 1.7	1830 0.5		
8 Tu	0300 1.8	1847 -0.1		
23 W	0307 1.7	0743 1.5	1035 1.6	1907 0.5
9 W	0328 1.7	0807 1.5	1102 1.6	1939 -0.1
24 Th	0315 1.7	0753 1.5	1148 1.6	1941 0.5
10 Th ○	0350 1.7	0827 1.4	1230 1.6	2027 0.1
25 F ●	0322 1.6	0813 1.4	1252 1.6	2016 0.6
11 F	0408 1.6	0857 1.2	1348 1.6	2113 0.3
26 Sa	0329 1.6	0839 1.3	1353 1.6	2051 0.7
12 Sa	0422 1.5	0934 1.0	1502 1.5	2156 0.6
27 Su	0337 1.6	0909 1.1	1455 1.6	2128 0.9
13 Su	0433 1.4	1016 0.9	1617 1.5	2237 0.8
28 M	0345 1.6	0943 1.0	1603 1.6	2209 1.1
14 M	0442 1.4	1101 0.8	1739 1.4	2317 1.0
29 Tu	0351 1.6	1022 0.8	1720 1.7	2253 1.3
15 Tu	0448 1.4	1035 0.6	1918 1.4	2354 1.3
30 W	0356 1.6	1108 0.7	1854 1.7	2343 1.5
31 Th	0356 1.6	1201 0.6	2052 1.8	

MEXICO

TIME MERIDIAN 90°W
Heights in feet are referenced to the chart datum of soundings.

0000h is midnight, 1200h is noon.

TAMPICO, MEXICO

HIGH & LOW WATER 1995

22°13'N 97°51'W

CENTRAL STANDARD TIME (GMT -6H)

SEPTEMBER

Day	Time	ft	Day	Time	ft
1 F	0052 / 0345 / 1304 / 2301	1.7 / 1.7 / 0.5 / 1.9	16 Sa)	1349	0.8
2 Sa (	1414	0.4	17 Su	0040 / 1500	1.8 / 0.8
3 Su	0022 / 1527	2.0 / 0.4	18 M	0106 / 1607	1.8 / 0.8
4 M	0108 / 1637	2.0 / 0.4	19 Tu	0119 / 1704	1.8 / 0.8
5 Tu	0141 / 1741	2.0 / 0.4	20 W	0128 / 0643 / 0950 / 1753	1.8 / 1.6 / 1.7 / 0.9
6 W	0205 / 0659 / 1034 / 1839	1.9 / 1.7 / 1.8 / 0.5	21 Th	0135 / 0647 / 1121 / 1837	1.8 / 1.5 / 1.7 / 0.9
7 Th	0223 / 0717 / 1207 / 1932	1.8 / 1.5 / 1.8 / 0.6	22 F	0142 / 0705 / 1231 / 1919	1.7 / 1.4 / 1.7 / 1.0
8 F O	0236 / 0746 / 1324 / 2021	1.7 / 1.3 / 1.8 / 0.8	23 Sa	0150 / 0729 / 1334 / 2002	1.7 / 1.2 / 1.8 / 1.1
9 Sa	0247 / 0819 / 1434 / 2107	1.7 / 1.1 / 1.9 / 1.0	24 Su ●	0158 / 0757 / 1434 / 2046	1.7 / 1.1 / 1.9 / 1.2
10 Su	0256 / 0855 / 1540 / 2151	1.6 / 1.0 / 1.9 / 1.2	25 M	0206 / 0829 / 1536 / 2133	1.7 / 0.9 / 1.9 / 1.4
11 M	0303 / 0933 / 1647 / 2234	1.6 / 0.8 / 1.9 / 1.4	26 Tu	0212 / 0906 / 1642 / 2225	1.7 / 0.7 / 2.0 / 1.5
12 Tu	0307 / 1013 / 1758 / 2317	1.6 / 0.8 / 1.8 / 1.6	27 W	0216 / 0948 / 1756 / 2325	1.7 / 0.6 / 2.0 / 1.7
13 W	0307 / 1057 / 1922	1.7 / 0.7 / 1.8	28 Th	0213 / 1036 / 1920	1.8 / 0.5 / 2.0
14 Th	0001 / 0259 / 1146 / 2114	1.7 / 1.7 / 0.7 / 1.8	29 F	1131 / 2055	0.4 / 2.1
15 F	0109 / 0219 / 1243 / 2337	1.8 / 1.8 / 0.8 / 1.8	30 Sa	1234 / 2222	0.4 / 2.1

OCTOBER

Day	Time	ft	Day	Time	ft
1 Su (	1345 / 2322	0.5 / 2.0	16 M)	1344 / 2315	0.8 / 1.7
2 M	1501	0.6	17 Tu	1452 / 2329	0.9 / 1.7
3 Tu	0001 / 1616	2.0 / 0.7	18 W	0625 / 0749 / 1559 / 2340	1.4 / 1.4 / 0.9 / 1.6
4 W	0026 / 0601 / 0956 / 1726	1.9 / 1.5 / 1.7 / 0.8	19 Th	0550 / 1028 / 1702 / 2351	1.3 / 1.4 / 1.0 / 1.6
5 Th	0043 / 0618 / 1142 / 1829	1.8 / 1.3 / 1.7 / 0.9	20 F	0602 / 1156 / 1801	1.1 / 1.5 / 1.1
6 F	0056 / 0645 / 1303 / 1926	1.7 / 1.1 / 1.8 / 1.1	21 Sa	0001 / 0624 / 1305 / 1858	1.6 / 0.9 / 1.7 / 1.2
7 Sa	0106 / 0717 / 1412 / 2020	1.6 / 0.9 / 1.9 / 1.3	22 Su	0011 / 0652 / 1407 / 1955	1.5 / 0.7 / 1.8 / 1.3
8 Su O	0113 / 0750 / 1513 / 2111	1.6 / 0.8 / 2.0 / 1.4	23 M ●	0020 / 0725 / 1506 / 2054	1.5 / 0.5 / 1.9 / 1.4
9 M	0118 / 0825 / 1612 / 2202	1.6 / 0.6 / 2.0 / 1.5	24 Tu	0026 / 0802 / 1606 / 2157	1.5 / 0.3 / 2.0 / 1.5
10 Tu	0120 / 0900 / 1710 / 2255	1.6 / 0.6 / 2.0 / 1.6	25 W	0029 / 0842 / 1709 / 2318	1.6 / 0.2 / 2.0 / 1.6
11 W	0114 / 0937 / 1811	1.7 / 0.5 / 1.9	26 Th	0015 / 0928 / 1816	1.6 / 0.1 / 2.0
12 Th	0009 / 1016 / 1919	1.7 / 0.6 / 1.9	27 F	1017 / 1926	0.1 / 2.0
13 F	1059 / 2039	0.6 / 1.8	28 Sa	1111 / 2033	0.1 / 1.9
14 Sa	1147 / 2158	0.7 / 1.8	29 Su	1211 / 2129	0.2 / 1.9
15 Su	1241 / 2249	0.7 / 1.8	30 M (	1317 / 2209	0.4 / 1.8
			31 Tu	1430 / 2236	0.6 / 1.6

NOVEMBER

Day	Time	ft	Day	Time	ft
1 W	0458 / 0855 / 1548 / 2255	1.2 / 1.3 / 0.8 / 1.5	16 Th	0453 / 0840 / 1439 / 2154	0.9 / 1.0 / 0.7 / 1.3
2 Th	0517 / 1108 / 1706 / 2308	1.0 / 1.4 / 0.9 / 1.4	17 F	0456 / 1101 / 1601 / 2207	0.7 / 1.1 / 0.9 / 1.3
3 F	0547 / 1241 / 1820 / 2318	0.7 / 1.5 / 1.1 / 1.4	18 Sa	0518 / 1229 / 1726 / 2218	0.5 / 1.2 / 1.0 / 1.2
4 Sa	0620 / 1352 / 1929 / 2324	0.5 / 1.6 / 1.2 / 1.4	19 Su	0547 / 1335 / 1847 / 2228	0.3 / 1.4 / 1.1 / 1.2
5 Su	0654 / 1452 / 2036 / 2326	0.3 / 1.7 / 1.3 / 1.4	20 M	0622 / 1434 / 2007 / 2233	0.0 / 1.6 / 1.2 / 1.3
6 M	0728 / 1546 / 2148 / 2316	0.2 / 1.6 / 1.4 / 1.4	21 Tu	0701 / 1531 / 2138	-0.2 / 1.7 / 1.3
7 Tu O	0803 / 1637	0.1 / 1.8	22 W ●	0743 / 1627	-0.4 / 1.8
8 W	0837 / 1727	0.1 / 1.7	23 Th	0828 / 1723	-0.5 / 1.8
9 Th	0912 / 1818	0.1 / 1.7	24 F	0916 / 1818	-0.5 / 1.7
10 F	0948 / 1909	0.2 / 1.6	25 Sa	1005 / 1908	-0.4 / 1.6
11 Sa	1024 / 1957	0.2 / 1.6	26 Su	1057 / 1951	-0.3 / 1.5
12 Su	1103 / 2037	0.3 / 1.5	27 M	1151 / 2023	-0.1 / 1.4
13 M	1145 / 2104	0.4 / 1.5	28 Tu	1248 / 2047	0.2 / 1.3
14 Tu	1232 / 2124	0.5 / 1.4	29 W (	0326 / 0721 / 1353 / 2105	0.8 / 0.9 / 0.4 / 1.2
15 W	1329 / 2140	0.6 / 1.4	30 Th)	0401 / 1007 / 1510 / 2118	0.5 / 0.9 / 0.7 / 1.1

DECEMBER

Day	Time	ft	Day	Time	ft
1 F	0439 / 1208 / 1642 / 2126	0.3 / 1.0 / 0.9 / 1.1	16 Sa	0358 / 1138 / 1501 / 2026	0.2 / 0.8 / 0.7 / 0.9
2 Sa	0518 / 1331 / 1821 / 2128	0.1 / 1.2 / 1.0 / 1.1	17 Su	0434 / 1302 / 1702 / 2032	-0.1 / 1.0 / 0.9 / 1.0
3 Su	0557 / 1433 / 2013	-0.1 / 1.3 / 1.1	18 M	0514 / 1402 / 1911 / 2024	-0.3 / 1.2 / 1.0 / 1.0
4 M	0635 / 1524	-0.2 / 1.4	19 Tu	0558 / 1455	-0.6 / 1.3
5 Tu	0712 / 1610	-0.3 / 1.4	20 W	0644 / 1545	-0.7 / 1.4
6 W O	0748 / 1653	-0.3 / 1.4	21 Th ●	0731 / 1632	-0.9 / 1.4
7 Th	0822 / 1734	-0.3 / 1.3	22 F	0819 / 1716	-0.9 / 1.4
8 F	0856 / 1810	-0.3 / 1.3	23 Sa	0908 / 1754 / 2319	-0.8 / 1.3 / 1.0
9 Sa	0928 / 1841	-0.3 / 1.2	24 Su	0041 / 0956 / 1826 / 2347	1.0 / -0.7 / 1.2 / 0.9
10 Su	0959 / 1905	-0.2 / 1.2	25 M	0214 / 1044 / 1850	0.9 / -0.5 / 1.1
11 M	1031 / 1922	-0.1 / 1.1	26 Tu	0030 / 0353 / 1132 / 1909	0.7 / 0.8 / -0.2 / 1.0
12 Tu	1104 / 1937	0.0 / 1.1	27 W	0121 / 0552 / 1220 / 1922	0.5 / 0.6 / 0.1 / 0.9
13 W	1142 / 1951	0.1 / 1.0	28 Th (	0214 / 0819 / 1313 / 1933	0.2 / 0.6 / 0.4 / 0.8
14 Th	0313 / 0558 / 1226 / 2004	0.6 / 0.6 / 0.3 / 1.0	29 F	0308 / 1100 / 1423 / 1938	-0.0 / 0.5 / 0.6 / 0.8
15 F	0328 / 0915 / 1326 / 2016	0.4 / 0.6 / 0.5 / 1.0	30 Sa	0359 / 1301 / 1623 / 1934	-0.2 / 0.9 / 0.8 / 0.9
			31 Su	0448 / 1409	-0.4 / 1.0

TIME MERIDIAN 90°W

0000h is midnight, 1200h is noon.

Heights in feet are referenced to the chart datum of soundings.

TIDE AND CURRENT DIFFERENCE TABLES

TIDE DIFFERENCES

The following pages provide information for calculating the tides at various locations around the Caribbean. Please note that this information is keyed to the tide tables for the primary tide reference stations found in Chapter 2, Coast Pilot.

This tide difference information has been created exclusively for Reed's. While Reed's has made every effort to ensure the table's accuracy and completeness, hydrographic data for the Caribbean is unfortunately sparse and less accurate than information available in the United States or Europe. Nonetheless, Reed's feels this easy-to-use table represents the best tidal information ever printed for the Caribbean.

For more information on Reed's tide tables, please refer to the introduction to Chapter 2. *Reed's Nautical Companion* also includes general information on tides and currents.

HOW TO USE THE TABLE

The table of tide differences is organized geographically by *tide difference reference stations*. It begins with Bermuda, moves south to Florida and the Bahamas, and then circles the entire Caribbean basin in a clockwise direction, from Cuba to Mexico.

In the **Place** column, locate the tide difference station in which you are interested. Then note the name of the *primary tide reference station* listed in bold type and centered on the page above the station you have chosen (e.g., ON MIAMI, FLORIDA). This is the table to which the differences for your location are keyed. The thirteen primary tide reference tables in Chapter 2 are marked on the margin index tabs to help you find them more easily (they are also listed in the book's index).

Under the **Position** heading, the next two columns list the tide difference station's approximate latitude and longitude.

The two **Time** columns give the *time differences* to be added or subtracted to the times given in the reference table for the day of the year in which you are interested. Note that all time differences are given in *hours* and *minutes*. The first column gives the time difference for *high tide*, and the second column gives the difference for *low tide*. A plus sign (+) indicates that the time should be added to the time listed in the primary reference tide table. A minus sign (–) indicates that the time should be subtracted from the reference time.

The two **Height** columns give the *height differences* for high and low tide that should be applied to the *tide heights* listed in the primary reference table. You compute the difference one of two ways, depending on how the data is presented in the tide difference table. If there are no parentheses around the entries, simply multiply when you see an asterisk (*), add when there is a plus sign (+), or subtract when there is a minus sign (–). The first difference applies to the high tide height from the reference table, and the second, to the low tide value from the reference table.

If parentheses enclose the numbers in the tide difference table, the tide height from the primary reference table must be multiplied by the first number inside the parentheses, which is preceded by an asterisk (*). The second value in the parentheses is then added to or subtracted from the value derived from the multiplication.

The heights derived using these tables must be applied to *chart soundings* to obtain *water depths*. In all cases, this tidal data is based on the *chart datum of soundings*. Some chart datums tend to be similar to the U.S. standard, which is Mean Lower Low Water. Others, however, are much lower, indicating that a 0 tide depth is an extremely rare event.

Bear in mind that local phenomena can greatly alter water depths. In some places, strong winds can affect tidal depths—for example, by as much as 3 feet along parts of the Mexican coast. Hurricanes can push surges more than 10 feet high ahead of them. Harbors at river mouths often experience seasonal fluctuations in depths, according to the amount of rainfall in the river's watershed.

The **Range** column gives the *average spring tide range* in feet for the tide difference station (where appropriate, this figure is the mean diurnal range). Keep in mind that these values are averages and that the actual range may be strongly influenced by local winds, rainfall, or other factors.

EXAMPLE

Suppose you want tidal information for Grand Turk in the Turks and Caicos on March 1, 1995. Find Grand Turk in the table (the Turks and Caicos follow the Bahamas in the listing). Note that differences for this station are keyed to the tide table for Nassau, Bahamas (found in Chapter 2, at the end of the coast pilot information for the Bahamas). The latitude and longitude of this tide position is 21° 26'N, 71° 09'W.

The time differences at Grand Turk for both high and low tide are the same: -15 minutes. On March 1, 1995, the tide will be low in Nassau at 0118, high at 0735, low at 1350, and high again at 1957. Therefore, by subtracting 15 minutes from each of these times, you determine that the tides at Grand Turk will be low at 0103, high at 0720, low at 1335, and high at 1942.

The height differences for Grand Turk are enclosed by parentheses (*0.64 – 0.14), so the tide heights from the Nassau tide table for March 1 must first be multiplied by the first number. Because the second number in parentheses is preceded by a minus sign (–), it is then subtracted from the result of the multiplication. On March 1, 1995, the first low tide at Grand Turk will be about 0.44 feet: multiply 0.9 feet (from the Nassau tide table for March 1) by 0.64 (from the Grand Turk tide difference table). From that value, subtract 0.14 (from the Grand Turk tide difference table). High tides will be about 2.55 feet and 2.42 feet, and the afternoon low, about 0.50 feet.

PLACE	POSITION		DIFFERENCES				RANGE
			Time		Height*		
	Latitude	Longitude	High	Low	High	Low	Spring
	North	West	h m	h m	ft	ft	ft

FLORIDA

Eastern Standard Time (GMT –5h)   Add 1 hour Daylight Saving April 2 – October 28

ON **MIAMI**, FLORIDA

PLACE	Latitude	Longitude	High	Low	High	Low	Spring
Ponce de Leon Inlet........................	29° 04'	80° 55'	+0 04	+0 21	*0.92	*0.94	2.7
Cape Canaveral..............................	28° 26'	80° 34'	−0 43	−0 40	*1.39	*1.38	4.1
Indian River							
Palm Bay..	28° 02'	80° 35'	+3 38	+4 20	*0.10	*0.10	0.2
Wabasso	27° 45'	80° 26'	+2 46	+3 20	*0.15	*0.19	0.5
Vero Beach	27° 38'	80° 22'	+3 19	+3 51	*0.34	*0.31	1.0
Fort Pierce.....................................	27° 27'	80° 19'	+1 06	+1 02	*0.48	*0.50	1.4
Jensen Beach	27° 14'	80° 13'	+2 38	+3 07	*0.41	*0.38	1.2
Sebastian Inlet	27° 52'	80° 27'	−0 26	−0 19	*0.81	*0.81	2.5
Vero Beach (ocean).......................	27° 40'	80° 22'	−0 33	−0 24	*1.35	*1.38	4.0
Fort Pierce Inlet, south jetty...........	27° 28'	80° 17'	−0 11	−0 13	*1.03	*1.06	3.1
St. Lucie River							
North Fork, St. Lucie River...........	27° 15'	80° 19'	+2 48	+3 30	*0.41	*0.38	1.2
Stuart, St. Lucie River	27° 12'	80° 16'	+2 35	+3 34	*0.37	*0.38	1.1
South Fork, St. Lucie River	27° 10'	80° 15'	+2 52	+3 35	*0.37	*0.38	1.1
Sewall Point, St. Lucie River........	27° 10'	80° 11'	+1 33	+2 12	*0.37	*0.38	1.1
Seminole Shores	27° 11'	80° 10'	−0 32	−0 13	*1.19	*1.19	3.6
Great Pocket..................................	27° 09'	80° 10'	+1 16	+1 52	*0.44	*0.44	1.3
Gomez, South Jupiter Narrows	27° 06'	80° 08'	+1 54	+2 42	*0.52	*0.50	1.6
Hobe Sound – State Park..............	27° 02'	80° 06'	+1 44	+2 23	*0.63	*0.63	1.9
Conch Bar, Jupiter Sound	26° 59'	80° 06'	+1 17	+1 39	*0.67	*0.63	2.0
Jupiter Sound, south end...............	26° 57'	80° 05'	+0 44	+0 50	*0.78	*0.75	2.4
Jupiter Inlet....................................	26° 57'	80° 04'	+0 13	+0 02	*1.00	*1.00	3.0
Loxahatchee River							
Tequesta	26° 57'	80° 06'	+1 16	+2 03	*0.71	*0.69	2.2
North Fork	26° 58'	80° 07'	+1 25	+2 00	*0.74	*0.75	2.3
Southwest Fork (spillway)	26° 56'	80° 09'	+1 13	+1 50	*0.79	*0.81	2.4
Northwest Fork...............................	26° 59'	80° 08'	+1 32	+2 11	*0.78	*0.81	2.4
Southwest Fork	26° 57'	80° 07'	+1 13	+1 48	*0.74	*0.75	2.3
Jupiter, Lake Worth Creek..............	26° 56'	80° 05'	+0 55	+1 17	*0.81	*0.81	2.5
Donald Ross Bridge........................	26° 53'	80° 04'	+0 41	+0 55	*0.92	*0.94	2.8
North Palm Beach, Lake Worth	26° 50'	80° 03'	+0 03	+0 18	*1.15	*1.19	3.4
Port of Palm Beach, Lake Worth	26° 46'	80° 03'	−0 02	+0 13	*1.04	*1.00	3.1
Palm Beach (ocean)	26° 43'	80° 02'	−0 23	−0 17	*1.11	*1.12	3.3
West Palm Beach Canal.................	26° 39'	80° 03'	+1 06	+1 37	*1.00	*1.00	2.8
Lake Worth Pier (ocean)................	26° 37'	80° 02'	−0 21	−0 16	*1.11	*1.12	3.3
Boynton Beach	26° 33'	80° 03'	+1 24	+2 10	*1.00	*1.00	2.8
Delray Beach	26° 28'	80° 04'	+1 43	+2 10	*1.00	*1.00	2.9
Yamato	26° 24'	80° 04'	+1 41	+2 00	*0.97	*0.94	2.8
Boca Raton....................................	26° 21'	80° 05'	+0 45	+1 14	*0.85	*0.88	2.5
Deerfield Beach	26° 19'	80° 05'	+0 49	+1 08	*0.96	*0.94	2.9
Hillsboro Beach, ICW	26° 16'	80° 05'	+0 24	+0 39	*1.11	*1.12	3.2
Hillsboro Inlet (inside)	26° 16'	80° 05'	+0 06	+0 07	*1.00	*1.00	2.9
Lauderdale–by–the–sea	26° 11'	80° 06'	−0 10	−0 07	*1.04	*1.06	3.1

*Heights of tides are found by multiplying heights from the Tide Tables by the *ratio listed here. When parenthesis are used, multiply heights by the *ratio and then add or subtract the second number as indicated.

PLACE	POSITION		DIFFERENCES				RANGE
			Time		Height*		
	Latitude	Longitude	High	Low	High	Low	Spring
	North	West	h m	h m	ft	ft	ft

FLORIDA (continued)

Eastern Standard Time (GMT –5h)   *Add 1 hour Daylight Saving April 2 – October 28*

ON MIAMI, FLORIDA

Fort Lauderdale

Bahía Mar Yacht Club	26° 07'	80° 06'	+0 17	+0 39	*0.94	*0.94	2.8
Andrews Ave Bridge, New River	26° 07'	80° 09'	+0 37	+0 57	*0.79	*0.81	2.4
Port Everglades	26° 06'	80° 07'	–0 08	–0 05	*1.05	*1.06	3.1
South Port Everglades	26° 05'	80° 07'	–0 02	+0 02	*1.00	*1.00	2.9
Hollywood Beach	26° 02'	80° 07'	+0 58	+1 09	*0.81	*0.81	2.4
Golden Beach	25° 58'	80° 08'	+1 34	+2 05	*0.81	*0.81	2.4
Sunny Isles, Biscayne Creek	25° 56'	80° 08'	+2 21	+2 28	*0.71	*0.69	2.2
North Miami Beach	25° 56'	80° 07'	–0 06	+0 01	*1.00	*1.00	3.0
Bakers Haulover Inlet (inside)	25° 54'	80° 08'	+1 15	+1 36	*0.78	*0.81	2.4
Indian Creek	25° 52'	80° 09'	+1 34	+1 51	*0.81	*0.81	2.5
Miami Beach	25° 46'	80° 08'	–0 02	+0 01	*1.00	*1.00	3.0
MIAMI HARBOR ENTRANCE	25° 46'	80° 08'	**Daily Predictions**				3.0

Biscayne Bay

Miami, 79th St. Causeway	25° 51'	80° 10'	+1 43	+2 14	*0.78	*0.75	2.4
Miami, Marina	25° 47'	80° 11'	+0 54	+1 18	*0.81	*0.81	2.4
Miami, Causeway (east end)	25° 46'	80° 09'	+1 17	+1 11	*0.78	*0.81	2.4
Dinner Key Marina	25° 44'	80° 14'	+1 17	+1 51	*0.74	*0.75	2.3

Florida Keys

Cape Florida (west), Key Biscayne	25° 40'	80° 10'	+0 47	+1 03	*0.67	*0.69	2.0
Cutler, Biscayne Bay	25° 37'	80° 18'	+1 23	+2 02	*0.78	*0.81	2.3
Soldier Key	25° 35'	80° 10'	+0 53	+1 20	*0.74	*0.75	2.3
Fowey Rocks	25° 35'	80° 06'	+0 01	+0 03	*0.97	*0.94	2.9
Ragged Keys, Biscayne Bay	25° 32'	80° 10'	+1 13	+1 45	*0.64	*0.64	1.9
Elliot Key (outside)	25° 29'	80° 11'	–0 04	+0 00	*0.93	*0.94	2.8
Elliot Key Harbor	25° 27'	80° 12'	+2 26	+3 25	*0.56	*0.56	1.6
Adams Key, Biscayne Bay	25° 24'	80° 14'	+2 48	+2 34	*0.52	*0.50	1.6
Christmas Point, Elliot Key	25° 24'	80° 14'	+0 35	+0 39	*0.72	*0.72	2.1
Turkey Point, Biscayne Bay	25° 26'	80° 20'	+2 33	+3 26	*0.60	*0.63	1.8
Totten Key	25° 23'	80° 15'	+2 48	+3 45	*0.49	*0.50	1.4
Ocean Reef Club, Key Largo	25° 18'	80° 17'	+0 11	+0 20	*0.93	*0.94	2.8
Garden Cove, Key Largo	25° 10'	80° 22'	+0 34	+1 10	*0.85	*0.88	2.6
Mosquito Bank	25° 04'	80° 24'	+0 22	+0 31	*0.85	*0.88	2.6
Molasses Reef	25° 01'	80° 23'	+0 14	+0 12	*0.88	*0.88	2.6
Pumpkin Key, Card Sound	25° 20'	80° 18'	+3 10	+3 16	*0.28	*0.28	0.8
Tavernier, Hawk Channel	25° 00'	80° 31'	+0 29	+0 28	*0.86	*0.50	2.6
Alligator Reef Light	24° 51'	80° 37'	+0 40	+0 34	*0.76	*0.76	2.3

ON KEY WEST, FLORIDA

Florida Bay

Channel Five, east	24° 50'	80° 46'	–0 55	–0 42	*0.81	*0.84	1.4
Channel Five, west	24° 50'	80° 47'	–0 59	–0 40	*0.90	*0.17	1.5
Long Key Channel, east	24° 48'	80° 51'	–1 10	–1 07	*0.84	*0.42	1.5
Long Key Channel, west	24° 48'	80° 53'	+5 58	+5 40	*0.79	*0.38	1.4

*Heights of tides are found by multiplying heights from the Tide Tables by the *ratio listed here. When parenthesis are used, multiply heights by the *ratio and then add or subtract the second number as indicated.

DIFFERENCES

PLACE	POSITION		DIFFERENCES				RANGE
			Time		Height*		
	Latitude	Longitude	High	Low	High	Low	Spring
	North	West	h m	h m	ft	ft	ft

FLORIDA (continued)

Eastern Standard Time (GMT –5h)   *Add 1 hour Daylight Saving April 2 – October 28*

ON KEY WEST, FLORIDA

PLACE	Latitude	Longitude	High	Low	High	Low	Spring
Duck Key	24° 46'	80° 55'	−1 11	−0 40	*0.96	*0.54	1.7
Grassy Key, north side	24° 46'	80° 56'	+5 38	+6 47	*0.72	*0.88	1.3
Grassy Key, south side	24° 45'	80° 58'	−1 07	−0 40	*1.20	*0.54	2.1
Flamingo	25° 09'	80° 56'	+5 35	+7 28	*1.48	*1.25	2.5
Fat Deer Key	24° 44'	81° 01'	+5 09	+6 26	*0.85	*0.79	1.5
Boot Key Harbor, Vaca Key	24° 42'	81° 06'	−1 04	−0 37	*1.12	*0.75	2.0
Sombrero Key	24° 38'	81° 07'	−1 01	−0 38	*1.17	*0.79	2.0
Knight Key Channel	24° 42'	81° 08'	+0 17	−0 18	*0.53	*0.53	1.0
Pigeon Key, south side	24° 42'	81° 09'	−1 09	−0 39	*0.81	*0.46	1.5
Pigeon Key, inside	24° 42'	81° 09'	−0 17	+0 18	*0.48	*0.58	1.0
Molasses Key	24° 41'	81° 12'	−0 50	−0 11	*0.77	*0.50	1.4
Money Key	24° 41'	81° 13'	+0 56	+1 42	*0.56	*0.46	1.1
West Bahía Honda Key	24° 47'	81° 16'	+3 59	+4 01	*0.97	*1.00	1.59
Horseshoe Keys, south end	24° 46'	81° 17'	+3 54	+3 09	*0.86	*1.00	1.36
Johnson Keys, south end	24° 45'	81° 18'	+3 36	+2 33	*0.72	*0.96	1.10
Johnson Keys, north end	24° 46'	81° 19'	+3 35	+4 22	*1.31	*1.38	2.12
Bahía Honda Key, Bahía Honda Ch	24° 39'	81° 17'	−0 45	−0 27	*0.86	*0.62	1.49
Spanish Harbor, Big Pine Key	24° 39'	81° 20'	−0 44	−0 03	*0.75	*0.42	1.34
Doctors Arm, Bogie Channel	24° 41'	81° 21'	+0 41	+1 47	*0.63	*0.71	1.00
Bogie Channel Bridge	24° 42'	81° 21'	+2 10	+2 11	*0.65	*0.83	1.00
No Name Key, e side, Bahía H Ch	24° 42'	81° 19'	+1 35	+1 33	*0.58	*0.83	0.88
Little Pine Key, south end	24° 43'	81° 18'	+1 07	+1 07	*0.56	*0.79	0.85
Porpoise Key, Big Spanish Chnl	24° 43'	81° 21'	+3 23	+2 29	*0.72	*1.00	1.10
Water Key, w end, Big Span Chnl	24° 44'	81° 21'	+3 23	+2 37	*0.81	*1.04	1.25
Mayo Key, Big Spanish Channel	24° 44'	81° 22'	+3 35	+3 01	*0.92	*1.08	1.46
Little Pine Key, north end	24° 45'	81° 20'	+3 38	+3 28	*1.05	*1.21	1.66
Big Pine Key, northeast shore	24° 44'	81° 23'	+3 19	+2 30	*0.86	*1.08	1.35
Crawl Key, Big Spanish Channel	24° 45'	81° 22'	+3 34	+4 13	*1.33	*1.33	2.18
Big Pine Key, north end	24° 45'	81° 24'	+4 24	+5 56	*0.96	*0.83	1.61
Annette Key, n end, Big Span Chnl	24° 46'	81° 23'	+3 30	+4 33	*1.44	*1.29	2.40
Little Spanish Key, Spanish Banks	24° 47'	81° 22'	+3 25	+4 30	*1.74	*1.62	2.88
Big Spanish Key	24° 47'	81° 25'	+3 19	+4 29	*1.97	*1.50	3.36
Munson Island, Newfound Hbr Ch	24° 37'	81° 24'	−0 40	−0 12	*0.98	*0.67	1.70
Ramrod Key, Newfound Harbor	24° 39'	81° 24'	−0 41	+0 05	*0.90	*0.50	1.60
Middle Torch Ky, Torch Ramrod C	24° 40'	81° 24'	−0 16	+1 29	*0.69	*0.38	1.22
Little Torch Key, Torch Channel	24° 40'	81° 24'	+0 11	+1 45	*0.57	*0.33	1.00
Big Pine Key, Newfound Harbor Ch	24° 39'	81° 23'	−0 09	+0 44	*0.82	*0.46	1.45
Big Pine Key, Coupon Bight	24° 39'	81° 21'	−0 20	+0 49	*0.87	*0.54	1.52
Little Torch Key, Pine Chnl Br, s	24° 40'	81° 23'	−0 15	+0 57	*0.68	*0.33	1.21
Little Torch Key, Pine Chnl Br, n	24° 40'	81° 23'	−0 13	+0 54	*0.69	*0.38	1.22
Big Pine Key, Pine Chnl Br, s	24° 40'	81° 22'	−0 13	+1 03	*0.67	*0.33	1.20
Big Pine Key, Pine Chnl Br, n	24° 40'	81° 22'	+0 03	+1 44	*0.57	*0.33	1.01
Big Pine Key, w side, Pine Chnl	24° 41'	81° 23'	+0 21	+1 52	*0.52	*0.42	0.89
Howe Key, s end, Harbor Chnl	24° 44'	81° 24'	+4 43	+4 49	*0.72	*0.62	1.20
Big Torch Key, Harbor Channel	24° 44'	81° 27'	+3 47	+5 51	*1.58	*1.29	2.68

*Heights of tides are found by multiplying heights from the Tide Tables by the *ratio listed here. When parenthesis are used, multiply heights by the *ratio and then add or subtract the second number as indicated.

PLACE	POSITION		DIFFERENCES				RANGE
			Time		Height*		
	Latitude	Longitude	High	Low	High	Low	Spring
	North	West	h m	h m	ft	ft	ft

FLORIDA (continued)
Eastern Standard Time (GMT –5h)   *Add 1 hour Daylight Saving April 2 – October 28*

ON KEY WEST, FLORIDA

Water Keys, s end, Harbor Chnl.....	24° 45'	81° 27'	+3 42	+5 41	*1.52	*1.00	2.64
Howe Key, northwest end...............	24° 46'	81° 26'	+3 29	+5 22	*1.68	*1.33	2.85
Summerland Key, Niles Channel S	24° 39'	81° 26'	–0 36	+0 11	*0.85	*0.71	1.42
Summerland Key, Niles Channel Br	24° 40'	81° 26'	–0 10	+0 56	*0.67	*0.58	1.12
Ramrod Key, Niles Channel Bridge	24° 40'	81° 25'	–0 13	+1 12	*0.67	*0.46	1.16
Big Torch Key, Niles Channel........	24° 42'	81° 26'	+3 15	+2 05	*0.61	*0.71	0.96
Knockemdown Key, north end........	24° 43'	81° 29'	+3 30	+4 54	*1.35	*1.21	2.25
Raccoon Key, east side.................	24° 45'	81° 29'	+3 20	+5 09	*1.50	*1.21	2.55
Content Key, Content Passage	24° 47'	81° 29'	+2 47	+3 50	*2.13	*1.83	3.58
Key Lois, southeast end	24° 36'	81° 28'	–1 15	–0 45	*1.06	*0.75	1.82
Sugarloaf Key, e side, Tarpon Cr ...	24° 38'	81° 31'	–0 41	+0 15	*0.89	*0.58	1.55
Gopher Key, Cudjoe Bay...............	24° 39'	81° 29'	–0 46	+0 17	*0.90	*0.71	1.52
Sugarloaf Key, Pirates Cove	24° 39'	81° 31'	–0 48	+1 41	*0.59	*0.75	0.92
Cudjoe Key, Cudjoe Bay	24° 40'	81° 30'	–0 38	+0 41	*0.87	*0.71	1.48
Summerland Ky, sw side, Kemp C	24° 39'	81° 27'	–0 26	+0 50	*0.81	*0.54	1.40
Cudjoe Key, north end, Kemp Chnl	24° 42'	81° 31'	+3 32	+4 40	*1.63	*1.46	2.71
Sugarloaf Key, ne side, Bow Chnl..	24° 40'	81° 32'	+3 47	+3 24	*1.01	*0.71	1.75
Cudjoe Key, Pirates Cove	24° 40'	81° 31'	+3 50	+2 55	*0.77	*0.79	1.26
Sugarloaf Key, n end, Bow Chnl.....	24° 42'	81° 33'	+3 37	+5 20	*1.29	*0.75	2.28
Pumpkin Key, Bow Channel	24° 43'	81° 34'	+3 17	+4 39	*1.56	*1.17	2.68
Sawyer Key, outside, Cudjoe Chnl .	24° 46'	81° 34'	+2 45	+5 24	*1.57	*0.50	2.90
Sawyer Key, inside, Cudjoe Chnl ...	24° 46'	81° 34'	+2 37	+5 19	*1.43	*0.50	2.62
Johnston Key, sw end, Turkey Bsn	24° 43'	81° 36'	+3 26	+5 38	*1.10	*0.50	1.99
Upper Sugarloaf Sound							
Perky.................................	24° 39'	81° 34'	+5 37	+8 25	*0.28	*0.08	0.52
Park Channel Bridge....................	24° 39'	81° 32'	+5 47	+8 33	*0.26	*0.29	0.42
North Harris Channel	24° 39'	81° 33'	+5 32	+8 04	*0.25	*0.25	0.41
Tarpon Creek	24° 38'	81° 31'	–0 29	+0 17	*0.35	*0.38	0.58
Snipe Keys							
Snipe Keys, se end, Inner Nrws....	24° 40'	81° 37'	+3 25	+5 39	*1.28	*0.83	2.24
Snipe Keys, Middle Narrows.........	24° 40'	81° 38'	+3 44	+5 54	*1.02	*0.67	1.78
Snipe Keys, Snipe Point...............	24° 42'	81° 40'	+2 15	+3 33	*1.69	*1.29	2.89
Waltz Key Basin							
Waltz Key....................................	24° 39'	81° 39'	+3 53	+5 33	*1.03	*0.96	1.70
Duck Key Point, Duck Key	24° 37'	81° 41'	+3 27	+4 57	*1.19	*0.96	2.01
O'Hara Key, north end	24° 37'	81° 39'	+3 53	+5 39	*1.03	*0.83	1.75
Saddlebunch Keys							
Saddlebunch Keys, Channel #5....	24° 37'	81° 38'	+4 32	+6 58	*0.66	*1.12	0.95
Saddlebunch Keys, Channel #4....	24° 37'	81° 37'	+4 35	+5 36	*0.54	*0.29	0.95
Saddlebunch Keys, Channel #3....	24° 37'	81° 36'	+1 44	–0 10	*0.43	*0.21	0.78
Similar Sound							
Bird Key.......................................	24° 35'	81° 38'	–0 21	+1 03	*0.59	*0.42	1.02
Shark Key, se end........................	24° 36'	81° 39'	+0 18	+1 51	*0.52	*0.46	0.88
Saddlebunch Keys	24° 36'	81° 37'	+0 39	+2 41	*0.37	*0.21	0.65
Big Coppitt Ky, ne side, Waltz Ky B	24° 36'	81° 39'	+4 21	+6 54	*0.84	*0.33	1.52

*Heights of tides are found by multiplying heights from the Tide Tables by the *ratio listed here. When parenthesis are used, multiply heights by the *ratio and then add or subtract the second number as indicated.

PLACE	POSITION		DIFFERENCES				RANGE
			Time		Height*		
	Latitude	Longitude	High	Low	High	Low	Spring
	North	West	h m	h m	ft	ft	ft

FLORIDA (continued)

Eastern Standard Time (GMT –5h)   *Add 1 hour Daylight Saving April 2 – October 28*

ON KEY WEST, Florida

Rockland Key, Rockland Chnl Br ...	24° 36'	81° 40'	+5 02	+6 06	*0.76	*0.88	1.21
Boca Chica Key, Long Point..........	24° 36'	81° 42'	+3 54	+5 22	*0.94	*0.71	1.60
Channel Key, west side	24° 36'	81° 44'	+3 09	+3 07	*0.70	*0.71	1.14
Boca Chica Channel Bridge	24° 35'	81° 43'	+1 23	+1 29	*0.57	*0.67	0.90
Key Haven – Stock Island Channel	24° 35'	81° 44'	+2 25	+2 57	*0.73	*0.79	1.18
Sigsbee Park, Garrison Bight Ch....	24° 35'	81° 47'	+1 59	+2 06	*0.81	*0.88	1.30
Key West, south side, Hawk Chnl ..	24° 33'	81° 47'	–0 52	–0 30	*1.07	*0.92	1.80
KEY WEST	24° 33'	81° 49'	**Daily Predictions**				1.64
Sand Key Lighthouse, Sand Ky Ch	24° 27'	81° 53'	–1 03	–0 39	*0.94	*0.79	1.58
Garden Key, Dry Tortugas.............	24° 38'	82° 52'	+0 29	+0 33	*0.94	*1.33	1.42
Cape Sable, East Cape	25° 07'	81° 05'	+3 56	+4 43	*2.26	*2.20	3.8
Shark River entrance.....................	25° 21'	81° 08'	+3 20	+4 38	*2.71	*2.50	4.5
Lostmans River entrance...............	25° 33'	81° 13'	+3 22	+4 42	*2.31	*2.31	3.9
Onion Key, Lostmans River............	25° 37'	81° 08'	+5 32	+7 46	*0.46	*0.46	0.9
Chatham River entrance................	25° 41'	81° 17'	+3 22	+4 46	*2.82	*2.50	4.2

BERMUDA

Atlantic Standard Time (GMT –4h)   *Add 1 hour Daylight Saving April 2 – October 28*

ON ST GEORGE'S, BERMUDA

ST GEORGE'S ISLAND	32° 23'	64° 42'	**Daily Predictions**				3.0
St. David's Island...........................	32° 22'	64° 39'	–0 07	–0 07	(*0.96+0.23)		2.6
Great Sound	32° 19'	64° 50'	+0 15	+0 15	(*1.08–0.14)		3.2

BAHAMA ISLANDS

Eastern Standard Time (GMT –5h)   *Add 1 hour Daylight Saving April 2 – October 28*

ON NASSAU, BAHAMAS

Grand Bahama							
Freeport Harbour............................	26° 31'	78° 46'	+0 00	+0 00	(*1.13–1.15)		3.3
Little Bahama Bank							
Memory Rock	26° 57'	79° 07'	+0 24	+0 29	*0.88	*0.88	2.7
Walkers Cay	27° 16'	78° 24'	+1 25	+1 25	(*0.95–0.64)		2.9
The Abacos							
Allans–Pensacola Cay....................	26° 59'	77° 40'	+0 35	+0 45	(*0.95–0.64)		2.9
Green Turtle Cay	26° 46'	77° 18'	+0 05	+0 05	(*1.00–0.95)		3.0
Pelican Harbour.............................	26° 23'	76° 58'	+0 25	+0 25	(*0.95–0.64)		2.9
Great Bahama Bank							
North Bimini....................................	25° 44'	79° 18'	+0 13	+0 25	*0.92	*0.92	2.9
Cat Cay	25° 33'	79° 17'	+0 23	+0 23	(*0.88–0.47)		2.6
South Riding Rock..........................	25° 14'	79° 10'	+0 40	+0 40	(*0.88–0.48)		2.6
Guinchos Cay	22° 45'	78° 07'	+0 14	+0 19	*0.81	*0.81	2.6
Cay Sal Bank							
Elbow Cay, Cay Sal Bank...............	23° 57'	80° 28'	+1 26	+1 31	*0.81	*0.81	2.6

*Heights of tides are found by multiplying heights from the Tide Tables by the *ratio listed here. When parenthesis are used, multiply heights by the *ratio and then add or subtract the second number as indicated.

PLACE	POSITION		DIFFERENCES				RANGE
			Time		Height*		
	Latitude	Longitude	High	Low	High	Low	Spring
	North	West	h m	h m	ft	ft	ft
BAHAMA ISLANDS (continued)							
Eastern Standard Time (GMT –5h)		*Add 1 hour Daylight Saving April 2 – October 28*					
			ON NASSAU, BAHAMAS				
The Berry Islands							
Great Stirrup Cay	24° 49’	77° 55’	+0 25	+0 25	(*0.88–0.48)		2.6
Andros Island							
Mastic Point	25° 03’	77° 58’	+0 05	+0 05	(*0.97–0.73)		2.6
Fresh Creek	24° 42’	77° 46’	+0 05	+0 05	(*1.08–0.77)		3.2
New Providence							
NASSAU, BAHAMAS	25° 05’	77° 21’	**Daily Predictions**				3.0
Eleuthera							
Royal Island Harbour	25° 31’	76° 51’	+0 05	+0 05	(*0.88–0.48)		2.6
Wide Opening	25° 25’	76° 41’	+0 25	+0 25	(*0.95–0.64)		2.9
Tracking Station	25° 15’	76° 19’	+2 17	+2 36	*0.92	*0.92	2.9
Eleuthera Island, east coast	24° 56’	76° 09’	+0 15	+0 18	(*0.88–0.47)		2.6
The Exumas							
Ship Channel	24° 52’	76° 48’	–0 15	–0 15	(*0.95–0.64)		2.9
Steventon	23° 40’	75° 58’	–0 05	–0 05	(*0.88–0.48)		2.6
George Town	23° 32’	75° 49’	–0 20	–0 20	(*0.83–0.30)		2.6
Long Island							
Clarence Harbour	23° 06’	74° 59’	+0 49	+0 54	*1.00	*1.00	3.1
Hard Bargain	23° 00’	74° 57’	+0 40	+0 40	(*0.76–0.15)		2.3
Jumentos Cays							
Nurse Channel	22° 31’	75° 51’	+0 15	+0 10	(*0.92–0.46)		2.9
Cat Island							
The Bight	24° 19’	75° 26’	–0 35	–0 35	(*0.92–0.46)		2.9
San Salvador	24° 06’	74° 26’	–0 35	–0 35	(*0.92–0.46)		2.9
Acklins Island							
Datum Bay	22° 10’	74° 18’	–0 15	–0 15	(*0.80–0.17)		2.6
Mayaguana							
Abraham Bay	22° 22’	73° 00’	+0 10	+0 13	*0.77	*0.77	2.5
Start Point	22° 20’	73° 03’	+0 25	+0 25	(*0.51+0.32)		1.6
Little Inagua	21° 27’	73° 01’	+0 10	+0 10	(*0.88–0.46)		2.6
Great Inagua							
Matthew Town	20° 57’	73° 41’	+0 15	+0 15	(*0.52+0.38)		1.6
TURKS & CAICOS							
Eastern Standard Time (GMT –5h)		*Add 1 hour Daylight Saving April 2 – October 28*					
			ON NASSAU, BAHAMAS				
Turks Islands							
Grand Turk	21° 26’	71° 09’	–0 15	–0 15	(*0.64–0.14)		1.9
Hawks Nest Anchorage	21° 26’	71° 07’	–0 19	–0 14	*0.81	*0.81	2.6
North Caicos Island							
Sandy Point	21° 56’	72° 03’	+0 38	+0 38	(*0.56–0.00)		1.6

***Heights of tides are found by multiplying heights from the Tide Tables by the *ratio listed here. When parenthesis are used, multiply heights by the *ratio and then add or subtract the second number as indicated.**

DIFFERENCES

PLACE	POSITION		DIFFERENCES				RANGE
			Time		Height*		
	Latitude	Longitude	High	Low	High	Low	Spring
	North	West	h m	h m	ft	ft	ft

CUBA

Eastern Standard Time (GMT –5h)   *Add 1 hour Daylight Saving April 2 – October 8*

ON **PORT OF SPAIN,** TRINIDAD

North Coast Cuba

Los Arroyos	22° 22'	84° 23'	+4 55	+6 05	(*0.31+0.18)		1.0

ON **SAN JUAN,** PUERTO RICO

La Coloma	22° 14'	83° 34'	+2 04	+ 2 23	*0.54	*0.54	0.9

ON **KEY WEST,** FLORIDA

Cabo San Antonio	21° 52'	84° 58'	−0 50	− 0 07	*0.92	*0.92	1.5
Bahía Honda..................................	22° 58'	83° 13'	−1 04	− 0 23	*0.76	*0.76	1.4
Havana	23° 09'	82° 20'	−0 48	− 0 40	*0.76	*0.76	1.5
Matanzas.......................................	23° 04'	81° 32'	−0 59	− 0 59	*0.92	*0.92	1.5
Cardenas	23° 04'	81° 12'	−0 11	+ 0 34	*1.08	*1.08	1.8

ON **NASSAU,** BAHAMAS

La Isabela.....................................	22° 56'	80° 00'	+1 41	+1 42	*0.62	*0.62	2.0
Cayo Paredon Grande....................	22° 29'	78° 09'	+0 15	+0 05	(*0.79−0.99)		2.6
Bahía Nuevitas							
Entrance	21° 38'	77° 07'	+1 15	+1 05	(*0.44−0.51)		1.3
Nuevitas..	21° 35'	77° 15'	+2 55	+2 55	(*0.51−0.67)		1.6
North Coast Cuba							
Puerto Padre	21° 12'	76° 36'	+1 25	+1 15	(*0.76−1.02)		2.3
Puerto Gibara	21° 06'	76° 08'	+0 25	+0 20	(*0.64−0.80)		2.0
Bahía Nipe							
Punta Caranero	20° 47'	75° 34'	+0 30	+0 25	(*0.76−1.02)		2.3
Antilla...	20° 50'	75° 44'	+0 50	+0 50	(*0.76−1.02)		2.3
North Coast Cuba							
Bahía de Levisa entrance...............	20° 45'	75° 28'	+0 18	+0 19	*0.74	*0.74	2.2
Puerto Tanamo..............................	20° 43'	75° 19'	+0 20	+0 20	(*0.64−0.80)		2.0
Baracoa	20° 21'	74° 30'	+0 10	+0 10	(*0.60−0.91)		1.9
Puerto Maysi..................................	20° 15'	74° 08'	+0 05	+0 05	(*0.79−0.99)		2.6

ON **SAN JUAN,** PUERTO RICO

South Coast Cuba							
Guantanamo Bay...........................	19° 54'	75° 09'	−0 27	−0 23	*0.89	*0.89	1.3
Puerto de Santiago de Cuba	19° 59'	75° 52'	+0 30	+0 17	*0.89	*0.89	1.2
Manzanillo	20° 21'	77° 07'	+1 41	+1 38	*1.39	*1.39	2.1
Ensenada de Mora							
Puerto de Pilon.............................	19° 54'	77° 19'	+0 11	+0 13	*0.72	*0.72	1.0
South Coast Cuba							
Casilda..	21° 45'	79° 59'	+1 04	+0 52	*0.65	*0.65	0.9
Bahía de Cienfuegos							
Punta Pasacaballos.......................	22° 04'	80° 27'	+0 49	+0 58	*0.80	*0.80	1.3
Cienfuegos	22° 08'	80° 27'	+0 51	+0 58	*0.81	*0.81	1.3

*Heights of tides are found by multiplying heights from the Tide Tables by the *ratio listed here. When parenthesis are used, multiply heights by the *ratio and then add or subtract the second number as indicated.

PLACE	POSITION		DIFFERENCES				RANGE
			Time		Height*		
	Latitude	Longitude	High	Low	High	Low	Spring
	North	West	h m	h m	ft	ft	ft

CUBA (continued)

Eastern Standard Time (GMT –5h)   *Add 1 hour Daylight Saving April 2 – October 8*

on **SAN JUAN, PUERTO RICO**

South Coast Cuba

Carapachibey, Isla de Pinos...........	21° 27'	82° 55'	+0 43	+0 52	*0.54	*0.54	0.9

on **KEY WEST, FLORIDA**

Cabo San Antonio	21° 52'	84° 58'	–0 50	– 0 07	*0.92	*0.92	1.5

CAYMAN ISLANDS

Eastern Standard Time (GMT –5h)   *Daylight Saving Time not observed*

on **CHARLOTTE AMALIE, USVI**

Grand Cayman	19° 20'	81° 20'	+0 11	+0 15	*1.63	*1.63	1.3

JAMAICA

Eastern Standard Time (GMT –5h)   *Daylight Saving Time not observed*

on **CHARLOTTE AMALIE, USVI**

North Coast

South Negril Point...........................	18° 18'	78° 24'	+5 25	+5 29	*3.88	*2.12	1.7
Montego Bay	18° 28'	77° 55'	+1 28	+1 36	*1.25	*1.25	1.0
St. Anns Bay.................................	18° 25'	77° 14'	+0 55	+0 59	*1.00	*1.00	0.8

on **CRISTÓBAL, PANAMA**

Port Antonio...................................	18° 11'	76°27°	–2 45	–3 00	(*0.89	+0.26)	0.9

South Coast

Port Morant...................................	17° 53'	76°19°	–1 55	–2 15	(*0.90	+0.63)	0.9
Port Royal.....................................	17° 57'	76°50°	–1 25	–1 40	(*0.60	+0.87)	0.6
Port Esquivel	17° 53'	77° 08'	–1 22	–1 45	(*0.70	+0.24)	0.6
Black River	18° 01'	77° 51'	–1 38	–2 15	(*0.58	+0.69)	0.6
Savanna la Mar	18° 12'	78° 08'	–1 53	–2 30	(*1.00	+0.67)	0.9

HAITI

Eastern Standard Time (GMT –5h)   *Add 1 hour Daylight Saving April 2 – October 28*

on **SAN JUAN, PUERTO RICO**

Massacre, Riviere du entrance.......	19° 43'	71° 46'	–1 01	–1 01	*1.45	*1.45	2.3
Port–au–Prince..............................	18° 33'	72° 21'	–0 32	–0 32	+0.1	+0.1	0.6

on **CHARLOTTE AMALIE, USVI**

Jacmel	18° 13'	72° 34'	–1 48	–1 44	(*2.68	–0.31)	1.3

*Heights of tides are found by multiplying heights from the Tide Tables by the *ratio listed here. When parenthesis are used, multiply heights by the *ratio and then add or subtract the second number as indicated.

DIFFERENCES

PLACE	POSITION		DIFFERENCES				RANGE
			Time		Height*		
	Latitude	Longitude	High	Low	High	Low	Spring
	North	West	h m	h m	ft	ft	ft

DOMINICAN REPUBLIC

Eastern Standard Time (GMT –5h)   *Daylight Saving Time not observed*

ON **SAN JUAN**, PUERTO RICO

Puerto Plata	19° 49'	70° 42'	−1 09	−1 14	*1.45	*1.45	2.3
Sanchez	19° 13'	69° 36'	−0 37	−0 37	*2.05	*2.05	3.3
Santa Barbara de Samana	19° 12'	69° 20'	−0 51	−0 47	*1.25	*1.25	2.0

ON **CHARLOTTE AMALIE, USVI**

Santo Domingo	18° 27'	69° 53'	+1 44	−2 45	*1.00	*1.00	0.8

PUERTO RICO

Atlantic Standard Time (GMT –4h)   *Daylight Saving Time not observed*

ON **SAN JUAN**, PUERTO RICO

West Coast – Puerto Rico

Puerto Real	18° 05'	67° 11'	−0 33	−0 26	*0.72	*0.72	1.2
Mayaguez	18° 13'	67° 09'	−0 30	−0 21	*0.99	*0.99	1.6

North Coast – Puerto Rico

SAN JUAN	18° 28'	66° 01'	**Daily Predictions**				1.6

East Coast – Puerto Rico

Playa de Fajardo	18° 20'	65° 38'	−0 10	−0 13	*1.00	*1.00	1.6
Roosevelt Roads	18° 14'	65° 37'	+0 02	+0 20	*0.63	*0.63	1.0

Culebra

Ensenada Honda	18° 18'	65° 17'	−0 34	−0 15	*0.99	*0.99	1.0

ON **CHARLOTTE AMALIE, USVI**

Culebrita, Isla	18° 19'	65° 14'	−0 57	+0 24	*1.39	*1.39	1.1

ON **SAN JUAN**, PUERTO RICO

Isla de Vieques

Punta Mulas	18° 09'	65° 26'	−0 14	−0 17	*0.72	*0.72	1.2

ON **CHARLOTTE AMALIE, USVI**

Puerto Ferro	18° 06'	65° 26'	−0 49	+0 45	*1.00	*1.00	0.8

South Coast – Puerto Rico

Puerto Maunabo	18° 00'	65° 53'	+0 41	−1 03	*0.88	*0.88	0.7
Arroyo	17° 58'	66° 04'	+2 29	−2 03	*1.00	*1.00	0.8
Playa Cortada	17° 59'	66° 27'	+1 15	−2 53	*1.00	*1.00	0.8
Playa de Ponce	17° 58'	66° 37'	+0 58	−2 29	*1.00	*1.00	0.8
Guanica	17° 58'	66° 55'	+0 15	−1 58	*0.88	*0.88	0.7
Magueyes Island	17° 58'	67° 03'	+1 35	−2 08	*0.88	*0.88	0.7

U.S. VIRGIN ISLANDS

Atlantic Standard Time (GMT –4h)   *Daylight Saving Time not observed*

ON **SAN JUAN**, PUERTO RICO

Magens Bay, St. Thomas	18° 22'	64° 55'	−0 16	−0 01	*0.91	*0.91	1.4

*Heights of tides are found by multiplying heights from the Tide Tables by the *ratio listed here. When parenthesis are used, multiply heights by the *ratio and then add or subtract the second number as indicated.

PLACE	POSITION		DIFFERENCES				RANGE
			Time		Height*		
	Latitude	Longitude	High	Low	High	Low	Spring
	North	West	h m	h m	ft	ft	ft

U.S. VIRGIN ISLANDS (continued)

Atlantic Standard Time (GMT –4h)   *Daylight Saving Time not observed*
ON **CHARLOTTE AMALIE, USVI**

CHARLOTTE AMALIE..............	18° 20'	64° 56'	**Daily Predictions**				0.8
St. John	18° 20'	64° 48'	+1 12	+1 16	(*0.82+0.31)		1.3
Christiansted, St. Croix..........	17° 45'	64° 42'	−1 05	−1 07	*1.00	*1.00	0.8

BRITISH VIRGIN ISLANDS

Atlantic Standard Time (GMT –4h)   *Daylight Saving Time not observed*
ON **CHARLOTTE AMALIE, USVI**

Tortola	18° 26'	64° 37'	+0 07	+0 11	(*0.82+1.01)		1.0
Anegada	18° 44'	64° 23'	−0 58	−0 04	(*2.33−0.48)		1.9

ANGUILLA

Atlantic Standard Time (GMT –4h)   *Daylight Saving Time not observed*
ON **CHARLOTTE AMALIE, USVI**

Road Bay	18° 12'	63° 06'	−0 18	−0 14	(*0.84+0.66)		1.3

ST. BARTHELEMY

Atlantic Standard Time (GMT –4h)   *Daylight Saving Time not observed*
ON **CHARLOTTE AMALIE, USVI**

St. Barthélemy..................	17° 54'	62° 51'	−1 48	−1 02	*1.75	*1.75	1.4

ANTIGUA

Atlantic Standard Time (GMT –4h)   *Daylight Saving Time not observed*
ON **CHARLOTTE AMALIE, USVI**

St. John's........................	17° 08'	61° 52'	+0 12	+0 12	(*0.81+0.62)		1.3

GUADELOUPE

Atlantic Standard Time (GMT –4h)   *Daylight Saving Time not observed*
ON **CHARLOTTE AMALIE, USVI**

Sainte Rose	16° 20'	61° 42'	−2 28	−2 24	(*1.28+0.67)		0.9
Pointe-à-Pitre...................	16° 14'	61° 32'	−1 58	−1 54	(*1.05+1.59)		0.9
Iles des Saintes	15° 52'	61° 36'	−3 33	−3 34	(*0.84+1.12)		0.6

DOMINICA

Atlantic Standard Time (GMT –4h)   *Daylight Saving Time not observed*
ON **CHARLOTTE AMALIE, USVI**

Portsmouth	15° 34'	61° 28'	+0 08	+0 06	(*1.09+1.33)		1.0
Woodbridge Bay...............	15° 19'	61° 24'	+0 12	+0 16	(*1.47+0.69)		1.3

*Heights of tides are found by multiplying heights from the Tide Tables by the *ratio listed here. When parenthesis are used, multiply heights by the *ratio and then add or subtract the second number as indicated.

PLACE	POSITION		DIFFERENCES				RANGE
			Time		Height*		
	Latitude	Longitude	High	Low	High	Low	Spring
	North	West	h m	h m	ft	ft	ft

DOMINICA

Atlantic Standard Time (GMT –4h)   *Daylight Saving Time not observed*

ON **FORT–DE–FRANCE,** MARTINIQUE

Roseau	15° 18'	61° 24'	+0 26	+0 13	*1.71	*1.71	1.2

MARTINIQUE

Atlantic Standard Time (GMT –4h)   *Daylight Saving Time not observed*

ON **FORT–DE–FRANCE,** MARTINIQUE

Fort–de–France, Martinique	14° 35'	61° 03'	**Daily Predictions**		0.5

SAINT LUCIA

Atlantic Standard Time (GMT –4h)   *Daylight Saving Time not observed*

ON **FORT–DE–FRANCE,** MARTINIQUE

Castries	14° 01'	61° 00'	−0 10	−0 52	(*1.14–0.65)	1.0
Vieux Fort Bay, St. Lucia	13° 44'	60° 58'	+0 53	+0 40	*1.82 *1.82	1.0

ST. VINCENT & THE GRENADINES

Atlantic Standard Time (GMT –4h)   *Daylight Saving Time not observed*

ON **FORT–DE–FRANCE,** MARTINIQUE

Kingstown, St. Vincent....................	13° 10'	61° 13'	−0 10	−1 12	(*0.35+1.12)	1.0
Mustique	12° 51'	61° 11'	+0 55	+0 23	(*1.50–1.88)	1.2
Charlestown Bay, Canouan............	12° 42'	61° 20'	+0 17	−0 32	(*1.50–1.23)	1.3
Tobago Cays	12° 38'	61° 21'	+0 30	−0 22	(*1.49–1.37)	1.3
Clifton Harbour, Union	12° 36'	61° 25'	+0 40	−0 44	(*1.14+0.01)	0.9

GRENADA

Atlantic Standard Time (GMT –4h)   *Daylight Saving Time not observed*

ON **FORT–DE–FRANCE,** MARTINIQUE

Hillsborough Bay, Carriacou...........	12° 29'	61° 27'	+0 10	−0 15	(*1.14–0.99)	0.9
St. George's Harbour......................	12° 03'	61° 45'	−0 10	−0 22	(*0.66+0.41)	0.7
Prickly Bay.....................................	12° 00'	61° 45'	+0 35	−0 34	(*1.60–1.36)	1.3

BARBADOS

Atlantic Standard Time (GMT –4h)   *Daylight Saving Time not observed*

ON **PORT OF SPAIN,** TRINIDAD

Carlisle Bay, Bridgetown	13° 06'	59° 37'	−0 35	−0 36	(*0.89–0.48)	1.9

*Heights of tides are found by multiplying heights from the Tide Tables by the *ratio listed here. When parenthesis are used, multiply heights by the *ratio and then add or subtract the second number as indicated.

PLACE	POSITION		DIFFERENCES				RANGE
			Time		Height*		
	Latitude	Longitude	High	Low	High	Low	Spring
	North	West	h m	h m	ft	ft	ft

TOBAGO

Atlantic Standard Time (GMT –4h)   *Daylight Saving Time not observed*

ON **PORT OF SPAIN,** TRINIDAD

Plymouth	11° 13'	60° 47'	−1 05	−1 05	(*0.87	+0.06)	2.0
Man of War Bay	11° 19'	60° 32'	−0 35	−0 35	(*0.98	−1.12)	2.3
Scarborough	11° 11'	60° 44'	−0 14	−0 13	(*0.98	−0.12)	2.3

TRINIDAD

Atlantic Standard Time (GMT –4h)   *Daylight Saving Time not observed*

ON **PORT OF SPAIN,** TRINIDAD

North Coast – Trinidad

Las Cuevas Bay	10° 47'	61° 24'	−1 01	−0 58	(*0.82	−0.20)	1.9
Toco	10° 50'	60° 56'	−1 10	−1 10	(*1.32	−0.61)	2.9

East Coast – Trinidad

Guayamare Point	10° 45'	60° 58'	−1 00	−1 00	(*1.39	−0.52)	3.0

ON **PUNTA GORDA,** VENEZUELA

Nariva River	10° 24'	61° 02'	−1 06	−2 16	(*0.41	+1.3)	3.1

South Coast – Trinidad

Erin Bay	10° 04'	61° 39'	−0 50	−1 41	−0.3	+1.2	5.6
Guayaguayare Bay	10° 09'	61° 01'	−1 32	−2 09	(*0.53	+1.3)	3.8

West Coast – Trinidad

Bonasse pier	10° 05'	61° 52'	−0 43	−1 15	−1.0	+1.4	4.4
Point Fortin	10° 11'	61° 42'	−0 54	−1 27	(*0.47	1.26)	3.6

ON **PORT OF SPAIN,** TRINIDAD

Lisas Point	10° 23'	61° 29'	−0 09	−0 08	(*1.42	−0.87)	3.2
PORT OF SPAIN	10° 39'	61° 31'	**Daily Predictions**				2.3
Carenage Bay	10° 41'	61° 36'	−0 58	−1 40	(*0.34	+1.6)	2.6
Staubles Bay	10° 41'	61° 39'	−1 07	−2 02	(*0.33	+1.7)	2.5

VENEZUELA

Atlantic Standard Time (GMT –4h)   *Daylight Saving Time not observed*

ON **PUNTA GORDA,** VENEZUELA

Río Orinoco

Isla Ramon Isidro	8° 39'	60° 35'	+0 07	−0 12	+0.2	+1.0	6.7

Gulf of Paria

PUNTA GORDA, Río San Juan	10° 10'	62° 38'	**Daily Predictions**				7.1
Barra de Maturin, channel entr	10° 18'	62° 31'	−0 22	−0 45	−1.0	+0.2	5.7
Boca Pedernales entrance	10° 01'	62° 12'	−0 03	−0 34	−1.3	+0.2	5.4
Puerto de Hierro	10° 37'	62° 05'	−0 46	−1 19	*0.59	*0.59	4.2
Macuro	10° 39'	61° 56'	−1 15	−2 05	*0.38	*0.38	2.7

ON **AMUAY,** VENEZUELA

Punta Penas to Amuay

Carúpano	10° 40'	63° 15'	−1 17	−0 42	+0.2	0.0	1.4

*Heights of tides are found by multiplying heights from the Tide Tables by the *ratio listed here. When parenthesis are used, multiply heights by the *ratio and then add or subtract the second number as indicated.

PLACE	POSITION		DIFFERENCES				RANGE
			Time		Height*		
	Latitude	Longitude	High	Low	High	Low	Spring
	North	West	h m	h m	ft	ft	ft

VENEZUELA (continued)

Atlantic Standard Time (GMT –4h) — *Daylight Saving Time not observed*
ON **AMUAY**, VENEZUELA

Porlamar, Isla de Margarita	10° 57'	63° 51'	–1 19	–0 59	+0.6	0.0	1.8
Cumaná	10° 28'	64° 11'	–2 37	–1 02	–0.1	0.0	1.1
Carenero	10° 32'	66° 07'	–1 51	–1 59	+0.8	+1.0	1.0
La Güaira	10° 36'	66° 56'	–2 29	–1 59	+0.8	+1.0	1.0
AMUAY	11° 45'	70° 13'	**Daily Predictions**				1.2

ON **MALECON**, VENEZUELA

Maracaibo

MALECON–ISLA ZAPARA	11° 00'	71° 35'	**Daily Predictions**				3.6
Bahía de Tablazos	10° 53'	71° 35'	+0 30	+0 11	*0.61	*0.31	2.3
Punta de Palmas	10° 48'	71° 37'	+0 35	+0 16	*0.49	*0.31	1.8

BONAIRE

Atlantic Standard Time (GMT –4h) — *Daylight Saving Time not observed*
ON **CRISTÓBAL**, PANAMA

Kralendijk	12° 09'	68° 17'	+0 35	+1 42	(*0.65+0.98)		1.0

CURAÇAO

Atlantic Standard Time (GMT –4h) — *Daylight Saving Time not observed*
ON **CRISTÓBAL**, PANAMA

Schottegat, Curaçao	12° 07'	68° 56'	+0 25	+1 09	*0.82	*0.82	0.9
Willemstad	12° 06'	68° 56'	+0 42	+1 38	(*0.65+0.98)		1.0

ARUBA

Atlantic Standard Time (GMT –4h) — *Daylight Saving Time not observed*
ON **CRISTÓBAL**, PANAMA

Oranjestad	12° 31'	70° 03'	+0 21	+1 16	(*0.65+0.98)		1.0
Malmok Bay	12° 36'	70° 03'	+0 33	+1 36	(*0.65+0.98)		1.0

COLOMBIA

Eastern Standard Time (GMT –5h) — *Daylight Saving Time not observed*
ON **CRISTÓBAL**, PANAMA

Río Hacha	11° 33'	72° 55'	–0 35	–0 35	(*1.01–0.18)		1.0
Santa Marta	11° 15'	74° 13'	–1 19	–1 08	(*0.99–0.06)		1.0
Puerto Colombia	11° 00'	74° 58'	–0 52	–1 08	(*1.29–0.16)		1.3
Cartagena	10° 26'	75° 34'	–1 16	–0 48	(*0.90–0.05)		1.0
Puerto Covenas	9° 20'	75° 40'	–1 06	–0 46	(*0.99–0.06)		1.0
Turbo	8° 10'	76° 45'	–0 49	–0 30	*1.43	*1.43	1.4
Punta Yarumal	8° 07'	76° 45'	–0 49	–0 30	(*1.62–0.16)		1.6

*Heights of tides are found by multiplying heights from the Tide Tables by the *ratio listed here. When parenthesis are used, multiply heights by the *ratio and then add or subtract the second number as indicated.

PLACE	POSITION		DIFFERENCES				RANGE
			Time		Height*		
	Latitude	Longitude	High	Low	High	Low	Spring
	North	West	h m	h m	ft	ft	ft

PANAMA

Eastern Standard Time (GMT –5h) *Daylight Saving Time not observed*

ON **CRISTÓBAL**, PANAMA

Puerto Caledonia............................	8° 54'	77° 41'	+0 12	0 00	(*1.01+0.04)		1.0
Puerto Mandinga	9° 30'	79° 03'	+0 08	–0 05	(*1.01+0.04)		1.0
CRISTÓBAL–COLÓN	9° 21'	79° 55'	**Daily Predictions**				1.1
Escudo de Veragua	9° 07'	81° 34'	+0 30	+0 15	(*0.89–0.07)		1.0
Boca del Toro	9° 21'	82° 15'	+0 20	+0 25	(*0.99–0.06)		1.0

COSTA RICA

Central Standard Time (GMT –6h) *Daylight Saving Time not observed*

ON **CRISTÓBAL**, PANAMA

Puerto Limon	10° 00'	83° 02'	–0 39	–0 37	(*0.90–0.02)		1.0

NICARAGUA

Central Standard Time (GMT –6h) *Daylight Saving Time not observed*

ON **PORT OF SPAIN**, TRINIDAD

Greytown (San Juan del Norte)	10° 55'	83° 42'	–2 30	–1 50	(*0.50–0.58)		1.3
Bluefields Bluff...............................	12° 00'	83° 40'	–2 35	–1 55	(*0.33–0.40)		1.0
Isla del Maiz Grande (Great Corn)	12° 10'	83° 03'	–1 55	–1 40	(*0.49–0.36)		1.3
Cayos del Perlas (Pearl Cays)	12° 25'	83° 25'	–1 40	–1 20	(*0.49–0.36)		1.3

ON **NASSAU**, BAHAMAS

Puerto Cabezas..............................	14° 01'	83° 23'	+4 26	+4 37	*0.54	*0.54	1.9
Cabo Gracias a Dios	15° 00'	83° 10'	+1 44	+0 54	*0.54	*0.54	1.6

HONDURAS

Central Standard Time (GMT –6h)Daylight Saving Time dates set yearly by government

ON **KEY WEST**, FLORIDA

Swan Island, Harbor Bay................	17° 24'	83° 42'	–1 18	–0 33	*0.51	*0.51	0.9
Isla de Guanaja (Bonacca)	16° 29'	85° 54'	–1 26	–1 42	*0.72	*0.72	1.3
Puerto Castilla	16° 00'	85° 54'	–0 48	–0 13	*0.46	*0.46	0.8
Isla de Roatán, Port Royal..............	16° 24'	86° 20'	–2 41	–2 35	*0.92	*0.92	1.4
Puerto Cortés	15° 50'	87° 57'	–0 43	–0 02	*0.38	*0.38	0.6

GUATEMALA

Central Standard Time (GMT –6h) *Daylight Saving Time not observed*

ON **KEY WEST**, FLORIDA

Río Dulce entrance........................	15° 50'	88° 49'	–1 25	–1 35	*0.92	*0.92	1.5

DIFFERENCES

*Heights of tides are found by multiplying heights from the Tide Tables by the *ratio listed here. When parenthesis are used, multiply heights by the *ratio and then add or subtract the second number as indicated.

PLACE	POSITION		DIFFERENCES				RANGE
			Time		Height*		
	Latitude	Longitude	High	Low	High	Low	Spring
	North	West	h m	h m	ft	ft	ft

BELIZE

Central Standard Time (GMT –6h)   *Daylight Saving Time not observed*
                                            ON **KEY WEST,** FLORIDA

Punta Gorda	16° 06'	88° 49'	–0 27	+0 30	*0.46	*0.46	0.8
Belize City	17° 30'	88° 11'	+0 14	+0 47	*0.46	*0.46	0.7

MEXICO

Central Standard Time (GMT –6h)   *Daylight Saving Time not observed*
                                            ON **TAMPICO,** MEXICO

Progreso	21° 18'	89° 40'	+1 19	+0 23	*1.29	*1.29	1.8
Campeche	19° 51'	90° 32'	–0 15	+0 50	(*2.14	–0.60)	2.0
Cuidad del Carmen	18° 40'	91° 51'	–0 40	+0 30	(*1.00	+0.70)	1.4
Frontera (Alvaro Mexico)	18° 32'	92° 39'	–0 18	–0 27	*1.14	*1.14	1.6
Coatzacoalcos (Puerto Mexico)	18° 09'	94° 25'	–0 40	+0 05	*1.07	*1.07	1.5
Alvarado	18° 46'	95° 46'	+0 51	+0 27	*0.93	*0.93	1.3
Veracruz	19° 12'	96° 08'	–0 19	–0 12	*1.21	*1.21	1.7
Tuxpan	21° 00'	97° 20'	+0 02	+0 04	*1.21	*1.21	1.7
TAMPICO HARBOR (Madero)	22° 13'	97° 51'	**Daily Predictions**				1.4
Matamoros	25° 53'	97° 31'	+0 55	+0 40	*1.00	*1.00	1.4

*Heights of tides are found by multiplying heights from the Tide Tables by the *ratio listed here. When parenthesis are used, multiply heights by the *ratio and then add or subtract the second number as indicated.

CURRENT DIFFERENCES

The current differences table that follows provides information for calculating tidal current information for various locations in Florida and Puerto Rico. This information must be used in conjunction with one of the current tables found at the end of the Florida and Puerto Rico sections of Chapter 2, Coast Pilot.

Unfortunately, tidal current data is extremely limited for most of the Caribbean. There is more information about general currents, however, and the introduction to Chapter 2 includes two current charts illustrating the trend of the average currents to be found in the Caribbean. Local currents are discussed in the appropriate country section of Chapter 2.

Mariners should bear in mind the effects of local winds and weather conditions. For instance, tidal currents off the Yucatan coast of Mexico can be reversed by a strong norther. Rivers often create local currents near their mouths that may reinforce coastal currents or may flow in opposition to local currents.

For more information on tides and currents in the Caribbean see the introduction to Chapter 2 and *Reed's Nautical Companion*.

HOW TO USE THE TABLE

The following current differences table for subordinate locations is organized geographically beginning with Florida and following with Puerto Rico.

In the first column, find the subordinate location in which you are interested. The name of the primary current reference table found in Chapter 2 to which your location is keyed is listed in bold type in the center of the page above the chosen location. The **Position** columns to the right of the location's name give its approximate latitude and longitude.

The **Time Differences** columns express the differences that must be applied to the times derived from the primary reference table. Differences are expressed in *hours* and *minutes*. The term *Slack* in the headings refers to the time when the current is at a minimum, before turning to flood or ebb.

The time differences for *Slack before flood* and *Slack before ebb* should be added or subtracted (as indicated by the plus + or minus - sign) to the times from the column labeled *Slack time* on the primary reference table. When determining *Slack before flood,* use the entry under *Slack time* that shows a current speed (in knots) under the *Flood* column, to the right of the *Max. time* column. When determining *Slack before ebb,* use the entry under *Slack time* that shows a current speed (in knots) under the *Ebb* column.

The **Speed Ratio** columns give ratios for determining approximate current speeds at subordinate locations for a specific day at the time of maximum flow. First apply the time differences from the subordinate location to times listed in the primary reference table to determine for a particular time whether the tide is flooding or ebbing, before or after the time of maximum flow. Then determine the approximate speed of maximum flow at the subordinate location by multiplying the corresponding maximum flood or ebb speed from the primary reference table by the relevant flood or ebb *speed ratio* given for the subordinate location.

The **Current Direction and Max Speed** columns give the average directions at the times of the maximum flood and ebb (in degrees true) for the subordinate location, with corresponding average speeds of maximum flood and ebb. Figures for these columns are read directly from the table, making it easy to make quick assessments of average local maximum currents.

EXAMPLE

Suppose you are interested in currents in Fajardo Harbor channel on March 27, 1995. The current differences for Fajardo Harbor channel are listed near the end of the current differences list. This location is keyed to the Vieques Passage current table found in Chapter 2 following the coast pilot information for Puerto Rico. The current differences are calculated for an approximate position in the Fajardo Harbor channel of 18° 20'N, 65° 37'W.

Now turn to the time and speed entries in the Vieques Passage current table for March 27, 1995. The current is at maximum ebb (0.6 knots) at 0150, slack at 0453, at maximum flood at 0801, slack at 1104, at maximum ebb at 1422, slack at 1741, at maximum flood at 2040, and slack again at 2343.

Fajardo Harbor's tide current difference of 1 hour, 13 minutes shown under the *Slack before flood* heading should be subtracted from the slack times before the floods noted above for Vieques Passage (0453 and 1741). In Fajardo minimum currents before floods will thus occur at 0340 and 1628.

Similarly, the tide current difference of 1 hour, 52 minutes shown under the *Max. flood* heading for Fajardo should be subtracted from the times of maximum floods shown in the Vieques Passage table. Maximum floods will occur at 0609 and 1848.

To find the time of slack before ebb in Fajardo, the tide current difference of 2 hours, 27 minutes under the *Slack before ebb* heading should be subtracted from the slack times before the ebbs (1104 and 2343) in the Vieques Passage table. Minimum currents before ebbs will occur at 0837 and 2116 in Fajardo.

Similarly, the tide current difference of 1 hour, 45 minutes shown under *Max. ebb* should be subtracted from the times of maximum ebb. Maximum ebbs will occur at 0005 and 1237.

The *Speed ratio* figures allow you to determine current speeds at the secondary location at the time of maximum flow for a specific day (which may differ from the *average* maximum flow speeds presented in the final two columns of the table). Applying the time differences to values listed for March 27 in Vieques Passage as before, maximum flood occurs in Fajardo at 0609 (0801 – 0152) and 1848 (2040 – 0152), and maximum ebb, at 0005 (0150 – 0145) and 1237 (1422 – 0145).

To figure the maximum flood speeds in Fajardo, multiply the maximum current speed under the *Fld* heading for the relevant times in Vieques Passage (0.6 for both max times) by the speed ratio for Fajardo given under the *Flood* heading (0.5). The result is 0.3 knots for both floods.

To compute maximum ebb speeds in Fajardo, multiply the speeds under the *Ebb* heading for Vieques Passage (0.6 for the first ebb and 0.7 for the second) by the speed ratio under the *Ebb* heading (1.6) for Fajardo. Current speed for the 0005 ebb is 1.0 knots; for the 1237 ebb, 1.1 knots.

DIFFERENCES

Current Differences

	POSITION		TIME DIFFERENCES				SPEED RATIOS		CURRENT DIRECTION & MAX SPEED			
	North latitude	West longitude	Slack before flood	Max flood	Slack before ebb	Max ebb	Flood	Ebb	Flood	Ebb	Flood	Ebb
			h m	h m	h m	h m			Dir	Dir	knots	knots
FLORIDA			*Eastern Standard Time (GMT –5h).*			*Add 1 hour Daylight Saving April 2 – October 28*						
			ON MIAMI HARBOR ENTRANCE, FLORIDA									
Ft. Pierce Inlet	27°28.30'	80°17.50'	+1:19	+0:39	+0:48	+0:35	1.5	2.0	250°	072°	2.6	3.1
Lake Worth Inlet (btwn jetties)	26°46.33'	80°02.13'	+0:13	–0:07	–0:01	0:00	1.3	2.3	273°	094°	2.4	3.6
Fort Lauderdale, New River	26°06.73'	80°07.18'	–0:43	–0:39	–0:06	–0:16	0.4	0.3	005°	130°	0.8	0.5
PORT EVERGLADES												
Entrance (between jetties)	26°05.58'	80°06.32'	–0:08	–0:49	–0:43	–0:34	0.3	0.4	275°	095°	0.6	0.7
Entrance from southward (canal)	26°05.20'	80°06.90'	+0:40	+0:07	+0:31	–0:09	0.7	1.1	167°	358°	1.3	1.7
Turning Basin	26°05.70'	80°07.05'	–1:01	–1:07	–1:02	–1:11	0.1	0.3	320°	155°	0.2	0.5
Turning Basin, 300 yards n of	26°05.80'	80°07.10'	–0:20	–1:09	–0:27	–0:14	0.5	1.1	349°	160°	0.9	1.8
17th Street Bridge	26°06.02'	80°07.13'	–0:38	–0:53	–0:28	–0:55	1.1	1.2	350°	170°	1.9	1.9
MIAMI HARBOR												
Bakers Haulover Cut	25°54.00'	80°07.40'	–0:01	+0:07	+0:14	–0:17	1.6	1.6	270°	090°	2.9	2.5
Government Cut												
East entrance, off n jetty	25°45.59'	80°07.35'	–0:02	–0:19	–0:08	–0:26	0.4	0.9	236°	092°	0.6	1.5
East entrance, inside s jetty	25°45.61'	80°07.66'	–0:07	–0:06	–0:04	0:00	1.2	1.1	343°	116°	2.1	1.8
Midway, n side	25°45.84'	80°07.96'	–0:12	–0:03	–0:07	–0:08	0.7	0.5	292°	108°	1.2	0.7
MIAMI HARBOR ENTRANCE ..	25°45.90'	80°08.17'	**Daily Predictions**						293°	112°	1.8	1.6
West entrance, s side	25°45.85'	80°08.25'	+0:09	+0:10	–0:04	+0:01	0.9	1.6	288°	100°	1.6	2.5
Main Channel												
Causeway I, 0.2 nm se of	25°46.06'	80°08.58'	+0:01	+0:23	–0:01	–0:14	0.8	0.4	306°	131°	1.4	0.7
Lummus I, ne corner	25°46.02'	80°08.70'	–0:07	–0:02	+0:06	–0:04	0.1	0.4	265°	104°	0.2	0.7
Lummus I, 0.18 nm off nw cor ...	25°46.32'	80°09.45'	–0:05	+0:50	+0:28	–0:08	0.3	0.3	285°	102°	0.5	0.5
Dodge I, 0.1 nm off nw corner ...	25°46.89'	80°10.90'	+0:17	–0:14	+0:01	+0:04	0.2	0.3	277°	093°	0.4	0.4
Fishermans Channel												
Lummus I, se corner	25°45.95'	80°08.71'	+0:08	+0:06	+0:19	–0:20	0.5	0.2	208°	086°	0.9	0.4
Fisher I, 0.2 nm nw of	25°45.87'	80°09.08'	+0:14	+0:38	+0:17	+0:39	0.6	0.7	280°	090°	1.0	1.1
Lummus I, 0.15 nm off sw cor ...	25°45.89'	80°09.69'	+0:20	–0:20	+0:10	+0:22	0.3	0.6	271°	095°	0.6	0.9
West end, sw of Dodge I	25°46.36'	80°10.74'	–0:05	–0:32	–0:15	–0:21	0.1	0.2	277°	089°	0.2	0.3
Miami River entrance............	25°46.21'	80°11.23'	+0:15	–0:02	–0:01	+0:46	0.1	0.4	261°	071°	0.2	0.6

Current Differences

Current Differences	POSITION North latitude	POSITION West longitude	TIME DIFFERENCES Slack before flood h m	TIME DIFFERENCES Max flood h m	TIME DIFFERENCES Slack before ebb h m	TIME DIFFERENCES Max ebb h m	SPEED RATIOS Flood	SPEED RATIOS Ebb	CURRENT DIRECTION & MAX SPEED Flood Dir	CURRENT DIRECTION & MAX SPEED Ebb Dir	CURRENT DIRECTION & MAX SPEED Flood knots	CURRENT DIRECTION & MAX SPEED Ebb knots
FLORIDA REEFS												
			ON KEY WEST, FLORIDA									
Caesar Creek, Biscayne Bay.....	25°23.20'	80°13.60'	+0:07	-0:08	-0:14	-0:05	1.2	1.0	316°	123°	1.2	1.8
Long Key, drawbridge east of....	24°50.40'	80°46.20'	+0:58	+1:27	+2:21	+1:33	1.1	0.7	000°	202°	1.1	1.2
Long Key Viaduct................	24°48.10'	80°51.90'	+1:34	+1:28	+2:02	+1:57	0.9	0.7	349°	170°	0.9	1.2
Moser Channel, swingbridge.....	24°42.00'	81°10.20'	+1:07	+1:30	+1:50	+1:47	1.4	1.0	339°	166°	1.4	1.8
Bahia Honda Harbor, bridge......	24°39.40'	81°17.30'	+1:01	+0:39	+1:53	+1:05	1.4	1.2	004°	182°	1.4	2.1
No Name Key, northeast of.......	24°42.30'	81°18.80'	+0:55	+1:24	+1:20	+0:53	0.7	0.5	312°	142°	0.7	0.9
Key West												
Main Ship Channel entrance...	24°28.40'	81°48.10'	-0:44	-0:12	+0:10	+0:10	0.2	0.3	040°	178°	0.2	0.4
Main Ship Channel...........	24°30.50'	81°48.30'	0:30	0:30	0:30	+0:30	0.1	0.2	064°	133°	-.-	0.4
			Daily Predictions									
KEY WEST, 0.3 nm w Ft. Taylor	24°32.90'	81°49.00'							022°	194°	1.0	1.7
Ft. Taylor, 0.6 nm north of ...	24°33.50'	81°48.60'	+0:20	-0:11	-0:11	+0:13	0.6	0.7	042°	202°	0.6	1.2
Turning Basin.................	24°34.00'	81°48.25'	+0:43	+0:44	+0:29	+1:06	0.8	0.6	048°	216°	0.8	1.1
Northwest Channel............	24°35.00'	81°50.90'	-0:08	-0:03	-0:09	-0:07	1.2	0.8	353°	162°	1.2	1.4
Northwest Channel............	24°37.30'	81°52.80'	-0:28	-0:19	-0:20	-0:20	0.6	0.4	346°	168°	0.6	0.6
Boca Grande Channel..........	24°34.00'	82°04.00'	-0:40	-0:45	-0:01	-0:06	1.1	0.8	353°	194°	1.1	1.2
New Ground.................	24°39.00'	82°25.00'	+1:36	+1:55	+1:28	+1:18	0.7	0.4	068°	244°	0.2	0.7
Isaac Shoal.................	24°33.50'	82°32.20'	+1:00	+0:54	+1:52	+1:55	1.0	0.5	002°	181°	1.0	0.8
Southeast Channel...........	24°37.62'	82°51.07'	-0:27	-0:06	+0:37	+0:36	0.6	0.4	004°	172°	0.6	0.6
Southwest Channel...........	24°36.92'	82°54.70'	+0:45	+0:59	+1:25	+2:04	0.4	0.4	001°	209°	0.4	0.6

Atlantic Standard Time (GMT −4h). Daylight Saving Time not observed

Current Differences	North latitude	West longitude	Slack before flood	Max flood	Slack before ebb	Max ebb	Flood	Ebb	Flood Dir	Ebb Dir	Flood knots	Ebb knots
PUERTO RICO												
			ON VIEQUES PASSAGE, PUERTO RICO									
Punta Ostiones, 1.5 nm w of ...	18°05.20'	67°13.60'	-0:26	-0:52	-0:04	-0:35	1.7	1.3	187°	001°	1.0	0.9
VIEQUES PASSAGE	18°11.30'	65°37.10'							250°	057°	0.6	0.7
			Daily Predictions									
Vieques Sound...............	18°15.87'	65°34.20'	-0:44	-1:16	-1:28	-1:05	0.7	0.9	180°	355°	0.4	0.6
Largo Shoals, w of...........	18°19.00'	65°35.00'	-0:52	-1:28	-1:33	-1:08	0.7	1.0	186°	330°	0.4	0.7
Ramos Cay, 0.3 nm se of......	18°18.60'	65°36.40'	-0:40	-0:42	-0:40	-0:44	0.3	0.1	120°	284°	0.2	0.1
Palominos I, 0.9 nm sw of.....	18°20.10'	65°34.80'	-0:40	-0:48	-0:40	-0:48	0.1	0.7	—°	307°	-.-	0.5
Fajardo Harbor (channel).....	18°20.00'	65°37.00'	-1:13	-1:52	-2:27	-1:45	0.5	1.6	162°	339°	0.3	1.1
Isla Marina, 0.2 nm w of......	18°20.50'	65°37.38'	-2:00	-2:00	-2:00	-2:06	0.1	1.0	—°	335°	-.-	0.7
Coronala Laja, 0.4 nm nw of....	18°21.60'	65°37.30'	-1:30	-1:30	-1:30	-1:33	0.0	0.4	—°	000°	-.-	0.3
Pasaje de San Juan...........	18°23.90'	65°36.90'	-1:10	-1:15	-1:10	-1:15	0.0	1.7	—°	310°	-.-	1.2

ELECTRONIC NAVIGATION AIDS

ELECTRONIC AIDS

RADIOBEACON REFERENCE MAP

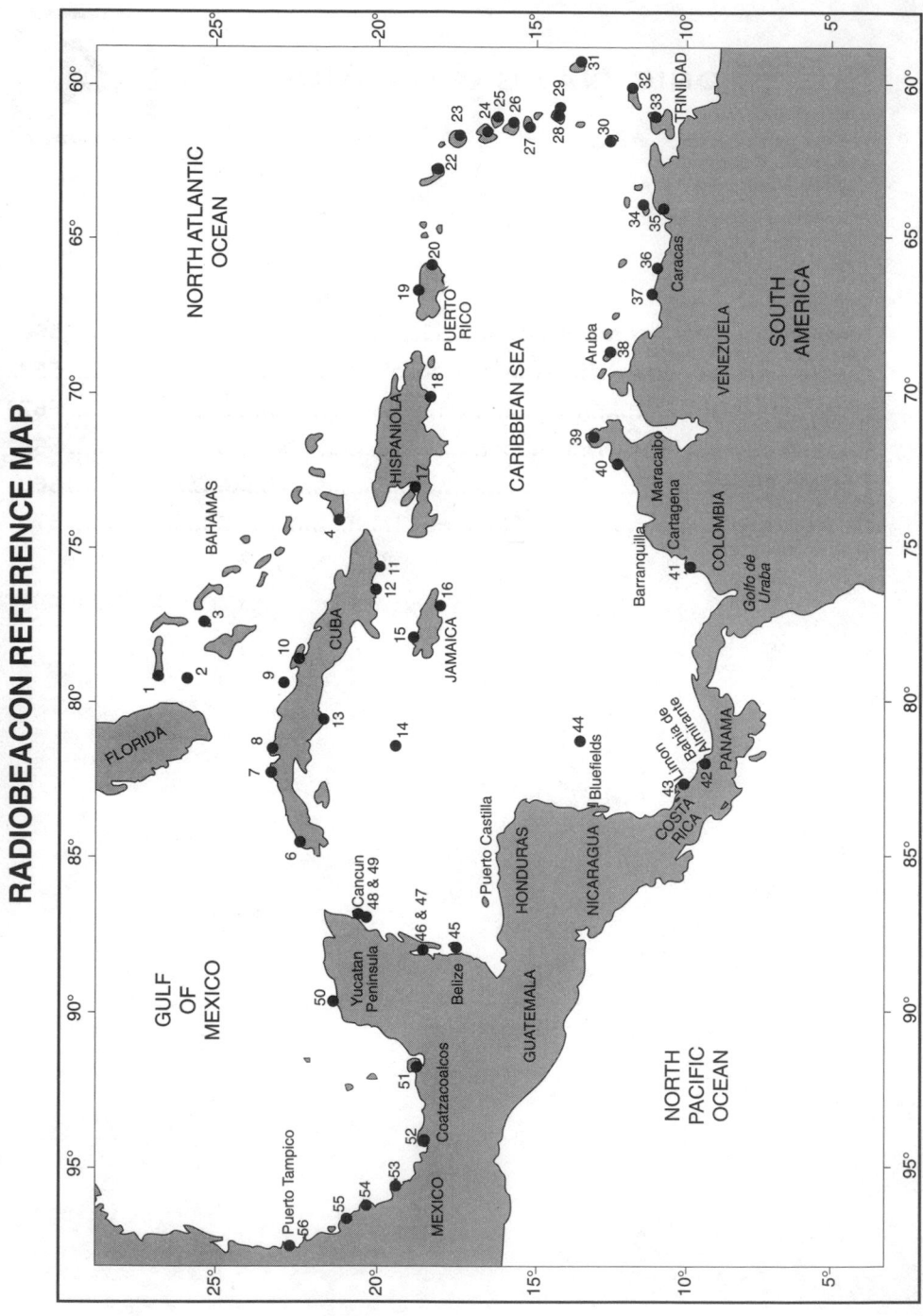

NORTH ATLANTIC OCEAN

BAHAMAS

FLORIDA

GULF OF MEXICO

CUBA

HISPANIOLA

PUERTO RICO

CARIBBEAN SEA

JAMAICA

NORTH PACIFIC OCEAN

Puerto Castilla

HONDURAS

GUATEMALA

NICARAGUA

Bluefields

COSTA RICA

Union de Bahia de Almirante

PANAMA

Golfo de Uraba

COLOMBIA

Cartagena

Barranquilla

Maracaibo

VENEZUELA

SOUTH AMERICA

Caracas

Aruba

TRINIDAD

MEXICO

Coatzacoalcos

Puerto Tampico

Yucatan Peninsula

Cancun

Belize

Radiobeacon Reference Map

MORSE CODE FOR IDENTIFICATION OF RADIOBEACONS

A ·–	I ··	Q ––·–	Y –·––	1 ·––––	9 ––––·
B –···	J ·–––	R ·–·	Z ––··	2 ··–––	0 –––––
C –·–·	K –·–	S ···		3 ···––	
D –··	L ·–··	T –		4 ····–	
E ·	M ––	U ··–		5 ·····	
F ··–·	N –·	V ···–		6 –····	
G ––·	O –––	W ·––		7 ––···	
H ····	P ·––·	X –··–		8 –––··	

RADIOBEACONS

The radiobeacon numbers refer to the map on the preceding page (there are no stations for numbers 5 and 21).

Most radiobeacons in the Caribbean are Aero beacons. These are located to best serve the needs of aircraft and should be used with caution. All radiobeacons are subject to interference and refraction errors. As with all aids to navigation in the Caribbean, users are cautioned that radiobeacons have been reported as unreliable.

When the distance to a radiobeacon is greater than 50 miles, a correction is usually applied to the bearing before plotting on a mercator chart. Refer to *Reed's Nautical Companion* for more information on radiobeacons.

BERMUDA

NOTE: The Bermuda radiobeacon is not shown on the radiobeacon reference map.
St. Davids Head, 32 22.0N, 64 38.9W. BSD (–··· ··· –··), 323kHz A2A, 150M.

FLORIDA

NOTE: The Florida radiobeacons are not shown on the radiobeacon reference map.
Jupiter Inlet Light Station, 27 04.6N, 80 07.1W. J (·–––), 294kHz A2A, 110M.
Miami, 25 44.0N, 80 09.6W. U (··–), 322kHz A2A, 100M.

BAHAMA ISLANDS

1) West End International Airport Aero, 26 41.3N, 78 58.7W. ZWE (––·· ·–– ·), 317kHz A2A, 100M.
2) Bimini Islands Aero, 25 42.5N, 79 16.3W. ZBB (––·· –··· –···), 396kHz A2A, 300M.
3) Nassau International Airport Aero, 25 02N, 77 28W. ZQA (––·· ––·– ·–), 251kHz A1A, 240M.
4) Great Inagua Aero, 20 57.6N, 73 40.5W. ZIN (––·· ·· –·), 376kHz A2A, 50M.

CUBA

6) San Julian Aero, 22 05N, 84 13W. USJ (··– ··· ·–––), 402kHz, 155M.
7) Havana Aero, 22 58N, 82 26W. A (·–), 339kHz, 256M.
8) Varder Aero, 23 05N, 81 22W. UVR (··– ···– ·–·), 272kHz A2A, 216M.
9) Cayo Caiman Grande, 22 41.1N, 78 53W. CCG (–·–· –·–· ––·), 290kHz N0N, A2A, 155M.
10) Punta Alegre, 22 22.5N, 78 47.3W. UPA (··– ·–––· ·–), 382kHz A2A, 70M.
11) Guantanamo Bay Aero, 19 54N, 75 10W. NBW (–· –··· ·––), 276.2kHz.
12) Santiago de Cuba Aero, 19 58N, 75 50W. UCU (··– –·–· ··–), 339kHz A2A, 70M.
13) Los Colorados Light Station, 22 02.1N, 80 26.5W. WY (·–– –·––), 298.8kHz N0N,

A2A. Transmits upon request through Central Territorial Hydrographic office (COX41) on 6818kHz during day or 3904kHz at night.

CAYMAN ISLANDS

14) Grand Cayman Aero, 19 17N, 81 23W. ZIY (−−·· ·· −·−−), 344kHz N0N, A2A, 240M.

JAMAICA

15) Montego Bay Aero, 18 30N, 77 55W. MBJ (−− −··· ·−−−) 248kHz N0N, A2A, 150M.

16) Kingston Aero, 17 58N, 76 53W. KIN (−·− ·· −·), 360kHz N0N, A2A, 250M.

HAITI

17) Port-au-Prince Aero, 18 35N, 72 17W. HHP (···· ···· ·−−·), 270kHz A2A, 240M.

DOMINICAN REPUBLIC

18) Punta Caucedo Aero, 18 27N, 69 40W. HIV (···· ·· ···−), 400kHz A2A, 240M.

PUERTO RICO

19) Dorado Aero (16 miles west of San Juan), 18 28N, 66 25 W. DDP (−·· −·· ·−−·), 391kHz N0N, A2A, 365M.

20) Roosevelt Roads Aero, 18 14N, 65 37W. NRR (−· ·−· ·−·), 264kHz N0N, A2A, 115M.

LEEWARD ISLANDS

22) Saint Barthelemy Aero, 17 54N, 62 51W. BY (−··· −·−−), 338kHz A1A, 50M.

23) Antigua (Coolidge) Aero, 17 07.5N, 61 47.6W. ZDX (−−·· −·· −·−·) 369kHz N0N, A2A, 256M.

24) Guadeloupe (Point-à-Pitre) Aero, 16 16N, 61 32W. FXG (··−· −·· −−·), 300kHz N0N, A2A, 250M.

25) Guadeloupe (Marie-Galante/Grand Bourg) Aero, 15 52N, 61 16W. MG (−− −−·), 376kHz A2A, 50M.

26) Dominica Aero, 15 32.8N, 61 18.4W. DOM (−·· −−− −−), 273kHz, 100M.

WINDWARD ISLANDS

27) Martinique (Fort de France) Aero, 14 36N, 61 06W, FXF (··−· −·−− ·−·) 314kHz A2A, 100M.

28) Saint Lucia (Hewanorra) Aero, 13 44N, 60 59W. BNE (−··· −· ·), 305kHz, 100M.

29) Saint Vincent (Arnos Vale) Aero, 13 09N, 61 13W. SV (··· ···−) 403kHz, 143M.

30) Grenada Aero, 12 00.5N, 61 46.8W. GND (−−· −· −··), 362kHz N0N, A2A, 115M.

BARBADOS

31) Barbados (Seawell Aerodome) Aero, 13 04N, 59 30W. BGI (−··· −−· ··), 345kHz N0N, A2A, 256M.

TOBAGO

32) Tobago (Crown Point) Aero, 11 09N, 60 51W. TAB (− ·− −··), 323kHz A2A, 100M.

TRINIDAD

33) Trinidad (Piarco) Aero, 10 36N, 61 26W. POS (·−−· −−− ···), 382kHz N0N A2A, 256M.

VENEZUELA

34) Margarita Aero, 10 55.3N, 63 57.4W. MTA (−− − ·−), 206kHz A2A, 100M.

35) Higuerote Aero, 10 28N, 66 05.7W. HOT (···· −−− −), 353kHz N0N A2A, 240M.

36) La Orchilla, 11 48N, 66 07W. ORC (−−− ·−· −·−·) 320kHZ A2A, 180M.

37) Maiquetia Aero, 10 37N, 66 59W. MIQ (−− ·· −−·−), 292kHz A2A, 130M.

NETHERLANDS ANTILLES

38) Curacao Aero, 12 13N, 69 04W. PJG (·−−· ·−−− −−·), 343kHz N0N, A2A, 150M.

COLOMBIA — ATLANTIC COAST

39) Portete Aero, 12 14.2N, 71 59.7W. PTE (·−−· − ·), 420kHz.

40) Riohacha Aero, 11 33N, 72 54W. RHC (·−· ···· −·−·), 295kHz N0N, A2A, 75M.

41) Isla Tierra Bomba Light Station, 10 20.6N, 75 34.8W. CG (−·−· −−·) period

540s, transmits 60s, silent 120s, repeats (2) 360s, 280kHz A2A, 100M. Transmits at 00 and 30 minutes past each hour.

PANAMA — ATLANTIC COAST

42) Almirante, 9 17.4N, 82 23.6W. B (−···), 290kHz A2A. Transmits continuously between 0500 and1300.

COSTA RICA

43) Limon (TIM), 10 00.1N, 83 01.6W. M (−−), period 600s, 290kHz A2A, 50M. Transmits upon request through Limon (TIM) at 00 and 30 minutes past the hour requested.

SAN ANDRES ISLAND — COLUMBIA

44) Isla San Andres, 12 35.1N, 81 42.3W. SPP (··· ·−−· ·−−·), 387kHz N0N, A2A, 40M.

BELIZE

45) Belize Aero, 17 32N, 88 18W. BZE (−··· −−·· ·), 392kHz N0N, A2A, 192M.

MEXICO

46) Chetumal Aero, 18 30N, 88 19W. CTM (−·−· − −−), 262.5kHz A2A, 256M.

47) Chetumal, 18 30N, 88 24W. XFP (−··− ··−· ·−−·), 293kHz A2A, 100M.

48) Cozumel, 20 28N, 86 59W. XFC (−··− ··−· −·−·), 319kHz A2A, 100M.

49) Cozumel Aero, 20 30.6N, 86 56.6W. CZM (−·−· −−·· −−), 330kHz A2A, 240M.

50) Progreso, 21 16N, 89 43W. XFN (−··− ··−· −·), 306kHz A2A, 100M.

51) Ciudad del Carmen Aero, 18 39.8N, 91 48.6W. CME (−·−· −− ·), 288kHz A2A, 256M.

52) Coatzacoalcos, 18 09.4N, 94 24.3W. XFF (−··− ··−· ··−·), 319kHz A2A, 100M.

53) Vera Cruz, 19 09.3N, 96 08.6W. XFU (−··− ··−· ··−), 296kHz A2A, 100M.

54) Nautla Aero, 20 12N, 96 46W. NAU (−· ·− ··−), 392kHz A2A, 256M.

55) Tuxpan Aero, 20 57N, 97 22W. TUX (− ··− −·−−), 262.5kHz A2A, 256M.

56) Tampico, 22 13.9N, 97 50.8W. XFS (−··− ··−· ···), 287kHz A2A.

RADAR BEACONS (RACONS)

Radar beacons (RACONs) are radar responder devices desgined to produce a distinctive image on the screens of ship's radar sets, thus enabling mariners to determine position with greater certainty than would be possible using a normal radar display alone.

The U.S. Coast Guard operates approximately 50 RACONS off U.S. coasts on maritime navigational aids; they are used to mark and identify points on shore; channel separation, LMB, and other buoys; channel entrances under bridges; and uncharted hazards to navigation (the Morse letter D—dash, dot, dash—has been reserved for this purpose). RACON marks displayed on a radar screen are Morse characters typically of length 1 to 2 miles, always start with a dash, and always extend radially outward from the radar target marked by the beacon. RACON locations and identifications are included in most marine navigational charts and in *Reed's* are noted in individual aid to navigation descriptions.

RACONs should be visible to most commercial shipboard radar systems on vessels 6 to 20 miles from the RACON installation, regardless of radar size. No additional receiving equipment is required. Some precautions are necessary, however, if use of RACONs is desired. Radars that operate in the 10cm band (2900–3100MHz) are usually installed as a second radar on larger vessels and may not respond to RACONs. The Coast Guard now installs dual-band (3cm and 10 cm) RACONs in most locations in U.S. waters. In addition, rain clutter control switches on radars must be switched off or, if necessary, on low to ensure that the RACON is visible. Finally, most RACONs operating in the U.S. are frequency-agile RACONs. Pulse correction circuitry (interference or clutter rejection on some radars) installed on most newer radars, if on, may prevent the radar from displaying some RACONs. This circuitry should be switched off.

LORAN-C STATUS

LORAN-C is of some use in the northern regions of the Caribbean. Groundwave coverage extends from the northern Bahamas to Cuba, to the Gulf of Honduras, and into the Gulf of Mexico along the Mexican coast.

Many users have reported good success in returning to positions where a LORAN reading was previously recorded. Even though the latitude/longitude readouts may be inaccurate, the readings received at a particular location have proven to be repeatable. The best results will be obtained by recording (or storing in the units memory) on-site Time Difference readings.

Keep in mind the possible differences between the NAD-83 Coordinate System and the NAD-27 System used on some Caribbean charts. Differences of over a mile have been reported when comparing latitude/longitude positions in the two systems. Government charts list the coordinate system used.

Skywave coverage is much less accurate and is subject to false readings. Skywave fixes must be used with great caution and should be confirmed with other navigational means. Skywaves may be usable as far southeast as the Virgin Islands; as far south as Maracaibo, Venezuela; and into Columbia, Panama, and Costa Rica. *Reed's* has received reports of usable signals being picked up throughout the Caribbean.

The Southeast U.S. 7980 Chain is in use in this area. It consists of the following broadcast sites:

Malone, FL, 31 00N, 85 10W. 7980 Master.
Grangeville, LA, 30 44N, 90 50W. 7980-W.
Raymondville, TX, 26 32N, 97 50W. 7980-X.
Jupiter, FL, 27 02N, 80 07W. 7980-Y.
Carolina Beach, NC, 34 04N, 77 55W. 7980-Z.

For current status information call the Coordinator of Chain Operations (COCO) in Malone, FL (205-899-5225).

For best use of LORAN-C in the Caribbean you should obtain charts with a LORAN grid overlay. Increased position accuracy is possible by plotting LORAN Time Differences on these charts. The latitude/longitude conversion programs on many LORAN sets have been found to be much less accurate in these waters than in the continental U.S.

GPS STATUS

As of June 8, 1994, the Global Positioning System (GPS) has reached initial operational capability. The GPS constellation consists of 25 satellites. Selective availability (SA) is on, offering approximately 100-meter accuracy.

Keep in mind the possible differences between the NAD-83 Coordinate System and the NAD-27 System used on some Caribbean charts. Differences of over a mile have been reported when comparing latitude/longitude positions in the two systems. Government charts will list the coordinate system used, and your GPS unit should be adjusted accordingly.

Differential GPS users are advised that the experimental DGPS reference stations are located in the NAD-83 Coordinate System. All users must use charts updated to NAD-83/WGS-84 to receive acceptable position results from DGPS.

For more information on GPS and the latest system status, contact the U.S. Coast Guard's Global Positioning Information Center (GPSIC): Commanding Officer, U.S. Coast Guard NAVCEN (Navigation Information Center), 7323 Telegraph Rd, Alexandria, VA 22310-3998. GPSIC watchstanders are available 24 hours a day to handle telephone, fax, and mail inquiries (phone, 703-313-5900; fax, -5920). A 24-hour voice recording (703-313-5907) provides access to a 90-second message of current status. Forecast outages, historical outages, and other changes in GPS are included as time permits.

A computer bulletin board system (BBS) provides GPS information such as GPS status messages, satellite almanacs, local Notices to Mariners, and general radionavigation information. Connection to the bulletin board can be made via phone (703-313-5910; handles speeds of 300–14,400bps; communications parameters: 8 data bits, no parity, 1 stop bit [8N1], aynchronous comms, full duplex), via SprintNet (#311020201328; users must set up their own accounts to access SprintNet), or via Internet (indirect, via the FedWorld BBS at Internet address "fedworld.gov"; from FedWorld, take gateway 54 to the GPSIC BBS).

The GPSIC also disseminates safety GPS Advisory Broadcast Messages through USCG broadcast stations. These may be heard by listening on VHF-FM voice, HF-SSB voice, and NAVTEX broadcasts. The broadcasts provide GPS users in the marine environment with the current status of the GPS satellite constellation, as well as any system outages that could affect GPS navigational accuracy. GPSIC also updates GPS information on the DMA NAVINFONET Database. Users must register off-line before they are allowed to use

NAVINFONET. To register, contact: Navigation Division, St D 44, DMA Hydrographic/Topographic Center, 4600 Sangamore Rd, Bethesda, MD 20816-5003.

Radio station WWV also broadcasts GPS status and outage reports at 14 and 15 minutes past the hour on 2.5, 5, 10, 15, and 20 MHz. WWVH broadcasts these reports at 43 and 44 minutes past the hour on 2.5, 5, 10, and 15 MHz. These reports are announced during the 40-second interval between time ticks. For more information on the WWV and WWVH time and weather broadcasts, see Chapter 5, Communications and Weather Services.

ELECTRONIC AIDS

COMMUNICATION & WEATHER SERVICES

SERVICES

CONTACTING THE U.S. COAST GUARD

In coastal waters of the United States, Puerto Rico, and the Virgin Islands, vessels may contact the Coast Guard on VHF channel 16. Channel 16 may be used only for distress and calling. Routine radio checks on this frequency are prohibited. After initial contact on channel 16 you will usually be asked to switch to channel 22A or channel 12.

The international hailing and distress frequency is 2182kHz in the medium-frequency band. This frequency is monitored by all Coast Guard stations, any vessel equipped with the proper equipment while underway, and many Coast Stations. After initial contact on 2182kHz you will usually be asked to switch to 2670kHz, which is the U.S. Coast Guard working frequency for weather broadcasts, Notices to Mariners, and marine safety broadcasts.

In August 1993, all United States Coast Guard communication stations and cutters discontinued watchkeeping on the distress frequency 500kHz and ceased all Morse code services in the medium-frequency radiotelegraphy band. More efficient telecommunication systems are now available to provide mariners with options for initiating or relaying distress alerts and passing and receiving maritime safety information. These options include INMARSAT, radio telex (SITOR), MF/HF single-sideband and VHF radiotelephone, satellite EPIRBS, INMARSAT Safetynet, NAVTEX and HF NAVTEX (SITOR).

NAVTEX broadcasts include the same Notice to Mariners, weather, search and rescue, and fixed fishing gear location products that have been provided by the MF Morse broadcasts. Distress and other calls to any U.S. Coast Guard communication station can also be made on the first four high-frequency single-sideband radiotelephone channels listed below in the section "Contact and Long-Range Liaison." Meteorological broadcasts are also made on these channels.

These options are believed to provide sufficient redundancy to ensure that adequate distress and safety communication capabilities are available.

EMERGENCY MEDICAL ADVICE

Contact the U.S. Coast Guard on 2182kHz or on one of the high-frequency channels listed below. In addition, High Seas Radiotelephone and Coastal Marine Operators can transfer emergency calls to the nearest Coast Guard station. There are no charges when the ship states the call is an emergency involving the safety of life or property at sea.

CONTACT AND LONG RANGE LIASON

The U.S. Coast Guard monitors the following frequencies as part of the CALL (Contact and Long Range Liason) system. Allow at least one minute for a response before switching channels. These frequencies are also used for voice weather broadcasts, navigation warnings, and medical communications. The Coast Guard monitors many channels at once and may not be able to respond immediately.

Channel	Transmit	Receive
424	4134kHz	4426kHz
601	6200kHz	6501kHz
816	8240kHz	8764kHz
1205	12242kHz	13089kHz
1625	16432kHz	17314kHz

VOICE RADIO BROADCASTS

NOTE: Most times in this section are in UTC (Universal Coordinated Time), which for all practical purposes is the same as GMT (Greenwich Mean Time).

NOAA Weather Radio operates VHF-FM radio stations on frequencies of 162.55, 162.40 and 162.475 MHz. These stations provide continuous weather broadcasts, including both regional and local weather. Broadcast tapes are generally updated every three hours during the day and at least every six hours.

Broadcasts vary, but generally include the following information:
1) Marine forecasts and warnings for coastal waters out to 60 miles

2) Offshore waters forecast for waters 60 to 250 miles from land
3) State forecasts and local forecasts
4) Selected weather observations from the Coast Guard, buoys, and other stations.

Whenever severe weather warnings are necessary, the tape is updated and the transmission devoted to "up-to-the-minute" information on storm dangers.

Outside the continental United States NOAA weather broadcasts are transmitted from Puerto Rico and the U.S. Virgin Islands. Bermuda, the Bahamas, and the British Virgin Islands have local VHF broadcasts as well.

WX-1: 162.55MHz
WX-2: 162.40MHz
WX-3: 162.475MHz

The United States Coast Guard also transmits navigation information on medium frequency (usually 2670.0kHz). The broadcast will be announced on 2182kHz and VHF channel 16 before commencing.

Coast Guard broadcasts usually include Notices to Mariners, marine warnings, hurricane information and weather. The Coast Guard's high-seas weather information is transmitted via station NMN (Chesapeake Bay, Virgina). For many mariners in the Caribbean, this is the best source of complete weather data.

Coast Stations should respond to calls on the international hailing and distress frequencys: VHF channel 16 or 2182kHz. These stations include pilots, port authorities, and public correspondence stations. The latter can be used for making telephone calls. Most stations monitoring 2182kHz also respond to calls on VHF channel 16. A partial list of coast stations follows; *Reed's* welcomes any additions to this material.

Commercial broadcast stations are listed below after weather broadcasts and Coast Stations listings. Whenever possible, English-language stations are listed in those countries where the predominant language is not English. Schedules and frequencies are subject to frequent change.

*Stations of particular interest to boaters are preceded by an asterix (*).

WWV

*MARINE STORM WARNINGS for the North Atlantic Ocean are broadcast by station WWV. They follow the regular time announcements at 8 and 9 minutes after the hour. Frequencies are 2500, 5000, 10000, 15000, and 20000 kHz. See the section "Time Signals" later in this chapter for more information on station WWV.

The National Weather Service issues warning updates at 0500, 1100, 1700, and 2300 UTC. The updates are announced at the next broadcast following time of issue. Topics include locations of storm centers, low-pressure systems, and hurricanes and their predicted positions for the next 12 to 24 hours.

PORTSMOUTH, VA

*Call sign NMN
U.S. Coast Guard, Chesapeake Bay, Virginia

NMN provides the most complete offshore weather information available in this region. Broadcasts include forecasts and a synopsis for New England, the West Central North Atlantic, the Southwest North Atlantic (including the Bahamas), the Gulf of Mexico, and the Caribbean.

0400, 0530, 1000 UTC on 4426.0, 6501.0, and 8764.0kHz
1130, 1600 UTC on 6501.0, 8764.0, and 13089.0kHz
1730 UTC on 8764.0, 13089.0, and 17314.0kHz.
2200 and 2330 UTC on 6501.0, 8764.0, and 13089.0kHz

VOICE OF AMERICA

Voice of America
330 Independence Avenue SW
Washington, DC 20547
202-619-2538

Directed to the Caribbean:
0000 to 0100 UTC on 930, 6130, 9455, and 11695 kHz
0100 to 0200 UTC on 5995, 6130, 7405, 9455, 9775, 11580, 15120, and 15205 kHz
0200 to 0300 UTC on 930kHz
1000 to 1100 UTC on 930, 7405, 9590, 11915, and 15120 kHz

SERVICES

1100 to 1200 UTC on 7405, 9590, 11915, and 15120 kHz

1200 to 1230 UTC on 930kHz

1700 to 1730 UTC on 930kHz

2100 to 2200 UTC on 930kHz

Directed to the American Republics (South America):

0000 to 0030 UTC on 5995, 7405, 9775, 11580, 15120, and 15205 kHz

0030 to 0100 UTC on 5995, 7405, 9775, 11580, 15120, and 15205 kHz.

0100 to 0200 UTC on 5995, 6130, 7405, 9455, 9775, 11580, 15120, and 15205 kHz.

0200 to 0400 UTC on 1530 and 1580 Tuesday through Saturday (English language)

0300 to 0400 UTC on 1530 and 1580 Sunday and Monday (English language)

Directed to northern Central America:

0030 to 0200 UTC on 1530 and 1580kHz

0100 to 0200 UTC on 930, 5995, 6130, 7405, 9455, 9775, 11580, 15120, and 15205kHz

0200 to 0230 UTC on 5995, 7405, 9775, 11580, 15120, and 15205kHz Tuesday through Saturday

BBC WORLD SERVICE

British Broadcasting Corporation
World Service
Bush House
London, WC2B 4PH, England
71-257-2875

Directed to the Caribbean:

0000 to 0330 UTC on 7325kHz

0020 to 0230 UTC on 9590kHz

0300 to 0330 UTC on 930kHz

0500 to 0820 UTC on 9640kHz

1100 to 1200 UTC on 930kHz

1200 to 1400 UTC on 15220kHz

1400 to 1620 UTC on 17840kHz

1600 to 1620 UTC on 930kHz

1800 to 1830 UTC on 930kHz

2100 to 0600 UTC on 5975kHz

2200 to 0330 UTC on 9915kHz

Directed to Central America and Mexico:

0000 to 0630 UTC on 5975kHz

0000 to 0430 UTC on 7325 and 9915 kHz

0030 to 0230 UTC on 9590kHz

0500 to 0630 UTC on 9640kHz

1100 to 1400 UTC on 15220kHz

1400 to 1615 UTC on 17840kHz

2300 to 2400 UTC on 5975, 7325, and 9915 kHz

BERMUDA

WEATHER

*Call sign: ZBM,** Bermuda Harbour Radio, St. Georges. VHF channel 07 at 0900 Local Time. VHF channel 27 and 2582kHz at 1235 and 2035 UTC

COAST STATIONS

Call sign: ZBM, Bermuda Harbour Radio, St. Georges. Stands by on VHF channel 16 and 2182kHz

Call sign: VRT, Bermuda Radio, Public Correspondence. VHF 16, switch to VHF channels 26 and 28

GENERAL BROADCAST STATIONS

ZBM, 1340kHz 1kW, FM 89.1MHz.

ZFB, 1230kHz 1kW, FM 94.9MHz.

VSB, 1160kHz, 1280kHz, 1450kHz 1kW, FM 106.2MHz

NORTHERN FLORIDA

WEATHER

Call sign: NMA-10, Mayport, U.S. Coast Guard. 0015 and 1215 UTC on VHF channel 22A. 0620 and 1820 UTC on 2670.0kHz

Call sign: KHB-39, Jacksonville, WX-1

Call sign: WXJ-60, Gainesville, WX-3

Call sign: KIH-26, Daytona Beach, WX-2

Call sign: KIH-63, Orlando, WX-3

Call sign: WXJ-70, Melbourne, WX-1

Call sign: KEC-50, West Palm Beach, WX-3

FT. LAUDERDALE, FL

WEATHER

*Call sign: W0M,** AT&T Coast Station. 1300 and 2300 UTC on 4363.0, 8722.0, 13092.0, 17242.0, and 22738.0 kHz

MIAMI, FL

WEATHER

Call sign: KHB-34, Miami, WX-1

Call sign: NCF, U.S. Coast Guard. 1230 and 2230 UTC on VHF channel 22A. 0350 and 1550 UTC on 2670.0kHz

KEY WEST, FL

WEATHER

Call sign: WXJ-95, Key West, WX-2

Call sign: NOK, U.S. Coast Guard. 1200 and 2200 UTC on VHF channel 22A

ST. PETERSBURG, FL
WEATHER
Call sign: NMA-21, U.S. Coast Guard. 1300 and 2300 UTC on VHF channel 22A. 0320 and 1420 UTC on 2670.0kHz

PANAMA CITY, FL
WEATHER
Call sign: NOQ-7, U.S. Coast Guard. 1035, 1635, and 2235 UTC on VHF channel 22A. 1005, 1205, 1605, and 2205 UTC on 2670.0kHz

MOBILE, AL
WEATHER
Call sign: NOQ, U.S. Coast Guard. 1020, 1220, 1620, and 2220 UTC on VHF channel 22A. 1020, 1220, 1620, and 2220 UTC on 2670.0kHz
Call sign: WLO, Mobile Coast Station. 0000, 0600, 1200, and 1800 UTC on 4369.0, 8788.0, 13110.0, 17362.0, and 22804.0kHz.

NEW ORLEANS, LA
WEATHER
Call sign: NMG-2, U.S. Coast Guard. 0100 and 1550 UTC on 432kHz. 1035, 1235, 1635, and 2235 UTC on VHF channel 22A and 2670.0kHz.

GALVESTON, TX
WEATHER
Call sign: NOY, U.S. Coast Guard. 1045, 1245, 1645 and 2245 UTC on VHF channel 22A. 1050, 1250, 1650, and 2250 UTC on 2670.0kHz.

CORPUS CHRISTI, TX
WEATHER
Call sign: NOY-8, U.S. Coast Guard. 1040, 1240, 1640, and 2240 UTC on VHF channel 22A and 2670.0kHz.

BAHAMAS
WEATHER
Call sign: C6N, Nassau. VHF channel 27 every even hour
*Radio Bahamas, 810 kHz 1kW, 1240kHz 1kW,1540kHz 20kW, FM 107.1MHz, FM 107.9MHz. Weather at 1230 and 2330 UTC and with the news on the hour.

COAST STATIONS
Numerous coast stations monitor VHF channel 16 in the Bahamas. Most marinas standing by, and there is always a boater willing to assist within radio range. A partial listing only of some widely used stations follows.

*Call sign: BASRA, Bahamas Air Sea Rescue Association. Contact on VHF channel 16 or 2182kHz
Call sign: Jack Tar, West End Marina. Contact on VHF channel 16
Call sign: Walker's Cay, Walker's Cay Marina. Contact on VHF channel 16.
Call sign: C6X2, Marsh Harbor Public Correspondence. Stands by on 2182kHz.
Call sign: Treasure Cay, Treasure Cay Marina. Contact on VHF channel 16.
Call sign: ZFP-81, Freeport Harbor Control. VHF channel 16 or 2182kHz.
Call sign: Bortow Pilots, Freeport pilots. Contact on VHF channels 6, 10, 13, 14, and 16.
Call sign: Borco Marine, The Bahamas Oil Refining Company, Freeport. Contact on VHF channel 16
Call sign: Cat Cay Club, Cat Cay, Bahamas. Contact on VHF channel 16
Call sign: Chub Cay, Chub Cay Marina. Contact on VHF channel 16
Call sign: Great Harbour Cay Marina, Great Harbour, Berry Islands. Contact on VHF channel 16
Call sign: Nassau Harbor Control. Contact on VHF channels 6, 10, 13, 14 and 16. Stands by on 2182kHz
Call sign: C6N3, Nassau Public Correspondence. VHF channel 27
Call sign: C6N2, Nassau Public Correspondence. Stands by on 2182kHz
Call sign: Wee Watin, Highborne Cay, Exumas. Contact on VHF channel 16
Call sign: Sampson, Sampson Cay, Exumas. Contact on VHF channel 16
Call sign: Stella Maris, Stella Maris Marina, Long Island. Contact on VHF channel 16
Call sign: Morton Salt, Commercial wharf on Great Inagua. Contact on VHF channel 16 or 2182kHz

TURKS AND CAICOS
Caicos Pilots, Contact on VHF channel 16
Call sign: VSI, Grand Turk Public Correspondence. VHF channel 16 or 2182kHz
Cockburn Town Pilots, Grand Turk. Contact on VHF channel 16
Radio Turks and Caicos, 1460kHz 2.5kW
Atlantic Beacon, 1570kHz 50kW
Coral Radio, 89.3MHz, 89.9MHz, 90.5MHz, FM 92.5MHz
WPRT Radio, FM 88.7MHz

SERVICES

CUBA

WEATHER

Call signs: CLT, CLA, Habana. 0105, 1305, 2005 and 2205 UTC on 476kHz and 500kHz. Broadcasts in Spanish

Call sign: CLX, Casa Blanca. 0145 UTC on 3560kHz. 1345, 1700, 1900, 1945, and 2200 on 6995kHz. Broadcasts in Spanish

COAST STATIONS

Call sign: Mariel Practice, Mariel Pilots. Contact on VHF channel 16

Call signs: CLT, CLA, Habana, Public Correspondence. Stands by on 2182kHz

Call sign: Habana Practicos, Habana Pilots. Contact on VHF channels 13 and 16

Call sign: Morro Habana, Habana port signal station. Contact on VHF channels 13, 16, and 68

Call sign: Habana Capitonia, Habana Port Captain. Contact on channels 16 and 68

Call sign: Terminales Contenedores, Container terminal. Contact on VHF channels 16 and 74

Call sign: CLX, Casa Blanca. Stands by on 2182kHz

Call sign: CLW, Cardenas, Public Correspondence. Stands by on 2182kHz

Call sign: CLC2, Isabela de Sagua, Public Correspondence. Stands by on 2182kHz

Isabela de Sagua Pilots. Contact on VHF channel 16

Call sign: CLG-50 Caiman, Old Bahama Channel Traffic Control. Contact on VHF channel 13

Call sign: CLG-60 Confites, Old Bahama Channel Traffic Control. Contact on VHF channel 13

Call sign: CLC3, Caibarien, Public Correspondence. Stands by on 2182kHz

Call sign: CLK, Nuevitas, Public Correspondence. Stands by on 2182kHz

Call sign: CLM4, Guardalabarca, Public Correspondence. Stands by on 2182kHz

Call sign: CLM3, Baracoa, Public Correspondence. Stands by on 2182kHz

Call sign: Guantanamo Port Control, Contact on VHF channel 12

Guantanamo Bay Pilots. Contact on VHF channel 74.

Call sign: CLM, Santiago de Cuba. Stands by on 2182kHz

Call sign: Santiago Practicos, Santiago de Cuba pilots. Contact on VHF channels 13 and 16

Call sign: Castilda Practicos, Golfo De Guancanayabo pilots. Contact on VHF channels 13 and 16

Call sign: CLK2, Santa Cruz del Sur, Public Correspondence. Stands by on 2182kHz

Call sign: CLC, Cienfuegos, Public Correspondence. Stands by on 2182kHz

Call sign: CLT2, Batabano, Public Correspondence. Stands by on 2182kHz

Call sign: CLT3, Nueva Gerona, Public Correspondence. Stands by on 2182kHz

Call sign: CLF3, El Morrillo, Public Correspondence. Stands by on 2182kHz

Call sign: CLF-2, Arroyos de Mantua. Stands by on 2182kHz

GENERAL BROADCASTS

There are dozens of Spanish language broadcast stations, on all segments of the dial.

Radio Taíno, 830kHz 300kW, 1160kHz 300kW. English language from 0100 to 0200, from 0300 to 0430, and from 2000 to 2200 UTC

Radio Habana, Shortwave. English 0000 to 0600 UTC on 11950kHz, 0200 to 0430 UTC on 5965kHz, and 0400 to 0600 UTC on 6180kHz and 11760kHz

AFRTS, Armed Forces Radio, Guantánamo Bay, 1340kHz 0.25kW, FM 102MHz, FM 103MHz.

CAYMAN ISLANDS

Call sign: Cayman Harbor, Cayman Brac Agent. Contact on VHF channel 16

Call sign: Cayman Energy, Cayman Brac operations control. Contact on VHF channel 16

Call sign: Bonito, Cayman Brac pilots. Contact on VHF channel 16

Radio Cayman, 1205kHz 1kW, 1555kHz 10kW, FM 89.9MHz, FM 91.9MHz, FM 105.3MHz

JAMAICA

WEATHER

*Call sign: 6YX, Jamaica Coast Guard. 0130, 1330, 1430, 1830, and 1900 UTC on VHF channel 13. 1330 and 1830 UTC on 2738kHz

COAST STATIONS

Call sign: 6YX, Kingston, Jamaica Coast Guard. Stands by on 2182kHz

Call sign: 6YI, Kingston, Public Correspondence. Stands by on 2182kHz

Kingston Pilots, Contact on VHF channels 11 and 16

Call sign: Silver Spray, Port Esquivel pilots. Contact on VHF channel 16

Port Antonio Pilots. Contact on VHF channel 16

Discovery Bay Pilots. Contact on VHF channel 16

Montego Bay Pilots. Contact on VHF channel 16

GENERAL BROADCASTS

Jamaica Broadcasting Corporation, 560kHz 5kW, 620kHz 5kW, 700kHz 10kW, 750kHz 10kW, 850kHz 10kW, 1090kHz 1kW, FM 91.1MHz, FM 92.1MHz, FM 93.3MHz, FM 97.1MHz, FM 97.3MHz, FM 98.7MHz, FM 99.7MHz, FM 100.3MHz, FM 103.9MHz, FM 105.7MHz. Weather and fishermen's forecast weekdays at 2248 UTC

Radio Jamaica, 550kHz 5kW, 580kHz 10kW, 720kHz 10kW, 770kHz 5kW, FM 90.5MHz, FM 91.5MHz, FM 92.7MHz, FM 92.9MHz, FM 94.5MHz, FM 95.7MHz, FM 98.1MHz, FM 101.3MHz, FM 104.5MHz

Island Broadcasting Services, KLAS, FM 89.3MHz

HAITI
COAST STATIONS

Call sign: MF, Port-au-Prince, Public Correspondence. Stands by on VHF channel 16 and 2182kHz

Port-au-Prince Pilots, Contact on VHF channel 16

Cap Haitién Pilots, Stands by on VHF channel 16

GENERAL BROADCASTS

There are dozens of French and Creole language stations in Haiti. This is a listing of English language broadcasts.

*Radio 4VEH, 1030kHz 10kW. Cap-Haitién. News and weather at 1200 UTC. English from 1100 to 1400 and from 2300 to 2400 UTC

DOMINICAN REPUBLIC

Call sign: HIA, Santo Domingo Piloto, Public Correspondence. Stands by on VHF channel 16 or on 2182kHz

Call sign: HIW 19, San Pedro de Macoris Pilots. Stands by on VHF channel 16 and 2182kHz

Call sign: HIW 20, Puerto de Haina Pilots. Stands by on VHF channel 16 or on 2182kHz

Call sign: HIW 9, Romano Pilots. Stands by on VHF channel 16

Call sign: HIW 8, Puerto Plata Pilots. Stands by on VHF channel 16

There are dozens of Spanish language broadcast stations, on all segments of the dial.

PUERTO RICO
WEATHER

*Call sign: WXJ-69, Marico, WX-1
*Call sign: WXJ-68, San Juan, WX-2
*Call sign: NMR-1, U.S. Coast Guard, San Juan. 1210 and 2210 UTC on VHF channel 22A. 0305 and 1505 UTC on 2670.0kHz
*WOSO, San Juan, 1030kHz 10kW. All English news and talk

COAST STATIONS

Call sign: KRV, Public Correspondence, Ponce Playa. VHF channel 28
Call sign: WHU 645, Public Correspondence, Luquillo. VHF channel 86
Call sign: WCU 243, Public Correspondence, Maricao. VHF channel 27
Call sign: WCT, Public Correspondence, Santurce. VHF channel 26
Call sign: KMD 214, Public Correspondence, San Juan. VHF channel 28

GENERAL BROADCASTS

There are dozens of Spanish language broadcast stations in Puerto Rico, on all segments of the dial. This is a partial list of English broadcasts:

*WOSO, San Juan, 1030kHz 10kW, All English news and talk
WBMJ, San Juan, 1190kHz, 10kW, 0930 to 0300 UTC, English and Spanish religious
WIVV, Vieques, 1370kHz, 5kW, 0925 to 0230 UTC, English and Spanish religious
AFRTS, Armed Forces Radio, U.S. Air Force, 780kHz 0.05kW Aguadilla, 1040kHz 0.05kW San Juan, 1200kHz 0.05kW Roosevelt Roads, 1460kHz

U.S. VIRGIN ISLANDS
WEATHER

*Call sign: WXM-96, St. Thomas, WX-3
*Call sign: WAH, Virgin Islands Radio, St. Thomas. VHF channels 28 and 85 at 0800 and 2000 UTC. 0600, 1400, and 2200 UTC on 2506.0, 4357.0, 4381.0, 6510.0, and 13077.0kHz.

COAST STATIONS

*Call sign: WAH, Virgin Islands Radio, Public Correspondence, St. Thomas. VHF channels 24, 25, 28, 84, 85, 87, and 88. Stands by on 2182kHz. See High Seas Radiotelephone Service

SERVICES

section later in this chapter for more information.

GENERAL BROADCASTS
WSTX, 970kHz 5kW, FM 100.3MHz
WVWI, 1000kHz 5kW
WGOD, 1090kHz 0.25kW, FM 97.9MHz
WRRA, 1290kHz 0.5kW
WSTA, 1340kHz 1kW
WIUJ, FM 88.9MHz
WDCM, FM 92.3MHz
WAVI, FM 93.5MHz

BRITISH VIRGIN ISLANDS
WEATHER
Call sign: Tortola Radio, VHF channel 27 at 1300 and 1600 UTC

COAST STATIONS
Call sign: Tortola Radio. Contact on VHF channel 16
Tortola Pilots. Contact on VHF channel 16

GENERAL BROADCASTS
ZBVI, 780kHz 10kW. Tortola
Caribbean Broadcasting System, FM 91.7MHz (Z Gold), FM 94.3MHz (The Heat), FM 103.7 (ZROD)

ANGUILLA
Radio Anguilla. 1505kHz 1kW
ZJF-FM. 105MHz
The Caribbean Beacon. 690kHz 15kW, 1610kHz 50kW, FM 100.1MHz

ST. MARTIN
Radiodiffusion Francaise D'Outre-Mer (RFO). FM 99.2MHz. Broadcasts in French
Radio Caraibes International. FM 104.7MHz. Broadcasts in French
Radio St. Martin. FM 95.3MHz. Broadcasts in French and English
Radio Voix Chretiennes de St. Martin. FM 106MHz. Broadcasts in French and English

ST. MAARTEN
Philipsburg Harbor Master. Contact on VHF channel 16

SABA
*Call sign: PJS, Saba Radio, Public Correspondence. This is the main communications service in the Leeward Islands, with a 200-mile range on VHF (its antenna is 3,083 feet above sea level). This area extends from the British Virgin Islands to Antigua. For emergencies Saba Radio is in contact with the U.S. Coast Guard and other rescue agencies. During hurricane season it broadcasts reports as received. Contact the station on VHF channels 16, 26, and 84, seven days a week from 0600 to 2400. The station accepts international phone credit cards (AT&T international charge numbers beginning with 891) or will place collect calls for you. To make shore-to-ship calls, dial 599-46-3402. For more information on Saba Radio's services, call 599-46-3211.

ST. EUSTATIUS
Oranjestad Pilots, Call on VHF channel 16

ST. CHRISTOPHER AND NEVIS
Basseterre Pilots and Port Authorities. Contact on VHF channel 16
Radio ZIZ. 555kHz 20kW, FM 90MHz
Radio Paradise. 825kHz 50kW
Voice of Nevis. 895kHz 10kW

MONTSERRAT
*Radio Antilles. 930kHz 20kw. Marine weather forecasts at 1335 and 2225 UTC. Radio Antilles is a good source of weather information for the Eastern Caribbean.

ANTIGUA AND BARBUDA
COAST STATIONS
*English Harbour Radio V2MA2, Nicholson Yacht Charters. Contact on VHF channel 68 or on 8294.0kHz. Monday through Friday 0900 to 1630 local time, Saturday 0900 until noon
English Harbour Port Authority. Contact on VHF channel 16
Saint John's Harbour Authorities. Contact on VHF channel 16 or 2182kHz
Call sign: Marine Center, Saint John's oil terminal. Contact on VHF channel 16 or 2182kHz

GENERAL BROADCASTS
Antigua and Barbuda Broadcast Service, 620kHz 10Kw
Radio ZDK, 1100kHz 10kW, FM 99.0MHz
Caribbean Radio Lighthouse, 1165kHz 10kW, FM 90.0MHz
BBC Relay Station, 5975 kHz, 6110kHz, 6195kHz, 9640kHz, 15205kHz, 15220kHz
VOA Relay Station, 1580kHz 50kW

GUADELOUPE

Pointe-à-Pitre Pilots. Contact on VHF channel 16
Basse-Terre Port Authority. Contact on VHF channel 16
Radiodiffusion Francaise D'Outre-Mer (RFO). 640kHz 40kW, 1420kHz 5kW, FM 97.0MHz. Broadcasts in French

DOMINICA

Roseau Pilots. Contact on VHF channel 16
Dominica Broadcasting Corporation, 595kHz 10kW, FM 88.1MHz
Gospel Broadcasting Corporation, ZGBC, 740kHz 10kW, FM 102.1MHz

MARTINIQUE

WEATHER
Call sign: FFP, Fort de France. Every odd hour on the half-hour on VHF channels 26 and 27. Every hour, 1218 and 2018 UTC on 435kHz. Every odd hour plus 33 minutes on 2545kHz. Broadcasts in French

COAST STATIONS
Call sign: FFP, Fort de France, Public Correspondence. Stands by on 2182kHz
Fort de France Port Authorities. Contact on VHF channels 13 and 16

GENERAL BROADCASTS
Société Nationale de Radio-Télévision Française d'Outre Mer. 1310kHz 20kW, FM 92MHz, FM 95MHz. Broadcasts in French
Radio Caraibes International. 1090kHz 20kW, FM 89.9MHz, FM 92.5MHz, FM 98.7MHz, FM 106.1MHz. Broadcasts in French

ST. LUCIA

COAST STATIONS
Call sign: Vieux Fort Lighthouse, Vieux Fort Port Officials. Contact on VHF channel 16 or 2182kHz
Call sign: Hess St. Lucia, Oil terminal in Grande Cul de Sac Bay. Contact on VHF channel 16
Call sign: Castries Lighthouse, Port Castries port authorities. Contact on VHF channel 16 or 2182kHz

GENERAL BROADCASTS
Radio St. Lucia, 660kHz 10kW, FM 97.3MHz, 99.5MHz, 107.3MHz. In English and Creole
Radio Caribbean International. 840kHz 20kW, FM 95.5MHz, FM 99.1MHz, FM 101.1MHz. In English and Creole

ST. VINCENT AND THE GRENADINES

Call sign: ZQS. Kingstown port authorities. Contact on VHF channel 16 and 2182kHz
St. Vincent and the Grenadines National Broadcasting Corporation, 705kHz 10kW

GRENADA

Call sign: J3YA, Saint George Port Control. Contact on VHF channel 16
Call sign: J3YB, Saint George Pilots. Contact on VHF channel 16
Radio Grenada. 535kHz 20kW

BARBADOS

COAST STATIONS
Call sign: 8PA, Bridgetown, Port Signal Station. Stands by on VHF channels 12 and 16. Monitors 2182kHz
Call sign: 8PO, Public Correspondence. Stands by on 2182kHz

GENERAL BROADCASTS
Caribbean Broadcasting. 900kHz 10kW, FM 98.1MHz
Radio Liberty. FM 98.1MHz
Barbados Rediffusion. 790kHz 20kW, FM 104.1MHz
Voice of Barbados. 790kHz
Yess Ten Four. FM 104.1MHz
Barbados Broadcasting. FM 90.7MHz, FM 102.1MHz

TRINIDAD AND TOBAGO

WEATHER
Call sign: 9YL, North Post. 1340 and 2040 UTC on VHF channels 24, 25, 26, and 27. 1250 and 1850 UTC on 3165kHz. 2300 UTC on 6470.5kHz. 0100, 0600, 0900, 1300, 1500, 1730, and 2130 on 8441kHz. 1330 and 2050 on 12885kHz. 1200 and 1530 UTC on 17184.8kHz

COAST STATION
Call sign: 9YL, North Post, Public Correspondence. Stands by on 2182kHz

GENERAL BROADCASTS
National Broadcasting Service. 610kHz 50kW, FM 98.9MHz, 100.0MHz
Trinidad Broadcasting Company. 730kHz 20kW, FM 91.1MHz, FM 95.1MHz, FM 105.1MHz

VENEZUELA

Call sign: YVG, La Guaira, Public Correspondence. Stands by on 2182kHz

SERVICES

Puerto Cabello Pilots. Monitor VHF channel 16

Puerto El Guamache, Isla de Margarita. Contact on VHF channel 16

Call sign: Meneven Puerto La Cruz, Puerto La Cruz pilots. Contact on VHF channel 16

Call sign: San Carlos Pilot, Pilots for Lago De Maracaibo. Contact on VHF channel 16

Puerto Cabello Pilots. Contact on VHF channel 16

There are hundreds of Spanish language general broadcast stations, on all segments of the dial.

BONAIRE

WEATHER

***Trans World Radio PJB,** 800kHz 500kW. News and weather in English 1230 UTC weekdays, 1300 UTC Saturday and Sunday, and 0300 UTC

COAST STATIONS

Pilots. Contact Curacao Coast Radio PJC
Goto Oil Terminal. Contact on VHF channel 16

GENERAL BROADCASTS

Trans World Radio PJB. See above.
Trans World Radio, Shortwave. English 0255 to 0430 UTC on 11930kHz, 0300 to 0430 UTC on 9535 kHz, and 1055 to 1330 UTC on 11815kHz and 15345kHz

CURACAO

Call sign: Fort Nassau, Port Operations, VHF channels 12 and 16

Call sign: PJC, Curacao Coast Radio, Public Correspondence. Stands by on 2182kHz

PJC-9, 1500kHz 3kW, FM 105.1MHz. Dutch and some English

PJL-3, 1100kHz 0.25kW. Voice of America News at 1800 UTC. Sunday religious broadcast in English from 1200 to 1400 and 2200 to 2300 UTC

Radio Korsou, FM 93.9MHz, FM 101.1MHz. English Tuesdays at 0000 UTC

ARUBA

Sint Nicolaas Baai Pilots. Contact on VHF channels 14 and 16

Oranjestad Port Radio. Contact on VHF channel 16

Radio Victoria. 960kHz 10kW, FM 93.1MHz. Dutch

Radio 1270. 1270kHz 1.5kW. Dutch

Voice of Aruba. 1320kHz 1kW, FM 89.9MHz. Dutch

Radio Kelkboom. 1440kHz 1kW, FM 106.7MHz. Dutch

Radio Caruso Booy. FM 97.9MHz. Dutch

Radio Carina. FM 103.5MHz. Dutch

COLOMBIA

Call sign: HKB, Barranquilla, Public Correspondence. Stands by on 2182kHz

Call sign: Puerto Bolivar, Port authorities. Contact on VHF channels 6 and 16

Cartagena Pilots. Contact on VHF channels 11 and 16

There are hundreds of Spanish language general broadcast stations, on all segments of the dial.

PANAMA

Puerto De Bahia De Las Minas Pilots. Contact on VHF channel 16

Puerto Cristobal Signal Station. Contact on VHF channel 12

Call sign: HPN, Canal Radio Station, Balboa. All vessels must communicate with the Port Captain through HPN. Other than emergency traffic and routine bridge-to-bridge VHF communications, no vessels in transit through the Canal shall communicate with any other station, local or distant. Contact on VHF channel 16 or 2182kHz

Call sign: HPP, Public Correspondence. Stands by on 2182kHz

There are dozens of Spanish language general broadcast stations, on all segments of the dial.

Call sign: Rambala Control, Oil terminal in Laguna de Chiriqui. Contact on VHF channel 16

Call sign: Chiriqui Grande Pilots, Laguna de Chiriqui. Contact on VHF channel 16

ACA20, 790kHz 10kW. AFRTS Armed Forces Radio, Southern Command Network, Ft. Clayton, Canal Zone

COSTA RICA

Call sign: TIM, Limon, Public Correspondence. Stands by on 2182kHz

Limon Pilots. Contact on VHF channel 16. There are dozens of Spanish language general broadcast stations, on all segments of the dial.

AWR, shortwave 5030kHz, 5970kHz, 6150kHz, 9725kHz, 11870kHz, 13750kHz and 15460kHz 50kW. English from 1100 to 1300 UTC and from 2300 to 0100 UTC. Saturday at 1230 UTC

NICARAGUA

Bluefields Pilots. Contact on VHF channel 16. There are dozens of Spanish language general broadcast stations, on all segments of the dial.

HONDURAS

Puerto Cortes Pilots. Contact on VHF channels 6 and 16
There are dozens of Spanish language general broadcast stations, on all segments of the dial.
La Voz Evangélica. 810kHz 1kW, 1310kHz 1kW, 1390kHz 10kW. Shortwave 4820.2kHz. English from 0300 to 0500 Monday. Religious

GUATEMALA

GENERAL BROADCASTS

There are dozens of Spanish language general broadcast stations, on all segments of the dial.
Radio Cultural. 730kHz 10kW. English from 0300 to 0430 UTC and Sundays from 2345 to 0430 UTC
Unión Radio. 1330kHz 10 kW. English from 0200 to 0400 UTC

BELIZE

WEATHER

*Radio Belize. 830kHz 10kW, 910kHz 1kW, 930kHz 1kW, 940kHz 1kW, FM 88.9MHz, FM 91.1MHz. News and weather in English at 0100, 0300, 1300, 1500, 1700, 1830, 2100, and 2300 UTC

COAST STATIONS

Belize Pilot Station. Stands by on 2182kHz.
Belize Customs Control. Stands by on 2750kHz
Belize City Pilots. Contact on VHF channel 16

GENERAL BROADCASTS

Radio Belize. See above
British Forces Broadcast Service. FM 93.1MHz, FM 99.1MHz
VOA Relay Station. 1530kHz 50kW, 1580kHz 50kW

MEXICO

WEATHER

Call sign: XFU, Veracruz. 0400, 1600, and 2100 UTC on 451kHz and 8656kHz

COAST STATIONS

Call sign: XFP, Chetumal, Public Correspondence. Stands by on 2182kHz
San Miguel de Cozumel Pilot. Contact on VHF channel 16
Call sign: XFC, Cozumel, Public Correspondence. Stands by on 2182kHz
Cayo Arcas Terminal. Contact on VHF channel 09
Call sign: XFN, Progreso, Public Correspondence. Stands by on 2182kHz

Call sign: XFF, Coatzacoalcos, Public Correspondence. Stands by on 2182kHz
Call sign: XFU, Puerto Veracruz, Public Correspondence. Stands by on 2182kHz
Call sign: XFS, Tampico, Public Correspondence. Stands by on 2182kHz

There are hundreds of Spanish language general broadcast stations on all segments of the dial.

NAVTEX

NAVTEX service of Maritime Safety Information (MSI) broadcasting under the Worldwide Navigational Warning Service is operational worldwide. NAVTEX is an internationally coordinated method of broadcasting distress, urgent, and safety messages and weather forecasts and warnings using small, low-cost printing receivers designed to be installed in the pilothouse of a vessel.

A series of coast stations transmit NAVTEX radio teletype safety messages on medium frequency 518kHz during preset time slots so as to minimize interference with one another. Routine messages are normally broadcast four to six times daily. Urgent messages are broadcast on receipt, provided that an adjacent station is not transmitting. The coverage of NAVTEX is reasonably continuous out to 200 nautical miles from the transmitting station. Interference from or receipt of stations farther away occasionally occurs at night. In the U.S., the Coast Guard is the responsible agency for NAVTEX operation.

Each NAVTEX message broadcast contains a four-character header describing identification of station, message content, and message serial number. The header allows NAVTEX receivers to screen incoming messages, inhibiting those that have been previously received or are of a category of no interest to the user, and print the rest on adding-machine-sized paper. NAVTEX not only provides marine information previously available only to those knowledgable in Morse code, but also allows any mariner who cannot man a radio full time (such as commercial fishermen) to receive safety information at any hour immediately. USCG voice broadcasts, often of more inshore and harbor information, on VHF channel 22A remain unaffected by NAVTEX.

SERVICES

To receive these broadcasts of notices and marine weather mariners need a special NAV-TEX receiver. Mariners who do not have NAV-TEX receivers but have SITOR radio equipment can also receive these broadcasts by operating it in the FEC mode and tuning to 518kHz.

Bermuda Harbour Radio ZBM, Identifier B. 0100, 0600, 1300, and 1900 UTC
Portsmouth, VA, NMN, Identifier N. 0130, 0530, 0930, 1330, 1730, and 2130 UTC
Miami, FL, NMA, Identifier A. 0000, 0400, 0800, 1200, 1600, and 2000 UTC
New Orleans, LA, NMG, Identifier G. 0300, 0700, 1100, 1500, 1900, and 2300 UTC
San Juan, PR, NMR, Identifier R. 0200, 0600, 1000, 1400, 1800, and 2200 UTC

WEATHER FACSIMILE

For best reception subtract 1.9kHz from the assigned frequencies. See your weather facsimile instructions for more information.

MARSHFIELD, MA

Call sign: NMF
Continuous on 6340.5 and 12750.0kHz

Time	UTC	Subject
0301	1730	Header
0305		Broadcast schedule
0315		Satellite Imagery
0325,	1735	Surface Analysis (Part I)
0338,	1748	Surface Analysis (Part II)
0351		500mb Analysis
	1835	Header
0401,	1840	Surface Analysis (Part I)
0414,	1853	Surface Analysis (Part II)
	1906	500mb Analysis
	1916	Sea State Analysis
	1926	500mb Prognosis, 96-Hour
	1936	Surface Prognosis, 96-Hour
	1946	Gulf Stream Analysis
0800	2015	Header
0805	2020	Weather Depiction Prognosis, 24-Hour
0815,	2030	Wind Wave Prognosis, 24-Hour
0825,	2040	Surface Prognosis, 48-Hour

Time	UTC	Subject
0845,	2100	Sea State Prognosis, 48-Hour
0835,	2050	500mb Prognosis, 48-Hour
0905		Header
0910		Legend
0920		Request for Comments
	2110	Satellite Imagery (Annotated)
0930,	2120	Surface Analysis (Part I)
0943,	2133	Surface Analysis (Part II)
0956		Satellite Imagery (Annotated)
1006		Gulf Stream Analysis (Part I)
1016		Gulf Stream Analysis (Part II)
1026	2146	Surface Analysis (Part I)
1039,	2159	Surface Analysis (Part II)

MOBILE, AL

Call sign: WLO
Continuous on 6852.0kHz (5kw)
1200 to 0000 UTC on 2572.0 and 9157.0kHz (both 5kw)

Time	UTC	Subject
0230,	1430	Gulf of Mexico Surface Analysis
	1500	Broadcast schedule
0735,	1910	United States Surface Analysis
0920,	2020	Gulf of Mexico Surface Analysis
	2100	Gulf of Mexico and Atlantic Sea Surface Temperature Analysis (Monday, Wednesday, Friday); Gulf of Mexico and Atlantic Gulf Stream Flow Analysis (Tuesday, Thursday, Saturday)
1100,	2300	High Seas Forecast
1145,	2345	Gulf of Mexico Surface Prognosis, 18-Hour/36-Hour

This broadcast originates from the National Hurricane Center of the National Weather Service. Gulf Stream Flow charts may not be available during the summer months due to weak isothermal conditions in the Gulf. For additional information about any of these charts, call the National Hurricane Center in Coral Gables, Florida (305-665-6640).

HIGH SEAS RADIOTELEPHONE SERVICE

AT&T High Seas Radiotelephone Service provides two-way voice communication between ships on the high seas or telephones on land, at sea, or in the air. The service is world-wide is scope. Three coast stations provide seven-day-a-week, 24-hour service. Vessel owners must meet a number of licensing requirements before lawfully transmitting any radiotelephone messages. According to FCC regulations, there must be on board: a valid ship's radiotelephone station license; a valid radiotelephone operator's license; and a radio station logbook. All persons using radio-telephones should be thoroughly familiar with approved radio communication procedures and operating features of the equipment.

AT&T COAST STATION WOO

P.O. Box 550
End of Beach Avenue
Manahawkin, NJ 08050
Technical information: (609) 597-2201

Digital Selective Calling ID: 00-366-0002

Shore-to-ship calls: 800-SEA-CALL
Individual registration set-up: 800-SEA-CALL
Ship registration set-up: 800-752-0279 or
407-850-4895 (collect)

Cost: $14.98 for the first 3 minutes, $4.98/addi-tional minute or fraction thereof (3-minute minimum charge per call). You are not charged until the person you request to speak to has come on the line.

Channel	Coast Station Transmit	Ship Station Transmit
232	2558.0kHz	2166.0kHz
242	2450.0	2366.0
410	4384.0	4092.0
411	4387.0	4095.0
416	4402.0	4110.0
422	4420.0	4128.0
808	8740.0	8216.0
811	8749.0	8225.0
815	8761.0	8237.0
826	8794.0	8270.0

Channel	Coast Station Transmit	Ship Station Transmit
1203	13083.0	12236.0
1210	13104.0	12257.0
1211	13107.0	12260.0
1228	13158.0	12311.0
1605	17254.0	16372.0
1620	17299.0	16417.0
1626	17317.0	16435.0
1631	17332.0	16450.0
2201	22696.0	22000.0
2205	22708.0	22012.0
2210	22723.0	22027.0
2236	22801.0	22105.0

Voice Broadcasts
Traffic lists broadcast on the hour every even hour UTC on channels 411 and 811

Weather broacasts from the National Weather Service: On channels 411 and 811 at 1200 and 2200 UTC

SITOR/Digital Selective Calling Data Broadcasts
Traffic list schedule pending FCC approval, on ITU channels 405, 629, 839, and 1307
Weather at 20 minutes past every even hour UTC

Morse Data Broadcasts
Transmit traffic lists continuously on channel 811

AT&T COAST STATION WOM

1340 N.W. 40th Avenue
Fort Lauderdale, FL 33313
Technical Information: 305-587-0910 (collect)

Digital Selective Calling ID: 00-366-0001

Shore-to-ship calls: 800-SEA-CALL
Individual registration set-up: 800-SEA-CALL
Ship registration set-up: 800-752-0279 or
407-850-4895 (collect)

Cost: $14.98 for the first 3 minutes, $4.98/addi-tional minute or fraction thereof (3-minute minimum charge per call). You are not charged until the person you request to speak to has come on the line.

Channel	Coast Station Transmit	Ship Station Transmit
209	2490.0kHz	2031.5kHz
221	2514.0	2118.0
245	2566.0	2390.0
247	2442.0	2406.0

SERVICES

Channel	Coast Station Transmit	Ship Station Transmit
403	4363.0	4071.0
412	4390.0	4098.0
417	4405.0	4113.0
423	4423.0	4131.0
802	8722.0	8198.0
805	8731.0	8207.0
810	8746.0	8222.0
814	8758.0	8234.0
825	8791.0	8267.0
831	8809.0	8285.0
1206	13092.0	12245.0
1208	13098.0	12251.0
1209	13101.0	12254.0
1215	13119.0	12272.0
1223	13143.0	12296.0
1230	13164.0	12317.0
1601	17242.0	16360.0
1609	17266.0	16384.0
1610	17269.0	16387.0
1611	17272.0	16390.0
1616	17287.0	16405.0
2215	22738.0	22042.0
2216	22741.0	22045.0
2222	22759.0	22063.0

Voice Broadcasts
Traffic lists on channels 403, 802, 1206, 1601, and 2215 on the hour every odd hour UTC

Weather from the National Weather Service: On channels 403, 802, 1206, 1601, and 2215 at 1300 and 2300 UTC and on request at no charge. Also , hurricane warnings broadcast with every traffic list when they are in effect

Sitor/Digital Selective Calling broadcasts
Pending FCC approval

AT&T COAST STATION KMI

P.O. Box 9
Inverness, CA 94937
Technical information: 415-669-1055 (collect)

Digital Selective Calling ID: 00-366-0000

Shore-to-ship calls: 800-SEA-CALL
Individual registration set-up: 800-SEA-CALL
Ship registration set-up: 800-752-0279 or
407-850-4895 (collect)

Cost: $14.98 for the first 3 minutes, $4.98/additional minute or fraction thereof (3-minute minimum charge per call). You are not

charged until the person you request to speak to has come on the line.

Channel	Coast Station Transmit	Ship Station Transmit
242	2450.0kHz	2003.0kHz
248	2506.0	2406.0
401	4357.0	4065.0
416	4402.0	4110.0
417	4405.0	4113.0
804	8728.0	18204.0
809	8743.0	8219.0
822	8782.0	8258.0
1201	13077.0	12230.0
1202	13080.0	12233.0
1203	13083.0	12236.0
1229	13161.0	12314.0
1602	17245.0	16363.0
1603	17248.0	16366.0
1624	17311.0	16429.0
2214	22735.0	22039.0
2223	22762.0	22066.0
2228	22777.0	22081.0
2236	22801.0	22105.0

Voice Broadcasts
Traffic lists on channels 416 and 1203 every hours on the hour

Weather from the National Weather Service: On channels 416 and 1203 at 0000 and 1200 UTC

SITOR/DSC Data Broadcasts
Frequency: 4215.8, 6324.8, and 12628.3, and 16868.3kHz
Traffic lists on the hour (pending FCC approval)
Weather at 20 minutes past every odd hour UTC

COAST STATION WLO

Coast Station WLO
Mobile Marine Radio, Inc.
7700 Rinla Avenue
Mobile, AL 36619

Technical information, SITOR, telegrams, telex, services: 800-633-1312 or 205-666-5110

Shore-to-ship calls: dial "O" and ask for the Mobile Alabama Marine Operator, or call WLO direct (800-633-1634; 205-666-2998, or 205-666-3555)

Channel	Coast Station Transmit	Ship Station Transmit
205	2572.0kHz	2430.0kHz
405	4369.0	4077.0
414	4396.0	4104.0
419	4411.0	4119.0
607	6519.0	6218.0
824	8788.0	8264.0
829	8803.0	8279.0
830	8806.0	8282.0
1212	13110.0	12263.0
1225	13149.0	12302.0
1226	13152.0	12305.0
1607	17260.0	16378.0
1641	17362.0	16480.0
1647	17380.0	16498.0
1807	19773.0	18798.0
2237	22804.0	22108.0

Voice Broadcasts

Traffic lists are broadcast every hour on the hour on channels 405, 824, 1212, 1641, and 2237

Weather Broadcasts: On channels 405, 824, 1212, 1641, and 2237 at 0000, 0600, 1200, and 1800 UTC

COAST STATION WAH

Virgin Islands Radio
Global Communication Corp.
7843 Mountain Top
St. Thomas, VI 00802

Shore-to-ship calls and information:
809-776-8282 or 800-LEEWARD (800-533-9273);
809-774-8204, fax

Cost $1.25/minute for radio time (3-minute minimum) plus the usual telephone rates. Forms of payment include: Visa, Master Card, American Express, Discover, telephone credit cards, collect calls, third-party billing, and marine identification numbers. VI Radio also offers fax and a full answering and message service.

Channel	Coast Station Transmit	Ship Station Transmit
Calling	2182.0kHz	2182.0kHz
Coastal	2506.0	2009.0
Coastal	2585.0	2086.0
401	4357.0	4065.0
409	4381.0	4089.0

Channel	Coast Station Transmit	Ship Station Transmit
604	6510.0	6209.0
605	6513.0	6212.0
804	8728.0	8204.0
809	8743.0	8219.0
1201	13077.0	12230.0
1202	13080.0	12233.0
1602	17245.0	16363.0
1603	17248.0	16366.0
2223	22762.0	22066.0

Voice Broadcasts

Traffic Lists are broadcast hourly on the hour. Even hours: channels 409, 604, 1201, and coastal 2506kHz
Odd hours: channels 401 and 1201

Weather Broadcasts: Offshore Caribbean weather on channels 401, 409, 604, 1201, and coastal 2506kHz at 0600, 1400, and 2200 UTC. Local VI and Puerto Rico marine weather on VHF 28 and 85 at 0800 and 2000 UTC.

TIME SIGNALS

The U.S. Naval Observatory (USNO) provides recorded time announcements by telephone (900-410-8463 or 202-653-1800; identical recordings both numbers).

Station WWV from Fort Collins, Colorado, and station WWVH from Keka'a, Kauai, Hawaii, broadcast continuous time announcements. WWV transmits on 2500, 5000, 10000, 15000, and 20000kHz. WWVH transmits on 2500, 5000, 10000, and 15000kHz. These broadcasts are prepared by the National Institute of Standards and Technology, Time and Frequency Division, Boulder, CO, 80303.

Time announcements are made every minute, commencing at 15 seconds before the minute on WWVH and 7 1/2 seconds before the minute on WWV. The time given is Coordinated Universal Time (UTC), which is essentially the same as Greenwich Mean Time (the time at the Prime Meridian, 0 longitude, Greenwich, England).

Reed's uses UTC whenever possible in listing radio broadcast times. See Chapter 6, Nautical Ephemeris, for a listing of local, or zone times, for most maritime nations of the world.

SERVICES

WWV and WWVH also broadcast storm warnings, which are explained in the section Voice Radio Broadcasts in this chapter, and GPS updates, which is discussed in Chapter 4.

AMATEUR RADIO

Many boaters are "hams," or amateur radio operators. Below is a list of some popular nets of interest to mariners. Some are informal nets and may have changed times, frequencies, and nature of traffic. It is up to the individual radio operator to determine if a particular net exists and will handle his or her traffic.

Many of these nets carry local weather reports and sea conditions. The East Coast Waterway Net is particularly popular among boaters. All times and frequencies are subject to change. The editors welcome current information on nets for this list.

UTC	Frequency MHz	Net Name, Area, Type of Information
0030	3.923	Tar Heel Emergency (North Carolina, WX/TFC)
0100	3.935	Gulf Coast Hurricane (Gulf, WX/TFC)
0200	14.334	Brazil, East U.S. TFC (WX/TFC)
0330	14.040	East Coast Maritime CW (East Coast U.S.)
0400	14.310	Maritime Emergency (Northeast Canada, TFC)
0630	14.313	International Maritime Mobile (TFC)
1030	3.815	Caribbean Weather (Caribbean, WX/TFC)
1100	3.750	Maritime Weather (Northeast Canada, WX/TFC)
1100	7.237	Caribbean Maritime (TFC)
1100	14.283	Caribus Traffic (East Coast, Caribbean, TFC)
1110	3.930	Puerto Rico Weather (Puerto Rico, Virgin Islands, WX/TFC)
1145	14.121	Mississauga (Eastern Canada, Atlantic, Caribbean, TFC)
1145	7.268	East Coast Waterway (East Coast, Caribbean, TFC)
1200	14.040	East Coast Maritime CW (East Coast United States)
1230	7.185	Barbados Info. (Caribbean, TFC)
1245	7.268	East Coast Waterway (East Coast, Caribbean, TFC)

UTC	Frequency MHz	Net Name, Area, Type of Information
1300	21.400	TransAtlantic (Atlantic, Mediterranean, Caribbean, TFC)
1345	3.968	East Coast Waterway (East Coast, Caribbean, TFC)
1400	7.085	Bluewater (East Atlantic, United States, TFC)
1400	7.292	Florida Coast (Florida, TFC)
1600	14.300	Maritime Mobile Service
	14.313	(Atlantic, Caribbean TFC)
1700	14.313	Intercontinental (Atlantic, Medieterranean, Caribbean, TFC)
1800	14.303	United Kingdom Maritime (Atlantic, Mediterranean, Caribbean, TFC)
1800	14.313	Maritime Mobile Service (Worldwide, TFC)
2130	14.290	East Coast Waterway (East Coast, Caribbean, TFC)
2200	3.930	West Indies SSB (Puerto Rico, Virgin Islands, TFC)
2230	3.815	Caribbean Weather (Caribbean, WX/TFC)
2230	3.958	Massachusetts, Rhode Island (TFC)
2310	3.930	Puerto Rico Weather (Puerto Rico, Virgin Islands, WX/TFC)
2400	14.313	Maritime Mobile Service (Worldwide, TFC)
2400	14.325	Hurricane (Atlantic, Caribbean, Pacific, Emergency, WX)

WX = Weather information
TFC = Traffic

OTHER SOURCES OF WEATHER INFORMATION

National Hurricane Center
Coral Gables, Florida
305-662-5702, recorded information
305-666-4612
305-661-0738, fax

The voice recording number provides current information on developing tropical storms and hurricanes. The 666 number is manned 24 hours a day. Use the fax number to receive current Gulf Stream information from south of

Cape Hatteras to the Straits of Florida and the Gulf of Mexico. Current speeds, water temperature, and eddy locations are included.

National Climatic Data Center
Federal Building
Asheville, NC 28801-2733
704-271-2733; 704-271-4876, fax

Detailed Gulf Stream charts and information from Nova Scotia to the Bahamas is available for a fee. You can receive data by mail or fax.

NOAA Information Hotline
800-662-6622, recorded information line
900-884-6622, recorded weather reports

Call the 900 number to receive hurricane reports, NOAA weather reports from around the U.S., or the WWV time signal. Know in advance the telephone area code for the region in which you are interested. The charge is $0.98 per minute. A touch-tone phone is necessary. The 800 number provides information on accessing the 900 number.

U.S. Naval Atlantic Meteorology Oceanography Facility
U.S. Naval Air Station, Bermuda
809-293-5339

Departure weather packages are available with 24 hours notice. You may call from the Bermuda Yacht Reporting Office on Ordnance Island. Packages include satellite photos, weatherfax charts, and detailed Gulf Stream information.

Note: This base is currently scheduled to close in September 1995.

Nassau Meteorological Service
Nassau, Bahamas

For up-to-date local weather forecasts, call 809-377-7040; in Nassau, dial only 915.

NAUTICAL EPHEMERIS

EPHEMERIS

AN INTRODUCTION TO REED'S NAUTICAL EPHEMERIS

The ephemeris section of *Reed's Nautical Almanac* continues to carry all the information necessary to calculate the position of a boat by celestial navigation.

The emhemeris is the functional equivalent of the *Nautical Almanac* published annually by the United States Naval Observatory, but it is organized in quite a different and more compact fashion. If you are familiar with the U.S. Almanac, please take a moment to read the following section and to reorient yourself.

In the U.S. Almanac, you are used to finding all the critical data presented three days at a time on a two-page table known as the "Daily Pages." *Reed's* presents the same information by *month*, in six pages of tables. In the U.S. book, most data is given hourly; in *Reed's*, the increment varies according to necessity. Some bodies are tabulated for every 2 hours, some for 6 hours, and some for 24 hours. Here is an overview of the **monthly tables**:

First page: Sun and Moon general information such as rises and sets, transit (meridian passage), and time of civil twilight. Several phenomenon are calculated for 52°N latitude (Greenwich) with corrections supplied for other latitudes.

Second page: Sixty navigation stars with not only the customary Declination and SHA but also GHA and the astronomers' Right Ascension. Note that a transit time is also supplied for each star (with daily corrections), a very useful aid for star identification.

Third and fourth pages: GHA and Declination of the Sun and Aries for every 2 hours.

Fifth page: GHA and Declination of the four navigation planets for each day of the month (Venus, Jupiter, Mars, and Saturn). A merdian passage time is also given.

Sixth page: GHA and Declination of the Moon for every 6 hours.

Reed's correction tables are also different. In the U.S. almanac you find "increments" pages where corrections for all bodies are presented in one continuous table, 2 minutes per page. *Reed's* has different correction tables for different bodies, and most present the correction in several parts. Also, Moon and Planet GHA and Dec corrections are all based on a rate of change given in the monthly tables, a concept somewhat like *v* and *d* corrections.

The various altitude correction tables are similar to the U.S. versions, except in many cases they nicely include the Dip correction. Also, both the Moon and Polaris tables are much easier to use.

In summation, users of the standard *U.S. Nautical Almanac* will find *Reed's* ephemeris foreign at first. It takes a little study to comprehend *Reed's* layout, and usually you will have to do a little more addition to compute your corrections. However, *Reed's* is quite compact, and it works!

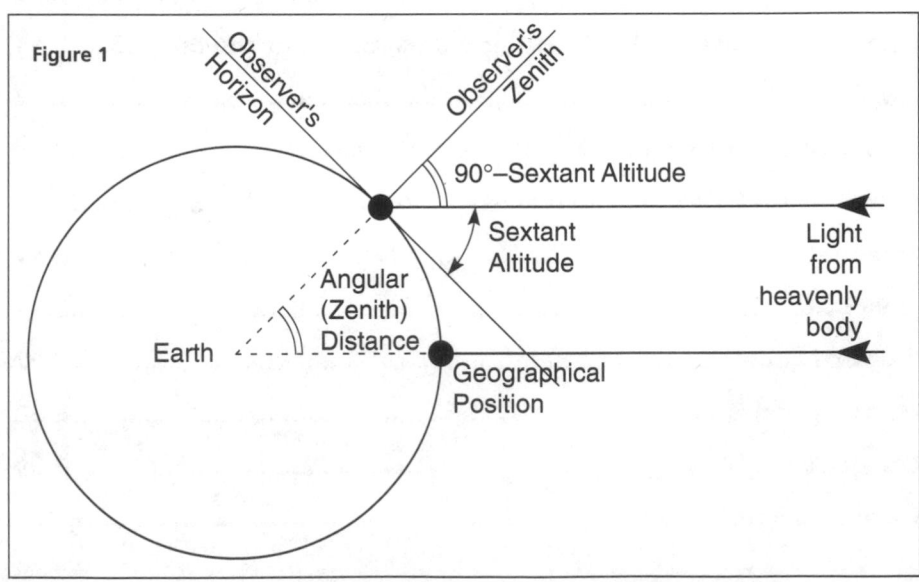

Figure 1

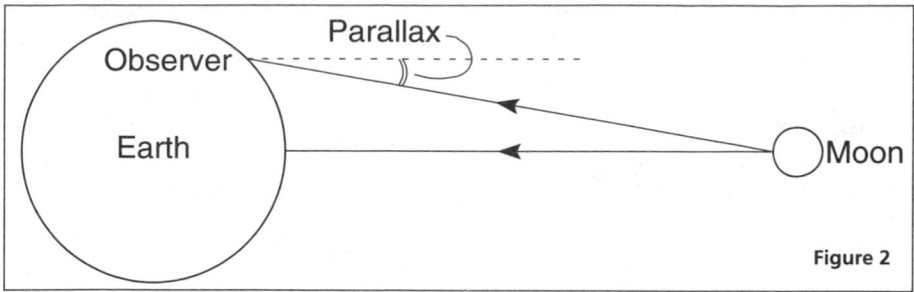

Figure 2

It is worth noting that *Reed's* habit of listing transit times of all bodies makes its ephemeris particularly good for general star-gazing.

CELESTIAL NAVIGATION

This section is intended as a brief overview of the principles and terminology of celestial navigation.

Figure 1 suggests that by measuring the angle between a heavenly body and the horizon, it is possible to find the angular distance, or *zenith distance* (ZD), between your position and the spot on the Earth's surface where the body is directly overhead (its *geographical position,* or GP). By definition, an arc from the center of the Earth along its surface can be converted directly to nautical miles. Hence, the ZD and GP provide a position line, just as the range of a charted terrestrial landmark can be used to derive a position line in coastal navigation. For instance, if the corrected sextant altitude in the figure was 42°, then the ZD would be 48° or a 2,880-nautical-mile range between your vessel and the body's GP (60 miles/degree x 48). For this information to be of any practical value, we must:

(a) be able to see a suitable heavenly body;
(b) know the body's geographical position;
(c) be able to correct the *sextant altitude* for errors such as atmospheric refraction; and
(d) be able to plot the position line on a chart.

FINDING THE POSITION OF A HEAVENLY BODY

By convention, celestial navigation assumes that the Sun, Moon, planets, and stars are located on the inner surface of a *celestial sphere* whose center is at the center of the Earth and whose poles, equator, and prime meridian are precisely aligned with their terrestrial counterparts. Latitude and longitude, however, are not used.

Declination (Dec) is the celestial equivalent of latitude: it is measured in degrees, north or south of the celestial equator.

Greenwich Hour Angle (GHA) is equivalent to longitude, except that it is always measured in a westerly direction. Therefore, a star whose Declination is N39° and whose GHA is 40° would appear overhead to an observer at 39°N 40°W, while one whose Declination is S17° and whose GHA is 219° would be overhead when seen from 17°S 141°E.

The ephemeris predicts the Declination and GHA of the Sun, the Moon, four planets, and sixty stars for every second of one year.

CORRECTING THE SEXTANT ALTITUDE

The *sextant altitude* (Hs) is subject to a number of errors.

Index error is caused by imperfect adjustment of the sextant. A quick check of index error can be achieved by moving the index arm until the horizon—seen through the sextant—appears as an unbroken line. The sextant should then read 0, but there is often a small discrepancy. Note the size of this discrepancy and whether it is "on the arc" (i.e., the index arm is to the left of 0) or "off the arc" (i.e., the index arm is to the right of 0).

To apply index error to the sextant altitude, the simple rule is "If it's on the arc, take it off; if it's off the arc, add it on"—i.e., an index error "on the arc" should be subtracted from the sextant altitude.

Dip correction arises from the fact that a perfect 90° horizon is always slightly below an observer whose *height of eye* is above sea level.

The result of applying Dip and Index error to the sextant altitude is called *apparent altitude* (Ha), the altitude shot with any sextant from any height deck. Apparent altitude is the common value needed to enter many tables in order to determine the final three corrections.

EPHEMERIS

Parallax is caused by the size of the Earth and the fact that the geometry of celestial navigation assumes that sights are taken from the center of the Earth (figures 1 and 2). Because the Earth is relatively tiny, parallax is only really significant in the case of the Moon.

Refraction is caused by the atmosphere distorting the light from heavenly bodies. It is greatest for bodies near the horizon, and as it can vary in extreme conditions, sights with altitudes of less than 10° should be regarded with skepticism.

Semi-diameter arises from the physical size of the body being observed and the fact that tabulated values refer to the center of the body concerned. In the case of the Sun and Moon, this is about 15' higher than the lower edge of the visible disc.

PLOTTING A POSITION LINE

Since an angular measurement through the Earth's surface from the center can be directly converted to nautical miles, the zenith distance gives the diameter in miles of a circular position line centered on the body's geographical position. In other words, 90° less the corrected altitude is the actual distance from the observor to the body. In practice, this distance is usually far too large to be plotted on a chart, so the results of sights have to be "reduced" to more manageable dimensions (see page E 6.) However, zenith distance is used in both the noon sights of the Sun and Pole Star sights to calculate and plot your latitude.

USING THE TABLES

The following subsections describe in more detail how to use the ephemeris tables to calculate the necessary data for various types of celestial problems.

SUN SIGHTS

Finding the Sun's position

The Declination and GHA of the Sun are given on the third and fourth pages of each monthly section, tabulated at 2-hour intervals for each day.

The Sun's declination changes so slowly that the necessary accuracy can be achieved by mental interpolation. The correction may be positive or negative according to the season. Its sign can be found by looking at the entry that

follows to see whether the declination is increasing (+) or decreasing (−).

For instance, if you take a sight at 0925 on January 1, you will observe that the declination is S23°01.7' at 0800 and S23°01.3' at 1000. Therefore, the rate of change is -0.4' every 2 hours. For 0925, you can interpolate a correction of -0.3' to apply to the 0800 value.

The Sun's GHA increases at a rate of 15° per hour, but to simplify the job of interpolating accurately, a GHA correction table for the Sun appears on page E 94. Note that the GHA correction must always be added because GHA is always measured to the west of Greenwich

Sun altitude corrections

Refraction, dip, and parallax tables are on page E 92, and the Sun's semi-diameter is given on the first page of each monthly section, but for convenience, all four corrections have been combined in the Sun Altitude Total Correction Table on page E 93. For greater accuracy, another small correction will be found at the foot of this table to account for the Sun's apparently changing diameter.

Note that the Sun Altitude Total Correction Table relates only to sights of the Sun's *lower limb*. Sights of the upper limb must be corrected either by using the separate tables or by subtracting twice the semi-diameter. Note also that the separate tables must be used for sun sights of less than 9°.

STAR SIGHTS

Finding the time of twilight

Star sights can be taken only when the star and the horizon are both visible—i.e., at *twilight*. Strictly speaking, *civil twilight* occurs when the Sun is 6° below the horizon and *nautical twilight* when it is 12° below the horizon. The best time to take star sights is around civil twilight, so this is the twilight listed in *Reed's Almanac*, on the first page of each monthly section.

The times given for twilight, sunrise, and sunset are correct for 52°N, 0°W (Greenwich, England). They must therefore be corrected to take account of your own latitude and longitude.

The *twilight latitude correction* is given in the subsidiary table on the righthand side of the same page. The *longitude correction* is found by adding 4 minutes for every degree of westerly longitude or subtracting 4 minutes for every degree of easterly longitude. The Arc into Time Table on page E 91 helps with this calculation.

Finding the position of a star

The essential information for sixty stars that are bright enough to be visible at twilight is given in the star list on the second page of each monthly section.

This list notes the GHA of each star at 0000 on the first day of the month. The tables on page E 94 can be used to correct this value for date and time.

An alternative method is to use the star's *Sidereal Hour Angle* (SHA), which gives its position measured westward relative to a meridian on the celestial equator called the *First Point of Aries*.

To find the GHA of a star, first find the GHA of Aries. This value is tabulated at 2-hour intervals on the third and fourth pages of each monthly section. The correction tables on page E 94 simplify the job of interpolation. To the GHA of Aries add the SHA listed for your chosen star. If the result is more than 360°, subtract 360°.

The *declinations* of stars change so slowly that for navigational purposes they can be regarded as being fixed throughout a month and can be taken directly from the monthly star list.

Right Ascension (RA) refers to the star's position measured eastward from the First Point of Aries and is usually given in terms of time (1 hour=15°). This value is useful in astronomy, where it is the common measurement of star positions.

Star altitude corrections

For stars, errors due to semi-diameter and parallax are negligible, so sextant altitudes need only be corrected for dip and refraction. It is possible to allow for each error individually, using the tables on page E 92. Both should be subtracted from the observed altitude. For convenience, refraction and dip have been combined into the Star or Planet Altitude Total Correction Table on page E 96.

PLANET SIGHTS

Of the planets, only Venus, Jupiter, Mars, and Saturn are of navigational significance. The section on Planets, pages E 14–15, gives you complete information on the visibility of these planets during the year.

Finding the position of a planet

The *Declination* and *GHA* of the navigational planets are presented on the fifth page of each monthly section. They are tabulated at midnight (00h0m) for each day.

The GHAs of planets increase at about 15° per hour: the rate of change on any particular day is given more accurately in the column headed

Mean Var. To save space, only the minutes are shown: a Mean Var of 3.2 means an hourly increase of 15°03.2', while a Mean Var of 59.4 means an hourly increase of 14°59.4'.

Once you know the Mean Var, the Planets GHA Correction Tables on pages E 101–102 allows you to interpolate to the nearest hour, while the table on page E 103 permits you to interpolate to minutes and seconds.

The Declination is also shown for midnight on each day, with the mean hourly variation. Its interpolation table is on pages E104–105. As with the Sun, it is important to note whether the declination of a planet is increasing or decreasing.

Planet Altitude Corrections

Corrections for planet sights are exactly the same as those for stars, page E 96.

MOON SIGHTS

Finding the position of the Moon

The Moon is so much closer to Earth than any other heavenly body and moves so much faster that finding its position and correcting its observed altitude are much more complicated and error-prone. The layout of the tables and the processes involved, however, are similar to those for the planets.

The Moon's *Declination* and *GHA* are given on the sixth page of each monthly section, tabulated at 6-hour intervals for each day.

The Moon's GHA increases at about 14°30' per hour. The precise rate of increase is given in the column headed *Mean Var,* but to save space only the minutes are shown. Therefore, a Mean Var of 27.7 means an hourly increase of 14°27.7'.

Knowing the Mean Var, you can use the Moon GHA Correction Table on page E 96 to interpolate to the nearest hour, while the table on pages E 97–98 allows you to interpolate to minutes and seconds.

Similarly, the Declination is shown along with its mean hourly variation. Hourly corrections are calculated by simply multiplying the number of hours times the variation, while the table on page E 99 interpolates for minutes.

Moon altitude corrections

The corrections to be applied to Moon sights can be found from the Moon Altitude Total Correction Table on page E 95.

First, however, you need to know the *horizontal parallax* (the parallax error that would occur if the observed altitude were 0°), which can be

EPHEMERIS

obtained from the first page of the monthly sections. Taking care to choose the correct part of the table—depending on whether the sight is of the upper or lower limb—find the column in the table corresponding to the value of horizontal parallax and the row corresponding to the sextant altitude. The correction obtained must be added, unless it is for an observation of the upper limb in excess of 64°, in which case it must be subtracted.

Finally, add the correction for *height of eye*, found from the subsidiary table on the same page.

Note: Do not use the standard Dip tables in conjunction with the Moon Altitude Total Correction Table.

THE NOON SIGHT

The so-called noon sight—taken at approximately noon local time—gives the simplest of all astro position lines. It is more correctly called a *Meridian Passage* sight, because it is taken at the moment when the Sun transits the observer's meridian—i.e., when it is at its highest and directly south or north of the observer.

The first step in taking a noon sight is to determine when meridian passage will occur. This time can be found from the column headed *Transit* in the top half of the first page in the appropriate monthly section. Here you will find the time (GMT) when the Sun crosses the Greenwich Meridian.

Figure 3

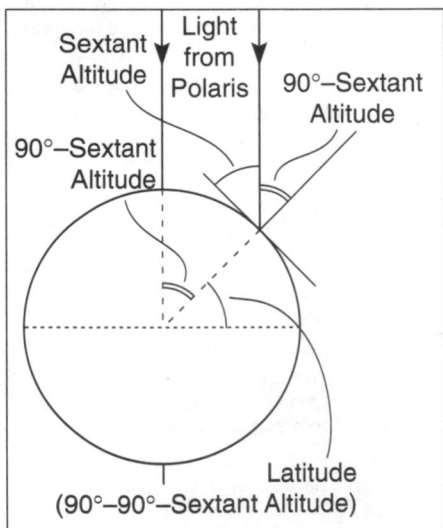

Use the Arc into Time table on page E 91, or calculate using 1°=4 minutes, to correct the time of transit for your *dead-reackoning (DR)* longitude. An approximation is all that is required, because in practice it is usual to measure the Sun's altitude a few minutes before the expected time and to repeat the observation at intervals until the Sun stops rising in the sky and starts to descend.

Having corrected the sextant altitude in the usual way, subtract the observed altitude from 90° to determine the *zenith distance*.

Latitude is then equal to either the sum or the difference of the Declination and the Zenith Distance (ZD). It is usually obvious whether declination should be added or subtracted, but if there is any ambiguity, note whether the Sun is to your north or south, and give the Zenith Distance the opposite name. If the Zenith Distance and Declination have the same name, add them together. If they have different names, take the smaller from the larger, and name the latitude after the larger.

LATITUDE BY POLARIS

If Polaris were perfectly aligned with the pole, as its alternative name of Pole Star suggests, its altitude (after correction for the usual errors) would be exactly the same as the observer's latitude. Figure 3 illustrates the principle. It is not, in fact, in perfect alignment but is sufficiently close that only minor arithmetical adjustments are required. Polaris is not a particularly bright star, but it can usually be found at twilight by setting the sextant index arm to your approximate latitude and scanning the northern sky with the sextant.

A table giving the correction to be applied to the observed altitude is on page E 90. It is first necessary to find the *Local Hour Angle of Aries*. This is done by finding the GHA of Aries and subtracting from it your longitude if you are west of Greenwich or adding to it your longitude if you are east of Greenwich.

SIGHT REDUCTION

The Intercept Method

Astro position lines, aside from Noon and Polaris latitude lines, are most easily plotted using the *Marc St. Hilaire, or Intercept, method.* This method involves calculating what the altitude of a heavenly body would be as seen from some convenient nearby position and comparing this value with its *observed altitude* (HO). If the observed altitude (Ho) is greater than the *calculated altitude* (Hc), the true position must be closer to the heavenly body from the *assumed position,* and vice versa. The size of the discrepancy shows how much closer (or farther away) and is called the *intercept.*

Figure 4 illustrates the whole celestial plot. The beauty of the intercept method is that only the *assumed postion* (AP), intercept, and position line need to be drawn, all of which can be done on a manageable scale. You do need to know the direction as well as the length of the intercept. This bearing will be the same as the actual bearing of the heavenly body, but it is easier and more accurate to calculate it than to measure it.

Figure 4 also illustrates the concept that although a range plotted directly from the *geographical position* (GP) would form a circle, this position circle is so big that a section up to about 60 miles in length can be regarded as a straight line that runs at right angles to the intercept.

The calculated altitude and bearing can both be found from precomputed tables such as the *Sight Reduction Tables for Air Navigation (H.O. 249);* by the more compact Versine and Log Cosine tables and the ABC tables, found in *Reed's* on pages E 112–131 and E 106–111 respectively; or with an electronic calculator.

Whichever method you choose, the calculations require the Declination of the body; the latitude of an assumed position (it is usually necessary to round out your DR to the nearest whole degree); and the *Local Hour Angle* (LHA).

The LHA is the difference in longitude between your assumed position and the geographical position of the heavenly body. It is found by subtracting westerly longitude from the GHA (+360° if necessary) or by adding easterly longitude (−360° if necessary). You will find it most convenient to make the assumed position (AP) such that LHA becomes a whole number of degrees. If the DR is 34°50'N, 36°40'W, for instance, and the GHA of the body is 110°35.4', a suitable AP would be 35°N, 36°35.4'W.

The various sight reduction methods will eventually give you a calculated altitude (Hc) and an azimuth. The azimuth given by the calculator method or *Reed's* tables is always less than 90° and is the bearing relative to the North or South Pole, measuring east or west. An azimuth of 70°, for instance, could correspond to a bearing of 070° (N70°E), 110° (S70°E), 250° (S70°W), or 290° (N70°W). The easiest way to decide which of the four is correct is to note the approximate bearing of the heavenly body at the time of the sight. Alternatively, it can be found from the rules at the end of the ABC tables (see page E 111).

ELECTRONIC SIGHT REDUCTION

For electronic sight reduction a calculator capable of handling trigonometric functions is essential, and at least one memory is useful, but be prepared to store data on a separate notepad as well.

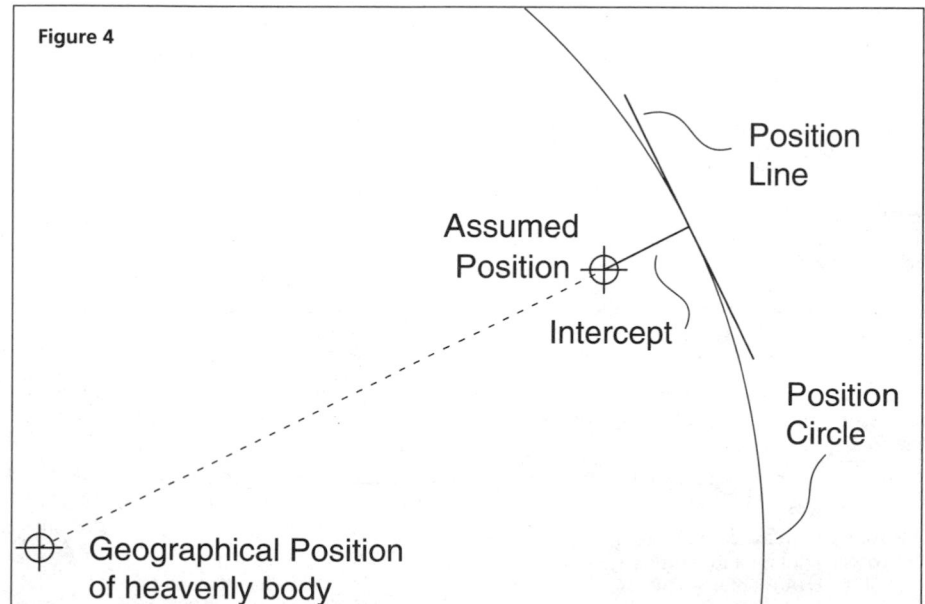

Figure 4

Position Line

Assumed Position

Intercept

Position Circle

Geographical Position of heavenly body

EPHEMERIS

The first task is to convert the declination into degrees and decimals and to select a suitable assumed position that gives a latitude and an LHA in whole degrees.

Then the calculated altitude (Hc) is given by the formula:

Sin Hc = Cos LHA x Cos Lat x Cos Dec ± Sin Lat x Sin Dec

(Note that if Lat and Dec have the same name, they should be added, and if they have opposite names, the smaller value should be subtracted.)

The *azimuth* is given by using the formula:

$$Sin\ Az = \frac{(Sin\ LHA\ x\ Cos\ Dec)}{Cos\ Hc}$$

The exact process required to carry out these calculations depends on the calculator being used. Some use "Polish Notation," some regular algebraic; some default to degrees, some to radians. The example on the next page should get you started.

SIGHT REDUCTION BY TABLES

The same formulae could be used in conjunction with a set of mathematical tables instead of a pocket calculator, but the calculations can be made simpler by applying the *versine formula* (the versine of an angle is equal to 1 minus its cosine):

Vers Zenith Distance = Vers LHA x Cos Lat x Cos Dec + Vers (Lat ± Dec)

(Note that if Lat and Dec have the same name, they should be *subtracted,* and if they have opposite names, they should be *added*).

Hc is then found by subtracting the Zenith Distance from 90°.

To simplify the multiplication process, *Reed's* Versine Tables (pages E112–125) include logarithms of versines in bold type, and the tables on pages E126–131 are log cosines. Adding logs is the equivalent of multiplying. You may subtract 10 as needed (as you would subtract 360° from an angle greater than 360°). Hence, the formula in terms of *Reed's* tables is:

Natural Versine Zenith Distance = Nat Vers (Log Vers LHA + Log Cos Lat + Log Cos Dec) + Nat Vers (Lat ± Dec)

The azimuth is calculated with the ABC Tables on pages E 106–111.

A is found from the A table, using LHA to find the correct column and latitude to find the row. If the LHA is between 90° and 270°, *A* is negative.

B is found from the B table, again with LHA determining the correct column, but this time with Declination determining the row. B is negative if the latitude and declination have the same name (i.e., are both South or both North).

The C table is used to convert the sum of *A* and *B* into the azimuth. If *C* is positive, the azimuth is the same name (north or south) as your latitude, and if the LHA is less than 180° the azimuth is westerly.

WORKED EXAMPLES

Noon Sight
Mer Pass September 10; DR: 35°00'N, 35°40'W
Sext Alt of Sun Lower Limb (LL): 59°38.2'
Index Error (IE), 0; Height of Eye (HE), 10ft

1. Find the time of Meridian Passage on September 10.

Transit (from page E 66)	1157
Correct for DR longitude	
35°40' to time (from page E 91)	223
	1420 GMT

2. Calculate Declination of Sun from the monthly ephemeris.

Dec at 1400 GMT (page E 68)	N 4°58.8'
Correct for 20min by interpolation	– 0.2'
(20m/2h = 1/6 x -1.3 (2h diff))= –0.2')	
Dec at 1420 GMT	N 4°58.6'

3. Calculate observed altitude (Ho).

Sextant altitude	59°38.2'
Total correction (from p E 93)	+ 12.4'
Monthly correction (from p E 93)	– 0.1'
Observed altitude (Ho)	59°50.5'

4. Calculate latitude.

Zenith	90°00.0'
subtract Ho	– 59°50.5'
Zenith Distance	(N) 30°09.5'
Declination	+N 4°58.6'
Latitude	35°08.1'N

Morning/Afternoon Sun Sight
15h 35m 42s GMT Sep 10; DR: 34°55'N, 35°50'W
Sext Alt of Sun LL: 55°08.8'
IE, O; HE, 10ft

1. Find the position of the Sun at 15h35m42s GMT on September 10 from the monthly ephemeris.

GHA at 1400 (from p E 68)	GHA 30°43.9'
Correct for 1h 35m (from p E 94)	23°45.0'
Correct for 42s (from p E 94)	10.5'
GHA at 15h 35m 42s	54°39.4'
Dec at 1400 (from p E 68)	N 4°58.8'
Correct for 1h 35m by interpolation	– 1.4'
Dec at 15h 35m 42s	N 4°57.4'

2. Correct the sextant altitude.

Sextant altitude	55°08.8'
Sun Total Corr (from p E 93)	+ 12.3'
Monthly correction (from p E 93)	– 0.1'
Observed altitude	55°21.0'

3. Determine the assumed position and calculate the LHA:

GHA	54°39.4'
Assumed longitude	35°39.4'W
Local Hour Angle	19°00.0'
Assumed latitude	35°N

4. Reduce the sight. Here we will use the calculator method. See next example for use of *Reed's* tables.

Convert declination to degrees and decimals:

4 degrees	4.000°
57.4 minutes ÷ 60	0.957°
	4.957°

Find the intercept. Depending on the particular calculator the key sequence looks something like this (remember to use degree notation).

LHA $\boxed{\text{COS}}$ $\boxed{\times}$ Lat $\boxed{\text{COS}}$ $\boxed{\times}$ Dec $\boxed{\text{COS}}$ $\boxed{=}$

19 $\boxed{\text{COS}}$ $\boxed{\times}$ 35 $\boxed{\text{COS}}$ $\boxed{\times}$ 4.957 $\boxed{\text{COS}}$ $\boxed{=}$

In this case the answer is 0.7716. Write down this interim answer (or use the store function of your calculator) for use in the next calculation (the + is because Lat and Dec are both N):

Lat $\boxed{\text{SIN}}$ $\boxed{\times}$ Dec $\boxed{\text{SIN}}$ $\boxed{+}$ 0.7716 $\boxed{=}$ Hc $\boxed{\text{ASIN}}$

35 $\boxed{\text{SIN}}$ $\boxed{\times}$ 4.957 $\boxed{\text{SIN}}$ $\boxed{+}$ 0.7716 $\boxed{=}$ Hc $\boxed{\text{ASIN}}$

In this case the answer is 55.201, which is the calculated altitude. Write it down (for safety), and then, with the answer still on the display, convert the decimal degrees to minutes:

$\boxed{-}$ 55 $\boxed{=}$ $\boxed{\times}$ 60 $\boxed{=}$ 12.1

Calculated altitude (Hc) =	55°12.1'
Observed altitude (Ho) =	55°21.0'
Intercept	Toward 8.9'

Find the azimuth/bearing:

LHA $\boxed{\text{SIN}}$ $\boxed{\times}$ Dec $\boxed{\text{COS}}$ $\boxed{/}$ Hc $\boxed{\text{COS}}$ $\boxed{=}$
Azimuth $\boxed{\text{ASIN}}$

19 $\boxed{\text{SIN}}$ $\boxed{\times}$ 4.957 $\boxed{\text{COS}}$ $\boxed{/}$ 55.201 $\boxed{\text{COS}}$ $\boxed{=}$
Azimuth $\boxed{\text{ASIN}}$

In this case the answer is 34.635, so the Azimuth is 35°—actually S35°W, or 215°.

Evening Stars/Planet Sight

2110 GMT Sep 10, DR: 34°30'N, 36°40'W
Sext Alt Jupiter: 29°59.9' at 21h 07m 26s GMT
Sext Alt Arcturus: 37°44.0' at 21h 11m 19s GMT
IE, 0; HE, 10ft

1. Find the time of evening twilight at 35°N, 36°W on September 10.

Twilight (from p E 66)	1902 GMT
Latitude correction (from p E 66)	– 0017
	1845 GMT
Longitude corr (from p E 91)	+ 0224
Corrected time of twilight	2109 GMT

2. Find the position of Jupiter at 21h07m26s GMT on September 10.

GHA at 0000 (from p E 70)	102°34.7'
Mean Var per hour 15°02.2'	
Correction for 21h (from p E 102)	315°46.2'
Correction for 07m (from p E 103)	1°45.2'
Correction for 26s (from p E 103)	6.5'
	420°12.6'
Value is over 360°, so subtract	-360°00.0'
GHA at 21h07m26s	60°12.6'
Dec at 0000	S 21°06.9'
Mean Var per hour	+ 0.0'
Correction for 21h07m (from p E 104)	+ 0.0'
Dec (by interpolation**)	S 21°07.9'

**when Mean Var = 0, interpolate to next day

3. Correct the sextant altitude.

Sextant altitude	29°59.9'
Planet total corr (from p E 96)	– 4.7'
Observed altitude	29°55.2'

4. Determine the assumed position and calculate the LHA.

GHA	60°12.6'
Assumed longitude	36°12.6'W
Local Hour Angle	24°00.0'
Assumed latitude	35°N

5. Reduce the sight with *Reed's* tables. Using the versine tables, find the intercept.

Log versine LHA (from page E 118)	8.9368
Log cos Lat (from page E 128)	9.9134
Log cos Dec (from page E 127)	9.9698
Total	28.8200
Delete tens digit	8.8200
Convert Log to Nat (from page E 114)	0.0661

Add Lat and Dec (because opposite names):	
Dec	S 21°07.9'
Lat	N 35°00.0'
	56°07.9'

Nat versine of 56°07.9'	0.4427
Add previous answer	0.0661
Nat versine Zenith Distance (p. E 120)	0.5088
Zenith Distance	60°35.0'
Subtract from 90° (=89° 60)	90°00.0'
Hc	29°25.0'
Ho	29°55.2'
Intercept	Toward 30.2'

6. Find the bearing:

A (from p E 107)	+ 1.57
B (from p E 107)	+ 0.944
A + B	2.514
C (from p E 110)	S26°W
Bearing	206°

7. Find the position of Arcturus at 21h11m19s GMT on Sep 10.

GHA Aries at 2000	289°22.9'
Correction for 1h11m (from p E 94)	17°48.0'
Correction for 19s (from p E 94)	4.8'
GHA Aries at 21h11m19s	307°15.7'

SHA Arcturus (from p E 67)	146°08.2'
GHA Arcturus	453°23.9'
less 360°	93°23.9'
Dec Arcturus	N 19°12.5'
Assumed longitude	W 36°23.9'
LHA	57°00.0'
Assumed latitude	N 35°

Calculate #7 by electronic or tabular methods. Intercept 4.4' towards, bearing 268°.

Latitude by Polaris

21h 13m GMT Sep 10, DR: 34°40'N, 36°50'W
Sext Alt Polaris: 34°09.1'
IE, 0; HE, 10ft

GHA Aries at 2000	289°22.9'
Correction for 1h13m (from p E 94)	18°18.0'

GHA Aries at 2113	307°40.9'
DR longitude	36°50.0'
LHA Aries	270°50.9'
Sextant altitude	34°09.1'
Star altitude correction (from p E 96)	– 4.4'
Observed altitude	34°04.7'
Polaris correction (from p 954)	+ 27.0
Latitude	34°31.7'

Moon Sight

23h 50m 07s GMT Sep 10, DR: 34°40'N, 36°40'W
Sext Alt Moon LL: 27°10.6'
IE, 0; HE, 10ft

GHA Moon at 1800 (from page E 71)	252°56.2'
Mean Var per hour 14°30.9' (E 71)	
Correction for 5h (from p E 96)	72°34.5'
Correction for 50m (from p 961)	12°06.5'
Correction for 07s (from p 961)	1.7'
GHA at 21h15m07s	337°38.9'

Dec at 1800 (from page E 71)	N 4°37.0'
Mean Var per hour +10.4'	
Correction for 5h (mental arithmetic)	+ 52.0'
Correction for 50m (from p 963)	+ 8.7'
Dec at 07h44m27s	N 5°37.7'

Calculate intercept by electronic or tabular methods:

AP: N 35° W 36° 38.9'
Intercept 13.7' away, bearing 104°.

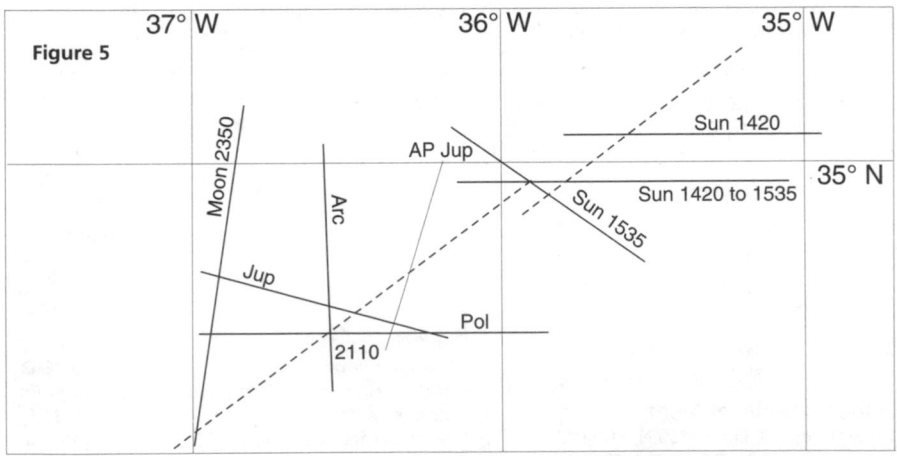

37° W   36° W   35° W

Figure 5

35° N

Moon 2350

AP Jup

Arc

Sun 1420

Sun 1420 to 1535

Sun 1535

Jup

Pol

2110

Figure 5 is a plot of the various example sights. For clarity, only the assumed positon and bearing line of the Jupiter sight is shown. Note also that the DR course is plotted but not the DR positions. The noon sun line was run with the DR to create a 15:35 running fix.

USING A CALCULATOR TO FIND GHA AND DECLINATION OF THE SUN

Greenwich Hour Angle (GHA) and Declination (Dec) of the Sun for 1995 can be calculated using an electronic calculator and the following sets of monthly polynomial coefficients.

The date and time in GMT are used to form the interpolation factor p. This can be expressed as $p = d/32$ where d is the sum of the month and decimal of a day. Then GHA–GMT in hours and Dec in degrees are calculated from polynomial expressions of the form:

$$a_0 + a_1 p + a_2 p^2 + a_3 p^3 + a_4 p^4$$

where p is the interpolating factor. The simplest way of evaluating this is to use the nested form:

$$(((a_4 p + a_3) p + a_2) p + a_1) p + a_0$$

Example. Calculate GHA and Dec of Sun on July 23, 1995, at 17h 02m 15s GMT.

GMT $= 17h.0375$ and the interpolation factor is

$p = (23 + 17.0375/24)/32 = 0.740934$

GHA – GMT $= 11h.94248 - 0h.10822p + 0h.03828p^2 + 0h.02631p^3 - 0h.00486p^4$

$= 11h.89255$

Hence, GHA $= 11h.89255 + $ GMT $= 11h.89255 + 17h.0375$

Remove multiples of 24h from GHA and multiply by 15 to convert from hours to degrees.

Then, GHA $= 73°.9507 = 73°.57.0'$

Dec $= 23°.2095 - 1°.7861p - 3°.4640p^2 + 0°.1393p^3 + 0°.0885p^4$

$= 20°.0678 = $ N20°.04.1'

Semi-diameter of the Sun

Jan 1– Feb 4	16.3'	Apr 20–May 14	1.9'	Oct 12–Nov 3	16.1'
Feb 5–Mar 5	16.2'	May 15–Aug 25	15.8'	Nov 4–Dec 2	16.2'
Mar 6–Mar 28	16.1'	Aug 26–Sep 19	15.9'	Dec 3–Dec 31	16.3'
Mar 29–Apr 19	16.0'	Sep 20–Oct 11	16.0'		

To correct for the effect of parallax of the Sun it is normally sufficient to add 0.1' to all observed altitudes less than 70°. If greater accuracy is required, the correction is 0.15' x cos altitude.

Monthly polynomial coefficients for the Sun, 1995

		JANUARY GHA–GMT h	Dec °	FEBRUARY GHA–GMT h	Dec °	MARCH GHA–GMT h	Dec °	APRIL GHA–GMT h	Dec °
Sun	a_0	11.95485	-23.1274	11.77754	-17.5685	11.78780	-8.2223	11.92549	3.8879
	a_1	-0.25765	2.2244	-0.08585	8.8343	0.09402	12.0623	0.15872	12.4243
	a_2	0.04030	3.9606	0.12306	2.6460	0.08040	1.0033	-0.00489	-0.6413
	a_3	0.05124	-0.2413	-0.00749	-0.6094	-0.03029	-0.5865	-0.03633	-0.5030
	a_4	-0.01377	-0.1063	-0.00652	-0.0025	-0.00151	0.0189	0.00550	0.0023
check sum		11.77497	-17.2900	11.80074	-6.7001	11.93042	4.2757	12.04849	15.1702

		MAY GHA–GMT h	Dec °	JUNE GHA–GMT h	Dec °	JULY GHA–GMT h	Dec °	AUGUST GHA–GMT h	Dec °
Sun	a_0	12.04432	14.5594	12.04128	21.8134	11.94248	23.2095	11.89323	18.4330
	a_1	0.07125	9.9035	-0.07612	4.6889	-0.10822	-1.7861	0.02173	-7.7863
	a_2	-0.06807	-2.0554	-0.05473	-3.2301	0.03828	-3.4640	0.09497	-2.5503
	a_3	-0.01980	-0.4955	0.01926	-0.3045	0.02631	0.1393	-0.01285	0.3973
	a_4	0.01113	0.0448	0.00620	0.1167	-0.00486	0.0885	-0.00168	0.0360
check sum		12.03883	21.9568	11.93589	23.0844	11.89399	18.1872	11.99540	8.5297

		SEPTEMBER GHA–GMT h	Dec °	OCTOBER GHA–GMT h	Dec °	NOVEMBER GHA–GMT h	Dec °	DECEMBER GHA–GMT h	Dec °
Sun	a_0	11.99025	8.8896	12.16193	-2.5278	12.27218	-13.8785	12.19422	-21.5258
	a_1	0.16306	-11.4804	0.17545	-12.4396	0.02625	-10.4519	-0.18847	-5.3485
	a_2	0.05387	-1.1774	-0.02836	0.2327	-0.10434	1.8735	-0.09465	3.4748
	a_3	-0.03830	0.4247	-0.04561	0.4848	-0.03077	0.6426	0.02642	0.5004
	a_4	0.00389	0.0393	0.00948	0.0466	0.01876	-0.0320	0.01141	-0.1733
check sum		12.17277	-3.3042	12.27289	-14.2033	12.18208	-21.8463	11.94893	-23.0724

Prepared by HM Nautical Almanac Office, Royal Greenwich Observatory, reproduced with permission from data supplied by the Science and Engineering Research Council.

EPHEMERIS

TIME

Zone, Standard, and Daylight Saving Times

Zone Time is a system that rigidly divides the world into 25 time zones, all relating to the Prime Meridian that passes through Greenwich, England. Zone Time 0 is also known as both Greenwich Mean Time (GMT) and Universal Coordinated Time (UTC).

Standard Time Zones are created by individual countries according to their needs. While Standard Times often equal Zone Times, they do not necessarily do so. The table on the opposite page lists all countries where Standard Time varies from Zone Time.

All the tables in this Ephemeris section are based on GMT. Some countries keep Daylight Saving Time during the summer months. When Daylight Saving Time is in effect, clocks are advanced one hour over Standard Time.

MEASUREMENT OF TIME

Definitions

Mean Time. The Earth does not orbit uniformly round the Sun, but for the purposes of time-keeping it is assumed that it does.

1 Mean Solar Day = 24 Mean Solar Hours. The average time taken for the Sun to make two successive transits of the same meridian. This represents slightly more than a 360° rotation of the Earth, because the Earth is constantly moving on in its orbit and will therefore have to revolve a little farther in order to present the same face to the Sun once more.

1 Sidereal Day = 23h 56m 04.1s of Mean Solar Time. The time taken for the Earth to complete a 360° rotation. Because the stars are so distant, Earth's progress along its orbit is relatively insignificant. The Sidereal Day can therefore be treated as the time taken for a star to make two transits of the same meridian.

1 Lunar Day = approx 24h 50m of Mean Solar Time (average).

1 Calendar Month = 28, 29, 30, or 31 days, depending on the month.

1 Lunar Month (or **Lunation**, or **Synodical Month**). The time interval between successive New Moons—about 29½ Mean Solar Days. As with the Mean Solar Day, this represents slightly more than a 360° rotation.

Common and Leap Years. Under the Gregorian calendar, a common year consists of 365 calendar days, a leap year of 366 caletndar days. This would suggest that with leap years

every four years, the average year works out at 365.25 days. In fact, this figure is close, but not close enough, to the length of the Mean Solar Year, so leap years are defined as those years that are divisible by 4 (as 1988, 1992, etc.), excluding century years unless they are divisible by 400; thus the year 2000 will be a leap year, but 2100 a common year. One complete cycle of the Gregorian calendar takes 400 years, in which there will be:

97 (leap) years of 366 days each	= 35,502
303 years of 365 days each	= 10,595
Therefore, the total number of days =	146,097

The mean length of year over the whole cycle will thus be 146,097/400 days, or 365.425 days. This is known as the Civil Year.

TIME ZONES

	0° Greenwich Meridian
ZONE 0	7°30'W
ZONE +1	22°30'W
ZONE +2	37°30'W
ZONE +3	52°30'W
ZONE +4	67°30'W
ZONE +5	82°30'W
ZONE +6	97°30'W
ZONE +7	112°30'W
ZONE +8	127°30'W
ZONE +9	142°30'W
ZONE +10	157°30'W
ZONE +11	172°30'W
ZONE +12	180°00' Intl Date Line
ZONE −12	172°30'E
ZONE −11	157°30'E
ZONE −10	142°30'E
ZONE −9	127°30'E
ZONE −8	112°30'E
ZONE −7	97°30'E
ZONE −6	82°30'E
ZONE −5	67°30'E
ZONE −4	52°30'E
ZONE −3	37°30'E
ZONE −2	22°30'E
ZONE −1	7°30'E
ZONE 0	0°Greenwich Meridian

Note that the International Date Line does not follow the 180° meridian throughout its length, but deviates in order to avoid populated areas.

STANDARD TIMES

Countries normally keeping GMT

Ascension Island
Burkina-Faso
* Canary Islands
† Channel Islands
* Faeroes
Gambia
Ghana
† Great Britain
Guinea-Bissau
Guinea Republic
Iceland
† Ireland, Northern
† Irish Republic
Ivory Coast
Liberia
* Madeira
Mali
Mauritania
Morocco
* Portugal
Principe
St Helena
São Tomé
Senegal
Sierra Leone
Togo Republic
Tristan da Cunha

* May keep Summer Time or Daylight Saving Time.
† British Summer Time, one hour in advance of GMT, is kept from March 27 0100h to Oct 23 0100h GMT.

Countries keeping times fast on GMT

Add to GMT to find Standard Time; subtract from Standard Time to find GMT.

* Albania 1h
Algeria 1h
Andaman Is 5½h
* Angola 1h
Australia:
* Victoria 10h
* NSW 10h
* Tasmania 10h
* Queensland 10h
* South 9½h
  N Territory 9½h
* West 8h
* Austria 1h
Bahrain 3h
* Balearic Is 1h
Bangladesh 6h
* Belgium 1h
* Bulgaria 2h
Burma 6½h
Cameroon 1h
* China 8h
Congo 1h
* Corsica 1h
* Crete 2h
* Cyprus 2h
* Czechoslovakia 1h
* Denmark 1h
* Egypt 2h
* Estonia 2h
Ethiopia 3h
Fiji 12h
* Finland 2h
* France 1h
* Germany 1h
* Gibraltar 1h
* Greece 2h
* Holland 1h
Hong Kong 8h
* Hungary 1h
India 5½h
* Iran 3½h
* Iraq 3h
* Israel 2h
* Italy 1h
Japan 9h
* Jordan 2h
Kenya 3h
Korea 9h
Laos 7h
* Latvia 2h
* Lebanon 2h
Libya 2h
* Liechtenstein 1h
* Lithuania 2h
* Luxembourg 1h
Madagascar 3h
Malawi 2h
Malaysia 8h
* Malta 1h
Marshall Is 12h
Mauritius 4h
* Monaco 1h
Mozambique 2h

* New Zealand 12h
Nigeria 1h
* Norway 1h
Pakistan 5h
Philippines 8h
* Poland 1h
* Romania 2h
Russia 3½h
Seychelles 4h
* Sicily 1h
Singapore 8h
Solomon Is 11h
Somalia 3h
South Africa 2h
* Spain 1h
Sri Lanka 5½h
* Sweden 1h
* Switzerland 1h
* Syria 2h
Taiwan 8h
Tanzania 3h
Thailand 7h
Tunisia 1h
* Turkey 2h
Uganda 3h
Vietnam 7h
* Yugoslavia 1h
Zambia 2h
Zimbabwe 2h

* May keep Summer Time or Daylight Saving Time.

Countries keeping times slow on GMT

Subtract from GMT to find Standard Time; add to Standard Time to find GMT.

* Argentina 3h
* Azores 1h
* Bahamas 5h
Barbados 4h
Belize 6h
* Bermuda 4h
Brazil E 3h
Brazil W 4h
Canada:
* Alberta 7h
* Brit Columbia 8h
* Labrador 4h
* Manitoba 6h
* Newfndland 3½h
* New Brunswick 4h
* Nova Scotia 4h
* Ontario 5h
* Quebec 5h
* Saskatchewan 6h
* Yukon 8h
Cape Verde Is 1h
* Chile 4h
Colombia 5h
* Cook Is 10h
* Costa Rica 6h
* Cuba 5h
Dominican Rep 4h
Ecuador 5h
* Easter Island 6h
El Salvador 6h
* Falkland Is 4h
French Guiana 3h
* Greenland 1–4h
Grenada 4h
Guadeloupe 4h
* Guatemala 6h
Guyana 3h
* Haiti 5h
Honduras 6h
Jamaica 5h
Leeward Is 4h
Mexico 6–8h
Midway Is 11h
Nicaragua 6h
Niue Is 11h
Panama 5h
* Paraguay 4h
Peru 5h
Puerto Rico 4h
* St Pierre and Miquelon 3h
Samoa 11h
South Georgia 2h
Trinidad and Tobago 4h
* Turks & Caicos Is 5h
United States:
* Eastern Zone 5h
* Central Zone 6h
* Pacific Zone 8h
* Mountain Zn 7h
* Alaska Zone 9hr
Hawaiian Is 10h
* Uruguay 3h
Venezuela 4h
Virgin Is 4h
Windward Is 4h

* May keep Summer Time or Daylight Saving Time.

EPHEMERIS

VISIBILITY OF PLANETS 1995

VENUS is a brilliant object in the morning sky from the beginning of the year until mid-July, when it becomes too close to the Sun for observation. During the last week in September it reappears in the evening sky, where it stays until the end of the year. Venus is in conjunction with Jupiter on January 14 and November 19, with Saturn on April 13, with Mercury on June 19 and September 28, and with Mars on November 22.

MARS rises well before midnight at the beginning of the year in Leo (passing 4° N of Regulus on January 28) and is at opposition on February 12, when it is visible all night as a bright, reddish object. Its eastward elongation gradually decreases, and from late May it is visible only in the evening until late December, when it becomes too close to the Sun for observation. It passes from Leo into Cancer, back into Leo (passing 1.1° N of Regulus on May 24), then moves through Virgo (passing 2° N of Spica on August 27), Libra, Scorpius, Ophiuchus (passing 4° N of Antares on November 2), and into Sagittarius at the end of November. Mars is in conjunction with Jupiter on November 16, with Venus on November 22, and with Mercury on December 23.

JUPITER rises well before sunrise at the beginning of the year in Scorpius, moving into Ophiuchus by mid-January (passing 5° N of Antares on January 23), and by early March can be seen for more than half the night. Its westward elongation gradually increases until on June 1 it is at opposition, when it is visible all night. Its eastward elongation then decreases as it passes from Ophiuchus (passing 5° N of Antares} on June 14), into Scorpius by early July, and returning to Ophiuchus in late August (passing 5° N of Antares on September 20, by which time it can be seen only in the evening sky), where it remains until early December, when it becomes too close to the Sun for observation. Jupiter is in conjunction with Venus on January 14 and November 19 and with Mars on November 16.

SATURN can be seen in the evening sky in Aquarius until mid-February; then it becomes too close to the Sun for observation. It reappears in the morning sky during the second half of March still in Aquarius, in which constellation it remains all year. Its westward elongation gradually increases until it is at opposition on September 14, when it is visible all night. Its eastward elongation then gradually decreases until mid-December when it can be seen only

in the evening sky. Saturn is in conjunction with Mercury on March 26 and with Venus on April 13.

MERCURY can be seen only low in the east before sunrise or low in the west after sunset (about the time of the beginning or end of civil twilight). It is visible in the mornings between the following approximate dates: February 10 (+2.2) to April 6 (-1.1); June 15 (+2.8) to July 20 (-1.5); October 12 (+1.5) to November 8 (-1.0) The planet is brighter at the end of each period. It is visible in the evenings between the following approximate dates: January 1 (-0.9) to January 29 (+1.7); April 22 (-1.6) to May 26 (+2.8); August 6 (-1.1) to September 29 (+2.4); December 10 (-0.7) to December 31 (-0.6). The planet is brighter at the beginning of each period. The figures in parentheses are the magnitudes.

PLANET DIAGRAM

The diagram opposite shows, in graphical form for any date during the year, the local mean time of meridian passage (transit) of the Sun, of the five major planets, and of each 30° of SHA. It is intended to provide a general picture of the availability of planets and stars for observation.

The trick to this graph is to select your day and then to read the meridian passages from bottom to top for 24 hours and to understand them as defining the relationships of the bodies throughout the day. For instance, observe the events of January 20:

Mars transits the meridian at about 0200, so it should be still fairly high in the western sky at dawn.

Venus and **Jupiter** both transit a little before 0900, 3 hours before the Sun. Therefore, they should be rising roughly 3 hours before dawn and should be fairly close together in the sky.

Mercury transits at 1330 and will be very low in the western sky at sunset.

Saturn transits at 1500 and hence will also be in the sunset sky, higher than Mercury.

Note the conjunction of **Jupiter, Mars,** and **Venus** that will take place about November 18. From the monthly pages, we know that this will be a moonless evening; so, given a clear sky, it should be a lovely planet show.

Note also that on each side of the line marking the time of meridian passage of the Sun is a band, 45 minutes wide, shaded to indicate that planets and stars setting or rising within 45 minutes of the Sun are too close for observation.

PLANETS, 1995

LOCAL MEAN TIME OF MERIDIAN PASSAGE

LOCAL MEAN TIME OF MERIDIAN PASSAGE

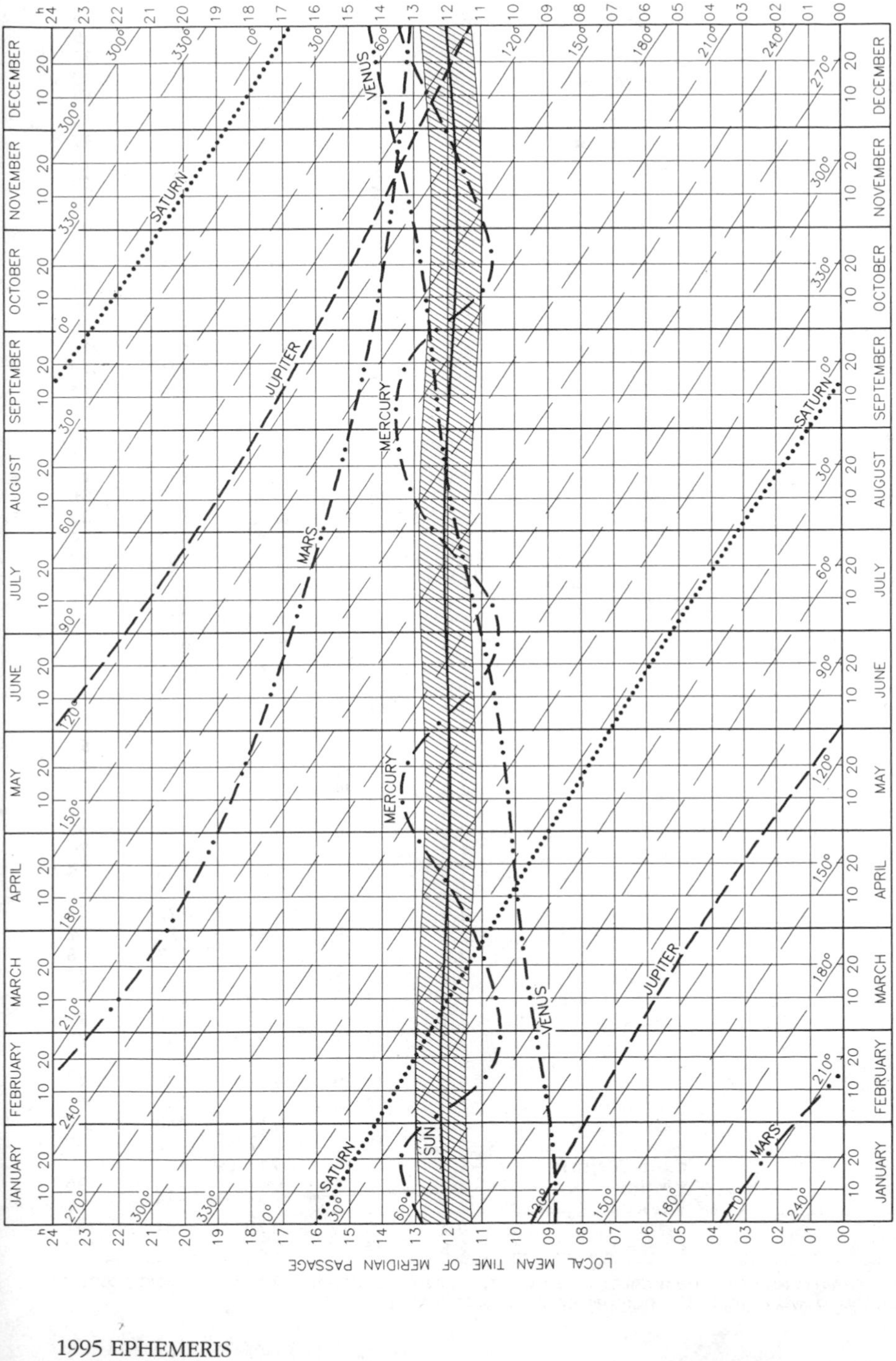

EPHEMERIS

ALPHABETICAL INDEX OF PRINCIPAL STARS
With their approximate places, 1995

Proper Name	Constellation Name	Mag	RA	Dec	SHA	No
Acamar	Eridani	3.1	2 58	S 40	315	8
Achernar	Eridani	0.6	1 37	S 57	336	5
Acrux	Crucis	1.1	12 26	S 63	173	32
Adhara	Canis Majoris	1.6	6 58	S 28	255	20
Aldebaran	Tauri	1.1	4 36	N 16	291	11
Alioth	Ursae Majoris	1.7	12 54	N 56	167	35
Alkaid	Ursae Majoris	1.9	13 47	N 49	153	37
Al Na'ir	Gruis	2.2	22 08	S 47	28	58
Alnilam	Orionis	1.8	5 36	S 1	276	16
Alphard	Hydrae	2.2	9 27	S 9	218	27
Alphecca	Coronae Bor	2.3	15 34	N 27	126	44
Alpheratz	Andromedae	2.2	0 08	N 29	358	1
Altair	Aquilae	0.9	19 50	N 9	62	54
Ankaa	Phoenicis	2.4	0 26	S 42	354	2
Antares	Scorpii	1.2	16 29	S 26	113	45
Arcturus	Bootis	0.2	14 15	N 19	146	40
Atria	Triang Aust	1.9	16 48	S 69	108	46
Avior	Carinae	1.7	8 22	S 59	234	24
Bellatrix	Orionis	1.7	5 25	N 6	279	14
Betelgeuse	Orionis	0.1-1.2	5 55	N 7	271	17
Canopus	Carinae	−0.9	6 24	S 53	264	18
Capella	Aurigae	0.2	5 16	N 46	281	13
Castor	Geminorum	1.6	7 34	N 32	246	21
Deneb	Cygni	1.3	20 41	N 45	50	56
Denebola	Leonis	2.2	11 49	N 15	183	30
Diphda	Ceti	2.2	0 43	S 18	349	4
Dubhe	Ursae Majoris	2.0	11 03	N 62	194	29
Elnath	Tauri	1.8	5 26	N 29	279	15
Eltanin	Draconis	2.4	17 56	N 51	91	50
Enif	Pegasi	2.5	21 44	N 10	34	57
Fomalhaut	Piscis Aust	1.3	22 57	S 30	16	59
Gacrux	Crucis	1.6	12 31	S 57	172	33
Gienah	Corvi	2.8	12 16	S 18	176	31
Hadar	Centauri	0.9	14 03	S 60	149	38
Hamal	Arietis	2.2	2 07	N 23	328	7
Kaus Aust	Sagittarii	2.0	18 24	S 34	84	51
Kochab	Ursae Minoris	2.2	14 51	N 74	137	43
Markab	Pegasi	2.6	23 04	N 15	14	60
Menkar	Ceti	2.8	3 02	N 4	315	9
Menkent	Centauri	2.3	14 06	S 36	148	39
Miaplacidus	Carinae	1.8	9 13	S 70	222	26
Mimosa	Crucis	1.5	12 47	S 60	168	34
Mirfak	Persei	1.9	3 24	N 50	309	10
Nunki	Sagittarii	2.1	18 55	S 26	76	53
Peacock	Pavonis	2.1	20 25	S 57	54	55
POLARIS	Ursae Minoris	2.1	2 26	N 89	323	6
Pollux	Geminorum	1.2	7 45	N 28	244	23
Procyon	Canis Minoris	0.5	7 39	N 5	245	22
Rasalhague	Ophiuchi	2.1	17 35	N 13	96	49
Regulus	Leonis	1.3	10 08	N 12	208	28
Rigel	Orionis	0.3	5 14	S 8	281	12
Rigil Kent	Centauri	0.1	14 39	S 61	140	41
Sabik	Ophiuchi	2.6	17 10	S 16	102	47
Schedar	Cassiopeiae	2.5	0 40	N 56	350	3
Shaula	Scorpii	1.7	17 33	S 37	97	48
Sirius	Canis Majoris	−1.6	6 45	S 17	259	19
Spica	Virginis	1.2	13 25	S 11	159	36
Suhail	Velorum	2.2	9 08	S 43	223	25
Vega	Lyrae	0.1	18 37	N 39	81	52
Zuben'ubi	Librae	2.9	14 51	S 16	137	42

The last column refers to the number given to the star in this almanac. The star's exact position may be found according to this number on the monthly pages.

CELESTIAL PHENOMENA 1995

SEASONS 1995

Vernal Equinox. Spring begins when Sun enters Aries, 02h14 March 21.

Summer Solstice. Summer begins when Sun enters Cancer, 20h34 June 21.

Autumn Equinox. Autumn begins when Sun enters Libra, 12h13 September 23.

Winter Solstice. Winter begins when Sun enters Capricorn, 08h17 December 22.

Earth is at Perihelion (closest to the Sun) 11h January 4; at Aphelion (farthest from the Sun), 02h July 4.

ECLIPSES 1995

There are two eclipses of the Sun and one of the Moon in 1995:

April 15. Partial eclipse of the Moon, begins 10h08, ends 14h28. Visible in Mexico, W half of N America, Pacific Ocean, Australasia, and E part of Asia.

April 29. Annular eclipse of the Sun, begins 14h33, ends 20h31. Visible in Pacific Ocean, Central America, S America except extreme S tip, Atlantic Ocean, and W Africa.

October 24. Total eclipse of the Sun, begins 01h51, ends 07h13. Visible in extreme NE Africa, Central and E Asia except NE part, N Indian Ocean, N half of Australia, and W Pacific Ocean.

Further celestial phenomena can be found in the Diary section on the second of each set of monthly pages. The phases of the moon are on the first page of each section.

1996 DATA

If the 1996 edition of *Reed's Nautical Almanac* is not available to you at the start of the year, it will be possible to use the data given in these tables for Sun and star sights. The details will be approximate but of quite sufficient accuracy for navigational purposes, as any error would be unlikely to exceed 0.4'.

It is not possible to use the 1995 data for 1996 observations of the Moon or planets.

INDEX OF TABLES

EPHEMERIS

JANUARY 1995 — SUN & MOON — GMT

SUN

Yr	Mth	Week	Equation of Time 0h	12h	Transit	Semi-diam	Lat 52°N Twilight	Sunrise	Sunset	Twilight	Lat Corr to Sunrise, Sunset etc — Lat	Twilight	Sunrise	Sunset	Twilight
			m s	m s	h m	′	h m	h m	h m	h m	°	h m	h m	h m	h m
1	1	Sun	+03 11	+03 26	12 03	16.3	07 28	08 08	15 59	16 39	N60	+0 33	+0 47	-0 47	-0 33
2	2	Mon	+03 40	+03 54	12 04	16.3	07 28	08 08	16 00	16 40	55	+0 11	+0 15	-0 15	-0 11
3	3	Tu	+04 08	+04 22	12 04	16.3	07 28	08 08	16 01	16 41	50	-0 06	-0 09	+0 09	+0 06
4	4	Wed	+04 36	+04 50	12 05	16.3	07 27	08 08	16 02	16 43	45	-0 20	-0 27	+0 27	+0 20
5	5	Th	+05 03	+05 17	12 05	16.3	07 27	08 07	16 03	16 44	N40	-0 32	-0 41	+0 41	+0 32
6	6	Fri	+05 30	+05 43	12 06	16.3	07 27	08 07	16 05	16 45	35	-0 42	-0 54	+0 54	+0 42
7	7	Sat	+05 57	+06 10	12 06	16.3	07 27	08 07	16 06	16 46	30	-0 52	-1 05	+1 05	+0 52
8	8	Sun	+06 23	+06 35	12 07	16.3	07 26	08 06	16 07	16 47	25	-1 00	-1 15	+1 15	+1 00
9	9	Mon	+06 48	+07 01	12 07	16.3	07 26	08 06	16 09	16 48	N20	-1 08	-1 24	+1 24	+1 08
10	10	Tu	+07 13	+07 25	12 07	16.3	07 25	08 05	16 10	16 50	15	-1 16	-1 32	+1 32	+1 16
11	11	Wed	+07 37	+07 49	12 08	16.3	07 25	08 05	16 11	16 51	10	-1 24	-1 40	+1 40	+1 24
12	12	Th	+08 01	+08 13	12 08	16.3	07 24	08 04	16 13	16 52	5	-1 31	-1 48	+1 48	+1 31
13	13	Fri	+08 24	+08 36	12 09	16.3	07 24	08 03	16 14	16 54	0	-1 39	-1 56	+1 56	+1 39
14	14	Sat	+08 47	+08 58	12 09	16.3	07 23	08 02	16 16	16 55	S 5	-1 47	-2 04	+2 04	+1 47
15	15	Sun	+09 09	+09 20	12 09	16.3	07 22	08 02	16 17	16 57	10	-1 55	-2 12	+2 12	+1 55
16	16	Mon	+09 30	+09 40	12 10	16.3	07 22	08 01	16 19	16 58	15	-2 04	-2 20	+2 20	+2 04
17	17	Tu	+09 51	+10 01	12 10	16.3	07 21	08 00	16 21	17 00	S20	-2 14	-2 29	+2 29	+2 14
18	18	Wed	+10 11	+10 20	12 10	16.3	07 20	07 59	16 22	17 01	25	-2 24	-2 38	+2 38	+2 24
19	19	Th	+10 30	+10 39	12 11	16.3	07 19	07 58	16 24	17 03	30	-2 36	-2 48	+2 48	+2 36
20	20	Fri	+10 48	+10 57	12 11	16.3	07 18	07 57	16 26	17 04	35	-2 50	-3 00	+3 00	+2 50
21	21	Sat	+11 06	+11 14	12 11	16.3	07 17	07 56	16 27	17 06	S40	-3 06	-3 13	+3 13	+3 06
22	22	Sun	+11 23	+11 31	12 12	16.3	07 16	07 54	16 29	17 07	45	-3 26	-3 29	+3 29	+3 26
23	23	Mon	+11 39	+11 47	12 12	16.3	07 15	07 53	16 31	17 09	50	-3 52	-3 49	+3 49	+3 52
24	24	Tu	+11 55	+12 02	12 12	16.3	07 14	07 52	16 33	17 10					
25	25	Wed	+12 09	+12 16	12 12	16.3	07 13	07 51	16 34	17 12					
26	26	Th	+12 23	+12 30	12 12	16.3	07 12	07 49	16 36	17 14					
27	27	Fri	+12 36	+12 43	12 13	16.3	07 11	07 48	16 38	17 15					
28	28	Sat	+12 49	+12 55	12 13	16.3	07 09	07 47	16 40	17 17					
29	29	Sun	+13 00	+13 06	12 13	16.3	07 08	07 45	16 42	17 19					
30	30	Mon	+13 11	+13 16	12 13	16.3	07 07	07 44	16 43	17 20					
31	31	Tu	+13 21	+13 26	12 13	16.3	07 05	07 42	16 45	17 22					

NOTES
Lat corrections are for mid-month.
Equation of Time is the excess of Mean Time over Apparent Time.

MOON

Yr	Mth	Week	Age	Transit (Upper)	Diff	Semi-diam	Hor Par	Lat 52°N Moonrise	Moonset	Phases of the Moon
			days	h m	m	′		h m	h m	d h m
1	1	Sun	30	12 05	59	16.5	60.5	07 40	16 34	● New Moon 1 10 56
2	2	Mon	01	13 04	55	16.3	59.9	08 24	17 51	☾ First Quarter 8 15 46
3	3	Tu	02	13 59	52	16.1	59.2	09 00	19 09	○ Full Moon 16 20 26
4	4	Wed	03	14 51	49	15.9	58.3	09 29	20 25	☽ Last Quarter 24 04 58
5	5	Th	04	15 40	47	15.6	57.4	09 54	21 38	● New Moon 30 22 48
6	6	Fri	05	16 27	44	15.4	56.5	10 17	22 48	
7	7	Sat	06	17 11	45	15.2	55.7	10 39	23 56	
8	8	Sun	07	17 56	44	15.0	55.1	11 01	— —	
9	9	Mon	08	18 40	45	14.9	54.6	11 25	01 02	Apogee 11 22
10	10	Tu	09	19 25	46	14.8	54.3	11 52	02 06	Perigee 27 23
11	11	Wed	10	20 11	47	14.7	54.1	12 22	03 08	
12	12	Th	11	20 58	49	14.8	54.1	12 58	04 08	
13	13	Fri	12	21 47	49	14.8	54.3	13 41	05 03	
14	14	Sat	13	22 36	49	14.9	54.5	14 31	05 52	
15	15	Sun	14	23 25	48	15.0	54.9	15 27	06 36	
16	16	Mon	15	24 13	—	15.1	55.3	16 30	07 14	
17	17	Tu	16	00 13	49	15.2	55.7	17 36	07 47	
18	18	Wed	17	01 02	47	15.3	56.2	18 45	08 15	
19	19	Th	18	01 49	48	15.4	56.7	19 56	08 41	
20	20	Fri	19	02 37	47	15.6	57.2	21 08	09 04	
21	21	Sat	20	03 24	49	15.7	57.7	22 22	09 28	**NOTES**
22	22	Sun	21	04 13	50	15.8	58.1	23 37	09 52	**Diff** equals daily change in
23	23	Mon	22	05 03	52	16.0	58.6	— —	10 18	transit time.
24	24	Tu	23	05 55	55	16.1	59.1	00 52	10 49	To correct Moonrise, Moonset,
25	25	Wed	24	06 50	58	16.2	59.4	02 08	11 26	or Transit times for Latitude
26	26	Th	25	07 48	59	16.3	59.7	03 21	12 11	and/or Longitude see page
27	27	Fri	26	08 47	61	16.3	59.9	04 28	13 06	E 100. For further information
28	28	Sat	27	09 48	59	16.3	59.9	05 26	14 11	about these tables see page E 4.
29	29	Sun	28	10 47	56	16.3	59.7	06 15	15 24	For Arc to Time correction see
30	30	Mon	29	11 43	54	16.2	59.3	06 55	16 41	page E 91.
31	31	Tu	01	12 37	51	16.0	58.7	07 27	17 58	

JANUARY 1995 — STARS — 0h GMT January 1

No	Name	Mag	Transit h m	Dec ° ′	GHA ° ′	RA h m	SHA ° ′
	ARIES................		17 16		100 10.7		
1	Alpheratz.........	2.2	17 25	N 29 04.0	98 08.6	0 08	357 57.9
2	Ankaa...............	2.4	17 42	S 42 20.2	93 40.2	0 26	353 29.5
3	Schedar	2.5	17 57	N 56 30.9	90 07.1	0 40	349 56.4
4	Diphda	2.2	18 00	S 18 00.9	89 20.5	0 43	349 09.8
5	Achernar...........	0.6	18 54	S 57 16.0	75 47.7	1 38	335 37.0
6	POLARIS	2.1	19 44	N 89 14.8	63 17.3	2 28	323 06.6
7	Hamal...............	2.2	19 23	N 23 26.4	68 27.0	2 07	328 16.3
8	Acamar.............	3.1	20 14	S 40 19.7	55 39.4	2 58	315 28.7
9	Menkar	2.8	20 18	N 4 04.2	54 40.1	3 02	314 29.4
10	Mirfak	1.9	20 40	N 49 50.8	49 10.6	3 24	308 59.9
11	Aldebaran.........	1.1	21 51	N 16 29.9	31 15.7	4 36	291 05.0
12	Rigel	0.3	22 30	S 8 12.6	21 35.8	5 14	281 25.1
13	Capella	0.2	22 32	N 45 59.6	21 05.2	5 16	280 54.5
14	Bellatrix	1.7	22 40	N 6 20.6	18 57.2	5 25	278 46.5
15	Elnath..............	1.8	22 42	N 28 36.1	18 40.4	5 26	278 29.7
16	Alnilam	1.8	22 52	S 1 12.5	16 10.8	5 36	276 00.1
17	Betelgeuse.......0.1-1.2		23 10	N 7 24.2	11 26.6	5 55	271 15.9
18	Canopus............	-0.9	23 39	S 52 41.8	4 12.4	6 24	264 01.7
19	Sirius	-1.6	0 04	S 16 42.7	358 56.2	6 45	258 45.5
20	Adhara	1.6	0 18	S 28 58.1	355 33.7	6 58	255 23.0
21	Castor	1.6	0 53	N 31 53.8	346 35.8	7 34	246 25.1
22	Procyon	0.5	0 58	N 5 14.1	345 24.5	7 39	245 13.8
23	Pollux	1.2	1 04	N 28 02.1	343 54.9	7 45	243 44.2
24	Avior	1.7	1 41	S 59 29.7	334 33.6	8 22	234 22.9
25	Suhail	2.2	2 27	S 43 24.8	323 12.8	9 08	223 02.1
26	Miaplacidus	1.8	2 32	S 69 41.8	321 52.3	9 13	221 41.6
27	Alphard............	2.2	2 46	S 8 38.4	318 20.0	9 27	218 09.3
28	Regulus	1.3	3 27	N 11 59.3	308 08.6	10 08	207 57.9
29	Dubhe	2.0	4 22	N 61 46.3	294 18.9	11 03	194 08.2
30	Denebola	2.2	5 07	N 14 35.8	282 58.3	11 49	182 47.6
31	Gienah	2.8	5 34	S 17 30.9	276 17.1	12 16	176 06.4
32	Acrux...............	1.1	5 45	S 63 04.1	273 35.2	12 26	173 24.5
33	Gacrux..............	1.6	5 49	S 57 04.9	272 26.8	12 31	172 16.1
34	Mimosa	1.5	6 06	S 59 39.5	268 18.7	12 47	168 08.0
35	Alioth	1.7	6 12	N 55 58.8	266 43.4	12 54	166 32.7
36	Spica................	1.2	6 43	S 11 08.2	258 56.5	13 25	158 45.8
37	Alkaid..............	1.9	7 05	N 49 20.0	253 20.5	13 47	153 09.8
38	Hadar	0.9	7 22	S 60 20.7	249 18.3	14 03	149 07.6
39	Menkent	2.3	7 24	S 36 20.6	248 34.6	14 06	148 23.9
40	Arcturus	0.2	7 33	N 19 12.3	246 19.1	14 15	146 08.4
41	Rigil Kent.	0.1	7 57	S 60 48.6	240 21.4	14 39	140 10.7
42	Zuben'ubi	2.9	8 09	S 16 01.2	237 31.5	14 51	137 20.8
43	Kochab	2.2	8 09	N 74 10.2	237 30.7	14 51	137 20.0
44	Alphecca	2.3	8 52	N 26 43.7	226 33.6	15 34	126 22.9
45	Antares	1.2	9 47	S 26 25.1	212 54.2	16 29	112 43.5
46	Atria	1.9	10 06	S 69 00.9	208 08.9	16 48	107 58.2
47	Sabik	2.6	10 28	S 15 43.0	202 39.4	17 10	102 28.7
48	Shaula	1.7	10 51	S 37 05.9	196 51.7	17 33	96 41.0
49	Rasalhague	2.1	10 52	N 12 33.8	196 30.3	17 35	96 19.6
50	Eltanin.............	2.4	11 14	N 51 29.3	191 03.8	17 56	90 53.1
51	Kaus Aust.	2.0	11 41	S 34 23.1	184 13.2	18 24	84 02.5
52	Vega	0.1	11 54	N 38 46.8	180 59.4	18 37	80 48.7
53	Nunki	2.1	12 12	S 26 18.1	176 26.5	18 55	76 15.8
54	Altair...............	0.9	13 08	N 8 51.4	162 32.7	19 51	62 22.0
55	Peacock	2.1	13 42	S 56 45.0	153 52.2	20 25	53 41.5
56	Deneb	1.3	13 58	N 45 15.9	149 52.0	20 41	49 41.3
57	Enif	2.5	15 01	N 9 51.2	134 11.7	21 44	34 01.0
58	Al Na'ir............	2.2	15 25	S 46 59.2	128 12.1	22 08	28 01.4
59	Fomalhaut	1.3	16 14	S 29 39.0	115 50.1	22 57	15 39.4
60	Markab	2.6	16 21	N 15 10.8	114 03.0	23 05	13 52.3

Stars Transit Corr Table

Date	Corr h m	Date	Corr h m
1	−0 00	17	−1 03
2	−0 04	18	−1 07
3	−0 08	19	−1 11
4	−0 12	20	−1 15
5	−0 16	21	−1 19
6	−0 20	22	−1 23
7	−0 24	23	−1 27
8	−0 28	24	−1 30
9	−0 31	25	−1 34
10	−0 35	26	−1 38
11	−0 39	27	−1 42
12	−0 43	28	−1 46
13	−0 47	29	−1 50
14	−0 51	30	−1 54
15	−0 55	31	−1 58
16	−0 59		

STAR TRANSIT

To find the approx time of transit of a star for any day of the month use above table. All corrections are subtractive.

If the value taken from the table is greater than the time of transit for the first of the month, add 23h 56min to the time of transit before subtracting the correction.

Example: What time will Adhara (No 20) transit the Meridian on January 30?

	h min
Transit on Jan 1	00 18
	+23 56
	24 14
Corr for Jan 30	−01 54
Transit on Jan 30	22 20

JANUARY DIARY

d h	
4 01	Mars stationary
4 11	Earth at perihelion
5 17	Saturn 7° S of Moon
13 12	Venus greatest elongation W(47°)
14 09	Venus 3° N of Jupiter
15 22	Venus 8° N of Antares
19 08	Mercury greatest elongation E(19°)
19 19	Mars 9° N of Moon
23 01	Jupiter 5° N of Antares
23 11	Spica 0.6° S of Moon
25 12	Mercury stationary
26 17	Jupiter 1.7° S of Moon
27 12	Venus 0.2° S of Moon
28 18	Mars 4° N of Regulus
29 20	Neptune 4° S of Moon

NOTES

Star declinations may be used as is for the whole month. To correct GHA for day, hour, minute and second see page E 92 and for further explanation of this table see page E 4.

JANUARY

JANUARY 1995 — SUN & ARIES — GMT

Band 1

Time	SUN GHA	Dec	ARIES GHA	Time	SUN GHA	Dec	ARIES GHA	Time	SUN GHA	Dec	ARIES GHA	Time
	Sunday, 1st January				Friday, 6th January				Wednesday, 11th January			
00	179 12.0	S23 03.2	100 10.7	00	178 37.3	S22 34.4	105 06.4	00	178 05.5	S21 54.4	110 02.1	00
02	209 11.4	23 02.9	130 15.7	02	208 36.8	22 33.8	135 11.3	02	208 05.0	21 53.6	140 07.0	02
04	239 10.8	23 02.5	160 20.6	04	238 36.2	22 33.2	165 16.3	04	238 04.5	21 52.9	170 12.0	04
06	269 10.2	23 02.1	190 25.5	06	268 35.6	22 32.6	195 21.2	06	268 04.0	21 52.1	200 16.9	06
08	299 09.6	23 01.7	220 30.4	08	298 35.1	22 32.1	225 26.1	08	298 03.5	21 51.3	230 21.8	08
10	329 09.0	23 01.3	250 35.4	10	328 34.5	22 31.5	255 31.1	10	328 03.0	21 50.6	260 26.8	10
12	359 08.4	23 00.9	280 40.3	12	358 34.0	22 30.9	285 36.0	12	358 02.5	21 49.8	290 31.7	12
14	29 07.8	23 00.5	310 45.2	14	28 33.4	22 30.3	315 40.9	14	28 02.0	21 49.0	320 36.6	14
16	59 07.2	23 00.0	340 50.2	16	58 32.9	22 29.7	345 45.8	16	58 01.5	21 48.2	350 41.5	16
18	89 06.7	22 59.6	10 55.1	18	88 32.3	22 29.1	15 50.8	18	88 01.0	21 47.5	20 46.5	18
20	119 06.1	22 59.2	41 00.0	20	118 31.8	22 28.5	45 55.7	20	118 00.5	21 46.7	50 51.4	20
22	149 05.5	S22 58.8	71 04.9	22	148 31.2	S22 27.9	76 00.6	22	148 00.1	S21 45.9	80 56.3	22

Band 2

Time	SUN GHA	Dec	ARIES GHA	Time	SUN GHA	Dec	ARIES GHA	Time	SUN GHA	Dec	ARIES GHA	Time
	Monday, 2nd January				Saturday, 7th January				Thursday, 12th January			
00	179 04.9	S22 58.4	101 09.9	00	178 30.7	S22 27.3	106 05.6	00	177 59.6	S21 45.1	111 01.3	00
02	209 04.3	22 58.0	131 14.8	02	208 30.1	22 26.6	136 10.5	02	207 59.1	21 44.3	141 06.2	02
04	239 03.7	22 57.5	161 19.7	04	238 29.6	22 26.0	166 15.4	04	237 58.6	21 43.5	171 11.1	04
06	269 03.1	22 57.1	191 24.6	06	268 29.1	22 25.4	196 20.3	06	267 58.1	21 42.7	201 16.0	06
08	299 02.5	22 56.7	221 29.6	08	298 28.5	22 24.8	226 25.3	08	297 57.6	21 41.9	231 21.0	08
10	329 01.9	22 56.2	251 34.5	10	328 28.0	22 24.2	256 30.2	10	327 57.1	21 41.1	261 25.9	10
12	359 01.4	22 55.8	281 39.4	12	358 27.4	22 23.5	286 35.1	12	357 56.7	21 40.3	291 30.8	12
14	29 00.8	22 55.3	311 44.4	14	28 26.9	22 22.9	316 40.1	14	27 56.2	21 39.5	321 35.7	14
16	59 00.2	22 54.9	341 49.3	16	58 26.3	22 22.3	346 45.0	16	57 55.7	21 38.7	351 40.7	16
18	88 59.6	22 54.4	11 54.2	18	88 25.8	22 21.6	16 49.9	18	87 55.2	21 37.8	21 45.6	18
20	118 59.0	22 54.0	41 59.1	20	118 25.3	22 21.0	46 54.8	20	117 54.7	21 37.0	51 50.5	20
22	148 58.4	S22 53.5	72 04.1	22	148 24.7	S22 20.3	76 59.8	22	147 54.3	S21 36.2	81 55.5	22

Band 3

Time	SUN GHA	Dec	ARIES GHA	Time	SUN GHA	Dec	ARIES GHA	Time	SUN GHA	Dec	ARIES GHA	Time
	Tuesday, 3rd January				Sunday, 8th January				Friday, 13th January			
00	178 57.8	S22 53.1	102 09.0	00	178 24.2	S22 19.7	107 04.7	00	177 53.8	S21 35.4	112 00.4	00
02	208 57.3	22 52.6	132 13.9	02	208 23.7	22 19.0	137 09.6	02	207 53.3	21 34.5	142 05.3	02
04	238 56.7	22 52.1	162 18.9	04	238 23.1	22 18.4	167 14.6	04	237 52.8	21 33.7	172 10.2	04
06	268 56.1	22 51.7	192 23.8	06	268 22.6	22 17.7	197 19.5	06	267 52.4	21 32.9	202 15.2	06
08	298 55.5	22 51.2	222 28.7	08	298 22.1	22 17.1	227 24.4	08	297 51.9	21 32.0	232 20.1	08
10	328 54.9	22 50.7	252 33.6	10	328 21.5	22 16.4	257 29.3	10	327 51.4	21 31.2	262 25.0	10
12	358 54.4	22 50.2	282 38.6	12	358 21.0	22 15.8	287 34.3	12	357 50.9	21 30.3	292 30.0	12
14	28 53.8	22 49.7	312 43.5	14	28 20.5	22 15.1	317 39.2	14	27 50.5	21 29.5	322 34.9	14
16	58 53.2	22 49.3	342 48.4	16	58 19.9	22 14.4	347 44.1	16	57 50.0	21 28.7	352 39.8	16
18	88 52.6	22 48.8	12 53.4	18	88 19.4	22 13.7	17 49.0	18	87 49.5	21 27.8	22 44.7	18
20	118 52.0	22 48.3	42 58.3	20	118 18.9	22 13.1	47 54.0	20	117 49.1	21 26.9	52 49.7	20
22	148 51.5	S22 47.8	73 03.2	22	148 18.4	S22 12.4	77 58.9	22	147 48.6	S21 26.1	82 54.6	22

Band 4

Time	SUN GHA	Dec	ARIES GHA	Time	SUN GHA	Dec	ARIES GHA	Time	SUN GHA	Dec	ARIES GHA	Time
	Wednesday, 4th January				Monday, 9th January				Saturday, 14th January			
00	178 50.9	S22 47.3	103 08.1	00	178 17.8	S22 11.7	108 03.8	00	177 48.1	S21 25.2	112 59.5	00
02	208 50.3	22 46.8	133 13.1	02	208 17.3	22 11.0	138 08.8	02	207 47.7	21 24.4	143 04.5	02
04	238 49.8	22 46.3	163 18.0	04	238 16.8	22 10.3	168 13.7	04	237 47.2	21 23.5	173 09.4	04
06	268 49.2	22 45.8	193 22.9	06	268 16.3	22 09.6	198 18.6	06	267 46.8	21 22.6	203 14.3	06
08	298 48.6	22 45.3	223 27.9	08	298 15.7	22 08.9	228 23.5	08	297 46.3	21 21.8	233 19.2	08
10	328 48.0	22 44.7	253 32.8	10	328 15.2	22 08.2	258 28.5	10	327 45.8	21 20.9	263 24.2	10
12	358 47.5	22 44.2	283 37.7	12	358 14.7	22 07.5	288 33.4	12	357 45.4	21 20.0	293 29.1	12
14	28 46.9	22 43.7	313 42.6	14	28 14.2	22 06.8	318 38.3	14	27 44.9	21 19.1	323 34.0	14
16	58 46.3	22 43.2	343 47.6	16	58 13.7	22 06.1	348 43.3	16	57 44.5	21 18.2	353 39.0	16
18	88 45.8	22 42.7	13 52.5	18	88 13.1	22 05.4	18 48.2	18	87 44.0	21 17.3	23 43.9	18
20	118 45.2	22 42.1	43 57.4	20	118 12.6	22 04.7	48 53.1	20	117 43.6	21 16.5	53 48.8	20
22	148 44.6	S22 41.6	74 02.4	22	148 12.1	S22 04.0	78 58.0	22	147 43.1	S21 15.6	83 53.7	22

Band 5

Time	SUN GHA	Dec	ARIES GHA	Time	SUN GHA	Dec	ARIES GHA	Time	SUN GHA	Dec	ARIES GHA	Time
	Thursday, 5th January				Tuesday, 10th January				Sunday, 15th January			
00	178 44.1	S22 41.1	104 07.3	00	178 11.6	S22 03.3	109 03.0	00	177 42.7	S21 14.7	113 58.7	00
02	208 43.5	22 40.5	134 12.2	02	208 11.1	22 02.5	139 07.9	02	207 42.2	21 13.8	144 03.6	02
04	238 42.9	22 40.0	164 17.1	04	238 10.6	22 01.8	169 12.8	04	237 41.8	21 12.9	174 08.5	04
06	268 42.4	22 39.4	194 22.1	06	268 10.1	22 01.1	199 17.8	06	267 41.3	21 12.0	204 13.5	06
08	298 41.8	22 38.9	224 27.0	08	298 09.6	22 00.3	229 22.7	08	297 40.9	21 11.1	234 18.4	08
10	328 41.2	22 38.3	254 31.9	10	328 09.0	21 59.6	259 27.6	10	327 40.4	21 10.2	264 23.3	10
12	358 40.7	22 37.8	284 36.8	12	358 08.5	21 58.9	289 32.5	12	357 40.0	21 09.2	294 28.2	12
14	28 40.1	22 37.2	314 41.8	14	28 08.0	21 58.1	319 37.5	14	27 39.6	21 08.3	324 33.2	14
16	58 39.5	22 36.7	344 46.7	16	58 07.5	21 57.4	349 42.4	16	57 39.1	21 07.4	354 38.1	16
18	88 39.0	22 36.1	14 51.6	18	88 07.0	21 56.6	19 47.3	18	87 38.7	21 06.5	24 43.0	18
20	118 38.4	22 35.5	44 56.6	20	118 06.5	21 55.9	49 52.3	20	117 38.2	21 05.6	54 47.9	20
22	148 37.9	S22 35.0	75 01.5	22	148 06.0	S21 55.1	79 57.2	22	147 37.8	S21 04.6	84 52.9	22

NOTES

Sun & Aries GHA corrections for additional hour, minutes, and seconds on page E 94.
Correct Sun Declination by interpolation. For example see page E 4.

JANUARY 1995 — SUN & ARIES — GMT

Monday, 16th January

Time	SUN GHA	Dec	ARIES GHA
00	177 37.4	S21 03.7	114 57.8
02	207 36.9	21 02.8	145 02.7
04	237 36.5	21 01.8	175 07.7
06	267 36.1	21 00.9	205 12.6
08	297 35.6	21 00.0	235 17.5
10	327 35.2	20 59.0	265 22.4
12	357 34.8	20 58.1	295 27.4
14	27 34.4	20 57.1	325 32.3
16	57 33.9	20 56.2	355 37.2
18	87 33.5	20 55.2	25 42.2
20	117 33.1	20 54.3	55 47.1
22	147 32.7	S20 53.3	85 52.0

Tuesday, 17th January

Time	SUN GHA	Dec	ARIES GHA
00	177 32.2	S20 52.3	115 56.9
02	207 31.8	20 51.4	146 01.9
04	237 31.4	20 50.4	176 06.8
06	267 31.0	20 49.4	206 11.7
08	297 30.6	20 48.5	236 16.7
10	327 30.1	20 47.5	266 21.6
12	357 29.7	20 46.5	296 26.5
14	27 29.3	20 45.5	326 31.4
16	57 28.9	20 44.6	356 36.4
18	87 28.5	20 43.6	26 41.3
20	117 28.1	20 42.6	56 46.2
22	147 27.7	S20 41.6	86 51.2

Wednesday, 18th January

Time	SUN GHA	Dec	ARIES GHA
00	177 27.3	S20 40.6	116 56.1
02	207 26.9	20 39.6	147 01.0
04	237 26.5	20 38.6	177 05.9
06	267 26.1	20 37.6	207 10.9
08	297 25.7	20 36.6	237 15.8
10	327 25.3	20 35.6	267 20.7
12	357 24.9	20 34.6	297 25.7
14	27 24.5	20 33.5	327 30.6
16	57 24.1	20 32.5	357 35.5
18	87 23.7	20 31.5	27 40.4
20	117 23.3	20 30.5	57 45.4
22	147 22.9	S20 29.5	87 50.3

Thursday, 19th January

Time	SUN GHA	Dec	ARIES GHA
00	177 22.5	S20 28.4	117 55.2
02	207 22.1	20 27.4	148 00.2
04	237 21.7	20 26.4	178 05.1
06	267 21.3	20 25.3	208 10.0
08	297 20.9	20 24.3	238 14.9
10	327 20.5	20 23.3	268 19.9
12	357 20.2	20 22.2	298 24.8
14	27 19.8	20 21.2	328 29.7
16	57 19.4	20 20.1	358 34.6
18	87 19.0	20 19.1	28 39.6
20	117 18.6	20 18.0	58 44.5
22	147 18.3	S20 16.9	88 49.4

Friday, 20th January

Time	SUN GHA	Dec	ARIES GHA
00	177 17.9	S20 15.9	118 54.4
02	207 17.5	20 14.8	148 59.3
04	237 17.1	20 13.8	179 04.2
06	267 16.8	20 12.7	209 09.1
08	297 16.4	20 11.6	239 14.1
10	327 16.0	20 10.6	269 19.0
12	357 15.6	20 09.5	299 23.9
14	27 15.3	20 08.4	329 28.9
16	57 14.9	20 07.3	359 33.8
18	87 14.5	20 06.2	29 38.7
20	117 14.2	20 05.1	59 43.6
22	147 13.8	S20 04.1	89 48.6

Saturday, 21st January

Time	SUN GHA	Dec	ARIES GHA
00	177 13.5	S20 03.0	119 53.5
02	207 13.1	20 01.9	149 58.4
04	237 12.7	20 00.8	180 03.4
06	267 12.4	19 59.7	210 08.3
08	297 12.0	19 58.6	240 13.2
10	327 11.7	19 57.5	270 18.1
12	357 11.3	19 56.4	300 23.1
14	27 11.0	19 55.3	330 28.0
16	57 10.6	19 54.1	0 32.9
18	87 10.3	19 53.0	30 37.9
20	117 09.9	19 51.9	60 42.8
22	147 09.6	S19 50.8	90 47.7

Sunday, 22nd January

Time	SUN GHA	Dec	ARIES GHA
00	177 09.2	S19 49.7	120 52.6
02	207 08.9	19 48.5	150 57.6
04	237 08.5	19 47.4	181 02.5
06	267 08.2	19 46.3	211 07.4
08	297 07.8	19 45.2	241 12.4
10	327 07.5	19 44.0	271 17.3
12	357 07.2	19 42.9	301 22.2
14	27 06.8	19 41.7	331 27.1
16	57 06.5	19 40.6	1 32.1
18	87 06.2	19 39.5	31 37.0
20	117 05.8	19 38.3	61 41.9
22	147 05.5	S19 37.2	91 46.8

Monday, 23rd January

Time	SUN GHA	Dec	ARIES GHA
00	177 05.2	S19 36.0	121 51.8
02	207 04.8	19 34.8	151 56.7
04	237 04.5	19 33.7	182 01.6
06	267 04.2	19 32.5	212 06.6
08	297 03.8	19 31.4	242 11.5
10	327 03.5	19 30.2	272 16.4
12	357 03.2	19 29.0	302 21.3
14	27 02.9	19 27.9	332 26.3
16	57 02.6	19 26.7	2 31.2
18	87 02.2	19 25.5	32 36.1
20	117 01.9	19 24.3	62 41.1
22	147 01.6	S19 23.2	92 46.0

Tuesday, 24th January

Time	SUN GHA	Dec	ARIES GHA
00	177 01.3	S19 22.0	122 50.9
02	207 01.0	19 20.8	152 55.8
04	237 00.7	19 19.6	183 00.8
06	267 00.4	19 18.4	213 05.7
08	297 00.0	19 17.2	243 10.6
10	326 59.7	19 16.0	273 15.6
12	356 59.4	19 14.8	303 20.5
14	26 59.1	19 13.6	333 25.4
16	56 58.8	19 12.4	3 30.3
18	86 58.5	19 11.2	33 35.3
20	116 58.2	19 10.0	63 40.2
22	146 57.9	S19 08.8	93 45.1

Wednesday, 25th January

Time	SUN GHA	Dec	ARIES GHA
00	176 57.6	S19 07.6	123 50.1
02	206 57.3	19 06.4	153 55.0
04	236 57.0	19 05.1	183 59.9
06	266 56.7	19 03.9	214 04.8
08	296 56.4	19 02.7	244 09.8
10	326 56.1	19 01.5	274 14.7
12	356 55.9	19 00.3	304 19.6
14	26 55.6	18 59.0	334 24.6
16	56 55.3	18 57.8	4 29.5
18	86 55.0	18 56.6	34 34.4
20	116 54.7	18 55.3	64 39.3
22	146 54.4	S18 54.1	94 44.3

Thursday, 26th January

Time	SUN GHA	Dec	ARIES GHA
00	176 54.1	S18 52.8	124 49.2
02	206 53.9	18 51.6	154 54.1
04	236 53.6	18 50.4	184 59.0
06	266 53.3	18 49.1	215 04.0
08	296 53.0	18 47.9	245 08.9
10	326 52.7	18 46.6	275 13.8
12	356 52.5	18 45.3	305 18.8
14	26 52.2	18 44.1	335 23.7
16	56 51.9	18 42.8	5 28.6
18	86 51.7	18 41.6	35 33.5
20	116 51.4	18 40.3	65 38.5
22	146 51.1	S18 39.0	95 43.4

Friday, 27th January

Time	SUN GHA	Dec	ARIES GHA
00	176 50.9	S18 37.8	125 48.3
02	206 50.6	18 36.5	155 53.3
04	236 50.3	18 35.2	185 58.2
06	266 50.1	18 33.9	216 03.1
08	296 49.8	18 32.7	246 08.0
10	326 49.5	18 31.4	276 13.0
12	356 49.3	18 30.1	306 17.9
14	26 49.0	18 28.8	336 22.8
16	56 48.8	18 27.5	6 27.8
18	86 48.5	18 26.2	36 32.7
20	116 48.3	18 24.9	66 37.6
22	146 48.0	S18 23.6	96 42.5

Saturday, 28th January

Time	SUN GHA	Dec	ARIES GHA
00	176 47.8	S18 22.3	126 47.5
02	206 47.5	18 21.0	156 52.4
04	236 47.3	18 19.7	186 57.3
06	266 47.0	18 18.4	217 02.3
08	296 46.8	18 17.1	247 07.2
10	326 46.5	18 15.8	277 12.1
12	356 46.3	18 14.5	307 17.0
14	26 46.1	18 13.2	337 22.0
16	56 45.8	18 11.9	7 26.9
18	86 45.6	18 10.6	37 31.8
20	116 45.3	18 09.2	67 36.8
22	146 45.1	S18 07.9	97 41.7

Sunday, 29th January

Time	SUN GHA	Dec	ARIES GHA
00	176 44.9	S18 06.6	127 46.6
02	206 44.7	18 05.3	157 51.5
04	236 44.4	18 03.9	187 56.5
06	266 44.2	18 02.6	218 01.4
08	296 44.0	18 01.3	248 06.3
10	326 43.7	17 59.9	278 11.3
12	356 43.5	17 58.6	308 16.2
14	26 43.3	17 57.2	338 21.1
16	56 43.1	17 55.9	8 26.0
18	86 42.9	17 54.6	38 31.0
20	116 42.6	17 53.2	68 35.9
22	146 42.4	S17 51.9	98 40.8

Monday, 30th January

Time	SUN GHA	Dec	ARIES GHA
00	176 42.2	S17 50.5	128 45.7
02	206 42.0	17 49.2	158 50.7
04	236 41.8	17 47.8	188 55.6
06	266 41.6	17 46.4	219 00.5
08	296 41.3	17 45.1	249 05.5
10	326 41.1	17 43.7	279 10.4
12	356 40.9	17 42.3	309 15.3
14	26 40.7	17 41.0	339 20.2
16	56 40.5	17 39.6	9 25.2
18	86 40.3	17 38.2	39 30.1
20	116 40.1	17 36.9	69 35.0
22	146 39.9	S17 35.5	99 40.0

Tuesday, 31st January

Time	SUN GHA	Dec	ARIES GHA
00	176 39.7	S17 34.1	129 44.9
02	206 39.5	17 32.7	159 49.8
04	236 39.3	17 31.3	189 54.7
06	266 39.1	S17 30.0	219 59.7
08	296 38.9	S17 28.6	250 04.6
10	326 38.7	17 27.2	280 09.5
12	356 38.6	17 25.8	310 14.5
14	26 38.4	S17 24.4	340 19.4
16	56 38.2	S17 23.0	10 24.3
18	86 38.0	17 21.6	40 29.2
20	116 37.8	17 20.2	70 34.2
22	146 37.6	S17 18.8	100 39.1

JANUARY

JANUARY 1995 — PLANETS — 0h GMT

VENUS / JUPITER

Mer Pass h m	GHA ° '	Mean Var/hr 14°+	Dec ° '	Mean Var/hr '	Note (Corrections on Page E 101)	GHA ° '	Mean Var/hr 15°+	Dec ° '	Mean Var/hr '	Mer Pass h m
08 49	227 46.2	0.1	S 15 13.9	0.5	1 SUN	217 15.3	1.9	S 20 20.1	0.1	09 30
08 49	227 49.8	0.1	S 15 26.4	0.5	2 Mon	218 01.9	1.9	S 20 22.2	0.1	09 27
08 48	227 52.8	0.1	S 15 38.9	0.5	3 Tu	218 48.5	1.9	S 20 24.3	0.1	09 24
08 48	227 55.0	0.1	S 15 51.4	0.5	4 Wed	219 35.1	2.0	S 20 26.5	0.1	09 20
08 48	227 56.6	0.0	S 16 04.0	0.5	5 Th	220 21.9	1.9	S 20 28.5	0.1	09 17
08 48	227 57.6	0.0	S 16 16.5	0.5	6 Fri	221 08.7	1.9	S 20 30.6	0.1	09 14
08 48	227 57.9	0.0	S 16 29.0	0.5	7 Sat	221 55.5	2.0	S 20 32.6	0.1	09 11
08 48	227 57.7	0.0	S 16 41.4	0.5	8 SUN	222 42.4	2.0	S 20 34.6	0.1	09 08
08 48	227 56.8	14	S 16 53.7	0.5	9 Mon	223 29.4	2.0	S 20 36.6	0.1	09 05
08 48	227 55.4	59.9	S 17 06.0	0.5	10 Tu	224 16.5	2.0	S 20 38.5	0.1	09 02
08 48	227 53.4	59.9	S 17 18.1	0.5	11 Wed	225 03.7	2.0	S 20 40.4	0.1	08 59
08 49	227 50.8	59.9	S 17 30.0	0.5	12 Th	225 50.9	2.0	S 20 42.3	0.1	08 55
08 49	227 47.6	59.8	S 17 41.8	0.5	13 Fri	226 38.2	2.0	S 20 44.2	0.1	08 52
08 49	227 43.9	59.8	S 17 53.4	0.5	14 Sat	227 25.5	2.0	S 20 46.0	0.1	08 49
08 49	227 39.7	59.8	S 18 04.8	0.5	15 SUN	228 13.0	2.0	S 20 47.8	0.1	08 46
08 50	227 35.0	59.8	S 18 16.0	0.5	16 Mon	229 00.5	2.0	S 20 49.5	0.1	08 43
08 50	227 29.8	59.8	S 18 27.0	0.4	17 Tu	229 48.1	2.0	S 20 51.3	0.1	08 40
08 51	227 24.0	59.7	S 18 37.7	0.4	18 Wed	230 35.9	2.0	S 20 53.0	0.1	08 36
08 51	227 17.8	59.7	S 18 48.1	0.4	19 Th	231 23.7	2.0	S 20 54.7	0.1	08 33
08 51	227 11.1	59.7	S 18 58.2	0.4	20 Fri	232 11.5	2.0	S 20 56.3	0.1	08 30
08 52	227 03.9	59.7	S 19 08.1	0.4	21 Sat	232 59.5	2.0	S 20 58.0	0.1	08 27
08 52	226 56.2	59.7	S 19 17.6	0.4	22 SUN	233 47.6	2.0	S 20 59.6	0.1	08 24
08 53	226 48.2	59.6	S 19 26.8	0.4	23 Mon	234 35.8	2.0	S 21 01.1	0.1	08 20
08 54	226 39.7	59.6	S 19 35.6	0.4	24 Tu	235 24.0	2.0	S 21 02.7	0.1	08 17
08 54	226 30.7	59.6	S 19 44.1	0.3	25 Wed	236 12.4	2.0	S 21 04.2	0.1	08 14
08 55	226 21.4	59.6	S 19 52.1	0.3	26 Th	237 00.9	2.0	S 21 05.7	0.1	08 11
08 55	226 11.7	59.6	S 19 59.8	0.3	27 Fri	237 49.4	2.0	S 21 07.2	0.1	08 08
08 56	226 01.6	59.6	S 20 07.1	0.3	28 Sat	238 38.1	2.0	S 21 08.6	0.1	08 04
08 57	225 51.2	59.6	S 20 14.0	0.3	29 SUN	239 26.9	2.0	S 21 10.0	0.1	08 01
08 58	225 40.4	59.5	S 20 20.5	0.3	30 Mon	240 15.8	2.0	S 21 11.4	0.1	07 58
08 58	225 29.3	59.5	S 20 26.5	0.2	31 Tu	241 04.8	2.0	S 21 12.8	0.1	07 55

VENUS, Av. Mag. -4.4
S.H.A. January
5 124; 10 119; 15 114; 20 108; 25 103; 30 97.

JUPITER, Av. Mag.-1.8
S.H.A. January
5 116; 10 115; 15 114; 20 113; 25 112; 30 112.

MARS / SATURN

Mer Pass h m	GHA ° '	Mean Var/hr 15°+	Dec ° '	Mean Var/hr '	Note (Corrections on Page E 101)	GHA ° '	Mean Var/hr 15°+	Dec ° '	Mean Var/hr '	Mer Pass h m
03 42	304 17.4	2.4	N 13 45.6	0.1	1 SUN	119 50.8	2.3	S 10 14.3	0.1	15 58
03 38	305 14.6	2.4	N 13 47.3	0.1	2 Mon	120 45.2	2.3	S 10 12.3	0.1	15 55
03 35	306 12.6	2.4	N 13 49.4	0.1	3 Tu	121 39.6	2.3	S 10 10.3	0.1	15 51
03 31	307 11.3	2.5	N 13 51.7	0.1	4 Wed	122 33.9	2.3	S 10 08.3	0.1	15 47
03 27	308 10.8	2.5	N 13 54.2	0.1	5 Th	123 28.1	2.3	S 10 06.2	0.1	15 44
03 23	309 11.1	2.5	N 13 57.1	0.1	6 Fri	124 22.3	2.3	S 10 04.2	0.1	15 40
03 19	310 12.1	2.6	N 14 00.2	0.1	7 Sat	125 16.4	2.3	S 10 02.1	0.1	15 37
03 15	311 13.8	2.6	N 14 03.7	0.1	8 SUN	126 10.5	2.3	S 9 59.9	0.1	15 33
03 10	312 16.4	2.6	N 14 07.3	0.2	9 Mon	127 04.5	2.2	S 9 57.8	0.1	15 29
03 06	313 19.7	2.7	N 14 11.3	0.2	10 Tu	127 58.4	2.2	S 9 55.6	0.1	15 26
03 02	314 23.8	2.7	N 14 15.6	0.2	11 Wed	128 52.3	2.2	S 9 53.4	0.1	15 22
02 58	315 28.6	2.7	N 14 20.1	0.2	12 Th	129 46.1	2.2	S 9 51.2	0.1	15 19
02 53	316 34.3	2.8	N 14 24.9	0.2	13 Fri	130 39.9	2.2	S 9 49.0	0.1	15 15
02 49	317 40.7	2.8	N 14 29.9	0.2	14 Sat	131 33.6	2.2	S 9 46.7	0.1	15 11
02 44	318 47.9	2.8	N 14 35.2	0.2	15 SUN	132 27.2	2.2	S 9 44.4	0.1	15 08
02 40	319 55.9	2.9	N 14 40.8	0.2	16 Mon	133 20.8	2.2	S 9 42.1	0.1	15 04
02 35	321 04.7	2.9	N 14 46.6	0.3	17 Tu	134 14.3	2.2	S 9 39.8	0.1	15 01
02 31	322 14.3	2.9	N 14 52.7	0.3	18 Wed	135 07.8	2.2	S 9 37.4	0.1	14 57
02 26	323 24.7	3.0	N 14 59.0	0.3	19 Th	136 01.2	2.2	S 9 35.0	0.1	14 54
02 21	324 35.8	3.0	N 15 05.6	0.3	20 Fri	136 54.6	2.2	S 9 32.7	0.1	14 50
02 16	325 47.7	3.0	N 15 12.3	0.3	21 Sat	137 48.0	2.2	S 9 30.2	0.1	14 47
02 12	327 00.4	3.1	N 15 19.3	0.3	22 SUN	138 41.2	2.2	S 9 27.8	0.1	14 43
02 07	328 13.8	3.1	N 15 26.5	0.3	23 Mon	139 34.5	2.2	S 9 25.4	0.1	14 40
02 02	329 27.9	3.1	N 15 33.8	0.3	24 Tu	140 27.7	2.2	S 9 22.9	0.1	14 36
01 57	330 42.8	3.1	N 15 41.4	0.3	25 Wed	141 20.8	2.2	S 9 20.4	0.1	14 32
01 52	331 58.3	3.2	N 15 49.1	0.3	26 Th	142 13.9	2.2	S 9 17.9	0.1	14 29
01 47	333 14.6	3.2	N 15 57.0	0.3	27 Fri	143 07.0	2.2	S 9 15.4	0.1	14 25
01 42	334 31.5	3.2	N 16 04.9	0.3	28 Sat	144 00.0	2.2	S 9 12.9	0.1	14 22
01 36	335 49.1	3.3	N 16 13.0	0.3	29 SUN	144 53.0	2.2	S 9 10.3	0.1	14 18
01 31	337 07.3	3.3	N 16 21.2	0.3	30 Mon	145 45.9	2.2	S 9 07.8	0.1	14 15
01 26	338 26.0	3.3	N 16 29.5	0.4	31 Tu	146 38.8	2.2	S 9 05.2	0.1	14 11

MARS, Av. Mag. -0.7
S.H.A. January
5 204; 10 204; 15 205; 20 206; 25 207; 30 208.

SATURN, Av. Mag.-+1.0
S.H.A. January
5 19; 10 19; 15 18; 20 18; 25 18; 30 17.

JANUARY 1995 — MOON

Day	GMT hr	GHA ° ′	Mean Var/hr 14°+	Dec ° ′	Mean Var/hr ′	Day	GMT hr	GHA ° ′	Mean Var/hr 14°+	Dec ° ′	Mean Var/hr ′
1 Sun	0	186 11.7	23.1	S 19 27.2	3.6	17 Tu	0	356 45.4	30.8	N 15 45.5	7.0
	6	272 30.6	23.5	S 19 05.8	4.4		6	83 49.6	30.9	N 15 03.7	7.5
	12	358 51.4	23.9	S 18 39.6	5.2		12	170 54.4	30.9	N 14 19.1	7.9
	18	85 14.2	24.2	S 18 08.7	5.9		18	257 59.7	30.9	N 13 31.8	8.3
2 Mon	0	171 39.5	24.7	S 17 33.4	6.7	18 Wed	0	345 05.5	31.0	N 12 41.9	8.8
	6	258 07.5	25.1	S 16 53.9	7.2		6	72 11.9	31.2	N 11 49.6	9.2
	12	344 38.3	25.7	S 16 10.6	7.9		12	159 18.7	31.2	N 10 55.1	9.5
	18	71 12.1	26.2	S 15 23.7	8.4		18	246 26.0	31.3	N 9 58.5	9.8
3 Tu	0	157 49.0	26.7	S 14 33.5	8.9	19 Th	0	333 33.6	31.3	N 8 59.9	10.0
	6	244 29.1	27.2	S 13 40.4	9.4		6	60 41.5	31.3	N 7 59.6	10.4
	12	331 12.3	27.8	S 12 44.6	9.7		12	147 49.6	31.3	N 6 57.6	10.6
	18	57 58.6	28.3	S 11 46.5	10.1		18	234 57.9	31.4	N 5 54.1	10.8
4 Wed	0	144 48.0	28.7	S 10 46.4	10.4	20 Fri	0	322 06.1	31.4	N 4 49.5	11.0
	6	231 40.4	29.3	S 9 44.6	10.6		6	49 14.3	31.3	N 3 43.7	11.2
	12	318 35.8	29.7	S 8 41.3	10.7		12	136 22.2	31.3	N 2 37.0	11.2
	18	45 33.9	30.2	S 7 36.9	10.9		18	223 29.7	31.2	N 1 29.7	11.4
5 Th	0	132 34.6	30.5	S 6 31.6	11.0	21 Sat	0	310 36.8	31.1	N 0 21.8	11.4
	6	219 37.8	31.0	S 5 25.6	11.0		6	37 43.1	30.9	S 0 46.4	11.4
	12	306 43.3	31.3	S 4 19.2	11.1		12	124 48.7	30.8	S 1 54.7	11.4
	18	33 50.9	31.6	S 3 12.6	11.1		18	211 53.3	30.5	S 3 02.9	11.3
6 Fri	0	121 00.5	32.0	S 2 06.0	11.0	22 Sun	0	298 56.7	30.4	S 4 10.7	11.2
	6	208 11.8	32.2	S 0 59.6	11.0		6	25 58.9	30.1	S 5 18.1	11.1
	12	295 24.8	32.4	N 0 06.5	10.9		12	112 59.7	29.8	S 6 24.7	10.9
	18	22 39.1	32.6	N 1 12.0	10.8		18	199 58.9	29.6	S 7 30.3	10.7
7 Sat	0	109 54.7	32.8	N 2 16.8	10.7	23 Mon	0	286 56.4	29.2	S 8 34.7	10.5
	6	197 11.2	32.9	N 3 20.8	10.5		6	13 52.0	28.9	S 9 37.6	10.2
	12	284 28.7	33.0	N 4 23.8	10.3		12	100 45.6	28.6	S 10 38.8	9.8
	18	11 46.8	33.1	N 5 25.7	10.1		18	187 37.1	28.2	S 11 38.2	9.5
8 Sun	0	99 05.5	33.2	N 6 26.3	9.9	24 Tu	0	274 26.4	27.8	S 12 35.3	9.0
	6	186 24.4	33.2	N 7 25.6	9.6		6	1 13.5	27.5	S 13 30.0	8.7
	12	273 43.6	33.3	N 8 23.4	9.3		12	87 58.2	27.0	S 14 22.0	8.2
	18	1 02.9	33.2	N 9 19.6	9.0		18	174 40.6	26.6	S 15 11.1	7.7
9 Mon	0	88 22.0	33.1	N 10 14.1	8.7	25 Wed	0	261 20.6	26.3	S 15 57.0	7.0
	6	175 40.9	33.1	N 11 06.8	8.4		6	347 58.3	25.8	S 16 39.5	6.4
	12	262 59.4	33.0	N 11 57.6	8.1		12	74 33.7	25.5	S 17 18.3	5.8
	18	350 17.5	32.9	N 12 46.4	7.8		18	161 06.9	25.1	S 17 53.2	5.1
10 Tu	0	77 34.9	32.8	N 13 33.1	7.3	26 Th	0	247 38.1	24.8	S 18 24.0	4.3
	6	164 51.7	32.6	N 14 17.6	7.0		6	334 07.4	24.6	S 18 50.5	3.6
	12	252 07.8	32.5	N 14 59.8	6.6		12	60 35.0	24.4	S 19 12.5	2.8
	18	339 23.0	32.4	N 15 39.6	6.2		18	147 01.2	24.1	S 19 29.9	2.0
11 Wed	0	66 37.3	32.2	N 16 16.9	5.8	27 Fri	0	233 26.1	24.0	S 19 42.5	1.2
	6	153 50.6	32.1	N 16 51.6	5.3		6	319 50.2	23.9	S 19 50.3	0.4
	12	241 03.0	31.9	N 17 23.7	4.8		12	46 13.6	23.9	S 19 53.1	0.4
	18	328 14.3	31.8	N 17 52.9	4.4		18	132 36.8	23.9	S 19 50.9	1.3
12 Th	0	55 24.7	31.5	N 18 19.4	3.8	28 Sat	0	219 00.0	23.9	S 19 43.8	2.1
	6	142 34.0	31.4	N 18 42.8	3.4		6	305 23.5	24.0	S 19 31.7	2.9
	12	229 42.4	31.2	N 19 03.3	2.9		12	31 47.8	24.2	S 19 14.8	3.7
	18	316 49.8	31.0	N 19 20.6	2.3		18	118 13.0	24.5	S 18 53.1	4.5
13 Fri	0	43 56.3	31.0	N 19 34.8	1.7	29 Sun	0	204 39.6	24.7	S 18 26.7	5.2
	6	131 02.0	30.8	N 19 45.7	1.2		6	291 07.7	25.0	S 17 55.9	5.9
	12	218 06.8	30.7	N 19 53.4	0.7		12	17 37.6	25.3	S 17 20.9	6.6
	18	305 11.0	30.6	N 19 57.7	0.1		18	104 09.5	25.7	S 16 41.7	7.2
14 Sat	0	32 14.5	30.5	N 19 58.6	0.5	30 Mon	0	190 43.6	26.1	S 15 58.8	7.8
	6	119 17.6	30.5	N 19 56.1	1.1		6	277 20.0	26.5	S 15 12.3	8.4
	12	206 20.2	30.3	N 19 50.2	1.6		12	3 58.9	26.9	S 14 22.6	8.9
	18	293 22.5	30.3	N 19 40.8	2.2		18	90 40.3	27.4	S 13 29.8	9.3
15 Sun	0	20 24.6	30.3	N 19 28.0	2.8	31 Tu	0	177 24.2	27.8	S 12 34.4	9.7
	6	107 26.6	30.3	N 19 11.8	3.4		6	264 10.7	28.2	S 11 36.5	10.0
	12	194 28.6	30.3	N 18 52.1	3.9		12	350 59.8	28.6	S 10 36.5	10.4
	18	281 30.6	30.4	N 18 29.1	4.4		18	77 51.3	29.0	S 9 34.6	10.6
16 Mon	0	8 32.9	30.5	N 18 02.7	4.9						
	6	95 35.4	30.5	N 17 33.1	5.5						
	12	182 38.3	30.6	N 17 00.3	6.0						
	18	269 41.6	30.7	N 16 24.4	6.6						

NOTE Moon GHA corrections for additional hours, minutes, and seconds on page E 96.
Moon Declination corrections on page E 99. Mean Var/Hr value needed for both corrections.

JANUARY

FEBRUARY 1995 — SUN & MOON — GMT

SUN

Day of			Equation of Time			Semi-	Lat 52°N				Lat Corr to Sunrise, Sunset etc				
Yr	Mth	Week	0h	12h	Transit	diam	Twi-light	Sun-rise	Sun-set	Twi-light	Lat	Twi-light	Sun-rise	Sun-set	Twi-light
			m s	m s	h m	'	h m	h m	h m	h m	°	h m	h m	h m	h m
32	1	Wed	+13 30	+13 34	12 14	16.3	07 04	07 41	16 47	17 24	N60	+0 15	+0 23	-0 23	-0 15
33	2	Th	+13 38	+13 42	12 14	16.3	07 03	07 39	16 49	17 25	55	+0 05	+0 08	-0 08	-0 05
34	3	Fri	+13 46	+13 49	12 14	16.3	07 01	07 38	16 51	17 27	50	-0 03	-0 05	+0 05	+0 03
35	4	Sat	+13 53	+13 56	12 14	16.3	07 00	07 36	16 53	17 29	45	-0 10	-0 14	+0 14	+0 10
36	5	Sun	+13 58	+14 01	12 14	16.2	06 58	07 34	16 54	17 31	N40	-0 15	-0 22	+0 22	+0 15
37	6	Mon	+14 03	+14 06	12 14	16.2	06 57	07 33	16 56	17 32	35	-0 21	-0 30	+0 30	+0 21
38	7	Tu	+14 08	+14 09	12 14	16.2	06 55	07 31	16 58	17 34	30	-0 25	-0 36	+0 36	+0 25
39	8	Wed	+14 11	+14 12	12 14	16.2	06 53	07 29	17 00	17 36	25	-0 30	-0 41	+0 41	+0 30
40	9	Th	+14 14	+14 15	12 14	16.2	06 52	07 27	17 02	17 38	N20	-0 34	-0 47	+0 47	+0 34
41	10	Fri	+14 15	+14 16	12 14	16.2	06 50	07 26	17 04	17 39	15	-0 39	-0 52	+0 52	+0 39
42	11	Sat	+14 16	+14 16	12 14	16.2	06 48	07 24	17 06	17 41	10	-0 43	-0 56	+0 56	+0 43
43	12	Sun	+14 16	+14 16	12 14	16.2	06 46	07 22	17 08	17 43	5	-0 47	-1 01	+1 01	+0 47
44	13	Mon	+14 16	+14 15	12 14	16.2	06 45	07 20	17 09	17 45	0	-0 52	-1 05	+1 05	+0 52
45	14	Tu	+14 15	+14 14	12 14	16.2	06 43	07 18	17 11	17 46	S 5	-0 57	-1 10	+1 10	+0 57
46	15	Wed	+14 12	+14 11	12 14	16.2	06 41	07 16	17 13	17 48	10	-1 01	-1 15	+1 15	+1 01
47	16	Th	+14 10	+14 08	12 14	16.2	06 39	07 14	17 15	17 50	15	-1 07	-1 20	+1 20	+1 07
48	17	Fri	+14 06	+14 04	12 14	16.2	06 37	07 12	17 17	17 52	S20	-1 13	-1 25	+1 25	+1 13
49	18	Sat	+14 02	+13 59	12 14	16.2	06 35	07 10	17 19	17 53	25	-1 19	-1 30	+1 30	+1 19
50	19	Sun	+13 57	+13 54	12 14	16.2	06 34	07 08	17 21	17 55	30	-1 26	-1 36	+1 36	+1 26
51	20	Mon	+13 51	+13 48	12 14	16.2	06 32	07 06	17 22	17 57	35	-1 35	-1 43	+1 43	+1 35
52	21	Tu	+13 45	+13 41	12 14	16.2	06 30	07 04	17 24	17 59	S40	-1 45	-1 51	+1 51	+1 45
53	22	Wed	+13 38	+13 34	12 14	16.2	06 28	07 02	17 26	18 00	45	-1 57	-2 00	+2 00	+1 57
54	23	Th	+13 30	+13 26	12 13	16.2	06 26	07 00	17 28	18 02	50	-2 11	-2 11	+2 11	+2 11
55	24	Fri	+13 22	+13 18	12 13	16.2	06 24	06 58	17 30	18 04					
56	25	Sat	+13 13	+13 09	12 13	16.2	06 22	06 56	17 32	18 06					
57	26	Sun	+13 04	+12 59	12 13	16.2	06 19	06 54	17 33	18 07					
58	27	Mon	+12 54	+12 49	12 13	16.2	06 17	06 51	17 35	18 09					
59	28	Tu	+12 44	+12 39	12 13	16.2	06 15	06 49	17 37	18 11					

NOTES

Lat corrections are for mid-month.
Equation of Time is the excess of
Mean Time over Apparent Time.

MOON

Day of				Transit	Diff	Semi-	Hor	Lat 52°N		Phases of the Moon			
Yr	Mth	Week	Age	(Upper)		diam	Par	Moon-rise	Moon-set				
			days	h m	m	'	'	h m	h m			d	h	m
32	1	Wed	02	13 28	49	15.8	58.0	07 55	19 13					
33	2	Th	03	14 17	46	15.6	57.2	08 19	20 26	(First Quarter	7	12	54
34	3	Fri	04	15 03	46	15.4	56.5	08 42	21 37	○ Full Moon	15	12	15
35	4	Sat	05	15 49	45	15.2	55.7	09 05	22 45	) Last Quarter	22	13	04
36	5	Sun	06	16 34	45	15.0	55.1	09 29	23 51				
37	6	Mon	07	17 19	46	14.9	54.7	09 55	— —				
38	7	Tu	08	18 05	47	14.8	54.4	10 24	00 54				
39	8	Wed	09	18 52	48	14.8	54.2	10 57	01 55				
40	9	Th	10	19 40	48	14.8	54.3	11 37	02 52	Apogee	8	18	
41	10	Fri	11	20 28	49	14.8	54.5	12 23	03 44	Perigee	23	02	
42	11	Sat	12	21 17	49	14.9	54.8	13 17	04 30				
43	12	Sun	13	22 06	49	15.1	55.3	14 16	05 11				
44	13	Mon	14	22 55	48	15.2	55.8	15 21	05 46				
45	14	Tu	15	23 43	49	15.4	56.4	16 30	06 16				
46	15	Wed	16	24 32	—	15.5	57.0	17 41	06 44				
47	16	Th	17	00 32	48	15.7	57.5	18 55	07 09				
48	17	Fri	18	01 20	49	15.8	58.0	20 09	07 33				
49	18	Sat	19	02 09	51	15.9	58.4	21 25	07 58				
50	19	Sun	20	03 00	52	16.0	58.8	22 41	08 24				
51	20	Mon	21	03 52	54	16.1	59.0	23 57	08 54				
52	21	Tu	22	04 46	57	16.1	59.1	— —	09 28				
53	22	Wed	23	05 43	57	16.1	59.2	01 10	10 10	**NOTES**			
54	23	Th	24	06 40	59	16.1	59.2	02 18	11 01	**Diff** equals daily change in			
55	24	Fri	25	07 39	58	16.1	59.2	03 18	12 01	transit time.			
56	25	Sat	26	08 37	56	16.1	59.0	04 09	13 09	To correct Moonrise, Moonset,			
57	26	Sun	27	09 33	53	16.0	58.7	04 51	14 21	or Transit times for Latitude			
58	27	Mon	28	10 26	52	15.9	58.4	05 25	15 36	and/or Longitude see page			
59	28	Tu	29	11 18	49	15.8	57.9	05 55	16 51	E 100. For further information			

NOTES

Diff equals daily change in transit time.
To correct Moonrise, Moonset, or Transit times for Latitude and/or Longitude see page E 100. For further information about these tables see page E 4. For Arc to Time correction see page E 91.

FEBRUARY 1995   STARS   0h GMT February 1

No	Name	Mag	Transit h m	Dec ° ′	GHA ° ′	RA h m	SHA ° ′
	ARIES................		15 15		130 44.0		
1	Alpheratz.........	2.2	15 23	N 29 03.9	128 42.0	0 08	357 58.0
2	Ankaa.............	2.4	15 41	S 42 20.1	124 13.6	0 26	353 29.6
3	Schedar...........	2.5	15 55	N 56 30.8	120 40.6	0 40	349 56.6
4	Diphda............	2.2	15 58	S 18 00.9	119 53.9	0 43	349 09.9
5	Achernar..........	0.6	16 52	S 57 16.0	106 21.3	1 38	335 37.3
6	POLARIS..........	2.1	17 41	N 89 14.9	94 02.0	2 27	323 18.0
7	Hamal.............	2.2	17 21	N 23 26.4	99 00.4	2 07	328 16.4
8	Acamar............	3.1	18 12	S 40 19.8	86 12.8	2 58	315 28.8
9	Menkar...........	2.8	18 16	N 4 04.1	85 13.5	3 02	314 29.5
10	Mirfak...........	1.9	18 38	N 49 50.8	79 44.1	3 24	309 00.1
11	Aldebaran........	1.1	19 49	N 16 29.9	61 49.1	4 36	291 05.1
12	Rigel............	0.3	20 28	S 8 12.7	52 09.1	5 14	281 25.1
13	Capella..........	0.2	20 30	N 45 59.6	51 38.6	5 16	280 54.6
14	Bellatrix........	1.7	20 39	N 6 20.6	49 30.6	5 25	278 46.6
15	Elnath...........	1.8	20 40	N 28 36.2	49 13.8	5 26	278 29.8
16	Alnilam..........	1.8	20 50	S 1 12.5	46 44.2	5 36	276 00.2
17	Betelgeuse.......	0.1-1.2	21 09	N 7 24.2	42 00.0	5 55	271 16.0
18	Canopus..........	-0.9	21 37	S 52 42.0	34 45.9	6 24	264 01.9
19	Sirius...........	-1.6	21 58	S 16 42.8	29 29.6	6 45	258 45.6
20	Adhara...........	1.6	22 12	S 28 58.2	26 07.0	6 58	255 23.0
21	Castor...........	1.6	22 48	N 31 53.8	17 09.1	7 34	246 25.1
22	Procyon..........	0.5	22 52	N 5 14.0	15 57.8	7 39	245 13.8
23	Pollux...........	1.2	22 58	N 28 02.1	14 28.2	7 45	243 44.2
24	Avior............	1.7	23 36	S 59 29.9	5 07.0	8 22	234 23.0
25	Suhail...........	2.2	0 25	S 43 25.0	353 46.1	9 08	223 02.1
26	Miaplacidus......	1.8	0 30	S 69 42.0	352 25.5	9 13	221 41.5
27	Alphard..........	2.2	0 44	S 8 38.5	348 53.3	9 27	218 09.3
28	Regulus..........	1.3	1 25	N 11 59.2	338 41.8	10 08	207 57.8
29	Dubhe............	2.0	2 20	N 61 46.4	324 51.9	11 03	194 07.9
30	Denebola.........	2.2	3 05	N 14 35.7	313 31.4	11 49	182 47.4
31	Gienah...........	2.8	3 32	S 17 31.0	306 50.2	12 16	176 06.2
32	Acrux............	1.1	3 43	S 63 04.2	304 08.1	12 26	173 24.1
33	Gacrux...........	1.6	3 47	S 57 05.1	302 59.8	12 31	172 15.8
34	Mimosa...........	1.5	4 04	S 59 39.6	298 51.7	12 47	168 07.7
35	Alioth...........	1.7	4 10	N 55 58.8	297 16.4	12 54	166 32.4
36	Spica............	1.2	4 41	S 11 08.2	289 29.6	13 25	158 45.6
37	Alkaid...........	1.9	5 04	N 49 19.9	283 53.5	13 47	153 09.5
38	Hadar............	0.9	5 20	S 60 20.8	279 51.2	14 04	149 07.2
39	Menkent..........	2.3	5 23	S 36 20.7	279 07.6	14 06	148 23.6
40	Arcturus.........	0.2	5 32	N 19 12.2	276 52.2	14 15	146 08.2
41	Rigil Kent.......	0.1	5 55	S 60 48.6	270 54.3	14 39	140 10.3
42	Zuben'ubi........	2.9	6 07	S 16 01.3	268 04.6	14 51	137 20.6
43	Kochab...........	2.2	6 07	N 74 10.2	268 03.4	14 51	137 19.4
44	Alphecca.........	2.3	6 50	N 26 43.7	257 06.7	15 34	126 22.7
45	Antares..........	1.2	7 45	S 26 25.2	243 27.2	16 29	112 43.2
46	Atria............	1.9	8 04	S 69 00.8	238 41.6	16 48	107 57.6
47	Sabik............	2.6	8 26	S 15 43.1	233 12.5	17 10	102 28.5
48	Shaula...........	1.7	8 49	S 37 05.9	227 24.8	17 33	96 40.8
49	Rasalhague.......	2.1	8 50	N 12 33.7	227 03.4	17 35	96 19.4
50	Eltanin..........	2.4	9 12	N 51 29.2	221 36.8	17 56	90 52.8
51	Kaus Aust........	2.0	9 39	S 34 23.1	214 46.3	18 24	84 02.3
52	Vega.............	0.1	9 52	N 38 46.6	211 32.6	18 37	80 48.6
53	Nunki............	2.1	10 10	S 26 18.1	206 59.6	18 55	76 15.6
54	Altair...........	0.9	11 06	N 8 51.3	193 05.9	19 51	62 21.9
55	Peacock..........	2.1	11 40	S 56 44.9	184 25.4	20 25	53 41.4
56	Deneb............	1.3	11 56	N 45 15.8	180 25.3	20 41	49 41.3
57	Enif.............	2.5	12 59	N 9 51.2	164 44.9	21 44	34 00.9
58	Al Na'ir.........	2.2	13 23	S 46 59.1	158 45.4	22 08	28 01.4
59	Fomalhaut........	1.3	14 12	S 29 38.9	146 23.5	22 57	15 39.5
60	Markab...........	2.6	14 19	N 15 10.8	144 36.3	23 05	13 52.3

Star Transit Corr Table

Date	Corr h m	Date	Corr h m
1	−0 00	17	−1 03
2	−0 04	18	−1 07
3	−0 08	19	−1 11
4	−0 12	20	−1 15
5	−0 16	21	−1 19
6	−0 20	22	−1 23
7	−0 24	23	−1 27
8	−0 28	24	−1 30
9	−0 31	25	−1 34
10	−0 35	26	−1 38
11	−0 39	27	−1 42
12	−0 43	28	−1 46
13	−0 47	29	−1 50
14	−0 51	30	−1 54
15	−0 55	31	−1 58
16	−0 59		

STAR TRANSIT

To find the approx time of transit of a star for any day of the month use above table. All corrections are subtractive.

If the value taken from the table is greater than the time of transit for the first of the month, add 23h 56min to the time of transit before subtracting the correction.

Example: What time will Suhail (No 25) transit the Meridian on February 30?

	h min
Transit on Feb 1	00 25
	+23 56
	24 21
Corr for Feb 30	−01 54
Transit on Feb 30	22 27

FEBRUARY DIARY

d h	
2 08	Saturn 6° S of Moon
12 03	Mars closest approach
12 03	Mars at oposition
15 10	Mars 10° N of Moon
15 19	Mercury stationary
19 17	Spica 0.9° S of Moon
23 05	Jupiter 2° S of Moon
26 05	Venus 4° S of Moon
26 05	Neptune 4° S of Moon
26 13	Uranus 6° S of Moon
27 11	Mercury 5° S of Moon

NOTES

Star declinations may be used as is for the whole month. To correct GHA for day, hour, minute and second see page E 92 and for further explanation of this table see page E 4.

FEBRUARY

FEBRUARY 1995 — SUN & ARIES — GMT

Wednesday, 1st February

Time	SUN GHA	Dec	ARIES GHA
00	176 37.4	S17 17.4	130 44.0
02	206 37.3	17 16.0	160 49.0
04	236 37.1	17 14.6	190 53.9
06	266 36.9	17 13.2	220 58.8
08	296 36.7	17 11.8	251 03.7
10	326 36.5	17 10.3	281 08.7
12	356 36.4	17 08.9	311 13.6
14	26 36.2	17 07.5	341 18.5
16	56 36.0	17 06.1	11 23.5
18	86 35.9	17 04.7	41 28.4
20	116 35.7	17 03.2	71 33.3
22	146 35.5	S17 01.8	101 38.2

Thursday, 2nd February

Time	SUN GHA	Dec	ARIES GHA
00	176 35.4	S17 00.4	131 43.2
02	206 35.2	16 59.0	161 48.1
04	236 35.0	16 57.5	191 53.0
06	266 34.9	16 56.1	221 57.9
08	296 34.7	16 54.6	252 02.9
10	326 34.6	16 53.2	282 07.8
12	356 34.4	16 51.8	312 12.7
14	26 34.3	16 50.3	342 17.7
16	56 34.1	16 48.9	12 22.6
18	86 33.9	16 47.4	42 27.5
20	116 33.8	16 46.0	72 32.4
22	146 33.6	S16 44.5	102 37.4

Friday, 3rd February

Time	SUN GHA	Dec	ARIES GHA
00	176 33.5	S16 43.1	132 42.3
02	206 33.4	16 41.6	162 47.2
04	236 33.2	16 40.2	192 52.2
06	266 33.1	16 38.7	222 57.1
08	296 32.9	16 37.2	253 02.0
10	326 32.8	16 35.8	283 06.9
12	356 32.6	16 34.3	313 11.9
14	26 32.5	16 32.8	343 16.8
16	56 32.4	16 31.4	13 21.7
18	86 32.2	16 29.9	43 26.7
20	116 32.1	16 28.4	73 31.6
22	146 32.0	S16 26.9	103 36.5

Saturday, 4th February

Time	SUN GHA	Dec	ARIES GHA
00	176 31.8	S16 25.5	133 41.4
02	206 31.7	16 24.0	163 46.4
04	236 31.6	16 22.5	193 51.3
06	266 31.5	16 21.0	223 56.2
08	296 31.3	16 19.5	254 01.2
10	326 31.2	16 18.0	284 06.1
12	356 31.1	16 16.6	314 11.0
14	26 31.0	16 15.1	344 15.9
16	56 30.8	16 13.6	14 20.9
18	86 30.7	16 12.1	44 25.8
20	116 30.6	16 10.6	74 30.7
22	146 30.5	S16 09.1	104 35.7

Sunday, 5th February

Time	SUN GHA	Dec	ARIES GHA
00	176 30.4	S16 07.6	134 40.6
02	206 30.3	16 06.1	164 45.5
04	236 30.2	16 04.6	194 50.4
06	266 30.0	16 03.1	224 55.4
08	296 29.9	16 01.6	255 00.3
10	326 29.8	16 00.0	285 05.2
12	356 29.7	15 58.5	315 10.2
14	26 29.6	15 57.0	345 15.1
16	56 29.5	15 55.5	15 20.0
18	86 29.4	15 54.0	45 24.9
20	116 29.3	15 52.5	75 29.9
22	146 29.2	S15 50.9	105 34.8

Monday, 6th February

Time	SUN GHA	Dec	ARIES GHA
00	176 29.1	S15 49.4	135 39.7
02	206 29.0	15 47.9	165 44.6
04	236 28.9	15 46.4	195 49.6
06	266 28.8	15 44.8	225 54.5
08	296 28.8	15 43.3	255 59.4
10	326 28.7	15 41.8	286 04.4
12	356 28.6	15 40.2	316 09.3
14	26 28.5	15 38.7	346 14.2
16	56 28.4	15 37.2	16 19.1
18	86 28.3	15 35.6	46 24.1
20	116 28.2	15 34.1	76 29.0
22	146 28.2	S15 32.5	106 33.9

Tuesday, 7th February

Time	SUN GHA	Dec	ARIES GHA
00	176 28.1	S15 31.0	136 38.9
02	206 28.0	15 29.4	166 43.8
04	236 27.9	15 27.9	196 48.7
06	266 27.9	15 26.3	226 53.6
08	296 27.8	15 24.8	256 58.6
10	326 27.7	15 23.2	287 03.5
12	356 27.6	15 21.7	317 08.4
14	26 27.6	15 20.1	347 13.4
16	56 27.5	15 18.5	17 18.3
18	86 27.4	15 17.0	47 23.2
20	116 27.4	15 15.4	77 28.1
22	146 27.3	S15 13.8	107 33.1

Wednesday, 8th February

Time	SUN GHA	Dec	ARIES GHA
00	176 27.2	S15 12.3	137 38.0
02	206 27.2	15 10.7	167 42.9
04	236 27.1	15 09.1	197 47.9
06	266 27.1	15 07.6	227 52.8
08	296 27.0	15 06.0	257 57.7
10	326 26.9	15 04.4	288 02.6
12	356 26.9	15 02.8	318 07.6
14	26 26.8	15 01.2	348 12.5
16	56 26.8	14 59.7	18 17.4
18	86 26.7	14 58.1	48 22.4
20	116 26.7	14 56.5	78 27.3
22	146 26.6	S14 54.9	108 32.2

Thursday, 9th February

Time	SUN GHA	Dec	ARIES GHA
00	176 26.6	S14 53.3	138 37.1
02	206 26.6	14 51.7	168 42.1
04	236 26.5	14 50.1	198 47.0
06	266 26.5	14 48.5	228 51.9
08	296 26.4	14 46.9	258 56.8
10	326 26.4	14 45.3	289 01.8
12	356 26.4	14 43.7	319 06.7
14	26 26.3	14 42.1	349 11.6
16	56 26.3	14 40.5	19 16.6
18	86 26.3	14 38.9	49 21.5
20	116 26.2	14 37.3	79 26.4
22	146 26.2	S14 35.7	109 31.3

Friday, 10th February

Time	SUN GHA	Dec	ARIES GHA
00	176 26.2	S14 34.1	139 36.3
02	206 26.1	14 32.5	169 41.2
04	236 26.1	14 30.9	199 46.1
06	266 26.1	14 29.3	229 51.1
08	296 26.1	14 27.6	259 56.0
10	326 26.0	14 26.0	290 00.9
12	356 26.0	14 24.4	320 05.8
14	26 26.0	14 22.8	350 10.8
16	56 26.0	14 21.2	20 15.7
18	86 26.0	14 19.5	50 20.6
20	116 26.0	14 17.9	80 25.6
22	146 25.9	S14 16.3	110 30.5

Saturday, 11th February

Time	SUN GHA	Dec	ARIES GHA
00	176 25.9	S14 14.6	140 35.4
02	206 25.9	14 13.0	170 40.3
04	236 25.9	14 11.4	200 45.3
06	266 25.9	14 09.7	230 50.2
08	296 25.9	14 08.1	260 55.1
10	326 25.9	14 06.5	291 00.1
12	356 25.9	14 04.8	321 05.0
14	26 25.9	14 03.2	351 09.9
16	56 25.9	14 01.5	21 14.8
18	86 25.9	13 59.9	51 19.8
20	116 25.9	13 58.3	81 24.7
22	146 25.9	S13 56.6	111 29.6

Sunday, 12th February

Time	SUN GHA	Dec	ARIES GHA
00	176 25.9	S13 55.0	141 34.6
02	206 25.9	13 53.3	171 39.5
04	236 25.9	13 51.7	201 44.4
06	266 25.9	13 50.0	231 49.3
08	296 25.9	13 48.3	261 54.3
10	326 25.9	13 46.7	291 59.2
12	356 25.9	13 45.0	322 04.1
14	26 25.9	13 43.4	352 09.0
16	56 26.0	13 41.7	22 14.0
18	86 26.0	13 40.0	52 18.9
20	116 26.0	13 38.4	82 23.8
22	146 26.0	S13 36.7	112 28.8

Monday, 13th February

Time	SUN GHA	Dec	ARIES GHA
00	176 26.0	S13 35.0	142 33.7
02	206 26.1	13 33.4	172 38.6
04	236 26.1	13 31.7	202 43.5
06	266 26.1	13 30.0	232 48.5
08	296 26.1	13 28.3	262 53.4
10	326 26.2	13 26.7	292 58.3
12	356 26.2	13 25.0	323 03.3
14	26 26.2	13 23.3	353 08.2
16	56 26.2	13 21.6	23 13.1
18	86 26.3	13 20.0	53 18.0
20	116 26.3	13 18.3	83 23.0
22	146 26.3	S13 16.6	113 27.9

Tuesday, 14th February

Time	SUN GHA	Dec	ARIES GHA
00	176 26.4	S13 14.9	143 32.8
02	206 26.4	13 13.2	173 37.8
04	236 26.5	13 11.5	203 42.7
06	266 26.5	13 09.8	233 47.6
08	296 26.5	13 08.1	263 52.5
10	326 26.6	13 06.4	293 57.5
12	356 26.6	13 04.7	324 02.4
14	26 26.7	13 03.0	354 07.3
16	56 26.7	13 01.3	24 12.3
18	86 26.8	12 59.6	54 17.2
20	116 26.8	12 57.9	84 22.1
22	146 26.9	S12 56.2	114 27.0

Wednesday, 15th February

Time	SUN GHA	Dec	ARIES GHA
00	176 26.9	S12 54.5	144 32.0
02	206 27.0	12 52.8	174 36.9
04	236 27.0	12 51.1	204 41.8
06	266 27.1	12 49.4	234 46.8
08	296 27.1	12 47.7	264 51.7
10	326 27.2	12 46.0	294 56.6
12	356 27.2	12 44.3	325 01.5
14	26 27.3	12 42.6	355 06.5
16	56 27.4	12 40.8	25 11.4
18	86 27.4	12 39.1	55 16.3
20	116 27.5	12 37.4	85 21.2
22	146 27.6	S12 35.7	115 26.2

NOTES

Sun & Aries GHA corrections for additional hour, minutes, and seconds on page E 94.
Correct Sun Declination by interpolation. For example see page E 4.

FEBRUARY 1995 — SUN & ARIES — GMT

Thursday, 16th February

Time	SUN GHA	Dec	ARIES GHA
00	176 27.6	S12 34.0	145 31.1
02	206 27.7	12 32.2	175 36.0
04	236 27.8	12 30.5	205 41.0
06	266 27.8	12 28.8	235 45.9
08	296 27.9	12 27.1	265 50.8
10	326 28.0	12 25.3	295 55.7
12	356 28.1	12 23.6	326 00.7
14	26 28.1	12 21.9	356 05.6
16	56 28.2	12 20.1	26 10.5
18	86 28.3	12 18.4	56 15.5
20	116 28.4	12 16.7	86 20.4
22	146 28.4	S12 14.9	116 25.3

Friday, 17th February

Time	SUN GHA	Dec	ARIES GHA
00	176 28.5	S12 13.2	146 30.2
02	206 28.6	12 11.5	176 35.2
04	236 28.7	12 09.7	206 40.1
06	266 28.8	12 08.0	236 45.0
08	296 28.9	12 06.2	266 50.0
10	326 28.9	12 04.5	296 54.9
12	356 29.0	12 02.7	326 59.8
14	26 29.1	12 01.0	357 04.7
16	56 29.2	11 59.2	27 09.7
18	86 29.3	11 57.5	57 14.6
20	116 29.4	11 55.7	87 19.5
22	146 29.5	S11 54.0	117 24.5

Saturday, 18th February

Time	SUN GHA	Dec	ARIES GHA
00	176 29.6	S11 52.2	147 29.4
02	206 29.7	11 50.5	177 34.3
04	236 29.8	11 48.7	207 39.2
06	266 29.9	11 47.0	237 44.2
08	296 30.0	11 45.2	267 49.1
10	326 30.1	11 43.4	297 54.0
12	356 30.2	11 41.7	327 59.0
14	26 30.3	11 39.9	358 03.9
16	56 30.4	11 38.2	28 08.8
18	86 30.5	11 36.4	58 13.7
20	116 30.6	11 34.6	88 18.7
22	146 30.7	S11 32.8	118 23.6

Sunday, 19th February

Time	SUN GHA	Dec	ARIES GHA
00	176 30.8	S11 31.1	148 28.5
02	206 30.9	11 29.3	178 33.5
04	236 31.1	11 27.5	208 38.4
06	266 31.2	11 25.8	238 43.3
08	296 31.3	11 24.0	268 48.2
10	326 31.4	11 22.2	298 53.2
12	356 31.5	11 20.4	328 58.1
14	26 31.6	11 18.7	359 03.0
16	56 31.8	11 16.9	29 07.9
18	86 31.9	11 15.1	59 12.9
20	116 32.0	11 13.3	89 17.8
22	146 32.1	S11 11.5	119 22.7

Monday, 20th February

Time	SUN GHA	Dec	ARIES GHA
00	176 32.2	S11 09.7	149 27.7
02	206 32.4	11 08.0	179 32.6
04	236 32.5	11 06.2	209 37.5
06	266 32.6	11 04.4	239 42.4
08	296 32.8	11 02.6	269 47.4
10	326 32.9	11 00.8	299 52.3
12	356 33.0	10 59.0	329 57.2
14	26 33.1	10 57.2	0 02.2
16	56 33.3	10 55.4	30 07.1
18	86 33.4	10 53.6	60 12.0
20	116 33.6	10 51.8	90 16.9
22	146 33.7	S10 50.0	120 21.9

Tuesday, 21st February

Time	SUN GHA	Dec	ARIES GHA
00	176 33.8	S10 48.2	150 26.8
02	206 34.0	10 46.4	180 31.7
04	236 34.1	10 44.6	210 36.7
06	266 34.2	10 42.8	240 41.6
08	296 34.4	10 41.0	270 46.5
10	326 34.5	10 39.2	300 51.4
12	356 34.7	10 37.4	330 56.4
14	26 34.8	10 35.6	1 01.3
16	56 35.0	10 33.8	31 06.2
18	86 35.1	10 32.0	61 11.2
20	116 35.3	10 30.2	91 16.1
22	146 35.4	S10 28.4	121 21.0

Wednesday, 22nd February

Time	SUN GHA	Dec	ARIES GHA
00	176 35.6	S10 26.6	151 25.9
02	206 35.7	10 24.7	181 30.9
04	236 35.9	10 22.9	211 35.8
06	266 36.0	10 21.1	241 40.7
08	296 36.2	10 19.3	271 45.7
10	326 36.3	10 17.5	301 50.6
12	356 36.5	10 15.7	331 55.5
14	26 36.6	10 13.8	2 00.4
16	56 36.8	10 12.0	32 05.4
18	86 37.0	10 10.2	62 10.3
20	116 37.1	10 08.4	92 15.2
22	146 37.3	S10 06.5	122 20.1

Thursday, 23rd February

Time	SUN GHA	Dec	ARIES GHA
00	176 37.4	S10 04.7	152 25.1
02	206 37.6	10 02.9	182 30.0
04	236 37.8	10 01.1	212 34.9
06	266 37.9	9 59.2	242 39.9
08	296 38.1	9 57.4	272 44.8
10	326 38.3	9 55.6	302 49.7
12	356 38.4	9 53.7	332 54.6
14	26 38.6	9 51.9	2 59.6
16	56 38.8	9 50.1	33 04.5
18	86 39.0	9 48.2	63 09.4
20	116 39.1	9 46.4	93 14.4
22	146 39.3	S 9 44.6	123 19.3

Friday, 24th February

Time	SUN GHA	Dec	ARIES GHA
00	176 39.5	S 9 42.7	153 24.2
02	206 39.7	9 40.9	183 29.1
04	236 39.8	9 39.0	213 34.1
06	266 40.0	9 37.2	243 39.0
08	296 40.2	9 35.4	273 43.9
10	326 40.4	9 33.5	303 48.9
12	356 40.6	9 31.7	333 53.8
14	26 40.7	9 29.8	3 58.7
16	56 40.9	9 28.0	34 03.6
18	86 41.1	9 26.1	64 08.6
20	116 41.3	9 24.3	94 13.5
22	146 41.5	S 9 22.4	124 18.4

Saturday, 25th February

Time	SUN GHA	Dec	ARIES GHA
00	176 41.7	S 9 20.6	154 23.4
02	206 41.9	9 18.7	184 28.3
04	236 42.1	9 16.9	214 33.2
06	266 42.2	9 15.0	244 38.1
08	296 42.4	9 13.2	274 43.1
10	326 42.6	9 11.3	304 48.0
12	356 42.8	9 09.5	334 52.9
14	26 43.0	9 07.6	4 57.9
16	56 43.2	9 05.7	35 02.8
18	86 43.4	9 03.9	65 07.7
20	116 43.6	9 02.0	95 12.6
22	146 43.8	S 9 00.2	125 17.6

Sunday, 26th February

Time	SUN GHA	Dec	ARIES GHA
00	176 44.0	S 8 58.3	155 22.5
02	206 44.2	8 56.4	185 27.4
04	236 44.4	8 54.6	215 32.3
06	266 44.6	8 52.7	245 37.3
08	296 44.8	8 50.8	275 42.2
10	326 45.0	8 49.0	305 47.1
12	356 45.2	8 47.1	335 52.1
14	26 45.4	8 45.2	5 57.0
16	56 45.6	8 43.4	36 01.9
18	86 45.8	8 41.5	66 06.8
20	116 46.1	8 39.6	96 11.8
22	146 46.3	S 8 37.7	126 16.7

Monday, 27th February

Time	SUN GHA	Dec	ARIES GHA
00	176 46.5	S 8 35.9	156 21.6
02	206 46.7	8 34.0	186 26.6
04	236 46.9	8 32.1	216 31.5
06	266 47.1	8 30.3	246 36.4
08	296 47.3	8 28.4	276 41.3
10	326 47.5	8 26.5	306 46.3
12	356 47.8	8 24.6	336 51.2
14	26 48.0	8 22.7	6 56.1
16	56 48.2	8 20.9	37 01.1
18	86 48.4	8 19.0	67 06.0
20	116 48.6	8 17.1	97 10.9
22	146 48.9	S 8 15.2	127 15.8

Tuesday, 28th February

Time	SUN GHA	Dec	ARIES GHA
00	176 49.1	S 8 13.3	157 20.8
02	206 49.3	8 11.4	187 25.7
04	236 49.5	8 09.6	217 30.6
06	266 49.7	8 07.7	247 35.6
08	296 50.0	8 05.8	277 40.5
10	326 50.2	8 03.9	307 45.4
12	356 50.4	8 02.0	337 50.3
14	26 50.7	8 00.1	7 55.3
16	56 50.9	7 58.2	38 00.2
18	86 51.1	7 56.3	68 05.1
20	116 51.3	7 54.5	98 10.1
22	146 51.6	S 7 52.6	128 15.0

FEBRUARY

FEBRUARY 1995 — PLANETS — 0h GMT

Mer Pass h m	GHA ° '	Mean Var/hr 14°+	Dec ° '	Mean Var/hr	Note Corrections on Page E 101	GHA ° '	Mean Var/hr 15°+	Dec ° '	Mean Var/hr	Mer Pass h m
	VENUS					**JUPITER**				
08 59	225 17.8	59.5	S 20 32.0	0.2	1 Wed	241 53.9	2.1	S 21 14.1	0.1	07 51
09 00	225 06.1	59.5	S 20 37.1	0.2	2 Th	242 43.2	2.1	S 21 15.4	0.1	07 48
09 01	224 54.0	59.5	S 20 41.7	0.2	3 Fri	243 32.5	2.1	S 21 16.7	0.1	07 45
09 02	224 41.7	59.5	S 20 45.9	0.1	4 Sat	244 22.0	2.1	S 21 17.9	0.0	07 41
09 02	224 29.1	59.5	S 20 49.5	0.1	5 SUN	245 11.6	2.1	S 21 19.1	0.1	07 38
09 03	224 16.3	59.5	S 20 52.7	0.1	6 Mon	246 01.3	2.1	S 21 20.3	0.0	07 35
09 04	224 03.2	59.4	S 20 55.3	0.1	7 Tu	246 51.1	2.1	S 21 21.5	0.0	07 32
09 05	223 50.0	59.4	S 20 57.5	0.1	8 Wed	247 41.1	2.1	S 21 22.6	0.0	07 28
09 06	223 36.5	59.4	S 20 59.1	0.0	9 Th	248 31.2	2.1	S 21 23.7	0.0	07 25
09 07	223 22.8	59.4	S 21 00.2	0.0	10 Fri	249 21.4	2.1	S 21 24.8	0.0	07 22
09 08	223 08.9	59.4	S 21 00.7	0.0	11 Sat	250 11.8	2.1	S 21 25.9	0.0	07 18
09 09	222 54.9	59.4	S 21 00.7	0.0	12 SUN	251 02.3	2.1	S 21 26.9	0.0	07 15
09 10	222 40.7	59.4	S 21 00.2	0.0	13 Mon	251 52.9	2.1	S 21 27.9	0.0	07 11
09 11	222 26.4	59.4	S 20 59.1	0.1	14 Tu	252 43.7	2.1	S 21 28.9	0.0	07 08
09 12	222 11.9	59.4	S 20 57.4	0.1	15 Wed	253 34.6	2.1	S 21 29.9	0.0	07 05
09 13	221 57.3	59.4	S 20 55.2	0.1	16 Th	254 25.7	2.1	S 21 30.8	0.0	07 01
09 14	221 42.6	59.4	S 20 52.5	0.1	17 Fri	255 16.9	2.1	S 21 31.7	0.0	06 58
09 15	221 27.9	59.4	S 20 49.1	0.2	18 Sat	256 08.2	2.1	S 21 32.6	0.0	06 54
09 16	221 13.0	59.4	S 20 45.2	0.2	19 SUN	256 59.7	2.1	S 21 33.5	0.0	06 51
09 17	220 58.1	59.4	S 20 40.8	0.2	20 Mon	257 51.3	2.2	S 21 34.3	0.0	06 48
09 18	220 43.2	59.4	S 20 35.7	0.2	21 Tu	258 43.1	2.2	S 21 35.1	0.0	06 44
09 19	220 28.2	59.4	S 20 30.2	0.3	22 Wed	259 35.1	2.2	S 21 35.9	0.0	06 41
09 20	220 13.2	59.4	S 20 24.0	0.3	23 Th	260 27.2	2.2	S 21 36.6	0.0	06 37
09 21	219 58.2	59.4	S 20 17.2	0.3	24 Fri	261 19.5	2.2	S 21 37.4	0.0	06 34
09 22	219 43.2	59.4	S 20 09.9	0.3	25 Sat	262 11.9	2.2	S 21 38.1	0.0	06 30
09 23	219 28.2	59.4	S 20 02.1	0.4	26 SUN	263 04.5	2.2	S 21 38.8	0.0	06 27
09 24	219 13.2	59.4	S 19 53.7	0.4	27 Mon	263 57.2	2.2	S 21 39.4	0.0	06 23
09 24	218 58.3	59.4	S 19 44.7	0.4	28 Tu	264 50.1	2.2	S 21 40.1	0.0	06 20

VENUS, Av. Mag. -4.2
S.H.A. February
5 90; 10 84; 15 78; 20 72; 25 65; 28 62.

JUPITER, Av. Mag.-2.0
S.H.A. February
5 111; 10 110; 15 109; 20 108; 25 108; 28 107.

Mer Pass h m	GHA ° '	Mean Var/hr 15°+	Dec ° '	Mean Var/hr	Note Corrections on Page E 101	GHA ° '	Mean Var/hr 15°+	Dec ° '	Mean Var/hr	Mer Pass h m
	MARS					**SATURN**				
01 21	339 45.3	3.3	N 16 37.9	0.3	1 Wed	147 31.7	2.2	S 9 02.6	0.1	14 08
01 15	341 05.2	3.3	N 16 46.3	0.4	2 Th	148 24.5	2.2	S 9 00.0	0.1	14 04
01 10	342 25.5	3.4	N 16 54.8	0.4	3 Fri	149 17.3	2.2	S 8 57.4	0.1	14 01
01 05	343 46.2	3.4	N 17 03.2	0.4	4 Sat	150 10.1	2.2	S 8 54.8	0.1	13 57
00 59	345 07.4	3.4	N 17 11.7	0.4	5 SUN	151 02.8	2.2	S 8 52.1	0.1	13 54
00 54	346 28.9	3.4	N 17 20.2	0.4	6 Mon	151 55.5	2.2	S 8 49.5	0.1	13 50
00 48	347 50.8	3.4	N 17 28.6	0.3	7 Tu	152 48.2	2.2	S 8 46.8	0.1	13 47
00 43	349 12.9	3.4	N 17 36.9	0.3	8 Wed	153 40.8	2.2	S 8 44.1	0.1	13 43
00 38	350 35.3	3.4	N 17 45.2	0.3	9 Th	154 33.4	2.2	S 8 41.4	0.1	13 40
00 32	351 57.9	3.4	N 17 53.4	0.3	10 Fri	155 26.0	2.2	S 8 38.7	0.1	13 36
00 27	353 20.6	3.5	N 18 01.5	0.3	11 Sat	156 18.6	2.2	S 8 36.0	0.1	13 33
00 21	354 43.5	3.5	N 18 09.4	0.3	12 SUN	157 11.1	2.2	S 8 33.3	0.1	13 29
00 16	356 06.4	3.5	N 18 17.2	0.3	13 Mon	158 03.6	2.2	S 8 30.6	0.1	13 26
00 10	357 29.3	3.5	N 18 24.9	0.3	14 Tu	158 56.1	2.2	S 8 27.8	0.1	13 22
00 05	358 52.2	3.5	N 18 32.3	0.3	15 Wed	159 48.6	2.2	S 8 25.1	0.1	13 19
23 54	0 15.0	3.4	N 18 39.6	0.3	16 Th	160 41.0	2.2	S 8 22.3	0.1	13 15
23 48	1 37.7	3.4	N 18 46.7	0.3	17 Fri	161 33.5	2.2	S 8 19.6	0.1	13 12
23 43	3 00.2	3.4	N 18 53.6	0.3	18 Sat	162 25.9	2.2	S 8 16.8	0.1	13 08
23 37	4 22.5	3.4	N 19 00.3	0.3	19 SUN	163 18.3	2.2	S 8 14.0	0.1	13 05
23 32	5 44.6	3.4	N 19 06.7	0.3	20 Mon	164 10.7	2.2	S 8 11.3	0.1	13 01
23 26	7 06.4	3.4	N 19 12.9	0.3	21 Tu	165 03.0	2.2	S 8 08.5	0.1	12 58
23 21	8 27.9	3.4	N 19 18.9	0.2	22 Wed	165 55.4	2.2	S 8 05.7	0.1	12 54
23 16	9 49.0	3.4	N 19 24.5	0.2	23 Th	166 47.7	2.2	S 8 02.9	0.1	12 51
23 10	11 09.6	3.3	N 19 30.0	0.2	24 Fri	167 40.0	2.2	S 8 00.1	0.1	12 47
23 05	12 29.9	3.3	N 19 35.1	0.2	25 Sat	168 32.4	2.2	S 7 57.3	0.1	12 44
23 00	13 49.6	3.3	N 19 40.0	0.2	26 SUN	169 24.7	2.2	S 7 54.5	0.1	12 41
22 54	15 08.9	3.3	N 19 44.6	0.2	27 Mon	170 17.0	2.2	S 7 51.7	0.1	12 37
22 49	16 27.5	3.3	N 19 48.9	0.2	28 Tu	171 09.3	2.2	S 7 48.9	0.1	12 34

MARS, Av. Mag. -1.1
S.H.A. February
5 210; 10 212; 15 214; 20 216; 25 218; 28 219.

SATURN, Av. Mag. +1.0
S.H.A. February
5 16; 10 16; 15 15; 20 15; 25 14; 28 14.

FEBRUARY 1995 — MOON

Day	GMT hr	GHA ° '	Mean Var/hr 14°+	Dec ° '	Mean Var/hr '	Day	GMT hr	GHA ° '	Mean Var/hr 14°+	Dec ° '	Mean Var/hr '
1 Wed	0	164 45.3	29.4	S 8 31.2	10.8	17 Fri	0	340 37.1	30.4	N 1 44.5	11.4
	6	251 41.7	29.8	S 7 26.5	11.0		6	67 39.9	30.4	N 0 35.8	11.5
	12	338 40.3	30.2	S 6 20.8	11.1		12	154 42.0	30.2	S 0 33.1	11.5
	18	65 41.1	30.5	S 5 14.4	11.1		18	241 43.4	30.1	S 1 42.2	11.5
2 Th	0	152 43.9	30.8	S 4 07.4	11.2	18 Sat	0	328 43.9	29.9	S 2 51.2	11.4
	6	239 48.6	31.1	S 3 00.2	11.3		6	55 43.4	29.7	S 3 59.8	11.3
	12	326 55.0	31.4	S 1 52.9	11.1		12	142 41.7	29.5	S 5 07.8	11.2
	18	54 03.1	31.6	S 0 45.8	11.1		18	229 38.9	29.3	S 6 15.0	11.0
3 Fri	0	141 12.6	31.9	N 0 20.9	11.0	19 Sun	0	316 34.7	29.1	S 7 21.2	10.8
	6	228 23.4	32.0	N 1 27.1	10.9		6	43 29.2	28.8	S 8 25.9	10.5
	12	315 35.4	32.1	N 2 32.5	10.7		12	130 22.0	28.5	S 9 29.1	10.2
	18	42 48.4	32.3	N 3 37.0	10.6		18	217 13.3	28.2	S 10 30.5	9.8
4 Sat	0	130 02.2	32.4	N 4 40.5	10.3	20 Mon	0	304 02.9	28.0	S 11 29.7	9.5
	6	217 16.8	32.5	N 5 42.7	10.2		6	30 50.7	27.6	S 12 26.7	9.0
	12	304 31.9	32.6	N 6 43.6	9.9		12	117 36.8	27.4	S 13 21.0	8.5
	18	31 47.4	32.7	N 7 43.0	9.6		18	204 21.0	27.0	S 14 12.6	8.0
5 Sun	0	119 03.4	32.6	N 8 40.8	9.3	21 Tu	0	291 03.5	26.7	S 15 01.1	7.5
	6	206 19.3	32.7	N 9 36.8	9.0		6	17 44.2	26.4	S 15 46.4	6.9
	12	293 35.3	32.7	N 10 31.0	8.6		12	104 23.1	26.2	S 16 28.1	6.3
	18	20 51.3	32.7	N 11 23.2	8.3		18	191 00.4	25.9	S 17 06.2	5.7
6 Mon	0	108 07.1	32.6	N 12 13.4	7.9	22 Wed	0	277 36.2	25.7	S 17 40.4	5.0
	6	195 22.6	32.5	N 13 01.4	7.5		6	4 10.5	25.5	S 18 10.6	4.3
	12	282 37.7	32.5	N 13 47.1	7.2		12	90 43.5	25.3	S 18 36.5	3.5
	18	9 52.4	32.4	N 14 30.5	6.8		18	177 15.4	25.2	S 18 58.2	2.8
7 Tu	0	97 06.5	32.2	N 15 11.5	6.4	23 Th	0	263 46.4	25.1	S 19 15.3	2.0
	6	184 20.1	32.1	N 15 49.9	5.9		6	350 16.7	25.0	S 19 27.9	1.3
	12	271 32.9	32.0	N 16 25.8	5.4		12	76 46.5	24.9	S 19 36.0	0.5
	18	358 45.1	31.9	N 16 58.9	5.0		18	163 16.0	24.9	S 19 39.3	0.3
8 Wed	0	85 56.5	31.7	N 17 29.2	4.5	24 Fri	0	249 45.6	25.0	S 19 38.0	1.1
	6	173 07.1	31.7	N 17 56.8	4.1		6	336 15.4	25.1	S 19 32.0	1.8
	12	260 17.0	31.5	N 18 21.4	3.6		12	62 45.6	25.2	S 19 21.4	2.6
	18	347 26.0	31.3	N 18 43.0	3.1		18	149 16.6	25.3	S 19 06.3	3.3
9 Th	0	74 34.3	31.2	N 19 01.5	2.6	25 Sat	0	235 48.6	25.5	S 18 46.6	4.1
	6	161 41.8	31.1	N 19 17.0	2.0		6	322 21.7	25.7	S 18 22.7	4.7
	12	248 48.6	31.0	N 19 29.2	1.4		12	48 56.2	26.0	S 17 54.5	5.4
	18	335 54.7	30.9	N 19 38.3	0.9		18	135 32.2	26.3	S 17 22.3	6.1
10 Fri	0	63 00.1	30.8	N 19 44.1	0.4	26 Sun	0	222 09.9	26.6	S 16 46.2	6.7
	6	150 04.9	30.7	N 19 46.5	0.2		6	308 49.5	27.0	S 16 06.4	7.3
	12	237 09.2	30.7	N 19 45.7	0.8		12	35 30.9	27.2	S 15 23.1	7.8
	18	324 13.0	30.7	N 19 41.4	1.3		18	122 14.3	27.6	S 14 36.7	8.3
11 Sat	0	51 16.3	30.5	N 19 33.8	1.9	27 Mon	0	208 59.8	28.0	S 13 47.2	8.8
	6	138 19.4	30.4	N 19 22.8	2.4		6	295 47.4	28.3	S 12 54.9	9.2
	12	225 22.1	30.4	N 19 08.4	3.0		12	22 37.0	28.6	S 12 00.1	9.5
	18	312 24.7	30.4	N 18 50.6	3.5		18	109 28.7	29.0	S 11 03.0	9.8
12 Sun	0	39 27.1	30.4	N 18 29.4	4.1	28 Tu	0	196 22.4	29.3	S 10 04.0	10.1
	6	126 29.5	30.4	N 18 05.0	4.7		6	283 18.2	29.7	S 9 03.1	10.4
	12	213 31.8	30.4	N 17 37.2	5.2		12	10 15.8	29.9	S 8 00.8	10.6
	18	300 34.3	30.4	N 17 06.2	5.7		18	97 15.3	30.2	S 6 57.1	10.8
13 Mon	0	27 36.8	30.5	N 16 32.0	6.3						
	6	114 39.5	30.5	N 15 54.6	6.8						
	12	201 42.4	30.5	N 15 14.3	7.2						
	18	288 45.5	30.6	N 14 31.1	7.8						
14 Tu	0	15 48.8	30.6	N 13 45.0	8.1						
	6	102 52.4	30.6	N 12 56.2	8.6						
	12	189 56.2	30.6	N 12 04.8	9.0						
	18	277 00.2	30.7	N 11 11.0	9.4						
15 Wed	0	4 04.4	30.7	N 10 15.0	9.7						
	6	91 08.7	30.7	N 9 16.7	10.1						
	12	178 13.1	30.7	N 8 16.5	10.4						
	18	265 17.5	30.7	N 7 14.6	10.6						
16 Th	0	352 21.9	30.7	N 6 11.0	10.8						
	6	79 26.1	30.6	N 5 06.0	11.1						
	12	166 30.1	30.6	N 3 59.7	11.2						
	18	253 33.8	30.6	N 2 52.5	11.4						

NOTE Moon GHA corrections for additional hours, minutes, and seconds on page E 96.
Moon Declination corrections on page E 99. Mean Var/Hr value needed for both corrections.

FEBRUARY

MARCH 1995   SUN & MOON   GMT

SUN

Day of Yr Mth Week	Equation of Time 0h	12h	Transit	Semi-diam	Lat 52°N Twi-light	Sun-rise	Sun-set	Twi-light	Lat	Lat Corr to Sunrise, Sunset etc Twi-light	Sun-rise	Sun-set	Twi-light
	m s	m s	h m	′	h m	h m	h m	h m	°	h m	h m	h m	h m
60 1 Wed	+12 33	+12 27	12 12	16.2	06 13	06 47	17 39	18 13	N60	-0 05	+0 03	-0 03	+0 05
61 2 Th	+12 22	+12 16	12 12	16.2	06 11	06 45	17 41	18 14	55	-0 02	+0 01	-0 01	+0 02
62 3 Fri	+12 10	+12 03	12 12	16.2	06 09	06 43	17 42	18 16	50	+0 01	-0 01	+0 01	-0 01
63 4 Sat	+11 57	+11 51	12 12	16.2	06 07	06 40	17 44	18 18	45	+0 03	-0 02	+0 02	-0 03
64 5 Sun	+11 44	+11 38	12 12	16.2	06 05	06 38	17 46	18 20	N40	+0 04	-0 03	+0 03	-0 04
65 6 Mon	+11 31	+11 24	12 11	16.1	06 02	06 36	17 48	18 22	35	+0 04	-0 04	+0 04	-0 04
66 7 Tu	+11 17	+11 10	12 11	16.1	06 00	06 34	17 50	18 23	30	+0 05	-0 05	+0 05	-0 05
67 8 Wed	+11 03	+10 56	12 11	16.1	05 58	06 31	17 51	18 25	25	+0 05	-0 05	+0 05	-0 05
68 9 Th	+10 48	+10 41	12 11	16.1	05 56	06 29	17 53	18 27	N20	+0 05	-0 06	+0 06	-0 05
69 10 Fri	+10 33	+10 26	12 10	16.1	05 53	06 27	17 55	18 29	15	+0 05	-0 07	+0 07	-0 05
70 11 Sat	+10 18	+10 10	12 10	16.1	05 51	06 25	17 57	18 30	10	+0 05	-0 08	+0 08	-0 04
71 12 Sun	+10 02	+09 54	12 10	16.1	05 49	06 22	17 58	18 32	5	+0 04	-0 09	+0 09	-0 04
72 13 Mon	+09 46	+09 38	12 10	16.1	05 47	06 20	18 00	18 34	0	+0 03	-0 09	+0 09	-0 03
73 14 Tu	+09 30	+09 22	12 09	16.1	05 44	06 18	18 02	18 36	S 5	+0 03	-0 10	+0 10	-0 03
74 15 Wed	+09 13	+09 05	12 09	16.1	05 42	06 16	18 04	18 37	10	+0 01	-0 11	+0 11	-0 01
75 16 Th	+08 56	+08 48	12 09	16.1	05 40	06 13	18 05	18 39	15	+0 00	-0 12	+0 12	-0 00
76 17 Fri	+08 39	+08 30	12 09	16.1	05 37	06 11	18 07	18 41	S20	-0 01	-0 13	+0 13	+0 01
77 18 Sat	+08 22	+08 13	12 08	16.1	05 35	06 09	18 09	18 42	25	-0 03	-0 14	+0 14	+0 03
78 19 Sun	+08 04	+07 55	12 08	16.1	05 33	06 06	18 11	18 44	30	-0 06	-0 15	+0 15	+0 06
79 20 Mon	+07 47	+07 38	12 08	16.1	05 30	06 04	18 12	18 46	35	-0 08	-0 16	+0 16	+0 08
80 21 Tu	+07 29	+07 20	12 07	16.1	05 28	06 02	18 14	18 48	S40	-0 12	-0 18	+0 18	+0 12
81 22 Wed	+07 11	+07 02	12 07	16.1	05 26	05 59	18 16	18 50	45	-0 16	-0 20	+0 20	+0 16
82 23 Th	+06 53	+06 44	12 07	16.1	05 23	05 57	18 17	18 51	50	-0 21	-0 22	+0 22	+0 21
83 24 Fri	+06 35	+06 26	12 06	16.1	05 21	05 55	18 19	18 53					
84 25 Sat	+06 17	+06 08	12 06	16.1	05 19	05 52	18 21	18 55					
85 26 Sun	+05 59	+05 50	12 06	16.1	05 16	05 50	18 23	18 57					
86 27 Mon	+05 41	+05 31	12 06	16.1	05 14	05 48	18 24	18 58					
87 28 Tu	+05 22	+05 13	12 05	16.0	05 11	05 45	18 26	19 00			NOTES		
88 29 Wed	+05 04	+04 55	12 05	16.0	05 09	05 43	18 28	19 02		Lat corrections are for mid-month.			
89 30 Th	+04 46	+04 37	12 05	16.0	05 07	05 41	18 29	19 04		**Equation of Time** is the excess of			
90 31 Fri	+04 28	+04 19	12 04	16.0	05 04	05 39	18 31	19 05		Mean Time over Apparent Time.			

MOON

Day of Yr Mth Week	Age	Transit (Upper)	Diff	Semi-diam	Hor Par	Lat 52°N Moon-rise	Moon-set	Phases of the Moon
	days	h m	m	′	′	h m	h m	d h m
60 1 Wed	00	12 07	47	15.6	57.3	06 21	18 04	
61 2 Th	01	12 54	46	15.5	56.7	06 44	19 16	● New Moon 1 11 48
62 3 Fri	02	13 40	46	15.3	56.1	07 08	20 25	☽ First Quarter 9 10 14
63 4 Sat	03	14 26	46	15.1	55.5	07 31	21 33	○ Full Moon 17 01 26
64 5 Sun	04	15 12	46	15.0	55.0	07 57	22 39	☾ Last Quarter 23 20 10
65 6 Mon	05	15 58	47	14.9	54.6	08 25	23 41	● New Moon 31 02 09
66 7 Tu	06	16 45	47	14.8	54.3	08 57	— —	
67 8 Wed	07	17 32	48	14.8	54.2	09 34	00 40	
68 9 Th	08	18 20	48	14.8	54.3	10 17	01 34	
69 10 Fri	09	19 08	48	14.9	54.5	11 07	02 22	Apogee 8 15
70 11 Sat	10	19 56	49	15.0	54.9	12 03	03 05	Perigee 20 13
71 12 Sun	11	20 45	48	15.1	55.5	13 05	03 42	
72 13 Mon	12	21 33	49	15.3	56.2	14 11	04 14	
73 14 Tu	13	22 22	49	15.5	56.9	15 21	04 43	
74 15 Wed	14	23 11	49	15.7	57.6	16 34	05 09	
75 16 Th	15	24 00	—	15.9	58.3	17 49	05 34	
76 17 Fri	16	00 00	52	16.1	58.9	19 06	06 00	
77 18 Sat	17	00 52	53	16.2	59.4	20 24	06 26	
78 19 Sun	18	01 45	55	16.3	59.7	21 42	06 56	
79 20 Mon	19	02 40	57	16.3	59.8	22 59	07 30	
80 21 Tu	20	03 37	59	16.3	59.7	— —	08 10	
81 22 Wed	21	04 36	58	16.2	59.5	00 10	08 59	NOTES
82 23 Th	22	05 34	58	16.1	59.2	01 13	09 56	**Diff** equals daily change in
83 24 Fri	23	06 32	56	16.0	58.8	02 06	11 01	transit time.
84 25 Sat	24	07 28	53	15.9	58.4	02 50	12 11	To correct Moonrise, Moonset,
85 26 Sun	25	08 21	51	15.8	58.0	03 26	13 24	or Transit times for Latitude
86 27 Mon	26	09 12	49	15.7	57.5	03 57	14 37	and/or Longitude see page
87 28 Tu	27	10 01	47	15.5	57.0	04 23	15 49	E 100. For further information
88 29 Wed	28	10 48	46	15.4	56.5	04 47	17 00	about these tables see page E 4.
89 30 Th	29	11 34	46	15.3	56.0	05 10	18 09	For Arc to Time correction see
90 31 Fri	00	12 20	45	15.1	55.6	05 34	19 17	page E 91.

MARCH 1995

STARS

0h GMT March 1

No	Name	Mag	Transit h m	Dec ° '	GHA ° '	RA h m	SHA ° '
	ARIES..................		13 24		158 19.9		
1	Alpheratz........ 2.2		13 33	N 29 03.8	156 17.9	0 08	357 58.0
2	Ankaa................ 2.4		13 50	S 42 20.0	151 49.5	0 26	353 29.6
3	Schedar 2.5		14 05	N 56 30.7	148 16.6	0 40	349 56.7
4	Diphda 2.2		14 08	S 18 00.9	147 29.8	0 43	349 09.9
5	Achernar 0.6		15 02	S 57 15.8	133 57.4	1 38	335 37.5
6	POLARIS 2.1		15 50	N 89 14.8	121 47.5	2 26	323 27.6
7	Hamal.............. 2.2		15 31	N 23 26.4	126 36.4	2 07	328 16.5
8	Acamar............. 3.1		16 22	S 40 19.7	113 48.9	2 58	315 29.0
9	Menkar 2.8		16 26	N 4 04.1	112 49.5	3 02	314 29.6
10	Mirfak 1.9		16 48	N 49 50.7	107 20.2	3 24	309 00.3
11	Aldebaran......... 1.1		17 59	N 16 29.9	89 25.1	4 36	291 05.2
12	Rigel 0.3		18 38	S 8 12.7	79 45.2	5 14	281 25.3
13	Capella 0.2		18 40	N 45 59.7	79 14.6	5 16	280 54.7
14	Bellatrix 1.7		18 48	N 6 20.5	77 06.6	5 25	278 46.7
15	Elnath 1.8		18 50	N 28 36.2	76 49.9	5 26	278 30.0
16	Alnilam 1.8		19 00	S 1 12.5	74 20.2	5 36	276 00.3
17	Betelgeuse 0.1-1.2		19 18	N 7 24.2	69 36.0	5 55	271 16.1
18	Canopus............-0.9		19 47	S 52 42.0	62 22.0	6 24	264 02.1
19	Sirius ....-1.6		20 08	S 16 42.9	57 05.6	6 45	258 45.7
20	Adhara 1.6		20 22	S 28 58.3	53 43.1	6 58	255 23.2
21	Castor............... 1.6		20 58	N 31 53.9	44 45.1	7 34	246 25.2
22	Procyon............ 0.5		21 02	N 5 14.0	43 33.8	7 39	245 13.9
23	Pollux 1.2		21 08	N 28 02.2	42 04.2	7 45	243 44.3
24	Avior 1.7		21 46	S 59 30.0	32 43.0	8 22	234 23.1
25	Suhail 2.2		22 31	S 43 25.1	21 22.1	9 08	223 02.2
26	Miaplacidus 1.8		22 36	S 69 42.2	20 01.6	9 13	221 41.7
27	Alphard............ 2.2		22 50	S 8 38.5	16 29.2	9 27	218 09.3
28	Regulus 1.3		23 31	N 11 59.2	6 17.7	10 08	207 57.8
29	Dubhe 2.0		0 30	N 61 46.5	352 27.7	11 03	194 07.8
30	Denebola 2.2		1 15	N 14 35.7	341 07.2	11 49	182 47.3
31	Gienah 2.8		1 42	S 17 31.1	334 26.0	12 16	176 06.1
32	Acrux................ 1.1		1 53	S 63 04.4	331 43.8	12 26	173 23.9
33	Gacrux.............. 1.6		1 57	S 57 05.2	330 35.5	12 31	172 15.6
34	Mimosa 1.5		2 14	S 59 39.8	326 27.3	12 48	168 07.4
35	Alioth 1.7		2 20	N 55 58.9	324 52.1	12 54	166 32.2
36	Spica................ 1.2		2 51	S 11 08.3	317 05.3	13 25	158 45.4
37	Alkaid............... 1.9		3 14	N 49 20.0	311 29.2	13 47	153 09.3
38	Hadar 0.9		3 30	S 60 20.9	307 26.8	14 04	149 06.9
39	Menkent 2.3		3 33	S 36 20.8	306 43.3	14 06	148 23.4
40	Arcturus........... 0.2		3 42	N 19 12.2	304 27.9	14 15	146 08.0
41	Rigil Kent. 0.1		4 05	S 60 48.8	298 29.8	14 39	140 09.9
42	Zuben'ubi 2.9		4 17	S 16 01.4	295 40.3	14 51	137 20.4
43	Kochab............. 2.2		4 17	N 74 10.3	295 38.7	14 51	137 18.8
44	Alphecca 2.3		5 00	N 26 43.6	284 42.3	15 35	126 22.4
45	Antares 1.2		5 55	S 26 25.2	271 02.9	16 29	112 43.0
46	Atria 1.9		6 14	S 69 00.8	266 17.0	16 48	107 57.1
47	Sabik 2.6		6 36	S 15 43.1	260 48.1	17 10	102 28.2
48	Shaula 1.7		6 59	S 37 05.9	255 00.4	17 33	96 40.5
49	Rasalhague 2.1		7 00	N 12 33.7	254 39.1	17 35	96 19.2
50	Eltanin............. 2.4		7 22	N 51 29.1	249 12.5	17 56	90 52.6
51	Kaus Aust. 2.0		7 49	S 34 23.1	242 22.0	18 24	84 02.1
52	Vega................. 0.1		8 02	N 38 46.6	239 08.2	18 37	80 48.3
53	Nunki 2.1		8 20	S 26 18.0	234 35.3	18 55	76 15.4
54	Altair 0.9		9 16	N 8 51.3	220 41.7	19 51	62 21.8
55	Peacock............ 2.1		9 50	S 56 44.8	212 01.1	20 25	53 41.2
56	Deneb 1.3		10 06	N 45 15.7	208 01.0	20 41	49 41.1
57	Enif.................. 2.5		11 09	N 9 51.1	192 20.8	21 44	34 00.9
58	Al Na'ir 2.2		11 33	S 46 59.0	186 21.2	22 08	28 01.3
59	Fomalhaut 1.3		12 22	S 29 38.9	173 59.3	22 57	15 39.4
60	Markab 2.6		12 29	N 15 10.7	172 12.2	23 05	13 52.3

Star Transit Corr Table

Date	Corr h m	Date	Corr h m
1	−0 00	17	−1 03
2	−0 04	18	−1 07
3	−0 08	19	−1 11
4	−0 12	20	−1 15
5	−0 16	21	−1 19
6	−0 20	22	−1 23
7	−0 24	23	−1 27
8	−0 28	24	−1 30
9	−0 31	25	−1 34
10	−0 35	26	−1 38
11	−0 39	27	−1 42
12	−0 43	28	−1 46
13	−0 47	29	−1 50
14	−0 51	30	−1 54
15	−0 55	31	−1 58
16	−0 59		

STAR TRANSIT

To find the approx time of transit of a star for any day of the month use above table. All corrections are subtractive.

If the value taken from the table is greater than the time of transit for the first of the month, add 23h 56min to the time of transit before subtracting the correction.

Example: What time will Dubhe (No 29) transit the Meridian on March 30?

	h min
Transit on Mar 1	00 30
	+23 56
	24 26
Corr for Mar 30	−01 54
Transit on Mar 30	22 32

MARCH DIARY

d h	
1 11	Mercury greatest elongation W(27°)
6 02	Saturn in conjunction with Sun
14 04	Mars 9° N of Moon
21 02	Equinox
22 14	Jupiter 2° S of Moon
25 12	Neptune 5° S of Moon
25 17	Mars stationary
25 21	Uranus 6° S of Moon
26 00	Mercury 0.6° S of Saturn
28 04	Venus 6° S of Moon
29 13	Saturn 6° S of Moon
30 01	Mercury 6° S of Moon

NOTES

Star declinations may be used as is for the whole month. To correct GHA for day, hour, minute and second see page E 92 and for further explanation of this table see page E 4.

MARCH

MARCH 1995 — SUN & ARIES — GMT

Wednesday, 1st March

Time	SUN GHA	Dec	ARIES GHA
00	176 51.8	S 7 50.7	158 19.9
02	206 52.0	7 48.8	188 24.8
04	236 52.3	7 46.9	218 29.8
06	266 52.5	7 45.0	248 34.7
08	296 52.7	7 43.1	278 39.6
10	326 53.0	7 41.2	308 44.5
12	356 53.2	7 39.3	338 49.5
14	26 53.5	7 37.4	8 54.4
16	56 53.7	7 35.5	38 59.3
18	86 53.9	7 33.6	69 04.3
20	116 54.2	7 31.7	99 09.2
22	146 54.4	S 7 29.8	129 14.1

Monday, 6th March

Time	SUN GHA	Dec	ARIES GHA
00	177 07.3	S 5 55.8	163 15.6
02	207 07.6	5 53.8	193 20.5
04	237 07.9	5 51.9	223 25.5
06	267 08.2	5 50.0	253 30.4
08	297 08.5	5 48.0	283 35.3
10	327 08.7	5 46.1	313 40.2
12	357 09.0	5 44.2	343 45.2
14	27 09.3	5 42.2	13 50.1
16	57 09.6	5 40.3	43 55.0
18	87 09.9	5 38.3	74 00.0
20	117 10.2	5 36.4	104 04.9
22	147 10.5	S 5 34.5	134 09.8

Saturday, 11th March

Time	SUN GHA	Dec	ARIES GHA
00	177 25.6	S 3 58.9	168 11.3
02	207 25.9	3 56.9	198 16.2
04	237 26.2	3 54.9	228 21.2
06	267 26.6	3 53.0	258 26.1
08	297 26.9	3 51.0	288 31.0
10	327 27.2	3 49.1	318 35.9
12	357 27.5	3 47.1	348 40.9
14	27 27.9	3 45.1	18 45.8
16	57 28.2	3 43.2	48 50.7
18	87 28.5	3 41.2	78 55.6
20	117 28.9	3 39.2	109 00.6
22	147 29.2	S 3 37.3	139 05.5

Thursday, 2nd March

Time	SUN GHA	Dec	ARIES GHA
00	176 54.7	S 7 27.9	159 19.0
02	206 54.9	7 26.0	189 24.0
04	236 55.2	7 24.1	219 28.9
06	266 55.4	7 22.2	249 33.8
08	296 55.6	7 20.3	279 38.8
10	326 55.9	7 18.4	309 43.7
12	356 56.1	7 16.5	339 48.6
14	26 56.4	7 14.6	9 53.5
16	56 56.6	7 12.6	39 58.5
18	86 56.9	7 10.7	70 03.4
20	116 57.1	7 08.8	100 08.3
22	146 57.4	S 7 06.9	130 13.3

Tuesday, 7th March

Time	SUN GHA	Dec	ARIES GHA
00	177 10.8	S 5 32.5	164 14.7
02	207 11.1	5 30.6	194 19.7
04	237 11.4	5 28.6	224 24.6
06	267 11.6	5 26.7	254 29.5
08	297 11.9	5 24.8	284 34.5
10	327 12.2	5 22.8	314 39.4
12	357 12.5	5 20.9	344 44.3
14	27 12.8	5 18.9	14 49.2
16	57 13.1	5 17.0	44 54.2
18	87 13.4	5 15.0	74 59.1
20	117 13.7	5 13.1	105 04.0
22	147 14.0	S 5 11.1	135 09.0

Sunday, 12th March

Time	SUN GHA	Dec	ARIES GHA
00	177 29.5	S 3 35.3	169 10.4
02	207 29.8	3 33.3	199 15.4
04	237 30.2	3 31.4	229 20.3
06	267 30.5	3 29.4	259 25.2
08	297 30.8	3 27.4	289 30.1
10	327 31.2	3 25.5	319 35.1
12	357 31.5	3 23.5	349 40.0
14	27 31.9	3 21.5	19 44.9
16	57 32.2	3 19.6	49 49.9
18	87 32.5	3 17.6	79 54.8
20	117 32.9	3 15.6	109 59.7
22	147 33.2	S 3 13.7	140 04.6

Friday, 3rd March

Time	SUN GHA	Dec	ARIES GHA
00	176 57.7	S 7 05.0	160 18.2
02	206 57.9	7 03.1	190 23.1
04	236 58.2	7 01.2	220 28.0
06	266 58.4	6 59.3	250 33.0
08	296 58.7	6 57.4	280 37.9
10	326 58.9	6 55.4	310 42.8
12	356 59.2	6 53.5	340 47.8
14	26 59.4	6 51.6	10 52.7
16	56 59.7	6 49.7	40 57.6
18	87 00.0	6 47.8	71 02.5
20	117 00.2	6 45.9	101 07.5
22	147 00.5	S 6 43.9	131 12.4

Wednesday, 8th March

Time	SUN GHA	Dec	ARIES GHA
00	177 14.3	S 5 09.2	165 13.9
02	207 14.6	5 07.3	195 18.8
04	237 14.9	5 05.3	225 23.7
06	267 15.2	5 03.4	255 28.7
08	297 15.5	5 01.4	285 33.6
10	327 15.8	4 59.5	315 38.5
12	357 16.1	4 57.5	345 43.4
14	27 16.4	4 55.6	15 48.4
16	57 16.7	4 53.6	45 53.3
18	87 17.1	4 51.7	75 58.2
20	117 17.4	4 49.7	106 03.2
22	147 17.7	S 4 47.8	136 08.1

Monday, 13th March

Time	SUN GHA	Dec	ARIES GHA
00	177 33.5	S 3 11.7	170 09.6
02	207 33.9	3 09.7	200 14.5
04	237 34.2	3 07.8	230 19.4
06	267 34.6	3 05.8	260 24.4
08	297 34.9	3 03.8	290 29.3
10	327 35.2	3 01.9	320 34.2
12	357 35.6	2 59.9	350 39.1
14	27 35.9	2 57.9	20 44.1
16	57 36.3	2 56.0	50 49.0
18	87 36.6	2 54.0	80 53.9
20	117 36.9	2 52.0	110 58.9
22	147 37.3	S 2 50.1	141 03.8

Saturday, 4th March

Time	SUN GHA	Dec	ARIES GHA
00	177 00.8	S 6 42.0	161 17.3
02	207 01.0	6 40.1	191 22.3
04	237 01.3	6 38.2	221 27.2
06	267 01.6	6 36.3	251 32.1
08	297 01.8	6 34.3	281 37.0
10	327 02.1	6 32.4	311 42.0
12	357 02.4	6 30.5	341 46.9
14	27 02.6	6 28.6	11 51.8
16	57 02.9	6 26.6	41 56.8
18	87 03.2	6 24.7	72 01.7
20	117 03.4	6 22.8	102 06.6
22	147 03.7	S 6 20.9	132 11.5

Thursday, 9th March

Time	SUN GHA	Dec	ARIES GHA
00	177 18.0	S 4 45.8	166 13.0
02	207 18.3	4 43.9	196 17.9
04	237 18.6	4 41.9	226 22.9
06	267 18.9	4 40.0	256 27.8
08	297 19.2	4 38.0	286 32.7
10	327 19.5	4 36.0	316 37.7
12	357 19.8	4 34.1	346 42.6
14	27 20.2	4 32.1	16 47.5
16	57 20.5	4 30.2	46 52.4
18	87 20.8	4 28.2	76 57.4
20	117 21.1	4 26.3	107 02.3
22	147 21.4	S 4 24.3	137 07.2

Tuesday, 14th March

Time	SUN GHA	Dec	ARIES GHA
00	177 37.6	S 2 48.1	171 08.7
02	207 38.0	2 46.1	201 13.6
04	237 38.3	2 44.1	231 18.6
06	267 38.7	2 42.2	261 23.5
08	297 39.0	2 40.2	291 28.4
10	327 39.4	2 38.2	321 33.4
12	357 39.7	2 36.3	351 38.3
14	27 40.1	2 34.3	21 43.2
16	57 40.4	2 32.3	51 48.1
18	87 40.8	2 30.3	81 53.1
20	117 41.1	2 28.4	111 58.0
22	147 41.5	S 2 26.4	142 02.9

Sunday, 5th March

Time	SUN GHA	Dec	ARIES GHA
00	177 04.0	S 6 18.9	162 16.5
02	207 04.3	6 17.0	192 21.4
04	237 04.5	6 15.1	222 26.3
06	267 04.8	6 13.2	252 31.2
08	297 05.1	6 11.2	282 36.2
10	327 05.4	6 09.3	312 41.1
12	357 05.6	6 07.4	342 46.0
14	27 05.9	6 05.4	12 51.0
16	57 06.2	6 03.5	42 55.9
18	87 06.5	6 01.6	73 00.8
20	117 06.8	5 59.6	103 05.7
22	147 07.0	S 5 57.7	133 10.7

Friday, 10th March

Time	SUN GHA	Dec	ARIES GHA
00	177 21.7	S 4 22.4	167 12.2
02	207 22.0	4 20.4	197 17.1
04	237 22.4	4 18.4	227 22.0
06	267 22.7	4 16.5	257 26.9
08	297 23.0	4 14.5	287 31.9
10	327 23.3	4 12.6	317 36.8
12	357 23.6	4 10.6	347 41.7
14	27 24.0	4 08.7	17 46.7
16	57 24.3	4 06.7	47 51.6
18	87 24.6	4 04.7	77 56.5
20	117 24.9	4 02.8	108 01.4
22	147 25.3	S 4 00.8	138 06.4

Wednesday, 15th March

Time	SUN GHA	Dec	ARIES GHA
00	177 41.8	S 2 24.4	172 07.8
02	207 42.2	2 22.5	202 12.8
04	237 42.5	2 20.5	232 17.7
06	267 42.9	2 18.5	262 22.6
08	297 43.2	2 16.5	292 27.6
10	327 43.6	2 14.6	322 32.5
12	357 43.9	2 12.6	352 37.4
14	27 44.3	2 10.6	22 42.3
16	57 44.6	2 08.6	52 47.3
18	87 45.0	2 06.7	82 52.2
20	117 45.3	2 04.7	112 57.1
22	147 45.7	S 2 02.7	143 02.1

NOTES

Sun & Aries GHA corrections for additional hour, minutes, and seconds on page E 94.
Correct Sun Declination by interpolation. For example see page E 4.

MARCH 1995 — SUN & ARIES — GMT

Thursday, 16th March

Time	SUN GHA	Dec	ARIES GHA
00	177 46.0	S 2 00.7	173 07.0
02	207 46.4	1 58.8	203 11.9
04	237 46.7	1 56.8	233 16.8
06	267 47.1	1 54.8	263 21.8
08	297 47.5	1 52.8	293 26.7
10	327 47.8	1 50.9	323 31.6
12	357 48.2	1 48.9	353 36.6
14	27 48.5	1 46.9	23 41.5
16	57 48.9	1 44.9	53 46.4
18	87 49.2	1 43.0	83 51.3
20	117 49.6	1 41.0	113 56.3
22	147 50.0	S 1 39.0	144 01.2

Friday, 17th March

Time	SUN GHA	Dec	ARIES GHA
00	177 50.3	S 1 37.0	174 06.1
02	207 50.7	1 35.1	204 11.1
04	237 51.0	1 33.1	234 16.0
06	267 51.4	1 31.1	264 20.9
08	297 51.8	1 29.1	294 25.8
10	327 52.1	1 27.2	324 30.8
12	357 52.5	1 25.2	354 35.7
14	27 52.8	1 23.2	24 40.6
16	57 53.2	1 21.2	54 45.6
18	87 53.6	1 19.3	84 50.5
20	117 53.9	1 17.3	114 55.4
22	147 54.3	S 1 15.3	145 00.3

Saturday, 18th March

Time	SUN GHA	Dec	ARIES GHA
00	177 54.6	S 1 13.3	175 05.3
02	207 55.0	1 11.4	205 10.2
04	237 55.4	1 09.4	235 15.1
06	267 55.7	1 07.4	265 20.1
08	297 56.1	1 05.4	295 25.0
10	327 56.5	1 03.5	325 29.9
12	357 56.8	1 01.5	355 34.8
14	27 57.2	0 59.5	25 39.8
16	57 57.6	0 57.5	55 44.7
18	87 57.9	0 55.6	85 49.6
20	117 58.3	0 53.6	115 54.5
22	147 58.7	S 0 51.6	145 59.5

Sunday, 19th March

Time	SUN GHA	Dec	ARIES GHA
00	177 59.0	S 0 49.6	176 04.4
02	207 59.4	0 47.6	206 09.3
04	237 59.8	0 45.7	236 14.3
06	268 00.1	0 43.7	266 19.2
08	298 00.5	0 41.7	296 24.1
10	328 00.9	0 39.7	326 29.0
12	358 01.2	0 37.8	356 34.0
14	28 01.6	0 35.8	26 38.9
16	58 02.0	0 33.8	56 43.8
18	88 02.3	0 31.8	86 48.8
20	118 02.7	0 29.9	116 53.7
22	148 03.1	S 0 27.9	146 58.6

Monday, 20th March

Time	SUN GHA	Dec	ARIES GHA
00	178 03.4	S 0 25.9	177 03.5
02	208 03.8	0 23.9	207 08.5
04	238 04.2	0 22.0	237 13.4
06	268 04.5	0 20.0	267 18.3
08	298 04.9	0 18.0	297 23.3
10	328 05.3	0 16.0	327 28.2
12	358 05.6	0 14.1	357 33.1
14	28 06.0	0 12.1	27 38.0
16	58 06.4	0 10.1	57 43.0
18	88 06.8	0 08.1	87 47.9
20	118 07.1	0 06.2	117 52.8
22	148 07.5	S 0 04.2	147 57.8

Tuesday, 21st March

Time	SUN GHA	Dec	ARIES GHA
00	178 07.9	S 0 02.2	178 02.7
02	208 08.2	0 00.2	208 07.6
04	238 08.6	N 0 01.7	238 12.5
06	268 09.0	0 03.7	268 17.5
08	298 09.4	0 05.7	298 22.4
10	328 09.7	0 07.7	328 27.3
12	358 10.1	0 09.6	358 32.3
14	28 10.5	0 11.6	28 37.2
16	58 10.9	0 13.6	58 42.1
18	88 11.2	0 15.6	88 47.0
20	118 11.6	0 17.5	118 52.0
22	148 12.0	N 0 19.5	148 56.9

Wednesday, 22nd March

Time	SUN GHA	Dec	ARIES GHA
00	178 12.3	N 0 21.5	179 01.8
02	208 12.7	0 23.5	209 06.7
04	238 13.1	0 25.4	239 11.7
06	268 13.5	0 27.4	269 16.6
08	298 13.8	0 29.4	299 21.5
10	328 14.2	0 31.4	329 26.5
12	358 14.6	0 33.3	359 31.4
14	28 15.0	0 35.3	29 36.3
16	58 15.3	0 37.3	59 41.2
18	88 15.7	0 39.3	89 46.2
20	118 16.1	0 41.2	119 51.1
22	148 16.5	N 0 43.2	149 56.0

Thursday, 23rd March

Time	SUN GHA	Dec	ARIES GHA
00	178 16.8	N 0 45.2	180 01.0
02	208 17.2	0 47.1	210 05.9
04	238 17.6	0 49.1	240 10.8
06	268 18.0	0 51.1	270 15.7
08	298 18.4	0 53.1	300 20.7
10	328 18.7	0 55.0	330 25.6
12	358 19.1	0 57.0	0 30.5
14	28 19.5	0 59.0	30 35.5
16	58 19.9	1 00.9	60 40.4
18	88 20.2	1 02.9	90 45.3
20	118 20.6	1 04.9	120 50.2
22	148 21.0	N 1 06.9	150 55.2

Friday, 24th March

Time	SUN GHA	Dec	ARIES GHA
00	178 21.4	N 1 08.8	181 00.1
02	208 21.8	1 10.8	211 05.0
04	238 22.1	1 12.8	241 10.0
06	268 22.5	1 14.7	271 14.9
08	298 22.9	1 16.7	301 19.8
10	328 23.3	1 18.7	331 24.7
12	358 23.6	1 20.6	1 29.7
14	28 24.0	1 22.6	31 34.6
16	58 24.4	1 24.6	61 39.5
18	88 24.8	1 26.6	91 44.5
20	118 25.1	1 28.5	121 49.4
22	148 25.5	N 1 30.5	151 54.3

Saturday, 25th March

Time	SUN GHA	Dec	ARIES GHA
00	178 25.9	N 1 32.5	181 59.2
02	208 26.3	1 34.4	212 04.2
04	238 26.6	1 36.4	242 09.1
06	268 27.0	1 38.4	272 14.0
08	298 27.4	1 40.3	302 18.9
10	328 27.8	1 42.3	332 23.9
12	358 28.1	1 44.3	2 28.8
14	28 28.5	1 46.2	32 33.7
16	58 28.9	1 48.2	62 38.7
18	88 29.3	1 50.2	92 43.6
20	118 29.7	1 52.1	122 48.5
22	148 30.0	N 1 54.1	152 53.4

Sunday, 26th March

Time	SUN GHA	Dec	ARIES GHA
00	178 30.4	N 1 56.1	182 58.4
02	208 30.8	1 58.0	213 03.3
04	238 31.2	2 00.0	243 08.2
06	268 31.5	2 02.0	273 13.2
08	298 31.9	2 03.9	303 18.1
10	328 32.3	2 05.9	333 23.0
12	358 32.7	2 07.8	3 27.9
14	28 33.1	2 09.8	33 32.9
16	58 33.4	2 11.8	63 37.8
18	88 33.8	2 13.7	93 42.7
20	118 34.2	2 15.7	123 47.7
22	148 34.6	N 2 17.7	153 52.6

Monday, 27th March

Time	SUN GHA	Dec	ARIES GHA
00	178 35.0	N 2 19.6	183 57.5
02	208 35.3	2 21.6	214 02.4
04	238 35.7	2 23.5	244 07.4
06	268 36.1	2 25.5	274 12.3
08	298 36.5	2 27.5	304 17.2
10	328 36.8	2 29.4	334 22.2
12	358 37.2	2 31.4	4 27.1
14	28 37.6	2 33.3	34 32.0
16	58 38.0	2 35.3	64 36.9
18	88 38.4	2 37.3	94 41.9
20	118 38.7	2 39.2	124 46.8
22	148 39.1	N 2 41.2	154 51.7

Tuesday, 28th March

Time	SUN GHA	Dec	ARIES GHA
00	178 39.5	N 2 43.1	184 56.7
02	208 39.9	2 45.1	215 01.6
04	238 40.3	2 47.0	245 06.5
06	268 40.6	2 49.0	275 11.4
08	298 41.0	2 51.0	305 16.4
10	328 41.4	2 52.9	335 21.3
12	358 41.8	2 54.9	5 26.2
14	28 42.1	2 56.8	35 31.1
16	58 42.5	2 58.8	65 36.1
18	88 42.9	3 00.7	95 41.0
20	118 43.3	3 02.7	125 45.9
22	148 43.7	N 3 04.6	155 50.9

Wednesday, 29th March

Time	SUN GHA	Dec	ARIES GHA
00	178 44.0	N 3 06.6	185 55.8
02	208 44.4	3 08.5	216 00.7
04	238 44.8	3 10.5	246 05.6
06	268 45.2	3 12.4	276 10.6
08	298 45.5	3 14.4	306 15.5
10	328 45.9	3 16.3	336 20.4
12	358 46.3	3 18.3	6 25.4
14	28 46.7	3 20.2	36 30.3
16	58 47.0	3 22.2	66 35.2
18	88 47.4	3 24.1	96 40.1
20	118 47.8	3 26.1	126 45.1
22	148 48.2	N 3 28.0	156 50.0

Thursday, 30th March

Time	SUN GHA	Dec	ARIES GHA
00	178 48.5	N 3 30.0	186 54.9
02	208 48.9	3 31.9	216 59.9
04	238 49.3	3 33.9	247 04.8
06	268 49.7	3 35.8	277 09.7
08	298 50.1	3 37.8	307 14.6
10	328 50.4	3 39.7	337 19.6
12	358 50.8	3 41.6	7 24.5
14	28 51.2	3 43.6	37 29.4
16	58 51.6	3 45.5	67 34.4
18	88 51.9	3 47.5	97 39.3
20	118 52.3	3 49.4	127 44.2
22	148 52.7	N 3 51.3	157 49.1

Friday, 31st March

Time	SUN GHA	Dec	ARIES GHA
00	178 53.0	N 3 53.3	187 54.1
02	208 53.4	3 55.2	217 59.0
04	238 53.8	3 57.2	248 03.9
06	268 54.2	N 3 59.1	278 08.9
08	298 54.5	N 4 01.0	308 13.8
10	328 54.9	4 03.0	338 18.7
12	358 55.3	4 04.9	8 23.6
14	28 55.7	N 4 06.9	38 28.6
16	58 56.0	N 4 08.8	68 33.5
18	88 56.4	4 10.7	98 38.4
20	118 56.8	4 12.7	128 43.3
22	148 57.2	N 4 14.6	158 48.3

MARCH

MARCH 1995   PLANETS   0h GMT

	VENUS				Note	JUPITER				
Mer Pass h m	GHA ° ′	Mean Var/hr 14°+	Dec ° ′	Mean Var/hr ′	Corrections on Page E 101	GHA ° ′	Mean Var/hr 15°+	Dec ° ′	Mean Var/hr ′	Mer Pass h m
09 25	218 43.5	59.4	S 19 35.1	0.4	1 Wed	265 43.2	2.2	S 21 40.7	0.0	06 16
09 26	218 28.7	59.4	S 19 25.0	0.4	2 Th	266 36.5	2.2	S 21 41.3	0.0	06 13
09 27	218 14.0	59.4	S 19 14.4	0.5	3 Fri	267 29.9	2.2	S 21 41.9	0.0	06 09
09 28	217 59.4	59.4	S 19 03.2	0.5	4 Sat	268 23.5	2.2	S 21 42.4	0.0	06 06
09 29	217 44.9	59.4	S 18 51.4	0.5	5 SUN	269 17.3	2.2	S 21 42.9	0.0	06 02
09 30	217 30.5	59.4	S 18 39.2	0.5	6 Mon	270 11.2	2.3	S 21 43.4	0.0	05 58
09 31	217 16.3	59.4	S 18 26.4	0.6	7 Tu	271 05.3	2.3	S 21 43.9	0.0	05 55
09 32	217 02.1	59.4	S 18 13.0	0.6	8 Wed	271 59.6	2.3	S 21 44.4	0.0	05 51
09 33	216 48.1	59.4	S 17 59.2	0.6	9 Th	272 54.1	2.3	S 21 44.8	0.0	05 48
09 34	216 34.2	59.4	S 17 44.8	0.6	10 Fri	273 48.8	2.3	S 21 45.2	0.0	05 44
09 35	216 20.5	59.4	S 17 30.0	0.6	11 Sat	274 43.6	2.3	S 21 45.6	0.0	05 40
09 36	216 07.0	59.4	S 17 14.6	0.7	12 SUN	275 38.6	2.3	S 21 46.0	0.0	05 37
09 37	215 53.5	59.4	S 16 58.8	0.7	13 Mon	276 33.8	2.3	S 21 46.3	0.0	05 33
09 38	215 40.3	59.5	S 16 42.5	0.7	14 Tu	277 29.2	2.3	S 21 46.7	0.0	05 29
09 39	215 27.2	59.5	S 16 25.7	0.7	15 Wed	278 24.8	2.3	S 21 47.0	0.0	05 26
09 39	215 14.3	59.5	S 16 08.4	0.7	16 Th	279 20.6	2.3	S 21 47.3	0.0	05 22
09 40	215 01.5	59.5	S 15 50.7	0.8	17 Fri	280 16.6	2.3	S 21 47.5	0.0	05 18
09 41	214 49.0	59.5	S 15 32.5	0.8	18 Sat	281 12.7	2.4	S 21 47.8	0.0	05 14
09 42	214 36.6	59.5	S 15 13.9	0.8	19 SUN	282 09.1	2.4	S 21 48.0	0.0	05 11
09 43	214 24.3	59.5	S 14 54.8	0.8	20 Mon	283 05.6	2.4	S 21 48.2	0.0	05 07
09 44	214 12.3	59.5	S 14 35.3	0.8	21 Tu	284 02.3	2.4	S 21 48.4	0.0	05 03
09 44	214 00.4	59.5	S 14 15.4	0.8	22 Wed	284 59.3	2.4	S 21 48.6	0.0	04 59
09 45	213 48.7	59.5	S 13 55.1	0.9	23 Th	285 56.4	2.4	S 21 48.8	0.0	04 55
09 46	213 37.2	59.5	S 13 34.4	0.9	24 Fri	286 53.7	2.4	S 21 48.9	0.0	04 52
09 47	213 25.9	59.5	S 13 13.3	0.9	25 Sat	287 51.2	2.4	S 21 49.0	0.0	04 48
09 47	213 14.8	59.5	S 12 51.8	0.9	26 SUN	288 48.9	2.4	S 21 49.1	0.0	04 44
09 48	213 03.8	59.6	S 12 30.0	0.9	27 Mon	289 46.9	2.4	S 21 49.1	0.0	04 40
09 49	212 53.0	59.6	S 12 07.8	0.9	28 Tu	290 45.0	2.4	S 21 49.2	0.0	04 36
09 49	212 42.4	59.6	S 11 45.3	1.0	29 Wed	291 43.3	2.4	S 21 49.2	0.0	04 32
09 50	212 31.9	59.6	S 11 22.4	1.0	30 Th	292 41.8	2.4	S 21 49.2	0.0	04 28
09 51	212 21.7	59.6	S 10 59.2	1.0	31 Fri	293 40.6	2.5	S 21 49.2	0.0	04 25

VENUS, Av. Mag. -4.1
S.H.A. March
5 55; 10 49; 15 43; 20 37; 25 31; 30 26.

JUPITER, Av. Mag.-2.2
S.H.A. March
5 107; 10 107; 15 106; 20 106; 25 106; 30 106.

	MARS				Note	SATURN				
Mer Pass h m	GHA ° ′	Mean Var/hr 15°+	Dec ° ′	Mean Var/hr ′	Corrections on Page E 101	GHA ° ′	Mean Var/hr 15°+	Dec ° ′	Mean Var/hr ′	Mer Pass h m
22 44	17 45.6	3.2	N 19 52.9	0.2	1 Wed	172 01.5	2.2	S 7 46.1	0.1	12 30
22 39	19 03.1	3.2	N 19 56.7	0.1	2 Th	172 53.8	2.2	S 7 43.2	0.1	12 27
22 34	20 19.9	3.2	N 20 00.1	0.1	3 Fri	173 46.1	2.2	S 7 40.4	0.1	12 23
22 29	21 36.1	3.1	N 20 03.3	0.1	4 Sat	174 38.4	2.2	S 7 37.6	0.1	12 20
22 24	22 51.5	3.1	N 20 06.1	0.1	5 SUN	175 30.6	2.2	S 7 34.8	0.1	12 16
22 19	24 06.3	3.1	N 20 08.7	0.1	6 Mon	176 22.9	2.2	S 7 32.0	0.1	12 13
22 14	25 20.3	3.1	N 20 11.0	0.1	7 Tu	177 15.2	2.2	S 7 29.2	0.1	12 09
22 09	26 33.6	3.0	N 20 13.0	0.1	8 Wed	178 07.5	2.2	S 7 26.4	0.1	12 06
22 05	27 46.1	3.0	N 20 14.7	0.1	9 Th	178 59.7	2.2	S 7 23.5	0.1	12 02
22 00	28 57.8	3.0	N 20 16.1	0.1	10 Fri	179 52.0	2.2	S 7 20.7	0.1	11 59
21 55	30 08.8	2.9	N 20 17.3	0.0	11 Sat	180 44.3	2.2	S 7 17.9	0.1	11 55
21 51	31 19.0	2.9	N 20 18.2	0.0	12 SUN	181 36.6	2.2	S 7 15.1	0.1	11 52
21 46	32 28.4	2.9	N 20 18.8	0.0	13 Mon	182 28.9	2.2	S 7 12.3	0.1	11 48
21 41	33 36.9	2.8	N 20 19.2	0.0	14 Tu	183 21.2	2.2	S 7 09.5	0.1	11 45
21 37	34 44.7	2.8	N 20 19.3	0.0	15 Wed	184 13.5	2.2	S 7 06.7	0.1	11 41
21 33	35 51.8	2.8	N 20 19.1	0.0	16 Th	185 05.8	2.2	S 7 04.0	0.1	11 38
21 28	36 58.0	2.7	N 20 18.7	0.0	17 Fri	185 58.1	2.2	S 7 01.2	0.1	11 34
21 24	38 03.4	2.7	N 20 18.1	0.0	18 Sat	186 50.5	2.2	S 6 58.4	0.1	11 31
21 20	39 08.0	2.7	N 20 17.2	0.0	19 SUN	187 42.8	2.2	S 6 55.6	0.1	11 27
21 15	40 11.9	2.6	N 20 16.1	0.1	20 Mon	188 35.2	2.2	S 6 52.9	0.1	11 24
21 11	41 15.0	2.6	N 20 14.8	0.1	21 Tu	189 27.6	2.2	S 6 50.1	0.1	11 21
21 07	42 17.3	2.6	N 20 13.3	0.1	22 Wed	190 20.0	2.2	S 6 47.4	0.1	11 17
21 03	43 18.8	2.5	N 20 11.5	0.1	23 Th	191 12.4	2.2	S 6 44.7	0.1	11 14
20 59	44 19.6	2.5	N 20 09.5	0.1	24 Fri	192 04.8	2.2	S 6 41.9	0.1	11 10
20 55	45 19.6	2.5	N 20 07.3	0.1	25 Sat	192 57.3	2.2	S 6 39.2	0.1	11 07
20 51	46 18.9	2.4	N 20 04.9	0.1	26 SUN	193 49.7	2.2	S 6 36.5	0.1	11 03
20 47	47 17.4	2.4	N 20 02.3	0.1	27 Mon	194 42.2	2.2	S 6 33.8	0.1	11 00
20 44	48 15.3	2.4	N 19 59.5	0.1	28 Tu	195 34.7	2.2	S 6 31.1	0.1	10 56
20 40	49 12.4	2.4	N 19 56.4	0.1	29 Wed	196 27.3	2.2	S 6 28.4	0.1	10 53
20 36	50 08.8	2.3	N 19 53.2	0.1	30 Th	197 19.8	2.2	S 6 25.8	0.1	10 49
20 33	51 04.5	2.3	N 19 49.8	0.2	31 Fri	198 12.4	2.2	S 6 23.1	0.1	10 46

MARS, Av. Mag. -0.6
S.H.A. March
5 221; 10 222; 15 223; 20 223; 25 223; 30 223.

SATURN, Av. Mag. +1.1
S.H.A. March
5 13; 10 13; 15 12; 20 12; 25 11; 30 10.

MARCH 1995   MOON

Day	GMT hr	GHA ° ′	Mean Var/hr 14°+	Dec ° ′	Mean Var/hr ′
1 Wed	0	184 16.5	30.5	S 5 52.5	10.9
	6	271 19.3	30.7	S 4 47.0	11.0
	12	358 23.7	31.0	S 3 41.1	11.0
	18	85 29.6	31.2	S 2 34.8	11.1
2 Th	0	172 36.7	31.4	S 1 28.4	11.1
	6	259 45.1	31.6	S 0 22.1	11.0
	12	346 54.5	31.8	N 0 43.9	10.9
	18	74 04.8	31.9	N 1 49.4	10.7
3 Fri	0	161 16.0	32.0	N 2 54.1	10.6
	6	248 27.9	32.1	N 3 58.0	10.4
	12	335 40.4	32.2	N 5 00.9	10.3
	18	62 53.4	32.2	N 6 02.5	10.0
4 Sat	0	150 06.7	32.2	N 7 02.7	9.8
	6	237 20.3	32.3	N 8 01.5	9.5
	12	324 34.0	32.3	N 8 58.6	9.2
	18	51 47.8	32.3	N 9 53.9	8.9
5 Sun	0	139 01.6	32.3	N 10 47.2	8.5
	6	226 15.3	32.2	N 11 38.6	8.1
	12	313 28.8	32.3	N 12 27.8	7.8
	18	40 42.0	32.2	N 13 14.7	7.4
6 Mon	0	127 54.9	32.1	N 13 59.3	7.0
	6	215 07.5	32.0	N 14 41.4	6.6
	12	302 19.6	31.9	N 15 21.0	6.1
	18	29 31.3	31.9	N 15 58.0	5.7
7 Tu	0	116 42.5	31.7	N 16 32.2	5.2
	6	203 53.1	31.6	N 17 03.7	4.8
	12	291 03.3	31.6	N 17 32.3	4.2
	18	18 12.9	31.5	N 17 58.0	3.7
8 Wed	0	105 22.0	31.4	N 18 20.7	3.2
	6	192 30.5	31.3	N 18 40.4	2.8
	12	279 38.5	31.2	N 18 56.9	2.2
	18	6 46.1	31.2	N 19 10.4	1.7
9 Th	0	93 53.2	31.1	N 19 20.7	1.2
	6	180 59.8	31.1	N 19 27.8	0.6
	12	268 06.1	31.0	N 19 31.6	0.1
	18	355 12.0	30.9	N 19 32.2	0.5
10 Fri	0	82 17.6	30.9	N 19 29.5	1.0
	6	169 22.9	30.8	N 19 23.5	1.6
	12	256 28.0	30.8	N 19 14.2	2.2
	18	343 32.9	30.8	N 19 01.7	2.7
11 Sat	0	70 37.7	30.8	N 18 45.8	3.3
	6	157 42.3	30.8	N 18 26.7	3.7
	12	244 46.9	30.7	N 18 04.3	4.4
	18	331 51.4	30.7	N 17 38.8	4.8
12 Sun	0	58 55.9	30.7	N 17 10.0	5.4
	6	146 00.4	30.7	N 16 38.1	5.8
	12	233 04.9	30.8	N 16 03.2	6.4
	18	320 09.5	30.8	N 15 25.2	6.8
13 Mon	0	47 14.0	30.7	N 14 44.3	7.3
	6	134 18.5	30.8	N 14 00.6	7.8
	12	221 23.1	30.8	N 13 14.0	8.3
	18	308 27.5	30.8	N 12 24.9	8.7
14 Tu	0	35 31.9	30.7	N 11 33.1	9.0
	6	122 36.2	30.7	N 10 39.0	9.4
	12	209 40.2	30.6	N 9 42.5	9.8
	18	296 44.0	30.6	N 8 43.9	10.1
15 Wed	0	23 47.5	30.5	N 7 43.2	10.4
	6	110 50.6	30.4	N 6 40.8	10.7
	12	197 53.2	30.4	N 5 36.7	11.0
	18	284 55.3	30.2	N 4 31.1	11.1
16 Th	0	11 56.7	30.0	N 3 24.2	11.3
	6	98 57.3	30.0	N 2 16.3	11.5
	12	185 57.0	29.8	N 1 07.6	11.6
	18	272 55.8	29.6	S 0 01.8	11.6

Day	GMT hr	GHA ° ′	Mean Var/hr 14°+	Dec ° ′	Mean Var/hr ′
17 Fri	0	359 53.4	29.4	S 1 11.5	11.6
	6	86 50.0	29.2	S 2 21.3	11.6
	12	173 45.2	28.9	S 3 31.0	11.5
	18	260 39.0	28.7	S 4 40.2	11.4
18 Sat	0	347 31.4	28.4	S 5 48.8	11.2
	6	74 22.2	28.2	S 6 56.3	11.0
	12	161 11.4	27.9	S 8 02.7	10.7
	18	247 58.9	27.6	S 9 07.4	10.4
19 Sun	0	334 44.7	27.3	S 10 10.4	10.1
	6	61 28.7	27.0	S 11 11.2	9.7
	12	148 10.9	26.7	S 12 09.7	9.2
	18	234 51.3	26.4	S 13 05.4	8.8
20 Mon	0	321 30.0	26.1	S 13 58.2	8.2
	6	48 07.1	25.9	S 14 47.8	7.6
	12	134 42.5	25.7	S 15 34.0	7.0
	18	221 16.4	25.4	S 16 16.5	6.4
21 Tu	0	307 49.0	25.2	S 16 55.2	5.7
	6	34 20.3	25.0	S 17 29.8	5.0
	12	120 50.6	24.9	S 18 00.1	4.3
	18	207 20.0	24.8	S 18 26.1	3.5
22 Wed	0	293 48.9	24.7	S 18 47.6	2.7
	6	20 17.3	24.7	S 19 04.5	2.0
	12	106 45.5	24.7	S 19 16.7	1.2
	18	193 13.9	24.8	S 19 24.3	0.5
23 Th	0	279 42.6	24.9	S 19 27.2	0.4
	6	6 11.9	25.0	S 19 25.4	1.1
	12	92 42.0	25.2	S 19 19.1	1.9
	18	179 13.1	25.4	S 19 08.2	2.6
24 Fri	0	265 45.5	25.7	S 18 52.8	3.3
	6	352 19.4	25.9	S 18 33.1	4.0
	12	78 54.9	26.3	S 18 09.3	4.7
	18	165 32.2	26.6	S 17 41.4	5.3
25 Sat	0	252 11.4	26.9	S 17 09.7	5.9
	6	338 52.5	27.2	S 16 34.3	6.5
	12	65 35.8	27.6	S 15 55.4	7.1
	18	152 21.1	28.0	S 15 13.3	7.6
26 Sun	0	239 08.6	28.3	S 14 28.2	8.0
	6	325 58.3	28.6	S 13 40.2	8.5
	12	52 50.0	29.0	S 12 49.6	8.9
	18	139 43.9	29.3	S 11 56.6	9.3
27 Mon	0	226 39.7	29.7	S 11 01.4	9.5
	6	313 37.6	30.0	S 10 04.3	9.9
	12	40 37.3	30.2	S 9 05.6	10.1
	18	127 38.7	30.5	S 8 05.3	10.2
28 Tu	0	214 41.9	30.8	S 7 03.7	10.4
	6	301 46.6	31.0	S 6 01.1	10.6
	12	28 52.7	31.3	S 4 57.6	10.7
	18	116 00.2	31.5	S 3 53.6	10.7
29 Wed	0	203 08.9	31.7	S 2 49.0	10.8
	6	290 18.6	31.8	S 1 44.3	10.8
	12	17 29.3	31.9	S 0 39.5	10.8
	18	104 40.9	32.0	N 0 25.1	10.7
30 Th	0	191 53.1	32.2	N 1 29.4	10.7
	6	279 05.9	32.2	N 2 33.1	10.5
	12	6 19.2	32.3	N 3 36.2	10.4
	18	93 32.8	32.3	N 4 38.4	10.2
31 Fri	0	180 46.6	32.4	N 5 39.5	10.0
	6	268 00.7	32.3	N 6 39.5	9.8
	12	355 14.7	32.3	N 7 38.0	9.5
	18	82 28.8	32.4	N 8 35.1	9.3

MARCH

NOTE Moon GHA corrections for additional hours, minutes, and seconds on page E 96.
Moon Declination corrections on page E 99. Mean Var/Hr value needed for both corrections.

APRIL 1995 — SUN & MOON — GMT

SUN

Day of Yr	Mth	Week	Equation of Time 0h	12h	Transit	Semi-diam	Twi-light	Sun-rise	Sun-set	Twi-light	Lat Corr to Sunrise, Sunset etc Lat	Twi-light	Sun-rise	Sun-set	Twi-light
			m s	m s	h m	'	h m	h m	h m	h m	°	h m	h m	h m	h m
91	1	Sat	+04 10	+04 01	12 04	16.0	05 02	05 36	18 33	19 07	N60	-0 30	-0 20	+0 20	+0 30
92	2	Sun	+03 52	+03 44	12 04	16.0	05 00	05 34	18 35	19 09	55	-0 10	-0 06	+0 06	+0 10
93	3	Mon	+03 35	+03 26	12 03	16.0	04 57	05 32	18 36	19 11	50	+0 06	+0 04	-0 04	-0 06
94	4	Tu	+03 17	+03 08	12 03	16.0	04 55	05 29	18 38	19 13	45	+0 17	+0 12	-0 12	-0 17
95	5	Wed	+03 00	+02 51	12 03	16.0	04 52	05 27	18 40	19 14	N40	+0 26	+0 19	-0 19	-0 26
96	6	Th	+02 43	+02 34	12 03	16.0	04 50	05 25	18 41	19 16	35	+0 34	+0 25	-0 25	-0 34
97	7	Fri	+02 25	+02 17	12 02	16.0	04 48	05 22	18 43	19 18	30	+0 41	+0 30	-0 30	-0 41
98	8	Sat	+02 08	+02 00	12 02	16.0	04 45	05 20	18 45	19 20	25	+0 47	+0 34	-0 34	-0 47
99	9	Sun	+01 52	+01 43	12 02	16.0	04 43	05 18	18 47	19 22	N20	+0 52	+0 38	-0 38	-0 52
100	10	Mon	+01 35	+01 27	12 01	16.0	04 41	05 16	18 48	19 24	15	+0 56	+0 42	-0 42	-0 56
101	11	Tu	+01 19	+01 11	12 01	16.0	04 38	05 13	18 50	19 25	10	+1 00	+0 46	-0 46	-1 00
102	12	Wed	+01 03	+00 55	12 01	16.0	04 36	05 11	18 52	19 27	5	+1 04	+0 49	-0 49	-1 04
103	13	Th	+00 47	+00 39	12 01	16.0	04 34	05 09	18 53	19 29	0	+1 07	+0 53	-0 53	-1 07
104	14	Fri	+00 32	+00 24	12 00	16.0	04 31	05 07	18 55	19 31	S 5	+1 11	+0 56	-0 56	-1 11
105	15	Sat	+00 17	+00 09	12 00	16.0	04 29	05 05	18 57	19 33	10	+1 14	+1 00	-1 00	-1 14
106	16	Sun	+00 02	-00 05	12 00	16.0	04 26	05 02	18 59	19 35	15	+1 17	+1 03	-1 03	-1 17
107	17	Mon	-00 13	-00 20	12 00	16.0	04 24	05 00	19 00	19 37	S20	+1 20	+1 07	-1 07	-1 20
108	18	Tu	-00 27	-00 33	11 59	16.0	04 22	04 58	19 02	19 38	25	+1 23	+1 11	-1 11	-1 23
109	19	Wed	-00 40	-00 47	11 59	15.9	04 20	04 56	19 04	19 40	30	+1 26	+1 15	-1 15	-1 26
110	20	Th	-00 53	-01 00	11 59	15.9	04 17	04 54	19 05	19 42	35	+1 29	+1 19	-1 19	-1 29
111	21	Fri	-01 06	-01 12	11 59	15.9	04 15	04 52	19 07	19 44	S40	+1 33	+1 24	-1 24	-1 33
112	22	Sat	-01 18	-01 24	11 59	15.9	04 13	04 50	19 09	19 46	45	+1 36	+1 30	-1 30	-1 36
113	23	Sun	-01 30	-01 36	11 58	15.9	04 10	04 47	19 10	19 48	50	+1 40	+1 37	-1 37	-1 40
114	24	Mon	-01 42	-01 47	11 58	15.9	04 08	04 45	19 12	19 50					
115	25	Tu	-01 53	-01 58	11 58	15.9	04 06	04 43	19 14	19 52					
116	26	Wed	-02 03	-02 08	11 58	15.9	04 04	04 41	19 16	19 53					
117	27	Th	-02 13	-02 18	11 58	15.9	04 01	04 39	19 17	19 55					
118	28	Fri	-02 22	-02 27	11 58	15.9	03 59	04 37	19 19	19 57					
119	29	Sat	-02 31	-02 35	11 57	15.9	03 57	04 35	19 21	19 59					
120	30	Sun	-02 40	-02 44	11 57	15.9	03 55	04 33	19 22	20 01					

Lat 52°N

NOTES
Lat corrections are for mid-month.
Equation of Time is the excess of Mean Time over Apparent Time.

MOON

Lat 52°N

Day of Yr	Mth	Week	Age	Transit (Upper)	Diff	Semi-diam	Hor Par	Moon-rise	Moon-set
			days	h m	m	'	'	h m	h m
91	1	Sat	01	13 05	46	15.0	55.1	05 59	20 24
92	2	Sun	02	13 51	47	14.9	54.7	06 26	21 28
93	3	Mon	03	14 38	47	14.8	54.4	06 56	22 28
94	4	Tu	04	15 25	48	14.8	54.2	07 31	23 24
95	5	Wed	05	16 13	48	14.8	54.1	08 12	— —
96	6	Th	06	17 01	47	14.8	54.2	08 59	00 15
97	7	Fri	07	17 48	48	14.8	54.5	09 52	00 59
98	8	Sat	08	18 36	47	15.0	54.9	10 51	01 38
99	9	Sun	09	19 23	48	15.1	55.5	11 54	02 12
100	10	Mon	10	20 11	48	15.3	56.2	13 01	02 42
101	11	Tu	11	20 59	49	15.6	57.1	14 11	03 08
102	12	Wed	12	21 48	50	15.8	58.0	15 24	03 34
103	13	Th	13	22 38	53	16.0	58.8	16 40	03 59
104	14	Fri	14	23 31	55	16.2	59.6	17 58	04 25
105	15	Sat	15	24 26	—	16.4	60.2	19 18	04 53
106	16	Sun	16	00 26	59	16.5	60.5	20 38	05 26
107	17	Mon	17	01 25	60	16.5	60.6	21 54	06 05
108	18	Tu	18	02 25	60	16.5	60.5	23 03	06 52
109	19	Wed	19	03 25	60	16.4	60.1	— —	07 48
110	20	Th	20	04 25	58	16.2	59.5	00 01	08 52
111	21	Fri	21	05 23	55	16.1	58.9	00 49	10 02
112	22	Sat	22	06 18	51	15.9	58.2	01 28	11 15
113	23	Sun	23	07 09	49	15.7	57.6	02 00	12 28
114	24	Mon	24	07 58	47	15.5	57.0	02 28	13 40
115	25	Tu	25	08 45	46	15.4	56.4	02 52	14 50
116	26	Wed	26	09 31	45	15.2	55.9	03 15	15 59
117	27	Th	27	10 16	45	15.1	55.4	03 38	17 06
118	28	Fri	28	11 01	46	15.0	55.0	04 02	18 12
119	29	Sat	29	11 47	46	14.9	54.6	04 28	19 17
120	30	Sun	01	12 33	47	14.8	54.4	04 57	20 19

Phases of the Moon

		d	h	m
(	First Quarter	8	05	35
O	Full Moon	15	12	08
)	Last Quarter	22	03	18
●	New Moon	29	17	36

	d	h
Apogee	5	10
Perigee	17	08

NOTES
Diff equals daily change in transit time.
To correct Moonrise, Moonset, or Transit times for Latitude and/or Longitude see page E 100. For further information about these tables see page E 4. For Arc to Time correction see page E 91.

APRIL 1995   STARS   0h GMT April 1

No	Name	Mag	Transit h m	Dec ° '	GHA ° '	RA h m	SHA ° '
	ARIES................		11 23		188 53.2		
1	Alpheratz..........	2.2	11 31	N 29 03.8	186 51.2	0 08	357 58.0
2	Ankaa...............	2.4	11 49	S 42 19.9	182 22.8	0 26	353 29.6
3	Schedar.............	2.5	12 03	N 56 30.6	178 49.9	0 40	349 56.7
4	Diphda..............	2.2	12 06	S 18 00.8	178 03.1	0 43	349 09.9
5	Achernar...........	0.6	13 00	S 57 15.7	164 30.7	1 38	335 37.5
6	POLARIS............	2.1	13 48	N 89 14.6	152 25.7	2 26	323 32.5
7	Hamal...............	2.2	13 29	N 23 26.3	157 09.7	2 07	328 16.5
8	Acamar.............	3.1	14 20	S 40 19.6	144 22.3	2 58	315 29.1
9	Menkar	2.8	14 24	N 4 04.1	143 22.9	3 02	314 29.7
10	Mirfak..............	1.9	14 46	N 49 50.7	137 53.6	3 24	309 00.4
11	Aldebaran.........	1.1	15 57	N 16 29.9	119 58.5	4 36	291 05.3
12	Rigel	0.3	16 36	S 8 12.7	110 18.6	5 14	281 25.4
13	Capella	0.2	16 38	N 45 59.6	109 48.1	5 16	280 54.9
14	Bellatrix	1.7	16 47	N 6 20.5	107 40.1	5 25	278 46.9
15	Elnath	1.8	16 48	N 28 36.1	107 23.3	5 26	278 30.1
16	Alnilam	1.8	16 58	S 1 12.5	104 53.6	5 36	276 00.4
17	Betelgeuse 0.1-1.2		17 17	N 7 24.2	100 09.4	5 55	271 16.2
18	Canopus...........-0.9		17 45	S 52 42.0	92 55.6	6 24	264 02.4
19	Sirius ....-1.6		18 06	S 16 42.9	87 39.0	6 45	258 45.8
20	Adhara	1.6	18 20	S 28 58.3	84 16.5	6 58	255 23.3
21	Castor...............	1.6	18 56	N 31 53.9	75 18.6	7 34	246 25.4
22	Procyon............	0.5	19 00	N 5 14.0	74 07.2	7 39	245 14.0
23	Pollux	1.2	19 06	N 28 02.2	72 37.6	7 45	243 44.4
24	Avior	1.7	19 44	S 59 30.1	63 16.6	8 22	234 23.4
25	Suhail	2.2	20 29	S 43 25.2	51 55.5	9 08	223 02.3
26	Miaplacidus	1.8	20 34	S 69 42.3	50 35.3	9 13	221 42.1
27	Alphard............	2.2	20 48	S 8 38.6	47 02.6	9 27	218 09.4
28	Regulus	1.3	21 29	N 11 59.2	36 51.1	10 08	207 57.9
29	Dubhe	2.0	22 24	N 61 46.6	23 01.1	11 03	194 07.9
30	Denebola	2.2	23 09	N 14 35.8	11 40.5	11 49	182 47.3
31	Gienah	2.8	23 36	S 17 31.2	4 59.3	12 16	176 06.1
32	Acrux...............	1.1	23 47	S 63 04.6	2 17.1	12 26	173 23.9
33	Gacrux..............	1.6	23 51	S 57 05.4	1 08.8	12 31	172 15.6
34	Mimosa	1.5	0 12	S 59 39.9	357 00.6	12 48	168 07.4
35	Alioth	1.7	0 18	N 55 59.1	355 25.4	12 54	166 32.2
36	Spica...............	1.2	0 49	S 11 08.4	347 38.5	13 25	158 45.3
37	Alkaid...............	1.9	1 12	N 49 20.1	342 02.4	13 47	153 09.2
38	Hadar...............	0.9	1 28	S 60 21.1	337 59.9	14 04	149 06.7
39	Menkent	2.3	1 31	S 36 20.9	337 16.5	14 06	148 23.3
40	Arcturus	0.2	1 40	N 19 12.3	335 01.1	14 15	146 07.9
41	Rigil Kent.	0.1	2 03	S 60 48.9	329 02.9	14 39	140 09.7
42	Zuben'ubi	2.9	2 15	S 16 01.4	326 13.5	14 51	137 20.3
43	Kochab.............	2.2	2 15	N 74 10.4	326 11.7	14 51	137 18.5
44	Alphecca	2.3	2 58	N 26 43.7	315 15.5	15 35	126 22.3
45	Antares	1.2	3 53	S 26 25.2	301 36.0	16 29	112 42.8
46	Atria	1.9	4 12	S 69 00.9	296 49.7	16 48	107 56.5
47	Sabik	2.6	4 34	S 15 43.1	291 21.2	17 10	102 28.0
48	Shaula	1.7	4 57	S 37 05.9	285 33.5	17 33	96 40.3
49	Rasalhague	2.1	4 58	N 12 33.7	285 12.2	17 35	96 19.0
50	Eltanin..............	2.4	5 20	N 51 29.2	279 45.5	17 57	90 52.3
51	Kaus Aust.	2.0	5 47	S 34 23.0	272 55.0	18 24	84 01.8
52	Vega	0.1	6 00	N 38 46.6	269 41.3	18 37	80 48.1
53	Nunki	2.1	6 18	S 26 18.0	265 08.4	18 55	76 15.2
54	Altair	0.9	7 14	N 8 51.3	251 14.8	19 51	62 21.6
55	Peacock	2.1	7 48	S 56 44.7	242 34.0	20 25	53 40.8
56	Deneb	1.3	8 04	N 45 15.6	238 34.1	20 41	49 40.9
57	Enif..................	2.5	9 07	N 9 51.1	222 53.9	21 44	34 00.7
58	Al Na'ir.............	2.2	9 31	S 46 58.8	216 54.3	22 08	28 01.1
59	Fomalhaut	1.3	10 20	S 29 38.8	204 32.5	22 57	15 39.3
60	Markab	2.6	10 27	N 15 10.7	202 45.4	23 05	13 52.2

Star Transit Corr Table

Date	Corr h m	Date	Corr h m
1	-0 00	17	-1 03
2	-0 04	18	-1 07
3	-0 08	19	-1 11
4	-0 12	20	-1 15
5	-0 16	21	-1 19
6	-0 20	22	-1 23
7	-0 24	23	-1 27
8	-0 28	24	-1 30
9	-0 31	25	-1 34
10	-0 35	26	-1 38
11	-0 39	27	-1 42
12	-0 43	28	-1 46
13	-0 47	29	-1 50
14	-0 51	30	-1 54
15	-0 55	31	-1 58
16	-0 59		

STAR TRANSIT

To find the approx time of transit of a star for any day of the month use above table. All corrections are subtractive.

If the value taken from the table is greater than the time of transit for the first of the month, add 23h 56min to the time of transit before subtracting the correction.

Example: What time will Spica (No 36) transit the Meridian on April 30?

	h min
Transit on Apr 1	00 49
	+23 56
	24 45
Corr for Apr 30	-01 54
Transit on Apr 30	22 51

APRIL DIARY

d h	
1 13	Jupiter stationary
10 14	Mars 8° N of Moon
13 17	Venus 0.6° N of Saturn
14 13	Mercury in superior conjunction
15 09	Spica 1° S of Moon
18 21	Jupiter 3° S of Moon
21 18	Neptune 5° S of Moon
22 04	Uranus 6° S of Moon
26 01	Saturn 6° S of Moon
27 05	Venus 4° S of Moon

NOTES

Star declinations may be used as is for the whole month. To correct GHA for day, hour, minute and second see page E 92 and for further explanation of this table see page E 4.

APRIL

APRIL 1995 — SUN & ARIES — GMT

Saturday, 1st April

Time	SUN GHA	Dec	ARIES GHA
00	178 57.5	N 4 16.5	188 53.2
02	208 57.9	4 18.5	218 58.1
04	238 58.3	4 20.4	249 03.1
06	268 58.6	4 22.3	279 08.0
08	298 59.0	4 24.3	309 12.9
10	328 59.4	4 26.2	339 17.8
12	358 59.8	4 28.1	9 22.8
14	29 00.1	4 30.1	39 27.7
16	59 00.5	4 32.0	69 32.6
18	89 00.9	4 33.9	99 37.6
20	119 01.2	4 35.8	129 42.5
22	149 01.6	N 4 37.8	159 47.4

Sunday, 2nd April

Time	SUN GHA	Dec	ARIES GHA
00	179 02.0	N 4 39.7	189 52.3
02	209 02.3	4 41.6	219 57.3
04	239 02.7	4 43.6	250 02.2
06	269 03.1	4 45.5	280 07.1
08	299 03.4	4 47.4	310 12.1
10	329 03.8	4 49.3	340 17.0
12	359 04.2	4 51.3	10 21.9
14	29 04.6	4 53.2	40 26.8
16	59 04.9	4 55.1	70 31.8
18	89 05.3	4 57.0	100 36.7
20	119 05.7	4 58.9	130 41.6
22	149 06.0	N 5 00.9	160 46.6

Monday, 3rd April

Time	SUN GHA	Dec	ARIES GHA
00	179 06.4	N 5 02.8	190 51.5
02	209 06.8	5 04.7	220 56.4
04	239 07.1	5 06.6	251 01.3
06	269 07.5	5 08.5	281 06.3
08	299 07.9	5 10.5	311 11.2
10	329 08.2	5 12.4	341 16.1
12	359 08.6	5 14.3	11 21.1
14	29 09.0	5 16.2	41 26.0
16	59 09.3	5 18.1	71 30.9
18	89 09.7	5 20.0	101 35.8
20	119 10.1	5 22.0	131 40.8
22	149 10.4	N 5 23.9	161 45.7

Tuesday, 4th April

Time	SUN GHA	Dec	ARIES GHA
00	179 10.8	N 5 25.8	191 50.6
02	209 11.1	5 27.7	221 55.5
04	239 11.5	5 29.6	252 00.5
06	269 11.9	5 31.5	282 05.4
08	299 12.2	5 33.4	312 10.3
10	329 12.6	5 35.3	342 15.3
12	359 13.0	5 37.2	12 20.2
14	29 13.3	5 39.1	42 25.1
16	59 13.7	5 41.1	72 30.0
18	89 14.1	5 43.0	102 35.0
20	119 14.4	5 44.9	132 39.9
22	149 14.8	N 5 46.8	162 44.8

Wednesday, 5th April

Time	SUN GHA	Dec	ARIES GHA
00	179 15.1	N 5 48.7	192 49.8
02	209 15.5	5 50.6	222 54.7
04	239 15.9	5 52.5	252 59.6
06	269 16.2	5 54.4	283 04.5
08	299 16.6	5 56.3	313 09.5
10	329 16.9	5 58.2	343 14.4
12	359 17.3	6 00.1	13 19.3
14	29 17.7	6 02.0	43 24.3
16	59 18.0	6 03.9	73 29.2
18	89 18.4	6 05.8	103 34.1
20	119 18.7	6 07.7	133 39.0
22	149 19.1	N 6 09.6	163 44.0

Thursday, 6th April

Time	SUN GHA	Dec	ARIES GHA
00	179 19.5	N 6 11.5	193 48.9
02	209 19.8	6 13.4	223 53.8
04	239 20.2	6 15.3	253 58.8
06	269 20.5	6 17.2	284 03.7
08	299 20.9	6 19.0	314 08.6
10	329 21.2	6 20.9	344 13.5
12	359 21.6	6 22.8	14 18.5
14	29 22.0	6 24.7	44 23.4
16	59 22.3	6 26.6	74 28.3
18	89 22.7	6 28.5	104 33.3
20	119 23.0	6 30.4	134 38.2
22	149 23.4	N 6 32.3	164 43.1

Friday, 7th April

Time	SUN GHA	Dec	ARIES GHA
00	179 23.7	N 6 34.2	194 48.0
02	209 24.1	6 36.0	224 53.0
04	239 24.4	6 37.9	254 57.9
06	269 24.8	6 39.8	285 02.8
08	299 25.2	6 41.7	315 07.8
10	329 25.5	6 43.6	345 12.7
12	359 25.9	6 45.5	15 17.6
14	29 26.2	6 47.3	45 22.5
16	59 26.6	6 49.2	75 27.5
18	89 26.9	6 51.1	105 32.4
20	119 27.3	6 53.0	135 37.3
22	149 27.6	N 6 54.9	165 42.2

Saturday, 8th April

Time	SUN GHA	Dec	ARIES GHA
00	179 28.0	N 6 56.7	195 47.2
02	209 28.3	6 58.6	225 52.1
04	239 28.7	7 00.5	255 57.0
06	269 29.0	7 02.4	286 02.0
08	299 29.4	7 04.2	316 06.9
10	329 29.7	7 06.1	346 11.8
12	359 30.1	7 08.0	16 16.7
14	29 30.4	7 09.9	46 21.7
16	59 30.8	7 11.7	76 26.6
18	89 31.1	7 13.6	106 31.5
20	119 31.5	7 15.5	136 36.5
22	149 31.8	N 7 17.3	166 41.4

Sunday, 9th April

Time	SUN GHA	Dec	ARIES GHA
00	179 32.2	N 7 19.2	196 46.3
02	209 32.5	7 21.1	226 51.2
04	239 32.8	7 22.9	256 56.2
06	269 33.2	7 24.8	287 01.1
08	299 33.5	7 26.7	317 06.0
10	329 33.9	7 28.5	347 11.0
12	359 34.2	7 30.4	17 15.9
14	29 34.6	7 32.2	47 20.8
16	59 34.9	7 34.1	77 25.7
18	89 35.3	7 36.0	107 30.7
20	119 35.6	7 37.8	137 35.6
22	149 35.9	N 7 39.7	167 40.5

Monday, 10th April

Time	SUN GHA	Dec	ARIES GHA
00	179 36.3	N 7 41.5	197 45.5
02	209 36.6	7 43.4	227 50.4
04	239 37.0	7 45.2	257 55.3
06	269 37.3	7 47.1	288 00.2
08	299 37.6	7 48.9	318 05.2
10	329 38.0	7 50.8	348 10.1
12	359 38.3	7 52.6	18 15.0
14	29 38.7	7 54.5	48 20.0
16	59 39.0	7 56.3	78 24.9
18	89 39.3	7 58.2	108 29.8
20	119 39.7	8 00.0	138 34.7
22	149 40.0	N 8 01.9	168 39.7

Tuesday, 11th April

Time	SUN GHA	Dec	ARIES GHA
00	179 40.3	N 8 03.7	198 44.6
02	209 40.7	8 05.6	228 49.5
04	239 41.0	8 07.4	258 54.4
06	269 41.4	8 09.3	288 59.4
08	299 41.7	8 11.1	319 04.3
10	329 42.0	8 12.9	349 09.2
12	359 42.4	8 14.8	19 14.2
14	29 42.7	8 16.6	49 19.1
16	59 43.0	8 18.5	79 24.0
18	89 43.4	8 20.3	109 28.9
20	119 43.7	8 22.1	139 33.9
22	149 44.0	N 8 24.0	169 38.8

Wednesday, 12th April

Time	SUN GHA	Dec	ARIES GHA
00	179 44.4	N 8 25.8	199 43.7
02	209 44.7	8 27.6	229 48.7
04	239 45.0	8 29.5	259 53.6
06	269 45.3	8 31.3	289 58.5
08	299 45.7	8 33.1	320 03.4
10	329 46.0	8 35.0	350 08.4
12	359 46.3	8 36.8	20 13.3
14	29 46.7	8 38.6	50 18.2
16	59 47.0	8 40.4	80 23.2
18	89 47.3	8 42.3	110 28.1
20	119 47.6	8 44.1	140 33.0
22	149 48.0	N 8 45.9	170 37.9

Thursday, 13th April

Time	SUN GHA	Dec	ARIES GHA
00	179 48.3	N 8 47.7	200 42.9
02	209 48.6	8 49.6	230 47.8
04	239 48.9	8 51.4	260 52.7
06	269 49.3	8 53.2	290 57.7
08	299 49.6	8 55.0	321 02.6
10	329 49.9	8 56.8	351 07.5
12	359 50.2	8 58.6	21 12.4
14	29 50.5	9 00.5	51 17.4
16	59 50.9	9 02.3	81 22.3
18	89 51.2	9 04.1	111 27.2
20	119 51.5	9 05.9	141 32.2
22	149 51.8	N 9 07.7	171 37.1

Friday, 14th April

Time	SUN GHA	Dec	ARIES GHA
00	179 52.1	N 9 09.5	201 42.0
02	209 52.5	9 11.3	231 46.9
04	239 52.8	9 13.1	261 51.9
06	269 53.1	9 14.9	291 56.8
08	299 53.4	9 16.7	322 01.7
10	329 53.7	9 18.5	352 06.6
12	359 54.0	9 20.3	22 11.6
14	29 54.4	9 22.1	52 16.5
16	59 54.7	9 23.9	82 21.4
18	89 55.0	9 25.7	112 26.4
20	119 55.3	9 27.5	142 31.3
22	149 55.6	N 9 29.3	172 36.2

Saturday, 15th April

Time	SUN GHA	Dec	ARIES GHA
00	179 55.9	N 9 31.1	202 41.1
02	209 56.2	9 32.9	232 46.1
04	239 56.5	9 34.7	262 51.0
06	269 56.8	9 36.5	292 55.9
08	299 57.2	9 38.3	323 00.9
10	329 57.5	9 40.1	353 05.8
12	359 57.8	9 41.9	23 10.7
14	29 58.1	9 43.7	53 15.6
16	59 58.4	9 45.5	83 20.6
18	89 58.7	9 47.3	113 25.5
20	119 59.0	9 49.0	143 30.4
22	149 59.3	N 9 50.8	173 35.4

NOTES

Sun & Aries GHA corrections for additional hour, minutes, and seconds on page E 94.
Correct Sun Declination by interpolation. For example see page E 4.

APRIL 1995 — SUN & ARIES — GMT

Sunday, 16th April

Time	SUN GHA	Dec	ARIES GHA
00	179 59.6	N 9 52.6	203 40.3
02	209 59.9	9 54.4	233 45.2
04	240 00.2	9 56.2	263 50.1
06	270 00.5	9 58.0	293 55.1
08	300 00.8	9 59.7	324 00.0
10	330 01.1	10 01.5	354 04.9
12	0 01.4	10 03.3	24 09.9
14	30 01.7	10 05.1	54 14.8
16	60 02.0	10 06.8	84 19.7
18	90 02.3	10 08.6	114 24.6
20	120 02.6	10 10.4	144 29.6
22	150 02.9	N10 12.2	174 34.5

Monday, 17th April

Time	SUN GHA	Dec	ARIES GHA
00	180 03.2	N10 13.9	204 39.4
02	210 03.5	10 15.7	234 44.4
04	240 03.8	10 17.5	264 49.3
06	270 04.1	10 19.2	294 54.2
08	300 04.4	10 21.0	324 59.1
10	330 04.7	10 22.8	355 04.1
12	0 05.0	10 24.5	25 09.0
14	30 05.3	10 26.3	55 13.9
16	60 05.5	10 28.0	85 18.8
18	90 05.8	10 29.8	115 23.8
20	120 06.1	10 31.6	145 28.7
22	150 06.4	N10 33.3	175 33.6

Tuesday, 18th April

Time	SUN GHA	Dec	ARIES GHA
00	180 06.7	N10 35.1	205 38.6
02	210 07.0	10 36.8	235 43.5
04	240 07.3	10 38.6	265 48.4
06	270 07.6	10 40.3	295 53.3
08	300 07.8	10 42.1	325 58.3
10	330 08.1	10 43.8	356 03.2
12	0 08.4	10 45.6	26 08.1
14	30 08.7	10 47.3	56 13.1
16	60 09.0	10 49.1	86 18.0
18	90 09.3	10 50.8	116 22.9
20	120 09.5	10 52.5	146 27.8
22	150 09.8	N10 54.3	176 32.8

Wednesday, 19th April

Time	SUN GHA	Dec	ARIES GHA
00	180 10.1	N10 56.0	206 37.7
02	210 10.4	10 57.8	236 42.6
04	240 10.7	10 59.5	266 47.6
06	270 10.9	11 01.2	296 52.5
08	300 11.2	11 03.0	326 57.4
10	330 11.5	11 04.7	357 02.3
12	0 11.8	11 06.4	27 07.3
14	30 12.0	11 08.2	57 12.2
16	60 12.3	11 09.9	87 17.1
18	90 12.6	11 11.6	117 22.1
20	120 12.9	11 13.4	147 27.0
22	150 13.1	N11 15.1	177 31.9

Thursday, 20th April

Time	SUN GHA	Dec	ARIES GHA
00	180 13.4	N11 16.8	207 36.8
02	210 13.7	11 18.5	237 41.8
04	240 13.9	11 20.3	267 46.7
06	270 14.2	11 22.0	297 51.6
08	300 14.5	11 23.7	327 56.6
10	330 14.7	11 25.4	358 01.5
12	0 15.0	11 27.1	28 06.4
14	30 15.3	11 28.9	58 11.3
16	60 15.5	11 30.6	88 16.3
18	90 15.8	11 32.3	118 21.2
20	120 16.1	11 34.0	148 26.1
22	150 16.3	N11 35.7	178 31.0

Friday, 21st April

Time	SUN GHA	Dec	ARIES GHA
00	180 16.6	N11 37.4	208 36.0
02	210 16.8	11 39.1	238 40.9
04	240 17.1	11 40.8	268 45.8
06	270 17.4	11 42.5	298 50.8
08	300 17.6	11 44.2	328 55.7
10	330 17.9	11 45.9	359 00.6
12	0 18.1	11 47.6	29 05.5
14	30 18.4	11 49.3	59 10.5
16	60 18.6	11 51.0	89 15.4
18	90 18.9	11 52.7	119 20.3
20	120 19.2	11 54.4	149 25.3
22	150 19.4	N11 56.1	179 30.2

Saturday, 22nd April

Time	SUN GHA	Dec	ARIES GHA
00	180 19.7	N11 57.8	209 35.1
02	210 19.9	11 59.5	239 40.0
04	240 20.2	12 01.2	269 45.0
06	270 20.4	12 02.9	299 49.9
08	300 20.7	12 04.6	329 54.8
10	330 20.9	12 06.3	359 59.8
12	0 21.2	12 08.0	30 04.7
14	30 21.4	12 09.6	60 09.6
16	60 21.6	12 11.3	90 14.5
18	90 21.9	12 13.0	120 19.5
20	120 22.1	12 14.7	150 24.4
22	150 22.4	N12 16.4	180 29.3

Sunday, 23rd April

Time	SUN GHA	Dec	ARIES GHA
00	180 22.6	N12 18.0	210 34.3
02	210 22.9	12 19.7	240 39.2
04	240 23.1	12 21.4	270 44.1
06	270 23.3	12 23.1	300 49.0
08	300 23.6	12 24.7	330 54.0
10	330 23.8	12 26.4	0 58.9
12	0 24.1	12 28.1	31 03.8
14	30 24.3	12 29.7	61 08.8
16	60 24.5	12 31.4	91 13.7
18	90 24.8	12 33.1	121 18.6
20	120 25.0	12 34.7	151 23.5
22	150 25.2	N12 36.4	181 28.5

Monday, 24th April

Time	SUN GHA	Dec	ARIES GHA
00	180 25.5	N12 38.1	211 33.4
02	210 25.7	12 39.7	241 38.3
04	240 25.9	12 41.4	271 43.2
06	270 26.2	12 43.0	301 48.2
08	300 26.4	12 44.7	331 53.1
10	330 26.6	12 46.3	1 58.0
12	0 26.8	12 48.0	32 03.0
14	30 27.1	12 49.6	62 07.9
16	60 27.3	12 51.3	92 12.8
18	90 27.5	12 52.9	122 17.7
20	120 27.7	12 54.6	152 22.7
22	150 28.0	N12 56.2	182 27.6

Tuesday, 25th April

Time	SUN GHA	Dec	ARIES GHA
00	180 28.2	N12 57.9	212 32.5
02	210 28.4	12 59.5	242 37.5
04	240 28.6	13 01.1	272 42.4
06	270 28.8	13 02.8	302 47.3
08	300 29.1	13 04.4	332 52.2
10	330 29.3	13 06.0	2 57.2
12	0 29.5	13 07.7	33 02.1
14	30 29.7	13 09.3	63 07.0
16	60 29.9	13 10.9	93 12.0
18	90 30.1	13 12.6	123 16.9
20	120 30.4	13 14.2	153 21.8
22	150 30.6	N13 15.8	183 26.7

Wednesday, 26th April

Time	SUN GHA	Dec	ARIES GHA
00	180 30.8	N13 17.4	213 31.7
02	210 31.0	13 19.1	243 36.6
04	240 31.2	13 20.7	273 41.5
06	270 31.4	13 22.3	303 46.5
08	300 31.6	13 23.9	333 51.4
10	330 31.8	13 25.5	3 56.3
12	0 32.0	13 27.2	34 01.2
14	30 32.2	13 28.8	64 06.2
16	60 32.4	13 30.4	94 11.1
18	90 32.6	13 32.0	124 16.0
20	120 32.9	13 33.6	154 21.0
22	150 33.1	N13 35.2	184 25.9

Thursday, 27th April

Time	SUN GHA	Dec	ARIES GHA
00	180 33.3	N13 36.8	214 30.8
02	210 33.5	13 38.4	244 35.7
04	240 33.7	13 40.0	274 40.7
06	270 33.9	13 41.6	304 45.6
08	300 34.1	13 43.2	334 50.5
10	330 34.3	13 44.8	4 55.4
12	0 34.4	13 46.4	35 00.4
14	30 34.6	13 48.0	65 05.3
16	60 34.8	13 49.6	95 10.2
18	90 35.0	13 51.2	125 15.2
20	120 35.2	13 52.8	155 20.1
22	150 35.4	N13 54.4	185 25.0

Friday, 28th April

Time	SUN GHA	Dec	ARIES GHA
00	180 35.6	N13 56.0	215 29.9
02	210 35.8	13 57.6	245 34.9
04	240 36.0	13 59.1	275 39.8
06	270 36.2	14 00.7	305 44.7
08	300 36.4	14 02.3	335 49.7
10	330 36.5	14 03.9	5 54.6
12	0 36.7	14 05.5	35 59.5
14	30 36.9	14 07.0	66 04.4
16	60 37.1	14 08.6	96 09.4
18	90 37.3	14 10.2	126 14.3
20	120 37.5	14 11.7	156 19.2
22	150 37.6	N14 13.3	186 24.2

Saturday, 29th April

Time	SUN GHA	Dec	ARIES GHA
00	180 37.8	N14 14.9	216 29.1
02	210 38.0	14 16.4	246 34.0
04	240 38.2	14 18.0	276 38.9
06	270 38.4	14 19.6	306 43.9
08	300 38.5	14 21.1	336 48.8
10	330 38.7	14 22.7	6 53.7
12	0 38.9	14 24.3	36 58.7
14	30 39.1	14 25.8	67 03.6
16	60 39.2	14 27.4	97 08.5
18	90 39.4	14 28.9	127 13.4
20	120 39.6	14 30.5	157 18.4
22	150 39.8	N14 32.0	187 23.3

Sunday, 30th April

Time	SUN GHA	Dec	ARIES GHA
00	180 39.9	N14 33.6	217 28.2
02	210 40.1	14 35.1	247 33.2
04	240 40.3	14 36.7	277 38.1
06	270 40.4	14 38.2	307 43.0
08	300 40.6	14 39.7	337 47.9
10	330 40.8	14 41.3	7 52.9
12	0 40.9	14 42.8	37 57.8
14	30 41.1	14 44.4	68 02.7
16	60 41.2	14 45.9	98 07.6
18	90 41.4	14 47.4	128 12.6
20	120 41.6	14 49.0	158 17.5
22	150 41.7	N14 50.5	188 22.4

APRIL

APRIL 1995 — PLANETS — 0h GMT

Mer Pass h m	GHA ° '	Mean Var/hr 14°+	Dec ° '	Mean Var/hr '	Note — Corrections on Page E 101	GHA ° '	Mean Var/hr 15°+	Dec ° '	Mean Var/hr '	Mer Pass h m
	VENUS					**JUPITER**				
09 51	212 11.6	59.6	S 10 35.7	1.0	1 Sat	294 39.5	2.5	S 21 49.2	0.0	04 21
09 52	212 01.7	59.6	S 10 11.9	1.0	2 SUN	295 38.6	2.5	S 21 49.1	0.0	04 17
09 53	211 51.9	59.6	S 9 47.8	1.0	3 Mon	296 38.0	2.5	S 21 49.1	0.0	04 13
09 53	211 42.3	59.6	S 9 23.4	1.0	4 Tu	297 37.5	2.5	S 21 49.0	0.0	04 09
09 54	211 32.9	59.6	S 8 58.8	1.0	5 Wed	298 37.2	2.5	S 21 48.9	0.0	04 05
09 55	211 23.6	59.6	S 8 33.9	1.1	6 Th	299 37.2	2.5	S 21 48.8	0.0	04 01
09 55	211 14.5	59.6	S 8 08.7	1.1	7 Fri	300 37.3	2.5	S 21 48.6	0.0	03 57
09 56	211 05.5	59.6	S 7 43.3	1.1	8 Sat	301 37.6	2.5	S 21 48.5	0.0	03 53
09 56	210 56.6	59.6	S 7 17.7	1.1	9 SUN	302 38.2	2.5	S 21 48.3	0.0	03 49
09 57	210 47.9	59.6	S 6 51.8	1.1	10 Mon	303 38.9	2.5	S 21 48.1	0.0	03 45
09 58	210 39.2	59.6	S 6 25.8	1.1	11 Tu	304 39.8	2.5	S 21 47.9	0.0	03 41
09 58	210 30.7	59.6	S 5 59.6	1.1	12 Wed	305 41.0	2.6	S 21 47.6	0.0	03 37
09 59	210 22.3	59.7	S 5 33.1	1.1	13 Th	306 42.3	2.6	S 21 47.4	0.0	03 33
09 59	210 14.0	59.7	S 5 06.5	1.1	14 Fri	307 43.8	2.6	S 21 47.1	0.0	03 28
10 00	210 05.8	59.7	S 4 39.7	1.1	15 Sat	308 45.5	2.6	S 21 46.8	0.0	03 24
10 00	209 57.7	59.7	S 4 12.8	1.1	16 SUN	309 47.4	2.6	S 21 46.5	0.0	03 20
10 01	209 49.6	59.7	S 3 45.8	1.1	17 Mon	310 49.5	2.6	S 21 46.2	0.0	03 16
10 01	209 41.6	59.7	S 3 18.6	1.1	18 Tu	311 51.8	2.6	S 21 45.8	0.0	03 12
10 02	209 33.7	59.7	S 2 51.3	1.1	19 Wed	312 54.3	2.6	S 21 45.4	0.0	03 08
10 02	209 25.8	59.7	S 2 23.8	1.1	20 Th	313 56.9	2.6	S 21 45.0	0.0	03 04
10 03	209 17.9	59.7	S 1 56.3	1.2	21 Fri	314 59.8	2.6	S 21 44.6	0.0	02 59
10 04	209 10.1	59.7	S 1 28.7	1.2	22 Sat	316 02.8	2.6	S 21 44.2	0.0	02 55
10 04	209 02.4	59.7	S 1 01.0	1.2	23 SUN	317 06.0	2.6	S 21 43.8	0.0	02 51
10 05	208 54.6	59.7	S 0 33.3	1.2	24 Mon	318 09.4	2.6	S 21 43.3	0.0	02 47
10 05	208 46.9	59.7	S 0 05.5	1.2	25 Tu	319 13.0	2.7	S 21 42.8	0.0	02 43
10 06	208 39.1	59.7	N 0 22.3	1.2	26 Wed	320 16.7	2.7	S 21 42.3	0.0	02 38
10 06	208 31.4	59.7	N 0 50.2	1.2	27 Th	321 20.6	2.7	S 21 41.8	0.0	02 34
10 07	208 23.6	59.7	N 1 18.1	1.2	28 Fri	322 24.7	2.7	S 21 41.3	0.0	02 30
10 07	208 15.8	59.7	N 1 46.0	1.2	29 Sat	323 28.9	2.7	S 21 40.7	0.0	02 26
10 08	208 08.0	59.7	N 2 13.9	1.2	30 SUN	324 33.3	2.7	S 21 40.1	0.0	02 21
20 29	51 59.5	2.3	N 19 46.2	0.2	1 Sat	199 05.0	2.2	S 6 20.5	0.1	10 42

VENUS, Av. Mag. -4.0
S.H.A. April
5 19; 10 13; 15 7; 20 2; 25 356; 30 351.

JUPITER, Av. Mag.-2.4
S.H.A. April
5 106; 10 106; 15 106; 20 106; 25 107; 30 107.

Mer Pass h m	GHA ° '	Mean Var/hr 15°+	Dec ° '	Mean Var/hr '	Note — Corrections on Page E 101	GHA ° '	Mean Var/hr 15°+	Dec ° '	Mean Var/hr '	Mer Pass h m
	MARS					**SATURN**				
20 25	52 53.8	2.2	N 19 42.4	0.2	2 SUN	199 57.6	2.2	S 6 17.8	0.1	10 39
20 22	53 47.5	2.2	N 19 38.5	0.2	3 Mon	200 50.3	2.2	S 6 15.2	0.1	10 35
20 18	54 40.5	2.2	N 19 34.4	0.2	4 Tu	201 43.0	2.2	S 6 12.6	0.1	10 32
20 15	55 32.8	2.2	N 19 30.1	0.2	5 Wed	202 35.7	2.2	S 6 10.0	0.1	10 28
20 11	56 24.5	2.1	N 19 25.6	0.2	6 Th	203 28.5	2.2	S 6 07.4	0.1	10 25
20 08	57 15.6	2.1	N 19 21.0	0.2	7 Fri	204 21.2	2.2	S 6 04.9	0.1	10 21
20 05	58 06.2	2.1	N 19 16.2	0.2	8 Sat	205 14.0	2.2	S 6 02.3	0.1	10 18
20 02	58 56.1	2.1	N 19 11.2	0.2	9 SUN	206 06.9	2.2	S 5 59.8	0.1	10 14
19 58	59 45.4	2.0	N 19 06.1	0.2	10 Mon	206 59.8	2.2	S 5 57.3	0.1	10 11
19 55	60 34.2	2.0	N 19 00.9	0.2	11 Tu	207 52.7	2.2	S 5 54.8	0.1	10 07
19 52	61 22.5	2.0	N 18 55.4	0.2	12 Wed	208 45.6	2.2	S 5 52.3	0.1	10 03
19 49	62 10.2	2.0	N 18 49.9	0.2	13 Th	209 38.6	2.2	S 5 49.8	0.1	10 00
19 46	62 57.4	1.9	N 18 44.1	0.2	14 Fri	210 31.6	2.2	S 5 47.4	0.1	09 56
19 43	63 44.1	1.9	N 18 38.3	0.3	15 Sat	211 24.7	2.2	S 5 44.9	0.1	09 53
19 39	64 30.2	1.9	N 18 32.3	0.3	16 SUN	212 17.8	2.2	S 5 42.5	0.1	09 49
19 36	65 15.9	1.9	N 18 26.1	0.3	17 Mon	213 11.0	2.2	S 5 40.1	0.1	09 46
19 33	66 01.2	1.9	N 18 19.8	0.3	18 Tu	214 04.1	2.2	S 5 37.7	0.1	09 42
19 31	66 45.9	1.9	N 18 13.4	0.3	19 Wed	214 57.4	2.2	S 5 35.4	0.1	09 39
19 28	67 30.3	1.8	N 18 06.8	0.3	20 Th	215 50.6	2.2	S 5 33.0	0.1	09 35
19 25	68 14.1	1.8	N 18 00.1	0.3	21 Fri	216 44.0	2.2	S 5 30.7	0.1	09 32
19 22	68 57.6	1.8	N 17 53.2	0.3	22 Sat	217 37.3	2.2	S 5 28.4	0.1	09 28
19 19	69 40.6	1.8	N 17 46.3	0.3	23 SUN	218 30.7	2.2	S 5 26.2	0.1	09 25
19 16	70 23.2	1.8	N 17 39.1	0.3	24 Mon	219 24.2	2.2	S 5 23.9	0.1	09 21
19 13	71 05.4	1.7	N 17 31.9	0.3	25 Tu	220 17.7	2.2	S 5 21.7	0.1	09 17
19 11	71 47.2	1.7	N 17 24.5	0.3	26 Wed	221 11.2	2.2	S 5 19.5	0.1	09 14
19 08	72 28.6	1.7	N 17 17.0	0.3	27 Th	222 04.8	2.2	S 5 17.3	0.1	09 10
19 05	73 09.7	1.7	N 17 09.4	0.3	28 Fri	222 58.5	2.2	S 5 15.1	0.1	09 07
19 03	73 50.4	1.7	N 17 01.6	0.3	29 Sat	223 52.2	2.2	S 5 13.0	0.1	09 03
19 00	74 30.7	1.7	N 16 53.7	0.3	30 SUN	224 45.9	2.2	S 5 10.9	0.1	09 00

MARS, Av. Mag. +0.2
S.H.A. April
5 223; 10 222; 15 221; 20 220; 25 219; 30 217.

SATURN, Av. Mag. +1.2
S.H.A. April
5 10; 10 9; 15 9; 20 8; 25 8; 30 7.

APRIL 1995   MOON

Day	GMT hr	GHA ° ′	Mean Var/hr 14°+	Dec ° ′	Mean Var/hr ′	Day	GMT hr	GHA ° ′	Mean Var/hr 14°+	Dec ° ′	Mean Var/hr ′
1 Sat	0	169 42.7	32.2	N 9 30.5	8.9	17 Mon	0	339 42.0	24.3	S 15 55.5	6.8
	6	256 56.4	32.2	N 10 24.2	8.6		6	66 08.1	24.1	S 16 36.8	6.1
	12	344 09.9	32.1	N 11 15.9	8.2		12	152 32.7	23.8	S 17 13.8	5.4
	18	71 23.0	32.2	N 12 05.5	7.8		18	238 56.0	23.7	S 17 46.4	4.6
2 Sun	0	158 35.8	32.1	N 12 53.0	7.5	18 Tu	0	325 18.2	23.5	S 18 14.5	3.8
	6	245 48.1	31.9	N 13 38.2	7.1		6	51 39.7	23.5	S 18 37.8	3.0
	12	333 00.1	31.9	N 14 21.0	6.7		12	138 00.8	23.5	S 18 56.2	2.2
	18	60 11.5	31.8	N 15 01.3	6.3		18	224 21.8	23.6	S 19 09.7	1.4
3 Mon	0	147 22.5	31.8	N 15 39.0	5.8	19 Wed	0	310 43.0	23.6	S 19 18.3	0.5
	6	234 33.0	31.7	N 16 14.1	5.4		6	37 04.7	23.8	S 19 21.9	0.3
	12	321 43.1	31.6	N 16 46.3	4.8		12	123 27.3	23.9	S 19 20.6	1.1
	18	48 52.6	31.5	N 17 15.7	4.4		18	209 51.1	24.3	S 19 14.4	1.9
4 Tu	0	136 01.8	31.4	N 17 42.2	3.8	20 Th	0	296 16.3	24.5	S 19 03.4	2.7
	6	223 10.4	31.4	N 18 05.5	3.3		6	22 43.3	24.8	S 18 47.8	3.4
	12	310 18.7	31.3	N 18 26.2	2.9		12	109 12.2	25.2	S 18 27.8	4.1
	18	37 26.7	31.3	N 18 43.6	2.3		18	195 43.3	25.6	S 18 03.4	4.8
5 Wed	0	124 34.3	31.2	N 18 57.9	1.8	21 Fri	0	282 16.7	26.0	S 17 35.0	5.5
	6	211 41.7	31.2	N 19 09.1	1.2		6	8 52.5	26.4	S 17 02.6	6.1
	12	298 48.8	31.1	N 19 17.0	0.8		12	95 30.9	26.9	S 16 26.6	6.6
	18	25 55.7	31.2	N 19 21.8	0.2		18	182 11.9	27.3	S 15 47.1	7.2
6 Th	0	113 02.5	31.1	N 19 23.3	0.3	22 Sat	0	268 55.5	27.7	S 15 04.5	7.6
	6	200 09.3	31.2	N 19 21.7	0.8		6	355 41.8	28.2	S 14 18.9	8.1
	12	287 16.0	31.2	N 19 16.8	1.4		12	82 30.8	28.6	S 13 30.5	8.5
	18	14 22.7	31.1	N 19 08.6	1.9		18	169 22.3	29.0	S 12 39.7	8.9
7 Fri	0	101 29.5	31.1	N 18 57.3	2.5	23 Sun	0	256 16.3	29.4	S 11 46.6	9.2
	6	188 36.3	31.1	N 18 42.8	3.0		6	343 12.7	29.8	S 10 51.5	9.5
	12	275 43.3	31.2	N 18 25.1	3.5		12	70 11.4	30.2	S 9 54.6	9.8
	18	2 50.4	31.2	N 18 04.3	4.0		18	157 12.4	30.5	S 8 56.2	9.9
8 Sat	0	89 57.6	31.3	N 17 40.4	4.5	24 Mon	0	244 15.3	30.9	S 7 56.4	10.1
	6	177 05.0	31.3	N 17 13.5	5.0		6	331 20.2	31.1	S 6 55.5	10.3
	12	264 12.6	31.2	N 16 43.5	5.5		12	58 26.9	31.4	S 5 53.6	10.5
	18	351 20.3	31.3	N 16 10.6	6.0		18	145 35.1	31.6	S 4 51.0	10.6
9 Sun	0	78 28.2	31.4	N 15 34.8	6.4	25 Tu	0	232 44.8	31.9	S 3 47.8	10.6
	6	165 36.1	31.3	N 14 56.2	6.9		6	319 55.9	32.1	S 2 44.3	10.7
	12	252 44.1	31.4	N 14 14.8	7.3		12	47 08.1	32.2	S 1 40.6	10.7
	18	339 52.1	31.4	N 13 30.7	7.8		18	134 21.2	32.3	S 0 36.9	10.6
10 Mon	0	67 00.1	31.3	N 12 44.0	8.3	26 Wed	0	221 35.3	32.4	N 0 26.6	10.5
	6	154 08.0	31.2	N 11 54.8	8.7		6	308 50.0	32.5	N 1 29.8	10.5
	12	241 15.7	31.3	N 11 03.1	9.1		12	36 05.3	32.6	N 2 32.5	10.3
	18	328 23.1	31.1	N 10 09.2	9.3		18	123 21.0	32.6	N 3 34.5	10.2
11 Tu	0	55 30.2	31.1	N 9 13.1	9.8	27 Th	0	210 37.0	32.7	N 4 35.7	10.0
	6	142 36.8	31.0	N 8 14.9	10.0		6	297 53.2	32.7	N 5 36.0	9.8
	12	229 42.8	30.9	N 7 14.8	10.4		12	25 09.4	32.6	N 6 35.1	9.6
	18	316 48.2	30.7	N 6 12.9	10.6		18	112 25.5	32.7	N 7 32.9	9.3
12 Wed	0	43 52.8	30.6	N 5 09.4	10.8	28 Fri	0	199 41.5	32.6	N 8 29.4	9.2
	6	130 56.4	30.4	N 4 04.3	11.0		6	286 57.2	32.6	N 9 24.3	8.9
	12	217 59.0	30.2	N 2 58.0	11.3		12	14 12.6	32.5	N 10 17.5	8.6
	18	305 00.5	30.0	N 1 50.6	11.4		18	101 27.6	32.4	N 11 08.9	8.2
13 Th	0	32 00.6	29.7	N 0 42.4	11.5	29 Sat	0	188 42.1	32.3	N 11 58.4	7.9
	6	118 59.3	29.5	S 0 26.6	11.5		6	275 56.0	32.2	N 12 45.7	7.5
	12	205 56.5	29.2	S 1 36.0	11.6		12	3 09.4	32.1	N 13 30.9	7.1
	18	292 51.9	28.9	S 2 45.6	11.6		18	Eclipse of the Sun occurs today			
14 Fri	0	19 45.6	28.6	S 3 55.1	11.6	30 Sun	0	177 34.4	31.9	N 14 54.3	6.3
	6	106 37.3	28.2	S 5 04.3	11.4		6	264 46.0	31.8	N 15 32.2	5.9
	12	193 27.0	27.9	S 6 12.8	11.3		12	351 56.9	31.7	N 16 07.6	5.4
	18	280 14.5	27.5	S 7 20.4	11.0		18	79 07.3	31.6	N 16 40.2	5.0
15 Sat	0	6 59.9	27.2	S 8 26.8	10.8						
	6	93 43.0	26.8	S 9 31.6	10.4						
	12	180 23.8	26.4	S 10 34.6	10.1						
	18	267 02.4	26.0	S 11 35.4	9.7						
16 Sun	0	353 38.6	25.6	S 12 33.6	9.2						
	6	80 12.6	25.2	S 13 29.1	8.7						
	12	166 44.4	25.0	S 14 21.4	8.1						
	18	253 14.2	24.6	S 15 10.3	7.5						

NOTE Moon GHA corrections for additional hours, minutes, and seconds on page E 96.
Moon Declination corrections on page E 99. Mean Var/Hr value needed for both corrections.

APRIL

MAY 1995 — SUN & MOON — GMT

SUN

Yr	Mth	Week	Equation of Time 0h	12h	Transit	Semi-diam	Lat 52°N Twi-light	Sun-rise	Sun-set	Twi-light	Lat Corr to Sunrise, Sunset etc Lat	Twi-light	Sun-rise	Sun-set	Twi-light
			m s	m s	h m	′	h m	h m	h m	h m	°	h m	h m	h m	h m
121	1	Mon	-02 47	-02 51	11 57	15.9	03 53	04 31	19 24	20 03	N60	-1 05	-0 44	+0 44	+1 05
122	2	Tu	-02 55	-02 58	11 57	15.9	03 51	04 29	19 26	20 05	55	-0 19	-0 14	+0 14	+0 19
123	3	Wed	-03 02	-03 05	11 57	15.9	03 49	04 28	19 27	20 07	50	+0 11	+0 08	-0 08	-0 11
124	4	Th	-03 08	-03 11	11 57	15.9	03 46	04 26	19 29	20 09	45	+0 33	+0 25	-0 25	-0 33
125	5	Fri	-03 14	-03 16	11 57	15.9	03 44	04 24	19 31	20 10	N40	+0 50	+0 39	-0 39	-0 50
126	6	Sat	-03 19	-03 21	11 57	15.9	03 42	04 22	19 32	20 12	35	+1 04	+0 50	-0 50	-1 04
127	7	Sun	-03 23	-03 26	11 57	15.9	03 40	04 20	19 34	20 14	30	+1 16	+1 00	-1 00	-1 16
128	8	Mon	-03 28	-03 29	11 57	15.9	03 38	04 19	19 36	20 16	25	+1 27	+1 09	-1 09	-1 27
129	9	Tu	-03 31	-03 33	11 56	15.9	03 36	04 17	19 37	20 18	N20	+1 36	+1 18	-1 18	-1 36
130	10	Wed	-03 34	-03 35	11 56	15.9	03 34	04 15	19 39	20 20	15	+1 44	+1 25	-1 25	-1 44
131	11	Th	-03 37	-03 38	11 56	15.9	03 32	04 13	19 40	20 22	10	+1 52	+1 33	-1 33	-1 52
132	12	Fri	-03 38	-03 39	11 56	15.9	03 31	04 12	19 42	20 23	5	+1 59	+1 40	-1 40	-1 59
133	13	Sat	-03 40	-03 40	11 56	15.9	03 29	04 10	19 44	20 25	0	+2 06	+1 46	-1 46	-2 06
134	14	Sun	-03 40	-03 41	11 56	15.9	03 27	04 09	19 45	20 27	S 5	+2 13	+1 53	-1 53	-2 13
135	15	Mon	-03 41	-03 40	11 56	15.8	03 25	04 07	19 47	20 29	10	+2 20	+2 00	-2 00	-2 20
136	16	Tu	-03 40	-03 40	11 56	15.8	03 23	04 05	19 48	20 31	15	+2 26	+2 07	-2 07	-2 26
137	17	Wed	-03 39	-03 39	11 56	15.8	03 21	04 04	19 50	20 33	S20	+2 33	+2 15	-2 15	-2 33
138	18	Th	-03 38	-03 37	11 56	15.8	03 20	04 03	19 51	20 34	25	+2 40	+2 22	-2 22	-2 40
139	19	Fri	-03 36	-03 34	11 56	15.8	03 18	04 01	19 53	20 36	30	+2 48	+2 31	-2 31	-2 48
140	20	Sat	-03 33	-03 31	11 56	15.8	03 16	04 00	19 54	20 38	35	+2 56	+2 41	-2 41	-2 56
141	21	Sun	-03 30	-03 28	11 57	15.8	03 15	03 58	19 56	20 39	S40	+3 04	+2 51	-2 51	-3 04
142	22	Mon	-03 26	-03 24	11 57	15.8	03 13	03 57	19 57	20 41	45	+3 14	+3 04	-3 04	-3 14
143	23	Tu	-03 22	-03 19	11 57	15.8	03 12	03 56	19 58	20 43	50	+3 26	+3 19	-3 19	-3 26
144	24	Wed	-03 17	-03 14	11 57	15.8	03 10	03 55	20 00	20 44					
145	25	Th	-03 11	-03 08	11 57	15.8	03 09	03 53	20 01	20 46					
146	26	Fri	-03 05	-03 02	11 57	15.8	03 07	03 52	20 02	20 48					
147	27	Sat	-02 59	-02 56	11 57	15.8	03 06	03 51	20 04	20 49					
148	28	Sun	-02 52	-02 49	11 57	15.8	03 05	03 50	20 05	20 51					
149	29	Mon	-02 45	-02 41	11 57	15.8	03 04	03 49	20 06	20 52					
150	30	Tu	-02 37	-02 33	11 57	15.8	03 02	03 48	20 07	20 53					
151	31	Wed	-02 29	-02 24	11 58	15.8	03 01	03 47	20 09	20 55					

NOTES
Lat corrections are for mid-month.
Equation of Time is the excess of Mean Time over Apparent Time.

MOON

Yr	Mth	Week	Age	Transit (Upper)	Diff	Semi-diam	Hor Par	Lat 52°N Moon-rise	Moon-set	Phases of the Moon
			days	h m	m	′	′	h m	h m	d h m
121	1	Mon	02	13 20	48	14.8	54.1	05 30	21 16	
122	2	Tu	03	14 08	47	14.7	54.0	06 09	22 09	(First Quarter 7 21 44
123	3	Wed	04	14 55	48	14.7	54.0	06 54	22 56	O Full Moon 14 20 48
124	4	Th	05	15 43	47	14.8	54.2	07 44	23 36	) Last Quarter 21 11 36
125	5	Fri	06	16 30	47	14.8	54.4	08 40	— —	● New Moon 29 09 27
126	6	Sat	07	17 17	46	14.9	54.8	09 41	00 12	
127	7	Sun	08	18 03	46	15.1	55.4	10 45	00 42	
128	8	Mon	09	18 49	47	15.3	56.1	11 52	01 10	
129	9	Tu	10	19 36	49	15.5	57.0	13 02	01 35	Apogee 3 01
130	10	Wed	11	20 25	51	15.8	57.9	14 14	01 59	Perigee 15 15
131	11	Th	12	21 16	53	16.0	58.9	15 30	02 24	Apogee 30 08
132	12	Fri	13	22 09	57	16.3	59.8	16 48	02 50	
133	13	Sat	14	23 06	60	16.5	60.5	18 08	03 20	
134	14	Sun	15	24 06	—	16.6	61.0	19 28	03 55	
135	15	Mon	16	00 06	62	16.7	61.2	20 43	04 39	
136	16	Tu	17	01 08	63	16.7	61.1	21 48	05 32	
137	17	Wed	18	02 11	61	16.5	60.7	22 43	06 35	
138	18	Th	19	03 12	58	16.4	60.1	23 27	07 46	
139	19	Fri	20	04 10	55	16.2	59.3	— —	09 01	
140	20	Sat	21	05 05	51	15.9	58.4	00 02	10 16	
141	21	Sun	22	05 56	48	15.7	57.6	00 32	11 29	NOTES
142	22	Mon	23	06 44	46	15.5	56.8	00 58	12 41	**Diff** equals daily change in
143	23	Tu	24	07 30	45	15.3	56.1	01 21	13 50	transit time.
144	24	Wed	25	08 15	45	15.1	55.5	01 44	14 58	To correct Moonrise, Moonset
145	25	Th	26	09 00	45	15.0	55.0	02 07	16 04	or Transit times for Latitude
146	26	Fri	27	09 45	46	14.9	54.6	02 32	17 09	and/or Longitude see page
147	27	Sat	28	10 31	47	14.8	54.3	03 00	18 11	E 100. For further information
148	28	Sun	29	11 17	47	14.7	54.1	03 31	19 10	about these tables see page E 4.
149	29	Mon	00	12 04	48	14.7	54.0	04 08	20 05	For Arc to Time correction see
150	30	Tu	01	12 52	48	14.7	53.9	04 50	20 54	page E 91.
151	31	Wed	02	13 40	47	14.7	54.0	05 39	21 37	

MAY 1995 — STARS — 0h GMT May 1

No	Name	Mag	Transit h m	Dec ° ′	GHA ° ′	RA h m	SHA ° ′
	ARIES.................		9 25		218 27.4		
1	Alpheratz.......... 2.2		9 33	N 29 03.7	216 25.2	0 08	357 57.8
2	Ankaa............... 2.4		9 51	S 42 19.7	211 56.8	0 26	353 29.4
3	Schedar 2.5		10 05	N 56 30.5	208 23.8	0 40	349 56.4
4	Diphda 2.2		10 08	S 18 00.7	207 37.2	0 43	349 09.8
5	Achernar 0.6		11 02	S 57 15.5	194 04.9	1 38	335 37.5
6	POLARIS 2.1		11 50	N 89 14.5	181 57.6	2 26	323 30.2
7	Hamal............... 2.2		11 31	N 23 26.3	186 43.9	2 07	328 16.5
8	Acamar............. 3.1		12 22	S 40 19.5	173 56.5	2 58	315 29.1
9	Menkar 2.8		12 26	N 4 04.2	172 57.0	3 02	314 29.6
10	Mirfak 1.9		12 48	N 49 50.6	167 27.8	3 24	309 00.4
11	Aldebaran........ 1.1		14 00	N 16 29.9	149 32.8	4 36	291 05.4
12	Rigel 0.3		14 38	S 8 12.6	139 52.9	5 14	281 25.5
13	Capella 0.2		14 40	N 45 59.5	139 22.4	5 16	280 55.0
14	Bellatrix 1.7		14 49	N 6 20.6	137 14.3	5 25	278 46.9
15	Elnath 1.8		14 50	N 28 36.1	136 57.6	5 26	278 30.2
16	Alnilam 1.8		15 00	S 1 12.5	134 27.9	5 36	276 00.5
17	Betelgeuse 0.1-1.2		15 19	N 7 24.2	129 43.7	5 55	271 16.3
18	Canopus...........-0.9		15 47	S 52 41.9	122 30.0	6 24	264 02.6
19	Sirius ....-1.6		16 08	S 16 42.8	117 13.3	6 45	258 45.9
20	Adhara 1.6		16 22	S 28 58.3	113 50.9	6 58	255 23.5
21	Castor.............. 1.6		16 58	N 31 53.9	104 52.9	7 34	246 25.5
22	Procyon 0.5		17 02	N 5 14.0	103 41.5	7 39	245 14.1
23	Pollux 1.2		17 08	N 28 02.2	102 12.0	7 45	243 44.6
24	Avior 1.7		17 46	S 59 30.1	92 51.1	8 22	234 23.7
25	Suhail 2.2		18 31	S 43 25.2	81 29.9	9 08	223 02.5
26	Miaplacidus 1.8		18 36	S 69 42.3	80 09.9	9 13	221 42.5
27	Alphard............ 2.2		18 50	S 8 38.6	76 36.9	9 27	218 09.5
28	Regulus............ 1.3		19 31	N 11 59.3	66 25.4	10 08	207 58.0
29	Dubhe 2.0		20 26	N 61 46.7	52 35.6	11 03	194 08.2
30	Denebola 2.2		21 12	N 14 35.8	41 14.8	11 49	182 47.4
31	Gienah 2.8		21 38	S 17 31.2	34 33.5	12 16	176 06.1
32	Acrux............... 1.1		21 49	S 63 04.7	31 51.4	12 26	173 24.0
33	Gacrux.............. 1.6		21 54	S 57 05.5	30 43.0	12 31	172 15.6
34	Mimosa 1.5		22 10	S 59 40.1	26 34.8	12 48	168 07.4
35	Alioth 1.7		22 16	N 55 59.2	24 59.6	12 54	166 32.2
36	Spica................ 1.2		22 47	S 11 08.4	17 12.7	13 25	158 45.3
37	Alkaid.............. 1.9		23 10	N 49 20.3	11 36.6	13 47	153 09.2
38	Hadar 0.9		23 26	S 60 21.2	7 34.0	14 04	149 06.6
39	Menkent 2.3		23 29	S 36 21.0	6 50.7	14 06	148 23.3
40	Arcturus........... 0.2		23 38	N 19 12.4	4 35.2	14 15	146 07.8
41	Rigil Kent......... 0.1		0 06	S 60 49.0	358 37.0	14 39	140 09.6
42	Zuben'ubi 2.9		0 17	S 16 01.4	355 47.6	14 51	137 20.2
43	Kochab............. 2.2		0 17	N 74 10.6	355 45.8	14 51	137 18.4
44	Alphecca 2.3		1 01	N 26 43.8	344 49.6	15 35	126 22.2
45	Antares 1.2		1 55	S 26 25.3	331 10.0	16 29	112 42.6
46	Atria 1.9		2 14	S 69 01.0	326 23.5	16 48	107 56.1
47	Sabik 2.6		2 36	S 15 43.1	320 55.2	17 10	102 27.8
48	Shaula 1.7		2 59	S 37 05.9	315 07.4	17 33	96 40.0
49	Rasalhague 2.1		3 00	N 12 33.8	314 46.2	17 35	96 18.8
50	Eltanin............. 2.4		3 22	N 51 29.3	309 19.4	17 57	90 52.0
51	Kaus Aust. 2.0		3 49	S 34 23.0	302 29.0	18 24	84 01.6
52	Vega................. 0.1		4 02	N 38 46.7	299 15.3	18 37	80 47.9
53	Nunki 2.1		4 20	S 26 18.0	294 42.3	18 55	76 14.9
54	Altair............... 0.9		5 16	N 8 51.4	280 48.7	19 51	62 21.3
55	Peacock............ 2.1		5 51	S 56 44.7	272 07.9	20 25	53 40.5
56	Deneb 1.3		6 06	N 45 15.7	268 08.0	20 41	49 40.6
57	Enif.................. 2.5		7 09	N 9 51.2	252 27.9	21 44	34 00.5
58	Al Na'ir............ 2.2		7 33	S 46 58.7	246 28.3	22 08	28 00.9
59	Fomalhaut 1.3		8 22	S 29 38.6	234 06.5	22 57	15 39.1
60	Markab 2.6		8 29	N 15 10.7	232 19.4	23 05	13 52.0

Star Transit Corr Table

Date	Corr h m	Date	Corr h m
1	−0 00	17	−1 03
2	−0 04	18	−1 07
3	−0 08	19	−1 11
4	−0 12	20	−1 15
5	−0 16	21	−1 19
6	−0 20	22	−1 23
7	−0 24	23	−1 27
8	−0 28	24	−1 30
9	−0 31	25	−1 34
10	−0 35	26	−1 38
11	−0 39	27	−1 42
12	−0 43	28	−1 46
13	−0 47	29	−1 50
14	−0 51	30	−1 54
15	−0 55	31	−1 58
16	−0 59		

STAR TRANSIT

To find the approx time of transit of a star for any day of the month use above table. All corrections are subtractive.

If the value taken from the table is greater than the time of transit for the first of the month, add 23h 56min to the time of transit before subtracting the correction.

Example: What time will Kochab (No 43) transit the Meridian on May 30?

	h min
Transit on May 1	00 17
	+23 56
	24 13
Corr for May 30	−01 54
Transit on May 30	22 19

MAY DIARY

d h	
1 05	Mercury 4° N of Moon
5 11	Uranus stationary
8 14	Mars 7° N of Moon
12 02	Mercury greatest elong. E(22°)
12 20	Spica 1° S of Moon
16 02	Jupiter 2° S of Moon
19 01	Neptune 5° S of Moon
19 10	Uranus 6° S of Moon
23 11	Saturn 6° S of Moon
24 07	Mars 1.1° N of Regulus
24 16	Mercury stationary
27 07	Venus 0.8° S of Moon

NOTES

Star declinations may be used as is for the whole month. To correct GHA for day, hour, minute and second see page E 92 and for further explanation of this table see page E 4.

MAY

MAY 1995 — SUN & ARIES — GMT

Monday, 1st May

Time	SUN GHA	Dec	ARIES GHA
00	180 41.9	N14 52.0	218 27.4
02	210 42.0	14 53.5	248 32.3
04	240 42.2	14 55.1	278 37.2
06	270 42.4	14 56.6	308 42.1
08	300 42.5	14 58.1	338 47.1
10	330 42.7	14 59.6	8 52.0
12	0 42.8	15 01.1	38 56.9
14	30 43.0	15 02.7	69 01.9
16	60 43.1	15 04.2	99 06.8
18	90 43.3	15 05.7	129 11.7
20	120 43.4	15 07.2	159 16.6
22	150 43.6	N15 08.7	189 21.6

Tuesday, 2nd May

Time	SUN GHA	Dec	ARIES GHA
00	180 43.7	N15 10.2	219 26.5
02	210 43.9	15 11.7	249 31.4
04	240 44.0	15 13.2	279 36.4
06	270 44.2	15 14.7	309 41.3
08	300 44.3	15 16.2	339 46.2
10	330 44.4	15 17.7	9 51.1
12	0 44.6	15 19.2	39 56.1
14	30 44.7	15 20.7	70 01.0
16	60 44.9	15 22.2	100 05.9
18	90 45.0	15 23.7	130 10.9
20	120 45.1	15 25.2	160 15.8
22	150 45.3	N15 26.7	190 20.7

Wednesday, 3rd May

Time	SUN GHA	Dec	ARIES GHA
00	180 45.4	N15 28.2	220 25.6
02	210 45.6	15 29.6	250 30.6
04	240 45.7	15 31.1	280 35.5
06	270 45.8	15 32.6	310 40.4
08	300 46.0	15 34.1	340 45.4
10	330 46.1	15 35.6	10 50.3
12	0 46.2	15 37.0	40 55.2
14	30 46.3	15 38.5	71 00.1
16	60 46.5	15 40.0	101 05.1
18	90 46.6	15 41.4	131 10.0
20	120 46.7	15 42.9	161 14.9
22	150 46.9	N15 44.4	191 19.9

Thursday, 4th May

Time	SUN GHA	Dec	ARIES GHA
00	180 47.0	N15 45.8	221 24.8
02	210 47.1	15 47.3	251 29.7
04	240 47.2	15 48.8	281 34.6
06	270 47.4	15 50.2	311 39.6
08	300 47.5	15 51.7	341 44.5
10	330 47.6	15 53.1	11 49.4
12	0 47.7	15 54.6	41 54.3
14	30 47.8	15 56.0	71 59.3
16	60 48.0	15 57.5	102 04.2
18	90 48.1	15 58.9	132 09.1
20	120 48.2	16 00.4	162 14.1
22	150 48.3	N16 01.8	192 19.0

Friday, 5th May

Time	SUN GHA	Dec	ARIES GHA
00	180 48.4	N16 03.3	222 23.9
02	210 48.5	16 04.7	252 28.8
04	240 48.6	16 06.2	282 33.8
06	270 48.8	16 07.6	312 38.7
08	300 48.9	16 09.0	342 43.6
10	330 49.0	16 10.5	12 48.6
12	0 49.1	16 11.9	42 53.5
14	30 49.2	16 13.3	72 58.4
16	60 49.3	16 14.7	103 03.3
18	90 49.4	16 16.2	133 08.3
20	120 49.5	16 17.6	163 13.2
22	150 49.6	N16 19.0	193 18.1

Saturday, 6th May

Time	SUN GHA	Dec	ARIES GHA
00	180 49.7	N16 20.4	223 23.1
02	210 49.8	16 21.9	253 28.0
04	240 49.9	16 23.3	283 32.9
06	270 50.0	16 24.7	313 37.8
08	300 50.1	16 26.1	343 42.8
10	330 50.2	16 27.5	13 47.7
12	0 50.3	16 28.9	43 52.6
14	30 50.4	16 30.3	73 57.6
16	60 50.5	16 31.7	104 02.5
18	90 50.6	16 33.1	134 07.4
20	120 50.7	16 34.5	164 12.3
22	150 50.8	N16 35.9	194 17.3

Sunday, 7th May

Time	SUN GHA	Dec	ARIES GHA
00	180 50.9	N16 37.3	224 22.2
02	210 51.0	16 38.7	254 27.1
04	240 51.1	16 40.1	284 32.1
06	270 51.1	16 41.5	314 37.0
08	300 51.2	16 42.9	344 41.9
10	330 51.3	16 44.3	14 46.8
12	0 51.4	16 45.7	44 51.8
14	30 51.5	16 47.0	74 56.7
16	60 51.6	16 48.4	105 01.6
18	90 51.7	16 49.8	135 06.5
20	120 51.7	16 51.2	165 11.5
22	150 51.8	N16 52.6	195 16.4

Monday, 8th May

Time	SUN GHA	Dec	ARIES GHA
00	180 51.9	N16 53.9	225 21.3
02	210 52.0	16 55.3	255 26.3
04	240 52.1	16 56.7	285 31.2
06	270 52.1	16 58.0	315 36.1
08	300 52.2	16 59.4	345 41.0
10	330 52.3	17 00.8	15 46.0
12	0 52.4	17 02.1	45 50.9
14	30 52.4	17 03.5	75 55.8
16	60 52.5	17 04.9	106 00.8
18	90 52.6	17 06.2	136 05.7
20	120 52.6	17 07.6	166 10.6
22	150 52.7	N17 08.9	196 15.5

Tuesday, 9th May

Time	SUN GHA	Dec	ARIES GHA
00	180 52.8	N17 10.3	226 20.5
02	210 52.9	17 11.6	256 25.4
04	240 52.9	17 13.0	286 30.3
06	270 53.0	17 14.3	316 35.3
08	300 53.1	17 15.7	346 40.2
10	330 53.1	17 17.0	16 45.1
12	0 53.2	17 18.3	46 50.0
14	30 53.2	17 19.7	76 55.0
16	60 53.3	17 21.0	106 59.9
18	90 53.4	17 22.3	137 04.8
20	120 53.4	17 23.7	167 09.8
22	150 53.5	N17 25.0	197 14.7

Wednesday, 10th May

Time	SUN GHA	Dec	ARIES GHA
00	180 53.5	N17 26.3	227 19.6
02	210 53.6	17 27.6	257 24.5
04	240 53.6	17 29.0	287 29.5
06	270 53.7	17 30.3	317 34.4
08	300 53.8	17 31.6	347 39.3
10	330 53.8	17 32.9	17 44.3
12	0 53.9	17 34.2	47 49.2
14	30 53.9	17 35.5	77 54.1
16	60 54.0	17 36.8	107 59.0
18	90 54.0	17 38.2	138 04.0
20	120 54.0	17 39.5	168 08.9
22	150 54.1	N17 40.8	198 13.8

Thursday, 11th May

Time	SUN GHA	Dec	ARIES GHA
00	180 54.1	N17 42.1	228 18.7
02	210 54.2	17 43.4	258 23.7
04	240 54.2	17 44.7	288 28.6
06	270 54.3	17 46.0	318 33.5
08	300 54.3	17 47.3	348 38.5
10	330 54.4	17 48.5	18 43.4
12	0 54.4	17 49.8	48 48.3
14	30 54.4	17 51.1	78 53.2
16	60 54.5	17 52.4	108 58.2
18	90 54.5	17 53.7	139 03.1
20	120 54.5	17 55.0	169 08.0
22	150 54.6	N17 56.2	199 13.0

Friday, 12th May

Time	SUN GHA	Dec	ARIES GHA
00	180 54.6	N17 57.5	229 17.9
02	210 54.6	17 58.8	259 22.8
04	240 54.7	18 00.1	289 27.7
06	270 54.7	18 01.3	319 32.7
08	300 54.7	18 02.6	349 37.6
10	330 54.8	18 03.9	19 42.5
12	0 54.8	18 05.1	49 47.5
14	30 54.8	18 06.4	79 52.4
16	60 54.8	18 07.7	109 57.3
18	90 54.9	18 08.9	140 02.2
20	120 54.9	18 10.2	170 07.2
22	150 54.9	N18 11.4	200 12.1

Saturday, 13th May

Time	SUN GHA	Dec	ARIES GHA
00	180 54.9	N18 12.7	230 17.0
02	210 55.0	18 13.9	260 22.0
04	240 55.0	18 15.2	290 26.9
06	270 55.0	18 16.4	320 31.8
08	300 55.0	18 17.7	350 36.7
10	330 55.0	18 18.9	20 41.7
12	0 55.0	18 20.1	50 46.6
14	30 55.1	18 21.4	80 51.5
16	60 55.1	18 22.6	110 56.5
18	90 55.1	18 23.8	141 01.4
20	120 55.1	18 25.1	171 06.3
22	150 55.1	N18 26.3	201 11.2

Sunday, 14th May

Time	SUN GHA	Dec	ARIES GHA
00	180 55.1	N18 27.5	231 16.2
02	210 55.1	18 28.8	261 21.1
04	240 55.1	18 30.0	291 26.0
06	270 55.1	18 31.2	321 30.9
08	300 55.1	18 32.4	351 35.9
10	330 55.1	18 33.6	21 40.8
12	0 55.2	18 34.8	51 45.7
14	30 55.2	18 36.0	81 50.7
16	60 55.2	18 37.3	111 55.6
18	90 55.2	18 38.5	142 00.5
20	120 55.2	18 39.7	172 05.4
22	150 55.2	N18 40.9	202 10.4

Monday, 15th May

Time	SUN GHA	Dec	ARIES GHA
00	180 55.2	N18 42.1	232 15.3
02	210 55.2	18 43.3	262 20.2
04	240 55.1	18 44.5	292 25.2
06	270 55.1	18 45.6	322 30.1
08	300 55.1	18 46.8	352 35.0
10	330 55.1	18 48.0	22 39.9
12	0 55.1	18 49.2	52 44.9
14	30 55.1	18 50.4	82 49.8
16	60 55.1	18 51.6	112 54.7
18	90 55.1	18 52.8	142 59.7
20	120 55.1	18 53.9	173 04.6
22	150 55.1	N18 55.1	203 09.5

NOTES

Sun & Aries GHA corrections for additional hour, minutes, and seconds on page E 94.
Correct Sun Declination by interpolation. For example see page E 4.

MAY 1995 — SUN & ARIES — GMT

Tuesday, 16th May

Time	SUN GHA	Dec	ARIES GHA
00	180 55.1	N18 56.3	233 14.4
02	210 55.0	18 57.5	263 19.4
04	240 55.0	18 58.6	293 24.3
06	270 55.0	18 59.8	323 29.2
08	300 55.0	19 01.0	353 34.2
10	330 55.0	19 02.1	23 39.1
12	0 54.9	19 03.3	53 44.0
14	30 54.9	19 04.4	83 48.9
16	60 54.9	19 05.6	113 53.9
18	90 54.9	19 06.7	143 58.8
20	120 54.9	19 07.9	174 03.7
22	150 54.8	N19 09.0	204 08.7

Wednesday, 17th May

Time	SUN GHA	Dec	ARIES GHA
00	180 54.8	N19 10.2	234 13.6
02	210 54.8	19 11.3	264 18.5
04	240 54.8	19 12.5	294 23.4
06	270 54.7	19 13.6	324 28.4
08	300 54.7	19 14.7	354 33.3
10	330 54.7	19 15.9	24 38.2
12	0 54.6	19 17.0	54 43.1
14	30 54.6	19 18.1	84 48.1
16	60 54.6	19 19.3	114 53.0
18	90 54.5	19 20.4	144 57.9
20	120 54.5	19 21.5	175 02.9
22	150 54.5	N19 22.6	205 07.8

Thursday, 18th May

Time	SUN GHA	Dec	ARIES GHA
00	180 54.4	N19 23.8	235 12.7
02	210 54.4	19 24.9	265 17.6
04	240 54.3	19 26.0	295 22.6
06	270 54.3	19 27.1	325 27.5
08	300 54.3	19 28.2	355 32.4
10	330 54.2	19 29.3	25 37.4
12	0 54.2	19 30.4	55 42.3
14	30 54.1	19 31.5	85 47.2
16	60 54.1	19 32.6	115 52.1
18	90 54.0	19 33.7	145 57.1
20	120 54.0	19 34.8	176 02.0
22	150 53.9	N19 35.9	206 06.9

Friday, 19th May

Time	SUN GHA	Dec	ARIES GHA
00	180 53.9	N19 37.0	236 11.9
02	210 53.8	19 38.1	266 16.8
04	240 53.8	19 39.2	296 21.7
06	270 53.7	19 40.3	326 26.6
08	300 53.7	19 41.4	356 31.6
10	330 53.6	19 42.4	26 36.5
12	0 53.6	19 43.5	56 41.4
14	30 53.5	19 44.6	86 46.4
16	60 53.5	19 45.7	116 51.3
18	90 53.4	19 46.7	146 56.2
20	120 53.3	19 47.8	177 01.1
22	150 53.3	N19 48.9	207 06.1

Saturday, 20th May

Time	SUN GHA	Dec	ARIES GHA
00	180 53.2	N19 49.9	237 11.0
02	210 53.2	19 51.0	267 15.9
04	240 53.1	19 52.0	297 20.9
06	270 53.0	19 53.1	327 25.8
08	300 53.0	19 54.2	357 30.7
10	330 52.9	19 55.2	27 35.6
12	0 52.8	19 56.3	57 40.6
14	30 52.8	19 57.3	87 45.5
16	60 52.7	19 58.3	117 50.4
18	90 52.6	19 59.4	147 55.3
20	120 52.6	20 00.4	178 00.3
22	150 52.5	N20 01.5	208 05.2

Sunday, 21st May

Time	SUN GHA	Dec	ARIES GHA
00	180 52.4	N20 02.5	238 10.1
02	210 52.3	20 03.5	268 15.1
04	240 52.3	20 04.6	298 20.0
06	270 52.2	20 05.6	328 24.9
08	300 52.1	20 06.6	358 29.8
10	330 52.0	20 07.6	28 34.8
12	0 52.0	20 08.7	58 39.7
14	30 51.9	20 09.7	88 44.6
16	60 51.8	20 10.7	118 49.6
18	90 51.7	20 11.7	148 54.5
20	120 51.6	20 12.7	178 59.4
22	150 51.6	N20 13.7	209 04.3

Monday, 22nd May

Time	SUN GHA	Dec	ARIES GHA
00	180 51.5	N20 14.7	239 09.3
02	210 51.4	20 15.7	269 14.2
04	240 51.3	20 16.7	299 19.1
06	270 51.2	20 17.7	329 24.1
08	300 51.1	20 18.7	359 29.0
10	330 51.0	20 19.7	29 33.9
12	0 50.9	20 20.7	59 38.8
14	30 50.8	20 21.7	89 43.8
16	60 50.8	20 22.7	119 48.7
18	90 50.7	20 23.7	149 53.6
20	120 50.6	20 24.7	179 58.6
22	150 50.5	N20 25.6	210 03.5

Tuesday, 23rd May

Time	SUN GHA	Dec	ARIES GHA
00	180 50.4	N20 26.6	240 08.4
02	210 50.3	20 27.6	270 13.3
04	240 50.2	20 28.6	300 18.3
06	270 50.1	20 29.5	330 23.2
08	300 50.0	20 30.5	0 28.1
10	330 49.9	20 31.5	30 33.1
12	0 49.8	20 32.4	60 38.0
14	30 49.7	20 33.4	90 42.9
16	60 49.6	20 34.4	120 47.8
18	90 49.5	20 35.3	150 52.8
20	120 49.4	20 36.3	180 57.7
22	150 49.3	N20 37.2	211 02.6

Wednesday, 24th May

Time	SUN GHA	Dec	ARIES GHA
00	180 49.2	N20 38.2	241 07.5
02	210 49.1	20 39.1	271 12.5
04	240 48.9	20 40.0	301 17.4
06	270 48.8	20 41.0	331 22.3
08	300 48.7	20 41.9	1 27.3
10	330 48.6	20 42.9	31 32.2
12	0 48.5	20 43.8	61 37.1
14	30 48.4	20 44.7	91 42.0
16	60 48.3	20 45.7	121 47.0
18	90 48.2	20 46.6	151 51.9
20	120 48.0	20 47.5	181 56.8
22	150 47.9	N20 48.4	212 01.8

Thursday, 25th May

Time	SUN GHA	Dec	ARIES GHA
00	180 47.8	N20 49.3	242 06.7
02	210 47.7	20 50.3	272 11.6
04	240 47.6	20 51.2	302 16.5
06	270 47.5	20 52.1	332 21.5
08	300 47.3	20 53.0	2 26.4
10	330 47.2	20 53.9	32 31.3
12	0 47.1	20 54.8	62 36.3
14	30 47.0	20 55.7	92 41.2
16	60 46.8	20 56.6	122 46.1
18	90 46.7	20 57.5	152 51.0
20	120 46.6	20 58.4	182 56.0
22	150 46.5	N20 59.3	213 00.9

Friday, 26th May

Time	SUN GHA	Dec	ARIES GHA
00	180 46.3	N21 00.2	243 05.8
02	210 46.2	21 01.1	273 10.8
04	240 46.1	21 01.9	303 15.7
06	270 45.9	21 02.8	333 20.6
08	300 45.8	21 03.7	3 25.5
10	330 45.7	21 04.6	33 30.5
12	0 45.5	21 05.4	63 35.4
14	30 45.4	21 06.3	93 40.3
16	60 45.3	21 07.2	123 45.3
18	90 45.1	21 08.1	153 50.2
20	120 45.0	21 08.9	183 55.1
22	150 44.9	N21 09.8	214 00.0

Saturday, 27th May

Time	SUN GHA	Dec	ARIES GHA
00	180 44.7	N21 10.6	244 05.0
02	210 44.6	21 11.5	274 09.9
04	240 44.4	21 12.3	304 14.8
06	270 44.3	21 13.2	334 19.7
08	300 44.2	21 14.0	4 24.7
10	330 44.0	21 14.9	34 29.6
12	0 43.9	21 15.7	64 34.5
14	30 43.7	21 16.6	94 39.5
16	60 43.6	21 17.4	124 44.4
18	90 43.4	21 18.2	154 49.3
20	120 43.3	21 19.1	184 54.2
22	150 43.1	N21 19.9	214 59.2

Sunday, 28th May

Time	SUN GHA	Dec	ARIES GHA
00	180 43.0	N21 20.7	245 04.1
02	210 42.8	21 21.6	275 09.0
04	240 42.7	21 22.4	305 14.0
06	270 42.5	21 23.2	335 18.9
08	300 42.4	21 24.0	5 23.8
10	330 42.2	21 24.8	35 28.7
12	0 42.1	21 25.6	65 33.7
14	30 41.9	21 26.5	95 38.6
16	60 41.8	21 27.3	125 43.5
18	90 41.6	21 28.1	155 48.5
20	120 41.5	21 28.9	185 53.4
22	150 41.3	N21 29.7	215 58.3

Monday, 29th May

Time	SUN GHA	Dec	ARIES GHA
00	180 41.2	N21 30.5	246 03.2
02	210 41.0	21 31.3	276 08.2
04	240 40.8	21 32.0	306 13.1
06	270 40.7	21 32.8	336 18.0
08	300 40.5	21 33.6	6 23.0
10	330 40.3	21 34.4	36 27.9
12	0 40.2	21 35.2	66 32.8
14	30 40.0	21 36.0	96 37.7
16	60 39.9	21 36.7	126 42.7
18	90 39.7	21 37.5	156 47.6
20	120 39.5	21 38.3	186 52.5
22	150 39.4	N21 39.1	216 57.5

Tuesday, 30th May

Time	SUN GHA	Dec	ARIES GHA
00	180 39.2	N21 39.8	247 02.4
02	210 39.0	21 40.6	277 07.3
04	240 38.9	21 41.3	307 12.2
06	270 38.7	21 42.1	337 17.2
08	300 38.5	21 42.9	7 22.1
10	330 38.3	21 43.6	37 27.0
12	0 38.2	21 44.4	67 31.9
14	30 38.0	21 45.1	97 36.9
16	60 37.8	21 45.8	127 41.8
18	90 37.6	21 46.6	157 46.7
20	120 37.5	21 47.3	187 51.7
22	150 37.3	N21 48.1	217 56.6

Wednesday, 31st May

Time	SUN GHA	Dec	ARIES GHA
00	180 37.1	N21 48.8	248 01.5
02	210 36.9	21 49.5	278 06.4
04	240 36.8	21 50.3	308 11.4
06	270 36.6	N21 51.0	338 16.3
08	300 36.4	N21 51.7	8 21.2
10	330 36.2	21 52.4	38 26.2
12	0 36.0	21 53.1	68 31.1
14	30 35.9	N21 53.9	98 36.0
16	60 35.7	N21 54.6	128 40.9
18	90 35.5	21 55.3	158 45.9
20	120 35.3	21 56.0	188 50.8
22	150 35.1	N21 56.7	218 55.7

MAY

MAY 1995 — PLANETS — 0h GMT

VENUS / JUPITER

Mer Pass h m	GHA ° '	Mean Var/hr 14°+	Dec ° '	Mean Var/hr '	Corrections on Page E 101		GHA ° '	Mean Var/hr 15°+	Dec ° '	Mean Var/hr '	Mer Pass h m
10 08	208 00.1	59.7	N 2 41.7	1.2	1	Mon	325 37.9	2.7	S 21 39.5	0.0	02 17
10 09	207 52.2	59.7	N 3 09.6	1.2	2	Tu	326 42.6	2.7	S 21 38.9	0.0	02 13
10 09	207 44.3	59.7	N 3 37.4	1.2	3	Wed	327 47.4	2.7	S 21 38.3	0.0	02 08
10 10	207 36.2	59.7	N 4 05.2	1.2	4	Th	328 52.4	2.7	S 21 37.7	0.0	02 04
10 10	207 28.1	59.7	N 4 32.9	1.2	5	Fri	329 57.6	2.7	S 21 37.0	0.0	02 00
10 11	207 19.9	59.7	N 5 00.5	1.2	6	Sat	331 02.9	2.7	S 21 36.3	0.0	01 55
10 11	207 11.7	59.6	N 5 28.1	1.1	7	SUN	332 08.3	2.7	S 21 35.6	0.0	01 51
10 12	207 03.3	59.6	N 5 55.5	1.1	8	Mon	333 13.9	2.7	S 21 34.9	0.0	01 47
10 13	206 54.8	59.6	N 6 22.9	1.1	9	Tu	334 19.6	2.7	S 21 34.2	0.0	01 42
10 13	206 46.2	59.6	N 6 50.1	1.1	10	Wed	335 25.4	2.7	S 21 33.5	0.0	01 38
10 14	206 37.5	59.6	N 7 17.2	1.1	11	Th	336 31.3	2.8	S 21 32.7	0.0	01 34
10 14	206 28.6	59.6	N 7 44.2	1.1	12	Fri	337 37.3	2.8	S 21 31.9	0.0	01 29
10 15	206 19.6	59.6	N 8 11.0	1.1	13	Sat	338 43.5	2.8	S 21 31.2	0.0	01 25
10 16	206 10.4	59.6	N 8 37.7	1.1	14	SUN	339 49.8	2.8	S 21 30.4	0.0	01 20
10 16	206 01.1	59.6	N 9 04.2	1.1	15	Mon	340 56.1	2.8	S 21 29.5	0.0	01 16
10 17	205 51.6	59.6	N 9 30.5	1.1	16	Tu	342 02.6	2.8	S 21 28.7	0.0	01 12
10 17	205 41.9	59.6	N 9 56.6	1.1	17	Wed	343 09.1	2.8	S 21 27.9	0.0	01 07
10 18	205 32.0	59.6	N 10 22.5	1.1	18	Th	344 15.8	2.8	S 21 27.0	0.0	01 03
10 19	205 22.0	59.6	N 10 48.2	1.1	19	Fri	345 22.5	2.8	S 21 26.2	0.0	00 58
10 20	205 11.7	59.6	N 11 13.7	1.1	20	Sat	346 29.3	2.8	S 21 25.3	0.0	00 54
10 20	205 01.2	59.6	N 11 38.9	1.0	21	SUN	347 36.1	2.8	S 21 24.4	0.0	00 49
10 21	204 50.5	59.5	N 12 03.8	1.0	22	Mon	348 43.0	2.8	S 21 23.5	0.0	00 45
10 22	204 39.6	59.5	N 12 28.5	1.0	23	Tu	349 50.0	2.8	S 21 22.6	0.0	00 41
10 22	204 28.5	59.5	N 12 52.9	1.0	24	Wed	350 57.1	2.8	S 21 21.7	0.0	00 36
10 23	204 17.1	59.5	N 13 17.1	1.0	25	Th	352 04.2	2.8	S 21 20.8	0.0	00 32
10 24	204 05.5	59.5	N 13 40.9	1.0	26	Fri	353 11.3	2.8	S 21 19.9	0.0	00 27
10 25	203 53.7	59.5	N 14 04.4	1.0	27	Sat	354 18.5	2.8	S 21 18.9	0.0	00 23
10 26	203 41.6	59.5	N 14 27.6	1.0	28	SUN	355 25.7	2.8	S 21 18.0	0.0	00 18
10 26	203 29.3	59.5	N 14 50.4	0.9	29	Mon	356 32.9	2.8	S 21 17.0	0.0	00 14
10 27	203 16.6	59.5	N 15 12.9	0.9	30	Tu	357 40.1	2.8	S 21 16.1	0.0	00 09
10 28	203 03.8	59.4	N 15 35.1	0.9	31	Wed	358 47.4	2.8	S 21 15.1	0.0	00 05

VENUS, Av. Mag. -3.9
S.H.A. May
5 345; 10 339; 15 334; 20 328; 25 322; 30 316.

JUPITER, Av. Mag.-2.5
S.H.A. May
5 108; 10 108; 15 109; 20 109; 25 110; 30 111.

MARS / SATURN

Mer Pass h m	GHA ° '	Mean Var/hr 15°+	Dec ° '	Mean Var/hr '	Corrections on Page E 101		GHA ° '	Mean Var/hr 15°+	Dec ° '	Mean Var/hr '	Mer Pass h m
18 57	75 10.7	1.6	N 16 45.7	0.3	1	Mon	225 39.7	2.2	S 5 08.8	0.1	08 56
18 55	75 50.3	1.6	N 16 37.0	0.3	2	Tu	226 33.6	2.2	S 5 06.8	0.1	08 52
18 52	76 29.6	1.6	N 16 29.3	0.3	3	Wed	227 27.5	2.3	S 5 04.7	0.1	08 49
18 49	77 08.6	1.6	N 16 20.9	0.4	4	Th	228 21.5	2.3	S 5 02.7	0.1	08 45
18 47	77 47.3	1.6	N 16 12.4	0.4	5	Fri	229 15.5	2.3	S 5 00.7	0.1	08 42
18 44	78 25.7	1.6	N 16 03.8	0.4	6	Sat	230 09.6	2.3	S 4 58.8	0.1	08 38
18 42	79 03.7	1.6	N 15 55.0	0.4	7	SUN	231 03.8	2.3	S 4 56.9	0.1	08 34
18 39	79 41.5	1.6	N 15 46.2	0.4	8	Mon	231 58.0	2.3	S 4 55.0	0.1	08 31
18 37	80 19.0	1.6	N 15 37.2	0.4	9	Tu	232 52.2	2.3	S 4 53.1	0.1	08 27
18 34	80 56.3	1.5	N 15 28.1	0.4	10	Wed	233 46.6	2.3	S 4 51.2	0.1	08 24
18 32	81 33.2	1.5	N 15 18.9	0.4	11	Th	234 41.0	2.3	S 4 49.4	0.1	08 20
18 29	82 09.9	1.5	N 15 09.6	0.4	12	Fri	235 35.4	2.3	S 4 47.6	0.1	08 16
18 27	82 46.4	1.5	N 15 00.1	0.4	13	Sat	236 29.9	2.3	S 4 45.9	0.1	08 13
18 25	83 22.6	1.5	N 14 50.6	0.4	14	SUN	237 24.5	2.3	S 4 44.2	0.1	08 09
18 22	83 58.6	1.5	N 14 40.9	0.4	15	Mon	238 19.2	2.3	S 4 42.5	0.1	08 05
18 20	84 34.3	1.5	N 14 31.2	0.4	16	Tu	239 13.9	2.3	S 4 40.8	0.1	08 02
18 18	85 09.8	1.5	N 14 21.3	0.4	17	Wed	240 08.7	2.3	S 4 39.1	0.1	07 58
18 15	85 45.1	1.5	N 14 11.3	0.4	18	Th	241 03.5	2.3	S 4 37.5	0.1	07 55
18 13	86 20.2	1.5	N 14 01.2	0.4	19	Fri	241 58.4	2.3	S 4 36.0	0.1	07 51
18 11	86 55.1	1.4	N 13 51.0	0.4	20	Sat	242 53.4	2.3	S 4 34.4	0.1	07 47
18 08	87 29.8	1.4	N 13 40.7	0.4	21	SUN	243 48.5	2.3	S 4 32.9	0.1	07 44
18 06	88 04.2	1.4	N 13 30.3	0.4	22	Mon	244 43.6	2.3	S 4 31.4	0.1	07 40
18 04	88 38.5	1.4	N 13 19.7	0.4	23	Tu	245 38.8	2.3	S 4 30.0	0.1	07 36
18 01	89 12.6	1.4	N 13 09.1	0.4	24	Wed	246 34.1	2.3	S 4 28.6	0.1	07 33
17 59	89 46.5	1.4	N 12 58.4	0.5	25	Th	247 29.5	2.3	S 4 27.2	0.1	07 29
17 57	90 20.2	1.4	N 12 47.6	0.5	26	Fri	248 24.9	2.3	S 4 25.8	0.1	07 25
17 55	90 53.7	1.4	N 12 36.6	0.5	27	Sat	249 20.4	2.3	S 4 24.5	0.1	07 22
17 53	91 27.1	1.4	N 12 25.6	0.5	28	SUN	250 16.0	2.3	S 4 23.3	0.1	07 18
17 50	92 00.3	1.4	N 12 14.5	0.5	29	Mon	251 11.6	2.3	S 4 22.0	0.1	07 14
17 48	92 33.3	1.4	N 12 03.2	0.5	30	Tu	252 07.3	2.3	S 4 20.8	0.0	07 10
17 46	93 06.1	1.4	N 11 51.9	0.5	31	Wed	253 03.1	2.3	S 4 19.6	0.0	07 07

MARS, Av. Mag. +0.7
S.H.A. May
5 215; 10 214; 15 212; 20 210; 25 208; 30 206.

SATURN, Av. Mag. +1.2
S.H.A. May
5 7; 10 6; 15 6; 20 6; 25 5; 30 5.

MAY 1995   MOON

Day	GMT hr	GHA ° ′	Mean Var/hr 14°+	Dec ° ′	Mean Var/hr ′	Day	GMT hr	GHA ° ′	Mean Var/hr 14°+	Dec ° ′	Mean Var/hr ′
1 Mon	0	166 17.0	31.5	N 17 10.0	4.5	17 Wed	0	328 35.3	22.7	S 19 19.4	1.5
	6	253 26.2	31.5	N 17 36.9	4.0		6	54 51.8	23.0	S 19 10.5	2.4
	12	340 34.9	31.4	N 18 00.9	3.4		12	141 10.0	23.4	S 18 56.5	3.2
	18	67 43.2	31.3	N 18 21.9	3.0		18	227 30.0	23.7	S 18 37.7	4.0
2 Tu	0	154 51.0	31.3	N 18 39.8	2.4	18 Th	0	313 52.3	24.2	S 18 14.2	4.8
	6	241 58.6	31.2	N 18 54.6	1.9		6	40 17.0	24.6	S 17 46.2	5.4
	12	329 05.8	31.2	N 19 06.3	1.4		12	126 44.4	25.1	S 17 14.0	6.1
	18	56 12.9	31.2	N 19 14.8	0.9		18	213 14.7	25.6	S 16 37.8	6.7
3 Wed	0	143 19.9	31.1	N 19 20.1	0.3	19 Fri	0	299 47.9	26.1	S 15 57.9	7.3
	6	230 26.8	31.2	N 19 22.2	0.2		6	26 24.2	26.6	S 15 14.6	7.8
	12	317 33.8	31.2	N 19 21.1	0.8		12	113 03.7	27.2	S 14 28.2	8.2
	18	44 40.8	31.2	N 19 16.7	1.3		18	199 46.2	27.6	S 13 38.8	8.7
4 Th	0	131 48.1	31.2	N 19 09.2	1.9	20 Sat	0	286 31.8	28.2	S 12 46.9	9.1
	6	218 55.5	31.3	N 18 58.5	2.3		6	13 20.4	28.7	S 11 52.7	9.4
	12	306 03.3	31.3	N 18 44.7	2.9		12	100 12.0	29.1	S 10 56.5	9.7
	18	33 11.3	31.4	N 18 27.8	3.3		18	187 06.4	29.5	S 9 58.4	9.9
5 Fri	0	120 19.8	31.5	N 18 07.7	3.9	21 Sun	0	274 03.4	30.0	S 8 58.9	10.1
	6	207 28.6	31.5	N 17 44.7	4.4		6	1 03.0	30.3	S 7 58.1	10.3
	12	294 37.8	31.6	N 17 18.7	4.8		12	88 05.0	30.7	S 6 56.2	10.4
	18	21 47.5	31.7	N 16 49.8	5.4		18	175 09.3	31.0	S 5 53.5	10.6
6 Sat	0	108 57.6	31.7	N 16 18.0	5.8	22 Mon	0	262 15.5	31.4	S 4 50.1	10.6
	6	196 08.0	31.8	N 15 43.5	6.2		6	349 23.7	31.7	S 3 46.4	10.7
	12	283 18.9	31.9	N 15 06.2	6.7		12	76 33.5	31.9	S 2 42.4	10.6
	18	10 30.0	31.9	N 14 26.3	7.1		18	163 44.9	32.2	S 1 38.3	10.6
7 Sun	0	97 41.4	32.0	N 13 43.9	7.5	23 Tu	0	250 57.5	32.3	S 0 34.4	10.6
	6	184 53.1	32.0	N 12 59.0	7.9		6	338 11.4	32.4	N 0 29.0	10.5
	12	272 04.8	31.9	N 12 11.7	8.3		12	65 26.2	32.6	N 1 32.5	10.4
	18	359 16.7	31.9	N 11 22.1	8.6		18	152 41.8	32.8	N 2 35.1	10.3
8 Mon	0	86 28.4	31.9	N 10 30.3	9.0	24 Wed	0	239 58.0	32.8	N 3 37.0	10.2
	6	173 40.1	31.9	N 9 36.4	9.3		6	327 14.8	32.9	N 4 38.0	10.0
	12	260 51.4	31.9	N 8 40.5	9.7		12	54 31.9	32.9	N 5 38.0	9.8
	18	348 02.4	31.8	N 7 42.8	9.9		18	141 49.2	32.9	N 6 36.8	9.6
9 Tu	0	75 12.8	31.6	N 6 43.3	10.2	25 Th	0	229 06.5	32.9	N 7 34.3	9.3
	6	162 22.5	31.5	N 5 42.2	10.4		6	316 23.8	32.9	N 8 30.4	9.1
	12	249 31.5	31.3	N 4 39.6	10.7		12	43 40.8	32.8	N 9 25.0	8.8
	18	336 39.4	31.1	N 3 35.6	10.8		18	130 57.6	32.7	N 10 17.9	8.4
10 Wed	0	63 46.3	30.9	N 2 30.5	11.1	26 Fri	0	218 14.1	32.6	N 11 09.0	8.2
	6	150 51.8	30.6	N 1 24.4	11.2		6	305 30.0	32.5	N 11 58.2	7.8
	12	237 55.9	30.4	N 0 17.4	11.3		12	32 45.4	32.4	N 12 45.3	7.5
	18	324 58.4	30.1	S 0 50.2	11.4		18	120 00.2	32.3	N 13 30.4	7.1
11 Th	0	51 59.1	29.8	S 1 58.2	11.4	27 Sat	0	207 14.4	32.2	N 14 13.1	6.7
	6	138 57.8	29.4	S 3 06.4	11.4		6	294 27.8	32.1	N 14 53.5	6.3
	12	225 54.5	29.1	S 4 14.6	11.3		12	21 40.6	32.0	N 15 31.5	5.9
	18	312 48.8	28.6	S 5 22.6	11.2		18	108 52.6	31.8	N 16 06.9	5.4
12 Fri	0	39 40.8	28.2	S 6 30.0	11.1	28 Sun	0	196 03.9	31.8	N 16 39.6	4.9
	6	126 30.2	27.8	S 7 36.5	10.9		6	283 14.5	31.6	N 17 09.6	4.5
	12	213 16.9	27.3	S 8 42.0	10.6		12	10 24.5	31.6	N 17 36.8	4.0
	18	300 01.0	26.8	S 9 46.0	10.3		18	97 33.8	31.5	N 18 01.1	3.5
13 Sat	0	26 42.2	26.3	S 10 48.3	10.0	29 Mon	0	184 42.5	31.4	N 18 22.4	3.0
	6	113 20.5	25.8	S 11 48.5	9.6		6	271 50.7	31.3	N 18 40.7	2.5
	12	199 55.9	25.4	S 12 46.3	9.1		12	358 58.5	31.3	N 18 55.8	1.9
	18	286 28.5	24.9	S 13 41.4	8.6		18	86 05.9	31.1	N 19 07.9	1.5
14 Sun	0	12 58.3	24.5	S 14 33.4	8.0	30 Tu	0	173 13.0	31.2	N 19 16.8	0.9
	6	99 25.4	24.0	S 15 21.9	7.4		6	260 19.9	31.1	N 19 22.5	0.4
	12	185 49.9	23.7	S 16 06.8	6.7		12	347 26.6	31.1	N 19 25.0	0.1
	18	272 12.1	23.3	S 16 47.7	6.0		18	74 33.4	31.1	N 19 24.3	0.7
15 Mon	0	358 32.1	23.0	S 17 24.2	5.3	31 Wed	0	161 40.2	31.2	N 19 20.3	1.3
	6	84 50.3	22.7	S 17 56.2	4.5		6	248 47.2	31.2	N 19 13.2	1.7
	12	171 06.9	22.5	S 18 23.5	3.7		12	335 54.4	31.3	N 19 02.9	2.3
	18	257 22.4	22.5	S 18 45.7	2.8		18	63 02.0	31.3	N 18 49.4	2.8
16 Tu	0	343 37.0	22.3	S 19 02.9	1.9						
	6	69 51.1	22.4	S 19 14.9	1.1						
	12	156 05.3	22.5	S 19 21.6	0.2						
	18	242 19.9	22.6	S 19 23.1	0.7						

NOTE Moon GHA corrections for additional hours, minutes, and seconds on page E 96. Moon Declination corrections on page E 99. Mean Var/hr value needed for both corrections.

MAY

JUNE 1995 — SUN & MOON — GMT

SUN

Day of			Equation of Time		Transit	Semi-diam	Lat 52°N				Lat Corr to Sunrise, Sunset etc				
Yr	Mth	Week	0h	12h			Twilight	Sunrise	Sunset	Twilight	Lat	Twilight	Sunrise	Sunset	Twilight
			m s	m s	h m	′	h m	h m	h m	h m	°	h m	h m	h m	h m
152	1	Th	-02 20	-02 15	11 58	15.8	03 00	03 46	20 10	20 56	N60	-1 57	-1 04	+1 04	+1 57
153	2	Fri	-02 11	-02 06	11 58	15.8	02 59	03 46	20 11	20 58	55	-0 28	-0 19	+0 19	+0 28
154	3	Sat	-02 01	-01 57	11 58	15.8	02 58	03 45	20 12	20 59	50	+0 15	+0 11	-0 11	-0 15
155	4	Sun	-01 52	-01 47	11 58	15.8	02 57	03 44	20 13	21 00	45	+0 44	+0 33	-0 33	-0 44
156	5	Mon	-01 41	-01 36	11 58	15.8	02 56	03 43	20 14	21 01	N40	+1 07	+0 51	-0 51	-1 07
157	6	Tu	-01 31	-01 25	11 59	15.8	02 55	03 43	20 15	21 02	35	+1 25	+1 06	-1 06	-1 25
158	7	Wed	-01 20	-01 15	11 59	15.8	02 55	03 42	20 16	21 03	30	+1 40	+1 19	-1 19	-1 40
159	8	Th	-01 09	-01 03	11 59	15.8	02 54	03 42	20 17	21 05	25	+1 53	+1 31	-1 31	-1 53
160	9	Fri	-00 58	-00 52	11 59	15.8	02 53	03 41	20 17	21 05	N20	+2 05	+1 41	-1 41	-2 05
161	10	Sat	-00 46	-00 40	11 59	15.8	02 53	03 41	20 18	21 06	15	+2 16	+1 51	-1 51	-2 16
162	11	Sun	-00 34	-00 28	12 00	15.8	02 52	03 40	20 19	21 07	10	+2 25	+2 00	-2 00	-2 25
163	12	Mon	-00 22	-00 16	12 00	15.8	02 52	03 40	20 20	21 08	5	+2 35	+2 09	-2 09	-2 35
164	13	Tu	-00 10	-00 04	12 00	15.8	02 51	03 40	20 20	21 09	0	+2 43	+2 18	-2 18	-2 43
165	14	Wed	+00 02	+00 09	12 00	15.8	02 51	03 40	20 21	21 10	S 5	+2 52	+2 26	-2 26	-2 52
166	15	Th	+00 15	+00 21	12 00	15.8	02 51	03 39	20 21	21 10	10	+3 00	+2 35	-2 35	-3 00
167	16	Fri	+00 28	+00 34	12 01	15.8	02 51	03 39	20 22	21 11	15	+3 09	+2 44	-2 44	-3 09
168	17	Sat	+00 40	+00 47	12 01	15.8	02 51	03 39	20 22	21 11	S20	+3 18	+2 53	-2 53	-3 18
169	18	Sun	+00 53	+01 00	12 01	15.8	02 50	03 39	20 23	21 12	25	+3 27	+3 03	-3 03	-3 27
170	19	Mon	+01 06	+01 13	12 01	15.8	02 50	03 39	20 23	21 12	30	+3 36	+3 14	-3 14	-3 36
171	20	Tu	+01 19	+01 26	12 01	15.8	02 51	03 39	20 23	21 12	35	+3 47	+3 27	-3 27	-3 47
172	21	Wed	+01 32	+01 39	12 02	15.8	02 51	03 40	20 24	21 13	S40	+3 59	+3 41	-3 41	-3 59
173	22	Th	+01 45	+01 52	12 02	15.8	02 51	03 40	20 24	21 13	45	+4 12	+3 57	-3 57	-4 12
174	23	Fri	+01 58	+02 05	12 02	15.8	02 51	03 40	20 24	21 13	50	+4 28	+4 18	-4 18	-4 28
175	24	Sat	+02 11	+02 18	12 02	15.8	02 51	03 40	20 24	21 13					
176	25	Sun	+02 24	+02 31	12 03	15.8	02 52	03 41	20 24	21 13					
177	26	Mon	+02 37	+02 44	12 03	15.8	02 52	03 41	20 24	21 13					
178	27	Tu	+02 50	+02 56	12 03	15.8	02 53	03 42	20 24	21 13					
179	28	Wed	+03 03	+03 09	12 03	15.8	02 53	03 42	20 24	21 13					
180	29	Th	+03 15	+03 21	12 03	15.8	02 54	03 43	20 24	21 12					
181	30	Fri	+03 27	+03 33	12 04	15.8	02 55	03 43	20 24	21 12					

NOTES

Lat corrections are for mid-month.
Equation of Time is the excess of Mean Time over Apparent Time.

MOON

Day of			Age	Transit (Upper)	Diff	Semi-diam	Hor Par	Lat 52°N		Phases of the Moon
Yr	Mth	Week						Moonrise	Moonset	
			days	h m	m	′	′	h m	h m	d h m
152	1	Th	03	14 27	46	14.8	54.2	06 33	22 14	
153	2	Fri	04	15 13	46	14.8	54.5	07 32	22 45	☾ First Quarter 6 10 26
154	3	Sat	05	15 59	46	14.9	54.9	08 34	23 13	○ Full Moon 13 04 03
155	4	Sun	06	16 45	46	15.1	55.4	09 39	23 39	☽ Last Quarter 19 22 01
156	5	Mon	07	17 31	46	15.3	56.1	10 47	— —	● New Moon 28 00 50
157	6	Tu	08	18 17	48	15.5	56.8	11 56	00 03	
158	7	Wed	09	19 05	50	15.7	57.7	13 08	00 26	
159	8	Th	10	19 55	54	16.0	58.7	14 23	00 50	
160	9	Fri	11	20 49	57	16.2	59.6	15 40	01 17	Perigee 13 01
161	10	Sat	12	21 46	61	16.5	60.4	16 59	01 49	Apogee 26 11
162	11	Sun	13	22 47	63	16.6	61.0	18 16	02 27	
163	12	Mon	14	23 50	63	16.7	61.4	19 27	03 14	
164	13	Tu	15	24 53	—	16.7	61.4	20 29	04 13	
165	14	Wed	16	00 53	62	16.6	61.1	21 20	05 21	
166	15	Th	17	01 55	58	16.5	60.5	22 00	06 36	
167	16	Fri	18	02 53	55	16.3	59.7	22 53	07 54	
168	17	Sat	19	03 48	50	16.0	58.7	23 02	09 12	
169	18	Sun	20	04 38	49	15.7	57.8	23 26	10 26	
170	19	Mon	21	05 27	46	15.5	56.9	23 50	11 39	
171	20	Tu	22	06 13	45	15.3	56.1	— —	12 48	
172	21	Wed	23	06 58	45	15.1	55.4	00 13	13 55	
173	22	Th	24	07 43	46	14.9	54.8	00 37	15 01	
174	23	Fri	25	08 29	46	14.8	54.4	01 04	16 04	
175	24	Sat	26	09 15	47	14.8	54.1	01 34	17 04	
176	25	Sun	27	10 02	47	14.7	54.0	02 08	18 00	
177	26	Mon	28	10 49	48	14.7	53.9	02 49	18 51	
178	27	Tu	29	11 37	47	14.7	54.0	03 35	19 36	
179	28	Wed	00	12 24	48	14.8	54.1	04 27	20 15	
180	29	Th	01	13 12	46	14.8	54.4	05 25	20 49	
181	30	Fri	02	13 58	46	14.9	54.7	06 26	21 19	

NOTES

Diff equals daily change in transit time.
To correct Moonrise, Moonset, or Transit times for Latitude and/or Longitude see page E 100. For further information about these tables see page E 4. For Arc to Time correction see page E 91.

JUNE 1995   STARS   0h GMT June 1

No	Name	Mag	Transit h m	Dec ° '	GHA ° '	RA h m	SHA ° '
	ARIES...............		7 23		249 00.7		
1	Alpheratz.........	2.2	7 31	N29 03.8	246 58.3	0 08	357 57.6
2	Ankaa.............	2.4	7 49	S 42 19.6	242 29.9	0 26	353 29.2
3	Schedar...........	2.5	8 03	N56 30.5	238 56.8	0 40	349 56.1
4	Diphda	2.2	8 06	S 18 00.6	238 10.3	0 43	349 09.6
5	Achernar..........	0.6	9 00	S 57 15.3	224 37.9	1 38	335 37.2
6	POLARIS	2.1	9 49	N89 14.4	212 22.9	2 27	323 22.2
7	Hamal.............	2.2	9 29	N23 26.3	217 17.0	2 07	328 16.3
8	Acamar............	3.1	10 20	S 40 19.3	204 29.7	2 58	315 29.0
9	Menkar	2.8	10 24	N 4 04.2	203 30.2	3 02	314 29.5
10	Mirfak	1.9	10 46	N49 50.5	198 00.9	3 24	309 00.2
11	Aldebaran........	1.1	11 58	N16 29.9	180 06.0	4 36	291 05.3
12	Rigel	0.3	12 36	S 8 12.5	170 26.1	5 14	281 25.4
13	Capella	0.2	12 38	N45 59.5	169 55.7	5 16	280 55.0
14	Bellatrix	1.7	12 47	N 6 20.6	167 47.6	5 25	278 46.9
15	Elnath.............	1.8	12 48	N28 36.1	167 30.8	5 26	278 30.1
16	Alnilam	1.8	12 58	S 1 12.4	165 01.2	5 36	276 00.5
17	Betelgeuse......0.1-1.2		13 17	N 7 24.2	160 17.0	5 55	271 16.3
18	Canopus...........-0.9		13 46	S 52 41.8	153 03.4	6 24	264 02.7
19	Sirius ....-1.6		14 07	S 16 42.8	147 46.7	6 45	258 46.0
20	Adhara	1.6	14 20	S 28 58.2	144 24.2	6 58	255 23.5
21	Castor.............	1.6	14 56	N31 53.8	135 26.2	7 34	246 25.5
22	Procyon...........	0.5	15 01	N 5 14.1	134 14.9	7 39	245 14.2
23	Pollux	1.2	15 06	N28 02.2	132 45.3	7 45	243 44.6
24	Avior	1.7	15 44	S 59 30.0	123 24.7	8 22	234 24.0
25	Suhail	2.2	16 29	S 43 25.2	112 03.3	9 08	223 02.6
26	Miaplacidus	1.8	16 34	S 69 42.3	110 43.6	9 13	221 42.9
27	Alphard...........	2.2	16 49	S 8 38.5	107 10.3	9 27	218 09.6
28	Regulus...........	1.3	17 29	N11 59.3	96 58.7	10 08	207 58.0
29	Dubhe	2.0	18 24	N61 46.7	83 09.1	11 03	194 08.4
30	Denebola	2.2	19 10	N14 35.8	71 48.2	11 49	182 47.5
31	Gienah	2.8	19 36	S 17 31.2	65 06.9	12 16	176 06.2
32	Acrux..............	1.1	19 47	S 63 04.8	62 24.9	12 26	173 24.2
33	Gacrux............	1.6	19 52	S 57 05.6	61 16.5	12 31	172 15.8
34	Mimosa	1.5	20 08	S 59 40.2	57 08.3	12 47	168 07.6
35	Alioth	1.7	20 14	N55 59.3	55 33.1	12 54	166 32.4
36	Spica...............	1.2	20 46	S 11 08.3	47 46.1	13 25	158 45.4
37	Alkaid.............	1.9	21 08	N49 20.4	42 10.0	13 47	153 09.3
38	Hadar	0.9	21 24	S 60 21.3	38 07.4	14 04	149 06.7
39	Menkent	2.3	21 27	S 36 21.0	37 24.0	14 06	148 23.3
40	Arcturus...........	0.2	21 36	N19 12.5	35 08.6	14 15	146 07.9
41	Rigil Kent.	0.1	22 00	S 60 49.1	29 10.4	14 39	140 09.7
42	Zuben'ubi	2.9	22 11	S 16 01.4	26 20.9	14 51	137 20.2
43	Kochab............	2.2	22 11	N74 10.7	26 19.4	14 51	137 18.7
44	Alphecca	2.3	22 55	N26 43.9	15 22.9	15 35	126 22.2
45	Antares	1.2	23 49	S 26 25.3	1 43.2	16 29	112 42.5
46	Atria	1.9	0 12	S 69 01.1	356 56.6	16 48	107 55.9
47	Sabik	2.6	0 34	S 15 43.1	351 28.4	17 10	102 27.7
48	Shaula	1.7	0 57	S 37 05.9	345 40.6	17 33	96 39.9
49	Rasalhague	2.1	0 59	N12 33.9	345 19.4	17 35	96 18.7
50	Eltanin.............	2.4	1 20	N51 29.5	339 52.6	17 57	90 51.9
51	Kaus Aust.	2.0	1 48	S 34 23.1	333 02.1	18 24	84 01.4
52	Vega	0.1	2 00	N38 46.8	329 48.4	18 37	80 47.7
53	Nunki	2.1	2 19	S 26 18.0	325 15.4	18 55	76 14.7
54	Altair	0.9	3 14	N 8 51.5	311 21.8	19 51	62 21.1
55	Peacock	2.1	3 49	S 56 44.7	302 40.8	20 25	53 40.1
56	Deneb	1.3	4 05	N45 15.8	298 41.0	20 41	49 40.3
57	Enif................	2.5	5 07	N 9 51.3	283 00.9	21 44	34 00.2
58	Al Na'ir...........	2.2	5 31	S 46 58.7	277 01.2	22 08	28 00.5
59	Fomalhaut	1.3	6 20	S 29 38.5	264 39.5	22 57	15 38.8
60	Markab	2.6	6 27	N15 10.8	262 52.5	23 05	13 51.8

Star Transit Corr Table

Date	Corr h m	Date	Corr h m
1	−0 00	17	−1 03
2	−0 04	18	−1 07
3	−0 08	19	−1 11
4	−0 12	20	−1 15
5	−0 16	21	−1 19
6	−0 20	22	−1 23
7	−0 24	23	−1 27
8	−0 28	24	−1 30
9	−0 31	25	−1 34
10	−0 35	26	−1 38
11	−0 39	27	−1 42
12	−0 43	28	−1 46
13	−0 47	29	−1 50
14	−0 51	30	−1 54
15	−0 55	31	−1 58
16	−0 59		

STAR TRANSIT

To find the approx time of transit of a star for any day of the month use above table. All corrections are subtractive.

If the value taken from the table is greater than the time of transit for the first of the month, add 23h 56min to the time of transit before subtracting the correction.

Example: What time will Atria (No 46) transit the Meridian on June 30?

	h min
Transit on Jun 1	00 12
	+23 56
	24 08
Corr for Jun 30	−01 54
Transit on Jun 30	22 14

JUNE DIARY

d h	
1 11	Jupiter at opposition
5 06	Mercury in inferior conjuction
5 20	Mars 6° N of Moon
9 06	Spica 1.1° S of Moon
12 08	Jupiter 2° S of Moon
14 14	Jupiter 5° N of Antares
15 10	Neptune 5° S of Moon
15 19	Uranus 6° S of Moon
15 21	Mercury 1.2° N of Aldebaran
17 06	Mercury stationary
19 05	Venus 5° N of Aldebaran
19 07	Mercury 4° S of Venus
19 19	Saturn 6° S of Moon

NOTES

Star declinations may be used as is for the whole month. To correct GHA for day, hour, minute and second see page E 92 and for further explanation of this table see page E 4.

JUNE

JUNE 1995 — SUN & ARIES — GMT

Thursday, 1st June

Time	SUN GHA	Dec	ARIES GHA	Time
00	180 34.9	N21 57.4	249 00.7	00
02	210 34.8	21 58.1	279 05.6	02
04	240 34.6	21 58.8	309 10.5	04
06	270 34.4	21 59.5	339 15.4	06
08	300 34.2	22 00.2	9 20.4	08
10	330 34.0	22 00.9	39 25.3	10
12	0 33.8	22 01.6	69 30.2	12
14	30 33.6	22 02.2	99 35.2	14
16	60 33.4	22 02.9	129 40.1	16
18	90 33.2	22 03.6	159 45.0	18
20	120 33.1	22 04.3	189 49.9	20
22	150 32.9	N22 05.0	219 54.9	22

Friday, 2nd June

Time	SUN GHA	Dec	ARIES GHA	Time
00	180 32.7	N22 05.6	249 59.8	00
02	210 32.5	22 06.3	280 04.7	02
04	240 32.3	22 07.0	310 09.7	04
06	270 32.1	22 07.6	340 14.6	06
08	300 31.9	22 08.3	10 19.5	08
10	330 31.7	22 08.9	40 24.4	10
12	0 31.5	22 09.6	70 29.4	12
14	30 31.3	22 10.2	100 34.3	14
16	60 31.1	22 10.9	130 39.2	16
18	90 30.9	22 11.5	160 44.1	18
20	120 30.7	22 12.2	190 49.1	20
22	150 30.5	N22 12.8	220 54.0	22

Saturday, 3rd June

Time	SUN GHA	Dec	ARIES GHA	Time
00	180 30.3	N22 13.5	250 58.9	00
02	210 30.1	22 14.1	281 03.9	02
04	240 29.9	22 14.7	311 08.8	04
06	270 29.7	22 15.4	341 13.7	06
08	300 29.5	22 16.0	11 18.6	08
10	330 29.3	22 16.6	41 23.6	10
12	0 29.1	22 17.2	71 28.5	12
14	30 28.9	22 17.8	101 33.4	14
16	60 28.7	22 18.5	131 38.4	16
18	90 28.5	22 19.1	161 43.3	18
20	120 28.3	22 19.7	191 48.2	20
22	150 28.0	N22 20.3	221 53.1	22

Sunday, 4th June

Time	SUN GHA	Dec	ARIES GHA	Time
00	180 27.8	N22 20.9	251 58.1	00
02	210 27.6	22 21.5	282 03.0	02
04	240 27.4	22 22.1	312 07.9	04
06	270 27.2	22 22.7	342 12.9	06
08	300 27.0	22 23.3	12 17.8	08
10	330 26.8	22 23.9	42 22.7	10
12	0 26.6	22 24.5	72 27.6	12
14	30 26.4	22 25.1	102 32.6	14
16	60 26.1	22 25.7	132 37.5	16
18	90 25.9	22 26.2	162 42.4	18
20	120 25.7	22 26.8	192 47.4	20
22	150 25.5	N22 27.4	222 52.3	22

Monday, 5th June

Time	SUN GHA	Dec	ARIES GHA	Time
00	180 25.3	N22 28.0	252 57.2	00
02	210 25.1	22 28.5	283 02.1	02
04	240 24.9	22 29.1	313 07.1	04
06	270 24.6	22 29.7	343 12.0	06
08	300 24.4	22 30.2	13 16.9	08
10	330 24.2	22 30.8	43 21.9	10
12	0 24.0	22 31.3	73 26.8	12
14	30 23.8	22 31.9	103 31.7	14
16	60 23.5	22 32.4	133 36.6	16
18	90 23.3	22 33.0	163 41.6	18
20	120 23.1	22 33.5	193 46.5	20
22	150 22.9	N22 34.1	223 51.4	22

Tuesday, 6th June

Time	SUN GHA	Dec	ARIES GHA	Time
00	180 22.7	N22 34.6	253 56.3	00
02	210 22.4	22 35.2	284 01.3	02
04	240 22.2	22 35.7	314 06.2	04
06	270 22.0	22 36.2	344 11.1	06
08	300 21.8	22 36.8	14 16.1	08
10	330 21.5	22 37.3	44 21.0	10
12	0 21.3	22 37.8	74 25.9	12
14	30 21.1	22 38.3	104 30.8	14
16	60 20.9	22 38.9	134 35.8	16
18	90 20.6	22 39.4	164 40.7	18
20	120 20.4	22 39.9	194 45.6	20
22	150 20.2	N22 40.4	224 50.6	22

Wednesday, 7th June

Time	SUN GHA	Dec	ARIES GHA	Time
00	180 20.0	N22 40.9	254 55.5	00
02	210 19.7	22 41.4	285 00.4	02
04	240 19.5	22 41.9	315 05.3	04
06	270 19.3	22 42.4	345 10.3	06
08	300 19.0	22 42.9	15 15.2	08
10	330 18.8	22 43.4	45 20.1	10
12	0 18.6	22 43.9	75 25.1	12
14	30 18.3	22 44.4	105 30.0	14
16	60 18.1	22 44.9	135 34.9	16
18	90 17.9	22 45.3	165 39.8	18
20	120 17.7	22 45.8	195 44.8	20
22	150 17.4	N22 46.3	225 49.7	22

Thursday, 8th June

Time	SUN GHA	Dec	ARIES GHA	Time
00	180 17.2	N22 46.8	255 54.6	00
02	210 17.0	22 47.2	285 59.6	02
04	240 16.7	22 47.7	316 04.5	04
06	270 16.5	22 48.2	346 09.4	06
08	300 16.2	22 48.6	16 14.3	08
10	330 16.0	22 49.1	46 19.3	10
12	0 15.8	22 49.6	76 24.2	12
14	30 15.5	22 50.0	106 29.1	14
16	60 15.3	22 50.5	136 34.1	16
18	90 15.1	22 50.9	166 39.0	18
20	120 14.8	22 51.4	196 43.9	20
22	150 14.6	N22 51.8	226 48.8	22

Friday, 9th June

Time	SUN GHA	Dec	ARIES GHA	Time
00	180 14.3	N22 52.2	256 53.8	00
02	210 14.1	22 52.7	286 58.7	02
04	240 13.9	22 53.1	317 03.6	04
06	270 13.6	22 53.5	347 08.6	06
08	300 13.4	22 54.0	17 13.5	08
10	330 13.1	22 54.4	47 18.4	10
12	0 12.9	22 54.8	77 23.3	12
14	30 12.7	22 55.2	107 28.3	14
16	60 12.4	22 55.7	137 33.2	16
18	90 12.2	22 56.1	167 38.1	18
20	120 11.9	22 56.5	197 43.0	20
22	150 11.7	N22 56.9	227 48.0	22

Saturday, 10th June

Time	SUN GHA	Dec	ARIES GHA	Time
00	180 11.4	N22 57.3	257 52.9	00
02	210 11.2	22 57.7	287 57.8	02
04	240 11.0	22 58.1	318 02.8	04
06	270 10.7	22 58.5	348 07.7	06
08	300 10.5	22 58.9	18 12.6	08
10	330 10.2	22 59.3	48 17.5	10
12	0 10.0	22 59.7	78 22.5	12
14	30 09.7	23 00.0	108 27.4	14
16	60 09.5	23 00.5	138 32.3	16
18	90 09.2	23 00.8	168 37.3	18
20	120 09.0	23 01.2	198 42.2	20
22	150 08.7	N23 01.6	228 47.1	22

Sunday, 11th June

Time	SUN GHA	Dec	ARIES GHA	Time
00	180 08.5	N23 02.0	258 52.0	00
02	210 08.2	23 02.3	288 57.0	02
04	240 08.0	23 02.7	319 01.9	04
06	270 07.7	23 03.1	349 06.8	06
08	300 07.5	23 03.4	19 11.8	08
10	330 07.2	23 03.8	49 16.7	10
12	0 07.0	23 04.2	79 21.6	12
14	30 06.7	23 04.5	109 26.5	14
16	60 06.5	23 04.9	139 31.5	16
18	90 06.2	23 05.2	169 36.4	18
20	120 06.0	23 05.5	199 41.3	20
22	150 05.7	N23 05.9	229 46.3	22

Monday, 12th June

Time	SUN GHA	Dec	ARIES GHA	Time
00	180 05.5	N23 06.2	259 51.2	00
02	210 05.2	23 06.6	289 56.1	02
04	240 05.0	23 06.9	320 01.0	04
06	270 04.7	23 07.2	350 06.0	06
08	300 04.5	23 07.6	20 10.9	08
10	330 04.2	23 07.9	50 15.8	10
12	0 04.0	23 08.2	80 20.8	12
14	30 03.7	23 08.5	110 25.7	14
16	60 03.5	23 08.8	140 30.6	16
18	90 03.2	23 09.2	170 35.5	18
20	120 02.9	23 09.5	200 40.5	20
22	150 02.7	N23 09.8	230 45.4	22

Tuesday, 13th June

Time	SUN GHA	Dec	ARIES GHA	Time
00	180 02.4	N23 10.1	260 50.3	00
02	210 02.2	23 10.4	290 55.2	02
04	240 01.9	23 10.7	321 00.2	04
06	270 01.7	23 11.0	351 05.1	06
08	300 01.4	23 11.3	21 10.0	08
10	330 01.1	23 11.6	51 15.0	10
12	0 00.9	23 11.9	81 19.9	12
14	30 00.6	23 12.1	111 24.8	14
16	60 00.4	23 12.4	141 29.7	16
18	90 00.1	23 12.7	171 34.7	18
20	119 59.9	23 13.0	201 39.6	20
22	149 59.6	N23 13.3	231 44.5	22

Wednesday, 14th June

Time	SUN GHA	Dec	ARIES GHA	Time
00	179 59.3	N23 13.5	261 49.5	00
02	209 59.1	23 13.8	291 54.4	02
04	239 58.8	23 14.1	321 59.3	04
06	269 58.6	23 14.3	352 04.2	06
08	299 58.3	23 14.6	22 09.2	08
10	329 58.0	23 14.8	52 14.1	10
12	359 57.8	23 15.1	82 19.0	12
14	29 57.5	23 15.3	112 24.0	14
16	59 57.3	23 15.6	142 28.9	16
18	89 57.0	23 15.8	172 33.8	18
20	119 56.7	23 16.1	202 38.7	20
22	149 56.5	N23 16.3	232 43.7	22

Thursday, 15th June

Time	SUN GHA	Dec	ARIES GHA	Time
00	179 56.2	N23 16.6	262 48.6	00
02	209 55.9	23 16.8	292 53.5	02
04	239 55.7	23 17.0	322 58.5	04
06	269 55.4	23 17.3	353 03.4	06
08	299 55.2	23 17.5	23 08.3	08
10	329 54.9	23 17.7	53 13.2	10
12	359 54.6	23 17.9	83 18.2	12
14	29 54.4	23 18.1	113 23.1	14
16	59 54.1	23 18.4	143 28.0	16
18	89 53.8	23 18.6	173 33.0	18
20	119 53.6	23 18.8	203 37.9	20
22	149 53.3	N23 19.0	233 42.8	22

NOTES

Sun & Aries GHA corrections for additional hour, minutes, and seconds on page E 94.
Correct Sun Declination by interpolation. For example see page E 4.

JUNE 1995 — SUN & ARIES — GMT

Friday, 16th June

Time	SUN GHA	Dec	ARIES GHA
00	179 53.0	N23 19.2	263 47.7
02	209 52.8	23 19.4	293 52.7
04	239 52.5	23 19.6	323 57.6
06	269 52.2	23 19.8	354 02.5
08	299 52.0	23 20.0	24 07.4
10	329 51.7	23 20.2	54 12.4
12	359 51.4	23 20.3	84 17.3
14	29 51.2	23 20.5	114 22.2
16	59 50.9	23 20.7	144 27.2
18	89 50.6	23 20.9	174 32.1
20	119 50.4	23 21.1	204 37.0
22	149 50.1	N23 21.2	234 41.9

Saturday, 17th June

Time	SUN GHA	Dec	ARIES GHA
00	179 49.8	N23 21.4	264 46.9
02	209 49.6	23 21.6	294 51.8
04	239 49.3	23 21.7	324 56.7
06	269 49.0	23 21.9	355 01.7
08	299 48.8	23 22.0	25 06.6
10	329 48.5	23 22.2	55 11.5
12	359 48.2	23 22.3	85 16.4
14	29 48.0	23 22.5	115 21.4
16	59 47.7	23 22.6	145 26.3
18	89 47.4	23 22.8	175 31.2
20	119 47.2	23 22.9	205 36.2
22	149 46.9	N23 23.1	235 41.1

Sunday, 18th June

Time	SUN GHA	Dec	ARIES GHA
00	179 46.6	N23 23.2	265 46.0
02	209 46.4	23 23.3	295 50.9
04	239 46.1	23 23.4	325 55.9
06	269 45.8	23 23.6	356 00.8
08	299 45.5	23 23.7	26 05.7
10	329 45.3	23 23.8	56 10.7
12	359 45.0	23 23.9	86 15.6
14	29 44.7	23 24.0	116 20.5
16	59 44.5	23 24.2	146 25.4
18	89 44.2	23 24.3	176 30.4
20	119 43.9	23 24.4	206 35.3
22	149 43.7	N23 24.5	236 40.2

Monday, 19th June

Time	SUN GHA	Dec	ARIES GHA
00	179 43.4	N23 24.6	266 45.2
02	209 43.1	23 24.7	296 50.1
04	239 42.8	23 24.8	326 55.0
06	269 42.6	23 24.9	356 59.9
08	299 42.3	23 24.9	27 04.9
10	329 42.0	23 25.0	57 09.8
12	359 41.8	23 25.1	87 14.7
14	29 41.5	23 25.2	117 19.6
16	59 41.2	23 25.3	147 24.6
18	89 40.9	23 25.3	177 29.5
20	119 40.7	23 25.4	207 34.4
22	149 40.4	N23 25.5	237 39.4

Tuesday, 20th June

Time	SUN GHA	Dec	ARIES GHA
00	179 40.1	N23 25.5	267 44.3
02	209 39.9	23 25.6	297 49.2
04	239 39.6	23 25.7	327 54.1
06	269 39.3	23 25.7	357 59.1
08	299 39.0	23 25.8	28 04.0
10	329 38.8	23 25.8	58 08.9
12	359 38.5	23 25.9	88 13.9
14	29 38.2	23 25.9	118 18.8
16	59 38.0	23 26.0	148 23.7
18	89 37.7	23 26.0	178 28.6
20	119 37.4	23 26.0	208 33.6
22	149 37.1	N23 26.1	238 38.5

Wednesday, 21st June

Time	SUN GHA	Dec	ARIES GHA
00	179 36.9	N23 26.1	268 43.4
02	209 36.6	23 26.1	298 48.4
04	239 36.3	23 26.2	328 53.3
06	269 36.0	23 26.2	358 58.2
08	299 35.8	23 26.2	29 03.1
10	329 35.5	23 26.2	59 08.1
12	359 35.2	23 26.2	89 13.0
14	29 35.0	23 26.2	119 17.9
16	59 34.7	23 26.2	149 22.9
18	89 34.4	23 26.2	179 27.8
20	119 34.1	23 26.3	209 32.7
22	149 33.9	N23 26.2	239 37.6

Thursday, 22nd June

Time	SUN GHA	Dec	ARIES GHA
00	179 33.6	N23 26.2	269 42.6
02	209 33.3	23 26.2	299 47.5
04	239 33.1	23 26.2	329 52.4
06	269 32.8	23 26.2	359 57.4
08	299 32.5	23 26.2	30 02.3
10	329 32.2	23 26.2	60 07.2
12	359 32.0	23 26.2	90 12.1
14	29 31.7	23 26.1	120 17.1
16	59 31.4	23 26.1	150 22.0
18	89 31.1	23 26.1	180 26.9
20	119 30.9	23 26.0	210 31.8
22	149 30.6	N23 26.0	240 36.8

Friday, 23rd June

Time	SUN GHA	Dec	ARIES GHA
00	179 30.3	N23 26.0	270 41.7
02	209 30.1	23 25.9	300 46.6
04	239 29.8	23 25.9	330 51.6
06	269 29.5	23 25.8	0 56.5
08	299 29.2	23 25.8	31 01.4
10	329 29.0	23 25.7	61 06.3
12	359 28.7	23 25.7	91 11.3
14	29 28.4	23 25.6	121 16.2
16	59 28.2	23 25.6	151 21.1
18	89 27.9	23 25.5	181 26.1
20	119 27.6	23 25.4	211 31.0
22	149 27.3	N23 25.4	241 35.9

Saturday, 24th June

Time	SUN GHA	Dec	ARIES GHA
00	179 27.1	N23 25.3	271 40.8
02	209 26.8	23 25.2	301 45.8
04	239 26.5	23 25.1	331 50.7
06	269 26.3	23 25.1	1 55.6
08	299 26.0	23 25.0	32 00.6
10	329 25.7	23 24.9	62 05.5
12	359 25.5	23 24.8	92 10.4
14	29 25.2	23 24.7	122 15.3
16	59 24.9	23 24.6	152 20.3
18	89 24.6	23 24.5	182 25.2
20	119 24.4	23 24.4	212 30.1
22	149 24.1	N23 24.3	242 35.1

Sunday, 25th June

Time	SUN GHA	Dec	ARIES GHA
00	179 23.8	N23 24.2	272 40.0
02	209 23.6	23 24.1	302 44.9
04	239 23.3	23 24.0	332 49.8
06	269 23.0	23 23.9	2 54.8
08	299 22.8	23 23.7	32 59.7
10	329 22.5	23 23.6	63 04.6
12	359 22.2	23 23.5	93 09.6
14	29 22.0	23 23.4	123 14.5
16	59 21.7	23 23.2	153 19.4
18	89 21.4	23 23.1	183 24.3
20	119 21.2	23 23.0	213 29.3
22	149 20.9	N23 22.8	243 34.2

Monday, 26th June

Time	SUN GHA	Dec	ARIES GHA
00	179 20.6	N23 22.7	273 39.1
02	209 20.4	23 22.5	303 44.0
04	239 20.1	23 22.4	333 49.0
06	269 19.8	23 22.2	3 53.9
08	299 19.6	23 22.1	33 58.8
10	329 19.3	23 21.9	64 03.8
12	359 19.0	23 21.8	94 08.7
14	29 18.8	23 21.6	124 13.6
16	59 18.5	23 21.5	154 18.5
18	89 18.2	23 21.3	184 23.5
20	119 18.0	23 21.1	214 28.4
22	149 17.7	N23 20.9	244 33.3

Tuesday, 27th June

Time	SUN GHA	Dec	ARIES GHA
00	179 17.4	N23 20.8	274 38.3
02	209 17.2	23 20.6	304 43.2
04	239 16.9	23 20.4	334 48.1
06	269 16.7	23 20.2	4 53.0
08	299 16.4	23 20.0	34 58.0
10	329 16.1	23 19.9	65 02.9
12	359 15.9	23 19.7	95 07.8
14	29 15.6	23 19.5	125 12.8
16	59 15.3	23 19.3	155 17.7
18	89 15.1	23 19.1	185 22.6
20	119 14.8	23 18.9	215 27.5
22	149 14.6	N23 18.7	245 32.5

Wednesday, 28th June

Time	SUN GHA	Dec	ARIES GHA
00	179 14.3	N23 18.4	275 37.4
02	209 14.0	23 18.2	305 42.3
04	239 13.8	23 18.0	335 47.3
06	269 13.5	23 17.8	5 52.2
08	299 13.3	23 17.6	35 57.1
10	329 13.0	23 17.4	66 02.0
12	359 12.7	23 17.1	96 07.0
14	29 12.5	23 16.9	126 11.9
16	59 12.2	23 16.7	156 16.8
18	89 12.0	23 16.4	186 21.8
20	119 11.7	23 16.2	216 26.7
22	149 11.5	N23 16.0	246 31.6

Thursday, 29th June

Time	SUN GHA	Dec	ARIES GHA
00	179 11.2	N23 15.7	276 36.5
02	209 10.9	23 15.5	306 41.5
04	239 10.7	23 15.2	336 46.4
06	269 10.4	23 15.0	6 51.3
08	299 10.2	23 14.7	36 56.2
10	329 09.9	23 14.4	67 01.2
12	359 09.7	23 14.2	97 06.1
14	29 09.4	23 13.9	127 11.0
16	59 09.2	23 13.7	157 16.0
18	89 08.9	23 13.4	187 20.9
20	119 08.7	23 13.1	217 25.8
22	149 08.4	N23 12.8	247 30.7

Friday, 30th June

Time	SUN GHA	Dec	ARIES GHA
00	179 08.2	N23 12.6	277 35.7
02	209 07.9	23 12.3	307 40.6
04	239 07.7	23 12.0	337 45.5
06	269 07.4	23 11.7	7 50.5
08	299 07.1	23 11.4	37 55.4
10	329 06.9	23 11.1	68 00.3
12	359 06.7	23 10.8	98 05.2
14	29 06.4	23 10.5	128 10.2
16	59 06.2	23 10.2	158 15.1
18	89 05.9	23 09.9	188 20.0
20	119 05.7	23 09.6	218 25.0
22	149 05.4	N23 09.3	248 29.9

JUNE

JUNE 1995 — PLANETS — 0h GMT

VENUS — Note — JUPITER

Mer Pass (h m)	GHA (° ')	Mean Var/hr 14°+	Dec (° ')	Mean Var/hr	Corrections on Page E 101	GHA (° ')	Mean Var/hr 15°+	Dec (° ')	Mean Var/hr	Mer Pass (h m)
10 29	202 50.6	59.4	N 15 56.8	0.9	1 Th	359 54.7	2.8	S 21 14.1	0.0	00 00
10 30	202 37.2	59.4	N 16 18.2	0.9	2 Fri	1 01.9	2.8	S 21 13.1	0.0	23 51
10 31	202 23.6	59.4	N 16 39.2	0.9	3 Sat	2 09.2	2.8	S 21 12.2	0.0	23 47
10 32	202 09.6	59.4	N 16 59.8	0.8	4 SUN	3 16.5	2.8	S 21 11.2	0.0	23 42
10 33	201 55.4	59.4	N 17 19.9	0.8	5 Mon	4 23.7	2.8	S 21 10.2	0.0	23 38
10 34	201 40.9	59.4	N 17 39.7	0.8	6 Tu	5 30.9	2.8	S 21 09.2	0.0	23 34
10 35	201 26.2	59.4	N 17 59.0	0.8	7 Wed	6 38.1	2.8	S 21 08.2	0.0	23 29
10 36	201 11.1	59.4	N 18 17.8	0.8	8 Th	7 45.3	2.8	S 21 07.3	0.0	23 25
10 37	200 55.8	59.4	N 18 36.2	0.7	9 Fri	8 52.5	2.8	S 21 06.3	0.0	23 20
10 38	200 40.2	59.3	N 18 54.1	0.7	10 Sat	9 59.5	2.8	S 21 05.3	0.0	23 16
10 39	200 24.4	59.3	N 19 11.5	0.7	11 SUN	11 06.6	2.8	S 21 04.3	0.0	23 11
10 40	200 08.2	59.3	N 19 28.4	0.7	12 Mon	12 13.6	2.8	S 21 03.3	0.0	23 07
10 41	199 51.8	59.3	N 19 44.8	0.7	13 Tu	13 20.5	2.8	S 21 02.4	0.0	23 02
10 42	199 35.1	59.3	N 20 00.7	0.6	14 Wed	14 27.4	2.8	S 21 01.4	0.0	22 58
10 43	199 18.2	59.3	N 20 16.0	0.6	15 Th	15 34.2	2.8	S 21 00.4	0.0	22 53
10 44	199 01.0	59.3	N 20 30.8	0.6	16 Fri	16 40.9	2.8	S 20 59.5	0.0	22 49
10 46	198 43.6	59.3	N 20 45.1	0.6	17 Sat	17 47.6	2.8	S 20 58.6	0.0	22 45
10 47	198 25.8	59.3	N 20 58.8	0.5	18 SUN	18 54.1	2.8	S 20 57.6	0.0	22 40
10 48	198 07.9	59.2	N 21 11.9	0.5	19 Mon	20 00.6	2.8	S 20 56.7	0.0	22 36
10 49	197 49.7	59.2	N 21 24.5	0.5	20 Tu	21 07.0	2.8	S 20 55.8	0.0	22 31
10 50	197 31.2	59.2	N 21 36.4	0.5	21 Wed	22 13.3	2.8	S 20 54.9	0.0	22 27
10 52	197 12.6	59.2	N 21 47.8	0.4	22 Th	23 19.4	2.8	S 20 54.0	0.0	22 23
10 53	196 53.7	59.2	N 21 58.6	0.4	23 Fri	24 25.5	2.8	S 20 53.1	0.0	22 18
10 54	196 34.6	59.2	N 22 08.7	0.4	24 Sat	25 31.5	2.7	S 20 52.3	0.0	22 14
10 56	196 15.3	59.2	N 22 18.3	0.4	25 SUN	26 37.4	2.7	S 20 51.4	0.0	22 09
10 57	195 55.7	59.2	N 22 27.2	0.3	26 Mon	27 43.1	2.7	S 20 50.6	0.0	22 05
10 58	195 36.1	59.2	N 22 35.5	0.3	27 Tu	28 48.7	2.7	S 20 49.8	0.0	22 01
11 00	195 16.2	59.2	N 22 43.1	0.3	28 Wed	29 54.2	2.7	S 20 49.0	0.0	21 56
11 01	194 56.2	59.2	N 22 50.1	0.3	29 Th	30 59.5	2.7	S 20 48.2	0.0	21 52
11 02	194 36.0	59.2	N 22 56.4	0.2	30 Fri	32 04.7	2.7	S 20 47.5	0.0	21 48

VENUS, Av. Mag. -3.9
S.H.A. June
5 309; 10 303; 15 296; 20 290; 25 284; 30 277.

JUPITER, Av. Mag. -2.6
S.H.A. June
5 111; 10 112; 15 113; 20 113; 25 114; 30 114.

MARS — Note — SATURN

Mer Pass (h m)	GHA (° ')	Mean Var/hr 15°+	Dec (° ')	Mean Var/hr	Corrections on Page E 101	GHA (° ')	Mean Var/hr 15°+	Dec (° ')	Mean Var/hr	Mer Pass (h m)
17 44	93 38.8	1.4	N 11 40.5	0.5	1 Th	253 59.0	2.3	S 4 18.5	0.0	07 03
17 42	94 11.3	1.4	N 11 29.0	0.5	2 Fri	254 55.0	2.3	S 4 17.4	0.0	06 59
17 40	94 43.7	1.3	N 11 17.4	0.5	3 Sat	255 51.0	2.3	S 4 16.3	0.0	06 56
17 37	95 15.9	1.3	N 11 05.7	0.5	4 SUN	256 47.2	2.3	S 4 15.3	0.0	06 52
17 35	95 48.0	1.3	N 10 53.9	0.5	5 Mon	257 43.4	2.3	S 4 14.3	0.0	06 48
17 33	96 19.9	1.3	N 10 42.0	0.5	6 Tu	258 39.6	2.4	S 4 13.3	0.0	06 44
17 31	96 51.7	1.3	N 10 30.0	0.5	7 Wed	259 36.0	2.4	S 4 12.4	0.0	06 41
17 29	97 23.4	1.3	N 10 17.9	0.5	8 Th	260 32.5	2.4	S 4 11.5	0.0	06 37
17 27	97 54.9	1.3	N 10 05.7	0.5	9 Fri	261 29.0	2.4	S 4 10.6	0.0	06 33
17 25	98 26.3	1.3	N 9 53.5	0.5	10 Sat	262 25.6	2.4	S 4 09.8	0.0	06 29
17 23	98 57.5	1.3	N 9 41.2	0.5	11 SUN	263 22.3	2.4	S 4 09.1	0.0	06 25
17 21	99 28.7	1.3	N 9 28.7	0.5	12 Mon	264 19.1	2.4	S 4 08.3	0.0	06 22
17 19	99 59.7	1.3	N 9 16.2	0.5	13 Tu	265 16.0	2.4	S 4 07.6	0.0	06 18
17 16	100 30.6	1.3	N 9 03.6	0.5	14 Wed	266 12.9	2.4	S 4 07.0	0.0	06 14
17 14	101 01.3	1.3	N 8 51.0	0.5	15 Th	267 10.0	2.4	S 4 06.3	0.0	06 10
17 12	101 32.0	1.3	N 8 38.2	0.5	16 Fri	268 07.1	2.4	S 4 05.7	0.0	06 07
17 10	102 02.6	1.3	N 8 25.4	0.5	17 Sat	269 04.4	2.4	S 4 05.2	0.0	06 03
17 08	102 33.0	1.3	N 8 12.5	0.5	18 SUN	270 01.7	2.4	S 4 04.7	0.0	05 59
17 06	103 03.3	1.3	N 7 59.5	0.5	19 Mon	270 59.1	2.4	S 4 04.2	0.0	05 55
17 04	103 33.5	1.3	N 7 46.4	0.5	20 Tu	271 56.6	2.4	S 4 03.8	0.0	05 51
17 02	104 03.7	1.3	N 7 33.3	0.5	21 Wed	272 54.1	2.4	S 4 03.4	0.0	05 47
17 00	104 33.7	1.2	N 7 20.1	0.6	22 Th	273 51.8	2.4	S 4 03.1	0.0	05 44
16 58	105 03.5	1.2	N 7 06.8	0.6	23 Fri	274 49.6	2.4	S 4 02.8	0.0	05 40
16 56	105 33.3	1.2	N 6 53.4	0.6	24 Sat	275 47.4	2.4	S 4 02.5	0.0	05 36
16 54	106 03.0	1.2	N 6 40.0	0.6	25 SUN	276 45.3	2.4	S 4 02.3	0.0	05 32
16 52	106 32.6	1.2	N 6 26.5	0.6	26 Mon	277 43.4	2.4	S 4 02.1	0.0	05 28
16 50	107 02.0	1.2	N 6 12.9	0.6	27 Tu	278 41.5	2.4	S 4 01.9	0.0	05 24
16 49	107 31.3	1.2	N 5 59.2	0.6	28 Wed	279 39.7	2.4	S 4 01.8	0.0	05 20
16 47	108 00.6	1.2	N 5 45.5	0.6	29 Th	280 38.0	2.4	S 4 01.8	0.0	05 17
16 45	108 29.7	1.2	N 5 31.7	0.6	30 Fri	281 36.4	2.4	S 4 01.7	0.0	05 13

MARS, Av. Mag. +1.1
S.H.A. June
5 203; 10 201; 15 198; 20 196; 25 193; 30 191.

SATURN, Av. Mag. +1.2
S.H.A. June
5 5; 10 5; 15 4; 20 4; 25 4; 30 4.

JUNE 1995　　　　　　　　　MOON

Day	GMT hr	GHA ° '	Mean Var/hr 14°+	Dec ° '	Mean Var/hr '	Day	GMT hr	GHA ° '	Mean Var/hr 14°+	Dec ° '	Mean Var/hr '
1 Th	0	150 09.9	31.4	N 18 32.8	3.3	17 Sat	0	305 07.3	28.3	S 10 28.0	10.2
	6	237 18.3	31.5	N 18 13.2	3.8		6	31 56.7	28.8	S 9 27.2	10.4
	12	324 27.2	31.6	N 17 50.5	4.3		12	118 49.0	29.2	S 8 24.9	10.5
	18	51 36.6	31.7	N 17 24.9	4.8		18	205 44.2	29.7	S 7 21.5	10.7
2 Fri	0	138 46.6	31.8	N 16 56.4	5.3	18 Sun	0	292 41.9	30.1	S 6 17.2	10.9
	6	225 57.2	31.9	N 16 25.1	5.7		6	19 42.2	30.5	S 5 12.2	11.0
	12	313 08.4	32.0	N 15 51.0	6.1		12	106 44.7	30.8	S 4 06.8	10.9
	18	40 20.2	32.0	N 15 14.3	6.6		18	193 49.4	31.2	S 3 01.2	10.9
3 Sat	0	127 32.5	32.2	N 14 35.1	7.0	19 Mon	0	280 56.0	31.5	S 1 55.6	10.9
	6	214 45.4	32.3	N 13 53.3	7.4		6	8 04.3	31.7	S 0 50.2	10.9
	12	301 58.8	32.3	N 13 09.2	7.8		12	95 14.3	31.9	N 0 14.9	10.8
	18	29 12.6	32.4	N 12 22.8	8.2		18	182 25.6	32.1	N 1 19.4	10.6
4 Sun	0	116 26.7	32.4	N 11 34.2	8.4	20 Tu	0	269 38.1	32.3	N 2 23.2	10.5
	6	203 41.1	32.4	N 10 43.5	8.8		6	356 51.6	32.4	N 3 26.2	10.3
	12	290 55.7	32.4	N 9 50.9	9.1		12	84 06.0	32.5	N 4 28.1	10.1
	18	18 10.3	32.4	N 8 56.4	9.4		18	171 21.1	32.7	N 5 29.0	9.9
5 Mon	0	105 24.9	32.4	N 8 00.2	9.6	21 Wed	0	258 36.7	32.6	N 6 28.5	9.7
	6	192 39.2	32.3	N 7 02.3	9.9		6	345 52.2	32.7	N 7 26.7	9.4
	12	279 53.3	32.3	N 6 02.9	10.1		12	73 08.9	32.7	N 8 23.3	9.1
	18	7 06.8	32.1	N 5 02.2	10.3		18	160 25.2	32.7	N 9 18.4	8.9
6 Tu	0	94 19.8	32.0	N 4 00.2	10.5	22 Th	0	247 41.4	32.6	N 10 11.6	8.5
	6	181 31.9	31.8	N 2 57.1	10.6		6	334 57.5	32.7	N 11 03.1	8.2
	12	268 43.0	31.7	N 1 53.0	10.9		12	62 13.3	32.6	N 11 52.6	7.9
	18	355 53.1	31.4	N 0 48.1	11.0		18	149 28.8	32.5	N 12 40.0	7.5
7 Wed	0	83 01.7	31.2	S 0 17.4	11.0	23 Fri	0	236 43.8	32.4	N 13 25.2	7.1
	6	170 08.9	30.9	S 1 23.3	11.1		6	323 58.3	32.3	N 14 08.2	6.8
	12	257 14.4	30.6	S 2 29.6	11.1		12	51 12.3	32.2	N 14 48.8	6.4
	18	344 18.1	30.3	S 3 35.9	11.1		18	138 25.6	32.1	N 15 27.0	5.9
8 Th	0	71 19.6	29.9	S 4 42.1	11.0	24 Sat	0	225 38.2	32.0	N 16 02.6	5.4
	6	158 19.0	29.4	S 5 48.0	10.9		6	312 50.2	31.9	N 16 35.6	5.0
	12	245 15.9	29.1	S 6 53.3	10.8		12	40 01.5	31.8	N 17 05.9	4.5
	18	332 10.3	28.5	S 7 57.7	10.5		18	127 12.2	31.7	N 17 33.4	4.0
9 Fri	0	59 01.9	28.1	S 9 01.1	10.3	25 Sun	0	214 22.1	31.5	N 17 58.0	3.6
	6	145 50.7	27.6	S 10 03.1	10.0		6	301 31.5	31.5	N 18 19.7	3.1
	12	232 36.6	27.1	S 11 03.5	9.7		12	28 40.2	31.4	N 18 38.4	2.5
	18	319 19.3	26.6	S 12 01.9	9.3		18	115 48.5	31.3	N 18 54.0	2.0
10 Sat	0	45 58.9	26.0	S 12 58.0	8.9	26 Mon	0	202 56.2	31.2	N 19 06.5	1.6
	6	132 35.4	25.5	S 13 51.5	8.4		6	290 03.5	31.2	N 19 15.9	1.0
	12	219 08.7	25.0	S 14 42.2	7.9		12	17 10.6	31.1	N 19 22.2	0.4
	18	305 39.0	24.5	S 15 29.6	7.3		18	104 17.4	31.1	N 19 25.2	0.1
11 Sun	0	32 06.1	24.0	S 16 13.5	6.6	27 Tu	0	191 24.0	31.1	N 19 25.0	0.6
	6	118 30.5	23.6	S 16 53.5	5.9		6	278 30.6	31.1	N 19 21.6	1.2
	12	204 52.1	23.1	S 17 29.4	5.1		12	5 37.2	31.2	N 19 14.9	1.6
	18	291 11.2	22.8	S 18 00.8	4.4		18	92 43.9	31.1	N 19 05.1	2.2
12 Mon	0	17 28.2	22.5	S 18 27.6	3.5	28 Wed	0	179 50.9	31.2	N 18 52.1	2.8
	6	103 43.4	22.3	S 18 49.5	2.7		6	266 58.1	31.3	N 18 36.0	3.3
	12	189 57.0	22.1	S 19 06.3	1.9		12	354 05.7	31.4	N 18 16.8	3.8
	18	276 09.6	22.0	S 19 17.9	0.9		18	81 13.8	31.5	N 17 54.5	4.2
13 Tu	0	2 21.5	22.0	S 19 24.1	0.0	29 Th	0	168 22.4	31.5	N 17 29.2	4.8
	6	88 33.2	22.0	S 19 25.0	0.9		6	255 31.5	31.6	N 17 01.0	5.2
	12	174 45.1	22.1	S 19 20.6	1.7		12	342 41.2	31.7	N 16 30.0	5.6
	18	260 57.7	22.3	S 19 10.8	2.6		18	69 51.5	31.9	N 15 56.2	6.1
14 Wed	0	347 11.4	22.5	S 18 55.7	3.4	30 Fri	0	157 02.5	32.0	N 15 19.7	6.5
	6	73 26.6	22.9	S 18 35.6	4.2		6	244 14.1	32.0	N 14 40.7	7.0
	12	159 43.7	23.3	S 18 10.6	5.0		12	331 26.4	32.2	N 13 59.2	7.3
	18	246 02.9	23.7	S 17 40.8	5.8		18	58 39.2	32.2	N 13 15.3	7.7
15 Th	0	332 24.7	24.1	S 17 06.6	6.5						
	6	58 49.2	24.7	S 16 28.3	7.1						
	12	145 16.6	25.1	S 15 46.0	7.7						
	18	231 47.1	25.7	S 15 00.1	8.2						
16 Fri	0	318 20.7	26.2	S 14 11.0	8.8						
	6	44 57.6	26.7	S 13 18.9	9.2						
	12	131 37.7	27.2	S 12 24.1	9.6						
	18	218 20.9	27.8	S 11 27.1	9.8						

NOTE Moon GHA corrections for additional hours, minutes, and seconds on page E 96. Moon Declination corrections on page E 99. Mean Var/Hr value needed for both corrections.

JUNE

JULY 1995 — SUN & MOON — GMT

SUN

Yr	Mth	Week	Equation of Time 0h	12h	Transit	Semi-diam	Twi-light	Sun-rise	Sun-set	Twi-light	Lat	Twi-light	Sun-rise	Sun-set	Twi-light
			m s	m s	h m	′	h m	h m	h m	h m	°	h m	h m	h m	h m
182	1	Sat	+03 39	+03 45	12 04	15.8	02 56	03 44	20 23	21 11	N60	-1 28	-0 55	+0 55	+1 28
183	2	Sun	+03 51	+03 57	12 04	15.8	02 56	03 45	20 23	21 11	55	-0 24	-0 17	+0 17	+0 24
184	3	Mon	+04 02	+04 08	12 04	15.8	02 57	03 45	20 22	21 10	50	+0 13	+0 10	-0 10	-0 13
185	4	Tu	+04 13	+04 19	12 04	15.8	02 58	03 46	20 22	21 10	45	+0 39	+0 30	-0 30	-0 39
186	5	Wed	+04 24	+04 29	12 04	15.8	02 59	03 47	20 22	21 09	N40	+1 00	+0 46	-0 46	-1 00
187	6	Th	+04 35	+04 40	12 05	15.8	03 00	03 48	20 21	21 08	35	+1 16	+1 00	-1 00	-1 16
188	7	Fri	+04 45	+04 50	12 05	15.8	03 01	03 49	20 20	21 08	30	+1 30	+1 12	-1 12	-1 30
189	8	Sat	+04 55	+04 59	12 05	15.8	03 02	03 50	20 20	21 07	25	+1 42	+1 22	-1 22	-1 42
190	9	Sun	+05 04	+05 08	12 05	15.8	03 04	03 51	20 19	21 06	N20	+1 53	+1 32	-1 32	-1 53
191	10	Mon	+05 13	+05 17	12 05	15.8	03 05	03 52	20 18	21 05	15	+2 03	+1 41	-1 41	-2 03
192	11	Tu	+05 21	+05 25	12 05	15.8	03 06	03 53	20 18	21 04	10	+2 12	+1 49	-1 49	-2 12
193	12	Wed	+05 29	+05 33	12 06	15.8	03 07	03 54	20 17	21 03	5	+2 20	+1 57	-1 57	-2 20
194	13	Th	+05 37	+05 40	12 06	15.8	03 09	03 55	20 16	21 02	0	+2 28	+2 05	-2 05	-2 28
195	14	Fri	+05 44	+05 47	12 06	15.8	03 10	03 56	20 15	21 01	S 5	+2 36	+2 13	-2 13	-2 36
196	15	Sat	+05 50	+05 54	12 06	15.8	03 11	03 57	20 14	20 59	10	+2 44	+2 21	-2 21	-2 44
197	16	Sun	+05 57	+06 00	12 06	15.8	03 13	03 58	20 13	20 58	15	+2 52	+2 29	-2 29	-2 52
198	17	Mon	+06 02	+06 05	12 06	15.8	03 14	04 00	20 12	20 57	S20	+3 00	+2 38	-2 38	-3 00
199	18	Tu	+06 07	+06 10	12 06	15.8	03 16	04 01	20 11	20 55	25	+3 08	+2 47	-2 47	-3 08
200	19	Wed	+06 12	+06 14	12 06	15.8	03 17	04 02	20 09	20 54	30	+3 17	+2 57	-2 57	-3 17
201	20	Th	+06 16	+06 18	12 06	15.8	03 19	04 04	20 08	20 52	35	+3 26	+3 08	-3 08	-3 26
202	21	Fri	+06 20	+06 21	12 06	15.8	03 21	04 05	20 07	20 51	S40	+3 37	+3 21	-3 21	-3 37
203	22	Sat	+06 23	+06 24	12 06	15.8	03 22	04 06	20 06	20 49	45	+3 49	+3 36	-3 36	-3 49
204	23	Sun	+06 25	+06 27	12 06	15.8	03 24	04 08	20 04	20 48	50	+4 03	+3 55	-3 55	-4 03
205	24	Mon	+06 27	+06 28	12 06	15.8	03 26	04 09	20 03	20 46					
206	25	Tu	+06 29	+06 29	12 06	15.8	03 27	04 10	20 02	20 45					
207	26	Wed	+06 30	+06 30	12 06	15.8	03 29	04 12	20 00	20 43					
208	27	Th	+06 30	+06 30	12 06	15.8	03 31	04 13	19 59	20 41					
209	28	Fri	+06 29	+06 29	12 06	15.8	03 32	04 15	19 57	20 39					
210	29	Sat	+06 28	+06 28	12 06	15.8	03 34	04 16	19 56	20 38					
211	30	Sun	+06 27	+06 26	12 06	15.8	03 36	04 18	19 54	20 36					
212	31	Mon	+06 25	+06 23	12 06	15.8	03 38	04 19	19 52	20 34					

Lat corrections are headed "Lat Corr to Sunrise, Sunset etc", "Lat 52°N"

NOTES
Lat corrections are for mid-month.
Equation of Time is the excess of Mean Time over Apparent Time.

MOON

Lat 52°N

Yr	Mth	Week	Age	Transit (Upper)	Diff	Semi-diam	Hor Par	Moon-rise	Moon-set
			days	h m	m	′		h m	h m
182	1	Sat	03	14 44	45	15.0	55.1	07 31	21 45
183	2	Sun	04	15 29	45	15.1	55.6	08 37	22 09
184	3	Mon	05	16 14	47	15.3	56.2	09 45	22 32
185	4	Tu	06	17 01	48	15.5	56.8	10 55	22 55
186	5	Wed	07	17 49	50	15.7	57.6	12 06	23 20
187	6	Th	08	18 39	54	15.9	58.4	13 20	23 49
188	7	Fri	09	19 33	57	16.1	59.2	14 35	— —
189	8	Sat	10	20 30	60	16.3	60.0	15 51	00 22
190	9	Sun	11	21 30	63	16.5	60.6	17 04	01 03
191	10	Mon	12	22 33	62	16.6	61.0	18 10	01 54
192	11	Tu	13	23 35	61	16.7	61.1	19 06	02 56
193	12	Wed	14	24 36	—	16.6	60.9	19 53	04 08
194	13	Th	15	00 36	57	16.5	60.5	20 30	05 26
195	14	Fri	16	01 33	54	16.3	59.8	21 02	06 45
196	15	Sat	17	02 27	51	16.0	58.9	21 29	08 03
197	16	Sun	18	03 18	49	15.8	57.9	21 54	09 19
198	17	Mon	19	04 07	47	15.5	57.0	22 18	10 32
199	18	Tu	20	04 54	46	15.3	56.2	22 42	11 42
200	19	Wed	21	05 40	46	15.1	55.4	23 08	12 49
201	20	Th	22	06 26	46	14.9	54.9	23 37	13 54
202	21	Fri	23	07 12	46	14.8	54.4	— —	14 55
203	22	Sat	24	07 58	47	14.8	54.2	00 10	15 53
204	23	Sun	25	08 45	48	14.7	54.1	00 48	16 46
205	24	Mon	26	09 33	48	14.7	54.1	01 32	17 34
206	25	Tu	27	10 21	47	14.8	54.2	02 22	18 15
207	26	Wed	28	11 08	47	14.8	54.4	03 18	18 51
208	27	Th	29	11 55	47	14.9	54.8	04 18	19 23
209	28	Fri	01	12 42	46	15.0	55.1	05 22	19 50
210	29	Sat	02	13 28	46	15.1	55.6	06 28	20 15
211	30	Sun	03	14 14	46	15.3	56.0	07 36	20 39
212	31	Mon	04	15 00	47	15.4	56.6	08 45	21 02

Phases of the Moon

		d	h	m
☾	First Quarter	5	20	02
○	Full Moon	12	10	49
☽	Last Quarter	19	11	10
●	New Moon	27	15	13
	Perigee	11	10	
	Apogee	23	20	

NOTES
Diff equals daily change in transit time.
To correct Moonrise, Moonset, or Transit times for Latitude and/or Longitude see page E 100. For further information about these tables see page E 4. For Arc to Time correction see page E 91.

JULY 1995   STARS   0h GMT July 1

No	Name	Mag	Transit h m	Dec ° '	GHA ° '	RA h m	SHA ° '
	ARIES................		5 25		278 34.8		
1	Alpheratz.........	2.2	5 33	N29 03.9	276 32.1	0 08	357 57.3
2	Ankaa...............	2.4	5 51	S 42 19.5	272 03.7	0 26	353 28.9
3	Schedar	2.5	6 05	N56 30.6	268 30.5	0 40	349 55.7
4	Diphda	2.2	6 08	S 18 00.5	267 44.1	0 43	349 09.3
5	Achernar	0.6	7 02	S 57 15.2	254 11.7	1 38	335 36.9
6	POLARIS	2.1	7 52	N89 14.3	241 45.3	2 27	323 10.5
7	Hamal...............	2.2	7 31	N23 26.4	246 50.8	2 07	328 16.0
8	Acamar.............	3.1	8 22	S 40 19.2	234 03.6	2 58	315 28.8
9	Menkar	2.8	8 26	N 4 04.3	233 04.1	3 02	314 29.3
10	Mirfak	1.9	8 48	N49 50.5	227 34.7	3 24	308 59.9
11	Aldebaran.........	1.1	10 00	N 16 29.9	209 39.9	4 36	291 05.1
12	Rigel	0.3	10 38	S 8 12.4	200 00.1	5 14	281 25.3
13	Capella	0.2	10 40	N45 59.4	199 29.6	5 16	280 54.8
14	Bellatrix	1.7	10 49	N 6 20.7	197 21.6	5 25	278 46.8
15	Elnath...............	1.8	10 50	N28 36.1	197 04.8	5 26	278 30.0
16	Alnilam	1.8	11 00	S 1 12.3	194 35.1	5 36	276 00.3
17	Betelgeuse	0.1-1.2	11 19	N 7 24.3	189 51.0	5 55	271 16.2
18	Canopus...........	-0.9	11 48	S 52 41.6	182 37.4	6 24	264 02.6
19	Sirius	-1.6	12 09	S 16 42.7	177 20.7	6 45	258 45.9
20	Adhara	1.6	12 22	S 28 58.0	173 58.3	6 58	255 23.5
21	Castor	1.6	12 58	N31 53.8	165 00.3	7 34	246 25.5
22	Procyon............	0.5	13 03	N 5 14.1	163 49.0	7 39	245 14.2
23	Pollux	1.2	13 09	N28 02.1	162 19.4	7 45	243 44.6
24	Avior	1.7	13 46	S 59 29.9	152 58.9	8 22	234 24.1
25	Suhail	2.2	14 31	S 43 25.1	141 37.5	9 08	223 02.7
26	Miaplacidus	1.8	14 36	S 69 42.2	140 18.0	9 13	221 43.2
27	Alphard............	2.2	14 51	S 8 38.5	136 44.4	9 27	218 09.6
28	Regulus	1.3	15 31	N11 59.3	126 32.9	10 08	207 58.1
29	Dubhe	2.0	16 26	N61 46.7	112 43.4	11 03	194 08.6
30	Denebola	2.2	17 12	N 14 35.9	101 22.3	11 49	182 47.5
31	Gienah	2.8	17 38	S 17 31.1	94 41.1	12 16	176 06.3
32	Acrux...............	1.1	17 49	S 63 04.8	91 59.2	12 26	173 24.4
33	Gacrux.............	1.6	17 54	S 57 05.6	90 50.8	12 31	172 16.0
34	Mimosa	1.5	18 10	S 59 40.2	86 42.6	12 47	168 07.8
35	Alioth	1.7	18 17	N55 59.3	85 07.4	12 54	166 32.6
36	Spica................	1.2	18 48	S 11 08.3	77 20.2	13 25	158 45.4
37	Alkaid..............	1.9	19 10	N49 20.4	71 44.3	13 47	153 09.5
38	Hadar	0.9	19 26	S 60 21.3	67 41.7	14 04	149 06.9
39	Menkent	2.3	19 29	S 36 21.0	66 58.2	14 06	148 23.4
40	Arcturus	0.2	19 38	N19 12.5	64 42.8	14 15	146 08.0
41	Rigil Kent........	0.1	20 02	S 60 49.2	58 44.6	14 39	140 09.8
42	Zuben'ubi	2.9	20 13	S 16 01.4	55 55.0	14 51	137 20.2
43	Kochab	2.2	20 13	N74 10.8	55 54.0	14 51	137 19.2
44	Alphecca	2.3	20 57	N26 44.0	44 57.0	15 35	126 22.2
45	Antares	1.2	21 51	S 26 25.3	31 17.3	16 29	112 42.5
46	Atria	1.9	22 10	S 69 01.3	26 30.8	16 48	107 56.0
47	Sabik	2.6	22 32	S 15 43.1	21 02.5	17 10	102 27.7
48	Shaula	1.7	22 55	S 37 06.0	15 14.6	17 33	96 39.8
49	Rasalhague	2.1	22 57	N12 34.0	14 53.5	17 35	96 18.7
50	Eltanin.............	2.4	23 18	N51 29.6	9 26.7	17 57	90 51.9
51	Kaus Aust.	2.0	23 46	S 34 23.1	2 36.1	18 24	84 01.3
52	Vega	0.1	0 02	N38 47.0	359 22.4	18 37	80 47.6
53	Nunki	2.1	0 21	S 26 18.0	354 49.4	18 55	76 14.6
54	Altair	0.9	1 16	N 8 51.6	340 55.8	19 51	62 21.0
55	Peacock	2.1	1 51	S 56 44.7	332 14.6	20 25	53 39.8
56	Deneb	1.3	2 07	N45 16.0	328 15.0	20 41	49 40.2
57	Enif	2.5	3 09	N 9 51.4	312 34.9	21 44	34 00.1
58	Al Na'ir............	2.2	3 33	S 46 58.6	306 35.1	22 08	28 00.3
59	Fomalhaut	1.3	4 22	S 29 38.5	294 13.4	22 57	15 38.6
60	Markab	2.6	4 30	N15 10.9	292 26.3	23 05	13 51.5

Star Transit Corr Table

Date	Corr h m	Date	Corr h m
1	−0 00	17	−1 03
2	−0 04	18	−1 07
3	−0 08	19	−1 11
4	−0 12	20	−1 15
5	−0 16	21	−1 19
6	−0 20	22	−1 23
7	−0 24	23	−1 27
8	−0 28	24	−1 30
9	−0 31	25	−1 34
10	−0 35	26	−1 38
11	−0 39	27	−1 42
12	−0 43	28	−1 46
13	−0 47	29	−1 50
14	−0 51	30	−1 54
15	−0 55	31	−1 58
16	−0 59		

STAR TRANSIT

To find the approx time of transit of a star for any day of the month use above table. All corrections are subtractive.

If the quantity taken from the table is greater than the time of transit for the first of the month, add 23h 56min to the time of transit before subtracting the correction.

Example: What time will Nunki (No 53) transit the Meridian on July 30?

	h min
Transit on Jul 1	00 21
	+23 56
	24 17
Corr for Jul 30	−01 54
Transit on Jul 30	22 23

JULY DIARY

d h	
4 02	Earth at aphelion
4 05	Mars 4° N of Moon
7 11	Saturn stationary
9 13	Jupiter 2° S of Moon
12 19	Neptune 4° S of Moon
13 03	Uranus 6° S of Moon
17 04	Saturn 6° S of Moon
17 05	Neptune at opposition
21 18	Uranus at opposition
28 02	Mercury in superior conjunction

NOTES

Star declinations may be used as is for the whole month. To correct GHA for day, hour, minute and second see page E 92 and for further explanation of this table see page E 4.

JULY

JULY 1995 — SUN & ARIES — GMT

Saturday, 1st July

Time	SUN GHA	Dec	ARIES GHA
00	179 05.2	N23 09.0	278 34.8
02	209 04.9	23 08.7	308 39.7
04	239 04.7	23 08.4	338 44.7
06	269 04.4	23 08.1	8 49.6
08	299 04.2	23 07.8	38 54.5
10	329 03.9	23 07.4	68 59.5
12	359 03.7	23 07.1	99 04.4
14	29 03.4	23 06.8	129 09.3
16	59 03.2	23 06.4	159 14.2
18	89 03.0	23 06.1	189 19.2
20	119 02.7	23 05.8	219 24.1
22	149 02.5	N23 05.4	249 29.0

Sunday, 2nd July

Time	SUN GHA	Dec	ARIES GHA
00	179 02.2	N23 05.1	279 34.0
02	209 02.0	23 04.7	309 38.9
04	239 01.7	23 04.4	339 43.8
06	269 01.5	23 04.0	9 48.7
08	299 01.3	23 03.7	39 53.7
10	329 01.0	23 03.3	69 58.6
12	359 00.8	23 02.9	100 03.5
14	29 00.6	23 02.6	130 08.4
16	59 00.3	23 02.2	160 13.4
18	89 00.1	23 01.8	190 18.3
20	118 59.9	23 01.5	220 23.2
22	148 59.6	N23 01.1	250 28.2

Monday, 3rd July

Time	SUN GHA	Dec	ARIES GHA
00	178 59.4	N23 00.7	280 33.1
02	208 59.2	23 00.3	310 38.0
04	238 58.9	22 59.9	340 42.9
06	268 58.7	22 59.5	10 47.9
08	298 58.5	22 59.2	40 52.8
10	328 58.2	22 58.8	70 57.7
12	358 58.0	22 58.4	101 02.7
14	28 57.8	22 58.0	131 07.6
16	58 57.5	22 57.6	161 12.5
18	88 57.3	22 57.2	191 17.4
20	118 57.1	22 56.8	221 22.4
22	148 56.8	N22 56.3	251 27.3

Tuesday, 4th July

Time	SUN GHA	Dec	ARIES GHA
00	178 56.6	N22 55.9	281 32.2
02	208 56.4	22 55.5	311 37.2
04	238 56.2	22 55.1	341 42.1
06	268 55.9	22 54.7	11 47.0
08	298 55.7	22 54.3	41 51.9
10	328 55.5	22 53.8	71 56.9
12	358 55.2	22 53.4	102 01.8
14	28 55.0	22 53.0	132 06.7
16	58 54.8	22 52.5	162 11.7
18	88 54.6	22 52.1	192 16.6
20	118 54.3	22 51.7	222 21.5
22	148 54.1	N22 51.2	252 26.4

Wednesday, 5th July

Time	SUN GHA	Dec	ARIES GHA
00	178 53.9	N22 50.8	282 31.4
02	208 53.7	22 50.3	312 36.3
04	238 53.5	22 49.9	342 41.2
06	268 53.2	22 49.4	12 46.2
08	298 53.0	22 49.0	42 51.1
10	328 52.8	22 48.5	72 56.0
12	358 52.6	22 48.0	103 00.9
14	28 52.4	22 47.6	133 05.9
16	58 52.1	22 47.1	163 10.8
18	88 51.9	22 46.6	193 15.7
20	118 51.7	22 46.2	223 20.6
22	148 51.5	N22 45.7	253 25.6

Thursday, 6th July

Time	SUN GHA	Dec	ARIES GHA
00	178 51.3	N22 45.2	283 30.5
02	208 51.1	22 44.7	313 35.4
04	238 50.8	22 44.3	343 40.4
06	268 50.6	22 43.8	13 45.3
08	298 50.4	22 43.3	43 50.2
10	328 50.2	22 42.8	73 55.1
12	358 50.0	22 42.3	104 00.1
14	28 49.8	22 41.8	134 05.0
16	58 49.6	22 41.3	164 09.9
18	88 49.4	22 40.8	194 14.9
20	118 49.2	22 40.3	224 19.8
22	148 48.9	N22 39.8	254 24.7

Friday, 7th July

Time	SUN GHA	Dec	ARIES GHA
00	178 48.7	N22 39.3	284 29.6
02	208 48.5	22 38.8	314 34.6
04	238 48.3	22 38.3	344 39.5
06	268 48.1	22 37.7	14 44.4
08	298 47.9	22 37.2	44 49.4
10	328 47.7	22 36.7	74 54.3
12	358 47.5	22 36.2	104 59.2
14	28 47.3	22 35.6	135 04.1
16	58 47.1	22 35.1	165 09.1
18	88 46.9	22 34.6	195 14.0
20	118 46.7	22 34.0	225 18.9
22	148 46.5	N22 33.5	255 23.9

Saturday, 8th July

Time	SUN GHA	Dec	ARIES GHA
00	178 46.3	N22 32.9	285 28.8
02	208 46.1	22 32.4	315 33.7
04	238 45.9	22 31.8	345 38.6
06	268 45.7	22 31.3	15 43.6
08	298 45.5	22 30.7	45 48.5
10	328 45.3	22 30.2	75 53.4
12	358 45.1	22 29.6	105 58.4
14	28 44.9	22 29.1	136 03.3
16	58 44.7	22 28.5	166 08.2
18	88 44.6	22 27.9	196 13.1
20	118 44.4	22 27.4	226 18.1
22	148 44.2	N22 26.8	256 23.0

Sunday, 9th July

Time	SUN GHA	Dec	ARIES GHA
00	178 44.0	N22 26.2	286 27.9
02	208 43.8	22 25.6	316 32.8
04	238 43.6	22 25.1	346 37.8
06	268 43.4	22 24.5	16 42.7
08	298 43.2	22 23.9	46 47.6
10	328 43.0	22 23.3	76 52.6
12	358 42.9	22 22.7	106 57.5
14	28 42.7	22 22.1	137 02.4
16	58 42.5	22 21.5	167 07.3
18	88 42.3	22 20.9	197 12.3
20	118 42.1	22 20.3	227 17.2
22	148 41.9	N22 19.7	257 22.1

Monday, 10th July

Time	SUN GHA	Dec	ARIES GHA
00	178 41.8	N22 19.1	287 27.1
02	208 41.6	22 18.5	317 32.0
04	238 41.4	22 17.9	347 36.9
06	268 41.2	22 17.3	17 41.8
08	298 41.0	22 16.6	47 46.8
10	328 40.9	22 16.0	77 51.7
12	358 40.7	22 15.4	107 56.6
14	28 40.5	22 14.8	138 01.6
16	58 40.3	22 14.1	168 06.5
18	88 40.2	22 13.5	198 11.4
20	118 40.0	22 12.9	228 16.3
22	148 39.8	N22 12.2	258 21.3

Tuesday, 11th July

Time	SUN GHA	Dec	ARIES GHA	Time
00	178 39.6	N22 11.6	288 26.2	00
02	208 39.5	22 11.0	318 31.1	02
04	238 39.3	22 10.3	348 36.1	04
06	268 39.1	22 09.7	18 41.0	06
08	298 39.0	22 09.0	48 45.9	08
10	328 38.8	22 08.4	78 50.8	10
12	358 38.6	22 07.7	108 55.8	12
14	28 38.5	22 07.0	139 00.7	14
16	58 38.3	22 06.4	169 05.6	16
18	88 38.1	22 05.7	199 10.6	18
20	118 38.0	22 05.1	229 15.5	20
22	148 37.8	N22 04.4	259 20.4	22

Wednesday, 12th July

Time	SUN GHA	Dec	ARIES GHA	Time
00	178 37.7	N22 03.7	289 25.3	00
02	208 37.5	22 03.0	319 30.3	02
04	238 37.3	22 02.4	349 35.2	04
06	268 37.2	22 01.7	19 40.1	06
08	298 37.0	22 01.0	49 45.0	08
10	328 36.9	22 00.3	79 50.0	10
12	358 36.7	21 59.6	109 54.9	12
14	28 36.5	21 58.9	139 59.8	14
16	58 36.4	21 58.3	170 04.8	16
18	88 36.2	21 57.6	200 09.7	18
20	118 36.1	21 56.9	230 14.6	20
22	148 35.9	N21 56.2	260 19.5	22

Thursday, 13th July

Time	SUN GHA	Dec	ARIES GHA	Time
00	178 35.8	N21 55.5	290 24.5	00
02	208 35.6	21 54.7	320 29.4	02
04	238 35.5	21 54.0	350 34.3	04
06	268 35.3	21 53.3	20 39.3	06
08	298 35.2	21 52.6	50 44.2	08
10	328 35.0	21 51.9	80 49.1	10
12	358 34.9	21 51.2	110 54.0	12
14	28 34.7	21 50.5	140 59.0	14
16	58 34.6	21 49.7	171 03.9	16
18	88 34.4	21 49.0	201 08.8	18
20	118 34.3	21 48.3	231 13.8	20
22	148 34.1	N21 47.5	261 18.7	22

Friday, 14th July

Time	SUN GHA	Dec	ARIES GHA	Time
00	178 34.0	N21 46.8	291 23.6	00
02	208 33.9	21 46.1	321 28.5	02
04	238 33.7	21 45.3	351 33.5	04
06	268 33.6	21 44.6	21 38.4	06
08	298 33.4	21 43.8	51 43.3	08
10	328 33.3	21 43.1	81 48.3	10
12	358 33.2	21 42.4	111 53.2	12
14	28 33.0	21 41.6	141 58.1	14
16	58 32.9	21 40.8	172 03.0	16
18	88 32.8	21 40.1	202 08.0	18
20	118 32.6	21 39.3	232 12.9	20
22	148 32.5	N21 38.6	262 17.8	22

Saturday, 15th July

Time	SUN GHA	Dec	ARIES GHA	Time
00	178 32.3	N21 37.8	292 22.8	00
02	208 32.2	21 37.0	322 27.7	02
04	238 32.1	21 36.3	352 32.6	04
06	268 32.0	21 35.5	22 37.5	06
08	298 31.8	21 34.7	52 42.5	08
10	328 31.7	21 33.9	82 47.4	10
12	358 31.6	21 33.2	112 52.3	12
14	28 31.4	21 32.4	142 57.2	14
16	58 31.3	21 31.6	173 02.2	16
18	88 31.2	21 30.8	203 07.1	18
20	118 31.1	21 30.0	233 12.0	20
22	148 30.9	N21 29.2	263 17.0	22

NOTES

Sun & Aries GHA corrections for additional hour, minutes, and seconds on page E 94.
Correct Sun Declination by interpolation. For example see page E 4.

JULY 1995 — SUN & ARIES — GMT

Sunday, 16th July

Time	SUN GHA	Dec	ARIES GHA
00	178 30.8	N21 28.4	293 21.9
02	208 30.7	21 27.6	323 26.8
04	238 30.6	21 26.8	353 31.7
06	268 30.5	21 26.0	23 36.7
08	298 30.3	21 25.2	53 41.6
10	328 30.2	21 24.4	83 46.5
12	358 30.1	21 23.6	113 51.5
14	28 30.0	21 22.8	143 56.4
16	58 29.9	21 22.0	174 01.3
18	88 29.7	21 21.1	204 06.2
20	118 29.6	21 20.3	234 11.2
22	148 29.5	N21 19.5	264 16.1

Monday, 17th July

Time	SUN GHA	Dec	ARIES GHA
00	178 29.4	N21 18.7	294 21.0
02	208 29.3	21 17.8	324 26.0
04	238 29.2	21 17.0	354 30.9
06	268 29.1	21 16.2	24 35.8
08	298 29.0	21 15.3	54 40.7
10	328 28.9	21 14.5	84 45.7
12	358 28.7	21 13.6	114 50.6
14	28 28.6	21 12.8	144 55.5
16	58 28.5	21 12.0	175 00.5
18	88 28.4	21 11.1	205 05.4
20	118 28.3	21 10.3	235 10.3
22	148 28.2	N21 09.4	265 15.2

Tuesday, 18th July

Time	SUN GHA	Dec	ARIES GHA
00	178 28.1	N21 08.5	295 20.2
02	208 28.0	21 07.7	325 25.1
04	238 27.9	21 06.8	355 30.0
06	268 27.8	21 06.0	25 35.0
08	298 27.7	21 05.1	55 39.9
10	328 27.6	21 04.2	85 44.8
12	358 27.5	21 03.4	115 49.7
14	28 27.4	21 02.5	145 54.7
16	58 27.3	21 01.6	175 59.6
18	88 27.2	21 00.7	206 04.5
20	118 27.1	20 59.8	236 09.5
22	148 27.0	N20 59.0	266 14.4

Wednesday, 19th July

Time	SUN GHA	Dec	ARIES GHA
00	178 27.0	N20 58.1	296 19.3
02	208 26.9	20 57.2	326 24.2
04	238 26.8	20 56.3	356 29.2
06	268 26.7	20 55.4	26 34.1
08	298 26.6	20 54.5	56 39.0
10	328 26.5	20 53.6	86 43.9
12	358 26.4	20 52.7	116 48.9
14	28 26.3	20 51.8	146 53.8
16	58 26.3	20 50.9	176 58.7
18	88 26.2	20 50.0	207 03.7
20	118 26.1	20 49.1	237 08.6
22	148 26.0	N20 48.2	267 13.5

Thursday, 20th July

Time	SUN GHA	Dec	ARIES GHA
00	178 25.9	N20 47.2	297 18.4
02	208 25.8	20 46.3	327 23.4
04	238 25.8	20 45.3	357 28.3
06	268 25.7	20 44.5	27 33.2
08	298 25.6	20 43.6	57 38.2
10	328 25.5	20 42.6	87 43.1
12	358 25.5	20 41.7	117 48.0
14	28 25.4	20 40.8	147 52.9
16	58 25.3	20 39.8	177 57.9
18	88 25.2	20 38.9	208 02.8
20	118 25.2	20 38.0	238 07.7
22	148 25.1	N20 37.0	268 12.7

Friday, 21st July

Time	SUN GHA	Dec	ARIES GHA
00	178 25.0	N20 36.1	298 17.6
02	208 24.9	20 35.1	328 22.5
04	238 24.9	20 34.2	358 27.4
06	268 24.8	20 33.2	28 32.4
08	298 24.7	20 32.3	58 37.3
10	328 24.7	20 31.3	88 42.2
12	358 24.6	20 30.4	118 47.2
14	28 24.6	20 29.4	148 52.1
16	58 24.5	20 28.4	178 57.0
18	88 24.4	20 27.5	209 01.9
20	118 24.4	20 26.5	239 06.9
22	148 24.3	N20 25.5	269 11.8

Saturday, 22nd July

Time	SUN GHA	Dec	ARIES GHA
00	178 24.3	N20 24.5	299 16.7
02	208 24.2	20 23.6	329 21.7
04	238 24.1	20 22.6	359 26.6
06	268 24.1	20 21.6	29 31.5
08	298 24.0	20 20.6	59 36.4
10	328 24.0	20 19.6	89 41.4
12	358 23.9	20 18.7	119 46.3
14	28 23.9	20 17.7	149 51.2
16	58 23.8	20 16.7	179 56.1
18	88 23.8	20 15.7	210 01.1
20	118 23.7	20 14.7	240 06.0
22	148 23.7	N20 13.7	270 10.9

Sunday, 23rd July

Time	SUN GHA	Dec	ARIES GHA
00	178 23.6	N20 12.7	300 15.9
02	208 23.6	20 11.7	330 20.8
04	238 23.5	20 10.7	0 25.7
06	268 23.5	20 09.7	30 30.6
08	298 23.4	20 08.7	60 35.6
10	328 23.4	20 07.6	90 40.5
12	358 23.4	20 06.6	120 45.4
14	28 23.3	20 05.6	150 50.4
16	58 23.3	20 04.6	180 55.3
18	88 23.2	20 03.6	211 00.2
20	118 23.2	20 02.5	241 05.1
22	148 23.2	N20 01.5	271 10.1

Monday, 24th July

Time	SUN GHA	Dec	ARIES GHA
00	178 23.1	N20 00.5	301 15.0
02	208 23.1	19 59.4	331 19.9
04	238 23.1	19 58.4	1 24.9
06	268 23.0	19 57.4	31 29.8
08	298 23.0	19 56.3	61 34.7
10	328 23.0	19 55.3	91 39.6
12	358 22.9	19 54.3	121 44.6
14	28 22.9	19 53.2	151 49.5
16	58 22.9	19 52.2	181 54.4
18	88 22.9	19 51.1	211 59.4
20	118 22.8	19 50.1	242 04.3
22	148 22.8	N19 49.0	272 09.2

Tuesday, 25th July

Time	SUN GHA	Dec	ARIES GHA
00	178 22.8	N19 47.9	302 14.1
02	208 22.8	19 46.9	332 19.1
04	238 22.7	19 45.8	2 24.0
06	268 22.7	19 44.8	32 28.9
08	298 22.7	19 43.7	62 33.9
10	328 22.7	19 42.6	92 38.8
12	358 22.7	19 41.6	122 43.7
14	28 22.7	19 40.5	152 48.6
16	58 22.6	19 39.4	182 53.6
18	88 22.6	19 38.3	212 58.5
20	118 22.6	19 37.2	243 03.4
22	148 22.6	N19 36.2	273 08.3

Wednesday, 26th July

Time	SUN GHA	Dec	ARIES GHA
00	178 22.6	N19 35.1	303 13.3
02	208 22.6	19 34.0	333 18.2
04	238 22.6	19 32.9	3 23.1
06	268 22.6	19 31.8	33 28.1
08	298 22.6	19 30.7	63 33.0
10	328 22.6	19 29.6	93 37.9
12	358 22.6	19 28.5	123 42.8
14	28 22.5	19 27.4	153 47.8
16	58 22.5	19 26.3	183 52.7
18	88 22.5	19 25.2	213 57.6
20	118 22.5	19 24.1	244 02.6
22	148 22.5	N19 23.0	274 07.5

Thursday, 27th July

Time	SUN GHA	Dec	ARIES GHA
00	178 22.5	N19 21.9	304 12.4
02	208 22.5	19 20.8	334 17.3
04	238 22.6	19 19.7	4 22.3
06	268 22.6	19 18.5	34 27.2
08	298 22.6	19 17.4	64 32.1
10	328 22.6	19 16.3	94 37.1
12	358 22.6	19 15.2	124 42.0
14	28 22.6	19 14.0	154 46.9
16	58 22.6	19 12.9	184 51.8
18	88 22.6	19 11.8	214 56.8
20	118 22.6	19 10.7	245 01.7
22	148 22.6	N19 09.5	275 06.6

Friday, 28th July

Time	SUN GHA	Dec	ARIES GHA
00	178 22.6	N19 08.4	305 11.6
02	208 22.7	19 07.2	335 16.5
04	238 22.7	19 06.1	5 21.4
06	268 22.7	19 05.0	35 26.3
08	298 22.7	19 03.8	65 31.3
10	328 22.7	19 02.7	95 36.2
12	358 22.8	19 01.5	125 41.1
14	28 22.8	19 00.4	155 46.1
16	58 22.8	18 59.2	185 51.0
18	88 22.8	18 58.0	215 55.9
20	118 22.9	18 56.9	246 00.8
22	148 22.9	N18 55.7	276 05.8

Saturday, 29th July

Time	SUN GHA	Dec	ARIES GHA
00	178 22.9	N18 54.6	306 10.7
02	208 22.9	18 53.4	336 15.6
04	238 23.0	18 52.2	6 20.5
06	268 23.0	18 51.1	36 25.5
08	298 23.0	18 49.9	66 30.4
10	328 23.1	18 48.7	96 35.3
12	358 23.1	18 47.5	126 40.3
14	28 23.1	18 46.4	156 45.2
16	58 23.2	18 45.2	186 50.1
18	88 23.2	18 44.0	216 55.0
20	118 23.2	18 42.8	247 00.0
22	148 23.3	N18 41.6	277 04.9

Sunday, 30th July

Time	SUN GHA	Dec	ARIES GHA
00	178 23.3	N18 40.4	307 09.8
02	208 23.4	18 39.2	337 14.8
04	238 23.4	18 38.0	7 19.7
06	268 23.4	18 36.8	37 24.6
08	298 23.5	18 35.6	67 29.5
10	328 23.5	18 34.4	97 34.5
12	358 23.6	18 33.2	127 39.4
14	28 23.6	18 32.0	157 44.3
16	58 23.7	18 30.8	187 49.3
18	88 23.7	18 29.6	217 54.2
20	118 23.8	18 28.4	247 59.1
22	148 23.8	N18 27.2	278 04.0

Monday, 31st July

Time	SUN GHA	Dec	ARIES GHA
00	178 23.9	N18 26.0	308 09.0
02	208 23.9	18 24.8	338 13.9
04	238 24.0	18 23.6	8 18.8
06	268 24.0	N18 22.3	38 23.8
08	298 24.1	N18 21.1	68 28.7
10	328 24.2	18 19.9	98 33.6
12	358 24.2	18 18.7	128 38.5
14	28 24.3	N18 17.4	158 43.5
16	58 24.3	N18 16.2	188 48.4
18	88 24.4	18 15.0	218 53.3
20	118 24.5	18 13.7	248 58.3
22	148 24.5	N18 12.5	279 03.2

JULY 1995 · PLANETS · 0h GMT

VENUS — Note — JUPITER

Mer Pass h m	GHA ° '	Mean Var/hr 14°+	Dec ° '	Mean Var/hr	Corrections on Page E 101	GHA ° '	Mean Var/hr 15°+	Dec ° '	Mean Var/hr	Mer Pass h m
11 04	194 15.7	59.1	N 23 02.1	0.2	1 Sat	33 09.8	2.7	S 20 46.8	0.0	21 43
11 05	193 55.3	59.1	N 23 07.1	0.2	2 SUN	34 14.7	2.7	S 20 46.0	0.0	21 39
11 06	193 34.8	59.1	N 23 11.5	0.1	3 Mon	35 19.5	2.7	S 20 45.4	0.0	21 35
11 08	193 14.2	59.1	N 23 15.1	0.1	4 Tu	36 24.2	2.7	S 20 44.7	0.0	21 31
11 09	192 53.5	59.1	N 23 18.1	0.1	5 Wed	37 28.6	2.7	S 20 44.0	0.0	21 26
11 10	192 32.7	59.1	N 23 20.4	0.1	6 Th	38 33.0	2.7	S 20 43.4	0.0	21 22
11 12	192 11.9	59.1	N 23 22.1	0.0	7 Fri	39 37.1	2.7	S 20 42.8	0.0	21 18
11 13	191 51.0	59.1	N 23 23.0	0.0	8 Sat	40 41.1	2.7	S 20 42.3	0.0	21 13
11 15	191 30.1	59.1	N 23 23.3	0.0	9 SUN	41 44.9	2.7	S 20 41.7	0.0	21 09
11 16	191 09.2	59.1	N 23 22.9	0.0	10 Mon	42 48.6	2.6	S 20 41.2	0.0	21 05
11 17	190 48.3	59.1	N 23 21.8	0.1	11 Tu	43 52.1	2.6	S 20 40.7	0.0	21 01
11 19	190 27.4	59.1	N 23 20.0	0.1	12 Wed	44 55.4	2.6	S 20 40.2	0.0	20 57
11 20	190 06.5	59.1	N 23 17.5	0.1	13 Th	45 58.6	2.6	S 20 39.8	0.0	20 52
11 22	189 45.6	59.1	N 23 14.3	0.2	14 Fri	47 01.6	2.6	S 20 39.4	0.0	20 48
11 23	189 24.8	59.1	N 23 10.5	0.2	15 Sat	48 04.4	2.6	S 20 39.0	0.0	20 44
11 24	189 04.1	59.1	N 23 05.9	0.2	16 SUN	49 07.0	2.6	S 20 38.6	0.0	20 40
11 26	188 43.4	59.1	N 23 00.7	0.2	17 Mon	50 09.5	2.6	S 20 38.3	0.0	20 36
11 27	188 22.8	59.1	N 22 54.8	0.3	18 Tu	51 11.7	2.6	S 20 38.0	0.0	20 32
11 28	188 02.3	59.2	N 22 48.2	0.3	19 Wed	52 13.8	2.6	S 20 37.7	0.0	20 28
11 30	187 42.0	59.2	N 22 41.0	0.3	20 Th	53 15.7	2.6	S 20 37.5	0.0	20 23
11 31	187 21.7	59.2	N 22 33.0	0.4	21 Fri	54 17.4	2.6	S 20 37.3	0.0	20 19
11 33	187 01.6	59.2	N 22 24.4	0.4	22 Sat	55 19.0	2.6	S 20 37.1	0.0	20 15
11 34	186 41.6	59.2	N 22 15.2	0.4	23 SUN	56 20.3	2.5	S 20 37.0	0.0	20 11
11 35	186 21.9	59.2	N 22 05.3	0.4	24 Mon	57 21.5	2.5	S 20 36.8	0.0	20 07
11 36	186 02.2	59.2	N 21 54.7	0.5	25 Tu	58 22.4	2.5	S 20 36.8	0.0	20 03
11 38	185 42.8	59.2	N 21 43.6	0.5	26 Wed	59 23.2	2.5	S 20 36.7	0.0	19 59
11 39	185 23.5	59.2	N 21 31.7	0.5	27 Th	60 23.8	2.5	S 20 36.7	0.0	19 55
11 40	185 04.5	59.2	N 21 19.3	0.5	28 Fri	61 24.1	2.5	S 20 36.7	0.0	19 51
11 42	184 45.7	59.2	N 21 06.2	0.6	29 Sat	62 24.3	2.5	S 20 36.8	0.0	19 47
11 43	184 27.0	59.2	N 20 52.5	0.6	30 SUN	63 24.3	2.5	S 20 36.8	0.0	19 43
11 44	184 08.7	59.2	N 20 38.2	0.6	31 Mon	64 24.1	2.5	S 20 36.9	0.0	19 39

VENUS, Av. Mag. -3.9
S.H.A. July
5 270; 10 264; 15 257; 20 250; 25 244; 30 237.

JUPITER, Av. Mag. -2.4
S.H.A. July
5 115; 10 115; 15 116; 20 116; 25 116; 30 116.

MARS — Note — SATURN

Mer Pass h m	GHA ° '	Mean Var/hr 15°+	Dec ° '	Mean Var/hr	Corrections on Page E 101	GHA ° '	Mean Var/hr 15°+	Dec ° '	Mean Var/hr	Mer Pass h m
16 43	108 58.8	1.2	N 5 17.9	0.6	1 Sat	282 34.9	2.4	S 4 01.7	0.0	05 09
16 41	109 27.7	1.2	N 5 04.0	0.6	2 SUN	283 33.5	2.4	S 4 01.8	0.0	05 05
16 39	109 56.6	1.2	N 4 50.0	0.6	3 Mon	284 32.2	2.5	S 4 01.9	0.0	05 01
16 37	110 25.3	1.2	N 4 36.0	0.6	4 Tu	285 31.0	2.5	S 4 02.0	0.0	04 57
16 35	110 54.0	1.2	N 4 21.9	0.6	5 Wed	286 29.8	2.5	S 4 02.2	0.0	04 53
16 33	111 22.5	1.2	N 4 07.7	0.6	6 Th	287 28.8	2.5	S 4 02.4	0.0	04 49
16 31	111 51.0	1.2	N 3 53.5	0.6	7 Fri	288 27.8	2.5	S 4 02.6	0.0	04 45
16 29	112 19.4	1.2	N 3 39.3	0.6	8 Sat	289 27.0	2.5	S 4 02.9	0.0	04 41
16 28	112 47.6	1.2	N 3 25.0	0.6	9 SUN	290 26.2	2.5	S 4 03.3	0.0	04 37
16 26	113 15.8	1.2	N 3 10.6	0.6	10 Mon	291 25.5	2.5	S 4 03.6	0.0	04 34
16 24	113 43.9	1.2	N 2 56.2	0.6	11 Tu	292 24.9	2.5	S 4 04.0	0.0	04 30
16 22	114 11.9	1.2	N 2 41.7	0.6	12 Wed	293 24.4	2.5	S 4 04.5	0.0	04 26
16 20	114 39.8	1.2	N 2 27.2	0.6	13 Th	294 24.0	2.5	S 4 04.9	0.0	04 22
16 18	115 07.7	1.2	N 2 12.6	0.6	14 Fri	295 23.7	2.5	S 4 05.5	0.0	04 18
16 16	115 35.4	1.2	N 1 58.0	0.6	15 Sat	296 23.5	2.5	S 4 06.0	0.0	04 14
16 15	116 03.0	1.2	N 1 43.3	0.6	16 SUN	297 23.4	2.5	S 4 06.6	0.0	04 10
16 13	116 30.6	1.1	N 1 28.6	0.6	17 Mon	298 23.4	2.5	S 4 07.3	0.0	04 06
16 11	116 58.0	1.1	N 1 13.9	0.6	18 Tu	299 23.4	2.5	S 4 07.9	0.0	04 02
16 09	117 25.4	1.1	N 0 59.1	0.6	19 Wed	300 23.6	2.5	S 4 08.6	0.0	03 58
16 07	117 52.7	1.1	N 0 44.3	0.6	20 Th	301 23.8	2.5	S 4 09.4	0.0	03 54
16 05	118 19.8	1.1	N 0 29.4	0.6	21 Fri	302 24.1	2.5	S 4 10.2	0.0	03 50
16 04	118 46.9	1.1	N 0 14.6	0.6	22 Sat	303 24.5	2.5	S 4 11.0	0.0	03 46
16 02	119 13.8	1.1	S 0 00.4	0.6	23 SUN	304 25.0	2.5	S 4 11.8	0.0	03 42
16 00	119 40.7	1.1	S 0 15.3	0.6	24 Mon	305 25.6	2.5	S 4 12.7	0.0	03 38
15 58	120 07.5	1.1	S 0 30.3	0.6	25 Tu	306 26.3	2.5	S 4 13.7	0.0	03 34
15 57	120 34.1	1.1	S 0 45.4	0.6	26 Wed	307 27.1	2.5	S 4 14.6	0.0	03 30
15 55	121 00.7	1.1	S 1 00.4	0.6	27 Th	308 27.9	2.5	S 4 15.6	0.0	03 26
15 53	121 27.2	1.1	S 1 15.5	0.6	28 Fri	309 28.8	2.5	S 4 16.7	0.0	03 22
15 51	121 53.5	1.1	S 1 30.6	0.6	29 Sat	310 29.9	2.5	S 4 17.7	0.0	03 17
15 50	122 19.8	1.1	S 1 45.7	0.6	30 SUN	311 31.0	2.5	S 4 18.8	0.1	03 13
15 48	122 46.0	1.1	S 2 00.9	0.6	31 Mon	312 32.1	2.6	S 4 20.0	0.0	03 09

MARS, Av. Mag. +1.3
S.H.A. July
5 188; 10 186; 15 183; 20 181; 25 178; 30 175.

SATURN, Av. Mag. +1.0
S.H.A. July
5 4; 10 4; 15 4; 20 4; 25 4; 30 4.

JULY 1995 — MOON

Day	GMT hr	GHA ° '	Mean Var/hr 14°+	Dec ° '	Mean Var/hr '	Day	GMT hr	GHA ° '	Mean Var/hr 14°+	Dec ° '	Mean Var/hr '
1 Sat	0	145 52.6	32.4	N 12 29.1	8.0	17 Mon	0	300 17.3	31.1	N 0 43.7	10.9
	6	233 06.6	32.4	N 11 40.8	8.4		6	27 24.3	31.4	N 1 49.3	10.8
	12	320 21.0	32.5	N 10 50.5	8.8		12	114 32.7	31.6	N 2 54.1	10.6
	18	47 35.8	32.5	N 9 58.2	9.0		18	201 42.2	31.7	N 3 57.8	10.4
2 Sun	0	134 50.8	32.5	N 9 04.2	9.3	18 Tu	0	288 52.8	31.9	N 5 00.3	10.2
	6	222 06.1	32.6	N 8 08.4	9.6		6	16 04.1	32.0	N 6 01.5	9.9
	12	309 21.5	32.5	N 7 11.2	9.8		12	103 16.2	32.1	N 7 01.3	9.7
	18	36 36.8	32.5	N 6 12.5	10.0		18	190 28.9	32.2	N 7 59.4	9.4
3 Mon	0	123 52.0	32.5	N 5 12.6	10.1	19 Wed	0	277 41.9	32.2	N 8 55.8	9.0
	6	211 06.9	32.4	N 4 11.5	10.4		6	4 55.3	32.2	N 9 50.3	8.7
	12	298 21.4	32.3	N 3 09.4	10.5		12	92 08.8	32.3	N 10 42.9	8.3
	18	25 35.3	32.2	N 2 06.5	10.6		18	179 22.3	32.2	N 11 33.5	8.1
4 Tu	0	112 48.4	32.0	N 1 02.9	10.7	20 Th	0	266 35.8	32.2	N 12 21.9	7.7
	6	200 00.6	31.9	S 0 01.2	10.8		6	353 49.1	32.2	N 13 08.0	7.3
	12	287 11.7	31.7	S 1 05.7	10.7		12	81 02.2	32.2	N 13 51.9	6.8
	18	14 21.6	31.4	S 2 10.4	10.8		18	168 15.0	32.1	N 14 33.3	6.5
5 Wed	0	101 30.1	31.1	S 3 15.2	10.7	21 Fri	0	255 27.4	32.0	N 15 12.2	6.1
	6	188 36.9	30.8	S 4 19.7	10.7		6	342 39.3	31.9	N 15 48.5	5.6
	12	275 41.9	30.5	S 5 23.9	10.6		12	69 50.8	31.8	N 16 22.1	5.1
	18	2 45.0	30.2	S 6 27.6	10.5		18	157 01.8	31.8	N 16 53.0	4.6
6 Th	0	89 45.9	29.7	S 7 30.5	10.3	22 Sat	0	244 12.3	31.7	N 17 21.2	4.1
	6	176 44.6	29.3	S 8 32.3	10.1		6	331 22.2	31.6	N 17 46.4	3.6
	12	263 40.8	28.9	S 9 33.0	9.8		12	58 31.7	31.5	N 18 07.7	3.2
	18	350 34.4	28.5	S 10 32.2	9.6		18	145 40.6	31.4	N 18 28.1	2.7
7 Fri	0	77 25.2	28.0	S 11 29.6	9.2	23 Sun	0	232 49.1	31.4	N 18 44.4	2.2
	6	164 13.2	27.4	S 12 25.1	8.8		6	319 57.1	31.3	N 18 57.6	1.6
	12	250 58.3	27.0	S 13 18.3	8.4		12	47 04.7	31.2	N 19 07.7	1.1
	18	337 40.5	26.5	S 14 09.0	7.9		18	134 12.0	31.2	N 19 14.7	0.6
8 Sat	0	64 19.6	26.0	S 14 56.8	7.4	24 Mon	0	221 19.0	31.1	N 19 18.5	0.1
	6	150 55.7	25.5	S 15 41.6	6.9		6	308 25.8	31.1	N 19 19.1	0.5
	12	237 28.8	25.0	S 16 23.0	6.2		12	35 32.4	31.1	N 19 16.5	1.0
	18	323 59.0	24.5	S 17 00.7	5.5		18	122 39.0	31.1	N 19 10.7	1.5
9 Sun	0	50 26.4	24.1	S 17 34.4	4.8	25 Tu	0	209 45.6	31.1	N 19 01.7	2.0
	6	136 51.3	23.7	S 18 04.0	4.1		6	296 52.3	31.1	N 18 49.6	2.6
	12	223 13.8	23.3	S 18 29.2	3.4		12	23 59.1	31.2	N 18 34.2	3.1
	18	309 34.1	23.1	S 18 49.7	2.6		18	111 06.1	31.2	N 18 15.8	3.6
10 Mon	0	35 52.6	22.9	S 19 05.4	1.7	26 Wed	0	198 13.5	31.3	N 17 54.3	4.2
	6	122 09.6	22.6	S 19 16.0	0.8		6	285 21.2	31.3	N 17 29.7	4.6
	12	208 25.4	22.5	S 19 21.6	0.0		12	12 29.3	31.4	N 17 02.2	5.1
	18	294 40.5	22.4	S 19 22.0	0.8		18	99 37.8	31.5	N 16 31.8	5.6
11 Tu	0	20 55.2	22.5	S 19 17.2	1.8	27 Th	0	186 46.8	31.5	N 15 58.6	6.1
	6	107 10.0	22.6	S 19 07.1	2.6		6	273 56.4	31.6	N 15 22.6	6.5
	12	193 25.2	22.7	S 18 51.9	3.5		12	1 06.5	31.8	N 14 44.0	6.9
	18	279 41.3	22.9	S 18 31.6	4.3		18	88 17.1	31.8	N 14 02.9	7.3
12 Wed	0	5 58.6	23.1	S 18 06.3	5.0	28 Fri	0	175 28.2	32.0	N 13 19.3	7.7
	6	92 17.5	23.4	S 17 36.3	5.8		6	262 39.8	32.1	N 12 33.4	8.1
	12	178 38.3	23.8	S 17 01.8	6.5		12	349 52.0	32.1	N 11 45.2	8.4
	18	265 01.2	24.2	S 16 23.0	7.2		18	77 04.5	32.2	N 10 55.0	8.8
13 Th	0	351 26.5	24.7	S 15 40.1	7.8	29 Sat	0	164 17.5	32.2	N 10 02.8	9.1
	6	77 54.4	25.1	S 14 53.5	8.4		6	251 30.7	32.3	N 9 08.8	9.3
	12	164 25.0	25.6	S 14 03.4	8.9		12	338 44.3	32.3	N 8 13.1	9.6
	18	250 58.5	26.1	S 13 10.2	9.4		18	65 58.0	32.3	N 7 15.9	9.8
14 Fri	0	337 34.8	26.6	S 12 14.3	9.7	30 Sun	0	153 11.8	32.3	N 6 17.3	10.1
	6	64 14.1	27.0	S 11 15.8	10.1		6	240 25.6	32.3	N 5 17.4	10.2
	12	150 56.2	27.5	S 10 15.2	10.4		12	327 39.2	32.3	N 4 16.3	10.4
	18	237 41.2	28.0	S 9 12.8	10.7		18	54 52.6	32.2	N 3 14.4	10.4
15 Sat	0	324 29.0	28.5	S 8 08.9	10.9	31 Mon	0	142 05.6	32.1	N 2 11.7	10.6
	6	51 19.5	28.9	S 7 03.8	11.1		6	229 18.1	32.0	N 1 08.3	10.7
	12	138 12.6	29.2	S 5 57.7	11.2		12	316 30.0	31.9	N 0 04.5	10.7
	18	225 08.1	29.6	S 4 51.0	11.2		18	43 41.1	31.6	S 0 59.6	10.7
16 Sun	0	312 06.0	30.0	S 3 43.9	11.2						
	6	39 06.0	30.4	S 2 36.7	11.2						
	12	126 08.0	30.6	S 1 29.5	11.2						
	18	213 11.8	30.9	S 0 22.7	11.0						

NOTE Moon GHA corrections for additional hours, minutes, and seconds on page E 96.
Moon Declination corrections on page E 99. Mean Var/Hr value needed for both corrections.

JULY

AUGUST 1995 — SUN & MOON — GMT

SUN

Day of Yr	Mth	Week	Equation of Time 0h (m s)	Equation of Time 12h (m s)	Transit (h m)	Semi-diam (′)	Lat 52°N Twilight (h m)	Lat 52°N Sunrise (h m)	Lat 52°N Sunset (h m)	Lat 52°N Twilight (h m)
213	1	Tu	+06 22	+06 20	12 06	15.8	03 39	04 21	19 51	20 32
214	2	Wed	+06 18	+06 16	12 06	15.8	03 41	04 22	19 49	20 30
215	3	Th	+06 14	+06 12	12 06	15.8	03 43	04 24	19 47	20 28
216	4	Fri	+06 09	+06 07	12 06	15.8	03 45	04 25	19 46	20 26
217	5	Sat	+06 04	+06 01	12 06	15.8	03 47	04 27	19 44	20 24
218	6	Sun	+05 58	+05 55	12 06	15.8	03 48	04 29	19 42	20 22
219	7	Mon	+05 51	+05 48	12 06	15.8	03 50	04 30	19 40	20 20
220	8	Tu	+05 44	+05 40	12 06	15.8	03 52	04 32	19 38	20 18
221	9	Wed	+05 36	+05 32	12 06	15.8	03 54	04 33	19 37	20 16
222	10	Th	+05 28	+05 24	12 05	15.8	03 56	04 35	19 35	20 14
223	11	Fri	+05 19	+05 14	12 05	15.8	03 57	04 37	19 33	20 12
224	12	Sat	+05 10	+05 05	12 05	15.8	03 59	04 38	19 31	20 10
225	13	Sun	+05 00	+04 54	12 05	15.8	04 01	04 40	19 29	20 07
226	14	Mon	+04 49	+04 43	12 05	15.8	04 03	04 41	19 27	20 05
227	15	Tu	+04 38	+04 32	12 05	15.8	04 05	04 43	19 25	20 03
228	16	Wed	+04 26	+04 20	12 04	15.8	04 07	04 45	19 23	20 01
229	17	Th	+04 14	+04 08	12 04	15.8	04 08	04 46	19 21	19 58
230	18	Fri	+04 01	+03 55	12 04	15.8	04 10	04 48	19 19	19 56
231	19	Sat	+03 48	+03 41	12 04	15.8	04 12	04 50	19 17	19 54
232	20	Sun	+03 34	+03 27	12 03	15.8	04 14	04 51	19 15	19 52
233	21	Mon	+03 20	+03 13	12 03	15.8	04 16	04 53	19 13	19 49
234	22	Tu	+03 06	+02 58	12 03	15.8	04 17	04 54	19 10	19 47
235	23	Wed	+02 50	+02 43	12 03	15.8	04 19	04 56	19 08	19 45
236	24	Th	+02 35	+02 27	12 02	15.8	04 21	04 58	19 06	19 42
237	25	Fri	+02 19	+02 11	12 02	15.8	04 23	04 59	19 04	19 40
238	26	Sat	+02 03	+01 54	12 02	15.9	04 25	05 01	19 02	19 38
239	27	Sun	+01 46	+01 37	12 02	15.9	04 26	05 03	19 00	19 35
240	28	Mon	+01 29	+01 20	12 01	15.9	04 28	05 04	18 57	19 33
241	29	Tu	+01 11	+01 02	12 01	15.9	04 30	05 06	18 55	19 31
242	30	Wed	+00 53	+00 44	12 01	15.9	04 32	05 08	18 53	19 28
243	31	Th	+00 35	+00 26	12 00	15.9	04 34	05 09	18 51	19 26

Lat Corr to Sunrise, Sunset etc

Lat (°)	Twilight (h m)	Sunrise (h m)	Sunset (h m)	Twilight (h m)
N60	-0 43	-0 30	+0 30	+0 43
55	-0 14	-0 10	+0 10	+0 14
50	+0 08	+0 06	-0 06	-0 08
45	+0 24	+0 18	-0 18	-0 24
N40	+0 37	+0 28	-0 28	-0 37
35	+0 48	+0 36	-0 36	-0 48
30	+0 57	+0 44	-0 44	-0 57
25	+1 05	+0 51	-0 51	-1 05
N20	+1 12	+0 57	-0 57	-1 12
15	+1 18	+1 02	-1 02	-1 18
10	+1 24	+1 08	-1 08	-1 24
5	+1 29	+1 13	-1 13	-1 29
0	+1 35	+1 18	-1 18	-1 35
S 5	+1 40	+1 23	-1 23	-1 40
10	+1 45	+1 28	-1 28	-1 45
15	+1 49	+1 33	-1 33	-1 49
S20	+1 54	+1 39	-1 39	-1 54
25	+1 59	+1 45	-1 45	-1 59
30	+2 04	+1 51	-1 51	-2 04
35	+2 10	+1 58	-1 58	-2 10
S40	+2 16	+2 06	-2 06	-2 16
45	+2 22	+2 15	-2 15	-2 22
50	+2 30	+2 26	-2 26	-2 30

NOTES

Lat corrections are for mid-month.
Equation of Time is the excess of Mean Time over Apparent Time.

MOON

Day of Yr	Mth	Week	Age (days)	Transit (Upper) (h m)	Diff (m)	Semi-diam (′)	Hor Par (′)	Lat 52°N Moonrise (h m)	Lat 52°N Moonset (h m)
213	1	Tu	05	15 47	49	15.6	57.1	09 56	21 27
214	2	Wed	06	16 36	51	15.7	57.7	11 08	21 53
215	3	Th	07	17 27	54	15.9	58.3	12 21	22 24
216	4	Fri	08	18 21	57	16.1	58.9	13 35	23 01
217	5	Sat	09	19 18	60	16.2	59.5	14 47	23 46
218	6	Sun	10	20 18	60	16.3	60.0	15 54	— —
219	7	Mon	11	21 18	60	16.4	60.3	16 53	00 41
220	8	Tu	12	22 18	59	16.5	60.4	17 43	01 46
221	9	Wed	13	23 17	55	16.4	60.3	18 24	02 59
222	10	Th	14	24 12	—	16.3	60.0	18 59	04 17
223	11	Fri	15	00 12	54	16.2	59.4	19 29	05 36
224	12	Sat	16	01 06	50	16.0	58.7	19 55	06 54
225	13	Sun	17	01 56	49	15.8	57.9	20 20	08 09
226	14	Mon	18	02 45	47	15.5	57.0	20 45	09 22
227	15	Tu	19	03 32	47	15.3	56.2	21 11	10 32
228	16	Wed	20	04 19	47	15.1	55.5	21 39	11 39
229	17	Th	21	05 06	47	15.0	54.9	22 11	12 43
230	18	Fri	22	05 53	47	14.8	54.5	22 47	13 43
231	19	Sat	23	06 40	48	14.8	54.3	23 29	14 38
232	20	Sun	24	07 28	47	14.8	54.2	— —	15 28
233	21	Mon	25	08 15	48	14.8	54.3	00 16	16 12
234	22	Tu	26	09 03	47	14.8	54.5	01 10	16 50
235	23	Wed	27	09 50	47	14.9	54.8	02 08	17 23
236	24	Th	28	10 37	47	15.0	55.2	03 11	17 53
237	25	Fri	29	11 24	46	15.2	55.7	04 17	18 19
238	26	Sat	00	12 10	47	15.3	56.2	05 25	18 44
239	27	Sun	01	12 57	48	15.5	56.7	06 34	19 08
240	28	Mon	02	13 45	48	15.6	57.3	07 45	19 33
241	29	Tu	03	14 33	51	15.7	57.7	08 58	19 59
242	30	Wed	04	15 24	53	15.8	58.2	10 11	20 29
243	31	Th	05	16 17	56	16.0	58.6	11 25	21 03

Phases of the Moon

		d h m
☾	First Quarter	4 03 16
○	Full Moon	10 18 15
☽	Last Quarter	18 03 04
●	New Moon	26 04 31
	Perigee	8 14
	Apogee	20 12

NOTES

Diff equals daily change in transit time.
To correct Moonrise, Moonset, or Transit times for Latitude and/or Longitude see page E 100. For further information about these tables see page E 4. For Arc to Time correction see page E 91.

AUGUST 1995   STARS   0h GMT August 1

No	Name	Mag	Transit h m	Dec ° '	GHA ° '	RA h m	SHA ° '
	ARIES..............		3 23		309 08.1		
1	Alpheratz..........	2.2	3 31	N 29 04.0	307 05.2	0 08	357 57.1
2	Ankaa..............	2.4	3 49	S 42 19.5	302 36.7	0 26	353 28.6
3	Schedar............	2.5	4 03	N 56 30.7	299 03.5	0 40	349 55.4
4	Diphda	2.2	4 06	S 18 00.4	298 17.2	0 43	349 09.1
5	Achernar..........	0.6	5 00	S 57 15.2	284 44.6	1 38	335 36.5
6	POLARIS	2.1	5 51	N 89 14.4	272 05.6	2 28	322 57.5
7	Hamal..............	2.2	5 30	N 23 26.5	277 23.9	2 07	328 15.8
8	Acamar.............	3.1	6 21	S 40 19.1	264 36.6	2 58	315 28.5
9	Menkar	2.8	6 24	N 4 04.4	263 37.2	3 02	314 29.1
10	Mirfak	1.9	6 46	N 49 50.5	258 07.7	3 24	308 59.6
11	Aldebaran........	1.1	7 58	N 16 30.0	240 13.0	4 36	291 04.9
12	Rigel................	0.3	8 36	S 8 12.4	230 33.2	5 14	281 25.1
13	Capella	0.2	8 38	N 45 59.4	230 02.6	5 16	280 54.5
14	Bellatrix	1.7	8 47	N 6 20.7	227 54.7	5 25	278 46.6
15	Elnath.............	1.8	8 48	N 28 36.1	227 37.9	5 26	278 29.8
16	Alnilam	1.8	8 58	S 1 12.3	225 08.3	5 36	276 00.2
17	Betelgeuse.......0.1-1.2		9 17	N 7 24.3	220 24.1	5 55	271 16.0
18	Canopus...........-0.9		9 46	S 52 41.5	213 10.6	6 24	264 02.5
19	Sirius ....-1.6		10 07	S 16 42.6	207 53.9	6 45	258 45.8
20	Adhara	1.6	10 20	S 28 57.9	204 31.5	6 58	255 23.4
21	Castor..............	1.6	10 56	N 31 53.8	195 33.5	7 34	246 25.4
22	Procyon	0.5	11 01	N 5 14.1	194 22.1	7 39	245 14.0
23	Pollux	1.2	11 07	N 28 02.1	192 52.6	7 45	243 44.5
24	Avior	1.7	11 44	S 59 29.7	183 32.1	8 22	234 24.0
25	Suhail	2.2	12 29	S 43 24.9	172 10.8	9 08	223 02.7
26	Miaplacidus	1.8	12 35	S 69 42.0	170 51.4	9 13	221 43.3
27	Alphard	2.2	12 49	S 8 38.4	167 17.7	9 27	218 09.6
28	Regulus	1.3	13 29	N 11 59.3	157 06.2	10 08	207 58.1
29	Dubhe	2.0	14 25	N 61 46.6	143 16.9	11 03	194 08.8
30	Denebola	2.2	15 10	N 14 35.9	131 55.7	11 49	182 47.6
31	Gienah	2.8	15 36	S 17 31.1	125 14.4	12 16	176 06.3
32	Acrux..............	1.1	15 47	S 63 04.7	122 32.8	12 26	173 24.7
33	Gacrux............	1.6	15 52	S 57 05.5	121 24.3	12 31	172 16.2
34	Mimosa	1.5	16 08	S 59 40.1	117 16.1	12 47	168 08.0
35	Alioth	1.7	16 15	N 55 59.3	115 40.9	12 54	166 32.8
36	Spica................	1.2	16 46	S 11 08.3	107 53.7	13 25	158 45.6
37	Alkaid..............	1.9	17 08	N 49 20.4	102 17.8	13 47	153 09.7
38	Hadar	0.9	17 24	S 60 21.3	98 15.2	14 04	149 07.1
39	Menkent	2.3	17 27	S 36 21.0	97 31.6	14 06	148 23.5
40	Arcturus...........	0.2	17 36	N 19 12.5	95 16.2	14 15	146 08.1
41	Rigil Kent.	0.1	18 00	S 60 49.2	89 18.2	14 39	140 10.1
42	Zuben'ubi	2.9	18 11	S 16 01.4	86 28.4	14 51	137 20.3
43	Kochab............	2.2	18 11	N 74 10.8	86 27.9	14 51	137 19.8
44	Alphecca	2.3	18 55	N 26 44.1	75 30.5	15 35	126 22.4
45	Antares	1.2	19 49	S 26 25.3	61 50.7	16 29	112 42.6
46	Atria	1.9	20 08	S 69 01.3	57 04.3	16 48	107 56.2
47	Sabik	2.6	20 30	S 15 43.0	51 35.9	17 10	102 27.8
48	Shaula	1.7	20 53	S 37 06.0	45 48.0	17 33	96 39.9
49	Rasalhague	2.1	20 55	N 12 34.1	45 26.8	17 35	96 18.7
50	Eltanin.............	2.4	21 16	N 51 29.8	40 00.1	17 57	90 52.0
51	Kaus Aust.	2.0	21 44	S 34 23.1	33 09.4	18 24	84 01.3
52	Vega................	0.1	21 57	N 38 47.1	29 55.8	18 37	80 47.7
53	Nunki	2.1	22 15	S 26 18.0	25 22.7	18 55	76 14.6
54	Altair	0.9	23 10	N 8 51.7	11 29.1	19 51	62 21.0
55	Peacock	2.1	23 45	S 56 44.8	2 47.9	20 25	53 39.8
56	Deneb	1.3	0 05	N 45 16.1	358 48.2	20 41	49 40.1
57	Enif	2.5	1 07	N 9 51.5	343 08.1	21 44	34 00.0
58	Al Na'ir.............	2.2	1 31	S 46 58.7	337 08.2	22 08	28 00.1
59	Fomalhaut	1.3	2 21	S 29 38.5	324 46.5	22 57	15 38.4
60	Markab	2.6	2 28	N 15 11.1	322 59.5	23 05	13 51.4

Star Transit Corr Table

Date	Corr h m	Date	Corr h m
1	−0 00	17	−1 03
2	−0 04	18	−1 07
3	−0 08	19	−1 11
4	−0 12	20	−1 15
5	−0 16	21	−1 19
6	−0 20	22	−1 23
7	−0 24	23	−1 27
8	−0 28	24	−1 30
9	−0 31	25	−1 34
10	−0 35	26	−1 38
11	−0 39	27	−1 42
12	−0 43	28	−1 46
13	−0 47	29	−1 50
14	−0 51	30	−1 54
15	−0 55	31	−1 58
16	−0 59		

STAR TRANSIT

To find the approx time of transit of a star for any day of the month use above table. All corrections are subtractive.

If the quantity taken from the table is greater than the time of transit for the first of the month, add 23h 56min to the time of transit before subtracting the correction.

Example: What time will Deneb (No 56) transit the Meridian on August 30?

	h min
Transit on Aug 1	00 05
	+23 56
	24 01
Corr for Aug 30	−01 54
Transit on Aug 30	22 17

AUGUST DIARY

d h
1 15 Mars 2° N of Moon
2 22 Jupiter stationary
5 20 Jupiter 2° S of Moon
9 04 Neptune 5° S of Moon
9 12 Uranus 6° S of Moon
9 16 Mercury 1.1° N of Regulus
13 11 Saturn 5° S of Moon
21 00 Venus in superior conjunction
27 13 Mars 2° N of Spica
28 07 Mercury 1.8° N of Moon
30 04 Mars 0.2° N of Moon

NOTES

Star declinations may be used as is for the whole month. To correct GHA for day, hour, minute and second see page E 92 and for further explanation of this table see page E 4.

AUGUST

AUGUST 1995   SUN & ARIES   GMT

Tuesday, 1st August

Time	SUN GHA	Dec	ARIES GHA
00	178 24.6	N18 11.2	309 08.1
02	208 24.7	18 10.0	339 13.0
04	238 24.7	18 08.8	9 18.0
06	268 24.8	18 07.5	39 22.9
08	298 24.9	18 06.3	69 27.8
10	328 25.0	18 05.0	99 32.7
12	358 25.0	18 03.8	129 37.7
14	28 25.1	18 02.5	159 42.6
16	58 25.2	18 01.3	189 47.5
18	88 25.2	18 00.0	219 52.5
20	118 25.3	17 58.7	249 57.4
22	148 25.4	N17 57.5	280 02.3

Wednesday, 2nd August

Time	SUN GHA	Dec	ARIES GHA
00	178 25.5	N17 56.2	310 07.2
02	208 25.6	17 54.9	340 12.2
04	238 25.6	17 53.7	10 17.1
06	268 25.7	17 52.4	40 22.0
08	298 25.8	17 51.1	70 27.0
10	328 25.9	17 49.9	100 31.9
12	358 26.0	17 48.6	130 36.8
14	28 26.1	17 47.3	160 41.7
16	58 26.1	17 46.0	190 46.7
18	88 26.2	17 44.7	220 51.6
20	118 26.3	17 43.5	250 56.5
22	148 26.4	N17 42.2	281 01.5

Thursday, 3rd August

Time	SUN GHA	Dec	ARIES GHA
00	178 26.5	N17 40.9	311 06.4
02	208 26.6	17 39.6	341 11.3
04	238 26.7	17 38.3	11 16.2
06	268 26.8	17 37.0	41 21.2
08	298 26.9	17 35.7	71 26.1
10	328 27.0	17 34.4	101 31.0
12	358 27.1	17 33.1	131 36.0
14	28 27.2	17 31.8	161 40.9
16	58 27.3	17 30.5	191 45.8
18	88 27.4	17 29.2	221 50.7
20	118 27.5	17 27.9	251 55.7
22	148 27.6	N17 26.6	282 00.6

Friday, 4th August

Time	SUN GHA	Dec	ARIES GHA
00	178 27.7	N17 25.3	312 05.5
02	208 27.8	17 23.9	342 10.5
04	238 27.9	17 22.6	12 15.4
06	268 28.0	17 21.3	42 20.3
08	298 28.1	17 20.0	72 25.2
10	328 28.2	17 18.7	102 30.2
12	358 28.3	17 17.3	132 35.1
14	28 28.5	17 16.0	162 40.0
16	58 28.6	17 14.7	192 44.9
18	88 28.7	17 13.4	222 49.9
20	118 28.8	17 12.0	252 54.8
22	148 28.9	N17 10.7	282 59.7

Saturday, 5th August

Time	SUN GHA	Dec	ARIES GHA
00	178 29.0	N17 09.4	313 04.7
02	208 29.2	17 08.0	343 09.6
04	238 29.3	17 06.7	13 14.5
06	268 29.4	17 05.3	43 19.4
08	298 29.5	17 04.0	73 24.4
10	328 29.6	17 02.7	103 29.3
12	358 29.8	17 01.3	133 34.2
14	28 29.9	17 00.0	163 39.2
16	58 30.0	16 58.6	193 44.1
18	88 30.1	16 57.3	223 49.0
20	118 30.3	16 55.9	253 53.9
22	148 30.4	N16 54.5	283 58.9

Sunday, 6th August

Time	SUN GHA	Dec	ARIES GHA
00	178 30.5	N16 53.2	314 03.8
02	208 30.7	16 51.8	344 08.7
04	238 30.8	16 50.5	14 13.7
06	268 30.9	16 49.1	44 18.6
08	298 31.1	16 47.7	74 23.5
10	328 31.2	16 46.4	104 28.4
12	358 31.3	16 45.0	134 33.4
14	28 31.5	16 43.6	164 38.3
16	58 31.6	16 42.3	194 43.2
18	88 31.8	16 40.9	224 48.2
20	118 31.9	16 39.5	254 53.1
22	148 32.0	N16 38.1	284 58.0

Monday, 7th August

Time	SUN GHA	Dec	ARIES GHA
00	178 32.2	N16 36.7	315 02.9
02	208 32.3	16 35.4	345 07.9
04	238 32.5	16 34.0	15 12.8
06	268 32.6	16 32.6	45 17.7
08	298 32.8	16 31.2	75 22.7
10	328 32.9	16 29.8	105 27.6
12	358 33.1	16 28.4	135 32.5
14	28 33.2	16 27.0	165 37.4
16	58 33.4	16 25.6	195 42.4
18	88 33.5	16 24.2	225 47.3
20	118 33.7	16 22.8	255 52.2
22	148 33.8	N16 21.4	285 57.1

Tuesday, 8th August

Time	SUN GHA	Dec	ARIES GHA
00	178 34.0	N16 20.0	316 02.1
02	208 34.1	16 18.6	346 07.0
04	238 34.3	16 17.2	16 11.9
06	268 34.5	16 15.8	46 16.9
08	298 34.6	16 14.4	76 21.8
10	328 34.8	16 13.0	106 26.7
12	358 34.9	16 11.6	136 31.6
14	28 35.1	16 10.1	166 36.6
16	58 35.3	16 08.7	196 41.5
18	88 35.4	16 07.3	226 46.4
20	118 35.6	16 05.9	256 51.4
22	148 35.8	N16 04.5	286 56.3

Wednesday, 9th August

Time	SUN GHA	Dec	ARIES GHA
00	178 35.9	N16 03.0	317 01.2
02	208 36.1	16 01.6	347 06.1
04	238 36.3	16 00.2	17 11.1
06	268 36.4	15 58.8	47 16.0
08	298 36.6	15 57.3	77 20.9
10	328 36.8	15 55.9	107 25.9
12	358 37.0	15 54.5	137 30.8
14	28 37.1	15 53.0	167 35.7
16	58 37.3	15 51.6	197 40.6
18	88 37.5	15 50.1	227 45.6
20	118 37.7	15 48.7	257 50.5
22	148 37.8	N15 47.2	287 55.4

Thursday, 10th August

Time	SUN GHA	Dec	ARIES GHA
00	178 38.0	N15 45.8	318 00.4
02	208 38.2	15 44.4	348 05.3
04	238 38.4	15 42.9	18 10.2
06	268 38.6	15 41.5	48 15.1
08	298 38.8	15 40.0	78 20.1
10	328 38.9	15 38.5	108 25.0
12	358 39.1	15 37.1	138 29.9
14	28 39.3	15 35.6	168 34.9
16	58 39.5	15 34.2	198 39.8
18	88 39.7	15 32.7	228 44.7
20	118 39.9	15 31.2	258 49.6
22	148 40.1	N15 29.8	288 54.6

Friday, 11th August

Time	SUN GHA	Dec	ARIES GHA
00	178 40.3	N15 28.3	318 59.5
02	208 40.5	15 26.8	349 04.4
04	238 40.7	15 25.4	19 09.3
06	268 40.9	15 23.9	49 14.3
08	298 41.0	15 22.4	79 19.2
10	328 41.2	15 20.9	109 24.1
12	358 41.4	15 19.5	139 29.1
14	28 41.6	15 18.0	169 34.0
16	58 41.8	15 16.5	199 38.9
18	88 42.0	15 15.0	229 43.8
20	118 42.2	15 13.5	259 48.8
22	148 42.4	N15 12.1	289 53.7

Saturday, 12th August

Time	SUN GHA	Dec	ARIES GHA
00	178 42.7	N15 10.6	319 58.6
02	208 42.9	15 09.1	350 03.6
04	238 43.1	15 07.6	20 08.5
06	268 43.3	15 06.1	50 13.4
08	298 43.5	15 04.6	80 18.3
10	328 43.7	15 03.1	110 23.3
12	358 43.9	15 01.6	140 28.2
14	28 44.1	15 00.1	170 33.1
16	58 44.3	14 58.6	200 38.1
18	88 44.5	14 57.1	230 43.0
20	118 44.7	14 55.6	260 47.9
22	148 45.0	N14 54.1	290 52.8

Sunday, 13th August

Time	SUN GHA	Dec	ARIES GHA
00	178 45.2	N14 52.6	320 57.8
02	208 45.4	14 51.1	351 02.7
04	238 45.6	14 49.6	21 07.6
06	268 45.8	14 48.1	51 12.6
08	298 46.0	14 46.5	81 17.5
10	328 46.3	14 45.0	111 22.4
12	358 46.5	14 43.5	141 27.3
14	28 46.7	14 42.0	171 32.3
16	58 46.9	14 40.5	201 37.2
18	88 47.2	14 38.9	231 42.1
20	118 47.4	14 37.4	261 47.1
22	148 47.6	N14 35.9	291 52.0

Monday, 14th August

Time	SUN GHA	Dec	ARIES GHA
00	178 47.8	N14 34.4	321 56.9
02	208 48.1	14 32.8	352 01.8
04	238 48.3	14 31.3	22 06.8
06	268 48.5	14 29.8	52 11.7
08	298 48.7	14 28.2	82 16.6
10	328 49.0	14 26.7	112 21.5
12	358 49.2	14 25.2	142 26.5
14	28 49.4	14 23.6	172 31.4
16	58 49.7	14 22.1	202 36.3
18	88 49.9	14 20.6	232 41.3
20	118 50.1	14 19.0	262 46.2
22	148 50.4	N14 17.5	292 51.1

Tuesday, 15th August

Time	SUN GHA	Dec	ARIES GHA
00	178 50.6	N14 15.9	322 56.0
02	208 50.9	14 14.4	353 01.0
04	238 51.1	14 12.8	23 05.9
06	268 51.3	14 11.1	53 10.8
08	298 51.6	14 09.7	83 15.8
10	328 51.8	14 08.2	113 20.7
12	358 52.1	14 06.6	143 25.6
14	28 52.3	14 05.0	173 30.5
16	58 52.6	14 03.5	203 35.5
18	88 52.8	14 01.9	233 40.4
20	118 53.0	14 00.4	263 45.3
22	148 53.3	N13 58.8	293 50.3

NOTES

Sun & Aries GHA corrections for additional hour, minutes, and seconds on page E 94.
Correct Sun Declination by interpolation. For example see page E 4.

AUGUST 1995 — SUN & ARIES — GMT

Time	SUN GHA	Dec	ARIES GHA
Wednesday, 16th August			
00	178 53.5	N13 57.2	323 55.2
02	208 53.8	13 55.7	354 00.1
04	238 54.0	13 54.1	24 05.0
06	268 54.3	13 52.5	54 10.0
08	298 54.5	13 51.0	84 14.9
10	328 54.8	13 49.4	114 19.8
12	358 55.1	13 47.8	144 24.8
14	28 55.3	13 46.2	174 29.7
16	58 55.6	13 44.7	204 34.6
18	88 55.8	13 43.1	234 39.5
20	118 56.1	13 41.5	264 44.5
22	148 56.3	N13 39.9	294 49.4
Thursday, 17th August			
00	178 56.6	N13 38.3	324 54.3
02	208 56.9	13 36.8	354 59.3
04	238 57.1	13 35.2	25 04.2
06	268 57.4	13 33.6	55 09.1
08	298 57.6	13 32.0	85 14.0
10	328 57.9	13 30.4	115 19.0
12	358 58.2	13 28.8	145 23.9
14	28 58.4	13 27.2	175 28.8
16	58 58.7	13 25.6	205 33.7
18	88 59.0	13 24.0	235 38.7
20	118 59.2	13 22.4	265 43.6
22	148 59.5	N13 20.8	295 48.5
Friday, 18th August			
00	178 59.8	N13 19.2	325 53.5
02	209 00.0	13 17.6	355 58.4
04	239 00.3	13 16.0	26 03.3
06	269 00.6	13 14.4	56 08.2
08	299 00.9	13 12.8	86 13.2
10	329 01.1	13 11.2	116 18.1
12	359 01.4	13 09.6	146 23.0
14	29 01.7	13 08.0	176 28.0
16	59 02.0	13 06.4	206 32.9
18	89 02.2	13 04.7	236 37.8
20	119 02.5	13 03.1	266 42.7
22	149 02.8	N13 01.5	296 47.7
Saturday, 19th August			
00	179 03.1	N12 59.9	326 52.6
02	209 03.4	12 58.3	356 57.5
04	239 03.6	12 56.6	27 02.5
06	269 03.9	12 55.0	57 07.4
08	299 04.2	12 53.4	87 12.3
10	329 04.5	12 51.8	117 17.2
12	359 04.8	12 50.1	147 22.2
14	29 05.1	12 48.5	177 27.1
16	59 05.3	12 46.9	207 32.0
18	89 05.6	12 45.3	237 37.0
20	119 05.9	12 43.6	267 41.9
22	149 06.2	N12 42.0	297 46.8
Sunday, 20th August			
00	179 06.5	N12 40.4	327 51.7
02	209 06.8	12 38.7	357 56.7
04	239 07.1	12 37.1	28 01.6
06	269 07.4	12 35.4	58 06.5
08	299 07.7	12 33.8	88 11.5
10	329 08.0	12 32.2	118 16.4
12	359 08.3	12 30.5	148 21.3
14	29 08.6	12 28.9	178 26.2
16	59 08.9	12 27.2	208 31.2
18	89 09.1	12 25.6	238 36.1
20	119 09.4	12 23.9	268 41.0
22	149 09.7	N12 22.3	298 46.0

Time	SUN GHA	Dec	ARIES GHA
Monday, 21st August			
00	179 10.0	N12 20.6	328 50.9
02	209 10.3	12 19.0	358 55.8
04	239 10.6	12 17.3	29 00.7
06	269 10.9	12 15.7	59 05.7
08	299 11.2	12 14.0	89 10.6
10	329 11.6	12 12.3	119 15.5
12	359 11.9	12 10.7	149 20.4
14	29 12.2	12 09.0	179 25.4
16	59 12.5	12 07.4	209 30.3
18	89 12.8	12 05.7	239 35.2
20	119 13.1	12 04.0	269 40.2
22	149 13.4	N12 02.4	299 45.1
Tuesday, 22nd August			
00	179 13.7	N12 00.7	329 50.0
02	209 14.0	11 59.0	359 54.9
04	239 14.3	11 57.3	29 59.9
06	269 14.6	11 55.7	60 04.8
08	299 14.9	11 54.0	90 09.7
10	329 15.3	11 52.3	120 14.7
12	359 15.6	11 50.6	150 19.6
14	29 15.9	11 49.0	180 24.5
16	59 16.2	11 47.3	210 29.4
18	89 16.5	11 45.6	240 34.4
20	119 16.8	11 43.9	270 39.3
22	149 17.2	N11 42.2	300 44.2
Wednesday, 23rd August			
00	179 17.5	N11 40.6	330 49.2
02	209 17.8	11 38.9	0 54.1
04	239 18.1	11 37.2	30 59.0
06	269 18.4	11 35.5	61 03.9
08	299 18.7	11 33.8	91 08.9
10	329 19.1	11 32.1	121 13.8
12	359 19.4	11 30.4	151 18.7
14	29 19.7	11 28.7	181 23.7
16	59 20.0	11 27.0	211 28.6
18	89 20.4	11 25.4	241 33.5
20	119 20.7	11 23.7	271 38.4
22	149 21.0	N11 22.0	301 43.4
Thursday, 24th August			
00	179 21.3	N11 20.3	331 48.3
02	209 21.7	11 18.6	1 53.2
04	239 22.0	11 16.9	31 58.2
06	269 22.3	11 15.2	62 03.1
08	299 22.7	11 13.4	92 08.0
10	329 23.0	11 11.7	122 12.9
12	359 23.3	11 10.0	152 17.9
14	29 23.7	11 08.3	182 22.8
16	59 24.0	11 06.6	212 27.7
18	89 24.3	11 04.9	242 32.6
20	119 24.7	11 03.2	272 37.6
22	149 25.0	N11 01.5	302 42.5
Friday, 25th August			
00	179 25.3	N10 59.8	332 47.4
02	209 25.7	10 58.1	2 52.4
04	239 26.0	10 56.3	32 57.3
06	269 26.3	10 54.6	63 02.2
08	299 26.7	10 52.9	93 07.1
10	329 27.0	10 51.2	123 12.1
12	359 27.4	10 49.5	153 17.0
14	29 27.7	10 47.7	183 21.9
16	59 28.0	10 46.0	213 26.9
18	89 28.4	10 44.3	243 31.8
20	119 28.7	10 42.6	273 36.7
22	149 29.1	N10 40.8	303 41.6

Time	SUN GHA	Dec	ARIES GHA
Saturday, 26th August			
00	179 29.4	N10 39.1	333 46.6
02	209 29.8	10 37.4	3 51.5
04	239 30.1	10 35.7	33 56.4
06	269 30.5	10 33.9	64 01.4
08	299 30.8	10 32.2	94 06.3
10	329 31.2	10 30.5	124 11.2
12	359 31.5	10 28.7	154 16.1
14	29 31.9	10 27.0	184 21.1
16	59 32.2	10 25.2	214 26.0
18	89 32.6	10 23.5	244 30.9
20	119 32.9	10 21.8	274 35.9
22	149 33.3	N10 20.0	304 40.8
Sunday, 27th August			
00	179 33.6	N10 18.3	334 45.7
02	209 34.0	10 16.5	4 50.6
04	239 34.3	10 14.8	34 55.6
06	269 34.7	10 13.1	65 00.5
08	299 35.0	10 11.3	95 05.4
10	329 35.4	10 09.6	125 10.4
12	359 35.7	10 07.8	155 15.3
14	29 36.1	10 06.1	185 20.2
16	59 36.5	10 04.3	215 25.1
18	89 36.8	10 02.6	245 30.1
20	119 37.2	10 00.8	275 35.0
22	149 37.5	N 9 59.0	305 39.9
Monday, 28th August			
00	179 37.9	N 9 57.3	335 44.8
02	209 38.3	9 55.5	5 49.8
04	239 38.6	9 53.8	35 54.7
06	269 39.0	9 52.0	65 59.6
08	299 39.4	9 50.3	96 04.6
10	329 39.7	9 48.5	126 09.5
12	359 40.1	9 46.7	156 14.4
14	29 40.4	9 45.0	186 19.3
16	59 40.8	9 43.2	216 24.3
18	89 41.2	9 41.4	246 29.2
20	119 41.5	9 39.7	276 34.1
22	149 41.9	N 9 37.9	306 39.1
Tuesday, 29th August			
00	179 42.3	N 9 36.1	336 44.0
02	209 42.7	9 34.4	6 48.9
04	239 43.0	9 32.6	36 53.8
06	269 43.4	9 30.8	66 58.8
08	299 43.8	9 29.1	97 03.7
10	329 44.1	9 27.3	127 08.6
12	359 44.5	9 25.5	157 13.6
14	29 44.9	9 23.7	187 18.5
16	59 45.3	9 22.0	217 23.4
18	89 45.6	9 20.2	247 28.3
20	119 46.0	9 18.4	277 33.3
22	149 46.4	N 9 16.6	307 38.2
Wednesday, 30th August			
00	179 46.8	N 9 14.8	337 43.1
02	209 47.1	9 13.1	7 48.1
04	239 47.5	9 11.3	37 53.0
06	269 47.9	9 09.5	67 57.9
08	299 48.3	9 07.7	98 02.8
10	329 48.6	9 05.9	128 07.8
12	359 49.0	9 04.1	158 12.7
14	29 49.4	9 02.3	188 17.6
16	59 49.8	9 00.6	218 22.6
18	89 50.2	8 58.8	248 27.5
20	119 50.6	8 57.0	278 32.4
22	149 50.9	N 8 55.2	308 37.3

Time	SUN GHA	Dec	ARIES GHA
Thursday, 31st August			
00	179 51.3	N 8 53.4	338 42.3
02	209 51.7	8 51.6	8 47.2
04	239 52.1	8 49.8	38 52.1
06	269 52.5	8 48.0	68 57.0
08	299 52.9	8 46.2	99 02.0
10	329 53.2	8 44.4	129 06.9
12	359 53.6	8 42.6	159 11.8
14	29 54.0	N 8 40.8	189 16.8
16	59 54.4	8 39.0	219 21.7
18	89 54.8	8 37.2	249 26.6
20	119 55.2	8 35.4	279 31.5
22	149 55.6	N 8 33.6	309 36.5

AUGUST

AUGUST 1995   PLANETS   0h GMT

VENUS Mer Pass h m	GHA ° '	Mean Var/hr 14°+	Dec ° '	Mean Var/hr '	Note Corrections on Page E 101		JUPITER GHA ° '	Mean Var/hr 15°+	Dec ° '	Mean Var/hr '	Mer Pass h m
11 45	183 50.5	59.3	N 20 23.4	0.6	1	Tu	65 23.7	2.5	S 20 37.1	0.0	19 35
11 46	183 32.6	59.3	N 20 07.9	0.7	2	Wed	66 23.1	2.5	S 20 37.3	0.0	19 31
11 48	183 14.9	59.3	N 19 51.9	0.7	3	Th	67 22.4	2.5	S 20 37.5	0.0	19 27
11 49	182 57.5	59.3	N 19 35.2	0.7	4	Fri	68 21.4	2.5	S 20 37.7	0.0	19 23
11 50	182 40.3	59.3	N 19 18.1	0.7	5	Sat	69 20.2	2.4	S 20 38.0	0.0	19 20
11 51	182 23.4	59.3	N 19 00.3	0.8	6	SUN	70 18.9	2.4	S 20 38.3	0.0	19 16
11 52	182 06.8	59.3	N 18 42.1	0.8	7	Mon	71 17.3	2.4	S 20 38.6	0.0	19 12
11 53	181 50.4	59.3	N 18 23.3	0.8	8	Tu	72 15.6	2.4	S 20 39.0	0.0	19 08
11 54	181 34.3	59.3	N 18 04.0	0.8	9	Wed	73 13.6	2.4	S 20 39.4	0.0	19 04
11 55	181 18.5	59.4	N 17 44.1	0.8	10	Th	74 11.5	2.4	S 20 39.8	0.0	19 00
11 56	181 02.9	59.4	N 17 23.8	0.9	11	Fri	75 09.2	2.4	S 20 40.3	0.0	18 56
11 57	180 47.6	59.4	N 17 03.0	0.9	12	Sat	76 06.6	2.4	S 20 40.7	0.0	18 53
11 58	180 32.6	59.4	N 16 41.7	0.9	13	SUN	77 03.9	2.4	S 20 41.3	0.0	18 49
11 59	180 17.8	59.4	N 16 20.0	0.9	14	Mon	78 01.0	2.4	S 20 41.8	0.0	18 45
12 00	180 03.3	59.4	N 15 57.8	0.9	15	Tu	78 58.0	2.4	S 20 42.4	0.0	18 41
12 01	179 49.1	59.4	N 15 35.1	1.0	16	Wed	79 54.7	2.4	S 20 43.0	0.0	18 37
12 02	179 35.1	59.4	N 15 12.1	1.0	17	Th	80 51.2	2.3	S 20 43.7	0.0	18 34
12 03	179 21.4	59.4	N 14 48.6	1.0	18	Fri	81 47.6	2.3	S 20 44.3	0.0	18 30
12 04	179 08.0	59.4	N 14 24.7	1.0	19	Sat	82 43.8	2.3	S 20 45.0	0.0	18 26
12 05	178 54.7	59.5	N 14 00.4	1.0	20	SUN	83 39.7	2.3	S 20 45.8	0.0	18 23
12 06	178 41.8	59.5	N 13 35.7	1.0	21	Mon	84 35.5	2.3	S 20 46.5	0.0	18 19
12 06	178 29.1	59.5	N 13 10.6	1.1	22	Tu	85 31.2	2.3	S 20 47.3	0.0	18 15
12 07	178 16.6	59.5	N 12 45.2	1.1	23	Wed	86 26.6	2.3	S 20 48.1	0.0	18 11
12 08	178 04.4	59.5	N 12 19.5	1.1	24	Th	87 21.9	2.3	S 20 48.9	0.0	18 08
12 09	177 52.4	59.5	N 11 53.4	1.1	25	Fri	88 16.9	2.3	S 20 49.8	0.0	18 04
12 10	177 40.6	59.5	N 11 26.9	1.1	26	Sat	89 11.8	2.3	S 20 50.7	0.0	18 00
12 10	177 29.0	59.5	N 11 00.2	1.1	27	SUN	90 06.6	2.3	S 20 51.6	0.0	17 57
12 11	177 17.6	59.5	N 10 33.2	1.1	28	Mon	91 01.1	2.3	S 20 52.6	0.0	17 53
12 12	177 06.5	59.5	N 10 05.8	1.1	29	Tu	91 55.5	2.3	S 20 53.5	0.0	17 50
12 13	176 55.5	59.6	N 9 38.2	1.2	30	Wed	92 49.7	2.3	S 20 54.5	0.0	17 46
12 13	176 44.8	59.6	N 9 10.4	1.2	31	Th	93 43.7	2.2	S 20 55.5	0.0	17 42

VENUS, Av. Mag. -3.9
S.H.A. August
5 230; 10 223; 15 217; 20 211; 25 205; 30 199.

JUPITER, Av. Mag.-2.2
S.H.A. August
5 116; 10 116; 15 116; 20 116; 25 115; 30 115.

MARS Mer Pass h m	GHA ° '	Mean Var/hr 15°+	Dec ° '	Mean Var/hr '	Note Corrections on Page E 101		SATURN GHA ° '	Mean Var/hr 15°+	Dec ° '	Mean Var/hr '	Mer Pass h m
15 46	123 12.0	1.1	S 2 16.1	0.6	1	Tu	313 33.4	2.6	S 4 21.1	0.0	03 05
15 44	123 38.0	1.1	S 2 31.3	0.6	2	Wed	314 34.8	2.6	S 4 22.3	0.1	03 01
15 43	124 03.8	1.1	S 2 46.5	0.6	3	Th	315 36.2	2.6	S 4 23.6	0.0	02 57
15 41	124 29.6	1.1	S 3 01.7	0.6	4	Fri	316 37.7	2.6	S 4 24.8	0.1	02 53
15 39	124 55.3	1.1	S 3 16.9	0.6	5	Sat	317 39.3	2.6	S 4 26.1	0.1	02 49
15 38	125 20.8	1.1	S 3 32.2	0.6	6	SUN	318 40.9	2.6	S 4 27.4	0.1	02 45
15 36	125 46.3	1.1	S 3 47.5	0.6	7	Mon	319 42.7	2.6	S 4 28.8	0.1	02 41
15 34	126 11.6	1.1	S 4 02.7	0.6	8	Tu	320 44.5	2.6	S 4 30.2	0.1	02 37
15 32	126 36.9	1.0	S 4 18.0	0.6	9	Wed	321 46.3	2.6	S 4 31.6	0.1	02 32
15 31	127 02.0	1.0	S 4 33.3	0.6	10	Th	322 48.3	2.6	S 4 33.0	0.1	02 28
15 29	127 27.0	1.0	S 4 48.6	0.6	11	Fri	323 50.3	2.6	S 4 34.5	0.1	02 24
15 27	127 51.9	1.0	S 5 03.9	0.6	12	Sat	324 52.4	2.6	S 4 36.0	0.1	02 20
15 26	128 16.7	1.0	S 5 19.2	0.6	13	SUN	325 54.6	2.6	S 4 37.5	0.1	02 16
15 24	128 41.4	1.0	S 5 34.5	0.6	14	Mon	326 56.8	2.6	S 4 39.0	0.1	02 12
15 23	129 06.0	1.0	S 5 49.7	0.6	15	Tu	327 59.1	2.6	S 4 40.6	0.1	02 08
15 21	129 30.5	1.0	S 6 05.0	0.6	16	Wed	329 01.4	2.6	S 4 42.2	0.1	02 04
15 19	129 54.8	1.0	S 6 20.3	0.6	17	Th	330 03.8	2.6	S 4 43.8	0.1	01 59
15 18	130 19.1	1.0	S 6 35.6	0.6	18	Fri	331 06.3	2.6	S 4 45.4	0.1	01 55
15 16	130 43.2	1.0	S 6 50.8	0.6	19	Sat	332 08.9	2.6	S 4 47.0	0.1	01 51
15 15	131 07.2	1.0	S 7 06.0	0.6	20	SUN	333 11.4	2.6	S 4 48.7	0.1	01 47
15 13	131 31.0	1.0	S 7 21.3	0.6	21	Mon	334 14.1	2.6	S 4 50.4	0.1	01 43
15 11	131 54.8	1.0	S 7 36.5	0.6	22	Tu	335 16.8	2.6	S 4 52.1	0.1	01 39
15 10	132 18.4	1.0	S 7 51.7	0.6	23	Wed	336 19.5	2.6	S 4 53.8	0.1	01 34
15 08	132 41.9	1.0	S 8 06.8	0.6	24	Th	337 22.3	2.6	S 4 55.6	0.1	01 30
15 07	133 05.3	1.0	S 8 22.0	0.6	25	Fri	338 25.2	2.6	S 4 57.3	0.1	01 26
15 05	133 28.5	1.0	S 8 37.1	0.6	26	Sat	339 28.1	2.6	S 4 59.1	0.1	01 22
15 04	133 51.6	1.0	S 8 52.2	0.6	27	SUN	340 31.0	2.6	S 5 00.9	0.1	01 18
15 02	134 14.6	0.9	S 9 07.2	0.6	28	Mon	341 34.0	2.6	S 5 02.7	0.1	01 14
15 01	134 37.4	1.0	S 9 22.2	0.6	29	Tu	342 37.0	2.6	S 5 04.5	0.1	01 09
14 59	135 00.2	0.9	S 9 37.2	0.6	30	Wed	343 40.1	2.6	S 5 06.3	0.1	01 05
14 58	135 22.7	0.9	S 9 52.2	0.6	31	Th	344 43.2	2.6	S 5 08.1	0.1	01 01

MARS, Av. Mag. +1.4
S.H.A. August
5 172; 10 169; 15 166; 20 163; 25 160; 30 157.

SATURN, Av. Mag. +0.9
S.H.A. August
5 5; 10 5; 15 5; 20 5; 25 6; 30 6.

AUGUST 1995 — MOON

Day	GMT hr	GHA ° '	Mean Var/hr 14°+	Dec ° '	Mean Var/hr '	Day	GMT hr	GHA ° '	Mean Var/hr 14°+	Dec ° '	Mean Var/hr '
1 Tu	0	130 51.2	31.5	S 2 03.7	10.7	17 Th	0	285 53.3	31.6	N 14 07.3	6.6
	6	218 00.3	31.2	S 3 07.8	10.6		6	13 03.4	31.7	N 14 47.4	6.2
	12	305 08.1	31.1	S 4 11.7	10.6		12	100 13.2	31.6	N 15 24.9	5.7
	18	32 14.6	30.8	S 5 15.0	10.4		18	187 22.9	31.6	N 15 59.7	5.3
2 Wed	0	119 19.5	30.5	S 6 17.7	10.3	18 Fri	0	274 32.3	31.6	N 16 31.7	4.8
	6	206 22.7	30.2	S 7 19.6	10.1		6	1 41.5	31.5	N 17 00.9	4.3
	12	293 24.2	29.9	S 8 20.4	9.9		12	88 50.3	31.4	N 17 27.1	3.9
	18	20 23.6	29.5	S 9 19.9	9.6		18	175 58.9	31.4	N 17 50.4	3.4
3 Th	0	107 21.0	29.1	S 10 17.9	9.4	19 Sat	0	263 07.2	31.4	N 18 10.7	2.9
	6	194 16.2	28.8	S 11 14.1	9.0		6	350 15.2	31.3	N 18 28.0	2.3
	12	281 09.0	28.3	S 12 08.4	8.6		12	77 23.0	31.2	N 18 42.2	1.8
	18	7 59.5	28.0	S 13 00.5	8.2		18	164 30.5	31.2	N 18 53.2	1.3
4 Fri	0	94 47.5	27.6	S 13 50.2	7.8	20 Sun	0	251 37.8	31.2	N 19 01.2	0.7
	6	181 33.0	27.2	S 14 37.2	7.3		6	338 45.0	31.2	N 19 06.0	0.2
	12	268 15.9	26.7	S 15 21.3	6.8		12	65 52.0	31.2	N 19 07.6	0.3
	18	354 56.3	26.3	S 16 02.2	6.2		18	152 59.0	31.2	N 19 06.1	0.8
5 Sat	0	81 34.2	25.9	S 16 39.7	5.6	21 Mon	0	240 05.9	31.2	N 19 01.4	1.3
	6	168 09.7	25.5	S 17 13.6	4.9		6	327 12.8	31.2	N 18 53.5	1.9
	12	254 42.8	25.2	S 17 43.7	4.3		12	54 19.8	31.2	N 18 42.5	2.4
	18	341 13.7	24.8	S 18 09.7	3.5		18	141 26.9	31.2	N 18 28.3	2.9
6 Sun	0	67 42.6	24.4	S 18 31.5	2.8	22 Tu	0	228 34.1	31.3	N 18 11.1	3.4
	6	154 09.7	24.2	S 18 48.9	2.0		6	315 41.6	31.3	N 17 50.8	4.0
	12	240 35.1	24.0	S 19 01.7	1.3		12	42 49.3	31.4	N 17 27.4	4.4
	18	326 59.2	23.8	S 19 09.8	0.5		18	129 57.2	31.4	N 17 01.1	4.9
7 Mon	0	53 22.1	23.7	S 19 13.1	0.3	23 Wed	0	217 05.5	31.5	N 16 31.9	5.4
	6	139 44.4	23.6	S 19 11.5	1.1		6	304 14.1	31.5	N 15 59.8	5.9
	12	226 06.1	23.6	S 19 05.1	1.9		12	31 23.0	31.5	N 15 24.9	6.3
	18	312 27.8	23.7	S 18 53.7	2.8		18	118 32.2	31.6	N 14 47.3	6.7
8 Tu	0	38 49.6	23.8	S 18 37.6	3.6	24 Th	0	205 41.8	31.6	N 14 07.1	7.2
	6	125 11.9	23.9	S 18 16.6	4.3		6	292 51.8	31.8	N 13 24.4	7.5
	12	211 35.0	24.1	S 17 50.9	5.1		12	20 02.0	31.8	N 12 39.3	8.0
	18	297 59.2	24.2	S 17 20.7	5.8		18	107 12.5	31.8	N 11 51.9	8.3
9 Wed	0	24 24.7	24.5	S 16 46.2	6.5	25 Fri	0	194 23.3	31.8	N 11 02.2	8.6
	6	110 51.9	24.8	S 16 07.5	7.2		6	281 34.3	31.8	N 10 10.5	9.0
	12	197 20.8	25.2	S 15 24.8	7.8		12	8 45.4	31.8	N 9 16.9	9.3
	18	283 51.7	25.5	S 14 38.5	8.3		18	95 56.7	31.9	N 8 21.5	9.5
10 Th	0	10 24.7	25.9	S 13 48.7	8.9	26 Sat	0	183 07.9	31.8	N 7 24.4	9.8
	6	96 59.9	26.3	S 12 55.9	9.4		6	270 19.2	31.9	N 6 25.8	10.0
	12	183 37.4	26.7	S 12 00.2	9.8		12	357 30.2	31.8	N 5 25.8	10.2
	18	270 17.3	27.0	S 11 01.9	10.1		18	84 41.1	31.7	N 4 24.7	10.3
11 Fri	0	356 59.5	27.5	S 10 01.5	10.4	27 Sun	0	171 51.6	31.7	N 3 22.5	10.5
	6	83 44.0	27.9	S 8 59.1	10.7		6	259 01.7	31.6	N 2 19.5	10.6
	12	170 30.8	28.2	S 7 55.1	10.9		12	346 11.2	31.4	N 1 15.9	10.7
	18	257 19.9	28.6	S 6 49.8	11.0		18	73 20.1	31.3	N 0 11.7	10.7
12 Sat	0	344 11.2	28.9	S 5 43.4	11.2	28 Mon	0	160 28.3	31.2	S 0 52.7	10.8
	6	71 04.5	29.2	S 4 36.4	11.2		6	247 35.5	31.0	S 1 57.3	10.8
	12	157 59.9	29.6	S 3 28.8	11.3		12	334 41.8	30.8	S 3 01.7	10.6
	18	244 57.1	29.9	S 2 21.1	11.3		18	61 46.9	30.6	S 4 05.9	10.6
13 Sun	0	331 56.0	30.1	S 1 13.3	11.2	29 Tu	0	148 50.8	30.4	S 5 09.5	10.5
	6	58 56.6	30.4	S 0 05.9	11.2		6	235 53.3	30.1	S 6 12.4	10.3
	12	145 58.7	30.6	N 1 01.0	11.0		12	322 54.4	29.9	S 7 14.3	10.1
	18	233 02.1	30.7	N 2 07.2	10.8		18	49 53.9	29.7	S 8 15.1	9.9
14 Mon	0	320 06.7	30.9	N 3 12.5	10.7	30 Wed	0	136 51.7	29.3	S 9 14.5	9.6
	6	47 12.5	31.1	N 4 16.7	10.5		6	223 47.8	29.0	S 10 12.3	9.3
	12	134 19.2	31.3	N 5 19.6	10.2		12	310 42.0	28.7	S 11 08.2	8.9
	18	221 26.7	31.4	N 6 21.0	9.9		18	37 34.3	28.3	S 12 02.0	8.6
15 Tu	0	308 34.9	31.4	N 7 20.9	9.7	31 Th	0	124 24.7	28.0	S 12 53.6	8.2
	6	35 43.7	31.6	N 8 19.0	9.4		6	211 13.0	27.7	S 13 42.6	7.7
	12	122 53.1	31.7	N 9 15.3	9.0		12	297 59.3	27.4	S 14 28.9	7.1
	18	210 02.7	31.6	N 10 09.6	8.7		18	24 43.6	27.0	S 15 12.2	6.7
16 Wed	0	297 12.7	31.7	N 11 01.7	8.3						
	6	24 22.8	31.7	N 11 51.7	7.9						
	12	111 33.0	31.7	N 12 39.3	7.5						
	18	198 43.2	31.7	N 13 24.5	7.1						

NOTE Moon GHA corrections for additional hours, minutes, and seconds on page E 96.
Moon Declination corrections on page E 99. Mean Var/Hr value needed for both corrections.

AUGUST

SEPTEMBER 1995 — SUN & MOON — GMT

SUN

| Day of | | | Equation of Time | | Transit | Semi-diam | Lat 52°N | | | | Lat Corr to Sunrise, Sunset etc | | | | |
Yr	Mth	Week	0h	12h			Twilight	Sunrise	Sunset	Twilight	Lat	Twilight	Sunrise	Sunset	Twilight
			m s	m s	h m	′	h m	h m	h m	h m	°	h m	h m	h m	h m
244	1	Fri	+00 17	+00 07	12 00	15.9	04 35	05 11	18 48	19 24	N60	-0 15	-0 07	+0 07	+0 15
245	2	Sat	-00 02	-00 12	12 00	15.9	04 37	05 12	18 46	19 21	55	-0 05	-0 02	+0 02	+0 05
246	3	Sun	-00 22	-00 31	11 59	15.9	04 39	05 14	18 44	19 19	50	+0 03	+0 01	-0 01	-0 03
247	4	Mon	-00 41	-00 51	11 59	15.9	04 41	05 16	18 42	19 16	45	+0 09	+0 04	-0 04	-0 09
248	5	Tu	-01 01	-01 11	11 59	15.9	04 42	05 17	18 39	19 14	N40	+0 14	+0 07	-0 07	-0 14
249	6	Wed	-01 21	-01 31	11 58	15.9	04 44	05 19	18 37	19 12	35	+0 17	+0 09	-0 09	-0 17
250	7	Th	-01 41	-01 51	11 58	15.9	04 46	05 21	18 35	19 09	30	+0 21	+0 11	-0 11	-0 21
251	8	Fri	-02 02	-02 12	11 58	15.9	04 47	05 22	18 32	19 07	25	+0 23	+0 12	-0 12	-0 23
252	9	Sat	-02 22	-02 33	11 57	15.9	04 49	05 24	18 30	19 04	N20	+0 25	+0 14	-0 14	-0 25
253	10	Sun	-02 43	-02 54	11 57	15.9	04 51	05 25	18 28	19 02	15	+0 27	+0 15	-0 15	-0 27
254	11	Mon	-03 04	-03 15	11 57	15.9	04 53	05 27	18 25	19 00	10	+0 29	+0 16	-0 16	-0 29
255	12	Tu	-03 25	-03 36	11 56	15.9	04 54	05 29	18 23	18 57	5	+0 30	+0 17	-0 17	-0 30
256	13	Wed	-03 46	-03 57	11 56	15.9	04 56	05 30	18 21	18 55	0	+0 32	+0 18	-0 18	-0 32
257	14	Th	-04 08	-04 18	11 56	15.9	04 58	05 32	18 18	18 52	S 5	+0 33	+0 20	-0 20	-0 33
258	15	Fri	-04 29	-04 40	11 55	15.9	04 59	05 34	18 16	18 50	10	+0 33	+0 21	-0 21	-0 33
259	16	Sat	-04 50	-05 01	11 55	15.9	05 01	05 35	18 14	18 48	15	+0 34	+0 22	-0 22	-0 34
260	17	Sun	-05 12	-05 23	11 55	15.9	05 03	05 37	18 11	18 45	S20	+0 35	+0 23	-0 23	-0 35
261	18	Mon	-05 33	-05 44	11 54	15.9	05 05	05 38	18 09	18 43	25	+0 35	+0 24	-0 24	-0 35
262	19	Tu	-05 55	-06 05	11 54	15.9	05 06	05 40	18 07	18 40	30	+0 35	+0 25	-0 25	-0 35
263	20	Wed	-06 16	-06 27	11 54	16.0	05 08	05 42	18 04	18 38	35	+0 35	+0 26	-0 26	-0 35
264	21	Th	-06 37	-06 48	11 53	16.0	05 10	05 43	18 02	18 36	S40	+0 35	+0 28	-0 28	-0 35
265	22	Fri	-06 59	-07 09	11 53	16.0	05 11	05 45	18 00	18 33	45	+0 34	+0 30	-0 30	-0 34
266	23	Sat	-07 20	-07 30	11 52	16.0	05 13	05 47	17 57	18 31	50	+0 33	+0 31	-0 31	-0 33
267	24	Sun	-07 41	-07 51	11 52	16.0	05 15	05 48	17 55	18 29					
268	25	Mon	-08 01	-08 12	11 52	16.0	05 16	05 50	17 53	18 26					
269	26	Tu	-08 22	-08 32	11 51	16.0	05 18	05 52	17 50	18 24					
270	27	Wed	-08 43	-08 53	11 51	16.0	05 20	05 53	17 48	18 22			**NOTES**		
271	28	Th	-09 03	-09 13	11 51	16.0	05 21	05 55	17 46	18 19					
272	29	Fri	-09 23	-09 33	11 50	16.0	05 23	05 57	17 43	18 17					
273	30	Sat	-09 43	-09 53	11 50	16.0	05 25	05 58	17 41	18 15					

NOTES

Lat corrections are for mid-month. **Equation of Time** is the excess of Mean Time over Apparent Time.

MOON

| Day of | | | Age | Transit (Upper) | Diff | Semi-diam | Hor Par | Lat 52°N | | Phases of the Moon | | | |
Yr	Mth	Week						Moon-rise	Moon-set				
			days	h m	m	′	′	h m	h m			d	h m
244	1	Fri	06	17 13	57	16.1	58.9	12 36	21 45	(	First Quarter	2	09 03
245	2	Sat	07	18 10	59	16.1	59.2	13 43	22 35	O	Full Moon	9	03 37
246	3	Sun	08	19 09	58	16.2	59.5	14 44	23 35	)	Last Quarter	16	21 09
247	4	Mon	09	20 07	58	16.2	59.6	15 36	— —	●	New Moon	24	16 55
248	5	Tu	10	21 05	55	16.2	59.6	16 20	00 43				
249	6	Wed	11	22 00	53	16.2	59.4	16 56	01 56				
250	7	Th	12	22 53	51	16.1	59.1	17 27	03 13				
251	8	Fri	13	23 44	50	16.0	58.7	17 55	04 30				
252	9	Sat	14	24 34	—	15.8	58.1	18 21	05 46		Perigee	5	01
253	10	Sun	15	00 34	49	15.7	57.4	18 46	07 00		Apogee	17	06
254	11	Mon	16	01 23	47	15.5	56.7	19 12	08 11		Perigee	30	04
255	12	Tu	17	02 10	48	15.3	56.0	19 40	09 21				
256	13	Wed	18	02 58	48	15.1	55.4	20 10	10 27				
257	14	Th	19	03 46	47	15.0	54.9	20 45	11 29				
258	15	Fri	20	04 33	48	14.9	54.5	21 25	12 27				
259	16	Sat	21	05 21	48	14.8	54.3	22 10	13 20				
260	17	Sun	22	06 09	47	14.8	54.2	23 01	14 06				
261	18	Mon	23	06 56	47	14.8	54.4	23 57	14 46				
262	19	Tu	24	07 43	47	14.9	54.7	— —	15 21				
263	20	Wed	25	08 30	47	15.0	55.1	00 57	15 52				
264	21	Th	26	09 17	46	15.2	55.6	02 02	16 20		**NOTES**		
265	22	Fri	27	10 03	47	15.3	56.3	03 09	16 46				
266	23	Sat	28	10 50	48	15.5	56.9	04 18	17 10				
267	24	Sun	29	11 38	50	15.7	57.5	05 29	17 35				
268	25	Mon	01	12 28	51	15.8	58.1	06 43	18 02				
269	26	Tu	02	13 19	53	16.0	58.6	07 57	18 31				
270	27	Wed	03	14 12	56	16.1	59.0	09 12	19 05				
271	28	Th	04	15 08	58	16.1	59.2	10 26	19 45				
272	29	Fri	05	16 06	58	16.2	59.3	11 36	20 33				
273	30	Sat	06	17 04	58	16.2	59.3	12 38	21 30				

NOTES

Diff equals daily change in transit time.
To correct Moonrise, Moonset, or Transit times for Latitude and/or Longitude see page E 100. For further information about these tables see page E 4. For Arc to Time correction see page E 91.

SEPTEMBER 1995 — STARS — 0h GMT September 1

No	Name	Mag	Transit h m	Dec ° ′	GHA ° ′	RA h m	SHA ° ′
	ARIES................		1 21		339 41.4		
1	Alpheratz..........	2.2	1 29	N 29 04.1	337 38.4	0 08	357 57.0
2	Ankaa...............	2.4	1 47	S 42 19.6	333 09.9	0 26	353 28.5
3	Schedar	2.5	2 01	N 56 30.9	329 36.6	0 40	349 55.2
4	Diphda	2.2	2 04	S 18 00.4	328 50.4	0 43	349 09.0
5	Achernar	0.6	2 58	S 57 15.3	315 17.7	1 38	335 36.3
6	POLARIS	2.1	3 50	N 89 14.5	302 27.5	2 29	322 46.1
7	Hamal...............	2.2	3 28	N 23 26.6	307 57.0	2 07	328 15.6
8	Acamar..............	3.1	4 19	S 40 19.1	295 09.7	2 58	315 28.3
9	Menkar	2.8	4 23	N 4 04.4	294 10.3	3 02	314 28.9
10	Mirfak	1.9	4 45	N 49 50.6	288 40.7	3 24	308 59.3
11	Aldebaran	1.1	5 56	N 16 30.0	270 46.1	4 36	291 04.7
12	Rigel	0.3	6 34	S 8 12.3	261 06.3	5 14	281 24.9
13	Capella	0.2	6 37	N 45 59.4	260 35.6	5 16	280 54.2
14	Bellatrix	1.7	6 45	N 6 20.7	258 27.8	5 25	278 46.4
15	Elnath	1.8	6 46	N 28 36.1	258 10.9	5 26	278 29.5
16	Alnilam	1.8	6 56	S 1 12.2	255 41.4	5 36	276 00.0
17	Betelgeuse........0.1-1.2		7 15	N 7 24.4	250 57.2	5 55	271 15.8
18	Canopus............	-0.9	7 44	S 52 41.4	243 43.6	6 24	264 02.2
19	Sirius	-1.6	8 05	S 16 42.5	238 27.0	6 45	258 45.6
20	Adhara	1.6	8 18	S 28 57.8	235 04.6	6 58	255 23.2
21	Castor...............	1.6	8 54	N 31 53.7	226 06.6	7 34	246 25.2
22	Procyon	0.5	8 59	N 5 14.1	224 55.3	7 39	245 13.9
23	Pollux	1.2	9 05	N 28 02.1	223 25.7	7 45	243 44.3
24	Avior	1.7	9 42	S 59 29.6	214 05.2	8 22	234 23.8
25	Suhail	2.2	10 27	S 43 24.8	202 44.0	9 08	223 02.6
26	Miaplacidus	1.8	10 33	S 69 41.9	201 24.5	9 13	221 43.1
27	Alphard	2.2	10 47	S 8 38.4	197 50.9	9 27	218 09.5
28	Regulus	1.3	11 27	N 11 59.3	187 39.4	10 08	207 58.0
29	Dubhe	2.0	12 23	N 61 46.4	173 50.1	11 03	194 08.7
30	Denebola	2.2	13 08	N 14 35.8	162 29.0	11 49	182 47.6
31	Gienah	2.8	13 35	S 17 31.0	155 47.8	12 16	176 06.4
32	Acrux................	1.1	13 45	S 63 04.6	153 06.2	12 26	173 24.8
33	Gacrux..............	1.6	13 50	S 57 05.4	151 57.7	12 31	172 16.3
34	Mimosa	1.5	14 06	S 59 40.0	147 49.6	12 47	168 08.2
35	Alioth	1.7	14 13	N 55 59.1	146 14.4	12 54	166 33.0
36	Spica................	1.2	14 44	S 11 08.2	138 27.0	13 25	158 45.6
37	Alkaid...............	1.9	15 06	N 49 20.3	132 51.3	13 47	153 09.9
38	Hadar	0.9	15 22	S 60 21.2	128 48.7	14 04	149 07.3
39	Menkent	2.3	15 25	S 36 20.9	128 05.0	14 06	148 23.6
40	Arcturus	0.2	15 34	N 19 12.5	125 49.6	14 15	146 08.2
41	Rigil Kent.	0.1	15 58	S 60 49.1	119 51.8	14 39	140 10.4
42	Zuben'ubi	2.9	16 09	S 16 01.3	117 01.8	14 51	137 20.4
43	Kochab..............	2.2	16 09	N 74 10.7	117 01.7	14 51	137 20.3
44	Alphecca	2.3	16 53	N 26 44.1	106 03.9	15 35	126 22.5
45	Antares	1.2	17 47	S 26 25.3	92 24.2	16 29	112 42.8
46	Atria	1.9	18 06	S 69 01.4	87 38.0	16 48	107 56.6
47	Sabik	2.6	18 28	S 15 43.0	82 09.3	17 10	102 27.9
48	Shaula	1.7	18 51	S 37 06.0	76 21.5	17 33	96 40.1
49	Rasalhague	2.1	18 53	N 12 34.1	76 00.3	17 35	96 18.9
50	Eltanin..............	2.4	19 15	N 51 29.8	70 33.7	17 57	90 52.3
51	Kaus Aust.	2.0	19 42	S 34 23.2	63 42.8	18 24	84 01.4
52	Vega.................	0.1	19 55	N 38 47.2	60 29.3	18 37	80 47.9
53	Nunki	2.1	20 13	S 26 18.0	55 56.1	18 55	76 14.7
54	Altair	0.9	21 08	N 8 51.7	42 02.5	19 51	62 21.1
55	Peacock	2.1	21 43	S 56 44.9	33 21.3	20 25	53 39.9
56	Deneb	1.3	21 59	N 45 16.3	29 21.6	20 41	49 40.2
57	Enif..................	2.5	23 01	N 9 51.6	13 41.3	21 44	33 59.9
58	Al Na'ir.............	2.2	23 25	S 46 58.8	7 41.5	22 08	28 00.1
59	Fomalhaut	1.3	0 19	S 29 38.5	355 19.8	22 57	15 38.4
60	Markab	2.6	0 26	N 15 11.1	353 32.7	23 05	13 51.3

Star Transit Corr Table

Date	Corr h m	Date	Corr h m
1	−0 00	17	−1 03
2	−0 04	18	−1 07
3	−0 08	19	−1 11
4	−0 12	20	−1 15
5	−0 16	21	−1 19
6	−0 20	22	−1 23
7	−0 24	23	−1 27
8	−0 28	24	−1 30
9	−0 31	25	−1 34
10	−0 35	26	−1 38
11	−0 39	27	−1 42
12	−0 43	28	−1 46
13	−0 47	29	−1 50
14	−0 51	30	−1 54
15	−0 55	31	−1 58
16	−0 59		

STAR TRANSIT

To find the approx time of transit of a star for any day of the month use above table. All corrections are subtractive.

If the quantity taken from the table is greater than the time of transit for the first of the month, add 23h 56min to the time of transit before subtracting the correction.

Example: What time will Fomalhaut (No 59) transit the Meridian on Sept. 30?

	h min
Transit on Sep 1	00 18
	+23 56
	24 14
Corr for Sep 30	−01 54
Transit on Sep 30	22 20

SEPTEMBER DIARY

d h	
2 04	Jupiter 3° S of Moon
5 11	Neptune 5° S of Moon
5 19	Uranus 6° S of Moon
9 17	Saturn 6° S of Moon
9 04	Mercury greatest elong. E(27°)
14 15	Saturn at opposition
20 07	Jupiter 5° N of Antares
22 06	Mercury stationary
23 12	Equinox
25 23	Mercury 3° S of Moon
27 18	Mars 2° S of Moon
28 21	Mercury 5° S of Venus
29 15	Jupiter 3° S of Moon

NOTES

Star declinations may be used as is for the whole month. To correct GHA for day, hour, minute and second see page E 92 and for further explanation of this table see page E 4.

SEPTEMBER

SEPTEMBER 1995 — SUN & ARIES — GMT

Time	SUN GHA ° '	Dec ° '	ARIES GHA ° '	Time	SUN GHA ° '	Dec ° '	ARIES GHA ° '	Time	SUN GHA ° '	Dec ° '	ARIES GHA ° '	Time
	Friday, 1st September				**Wednesday, 6th September**				**Monday, 11th September**			
00	179 56.0	N 8 31.8	339 41.4	00	180 20.3	N 6 41.9	344 37.1	00	180 46.1	N 4 49.3	349 32.8	00
02	209 56.4	8 30.0	9 46.3	02	210 20.7	6 40.1	14 42.0	02	210 46.6	4 47.4	19 37.7	02
04	239 56.7	8 28.2	39 51.3	04	240 21.2	6 38.2	44 47.0	04	240 47.0	4 45.5	49 42.6	04
06	269 57.1	8 26.4	69 56.2	06	270 21.6	6 36.4	74 51.9	06	270 47.4	4 43.6	79 47.6	06
08	299 57.5	8 24.6	100 01.1	08	300 22.0	6 34.5	104 56.8	08	300 47.9	4 41.7	109 52.5	08
10	329 57.9	8 22.8	130 06.0	10	330 22.4	6 32.6	135 01.7	10	330 48.3	4 39.8	139 57.4	10
12	359 58.3	8 21.0	160 11.0	12	0 22.8	6 30.8	165 06.7	12	0 48.8	4 37.9	170 02.4	12
14	29 58.7	8 19.1	190 15.9	14	30 23.3	6 28.9	195 11.6	14	30 49.2	4 36.0	200 07.3	14
16	59 59.1	8 17.3	220 20.8	16	60 23.7	6 27.1	225 16.5	16	60 49.6	4 34.1	230 12.2	16
18	89 59.5	8 15.5	250 25.8	18	90 24.1	6 25.2	255 21.4	18	90 50.1	4 32.2	260 17.1	18
20	119 59.9	8 13.7	280 30.7	20	120 24.5	6 23.3	285 26.4	20	120 50.5	4 30.3	290 22.1	20
22	150 00.3	N 8 11.9	310 35.6	22	150 25.0	N 6 21.5	315 31.3	22	150 51.0	N 4 28.4	320 27.0	22
	Saturday, 2nd September				**Thursday, 7th September**				**Tuesday, 12th September**			
00	180 00.7	N 8 10.1	340 40.5	00	180 25.4	N 6 19.6	345 36.2	00	180 51.4	N 4 26.5	350 31.9	00
02	210 01.1	8 08.3	10 45.5	02	210 25.8	6 17.7	15 41.2	02	210 51.8	4 24.6	20 36.9	02
04	240 01.5	8 06.4	40 50.4	04	240 26.2	6 15.9	45 46.1	04	240 52.3	4 22.7	50 41.8	04
06	270 01.9	8 04.6	70 55.3	06	270 26.7	6 14.0	75 51.0	06	270 52.7	4 20.8	80 46.7	06
08	300 02.3	8 02.8	101 00.3	08	300 27.1	6 12.1	105 55.9	08	300 53.2	4 18.9	110 51.6	08
10	330 02.7	8 01.0	131 05.2	10	330 27.5	6 10.3	136 00.9	10	330 53.6	4 17.0	140 56.6	10
12	0 03.1	7 59.2	161 10.1	12	0 27.9	6 08.4	166 05.8	12	0 54.1	4 15.1	171 01.5	12
14	30 03.5	7 57.3	191 15.0	14	30 28.4	6 06.5	196 10.7	14	30 54.5	4 13.2	201 06.4	14
16	60 03.9	7 55.5	221 20.0	16	60 28.8	6 04.7	226 15.7	16	60 54.9	4 11.3	231 11.4	16
18	90 04.3	7 53.7	251 24.9	18	90 29.2	6 02.8	256 20.6	18	90 55.4	4 09.4	261 16.3	18
20	120 04.7	7 51.9	281 29.8	20	120 29.6	6 00.9	286 25.5	20	120 55.8	4 07.5	291 21.2	20
22	150 05.1	N 7 50.0	311 34.8	22	150 30.1	N 5 59.0	316 30.4	22	150 56.3	N 4 05.6	321 26.1	22
	Sunday, 3rd September				**Friday, 8th September**				**Wednesday, 13th September**			
00	180 05.5	N 7 48.2	341 39.7	00	180 30.5	N 5 57.2	346 35.4	00	180 56.7	N 4 03.6	351 31.1	00
02	210 05.9	7 46.4	11 44.6	02	210 30.9	5 55.3	16 40.3	02	210 57.2	4 01.7	21 36.0	02
04	240 06.3	7 44.6	41 49.5	04	240 31.4	5 53.4	46 45.2	04	240 57.6	3 59.8	51 40.9	04
06	270 06.7	7 42.7	71 54.5	06	270 31.8	5 51.5	76 50.2	06	270 58.0	3 57.9	81 45.9	06
08	300 07.1	7 40.9	101 59.4	08	300 32.2	5 49.7	106 55.1	08	300 58.5	3 56.0	111 50.8	08
10	330 07.5	7 39.1	132 04.3	10	330 32.7	5 47.8	137 00.0	10	330 58.9	3 54.1	141 55.7	10
12	0 07.9	7 37.2	162 09.2	12	0 33.1	5 45.9	167 04.9	12	0 59.4	3 52.2	172 00.6	12
14	30 08.3	7 35.4	192 14.2	14	30 33.5	5 44.0	197 09.9	14	30 59.8	3 50.3	202 05.6	14
16	60 08.7	7 33.6	222 19.1	16	60 33.9	5 42.2	227 14.8	16	61 00.3	3 48.4	232 10.5	16
18	90 09.1	7 31.7	252 24.0	18	90 34.4	5 40.3	257 19.7	18	91 00.7	3 46.4	262 15.4	18
20	120 09.6	7 29.9	282 29.0	20	120 34.8	5 38.4	287 24.7	20	121 01.2	3 44.5	292 20.3	20
22	150 10.0	N 7 28.1	312 33.9	22	150 35.2	N 5 36.5	317 29.6	22	151 01.6	N 3 42.6	322 25.3	22
	Monday, 4th September				**Saturday, 9th September**				**Thursday, 14th September**			
00	180 10.4	N 7 26.2	342 38.8	00	180 35.7	N 5 34.6	347 34.5	00	181 02.0	N 3 40.7	352 30.2	00
02	210 10.8	7 24.4	12 43.7	02	210 36.1	5 32.8	17 39.4	02	211 02.5	3 38.8	22 35.1	02
04	240 11.2	7 22.6	42 48.7	04	240 36.5	5 30.9	47 44.4	04	241 02.9	3 36.9	52 40.1	04
06	270 11.6	7 20.7	72 53.6	06	270 37.0	5 29.0	77 49.3	06	271 03.4	3 35.0	82 45.0	06
08	300 12.0	7 18.9	102 58.5	08	300 37.4	5 27.1	107 54.2	08	301 03.8	3 33.0	112 49.9	08
10	330 12.4	7 17.0	133 03.5	10	330 37.8	5 25.2	137 59.2	10	331 04.3	3 31.1	142 54.8	10
12	0 12.8	7 15.2	163 08.4	12	0 38.3	5 23.3	168 04.1	12	1 04.7	3 29.2	172 59.8	12
14	30 13.2	7 13.4	193 13.3	14	30 38.7	5 21.5	198 09.0	14	31 05.2	3 27.3	203 04.7	14
16	60 13.7	7 11.5	223 18.2	16	60 39.1	5 19.6	228 13.9	16	61 05.6	3 25.4	233 09.6	16
18	90 14.1	7 09.7	253 23.2	18	90 39.6	5 17.7	258 18.9	18	91 06.0	3 23.5	263 14.6	18
20	120 14.5	7 07.8	283 28.1	20	120 40.0	5 15.8	288 23.8	20	121 06.5	3 21.5	293 19.5	20
22	150 14.9	N 7 06.0	313 33.0	22	150 40.4	N 5 13.9	318 28.7	22	151 06.9	N 3 19.6	323 24.4	22
	Tuesday, 5th September				**Sunday, 10th September**				**Friday, 15th September**			
00	180 15.3	N 7 04.1	343 38.0	00	180 40.9	N 5 12.0	344 33.6	00	181 07.4	N 3 17.7	353 29.3	00
02	210 15.7	7 02.3	13 42.9	02	210 41.3	5 10.1	18 38.6	02	211 07.8	3 15.8	23 34.3	02
04	240 16.1	7 00.4	43 47.8	04	240 41.8	5 08.2	48 43.5	04	241 08.3	3 13.9	53 39.2	04
06	270 16.6	6 58.6	73 52.7	06	270 42.2	5 06.3	78 48.4	06	271 08.7	3 11.9	83 44.1	06
08	300 17.0	6 56.7	103 57.7	08	300 42.6	5 04.5	108 53.4	08	301 09.2	3 10.0	113 49.1	08
10	330 17.4	6 54.9	134 02.6	10	330 43.1	5 02.6	138 58.3	10	331 09.6	3 08.1	143 54.0	10
12	0 17.8	6 53.0	164 07.5	12	0 43.5	5 00.7	169 03.2	12	1 10.1	3 06.2	173 58.9	12
14	30 18.2	6 51.2	194 12.5	14	30 43.9	4 58.8	199 08.1	14	31 10.5	3 04.2	204 03.8	14
16	60 18.6	6 49.3	224 17.4	16	60 44.4	4 56.9	229 13.1	16	61 10.9	3 02.3	234 08.8	16
18	90 19.1	6 47.5	254 22.3	18	90 44.8	4 55.0	259 18.0	18	91 11.4	3 00.4	264 13.7	18
20	120 19.5	6 45.6	284 27.2	20	120 45.3	4 53.1	289 22.9	20	121 11.8	2 58.5	294 18.6	20
22	150 19.9	N 6 43.8	314 32.2	22	150 45.7	N 4 51.2	319 27.9	22	151 12.3	N 2 56.6	324 23.6	22

NOTES

Sun & Aries GHA corrections for additional hour, minutes, and seconds on page E 94.
Correct Sun Declination by interpolation. For example see page E 4.

SEPTEMBER 1995 — SUN & ARIES — GMT

Saturday, 16th September | Thursday, 21st September | Tuesday, 26th September

Time	SUN GHA	Dec	ARIES GHA	Time	SUN GHA	Dec	ARIES GHA	Time	SUN GHA	Dec	ARIES GHA	Time
00	181 12.7	N 2 54.6	354 28.5	00	181 39.4	N 0 58.6	359 24.2	00	182 05.6	S 0 58.2	4 19.9	00
02	211 13.2	2 52.7	24 33.4	02	211 39.9	0 56.6	29 29.1	02	212 06.1	1 00.2	34 24.8	02
04	241 13.6	2 50.8	54 38.3	04	241 40.3	0 54.7	59 34.0	04	242 06.5	1 02.1	64 29.7	04
06	271 14.1	2 48.9	84 43.3	06	271 40.8	0 52.7	89 39.0	06	272 06.9	1 04.1	94 34.7	06
08	301 14.5	2 46.9	114 48.2	08	301 41.2	0 50.8	119 43.9	08	302 07.3	1 06.0	124 39.6	08
10	331 15.0	2 45.0	144 53.1	10	331 41.7	0 48.8	149 48.8	10	332 07.8	1 08.0	154 44.5	10
12	1 15.4	2 43.1	174 58.1	12	1 42.1	0 46.9	179 53.7	12	2 08.2	1 09.9	184 49.4	12
14	31 15.9	2 41.1	205 03.0	14	31 42.5	0 44.9	209 58.7	14	32 08.6	1 11.9	214 54.4	14
16	61 16.3	2 39.2	235 07.9	16	61 43.0	0 43.0	240 03.6	16	62 09.0	1 13.8	244 59.3	16
18	91 16.7	2 37.3	265 12.8	18	91 43.4	0 41.1	270 08.5	18	92 09.5	1 15.8	275 04.2	18
20	121 17.2	2 35.4	295 17.8	20	121 43.9	0 39.1	300 13.5	20	122 09.9	1 17.7	305 09.1	20
22	151 17.6	N 2 33.4	325 22.7	22	151 44.3	N 0 37.2	330 18.4	22	152 10.3	S 1 19.7	335 14.1	22

Sunday, 17th September | Friday, 22nd September | Wednesday, 27th September

Time	SUN GHA	Dec	ARIES GHA	Time	SUN GHA	Dec	ARIES GHA	Time	SUN GHA	Dec	ARIES GHA	Time
00	181 18.1	N 2 31.5	355 27.6	00	181 44.7	N 0 35.2	0 23.3	00	182 10.7	S 1 21.6	5 19.0	00
02	211 18.5	2 29.6	25 32.5	02	211 45.2	0 33.3	30 28.2	02	212 11.2	1 23.5	35 23.9	02
04	241 19.0	2 27.6	55 37.5	04	241 45.6	0 31.3	60 33.2	04	242 11.6	1 25.5	65 28.9	04
06	271 19.4	2 25.7	85 42.4	06	271 46.1	0 29.4	90 38.1	06	272 12.0	1 27.4	95 33.8	06
08	301 19.9	2 23.8	115 47.3	08	301 46.5	0 27.4	120 43.0	08	302 12.4	1 29.4	125 38.7	08
10	331 20.3	2 21.9	145 52.3	10	331 46.9	0 25.5	150 48.0	10	332 12.9	1 31.3	155 43.6	10
12	1 20.8	2 19.9	175 57.2	12	1 47.4	0 23.6	180 52.9	12	2 13.3	1 33.3	185 48.6	12
14	31 21.2	2 18.0	206 02.1	14	31 47.8	0 21.6	210 57.8	14	32 13.7	1 35.2	215 53.5	14
16	61 21.7	2 16.1	236 07.0	16	61 48.3	0 19.7	241 02.7	16	62 14.1	1 37.2	245 58.4	16
18	91 22.1	2 14.1	266 12.0	18	91 48.7	0 17.7	271 07.7	18	92 14.6	1 39.1	276 03.4	18
20	121 22.5	2 12.2	296 16.9	20	121 49.1	0 15.8	301 12.6	20	122 15.0	1 41.1	306 08.3	20
22	151 23.0	N 2 10.3	326 21.8	22	151 49.6	N 0 13.8	331 17.5	22	152 15.4	S 1 43.0	336 13.2	22

Monday, 18th September | Saturday, 23rd September | Thursday, 28th September

Time	SUN GHA	Dec	ARIES GHA	Time	SUN GHA	Dec	ARIES GHA	Time	SUN GHA	Dec	ARIES GHA	Time
00	181 23.4	N 2 08.3	356 26.8	00	181 50.0	N 0 11.9	1 22.5	00	182 15.8	S 1 45.0	6 18.1	00
02	211 23.9	2 06.4	26 31.7	02	211 50.4	0 09.9	31 27.4	02	212 16.2	1 46.9	36 23.1	02
04	241 24.3	2 04.5	56 36.6	04	241 50.9	0 08.0	61 32.3	04	242 16.7	1 48.9	66 28.0	04
06	271 24.8	2 02.5	86 41.5	06	271 51.3	0 06.0	91 37.2	06	272 17.1	1 50.8	96 32.9	06
08	301 25.2	2 00.6	116 46.5	08	301 51.8	0 04.1	121 42.2	08	302 17.5	1 52.8	126 37.9	08
10	331 25.6	1 58.7	146 51.4	10	331 52.2	0 02.2	151 47.1	10	332 17.9	1 54.7	156 42.8	10
12	1 26.1	1 56.7	176 56.3	12	1 52.6	0 00.2	181 52.0	12	2 18.3	1 56.6	186 47.7	12
14	31 26.6	1 54.8	207 01.3	14	31 53.1	S 0 01.7	211 56.9	14	32 18.8	1 58.6	216 52.6	14
16	61 27.0	1 52.8	237 06.2	16	61 53.5	0 03.7	242 01.9	16	62 19.2	2 00.5	246 57.6	16
18	91 27.5	1 50.9	267 11.1	18	91 53.9	0 05.6	272 06.8	18	92 19.6	2 02.5	277 02.5	18
20	121 27.9	1 49.0	297 16.0	20	121 54.4	0 07.6	302 11.7	20	122 20.0	2 04.4	307 07.4	20
22	151 28.3	N 1 47.0	327 21.0	22	151 54.8	S 0 09.5	332 16.7	22	152 20.4	S 2 06.4	337 12.4	22

Tuesday, 19th September | Sunday, 24th September | Friday, 29th September

Time	SUN GHA	Dec	ARIES GHA	Time	SUN GHA	Dec	ARIES GHA	Time	SUN GHA	Dec	ARIES GHA	Time
00	181 28.8	N 1 45.1	357 25.9	00	181 55.3	S 0 11.5	2 21.6	00	182 20.9	S 2 08.3	7 17.3	00
02	211 29.2	1 43.2	27 30.8	02	211 55.7	0 13.4	32 26.5	02	212 21.3	2 10.3	37 22.2	02
04	241 29.7	1 41.2	57 35.8	04	241 56.1	0 15.4	62 31.4	04	242 21.7	2 12.2	67 27.1	04
06	271 30.1	1 39.3	87 40.7	06	271 56.6	0 17.3	92 36.4	06	272 22.1	2 14.2	97 32.1	06
08	301 30.6	1 37.4	117 45.6	08	301 57.0	0 19.3	122 41.3	08	302 22.5	2 16.1	127 37.0	08
10	331 31.0	1 35.4	147 50.5	10	331 57.4	0 21.2	152 46.2	10	332 22.9	2 18.1	157 41.9	10
12	1 31.5	1 33.5	177 55.5	12	1 57.9	0 23.2	182 51.2	12	2 23.3	2 20.0	187 46.9	12
14	31 31.9	1 31.5	208 00.4	14	31 58.3	0 25.1	212 56.1	14	32 23.8	2 21.9	217 51.8	14
16	61 32.3	1 29.6	238 05.3	16	61 58.7	0 27.1	243 01.0	16	62 24.2	2 23.9	247 56.7	16
18	91 32.8	1 27.7	268 10.3	18	91 59.2	0 29.0	273 05.9	18	92 24.6	2 25.8	278 01.6	18
20	121 33.2	1 25.7	298 15.2	20	121 59.6	0 31.0	303 10.9	20	122 25.0	2 27.8	308 06.6	20
22	151 33.7	N 1 23.8	328 20.1	22	152 00.0	S 0 32.9	333 15.8	22	152 25.4	S 2 29.7	338 11.5	22

Wednesday, 20th September | Monday, 25th September | Saturday, 30th September

Time	SUN GHA	Dec	ARIES GHA	Time	SUN GHA	Dec	ARIES GHA	Time	SUN GHA	Dec	ARIES GHA	Time
00	181 34.1	N 1 21.8	358 25.0	00	182 00.5	S 0 34.8	3 20.7	00	182 25.8	S 2 31.7	8 16.4	00
02	211 34.6	1 19.9	28 30.0	02	212 00.9	0 36.8	33 25.7	02	212 26.2	2 33.6	38 21.4	02
04	241 35.0	1 18.0	58 34.9	04	242 01.3	0 38.7	63 30.6	04	242 26.7	2 35.5	68 26.3	04
06	271 35.5	1 16.0	88 39.8	06	272 01.8	0 40.7	93 35.5	06	272 27.1	2 37.5	98 31.2	06
08	301 35.9	1 14.1	118 44.7	08	302 02.2	0 42.6	123 40.4	08	302 27.5	2 39.4	128 36.1	08
10	331 36.3	1 12.1	148 49.7	10	332 02.6	0 44.6	153 45.4	10	332 27.9	2 41.4	158 41.1	10
12	1 36.8	1 10.2	178 54.6	12	2 03.0	0 46.5	183 50.3	12	2 28.3	2 43.3	188 46.0	12
14	31 37.2	1 08.3	208 59.5	14	32 03.5	0 48.5	213 55.2	14	32 28.7	2 45.3	218 50.9	14
16	61 37.6	1 06.3	239 04.5	16	62 03.9	0 50.4	244 00.2	16	62 29.1	2 47.2	248 55.8	16
18	91 38.1	1 04.4	269 09.4	18	92 04.3	0 52.4	274 05.1	18	92 29.5	2 49.1	279 00.8	18
20	121 38.6	1 02.4	299 14.3	20	122 04.8	0 54.3	304 10.0	20	122 29.9	2 51.1	309 05.7	20
22	151 39.0	N 1 00.5	329 19.2	22	152 05.2	S 0 56.3	334 14.9	22	152 30.3	S 2 53.0	339 10.6	22

SEPTEMBER

SEPTEMBER 1995 — PLANETS — 0h GMT

VENUS / JUPITER

Mer Pass h m	GHA ° '	Mean Var/hr 14°+	Dec ° '	Mean Var/hr '	Note Corrections on Page E 101	GHA ° '	Mean Var/hr 15°+	Dec ° '	Mean Var/hr '	Mer Pass h m
12 14	176 34.2	59.6	N 8 42.3	1.2	1 Fri	94 37.5	2.2	S 20 56.6	0.0	17 39
12 15	176 23.8	59.6	N 8 13.9	1.2	2 Sat	95 31.2	2.2	S 20 57.6	0.0	17 35
12 15	176 13.5	59.6	N 7 45.3	1.2	3 SUN	96 24.7	2.2	S 20 58.7	0.0	17 32
12 16	176 03.4	59.6	N 7 16.6	1.2	4 Mon	97 18.1	2.2	S 20 59.8	0.0	17 28
12 17	175 53.5	59.6	N 6 47.6	1.2	5 Tu	98 11.3	2.2	S 21 00.9	0.0	17 25
12 17	175 43.7	59.6	N 6 18.4	1.2	6 Wed	99 04.3	2.2	S 21 02.1	0.1	17 21
12 18	175 34.0	59.6	N 5 49.0	1.2	7 Th	99 57.1	2.2	S 21 03.3	0.0	17 18
12 19	175 24.5	59.6	N 5 19.5	1.2	8 Fri	100 49.8	2.2	S 21 04.4	0.0	17 14
12 19	175 15.0	59.6	N 4 49.8	1.2	9 Sat	101 42.3	2.2	S 21 05.6	0.1	17 11
12 20	175 05.7	59.6	N 4 20.0	1.3	10 SUN	102 34.7	2.2	S 21 06.9	0.0	17 07
12 21	174 56.5	59.6	N 3 50.0	1.3	11 Mon	103 26.9	2.2	S 21 08.1	0.1	17 04
12 21	174 47.3	59.6	N 3 20.0	1.3	12 Tu	104 19.0	2.2	S 21 09.4	0.0	17 00
12 22	174 38.2	59.6	N 2 49.8	1.3	13 Wed	105 10.9	2.2	S 21 10.6	0.1	16 57
12 22	174 29.2	59.6	N 2 19.5	1.3	14 Th	106 02.7	2.1	S 21 11.9	0.1	16 53
12 23	174 20.2	59.6	N 1 49.2	1.3	15 Fri	106 54.3	2.1	S 21 13.2	0.1	16 50
12 24	174 11.3	59.6	N 1 18.8	1.3	16 Sat	107 45.7	2.1	S 21 14.6	0.1	16 47
12 24	174 02.4	59.6	N 0 48.3	1.3	17 SUN	108 37.0	2.1	S 21 15.9	0.1	16 43
12 25	173 53.5	59.6	N 0 17.8	1.3	18 Mon	109 28.2	2.1	S 21 17.3	0.1	16 40
12 25	173 44.6	59.6	S 0 12.8	1.3	19 Tu	110 19.2	2.1	S 21 18.6	0.1	16 36
12 26	173 35.7	59.6	S 0 43.3	1.3	20 Wed	111 10.1	2.1	S 21 20.0	0.1	16 33
12 27	173 26.8	59.6	S 1 13.9	1.3	21 Th	112 00.8	2.1	S 21 21.4	0.1	16 30
12 27	173 17.8	59.6	S 1 44.5	1.3	22 Fri	112 51.4	2.1	S 21 22.8	0.1	16 26
12 28	173 08.9	59.6	S 2 15.1	1.3	23 Sat	113 41.9	2.1	S 21 24.2	0.1	16 23
12 28	172 59.9	59.6	S 2 45.6	1.3	24 SUN	114 32.2	2.1	S 21 25.6	0.1	16 20
12 29	172 50.8	59.6	S 3 16.1	1.3	25 Mon	115 22.4	2.1	S 21 27.0	0.1	16 16
12 30	172 41.6	59.6	S 3 46.5	1.3	26 Tu	116 12.4	2.1	S 21 28.5	0.1	16 13
12 30	172 32.4	59.6	S 4 16.9	1.3	27 Wed	117 02.3	2.1	S 21 29.9	0.1	16 10
12 31	172 23.1	59.6	S 4 47.2	1.3	28 Th	117 52.1	2.1	S 21 31.4	0.1	16 06
12 31	172 13.7	59.6	S 5 17.4	1.3	29 Fri	118 41.7	2.1	S 21 32.8	0.1	16 03
12 32	172 04.2	59.6	S 5 47.5	1.3	30 Sat	119 31.3	2.1	S 21 34.3	0.1	16 00

VENUS, Av. Mag. -3.9
S.H.A. September
5 192; 10 187; 15 181; 20 175; 25 170; 30 164.

JUPITER, Av. Mag. -2.0
S.H.A. September
5 115; 10 114; 15 113; 20 113; 25 112; 30 111.

MARS / SATURN

Mer Pass h m	GHA ° '	Mean Var/hr 15°+	Dec ° '	Mean Var/hr '	Note Corrections on Page E 101	GHA ° '	Mean Var/hr 15°+	Dec ° '	Mean Var/hr '	Mer Pass h m
14 56	135 45.2	0.9	S 10 07.1	0.6	1 Fri	345 46.3	2.6	S 5 10.0	0.1	00 57
14 55	136 07.5	0.9	S 10 22.0	0.6	2 Sat	346 49.5	2.6	S 5 11.8	0.1	00 53
14 53	136 29.7	0.9	S 10 36.8	0.6	3 SUN	347 52.6	2.6	S 5 13.7	0.1	00 48
14 52	136 51.7	0.9	S 10 51.6	0.6	4 Mon	348 55.9	2.6	S 5 15.5	0.1	00 44
14 50	137 13.6	0.9	S 11 06.3	0.6	5 Tu	349 59.1	2.6	S 5 17.4	0.1	00 40
14 49	137 35.4	0.9	S 11 21.0	0.6	6 Wed	351 02.4	2.6	S 5 19.3	0.1	00 36
14 47	137 57.0	0.9	S 11 35.7	0.6	7 Th	352 05.7	2.6	S 5 21.1	0.1	00 32
14 46	138 18.5	0.9	S 11 50.2	0.6	8 Fri	353 09.0	2.6	S 5 23.0	0.1	00 27
14 44	138 39.9	0.9	S 12 04.8	0.6	9 Sat	354 12.3	2.6	S 5 24.9	0.1	00 23
14 43	139 01.1	0.9	S 12 19.2	0.6	10 SUN	355 15.7	2.6	S 5 26.8	0.1	00 19
14 42	139 22.1	0.9	S 12 33.6	0.6	11 Mon	356 19.0	2.6	S 5 28.7	0.1	00 15
14 40	139 43.0	0.9	S 12 48.0	0.6	12 Tu	357 22.4	2.6	S 5 30.6	0.1	00 10
14 39	140 03.8	0.9	S 13 02.3	0.6	13 Wed	358 25.8	2.6	S 5 32.4	0.1	00 06
14 38	140 24.4	0.9	S 13 16.5	0.6	14 Th	359 29.1	2.6	S 5 34.3	0.1	00 02
14 36	140 44.9	0.8	S 13 30.6	0.6	15 Fri	0 32.5	2.6	S 5 36.2	0.1	23 54
14 35	141 05.2	0.8	S 13 44.7	0.6	16 Sat	1 35.9	2.6	S 5 38.0	0.1	23 49
14 34	141 25.3	0.8	S 13 58.6	0.6	17 SUN	2 39.3	2.6	S 5 39.9	0.1	23 45
14 32	141 45.3	0.8	S 14 12.5	0.6	18 Mon	3 42.7	2.6	S 5 41.8	0.1	23 41
14 31	142 05.1	0.8	S 14 26.4	0.6	19 Tu	4 46.1	2.6	S 5 43.6	0.1	23 37
14 30	142 24.8	0.8	S 14 40.1	0.6	20 Wed	5 49.4	2.6	S 5 45.4	0.1	23 33
14 28	142 44.3	0.8	S 14 53.7	0.6	21 Th	6 52.8	2.6	S 5 47.3	0.1	23 28
14 27	143 03.7	0.8	S 15 07.3	0.6	22 Fri	7 56.2	2.6	S 5 49.1	0.1	23 24
14 26	143 22.9	0.8	S 15 20.8	0.6	23 Sat	8 59.5	2.6	S 5 50.9	0.1	23 20
14 24	143 41.9	0.8	S 15 34.1	0.6	24 SUN	10 02.8	2.6	S 5 52.7	0.1	23 16
14 23	144 00.8	0.8	S 15 47.4	0.5	25 Mon	11 06.1	2.6	S 5 54.4	0.1	23 12
14 22	144 19.5	0.8	S 16 00.6	0.5	26 Tu	12 09.4	2.6	S 5 56.2	0.1	23 07
14 21	144 38.0	0.8	S 16 13.6	0.5	27 Wed	13 12.7	2.6	S 5 58.0	0.1	23 03
14 20	144 56.4	0.8	S 16 26.6	0.5	28 Th	14 15.9	2.6	S 5 59.7	0.1	22 59
14 18	145 14.6	0.8	S 16 39.5	0.5	29 Fri	15 19.1	2.6	S 6 01.4	0.1	22 55
14 17	145 32.6	0.7	S 16 52.2	0.5	30 Sat	16 22.3	2.6	S 6 03.1	0.1	22 51

MARS, Av. Mag. +1.4
S.H.A. September
5 154; 10 150; 15 147; 20 144; 25 141; 30 137.

SATURN, Av. Mag. +0.7
S.H.A. September
5 6; 10 7; 15 7; 20 7; 25 8; 30 8.

SEPTEMBER 1995   MOON

Day	GMT hr	GHA ° ′	Mean Var/hr 14°+	Dec ° ′	Mean Var/hr ′	Day	GMT hr	GHA ° ′	Mean Var/hr 14°+	Dec ° ′	Mean Var/hr ′
1 Fri	0	111 25.9	26.7	S 15 52.4	6.1	17 Sun	0	270 48.4	31.2	N 18 55.5	0.6
	6	198 06.3	26.3	S 16 29.1	5.5		6	357 55.6	31.2	N 18 51.9	1.2
	12	284 44.8	26.1	S 17 02.3	4.9		12	85 02.9	31.2	N 18 45.3	1.7
	18	11 21.5	25.8	S 17 31.7	4.2		18	172 10.5	31.3	N 18 35.5	2.1
2 Sat	0	97 56.5	25.6	S 17 57.2	3.5	18 Mon	0	259 18.3	31.4	N 18 22.6	2.7
	6	184 30.0	25.3	S 18 18.6	2.8		6	346 26.4	31.4	N 18 06.7	3.2
	12	271 02.2	25.2	S 18 35.8	2.1		12	73 34.7	31.5	N 17 47.8	3.7
	18	357 33.2	25.0	S 18 48.6	1.4		18	160 43.4	31.5	N 17 25.8	4.2
3 Sun	0	84 03.2	24.9	S 18 57.0	0.6	19 Tu	0	247 52.3	31.5	N 17 01.0	4.7
	6	170 32.6	24.8	S 19 00.8	0.2		6	335 01.6	31.6	N 16 33.3	5.1
	12	257 01.4	24.8	S 19 00.2	1.0		12	62 11.1	31.6	N 16 02.7	5.6
	18	343 30.0	24.8	S 18 54.9	1.7		18	149 20.9	31.6	N 15 29.4	6.1
4 Mon	0	69 58.5	24.8	S 18 45.0	2.5	20 Wed	0	236 31.0	31.7	N 14 53.3	6.4
	6	156 27.3	24.9	S 18 30.7	3.2		6	323 41.4	31.8	N 14 14.7	6.9
	12	242 56.5	25.0	S 18 11.8	3.9		12	50 52.0	31.8	N 13 33.5	7.3
	18	329 26.5	25.1	S 17 48.5	4.6		18	138 02.7	31.8	N 12 49.9	7.7
5 Tu	0	55 57.3	25.4	S 17 21.0	5.3	21 Th	0	225 13.5	31.8	N 12 03.9	8.1
	6	142 29.2	25.5	S 16 49.3	6.0		6	312 24.5	31.8	N 11 15.6	8.5
	12	229 02.4	25.8	S 16 13.7	6.6		12	39 35.4	31.8	N 10 25.2	8.8
	18	315 37.1	26.0	S 15 34.3	7.2		18	126 46.3	31.8	N 9 32.7	9.1
6 Wed	0	42 13.2	26.3	S 14 51.2	7.7	22 Fri	0	213 57.1	31.7	N 8 38.4	9.4
	6	128 51.1	26.6	S 14 04.8	8.3		6	301 07.6	31.7	N 7 42.2	9.7
	12	215 30.7	27.0	S 13 15.3	8.8		12	28 17.9	31.6	N 6 44.4	9.9
	18	302 12.1	27.2	S 12 22.8	9.2		18	115 27.7	31.6	N 5 45.0	10.2
7 Th	0	28 55.3	27.5	S 11 27.7	9.6	23 Sat	0	202 37.1	31.4	N 4 44.4	10.4
	6	115 40.4	27.8	S 10 30.2	10.0		6	289 45.9	31.3	N 3 42.5	10.5
	12	202 27.3	28.2	S 9 30.7	10.2		12	16 54.0	31.2	N 2 39.6	10.6
	18	289 16.0	28.5	S 8 29.2	10.5		18	104 01.3	31.1	N 1 35.9	10.7
8 Fri	0	16 06.5	28.7	S 7 26.2	10.8	24 Sun	0	191 07.7	30.9	N 0 31.5	10.8
	6	102 58.7	29.0	S 6 21.9	10.9		6	278 13.1	30.7	S 0 33.4	10.9
	12	189 52.6	29.2	S 5 16.5	11.0		12	5 17.4	30.5	S 1 38.5	10.9
	18	276 48.0	29.5	S 4 10.4	11.1		18	92 20.4	30.3	S 2 43.6	10.8
9 Sat	0	3 44.9	29.7	S 3 03.8	11.1	25 Mon	0	179 22.1	30.0	S 3 48.5	10.7
	6	90 43.2	29.9	S 1 56.8	11.2		6	266 22.3	29.7	S 4 53.1	10.7
	12	177 42.7	30.1	S 0 49.9	11.1		12	353 21.0	29.5	S 5 57.0	10.5
	18	264 43.5	30.3	N 0 16.8	11.0		18	80 18.1	29.2	S 7 00.0	10.2
10 Sun	0	351 45.3	30.5	N 1 23.0	10.8	26 Tu	0	167 13.5	28.9	S 8 01.8	10.0
	6	78 48.1	30.6	N 2 28.6	10.8		6	254 07.0	28.6	S 9 02.3	9.8
	12	165 51.8	30.7	N 3 33.4	10.6		12	340 58.8	28.2	S 10 01.1	9.4
	18	252 56.2	30.9	N 4 37.0	10.4		18	67 48.7	27.9	S 10 58.1	9.1
11 Mon	0	340 01.3	31.0	N 5 39.4	10.1	27 Wed	0	154 36.6	27.6	S 11 52.9	8.7
	6	67 06.9	31.1	N 6 40.4	9.9		6	241 22.6	27.3	S 12 45.3	8.2
	12	154 13.1	31.1	N 7 39.7	9.6		12	328 06.7	27.0	S 13 35.1	7.8
	18	241 19.6	31.1	N 8 37.3	9.2		18	54 49.0	26.7	S 14 22.0	7.3
12 Tu	0	328 26.4	31.2	N 9 33.0	8.9	28 Th	0	141 29.3	26.4	S 15 05.8	6.7
	6	55 33.5	31.2	N 10 26.6	8.5		6	228 08.0	26.1	S 15 46.3	6.1
	12	142 40.8	31.3	N 11 18.0	8.2		12	314 44.9	25.9	S 16 23.2	5.5
	18	229 48.1	31.2	N 12 07.2	7.7		18	41 20.4	25.7	S 16 56.4	4.8
13 Wed	0	316 55.6	31.2	N 12 53.9	7.3	29 Fri	0	127 54.4	25.5	S 17 25.7	4.2
	6	44 03.0	31.3	N 13 38.2	6.9		6	214 27.2	25.2	S 17 50.9	3.5
	12	131 10.5	31.2	N 14 19.8	6.5		12	300 58.9	25.1	S 18 12.0	2.7
	18	218 17.8	31.2	N 14 58.8	6.0		18	27 29.8	25.0	S 18 28.7	2.0
14 Th	0	305 25.1	31.2	N 15 34.9	5.5	30 Sat	0	114 00.1	25.0	S 18 41.1	1.2
	6	32 32.4	31.2	N 16 08.3	5.0		6	200 29.9	24.9	S 18 48.9	0.5
	12	119 39.5	31.2	N 16 38.8	4.5		12	286 59.6	24.9	S 18 52.3	0.2
	18	206 46.5	31.2	N 17 06.3	4.1		18	13 29.4	25.0	S 18 51.2	1.0
15 Fri	0	293 53.5	31.2	N 17 30.8	3.6						
	6	21 00.4	31.1	N 17 52.3	3.0						
	12	108 07.2	31.1	N 18 10.7	2.5						
	18	195 14.0	31.1	N 18 26.0	2.0						
16 Sat	0	282 20.8	31.1	N 18 38.2	1.5						
	6	9 27.6	31.1	N 18 47.2	0.9						
	12	96 34.4	31.2	N 18 53.1	0.4						
	18	183 41.3	31.2	N 18 55.9	0.1						

NOTE Moon GHA corrections for additional hours, minutes, and seconds on page E 96.
Moon Declination corrections on page E 99. Mean Var/Hr value needed for both corrections.

SEPTEMBER

OCTOBER 1995 — SUN & MOON — GMT

SUN

Day of Yr	Mth	Week	Eq. of Time 0h	Eq. of Time 12h	Transit	Semi-diam	Lat 52°N Twilight	Sunrise	Sunset	Twilight	Lat	Twilight	Sunrise	Sunset	Twilight
			m s	m s	h m	′	h m	h m	h m	h m	°	h m	h m	h m	h m
274	1	Sun	-10 03	-10 12	11 50	16.0	05 26	06 00	17 39	18 12	N60	+0 06	+0 14	-0 14	-0 06
275	2	Mon	-10 22	-10 32	11 49	16.0	05 28	06 02	17 36	18 10	55	+0 02	+0 05	-0 05	-0 02
276	3	Tu	-10 41	-10 51	11 49	16.0	05 30	06 03	17 34	18 08	50	-0 01	-0 03	+0 03	+0 01
277	4	Wed	-11 00	-11 09	11 49	16.0	05 31	06 05	17 32	18 05	45	-0 04	-0 09	+0 09	+0 04
278	5	Th	-11 19	-11 28	11 49	16.0	05 33	06 07	17 30	18 03	N40	-0 07	-0 14	+0 14	+0 07
279	6	Fri	-11 37	-11 46	11 48	16.0	05 35	06 08	17 27	18 01	35	-0 10	-0 18	+0 18	+0 10
280	7	Sat	-11 55	-12 03	11 48	16.0	05 36	06 10	17 25	17 59	30	-0 12	-0 22	+0 22	+0 12
281	8	Sun	-12 12	-12 21	11 48	16.0	05 38	06 12	17 23	17 56	25	-0 15	-0 26	+0 26	+0 15
282	9	Mon	-12 29	-12 37	11 47	16.0	05 40	06 13	17 20	17 54	N20	-0 17	-0 29	+0 29	+0 17
283	10	Tu	-12 46	-12 54	11 47	16.0	05 41	06 15	17 18	17 52	15	-0 20	-0 32	+0 32	+0 20
284	11	Wed	-13 02	-13 10	11 47	16.0	05 43	06 17	17 16	17 50	10	-0 23	-0 35	+0 35	+0 23
285	12	Th	-13 18	-13 25	11 47	16.1	05 45	06 19	17 14	17 48	5	-0 25	-0 38	+0 38	+0 25
286	13	Fri	-13 33	-13 40	11 46	16.1	05 46	06 20	17 12	17 45	0	-0 28	-0 41	+0 41	+0 28
287	14	Sat	-13 47	-13 54	11 46	16.1	05 48	06 22	17 09	17 43	S 5	-0 31	-0 44	+0 44	+0 31
288	15	Sun	-14 01	-14 08	11 46	16.1	05 50	06 24	17 07	17 41	10	-0 35	-0 47	+0 47	+0 35
289	16	Mon	-14 15	-14 21	11 46	16.1	05 51	06 25	17 05	17 39	15	-0 38	-0 50	+0 50	+0 38
290	17	Tu	-14 28	-14 34	11 45	16.1	05 53	06 27	17 03	17 37	S20	-0 42	-0 54	+0 54	+0 42
291	18	Wed	-14 40	-14 46	11 45	16.1	05 55	06 29	17 01	17 35	25	-0 47	-0 57	+0 57	+0 47
292	19	Th	-14 52	-14 58	11 45	16.1	05 56	06 31	16 59	17 33	30	-0 52	-1 01	+1 01	+0 52
293	20	Fri	-15 03	-15 08	11 45	16.1	05 58	06 32	16 56	17 31	35	-0 58	-1 06	+1 06	+0 58
294	21	Sat	-15 14	-15 18	11 45	16.1	06 00	06 34	16 54	17 29	S40	-1 05	-1 11	+1 11	+1 05
295	22	Sun	-15 23	-15 28	11 45	16.1	06 01	06 36	16 52	17 27	45	-1 13	-1 17	+1 17	+1 13
296	23	Mon	-15 32	-15 37	11 44	16.1	06 03	06 38	16 50	17 25	50	-1 24	-1 24	+1 24	+1 24
297	24	Tu	-15 41	-15 45	11 44	16.1	06 05	06 40	16 48	17 23					
298	25	Wed	-15 49	-15 52	11 44	16.1	06 06	06 41	16 46	17 21					
299	26	Th	-15 56	-15 59	11 44	16.1	06 08	06 43	16 44	17 19					
300	27	Fri	-16 02	-16 05	11 44	16.1	06 10	06 45	16 42	17 17					
301	28	Sat	-16 08	-16 10	11 44	16.1	06 12	06 47	16 40	17 15					
302	29	Sun	-16 12	-16 15	11 44	16.1	06 13	06 48	16 38	17 13					
303	30	Mon	-16 16	-16 18	11 44	16.1	06 15	06 50	16 36	17 12					
304	31	Tu	-16 20	-16 21	11 44	16.1	06 17	06 52	16 34	17 10					

NOTES

Lat corrections are for mid-month. **Equation of Time** is the excess of Mean Time over Apparent Time.

MOON

Lat 52°N

Day of Yr	Mth	Week	Age	Transit (Upper)	Diff	Semi-diam	Hor Par	Moonrise	Moonset	Phases of the Moon
			days	h m	m	′	′	h m	h m	d h m
274	1	Sun	07	18 02	57	16.1	59.3	13 33	22 34	(First Quarter 1 14 36
275	2	Mon	08	18 59	54	16.1	59.1	14 18	23 45	O Full Moon 8 15 52
276	3	Tu	09	19 53	53	16.0	58.9	14 56	— —	) Last Quarter 16 16 26
277	4	Wed	10	20 46	50	16.0	58.6	15 28	00 59	● New Moon 24 04 36
278	5	Th	11	21 36	50	15.9	58.2	15 56	02 13	(First Quarter 30 21 17
279	6	Fri	12	22 26	48	15.7	57.8	16 22	03 28	
280	7	Sat	13	23 14	48	15.6	57.3	16 47	04 41	
281	8	Sun	14	24 02	—	15.5	56.8	17 13	05 52	
282	9	Mon	15	00 02	47	15.3	56.2	17 40	07 03	Apogee 15 02
283	10	Tu	16	00 49	48	15.2	55.6	18 09	08 10	Perigee 26 21
284	11	Wed	17	01 37	48	15.0	55.1	18 42	09 15	
285	12	Th	18	02 25	48	14.9	54.7	19 20	10 15	
286	13	Fri	19	03 13	48	14.8	54.4	20 03	11 10	
287	14	Sat	20	04 01	48	14.8	54.2	20 52	11 59	
288	15	Sun	21	04 49	47	14.8	54.2	21 46	12 42	
289	16	Mon	22	05 36	46	14.8	54.4	22 44	13 19	
290	17	Tu	23	06 22	46	14.9	54.7	23 46	13 51	
291	18	Wed	24	07 08	46	15.0	55.2	— —	14 20	
292	19	Th	25	07 54	46	15.2	55.8	00 51	14 46	**NOTES**
293	20	Fri	26	08 40	47	15.4	56.6	01 58	15 11	
294	21	Sat	27	09 27	49	15.6	57.4	03 08	15 35	**Diff** equals daily change in
295	22	Sun	28	10 16	51	15.9	58.2	04 20	16 01	transit time.
296	23	Mon	29	11 07	54	16.1	58.9	05 35	16 29	To correct Moonrise, Moonset,
297	24	Tu	00	12 01	57	16.2	59.5	06 52	17 02	or Transit times for Latitude
298	25	Wed	01	12 58	58	16.3	59.9	08 08	17 40	and/or Longitude see page
299	26	Th	02	13 56	60	16.4	60.1	09 22	18 27	E 100. For further information
300	27	Fri	03	14 56	60	16.4	60.1	10 30	19 22	about these tables see page E 4.
301	28	Sat	04	15 56	58	16.3	59.9	11 29	20 26	For Arc to Time correction see
302	29	Sun	05	16 54	56	16.2	59.5	12 18	21 36	page E 91.
303	30	Mon	06	17 50	53	16.1	59.1	12 58	22 49	
304	31	Tu	07	18 43	50	16.0	58.6	13 31	— —	

OCTOBER 1995   STARS   0h GMT October 1

No	Name	Mag	Transit h m	Dec ° '	GHA ° '	RA h m	SHA ° '
	ARIES..................		23 19		9 15.6		
1	Alpheratz..........	2.2	23 27	N 29 04.2	7 12.5	0 08	357 56.9
2	Ankaa................	2.4	23 45	S 42 19.7	2 44.1	0 26	353 28.5
3	Schedar	2.5	0 03	N 56 31.0	359 10.7	0 40	349 55.1
4	Diphda	2.2	0 06	S 18 00.5	358 24.5	0 43	349 08.9
5	Achernar	0.6	1 00	S 57 15.4	344 51.7	1 38	335 36.1
6	POLARIS	2.1	1 52	N 89 14.6	331 54.1	2 29	322 38.5
7	Hamal................	2.2	1 30	N 23 26.6	337 31.1	2 07	328 15.5
8	Acamar	3.1	2 21	S 40 19.2	324 43.7	2 58	315 28.1
9	Menkar	2.8	2 25	N 4 04.5	323 44.3	3 02	314 28.7
10	Mirfak	1.9	2 47	N 49 50.7	318 14.6	3 24	308 59.0
11	Aldebaran.........	1.1	3 58	N 16 30.0	300 20.1	4 36	291 04.5
12	Rigel	0.3	4 37	S 8 12.3	290 40.3	5 14	281 24.7
13	Capella	0.2	4 39	N 45 59.4	290 09.5	5 16	280 53.9
14	Bellatrix	1.7	4 47	N 6 20.7	288 01.7	5 25	278 46.1
15	Elnath...............	1.8	4 48	N 28 36.1	287 44.9	5 26	278 29.3
16	Alnilam	1.8	4 58	S 1 12.3	285 15.3	5 36	275 59.7
17	Betelgeuse........	0.1-1.2	5 17	N 7 24.4	280 31.2	5 55	271 15.6
18	Canopus............	-0.9	5 46	S 52 41.4	273 17.5	6 24	264 01.9
19	Sirius................	-1.6	6 07	S 16 42.5	268 01.0	6 45	258 45.4
20	Adhara	1.6	6 20	S 28 57.8	264 38.5	6 58	255 22.9
21	Castor...............	1.6	6 56	N 31 53.7	255 40.5	7 34	246 24.9
22	Procyon	0.5	7 01	N 5 14.1	254 29.3	7 39	245 13.7
23	Pollux	1.2	7 07	N 28 02.0	252 59.6	7 45	243 44.0
24	Avior	1.7	7 44	S 59 29.6	243 39.1	8 22	234 23.5
25	Suhail	2.2	8 29	S 43 24.8	232 18.0	9 08	223 02.4
26	Miaplacidus	1.8	8 35	S 69 41.8	230 58.3	9 13	221 42.7
27	Alphard.............	2.2	8 49	S 8 38.4	227 24.9	9 27	218 09.3
28	Regulus.............	1.3	9 30	N 11 59.2	217 13.5	10 08	207 57.9
29	Dubhe	2.0	10 25	N 61 46.2	203 24.2	11 03	194 08.6
30	Denebola	2.2	11 10	N 14 35.8	192 03.1	11 49	182 47.5
31	Gienah	2.8	11 37	S 17 31.0	185 21.9	12 16	176 06.3
32	Acrux................	1.1	11 47	S 63 04.4	182 40.4	12 26	173 24.8
33	Gacrux..............	1.6	11 52	S 57 05.3	181 31.9	12 31	172 16.3
34	Mimosa	1.5	12 08	S 59 39.8	177 23.8	12 47	168 08.2
35	Alioth	1.7	12 15	N 55 59.0	175 48.6	12 54	166 33.0
36	Spica.................	1.2	12 46	S 11 08.2	168 01.2	13 25	158 45.6
37	Alkaid...............	1.9	13 08	N 49 20.2	162 25.5	13 47	153 09.9
38	Hadar	0.9	13 24	S 60 21.1	158 23.0	14 04	149 07.4
39	Menkent	2.3	13 27	S 36 20.9	157 39.3	14 06	148 23.7
40	Arcturus	0.2	13 36	N 19 12.4	155 23.8	14 15	146 08.2
41	Rigil Kent.	0.1	14 00	S 60 49.0	149 26.1	14 39	140 10.5
42	Zuben'ubi	2.9	14 11	S 16 01.3	146 36.1	14 51	137 20.5
43	Kochab.............	2.2	14 11	N 74 10.6	146 36.3	14 51	137 20.7
44	Alphecca	2.3	14 55	N 26 44.0	135 38.2	15 34	126 22.6
45	Antares	1.2	15 50	S 26 25.3	121 58.5	16 29	112 42.9
46	Atria	1.9	16 09	S 69 01.3	117 12.6	16 48	107 57.0
47	Sabik	2.6	16 30	S 15 43.0	111 43.6	17 10	102 28.0
48	Shaula	1.7	16 54	S 37 06.0	105 55.8	17 33	96 40.2
49	Rasalhague	2.1	16 55	N 12 34.1	105 34.6	17 35	96 19.0
50	Eltanin.............	2.4	17 17	N 51 29.8	100 08.1	17 57	90 52.5
51	Kaus Aust.	2.0	17 44	S 34 23.2	93 17.2	18 24	84 01.6
52	Vega.................	0.1	17 57	N 38 47.2	90 03.7	18 37	80 48.1
53	Nunki	2.1	18 15	S 26 18.0	85 30.5	18 55	76 14.9
54	Altair	0.9	19 10	N 8 51.7	71 36.8	19 51	62 21.2
55	Peacock	2.1	19 45	S 56 45.0	62 55.7	20 25	53 40.1
56	Deneb	1.3	20 01	N 45 16.3	58 56.0	20 41	49 40.4
57	Enif...................	2.5	21 04	N 9 51.6	43 15.6	21 44	34 00.0
58	Al Na'ir.............	2.2	21 27	S 46 58.9	37 15.8	22 08	28 00.2
59	Fomalhaut	1.3	22 17	S 29 38.6	24 54.0	22 57	15 38.4
60	Markab	2.6	22 24	N 15 11.2	23 06.9	23 05	13 51.3

Star Transit Corr Table

Date	Corr h m	Date	Corr h m
1	–0 00	17	–1 03
2	–0 04	18	–1 07
3	–0 08	19	–1 11
4	–0 12	20	–1 15
5	–0 16	21	–1 19
6	–0 20	22	–1 23
7	–0 24	23	–1 27
8	–0 28	24	–1 30
9	–0 31	25	–1 34
10	–0 35	26	–1 38
11	–0 39	27	–1 42
12	–0 43	28	–1 46
13	–0 47	29	–1 50
14	–0 51	30	–1 54
15	–0 55	31	–1 58
16	–0 59		

STAR TRANSIT

To find the approx time of transit of a star for any day of the month use above table. All corrections are subtractive.

If the quantity taken from the table is greater than the time of transit for the first of the month, add 23h 56min to the time of transit before subtracting the correction.

Example: What time will Schedar (No 3) transit the Meridian on October 30?

	h min
Transit on Oct 1	00 03
	+23 56
	23 59
Corr for Oct 30	–01 54
Transit on Oct 30	22 05

OCTOBER DIARY

d h	
2 17	Neptune 5° S of Moon
3 00	Uranus 6° S of Moon
4 09	Venus 3° N of Spica
5 00	Neptune stationary
6 15	Uranus stationary
6 22	Saturn 6° S of Moon
13 09	Mercury stationary
20 14	Mercury greatest elong. W (18°)
22 22	Mercury 4° N of Moon
25 11	Venus 1.9° S of Moon
26 11	Mars 4° S of Moon
27 06	Jupiter 4° S of Moon
29 23	Neptune 5° S of Moon
30 06	Uranus 6° S of Moon
30 13	Mercury 4° N of Spica

NOTES

Star declinations may be used as is for the whole month. To correct GHA for day, hour, minute and second see page E 92 and for further explanation of this table see page E 4.

OCTOBER

OCTOBER 1995 — SUN & ARIES — GMT

Sunday, 1st October

Time	SUN GHA	Dec	ARIES GHA
00	182 30.7	S 2 55.0	9 15.6
02	212 31.2	2 56.9	39 20.5
04	242 31.6	2 58.9	69 25.4
06	272 32.0	3 00.8	99 30.3
08	302 32.4	3 02.7	129 35.3
10	332 32.8	3 04.7	159 40.2
12	2 33.2	3 06.6	189 45.1
14	32 33.6	3 08.6	219 50.1
16	62 34.0	3 10.5	249 55.0
18	92 34.4	3 12.4	279 59.9
20	122 34.8	3 14.4	310 04.8
22	152 35.2	S 3 16.3	340 09.8

Monday, 2nd October

Time	SUN GHA	Dec	ARIES GHA
00	182 35.6	S 3 18.3	10 14.7
02	212 36.0	3 20.2	40 19.6
04	242 36.4	3 22.1	70 24.6
06	272 36.8	3 24.1	100 29.5
08	302 37.2	3 26.0	130 34.4
10	332 37.6	3 27.9	160 39.3
12	2 38.0	3 29.9	190 44.3
14	32 38.4	3 31.8	220 49.2
16	62 38.8	3 33.8	250 54.1
18	92 39.2	3 35.7	280 59.1
20	122 39.6	3 37.6	311 04.0
22	152 40.0	S 3 39.6	341 08.9

Tuesday, 3rd October

Time	SUN GHA	Dec	ARIES GHA
00	182 40.4	S 3 41.5	11 13.8
02	212 40.8	3 43.4	41 18.8
04	242 41.2	3 45.4	71 23.7
06	272 41.6	3 47.3	101 28.6
08	302 42.0	3 49.2	131 33.6
10	332 42.4	3 51.2	161 38.5
12	2 42.7	3 53.1	191 43.4
14	32 43.1	3 55.0	221 48.3
16	62 43.5	3 57.0	251 53.3
18	92 43.9	3 58.9	281 58.2
20	122 44.3	4 00.8	312 03.1
22	152 44.7	S 4 02.8	342 08.0

Wednesday, 4th October

Time	SUN GHA	Dec	ARIES GHA
00	182 45.1	S 4 04.7	12 13.0
02	212 45.5	4 06.6	42 17.9
04	242 45.9	4 08.6	72 22.8
06	272 46.3	4 10.5	102 27.8
08	302 46.6	4 12.4	132 32.7
10	332 47.0	4 14.3	162 37.6
12	2 47.4	4 16.3	192 42.5
14	32 47.8	4 18.2	222 47.5
16	62 48.2	4 20.1	252 52.4
18	92 48.6	4 22.1	282 57.3
20	122 49.0	4 24.0	313 02.3
22	152 49.4	S 4 25.9	343 07.2

Thursday, 5th October

Time	SUN GHA	Dec	ARIES GHA
00	182 49.7	S 4 27.8	13 12.1
02	212 50.1	4 29.8	43 17.0
04	242 50.5	4 31.7	73 22.0
06	272 50.9	4 33.6	103 26.9
08	302 51.3	4 35.5	133 31.8
10	332 51.6	4 37.5	163 36.8
12	2 52.0	4 39.4	193 41.7
14	32 52.4	4 41.3	223 46.6
16	62 52.8	4 43.2	253 51.5
18	92 53.2	4 45.2	283 56.5
20	122 53.5	4 47.1	314 01.4
22	152 53.9	S 4 49.0	344 06.3

Friday, 6th October

Time	SUN GHA	Dec	ARIES GHA
00	182 54.3	S 4 50.9	14 11.3
02	212 54.7	4 52.9	44 16.2
04	242 55.0	4 54.8	74 21.1
06	272 55.4	4 56.7	104 26.0
08	302 55.8	4 58.6	134 31.0
10	332 56.2	5 00.5	164 35.9
12	2 56.5	5 02.5	194 40.8
14	32 56.9	5 04.4	224 45.8
16	62 57.3	5 06.3	254 50.7
18	92 57.6	5 08.2	284 55.6
20	122 58.0	5 10.1	315 00.5
22	152 58.4	S 5 12.0	345 05.5

Saturday, 7th October

Time	SUN GHA	Dec	ARIES GHA
00	182 58.7	S 5 14.0	15 10.4
02	212 59.1	5 15.9	45 15.3
04	242 59.5	5 17.8	75 20.2
06	272 59.8	5 19.7	105 25.2
08	303 00.2	5 21.6	135 30.1
10	333 00.6	5 23.5	165 35.0
12	3 00.9	5 25.5	195 40.0
14	33 01.3	5 27.4	225 44.9
16	63 01.7	5 29.3	255 49.8
18	93 02.0	5 31.2	285 54.7
20	123 02.4	5 33.1	315 59.7
22	153 02.8	S 5 35.0	346 04.6

Sunday, 8th October

Time	SUN GHA	Dec	ARIES GHA
00	183 03.1	S 5 36.9	16 09.5
02	213 03.5	5 38.8	46 14.5
04	243 03.8	5 40.7	76 19.4
06	273 04.2	5 42.7	106 24.3
08	303 04.5	5 44.6	136 29.2
10	333 04.9	5 46.5	166 34.2
12	3 05.3	5 48.4	196 39.1
14	33 05.6	5 50.3	226 44.0
16	63 06.0	5 52.2	256 49.0
18	93 06.3	5 54.1	286 53.9
20	123 06.7	5 56.0	316 58.8
22	153 07.0	S 5 57.9	347 03.7

Monday, 9th October

Time	SUN GHA	Dec	ARIES GHA
00	183 07.4	S 5 59.8	17 08.7
02	213 07.8	6 01.7	47 13.6
04	243 08.1	6 03.6	77 18.5
06	273 08.4	6 05.5	107 23.5
08	303 08.8	6 07.4	137 28.4
10	333 09.1	6 09.3	167 33.3
12	3 09.4	6 11.2	197 38.2
14	33 09.8	6 13.1	227 43.2
16	63 10.1	6 15.0	257 48.1
18	93 10.5	6 16.9	287 53.0
20	123 10.8	6 18.8	317 58.0
22	153 11.2	S 6 20.7	348 02.9

Tuesday, 10th October

Time	SUN GHA	Dec	ARIES GHA
00	183 11.5	S 6 22.6	18 07.8
02	213 11.8	6 24.5	48 12.7
04	243 12.2	6 26.4	78 17.7
06	273 12.5	6 28.3	108 22.6
08	303 12.9	6 30.2	138 27.5
10	333 13.2	6 32.1	168 32.4
12	3 13.5	6 34.0	198 37.4
14	33 13.9	6 35.9	228 42.3
16	63 14.2	6 37.8	258 47.2
18	93 14.5	6 39.7	288 52.2
20	123 14.9	6 41.6	318 57.1
22	153 15.2	S 6 43.5	349 02.0

Wednesday, 11th October

Time	SUN GHA	Dec	ARIES GHA
00	183 15.5	S 6 45.4	19 06.9
02	213 15.9	6 47.2	49 11.9
04	243 16.2	6 49.1	79 16.8
06	273 16.5	6 51.0	109 21.7
08	303 16.9	6 52.9	139 26.7
10	333 17.2	6 54.8	169 31.6
12	3 17.5	6 56.7	199 36.5
14	33 17.8	6 58.6	229 41.4
16	63 18.2	7 00.5	259 46.4
18	93 18.5	7 02.3	289 51.3
20	123 18.8	7 04.2	319 56.2
22	153 19.1	S 7 06.1	350 01.2

Thursday, 12th October

Time	SUN GHA	Dec	ARIES GHA
00	183 19.5	S 7 08.0	20 06.1
02	213 19.8	7 09.9	50 11.0
04	243 20.1	7 11.8	80 15.9
06	273 20.4	7 13.6	110 20.9
08	303 20.7	7 15.5	140 25.8
10	333 21.1	7 17.4	170 30.7
12	3 21.4	7 19.3	200 35.7
14	33 21.7	7 21.2	230 40.6
16	63 22.0	7 23.0	260 45.5
18	93 22.3	7 24.9	290 50.4
20	123 22.6	7 26.8	320 55.4
22	153 22.9	S 7 28.7	351 00.3

Friday, 13th October

Time	SUN GHA	Dec	ARIES GHA
00	183 23.2	S 7 30.5	21 05.2
02	213 23.5	7 32.4	51 10.2
04	243 23.9	7 34.3	81 15.1
06	273 24.2	7 36.2	111 20.0
08	303 24.5	7 38.0	141 24.9
10	333 24.8	7 39.9	171 29.9
12	3 25.1	7 41.8	201 34.8
14	33 25.4	7 43.6	231 39.7
16	63 25.7	7 45.5	261 44.7
18	93 26.0	7 47.4	291 49.6
20	123 26.3	7 49.3	321 54.5
22	153 26.6	S 7 51.1	351 59.4

Saturday, 14th October

Time	SUN GHA	Dec	ARIES GHA
00	183 26.9	S 7 53.0	22 04.4
02	213 27.2	7 54.9	52 09.3
04	243 27.5	7 56.7	82 14.2
06	273 27.8	7 58.6	112 19.1
08	303 28.1	8 00.4	142 24.1
10	333 28.4	8 02.3	172 29.0
12	3 28.7	8 04.2	202 33.9
14	33 29.0	8 06.0	232 38.9
16	63 29.3	8 07.9	262 43.8
18	93 29.5	8 09.8	292 48.7
20	123 29.8	8 11.6	322 53.6
22	153 30.1	S 8 13.5	352 58.6

Sunday, 15th October

Time	SUN GHA	Dec	ARIES GHA
00	183 30.4	S 8 15.3	23 03.5
02	213 30.7	8 17.2	53 08.4
04	243 31.0	8 19.0	83 13.4
06	273 31.3	8 20.9	113 18.3
08	303 31.6	8 22.7	143 23.2
10	333 31.8	8 24.6	173 28.1
12	3 32.1	8 26.5	203 33.1
14	33 32.4	8 28.3	233 38.0
16	63 32.7	8 30.2	263 42.9
18	93 33.0	8 32.0	293 47.9
20	123 33.2	8 33.9	323 52.8
22	153 33.5	S 8 35.7	353 57.7

NOTES

Sun & Aries GHA corrections for additional hour, minutes, and seconds on page E 94.
Correct Sun Declination by interpolation. For example see page E 4.

OCTOBER 1995 — SUN & ARIES — GMT

Monday, 16th October

Time	SUN GHA	Dec	ARIES GHA
00	183 33.8	S 8 37.6	24 02.6
02	213 34.1	8 39.4	54 07.6
04	243 34.3	8 41.2	84 12.5
06	273 34.6	8 43.1	114 17.4
08	303 34.9	8 44.9	144 22.4
10	333 35.2	8 46.8	174 27.3
12	3 35.4	8 48.6	204 32.2
14	33 35.7	8 50.5	234 37.1
16	63 36.0	8 52.3	264 42.1
18	93 36.2	8 54.1	294 47.0
20	123 36.5	8 56.0	324 51.9
22	153 36.8	S 8 57.8	354 56.9

Tuesday, 17th October

Time	SUN GHA	Dec	ARIES GHA
00	183 37.0	S 8 59.7	25 01.8
02	213 37.3	9 01.5	55 06.7
04	243 37.6	9 03.3	85 11.6
06	273 37.8	9 05.2	115 16.6
08	303 38.1	9 07.0	145 21.5
10	333 38.3	9 08.8	175 26.4
12	3 38.6	9 10.7	205 31.3
14	33 38.8	9 12.5	235 36.3
16	63 39.1	9 14.3	265 41.2
18	93 39.4	9 16.2	295 46.1
20	123 39.6	9 18.0	325 51.1
22	153 39.9	S 9 19.8	355 56.0

Wednesday, 18th October

Time	SUN GHA	Dec	ARIES GHA
00	183 40.1	S 9 21.6	26 00.9
02	213 40.4	9 23.5	56 05.8
04	243 40.6	9 25.3	86 10.8
06	273 40.9	9 27.1	116 15.7
08	303 41.1	9 28.9	146 20.6
10	333 41.4	9 30.8	176 25.6
12	3 41.6	9 32.6	206 30.5
14	33 41.8	9 34.4	236 35.4
16	63 42.1	9 36.2	266 40.3
18	93 42.3	9 38.0	296 45.3
20	123 42.6	9 39.8	326 50.2
22	153 42.8	S 9 41.7	356 55.1

Thursday, 19th October

Time	SUN GHA	Dec	ARIES GHA
00	183 43.0	S 9 43.5	27 00.1
02	213 43.3	9 45.3	57 05.0
04	243 43.5	9 47.1	87 09.9
06	273 43.8	9 48.9	117 14.8
08	303 44.0	9 50.7	147 19.8
10	333 44.2	9 52.5	177 24.7
12	3 44.5	9 54.3	207 29.6
14	33 44.7	9 56.2	237 34.6
16	63 44.9	9 58.0	267 39.5
18	93 45.1	9 59.8	297 44.4
20	123 45.4	10 01.6	327 49.3
22	153 45.6	S10 03.4	357 54.3

Friday, 20th October

Time	SUN GHA	Dec	ARIES GHA
00	183 45.8	S10 05.2	27 59.2
02	213 46.0	10 07.0	58 04.1
04	243 46.3	10 08.8	88 09.1
06	273 46.5	10 10.6	118 14.0
08	303 46.7	10 12.4	148 18.9
10	333 46.9	10 14.2	178 23.8
12	3 47.1	10 16.0	208 28.8
14	33 47.4	10 17.8	238 33.7
16	63 47.6	10 19.6	268 38.6
18	93 47.8	10 21.4	298 43.5
20	123 48.0	10 23.2	328 48.5
22	153 48.2	S10 24.9	358 53.4

Saturday, 21st October

Time	SUN GHA	Dec	ARIES GHA
00	183 48.4	S10 26.7	28 58.3
02	213 48.6	10 28.5	59 03.3
04	243 48.9	10 30.3	89 08.2
06	273 49.1	10 32.1	119 13.1
08	303 49.3	10 33.9	149 18.0
10	333 49.5	10 35.7	179 23.0
12	3 49.7	10 37.5	209 27.9
14	33 49.9	10 39.2	239 32.8
16	63 50.1	10 41.0	269 37.8
18	93 50.3	10 42.8	299 42.7
20	123 50.5	10 44.6	329 47.6
22	153 50.7	S10 46.4	359 52.5

Sunday, 22nd October

Time	SUN GHA	Dec	ARIES GHA
00	183 50.9	S10 48.1	29 57.5
02	213 51.1	10 49.9	60 02.4
04	243 51.3	10 51.7	90 07.3
06	273 51.5	10 53.5	120 12.3
08	303 51.7	10 55.2	150 17.2
10	333 51.8	10 57.0	180 22.1
12	3 52.0	10 58.8	210 27.0
14	33 52.2	11 00.5	240 32.0
16	63 52.4	11 02.3	270 36.9
18	93 52.6	11 04.1	300 41.8
20	123 52.8	11 05.8	330 46.8
22	153 53.0	S11 07.6	0 51.7

Monday, 23rd October

Time	SUN GHA	Dec	ARIES GHA
00	183 53.2	S11 09.4	30 56.6
02	213 53.3	11 11.1	61 01.5
04	243 53.5	11 12.9	91 06.5
06	273 53.7	11 14.7	121 11.4
08	303 53.9	11 16.4	151 16.3
10	333 54.0	11 18.2	181 21.3
12	3 54.2	11 19.9	211 26.2
14	33 54.4	11 21.7	241 31.1
16	63 54.6	11 23.4	271 36.0
18	93 54.7	11 25.2	301 41.0
20	123 54.9	11 26.9	331 45.9
22	153 55.1	S11 28.7	1 50.8

Tuesday, 24th October

Time	SUN GHA	Dec	ARIES GHA
00	183 55.3	S11 30.4	31 55.7
02	213 55.4	11 32.2	62 00.7
04	243 55.6	11 33.9	92 05.6
06	273 55.7	11 35.7	122 10.5
08	303 55.9	11 37.4	152 15.5
10	333 56.1	11 39.2	182 20.4
12	3 56.2	11 40.9	212 25.3
14	33 56.4	11 42.7	242 30.2
16	63 56.6	11 44.4	272 35.2
18	93 56.7	11 46.1	302 40.1
20	123 56.9	11 47.9	332 45.0
22	153 57.0	S11 49.6	2 50.0

Wednesday, 25th October

Time	SUN GHA	Dec	ARIES GHA
00	183 57.2	S11 51.3	32 54.9
02	213 57.3	11 53.1	62 59.8
04	243 57.5	11 54.8	93 04.7
06	273 57.6	11 56.5	123 09.7
08	303 57.8	11 58.3	153 14.6
10	333 57.9	12 00.0	183 19.5
12	3 58.1	12 01.7	213 24.5
14	33 58.2	12 03.4	243 29.4
16	63 58.4	12 05.2	273 34.3
18	93 58.5	12 06.9	303 39.2
20	123 58.7	12 08.6	333 44.2
22	153 58.8	S12 10.3	3 49.1

Thursday, 26th October

Time	SUN GHA	Dec	ARIES GHA
00	183 58.9	S12 12.1	33 54.0
02	213 59.1	12 13.8	63 59.0
04	243 59.2	12 15.5	94 03.9
06	273 59.3	12 17.2	124 08.8
08	303 59.5	12 18.9	154 13.7
10	333 59.6	12 20.6	184 18.7
12	3 59.7	12 22.3	214 23.6
14	33 59.9	12 24.1	244 28.5
16	64 00.0	12 25.8	274 33.5
18	94 00.1	12 27.5	304 38.4
20	124 00.3	12 29.2	334 43.3
22	154 00.4	S12 30.9	4 48.2

Friday, 27th October

Time	SUN GHA	Dec	ARIES GHA
00	184 00.5	S12 32.6	34 53.2
02	214 00.6	12 34.3	64 58.1
04	244 00.8	12 36.0	95 03.0
06	274 00.9	12 37.7	125 08.0
08	304 01.0	12 39.4	155 12.9
10	334 01.1	12 41.1	185 17.8
12	4 01.2	12 42.8	215 22.7
14	34 01.3	12 44.5	245 27.7
16	64 01.5	12 46.2	275 32.6
18	94 01.6	12 47.9	305 37.5
20	124 01.7	12 49.5	335 42.4
22	154 01.8	S12 51.2	5 47.4

Saturday, 28th October

Time	SUN GHA	Dec	ARIES GHA
00	184 01.9	S12 52.9	35 52.3
02	214 02.0	12 54.6	65 57.2
04	244 02.1	12 56.3	96 02.2
06	274 02.2	12 58.0	126 07.1
08	304 02.3	12 59.7	156 12.0
10	334 02.4	13 01.3	186 16.9
12	4 02.5	13 03.0	216 21.9
14	34 02.6	13 04.7	246 26.8
16	64 02.7	13 06.4	276 31.7
18	94 02.8	13 08.0	306 36.7
20	124 02.9	13 09.7	336 41.6
22	154 03.0	S13 11.4	6 46.5

Sunday, 29th October

Time	SUN GHA	Dec	ARIES GHA
00	184 03.1	S13 13.1	36 51.4
02	214 03.2	13 14.7	66 56.4
04	244 03.3	13 16.4	97 01.3
06	274 03.4	13 18.1	127 06.2
08	304 03.5	13 19.7	157 11.2
10	334 03.6	13 21.4	187 16.1
12	4 03.7	13 23.0	217 21.0
14	34 03.7	13 24.7	247 25.9
16	64 03.8	13 26.4	277 30.9
18	94 03.9	13 28.0	307 35.8
20	124 04.0	13 29.7	337 40.7
22	154 04.1	S13 31.3	7 45.7

Monday, 30th October

Time	SUN GHA	Dec	ARIES GHA
00	184 04.1	S13 33.0	37 50.6
02	214 04.2	13 34.6	67 55.5
04	244 04.3	13 36.3	98 00.4
06	274 04.4	13 37.9	128 05.4
08	304 04.4	13 39.6	158 10.3
10	334 04.5	13 41.2	188 15.2
12	4 04.6	13 42.9	218 20.2
14	34 04.7	13 44.5	248 25.1
16	64 04.7	13 46.1	278 30.0
18	94 04.8	13 47.8	308 34.9
20	124 04.9	13 49.4	338 39.9
22	154 04.9	S13 51.1	8 44.8

Tuesday, 31st October

Time	SUN GHA	Dec	ARIES GHA	Time	SUN GHA	Dec	ARIES GHA	Time	SUN GHA	Dec	ARIES GHA
00	184 05.0	S13 52.7	38 49.7	08	304 05.2	S13 59.2	159 09.4	16	64 05.4	S14 05.7	279 29.1
02	214 05.0	13 54.3	68 54.6	10	334 05.3	14 00.8	189 14.4	18	94 05.5	14 07.3	309 34.1
04	244 05.1	13 56.0	98 59.6	12	4 05.3	14 02.5	219 19.3	20	124 05.5	14 09.0	339 39.0
06	274 05.1	S13 57.6	129 04.5	14	34 05.4	S14 04.1	249 24.2	22	154 05.6	S14 10.6	9 43.9

OCTOBER

OCTOBER 1995 — PLANETS — 0h GMT

VENUS / Note / JUPITER

Mer Pass h m	GHA ° '	Mean Var/hr 14°+	Dec ° '	Mean Var/hr	Corrections on Page E 101		GHA ° '	Mean Var/hr 15°+	Dec ° '	Mean Var/hr	Mer Pass h m
12 33	171 54.6	59.6	S 6 17.5	1.2	1	SUN	120 20.6	2.1	S 21 35.8	0.1	15 56
12 33	171 44.8	59.6	S 6 47.4	1.2	2	Mon	121 09.9	2.0	S 21 37.3	0.1	15 53
12 34	171 34.9	59.6	S 7 17.1	1.2	3	Tu	121 59.0	2.0	S 21 38.8	0.1	15 50
12 35	171 24.9	59.6	S 7 46.7	1.2	4	Wed	122 48.1	2.0	S 21 40.2	0.1	15 47
12 35	171 14.7	59.6	S 8 16.1	1.2	5	Th	123 37.0	2.0	S 21 41.7	0.1	15 43
12 36	171 04.4	59.6	S 8 45.3	1.2	6	Fri	124 25.7	2.0	S 21 43.2	0.1	15 40
12 37	170 53.9	59.6	S 9 14.3	1.2	7	Sat	125 14.4	2.0	S 21 44.7	0.1	15 37
12 38	170 43.2	59.5	S 9 43.1	1.2	8	SUN	126 03.0	2.0	S 21 46.2	0.1	15 34
12 38	170 32.2	59.5	S 10 11.7	1.2	9	Mon	126 51.4	2.0	S 21 47.7	0.1	15 30
12 39	170 21.1	59.5	S 10 40.1	1.2	10	Tu	127 39.7	2.0	S 21 49.2	0.1	15 27
12 40	170 09.8	59.5	S 11 08.2	1.2	11	Wed	128 28.0	2.0	S 21 50.7	0.1	15 24
12 41	169 58.3	59.5	S 11 36.1	1.2	12	Th	129 16.1	2.0	S 21 52.2	0.1	15 21
12 41	169 46.5	59.5	S 12 03.7	1.1	13	Fri	130 04.1	2.0	S 21 53.7	0.1	15 18
12 42	169 34.5	59.5	S 12 31.0	1.1	14	Sat	130 52.0	2.0	S 21 55.2	0.1	15 15
12 43	169 22.2	59.5	S 12 58.0	1.1	15	SUN	131 39.8	2.0	S 21 56.7	0.1	15 11
12 44	169 09.7	59.5	S 13 24.7	1.1	16	Mon	132 27.5	2.0	S 21 58.2	0.1	15 08
12 45	168 56.9	59.5	S 13 51.1	1.1	17	Tu	133 15.0	2.0	S 21 59.7	0.1	15 05
12 46	168 43.9	59.4	S 14 17.2	1.1	18	Wed	134 02.5	2.0	S 22 01.2	0.1	15 02
12 46	168 30.5	59.4	S 14 42.9	1.1	19	Th	134 49.9	2.0	S 22 02.7	0.1	14 59
12 47	168 16.9	59.4	S 15 08.2	1.0	20	Fri	135 37.2	2.0	S 22 04.2	0.1	14 56
12 48	168 03.0	59.4	S 15 33.2	1.0	21	Sat	136 24.4	2.0	S 22 05.6	0.1	14 52
12 49	167 48.8	59.4	S 15 57.8	1.0	22	SUN	137 11.5	2.0	S 22 07.1	0.1	14 49
12 50	167 34.4	59.4	S 16 21.9	1.0	23	Mon	137 58.5	2.0	S 22 08.6	0.1	14 46
12 51	167 19.6	59.4	S 16 45.7	1.0	24	Tu	138 45.4	1.9	S 22 10.0	0.1	14 43
12 52	167 04.5	59.4	S 17 09.0	1.0	25	Wed	139 32.2	1.9	S 22 11.5	0.1	14 40
12 53	166 49.1	59.3	S 17 31.9	0.9	26	Th	140 19.0	1.9	S 22 12.9	0.1	14 37
12 54	166 33.4	59.3	S 17 54.4	0.9	27	Fri	141 05.6	1.9	S 22 14.3	0.1	14 34
12 55	166 17.4	59.3	S 18 16.3	0.9	28	Sat	141 52.2	1.9	S 22 15.8	0.1	14 31
12 57	166 01.1	59.3	S 18 37.8	0.9	29	SUN	142 38.7	1.9	S 22 17.2	0.1	14 28
12 58	165 44.5	59.3	S 18 58.8	0.9	30	Mon	143 25.1	1.9	S 22 18.6	0.1	14 24
12 59	165 27.6	59.3	S 19 19.3	0.8	31	Tu	144 11.4	1.9	S 22 20.0	0.1	14 21

VENUS, Av. Mag. -3.9
S.H.A. October
5 158; 10 152; 15 146; 20 140; 25 134; 30 128.

JUPITER, Av. Mag.-1.9
S.H.A. October
5 110; 10 110; 15 109; 20 108; 25 107; 30 106.

MARS / Note / SATURN

Mer Pass h m	GHA ° '	Mean Var/hr 15°+	Dec ° '	Mean Var/hr	Corrections on Page E 101		GHA ° '	Mean Var/hr 15°+	Dec ° '	Mean Var/hr	Mer Pass h m
14 16	145 50.5	0.7	S 17 04.8	0.5	1	SUN	17 25.4	2.6	S 6 04.8	0.1	22 46
14 15	146 08.2	0.7	S 17 17.3	0.5	2	Mon	18 28.5	2.6	S 6 06.4	0.1	22 42
14 14	146 25.7	0.7	S 17 29.7	0.5	3	Tu	19 31.6	2.6	S 6 08.0	0.1	22 38
14 12	146 43.1	0.7	S 17 42.0	0.5	4	Wed	20 34.6	2.6	S 6 09.7	0.1	22 34
14 11	147 00.3	0.7	S 17 54.1	0.5	5	Th	21 37.6	2.6	S 6 11.2	0.1	22 30
14 10	147 17.4	0.7	S 18 06.1	0.5	6	Fri	22 40.5	2.6	S 6 12.8	0.1	22 25
14 09	147 34.2	0.7	S 18 18.0	0.5	7	Sat	23 43.4	2.6	S 6 14.3	0.1	22 21
14 08	147 50.9	0.7	S 18 29.7	0.5	8	SUN	24 46.3	2.6	S 6 15.8	0.1	22 17
14 07	148 07.5	0.7	S 18 41.3	0.5	9	Mon	25 49.1	2.6	S 6 17.3	0.1	22 13
14 06	148 23.9	0.7	S 18 52.8	0.5	10	Tu	26 51.9	2.6	S 6 18.8	0.1	22 09
14 05	148 40.0	0.7	S 19 04.1	0.5	11	Wed	27 54.6	2.6	S 6 20.2	0.1	22 05
14 04	148 56.1	0.7	S 19 15.3	0.5	12	Th	28 57.2	2.6	S 6 21.6	0.1	22 00
14 03	149 11.9	0.7	S 19 26.3	0.4	13	Fri	29 59.8	2.6	S 6 23.0	0.1	21 56
14 02	149 27.6	0.6	S 19 37.1	0.4	14	Sat	31 02.3	2.6	S 6 24.3	0.1	21 52
14 01	149 43.1	0.6	S 19 47.8	0.4	15	SUN	32 04.8	2.6	S 6 25.7	0.0	21 48
14 00	149 58.5	0.6	S 19 58.4	0.4	16	Mon	33 07.2	2.6	S 6 26.9	0.1	21 44
13 59	150 13.7	0.6	S 20 08.8	0.4	17	Tu	34 09.6	2.6	S 6 28.2	0.0	21 40
13 58	150 28.7	0.6	S 20 19.0	0.4	18	Wed	35 11.9	2.6	S 6 29.4	0.1	21 35
13 57	150 43.5	0.6	S 20 29.0	0.4	19	Th	36 14.1	2.6	S 6 30.6	0.0	21 31
13 56	150 58.1	0.6	S 20 38.9	0.4	20	Fri	37 16.2	2.6	S 6 31.8	0.0	21 27
13 55	151 12.6	0.6	S 20 48.6	0.4	21	Sat	38 18.3	2.6	S 6 32.9	0.0	21 23
13 54	151 26.9	0.6	S 20 58.2	0.4	22	SUN	39 20.3	2.6	S 6 34.0	0.0	21 19
13 53	151 41.1	0.6	S 21 07.5	0.4	23	Mon	40 22.2	2.6	S 6 35.0	0.0	21 15
13 52	151 55.0	0.6	S 21 16.7	0.4	24	Tu	41 24.1	2.6	S 6 36.0	0.0	21 11
13 51	152 08.8	0.6	S 21 25.7	0.4	25	Wed	42 25.9	2.6	S 6 37.0	0.0	21 07
13 50	152 22.5	0.6	S 21 34.6	0.4	26	Th	43 27.6	2.6	S 6 38.0	0.0	21 03
13 49	152 36.0	0.6	S 21 43.1	0.4	27	Fri	44 29.2	2.6	S 6 38.9	0.0	20 58
13 48	152 49.3	0.6	S 21 51.5	0.3	28	Sat	45 30.8	2.6	S 6 39.7	0.0	20 54
13 47	153 02.5	0.5	S 21 59.7	0.3	29	SUN	46 32.2	2.6	S 6 40.6	0.0	20 50
13 46	153 15.5	0.5	S 22 07.7	0.3	30	Mon	47 33.6	2.6	S 6 41.3	0.0	20 46
13 46	153 28.4	0.5	S 22 15.5	0.3	31	Tu	48 34.9	2.6	S 6 42.1	0.0	20 42

MARS, Av. Mag. +1.4
S.H.A. October
5 134; 10 130; 15 127; 20 123; 25 119; 30 115.

SATURN, Av. Mag. +0.8
S.H.A. October
5 8; 10 9; 15 9; 20 9; 25 10; 30 10.

OCTOBER 1995 — MOON

Day	GMT hr	GHA (° ')	Mean Var/hr 14°+	Dec (° ')	Mean Var/hr '
1 Sun	0	99 59.4	25.1	S 18 45.5	1.8
	6	186 29.9	25.2	S 18 35.5	2.5
	12	273 01.2	25.4	S 18 21.0	3.2
	18	359 33.4	25.5	S 18 02.2	3.9
2 Mon	0	86 06.8	25.8	S 17 39.2	4.6
	6	172 41.4	26.0	S 17 12.1	5.2
	12	259 17.5	26.3	S 16 41.2	5.8
	18	345 55.1	26.6	S 16 06.4	6.4
3 Tu	0	72 34.4	26.8	S 15 28.1	7.0
	6	159 15.4	27.2	S 14 46.5	7.5
	12	245 58.2	27.5	S 14 01.6	8.1
	18	332 42.7	27.8	S 13 13.8	8.4
4 Wed	0	59 29.2	28.1	S 12 23.2	8.9
	6	146 17.4	28.4	S 11 30.2	9.3
	12	233 07.4	28.6	S 10 34.8	9.6
	18	319 59.1	28.9	S 9 37.4	9.9
5 Th	0	46 52.5	29.2	S 8 38.2	10.1
	6	133 47.4	29.4	S 7 37.5	10.4
	12	220 43.9	29.7	S 6 35.3	10.6
	18	307 41.8	29.9	S 5 32.1	10.7
6 Fri	0	34 41.0	30.1	S 4 28.0	10.8
	6	121 41.5	30.3	S 3 23.3	10.9
	12	208 43.0	30.4	S 2 18.1	10.9
	18	295 45.5	30.5	S 1 12.8	10.9
7 Sat	0	22 49.0	30.7	S 0 07.5	10.9
	6	109 53.2	30.9	N 0 57.6	10.8
	12	196 58.0	30.9	N 2 02.2	10.7
	18	284 03.5	31.0	N 3 06.2	10.5
8 Sun	0	11 09.4	31.0	N 4 09.3	10.4
	6	98 15.7	31.1	N 5 11.4	10.2
	12	185 22.2	31.1	N 6 12.3	9.9
	18	272 29.0	31.2	N 7 11.8	9.6
9 Mon	0	359 35.9	31.2	N 8 09.6	9.4
	6	86 42.8	31.1	N 9 05.8	9.0
	12	173 49.7	31.1	N 10 00.1	8.7
	18	260 56.6	31.1	N 10 52.3	8.3
10 Tu	0	348 03.4	31.1	N 11 42.3	8.0
	6	75 10.1	31.1	N 12 30.1	7.5
	12	162 16.6	31.0	N 13 15.4	7.1
	18	249 22.9	31.0	N 13 58.2	6.6
11 Wed	0	336 29.1	31.0	N 14 38.4	6.2
	6	63 35.1	31.0	N 15 15.8	5.7
	12	150 40.9	31.0	N 15 50.5	5.3
	18	237 46.7	30.9	N 16 22.2	4.7
12 Th	0	324 52.3	30.9	N 16 51.0	4.2
	6	51 57.8	30.9	N 17 16.8	3.7
	12	139 03.3	30.9	N 17 39.5	3.2
	18	226 08.8	30.9	N 17 59.1	2.7
13 Fri	0	313 14.4	31.0	N 18 15.6	2.2
	6	40 20.1	30.9	N 18 28.9	1.6
	12	127 25.9	31.0	N 18 39.1	1.1
	18	214 31.9	31.1	N 18 46.1	0.6
14 Sat	0	301 38.2	31.1	N 18 49.9	0.0
	6	28 44.8	31.2	N 18 50.6	0.5
	12	115 51.8	31.2	N 18 48.2	1.0
	18	202 59.1	31.3	N 18 42.6	1.5
15 Sun	0	290 06.9	31.4	N 18 33.9	2.0
	6	17 15.1	31.4	N 18 22.2	2.5
	12	104 23.8	31.6	N 18 07.4	3.0
	18	191 33.0	31.6	N 17 49.7	3.5
16 Mon	0	278 42.7	31.8	N 17 29.0	3.9
	6	5 52.9	31.8	N 17 05.5	4.5
	12	93 03.6	31.8	N 16 39.1	4.9
	18	180 14.8	31.9	N 16 10.0	5.4
17 Tu	0	267 26.5	32.0	N 15 38.2	5.7
	6	354 38.5	32.1	N 15 03.8	6.2
	12	81 50.9	32.1	N 14 26.8	6.7
	18	169 03.7	32.2	N 13 47.3	7.0
18 Wed	0	256 16.7	32.2	N 13 05.4	7.4
	6	343 29.0	32.2	N 12 21.2	7.8
	12	70 43.2	32.2	N 11 34.8	8.1
	18	157 56.6	32.2	N 10 46.2	8.5
19 Th	0	245 09.8	32.2	N 9 55.5	8.8
	6	332 22.9	32.1	N 9 03.0	9.1
	12	59 35.8	32.0	N 8 08.5	9.4
	18	146 48.2	31.9	N 7 12.4	9.6
20 Fri	0	234 00.2	31.9	N 6 14.6	9.9
	6	321 11.5	31.8	N 5 15.4	10.1
	12	48 22.0	31.6	N 4 14.9	10.3
	18	135 31.7	31.5	N 3 13.1	10.4
21 Sat	0	222 40.3	31.3	N 2 10.3	10.6
	6	309 47.8	31.0	N 1 06.7	10.7
	12	36 54.0	30.8	N 0 02.4	10.8
	18	123 58.8	30.5	S 1 02.4	10.8
22 Sun	0	211 02.0	30.3	S 2 07.5	10.9
	6	298 03.6	29.9	S 3 12.7	10.8
	12	25 03.3	29.6	S 4 17.8	10.7
	18	112 01.1	29.2	S 5 22.4	10.7
23 Mon	0	198 56.9	28.9	S 6 26.5	10.5
	6	285 50.6	28.6	S 7 29.6	10.3
	12	12 42.0	28.2	S 8 31.6	10.1
	18	99 31.1	27.8	S 9 32.2	9.8
24 Tu	0	Eclipse of the Sun occurs today			
	6	273 02.4	27.0	S 11 27.9	9.1
	12	359 44.5	26.5	S 12 22.5	8.6
	18	86 24.2	26.3	S 13 14.5	8.2
25 Wed	0	173 01.7	25.8	S 14 03.7	7.6
	6	259 36.9	25.5	S 14 49.8	7.0
	12	346 10.0	25.1	S 15 32.5	6.4
	18	72 41.2	24.9	S 16 11.6	5.9
26 Th	0	159 10.6	24.7	S 16 46.8	5.2
	6	245 38.4	24.4	S 17 17.9	4.4
	12	332 04.8	24.2	S 17 44.8	3.6
	18	58 30.1	24.0	S 18 07.2	2.9
27 Fri	0	144 54.5	24.0	S 18 25.1	2.1
	6	231 18.4	23.9	S 18 38.4	1.3
	12	317 42.1	24.0	S 18 47.0	0.5
	18	44 05.8	24.0	S 18 50.8	0.2
28 Sat	0	130 29.9	24.1	S 18 49.8	1.0
	6	216 54.6	24.3	S 18 44.2	1.8
	12	303 20.3	24.5	S 18 33.9	2.5
	18	29 47.2	24.8	S 18 19.1	3.2
29 Sun	0	116 15.5	25.0	S 17 59.9	4.0
	6	202 45.5	25.4	S 17 36.3	4.6
	12	289 17.3	25.7	S 17 08.7	5.3
	18	15 51.1	26.0	S 16 37.1	5.9
30 Mon	0	102 27.0	26.4	S 16 01.8	6.6
	6	189 05.1	26.7	S 15 23.0	7.1
	12	275 45.5	27.2	S 14 40.9	7.5
	18	2 28.3	27.5	S 13 55.8	8.0
31 Tu	0	89 13.3	27.9	S 13 07.8	8.5
	6	176 00.5	28.3	S 12 17.2	8.8
	12	262 50.1	28.7	S 11 24.3	9.2
	18	349 41.7	29.0	S 10 29.2	9.5

NOTE Moon GHA corrections for additional hours, minutes, and seconds on page E 96.
Moon Declination corrections on page E 99. Mean Var/Hr value needed for both corrections.

OCTOBER

NOVEMBER 1995   SUN & MOON   GMT

SUN

| Day of | | | Equation of Time | | Transit | Semi-diam | Lat 52°N | | | | Lat Corr to Sunrise, Sunset etc | | | | |
Yr	Mth	Week	0h	12h			Twi-light	Sun-rise	Sun-set	Twi-light	Lat	Twi-light	Sun-rise	Sun-set	Twi-light
			m s	m s	h m	′	h m	h m	h m	h m	°	h m	h m	h m	h m
305	1	Wed	-16 22	-16 23	11 44	16.1	06 18	06 54	16 33	17 08	N60	+0 26	+0 38	-0 38	-0 26
306	2	Th	-16 24	-16 25	11 44	16.1	06 20	06 56	16 31	17 06	55	+0 09	+0 12	-0 12	-0 09
307	3	Fri	-16 25	-16 26	11 44	16.1	06 22	06 57	16 29	17 05	50	-0 05	-0 07	+0 07	+0 05
308	4	Sat	-16 26	-16 25	11 44	16.2	06 23	06 59	16 27	17 03	45	-0 16	-0 22	+0 22	+0 16
309	5	Sun	-16 25	-16 25	11 44	16.2	06 25	07 01	16 25	17 01	N40	-0 26	-0 34	+0 34	+0 26
310	6	Mon	-16 24	-16 23	11 44	16.2	06 27	07 03	16 24	17 00	35	-0 35	-0 45	+0 45	+0 35
311	7	Tu	-16 22	-16 20	11 44	16.2	06 28	07 05	16 22	16 58	30	-0 42	-0 54	+0 54	+0 42
312	8	Wed	-16 19	-16 17	11 44	16.2	06 30	07 06	16 20	16 57	25	-0 49	-1 03	+1 03	+0 49
313	9	Th	-16 15	-16 12	11 44	16.2	06 32	07 08	16 19	16 55	N20	-0 56	-1 10	+1 10	+0 56
314	10	Fri	-16 10	-16 07	11 44	16.2	06 33	07 10	16 17	16 54	15	-1 03	-1 18	+1 18	+1 03
315	11	Sat	-16 04	-16 01	11 44	16.2	06 35	07 12	16 15	16 52	10	-1 09	-1 24	+1 24	+1 09
316	12	Sun	-15 58	-15 55	11 44	16.2	06 37	07 14	16 14	16 51	5	-1 16	-1 31	+1 31	+1 16
317	13	Mon	-15 51	-15 47	11 44	16.2	06 38	07 15	16 12	16 50	0	-1 22	-1 38	+1 38	+1 22
318	14	Tu	-15 43	-15 38	11 44	16.2	06 40	07 17	16 11	16 48	S 5	-1 29	-1 45	+1 45	+1 29
319	15	Wed	-15 34	-15 29	11 45	16.2	06 42	07 19	16 10	16 47	10	-1 36	-1 51	+1 51	+1 36
320	16	Th	-15 24	-15 18	11 45	16.2	06 43	07 21	16 08	16 46	15	-1 44	-1 58	+1 58	+1 44
321	17	Fri	-15 13	-15 07	11 45	16.2	06 45	07 22	16 07	16 44	S20	-1 52	-2 06	+2 06	+1 52
322	18	Sat	-15 01	-14 55	11 45	16.2	06 46	07 24	16 06	16 43	25	-2 01	-2 14	+2 14	+2 01
323	19	Sun	-14 49	-14 42	11 45	16.2	06 48	07 26	16 04	16 42	30	-2 12	-2 23	+2 23	+2 12
324	20	Mon	-14 35	-14 29	11 46	16.2	06 49	07 28	16 03	16 41	35	-2 23	-2 33	+2 33	+2 23
325	21	Tu	-14 21	-14 14	11 46	16.2	06 51	07 29	16 02	16 40	S40	-2 37	-2 44	+2 44	+2 37
326	22	Wed	-14 06	-13 59	11 46	16.2	06 52	07 31	16 01	16 39	45	-2 54	-2 57	+2 57	+2 54
327	23	Th	-13 51	-13 42	11 46	16.2	06 54	07 33	16 00	16 38	50	-3 16	-3 14	+3 14	+3 16
328	24	Fri	-13 34	-13 26	11 47	16.2	06 55	07 34	15 59	16 37					
329	25	Sat	-13 17	-13 08	11 47	16.2	06 57	07 36	15 58	16 36					
330	26	Sun	-12 59	-12 49	11 47	16.2	06 58	07 37	15 57	16 36					
331	27	Mon	-12 40	-12 30	11 47	16.2	07 00	07 39	15 56	16 35					
332	28	Tu	-12 20	-12 10	11 48	16.2	07 01	07 40	15 55	16 34					
333	29	Wed	-12 00	-11 50	11 48	16.2	07 03	07 42	15 54	16 33					
334	30	Th	-11 39	-11 29	11 49	16.2	07 04	07 43	15 53	16 33					

NOTES
Lat corrections are for mid-month.
Equation of Time is the excess of Mean Time over Apparent Time.

MOON

| Day of | | | Age | Transit (Upper) | Diff | Semi-diam | Hor Par | Lat 52°N | | Phases of the Moon | | |
Yr	Mth	Week						Moon-rise	Moon-set			
			days	h m	m	′	′	h m	h m		d	h m
305	1	Wed	08	19 33	49	15.8	58.0	14 00	00 03	O Full Moon	7	07 20
306	2	Th	09	20 22	47	15.7	57.5	14 26	01 17	☽ Last Quarter	15	11 40
307	3	Fri	10	21 09	47	15.5	57.0	14 51	02 29	● New Moon	22	15 43
308	4	Sat	11	21 56	47	15.4	56.5	15 16	03 39	☾ First Quarter	29	06 28
309	5	Sun	12	22 43	48	15.3	56.0	15 41	04 49			
310	6	Mon	13	23 31	47	15.1	55.6	16 09	05 57			
311	7	Tu	14	24 18	—	15.0	55.1	16 41	07 02			
312	8	Wed	15	00 18	48	14.9	54.7	17 17	08 04			
313	9	Th	16	01 06	49	14.8	54.4	17 58	09 02	Apogee	11	21
314	10	Fri	17	01 55	47	14.8	54.2	18 44	09 53	Perigee	23	23
315	11	Sat	18	02 42	48	14.7	54.1	19 36	10 38			
316	12	Sun	19	03 30	46	14.7	54.1	20 32	11 18			
317	13	Mon	20	04 16	46	14.8	54.3	21 32	11 51			
318	14	Tu	21	05 02	45	14.9	54.6	22 35	12 21			
319	15	Wed	22	05 47	45	15.0	55.1	23 40	12 47			
320	16	Th	23	06 32	45	15.2	55.8	— —	13 12			
321	17	Fri	24	07 17	47	15.4	56.6	00 47	13 36			
322	18	Sat	25	08 04	49	15.7	57.5	01 56	14 00			
323	19	Sun	26	08 53	52	15.9	58.4	03 09	14 27			
324	20	Mon	27	09 45	55	16.2	59.3	04 24	14 56			
325	21	Tu	28	10 40	59	16.4	60.1	05 41	15 32			
326	22	Wed	29	11 39	61	16.5	60.6	06 58	16 14			
327	23	Th	01	12 40	62	16.6	60.9	08 11	17 07			
328	24	Fri	02	13 42	62	16.6	60.9	09 16	18 09			
329	25	Sat	03	14 44	58	16.5	60.6	10 12	19 20			
330	26	Sun	04	15 42	56	16.4	60.1	10 57	20 35			
331	27	Mon	05	16 38	52	16.2	59.4	11 34	21 51			
332	28	Tu	06	17 30	50	16.0	58.7	12 05	23 06			
333	29	Wed	07	18 20	48	15.8	57.9	12 32	— —			
334	30	Th	08	19 08	47	15.6	57.2	12 57	00 19			

NOTES
Diff equals daily change in transit time.
To correct Moonrise, Moonset, or Transit times for Latitude and/or Longitude see page E 100. For further information about these tables see page E 4. For Arc to Time correction see page E 91.

NOVEMBER 1995   STARS   0h GMT November 1

No	Name	Mag	Transit h m	Dec ° '	GHA ° '	RA h m	SHA ° '
	ARIES.................		21 17		39 48.9		
1	Alpheratz.........	2.2	21 25	N 29 04.3	37 45.9	0 08	357 57.0
2	Ankaa..............	2.4	21 43	S 42 19.8	33 17.4	0 26	353 28.5
3	Schedar............	2.5	21 57	N 56 31.1	29 44.1	0 40	349 55.2
4	Diphda	2.2	22 01	S 18 00.5	28 57.9	0 43	349 09.0
5	Achernar..........	0.6	22 55	S 57 15.6	15 25.1	1 38	335 36.2
6	POLARIS	2.1	23 46	N 89 14.8	2 25.1	2 30	322 36.2
7	Hamal...............	2.2	23 24	N 23 26.7	8 04.3	2 07	328 15.4
8	Acamar............	3.1	0 19	S 40 19.3	355 16.9	2 58	315 28.0
9	Menkar	2.8	0 23	N 4 04.4	354 17.5	3 02	314 28.6
10	Mirfak	1.9	0 45	N 49 50.8	348 47.8	3 24	308 58.9
11	Aldebaran........	1.1	1 56	N 16 30.0	330 53.2	4 36	291 04.3
12	Rigel	0.3	2 35	S 8 12.4	321 13.4	5 14	281 24.5
13	Capella	0.2	2 37	N 45 59.5	320 42.5	5 16	280 53.6
14	Bellatrix	1.7	2 45	N 6 20.7	318 34.9	5 25	278 46.0
15	Elnath	1.8	2 46	N 28 36.1	318 18.0	5 26	278 29.1
16	Alnilam	1.8	2 56	S 1 12.3	315 48.5	5 36	275 59.6
17	Betelgeuse	0.1-1.2	3 15	N 7 24.3	311 04.3	5 55	271 15.4
18	Canopus...........	-0.9	3 44	S 52 41.5	303 50.5	6 24	264 01.6
19	Sirius	-1.6	4 05	S 16 42.6	298 34.1	6 45	258 45.2
20	Adhara	1.6	4 19	S 28 57.9	295 11.6	6 58	255 22.7
21	Castor..............	1.6	4 54	N 31 53.6	286 13.6	7 34	246 24.7
22	Procyon	0.5	4 59	N 5 14.1	285 02.3	7 39	245 13.4
23	Pollux	1.2	5 05	N 28 02.0	283 32.7	7 45	243 43.8
24	Avior	1.7	5 42	S 59 29.6	274 12.0	8 22	234 23.1
25	Suhail	2.2	6 28	S 43 24.8	262 51.0	9 08	223 02.1
26	Miaplacidus	1.8	6 33	S 69 41.8	261 31.1	9 13	221 42.2
27	Alphard...........	2.2	6 47	S 8 38.4	257 58.0	9 27	218 09.1
28	Regulus	1.3	7 28	N 11 59.2	247 46.6	10 08	207 57.7
29	Dubhe	2.0	8 23	N 61 46.1	233 57.2	11 03	194 08.3
30	Denebola	2.2	9 08	N 14 35.7	222 36.3	11 49	182 47.4
31	Gienah	2.8	9 35	S 17 31.0	215 55.1	12 16	176 06.2
32	Acrux...............	1.1	9 46	S 63 04.3	213 13.4	12 26	173 24.5
33	Gacrux.............	1.6	9 50	S 57 05.2	212 05.0	12 31	172 16.1
34	Mimosa	1.5	10 07	S 59 39.7	207 56.9	12 47	168 08.0
35	Alioth	1.7	10 13	N 55 58.8	206 21.7	12 54	166 32.8
36	Spica................	1.2	10 44	S 11 08.3	198 34.4	13 25	158 45.5
37	Alkaid	1.9	11 06	N 49 20.0	192 58.8	13 47	153 09.9
38	Hadar	0.9	11 22	S 60 21.0	188 56.2	14 04	149 07.3
39	Menkent	2.3	11 25	S 36 20.8	188 12.5	14 06	148 23.6
40	Arcturus	0.2	11 34	N 19 12.3	185 57.1	14 15	146 08.2
41	Rigil Kent.	0.1	11 58	S 60 48.9	179 59.3	14 39	140 10.4
42	Zuben'ubi	2.9	12 09	S 16 01.3	177 09.4	14 51	137 20.5
43	Kochab............	2.2	12 09	N 74 10.4	177 09.8	14 51	137 20.9
44	Alphecca	2.3	12 53	N 26 43.9	166 11.5	15 34	126 22.6
45	Antares	1.2	13 48	S 26 25.2	152 31.8	16 29	112 42.9
46	Atria	1.9	14 07	S 69 01.2	147 46.1	16 48	107 57.2
47	Sabik	2.6	14 28	S 15 43.0	142 17.0	17 10	102 28.1
48	Shaula	1.7	14 52	S 37 06.0	136 29.2	17 33	96 40.3
49	Rasalhague	2.1	14 53	N 12 34.0	136 08.0	17 35	96 19.1
50	Eltanin.............	2.4	15 15	N 51 29.7	130 41.7	17 56	90 52.8
51	Kaus Aust.	2.0	15 42	S 34 23.1	123 50.6	18 24	84 01.7
52	Vega................	0.1	15 55	N 38 47.1	120 37.1	18 37	80 48.2
53	Nunki	2.1	16 13	S 26 18.0	116 03.9	18 55	76 15.0
54	Altair	0.9	17 09	N 8 51.7	102 10.2	19 51	62 21.3
55	Peacock	2.1	17 43	S 56 45.0	93 29.2	20 25	53 40.3
56	Deneb	1.3	17 59	N 45 16.4	89 29.5	20 41	49 40.6
57	Enif..................	2.5	19 02	N 9 51.6	73 49.0	21 44	34 00.1
58	Al Na'ir	2.2	19 26	S 46 59.0	67 49.2	22 08	28 00.3
59	Fomalhaut	1.3	20 15	S 29 38.7	55 27.4	22 57	15 38.5
60	Markab	2.6	20 22	N 15 11.2	53 40.3	23 05	13 51.4

Star Transit Corr Table

Date	Corr h m	Date	Corr h m
1	-0 00	17	-1 03
2	-0 04	18	-1 07
3	-0 08	19	-1 11
4	-0 12	20	-1 15
5	-0 16	21	-1 19
6	-0 20	22	-1 23
7	-0 24	23	-1 27
8	-0 28	24	-1 30
9	-0 31	25	-1 34
10	-0 35	26	-1 38
11	-0 39	27	-1 42
12	-0 43	28	-1 46
13	-0 47	29	-1 50
14	-0 51	30	-1 54
15	-0 55	31	-1 58
16	-0 59		

STAR TRANSIT

To find the approx time of transit of a star for any day of the month use above table. All corrections are subtractive.

If the quantity taken from the table is greater than the time of transit for the first of the month, add 23h 56min to the time of transit before subtracting the correction.

Example: What time will Acamar (No 8) transit the Meridian on November 30?

	h min
Transit on Nov 1	00 19
	+23 56
	24 15
Corr for Nov 30	-01 54
Transit on Nov 30	22 21

NOVEMBER DIARY

d h	
2 12	Mars 4° N of Antares
3 02	Saturn 6° S of Moon
10 18	Venus 4° N of Antares
16 08	Mars 1.2° S of Jupiter
19 12	Venus 1.3° S of Jupiter
22 14	Saturn stationary
22 22	Venus 0.2° S of Mars
23 05	Mercury in superior conjunction
24 01	Jupiter 4° S of Moon
24 08	Mars 5° S of Moon
24 09	Venus 6° S of Moon
26 07	Neptune 5° S of Moon
26 14	Uranus 6° S of Moon
30 07	Saturn 6° S of Moon

NOTES

Star declinations may be used as is for the whole month. To correct GHA for day, hour, minute and second see page E 92 and for further explanation of this table see page E 4.

NOVEMBER

NOVEMBER 1995   SUN & ARIES   GMT

Wednesday, 1st November

Time	SUN GHA ° '	Dec ° '	ARIES GHA ° '
00	184 05.6	S14 12.2	39 48.9
02	214 05.7	14 13.8	69 53.8
04	244 05.7	14 15.4	99 58.7
06	274 05.8	14 17.0	130 03.6
08	304 05.8	14 18.6	160 08.6
10	334 05.8	14 20.2	190 13.5
12	4 05.9	14 21.8	220 18.4
14	34 05.9	14 23.4	250 23.4
16	64 06.0	14 25.1	280 28.3
18	94 06.0	14 26.7	310 33.2
20	124 06.0	14 28.3	340 38.1
22	154 06.1	S14 29.8	10 43.1

Thursday, 2nd November

Time	SUN GHA ° '	Dec ° '	ARIES GHA ° '
00	184 06.1	S14 31.4	40 48.0
02	214 06.1	14 33.0	70 52.9
04	244 06.1	14 34.6	100 57.9
06	274 06.2	14 36.2	131 02.8
08	304 06.2	14 37.8	161 07.7
10	334 06.2	14 39.4	191 12.6
12	4 06.2	14 41.0	221 17.6
14	34 06.3	14 42.6	251 22.5
16	64 06.3	14 44.2	281 27.4
18	94 06.3	14 45.7	311 32.4
20	124 06.3	14 47.3	341 37.3
22	154 06.3	S14 48.9	11 42.2

Friday, 3rd November

Time	SUN GHA ° '	Dec ° '	ARIES GHA ° '
00	184 06.3	S14 50.5	41 47.1
02	214 06.4	14 52.0	71 52.1
04	244 06.4	14 53.6	101 57.0
06	274 06.4	14 55.2	132 01.9
08	304 06.4	14 56.8	162 06.8
10	334 06.4	14 58.3	192 11.8
12	4 06.4	14 59.9	222 16.7
14	34 06.4	15 01.5	252 21.6
16	64 06.4	15 03.0	282 26.6
18	94 06.4	15 04.6	312 31.5
20	124 06.4	15 06.1	342 36.4
22	154 06.4	S15 07.7	12 41.3

Saturday, 4th November

Time	SUN GHA ° '	Dec ° '	ARIES GHA ° '
00	184 06.4	S15 09.3	42 46.3
02	214 06.4	15 10.8	72 51.2
04	244 06.4	15 12.4	102 56.1
06	274 06.4	15 13.9	133 01.1
08	304 06.4	15 15.5	163 06.0
10	334 06.4	15 17.0	193 10.9
12	4 06.4	15 18.6	223 15.8
14	34 06.4	15 20.1	253 20.8
16	64 06.3	15 21.6	283 25.7
18	94 06.3	15 23.2	313 30.6
20	124 06.3	15 24.7	343 35.6
22	154 06.3	S15 26.3	13 40.5

Sunday, 5th November

Time	SUN GHA ° '	Dec ° '	ARIES GHA ° '
00	184 06.3	S15 27.8	43 45.4
02	214 06.3	15 29.3	73 50.3
04	244 06.2	15 30.9	103 55.3
06	274 06.2	15 32.4	134 00.2
08	304 06.2	15 33.9	164 05.1
10	334 06.2	15 35.5	194 10.1
12	4 06.1	15 37.0	224 15.0
14	34 06.1	15 38.5	254 19.9
16	64 06.1	15 40.0	284 24.8
18	94 06.0	15 41.5	314 29.8
20	124 06.0	15 43.1	344 34.7
22	154 06.0	S15 44.6	14 39.6

Monday, 6th November

Time	SUN GHA ° '	Dec ° '	ARIES GHA ° '
00	184 05.9	S15 46.1	44 44.6
02	214 05.9	15 47.6	74 49.5
04	244 05.9	15 49.1	104 54.4
06	274 05.8	15 50.6	134 59.3
08	304 05.8	15 52.1	165 04.3
10	334 05.7	15 53.6	195 09.2
12	4 05.7	15 55.1	225 14.1
14	34 05.6	15 56.6	255 19.1
16	64 05.6	15 58.1	285 24.0
18	94 05.5	15 59.6	315 28.9
20	124 05.5	16 01.1	345 33.8
22	154 05.4	S16 02.6	15 38.8

Tuesday, 7th November

Time	SUN GHA ° '	Dec ° '	ARIES GHA ° '
00	184 05.4	S16 04.1	45 43.7
02	214 05.3	16 05.6	75 48.6
04	244 05.3	16 07.1	105 53.5
06	274 05.2	16 08.6	135 58.5
08	304 05.2	16 10.1	166 03.4
10	334 05.1	16 11.5	196 08.3
12	4 05.0	16 13.0	226 13.3
14	34 05.0	16 14.5	256 18.2
16	64 04.9	16 16.0	286 23.1
18	94 04.8	16 17.5	316 28.0
20	124 04.8	16 18.9	346 33.0
22	154 04.7	S16 20.4	16 37.9

Wednesday, 8th November

Time	SUN GHA ° '	Dec ° '	ARIES GHA ° '
00	184 04.6	S16 21.9	46 42.8
02	214 04.6	16 23.3	76 47.8
04	244 04.5	16 24.8	106 52.7
06	274 04.4	16 26.3	136 57.6
08	304 04.3	16 27.7	167 02.5
10	334 04.3	16 29.2	197 07.5
12	4 04.2	16 30.6	227 12.4
14	34 04.1	16 32.1	257 17.3
16	64 04.0	16 33.6	287 22.3
18	94 03.9	16 35.0	317 27.2
20	124 03.8	16 36.5	347 32.1
22	154 03.8	S16 37.9	17 37.0

Thursday, 9th November

Time	SUN GHA ° '	Dec ° '	ARIES GHA ° '
00	184 03.7	S16 39.3	47 42.0
02	214 03.6	16 40.8	77 46.9
04	244 03.5	16 42.2	107 51.8
06	274 03.4	16 43.7	137 56.8
08	304 03.3	16 45.1	168 01.7
10	334 03.2	16 46.6	198 06.6
12	4 03.1	16 48.0	228 11.5
14	34 03.0	16 49.4	258 16.5
16	64 02.9	16 50.8	288 21.4
18	94 02.8	16 52.3	318 26.3
20	124 02.7	16 53.7	348 31.3
22	154 02.6	S16 55.1	18 36.2

Friday, 10th November

Time	SUN GHA ° '	Dec ° '	ARIES GHA ° '
00	184 02.5	S16 56.6	48 41.1
02	214 02.4	16 58.0	78 46.0
04	244 02.3	16 59.4	108 51.0
06	274 02.2	17 00.8	138 55.9
08	304 02.0	17 02.2	169 00.8
10	334 01.9	17 03.6	199 05.7
12	4 01.8	17 05.0	229 10.7
14	34 01.7	17 06.5	259 15.6
16	64 01.6	17 07.9	289 20.5
18	94 01.5	17 09.3	319 25.5
20	124 01.3	17 10.7	349 30.4
22	154 01.2	S17 12.1	19 35.3

Saturday, 11th November

Time	SUN GHA ° '	Dec ° '	ARIES GHA ° '
00	184 01.1	S17 13.5	49 40.2
02	214 01.0	17 14.9	79 45.2
04	244 00.8	17 16.3	109 50.1
06	274 00.7	17 17.6	139 55.0
08	304 00.6	17 19.0	170 00.0
10	334 00.4	17 20.4	200 04.9
12	4 00.3	17 21.8	230 09.8
14	34 00.2	17 23.2	260 14.7
16	64 00.0	17 24.6	290 19.7
18	93 59.9	17 26.0	320 24.6
20	123 59.8	17 27.3	350 29.5
22	153 59.6	S17 28.7	20 34.5

Sunday, 12th November

Time	SUN GHA ° '	Dec ° '	ARIES GHA ° '
00	183 59.5	S17 30.1	50 39.4
02	213 59.3	17 31.5	80 44.3
04	243 59.2	17 32.8	110 49.2
06	273 59.0	17 34.2	140 54.2
08	303 58.9	17 35.6	170 59.1
10	333 58.7	17 36.9	201 04.0
12	3 58.6	17 38.3	231 09.0
14	33 58.4	17 39.6	261 13.9
16	63 58.3	17 41.0	291 18.8
18	93 58.1	17 42.3	321 23.7
20	123 58.0	17 43.7	351 28.7
22	153 57.8	S17 45.0	21 33.6

Monday, 13th November

Time	SUN GHA ° '	Dec ° '	ARIES GHA ° '
00	183 57.6	S17 46.4	51 38.5
02	213 57.5	17 47.7	81 43.5
04	243 57.3	17 49.1	111 48.4
06	273 57.2	17 50.4	141 53.3
08	303 57.0	17 51.8	171 58.2
10	333 56.8	17 53.1	202 03.2
12	3 56.7	17 54.4	232 08.1
14	33 56.5	17 55.8	262 13.0
16	63 56.3	17 57.1	292 17.9
18	93 56.1	17 58.4	322 22.9
20	123 56.0	17 59.8	352 27.8
22	153 55.8	S18 01.1	22 32.7

Tuesday, 14th November

Time	SUN GHA ° '	Dec ° '	ARIES GHA ° '
00	183 55.6	S18 02.4	52 37.7
02	213 55.4	18 03.7	82 42.6
04	243 55.2	18 05.0	112 47.5
06	273 55.1	18 06.4	142 52.4
08	303 54.9	18 07.7	172 57.4
10	333 54.7	18 09.0	203 02.3
12	3 54.5	18 10.3	233 07.2
14	33 54.3	18 11.6	263 12.2
16	63 54.1	18 12.9	293 17.1
18	93 53.9	18 14.2	323 22.0
20	123 53.7	18 15.5	353 26.9
22	153 53.5	S18 16.8	23 31.9

Wednesday, 15th November

Time	SUN GHA ° '	Dec ° '	ARIES GHA ° '
00	183 53.3	S18 18.1	53 36.8
02	213 53.1	18 19.4	83 41.7
04	243 52.9	18 20.7	113 46.7
06	273 52.7	18 22.0	143 51.6
08	303 52.5	18 23.3	173 56.5
10	333 52.3	18 24.5	204 01.4
12	3 52.1	18 25.8	234 06.4
14	33 51.9	18 27.1	264 11.3
16	63 51.7	18 28.4	294 16.2
18	93 51.5	18 29.7	324 21.2
20	123 51.3	18 30.9	354 26.1
22	153 51.1	S18 32.2	24 31.0

NOTES

Sun & Aries GHA corrections for additional hour, minutes, and seconds on page E 94.
Correct Sun Declination by interpolation. For example see page E 4.

NOVEMBER 1995 — SUN & ARIES — GMT

Thursday, 16th November

Time	SUN GHA	Dec	ARIES GHA
00	183 50.9	S18 33.5	54 35.9
02	213 50.6	18 34.7	84 40.0
04	243 50.4	18 36.0	114 45.8
06	273 50.2	18 37.3	144 50.7
08	303 50.0	18 38.5	174 55.7
10	333 49.8	18 39.8	205 00.6
12	3 49.5	18 41.0	235 05.5
14	33 49.3	18 42.3	265 10.4
16	63 49.1	18 43.5	295 15.4
18	93 48.9	18 44.8	325 20.3
20	123 48.6	18 46.0	355 25.2
22	153 48.4	S18 47.3	25 30.2

Friday, 17th November

Time	SUN GHA	Dec	ARIES GHA
00	183 48.2	S18 48.5	55 35.1
02	213 47.9	18 49.8	85 40.0
04	243 47.7	18 51.0	115 44.9
06	273 47.5	18 52.2	145 49.9
08	303 47.2	18 53.5	175 54.8
10	333 47.0	18 54.7	205 59.7
12	3 46.7	18 55.9	236 04.6
14	33 46.5	18 57.1	266 09.6
16	63 46.2	18 58.4	296 14.5
18	93 46.0	18 59.6	326 19.4
20	123 45.8	19 00.8	356 24.4
22	153 45.5	S19 02.0	26 29.3

Saturday, 18th November

Time	SUN GHA	Dec	ARIES GHA
00	183 45.3	S19 03.2	56 34.2
02	213 45.0	19 04.4	86 39.1
04	243 44.7	19 05.7	116 44.1
06	273 44.5	19 06.9	146 49.0
08	303 44.2	19 08.1	176 53.9
10	333 44.0	19 09.3	206 58.9
12	3 43.7	19 10.5	237 03.8
14	33 43.5	19 11.7	267 08.7
16	63 43.2	19 12.9	297 13.6
18	93 42.9	19 14.0	327 18.6
20	123 42.7	19 15.2	357 23.5
22	153 42.4	S19 16.4	27 28.4

Sunday, 19th November

Time	SUN GHA	Dec	ARIES GHA
00	183 42.1	S19 17.6	57 33.4
02	213 41.9	19 18.8	87 38.3
04	243 41.6	19 20.0	117 43.2
06	273 41.3	19 21.1	147 48.1
08	303 41.0	19 22.3	177 53.1
10	333 40.8	19 23.5	207 58.0
12	3 40.5	19 24.7	238 02.9
14	33 40.2	19 25.8	268 07.9
16	63 39.9	19 27.0	298 12.8
18	93 39.7	19 28.2	328 17.7
20	123 39.4	19 29.3	358 22.6
22	153 39.1	S19 30.5	28 27.6

Monday, 20th November

Time	SUN GHA	Dec	ARIES GHA
00	183 38.8	S19 31.6	58 32.5
02	213 38.5	19 32.8	88 37.4
04	243 38.2	19 33.9	118 42.4
06	273 37.9	19 35.1	148 47.3
08	303 37.6	19 36.2	178 52.2
10	333 37.3	19 37.4	208 57.1
12	3 37.1	19 38.5	239 02.1
14	33 36.8	19 39.7	269 07.0
16	63 36.5	19 40.8	299 11.9
18	93 36.2	19 41.9	329 16.8
20	123 35.9	19 43.1	359 21.8
22	153 35.6	S19 44.2	29 26.7

Tuesday, 21st November

Time	SUN GHA	Dec	ARIES GHA
00	183 35.3	S19 45.3	59 31.6
02	213 35.0	19 46.4	89 36.6
04	243 34.7	19 47.6	119 41.5
06	273 34.3	19 48.7	149 46.4
08	303 34.0	19 49.8	179 51.3
10	333 33.7	19 50.9	209 56.3
12	3 33.4	19 52.0	240 01.2
14	33 33.1	19 53.1	270 06.1
16	63 32.8	19 54.2	300 11.1
18	93 32.5	19 55.3	330 16.0
20	123 32.2	19 56.4	0 20.9
22	153 31.8	S19 57.5	30 25.8

Wednesday, 22nd November

Time	SUN GHA	Dec	ARIES GHA
00	183 31.5	S19 58.6	60 30.8
02	213 31.2	19 59.7	90 35.7
04	243 30.9	20 00.8	120 40.6
06	273 30.6	20 01.9	150 45.6
08	303 30.2	20 03.0	180 50.5
10	333 29.9	20 04.1	210 55.4
12	3 29.6	20 05.1	241 00.3
14	33 29.2	20 06.2	271 05.3
16	63 28.9	20 07.3	301 10.2
18	93 28.6	20 08.4	331 15.1
20	123 28.2	20 09.4	1 20.1
22	153 27.9	S20 10.5	31 25.0

Thursday, 23rd November

Time	SUN GHA	Dec	ARIES GHA
00	183 27.6	S20 11.6	61 29.9
02	213 27.2	20 12.6	91 34.8
04	243 26.9	20 13.7	121 39.8
06	273 26.6	20 14.8	151 44.7
08	303 26.2	20 15.8	181 49.6
10	333 25.9	20 16.9	211 54.6
12	3 25.5	20 17.9	241 59.5
14	33 25.2	20 19.0	272 04.4
16	63 24.8	20 20.0	302 09.3
18	93 24.5	20 21.0	332 14.3
20	123 24.1	20 22.1	2 19.2
22	153 23.8	S20 23.1	32 24.1

Friday, 24th November

Time	SUN GHA	Dec	ARIES GHA
00	183 23.4	S20 24.2	62 29.1
02	213 23.1	20 25.2	92 34.0
04	243 22.7	20 26.2	122 38.9
06	273 22.4	20 27.2	152 43.8
08	303 22.0	20 28.3	182 48.8
10	333 21.7	20 29.3	212 53.7
12	3 21.3	20 30.3	242 58.6
14	33 20.9	20 31.3	273 03.5
16	63 20.6	20 32.3	303 08.5
18	93 20.2	20 33.3	333 13.4
20	123 19.8	20 34.4	3 18.3
22	153 19.5	S20 35.4	33 23.3

Saturday, 25th November

Time	SUN GHA	Dec	ARIES GHA
00	183 19.1	S20 36.4	63 28.2
02	213 18.7	20 37.4	93 33.1
04	243 18.4	20 38.4	123 38.0
06	273 18.0	20 39.4	153 43.0
08	303 17.6	20 40.3	183 47.9
10	333 17.2	20 41.3	213 52.8
12	3 16.9	20 42.3	243 57.8
14	33 16.5	20 43.3	274 02.7
16	63 16.1	20 44.3	304 07.6
18	93 15.7	20 45.3	334 12.5
20	123 15.4	20 46.2	4 17.5
22	153 15.0	S20 47.2	34 22.4

Sunday, 26th November

Time	SUN GHA	Dec	ARIES GHA
00	183 14.6	S20 48.2	64 27.3
02	213 14.2	20 49.1	94 32.3
04	243 13.8	20 50.1	124 37.2
06	273 13.4	20 51.1	154 42.1
08	303 13.0	20 52.0	184 47.0
10	333 12.6	20 53.0	214 52.0
12	3 12.3	20 53.9	244 56.9
14	33 11.9	20 54.9	275 01.8
16	63 11.5	20 55.8	305 06.8
18	93 11.1	20 56.8	335 11.7
20	123 10.7	20 57.7	5 16.6
22	153 10.3	S20 58.7	35 21.5

Monday, 27th November

Time	SUN GHA	Dec	ARIES GHA
00	183 09.9	S20 59.6	65 26.5
02	213 09.5	21 00.5	95 31.4
04	243 09.1	21 01.5	125 36.3
06	273 08.7	21 02.4	155 41.3
08	303 08.3	21 03.3	185 46.2
10	333 07.9	21 04.3	215 51.1
12	3 07.5	21 05.2	245 56.0
14	33 07.1	21 06.1	276 01.0
16	63 06.6	21 07.0	306 05.9
18	93 06.2	21 07.9	336 10.8
20	123 05.8	21 08.8	6 15.7
22	153 05.4	S21 09.7	36 20.7

Tuesday, 28th November

Time	SUN GHA	Dec	ARIES GHA
00	183 05.0	S21 10.7	66 25.6
02	213 04.6	21 11.6	96 30.5
04	243 04.2	21 12.5	126 35.5
06	273 03.8	21 13.4	156 40.4
08	303 03.3	21 14.2	186 45.3
10	333 02.9	21 15.1	216 50.2
12	3 02.5	21 16.0	246 55.2
14	33 02.1	21 16.9	277 00.1
16	63 01.6	21 17.8	307 05.0
18	93 01.2	21 18.7	337 10.0
20	123 00.8	21 19.5	7 14.9
22	153 00.4	S21 20.4	37 19.8

Wednesday, 29th November

Time	SUN GHA	Dec	ARIES GHA
00	182 59.9	S21 21.3	67 24.7
02	212 59.5	21 22.2	97 29.7
04	242 59.1	21 23.0	127 34.6
06	272 58.7	21 23.9	157 39.5
08	302 58.2	21 24.8	187 44.5
10	332 57.8	21 25.6	217 49.4
12	2 57.3	21 26.5	247 54.3
14	32 56.9	21 27.3	277 59.2
16	62 56.5	21 28.2	308 04.2
18	92 56.0	21 29.0	338 09.1
20	122 55.6	21 29.9	8 14.0
22	152 55.2	S21 30.7	38 19.0

Thursday, 30th November

Time	SUN GHA	Dec	ARIES GHA
00	182 54.7	S21 31.5	68 23.9
02	212 54.3	21 32.4	98 28.8
04	242 53.8	21 33.2	128 33.7
06	272 53.4	21 34.0	158 38.7
08	302 52.9	21 34.9	188 43.6
10	332 52.5	21 35.7	218 48.5
12	2 52.0	21 36.5	248 53.5
14	32 51.6	21 37.3	278 58.4
16	62 51.1	21 38.1	309 03.3
18	92 50.7	21 38.9	339 08.2
20	122 50.2	21 39.8	9 13.2
22	152 49.8	S21 40.6	39 18.1

NOVEMBER

NOVEMBER 1995 — PLANETS — 0h GMT

VENUS / JUPITER

Mer Pass h m	GHA ° '	Mean Var/hr 14°+	Dec ° '	Mean Var/hr	Note Corrections on Page E 101	GHA ° '	Mean Var/hr 15°+	Dec ° '	Mean Var/hr	Mer Pass h m
13 00	165 10.4	59.3	S 19 39.2	0.8	1 Wed	144 57.6	1.9	S 22 21.4	0.1	14 18
13 01	164 52.8	59.3	S 19 58.7	0.8	2 Th	145 43.8	1.9	S 22 22.7	0.1	14 15
13 02	164 35.0	59.2	S 20 17.6	0.8	3 Fri	146 29.9	1.9	S 22 24.1	0.1	14 12
13 04	164 16.8	59.2	S 20 35.9	0.7	4 Sat	147 15.9	1.9	S 22 25.4	0.1	14 09
13 05	163 58.4	59.2	S 20 53.7	0.7	5 SUN	148 01.9	1.9	S 22 26.8	0.1	14 06
13 06	163 39.7	59.2	S 21 10.8	0.7	6 Mon	148 47.7	1.9	S 22 28.1	0.1	14 03
13 07	163 20.7	59.2	S 21 27.4	0.7	7 Tu	149 33.5	1.9	S 22 29.4	0.1	14 00
13 09	163 01.4	59.2	S 21 43.4	0.6	8 Wed	150 19.3	1.9	S 22 30.7	0.1	13 57
13 10	162 41.8	59.2	S 21 58.8	0.6	9 Th	151 04.9	1.9	S 22 32.0	0.0	13 54
13 11	162 21.9	59.2	S 22 13.5	0.6	10 Fri	151 50.5	1.9	S 22 33.2	0.1	13 51
13 13	162 01.8	59.2	S 22 27.6	0.6	11 Sat	152 36.1	1.9	S 22 34.5	0.0	13 48
13 14	161 41.4	59.1	S 22 41.1	0.5	12 SUN	153 21.6	1.9	S 22 35.7	0.1	13 45
13 15	161 20.8	59.1	S 22 53.9	0.5	13 Mon	154 07.0	1.9	S 22 36.9	0.0	13 42
13 17	160 59.9	59.1	S 23 06.1	0.5	14 Tu	154 52.3	1.9	S 22 38.1	0.1	13 39
13 18	160 38.8	59.1	S 23 17.5	0.5	15 Wed	155 37.6	1.9	S 22 39.3	0.0	13 36
13 20	160 17.5	59.1	S 23 28.3	0.4	16 Th	156 22.9	1.9	S 22 40.5	0.0	13 33
13 21	159 55.9	59.1	S 23 38.4	0.4	17 Fri	157 08.1	1.9	S 22 41.6	0.1	13 30
13 23	159 34.2	59.1	S 23 47.8	0.4	18 Sat	157 53.2	1.9	S 22 42.8	0.0	13 27
13 24	159 12.3	59.1	S 23 56.5	0.3	19 SUN	158 38.3	1.9	S 22 43.9	0.0	13 24
13 25	158 50.2	59.1	S 24 04.4	0.3	20 Mon	159 23.4	1.9	S 22 45.0	0.0	13 21
13 27	158 28.0	59.1	S 24 11.7	0.3	21 Tu	160 08.3	1.9	S 22 46.0	0.0	13 18
13 28	158 05.6	59.1	S 24 18.2	0.2	22 Wed	160 53.3	1.9	S 22 47.1	0.0	13 15
13 30	157 43.1	59.1	S 24 24.0	0.2	23 Th	161 38.2	1.9	S 22 48.1	0.0	13 12
13 31	157 20.5	59.1	S 24 29.1	0.2	24 Fri	162 23.0	1.9	S 22 49.2	0.0	13 09
13 33	156 57.8	59.1	S 24 33.4	0.1	25 Sat	163 07.9	1.9	S 22 50.2	0.0	13 06
13 35	156 35.1	59.0	S 24 37.0	0.1	26 SUN	163 52.6	1.9	S 22 51.1	0.0	13 03
13 36	156 12.2	59.1	S 24 39.8	0.1	27 Mon	164 37.4	1.9	S 22 52.1	0.0	13 00
13 38	155 49.4	59.0	S 24 41.9	0.1	28 Tu	165 22.1	1.9	S 22 53.0	0.0	12 57
13 39	155 26.5	59.0	S 24 43.2	0.0	29 Wed	166 06.7	1.9	S 22 53.9	0.0	12 54
13 41	155 03.6	59.0	S 24 43.8	0.0	30 Th	166 51.4	1.9	S 22 54.8	0.0	12 51

VENUS, Av. Mag. -3.9
S.H.A. November
5 120; 10 114; 15 107; 20 100; 25 93; 30 87.

JUPITER, Av. Mag.-1.8
S.H.A. November
5 104; 10 103; 15 102; 20 101; 25 100; 30 98.

MARS / SATURN

Mer Pass h m	GHA ° '	Mean Var/hr 15°+	Dec ° '	Mean Var/hr	Note Corrections on Page E 101	GHA ° '	Mean Var/hr 15°+	Dec ° '	Mean Var/hr	Mer Pass h m
13 45	153 41.1	0.5	S 22 23.1	0.3	1 Wed	49 36.1	2.5	S 6 42.8	0.0	20 38
13 44	153 53.6	0.5	S 22 30.5	0.3	2 Th	50 37.2	2.5	S 6 43.5	0.0	20 34
13 43	154 06.0	0.5	S 22 37.7	0.3	3 Fri	51 38.3	2.5	S 6 44.1	0.0	20 30
13 42	154 18.3	0.5	S 22 44.7	0.3	4 Sat	52 39.2	2.5	S 6 44.7	0.0	20 26
13 42	154 30.4	0.5	S 22 51.4	0.3	5 SUN	53 40.1	2.5	S 6 45.3	0.0	20 22
13 41	154 42.4	0.5	S 22 57.9	0.3	6 Mon	54 40.8	2.5	S 6 45.8	0.0	20 18
13 40	154 54.2	0.5	S 23 04.3	0.3	7 Tu	55 41.5	2.5	S 6 46.2	0.0	20 14
13 39	155 05.9	0.5	S 23 10.3	0.2	8 Wed	56 42.1	2.5	S 6 46.7	0.0	20 10
13 38	155 17.4	0.5	S 23 16.2	0.2	9 Th	57 42.6	2.5	S 6 47.1	0.0	20 06
13 38	155 28.8	0.5	S 23 21.8	0.2	10 Fri	58 43.0	2.5	S 6 47.4	0.0	20 02
13 37	155 40.1	0.5	S 23 27.2	0.2	11 Sat	59 43.3	2.5	S 6 47.7	0.0	19 58
13 36	155 51.3	0.5	S 23 32.4	0.2	12 SUN	60 43.5	2.5	S 6 48.0	0.0	19 54
13 35	156 02.3	0.5	S 23 37.3	0.2	13 Mon	61 43.6	2.5	S 6 48.2	0.0	19 50
13 35	156 13.2	0.4	S 23 42.0	0.2	14 Tu	62 43.7	2.5	S 6 48.4	0.0	19 46
13 34	156 23.9	0.4	S 23 46.5	0.2	15 Wed	63 43.6	2.5	S 6 48.5	0.0	19 42
13 33	156 34.6	0.4	S 23 50.7	0.2	16 Th	64 43.4	2.5	S 6 48.6	0.0	19 38
13 33	156 45.1	0.4	S 23 54.7	0.2	17 Fri	65 43.2	2.5	S 6 48.7	0.0	19 34
13 32	156 55.5	0.4	S 23 58.4	0.1	18 Sat	66 42.8	2.5	S 6 48.7	0.0	19 30
13 31	157 05.8	0.4	S 24 01.8	0.1	19 SUN	67 42.3	2.5	S 6 48.7	0.0	19 26
13 31	157 16.0	0.4	S 24 05.0	0.1	20 Mon	68 41.8	2.5	S 6 48.6	0.0	19 22
13 30	157 26.1	0.4	S 24 08.0	0.1	21 Tu	69 41.1	2.5	S 6 48.5	0.0	19 18
13 29	157 36.1	0.4	S 24 10.7	0.1	22 Wed	70 40.4	2.5	S 6 48.3	0.0	19 14
13 29	157 46.0	0.4	S 24 13.2	0.1	23 Th	71 39.5	2.5	S 6 48.1	0.0	19 10
13 28	157 55.8	0.4	S 24 15.4	0.1	24 Fri	72 38.5	2.5	S 6 47.9	0.0	19 06
13 27	158 05.5	0.4	S 24 17.3	0.1	25 Sat	73 37.5	2.5	S 6 47.6	0.0	19 02
13 27	158 15.1	0.4	S 24 19.0	0.1	26 SUN	74 36.3	2.5	S 6 47.2	0.0	18 58
13 26	158 24.7	0.4	S 24 20.4	0.0	27 Mon	75 35.1	2.4	S 6 46.9	0.0	18 55
13 25	158 34.2	0.4	S 24 21.5	0.0	28 Tu	76 33.7	2.4	S 6 46.5	0.0	18 51
13 25	158 43.6	0.4	S 24 22.4	0.0	29 Wed	77 32.3	2.4	S 6 46.0	0.0	18 47
13 24	158 52.9	0.4	S 24 23.0	0.0	30 Th	78 30.7	2.4	S 6 45.5	0.0	18 43

MARS, Av. Mag. +1.3
S.H.A. November
5 111; 10 107; 15 103; 20 99; 25 95; 30 90.

SATURN, Av. Mag. +0.9
S.H.A. November
5 10; 10 10; 15 10; 20 10; 25 10; 30 10.

NOVEMBER 1995 — MOON

Day	GMT hr	GHA ° ′	Mean Var/hr 14°+	Dec ° ′	Mean Var/hr ′	Day	GMT hr	GHA ° ′	Mean Var/hr 14°+	Dec ° ′	Mean Var/hr ′
1 Wed	0	76 35.5	29.4	S 9 32.3	9.8	17 Fri	0	254 04.7	32.3	N 3 50.9	10.1
	6	163 31.2	29.7	S 8 33.7	10.0		6	341 18.1	32.0	N 2 50.0	10.3
	12	250 28.9	29.9	S 7 33.6	10.3		12	68 30.4	31.8	N 1 48.1	10.5
	18	337 28.2	30.2	S 6 32.4	10.4		18	155 41.4	31.6	N 0 45.4	10.6
2 Th	0	64 29.2	30.5	S 5 30.2	10.5	18 Sat	0	242 51.0	31.3	S 0 17.9	10.6
	6	151 31.6	30.6	S 4 27.2	10.7		6	329 59.0	31.0	S 1 21.6	10.7
	12	238 35.4	30.8	S 3 23.6	10.7		12	57 05.3	30.7	S 2 25.7	10.7
	18	325 40.4	31.0	S 2 19.7	10.7		18	144 09.6	30.4	S 3 29.9	10.7
3 Fri	0	52 46.5	31.2	S 1 15.6	10.7	19 Sun	0	231 11.9	30.0	S 4 34.0	10.6
	6	139 53.4	31.3	S 0 11.5	10.6		6	318 11.9	29.5	S 5 37.8	10.5
	12	227 01.1	31.4	N 0 52.4	10.5		12	45 09.6	29.2	S 6 41.1	10.4
	18	314 09.5	31.5	N 1 55.8	10.5		18	132 04.7	28.7	S 7 43.6	10.3
4 Sat	0	41 18.4	31.5	N 2 58.7	10.4	20 Mon	0	218 57.1	28.3	S 8 45.0	10.0
	6	128 27.6	31.6	N 4 00.8	10.2		6	305 46.8	27.8	S 9 45.1	9.7
	12	215 37.2	31.6	N 5 02.0	10.0		12	32 33.7	27.3	S 10 43.6	9.4
	18	302 46.8	31.6	N 6 02.0	9.8		18	119 17.6	26.8	S 11 40.3	9.0
5 Sun	0	29 56.5	31.6	N 7 00.8	9.5	21 Tu	0	205 58.6	26.3	S 12 34.7	8.6
	6	117 06.2	31.6	N 7 58.2	9.2		6	292 36.6	25.8	S 13 26.6	8.1
	12	204 15.8	31.5	N 8 54.0	9.0		12	19 11.8	25.4	S 14 15.8	7.6
	18	291 25.1	31.5	N 9 48.0	8.7		18	105 44.0	24.9	S 15 01.8	7.0
6 Mon	0	18 34.2	31.5	N 10 40.2	8.3	22 Wed	0	192 13.5	24.5	S 15 44.5	6.5
	6	105 42.9	31.4	N 11 30.3	7.9		6	278 40.5	24.1	S 16 23.4	5.8
	12	192 51.3	31.3	N 12 18.3	7.6		12	5 05.0	23.7	S 16 58.4	5.1
	18	279 59.4	31.3	N 13 04.0	7.2		18	91 27.3	23.3	S 17 29.1	4.3
7 Tu	0	7 07.0	31.2	N 13 47.3	6.7	23 Th	0	177 47.7	23.2	S 17 55.4	3.5
	6	94 14.2	31.1	N 14 28.0	6.4		6	264 06.6	22.9	S 18 17.1	2.8
	12	181 21.0	31.0	N 15 06.2	5.9		12	350 24.2	22.8	S 18 34.0	2.0
	18	268 27.5	31.1	N 15 41.6	5.4		18	76 40.8	22.6	S 18 45.9	1.0
8 Wed	0	355 33.5	30.9	N 16 14.2	5.0	24 Fri	0	162 57.0	22.7	S 18 52.8	0.3
	6	82 39.3	30.9	N 16 43.9	4.4		6	249 13.1	22.7	S 18 54.6	0.6
	12	169 44.9	30.9	N 17 10.7	4.0		12	335 29.4	22.8	S 18 51.4	1.5
	18	256 50.2	30.8	N 17 34.4	3.4		18	61 46.4	23.1	S 18 43.1	2.2
9 Th	0	343 55.4	30.9	N 17 55.1	2.9	25 Sat	0	148 04.4	23.3	S 18 29.9	3.1
	6	71 00.5	30.9	N 18 12.6	2.4		6	234 23.8	23.6	S 18 11.9	3.8
	12	158 05.6	30.9	N 18 27.0	1.8		12	320 44.9	23.9	S 17 49.2	4.6
	18	245 10.8	30.9	N 18 38.2	1.3		18	47 08.0	24.2	S 17 22.0	5.3
10 Fri	0	332 16.2	30.9	N 18 46.3	0.7	26 Sun	0	133 33.3	24.6	S 16 50.6	5.9
	6	59 21.8	31.0	N 18 51.1	0.3		6	220 01.1	25.1	S 16 15.1	6.6
	12	146 27.8	31.1	N 18 52.8	0.3		12	306 31.4	25.5	S 15 35.9	7.2
	18	233 34.1	31.1	N 18 51.3	0.8		18	33 04.5	26.0	S 14 53.1	7.7
11 Sat	0	320 41.0	31.2	N 18 46.6	1.4	27 Mon	0	119 40.3	26.4	S 14 07.0	8.2
	6	47 48.3	31.4	N 18 38.9	1.9		6	206 18.9	27.0	S 13 18.1	8.6
	12	134 56.3	31.4	N 18 28.1	2.3		12	293 00.4	27.4	S 12 26.4	9.0
	18	222 04.9	31.6	N 18 14.3	2.8		18	19 44.7	27.8	S 11 32.3	9.4
12 Sun	0	309 14.1	31.7	N 17 57.4	3.3	28 Tu	0	106 31.7	28.3	S 10 36.1	9.7
	6	36 24.1	31.8	N 17 37.7	3.8		6	193 21.4	28.7	S 9 38.0	10.0
	12	123 34.8	31.9	N 17 15.2	4.2		12	280 13.6	29.1	S 8 38.4	10.2
	18	210 46.2	32.0	N 16 49.8	4.7		18	7 08.2	29.5	S 7 37.4	10.3
13 Mon	0	297 58.4	32.1	N 16 21.7	5.2	29 Wed	0	94 05.1	29.9	S 6 35.2	10.5
	6	25 11.2	32.3	N 15 51.0	5.6		6	181 04.1	30.2	S 5 32.3	10.6
	12	112 24.8	32.3	N 15 17.7	6.0		12	268 05.1	30.5	S 4 28.6	10.7
	18	199 38.9	32.4	N 14 42.0	6.4		18	355 07.9	30.7	S 3 24.6	10.7
14 Tu	0	286 53.7	32.6	N 14 03.8	6.7	30 Th	0	82 12.4	31.0	S 2 20.3	10.7
	6	14 09.0	32.7	N 13 23.3	7.1		6	169 18.3	31.2	S 1 16.0	10.6
	12	101 24.8	32.7	N 12 40.6	7.5		12	256 25.5	31.4	S 0 11.8	10.6
	18	188 40.9	32.7	N 11 55.7	7.9		18	343 33.8	31.6	N 0 52.0	10.5
15 Wed	0	275 57.3	32.8	N 11 08.8	8.1						
	6	3 13.9	32.7	N 10 19.9	8.5						
	12	90 30.6	32.8	N 9 29.1	8.8						
	18	177 47.2	32.7	N 8 36.5	9.0						
16 Th	0	265 03.6	32.7	N 7 42.3	9.3						
	6	352 19.8	32.6	N 6 46.5	9.6						
	12	79 35.4	32.5	N 5 49.3	9.8						
	18	166 50.4	32.4	N 4 50.7	10.0						

NOTE Moon GHA corrections for additional hours, minutes, and seconds on page E 96.
Moon Declination corrections on page E 99. Mean Var/Hr value needed for both corrections.

NOVEMBER

DECEMBER 1995   SUN & MOON   GMT

SUN

Yr	Mth	Week	Equation of Time 0h	12h	Transit	Semi-diam	Lat 52°N Twi-light	Sun-rise	Sun-set	Twi-light		Lat Corr to Sunrise, Sunset etc Lat	Twi-light	Sun-rise	Sun-set	Twi-light
			m s	m s	h m	′	h m	h m	h m	h m		°	h m	h m	h m	h m
335	1	Fri	-11 18	-11 07	11 49	16.2	07 05	07 45	15 53	16 32		N60	+0 39	+0 55	-0 55	-0 39
336	2	Sat	-10 56	-10 44	11 49	16.2	07 07	07 46	15 52	16 32		55	+0 12	+0 17	-0 17	-0 12
337	3	Sun	-10 33	-10 21	11 50	16.3	07 08	07 48	15 51	16 31		50	-0 07	-0 10	+0 10	+0 07
338	4	Mon	-10 09	-09 57	11 50	16.3	07 09	07 49	15 51	16 31		45	-0 23	-0 30	+0 30	+0 23
339	5	Tu	-09 45	-09 33	11 50	16.3	07 10	07 50	15 50	16 30		N40	-0 37	-0 47	+0 47	+0 37
340	6	Wed	-09 21	-09 08	11 51	16.3	07 11	07 52	15 50	16 30		35	-0 48	-1 01	+1 01	+0 48
341	7	Th	-08 56	-08 43	11 51	16.3	07 13	07 53	15 49	16 30		30	-0 59	-1 13	+1 13	+0 59
342	8	Fri	-08 30	-08 17	11 52	16.3	07 14	07 54	15 49	16 29		25	-1 08	-1 24	+1 24	+1 08
343	9	Sat	-08 04	-07 51	11 52	16.3	07 15	07 55	15 49	16 29		N20	-1 18	-1 34	+1 34	+1 18
344	10	Sun	-07 37	-07 24	11 53	16.3	07 16	07 56	15 49	16 29		15	-1 26	-1 44	+1 44	+1 26
345	11	Mon	-07 10	-06 57	11 53	16.3	07 17	07 57	15 48	16 29		10	-1 35	-1 53	+1 53	+1 35
346	12	Tu	-06 43	-06 29	11 54	16.3	07 18	07 58	15 48	16 29		5	-1 43	-2 01	+2 01	+1 43
347	13	Wed	-06 15	-06 01	11 54	16.3	07 19	07 59	15 48	16 29		0	-1 52	-2 10	+2 10	+1 52
348	14	Th	-05 47	-05 32	11 54	16.3	07 20	08 00	15 48	16 29		S 5	-2 01	-2 18	+2 18	+2 01
349	15	Fri	-05 18	-05 04	11 55	16.3	07 20	08 01	15 48	16 29		10	-2 10	-2 27	+2 27	+2 10
350	16	Sat	-04 49	-04 35	11 55	16.3	07 21	08 02	15 49	16 29		15	-2 20	-2 36	+2 36	+2 20
351	17	Sun	-04 20	-04 05	11 56	16.3	07 22	08 03	15 49	16 30		S20	-2 30	-2 46	+2 46	+2 30
352	18	Mon	-03 51	-03 36	11 56	16.3	07 23	08 04	15 49	16 30		25	-2 42	-2 57	+2 57	+2 42
353	19	Tu	-03 21	-03 06	11 57	16.3	07 23	08 04	15 49	16 30		30	-2 55	-3 08	+3 08	+2 55
354	20	Wed	-02 52	-02 37	11 57	16.3	07 24	08 05	15 50	16 31		35	-3 10	-3 21	+3 21	+3 10
355	21	Th	-02 22	-02 07	11 58	16.3	07 25	08 06	15 50	16 31		S40	-3 28	-3 36	+3 36	+3 28
356	22	Fri	-01 52	-01 37	11 58	16.3	07 25	08 06	15 51	16 32		45	-3 50	-3 54	+3 54	+3 50
357	23	Sat	-01 22	-01 07	11 59	16.3	07 26	08 07	15 51	16 32		50	-4 20	-4 16	+4 16	+4 20
358	24	Sun	-00 52	-00 37	11 59	16.3	07 26	08 07	15 52	16 33						
359	25	Mon	-00 22	-00 07	12 00	16.3	07 26	08 07	15 52	16 33						
360	26	Tu	+00 08	+00 23	12 00	16.3	07 27	08 08	15 53	16 34						
361	27	Wed	+00 38	+00 53	12 01	16.3	07 27	08 08	15 54	16 35			NOTES			
362	28	Th	+01 08	+01 22	12 01	16.3	07 27	08 08	15 55	16 36			Lat corrections are for mid-month.			
363	29	Fri	+01 37	+01 52	12 02	16.3	07 27	08 08	15 56	16 36			**Equation of Time** is the excess of			
364	30	Sat	+02 06	+02 21	12 02	16.3	07 28	08 08	15 57	16 37			Mean Time over Apparent Time.			
365	31	Sun	+02 35	+02 50	12 03	16.3	07 28	08 08	15 58	16 38						

MOON

Yr	Mth	Week	Age	Transit (Upper)	Diff	Semi-diam	Hor Par	Lat 52°N Moon-rise	Moon-set	Phases of the Moon		
			days	h m	m	′	′	h m	h m		d h m	
335	1	Fri	09	19 55	46	15.4	56.5	13 21	01 30	○ Full Moon	7 01 27	
336	2	Sat	10	20 41	46	15.2	55.9	13 46	02 40	◗ Last Quarter	15 05 31	
337	3	Sun	11	21 27	47	15.1	55.4	14 13	03 47	● New Moon	22 02 22	
338	4	Mon	12	22 14	48	15.0	55.0	14 42	04 53	◖ First Quarter	28 19 06	
339	5	Tu	13	23 02	48	14.9	54.6	15 16	05 55			
340	6	Wed	14	23 50	48	14.8	54.4	15 55	06 54			
341	7	Th	15	24 38	—	14.8	54.1	16 39	07 48			
342	8	Fri	16	00 38	47	14.7	54.0	17 29	08 36			
343	9	Sat	17	01 25	47	14.7	54.0	18 24	09 18	Apogee	9 10	
344	10	Sun	18	02 12	46	14.7	54.0	19 22	09 53	Perigee	22 10	
345	11	Mon	19	02 58	45	14.8	54.2	20 23	10 24			
346	12	Tu	20	03 43	44	14.9	54.5	21 27	10 52			
347	13	Wed	21	04 27	44	15.0	55.0	22 32	11 16			
348	14	Th	22	05 11	45	15.2	55.6	23 38	11 40			
349	15	Fri	23	05 56	47	15.4	56.4	— —	12 03			
350	16	Sat	24	06 43	48	15.6	57.3	00 47	12 27			
351	17	Sun	25	07 31	52	15.9	58.2	01 59	12 54			
352	18	Mon	26	08 23	56	16.1	59.2	03 13	13 25			
353	19	Tu	27	09 19	59	16.4	60.1	04 28	14 02			
354	20	Wed	28	10 18	62	16.6	60.8	05 43	14 49			
355	21	Th	29	11 20	64	16.7	61.3	06 54	15 46	NOTES		
356	22	Fri	00	12 24	62	16.7	61.5	07 56	16 54	**Diff** equals daily change in		
357	23	Sat	01	13 26	59	16.7	61.3	08 48	18 09	transit time.		
358	24	Sun	02	14 25	57	16.6	60.7	09 31	19 28	To correct Moonrise, Moonset,		
359	25	Mon	03	15 22	52	16.3	60.0	10 06	20 47	or Transit times for Latitude		
360	26	Tu	04	16 14	50	16.1	59.1	10 36	22 04	and/or Longitude see page		
361	27	Wed	05	17 04	48	15.9	58.2	11 02	23 18	E 100. For further information		
362	28	Th	06	17 52	47	15.6	57.3	11 27	— —	about these tables see page E 4.		
363	29	Fri	07	18 39	47	15.4	56.5	11 52	00 29	For Arc to Time correction see		
364	30	Sat	08	19 26	46	15.2	55.7	12 18	01 38	page E 91.		
365	31	Sun	09	20 12	47	15.0	55.1	12 46	02 44			

DECEMBER 1995   STARS   0h GMT December 1

No	Name	Mag	Transit h m	Dec ° ′	GHA ° ′	RA h m	SHA ° ′
	ARIES................		19 19		69 23.0		
1	Alpheratz..........	2.2	19 27	N 29 04.3	67 20.1	0 08	357 57.1
2	Ankaa..............	2.4	19 45	S 42 19.9	62 51.7	0 26	353 28.7
3	Schedar............	2.5	19 59	N 56 31.2	59 18.3	0 40	349 55.3
4	Diphda.............	2.2	20 03	S 18 00.6	58 32.0	0 43	349 09.0
5	Achernar..........	0.6	20 57	S 57 15.7	44 59.3	1 38	335 36.3
6	POLARIS...........	2.1	21 48	N 89 15.0	32 03.7	2 29	322 40.7
7	Hamal..............	2.2	21 26	N 23 26.7	37 38.4	2 07	328 15.4
8	Acamar............	3.1	22 17	S 40 19.5	24 51.0	2 58	315 28.0
9	Menkar............	2.8	22 21	N 4 04.4	23 51.6	3 02	314 28.6
10	Mirfak.............	1.9	22 43	N 49 50.9	18 21.8	3 24	308 58.8
11	Aldebaran........	1.1	23 54	N 16 30.0	0 27.2	4 36	291 04.2
12	Rigel...............	0.3	0 37	S 8 12.5	350 47.4	5 14	281 24.4
13	Capella............	0.2	0 39	N 45 59.5	350 16.5	5 16	280 53.5
14	Bellatrix..........	1.7	0 47	N 6 20.7	348 08.8	5 25	278 45.8
15	Elnath..............	1.8	0 48	N 28 36.1	347 51.9	5 26	278 28.9
16	Alnilam............	1.8	0 58	S 1 12.4	345 22.4	5 36	275 59.4
17	Betelgeuse.......0.1-1.2		1 17	N 7 24.3	340 38.3	5 55	271 15.3
18	Canopus............	-0.9	1 46	S 52 41.7	333 24.4	6 24	264 01.4
19	Sirius	-1.6	2 07	S 16 42.7	328 08.0	6 45	258 45.0
20	Adhara.............	1.6	2 21	S 28 58.1	324 45.5	6 59	255 22.5
21	Castor..............	1.6	2 56	N 31 53.6	315 47.4	7 34	246 24.4
22	Procyon............	0.5	3 01	N 5 14.0	314 36.2	7 39	245 13.2
23	Pollux..............	1.2	3 07	N 28 01.9	313 06.6	7 45	243 43.6
24	Avior...............	1.7	3 44	S 59 29.7	303 45.8	8 22	234 22.8
25	Suhail..............	2.2	4 30	S 43 24.9	292 24.8	9 08	223 01.8
26	Miaplacidus......	1.8	4 35	S 69 41.9	291 04.7	9 13	221 41.7
27	Alphard............	2.2	4 49	S 8 38.5	287 31.9	9 27	218 08.9
28	Regulus............	1.3	5 30	N 11 59.1	277 20.4	10 08	207 57.4
29	Dubhe	2.0	6 25	N 61 46.0	263 30.8	11 03	194 07.8
30	Denebola..........	2.2	7 10	N 14 35.6	252 10.2	11 49	182 47.2
31	Gienah	2.8	7 37	S 17 31.1	245 29.0	12 16	176 06.0
32	Acrux...............	1.1	7 48	S 63 04.3	242 47.1	12 26	173 24.1
33	Gacrux.............	1.6	7 52	S 57 05.2	241 38.7	12 31	172 15.7
34	Mimosa	1.5	8 09	S 59 39.7	237 30.6	12 47	168 07.6
35	Alioth...............	1.7	8 15	N 55 58.6	235 55.6	12 54	166 32.6
36	Spica...............	1.2	8 46	S 11 08.3	228 08.3	13 25	158 45.3
37	Alkaid..............	1.9	9 08	N 49 19.8	222 32.7	13 47	153 09.7
38	Hadar	0.9	9 24	S 60 20.9	218 30.0	14 04	149 07.0
39	Menkent..........	2.3	9 27	S 36 20.8	217 46.4	14 06	148 23.4
40	Arcturus..........	0.2	9 36	N 19 12.2	215 31.0	14 15	146 08.0
41	Rigil Kent.........	0.1	10 00	S 60 48.8	209 33.2	14 39	140 10.2
42	Zuben'ubi	2.9	10 11	S 16 01.4	206 43.3	14 51	137 20.3
43	Kochab............	2.2	10 11	N 74 10.2	206 43.6	14 51	137 20.6
44	Alphecca	2.3	10 55	N 26 43.7	195 45.5	15 35	126 22.5
45	Antares............	1.2	11 50	S 26 25.2	182 05.8	16 29	112 42.8
46	Atria................	1.9	12 09	S 69 01.0	177 20.1	16 48	107 57.1
47	Sabik...............	2.6	12 31	S 15 43.0	171 51.1	17 10	102 28.1
48	Shaula	1.7	12 54	S 37 05.9	166 03.3	17 33	96 40.3
49	Rasalhague	2.1	12 55	N 12 33.9	165 42.1	17 35	96 19.1
50	Eltanin.............	2.4	13 17	N 51 29.5	160 15.8	17 56	90 52.8
51	Kaus Aust.	2.0	13 44	S 34 23.1	153 24.7	18 24	84 01.7
52	Vega................	0.1	13 57	N 38 47.0	150 11.3	18 37	80 48.3
53	Nunki..............	2.1	14 15	S 26 18.0	145 38.0	18 55	76 15.0
54	Altair	0.9	15 11	N 8 51.6	131 44.4	19 51	62 21.4
55	Peacock...........	2.1	15 45	S 56 44.9	123 03.5	20 25	53 40.5
56	Deneb	1.3	16 01	N 45 16.3	119 03.8	20 41	49 40.8
57	Enif.................	2.5	17 04	N 9 51.6	103 23.2	21 44	34 00.2
58	Al Na'ir...........	2.2	17 28	S 46 59.0	97 23.5	22 08	28 00.5
59	Fomalhaut	1.3	18 17	S 29 38.7	85 01.6	22 57	15 38.6
60	Markab	2.6	18 24	N 15 11.2	83 14.5	23 05	13 51.5

Star Transit Corr Table

Date	Corr h m	Date	Corr h m
1	−0 00	17	−1 03
2	−0 04	18	−1 07
3	−0 08	19	−1 11
4	−0 12	20	−1 15
5	−0 16	21	−1 19
6	−0 20	22	−1 23
7	−0 24	23	−1 27
8	−0 28	24	−1 30
9	−0 31	25	−1 34
10	−0 35	26	−1 38
11	−0 39	27	−1 42
12	−0 43	28	−1 46
13	−0 47	29	−1 50
14	−0 51	30	−1 54
15	−0 55	31	−1 58
16	−0 59		

STAR TRANSIT

To find the approx time of transit of a star for any day of the month use above table. All corrections are subtractive.

If the quantity taken from the table is greater than the time of transit for the first of the month, add 23h 56min to the time of transit before subtracting the correction.

Example: What time will Rigel (No 12) transit the Meridian on December30?

	h min
Transit on Dec 1	00 37
	+23 56
	24 33
Corr for Dec 30	−01 54
Transit on Dec 30	22 39

DECEMBER DIARY

d	h	
16	17	Venus 2° S of Neptune
18	22	Jupiter in conjunction with Sun
20	13	Venus 1.3° S of Uranus
22	08	Solstice
23	07	Mercury 7° S of Moon
23	07	Mars 6° S of Moon
23	09	Mercury 1.1° S of Mars
23	18	Neptune 5° S of Moon
24	02	Uranus 6° S of Moon
24	10	Venus 7° S of Moon
27	15	Saturn 5° S of Moon
28	02	Mercury 2° S of Neptune

NOTES

Star declinations may be used as is for the whole month. To correct GHA for day, hour, minute and second see page E 92 and for further explanation of this table see page E 4.

DECEMBER

DECEMBER 1995 — SUN & ARIES — GMT

Friday, 1st December

Time	SUN GHA	Dec	ARIES GHA
00	182 49.3	S21 41.4	69 23.0
02	212 48.9	21 42.2	99 27.9
04	242 48.4	21 43.0	129 32.9
06	272 47.9	21 43.8	159 37.8
08	302 47.5	21 44.5	189 42.7
10	332 47.0	21 45.3	219 47.7
12	2 46.6	21 46.1	249 52.6
14	32 46.1	21 46.9	279 57.5
16	62 45.6	21 47.7	310 02.4
18	92 45.2	21 48.5	340 07.4
20	122 44.7	21 49.2	10 12.3
22	152 44.2	S21 50.0	40 17.2

Saturday, 2nd December

Time	SUN GHA	Dec	ARIES GHA
00	182 43.8	S21 50.8	70 22.2
02	212 43.3	21 51.5	100 27.1
04	242 42.8	21 52.3	130 32.0
06	272 42.4	21 53.1	160 36.9
08	302 41.9	21 53.8	190 41.9
10	332 41.4	21 54.6	220 46.8
12	2 40.9	21 55.3	250 51.7
14	32 40.5	21 56.1	280 56.7
16	62 40.0	21 56.8	311 01.6
18	92 39.5	21 57.6	341 06.5
20	122 39.0	21 58.3	11 11.4
22	152 38.5	S21 59.0	41 16.4

Sunday, 3rd December

Time	SUN GHA	Dec	ARIES GHA
00	182 38.1	S21 59.8	71 21.3
02	212 37.6	22 00.5	101 26.2
04	242 37.1	22 01.2	131 31.2
06	272 36.6	22 02.0	161 36.1
08	302 36.1	22 02.7	191 41.0
10	332 35.6	22 03.4	221 45.9
12	2 35.1	22 04.1	251 50.9
14	32 34.7	22 04.8	281 55.8
16	62 34.2	22 05.5	312 00.7
18	92 33.7	22 06.2	342 05.7
20	122 33.2	22 06.9	12 10.6
22	152 32.7	S22 07.6	42 15.5

Monday, 4th December

Time	SUN GHA	Dec	ARIES GHA
00	182 32.3	S22 08.3	72 20.4
02	212 31.7	22 09.0	102 25.4
04	242 31.2	22 09.7	132 30.3
06	272 30.7	22 10.4	162 35.2
08	302 30.2	22 11.1	192 40.2
10	332 29.7	22 11.8	222 45.1
12	2 29.2	22 12.5	252 50.0
14	32 28.7	22 13.1	282 54.9
16	62 28.2	22 13.8	312 59.9
18	92 27.7	22 14.5	343 04.8
20	122 27.2	22 15.2	13 09.7
22	152 26.7	S22 15.8	43 14.6

Tuesday, 5th December

Time	SUN GHA	Dec	ARIES GHA
00	182 26.2	S22 16.5	73 19.6
02	212 25.7	22 17.1	103 24.5
04	242 25.2	22 17.8	133 29.4
06	272 24.7	22 18.5	163 34.4
08	302 24.2	22 19.1	193 39.3
10	332 23.6	22 19.8	223 44.2
12	2 23.1	22 20.4	253 49.1
14	32 22.6	22 21.0	283 54.1
16	62 22.1	22 21.7	313 59.0
18	92 21.6	22 22.3	344 03.9
20	122 21.1	22 22.9	14 08.9
22	152 20.6	S22 23.6	44 13.8

Wednesday, 6th December

Time	SUN GHA	Dec	ARIES GHA
00	182 20.0	S22 24.2	74 18.7
02	212 19.5	22 24.8	104 23.6
04	242 19.0	22 25.4	134 28.6
06	272 18.5	22 26.1	164 33.5
08	302 18.0	22 26.7	194 38.4
10	332 17.4	22 27.3	224 43.4
12	2 16.9	22 27.9	254 48.3
14	32 16.4	22 28.5	284 53.2
16	62 15.9	22 29.1	314 58.1
18	92 15.3	22 29.7	345 03.1
20	122 14.8	22 30.3	15 08.0
22	152 14.3	S22 30.9	45 12.9

Thursday, 7th December

Time	SUN GHA	Dec	ARIES GHA
00	182 13.8	S22 31.5	75 17.9
02	212 13.2	22 32.1	105 22.8
04	242 12.7	22 32.6	135 27.7
06	272 12.2	22 33.2	165 32.6
08	302 11.6	22 33.8	195 37.6
10	332 11.1	22 34.4	225 42.5
12	2 10.6	22 35.0	255 47.4
14	32 10.0	22 35.5	285 52.4
16	62 09.5	22 36.1	315 57.3
18	92 09.0	22 36.6	346 02.2
20	122 08.4	22 37.2	16 07.1
22	152 07.9	S22 37.8	46 12.1

Friday, 8th December

Time	SUN GHA	Dec	ARIES GHA
00	182 07.4	S22 38.3	76 17.0
02	212 06.8	22 38.9	106 21.9
04	242 06.3	22 39.4	136 26.8
06	272 05.7	22 40.0	166 31.8
08	302 05.2	22 40.5	196 36.7
10	332 04.6	22 41.0	226 41.6
12	2 04.1	22 41.6	256 46.6
14	32 03.6	22 42.1	286 51.5
16	62 03.0	22 42.6	316 56.4
18	92 02.5	22 43.2	347 01.3
20	122 01.9	22 43.7	17 06.3
22	152 01.4	S22 44.2	47 11.2

Saturday, 9th December

Time	SUN GHA	Dec	ARIES GHA
00	182 00.8	S22 44.7	77 16.1
02	212 00.3	22 45.2	107 21.1
04	241 59.7	22 45.7	137 26.0
06	271 59.2	22 46.2	167 30.9
08	301 58.6	22 46.7	197 35.8
10	331 58.1	22 47.2	227 40.8
12	1 57.5	22 47.7	257 45.7
14	31 57.0	22 48.2	287 50.6
16	61 56.4	22 48.7	317 55.6
18	91 55.8	22 49.2	348 00.5
20	121 55.3	22 49.7	18 05.4
22	151 54.7	S22 50.2	48 10.3

Sunday, 10th December

Time	SUN GHA	Dec	ARIES GHA
00	181 54.2	S22 50.7	78 15.3
02	211 53.6	22 51.1	108 20.2
04	241 53.1	22 51.6	138 25.1
06	271 52.5	22 52.1	168 30.1
08	301 51.9	22 52.5	198 35.0
10	331 51.4	22 53.0	228 39.9
12	1 50.8	22 53.5	258 44.8
14	31 50.2	22 53.9	288 49.8
16	61 49.7	22 54.4	318 54.7
18	91 49.1	22 54.8	348 59.6
20	121 48.5	22 55.3	19 04.6
22	151 48.0	S22 55.7	49 09.5

Monday, 11th December

Time	SUN GHA	Dec	ARIES GHA
00	181 47.4	S22 56.2	79 14.4
02	211 46.8	22 56.6	109 19.3
04	241 46.3	22 57.0	139 24.3
06	271 45.7	22 57.5	169 29.2
08	301 45.1	22 57.9	199 34.1
10	331 44.6	22 58.3	229 39.1
12	1 44.0	22 58.7	259 44.0
14	31 43.4	22 59.1	289 48.9
16	61 42.8	22 59.6	319 53.8
18	91 42.3	23 00.0	349 58.8
20	121 41.7	23 00.4	20 03.7
22	151 41.1	S23 00.8	50 08.6

Tuesday, 12th December

Time	SUN GHA	Dec	ARIES GHA
00	181 40.5	S23 01.2	80 13.5
02	211 40.0	23 01.6	110 18.5
04	241 39.4	23 02.0	140 23.4
06	271 38.8	23 02.4	170 28.3
08	301 38.2	23 02.8	200 33.3
10	331 37.6	23 03.2	230 38.2
12	1 37.1	23 03.5	260 43.1
14	31 36.5	23 03.9	290 48.0
16	61 35.9	23 04.3	320 53.0
18	91 35.3	23 04.7	350 57.9
20	121 34.7	23 05.0	21 02.8
22	151 34.2	S23 05.4	51 07.8

Wednesday, 13th December

Time	SUN GHA	Dec	ARIES GHA
00	181 33.6	S23 05.8	81 12.7
02	211 33.0	23 06.1	111 17.6
04	241 32.4	23 06.5	141 22.5
06	271 31.8	23 06.9	171 27.5
08	301 31.2	23 07.2	201 32.4
10	331 30.6	23 07.6	231 37.3
12	1 30.1	23 07.9	261 42.3
14	31 29.5	23 08.2	291 47.2
16	61 28.9	23 08.6	321 52.1
18	91 28.3	23 08.9	351 57.0
20	121 27.7	23 09.3	22 02.0
22	151 27.1	S23 09.6	52 06.9

Thursday, 14th December

Time	SUN GHA	Dec	ARIES GHA
00	181 26.5	S23 09.9	82 11.8
02	211 25.9	23 10.2	112 16.8
04	241 25.3	23 10.6	142 21.7
06	271 24.7	23 10.9	172 26.6
08	301 24.1	23 11.2	202 31.5
10	331 23.6	23 11.5	232 36.5
12	1 23.0	23 11.8	262 41.4
14	31 22.4	23 12.1	292 46.3
16	61 21.8	23 12.4	322 51.3
18	91 21.2	23 12.7	352 56.2
20	121 20.6	23 13.0	23 01.1
22	151 20.0	S23 13.3	53 06.0

Friday, 15th December

Time	SUN GHA	Dec	ARIES GHA
00	181 19.4	S23 13.6	83 11.0
02	211 18.8	23 13.9	113 15.9
04	241 18.2	23 14.1	143 20.8
06	271 17.6	23 14.4	173 25.7
08	301 17.0	23 14.7	203 30.7
10	331 16.4	23 15.0	233 35.6
12	1 15.8	23 15.2	263 40.5
14	31 15.2	23 15.5	293 45.5
16	61 14.6	23 15.8	323 50.4
18	91 14.0	23 16.0	353 55.3
20	121 13.4	23 16.3	24 00.2
22	151 12.8	S23 16.5	54 05.2

NOTES

Sun & Aries GHA corrections for additional hour, minutes, and seconds on page E 94.
Correct Sun Declination by interpolation. For example see page E 4.

DECEMBER 1995 — SUN & ARIES — GMT

Saturday, 16th December

Time	SUN GHA	Dec	ARIES GHA
00	181 12.2	S23 16.8	84 10.1
02	211 11.6	23 17.0	114 15.0
04	241 11.0	23 17.3	144 20.0
06	271 10.3	23 17.5	174 24.9
08	301 09.7	23 17.7	204 29.8
10	331 09.1	23 18.0	234 34.7
12	1 08.5	23 18.2	264 39.7
14	31 07.9	23 18.4	294 44.6
16	61 07.3	23 18.7	324 49.5
18	91 06.7	23 18.9	354 54.5
20	121 06.1	23 19.1	24 59.4
22	151 05.5	S23 19.3	55 04.3

Sunday, 17th December

Time	SUN GHA	Dec	ARIES GHA
00	181 04.9	S23 19.5	85 09.2
02	211 04.3	23 19.7	115 14.2
04	241 03.7	23 19.9	145 19.1
06	271 03.1	23 20.1	175 24.0
08	301 02.4	23 20.3	205 29.0
10	331 01.8	23 20.5	235 33.9
12	1 01.2	23 20.7	265 38.8
14	31 00.6	23 20.9	295 43.7
16	61 00.0	23 21.1	325 48.7
18	90 59.4	23 21.3	355 53.6
20	120 58.8	23 21.5	25 58.5
22	150 58.2	S23 21.6	56 03.5

Monday, 18th December

Time	SUN GHA	Dec	ARIES GHA
00	180 57.5	S23 21.8	86 08.4
02	210 56.9	23 22.0	116 13.3
04	240 56.3	23 22.1	146 18.2
06	270 55.7	23 22.3	176 23.2
08	300 55.1	23 22.5	206 28.1
10	330 54.5	23 22.6	236 33.0
12	0 53.9	23 22.8	266 38.0
14	30 53.2	23 22.9	296 42.9
16	60 52.6	23 23.1	326 47.8
18	90 52.0	23 23.2	356 52.7
20	120 51.4	23 23.3	26 57.7
22	150 50.8	S23 23.5	57 02.6

Tuesday, 19th December

Time	SUN GHA	Dec	ARIES GHA
00	180 50.2	S23 23.6	87 07.5
02	210 49.5	23 23.7	117 12.4
04	240 48.9	23 23.9	147 17.4
06	270 48.3	23 24.0	177 22.3
08	300 47.7	23 24.1	207 27.2
10	330 47.1	23 24.2	237 32.2
12	0 46.4	23 24.3	267 37.1
14	30 45.8	23 24.4	297 42.0
16	60 45.2	23 24.5	327 46.9
18	90 44.6	23 24.6	357 51.9
20	120 44.0	23 24.7	27 56.8
22	150 43.3	23 24.8	58 01.7

Wednesday, 20th December

Time	SUN GHA	Dec	ARIES GHA
00	180 42.7	S23 24.9	88 06.7
02	210 42.1	23 25.0	118 11.6
04	240 41.5	23 25.1	148 16.5
06	270 40.9	23 25.2	178 21.4
08	300 40.2	23 25.3	208 26.4
10	330 39.6	23 25.4	238 31.3
12	0 39.0	23 25.4	268 36.2
14	30 38.4	23 25.5	298 41.2
16	60 37.7	23 25.6	328 46.1
18	90 37.1	23 25.6	358 51.0
20	120 36.5	23 25.7	28 55.9
22	150 35.9	S23 25.8	59 00.9

Thursday, 21st December

Time	SUN GHA	Dec	ARIES GHA
00	180 35.3	S23 25.8	89 05.8
02	210 34.6	23 25.9	119 10.7
04	240 34.0	23 25.9	149 15.7
06	270 33.4	23 25.9	179 20.6
08	300 32.8	23 26.0	209 25.5
10	330 32.1	23 26.0	239 30.4
12	0 31.5	23 26.1	269 35.4
14	30 30.9	23 26.1	299 40.3
16	60 30.3	23 26.1	329 45.2
18	90 29.6	23 26.1	359 50.2
20	120 29.0	23 26.2	29 55.1
22	150 28.4	S23 26.2	60 00.0

Friday, 22nd December

Time	SUN GHA	Dec	ARIES GHA
00	180 27.8	S23 26.2	90 04.9
02	210 27.2	23 26.2	120 09.9
04	240 26.5	23 26.2	150 14.8
06	270 25.9	23 26.2	180 19.7
08	300 25.3	23 26.2	210 24.7
10	330 24.7	23 26.2	240 29.6
12	0 24.0	23 26.2	270 34.5
14	30 23.4	23 26.2	300 39.4
16	60 22.8	23 26.2	330 44.4
18	90 22.2	23 26.2	0 49.3
20	120 21.5	23 26.2	30 54.2
22	150 20.9	S23 26.2	60 59.1

Saturday, 23rd December

Time	SUN GHA	Dec	ARIES GHA
00	180 20.3	S23 26.1	91 04.1
02	210 19.7	23 26.1	121 09.0
04	240 19.0	23 26.1	151 13.9
06	270 18.4	23 26.0	181 18.9
08	300 17.8	23 26.0	211 23.8
10	330 17.2	23 26.0	241 28.7
12	0 16.5	23 25.9	271 33.6
14	30 15.9	23 25.9	301 38.6
16	60 15.3	23 25.8	331 43.5
18	90 14.7	23 25.8	1 48.4
20	120 14.0	23 25.7	31 53.4
22	150 13.4	S23 25.6	61 58.3

Sunday, 24th December

Time	SUN GHA	Dec	ARIES GHA
00	180 12.8	S23 25.6	92 03.2
02	210 12.2	23 25.5	122 08.1
04	240 11.5	23 25.4	152 13.1
06	270 10.9	23 25.4	182 18.0
08	300 10.3	23 25.3	212 22.9
10	330 09.7	23 25.2	242 27.9
12	0 09.0	23 25.1	272 32.8
14	30 08.4	23 25.0	302 37.7
16	60 07.8	23 25.0	332 42.6
18	90 07.2	23 24.9	2 47.6
20	120 06.5	23 24.8	32 52.5
22	150 05.9	S23 24.7	62 57.4

Monday, 25th December

Time	SUN GHA	Dec	ARIES GHA
00	180 05.3	S23 24.6	93 02.4
02	210 04.7	23 24.5	123 07.3
04	240 04.0	23 24.4	153 12.2
06	270 03.4	23 24.2	183 17.1
08	300 02.8	23 24.1	213 22.1
10	330 02.2	23 24.0	243 27.0
12	0 01.6	23 23.9	273 31.9
14	30 00.9	23 23.8	303 36.9
16	60 00.3	23 23.8	333 41.8
18	89 59.7	23 23.5	3 46.7
20	119 59.1	23 23.4	33 51.6
22	149 58.4	S23 23.2	63 56.6

Tuesday, 26th December

Time	SUN GHA	Dec	ARIES GHA
00	179 57.8	S23 23.1	94 01.5
02	209 57.2	23 22.9	124 06.4
04	239 56.6	23 22.8	154 11.3
06	269 56.0	23 22.6	184 16.3
08	299 55.3	23 22.5	214 21.2
10	329 54.7	23 22.3	244 26.1
12	359 54.1	23 22.2	274 31.1
14	29 53.5	23 22.0	304 36.0
16	59 52.9	23 21.8	334 40.9
18	89 52.2	23 21.7	4 45.8
20	119 51.6	23 21.5	34 50.8
22	149 51.0	S23 21.3	64 55.7

Wednesday, 27th December

Time	SUN GHA	Dec	ARIES GHA
00	179 50.4	S23 21.1	95 00.6
02	209 49.8	23 20.9	125 05.6
04	239 49.1	23 20.8	155 10.5
06	269 48.5	23 20.6	185 15.4
08	299 47.9	23 20.4	215 20.3
10	329 47.3	23 20.2	245 25.3
12	359 46.7	23 20.0	275 30.2
14	29 46.0	23 19.8	305 35.1
16	59 45.4	23 19.6	335 40.1
18	89 44.8	23 19.4	5 45.0
20	119 44.2	23 19.1	35 49.9
22	149 43.6	S23 18.9	65 54.8

Thursday, 28th December

Time	SUN GHA	Dec	ARIES GHA
00	179 43.0	S23 18.7	95 59.8
02	209 42.3	23 18.5	126 04.7
04	239 41.7	23 18.3	156 09.6
06	269 41.1	23 18.0	186 14.6
08	299 40.5	23 17.8	216 19.5
10	329 39.9	23 17.6	246 24.4
12	359 39.3	23 17.3	276 29.3
14	29 38.7	23 17.1	306 34.3
16	59 38.0	23 16.8	336 39.2
18	89 37.4	23 16.6	6 44.1
20	119 36.8	23 16.3	36 49.1
22	149 36.2	S23 16.1	66 54.0

Friday, 29th December

Time	SUN GHA	Dec	ARIES GHA
00	179 35.6	S23 15.8	96 58.9
02	209 35.0	23 15.5	127 03.8
04	239 34.4	23 15.3	157 08.8
06	269 33.8	23 15.0	187 13.7
08	299 33.2	23 14.7	217 18.6
10	329 32.5	23 14.5	247 23.6
12	359 31.9	23 14.2	277 28.5
14	29 31.3	23 13.9	307 33.4
16	59 30.7	23 13.6	337 38.3
18	89 30.1	23 13.3	7 43.3
20	119 29.5	23 13.0	37 48.2
22	149 28.9	S23 12.7	67 53.1

Saturday, 30th December

Time	SUN GHA	Dec	ARIES GHA
00	179 28.3	S23 12.4	97 58.0
02	209 27.7	23 12.1	128 03.0
04	239 27.1	23 11.8	158 07.9
06	269 26.5	23 11.5	188 12.8
08	299 25.9	23 11.2	218 17.8
10	329 25.3	23 10.9	248 22.7
12	359 24.7	23 10.6	278 27.6
14	29 24.1	23 10.3	308 32.5
16	59 23.4	23 10.0	338 37.5
18	89 22.8	23 09.6	8 42.4
20	119 22.2	23 09.3	38 47.3
22	149 21.6	S23 09.0	68 52.3

Sunday, 31st December

Time	SUN GHA	Dec	ARIES GHA
00	179 21.0	S23 08.6	98 57.2
02	209 20.4	23 08.3	129 02.1
04	239 19.8	23 07.9	159 07.0
06	269 19.2	S23 07.6	189 12.0
08	299 18.6	S23 07.2	219 16.9
10	329 18.0	23 06.9	249 21.8
12	359 17.4	23 06.5	279 26.8
14	29 16.8	S23 06.2	309 31.7
16	59 16.2	S23 05.8	339 36.6
18	89 15.6	23 05.5	9 41.5
20	119 15.1	23 05.1	39 46.5
22	149 14.5	S23 04.7	69 51.4

DECEMBER 1995 — PLANETS — 0h GMT

VENUS / JUPITER

Mer Pass h m	GHA ° '	Mean Var/hr 14°+	Dec ° '	Mean Var/hr '	Corrections on Page E 101		GHA ° '	Mean Var/hr 15°+	Dec ° '	Mean Var/hr '	Mer Pass h m
13 42	154 40.7	59.0	S 24 43.6	0.0	1	Fri	167 35.9	1.9	S 22 55.7	0.0	12 48
13 44	154 17.8	59.1	S 24 42.7	0.1	2	Sat	168 20.5	1.9	S 22 56.6	0.0	12 45
13 45	153 55.0	59.1	S 24 41.0	0.1	3	SUN	169 05.0	1.9	S 22 57.4	0.0	12 42
13 47	153 32.3	59.1	S 24 38.6	0.1	4	Mon	169 49.5	1.9	S 22 58.2	0.0	12 39
13 48	153 09.6	59.1	S 24 35.4	0.2	5	Tu	170 34.0	1.9	S 22 59.0	0.0	12 36
13 50	152 47.0	59.1	S 24 31.4	0.2	6	Wed	171 18.5	1.9	S 22 59.8	0.0	12 33
13 51	152 24.6	59.1	S 24 26.8	0.2	7	Th	172 02.9	1.8	S 23 00.5	0.0	12 30
13 53	152 02.3	59.1	S 24 21.3	0.3	8	Fri	172 47.3	1.9	S 23 01.2	0.0	12 27
13 54	151 40.1	59.1	S 24 15.2	0.3	9	Sat	173 31.7	1.8	S 23 01.9	0.0	12 24
13 56	151 18.1	59.1	S 24 08.3	0.3	10	SUN	174 16.1	1.8	S 23 02.6	0.0	12 21
13 57	150 56.2	59.1	S 24 00.6	0.3	11	Mon	175 00.4	1.8	S 23 03.2	0.0	12 18
13 59	150 34.6	59.1	S 23 52.3	0.4	12	Tu	175 44.7	1.8	S 23 03.9	0.0	12 16
14 00	150 13.1	59.1	S 23 43.2	0.4	13	Wed	176 29.1	1.8	S 23 04.5	0.0	12 13
14 01	149 51.9	59.1	S 23 33.4	0.4	14	Th	177 13.4	1.8	S 23 05.1	0.0	12 10
14 03	149 30.9	59.1	S 23 22.9	0.5	15	Fri	177 57.7	1.8	S 23 05.6	0.0	12 07
14 04	149 10.1	59.1	S 23 11.8	0.5	16	Sat	178 41.9	1.8	S 23 06.1	0.0	12 04
14 05	148 49.6	59.2	S 22 59.9	0.5	17	SUN	179 26.2	1.8	S 23 06.7	0.0	12 01
14 07	148 29.4	59.2	S 22 47.3	0.6	18	Mon	180 10.5	1.8	S 23 07.1	0.0	11 58
14 08	148 09.4	59.2	S 22 34.1	0.6	19	Tu	180 54.7	1.8	S 23 07.6	0.0	11 55
14 09	147 49.7	59.2	S 22 20.2	0.6	20	Wed	181 39.0	1.8	S 23 08.0	0.0	11 52
14 11	147 30.3	59.2	S 22 05.7	0.6	21	Th	182 23.3	1.8	S 23 08.5	0.0	11 49
14 12	147 11.2	59.2	S 21 50.5	0.7	22	Fri	183 07.5	1.8	S 23 08.8	0.0	11 46
14 13	146 52.5	59.2	S 21 34.7	0.7	23	Sat	183 51.8	1.8	S 23 09.2	0.0	11 43
14 14	146 34.0	59.2	S 21 18.3	0.7	24	SUN	184 36.0	1.8	S 23 09.6	0.0	11 40
14 16	146 15.9	59.3	S 21 01.2	0.7	25	Mon	185 20.3	1.8	S 23 09.9	0.0	11 37
14 17	145 58.1	59.3	S 20 43.6	0.8	26	Tu	186 04.6	1.8	S 23 10.2	0.0	11 34
14 18	145 40.7	59.3	S 20 25.3	0.8	27	Wed	186 48.8	1.8	S 23 10.4	0.0	11 31
14 19	145 23.6	59.3	S 20 06.5	0.8	28	Th	187 33.1	1.8	S 23 10.7	0.0	11 28
14 20	145 06.8	59.3	S 19 47.2	0.8	29	Fri	188 17.4	1.8	S 23 10.9	0.0	11 25
14 21	144 50.5	59.3	S 19 27.2	0.8	30	Sat	189 01.7	1.8	S 23 11.1	0.0	11 22
14 22	144 34.4	59.3	S 19 06.8	0.9	31	SUN	189 46.1	1.8	S 23 11.3	0.0	11 20

VENUS, Av. Mag. -4.0
S.H.A. December
5 80; 10 73; 15 66; 20 60; 25 53; 30 47.

JUPITER, Av. Mag.-1.8
S.H.A. December
5 97; 10 96; 15 95; 20 94; 25 92; 30 91.

MARS / SATURN

Mer Pass h m	GHA ° '	Mean Var/hr 15°+	Dec ° '	Mean Var/hr '	Corrections on Page E 101		GHA ° '	Mean Var/hr 15°+	Dec ° '	Mean Var/hr '	Mer Pass h m
13 24	159 02.2	0.4	S 24 23.4	0.0	1	Fri	79 29.1	2.4	S 6 45.0	0.0	18 39
13 23	159 11.4	0.4	S 24 23.4	0.0	2	Sat	80 27.4	2.4	S 6 44.4	0.0	18 35
13 22	159 20.5	0.4	S 24 23.2	0.0	3	SUN	81 25.5	2.4	S 6 43.8	0.0	18 31
13 22	159 29.7	0.4	S 24 22.8	0.0	4	Mon	82 23.6	2.4	S 6 43.1	0.0	18 27
13 21	159 38.7	0.4	S 24 22.1	0.0	5	Tu	83 21.5	2.4	S 6 42.4	0.0	18 24
13 20	159 47.7	0.4	S 24 21.1	0.1	6	Wed	84 19.4	2.4	S 6 41.6	0.0	18 20
13 20	159 56.7	0.4	S 24 19.8	0.1	7	Th	85 17.2	2.4	S 6 40.8	0.0	18 16
13 19	160 05.7	0.4	S 24 18.2	0.1	8	Fri	86 14.8	2.4	S 6 40.0	0.0	18 12
13 19	160 14.6	0.4	S 24 16.4	0.1	9	Sat	87 12.4	2.4	S 6 39.2	0.0	18 08
13 18	160 23.5	0.4	S 24 14.3	0.1	10	SUN	88 09.9	2.4	S 6 38.2	0.0	18 04
13 18	160 32.3	0.4	S 24 12.0	0.1	11	Mon	89 07.3	2.4	S 6 37.3	0.0	18 01
13 17	160 41.2	0.4	S 24 09.3	0.1	12	Tu	90 04.6	2.4	S 6 36.3	0.0	17 57
13 16	160 50.0	0.4	S 24 06.4	0.1	13	Wed	91 01.8	2.4	S 6 35.3	0.0	17 53
13 16	160 58.8	0.4	S 24 03.2	0.1	14	Th	91 58.8	2.4	S 6 34.2	0.0	17 49
13 15	161 07.6	0.4	S 23 59.8	0.2	15	Fri	92 55.9	2.4	S 6 33.1	0.0	17 45
13 15	161 16.5	0.4	S 23 56.0	0.2	16	Sat	93 52.8	2.4	S 6 31.9	0.0	17 42
13 14	161 25.3	0.4	S 23 52.0	0.2	17	SUN	94 49.6	2.4	S 6 30.8	0.1	17 38
13 13	161 34.1	0.4	S 23 47.8	0.2	18	Mon	95 46.3	2.4	S 6 29.5	0.1	17 34
13 13	161 42.9	0.4	S 23 43.2	0.2	19	Tu	96 42.9	2.4	S 6 28.3	0.1	17 30
13 12	161 51.7	0.4	S 23 38.4	0.2	20	Wed	97 39.5	2.3	S 6 27.0	0.1	17 27
13 12	162 00.6	0.4	S 23 33.3	0.2	21	Th	98 35.9	2.3	S 6 25.6	0.1	17 23
13 11	162 09.5	0.4	S 23 28.0	0.2	22	Fri	99 32.3	2.3	S 6 24.3	0.1	17 19
13 10	162 18.4	0.4	S 23 22.4	0.2	23	Sat	100 28.6	2.3	S 6 22.9	0.1	17 15
13 10	162 27.3	0.4	S 23 16.5	0.3	24	SUN	101 24.7	2.3	S 6 21.4	0.1	17 12
13 09	162 36.3	0.4	S 23 10.3	0.3	25	Mon	102 20.8	2.3	S 6 19.9	0.1	17 08
13 09	162 45.3	0.4	S 23 03.9	0.3	26	Tu	103 16.9	2.3	S 6 18.4	0.1	17 04
13 08	162 54.3	0.4	S 22 57.2	0.3	27	Wed	104 12.8	2.3	S 6 16.9	0.1	17 01
13 07	163 03.4	0.4	S 22 50.3	0.3	28	Th	105 08.6	2.3	S 6 15.3	0.1	16 57
13 07	163 12.5	0.4	S 22 43.1	0.3	29	Fri	106 04.4	2.3	S 6 13.7	0.1	16 53
13 06	163 21.7	0.4	S 22 35.6	0.3	30	Sat	107 00.0	2.3	S 6 12.0	0.1	16 49
13 06	163 30.9	0.4	S 22 27.9	0.3	31	SUN	107 55.6	2.3	S 6 10.3	0.1	16 46

MARS, Av. Mag. +1.3
S.H.A. December
5 86; 10 82; 15 78; 20 74; 25 70; 30 65.

SATURN, Av. Mag. +1.1
S.H.A. December
5 10; 10 10; 15 10; 20 10; 25 9; 30 9.

DECEMBER 1995 — MOON

Day	GMT hr	GHA ° '	Mean Var/hr 14°+	Dec ° '	Mean Var/hr '	Day	GMT hr	GHA ° '	Mean Var/hr 14°+	Dec ° '	Mean Var/hr '
1 Fri	0	70 43.1	31.7	N 1 55.3	10.5	17 Sun	0	250 56.9	30.1	S 6 55.4	10.1
	6	157 53.2	31.7	N 2 58.0	10.3		6	337 57.2	29.6	S 7 56.0	9.9
	12	245 03.9	31.9	N 3 59.8	10.1		12	64 54.8	29.1	S 8 55.6	9.7
	18	332 15.1	31.9	N 5 00.6	10.0		18	151 49.6	28.6	S 9 54.0	9.5
2 Sat	0	59 26.7	32.0	N 6 00.2	9.7	18 Mon	0	238 41.5	28.1	S 10 50.9	9.1
	6	146 38.5	32.0	N 6 58.6	9.5		6	325 30.3	27.5	S 11 46.0	8.9
	12	233 50.3	31.9	N 7 55.5	9.2		12	52 15.9	27.0	S 12 39.1	8.5
	18	321 02.2	31.9	N 8 50.9	8.9		18	138 58.3	26.4	S 13 29.9	8.0
3 Sun	0	48 13.9	31.9	N 9 44.6	8.6	19 Tu	0	225 37.4	25.9	S 14 18.1	7.5
	6	135 25.4	31.8	N 10 36.4	8.3		6	312 13.3	25.4	S 15 03.4	7.0
	12	222 36.6	31.8	N 11 26.3	8.0		12	38 46.0	24.9	S 15 45.5	6.4
	18	309 47.5	31.8	N 12 14.1	7.6		18	125 15.5	24.4	S 16 24.1	5.7
4 Mon	0	36 57.9	31.7	N 12 59.7	7.2	20 Wed	0	211 42.0	23.9	S 16 59.0	5.1
	6	124 07.8	31.6	N 13 42.9	6.7		6	298 05.7	23.5	S 17 29.8	4.4
	12	211 17.3	31.5	N 14 23.8	6.3		12	24 26.8	23.1	S 17 56.2	3.6
	18	298 26.2	31.4	N 15 02.1	5.9		18	110 45.6	22.8	S 18 18.1	2.8
5 Tu	0	25 34.6	31.3	N 15 37.8	5.4	21 Th	0	197 02.3	22.5	S 18 35.2	1.9
	6	112 42.6	31.3	N 16 10.8	5.0		6	283 17.4	22.3	S 18 47.4	1.2
	12	199 50.0	31.1	N 16 41.0	4.5		12	9 31.2	22.1	S 18 54.6	0.2
	18	286 57.0	31.1	N 17 08.3	4.0		18	95 44.2	22.0	S 18 56.5	0.6
6 Wed	0	14 03.6	31.0	N 17 32.7	3.5	22 Fri	0	181 56.7	22.1	S 18 53.3	1.5
	6	101 09.9	31.0	N 17 54.1	3.0		6	268 09.2	22.2	S 18 44.8	2.4
	12	188 15.9	31.0	N 18 12.4	2.5		12	354 22.1	22.3	S 18 31.1	3.2
	18	275 21.7	30.9	N 18 27.6	1.9		18	80 35.8	22.5	S 18 12.4	4.0
7 Th	0	2 27.4	30.9	N 18 39.6	1.4	23 Sat	0	166 50.8	22.7	S 17 48.7	4.8
	6	89 33.1	30.9	N 18 48.5	0.9		6	253 07.4	23.2	S 17 20.2	5.5
	12	176 38.9	31.0	N 18 54.2	0.4		12	339 25.8	23.5	S 16 47.2	6.3
	18	263 44.8	31.0	N 18 56.8	0.2		18	65 46.6	23.9	S 16 09.8	7.0
8 Fri	0	350 51.0	31.1	N 18 56.2	0.7	24 Sun	0	152 09.7	24.3	S 15 28.4	7.6
	6	77 57.5	31.1	N 18 52.4	1.2		6	238 35.5	24.8	S 14 43.2	8.2
	12	165 04.5	31.2	N 18 45.5	1.7		12	325 04.1	25.3	S 13 54.6	8.6
	18	252 12.0	31.3	N 18 35.5	2.2		18	51 35.6	25.7	S 13 02.9	9.2
9 Sat	0	339 20.1	31.5	N 18 22.5	2.7	25 Mon	0	138 10.1	26.3	S 12 08.4	9.5
	6	66 28.9	31.6	N 18 06.4	3.2		6	224 47.5	26.8	S 11 11.3	9.9
	12	153 38.3	31.7	N 17 47.5	3.7		12	311 27.9	27.2	S 10 12.1	10.2
	18	240 48.6	31.9	N 17 25.6	4.1		18	38 11.2	27.7	S 9 11.1	10.4
10 Sun	0	327 59.7	32.0	N 17 01.0	4.6	26 Tu	0	124 57.3	28.2	S 8 08.5	10.7
	6	55 11.6	32.2	N 16 33.6	5.0		6	211 46.1	28.6	S 7 04.7	10.8
	12	142 24.3	32.3	N 16 03.6	5.5		12	298 37.5	29.0	S 5 59.9	10.9
	18	229 37.9	32.4	N 15 31.0	5.9		18	25 31.4	29.4	S 4 54.5	11.0
11 Mon	0	316 52.3	32.5	N 14 55.9	6.2	27 Wed	0	112 27.6	29.8	S 3 48.6	11.0
	6	44 07.6	32.7	N 14 18.5	6.6		6	199 26.0	30.1	S 2 42.4	11.0
	12	131 23.6	32.8	N 13 38.8	7.0		12	286 26.3	30.3	S 1 36.4	11.0
	18	218 40.3	32.9	N 12 56.9	7.4		18	13 28.4	30.7	S 0 30.5	10.9
12 Tu	0	305 57.6	33.0	N 12 13.0	7.7	28 Th	0	100 32.2	30.9	N 0 34.9	10.8
	6	33 15.6	33.1	N 11 27.0	8.0		6	187 37.4	31.1	N 1 39.6	10.7
	12	120 34.0	33.1	N 10 39.1	8.3		12	274 43.9	31.3	N 2 43.6	10.5
	18	207 52.8	33.2	N 9 49.5	8.6		18	1 51.6	31.5	N 3 46.5	10.3
13 Wed	0	295 11.9	33.3	N 8 58.2	8.9	29 Fri	0	89 00.1	31.6	N 4 48.4	10.1
	6	22 31.2	33.3	N 8 05.3	9.1		6	176 09.5	31.7	N 5 49.0	9.8
	12	109 50.5	33.2	N 7 11.0	9.3		12	263 19.5	31.7	N 6 48.1	9.6
	18	197 09.7	33.2	N 6 15.3	9.5		18	350 30.0	31.8	N 7 45.7	9.3
14 Th	0	284 28.7	33.1	N 5 18.3	9.7	30 Sat	0	77 40.8	31.9	N 8 41.6	9.0
	6	11 47.2	33.0	N 4 20.2	9.9		6	164 51.9	31.9	N 9 35.7	8.7
	12	99 05.3	32.9	N 3 21.1	10.0		12	252 03.1	31.9	N 10 27.9	8.3
	18	186 22.6	32.7	N 2 21.1	10.1		18	339 14.3	31.8	N 11 18.0	8.0
15 Fri	0	273 39.0	32.6	N 1 20.4	10.2	31 Sun	0	66 25.4	31.8	N 12 06.1	7.6
	6	0 54.4	32.3	N 0 19.0	10.3		6	153 36.4	31.8	N 12 51.9	7.2
	12	88 08.5	32.1	S 0 42.9	10.4		12	240 47.1	31.7	N 13 35.3	6.8
	18	175 21.2	31.9	S 1 45.1	10.4		18	327 57.5	31.7	N 14 16.3	6.4
16 Sat	0	262 32.3	31.5	S 2 47.5	10.4						
	6	349 41.6	31.2	S 3 49.9	10.4						
	12	76 48.9	30.8	S 4 52.2	10.3						
	18	163 54.1	30.4	S 5 54.1	10.3						

NOTE Moon GHA corrections for additional hours, minutes, and seconds on page E 96.
Moon Declination corrections on page E 99. Mean Var/Hr value needed for both corrections.

DECEMBER

POLARIS (POLE STAR) TABLE, 1995

LHA Aries	Q	LHA Aries	Q	LHA Aries	Q	LHA Aries	Q	LHA Aries	Q	LHA Aries	Q	LHA Aries	Q	LHA Aries	Q
358 46	-36	86 00	-29	120 50	-4	153 30	+21	227 46	+44	281 46	+19	314 17	-6	349 32	-31
0 50	-37	87 38	-28	122 07	-3	154 56	+22	233 14	+43	283 10	+18	315 33	-7	351 16	-32
3 01	-38	89 14	-27	123 23	-2	156 23	+23	237 18	+42	284 32	+17	316 50	-8	353 02	-33
5 20	-39	90 49	-26	124 39	-1	157 51	+24	240 42	+41	285 55	+16	318 07	-9	354 53	-34
7 48	-40	92 21	-25	125 54	0	159 21	+25	243 42	+40	287 16	+15	319 24	-10	356 47	-35
10 29	-41	93 52	-24	127 11	+1	160 53	+26	246 25	+39	288 36	+14	320 42	-11	358 46	-36
13 27	-42	95 21	-23	128 27	+2	162 26	+27	248 55	+38	289 56	+13	322 00	-12	0 50	-37
16 49	-43	96 49	-22	129 43	+3	164 01	+28	251 15	+37	291 16	+12	323 19	-13	3 01	-38
20 50	-44	98 15	-21	130 59	+4	165 37	+29	253 28	+36	292 35	+11	324 38	-14	5 20	-39
26 13	-45	99 40	-20	132 16	+5	167 17	+30	255 33	+35	293 53	+10	325 57	-15	7 48	-40
47 38	-44	101 05	-19	133 32	+6	168 58	+31	257 34	+34	295 11	+9	327 18	-16	10 29	-41
53 01	-43	102 28	-18	134 49	+7	170 43	+32	259 29	+33	296 28	+8	328 39	-17	13 27	-42
57 02	-42	103 51	-17	136 05	+8	172 31	+33	261 20	+32	297 46	+7	330 00	-18	16 49	-43
60 24	-41	105 12	-16	137 23	+9	174 22	+34	263 08	+31	299 02	+6	331 23	-19	20 50	-44
63 22	-40	106 33	-15	138 40	+10	176 17	+35	264 53	+30	300 19	+5	332 46	-20	26 13	-45
66 03	-39	107 54	-14	139 58	+11	178 18	+36	266 34	+29	301 35	+4	334 11	-21	47 38	-44
68 31	-38	109 13	-13	141 16	+12	180 23	+37	268 14	+28	302 52	+3	335 36	-22	53 01	-43
70 50	-37	110 32	-12	142 35	+13	182 36	+38	269 50	+27	304 08	+2	337 02	-23	57 02	-42
73 01	-36	111 51	-11	143 55	+14	184 56	+39	271 25	+26	305 24	+1	338 30	-24	60 24	-41
75 05	-35	113 09	-10	145 15	+15	187 26	+40	272 58	+25	306 40	0	339 59	-25	63 22	-40
77 04	-34	114 27	-9	146 35	+16	190 09	+41	274 30	+24	307 57	-1	341 30	-26	66 03	-39
78 58	-33	115 44	-8	147 56	+17	193 09	+42	276 00	+23	309 12	-2	343 02	-27	68 31	-38
80 49	-32	117 01	-7	149 19	+18	196 33	+43	277 28	+22	310 28	-3	344 37	-28	70 50	-37
82 35	-31	118 18	-6	150 41	+19	200 37	+44	278 55	+21	311 44	-4	346 13	-29	73 01	-36
84 19	-30	119 34	-5	152 05	+20	206 05	+45	280 21	+20	313 01	-5	347 51	-30	75 05	-35
86 00		120 50		153 30		227 46		281 46		314 17		349 32		77 04	

NOTES: The table above can be used to find Latitude directly from an observation of Polaris. Find LHA of Aries from the monthly pages, and apply correction Q to the Observed Altitude (Sextant Altitude corrected on p. E 96). In critical cases (when LHA Aries equals tabulated number), use the higher Q value.

AZIMUTH OF POLARIS, 1995

LHA Aries	Latitude (N)							LHA Aries	Latitude (N)						
	0°	30°	50°	55°	60°	65°	70°		0°	30°	50°	55°	60°	65°	70°
0	0.5	0.5	0.7	0.8	0.9	1.1	1.4	180	359.5	359.5	359.3	359.2	359.1	359.0	358.7
10	0.3	0.4	0.5	0.6	0.7	0.8	1.0	190	359.7	359.6	359.5	359.4	359.3	359.2	359.0
20	0.2	0.3	0.3	0.4	0.4	0.5	0.7	200	359.8	359.7	359.7	359.6	359.6	359.5	359.4
30	0.1	0.1	0.1	0.2	0.2	0.2	0.3	210	359.9	359.9	359.9	359.8	359.8	359.8	359.7
40	0.0	0.0	359.9	359.9	359.9	359.9	359.9	220	0.0	0.0	0.1	0.1	0.1	0.1	0.1
50	359.8	359.8	359.7	359.7	359.7	359.6	359.5	230	0.2	0.2	0.3	0.3	0.3	0.4	0.5
60	359.7	359.7	359.5	359.5	359.4	359.3	359.1	240	0.3	0.3	0.5	0.5	0.6	0.7	0.8
70	359.6	359.5	359.4	359.3	359.2	359.0	358.8	250	0.4	0.5	0.6	0.7	0.8	1.0	1.2
80	359.5	359.4	359.2	359.1	359.0	358.8	358.5	260	0.5	0.6	0.8	0.9	1.0	1.2	1.5
90	359.4	359.3	359.1	358.9	358.8	358.5	358.2	270	0.6	0.7	0.9	1.0	1.2	1.4	1.7
100	359.3	359.2	358.9	358.8	358.6	358.4	358.0	280	0.7	0.8	1.0	1.2	1.3	1.6	1.9
110	359.3	359.2	358.9	358.7	358.5	358.3	357.9	290	0.7	0.8	1.1	1.3	1.4	1.7	2.1
120	359.3	359.1	358.8	358.7	358.5	358.2	357.8	300	0.7	0.9	1.2	1.3	1.5	1.8	2.2
130	359.2	359.1	358.8	358.7	358.5	358.2	357.8	310	0.8	0.9	1.2	1.3	1.5	1.8	2.2
140	359.3	359.2	358.9	358.7	358.5	358.3	357.9	320	0.7	0.9	1.1	1.3	1.5	1.8	2.2
150	359.3	359.2	358.9	358.8	358.6	358.4	358.0	330	0.7	0.8	1.1	1.2	1.4	1.7	2.1
160	359.4	359.3	359.0	358.9	358.8	358.5	358.2	340	0.6	0.7	1.0	1.1	1.3	1.5	1.9
170	359.4	359.4	359.2	359.1	358.9	358.7	358.4	350	0.6	0.6	0.9	1.0	1.1	1.3	1.7
180	359.5	359.5	359.3	359.2	359.1	359.0	358.7	360	0.5	0.5	0.7	0.8	0.9	1.1	1.4

Rule of thumb: When Cassiopeia is left (right), Polaris is west (east).

ARC INTO TIME CONVERSION TABLE

Arc °	Time h m	Arc °	Time h m	Arc °	Time h m	Arc °	Time h m	Arc °	Time h m	Arc °	Time h m	Arc ′	Time m s	Arc ″	Time s
0	0 0	60	4 0	120	8 0	180	12 0	240	16 0	300	20 0	0	0 0	0=0.0	0.00
1	0 4	61	4 4	121	8 4	181	12 4	241	16 4	301	20 4	1	0 4	1	0.07
2	0 8	62	4 8	122	8 8	182	12 8	242	16 8	302	20 8	2	0 8	2	0.13
3	0 12	63	4 12	123	8 12	183	12 12	243	16 12	303	20 12	3	0 12	3	0.20
4	0 16	64	4 16	124	8 16	184	12 16	244	16 16	304	20 16	4	0 16	4	0.27
5	0 20	65	4 20	125	8 20	185	12 20	245	16 20	305	20 20	5	0 20	5	0.33
6	0 24	66	4 24	126	8 24	186	12 24	246	16 24	306	20 24	6	0 24	6=0.1	0.40
7	0 28	67	4 28	127	8 28	187	12 28	247	16 28	307	20 28	7	0 28	7	0.47
8	0 32	68	4 32	128	8 32	188	12 32	248	16 32	308	20 32	8	0 32	8	0.53
9	0 36	69	4 36	129	8 36	189	12 36	249	16 36	309	20 36	9	0 36	9	0.60
10	0 40	70	4 40	130	8 40	190	12 40	250	16 40	310	20 40	10	0 40	10	0.67
11	0 44	71	4 44	131	8 44	191	12 44	251	16 44	311	20 44	11	0 44	11	0.73
12	0 48	72	4 48	132	8 48	192	12 48	252	16 48	312	20 48	12	0 48	12=0.2	0.80
13	0 52	73	4 52	133	8 52	193	12 52	253	16 52	313	20 52	13	0 52	13	0.87
14	0 56	74	4 56	134	8 56	194	12 56	254	16 56	314	20 56	14	0 56	14	0.93
15	1 0	75	5 0	135	9 0	195	13 0	255	17 0	315	21 0	15	1 0	15	1.00
16	1 4	76	5 4	136	9 4	196	13 4	256	17 4	316	21 4	16	1 4	16	1.07
17	1 8	77	5 8	137	9 8	197	13 8	257	17 8	317	21 8	17	1 8	17	1.13
18	1 12	78	5 12	138	9 12	198	13 12	258	17 12	318	21 12	18	1 12	18=0.3	1.20
19	1 16	79	5 16	139	9 16	199	13 16	259	17 16	319	21 16	19	1 16	19	1.27
20	1 20	80	5 20	140	9 20	200	13 20	260	17 20	320	21 20	20	1 20	20	1.33
21	1 24	81	5 24	141	9 24	201	13 24	261	17 24	321	21 24	21	1 24	21	1.40
22	1 28	82	5 28	142	9 28	202	13 28	262	17 28	322	21 28	22	1 28	22	1.47
23	1 32	83	5 32	143	9 32	203	13 32	263	17 32	323	21 32	23	1 32	23	1.53
24	1 36	84	5 36	144	9 36	204	13 36	264	17 36	324	21 36	24	1 36	24=0.4	1.60
25	1 40	85	5 40	145	9 40	205	13 40	265	17 40	325	21 40	25	1 40	25	1.67
26	1 44	86	5 44	146	9 44	206	13 44	266	17 44	326	21 44	26	1 44	26	1.73
27	1 48	87	5 48	147	9 48	207	13 48	267	17 48	327	21 48	27	1 48	27	1.80
28	1 52	88	5 52	148	9 52	208	13 52	268	17 52	328	21 52	28	1 52	28	1.87
29	1 56	89	5 56	149	9 56	209	13 56	269	17 56	329	21 56	29	1 56	29	1.93
30	2 0	90	6 0	150	10 0	210	14 0	270	18 0	330	22 0	30	2 0	30=0.5	2.00
31	2 4	91	6 4	151	10 4	211	14 4	271	18 4	331	22 4	31	2 4	31	2.07
32	2 8	92	6 8	152	10 8	212	14 8	272	18 8	332	22 8	32	2 8	32	2.13
33	2 12	93	6 12	153	10 12	213	14 12	273	18 12	333	22 12	33	2 12	33	2.20
34	2 16	94	6 16	154	10 16	214	14 16	274	18 16	334	22 16	34	2 16	34	2.27
35	2 20	95	6 20	155	10 20	215	14 20	275	18 20	335	22 20	35	2 20	35	2.33
36	2 24	96	6 24	156	10 24	216	14 24	276	18 24	336	22 24	36	2 24	36=0.6	2.40
37	2 28	97	6 28	157	10 28	217	14 28	277	18 28	337	22 28	37	2 28	37	2.47
38	2 32	98	6 32	158	10 32	218	14 32	278	18 32	338	22 32	38	2 32	38	2.53
39	2 36	99	6 36	159	10 36	219	14 36	279	18 36	339	22 36	39	2 36	39	2.60
40	2 40	100	6 40	160	10 40	220	14 40	280	18 40	340	22 40	40	2 40	40	2.67
41	2 44	101	6 44	161	10 44	221	14 44	281	18 44	341	22 44	41	2 44	41	2.73
42	2 48	102	6 48	162	10 48	222	14 48	282	18 48	342	22 48	42	2 48	42=0.7	2.80
43	2 52	103	6 52	163	10 52	223	14 52	283	18 52	343	22 52	43	2 52	43	2.87
44	2 56	104	6 56	164	10 56	224	14 56	284	18 56	344	22 56	44	2 56	44	2.93
45	3 0	105	7 0	165	11 0	225	15 0	285	19 0	345	23 0	45	3 0	45	3.00
46	3 4	106	7 4	166	11 4	226	15 4	286	19 4	346	23 4	46	3 4	46	3.07
47	3 8	107	7 8	167	11 8	227	15 8	287	19 8	347	23 8	47	3 8	47	3.13
48	3 12	108	7 12	168	11 12	228	15 12	288	19 12	348	23 12	48	3 12	48=0.8	3.20
49	3 16	109	7 16	169	11 16	229	15 16	289	19 16	349	23 16	49	3 16	49	3.27
50	3 20	110	7 20	170	11 20	230	15 20	290	19 20	350	23 20	50	3 20	50	3.33
51	3 24	111	7 24	171	11 24	231	15 24	291	19 24	351	23 24	51	3 24	51	3.40
52	3 28	112	7 28	172	11 28	232	15 28	292	19 28	352	23 28	52	3 28	52	3.47
53	3 32	113	7 32	173	11 32	233	15 32	293	19 32	353	23 32	53	3 32	53	3.53
54	3 36	114	7 36	174	11 36	234	15 36	294	19 36	354	23 36	54	3 36	54=0.9	3.60
55	3 40	115	7 40	175	11 40	235	15 40	295	19 40	355	23 40	55	3 40	55	3.67
56	3 44	116	7 44	176	11 44	236	15 44	296	19 44	356	23 44	56	3 44	56	3.73
57	3 48	117	7 48	177	11 48	237	15 48	297	19 48	357	23 48	57	3 48	57	3.80
58	3 52	118	7 52	178	11 52	238	15 52	298	19 52	358	23 52	58	3 52	58	3.87
59	3 56	119	7 56	179	11 56	239	15 56	299	19 56	359	23 56	59	3 56	59	3.93
60	4 00	120	8 00	180	12 00	240	16 00	300	20 00	360	24 00	60	4 00	60=1.0	4.00

CORRECTIONS

REFRACTION, DIP, AND SUN PARALLAX TABLES

Mean Refraction
Subtract

App Alt ° '	Refr '	App Alt ° '	Refr '
0 00	34.9	10 00	5.3
10	32.8	10	5.2
20	30.9	20	5.1
30	29.1	30	5.0
40	27.4	40	5.0
50	25.8	50	4.9
1 00	24.4	11 00	4.8
10	23.1	10	4.7
20	21.9	20	4.7
30	20.9	30	4.6
40	19.9	40	4.5
50	19.0	50	4.5
2 00	18.1	12 00	4.4
10	17.4	10	4.4
20	16.7	20	4.3
30	16.0	30	4.2
40	15.4	40	4.2
50	14.8	50	4.1
3 00	14.2	13 00	4.1
10	13.7	10	4.0
20	13.3	20	4.0
30	12.8	30	3.9
40	12.4	40	3.9
50	12.0	50	3.8
4 00	11.7	14 00	3.8
10	11.3	20	3.7
20	11.0	40	3.6
30	10.7	15 00	3.5
40	10.4	30	3.4
50	10.1	16 00	3.3
5 00	9.8	30	3.2
10	9.5	17 00	3.1
20	9.3	30	3.0
30	9.0	18 00	2.9
40	8.8	30	2.9
50	8.6	19 00	2.8
6 00	8.4	20 00	2.6
10	8.2	21 00	2.5
20	8.0	22 00	2.4
30	7.8	23 00	2.3
40	7.7	24 00	2.2
50	7.5	26 00	2.0
7 00	7.3	28 00	1.8
10	7.2	30 00	1.7
20	7.0	32 00	1.5
30	6.9	34 00	1.4
40	6.8	36 00	1.3
50	6.6	38 00	1.2
8 00	6.5	40 00	1.1
10	6.4	43 00	1.0
20	6.3	46 00	0.9
30	6.1	50 00	0.8
40	6.0	55 00	0.7
50	5.9	60 00	0.6
9 00	5.8	65 00	0.5
10	5.7	70 00	0.4
20	5.6	75 00	0.3
30	5.5	80 00	0.2
40	5.4	85 00	0.1
50	5.4	90 00	0.0

Dip of Sea Horizon
Subtract

HE ft	Dip '	HE m
2	1.5	0.6
3	1.8	0.9
4	2.0	1.2
5	2.2	1.5
6	2.4	1.8
7	2.6	2.1
8	2.8	2.4
9	2.9	2.7
10	3.1	3.0
11	3.3	3.4
12	3.4	3.7
13	3.5	4.0
14	3.7	4.3
15	3.8	4.6
16	3.9	4.9
17	4.0	5.2
18	4.2	5.5
19	4.3	5.8
20	4.4	6.1
22	4.6	6.7
24	4.8	7.3
26	5.0	7.9
28	5.2	8.5
30	5.4	9.1
32	5.5	9.8
34	5.7	10.4
36	5.9	11.0
38	6.0	11.6
40	6.2	12.2
42	6.4	12.8
44	6.5	13.4
46	6.7	14.0
48	6.8	14.6
50	6.9	15.2
52	7.1	15.9
54	7.2	16.5
56	7.3	17.0
58	7.5	17.7
60	7.6	18.3
65	7.9	19.8
70	8.2	21.3
80	8.8	24.4
90	9.3	27.4
100	9.8	30.5
120	10.7	36.6
140	11.6	42.7
160	12.4	49.8
180	13.2	54.9
200	13.7	61.0
220	14.5	67.1
240	15.2	73.2
260	15.8	79.3
280	16.4	85.3
300	17.0	91.4
350	18.3	107
400	19.6	122
450	20.8	137
500	21.9	152

Sun's Parallax in Altitude
Add

App Alt °	Parallax '
0	0.15
5	0.15
10	0.14
15	0.14
20	0.14
25	0.13
30	0.12
40	0.11
50	0.10
60	0.08
70	0.06
80	0.03
90	0.00

Notes:

This table is primarily useful for correcting sun sights with sextant altitudes of less than 9°.

For more conventional sun sights, you will find the table on the opposite page much quicker.

To use this table, first correct your sextant altitude (Hs) for dip, and then use the resulting apparent altitude (Ha) to figure corrections for refraction and parallax. Finally, get the Sun's semi-diameter from the first page of the appropriate monthly pages and add it if you shot the lower limb of the Sun, subtract if upper limb.

SUN ALTITUDE TOTAL CORRECTION TABLE (LOWER LIMB)

Always add

					Height of eye above sea level											
m	**0.9**	**1.8**	**2.4**	**3.0**	**3.7**	**4.3**	**4.9**	**5.5**	**6.0**	**7.6**	**9.0**	**12**	**15**	**18**	**21**	**24**
ft	**3**	**6**	**8**	**10**	**12**	**14**	**16**	**18**	**20**	**25**	**30**	**40**	**50**	**60**	**70**	**80**
°	′	′	′	′	′	′	′	′	′	′	′	′	′	′	′	′
9	8.6	8.0	7.6	7.2	6.9	6.6	6.4	6.2	5.9	5.4	4.9	4.1	3.4	2.7	2.1	1.5
10	9.1	8.5	8.1	7.9	7.5	7.2	7.0	6.7	6.6	6.0	5.5	4.7	3.9	3.3	2.7	2.1
11	9.6	9.0	8.6	8.3	8.0	7.7	7.4	7.2	7.0	6.4	6.0	5.2	4.4	3.7	3.1	2.5
12	10.0	9.4	9.0	8.7	8.4	8.1	7.8	7.6	7.4	6.8	6.4	5.6	4.8	4.1	3.5	2.9
13	10.3	9.7	9.3	9.0	8.7	8.4	8.2	7.9	7.7	7.2	6.7	5.9	5.2	4.5	3.9	3.3
14	10.6	10.0	9.6	9.3	9.0	8.7	8.5	8.2	8.0	7.5	7.0	6.2	5.5	4.8	4.2	3.6
15	10.9	10.2	9.9	9.5	9.2	9.0	8.7	8.5	8.2	7.7	7.2	6.4	5.7	5.0	4.4	3.8
16	11.1	10.5	10.1	9.7	9.5	9.2	8.9	8.7	8.5	7.9	7.5	6.7	5.9	5.2	4.6	4.1
17	11.3	10.7	10.3	10.0	9.7	9.4	9.1	8.9	8.7	8.2	7.7	6.9	6.1	5.5	4.9	4.3
18	11.5	10.8	10.5	10.1	9.9	9.6	9.3	9.1	8.9	8.3	7.9	7.0	6.3	5.6	5.0	4.5
19	11.6	11.0	10.6	10.3	10.0	9.7	9.5	9.2	9.0	8.5	8.0	7.2	6.5	5.8	5.2	4.6
20	11.8	11.2	10.8	10.4	10.2	9.9	9.6	9.4	9.2	8.6	8.2	7.4	6.6	5.9	5.3	4.8
21	11.9	11.3	10.9	10.6	10.3	10.0	9.8	9.5	9.3	8.8	8.3	7.5	6.8	6.1	5.5	4.9
22	12.0	11.4	11.0	10.7	10.4	10.1	9.9	9.7	9.4	8.9	8.4	7.6	6.9	6.2	5.6	5.0
23	12.1	11.5	11.1	10.8	10.5	10.2	10.0	9.8	9.5	9.0	8.5	7.7	7.0	6.3	5.7	5.1
24	12.2	11.6	11.2	10.9	10.6	10.3	10.1	9.9	9.6	9.1	8.6	7.8	7.1	6.4	5.8	5.2
25	12.3	11.7	11.3	11.0	10.7	10.4	10.2	10.0	9.7	9.2	8.7	7.9	7.2	6.5	5.9	5.3
26	12.4	11.8	11.4	11.1	10.8	10.5	10.3	10.1	9.8	9.3	8.8	8.0	7.3	6.6	6.0	5.4
27	12.5	11.9	11.5	11.2	10.9	10.6	10.4	10.1	9.9	9.4	8.9	8.1	7.4	6.7	6.1	5.5
28	12.6	12.0	11.6	11.3	11.0	10.7	10.4	10.2	10.0	9.5	9.0	8.2	7.4	6.8	6.2	5.6
30	12.7	12.1	11.7	11.4	11.1	10.8	10.6	10.4	10.1	9.6	9.1	8.3	7.6	6.9	6.3	5.7
32	12.9	12.2	11.9	11.5	11.2	11.0	10.7	10.5	10.2	9.7	9.3	8.4	7.7	7.0	6.4	5.8
34	13.0	12.3	12.0	11.6	11.3	11.1	10.8	10.6	10.3	9.8	9.4	8.5	7.8	7.1	6.5	5.9
36	13.1	12.4	12.1	11.7	11.4	11.2	10.9	10.7	10.4	9.9	9.5	8.6	7.9	7.2	6.6	6.0
38	13.2	12.5	12.1	11.8	11.5	11.2	11.0	10.8	10.5	10.0	9.5	8.7	8.0	7.3	6.7	6.1
40	13.3	12.6	12.2	11.9	11.6	11.3	11.1	10.8	10.6	10.1	9.6	8.8	8.1	7.4	6.8	6.2
42	13.4	12.7	12.3	12.0	11.7	11.4	11.2	10.9	10.7	10.2	9.7	8.9	8.2	7.5	6.9	6.3
44	13.4	12.7	12.4	12.0	11.7	11.5	11.2	11.0	10.7	10.2	9.8	8.9	8.2	7.5	6.9	6.3
46	13.5	12.8	12.4	12.1	11.8	11.5	11.3	11.0	10.8	10.3	9.8	9.0	8.3	7.6	7.0	6.4
48	13.6	12.9	12.5	12.2	11.9	11.6	11.3	11.1	10.9	10.4	9.9	9.1	8.3	7.7	7.1	6.4
50	13.6	12.9	12.5	12.2	11.9	11.6	11.4	11.1	10.9	10.4	9.9	9.1	8.4	7.7	7.1	6.5
52	13.6	13.0	12.6	12.3	12.0	11.7	11.4	11.2	11.0	10.5	10.0	9.2	8.4	7.8	7.2	6.5
54	13.7	13.0	12.6	12.3	12.0	11.7	11.5	11.3	11.0	10.5	10.0	9.2	8.5	7.8	7.2	6.6
56	13.7	13.1	12.7	12.4	12.1	11.8	11.5	11.3	11.1	10.6	10.1	9.3	8.5	7.9	7.3	6.7
58	13.8	13.1	12.7	12.4	12.1	11.8	11.6	11.3	11.1	10.6	10.1	9.3	8.6	7.9	7.3	6.8
60	13.8	13.1	12.8	12.4	12.1	11.9	11.6	11.4	11.1	10.6	10.2	9.3	8.6	7.9	7.3	6.8
62	13.9	13.2	12.8	12.5	12.2	11.9	11.7	11.4	11.2	10.7	10.2	9.4	8.7	8.0	7.4	6.8
64	13.9	13.2	12.8	12.5	12.2	11.9	11.7	11.5	11.2	10.7	10.2	9.4	8.7	8.0	7.4	6.9
66	14.0	13.2	12.9	12.5	12.3	12.0	11.7	11.5	11.3	10.7	10.3	9.5	8.7	8.1	7.5	7.0
70	14.1	13.3	12.9	12.6	12.3	12.0	11.8	11.6	11.3	10.8	10.3	9.5	8.8	8.1	7.5	7.0
80	14.2	13.5	13.1	12.8	12.5	12.2	11.9	11.7	11.5	11.0	10.5	9.7	8.9	8.3	7.7	7.1
90	14.3	13.6	13.2	12.9	12.6	12.3	12.1	11.9	11.6	11.1	10.6	9.8	9.1	8.4	7.8	7.2

MONTHLY CORRECTION

Jan	Feb	Mar	Apr	May	Jun	Jul	Aug	Sep	Oct	Nov	Dec
+0.3′	+0.2′	+0.1′	+0.0′	−0.1′	−0.2′	−0.2′	−0.2′	−0.1′	+0.1′	+0.2′	+0.3′

Notes:

For lower limb Sun sights greater than 9°, this table combines the corrections for refraction, dip, and parallax together with a correction for the Sun's semi-diameter. Simply add the one correction to obtain your Ho.

For slightly greater precision, also add or subtract the monthly correction, which compensates for slight changes in the Sun's semi-diameter.

If used to correct a sight of the **upper limb**, it is necessary to subtract twice the Sun's semi-diameter (given on the monthly pages) from the sextant altitude before entering the table.

CORRECTIONS

SUN, STAR AND ARIES GHA CORRECTION TABLES

Always add

SUN

Hours, minutes or seconds (α)	α mins	1h+ α mins	α secs
0	0 00.0	15 00.0	0.0
1	0 15.0	15 15.0	0.3
2	0 30.0	15 30.0	0.5
3	0 45.0	15 45.0	0.8
4	1 00.0	16 00.0	1.0
5	1 15.0	16 15.0	1.3
6	1 30.0	16 30.0	1.5
7	1 45.0	16 45.0	1.8
8	2 00.0	17 00.0	2.0
9	2 15.0	17 15.0	2.3
10	2 30.0	17 30.0	2.5
11	2 45.0	17 45.0	2.8
12	3 00.0	18 00.0	3.0
13	3 15.0	18 15.0	3.3
14	3 30.0	18 30.0	3.5
15	3 45.0	18 45.0	3.8
16	4 00.0	19 00.0	4.0
17	4 15.0	19 15.0	4.3
18	4 30.0	19 30.0	4.5
19	4 45.0	19 45.0	4.8
20	5 00.0	20 00.0	5.0
21	5 15.0	20 15.0	5.3
22	5 30.0	20 30.0	5.5
23	5 45.0	20 45.0	5.8
24	6 00.0	21 00.0	6.0
25	6 15.0	21 15.0	6.3
26	6 30.0	21 30.0	6.5
27	6 45.0	21 45.0	6.8
28	7 00.0	22 00.0	7.0
29	7 15.0	22 15.0	7.3
30	7 30.0	22 30.0	7.5
31	7 45.0	22 45.0	7.8
32	8 00.0	23 00.0	8.0
33	8 15.0	23 15.0	8.3
34	8 30.0	23 30.0	8.5
35	8 45.0	23 45.0	8.8
36	9 00.0	24 00.0	9.0
37	9 15.0	24 15.0	9.3
38	9 30.0	24 30.0	9.5
39	9 45.0	24 45.0	9.8
40	10 00.0	25 00.0	10.0
41	10 15.0	25 15.0	10.3
42	10 30.0	25 30.0	10.5
43	10 45.0	25 45.0	10.8
44	11 00.0	26 00.0	11.0
45	11 15.0	26 15.0	11.3
46	11 30.0	26 30.0	11.5
47	11 45.0	26 45.0	11.8
48	12 00.0	27 00.0	12.0
49	12 15.0	27 15.0	12.3
50	12 30.0	27 30.0	12.5
51	12 45.0	27 45.0	12.8
52	13 00.0	28 00.0	13.0
53	13 15.0	28 15.0	13.3
54	13 30.0	28 30.0	13.5
55	13 45.0	28 45.0	13.8
56	14 00.0	29 00.0	14.0
57	14 15.0	29 15.0	14.3
58	14 30.0	29 30.0	14.5
59	14 45.0	29 45.0	14.8
60	15 00.0	30 00.0	15.0

STAR AND ARIES

Date GMT	Corr for Date	α hours	1h+ α mins	α mins	α secs	
1st	0 00.0	0 00.0	15 02.5	0 00.0	0.0	0
2nd	0 59.1	15 02.5	15 17.5	0 15.0	0.3	1
3rd	1 58.2	30 04.9	15 32.6	0 30.1	0.5	2
4th	2 57.3	45 07.4	15 47.6	0 45.1	0.8	3
5th	3 56.5	60 09.9	16 02.7	1 00.2	1.0	4
6th	4 55.6	75 12.3	16 17.7	1 15.2	1.3	5
7th	5 54.8	90 14.8	16 32.7	1 30.2	1.5	6
8th	6 54.0	105 17.2	16 47.8	1 45.3	1.8	7
9th	7 53.1	120 19.7	17 02.8	2 00.3	2.0	8
10th	8 52.2	135 22.2	17 17.9	2 15.4	2.3	9
11th	9 51.4	150 24.6	17 32.9	2 30.4	2.5	10
12th	10 50.5	165 27.1	17 48.0	2 45.5	2.8	11
13th	11 49.6	180 29.6	18 03.0	3 00.5	3.0	12
14th	12 48.8	195 32.0	18 18.0	3 15.5	3.3	13
15th	13 48.0	210 34.5	18 33.1	3 30.6	3.5	14
16th	14 47.1	225 37.0	18 48.1	3 45.6	3.8	15
17th	15 46.2	240 39.4	19 03.2	4 00.7	4.0	16
18th	16 45.3	255 41.9	19 18.2	4 15.7	4.3	17
19th	17 44.5	270 44.4	19 33.2	4 30.7	4.5	18
20th	18 43.6	285 46.8	19 48.3	4 45.8	4.8	19
21st	19 42.7	300 49.3	20 03.3	5 00.8	5.0	20
22nd	20 41.9	315 51.7	20 18.4	5 15.9	5.3	21
23rd	21 41.0	330 54.2	20 33.4	5 30.9	5.5	22
24th	22 40.1	345 56.7	20 48.4	5 45.9	5.8	23
25th	23 39.3	360 59.1	21 03.5	6 01.0	6.0	24
26th	24 38.4		21 18.5	6 16.0	6.3	25
27th	25 37.6		21 33.6	6 31.1	6.5	26
28th	26 36.7		21 48.6	6 46.1	6.8	27
29th	27 35.8		22 03.6	7 01.1	7.0	28
30th	28 35.0		22 18.7	7 16.2	7.3	29
31st	29 34.1		22 33.7	7 31.2	7.5	30
			22 48.8	7 46.3	7.8	31
			23 03.8	8 01.3	8.0	32
			23 18.9	8 16.4	8.3	33
			23 33.9	8 31.4	8.5	34
			23 48.9	8 46.4	8.8	35
			24 04.0	9 01.5	9.0	36
			24 19.0	9 16.5	9.3	37
			24 34.1	9 31.6	9.5	38
			24 49.1	9 46.6	9.8	39
			25 04.1	10 01.6	10.0	40
			25 19.2	10 16.7	10.3	41
			25 34.2	10 31.7	10.5	42
			25 49.3	10 46.8	10.8	43
			26 04.3	11 01.8	11.0	44
			26 19.3	11 16.8	11.3	45
			26 34.4	11 31.9	11.5	46
			26 49.4	11 46.9	11.8	47
			27 04.5	12 02.0	12.0	48
			27 19.5	12 17.0	12.3	49
			27 34.6	12 32.1	12.5	50
			27 49.6	12 47.1	12.8	51
			28 04.6	13 02.1	13.0	52
			28 19.7	13 17.2	13.3	53
			28 34.7	13 32.2	13.5	54
			28 49.8	13 47.3	13.8	55
			29 04.8	14 02.3	14.0	56
			29 19.8	14 17.3	14.3	57
			29 34.9	14 32.4	14.5	58
			29 49.9	14 47.4	14.8	59
			30 04.9	15 02.5	15.0	60

Examples:

GHA Sun 15:13:25 GMT 1/12/95

from p. E 20	14:00	27 44.9
from 1H+Min column	1:13	18 15.0
from secs col.	25	6.3
GHA Sun.....................		46 06.2

GHA Sirius same time & date:

from p. E 19		358 56.2
from date col	12th	13 48.0
from hours col	15	225 37.0
from min col	13	3 15.5
from secs col	25	6.3
GHA Sirius.................		591 44.9
less 360°		231 44.9

MOON ALTITUDE TOTAL CORRECTION TABLE

Add/subtract as indicated

Sextant Altitude	Upper Limb — Add above line / Subtract below line								Hor Par (Lower)	Lower Limb Add							
Hor Par	54'	55'	56'	57'	58'	59'	60'	61'		54'	55'	56'	57'	58'	59'	60'	61'
°									°								
10	23.4	24.0	24.6	25.5	26.0	26.7	27.5	28.3	10	52.7	54.0	55.3	56.5	57.7	59.0	60.2	61.5
12	23.8	24.6	25.2	26.0	26.5	27.2	28.0	28.7	12	53.2	54.5	55.7	57.0	58.4	59.5	60.7	62.0
14	24.0	24.8	25.4	26.1	26.7	27.5	28.3	29.0	14	53.5	54.7	56.0	57.3	58.5	59.8	61.0	62.3
16	24.0	24.8	25.5	26.1	26.7	27.5	28.3	28.8	16	53.5	54.6	56.0	57.3	58.5	59.8	61.0	62.2
18	23.8	24.6	25.2	26.0	26.5	27.3	28.0	28.6	18	53.4	54.6	55.7	57.0	58.4	59.5	60.6	62.0
20	23.6	24.2	25.0	25.5	26.2	27.0	27.5	28.2	20	53.0	54.4	55.5	56.8	58.0	59.0	60.4	61.5
22	23.2	23.8	24.6	25.0	25.7	26.5	27.0	27.8	22	52.5	53.7	55.0	56.3	57.5	58.8	60.0	61.0
24	22.7	23.2	24.0	24.5	25.3	25.8	26.5	27.0	24	52.0	53.3	54.5	55.5	56.7	58.0	59.4	60.5
26	22.0	22.6	23.4	24.0	24.5	25.0	25.7	26.5	26	51.5	52.5	53.7	55.0	56.3	57.5	58.0	59.8
28	21.4	22.0	22.6	23.3	23.8	24.5	25.0	25.5	28	50.7	52.0	53.0	54.4	55.5	56.5	57.8	59.0
30	20.6	21.2	21.8	22.3	23.0	23.5	24.3	24.7	30	50.0	51.0	52.3	53.5	54.5	55.7	57.0	58.0
32	19.8	20.2	21.0	21.3	22.0	22.5	23.2	23.7	32	49.3	50.4	51.3	52.5	53.7	54.8	56.0	57.0
34	19.0	19.4	20.0	20.5	21.0	21.5	22.2	22.7	34	48.3	49.5	50.5	51.5	52.7	53.7	55.0	56.0
36	18.0	18.4	19.0	19.5	20.0	20.5	21.0	21.7	36	47.3	48.5	49.5	50.5	51.7	52.7	54.0	55.0
38	16.8	17.4	17.8	18.5	19.0	19.5	20.0	20.4	38	46.4	47.4	48.5	49.5	50.5	51.5	52.7	53.8
40	15.8	16.2	16.8	17.3	17.7	18.2	18.8	19.2	40	45.3	46.3	47.3	48.3	49.5	50.5	51.5	52.5
42	14.7	15.2	15.6	16.0	16.5	17.0	17.5	18.0	42	44.0	45.0	46.0	47.0	48.0	49.0	50.0	51.0
44	13.5	13.8	14.2	14.6	15.0	15.5	16.0	16.5	44	42.7	43.7	44.7	45.7	46.7	47.7	48.7	49.7
46	12.0	12.6	13.0	13.4	13.8	14.2	14.5	15.0	46	41.5	42.5	43.5	44.5	45.5	46.5	47.5	48.5
48	10.5	11.2	11.6	12.0	12.4	12.8	13.2	13.5	48	40.2	41.2	42.2	43.0	44.0	45.0	46.0	47.0
50	9.3	10.0	10.2	10.6	11.0	11.3	11.7	12.0	50	39.0	40.0	41.0	41.8	42.6	43.6	44.5	45.5
52	8.0	8.4	8.6	9.2	9.5	9.7	10.0	10.5	52	37.5	38.5	39.3	40.2	41.0	42.0	42.8	43.7
54	6.7	6.8	7.2	7.5	7.8	8.2	8.5	8.7	54	36.0	37.0	38.0	38.8	39.5	40.5	41.3	42.0
56	5.2	5.5	5.6	6.0	6.3	6.5	7.0	7.0	56	34.5	35.5	36.2	37.0	38.0	38.7	39.5	40.5
58	3.7	3.7	4.2	4.5	4.5	5.0	5.0	5.5	58	33.0	34.0	34.7	35.5	36.3	37.0	38.0	38.8
60	2.0	2.2	2.5	2.7	3.0	3.2	3.5	3.5	60	31.5	32.4	33.0	34.0	34.5	35.5	36.0	37.0
62	+0.5	+0.7	+0.8	+1.0	+1.2	+1.5	+1.5	+1.7	62	30.0	30.5	31.5	32.0	33.0	33.5	34.5	35.0
64	−1.2	−1.0	−1.0	−0.8	−0.6	−0.5	−0.3	−0.1	64	28.3	29.0	29.6	30.5	31.0	31.8	32.5	33.3
66	3.0	2.8	2.6	2.5	2.4	2.3	2.0	2.0	66	26.5	27.3	28.0	28.5	29.3	30.0	30.7	31.5
68	4.5	4.5	4.4	4.3	4.2	4.0	4.0	4.0	68	25.0	25.5	26.3	26.8	27.5	28.0	28.8	29.5
70	6.3	6.2	6.2	6.1	6.0	6.0	5.8	5.8	70	23.3	23.8	24.5	25.0	25.5	26.2	27.0	27.5
72	8.0	8.0	8.0	8.0	8.0	8.0	7.8	7.8	72	21.5	22.0	22.5	23.3	23.8	24.5	25.0	25.5
74	9.7	9.7	9.7	9.7	9.7	9.7	9.7	9.7	74	19.7	20.3	20.7	21.2	22.0	22.5	23.0	23.5
76	11.5	11.5	11.5	11.5	11.6	11.7	11.7	11.7	76	18.0	18.5	19.0	19.5	20.0	20.5	21.0	21.5
78	13.5	13.5	13.5	13.6	13.6	13.7	13.7	13.7	78	16.0	16.5	17.0	17.5	18.0	18.5	19.0	19.5
80	15.4	15.4	15.4	15.5	15.6	15.7	15.7	16.0	80	14.2	14.7	15.3	15.5	16.0	16.5	17.0	17.5
82	17.0	17.0	17.2	17.3	17.5	17.7	17.8	18.0	82	12.5	13.0	13.3	13.5	14.0	14.5	15.0	15.5
84	18.8	19.0	19.2	19.3	19.5	19.7	19.9	20.0	84	10.5	11.0	11.5	11.7	12.0	12.5	13.0	13.4
86	20.8	21.0	21.0	21.2	21.5	21.7	22.0	22.0	86	8.8	9.0	9.5	9.8	10.0	10.5	11.0	11.3
88	22.6	22.8	23.0	23.2	23.4	23.7	24.0	24.2	88	7.0	7.2	7.5	8.0	8.3	8.5	8.7	9.0
90									90								

HEIGHT OF EYE CORRECTION (Moon Only)

Add

Height of eye (m)	0	1.5	3	4.6	6	7.6	9	10.7	12	14	15	17	18	20	21	23	24	26	30
Height of eye (ft)	0	5	10	15	20	25	30	35	40	45	50	55	60	65	70	75	80	85	100
Corr		9.8'	7.6'	6.7'	6.0'	5.5'	5.0'	4.5'	4.0'	3.5'	3.2'	3.0'	2.5'	2.3'	2.0'	1.7'	1.3'	1.0'	0.8'	0.0'

Notes:

This table is in two parts. The upper table corrects for semi-diameter, parallax, and refraction. The Horizontal Parallax figure required for the top line varies daily and can be found on the first of the monthly pages. The lower table is especially formulated to go with the upper table so that dip is always added.

CORRECTIONS

STAR OR PLANET ALTITUDE TOTAL CORRECTION TABLE
Always subtract

		1.5	3.0	4.6	Height of eye above sea level									
	m	1.5	3.0	4.6	6.0	7.6	9.0	10.7	12	13.7	15	16.8	18	21.3
	ft	5	10	15	20	25	30	35	40	45	50	55	60	70
	°	′	′	′	′	′	′	′	′	′	′	′	′	′
	9	8.0	8.9	9.6	10.3	10.7	11.2	11.6	12.0	12.4	12.8	13.1	13.5	14.1
	10	7.4	8.4	9.1	9.7	10.2	10.6	11.1	11.5	11.8	12.2	12.5	12.9	13.5
	11	7.0	7.9	8.6	9.2	9.7	10.2	10.6	11.0	11.4	11.8	12.0	12.4	13.0
	12	6.6	7.5	8.2	8.8	9.3	9.8	10.2	10.6	11.0	11.4	11.6	12.0	12.6
	13	6.2	7.2	7.9	8.4	9.0	9.4	9.9	10.3	10.6	11.0	11.3	11.6	12.3
	14	5.9	6.9	7.6	8.1	8.6	9.2	9.6	10.0	10.3	10.7	11.0	11.3	12.0
	15	5.7	6.6	7.3	7.9	8.4	8.9	9.3	9.7	10.1	10.4	10.8	11.1	11.7
	16	5.5	6.4	7.1	7.7	8.2	8.7	9.1	9.5	9.9	10.2	10.5	10.9	11.5
	17	5.3	6.2	6.9	7.5	8.0	8.5	8.9	9.3	9.7	10.0	10.3	10.7	11.3
Sextant Altitude	18	5.1	6.0	6.7	7.3	7.8	8.3	8.7	9.1	9.5	9.8	10.2	10.5	11.1
	19	4.9	5.8	6.5	7.1	7.6	8.1	8.5	8.9	9.3	9.7	10.0	11.0	11.0
	20	4.8	5.7	6.4	7.0	7.5	8.0	8.4	8.8	9.2	9.6	9.9	10.2	10.8
	25	4.2	5.1	5.8	6.4	6.9	7.4	7.8	8.2	8.6	9.0	9.3	9.6	10.2
	30	3.8	4.7	5.4	6.0	6.5	7.0	7.4	7.8	8.2	8.6	8.9	9.2	9.8
	35	3.5	4.4	5.1	5.7	6.3	6.7	7.2	7.6	7.9	8.3	8.6	8.9	9.5
	40	3.3	4.2	4.9	5.5	6.0	6.5	6.9	7.3	7.7	8.1	8.4	8.7	9.3
	50	3.0	3.9	4.6	5.2	5.7	6.2	6.6	7.0	7.4	7.7	8.1	8.4	9.0
	60	2.7	3.6	4.4	4.9	5.5	5.9	6.4	6.8	7.1	7.5	7.8	8.1	8.8
	70	2.5	3.4	4.1	4.7	5.3	5.7	6.2	6.6	6.9	7.3	7.6	7.9	8.6
	80	2.3	3.3	4.0	4.6	5.1	5.5	6.0	6.4	6.7	7.1	7.4	7.8	8.4
	90	2.2	3.1	3.8	4.4	4.9	5.4	5.8	6.2	6.6	6.9	7.3	7.6	8.2

Note: This table combines the corrections for refraction and dip included in the table on page E 92, but not parallax or semi-diameter since these are of no significance in the case of star or planet sights.

MOON GHA CORRECTION TABLE (HOURS)
Always add

Var/hr 14°20′	14°20.5′	14°21′	14°21.5′	14°22′	14°22.5′	14°23′	14°23.5′	14°24′	14°24.5′	14°25′	14°25.5′
° ′	° ′	° ′	° ′	° ′	° ′	° ′	° ′	° ′	° ′	° ′	° ′
1 14 20.0	14 20.5	14 21.0	14 21.5	14 22.0	14 22.5	14 23.0	14 23.5	14 24.0	14 24.5	14 25.0	14 25.5
2 28 40.0	28 41.0	28 42.0	28 43.0	28 44.0	28 45.0	28 46.0	28 47.0	28 48.0	28 49.0	28 50.0	28 51.0
3 43 00.0	43 01.5	43 03.0	43 04.5	43 06.0	43 07.5	43 09.0	43 10.5	43 12.0	43 13.5	43 15.0	43 16.5
4 57 20.0	57 22.0	57 24.0	57 26.0	57 28.0	57 30.0	57 32.0	57 34.0	57 36.0	57 38.0	57 40.0	57 42.0
5 71 40.0	71 42.5	71 45.0	71 47.5	71 50.0	71 52.5	71 55.0	71 57.5	72 00.0	72 02.5	72 05.0	72 07.5

Hours

Var/hr 14°26′	14°26.5′	14°27′	14°27.5′	14°28′	14°28.5′	14°29′	14°29.5′	14°30′	14°30.5′	14°31′	14°31.5′
1 14 26.0	14 26.5	14 27.0	14 27.5	14 28.0	14°28.5	14 29.0	14 29.5	14 30.0	14 30.5	14 31.0	14 31.5
2 28 52.0	28 53.0	28 54.0	28 55.0	28 56.0	28 57.0	28 58.0	28 59.0	29 00.0	29 01.0	29 02.0	29 03.0
3 43 18.0	43 19.5	43 21.0	43 22.5	43 24.0	43 25.5	43 27.0	43 28.5	43 30.0	43 31.5	43 33.0	43 34.5
4 57 44.0	57 46.0	57 48.0	57 50.0	57 52.0	57 54.0	57 56.0	57 58.0	58 00.0	58 02.0	58 04.0	58 06.0
5 72 10.0	72 12.5	72 15.0	72 17.5	72 20.0	72 22.5	72 25.0	72 27.5	72 30.0	72 32.5	72 35.0	72 37.5

Hours

Var/hr 14°32′	14°32.5′	14°33′	14°33.5′	14°34′	14°34.5′	14°35′	14°35.5′	14°36′	14°36.5′	14°37′	14°37.5′
1 14 32.0	14 32.5	14 33.0	14 33.5	14 34.0	14 34.5	14 35.0	14 35.5	14 36.0	14 36.5	14 37.0	14 37.5
2 29 04.0	29 05.0	29 06.0	29 07.0	29 08.0	29 09.0	29 10.0	29 11.0	29 12.0	29 13.0	29 14.0	29 15.0
3 43 36.0	43 37.5	43 39.0	43 40.5	43 42.0	43 43.5	43 45.0	43 46.5	43 48.0	43 49.5	43 51.0	43 52.5
4 58 08.0	58 10.0	58 12.0	58 14.0	58 16.0	58 18.0	58 20.0	58 22.0	58 24.0	58 26.0	58 28.0	58 30.0
5 72 40.0	72 42.5	72 45.0	72 47.5	72 50.0	72 52.5	72 55.0	72 57.5	73 00.0	73 02.5	73 05.0	73 07.5

Hours

Note: The correction for Moon GHA is taken in three parts. Using the figure for variation per hour given in the monthly pages, you get the correction for hours from the table above and the correction for minutes from the tables on the next two pages. Finally, take the correction for seconds from the righthand side of whichever minute table you used.

MOON GHA CORRECTION TABLE (MINUTES)

Var/hr	14°20'	14°21'	14°22'	14°23'	14°24'	14°25'	14°26'	14°27'	14°28'	Diff 1'	Sec	Corr
0	0 00.0	0 00.0	0 00.0	0 00.0	0 00.0	0 00.0	0 00.0	0 00.0	0 00.0	0.0	0	0.0
1	0 14.3	0 14.4	0 14.4	0 14.4	0 14.4	0 14.4	0 14.4	0 14.4	0 14.5	0.0	1	0.2
2	0 28.7	0 28.7	0 28.7	0 28.8	0 28.8	0 28.8	0 28.9	0 28.9	0 28.9	0.0	2	0.5
3	0 43.0	0 43.0	0 43.1	0 43.2	0 43.2	0 43.2	0 43.3	0 43.3	0 43.4	0.0	3	0.7
4	0 57.3	0 57.4	0 57.5	0 57.5	0 57.6	0 57.7	0 57.7	0 57.8	0 57.9	0.1	4	1.0
5	1 11.7	1 11.8	1 11.8	1 11.9	1 12.0	1 12.1	1 12.2	1 12.2	1 12.3	0.1	5	1.2
6	1 26.0	1 26.1	1 26.2	1 26.3	1 26.4	1 26.5	1 26.6	1 26.7	1 26.8	0.1	6	1.4
7	1 40.3	1 40.4	1 40.6	1 40.7	1 40.8	1 40.9	1 41.2	1 41.2	1 41.3	0.1	7	1.7
8	1 54.7	1 54.8	1 54.9	1 55.1	1 55.2	1 55.3	1 55.5	1 55.6	1 55.7	0.1	8	1.9
9	2 09.0	2 09.2	2 09.3	2 09.4	2 09.6	2 09.8	2 09.9	2 10.0	2 10.2	0.2	9	2.2
10	2 23.3	2 23.5	2 23.7	2 23.8	2 24.0	2 24.2	2 24.3	2 24.5	2 24.7	0.2	10	2.4
11	2 37.7	2 37.8	2 38.0	2 38.2	2 38.4	2 38.6	2 38.8	2 39.0	2 39.1	0.2	11	2.6
12	2 52.0	2 52.2	2 52.4	2 52.6	2 52.8	2 53.0	2 53.2	2 53.4	2 53.6	0.2	12	2.9
13	3 06.3	3 06.6	3 06.8	3 07.0	3 07.2	3 07.4	3 07.6	3 07.8	3 08.1	0.2	13	3.1
14	3 20.7	3 20.9	3 21.1	3 21.4	3 21.6	3 21.8	3 22.1	3 22.3	3 22.5	0.2	14	3.4
15	3 35.0	3 35.2	3 35.5	3 35.8	3 36.0	3 36.2	3 36.5	3 36.8	3 37.0	0.2	15	3.6
16	3 49.3	3 49.6	3 49.9	3 50.1	3 50.4	3 50.7	3 50.9	3 51.2	3 51.5	0.3	16	3.8
17	4 03.7	4 04.0	4 04.2	4 04.5	4 04.8	4 05.1	4 05.4	4 05.6	4 05.9	0.3	17	4.1
18	4 18.0	4 18.3	4 18.6	4 18.9	4 19.2	4 19.5	4 19.8	4 20.1	4 20.4	0.3	18	4.3
19	4 32.3	4 32.6	4 33.0	4 33.3	4 33.6	4 33.9	4 34.2	4 34.6	4 34.9	0.3	19	4.6
20	4 46.7	4 47.0	4 47.3	4 47.7	4 48.0	4 48.3	4 48.7	4 49.0	4 49.3	0.3	20	4.8
21	5 01.0	5 01.4	5 01.7	5 02.0	5 02.4	5 02.8	5 03.1	5 03.4	5 03.8	0.4	21	5.0
22	5 15.3	5 15.7	5 16.1	5 16.4	5 16.8	5 17.2	5 17.5	5 17.9	5 18.3	0.4	22	5.3
23	5 29.7	5 30.0	5 30.4	5 30.8	5 31.2	5 31.6	5 32.0	5 32.4	5 32.7	0.4	23	5.5
24	5 44.0	5 44.4	5 44.8	5 45.2	5 45.6	5 46.0	5 46.4	5 46.8	5 47.2	0.4	24	5.8
25	5 58.3	5 58.8	5 59.2	5 59.6	6 00.0	6 00.4	6 00.8	6 01.2	6 01.7	0.4	25	6.0
26	6 12.7	6 13.1	6 13.5	6 14.0	6 14.4	6 14.8	6 15.3	6 15.7	5 16.1	0.4	26	6.2
27	6 27.0	6 27.4	6 27.9	6 28.4	6 28.8	6 29.2	6 29.7	6 30.2	6 30.6	0.4	27	6.5
28	6 41.3	6 41.8	6 42.3	6 42.7	6 43.2	6 43.7	6 44.1	6 44.6	6 45.1	0.5	28	6.7
29	6 55.7	6 56.2	6 56.6	6 57.1	6 57.6	6 58.1	6 58.6	6 59.0	6 59.5	0.5	29	7.0
30	7 10.0	7 10.5	7 11.0	7 11.5	7 12.0	7 12.5	7 13.0	7 13.5	7 14.0	0.5	30	7.2
31	7 24.3	7 24.8	7 25.4	7 25.9	7 26.4	7 26.9	7 27.4	7 28.0	7 28.5	0.5	31	7.4
32	7 38.7	7 39.2	7 39.7	7 40.3	7 40.8	7 41.3	7 41.9	7 42.4	7 42.9	0.5	32	7.7
33	7 53.0	7 53.6	7 54.1	7 54.6	7 55.2	7 55.8	7 56.3	7 56.8	7 57.4	0.6	33	7.9
34	8 07.3	8 07.9	8 08.5	8 09.0	8 09.6	8 10.2	8 10.7	8 11.3	8 11.9	0.6	34	8.2
35	8 21.7	8 22.2	8 22.8	8 23.4	8 24.0	8 24.6	8 25.2	8 25.8	8 26.3	0.6	35	8.4
36	8 36.0	8 36.6	8 37.2	8 37.8	8 38.4	8 39.0	8 39.6	8 40.2	8 40.8	0.6	36	8.6
37	8 50.3	8 51.0	8 51.6	8 52.2	8 52.8	8 53.4	8 54.0	8 54.6	8 55.3	0.6	37	8.9
38	9 04.7	9 05.3	9 05.9	9 06.6	9 07.2	9 07.8	9 08.5	9 09.1	9 09.7	0.6	38	9.1
39	9 19.0	9 19.6	9 20.3	9 21.0	9 21.6	9 22.2	9 22.9	9 23.6	9 24.2	0.6	39	9.4
40	9 33.3	9 34.0	9 34.7	9 35.3	9 36.0	9 36.7	9 37.3	9 38.0	9 38.7	0.7	40	9.6
41	9 47.7	9 48.4	9 49.0	9 49.7	9 50.4	9 51.1	9 51.8	9 52.4	9 53.1	0.7	41	9.8
42	10 02.0	10 02.7	10 03.4	10 04.1	10 04.8	10 05.5	10 06.2	10 06.9	10 07.6	0.7	42	10.1
43	10 16.3	10 17.0	10 17.8	10 18.5	10 19.2	10 19.9	10 20.6	10 21.4	10 22.1	0.7	43	10.3
44	10 30.7	10 31.4	10 32.1	10 32.9	10 33.6	10 34.3	10 35.1	10 35.8	10 36.5	0.7	44	10.6
45	10 45.0	10 45.8	10 46.5	10 47.2	10 48.0	10 48.8	10 49.5	10 50.2	10 51.0	0.8	45	10.8
46	10 59.3	11 00.1	11 00.9	11 01.6	11 02.4	11 03.2	11 03.9	11 04.7	11 05.5	0.8	46	11.0
47	11 13.7	11 14.4	11 15.2	11 16.0	11 16.8	11 17.6	11 18.4	11 19.2	11 19.9	0.8	47	11.3
48	11 28.0	11 28.8	11 29.6	11 30.4	11 31.2	11 32.0	11 32.8	11 33.6	11 34.4	0.8	48	11.5
49	11 42.3	11 43.2	11 44.0	11 44.8	11 45.6	11 46.4	11 47.2	11 48.0	11 48.9	0.8	49	11.8
50	11 56.7	11 57.5	11 58.3	11 59.2	12 00.0	12 00.8	12 01.7	12 02.5	12 03.3	0.8	50	12.0
51	12 11.0	12 11.8	12 12.7	12 13.6	12 14.4	12 15.2	12 16.1	12 17.0	12 17.8	0.8	51	12.2
52	12 25.3	12 26.2	12 27.1	12 27.9	12 28.8	12 29.7	12 30.5	12 31.4	12 32.3	0.9	52	12.5
53	12 39.7	12 40.6	12 41.4	12 42.3	12 43.2	12 44.1	12 45.0	12 45.8	12 46.7	0.9	53	12.7
54	12 54.0	12 54.9	12 55.8	12 56.7	12 57.6	12 58.5	12 59.4	13 00.3	13 01.2	0.9	54	13.0
55	13 08.3	13 09.2	13 10.2	13 11.1	13 12.0	13 12.9	13 13.8	13 14.8	13 15.7	0.9	55	13.2
56	13 22.7	13 23.6	13 24.5	13 25.5	13 26.4	13 27.3	13 28.3	13 29.2	13 30.1	0.9	56	13.4
57	13 37.0	13 38.0	13 38.9	13 39.8	13 40.8	13 41.8	13 42.7	13 43.6	13 44.6	1.0	57	13.7
58	13 51.3	13 52.3	13 53.3	13 54.2	13 55.2	13 56.2	13 57.1	13 58.1	13 59.1	1.0	58	13.9
59	14 05.7	14 06.6	14 07.6	14 08.6	14 09.6	14 10.6	14 11.6	14 12.6	14 13.5	1.0	59	14.1
60	14 20.0	14 21.0	14 22.0	14 23.0	14 24.0	14 25.0	14 26.0	14 27.0	14 28.0	1.0	60	14.4

Minutes

CORRECTIONS

MOON GHA CORRECTION TABLE (MINUTES)

Var/hr	14°29'	14°30'	14°31'	14°32'	14°33'	14°34'	14°35'	14°36'	14°37'	Diff 1'	Sec	Corr
0	0 00.0	0 00.0	0 00.0	0 00.0	0 00.0	0 00.0	0 00.0	0 00.0	0 00.0	0.0	0	0.0
1	0 14.5	0 14.5	0 14.5	0 14.6	0 14.6	0 14.6	0 14.6	0 14.6	0 14.6	0.0	1	0.2
2	0 29.0	0 29.0	0 29.0	0 29.1	0 29.1	0 29.1	0 29.2	0 29.2	0 29.2	0.0	2	0.5
3	0 43.4	0 43.5	0 43.6	0 43.6	0 43.6	0 43.7	0 43.8	0 43.8	0 43.8	0.0	3	0.7
4	0 57.9	0 58.0	0 58.1	0 58.1	0 58.2	0 58.3	0 58.3	0 58.4	0 58.5	0.1	4	1.0
5	1 12.4	1 12.5	1 12.6	1 12.7	1 12.8	1 12.8	1 12.9	1 13.0	1 13.1	0.1	5	1.2
6	1 26.9	1 27.0	1 27.1	1 27.2	1 27.3	1 27.4	1 27.5	1 27.6	1 27.7	0.1	6	1.5
7	1 41.4	1 41.5	1 41.6	1 41.7	1 41.8	1 42.0	1 42.1	1 42.2	1 42.3	0.1	7	1.7
8	1 55.9	1 56.0	1 56.1	1 56.3	1 56.4	1 56.5	1 56.7	1 56.8	1 56.9	0.1	8	1.9
9	2 10.4	2 10.5	2 10.6	2 10.8	2 11.0	2 11.1	2 11.2	2 11.4	2 11.6	0.2	9	2.2
10	2 24.8	2 25.0	2 25.2	2 25.2	2 25.5	2 25.7	2 25.8	2 26.0	2 26.2	0.2	10	2.4
11	2 39.3	2 39.5	2 39.7	2 39.9	2 40.0	2 40.2	2 40.4	2 40.6	2 40.8	0.2	11	2.7
12	2 53.8	2 54.0	2 54.2	2 54.4	2 54.6	2 54.8	2 55.0	2 55.2	2 55.4	0.2	12	2.9
13	3 08.3	3 08.5	3 08.7	3 08.9	3 09.2	3 09.4	3 09.6	3 09.8	3 10.0	0.2	13	3.2
14	3 22.8	3 23.0	3 23.2	3 23.5	3 23.7	3 23.9	3 24.2	3 24.4	3 24.6	0.2	14	3.4
15	3 37.2	3 37.5	3 37.8	3 38.0	3 38.2	3 38.5	3 38.8	3 39.0	3 39.2	0.2	15	3.6
16	3 51.7	3 52.0	3 52.3	3 52.5	3 52.8	3 53.1	3 53.3	3 53.6	3 53.9	0.3	16	3.9
17	4 06.2	4 06.5	4 06.8	4 07.1	4 07.4	4 07.6	4 07.9	4 08.2	4 08.5	0.3	17	4.1
18	4 20.7	4 21.0	4 21.3	4 21.6	4 21.9	4 22.2	4 22.5	4 22.8	4 23.1	0.3	18	4.4
19	4 35.2	4 35.5	4 35.8	4 36.1	4 36.4	4 36.8	4 37.1	4 37.4	4 37.7	0.3	19	4.6
20	4 49.7	4 50.0	4 50.3	4 50.7	4 51.0	4 51.3	4 51.7	4 52.0	4 52.3	0.3	20	4.9
21	5 04.2	5 04.5	5 04.8	5 05.2	5 05.6	5 05.9	5 06.2	5 06.6	5 07.0	0.4	21	5.1
22	5 18.6	5 19.0	5 19.4	5 19.7	5 20.1	5 20.5	5 20.8	5 21.2	5 21.6	0.4	22	5.3
23	5 33.1	5 33.5	5 33.9	5 34.3	5 34.6	5 35.0	5 35.4	5 35.8	5 36.2	0.4	23	5.6
24	5 47.6	5 48.0	5 48.4	5 48.8	5 49.2	5 49.6	5 50.0	5 50.4	5 50.8	0.4	24	5.8
25	6 02.1	6 02.5	6 02.9	6 03.3	6 03.8	6 04.2	6 04.6	6 05.0	6 05.4	0.4	25	6.1
26	6 16.6	6 17.0	6 17.4	6 17.9	6 18.3	6 18.7	6 19.2	6 19.6	6 20.0	0.4	26	6.3
27	6 31.0	6 31.5	6 32.0	6 32.4	6 32.8	6 33.3	6 33.8	6 34.2	6 34.6	0.4	27	6.5
28	6 45.5	6 46.0	6 46.5	6 46.9	6 47.4	6 47.9	6 48.3	6 48.8	6 49.3	0.5	28	6.8
29	7 00.0	7 00.5	7 01.0	7 01.5	7 02.0	7 02.4	7 02.9	7 03.4	7 03.9	0.5	29	7.0
30	7 14.5	7 15.0	7 15.5	7 16.0	7 16.5	7 17.0	7 17.5	7 18.0	7 18.5	0.5	30	7.3
31	7 29.0	7 29.5	7 30.0	7 30.5	7 31.0	7 31.6	7 32.1	7 32.6	7 33.1	0.5	31	7.5
32	7 43.5	7 44.0	7 44.5	7 45.1	7 45.6	7 46.1	7 46.7	7 47.2	7 47.7	0.5	32	7.8
33	7 58.0	7 58.5	7 59.0	7 59.6	8 00.2	8 00.7	8 01.2	8 01.8	8 02.4	0.6	33	8.0
34	8 12.4	8 13.0	8 13.6	8 14.1	8 14.7	8 15.3	8 15.8	8 16.4	8 17.0	0.6	34	8.2
35	8 26.9	8 27.5	8 28.1	8 28.7	8 29.2	8 29.8	8 30.4	8 31.0	8 31.6	0.6	35	8.5
36	8 41.4	8 42.0	8 42.6	8 43.2	8 43.8	8 44.4	8 45.0	8 45.6	8 46.2	0.6	36	8.7
37	8 55.9	8 56.5	8 57.1	8 57.7	8 58.4	8 59.0	8 59.6	9 00.2	9 00.8	0.6	37	9.0
38	9 10.4	9 11.0	9 11.6	9 12.3	9 12.9	9 13.5	9 14.2	9 14.8	9 15.4	0.6	38	9.2
39	9 24.8	9 25.5	9 26.2	9 26.8	9 27.4	9 28.1	9 28.8	9 29.4	9 30.0	0.6	39	9.5
40	9 39.3	9 40.0	9 40.7	9 41.3	9 42.0	9 42.7	9 43.3	9 44.0	9 44.7	0.7	40	9.7
41	9 53.8	9 54.5	9 55.2	9 55.9	9 56.6	9 57.2	9 57.9	9 58.6	9 59.3	0.7	41	9.9
42	10 08.3	10 09.0	10 09.7	10 10.4	10 11.1	10 11.8	10 12.5	10 13.2	10 13.9	0.7	42	10.2
43	10 22.8	10 23.5	10 24.2	10 24.9	10 25.6	10 26.4	10 27.1	10 27.8	10 28.5	0.7	43	10.4
44	10 37.3	10 38.0	10 38.7	10 39.5	10 40.2	10 40.9	10 41.7	10 42.2	10 43.1	0.7	44	10.7
45	10 51.8	10 52.5	10 53.2	10 54.0	10 54.8	10 55.5	10 56.2	10 57.0	10 57.8	0.8	45	10.9
46	11 06.2	11 07.0	11 07.8	11 08.5	11 09.3	11 10.1	11 10.8	11 11.6	11 12.4	0.8	46	11.2
47	11 20.7	11 21.5	11 22.3	11 23.1	11 23.8	11 24.6	11 25.4	11 26.2	11 27.0	0.8	47	11.4
48	11 35.2	11 36.0	11 36.8	11 37.6	11 38.4	11 39.2	11 40.0	11 40.8	11 41.6	0.8	48	11.6
49	11 49.7	11 50.5	11 51.3	11 52.1	11 53.0	11 53.8	11 54.6	11 55.4	11 56.2	0.8	49	11.9
50	12 04.2	12 05.0	12 05.8	12 06.7	12 07.5	12 08.3	12 09.2	12 10.0	12 10.8	0.8	50	12.1
51	12 18.6	12 19.5	12 20.4	12 21.2	12 22.0	12 22.9	12 23.8	12 24.6	12 25.4	0.8	51	12.4
52	12 33.1	12 34.0	12 34.9	12 35.7	12 36.6	12 37.5	12 38.3	12 39.2	12 40.1	0.9	52	12.6
53	12 47.6	12 48.5	12 49.4	12 50.3	12 51.2	12 52.0	12 52.9	12 53.8	12 54.7	0.9	53	12.9
54	13 02.1	13 03.0	13 03.9	13 04.8	13 05.7	13 06.6	13 07.5	13 08.4	13 09.3	0.9	54	13.1
55	13 16.6	13 17.5	13 18.4	13 19.3	13 20.2	13 21.2	13 22.1	13 23.0	13 23.9	0.9	55	13.3
56	13 31.1	13 32.0	13 32.9	13 33.9	13 34.8	13 35.7	13 36.7	13 37.6	13 38.5	0.9	56	13.6
57	13 45.6	13 46.5	13 47.4	13 48.4	13 49.4	13 50.3	13 51.2	13 52.2	13 53.2	1.0	57	13.9
58	14 00.0	14 01.0	14 02.0	14 02.9	14 03.9	14 04.9	14 05.8	14 06.8	14 07.8	1.0	58	14.1
59	14 14.5	14 15.5	14 16.5	14 17.5	14 18.4	14 19.4	14 20.4	14 21.4	14 22.4	1.0	59	14.3
60	14 29.0	14 30.0	14 31.0	14 32.0	14 33.0	14 34.0	14 35.0	14 36.0	14 37.0	1.0	60	14.6

Minutes

MOON DECLINATION CORRECTION TABLE

Var/hr	0.0'	1.0'	2.0'	3.0'	4.0'	5.0'	6.0'	7.0'	8.0'	9.0'	10.0'	11.0'	12.0'	13.0'	14.0'	15.0'	16.0'	17.0'	18.0'
0	0.0	0.0	0.0	0.0	0.0	0.0	0.0	0.0	0.0	0.0	0.0	0.0	0.0	0.0	0.0	0.0	0.0	0.0	0.0
1	0.0	0.0	0.0	0.0	0.1	0.1	0.1	0.1	0.1	0.2	0.2	0.2	0.2	0.2	0.2	0.2	0.3	0.3	0.3
2	0.0	0.0	0.1	0.1	0.1	0.2	0.2	0.2	0.3	0.3	0.3	0.4	0.4	0.4	0.5	0.5	0.5	0.6	0.6
3	0.0	0.0	0.1	0.2	0.2	0.2	0.3	0.4	0.4	0.4	0.5	0.6	0.6	0.6	0.7	0.8	0.8	0.8	0.9
4	0.0	0.1	0.1	0.2	0.3	0.3	0.4	0.5	0.5	0.6	0.7	0.7	0.8	0.9	0.9	1.0	1.1	1.1	1.2
5	0.0	0.1	0.2	0.2	0.3	0.4	0.5	0.6	0.7	0.8	0.8	0.9	1.0	1.1	1.2	1.2	1.3	1.4	1.5
6	0.0	0.1	0.2	0.3	0.4	0.5	0.6	0.7	0.8	0.9	1.0	1.1	1.2	1.3	1.4	1.5	1.6	1.7	1.8
7	0.0	0.1	0.2	0.4	0.5	0.6	0.7	0.8	0.9	1.0	1.2	1.3	1.4	1.5	1.6	1.8	1.9	2.0	2.1
8	0.0	0.1	0.3	0.4	0.5	0.7	0.8	0.9	1.1	1.2	1.3	1.5	1.6	1.7	1.9	2.0	2.1	2.3	2.4
9	0.0	0.2	0.3	0.4	0.6	0.8	0.9	1.0	1.2	1.4	1.5	1.6	1.8	2.0	2.1	2.2	2.4	2.6	2.7
10	0.0	0.2	0.3	0.5	0.7	0.8	1.0	1.2	1.3	1.5	1.7	1.8	2.0	2.2	2.3	2.5	2.7	2.8	3.0
11	0.0	0.2	0.4	0.6	0.7	0.9	1.1	1.3	1.5	1.6	1.8	2.0	2.2	2.4	2.6	2.8	2.9	3.1	3.3
12	0.0	0.2	0.4	0.6	0.8	1.0	1.2	1.4	1.6	1.8	2.0	2.2	2.4	2.6	2.8	3.0	3.2	3.4	3.6
13	0.0	0.2	0.4	0.6	0.9	1.1	1.3	1.5	1.7	2.0	2.2	2.4	2.6	2.8	3.0	3.2	3.5	3.7	3.9
14	0.0	0.2	0.5	0.7	0.9	1.2	1.4	1.6	1.9	2.1	2.3	2.6	2.8	3.0	3.3	3.5	3.7	4.0	4.2
15	0.0	0.2	0.5	0.8	1.0	1.2	1.5	1.8	2.0	2.2	2.5	2.8	3.0	3.2	3.5	3.8	4.0	4.2	4.5
16	0.0	0.3	0.5	0.8	1.1	1.3	1.6	1.9	2.1	2.4	2.7	2.9	3.2	3.5	3.7	4.0	4.3	4.5	4.8
17	0.0	0.3	0.6	0.8	1.1	1.4	1.7	2.0	2.3	2.6	2.8	3.1	3.4	3.7	4.0	4.2	4.5	4.8	5.1
18	0.0	0.3	0.6	0.9	1.2	1.5	1.8	2.1	2.4	2.7	3.0	3.3	3.6	3.9	4.2	4.5	4.8	5.1	5.4
19	0.0	0.3	0.6	1.0	1.3	1.6	1.9	2.2	2.5	2.8	3.2	3.5	3.8	4.1	4.4	4.8	5.1	5.4	5.7
20	0.0	0.3	0.7	1.0	1.3	1.7	2.0	2.3	2.7	3.0	3.3	3.7	4.0	4.3	4.7	5.0	5.3	5.7	6.0
21	0.0	0.4	0.7	1.0	1.4	1.8	2.1	2.4	2.8	3.2	3.5	3.8	4.2	4.6	4.9	5.2	5.6	6.0	6.3
22	0.0	0.4	0.7	1.1	1.5	1.8	2.2	2.6	2.9	3.3	3.7	4.0	4.4	4.8	5.1	5.5	5.9	6.2	6.6
23	0.0	0.4	0.8	1.2	1.5	1.9	2.3	2.7	3.1	3.4	3.8	4.2	4.6	5.0	5.4	5.8	6.1	6.5	6.9
24	0.0	0.4	0.8	1.2	1.6	2.0	2.4	2.8	3.2	3.6	4.0	4.4	4.8	5.2	5.6	6.0	6.4	6.8	7.2
25	0.0	0.4	0.8	1.2	1.7	2.1	2.5	2.9	3.3	3.8	4.2	4.6	5.0	5.4	5.8	6.2	6.7	7.1	7.5
26	0.0	0.4	0.9	1.3	1.7	2.2	2.6	3.0	3.5	3.9	4.3	4.8	5.2	5.6	6.1	6.5	6.9	7.4	7.8
27	0.0	0.4	0.9	1.3	1.8	2.2	2.7	3.2	3.6	4.0	4.5	5.0	5.4	5.8	6.3	6.8	7.2	7.6	8.1
28	0.0	0.5	0.9	1.4	1.9	2.3	2.8	3.3	3.7	4.2	4.7	5.1	5.6	6.1	6.5	7.0	7.5	7.9	8.4
29	0.0	0.5	1.0	1.4	1.9	2.4	2.9	3.4	3.9	4.4	4.8	5.3	5.8	6.3	6.8	7.2	7.7	8.2	8.7
30	0.0	0.5	1.0	1.5	2.0	2.5	3.0	3.5	4.0	4.5	5.0	5.5	6.0	6.5	7.0	7.5	8.0	8.5	9.0
31	0.0	0.5	1.0	1.6	2.1	2.6	3.1	3.6	4.1	4.6	5.2	5.7	6.2	6.7	7.2	7.8	8.3	8.8	9.3
32	0.0	0.5	1.1	1.6	2.1	2.7	3.2	3.7	4.3	4.8	5.3	5.9	6.4	6.9	7.5	8.0	8.5	9.1	9.6
33	0.0	0.6	1.1	1.6	2.2	2.8	3.3	3.8	4.4	5.0	5.5	6.0	6.6	7.2	7.7	8.2	8.8	9.4	9.9
34	0.0	0.6	1.1	1.7	2.3	2.8	3.4	4.0	4.5	5.1	5.7	6.2	6.8	7.4	7.9	8.5	9.1	9.6	10.2
35	0.0	0.6	1.2	1.8	2.3	2.9	3.5	4.1	4.7	5.2	5.8	6.4	7.0	7.6	8.2	8.8	9.3	9.9	10.5
36	0.0	0.6	1.2	1.8	2.4	3.0	3.6	4.2	4.8	5.4	6.0	6.6	7.2	7.8	8.4	9.0	9.6	10.2	10.8
37	0.0	0.6	1.2	1.8	2.5	3.1	3.7	4.3	4.9	5.6	6.2	6.8	7.4	8.0	8.6	9.2	9.9	10.5	11.1
38	0.0	0.6	1.3	1.9	2.5	3.2	3.8	4.4	5.1	5.7	6.3	7.0	7.6	8.2	8.9	9.5	10.1	10.8	11.4
39	0.0	0.6	1.3	2.0	2.6	3.2	3.9	4.6	5.2	5.8	6.5	7.2	7.8	8.4	9.1	9.8	10.4	11.0	11.7
40	0.0	0.7	1.3	2.0	2.7	3.3	4.0	4.7	5.3	6.0	6.7	7.3	8.0	8.7	9.3	10.0	10.7	11.3	12.0
41	0.0	0.7	1.4	2.0	2.7	3.4	4.1	4.8	5.5	6.2	6.8	7.5	8.2	8.9	9.6	10.2	10.9	11.6	12.3
42	0.0	0.7	1.4	2.1	2.8	3.5	4.2	4.9	5.6	6.3	7.0	7.7	8.4	9.1	9.8	10.5	11.2	11.9	12.6
43	0.0	0.7	1.4	2.2	2.9	3.6	4.3	5.0	5.7	6.4	7.2	7.9	8.6	9.3	10.0	10.8	11.5	12.2	12.9
44	0.0	0.7	1.5	2.2	2.9	3.7	4.4	5.1	5.9	6.6	7.3	8.1	8.8	9.5	10.3	11.0	11.7	12.5	13.2
45	0.0	0.7	1.5	2.2	3.0	3.8	4.5	5.2	6.0	6.8	7.5	8.2	9.0	9.8	10.5	11.2	12.0	12.8	13.5
46	0.0	0.8	1.5	2.3	3.1	3.8	4.6	5.4	6.1	6.9	7.7	8.4	9.2	10.0	10.7	11.5	12.3	13.0	13.8
47	0.0	0.8	1.6	2.4	3.1	3.9	4.7	5.5	6.3	7.0	7.8	8.6	9.4	10.2	11.0	11.8	12.5	13.3	14.1
48	0.0	0.8	1.6	2.4	3.2	4.0	4.8	5.6	6.4	7.2	8.0	8.8	9.6	10.4	11.2	12.0	12.8	13.6	14.4
49	0.0	0.8	1.6	2.4	3.3	4.1	4.9	5.7	6.5	7.4	8.2	9.0	9.8	10.6	11.4	12.2	13.1	13.9	14.7
50	0.0	0.8	1.7	2.5	3.3	4.2	5.0	5.8	6.7	7.5	8.3	9.2	10.0	10.8	11.7	12.5	13.3	14.2	15.0
51	0.0	0.8	1.7	2.6	3.4	4.2	5.1	6.0	6.8	7.6	8.5	9.4	10.2	11.0	11.9	12.8	13.6	14.4	15.3
52	0.0	0.9	1.7	2.6	3.5	4.3	5.2	6.1	6.9	7.8	8.7	9.5	10.4	11.3	12.1	13.0	13.9	14.7	15.6
53	0.0	0.9	1.8	2.6	3.5	4.4	5.3	6.2	7.1	8.0	8.8	9.7	10.6	11.5	12.4	13.2	14.1	15.0	15.9
54	0.0	0.9	1.8	2.7	3.6	4.5	5.4	6.3	7.2	8.1	9.0	9.9	10.8	11.7	12.6	13.5	14.4	15.3	16.2
55	0.0	0.9	1.8	2.8	3.7	4.6	5.5	6.4	7.3	8.2	9.2	10.1	11.0	11.9	12.8	13.8	14.7	15.6	16.5
56	0.0	0.9	1.9	2.8	3.7	4.7	5.6	6.5	7.5	8.4	9.3	10.3	11.2	12.1	13.1	14.0	14.9	15.9	16.8
57	0.0	1.0	1.9	2.8	3.8	4.8	5.7	6.6	7.6	8.6	9.5	10.4	11.4	12.4	13.3	14.2	15.2	16.2	17.1
58	0.0	1.0	1.9	2.9	3.9	4.8	5.8	6.8	7.7	8.7	9.7	10.6	11.6	12.6	13.5	14.5	15.5	16.4	17.4
59	0.0	1.0	2.0	3.0	3.9	4.9	5.9	6.9	7.9	8.8	9.8	10.8	11.8	12.8	13.8	14.8	15.7	16.7	17.7
60	0.0	1.0	2.0	3.0	4.0	5.0	6.0	7.0	8.0	9.0	10.0	11.0	12.0	13.0	14.0	15.0	16.0	17.0	18.0

Minutes (row label, left margin)

Note: The table above gives a Moon declination correction for minutes based on the Var/Hr taken from the monthly page. The correction for hours is simply Var/Hr multiplied by hours.

CORRECTIONS

MOON MERIDIAN PASSAGE TRANSIT CORRECTION TABLE

	Daily difference of Meridian Passage											
Minutes	39	42	45	48	51	54	57	60	63	66	69	
Longitude E/W												
0°	0	0	0	0	0	0	0	0	0	0	0	**0°**
10°	1	1	1	1	1	1	2	2	2	2	2	**10°**
20°	2	2	2	3	3	3	3	3	3	4	4	**20°**
30°	3	3	4	4	4	4	5	5	5	5	6	**30°**
40°	4	5	5	5	6	6	6	7	7	7	8	**40°**
50°	5	6	6	7	7	7	8	8	9	9	10	**50°**
60°	6	7	7	8	8	9	9	10	10	11	11	**60°**
70°	8	8	9	9	10	10	11	12	12	13	13	**70°**
80°	9	9	10	11	11	12	13	13	14	15	15	**80°**
90°	10	10	11	12	13	13	14	15	16	16	17	**90°**
100°	11	12	12	13	14	15	16	17	17	18	19	**100°**
110°	12	13	14	15	16	16	17	18	19	20	21	**110°**
120°	13	14	15	16	17	18	19	20	21	22	23	**120°**
130°	14	15	16	17	18	19	21	22	23	24	25	**130°**
140°	15	16	17	19	20	21	22	23	24	26	27	**140°**
150°	16	17	19	20	21	22	24	25	26	27	29	**150°**
160°	17	19	20	21	23	24	25	27	28	29	31	**160°**
170°	18	20	21	23	24	25	27	28	30	31	33	**170°**
180°	19	21	22	24	25	27	28	30	31	33	34	**180°**

Note: Apply correction in **minutes** to Time of Meridian Passage given in the monthly pages.
Add if longitude is West; **Subtract** if longitude is East.

MOON RISING AND SETTING CORRECTION TABLE

Dec (N/S)	2°	4°	6°	8°	10°	12°	14°	16°	18°	20°	22°	24°	26°	28°	
Latitude °N															
0	10	21	31	41	52	63	74	86	98	111	125	139	155	172	**0**
2	10	20	30	40	51	61	72	84	96	108	121	135	151	167	**2**
4	10	19	29	39	49	60	70	82	93	105	118	132	147	163	**4**
6	9	19	28	38	48	58	68	79	90	102	115	128	143	159	**6**
8	9	18	28	37	46	56	66	77	88	99	112	125	139	154	**8**
10	9	18	27	36	45	55	64	75	85	96	108	121	135	150	**10**
12	9	17	26	35	44	53	62	72	82	93	105	117	131	146	**12**
14	8	17	25	33	42	51	60	70	80	90	101	113	127	141	**14**
16	8	16	24	32	41	49	58	67	77	87	98	110	122	136	**16**
18	8	15	23	31	39	47	56	65	74	84	94	106	118	132	**18**
20	7	15	22	30	37	45	54	62	71	81	91	102	114	127	**20**
22	7	14	21	28	36	43	51	60	68	77	87	98	109	122	**22**
24	7	13	20	27	34	41	49	57	65	74	83	93	104	117	**24**
26	6	13	19	26	32	39	47	54	62	70	79	89	99	111	**26**
28	6	12	18	24	31	37	44	51	59	66	75	84	94	106	**28**
30	6	11	17	23	29	35	41	48	55	63	71	79	89	100	**30**
32	5	11	16	21	27	33	39	45	51	58	66	74	84	94	**32**
34	5	10	15	20	25	30	36	42	48	54	61	69	78	87	**34**
36	4	9	13	18	23	28	33	38	44	50	56	63	71	81	**36**
38	4	8	12	16	21	25	30	34	39	45	51	58	65	73	**38**
40	4	7	11	14	18	22	26	30	35	40	45	51	58	66	**40**
42	3	6	9	12	16	19	23	26	30	35	39	44	50	57	**42**
44	3	5	8	10	13	16	19	22	25	29	33	37	42	48	**44**
46	2	4	6	8	10	12	15	17	20	22	26	29	33	38	**46**
48	1	3	4	6	7	9	10	12	14	16	18	20	23	27	**48**
50	1	1	2	3	4	4	5	6	7	8	9	11	12	14	**50**
52	0	0	0	0	0	0	0	0	0	0	0	0	0	0	**52**
54	1	2	2	3	4	5	6	7	8	9	11	12	14	17	**54**
56	2	3	5	7	8	10	12	15	17	20	23	26	31	37	**56**
58	3	5	8	11	13	16	20	23	27	31	37	43	51	62	**58**

Note: This table corrects the times of Moon Rise or Set for your latitude. Find the moon's approximate declination from the Moon table on the sixth page of the month.
All corrections are in **minutes** and are to be applied as follows:

From Latitude **0°N to 52°N** with Declination **N**:	**Add** to Moonrise, **Subtract** from Moonset
From Latitude **0°N to 52°N** with Declination **S**:	**Subtract** from Moonrise, **Add** to Moonset
From Latitude **52°N to 58°N** with Declination **N**:	**Subtract** from Moonrise, **Add** to Moonset
From Latitude **52°N to 58°N** with Declination **S**:	**Add** to Moonrise, **Subtract** from Moonset

For greatest precision, also apply daily change (Diff) correction for your longitude from table at top of page.

PLANETS GHA CORRECTION TABLE (HOURS)

Always add

Var/hr	14°58.8′	14°59.0′	14°59.1′	14°59.3′	14°59.4′	14°59.6′	14°59.7′	14°59.9′	15°0.0′
	° ′	° ′	° ′	° ′	° ′	° ′	° ′	° ′	° ′
0	0 00.0	0 00.0	0 00.0	0 00.0	0 00.0	0 00.0	0 00.0	0 00.0	0 00.0
1	14 58.8	14 59.0	14 59.1	14 59.3	14 59.4	14 59.6	14 59.7	14 59.9	15 00.0
2	29 57.6	29 58.0	29 58.2	29 58.6	29 58.8	29 59.2	29 59.4	29 59.8	30 00.0
3	44 56.4	44 57.0	44 57.3	44 57.9	44 58.2	44 58.8	44 59.1	44 59.7	45 00.0
4	59 55.2	59 56.0	59 56.4	59 57.2	59 57.6	59 58.4	59 58.8	59 59.6	60 00.0
5	74 54.0	74 55.0	74 55.5	74 56.5	74 57.0	74 58.0	74 58.5	74 59.5	75 00.0
6	89 52.8	89 54.0	89 54.6	89 55.8	89 56.4	89 57.6	89 58.2	89 59.4	90 00.0
7	104 51.6	104 53.0	104 53.7	104 55.1	104 55.8	104 57.2	104 57.9	104 59.3	105 00.0
8	119 50.4	119 52.0	119 52.8	119 54.4	119 55.2	119 56.8	119 57.6	119 59.2	120 00.0
9	134 49.2	134 51.0	134 51.9	134 53.7	134 54.6	134 56.4	134 57.3	134 59.1	135 00.0
10	149 48.0	149 50.0	149 51.0	149 53.0	149 54.0	149 56.0	149 57.0	149 59.0	150 00.0
11	164 46.8	164 49.0	164 50.1	164 52.3	164 53.4	164 55.6	164 56.7	164 58.9	165 00.0
12	179 45.6	179 48.0	179 49.2	179 51.6	179 52.8	179 55.2	179 56.4	179 58.8	180 00.0
13	194 44.4	194 47.0	194 48.3	194 50.9	194 52.2	194 54.8	194 56.1	194 58.7	195 00.0
14	209 43.2	209 46.0	209 47.4	209 50.2	209 51.6	209 54.4	209 55.8	209 58.6	210 00.0
15	224 42.0	224 45.0	224 46.5	224 49.5	224 51.0	224 54.0	224 55.5	224 58.5	225 00.0
16	239 40.8	239 44.0	239 45.6	239 48.8	239 50.4	239 53.6	239 55.2	239 58.4	240 00.0
17	254 39.6	254 43.0	254 44.7	254 48.1	254 49.8	254 53.2	254 54.9	254 58.3	255 00.0
18	269 38.4	269 42.0	269 43.8	269 47.4	269 49.2	269 52.8	269 54.6	269 58.2	270 00.0
19	284 37.2	284 41.0	284 42.9	284 46.7	284 48.6	284 52.4	284 54.3	284 58.1	285 00.0
20	299 36.0	299 40.0	299 42.0	299 46.0	299 48.0	299 52.0	299 54.0	299 58.0	300 00.0
21	314 34.8	314 39.0	314 41.1	314 45.3	314 47.4	314 51.6	314 53.7	314 57.9	315 00.0
22	329 33.6	329 38.0	329 40.2	329 44.6	329 46.8	329 51.2	329 53.4	329 57.8	330 00.0
23	344 32.4	344 37.0	344 39.3	344 43.7	344 46.2	344 50.8	344 53.1	344 57.7	345 00.0
24	359 31.2	359 36.0	359 38.4	359 43.2	359 45.6	359 50.4	359 52.8	359 57.6	0 00.0

Var/hr	15°00.2′	15°00.3′	15°00.5′	15°00.6′	15°00.8′	15°00.9′	15°01.1′	15°01.2′	15°01.4′
	° ′	° ′	° ′	° ′	° ′	° ′	° ′	° ′	° ′
0	0 00.0	0 00.0	0 00.0	0 00.0	0 00.0	0 00.0	0 00.0	0 00.0	0 00.0
1	15 00.2	15 00.3	15 00.5	15 00.6	15 00.8	15 00.9	15 01.1	15 01.2	15 01.4
2	30 00.4	30 00.6	30 01.0	30 01.2	30 01.6	30 01.8	30 02.2	30 02.4	30 02.8
3	45 00.6	45 00.9	45 01.5	45 01.8	45 02.4	45 02.7	45 03.3	45 03.6	45 04.2
4	60 00.8	60 01.2	60 02.0	60 02.4	60 03.2	60 03.6	60 04.4	60 04.8	60 05.6
5	75 01.0	75 01.5	75 02.5	75 03.0	75 04.0	75 04.5	75 05.5	75 06.0	75 07.0
6	90 01.2	90 01.8	90 03.0	90 03.6	90 04.8	90 05.4	90 06.6	90 07.2	90 08.4
7	105 01.4	105 02.1	105 03.5	105 04.2	105 05.6	105 06.3	105 07.7	105 08.4	105 09.8
8	120 01.6	120 02.4	120 04.0	120 04.8	120 06.4	120 07.2	120 08.8	120 09.6	120 11.2
9	135 01.8	135 02.7	135 04.5	135 05.4	135 07.2	135 08.1	135 09.9	135 10.8	135 12.6
10	150 02.0	150 03.0	150 05.0	150 06.0	150 08.0	150 09.0	150 11.0	150 12.0	150 14.0
11	165 02.2	165 03.3	165 05.5	165 06.6	165 08.8	165 09.9	165 12.1	165 13.2	165 15.4
12	180 02.4	180 03.6	180 06.0	180 07.2	180 09.6	180 10.8	180 13.2	180 14.4	180 16.8
13	195 02.6	195 03.9	190 06.5	195 07.8	195 10.4	195 11.7	195 14.3	195 15.6	195 18.2
14	210 02.8	210 04.2	210 07.0	210 08.4	210 11.2	210 12.6	210 15.4	210 16.8	210 19.6
15	225 03.0	225 04.5	225 07.5	225 09.0	225 12.0	225 13.5	225 16.5	225 18.5	225 21.0
16	240 03.2	240 04.8	240 08.0	240 09.6	240 12.8	240 14.4	240 17.6	240 19.2	240 22.4
17	255 03.4	255 05.1	255 08.5	255 10.2	255 13.6	255 15.3	255 18.7	255 20.4	255 23.8
18	270 03.6	270 05.4	270 09.0	270 10.8	270 14.4	270 16.2	270 19.8	270 21.6	270 25.2
19	285 03.8	285 05.7	285 09.5	285 11.4	285 15.2	285 17.1	285 20.9	285 22.8	285 26.6
20	300 04.0	300 06.0	300 10.0	300 12.0	300 16.0	300 18.0	300 22.0	300 24.0	300 28.0
21	315 04.2	315 06.3	315 10.5	315 12.6	315 16.8	315 18.9	315 23.1	315 25.2	315 29.4
22	330 04.4	330 06.6	330 11.0	330 13.2	330 17.6	330 19.8	330 24.2	330 26.4	330 30.8
23	345 04.6	345 06.9	345 11.5	345 13.8	345 18.4	345 20.7	345 25.3	345 27.6	345 32.2
24	0 04.8	0 07.2	0 12.0	0 14.4	0 19.2	0 21.6	0 26.4	0 28.8	0 33.6

Note: The correction for Planet GHA is taken in three parts. Using the daily figure for variation per hour given on the monthly page, you get the correction for hours from the table on this or the following page, and then the correction for minutes from the table on page E 103. Finally, take the correction for seconds from the righthand side of the minute table.

CORRECTIONS

PLANETS GHA CORRECTION TABLE (HOURS)

Always add

Var/hr	15°01.5′	15°01.7′	15°01.8′	15°02.0′	15°02.1′	15°02.3′	15°02.4′	15°02.6′	15°02.7′
	° ′	° ′	° ′	° ′	° ′	° ′	° ′	° ′	° ′
0	0 00.0	0 00.0	0 00.0	0 00.0	0 00.0	0 00.0	0 00.0	0 00.0	0 00.0
1	15 01.5	15 01.7	15 01.8	15 02.0	15 02.1	15 02.3	15 02.4	15 02.6	15 02.7
2	30 03.0	30 03.4	30 03.6	30 04.0	30 04.2	30 04.6	30 04.8	30 05.2	30 05.4
3	45 04.5	45 05.1	45 05.4	45 06.0	45 06.3	45 06.9	45 07.2	45 07.8	45 08.1
4	60 06.0	60 06.8	60 07.2	60 08.0	60 08.4	60 09.2	60 09.6	60 10.4	60 10.8
5	75 07.5	75 08.5	75 09.0	75 10.0	75 10.5	75 11.5	75 12.0	75 13.0	75 13.5
6	90 09.0	90 10.2	90 10.8	90 12.0	90 12.6	90 13.8	90 14.4	90 15.6	90 16.2
7	105 10.5	105 11.9	105 12.6	105 14.0	105 14.7	105 16.1	105 16.8	105 18.2	105 18.9
8	120 12.0	120 13.6	120 14.4	120 16.0	120 16.8	120 18.4	120 19.2	120 20.8	120 21.6
9	135 13.5	135 15.3	135 16.2	135 18.0	135 18.9	135 20.7	135 21.6	135 23.4	135 24.3
10	150 15.0	150 17.0	150 18.0	150 20.0	150 21.0	150 23.0	150 24.0	150 26.0	150 27.0
11	165 16.5	165 18.7	165 19.8	165 22.0	165 23.1	165 25.3	165 26.4	165 28.6	165 29.7
12	180 18.0	180 20.4	180 21.6	180 24.0	180 25.2	180 27.6	180 28.8	180 31.2	180 32.4
13	195 19.5	195 22.1	195 23.4	195 26.0	195 27.3	195 29.9	195 31.2	195 33.8	195 35.1
14	210 21.0	210 23.8	210 25.2	210 28.0	210 29.4	210 32.2	210 33.6	210 36.4	210 37.8
15	225 22.5	225 25.5	225 27.0	225 30.0	225 31.5	225 34.5	225 36.0	225 39.0	225 40.5
16	240 24.0	240 27.2	240 28.8	240 32.0	240 33.6	240 36.8	240 38.4	240 41.6	240 43.2
17	255 25.5	255 28.9	255 30.6	255 34.0	255 35.7	255 39.1	255 40.8	255 44.2	255 45.9
18	270 27.0	270 30.6	270 32.4	270 36.0	270 37.8	270 41.4	270 43.2	270 46.8	270 48.6
19	285 28.5	285 32.3	285 34.2	285 38.0	285 39.9	285 43.7	285 45.6	285 49.4	285 51.3
20	300 30.0	300 34.0	300 36.0	300 40.0	300 42.0	300 46.0	300 48.0	300 52.0	300 54.0
21	315 31.5	315 35.7	315 37.8	315 42.0	315 44.1	315 48.3	315 50.4	315 54.6	315 56.7
22	330 33.0	330 37.4	330 39.6	330 44.0	330 46.2	330 50.6	330 52.8	330 57.2	330 59.4
23	345 34.5	345 39.1	345 41.4	345 46.0	345 48.3	345 52.9	345 55.2	345 59.8	346 02.1
24	0 36.0	0 40.8	0 43.2	0 48.0	0 50.4	0 55.2	0 57.6	1 02.4	1 04.8

Hours

Var/hr	15°02.9′	15°03.0′	15°03.2′	15°03.3′	15°03.5′	15°03.6′	15°03.8′	15°03.9′	15°04.1′
	° ′	° ′	° ′	° ′	° ′	° ′	° ′	° ′	° ′
0	0 00.0	0 00.0	0 00.0	0 00.0	0 00.0	0 00.0	0 00.0	0 00.0	0 00.0
1	15 02.9	15 03.0	15 03.2	15 03.3	15 03.5	15 03.6	15 03.8	15 03.9	15 04.1
2	30 05.8	30 06.0	30 06.4	30 06.6	30 07.0	30 07.2	30 07.6	30 07.8	30 08.2
3	45 08.7	45 09.0	45 09.6	45 09.9	45 10.5	45 10.8	45 11.4	45 11.7	45 12.3
4	60 11.6	60 12.0	60 12.8	60 13.2	60 14.0	60 14.4	60 15.2	60 15.6	60 16.4
5	75 14.5	75 15.0	75 16.0	75 16.5	75 17.5	75 18.0	75 19.0	75 19.5	75 20.5
6	90 17.4	90 18.0	90 19.2	90 19.8	90 21.0	90 21.6	90 22.8	90 23.4	90 24.6
7	105 20.3	105 21.0	105 22.4	105 23.1	105 24.5	105 25.2	105 26.6	105 27.3	105 28.7
8	120 23.2	120 24.0	120 25.6	120 26.4	120 28.0	120 28.8	120 30.4	120 31.2	120 32.8
9	135 26.1	135 27.0	135 28.8	135 29.7	135 31.5	135 32.4	135 34.2	135 35.1	135 36.9
10	150 29.0	150 30.0	150 32.0	150 33.0	150 35.0	150 36.0	150 38.0	150 39.0	150 41.0
11	165 31.9	165 33.0	165 35.2	165 36.3	165 38.5	165 39.6	165 41.8	165 42.9	165 45.1
12	180 34.8	180 36.0	180 38.4	180 39.6	180 42.0	180 43.2	180 45.6	180 46.8	180 49.2
13	195 37.7	195 39.0	195 41.6	195 42.9	195 45.5	195 46.8	195 49.4	195 50.7	195 53.3
14	210 40.6	210 42.0	210 44.8	210 46.2	210 49.0	210 50.4	210 53.2	210 54.6	210 57.4
15	225 43.5	225 45.0	225 48.0	225 49.5	225 52.5	225 54.0	225 57.0	225 58.5	226 01.5
16	240 46.4	240 48.0	240 51.2	240 52.8	240 56.0	240 57.6	241 00.8	241 02.4	241 05.6
17	255 49.3	255 51.0	255 54.4	255 56.1	255 59.5	256 01.2	256 04.6	256 06.3	256 09.7
18	270 52.2	270 54.0	270 57.6	270 59.4	271 03.0	271 04.8	271 08.4	271 10.2	271 13.8
19	285 55.1	285 57.0	286 00.8	286 02.7	286 06.5	286 08.4	286 12.2	286 14.1	286 17.9
20	300 58.0	301 00.0	301 04.0	301 06.0	301 10.0	301 12.0	301 16.0	301 18.0	301 22.0
21	316 00.9	316 03.0	316 07.2	316 09.3	316 13.5	316 15.6	316 19.8	316 21.9	316 26.1
22	331 03.8	331 06.0	331 10.4	331 12.6	331 17.0	331 19.2	331 23.6	331 25.8	331 30.2
23	346 06.7	346 09.0	346 13.6	346 15.9	346 20.5	346 22.8	346 27.4	346 29.7	346 34.3
24	001 09.6	001 12.0	001 16.8	001 19.2	001 24.0	001 26.4	001 31.2	001 33.6	001 38.4

Hours

Note: The correction for Planet GHA is taken in three parts. Using the daily figure for variation per hour given on the monthly page, you get the correction for hours from the table on this or the preceding page, and then the correction for minutes from the table on the opposite page. Finally, take the correction for seconds from the righthand side of the minute table.

PLANETS GHA CORRECTION TABLE (MINUTES)

Always add

Var/hr	14°58.8'	14°59.4'	15°00.0'	15°00.6'	15°01.2'	15°01.8'	15°02.4'	15°03.0'	15°03.6'	Sec	
	° '	° '	° '	° '	° '	° '	° '	° '	° '		'
0	0 00.0	0 00.0	0 00.0	0 00.0	0 00.0	0 00.0	0 00.0	0 00.0	0 00.0	0	0.0
1	0 15.0	0 15.0	0 15.0	0 15.0	0 15.0	0 15.0	0 15.0	0 15.0	0 15.1	1	0.3
2	0 30.0	0 30.0	0 30.0	0 30.0	0 30.0	0 30.1	0 30.1	0 30.1	0 30.1	2	0.5
3	0 44.9	0 45.0	0 45.0	0 45.0	0 45.1	0 45.1	0 45.1	0 45.1	0 45.2	3	0.8
4	0 59.9	1 00.0	1 00.0	1 00.0	1 00.1	1 00.1	1 00.2	1 00.2	1 00.2	4	1.0
5	1 14.9	1 14.9	1 15.0	1 15.0	1 15.1	1 15.2	1 15.2	1 15.2	1 15.3	5	1.3
6	1 29.9	1 29.9	1 30.0	1 30.1	1 30.1	1 30.2	1 30.2	1 30.3	1 30.4	6	1.5
7	1 44.9	1 44.9	1 45.0	1 45.1	1 45.1	1 45.2	1 45.3	1 45.3	1 45.4	7	1.8
8	1 59.8	1 59.9	2 00.0	2 00.1	2 00.2	2 00.2	2 00.3	2 00.4	2 00.5	8	2.0
9	2 14.8	2 14.9	2 15.0	2 15.1	2 15.2	2 15.3	2 15.4	2 15.4	2 15.5	9	2.3
10	2 29.8	2 29.9	2 30.0	2 30.1	2 30.2	2 30.3	2 30.4	2 30.5	2 30.6	10	2.5
11	2 44.8	2 44.9	2 45.0	2 45.1	2 45.2	2 45.3	2 45.4	2 45.5	2 45.7	11	2.8
12	2 59.8	2 59.9	3 00.0	3 00.1	3 00.2	3 00.4	3 00.5	3 00.6	3 00.7	12	3.0
13	3 14.7	3 14.9	3 15.0	3 15.1	3 15.3	3 15.4	3 15.5	3 15.6	3 15.8	13	3.3
14	3 29.7	3 29.9	3 30.0	3 30.1	3 30.3	3 30.4	3 30.6	3 30.7	3 30.8	14	3.5
15	3 44.7	3 44.8	3 45.0	3 45.2	3 45.3	3 45.4	3 45.6	3 45.7	3 45.9	15	3.8
16	3 59.7	3 59.8	4 00.0	4 00.2	4 00.3	4 00.5	4 00.6	4 00.8	4 01.0	16	4.0
17	4 14.7	4 14.8	4 15.0	4 15.2	4 15.3	4 15.5	4 15.7	4 15.8	4 16.0	17	4.3
18	4 29.6	4 29.8	4 30.0	4 30.2	4 30.4	4 30.5	4 30.7	4 30.9	4 31.1	18	4.5
19	4 44.6	4 44.8	4 45.0	4 45.2	4 45.4	4 45.6	4 45.8	4 45.9	4 46.1	19	4.8
20	4 59.6	4 59.8	5 00.0	5 00.2	5 00.4	5 00.6	5 00.8	5 01.0	5 01.2	20	5.0
21	5 14.6	5 14.8	5 15.0	5 15.2	5 15.4	5 15.6	5 15.8	5 16.0	5 16.3	21	5.3
22	5 29.6	5 29.8	5 30.0	5 30.2	5 30.4	5 30.7	5 30.9	5 31.1	5 31.3	22	5.5
23	5 44.5	5 44.8	5 45.0	5 45.2	5 45.5	5 45.7	5 45.9	5 46.1	5 46.4	23	5.8
24	5 59.5	5 59.8	6 00.0	6 00.2	6 00.5	6 00.7	6 01.0	6 01.2	6 01.4	24	6.0
25	6 14.5	6 14.8	6 15.0	6 15.2	6 15.5	6 15.7	6 16.0	6 16.2	6 16.5	25	6.3
26	6 29.5	6 29.7	6 30.0	6 30.3	6 30.5	6 30.8	6 31.0	6 31.3	6 31.6	26	6.5
27	6 04.5	6 44.7	6 45.0	6 45.3	6 45.5	6 45.8	6 46.1	6 46.3	6 46.6	27	6.8
28	6 59.4	6 59.7	7 00.0	7 00.3	7 00.6	7 00.8	7 01.1	7 01.4	7 01.7	28	7.0
29	7 14.4	7 14.7	7 15.0	7 15.3	7 15.6	7 15.9	7 16.2	7 16.4	7 16.7	29	7.3
30	7 29.4	7 29.7	7 30.0	7 30.3	7 30.6	7 30.9	7 31.2	7 31.5	7 31.8	30	7.5
31	7 44.4	7 44.7	7 45.0	7 45.3	7 45.6	7 45.9	7 46.2	7 46.5	7 46.9	31	7.8
32	7 59.4	7 59.7	8 00.0	8 00.3	8 00.6	8 01.0	8 01.3	8 01.6	8 01.9	32	8.0
33	8 14.3	8 14.7	8 15.0	8 15.3	8 15.7	8 16.0	8 16.3	8 16.6	8 17.0	33	8.3
34	8 29.3	8 29.7	8 30.0	8 30.3	8 30.7	8 31.0	8 31.4	8 31.7	8 32.0	34	8.5
35	8 44.3	8 44.6	8 45.0	8 45.5	8 45.7	8 46.0	8 46.4	8 46.7	8 47.1	35	8.8
36	8 59.3	8 59.6	9 00.0	9 00.4	9 00.7	9 01.1	9 01.4	9 01.8	9 02.2	36	9.0
37	9 14.3	9 14.6	9 15.0	9 15.4	9 15.7	9 16.1	9 16.5	9 16.8	9 17.2	37	9.3
38	9 29.2	9 29.6	9 30.0	9 30.4	9 30.8	9 31.1	9 31.5	9 31.9	9 32.3	38	9.5
39	9 44.2	9 44.6	9 45.0	9 45.4	9 45.8	9 46.2	9 46.6	9 46.9	9 47.3	39	9.8
40	9 59.2	9 59.6	10 00.0	10 00.4	10 00.8	10 01.2	10 01.6	10 02.0	10 02.4	40	10.0
41	10 14.2	10 14.6	10 15.0	10 15.4	10 15.8	10 16.2	10 16.6	10 17.0	10 17.5	41	10.3
42	10 29.2	10 29.6	10 30.0	10 30.4	10 30.8	10 31.3	10 31.7	10 32.1	10 32.5	42	10.5
43	10 44.1	10 44.6	10 45.0	10 45.4	10 45.9	10 46.3	10 46.7	10 47.1	10 47.6	43	10.8
44	10 59.1	10 59.6	11 00.0	11 00.4	11 00.9	11 01.3	11 01.8	11 02.2	11 02.6	44	11.0
45	11 14.1	11 14.6	11 15.0	11 15.4	11 15.9	11 16.3	11 16.8	11 17.2	11 17.7	45	11.3
46	11 29.1	11 29.5	11 30.0	11 30.5	11 30.9	11 31.4	11 31.8	11 32.3	11 32.8	46	11.5
47	11 44.1	11 44.5	11 45.0	11 45.5	11 45.9	11 46.4	11 46.9	11 47.3	11 47.8	47	11.8
48	11 59.0	11 59.5	12 00.0	12 00.5	12 01.0	12 01.4	12 01.9	12 02.4	12 02.9	48	12.0
49	12 14.0	12 14.5	12 15.0	12 15.5	12 16.0	12 16.5	12 17.0	12 17.4	12 17.9	49	12.3
50	12 29.0	12 29.5	12 30.0	12 30.5	12 31.0	12 31.5	12 32.0	12 32.5	12 33.0	50	12.5
51	12 44.0	12 44.5	12 45.0	12 45.5	12 46.0	12 46.5	12 47.0	12 47.5	12 48.1	51	12.8
52	12 59.0	12 59.5	13 00.0	13 00.5	13 01.0	13 01.6	13 02.1	13 02.6	13 03.1	52	13.1
53	13 13.9	13 14.5	13 15.0	13 15.5	13 16.1	13 16.6	13 17.1	13 17.6	13 18.2	53	13.3
54	13 28.9	13 29.5	13 30.0	13 30.5	13 31.1	13 31.6	13 32.2	13 32.7	13 33.2	54	13.5
55	13 43.9	13 44.4	13 45.0	13 45.6	13 46.1	13 46.6	13 47.2	13 47.7	13 48.3	55	13.8
56	13 58.9	13 59.4	14 00.0	14 00.6	14 01.1	14 01.7	17 02.2	14 02.8	14 03.4	56	14.0
57	14 13.9	14 14.4	14 15.0	14 15.6	14 16.1	14 16.7	14 17.3	14 17.8	14 18.4	57	14.3
58	14 28.8	14 29.4	14 30.0	14 30.6	14 31.2	14 31.7	14 32.3	14 32.9	14 33.5	58	14.5
59	14 43.8	14 44.4	14 45.0	14 45.6	14 46.2	14 46.8	14 47.4	14 47.9	14 48.5	59	14.8
60	14 58.8	14 59.4	15 00.0	15 00.6	15 01.2	15 01.8	15 02.4	15 03.0	15 03.6	60	15.0

CORRECTIONS

PLANETS DECLINATION CORRECTION TABLE

Var/hr	0.0'	0.1'	0.2'	0.3'	0.4'	0.5'	0.6'	0.7'	0.8'	0.9'	1.0'	1.1'	1.2'	1.3'	1.4'	1.5'
h m	'	'	'	'	'	'	'	'	'	'	'	'	'	'	'	'
0 00	0.0	0.0	0.0	0.0	0.0	0.0	0.0	0.0	0.0	0.0	0.0	0.0	0.0	0.0	0.0	0.0
12	0.0	0.0	0.0	0.1	0.1	0.1	0.1	0.1	0.2	0.2	0.2	0.2	0.2	0.3	0.3	0.3
24	0.0	0.0	0.1	0.1	0.2	0.2	0.2	0.3	0.3	0.4	0.4	0.4	0.5	0.5	0.6	0.6
36	0.0	0.1	0.1	0.2	0.2	0.3	0.4	0.4	0.5	0.5	0.6	0.7	0.7	0.8	0.8	0.9
48	0.0	0.1	0.2	0.2	0.3	0.4	0.5	0.6	0.6	0.7	0.8	0.9	1.0	1.0	1.1	1.2
1 00	0.0	0.1	0.2	0.3	0.4	0.5	0.6	0.7	0.8	0.9	1.0	1.1	1.2	1.3	1.4	1.5
12	0.0	0.1	0.2	0.4	0.5	0.6	0.7	0.8	1.0	1.1	1.2	1.3	1.4	1.6	1.7	1.8
24	0.0	0.1	0.3	0.4	0.6	0.7	0.8	1.0	1.1	1.3	1.4	1.5	1.7	1.8	2.0	2.1
36	0.0	0.2	0.3	0.5	0.6	0.8	1.0	1.1	1.3	1.4	1.6	1.8	1.9	2.1	2.2	2.4
48	0.0	0.2	0.4	0.5	0.7	0.9	1.1	1.3	1.4	1.6	1.8	2.0	2.2	2.3	2.5	2.7
2 00	0.0	0.2	0.4	0.6	0.8	1.0	1.2	1.4	1.6	1.8	2.0	2.2	2.4	2.6	2.8	3.0
12	0.0	0.2	0.4	0.7	0.9	1.1	1.3	1.5	1.8	2.0	2.2	2.4	2.6	2.9	3.1	3.3
24	0.0	0.2	0.5	0.7	1.0	1.2	1.4	1.7	1.9	2.2	2.4	2.6	2.9	3.1	3.4	3.6
36	0.0	0.3	0.5	0.8	1.0	1.3	1.6	1.8	2.1	2.3	2.6	2.9	3.1	3.4	3.6	3.9
48	0.0	0.3	0.6	0.8	1.1	1.4	1.7	2.0	2.2	2.5	2.8	3.1	3.4	3.6	3.9	4.2
3 00	0.0	0.3	0.6	0.9	1.2	1.5	1.8	2.1	2.4	2.7	3.0	3.3	3.6	3.9	4.2	4.5
12	0.0	0.3	0.6	1.0	1.3	1.6	1.9	2.2	2.6	2.9	3.2	3.5	3.8	4.2	4.5	4.8
24	0.0	0.3	0.7	1.0	1.4	1.7	2.0	2.4	2.7	3.1	3.4	3.7	4.1	4.4	4.8	5.1
36	0.0	0.4	0.7	1.1	1.4	1.8	2.2	2.5	2.9	3.2	3.6	4.0	4.3	4.7	5.0	5.4
48	0.0	0.4	0.8	1.1	1.5	1.9	2.3	2.7	3.0	3.4	3.8	4.2	4.6	4.9	5.3	5.7
4 00	0.0	0.4	0.8	1.2	1.6	2.0	2.4	2.8	3.2	3.6	4.0	4.4	4.8	5.2	5.6	6.0
12	0.0	0.4	0.8	1.3	1.7	2.1	2.5	2.9	3.4	3.8	4.2	4.6	5.0	5.5	5.9	6.3
24	0.0	0.4	0.9	1.3	1.8	2.2	2.6	3.1	3.5	4.0	4.4	4.8	5.3	5.7	6.2	6.6
36	0.0	0.5	0.9	1.4	1.8	2.3	2.8	3.2	3.7	4.1	4.6	5.1	5.5	6.0	6.4	6.9
48	0.0	0.5	1.0	1.4	1.9	2.4	2.9	3.4	3.8	4.3	4.8	5.3	5.8	6.2	6.7	7.2
5 00	0.0	0.5	1.0	1.5	2.0	2.5	3.0	3.5	4.0	4.5	5.0	5.5	6.0	6.5	7.0	7.5
12	0.0	0.5	1.0	1.6	2.1	2.6	3.1	3.6	4.2	4.7	5.2	5.7	6.2	6.8	7.3	7.8
24	0.0	0.5	1.1	1.6	2.2	2.7	3.2	3.8	4.3	4.9	5.4	5.9	6.5	7.0	7.6	8.1
36	0.0	0.6	1.1	1.7	2.2	2.8	3.4	3.9	4.5	5.0	5.6	6.2	6.7	7.3	7.8	8.4
48	0.0	0.6	1.2	1.7	2.3	2.9	3.5	4.1	4.6	5.2	5.8	6.4	7.0	7.5	8.1	8.7
6 00	0.0	0.6	1.2	1.8	2.4	3.0	3.6	4.2	4.8	5.4	6.0	6.6	7.2	7.8	8.4	9.0
12	0.0	0.6	1.2	1.9	2.5	3.1	3.7	4.3	5.0	5.6	6.2	6.8	7.4	8.1	8.7	9.3
24	0.0	0.6	1.3	1.9	2.6	3.2	3.8	4.5	5.1	5.8	6.4	7.0	7.7	8.3	9.0	9.6
36	0.0	0.7	1.3	2.0	2.6	3.3	4.0	4.6	5.3	5.9	6.6	7.3	7.9	8.6	9.2	9.9
48	0.0	0.7	1.4	2.0	2.7	3.4	4.1	4.8	5.4	6.1	6.8	7.5	8.2	8.8	9.5	10.2
7 00	0.0	0.7	1.4	2.1	2.8	3.5	4.2	4.9	5.6	6.3	7.0	7.7	8.4	9.1	9.8	10.5
12	0.0	0.7	1.4	2.2	2.9	3.6	4.3	5.0	5.8	6.5	7.2	7.9	8.6	9.4	10.1	10.8
24	0.0	0.7	1.5	2.2	3.0	3.7	4.4	5.2	5.9	6.7	7.4	8.1	8.9	9.6	10.4	11.1
36	0.0	0.8	1.5	2.3	3.0	3.8	4.6	5.3	6.1	6.8	7.6	8.4	9.1	9.9	10.6	11.4
48	0.0	0.8	1.6	2.3	3.1	3.9	4.7	5.5	6.2	7.0	7.8	8.6	9.4	10.1	10.9	11.7
8 00	0.0	0.8	1.6	2.4	3.2	4.0	4.8	5.6	6.4	7.2	8.0	8.8	9.6	10.4	11.2	12.0
12	0.0	0.8	1.6	2.5	3.3	4.1	4.9	5.7	6.6	7.4	8.2	9.0	9.8	10.7	11.5	12.3
24	0.0	0.8	1.7	2.5	3.4	4.2	5.0	5.9	6.7	7.6	8.4	9.2	10.1	10.9	11.8	12.6
36	0.0	0.9	1.7	2.6	3.4	4.3	5.2	6.0	6.9	7.7	8.6	9.5	10.3	11.2	12.0	12.9
48	0.0	0.9	1.8	2.6	3.5	4.4	5.3	6.2	7.0	7.9	8.8	9.7	10.6	11.4	12.3	13.2
9 00	0.0	0.9	1.8	2.7	3.6	4.5	5.4	6.3	7.2	8.1	9.0	9.9	10.8	11.7	12.6	13.5
12	0.0	0.9	1.8	2.8	3.7	4.6	5.5	6.4	7.4	8.3	9.2	10.1	11.0	12.0	12.9	13.8
24	0.0	0.9	1.9	2.8	3.8	4.7	5.6	6.6	7.5	8.5	9.4	10.3	11.3	12.2	13.2	14.1
36	0.0	1.0	1.9	2.9	3.8	4.8	5.8	6.7	7.7	8.6	9.6	10.6	11.5	12.5	13.4	14.4
48	0.0	1.0	2.0	2.9	3.9	4.9	5.9	6.9	7.8	8.8	9.8	10.8	11.8	12.7	13.7	14.7
10 00	0.0	1.0	2.0	3.0	4.0	5.0	6.0	7.0	8.0	9.0	10.0	11.0	12.0	13.0	14.0	15.0
12	0.0	1.0	2.0	3.1	4.1	5.1	6.1	7.1	8.2	9.2	10.2	11.2	12.2	13.2	14.3	15.3
24	0.0	1.0	2.1	3.1	4.2	5.2	6.2	7.3	8.3	9.4	10.4	11.4	12.5	13.5	14.6	15.6
36	0.0	1.1	2.1	3.2	4.2	5.3	6.4	7.4	8.5	9.5	10.6	11.7	12.7	13.8	14.8	15.9
48	0.0	1.1	2.2	3.2	4.3	5.4	6.5	7.6	8.6	9.7	10.8	11.9	13.0	14.0	15.1	16.2
11 00	0.0	1.1	2.2	3.3	4.4	5.5	6.6	7.7	8.8	9.9	11.0	12.1	13.2	14.3	15.4	16.5
12	0.0	1.1	2.2	3.4	4.5	5.6	6.7	7.8	9.0	10.1	11.2	12.3	13.4	14.6	15.7	16.8
24	0.0	1.1	2.3	3.4	4.6	5.7	6.8	8.0	9.1	10.3	11.4	12.5	13.7	14.8	16.0	17.1
36	0.0	1.2	2.3	3.5	4.6	5.8	7.0	8.1	9.3	10.4	11.6	12.8	13.9	15.1	16.2	17.4
48	0.0	1.2	2.4	3.5	4.7	5.9	7.1	8.3	9.4	10.6	11.8	13.0	14.2	15.3	16.5	17.7
12 00	0.0	1.2	2.4	3.6	4.8	6.0	7.2	8.4	9.6	10.8	12.0	13.2	14.4	15.6	16.8	18.0

PLANETS DECLINATION CORRECTION TABLE

Var/hr	0.0′	0.1′	0.2′	0.3′	0.4′	0.5′	0.6′	0.7′	0.8′	0.9′	1.0′	1.1′	1.2′	1.3′	1.4′	1.5′
h m	′	′	′	′	′	′	′	′	′	′	′	′	′	′	′	′
12 00	0.0	1.2	2.4	3.6	4.8	6.0	7.2	8.4	9.6	10.8	12.0	13.2	14.4	15.6	16.8	18.0
12	0.0	1.2	2.4	3.7	4.9	6.1	7.3	8.5	9.8	11.0	12.2	13.4	14.6	15.9	17.1	18.3
24	0.0	1.2	2.5	3.7	5.0	6.2	7.4	8.7	9.9	11.2	12.4	13.6	14.9	16.1	17.4	18.6
36	0.0	1.3	2.5	3.8	5.0	6.3	7.6	8.8	10.1	11.3	12.6	13.9	15.1	16.4	17.6	18.9
48	0.0	1.3	2.6	3.8	5.1	6.4	7.7	9.0	10.2	11.5	12.8	14.1	15.4	16.6	17.9	19.2
13 00	0.0	1.3	2.6	3.9	5.2	6.5	7.8	9.1	10.4	11.7	13.0	14.3	15.6	16.9	18.2	19.5
12	0.0	1.3	2.6	4.0	5.3	6.6	7.9	9.2	10.6	11.9	13.2	14.5	15.8	17.2	18.5	19.8
24	0.0	1.3	2.7	4.0	5.4	6.7	8.0	9.4	10.7	12.1	13.4	14.7	16.1	17.4	18.8	20.1
36	0.0	1.4	2.7	4.1	5.4	6.8	8.2	9.5	10.9	12.2	13.6	15.0	16.3	17.7	19.0	20.4
48	0.0	1.4	2.8	4.1	5.5	6.9	8.3	9.7	11.0	12.4	13.8	15.2	16.6	17.9	19.3	20.7
14 00	0.0	1.4	2.8	4.2	5.6	7.0	8.4	9.8	11.2	12.6	14.0	15.4	16.8	18.2	19.6	21.0
12	0.0	1.4	2.8	4.3	5.7	7.1	8.5	9.9	11.4	12.8	14.2	15.6	17.0	18.5	19.9	21.3
24	0.0	1.4	2.9	4.3	5.8	7.2	8.6	10.1	11.5	13.0	14.4	15.8	17.3	18.7	20.2	21.6
36	0.0	1.5	2.9	4.4	5.8	7.3	8.8	10.2	11.7	13.1	14.6	16.1	17.5	19.0	20.4	21.9
48	0.0	1.5	3.0	4.4	5.9	7.4	8.9	10.4	11.8	13.3	14.8	16.3	17.8	19.2	20.7	22.2
15 00	0.0	1.5	3.0	4.5	6.0	7.5	9.0	10.5	12.0	13.5	15.0	16.5	18.0	19.5	21.0	22.5
12	0.0	1.5	3.0	4.6	6.1	7.6	9.1	10.6	12.2	13.7	15.2	16.7	18.2	19.8	21.3	22.8
24	0.0	1.5	3.1	4.6	6.2	7.7	9.2	10.8	12.3	13.9	15.4	16.9	18.5	20.0	21.6	23.1
36	0.0	1.6	3.1	4.7	6.2	7.8	9.4	10.9	12.5	14.0	15.6	17.2	18.7	20.3	21.8	23.4
48	0.0	1.6	3.2	4.7	6.3	7.9	9.5	11.1	12.6	14.2	15.8	17.4	19.0	20.5	22.1	23.7
16 00	0.0	1.6	3.2	4.8	6.4	8.0	9.6	11.2	12.8	14.4	16.0	17.6	19.2	20.8	22.4	24.0
12	0.0	1.6	3.2	4.9	6.5	8.1	9.7	11.3	13.0	14.6	16.2	17.8	19.4	21.1	22.7	24.3
24	0.0	1.6	3.3	4.9	6.6	8.2	9.8	11.5	13.1	14.8	16.4	18.0	19.7	21.3	23.0	24.6
36	0.0	1.7	3.3	5.0	6.6	8.3	10.0	11.6	13.3	15.0	16.6	18.3	19.9	21.6	23.2	24.9
48	0.0	1.7	3.4	5.0	6.7	8.4	10.1	11.8	13.4	15.1	16.8	18.5	20.2	21.8	23.5	25.2
17 00	0.0	1.7	3.4	5.1	6.8	8.5	10.2	11.9	13.6	15.3	17.0	18.7	20.4	22.1	23.8	25.5
12	0.0	1.7	3.4	5.2	6.9	8.6	10.3	12.0	13.8	15.5	17.2	18.9	20.6	22.4	24.1	25.8
24	0.0	1.7	3.5	5.2	7.0	8.7	10.4	12.2	13.9	15.7	17.4	19.1	20.9	22.6	24.4	26.1
36	0.0	1.8	3.5	5.3	7.0	8.8	10.6	12.3	14.1	15.8	17.6	19.4	21.1	22.9	24.6	26.4
48	0.0	1.8	3.6	5.3	7.1	8.9	10.7	12.5	14.2	16.0	17.8	19.6	21.4	23.1	24.9	26.7
18 00	0.0	1.8	3.6	5.4	7.2	9.0	10.8	12.6	14.4	16.2	18.0	19.8	21.6	23.4	25.2	27.0
12	0.0	1.8	3.6	5.5	7.3	9.1	10.9	12.7	14.6	16.4	18.2	20.0	21.8	23.7	25.5	27.3
24	0.0	1.8	3.7	5.5	7.4	9.2	11.0	12.9	14.7	16.6	18.4	20.2	22.1	23.9	25.8	27.6
36	0.0	1.9	3.7	5.6	7.4	9.3	11.2	13.0	14.9	16.7	18.6	20.5	22.3	24.2	26.0	27.9
48	0.0	1.9	3.8	5.6	7.5	9.4	11.3	13.2	15.0	16.9	18.8	20.7	22.6	24.4	26.3	28.2
19 00	0.0	1.9	3.8	5.7	7.6	9.5	11.4	13.3	15.2	17.1	19.0	20.9	22.8	24.7	26.6	28.5
12	0.0	1.9	3.8	5.8	7.7	9.6	11.5	13.4	15.4	17.3	19.2	21.1	23.0	25.0	26.9	28.8
24	0.0	1.9	3.9	5.8	7.8	9.7	11.6	13.6	15.5	17.5	19.4	21.3	23.3	25.2	27.2	29.1
36	0.0	2.0	3.9	5.9	7.8	9.8	11.8	13.7	15.7	17.6	19.6	21.6	23.5	25.5	27.4	29.4
48	0.0	2.0	4.0	5.9	7.9	9.9	11.9	13.9	15.8	17.8	19.8	21.8	23.8	25.7	27.7	29.7
20 00	0.0	2.0	4.0	6.0	8.0	10.0	12.0	14.0	16.0	18.0	20.0	22.0	24.0	26.0	28.0	30.0
12	0.0	2.0	4.0	6.1	8.1	10.1	12.1	14.1	16.2	18.2	20.2	22.2	24.2	26.3	28.3	30.3
24	0.0	2.0	4.1	6.1	8.2	10.2	12.2	14.3	16.3	18.4	20.4	22.4	24.5	26.5	28.6	30.6
36	0.0	2.1	4.1	6.2	8.2	10.3	12.4	14.4	16.5	18.5	20.6	22.7	24.7	26.8	28.8	30.9
48	0.0	2.1	4.2	6.2	8.3	10.4	12.5	14.6	16.6	18.7	20.8	22.9	25.0	27.0	29.1	31.2
21 00	0.0	2.1	4.2	6.3	8.4	10.5	12.6	14.7	16.8	18.9	21.0	23.1	25.2	27.3	29.4	31.5
12	0.0	2.1	4.2	6.4	8.5	10.6	12.7	14.8	17.0	19.1	21.2	23.3	25.4	27.6	29.7	31.8
24	0.0	2.1	4.3	6.4	8.6	10.7	12.8	15.0	17.1	19.3	21.4	23.5	25.7	27.8	30.0	32.1
36	0.0	2.2	4.3	6.5	8.6	10.8	13.0	15.1	17.3	19.4	21.6	23.8	25.9	28.1	30.2	32.4
48	0.0	2.2	4.4	6.5	8.7	10.9	13.1	15.3	17.4	19.6	21.8	24.0	26.2	28.3	30.5	32.7
22 00	0.0	2.2	4.4	6.6	8.8	11.0	13.2	15.4	17.6	19.8	22.0	24.2	26.4	28.6	30.8	33.0
12	0.0	2.2	4.4	6.7	8.9	11.1	13.3	15.5	17.8	20.0	22.2	24.4	26.6	28.9	31.1	33.3
24	0.0	2.2	4.5	6.7	9.0	11.2	13.4	15.7	17.9	20.2	22.4	24.6	26.9	29.1	31.4	33.6
36	0.0	2.3	4.5	6.8	9.0	11.3	13.6	15.8	18.1	20.3	22.6	24.9	27.1	29.4	31.6	33.9
48	0.0	2.3	4.6	6.8	9.1	11.4	13.7	16.0	18.2	20.5	22.8	25.1	27.4	29.6	31.9	34.2
23 00	0.0	2.3	4.6	6.9	9.2	11.5	13.8	16.1	18.4	20.7	23.0	25.3	27.6	29.9	32.2	34.5
12	0.0	2.3	4.6	7.0	9.3	11.6	13.9	16.2	18.6	20.9	23.2	25.5	27.8	30.2	32.5	34.8
24	0.0	2.3	4.7	7.0	9.4	11.7	14.0	16.4	18.7	21.1	23.4	25.7	28.1	30.4	32.8	35.1
36	0.0	2.4	4.7	7.1	9.4	11.8	14.2	16.5	18.9	21.2	23.6	26.0	28.3	30.7	33.0	35.4
48	0.0	2.4	4.8	7.1	9.5	11.9	14.3	16.7	19.0	21.4	23.8	26.2	28.6	30.9	33.3	35.7
24 00	0.0	2.4	4.8	7.2	9.6	12.0	14.4	16.8	19.2	21.6	24.0	26.4	28.8	31.2	33.6	36.0

CORRECTIONS

ABC TABLES

A
+ if hour angle is listed at top
− if hour angle is listed at bottom

LHA	1°/359°	2°/358°	3°/357°	4°/356°	5°/355°	6°/354°	7°/353°	8°/352°	9°/351°	10°/350°	11°/349°	12°/348°	13°/347°	14°/346°	15°/345°
0	0.00	.000	.000	.000	.000	.000	.000	.000	.000	.000	.000	.000	.000	.000	.000
3	3.00	1.50	1.00	.749	.599	.499	.427	.373	.331	.297	.270	.247	.227	.210	.196
6	6.02	3.01	2.01	1.50	1.20	1.00	.856	.748	.664	.596	.541	.494	.455	.422	.392
9	9.07	4.54	3.02	2.27	1.81	1.51	1.29	1.13	1.00	.898	.815	.745	.686	.635	.591
12	12.2	6.09	4.06	3.04	2.43	2.02	1.73	1.51	1.34	1.21	1.09	1.00	.921	.853	.793
15	15.4	7.67	5.11	3.83	3.06	2.55	2.18	1.91	1.69	1.52	1.38	1.26	1.16	1.07	1.00
18	18.6	9.30	6.20	4.65	3.71	3.09	2.65	2.31	2.05	1.84	1.67	1.53	1.41	1.30	1.21
21	22.0	11.0	7.32	5.49	4.39	3.65	3.13	2.73	2.42	2.18	1.97	1.81	1.66	1.54	1.43
24	25.5	12.7	8.50	6.37	5.09	4.24	3.63	3.17	2.81	2.53	2.29	2.09	1.93	1.79	1.66
27	29.2	14.6	9.72	7.29	5.82	4.85	4.15	3.63	3.22	2.89	2.62	2.40	2.21	2.04	1.90
30	33.1	16.5	11.0	8.26	6.60	5.49	4.70	4.11	3.65	3.27	2.97	2.72	2.50	2.32	2.15
33	37.2	18.6	12.4	9.29	7.42	6.18	5.29	4.62	4.10	3.68	3.34	3.06	2.81	2.61	2.42
36	41.6	20.8	13.9	10.4	8.30	6.91	5.92	5.17	4.59	4.12	3.74	3.42	3.15	2.91	2.71
38	44.8	22.4	14.9	11.2	8.93	7.43	6.36	5.56	4.93	4.43	4.02	3.68	3.38	3.13	2.92
40	48.1	24.0	16.0	12.0	9.59	7.98	6.83	5.97	5.30	4.76	4.32	3.95	3.63	3.37	3.13
42	51.6	25.8	17.2	12.9	10.3	8.57	7.33	6.41	5.69	5.11	4.63	4.24	3.90	3.61	3.36
44	55.3	27.7	18.4	13.8	11.0	9.19	7.86	6.87	6.10	5.48	4.97	4.54	4.18	3.87	3.60
46	59.3	29.7	19.8	14.8	11.8	9.85	8.43	7.37	6.54	5.87	5.33	4.87	4.49	4.15	3.86
48	63.6	31.8	21.2	15.9	12.7	10.6	9.05	7.90	7.01	6.30	5.71	5.23	4.81	4.45	4.14
50	68.3	34.1	22.7	17.0	13.6	11.3	9.71	8.48	7.52	6.76	6.13	5.61	5.16	4.78	4.45
52	73.3	36.7	24.4	18.3	14.6	12.2	10.4	9.11	8.08	7.26	6.58	6.02	5.55	5.13	4.78
54	78.9	39.4	26.3	19.7	15.7	13.1	11.2	9.79	8.69	7.81	7.08	6.48	5.96	5.52	5.14
56	84.9	42.5	28.3	21.2	16.9	14.1	12.1	10.5	9.36	8.41	7.63	6.97	6.42	5.95	5.53
58	91.7	45.8	30.5	22.9	18.3	15.2	13.0	11.4	10.1	9.08	8.23	7.53	6.93	6.42	5.97
60	99.2	49.6	33.0	24.8	19.8	16.5	14.1	12.3	10.9	9.82	8.91	8.15	7.50	6.95	6.46
62	108	53.9	35.9	26.9	21.5	17.9	15.3	13.4	11.9	10.7	9.68	8.85	8.15	7.54	7.02
64	117	58.7	39.1	29.3	23.4	19.5	16.7	14.6	12.9	11.6	10.5	9.65	8.88	8.22	7.65
66	129	64.3	42.9	32.1	25.7	21.4	18.3	16.0	14.2	12.7	11.6	10.6	9.72	9.01	8.38
LHA	179°/181°	178°/182°	177°/183°	176°/184°	175°/185°	174°/186°	173°/187°	172°/188°	171°/189°	170°/190°	169°/191°	168°/192°	167°/193°	166°/194°	165°/195°

Latitude (°N/S)

B
− if Lat and Dec have same name
+ if Lat and Dec have different names

LHA	1°/359°	2°/358°	3°/357°	4°/356°	5°/355°	6°/354°	7°/353°	8°/352°	9°/351°	10°/350°	11°/349°	12°/348°	13°/347°	14°/346°	15°/345°
0	0.00	.000	.000	.000	.000	.000	.000	.000	.000	.000	.000	.000	.000	.000	.000
3	3.00	1.50	1.00	.751	.601	.501	.430	.377	.335	.302	.275	.252	.233	.217	.202
6	6.02	3.01	2.01	1.51	1.21	1.01	.862	.755	.672	.605	.551	.506	.467	.434	.406
9	9.08	4.54	3.03	2.27	1.82	1.52	1.30	1.14	1.01	.912	.830	.762	.704	.655	.612
12	12.2	6.09	4.06	3.05	2.44	2.03	1.74	1.53	1.36	1.22	1.11	1.02	.945	.879	.821
15	15.4	7.68	5.12	3.84	3.07	2.56	2.20	1.93	1.71	1.54	1.40	1.29	1.19	1.11	1.04
18	18.6	9.31	6.21	4.66	3.73	3.11	2.67	2.33	2.08	1.87	1.70	1.56	1.44	1.34	1.26
21	22.0	11.0	7.33	5.50	4.40	3.67	3.15	2.76	2.45	2.21	2.01	1.85	1.71	1.59	1.48
24	25.5	12.8	8.51	6.38	5.11	4.26	3.65	3.20	2.85	2.56	2.33	2.14	1.98	1.84	1.72
27	29.2	14.6	9.74	7.30	5.85	4.87	4.18	3.66	3.26	2.93	2.67	2.45	2.27	2.11	1.97
30	33.1	16.5	11.0	8.28	6.62	5.52	4.74	4.15	3.69	3.32	3.03	2.78	2.57	2.39	2.23
33	37.2	18.6	12.4	9.31	7.45	6.21	5.33	4.67	4.15	3.74	3.40	3.12	2.89	2.68	2.51
36	41.6	20.8	13.9	10.4	8.34	6.95	5.96	5.22	4.64	4.18	3.81	3.49	3.23	3.00	2.81
38	44.8	22.4	14.9	11.2	8.96	7.47	6.41	5.61	4.99	4.50	4.09	3.76	3.47	3.23	3.02
40	48.1	24.0	16.0	12.0	9.63	8.03	6.89	6.03	5.36	4.83	4.40	4.04	3.73	3.47	3.24
42	51.6	25.8	17.2	12.9	10.3	8.61	7.39	6.47	5.76	5.19	4.72	4.33	4.00	3.72	3.48
44	55.3	27.7	18.5	13.8	11.1	9.24	7.92	6.94	6.17	5.56	5.06	4.64	4.29	3.99	3.73
46	59.3	29.7	19.8	14.8	11.9	9.91	8.50	7.44	6.62	5.96	5.43	4.98	4.60	4.28	4.00
48	63.6	31.8	21.2	15.9	12.7	10.6	9.11	7.98	7.10	6.40	5.82	5.34	4.94	4.59	4.29
50	68.3	34.1	22.8	17.1	13.7	11.4	9.78	8.56	7.62	6.86	6.25	5.73	5.30	4.93	4.60
52	73.3	36.7	24.5	18.3	14.7	12.2	10.5	9.20	8.18	7.37	6.71	6.16	5.69	5.29	4.95
54	78.9	39.4	26.3	19.7	15.8	13.2	11.3	9.89	8.80	7.93	7.21	6.62	6.12	5.69	5.32
56	84.9	42.5	28.3	21.3	17.0	14.2	12.2	10.7	9.48	8.54	7.77	7.13	6.59	6.13	5.73
58	91.7	45.9	30.6	22.9	18.4	15.3	13.1	11.5	10.2	9.22	8.39	7.70	7.11	6.62	6.18
60	99.2	49.6	33.1	24.8	19.9	16.6	14.2	12.5	11.1	9.97	9.08	8.33	7.70	7.16	6.69
62	108	53.9	35.9	27.0	21.6	18.0	15.4	13.5	12.0	10.8	9.86	9.05	8.36	7.77	7.27
LHA	179°/181°	178°/182°	177°/183°	176°/184°	175°/185°	174°/186°	173°/187°	172°/188°	171°/189°	170°/190°	169°/191°	168°/192°	167°/193°	166°/194°	165°/195°

Declination (°N/S)

ABC TABLES

A   + if hour angle is listed at top
     − if hour angle is listed at bottom

LHA	16° 344°	17° 343°	18° 342°	19° 341°	20° 340°	21° 339°	22° 338°	23° 337°	24° 336°	25° 335°	26° 334°	27° 333°	28° 332°	29° 331°	30° 330°
0	.000	.000	.000	.000	.000	.000	.000	.000	.000	.000	.000	.000	.000	.000	.000
3	.183	.171	.161	.152	.144	.137	.130	.123	.118	.112	.107	.103	.099	.095	.091
6	.367	.344	.323	.305	.289	.274	.260	.248	.236	.225	.215	.206	.198	.190	.182
9	.552	.518	.487	.460	.435	.413	.392	.373	.356	.340	.325	.311	.298	.286	.274
12	.741	.695	.654	.617	.584	.554	.526	.501	.477	.456	.436	.417	.400	.383	.368
15	.934	.876	.825	.778	.736	.698	.663	.631	.602	.575	.549	.526	.504	.483	.464
18	1.13	1.06	1.00	.944	.893	.846	.804	.765	.730	.697	.666	.638	.611	.586	.563
21	1.34	1.26	1.18	1.11	1.05	1.00	.950	.904	.862	.823	.787	.753	.722	.693	.665
24	1.55	1.46	1.37	1.29	1.22	1.16	1.10	1.05	1.00	.955	.913	.874	.837	.803	.771
27	1.78	1.67	1.57	1.48	1.40	1.33	1.26	1.20	1.14	1.09	1.04	1.00	.958	.919	.883
30	2.01	1.89	1.78	1.68	1.59	1.50	1.43	1.36	1.30	1.24	1.18	1.13	1.09	1.04	1.00
33	2.26	2.12	2.00	1.89	1.78	1.69	1.61	1.53	1.46	1.39	1.33	1.27	1.22	1.17	1.12
36	2.53	2.38	2.24	2.11	2.00	1.89	1.80	1.71	1.63	1.56	1.49	1.43	1.37	1.31	1.26
38	2.72	2.56	2.40	2.27	2.15	2.04	1.93	1.84	1.75	1.68	1.60	1.53	1.47	1.41	1.35
40	2.93	2.74	2.58	2.44	2.31	2.19	2.08	1.98	1.88	1.80	1.72	1.65	1.58	1.51	1.45
42	3.14	2.95	2.77	2.61	2.47	2.35	2.23	2.12	2.02	1.93	1.85	1.77	1.69	1.62	1.56
44	3.37	3.16	2.97	2.80	2.65	2.52	2.39	2.28	2.17	2.07	1.98	1.90	1.82	1.74	1.67
46	3.61	3.39	3.19	3.01	2.85	2.70	2.56	2.44	2.33	2.22	2.12	2.03	1.95	1.87	1.79
48	3.87	3.63	3.42	3.23	3.05	2.89	2.75	2.62	2.49	2.38	2.28	2.18	2.09	2.00	1.92
50	4.16	3.90	3.67	3.46	3.27	3.10	2.95	2.81	2.68	2.56	2.44	2.34	2.24	2.15	2.06
52	4.46	4.19	3.94	3.72	3.52	3.33	3.17	3.02	2.87	2.74	2.62	2.51	2.41	2.31	2.22
54	4.80	4.50	4.24	4.00	3.78	3.59	3.41	3.24	3.09	2.95	2.82	2.70	2.59	2.48	2.38
56	5.17	4.85	4.56	4.31	4.07	3.86	3.67	3.49	3.33	3.18	3.04	2.91	2.79	2.67	2.57
58	5.58	5.23	4.93	4.65	4.40	4.17	3.96	3.77	3.59	3.43	3.28	3.14	3.01	2.89	2.77
60	6.04	5.67	5.33	5.03	4.76	4.51	4.29	4.08	3.89	3.71	3.55	3.40	3.26	3.12	3.00
62	6.56	6.15	5.79	5.46	5.17	4.90	4.65	4.43	4.22	4.03	3.86	3.69	3.54	3.39	3.26
64	7.15	6.71	6.31	5.95	5.63	5.34	5.07	4.83	4.61	4.40	4.20	4.02	3.86	3.70	3.55
66	7.83	7.35	6.91	6.52	6.17	5.85	5.56	5.29	5.04	4.82	4.61	4.41	4.22	4.05	3.89
LHA	164° 196°	163° 197°	162° 198°	161° 199°	160° 200°	159° 201°	158° 202°	157° 203°	156° 204°	155° 205°	154° 206°	153° 207°	152° 208°	151° 209°	150° 210°

Latitude (°N/S)

B   − if Lat and Dec have same name
     + if Lat and Dec have different names

LHA	16° 344°	17° 343°	18° 342°	19° 341°	20° 340°	21° 339°	22° 338°	23° 337°	24° 336°	25° 335°	26° 334°	27° 333°	28° 332°	29° 331°	30° 330°
0	.000	.000	.000	.000	.000	.000	.000	.000	.000	.000	.000	.000	.000	.000	.000
3	.190	.179	.170	.161	.153	.146	.140	.134	.129	.124	.120	.115	.112	.108	.105
6	.381	.359	.340	.323	.307	.293	.281	.269	.258	.249	.240	.232	.224	.217	.210
9	.575	.542	.513	.486	.463	.442	.423	.405	.389	.375	.361	.349	.337	.327	.317
12	.771	.727	.688	.653	.621	.593	.567	.544	.523	.503	.485	.468	.453	.438	.425
15	.972	.916	.867	.823	.783	.748	.715	.686	.659	.634	.611	.590	.571	.553	.536
18	1.18	1.11	1.05	.998	.950	.907	.867	.832	.799	.769	.741	.716	.692	.670	.650
21	1.39	1.31	1.24	1.18	1.12	1.07	1.02	.982	.944	.908	.876	.846	.818	.792	.768
24	1.62	1.52	1.44	1.37	1.30	1.24	1.19	1.14	1.09	1.05	1.02	.981	.948	.918	.890
27	1.85	1.74	1.65	1.57	1.49	1.42	1.36	1.30	1.25	1.21	1.16	1.12	1.09	1.05	1.02
30	2.09	1.97	1.87	1.77	1.69	1.61	1.54	1.48	1.42	1.37	1.32	1.27	1.23	1.19	1.15
33	2.36	2.22	2.10	1.99	1.90	1.81	1.73	1.66	1.60	1.54	1.48	1.43	1.38	1.34	1.30
36	2.64	2.48	2.32	2.23	2.12	2.03	1.94	1.86	1.79	1.72	1.66	1.60	1.55	1.50	1.45
38	2.83	2.67	2.53	2.40	2.28	2.18	2.09	2.00	1.92	1.85	1.78	1.72	1.66	1.61	1.56
40	3.04	2.87	2.72	2.58	2.45	2.34	2.24	2.15	2.06	1.99	1.91	1.85	1.79	1.73	1.68
42	3.27	3.08	2.91	2.77	2.63	2.51	2.40	2.30	2.21	2.13	2.05	1.98	1.92	1.86	1.80
44	3.50	3.30	3.13	2.97	2.82	2.69	2.58	2.47	2.37	2.29	2.20	2.13	2.06	1.99	1.93
46	3.76	3.54	3.35	3.18	3.03	2.89	2.76	2.65	2.55	2.45	2.36	2.28	2.21	2.14	2.07
48	4.03	3.80	3.59	3.41	3.25	3.10	2.96	2.84	2.73	2.63	2.53	2.45	2.37	2.29	2.22
50	4.32	4.08	3.86	3.66	3.48	3.33	3.18	3.05	2.93	2.82	2.72	2.63	2.54	2.46	2.38
52	4.64	4.38	4.14	3.93	3.74	3.57	3.42	3.28	3.15	3.03	2.92	2.82	2.73	2.64	2.56
54	4.99	4.71	4.45	4.23	4.02	3.84	3.67	3.52	3.38	3.26	3.14	3.03	2.93	2.84	2.75
56	5.38	5.07	4.80	4.55	4.33	4.14	3.96	3.79	3.65	3.51	3.38	3.27	3.16	3.06	2.97
58	5.81	5.47	5.18	4.92	4.68	4.47	4.27	4.10	3.93	3.79	3.65	3.53	3.41	3.30	3.20
60	6.28	5.92	5.61	5.32	5.06	4.83	4.62	4.43	4.26	4.10	3.95	3.82	3.69	3.57	3.46
62	6.82	6.43	6.09	5.78	5.50	5.25	5.02	4.81	4.62	4.45	4.29	4.14	4.01	3.88	3.76
LHA	164° 196°	163° 197°	162° 198°	161° 199°	160° 200°	159° 201°	158° 202°	157° 203°	156° 204°	155° 205°	154° 206°	153° 207°	152° 208°	151° 209°	150° 210°

Declination (°N/S)

ABC TABLES

ABC TABLES

A + if hour angle is listed at top
− if hour angle is listed at bottom

LHA	32° 328°	34° 326°	36° 324°	38° 322°	40° 320°	42° 318°	44° 316°	46° 314°	48° 312°	50° 310°	52° 308°	54° 306°	56° 304°	58° 302°	60° 300°
0	.000	.000	.000	.000	.000	.000	.000	.000	.000	.000	.000	.000	.000	.000	.000
3	.084	.078	.072	.067	.062	.058	.054	.051	.047	.044	.041	.038	.035	.033	.030
6	.168	.156	.145	.135	.125	.117	.109	.101	.095	.088	.082	.076	.071	.066	.061
9	.253	.235	.218	.203	.189	.176	.164	.153	.143	.133	.124	.115	.107	.099	.091
12	.340	.315	.293	.272	.253	.236	.220	.205	.191	.178	.166	.154	.143	.133	.123
15	.429	.397	.369	.343	.319	.298	.277	.259	.241	.225	.209	.195	.181	.167	.155
18	.520	.482	.447	.416	.387	.361	.336	.314	.293	.273	.254	.236	.219	.203	.188
21	.614	.569	.528	.491	.457	.426	.398	.371	.346	.322	.300	.279	.259	.240	.222
24	.713	.660	.613	.570	.531	.494	.461	.430	.401	.374	.348	.323	.300	.278	.257
27	.815	.755	.701	.652	.607	.566	.528	.492	.459	.428	.398	.370	.344	.318	.294
30	.924	.856	.795	.739	.688	.641	.598	.558	.520	.484	.451	.419	.389	.361	.333
33	1.04	.963	.894	.831	.774	.721	.672	.627	.585	.545	.507	.472	.438	.406	.375
36	1.16	1.08	1.00	.930	.866	.807	.752	.702	.654	.610	.568	.528	.490	.454	.419
38	1.25	1.16	1.08	1.00	.931	.868	.809	.754	.703	.656	.610	.568	.527	.488	.451
40	1.34	1.24	1.15	1.07	1.00	.932	.869	.810	.756	.704	.656	.610	.566	.524	.484
42	1.44	1.33	1.24	1.15	1.07	1.00	.932	.870	.811	.756	.703	.654	.607	.563	.520
44	1.55	1.43	1.33	1.24	1.15	1.07	1.00	.933	.870	.810	.754	.702	.651	.603	.558
46	1.66	1.54	1.43	1.33	1.23	1.15	1.07	1.00	.932	.869	.809	.752	.698	.647	.598
48	1.78	1.65	1.53	1.42	1.32	1.23	1.15	1.07	1.00	.932	.868	.807	.749	.694	.641
50	1.91	1.77	1.64	1.53	1.42	1.32	1.23	1.15	1.07	1.00	.931	.866	.804	.745	.688
52	2.05	1.90	1.76	1.64	1.53	1.42	1.33	1.24	1.15	1.07	1.00	.930	.863	.800	.739
54	2.20	2.04	1.89	1.76	1.64	1.53	1.43	1.33	1.24	1.15	1.08	1.00	.928	.860	.795
56	2.37	2.20	2.04	1.90	1.77	1.65	1.54	1.43	1.33	1.24	1.16	1.08	1.00	.926	.856
58	2.56	2.37	2.20	2.05	1.91	1.78	1.66	1.55	1.44	1.34	1.25	1.16	1.08	1.00	.924
60	2.77	2.57	2.38	2.22	2.06	1.92	1.79	1.67	1.56	1.45	1.35	1.26	1.17	1.08	1.00
62	3.01	2.79	2.59	2.41	2.24	2.09	1.95	1.82	1.69	1.58	1.47	1.37	1.27	1.18	1.09
64	3.28	3.04	2.82	2.62	2.44	2.28	2.12	1.98	1.85	1.72	1.60	1.49	1.38	1.28	1.18
66	3.59	3.33	3.09	2.87	2.68	2.49	2.33	2.17	2.02	1.88	1.75	1.63	1.52	1.40	1.30
LHA	148° 212°	146° 214°	144° 216°	142° 218°	140° 220°	138° 222°	136° 224°	134° 226°	132° 228°	130° 230°	128° 232°	126° 234°	124° 236°	122° 238°	120° 240°

Latitude (°N/S)

B − if Lat and Dec have same name
+ if Lat and Dec have different names

LHA	32° 328°	34° 326°	36° 324°	38° 322°	40° 320°	42° 318°	44° 316°	46° 314°	48° 312°	50° 310°	52° 308°	54° 306°	56° 304°	58° 302°	60° 300°
0	.000	.000	.000	.000	.000	.000	.000	.000	.000	.000	.000	.000	.000	.000	.000
3	.099	.094	.089	.085	.082	.078	.075	.073	.071	.068	.067	.065	.063	.062	.061
6	.198	.188	.179	.171	.164	.157	.151	.146	.141	.137	.133	.130	.127	.124	.121
9	.299	.283	.269	.257	.246	.237	.228	.220	.213	.207	.201	.196	.191	.187	.183
12	.401	.380	.362	.345	.331	.318	.306	.295	.286	.277	.270	.263	.256	.251	.245
15	.506	.479	.456	.435	.417	.400	.386	.372	.361	.350	.340	.331	.323	.316	.309
18	.613	.581	.553	.528	.505	.486	.468	.452	.437	.424	.412	.402	.392	.383	.375
21	.724	.686	.653	.623	.597	.574	.553	.534	.517	.501	.487	.474	.463	.453	.443
24	.840	.796	.757	.723	.693	.665	.641	.619	.599	.581	.565	.550	.537	.525	.514
27	.962	.911	.867	.828	.793	.761	.733	.708	.686	.665	.647	.630	.615	.601	.588
30	1.09	1.03	.982	.938	.898	.863	.831	.803	.777	.754	.733	.714	.696	.681	.667
33	1.23	1.16	1.11	1.05	1.01	`.971	.935	.903	.874	.848	.824	.803	.783	.766	.750
36	1.37	1.30	1.24	1.18	1.13	1.09	1.05	1.01	.978	.948	.922	.898	.876	.857	.839
38	1.47	1.40	1.33	1.27	1.22	1.17	1.12	1.09	1.05	1.02	.991	.966	.942	.921	.902
40	1.58	1.50	1.43	1.36	1.31	1.25	1.21	1.17	1.13	1.10	1.06	1.04	1.01	.989	.969
42	1.70	1.61	1.53	1.46	1.40	1.35	1.30	1.25	1.21	1.18	1.14	1.11	1.09	1.06	1.04
44	1.82	1.73	1.64	1.57	1.50	1.44	1.39	1.34	1.30	1.26	1.23	1.19	1.16	1.14	1.12
46	1.95	1.85	1.76	1.68	1.61	1.55	1.49	1.44	1.39	1.35	1.31	1.28	1.25	1.22	1.20
48	2.10	1.99	1.89	1.80	1.73	1.66	1.60	1.54	1.49	1.45	1.41	1.37	1.34	1.31	1.28
50	2.25	2.13	2.03	1.94	1.85	1.78	1.72	1.66	1.60	1.56	1.51	1.47	1.44	1.41	1.38
52	2.42	2.29	2.18	2.08	1.99	1.91	1.84	1.78	1.72	1.67	1.62	1.58	1.54	1.51	1.48
54	2.60	2.46	2.34	2.24	2.14	2.06	1.98	1.91	1.85	1.80	1.75	1.70	1.66	1.62	1.59
56	2.80	2.65	2.52	2.41	2.31	2.22	2.13	2.06	2.00	1.94	1.88	1.83	1.79	1.75	1.71
58	3.02	2.86	2.72	2.60	2.49	2.39	2.30	2.22	2.15	2.09	2.03	1.98	1.93	1.89	1.85
60	3.27	3.10	2.95	2.81	2.69	2.59	2.49	2.41	2.33	2.26	2.20	2.14	2.09	2.04	2.00
62	3.55	3.36	3.20	3.05	2.93	2.81	2.71	2.61	2.53	2.46	2.39	2.32	2.27	2.22	2.17
LHA	148° 212°	146° 214°	144° 216°	142° 218°	140° 220°	138° 222°	136° 224°	134° 226°	132° 228°	130° 230°	128° 232°	126° 234°	124° 236°	122° 238°	120° 240°

Declination (°N/S)

ABC TABLES

A
+ if hour angle is listed at top
− if hour angle is listed at bottom

LHA	62° 298°	64° 296°	66° 294°	68° 292°	70° 290°	72° 288°	74° 286°	76° 284°	78° 282°	80° 280°	82° 278°	84° 276°	86° 274°	88° 272°	90° 270°
0	.000	.000	.000	.000	.000	.000	.000	.000	.000	.000	.000	.000	.000	.000	.000
3	.028	.026	.023	.021	.019	.017	.015	.013	.011	.009	.007	.006	.004	.002	.000
6	.056	.051	.047	.043	.038	.034	.030	.026	.022	.019	.015	.011	.007	.004	.000
9	.084	.077	.071	.064	.058	.051	.045	.039	.034	.028	.022	.017	.011	.006	.000
12	.113	.104	.065	.086	.077	.069	.061	.053	.045	.037	.030	.022	.015	.007	.000
15	.142	.131	.119	.108	.098	.087	.077	.067	.057	.047	.038	.028	.019	.009	.000
18	.173	.158	.145	.131	.118	.106	.093	.081	.069	.057	.046	.034	.023	.012	.000
21	.204	.187	.171	.155	.140	.125	.110	.096	.082	.068	.054	.040	.027	.013	.000
24	.237	.217	.198	.180	.162	.145	.128	.111	.095	.079	.063	.047	.031	.016	.000
27	.271	.249	.227	.206	.185	.166	.146	.127	.108	.090	.072	.054	.036	.018	.000
30	.307	.282	.257	.233	.210	.188	.166	.144	.123	.102	.081	.061	.040	.020	.000
33	.345	.317	.289	.262	.236	.211	.186	.162	.138	.115	.091	.068	.045	.023	.000
36	.386	.354	.323	.294	.264	.236	.208	.181	.154	.128	.102	.076	.051	.025	.000
38	.415	.381	.348	.316	.284	.254	.224	.195	.166	.138	.110	.082	.055	.027	.000
40	.446	.409	.374	.339	.305	.273	.241	.209	.178	.148	.118	.088	.059	.029	.000
42	.479	.439	.401	.364	.328	.293	.258	.224	.191	.159	.127	.095	.063	.031	.000
44	.513	.471	.430	.390	.351	.314	.277	.241	.205	.170	.136	.101	.068	.034	.000
46	.551	.505	.461	.418	.377	.336	.297	.258	.220	.183	.146	.109	.072	.036	.000
48	.591	.542	.494	.449	.404	.361	.318	.277	.236	.196	.156	.1147	.078	.039	.000
50	.634	.581	.531	.481	.434	.387	.342	.297	.253	.210	.167	.125	.083	.042	.000
52	.681	.624	.570	.517	.466	.416	.367	.319	.272	.226	.180	.135	.090	.045	.000
54	.732	.671	.613	.556	.501	.447	.395	.343	.293	.243	.193	.145	.096	.048	.000
56	.788	.723	.660	.559	.540	.482	.425	.370	.315	.261	.208	.156	.104	.052	.000
58	.851	.781	.713	.647	.582	.520	.459	.399	.340	.282	.225	.168	.112	.056	.000
60	.921	.845	.771	.700	.630	.563	.497	.432	.368	.305	.243	.182	.121	.060	.000
62	1.00	.917	.837	.760	.685	.611	.539	.469	.400	.332	.264	.198	.132	.066	.000
64	1.09	1.00	.913	.828	.746	.666	.588	.511	.436	.362	.288	.215	.143	.072	.000
66	1.19	1.10	1.00	.907	.817	.730	.644	.560	.477	.396	.316	.236	.157	.078	.000
LHA	118° 242°	116° 244°	114° 246°	112° 248°	110° 250°	108° 252°	106° 254°	104° 256°	102° 258°	100° 260°	98° 262°	96° 264°	94° 266°	92° 268°	90° 270°

(Latitude (°N/S))

B
− if Lat and Dec have same name
+ if Lat and Dec have different names

LHA	62° 298°	64° 296°	66° 294°	68° 292°	70° 290°	72° 288°	74° 286°	76° 284°	78° 282°	80° 280°	82° 278°	84° 276°	86° 274°	88° 272°	90° 270°
0	.000	.000	.000	.000	.000	.000	.000	.000	.000	.000	.000	.000	.000	.000	.000
3	.059	.058	.057	.057	.056	.055	.055	.054	.054	.053	.053	.053	.053	.052	.052
6	.119	.117	.115	.113	.112	.111	.109	.108	.107	.107	.106	.106	.105	.105	.105
9	.179	.176	.173	.171	.169	.167	.165	.163	.162	.161	.160	.159	.159	.158	.158
12	.241	.236	.233	.229	.226	.223	.221	.219	.217	.216	.215	.214	.213	.213	.213
15	.303	.298	.293	.289	.285	.282	.279	.276	.274	.272	.271	.269	.269	.268	.268
18	.368	.362	.356	.350	.346	.342	.338	.335	.332	.330	.328	.327	.326	.325	.325
21	.435	.427	.420	.414	.408	.404	.399	.396	.392	.390	.388	.386	.385	.384	.384
24	.504	.495	.487	.480	.474	.468	.463	.459	.455	.452	.450	.448	.446	.446	.445
27	.577	.567	.558	.550	.542	.536	.530	.525	.521	.517	.515	.512	.511	.510	.510
30	.654	.642	.632	.623	.614	.607	.601	.595	.590	.586	.583	.581	.579	.578	.577
33	.735	.723	.711	.700	.691	.683	.676	.669	.664	.659	.656	.653	.651	.650	.649
36	.823	.808	.795	.784	.773	.764	.756	.749	.743	.738	.734	.731	.728	.727	.727
38	.885	.869	.855	.843	.831	.821	.813	.805	.799	.793	.789	.786	.783	.782	.781
40	.950	.934	.919	.905	.893	.882	.873	.865	.858	.852	.847	.844	.841	.840	.839
42	1.02	1.00	.986	.971	.958	.947	.937	.928	.921	.914	.909	.905	.903	.901	.900
44	1.09	1.07	1.06	1.04	1.03	1.02	1.00	.995	.987	.981	.975	.971	.968	.966	.966
46	1.17	1.15	1.13	1.12	1.10	1.09	1.08	1.07	1.06	1.05	1.05	1.04	1.04	1.04	1.04
48	1.26	1.24	1.22	1.20	1.18	1.17	1.16	1.14	1.14	1.13	1.12	1.12	1.11	1.11	1.11
50	1.35	1.33	1.30	1.29	1.27	1.25	1.24	1.23	1.22	1.21	1.20	1.20	1.19	1.19	1.19
52	1.45	1.42	1.40	1.38	1.36	1.35	1.33	1.32	1.31	1.30	1.29	1.29	1.28	1.28	1.28
54	1.56	1.53	1.51	1.48	1.46	1.45	1.43	1.42	1.41	1.40	1.39	1.38	1.38	1.38	1.38
56	1.68	1.65	1.62	1.60	1.58	1.56	1.54	1.53	1.52	1.51	1.50	1.49	1.49	1.48	1.48
58	1.81	1.78	1.75	1.73	1.70	1.68	1.66	1.65	1.64	1.63	1.62	1.61	1.60	1.60	1.60
60	1.96	1.93	1.90	1.87	1.84	1.82	1.80	1.79	1.77	1.76	1.75	1.74	1.74	1.73	1.73
62	2.13	2.09	2.06	2.03	2.00	1.98	1.96	1.94	1.92	1.91	1.90	1.89	1.89	1.88	1.88
LHA	118° 242°	116° 244°	114° 246°	112° 248°	110° 250°	108° 252°	106° 254°	104° 256°	102° 258°	100° 260°	98° 262°	96° 264°	94° 266°	92° 268°	90° 270°

(Declination (°N/S))

ABC TABLES

ABC TABLES

C $= A \pm B$

C	.00	.05	.10	.15	.20	.25	.30	.35	.40	.45	.50	.55	.60	.70
Lat °	°	°	°	°	°	°	°	°	°	°	°	°	°	°
0	90.0	87.1	84.3	81.5	78.7	76.0	73.3	70.7	68.2	65.8	63.4	61.2	59.0	55.0
10	90.0	87.2	84.4	81.6	78.9	76.2	73.5	71.0	68.5	66.1	63.8	61.6	59.4	55.4
20	90.0	87.3	84.6	82.0	79.4	76.8	74.3	71.8	69.4	67.1	64.8	62.7	60.6	56.7
24	90.0	87.4	84.8	82.2	79.6	77.1	74.7	72.3	69.9	67.7	65.5	63.3	61.3	57.4
28	90.0	87.5	85.0	82.5	80.0	77.6	75.2	72.8	70.5	68.3	66.2	64.1	62.1	58.3
30	90.0	87.5	85.1	82.6	80.2	77.8	75.4	73.1	70.9	68.7	66.6	64.5	62.5	58.8
32	90.0	87.6	85.2	82.8	80.4	78.0	75.7	73.5	71.3	69.1	67.0	65.0	63.0	59.3
34	90.0	87.6	85.3	82.9	80.6	78.3	76.0	73.8	71.7	69.5	67.5	65.5	63.6	59.9
36	90.0	87.7	85.4	83.1	80.8	78.6	76.4	74.2	72.1	70.0	68.0	66.0	64.1	60.5
38	90.0	87.7	85.5	83.3	81.0	78.9	76.7	74.6	72.5	70.5	68.5	66.6	64.7	61.1
40	90.0	87.8	85.6	83.4	81.3	79.2	77.1	75.0	73.0	71.0	69.0	67.2	65.3	61.8
42	90.0	87.9	85.7	83.6	81.5	79.5	77.4	75.4	73.4	71.5	69.6	67.8	66.0	62.5
44	90.0	87.9	85.9	83.8	81.8	79.8	77.8	75.9	73.9	72.1	70.2	68.4	66.7	63.3
46	90.0	88.0	86.0	84.1	82.1	80.1	78.2	76.3	74.5	72.6	70.8	69.1	67.4	64.1
48	90.0	88.1	86.2	84.3	82.4	80.5	78.6	76.8	75.0	73.2	71.5	69.8	68.1	64.9
50	90.0	88.2	86.3	84.5	82.7	80.9	79.1	77.3	75.6	73.9	72.2	70.5	68.9	65.8
52	90.0	88.2	86.5	84.7	83.0	81.2	79.5	77.8	76.2	74.5	72.9	71.3	69.7	66.7
54	90.0	88.3	86.6	85.0	83.3	81.6	80.0	78.4	76.8	75.2	73.6	72.1	70.6	67.6
56	90.0	88.4	86.8	85.2	83.6	82.0	80.5	78.9	77.4	75.9	74.4	72.9	71.5	68.6
58	90.0	88.5	87.0	85.5	84.0	82.5	81.0	79.5	78.0	76.6	75.2	73.8	72.4	69.6
60	90.0	88.6	87.1	85.7	84.3	82.9	81.5	80.1	78.7	77.3	76.0	74.6	73.3	70.7
62	90.0	88.7	87.3	86.0	84.6	83.3	82.0	80.7	79.4	78.1	76.8	75.5	74.3	71.8
64	90.0	88.7	87.5	86.2	85.0	83.7	82.5	81.3	80.1	78.8	77.6	76.4	75.3	72.9
66	90.0	88.8	87.7	86.5	85.3	84.2	83.0	81.9	80.8	79.6	78.5	77.4	76.3	74.1
68	90.0	88.9	87.9	86.8	85.7	84.6	83.6	82.5	81.5	80.4	79.4	78.4	77.3	75.3
	.00	.05	.10	.15	.20	.25	.30	.35	.40	.45	.50	.55	.60	.70

C	.80	.90	1.00	1.10	1.20	1.40	1.60	1.80	2.00	2.20	2.40	2.60	2.80
Lat °	°	°	°	°	°	°	°	°	°	°	°	°	°
0	51.3	48.0	45.0	42.3	39.8	35.5	32.0	29.1	26.6	24.4	22.6	21.0	19.7
10	51.8	48.4	45.4	42.7	40.2	36.0	32.4	29.4	26.9	24.8	22.9	21.3	19.9
20	53.1	49.8	46.8	44.1	41.6	37.2	33.6	30.6	28.0	25.8	23.9	22.3	20.8
24	53.8	50.6	47.6	44.9	42.4	38.0	34.4	31.3	28.7	26.5	24.5	22.8	21.4
28	54.8	51.5	48.6	45.8	43.3	39.0	35.3	32.2	29.55	27.2	25.3	23.5	22.0
30	55.3	52.1	49.1	46.4	43.9	39.5	35.8	32.7	30.0	27.7	25.7	23.9	22.4
32	55.8	52.7	49.7	47.0	44.5	40.1	36.4	33.2	30.5	28.2	26.2	24.4	22.8
34	56.4	53.3	50.3	47.6	45.1	40.7	37.0	33.8	31.1	28.7	26.7	24.9	23.3
36	57.1	53.9	51.0	48.3	45.8	41.4	37.7	34.5	31.7	29.3	27.3	25.4	23.8
38	57.8	54.7	51.8	49.1	46.6	42.2	38.4	35.2	32.4	30.0	27.9	26.0	24.4
40	58.5	55.4	52.5	49.9	47.4	43.0	39.2	36.0	33.1	30.7	28.5	26.7	25.0
42	59.3	56.2	53.4	50.7	48.3	43.9	40.1	36.8	33.9	31.5	29.3	27.4	25.7
44	60.1	57.1	54.3	51.6	49.2	44.8	41.0	37.7	34.8	32.3	30.1	28.1	26.4
46	60.9	58.0	55.2	52.6	50.2	45.8	42.0	38.7	35.7	33.2	31.0	29.0	27.2
48	61.8	58.9	56.2	53.6	51.2	46.9	43.0	39.7	36.8	34.2	31.9	29.9	28.1
50	62.8	60.0	57.3	54.7	52.4	48.0	44.2	40.8	37.9	35.3	33.0	30.9	29.1
52	63.8	61.0	58.4	55.9	53.5	49.2	45.4	42.1	39.1	36.4	34.1	32.0	30.1
54	64.8	62.1	59.6	57.1	54.8	50.6	46.8	43.4	40.4	37.7	35.3	33.2	31.3
56	65.9	63.3	60.8	58.4	56.1	51.9	48.2	44.8	41.8	39.1	36.7	34.5	32.6
58	67.0	64.5	62.1	59.8	57.5	53.4	49.7	46.4	43.4	40.6	38.2	36.0	34.0
60	68.2	65.8	63.4	61.2	59.0	55.0	51.3	48.0	45.0	42.3	39.8	37.6	35.5
62	69.4	67.1	64.9	62.7	60.6	56.7	53.1	49.8	46.8	44.1	41.6	39.3	37.3
64	70.7	68.5	66.3	64.3	62.3	58.5	55.0	51.7	48.8	46.0	43.5	41.3	39.2
66	72.0	69.9	67.9	65.9	64.0	60.3	56.9	53.8	50.9	48.2	45.7	43.4	41.3
68	73.3	71.4	69.5	67.6	65.8	62.3	59.1	56.0	53.2	50.5	48.0	45.8	43.6
	.80	.90	1.00	1.10	1.20	1.40	1.60	1.80	2.00	2.20	2.40	2.60	2.80

Naming the Azimuth: If answer is **+**, azimuth is **South** in North latitudes and **North** in South latitudes; if answer is **–**, azimuth is **North** in North latitudes and **South** in South latitudes. If Hour Angle is **less than 180°**, azimuth is **West**; if **more than 180°**, azimuth is **East**.

ABC TABLES

C = A±B

C	3.20	3.60	4.00	4.50	5.00	6.00	7.00	8.00	9.00	10.0	15.0	20.0	40.0
Lat	°	°	°	°	°	°	°	°	°	°	°	°	°
0	17.4	15.5	14.0	12.5	11.3	9.5	8.1	7.1	6.3	5.7	3.8	2.9	1.4
10	17.6	15.8	14.2	12.7	11.5	9.6	8.3	7.2	6.4	5.8	3.9	2.9	1.5
20	18.4	16.5	14.9	13.3	12.0	10.1	8.6	7.6	6.7	6.1	4.1	3.0	1.5
24	18.9	16.9	15.3	13.7	12.3	10.3	8.9	7.8	6.9	6.2	4.2	3.1	1.6
28	19.5	17.5	15.8	14.1	12.8	10.7	9.2	8.1	7.2	6.5	4.3	3.2	1.6
30	19.8	17.8	16.1	14.4	13.0	10.9	9.4	8.2	7.3	6.6	4.4	3.3	1.7
32	20.2	18.1	16.4	14.7	13.3	11.1	9.6	8.4	7.5	6.7	4.5	3.4	1.7
34	20.7	18.5	16.8	15.0	13.6	11.4	9.8	8.6	7.6	6.9	4.6	3.5	1.7
36	21.1	19.0	17.2	15.4	13.9	11.6	10.0	8.8	7.8	7.0	4.7	3.5	1.8
38	21.6	19.4	17.6	15.8	14.2	11.9	10.3	9.0	8.0	7.2	4.8	3.6	1.8
40	22.2	19.9	18.1	16.2	14.6	12.3	10.6	9.3	8.3	7.4	5.0	3.7	1.9
42	22.8	20.5	18.6	16.7	15.1	12.6	10.9	9.5	8.5	7.7	5.1	3.8	1.9
44	23.5	21.1	19.2	17.2	15.5	13.0	11.2	9.9	8.8	7.9	5.3	4.0	2.0
46	24.2	21.8	19.8	17.8	16.1	13.5	11.6	10.2	9.1	8.2	5.5	4.1	2.1
48	25.0	22.5	20.5	18.4	16.6	14.0	12.1	10.6	9.4	8.5	5.7	4.3	2.1
50	25.9	23.4	21.3	19.1	17.3	14.5	12.5	11.0	9.8	8.8	5.9	4.4	2.2
52	26.9	24.3	22.1	19.9	18.0	15.1	13.1	11.5	10.2	9.2	6.2	4.6	2.3
54	28.0	25.3	23.1	20.7	18.8	15.8	13.7	12.0	10.7	9.7	6.5	4.9	2.4
56	29.2	26.4	24.1	21.7	19.7	16.6	14.3	12.6	11.2	10.1	6.8	5.1	2.6
58	30.5	27.7	25.3	22.8	20.7	17.5	15.1	13.3	11.8	10.7	7.2	5.4	2.7
60	32.0	29.1	26.6	24.0	21.8	18.4	15.9	14.0	12.5	11.3	7.6	5.7	2.9
62	33.6	30.6	28.0	25.3	23.1	19.6	16.9	14.9	13.3	12.0	8.1	6.1	3.0
64	35.5	32.4	29.7	26.9	24.5	20.8	18.1	15.9	14.2	12.9	8.6	6.5	3.3
66	37.6	34.3	31.6	28.7	26.2	22.3	19.4	17.1	15.3	13.8	9.3	7.0	3.5
68	39.8	36.6	33.7	30.7	28.1	24.0	20.9	18.5	16.5	14.9	10.1	7.6	3.8
	3.20	3.60	4.00	4.50	5.00	6.00	7.00	8.00	9.00	10.0	15.0	20.0	40.0

Naming the Azimuth: If answer is **+**, azimuth is **South** in North latitudes and **North** in South latitudes; if answer is **–**, azimuth is **North** in North latitudes and **South** in South latitudes. If Hour Angle is **less than 180°**, azimuth is **West**; if **more than 180°**, azimuth is **East**.

VERSINES

′	0° Log	Nat	1° Log	Nat	2° Log	Nat	3° Log	Nat	4° Log	Nat	5° Log	Nat	6° Log	Nat	′
0′	∞	0.0000	1827	0002	6.7847	0006	1369	0014	7.3867	0024	5804	0038	7.7386	0.0055	60
1	2.6264	0.0000	1971	0002	6.7919	0006	1417	0014	7.3903	0025	5833	0038	7.7410	0.0055	59
2	3.2285	0.0000	2112	0002	6.7991	0006	1465	0014	7.3939	0025	5862	0039	7.7434	0.0055	58
3	3.5807	0.0000	2251	0002	6.8062	0006	1512	0014	7.3975	0025	5890	0039	7.7458	0.0056	57
4	3.8305	0.0000	2388	0002	6.8132	0007	1560	0014	7.4010	0025	5919	0039	7.7482	0.0056	56
5	4.0244	0.0000	2522	0002	6.8202	0007	1607	0014	7.4046	0025	5947	0039	7.7506	0.0056	55
6	4.1827	0.0000	2655	0002	6.8271	0007	1653	0015	7.4081	0026	5976	0040	7.7530	0.0057	54
7	4.3166	0.0000	2786	0002	6.8340	0007	1700	0015	7.4116	0026	6004	0040	7.7553	0.0057	53
8	4.4326	0.0000	2914	0002	6.8408	0007	1746	0015	7.4151	0026	6032	0040	7.7577	0.0057	52
9	4.5349	0.0000	3041	0002	6.8476	0007	1792	0015	7.4186	0026	6060	0040	7.7601	0.0058	51
10	4.6264	0.0000	3166	0002	6.8543	0007	1838	0015	7.4221	0026	6089	0041	7.7624	0.0058	50
11	4.7092	0.0000	3289	0002	6.8609	0007	1884	0015	7.4256	0027	6116	0041	7.7647	0.0058	49
12	4.7848	0.0000	3411	0002	6.8675	0007	1929	0016	7.4290	0027	6144	0041	7.7671	0.0058	48
13	4.8543	0.0000	3531	0002	6.8741	0007	1974	0016	7.4325	0027	6172	0041	7.7694	0.0059	47
14	4.9187	0.0000	3649	0002	6.8806	0008	2019	0016	7.4359	0027	6200	0042	7.7717	0.0059	46
15	4.9786	0.0000	3765	0002	6.8870	0008	2064	0016	7.4393	0027	6227	0042	7.7741	0.0059	45
16	5.0347	0.0000	3880	0002	6.8934	0008	2108	0016	7.4427	0028	6255	0042	7.7764	0.0060	44
17	5.0873	0.0000	3994	0002	6.8998	0008	2152	0016	7.4461	0028	6282	0042	7.7787	0.0060	43
18	5.1370	0.0000	4106	0003	6.9061	0008	2196	0017	7.4495	0028	6310	0043	7.7810	0.0060	42
19	5.1839	0.0000	4217	0003	6.9124	0008	2240	0017	7.4528	0028	6337	0043	7.7833	0.0061	41
20	5.2285	0.0000	4326	0003	6.9186	0008	2284	0017	7.4562	0029	6364	0043	7.7855	0.0061	40
21	5.2709	0.0000	4434	0003	6.9248	0008	2327	0017	7.4595	0029	6391	0044	7.7878	0.0061	39
22	5.3113	0.0000	4540	0003	6.9309	0009	2370	0017	7.4628	0029	6418	0044	7.7901	0.0062	38
23	5.3499	0.0000	4646	0003	6.9370	0009	2413	0017	7.4661	0029	6445	0044	7.7924	0.0062	37
24	5.3868	0.0000	4750	0003	6.9431	0009	2456	0018	7.4694	0029	6472	0044	7.7946	0.0062	36
25	5.4223	0.0000	4852	0003	6.9491	0009	2498	0018	7.4727	0030	6499	0045	7.7969	0.0063	35
26	5.4564	0.0000	4954	0003	6.9551	0009	2540	0018	7.4760	0030	6525	0045	7.7991	0.0063	34
27	5.4891	0.0000	5054	0003	6.9610	0009	2582	0018	7.4792	0030	6552	0045	7.8014	0.0063	33
28	5.5207	0.0000	5154	0003	6.9669	0009	2624	0018	7.4825	0030	6578	0045	7.8036	0.0064	32
29	5.5512	0.0000	5252	0003	6.9727	0009	2666	0018	7.4857	0031	6605	0046	7.8059	0.0064	31
30	5.5807	0.0000	5349	0003	6.9785	0010	2707	0019	7.4889	0031	6631	0046	7.8081	0.0064	30
31	5.6091	0.0000	5445	0004	6.9843	0010	2749	0019	7.4921	0031	6657	0046	7.8103	0.0065	29
32	5.6367	0.0000	5540	0004	6.9900	0010	2790	0019	7.4953	0031	6684	0047	7.8125	0.0065	28
33	5.6634	0.0000	5634	0004	6.9957	0010	2830	0019	7.4985	0032	6710	0047	7.8147	0.0065	27
34	5.6894	0.0000	5727	0004	7.0014	0010	2871	0019	7.5017	0032	6736	0047	7.8169	0.0066	26
35	5.7146	0.0001	5818	0004	7.0070	0010	2912	0020	7.5049	0032	6762	0047	7.8191	0.0066	25
36	5.7390	0.0001	5909	0004	7.0126	0010	2952	0020	7.5080	0032	6788	0048	7.8213	0.0066	24
37	5.7628	0.0001	5999	0004	7.0181	0010	2992	0020	7.5111	0032	6813	0048	7.8235	0.0067	23
38	5.7860	0.0001	6088	0004	7.0237	0011	3032	0020	7.5143	0033	6839	0048	7.8257	0.0067	22
39	5.8085	0.0001	6177	0004	7.0291	0011	3072	0020	7.5174	0033	6865	0049	7.8279	0.0067	21
40	5.8305	0.0001	6264	0004	7.0346	0011	3111	0020	7.5205	0033	6890	0049	7.8301	0.0068	20
41	5.8520	0.0001	6350	0004	7.0400	0011	3151	0021	7.5236	0033	6916	0049	7.8322	0.0068	19
42	5.8729	0.0001	6436	0004	7.0454	0011	3190	0021	7.5267	0034	6941	0049	7.8344	0.0068	18
43	5.8934	0.0001	6521	0004	7.0507	0011	3229	0021	7.5297	0034	6967	0050	7.8365	0.0069	17
44	5.9133	0.0001	6605	0005	7.0560	0011	3268	0021	7.5328	0034	6992	0050	7.8387	0.0069	16
45	5.9328	0.0001	6688	0005	7.0613	0012	3306	0021	7.5359	0034	7017	0050	7.8408	0.0069	15
46	5.9519	0.0001	6770	0005	7.0666	0012	3345	0022	7.5389	0035	7042	0051	7.8430	0.0070	14
47	5.9706	0.0001	6852	0005	7.0718	0012	3383	0022	7.5419	0035	7067	0051	7.8451	0.0070	13
48	5.9889	0.0001	6932	0005	7.0770	0012	3421	0022	7.5450	0035	7092	0051	7.8472	0.0070	12
49	6.0068	0.0001	7012	0005	7.0821	0012	3459	0022	7.5480	0035	7117	0051	7.8494	0.0071	11
50	6.0244	0.0001	7092	0005	7.0872	0012	3497	0022	7.5510	0036	7142	0052	7.8515	0.0071	10
51	6.0416	0.0001	7170	0005	7.0923	0012	3535	0023	7.5539	0036	7167	0052	7.8536	0.0071	9
52	6.0584	0.0001	7248	0005	7.0974	0013	3572	0023	7.5569	0036	7191	0052	7.8557	0.0072	8
53	6.0750	0.0001	7325	0005	7.1024	0013	3610	0023	7.5599	0036	7216	0053	7.8578	0.0072	7
54	6.0912	0.0001	7402	0005	7.1074	0013	3647	0023	7.5629	0037	7240	0053	7.8599	0.0072	6
55	6.1071	0.0001	7478	0006	7.1124	0013	3684	0023	7.5658	0037	7265	0053	7.8620	0.0073	5
56	6.1228	0.0001	7553	0006	7.1174	0013	3721	0024	7.5687	0037	7289	0054	7.8641	0.0073	4
57	6.1382	0.0001	7628	0006	7.1223	0013	3757	0024	7.5717	0037	7314	0054	7.8662	0.0073	3
58	6.1533	0.0001	7701	0006	7.1272	0013	3794	0024	7.5746	0038	7338	0054	7.8682	0.0074	2
59	6.1681	0.0001	7775	0006	7.1320	0014	3830	0024	7.5775	0038	7362	0054	7.8703	0.0074	1
60	6.1827	0.0002	7847	0006	7.1369	0014	3867	0024	7.5804	0038	7386	0055	7.8724	0.0075	0
′	Log	Nat	Log	Nat	Log	Nat	Log	Nat	Log	Nat	Log	Nat	Log	Nat	′
	359°		**358°**		**357°**		**356°**		**355°**		**354°**		**353°**		

Note: For compactness, the leading digit has been dropped from alternate columns. Scan preceding column and row for necessary digit.

NAUTICAL EPHEMERIS

VERSINES

′	7° Log	Nat	8° Log	Nat	9° Log	Nat	10° Log	Nat	11° Log	Nat	12° Log	Nat	13° Log	Nat	′
0	7.8724	0.0075	9882	0097	8.0903	0123	1816	0152	8.2642	0184	3395	0219	8.4087	0.0256	60
1	7.8744	0.0075	9900	0098	8.0919	0124	1831	0152	8.2655	0184	3407	0219	8.4099	0.0257	59
2	7.8765	0.0075	9918	0098	8.0935	0124	1845	0153	8.2668	0185	3419	0220	8.4110	0.0258	58
3	7.8786	0.0076	9936	0099	8.0951	0124	1859	0153	8.2681	0185	3431	0220	8.4121	0.0258	57
4	7.8806	0.0076	9954	0099	8.0967	0125	1874	0154	8.2694	0186	3443	0221	8.4132	0.0259	56
5	7.8826	0.0076	9972	0099	8.0983	0125	1888	0154	8.2707	0187	3455	0222	8.4143	0.0260	55
6	7.8847	0.0077	9990	0100	8.0999	0126	1902	0155	8.2720	0187	3467	0222	8.4154	0.0260	54
7	7.8867	0.0077	0008	0100	8.1015	0126	1917	0155	8.2733	0188	3479	0223	8.4165	0.0261	53
8	7.8887	0.0077	0025	0101	8.1031	0127	1931	0156	8.2746	0188	3491	0223	8.4176	0.0262	52
9	7.8908	0.0078	0043	0101	8.1046	0127	1945	0157	8.2759	0189	3502	0224	8.4187	0.0262	51
10	7.8928	0.0078	0061	0101	8.1062	0128	1959	0157	8.2772	0189	3514	0225	8.4198	0.0263	50
11	7.8948	0.0078	0078	0102	8.1078	0128	1974	0158	8.2785	0190	3526	0225	8.4209	0.0264	49
12	7.8968	0.0079	0096	0102	8.1094	0129	1988	0158	8.2798	0190	3538	0226	8.4220	0.0264	48
13	7.8988	0.0079	0114	0103	8.1109	0129	2002	0159	8.2811	0191	3550	0226	8.4230	0.0265	47
14	7.9008	0.0080	0131	0103	8.1125	0130	2016	0159	8.2824	0192	3562	0227	8.4241	0.0266	46
15	7.9028	0.0080	0149	0103	8.1141	0130	2030	0160	8.2836	0192	3573	0228	8.4252	0.0266	45
16	7.9048	0.0080	0166	0104	8.1156	0131	2044	0160	8.2849	0193	3585	0228	8.4263	0.0267	44
17	7.9068	0.0081	0184	0104	8.1172	0131	2058	0161	8.2862	0193	3597	0229	8.4274	0.0268	43
18	7.9088	0.0081	0201	0105	8.1187	0131	2072	0161	8.2875	0194	3609	0230	8.4285	0.0268	42
19	7.9108	0.0081	0219	0105	8.1203	0132	2086	0162	8.2887	0194	3620	0230	8.4296	0.0269	41
20	7.9127	0.0082	0236	0106	8.1218	0132	2100	0162	8.2900	0195	3632	0231	8.4306	0.0270	40
21	7.9147	0.0082	0253	0106	8.1234	0133	2114	0163	8.2913	0196	3644	0231	8.4317	0.0270	39
22	7.9167	0.0083	0271	0106	8.1249	0133	2128	0163	8.2926	0196	3655	0232	8.4328	0.0271	38
23	7.9186	0.0083	0288	0107	8.1265	0134	2142	0164	8.2938	0197	3667	0233	8.4339	0.0272	37
24	7.9206	0.0083	0305	0107	8.1280	0134	2156	0164	8.2951	0197	3679	0233	8.4350	0.0272	36
25	7.9225	0.0084	0322	0108	8.1295	0135	2170	0165	8.2964	0198	3690	0234	8.4360	0.0273	35
26	7.9245	0.0084	0339	0108	8.1311	0135	2184	0165	8.2976	0198	3702	0235	8.4371	0.0274	34
27	7.9264	0.0084	0357	0109	8.1326	0136	2198	0166	8.2989	0199	3714	0235	8.4382	0.0274	33
28	7.9284	0.0085	0374	0109	8.1341	0136	2211	0166	8.3001	0200	3725	0236	8.4392	0.0275	32
29	7.9303	0.0085	0391	0109	8.1357	0137	2225	0167	8.3014	0200	3737	0236	8.4403	0.0276	31
30	7.9322	0.0086	0408	0110	8.1372	0137	2239	0167	8.3027	0201	3748	0237	8.4414	0.0276	30
31	7.9342	0.0086	0425	0110	8.1387	0138	2253	0168	8.3039	0201	3760	0238	8.4424	0.0277	29
32	7.9361	0.0086	0442	0111	8.1402	0138	2266	0169	8.3052	0202	3771	0238	8.4435	0.0278	28
33	7.9380	0.0087	0459	0111	8.1417	0139	2280	0169	8.3064	0202	3783	0239	8.4446	0.0278	27
34	7.9399	0.0087	0475	0112	8.1432	0139	2294	0170	8.3077	0203	3794	0240	8.4456	0.0279	26
35	7.9418	0.0087	0492	0112	8.1447	0140	2307	0170	8.3089	0204	3806	0240	8.4467	0.0280	25
36	7.9437	0.0088	0509	0112	8.1463	0140	2321	0171	8.3102	0204	3817	0241	8.4478	0.0280	24
37	7.9456	0.0088	0526	0113	8.1478	0141	2335	0171	8.3114	0205	3829	0241	8.4488	0.0281	23
38	7.9475	0.0089	0543	0113	8.1493	0141	2348	0172	8.3126	0205	3840	0242	8.4499	0.0282	22
39	7.9494	0.0089	0559	0114	8.1508	0141	2362	0172	8.3139	0206	3851	0243	8.4509	0.0282	21
40	7.9513	0.0089	0576	0114	8.1522	0142	2375	0173	8.3151	0207	3863	0243	8.4520	0.0283	20
41	7.9532	0.0090	0593	0115	8.1537	0142	2389	0173	8.3164	0207	3874	0244	8.4530	0.0284	19
42	7.9551	0.0090	0609	0115	8.1552	0143	2402	0174	8.3176	0208	3886	0245	8.4541	0.0285	18
43	7.9569	0.0091	0626	0116	8.1567	0143	2416	0174	8.3188	0208	3897	0245	8.4551	0.0285	17
44	7.9588	0.0091	0642	0116	8.1582	0144	2429	0175	8.3200	0209	3908	0246	8.4562	0.0286	16
45	7.9607	0.0091	0659	0116	8.1597	0144	2443	0175	8.3213	0210	3920	0247	8.4572	0.0287	15
46	7.9625	0.0092	0675	0117	8.1612	0145	2456	0176	8.3225	0210	3931	0247	8.4583	0.0287	14
47	7.9644	0.0092	0692	0117	8.1626	0145	2469	0177	8.3237	0211	3942	0248	8.4593	0.0288	13
48	7.9662	0.0093	0708	0118	8.1641	0146	2483	0177	8.3250	0211	3953	0249	8.4604	0.0289	12
49	7.9681	0.0093	0725	0118	8.1656	0146	2496	0178	8.3262	0212	3965	0249	8.4614	0.0289	11
50	7.9699	0.0093	0741	0119	8.1671	0147	2510	0178	8.3274	0213	3976	0250	8.4625	0.0290	10
51	7.9718	0.0094	0757	0119	8.1685	0147	2523	0179	8.3286	0213	3987	0250	8.4635	0.0291	9
52	7.9736	0.0094	0774	0120	8.1700	0148	2536	0179	8.3298	0214	3998	0251	8.4645	0.0291	8
53	7.9755	0.0095	0790	0120	8.1715	0148	2549	0180	8.3310	0214	4010	0252	8.4656	0.0292	7
54	7.9773	0.0095	0806	0120	8.1729	0149	2563	0180	8.3323	0215	4021	0252	8.4666	0.0293	6
55	7.9791	0.0095	0823	0121	8.1744	0149	2576	0181	8.3335	0216	4032	0253	8.4677	0.0294	5
56	7.9809	0.0096	0839	0121	8.1758	0150	2589	0182	8.3347	0216	4043	0254	8.4687	0.0294	4
57	7.9828	0.0096	0855	0122	8.1773	0150	2602	0182	8.3359	0217	4054	0254	8.4697	0.0295	3
58	7.9846	0.0097	0871	0122	8.1787	0151	2615	0183	8.3371	0217	4065	0255	8.4708	0.0296	2
59	7.9864	0.0097	0887	0123	8.1802	0151	2629	0183	8.3383	0218	4076	0256	8.4718	0.0296	1
60	7.9882	0.0097	0903	0123	8.1816	0152	2642	0184	8.3395	0219	4087	0256	8.4728	0.0297	0
′	Log	Nat	Log	Nat	Log	Nat	Log	Nat	Log	Nat	Log	Nat	Log	Nat	′
	352°		351°		350°		349°		348°		347°		346°		

VERSINES

Note: For compactness, the leading digit has been dropped from alternate columns. Scan preceding column and row for necessary digit.

VERSINES

′	14° Log	Nat	15° Log	Nat	16° Log	Nat	17° Log	Nat	18° Log	Nat	19° Log	Nat	20° Log	Nat	′
0	8.4728	0.0297	5324	0341	8.5881	0387	6404	0437	8.6897	0489	7362	0545	8.7804	0.0603	60
1	8.4738	0.0298	5334	0341	8.5890	0388	6413	0438	8.6905	0490	7370	0546	8.7811	0.0604	59
2	8.4749	0.0298	5343	0342	8.5899	0389	6421	0439	8.6913	0491	7378	0547	8.7818	0.0605	58
3	8.4759	0.0299	5353	0343	8.5908	0390	6430	0440	8.6921	0492	7385	0548	8.7825	0.0606	57
4	8.4769	0.0300	5363	0344	8.5917	0391	6438	0440	8.6929	0493	7393	0549	8.7832	0.0607	56
5	8.4779	0.0301	5372	0345	8.5926	0391	6447	0441	8.6937	0494	7400	0550	8.7839	0.0608	55
6	8.4790	0.0301	5382	0345	8.5935	0392	6455	0442	8.6945	0495	7408	0551	8.7847	0.0609	54
7	8.4800	0.0302	5391	0346	8.5944	0393	6463	0443	8.6953	0496	7415	0551	8.7854	0.0610	53
8	8.4810	0.0303	5401	0347	8.5953	0394	6472	0444	8.6961	0497	7423	0552	8.7861	0.0611	52
9	8.4820	0.0303	5410	0348	8.5962	0395	6480	0445	8.6968	0498	7430	0553	8.7868	0.0612	51
10	8.4830	0.0304	5420	0348	8.5971	0395	6488	0445	8.6976	0498	7438	0554	8.7875	0.0613	50
11	8.4841	0.0305	5429	0349	8.5980	0396	6497	0446	8.6984	0499	7445	0555	8.7882	0.0614	49
12	8.4851	0.0306	5439	0350	8.5989	0397	6505	0447	8.6992	0500	7453	0556	8.7889	0.0615	48
13	8.4861	0.0306	5448	0351	8.5997	0398	6514	0448	8.7000	0501	7460	0557	8.7896	0.0616	47
14	8.4871	0.0307	5458	0351	8.6006	0399	6522	0449	8.7008	0502	7468	0558	8.7903	0.0617	46
15	8.4881	0.0308	5467	0352	8.6015	0400	6530	0450	8.7016	0503	7475	0559	8.7910	0.0618	45
16	8.4891	0.0308	5476	0353	8.6024	0400	6539	0451	8.7024	0504	7482	0560	8.7918	0.0619	44
17	8.4901	0.0309	5486	0354	8.6033	0401	6547	0452	8.7031	0505	7490	0561	8.7925	0.0620	43
18	8.4911	0.0310	5495	0354	8.6042	0402	6555	0452	8.7039	0506	7497	0562	8.7932	0.0621	42
19	8.4921	0.0311	5505	0355	8.6051	0403	6563	0453	8.7047	0507	7505	0563	8.7939	0.0622	41
20	8.4932	0.0311	5514	0356	8.6059	0404	6572	0454	8.7055	0508	7512	0564	8.7946	0.0623	40
21	8.4942	0.0312	5523	0357	8.6068	0404	6580	0455	8.7063	0508	7520	0565	8.7953	0.0624	39
22	8.4952	0.0313	5533	0358	8.6077	0405	6588	0456	8.7071	0509	7527	0566	8.7960	0.0625	38
23	8.4962	0.0313	5542	0358	8.6086	0406	6597	0457	8.7078	0510	7534	0567	8.7967	0.0626	37
24	8.4972	0.0314	5552	0359	8.6094	0407	6605	0458	8.7086	0511	7542	0568	8.7974	0.0627	36
25	8.4982	0.0315	5561	0360	8.6103	0408	6613	0458	8.7094	0512	7549	0569	8.7981	0.0628	35
26	8.4992	0.0316	5570	0361	8.6112	0409	6621	0459	8.7102	0513	7557	0570	8.7988	0.0629	34
27	8.5002	0.0316	5579	0361	8.6121	0409	6630	0460	8.7110	0514	7564	0571	8.7995	0.0630	33
28	8.5012	0.0317	5589	0362	8.6129	0410	6638	0461	8.7117	0515	7571	0572	8.8002	0.0631	32
29	8.5021	0.0318	5598	0363	8.6138	0411	6646	0462	8.7125	0516	7579	0573	8.8009	0.0632	31
30	8.5031	0.0319	5607	0364	8.6147	0412	6654	0463	8.7133	0517	7586	0574	8.8016	0.0633	30
31	8.5041	0.0319	5617	0364	8.6156	0413	6662	0464	8.7141	0518	7593	0575	8.8023	0.0634	29
32	8.5051	0.0320	5626	0365	8.6164	0413	6671	0465	8.7148	0519	7601	0576	8.8030	0.0635	28
33	8.5061	0.0321	5635	0366	8.6173	0414	6679	0465	8.7156	0520	7608	0577	8.8037	0.0636	27
34	8.5071	0.0321	5644	0367	8.6182	0415	6687	0466	8.7164	0520	7615	0577	8.8044	0.0637	26
35	8.5081	0.0322	5654	0368	8.6190	0416	6695	0467	8.7172	0521	7623	0578	8.8051	0.0638	25
36	8.5091	0.0323	5663	0368	8.6199	0417	6703	0468	8.7179	0522	7630	0579	8.8058	0.0639	24
37	8.5101	0.0324	5672	0369	8.6208	0418	6711	0469	8.7187	0523	7637	0580	8.8065	0.0640	23
38	8.5110	0.0324	5681	0370	8.6216	0418	6720	0470	8.7195	0524	7645	0581	8.8072	0.0641	22
39	8.5120	0.0325	5691	0371	8.6225	0419	6728	0471	8.7202	0525	7652	0582	8.8079	0.0642	21
40	8.5130	0.0326	5700	0372	8.6234	0420	6736	0472	8.7210	0526	7659	0583	8.8086	0.0644	20
41	8.5140	0.0327	5709	0372	8.6242	0421	6744	0473	8.7218	0527	7666	0584	8.8092	0.0645	19
42	8.5150	0.0327	5718	0373	8.6251	0422	6752	0473	8.7225	0528	7674	0585	8.8099	0.0646	18
43	8.5160	0.0328	5727	0374	8.6259	0423	6760	0474	8.7233	0529	7681	0586	8.8106	0.0647	17
44	8.5169	0.0329	5736	0375	8.6268	0423	6768	0475	8.7241	0530	7688	0587	8.8113	0.0648	16
45	8.5179	0.0330	5745	0375	8.6277	0424	6776	0476	8.7248	0531	7696	0588	8.8120	0.0649	15
46	8.5189	0.0330	5755	0376	8.6285	0425	6785	0477	8.7256	0532	7703	0589	8.8127	0.0650	14
47	8.5199	0.0331	5764	0377	8.6294	0426	6793	0478	8.7264	0533	7710	0590	8.8134	0.0651	13
48	8.5208	0.0332	5773	0378	8.6302	0427	6801	0479	8.7271	0534	7717	0591	8.8141	0.0652	12
49	8.5218	0.0333	5782	0379	8.6311	0428	6809	0480	8.7279	0534	7725	0592	8.8148	0.0653	11
50	8.5228	0.0333	5791	0379	8.6319	0428	6817	0480	8.7287	0535	7732	0593	8.8155	0.0654	10
51	8.5237	0.0334	5800	0380	8.6328	0429	6825	0481	8.7294	0536	7739	0594	8.8161	0.0655	9
52	8.5247	0.0335	5809	0381	8.6336	0430	6833	0482	8.7302	0537	7746	0595	8.8168	0.0656	8
53	8.5257	0.0335	5818	0382	8.6345	0431	6841	0483	8.7309	0538	7753	0596	8.8175	0.0657	7
54	8.5266	0.0336	5827	0383	8.6353	0432	6849	0484	8.7317	0539	7761	0597	8.8182	0.0658	6
55	8.5276	0.0337	5836	0383	8.6362	0433	6857	0485	8.7325	0540	7768	0598	8.8189	0.0659	5
56	8.5286	0.0338	5845	0384	8.6370	0434	6865	0486	8.7332	0541	7775	0599	8.8196	0.0660	4
57	8.5295	0.0338	5854	0385	8.6379	0434	6873	0487	8.7340	0542	7782	0600	8.8202	0.0661	3
58	8.5305	0.0339	5863	0386	8.6387	0435	6881	0488	8.7347	0543	7789	0601	8.8209	0.0662	2
59	8.5315	0.0340	5872	0387	8.6396	0436	6889	0489	8.7355	0544	7797	0602	8.8216	0.0663	1
60	8.5324	0.0341	5881	0387	8.6404	0437	6897	0489	8.7362	0545	7804	0603	8.8223	0.0664	0

′	Log	Nat	Log	Nat	Log	Nat	Log	Nat	Log	Nat	Log	Nat	Log	Nat	′
	345°		344°		343°		342°		341°		340°		339°		

Note: For compactness, the leading digit has been dropped from alternate columns. Scan preceding column and row for necessary digit.

VERSINES

′	21° Log	Nat	22° Log	Nat	23° Log	Nat	24° Log	Nat	25° Log	Nat	26° Log	Nat	27° Log	Nat	′
0	8.8223	0.0664	8622	0728	8.9003	0795	9368	0865	8.9717	0937	0052	1012	9.0374	0.1090	60
1	8.8230	0.0665	8629	0729	8.9010	0796	9374	0866	8.9723	0938	0058	1013	9.0379	0.1091	59
2	8.8237	0.0666	8635	0730	8.9016	0797	9380	0867	8.9728	0939	0063	1015	9.0385	0.1093	58
3	8.8243	0.0667	8642	0731	8.9022	0798	9386	0868	8.9734	0941	0068	1016	9.0390	0.1094	57
4	8.8250	0.0668	8648	0733	8.9028	0800	9392	0869	8.9740	0942	0074	1017	9.0395	0.1095	56
5	8.8257	0.0669	8655	0734	8.9034	0801	9398	0870	8.9745	0943	0079	1018	9.0400	0.1097	55
6	8.8264	0.0670	8661	0735	8.9041	0802	9403	0872	8.9751	0944	0085	1020	9.0406	0.1098	54
7	8.8271	0.0672	8668	0736	8.9047	0803	9409	0873	8.9757	0946	0090	1021	9.0411	0.1099	53
8	8.8277	0.0673	8674	0737	8.9053	0804	9415	0874	8.9762	0947	0096	1022	9.0416	0.1101	52
9	8.8284	0.0674	8681	0738	8.9059	0805	9421	0875	8.9768	0948	0101	1024	9.0421	0.1102	51
10	8.8291	0.0675	8687	0739	8.9065	0806	9427	0876	8.9774	0949	0107	1025	9.0426	0.1103	50
11	8.8298	0.0676	8693	0740	8.9071	0808	9433	0878	8.9779	0950	0112	1026	9.0432	0.1105	49
12	8.8304	0.0677	8700	0741	8.9078	0809	9439	0879	8.9785	0952	0117	1027	9.0437	0.1106	48
13	8.8311	0.0678	8706	0742	8.9084	0810	9445	0880	8.9791	0953	0123	1029	9.0442	0.1107	47
14	8.8318	0.0679	8713	0743	8.9090	0811	9451	0881	8.9796	0954	0128	1030	9.0447	0.1108	46
15	8.8325	0.0680	8719	0745	8.9096	0812	9457	0882	8.9802	0955	0134	1031	9.0453	0.1110	45
16	8.8331	0.0681	8726	0746	8.9102	0813	9462	0884	8.9808	0957	0139	1033	9.0458	0.1111	44
17	8.8338	0.0682	8732	0747	8.9108	0814	9468	0885	8.9813	0958	0145	1034	9.0463	0.1112	43
18	8.8345	0.0683	8738	0748	8.9114	0816	9474	0886	8.9819	0959	0150	1035	9.0468	0.1114	42
19	8.8351	0.0684	8745	0749	8.9121	0817	9480	0887	8.9825	0960	0155	1036	9.0473	0.1115	41
20	8.8358	0.0685	8751	0750	8.9127	0818	9486	0888	8.9830	0962	0161	1038	9.0479	0.1116	40
21	8.8365	0.0686	8758	0751	8.9133	0819	9492	0890	8.9836	0963	0166	1039	9.0484	0.1118	39
22	8.8372	0.0687	8764	0752	8.9139	0820	9498	0891	8.9841	0964	0172	1040	9.0489	0.1119	38
23	8.8378	0.0688	8770	0753	8.9145	0821	9503	0892	8.9847	0965	0177	1042	9.0494	0.1121	37
24	8.8385	0.0689	8777	0755	8.9151	0822	9509	0893	8.9853	0967	0182	1043	9.0499	0.1122	36
25	8.8392	0.0691	8783	0756	8.9157	0824	9515	0894	8.9858	0968	0188	1044	9.0505	0.1123	35
26	8.8398	0.0692	8790	0757	8.9163	0825	9521	0896	8.9864	0969	0193	1045	9.0510	0.1125	34
27	8.8405	0.0693	8796	0758	8.9169	0826	9527	0897	8.9869	0970	0198	1047	9.0515	0.1126	33
28	8.8412	0.0694	8802	0759	8.9175	0827	9533	0898	8.9875	0972	0204	1048	9.0520	0.1127	32
29	8.8418	0.0695	8809	0760	8.9182	0828	9538	0899	8.9881	0973	0209	1049	9.0525	0.1129	31
30	8.8425	0.0696	8815	0761	8.9188	0829	9544	0900	8.9886	0974	0215	1051	9.0530	0.1130	30
31	8.8432	0.0697	8821	0762	8.9194	0831	9550	0902	8.9892	0975	0220	1052	9.0536	0.1131	29
32	8.8438	0.0698	8828	0763	8.9200	0832	9556	0903	8.9897	0977	0225	1053	9.0541	0.1133	28
33	8.8445	0.0699	8834	0765	8.9206	0833	9562	0904	8.9903	0978	0231	1055	9.0546	0.1134	27
34	8.8452	0.0700	8840	0766	8.9212	0834	9568	0905	8.9909	0979	0236	1056	9.0551	0.1135	26
35	8.8458	0.0701	8847	0767	8.9218	0835	9573	0906	8.9914	0980	0241	1057	9.0556	0.1137	25
36	8.8465	0.0702	8853	0768	8.9224	0836	9579	0908	8.9920	0982	0247	1058	9.0561	0.1138	24
37	8.8471	0.0703	8859	0769	8.9230	0838	9585	0909	8.9925	0983	0252	1060	9.0566	0.1139	23
38	8.8478	0.0704	8866	0770	8.9236	0839	9591	0910	8.9931	0984	0257	1061	9.0572	0.1141	22
39	8.8485	0.0705	8872	0771	8.9242	0840	9596	0911	8.9936	0985	0263	1062	9.0577	0.1142	21
40	8.8491	0.0707	8878	0772	8.9248	0841	9602	0912	8.9942	0987	0268	1064	9.0582	0.1143	20
41	8.8498	0.0708	8885	0773	8.9254	0842	9608	0914	8.9947	0988	0273	1065	9.0587	0.1145	19
42	8.8504	0.0709	8891	0775	8.9260	0843	9614	0915	8.9953	0989	0279	1066	9.0592	0.1146	18
43	8.8511	0.0710	8897	0776	8.9266	0845	9620	0916	8.9959	0990	0284	1068	9.0597	0.1147	17
44	8.8518	0.0711	8903	0777	8.9272	0846	9625	0917	8.9964	0992	0289	1069	9.0602	0.1149	16
45	8.8524	0.0712	8910	0778	8.9278	0847	9631	0919	8.9970	0993	0295	1070	9.0607	0.1150	15
46	8.8531	0.0713	8916	0779	8.9284	0848	9637	0920	8.9975	0994	0300	1072	9.0613	0.1151	14
47	8.8537	0.0714	8922	0780	8.9290	0849	9643	0921	8.9981	0996	0305	1073	9.0618	0.1153	13
48	8.8544	0.0715	8929	0781	8.9296	0850	9648	0922	8.9986	0997	0311	1074	9.0623	0.1154	12
49	8.8550	0.0716	8935	0782	8.9302	0852	9654	0923	8.9992	0998	0316	1075	9.0628	0.1156	11
50	8.8557	0.0717	8941	0784	8.9308	0853	9660	0925	8.9997	0999	0321	1077	9.0633	0.1157	10
51	8.8564	0.0718	8947	0785	8.9314	0854	9666	0926	9.0003	1001	0327	1078	9.0638	0.1158	9
52	8.8570	0.0719	8954	0786	8.9320	0855	9671	0927	9.0008	1002	0332	1079	9.0643	0.1160	8
53	8.8577	0.0721	8960	0787	8.9326	0856	9677	0928	9.0014	1003	0337	1081	9.0648	0.1161	7
54	8.8583	0.0722	8966	0788	8.9332	0857	9683	0930	9.0019	1004	0342	1082	9.0653	0.1162	6
55	8.8590	0.0723	8972	0789	8.9338	0859	9688	0931	9.0025	1006	0348	1083	9.0658	0.1164	5
56	8.8596	0.0724	8979	0790	8.9344	0860	9694	0932	9.0030	1007	0353	1085	9.0664	0.1165	4
57	8.8603	0.0725	8985	0792	8.9350	0861	9700	0933	9.0036	1008	0358	1086	9.0669	0.1166	3
58	8.8609	0.0726	8991	0793	8.9356	0862	9706	0934	9.0041	1010	0363	1087	9.0674	0.1168	2
59	8.8616	0.0727	8997	0794	8.9362	0863	9711	0936	9.0047	1011	0369	1089	9.0679	0.1169	1
60	8.8622	0.0728	9003	0795	8.9368	0865	9717	0937	9.0052	1012	0374	1090	9.0684	0.1171	0
′	Log	Nat	Log	Nat	Log	Nat	Log	Nat	Log	Nat	Log	Nat	Log	Nat	′
	338°		337°		336°		335°		334°		333°		332°		

Note: For compactness, the leading digit has been dropped from alternate columns. Scan preceding column and row for necessary digit.

VERSINES

VERSINES

′	28° Log	Nat	29° Log	Nat	30° Log	Nat	31° Log	Nat	32° Log	Nat	33° Log	Nat	34° Log	Nat	′
0	9.0684	0.1171	0982	1254	9.1270	1340	1548	1428	9.1817	1520	2077	1613	9.2329	0.1710	60
1	9.0689	0.1172	0987	1255	9.1275	1341	1553	1430	9.1821	1521	2081	1615	9.2333	0.1711	59
2	9.0694	0.1173	0992	1257	9.1280	1343	1557	1431	9.1826	1523	2086	1616	9.2337	0.1713	58
3	9.0699	0.1175	0997	1258	9.1284	1344	1562	1433	9.1830	1524	2090	1618	9.2341	0.1715	57
4	9.0704	0.1176	1002	1259	9.1289	1346	1566	1434	9.1835	1526	2094	1620	9.2346	0.1716	56
5	9.0709	0.1177	1007	1261	9.1294	1347	1571	1436	9.1839	1527	2098	1621	9.2350	0.1718	55
6	9.0714	0.1179	1012	1262	9.1298	1348	1576	1437	9.1843	1529	2103	1623	9.2354	0.1719	54
7	9.0719	0.1180	1016	1264	9.1303	1350	1580	1439	9.1848	1530	2107	1624	9.2358	0.1721	53
8	9.0724	0.1181	1021	1265	9.1308	1351	1585	1440	9.1852	1532	2111	1626	9.2362	0.1723	52
9	9.0729	0.1183	1026	1267	9.1313	1353	1589	1442	9.1857	1533	2115	1628	9.2366	0.1724	51
10	9.0734	0.1184	1031	1268	9.1317	1354	1594	1443	9.1861	1535	2120	1629	9.2370	0.1726	50
11	9.0739	0.1186	1036	1269	9.1322	1356	1598	1445	9.1865	1537	2124	1631	9.2374	0.1728	49
12	9.0744	0.1187	1041	1271	9.1327	1357	1603	1446	9.1870	1538	2128	1632	9.2378	0.1729	48
13	9.0749	0.1188	1046	1272	9.1331	1359	1607	1448	9.1874	1540	2132	1634	9.2383	0.1731	47
14	9.0754	0.1190	1050	1274	9.1336	1360	1612	1449	9.1879	1541	2137	1636	9.2387	0.1732	46
15	9.0759	0.1191	1055	1275	9.1341	1362	1616	1451	9.1883	1543	2141	1637	9.2391	0.1734	45
16	9.0764	0.1192	1060	1276	9.1345	1363	1621	1452	9.1887	1544	2145	1639	9.2395	0.1736	44
17	9.0769	0.1194	1065	1278	9.1350	1365	1625	1454	9.1892	1546	2149	1640	9.2399	0.1737	43
18	9.0775	0.1195	1070	1279	9.1355	1366	1630	1455	9.1896	1547	2154	1642	9.2403	0.1739	42
19	9.0780	0.1197	1075	1281	9.1359	1368	1634	1457	9.1900	1549	2158	1644	9.2407	0.1741	41
20	9.0785	0.1198	1079	1282	9.1364	1369	1639	1458	9.1905	1550	2162	1645	9.2411	0.1742	40
21	9.0790	0.1199	1084	1284	9.1369	1370	1643	1460	9.1909	1552	2166	1647	9.2415	0.1744	39
22	9.0795	0.1201	1089	1285	9.1373	1372	1648	1461	9.1913	1554	2170	1648	9.2419	0.1746	38
23	9.0800	0.1202	1094	1286	9.1378	1373	1652	1463	9.1918	1555	2175	1650	9.2423	0.1747	37
24	9.0805	0.1204	1099	1288	9.1383	1375	1657	1464	9.1922	1557	2179	1652	9.2428	0.1749	36
25	9.0810	0.1205	1104	1289	9.1387	1376	1661	1466	9.1926	1558	2183	1653	9.2432	0.1751	35
26	9.0814	0.1206	1108	1291	9.1392	1378	1666	1468	9.1931	1560	2187	1655	9.2436	0.1752	34
27	9.0819	0.1208	1113	1292	9.1397	1379	1670	1469	9.1935	1561	2191	1656	9.2440	0.1754	33
28	9.0824	0.1209	1118	1294	9.1401	1381	1675	1471	9.1939	1563	2196	1658	9.2444	0.1755	32
29	9.0829	0.1210	1123	1295	9.1406	1382	1679	1472	9.1944	1565	2200	1660	9.2448	0.1757	31
30	9.0834	0.1212	1128	1296	9.1410	1384	1684	1474	9.1948	1566	2204	1661	9.2452	0.1759	30
31	9.0839	0.1213	1132	1298	9.1415	1385	1688	1475	9.1952	1568	2208	1663	9.2456	0.1760	29
32	9.0844	0.1215	1137	1299	9.1420	1387	1693	1477	9.1957	1569	2212	1664	9.2460	0.1762	28
33	9.0849	0.1216	1142	1301	9.1424	1388	1697	1478	9.1961	1571	2217	1666	9.2464	0.1764	27
34	9.0854	0.1217	1147	1302	9.1429	1390	1702	1480	9.1965	1572	2221	1668	9.2468	0.1765	26
35	9.0859	0.1219	1151	1304	9.1434	1391	1706	1481	9.1970	1574	2225	1669	9.2472	0.1767	25
36	9.0864	0.1220	1156	1305	9.1438	1393	1711	1483	9.1974	1575	2229	1671	9.2476	0.1769	24
37	9.0869	0.1222	1161	1306	9.1443	1394	1715	1484	9.1978	1577	2233	1672	9.2480	0.1770	23
38	9.0874	0.1223	1166	1308	9.1447	1396	1720	1486	9.1983	1579	2238	1674	9.2484	0.1772	22
39	9.0879	0.1224	1171	1309	9.1452	1397	1724	1487	9.1987	1580	2242	1676	9.2489	0.1774	21
40	9.0884	0.1226	1175	1311	9.1457	1399	1728	1489	9.1991	1582	2246	1677	9.2493	0.1775	20
41	9.0889	0.1227	1180	1312	9.1461	1400	1733	1490	9.1996	1583	2250	1679	9.2497	0.1777	19
42	9.0894	0.1229	1185	1314	9.1466	1401	1737	1492	9.2000	1585	2254	1680	9.2501	0.1779	18
43	9.0899	0.1230	1190	1315	9.1470	1403	1742	1493	9.2004	1586	2258	1682	9.2505	0.1780	17
44	9.0904	0.1231	1194	1317	9.1475	1404	1746	1495	9.2009	1588	2263	1684	9.2509	0.1782	16
45	9.0909	0.1233	1199	1318	9.1480	1406	1751	1496	9.2013	1590	2267	1685	9.2513	0.1784	15
46	9.0914	0.1234	1204	1319	9.1484	1407	1755	1498	9.2017	1591	2271	1687	9.2517	0.1785	14
47	9.0919	0.1236	1209	1321	9.1489	1409	1760	1500	9.2021	1593	2275	1689	9.2521	0.1787	13
48	9.0923	0.1237	1213	1322	9.1493	1410	1764	1501	9.2026	1594	2279	1690	9.2525	0.1789	12
49	9.0928	0.1238	1218	1324	9.1498	1412	1768	1503	9.2030	1596	2283	1692	9.2529	0.1790	11
50	9.0933	0.1240	1223	1325	9.1503	1413	1773	1504	9.2034	1597	2288	1693	9.2533	0.1792	10
51	9.0938	0.1241	1228	1327	9.1507	1415	1777	1506	9.2039	1599	2292	1695	9.2537	0.1793	9
52	9.0943	0.1243	1232	1328	9.1512	1416	1782	1507	9.2043	1601	2296	1697	9.2541	0.1795	8
53	9.0948	0.1244	1237	1330	9.1516	1418	1786	1509	9.2047	1602	2300	1698	9.2545	0.1797	7
54	9.0953	0.1245	1242	1331	9.1521	1419	1791	1510	9.2052	1604	2304	1700	9.2549	0.1798	6
55	9.0958	0.1247	1247	1332	9.1525	1421	1795	1512	9.2056	1605	2308	1701	9.2553	0.1800	5
56	9.0963	0.1248	1251	1334	9.1530	1422	1799	1513	9.2060	1607	2312	1703	9.2557	0.1802	4
57	9.0968	0.1250	1256	1335	9.1535	1424	1804	1515	9.2064	1609	2317	1705	9.2561	0.1803	3
58	9.0973	0.1251	1261	1337	9.1539	1425	1808	1516	9.2069	1610	2321	1706	9.2565	0.1805	2
59	9.0977	0.1252	1266	1338	9.1544	1427	1813	1518	9.2073	1612	2325	1708	9.2569	0.1807	1
60	9.0982	0.1254	1270	1340	9.1548	1428	1817	1520	9.2077	1613	2329	1710	9.2573	0.1808	0
′	Log	Nat	Log	Nat	Log	Nat	Log	Nat	Log	Nat	Log	Nat	Log	Nat	′
	331°		330°		329°		328°		327°		326°		325°		

Note: For compactness, the leading digit has been dropped from alternate columns. Scan preceding column and row for necessary digit.

VERSINES

/	35° Log	Nat	36° Log	Nat	37° Log	Nat	38° Log	Nat	39° Log	Nat	40° Log	Nat	41° Log	Nat	/
0	9.2573	0.1808	2810	1910	9.3040	2014	3263	2120	9.3480	2229	3691	2340	9.3897	0.2453	60
1	9.2577	0.1810	2814	1912	9.3044	2015	3267	2122	9.3484	2230	3695	2341	9.3900	0.2455	59
2	9.2581	0.1812	2818	1913	9.3047	2017	3270	2123	9.3487	2232	3698	2343	9.3904	0.2457	58
3	9.2585	0.1813	2822	1915	9.3051	2019	3274	2125	9.3491	2234	3702	2345	9.3907	0.2459	57
4	9.2589	0.1815	2825	1917	9.3055	2021	3278	2127	9.3494	2236	3705	2347	9.3910	0.2461	56
5	9.2593	0.1817	2829	1918	9.3059	2022	3281	2129	9.3498	2238	3709	2349	9.3914	0.2462	55
6	9.2597	0.1819	2833	1920	9.3062	2024	3285	2131	9.3502	2240	3712	2351	9.3917	0.2464	54
7	9.2601	0.1820	2837	1922	9.3066	2026	3289	2132	9.3505	2241	3716	2353	9.3920	0.2466	53
8	9.2605	0.1822	2841	1924	9.3070	2028	3292	2134	9.3509	2243	3719	2355	9.3924	0.2468	52
9	9.2609	0.1824	2845	1925	9.3074	2029	3296	2136	9.3512	2245	3723	2356	9.3927	0.2470	51
10	9.2613	0.1825	2849	1927	9.3077	2031	3300	2138	9.3516	2247	3726	2358	9.3931	0.2472	50
11	9.2617	0.1827	2853	1929	9.3081	2033	3303	2140	9.3519	2249	3729	2360	9.3934	0.2474	49
12	9.2621	0.1829	2856	1930	9.3085	2035	3307	2141	9.3523	2251	3733	2362	9.3937	0.2476	48
13	9.2625	0.1830	2860	1932	9.3089	2036	3311	2143	9.3526	2252	3736	2364	9.3941	0.2478	47
14	9.2629	0.1832	2864	1934	9.3093	2038	3314	2145	9.3530	2254	3740	2366	9.3944	0.2480	46
15	9.2633	0.1834	2868	1936	9.3096	2040	3318	2147	9.3534	2256	3743	2368	9.3947	0.2482	45
16	9.2637	0.1835	2872	1937	9.3100	2042	3322	2149	9.3537	2258	3747	2370	9.3951	0.2484	44
17	9.2641	0.1837	2876	1939	9.3104	2044	3325	2150	9.3541	2260	3750	2371	9.3954	0.2485	43
18	9.2645	0.1839	2880	1941	9.3107	2045	3329	2152	9.3544	2262	3754	2373	9.3957	0.2487	42
19	9.2649	0.1840	2883	1942	9.3111	2047	3333	2154	9.3548	2263	3757	2375	9.3961	0.2489	41
20	9.2653	0.1842	2887	1944	9.3115	2049	3336	2156	9.3551	2265	3760	2377	9.3964	0.2491	40
21	9.2657	0.1844	2891	1946	9.3119	2051	3340	2158	9.3555	2267	3764	2379	9.3967	0.2493	39
22	9.2661	0.1845	2895	1948	9.3122	2052	3343	2159	9.3558	2269	3767	2381	9.3971	0.2495	38
23	9.2665	0.1847	2899	1949	9.3126	2054	3347	2161	9.3562	2271	3771	2383	9.3974	0.2497	37
24	9.2669	0.1849	2903	1951	9.3130	2056	3351	2163	9.3565	2273	3774	2385	9.3977	0.2499	36
25	9.2673	0.1850	2907	1953	9.3134	2058	3354	2165	9.3569	2275	3778	2387	9.3981	0.2501	35
26	9.2677	0.1852	2910	1955	9.3137	2059	3358	2167	9.3572	2276	3781	2388	9.3984	0.2503	34
27	9.2681	0.1854	2914	1956	9.3141	2061	3362	2168	9.3576	2278	3784	2390	9.3987	0.2505	33
28	9.2685	0.1855	2918	1958	9.3145	2063	3365	2170	9.3579	2280	3788	2392	9.3991	0.2507	32
29	9.2688	0.1857	2922	1960	9.3149	2065	3369	2172	9.3583	2282	3791	2394	9.3994	0.2509	31
30	9.2692	0.1859	2926	1961	9.3152	2066	3372	2174	9.3586	2284	3795	2396	9.3998	0.2510	30
31	9.2696	0.1861	2930	1963	9.3156	2068	3376	2176	9.3590	2286	3798	2398	9.4001	0.2512	29
32	9.2700	0.1862	2933	1965	9.3160	2070	3380	2178	9.3594	2287	3802	2400	9.4004	0.2514	28
33	9.2704	0.1864	2937	1967	9.3163	2072	3383	2179	9.3597	2289	3805	2402	9.4008	0.2516	27
34	9.2708	0.1866	2941	1968	9.3167	2074	3387	2181	9.3601	2291	3808	2404	9.4011	0.2518	26
35	9.2712	0.1867	2945	1970	9.3171	2075	3390	2183	9.3604	2293	3812	2405	9.4014	0.2520	25
36	9.2716	0.1869	2949	1972	9.3175	2077	3394	2185	9.3608	2295	3815	2407	9.4017	0.2522	24
37	9.2720	0.1871	2953	1974	9.3178	2079	3398	2187	9.3611	2297	3819	2409	9.4021	0.2524	23
38	9.2724	0.1872	2956	1975	9.3182	2081	3401	2188	9.3615	2299	3822	2411	9.4024	0.2526	22
39	9.2728	0.1874	2960	1977	9.3186	2082	3405	2190	9.3618	2300	3826	2413	9.4027	0.2528	21
40	9.2732	0.1876	2964	1979	9.3189	2084	3409	2192	9.3622	2302	3829	2415	9.4031	0.2530	20
41	9.2736	0.1877	2968	1981	9.3193	2086	3412	2194	9.3625	2304	3832	2417	9.4034	0.2532	19
42	9.2740	0.1879	2972	1982	9.3197	2088	3416	2196	9.3629	2306	3836	2419	9.4037	0.2534	18
43	9.2744	0.1881	2975	1984	9.3201	2090	3419	2198	9.3632	2308	3839	2421	9.4041	0.2536	17
44	9.2747	0.1883	2979	1986	9.3204	2091	3423	2199	9.3636	2310	3843	2422	9.4044	0.2537	16
45	9.2751	0.1884	2983	1987	9.3208	2093	3427	2201	9.3639	2312	3846	2424	9.4047	0.2539	15
46	9.2755	0.1886	2987	1989	9.3212	2095	3430	2203	9.3643	2313	3849	2426	9.4051	0.2541	14
47	9.2759	0.1888	2991	1991	9.3215	2097	3434	2205	9.3646	2315	3853	2428	9.4054	0.2543	13
48	9.2763	0.1889	2994	1993	9.3219	2098	3437	2207	9.3650	2317	3856	2430	9.4057	0.2545	12
49	9.2767	0.1891	2998	1994	9.3223	2100	3441	2208	9.3653	2319	3860	2432	9.4061	0.2547	11
50	9.2771	0.1893	3002	1996	9.3226	2102	3444	2210	9.3657	2321	3863	2434	9.4064	0.2549	10
51	9.2775	0.1894	3006	1998	9.3230	2104	3448	2212	9.3660	2323	3866	2436	9.4067	0.2551	9
52	9.2779	0.1896	3010	2000	9.3234	2106	3452	2214	9.3664	2325	3870	2438	9.4071	0.2553	8
53	9.2783	0.1898	3013	2001	9.3237	2107	3455	2216	9.3667	2326	3873	2440	9.4074	0.2555	7
54	9.2787	0.1900	3017	2003	9.3241	2109	3459	2218	9.3670	2328	3877	2441	9.4077	0.2557	6
55	9.2790	0.1901	3021	2005	9.3245	2111	3462	2219	9.3674	2330	3880	2443	9.4080	0.2559	5
56	9.2794	0.1903	3025	2007	9.3248	2113	3466	2221	9.3677	2332	3883	2445	9.4084	0.2561	4
57	9.2798	0.1905	3028	2008	9.3252	2115	3469	2223	9.3681	2334	3887	2447	9.4087	0.2563	3
58	9.2802	0.1906	3032	2010	9.3256	2116	3473	2225	9.3684	2336	3890	2449	9.4090	0.2565	2
59	9.2806	0.1908	3036	2012	9.3259	2118	3477	2227	9.3688	2338	3893	2451	9.4094	0.2567	1
60	9.2810	0.1910	3040	2014	9.3263	2120	3480	2229	9.3691	2340	3897	2453	9.4097	0.2569	0
/	Log	Nat	Log	Nat	Log	Nat	Log	Nat	Log	Nat	Log	Nat	Log	Nat	/
	324°		323°		322°		321°		320°		319°		318°		

Note: For compactness, the leading digit has been dropped from alternate columns. Scan preceding column and row for necessary digit.

VERSINES

VERSINES

/	42° Log	Nat	43° Log	Nat	44° Log	Nat	45° Log	Nat	46° Log	Nat	47° Log	Nat	48° Log	Nat	/
0	9.4097	0.2569	4292	2686	9.4482	2807	4667	2929	9.4848	3053	5024	3180	9.5197	0.3309	60
1	9.4100	0.2570	4295	2688	9.4485	2809	4670	2931	9.4851	3056	5027	3182	9.5199	0.3311	59
2	9.4103	0.2572	4298	2690	9.4488	2811	4673	2933	9.4854	3058	5030	3184	9.5202	0.3313	58
3	9.4107	0.2574	4301	2692	9.4491	2813	4676	2935	9.4857	3060	5033	3186	9.5205	0.3315	57
4	9.4110	0.2576	4305	2694	9.4494	2815	4679	2937	9.4860	3062	5036	3189	9.5208	0.3317	56
5	9.4113	0.2578	4308	2696	9.4497	2817	4682	2939	9.4863	3064	5039	3191	9.5211	0.3320	55
6	9.4117	0.2580	4311	2698	9.4501	2819	4685	2941	9.4866	3066	5042	3193	9.5214	0.3322	54
7	9.4120	0.2582	4314	2700	9.4504	2821	4688	2943	9.4869	3068	5045	3195	9.5216	0.3324	53
8	9.4123	0.2584	4317	2702	9.4507	2823	4691	2945	9.4872	3070	5048	3197	9.5219	0.3326	52
9	9.4126	0.2586	4321	2704	9.4510	2825	4694	2947	9.4875	3072	5050	3199	9.5222	0.3328	51
10	9.4130	0.2588	4324	2706	9.4513	2827	4698	2950	9.4878	3074	5053	3201	9.5225	0.3330	50
11	9.4133	0.2590	4327	2708	9.4516	2829	4701	2952	9.4881	3076	5056	3203	9.5228	0.3333	49
12	9.4136	0.2592	4330	2710	9.4519	2831	4704	2954	9.4883	3079	5059	3206	9.5231	0.3335	48
13	9.4140	0.2594	4333	2712	9.4522	2833	4707	2956	9.4886	3081	5062	3208	9.5233	0.3337	47
14	9.4143	0.2596	4337	2714	9.4525	2835	4710	2958	9.4889	3083	5065	3210	9.5236	0.3339	46
15	9.4146	0.2598	4340	2716	9.4529	2837	4713	2960	9.4892	3085	5068	3212	9.5239	0.3341	45
16	9.4149	0.2600	4343	2718	9.4532	2839	4716	2962	9.4895	3087	5071	3214	9.5242	0.3343	44
17	9.4153	0.2602	4346	2720	9.4535	2841	4719	2964	9.4898	3089	5074	3216	9.5245	0.3346	43
18	9.4156	0.2604	4349	2722	9.4538	2843	4722	2966	9.4901	3091	5076	3218	9.5247	0.3348	42
19	9.4159	0.2606	4352	2724	9.4541	2845	4725	2968	9.4904	3093	5079	3221	9.5250	0.3350	41
20	9.4162	0.2608	4356	2726	9.4544	2847	4728	2970	9.4907	3095	5082	3223	9.5253	0.3352	40
21	9.4166	0.2610	4359	2728	9.4547	2849	4731	2972	9.4910	3097	5085	3225	9.5256	0.3354	39
22	9.4169	0.2612	4362	2730	9.4550	2851	4734	2974	9.4913	3100	5088	3227	9.5259	0.3356	38
23	9.4172	0.2613	4365	2732	9.4553	2853	4737	2976	9.4916	3102	5091	3229	9.5262	0.3359	37
24	9.4175	0.2615	4368	2734	9.4556	2855	4740	2978	9.4919	3104	5094	3231	9.5264	0.3361	36
25	9.4179	0.2617	4372	2736	9.4560	2857	4743	2981	9.4922	3106	5097	3233	9.5267	0.3363	35
26	9.4182	0.2619	4375	2738	9.4563	2859	4746	2983	9.4925	3108	5099	3236	9.5270	0.3365	34
27	9.4185	0.2621	4378	2740	9.4566	2861	4749	2985	9.4928	3110	5102	3238	9.5273	0.3367	33
28	9.4188	0.2623	4381	2742	9.4569	2863	4752	2987	9.4931	3112	5105	3240	9.5276	0.3369	32
29	9.4192	0.2625	4384	2744	9.4572	2865	4755	2989	9.4934	3114	5108	3242	9.5278	0.3372	31
30	9.4195	0.2627	4387	2746	9.4575	2867	4758	2991	9.4937	3116	5111	3244	9.5281	0.3374	30
31	9.4198	0.2629	4391	2748	9.4578	2870	4761	2993	9.4940	3119	5114	3246	9.5284	0.3376	29
32	9.4201	0.2631	4394	2750	9.4581	2872	4764	2995	9.4942	3121	5117	3248	9.5287	0.3378	28
33	9.4205	0.2633	4397	2752	9.4584	2874	4767	2997	9.4945	3123	5120	3251	9.5290	0.3380	27
34	9.4208	0.2635	4400	2754	9.4587	2876	4770	2999	9.4948	3125	5122	3253	9.5292	0.3383	26
35	9.4211	0.2637	4403	2756	9.4590	2878	4773	3001	9.4951	3127	5125	3255	9.5295	0.3385	25
36	9.4214	0.2639	4406	2758	9.4594	2880	4776	3003	9.4954	3129	5128	3257	9.5298	0.3387	24
37	9.4218	0.2641	4410	2760	9.4597	2882	4779	3005	9.4957	3131	5131	3259	9.5301	0.3389	23
38	9.4221	0.2643	4413	2762	9.4600	2884	4782	3008	9.4960	3133	5134	3261	9.5304	0.3391	22
39	9.4224	0.2645	4416	2764	9.4603	2886	4785	3010	9.4963	3135	5137	3263	9.5306	0.3393	21
40	9.4227	0.2647	4419	2766	9.4606	2888	4788	3012	9.4966	3138	5140	3266	9.5309	0.3396	20
41	9.4231	0.2649	4422	2768	9.4609	2890	4791	3014	9.4969	3140	5142	3268	9.5312	0.3398	19
42	9.4234	0.2651	4425	2770	9.4612	2892	4794	3016	9.4972	3142	5145	3270	9.5315	0.3400	18
43	9.4237	0.2653	4428	2772	9.4615	2894	4797	3018	9.4975	3144	5148	3272	9.5318	0.3402	17
44	9.4240	0.2655	4432	2774	9.4618	2896	4800	3020	9.4978	3146	5151	3274	9.5320	0.3404	16
45	9.4244	0.2657	4435	2776	9.4621	2898	4803	3022	9.4981	3148	5154	3276	9.5323	0.3407	15
46	9.4247	0.2659	4438	2778	9.4624	2900	4806	3024	9.4984	3150	5157	3278	9.5326	0.3409	14
47	9.4250	0.2661	4441	2780	9.4627	2902	4809	3026	9.4986	3152	5160	3281	9.5329	0.3411	13
48	9.4253	0.2663	4444	2782	9.4630	2904	4812	3028	9.4989	3155	5162	3283	9.5331	0.3413	12
49	9.4256	0.2665	4447	2784	9.4633	2906	4815	3030	9.4992	3157	5165	3285	9.5334	0.3415	11
50	9.4260	0.2667	4450	2786	9.4637	2908	4818	3033	9.4995	3159	5168	3287	9.5337	0.3417	10
51	9.4263	0.2669	4454	2788	9.4640	2910	4821	3035	9.4998	3161	5171	3289	9.5340	0.3420	9
52	9.4266	0.2671	4457	2790	9.4643	2912	4824	3037	9.5001	3163	5174	3291	9.5343	0.3422	8
53	9.4269	0.2673	4460	2792	9.4646	2915	4827	3039	9.5004	3165	5177	3294	9.5345	0.3424	7
54	9.4273	0.2675	4463	2794	9.4649	2917	4830	3041	9.5007	3167	5180	3296	9.5348	0.3426	6
55	9.4276	0.2677	4466	2797	9.4652	2919	4833	3043	9.5010	3169	5182	3298	9.5351	0.3428	5
56	9.4279	0.2679	4469	2799	9.4655	2921	4836	3045	9.5013	3172	5185	3300	9.5354	0.3431	4
57	9.4282	0.2681	4472	2801	9.4658	2923	4839	3047	9.5016	3174	5188	3302	9.5357	0.3433	3
58	9.4285	0.2682	4476	2803	9.4661	2925	4842	3049	9.5018	3176	5191	3304	9.5359	0.3435	2
59	9.4289	0.2684	4479	2805	9.4664	2927	4845	3051	9.5021	3178	5194	3307	9.5362	0.3437	1
60	9.4292	0.2686	4482	2807	9.4667	2929	4848	3053	9.5024	3180	5197	3309	9.5365	0.3439	0
/	Log	Nat	Log	Nat	Log	Nat	Log	Nat	Log	Nat	Log	Nat	Log	Nat	/
	317°		316°		315°		314°		313°		312°		311°		

Note: For compactness, the leading digit has been dropped from alternate columns. Scan preceding column and row for necessary digit.

VERSINES

/	49° Log	Nat	50° Log	Nat	51° Log	Nat	52° Log	Nat	53° Log	Nat	54° Log	Nat	55° Log	Nat	/
0	9.5365	0.3439	5529	3572	9.5690	3707	5847	3843	9.6001	3982	6151	4122	9.6298	0.4264	60
1	9.5368	0.3442	5532	3574	9.5693	3709	5850	3846	9.6003	3984	6154	4125	9.6301	0.4267	59
2	9.5370	0.3444	5535	3577	9.5695	3711	5852	3848	9.6006	3986	6156	4127	9.6303	0.4269	58
3	9.5373	0.3446	5537	3579	9.5698	3714	5855	3850	9.6008	3989	6159	4129	9.6306	0.4271	57
4	9.5376	0.3448	5540	3581	9.5701	3716	5857	3853	9.6011	3991	6161	4132	9.6308	0.4274	56
5	9.5379	0.3450	5543	3583	9.5703	3718	5860	3855	9.6014	3993	6164	4134	9.6311	0.4276	55
6	9.5381	0.3453	5546	3586	9.5706	3720	5863	3857	9.6016	3996	6166	4136	9.6313	0.4279	54
7	9.5384	0.3455	5548	3588	9.5709	3723	5865	3859	9.6019	3998	6169	4139	9.6315	0.4281	53
8	9.5387	0.3457	5551	3590	9.5711	3725	5868	3862	9.6021	4000	6171	4141	9.6318	0.4283	52
9	9.5390	0.3459	5554	3592	9.5714	3727	5870	3864	9.6024	4003	6174	4143	9.6320	0.4286	51
10	9.5393	0.3461	5556	3594	9.5716	3729	5873	3866	9.6026	4005	6176	4146	9.6323	0.4288	50
11	9.5395	0.3464	5559	3597	9.5719	3732	5876	3869	9.6029	4007	6178	4148	9.6325	0.4290	49
12	9.5398	0.3466	5562	3599	9.5722	3734	5878	3871	9.6031	4010	6181	4150	9.6327	0.4293	48
13	9.5401	0.3468	5564	3601	9.5724	3736	5881	3873	9.6034	4012	6183	4153	9.6330	0.4295	47
14	9.5404	0.3470	5567	3603	9.5727	3738	5883	3876	9.6036	4014	6186	4155	9.6332	0.4298	46
15	9.5406	0.3472	5570	3606	9.5730	3741	5886	3878	9.6039	4017	6188	4158	9.6335	0.4300	45
16	9.5409	0.3475	5572	3608	9.5732	3743	5888	3880	9.6041	4019	6191	4160	9.6337	0.4302	44
17	9.5412	0.3477	5575	3610	9.5735	3745	5891	3882	9.6044	4021	6193	4162	9.6340	0.4305	43
18	9.5415	0.3479	5578	3612	9.5738	3748	5894	3885	9.6046	4024	6196	4165	9.6342	0.4307	42
19	9.5417	0.3481	5581	3615	9.5740	3750	5896	3887	9.6049	4026	6198	4167	9.6344	0.4310	41
20	9.5420	0.3483	5583	3617	9.5743	3752	5899	3889	9.6051	4028	6201	4169	9.6347	0.4312	40
21	9.5423	0.3486	5586	3619	9.5745	3754	5901	3892	9.6054	4031	6203	4172	9.6349	0.4314	39
22	9.5426	0.3488	5589	3621	9.5748	3757	5904	3894	9.6056	4033	6206	4174	9.6352	0.4317	38
23	9.5428	0.3490	5591	3624	9.5751	3759	5906	3896	9.6059	4035	6208	4176	9.6354	0.4319	37
24	9.5431	0.3492	5594	3626	9.5753	3761	5909	3899	9.6061	4038	6210	4179	9.6356	0.4322	36
25	9.5434	0.3494	5597	3628	9.5756	3763	5912	3901	9.6064	4040	6213	4181	9.6359	0.4324	35
26	9.5437	0.3497	5599	3630	9.5759	3766	5914	3903	9.6066	4042	6215	4184	9.6361	0.4326	34
27	9.5439	0.3499	5602	3632	9.5761	3768	5917	3905	9.6069	4045	6218	4186	9.6364	0.4329	33
28	9.5442	0.3501	5605	3635	9.5764	3770	5919	3908	9.6071	4047	6220	4188	9.6366	0.4331	32
29	9.5445	0.3503	5607	3637	9.5766	3773	5922	3910	9.6074	4049	6223	4191	9.6368	0.4334	31
30	9.5448	0.3506	5610	3639	9.5769	3775	5924	3912	9.6076	4052	6225	4193	9.6371	0.4336	30
31	9.5450	0.3508	5613	3641	9.5772	3777	5927	3915	9.6079	4054	6228	4195	9.6373	0.4338	29
32	9.5453	0.3510	5615	3644	9.5774	3779	5930	3917	9.6081	4056	6230	4198	9.6376	0.4341	28
33	9.5456	0.3512	5618	3646	9.5777	3782	5932	3919	9.6084	4059	6233	4200	9.6378	0.4343	27
34	9.5458	0.3514	5621	3648	9.5779	3784	5935	3922	9.6086	4061	6235	4202	9.6380	0.4346	26
35	9.5461	0.3517	5623	3650	9.5782	3786	5937	3924	9.6089	4063	6237	4205	9.6383	0.4348	25
36	9.5464	0.3519	5626	3653	9.5785	3789	5940	3926	9.6091	4066	6240	4207	9.6385	0.4350	24
37	9.5467	0.3521	5629	3655	9.5787	3791	5942	3929	9.6094	4068	6242	4210	9.6388	0.4353	23
38	9.5469	0.3523	5631	3657	9.5790	3793	5945	3931	9.6096	4070	6245	4212	9.6390	0.4355	22
39	9.5472	0.3525	5634	3659	9.5793	3795	5947	3933	9.6099	4073	6247	4214	9.6392	0.4358	21
40	9.5475	0.3528	5637	3662	9.5795	3798	5950	3935	9.6101	4075	6250	4217	9.6395	0.4360	20
41	9.5478	0.3530	5639	3664	9.5798	3800	5953	3938	9.6104	4078	6252	4219	9.6397	0.4362	19
42	9.5480	0.3532	5642	3666	9.5800	3802	5955	3940	9.6106	4080	6255	4221	9.6400	0.4365	18
43	9.5483	0.3534	5645	3668	9.5803	3804	5958	3942	9.6109	4082	6257	4224	9.6402	0.4367	17
44	9.5486	0.3537	5647	3671	9.5806	3807	5960	3945	9.6111	4085	6259	4226	9.6404	0.4370	16
45	9.5489	0.3539	5650	3673	9.5808	3809	5963	3947	9.6114	4087	6262	4229	9.6407	0.4372	15
46	9.5491	0.3541	5653	3675	9.5811	3811	5965	3949	9.6116	4089	6264	4231	9.6409	0.4374	14
47	9.5494	0.3543	5655	3677	9.5813	3814	5968	3952	9.6119	4092	6267	4233	9.6412	0.4377	13
48	9.5497	0.3545	5658	3680	9.5816	3816	5970	3954	9.6121	4094	6269	4236	9.6414	0.4379	12
49	9.5499	0.3548	5661	3682	9.5819	3818	5973	3956	9.6124	4096	6272	4238	9.6416	0.4382	11
50	9.5502	0.3550	5663	3684	9.5821	3820	5975	3959	9.6126	4099	6274	4240	9.6419	0.4384	10
51	9.5505	0.3552	5666	3686	9.5824	3823	5978	3961	9.6129	4101	6277	4243	9.6421	0.4386	9
52	9.5508	0.3554	5669	3689	9.5826	3825	5981	3963	9.6131	4103	6279	4245	9.6423	0.4389	8
53	9.5510	0.3557	5671	3691	9.5829	3827	5983	3966	9.6134	4106	6281	4248	9.6426	0.4391	7
54	9.5513	0.3559	5674	3693	9.5832	3830	5986	3968	9.6136	4108	6284	4250	9.6428	0.4394	6
55	9.5516	0.3561	5677	3695	9.5834	3832	5988	3970	9.6139	4110	6286	4252	9.6431	0.4396	5
56	9.5518	0.3563	5679	3698	9.5837	3834	5991	3973	9.6141	4113	6289	4255	9.6433	0.4398	4
57	9.5521	0.3565	5682	3700	9.5839	3837	5993	3975	9.6144	4115	6291	4257	9.6435	0.4401	3
58	9.5524	0.3568	5685	3702	9.5842	3839	5996	3977	9.6146	4117	6294	4259	9.6438	0.4403	2
59	9.5527	0.3570	5687	3705	9.5845	3841	5998	3980	9.6149	4120	6296	4262	9.6440	0.4406	1
60	9.5529	0.3572	5690	3707	9.5847	3843	6001	3982	9.6151	4122	6298	4264	9.6442	0.4408	0
/	Log	Nat	Log	Nat	Log	Nat	Log	Nat	Log	Nat	Log	Nat	Log	Nat	/
	310°		309°		308°		307°		306°		305°		304°		

VERSINES

Note: For compactness, the leading digit has been dropped from alternate columns. Scan preceding column and row for necessary digit.

VERSINES

/	56° Log	56° Nat	57° Log	57° Nat	58° Log	58° Nat	59° Log	59° Nat	60° Log	60° Nat	61° Log	61° Nat	62° Log	62° Nat	/
0	9.6442	0.4408	6584	4554	9.6722	4701	6857	4850	9.6990	5000	7120	5152	9.7247	0.5305	60
1	9.6445	0.4410	6586	4556	9.6724	4703	6859	4852	9.6992	5003	7122	5154	9.7249	0.5308	59
2	9.6447	0.4413	6588	4558	9.6726	4706	6862	4855	9.6994	5005	7124	5157	9.7251	0.5310	58
3	9.6450	0.4415	6591	4561	9.6729	4708	6864	4857	9.6996	5008	7126	5160	9.7253	0.5313	57
4	9.6452	0.4418	6593	4563	9.6731	4711	6866	4860	9.6998	5010	7128	5162	9.7255	0.5316	56
5	9.6454	0.4420	6595	4566	9.6733	4713	6868	4862	9.7001	5013	7130	5165	9.7258	0.5318	55
6	9.6457	0.4423	6598	4568	9.6735	4716	6870	4865	9.7003	5015	7133	5167	9.7260	0.5321	54
7	9.6459	0.4425	6600	4571	9.6738	4718	6873	4867	9.7005	5018	7135	5170	9.7262	0.5323	53
8	9.6461	0.4427	6602	4573	9.6740	4721	6875	4870	9.7007	5020	7137	5172	9.7264	0.5326	52
9	9.6464	0.4430	6604	4576	9.6742	4723	6877	4872	9.7009	5023	7139	5175	9.7266	0.5328	51
10	9.6466	0.4432	6607	4578	9.6744	4725	6879	4875	9.7012	5025	7141	5177	9.7268	0.5331	50
11	9.6469	0.4435	6609	4580	9.6747	4728	6882	4877	9.7014	5028	7143	5180	9.7270	0.5334	49
12	9.6471	0.4437	6611	4583	9.6749	4730	6884	4880	9.7016	5030	7145	5182	9.7272	0.5336	48
13	9.6473	0.4439	6614	4585	9.6751	4733	6886	4882	9.7018	5033	7147	5185	9.7274	0.5339	47
14	9.6476	0.4442	6616	4588	9.6754	4735	6888	4885	9.7020	5035	7150	5188	9.7276	0.5341	46
15	9.6478	0.4444	6618	4590	9.6756	4738	6890	4887	9.7022	5038	7152	5190	9.7279	0.5344	45
16	9.6480	0.4447	6621	4593	9.6758	4740	6893	4890	9.7025	5040	7154	5193	9.7281	0.5346	44
17	9.6483	0.4449	6623	4595	9.6760	4743	6895	4892	9.7027	5043	7156	5195	9.7283	0.5349	43
18	9.6485	0.4452	6625	4598	9.6763	4745	6897	4895	9.7029	5045	7158	5198	9.7285	0.5352	42
19	9.6487	0.4454	6628	4600	9.6765	4748	6899	4897	9.7031	5048	7160	5200	9.7287	0.5354	41
20	9.6490	0.4456	6630	4602	9.6767	4750	6902	4900	9.7033	5050	7162	5203	9.7289	0.5357	40
21	9.6492	0.4459	6632	4605	9.6769	4753	6904	4902	9.7035	5053	7165	5205	9.7291	0.5359	39
22	9.6495	0.4461	6635	4607	9.6772	4755	6906	4905	9.7038	5056	7167	5208	9.7293	0.5362	38
23	9.6497	0.4464	6637	4610	9.6774	4758	6908	4907	9.7040	5058	7169	5211	9.7295	0.5364	37
24	9.6499	0.4466	6639	4612	9.6776	4760	6910	4910	9.7042	5061	7171	5213	9.7297	0.5367	36
25	9.6502	0.4469	6641	4615	9.6778	4763	6913	4912	9.7044	5063	7173	5216	9.7299	0.5370	35
26	9.6504	0.4471	6644	4617	9.6781	4765	6915	4915	9.7046	5066	7175	5218	9.7302	0.5372	34
27	9.6506	0.4473	6646	4620	9.6783	4768	6917	4917	9.7049	5068	7177	5221	9.7304	0.5375	33
28	9.6509	0.4476	6648	4622	9.6785	4770	6919	4920	9.7051	5071	7179	5223	9.7306	0.5377	32
29	9.6511	0.4478	6651	4625	9.6787	4773	6922	4922	9.7053	5073	7182	5226	9.7308	0.5380	31
30	9.6513	0.4481	6653	4627	9.6790	4775	6924	4925	9.7055	5076	7184	5228	9.7310	0.5383	30
31	9.6516	0.4483	6655	4629	9.6792	4777	6926	4927	9.7057	5078	7186	5231	9.7312	0.5385	29
32	9.6518	0.4485	6658	4632	9.6794	4780	6928	4930	9.7059	5081	7188	5234	9.7314	0.5388	28
33	9.6520	0.4488	6660	4634	9.6797	4782	6930	4932	9.7062	5083	7190	5236	9.7316	0.5390	27
34	9.6523	0.4490	6662	4637	9.6799	4785	6933	4935	9.7064	5086	7192	5239	9.7318	0.5393	26
35	9.6525	0.4493	6665	4639	9.6801	4787	6935	4937	9.7066	5088	7194	5241	9.7320	0.5395	25
36	9.6527	0.4495	6667	4642	9.6803	4790	6937	4940	9.7068	5091	7196	5244	9.7322	0.5398	24
37	9.6530	0.4498	6669	4644	9.6806	4792	6939	4942	9.7070	5093	7199	5246	9.7324	0.5401	23
38	9.6532	0.4500	6671	4647	9.6808	4795	6941	4945	9.7072	5096	7201	5249	9.7326	0.5403	22
39	9.6535	0.4502	6674	4649	9.6810	4797	6944	4947	9.7074	5099	7203	5251	9.7329	0.5406	21
40	9.6537	0.4505	6676	4652	9.6812	4800	6946	4950	9.7077	5101	7205	5254	9.7331	0.5408	20
41	9.6539	0.4507	6678	4654	9.6815	4802	6948	4952	9.7079	5104	7207	5257	9.7333	0.5411	19
42	9.6542	0.4510	6681	4656	9.6817	4805	6950	4955	9.7081	5106	7209	5259	9.7335	0.5414	18
43	9.6544	0.4512	6683	4659	9.6819	4807	6952	4957	9.7083	5109	7211	5262	9.7337	0.5416	17
44	9.6546	0.4515	6685	4661	9.6821	4810	6955	4960	9.7085	5111	7213	5264	9.7339	0.5419	16
45	9.6549	0.4517	6687	4664	9.6823	4812	6957	4962	9.7087	5114	7215	5267	9.7341	0.5421	15
46	9.6551	0.4520	6690	4666	9.6826	4815	6959	4965	9.7090	5116	7218	5269	9.7343	0.5424	14
47	9.6553	0.4522	6692	4669	9.6828	4817	6961	4967	9.7092	5119	7220	5272	9.7345	0.5426	13
48	9.6556	0.4524	6694	4671	9.6830	4820	6963	4970	9.7094	5121	7222	5274	9.7347	0.5429	12
49	9.6558	0.4527	6697	4674	9.6832	4822	6966	4972	9.7096	5124	7224	5277	9.7349	0.5432	11
50	9.6560	0.4529	6699	4676	9.6835	4825	6968	4975	9.7098	5126	7226	5280	9.7351	0.5434	10
51	9.6563	0.4532	6701	4679	9.6837	4827	6970	4977	9.7100	5129	7228	5282	9.7353	0.5437	9
52	9.6565	0.4534	6703	4681	9.6839	4830	6972	4980	9.7102	5132	7230	5285	9.7355	0.5439	8
53	9.6567	0.4537	6706	4684	9.6841	4832	6974	4982	9.7105	5134	7232	5287	9.7358	0.5442	7
54	9.6570	0.4539	6708	4686	9.6844	4835	6977	4985	9.7107	5137	7234	5290	9.7360	0.5445	6
55	9.6572	0.4541	6710	4688	9.6846	4837	6979	4987	9.7109	5139	7237	5292	9.7362	0.5447	5
56	9.6574	0.4544	6713	4691	9.6848	4840	6981	4990	9.7111	5142	7239	5295	9.7364	0.5450	4
57	9.6577	0.4546	6715	4693	9.6850	4842	6983	4992	9.7113	5144	7241	5298	9.7366	0.5452	3
58	9.6579	0.4549	6717	4696	9.6853	4845	6985	4995	9.7115	5147	7243	5300	9.7368	0.5455	2
59	9.6581	0.4551	6719	4698	9.6855	4847	6988	4997	9.7118	5149	7245	5303	9.7370	0.5458	1
60	9.6584	0.4554	6722	4701	9.6857	4850	6990	5000	9.7120	5152	7247	5305	9.7372	0.5460	0

/	Log	Nat	Log	Nat	Log	Nat	Log	Nat	Log	Nat	Log	Nat	Log	Nat	/
	303°		302°		301°		300°		299°		298°		297°		

Note: For compactness, the leading digit has been dropped from alternate columns. Scan preceding column and row for necessary digit.

VERSINES

′	63° Log	Nat	64° Log	Nat	65° Log	Nat	66° Log	Nat	67° Log	Nat	68° Log	Nat	69° Log	Nat	′
0	9.7372	0.5460	7494	5616	9.7615	5774	7732	5933	9.7848	6093	7962	6254	9.8073	0.6416	60
4	9.7380	0.5470	7503	5627	9.7623	5784	7740	5943	9.7856	6103	7969	6265	9.8080	0.6427	56
8	9.7388	0.5481	7511	5637	9.7630	5795	7748	5954	9.7863	6114	7976	6276	9.8088	0.6438	52
12	9.7397	0.5491	7519	5648	9.7638	5805	7756	5965	9.7871	6125	7984	6286	9.8095	0.6449	48
16	9.7405	0.5502	7527	5658	9.7646	5816	7764	5975	9.7879	6136	7991	6297	9.8102	0.6460	44
20	9.7413	0.5512	7535	5669	9.7654	5827	7771	5986	9.7886	6146	7999	6308	9.8110	0.6471	40
24	9.7421	0.5522	7543	5679	9.7662	5837	7779	5997	9.7894	6157	8006	6319	9.8117	0.6482	36
28	9.7429	0.5533	7551	5690	9.7670	5848	7787	6007	9.7901	6168	8014	6330	9.8124	0.6492	32
32	9.7438	0.5543	7559	5700	9.7678	5858	7794	6018	9.7909	6179	8021	6340	9.8131	0.6503	28
36	9.7446	0.5554	7567	5711	9.7686	5869	7802	6029	9.7916	6189	8029	6351	9.8139	0.6514	24
40	9.7454	0.5564	7575	5721	9.7693	5880	7810	6039	9.7924	6200	8036	6362	9.8146	0.6525	20
44	9.7462	0.5575	7583	5732	9.7701	5890	7817	6050	9.7931	6211	8043	6373	9.8153	0.6536	16
48	9.7470	0.5585	7591	5742	9.7709	5901	7825	6061	9.7939	6222	8051	6384	9.8160	0.6547	12
52	9.7478	0.5595	7599	5753	9.7717	5911	7833	6071	9.7947	6232	8058	6395	9.8168	0.6558	8
56	9.7486	0.5606	7607	5763	9.7725	5922	7840	6082	9.7954	6243	8066	6405	9.8175	0.6569	4
60	9.7494	0.5616	7615	5774	9.7732	5933	7848	6093	9.7962	6254	8073	6416	9.8182	0.6580	0

| | 296° | | 295° | | 294° | | 293° | | 292° | | 291° | | 290° | | |

′	70° Log	Nat	71° Log	Nat	72° Log	Nat	73° Log	Nat	74° Log	Nat	75° Log	Nat	76° Log	Nat	′
0	9.8182	0.6580	8289	6744	9.8395	6910	8498	7076	9.8600	7244	8699	7412	9.8797	0.7581	60
4	9.8189	0.6591	8296	6755	9.8402	6921	8505	7087	9.8606	7255	8706	7423	9.8804	0.7592	56
8	9.8197	0.6602	8304	6766	9.8409	6932	8512	7099	9.8613	7266	8712	7434	9.8810	0.7603	52
12	9.8204	0.6613	8311	6777	9.8416	6943	8519	7110	9.8620	7277	8719	7446	9.8817	0.7615	48
16	9.8211	0.6624	8318	6788	9.8422	6954	8525	7121	9.8626	7288	8726	7457	9.8823	0.7626	44
20	9.8218	0.6635	8325	6799	9.8429	6965	8532	7132	9.8633	7300	8732	7468	9.8829	0.7637	40
24	9.8225	0.6645	8332	6810	9.8436	6976	8539	7143	9.8640	7311	8739	7479	9.8836	0.7649	36
28	9.8232	0.6656	8339	6821	9.8443	6987	8546	7154	9.8646	7322	8745	7491	9.8842	0.7660	32
32	9.8240	0.6667	8346	6832	9.8450	6998	8552	7165	9.8653	7333	8752	7502	9.8849	0.7671	28
36	9.8247	0.6678	8353	6844	9.8457	7010	8559	7177	9.8660	7344	8758	7513	9.8855	0.7683	24
40	9.8254	0.6689	8360	6855	9.8464	7021	8566	7188	9.8666	7356	8765	7524	9.8861	0.7694	20
44	9.8261	0.6700	8367	6866	9.8471	7032	8573	7199	9.8673	7367	8771	7536	9.8868	0.7705	16
48	9.8268	0.6711	8374	6877	9.8478	7043	8579	7210	9.8679	7378	8778	7547	9.8874	0.7716	12
52	9.8275	0.6722	8381	6888	9.8484	7054	8586	7221	9.8686	7389	8784	7558	9.8881	0.7728	8
56	9.8282	0.6733	8388	6899	9.8491	7065	8593	7232	9.8693	7401	8791	7569	9.8887	0.7739	4
60	9.8289	0.6744	8395	6910	9.8498	7076	8600	7244	9.8699	7412	8797	7581	9.8893	0.7750	0

| | 289° | | 288° | | 287° | | 286° | | 285° | | 284° | | 283° | | |

′	77° Log	Nat	78° Log	Nat	79° Log	Nat	80° Log	Nat	81° Log	Nat	82° Log	Nat	83° Log	Nat	′
0	9.8893	0.7750	8988	7921	9.9081	8092	9172	8264	9.9261	8436	9349	8608	9.9436	0.8781	60
4	9.8900	0.7762	8994	7932	9.9087	8103	9178	8275	9.9267	8447	9355	8620	9.9441	0.8793	56
8	9.8906	0.7773	9000	7944	9.9093	8115	9184	8286	9.9273	8459	9361	8631	9.9447	0.8804	52
12	9.8912	0.7785	9006	7955	9.9099	8126	9190	8298	9.9279	8470	9367	8643	9.9453	0.8816	48
16	9.8919	0.7796	9013	7966	9.9105	8138	9196	8309	9.9285	8482	9372	8654	9.9458	0.8828	44
20	9.8925	0.7807	9019	7978	9.9111	8149	9202	8321	9.9291	8493	9378	8666	9.9464	0.8839	40
24	9.8931	0.7819	9025	7989	9.9117	8160	9208	8332	9.9297	8505	9384	8677	9.9470	0.8851	36
28	9.8938	0.7830	9031	8001	9.9123	8172	9214	8344	9.9302	8516	9390	8689	9.9475	0.8862	32
32	9.8944	0.7841	9037	8012	9.9129	8183	9220	8355	9.9308	8528	9395	8701	9.9481	0.8874	28
36	9.8950	0.7853	9044	8023	9.9135	8195	9226	8367	9.9314	8539	9401	8712	9.9487	0.8885	24
40	9.8956	0.7864	9050	8035	9.9141	8206	9232	8378	9.9320	8551	9407	8724	9.9492	0.8897	20
44	9.8963	0.7875	9056	8046	9.9148	8218	9237	8390	9.9326	8562	9413	8735	9.9498	0.8908	16
48	9.8969	0.7887	9062	8058	9.9154	8229	9243	8401	9.9332	8574	9418	8747	9.9504	0.8920	12
52	9.8975	0.7898	9068	8069	9.9160	8241	9249	8413	9.9338	8585	9424	8758	9.9509	0.8932	8
56	9.8981	0.7910	9074	8080	9.9166	8252	9255	8424	9.9343	8597	9430	8770	9.9515	0.8943	4
60	9.8988	0.7921	9081	8092	9.9172	8264	9261	8436	9.9349	8608	9436	8781	9.9521	0.8955	0

| ′ | 282° | | 281° | | 280° | | 279° | | 278° | | 277° | | 276° | | ′ |

VERSINES

Note: For compactness, the leading digit has been dropped from alternate columns. Scan preceding column and row for necessary digit.

VERSINES

/	84° Log	Nat	85° Log	Nat	86° Log	Nat	87° Log	Nat	88° Log	Nat	89° Log	Nat	90° Log	Nat	/
0	9.9521	0.8955	9604	9128	9.9686	9302	9767	9477	9.9846	9651	9924	9825	0.0000	1.0000	60
4	9.9526	0.8966	9609	9140	9.9691	9314	9772	9488	9.9851	9663	9929	9837	0.0005	1.0012	56
8	9.9532	0.8978	9615	9152	9.9697	9326	9777	9500	9.9856	9674	9934	9849	0.0010	1.0023	52
12	9.9537	0.8989	9620	9163	9.9702	9337	9782	9512	9.9861	9686	9939	9860	0.0015	1.0035	48
16	9.9543	0.9001	9626	9175	9.9708	9349	9788	9523	9.9867	9698	9944	9872	0.0020	1.0047	44
20	9.9548	0.9013	9631	9186	9.9713	9360	9793	9535	9.9872	9709	9949	9884	0.0025	1.0058	40
24	9.9554	0.9024	9637	9198	9.9718	9372	9798	9546	9.9877	9721	9954	9895	0.0030	1.0070	36
28	9.9560	0.9036	9642	9210	9.9724	9384	9804	9558	9.9882	9732	9959	9907	0.0035	1.0081	32
32	9.9565	0.9047	9648	9221	9.9729	9395	9809	9570	9.9887	9744	9964	9919	0.0040	1.0093	28
36	9.9571	0.9059	9653	9233	9.9734	9407	9814	9581	9.9893	9756	9970	9930	0.0045	1.0105	24
40	9.9576	0.9071	9659	9244	9.9740	9419	9819	9593	9.9898	9767	9975	9942	0.0050	1.0116	20
44	9.9582	0.9082	9664	9256	9.9745	9430	9825	9604	9.9903	9779	9980	9953	0.0055	1.0128	16
48	9.9587	0.9094	9670	9268	9.9751	9442	9830	9616	9.9908	9791	9985	9965	0.0060	1.0140	12
52	9.9593	0.9105	9675	9279	9.9756	9453	9835	9628	9.9913	9802	9990	9977	0.0065	1.0151	8
56	9.9598	0.9117	9681	9291	9.9761	9465	9840	9639	9.9918	9814	9995	9988	0.0070	1.0163	4
60	9.9604	0.9128	9686	9302	9.9767	9477	9846	9651	9.9924	9825	0000	0000	0.0075	1.0175	0

275°	274°	273°	272°	271°	270°	269°

0′	91° Log	Nat	92° Log	Nat	93° Log	Nat	94° Log	Nat	95° Log	Nat	96° Log	Nat	97° Log	Nat	/
0′	0.0075	1.0175	0149	0349	0.0222	0523	0293	0698	0.0363	0872	0432	1045	0.0499	1.1219	60
4	0.0080	1.0186	0154	0361	0.0226	0535	0298	0709	0.0368	0883	0436	1057	0.0504	1.1230	56
8	0.0085	1.0198	0159	0372	0.0231	0547	0302	0721	0.0372	0895	0441	1068	0.0508	1.1242	52
12	0.0090	1.0209	0164	0384	0.0236	0558	0307	0732	0.0377	0906	0445	1080	0.0513	1.1253	48
16	0.0095	1.0221	0168	0396	0.0241	0570	0312	0744	0.0381	0918	0450	1092	0.0517	1.1265	44
20	0.0100	1.0233	0173	0407	0.0245	0581	0316	0756	0.0386	0929	0454	1103	0.0522	1.1276	40
24	0.0105	1.0244	0178	0419	0.0250	0593	0321	0767	0.0391	0941	0459	1115	0.0526	1.1288	36
28	0.0110	1.0256	0183	0430	0.0255	0605	0326	0779	0.0395	0953	0463	1126	0.0531	1.1299	32
32	0.0115	1.0268	0188	0442	0.0260	0616	0330	0790	0.0400	0964	0468	1138	0.0535	1.1311	28
36	0.0120	1.0279	0193	0454	0.0264	0628	0335	0802	0.0404	0976	0473	1149	0.0539	1.1323	24
40	0.0125	1.0291	0197	0465	0.0269	0640	0340	0814	0.0409	0987	0477	1161	0.0544	1.1334	20
44	0.0129	1.0302	0202	0477	0.0274	0651	0344	0825	0.0414	0999	0481	1172	0.0548	1.1346	16
48	0.0134	1.0314	0207	0488	0.0279	0663	0349	0837	0.0418	1011	0486	1184	0.0553	1.1357	12
52	0.0139	1.0326	0212	0500	0.0283	0674	0354	0848	0.0423	1022	0490	1196	0.0557	1.1369	8
56	0.0144	1.0337	0217	0512	0.0288	0686	0358	0860	0.0427	1034	0495	1207	0.0562	1.1380	4
60	0.0149	1.0349	0222	0523	0.0293	0698	0363	0872	0.0432	1045	0499	1219	0.0566	1.1392	0

268°	267°	266°	265°	264°	263°	262°

0′	98° Log	Nat	99° Log	Nat	100° Log	Nat	101° Log	Nat	102° Log	Nat	103° Log	Nat	104° Log	Nat	/
0′	0.0566	1.1392	0631	1564	0.0695	1736	0758	1908	0.0820	2079	0881	2250	0.0941	1.2419	60
4	0.0570	1.1403	0636	1576	0.0700	1748	0763	1920	0.0824	2090	0885	2261	0.0945	1.2431	56
8	0.0575	1.1415	0640	1587	0.0704	1759	0767	1931	0.0829	2102	0889	2272	0.0949	1.2442	52
12	0.0579	1.1426	0644	1599	0.0708	1771	0771	1942	0.0833	2113	0893	2284	0.0953	1.2453	48
16	0.0583	1.1438	0648	1610	0.0712	1782	0775	1954	0.0837	2125	0897	2295	0.0957	1.2464	44
20	0.0588	1.1449	0653	1622	0.0717	1794	0779	1965	0.0841	2136	0901	2306	0.0961	1.2476	40
24	0.0592	1.1461	0657	1633	0.0721	1805	0783	1977	0.0845	2147	0905	2317	0.0965	1.2487	36
28	0.0597	1.1472	0661	1645	0.0725	1817	0787	1988	0.0849	2159	0909	2329	0.0968	1.2498	32
32	0.0601	1.1484	0666	1656	0.0729	1828	0792	1999	0.0853	2170	0913	2340	0.0972	1.2509	28
36	0.0605	1.1495	0670	1668	0.0733	1840	0796	2011	0.0857	2181	0917	2351	0.0976	1.2521	24
40	0.0610	1.1507	0674	1679	0.0738	1851	0800	2022	0.0861	2193	0921	2363	0.0980	1.2532	20
44	0.0614	1.1518	0678	1691	0.0742	1862	0804	2034	0.0865	2204	0925	2374	0.0984	1.2543	16
48	0.0618	1.1530	0683	1702	0.0746	1874	0808	2045	0.0869	2215	0929	2385	0.0988	1.2554	12
52	0.0623	1.1541	0687	1714	0.0750	1885	0812	2056	0.0873	2227	0933	2397	0.0992	1.2566	8
56	0.0627	1.1553	0691	1725	0.0754	1897	0816	2068	0.0877	2238	0937	2408	0.0996	1.2577	4
60	0.0631	1.1564	0695	1736	0.0758	1908	0820	2079	0.0881	2250	0941	2419	0.1000	1.2588	0

261°	260°	259°	258°	257°	256°	255°

Note: For compactness, the leading digit has been dropped from alternate columns. Scan preceding column and row for necessary digit.

VERSINES

105°–111° / 254°–248°

′	105° Log	Nat	106° Log	Nat	107° Log	Nat	108° Log	Nat	109° Log	Nat	110° Log	Nat	111° Log	Nat	′
0	0.1000	1.2588	1057	2756	0.1114	2924	1169	3090	0.1224	3256	1278	3420	0.1330	1.3584	60
4	0.1004	1.2599	1061	2768	0.1118	2935	1173	3101	0.1228	3267	1281	3431	0.1334	1.3595	56
8	0.1007	1.2611	1065	2779	0.1121	2946	1177	3112	0.1231	3278	1285	3442	0.1337	1.3605	52
12	0.1011	1.2622	1069	2790	0.1125	2957	1180	3123	0.1235	3289	1288	3453	0.1341	1.3616	48
16	0.1015	1.2633	1072	2801	0.1129	2968	1184	3134	0.1238	3300	1292	3464	0.1344	1.3627	44
20	0.1019	1.2644	1076	2812	0.1133	2979	1188	3145	0.1242	3311	1295	3475	0.1347	1.3638	40
24	0.1023	1.2656	1080	2823	0.1136	2990	1191	3156	0.1246	3322	1299	3486	0.1351	1.3649	36
28	0.1027	1.2667	1084	2835	0.1140	3002	1195	3168	0.1249	3333	1302	3497	0.1354	1.3660	32
32	0.1031	1.2678	1088	2846	0.1144	3013	1199	3179	0.1253	3344	1306	3508	0.1358	1.3670	28
36	0.1034	1.2689	1091	2857	0.1147	3024	1202	3190	0.1256	3355	1309	3518	0.1361	1.3681	24
40	0.1038	1.2700	1095	2868	0.1151	3035	1206	3201	0.1260	3365	1313	3529	0.1365	1.3692	20
44	0.1042	1.2712	1099	2879	0.1155	3046	1210	3212	0.1263	3376	1316	3540	0.1368	1.3703	16
48	0.1046	1.2723	1103	2890	0.1158	3057	1213	3223	0.1267	3387	1320	3551	0.1372	1.3714	12
52	0.1050	1.2734	1106	2901	0.1162	3068	1217	3234	0.1271	3398	1323	3562	0.1375	1.3724	8
56	0.1053	1.2745	1110	2913	0.1166	3079	1220	3245	0.1274	3409	1327	3573	0.1378	1.3735	4
60	0.1057	1.2756	1114	2924	0.1169	3090	1224	3256	0.1278	3420	1330	3584	0.1382	1.3746	0

Bottom headers: 254° 253° 252° 251° 250° 249° 248°

112°–118° / 247°–241°

′	112° Log	Nat	113° Log	Nat	114° Log	Nat	115° Log	Nat	116° Log	Nat	117° Log	Nat	118° Log	Nat	′
0	0.1382	1.3746	1432	3907	0.1482	4067	1531	4226	0.1579	4384	1626	4540	0.1672	1.4695	60
4	0.1385	1.3757	1436	3918	0.1485	4078	1534	4237	0.1582	4394	1629	4550	0.1675	1.4705	56
8	0.1389	1.3768	1439	3929	0.1489	4089	1537	4247	0.1585	4405	1632	4561	0.1678	1.4715	52
12	0.1392	1.3778	1442	3939	0.1492	4099	1541	4258	0.1588	4415	1635	4571	0.1681	1.4726	48
16	0.1395	1.3789	1446	3950	0.1495	4110	1544	4268	0.1591	4425	1638	4581	0.1684	1.4736	44
20	0.1399	1.3800	1449	3961	0.1498	4120	1547	4279	0.1594	4436	1641	4592	0.1687	1.4746	40
24	0.1402	1.3811	1452	3971	0.1502	4131	1550	4289	0.1598	4446	1644	4602	0.1690	1.4756	36
28	0.1406	1.3821	1456	3982	0.1505	4142	1553	4300	0.1601	4457	1647	4612	0.1693	1.4766	32
32	0.1409	1.3832	1459	3993	0.1508	4152	1557	4310	0.1604	4467	1650	4623	0.1696	1.4777	28
36	0.1412	1.3843	1462	4003	0.1511	4163	1560	4321	0.1607	4478	1653	4633	0.1699	1.4787	24
40	0.1416	1.3854	1466	4014	0.1515	4173	1563	4331	0.1610	4488	1656	4643	0.1702	1.4797	20
44	0.1419	1.3864	1469	4025	0.1518	4184	1566	4342	0.1613	4498	1659	4654	0.1705	1.4807	16
48	0.1422	1.3875	1472	4035	0.1521	4195	1569	4352	0.1616	4509	1662	4664	0.1708	1.4818	12
52	0.1426	1.3886	1476	4046	0.1524	4205	1572	4363	0.1619	4519	1666	4674	0.1711	1.4828	8
56	0.1429	1.3897	1479	4057	0.1528	4216	1576	4373	0.1623	4530	1669	4684	0.1714	1.4838	4
60	0.1432	1.3907	1482	4067	0.1531	4226	1579	4384	0.1626	4540	1672	4695	0.1717	1.4848	0

Bottom headers: 247° 246° 245° 244° 243° 242° 241°

119°–125° / 240°–234°

′	119° Log	Nat	120° Log	Nat	121° Log	Nat	122° Log	Nat	123° Log	Nat	124° Log	Nat	125° Log	Nat	′
0	0.1717	1.4848	1761	5000	0.1804	5150	1847	5299	0.1888	5446	1929	5592	0.1969	1.5736	60
4	0.1720	1.4858	1764	5010	0.1807	5160	1849	5309	0.1891	5456	1932	5602	0.1972	1.5745	56
8	0.1723	1.4868	1767	5020	0.1810	5170	1852	5319	0.1894	5466	1934	5611	0.1974	1.5755	52
12	0.1726	1.4879	1770	5030	0.1813	5180	1855	5329	0.1896	5476	1937	5621	0.1977	1.5764	48
16	0.1729	1.4889	1773	5040	0.1816	5190	1858	5339	0.1899	5485	1940	5630	0.1979	1.5774	44
20	0.1732	1.4899	1775	5050	0.1818	5200	1861	5348	0.1902	5495	1942	5640	0.1982	1.5783	40
24	0.1734	1.4909	1778	5060	0.1821	5210	1863	5358	0.1905	5505	1945	5650	0.1985	1.5793	36
28	0.1737	1.4919	1781	5070	0.1824	5220	1866	5368	0.1907	5515	1948	5659	0.1987	1.5802	32
32	0.1740	1.4929	1784	5080	0.1827	5230	1869	5378	0.1910	5524	1950	5669	0.1990	1.5812	28
36	0.1743	1.4939	1787	5090	0.1830	5240	1872	5388	0.1913	5534	1953	5678	0.1992	1.5821	24
40	0.1746	1.4950	1790	5100	0.1833	5250	1875	5398	0.1916	5544	1956	5688	0.1995	1.5831	20
44	0.1749	1.4960	1793	5110	0.1835	5260	1877	5407	0.1918	5553	1958	5698	0.1998	1.5840	16
48	0.1752	1.4970	1796	5120	0.1838	5270	1880	5417	0.1921	5563	1961	5707	0.2000	1.5850	12
52	0.1755	1.4980	1799	5130	0.1841	5279	1883	5427	0.1924	5573	1964	5717	0.2003	1.5859	8
56	0.1758	1.4990	1801	5140	0.1844	5289	1886	5437	0.1926	5582	1966	5726	0.2005	1.5868	4
60	0.1761	1.5000	1804	5150	0.1847	5299	1888	5446	0.1929	5592	1969	5736	0.2008	1.5878	0

Bottom headers: 240° 239° 238° 237° 236° 235° 234°

VERSINES

Note: For compactness, the leading digit has been dropped from alternate columns. Scan preceding column and row for necessary digit.

VERSINES

/	126° Log	Nat	127° Log	Nat	128° Log	Nat	129° Log	Nat	130° Log	Nat	131° Log	Nat	132° Log	Nat	/
0	0.2008	1.5878	2046	6018	0.2084	6157	2120	6293	0.2156	6428	2191	6561	0.2225	1.6691	60
6	0.2012	1.5892	2050	6032	0.2087	6170	2124	6307	0.2159	6441	2194	6574	0.2228	1.6704	54
12	0.2016	1.5906	2054	6046	0.2091	6184	2127	6320	0.2163	6455	2198	6587	0.2232	1.6717	48
18	0.2019	1.5920	2057	6060	0.2095	6198	2131	6334	0.2166	6468	2201	6600	0.2235	1.6730	42
24	0.2023	1.5934	2061	6074	0.2098	6211	2134	6347	0.2170	6481	2205	6613	0.2238	1.6743	36
30	0.2027	1.5948	2065	6088	0.2102	6225	2138	6361	0.2173	6494	2208	6626	0.2242	1.6756	30
36	0.2031	1.5962	2069	6101	0.2106	6239	2142	6374	0.2177	6508	2211	6639	0.2245	1.6769	24
42	0.2035	1.5976	2072	6115	0.2109	6252	2145	6388	0.2180	6521	2215	6652	0.2248	1.6782	18
48	0.2039	1.5990	2076	6129	0.2113	6266	2149	6401	0.2184	6534	2218	6665	0.2252	1.6794	12
54	0.2042	1.6004	2080	6143	0.2116	6280	2152	6414	0.2187	6547	2222	6678	0.2255	1.6807	6
60	0.2046	1.6018	2084	6157	0.2120	6293	2156	6428	0.2191	6561	2225	6691	0.2258	1.6820	0

	Log	Nat	Log	Nat	Log	Nat	Log	Nat	Log	Nat	Log	Nat	Log	Nat	
	233°		232°		231°		230°		229°		228°		227°		

/	133° Log	Nat	134° Log	Nat	135° Log	Nat	136° Log	Nat	137° Log	Nat	138° Log	Nat	139° Log	Nat	/
0	0.2258	1.6820	2291	6947	0.2323	7071	2354	7193	0.2384	7314	2413	7431	0.2442	1.7547	60
6	0.2262	1.6833	2294	6959	0.2326	7083	2357	7206	0.2387	7325	2416	7443	0.2445	1.7559	54
12	0.2265	1.6845	2297	6972	0.2329	7096	2360	7218	0.2390	7337	2419	7455	0.2448	1.7570	48
18	0.2268	1.6858	2300	6984	0.2332	7108	2363	7230	0.2393	7349	2422	7466	0.2451	1.7581	42
24	0.2271	1.6871	2304	6997	0.2335	7120	2366	7242	0.2396	7361	2425	7478	0.2453	1.7593	36
30	0.2275	1.6884	2307	7009	0.2338	7133	2369	7254	0.2399	7373	2428	7490	0.2456	1.7604	30
36	0.2278	1.6896	2310	7022	0.2341	7145	2372	7266	0.2402	7385	2431	7501	0.2459	1.7615	24
42	0.2281	1.6909	2313	7034	0.2344	7157	2375	7278	0.2405	7396	2434	7513	0.2462	1.7627	18
48	0.2284	1.6921	2316	7046	0.2347	7169	2378	7290	0.2408	7408	2436	7524	0.2464	1.7638	12
54	0.2288	1.6934	2319	7059	0.2351	7181	2381	7302	0.2410	7420	2439	7536	0.2467	1.7649	6
60	0.2291	1.6947	2323	7071	0.2354	7193	2384	7314	0.2413	7431	2442	7547	0.2470	1.7660	0

	Log	Nat	Log	Nat	Log	Nat	Log	Nat	Log	Nat	Log	Nat	Log	Nat	
	226°		225°		224°		223°		222°		221°		220°		

/	140° Log	Nat	141° Log	Nat	142° Log	Nat	143° Log	Nat	144° Log	Nat	145° Log	Nat	146° Log	Nat	/
0	0.2470	1.7660	2497	7771	0.2524	7880	2549	7986	0.2574	8090	2599	8192	0.2622	1.8290	60
6	0.2473	1.7672	2500	7782	0.2526	7891	2552	7997	0.2577	8100	2601	8202	0.2625	1.8300	54
12	0.2476	1.7683	2503	7793	0.2529	7902	2554	8007	0.2579	8111	2603	8211	0.2627	1.8310	48
18	0.2478	1.7694	2505	7804	0.2531	7912	2557	8018	0.2582	8121	2606	8221	0.2629	1.8320	42
24	0.2481	1.7705	2508	7815	0.2534	7923	2560	8028	0.2584	8131	2608	8231	0.2631	1.8329	36
30	0.2484	1.7716	2511	7826	0.2537	7934	2562	8039	0.2587	8141	2611	8241	0.2634	1.8339	30
36	0.2486	1.7727	2513	7837	0.2539	7944	2565	8049	0.2589	8151	2613	8251	0.2636	1.8348	24
42	0.2489	1.7738	2516	7848	0.2542	7955	2567	8059	0.2591	8161	2615	8261	0.2638	1.8358	18
48	0.2492	1.7749	2518	7859	0.2544	7965	2569	8070	0.2594	8171	2618	8271	0.2641	1.8368	12
54	0.2495	1.7760	2521	7869	0.2547	7976	2572	8080	0.2596	8181	2620	8281	0.2643	1.8377	6
60	0.2497	1.7771	2524	7880	0.2549	7986	2574	8090	0.2599	8192	2622	8290	0.2645	1.8387	0

	Log	Nat	Log	Nat	Log	Nat	Log	Nat	Log	Nat	Log	Nat	Log	Nat	
	219°		218°		217°		216°		215°		214°		213°		

/	147° Log	Nat	148° Log	Nat	149° Log	Nat	150° Log	Nat	151° Log	Nat	152° Log	Nat	153° Log	Nat	/
0	0.2645	1.8387	2667	8480	0.2689	8572	2709	8660	0.2729	8746	2748	8829	0.2767	1.8910	60
6	0.2647	1.8396	2669	8490	0.2691	8581	2711	8669	0.2731	8755	2750	8838	0.2769	1.8918	54
12	0.2650	1.8406	2671	8499	0.2693	8590	2713	8678	0.2733	8763	2752	8846	0.2771	1.8926	48
18	0.2652	1.8415	2674	8508	0.2695	8599	2715	8686	0.2735	8771	2754	8854	0.2772	1.8934	42
24	0.2654	1.8425	2676	8517	0.2697	8607	2717	8695	0.2737	8780	2756	8862	0.2774	1.8942	36
30	0.2656	1.8434	2678	8526	0.2699	8616	2719	8704	0.2739	8788	2758	8870	0.2776	1.8949	30
36	0.2658	1.8443	2680	8536	0.2701	8625	2721	8712	0.2741	8796	2760	8878	0.2778	1.8957	24
42	0.2661	1.8453	2682	8545	0.2703	8634	2723	8721	0.2743	8805	2761	8886	0.2779	1.8965	18
48	0.2663	1.8462	2684	8554	0.2705	8643	2725	8729	0.2745	8813	2763	8894	0.2781	1.8973	12
54	0.2665	1.8471	2686	8563	0.2707	8652	2727	8738	0.2746	8821	2765	8902	0.2783	1.8980	6
60	0.2667	1.8480	2689	8572	0.2709	8660	2729	8746	0.2748	8829	2767	8910	0.2785	1.8988	0

/	Log	Nat	Log	Nat	Log	Nat	Log	Nat	Log	Nat	Log	Nat	Log	Nat	/
	212°		211°		210°		209°		208°		207°		206°		

VERSINES

/	154° Log	Nat	155° Log	Nat	156° Log	Nat	157° Log	Nat	158° Log	Nat	159° Log	Nat	160° Log	Nat	/
0	0.2785	1.8988	2802	9063	0.2818	9135	2834	9205	0.2849	9272	2864	9336	0.2877	1.9397	60
6	0.2787	1.8996	2804	9070	0.2820	9143	2836	9212	0.2851	9278	2865	9342	0.2879	1.9403	54
12	0.2788	1.9003	2805	9078	0.2822	9150	2837	9219	0.2852	9285	2866	9348	0.2880	1.9409	48
18	0.2790	1.9011	2807	9085	0.2823	9157	2839	9225	0.2854	9291	2868	9354	0.2881	1.9415	42
24	0.2792	1.9018	2809	9092	0.2825	9164	2840	9232	0.2855	9298	2869	9361	0.2883	1.9421	36
30	0.2793	1.9026	2810	9100	0.2826	9171	2842	9239	0.2857	9304	2871	9367	0.2884	1.9426	30
36	0.2795	1.9033	2812	9107	0.2828	9178	2843	9245	0.2858	9311	2872	9373	0.2885	1.9432	24
42	0.2797	1.9041	2814	9114	0.2829	9184	2845	9252	0.2859	9317	2873	9379	0.2887	1.9438	18
48	0.2799	1.9048	2815	9121	0.2831	9191	2846	9259	0.2861	9323	2875	9385	0.2888	1.9444	12
54	0.2800	1.9056	2817	9128	0.2833	9198	2848	9265	0.2862	9330	2876	9391	0.2889	1.9449	6
60	0.2802	1.9063	2818	9135	0.2834	9205	2849	9272	0.2864	9336	2877	9397	0.2890	1.9455	0
	Log	Nat	Log	Nat	Log	Nat	Log	Nat	Log	Nat	Log	Nat	Log	Nat	
	205°		204°		203°		202°		201°		200°		199°		

/	161° Log	Nat	162° Log	Nat	163° Log	Nat	164° Log	Nat	165° Log	Nat	166° Log	Nat	167° Log	Nat	/
0	0.2890	1.9455	2903	9511	0.2914	9563	2925	9613	0.2936	9659	2945	9703	0.2954	1.9744	60
6	0.2892	1.9461	2904	9516	0.2915	9568	2926	9617	0.2937	9664	2946	9707	0.2955	1.9748	54
12	0.2893	1.9466	2905	9521	0.2917	9573	2927	9622	0.2938	9668	2947	9711	0.2956	1.9751	48
18	0.2894	1.9472	2906	9527	0.2918	9578	2929	9627	0.2939	9673	2948	9715	0.2957	1.9755	42
24	0.2895	1.9478	2907	9532	0.2919	9583	2930	9632	0.2940	9677	2949	9720	0.2958	1.9759	36
30	0.2897	1.9483	2909	9537	0.2920	9588	2931	9636	0.2941	9681	2950	9724	0.2959	1.9763	30
36	0.2898	1.9489	2910	9542	0.2921	9593	2932	9641	0.2942	9686	2951	9728	0.2959	1.9767	24
42	0.2899	1.9494	2911	9548	0.2922	9598	2933	9646	0.2942	9690	2952	9732	0.2960	1.9770	18
48	0.2900	1.9500	2912	9553	0.2923	9603	2934	9650	0.2943	9694	2953	9736	0.2961	1.9774	12
54	0.2901	1.9505	2913	9558	0.2924	9608	2935	9655	0.2944	9699	2953	9740	0.2962	1.9778	6
60	0.2903	1.9511	2914	9563	0.2925	9613	2936	9659	0.2945	9703	2954	9744	0.2963	1.9781	0
	Log	Nat	Log	Nat	Log	Nat	Log	Nat	Log	Nat	Log	Nat	Log	Nat	
	198°		197°		196°		195°		194°		193°		192°		

/	168° Log	Nat	169° Log	Nat	170° Log	Nat	171° Log	Nat	172° Log	Nat	173° Log	Nat	174° Log	Nat	/
0	0.2963	1.9781	2970	9816	0.2977	9848	2983	9877	0.2989	9903	2994	9925	0.2998	1.9945	60
6	0.2963	1.9785	2971	9820	0.2978	9851	2984	9880	0.2990	9905	2995	9928	0.2999	1.9947	54
12	0.2964	1.9789	2972	9823	0.2978	9854	2985	9882	0.2990	9907	2995	9930	0.2999	1.9949	48
18	0.2965	1.9792	2972	9826	0.2979	9857	2985	9885	0.2991	9910	2995	9932	0.3000	1.9951	42
24	0.2966	1.9796	2973	9829	0.2980	9860	2986	9888	0.2991	9912	2996	9934	0.3000	1.9952	36
30	0.2966	1.9799	2974	9833	0.2980	9863	2986	9890	0.2992	9914	2996	9936	0.3000	1.9954	30
36	0.2967	1.9803	2974	9836	0.2981	9866	2987	9893	0.2992	9917	2997	9938	0.3001	1.9956	24
42	0.2968	1.9806	2975	9839	0.2982	9869	2987	9895	0.2993	9919	2997	9940	0.3001	1.9957	18
48	0.2969	1.9810	2976	9842	0.2982	9871	2988	9898	0.2993	9921	2998	9942	0.3001	1.9959	12
54	0.2969	1.9813	2977	9845	0.2983	9874	2989	9900	0.2994	9923	2998	9943	0.3002	1.9960	6
60	0.2970	1.9816	2977	9848	0.2983	9877	2989	9903	0.2994	9925	2998	9945	0.3002	1.9962	0
	Log	Nat	Log	Nat	Log	Nat	Log	Nat	Log	Nat	Log	Nat	Log	Nat	
	191°		190°		189°		188°		187°		186°		185°		

/	175° Log	Nat	176° Log	Nat	177° Log	Nat	178° Log	Nat	179° Log	Nat	/
0	0.3002	1.9962	3005	9976	0.3007	9986	3009	9994	0.3010	9998	60
6	0.3002	1.9963	3005	9977	0.3008	9987	3009	9995	0.3010	9999	54
12	0.3003	1.9965	3006	9978	0.3008	9988	3009	9995	0.3010	9999	48
18	0.3003	1.9966	3006	9979	0.3008	9989	3009	9996	0.3010	9999	42
24	0.3003	1.9968	3006	9980	0.3008	9990	3009	9996	0.3010	9999	36
30	0.3004	1.9969	3006	9981	0.3008	9990	3010	9997	0.3010	0000	30
36	0.3004	1.9971	3006	9982	0.3008	9991	3010	9997	0.3010	0000	24
42	0.3004	1.9972	3007	9983	0.3009	9992	3010	9997	0.3010	0000	18
48	0.3004	1.9973	3007	9984	0.3009	9993	3010	9998	0.3010	0000	12
54	0.3005	1.9974	3007	9985	0.3009	9993	3010	9998	0.3010	0000	6
60	0.3005	1.9976	3007	9986	0.3009	9994	3010	9998	0.3010	0000	0
/	Log	Nat	Log	Nat	Log	Nat	Log	Nat	Log	Nat	/
	184°		183°		182°		181°		180°		

VERSINES

LOG COSINES

	0°	1°	2°	3°	4°	5°	6°	7°	8°	9°	10°	11°	12°	13°	14°	
0	0.0000	9999	9997	9994	9989	9.9983	9976	9968	9958	9.9946	9934	9919	9904	9887	9.9869	60
1	0.0000	9999	9997	9994	9989	9.9983	9976	9967	9957	9.9946	9933	9919	9904	9887	9.9869	59
2	0.0000	9999	9997	9994	9989	9.9983	9976	9967	9957	9.9946	9933	9919	9904	9887	9.9868	58
3	0.0000	9999	9997	9994	9989	9.9983	9976	9967	9957	9.9946	9933	9918	9903	9886	9.9868	57
4	0.0000	9999	9997	9994	9989	9.9983	9976	9967	9957	9.9945	9933	9918	9903	9886	9.9868	56
5	0.0000	9999	9997	9994	9989	9.9983	9975	9967	9957	9.9945	9932	9918	9903	9886	9.9867	55
6	0.0000	9999	9997	9994	9989	9.9983	9975	9967	9956	9.9945	9932	9918	9902	9885	9.9867	54
7	0.0000	9999	9997	9994	9989	9.9983	9975	9966	9956	9.9945	9932	9918	9902	9885	9.9867	53
8	0.0000	9999	9997	9994	9989	9.9983	9975	9966	9956	9.9945	9932	9917	9902	9885	9.9867	52
9	0.0000	9999	9997	9993	9989	9.9982	9975	9966	9956	9.9944	9931	9917	9902	9885	9.9866	51
10	0.0000	9999	9997	9993	9989	9.9982	9975	9966	9956	9.9944	9931	9917	9901	9884	9.9866	50
11	0.0000	9999	9997	9993	9988	9.9982	9975	9966	9955	9.9944	9931	9917	9901	9884	9.9866	49
12	0.0000	9999	9997	9993	9988	9.9982	9975	9966	9955	9.9944	9931	9916	9901	9884	9.9865	48
13	0.0000	9999	9997	9993	9988	9.9982	9974	9965	9955	9.9944	9931	9916	9901	9883	9.9865	47
14	0.0000	9999	9997	9993	9988	9.9982	9974	9965	9955	9.9943	9930	9916	9900	9883	9.9865	46
15	0.0000	9999	9997	9993	9988	9.9982	9974	9965	9955	9.9943	9930	9916	9900	9883	9.9864	45
16	0.0000	9999	9997	9993	9988	9.9982	9974	9965	9955	9.9943	9930	9915	9900	9883	9.9864	44
17	0.0000	9999	9997	9993	9988	9.9982	9974	9965	9954	9.9943	9930	9915	9899	9882	9.9864	43
18	0.0000	9999	9996	9993	9988	9.9981	9974	9965	9954	9.9943	9929	9915	9899	9882	9.9863	42
19	0.0000	9999	9996	9993	9988	9.9981	9974	9964	9954	9.9942	9929	9915	9899	9882	9.9863	41
20	0.0000	9999	9996	9993	9988	9.9981	9973	9964	9954	9.9942	9929	9914	9899	9881	9.9863	40
21	0.0000	9999	9996	9993	9987	9.9981	9973	9964	9954	9.9942	9929	9914	9898	9881	9.9862	39
22	0.0000	9999	9996	9992	9987	9.9981	9973	9964	9954	9.9942	9929	9914	9898	9881	9.9862	38
23	0.0000	9999	9996	9992	9987	9.9981	9973	9964	9953	9.9941	9928	9914	9898	9880	9.9862	37
24	0.0000	9999	9996	9992	9987	9.9981	9973	9964	9953	9.9941	9928	9913	9897	9880	9.9861	36
25	0.0000	9999	9996	9992	9987	9.9981	9973	9964	9953	9.9941	9928	9913	9897	9880	9.9861	35
26	0.0000	9999	9996	9992	9987	9.9980	9973	9963	9953	9.9941	9928	9913	9897	9880	9.9861	34
27	0.0000	9999	9996	9992	9987	9.9980	9972	9963	9953	9.9941	9927	9913	9897	9879	9.9860	33
28	0.0000	9999	9996	9992	9987	9.9980	9972	9963	9952	9.9940	9927	9912	9896	9879	9.9860	32
29	0.0000	9999	9996	9992	9987	9.9980	9972	9963	9952	9.9940	9927	9912	9896	9879	9.9860	31
30	0.0000	9999	9996	9992	9987	9.9980	9972	9963	9952	9.9940	9927	9912	9896	9878	9.9859	30
31	0.0000	9998	9996	9992	9986	9.9980	9972	9963	9952	9.9940	9926	9912	9896	9878	9.9859	29
32	0.0000	9998	9996	9992	9986	9.9980	9972	9962	9952	9.9940	9926	9911	9895	9878	9.9859	28
33	0.0000	9998	9996	9992	9986	9.9980	9972	9962	9951	9.9939	9926	9911	9895	9877	9.9858	27
34	0.0000	9998	9996	9992	9986	9.9979	9971	9962	9951	9.9939	9926	9911	9895	9877	9.9858	26
35	0.0000	9998	9996	9992	9986	9.9979	9971	9962	9951	9.9939	9925	9911	9894	9877	9.9858	25
36	0.0000	9998	9996	9991	9986	9.9979	9971	9962	9951	9.9939	9925	9910	9894	9876	9.9857	24
37	0.0000	9998	9995	9991	9986	9.9979	9971	9962	9951	9.9939	9925	9910	9894	9876	9.9857	23
38	0.0000	9998	9995	9991	9986	9.9979	9971	9961	9951	9.9938	9925	9910	9894	9876	9.9857	22
39	0.0000	9998	9995	9991	9986	9.9979	9971	9961	9950	9.9938	9925	9910	9893	9876	9.9856	21
40	0.0000	9998	9995	9991	9986	9.9979	9971	9961	9950	9.9938	9924	9909	9893	9875	9.9856	20
41	0.0000	9998	9995	9991	9985	9.9979	9970	9961	9950	9.9938	9924	9909	9893	9875	9.9856	19
42	0.0000	9998	9995	9991	9985	9.9978	9970	9961	9950	9.9937	9924	9909	9892	9875	9.9855	18
43	0.0000	9998	9995	9991	9985	9.9978	9970	9960	9950	9.9937	9924	9909	9892	9874	9.9855	17
44	0.0000	9998	9995	9991	9985	9.9978	9970	9960	9949	9.9937	9923	9908	9892	9874	9.9855	16
45	0.0000	9998	9995	9991	9985	9.9978	9970	9960	9949	9.9937	9923	9908	9892	9874	9.9854	15
46	0.0000	9998	9995	9991	9985	9.9978	9970	9960	9949	9.9937	9923	9908	9891	9873	9.9854	14
47	0.0000	9998	9995	9991	9985	9.9978	9969	9960	9949	9.9936	9923	9908	9891	9873	9.9854	13
48	0.0000	9998	9995	9990	9985	9.9978	9969	9960	9949	9.9936	9922	9907	9891	9873	9.9853	12
49	0.0000	9998	9995	9990	9985	9.9978	9969	9959	9948	9.9936	9922	9907	9890	9872	9.9853	11
50	0.0000	9998	9995	9990	9985	9.9977	9969	9959	9948	9.9936	9922	9907	9890	9872	9.9853	10
51	0.0000	9998	9995	9990	9984	9.9977	9969	9959	9948	9.9936	9922	9906	9890	9872	9.9852	9
52	0.0000	9998	9995	9990	9984	9.9977	9969	9959	9948	9.9935	9921	9906	9890	9872	9.9852	8
53	9.9999	9998	9994	9990	9984	9.9977	9969	9959	9948	9.9935	9921	9906	9889	9871	9.9852	7
54	9.9999	9998	9994	9990	9984	9.9977	9968	9959	9947	9.9935	9921	9906	9889	9871	9.9851	6
55	9.9999	9998	9994	9990	9984	9.9977	9968	9958	9947	9.9935	9921	9905	9889	9871	9.9851	5
56	9.9999	9998	9994	9990	9984	9.9977	9968	9958	9947	9.9934	9920	9905	9888	9870	9.9851	4
57	9.9999	9997	9994	9990	9984	9.9977	9968	9958	9947	9.9934	9920	9905	9888	9870	9.9850	3
58	9.9999	9997	9994	9990	9984	9.9976	9968	9958	9947	9.9934	9920	9905	9888	9870	9.9850	2
59	9.9999	9997	9994	9989	9984	9.9976	9968	9958	9946	9.9934	9920	9904	9888	9869	9.9850	1
60	9.9999	9997	9994	9989	9983	9.9976	9968	9958	9946	9.9934	9919	9904	9887	9869	9.9849	0
	89°	88°	87°	86°	85°	84°	83°	82°	81°	80°	79°	78°	77°	76°	75°	

LOG SINES

LOG COSINES

	15°	16°	17°	18°	19°	20°	21°	22°	23°	24°	25°	26°	27°	28°	29°	
0	9.9849	9828	9806	9782	9757	9.9730	9702	9672	9640	9.9607	9573	9537	9499	9459	9.9418	60
1	9.9849	9828	9806	9782	9756	9.9729	9701	9671	9640	9.9607	9572	9536	9498	9459	9.9417	59
2	9.9849	9828	9805	9781	9756	9.9729	9701	9671	9639	9.9606	9572	9535	9498	9458	9.9417	58
3	9.9848	9827	9805	9781	9755	9.9728	9700	9670	9639	9.9606	9571	9535	9497	9457	9.9416	57
4	9.9848	9827	9804	9780	9755	9.9728	9700	9670	9638	9.9605	9570	9534	9496	9457 ·	9.9415	56
5	9.9848	9827	9804	9780	9755	9.9728	9699	9669	9638	9.9604	9570	9534	9496	9456	9.9415	55
6	9.9847	9826	9804	9780	9754	9.9727	9699	9669	9637	9.9604	9569	9533	9495	9455	9.9414	54
7	9.9847	9826	9803	9779	9754	9.9727	9698	9668	9636	9.9603	9569	9532	9494	9455	9.9413	53
8	9.9847	9826	9803	9779	9753	9.9726	9698	9668	9636	9.9603	9568	9532	9494	9454	9.9413	52
9	9.9846	9825	9802	9778	9753	9.9726	9697	9667	9635	9.9602	9567	9531	9493	9453	9.9412	51
10	9.9846	9825	9802	9778	9752	9.9725	9697	9667	9635	9.9602	9567	9530	9492	9453	9.9411	50
11	9.9846	9824	9802	9778	9752	9.9725	9696	9666	9634	9.9601	9566	9530	9492	9452	9.9410	49
12	9.9845	9824	9801	9777	9751	9.9724	9696	9666	9634	9.9601	9566	9529	9491	9451	9.9410	48
13	9.9845	9824	9801	9777	9751	9.9724	9695	9665	9633	9.9600	9565	9529	9490	9451	9.9409	47
14	9.9845	9823	9801	9776	9751	9.9723	9695	9664	9633	9.9599	9564	9528	9490	9450	9.9408	46
15	9.9844	9823	9800	9776	9750	9.9723	9694	9664	9632	9.9599	9564	9527	9489	9449	9.9408	45
16	9.9844	9823	9800	9775	9750	9.9722	9694	9663	9632	9.9598	9563	9527	9488	9449	9.9407	44
17	9.9844	9822	9799	9775	9749	9.9722	9693	9663	9631	9.9598	9563	9526	9488	9448	9.9406	43
18	9.9843	9822	9799	9775	9749	9.9722	9693	9662	9631	9.9597	9562	9525	9487	9447	9.9406	42
19	9.9843	9821	9799	9774	9748	9.9721	9692	9662	9630	9.9597	9561	9525	9486	9447	9.9405	41
20	9.9843	9821	9798	9774	9748	9.9721	9692	9661	9629	9.9596	9561	9524	9486	9446	9.9404	40
21	9.9842	9821	9798	9773	9747	9.9720	9691	9661	9629	9.9595	9560	9524	9485	9445	9.9403	39
22	9.9842	9820	9797	9773	9747	9.9720	9691	9660	9628	9.9595	9560	9523	9485	9444	9.9403	38
23	9.9842	9820	9797	9773	9747	9.9719	9690	9660	9628	9.9594	9559	9522	9484	9444	9.9402	37
24	9.9841	9820	9797	9772	9746	9.9719	9690	9659	9627	9.9594	9558	9522	9483	9443	9.9401	36
25	9.9841	9819	9796	9772	9746	9.9718	9689	9659	9627	9.9593	9558	9521	9483	9442	9.9401	35
26	9.9841	9819	9796	9771	9745	9.9718	9689	9658	9626	9.9593	9557	9520	9482	9442	9.9400	34
27	9.9840	9819	9795	9771	9745	9.9717	9688	9658	9626	9.9592	9557	9520	9481	9441	9.9399	33
28	9.9840	9818	9795	9770	9744	9.9717	9688	9657	9625	9.9591	9556	9519	9481	9440	9.9398	32
29	9.9839	9818	9795	9770	9744	9.9716	9687	9657	9625	9.9591	9555	9519	9480	9440	9.9398	31
30	9.9839	9817	9794	9770	9743	9.9716	9687	9656	9624	9.9590	9555	9518	9479	9439	9.9397	30
31	9.9839	9817	9794	9769	9743	9.9715	9686	9656	9623	9.9590	9554	9517	9479	9438	9.9396	29
32	9.9838	9817	9793	9769	9743	9.9715	9686	9655	9623	9.9589	9554	9517	9478	9438	9.9396	28
33	9.9838	9816	9793	9768	9742	9.9714	9685	9655	9622	9.9589	9553	9516	9477	9437	9.9395	27
34	9.9838	9816	9793	9768	9742	9.9714	9685	9654	9622	9.9588	9552	9515	9477	9436	9.9394	26
35	9.9837	9815	9792	9767	9741	9.9714	9684	9654	9621	9.9587	9552	9515	9476	9436	9.9393	25
36	9.9837	9815	9792	9767	9741	9.9713	9684	9653	9621	9.9587	9551	9514	9475	9435	9.9393	24
37	9.9837	9815	9791	9767	9740	9.9713	9683	9652	9620	9.9586	9551	9513	9475	9434	9.9392	23
38	9.9836	9814	9791	9766	9740	9.9712	9683	9652	9620	9.9586	9550	9513	9474	9433	9.9391	22
39	9.9836	9814	9791	9766	9739	9.9712	9682	9651	9619	9.9585	9549	9512	9473	9433	9.9391	21
40	9.9836	9814	9790	9765	9739	9.9711	9682	9651	9618	9.9584	9549	9512	9473	9432	9.9390	20
41	9.9835	9813	9790	9765	9739	9.9711	9681	9650	9618	9.9584	9548	9511	9472	9431	9.9389	19
42	9.9835	9813	9789	9764	9738	9.9710	9681	9650	9617	9.9583	9548	9510	9471	9431	9.9388	18
43	9.9835	9812	9789	9764	9738	9.9710	9680	9649	9617	9.9583	9547	9510	9471	9430	9.9388	17
44	9.9834	9812	9789	9764	9737	9.9709	9680	9649	9616	9.9582	9546	9509	9470	9429	9.9387	16
45	9.9834	9812	9788	9763	9737	9.9709	9679	9648	9616	9.9582	9546	9508	9469	9429	9.9386	15
46	9.9833	9811	9788	9763	9736	9.9708	9679	9648	9615	9.9581	9545	9508	9469	9428	9.9385	14
47	9.9833	9811	9787	9762	9736	9.9708	9678	9647	9615	9.9580	9545	9507	9468	9427	9.9385	13
48	9.9833	9811	9787	9762	9735	9.9707	9678	9647	9614	9.9580	9544	9506	9467	9427	9.9384	12
49	9.9832	9810	9787	9761	9735	9.9707	9677	9646	9613	9.9579	9543	9506	9467	9426	9.9383	11
50	9.9832	9810	9786	9761	9734	9.9706	9677	9646	9613	9.9579	9543	9505	9466	9425	9.9383	10
51	9.9832	9809	9786	9761	9734	9.9706	9676	9645	9612	9.9578	9542	9505	9465	9424	9.9382	9
52	9.9831	9809	9785	9760	9734	9.9705	9676	9645	9612	9.9577	9542	9504	9465	9424	9.9381	8
53	9.9831	9809	9785	9760	9733	9.9705	9675	9644	9611	9.9577	9541	9503	9464	9423	9.9380	7
54	9.9831	9808	9785	9759	9733	9.9704	9675	9643	9611	9.9576	9540	9503	9463	9422	9.9380	6
55	9.9830	9808	9784	9759	9732	9.9704	9674	9643	9610	9.9576	9540	9502	9463	9422	9.9379	5
56	9.9830	9808	9784	9758	9732	9.9703	9674	9642	9610	9.9575	9539	9501	9462	9421	9.9378	4
57	9.9830	9807	9783	9758	9731	9.9703	9673	9642	9609	9.9575	9538	9501	9461	9420	9.9377	3
58	9.9829	9807	9783	9758	9731	9.9702	9673	9641	9608	9.9574	9538	9500	9461	9420	9.9377	2
59	9.9829	9806	9782	9757	9730	9.9702	9672	9641	9608	9.9573	9537	9499	9460	9419	9.9376	1
60	9.9828	9806	9782	9757	9730	9.9702	9672	9640	9607	9.9573	9537	9499	9459	9418	9.9375	0
	74°	73°	72°	71°	70°	69°	68°	67°	66°	65°	64°	63°	62°	61°	60°	

LOG SINES

COSINES

LOG COSINES

	30°	31°	32°	33°	34°	35°	36°	37°	38°	39°	40°	41°	42°	43°	44°	
0	9.9375	9331	9284	9236	9186	9.9134	9080	9023	8965	9.8905	8843	8778	8711	8641	9.8569	60
1	9.9375	9330	9283	9235	9185	9.9133	9079	9023	8964	9.8904	8841	8777	8710	8640	9.8568	59
2	9.9374	9329	9283	9234	9184	9.9132	9078	9022	8963	9.8903	8840	8776	8708	8639	9.8567	58
3	9.9373	9328	9282	9233	9183	9.9131	9077	9021	8962	9.8902	8839	8775	8707	8638	9.8566	57
4	9.9372	9328	9281	9233	9182	9.9130	9076	9020	8961	9.8901	8838	8773	8706	8637	9.8564	56
5	9.9372	9327	9280	9232	9181	9.9129	9075	9019	8960	9.8900	8837	8772	8705	8635	9.8563	55
6	9.9371	9326	9279	9231	9181	9.9128	9074	9018	8959	9.8899	8836	8771	8704	8634	9.8562	54
7	9.9370	9325	9279	9230	9180	9.9127	9073	9017	8958	9.8898	8835	8770	8703	8633	9.8561	53
8	9.9369	9325	9278	9229	9179	9.9127	9072	9016	8957	9.8897	8834	8769	8702	8632	9.8560	52
9	9.9369	9324	9277	9229	9178	9.9126	9071	9015	8956	9.8896	8833	8768	8700	8631	9.8558	51
10	9.9368	9323	9276	9228	9177	9.9125	9070	9014	8955	9.8895	8832	8767	8699	8629	9.8557	50
11	9.9367	9322	9275	9227	9176	9.9124	9069	9013	8954	9.8894	8831	8766	8698	8628	9.8556	49
12	9.9367	9322	9275	9226	9175	9.9123	9069	9012	8953	9.8893	8830	8765	8697	8627	9.8555	48
13	9.9366	9321	9274	9225	9175	9.9122	9068	9011	8952	9.8892	8829	8763	8696	8626	9.8553	47
14	9.9365	9320	9273	9224	9174	9.9121	9067	9010	8951	9.8891	8828	8762	8695	8625	9.8552	46
15	9.9364	9319	9272	9224	9173	9.9120	9066	9009	8950	9.8890	8827	8761	8694	8624	9.8551	45
16	9.9364	9318	9272	9223	9172	9.9119	9065	9008	8949	9.8889	8825	8760	8692	8622	9.8550	44
17	9.9363	9318	9271	9222	9171	9.9119	9064	9007	8948	9.8888	8824	8759	8691	8621	9.8549	43
18	9.9362	9317	9270	9221	9170	9.9118	9063	9006	8947	9.8887	8823	8758	8690	8620	9.8547	42
19	9.9361	9316	9269	9220	9169	9.9117	9062	9005	8946	9.8885	8822	8757	8689	8619	9.8546	41
20	9.9361	9315	9268	9219	9169	9.9116	9061	9004	8945	9.8884	8821	8756	8688	8618	9.8545	40
21	9.9360	9315	9268	9219	9168	9.9115	9060	9003	8944	9.8883	8820	8755	8687	8616	9.8544	39
22	9.9359	9314	9267	9218	9167	9.9114	9059	9002	8943	9.8882	8819	8753	8686	8615	9.8542	38
23	9.9358	9313	9266	9217	9166	9.9113	9058	9001	8942	9.8881	8818	8752	8684	8614	9.8541	37
24	9.9358	9312	9265	9216	9165	9.9112	9057	9000	8941	9.8880	8817	8751	8683	8613	9.8540	36
25	9.9357	9312	9264	9215	9164	9.9111	9056	9000	8940	9.8879	8816	8750	8682	8612	9.8539	35
26	9.9356	9311	9264	9214	9163	9.9110	9056	8999	8939	9.8878	8815	8749	8681	8610	9.8537	34
27	9.9355	9310	9263	9214	9163	9.9110	9055	8998	8938	9.8877	8814	8748	8680	8609	9.8536	33
28	9.9355	9309	9262	9213	9162	9.9109	9054	8997	8937	9.8876	8813	8747	8679	8608	9.8535	32
29	9.9354	9308	9261	9212	9161	9.9108	9053	8996	8936	9.8875	8812	8746	8677	8607	9.8534	31
30	9.9353	9308	9260	9211	9160	9.9107	9052	8995	8935	9.8874	8810	8745	8676	8606	9.8532	30
31	9.9352	9307	9259	9210	9159	9.9106	9051	8994	8934	9.8873	8809	8743	8675	8604	9.8531	29
32	9.9352	9306	9259	9209	9158	9.9105	9050	8993	8933	9.8872	8808	8742	8674	8603	9.8530	28
33	9.9351	9305	9258	9209	9157	9.9104	9049	8992	8932	9.8871	8807	8741	8673	8602	9.8529	27
34	9.9350	9305	9257	9208	9156	9.9103	9048	8991	8931	9.8870	8806	8740	8672	8601	9.8527	26
35	9.9349	9304	9256	9207	9156	9.9102	9047	8990	8930	9.8869	8805	8739	8671	8600	9.8526	25
36	9.9349	9303	9255	9206	9155	9.9101	9046	8989	8929	9.8868	8804	8738	8669	8598	9.8525	24
37	9.9348	9302	9255	9205	9154	9.9101	9045	8988	8928	9.8867	8803	8737	8668	8597	9.8524	23
38	9.9347	9301	9254	9204	9153	9.9100	9044	8987	8927	9.8866	8802	8736	8667	8596	9.8522	22
39	9.9346	9301	9253	9204	9152	9.9099	9043	8986	8926	9.8865	8801	8734	8666	8595	9.8521	21
40	9.9346	9300	9252	9203	9151	9.9098	9042	8985	8925	9.8864	8800	8733	8665	8594	9.8520	20
41	9.9345	9299	9251	9202	9150	9.9097	9041	8984	8924	9.8863	8799	8732	8664	8592	9.8519	19
42	9.9344	9298	9251	9201	9149	9.9096	9041	8983	8923	9.8862	8797	8731	8662	8591	9.8517	18
43	9.9343	9298	9250	9200	9149	9.9095	9040	8982	8922	9.8860	8796	8730	8661	8590	9.8516	17
44	9.9343	9297	9249	9199	9148	9.9094	9039	8981	8921	9.8859	8795	8729	8660	8589	9.8515	16
45	9.9342	9296	9248	9198	9147	9.9093	9038	8980	8920	9.8858	8794	8728	8659	8588	9.8514	15
46	9.9341	9295	9247	9198	9146	9.9092	9037	8979	8919	9.8857	8793	8727	8658	8586	9.8512	14
47	9.9340	9294	9247	9197	9145	9.9091	9036	8978	8918	9.8856	8792	8725	8657	8585	9.8511	13
48	9.9340	9294	9246	9196	9144	9.9091	9035	8977	8917	9.8855	8791	8724	8655	8584	9.8510	12
49	9.9339	9293	9245	9195	9143	9.9090	9034	8976	8916	9.8854	8790	8723	8654	8583	9.8509	11
50	9.9338	9292	9244	9194	9142	9.9089	9033	8975	8915	9.8853	8789	8722	8653	8582	9.8507	10
51	9.9337	9291	9243	9193	9142	9.9088	9032	8974	8914	9.8852	8788	8721	8652	8580	9.8506	9
52	9.9337	9291	9242	9193	9141	9.9087	9031	8973	8913	9.8851	8787	8720	8651	8579	9.8505	8
53	9.9336	9290	9242	9192	9140	9.9086	9030	8972	8912	9.8850	8785	8719	8650	8578	9.8504	7
54	9.9335	9289	9241	9191	9139	9.9085	9029	8971	8911	9.8849	8784	8718	8648	8577	9.8502	6
55	9.9334	9288	9240	9190	9138	9.9084	9028	8970	8910	9.8848	8783	8716	8647	8575	9.8501	5
56	9.9334	9287	9239	9189	9137	9.9083	9027	8969	8909	9.8847	8782	8715	8646	8574	9.8500	4
57	9.9333	9287	9238	9188	9136	9.9082	9026	8968	8908	9.8846	8781	8714	8645	8573	9.8499	3
58	9.9332	9286	9238	9187	9135	9.9081	9025	8967	8907	9.8845	8780	8713	8644	8572	9.8497	2
59	9.9331	9285	9237	9187	9135	9.9080	9024	8966	8906	9.8844	8779	8712	8642	8571	9.8496	1
60	9.9331	9284	9236	9186	9134	9.9080	9023	8965	8905	9.8843	8778	8711	8641	8569	9.8495	0
	59°	58°	57°	56°	55°	54°	53°	52°	51°	50°	49°	48°	47°	46°	45°	

LOG SINES

LOG COSINES

	45°	46°	47°	48°	49°	50°	51°	52°	53°	54°	55°	56°	57°	58°	59°	
0	9.8495	8418	8338	8255	8169	9.8081	7989	7893	7795	9.7692	7586	7476	7361	7242	9.7118	60
1	9.8494	8416	8336	8254	8168	9.8079	7987	7892	7793	9.7690	7584	7474	7359	7240	9.7116	59
2	9.8492	8415	8335	8252	8167	9.8078	7986	7890	7791	9.7689	7582	7472	7357	7238	9.7114	58
3	9.8491	8414	8334	8251	8165	9.8076	7984	7889	7790	9.7687	7580	7470	7355	7236	9.7112	57
4	9.8490	8412	8332	8249	8164	9.8075	7982	7887	7788	9.7685	7579	7468	7353	7234	9.7110	56
5	9.8489	8411	8331	8248	8162	9.8073	7981	7885	7786	9.7683	7577	7466	7351	7232	9.7108	55
6	9.8487	8410	8330	8247	8161	9.8072	7979	7884	7785	9.7682	7575	7464	7349	7230	9.7106	54
7	9.8486	8409	8328	8245	8159	9.8070	7978	7882	7783	9.7680	7573	7462	7347	7228	9.7104	53
8	9.8485	8407	8327	8244	8158	9.8069	7976	7880	7781	9.7678	7571	7461	7345	7226	9.7102	52
9	9.8483	8406	8326	8242	8156	9.8067	7975	7879	7780	9.7676	7570	7459	7344	7224	9.7099	51
10	9.8482	8405	8324	8241	8155	9.8066	7973	7877	7778	9.7675	7568	7457	7342	7222	9.7097	50
11	9.8481	8403	8323	8240	8153	9.8064	7972	7876	7776	9.7673	7566	7455	7340	7220	9.7095	49
12	9.8480	8402	8322	8238	8152	9.8063	7970	7874	7774	9.7671	7564	7453	7338	7218	9.7093	48
13	9.8478	8401	8320	8237	8150	9.8061	7968	7872	7773	9.7669	7562	7451	7336	7216	9.7091	47
14	9.8477	8399	8319	8235	8149	9.8060	7967	7871	7771	9.7668	7561	7449	7334	7214	9.7089	46
15	9.8476	8398	8317	8234	8148	9.8058	7965	7869	7769	9.7666	7559	7447	7332	7212	9.7087	45
16	9.8475	8397	8316	8233	8146	9.8056	7964	7867	7768	9.7664	7557	7445	7330	7210	9.7085	44
17	9.8473	8395	8315	8231	8145	9.8055	7962	7866	7766	9.7662	7555	7444	7328	7208	9.7082	43
18	9.8472	8394	8313	8230	8143	9.8053	7960	7864	7764	9.7661	7553	7442	7326	7205	9.7080	42
19	9.8471	8393	8312	8228	8142	9.8052	7959	7863	7763	9.7659	7551	7440	7324	7203	9.7078	41
20	9.8469	8391	8311	8227	8140	9.8050	7957	7861	7761	9.7657	7550	7438	7322	7201	9.7076	40
21	9.8468	8390	8309	8225	8139	9.8049	7956	7859	7759	9.7655	7548	7436	7320	7199	9.7074	39
22	9.8467	8389	8308	8224	8137	9.8047	7954	7858	7758	9.7654	7546	7434	7318	7197	9.7072	38
23	9.8466	8387	8306	8223	8136	9.8046	7953	7856	7756	9.7652	7544	7432	7316	7195	9.7070	37
24	9.8464	8386	8305	8221	8134	9.8044	7951	7854	7754	9.7650	7542	7430	7314	7193	9.7068	36
25	9.8463	8385	8304	8220	8133	9.8043	7949	7853	7752	9.7648	7540	7428	7312	7191	9.7065	35
26	9.8462	8383	8302	8218	8131	9.8041	7948	7851	7751	9.7647	7539	7427	7310	7189	9.7063	34
27	9.8460	8382	8301	8217	8130	9.8040	7946	7849	7749	9.7645	7537	7425	7308	7187	9.7061	33
28	9.8459	8381	8300	8215	8128	9.8038	7945	7848	7747	9.7643	7535	7423	7306	7185	9.7059	32
29	9.8458	8379	8298	8214	8127	9.8037	7943	7846	7746	9.7641	7533	7421	7304	7183	9.7057	31
30	9.8457	8378	8297	8213	8125	9.8035	7941	7844	7744	9.7640	7531	7419	7302	7181	9.7055	30
31	9.8455	8377	8295	8211	8124	9.8034	7940	7843	7742	9.7638	7529	7417	7300	7179	9.7053	29
32	9.8454	8375	8294	8210	8122	9.8032	7938	7841	7740	9.7636	7528	7415	7298	7177	9.7050	28
33	9.8453	8374	8293	8208	8121	9.8031	7937	7840	7739	9.7634	7526	7413	7296	7175	9.7048	27
34	9.8451	8373	8291	8207	8120	9.8029	7935	7838	7737	9.7632	7524	7411	7294	7173	9.7046	26
35	9.8450	8371	8290	8205	8118	9.8027	7934	7836	7735	9.7631	7522	7409	7292	7171	9.7044	25
36	9.8449	8370	8289	8204	8117	9.8026	7932	7835	7734	9.7629	7520	7407	7290	7168	9.7042	24
37	9.8448	8369	8287	8203	8115	9.8024	7930	7833	7732	9.7627	7518	7406	7288	7166	9.7040	23
38	9.8446	8367	8286	8201	8114	9.8023	7929	7831	7730	9.7625	7517	7404	7286	7164	9.7037	22
39	9.8445	8366	8284	8200	8112	9.8021	7927	7830	7728	9.7624	7515	7402	7284	7162	9.7035	21
40	9.8444	8365	8283	8198	8111	9.8020	7926	7828	7727	9.7622	7513	7400	7282	7160	9.7033	20
41	9.8442	8363	8282	8197	8109	9.8018	7924	7826	7725	9.7620	7511	7398	7280	7158	9.7031	19
42	9.8441	8362	8280	8195	8108	9.8017	7922	7825	7723	9.7618	7509	7396	7278	7156	9.7029	18
43	9.8440	8361	8279	8194	8106	9.8015	7921	7823	7722	9.7616	7507	7394	7276	7154	9.7027	17
44	9.8439	8359	8277	8193	8105	9.8014	7919	7821	7720	9.7615	7505	7392	7274	7152	9.7025	16
45	9.8437	8358	8276	8191	8103	9.8012	7918	7820	7718	9.7613	7504	7390	7272	7150	9.7022	15
46	9.8436	8357	8275	8190	8102	9.8010	7916	7818	7716	9.7611	7502	7388	7270	7148	9.7020	14
47	9.8435	8355	8273	8188	8100	9.8009	7914	7816	7715	9.7609	7500	7386	7268	7146	9.7018	13
48	9.8433	8354	8272	8187	8099	9.8007	7913	7815	7713	9.7607	7498	7384	7266	7144	9.7016	12
49	9.8432	8353	8270	8185	8097	9.8006	7911	7813	7711	9.7606	7496	7382	7264	7141	9.7014	11
50	9.8431	8351	8269	8184	8096	9.8004	7910	7811	7710	9.7604	7494	7380	7262	7139	9.7012	10
51	9.8429	8350	8268	8182	8094	9.8003	7908	7810	7708	9.7602	7492	7379	7260	7137	9.7009	9
52	9.8428	8349	8266	8181	8093	9.8001	7906	7808	7706	9.7600	7491	7377	7258	7135	9.7007	8
53	9.8427	8347	8265	8180	8091	9.8000	7905	7806	7704	9.7599	7489	7375	7256	7133	9.7005	7
54	9.8426	8346	8264	8178	8090	9.7998	7903	7805	7703	9.7597	7487	7373	7254	7131	9.7003	6
55	9.8424	8345	8262	8177	8088	9.7997	7901	7803	7701	9.7595	7485	7371	7252	7129	9.7001	5
56	9.8423	8343	8261	8175	8087	9.7995	7900	7801	7699	9.7593	7483	7369	7250	7127	9.6998	4
57	9.8422	8342	8259	8174	8085	9.7993	7898	7800	7697	9.7591	7481	7367	7248	7125	9.6996	3
58	9.8420	8341	8258	8172	8084	9.7992	7897	7798	7696	9.7590	7479	7365	7246	7123	9.6994	2
59	9.8419	8339	8257	8171	8082	9.7990	7895	7796	7694	9.7588	7477	7363	7244	7120	9.6992	1
60	9.8418	8338	8255	8169	8081	9.7989	7893	7795	7692	9.7586	7476	7361	7242	7118	9.6990	0
	44°	43°	42°	41°	40°	39°	38°	37°	36°	35°	34°	33°	32°	31°	30°	

LOG SINES

COSINES

LOG COSINES

	60°	61°	62°	63°	64°	65°	66°	67°	68°	69°	70°	71°	72°	73°	74°	
0	9.6990	6856	6716	6570	6418	9.6259	6093	5919	5736	9.5543	5341	5126	4900	4659	9.4403	60
1	9.6988	6853	6714	6568	6416	9.6257	6090	5916	5733	9.5540	5337	5123	4896	4655	9.4399	59
2	9.6985	6851	6711	6566	6413	9.6254	6087	5913	5729	9.5537	5334	5119	4892	4651	9.4395	58
3	9.6983	6849	6709	6563	6411	9.6251	6085	5910	5726	9.5533	5330	5115	4888	4647	9.4390	57
4	9.6981	6847	6707	6561	6408	9.6249	6082	5907	5723	9.5530	5327	5112	4884	4643	9.4386	56
5	9.6979	6844	6704	6558	6405	9.6246	6079	5904	5720	9.5527	5323	5108	4880	4639	9.4381	55
6	9.6977	6842	6702	6556	6403	9.6243	6076	5901	5717	9.5524	5320	5104	4876	4634	9.4377	54
7	9.6974	6840	6699	6553	6400	9.6240	6073	5898	5714	9.5520	5316	5101	4873	4630	9.4372	53
8	9.6972	6837	6697	6551	6398	9.6238	6070	5895	5711	9.5517	5313	5097	4869	4626	9.4368	52
9	9.6970	6835	6695	6548	6395	9.6235	6068	5892	5708	9.5514	5309	5093	4865	4622	9.4364	51
10	9.6968	6833	6692	6546	6392	9.6232	6065	5889	5704	9.5510	5306	5090	4861	4618	9.4359	50
11	9.6966	6831	6690	6543	6390	9.6230	6062	5886	5701	9.5507	5302	5086	4857	4614	9.4355	49
12	9.6963	6828	6687	6541	6387	9.6227	6059	5883	5698	9.5504	5299	5082	4853	4609	9.4350	48
13	9.6961	6826	6685	6538	6385	9.6224	6056	5880	5695	9.5500	5295	5078	4849	4605	9.4346	47
14	9.6959	6824	6683	6536	6382	9.6221	6053	5877	5692	9.5497	5292	5075	4845	4601	9.4341	46
15	9.6957	6821	6680	6533	6379	9.6219	6050	5874	5689	9.5494	5288	5071	4841	4597	9.4337	45
16	9.6955	6819	6678	6531	6377	9.6216	6047	5871	5685	9.5490	5285	5067	4837	4593	9.4332	44
17	9.6952	6817	6675	6528	6374	9.6213	6045	5868	5682	9.5487	5281	5064	4833	4588	9.4328	43
18	9.6950	6814	6673	6526	6371	9.6210	6042	5865	5679	9.5484	5278	5060	4829	4584	9.4323	42
19	9.6948	6812	6671	6523	6369	9.6208	6039	5862	5676	9.5480	5274	5056	4825	4580	9.4319	41
20	9.6946	6810	6668	6521	6366	9.6205	6036	5859	5673	9.5477	5270	5052	4821	4576	9.4314	40
21	9.6943	6808	6666	6518	6364	9.6202	6033	5856	5670	9.5474	5267	5049	4817	4572	9.4310	39
22	9.6941	6805	6663	6515	6361	9.6199	6030	5853	5666	9.5470	5263	5045	4813	4567	9.4305	38
23	9.6939	6803	6661	6513	6358	9.6197	6027	5850	5663	9.5467	5260	5041	4809	4563	9.4301	37
24	9.6937	6801	6659	6510	6356	9.6194	6024	5847	5660	9.5463	5256	5037	4805	4559	9.4296	36
25	9.6935	6798	6656	6508	6353	9.6191	6021	5844	5657	9.5460	5253	5034	4801	4555	9.4292	35
26	9.6932	6796	6654	6505	6350	9.6188	6019	5841	5654	9.5457	5249	5030	4797	4550	9.4287	34
27	9.6930	6794	6651	6503	6348	9.6186	6016	5838	5650	9.5453	5246	5026	4793	4546	9.4283	33
28	9.6928	6791	6649	6500	6345	9.6183	6013	5834	5647	9.5450	5242	5022	4789	4542	9.4278	32
29	9.6926	6789	6646	6498	6342	9.6180	6010	5831	5644	9.5447	5239	5019	4785	4538	9.4274	31
30	9.6923	6787	6644	6495	6340	9.6177	6007	5828	5641	9.5443	5235	5015	4781	4533	9.4269	30
31	9.6921	6784	6642	6493	6337	9.6175	6004	5825	5638	9.5440	5231	5011	4777	4529	9.4264	29
32	9.6919	6782	6639	6490	6335	9.6172	6001	5822	5634	9.5437	5228	5007	4773	4525	9.4260	28
33	9.6917	6780	6637	6488	6332	9.6169	5998	5819	5631	9.5433	5224	5003	4769	4521	9.4255	27
34	9.6914	6777	6634	6485	6329	9.6166	5995	5816	5628	9.5430	5221	5000	4765	4516	9.4251	26
35	9.6912	6775	6632	6483	6327	9.6163	5992	5813	5625	9.5426	5217	4996	4761	4512	9.4246	25
36	9.6910	6773	6629	6480	6324	9.6161	5990	5810	5621	9.5423	5213	4992	4757	4508	9.4242	24
37	9.6908	6770	6627	6477	6321	9.6158	5987	5807	5618	9.5420	5210	4988	4753	4503	9.4237	23
38	9.6905	6768	6625	6475	6319	9.6155	5984	5804	5615	9.5416	5206	4984	4749	4499	9.4232	22
39	9.6903	6766	6622	6472	6316	9.6152	5981	5801	5612	9.5413	5203	4981	4745	4495	9.4228	21
40	9.6901	6763	6620	6470	6313	9.6149	5978	5798	5609	9.5409	5199	4977	4741	4491	9.4223	20
41	9.6899	6761	6617	6467	6311	9.6147	5975	5795	5605	9.5406	5196	4973	4737	4486	9.4219	19
42	9.6896	6759	6615	6465	6308	9.6144	5972	5792	5602	9.5403	5192	4969	4733	4482	9.4214	18
43	9.6894	6756	6612	6462	6305	9.6141	5969	5789	5599	9.5399	5188	4965	4729	4478	9.4209	17
44	9.6892	6754	6610	6460	6303	9.6138	5966	5785	5596	9.5396	5185	4962	4725	4473	9.4205	16
45	9.6890	6752	6607	6457	6300	9.6135	5963	5782	5592	9.5392	5181	4958	4721	4469	9.4200	15
46	9.6887	6749	6605	6454	6297	9.6133	5960	5779	5589	9.5389	5177	4954	4717	4465	9.4195	14
47	9.6885	6747	6603	6452	6295	9.6130	5957	5776	5586	9.5385	5174	4950	4713	4460	9.4191	13
48	9.6883	6744	6600	6449	6292	9.6127	5954	5773	5583	9.5382	5170	4946	4709	4456	9.4186	12
49	9.6881	6742	6598	6447	6289	9.6124	5951	5770	5579	9.5379	5167	4942	4705	4452	9.4182	11
50	9.6878	6740	6595	6444	6286	9.6121	5948	5767	5576	9.5375	5163	4939	4700	4447	9.4177	10
51	9.6876	6737	6593	6442	6284	9.6119	5945	5764	5573	9.5372	5159	4935	4696	4443	9.4172	9
52	9.6874	6735	6590	6439	6281	9.6116	5943	5761	5570	9.5368	5156	4931	4692	4438	9.4168	8
53	9.6872	6733	6588	6437	6278	9.6113	5940	5758	5566	9.5365	5152	4927	4688	4434	9.4163	7
54	9.6869	6730	6585	6434	6276	9.6110	5937	5754	5563	9.5361	5148	4923	4684	4430	9.4158	6
55	9.6867	6728	6583	6431	6273	9.6107	5934	5751	5560	9.5358	5145	4919	4680	4425	9.4153	5
56	9.6865	6726	6580	6429	6270	9.6104	5931	5748	5556	9.5354	5141	4915	4676	4421	9.4149	4
57	9.6863	6723	6578	6426	6268	9.6102	5928	5745	5553	9.5351	5137	4911	4672	4417	9.4144	3
58	9.6860	6721	6575	6424	6265	9.6099	5925	5742	5550	9.5347	5134	4908	4668	4412	9.4139	2
59	9.6858	6718	6573	6421	6262	9.6096	5922	5739	5547	9.5344	5130	4904	4663	4408	9.4135	1
60	9.6856	6716	6570	6418	6259	9.6093	5919	5736	5543	9.5341	5126	4900	4659	4403	9.4130	0
	29°	28°	27°	26°	25°	24°	23°	22°	21°	20°	19°	18°	17°	16°	15°	

LOG SINES

LOG COSINES

	75°	76°	77°	78°	79°	80°	81°	82°	83°	84°	85°	86°	87°	88°	89°	
0	9.4130	3837	3521	3179	2806	9.2397	1943	1436	0859	9.0192	0597	1564	2812	4572	8.2419	60
1	9.4125	3832	3515	3173	2799	9.2390	1935	1427	0849	9.0180	0612	1582	2836	4608	8.2346	59
2	9.4121	3827	3510	3167	2793	9.2382	1927	1418	0838	9.0168	0626	1600	2860	4645	8.2272	58
3	9.4116	3822	3504	3161	2786	9.2375	1919	1409	0828	9.0156	0641	1619	2885	4682	8.2196	57
4	9.4111	3816	3499	3155	2780	9.2368	1911	1399	0818	9.0144	0655	1637	2910	4719	8.2119	56
5	9.4106	3811	3493	3149	2773	9.2361	1903	1390	0807	9.0132	0670	1655	2934	4757	8.2041	55
6	9.4102	3806	3488	3143	2767	9.2354	1895	1381	0797	9.0120	0685	1674	2959	4794	8.1961	54
7	9.4097	3801	3482	3137	2760	9.2346	1887	1372	0786	9.0107	0699	1693	2984	4833	8.1880	53
8	9.4092	3796	3477	3131	2754	9.2339	1879	1363	0776	9.0095	0714	1711	3009	4871	8.1798	54
9	9.4087	3791	3471	3125	2747	9.2332	1871	1354	0765	9.0083	0729	1730	3035	4910	8.1713	51
10	9.4083	3786	3466	3119	2740	9.2324	1863	1345	0755	9.0070	0744	1749	3060	4950	8.1627	50
11	9.4078	3781	3460	3113	2734	9.2317	1855	1336	0744	9.0058	0759	1768	3086	4989	8.1539	49
12	9.4073	3775	3455	3107	2727	9.2310	1847	1326	0734	9.0046	0774	1787	3111	5029	8.1450	48
13	9.4068	3770	3449	3101	2721	9.2303	1838	1317	0723	9.0033	0789	1806	3137	5070	8.1359	47
14	9.4063	3765	3444	3095	2714	9.2295	1830	1308	0712	9.0021	0804	1825	3163	5110	8.1265	46
15	9.4059	3760	3438	3089	2707	9.2288	1822	1299	0702	9.0008	0819	1844	3190	5152	8.1170	45
16	9.4054	3755	3432	3083	2701	9.2281	1814	1289	0691	8.9996	0834	1863	3216	5193	8.1072	44
17	9.4049	3750	3427	3077	2694	9.2273	1806	1280	0680	8.9983	0850	1883	3242	5235	8.0972	43
18	9.4044	3745	3421	3070	2687	9.2266	1797	1271	0670	8.9970	0865	1902	3269	5277	8.0870	42
19	9.4039	3739	3416	3064	2681	9.2258	1789	1261	0659	8.9958	0881	1922	3296	5320	8.0765	41
20	9.4035	3734	3410	3058	2674	9.2251	1781	1252	0648	8.9945	0896	1941	3323	5363	8.0658	40
21	9.4030	3729	3404	3052	2667	9.2244	1772	1242	0637	8.9932	0911	1961	3350	5407	8.0548	39
22	9.4025	3724	3399	3046	2661	9.2236	1764	1233	0626	8.9919	0927	1981	3378	5451	8.0436	38
23	9.4020	3719	3393	3040	2654	9.2229	1756	1224	0616	8.9907	0943	2001	3405	5496	8.0320	37
24	9.4015	3713	3387	3034	2647	9.2221	1747	1214	0605	8.9894	0958	2021	3433	5541	8.0201	36
25	9.4010	3708	3382	3027	2640	9.2214	1739	1205	0594	8.9881	0974	2041	3461	5586	8.0078	35
26	9.4006	3703	3376	3021	2634	9.2206	1731	1195	0583	8.9868	0990	2061	3489	5632	7.9953	34
27	9.4001	3698	3370	3015	2627	9.2199	1722	1186	0572	8.9855	1006	2082	3517	5678	7.9823	33
28	9.3996	3692	3365	3009	2620	9.2191	1714	1176	0561	8.9842	1022	2102	3546	5725	7.9689	32
29	9.3991	3687	3359	3003	2613	9.2184	1705	1167	0550	8.9829	1038	2123	3574	5773	7.9551	31
30	9.3986	3682	3353	2997	2606	9.2176	1697	1157	0539	8.9816	1054	2143	3603	5821	7.9409	30
31	9.3981	3677	3348	2990	2600	9.2169	1689	1147	0527	8.9803	1070	2164	3632	5869	7.9262	29
32	9.3976	3671	3342	2984	2593	9.2161	1680	1138	0516	8.9789	1086	2185	3661	5918	7.9109	28
33	9.3971	3666	3336	2978	2586	9.2153	1672	1128	0505	8.9776	1102	2206	3691	5968	7.8952	27
34	9.3966	3661	3331	2972	2579	9.2146	1663	1118	0494	8.9763	1118	2227	3721	6018	7.8788	26
35	9.3962	3655	3325	2965	2572	9.2138	1655	1109	0483	8.9750	1135	2248	3750	6069	7.8617	25
36	9.3957	3650	3319	2959	2565	9.2131	1646	1099	0472	8.9736	1151	2269	3780	6120	7.8440	24
37	9.3952	3645	3313	2953	2558	9.2123	1637	1089	0460	8.9723	1167	2290	3811	6172	7.8255	23
38	9.3947	3640	3308	2947	2551	9.2115	1629	1080	0449	8.9710	1184	2312	3841	6225	7.8062	22
39	9.3942	3634	3302	2940	2545	9.2108	1620	1070	0438	8.9696	1201	2333	3872	6278	7.7860	21
40	9.3937	3629	3296	2934	2538	9.2100	1612	1060	0426	8.9683	1217	2355	3903	6332	7.7649	20
41	9.3932	3624	3290	2928	2531	9.2092	1603	1050	0415	8.9669	1234	2377	3934	6387	7.7426	19
42	9.3927	3618	3284	2921	2524	9.2085	1594	1040	0403	8.9655	1251	2398	3965	6442	7.7191	18
43	9.3922	3613	3279	2915	2517	9.2077	1586	1030	0392	8.9642	1267	2420	3997	6498	7.6943	17
44	9.3917	3608	3273	2909	2510	9.2069	1577	1020	0380	8.9628	1284	2443	4028	6555	7.6680	16
45	9.3912	3602	3267	2902	2503	9.2061	1568	1011	0369	8.9614	1301	2465	4061	6612	7.6399	15
46	9.3907	3597	3261	2896	2496	9.2054	1560	1001	0357	8.9601	1318	2487	4093	6671	7.6100	14
47	9.3902	3591	3255	2890	2489	9.2046	1551	0991	0346	8.9587	1335	2509	4125	6730	7.5778	13
48	9.3897	3586	3250	2883	2482	9.2038	1542	0981	0334	8.9573	1353	2532	4158	6790	7.5431	12
49	9.3892	3581	3244	2877	2475	9.2030	1533	0971	0323	8.9559	1370	2555	4191	6850	7.5053	11
50	9.3887	3575	3238	2870	2468	9.2022	1525	0961	0311	8.9545	1387	2577	4224	6912	7.4639	10
51	9.3882	3570	3232	2864	2461	9.2015	1516	0951	0299	8.9531	1405	2600	4258	6975	7.4182	9
52	9.3877	3564	3226	2858	2454	9.2007	1507	0940	0287	8.9517	1422	2623	4292	7038	7.3671	8
53	9.3872	3559	3220	2851	2447	9.1999	1498	0930	0276	8.9503	1440	2646	4326	7102	7.3091	7
54	9.3867	3554	3214	2845	2439	9.1991	1489	0920	0264	8.9489	1457	2670	4360	7168	7.2422	6
55	9.3862	3548	3208	2838	2432	9.1983	1480	0910	0252	8.9475	1475	2693	4395	7234	7.1631	5
56	9.3857	3543	3202	2832	2425	9.1975	1471	0900	0240	8.9460	1492	2717	4429	7301	7.0663	4
57	9.3852	3537	3197	2825	2418	9.1967	1462	0890	0228	8.9446	1510	2740	4465	7370	6.9415	3
58	9.3847	3532	3191	2819	2411	9.1959	1453	0879	0216	8.9432	1528	2764	4500	7439	6.7657	2
59	9.3842	3526	3185	2812	2404	9.1951	1445	0869	0204	8.9417	1546	2788	4536	7510	6.4657	1
60	9.3837	3521	3179	2806	2397	9.1943	1436	0859	0192	8.9403	1564	2812	4572	7581	4.1228	0
	14°	13°	12°	11°	10°	9°	8°	7°	6°	5°	4°	3°	2°	1°	0°	

LOG SINES

COSINES

MULTILANGUAGE GLOSSARY

APPENDICES

Translations are given under the following headings:

ENGLISH	FRENCH	SPANISH	DUTCH
1 PROHIBITIONS	Interdictions	Prohibiciones	Verbouwen
2 TYPES OF VESSEL	Types du bateau	Typos de barco	Scheepstypen
3 PARTS OF VESSEL	Parties du bateau	Partes del barco	Scheeps onderdelen
4 MASTS & SPARS	Mâts	Mástiles y palos	Masten
5 RIGGING	Gréement	Aparejo	Tuigage
6 SAILS	Voilure	Velas	Zeilen
7 BELOW DECK	Cabine	Alcázar	Onderdeks
8 NAVIGATION EQUIPMENT	Equipement de navigation	Equipo de navigación	Navigatie uitrusting
9 ENGINES	Moteurs	Motores	Motoren
10 ENGINE ACCESSORIES	Accessoires moteur	Máquina accesorio	Onderdelen van motoren
11 ELECTRICS	Electricité	Electricidad	Elektriciteit
12 FUEL AND OIL	Combusitibles	Gazolina	Div brandstoffen
13 METALS	Métaux	Metales	Metalen
14 LIGHTS	Lumières	Luz	Lichten
15 SHIP'S PAPERS	Papiers du bateau	Papeles del barco	Scheepspapieren
16 TOOLS	Outils	Herramientas	Gereedschap
17 CHANDLERY	Ship chandler	Pertrechos	Scheepsbehoeften
18 FOOD	Nourriture	Comida	Proviand
19 SHOPS AND PLACES ASHORE	Boutiques et endroio divers	Tiendas y sitios en tierra	Winkels & plaatsen aan land
20 IN HARBOR	Au port	En el puerto	In de haven
21 FIRST AID	Premiers secours	Primero socorro	Eerste hulp bij ongelukken

1 PROHIBITIONS

Prohibited area	Zone interdite	Zona prohibida	Verboden gebied
Anchoring prohibited	Defense de mouiller	Fondeadero prohibido	Verboden ankerplaats
Mooring prohibited	Accostage interdite	Amarradero prohibido	Verboden aan te leggen

2 TYPES OF VESSEL

PRIVATE

Sloop	Sloop	Balandra	Sloep
Cutter	Cotre	Cúter	Kotter
Ketch	Ketch	Queche	Kits
Yawl	Yawl	Yola	Yaw
Schooner	Goélette	Goleta	Schoener
Motorsailer	Bateau mixte	Moto-velero	Motorzeiljacht
Dinghy	Youyou, prame	Balandro	Jol, bijboot
Launch	Chaloupe	Lancha	Barkas
Motorboat	Bateau à moteur	Motora, bote a motor	Motorboot
Lifeboat	Bateau, canot de sauvetage	Bote salvadidas	Reddingboot

ENGLISH	FRENCH	SPANISH	DUTCH
		COMMERCIAL	
Trawler	Chalutier	Pesquero	Stoomtreiler
Tanker	Bateau-citerne	Petrolero	Tankschip
Merchantman	Navire marchand	Buque mercante	Koopvaardijschip
Ferry	Transbordeur, bac	Transbordador	Pont, veerboot
Tug	Remorqueur	Remolcador	Sleepboot

3 PARTS OF VESSEL

Stem	Étrave	Roda	Voorsteven
Stern	Poupe	Popa	Achtersteven
Forecastle (fo'c's'le)	Gaillard d'avant	Castillo de proa	Vooronder
Forepeak	Pic avant	Pique de proa	Voorpiek
Cabin	Cabine	Camarote	Kajuit
Chain locker	Puits à chaines	Caja de cadenas	Kettingbak
Heads	Toilette	Retrete	W.C.
Galley	Cuisine	Cocina	Kombuis
Chartroom	Salle des cartes	Caseta de derrota	Kaartenkamer
Bunk	Couchette	Litera	Kooi
Pipe cot	Cadre	Catre	Pijkooi
Engine room	Chambre des machines	Cámara de máquinas	Motorruim
Locker	Coffre	Taquilla	Kastje
Bulkhead	Cloison	Mamparo	Schot
Hatch	Écoutille	Escotilla	Luik
Cockpit	Cockpit	Cabina	Kuip
Sail locker	Soute à voiles	Panol de velas	Zeilkooi
Freshwater tank	Reservoir d'eau douce	Tanque de agua potable	Drinkwatertank
Rudder	Gouvernail	Timón	Roer
Propeller	Hélice	Hélice	Schroef
Bilges	Cale	Sentina	Kim
Keel	Quille	Quilla	Kiel
Gunwale (also gunnel)	Plat-bord	Borda, regala	Dolboord
Rubbing strake	Bourrelet de défense	Verduguillo	Berghout
Tiller	Barre	Cana	Helmstok
Stanchion	Chandelier	Candelero	Scepters
Bilgepump	Pompe de cale	Bombas de achique de sentina	Lenspomp
Pulpit	Balcon avant	Pülpito	Preekstoel
Pushpit	Balcon arrière	Púlpito de popa	Hekstoel

4 MASTS AND SPARS

Mast	Mât	Palo	Mast
Foremast	Mât de misaine	Trinquete	Fokkemast
Mizzen mast	Mât d'artimon	Palo mesana	Bezaansmast
Boom	Bôme	Botavara	Giek
Bowsprit	Beaupré	Baupres	Boegspriet
Bumpkin	Bout-dehors	Pescante amura trinquette	Papegaaistok
Spinnaker boom	Tangon de spi	Tangon del espinaquer	Nagel-of spinnakerboom
Gaff	Corne	Pico (de vela cangreja)	Gaffel
Spreaders	Barres de flèche	Crucetas	Dwarszaling
Jumper strut	Guignol	Contrete	Knikstagen

APPENDICES

ENGLISH	FRENCH	SPANISH	DUTCH
Truck	Pomme	Tope (galleta)	Top
Slide	Coulisseau	Corredera	Slede
Roller reefing	Bôme à rouleau	Rizo de catalina	Patentrif
Worm gear	Vis sans fin	Husillo	Worm en wormwiel
Solid	Massif	Macizo	Massief
Hollow	Creux	Hueco	Hol
Derrick	Grue	Pluma de carga	Dirk of Kraanlijn

5 RIGGING

STANDING

Forestay	Étai avant, étai de trinquette	Estay de proa	Voorstag
Aft stay	Étai arriere	Stay de popa	Achterstag
Shrouds	Haubans	Obenques	Want
Stay	Étai	Estay	Stag
Bobstay	Sous-barbe	Barbiquejo	Waterstag
Backstay	Galhauban	Brandal	Pakstagen
Guy	Retenue	Retenida (Cabo de retenida viento)	Bulletalie

RUNNING

Halyard	Drisse	Driza	Val
Foresail halyard	Drisse de misaine	Driza de trinquetilla	Voorzeil val
Throat halyard	Attache de drisse	Driza de boca	Klauwval
Peak halyard	Drisse de pic	Driza de pico	Piekeval
Burgee halyard	Drisse de guidon	Driza de grimpola	Clubstandaardval
Topping lift	Balancine	Amantillo	Dirk
Main sheet	Écoute de grand voile	Escota mayor	Grootschoot
Foresail sheet	Écoute de Misaine	Trinquetilla (escota de)	Voorzeil of Fokkeschoot
Boom vang	Hale-bas de bôme	Trapa	Neerhouder
Rope	Cordage	Cabulleria	Touw
Single block	Poule simple	Motón de una cajera	Eenschijfsblok
Double block	Poulie double	Motón de dos cajeras	Tweeschijfsblok
Sheave	Réa	Roldana	Schijf
Shackle	Manille	Grillete	Sluiting
Pin	Goupille	Perno, cabilla	Bout
"D" shackle	Manille Droite	Grillete en D	Harpsluiting
Snapshackle	Manille rapide	Grillete de escape	Patentsluiting

6 SAILS

Mainsail	Grand voile	Vela mayor	Grootzeil
Foresail	Voile de misaine	Vela trinquete	Voorzeil
Jib	Foc	Foque	Fok
Storm jib	Tourmetin	Foque de capa	Stormfok
Trysail	Voile de cape	Vela de cangrejo	Stormzeil
Genoa	Génois	Foque génova	Genua
Spinnaker	Spinnaker	Espinaquer (foque balón)	Spinnaker
Topsail	Flèche	Gavia	Topzeil
Mizzen sail	Artimon	Mesana	Druil of bezaan
Lugsail	Boile de fortune	Vela al tercio	Emmerzeil

ENGLISH	FRENCH	SPANISH	DUTCH
		PARTS OF SAIL	
Head	Point de drisse	Puno de driza	Top
Tack	Point d'amure	Puno de amura	Hals
Clew	Point d'écoute	Puno de escota	Schoothoorn
Luff	Guidant	Gratil	Voorlijk
Leech	Chute arrière	Apagapenol	Achterlijk
Foot	Bordure	Pujamen	Onderlijk
Roach	Rond échancrure	Alunamiento	Gilling
Peak	Pic	Pico	Piek
Throat	Gorge	Puno de driza	Klauw
Batten pocket	Étui, gaine de latte	Bolsa del sable	Zeillatzak
Batten	Latte	Enjaretado	Zeillat
Cringle	Anneau, patte de bouline	Garruncho de cabo	Grommer
Seam	Couture	Costura	Naad
Sailbag	Sac à voile	Saco de vela	Zeilzak

7 BELOW DECK

Toilet	Toilette	Retretes	W.C.
Toilet paper	Papier hygiénique	Papel higiénico	Toilet-papier
Towel	Serviette	Toalla	Handdoek
Soap	Savon	Jabón	Zeep
Cabin	Cabine	Camarote	Kajuit
Mattress	Matelas	Colchón	Matras
Sleeping bag	Sac de couchage	Saco de dormir	Slaapzak
Sheet	Drap	Sábana	Laken
Blanket	Couverture	Manta	Wollen deken
Galley	Cuisine	Cocina	Kombuis
Cook stove	Cuisinière	Fogón	Kookpan
Frying pan	Poêle à frire	Sartén	Braadpan
Saucepan	Casserole	Cacerola	Steelpan of Stoofpanl
Kettle	Bouilloire	Caldero	Ketel
Tea pot	Théière	Tetera	Theepot
Coffee pot	Cafetière	Cafetera	Koffiepot
Knives	Couteaux	Cuchillos	Messen
Forks	Fourchettes	Tenedores	Vorken
Spoons	Cuillères	Cucharas	Lepels
Can opener	Ouvre-boites	Abrelatas	Blikopener
Corkscrew	Tire-bouchon	Sacacorchos	Kurketrekker
Matches	Allumettes	Cerillas	Lucifers
Dishwashing liquid	Détergent	Detergente	Afwasmiddel

8 NAVIGATION EQUIPMENT

Chart table	Table à cartes	Planero	Kaartentafel
Chart	Carte marine	Carta Náutica	Zeekaarta
Parallel ruler	Règles parallèles	Regla de paralelas	Parallel Liniaal
Protractor	Rapporteur	Transportador	Gradenboog
Pencil	Crayon	Lápiz	Potlood
Eraser	Gomme	Goma	Vlakgom
Dividers	Pointes sèches	Compas de puntas	Verdeelpasser
Binoculars	Jumelles	Gemelos	Kijker
Compass	Compas	Compás	Kompas
Handbearing compass	Compas de relèvement	Alidada	Handpeilkompas
Depthsounder	Echosondeur	Sondador acústico	Echolood
Radio receiver	Poste récepteur	Receptor de radio	Radio-ontvangtoestel

APPENDICES

ENGLISH	FRENCH	SPANISH	DUTCH
Radio direction finder	Récepteur goniométrique	Radio goniómetro	Radiopeiltoestel
Patent log	Loch enregistreur	Coredera de patente	Patent log
Sextant	Sextant	Sextante	Sextant

9 ENGINES

Gas engine	Moteur à essence	Motor de gasolina	Benzinemotor
Diesel engine	Moteur diesel	Motor diesel	Dieselmotor
Two-stroke	À deuxtemps	Dos tiempos	Tweetakt
Four-stroke	À quartre temps	Cuatro tiempos	Viertakt
Exhaust pipe	Tuyau déchappement	Tubo de escape	Uitlaatpijp
Gearbox	Boîte de vitesse	Caja de engranajes	Versnelligsbak
Gear lever	Levier des vitesses	Palanca de cambio	Versnellingshendel
Throttle	Accelérateur	Estrangulador	Manette
Clutch	Embrayage	Embrague	Koppeling
Stern tube	Tube d'étambot, arbre	Bocina	Schroefaskoker
Fuel pump	Pompe à combustible	Bomba de alimentación	Brandstofpomp
Carburetor	Carburateur	Carburado	Carburateur
Fuel tank	Réservoir de combustible	Tanque de combustible	Brandstoftank

10 ENGINE ACCESSORIES

Cylinder head	Culasse	Culata	Cilinderkop
Jointing compound	Pâte à joint	Junta de culata	Vloeibare pakking
Nut	Ecrou	Tuerca	Moer
Bolt	Boulon	Perno	Bout
Washer	Rondelle	Arandela	Ring
Split pin	Coupille fendue	Pasador abierto	Splitpen
Asbestos tape	Ruban d'amiante	Cinta de amianto	Asbestband
Copper pipe	Tuyau de cuivre	Tubo de cobre	Koperpijp
Plastic pipe	Tuyau de plastique	Tubo de plastico	Plastikpijp

11 ELECTRICS

Voltage	Tension	Voltaje	Spanning
Amp	Ampères	Amperio	Ampère
Spark plug	Bougie	Bujia	Bougie
Dynamo	Dynamo	Dinamo	Dynamo
Magneto	Magnéto	Magneto	Magneet
Dynamo belt	Courroi de dynamo	Correa de dinamo	Dynamo-riem
Battery	Accumulateur	Bateria	Accu
Contact breaker	Interrupteur	Disyuntor	Contactonderbreker
Fuse box	Boîte à fusibles	Caja de fusibles	Zekeringskast
Switch	Commutateur	Interruptor	Schakelaar
Bulb	Ampoule	Bombilla	Lampje
Copper wire	File de cuivre	Cable de cobre	Koperdraad
Distilled water	Eau distillée	Agua destilada	Gedistilleerd water
Solder	Soudure	Soldadura	Soldeer
Flux	Flux	Flux	Smeltmiddel
Insulating tape	Ruban isolant	Cinta aislante	Isolatieband

ENGLISH	FRENCH	SPANISH	DUTCH
12 FUEL AND OIL			
Gasoline	Essence	Gasolina	Benzine
Kerosene	Pétrole lampant	Petroleo	Petroleum
Diesel oil	Gas-oil	Gasoil	Dieselolie
Alcohol	Alcool à brûler	Alcool desnaturalizado	Spiritus
Lubricating oil	Huile	Aceite de lubricación	Smeerolie
Two-stroke oil	Huile deux temps	Aceite de motor 2 tiempos	Tweetaktolie
Penetrating oil	Huile penetrante, dégrippant	Aceite penetrante	Kruipolie
Grease	Graisse	Grasa	Vet
13 METALS			
Galvanized iron	Fer galvanisé	Hierro galvanizado	Gegalvaniseerd Ijzer
Stainless steel	Acier inoxydable	Acero inoxidable	Roestvrij staal
Iron	Fer	Hierro	Ijzer
Steel	Acier	Acero	Staal
Copper	Cuivre	Cobre	Koper
Brass	Laiton	Latón	Messing
Aluminum	Aluminium	Aluminio	Aluminium
Bronze	Bronze	Bronce	Brons
14 LIGHTS			
Navigation lights	Feux de bord	Luces de navegación	Navigatie lichten
Masthead light	Fue de téte de mât	Luz del tope de proa	Toplicht
Spreader light	Feu de barre de flèche	Luz de verga	Zalinglicht
Port light	Feu de babord	Luz de babor	Bakboordlicht
Starboard light	Feu de tribord	Luz de estribor	Stuurboordlicht
Stern light	Feu arrière	Luz de alcance	Heklicht
Cabin lamp	Lampe de cabine	Lámpera de camarote	Kajuitlamp
Lamp glass	Verre de lampe	Lámpara de cristal	Lampeglas
Wick	Mèche	Mecha (para engrase)	Kous
15 SHIP'S PAPERS			
Certificate of Registry	Acte de francisation	Patente de Navegación	Zeebrief
Pratique	Libre-pratique	Plática	Verlof tot ontscheping
Ship's log	Livre de bord	Cuaderno de bitácora	Journaal
Insurance certificate	Certificat d'assurance	Poliza de seguro	Verzekeringsbewijs
Passport	Passeport	Passaporte	Paspoort
Customs clearance	Dédouanement	Despacho de aduana	Bewijs van inklaring door douane
16 TOOLS			
Hammer	Marteau	Martillo	Hamer
Wood chisel	Ciseau à bois	Formón	Beitel
Cold chisel	Ciseau à froid	Cortafrio	Koubeitel
Screwdriver	Tournevis	Destornillador	Schroevedraaier
Wrench (also spanner)	Clé	Llave para tuercas	Sleutel
Adjustable wrench	Clé anglaise	Llave adjustable	Verstelbare sleutel
Saw	Scie	Sierra	Zaag
Hacksaw	Scie à métaux	Sierra para metal	IJzerzaag
Hand drill	Chignolle à main	Taladro de mano	Handboor

APPENDICES

ENGLISH	FRENCH	SPANISH	DUTCH
File	Lime	Lima	Vijl
Wire cutters	Pinces coupantes	Cortador de alambre	Draadschaar
Pliers	Pinces	Alicates	Buigtang
Wrench	Tourne-à-gauche	Llave de boca	Waterpomptang

17 CHANDLERY

ENGLISH	FRENCH	SPANISH	DUTCH
Burgee	Guidon	Grimpola	Clubstandaard
Ensign	Pavillon	Pabellón	Natie vlag
Courtesy flag	Fanion de courtoisie	Pabellón extranjero	Vreemde natievlag
Q flag	Pavillon Q	Bandera Q	Quarantaine Vlag
Signal flag	Pavillon (alphabetique)	Bandera de senales	Seinvlag
Anchor	Ancre	Ancla	Anker
Anchor chain	Chaîne d'ancre	Cadena del ancla	Ankerketting
Rope	Cordage	Cabulleria	Touw
Hawser	Cable d'acier	Estacha, amarra	Staaldraad
Synthetic rope	Cordage synthétique	Cabullería sintetica	Synthetisch touw
Nylon rope	Cordage de nylon	Cabullería de nylon	Nylon touw
Dacron	Cordage de Tergal	Cabullería de terylene	Terylene touw
Hemp rope	Cordage de chanvre	Cabullería de canamo	Henneptouw
Fender	Defense	Defensa	Stootkussen
Lifebuoy	Bouée sauvetage	Guindola	Redding boei
Cleat	Taquet	Cornamusa	Klamp
Winch	Winch	Chigre	Lier
Boat hook	Gaffe	Bichero	Pikhaak
Oar	Aviron	Remo	Riem
Fairlead	Chaumard	Guía	Verhaalkam
Eye bolt	Piton de filière	Cáncamo	Oogbout
Paint	Peinture	Pintura	Verf
Varnish	Vernis	Barniz	Lak
Sandpaper	Papier de verre	Papel de lija	Schuurpapier
Foghorn	Corne de brume	Bocina de niebla	Misthoorn

18 FOOD

ENGLISH	FRENCH	SPANISH	DUTCH
Cheese	Fromage	Queso	Kaas
Butter	Beurre	Mantequilla	Boter
Bread	Pain	Pan	Brood
Milk	Lait	Leche	Melk
Jam	Confiture	Compota	Jam
Marmalade	Confiture d'oranges	Marmelada	Marmelade
Mustard	Moutarde	Mostaza	Mosterd
Salt	Sel	Sal	Zout
Pepper	Poivre	Pimienta	Peper
Vinegar	Vinaigre	Vinagre	Azjin
Meat	Viande	Carne	Vlees
Fish	Poisson	Pescado	Vis
Fruit	Fruits	Frutas	Fruit
Vegetables	Légumes	Legumbres	Groenten
Sausages	Saucisses	Embutidos	Worstjes
Ham	Jambon	Jamón	Ham
Beef	Boeuf	Carne de vaca	Rundvlees
Pork	Porc	Carne de cerdo	Varkensvlees
Lamb	Mouton	Carne de cernero	Schapenvlees
Bacon	Lard fumé	Tocino	Spek
Eggs	Oeufs	Huevos	Eieren
Fresh water	Eau douce	Agua dulce	Zoetwater

ENGLISH	FRENCH	SPANISH	DUTCH
19 SHOPS AND PLACES ASHORE			
Grocer	Épicier	Tendero de Comestibles	Kruidenier
Greengrocer	Marchand de légumes	Verdulero	Groente handelaar
Butcher	Boucher	Carnicero	Slager
Baker	Boulanger	Panadero	Bakker
Fishmonger	Quincaillerie	Ferretero	Ljzerwarenwinkel
Supermarket	Supermarché	Supermercado	Supermarkt
Market	Marché	Mercado	Markt
Yacht chandler	Fournisseur de marine	Almacén de efectos navales	Scheepsleverancier
Sailmaker	Voilier	Velero	Zeilmakeri
Garage	Garage	Garaje	Garage
Railway station	Gare	Estación	Station
Bus	Autobus	Autobus	Bus
Post Office	Poste	Correos	Postkantoor
Bank	Banque	Banco	Bank
Pharmacist	Pharmacien	Farmaceútico	Apotheek
Hospital	Hôpital	Hospital	Ziekenhuis
Doctor	Médecin	Medico	Dokter
Dentist	Dentiste	Dentista	Tandarts
20 IN HARBOR			
Harbor	Bassin	Puerto	Haven
Yacht harbor	Bassin pour yachts	Puerto de yates	Jachthaven
Fishing harbor	Port de pêche	Puerto pesquero	Vissershaven
Harbor master	Capitaine de port	Capitan de puerto	Havenmeester
Harbor master's office	Bureau de Capitaine de port	Comandacia de puerto	Havenkantoor
Immigration officer	Agent du service de l'immigration	Oficial de inmigración	Immigratie beamte
Customs office	Bureau de douane	Aduana	Douanekantoor
Prohibited area	Zone interdite	Zona prohibida	Verboden gebied
Anchoring prohibited	Défense de mouiller	Fondeadero prohibido	Verboden ankerplaats
Mooring prohibited	Accostage interdit	Amarradero prohibido	Verboden aan te leggen
Lock	Écluse	Esclusa	Sluis
Canal	Canal	Canal	Kanaal
Mooring place	Point d'accostage	Amarradero	Aanlegplaats
Movable bridge	Pont mobile	Puente móvil	Beweegbare brug
Swing bridge	Pont tourant	Puente giratorio	Draaibrug
Lifting bridge	Pont basculant	Puente levadizo	Hefbrug
Ferry	Bac	Transbordador	Veer
Harbor steps	Éscalier du quai	Escala Real	Haventrappen
21 FIRST AID			
Bandage	Bandage	Venda	Verband
Gauze (also lint)	Pansement	Hilacha	Verbandgaas
Adhesive bandage	Pansement adhésif	Esparadrapo	Kleefpleister
Scissors	Ciseaux	Tijeras	Schaar
Safety pin	Épingle de sûreté	Imperidibles	Veiligheidsspeld
Tweezers	Pince à échardes	Pinzas	Pincet
Thermometer	Thermométre	Termómetro	Thermometer
Disinfectant	Désinfectant	Desinfectante	Desinfecterend-middel
Aspirin tablets	Aspirine	Pastillas de aspirina	Aspirine
Laxative	Laxatif	Laxante	Laxeermiddel

APPENDICES

ENGLISH	FRENCH	SPANISH	DUTCH
Indigestion tablets	Pillules contre l'indigestion	Pastillas laxantes	Laxeertabletten
Antiseptic cream	Onguent antiseptique	Pomada antiséptica	Antiseptische zalf
Anti-seasickness pills	Remède contre le mal de mer	Pildoras contra el mareo	Pillen tegen zeeziekte
Calamine lotion	Lotion à la calamine	Locion de calamina	Anti-jeuk middel
Wound dressing	Pansement stérilisé	Botiquin para heridas	Noodverband
Stomach upset	Mal à l'estomac	Corte de digestion	Last van de maag

CHART TERMS
1 LIGHT CHARACTERISTICS

F.	Fixe	f.	v.
Oc.	Occ.	Oc.	O.
Iso	Iso	Iso./Isof.	Iso.
Fl.	É	D.	S.
Q	Scint	Ct.	Fl.
IQ	Scint. dis.	Gp. Ct.	Int. Fl.
Al.	Alt.	Alt.	Alt.
Oc.(..)	… Occ.	Gp. Oc. Gr. Oc.	GO.
Fl.(..)	… É	Gp. D.	GS.
Mo	-	Mo	-
FFI	Fixe É	F.D.	V & S
FFI.(..)	Fixe .. É	F. Gp. D./Gp. DyF.	V & GS

2 COMPASS POINTS

North (N) South (S)	Nord (N) Sud (S)	Norte (N) Sur (S)	Noord (N) Zuid (Z)
East (E) West (W)	Est (E) Ouest (O)	Este, Leste (E) Oeste (W)	Oost (O) West (W))
Northeast (NE)	Nordé (NE)	Nordeste (NE)	Noord-oost (NO)
North-Northeast (NNE)	Nord-Nordé (NNE)	Nornordeste (NNE)	Noord-noord-oost (NNO)
North by East	Nord quart Nordé	Norte cuarta al Este (N4NE)	Noord ten oosten (N-t-O)

3 COLORS

Black	Noir (n)	Negro (n)	Zwart (Z)
Red	Rouge (r)	Rojo (r)	Rood (R)
Green	Vert (v)	Verde (v)	Groen (Gn)
Yellow	Jaune (j)	Amarillo (am)	Geel (Gl)
White	Blanc (b)	Blanco (b)	Wit (w)
Orange	Orange (org)	Naranja	Oranje (or)
Blue	Bleu (bl)	Azul (az)	Blauw (B)
Brown	Brun	Pardo (p)	Bruin
Violet	Violet (vio)	Violeta	Violet (Vi)

4 RADIO AND AURAL AIDS

Radiobeacon	Radiophare	Radiofaro	Radiobaken
Diaphone	Diaphone	Diafono	Diafoon
Horn	Nautophone	Nautofono	Nautofoon
Siren	Siène	Sirena	Mistsirene
Reed	Trompette	Bocina	Mistfluit
Explosive	Explosion	Explosivo	Knalsignaal
Bell	Cloche	Campana	Mistklok
Gong	Gong	Gong	Mistgong
Whistle	Sifflet	Silbato	Mistfluit

ENGLISH	FRENCH	SPANISH	DUTCH
		5 STRUCTURE OR FLOAT	
Dolphin	Duc d'Albe	Dague de Alba	Ducdalf
Light	Feu	Luz	Licht
Lighthouse	Phare	Faro	Lichttoren
Light vessel	Bateau feu	Faro flotanto	Lichtschip
Light float	Feu flottant	Luzflotante	Lichtvlot
Beacon	Balise	Baliza	Baken
Column	Colonne	Columna	Lantaarnpaal
Dwelling	Maison	Casa	Huis
Framework Tower	Pylone	Armazon	Traliemast
House	Bâtiment	Casa	Huis
Hut	Cabane	Caseta	Huisje
Mast	Mât	Mastil	Mast
Post	Poteau	Poste	Lantaarnpaal
Tower	Tour	Torre	Toren
Mooring buoy	Boueé de corps-mort	Boya de amarre muerto	Meerboei
Buoy	Bouée	Boya	Ton
		6 TYPE OF MARKING	
Band	Bande	Fajas horizontales	Horizontaal gestreept
Stripe	Raie	Fajas verticales	Vertikaal gestreept
Checkered	à damier	Damero	Geblokt
Top mark	Voyant	Marea de Tope	Topteken
		7 SHAPE	
Round	Circulaire	Redondo	Rond
Conical	Conique	Conico	Kegelvormig
Diamond	Losange	Rombo	Ruitvormig
Square	Carré	Cuadrangular	Vierkant
Triangle	Triangle	Triangulo	Driehoek
		8 DESCRIPTION	
Destroyed	Détruit	Destruido	Vernield
Occasional	Feu occasionnel	Ocasional	Facultatief
Temporary	Temporaire	Temporal	Tijdelijk
Extinguished	Éteint	Apagada	Gedoofd
		9 TIDE	
High water	Pleine mer	Pleamar	Hoog water
Low water	Basse mer	Bajamar	Lagg watery
Flood	Marée montante	Entrante	Vloed
Ebb	Marée decendante	Vaciante	Eb
Stand	Étale	Margen	Stil water
Range	Amplitude	Repunte	Verval
Spring tide	Vive eau	Marea viva	Springtij
Neap tide	Morte eau	Aguas Muertas	Doodtij
Sea level	Niveau	Nivel	Waterstand
Mean	Moyen	Media	Gemiddeld
Current	Courant	Corriente	Stroomt
		10 CHART DANGERS	
Sunken rock	Roche subergée	Roca siempre cubierta	Blinde klip
Wreck	Épave	Naufragio (Nauf)	Wrak
Shoal	Haut fond (Ht. Fd.)	Bajo (Bo)	Droogte, ondiepte (Dre.)
Obstruction	Obstruction (Obs.)	Obstrución (Obston.)	Belemmering van de vaart, hindernis (Obstr.)

APPENDICES

ENGLISH	FRENCH	SPANISH	DUTCH
Overfalls	Remous et clapotis	Escarceos, hileros	Waterrafel
Dries	Assèche	Que vela en bajmar	Droogvallend
Isolated Danger	Danger isolé	Peligro aislado	Losliggend gevaar

11 WEATHER

ENGLISH	FRENCH	SPANISH	DUTCH
Weather Forecast	Prévions météo	Previsión meteorologica	Weersvoorspelling
Gale	Coup de vent	Duro	Storm
Squall	Grain	Turbonada	Bui
Fog	Brouillard	Niebla	Mist
Mist	Brume légere ou mouillée	Neblina	Nevel

12 DIMENSIONS

ENGLISH	FRENCH	SPANISH	DUTCH
Height	Tirant d'air	Altura	Doorvaarthoogte
Width	Largeur, de large	Ancho, anchura	Breedte
Depth	Profondeur	Fondo, profundidad	Diepte
Draft	Tirant d'eau	Calado	Diepgang

SIMPLE FORM OF SALVAGE AGREEMENT

"No Cure — No Pay"
(Incorporating Lloyd's Open Form)

DATE:_____

It is Hereby Agreed Between_____

for and on behalf of the Owners of the _____
(Hereinafter called "the Owners")

And_____ for and on behalf of _____
(Hereinafter called "the Contractor")

1) That the Contractor will use his best endeavors to salve the _____
and take her into_____
or such other place as may hereinafter be agreed, or if no place is named or agreed, to a place of safety.

2) That the services shall be rendered by the Contractor and accepted by the owner as salvage services upon the principal of "No cure — No pay," subject to the terms, conditions, and provisions (including those relating to arbitration and the providing of security) of the current Standard Form of Salvage Agreement approved and published by the Council of Lloyd's of London and known as Lloyd's Open Form.

3) In the event of success, the Contractor's remuneration shall be $_____, or if no sum be mutually agreed between the parties or entered herein, same shall be fixed by arbitration in London in the manner prescribed in Lloyd's Open Form.

4) The Owners, their servants and agents, shall cooperate fully with the Contractor in and about the salvage including obtaining entry to the place named in Clause 1 hereof or the place of safety. The Contractor may make reasonable use of the vessel's machinery, gear, equipment, anchors, chains, stores, and other appurtenances during and for the purpose of the services free of expense, but shall not unnecessarily damage, abandon, or sacrifice the same, or any property, the subject of this Agreement.

For and on behalf of the Owners of property to be salved

_____

For and on behalf of the Contractor

_____

Note: Full copies of the Lloyd's Open Form Salvage Agreement can be obtained from the Salvage Arbitration Branch, Lloyd's of London, One Lime Street, London EC3M 7HA, England; telephone: (0)71 623 7100, extension 5849, who should be notified of the services only when no agreement can be reached as to remuneration.

INDEX

INDEX

INDEX

INDEX

INDEX

INDEX

INDEX

INDEX

INDEX